The Princeton Review®

PrincetonReview.com

THE BEST 392 COLLEGES

2027 Edition

By Robert Franek, David Soto,

Stephen Koch, Aaron Riccio, Laura Rose,

and The Staff of The Princeton Review

Penguin Random House

The Princeton Review
110 East 42nd Street, 7th Floor
New York, NY 10017
princetonreview.com
penguinrandomhouse.com

Published in the United States by Penguin Random House LLC, New York.

ISBN: 979-8-217-12523-4

Editors: Aaron Riccio and Laura Rose
Production Artist: Deborah Weber
Content Contributors: Jen Adams, Corinne Dolci, and Andrea Kornstein

Manufactured in the United States of America

10 9 8 7 6 5 4 3 2 1

2027 Edition

EU Contact:
Penguin Random House Ireland
32 Nassau Street
Dublin D02 YH68
https://eu-contact.penguin.ie

The Princeton Review Publishing Team
Rob Franek, Editor-in-Chief
David Soto, Senior Director, Data Operations
Stephen Koch, Senior Manager, Data Operations
Deborah Weber, Director of Production
Jason Ullmeyer, Production Design Manager
Jennifer Chapman, Senior Production Artist
Selena Coppock, Director of Editorial
Aaron Riccio, Director, Editorial Admissions Content
Orion McBean, Senior Editor
Meave Shelton, Senior Editor
Laura Rose, Editor
Isabelle Appleton, Editorial Assistant

Penguin Random House Publishing Team
Tom Russell, VP, Publisher
Alison Stoltzfus, Senior Director, Publishing
Emily Hoffman, Managing Editor
Mary Ellen Owens, Assistant Director of Production
Suzanne Lee, Senior Designer
Eugenia Lo, Publishing Assistant

For customer service, please contact **editorialsupport@review.com**, and be sure to include:

- full title of the book
- ISBN
- page number

Acknowledgments

Each year we assemble an awesomely talented group of colleagues who work together to produce our newest Best Colleges edition. It requires synchronized, Herculean efforts annually to update our college profiles in their component parts—narrative, surveys, rankings, ratings, stats, etc.,—and this, our 35th edition, is no exception. Everyone involved in this effort—authors, editors, data managers, production specialists, and designers—goes above and beyond to make *The Best 392 Colleges* an exceptional student resource guide. For over 30 years, we've worked to collect and publish what prospective college students really want: The most honest, accessible, and pertinent information about the colleges they are considering attending.

My sincere thanks go to everybody who has contributed to this tremendous project over the course of more than a quarter-century. A special thank you goes to our authors, Jen Adams, Cathy Cuthbertson, Corinne Dolci, Selena Fragassi, Lynne Hayes, Andrea Kornstein, Amanda Krupman, Christine Lindwall, Suzanne McKenzie, Nina Mozes, Pamela Ross, Hazel Schaffer, Marc Sheforgen, Olivia Tejeda, Catherine Thomas, Tina Tuminaro, and Ysabel Yates for their dedication in poring through tens of thousands of surveys to produce the campus culture narratives of each school we profiled. Very special thanks goes to Aaron Riccio and Laura Rose for their editorial commitment and vision, and to Stephen Koch, who continues to work in partnership with school administrators and students. My continued thanks go to our data guru, David Soto, for his successful efforts in collecting and accurately representing the statistical data that appear with each college profile. The scope of this project and its deadline constraints could not have been realized without the calm presence of our director of production, Deborah Weber—her dedication, focus, and attention to detail continues to impress and remind me of what a pleasure it is to work on this project each year. Special thanks also go to Jeanne Krier, my trusted colleague, media advisor, and friend, for the dedicated work she has done on this book and the overall series since its inception. Finally, I would like to make special mention of Tom Russell and Alison Stoltzfus, our Penguin Random House publishing team, for their continuous investment and faith in our ideas.

Robert Franek
Editor-in-Chief
Lead Author—*The Best 392 Colleges*

Contents

Get More (Free) Content

at PrincetonReview.com/guidebooks

As easy as 1•2•3

1 Go to PrincetonReview.com/guidebooks or scan the **QR code** and enter the following ISBN to register your book: **9798217125234**

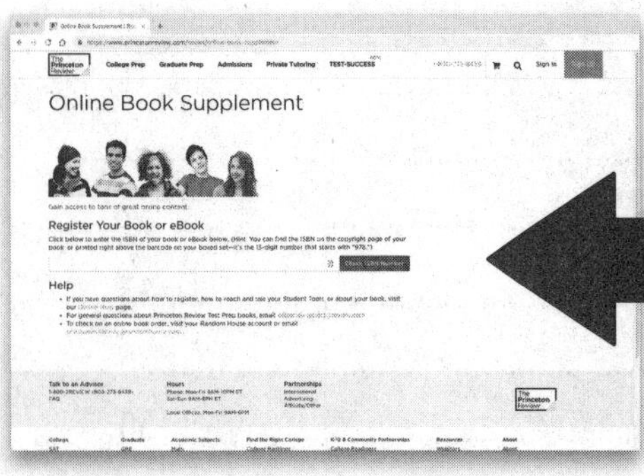

2 Answer a few simple questions to set up an exclusive Princeton Review account. *(If you already have one, you can just log in.)*

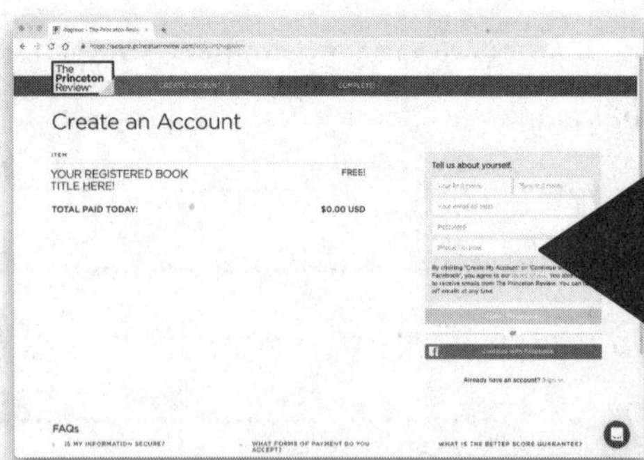

3 Enjoy access to your **FREE** content!

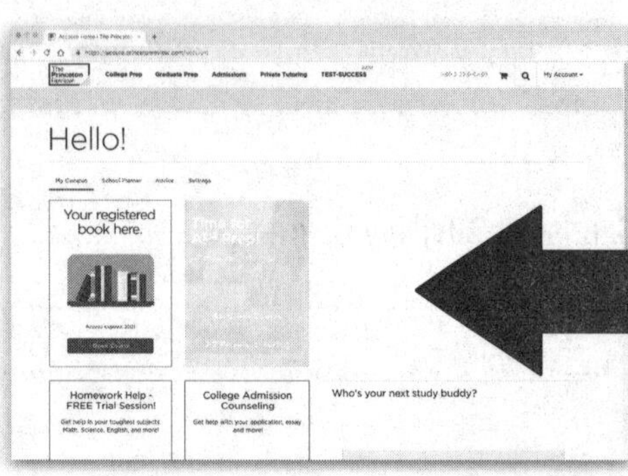

Once you've registered, you can...

- Take a full-length practice SAT® and ACT®
- Get valuable advice about applying to college, including our 26 Financial Aid Tips
- Complete and submit our interactive CH&W survey for a chance to win a $3,500 scholarship
- Access a printable copy of the index for ease of use
- Check for any post-print updates or errata

Need to report a potential **content** issue?

Contact **EditorialSupport@review.com** and include:

- full title of the book
- ISBN
- page number

Need to report a **technical** issue?

Contact **TPRStudentTech@review.com** and provide:

- your full name
- email address used to register the book
- full book title and ISBN
- Operating system (Mac/PC) and browser (Chrome, Firefox, Safari, etc.)

PART 1

Introduction

35 Years of The Princeton Review's College Rankings

1992	Edition	2027
250	Colleges profiled	392
30,000	Student surveys	172,000
120	Average surveys per campus	439
67	Survey questions	98

"There was a void in the college guide market and we have filled it with this book."

Over 30 years ago, The Princeton Review opened the first edition of *The Best Colleges* with this bold statement. In 1992, no other book provided in-depth descriptions of schools alongside statistics covering admissions, financial aid, and student body demographics.

Then, as now, no other guide was based on the input of so many students. Then, as now, we at The Princeton Review believe that current students are the real experts about life at a particular college or university—only they can give you the most candid and informed feedback on what life is really like on campus. More than two million students have participated in our surveys over the past quarter century, and we are pleased to continue to publish what we believe is the most substantive resource you need to find the college that will fit you best.

We've added (and dropped) schools from the book, we've exponentially increased our student survey results, and we've changed or renamed many of the categories in which we've used student feedback to rank 25 top colleges in each of 50 fields. Our guiding conviction, however, remains the same: there is no single "best" college, only the best college for you. The profiles and ranking lists in this book can help you find the school that best fits your unique personality and goals.

What college is right for me?

We encourage students to consider their wants and needs across five categories: academics, campus culture, financial aid, career services, and health services.

Academics

Does the college you're considering offer classes and learning opportunities that interest you? You don't need to declare a college major until your junior year of college—but you're more likely to succeed if you're excited about and engaged by the options available to you. Consider your learning style: Do you prefer informative lectures or lively discussions? Research and analysis, or hands-on experience and practice? Writing papers or working in small groups? Look for the academic experience you'll need to feel challenged and engaged, and what support you'll need for success—peer tutoring, accessible professors, mentorship, and career services are just some of the options you might find on campus. Check out course and program descriptions, reviews of professors, and sit in on some classes if you're able to visit campus.

Campus Culture

Do you want a big school or a small one? A bustling urban campus or a verdant quad in the country? A college where everyone cheers on the basketball team, or one where every theater production gets a standing ovation? Every college has its own special vibe.

You can start narrowing down your list by making some decisions about the size of the student body and geographical location, and then move on to aspects you can identify by visiting campus, talking to current students, and trusting your gut instincts: the personalities, politics, and interests of the student body. Take quality of life into account, too, and try to check out the dorms, food, and recreational facilities on campus, as well as any health services they offer.

Financial Aid

The cost of college is one of the biggest concerns for students, parents, and counselors. We hear that from the students we work with and see it on our annual College Hopes & Worries Survey. It's important to be realistic about your family's finances and to avoid taking on unreasonable debts in the name of your education—but it's also important not to cross a school off your list because of a scary sticker price.

Many colleges and universities make incredible financial aid offers (sometimes as a combination of grants and scholarships, which means no debt at all!). Raising your grades and your SAT or ACT scores will help you become more eligible for merit-based financial aid. And more and more data on college outcomes—that is, career placement rates and average starting salaries—is becoming available, which can help you assess the value of investing your tuition dollars in a particular college.

You can check out our list of 209 "Best Value" schools in Part 2 of this book, and read more about them in our searchable online listings at princetonreview.com/college-rankings/best-value-colleges.

Career Development

Visit or contact the career development center at all the schools you're considering. Find out how each supports students in preparing for the professional world. Do they offer résumé writing workshops? Practice interviews? Networking events with alumni? If you foresee yourself in a particular field, location, or specific workplace, ask about past students' track records of finding internships, getting accepted to grad school, or landing entry-level jobs in those areas.

College admission officers and career counselors are more than happy to highlight their institutions' success stories—as well as the unique skill-building programs and experiences their campuses have to offer.

Health

In conjunction with all of the above categories, a student's overall well-being while away at college is also a vital consideration, as it becomes more difficult to have a fruitful experience when in a stressed or unhealthy situation. In conjunction with The Ruderman Foundation, The Princeton Review began surveying schools in 2024 to get a sense of their available mental health services. Those results can be found here (princetonreview.com/mental-health-on-college-campus), and is a topic that you should bring up with any college you're applying to, so that you can be sure that your needs can and will be met.

Getting into Selective Colleges: An Overview for High School Students

6 STEPS TO GETTING INTO COLLEGE

Putting some effort into your schoolwork and extracurricular experiences can make applying to your choice colleges a lot less stressful. Though they might sound obvious, the following steps are extremely important! (Many of these are true even at schools that have adopted Test Optional policies, as submitting a test may help for other considerations, and at a Test Free school, you may want to focus even more on the non-test steps below.)

1. Work hard for good grades.
2. Enroll in challenging courses.
3. Spend time preparing for the ACT® or SAT®.
4. Polish your writing skills.
5. Establish relationships with teachers and advisors who can write strong letters of recommendation for you.
6. Get involved in some activities, community service, or work experiences that will enable you to show your values, talents, and skills.

College admission is all about compatibility. As an applicant, you are looking for an environment where you can thrive academically and personally, and it is the job of an admission officer to identify students who will make great additions to a unique campus community.

Your path to college begins your first year in high school. Grades and test scores are important factors in college admission, but admissions officers are also looking for curious and engaged candidates who will round out a diverse first-year class.

Grades

Most admissions officers report that your GPA and the rigor of your high school curriculum are the most important elements of your college application.

- Choose your high school classes carefully. Challenge yourself with honors, AP®, and IB® courses when they are available.
- Your grades count for all four years of high school. When colleges review your transcript, they often look at grade trends across subjects and course levels.
- Even if you had a rough first year of high school, there's still time to turn your grades around. Many schools will reward your upward trajectory.

Test Scores

SAT and/or ACT scores take the lead, but admissions officers consider your performance on other standardized tests as well.

- The PSAT® is optional your sophomore year, but your junior year PSAT scores can qualify you for scholarship programs such as the National Merit® Scholarship, which can help cover the cost of tuition and get you into a great college. Learning the digital PSAT format will also help prepare you for the SAT, which is very similar.
- Strong performances on AP Exams can indicate your potential for academic achievement to college admission officers. More than 2,100 colleges and universities accept high scores on AP Exams for course credits.
- Most schools view the ACT and SAT equally, so it's completely up to you which test you take (you can even take both!). The ACT's Writing section is optional, but some colleges may require it.
- Test Optional schools: Schools that are Test Optional do not require standardized test scores as part of a complete application. (Some exceptions apply if your GPA falls below a certain threshold.) Since your test scores could qualify you for merit scholarships even at Test Optional schools, it's still a smart idea to take (and prep for!) at least one standardized test. Be advised that while many schools adopted a Test Optional policy during the 2020–2021 height of COVID, many prestigious schools are once again starting to require it, pointing to data from a study that suggests that high scores on a standardized test may be the best predictor of student success in college.

Extracurriculars

What you do with your time shows colleges who you are and what qualities you'll bring to campus.

- Commitment to a sport, hobby, religious organization, or job over four years of high school is key. Colleges would much rather see you excited about a few worthwhile endeavors than marginally involved with a ton of clubs.
- If an after-school job is cutting into your extracurricular time, don't worry! Work experience demonstrates maturity and responsibility on your college application.
- Make your summer count! Some students enroll in university programs to start earning college credits. Others volunteer or find a summer job. Whatever you do, your experience can make your college application rise to the top of a competitive applicant pool.

What Should You Do This Summer?

Ahhh, summer. The possibilities seem endless. You can get a job, intern, travel, study, volunteer, or do nothing at all. Here are a few ideas to get you started:

- **Go to college:** No, not for real. However, you can participate in summer programs at colleges and universities at home and abroad. Programs can focus on anything from academics (stretch your brain by taking an intensive science or language course) to sports to admissions guidance. This is also a great opportunity to explore college life firsthand, especially if you get to stay in a dorm. Summer is also a time when families on vacations can squeeze in a college visit while they're in "the neighborhood." Even if classes aren't in session when you are able to tour a campus, the more colleges you can visit, the better informed your final college choice will be.
- **Prep for the PSAT, SAT, or ACT:** Even at Test Optional schools—and especially if you're seeking to maximize financial aid—test scores can help to round out your overall application. Getting this valuable prep-work done during a less busy part of your year can also help you to keep your full focus on your grades and extracurriculars when school resumes.
- **Research scholarships:** College is expensive. While you should never rule out a school based on cost, the more scholarship money you can secure beforehand, the more college options you will have. You'll find loads of info on financial aid and scholarships on our site, princetonreview.com/college-advice/how-to-pay-for-college.

Applying for Financial Aid

The cost of college has been the biggest concern among respondents to our annual College Hopes & Worries survey for the past five years. Educate yourself about the financial aid system before you submit forms to get the best outcome for you and your family.

- Be aware that applying to college and applying for financial aid are two separate processes.
- The U.S. Department of Education (USDOE) requires all schools that offer federal aid to provide a net-price calculator (but does not audit them for accuracy). Use this tool on each prospective school's financial aid website, but be aware that these estimates are non-binding and can be off by $10,000 or more.
- Make sure you submit the 2027–2028 FAFSA. It's a good idea to start filling it out early in case you need to get help answering any of the questions; it is usually available on October 1. Please visit the websites of any school to which you are applying if you need specific advice on what to file.
- In addition to the FAFSA, many schools require the College Board's CSS Profile® and/or their own aid forms to be completed to be considered for institutional aid. The CSS Profile should be available on October 1. Those applying for Early Decision (and for some schools, Early Action as well), may need to complete this and other aid forms before the FAFSA is released.
- Your financial aid offer is intended to meet your need and can consist of:
    - grants and scholarships (which do not need to be paid back)
    - federal work-study (a job)
    - student loans
- Outside organizations offer scholarships tailored to academic interests, talents, extracurricular activities, career goals, geographic location, and many more factors. Keep an eye on deadlines, which could fall as early as the summer before senior year.

Some of Our Other Helpful Books

The 2027 Edition of The Princeton Review's *Paying for College* contains line-by-line strategies for completing the 2027–2028 versions of the FAFSA and CSS Profile to your best advantage. It explains how the financial aid process works and reveals strategies for maximizing your eligibility for aid. Authored by Kal Chany, one of the nation's most widely sourced experts on college funding, it also includes annually updated information on education tax breaks, college savings programs, and student and parent loans. Check out Kal Chany's "26 Tips for Getting Financial Aid . . ." online in your student tools.

College Admission 101 presents simple answers to your toughest questions about the college admissions process, figuring out financial aid, and getting into the school of your choice.

The Complete College Planner provides high-school students with a comprehensive and activity-filled planner to help you map out all the important tasks and information you'll want to gather before and during your college search.

The Complete Guide to College Application Essays recognizes the increasing importance of your personal application statement and walks you through every step of how to prepare, brainstorm, draft, and revise your application essays.

The Ultimate Guide to HBCUs provides a thorough look at all 101 Historically Black Colleges and Universities to make sure that students aren't missing out on a potentially ideal opportunity.

Great Schools for 22 of the Most Popular Undergraduate Majors

Worried about having to declare a major on your college application? Relax. Most colleges won't require you to declare a major until the end of your sophomore year, giving you plenty of time to explore your options. However, problems may arise if you are thinking about majoring in a program that limits its enrollment—meaning that if you don't declare that major early on, you might not get into that program at a later date.

On the flip side, some students declare a major on their application because they believe it will boost their chances of gaining admission. This can be problematic, however, if you later decide to change your major. It involves switching from one school within the college to another (e.g., from the school of arts and sciences to the school of business), which can be difficult.

While it may be tempting to choose a college based on the prestige of a given program, keep in mind that as you are exposed to new ideas and learning experiences, you may change your mind. (Choosing a school based on program availability is a different story.) You may also want to investigate opportunities to design your own major. A commitment to a major would limit you in many ways.

How Did We Compile These Lists?

Each year we collect data from more than 2,000 colleges on the subject of—among many other things—undergraduate academic offerings. We ask colleges to report not only which undergraduate majors they offer, but also which of their majors have the highest enrollment and the number of bachelor's degrees each school awarded in these areas. The list below identifies (in alphabetical order) 22 of the 40 "most popular" majors that the schools responding to our survey reported to us. We also conduct our own research on college majors. We look at institutional data, and we consult with our in-house college admissions experts as well as our National College Counselor Advisory Board (whom we list on page 863) for their input on schools offering great programs in these majors. We thank them and all of the guidance counselors, college admissions counselors, and education experts across the country whose recommendations we considered in developing these lists. Of the nearly 2,800 four-year colleges across the United States, those on these lists represent only a snapshot of the many offering great programs in these majors. Use our lists as a starting point for further research.

Great Schools for Accounting Majors

- Agnes Scott College
- Alfred University
- Assumption University
- Auburn University
- Babson College
- Baylor University
- Bentley University
- Boston College
- Boston University
- Brigham Young University (UT)
- Bryant University
- Bucknell University
- Calvin University
- City University of New York—Baruch College
- City University of New York—Brooklyn College
- City University of New York—Hunter College
- City University of New York—Queens College
- Claremont McKenna College
- Clemson University
- College of Charleston
- College of Saint Benedict/Saint John's University
- Cornell University
- DePaul University
- Drexel University
- Duquesne University
- Elon University
- Emory University
- Fairfield University
- Fordham University
- George Mason University
- Georgetown University
- Hofstra University
- Illinois Wesleyan University
- Indiana University—Bloomington
- Iowa State University
- James Madison University
- Lehigh University
- Le Moyne College
- Marquette University
- Miami University
- Moravian University
- New York University
- Northeastern University
- Pace University
- Penn State University Park
- Pepperdine University
- Rider University
- Rochester Institute of Technology
- St. Bonaventure University
- Seton Hall University
- Siena University
- Southern Methodist University
- Stonehill College
- Suffolk University
- Temple University
- Texas A&M University—College Station
- Transylvania University
- The University of Alabama at Birmingham
- University of Florida
- University of Houston
- University of Illinois at Urbana-Champaign
- University of Michigan—Ann Arbor
- University of Mississippi
- University of Oklahoma
- University of Pennsylvania
- University of Southern California
- University of Texas at Austin
- The University of Texas at Dallas
- Washington & Jefferson College
- Washington and Lee University

Great Schools for Agriculture Majors

- Angelo State University
- Auburn University
- Berea College
- Clemson University
- College of the Ozarks
- Colorado State University
- Cornell University
- Illinois Institute of Technology
- Iowa State University
- Kansas State University
- Louisiana State University—Baton Rouge
- Michigan State University
- Middle Tennessee State University
- North Carolina State University
- The Ohio State University—Columbus
- Oregon State University
- Penn State University Park
- Purdue University—West Lafayette
- Texas A&M University—College Station
- University of Arizona
- University of Arkansas—Fayetteville
- University of California—Davis
- University of Connecticut
- University of Florida
- University of Georgia
- University of Hawaii—Manoa
- University of Idaho
- University of Illinois at Urbana-Champaign
- University of Kentucky
- University of Maine
- University of Maryland, College Park
- University of Massachusetts—Amherst
- University of Minnesota—Twin Cities
- University of Missouri
- University of Nebraska—Lincoln
- University of Rhode Island
- University of Tennessee—Knoxville
- University of Vermont
- University of Wisconsin—Madison
- University of Wyoming
- Virginia Tech
- Washington State University
- West Virginia University

Great Schools for Artificial Intelligence Majors

- Arizona State University
- California Institute of Technology
- Carnegie Mellon University
- Columbia University
- Cornell University
- Duke University
- Eastern Michigan University
- Georgia Institute of Technology
- Harvard College
- Illinois Institute of Technology
- Indiana University—Bloomington
- Johns Hopkins University
- Massachusetts Institute of Technology
- Nazareth University
- Penn State University Park
- Purdue University—West Lafayette
- Rochester Institute of Technology
- Stanford University
- University of Arizona
- University of California—Berkeley
- University of California—San Diego
- University of Colorado Boulder
- University of Georgia
- University of Illinois at Urbana-Champaign
- University of Miami
- University of Michigan—Ann Arbor
- University of Pennsylvania
- University of Southern California
- University of Tennessee—Knoxville
- University of Texas at Austin
- The University of Texas at Dallas
- University of Washington

Great Schools for Biology Majors

- Agnes Scott College
- Albion College
- Allegheny College
- Amherst College
- Appalachian State University
- Auburn University
- Austin College
- Bates College
- Baylor University
- Berea College
- Berry College
- Boston College
- Boston University
- Bowdoin College
- Brandeis University
- Brigham Young University (UT)
- Brown University
- Bryn Mawr College
- Bucknell University
- Carleton College
- Case Western Reserve University
- Christopher Newport University
- City University of New York—City College
- Clark University
- Clemson University
- Coe College
- Colby College
- Colgate University
- College of Charleston
- The College of New Jersey
- College of Saint Benedict/Saint John's University
- The College of Wooster
- Colorado College
- Colorado State University
- Connecticut College
- Cornell University
- Creighton University
- Dartmouth College
- Davidson College
- Denison University
- DePauw University
- Dickinson College
- Drew University
- Drury University
- Duke University
- Duquesne University
- Earlham College
- Eckerd College
- Emory University
- Florida Southern College
- Franklin & Marshall College
- George Mason University
- Gettysburg College
- Gonzaga University
- Gordon College
- Grinnell College
- Hamilton College
- Hampden-Sydney College
- Hampton University
- Hanover College
- Harvard College
- Haverford College
- Hofstra University
- Howard University
- Johns Hopkins University
- Juniata College
- Kalamazoo College
- Knox College
- Lafayette College
- Lake Forest College
- Lawrence University
- Le Moyne College
- Lewis & Clark College
- Louisiana State University—Baton Rouge
- Loyola University Chicago
- Lycoming College
- Marquette University
- Michigan State University
- Middlebury College
- Mount Holyoke College

- Muhlenberg College
- North Carolina State University
- Oberlin College
- Occidental College
- Ohio Wesleyan University
- Pomona College
- Princeton University
- Randolph College
- Randolph-Macon College
- Reed College
- Rhodes College
- Rice University
- Ripon College
- Sacred Heart University
- Saint Louis University
- Saint Michael's College
- Scripps College
- Seton Hall University
- Siena University
- Skidmore College
- Smith College
- Southwestern University
- Spelman College
- St. John's University (NY)
- St. Mary's College of Maryland
- St. Olaf College
- State University of New York—Binghamton University
- State University of New York—College of Environmental Science and Forestry
- State University of New York at Geneseo
- State University of New York—Stony Brook University
- Susquehanna University
- Swarthmore College
- Temple University
- Transylvania University
- Trinity College (CT)
- Trinity University
- Truman State University
- Tufts University
- Union College (NY)
- The University of the South
- The University of Alabama at Birmingham
- University of California—Berkeley
- University of California—Davis
- University of California—Irvine
- University of California—Los Angeles
- University of California—Merced
- University of California—Riverside
- University of California—San Diego
- University of California—Santa Barbara
- University of California—Santa Cruz
- The University of Chicago
- University of Colorado Boulder
- University of Dallas
- University of Delaware
- University of Florida
- University of Georgia
- University of Hawaii—Manoa
- University of Houston
- University of Lynchburg
- University of Mary Washington
- University of Maryland, Baltimore County
- University of Massachusetts—Amherst
- University of Miami
- University of Michigan—Ann Arbor
- University of Minnesota—Twin Cities
- The University of Montana—Missoula
- University of New England
- University of New Hampshire
- University of North Carolina at Chapel Hill
- University of Pittsburgh—Pittsburgh Campus
- University of Rochester
- University of San Diego
- The University of Scranton
- University of South Carolina—Columbia
- University of South Florida
- University of Texas at Austin
- The University of Texas at Dallas
- University of Vermont
- University of Washington
- University of Wisconsin—Madison
- Ursinus College
- Vassar College
- Warren Wilson College
- Washington College
- Washington University in St. Louis
- Wellesley College
- Wheaton College (MA)
- Whitman College
- William & Mary
- Wofford College
- Xavier University of Louisiana
- Yale University

Great Schools for Business/Finance Majors

- Alfred University
- Arizona State University
- Babson College
- Bentley University
- Berea College
- Boston College
- Brigham Young University (UT)
- Bradley University
- Bryant University
- Butler University
- California State University, Stanislaus
- Calvin University
- Carnegie Mellon University
- Catawba College
- Champlain College
- Chapman University
- Christopher Newport University
- City University of New York—Baruch College
- City University of New York—Brooklyn College
- College of Charleston
- Cornell University
- Creighton University

- DePaul University
- Drexel University
- Elon University
- Emory University
- Fairfield University
- Florida International University
- Florida State University
- Fordham University
- High Point University
- Indiana University—Bloomington
- Iona University
- Iowa State University
- John Carroll University
- Lehigh University
- Lycoming College
- Marquette University
- Massachusetts Institute of Technology
- McDaniel College
- Mercer University
- Miami University
- Michigan State University
- Middle Tennessee State University
- Montclair State University
- New York University
- Northwestern University
- Ohio University—Athens
- Oregon State University
- Pace University
- Portland State University
- Rice University
- Roanoke College
- Rollins College
- Rowan University
- Rutgers University—New Brunswick
- Seattle University
- San Diego State University
- Saint Joseph's University (PA)
- Saint Mary's College of California
- Saint Michael's College
- Santa Clara University
- Siena University
- Southwestern University
- State University of New York—University at Albany
- Stetson University
- Suffolk University
- Texas State University
- University of Arkansas—Fayetteville
- University of California—Berkeley
- University of California—Irvine
- University of California—Los Angeles
- The University of Chicago
- University of Florida
- University of Houston
- University of Illinois at Urbana-Champaign
- University of Michigan—Ann Arbor
- University of North Carolina at Charlotte
- University of North Carolina at Greensboro
- University of Notre Dame
- University of Pennsylvania
- University of Richmond
- University of St. Thomas (MN)
- University of San Diego
- University of San Francisco
- University of Southern California
- University of Texas at Austin
- The University of Texas at Dallas
- The University of Tulsa
- University of Virginia
- Villanova University
- Washington and Lee University
- Washington University in St. Louis
- William & Mary
- Wittenberg University

Great Schools for Communications Majors

- American University
- Baylor University
- Boston College
- Boston University
- Bradley University
- Butler University
- City University of New York—City College
- City University of New York—Hunter College
- Clemson University
- College of Charleston
- Cornell University
- Denison University
- DePaul University
- DePauw University
- Duquesne University
- Eckerd College
- Elon University
- Emerson College
- Eugene Lang College of Liberal Arts at The New School
- Fairfield University
- Fordham University
- Gonzaga University
- High Point University
- Hollins University
- Hofstra University
- Howard University
- Indiana University—Bloomington
- Iowa State University
- Ithaca College
- James Madison University
- Lake Forest College
- Loyola University Maryland
- Loyola University New Orleans
- Marist University
- Manhattanville University
- Muhlenberg College
- New York University
- Northwestern University
- Pace University
- Pepperdine University
- Quinnipiac University
- Ripon College

- Salisbury University
- Seton Hall University
- St. Bonaventure University
- St. John's University (NY)
- Stanford University
- State University of New York—Purchase College
- Suffolk University
- Susquehanna University
- Syracuse University
- Texas Christian University
- University of Arizona
- University of California—San Diego
- University of California—Santa Barbara
- University of Iowa
- University of Maryland, College Park
- University of San Diego
- University of Southern California
- The University of Tampa
- University of Texas at Austin
- University of Utah

Great Schools for Computer Science/Computer Engineering Majors

- Arizona State University
- Boston University
- Brown University
- California Institute of Technology
- Carleton College
- Carnegie Mellon University
- Case Western Reserve University
- City University of New York—Brooklyn College
- City University of New York—Hunter College
- Colby College
- Colorado State University
- Columbia University
- Cornell University
- DePaul University
- Duke University
- George Mason University
- Georgia Institute of Technology
- Harvey Mudd College
- Harvard College
- Illinois Institute of Technology
- Johns Hopkins University
- Kettering University
- Lehigh University
- Massachusetts Institute of Technology
- Miami University
- Middlebury College
- Missouri University of Science and Technology
- New Jersey Institute of Technology
- Northwestern University
- Oregon State University
- Princeton University
- Purdue University—West Lafayette
- Rice University
- Rensselaer Polytechnic Institute
- Rochester Institute of Technology
- Rose-Hulman Institute of Technology
- Stanford University
- Stevens Institute of Technology
- Swarthmore College
- University of Arizona
- University of California—Berkeley
- University of California—Irvine
- University of California—Los Angeles
- University of California—Riverside
- University of Illinois at Urbana-Champaign
- University of Maryland, Baltimore County
- University of Massachusetts—Amherst
- University of Michigan—Ann Arbor
- University of Texas at Austin
- The University of Texas at Dallas
- University of Washington
- Washington University in St. Louis
- Worcester Polytechnic Institute

Great Schools for Criminology Majors

- American University
- Angelo State University
- Arizona State University
- Auburn University
- Batten University
- California State University, Stanislaus
- Champlain College
- Florida State University
- George Mason University
- Indiana University of Pennsylvania
- Loyola University New Orleans
- Michigan State University
- North Carolina State University
- The Ohio State University—Columbus
- Ohio University—Athens
- Penn State University Park
- Quinnipiac University
- St. John's University (NY)
- State University of New York—University at Albany
- Stonehill College
- Suffolk University
- University of California—Irvine
- University of Cincinnati
- University of Delaware
- University of Denver
- University of Louisville
- University of Maryland, College Park
- University of Miami
- University of New Hampshire
- University of New Haven
- University of South Carolina—Columbia
- University of South Florida
- The University of Tampa
- University of Utah
- Whittier College

Great Schools for Education Majors

- Alfred University
- Auburn University
- Barnard College
- Bucknell University
- Calvin University
- Catawba College
- City University of New York—Brooklyn College
- City University of New York—Hunter College
- Colgate University
- The College of New Jersey
- College of the Ozarks
- Columbia University
- Cornell College
- Cornell University
- Duquesne University
- East Carolina University
- Elmira College
- Elon University
- Gonzaga University
- Goucher College
- Hillsdale College
- Indiana University—Bloomington
- Juniata College
- Knox College
- Loyola Marymount University
- Manhattan University
- Marquette University
- Miami University
- Monmouth University (NJ)
- Nazareth University
- New York University
- Northeastern University
- Northwestern University
- The Ohio State University—Columbus
- Rider University
- Ripon College
- Rowan University
- St. Bonaventure University
- Salisbury University
- Salve Regina University
- Simmons University
- Skidmore College
- Smith College
- State University of New York at Geneseo
- Taylor University
- Trinity University
- University of Maine
- University of Mississippi
- The University of Montana—Missoula
- The University of South Dakota
- Vanderbilt University
- Villanova University
- Wagner College
- Wellesley College
- William Jewell College
- William & Mary
- Wittenberg University
- Xavier University (OH)

Great Schools for Engineering Majors

- California Institute of Technology
- Carnegie Mellon University
- Case Western Reserve University
- Columbia University
- The Cooper Union for the Advancement of Science and Art
- Clarkson University
- Cornell University
- Drexel University
- Duke University
- Franklin W. Olin College of Engineering
- Georgia Institute of Technology
- Harvard College
- Harvey Mudd College
- Illinois Institute of Technology
- Johns Hopkins University
- Kettering University
- Lawrence Technological University
- Manhattan University
- Massachusetts Institute of Technology
- Michigan Technological University
- Missouri University of Science and Technology
- Montana Technological University
- New Jersey Institute of Technology
- Penn State University Park
- Princeton University
- Purdue University—West Lafayette
- Rensselaer Polytechnic Institute
- Rice University
- Rochester Institute of Technology
- Rose-Hulman Institute of Technology
- Stanford University
- Stevens Institute of Technology
- Texas A&M University—College Station
- United States Military Academy
- United States Naval Academy
- University of California—Berkeley
- University of California—Los Angeles
- University of California—Merced
- University of Illinois at Urbana-Champaign
- University of Michigan—Ann Arbor
- University of Texas at Austin
- University of Wisconsin—Madison
- Virginia Tech
- Webb Institute
- Worcester Polytechnic Institute

Great Schools for English Literature and Language Majors

- Alfred University
- Amherst College
- Bard College
- Barnard College
- Bates College
- Beloit College
- Bennington College
- Bowdoin College
- Brown University
- Bryn Mawr College
- City University of New York—Hunter College
- Colby College
- Colgate University
- Columbia University
- Cornell University
- Dartmouth College
- Davidson College
- Denison University
- DePauw University
- Duke University
- Emerson College
- Emory University
- Eugene Lang College of Liberal Arts at The New School
- Fordham University
- Gettysburg College
- Georgetown University
- Grinnell College
- Hanover College
- Harvard College
- Haverford College
- Hollins University
- Iowa State University
- Johns Hopkins University
- Kalamazoo College
- Kenyon College
- Knox College
- Lawrence University
- Lewis & Clark College
- Northwestern University
- Oberlin College
- Pitzer College
- Pomona College
- Princeton University
- Reed College
- St. Lawrence University
- St. Olaf College
- Smith College
- Spelman College
- Stanford University
- St. Mary's College of Maryland
- Syracuse University
- Trinity College (CT)
- Truman State University
- Tufts University
- University of California—Berkeley
- University of California—Los Angeles
- The University of Chicago
- University of Michigan—Ann Arbor
- University of North Carolina Asheville
- University of Notre Dame
- University of Pennsylvania
- The University of the South
- University of Utah
- Vassar College
- Washington University in St. Louis
- Wellesley College
- Wesleyan University
- Williams College
- Yale University

Great Schools for Environmental Studies Majors

- Allegheny College
- Bates College
- Bowdoin College
- Colby College
- College of the Atlantic
- Colorado College
- Dickinson College
- Eckerd College
- Emory University
- Flagler College
- Harvard College
- Hobart and William Smith Colleges
- Juniata College
- Middlebury College
- New College of Florida
- Northeastern University
- Oberlin College
- Occidental College
- Pitzer College
- Pomona College
- Portland State University
- St. Mary's College of Maryland
- Stanford University
- State University of New York—Binghamton University
- State University of New York—College of Environmental Science and Forestry
- University of California—Berkeley
- University of California—Santa Cruz
- University of Colorado Boulder
- University of Idaho
- The University of Montana—Missoula
- University of New Hampshire
- University of North Carolina Asheville
- University of North Carolina at Chapel Hill
- University of Oregon
- University of Redlands
- The University of the South
- University of Vermont
- University of Washington
- Warren Wilson College
- Washington College
- Yale University

Great Schools for Health Services Majors

- Adelphi University
- Agnes Scott College
- Bellarmine University
- Boston University
- Capital University
- Clemson University
- College of the Ozarks
- Creighton University
- Drexel University
- Duquesne University
- East Carolina University
- Eastern Michigan University
- Elmira College
- Fairfield University
- Furman University
- Gettysburg College
- Grove City College
- Hampton University
- Howard University
- Iona University
- Ithaca College
- James Madison University
- Johns Hopkins University
- Kalamazoo College
- Loyola University Chicago
- Manhattanville University
- Mercer University
- Monmouth University (NJ)
- Montana Technological University
- Moravian University
- Nazareth University
- Northeastern University
- Ohio University—Athens
- Purdue University—West Lafayette
- Quinnipiac University
- Sacred Heart University
- Saint Anselm College
- Saint Louis University
- Salve Regina University
- Seton Hall University
- Simmons University
- Spelman College
- State University of New York—Stony Brook University
- Suffolk University
- Texas A&M University—College Station
- Texas Christian University
- Texas State University
- Tulane University
- The University of Alabama at Birmingham
- University of Central Florida
- University of Cincinnati
- University of Delaware
- University of Florida
- University of Houston
- University of Louisville
- University of Lynchburg
- University of Miami
- University of New England
- University of North Dakota
- University of Oklahoma
- University of Portland
- University of Rhode Island
- University of St. Francis (IL)
- The University of South Dakota
- University of South Florida
- University of Utah
- University of Wyoming
- Wagner College
- Washington University in St. Louis
- West Virginia University
- Westminster University
- Wheaton College (IL)
- William Jewell College
- Xavier University (OH)

Great Schools for History Majors

- Bates College
- Bowdoin College
- Brown University
- Centre College
- Colgate University
- College of the Holy Cross
- The College of Wooster
- Columbia University
- Davidson College
- Drew University
- Furman University
- Georgetown University
- Grinnell College
- Hampden-Sydney College
- Harvard College
- Haverford College
- Hillsdale College
- Kenyon College
- Oberlin College
- Princeton University
- Ripon College
- Stanford University
- Tulane University
- University of California—Berkeley
- University of California—Los Angeles
- The University of Chicago
- University of Dallas
- University of Michigan—Ann Arbor
- University of Virginia
- Wabash College
- Williams College
- Yale University

Great Schools for International Relations and Affairs Majors

- American University
- Bucknell University
- Claremont McKenna College
- Clark University
- Connecticut College
- The George Washington University
- Georgetown University
- Gettysburg College
- Hamilton College
- Harvard College
- Lafayette College
- Lewis & Clark College
- Middlebury College
- Occidental College
- Tufts University
- The University of Chicago
- Yale University

Great Schools for Journalism Majors

- American University
- Arizona State University
- Auburn University
- Boston University
- Carleton College
- Duke University
- Emerson College
- The George Washington University
- Hampton University
- Howard University
- Indiana University—Bloomington
- Iowa State University
- Ithaca College
- Kansas State University
- Loyola University New Orleans
- Michigan State University
- New York University
- Northwestern University
- Ohio University—Athens
- Penn State University Park
- St. Bonaventure University
- State University of New York—Purchase College
- State University of New York—Stony Brook University
- Syracuse University
- Temple University
- The University of Alabama—Tuscaloosa
- University of Arizona
- University of Arkansas—Fayetteville
- University of Florida
- University of Georgia
- University of Kansas
- University of Kentucky
- University of Idaho
- University of Illinois at Urbana-Champaign
- University of Iowa
- University of Maryland, College Park
- University of Minnesota—Twin Cities
- University of Mississippi
- University of Missouri
- The University of Montana—Missoula
- University of Nebraska—Lincoln
- University of North Carolina at Chapel Hill
- University of Oklahoma
- University of Oregon
- University of Southern California
- University of Texas at Austin
- University of Wisconsin—Madison
- Washington State University
- West Virginia University

Great Schools for Marketing and Sales Majors

- Babson College
- Baylor University
- Bentley University
- Bryant University
- Butler University
- DePaul University
- Drury University
- Duquesne University
- Fairfield University
- Hofstra University
- Indiana University—Bloomington
- Iowa State University
- James Madison University
- Loyola Marymount University
- Manhattan University
- Miami University
- Providence College
- Saint Joseph's University (PA)
- San Diego State University
- Seattle University
- Siena University
- Syracuse University
- Texas A&M University—College Station
- The University of Alabama—Tuscaloosa
- University of Central Florida
- University of Cincinnati
- University of Dayton
- University of Michigan—Ann Arbor
- University of Mississippi
- University of Pennsylvania
- University of South Florida
- University of Texas at Austin

Great Schools for Mathematics & Statistics Majors

- Amherst College
- Agnes Scott College
- Bowdoin College
- Brown University
- Bryant University
- Bryn Mawr College
- California Institute of Technology
- Carleton College
- Carnegie Mellon University
- College of the Holy Cross
- Columbia University
- Grinnell College
- Hamilton College
- Hampton University
- Harvard College
- Harvey Mudd College
- Haverford College
- Macalester College
- Massachusetts Institute of Technology
- New York University
- Pomona College
- Princeton University
- Randolph College
- Reed College
- Rice University
- St. Lawrence University
- St. Olaf College
- Stanford University
- United States Coast Guard Academy
- University of California—Berkeley
- University of California—Los Angeles
- The University of Chicago
- University of Rochester
- Wabash College
- Williams College

Great Schools for Mechanical Engineering Majors

- Auburn University
- Bradley University
- California Institute of Technology
- Case Western Reserve University
- Clarkson University
- Colorado State University
- The Cooper Union for the Advancement of Science and Art
- Drexel University
- Franklin W. Olin College of Engineering
- Georgia Institute of Technology
- Grove City College
- Harvey Mudd College
- Illinois Institute of Technology
- Iowa State University
- Lafayette College
- Lehigh University
- Massachusetts Institute of Technology
- Michigan Technological University
- Missouri University of Science and Technology
- Montana Technological University
- New Jersey Institute of Technology
- North Carolina State University
- Ohio Northern University
- Oregon State University
- Princeton University
- Purdue University—West Lafayette
- Rochester Institute of Technology
- Rose-Hulman Institute of Technology
- Stanford University
- Stevens Institute of Technology
- United States Military Academy
- University of California—Berkeley
- University of Illinois at Urbana-Champaign
- University of Maryland, Baltimore County
- University of Michigan—Ann Arbor
- Virginia Tech
- Worcester Polytechnic Institute

Great Schools for Nursing Majors

- Angelo State University
- Baylor University
- Bellarmine University
- Creighton University
- Calvin University
- The Catholic University of America
- Drexel University
- Duke University
- Duquesne University
- East Carolina University
- Emory University
- Fairfield University
- Florida Southern College
- Indiana University of Pennsylvania
- Loyola University Chicago
- Montana Technological University
- Ohio Northern University
- The Ohio State University—Columbus
- Saint Anselm College
- Saint Louis University
- Salve Regina University
- Texas Christian University
- The University of Alabama—Tuscaloosa
- University of Delaware
- University of Louisville
- University of North Carolina at Chapel Hill
- University of North Dakota
- University of Pennsylvania
- University of Rhode Island
- University of Wyoming
- Villanova University
- Washington State University
- Xavier University (OH)

Great Schools for Political Science/Government Majors

- American University
- Amherst College
- Bard College
- Bates College
- Bowdoin College
- Brigham Young University (UT)
- Bryn Mawr College
- Bucknell University
- Carleton College
- Claremont McKenna College
- Clark University
- Colby College
- College of the Holy Cross
- Colorado College
- Columbia University
- Connecticut College
- Dartmouth College
- Davidson College
- Dickinson College
- Drew University
- Franklin & Marshall College
- Furman University
- George Mason University
- The George Washington University
- Georgetown University
- Gettysburg College
- Gonzaga University
- Grinnell College
- Harvard College
- Kenyon College
- Macalester College
- Princeton University
- Scripps College
- Skidmore College
- Stanford University
- Swarthmore College
- Syracuse University
- Trinity College (CT)
- University of Arizona
- University of California—Berkeley
- University of California—Los Angeles
- University of Washington
- University of Wisconsin—Madison
- Vassar College
- Wake Forest University
- Washington and Lee University
- William & Mary
- Yale University

Great Schools for Psychology Majors

- Agnes Scott College
- Albion College
- Allegheny College
- Assumption University
- Barnard College
- Bates College
- Bucknell University
- Carleton College
- Carnegie Mellon University
- Christopher Newport University
- City University of New York—Brooklyn College
- City University of New York—City College
- City University of New York—Hunter College
- City University of New York—Queens College
- Clark University
- Coe College
- College of the Holy Cross
- Colorado State University
- Columbia University
- Cornell University
- Dartmouth College
- DePaul University
- Duke University
- Earlham College
- Eugene Lang College of Liberal Arts at The New School
- Flagler College
- Florida State University
- Franklin & Marshall College
- George Mason University
- Gettysburg College
- Hampton University
- Hanover College
- Harvard College
- James Madison University
- Le Moyne College
- Lewis & Clark College
- Loyola University Chicago
- Loyola University New Orleans
- Moravian University
- Mount Holyoke College
- New York University
- The Ohio State University—Columbus
- Ohio Wesleyan University
- Pitzer College
- Portland State University
- Princeton University
- Quinnipiac University
- Randolph College
- Roanoke College
- Rowan University
- St. Mary's College of Maryland
- Siena University
- Simmons University
- Smith College
- Spelman College
- Stanford University
- State University of New York at Geneseo
- State University of New York—University at Albany
- Stetson University
- Stonehill College
- Temple University
- Texas A&M University—College Station
- Union College (NY)
- University of Arizona

- University of California—Davis
- University of California—Los Angeles
- University of California—Merced
- University of California—Riverside
- University of California—Santa Barbara
- University of California—Santa Cruz
- University of Connecticut
- University of Florida
- University of Houston
- University of Idaho
- University of Mary Washington
- University of Maryland, College Park
- University of Massachusetts—Amherst
- University of Michigan—Ann Arbor
- University of Minnesota—Twin Cities
- The University of Montana—Missoula
- University of Nebraska—Lincoln
- University of Pittsburgh—Pittsburgh Campus
- University of Puget Sound
- University of San Francisco
- The University of South Dakota
- University of South Florida
- University of Southern California
- University of Tennessee—Knoxville
- University of Texas at Austin
- University of Utah
- Vassar College
- Washington & Jefferson College
- Washington College
- Washington University in St. Louis
- Wesleyan University
- Xavier University of Louisiana
- Yale University

How We Produce This Book

This Year's Edition

In the 35 years since the first edition of this book, our *Best Colleges* guide has grown considerably. We've added more than 140 colleges to the guide and deleted a fair share along the way. How we choose the schools for the book, and how we produce it, however, has not changed significantly over the years (with the exception of how we conduct our student survey—more on this follows).

To determine which schools will be in each edition, we don't use mathematical calculations or formulas. Instead we rely on a wide range of input, both quantitative and qualitative. Every year we collect data from more than 2,000 colleges that we use for our complete search index of colleges (princetonreview.com/college-search) and *Best Value Colleges* (princetonreview.com/college-rankings/best-value-colleges), this book, and our online profiles of schools. We visit dozens of colleges and meet with their admissions officers, deans, presidents, and college students. We talk with hundreds of high school counselors, parents, and students. Colleges also submit information to us requesting consideration for inclusion in the book. As a result, we are able to maintain a constantly evolving list of colleges to consider adding to the book. Any college we add to the guide, however, must agree to support our efforts to survey its students via our anonymous student survey. (Sometimes a college's administrative protocols will not allow it to participate in our student survey; this has caused some academically outstanding schools to be absent from the guide.) Finally, we work to ensure that our roster of colleges in the book presents a wide representation of institutions by region, character, and type. Here you'll find profiles of public and private schools, Historically Black Colleges and Universities, men's and women's colleges, science- and technology-focused institutions, nontraditional colleges, highly selective schools, and some with virtually open-door admissions policies.

"We worked to create a guide that would help people who couldn't always get to the campus nonetheless get in-depth campus feedback to find the schools best for them."

For this year's edition, we added four schools to this guide: Adelphi University, Capital University, Montclair State University, and The University of North Carolina—Charlotte.

The narratives in this edition are based on our surveys of 172,000 students attending the 392 colleges in the book. We surveyed about 439 students per campus on average, though that number varies depending on the size of the student population. We've surveyed thousands of students from institutions of many different sizes and types, including Clemson University, the University of Virginia, and the United States Naval Academy.

All of the institutions in this guide are academically terrific in our opinion. The 392 schools featured—our picks of the cream of the crop colleges and universities—comprise only the top 14 percent of the approximately 2,800 four-year colleges in the nation. These are all very different schools with many different and wonderful things to offer. We hope you will use this book as a starting point (it will certainly give you a snapshot of what life is like at these schools), but not as the final word on any one school. Check out other resources. Visit as many colleges as you can. Talk to students at those colleges—ask what they love and what bothers them most about their schools. Finally, form your own opinions about the colleges you are considering. At the end of the day, it's what YOU think about the schools that matters most, and that will enable you to answer that all-important question: "Which college is best for me?"

About Our Student Survey for Our *Best Colleges* Books

Surveying tens of thousands of students on hundreds of campuses is a large undertaking. In 1992, when we published the first edition of this book, we had surveyed an average of 120 students on each of the 250 campuses we profiled. We conducted that survey in person on the college campuses, setting up tables in central locations at which students filled out the surveys. Sometimes in order for us to collect surveys from a wide range of students, first years to seniors, this process took place over several days and at a variety of campus locations.

As you might imagine, today all of our surveys are completed online. The process is more efficient, secure, and representative, and we are able to gather opinions from far more students per college than we had reached previously. The average number of student surveys (per college) upon which our ranking lists are annually tallied is now 439 students per campus (and at some schools we hear from more than 5,000 students).

Our student survey is also now a continuous process. Students submit surveys online from all schools in the book and they can submit their surveys at any time during the academic year at princetonreview.com/studentsurvey. (Our site will accept only one survey from a student per academic year per school.) We also officially conduct surveys of students at each school in the book once every three years, on average, working with administrators to reach out to their students. We conduct these surveys more often than once every three years if the colleges request that we do so (and we can accommodate their request) or if we deem it necessary to capture dramatic changes on a campus. And of course, surveys we receive from students outside of their schools' normal survey cycles are always factored into the subsequent year's ranking calculations, so our pool of student survey data is continuously refreshed.

The survey has almost 100 questions in four main sections: "About Yourself," "Your School's Academics/Administration," "Students," and "Life at Your School." We ask about all sorts of things, from "How many out-of-class hours do you spend studying each day?" to "How do you rate your campus food?" Most questions offer an answer choice on a five-point scale: students fill in one of five boxes on a grid with headers varying by topic (e.g., a range from "Excellent" to "Awful"). Once the surveys have been completed and responses stored in our database, every college is given a score (similar to a GPA) for its students' answers to each question. This score enables us to compare student opinions from college to college and to tally the ranking lists. Most of the lists are based on students' answers to one survey question; some lists are based on answers to several survey questions. But all of our 50 ranking lists are based entirely on our student survey results.

Once we have the student survey information in hand, we write the college profiles. Student quotations in each profile come from our surveys (eight survey questions invite the students to tell us in their own words what they think about various aspects of their student body and campus experiences). We chose quotations that represent sentiments expressed by the majority of survey respondents from the college, or that illustrate one side or another of a mixed bag of student opinion, in which case there will also appear a counterpoint within the text. We send draft profiles to administrative contacts at each school for comments and corrections. We take careful measures to review the school's suggestions against the student survey data we collected and make appropriate changes when warranted.

How This Book Is Organized

Each of the colleges and universities in this book has its own two-page profile. To make it easier to find and compare information about the schools, we've used the same profile format for every school. At the very top of the profile, you will see the school's address and telephone number for the admissions office, the telephone number for the financial aid office, and the school's website and/or email address. On the right-hand side of the first page, you'll see a Survey Snapshot that provides three topics that students showed a higher consensus of opinion about when answering their surveys. On the second page, you'll see a QR code that will take you directly to our online profile of the school, where you can save and compare schools. On the outside of each page is a sidebar (narrow column) primarily containing statistics. These two sidebars are divided into six categories: Ratings, Campus Life, Campus Mental Health Services, Academics, Selectivity, and Financial Facts. The remainder of each page contains the school's narrative profile, divided into three sections—Students Say, The Princeton Review Says, and The School Says—drawing from student voices, our analysis of the data, and the school's own perspective.

What Each Section Covers

Each school profile is made up of four sections: The Sidebars, Students Say, The Princeton Review Says, and The School Says. Here's what you'll find in each part:

The Sidebars

The sidebars contain various statistics culled from our surveys of students attending the school and from questionnaires that school administrators complete at our request in the fall of each year. The six categories shown in the sidebars are in all caps, each followed by its associated data fields and descriptions. Keep in mind that not all data fields will appear for every school—in some cases, the information is not reported or not applicable. An NR (Not Reported) in the sidebars indicates that the school did not provide data for that field.

RATINGS

We compile the eight ratings—Quality of Life, Fire Safety, Green, Academic, Profs Interesting, Profs Accessible, Admissions, and Financial Aid—listed in the sidebars based on the results from our student surveys and/or institutional data we collect from school administrators.

Ratings are on a scale of 60–99. A rating of 60* (60 with an asterisk) means the school did not report enough underlying data points by our deadline for us to calculate an accurate rating. (These data points are described in the ratings explanations.)

Note that because the Admission Rating is a factor used to calculate the Academic Rating, a school with a 60* Admissions Rating may have an Academic Rating that is lower than it might otherwise have been.

Ratings are designed to compare colleges within this edition only. Because our calculation methods may change from year to year, ratings from this edition should not be compared to those in any previous or future edition.

These ratings are numerical measures that show how each school compares to others on a fixed scale.

Quality of Life Rating

On a scale of 60–99, this rating measures how happy students are with their campus experience outside the classroom. It is based on students' survey responses across the following factors:

- Overall happiness; campus beauty, safety, and location; dorm comfort; food quality; ease of navigating campus and administration; student friendliness; and interaction among different student groups and the wider community

Fire Safety Rating

On a scale of 60–99, this rating measures how well prepared a school is to prevent or respond to campus fires, specifically in residence halls. We asked schools several questions about their efforts to ensure fire safety for campus residents. We developed the questions in consultation with the Center for Campus Fire Safety (myccfs.org). Each school's responses to seven questions were considered when calculating its Fire Safety Rating. They cover:

1. The percentage of student housing sleeping rooms protected by an automatic fire sprinkler system with a fire sprinkler head located in the individual sleeping rooms
2. The percentage of student housing sleeping rooms equipped with a smoke detector connected to a supervised fire alarm system
3. The number of malicious fire alarms that occur in student housing per year
4. The number of unwanted fire alarms that occur in student housing per year
5. The banning of certain hazardous items and activities in residence halls, like candles, smoking, halogen lamps, etc.
6. The percentage of student housing fire alarm systems that, if activated, result in a signal being transmitted to a monitored location, where security investigates before notifying the fire department
7. The percentage of student housing fire alarm systems that, if activated, result in a signal being transmitted immediately to a continuously monitored location

Schools that did not report answers to a sufficient number of questions receive a Fire Safety Rating of 60* (60 with an asterisk). On page 50 of this book, you'll find a list of the schools with a score of 99 (the highest score) in this category.

Green Rating

Each year, we ask schools a series of questions to assess their overall commitment to environmental responsibility. The questions cover three areas:

- Whether students enjoy a healthy and sustainable quality of life on campus
- How well the school prepares students for careers in the clean energy economy and for engaged citizenship in a world facing environmental challenges
- How environmentally responsible the school's policies are

Additionally, The Princeton Review has partnered with the Association for the Advancement of Sustainability in Higher Education (AASHE) to streamline the reporting process for schools that participate in multiple higher education sustainability assessments, reducing the time campus staff spend tracking data and completing surveys.

The Princeton Review's Green Rating, on a scale of 60–99, is calculated from schools' responses to the following questions:

1. **Food sourcing:** What percentage of food expenditures goes toward local, organic, or otherwise environmentally preferable food?
2. **Transportation options:** Does the school offer programs such as mass transit, bike sharing, car sharing, carpooling, carpool/vanpool matching, cash-out parking, anti-idling policies, telecommuting, or condensed work weeks?
3. **Sustainability committee:** Does the school have a formal sustainability committee that includes student participation?
4. **Green building standards:** Were buildings constructed or majorly renovated in the past three years LEED (Leadership in Energy and Environmental Design) certified?
5. **Waste diversion:** What is the school's overall waste-diversion rate?
6. **Environmental studies:** Does the school offer an environmental studies major, minor, or concentration?
7. **Sustainability outcomes:** Do any degree programs include sustainability as a required learning outcome?
8. **Greenhouse gas plan:** Does the school have a formal plan to reduce its greenhouse gas emissions?
9. **Renewable energy:** What percentage of the school's energy consumption comes from renewable sources?
10. **Sustainability officer:** Does the school employ a dedicated full-time sustainability officer?

Schools that did not provide sufficient responses to allow a fair comparison receive a Green Rating of 60*. On page 51 of this book and on our website at princetonreview.com/college-rankings/green-guide/green-honor-roll, you'll find a list of the schools with 99 (the highest score) Green Ratings.

Check out our free resource, The Princeton Review's Guide to Green Colleges at princetonreview.com/green-guide.

Academic Rating

On a scale of 60–99, this rating measures academic intensity: how hard students work and how strong the overall learning environment is. It is based on student surveys and administrator data, and takes into account:

- Hours students report studying outside of class each day
- Students' assessments of professors' teaching ability and accessibility
- Quality of school facilities
- Student-to-faculty ratio
- Amount of class time spent in discussion
- Caliber of the student body, as measured by admissions statistics

Profs Interesting Rating

On a scale of 60–99, this rating is based on levels of surveyed students' agreement or disagreement with this statement: "Your instructors are good teachers."

Profs Accessible Rating

On a scale of 60–99, this rating is based on levels of surveyed students' agreement or disagreement with this statement: "Your instructors are accessible outside the classroom."

Admissions Rating

On a scale of 60–99, this rating is a measure of how competitive admission is at the school. This rating is determined by several factors, including the high school class rank of entering first-year students, test scores, and percentage of applicants accepted.

Financial Aid Rating

On a scale of 60–99, this rating measures both the financial aid a school awards and students' satisfaction with their aid packages. It is based on school-reported financial aid data and students' survey responses to, "If you receive financial aid, how satisfied are you with your financial aid package?" A list of schools with a score of 99 (highest score) can be found on page 50. Tuition-free schools are not rated.

CAMPUS LIFE

Type of school

Whether the school is public or private.

Affiliation

Any religious order with which the school is affiliated.

Environment

The type of school environment, based on population and setting.

- Rural (In or near a rural community, pop. under 5,000)
- Village (In a small town, pop. 5,000–24,999, or near a small town)
- Town (In a large town, pop. 25,000–74,999, or near a large town)
- City (In a small/medium city, pop. 75,000–299,999, or within its metropolitan area)
- Metropolis (In a major city, pop. 300,000 or more, or within its metropolitan area)

Students

Degree-seeking undergrad enrollment

The total number of degree-seeking undergraduates who attend the school.

"% male / female / not reported" through "# countries represented"

This section provides demographic and other information about the degree-seeking undergraduate student body, including:

- Ethnicity
- Number of countries represented
- Percentages of students who are from in state, out of state, attended a public high school, live on campus as first-year students, and belong to Greek organizations

Please note that the Common Data Set does not offer "another gender" as an option, and so we are only able to provide "male," "female," or "not reported" as responses, and these numbers, which are rounded, may not always add up to 100%. Additionally, while the data in this book generally serves as an accurate project for the coming years, judicial and executive branch shifts with regard to affirmative action and DEI may result in unexpected demographic shifts.

CAMPUS MENTAL HEALTH SERVICES

Six services are listed—ranging from "Offers mental health/wellness program" to "Mental health/well-being courses"—with a yes/no indicator of whether that service or program is available. This data has been collected annually in partnership with the Ruderman Foundation since 2024. Schools that did not respond are marked NR (Not Reported).

ACADEMICS

% students returning for sophomore year

The percentage of degree-seeking first-year students returning for sophomore year.

% students graduating within 4 years

The percentage of degree-seeking undergraduate students graduating in four years or less.

% students graduating within 6 years

The percentage of degree-seeking undergraduate students graduating in six years or less.

Calendar

Academic calendar format or schedule:

- **Semester:** Two long terms, typically starting in September and January
- **Trimester:** Three terms, usually one before winter break and two after
- **Quarter:** Four terms, each typically lasting nine or ten weeks, including exams
- **4-1-4:** Two standard semesters with a month-long term in between
- **4-4-1:** Two longer semesters followed by a short term

For details, contact the school's admissions office.

Student/faculty ratio

The ratio of full-time undergraduate instructional faculty members to all undergraduates.

Most common class size; Most common lab size

The most common class size for regular courses and for labs/discussion sections, and the percentage of all classes that fall into that size range.

Most Popular Majors

The three majors with the highest enrollments at the school.

Applicants Also Look At

These lists show schools that applicants also look at and often, sometimes, and rarely choose over this school. The data comes directly from colleges, which track where their accepted applicants also applied and which school those applicants ultimately chose. Admissions officers can review and update these lists each year.

SELECTIVITY

of applicants (total / in-state / out-of-state / international)

The total number of all applicants, as well as the total number of in-state, out-of-state, and international applicants.

% of applicants accepted (total / in-state / out-of-state / international)

The percentage of applicants accepted for each group, based on that group's total number of applicants: overall, in-state, out-of-state, and international.

% of total acceptees attending

The percentage of accepted students who enrolled at the school.

of early decision applicants

The number of students who applied under the college's early decision plan.

% of early decision applicants accepted

The percentage of early decision applicants who were admitted under this plan. Since early decision is binding, nearly all admitted students enroll.

offered a place on the wait list

The number of qualified applicants offered a place on a college's wait list.

admitted from wait list

The number of waitlisted applicants who were offered admission. This figure varies widely by school and is worth considering when deciding whether to accept a place on a waitlist.

First-Year Profile

The numbers in this section apply only to the students who were accepted and chose to attend.

Testing policy

Some colleges require certain applicants, like homeschooled or international students, to submit scores, so check the testing policies of the schools you're applying to.

Test Flexible allows students to choose which type of test(s) to submit, such as SAT, AP, IB, and other exam scores. You should check with those schools on a case-by-case basis.

Test Free, sometimes referred to as Test Blind, means that the school will not look at or consider your scores in any capacity.

Test Optional means that schools will consider your scores if you choose to submit them, and we recommend that students do so, as this can sometimes be key in discussions of merit aid. There are a few schools designated as Test Optional with an exclamation point (**!**), meaning students can apply without submitting test scores as long as meet certain requirements.

Test Required means that one of the tests listed (usually SAT, ACT, or CLT) is required for your application.

Range of SAT and ACT scores

The middle 50 percent range of test scores for entering first-year students. (EBRW refers to the Evidence-Based Reading and Writing section.)

We made the above information available to contacts at each school for review and approval. You may also cross-reference our print profiles with our online school profiles at PrincetonReview.com, which list the most up-to-date data as reported by schools.

Don't be discouraged from applying to the school of your choice even if your combined test scores are below the average, because you may still have a chance of getting in. Remember that many schools value other aspects of your application (e.g., your grades, how good a match you make with the school) more heavily than test scores.

% submitting SAT / ACT scores

The percentage of applicants who submitted SAT or ACT scores for admission.

Average HS GPA / % submitting HS GPA

The average grade point average of entering first-year students, typically reported on an unweighted 1.0–4.0 scale, though some schools use a weighted 1.0–5.0 scale. (A few of the schools report averages on a 100-point scale.) GPA is one of the key factors in college admissions. The percentage indicates the share of students who submitted one.

% graduated top 10%, top 25%, top 50% of class

Of those students for whom class rank was reported, the percentage of entering first-year students who ranked in the top tenth, quarter, and half of their high school classes.

% submitting high school rank

The percentage of students who submitted their rank in their applications.

Important Dates

Early decision, early action, and regular application deadlines / notifications

The dates by which all materials must be postmarked (we suggest "received in the office") in order to be considered for admission under each particular admissions option/cycle for matriculation in the fall term. This section also includes, if schools provide it, the expected dates for notifications about a decision on your application.

Rolling admission means that applications will be evaluated as they are received versus the school waiting to review all applications until after a hard deadline. Rolling notification means that students will be notified of admission on an ongoing basis. If a specific date is listed, that is the date on which rolling reviews or notifications begin.

Nonfall registration

Whether or not the school allows students to enroll at times other than the fall term.

FINANCIAL FACTS

Throughout this section, if two numbers are given, one in parentheses, the first number is for the overall population of undergrads and the second number is more specifically for first-years. Data marked with a star (*) reflect the most recent available figures, which may not correspond to the current reporting period.

Annual tuition

The tuition at the school. For public colleges, the cost of tuition is provided for both residents of that school's state and for nonresidents. In-state tuition is typically much lower than out-of-state tuition.

Food and housing

Estimated annual costs.

Required fees

Any additional costs students must pay beyond tuition and housing in order to attend the school. These typically include fees such as a student activity fee or a technology fee. In a few rare cases, this field may also bundle in books and supplies, housing, tuition, or other expenses, and may be called a comprehensive fee. If the amount in this field seems unusually large, contact the school for an exact breakdown.

Books and supplies

Estimated annual cost of necessary textbooks and/or supplies.

Average need-based scholarship

The average need-based scholarship and grant aid awarded to students with financial need.

% students with need receiving need-based scholarship or grant aid

The percentage of all degree-seeking undergraduates who were determined to have financial need and received any need-based scholarship or grant.

% students with need receiving non-need-based scholarship or grant aid

The percentage of all degree-seeking undergraduates, determined to have financial need, receiving any non-need-based scholarship or grant aid.

% students with need receiving need-based self-help aid

The percentage of all degree-seeking undergraduates, determined to have financial need, who received any need-based self-help aid (essentially loans or work-study or jobs from institutional, state, or federal sources).

% students receiving any financial aid

The percentage of all degree-seeking undergraduate students receiving any financial aid (need-based, merit-based, gift aid).

% UG borrow to pay for school

The percentage who borrowed at any time through any loan programs (institutional, state, Federal Perkins, Federal Subsidized and Unsubsidized, private loans that were certified by your institution, etc., excluding parent loans). Includes both Federal Direct Student Loans and Federal Family Education Loans.

Average cumulative indebtedness

The average cumulative principal borrowed by those undergraduates who took out any loan at any time (Federal Perkins, Federal Subsidized and Unsubsidized, Federal Direct Student Loans, Federal Family Loans, and any institutional, state, or private loans that institution is aware of).

The statistical data reported in this book, unless otherwise noted, was collected from the profiled colleges from the fall of 2025 through the spring of 2026. In some cases, schools did not provide the necessary data in time for publication despite our repeated requests. Because enrollment figures, financial statistics, and application and financial aid deadlines change from year to year, we recommend verifying all information directly with the school before applying.

% of students with need fully met

The percentage of students, determined to have financial need, whose needs were fully met (excludes PLUS loans, unsubsidized loans, and private alternative loans).

Average % of student need met

On average, the percentage of financial need that was met for students who were awarded any need-based aid. Excludes any aid that was awarded in excess of need as well as any resources that were awarded to replace EFC (PLUS loans, unsubsidized loans, and private alternative loans).

STUDENTS SAY

This section shares the straight-from-the-campus feedback we get from the school's most important customers: the students attending them. It summarizes opinions from surveyed students, from first-years through seniors, and includes direct quotes from them and school-provided statistics where relevant. Students Say is divided into three subsections:

Academics

How hard students work and how satisfied they are with their education, including which programs and departments received the highest marks, how professors interact with students, and student opinions on school resources and career guidance

Campus Life

Life outside the classroom, covering everything from food quality to the popularity of Greek life, with students describing their on- and off-campus social lives

Student Body

The types of students the school attracts, how competitive or collaborative the student culture is, and how students perceive interaction among different groups

THE PRINCETON REVIEW SAYS

Admissions

This section lets you know which aspects of your application are most important to the admissions officers at the school. It also lists the high school curricular prerequisites for applicants, which standardized tests (if any) are required, and special information about the school's admissions process (e.g., do minority students and legacies, for example, receive special consideration?).

Financial Aid

Here you'll find out what you need to know about the financial aid process at the school, namely what forms you need and what types of merit-based aid and loans are available. Information about need-based aid is contained in the financial aid sidebar. This section includes specific deadline dates for submission of materials as reported by the colleges. We strongly encourage students seeking financial aid to file all forms—federal, state, and institutional—carefully, fully, and on time.

The Inside Word

This section gives you the inside scoop on what it takes to gain admission to the school. It reflects our own insights about each school's admissions process and acceptance trends. (We visit scores of colleges each year and talk with hundreds of admissions officers in order to glean this info.) It also incorporates information from institutional data we collect and our surveys over the years of students at the school.

THE SCHOOL SAYS

From the Admissions Office

This section, written by the school's admissions office, highlights what they most want prospective students to know about the institution.

About Our College Ranking Lists

Finding a college with terrific academics is easy. Out of the thousands of schools you might attend, there are hundreds that offer high-level courses across the board. Hundreds more have specialized programs that are among the best in their field. Finding those schools is sometimes just a matter of searching out professors that you want to learn from or research with, majors that fascinate you, or unique learning opportunities—such as experiential curricula or studying abroad. Our 392 school profiles in this book note such opportunities—and more. Where those schools differ, however, is in their campus cultures, student bodies, and non-academic offerings. To that end, we feature in this book dozens of unique categories of ranking lists. They reveal distinctions about the colleges in matters that may be vitally important to you.

Our 50 ranking lists are entirely based on our surveys of 172,000 students at the colleges in our book.

Though some members of the media, the public, and school administrators attribute these rankings to us at The Princeton Review (indeed, we are the company that tallies and reports them), these lists do not reflect our opinion of the schools. It's the way in which students communicate to us what they think of their experiences at their schools that determine on which lists schools appear. Our lists are not based on *our* estimate of how interesting a school's professors are or how generous the school is with financial aid or how good the campus food is.

Our 50 ranking lists are entirely based on our *surveys of the 172,000 students at the colleges* in our book. We ask them almost 100 questions about everything from how they rate their campus experiences to their POV about their school's campus culture and student body. (You'll find detailed information about our student survey and the methodology for our ranking lists on our website at princetonreview.com/college-rankings/ranking-methodology.)

It is *what their students tell us* about their experiences at these schools that determines on which lists the schools appear.

Note: our *choice* of the 392 schools in this book *is* largely based on our opinion of the schools' academics. Only about 14 percent of the nation's four-year colleges are in the book. *In our view,* each one offers an outstanding undergraduate education. We consider these schools the "best" in the nation—academically (hence the word "Best" in our book's title). It is *what their students tell us* about their experiences at these schools that determines on which lists the schools appear.

The way in which we report our ranking lists has also evolved over time. Based on over 9,000 responses from our annual College Hopes & Worries Surveys, we focused on the 10 campus topics that mattered most to those searching for a best-fit college. The areas they indicated were of highest importance to them were academics, financial aid, amenities and facilities, campus services (including career, health, and wellness), and insights about the campus culture and student body. From that feedback, we have developed new lists. In 2025, we added a list for the "Most Politically Moderate Students," and this year, we've added one for "Great Outdoors: Students Get Outside."

We have also made two significant changes in our remaining ranking lists. First, we trimmed the number of them from 62 to 50 (and renamed some for clarity). Then, for the remaining lists, we increased the number of schools on each from 20 to 25. Because this allowed us to name more schools per category, we were able to better shine a light on some Best schools that hadn't made our previous lists. (More than two-thirds of the 392 schools in this book appear on one of our "top 25" lists.)

These decisions are compatible with our long-standing commitment to *not* rank the colleges in this book hierarchically on academics or on any other topic (in the case of this edition from 1 to 392). Our 50 categories of lists of top 25 ranking colleges in this book are presented as an alternative to mega-list one-topic-fits-all rankings. As Rob Franek, our editor-in-chief and lead author of this book, has said for many years, hundreds of times in interviews as well as in talks he gives to college applicants and their parents, "It's not, 'Which college is best?' but 'Which college is best for YOU' that matters."

This book exists to give applicants and parents information that goes beyond academics and that provides more focused information about a college's offerings and character to help an applicant decide—on a very personal level—whether it's the right (or wrong!) school for them.

This book exists to give applicants and parents information that goes beyond academics and that provides more focused information about a college's offerings and character to help an applicant decide—on a very personal level—whether it's the right (or wrong!) school for them.

We close with a grateful note to the college officials, counselors, advisors, students, and parents who have made this annual guide possible for thirty-plus years. Our ranking lists, rating scores, and profiles have factored in data from more than 2 million students and tens of thousands of administrators. To all who have completed our past surveys and all who will complete them this year: thank you. Your input is essential to our book. We have heard from many students who told us that without our book, they might never have considered the schools that were their "best fit" colleges, schools which they have since become outstanding applicants to and alumni of!

We wish you all the best *on your* college journey.

WE WANT TO HEAR FROM YOU

To all of our readers, we welcome your feedback on how we can continue to improve this guide. We hope you will share with us your comments, questions, and suggestions. Please contact us at editorialsupport@review.com. We welcome it.

To college applicants, we wish you all the best in your college search. And when you get to your campuses and settle in to your college life, come back to us online; participate in our survey for this book at princetonreview.com/college-rankings/student-survey. Let your honest comments about your schools guide prospective students who want your help answering the $64,000 question (goodness knows, the sticker price at some schools may be that high or even higher!): "Which is the best college for me?"

PART 2

School Rankings and Lists

We present our 50 "Top 25" ranking lists in seven categories.

Academics/Administration

Quality of Life

Politics

Campus Life

Town Life

Extracurriculars

Social Scene

Honor Rolls

Best Value Colleges

Best Colleges for Game Design Rankings

Best Colleges for Entrepreneurship Studies Rankings

Under each list heading, we tell you the survey question or assessment that we used to tabulate the list. We tally student responses to several questions on our survey for our lists "Best Classroom Experience," "Best Quality of Life," and "Green Matters: Everyone Cares About Conservation." Be aware that these 50 ranking lists are based entirely on student surveys. They do not reflect our opinions of the schools. They are entirely the result of what students attending these schools tell us about them: It's how students rate their own schools and what they report to us about their campus experiences at them that make our ranking lists so unusual. After all, what better way is there to judge a school than by what its customers—its students—say about it?

ACADEMICS/ADMINISTRATION

Best Classroom Experience

Based on student ratings of their professors, lab facilities, the percent of classes they attend, and the amount of in-class discussion.

1. Reed College
2. Franklin W. Olin College of Engineering
3. Carleton College
4. Elon University
5. Washington and Lee University
6. Wellesley College
7. Bennington College
8. St. Olaf College
9. Denison University
10. Claremont McKenna College
11. Earlham College
12. Thomas Aquinas College (CA)
13. Wabash College
14. University of Richmond
15. The University of the South
16. Harvey Mudd College
17. Grinnell College
18. Bryn Mawr College
19. St. John's College (MD)
20. Sarah Lawrence College
21. Pitzer College
22. Rollins College
23. United States Naval Academy
24. Wofford College
25. High Point University

Students Study the Most

Based on student ratings of how many hours they spend studying outside of class each day.

1. Massachusetts Institute of Technology
2. California Institute of Technology
3. Harvey Mudd College
4. Franklin W. Olin College of Engineering
5. Princeton University
6. Claremont McKenna College
7. Williams College
8. Reed College
9. Carleton College
10. Rose-Hulman Institute of Technology
11. Wellesley College
12. Grinnell College
13. Middlebury College
14. Amherst College
15. Bowdoin College
16. Centre College
17. College of the Atlantic
18. Lafayette College
19. Washington University in St. Louis
20. The University of Chicago
21. Rice University
22. Bryn Mawr College
23. St. John's College (NM)
24. Hillsdale College
25. Wesleyan University

Professors Get High Marks

Based on student ratings of their professors.

1. Franklin W. Olin College of Engineering
2. Reed College
3. Wesleyan University
4. Sarah Lawrence College
5. Bard College
6. Southwestern University
7. Middlebury College
8. Carleton College
9. Harvey Mudd College
10. Claremont McKenna College
11. Thomas Aquinas College (CA)
12. St. John's College (NM)
13. University of San Diego
14. St. John's College (MD)
15. University of Dallas
16. Bennington College
17. Macalester College
18. The University of the South
19. Earlham College
20. Wellesley College
21. Mount Holyoke College
22. Washington and Lee University
23. Elon University
24. College of the Atlantic
25. Smith College

Most Accessible Professors

Based on student ratings of how accessible their professors are outside of the classroom.

1. Middlebury College
2. St. John's College (MD)
3. United States Naval Academy
4. Thomas Aquinas College (CA)
5. Claremont McKenna College
6. Juniata College
7. Hobart and William Smith Colleges
8. Harvey Mudd College
9. Wabash College
10. Denison University
11. Washington and Lee University
12. Earlham College
13. Vanderbilt University
14. Lafayette College
15. The University of the South
16. University of Richmond
17. St. Lawrence University
18. Carleton College
19. Colby College
20. Allegheny College
21. Franklin W. Olin College of Engineering
22. University of San Diego
23. Grove City College
24. Reed College
25. Mount Holyoke College

Best Science Lab Facilities

Based on student ratings of their school's science lab facilities.

1. Union College (NY)
2. St. Lawrence University
3. California Institute of Technology
4. Harvey Mudd College
5. Ripon College
6. Claremont McKenna College
7. Denison University
8. United States Naval Academy
9. Hampden-Sydney College
10. Lehigh University
11. Trinity University
12. University of St. Francis (IL)
13. Bates College
14. Rose-Hulman Institute of Technology
15. College of Wooster
16. Carleton College
17. Santa Clara University
18. The University of Chicago
19. Washington University in St. Louis
20. Hamilton College
21. Juniata College
22. Skidmore College
23. Pitzer College
24. University of San Diego
25. Lafayette College

Best Health Services

Based on student ratings of the health services on campus.

1. The University of Chicago
2. University of Virginia
3. Vanderbilt University
4. University of San Diego
5. Wabash College
6. Salve Regina University
7. Rollins College
8. University of Richmond
9. California Institute of Technology
10. Xavier University (OH)
11. Lake Forest College
12. University of Arizona
13. Claremont McKenna College
14. University of Mary Washington
15. University of Texas at Austin
16. Washington State University
17. Babson College
18. James Madison University
19. Carleton College
20. Marquette University
21. Ripon College
22. Florida International University
23. California State University, Stanislaus
24. Gonzaga University
25. Trinity University

Best Student Support and Counseling Services

Based on students' assessments of counseling services available on campus.

1. Macalester College
2. Stevens Institute of Technology
3. The University of the South
4. St. Lawrence University
5. Seton Hall University
6. Elon University
7. Skidmore College
8. Xavier University (OH)
9. Texas Christian University
10. Columbia University
11. Sacred Heart University
12. Grove City College
13. Babson College
14. Rollins College
15. High Point University
16. Moravian University
17. Bentley University
18. Rice University
19. Nazareth University
20. John Carroll University
21. Mercer University
22. Hampden-Sydney College
23. Michigan Technological University
24. Worcester Polytechnic Institute
25. Wesleyan University

Best Career Services

Based on student ratings of their school's career and job placement services.

1. Bentley University
2. Washington and Lee University
3. Denison University
4. Claremont McKenna College
5. Lafayette College
6. St. Lawrence University
7. Rose-Hulman Institute of Technology
8. Northeastern University
9. Bryant University
10. Clemson University
11. University of San Diego
12. Elon University
13. Randolph-Macon College
14. High Point University
15. Grove City College
16. Coe College
17. Moravian University
18. Southwestern University
19. Wabash College
20. Washington University in St. Louis
21. Hampden-Sydney College
22. Fairfield University
23. The University of Chicago
24. Sacred Heart University
25. Brigham Young University (UT)

Best College Library

Based on student ratings of their library facilities.

1. Brigham Young University (UT)
2. Boston College
3. William & Mary
4. The University of Chicago
5. Hampden-Sydney College
6. The Ohio State University—Columbus
7. Lafayette College
8. Mount Holyoke College
9. Columbia University
10. University of San Diego
11. Reed College
12. University of Denver
13. Denison University
14. Lehigh University
15. Texas Christian University
16. Loyola Marymount University
17. Smith College
18. College of Wooster
19. Bryant University
20. United States Naval Academy
21. St. Lawrence University
22. Salve Regina University
23. University of Rochester
24. Clemson University
25. St. John's College (NM)

Great Financial Aid

Based on student ratings of overall satisfaction with their financial aid packages.

1. Washington and Lee University
2. Juniata College
3. Princeton University
4. Amherst College
5. Reed College
6. Vanderbilt University
7. Gettysburg College
8. Franklin W. Olin College of Engineering
9. St. Olaf College
10. Lafayette College
11. Columbia University
12. Washington University in St. Louis
13. Rice University
14. Denison University
15. Dickinson College
16. Trinity University
17. Thomas Aquinas College (CA)
18. Macalester College
19. College of the Atlantic
20. Gonzaga University
21. Kalamazoo College
22. Randolph-Macon College
23. St. Lawrence University
24. University of Dayton
25. Grinnell College

Financial Aid Not So Great

Based on student ratings of overall satisfaction with their financial aid packages.

1. New York University
2. University of Pittsburgh—Pittsburgh Campus
3. Michigan State University
4. University of California—Irvine
5. James Madison University
6. Eugene Lang College of Liberal Arts at The New School
7. Emerson College
8. University of California—Santa Cruz
9. Loyola Marymount University
10. State University of New York—Stony Brook University
11. Colorado State University
12. University of Massachusetts—Amherst
13. University of Utah
14. University of Oregon
15. University of Houston
16. State University of New York—University at Albany
17. University of Mary Washington
18. California State University, Stanislaus
19. University of Cincinnati
20. Clemson University
21. East Carolina University
22. Ohio University—Athens
23. Grove City College
24. William & Mary
25. Salisbury University

Best-Run Colleges

Based on student ratings of how smoothly their colleges are run.

1. Claremont McKenna College
2. United States Naval Academy
3. High Point University
4. Denison University
5. Bentley University
6. St. Lawrence University
7. Washington and Lee University
8. Rose-Hulman Institute of Technology
9. Brigham Young University (UT)
10. Clemson University
11. Texas Christian University
12. Elon University
13. Grove City College
14. Marquette University
15. University of Richmond
16. Bryant University
17. Randolph-Macon College
18. Coe College
19. Moravian University
20. Wabash College
21. Washington University in St. Louis
22. Hampden-Sydney College
23. The University of Chicago
24. Rice University
25. Taylor University

Green Matters: Everyone Cares About Conservation

Based on students' answers to survey questions, including how they rate administration and student support for environmental awareness and conservation efforts.

1. College of the Atlantic
2. State University of New York—College of Environmental Science and Forestry
3. Pitzer College
4. University of San Diego
5. St. Lawrence University
6. Mount Holyoke College
7. Macalester College
8. The University of the South
9. University of Vermont
10. Carleton College
11. Middlebury College
12. Warren Wilson College
13. Oberlin College
14. Harvey Mudd College
15. Smith College
16. Dickinson College
17. Bennington College
18. Gonzaga University
19. Skidmore College
20. Bowdoin College
21. American University
22. Wesleyan University
23. Colby College
24. Earlham College
25. Elon University

Their Students Love These Colleges

Based on student ratings of their overall satisfaction with their schools.

1. Vanderbilt University
2. University of San Diego
3. Juniata College
4. United States Naval Academy
5. Mount Holyoke College
6. Washington State University
7. Boston College
8. St. Lawrence University
9. Denison University
10. Elon University
11. Wabash College
12. Claremont McKenna College
13. Harvey Mudd College
14. James Madison University
15. William & Mary
16. Hillsdale College
17. Rice University
18. Carleton College
19. Babson College
20. The University of the South
21. Washington and Lee University
22. The University of Chicago
23. Bentley University
24. Texas Christian University
25. Clemson University

QUALITY OF LIFE

Happiest Students

Based on students' assessments of their own happiness.

1. Vanderbilt University
2. University of San Diego
3. Denison University
4. Taylor University
5. St. John's College (MD)
6. William & Mary
7. Washington and Lee University
8. Elon University
9. Texas Christian University
10. Hobart and William Smith Colleges
11. Clemson University
12. Boston College
13. Lafayette College
14. Thomas Aquinas College (CA)
15. Washington State University
16. Bryant University
17. University of Dallas
18. St. Lawrence University
19. Juniata College
20. The University of the South
21. James Madison University
22. Hillsdale College
23. Mount Holyoke College
24. University of Texas at Austin
25. Gonzaga University

Most Beautiful Campus

Based on student ratings of the beauty of their campuses.

1. University of San Diego
2. The University of the South
3. High Point University
4. Mount Holyoke College
5. Vanderbilt University
6. Salve Regina University
7. Lewis & Clark College
8. Rhodes College
9. Elon University
10. Texas Christian University
11. Berry College
12. Pepperdine University
13. Scripps College
14. James Madison University
15. Thomas Aquinas College (CA)
16. Reed College
17. Bennington College
18. Bryn Mawr College
19. University of California—Santa Cruz
20. College of the Atlantic
21. Washington University in St. Louis
22. University of Richmond
23. The University of Chicago
24. Rollins College
25. Loyola Marymount University

Great Outdoors: Students Get Outside

Based on students' answers to survey question: students take advantage of the outdoors

1. The University of the South
2. St. Lawrence University
3. College of the Atlantic
4. Washington and Lee University
5. United States Naval Academy
6. Colby College
7. Pitzer College
8. Bowdoin College
9. Middlebury College
10. Brigham Young University (UT)
11. Gonzaga University
12. University of Vermont
13. State University of New York—College of Environmental Science and Forestry
14. Clemson University
15. University of Portland
16. Berry College
17. William & Mary
18. Skidmore College
19. Florida Southern College
20. The University of Scranton
21. State University of New York at Geneseo
22. Quinnipiac University
23. McDaniel College
24. University of Oregon
25. Carleton College

Best Campus Food

Based on student ratings of the food at their colleges.

1. University of Massachusetts—Amherst
2. Bowdoin College
3. James Madison University
4. Harvey Mudd College
5. College of the Atlantic
6. University of San Diego
7. Vanderbilt University
8. Cornell University
9. Virginia Tech
10. Rollins College
11. Elon University
12. University of Richmond
13. Bates College
14. Sacred Heart University
15. University of Dayton
16. Mount Holyoke College
17. Fairfield University
18. Wesleyan University
19. University of Oregon
20. Florida International University
21. Bennington College
22. Whitman College
23. Claremont McKenna College
24. Rice University
25. Michigan State University

Campus Food Not So Tasty

Based on student ratings of the food on their campuses.

1. Clarkson University
2. Ohio Wesleyan University
3. Catawba College
4. Saint Joseph's University (PA)
5. Sarah Lawrence College
6. Hampden-Sydney College
7. Washington & Jefferson College
8. Lycoming College
9. Warren Wilson College
10. Randolph-Macon College
11. Connecticut College
12. Spelman College
13. Rensselaer Polytechnic Institute
14. University of California—Santa Cruz
15. Xavier University of Louisiana
16. William & Mary
17. Salve Regina University
18. Kettering University
19. Grinnell College
20. Trinity College (CT)
21. Coe College
22. Nazareth University
23. University of California—Merced
24. Macalester College
25. Worcester Polytechnic Institute

Best College Dorms

Based on student ratings of their dorms and residence halls.

1. Bowdoin College
2. Washington University in St. Louis
3. High Point University
4. Vanderbilt University
5. Washington and Lee University
6. Elon University
7. Franklin W. Olin College of Engineering
8. Mount Holyoke College
9. Scripps College
10. Sacred Heart University
11. Brigham Young University (UT)
12. The University of Chicago
13. University of San Diego
14. Pitzer College
15. Texas Christian University
16. Reed College
17. Washington State University
18. Bennington College
19. Rice University
20. Rose-Hulman Institute of Technology
21. Butler University
22. James Madison University
23. Rollins College
24. Amherst College
25. University of Oregon

College Dorms Not So Fancy

Based on student ratings of their dorms and residence halls.

1. New College of Florida
2. Xavier University of Louisiana
3. Catawba College
4. Simmons University
5. Connecticut College
6. Clarkson University
7. Warren Wilson College
8. Spelman College
9. University of California—Santa Cruz
10. Ohio Wesleyan University
11. Rochester Institute of Technology
12. Austin College
13. Rider University
14. Albion College
15. Siena University
16. Coe College
17. Michigan Technological University
18. Randolph-Macon College
19. Trinity College (CT)
20. Case Western Reserve University
21. University of Vermont
22. Rensselaer Polytechnic Institute
23. Dickinson College
24. Lycoming College
25. Ripon College

Best Quality of Life

Based on student ratings of the beauty, safety, and friendliness on campus, among other ratings.

1. University of San Diego
2. Vanderbilt University
3. Washington University in St. Louis
4. Texas Christian University
5. Claremont McKenna College
6. Denison University
7. Washington and Lee University
8. College of the Atlantic
9. Kansas State University
10. Brigham Young University (UT)
11. Rice University
12. University of Richmond
13. Taylor University
14. Emory University
15. United States Naval Academy
16. Boston College
17. Auburn University
18. Thomas Aquinas College (CA)
19. Grove City College
20. Harvey Mudd College
21. Stevens Institute of Technology
22. Rollins College
23. Clemson University
24. Elon University
25. Colorado State University

Friendliest Students

Based on how strongly students agree that their fellow students are extremely friendly.

1. William & Mary
2. Claremont McKenna College
3. Taylor University
4. St. Lawrence University
5. Carleton College
6. Denison University
7. Grove City College
8. Vanderbilt University
9. Rice University
10. Clemson University
11. Wabash College
12. Gonzaga University
13. Washington and Lee University
14. Hampden-Sydney College
15. United States Naval Academy
16. Washington State University
17. Hillsdale College
18. College of the Atlantic
19. Harvey Mudd College
20. The University of the South
21. Earlham College
22. Bowdoin College
23. Bryant University
24. Berry College
25. Mercer University

POLITICS

Most Politically Conservative Students

Based on students' assessments of their personal political views.

1. Texas Christian University
2. Hillsdale College
3. Grove City College
4. College of the Ozarks
5. Taylor University
6. University of Dallas
7. United States Naval Academy
8. The Catholic University of America
9. Hampden-Sydney College
10. Wabash College
11. Thomas Aquinas College (CA)
12. Baylor University
13. Florida Southern College
14. Clemson University
15. Bryant University
16. Brigham Young University (UT)
17. Pepperdine University
18. Randolph-Macon College
19. East Carolina University
20. Iona University
21. Xavier University (OH)
22. Juniata College
23. Monmouth University (NJ)
24. John Carroll University
25. Wofford College

Most Politically Liberal Students

Based on students' assessments of their personal political views.

1. Bennington College
2. Reed College
3. Mount Holyoke College
4. Bryn Mawr College
5. Lewis & Clark College
6. Sarah Lawrence College
7. Pitzer College
8. State University of New York—College of Environmental Science and Forestry
9. Eugene Lang College of Liberal Arts at The New School
10. Macalester College
11. Warren Wilson College
12. College of the Atlantic
13. Hollins University
14. Wesleyan University
15. Carleton College
16. Oberlin College
17. Skidmore College
18. University of Oregon
19. American University
20. University of Vermont
21. Clark University
22. University of Mary Washington
23. College of Wooster
24. Bowdoin College
25. Grinnell College

Most Politically Moderate Students

Based on students' assessments of their personal political views.

1. Manhattan University
2. James Madison University
3. Austin College
4. St. Lawrence University
5. University of Richmond
6. Lycoming College
7. Bucknell University
8. University of Houston
9. Coe College
10. University of New England
11. New Jersey Institute of Technology
12. The Ohio State University—Columbus
13. Stevens Institute of Technology
14. Rowan University
15. University of Cincinnati
16. Saint Joseph's University (PA)
17. The University of North Carolina—Charlotte
18. Wagner College
19. North Carolina State University
20. Moravian University
21. Fairfield University
22. Bradley University
23. Michigan State University
24. Stetson University
25. Gonzaga University

Most Politically Active Students

Based on student ratings of their own levels of political awareness.

1. George Washington University
2. American University
3. Macalester College
4. Reed College
5. Middlebury College
6. Mount Holyoke College
7. Bennington College
8. Claremont McKenna College
9. Pitzer College
10. Sarah Lawrence College
11. Wesleyan University
12. Dickinson College
13. Emerson College
14. Denison University
15. Lewis & Clark College
16. Rhodes College
17. College of the Atlantic
18. State University of New York—College of Environmental Science and Forestry
19. Clark University
20. Eugene Lang College of Liberal Arts at The New School
21. Washington and Lee University
22. Carleton College
23. The University of North Carolina—Asheville
24. Oberlin College
25. Marist University

CAMPUS LIFE

Lots of Race/Class Interaction

Based on how strongly students agree that students from different racial, ethnic, and socioeconomic backgrounds interact frequently and easily.

1. Rice University
2. United States Naval Academy
3. Loyola University New Orleans
4. Wabash College
5. Claremont McKenna College
6. The University of Chicago
7. Harvey Mudd College
8. Hampden-Sydney College
9. The College of Wooster
10. University of North Carolina at Charlotte
11. Wesleyan University
12. Rhodes College
13. College of the Atlantic
14. Rose-Hulman Institute of Technology
15. Sacred Heart University
16. St. John's College (NM)
17. Loyola Marymount University
18. Macalester College
19. Juniata College
20. Mount Holyoke College
21. Babson College
22. University of South Florida
23. Worcester Polytechnic Institute
24. California State University, Stanislaus
25. Pace University

Little Race/Class Interaction

Based on how strongly students agree that students from different racial, ethnic, and socioeconomic backgrounds interact frequently and easily.

1. Fairfield University
2. Lewis & Clark College
3. Washington & Jefferson College
4. Duquesne University
5. Warren Wilson College
6. Muhlenberg College
7. Clarkson University
8. Santa Clara University
9. Monmouth University (NJ)
10. Trinity College (CT)
11. Case Western Reserve University
12. Bucknell University
13. Connecticut College
14. University of New Hampshire
15. Simmons University
16. University of Richmond
17. The Catholic University of America
18. Seattle University
19. Ithaca College
20. Sarah Lawrence College
21. University of Virginia
22. University of California—Santa Cruz
23. Bentley University
24. State University of New York—University at Albany
25. Bowdoin College

LGBTQ-Friendly

Based on how strongly students agree that their fellow students treat all persons equally, regardless of their sexual orientation and gender identity/expression.

1. University of Vermont
2. College of the Atlantic
3. Smith College
4. Mount Holyoke College
5. Reed College
6. Harvey Mudd College
7. Macalester College
8. State University of New York—College of Environmental Science and Forestry
9. Pitzer College
10. Carleton College
11. Claremont McKenna College
12. Bennington College
13. Wellesley College
14. Bryn Mawr College
15. Earlham College
16. Wesleyan University
17. Columbia University
18. California Institute of Technology
19. Emerson College
20. William & Mary
21. Oberlin College
22. Grinnell College
23. American University
24. The University of Chicago
25. University of Mary Washington

LGBTQ-Unfriendly

Based on how strongly students disagree that their fellow students treat all persons equally, regardless of their sexual orientation and gender identity/expression.

1. Grove City College
2. College of the Ozarks
3. University of Tennessee—Knoxville
4. Indiana University of Pennsylvania
5. University of Dallas
6. Hillsdale College
7. Baylor University
8. East Carolina University
9. Salisbury University
10. Duquesne University
11. Berry College
12. Rowan University
13. Fairfield University
14. Santa Clara University
15. Eastern Michigan University
16. Albion College
17. Randolph College
18. The Catholic University of America
19. Brigham Young University (UT)
20. Monmouth University (NJ)
21. Moravian University
22. State University of New York—University at Albany
23. Bentley University
24. Manhattan University
25. University of Louisville

Most Religious Students

Based on how strongly students agree that their fellow students are very religious.

1. Brigham Young University (UT)
2. University of Dallas
3. Taylor University
4. The Catholic University of America
5. Grove City College
6. Hillsdale College
7. Thomas Aquinas College (CA)
8. College of the Ozarks
9. Sacred Heart University
10. Clemson University
11. Pepperdine University
12. St. John's College (MD)
13. Baylor University
14. Fairfield University
15. Iona University
16. Berry College
17. Marquette University
18. Wofford College
19. John Carroll University
20. Mercer University
21. Stonehill College
22. Boston College
23. Bellarmine University
24. Hampden-Sydney College
25. Texas Christian University

Least Religious Students

Based on how strongly students disagree that their fellow students are very religious.

1. Mount Holyoke College
2. Reed College
3. Lewis & Clark College
4. Grinnell College
5. Bennington College
6. Wheaton College (MA)
7. Smith College
8. Eugene Lang College of Liberal Arts at The New School
9. Pitzer College
10. Sarah Lawrence College
11. Franklin W. Olin College of Engineering
12. Harvey Mudd College
13. State University of New York—College of Environmental Science and Forestry
14. University of Vermont
15. Middlebury College
16. University of California—Santa Cruz
17. College of the Atlantic
18. Connecticut College
19. California Institute of Technology
20. Oberlin College
21. Wesleyan University
22. Claremont McKenna College
23. Rensselaer Polytechnic Institute
24. Macalester College
25. Clark University

TOWN LIFE

College City Gets High Marks

Based on student ratings of the towns and cities where their schools are located.

1. Columbia University
2. United States Naval Academy
3. Stevens Institute of Technology
4. University of San Diego
5. Boston College
6. American University
7. Tulane University
8. Vanderbilt University
9. The George Washington University
10. Simmons University
11. Salve Regina University
12. University of Denver
13. New York University
14. Fairfield University
15. The University of Chicago
16. Rollins College
17. University of Texas at Austin
18. University of Wisconsin—Madison
19. Emerson College
20. Eugene Lang College of Liberal Arts at The New School
21. Suffolk University
22. Illinois Institute of Technology
23. Skidmore College
24. Macalester College
25. Texas Christian University

Town-Gown Relations Are Great

Based on student ratings of how well they get along with the local community.

1. Denison University
2. United States Naval Academy
3. Brigham Young University (UT)
4. Vanderbilt University
5. Clemson University
6. Washington and Lee University
7. Bryant University
8. Randolph-Macon College
9. Grove City College
10. Taylor University
11. St. Lawrence University
12. Hobart and William Smith Colleges
13. Salve Regina University
14. Florida International University
15. Macalester College
16. Sacred Heart University
17. Florida Southern College
18. University of Mary Washington
19. Gonzaga University
20. Claremont McKenna College
21. Moravian University
22. Berry College
23. College of the Atlantic
24. Rollins College
25. John Carroll University

EXTRACURRICULARS

Best Athletic Facilities

Based on student ratings of the recreational and athletic facilities at their schools.

1. Colby College
2. Auburn University
3. James Madison University
4. Denison University
5. The University of Alabama—Tuscaloosa
6. Washington State University
7. The Ohio State University—Columbus
8. Gettysburg College
9. University of Oregon
10. North Carolina State University
11. Texas Christian University
12. Clemson University
13. University of Richmond
14. Ripon College
15. Roanoke College
16. Vanderbilt University
17. Skidmore College
18. Wabash College
19. Florida State University
20. University of Pittsburgh—Pittsburgh Campus
21. University of Denver
22. Tulane University
23. University of Puget Sound
24. Washington and Lee University
25. Quinnipiac University

Students Love Their School Teams

Based on student assessments of the popularity of intercollegiate sports at their schools.

1. The Ohio State University—Columbus
2. Gonzaga University
3. Brigham Young University (UT)
4. University of Dayton
5. Clemson University
6. University of Tennessee—Knoxville
7. Hampden-Sydney College
8. United States Naval Academy
9. James Madison University
10. Wabash College
11. Xavier University (OH)
12. Taylor University
13. Seton Hall University
14. Baylor University
15. Texas Christian University
16. University of Virginia
17. Mercer University
18. North Carolina State University
19. Michigan State University
20. University of Oregon
21. Marquette University
22. William & Mary
23. University of New Haven
24. Fairfield University
25. The University of Scranton

Everyone Plays Intramural Sports

Based on student ratings of the popularity of intramural sports at their schools.

1. Washington and Lee University
2. Texas Christian University
3. Gettysburg College
4. The University of the South
5. Wabash College
6. University of Arizona
7. Sacred Heart University
8. Hampden-Sydney College
9. Elon University
10. Albion College
11. James Madison University
12. Lehigh University
13. Clemson University
14. University of Delaware
15. East Carolina University
16. University of Virginia
17. Spelman College
18. Washington State University
19. Rose-Hulman Institute of Technology
20. Worcester Polytechnic Institute
21. Michigan State University
22. High Point University
23. Indiana University of Pennsylvania
24. Baylor University
25. Southwestern University

Best College Radio Station

Based on student ratings of their campus radio stations.

1. Seton Hall University
2. Reed College
3. Carleton College
4. Eckerd College
5. Hillsdale College
6. Emerson College
7. Earlham College
8. Washington and Lee University
9. Denison University
10. Chapman University
11. Smith College
12. Mount Holyoke College
13. Columbia University
14. Arizona State University
15. Hofstra University
16. Bennington College
17. John Carroll University
18. Whitman College
19. University of Puget Sound
20. Bowdoin College
21. Rider University
22. Skidmore College
23. Ithaca College
24. Rice University
25. University of South Florida

Best College Newspaper

Based on student ratings of their campus newspaper.

1. Columbia University
2. American University
3. Rice University
4. Vanderbilt University
5. Tulane University
6. Oberlin College
7. Washington and Lee University
8. Ithaca College
9. Loyola Marymount University
10. Wabash College
11. Grinnell College
12. Mount Holyoke College
13. Macalester College
14. Sacred Heart University
15. Reed College
16. George Washington University
17. Emerson College
18. Princeton University
19. Lehigh University
20. William & Mary
21. Wesleyan University
22. Bowdoin College
23. Taylor University
24. Fairfield University
25. Loyola University New Orleans

Best College Theater

Based on student ratings of their campus theater productions.

1. Elon University
2. Wagner College
3. State University of New York—Purchase College
4. Bennington College
5. Muhlenberg College
6. Emerson College
7. Wesleyan University
8. Drew University
9. New York University
10. Northwestern University
11. Sarah Lawrence College
12. University of Mary Washington
13. Ithaca College
14. Denison University
15. Carnegie Mellon University
16. Lafayette College
17. Oberlin College
18. High Point University
19. Rollins College
20. Nazareth University
21. Chapman University
22. Loyola Marymount University
23. Butler University
24. Sacred Heart University
25. Florida Southern College

Students Most Engaged in Community Service

Based on how strongly students agree that the students at their schools are committed to community service.

1. Marquette University
2. Brigham Young University (UT)
3. United States Naval Academy
4. Hobart and William Smith Colleges
5. Hillsdale College
6. Tulane University
7. Gonzaga University
8. Salve Regina University
9. John Carroll University
10. Randolph-Macon College
11. Sacred Heart University
12. College of the Atlantic
13. Washington and Lee University
14. Wabash College
15. Berry College
16. The Catholic University of America
17. Loyola Marymount University
18. State University of New York—College of Environmental Science and Forestry
19. Hampden-Sydney College
20. Warren Wilson College
21. William & Mary
22. Vanderbilt University
23. Grove City College
24. The University of Scranton
25. Taylor University

Most Active Student Government

Based on how strongly students agree that their student governments have an active presence and a tremendous impact on campus.

1. Hampden-Sydney College
2. Wabash College
3. Bryn Mawr College
4. Pitzer College
5. Washington and Lee University
6. College of the Atlantic
7. Claremont McKenna College
8. Harvey Mudd College
9. St. Lawrence University
10. Hobart and William Smith Colleges
11. Mount Holyoke College
12. Smith College
13. State University of New York—College of Environmental Science and Forestry
14. Washington State University
15. Hollins University
16. High Point University
17. Rollins College
18. Elon University
19. Skidmore College
20. Seton Hall University
21. St. John's College (MD)
22. The University of the South
23. Reed College
24. Centre College
25. Babson College

SOCIAL SCENE

Lots of Greek Life

Based on student ratings of the popularity of fraternities and sororities at their schools.

1. Wofford College
2. Bucknell University
3. Butler University
4. Auburn University
5. Wabash College
6. Texas Christian University
7. Baylor University
8. University of Georgia
9. University of Tennessee—Knoxville
10. Sacred Heart University
11. Washington and Lee University
12. Clemson University
13. The University of the South
14. Vanderbilt University
15. DePauw University
16. University of Mississippi
17. Transylvania University
18. University of South Carolina—Columbia
19. Tulane University
20. Rhodes College
21. Centre College
22. Hampden-Sydney College
23. Southwestern University
24. Washington State University
25. University of Oklahoma

Lots of Beer

Based on student ratings of how widely beer is used at their schools.

1. Colby College
2. Gettysburg College
3. Bucknell University
4. University of Wisconsin—Madison
5. The University of the South
6. Tulane University
7. Trinity College (CT)
8. St. Lawrence University
9. Washington and Lee University
10. Syracuse University
11. Juniata College
12. Providence College
13. University of Florida
14. University of Dayton
15. West Virginia University
16. Claremont McKenna College
17. Hampden-Sydney College
18. University of New Hampshire
19. Lafayette College
20. Colgate University
21. Bryant University
22. Grinnell College
23. Denison University
24. University of Delaware
25. Ohio University—Athens

Cancel the Keg

Based on student ratings of how widely beer is used at their schools.

1. Brigham Young University (UT)
2. City College of New York of The City University of New York
3. College of the Ozarks
4. Taylor University
5. Spelman College
6. City University of New York—Brooklyn College
7. California State University, Stanislaus
8. Pepperdine University
9. Pace University
10. Grove City College
11. Florida International University
12. United States Naval Academy
13. Adelphi University
14. Iona University
15. Baylor University
16. University of California—Merced
17. Montclair State University
18. State University of New York—Stony Brook University
19. University of California—Irvine
20. Bellarmine University
21. Simmons University
22. University of St. Francis (IL)
23. University of South Florida
24. University of Maryland, Baltimore County
25. Middle Tennessee State University

Lots of Hard Liquor

Based on students' answers to the survey question, "How widely is hard liquor used at your school?"

1. Tulane University
2. University of Wisconsin—Madison
3. Providence College
4. Wake Forest University
5. Bucknell University
6. Grinnell College
7. Syracuse University
8. St. Lawrence University
9. The University of the South
10. University of Florida
11. Colgate University
12. Penn State University Park
13. Juniata College
14. Gettysburg College
15. West Virginia University
16. Trinity College (CT)
17. Washington and Lee University
18. Ohio University—Athens
19. University of New Hampshire
20. Claremont McKenna College
21. Bennington College
22. University of Dayton
23. Harvey Mudd College
24. Hamilton College
25. Eckerd College

Scotch and Soda, Hold the Scotch

Based on students' answers to the survey question, "How widely is hard liquor used at your school?"

1. Brigham Young University (UT)
2. College of the Ozarks
3. Taylor University
4. City College of New York of The City University of New York
5. City University of New York—Brooklyn College
6. California State University, Stanislaus
7. United States Naval Academy
8. Spelman College
9. Pepperdine University
10. Pace University
11. Grove City College
12. Iona University
13. Adelphi University
14. Baylor University
15. University of St. Francis (IL)
16. Montclair State University
17. Bellarmine University
18. State University of New York—Stony Brook University
19. Berry College
20. University of California—Irvine
21. University of South Florida
22. The University of North Carolina—Charlotte
23. University of Mary Washington
24. University of California—Merced
25. Hofstra University

Reefer Madness

Based on student ratings concerning the use of marijuana at their schools.

1. Skidmore College
2. Lewis & Clark College
3. University of Vermont
4. Pitzer College
5. Bennington College
6. Reed College
7. Sarah Lawrence College
8. University of Colorado Boulder
9. Grinnell College
10. University of Rhode Island
11. Colorado College
12. Syracuse University
13. Emerson College
14. Wesleyan University
15. Oberlin College
16. Warren Wilson College
17. Tulane University
18. St. Lawrence University
19. Brown University
20. University of Oregon
21. Bates College
22. University of Denver
23. Ohio University—Athens
24. West Virginia University
25. University of California—Santa Cruz

Pot's Not Hot

Based on student ratings concerning the use of marijuana at their schools.

1. United States Naval Academy
2. United States Military Academy
3. United States Air Force Academy
4. Brigham Young University (UT)
5. Thomas Aquinas College (CA)
6. College of the Ozarks
7. Taylor University
8. Grove City College
9. Princeton University
10. City University of New York—Baruch College
11. City University of New York—Brooklyn College
12. California State University, Stanislaus
13. Pepperdine University
14. City College of New York of The City University of New York
15. Spelman College
16. Hillsdale College
17. Iona University
18. Baylor University
19. Berry College
20. Florida International University
21. Pace University
22. Florida Southern College
23. Rose-Hulman Institute of Technology
24. University of Dallas
25. Bellarmine University

THE PRINCETON REVIEW'S HONOR ROLLS

We salute these schools that received a 99 (the highest score) in the tallies for our "Financial Aid," "Fire Safety," and "Green" Ratings. Our school ratings are numerical scores (not ranking lists) that show how a school "sizes up" on a fixed scale. They are comparable to grades and based primarily on institutional data we collect directly from the colleges. Note that schools with an asterisk after them do not appear in this book. You can find more about them in in our free online listings at princetonreview.com/college-search.

Financial Aid Honor Roll

Schools are listed in alphabetical order. See page 25 for information on how our "Financial Aid Rating" is determined.

Amherst College
Bates College
Bowdoin College
California Institute of Technology
Carleton College
Colby College
Grinnell College Harvard College
Kenyon College
Mount Holyoke College
Oberlin College
Pomona College
Princeton University
Reed College
Swarthmore College
The University of Chicago
Union College (NY)
Vassar College
Washington and Lee University
Wesleyan University
Williams College
Yale University

Fire Safety Honor Roll

Schools are listed in alphabetical order. See page 23 for information on how our "Fire Safety Rating" is determined.

Adelphi University
Alfred University
Barton College*
Bentley University
Bowdoin College
Brenau University*
Bridgewater State University*
Carleton College
Champlain College
City University of New York—Queens College
College of Saint Benedict/Saint John's University
Dean College*
Denison University
Duquesne University
East Carolina University
Elmhurst University*
Emmanuel College*
Farmingdale State College, State University of New York*
Fordham University
Framingham State University*
Hofstra University
Ithaca College
Louisiana State University—Baton Rouge
Loyola University New Orleans
Macalester College
Marquette University
Millikin University*
Monmouth University (NJ)
Moravian University
Mount Saint Mary's University*
Muhlenberg College
New York University
North Carolina State University
Ohio Wesleyan University
Quinnipiac University
Skidmore College
St. John's University (NY)
State University of New York—College of Environmental Science and Forestry
State University of New York at Geneseo
Stockton University*
Texas State University
The College of New Jersey
The University of North Carolina—Charlotte
The University of North Carolina—Greensboro
Towson University*
Truman State University
United States Air Force Academy
University of Arizona
University of Maine
University of Maryland, Baltimore County
University of New Hampshire
University of North Carolina at Chapel Hill
University of South Florida
University of St. Francis (IL)
University of Vermont
Wagner College
Washington College
Webb Institute
Weber State University*
West Chester University of Pennsylvania*
Worcester State University*
Xavier University of Louisiana

Green Honor Roll

Schools are listed in alphabetical order. See page 23 for information on how our "Green Rating" is determined.

American University
California State University, San Bernardino*
Carnegie Mellon University
College of the Atlantic
Colorado State University
Cornell University
École de Technologie Supérieure Reports*
Lehigh University
Loyola Marymount University
Loyola University Chicago
Queen's University Belfast*
Randolph College
Red River College Polytechnic*
Southern Oregon University*
Stanford University
State University of New York—College of Environmental Science and Forestry
Stevens Institute of Technology
Tecnologico de Monterrey Campus Guadalajara*
Tecnologico de Monterrey Campus Monterrey*
The American College of Greece*
The Catholic University of America
University at Buffalo*
University College Cork—National University of Ireland, Cork*
University of California, Berkeley
University of California, Santa Barbara
University of California, Santa Cruz
University of Miami
University of Northern British Columbia*
University of Victoria*
University of Washington, Bothell*
Victoria University of Wellington*
Virginia Tech
York University*

Tuition-Free Schools Honor Roll[1]

The following schools have been excluded from our ranking and ratings dealing with financial aid:

Berea College
College of the Ozarks
Deep Springs College*
United States Air Force Academy
United States Coast Guard Academy
United States Merchant Marine Academy*
United States Military Academy
United States Naval Academy
Webb Institute

Mental Health Services Honor Roll

Schools are listed in alphabetical order. Each was selected based on their performance in three key categories selected by a panel of experts in higher education mental health practices. Out of an initial pool of 250 respondents, these were the ones that showed an especially strong commitment to their students' mental health and well-being.

Arizona State University
Boston University
Coastal Carolina University*
Colorado State University
Columbia University
Dartmouth College
Florida Institute of Technology*
Massachusetts Institute of Technology
Mercer University
Michigan Technological University
Molloy University
Nazareth University
New York University
Northern Michigan University
Pace University
Princeton University
Rice University
Samford University*
St. John's University (NY)
State University of New York—Stony Brook University
State University of New York—University at Albany
Stevens Institute of Technology
Syracuse University
Texas Christian University
The University of North Carolina—Greensboro
University of Florida
University of North Dakota
Weber State University*
William & Mary
Worcester Polytechnic Institute

[1] We commend these schools on their ability to do the seemingly impossible: not charge tuition. While some charge students for food and housing and other fees, the overall cost of attendance at these schools is very low, and at some schools: free! (Note: We do not include these schools in our ranking lists dealing with financial aid, since they would have an unfair advantage over schools that charge even a moderate tuition.)

In collaboration with the Ruderman Family Foundation, our first annual 2024 Campus Mental Health Survey invited nearly all 4-year colleges and universities to participate early in the year. A portion of the results from respondents are listed for all applicable schools in this book. They can also be found on each school's online profile (princetonreview.com/college-search) and our dedicated Mental Health hub (princetonreview.com/mental-health-on-college-campus).

The questions covered included:

1. **What types of training are available for students and faculty/staff?**
   OUR PANEL NOTES: The wider the range of training, the more the school can cover mental health issues that first occur in those between the ages of 18 and 24.
2. **Is there a Chief Behavioral Health Officer (or similar) to advise and implement mental health policies and programs?**
   OUR PANEL NOTES: "These positions not only demonstrate a commitment to collegiate mental health but show a respect among colleagues in various roles throughout campus for the expertise of an experienced mental health professional."
3. **Are clinicians trained to provide care to specific groups?**
   OUR PANEL NOTES: "It is critical to include the thoughts, opinions, and experiences of students, faculty, and staff to ensure that services and resources meet their needs."
4. **How often is a wellness screening and assessment of all students conducted?**
   OUR PANEL NOTES: Regular, widespread screening is preferred because it "introduces students to available resources and supports they may not have sought out on their own" and helps to "destigmatize any negative perceptions about seeking services."
5. **Are there peer-to-peer offerings relating to mental health?**
   OUR PANEL NOTES: "Some students may feel more comfortable speaking with a fellow classmate" and they "may be more willing to take issues that they deem less serious (although not necessarily objectively less serious) to a peer."
6. **Is mental health and wellness a part of the residential experience?**
   OUR PANEL NOTES: Residential communities have a "natural infrastructure" that helps to "support campaigns and programming that normalizes healthy communication, sleep, eating, and self-care" all of which is foundational to academic rigor.
7. **Are counseling, referral, and well-being services available to all students?**
   OUR PANEL NOTES: With no way to predict the services students need, a "robust referral network is a key part of a counseling center's network of care" and ensures that there's "targeted expertise in a variety of specialty areas."
8. **Is there a website that consolidates information about the institution's mental health offerings?**
   OUR PANEL NOTES: "Websites are essential in dispensing clear and concise messaging regarding mental health resources, wayfinding, screening tools, and asynchronous learning."
9. **Is there for-credit or non-credit mental health/well-being education for students?**
   OUR PANEL NOTES: In addition to normalizing help-seeking, this gives faculty the chance to "model discussing mental health topics, which allows them to appear more approachable and less intimidating to students."
10. **Is the counseling center accredited?**
    OUR PANEL NOTES: This shows external verification of services that meet the highest standards in the field.
11. **Is there an official support program for students returning from a mental health leave of absence?**
    OUR PANEL NOTES: It is important that students have the freedom to choose what their wellness goals are and how they want to achieve them. Support programs allow students to make informed decisions about leaving and returning.
12. **Is the counseling center open and fully staffed year-round?**
    OUR PANEL NOTES: It is useful for students to know when they will be reliably able to seek counseling, and whether there are alternatives for continued care.

THE PRINCETON REVIEW'S 209 BEST VALUE COLLEGES FOR 2025

This is The Princeton Review's list of Best Value Colleges from June 2025. We selected the 209 schools based on 40 weighted data points, including academics, cost, financial aid, and student debt to statistics on graduation rates, alumni salaries, and job satisfaction. Alumni survey information was provided by PayScale.com. For detailed profiles, and the 2026 Best Value list (once released), see PrincetonReview.com/best-value-colleges.

Albion College
Allegheny College
Amherst College
Arizona State University
Austin College
Babson College
Barnard College
Bates College
Baylor University
Bentley University
Berea College
Berry College
Bowdoin College
Bradley University
Brandeis University
Brigham Young University (UT)
Brown University
Bryant University
Bryn Mawr College
Bucknell University
California Institute of Technology
California State University, Stanislaus
Carleton College
Carnegie Mellon University
Case Western Reserve University
Centre College
City College of New York of The City University of New York
City University of New York—Baruch College
City University of New York—Brooklyn College
City University of New York—Hunter College
Claremont McKenna College
Clark University
Clarkson University
Clemson University
Colby College
Colgate University
College of the Ozarks
College of Wooster
Colorado College
Columbia University
Connecticut College
Cornell University
Dartmouth College
Davidson College
Deep Springs College
Denison University
Dickinson College
Drew University
Duke University
Elon University
Emory University
Fairfield University
Florida International University
Florida State University
Fordham University
Franklin & Marshall College
Franklin W. Olin College of Engineering
George Washington University
Georgetown University
Georgia Institute of Technology
Gettysburg College
Grinnell College
Grove City College
Hamilton College
Hampden-Sydney College
Harvard College
Harvey Mudd College
Haverford College
Hobart and William Smith Colleges
Hofstra University
Illinois Institute of Technology
James Madison University
John Carroll University
Johns Hopkins University
Kalamazoo College
Kenyon College
Lafayette College
Lake Forest College
Lawrence University
Lehigh University
Loyola Marymount University
Macalester College
Marquette University
Massachusetts Institute of Technology
McDaniel College
Mercer University
Miami University
Michigan State University
Michigan Technological University
Middlebury College
Missouri University of Science and Technology
Mount Holyoke College
Muhlenberg College
New College of Florida
New Jersey Institute of Technology
New York University
North Carolina State University
Northeastern University
Northwestern University
Occidental College
Ohio Wesleyan University
Oregon State University
Pitzer College

Pomona College
Princeton University
Purdue University—West Lafayette
Reed College
Rensselaer Polytechnic Institute
Rhodes College
Rice University
Rose-Hulman Institute of Technology
Saint Louis University
Salisbury University
Santa Clara University
Sarah Lawrence College
Scripps College
Simmons University
Skidmore College
Smith College
Southwestern University
St. John's College (MD)
St. John's College (NM)
St. Lawrence University
St. Mary's College of Maryland
St. Olaf College
Stanford University
State University of New York—Binghamton University
State University of New York—Stony Brook University
State University of New York at Geneseo
Stevens Institute of Technology
Swarthmore College
Taylor University
Texas A&M University—College Station
Texas Christian University
The Cooper Union for the Advancement of Science and Art
The Ohio State University–Columbus
The University of Chicago
The University of Texas at Dallas
The University of the South
Thomas Aquinas College (CA)
Trinity College (CT)
Trinity University
Truman State University
Tufts University
Tulane University
Union College (NY)
United States Air Force Academy
United States Coast Guard Academy
United States Merchant Marine Academy
United States Military Academy
United States Naval Academy
University of Arizona
University of California—Berkeley
University of California—Davis
University of California—Irvine
University of California—Los Angeles
University of California—Riverside
University of California—San Diego
University of California—Santa Barbara
University of California—Santa Cruz
University of Central Florida
University of Cincinnati
University of Colorado—Boulder
University of Dallas
University of Dayton
University of Delaware
University of Denver
University of Florida
University of Georgia
University of Houston
University of Illinois at Urbana-Champaign
University of Mary Washington
University of Maryland, Baltimore County
University of Massachusetts—Amherst
University of Michigan—Ann Arbor
University of Minnesota—Twin Cities
University of North Carolina at Chapel Hill
University of Notre Dame
University of Pennsylvania
University of Pittsburgh—Pittsburgh Campus
University of Portland
University of Puget Sound
University of Richmond
University of Rochester
University of Tennessee at Knoxville
University of Texas at Austin
University of Utah
University of Vermont
University of Virginia
University of Washington
University of Wisconsin—Madison
Vanderbilt University
Vassar College
Virginia Tech
Wabash College
Wake Forest University
Washington and Lee University
Washington State University
Washington University in St. Louis
Webb Institute
Wellesley College
Wesleyan University
Whitman College
William & Mary
William Jewell College
Williams College
Wofford College
Worcester Polytechnic Institute
Yale University

The Best Value Colleges contains 14 ranking lists, all of which focus on different aspects of financial aid and career preparation. Because this book already contains a Financial Aid Honors Roll, we've included 12 of those lists here.

Top 50 Best Value Colleges (Private Schools)

The fifty private schools that received the highest overall rating used to determine inclusion in *The Best Value Colleges.*

1. Princeton University
2. California Institute of Technology
3. Massachusetts Institute of Technology
4. Harvey Mudd College
5. Stanford University
6. Columbia University
7. Williams College
8. Harvard College
9. Dartmouth College
10. Yale University
11. University of Pennsylvania
12. Cornell University
13. Duke University
14. Rice University
15. Washington and Lee University
16. Johns Hopkins University
17. Pomona College
18. Carnegie Mellon University
19. Haverford College
20. The Cooper Union for the Advancement of Science and Art
21. Brown University
22. Wellesley College
23. Claremont McKenna College
24. Wesleyan University
25. Lehigh University
26. Bowdoin College
27. Brigham Young University (UT)
28. Vanderbilt University
29. Amherst College
30. Washington University in St. Louis
31. Franklin W. Olin College of Engineering
32. Colgate University
33. University of Notre Dame
34. The University of Chicago
35. Carleton College
36. Swarthmore College
37. Lafayette College
38. Rose-Hulman Institute of Technology
39. Union College (NY)
40. Wabash College
41. Babson College
42. Grinnell College
43. St. Olaf College
44. Colby College
45. Trinity College (CT)
46. Trinity University
47. Middlebury College
48. Northwestern University
49. Barnard College
50. Tufts University

Top 50 Best Value Colleges (Public Schools)

The fifty public schools that received the highest overall rating used to determine inclusion in *The Best Value Colleges.*

1. Georgia Institute of Technology
2. University of Virginia
3. University of North Carolina at Chapel Hill
4. University of California—Irvine
5. University of California—Berkeley
6. University of California—San Diego
7. University of Michigan—Ann Arbor
8. University of Washington
9. North Carolina State University
10. University of Illinois at Urbana-Champaign
11. William & Mary
12. University of Georgia
13. University of California—Santa Barbara
14. University of Texas at Austin
15. University of California—Los Angeles
16. State University of New York—Binghamton University
17. University of Wisconsin—Madison
18. Texas A&M University—College Station
19. City University of New York—Baruch College
20. Purdue University—West Lafayette
21. Missouri University of Science and Technology
22. Florida State University
23. University of Florida
24. New College of Florida
25. University of California—Davis
26. State University of New York—Stony Brook University
27. New Jersey Institute of Technology
28. Truman State University
29. University of Maryland, Baltimore County
30. The Ohio State University–Columbus
31. Michigan Technological University
32. University of Minnesota—Twin Cities
33. University of California—Riverside
34. University of Colorado—Boulder
35. Miami University
36. University of Utah
37. Florida International University
38. Clemson University
39. Virginia Tech
40. The University of Texas at Dallas
41. University of Massachusetts—Amherst
42. University of Houston
43. University of Central Florida
44. City University of New York—Hunter College
45. St. Mary's College of Maryland
46. Washington State University
47. James Madison University
48. University of California—Santa Cruz
49. University of Pittsburgh—Pittsburgh Campus
50. University of Tennessee at Knoxville

Top 20 Best Value Colleges for Students With No Demonstrated Need (Private)

To create this list, we used the same methodology for our ROI rating, but removed need-based aid information. If you don't qualify for financial aid, these are your twenty-five best value private schools.

1. Massachusetts Institute of Technology
2. Harvey Mudd College
3. Stanford University
4. Brigham Young University (UT)
5. Princeton University
6. California Institute of Technology
7. Cornell University
8. Williams College
9. Columbia University
10. Dartmouth College
11. Harvard College
12. Yale University
13. Duke University
14. Carnegie Mellon University
15. University of Pennsylvania
16. Colgate University
17. Johns Hopkins University
18. Rice University
19. Claremont McKenna College
20. The Cooper Union for the Advancement of Science and Art

Top 20 Best Value Colleges for Students With No Demonstrated Need (Public)

To create this list, we used the same methodology for our ROI rating, but removed need-based aid information. If you don't qualify for financial aid, these are your twenty-five best value public schools.

1. Georgia Institute of Technology
2. University of North Carolina at Chapel Hill
3. University of Michigan—Ann Arbor
4. University of Illinois at Urbana-Champaign
5. University of California—Berkeley
6. North Carolina State University
7. Purdue University—West Lafayette
8. University of Virginia
9. State University of New York—Binghamton University
10. University of California—San Diego
11. University of Florida
12. University of Washington
13. William & Mary
14. University of Georgia
15. University of California—Irvine
16. Florida State University
17. Texas A&M University—College Station
18. University of Texas at Austin
19. Virginia Tech
20. University of California—Los Angeles

Top 20 Best Alumni Network (Private)

These twenty private schools have the strongest and most active alumni networks, based on current students' ratings of alumni activity and visibility on campus.

1. St. Lawrence University
2. Hampden-Sydney College
3. Washington and Lee University
4. University of Notre Dame
5. Wabash College
6. Dartmouth College
7. Davidson College
8. Claremont McKenna College
9. Colgate University
10. Hobart and William Smith Colleges
11. Massachusetts Institute of Technology
12. The University of the South
13. Wellesley College
14. Agnes Scott College
15. Stanford University
16. Georgetown University
17. Texas Christian University
18. Bryn Mawr College
19. Williams College
20. Lehigh University

Top 20 Best Alumni Network (Public)

These twenty public schools have the strongest and most active alumni networks, based on current students' ratings of alumni activity and visibility on campus.

1. University of Michigan—Ann Arbor
2. Virginia Tech
3. University of Texas at Austin
4. Georgia Institute of Technology
5. University of Florida
6. Clemson University
7. Washington State University
8. University of Georgia
9. University of Virginia
10. Purdue University—West Lafayette
11. North Carolina State University
12. The University of Alabama—Tuscaloosa
13. Florida State University
14. University of Wisconsin—Madison
15. University of North Carolina at Chapel Hill
16. City University of New York—Baruch College
17. University of California—Los Angeles
18. William & Mary
19. The Ohio State University–Columbus
20. James Madison University

Top 20 Best Schools for Internships (Private)

This top twenty private school list is based on students' ratings of accessibility of internships at their school.

1. Northeastern University
2. Wabash College
3. Washington and Lee University
4. St. Lawrence University
5. Claremont McKenna College
6. Denison University
7. Harvey Mudd College
8. Brigham Young University (UT)
9. University of Richmond
10. Stanford University
11. Franklin W. Olin College of Engineering
12. Hobart and William Smith Colleges
13. Wake Forest University
14. Marquette University
15. Austin College
16. Hampden-Sydney College
17. College of Wooster
18. Rhodes College
19. Dartmouth College
20. Worcester Polytechnic Institute

Top 20 Best Schools for Internships (Public)

This top twenty public school list is based on students' ratings of accessibility of internships at their school.

1. University of Michigan—Ann Arbor
2. Georgia Institute of Technology
3. The University of Texas at Dallas
4. Purdue University—West Lafayette
5. Missouri University of Science and Technology
6. William & Mary
7. Washington State University
8. University of Washington
9. University of Texas at Austin
10. Miami University
11. Clemson University
12. University of Cincinnati
13. Florida State University
14. Michigan Technological University
15. North Carolina State University
16. University of Georgia
17. Virginia Tech
18. University of Mary Washington
19. Oregon State University
20. The Ohio State University–Columbus

Top 20 Best Career Placement (Private)

This top twenty list of private schools is based on students' ratings of career services at their school, and on PayScale.com's median starting and mid-career salary information.

1. Massachusetts Institute of Technology
2. Harvey Mudd College
3. California Institute of Technology
4. Stanford University
5. Princeton University
6. Harvard College
7. Carnegie Mellon University
8. University of Pennsylvania
9. Claremont McKenna College
10. Dartmouth College
11. Yale University
12. Stevens Institute of Technology
13. Santa Clara University
14. Babson College
15. Worcester Polytechnic Institute
16. Rose-Hulman Institute of Technology
17. Lehigh University
18. Cornell University
19. Colgate University
20. Columbia University

Top 20 Best Career Placement (Public)

This top twenty list of public schools is based on students' ratings of career services at their school, and on PayScale.com's median starting and mid-career salary information.

1. Georgia Institute of Technology
2. University of California—Berkeley
3. Missouri University of Science and Technology
4. University of Michigan—Ann Arbor
5. University of Virginia
6. University of Illinois at Urbana-Champaign
7. University of California—San Diego
8. Virginia Tech
9. University of California—Los Angeles
10. New Jersey Institute of Technology
11. University of Washington
12. University of California—Santa Barbara
13. Michigan Technological University
14. University of California—Davis
15. Texas A&M University—College Station
16. University of California—Irvine
17. University of Texas at Austin
18. William & Mary
19. Purdue University—West Lafayette
20. City University of New York—Baruch College

Top 20 Best Schools for Making an Impact (Private)

These twenty private schools were selected based on student ratings and responses to our survey questions covering community service opportunities at their school, student government, sustainability efforts, and on-campus student engagement. We also considered PayScale.com's percentage of alumni from each school that reported that they had high job meaning.

1. Pitzer College
2. Agnes Scott College
3. Harvey Mudd College
4. Emory University
5. Allegheny College
6. Mount Holyoke College
7. Brown University
8. Claremont McKenna College
9. Hobart and William Smith Colleges
10. University of San Diego
11. Macalester College
12. Colby College
13. Brandeis University
14. Skidmore College
15. Mercer University
16. Clark University
17. Wellesley College
18. Wesleyan University
19. Washington and Lee University
20. St. Lawrence University

Top 20 Best Schools for Making an Impact (Public)

These twenty public schools were selected based on student ratings and responses to our survey questions covering community service opportunities at their school, student government, sustainability efforts, and on-campus student engagement. We also considered PayScale.com's percentage of alumni from each school that reported that they had high job meaning.

1. University of Vermont
2. St. Mary's College of Maryland
3. University of Michigan—Ann Arbor
4. University of Washington
5. University of California—Riverside
6. University of California—Davis
7. Georgia Institute of Technology
8. University of North Carolina at Chapel Hill
9. California State University, Stanislaus
10. Virginia Tech
11. University of Mary Washington
12. Washington State University
13. City College of New York of The City University of New York
14. University of Maryland, Baltimore County
15. Arizona State University
16. University of Wisconsin—Madison
17. The Ohio State University–Columbus
18. Oregon State University
19. William & Mary
20. University of Pittsburgh—Pittsburgh Campus

Top 50 Undergraduate Colleges for Game Design

We surveyed 150 institutions and ranked the best schools for game design majors in 2025. Below are those Top 50 schools. Please find more information on this project here: princetonreview.com/game-design.

1. New York University
2. University of Southern California
3. University of Central Florida
4. Rochester Institute of Technology
5. Abertay University
6. DigiPen Institute of Technology
7. Clark University
8. University of Utah
9. Savannah College of Art and Design
10. Michigan State University
11. Champlain College
12. Drexel University
13. Worcester Polytechnic Institute
14. Northeastern University
15. Purdue University
16. Falmouth University
17. Shawnee State University
18. University of Florida
19. Full Sail University
20. Vancouver Film School
21. Quinnipiac University
22. New England Institute of Technology
23. Bradley University
24. Miami University
25. DePaul University
26. Howest University of Applied Sciences
27. Rensselaer Polytechnic Institute
28. University of California, Santa Barbara
29. Abilene Christian University
30. Kent State University
31. Marist University
32. University of California, Irvine
33. LaSalle College Vancouver
34. Academy of Art University
35. University of Miami
36. Northern Arizona University
37. Dakota State University
38. University of Michigan-Dearborn
39. New Jersey Institute of Technology
40. University of Wisconsin-Stout
41. Stetson University
42. Oklahoma Christian University
43. Bloomfield College of Montclair State University
44. Indiana University Bloomington
45. University of Massachusetts Dartmouth
46. ArtCenter College of Design
47. Louisiana State University
48. Oklahoma City University
49. Cleveland Institute of Art
50. New York Film Academy

Top 50 Undergraduate Colleges for Entrepreneurship

We surveyed nearly 300 schools with entrepreneurship studies so we can tell you which schools have the best opportunities. Below are those Top 50 schools. Please find more information on this project here: princetonreview.com/entrepreneur.

1. University of Houston
2. The University of Texas at Austin
3. Babson College
4. The University of Michigan, Ann Arbor
5. University of Washington
6. Washington University in St. Louis
7. University of Maryland
8. Michigan State University
9. Iowa State University
10. Tecnológico de Monterrey
11. The University of St. Thomas
12. Erasmus University Rotterdam
13. Syracuse University
14. Northeastern University
15. DePaul University
16. The University of Miami
17. The University of Iowa
18. Florida State University
19. Florida Atlantic University
20. Drexel University
21. The University of Texas at Dallas
22. University of Utah
23. Purdue University
24. University of South Florida
25. University of Delaware
26. The University of Tampa
27. The Pennsylvania State University
28. Texas Christian University
29. East Carolina University
30. University of Arizona
31. University of Connecticut
32. Saint Louis University
33. New Jersey Institute of Technology
34. Belmont University
35. University of Nebraska—Lincoln
36. Boston University
37. Savannah College of Art and Design (SCAD)
38. University of Dayton
39. Rowan University
40. Fordham University
41. Auburn University
42. The University of Tulsa
43. The George Washington University
44. Florida Gulf Coast University
45. University of Minnesota
46. Temple University
47. University at Buffalo
48. American University
49. University of Cincinnati
50. The University of Tennessee, Knoxville

STATISTICAL STAND-OUT SCHOOLS FOR 2027

We present this new list to highlight colleges with impressive stats—from lowest tuition & fees to highest 4-year graduation rate—based on data from our institutional surveys. We chose these categories based on our surveys of college applicants and their parents.

MONEY MATTERS

THE LOWEST ANNUAL TUITION & FEES

$5,954* Public College (in-state)
University of Central Florida (page 638)

$23,650* Private College
William Jewell College (page 832)

*Annual tuition and fees (first-year)

THE HIGHEST AVERAGE NEED-BASED SCHOLARSHIPS

$80,837

Princeton University (page 458)

THE LOWEST AVERAGE UNDERGRAD DEBT

$7,849
(14% borrowed)

CUNY–City College (page 166)

GRADUATION KUDOS

97% HIGHEST 6-YEAR GRADUATION RATE

Duke University (page 234)
Franklin W. Olin College of Engineering (page 270)
Harvard College (page 302)
Princeton University (page 458)
University of Pennsylvania (page 726)

92% HIGHEST 4-YEAR GRADUATION RATE

United States Naval Academy (page 610)

DEMOGRAPHIC DISTINCTIONS

THE MOST APPLICATIONS

145,086 Public College
University of California–Los Angeles (page 626)

114,125 Private College
New York University (page 424)

HIGHEST YIELD RATE (Percent of admitted students who enroll)

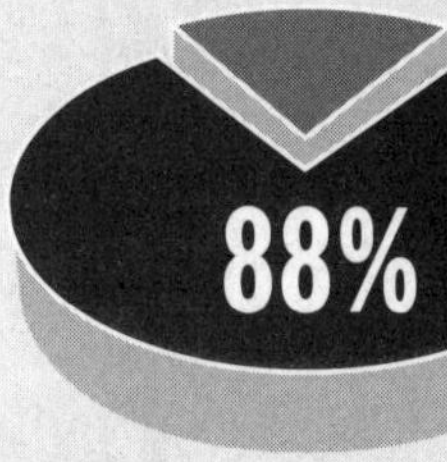

University of Chicago (page 640)

THE LOWEST STUDENT FACULTY RATIO

California Institute of Technology (page 136)
Massachusetts Institute of Technology (page 388)

98% **HIGHEST PERCENTAGE OF STUDENTS FROM OUT OF STATE**
Dartmouth College (page 216)

168 **MOST COUNTRIES REPRESENTED**
CUNY–Baruch College (page 162)

LARGEST UNDERGRADUATE ENROLLMENT

63,906
Public College
Arizona State University (page 82)

32,952
Private College
Brigham Young University (UT) (page 124)

MOST DIVERSE STUDENT BODY

CUNY–Brooklyn College
(page 164)

General Note: Only institutions confirming their 2026–2027 data by March 1, 2026, were considered for these lists. Tuition-free institutions were excluded from "lowest tuition."

PART 3

The Best 392 Colleges

Adelphi University

1 South Avenue, Garden City, NY 11530 • Admissions: 516-877-3050

Survey Snapshot
Students love Garden City, NY
Great off-campus food
Easy to get around campus

RATINGS

Quality of Life	**86**
Fire Safety	**99**
Green	**60***
Academic	**76**
Profs Interesting	**84**
Profs Accessible	**87**
Admissions	**85**
Financial Aid	**83**

CAMPUS LIFE

Type of school	Private
Environment	Metropolis

Students

Degree-seeking undergrad enrollment	5,046
% male/female/not reported	33/67/0
% from out of state	7
% First-year live on campus	27
% Ugrads live on campus	17
# of fraternities (% join)	8 (NR)
# of sororities (% join)	10 (NR)
% Asian	15
% Black or African American	10
% Hispanic	24
% Native American	<1
% Pacific Islander	<1
% Race and/or ethnicity unknown	3
% Two or more races	3
% White	40
% International	4
# of countries represented	66

CAMPUS MENTAL HEALTH SERVICES

Offers mental health/wellness program	Yes
Mental health training available to students	Yes
Employs Chief Wellness Officer	No
Peer-to-peer mental health offerings	Yes
Counseling center has guidelines or accreditation	Yes
Mental health/well-being courses	Yes, for-credit

ACADEMICS

% students returning for sophomore year	83
% students graduating within 4 years	61
% students graduating within 6 years	71
Calendar	Semester
Student/faculty ratio	11:1
Most common class size 20–29.	(38%)
Most common lab/discussion size 20–29.	(49%)

Most Popular Majors
Biology/Biological Sciences; Registered Nursing/Registered Nurse; Psychology

Applicants Often Prefer
Hofstra University, Saint John's University, State University of New York—Stony Brook University

Applicants Sometimes Prefer
City University of New York—Hunter College, City University of New York—Queens College

Applicants Rarely Prefer
Long Island University, Molloy University, New York University

STUDENTS SAY "..."

Academics

At Adelphi University, "students are encouraged to grow both academically and personally." Thanks to "small class sizes," students say, "you really get a feel for your professor and aren't just another number in a huge lecture hall." Many also highlight the school's "strong nursing program," which is "very inclusive and accommodating," and offers opportunities like "clinical lab simulations." Other majors also praise how "technology is integrated into a lot of courses." One notes how access to virtual reality lets them "explore everything from ancient cities to chemistry labs," while another brings up an "innovative" class where "the vast majority of...time was spent learning to fly and recording videos using the drones." Despite these exciting tools, a handful of students do complain that some professors "simply lecture the whole time." However, undergrads in the Honors College emphasize that their seminar courses tend to "prioritize class discussion above all." Outside of the classroom, "there are great opportunities for hands-on learning through internships and research programs." There's also "a tremendous amount of support [available] for students," with many applauding "the C.A.S.E. tutoring center" specifically. When it comes down to it, Adelphi delivers "strong academic programs [with] professors [that] genuinely want you to succeed."

Campus Life

Adelphi has many commuter students, and some admit that it can feel like "those who commute tend to have a lesser social life on campus." Nevertheless, the university is often buzzing with activities that everyone can enjoy. There are plenty of "one-off events...like goat yoga and formal etiquette class. It's very exciting trying something new, especially for free." Students also look forward to campus traditions like "Fall Carnival during Spirit Weekend, Casino Night, Panther Madness (our version of homecoming), and the winter lighting" along with "daily fun things like trivia nights, movie nights [and]...lots of performances." Many also note that "athletics are big," since "Adelphi fields numerous NCAA Division II teams." Undergrads can find groups for nearly any interest. One student makes time for "fiber arts club, artivism club, students with disabilities club, [and] dungeons and dragons club." And if you're one of those who prioritize academics, you're not alone: "One of my favorite extracurricular activities is participating in a work-study group with my classmates." Undergrads appreciate being "just a train ride from Manhattan, giving students immediate access to internships, cultural events, and industry connections" while living on "a close-knit, suburban" campus. Overall, students find the school's activities to be a good way to "explore new interests, collaborate with diverse peers, and add a fun, purposeful rhythm to student life."

Student Body

Students suggest that Adelphi's the place where "everybody has a smile and is always kind," not to mention "supportive...smart and ambitious." As one student details, "Everyone looks out for each other, whether it is sharing notes, preparing for exams together, or talking through career goals and personal challenges. What makes our student body unique is that the support is never competitive; it is truly communal." Additionally, undergrads note that while many classmates are "from the surrounding Long Island and New York City areas," you'll also find "students from across the country and abroad." This "wide range of backgrounds, interests, and life experiences...creates a campus environment that feels both diverse and very community-oriented." Students also value the fact that their "peers are not only academically driven but...deeply engaged in pursuits beyond the classroom—whether that's athletics, arts, activism, or entrepreneurship." Plus, the school's relatively small size means that "people recognize one another quickly, classmates become familiar faces across departments, and conversations started in a seminar often continue in the library, the science building, or over coffee." As this student concludes, "I have met so many new people who I love from Adelphi and believe it is truly a school where there is something for everyone."

Adelphi University

Financial Aid: 516-877-3080 • E-Mail: admissions@adelphi.edu • Website: www.adelphi.edu

THE PRINCETON REVIEW SAYS

Admissions

The school reports that its standardized testing policy for use in admission for Fall 2026 is Test Optional. The Princeton Review suggests that interested applicants consult with the school for the most up-to-date standardized testing policies. *Very important factors considered include:* rigor of secondary school record. *Important factors considered include:* academic GPA, standardized test scores, application essay, recommendation(s), extracurricular activities, talent/ability, character/personal qualities, volunteer work. *Other factors considered include:* interview, first generation, geographical residence, work experience, level of applicant's interest. High school diploma is required and GED is accepted. *Academic units required:* 4 English, 3 math, 3 science, 2 language (other than English), 1 social studies, 1 history, 2 academic electives.

Financial Aid

Students should submit: FAFSA; State aid form. Priority filing deadline is 3/1. The Princeton Review suggests that all financial aid forms be submitted as soon as possible. *Need-based scholarships/grants offered:* Federal Pell; Federal SEOG; State scholarships/grants; Private scholarships; College/university scholarship or grant aid from institutional funds. *Loan aid offered:* Federal Direct Subsidized Loans; Federal Direct Unsubsidized Loans; Direct PLUS loans. Admitted students will be notified of awards on a rolling basis beginning 1/15. Federal Work-Study Program available. Institutional employment available.

The Inside Word

Applying early action gives you a competitive edge, as you'll be among the first considered for generous scholarships and need-based aid, with no binding commitment.

THE SCHOOL SAYS

From the Admissions Office

"Adelphi University is a highly respected, nationally recognized university where academic rigor meets measurable outcomes. Located in Garden City, New York—just a short train ride from New York City—Adelphi offers a personalized campus experience with direct access to one of the most competitive career markets in the world. With nearly 8,000 undergraduate and graduate students, Adelphi delivers an individualized academic experience across more than 70 undergraduate programs. Students learn within distinguished schools, including the College of Nursing and Public Health, the Gordon F. Derner School of Psychology, the School of Social Work, the Robert B. Willumstad School of Business, and the Honors College. An 11:1 student-to-faculty ratio ensures that students are known, challenged, and supported by faculty who are deeply invested in their success.

"Adelphi's strength is not just in what students learn—but in what they achieve. Ninety-two percent of graduates are employed, continuing their education, or engaged in meaningful opportunities within one year of graduation, and alumni report salaries that are competitive with national benchmarks. Through internships, clinical placements, and research—many connected to New York City—students graduate with both experience and a clear competitive edge. National recognition reinforces this impact. Adelphi is recognized by Times Higher Education among a select group of U.S. institutions included in its global rankings—placing the University within approximately the top 8% of colleges and universities evaluated nationwide. Adelphi is also ranked the top private university on Long Island by Forbes and is consistently recognized for strong student outcomes, value, and social mobility.

"Adelphi takes a holistic approach to admission, seeking students who are motivated, curious, and ready to grow. Through rigorous academics, individualized support, and intentional career preparation, Adelphi ensures that students graduate not just with a degree—but with direction, experience, and long-term opportunity."

SELECTIVITY

# of total applicants	17,233
% of total applicants accepted	72
% of total acceptees attending	8
# offered a place on the wait list	193
# admitted from wait list	6

First-Year Profile

Testing policy	Test Optional
Range SAT composite	1140–1330
Range SAT EBRW	570–680
Range SAT math	550–670
Range ACT composite	23–31
% submitting SAT scores	22
% submitting ACT scores	2
Average HS GPA	3.7
% submitting high school GPA	100

Important Dates

Early action	
Apply by	11/1
Notified by	12/31
Regular	
Apply by	Rolling
Notified by	Rolling, 11/15
Nonfall registration?	Yes

FINANCIAL FACTS

Annual tuition	$50,110
Food and housing	$22,850
Required fees	$1,940
Books and supplies	$1,200
Average need-based scholarship (First-year)	$33,301 ($36,277)
% students with need rec. need-based scholarship or grant aid (First-year)	84 (82)
% students with need rec. non-need-based scholarship or grant aid (First-year)	19 (23)
% students with need rec. need-based self-help aid (First-year)	72 (76)
% students rec. any financial aid (First-year)	95 (99)
% UG borrow to pay for school	57
Average cumulative indebtedness	$23,381
% of students with need fully met (First-year)	16 (20)
Average % of student need met (First-year)	55 (59)

AGNES SCOTT COLLEGE

141 East College Avenue, Decatur, GA 30030 • Admissions: 404-471-6285

Survey Snapshot
Students are happy
Lab facilities are great
Great library

RATINGS

Quality of Life	89
Fire Safety	93
Green	90
Academic	91
Profs Interesting	93
Profs Accessible	96
Admissions	87
Financial Aid	87

CAMPUS LIFE

Type of school	Private
Affiliation	Presbyterian
Environment	Metropolis

Students

Degree-seeking undergrad enrollment	721
% male/female/not reported	0/100/0
% from out of state	33
% First-year live on campus	87
% Ugrads live on campus	83
# of sororities (% join)	NR
% Asian	4
% Black or African American	35
% Hispanic	15
% Native American	<1
% Pacific Islander	<1
% Race and/or ethnicity unknown	<1
% Two or more races	7
% White	36
% International	2
# of countries represented	12

CAMPUS MENTAL HEALTH SERVICES

Offers mental health/wellness program	Yes
Mental health training available to students	No
Employs Chief Wellness Officer	NR
Peer-to-peer mental health offerings	NR
Counseling center has guidelines or accreditation	No
Mental health/well-being courses	NR

ACADEMICS

% students returning for sophomore year	74
% students graduating within 4 years	63
% students graduating within 6 years	68
Calendar	Semester
Student/faculty ratio	10:1
Most common class size 10–19.	(47%)
Most common lab/discussion size 20–29.	(43%)

Most Popular Majors
Psychology; Public Health; Business Administration and Management

Applicants Often Prefer
Georgia State University, University of Georgia

Applicants Sometimes Prefer
Mount Holyoke College

STUDENTS SAY "..."

Academics

Agnes Scott College is a liberal arts college dedicated to fostering a "supportive community of strong women working to create change in the world." The school's unique SUMMIT curriculum offers an individualized course of study, immersion, and experiences under the guidance of a personal advisor. The program is designed "to engage [students] in the social challenges of our times while providing context for a variety of viewpoints, whether that is various global, religious, or political perspectives." Throughout their time here, all students participate in co-curricular development activities, such as Peak Week, a period in the spring where students take part in events like Global Journeys (faculty-led trips), career experiences, and SCALE, where second-years collaborate with Atlanta businesses and nonprofits. One student highlights the autonomy of the curriculum as a major reason for choosing Agnes Scott: "I have the power to create the program. That is a wonderful opportunity," adding, "I [will] leave an impact on my college." The academics here are "rigorous but rewarding," and "students are expected to work hard outside of the classroom so that class time can be spent valuably." To this end, professors "create thoughtful syllabi" and "classes are interactive and engaging because [professors] are open to different teaching styles and making sure all students can bring their own perspective into the discussion." The administration "really tries to get the student's perspective on all aspects of campus life" and is "inclusive and open to addressing problems within the student body." The college "prepares its students to face the world head-on," providing valuable leadership opportunities and "creating a living-and-learning community...[while] preparing women to be a part of the global community."

Campus Life

"The campus is absolutely beautiful," and "the energy and vibe here is unique. We get the experience of a large city but have the community of a close-knit town." Admittedly, "there isn't much free time because students...tend to have work study, jobs, hard classes, volunteer, extracurricular, and internships to keep them busy all week." Fortunately, the "student-led Programing Board offers weekly events," and there are "constantly events on campus put on by student clubs." One very popular event is Pancake Jam, where the night before exams, "faculty and staff serve us breakfast food so students can sing, dance, and destress." When students want a break from campus, they can "hang out in downtown Decatur since it is a quick walk from campus," and it's a "cute and a safe little town." Additionally, "the MARTA subway system is a five-minute walk, so you can [visit] almost anywhere in Atlanta." Students enjoy Atlanta's "vibrant culture...by eating at restaurants, visiting museums, attending music events, and visiting art galleries." Closer to home, the campus features numerous hammocks for students, so when the weather is nice, it's common to "see us hanging out in between classes" or enjoying a good book in them.

Student Body

Agnes Scott "is an incredibly diverse campus of students," representing a wide range of backgrounds and viewpoints. Students value the "inclusivity created by the campus community," which actively "welcomes students of all identities" and encourages students to be "inquisitive and forward-thinking," ensuring that "there is never a Scottie that is alone here." The school is described as having "both a competitive and loving environment. Every student is so understanding and willing to cooperate with everyone else." For instance, "It is very easy to form study groups or collaborate with others on projects." Within this supportive student body, "everyone finds their group and niche on campus."

Agnes Scott College

Financial Aid: 404-471-6395 • E-Mail: admission@agnesscott.edu • Website: www.agnesscott.edu

THE PRINCETON REVIEW SAYS

Admissions

The school reports that its standardized testing policy for use in admission for Fall 2026 is Test Optional. The Princeton Review suggests that interested applicants consult with the school for the most up-to-date standardized testing policies. *Very important factors considered include:* rigor of secondary school record, academic GPA. *Important factors considered include:* application essay, recommendation(s), extracurricular activities, talent/ability, volunteer work. *Other factors considered include:* class rank, standardized test scores, interview, character/personal qualities, first generation, alumni/ae relation, geographical residence, state residency, work experience, level of applicant's interest. High school diploma is required and GED is accepted. *Academic units recommended:* 4 English, 4 math, 4 science, 2 science labs, 2 language (other than English), 2 social studies.

Financial Aid

Students should submit: FAFSA. Priority filing deadline is 2/15. The Princeton Review suggests that all financial aid forms be submitted as soon as possible. *Need-based scholarships/grants offered:* Federal Pell; Federal SEOG; State scholarships/grants; Private scholarships; College/university scholarship or grant aid from institutional funds. *Loan aid offered:* Federal Direct Subsidized Loans; Federal Direct Unsubsidized Loans; Direct PLUS loans. Admitted students will be notified of awards on a rolling basis beginning 3/1. Federal Work-Study Program available. Institutional employment available.

The Inside Word

Admissions officers at Agnes Scott College happily take a holistic approach to their process. They seek to create an incoming class that's diverse and reflective of many interests and ideas. They also realize that potential can be measured in a variety of ways. If you want to give yourself a bit of a leg up, the college highly recommends that you take advantage of the opportunity for an interview with an admissions counselor.

THE SCHOOL SAYS

From the Admissions Office

"This is your liberal arts education, reimagined, at Agnes Scott College. During your four years here, you'll grow as a person, a student and a leader. Through SUMMIT, our signature experience for all students, you'll take on a rigorous curriculum focused on leadership, global citizenship and professional success. You will be able to shape your academic experience within your major with experiential opportunities (study abroad, research and internships) to ensure you are learning what you want to learn for your goals.

"Your classrooms will be small but big on community. You will learn from diverse perspectives; there is no racial or ethnic majority on campus. You'll make lifelong friendships in residence halls and while taking part in 60+ clubs and organizations. You will have the chance to explore the Atlanta community, as one of the best southern cities for culture, cuisine and internship opportunities. And you'll explore the world through class experiences and on your own as an informed global citizen."

SELECTIVITY

# of total applicants	2,070
% of total applicants accepted	64
% of total acceptees attending	15
# of in-state applicants	1,049
% of in-state applicants accepted	75
# of out-of-state-applicants	613
% of applicants accepted from out of state	73
# of international applicants	408
% of international applicants accepted	18
# of early decision applicants	8
% of early decision applicants accepted	75
# offered a place on the wait list	0

First-Year Profile

Testing policy	Test Optional
Range SAT composite	1120–1280
Range SAT EBRW	570–670
Range SAT math	510–610
Range ACT composite	25–31
% submitting SAT scores	29
% submitting ACT scores	11
Average HS GPA	3.6
% submitting high school GPA	98
% graduated top 10% of class	13
% graduated top 25% of class	47
% graduated top 50% of class	74
% submitting high school rank	44

Important Dates

Early decision	
Apply by	11/1
Notified by	12/1
Early action	
Apply by	11/15
Notified by	12/15
Regular	
Apply by	5/1
Notified by	Rolling, 12/15
Nonfall registration?	No

FINANCIAL FACTS

Annual tuition	$53,256
Food and housing	$14,079
Required fees	$350
Books and supplies	$1,000
Average need-based scholarship (First-year)	$39,479 ($43,398)
% students with need rec. need-based scholarship or grant aid (First-year)	100 (100)
% students with need rec. non-need-based scholarship or grant aid (First-year)	2 (7)
% students with need rec. need-based self-help aid (First-year)	63 (69)
% UG borrow to pay for school	60
Average cumulative indebtedness	$32,452
% of students with need fully met (First-year)	3 (8)
Average % of student need met (First-year)	62 (70)

ALBION COLLEGE

611 E. Porter Street, Albion, MI 49224 • Admissions: 517-629-0321

Survey Snapshot
Lab facilities are great
Frats and sororities are popular
Intramural sports are popular

RATINGS

Quality of Life	**77**
Fire Safety	**88**
Green	**87**
Academic	**83**
Profs Interesting	**92**
Profs Accessible	**95**
Admissions	**74**
Financial Aid	**91**

CAMPUS LIFE

Type of school	Private
Environment	Village

Students

Degree-seeking undergrad enrollment	1,163
% male/female/not reported	48/52/<1
% from out of state	23
% First-year live on campus	100
% Ugrads live on campus	93
# of fraternities (% join)	9 (25)
# of sororities (% join)	8 (26)
% Asian	2
% Black or African American	14
% Hispanic	11
% Native American	<1
% Pacific Islander	0
% Race and/or ethnicity unknown	7
% Two or more races	5
% White	55
% International	6
# of countries represented	24

CAMPUS MENTAL HEALTH SERVICES

Offers mental health/wellness program	Yes
Mental health training available to students	Yes
Employs Chief Wellness Officer	Yes
Peer-to-peer mental health offerings	No
Counseling center has guidelines or accreditation	Yes
Mental health/well-being courses	Yes, for-credit

ACADEMICS

% students returning for sophomore year	68
% students graduating within 4 years	45
% students graduating within 6 years	57
Calendar	Semester
Student/faculty ratio	11:1
Most common class size 10–19.	(43%)
Most common lab/discussion size 10–19.	(52%)

Most Popular Majors

Biology/Biological Sciences; Exercise Science and Kinesiology; Research and Experimental Psychology

Applicants Also Look At

Grand Valley State University, Michigan State University, University of Michigan—Ann Arbor

STUDENTS SAY "..."

Academics

Albion College is known for its "great academics" and supportive, "close-knit community." According to students, the college's liberal arts education is outstanding, with "plenty of academic and research opportunities for students." One student notes that they've been involved with active science research projects "since my freshman year, and I have learned so much." Strong programs like the Wilson Medical Institute, which "has a very high rate of students being accepted into medical school," and the Gerstacker Business Institute allow students to "gain real-world experience." Some students note that while "classes are challenging," they appreciate that Albion fosters an environment that "encourages questions [and] thinking" while offering "personal attention to each student." Small class sizes "make it easier to learn" and foster "connections with your classmates and professors." In general, classes "include more discussion than lecture," allowing students to express their "own opinions and values and see others' views." Many Albion undergrads are full of praise for their professors. "The professors here are…the true highlight of this campus!" As one student explains, "They make themselves available outside of class and encourage students to ask for help." Another student adds, "I have had access to opportunities I never knew existed because of the help and support I get from professors." Concludes one student, "I've had lots of amazing professional development, networking, and research experiences, the mentoring here is super helpful…they have all the resources to help you succeed."

Campus Life

Albion College offers a wide range of clubs, organizations, and events, and "everyone is very involved on campus," often taking part in multiple activities, such as Greek life, service groups, or sports. In addition, the "Union Board hosts a lot of events for students," including comedy shows and concerts. Sports also play an important role. As one student puts it, "Athletic culture at Albion is huge." From swimming, basketball, track, and volleyball to the popular equestrian center, there are endless opportunities to stay active, and spectator sports draw large crowds. For those who enjoy being outside, "the Nature Center is really good for hiking and outdoor activities" like relaxing in a hammock or swimming in the creek. Beyond these activities, many students join volunteer and social groups. The popular Student Volunteer Bureau, for example, "focuses on helping out the local community," and Greek life brings students together "with great opportunities for service, building friendships, and contributing to the community." Others pursue passions in music, theater, politics, or clubs tied to their academic interests. As one undergraduate shares, "I think there is a club or niche here where everyone can find a group of people they fit in with."

Student Body

Students at Albion College describe their peers as warm, involved, and eager to support one another. "One of my favorite things [about Albion] is the people," says one undergrad, reflecting a common view that the small campus feels like "one big family." In fact, the "very small and close-knit" community "leads to a great energy on campus," where students say it's easy to form friendships and feel recognized. One student notes, "I have met all kinds of people...from a multitude of different backgrounds," while others highlight the "diverse point[s] of view" that enrich discussions and campus life. The Albion community is "very open and accepting and everyone can find people to vibe with on this campus." In addition, as one student shares, "I love that everyone seems to be so engaged in everything that is going on and that there [is] always room for anyone."

Albion College

Financial Aid: 517-629-0440 • E-Mail: admission@albion.edu • Website: www.albion.edu

THE PRINCETON REVIEW SAYS

Admissions

The school reports that its standardized testing policy for use in admission for Fall 2026 is Test Optional. The Princeton Review suggests that interested applicants consult with the school for the most up-to-date standardized testing policies. *Important factors considered include:* academic GPA. *Other factors considered include:* rigor of secondary school record, class rank, recommendation(s). High school diploma is required and GED is accepted.

Financial Aid

Students should submit: FAFSA. Priority filing deadline is 12/1. The Princeton Review suggests that all financial aid forms be submitted as soon as possible. *Need-based scholarships/grants offered:* Federal Pell; Federal SEOG; State scholarships/grants; Private scholarships; College/university scholarship or grant aid from institutional funds. *Loan aid offered:* Federal Direct Subsidized Loans; Federal Direct Unsubsidized Loans; Direct PLUS loans. Admitted students will be notified of awards on a rolling basis beginning 12/1. Federal Work-Study Program available. Institutional employment available.

The Inside Word

Keep in mind when applying to Albion that academic success takes precedence, and applicants should have taken a challenging high school curriculum, including some honors and AP courses. Of course, admissions officers are also concerned about maintaining a vibrant community, so careful attention will also be paid to extracurricular activities.

THE SCHOOL SAYS

From the Admissions Office

"At Albion College, we believe in preparing students to make an immediate impact—through a highly applied liberal arts education, a welcoming residential community, and focused career development. Albion offers nearly 100 areas of study with no waiting lists for majors, along with dual degree programs in engineering, teacher certification options, and a BFA in art.

"Every student is assigned a dedicated advisor from day one to help navigate academics, long-term goals, and new interests. Career preparation is woven throughout the student experience—through internships, course-embedded experiential learning, off-campus study, paid consulting work, grant-funded research, and volunteer placements.

"Our renowned institutes and centers support real-world learning in business and management, public policy and service, sustainability, medicine and health sciences, education, and social change. Students in the Prentiss M. Brown Honors Program explore small, interdisciplinary seminars and complete a capstone research or creative project.

"Albion provides the most diverse campus experience, the best student experience, and the greatest social mobility for its graduates of any school in Michigan. Campus life is vibrant and inclusive, with 100+ student-led organizations, a spirited Greek system, and exciting traditions like Drip Ball and the Day of Woden. Albion competes in the NCAA Division III Michigan Intercollegiate Athletic Association with 24 varsity teams—including equestrian, wrestling, and esports.

"Set along the scenic Kalamazoo River and just two blocks from a charming downtown, Albion combines natural beauty with urban access via our Amtrak station and proximity to Lansing, Kalamazoo, Ann Arbor, and Detroit."

SELECTIVITY

# of total applicants	8,048
% of total applicants accepted	74
% of total acceptees attending	6
# of in-state applicants	3,278
% of in-state applicants accepted	79
# of out-of-state-applicants	3,038
% of applicants accepted from out of state	82
# of international applicants	1,063
% of international applicants accepted	48
# of early decision applicants	324
% of early decision applicants accepted	49
# offered a place on the wait list	0
# admitted from wait list	0

First-Year Profile

Testing policy	Test Optional
Average HS GPA	3.5
% submitting high school GPA	88

Important Dates

Early decision	
Apply by	11/1
Notified by	Rolling
Early action	
Apply by	12/1
Notified by	2/1
Regular	
Apply by	Rolling
Notified by	Rolling
Nonfall registration?	Yes

FINANCIAL FACTS

Annual tuition	$59,620
Food and housing	$13,210
Required fees (First-year)	$640 ($825)
Books and supplies	$850
Average need-based scholarship (First-year)	$51,364 ($52,128)
% students with need rec. need-based scholarship or grant aid (First-year)	100 (100)
% students with need rec. non-need-based scholarship or grant aid (First-year)	98 (97)
% students with need rec. need-based self-help aid (First-year)	72 (71)
% students rec. any financial aid (First-year)	100 (100)
% UG borrow to pay for school	69
Average cumulative indebtedness	$36,857
% of students with need fully met (First-year)	37 (38)
Average % of student need met (First-year)	93 (95)

ALFRED UNIVERSITY

One Saxon Drive, Alfred, NY 14802-1205 • Admissions: 607-871-2115

Survey Snapshot
Students are happy
Great library
Diverse student types interact on campus

RATINGS

Quality of Life	**84**
Fire Safety	**99**
Green	**60***
Academic	**82**
Profs Interesting	**89**
Profs Accessible	**93**
Admissions	**89**
Financial Aid	**90**

CAMPUS LIFE

Type of school	Private
Environment	Rural

Students

Degree-seeking undergrad enrollment	1,448
% male/female/not reported	46/53/1
% from out of state	25
# of fraternities	0
# of sororities	0
% Asian	1
% Black or African American	7
% Hispanic	9
% Native American	<1
% Pacific Islander	<1
% Race and/or ethnicity unknown	3
% Two or more races	4
% White	65
% International	10
# of countries represented	32

CAMPUS MENTAL HEALTH SERVICES

Offers mental health/wellness program	Yes
Mental health training available to students	Yes
Employs Chief Wellness Officer	Yes
Peer-to-peer mental health offerings	No
Counseling center has guidelines or accreditation	Yes
Mental health/well-being courses	No

ACADEMICS

% students returning for sophomore year	76
% students graduating within 4 years	35
% students graduating within 6 years	46
Calendar	Semester
Most common class size 10–19.	(41%)
Most common lab/discussion size 10–19.	(52%)

Applicants Sometimes Prefer
Rochester Institute of Technology, State University of New York—Buffalo State University, State University of New York—University at Buffalo, University of Rochester

Applicants Rarely Prefer
St. Ambrose University, St. Lawrence University

STUDENTS SAY "..."

Academics

Flexibility is paramount to an Alfred University education and the school wants its Saxons to avail themselves of the "variety of academic opportunities" it offers in order to create a truly individual curriculum. While known for its "excellent art program"—especially ceramics and glass—students confirm that it's "easy to take subjects outside your major," and they value the number of "other majors versus a traditional art [school] setting" that are available. As one art student attests, "If I had decided to change majors, Alfred has almost every opportunity."

With fewer than 2,000 undergraduates on its sprawling upstate campus, students find "the classroom size is perfect for a more personalized education." As one student says, "It is the closest to one-on-one teaching you can get." Students also have access to hands-on facilities such as outdoor kilns and wind tunnels, as well as built-in funding for real-world experiences via the Alfred University Applied and Experiential Learning Program (APEX). For those who do conduct their own research or experiments, professors are "always willing to put time into student independent projects." Classes at Alfred are headed by "outstanding, talented, dedicated" professors who "are always pushing you to reach your full potential" and they "bring a level of vibrancy and academic encouragement through enthusiasm to the classroom."

Campus Life

Alfred is the second-oldest coed institution in the country, and the school has a long history of often quirky traditions, such as the Pine Hill Derby (soap box racing) and Hot Dog Day (just what it sounds like). School spirit is strong, with students donning purple and gold for Saxon Fridays, and "every sports team is supported, and superfans are at every event." Part of the reason for this strong "sense of community" is the school's "somewhat rural location" in the southern tier of New York, where the "beautiful" campus hums with activities. Students say "there are so many clubs and options that you can find something to do" regardless of the day of week. This includes the "strong equestrian program," as well as "student club productions...and fundraisers and an excellent selection of movies shown on campus." As far as infrastructure goes, "the facilities are amazing," particularly those for art and engineering. That's a good thing, because it means that although "it snows constantly" in this bucolic location, students can carry on with their activities.

Student Body

Alfred's students freely mix and move between the traditional major-related groups to become "well-acquainted with people from a variety of studies and backgrounds and with a variety of interests." All first-year and transfer students participate in Alfred's Common Ground program, taking part in small group discussions to learn about different backgrounds and assumptions they might have. While some say there is "a pretty significant gap between the prevalent, spunky art students and the more reclusive engineers," most easily socialize across academic lines and "more often than not, you'll see engineers rubbing elbows with philosophy majors and artists chilling with math and chemistry majors." The art program draws a large creative component to campus, and while "everyone finds their own little niche" in this "warm" environment, it "definitely does not mean they stay there—you are allowed to float between everything." Saxons are, as a whole, "friendly, outgoing, and involved," and "you can't go down the street without receiving a smile."

ALFRED UNIVERSITY

Financial Aid: 607-871-2159 • E-Mail: admissions@alfred.edu • Website: www.alfred.edu

THE PRINCETON REVIEW SAYS

Admissions

The school reports that its standardized testing policy for use in admission for Fall 2026 is Test Optional. The Princeton Review suggests that interested applicants consult with the school for the most up-to-date standardized testing policies. *Very important factors considered include:* rigor of secondary school record, class rank, academic GPA, extracurricular activities, character/personal qualities. *Important factors considered include:* standardized test scores, application essay, recommendation(s), interview, volunteer work, work experience. *Other factors considered include:* talent/ability, first generation, level of applicant's interest. High school diploma is required and GED is accepted. *Academic units required:* 4 English, 3 math, 2 science, 2 science labs, 2 social studies, 3 academic electives. *Academic units recommended:* 4 English, 4 math, 3 science, 3 science labs, 1 language (other than English), 3 social studies.

Financial Aid

Students should submit: FAFSA; State aid form. Priority filing deadline is 3/15. The Princeton Review suggests that all financial aid forms be submitted as soon as possible. *Need-based scholarships/grants offered:* Federal Pell; Federal SEOG; State scholarships/grants; Private scholarships; College/university scholarship or grant aid from institutional funds. *Loan aid offered:* Federal Direct Subsidized Loans; Federal Direct Unsubsidized Loans; Direct PLUS loans; College/university loans from institutional funds. Admitted students will be notified of awards on a rolling basis beginning 2/15. Federal Work-Study Program available. Institutional employment available.

The Inside Word

Alfred is a fine university with a solid local reputation. The allure for arts students is obvious—Alfred's programs in the arts are especially well-regarded—and as a result, competition is fierce among applicants for these programs. A stellar portfolio, even more than great grades and standardized test scores (if submitting), is your most likely ticket in. Competition for the engineering school is also tight. Applicants will need to have thrived in a rigorous high school program.

THE SCHOOL SAYS

From the Admissions Office

"The admissions process at Alfred University is the foundation for the personal attention each student can expect during their time at AU. Each applicant is evaluated individually and receives genuine, individual care and consideration.

"The best way to discover all Alfred University has to offer is to come to campus. We truly have something for everyone with more than forty courses of study, twenty-one NCAA Division III sports and two IHSA sports, and over eighty student-run clubs and organizations. You can tour campus; meet current students, faculty, coaches and staff; attend a class; and eat in our dining hall-experience firsthand what life at AU is like.

"Alfred University is a place where students are free to pursue their interests—all of them—no matter how varied or different. Academics, athletics, co-ops, study abroad, internships, special interests—they're all part of what makes you who you are and who you are going to become."

SELECTIVITY

# of total applicants	7,271
% of total applicants accepted	48
% of total acceptees attending	12
# of in-state applicants	3,302
% of in-state applicants accepted	56
# of out-of-state-applicants	2,034
% of applicants accepted from out of state	61
# of international applicants	1,928
% of international applicants accepted	20

First-Year Profile

Testing policy	Test Optional
Range SAT composite	1130–1310
Range SAT EBRW	560–660
Range SAT math	560–660
Range ACT composite	24–30
% submitting SAT scores	26
% submitting ACT scores	4
Average HS GPA	3.5
% submitting high school GPA	100
% graduated top 10% of class	21
% graduated top 25% of class	53
% graduated top 50% of class	90
% submitting high school rank	40

Important Dates

Early action	
Apply by	12/1
Notified by	Rolling
Regular	
Apply by	8/1
Notified by	Rolling, 11/15
Nonfall registration?	Yes

FINANCIAL FACTS

Annual tuition	$44,300
Food and housing	$16,960
Required fees	$1,450
Books and supplies	$1,300
Average need-based scholarship (First-year)	$31,740 ($33,683)
% students with need rec. need-based scholarship or grant aid (First-year)	99 (100)
% students with need rec. non-need-based scholarship or grant aid (First-year)	87 (94)
% students with need rec. need-based self-help aid (First-year)	75 (75)
% UG borrow to pay for school	86
Average cumulative indebtedness	$26,966
% of students with need fully met (First-year)	28 (31)
Average % of student need met (First-year)	83 (86)

Allegheny College

520 North Main Street, Meadville, PA 16335 • Admissions: 814-332-4351

Survey Snapshot
Students environmentally aware
Students take advantage of the outdoors
Active student government

RATINGS

Quality of Life	86
Fire Safety	85
Green	60*
Academic	87
Profs Interesting	94
Profs Accessible	96
Admissions	87
Financial Aid	93

CAMPUS LIFE

Type of school	Private
Affiliation	United Methodist
Environment	Town

Students

Degree-seeking undergrad enrollment	1,099
% male/female/not reported	48/52/0
% from out of state	55
% First-year from public high school	88
% First-year live on campus	96
% Ugrads live on campus	88
# of fraternities (% join)	4 (11)
# of sororities (% join)	6 (21)
% Asian	2
% Black or African American	9
% Hispanic	7
% Native American	<1
% Pacific Islander	<1
% Race and/or ethnicity unknown	2
% Two or more races	4
% White	69
% International	6
# of countries represented	32

CAMPUS MENTAL HEALTH SERVICES

Offers mental health/wellness program	Yes
Mental health training available to students	Yes
Employs Chief Wellness Officer	Yes
Peer-to-peer mental health offerings	No
Counseling center has guidelines or accreditation	No
Mental health/well-being courses	Yes, non-credit

ACADEMICS

% students returning for sophomore year	80
% students graduating within 4 years	67
% students graduating within 6 years	73
Calendar	Semester
Student/faculty ratio	8:1
Most common class size 10–19.	(56%)
Most common lab/discussion size 10–19.	(58%)

Most Popular Majors

Biology/Biological Sciences; Sustainability Studies; Psychology

Applicants Sometimes Prefer

Duquesne University, John Carroll University, Kent State University— Kent Campus, Ohio University—Athens, Penn State University Park, Temple University, University of Pittsburgh—Pittsburgh Campus, Westminster College (PA)

Applicants Rarely Prefer

Washington & Jefferson College

STUDENTS SAY "..."

Academics

Students at Allegheny College feel encouraged by the school's distinctive and flexible approach to education to mix and match different fields of interest: "You have students who major in neuroscience and minor in English, or major in economics and minor in philosophy." This speaks to the school's rigorous and rewarding academic program, which emphasizes "achieving personal intellectual growth." This is proven in the classroom, where it's said that "students often ask questions in class and actively engage in discussions," and this "passion for education makes class discussion lively and enhances the overall experience of an education." Students note that "the majority of professors at Allegheny are wonderful and extremely helpful," and the small class sizes create opportunities for meaningful interaction and guidance. Many students emphasize the accessibility of faculty: "I love the fact that I can go speak to any of my professors about anything and get the help I need." Another hallmark of the Allegheny experience is the required senior research project. One student explains, "The senior research project we are required to complete before graduating does a lot to bolster résumés and prep students for graduate schools." Beyond strengthening academic and professional credentials, the project serves as a unifying experience that "inspires a level of camaraderie and cooperation unusual for a college." As one student says, "Allegheny does a good job of making us think critically, while also allowing us to still enjoy our college experience."

Campus Life

"The campus is very lively," thanks in part to the requirement that students live in on-campus housing for four years, or eight full semesters. "In addition to going to classes and studying in between, most students try to get actively involved with campus life" and weekends often center around on-campus activities. And with numerous school-sponsored clubs and organizations, "everyone can find something [they're] passionate about at Allegheny." Students also take advantage of the "natural beauty of this region" through outdoor activities. Popular choices include Outing Club events, which range from backpacking and skiing to canoeing and white-water rafting. "Community service and volunteer work are also important" aspects of student life, along with athletics—"games are well attended and tailgating is popular among students on the weekends." For those interested, Greek life is also available "if you want it to be a part of your experience." Overall, the campus is a tight-knit community that is "small enough that you will see a familiar face wherever you go, without feeling like you know everyone on campus."

Student Body

Allegheny College has a "very welcoming, judgment-free student body," where "generally people are accepting of your identity, restrictions and boundaries." Students appreciate the school's commitment to admitting "students from different cultures and a general acceptance of varying creeds, sexual orientations, gender identities, and races," and view Allegheny as an "excellent melting pot of ideas, experiences and identities." On the whole, "academics are important to Allegheny students," who are "incredibly involved, engaged, and passionate about what they do." The "majority of [the] student body prides itself on social justice and service work," with one student sharing, "Just being on this campus is an education in politics...and environmentalism." Students routinely refer to their peers as unique, "all with their own very different interests," forming a "diverse community that offers many viewpoints, backgrounds, and experiences." However, one thing that Allegheny students share is a strong sense of connection and belonging, often pointing to the college's "family-like atmosphere" as one of its defining and best qualities.

ALLEGHENY COLLEGE

Financial Aid: 800-835-7780 • E-Mail: admissions@allegheny.edu • Website: allegheny.edu

THE PRINCETON REVIEW SAYS

Admissions

The school reports that its standardized testing policy for use in admission for Fall 2026 is Test Optional. The Princeton Review suggests that interested applicants consult with the school for the most up-to-date standardized testing policies. *Very important factors considered include:* rigor of secondary school record, academic GPA. *Important factors considered include:* standardized test scores, extracurricular activities, character/personal qualities. *Other factors considered include:* class rank, application essay, recommendation(s), interview, talent/ability, first generation, geographical residence, volunteer work, work experience, level of applicant's interest. High school diploma is required and GED is accepted. *Academic units required:* 4 English, 3 math, 3 science, 2 language (other than English), 3 social studies, 1 visual/performing arts.

Financial Aid

Students should submit: FAFSA. Priority filing deadline is 2/15. The Princeton Review suggests that all financial aid forms be submitted as soon as possible. *Need-based scholarships/grants offered:* Federal Pell; Federal SEOG; State scholarships/grants; Private scholarships; College/university scholarship or grant aid from institutional funds. *Loan aid offered:* Federal Direct Subsidized Loans; Federal Direct Unsubsidized Loans; Direct PLUS loans; State Loans; College/university loans from institutional funds. Admitted students will be notified of awards on a rolling basis beginning 11/15. Federal Work-Study Program available. Institutional employment available.

The Inside Word

Students seeking admission to Allegheny would be well-served by having an average GPA of at least 3.5, but as the school puts it of their holistic and thorough review process: "no single grade, factor, or score" determines admission. In addition to grades, admission officers look closely at recommendation letters, essays, community involvement, and students' other talents, and because the school is Test Optional, it strongly recommends an on-campus or online interview to help provide a more complete picture. The school has two early decision dates, in addition to early action and regular decision deadlines.

THE SCHOOL SAYS

From the Admissions Office

"Allegheny is looking for students who aren't focused on just one thing, who aren't content to follow a simple straightforward path. Our students tap into all of their talent and interests, no matter how unusual the combinations.

"A typical Allegheny student might study biochemistry, economics or filmmaking while preparing for medical school, but also play club soccer, report for the newspaper, intern at the hospital, and learn to ski—all in the same week!

"Allegheny provides the freedom to select majors and minors of unusual combinations, cultivating creative, "big picture" thinking others often stifle.

"So, if you feel you have combinations of interests that others might consider unusual—we want to celebrate that with you! We think of that as a compliment, one that recognizes the complexity possible in all of us."

SELECTIVITY

# of total applicants	6,151
% of total applicants accepted	59
% of total acceptees attending	9
# of in-state applicants	1,435
% of in-state applicants accepted	83
# of out-of-state-applicants	2,855
% of applicants accepted from out of state	77
# of international applicants	1,861
% of international applicants accepted	13
# of early decision applicants	135
% of early decision applicants accepted	50
# offered a place on the wait list	220
# admitted from wait list	3

First-Year Profile

Testing policy	Test Optional
Range SAT composite	1160–1360
Range SAT EBRW	610–670
Range SAT math	540–660
Range ACT composite	21–28
% submitting SAT scores	31
% submitting ACT scores	9
Average HS GPA	3.6
% submitting high school GPA	4
% graduated top 10% of class	25
% graduated top 25% of class	50
% graduated top 50% of class	80

Important Dates

Early decision	
Apply by	11/15
Notified by	11/30
Other ED apply by	2/1
Other ED notified by	2/15
Early action	
Apply by	12/1
Notified by	1/1
Regular	
Apply by	2/15
Notified by	3/15
Nonfall registration?	Yes

FINANCIAL FACTS

Annual tuition	$59,050
Food and housing	$15,760
Required fees	$740
Books and supplies	$500
Average need-based scholarship (First-year)	$39,803 ($39,803)
% students with need rec. need-based scholarship or grant aid (First-year)	100 (100)
% students with need rec. non-need-based scholarship or grant aid (First-year)	24 (24)
% students with need rec. need-based self-help aid (First-year)	74 (74)
% students rec. any financial aid (First-year)	100 (100)
% UG borrow to pay for school	87
Average cumulative indebtedness	$45,567
% of students with need fully met (First-year)	37 (37)
Average % of student need met (First-year)	94 (94)

AMERICAN UNIVERSITY

4400 Massachusetts Ave., NW, Washington, DC 20016 • Admissions: 202-885-6000

Survey Snapshot
Lots of liberal students
Students environmentally aware
Students love Washington, DC

RATINGS

Quality of Life	**92**
Fire Safety	**89**
Green	**99**
Academic	**84**
Profs Interesting	**90**
Profs Accessible	**91**
Admissions	**88**
Financial Aid	**89**

CAMPUS LIFE

Type of school	Private
Affiliation	Methodist
Environment	Metropolis

Students

Degree-seeking undergrad enrollment	6,559
% male/female/not reported	38/62/0
% from out of state	97
% First-year live on campus	96
# of fraternities (% join)	14 (NR)
# of sororities (% join)	11 (NR)
% Asian	7
% Black or African American	10
% Hispanic	16
% Native American	<1
% Pacific Islander	<1
% Race and/or ethnicity unknown	4
% Two or more races	6
% White	52
% International	6
# of countries represented	70

CAMPUS MENTAL HEALTH SERVICES

Offers mental health/wellness program	Yes
Mental health training available to students	Yes
Employs Chief Wellness Officer	Yes
Peer-to-peer mental health offerings	Yes
Counseling center has guidelines or accreditation	Yes
Mental health/well-being courses	Yes, for-credit

ACADEMICS

% students returning for sophomore year	87
% students graduating within 4 years	66
% students graduating within 6 years	75
Calendar	Semester
Student/faculty ratio	10:1
Most common class size 10–19.	(54%)

Most Popular Majors

International Relations and Affairs; Business Administration and Management; Political Science and Government

Applicants Also Look At

Boston College, Boston University, Fordham University, The George Washington University, Georgetown University, New York University, Northeastern University, Syracuse University

STUDENTS SAY "..."

Academics

American University leverages its Washington, DC, location to deliver "global exposure and access to opportunities outside the classroom," including internships, volunteer work, and professional experiences. As one student shares, "I can connect what I learn in class to real-world settings, which makes my education feel practical and relevant." Favorite class experiences include student-run communications firms, on-the-ground journalism classes that build on data and interviews from local elections, and visits to the Superior Court of DC. With "so many" programs available, "study abroad is a huge culture here." One student studying at the AU campus in Brussels "visited close to a dozen international law and policy institutions with speakers and interactive visits." Another huge part of the AU culture is professors who "bring interdisciplinary expertise and a genuine passion for teaching undergraduates." For instance, a student in the popular School of International Service points to educators who are "incredibly well-connected, [and] diverse in opinion and research opportunities." In addition to SIS and political science, students highlight AU's communications, business, and economics programs. Many professors go "above and beyond for their students...They are also willing and able to provide valuable connections to those in your field." And importantly, "the professors use DC as our campus, often taking students on visits to the institutions or places we are learning about to enrich our learning." Many agree: "The faculty and location are just about unbeatable for political science and international relations," allowing AU to be "a school where you DO while you learn."

Campus Life

The name for students, Eagles, gives rise to a punny tradition—"Thank Clawed it's Wednesday!" Starting in late-February, the quad transforms into a midday party with pop-up markets, food trucks, and giveaways for those decked out in AU colors—red, white, and blue. Other traditions include "student published media organizations, which are a large part of campus life," and a student radio host reports: "The community for the station was great, the training was comprehensive and facilities and equipment were nice." Student writers also enjoy a variety of opportunities at both the official student paper and "an unaffiliated but student-run newspaper and satire site." AU also has intramural sports, Greek life, and "tons of clubs on lots of things," such as Model United Nations, which the members appreciate, "whether it's organizing the conferences, being on a team, or visiting embassies and ambassadors." It helps, too, that whether visiting political, cultural, or just foodie landmarks, students get free Metro passes. Such perks ensure that students can explore the overall "beauty of DC. There are so many opportunities and experiences readily available to us to encourage and inspire our learning."

Student Body

American University fosters "a very community-oriented campus," drawing students with "strong political interests and eagerness to be involved in issues on and around the campus." Overall, students "are very dedicated, driven individuals who take on a lot—academically, professionally, and socially. I know very few people who aren't taking a full load, double majoring, with an internship, and part of multiple clubs." Additionally, students are commonly "very interdisciplinary individuals!" One Eagle emphasizes: "Most students who double major/minor/etc. are taking them in wildly different subjects or have club interests outside of their major." Another student agrees, saying, "This truly is a school for those who are intellectually curious and question everything." This curiosity includes self-reflection, and many acknowledge that views on campus skew left-leaning. One student points out: "My peers are very enthusiastic about change, whether it be climate or social and racial justice." Regardless of political views, "the common thread seems to be that students place their career goals very high on their priority list." All in all, Eagles "are very interested in how the world works and wish to be active members of society."

AMERICAN UNIVERSITY

Financial Aid: 202-885-6500 • E-Mail: admissions@american.edu • Website: www.american.edu

THE PRINCETON REVIEW SAYS

Admissions

The school reports that its standardized testing policy for use in admission for Fall 2026 is Test Optional. The Princeton Review suggests that interested applicants consult with the school for the most up-to-date standardized testing policies. *Very important factors considered include:* rigor of secondary school record, academic GPA, level of applicant's interest. *Important factors considered include:* application essay, recommendation(s), extracurricular activities, talent/ability, character/personal qualities, volunteer work. *Other factors considered include:* standardized test scores, first generation, geographical residence, work experience. High school diploma is required and GED is accepted. *Academic units required:* 4 English, 3 math, 3 science, 2 science labs, 2 language (other than English), 2 social studies. *Academic units recommended:* 4 English, 4 math, 4 science, 3 language (other than English), 4 social studies.

Financial Aid

Students should submit: FAFSA; CSS PROFILE. Priority filing deadline is 11/15. The Princeton Review suggests that all financial aid forms be submitted as soon as possible. *Need-based scholarships/grants offered:* Federal Pell; Federal SEOG; Private scholarships; College/university scholarship or grant aid from institutional funds; State scholarships/grants. *Loan aid offered:* Federal Direct Subsidized Loans; Federal Direct Unsubsidized Loans; Direct PLUS loans. Admitted students will be notified of awards on or about 4/1. Federal Work-Study Program available. Institutional employment available.

The Inside Word

Admissions officers at American University take a holistic approach, carefully reviewing each component of an application. Your academic transcript carries the most weight, and a rigorous college prep curriculum will strengthen your candidacy. American is also a Test Optional school, and opting out of test scores will not affect your eligibility for merit awards or entrance to the Honors Program.

THE SCHOOL SAYS

From the Admissions Office

"At American University, passion inspires meaningful impact, changemakers find community, and the world's greatest challenges meet their match. Our undergraduate experience centers on empowering lives of purpose, advancing knowledge through experiential learning, and partnering with our home city of Washington, DC. Whatever your passion, an AU education is a launching pad for those who want to lead the way toward positive change.

"AU's rigorous curriculum features high-impact educational experiences that combine in-depth theoretical study with meaningful real-world experiences. Regardless of your choice of major, you'll acquire a solid foundation in liberal arts while pursuing thorough study in your chosen field. The flexibility of our programs and the breadth of our faculty expertise help you focus your studies on what drives you.

"Our community is filled with ambitious visionaries and practitioners who use their passion and purpose to make an impact in this changing world. Our students learn outside of the classroom as much as they do inside through experiences made possible in our home city, where pivotal national and global decisions are made. Our network of world-class faculty and visiting scholars brings deep connections to influential companies and organizations in the public, private, and non-profit sectors and enhance the excellence of our programs.

"We are a university driven to make a difference. We step up, we show up, and we say "challenge accepted" to the issues that matter most to us—and our communities. Are you ready to join us?"

SELECTIVITY

# of total applicants	20,960
% of total applicants accepted	66
% of total acceptees attending	11
# of early decision applicants	392
% of early decision applicants accepted	81
# offered a place on the wait list	4,928
# admitted from wait list	1,182

First-Year Profile

Testing policy	Test Optional
Range SAT composite	1320–1440
Range SAT EBRW	630–710
Range SAT math	680–740
Range ACT composite	30–33
% submitting SAT scores	16
% submitting ACT scores	6

Important Dates

Early decision	
Apply by	11/15
Notified by	12/31
Other ED apply by	1/15
Other ED notified by	2/15
Early action	
Apply by	11/1
Notified by	1/31
Regular	
Apply by	1/15
Notified by	4/1
Nonfall registration?	Yes

FINANCIAL FACTS

Annual tuition	$62,680
Food and housing	$19,104
Required fees (First-year)	$1,722 ($1,972)
Books and supplies	$1,200
Average need-based scholarship (First-year)	$34,870 ($40,439)
% students with need rec. need-based scholarship or grant aid (First-year)	96 (97)
% students with need rec. non-need-based scholarship or grant aid (First-year)	47 (45)
% students with need rec. need-based self-help aid (First-year)	87 (88)
% of students with need fully met (First-year)	23 (42)
Average % of student need met (First-year)	78 (88)

Amherst College

220 South Pleasant Street, Amherst, MA 01002 • Admissions: 413-542-2328

Survey Snapshot
Students are happy
Active minority support groups
Students always studying

RATINGS

Quality of Life	85
Fire Safety	79
Green	95
Academic	91
Profs Interesting	90
Profs Accessible	92
Admissions	98
Financial Aid	99

CAMPUS LIFE

Type of school	Private
Environment	Town

Students

Degree-seeking undergrad enrollment	1,901
% male/female/not reported	45/55/<1
% from out of state	85
% First-year from public high school	52
% First-year live on campus	100
% Ugrads live on campus	94
# of fraternities	0
# of sororities	0
% Asian	16
% Black or African American	8
% Hispanic	13
% Native American	<1
% Pacific Islander	0
% Race and/or ethnicity unknown	4
% Two or more races	9
% White	37
% International	13
# of countries represented	76

CAMPUS MENTAL HEALTH SERVICES

Offers mental health/wellness program	Yes
Mental health training available to students	No
Employs Chief Wellness Officer	Yes
Peer-to-peer mental health offerings	Yes
Counseling center has guidelines or accreditation	Yes
Mental health/well-being courses	NR

ACADEMICS

% students returning for sophomore year	98
% students graduating within 4 years	73
% students graduating within 6 years	93
Calendar	Semester
Student/faculty ratio	7:1
Most common class size 10–19.	(33%)
Most common lab/discussion size 10–19.	(54%)

Most Popular Majors

Mathematics; Econometrics and Quantitative Economics

Applicants Also Look At

Brown University, Columbia University, Dartmouth College, Harvard College, Princeton University, Stanford University, University of Pennsylvania, Williams College, Yale University

STUDENTS SAY "…"

Academics

Amherst College's open curriculum keeps the focus on what undergraduates want, dispensing with general requirements so that students can have "control over their own education" and "take classes that they actually love," forging their own intellectual path in one of the numerous undergraduate majors offered. And while there may not be mandatory core classes, the course catalog offers over 850 options, with more available through partner schools in the Five College Consortium: as one student puts it, "Every year at Amherst I have gotten more and more intellectually curious". Add the school's numerous research opportunities, and you've got an "academically rigorous undergraduate education" that is supported by multiple resource centers to foster awareness and identity. In addition to campus resources, the "professors on campus really care about the academic experience of their students." They "format their classes in a way that makes it entertaining and engaging to learn even the most difficult material." That's important to many attendees, for while "challenging" is used to describe the overall education, that's matched by an acknowledgment of how "supportive and manageable" it all is, thanks to the school's resources and its "very flexible and understanding" professors. One student shares, "They really do care about their students; one time I got a personal email from a professor after missing class due to an illness for a couple days." To these students, "Amherst feel[s] like a place where I am taken care of and cared for."

Campus Life

Students describe weekdays as fairly busy—"balancing our schoolwork, clubs, work-study jobs, sports, and more"—so much so that a lot of socializing is built around study sessions and the dining hall. That said, "Outside of class, people attend campus events (like watching the improv group every Monday night) and when the weather cooperates, "people will be found lounging in the grassy quads, playing Frisbee, [and] going out to nearby towns or ponds [and] mini-beaches." On the weekends, "life is usually going to a sports event or another event during the day and homework and then going out at night," or as one undergraduate explains, "Whenever a party can be thrown, there will be a party." Students also point to the school's savvy event planning, which includes mainstays like trivia but also activities like build-a-bear and axe-throwing. The common theme is that students "are constantly moving and busy with packed schedules that encompass a variety of activities."

Student Body

The key qualities of the average Amherst student, regardless of their specific interests ("Everyone has their 'thing'"), are being "diverse, curious and extremely motivated." That shared passion creates a "very collaboration-driven" community that some call "extremely non-competitive." Amherst students are described as being incredibly generous, who "help each other because they want the best for one another." The productive nature of the school and the "quite varied interests" of the student body make for a naturally eclectic group: "There are introverts, extroverts, partiers, and those that like to just stay in and play games on the weekends…I would say that Amherst students are kind and accept everyone, even when they are completely different from themselves."

AMHERST COLLEGE

Financial Aid: 413-542-2296 • E-Mail: admission@amherst.edu • Website: www.amherst.edu

THE PRINCETON REVIEW SAYS

Admissions

The school reports that its standardized testing policy for use in admission for Fall 2026 is Test Optional. The Princeton Review suggests that interested applicants consult with the school for the most up-to-date standardized testing policies. *Very important factors considered include:* rigor of secondary school record, academic GPA, standardized test scores, application essay, recommendation(s), extracurricular activities, talent/ability. *Important factors considered include:* class rank, character/personal qualities, first generation, volunteer work, work experience. *Other factors considered include:* geographical residence. High school diploma or equivalent is not required. *Academic units recommended:* 4 English, 4 math, 4 science, 2 science labs, 3 language (other than English), 2 social studies, 2 history.

Financial Aid

Students should submit: FAFSA; CSS PROFILE. Priority filing deadline is 1/15. The Princeton Review suggests that all financial aid forms be submitted as soon as possible. *Need-based scholarships/grants offered:* Federal Pell; Federal SEOG; State scholarships/grants; Private scholarships; College/university scholarship or grant aid from institutional funds. *Loan aid offered:* Federal Direct Subsidized Loans; Federal Direct Unsubsidized Loans; Direct PLUS loans; College/university loans from institutional funds. Admitted students will be notified of awards on or about 4/1. Federal Work-Study Program available. Institutional employment available.

The Inside Word

Membership certainly has its benefits at the highly selective Amherst College. For the price of entry to this school, students also gain entrance to the prestigious Five College Consortium, which allows enrolled students to take courses for credit at no additional cost at any of the four other participating consortium members (Hampshire College, Mount Holyoke College, Smith College, and the University of Massachusetts Amherst). And this deal isn't just confined to the classroom: students can use other schools' libraries, eat meals at the other cafeterias, and participate in extracurricular activities offered at the other schools. And don't worry about how you'll get there—your bus fare is covered too.

THE SCHOOL SAYS

From the Admissions Office

"Founded in 1821, Amherst College is considered one of the premier liberal arts colleges in the nation, enrolling 1,900 bright, talented, energetic and curious young people. A commitment to diversity, defined in its broadest sense, is fundamental to Amherst's mission. Need-blind admission for all applicants (domestic and international) and generous, no-loan financial aid offers ensure that exceptional students from across the country and around the world are admitted to Amherst based on accomplishment and promise, regardless of family income. Located in Amherst, Massachusetts, a town of 35,000 people in an area of great natural beauty, the College's 1,000-acre campus offers top-notch academic, athletic and residential facilities, including a new state-of-the-art science center designed to facilitate interdisciplinary research. Awarding the BA degree in forty-three majors in the humanities, social sciences and natural sciences, Amherst offers an Open Curriculum, allowing students unusual independence and flexibility in designing their educational programs, unconstrained by distribution or area requirements. Through the Five College Consortium, Amherst students can also take courses and participate in activities at Smith College, Mount Holyoke, Hampshire College, and the University of Massachusetts Amherst, providing access to a remarkably broad collection of curricular and extracurricular options. Amherst's small classes and low student-faculty ratio foster close, one-to-one interactions with professors and fellow students and provide exceptional opportunities for undergraduate research with highly talented, accomplished faculty, contributing to an uncommonly engaging intellectual and personal experience within a lively community."

SELECTIVITY

# of total applicants	15,819
% of total applicants accepted	8
% of total acceptees attending	40
# of in-state applicants	1,061
% of in-state applicants accepted	12
# of out-of-state-applicants	8,412
% of applicants accepted from out of state	12
# of international applicants	6,346
% of international applicants accepted	1
# of early decision applicants	971
% of early decision applicants accepted	22
# offered a place on the wait list	1,294
# admitted from wait list	44

First-Year Profile

Testing policy	Test Optional
Range SAT composite	1470–1540
Range SAT EBRW	730–770
Range SAT math	730–790
Range ACT composite	33–35
% submitting SAT scores	40
% submitting ACT scores	16
% graduated top 10% of class	88
% graduated top 25% of class	96
% graduated top 50% of class	100
% submitting high school rank	28

Important Dates

Early decision	
Apply by	11/7
Notified by	12/15
Regular	
Apply by	1/5
Notified by	4/1
Nonfall registration?	No

FINANCIAL FACTS

Annual tuition	$73,140
Food and housing	$19,260
Required fees	$690
Average need-based scholarship (First-year)	$75,199 ($76,445)
% students with need rec. need-based scholarship or grant aid (First-year)	100 (100)
% students with need rec. non-need-based scholarship or grant aid (First-year)	0 (0)
% students with need rec. need-based self-help aid (First-year)	81 (77)
% students rec. any financial aid (First-year)	59 (57)
% UG borrow to pay for school	19
Average cumulative indebtedness	$29,149
% of students with need fully met (First-year)	100 (100)
Average % of student need met (First-year)	100 (100)

Angelo State University

ASU Station #11014, San Angelo, TX 76909 • Admissions: 325-942-2041

Survey Snapshot
Lots of conservative students
School is well run
Diverse student types interact on campus

RATINGS

Quality of Life	**91**
Fire Safety	**89**
Green	**60***
Academic	**81**
Profs Interesting	**91**
Profs Accessible	**93**
Admissions	**83**
Financial Aid	**87**

CAMPUS LIFE

Type of school	Public
Environment	City

Students

Degree-seeking undergrad enrollment	5,886
% male/female/not reported	44/56/<1
% from out of state	3
% First-year live on campus	69
% Ugrads live on campus	18
# of fraternities (% join)	5 (3)
# of sororities (% join)	3 (3)
% Asian	1
% Black or African American	6
% Hispanic	42
% Native American	<1
% Pacific Islander	<1
% Race and/or ethnicity unknown	1
% Two or more races	3
% White	42
% International	5
# of countries represented	33

CAMPUS MENTAL HEALTH SERVICES

Offers mental health/wellness program	Yes
Mental health training available to students	No
Employs Chief Wellness Officer	No
Peer-to-peer mental health offerings	No
Counseling center has guidelines or accreditation	No
Mental health/well-being courses	NR

ACADEMICS

% students returning for sophomore year	73
% students graduating within 4 years	33
% students graduating within 6 years	45
Calendar	Semester
Student/faculty ratio	19:1
Most common class size 20–29.	(35%)
Most common lab/discussion size 10–19.	(50%)

Most Popular Majors

Multi-/Interdisciplinary Studies; Registered Nursing/Registered Nurse; Business Administration and Management

STUDENTS SAY "…"

Academics

Angelo State University creates "a place to enhance your education while gaining a large extended family of peers and faculty." From "financial aid to instruction and tutoring programs, [the school] is focused on helping its students matriculate and succeed in their future endeavors." One student adds, "We have a great administration staff here with open doors…for the students who may have questions or concerns or just want to chat." ASU is committed to making "college affordable to everyone," as evidenced by the fact that nearly 85 percent of students receive some form of aid that does not need to be repaid after graduation. Classes at ASU are taught by instructors who are "attentive to students' needs and experiences in and outside of the classroom" and "help prepare us for our careers upon graduation." Students also appreciate the smaller class sizes, noting that "it really helps to have the one-on-one help and communication with a professor to learn the specific subject." Professors don't just teach; they "encourage students to achieve greatness and successfully complete their schooling to the best of their abilities." They also support their students by "explaining concepts outside of class time, offering advice of which courses to take, or even offering career advice." The faculty genuinely care about students' success; they "all have your best interest and will work with you, yet still hold you accountable."

Campus Life

"Life at ASU is pretty laid back," and the "course schedule is flexible enough with breaks, which gives [us] time enough to eat, work, chit-chat, study or do other things." There are "activities going on at all times," including events like haunted houses, sports games, Ram Jam, club meetings, art events, and volunteer work. Student organizations "are fully committed to making the campus atmosphere fun and exciting," with a variety of options available: departmental organizations for students within their major, religious and secular organizations, and "fraternities and sororities that are about community engagement." Intramural sports are very popular here, and many students "have spent countless hours on the fields at ASU." This is a Division II school, and the "athletics teams here are outstanding and the games are a blast to attend." You don't need to be an athlete to "spend a lot of time in the CHP" (Center for Human Performance), which has a "new and very nice gym" complete with a basketball court, a large weight room, a rock-climbing wall, racquetball rooms, and other options for recreation and exercise. For those who enjoy nature, the university offers a lake facility where students can rent kayaks and bikes and enjoy a scenic picnic area.

Student Body

At ASU, "there are so many opportunities to meet people and make long-lasting friendships and connections." The students are "friendly and accommodating" and they've "all got the kind Texan heart, although not all of them are native Texans." Indeed, the population is "an amazingly diverse mixture of traditional and non-traditional students" from "so many different countries, states and towns." Many students are first-generation, and many "are from around the San Angelo area, so the small-town feel is very much present." The university is designated as a Hispanic Serving Institution (HSI), and "there is a lot of Hispanic culture in San Angelo." One student notes, "Everyone has a different story on why they are earning a degree." The Ram Fam, as the community is known, is "dedicated to a culture of excellence in not only education but in every aspect, from sports to community service." ASU also has "a tremendous reputation of making students feel welcome and helping them fit into their role as a student and cherished member of this university."

ANGELO STATE UNIVERSITY

Financial Aid: 325-942-2246 • E-Mail: admissions@angelo.edu • Website: www.angelo.edu

THE PRINCETON REVIEW SAYS

Admissions

The school reports that its standardized testing policy for use in admission for Fall 2026 will require applicants to submit either the SAT or ACT. The Princeton Review suggests that interested applicants consult with the school for the most up-to-date standardized testing policies. *Very important factors considered include:* class rank, standardized test scores. *Other factors considered include:* rigor of secondary school record, academic GPA, extracurricular activities, talent/ability, character/personal qualities, first generation, geographical residence, state residency, volunteer work, work experience, level of applicant's interest. High school diploma is required and GED is accepted. *Academic units recommended:* 4 English, 4 math, 4 science, 2 language (other than English), 4 social studies, 6 academic electives, 1 visual/performing arts.

Financial Aid

Students should submit: FAFSA. Priority filing deadline is 1/15. The Princeton Review suggests that all financial aid forms be submitted as soon as possible. *Need-based scholarships/grants offered:* Federal Pell; Federal SEOG; State scholarships/grants; Private scholarships; College/university scholarship or grant aid from institutional funds. *Loan aid offered:* Federal Direct Subsidized Loans; Federal Direct Unsubsidized Loans; Direct PLUS loans. Admitted students will be notified of awards on a rolling basis beginning 1/15. Federal Work-Study Program available. Institutional employment available.

The Inside Word

When accepting new students to Angelo State University, the admissions department places a strong emphasis on academic achievement and the desire for students to "find what drives" them. Students are guaranteed admission to Angelo State if they are graduating from an accredited high school and meet certain qualifications (mainly based on high school class rank). To find out the exact criteria, please visit the school's website. Even if a student does not meet the guaranteed admission requirements, their application will be holistically reviewed by the school.

THE SCHOOL SAYS

From the Admissions Office

"Angelo State University is widely known as the premier regional university in West Texas. The university maintains a commitment to excellence for our students by emphasizing a strong set of core values and providing endless opportunities through hands-on, experiential learning in smaller classes. ASU shines with superb records of graduates' acceptance into professional schools. Eighty percent of pre-med students are accepted into medical school, well above the national average of 41 percent. Ninety percent of students who complete the pre-veterinary program and receive the highest recommendations from ASU faculty are accepted into veterinary school. Over 95 percent of agriculture, biology, chemistry and biochemistry majors who apply are accepted into graduate school. ASU nursing students have a pass rate of over 92 percent on the NCLEX-RN licensure exam. Pointing to the future, ASU has joined the Southwest Airlines Destination 225 program that provides career pathways for commercial aviation students, and is developing a Cybersecurity and Artificial Intelligence Center of Excellence through our Kay Bailey Hutchison Center for Cyber Intelligence, Innovation, and Security Studies.

"Annually awarding over $12 million in scholarships, ASU remains one of the top educational values in Texas. About 90 percent of ASU students receive some form of financial support, and over 45 percent graduate debt free. ASU also encourages healthy student lifestyles while fostering leadership development through 100-plus student organizations, a thriving intramurals and club sports program that includes the new ASU Rodeo Team, and modern recreation and fitness facilities. ASU student-athletes compete in newly-renovated, state-of-the-art facilities."

SELECTIVITY

# of total applicants	6,865
% of total applicants accepted	80
% of total acceptees attending	25
# of in-state applicants	6,547
% of in-state applicants accepted	80
# of out-of-state-applicants	261
% of applicants accepted from out of state	76
# of international applicants	57
% of international applicants accepted	96

First-Year Profile

Testing policy	SAT or ACT Required
Range SAT composite	860–1130
Range SAT EBRW	440–580
Range SAT math	420–550
Range ACT composite	18–24
% submitting SAT scores	29
% submitting ACT scores	44
Average HS GPA	3.7
% submitting high school GPA	89
% graduated top 10% of class	17
% graduated top 25% of class	42
% graduated top 50% of class	74
% submitting high school rank	78

Important Dates

Regular	
Notified by	Rolling, 9/1
Nonfall registration?	Yes

FINANCIAL FACTS

Annual in-state tuition	$5,619
Annual out-of-state tuition	$17,919
Food and housing	$10,820
Required fees	$3,965
Books and supplies	$1,200
Average need-based scholarship (First-year)	$9,865 ($11,302)
% students with need rec. need-based scholarship or grant aid (First-year)	92 (91)
% students with need rec. non-need-based scholarship or grant aid (First-year)	70 (80)
% students with need rec. need-based self-help aid (First-year)	45 (42)
% UG borrow to pay for school	50
Average cumulative indebtedness	$23,911
% of students with need fully met (First-year)	4 (5)
Average % of student need met (First-year)	85 (89)

Appalachian State University

287 Rivers St., Boone, NC 28608 • Admissions: 828-262-2120

Survey Snapshot
Students are friendly
Students environmentally aware
Students love Boone, NC

RATINGS

Quality of Life	86
Fire Safety	90
Green	88
Academic	79
Profs Interesting	87
Profs Accessible	90
Admissions	82
Financial Aid	80

CAMPUS LIFE

Type of school	Public
Environment	Village

Students

Degree-seeking undergrad enrollment	19,621
% male/female/not reported	45/55/0
% from out of state	10
% First-year from public high school	89
% First-year live on campus	96
% Ugrads live on campus	31
# of fraternities (% join)	18 (6)
# of sororities (% join)	13 (8)
% Asian	2
% Black or African American	3
% Hispanic	9
% Native American	<1
% Pacific Islander	<1
% Race and/or ethnicity unknown	1
% Two or more races	5
% White	81
% International	<1
# of countries represented	60

CAMPUS MENTAL HEALTH SERVICES

Offers mental health/wellness program	Yes
Mental health training available to students	No
Employs Chief Wellness Officer	NR
Peer-to-peer mental health offerings	NR
Counseling center has guidelines or accreditation	No
Mental health/well-being courses	NR

ACADEMICS

% students returning for sophomore year	84
% students graduating within 4 years	55
% students graduating within 6 years	71
Calendar	Semester
Student/faculty ratio	16:1
Most common class size 20–29.	(34%)
Most common lab/discussion size 20–29.	(51%)

Most Popular Majors

Biology/Biological Sciences; Sports, Kinesiology, and Physical Education/Fitness; Psychology

Applicants Also Look At

North Carolina State University, University of North Carolina at Chapel Hill

STUDENTS SAY "..."

Academics

It's easy for Appalachian State University to attract undergraduates. Not only is the school "exceedingly affordable," but it offers "gorgeous scenery" and "a strong sense of community that makes all its students feel like they have found their place." Undergrads also appreciate the resources provided to facilitate everyone's experience, such as the school's textbook rental program, which "saves most students hundreds of dollars per semester" and tries to ensure that students "do not have to stress about purchasing too many books." Additionally, App State provides "great continuing education scholarships."

The university touts a "terrific Honors College" as well as "a wide range of majors." Plus, all undergrads here benefit from "class sizes [that] are small enough to allow a more personal learning experience while remaining large enough to allow all students to get the classes they need." Many applaud the fact that their professors are "all highly educated experts in their respective fields and do not rely on TAs to teach their courses." And speaking of the faculty, students find that most of them "genuinely seem to love teaching." They are also "exceedingly knowledgeable" and provide students with "great resources that really help [them] to understand and apply material." All in all, "App [has] the greatest professional staff that I have ever encountered. From advisors, professors, or even the people working in the kitchen, everyone legitimately wants to see you succeed."

Campus Life

Simply put, you'd have to work really hard to be bored at App State. For starters, "attending football games and tailgating" is always a big draw. "There are [also] many, many clubs you can join and participate in" like the App State Running club, the Finance Student Association, and theater and music group. Students also note that both "Greek life and religious life [are] common, but not overbearing."

App State also has a fair number of students who gravitate toward the outdoors. In the warmer months, you'll find undergrads "lounging in hammocks or playing [various] outdoor sports." Of course, "once the snow falls, kids have snowball fights, or sled down the hills, taking advantage of the winter fun." And for the adventurous type, you can certainly find plenty here. Perhaps unsurprisingly, the university offers robust Outdoor Programs, organizing exciting trips such as "canoeing [and] stand-up paddle boarding" and "skiing and snowboarding in the winter." There are also "many hiking trails a short drive from campus." Given the school's proximity to the Blue Ridge Parkway, it makes sense that "rock climbing is very popular here and you can often hear rock climbers hooting and hollering as you hike a trail."

Student Body

App State seems to attract "laid-back and casual" individuals who typically give off a "relaxed, accepting vibe" peppered with a "tinge...[of] hippie." A large percentage of students "are extremely passionate about sustainability...and their impact on the environment" as well. Moreover, undergrads see their peers as "open-minded" people who "are very accepting of ideas and identities that do not fit the status quo," though some students do report their peers to lean "more on the liberal side" of the political spectrum. Perhaps more critically, students underscore the fact that their classmates are "kind and genuine." Indeed, "if you need help, almost anyone you find walking down the hallway would go out of their way to lend a helping hand." While some say it can feel like "most of the students are white" and a "vast majority of people...com[e] from North Carolina and other southern states," others counter that you can still meet "students from all around the country and world." Overall, "App State truly has such a welcoming and accepting student body that it would be hard to come across someone that you absolutely just didn't like or didn't enjoy talking to."

APPALACHIAN STATE UNIVERSITY

Financial Aid: 828-262-2190 • E-Mail: admissions@appstate.edu • Website: www.appstate.edu

THE PRINCETON REVIEW SAYS

Admissions

While the school reports that its standardized testing policy for Fall 2026 is Test Optional, applicants with a weighted high school GPA below 2.8 must submit an ACT or SAT score. *Very important factors considered include:* rigor of secondary school record, class rank, academic GPA. *Important factors considered include:* standardized test scores, interview, extracurricular activities, talent/ability, volunteer work, work experience, level of applicant's interest. *Other factors considered include:* application essay, character/personal qualities, first generation. High school diploma is required and GED is accepted. *Academic units required:* 4 English, 4 math, 3 science, 1 science lab, 2 language (other than English), 1 social studies, 1 history.

Financial Aid

Students should submit: FAFSA. The Princeton Review suggests that all financial aid forms be submitted as soon as possible. *Need-based scholarships/grants offered:* Federal Pell; Federal SEOG; State scholarships/grants; Private scholarships; College/university scholarship or grant aid from institutional funds. *Loan aid offered:* Federal Direct Subsidized Loans; Federal Direct Unsubsidized Loans; Direct PLUS loans. Admitted students will be notified of awards on a rolling basis beginning 3/15. Federal Work-Study Program available. Institutional employment available.

The Inside Word

The folks in Appalachian State's admissions office are looking for individuals who want to fully engage with both campus life and the world at large. To find such candidates, they take a holistic approach to their decision making and closely examine all application facets, from academic rigor to leadership roles in extracurriculars. So don't cut any corners! Of course, academics will still take top priority, but the most competitive students will definitely have some honors and AP or IB courses sprinkled throughout their transcript and the school recommends that you keep a "brag file" that'll help you spotlight your special skills.

THE SCHOOL SAYS

From the Admissions Office

"App State is known as the "premier public undergraduate institution in the state of North Carolina," and is one of 17 campuses in the University of North Carolina System. The university enrolls more than 20,000 students and offers more than 150 undergraduate and graduate majors, but the student-to-faculty ratio is low, so professors also serve as mentors. The university is located in the Blue Ridge Mountains, one of the country's most beautiful locations—and the perfect setting for students to strengthen their academic focus, discover their passions, enhance their leadership skills and take the next step in their life's journey. The vibrant downtown of Boone is just a block from campus, and the town enjoys the ranking of one of the safest cities in the state. From the moment students begin their studies at App State, they are expected to develop as critical and creative thinkers, effective communicators and inquisitive local-to-global learners. App State alumni go on to earn advanced degrees, start businesses, build distinguished military careers, work overseas and develop careers that take them in many directions, all while giving back to the communities in which they live and work."

SELECTIVITY

# of total applicants	22,184
% of total applicants accepted	94
% of total acceptees attending	19
# of in-state applicants	14,955
% of in-state applicants accepted	94
# of out-of-state-applicants	6,678
% of applicants accepted from out of state	93
# of international applicants	551
% of international applicants accepted	89
# offered a place on the wait list	446
# admitted from wait list	192

First-Year Profile

Testing policy	Test Optional !
Range SAT composite	1110–1270
Range SAT EBRW	560–660
Range SAT math	540–630
Range ACT composite	20–27
% submitting SAT scores	7
% submitting ACT scores	20
Average HS GPA	3.8
% submitting high school GPA	100
% graduated top 10% of class	9
% graduated top 25% of class	30
% graduated top 50% of class	67
% submitting high school rank	84

Important Dates

Regular	
Notified by	Rolling, 3/16
Nonfall registration?	Yes

FINANCIAL FACTS

Annual in-state tuition	$4,242
Annual out-of-state tuition	$21,238
Food and housing	$12,258
Required fees	$3,299
Books and supplies	$800
Average need-based scholarship (First-year)	$11,203 ($10,715)
% students with need rec. need-based scholarship or grant aid (First-year)	83 (85)
% students with need rec. non-need-based scholarship or grant aid (First-year)	3 (5)
% students with need rec. need-based self-help aid (First-year)	61 (57)
% students rec. any financial aid (First-year)	63 (70)
% UG borrow to pay for school	49
Average cumulative indebtedness	$25,442
% of students with need fully met (First-year)	3 (5)
Average % of student need met (First-year)	53 (55)

! Test Optional if you have a GPA of 2.8 or higher.

Arizona State University

Admissions Services, PO Box 871004, Tempe, AZ 85287-1004 • Admissions: 480-965-7788

Survey Snapshot
Students love Tempe, AZ
Everyone loves the Sun Devils
College radio is popular

RATINGS

Quality of Life	84
Fire Safety	88
Green	97
Academic	75
Profs Interesting	83
Profs Accessible	89
Admissions	78
Financial Aid	86

CAMPUS LIFE

Type of school	Public
Environment	Metropolis

Students

Degree-seeking undergrad enrollment	63,906
% male/female/not reported	51/49/0
% from out of state	26
% First-year live on campus	68
% Ugrads live on campus	24
# of fraternities (% join)	35 (8)
# of sororities (% join)	31 (12)
% Asian	9
% Black or African American	5
% Hispanic	28
% Native American	1
% Pacific Islander	<1
% Race and/or ethnicity unknown	4
% Two or more races	6
% White	39
% International	8
# of countries represented	131

CAMPUS MENTAL HEALTH SERVICES

Offers mental health/wellness program	Yes
Mental health training available to students	Yes
Employs Chief Wellness Officer	Yes
Peer-to-peer mental health offerings	Yes
Counseling center has guidelines or accreditation	Yes
Mental health/well-being courses	Yes, for-credit

ACADEMICS

% students returning for sophomore year	87
% students graduating within 4 years	55
% students graduating within 6 years	69
Calendar	Semester
Student/faculty ratio	18:1
Most common class size 20–29.	(28%)
Most common lab/discussion size 20–29.	(29%)

Most Popular Majors
Computer Science; Biology/Biological Sciences; Business, Management, Marketing, and Related Support Services

STUDENTS SAY "..."

Academics

Having managed to "personalize every student's experience" and offering "endless... opportunities for success," Arizona State University is all about helping its undergraduates find their place in a diverse and dynamic community. To that end, it offers a wide range of exceptional academic departments and programs, including the "renowned business school, school of journalism, [and] Thunderbird School of Global Management," and an "innovative engineering program with lots of hands-on learning experiences." Many students describe "endless...opportunities for success," including study abroad programs, internships, and undergraduate research through programs like the Fulton Undergraduate Research Initiative (FURI). There's an "abundance of resources" and support that is much appreciated: "We have funding, students, professors, grants...you name it. Being the large university means having EVERYTHING at your fingertips." Professors are described as "enthusiastic, supportive, and engaged," often incorporating their "research interests and experiences" into coursework. As with any large university, the quality of instruction can vary across departments, but as one student shares, "Most of my professors would bend over backward to help me out—even when the issue wasn't in their particular class," and another adds, "I've met some stellar faculty throughout my journey at ASU and couldn't be more thankful."

Campus Life

Life at Arizona State University is lively, and students fill their days with classes, activities, and social events. In addition, "Since it is always warm, we are very active and spend a lot of time outdoors." One student adds, "There are always people out at the pools, exercising in the gym, playing sports on the sand volleyball courts or soccer fields, or riding bikes or long boards." For those who prefer to stay indoors, ASU offers a "very strong gaming community," as well as "really interesting lectures." There are also "endless clubs and many athletic events," and the "programming board... host[s] events every week, including free films and food" that keep campus life fresh and engaging. Off campus, downtown Tempe provides plenty of entertainment, including "a thriving alternative music and DIY scene in the Maple-Ash district... with ties to the local arts communities, political activism, and house shows where local bands play." Greek life is also a vibrant part of the ASU experience. One undergrad shares that it's "really fun [and] not as party-oriented as it used to be," adding that "fraternities and sororities get involved around campus" through community service, philanthropy, and intramural games. Altogether, ASU offers an environment that encourages students to connect, get involved, and make the most of their college experience.

Student Body

At ASU, students describe their peers as having a "unique blend of intelligence and fun" and being "nice and welcoming." As one student puts it, "Every person you meet has a smile on their face, ready to help." In addition to being friendly, another student reports that ASU undergraduates "are excellent at getting involved in community activities and speaking up for what they believe in...[as well as] spread[ing] awareness about important issues." One student points out that "since there are so many students [at ASU],...it also allows you to meet people with a variety of different perspectives, backgrounds, and interests." Consequently, "everyone who comes to ASU is absolutely able to find other people with the same interests, passions, beliefs, and world views, as well as countless others who see the world very differently," says one student, adding, "No matter who you are, you can find a community of peers" at ASU.

ARIZONA STATE UNIVERSITY

Financial Aid: 855-278-5080 • E-Mail: admissions@asu.edu • Website: www.asu.edu

THE PRINCETON REVIEW SAYS

Admissions

The school reports that its standardized testing policy for use in admission for Fall 2026 is Test Optional. The Princeton Review suggests that interested applicants consult with the school for the most up-to-date standardized testing policies. *Very important factors considered include:* academic GPA. *Important factors considered include:* rigor of secondary school record, class rank. *Other factors considered include:* standardized test scores, state residency. High school diploma is required and GED is accepted. *Academic units required:* 4 English, 4 math, 3 science, 3 science labs, 2 language (other than English), 2 social sciences (1 history), 1 fine arts or career/technical.

Financial Aid

Students should submit: FAFSA. Priority filing deadline is 1/15. The Princeton Review suggests that all financial aid forms be submitted as soon as possible. *Need-based scholarships/grants offered:* Federal Pell; Federal SEOG; State scholarships/grants; Private scholarships; College/university scholarship or grant aid from institutional funds; United Negro College Fund; Federal Nursing Scholarships. *Loan aid offered:* Federal Direct Subsidized Loans; Federal Direct Unsubsidized Loans; Direct PLUS loans; Federal Nursing Loans; State Loans; College/university loans from institutional funds; Private loans. Admitted students will be notified of awards on a rolling basis beginning 12/1. Federal Work-Study Program available. Institutional employment available.

The Inside Word

Admission officers at Arizona State University strive to build an incoming class that reflects diverse backgrounds and interests. The school takes a fairly straightforward approach to the admission process. Applicants must have or meet at least one of the following: minimum 3.00 GPA (4.00 scale), top 25 percent of their graduating class, or a minimum ACT score of 22 (24 for nonresidents) or an SAT score of 1120 (1180 for nonresidents).

THE SCHOOL SAYS

From the Admissions Office

"ASU is a public research university that measures itself by whom it includes and how they succeed. As one university in many places, serving over 160,000 students in Fall 2025, ASU offers campuses and learning locations in Arizona and around the world so students can choose the learning environment that works for them. ASU offers four campuses in metropolitan Phoenix. The Downtown Phoenix campus hosts more than 10,700 students studying journalism, health care, public service, and more, and will be home to the John Shufeldt School of Medicine and Medical Engineering in fall 2026. The Polytechnic campus, located in Mesa, Arizona, is home to more than 6,100 students who are exploring professional and technical programs in a hands-on learning environment. More than 55,300 students study business, engineering, design and arts, sustainability, science, education and more at the historic Tempe campus. At the epicenter of the thriving West Valley is ASU's West Valley campus, offering business, engineering, education, health, and interdisciplinary arts and science programs, and opportunities to explore entrepreneurship through experiential learning to more than 5,200 students. Other Arizona locations include ASU at Mesa City Center, home to the MIX Center, where students enjoy an immersive media experience. At the Health Futures Center, a collaboration with Mayo Clinic, students conduct innovative medical research. To increase opportunities for California learners, the ASU California Center Broadway hosts ASU's film and journalism schools, as well as ASU Local—Los Angeles, while the ASU California Center Grand hosts ASU FIDM—ASU's premier fashion program, offering a career-focused art school environment with locations including London, as well as online. Both centers offer a career-focused art school environment with high-tech studios and equipment and access to industry professionals. Zooming out, Arizona State University offers learning opportunities in diverse locations including Hawaii, Washington, D.C., London, and Bermuda, as well as online. Across all campuses and throughout the academic year, ASU enrolls more than 194,400 students."

SELECTIVITY

# of total applicants	69,617
% of total applicants accepted	88
% of total acceptees attending	22
# of in-state applicants	20,323
% of in-state applicants accepted	90
# of out-of-state-applicants	40,388
% of applicants accepted from out of state	87
# of international applicants	8,906
% of international applicants accepted	90

First-Year Profile

Testing policy	Test Optional
Average HS GPA	3.5
% submitting high school GPA	98
% graduated top 10% of class	30
% graduated top 25% of class	60
% graduated top 50% of class	87
% submitting high school rank	52

Important Dates

Regular	
Apply by	1/15
Notified by	Rolling, 8/1
Nonfall registration?	Yes

FINANCIAL FACTS

Annual in-state tuition	$12,172
Annual out-of-state tuition	$34,364
Food and housing	$17,754
Required fees	$803
Books and supplies	$1,320
Average need-based scholarship (First-year)	$14,286 ($16,089)
% students with need rec. need-based scholarship or grant aid (First-year)	95 (97)
% students with need rec. non-need-based scholarship or grant aid (First-year)	9 (11)
% students with need rec. need-based self-help aid (First-year)	44 (39)
% students rec. any financial aid (First-year)	87 (95)
% UG borrow to pay for school	36
Average cumulative indebtedness	$25,659
% of students with need fully met (First-year)	15 (15)
Average % of student need met (First-year)	59 (62)

ASSUMPTION UNIVERSITY

500 Salisbury St., Worcester, MA 01609-1296 • Admissions: 508-767-7285

Survey Snapshot
Students get along with local community
Students involved in community service
Lots of conservative students

RATINGS

Quality of Life	**88**
Fire Safety	**60***
Green	**60***
Academic	**80**
Profs Interesting	**89**
Profs Accessible	**94**
Admissions	**75**
Financial Aid	**91**

CAMPUS LIFE

Type of school	Private
Affiliation	Roman Catholic
Environment	City

Students

Degree-seeking undergrad enrollment	1,734
% male/female/not reported	44/56/0
% from out of state	28
% First-year from public high school	78
% First-year live on campus	88
% Ugrads live on campus	83
# of fraternities	0
# of sororities	0
% Asian	2
% Black or African American	7
% Hispanic	15
% Native American	<1
% Pacific Islander	<1
% Race and/or ethnicity unknown	1
% Two or more races	4
% White	69
% International	3
# of countries represented	23

CAMPUS MENTAL HEALTH SERVICES

Offers mental health/wellness program	Yes
Mental health training available to students	No
Employs Chief Wellness Officer	NR
Peer-to-peer mental health offerings	NR
Counseling center has guidelines or accreditation	No
Mental health/well-being courses	NR

ACADEMICS

% students returning for sophomore year	82
% students graduating within 4 years	68
% students graduating within 6 years	73
Calendar	Semester
Student/faculty ratio	11:1
Most common class size 20–29.	(44%)
Most common lab/discussion size 10–19.	(74%)

Most Popular Majors

Nursing; Psychology; Business Administration and Management

STUDENTS SAY "..."

Academics

Curiosity, faith, and learning are cornerstones of an Assumption University education, which "helps foster well-rounded, creative, intelligent and caring young adults to be successful and morally sound in their future endeavors." The Catholic school's curriculum begins with the Foundations Program, a 13-course program that encourages self-exploration and introspection to help students discover who they want to become; this is achieved through "service, meaningful discussions, and liberal arts classes." Assumption is a "very welcoming and inclusive institution" that focuses both on education and "core values." Experiential learning is emphasized, with the idea that students "receive a greater impact" through the application of skills via service learning, study abroad (the school has a campus in Rome), and internships; campus jobs represent another avenue for experience and are said to be "abundant." Within the classroom, the "beyond helpful" professors are engaging and approachable, "willing to talk to you whenever you need it and [caring] about your wellbeing." Their "diversity of teaching styles," complemented by a variety of backgrounds, allows them to "bring their personal experiences into the classroom" and make classes "interesting and enjoyable." Students take note of these efforts: "the professors here at Assumption all love what they do, and it is obvious in the classroom." This level of support extends to all arms of the university, including the Academic Support Center (which provides tutoring) and the Career Development and Internship Center. As far as students are concerned, this level of care and support is "truly a blessing."

Campus Life

Students love their "beautiful, diverse, and secured campus," and most attendees choose to remain on their picture-perfect campus thanks to a four-year housing guarantee. Assumption has "a tight-knit, faith-based community where everyone is part of a family" and students feel that "there is a great sense of belonging" that makes it "easy to meet new people," especially for those who are "very invested in academics, sports, extracurriculars, and social experiences." The town of Worcester, Massachusetts, is a New England college hub, so there is "always something to do if you want to get off campus" or want to socially mix with students at other nearby schools. This may actually be too true in some cases where students note that as the Thursday weekend rolls around, the on-campus scene gets quiet, with many of the older students heading off-campus, because Assumption is "strict as far as drinking goes." That said, students describe local activities "like Bingo Nights, movie nights, trivia, [and] Family Feud" as being "really fun."

Student Body

Hound Nation "is like no other" in terms of community and manners, and everyone is "courteous and [will] hold doors open or lend you a calculator in class if your forgot yours." According to their peers, students tend to be "generally middle-class Caucasians [who] are heterosexual" and the school has "a very conservative feel." While the school itself is described as "very Catholic," students qualify this as meaning that most undergraduates "come from Catholic upbringings or have attended Catholic school but are not necessarily religious." The biggest separation between students seems to be whether they're athletes or not, but even in this case, everyone remains "generally happy" and "very sociable and approachable," with no airs put on. In short, people here "genuinely care about each other and it makes for a wonderful experience."

ASSUMPTION UNIVERSITY

Financial Aid: 508-767-7158 • E-Mail: admiss@assumption.edu • Website: www.assumption.edu

THE PRINCETON REVIEW SAYS

Admissions

The school reports that its standardized testing policy for use in admission for Fall 2026 is Test Optional. The Princeton Review suggests that interested applicants consult with the school for the most up-to-date standardized testing policies. *Very important factors considered include:* academic GPA, application essay. *Important factors considered include:* rigor of secondary school record, recommendation(s), interview, volunteer work, level of applicant's interest. *Other factors considered include:* class rank, standardized test scores, extracurricular activities, talent/ability, character/personal qualities, first generation, alumni/ae relation. High school diploma is required and GED is accepted. *Academic units required:* 4 English, 3 math, 2 science, 2 language (other than English), 2 history, 5 academic electives.

Financial Aid

Students should submit: FAFSA. Priority filing deadline is 3/15. The Princeton Review suggests that all financial aid forms be submitted as soon as possible. *Need-based scholarships/grants offered:* Federal Pell; Federal SEOG; State scholarships/grants; Private scholarships; College/university scholarship or grant aid from institutional funds. *Loan aid offered:* Federal Direct Subsidized Loans; Federal Direct Unsubsidized Loans; Direct PLUS loans; State Loans. Admitted students will be notified of awards on a rolling basis beginning 11/15. Federal Work-Study Program available. Institutional employment available.

The Inside Word

Over three-quarters of those who apply to Assumption are admitted; keeping in mind that the applicant pool is somewhat self-selective, academically average students shouldn't have a hard time getting in. Assumption uses the Common Application and submitting standardized test scores is optional. Please note that international students who do not have English as a first language will need to provide English proficiency scores and should visit the school's website for requirements and details.

THE SCHOOL SAYS

From the Admissions Office

"Students flourish at Assumption University. The D'Amour College of Liberal Arts and Sciences, the Grenon School of Business, the Froelich School of Nursing, the School of Health Professions, and the School of Graduate Studies offers students many degree options, as well as dual and accelerated bachelor's/master's programs. Established in 1904 by the Augustinians of the Assumption, the University is a Catholic, liberal arts coeducational institution offering an educational experience that cultivates academic excellence and a holistic approach to the formation of the whole person. Approximately 1,700 undergraduates choose from among 35 majors and 48 minors, gaining a foundation for lifelong success. Students engage with highly credentialed faculty and staff in a community that fosters critical intelligence, thoughtful citizenship, and compassionate service. With a student/faculty ratio of just 11:1, Assumption's professors challenge students to ask questions and "seek the truth in the company of friends." In the past six years, 90% of Assumption's graduates were employed, enlisted in the military, enrolled in additional education, or participated in post-graduate service opportunities.

"Assumption's beautiful 185-acre campus is situated in a residential neighborhood just minutes from thriving downtown Worcester, Massachusetts. The campus is lively seven days a week with academic programming, activities sponsored by more than 60 student clubs and organizations, community service opportunities, campus ministry programs; and intercollegiate, intramural, and club sports. The University's campus in Rome, Italy, a ranked Top 10 study abroad program in America, utilizes the city as the classroom and enriches students' academic and cultural pursuits."

SELECTIVITY

# of total applicants	5,695
% of total applicants accepted	85
% of total acceptees attending	11
# of early decision applicants	79
% of early decision applicants accepted	81

First-Year Profile

Testing policy	Test Optional
Average HS GPA	3.6
% submitting high school GPA	94
% graduated top 10% of class	14
% graduated top 25% of class	34
% graduated top 50% of class	77
% submitting high school rank	42

Important Dates

Early decision	
Apply by	11/1
Notified by	Two weeks from submission
Early action	
Apply by	11/15
Notified by	Two weeks from submission
Regular	
Apply by	4/1
Notified by	Two weeks from submission
Nonfall registration?	Yes

FINANCIAL FACTS

Annual tuition	$54,070
Food and housing	$17,050
Required fees	$960
Books and supplies	$1,000
Average need-based scholarship (First-year)	$37,352 ($40,709)
% students with need rec. need-based scholarship or grant aid (First-year)	98 (100)
% students with need rec. non-need-based scholarship or grant aid (First-year)	27 (27)
% students with need rec. need-based self-help aid (First-year)	74 (77)
% UG borrow to pay for school	82
Average cumulative indebtedness	$41,331
% of students with need fully met (First-year)	34 (31)
Average % of student need met (First-year)	82 (85)

AUBURN UNIVERSITY

The Quad Center, Auburn, AL 36849-1111 • Admissions: 334-844-6425

Survey Snapshot
Lots of conservative students
Students are happy
Students get along with local community

RATINGS

Quality of Life	94
Fire Safety	60*
Green	60*
Academic	81
Profs Interesting	86
Profs Accessible	92
Admissions	90
Financial Aid	83

CAMPUS LIFE

Type of school	Public
Environment	Town

Students

Degree-seeking undergrad enrollment	27,627
% male/female/not reported	49/51/0
% from out of state	43
% First-year live on campus	59
% Ugrads live on campus	17
# of fraternities (% join)	30 (30)
# of sororities (% join)	21 (53)
% Asian	3
% Black or African American	4
% Hispanic	5
% Native American	<1
% Pacific Islander	<1
% Race and/or ethnicity unknown	<1
% Two or more races	3
% White	83
% International	1
# of countries represented	68

CAMPUS MENTAL HEALTH SERVICES

Offers mental health/wellness program	Yes
Mental health training available to students	No
Employs Chief Wellness Officer	NR
Peer-to-peer mental health offerings	NR
Counseling center has guidelines or accreditation	No
Mental health/well-being courses	NR

ACADEMICS

% students returning for sophomore year	94
% students graduating within 4 years	62
% students graduating within 6 years	82
Calendar	Semester
Student/faculty ratio	21:1
Most common class size 20–29.	(27%)
Most common lab/discussion size 10–19.	(30%)

Most Popular Majors

Mechanical Engineering; Business Administration and Management

Applicants Sometimes Prefer

Clemson University, Georgia Institute of Technology, The University of Alabama—Tuscaloosa, University of Florida, University of Georgia, University of Tennessee—Knoxville

STUDENTS SAY "..."

Academics

As one of the South's largest universities, Auburn University provides its students with more than 150 majors across 12 schools and colleges, which undergraduates declare to be an "excellent diversity in courses/majors." The R1 research university also offers numerous opportunities for student research, as well as "many internship/co-op opportunities advertised and available." The school is also a Carnegie-recognized Community Engaged Institution, and its focus on outreach and engagement has led to numerous partnerships with schools, businesses, and communities, including the AuburnServes Network and Campus Kitchens Project. The school's longstanding reputation is rooted in an institutional support system that "provides you plenty of resources and opportunities to get a top-notch education," and students find that "nurturing education, extracurricular involvement opportunities, and professional skill development."

Auburn's history, traditions, and "challenging, captivating, unique and yet still timeless" environment extends to the classroom, where "approachable" professors "bring material to life." The plethora of learning pathways available through the sheer number of courses (which include some "very challenging engineering programs") may be daunting, "but the work pays off." Professors are proud instructors (and often researchers) who students say "make it clear that they are here to teach [us]" and "go out of their way to help you learn if you ask them." For those classes requiring additional support, "graduate student assistants are helpful in assisting professors in understanding how to make material more exciting to learn." Whatever the course of study, students feel that those in charge are "always very intelligent on the subjects at hand," and one simply says "I have received a wonderful education."

Campus Life

Student input is "very respected" at Auburn, so the "Old South small town feeling" of campus life has an easy flow. The facilities themselves, like the recreation center, are "amazing" and there's a "good food atmosphere in the community." There's also a nearby state park that provides a fun respite from university life (as do the nearby cities of Birmingham and Atlanta), and the city of Auburn "has a safe downtown area where students can go to bars" on weekends as well. Extracurricular activities abound with more than 600 student organizations, and Greek life is popular as well, though students say that "it's definitely possible to fit in without being a part of Greek life." Moreover, attendees have direct input in the abundant campus offerings, as the Student Government Association "is very strong at Auburn" and "student involvement is high." And so far as participation goes, everybody loves Aubie the Tiger—"Football Saturdays at Auburn are second to none"—which means that the university's legendary athletics "drive a ton of campus life and help unite the student body."

Student Body

Two things are typical of the average Auburn student: they're the sort "who would say 'hello' walking along the concourse to class," and they're also filled with "so much school spirit" that some might consider them to be "highly obsessed with football." Many students hail from Alabama and are described as both "friendly" and loyal: "Alabama students love Alabama football; Auburn students love Auburn." This devotion lays a strong foundation in which even the meekest voice "can cause tangible change" knowing that "the Auburn Family has your back." The certainty of support makes Auburn a "welcoming place" where any student "would lend a hand in a time of need."

AUBURN UNIVERSITY

Financial Aid: 334-844-4634 • E-Mail: admissions@auburn.edu • Website: www.auburn.edu

THE PRINCETON REVIEW SAYS

Admissions

The school reports that its standardized testing policy for use in admission for Fall 2026 will require applicants to submit either the SAT or ACT. The Princeton Review suggests that interested applicants consult with the school for the most up-to-date standardized testing policies. *Very important factors considered include:* academic GPA, standardized test scores. *Important factors considered include:* rigor of secondary school record. *Other factors considered include:* state residency. High school diploma is required and GED is accepted. *Academic units required:* 4 English, 3 math, 2 science, 1 science lab, 3 social studies. *Academic units recommended:* 2 science labs, 1 language (other than English), 4 social studies.

Financial Aid

Students should submit: FAFSA. Priority filing deadline is 3/28. The Princeton Review suggests that all financial aid forms be submitted as soon as possible. *Need-based scholarships/grants offered:* Federal Pell; Federal SEOG; State scholarships/grants; Private scholarships; College/university scholarship or grant aid from institutional funds. *Loan aid offered:* Federal Direct Subsidized Loans; Federal Direct Unsubsidized Loans; Direct PLUS loans; College/university loans from institutional funds. Admitted students will be notified of awards on a rolling basis beginning 4/15. Federal Work-Study Program available. Institutional employment available.

The Inside Word

Auburn admissions officers have approximately 60,000 applications to sort through each year, and admission here is somewhat selective. Applicants are evaluated as individuals, and those who fall short of the average GPA, curricular, and standardized test score standards for incoming first-years should know that the admissions committee is also looking for those with unique talents and abilities that will contribute substantially to campus life. Letters of recommendation, essays, and extracurricular activities are the make-or-break point for borderline candidates.

THE SCHOOL SAYS

From the Admissions Office

"Auburn University is a comprehensive land, sea, and space-grant university serving Alabama and the nation. The university is especially charged with the responsibility of enhancing the economic, social, and cultural development of the state through its instruction, research, and extension programs. In all of these programs, the university is committed to the pursuit of excellence. The university assumes an obligation to provide an environment of learning in which the individual and society are enriched by the discovery, preservation, transmission, and application of knowledge; in which students grow intellectually as they study and do research under the guidance of competent faculty; and in which the faculty develop professionally and contribute fully to the intellectual life of the institution, community, and state. This obligation unites Auburn University's continuing commitment to its land-grant traditions and the institution's role as a dynamic and complex, comprehensive university."

SELECTIVITY

# of total applicants	59,121
% of total applicants accepted	47
% of total acceptees attending	22
# of in-state applicants	12,498
% of in-state applicants accepted	62
# of out-of-state-applicants	45,127
% of applicants accepted from out of state	44
# of international applicants	1,496
% of international applicants accepted	9

First-Year Profile

Testing policy	SAT or ACT Required
Range SAT composite	1280–1370
Range SAT EBRW	640–700
Range SAT math	630–700
Range ACT composite	27–31
% submitting SAT scores	22
% submitting ACT scores	78
Average HS GPA	4.1
% submitting high school GPA	100
% graduated top 10% of class	35
% graduated top 25% of class	65
% graduated top 50% of class	93
% submitting high school rank	34

Important Dates

Early action	
Apply by	12/1
Notified by	2/1
Regular	
Apply by	2/1
Notified by	Rolling, 3/1
Nonfall registration?	Yes

FINANCIAL FACTS

Annual in-state tuition	$13,306
Annual out-of-state tuition	$35,986
Food and housing	$17,210
Required fees	$1,966
Books and supplies	$1,200
Average need-based scholarship (First-year)	$11,467 ($12,204)
% students with need rec. need-based scholarship or grant aid (First-year)	83 (91)
% students with need rec. non-need-based scholarship or grant aid (First-year)	15 (19)
% students with need rec. need-based self-help aid (First-year)	63 (53)
% students rec. any financial aid (First-year)	63 (73)
% UG borrow to pay for school	36
Average cumulative indebtedness	$36,136
% of students with need fully met (First-year)	16 (20)
Average % of student need met (First-year)	51 (56)

Austin College

900 N. Grand Avenue, Sherman, TX 75090 • Admissions: 903-813-3000

Survey Snapshot
Internships are widely available
Diverse student types interact on campus
Students environmentally aware

RATINGS

Quality of Life	81
Fire Safety	78
Green	93
Academic	85
Profs Interesting	91
Profs Accessible	93
Admissions	89
Financial Aid	93

CAMPUS LIFE

Type of school	Private
Affiliation	Presbyterian
Environment	Town

Students

Degree-seeking undergrad enrollment	1,170
% male/female/not reported	48/49/3
% from out of state	7
% First-year live on campus	95
% Ugrads live on campus	85
# of fraternities (% join)	9 (NR)
# of sororities (% join)	8 (NR)
% Asian	9
% Black or African American	8
% Hispanic	29
% Native American	1
% Pacific Islander	<1
% Race and/or ethnicity unknown	1
% Two or more races	5
% White	47
% International	1
# of countries represented	16

CAMPUS MENTAL HEALTH SERVICES

Offers mental health/wellness program	Yes
Mental health training available to students	Yes
Employs Chief Wellness Officer	Yes
Peer-to-peer mental health offerings	Yes
Counseling center has guidelines or accreditation	No
Mental health/well-being courses	No

ACADEMICS

% students returning for sophomore year	79
% students graduating within 4 years	63
% students graduating within 6 years	67
Calendar	4-1-4
Student/faculty ratio	11:1
Most common class size 10–19.	(43%)
Most common lab/discussion size 10–19.	(58%)

Most Popular Majors
Biology/Biological Sciences; Psychology; Business/Commerce

Applicants Sometimes Prefer
Southwestern University, Texas A&M University—College Station, University of Houston, University of North Texas UNT, University of Texas at Austin, The University of Texas at Dallas

STUDENTS SAY "…"

Academics

Located about an hour north of Dallas, Austin College is a small private liberal arts school that places applied learning at the forefront of the curriculum. A mandatory First-Year Experience program helps to introduce new 'Roos to all that the school has to offer in this respect, while a month-long JanTerm course each year—some of which are offered abroad—helps "encourage [students] to try classes outside of their majors." As one student reports, "I was able to spend the month of January doing an internship that counted as my course... [a] practical experience that was truly beneficial." As students put it, "The sheer amount of hands-on learning experiences that we have here at Austin College is phenomenal." Students are given many "unique opportunities that are unlike any other institution," including undergraduate research opportunities through the Center for Research, Experiential, Artistic & Transformative Education (CREATE).

Professors are accessible and "emblematic of the liberal arts experience, managing to create courses that are applicable and/or explore a number of disciplines." This means that "there are tons of fun classes that may have a lot of work, but the work feels like a game or the professor works to include very interesting and attention-grabbing activities." One student specifies, "I got to go taste food at local restaurants and learned how to critique said food, I got to help with a local charity for a class." In summary, "all of the core areas that you want a college to succeed in, Austin College excels at."

Campus Life

Part of the beauty of a small campus [is] you can be a part of anything and everything, and the "sense of pride and community runs rampant with all of our students and faculty." Students can expect to be busy, as many "have a full schedule with classes, frats/sororities, student organizations, clubs, internships, and on campus jobs (AC is full of opportunities for students to earn money working on the campus)." Luckily the campus itself "is small, so there is not much competition for parking and traveling to class is very easy." The Campus Activities Board "[has] these weekly and monthly events all year long that [keep] us students entertained at full max," including offerings such as "an escape room off campus (free of charge), or a HUGE Texas-fest carnival with a big ride." There are also particularly strong international opportunities at Austin, and "it's so easy to travel abroad with the school (with scholarship)!" Another student illustrates: "After I graduate, I'll have traveled four times through AC: twice domestic and twice abroad, all pretty much funded by a scholarship I received on campus my freshman year. The school really wants its students to explore and have an experience that you can't get at any other university."

Student Body

This group is "diverse in our languages, races, religions, political views," with almost half of the students representing an ethnic minority group. "Everyone here is very open and accepting" and "all bounce off from one another learning new things all the time." As a student says, "We are small, but a mighty community, and a group can truly be found for all." The college "fosters an environment of inclusion and openness for new ideas and community," and while "there are naturally formed friend groups/cliques, as well as Greek life, students tend to mix regardless of their connections." An additional benefit to the school's size "means basically everyone knows each other and we are able to create a special environment at events because of the comfortability with each other." Another student concurs: "It is very easy to make friends with other students, [and] everyone is always willing to talk and say hello, even if they have met you only a few times."

AUSTIN COLLEGE

Financial Aid: 903-813-2900 • E-Mail: admission@austincollege.edu • Website: www.austincollege.edu

THE PRINCETON REVIEW SAYS

Admissions

The school reports that its standardized testing policy for use in admission for Fall 2026 is Test Optional. The Princeton Review suggests that interested applicants consult with the school for the most up-to-date standardized testing policies. *Very important factors considered include:* rigor of secondary school record, academic GPA. *Important factors considered include:* application essay. *Other factors considered include:* class rank, standardized test scores, recommendation(s), interview, extracurricular activities, talent/ability, character/personal qualities, first generation, alumni/ae relation, volunteer work, work experience, level of applicant's interest. High school diploma is required and GED is accepted. *Academic units required:* 4 English, 3 math, 3 science, 1 science lab, 2 language (other than English), 2 social studies, 1 visual/performing arts. *Academic units recommended:* 4 English, 4 math, 4 science, 2 science labs, 2 language (other than English), 4 social studies, 2 visual/performing arts.

Financial Aid

Students should submit: FAFSA. Priority filing deadline is 3/1. The Princeton Review suggests that all financial aid forms be submitted as soon as possible. *Need-based scholarships/grants offered:* Federal Pell; Federal SEOG; State scholarships/grants; Private scholarships; College/university scholarship or grant aid from institutional funds. *Loan aid offered:* Federal Direct Subsidized Loans; Federal Direct Unsubsidized Loans; Direct PLUS loans; State Loans. Admitted students will be notified of awards on a rolling basis beginning 12/1. Federal Work-Study Program available. Institutional employment available.

The Inside Word

Austin College takes a holistic approach to the admissions game. Indeed, the school does its best to get a feel for who each applicant is beyond their GPA and transcript. Therefore, expect your recommendations, extracurricular activities, and essay to be heavily vetted. Additionally, the college is impressed with students who challenge themselves academically. Admissions officers are frequently more impressed with a B in an honors course than an A in a standard class.

THE SCHOOL SAYS

From the Admissions Office

"If you want to be anonymous, choose a different school. But if you dream of connecting with others, exploring the world, and discovering more about yourself, then Austin College is exactly where you belong.

"Learning happens in classroom discussions led by talented professors, dedicated to teaching and passionate about their work, who act as partners in education with students. Faculty and students often work together in research projects and learning opportunities in which sometimes the answers discovered aren't as important as the process of inquiry and discovery.

"Students come to Austin College for exceptional academic offerings in more than 57 areas of study in the humanities, sciences, and social sciences. Over the past five years, 82 percent of graduates completed an internship as career preparation. 94 percent of our graduates are attending graduate or professional school or are employed within a year of graduation. The highest number of students enroll in medical and law schools. Many graduates receive prestigious honors like Fulbright grants or Teach for America positions. "From Deposit to Your Graduation in Four Years: Our Commitment to Your Success Is Guaranteed.

"We are confident in our academic programs and personalized mentoring; we promise that any full-time student who meets the Finish in Four Guarantee requirements in effect at the time of their enrollment will graduate in four calendar years. And, if you don't, Austin College will waive tuition costs for any courses you need to complete your degree. Guaranteed."

SELECTIVITY

# of total applicants	5,084
% of total applicants accepted	47
% of total acceptees attending	15

First-Year Profile

Testing policy	Test Optional
Range SAT composite	1110–1210
Range SAT EBRW	550–660
Range SAT math	550–650
Range ACT composite	23–29
% submitting SAT scores	24
% submitting ACT scores	8
Average HS GPA	3.6
% submitting high school GPA	99
% graduated top 10% of class	20
% graduated top 25% of class	47
% graduated top 50% of class	84
% submitting high school rank	50

Important Dates

Early decision	
Apply by	11/1
Notified by	1/15
Other ED apply by	2/1
Other ED notified by	3/1
Early action	
Apply by	11/1
Notified by	1/15
Regular	
Apply by	8/15
Notified by	Rolling, 11/15
Nonfall registration?	No

FINANCIAL FACTS

Annual tuition	$51,308
Food and housing	$14,929
Required fees	$210
Average need-based scholarship (First-year)	$39,952 ($43,565)
% students with need rec. need-based scholarship or grant aid (First-year)	100 (100)
% students with need rec. non-need-based scholarship or grant aid (First-year)	22 (20)
% students with need rec. need-based self-help aid (First-year)	66 (66)
% students rec. any financial aid (First-year)	100 (100)
% UG borrow to pay for school	55
Average cumulative indebtedness	$35,337
% of students with need fully met (First-year)	45 (41)
Average % of student need met (First-year)	90 (91)

BABSON COLLEGE

231 Forest Street, Babson Park, MA 02457 • Admissions: 781-239-5522

Survey Snapshot
Career services are great
Internships are widely available
School is well run

RATINGS

Quality of Life	**90**
Fire Safety	**94**
Green	**82**
Academic	**81**
Profs Interesting	**90**
Profs Accessible	**92**
Admissions	**96**
Financial Aid	**96**

CAMPUS LIFE

Type of school	Private
Environment	Village

Students

Degree-seeking undergrad enrollment	2,780
% male/female/not reported	57/43/0
% from out of state	78
% First-year live on campus	100
% Ugrads live on campus	76
# of fraternities (% join)	4 (14)
# of sororities (% join)	3 (15)
% Asian	13
% Black or African American	4
% Hispanic	18
% Native American	0
% Pacific Islander	0
% Race and/or ethnicity unknown	8
% Two or more races	3
% White	26
% International	27
# of countries represented	84

CAMPUS MENTAL HEALTH SERVICES

Offers mental health/wellness program	Yes
Mental health training available to students	Yes
Employs Chief Wellness Officer	Yes
Peer-to-peer mental health offerings	Yes
Counseling center has guidelines or accreditation	Yes
Mental health/well-being courses	No

ACADEMICS

% students returning for sophomore year	97
% students graduating within 4 years	87
% students graduating within 6 years	92
Calendar	Semester
Student/faculty ratio	16:1
Most common class size 30–39.	(29%)

Most Popular Majors

Business Administration and Management

Applicants Also Look At

Bentley University, Boston College, Boston University, New York University, Northeastern University

STUDENTS SAY "..."

Academics

Babson College, with its focus on business, serves as a launching pad for "the professional careers of their students." That begins with a first-year Foundations of Management and Entrepreneurship (FME) that, as the school puts it, teaches "how to lead, work in a team, manage obstacles, take risks, navigate uncertainty, and see a plan through to completion." Students agree that "not only does this create a great foundation, but it teaches a lot about running a business." Babson provides "amazing funding for students" through the eTower entrepreneurial incubator and investment-based courses with "$3,000 to launch the venture [you design], and your grade is based on how effectively you execute and generate revenue," or with "$7 million of the school's actual endowment in the stock market." These classes "prepare students through meaningful, hands-on responsibility rather than purely theoretical work." In addition to the "huge emphasis on learning by doing," Babson offers "so much opportunity for growth and exploration in business through various clubs and internships offered around campus. The career fairs and frequent speakers allow you to build your network for the future and gauge what areas of business you might want to be involved in." Overall, "Babson's greatest strength is how it turns students into operators, not just learners. The culture pushes you to take ideas seriously enough to execute them—build, test, sell, measure, iterate...You learn to be comfortable with ambiguity, make decisions with imperfect information, and still move things forward."

Campus Life

Babson students are "devoted to [their] professional clubs on campus." These organizations "are one of the best ways to meet people and build strong connections, and nearly everyone participates in at least one." And many look to clubs to further their executive functioning skills. For example, one student appreciates "serving as president of a major finance organization [and] leading another branch of a large finance group." Also popular is "anything music-related," such as theater, a cappella, and jazz. One student enthuses about the Babson Dance Ensemble: "This club means a lot to me as it allowed me to grow and experiment as a choreographer, develop a network of talented dancers, and grow my leadership skills." Exercise is another way students connect. "The intramural sports are really good" and feature teams that range from "equestrian and e-sports to pickleball and polo." Students report that the recreation center itself, with "many courts for basketball and volleyball players, a complete gym with bodybuilding and cardio, [and an] Olympic-size pool," is a major campus hub. Taken together, these clubs, teams, and campus spaces allow for "a great balance of work and fun."

Student Body

Babson draws ambitious, focused students eager to build something great. "Some students choose to grind academically, while others focus more on building their own businesses, but everyone is always building something," says one student. Having this shared goal in common creates a "collective uplifting" across campus, with one student sharing, "The reason I was successful throughout my college career was because of the energy of the student body." Another describes their peers as "the type of people who will listen to your business pitch at 11:00 pm in the library,...invite you to sit beside them if you are sitting alone..., [and are] some of the most inspiring, hard-working, ambitious friends, leaders, and business owners who inspire me to consistently hold myself to the highest standard." Many say that this collaborative energy results from being "surrounded by students from different backgrounds and walks of life, all of whom enrich our discussions and make them more engaging and insightful. I have friends from...many other countries, each of whom has broadened my understanding of global socio-economic issues." In short, "everyone here is working towards something great, wants to succeed, and do big things in their life and career."

BABSON COLLEGE

Financial Aid: 781-239-4219 • E-Mail: ugradadmission@babson.edu • Website: www.babson.edu

THE PRINCETON REVIEW SAYS

Admissions

The school reports that its standardized testing policy for use in admission for Fall 2026 is Test Optional. The Princeton Review suggests that interested applicants consult with the school for the most up-to-date standardized testing policies. *Very important factors considered include:* rigor of secondary school record, class rank, academic GPA, standardized test scores, application essay, recommendation(s), extracurricular activities, character/personal qualities. *Other factors considered include:* interview, talent/ability, first generation, alumni/ae relation, geographical residence, state residency, volunteer work, work experience, level of applicant's interest. High school diploma is required and GED is accepted. *Academic units required:* 4 English, 4 math, 3 science, 4 social studies. *Academic units recommended:* 4 English, 4 math, 3 science, 4 language (other than English), 4 social studies.

Financial Aid

Students should submit: FAFSA; CSS PROFILE. Priority filing deadline is 2/1. The Princeton Review suggests that all financial aid forms be submitted as soon as possible. *Need-based scholarships/grants offered:* Federal Pell; Federal SEOG; State scholarships/grants; Private scholarships; College/university scholarship or grant aid from institutional funds. *Loan aid offered:* Federal Direct Subsidized Loans; Federal Direct Unsubsidized Loans; Direct PLUS loans; State Loans. Admitted students will be notified of awards on or about 4/1. Federal Work-Study Program available. Institutional employment available.

The Inside Word

Babson's prominence as a noteworthy undergraduate business school continues to rise. Incoming students are evaluated on their academic performance (high school GPAs and standardized test scores, if submitted) as well as nonacademic factors including leadership, involvement, and enthusiasm. Writing ability is a valued commodity, and prospective students should be ready for the supplemental writing section of the application. Besides Regular Decision application, Babson offers three fall application plans for first-years—Early Decision I, Early Decision II, and Early Action—in addition to January G.A.P. Enrollment, which allows students to apply for the spring semester.

THE SCHOOL SAYS

From the Admissions Office

"Nationally recognized as the number one school in entrepreneurship for 29 times, Babson College is the premier institution for entrepreneurship education. Through our entrepreneurial thought and action methodology, we teach our students to think and act entrepreneurially to pursue their passions and create a path to success, no matter where that path might lead. As a result, Babson graduates are entrepreneurial leaders, with a mindset and skillset to impact communities and organizations around the world. Our immersive, hands-on curriculum blends the liberal arts and sciences with business courses providing students with the ability to adapt to ever-changing business environments, the experience to hit the ground running upon graduation, and the know-how to discover opportunities that will create economic and social value everywhere.

"With an average class size of thirty to thirty-nine students and a student/faculty ratio of 16:1, Babson's tight-knit community provides students with the opportunity to form close relationships with faculty and staff. With about 84 percent holding a doctoral degree, these accomplished business executives, authors, entrepreneurs, scholars, researchers, and artists bring intellectual diversity and real-world experiences that add depth to Babson's programs. Most importantly, faculty members teach 100 percent of the courses.

"At Babson, students receive a world-class education that is innovative and creative, yet practical. They study business, liberal arts and sciences, learn about leadership, and undertake a transformative life experience preparing them to create an authentic, powerful brand of success. Our students make friends, find mentors, and develop long-lasting relationships that will thrive long after graduation."

SELECTIVITY

# of total applicants	10,552
% of total applicants accepted	16
% of total acceptees attending	41
# of early decision applicants	1,339
% of early decision applicants accepted	25
# offered a place on the wait list	3,551
# admitted from wait list	163

First-Year Profile

Testing policy	Test Optional
Range SAT composite	1410–1510
Range SAT EBRW	680–740
Range SAT math	720–780
Range ACT composite	30–34
% submitting SAT scores	24
% submitting ACT scores	4

Important Dates

Early decision	
Apply by	11/1
Notified by	12/15
Other ED apply by	1/2
Other ED notified by	2/15
Early action	
Apply by	11/1
Notified by	1/1
Regular	
Apply by	1/2
Notified by	4/1
Nonfall registration?	Yes

FINANCIAL FACTS

Annual tuition	$60,288
Food and housing	$23,228
Books and supplies	$1,300
Average need-based scholarship (First-year)	$52,926 ($50,696)
% students with need rec. need-based scholarship or grant aid (First-year)	98 (98)
% students with need rec. non-need-based scholarship or grant aid (First-year)	13 (7)
% students with need rec. need-based self-help aid (First-year)	68 (76)
% students rec. any financial aid (First-year)	40 (39)
% UG borrow to pay for school	34
Average cumulative indebtedness	$40,846
% of students with need fully met (First-year)	95 (100)
Average % of student need met (First-year)	96 (100)

Bard College

PO Box 5000, Annandale-on-Hudson, NY 12504 • Admissions: 845-758-7472

Survey Snapshot
Lots of liberal students
Lab facilities are great
Class discussions encouraged

RATINGS

Quality of Life	**84**
Fire Safety	**60***
Green	**89**
Academic	**91**
Profs Interesting	**98**
Profs Accessible	**96**
Admissions	**88**
Financial Aid	**80**

CAMPUS LIFE

Type of school	Private
Environment	Rural

Students

Degree-seeking undergrad enrollment	1,804
% male/female/not reported	41/59/0
% from out of state	66
% First-year from public high school	58
% First-year live on campus	99
% Ugrads live on campus	75
# of fraternities	0
# of sororities	0
% Asian	4
% Black or African American	6
% Hispanic	10
% Native American	<1
% Pacific Islander	0
% Race and/or ethnicity unknown	6
% Two or more races	5
% White	57
% International	11
# of countries represented	57

CAMPUS MENTAL HEALTH SERVICES

Offers mental health/wellness program	Yes
Mental health training available to students	No
Employs Chief Wellness Officer	NR
Peer-to-peer mental health offerings	NR
Counseling center has guidelines or accreditation	No
Mental health/well-being courses	NR

ACADEMICS

% students returning for sophomore year	85
% students graduating within 4 years	62
% students graduating within 6 years	74
Calendar	Semester
Student/faculty ratio	10:1
Most common class size 10–19.	(44%)

Most Popular Majors

English Language and Literature; Visual and Performing Arts; Social Sciences

Applicants Often Prefer

Barnard College, Boston University, Columbia University, Johns Hopkins University, New York University, Northeastern University, Oberlin College, Princeton University, Reed College, Sarah Lawrence College, Tufts University, University of California—Santa Cruz, The University of Chicago

Applicants Sometimes Prefer

Bates College, Bowdoin College, Brandeis University, Brown University, Connecticut College, Grinnell College, Haverford College, Kenyon College, Macalester College, Occidental College, Scripps College, Swarthmore College, Vassar College, Wesleyan University

STUDENTS SAY "..."

Academics

Bard College, located in the picturesque Hudson Valley, is an institution that truly pushes its undergraduates to "think critically, ask questions...and follow those questions through." Students love the "small and intimate" class sizes, and they consistently find their course materials to be "intriguing, relevant, and challenging." Indeed, the academics are rigorous and culminate in a senior project "required by all students." Many undergrads truly appreciate this requirement, noting it's "a phenomenal opportunity to get hands-on experience working with professionals in the field," and "students end up producing amazing pieces of literature, theater, music, art, [and] scientific research." Bardians also benefit from professors who are "extremely invested in what they are teaching and really want the students to learn as much as they can from them." That means that the faculty "expect a lot from all students, in their assignments, in the depth with which they explore the material, and in the level of discussion." Fortunately, it's "rare to find a teacher that doesn't have time to sit down with the individual student to discuss class work and personal matters." Professors are "well connected in their given fields, they are also great resources for research, internships, and networking." As one student aptly says, "The classes at Bard and the professors are truly amazing."

Campus Life

Given the emphasis on academics at Bard, it's not unusual to find students enjoying "intellectual conversations and...rehashing class topics" even after class. However, there is also plenty of extracurricular fun to be had. "There are always events happening on campus, including concerts, dance performances, student theater pieces, community dinners, guest lectures, and yoga classes." One student sings the praises of the music scene, noting it's "terrific, both in terms of student bands and outside acts that perform on campus." Of course, "there are also various student clubs like the Surrealist Training Circus and the Bard Free Press that meet weekly." Bard's drinking scene is fairly low-key; "on the weekends you can find "some parties, but if you have a good group of friends, you'll often stay in with wine or beer and listen to good music." As this student explains, "Bard is a place where often the best night out is time spent with friends." For those who appreciate spending time outdoors, the school is "in the middle of a forest in the Hudson Valley, so there are some absolutely gorgeous spots and hiking trails on campus." There's even one that provides "easy access to our own private waterfall!"

Student Body

When asked about their classmates, students quickly assert that "the only thing consistent from one Bardian to the next is that they will always surprise you." Nevertheless, while they may be "incredibly diverse in terms of [their] interests and passions," there's still plenty that unites these "creative and brilliant" individuals. To begin with, they tend to be "deep thinkers." As one undergrad explains, "If you're the kind of person who liked to think about big ideas in high school and felt left out when people around you were not moved by them, then Bard is the perfect place [for you]." Students are often described as "very accepting and liberal. They try to make everyone feel included regardless of gender, sexuality, race, etc." Another student concurs, adding, "Bard students are activists; we revel in politics, culture, education, and human rights." Undergrads appreciate that "there isn't much competition between students when it comes to grades or classes. People are just supportive of the projects their peers are working on." Ultimately, Bard is a place where "you can be a musical mathematician or a written arts and economics major, you can dance, sing, paint or be an athlete or none or all of the above, and people will be excited to hear your story."

Bard College

Financial Aid: 845-758-7526 • E-Mail: admissions@bard.edu • Website: www.bard.edu

THE PRINCETON REVIEW SAYS

Admissions

The school reports that its standardized testing policy for use in admission for Fall 2026 is Test Optional. The Princeton Review suggests that interested applicants consult with the school for the most up-to-date standardized testing policies. *Very important factors considered include:* rigor of secondary school record, academic GPA, application essay, recommendation(s), extracurricular activities, talent/ability, character/personal qualities. *Important factors considered include:* volunteer work, work experience. *Other factors considered include:* class rank, standardized test scores, interview, first generation, alumni/ae relation, geographical residence, state residency, religious affiliation/commitment, level of applicant's interest. High school diploma is required and GED is accepted. *Academic units recommended:* 4 English, 4 math, 4 science, 3 science labs, 4 language (other than English), 4 social studies, 4 history.

Financial Aid

Students should submit: FAFSA; CSS PROFILE. The Princeton Review suggests that all financial aid forms be submitted as soon as possible. *Need-based scholarships/grants offered:* Federal Pell; Federal SEOG; State scholarships/grants; Private scholarships; College/university scholarship or grant aid from institutional funds. *Loan aid offered:* Federal Direct Subsidized Loans; Federal Direct Unsubsidized Loans; Direct PLUS loans. Admitted students will be notified of awards on or about 3/20. Federal Work-Study Program available. Institutional employment available.

The Inside Word

Successful applicants tend to have high school transcripts rife with honors and AP courses, and a strong college prep curriculum is clearly a must. Beyond that, admissions officers want students who appear to be independent thinkers with a thirst for knowledge. It's a good idea to submit ACT or SAT scores, although optional. Above all, if you are set on Bard but concerned that your application alone won't give the whole story, consider Bard's Immediate Decision Plan, an all-day process that includes an interview, which yields a decision 48 hours later. The application deadline for Immediate Decision is November 1.

THE SCHOOL SAYS

From the Admissions Office

"An alliance with Rockefeller University, the renowned graduate scientific research institution, gives Bardians access to Rockefeller's professors and laboratories and to places in Rockefeller's Summer Research Fellows Program. Almost all our math and science graduates pursue graduate or professional studies; 90 percent of our applicants to medical and health professional schools are accepted.

"The Globalization and International Affairs (BGIA) Program is a residential program in the heart of New York City that offers undergraduates a unique opportunity to undertake specialized study with leading practitioners and scholars in international affairs and to gain internship experience with international-affairs organizations. Topics in the curriculum include human rights, international economics, global environmental issues, international justice, managing international risk, and writing on international affairs, among others. Internships/tutorials are tailored to students' particular fields of study.

"Civic engagement has become a large and growing part of student life at Bard, with a high percentage of students participating in a wide variety of local, national, and international programs sponsored by the college or initiated by students.

"Beyond the central campus, Bard has created global programs and satellite campuses from Berlin to the West Bank, offering students unique opportunities for study abroad and making Bard's student body strongly international."

SELECTIVITY

# of total applicants	5,141
% of total applicants accepted	65
% of total acceptees attending	15
# of early decision applicants	46
% of early decision applicants accepted	89

First-Year Profile

Testing policy	Test Optional
Range ACT composite	27–31
% submitting ACT scores	17
% graduated top 10% of class	41
% graduated top 25% of class	69
% graduated top 50% of class	94
% submitting high school rank	25

Important Dates

Early decision	
Apply by	11/1
Notified by	1/1
Early action	
Apply by	11/1
Notified by	1/1
Regular	
Apply by	1/1
Notified by	Rolling, 4/1
Nonfall registration?	No

FINANCIAL FACTS

Annual tuition	$55,566
Food and housing	$17,500
Required fees	$470
Books and supplies	$1,100
Average need-based scholarship (First-year)	$44,444 ($47,022)
% students with need rec. need-based scholarship or grant aid (First-year)	96 (97)
% students with need rec. non-need-based scholarship or grant aid (First-year)	0 (0)
% students with need rec. need-based self-help aid (First-year)	81 (82)
% students rec. any financial aid (First-year)	68 (69)
% UG borrow to pay for school	57
Average cumulative indebtedness	$27,726
% of students with need fully met (First-year)	22 (25)
Average % of student need met (First-year)	79 (81)

Barnard College

3009 Broadway, New York, NY 10027 • Admissions: 212-854-2014

Survey Snapshot
Lots of liberal students
Great library
Students love New York, NY

RATINGS

Quality of Life	**91**
Fire Safety	**75**
Green	**94**
Academic	**91**
Profs Interesting	**91**
Profs Accessible	**94**
Admissions	**99**
Financial Aid	**97**

CAMPUS LIFE

Type of school	Private
Environment	Metropolis

Students

Degree-seeking undergrad enrollment	3,217
% male/female/not reported	0/100/0
% from out of state	68
% First-year from public high school	50
% First-year live on campus	97
% Ugrads live on campus	75
# of sororities (% join)	10 (8)
% Asian	24
% Black or African American	5
% Hispanic	14
% Native American	<1
% Pacific Islander	0
% Race and/or ethnicity unknown	3
% Two or more races	7
% White	30
% International	17
# of countries represented	63

CAMPUS MENTAL HEALTH SERVICES

Offers mental health/wellness program	Yes
Mental health training available to students	Yes
Employs Chief Wellness Officer	Yes
Peer-to-peer mental health offerings	Yes
Counseling center has guidelines or accreditation	Yes
Mental health/well-being courses	Yes, non-credit

ACADEMICS

% students returning for sophomore year	97
% students graduating within 4 years	81
% students graduating within 6 years	92
Calendar	Semester
Student/faculty ratio	9:1
Most common class size 10–19.	(48%)

Most Popular Majors

Psychology; Economics; Computer Science

Applicants Also Look At

Boston University, Brown University, Columbia University, Cornell University, New York University, Northwestern University, Princeton University, The University of Chicago, Wellesley College, Wesleyan University, Yale University

STUDENTS SAY "..."

Academics

Barnard College, a celebrated private women's liberal arts college, offers students "the best of both worlds" with both a "small academic setting" and "full access to the Ivy League institution (Columbia University) right across the street. The school's "close community" offers a familiarity that carries beyond the walls of the classroom into the real world, where 37,000 alumnae form an empowering web that provides internships, career opportunities, and guidance through a variety of programs such as Mentor-in-Residence. Through this vast support network and Barnard's plentiful resources (for instance, the school spends $750,000 annually to aid students wishing to take unpaid internships), students seamlessly undergo a "transition from a young female college student to an adjusted global citizen."

This is due in no small part to Barnard's faculty, who are "really engaging and make the material approachable and interesting" and advise in further capacities through the school's numerous research and fellowship programs. No matter the area of study or size of the class, professors "definitely make time for students to come talk to them." Classes are a mix of lectures and discussions, and Barnard was one of the first colleges to institute a digital fluency requirement that imparts data manipulation skills and unites disciplines using digital tools. Even for those who may be nervous to tackle an unfamiliar topic or requirement, students say educators here are adept at "creating an environment to learn from and be inspired by classmates through the discussions held." The "phenomenal" education experience may be "challenging and very stressful" at times, but students are "so grateful" to be under the Barnard umbrella.

Campus Life

Students at Barnard live in "one of the greatest cities on Earth," where they're not just given free admission to many of New York City's legendary institutions, but have the opportunity to study with local artists, curators, and scientists, often at the museums or labs in which they work. Of course, the beauty of the school's uptown location is that it provides a whole city to explore while also being just removed enough to allow "a lot of fun events [to] take place on campus." And while there are over 600 clubs between Barnard and Columbia, it's not unusual to find students "just chilling"—that is, when they're not "working or going to office hours, or pursuing an internship, a personal job, etc." Even with rigorous classes and a city filled with theaters, museums, and more restaurants than one can healthily visit in a lifetime—plus traditional and "phenomenal Greek life" opportunities across the street at Columbia—students are "intensely dedicated to pursuing their interests, whether that be artistic, academic, pre-professional, or athletic ones."

Student Body

Barnard College is filled with "driven, intelligent" students who are "extremely interested, dedicated, and passionate" in everything: "biology, dance, theatre, architecture, economics, international relations" (just to name a few). Undergrads suggest that there's a "tendency to overload," but qualify that by explaining that's not a bad thing, as they are "very proactive and use all resources available...to achieve their goals." Moreover, while students here are "ambitious, driven, and hard workers," it is "not at the cost of physical or mental health: they know how to have fun, too." The result is a group of women that is "smart, independent, and ready to take on the world." These "cool, creative, confident, well-spoken, and determined" women are well aware of what's been said about their "cosmopolitan" location: those who make it here can make it anywhere.

Barnard College

Financial Aid: 212-854-2154 • E-Mail: admissions@barnard.edu • Website: www.barnard.edu

THE PRINCETON REVIEW SAYS

Admissions

The school reports that its standardized testing policy for use in admission for Fall 2026 is Test Optional. The Princeton Review suggests that interested applicants consult with the school for the most up-to-date standardized testing policies. *Very important factors considered include:* rigor of secondary school record, academic GPA, application essay, recommendation(s), character/personal qualities. *Important factors considered include:* class rank, extracurricular activities, talent/ability, volunteer work, work experience. *Other factors considered include:* standardized test scores, interview, first generation, alumni/ae relation, geographical residence, level of applicant's interest. High school diploma is required and GED is accepted. *Academic units recommended:* 4 English, 3 math, 3 science, 3 language (other than English), 3 history.

Financial Aid

Students should submit: FAFSA; CSS PROFILE; State aid form; Business/Farm Supplement. Priority filing deadline is 11/1. The Princeton Review suggests that all financial aid forms be submitted as soon as possible. *Need-based scholarships/grants offered:* Federal Pell; Federal SEOG; State scholarships/grants; College/university scholarship or grant aid from institutional funds. *Loan aid offered:* Federal Direct Subsidized Loans; Federal Direct Unsubsidized Loans; Direct PLUS loans. Admitted students will be notified of awards on a rolling basis. Federal Work-Study Program available. Institutional employment available.

The Inside Word

Barnard may have a highly competitive selection process—indeed, early decision applications have increased dramatically in recent years—but you wouldn't know it based on the admissions staff, who are surprisingly open and accessible. It comes as no surprise that the admission committee's expectations are high, given the school's long and impressive tradition of excellence, but those expectations reflect a genuine interest in who potential students are and what's on their minds.

THE SCHOOL SAYS

From the Admissions Office

"Barnard College is a small, distinguished liberal arts college for women that is partnered with Columbia University and located in the heart of New York City. Barnard students are wide ranging in their interests and passions, but they also share in a distinctive experience that creates an enduring bond: they live and learn in an environment where women always come first, where they're surrounded by other smart and inspiring women, and where they have access to a wide array of opportunities, both on and off campus. The Barnard community thrives on high expectations. By setting rigorous academic standards and giving students the support they need to meet those standards, Barnard enables them to discover their own capabilities.

"The college enrolls women from all over the United States and around the world. More than sixty countries, including Australia, Brazil, China, Denmark, France, India, Morocco, Russia, Turkey, and Zimbabwe are represented in the student body. Students pursue their academic studies in more than forty majors, are able to cross register at Columbia University, and have access to several combined 4+1 BA/MA programs at Columbia.

"Students may participate in Division I Varsity Columbia University athletic teams, in more than thirty club sports, and in a wide variety of intramural sports, and have access to over 500 student clubs and organizations at Barnard and Columbia."

SELECTIVITY

# of total applicants	10,426
% of total applicants accepted	10
% of total acceptees attending	67
# of early decision applicants	1,437
% of early decision applicants accepted	33
# offered a place on the wait list	2,173
# admitted from wait list	153

First-Year Profile

Testing policy	Test Optional
Range SAT composite	1480–1540
Range SAT EBRW	730–760
Range SAT math	730–790
Range ACT composite	32–35
% submitting SAT scores	38
% submitting ACT scores	16

Important Dates

Early decision	
Apply by	11/1
Notified by	12/15
Regular	
Apply by	1/2
Notified by	4/1
Nonfall registration?	No

FINANCIAL FACTS

Annual tuition	$70,644
Food and housing	$22,691
Required fees	$2,168
Books and supplies	$1,200
Average need-based scholarship (First-year)	$57,173 ($60,320)
% students with need rec. need-based scholarship or grant aid (First-year)	100 (100)
% students with need rec. non-need-based scholarship or grant aid (First-year)	0 (0)
% students with need rec. need-based self-help aid (First-year)	96 (98)
% students rec. any financial aid (First-year)	33 (35)
% UG borrow to pay for school	37
Average cumulative indebtedness	$24,784
% of students with need fully met (First-year)	96 (98)
Average % of student need met (First-year)	100 (100)

BATES COLLEGE

2 Andrews Road, Lewiston, ME 04240 • Admissions: 207-786-6000

Survey Snapshot
Lots of liberal students
Students are happy
Great food on campus

RATINGS

Quality of Life	**83**
Fire Safety	**60***
Green	**97**
Academic	**88**
Profs Interesting	**91**
Profs Accessible	**94**
Admissions	**96**
Financial Aid	**99**

CAMPUS LIFE

Type of school	Private
Environment	Town

Students

Degree-seeking undergrad enrollment	1,736
% male/female/not reported	48/49/3
% from out of state	89
% First-year from public high school	50
% First-year live on campus	100
% Ugrads live on campus	93
# of fraternities	0
# of sororities	0
% Asian	7
% Black or African American	4
% Hispanic	9
% Native American	<1
% Pacific Islander	<1
% Race and/or ethnicity unknown	1
% Two or more races	9
% White	63
% International	9
# of countries represented	92

CAMPUS MENTAL HEALTH SERVICES

Offers mental health/wellness program	Yes
Mental health training available to students	No
Employs Chief Wellness Officer	NR
Peer-to-peer mental health offerings	NR
Counseling center has guidelines or accreditation	No
Mental health/well-being courses	NR

ACADEMICS

% students returning for sophomore year	92
% students graduating within 4 years	83
% students graduating within 6 years	88
Calendar	4-4-1
Student/faculty ratio	9:1
Most common class size 10–19.	(42%)

Most Popular Majors

History; Political Science and Government; Psychology

STUDENTS SAY "..."

Academics

Maine's Bates College is a small liberal arts college that celebrates an "unbelievably tight-knit community" of students, professors, and the surrounding area. In fact, half of all students participate in a community-engaged, hands-on course each year, such as one where "French-speaking African immigrants met with Franco-Americans and we worked with the two groups to help the New Mainers learn English." Bates offers a "very holistic education" with an emphasis on critical thinking where everyone is "challenged to express their opinions, try something new, and stand up for a cause." As one student observes, "The most important thing I've learned so far is how to come up with an intelligent stance on an issue or idea." The opportunity for such realizations comes because "classes are mostly centered around personal progress rather than comparing students to one another."

The "flexible calendar" at Bates includes a springtime Short Term, in which students have four weeks to travel off-campus, complete fieldwork, or focus on just one class (the school says that "professors have a blast coming up with the topics"). Professors are universally beloved and "like to challenge students, and ask questions to encourage students to flesh out their opinions," and "make you think and come up with your own opinion about issues." A student sums up their Bates experience: "I couldn't ask for more helpful professors, a more helpful administration, or a variety of classes that suit the needs and requirements of my major."

Campus Life

For the entertainment-minded, Bates features "a multitude of...events to go to any day of the week," including "workshops for dance, fashion shows, and awesome days for food where the culinary staff brings themed food." Speaking of which, for those into food, the school's one dining hall is not only "absolutely amazing" but is also a popular gathering place "where students spend hours per day talking to many different people." And as for those focused on socializing or studying, the "library is also a large social hub where people like to talk while doing work." Above all, students are "always balancing academics with extracurriculars," and for them, there's a "huge amount of clubs and opportunities to get involved in the community," as well as traditions such as the Village Club Series on Thursdays, when musical groups play on campus. "Every time there is an a cappella concert, you will see the seats packed, and everyone cheering for each group." Portland and Boston are close by, so "you can always switch up your scenery when you need city life." Students also "regularly explore other parts of Maine," both on their own and through organizations like the Outing Club, which "hosts events every weekend, from skiing at our nearby mountains to sunrise paddles to backpacking trips" and "has a room full of gear that's free to check out."

Student Body

As one student notes, "My peers are enthusiastic about learning, being outdoors, and making connections." Students are very scholastically motivated and there is "a lot of variability in academic interests and how people spend their time." While "everyone has their own passions and is very chill at the same time," students say that "one of [Bates'] most unique features" is that "students are also extremely social" with the result being an atmosphere that is "very collaborative and kind." With such a focus on community engagement, this is a group that is "incredibly curious, friendly, and involved around campus and the greater Lewiston area." Most everyone is "involved in things outside of academics, whether that be sports teams, volunteering, or extracurricular clubs," and there "is a ton of crossover and interaction between different people." All in all, Bates holds a special place in the hearts of its classes, a college that in turn helps to make "everyone very special."

BATES COLLEGE

Financial Aid: 207-786-6096 • E-Mail: admission@bates.edu • Website: www.bates.edu

THE PRINCETON REVIEW SAYS

Admissions

The school reports that its standardized testing policy for use in admission for Fall 2026 is Test Optional. *Very important factors considered include:* rigor of secondary school record, class rank, academic GPA, application essay, recommendation(s), extracurricular activities, talent/ability, character/personal qualities. *Important factors considered include:* first generation, geographical residence, state residency, level of applicant's interest. *Other factors considered include:* standardized test scores (if submitted), alumni/ae relation, volunteer work, home obligations, and work experience. High school diploma is required and GED is not accepted. *Academic units required:* 4 English, 3 math, 3 science, 2 science labs, 2 language (other than English), 3 social studies, 3 history. *Academic units recommended:* 4 English, 4 math, 4 science, 3 science labs, 4 language (other than English), 4 social studies, 4 history.

Financial Aid

Students should submit: FAFSA; CSS PROFILE. *Need-based scholarships/grants offered:* Federal Pell; Federal SEOG; State scholarships/grants; Private scholarships; College/university scholarship or grant aid from institutional funds. *Loan aid offered:* Federal Direct Subsidized Loans; Direct PLUS loans; Federal Direct Unsubsidized Loans. Admitted students will be notified of awards on or about 3/15. Federal Work-Study Program available. Institutional employment available.

The Inside Word

Bates looks for students who challenge themselves in the classroom and beyond. A student's academic rigor, essays, and recommendations may be even more important than their GPA and test scores. The essay, in particular, is a chance to stand out—Bates is most interested in what has changed and inspired their applicants. Alumni conversations are available to prospective students upon request. These alumni conversations are not interviews, and they are both optional and informational—meaning prospective students are not being evaluated as part of the application process.

THE SCHOOL SAYS

From the Admissions Office

"Bates College in Lewiston, Maine, is recognized as one of the nation's finest liberal arts colleges. Bates is defined by academic excellence and its supportive, kind, collaborative community. Since 1855, Bates has welcomed students of all backgrounds, fostering a culture of inclusion that prepares its students to thrive personally and professionally after graduation.

"Our curriculum bridges the liberal arts with professional readiness. Bates offers small, seminar-style classes where students build critical thinking skills, knowledge, and close relationships with their classmates and dedicated professors. Each student's academic journey includes four years of integrated advising and opportunities for community-engaged learning and study abroad. This journey culminates in the Senior Thesis or Capstone project, a hallmark of our many opportunities for mentored research and student-faculty collaboration.

"Central to the experience is our unique Purposeful Work program. This signature initiative ensures that students align their interests with career outcomes through internships, practitioner-taught courses, job shadowing, and professional advising.

"Beyond the classroom, students enjoy a vibrant campus life, participating in varsity and club sports, exceptional arts programs, and over 100 student-run clubs, all while enjoying Maine's unique landscape and culture. Bates is committed to access, meeting 100% of demonstrated financial need to minimize student debt. Our holistic admission process prioritizes a student's experiences and abilities; notably, Bates has been test-optional for more than four decades.

"Bates is dedicated to preparing leaders sustained by a love of learning and a commitment to responsible stewardship of the wider world, Bates is a college for coming times."

SELECTIVITY

# of total applicants	9,660
% of total applicants accepted	15
% of total acceptees attending	34
# of in-state applicants	356
% of in-state applicants accepted	27
# of out-of-state-applicants	4,262
% of applicants accepted from out of state	28
# of international applicants	5,039
% of international applicants accepted	3
# of early decision applicants	949
% of early decision applicants accepted	34
# offered a place on the wait list	2,103
# admitted from wait list	39

First-Year Profile

Testing policy	Test Optional
Range SAT composite	1330–1510
Range SAT EBRW	670–750
Range SAT math	620–770
Range ACT composite	31–34
% submitting SAT scores	13
% submitting ACT scores	8

Important Dates

Early decision	
Apply by	11/15
Notified by	12/20
Other ED apply by	1/10
Other ED notified by	2/15
Regular	
Apply by	1/10
Notified by	4/1
Nonfall registration?	No

FINANCIAL FACTS*

Annual tuition	$70,146
Food and housing	$19,784
Required fees (First-year)	$0 ($450)
Books and supplies	$900
Average need-based scholarship (First-year)	$61,074 ($59,701)
% students with need rec. need-based scholarship or grant aid (First-year)	100 (100)
% students with need rec. non-need-based scholarship or grant aid (First-year)	0 (0)
% students with need rec. need-based self-help aid (First-year)	94 (92)
% students rec. any financial aid (First-year)	44 (45)
% UG borrow to pay for school	23
Average cumulative indebtedness	$35,206
% of students with need fully met (First-year)	100 (100)
Average % of student need met (First-year)	100 (100)

* Most recently reported data at time of printing. Scan the QR code to find the latest updates.

Batten University

5817 Wesleyan Drive, Virginia Beach, VA 23455 • Admissions: 757-455-3208

Survey Snapshot
Students are happy
Everyone loves the Blue Marlins
Campus newspaper is popular

RATINGS

Quality of Life	86
Fire Safety	79
Green	84
Academic	82
Profs Interesting	91
Profs Accessible	94
Admissions	76
Financial Aid	84

CAMPUS LIFE

Type of school	Private
Affiliation	Methodist
Environment	Metropolis

Students

Degree-seeking undergrad enrollment	1,256
% male/female/not reported	43/57/0
% from out of state	21
% First-year live on campus	81
% Ugrads live on campus	54
# of fraternities (% join)	4 (NR)
# of sororities (% join)	5 (NR)
% Asian	3
% Black or African American	20
% Hispanic	8
% Native American	2
% Pacific Islander	0
% Race and/or ethnicity unknown	20
% Two or more races	5
% White	39
% International	3
# of countries represented	22

CAMPUS MENTAL HEALTH SERVICES

Offers mental health/wellness program	Yes
Mental health training available to students	Yes
Employs Chief Wellness Officer	Yes
Peer-to-peer mental health offerings	Yes
Counseling center has guidelines or accreditation	Yes
Mental health/well-being courses	Yes, non-credit

ACADEMICS

% students returning for sophomore year	74
% students graduating within 4 years	36
% students graduating within 6 years	42
Calendar	Continuous
Student/faculty ratio	15:1
Most common class size 10–19.	(52%)

Most Popular Majors
Criminal Justice/Safety Studies; Social Sciences; Business Administration and Management

On July 1, 2026, Virginia Wesleyan University became Batten University.

STUDENTS SAY "..."

Academics

Students enjoy the "small classes" at Batten University, a liberal arts school where "you're more than a number." Flexibility is the key to "making every single student feel as though this is their second home, and that every person they come into contact with is looking out for [their] best interest." That can be seen in the research and internship opportunities but is most keenly felt in course offerings, which extend from "study away" programs ranging from one week to one year to a single-course-focused three-week January term—required for first- and second-years but open to all—and a discounted summer session to catch up, get ahead, or simply explore. Across the 42 majors, students find many classes to be "discussion or interaction-based" and "always taught by...professors" rather than teaching assistants. The professors here seem to "genuinely care about their students and are approachable outside the classroom." It's an environment where "professors make lifelong connections with students." As one student emphasizes, "I have never met a faculty so invested in my own personal success." This supportive environment is one of the school's top strengths. As one student says, "I have never experienced [a] learning environment like this one. Professors not only care about their students, but they go above and beyond to ensure that every student understands the material."

Campus Life

Batten's beautiful, 300-acre coastal campus offers many activities across numerous interests—one student lists activities across "Greek life, music, arts, religion, sciences, business, etc." Because students are mostly required to live on campus, it is a hub for student organizations, volunteering opportunities, or just hangouts, and the student activity committee offers everything from bingo to laser tag and goat yoga. Other ways to relax include recreational activities like using "the pool, the rock wall, the indoor track, the gymnasium, and the pool table in the student center." When the weather is nice, students spend time outside at Chick's Beach, and many students enjoy trying the "delicious restaurants around Norfolk" and Virginia Beach. There are big parties, but students describe a more casual culture in which "social gatherings are huge" and where students "love inviting [their] friends and teammates over to get over a stressful week of studying and homework."

Student Body

Students "can easily build strong relationship[s]" among this "close-knit community" of "laid back" yet "friendly and outgoing" peers who are "open to new things." The average Batten student tends to be "very busy" and "involved in several different clubs and community service groups." Many people here "join one of the Greek organizations available" or become "a member of a sports team" to make friends, though there are plenty of other ways to bond with classmates. As one student says, "Whatever you are interested in, you can easily find a group of people that connect with you. Our school is so inviting that it's hard to not fit in somewhere." Another student emphasizes the inclusive nature of the student body, saying, "I feel like my school is extremely accepting, and we have events for all cultures, beliefs, and extracurricular [activities] all the time." In addition to attending events and getting involved in extracurriculars, coursework also tends to be a high priority among this crowd. As one enrollee describes their peers, "Students are generally pretty spirited and helpful, and most [people] seem to genuinely care about their academics."

BATTEN UNIVERSITY

Financial Aid: 757-455-3345 • E-Mail: admissions@vwu.edu • Website: www.vwu.edu

THE PRINCETON REVIEW SAYS

Admissions

The school reports that its standardized testing policy for use in admission for Fall 2026 is Test Optional. The Princeton Review suggests that interested applicants consult with the school for the most up-to-date standardized testing policies. *Very important factors considered include:* rigor of secondary school record, academic GPA, level of applicant's interest. *Important factors considered include:* extracurricular activities. *Other factors considered include:* standardized test scores, recommendation(s), interview, talent/ability, character/personal qualities, first generation, alumni/ae relation, volunteer work, work experience. High school diploma is required and GED is accepted. *Academic units required:* 4 English, 3 math, 2 science, 2 science labs, 2 language (other than English), 1 history, 1 computer science. *Academic units recommended:* 4 English, 3 math, 2 science, 2 science labs, 2 language (other than English), 1 history, 4 academic electives, 1 computer science.

Financial Aid

Students should submit: FAFSA; State aid form. Priority filing deadline is 3/1. The Princeton Review suggests that all financial aid forms be submitted as soon as possible. *Need-based scholarships/grants offered:* Federal Pell; Federal SEOG; State scholarships/grants; Private scholarships; College/university scholarship or grant aid from institutional funds. *Loan aid offered:* Federal Direct Subsidized Loans; Federal Direct Unsubsidized Loans; Direct PLUS loans. Admitted students will be notified of awards on a rolling basis beginning 10/15. Federal Work-Study Program available. Institutional employment available.

The Inside Word

As the university's profile rises, so too does the number of applications it receives. And each year, competition for admission increases. Therefore, to be accepted, applicants need to have earned strong grades in college prep courses. Additionally, given the college's small size, admissions officers are on the lookout for students who will contribute to campus life. Therefore, active and sustained participation in a handful of extracurricular activities helps candidates appear more attractive to the admissions committee.

THE SCHOOL SAYS

From the Admissions Office

"Batten University seeks to enroll qualified students from diverse social, religious, racial, economic, and geographic backgrounds. Admission is based solely on the applicant's academic and personal qualifications. Factors considered include grades, recommendations, standardized test scores, and extracurricular activities. Batten is using a Test Optional admissions process, but we will accept SAT or ACT scores for use in placement and advising. A high school diploma is required (GED accepted) and proof of English proficiency is required for all international applicants. Batten University considers applications on a rolling admissions basis. Applicants can typically expect notification within two to three weeks after we receive your completed application and supporting documents. Prospective students are encouraged to visit our beautiful 300-acre wooded campus for a tour and to meet with an enrollment counselor. Learn more about admissions at www.vwu.edu."

SELECTIVITY

# of total applicants	3,808
% of total applicants accepted	73
% of total acceptees attending	12

First-Year Profile

Testing policy	Test Optional
Average HS GPA	3.3
% submitting high school GPA	91

Important Dates

Regular	
Notified by	Rolling, 9/15
Nonfall registration?	Yes

FINANCIAL FACTS

Annual tuition	$38,776
Food and housing	$13,174
Required fees	$2,642
Books and supplies	$0
Average need-based scholarship (First-year)	$6,886 ($8,635)
% students with need rec. need-based scholarship or grant aid (First-year)	58 (67)
% students with need rec. non-need-based scholarship or grant aid (First-year)	96 (100)
% students with need rec. need-based self-help aid (First-year)	70 (70)
% UG borrow to pay for school	70
Average cumulative indebtedness	$39,613
% of students with need fully met (First-year)	22 (24)
Average % of student need met (First-year)	81 (84)

BAYLOR UNIVERSITY

One Bear Place #97056, Waco, TX 76798 • Admissions: 254-710-3435

Survey Snapshot
Lots of conservative students
Students are very religious
Everyone loves the Bears

RATINGS

Quality of Life	**85**
Fire Safety	**90**
Green	**60***
Academic	**82**
Profs Interesting	**88**
Profs Accessible	**92**
Admissions	**89**
Financial Aid	**86**

CAMPUS LIFE

Type of school	Private
Affiliation	Baptist
Environment	City

Students

Degree-seeking undergrad enrollment	14,089
% male/female/not reported	40/60/0
% from out of state	32
% First-year from public high school	63
% First-year live on campus	98
% Ugrads live on campus	34
# of fraternities (% join)	15 (NR)
# of sororities (% join)	17 (NR)
% Asian	9
% Black or African American	6
% Hispanic	19
% Native American	<1
% Pacific Islander	<1
% Race and/or ethnicity unknown	1
% Two or more races	5
% White	57
% International	3
# of countries represented	90

CAMPUS MENTAL HEALTH SERVICES

Offers mental health/wellness program	Yes
Mental health training available to students	No
Employs Chief Wellness Officer	NR
Peer-to-peer mental health offerings	NR
Counseling center has guidelines or accreditation	No
Mental health/well-being courses	NR

ACADEMICS

% students returning for sophomore year	89
% students graduating within 4 years	71
% students graduating within 6 years	82
Calendar	Semester
Student/faculty ratio	14:1
Most common class size 10–19.	(38%)
Most common lab/discussion size 10–19.	(46%)

Most Popular Majors

Biology/Biological Sciences; Health/Medical Preparatory Programs; Registered Nursing/ Registered Nurse

Applicants Also Look At

Texas A&M University—College Station, Texas Christian University, Texas Tech University, University of Arkansas—Fayetteville, University of Texas at Austin

STUDENTS SAY "..."

Academics

Academics at Baylor are rigorous and highly personalized, with academics held "to a high standard." Students note that those pursuing a competitive track should "be prepared to be tested to the limit." Despite these high stakes, "the professors are there for you and actually care about your academics, and most even about your well-being." Students also consider Baylor's Christian mission to be uplifting: "My professors are all passionate people and they do not push faith, but they do involve it in the classroom in an inspirational way." Baylor's courses also include discussion-based learning and hands-on field trips. "In my Introduction to Teaching course, we tutored students in a local elementary school. My environmental science class took field trips to the Waco wetlands." Practical research and volunteer opportunities are particularly useful to those in specialized fields: "I am in a laparoscopy lab that enables pre-med students to learn about the research process. There is also a surgical skills class that allows pre-health students to learn skills often used in the world of healthcare." Liberal arts students enjoy unique projects like the "UnEssay" that give them "a lot of freedom to incorporate things we like into an English class."

Campus Life

Baylor's "beautiful" campus is home to a "very close-knit community where you feel accepted very easily" and offers lots of "opportunities to find groups of people to belong to." One student explains how "at the beginning of the fall semester we have this event called 'Late Night' where all the clubs, including, frats, sororities, and sporting clubs enable you to see all [that is] available on campus." As a NCAA Division I school, many students list football and basketball games among their favorite activities. As one first-year student describes it: "Everyone is excited to go to the football and basketball games, and the student section at Baylor is unlike any other." Baylor's "unapologetically Christian" ethos is also celebrated throughout campus life. "Every Monday night there is Vertical, which is an amazing worship and sermon. When I imagined what a Christian college would look like, Vertical is what I imagined," explains one student. Popular school-sponsored events abound throughout the academic year, including All University Thanksgiving, Homecoming, Christmas on 5th Street, and Diadeloso. Students also rave about weekly Dr Pepper Hour, the rock-climbing wall in the student center, and gathering at coffee shops around Waco on the weekends. Finally, professional organizations, like those for the pre-med world, not only provide vital career opportunities but keep the school feeling "more like a community than a competition."

Student Body

"My peers at Baylor University are the kindest and most loving group of people I have ever known." Adds another student, "When I think of 'Southern hospitality,' the way my peers treat one another comes immediately to mind." Baylor students also describe each other as goal-oriented, focused, and engaged with religious and social communities. "Everyone at Baylor is out and about doing things on campus and interacting with the people around them," says one student. And "everyone here at Baylor is aiming for success in their own way." Further, many students cherish that "intellectual diversity and open mindedness are abundant" among professors and students, and many make note of the variety of identities celebrated on campus: "The student body at Baylor is generally Christian, but from a diverse selection of denominations. I also have many nonChristian friends. There is lots of ideological diversity as well, including a thriving LGBTQIA+ community that I myself am a part of."

BAYLOR UNIVERSITY

Financial Aid: 254-710-2611 • E-Mail: admissions@baylor.edu • Website: www.baylor.edu

THE PRINCETON REVIEW SAYS

Admissions

The school reports that its standardized testing policy for use in admission for Fall 2026 is Test Optional. The Princeton Review suggests that interested applicants consult with the school for the most up-to-date standardized testing policies. *Very important factors considered include:* academic GPA, standardized test scores. *Important factors considered include:* rigor of secondary school record, application essay. *Other factors considered include:* class rank, recommendation(s), extracurricular activities, talent/ability, character/personal qualities, first generation, alumni/ae relation, geographical residence, state residency, religious affiliation/commitment, volunteer work, work experience, level of applicant's interest. High school diploma is required and GED is accepted. *Academic units recommended:* 4 English, 4 math, 4 science, 2 science labs, 2 language (other than English), 2 social studies, 1 history.

Financial Aid

Students should submit: CSS PROFILE. Priority filing deadline is 11/1. The Princeton Review suggests that all financial aid forms be submitted as soon as possible. *Need-based scholarships/grants offered:* Federal Pell; Federal SEOG; State scholarships/grants; College/university scholarship or grant aid from institutional funds. *Loan aid offered:* Federal Direct Subsidized Loans; Federal Direct Unsubsidized Loans; Direct PLUS loans; State Loans; College/university loans from institutional funds. Admitted students will be notified of awards on a rolling basis beginning 2/1. Federal Work-Study Program available. Institutional employment available.

The Inside Word

Those who want to attend Baylor will need more than GPA, class rank, and optional test scores—they'll need to show a desire to be part of a community that also values faith and personal calling. Admissions officers will consider an essay, recommendation letters, short answer responses, and a résumé to determine which students are a good fit for their mission. They are also looking for those who express a true interest in becoming a Baylor Bear. Certain majors (such as Engineering and the Baylor Business Fellows program) have additional requirements, and those who plan to apply should investigate requirements thoroughly before doing so.

THE SCHOOL SAYS

From the Admissions Office

"Baylor's mission is to educate men and women for worldwide leadership and service by integrating academic excellence and Christian commitment within a caring community. Our professors share a commitment to research and teaching. That means Baylor faculty include some of the nation's foremost scholars who also have a passion for helping you succeed. In 2021, Baylor University was named a Research 1 university by the Carnegie Classification of Institutions of Higher Education, joining the nation's top-tier research institutions as a doctoral university with very high research activity and elevating Baylor as a preeminent Christian research university. What else makes Baylor unique? Our belief that the world needs a preeminent research university that is distinctly Christian. This allows academics, research, and faith to work together. The outcome? Baylor students find both their career and calling in life. Many majors boast a 100 percent 'success rate,' meaning students find jobs or start graduate school within 90 days of graduation. When you become a Baylor student, you join the Baylor family. Professors and classmates become lifelong friends and your biggest cheerleaders. They will inspire you. Embolden you. Challenge you and walk with you. And you'll do the same for them; after all, you're family. Traditions bind generations of Baylor students together by a shared experience that transcends culture, trends and time. That's why, after graduation, you'll want to return 'home' each fall for one of our favorite traditions: Baylor Homecoming."

SELECTIVITY

# of total applicants	44,924
% of total applicants accepted	52
% of total acceptees attending	12
# of in-state applicants	28,416
% of in-state applicants accepted	52
# of out-of-state-applicants	12,955
% of applicants accepted from out of state	55
# of international applicants	3,553
% of international applicants accepted	50

First-Year Profile

Testing policy	Test Optional
Range SAT composite	1190–1370
Range SAT EBRW	600–690
Range SAT math	590–690
Range ACT composite	26–32
% submitting SAT scores	47
% submitting ACT scores	22
% graduated top 10% of class	42
% graduated top 25% of class	76
% graduated top 50% of class	95
% submitting high school rank	49

Important Dates

Early decision	
Apply by	11/1
Notified by	12/15
Early action	
Apply by	11/1
Notified by	2/1
Regular	
Apply by	2/15
Notified by	4/10
Nonfall registration?	Yes

FINANCIAL FACTS

Annual tuition	$67,756
Food and housing	$15,318
Books and supplies	$1,438
Average need-based scholarship (First-year)	$35,975 ($39,483)
% students with need rec. need-based scholarship or grant aid (First-year)	95 (98)
% students with need rec. non-need-based scholarship or grant aid (First-year)	16 (14)
% students with need rec. need-based self-help aid (First-year)	75 (75)
% students rec. any financial aid (First-year)	92 (98)
% UG borrow to pay for school	42
Average cumulative indebtedness	$57,257
% of students with need fully met (First-year)	20 (18)
Average % of student need met (First-year)	66 (71)

BELLARMINE UNIVERSITY

2001 Newburg Road, Louisville, KY 40205 • Admissions: 502-272-8131

Survey Snapshot
Internships are widely available
Great library
Active minority support groups

RATINGS

Quality of Life	**86**
Fire Safety	**95**
Green	**81**
Academic	**81**
Profs Interesting	**89**
Profs Accessible	**94**
Admissions	**82**
Financial Aid	**90**

CAMPUS LIFE

Type of school	Private
Affiliation	Roman Catholic
Environment	Metropolis

Students

Degree-seeking undergrad enrollment	2,161
% male/female/not reported	39/60/2
% from out of state	30
% First-year from public high school	73
% First-year live on campus	68
% Ugrads live on campus	46
# of fraternities (% join)	1 (1)
# of sororities (% join)	1 (4)
% Asian	3
% Black or African American	11
% Hispanic	10
% Native American	<1
% Pacific Islander	<1
% Race and/or ethnicity unknown	1
% Two or more races	5
% White	67
% International	2
# of countries represented	36

CAMPUS MENTAL HEALTH SERVICES

Offers mental health/wellness program	Yes
Mental health training available to students	Yes
Employs Chief Wellness Officer	No
Peer-to-peer mental health offerings	Yes
Counseling center has guidelines or accreditation	Yes
Mental health/well-being courses	Yes, non-credit

ACADEMICS

% students returning for sophomore year	75
% students graduating within 4 years	57
% students graduating within 6 years	64
Calendar	Semester
Student/faculty ratio	12:1
Most common class size 10–19.	(39%)
Most common lab/discussion size 10–19.	(81%)

Most Popular Majors
Psychology; Registered Nursing/Registered Nurse; Business Administration and Management

Applicants Often Prefer
University of Kentucky, University of Louisville

STUDENTS SAY "..."

Academics

"Whether it's academically, mentally, spiritually, or physically," students note that Bellarmine University's staff (and students) are "always willing to do whatever they need to help you be your best." Undergraduates report that they feel "academically challenged but not overwhelmed," thanks in large part to creative professors who offer "take the time to offer extra help, provide mentorship, and connect course material to real-world applications." Bellarmine offers "a wide variety of fascinating discussion-based classes" and "encourages students to get out in the community and experience new things that may supplement their education." There are "support systems everywhere...as one of Bellarmine's goals is to provide a holistic education." There's even a Pioneer Scholars program that makes this "a great school for first-generation college students." Regardless of your needs, "students receive personal attention, and there is a strong sense of teamwork and belonging on campus," bolstered by a belief that "the staff members are just as motivated to be here as the students." Small class sizes enhance the time spent with "truly wonderful professors who have challenged my thinking and taken the time to give one-on-one help and develop meaningful relationships." Overall, students "feel seen, valued, and encouraged to grow...[with] a well-rounded educational experience that prepares students not just for careers, but for life beyond college."

Campus Life

Bellarmine undergrads "care deeply about their academic life but aren't consumed by it" and are happy to immerse themselves in numerous extracurricular opportunities. For starters, "there are various sports events, carnivals, fairs, and festivals [that] provide [relaxing] environments." It's also very common for students to "attend workshops, volunteer in the community, or take part in...talent shows or cultural celebrations." One student chimes in, "I love all the events hosted by our Student Activity Center. A lot of them...involve winning prizes, free food, or fun crafts!" Bellarmine undergrads are also a pretty active lot, and they note "the pickleball courts, tennis courts, and access to Joe Creason Park." Additionally, intramural sports are popular and "many students...build fitness into their routines, often spending time at the SURF, our campus gym, either working out or working shifts there." Beyond athletics, undergrads can attend activities like "violin and art sessions." Another student adds, "I enjoy open mic nights hosted by student organizations, getting involved in our literary magazine, and joining hands with other creatives to create big events that celebrate the arts at Bellarmine." And of course, there are a range of clubs, including climbing, psychology, mock trial, Muay Thai, and boxing. All in all, "the campus is frequently lively and the students' lives consist of hard work and enjoyment of the facilities offered."

Student Body

Bellarmine is a Catholic school that cultivates a "very welcoming and vibrant" student body," including those "with strong religious backgrounds and more secular [ones]." Students appreciate that they've "encountered and participated in a lot of productive dialogue between different groups." There are also a substantial number of "nontraditional students—parents, caregivers, first-generation college students, and career-changers—who bring resilience, maturity, and purpose into the classroom." And given the school's small size, "it is not uncommon to see familiar faces often, so relationships are often built through that." Many also point to a friendliness that pervades the campus. Undergrads say their classmates are "always eager to start a conversation," and another student shares, "I never have a fear of being judged for saying the wrong answer because I know that everyone is so supportive and wants to watch you grow into the person you want to be." Truly, a Bellarmine education means you'll forge "connections and friendships that last a lifetime."

Bellarmine University

Financial Aid: 502-272-4723 • E-Mail: admissions@bellarmine.edu • Website: www.bellarmine.edu

THE PRINCETON REVIEW SAYS

Admissions

The school reports that its standardized testing policy for use in admission for Fall 2026 is Test Optional. The Princeton Review suggests that interested applicants consult with the school for the most up-to-date standardized testing policies. *Very important factors considered include:* rigor of secondary school record, academic GPA, recommendation(s), character/personal qualities, level of applicant's interest. *Important factors considered include:* class rank, extracurricular activities. *Other factors considered include:* standardized test scores, application essay, interview, talent/ability, first generation, alumni/ae relation, geographical residence, state residency, volunteer work, work experience. High school diploma is required and GED is accepted. *Academic units required:* 4 English, 3 math, 3 science, 2 science labs, 2 language (other than English), 2 social studies, 1 history, 5 academic electives.

Financial Aid

Students should submit: FAFSA. Priority filing deadline is 11/1. The Princeton Review suggests that all financial aid forms be submitted as soon as possible. *Need-based scholarships/grants offered:* Federal Pell; Federal SEOG; State scholarships/grants; Private scholarships; College/university scholarship or grant aid from institutional funds. *Loan aid offered:* Federal Direct Subsidized Loans; Federal Direct Unsubsidized Loans; Direct PLUS loans; College/university loans from institutional funds. Admitted students will be notified of awards on a rolling basis beginning 1/31. Federal Work-Study Program available. Institutional employment available.

The Inside Word

Admissions at Bellarmine University takes a holistic approach in the search for a well-rounded candidate whose qualifications reflect more than the sum total of a GPA and transcript. Recommendations and personal statements—which should present a strong picture of the student's educational goals—volunteer experiences, and extracurricular commitments, hold significant weight. Candidates with strong grades and diverse interests are likely to earn acceptance.

THE SCHOOL SAYS

From the Admissions Office

"Bellarmine University prepares students for success through a liberal arts education, combined with training for mastery in a specialized area. We offer more than fifty majors in the arts and sciences, humanities, education, communication, business, environmental studies, nursing and health science, plus graduate programs in nursing, education, physical therapy, business and communication. We engage students in state-of-the-art classrooms and expand their horizons through internship and study abroad opportunities. Bellarmine delivers this world-class education just five miles from downtown Louisville, the nation's sixteenth largest city. The 175-acre campus is set in a safe, historic and eclectic neighborhood, and features a fitness center, tennis courts, athletic fields and two new dining halls. With more than fifty clubs and organizations, twenty NCAA Division II athletic teams, plus Division I men's lacrosse, Bellarmine offers a variety of recreational opportunities for all students. Students who reside on campus also find a Bellarmine difference in the living arrangements. From traditional residence halls to apartment-style and suite living arrangements, students have many housing options to choose from; the newest residence halls surround a Tuscan-style piazza. As Bellarmine attracts more residential students, the university has created more gathering spaces for them, such as the Café on the ground floor of the Siena Primo residence hall. New learning communities cater to residents and commuters alike, offering opportunities for focused, collaborative studies on topics such as leadership, healthcare, science and technology."

SELECTIVITY

# of total applicants	4,761
% of total applicants accepted	86
% of total acceptees attending	13

First-Year Profile

Testing policy	Test Optional
Range SAT composite	1030–1230
Range SAT EBRW	520–630
Range SAT math	510–620
Range ACT composite	19–26
% submitting SAT scores	8
% submitting ACT scores	45
Average HS GPA	3.5
% submitting high school GPA	100

Important Dates

Early action	
Apply by	11/1
Notified by	11/15
Regular	
Apply by	8/15
Notified by	Rolling, 9/1
Nonfall registration?	Yes

FINANCIAL FACTS

Annual tuition	$48,900
Food and housing	$11,310
Required fees (First-year)	$1,590 ($1,990)
Books and supplies	$500
Average need-based scholarship (First-year)	$33,520 ($36,241)
% students with need rec. need-based scholarship or grant aid (First-year)	98 (99)
% students with need rec. non-need-based scholarship or grant aid (First-year)	34 (30)
% students with need rec. need-based self-help aid (First-year)	72 (76)
% UG borrow to pay for school	60
Average cumulative indebtedness	$27,609
% of students with need fully met (First-year)	28 (23)
Average % of student need met (First-year)	86 (87)

BELOIT COLLEGE

700 College St., Beloit, WI 53511 • Admissions: 608-363-2500

Survey Snapshot
Great library
Easy to get around campus
Career services are great

RATINGS

Quality of Life	**84**
Fire Safety	**82**
Green	**60***
Academic	**85**
Profs Interesting	**92**
Profs Accessible	**91**
Admissions	**88**
Financial Aid	**91**

CAMPUS LIFE

Type of school	Private
Environment	Town

Students

Degree-seeking undergrad enrollment	898
% male/female/not reported	49/51/0
% from out of state	77
% First-year from public high school	64
% First-year live on campus	95
% Ugrads live on campus	90
# of fraternities (% join)	3 (NR)
# of sororities (% join)	3 (NR)
% Asian	2
% Black or African American	8
% Hispanic	18
% Native American	0
% Pacific Islander	0
% Race and/or ethnicity unknown	2
% Two or more races	4
% White	50
% International	14
# of countries represented	43

CAMPUS MENTAL HEALTH SERVICES

Offers mental health/wellness program	Yes
Mental health training available to students	No
Employs Chief Wellness Officer	NR
Peer-to-peer mental health offerings	NR
Counseling center has guidelines or accreditation	No
Mental health/well-being courses	NR

ACADEMICS

% students returning for sophomore year	86
% students graduating within 4 years	57
% students graduating within 6 years	67
Calendar	Semester
Student/faculty ratio	11:1
Most common class size 10–19.	(51%)

Most Popular Majors

Biology; Psychology; Sociology

Applicants Sometimes Prefer

Carleton College, The College of Wooster, DePauw University, Earlham College, Grinnell College, Illinois Wesleyan University, Kalamazoo College, Kenyon College, Knox College, Lawrence University, Lewis & Clark College, Macalester College, Oberlin College, St. Olaf College, University of Wisconsin—Madison

STUDENTS SAY "..."

Academics

Beloit College is a private liberal arts school that provides a global, experiential education and "consistently encourages students to follow their interests both in and out of class in creative ways." The college's flexible curriculum offers students the "freedom to study what they are passionate about" and student-designed "academic paths [that] can be customized to suit every student's needs, interests, and goals." These experiences include Impact Beloit, which offers a variety of career-readiness and community-based learning programs, including internships within the town of Beloit. One student says, "It has placed me in a local business, working 10–20 hours a week while earning credit and getting paid. I have been able to directly apply what I've learned in the classroom and learn so much more." Students appreciate that their professors are "dynamic and knowledgeable" and "bring unique perspectives to class material." The "structure of the classes is very interactive" and "a significant amount [of] classes at Beloit are discussion-based." Small class sizes create an environment where "every student gets to participate and collaborate with one another," and there is a good deal of "intensive essay writing and an emphasis on self-identity." The college has "very good resources for helping you with research, internships, and graduate school applications and program decisions" and excels at "connecting us to local professionals and [alumni]." These opportunities give students valuable "experience that'll separate them from the herd of job applicants," resulting in 93 percent of students being employed or in graduate school within six months of graduation.

Campus Life

At Beloit, "there is always something going on." During the warmer months, "there are a lot of spaces on campus to sit outside, play pick-up, and just overall enjoy the outdoors, and the college facilitates a lot of outside activities." Clubs and organizations "are always throwing events and encourage students to try something new," and "everyone is a part of at least one club, and usually several," with options from theater to powerlifting club. One undergrad observes, "I really enjoy the ways athletics, intramurals, and SAAC [Student Athlete Advisory Committee] connect you with other students." Another great opportunity to bring students together is with traditions like "Spring Day (a day off of school where we have a carnival, free food, and outdoor games)." A popular spot to hang out with friends, play games, or grab a bite is the Powerhouse, a 120,000-square-foot facility that houses the student union and athletic center. On weekends, "there are usually parties or events," and "many people enjoy the cafe on campus and will spend their time studying or having fun with friends there."

Student Body

The student body at Beloit is "a unique blend of athletes, academics, and people...fitting together on one small campus." The community is welcoming and open-minded, with students who "aren't afraid to express themselves and stand out in different ways." At Beloit, "you will find athletes passionate about theater, classicists that translate Star Wars into Latin, and Japanese majors that study queer themes in medieval literature." For a small school, the student body "is extremely diverse, with students from not only all over the country but all over the world," which leads to "a lot of different perspectives coming together." A common trait among students is that they "care a lot about their community" and are "very engaged students and citizens who are passionate about various causes and their academics." As one student shares, "All in all, I believe Beloit is a great place to find a more unique, open-minded, and interesting group of people."

BELOIT COLLEGE

Financial Aid: 608-363-2663 • E-Mail: admissions@beloit.edu • Website: www.beloit.edu

THE PRINCETON REVIEW SAYS

Admissions

The school reports that its standardized testing policy for use in admission for Fall 2026 is Test Optional. The Princeton Review suggests that interested applicants consult with the school for the most up-to-date standardized testing policies. *Very important factors considered include:* rigor of secondary school record, academic GPA, application essay, recommendation(s). *Important factors considered include:* extracurricular activities, talent/ability, character/personal qualities. *Other factors considered include:* class rank, standardized test scores, interview, first generation, alumni/ae relation, volunteer work, work experience, level of applicant's interest. High school diploma is required and GED is accepted. *Academic units recommended:* 4 English, 3 math, 3 science, 3 science labs, 2 language (other than English), 3 social studies.

Financial Aid

Students should submit: FAFSA. Priority filing deadline is 11/1. The Princeton Review suggests that all financial aid forms be submitted as soon as possible. *Need-based scholarships/grants offered:* Federal Pell; Federal SEOG; State scholarships/grants; Private scholarships; College/university scholarship or grant aid from institutional funds. *Loan aid offered:* Federal Direct Subsidized Loans; Federal Direct Unsubsidized Loans; Direct PLUS loans. Admitted students will be notified of awards on a rolling basis. Federal Work-Study Program available. Institutional employment available.

The Inside Word

Beloit wants to see a rigorous academic transcript but also emphasizes a holistic approach that focuses on getting to know the student behind the application. The admission office prefers to receive a letter of recommendation from a teacher who taught you during your junior year, but it is most important to select someone who can provide the most insight to you as a student.

THE SCHOOL SAYS

From the Admissions Office

"There's a difference between getting an education and being so immersed, so transformed, so enthralled with living and learning that your education never really stops. That's the Beloit College experience.

"Beloiters learn in every nook and cranny of campus. Our flexible curriculum offers 40+ majors and minors, allowing you to become your best self-entrepreneur, activist, scholar, human. And your trusted advisors and mentors will give you support and encouragement along the way.

"With a Beloit College education under your belt, you'll be prepared for wherever life takes you, from your first job to your future career and everywhere in between. Our five schools—Business, Environment & Sustainability, Global & Public Service, Health Sciences, and Media & the Arts—bring career pathways to the center of your college experience. Discover what you love, translate it into a fulfilling career, and connect your passions and academic interests.

"With 21 NCAA Division III athletic teams, countless performances, and dozens of clubs to choose from—and the ability to create your own—you won't stay still for long. Your peers will show up for your productions, games, and events, because they care. There's also plenty of spaces across campus and in the city for you to experience something new—open mics, pub trivia, and art installations, to name a few.

"Choosing Beloit College means becoming a part of our close-knit, inclusive community built on relationships developed in and out of the classroom. You'll build strong connections, engage in time-honored traditions, and make friends for life."

SELECTIVITY

# of total applicants	3,914
% of total applicants accepted	57
% of total acceptees attending	10
# of in-state applicants	246
% of in-state applicants accepted	85
# of out-of-state-applicants	1,951
% of applicants accepted from out of state	84
# of international applicants	1,717
% of international applicants accepted	23
# of early decision applicants	1,750
% of early decision applicants accepted	71

First-Year Profile

Testing policy	Test Optional
Range SAT composite	1250–1280
Range SAT EBRW	630–720
Range SAT math	580–640
Range ACT composite	26–31
% submitting SAT scores	8
% submitting ACT scores	9
Average HS GPA	3.4
% submitting high school GPA	100
% graduated top 10% of class	30
% graduated top 25% of class	55
% graduated top 50% of class	82
% submitting high school rank	37

Important Dates

Early action	
Apply by	11/1
Notified by	12/1
Regular	
Notified by	Rolling, 11/1
Nonfall registration?	Yes

FINANCIAL FACTS

Annual tuition	$60,364
Food and housing	$11,263
Required fees	$522
Books and supplies	$1,154
Average need-based scholarship (First-year)	$37,603 ($39,493)
% students with need rec. need-based scholarship or grant aid (First-year)	98 (99)
% students with need rec. non-need-based scholarship or grant aid (First-year)	50 (47)
% students with need rec. need-based self-help aid (First-year)	83 (80)
% students rec. any financial aid (First-year)	99 (99)
% UG borrow to pay for school	61
Average cumulative indebtedness	$23,534
% of students with need fully met (First-year)	31 (32)
Average % of student need met (First-year)	95 (96)

BENNINGTON COLLEGE

One College Drive, Bennington, VT 05201 • Admissions: 802-440-4312

Survey Snapshot
Theater is popular
Students environmentally aware
Easy to get around campus

RATINGS

Quality of Life	**85**
Fire Safety	**97**
Green	**60***
Academic	**89**
Profs Interesting	**97**
Profs Accessible	**93**
Admissions	**92**
Financial Aid	**89**

CAMPUS LIFE

Type of school	Private
Environment	Village

Students

Degree-seeking undergrad enrollment	695
% male/female/not reported	27/72/1
% from out of state	95
% First-year from public high school	60
% First-year live on campus	99
% Ugrads live on campus	98
# of fraternities	0
# of sororities	0
% Asian	2
% Black or African American	4
% Hispanic	9
% Native American	<1
% Pacific Islander	0
% Race and/or ethnicity unknown	1
% Two or more races	6
% White	65
% International	13
# of countries represented	42

CAMPUS MENTAL HEALTH SERVICES

Offers mental health/wellness program	Yes
Mental health training available to students	Yes
Employs Chief Wellness Officer	Yes
Peer-to-peer mental health offerings	No
Counseling center has guidelines or accreditation	Yes
Mental health/well-being courses	Yes, non-credit

ACADEMICS

% students returning for sophomore year	88
% students graduating within 4 years	63
% students graduating within 6 years	70
Calendar	Semester
Student/faculty ratio	8:1
Most common class size 10–19.	(62%)

Most Popular Majors

Visual and Performing Arts; English Language and Literature; Foreign Languages and Literatures

Applicants Also Look At

Bard College, Mount Holyoke College, New York University, Oberlin College, Sarah Lawrence College, Skidmore College, Smith College, University of Connecticut, University of Vermont, Vassar College

STUDENTS SAY "..."

Academics

Bennington College emphasizes a "Socratic, discussion-driven classroom structure," meaning "there are almost no traditional lecture classes or seminars" (with a few exceptions, like neuroscience). On the whole, these "small and generally engaging" classes provide "excellent, hands-on opportunities to use their knowledge in a field that moves them," helping them better understand "what their strengths are in the working world." This approach is supported by Bennington's distinctive Plan process, which eschews official majors in favor of a program tailored "toward the individual student's interests and goals." Students note that those who benefit the most from this educational model tend to be "self-driven, focused, and have a clear idea of how to apply one's learning beyond Bennington." In other words, the school's "adaptable and creatively rigorous" Plan process is "exactly what you make of it." Another hallmark of a Bennington education is its nearly 100-year-old Field Work Term program, during which students spend six weeks each year in what the school calls a "high-impact learning experience," ranging from internships to independent research. In this independent, yet supportive environment, it's assuring to hear that the professors "all love teaching, are enthusiastic about our contributions to courses." These teachers "make learning fun and engaging in a way that encourages deep and critical thinking as well as providing resources and opportunities to students who ask for them." Ultimately, the school works to "support and nurture the endeavors of every student," and as Bennington's biggest fans put it, these "life-changing" academics and teachers result in "incredible work being created on campus every single day."

Campus Life

Bennington is a "beautiful hilltop with access to pathways and hiking trails," and students say that "students, staff, and faculty make [the school] come alive in our small part of the woods." Consequently, "in the spring and fall, folks will be on the lawn, picnicking or playing instruments," alongside pickup volleyball and soccer games. (There's not a lot of talk about sports beyond that they've "only recently become a thing" in some circles.) And while there's no Greek life, "club culture is big." This emphasis on campus-based activities suits students, who "spend a lot of time practicing their craft and sharing it with others." Moreover, because the school doesn't have traditional dorms and instead places students in cooperative houses of between 30 and 45 students, there tend to be a lot of house activities. Some houses host "parties on campus every week, which most of the campus attends," thanks to their "very strong and unique themes," with annual standouts like "Dewey's wedding theme" and the "Swalloween Halloween party." No wonder, then, that there's not a lot of traveling into town or nearby Albany: "the vast majority stay on campus." Those who look for things to do will find plenty of support and, through the constant events, "opportunities to come together as a community."

Student Body

Bennington is driven by the particular blend of "artistic, funny, creative, and engaged" enrollees in any given term, so the focus of activities is "constantly changing." That's not a negative; students "make the environment their own and are not afraid of shaking expectations and the status quo." At the same time, certain core values remain consistent. The school is widely described as inclusive and "queer-friendly." It's also said that "international students play a huge role in the soul of the Bennington community," and "unity in diversity" is emphasized. Students describe themselves as "kind and supportive and a little bit weird in the best way possible." Many of these characteristics also lead to a robust sense of activism: "We have deep ethical and political commitments." Bennington is made up of people who "genuinely want to be here," creating an environment where students feel free to "be yourself and be as creative as you want."

BENNINGTON COLLEGE

Financial Aid: 800-833-6845 • E-Mail: admissions@bennington.edu • Website: www.bennington.edu

THE PRINCETON REVIEW SAYS

Admissions

The school reports that its standardized testing policy for use in admission for Fall 2026 is Test Optional. The Princeton Review suggests that interested applicants consult with the school for the most up-to-date standardized testing policies. *Very important factors considered include:* rigor of secondary school record, academic GPA, application essay, recommendation(s), talent/ability, character/personal qualities. *Important factors considered include:* interview. *Other factors considered include:* class rank, standardized test scores, extracurricular activities, first generation, volunteer work, work experience. High school diploma is required and GED is accepted. *Academic units required:* 4 English. *Academic units recommended:* 4 math, 4 science, 3 science labs, 3 language (other than English), 3 social studies.

Financial Aid

Students should submit: FAFSA; CSS PROFILE. Priority filing deadline is 11/1. The Princeton Review suggests that all financial aid forms be submitted as soon as possible. *Need-based scholarships/grants offered:* Federal Pell; Federal SEOG; State scholarships/grants; Private scholarships. *Loan aid offered:* Federal Direct Subsidized Loans; Federal Direct Unsubsidized Loans; Direct PLUS loans; State Loans. Admitted students will be notified of awards on or about 3/20. Federal Work-Study Program available. Institutional employment available.

The Inside Word

Bennington accepts both the Common Application and the Coalition Application on Scoir. While the interview is optional, the school strongly encourages it as a way for applicants to share more about themselves. The school works with all admitted students to craft affordable, workable finance plans, and 95 percent of Bennington students receive some form of financial aid.

THE SCHOOL SAYS

From the Admissions Office

"Bennington will change the way you learn.

For nearly a century, Bennington College has done education differently. Instead of saying, "Choose your major, and we'll give you a list of required courses," we ask, "What do you want to explore, and how far can we take your ideas?"

"We call this the Plan process. You won't just build your own major—you'll create a completely unique academic path. No core curriculum, no cookie-cutter prerequisites, no preset path. You'll design the education you've always wanted on our stunningly beautiful Vermont campus.

"While most colleges talk about real-world experience, Bennington guarantees it. For six weeks each year, you'll leave campus and chase your ideas out into the world. This is Field Work Term: the nation's only guaranteed annual internship. You'll build confidence, skills, and a résumé that reflects your goals.

"You'll also collaborate with practicing artists, scientists, writers, and designers: our faculty take student work as seriously as their own. They'll provide you with individual mentorship and balance challenge with support. And, since most Bennington classes have fewer than 15 students, your voice will be heard.

"Weirdness is welcome here. Curiosity is expected. Conversations carry from classrooms to studios to dining halls, last late into the evening, and jump from playlists to politics to poetry. You'll find a tight-knit creative community, brimming with unapologetically wacky clubs and social events. College is about more than getting you the job you want: it's about creating the life you've only begun to imagine. Inquire. Apply. Enroll."

SELECTIVITY

# of total applicants	2,709
% of total applicants accepted	37
% of total acceptees attending	16
# of in-state applicants	36
% of in-state applicants accepted	72
# of out-of-state-applicants	1,242
% of applicants accepted from out of state	70
# of international applicants	1,431
% of international applicants accepted	8
# of early decision applicants	264
% of early decision applicants accepted	17
# offered a place on the wait list	123
# admitted from wait list	43

First-Year Profile

Testing policy	Test Optional
Range SAT composite	1340–1480
Range SAT EBRW	680–750
Range SAT math	620–730
Range ACT composite	33–34
% submitting SAT scores	14
% submitting ACT scores	4
Average HS GPA	3.7
% submitting high school GPA	35
% graduated top 10% of class	31
% graduated top 25% of class	67
% graduated top 50% of class	98
% submitting high school rank	26

Important Dates

Early decision	
Apply by	11/1
Notified by	12/15
Other ED apply by	1/10
Other ED notified by	2/15
Early action	
Apply by	11/1
Notified by	1/31
Regular	
Apply by	1/10
Notified by	3/31
Nonfall registration?	Yes

FINANCIAL FACTS

Annual tuition	$71,700
Food and housing	$20,100
Required fees (First-year)	$1,200 ($1,700)
Books and supplies	$2,000
Average need-based scholarship (First-year)	$60,318 ($67,530)
% students with need rec. need-based scholarship or grant aid (First-year)	100 (100)
% students with need rec. non-need-based scholarship or grant aid (First-year)	18 (19)
% students with need rec. need-based self-help aid (First-year)	87 (88)
% students rec. any financial aid (First-year)	95 (100)
% UG borrow to pay for school	61
Average cumulative indebtedness	$30,829
% of students with need fully met (First-year)	8 (13)
Average % of student need met (First-year)	88 (93)

Bentley University

175 Forest Street, Waltham, MA 02452 • Admissions: 781-891-2244

Survey Snapshot
Great library
Internships are widely available
Career services are great

RATINGS

Quality of Life	90
Fire Safety	99
Green	98
Academic	82
Profs Interesting	90
Profs Accessible	92
Admissions	91
Financial Aid	88

CAMPUS LIFE

Type of school	Private
Environment	Town

Students

Degree-seeking undergrad enrollment	4,563
% male/female/not reported	61/39/<1
% from out of state	52
% First-year from public high school	61
% First-year live on campus	96
% Ugrads live on campus	72
# of fraternities (% join)	8 (12)
# of sororities (% join)	6 (20)
% Asian	11
% Black or African American	5
% Hispanic	16
% Native American	<1
% Pacific Islander	<1
% Race and/or ethnicity unknown	1
% Two or more races	3
% White	50
% International	13
# of countries represented	88

CAMPUS MENTAL HEALTH SERVICES

Offers mental health/wellness program	Yes
Mental health training available to students	Yes
Employs Chief Wellness Officer	Yes
Peer-to-peer mental health offerings	Yes
Counseling center has guidelines or accreditation	Yes
Mental health/well-being courses	No

ACADEMICS

% students returning for sophomore year	93
% students graduating within 4 years	82
% students graduating within 6 years	88
Calendar	Semester
Student/faculty ratio	12:1
Most common class size 30–39.	(44%)

Most Popular Majors

Finance; Marketing/Marketing Management; Business Administration and Management

Applicants Sometimes Prefer

Babson College, Bryant University, Northeastern University, Stonehill College, University of Connecticut, University of Massachusetts—Amherst

STUDENTS SAY "..."

Academics

Bentley University is "well-known for preparing students for careers in business," and students say that "even the General Education subjects are designed to be applicable in the corporate world." The "excellent technical knowledge and skills" students gain and the focus on real-world application show in the school's placement rates: 98 percent of students are employed or in graduate school within six months of graduation. There are numerous business programs with "niches for any unique students," as well as the most up-to-date courses and majors like *Artificial Intelligence for Innovation.* Many classes focus on "growing students' soft skills," such as collaboration, by incorporating multiple group projects. Some classes run in conjunction with others, "enhancing what students learn," and many include presentations from industry professionals who share valuable insights. Overall, "the professors are very helpful and want their students to succeed." Many instructors are "from the top of their field and provide an amazing network as well as very applicable knowledge going far beyond what a book can teach." Faculty members have been known to "help corporations recruit high-performing students and encourage the student body to apply to certain companies that they have relationships with." Most students agree that Bentley "does a great job of prepping students for life" beyond the classroom. As one student says, "The amount of resources they offer (jobs on campus, internship support, clubs that support you, peer mentorship, networking opportunities) is actually unreal."

Campus Life

Life on campus is busy, and many Bentley students have "a strong focus on jobs, internships, and résumé building." Consequently, there are numerous interest-based clubs and activities, such as the student-run Bentley Investment Group (BIG), which offers students "a great opportunity to get involved and meet a ton of other investment enthusiasts." The drive to network also means that most students are "part of an organization, whether it be Greek life or a club." Intramural and club-level sports are also popular: "Intramural sports are my favorite because I have met so many new friends trying out new activities," explains one undergrad. Parties are certainly "a major factor of social life on campus" for some students, especially on the weekends, but "there is no pressure to go," and the campus activities board "makes sure there are events throughout the week and weekends for people to attend that are school-sanctioned." Other fun activities include attending Division I hockey games in the school's sports complex, as well as the "Spring Day concert with big names like Jack Harlow and Diplo," bingo tournaments, and the ski and snowboarding club's weekend trip. As one student says of Bentley, students are "involved,...enjoy campus [life], and are generally happy!"

Student Body

Bentley students overwhelmingly describe their peers as "focused and highly motivated." On the whole, students "take their schoolwork seriously," and "are very career-focused," but show "a sense of mutual respect." One student notes that "Many have started their own businesses and go above and beyond academically." The university is about more than just studying and careers. People here "like to have fun outside of the classroom" and are "very outgoing and involved in a range of activities on campus." One undergrad says, "Socially, there is a crowd for everyone," but adds that there are fewer options "when it comes to arts-oriented people." The student body has a significant number of international students and is "diverse in culture and educational experience, with broad perspectives from industries and countries across the world." One student sums up the student body, saying, "We balance ambition with fun, and that's what makes life here special."

Bentley University

Financial Aid: 781-891-3441 • E-Mail: ugadmission@bentley.edu • Website: www.bentley.edu

THE PRINCETON REVIEW SAYS

Admissions

The school reports that its standardized testing policy for use in admission for Fall 2026 is Test Optional. The Princeton Review suggests that interested applicants consult with the school for the most up-to-date standardized testing policies. *Very important factors considered include:* rigor of secondary school record. *Important factors considered include:* academic GPA, application essay, recommendation(s), extracurricular activities, talent/ability, character/personal qualities, volunteer work, level of applicant's interest. *Other factors considered include:* standardized test scores, interview, first generation, alumni/ae relation, geographical residence, state residency, work experience. High school diploma is required and GED is accepted. *Academic units required:* 4 English, 4 math, 3 science, 3 science labs, 3 language (other than English), 3 social studies. *Academic units recommended:* 4 English, 4 math, 3 science, 3 science labs, 3 language (other than English), 3 social studies.

Financial Aid

Students should submit: FAFSA; CSS PROFILE; Business/Farm Supplement; Noncustodial Profile. Priority filing deadline is 11/15. The Princeton Review suggests that all financial aid forms be submitted as soon as possible. *Need-based scholarships/grants offered:* Federal Pell; Federal SEOG; State scholarships/grants; Private scholarships; College/university scholarship or grant aid from institutional funds. *Loan aid offered:* Federal Direct Subsidized Loans; Federal Direct Unsubsidized Loans; Direct PLUS loans; State Loans. Admitted students will be notified of awards on or about Late March. Federal Work-Study Program available. Institutional employment available.

The Inside Word

Bentley may be known as a business school, but don't rush to stack your senior-year electives with business classes to impress the admissions officers. Instead, focus on taking a broad array of classes that challenge your skills, including honors, AP, and IB classes if possible. The admissions committee wants to see academic diversity, whether it's in English, history, social sciences, math, lab sciences, or foreign languages. Additionally, if your standardized test scores fall within the school's average admission range or higher, consider submitting those scores to boost your application.

THE SCHOOL SAYS

From the Admissions Office

"Bentley University is one of the nation's leading business schools, dedicated to preparing graduates who will transform business and the world for the better. Students develop well-rounded skills that lead to successful and rewarding careers and become a powerful force in whatever field they choose. Bentley students have the technical skills, global perspective and high ethical standards required for personal and professional success and are highly sought-after by today's leading organizations.

"In 2025, 98% of all Bentley graduates were employed or enrolled in graduate school within six months of graduation. This success is recognized annually by The Princeton Review, which has ranked the university's career services office among the top five in the nation for seven consecutive years.

"Approximately 96 percent of freshmen live on campus. Students live and learn in a diverse environment that prepares them to thrive in today's diverse work world. International students representing over 80 countries are part of the Bentley community. There are more than 100 student organizations, as well as abundant intramurals, recreational sports, and over 20 varsity teams in NCAA Divisions I and II. Bentley's location in Waltham, Massachusetts—minutes from Boston—puts the city's many resources within easy reach. Bentley's free shuttle makes regular trips to Harvard Square in Cambridge, just a subway ride from the heart of Boston. Boston also offers students many opportunities for internships and jobs after graduation."

SELECTIVITY

# of total applicants	11,403
% of total applicants accepted	47
% of total acceptees attending	21
# of in-state applicants	3,868
% of in-state applicants accepted	50
# of out-of-state-applicants	5,290
% of applicants accepted from out of state	50
# of international applicants	1,895
% of international applicants accepted	35
# of early decision applicants	719
% of early decision applicants accepted	64
# offered a place on the wait list	1,568
# admitted from wait list	101

First-Year Profile

Testing policy	Test Optional
Range SAT composite	1230–1370
Range SAT EBRW	610–690
Range SAT math	610–710
Range ACT composite	29–33
% submitting SAT scores	29
% submitting ACT scores	4
% graduated top 10% of class	29
% graduated top 25% of class	67
% graduated top 50% of class	91
% submitting high school rank	16

Important Dates

Early decision	
Apply by	11/15
Notified by	Late December
Other ED apply by	1/15
Other ED notified by	2/1
Regular	
Apply by	1/15
Notified by	3/15
Nonfall registration?	Yes

FINANCIAL FACTS

Annual tuition	$65,860
Food and housing	$22,010
Required fees	$520
Books and supplies	$1,200
Average need-based scholarship (First-year)	$45,945 ($47,954)
% students with need rec. need-based scholarship or grant aid (First-year)	99 (99)
% students with need rec. non-need-based scholarship or grant aid (First-year)	16 (19)
% students with need rec. need-based self-help aid (First-year)	72 (68)
% students rec. any financial aid (First-year)	83 (84)
% UG borrow to pay for school	53
Average cumulative indebtedness	$48,727
% of students with need fully met (First-year)	22 (25)
Average % of student need met (First-year)	82 (87)

Berea College

101 Chestnut Street, Berea, KY 40404 • Admissions: 859-985-3500

Survey Snapshot
Great financial aid
Diverse student types interact on campus
Students environmentally aware

RATINGS

Quality of Life	83
Fire Safety	95
Green	60*
Academic	87
Profs Interesting	89
Profs Accessible	92
Admissions	95
Financial Aid	60*

CAMPUS LIFE

Type of school	Private
Environment	Village

Students

Degree-seeking undergrad enrollment	1,500
% male/female/not reported	41/59/0
% from out of state	55
% First-year live on campus	100
% Ugrads live on campus	96
# of fraternities	0
# of sororities	0
% Asian	3
% Black or African American	20
% Hispanic	18
% Native American	0
% Pacific Islander	<1
% Race and/or ethnicity unknown	<1
% Two or more races	6
% White	44
% International	9
# of countries represented	64

CAMPUS MENTAL HEALTH SERVICES

Offers mental health/wellness program	Yes
Mental health training available to students	Yes
Employs Chief Wellness Officer	Yes
Peer-to-peer mental health offerings	Yes
Counseling center has guidelines or accreditation	No
Mental health/well-being courses	NR

ACADEMICS

% students returning for sophomore year	79
% students graduating within 4 years	44
% students graduating within 6 years	66
Calendar	Semester
Student/faculty ratio	10:1
Most common class size 10–19.	(64%)

Most Popular Majors

Biology/Biological Sciences; Communication; Business/Commerce; Computer and Information Sciences

STUDENTS SAY "..."

Academics

Since 1892, tuition-free Berea College has been turning out "well-rounded, hardworking students fully prepared for grad school or the workforce." This federally recognized work college only admits academically strong individuals "who otherwise couldn't afford college but who are deserving." Each student earns a scholarship disbursement for their ten mandatory work hours per week while developing professional skills—an experience widely regarded as a "wonderful opportunity." Additionally, the college offers "a huge scholarship to study abroad," an opportunity many students pursue. The skills acquired through the work they do can be applied to real-world settings at the college (such as Berea's College Farm or retail outlets), meaning that "if the labor program is used to its fullest extent, each student has the opportunity to graduate with a fantastic résumé and many network connections." The uniqueness of the program also creates "truly a different world when it comes to the atmosphere of the college," fueled by the pool of students and faculty that are drawn to it.

Professors here are equally excited about the opportunity being presented, and are "lively and passionate about their subjects, and it is very evident within their classrooms." A student vouches, "If you miss a class, professors will email you to find out why." Small student-to-faculty ratios "[allow] them to adapt to their students' needs" and affords the bandwidth to "care about not just your learning but also about who you are as an individual." All students at this liberal arts school appreciate the rigorous academic and practical efforts required to complete their education, including one who says "I've never felt more challenged than when I stepped foot in a Berea classroom."

Campus Life

Make sure there's coffee brewing, because "naps are rare" at Berea, and undergraduates confess that they "usually don't sleep in because there is just so much to do." In addition to their work and regular study, each student is also expected to attend seven Convocations—supplemental lectures, concerts, and performances—during their fall term (except during graduation term). Students look to one another for entertainment, noting that you have to "make something happen" through one of the more than sixty clubs and student organizations. The town of Berea is similarly lowkey ("a calm place"), though as the Folk Arts & Crafts Capital of Kentucky, there are plenty of artisans, crafts, and heritage activities such as Contra dancing available for those looking to explore local roots. For those looking for a little more urban shopping and dining (which some students stress "is a must"), the town of Richmond is a 15-minute drive or campus shuttle ride away, with the city of Lexington just a bit further. Beyond that, "there isn't a big party scene"—a ban on the sale of alcohol in Berea was only recently lifted and remains controversial, and it remains against school rules to have alcohol on campus. This doesn't seem to bother undergraduates, who mention that they're "constantly holding events" that include "movie nights, game nights, dances, [and] bowling."

Student Body

Though founded in 1855, this progressive school is "very deeply rooted in Appalachian culture and history, but unafraid to address issues outside of that." You don't just stumble by a free education and stacked résumé without some sort of otherworldly drive: "the one thing that ties us all together is the fact that we had to work so hard to get into Berea." Many from this "creative" and "incredibly resilient" group are first-generation college students "from the Appalachian region," all of which makes for a particular sort of academically driven and serious student. That said, some note that this quality also spills over into personal relationships, as there seem to be "a lot of couples on campus." Overall, if you look around you're most likely to see "an overworked, but generally content student shuffling between classes and work."

BEREA COLLEGE

Financial Aid: 859-985-3314 • E-Mail: admissions@berea.edu • Website: www.berea.edu

THE PRINCETON REVIEW SAYS

Admissions

The school reports that its standardized testing policy for use in admission for Fall 2026 is Test Optional. The Princeton Review suggests that interested applicants consult with the school for the most up-to-date standardized testing policies. *Very important factors considered include:* interview. *Important factors considered include:* rigor of secondary school record, class rank, academic GPA, standardized test scores, application essay, character/personal qualities. *Other factors considered include:* recommendation(s), extracurricular activities, talent/ability, first generation, geographical residence, state residency, volunteer work, work experience, level of applicant's interest. High school diploma is required and GED is accepted. *Academic units recommended:* 4 English, 3 math, 2 science, 2 science labs, 2 language (other than English), 2 social studies.

Financial Aid

Students should submit: FAFSA. Priority filing deadline is 10/31. The Princeton Review suggests that all financial aid forms be submitted as soon as possible. *Need-based scholarships/grants offered:* Federal Pell; Federal SEOG; State scholarships/grants; Private scholarships; College/university scholarship or grant aid from institutional funds. *Loan aid offered:* Federal Direct Subsidized Loans; Federal Direct Unsubsidized Loans; Direct PLUS loans; College/university loans from institutional funds. Admitted students will be notified of awards on a rolling basis beginning 3/1. Federal Work-Study Program available.

The Inside Word

The Tuition Promise Scholarship that every student receives understandably attracts a lot of applicants. Competition among candidates is intense. To be considered, applicants must meet Berea's financial eligibility requirement. It is recommended that you check out the financial eligibility estimator on the school's website to see if you qualify before applying to the school. Berea has rolling admissions, but strongly suggests that you submit your application as early as possible.

THE SCHOOL SAYS

From the Admissions Office

"Since its founding in 1855, Berea College has provided a high quality, low-cost education to students of all races. As the first interracial and co-educational college in the South, Berea admits students with great academic promise but limited financial means. Over the past 150 years, Berea has evolved into one of the most distinctive colleges in the United States serving students primarily from the Appalachian region.

"All admitted students receive a Tuition Promise Scholarship, which completely covers the cost of tuition after other forms of grant and scholarship aid are applied. This leaves only minimal expenses for housing, meals, and other expenses. Students graduate with one of the lowest rates of student educational debt in the nation, and one in three students graduate debt free. In addition to the Scholarship, students receive a laptop computer and a paid on-campus job to assist with educational and personal expenses as well as gain valuable work experience before graduation.

"As a result of this combination of academic reputation and generous financial assistance, Berea attracts many more applicants than are able to be accepted, so admission is competitive. The best means of improving the chances for admission is to complete the application process as early as possible, preferably by October 31 of the senior year."

SELECTIVITY

# of total applicants	4,633
% of total applicants accepted	16
% of total acceptees attending	55

First-Year Profile

Testing policy	Test Optional
Range SAT composite	1120–1260
Range SAT EBRW	550–680
Range SAT math	520–630
Range ACT composite	22–28
% submitting SAT scores	4
% submitting ACT scores	35
Average HS GPA	3.6
% submitting high school GPA	91
% graduated top 10% of class	30
% graduated top 25% of class	65
% graduated top 50% of class	95
% submitting high school rank	58

Important Dates

Regular	
Apply by	3/31
Notified by	Rolling, 11/15
Nonfall registration?	No

FINANCIAL FACTS*

Annual tuition	$54,700
Food and housing	$9,142
Required fees	$780
Books and supplies	$750
Average need-based scholarship (First-year)	$59,792 ($60,297)
% students with need rec. need-based scholarship or grant aid (First-year)	100 (100)
% students with need rec. non-need-based scholarship or grant aid (First-year)	0 (0)
% students with need rec. need-based self-help aid (First-year)	100 (100)
% students rec. any financial aid (First-year)	100 (100)
% UG borrow to pay for school	33
Average cumulative indebtedness	$6,134
% of students with need fully met (First-year)	3 (2)
Average % of student need met (First-year)	94 (95)

* Most recently reported data at time of printing. Scan the QR code to find the latest updates.

Berry College

2277 Martha Berry Hwy, NW, Mount Berry, GA 30149 • Admissions: 706-236-2215

Survey Snapshot
Internships are widely available
Students take advantage of the outdoors
Career services are great

RATINGS

Quality of Life	88
Fire Safety	95
Green	60*
Academic	84
Profs Interesting	92
Profs Accessible	94
Admissions	84
Financial Aid	91

CAMPUS LIFE

Type of school	Private
Environment	Town

Students

Degree-seeking undergrad enrollment	2,252
% male/female/not reported	37/63/0
% from out of state	25
% First-year live on campus	93
% Ugrads live on campus	87
# of fraternities	0
# of sororities	0
% Asian	2
% Black or African American	8
% Hispanic	13
% Native American	<1
% Pacific Islander	<1
% Race and/or ethnicity unknown	1
% Two or more races	5
% White	70
% International	<1
# of countries represented	4

CAMPUS MENTAL HEALTH SERVICES

Offers mental health/wellness program	Yes
Mental health training available to students	Yes
Employs Chief Wellness Officer	No
Peer-to-peer mental health offerings	Yes
Counseling center has guidelines or accreditation	No
Mental health/well-being courses	Yes, non-credit

ACADEMICS

% students returning for sophomore year	85
% students graduating within 4 years	65
% students graduating within 6 years	71
Calendar	Semester
Student/faculty ratio	12:1
Most common class size 10–19.	(39%)
Most common lab/discussion size 10–19.	(59%)

Most Popular Majors

Biology/Biological Sciences; Zoology/ Animal Biology; Psychology

STUDENTS SAY "…"

Academics

Berry College is ideal for students with "ambitious goals," offering academics "designed to set you up for success" in your career or advanced degree—"as long as you are willing to put in the work." The college offers over 75 areas of study, including a "very hands-on" Animal Science major that allows students to work directly with live animals. While academics are described as "usually demanding," they are balanced by a "very strong" support system that begins as early as first-year orientation. During their orientation class, students create "a detailed plan" for their entire academic career and receive feedback from both their advisor and peer mentor. Beyond the classroom, students have access to numerous "mentorship, networking, career, and research opportunities," making it easy to gain experience that both "looks great in your résumé" and "helps you grow." One example is Berry's Cultural Events Program, which hosts lectures, panel discussions, and concerts. While participation is required, many students view it as a favorite extracurricular activity. As one student explains, "So many are held each semester that I can always count on there being enough on topics I'm interested in." Overall, Berry provides a well-rounded environment where students feel "supported and confident." This is due in large part to the professors, who "push you to be your very best" while also being "very understanding." The faculty "want you to succeed" and "make an effort to help students every way they can."

Campus Life

Students are awed by all 27,000 acres of Berry (the "world's largest campus"): "The beauty...absolutely amazes me. Plus, there's cows!" There's plenty to see and do, including the LifeWorks program, which gives students professional experience across a wide variety of on-campus jobs: "It is common for students to have two to three jobs." In addition, because "it's easy to start" an activity, "there's always a club for whatever someone may be interested in." While Berry is not officially a religious school, it "was founded on Christian principles," and attending church services and Bible studies are popular activities for many students. Students also enjoy playing intramurals and taking day trips with the outdoors club to rock climb or explore nearby caves. Sporting events are "very exciting to attend because the campus is small, so you typically know the players and have plenty of friends in the stands." With few exceptions, full-time students live on campus, and while some would like to see dorm and parking upgrades, the residential nature of the school creates a close-knit community. Overall, students like living in the "Berry Bubble," and say it "feels like family."

Student Body

Berry's "very dedicated" students want to do it all and playfully describe how "everyone is involved with everything all the time" as being "Berry Busy." Thankfully, this still allows students to be "thoughtful, caring, and hardworking" and, perhaps most importantly, "very friendly." There is, in fact, a "Good Neighbor Culture" at the school, and this results in peers who are "encouraging, supportive, and bring out the best in me." The student body is a tight-knit group, and classes, extracurriculars, and the LifeWorks program, allow them to "get to know people more in-depth." As one student explains, "the different environments bring out different parts of people's personalities." Many students here are Christian, though not exclusively. One student adds that there are also "many students [who] ascribe to different religious traditions" as well as "a significant number of atheist students." Students note "how welcoming everyone is" and describe the school as a place where their peers are willing "to help each other succeed." As one student sums up, "We look out for those beside us and treat our community with care and intentionality."

Berry College

Financial Aid: 706-236-1714 • E-Mail: admissions@berry.edu • Website: www.berry.edu

THE PRINCETON REVIEW SAYS

Admissions

The school reports that its standardized testing policy for use in admission for Fall 2026 is Test Free. The Princeton Review suggests that interested applicants consult with the school for the most up-to-date standardized testing policies. *Very important factors considered include:* rigor of secondary school record, academic GPA. *Important factors considered include:* application essay, extracurricular activities. *Other factors considered include:* recommendation(s), interview, talent/ability, character/personal qualities, volunteer work, work experience. High school diploma is required and GED is accepted. *Academic units required:* 4 English, 4 math, 3 science, 2 language (other than English), 3 social studies, 4 academic electives.

Financial Aid

Students should submit: FAFSA; State aid form. Priority filing deadline is 2/15. The Princeton Review suggests that all financial aid forms be submitted as soon as possible. *Need-based scholarships/grants offered:* Federal Pell; Federal SEOG; College/university scholarship or grant aid from institutional funds. *Loan aid offered:* Federal Direct Subsidized Loans; Federal Direct Unsubsidized Loans; Direct PLUS loans; College/university loans from institutional funds. Admitted students will be notified of awards on a rolling basis beginning 11/1. Federal Work-Study Program available. Institutional employment available.

The Inside Word

Admissions officers at Berry College do their best to get to know and wholly consider each candidate. Of course, a solid college prep curriculum is a must. Students have the option of submitting either a Common App or using Berry's own application; both are given equal weight. Better yet, both are free. Standardized test scores are only required for Georgia residents who wish to be considered for the Zell Miller Scholarship. Finally, applicants who are sure that Berry is their top choice are encouraged to apply early action.

THE SCHOOL SAYS

From the Admissions Office

"Berry College offers approximately 2,200 undergraduates and 200 graduates a one-of-a-kind educational experience saying Comparisons fail, "There's no place like Berry." With 27,000 acres it's the largest campus in the world where science students conduct field research alongside professors; animal science majors get hands-on experience on a working farm; and everyone connects to nature whether hiking or biking 88 miles of trails or simply hanging a hammock. Ongoing development of state-of-the-art facilities is a priority with recent additions such as a new animal science building and a new building to house nursing and physician's associate programs. 97% of students participate in Berry's LifeWorks program which provides eight semesters of paid professional development. The Center for Personal and Professional Development matches students with on-campus positions where they apply classroom knowledge in practical way; build transferable skills like leadership, teamwork, and critical thinking; and connect with a nationwide network of alumni. With rigorous academics across 75+ majors, minors and pre-professional programs, Berry averages 18 students per class; 82% of students complete a significant research or internship experience. Student/faculty interaction was ranked in the top 10% nationally by freshmen completing the National Survey of Student Engagement. Through The Berry Journey, our signature approach to collaborating with students, students have a series of connected courses and guided learning experiences with the support of trusted faculty, mentors and peers that will help you test out your direction, reflect on your experiences, adopt your plans and graduate equipped for your purposeful next steps."

SELECTIVITY

# of total applicants	5,929
% of total applicants accepted	73
% of total acceptees attending	16

First-Year Profile

Testing policy	Test Free
Average HS GPA	3.9
% submitting high school GPA	100

Important Dates

Early action	
Apply by	11/1
Notified by	12/1
Regular	
Apply by	1/15
Notified by	Rolling, 11/1
Nonfall registration?	Yes

FINANCIAL FACTS

Annual tuition	$44,190
Food and housing	$14,980
Required fees	$376
Books and supplies	$1,000
Average need-based scholarship (First-year)	$34,889 ($34,893)
% students with need rec. need-based scholarship or grant aid (First-year)	100 (100)
% students with need rec. non-need-based scholarship or grant aid (First-year)	29 (27)
% students with need rec. need-based self-help aid (First-year)	67 (67)
% students rec. any financial aid (First-year)	99 (100)
% UG borrow to pay for school	46
Average cumulative indebtedness	$24,894
% of students with need fully met (First-year)	34 (36)
Average % of student need met (First-year)	86 (85)

Boston College

140 Commonwealth Avenue, Chestnut Hill, MA 02467 • Admissions: 617-552-3100

Survey Snapshot
Great library
Students love Boston, MA
Everyone loves the Eagles

RATINGS

Quality of Life	**94**
Fire Safety	**95**
Green	**60***
Academic	**90**
Profs Interesting	**94**
Profs Accessible	**96**
Admissions	**98**
Financial Aid	**95**

CAMPUS LIFE

Type of school	Private
Affiliation	Roman Catholic
Environment	City

Students

Degree-seeking undergrad enrollment	9,677
% male/female/not reported	47/53/0
% from out of state	76
% First-year from public high school	46
% First-year live on campus	99
% Ugrads live on campus	78
# of fraternities	0
# of sororities	0
% Asian	12
% Black or African American	5
% Hispanic	12
% Native American	<1
% Pacific Islander	<1
% Race and/or ethnicity unknown	2
% Two or more races	6
% White	56
% International	7
# of countries represented	79

CAMPUS MENTAL HEALTH SERVICES

Offers mental health/wellness program	Yes
Mental health training available to students	Yes
Employs Chief Wellness Officer	Yes
Peer-to-peer mental health offerings	Yes
Counseling center has guidelines or accreditation	No
Mental health/well-being courses	Yes, for-credit

ACADEMICS

% students returning for sophomore year	96
% students graduating within 4 years	86
% students graduating within 6 years	91
Calendar	Semester
Student/faculty ratio	10:1
Most common class size 10–19.	(36%)

Most Popular Majors

Biology; Economics; Finance

Applicants Often Prefer

Brown University, Columbia University, Cornell University, Dartmouth College, Duke University, Harvard College, Tufts University, University of California—Berkeley, University of California—Los Angeles, University of Michigan—Ann Arbor, University of Notre Dame, University of Pennsylvania, University of Southern California, University of Virginia, Vanderbilt University, Yale University

Applicants Rarely Prefer

Boston University, College of the Holy Cross, Fordham University, The George Washington University, New York University, Northeastern University, Providence College, University of Massachusetts—Amherst, Villanova University

STUDENTS SAY "..."

Academics

Boston College is a small private Jesuit college that has long been delivering a "prestigious" liberal arts education with a holistic focus on sending "well-rounded" individuals out into the world. That goal is furthered by a strong core curriculum spread across a variety of disciplines and "phenomenal professors" who work to make sure each individual has a "great experience academically." One student vouches for the faculty: "Boston College's professors are truly exceptional and are devoted to undergraduate learning." Even outside of the classroom, a student-to-faculty ratio of 10:1 provides plenty of face time, and students find that professors are "easily accessible outside of classes" and "engaging, challenging, and understanding, [and] are genuinely interested in the student as a whole person." Post-graduation, BCers say that their "well-connected" teachers are happy to help with the job search, which is buoyed by a strong network of more than 200,000 alumni. Though the entire experience comes with "high expectations," students find that the support and knowledge are easily found on the BC journey, and they "feel prepared for whatever is next" after graduation. "I have always revered Boston College's academic and athletic reputation, and coming here, I have not been disappointed," says a student.

Campus Life

Located on the outskirts of Boston in a "perfect" suburban location, BC's "gorgeous campus" is the home to 31 "incredible [Division I] sports teams" and more than 40 intramural teams. Accordingly, there are "superfans at every event" and in general "just so much school spirit and love for the university!" Boston College offers a "plethora of extracurricular activities"—more than 300 student organizations, as a matter of fact—and students believe that "there's a club or group for everyone here." Students can easily head to Downtown Boston to partake in concerts, museums, and other cultural activities, but they seem equally as content to return to their "close-knit college" where they "feel very at home." That said, the school's Jesuit mission of faith and service means that "there is also a large service component" that supplements the college's academics, and students often "serve the community in Boston and communities all around the world." Ultimately, students laud the "great facilities" and "state-of-the-art resources" provided to them at every turn.

Student Body

Each year, Boston College "becomes more and more diverse," moving away from its old nickname as "J. Crew U" to a present where one-third of students now identify as AHANA (African, Hispanic, Asian and Native American descent). The school's Jesuit affiliation continues to bring in "a large religious/spiritual community," but "it is only one group of many" among the greater pool of "really ambitious" and "hardworking" BC students. "The majority of students seem intelligent and academically driven as well as dedicated to and passionate about one or more extracurricular activities," and indeed the plethora of sports teams and extracurriculars makes it easy to mingle from the get-go. As one student puts it, "once you've settled in, you'll find that it's not at all difficult to find a group of friends." It helps, of course, to share a similar "work hard, play hard mentality" among this "academically oriented bunch," but ultimately, everyone "definitely [has] school as a top priority. They just also happen to be "into having a good time" and making the most of their college experience and location.

BOSTON COLLEGE

Financial Aid: 617-552-3300 • E-Mail: admission@bc.edu • Website: www.bc.edu

THE PRINCETON REVIEW SAYS

Admissions

The school reports that its standardized testing policy for use in admission for Fall 2026 is Test Optional. The Princeton Review suggests that interested applicants consult with the school for the most up-to-date standardized testing policies. *Very important factors considered include:* rigor of secondary school record, academic GPA. *Important factors considered include:* class rank, application essay, recommendation(s), extracurricular activities, talent/ability, character/personal qualities, religious affiliation/commitment, volunteer work. *Other factors considered include:* standardized test scores, first generation, work experience. High school diploma is required and GED is accepted. *Academic units recommended:* 4 English, 4 math, 4 science, 4 science labs, 4 language (other than English), 4 social studies, 4 history.

Financial Aid

Students should submit: FAFSA; CSS PROFILE; Business/Farm Supplement. Priority filing deadline is 2/1. The Princeton Review suggests that all financial aid forms be submitted as soon as possible. *Need-based scholarships/grants offered:* Federal Pell; Federal SEOG; State scholarships/grants; Private scholarships; College/university scholarship or grant aid from institutional funds. *Loan aid offered:* Federal Direct Subsidized Loans; Federal Direct Unsubsidized Loans; Direct PLUS loans; State Loans. Admitted students will be notified of awards on or about 4/1. Federal Work-Study Program available. Institutional employment available.

The Inside Word

Boston College is one of many selective schools that eschew set admissions formulae. While a challenging high school curriculum and strong grades are essential for any serious candidate, the college seeks students who are passionate and make connections between academic pursuits and extracurricular activities. The application process should reveal a distinct, mature voice and a student whose interest in education goes beyond the simple desire to earn an A.

THE SCHOOL SAYS

From the Admissions Office

"Boston College undergraduate students achieve at the highest levels with honors in the past ten years including 1 Rhodes Scholarship winner, 114 Fulbrights, 1 Marshall, 7 Goldwaters, 6 Beckmans, and 6 Truman Postgraduate Fellowship Programs. Junior Year Abroad and Scholar of the College Program offer students flexibility within the curriculum. Facilities opened in the past ten years include: Stokes Hall, Cadigan Alumni Center, Thomas More Apartments, Fish Field House, Margot Connell Recreation Center, and the new Schiller Institute for Integrated Sciences and Society. Students enjoy the vibrant location in Chestnut Hill with easy access to the cultural and historical richness of Boston."

SELECTIVITY

# of total applicants	38,658
% of total applicants accepted	14
% of total acceptees attending	45
# of in-state applicants	5,827
% of in-state applicants accepted	15
# of out-of-state-applicants	28,582
% of applicants accepted from out of state	14
# of international applicants	4,235
% of international applicants accepted	13
# of early decision applicants	4,911
% of early decision applicants accepted	32

First-Year Profile

Testing policy	Test Optional
Range SAT composite	1440–1520
Range SAT EBRW	710–760
Range SAT math	720–780
Range ACT composite	33–35
% submitting SAT scores	41
% submitting ACT scores	19
% graduated top 10% of class	93
% graduated top 25% of class	99
% graduated top 50% of class	99

Important Dates

Early decision	
Apply by	11/1
Notified by	12/15
Other ED apply by	1/1
Other ED notified by	2/15
Regular	
Apply by	1/2
Notified by	4/1
Nonfall registration?	Yes

FINANCIAL FACTS

Annual tuition	$72,180
Food and housing	$19,290
Required fees	$1,328
Books and supplies	$1,250
Average need-based scholarship (First-year)	$57,690 ($60,503)
% students with need rec. need-based scholarship or grant aid (First-year)	90 (90)
% students with need rec. non-need-based scholarship or grant aid (First-year)	3 (3)
% students with need rec. need-based self-help aid (First-year)	93 (91)
% students rec. any financial aid (First-year)	67 (NR)
% UG borrow to pay for school	38
Average cumulative indebtedness	$24,892
% of students with need fully met (First-year)	100 (100)
Average % of student need met (First-year)	100 (100)

Boston University

One Silber Way, Boston, MA 02215 • Admissions: 617-353-2300

Survey Snapshot
Students love Boston, MA
Great food on campus
Recreation facilities are great

RATINGS

Quality of Life	82
Fire Safety	95
Green	95
Academic	88
Profs Interesting	89
Profs Accessible	94
Admissions	97
Financial Aid	91

CAMPUS LIFE

Type of school	Private
Environment	Metropolis

Students

Degree-seeking undergrad enrollment	17,628
% male/female/not reported	41/59/0
% from out of state	79
% First-year from public high school	71
% First-year live on campus	99
% Ugrads live on campus	57
# of fraternities (% join)	8 (NR)
# of sororities (% join)	10 (11)
% Asian	21
% Black or African American	6
% Hispanic	12
% Native American	<1
% Pacific Islander	<1
% Race and/or ethnicity unknown	4
% Two or more races	5
% White	30
% International	21
# of countries represented	112

CAMPUS MENTAL HEALTH SERVICES

Offers mental health/wellness program	Yes
Mental health training available to students	Yes
Employs Chief Wellness Officer	Yes
Peer-to-peer mental health offerings	Yes
Counseling center has guidelines or accreditation	Yes
Mental health/well-being courses	Yes, for-credit

ACADEMICS

% students returning for sophomore year	94
% students graduating within 4 years	82
% students graduating within 6 years	90
Calendar	Semester
Student/faculty ratio	10:1
Most common class size 10–19.	(40%)
Most common lab/discussion size 20–29.	(46%)

Most Popular Majors

Economics; Business Administration and Management; Computer Science

Applicants Also Look At

Boston College, Columbia University, New York University, Northeastern University, Northwestern University, Tufts University, University of California—Berkeley, University of California—Los Angeles, University of Michigan—Ann Arbor, University of Pennsylvania, University of Southern California

STUDENTS SAY "..."

Academics

The undergraduates of Boston University say "the range and diversity of opportunities at Boston University allows you to Be You," with the freedom to assemble the more than 300 courses of study into a unique curriculum that is "equal parts liberal arts education and pre-professional experience." Study abroad is encouraged to supplement the classroom experience (there are more than 170 programs available in 20 countries), and the 10 undergraduate "schools and colleges within Boston University provide students with access to almost every imaginable program of study." Students also laud the "research opportunities" (the school spends more than half a billion dollars each year on research), and the access that comes both from the school's reputation and relationships as well as from its prime location in one of the country's biggest biotech and healthcare hubs. This experience is also embodied by the world-class faculty, who are "actively pursuing research in their field" and "constantly striving to be better for the student's benefit." Their "interesting backgrounds...fuel class discussions in a variety of academic areas" and encourage discourse and participation among classes of all levels. A student notes that in this capacity, professors act as "engaging partners in my academic experience."

Campus Life

Students love the university's "urban campus" in Boston's Back Bay, where they can "run along the Charles River," go "shopping on Newbury or in Harvard Square," or frequent "plays and ballets and museums" and the many local "clubs and bars." Boston is the epitome of a college town, and three-quarters of students live on campus in "the heart of Boston," enjoying the "wonderful" support structure of campus life with the pulse of the city just outside their door, as well as the ability to make friends at all of the nearby colleges in Cambridge, Somerville, Allston, and Brookline. A student remarks: "The city itself is like our campus." Campus itself has "a lot of clubs and activities to get involved in," as well as "house parties," "BU hockey games," and "frat parties," and "there is more to do than you will be able to find the time for." As "there's always something interesting going on on- and off-campus," students don't have to work hard to fill the hours, but they make sure to keep a balance in doing so and take pride in "being able to find balance in living strong academic lives and exciting social lives as well." One student sums up: "Life at BU is anything you want it to be."

Student Body

The student body is vastly diverse in terms of makeup (partially "because we are an international university"), but most here are said to be "motivated, culturally aware, intelligent, adventurous," "driven and involved," and "very passionate." Perhaps these common traits are why one student remarks that "there is a great sense of diversity, yet an overwhelming feeling of unity." With more than 450 student organizations (including 80 religious and cultural ones), BUers are easily able to have "a wide range of interests both inside and outside the classroom" and are happy to keep a busy pace. A student says, "My life at BU is quite packed because I chose to make it that way." These pursuits and passions also fuel the dialogue around campus, and students are known to be "intellectually stimulating in conversations" and enjoy finding others that share their interests. The highest value seems to be placed on "diversity of thought," as "originality is valued highly at BU."

BOSTON UNIVERSITY

Financial Aid: 617-353-4176 • E-Mail: admissions@bu.edu; intadmis@bu.edu • Website: www.bu.edu

THE PRINCETON REVIEW SAYS

Admissions

The school reports that its standardized testing policy for use in admission for Fall 2026 is Test Optional. The Princeton Review suggests that interested applicants consult with the school for the most up-to-date standardized testing policies. *Very important factors considered include:* rigor of secondary school record, academic GPA. *Important factors considered include:* class rank, application essay, recommendation(s), extracurricular activities, character/personal qualities. *Other factors considered include:* standardized test scores, first generation, geographical residence, state residency, volunteer work, work experience, level of applicant's interest. High school diploma is required and GED is accepted. *Academic units required:* 4 English, 3 math, 3 science, 3 science labs, 2 language (other than English), 3 social studies. *Academic units recommended:* 4 English, 4 math, 4 science, 4 science labs, 4 language (other than English), 4 social studies.

Financial Aid

Students should submit: FAFSA; CSS PROFILE. The Princeton Review suggests that all financial aid forms be submitted as soon as possible. *Need-based scholarships/grants offered:* Federal Pell; Federal SEOG; State scholarships/grants; Private scholarships; College/university scholarship or grant aid from institutional funds. *Loan aid offered:* Federal Direct Subsidized Loans; Federal Direct Unsubsidized Loans; Direct PLUS loans; State Loans. Admitted students will be notified of awards on or about Late March (Dec 15 for ED). Federal Work-Study Program available. Institutional employment available.

The Inside Word

BU can afford to stay competitive, and they strongly emphasize high school academic performance as the key indicator of a student's admissibility to the university. BU values students who take on a challenging high school curriculum (especially AP and IB classes, or whatever the most challenging course load available is). The personal essay, recommendations, and extracurricular activities are also important factors in assessing applicants. BU meets the full demonstrated need for admitted first-year students who are U.S. citizens or permanent residents.

THE SCHOOL SAYS

From the Admissions Office

"In the heart of Boston, Boston University serves as a standard for research, academic excellence, and dauntless passion to pursue knowledge without limits. With guidance from academic scholars and faculty at 10 schools and colleges, students can choose from more than 300 programs to create their own journey and path to success. A 10:1 student-to-faculty ratio, and average class size of 30 means that professors know their students by name. BU meets full demonstrated need for admitted first-year students who are US citizens or permanent residents.

"Grounded in a rigorous academic experience, Boston University is a member of the prestigious Association of American Universities, placing it among the top research universities in the world. From their first-year, BU students can access resources and find opportunities to explore their passion and turn it into a career. And, with 170+ study abroad programs, a global education is part of the BU package.

"Back on campus, students can engage with 450 student organizations, a 100% fossil fuel building named the Duan Family Center for Computing & Data Sciences, and dedicated community spaces like The LGBTQIA+ Center, The Newbury Center and The Howard Thurman Center. BU students can pursue their interests beyond the classroom and find a community that makes BU feel like home. A diverse student body from all 50 states and more than 148 countries around the world comes together to create a vibrant campus, where students are guaranteed four years of housing. With 87% of students completing at least one experiential learning opportunity while at BU, it's no surprise that the University is ranked #13 for most employable graduates by Times Higher Ed."

SELECTIVITY

# of total applicants	76,776
% of total applicants accepted	13
% of total acceptees attending	35
# of in-state applicants	8,062
% of in-state applicants accepted	13
# of out-of-state-applicants	50,764
% of applicants accepted from out of state	12
# of international applicants	15,794
% of international applicants accepted	16
# of early decision applicants	6,907
% of early decision applicants accepted	31
# offered a place on the wait list	15,751
# admitted from wait list	95

First-Year Profile

Testing policy	Test Optional
Range SAT composite	1420–1510
Range SAT EBRW	700–750
Range SAT math	720–780
Range ACT composite	33–34
% submitting SAT scores	36
% submitting ACT scores	10
Average HS GPA	3.9
% submitting high school GPA	100
% graduated top 10% of class	86
% graduated top 25% of class	98
% graduated top 50% of class	100
% submitting high school rank	14

Important Dates

Early decision	
Apply by	11/1
Notified by	12/15
Other ED apply by	1/5
Other ED notified by	2/15
Regular	
Apply by	1/5
Notified by	4/1
Nonfall registration?	Yes

FINANCIAL FACTS

Annual tuition	$73,024
Food and housing	$20,740
Required fees	$1,570
Books and supplies	$1,000
Average need-based scholarship (First-year)	$65,706 ($66,926)
% students with need rec. need-based scholarship or grant aid (First-year)	99 (100)
% students with need rec. non-need-based scholarship or grant aid (First-year)	32 (49)
% students with need rec. need-based self-help aid (First-year)	65 (67)
% students rec. any financial aid (First-year)	53 (52)
% UG borrow to pay for school	34
Average cumulative indebtedness	$36,774
% of students with need fully met (First-year)	37 (53)
Average % of student need met (First-year)	92 (98)

Bowdoin College

255 Maine Street, Brunswick, ME 04011-8448 • Admissions: 207-725-3100

Survey Snapshot
Great food on campus
Students take advantage of the outdoors
Dorms are like palaces

RATINGS

Quality of Life	91
Fire Safety	99
Green	95
Academic	91
Profs Interesting	92
Profs Accessible	95
Admissions	98
Financial Aid	99

CAMPUS LIFE

Type of school	Private
Environment	Village

Students

Degree-seeking undergrad enrollment	1,837
% male/female/not reported	47/53/0
% from out of state	90
% First-year from public high school	52
% First-year live on campus	100
% Ugrads live on campus	95
# of fraternities	0
# of sororities	0
% Asian	10
% Black or African American	5
% Hispanic	15
% Native American	<1
% Pacific Islander	<1
% Race and/or ethnicity unknown	1
% Two or more races	9
% White	53
% International	6
# of countries represented	57

CAMPUS MENTAL HEALTH SERVICES

Offers mental health/wellness program	Yes
Mental health training available to students	No
Employs Chief Wellness Officer	NR
Peer-to-peer mental health offerings	NR
Counseling center has guidelines or accreditation	No
Mental health/well-being courses	NR

ACADEMICS

% students returning for sophomore year	98
% students graduating within 4 years	72
% students graduating within 6 years	93
Calendar	Semester
Student/faculty ratio	8:1
Most common class size 10–19.	(45%)

Most Popular Majors
Political Science and Government; Economics; Biology/Biological Sciences

Applicants Often Prefer
Brown University, Harvard College, Yale University

Applicants Sometimes Prefer
Amherst College, Cornell University, Dartmouth College, Swarthmore College, Williams College

Applicants Rarely Prefer
Middlebury College, Wesleyan University

STUDENTS SAY "..."

Academics

Bowdoin College, a liberal arts school on the coast of Maine, has produced luminary alumni like Nathaniel Hawthorne, Henry Wadsworth Longfellow, and Franklin Pierce. This rich history has shaped its current and traditional academic vision of a well-rounded education. New students are required to take a writing seminar, and at least one full-credit course in each of five subjects: mathematical, computational, or statistical reasoning; inquiry in the natural sciences; difference, power, and inequity; international perspectives; and visual and performing arts. Sophomores can then choose their majors from a wide variety of over 40 subjects, ranging from traditional fields such as history, physics, and English to modern focuses such as Digital and Computational Studies. Bowdoin encourages academic exploration so that students have the time to take courses outside their main areas of study. Small classes and a low student-faculty ratio reflect one of Bowdoin's greatest strengths: excellent, dedicated professors who foster thoughtful discussion and provide personalized support. "I'm really grateful to go to a liberal arts college where I can get so much more attention from professors...they are only here to teach and they love it." As another explains, Bowdoin offers "amazing professors who are passionate and smart and who care deeply about their students.

Campus Life

Bowdoin's architecturally distinct New England campus stands out whether it is dotted with Maine's celebrated foliage in autumn or dusted with snow in winter. The natural surroundings are a great draw; some students have come to love the outdoors through the Bowdoin Outing Club (BOC), a student organization that hosts over 150 events each year. "I came here without ANY experience in the outdoors at all...but now I've done whitewater canoeing/rafting, mountain biking, skiing, backpacking, etc.!" First-year and second-year students are required to live on campus and most choose to stay until they graduate. As there is no Greek life at Bowdoin, the many clubs and extracurricular activities, which include environmental advocacy, sports, and the student newspaper, are central to life at the college. "Most students are involved in multiple on-campus activities—I don't know anyone who doesn't do several other things outside of classes." Students can also be found perusing the renowned Bowdoin College Museum of Art, which houses over 20,000 artworks in its collection.

Student Body

The Bowdoin community is known for its camaraderie. "Bowdoin's student body is small enough that walking on campus means saying 'hi' to a lot of familiar faces." The "Bowdoin hello," a longstanding tradition by which students greet each other enthusiastically on campus, represents the sense of unity and friendliness often observed. "One thing I love about Bowdoin, and that drew me to the school in my college search, was the supportive and collaborative atmosphere." This community spirit is reflected in students' support for school athletics, which has a strong presence on campus. Varsity football, basketball, baseball, and ice hockey games are routinely filled with groups of Bowdoin "Polar Bears" excitedly cheering in support of their teams.

Students also suggest that their peers "care very strongly about forming community and bridging connections." Many describe their classmates as academically competitive in general, yet extremely supportive. "I appreciate the community here, as people want others to succeed with them and are more than willing to offer help to get you where you want to be." The helpfulness of fellow students is frequently cited as a significant factor in the school's academic success. "I feel I can grow more as a student with collaborative peers rather than [with] peers who are trying to compete with me."

BOWDOIN COLLEGE

Financial Aid: 207-725-3144 • E-Mail: admissions@bowdoin.edu • Website: www.bowdoin.edu

THE PRINCETON REVIEW SAYS

Admissions

The school reports that its standardized testing policy for use in admission for Fall 2026 is Test Optional. The Princeton Review suggests that interested applicants consult with the school for the most up-to-date standardized testing policies. *Very important factors considered include:* rigor of secondary school record, class rank, academic GPA, application essay, recommendation(s), extracurricular activities, talent/ability, character/personal qualities. *Other factors considered include:* standardized test scores, interview, first generation, alumni/ae relation, geographical residence, state residency, volunteer work, work experience, level of applicant's interest. High school diploma is required and GED is accepted. *Academic units recommended:* 4 English, 4 math, 4 science, 3 science labs, 4 language (other than English), 4 social studies.

Financial Aid

Students should submit: FAFSA; CSS PROFILE; Business/Farm Supplement. The Princeton Review suggests that all financial aid forms be submitted as soon as possible. *Need-based scholarships/grants offered:* Federal Pell; Federal SEOG; State scholarships/grants; Private scholarships; College/university scholarship or grant aid from institutional funds. *Loan aid offered:* Federal Direct Subsidized Loans; Federal Direct Unsubsidized Loans; State Loans. Admitted students will be notified of awards on or about 4/1. Federal Work-Study Program available. Institutional employment available.

The Inside Word

Admissions officers at Bowdoin are looking for students who are curious, thoughtful, and engaged. Bowdoin looks at student grades relative to the respective school's level of difficulty, recommendations from teachers and counselors, writing samples, school and community involvement, character, and overall academic potential. A personal interview isn't required but is recommended. To help you introduce yourself to the school, you have the option to submit a two-minute video response to a randomly selected question, such as, "What is the best thing that has happened to you in the past year?" Bowdoin has had a Test Optional policy since 1969.

THE SCHOOL SAYS

From the Admissions Office

"Bowdoin is a welcoming and diverse community of students, faculty, and staff who care about and support each other through four years of learning, exploration, and growth. We are dedicated to the liberal arts, deep intellectual inquiry, and discourse and debate on the toughest issues. All this takes place in the vibrant and accessible town of Brunswick amid one of the most beautiful settings anywhere—the extraordinary coast of Maine.

"Bowdoin combines a 224-year tradition of serving the common good with a wide range of curricular and extracurricular opportunities. A leader in the teaching and study of the environment for over fifty years, the College supports its interdisciplinary approach with unparalleled facilities and field stations for place-based research. Every student receives a MacBook Pro, iPad mini, Apple Pencil, and course-specific software, equipping them to learn and lead in a digital world. One of the most active research liberal arts colleges, Bowdoin is classified as a "Research College" by the Carnegie Foundation. Through the Hastings Initiative for AI and Humanity, Bowdoin empowers students and faculty to critically examine, thoughtfully use, and ethically shape AI's future.

"Bowdoin is one of only ten colleges or universities that accept students on a need-blind basis with a commitment to meet full demonstrated need for all four years without the use of loans. Nearly half of our students receive scholarship assistance from the College, and Bowdoin stands firm in its decision to eliminate loans from aid packages."

SELECTIVITY

# of total applicants	14,045
% of total applicants accepted	7
% of total acceptees attending	54
# of in-state applicants	540
% of in-state applicants accepted	14
# of out-of-state-applicants	7,464
% of applicants accepted from out of state	11
# of international applicants	6,041
% of international applicants accepted	1
# of early decision applicants	1,985
% of early decision applicants accepted	15
# admitted from wait list	5

First-Year Profile

Testing policy	Test Optional
Range SAT composite	1470–1540
Range SAT EBRW	730–770
Range SAT math	730–780
Range ACT composite	33–35
% submitting SAT scores	35
% submitting ACT scores	17
% graduated top 10% of class	89
% graduated top 25% of class	100
% graduated top 50% of class	100
% submitting high school rank	27

Important Dates

Early decision	
Apply by	11/15
Notified by	12/15
Other ED apply by	1/5
Other ED notified by	2/15
Regular	
Apply by	1/5
Notified by	Mid-March
Nonfall registration?	No

FINANCIAL FACTS

Annual tuition	$71,070
Food and housing	$19,560
Required fees	$670
Books and supplies	$840
Average need-based scholarship (First-year)	$70,968 ($70,186)
% students with need rec. need-based scholarship or grant aid (First-year)	100 (100)
% students with need rec. non-need-based scholarship or grant aid (First-year)	0 (0)
% students with need rec. need-based self-help aid (First-year)	99 (100)
% students rec. any financial aid (First-year)	52 (52)
% UG borrow to pay for school	15
Average cumulative indebtedness	$33,910
% of students with need fully met (First-year)	100 (100)
Average % of student need met (First-year)	100 (100)

Bradley University

1501 W. Bradley Avenue, Peoria, IL 61625 • Admissions: 309-677-1000

Survey Snapshot
Easy to get around campus
Intramural sports are popular
Internships are widely available

RATINGS

Quality of Life	85
Fire Safety	93
Green	60*
Academic	80
Profs Interesting	87
Profs Accessible	91
Admissions	84
Financial Aid	88

CAMPUS LIFE

Type of school	Private
Environment	City

Students

Degree-seeking undergrad enrollment	3,231
% male/female/not reported	49/51/0
% from out of state	12
% First-year live on campus	75
% Ugrads live on campus	64
# of fraternities (% join)	19 (29)
# of sororities (% join)	11 (21)
% Asian	4
% Black or African American	13
% Hispanic	15
% Native American	<1
% Pacific Islander	<1
% Race and/or ethnicity unknown	9
% Two or more races	2
% White	55
% International	2
# of countries represented	37

CAMPUS MENTAL HEALTH SERVICES

Offers mental health/wellness program	Yes
Mental health training available to students	Yes
Employs Chief Wellness Officer	No
Peer-to-peer mental health offerings	Yes
Counseling center has guidelines or accreditation	No
Mental health/well-being courses	No

ACADEMICS

% students returning for sophomore year	82
% students graduating within 4 years	62
% students graduating within 6 years	73
Calendar	Semester
Student/faculty ratio	10:1
Most common class size 10–19.	(33%)
Most common lab/discussion size 10–19.	(44%)

Most Popular Majors

Engineering; Health Professions and Related Programs; Business, Management, Marketing, And Related Support Services

Applicants Often Prefer

Illinois State University, University of Illinois at Urbana—Champaign

Applicants Sometimes Prefer

DePaul University, Loyola University Chicago, Marquette University, University of Illinois at Chicago

STUDENTS SAY "…"

Academics

Bradley University's core curriculum "is always promoting ways to help yourself and get out there." Curious, critical thinkers are encouraged through the completion of at least two experiential learning opportunities, including service learning, study abroad, or capstone experiences; in particular, "the amount of internship opportunities that the campus has access to is extremely helpful for students who need real-world experiences in their field." Students say the "small class sizes and individualized experiences" are "what the school majorly excels at," along with things like affordability. Students also highlight the "resources to improve grades or help when you are struggling," as well as "vast opportunities for growth in students' personal and professional development." These doors open in part thanks to the "talented professors who do a good job of explaining the course material and instilling their passion." As one enrollee explains, "One of my professors incorporates class discussions, documentaries, guest speakers, and field trips into each of her classes." Another concludes: "The university promises and delivers practical experiences and education that go beyond normal academics to teach worthwhile lessons."

Campus Life

Bradley students tend to be "involved in the school, whether being in Greek life, attending sporting events, [or] going to school events." Many students "are involved in one club or class that engages a form of visual or performing art," and "there are almost always musical performances, art galleries, and exhibitions showcasing student work." In fact, students say there "are pretty much always events happening," not to mention meetings and practices for more than 200 student organizations. To top it off, all of the clubs and extracurriculars "are also really flexible which allows students to not only participate in a wide variety of activities but also hold many different leadership positions or paid job opportunities." Everything is "either within…walking distance or within a 5–10 minute drive" of the Peoria, Illinois, campus, and when the weather is nice, "students will spend time on the quads, reading while sitting in chairs, climbing trees, playing soccer or football, or playing lawn games." Many people make use of the gym, and "there'll usually be people playing sports on the basketball court in there." One student says of their simple but satisfying formula, "Life is excellent. My days are full, with activities, classes, and hanging out with friends."

Student Body

Bradley students are "highly motivated and artistically inclined," and while they "care about academics and preparing themselves for the future,…they don't let that get in the way of having a fun and fulfilling college experience." This student body is "very diverse while still being tight-knit," and there is a large "mix of personalities and passions, which means lots of unique clubs." The university is "great at creating a welcoming environment for new and old students alike," and those students are "very friendly and open, which makes it a good environment to learn and connect with others." Everyone is "very supportive and very encouraging," and are usually "engaged in discussions and very social with each other." Many agree that the people are as foundational as the academics: "Everyone really does do their best to help each other out…the student body really [makes] being at Bradley truly worth it."

BRADLEY UNIVERSITY

Financial Aid: 309-677-3089 • E-Mail: admissions@bradley.edu • Website: www.bradley.edu

THE PRINCETON REVIEW SAYS

Admissions

The school reports that its standardized testing policy for use in admission for Fall 2026 is Test Free. The Princeton Review suggests that interested applicants consult with the school for the most up-to-date standardized testing policies. *Very important factors considered include:* rigor of secondary school record, academic GPA. *Important factors considered include:* class rank. *Other factors considered include:* application essay, recommendation(s), interview, extracurricular activities, talent/ability, character/personal qualities, first generation, alumni/ae relation, volunteer work, work experience, level of applicant's interest. High school diploma is required and GED is accepted. *Academic units required:* 4 English, 3 math, 2 science, 2 science labs, 2 social studies. *Academic units recommended:* 4 English, 4 math, 3 science, 2 science labs, 3 social studies, 2 history.

Financial Aid

Students should submit: FAFSA. The Princeton Review suggests that all financial aid forms be submitted as soon as possible. *Need-based scholarships/grants offered:* Federal Pell; Federal SEOG; State scholarships/grants; Private scholarships; College/university scholarship or grant aid from institutional funds; United Negro College Fund. *Loan aid offered:* Federal Direct Subsidized Loans; Federal Direct Unsubsidized Loans; Direct PLUS loans. Admitted students will be notified of awards on a rolling basis beginning 11/15. Federal Work-Study Program available. Institutional employment available.

The Inside Word

Bradley has a strong regional pull, which leads to an undergraduate population of mostly Illinois residents. However, out-of-staters who dream of attaining their ever-popular business or health care degrees shouldn't worry! This university has a history of eagerly admitting above-average students who want to get an excellent education, without the grueling admission process other private schools put applicants through. Just make sure you keep your application deadlines straight, as there are three separate application deadlines to choose from (early action, regular, and extended).

THE SCHOOL SAYS

From the Admissions Office

"Bradley offers nearly 5,000 students a broad range of academic programs enhanced by required experiential learning. The university prepares students for immediate and substantial career success by offering resources not found at small colleges and more personalized experiences than large universities. Great academic variety leads to choices of majors, minors and graduate programs that are uncommon at most private universities. More than 100 academic programs are available in business, communications, education, engineering, fine and performing arts, health sciences, liberal arts, science and technology. Unique programs include entrepreneurship, game design, sports communication and physical therapy. Located less than three hours from Chicago, St. Louis and Indianapolis, the ninety-seven acre residential campus is located in a historic neighborhood just one mile from downtown Peoria, the largest metropolitan area in downstate Illinois.

"Bradley students develop leadership skills in more than 200 student organizations, with more than 60 dedicated to student leadership and community service. Students may also participate in the nation's most winning speech team, fraternities and sororities, and NCAA Division I athletics. Bradley graduates are well prepared for a career or direct entry to graduate school with 93 percent employed, continuing their education or pursuing other postgraduate experiences within six months of graduation. In addition to academic advising, each student has a dedicated career advisor to facilitate their planning, so that 94 percent of graduates have participated in an internship, practicum, undergraduate research, community service or study abroad.

"The Princeton Review rates Bradley's internship opportunities among the top 20 for private schools in the nation, and the video game design program as among the top 20 in the nation."

SELECTIVITY

# of total applicants	8,539
% of total applicants accepted	75
% of total acceptees attending	10
# of in-state applicants	6,341
% of in-state applicants accepted	82
# of out-of-state-applicants	1,369
% of applicants accepted from out of state	70
# of international applicants	827
% of international applicants accepted	29
# offered a place on the wait list	0
# admitted from wait list	0

First-Year Profile

Testing policy	Test Free
Average HS GPA	3.8
% submitting high school GPA	100
% graduated top 10% of class	23
% graduated top 25% of class	51
% graduated top 50% of class	82
% submitting high school rank	33

Important Dates

Regular	
Notified by	Rolling, 10/1

FINANCIAL FACTS

Annual tuition	$42,860
Food and housing	$14,050
Required fees	$990
Books and supplies	$1,300
Average need-based scholarship (First-year)	$30,518 ($32,769)
% students with need rec. need-based scholarship or grant aid (First-year)	99 (100)
% students with need rec. non-need-based scholarship or grant aid (First-year)	16 (21)
% students with need rec. need-based self-help aid (First-year)	81 (76)
% students rec. any financial aid (First-year)	97 (100)
% UG borrow to pay for school	72
Average cumulative indebtedness	$35,026
% of students with need fully met (First-year)	20 (24)
Average % of student need met (First-year)	78 (80)

Brandeis University

415 South Street, Waltham, MA 02453 • Admissions: 781-736-3500

Survey Snapshot
Lots of liberal students
Lab facilities are great
Students involved in community service

RATINGS

Quality of Life	84
Fire Safety	60*
Green	60*
Academic	89
Profs Interesting	92
Profs Accessible	94
Admissions	92
Financial Aid	93

CAMPUS LIFE

Type of school	Private
Environment	Metropolis

Students

Degree-seeking undergrad enrollment	3,342
% male/female/not reported	43/57/<1
% from out of state	67
% First-year from public high school	57
% First-year live on campus	99
% Ugrads live on campus	70
# of fraternities	0
# of sororities	0
% Asian	19
% Black or African American	7
% Hispanic	11
% Native American	0
% Pacific Islander	0
% Race and/or ethnicity unknown	3
% Two or more races	5
% White	40
% International	16
# of countries represented	52

CAMPUS MENTAL HEALTH SERVICES

Offers mental health/wellness program	Yes
Mental health training available to students	Yes
Employs Chief Wellness Officer	No
Peer-to-peer mental health offerings	No
Counseling center has guidelines or accreditation	Yes
Mental health/well-being courses	Yes, non-credit

ACADEMICS

% students returning for sophomore year	86
% students graduating within 4 years	74
% students graduating within 6 years	81
Calendar	Semester
Student/faculty ratio	8:1
Most common class size 10–19.	(47%)

Most Popular Majors

Biology/Biological Sciences; Economics; Business/Commerce

Applicants Also Look At

Boston College, Boston University, Cornell University, The George Washington University, New York University, Northeastern University, State University of New York—Binghamton University, Tufts University, University of California—Berkeley, University of California—Los Angeles, University of California—San Diego, University of Massachusetts—Amherst, University of Michigan—Ann Arbor, University of Rochester, University of Southern California

STUDENTS SAY "..."

Academics

Conveniently located just outside of Boston, Brandeis University teaches students "the value of hard work, cultivates curiosity and [an] interest in learning, and introduces one to various perspectives." The university is known for its academic flexibility, which allows students "to study whatever they want" and pursue multiple passions. Undergraduates appreciate that Brandeis provides "the opportunity to explore every possible interest...with the overwhelming support of faculty and peers." This supportive environment is reinforced by "an abundance of undergraduate research opportunities in all majors," encouraging students to apply what they learn beyond the classroom. The academics are "definitely challenging but manageable" because "all departments at Brandeis" have faculty "who care about helping students learn and succeed." In fact, students consistently report that the professors are one of the school's greatest strengths and the majority are "engaging, insightful, and responsive," and many go out of their way to mentor students. One student calls them "passionate about the topic they are teaching." Another adds, "Brandeis attracts some of the best professors and they are very motivating and helpful." As one student simply says, "My academic experience has been fantastic."

Campus Life

While academics are central to the student experience, "Brandeis thrives on its campus club and student activities culture." Students describe an atmosphere where involvement is the norm rather than the exception. "We have so many students who get involved on campus and participate in clubs and other activities," one student explains, while another notes that "volunteer-work is a big deal here." There are numerous opportunities for engagement—ranging from community service clubs and cultural or religious organizations to special-interest groups, theater productions, musical ensembles, and sports teams. "Most clubs don't have any barriers to entry so it's really easy to get involved." When they're not attending class or club meetings, students "enjoy the green spaces on campus and have fun connecting with other students." Weekends are lively, as "there are always shows going on, whether it's theatre, a cappella, or improv," as wells as "sports events and guest lecturers." Some undergrads also enjoy "Greek life events off campus," and many appreciate the school's "[close] proximity" to Cambridge and Boston." Brandeis is a vibrant, fast-paced community where, as one student puts it, "the average person would probably tell you they are a part of five clubs or groups, have a job, and have a very active social life. It's kind of crazy, but I love it."

Student Body

Students at Brandeis describe their peers as "very engaged and involved," and "completely passionate about whatever it is they commit themselves to." The "student body is special in that it is truly a community" full of "unique, interesting, passionate, motivated, inspiring, and intelligent" individuals. Indeed, one student reports, "Everyone here is very welcoming and supportive," with another adding, "It was surprisingly easy to make a ton of friends on this campus." While some undergrads readily admit that they "do have the tendency to be a little more on the introverted and nerdy side," they are also "very caring, genuine people" who are "quirky and a little weird in the best way possible." As one student explains, "I love that...everyone's attitude is kind of 'do whatever you want to/need to do.'" Ultimately, "the best part of Brandeis is the people." As one student shares, "We are a quirky campus, where no two students are alike, but the student body is collectively [filled with] down-to-earth, driven knowledge-seekers who care about the community and the world at large."

BRANDEIS UNIVERSITY

Financial Aid: 781-736-3700 • E-Mail: admissions@brandeis.edu • Website: www.brandeis.edu

THE PRINCETON REVIEW SAYS

Admissions

The school reports that its standardized testing policy for use in admission for Fall 2026 is Test Optional. The Princeton Review suggests that interested applicants consult with the school for the most up-to-date standardized testing policies. *Very important factors considered include:* rigor of secondary school record, class rank, academic GPA, first generation. *Important factors considered include:* application essay, recommendation(s), extracurricular activities, talent/ability. *Other factors considered include:* standardized test scores, interview, alumni/ae relation, geographical residence, state residency, religious affiliation/commitment, volunteer work, work experience, level of applicant's interest. High school diploma is required and GED is accepted. *Academic units recommended:* 4 English, 4 math, 4 science, 2 science labs, 4 language (other than English), 4 social studies.

Financial Aid

Students should submit: FAFSA; CSS PROFILE. The Princeton Review suggests that all financial aid forms be submitted as soon as possible. *Need-based scholarships/grants offered:* Federal Pell; Federal SEOG; State scholarships/grants; Private scholarships; College/university scholarship or grant aid from institutional funds. *Loan aid offered:* Federal Direct Subsidized Loans; Federal Direct Unsubsidized Loans; Direct PLUS loans; College/university loans from institutional funds. Admitted students will be notified of awards on or about 4/1. Federal Work-Study Program available. Institutional employment available.

The Inside Word

Admissions to Brandeis is selective. Therefore, it's imperative that applicants have taken a challenging course load that includes a handful of honors, AP, or IB classes (if and when possible). However, admissions officers are also looking for students who will thrive in and contribute to campus life. Hence, personal statements, letters of recommendation, and extracurricular activities also hold some weight.

THE SCHOOL SAYS

From the Admissions Office

"At Brandeis, learning goes beyond the classroom. Our liberal arts education has always been defined by curiosity, rigor and a commitment to social justice and inclusivity. Today, it's also shaped by real-world experience and career readiness for the digital age.

"Through the Brandeis Plan to Reinvent the Liberal Arts, you'll pair big ideas with hands-on learning, building career-ready credentials and sought-after skills. From your first semester, you'll work with both an academic and a career advisor to chart your path—linking your studies to the skills that employers and graduate schools value most.

"Along your academic journey, you'll earn microcredentials that highlight your achievements, from research and innovation to digital tools, creating a verified second transcript of your strengths alongside your academic transcript. This proof of your skills and leadership will show future employers or graduate school programs that you have what it takes to succeed.

"At the heart of this experience is the Center for Careers and Applied Liberal Arts, a vibrant hub that brings together advising, internships, mentors, alumni and emerging technologies such as AI and virtual reality.

"By the time you graduate, you'll have completed internships and built the confidence, connections and clarity to thrive—whether you're launching a career, pursuing graduate study or making an impact on the world.

At Brandeis, you don't just earn a liberal arts degree. You graduate with proof of what you know, what you can do, and the difference you're ready to make."

SELECTIVITY

# of total applicants	9,756
% of total applicants accepted	45
% of total acceptees attending	17
# of in-state applicants	1,858
% of in-state applicants accepted	56
# of out-of-state-applicants	4,322
% of applicants accepted from out of state	64
# of international applicants	3,576
% of international applicants accepted	18
# of early decision applicants	680
% of early decision applicants accepted	36
# offered a place on the wait list	1,717
# admitted from wait list	206

First-Year Profile

Testing policy	Test Optional
Range SAT composite	1370–1470
Range SAT EBRW	670–740
Range SAT math	660–750
Range ACT composite	31–34
% submitting SAT scores	28
% submitting ACT scores	8
Average HS GPA	3.8
% submitting high school GPA	87
% graduated top 10% of class	39
% graduated top 25% of class	77
% graduated top 50% of class	97
% submitting high school rank	19

Important Dates

Early decision	
Apply by	11/3
Notified by	12/11
Other ED apply by	1/15
Other ED notified by	2/5
Early action	
Apply by	11/3
Notified by	1/29
Regular	
Apply by	1/15
Notified by	3/19
Nonfall registration?	Yes

FINANCIAL FACTS

Annual tuition	$69,934
Food and housing	$19,384
Required fees (First-year)	$598 ($2,023)
Books and supplies	$1,000
Average need-based scholarship (First-year)	$59,009 ($62,952)
% students with need rec. need-based scholarship or grant aid (First-year)	98 (98)
% students with need rec. non-need-based scholarship or grant aid (First-year)	13 (17)
% students with need rec. need-based self-help aid (First-year)	84 (82)
% students rec. any financial aid (First-year)	70 (82)
% UG borrow to pay for school	33
Average cumulative indebtedness	$28,880
% of students with need fully met (First-year)	61 (70)
Average % of student need met (First-year)	94 (97)

Brigham Young University (UT)

Brigham Young University, Provo, UT 84602 • Admissions: 801-422-2507

Survey Snapshot
Students are very religious
Students take advantage of the outdoors
Great library

RATINGS	
Quality of Life	95
Fire Safety	60*
Green	92
Academic	85
Profs Interesting	94
Profs Accessible	92
Admissions	91
Financial Aid	80

CAMPUS LIFE

Type of school	Private
Affiliation	Church of Jesus Christ of Latter-day Saints
Environment	City

Students

Degree-seeking undergrad enrollment	32,952
% male/female/not reported	48/52/0
% from out of state	80
% First-year live on campus	75
% Ugrads live on campus	18
# of fraternities	0
# of sororities	0
% Asian	2
% Black or African American	<1
% Hispanic	8
% Native American	<1
% Pacific Islander	1
% Race and/or ethnicity unknown	2
% Two or more races	4
% White	81
% International	3
# of countries represented	121

CAMPUS MENTAL HEALTH SERVICES

Offers mental health/wellness program	Yes
Mental health training available to students	No
Employs Chief Wellness Officer	NR
Peer-to-peer mental health offerings	NR
Counseling center has guidelines or accreditation	No
Mental health/well-being courses	NR

ACADEMICS

% students returning for sophomore year	91
% students graduating within 4 years	27
% students graduating within 6 years	81
Calendar	Semester
Student/faculty ratio	22:1
Most common class size 20–29.	(26%)

Most Popular Majors

Business/Commerce; Elementary Education and Teaching; Exercise Physiology

STUDENTS SAY "..."

Academics

Brigham Young University works with the Church of Jesus Christ of Latter-day Saints to provide undergraduates with a "very uplifting and spiritual" community. Students truly appreciate the school's focus on "character building" activities and "long-term service. Many undergrads also like that BYU has placed an equal emphasis "on being affordable." Of course, BYU's "greatest strength [just might be] the academic rigor of the university. Regardless of your department, you are guaranteed to get a strong education in your field." Indeed, there are "many great nationally regarded programs;" a few "that stand out are the accountancy and animation [departments]." No matter your course of study, "the workload at BYU is intense, and that is something one should be prepared for." Fortunately, professors "tend to be really encouraging and look to help students do the best they can." They truly "embody the values of the school and are inclusive and collaborative." It's also evident that most professors here "have a passion for what they teach which makes it easier to learn." As this satisfied undergrad exclaims, "BYU only hires the best!" Just as critical, undergrads can rest assured that they'll leave college ready for the real world. Students attribute this to having "fantastic internship opportunities" along with "many resources for getting hands-on experience" through experiential learning. This involves everything from conducting field research and attending symposiums to studying abroad and completing capstone projects.

Campus Life

Brigham Young University has close ties to the Church of Jesus Christ of Latter-day Saints, and there are consequently many faith-based extracurriculars. For example, "students attend church services all over campus for two hours each Sunday [and] many...participate in temple worship (a little more sacred than a regular church service)." Those looking for secular activities will find that "there are always lots of events and clubs and festive things going on around campus and the great thing is you don't have to be a member or anything to join in." These include everything from folk and ballroom dancing to volunteer service projects and marching band. Sports—including "the pickleball obsession...we all love to play"—are also quite popular. As one undergrad shares, "there are tons of intramurals that students join that are fun and competitive." In addition, there are "lots of outdoorsy activities such as hiking, Frisbee, [and] spikeball [along with a large] amount of board games and Harry Potter in the winter months." Students also like taking a break from campus life periodically. Stroll around downtown Provo and you're bound to spot some BYU undergrads attending "local community events such as farmer's markets or holiday activities."

Student Body

Many Brigham Young undergrads recognize that "the most obvious thing that's unique about BYU is the percentage of the student body that is a member of the Church of Jesus Christ of Latter-day Saints." As this undergrad explains, "BYU is very faith-based, so many of my peers hold strong religious opinions and motivations." This helps to establish "a common set of core values" among students and fosters "a genuinely fun, wholesome, and productive learning and social environment." Another classmate concurs: "The students are kind and outgoing, and they always strive for the highest level of excellence academically and spiritually." Some students disagree on the extent of the "predominantly white" community being "very loving and inclusive," with a few noting a "small but extremely vocal population of hyper-conservatism, and a relatively conservative majority who do not step in to protect the interests of the minorities." Others assert that "you can start a conversation with anyone, anywhere." As this undergrad concludes, "My peers are actually a huge inspiration to me. It's evident that everyone is doing their best to be a good person [and a] real contributor to society and it motivates me to try harder every day."

Brigham Young University (UT)

Financial Aid: 801-422-8153 • E-Mail: admissions@byu.edu • Website: www.byu.edu

THE PRINCETON REVIEW SAYS

Admissions

The school reports that its standardized testing policy for use in admission for Fall 2026 is Test Optional. The Princeton Review suggests that interested applicants consult with the school for the most up-to-date standardized testing policies. *Very important factors considered include:* rigor of secondary school record, academic GPA, standardized test scores, application essay, recommendation(s), extracurricular activities, talent/ability, character/personal qualities, religious affiliation/commitment, volunteer work, work experience. *Important factors considered include:* first generation. *Other factors considered include:* level of applicant's interest. High school diploma is required and GED is accepted. *Academic units recommended:* 4 English, 4 math, 3 science, 2 language (other than English), 2 history.

Financial Aid

Students should submit: FAFSA. Priority filing deadline is 2/1. The Princeton Review suggests that all financial aid forms be submitted as soon as possible. *Need-based scholarships/grants offered:* Federal Pell; Private scholarships; College/university scholarship or grant aid from institutional funds; State scholarships/grants. *Loan aid offered:* Federal Direct Subsidized Loans; Federal Direct Unsubsidized Loans; Direct PLUS loans; College/university loans from institutional funds. Admitted students will be notified of awards on a rolling basis beginning April 15th.

The Inside Word

Students at Brigham Young University tend to be a self-selecting bunch: approximately four-fifths of those who get accepted to the school end up attending. That dedication manifests in many ways throughout the application process, but admissions officers certainly appreciate seeing students who embrace LDS principles. That goes the other way too: the Church of Jesus Christ of Latter-day Saints supports BYU students by helping to subsidize tuition prices, so much so that—per the school—it's as if "each student attending BYU is on scholarship."

THE SCHOOL SAYS

From the Admissions Office

"The mission of Brigham Young University-founded, supported, and guided by The Church of Jesus Christ of Latter-day Saints—is to assist individuals in their quest for perfection and eternal life. That assistance should provide a period of intensive learning in a stimulating setting where a commitment to excellence is expected and the full realization of human potential is pursued. All instruction, programs, and services at BYU, including a wide variety of extracurricular experiences, should make their own contribution toward the balanced development of the total person. Such a broadly prepared individual will not only be capable of meeting personal challenge and change but will also bring strength to others in the tasks of home and family life, social relationships, civic duty, and service to mankind."

SELECTIVITY

# of total applicants	11,698
% of total applicants accepted	68
% of total acceptees attending	78
# of in-state applicants	4,306
% of in-state applicants accepted	71
# of out-of-state-applicants	7,185
% of applicants accepted from out of state	66
# of international applicants	207
% of international applicants accepted	59

First-Year Profile

Testing policy	Test Optional
Range SAT composite	1290–1370
Range SAT EBRW	650–720
Range SAT math	640–730
Range ACT composite	28–32
Average HS GPA	3.9
% submitting high school GPA	99
% graduated top 10% of class	55
% graduated top 25% of class	87
% graduated top 50% of class	99
% submitting high school rank	55

Important Dates

Regular	
Apply by	12/15
Notified by	2/19
Nonfall registration?	Yes

FINANCIAL FACTS

Annual tuition	$6,688
Food and housing	$10,396
Books and supplies	$392
Average need-based scholarship (First-year)	$7,024 ($3,832)
% students with need rec. need-based scholarship or grant aid (First-year)	76 (70)
% students with need rec. non-need-based scholarship or grant aid (First-year)	60 (28)
% students with need rec. need-based self-help aid (First-year)	17 (19)
% students rec. any financial aid (First-year)	43 (27)
% UG borrow to pay for school	18
Average cumulative indebtedness	$12,839
% of students with need fully met (First-year)	6 (0)
Average % of student need met (First-year)	41 (25)

Brown University

One Prospect Street, Providence, RI 02912 • Admissions: 401-863-2378

Survey Snapshot
Lots of liberal students
Students always studying
Students are happy

RATINGS

Quality of Life	89
Fire Safety	60*
Green	60*
Academic	93
Profs Interesting	95
Profs Accessible	95
Admissions	99
Financial Aid	96

CAMPUS LIFE

Type of school	Private
Environment	City

Students

Degree-seeking undergrad enrollment	7,196
% male/female/not reported	49/51/0
% from out of state	94
% First-year from public high school	55
% First-year live on campus	98
% Ugrads live on campus	75
# of fraternities (% join)	9 (3)
# of sororities (% join)	7 (3)
% Asian	24
% Black or African American	8
% Hispanic	12
% Native American	<1
% Pacific Islander	<1
% Race and/or ethnicity unknown	4
% Two or more races	8
% White	31
% International	13
# of countries represented	132

CAMPUS MENTAL HEALTH SERVICES

Offers mental health/wellness program	Yes
Mental health training available to students	Yes
Employs Chief Wellness Officer	Yes
Peer-to-peer mental health offerings	Yes
Counseling center has guidelines or accreditation	Yes
Mental health/well-being courses	No

ACADEMICS

% students returning for sophomore year	99
% students graduating within 4 years	75
% students graduating within 6 years	96
Calendar	Semester
Student/faculty ratio	8:1
Most common class size 1–9.	(34%)

Most Popular Majors

Biology/Biological Sciences, General; Applied Mathematics, General; Econometrics and Quantitative Economics

Applicants Also Look At

Columbia University, Cornell University, Dartmouth College, Duke University, Harvard College, Northwestern University, Princeton University, Stanford University, University of Pennsylvania, Yale University

STUDENTS SAY "..."

Academics

Interdisciplinary-focused Brown University, in Providence, Rhode Island, is dedicated to undergraduate freedom, meaning students must take responsibility for designing their own courses of study via the Open Curriculum. Students sing the praises of the academic flexibility at this Ivy League institution and the accompanying emphasis on social action. "We would not be...strong students and teachers without a proper system in place to encourage that," says one undergrad. Those who roam these hallowed halls are "constantly questioning what could make the world and our school a better place." Every person "has their own interests and pursues it without any push from others," which is why Brown can be a "very intense" place to go to school—not because students are competing academically with each other, but "because there are so many people doing so much and fighting so hard for it."

Brown's faculty "are at the top of their fields and are working on research that pushes those fields forward." The "engaging, personal, and incredibly dedicated" professors are "the heart and soul of our strongest departments." They "care so much about what they do and connect with students on a very human level." Undergraduates come first here, and Brown encourages students to "explore their academic interests independently in order to experience everything that academics have to offer." As one enrollee explains it, "No other school I had looked at allowed students to...build their own academic journey without any general requirements." Graduates tend to "not just go to the normative career options," and "career and internship placement has become a top priority of the new university administration."

Campus Life

Students describe a nice balance between work and play at Brown—academia rules during a week that is "filled with countless hours of study," but it's also an "exciting" and "very happy place with many activities and events going on all the time." Some go to parties or "downtown for the weekend," while others make the most of the constant "lectures, movie screenings, improv shows, dance performances, [and] a cappella showcases." Many here also do "intellectual activities or athletics over breaks," and "community clubs and special interest clubs (such as international student groups)" are extremely popular. Students also often go to the lounges in the dorms to watch movies with friends. And, "beautiful" as the campus is, students can easily walk one minute to Thayer Street and "enjoy restaurants and excellent dining" or walk 20 minutes to Providence Place Mall. Boston and New York are very close, but "Providence is busy enough that Brown never completely empties out."

Student Body

This "knowledgeable and inspiring" community is made up of people who are "very intelligent, care about global issues, and possess one or two quirks." The school "has a way of molding people into their best selves," and the most common trait is "a true zeal for whatever it is that we care most about." Although this is a liberal campus, there are "a handful of conservatives," and "the entire body has a general chilled-out vibe." As one student puts it, "I've never experienced so many people willing to have a conversation about topics that usually make people uncomfortable." There is "a prevailing intolerance of intolerance on campus," and the culture of activism "bespeaks an idealism and a strong moral code that drives a lot of the work students do on campus."

Brown University

Financial Aid: 401-863-2721 • E-Mail: admission@brown.edu • Website: www.brown.edu

THE PRINCETON REVIEW SAYS

Admissions

The school reports that its standardized testing policy for use in admission for Fall 2026 will require applicants to submit either the SAT or ACT. The Princeton Review suggests that interested applicants consult with the school for the most up-to-date standardized testing policies. *Very important factors considered include:* rigor of secondary school record, class rank, academic GPA, standardized test scores, application essay, recommendation(s), talent/ability, character/personal qualities. *Important factors considered include:* extracurricular activities. *Other factors considered include:* first generation, alumni/ae relation, geographical residence, state residency, volunteer work, work experience. High school diploma is required and GED is accepted. *Academic units required:* 4 English, 4 math, 3 science (including 2 lab science), 3 language (other than English), 2 history, 1 academic elective. *Academic units recommended:* 4 English, 4 math, 4 science (including 3 lab science), 4 language (other than English), 1 social studies, 3 history, 1 academic elective, 1 visual/performing arts.

Financial Aid

Students should submit: FAFSA, CSS PROFILE. Priority filing deadline is 2/1. The Princeton Review suggests that all financial aid forms be submitted as soon as possible. *Need-based scholarships/grants offered:* Federal Pell Grants; Federal SEOG; state scholarships/grants; private scholarships; college/university scholarships or grant aid from institutional funds. *Loan aid offered:* Federal Direct Subsidized Loans; Federal Direct Unsubsidized Loans; Federal Direct PLUS Loans. Federal Work-Study Program available. Institutional employment available.

The Inside Word

The cream of just about every crop applies to Brown, and admission is extremely competitive. Gaining admission requires more than just a superior academic profile from high school. Candidates from states that are overrepresented in the applicant pool, such as New York, have to be particularly distinguished in order to have the best chance at admission. Brown accepts the Common Application, with additional writing supplements for all firstyear students, and requires some additional statements from students who apply to the Program in Liberal Medical Education or the Dual Degree Program with Rhode Island School of Design.

THE SCHOOL SAYS

From the Admissions Office

"Brown University is the nation's seventh oldest institution and a member of the Ivy League. The University is known for its academic rigor rooted in its Open Curriculum. Brown has no distribution requirements that students must complete to graduate, which attracts self-motivated students committed to being the architects of their own education. Students like to say that only Brown offers absolute freedom to study what they love, and only what they love. Students are challenged by their own experiences, peers, and advisors to expand their notions of "what they love." Students sample a range of courses before immersing themselves in more than 80 academic concentrations, with the option of independent study. Brown offers unparalleled opportunities for research collaboration with faculty who lead in their fields; the best in educational innovation, and leading-edge scholarship; and opportunities for community-based service learning. This contributes to a reputation for graduating entrepreneurial, mission-oriented students who make an impact in their communities and the world. Brown prioritizes giving students the skills to successfully prepare for and navigate a lifetime of career opportunities. Brown has among the highest rates nationally of admission to law school and medical school, and graduates successfully begin careers in areas of science and engineering, the arts, policy, medicine and many other fields. The Warren Alpert Medical School and the Brown University School of Public Health are the only medical school and public health school in Rhode Island, offering medical training and leading research into therapies and cures and areas of population health."

SELECTIVITY

# of total applicants	42,774
% of total applicants accepted	6
% of total acceptees attending	63
# of in-state applicants	559
% of in-state applicants accepted	11
# of out-of-state-applicants	32,351
% of applicants accepted from out of state	7
# of international applicants	9,861
% of international applicants accepted	4
# of early decision applicants	5,062
% of early decision applicants accepted	18
# admitted from wait list	295

First-Year Profile

Testing policy	SAT or ACT Required
Range SAT composite	1470–1550
Range SAT EBRW	730–770
Range SAT math	730–790
Range ACT composite	33–35
% submitting SAT scores	77
% submitting ACT scores	28
% graduated top 10% of class	93
% graduated top 25% of class	98
% graduated top 50% of class	100
% submitting high school rank	29

Important Dates

Early decision	
Apply by	11/1
Notified by	12/15
Regular	
Apply by	1/5
Notified by	3/31
Nonfall registration?	No

FINANCIAL FACTS

Annual tuition	$74,568
Food and housing	$19,464
Required fees (First-year)	$2,850 ($3,084)
Average need-based scholarship (First-year)	$68,394 ($68,640)
% students with need rec. need-based scholarship or grant aid (First-year)	99 (98)
% students with need rec. non-need-based scholarship or grant aid (First-year)	0 (0)
% students with need rec. need-based self-help aid (First-year)	84 (80)
% students rec. any financial aid (First-year)	56 (61)
% UG borrow to pay for school	20
Average cumulative indebtedness	$36,263
% of students with need fully met (First-year)	100 (100)
Average % of student need met (First-year)	100 (100)

BRYANT UNIVERSITY

1150 Douglas Pike, Smithfield, RI 02917 • Admissions: 401-232-6100

Survey Snapshot
Internships are widely available
Students are happy
Great library

RATINGS

Quality of Life	**91**
Fire Safety	**89**
Green	**89**
Academic	**82**
Profs Interesting	**93**
Profs Accessible	**95**
Admissions	**86**
Financial Aid	**90**

CAMPUS LIFE

Type of school	Private
Environment	Village

Students

Degree-seeking undergrad enrollment	3,503
% male/female/not reported	64/36/0
% from out of state	84
% First-year from public high school	76
% First-year live on campus	90
% Ugrads live on campus	84
# of fraternities (% join)	3 (7)
# of sororities (% join)	4 (10)
% Asian	4
% Black or African American	5
% Hispanic	10
% Native American	<1
% Pacific Islander	<1
% Race and/or ethnicity unknown	1
% Two or more races	2
% White	72
% International	5
# of countries represented	50

CAMPUS MENTAL HEALTH SERVICES

Offers mental health/wellness program	Yes
Mental health training available to students	Yes
Employs Chief Wellness Officer	Yes
Peer-to-peer mental health offerings	No
Counseling center has guidelines or accreditation	No
Mental health/well-being courses	No

ACADEMICS

% students returning for sophomore year	85
% students graduating within 4 years	78
% students graduating within 6 years	81
Calendar	Semester
Student/faculty ratio	14:1
Most common class size 30–39.	(42%)
Most common lab/discussion size 10–19.	(46%)

Most Popular Majors

Accounting; Finance; Marketing/Marketing Management

Applicants Often Prefer

Babson College, Bentley University, Boston College, Boston University, University of Connecticut, University of Massachusetts—Amherst

Applicants Sometimes Prefer

Fairfield University, Fordham University, Loyola University Maryland, Marist University, Northeastern University, Providence College, University of Vermont

Applicants Rarely Prefer

Assumption University, Merrimack College, Quinnipiac University, Roger Williams University, Sacred Heart University, Saint Joseph's University (PA), Stonehill College, Suffolk University, University of New Hampshire, University of Rhode Island

STUDENTS SAY "..."

Academics

At Bryant University in Rhode Island, learning doesn't happen in silos. The school brings together business, humanities and social science, and health and behavioral sciences in ways that encourage students to "think dynamically." That mix of disciplines—paired with plenty of real-world experience—is what many say makes Bryant stand out. "The school truly prepares us for business and leadership," one student explains, while another notes, "It is very hard to not get a job within six months of graduating." Part of the reason for this is that the school "excels in its ability to provide hands-on academic experiences." The first-year Bryant IDEA Program, for example, is "a three-day intensive program that teaches design thinking" to solve real-world problems. Students can also take part in experiences like Walk on Wall Street, semester-long study abroad, or short-term faculty-led study abroad trips tied to academic courses. Overall, students describe an "academic experience...focused on learning rather than getting a grade" and where everyone is "very willing to offer extra help when it is needed," making it "hard [for a student] to fall through the cracks." Many of the faculty are "professionals in their industry" who "bring great insight into various industries" and "apply their real-world experience" to the classroom. While some students express mixed feelings about the professors, for the most part, the professors are "super friendly, accessible, and encourage discussion both inside and outside of the classroom." One student shares, "I feel incredibly supported by my professors and they continuously push me to be my best self." And for many, the academics, career resources, and industry connections offered by the university pay off. As one student declares, "The ROI for Bryant is one of the best, and I know I will be set up for a successful career after graduation."

Campus Life

On this "very busy" campus, "there's almost always some event going on where you can get free food, play games, get free stuff, or watch a performance." Bryant Bulldogs "tend to fill the days with different club meetings, classes, study sessions, spending time with friends, and attending different events on campus." And there are intramural sports, clubs, and organizations for nearly every interest. Many students are "very involved on campus...[and] have multiple extracurriculars," which one student says, "have introduced me to a new group of people and exposed me to new ways of thinking." When the weather is nice, students like to "sit and do homework by the pond." The student programming board hosts events "almost every weekend, starting on Thursday and going until Sunday, so there is rarely a boring moment." Off campus, students "enjoy exploring downtown Providence" for its restaurants, nightlife, and shopping. Overall, students find the campus "extremely welcoming" and say that Bryant has the "perfect balance of academics, recreation, and extracurricular activities."

Student Body

"The Bryant community is very tight knit and helps make you feel at home on campus." The student body is often described as "motivated, hardworking, kind, fun," and diverse "in terms of background and occupational interest." They "offer a wide array of perspectives on the world," while remaining "one big community." One undergrad shares, "I have been able to meet some of the best people during my time at Bryant." Undergrads are "driven to succeed in their careers after college," and "almost everyone who can is employed in a summer internship." In general, students are "very involved and very competitive," but are also supportive of one another and "push each other to be better." The result is a campus teeming with "different types of leaders who are each striving for their individual goals but are also devoted to maintaining a strong, cohesive student body." One student adds, "If entrepreneurship was [a] person, it would be a Bryant student."

Bryant University

Financial Aid: 401-232-6020 • E-Mail: admission@bryant.edu • Website: www.bryant.edu

THE PRINCETON REVIEW SAYS

Admissions

The school reports that its standardized testing policy for use in admission for Fall 2026 is Test Optional. The Princeton Review suggests that interested applicants consult with the school for the most up-to-date standardized testing policies. *Very important factors considered include:* rigor of secondary school record, academic GPA, application essay, recommendation(s). *Important factors considered include:* class rank, standardized test scores. *Other factors considered include:* interview, extracurricular activities, talent/ability, character/personal qualities, first generation, alumni/ae relation, geographical residence, state residency, volunteer work, work experience, level of applicant's interest. High school diploma is required and GED is accepted. *Academic units required:* 2 English, 4 math, 2 science, 2 science labs, 2 language (other than English), 2 social studies. *Academic units recommended:* 4 English, 4 math, 3 science, 2 science labs, 2 language (other than English), 3 social studies.

Financial Aid

Students should submit: FAFSA. Priority filing deadline is 2/1. The Princeton Review suggests that all financial aid forms be submitted as soon as possible. *Need-based scholarships/grants offered:* Federal Pell; Federal SEOG; State scholarships/grants; Private scholarships; College/university scholarship or grant aid from institutional funds. *Loan aid offered:* Federal Direct Subsidized Loans; Federal Direct Unsubsidized Loans; Direct PLUS loans; State Loans. Admitted students will be notified of awards on or about 3/15. Federal Work-Study Program available. Institutional employment available.

The Inside Word

The admissions process at Bryant University is wholly comprehensive. To begin, the school wants students who have taken a challenging college prep curriculum (including honors, AP, and IB courses when possible). Of course, letters of recommendation and extracurricular involvement are also important. Applicants wary of standardized tests will be delighted to learn that Bryant is a Test Optional school.

THE SCHOOL SAYS

From the Admissions Office

"To be a Bryant Bulldog is to be in—in demand, in the room, and in the know. You'll be immersed in hands-on experiences from day one, and a solid foundation of design thinking and AI will prepare you to solve complex problems, innovate, and lead. At Bryant, you'll work together with peers, faculty, and industry partners, turning challenges into opportunities to go farther than you ever imagined. Our graduates are consistently ranked in the top 1% for career outcomes, which proves the long-term value of a Bryant degree. Bryant is a national leader in return on higher education investment, delivering exceptional earnings potential and economic mobility outcomes. According to the newly released Georgetown University Center on Education and the Workforce scorecard, Bryant ranks in the top 1% of 4,600 schools nationwide for a 40-year return on investment. In addition, 98% of our alumni are employed or in graduate school within six months of graduation with a median starting salary of $77,000.

"As a Bulldog, you'll be part of a close-knit community of over 3,600 students from nearly 40 states and 40 countries. Our campus is buzzing with energy—it's where you'll cheer on Division I teams, make discoveries in state-of-the-art labs, and have meaningful conversations inside and outside of class. Collaboration is at the heart of everything we do, and when you're ready to branch out, Providence, Boston, and New York City are nearby, offering endless opportunities for internships, culture, and exploration.

"And here's the best part: being a Bryant Bulldog sets you up for a lifetime of success. With the support of dedicated faculty mentors and a strong alumni network, you'll leave here ready to lead, make an impact, and achieve your goals.

"This is your in."

SELECTIVITY

# of total applicants	9,606
% of total applicants accepted	65
% of total acceptees attending	17
# of in-state applicants	940
% of in-state applicants accepted	71
# of out-of-state-applicants	7,859
% of applicants accepted from out of state	65
# of international applicants	807
% of international applicants accepted	59
# of early decision applicants	NR
% of early decision applicants accepted	NR
# offered a place on the wait list	343
# admitted from wait list	9

First-Year Profile

Testing policy	Test Optional
Range SAT composite	1190–1330
Range SAT EBRW	590–660
Range SAT math	590–670
Range ACT composite	25–32
% submitting SAT scores	10
% submitting ACT scores	1
Average HS GPA	3.5
% submitting high school GPA	100
% graduated top 10% of class	19
% graduated top 25% of class	47
% graduated top 50% of class	84
% submitting high school rank	26

Important Dates

Early decision	
Apply by	11/1
Notified by	12/8
Other ED apply by	1/15
Other ED notified by	2/15
Early action	
Apply by	11/15
Notified by	1/15
Regular	
Apply by	2/1
Notified by	3/15
Nonfall registration?	Yes

FINANCIAL FACTS

Annual tuition	$54,934
Food and housing	$19,004
Required fees	$1,304
Books and supplies	$1,200
Average need-based scholarship (First-year)	$11,472 ($26,354)
% students with need rec. need-based scholarship or grant aid (First-year)	100 (100)
% students with need rec. non-need-based scholarship or grant aid (First-year)	24 (28)
% students with need rec. need-based self-help aid (First-year)	92 (88)
% UG borrow to pay for school	30
Average cumulative indebtedness	$68,886
% of students with need fully met (First-year)	28 (31)
Average % of student need met (First-year)	22 (73)

Bryn Mawr College

101 N. Merion Avenue, Bryn Mawr, PA 19010-2899 • Admissions: 610-526-5152

Survey Snapshot
Active student government
Active minority support groups
Great library

RATINGS

Quality of Life	89
Fire Safety	82
Green	88
Academic	91
Profs Interesting	94
Profs Accessible	94
Admissions	94
Financial Aid	98

CAMPUS LIFE

Type of school	Private
Environment	Metropolis

Students

Degree-seeking undergrad enrollment	1,363
% male/female/not reported	0/100/0
% from out of state	88
% First-year from public high school	54
% First-year live on campus	100
% Ugrads live on campus	90
# of sororities	0
% Asian	12
% Black or African American	5
% Hispanic	9
% Native American	<1
% Pacific Islander	<1
% Race and/or ethnicity unknown	4
% Two or more races	7
% White	51
% International	13
# of countries represented	44

CAMPUS MENTAL HEALTH SERVICES

Offers mental health/wellness program	Yes
Mental health training available to students	No
Employs Chief Wellness Officer	NR
Peer-to-peer mental health offerings	NR
Counseling center has guidelines or accreditation	No
Mental health/well-being courses	NR

ACADEMICS

% students returning for sophomore year	92
% students graduating within 4 years	88
% students graduating within 6 years	82
Calendar	Semester
Student/faculty ratio	8:1
Most common class size 10–19.	(47%)

Most Popular Majors

Mathematics; Psychology; English Language and Literature

Applicants Also Look At

Barnard College, Boston University, Brown University, Haverford College, Mount Holyoke College, Smith College, Swarthmore College, The University of Chicago, Wellesley College, Wesleyan University

STUDENTS SAY "..."

Academics

Bryn Mawr College, one of the Seven Sisters, is "a prestigious" institution "where you will work harder than you thought was possible, you'll learn more than you've ever learned before, and you'll feel...welcomed every step of the way." Mawrters are part of a "very inclusive and...empowering" sisterhood, one that's "collaborative rather than competitive." Although the college is "academically rigorous," it provides "the support [students] need to meet these high standards." This includes access to the Tri-Co and Quaker Consortium, through which students can take classes at schools like Haverford and UPenn. It also means that Bryn Mawr itself is able to keep its class sizes small, and when "a majority of [your] classes are 20 people or less...you really get to know your peers and your professors/advisors." That's even more of a positive, given that most teachers are described as "enthusiastic, knowledgeable...and very invested in their students' learning." Another student agrees, noting, "Every professor I've had has been more than willing to help me when I need help understanding something or need an accommodation on an assignment." They also "encourage you to share your opinion in class and contribute to the content of the discussion." That's a rewarding experience that helps students graduate ahead of the game: "I have very much benefited from this level of rigor."

Campus Life

Bryn Mawr students are a diligent lot. Therefore, it's common for undergrads here to "spend a lot of time studying and working either at on-campus or off-campus jobs." Despite their busy schedules, they still manage to find time for extracurriculars, and the wide range of them, "from equestrian to knitting to anime," means there's truly something for everyone. For instance, "a cappella groups are very big on campus [and] a lot of students are involved with student government." Additionally, "the student activities office plans a lot of events," such as movie screenings, tie-dye parties, concerts, pumpkin decorating, and more. Even the school president gets in on the action by hosting "'Presidential PopUps' where they will bring in, say, an ice cream truck, and everyone gets free ice cream." Students say that "partying does happen, but you have to seek it out," as it's generally not on campus. As a result, when the weekend rolls around, students often head to "Philadelphia for dinner and nightlife since it is so close" and note that "the surrounding towns have fabulous restaurants as well, so good dining options are never in short supply." In short, the vibe is that "everyone ends up involving themselves in multiple clubs or projects. It's hectic sometimes but fun."

Student Body

Bryn Mawr attracts "brilliantly smart...and intensely academic" students who are deeply curious about the world around them. Indeed, "not a day goes by that I don't overhear a conversation about current events, politics, or other scholarly topics in the dining hall." Fortunately, there are "not many people here who have an 'I am smarter than you' attitude." In fact, students report that their classmates are "extraordinarily friendly and welcoming, especially to first-years." One undergrad says, "Whether you're dressed from an L.L. Bean catalog or you prefer cosplay in daily life, everyone is welcome and celebrated and part of this place." Many Mawrters also appreciate the diversity among their peers, particularly regarding gender identity, noting that you'll find "many queer and gender non-conforming students." Additionally, a number of students identify as "staunch feminists" and "are very into social justice." As this undergrad explains, "People care deeply about issues and strive toward making the world a better place." Ultimately, Mawrters are a close-knit community where "each student strives to be their very best while making sure every person around them also succeeds."

BRYN MAWR COLLEGE

Financial Aid: 610-526-5245 • E-Mail: admissions@brynmawr.edu • Website: www.brynmawr.edu

THE PRINCETON REVIEW SAYS

Admissions

The school reports that its standardized testing policy for use in admission for Fall 2026 is Test Optional. The Princeton Review suggests that interested applicants consult with the school for the most up-to-date standardized testing policies. *Very important factors considered include:* rigor of secondary school record, class rank, application essay, recommendation(s). *Important factors considered include:* academic GPA, interview, extracurricular activities, character/personal qualities. *Other factors considered include:* standardized test scores, talent/ability, first generation, geographical residence, state residency, volunteer work, work experience. High school diploma is required and GED is accepted. *Academic units recommended:* 4 English, 4 math, 4 science, 1 science lab, 4 language (other than English), 2 social studies, 2 history, 2 computer science.

Financial Aid

Students should submit: FAFSA; CSS PROFILE. The Princeton Review suggests that all financial aid forms be submitted as soon as possible. *Need-based scholarships/grants offered:* Federal Pell; Federal SEOG; College/university scholarship or grant aid from institutional funds. *Loan aid offered:* Federal Direct Subsidized Loans; Direct PLUS loans. Federal Work-Study Program available. Institutional employment available.

The Inside Word

Bryn Mawr College is very competitive and applicants need to find a way to stand out from the crowd. In addition to submitting the Common Application, incoming first-year students should check the school's website for all additional requirements, such as writing supplements, a mid-year report, and other items. While not required, students are also encouraged to interview with an alum or admissions officer.

THE SCHOOL SAYS

From the Admissions Office

"Bryn Mawr, a selective women's college with 1,402 undergraduates, is renowned for its academic excellence, diverse and close-knit community, and engagement with the world.

"On an historic campus just outside of Philadelphia, Bryn Mawr students find challenging courses and research; strong bonds with faculty, students, and alumnae/i; innovative programs that connect study with action; and top-tier partnerships that expand options.

"Critical, creative, and collaborative, Bryn Mawr alumnae/i are agents of change in every arena—and forever members of a community founded on respect for individuals.

"Minutes outside of Philadelphia and only two hours by train from New York City and Washington, D.C., Bryn Mawr is recognized by many as one of the most stunning college campuses in the United States.

"Standardized test scores for U.S. applicants or U.S. permanent residents are not required. Non-U.S. citizens and Non-U.S. permanent residents are required to submit standardized test scores (SAT or ACT) as well as either the TOEFL or IELTS if their primary language is not English and/or their language of instruction over the last four years has not been English."

SELECTIVITY

# of total applicants	4,094
% of total applicants accepted	29
% of total acceptees attending	32
# of in-state applicants	396
% of in-state applicants accepted	27
# of out-of-state-applicants	2,423
% of applicants accepted from out of state	40
# of international applicants	1,275
% of international applicants accepted	9
# of early decision applicants	456
% of early decision applicants accepted	37
# offered a place on the wait list	494
# admitted from wait list	23

First-Year Profile

Testing policy	Test Optional
Range SAT composite	1290–1490
Range SAT EBRW	660–750
Range SAT math	620–760
Range ACT composite	29–33
% submitting SAT scores	64
% submitting ACT scores	21
% graduated top 10% of class	66
% graduated top 25% of class	93
% graduated top 50% of class	100
% submitting high school rank	20

Important Dates

Early decision	
Apply by	11/15
Notified by	1/1
Regular	
Apply by	1/15
Notified by	4/1

FINANCIAL FACTS

Annual tuition	$61,190
Food and housing	$18,690
Required fees	$970
Books and supplies	$1,000
Average need-based scholarship (First-year)	$59,201 ($60,057)
% students with need rec. need-based scholarship or grant aid (First-year)	98 (100)
% students with need rec. non-need-based scholarship or grant aid (First-year)	82 (30)
% students with need rec. need-based self-help aid (First-year)	98 (80)
% students rec. any financial aid (First-year)	74 (72)
% UG borrow to pay for school	44
Average cumulative indebtedness	$27,434
% of students with need fully met (First-year)	100 (100)
Average % of student need met (First-year)	100 (100)

Bucknell University

1 Dent Drive, Lewisburg, PA 17837 • Admissions: 570-577-3000

Survey Snapshot
Intramural sports are popular
Frats and sororities are popular
Alumni active on campus

RATINGS

Quality of Life	**82**
Fire Safety	**92**
Green	**93**
Academic	**90**
Profs Interesting	**93**
Profs Accessible	**94**
Admissions	**93**
Financial Aid	**89**

CAMPUS LIFE

Type of school	Private
Environment	Village

Students

Degree-seeking undergrad enrollment	3,888
% male/female/not reported	48/52/<1
% from out of state	78
% First-year from public high school	59
% First-year live on campus	100
% Ugrads live on campus	88
# of fraternities (% join)	7 (30)
# of sororities (% join)	9 (45)
% Asian	4
% Black or African American	4
% Hispanic	10
% Native American	<1
% Pacific Islander	<1
% Race and/or ethnicity unknown	<1
% Two or more races	4
% White	73
% International	4
# of countries represented	50

CAMPUS MENTAL HEALTH SERVICES

Offers mental health/wellness program	Yes
Mental health training available to students	Yes
Employs Chief Wellness Officer	Yes
Peer-to-peer mental health offerings	NR
Counseling center has guidelines or accreditation	Yes
Mental health/well-being courses	Yes, non-credit

ACADEMICS

% students returning for sophomore year	91
% students graduating within 4 years	80
% students graduating within 6 years	85
Calendar	Semester
Student/faculty ratio	9:1
Most common class size 10–19.	(41%)
Most common lab/discussion size 10–19.	(54%)

Most Popular Majors
Psychology; Economics; Biology

Applicants Often Prefer
Cornell University, Dartmouth College, Tufts University, University of Pennsylvania, University of Virginia

Applicants Sometimes Prefer
Boston College, Colgate University, Lehigh University, University of Richmond, Wake Forest University

Applicants Rarely Prefer
Elon University, Lafayette College, Northeastern University, Penn State University Park, Villanova University

STUDENTS SAY "..."

Academics

To students, Bucknell University is a Goldilocks school: not too big or small, but "just right." The 445-acre campus is glowingly, goldenly described as well: "A beautiful campus...the sunset is unbeatable and the buildings are so technologically advanced." Curiosity is a pillar of learning at Bucknell, where the administration "ensure[s] a well-rounded education with experiential learning." Enrollees are welcome "to study far beyond my chosen major" in all three schools—such that biomedical engineers note their work with orthopedic surgeons on device prototypes; Markets, Innovation & Design students examine sustainability for renovations on campus; and management students treat $3 million of Bucknell's endowment like their own investment company. All this "simulates a real-life work environment while also being centered around serving the Lewisburg community."

Bucknell professors are "all leaders in their field," and devote time to share their expertise: "[They] are very dedicated and willing to engage with students...on an academic level or just grabbing a coffee to chat." The student-teacher ratio sets the bar for dynamic discussion in small classes, as one observes, "Get[ting] to know my professors personally... makes me more likely to ask questions." Even with all the attention, students still feel they are allowed the autonomy to learn and make mistakes. They rise to the challenges of "academically rigorous" and "truly stellar" instruction, which fuels the inquisitive mind: "Everyday class life has proved to keep me motivated and constantly trying to learn in different disciplines."

Campus Life

The vibrant campus life at Bucknell "has the perfect balance of challenging academics and a plethora of fun activities [with which] to let off steam." There are weekly events: arts and entertainment with concerts and gallery shows; others advance education and careers with guest speakers who are often alumni, a network that "genuinely wants to help out the community that helped them." Students embrace the cooperative spirit with their "highly involved" leadership and outreach. Many are "committed to making change," with "amazing research opportunities" starting their first year, like Bucknell's chapter of "e-NABLE," where students rev up MakerSpace's 3-D printer to fabricate upper limb prosthetics for those in need, and in turn see "a great chance to support and get to know the local community."

On the weekend, students kick back with a movie, break a sweat on a hike, or venture off the quad to "let loose" outside of campus. Many partake in Super Saturday, "an all-day party hosted by the fraternities where everyone is welcome." Bucknellians can "easily walk downtown" for the restaurant and bar scene or go kayaking and biking. Whatever the interest, group camaraderie abounds: "There is always someone who will happily join you."

Student Body

Students at Bucknell work together in a wide variety of ways to study, improve the school, and advance their "collaborative living and learning environment." The collegiate atmosphere, described as "extremely supportive and smart, but not overly competitive," motivates students—"I feel compelled by my peers to work hard"—and the many study groups help to keep "an emphasis on teamwork."

Students also "prioritize health," which means many can be found together on the field, from gym workouts to Division I sports. "Many of my peers are athletes," notes a student; a few have even gone on to become Olympians. A "work hard, play hard" mantra also cultivates a "strong community bond" among students that explains why diversity and equity are so important to students. One student has already taken notice: "I feel...the student body became more diverse...from the time I was a freshman to a senior." Regardless of similarities and differences, Bucknellians are confident about what unites them, declaring, "[We] all share the same goal: to learn."

BUCKNELL UNIVERSITY

Financial Aid: 570-577-1331 • E-Mail: admissions@bucknell.edu • Website: www.bucknell.edu

THE PRINCETON REVIEW SAYS

Admissions

The school reports that its standardized testing policy for use in admission for Fall 2026 is Test Optional. The Princeton Review suggests that interested applicants consult with the school for the most up-to-date standardized testing policies. *Very important factors considered include:* rigor of secondary school record, academic GPA, application essay, extracurricular activities, talent/ability, character/personal qualities. *Important factors considered include:* standardized test scores, recommendation(s), volunteer work, work experience. *Other factors considered include:* class rank, first generation, alumni/ae relation, geographical residence, religious affiliation/commitment, level of applicant's interest. High school diploma is required and GED is accepted. *Academic units required:* 4 English, 3 math, 3 science, 2 language (other than English), 3 social studies, 3 history. *Academic units recommended:* 4 English, 4 math, 4 science, 2 science labs, 4 language (other than English), 2 social studies, 2 history, 1 academic elective.

Financial Aid

Students should submit: FAFSA. Priority filing deadline is 11/15. The Princeton Review suggests that all financial aid forms be submitted as soon as possible. *Need-based scholarships/grants offered:* Federal Pell; Federal SEOG; State scholarships/grants; Private scholarships; College/university scholarship or grant aid from institutional funds. *Loan aid offered:* Federal Direct Subsidized Loans; Federal Direct Unsubsidized Loans; Direct PLUS loans. Admitted students will be notified of awards on or about 12/15 ED; 2/15 ED2, 3/15 RD. Federal Work-Study Program available. Institutional employment available.

The Inside Word

A well-rounded, extremely polished application is non-negotiable for the hopeful Bucknell applicant, as the school gets more competitive every year. Admissions officers strive to consider all facets of the applications they receive—essays, recommendations, transcripts, test scores—so make sure you consider all of them carefully. In particular, the admission committee is looking for applicants who can demonstrate how they are bold, thoughtful, and compassionate leaders. Bucknell accepts the Common Application.

THE SCHOOL SAYS

From the Admissions Office

"Bucknell University offers more than 60 majors and 70 minors in the College of Arts & Sciences, College of Engineering and Freeman College of Management. Your professors will be mentors and innovators in their fields who will challenge you to think critically, develop your ideas thoughtfully and apply what you learn. Bucknell is a residential university, so most students live on campus, but learning, service, research and recreation extend off campus. You will have the opportunity to volunteer as close as the local nursing home, community center and sustainable farm, and as far away as New Orleans and Nicaragua. Every year, students also travel off campus to conduct research with faculty mentors. Destinations have included Alaska, Suriname and Australia.

"At Bucknell, you'll take advantage of career services such as advising, networking, mock interviews and employer fairs. You can explore your career options and network with alumni through summer internships with corporations, government organizations and nonprofits locally, nationally and internationally. An externship program provides job-shadowing opportunities for sophomores.

"With its green spaces, brick buildings and striking vistas, Bucknell's 450-acre campus is a quintessential college environment in the heart of scenic central Pennsylvania. The restaurants and shops of downtown Lewisburg—including the Barnes & Noble at Bucknell University and the historic Campus Theatre—lie within walking distance of campus. The University is located within three- to four-hours' driving distance of Baltimore, New York City, Philadelphia, Pittsburgh and Washington, D.C."

SELECTIVITY

# of total applicants	11,561
% of total applicants accepted	32
% of total acceptees attending	28
# of in-state applicants	2,044
% of in-state applicants accepted	37
# of out-of-state-applicants	6,884
% of applicants accepted from out of state	41
# of international applicants	2,631
% of international applicants accepted	6
# of early decision applicants	1,200
% of early decision applicants accepted	55
# offered a place on the wait list	2,908
# admitted from wait list	150

First-Year Profile

Testing policy	Test Optional
Range SAT composite	1170–1360
Range SAT EBRW	590–690
Range SAT math	570–680
Range ACT composite	25–32
% submitting SAT scores	68
% submitting ACT scores	18
Average HS GPA	3.6
% submitting high school GPA	100
% graduated top 10% of class	56
% graduated top 25% of class	85
% graduated top 50% of class	98
% submitting high school rank	18

Important Dates

Early decision	
Apply by	11/1
Notified by	12/15
Other ED apply by	1/10
Other ED notified by	2/15
Regular	
Apply by	1/15
Notified by	4/1
Nonfall registration?	No

FINANCIAL FACTS

Annual tuition	$72,600
Food and housing	$18,380
Required fees	$900
Books and supplies	$900
Average need-based scholarship (First-year)	$49,313 ($51,981)
% students with need rec. need-based scholarship or grant aid (First-year)	96 (98)
% students with need rec. non-need-based scholarship or grant aid (First-year)	12 (21)
% students with need rec. need-based self-help aid (First-year)	70 (60)
% students rec. any financial aid (First-year)	64 (67)
% UG borrow to pay for school	44
Average cumulative indebtedness	$43,060
% of students with need fully met (First-year)	25 (29)
Average % of student need met (First-year)	89 (93)

Butler University

4600 Sunset Avenue, Indianapolis, IN 46208 • Admissions: 317-940-8100

Survey Snapshot
Everyone loves the Bulldogs
Frats and sororities are popular
Recreation facilities are great

RATINGS

Quality of Life	**85**
Fire Safety	**90**
Green	**96**
Academic	**84**
Profs Interesting	**92**
Profs Accessible	**95**
Admissions	**87**
Financial Aid	**86**

CAMPUS LIFE

Type of school	Private
Environment	Metropolis

Students

Degree-seeking undergrad enrollment	4,367
% male/female/not reported	39/61/0
% from out of state	46
% First-year from public high school	72
% First-year live on campus	86
% Ugrads live on campus	66
# of fraternities (% join)	11 (25)
# of sororities (% join)	11 (31)
% Asian	4
% Black or African American	6
% Hispanic	8
% Native American	<1
% Pacific Islander	0
% Race and/or ethnicity unknown	1
% Two or more races	4
% White	75
% International	2
# of countries represented	41

CAMPUS MENTAL HEALTH SERVICES

Offers mental health/wellness program	Yes
Mental health training available to students	Yes
Employs Chief Wellness Officer	Yes
Peer-to-peer mental health offerings	Yes
Counseling center has guidelines or accreditation	Yes
Mental health/well-being courses	No

ACADEMICS

% students returning for sophomore year	85
% students graduating within 4 years	69
% students graduating within 6 years	77
Calendar	Semester
Student/faculty ratio	11:1
Most common class size 20–29.	(39%)
Most common lab/discussion size 10–19.	(50%)

Most Popular Majors

Psychology; Finance; Marketing/Marketing Management

Applicants Also Look At

Ball State University, Indiana University—Bloomington, Indiana University—Indianapolis, Ivy Tech State College—Indianapolis, Marquette University, Miami University, Michigan State University, Purdue University—West Lafayette, University of Cincinnati, University of Illinois at Urbana—Champaign, University of Iowa

STUDENTS SAY "..."

Academics

Centrally located in the heart of Indianapolis, Butler University combines city living with a personalized academic experience. Offering "a large mix of majors and minors," the university does a "great job at providing connections and opportunities from undergraduate research...to outstanding internships." Butler's academic excellence can also be seen in programs like Dance, Pharmacy, and Business that are "extremely well done and nationally known." Across departments, many enrollees agree that the school "goes above and beyond to promote an outstanding environment of learning and growing for its students." Undergrads tout the benefits of small classes and a low student-to-faculty ratio, which "create[s] the perfect atmosphere to get one-on-one time with professors" and "develop a greater understanding of the material."

The hands-on educational experience is made more valuable by the "high quality of academic faculty," especially those who "are passionate and have a genuine interest in students' learning." As one enrollee notes, "Professors at Butler care about who you are as a person, not just [as] a student." The "attentive and engaging" faculty "make learning fun" while also being ever-ready to "help a student out and give them support both academically and personally. With "ample opportunity to work with the professors and get great experience for grad school," many enrollees find that the university provides a "high level of education" that they were looking for.

Campus Life

Many students, affectionately known as Bulldogs, consider Butler's 300-acre campus to be "very beautiful, which makes it enjoyable to be outside when the weather is nice." A variety of extracurricular options, including "hundreds of clubs as well as Greek life [helps] keep the whole campus united." In fact, Greek life tops the charts as a "fun way to meet new people and get one's mind off school." Bulldogs also "enjoy participating in intramural sports" and mention that "it's a huge part of Butler culture to attend basketball games." In addition to all of the campus activities, undergrads are all involved with the local community via the university's unique "'Indianapolis Community Requirement' that has students take one class connecting them with the Indianapolis area and often centers around community service." One undergrad sums it up nicely, saying, "everyone is involved in something,"

At Butler, you get the best of both worlds with "great access to a big city while still being far away enough to not be fully encompassed by [it]." Students agree that "Indianapolis itself is very cool to explore," and specifically note enjoying the nice restaurants and gardens, as well as "going to Broad Ripple (a small trendy area of town)." Additionally, "downtown Indy and the river walk are also very common spots on the weekends for students to go and hangout at or visit." As one student puts it, "being so close to Indy gives you a lot of opportunities for fun."

Student Body

Butler's student population continues to emit Hoosier Hospitality. If any student is ever in need of help, they always have someone to go to. The majority of students agree, describing the university as a "very tight knit community," with one person expressing, "Butler students are very friendly," and "[it's] easier to find a kind student at Butler than an unkind one." In terms of diversity, while some find the student body to be "overwhelming majority white," others feel that "Butler is making an effort to [create] an inclusive and diverse environment." As one student puts it, "Although there are many different political beliefs and divides, my peers all come together to celebrate our school and our community." At Butler, "everyone does a great job of making sure people fit in." That's in large part due to what respondents describe as "Hoosier Hospitality," in that "if any student is ever in need of help, they always have someone to go to."

Butler University

Financial Aid: 317-940-8200 • E-Mail: admission@butler.edu • Website: www.butler.edu

THE PRINCETON REVIEW SAYS

Admissions

The school reports that its standardized testing policy for use in admission for Fall 2026 is Test Optional. The Princeton Review suggests that interested applicants consult with the school for the most up-to-date standardized testing policies. *Very important factors considered include:* rigor of secondary school record, academic GPA, standardized test scores. *Important factors considered include:* application essay, extracurricular activities. *Other factors considered include:* class rank, recommendation(s), talent/ability, character/personal qualities, first generation, volunteer work, work experience, level of applicant's interest. High school diploma is required and GED is accepted. *Academic units required:* 4 English, 3 math, 3 science, 2 social studies. *Academic units recommended:* 2 language (other than English).

Financial Aid

Students should submit: FAFSA. Priority filing deadline is 12/1. The Princeton Review suggests that all financial aid forms be submitted as soon as possible. *Need-based scholarships/grants offered:* Federal Pell; Federal SEOG; State scholarships/grants; Private scholarships; College/university scholarship or grant aid from institutional funds. *Loan aid offered:* Federal Direct Subsidized Loans; Federal Direct Unsubsidized Loans; Direct PLUS loans. Admitted students will be notified of awards on a rolling basis beginning 2/1. Federal Work-Study Program available. Institutional employment available.

The Inside Word

Butler tries to make the application process as easy as possible by allowing potential undergrads to apply via the Common App. Supplemental requirements vary based on if you're a first-year applicant, transfer student, or international student, so make sure you double check the applicable required and optional checklists provided by the university. Additionally, when it comes to test scores, you get to choose whether you apply with or without test scores. Ultimately, the admissions department seeks applicants who are accomplished in their academics, involved in their school or community, and are ambitious about their future endeavors.

SELECTIVITY

# of total applicants	11,139
% of total applicants accepted	82
% of total acceptees attending	14
# of in-state applicants	5,481
% of in-state applicants accepted	78
# of out-of-state-applicants	5,255
% of applicants accepted from out of state	89
# of international applicants	403
% of international applicants accepted	46
# of early decision applicants	20
% of early decision applicants accepted	85
# offered a place on the wait list	0
# admitted from wait list	0

First-Year Profile

Testing policy	Test Optional
Range SAT composite	1160–1330
Range SAT EBRW	590–680
Range SAT math	570–660
Range ACT composite	26–31
% submitting SAT scores	38
% submitting ACT scores	14
Average HS GPA	3.8
% submitting high school GPA	100
% graduated top 10% of class	41
% graduated top 25% of class	67
% graduated top 50% of class	92
% submitting high school rank	40

Important Dates

Early decision	
Apply by	11/1
Notified by	12/12
Early action	
Apply by	11/1
Notified by	12/20
Regular	
Apply by	8/1
Notified by	2/1
Nonfall registration?	Yes

FINANCIAL FACTS

Annual tuition	$50,860
Food and housing	$17,730
Required fees	$990
Books and supplies	$1,100
Average need-based scholarship (First-year)	$30,603 ($32,295)
% students with need rec. need-based scholarship or grant aid (First-year)	94 (100)
% students with need rec. non-need-based scholarship or grant aid (First-year)	21 (25)
% students with need rec. need-based self-help aid (First-year)	69 (68)
% students rec. any financial aid (First-year)	97 (99)
% UG borrow to pay for school	51
Average cumulative indebtedness	$44,645
% of students with need fully met (First-year)	14 (14)
Average % of student need met (First-year)	73 (72)

California Institute of Technology

1200 East California Boulevard, Pasadena, CA 91125 • Admissions: 626-395-6341

Survey Snapshot
Students always studying
Lab facilities are great
Great financial aid

RATINGS	
Quality of Life	**86**
Fire Safety	**89**
Green	**60***
Academic	**91**
Profs Interesting	**84**
Profs Accessible	**88**
Admissions	**99**
Financial Aid	**99**

CAMPUS LIFE

Type of school	Private
Environment	City

Students

Degree-seeking undergrad enrollment	971
% male/female/not reported	54/46/0
% from out of state	64
% First-year from public high school	609
% First-year live on campus	99
% Ugrads live on campus	93
# of fraternities	0
# of sororities	0
% Asian	40
% Black or African American	4
% Hispanic	13
% Native American	0
% Pacific Islander	<1
% Race and/or ethnicity unknown	<1
% Two or more races	7
% White	20
% International	16
# of countries represented	48

CAMPUS MENTAL HEALTH SERVICES

Offers mental health/wellness program	Yes
Mental health training available to students	Yes
Employs Chief Wellness Officer	Yes
Peer-to-peer mental health offerings	Yes
Counseling center has guidelines or accreditation	No
Mental health/well-being courses	Yes, for-credit

ACADEMICS

% students returning for sophomore year	96
% students graduating within 4 years	77
% students graduating within 6 years	90
Calendar	Quarter
Student/faculty ratio	3:1
Most common class size 10–19.	(38%)
Most common lab/discussion size 10–19.	(50%)

Most Popular Majors

Computer Science; Mechanical Engineering; Physics

STUDENTS SAY "..."

Academics

The California Institute of Technology is a world-renowned bastion of innovation, and not just in the realm of science and engineering (though it is undoubtedly "geared toward training tomorrow's leaders and pioneers in the field of science"). Students at Caltech are encouraged to learn how to think and address challenges, and the school excels at "keeping students occupied and entertained while at the same time cramming a ridiculous amount of information into our heads." Interdisciplinary study and teamwork are woven throughout the academic experience, or as one student cheers: "Cross-collaboration of ideas and ingenuity leads to epic-ness!" While the "intense" academic experience can seem overwhelming to the outside eye, resources are thickly spread across the 1,000-or-so undergraduate students—there's a 3:1 student-to-faculty ratio, which means that "classes are small and it's often easy to form tight bonds with the professors." There are "lots of funding opportunities (for instance, the Housner Fund and the Moore-Hufstedler Fund) for projects outside of the classroom," and guidance is easily found. That's a crucial part of the Caltech puzzle, given the rigorous and thorough core curriculum, which incorporates science, humanities, math, and social science and is designed to "[expose] each student to a broad range of subjects." According to one student, it's "an extremely difficult whirlwind of humbling and fascinating knowledge," especially, adds another, in the case of a few professors who are "Nobel Prize winners, [but that] does not make them good lecturers." Far more than not, students claim "you'll love what you learn," and that Caltech is where students "work together to solve the problems of tomorrow, while enjoying great weather."

Campus Life

The beating heart of undergraduate life at Caltech is its distinctive house system, which places first-year students into one of nine residential communities and makes it so they "immediately are integrated into a close social network/safety net. Basically, each student automatically gets ~100 friends." There is plenty of intermingling between the different house cultures (and between undergrads and grads or students and faculty), and "most people find that they identify strongly with at least one of the cultures." One engineering student testifies to his crafty house's DIY nature: "My house has a tool room and turned down the housing office's offer to buy us a TV." Houses all sit down to their own family-style meal on weeknights, and each also hosts one elaborate "interhouse" party during the year, often involving elaborately engineered themes, light shows, and decorations. Traditions (and pranks) speak to the creativity of each house, like the one whose members experimentally "freeze pumpkins in liquid nitrogen and drop them off of [Caltech Hall]" each Halloween, and the school's Honor Code provides a lot of trust for such well-intentioned shenanigans. Ultimately, while some students do find the time to "take trips to the beach and LA," most say that "[problem] sets and extracurriculars keep us pretty close to campus."

Student Body

While the house system provides both "a family-like support network for students" and a quick shorthand to students' particular cultures, "there is a wide range in personality within the student body." Almost everyone seems to have "an odd sense of humor and a serious hobby, whether it be Minecraft, building lasers, or rock climbing." This is a "beautiful, small campus" in which "everyone knows each other," and there is "complete trust within the student body," which allows people to take a breather from the "extreme academic pressures" of the workload. "There's no way around it," writes one student: if you self-identify as "nerdier than average," you'll likely fit right in.

California Institute of Technology

Financial Aid: 626-395-6280 • E-Mail: ugadmissions@caltech.edu • Website: www.caltech.edu

THE PRINCETON REVIEW SAYS

Admissions

The school reports that its standardized testing policy for use in admission for Fall 2026 will require applicants to submit either the SAT or ACT. The Princeton Review suggests that interested applicants consult with the school for the most up-to-date standardized testing policies. *Very important factors considered include:* rigor of secondary school record, standardized test scores, application essay, recommendation(s), character/personal qualities. *Important factors considered include:* class rank, academic GPA, extracurricular activities. *Other factors considered include:* talent/ability, first generation, geographical residence, volunteer work, work experience. High school diploma or equivalent is not required. *Academic units required:* 4 English, 4 math, 2 science; 2 history and/or social science. *Academic units recommended:* 3 science; 3 history and/or social science.

Financial Aid

Students should submit: FAFSA; Institution's own financial aid form; CSS PROFILE; Business/Farm Supplement; State aid form. Priority filing deadline is 3/15. The Princeton Review suggests that all financial aid forms be submitted as soon as possible. *Need-based scholarships/grants offered:* Federal Pell; Federal SEOG; State scholarships/grants; Private scholarships; College/university scholarship or grant aid from institutional funds. *Loan aid offered:* Federal Direct Subsidized Loans; Federal Direct Unsubsidized Loans; Direct PLUS loans; College/university loans from institutional funds. Admitted students will be notified of awards on or about 4/15. Federal Work-Study Program available. Institutional employment available.

The Inside Word

The Undergraduate Admissions Committee has faculty on it, so keep that in mind when submitting your application and showcase your creativity and intellect: no student is admitted to the school unless they receive a positive review from a faculty member. Stellar academic credentials are a necessity for this extremely selective school, and prospective students must display an aptitude for math and science.

THE SCHOOL SAYS

From the Admissions Office

"Successful applicants to Caltech are multifaceted individuals deeply passionate about STEM, they seek out the most challenging classes available to them, creatively solve problems, and are tenacious every day. Their intrinsic curiosity propels them to explore STEM in and outside of the classroom while also appreciating humanities and social sciences. At Caltech, students do not study just one thing and a passion for all STEM fields is necessary to be successful.

"Applications are reviewed holistically; meaning, each required component of an application is evaluated and used by the admissions committee to reach a decision. Our review process allows multiple admissions officers and faculty committee members to read and discuss the most competitive applications. Admissions officers move the most competitive application onto a faculty review who do a full read of a student's application materials. The context of an applicant's individual circumstances allows us to get to know them and assess their prior attainment and potential. Each applicant is considered as a whole person, therefore, there is no single admissions requirement that is deemed more important than others. Visit our website to learn more about how we review applications, preparing for Caltech, and learn what we look for."

SELECTIVITY

# of total applicants	11,285
% of total applicants accepted	4
% of total acceptees attending	58
# offered a place on the wait list	263
# admitted from wait list	1

First-Year Profile

Testing policy	SAT or ACT Required
Range SAT EBRW	760–780
Range SAT math	790–800
Range ACT composite	35–36
% submitting SAT scores	78
% submitting ACT scores	22
% graduated top 10% of class	97
% graduated top 25% of class	100
% submitting high school rank	15

Important Dates

Early action	
Apply by	11/1
Notified by	12/15
Regular	
Apply by	1/3
Notified by	3/15
Nonfall registration?	No

FINANCIAL FACTS

Annual tuition	$68,574
Food and housing	$21,996
Required fees (First-year)	$2,665 ($3,265)
Books and supplies	$1,428
Average need-based scholarship (First-year)	$72,099 ($66,645)
% students with need rec. need-based scholarship or grant aid (First-year)	100 (100)
% students with need rec. non-need-based scholarship or grant aid (First-year)	0 (0)
% students with need rec. need-based self-help aid (First-year)	61 (68)
% students rec. any financial aid (First-year)	42 (48)
% UG borrow to pay for school	23
Average cumulative indebtedness	$28,935
% of students with need fully met (First-year)	100 (100)
Average % of student need met (First-year)	100 (100)

CALIFORNIA STATE UNIVERSITY, STANISLAUS

One University Circle, Turlock, CA 95382 • Admissions: 209-667-3070

Survey Snapshot
Students are happy
Diverse student types interact on campus
Great library

RATINGS

Quality of Life	86
Fire Safety	96
Green	85
Academic	74
Profs Interesting	86
Profs Accessible	87
Admissions	71
Financial Aid	86

CAMPUS LIFE

Type of school	Public
Environment	City

Students

Degree-seeking undergrad enrollment	8,374
% male/female/not reported	35/65/0
% from out of state	0
% First-year from public high school	96
% First-year live on campus	14
% Ugrads live on campus	20
# of fraternities (% join)	4 (1)
# of sororities (% join)	6 (1)
% Asian	9
% Black or African American	3
% Hispanic	62
% Native American	<1
% Pacific Islander	1
% Race and/or ethnicity unknown	4
% Two or more races	3
% White	18
% International	1
# of countries represented	24

CAMPUS MENTAL HEALTH SERVICES

Offers mental health/wellness program	Yes
Mental health training available to students	Yes
Employs Chief Wellness Officer	Yes
Peer-to-peer mental health offerings	Yes
Counseling center has guidelines or accreditation	Yes
Mental health/well-being courses	Yes, for-credit

ACADEMICS

% students returning for sophomore year	85
% students graduating within 4 years	30
% students graduating within 6 years	52
Calendar	Semester
Student/faculty ratio	17:1
Most common class size 20–29.	(42%)
Most common lab/discussion size 10–19.	(28%)

Most Popular Majors

Business Administration and Management; Psychology; Liberal Arts and Sciences/Liberal Studies

Applicants Also Look At

California State University, Fresno, California State University, Sacramento, San Jose State University

STUDENTS SAY "..."

Academics

California State University, Stanislaus delivers a supportive, "student-centric" education at a great value. "The quality of education per dollar is incredible," says one student, and the university reports that "eight in ten students earn grants or scholarships—and more than half finish their degree debt-free." And this has no impact on the number of educational experiences available: students enjoy plenty of "completely interactive and student-directed labs," as well as "innovative learning approaches such as business simulations, real-world case studies, and group projects." One student is particularly impressed by "how many professors come from different cultural backgrounds and integrate their identities into lectures, allowing me to learn about business concepts while also gaining cultural and global perspectives." As one student puts it, courses are "both challenging and rewarding" and "push me to think critically while still providing the guidance and resources needed to succeed." One student was so taken with the personalized accommodations they received that it "renewed my confidence in pursuing higher education—so much so that I'm now considering a master's degree." Students also credit academic clubs, especially among the popular STEM and health science majors, with their success. Explains one student: "As a dual STEM major, I found that clubs related to these majors are extremely helpful since professors that teach courses in those majors sometimes attend them as well, making it easy to ask questions and get help with both classwork and future planning for post-graduation." Overall, Stan State students know "the school is willing to help students in any way that they can."

Campus Life

Warrior Wednesdays are at the heart of Stan State—they "bring students together," advancing the "sense of community" that students say is one of the school's greatest strengths. Located in the quad, "these events allow students to get information on different clubs on campus, different resources, and meet new people." They feature DIY activities and food trucks, and students look forward to hanging out with faculty and friends. Other favorite on-campus activities include plant sales, movie nights, astronomy nights and morning bird walks. Students can also be found hanging out in the Fab Lab, "a hobby shop which is popular with 3D printing." One student enthuses: "There's some nice benches outside the library, too, where I can meet up with friends and be loud and play games. The Warrior Cross Cultural Center also provides board games and cozy bean bags...Turlock is definitely not a party town, and my friends and I all commute, but it's amazing that this university is what unites us and we use campus as our meeting spot." One student sums it up, saying "I love Stan State and I have had a wonderful time here."

Student Body

"At Stanislaus State University, the student body feels like a community rather than just a collection of individuals." Located east of the Bay Area in California's Central Valley, the school attracts "a diverse population" with "a variety of first-generation college students, transfer students from surrounding areas, older students returning to school to finish their higher education, as well as master's students studying to be experts in their field." In the classroom, "discussions turn into collaborative projects, study groups become close communities, and classmates from very different backgrounds learn from one another." These different professional backgrounds and life experiences bring "a wide range of perspectives to every conversation." Students further celebrate "the main demographic being POC," with one student noting that they "feel at home" being "working class and a minority." All told, it's common to see members of the student body "smiling ear to ear" from the way "our peers uplift each other."

California State University, Stanislaus

Financial Aid: 209-667-3336 • E-Mail: Outreach_help_desk@csustan.edu • Website: www.csustan.edu

THE PRINCETON REVIEW SAYS

Admissions

The school reports that its standardized testing policy for use in admission for Fall 2026 is Test Optional. The Princeton Review suggests that interested applicants consult with the school for the most up-to-date standardized testing policies. *Very important factors considered include:* rigor of secondary school record, academic GPA. *Other factors considered include:* extracurricular activities, character/personal qualities, first generation, volunteer work, work experience. High school diploma is required and GED is accepted. *Academic units required:* 4 English, 3 math, 2 science, 2 science labs, 2 language (other than English), 1 social studies, 1 history, 1 academic elective, 1 visual/performing arts. *Academic units recommended:* 4 English, 3 math, 2 science, 2 science labs, 2 language (other than English), 1 social studies, 1 history, 1 academic elective, 1 visual/performing arts.

Financial Aid

Students should submit: FAFSA; State aid form. Priority filing deadline is 3/2. The Princeton Review suggests that all financial aid forms be submitted as soon as possible. *Need-based scholarships/grants offered:* Federal Pell; Federal SEOG; State scholarships/grants; Private scholarships; College/university scholarship or grant aid from institutional funds. *Loan aid offered:* Federal Direct Subsidized Loans; Federal Direct Unsubsidized Loans; Direct PLUS loans; State Loans. Admitted students will be notified of awards on a rolling basis beginning 4/1. Federal Work-Study Program available. Institutional employment available.

The Inside Word

California State University, Stanislaus, accepts students from all kinds of backgrounds with a wide variety of life experiences to bring to the campus. The university is committed to providing an education that is both accessible and outstanding. Hence, it's safe to say that when evaluating potential new students, both strong academics and character play a strong role in admissions. The best contenders will have a strong GPA, challenge themselves academically, and demonstrate what they can bring to the CSU community.

THE SCHOOL SAYS

From the Admissions Office

"For over sixty years, California State University, Stanislaus, has welcomed students from California's Central Valley and worldwide. Stanislaus State continues to distinguish itself as an institution that provides top-quality degree programs with a high level of personal attention, offering forty-seven majors, forty-eight minors and more than 100 areas of concentration, along with eighteen master's degree programs, seven credential programs, and a doctorate in educational leadership. With a student-to-faculty ratio of 17:1, Stanislaus State demonstrates its commitment to individualized instruction over the more common lecture-hall style of many larger universities. The university enjoys an ideal location in the Northern San Joaquin Valley, a short distance from the San Francisco Bay Area, Monterey, Big Sur, the Sierra Nevada Mountains, and the state capital of Sacramento. The main campus is located in the city of Turlock, a community that prides itself on its small-town atmosphere, clean living space, excellent schools, and low crime rate. Degree programs in these disciplines have earned specialized accreditation: art, business administration, education, music, nursing, psychology, public administration, social work, and theater. The College of Business Administration and the College of Education, Kinesiology and Social Work have also earned prestigious state and national accreditation. Over $79 million in merit- and need-based grants and scholarships were awarded for the 2024–25 school year, and over 76 percent of undergraduates receive need-based aid."

SELECTIVITY

# of total applicants	5,436
% of total applicants accepted	96
% of total acceptees attending	20
# of in-state applicants	5,335
% of in-state applicants accepted	96
# of out-of-state-applicants	50
% of applicants accepted from out of state	82
# of international applicants	51
% of international applicants accepted	84

First-Year Profile

Testing policy	Test Optional
Average HS GPA	3.5
% submitting high school GPA	99

Important Dates

Regular	
Apply by	7/31
Notified by	Rolling, 11/1
Nonfall registration?	Yes

FINANCIAL FACTS

Annual in-state tuition	$6,838
Annual out-of-state tuition	$20,968
Food and housing	$14,414
Required fees	$2,308
Books and supplies	$1,158
Average need-based scholarship (First-year)	$13,766 ($14,041)
% students with need rec. need-based scholarship or grant aid (First-year)	98 (100)
% students with need rec. non-need-based scholarship or grant aid (First-year)	7 (11)
% students with need rec. need-based self-help aid (First-year)	89 (85)
% students rec. any financial aid (First-year)	82 (92)
% UG borrow to pay for school	29
Average cumulative indebtedness	$15,765
% of students with need fully met (First-year)	7 (9)
Average % of student need met (First-year)	76 (81)

Calvin University

3201 Burton Street S.E., Grand Rapids, MI 49546 • Admissions: 616-526-6106

Survey Snapshot
Students are happy
Lab facilities are great
Internships are widely available

RATINGS

Quality of Life	87
Fire Safety	82
Green	60*
Academic	84
Profs Interesting	93
Profs Accessible	95
Admissions	87
Financial Aid	91

CAMPUS LIFE

Type of school	Private
Affiliation	Christian Reformed
Environment	Metropolis

Students

Degree-seeking undergrad enrollment	3,173
% male/female/not reported	51/49/0
% from out of state	30
% First-year from public high school	52
% First-year live on campus	93
% Ugrads live on campus	66
# of fraternities	0
# of sororities	0
% Asian	3
% Black or African American	6
% Hispanic	5
% Native American	<1
% Pacific Islander	<1
% Race and/or ethnicity unknown	1
% Two or more races	2
% White	67
% International	15
# of countries represented	63

CAMPUS MENTAL HEALTH SERVICES

Offers mental health/wellness program	Yes
Mental health training available to students	No
Employs Chief Wellness Officer	NR
Peer-to-peer mental health offerings	NR
Counseling center has guidelines or accreditation	Yes
Mental health/well-being courses	NR

ACADEMICS

% students returning for sophomore year	88
% students graduating within 4 years	64
% students graduating within 6 years	77
Calendar	Semester
Student/faculty ratio	14:1
Most common class size 20–29.	(41%)
Most common lab/discussion size 10–19.	(38%)

Most Popular Majors

Engineering; Registered Nursing/Registered Nurse; Business Administration and Management

Applicants Often Prefer

University of Michigan—Ann Arbor, Wheaton College (IL)

Applicants Sometimes Prefer

Cedarville University, Central Michigan University, Grand Valley State University, Hope College, Michigan State University, Purdue University—West Lafayette, Taylor University

Applicants Rarely Prefer

Cornerstone University, Indiana Wesleyan University, Olivet Nazarene University, Spring Arbor University, Trinity Christian College, Western Michigan University

STUDENTS SAY "..."

Academics

To attend Calvin University is to immerse oneself in "a Christian learning atmosphere where faith is woven into all areas of study." Calvin is a "fantastic academic institution that tries to foster the development of the heart and mind." The university helps students build their "relationship with God while also challenging them in a rigorous academic environment to enable them to be agents of change and renewal in the world." Classes at Calvin are demanding, with one student sharing, "I have been challenged academically, intellectually, and spiritually in every class I've had, and that's made me a better person and has prepared me for graduate school and beyond." Outside the classroom, students participate in "study groups and Bible studies to help each other grow toward academic and spiritual goals." Many students report that the professors "are arguably Calvin's strongest asset." They "are interested not only in who you are as a student but also who you are as a person" and "want to see [you] succeed." These teachers achieve a well-received mix of being "devoted to [their] subjects" and serving as "great role models for how to be Christian professionals" who "pushed me to grow" and, in at least one specific case, "inspired me even more in my pursuit of an environmental science major." Reflecting on their experience, another student says, "Calvin is all about Christ, community, and challenging yourself."

Campus Life

Dorm life, a requirement for at least two years at Calvin, "is vibrant" and, thanks to an active Student Activities Organization, filled with "many dorm activities each week as well as school-wide events each weekend." Among the most popular features are "concerts from some popular performers and some who are up-and-coming" and frequent "showings of new movies for discounted prices." The school also hosts carnivals, dances, intramurals, concerts, sporting events, comedy skits, and "fun things at the dining halls." For those seeking to use their artistic or athletic talents, there's "a wide variety of student ensembles for singing and for instrumental groups," and "intramurals are very popular when people have free time." While some students "may be frustrated with the dry campus policy," it is noted that "the number of students who want to party is very small" and they tend to head off-campus. For those looking to explore beyond campus (and have cars), downtown Grand Rapids "has a lot to offer," including "a ton of unique, local coffee shops" that students love to visit. The city "is close enough to Chicago that we sometimes spend the day there," and many "backpack, hike, and go to Lake Michigan." Whether it's Bible study, gym workouts, study sessions, or extracurriculars, students suggest that "a lot of life on campus at Calvin University is focused on community and interacting with fellow students."

Student Body

"People at Calvin are generally quite friendly and approachable" in addition to being "hardworking and quite smart." The student body is "small enough that Calvin begins to feel like home, but large enough that you don't know everyone." While most students "are Christians and come from somewhere in the Midwest," the school is "intentionally inclusive of all different views and perspectives" and "doesn't force religion upon anyone." One student says, "I feel I can appropriately express my opinions and views without the condemnation of others." Calvin "is very community-oriented," and students can easily "find someone to connect with, whether through classes, residence halls, or clubs." Students are "very caring, generous, and respectful," and many choose to come here out of a desire to "explore and live out their Christian faith in their studies and future careers."

CALVIN UNIVERSITY

Financial Aid: 800-688-0122 • E-Mail: admissions@calvin.edu • Website: www.calvin.edu

THE PRINCETON REVIEW SAYS

Admissions

The school reports that its standardized testing policy for use in admission for Fall 2026 is Test Optional. The Princeton Review suggests that interested applicants consult with the school for the most up-to-date standardized testing policies. *Very important factors considered include:* rigor of secondary school record, academic GPA. *Important factors considered include:* standardized test scores, application essay, recommendation(s), extracurricular activities, character/personal qualities, religious affiliation/commitment. *Other factors considered include:* class rank, volunteer work, work experience, level of applicant's interest. High school diploma is required and GED is accepted. *Academic units required:* 3 English, 2 math, 2 science, 2 social studies. *Academic units recommended:* 4 English, 3 math, 2 science, 2 language (other than English), 3 social studies.

Financial Aid

Students should submit: FAFSA. The Princeton Review suggests that all financial aid forms be submitted as soon as possible. *Need-based scholarships/grants offered:* Federal Pell; Federal SEOG; State scholarships/grants; Private scholarships; College/university scholarship or grant aid from institutional funds; United Negro College Fund. *Loan aid offered:* Federal Direct Subsidized Loans; Federal Direct Unsubsidized Loans; Direct PLUS loans. Admitted students will be notified of awards on a rolling basis beginning 2/25 of a given year. Federal Work-Study Program available. Institutional employment available.

The Inside Word

Admissions officers at Calvin are interested in candidates who will flourish within the school's academic and social community. Just as importantly, they seek applicants who are looking to deepen and affirm their Christian faith. The college accepts over 70 percent of their applicant pool, so students who maintain solid transcripts should not have too much difficulty getting in. Bear in mind, though, that the high acceptance rate is partially due to the self-selecting nature of Calvin's applicant cohort.

THE SCHOOL SAYS

From the Admissions Office

"Choosing a college isn't just about picking a major. It's about choosing the kind of person you want to become.

"At Calvin University, you'll step into an education designed to help you reimagine what your work can be, refine your calling, and discover how to renew the world around you.

"Education doesn't just happen in the classroom. Through internships, research, service learning, and real-world experiences, you won't just get knowledge—you'll learn how to apply it with confidence. Whether you're studying engineering, nursing, business, or education, you'll graduate with meaningful, hands-on experience.

"At the same time, a liberal arts foundation broadens your perspective and teaches you to think creatively and communicate effectively. It's the kind of preparation that sets you apart in a competitive job market and equips you to lead with purpose.

"Here, your faith is part of everything you do. Rooted in the Reformed Christian tradition, Calvin challenges you to think deeply, ask hard questions, and wrestle with how your beliefs connect to your work, your studies, and the needs of your community.

"You'll learn from professors who are deeply committed Christians with world-class expertise and alongside students from across the U.S. and around the globe. Their perspectives will challenge and inspire you.

"At Calvin, you're not just preparing for a job. You're preparing for a life of impact, equipped to restore what's broken, strengthen what's good, and lead with courage and confidence."

SELECTIVITY

# of total applicants	5,687
% of total applicants accepted	68
% of total acceptees attending	19
# of in-state applicants	2,308
% of in-state applicants accepted	82
# of out-of-state-applicants	1,425
% of applicants accepted from out of state	85
# of international applicants	1,954
% of international applicants accepted	38

First-Year Profile

Testing policy	Test Optional
Range SAT composite	1110–1330
Range SAT EBRW	560–680
Range SAT math	540–660
Range ACT composite	26–31
% submitting SAT scores	51
% submitting ACT scores	8
Average HS GPA	3.8
% submitting high school GPA	100
% graduated top 10% of class	40
% graduated top 25% of class	48
% graduated top 50% of class	80
% submitting high school rank	21

Important Dates

Regular	
Apply by	8/15
Notified by	Rolling, 11/1
Nonfall registration?	Yes

FINANCIAL FACTS

Annual tuition	$42,120
Food and housing	$13,080
Books and supplies	$1,000
Average need-based scholarship (First-year)	$28,845 ($31,644)
% students with need rec. need-based scholarship or grant aid (First-year)	100 (100)
% students with need rec. non-need-based scholarship or grant aid (First-year)	35 (34)
% students with need rec. need-based self-help aid (First-year)	49 (45)
% students rec. any financial aid (First-year)	97 (100)
% UG borrow to pay for school	49
Average cumulative indebtedness	$27,114
% of students with need fully met (First-year)	37 (36)
Average % of student need met (First-year)	85 (88)

Capital University

1 College and Main, Columbus, OH 43209 • Admissions: 614-236-6101

Survey Snapshot
Students are happy
Great off-campus food
Easy to get around campus

RATINGS

Quality of Life	**83**
Fire Safety	**84**
Green	**60***
Academic	**77**
Profs Interesting	**86**
Profs Accessible	**89**
Admissions	**84**
Financial Aid	**88**

CAMPUS LIFE

Type of school	Private
Affiliation	Lutheran
Environment	Metropolis

Students

Degree-seeking undergrad enrollment	1,624
% male/female/not reported	44/56/0
% from out of state	7
% First-year from public high school	92
% First-year live on campus	78
% Ugrads live on campus	53
# of fraternities (% join)	5 (10)
# of sororities (% join)	5 (13)
% Asian	2
% Black or African American	17
% Hispanic	7
% Native American	<1
% Pacific Islander	0
% Race and/or ethnicity unknown	2
% Two or more races	5
% White	63
% International	2
# of countries represented	15

CAMPUS MENTAL HEALTH SERVICES

Offers mental health/wellness program	NR
Mental health training available to students	No
Employs Chief Wellness Officer	NR
Peer-to-peer mental health offerings	NR
Counseling center has guidelines or accreditation	No
Mental health/well-being courses	NR

ACADEMICS

% students returning for sophomore year	73
% students graduating within 4 years	51
% students graduating within 6 years	57
Calendar	Semester
Student/faculty ratio	11:1
Most common class size 10–19.	(44%)
Most common lab/discussion size 10–19.	(59%)

Most Popular Majors

Education; Registered Nursing/Registered Nurse; Business Administration and Management

Applicants Also Look At

Bowling Green State University, Columbus State Community College, The Ohio State University—Columbus, The Ohio State University–Newark, Ohio University—Athens, Otterbein University, University of Cincinnati

STUDENTS SAY "..."

Academics

Capital University is a private liberal arts institution that provides an array of study and student experiences that lead to responses like "I feel like I'm set up for success in my major/program and my future career." Students note the school does "a brilliant job at focusing on the student as an individual," with support to back that up, and there are "a number of interesting courses offered," and adding majors is "encouraged and simple." Additionally, the Columbus, Ohio, location provides a "small school setting, while also getting access to big city amenities and opportunities," which the university "does a very good job" of promoting, including "guest lectures from many amazing writers and speakers." Experiential learning is a key component of the curriculum, and there are "lots of opportunities for field work and observation/hands-on learning early on in programs in order to give students lots of experience." Professors are "very good at making you feel like you matter in the classroom" and "want to see you succeed in whatever endeavors you choose." They "are determined to give [a] good education to the students and show up outside of the classroom consistently." Small class sizes "make it easy to ask questions," and "there are many opportunities for individuals to take on leadership opportunities and network with professors and their connections." Many classes "include a significant prioritization of student discussion combined with traditional lecture," as well as opportunities "to take what you have learned in class and make a whole research project out of it." As one student shares, "Capital really [encourages] students to strive for excellence."

Campus Life

"Life at school is lively and there is always something going on." Many students attend the free or low-cost events put on by the Office of Student and Community Engagement and the Campus Activities Board, which "are often large, with free food and activities, and sometimes...excursions off campus, such as to a hockey game, a gaming center...or even amusement parks." The gym is popular, as are the numerous athletes who "get support from all students." Greek life is also big and allows "for students to get involved on campus, in their community, and even in broader communities." The "outdoor campus is well-maintained and beautiful," and there is easy access to downtown Columbus. Students note that while "a lot of people go home on the weekends," the university is "good at finding an interest for everyone and makes sure to have commuter-specific events." There are more than 90 student organizations, ranging from philanthropic and cultural organizations to interest-based organizations and even clubs for specific games. "It's so easy to get involved in a variety of organizations, from recreational, professional, and social," says one student.

Student Body

Students feel that their "very open, intelligent, helpful, and welcoming" peers are a big part of what makes "going to college at Capital University a great experience." While a majority of students are white, respondents point to a "very diverse" environment in practice, particularly through "a good showing for cultural diversity with events." There's also a nice mix of backgrounds: "musicians, athletes, transfer students, [and] international students who are always friendly and welcoming." For the most part, "all of the students get along pretty well and really embody a positive environment." And because there are under 2,000 students, "you are able to see your friends all the time and learn to be a more social person overall." As one student happily summarizes: "My peers have humor and wit. Both combined, they [make] for amazing academic resources and friends that help along the way towards graduation here at Capital."

Capital University

Financial Aid: 614-236-6511 • E-Mail: admission@capital.edu • Website: www.capital.edu

THE PRINCETON REVIEW SAYS

Admissions

The school reports that its standardized testing policy for use in admission for Fall 2026 is Test Optional. The Princeton Review suggests that interested applicants consult with the school for the most up-to-date standardized testing policies. *Very important factors considered include:* academic GPA. *Other factors considered include:* rigor of secondary school record, standardized test scores, application essay, recommendation(s). High school diploma is required and GED is accepted. *Academic units recommended:* 4 English, 3 math, 3 science, 2 science labs, 2 language (other than English), 3 social studies, 1 visual/performing arts.

Financial Aid

Students should submit: FAFSA. The Princeton Review suggests that all financial aid forms be submitted as soon as possible. *Need-based scholarships/grants offered:* Federal Pell; Federal SEOG; State scholarships/grants; Private scholarships; College/university scholarship or grant aid from institutional funds. *Loan aid offered:* Federal Direct Subsidized Loans; Federal Direct Unsubsidized Loans; Direct PLUS loans; State Loans. Admitted students will be notified of awards on a rolling basis beginning 10/15. Federal Work-Study Program available. Institutional employment available.

The Inside Word

While test scores, cumulative GPA, and high school curriculum are all important factors in the decision-making process, Capital University also places emphasis on an applicant's life experiences and potential to contribute to the community. Students applying to the music or nursing programs, or those entering as home-schooled students, will need to meet some additional requirements. To help navigate it all, each applicant is assigned an admissions counselor who can answer questions about majors, scholarships, and student life. Best of all, there is no fee to apply.

THE SCHOOL SAYS

From the Admissions Office

"Capital University offers a personal, career-connected education in the heart of Columbus, Ohio, where students benefit from both a close-knit campus community and access to one of the Midwest's most opportunity-rich cities.

"From the moment they arrive, students engage in internships, research, and partnerships with leading employers across healthcare, business, government, and the arts. These experiences, combined with Capital's Signature Learning curriculum, ensure students develop the knowledge and the human skills employers value most, including communication, ethical leadership, problem-solving, and adaptability.

"At Capital, students are known by name and supported by faculty who are invested in their success. This personalized approach helps students connect their academic experience to meaningful career paths. Outside the classroom, students can find their place and build community through more than 100 student organizations, 13 fraternities and sororities, and 23 varsity athletic programs, including emerging opportunities like esports.

"The outcomes reflect this commitment. Over 93% of graduates are employed or enrolled in graduate school within six months, and nearly all students complete at least one internship or field experience. Many of Capital's health and professional programs report strong licensure pass rates and graduate school placement, reinforcing the university's focus on career readiness and long-term success.

"With nearly 200 years of trusted results and strong ties across Columbus, Capital provides students with both a supportive community and a clear path forward. At Capital, students gain more than a degree. They gain direction, experience, and the confidence to succeed."

SELECTIVITY

# of total applicants	5,382
% of total applicants accepted	65
% of total acceptees attending	13

First-Year Profile

Testing policy	Test Optional
Range SAT composite	900–1120
Range SAT EBRW	440–560
Range SAT math	430–560
Range ACT composite	17–24
% submitting SAT scores	12
% submitting ACT scores	27
Average HS GPA	3.5
% submitting high school GPA	100
% graduated top 10% of class	18
% graduated top 25% of class	44
% graduated top 50% of class	76
% submitting high school rank	64

Important Dates

Regular	
Notified by	Rolling, 10/1
Nonfall registration?	Yes

FINANCIAL FACTS

Annual tuition	$45,600
Food and housing	$13,388
Required fees	$490
Books and supplies	$2,238
Average need-based scholarship (First-year)	$11,585 ($12,200)
% students with need rec. need-based scholarship or grant aid (First-year)	99 (75)
% students with need rec. non-need-based scholarship or grant aid (First-year)	96 (100)
% students with need rec. need-based self-help aid (First-year)	66 (61)
% students rec. any financial aid (First-year)	98 (99)
% UG borrow to pay for school	88
Average cumulative indebtedness	$34,479
% of students with need fully met (First-year)	22 (20)
Average % of student need met (First-year)	78 (80)

CARLETON COLLEGE

One North College Street, Northfield, MN 55057 • Admissions: 507-222-4190

Survey Snapshot
Lots of liberal students
Students always studying
Students take advantage of the outdoors

RATINGS

Quality of Life	90
Fire Safety	99
Green	60*
Academic	97
Profs Interesting	98
Profs Accessible	96
Admissions	95
Financial Aid	99

CAMPUS LIFE

Type of school	Private
Environment	Village

Students

Degree-seeking undergrad enrollment	1,911
% male/female/not reported	49/51/<1
% from out of state	78
% First-year from public high school	64
% First-year live on campus	100
% Ugrads live on campus	92
# of fraternities	0
# of sororities	0
% Asian	11
% Black or African American	5
% Hispanic	10
% Native American	<1
% Pacific Islander	<1
% Race and/or ethnicity unknown	3
% Two or more races	8
% White	51
% International	10
# of countries represented	73

CAMPUS MENTAL HEALTH SERVICES

Offers mental health/wellness program	Yes
Mental health training available to students	Yes
Employs Chief Wellness Officer	No
Peer-to-peer mental health offerings	Yes
Counseling center has guidelines or accreditation	No
Mental health/well-being courses	Yes, for-credit

ACADEMICS

% students returning for sophomore year	94
% students graduating within 4 years	81
% students graduating within 6 years	89
Calendar	Trimester
Student/faculty ratio	8:1
Most common class size 10–19.	(55%)
Most common lab/discussion size 10–19.	(70%)

Most Popular Majors
Computer Science; Biology/Biological Sciences

Applicants Often Prefer
Brown University, Pomona College, Williams College, Yale University

Applicants Sometimes Prefer
Bowdoin College, Swarthmore College

Applicants Rarely Prefer
Grinnell College, Macalester College, Middlebury College

STUDENTS SAY "..."

Academics

Carleton College provides a liberal arts education known for its "academic rigor," and while the trimester schedule means that "classes move quick and can become overwhelming," students say peers are "supportive and won't hesitate to help each other with assignments." One standout program "connects students with upper-classmen" in the health sciences and "plans a lot of engaging and informative events." Students appreciate opportunities to be innovative and self-directed. One explains, "I'm combining political science with visual arts, [by] using poetry from political prisoners in a stop motion animation short film." And unlike many schools, all courses at Carleton are taught by professors. Overall, professors are described as "absolutely phenomenal and…very dedicated." One student shares, "I've had multiple professors who have been willing to give up time on weekends...to discuss class work and…attend student events." Students, known across campus as Carls, also get the chance to mingle with instructors as part of the Carleton Convocations Program, a campus-wide weekly speaker series featuring experts from a wide array of disciplines sharing research and insights to "stimulate thought and conversation." Students "are encouraged to attend and meet with each speaker," and widely report that convocations are "a really nice way to learn something new and enrich our experience." In short, Carleton is a place for "genuine scholars" who value a "very strong sense of community where your peers and teachers all want to support you and help you reach your fullest potential."

Campus Life

During the week, students focus on academics but make a point to "fit in as many other activities as we can," thanks to the school's "rich club culture." There are "many clubs and athletic teams of varying levels that students join," and many note that "Frisbee is an especially popular activity on campus." Students spend "a lot of time outside, working, playing sports, and hanging out." Colder months find Carls "ice skating in the quad," cross-country skiing, and snowshoeing through the Arboretum. And "on the weekends, there's usually somewhere on campus to party." Carls are "not afraid to be goofy or engage in any of our many ridiculous traditions," whether that's blowing bubbles on professors at convocations, letting out a primal scream at 10 pm the night before finals start, or dressing to impress for Midwinter Ball. Friday flower sales near the student mailboxes are a tradition that strengthens friendships and encourages "a sense of community and belonging." As one student attests, "The feeling of having a busy week and finding a flower in your mailbox just elevates the whole mood." Carleton is a community where students "feel comfortable, supported, and connected" on a campus "that truly feels like home."

Student Body

Students at Carleton tend to share one defining feature: "It might be a strange hobby, a niche academic passion, or just a funny little personality trait, but it's something people embrace rather than hide. It creates a campus atmosphere where individuality feels normal and celebrated." As a result, students can "sit down in the dining hall or walk into a study space and end up in the most unexpected, interesting conversations—sometimes about classes, but just as often about random curiosities or big ideas. The student body is curious, open-minded, and excited to connect with one another." One student describes the overall vibe as "crunchy casual," and students are known to "work hard and study frequently," and challenge each other intellectually. "The Carleton student body runs on the liberal side, but everyone is open to differing viewpoints, and no one criticizes others whose opinions may differ from their own." At Carleton, personal differences are celebrated: "Carleton students are often described as quirky, and I think people have really embraced that—being weird and being yourself are important."

CARLETON COLLEGE

Financial Aid: 507-222-4138 • E-Mail: admissions@carleton.edu • Website: www.carleton.edu

THE PRINCETON REVIEW SAYS

Admissions

The school reports that its standardized testing policy for use in admission for Fall 2026 is Test Optional. The Princeton Review suggests that interested applicants consult with the school for the most up-to-date standardized testing policies. *Very important factors considered include:* rigor of secondary school record, class rank, academic GPA, application essay, recommendation(s), extracurricular activities, talent/ability, character/personal qualities. *Other factors considered include:* standardized test scores, interview, first generation, geographical residence, volunteer work, work experience. High school diploma is required and GED is accepted. *Academic units recommended:* 4 English, 3 math, 3 science, 1 science lab, 3 language (other than English), 3 social studies.

Financial Aid

Students should submit: FAFSA; CSS PROFILE. Priority filing deadline is 1/15. The Princeton Review suggests that all financial aid forms be submitted as soon as possible. *Need-based scholarships/grants offered:* Federal Pell; Federal SEOG; State scholarships/grants; Private scholarships; College/university scholarship or grant aid from institutional funds; United Negro College Fund. *Loan aid offered:* Federal Direct Subsidized Loans; Federal Direct Unsubsidized Loans; Direct PLUS loans; State Loans; College/university loans from institutional funds. Admitted students will be notified of awards on or about 3/15. Federal Work-Study Program available. Institutional employment available.

The Inside Word

Gaining admission to Carleton is highly competitive. While it is possible to get in without stellar high school grades, showing tremendous promise, or having an exceptional talent, most successful applicants demonstrate all of these qualities. High school records are weighed most heavily here, and your personal essay is also very important. Given the importance of community at Carleton, interviews are strongly recommended.

THE SCHOOL SAYS

From the Admissions Office

"While Carleton students are curious and ambitious, they don't take themselves too seriously and are always there to help each other out. Carleton offers 33 majors and 38 minors, and students don't declare a major until spring of their sophomore year. Outside of the classroom, Carleton students are active in over 200 student-led clubs, from KRLX (the student-run radio station) to K-Pop to juggling. About 70% of Carleton students study abroad, 69% participate in community or civic engagement, and 77% are engaged in research. The college is committed to meeting 100% of demonstrated family financial need and keeping loans to a manageable amount; nearly 3 out of 5 students receive need-based financial aid and 13% are among the first in their families to attend college. Carleton grads go on to success across sectors, whether they become astrophysicists photographing black holes, ecology researchers tracking bird migration, Pulitzer Prize-winning editorial writers, developers at Google, doctors providing care to communities most in need, or Academy Award-winning film directors. Carleton is also a top Fulbright-producing school. You'll find Carleton alumni serving in the Peace Corps, leading Fortune 500 companies, and pursuing grad school (about 70% go on to graduate school). It has a uniquely loyal alumni network of 25,000, and grads are always willing to help other Carls."

SELECTIVITY

# of total applicants	6,796
% of total applicants accepted	22
% of total acceptees attending	35
# of in-state applicants	636
% of in-state applicants accepted	35
# of out-of-state-applicants	2,870
% of applicants accepted from out of state	39
# of international applicants	3,290
% of international applicants accepted	4
# of early decision applicants	760
% of early decision applicants accepted	35
# offered a place on the wait list	675
# admitted from wait list	33

First-Year Profile

Testing policy	Test Optional
Range SAT composite	1460–1530
Range SAT EBRW	730–770
Range SAT math	720–780
Range ACT composite	32–35
% submitting SAT scores	39
% submitting ACT scores	25
% graduated top 10% of class	77
% graduated top 25% of class	94
% graduated top 50% of class	100
% submitting high school rank	31

Important Dates

Early decision	
Apply by	11/15
Notified by	12/15
Other ED apply by	1/15
Other ED notified by	2/15
Regular	
Apply by	1/15
Notified by	3/31
Nonfall registration?	No

FINANCIAL FACTS

Annual tuition	$75,186
Food and housing	$19,314
Required fees	$486
Books and supplies	$1,101
Average need-based scholarship (First-year)	$65,579 ($66,762)
% students with need rec. need-based scholarship or grant aid (First-year)	100 (100)
% students with need rec. non-need-based scholarship or grant aid (First-year)	0 (0)
% students with need rec. need-based self-help aid (First-year)	98 (98)
% students rec. any financial aid (First-year)	61 (65)
% UG borrow to pay for school	35
Average cumulative indebtedness	$21,075
% of students with need fully met (First-year)	100 (100)
Average % of student need met (First-year)	100 (100)

Carnegie Mellon University

5000 Forbes Avenue, Pittsburgh, PA 15213 • Admissions: 412-268-2082

Survey Snapshot
Students always studying
Students are happy
Students love Pittsburgh, PA

RATINGS

Quality of Life	86
Fire Safety	97
Green	99
Academic	91
Profs Interesting	89
Profs Accessible	93
Admissions	99
Financial Aid	97

CAMPUS LIFE

Type of school	Private
Environment	Metropolis

Students

Degree-seeking undergrad enrollment	7,620
% male/female/not reported	52/48/0
% from out of state	88
% First-year live on campus	100
% Ugrads live on campus	47
# of fraternities (% join)	18 (15)
# of sororities (% join)	20 (17)
% Asian	35
% Black or African American	4
% Hispanic	8
% Native American	<1
% Pacific Islander	<1
% Race and/or ethnicity unknown	6
% Two or more races	5
% White	19
% International	22
# of countries represented	85

CAMPUS MENTAL HEALTH SERVICES

Offers mental health/wellness program	Yes
Mental health training available to students	Yes
Employs Chief Wellness Officer	Yes
Peer-to-peer mental health offerings	Yes
Counseling center has guidelines or accreditation	Yes
Mental health/well-being courses	Yes, for-credit

ACADEMICS

% students returning for sophomore year	97
% students graduating within 4 years	80
% students graduating within 6 years	94
Calendar	Semester
Student/faculty ratio	6:1
Most common class size 1–9.	(37%)
Most common lab/discussion size 20–29.	(36%)

Most Popular Majors

Computer Science; Electrical and Electronics Engineering; Business Administration and Management

Applicants Also Look At

Brown University, Cornell University, Georgia Institute of Technology, Harvard College, Massachusetts Institute of Technology, Princeton University, Stanford University, University of California—Berkeley, University of California—Los Angeles, University of Pennsylvania, Yale University

STUDENTS SAY "..."

Academics

It's easy to understand why students feel Carnegie Mellon is "one of the brightest universities in the country." After all, the university offers "unlimited opportunities for academic exploration and mastery." Indeed, CMU undergrads value "the interdisciplinary nature of many departments here" as it certainly "enhances [their] education." One individual elaborates, "I like that it allows students of different majors to collaborate and get to know each other, expanding general knowledge" in the process. Academically, the engineering and computer science programs are popular and "rank very highly." Another student shares, "The curriculum is very advanced in all the STEM courses so people graduate with the most up-to-date knowledge and skills." Though the vast majority of classes at CMU are on the smaller side, some students observe that "lower-level classes tend to be large lectures." That said, classes overall put a "huge focus on problem-solving, rather than memorization," which students appreciate. And while some admit there are some courses "incredibly difficult and at many times overwhelming," the overall "academic experience itself [is] enriching." And for many, a few grueling classes is worth it, as "CMU is very well-connected to many industries and organizations, and it is very feasible for CMU students to use the university as a launching pad into their interests."

Campus Life

Life at Carnegie Mellon moves at a frenetic pace. "There's always something to do and experience." As one undergrad explains, "Whether it's programming, singing a cappella, dancing Bhangra, driving in Buggy races, we invest and spend a lot of time in everything we do." Of course, it helps that "the school's extracurriculars are sensational." Many feel "there's such a wide variety of...clubs, events, and traditions" that there's something for everyone. "I have enjoyed academic bowl, model UN, ultimate Frisbee, and the Black student organization. There are also professional and other minority organizations, mock trial, intramural and club sports, a newspaper and other policy magazines," one student notes.

When the weekend rolls around, you can always find "some sort of party" or a handful of students heading "out to bars and clubs," though many people are also content with "movie and game nights." Finally, CMU undergrads also love to experience all that Pittsburgh has to offer. You can often find people "heading into the neighboring areas of Oakland, Squirrel Hill, and Shadyside to grab food and hang out." Plus, the city has tons "of cool museums," and the university is "situated between two nice parks" which are always great for a stroll.

Student Body

Students at Carnegie Mellon immediately note that their peers tend to be incredibly "academically focused" and "set themselves to a very high standard in their work." Fortunately, they still know how to foster "a supportive learning environment where students help each other grow. There's no toxic competition among us." But there is no denying that many are "intensely working for internships and jobs which will carry us in the future." This type of dedication to excellence extends beyond the classroom as well, with students saying their peers are "really passionate about things they do," including their extracurriculars. Though a few individuals do lament that some classmates "find that participating in other organizations is only a means to add things to a résumé, rather than have fun in school," most feel it's "more important to have a healthy work-life balance."

Socially, "many people [at CMU] are introverts." Although people like to stick to their groups—like athletes or international students—"the student body can be diverse if you don't stay in your bubble." At CMU, "everyone is a quirky kid" and has "unique interests and hobbies that you wouldn't expect." As one student notes, "You can have a good conversation with almost anyone about their courses, their departments, homework, different professors, etc."

Carnegie Mellon University

Financial Aid: 412-268-8186 • E-Mail: admission@andrew.cmu.edu • Website: www.cmu.edu

THE PRINCETON REVIEW SAYS

Admissions

The school reports that its standardized testing policy for use in admission for Fall 2026 is Test Flexible. The Princeton Review suggests that interested applicants consult with the school for the most up-to-date standardized testing policies. *Very important factors considered include:* rigor of secondary school record, class rank, academic GPA, extracurricular activities, character/personal qualities, volunteer work. *Important factors considered include:* application essay, recommendation(s), talent/ability, first generation. *Other factors considered include:* standardized test scores, geographical residence, work experience. High school diploma is required and GED is accepted. *Academic units required:* 4 English, 4 math, 3 science, 2 language (other than English), 3 academic electives.

Financial Aid

Students should submit: FAFSA; CSS PROFILE. The Princeton Review suggests that all financial aid forms be submitted as soon as possible. *Need-based scholarships/grants offered:* Federal Pell; Federal SEOG; State scholarships/grants; Private scholarships; College/university scholarship or grant aid from institutional funds. *Loan aid offered:* Federal Direct Subsidized Loans; Federal Direct Unsubsidized Loans; Direct PLUS loans; College/university loans from institutional funds. Admitted students will be notified of awards on or about 4/1. Federal Work-Study Program available. Institutional employment available.

The Inside Word

Carnegie Mellon draws a strong applicant pool, making admission highly competitive. Testing requirements vary by program, so be sure to check the school's website. The School of Computer Science requires the SAT or ACT, while several colleges and programs follow a test-flexible policy, allowing you to choose from options like the SAT, ACT, AP, or IB. The College of Fine Arts is test optional and requires portfolios or auditions instead.

THE SCHOOL SAYS

From the Admissions Office

"Carnegie Mellon is a world-class, innovative university, rich with tradition and culture. Our interdisciplinary approach to education sharpens students' problem-solving, critical thinking, analytical and quantitative skills. With more than 90 majors and minors, our premier fine arts, business and humanities programs are equally matched by top-ranked technology, science and computer science programs. Our students and faculty are world changers in problem-solving, leadership and communication. Graduates leave Carnegie Mellon equipped with the skills to impact society in a transformative way.

"We take pride in our academics, but also realize the importance of life outside the classroom. Campus life at Carnegie Mellon is vibrant, with opportunities spanning Fraternity and Sorority life and service, clubs and organizations, and intramurals and athletics. Though we're in the midst of the city of Pittsburgh, we have a 120-acre campus bordered by 500-acre Schenley Park—there's plenty of green space in every direction. With hundreds of ways to spend a study break, students take advantage of our culturally rich surroundings and get involved in the Pittsburgh community. And with three of the best athletic teams around (the Penguins, Pirates and Steelers!) here in our city, we know you'll love being a Pittsburgher as much as we do."

SELECTIVITY

# of total applicants	34,867
% of total applicants accepted	11
% of total acceptees attending	47
# of early decision applicants	2,680
% of early decision applicants accepted	21
# offered a place on the wait list	12,048
# admitted from wait list	38

First-Year Profile

Testing policy	Test Flexible
Range SAT composite	1500–1560
Range SAT EBRW	730–770
Range SAT math	770–800
Range ACT composite	34–36
% submitting SAT scores	65
% submitting ACT scores	18
Average HS GPA	3.9
% submitting high school GPA	19
% graduated top 10% of class	83
% graduated top 25% of class	94
% graduated top 50% of class	99
% submitting high school rank	99

Important Dates

Early decision	
Apply by	11/1
Notified by	12/15
Regular	
Apply by	1/1
Notified by	4/1
Nonfall registration?	No

FINANCIAL FACTS

Annual tuition	$69,702
Food and housing	$19,560
Required fees (First-year)	$1,114 ($1,862)
Books and supplies	$1,000
Average need-based scholarship (First-year)	$65,194 ($62,154)
% students with need rec. need-based scholarship or grant aid (First-year)	97 (96)
% students with need rec. non-need-based scholarship or grant aid (First-year)	6 (6)
% students with need rec. need-based self-help aid (First-year)	78 (84)
% students rec. any financial aid (First-year)	40 (45)
% UG borrow to pay for school	29
Average cumulative indebtedness	$31,336
% of students with need fully met (First-year)	96 (97)
Average % of student need met (First-year)	100 (100)

Case Western Reserve University

10900 Euclid Avenue, Cleveland, OH 44106 • Admissions: 216-368-4450

Survey Snapshot
Frats and sororities are popular
Theater is popular
Active minority support groups

RATINGS

Quality of Life	**78**
Fire Safety	**84**
Green	**96**
Academic	**81**
Profs Interesting	**83**
Profs Accessible	**86**
Admissions	**95**
Financial Aid	**95**

CAMPUS LIFE

Type of school	Private
Environment	Metropolis

Students

Degree-seeking undergrad enrollment	6,437
% male/female/not reported	52/48/<1
% from out of state	83
% First-year from public high school	70
% First-year live on campus	98
% Ugrads live on campus	72
# of fraternities (% join)	18 (20)
# of sororities (% join)	9 (19)
% Asian	30
% Black or African American	6
% Hispanic	12
% Native American	<1
% Pacific Islander	<1
% Race and/or ethnicity unknown	1
% Two or more races	5
% White	34
% International	11
# of countries represented	46

CAMPUS MENTAL HEALTH SERVICES

Offers mental health/wellness program	Yes
Mental health training available to students	No
Employs Chief Wellness Officer	NR
Peer-to-peer mental health offerings	NR
Counseling center has guidelines or accreditation	No
Mental health/well-being courses	NR

ACADEMICS

% students returning for sophomore year	93
% students graduating within 4 years	75
% students graduating within 6 years	87
Calendar	Semester
Student/faculty ratio	10:1
Most common class size 10–19.	(38%)
Most common lab/discussion size 10–19.	(40%)

Most Popular Majors

Bioengineering and Biomedical Engineering; Mechanical Engineering; Biology/Biological Sciences

Applicants Often Prefer

Carnegie Mellon University, Washington University in St. Louis

Applicants Sometimes Prefer

The Ohio State University—Columbus, University of Michigan—Ann Arbor, University of Pittsburgh—Pittsburgh Campus

* Demographic data is the latest available at time of printing. Scan the QR code to find the latest updates.

STUDENTS SAY "..."

Academics

Case Western Reserve University is a nationally recognized research university offering a "hands-on interface between curriculum and real-world situations." It is also a "very interdisciplinary school that encourages multiple majors/minors" and, to that end, offers "research opportunities in very different fields, various opportunities for publications and conference presentations, [and] experiential evidence-based learning strategies." CWRU has particularly strong engineering and medical programs, and "the academics and education provided by CWRU are excellent and intensive, which draws attention from employers." Students also note that "the Undergraduate Research Office is extremely helpful in finding research offices, and most hospitals are open to students getting involved in volunteering and research."

Classes tap into a variety of teaching methods, including "recitation sections, where students ask questions and work through practice problems in small group settings...and are a way of connecting with peers," and "reverse lectures where you watch lectures on your study time and then go to the lecture time for questions." One student gives an example from their intro engineering course's labs, which "involve working in groups of 4 to design prototypes for problems involving different types of engineering, such [as] designing a set of wheel-legs...for a robotic car to help it traverse obstacles." The professors at CWRU are "extremely enthusiastic about the material they are teaching, which goes a long way to making the class engaging." As one student notes, "the amount of professors at CWRU that are incredibly knowledgeable, passionate, and excited to teach is far greater than the number that are not." In addition, "For introductory classes, additional resources like teaching assistants, supplemental instructors, and tutors are easily accessible and helpful." Another student says, "Overall, this school and the professors have fostered my passions and are what led me to end up pursuing medicine as a career."

Campus Life

CWRU students "find a lot of meaning outside of the classroom," and "everyone is in at least one club but often more, [and] many people are working or are in a research lab." As some students note, since "everyone is so intensely busy, most socializing happens either during extracurriculars or at weekend parties." In addition, the student board provides activities such as "trips to New York on breaks, food tours around the city, and many fun giveaways." Many students "are also part of varsity sports or intramural sports. Our school's ultimate Frisbee team is quite competitive." As for getting off campus, the school is located in Cleveland's booming Arts District, and students say that "going to the CMA [Cleveland Museum of Art], MOCA [Museum of Contemporary Art], the Botanical Garden, and History Museum are huge." They also like "to eat out at the various restaurants throughout Cleveland and go out to areas such as Little Italy, Ohio City, and the Flats." Between the city and the "myriad of clubs and organizations on campus," students express that "there is truly a place that everybody belongs."

Student Body

Students at CWRU are described as the sort of overachiever who is "probably minoring in like 2–3 different things if not double majoring already because just having your major isn't enough." Luckily, this is a "very supportive environment of peers pushing each other to be their best," and that "is what makes the experience enjoyable." Additionally, the size of the school makes it so "the student body as a whole is very connected within themselves and it's impossible to go a day without seeing someone you know on campus." Attendees also speak toward the school's diversity, in that "you will meet people of lots of different backgrounds and countries," all of whom bring "the best of their cultures and [aren't] afraid to express themselves." This active "community really motivates others to work hard for their professional goals," and provides not only "a lot of ways to relax and have fun, but plenty of people to study with as well."

Case Western Reserve University

Financial Aid: 216-368-4530 • E-Mail: admission@case.edu • Website: www.case.edu

THE PRINCETON REVIEW SAYS

Admissions

The school reports that its standardized testing policy for use in admission for Fall 2026 is Test Optional. The Princeton Review suggests that interested applicants consult with the school for the most up-to-date standardized testing policies. *Very important factors considered include:* rigor of secondary school record, class rank, academic GPA, extracurricular activities. *Important factors considered include:* application essay, recommendation(s), interview, talent/ability, character/personal qualities, volunteer work. *Other factors considered include:* standardized test scores, first generation, alumni/ae relation, work experience, level of applicant's interest. High school diploma is required and GED is accepted. *Academic units required:* 4 English, 3 math, 3 science, 2 science labs, 2 language (other than English), 2 social studies. *Academic units recommended:* 4 math, 3 science labs, 3 language (other than English), 3 social studies.

Financial Aid

Students should submit: FAFSA; Institution's own financial aid form; CSS PROFILE. Priority filing deadline is 1/15. The Princeton Review suggests that all financial aid forms be submitted as soon as possible. *Need-based scholarships/grants offered:* Federal Pell; Federal SEOG; State scholarships/grants; Private scholarships; College/university scholarship or grant aid from institutional funds. *Loan aid offered:* Federal Direct Subsidized Loans; Federal Direct Unsubsidized Loans; Direct PLUS loans; College/university loans from institutional funds. Admitted students will be notified of awards on a rolling basis. Federal Work-Study Program available. Institutional employment available.

The Inside Word

CWRU is a school with a growing profile, which means that the number of applications keeps increasing and competition is getting stiffer. CWRU uses a "single-door admission policy," meaning students apply to the whole school rather than individual departments. Once accepted, you can change majors without reapplying. CWRU accepts the Common Application and Coalition with Scoir.

THE SCHOOL SAYS

From the Admissions Office

"Challenging and innovative academic programs, next-level technology, experiential learning, real-world environments, and faculty mentors are at the core of the Case Western Reserve University experience. CWRU's faculty challenges and supports all students, and its partnerships with world-class cultural, educational, and scientific institutions ensure that your education extends beyond the classroom. CWRU offers more than 100 academic programs and a single-door admission policy; once admitted to CWRU, you can major in any of our programs, or double and even triple major in several of them. Our 10:1 student-to-faculty ratio, among the best in the nation, allows students to have close interaction with professors. Co-ops, internships, research, creative endeavors, study abroad, and other opportunities bring theory to life in amazing settings, and 99 percent of students participate in these experiential learning opportunities. With 80 percent of students living on campus, CWRU has a residential feel unique to urban universities. First-year students live together in one of four residential communities. Advisors offer students guidance, helping them learn about and gain access to everything CWRU has to offer, in order to situate students for success."

SELECTIVITY

# of total applicants	37,082
% of total applicants accepted	38
% of total acceptees attending	12
# of in-state applicants	3,444
% of in-state applicants accepted	30
# of out-of-state-applicants	23,059
% of applicants accepted from out of state	46
# of international applicants	10,579
% of international applicants accepted	23
# of early decision applicants	1,053
% of early decision applicants accepted	25
# offered a place on the wait list	9,168
# admitted from wait list	688

First-Year Profile

Testing policy	Test Optional
Range SAT composite	1440–1530
Range SAT EBRW	710–760
Range SAT math	730–780
Range ACT composite	32–34
% submitting SAT scores	52
% submitting ACT scores	15
Average HS GPA	3.8
% submitting high school GPA	92
% graduated top 10% of class	70
% graduated top 25% of class	93
% graduated top 50% of class	100
% submitting high school rank	17

Important Dates

Early decision	
Apply by	11/1
Notified by	12/5
Early action	
Apply by	11/1
Notified by	12/21
Regular	
Apply by	1/15
Notified by	3/19
Nonfall registration?	Yes

FINANCIAL FACTS

Annual tuition	$71,410
Food and housing	$18,620
Required fees	$1,285
Books and supplies	$1,200
Average need-based scholarship (First-year)	$49,959 ($49,293)
% students with need rec. need-based scholarship or grant aid (First-year)	97 (97)
% students with need rec. non-need-based scholarship or grant aid (First-year)	18 (35)
% students with need rec. need-based self-help aid (First-year)	91 (91)
% UG borrow to pay for school	46
Average cumulative indebtedness	$29,079
% of students with need fully met (First-year)	81 (82)
Average % of student need met (First-year)	98 (100)

CATAWBA COLLEGE

2300 W. Innes Street, Salisbury, NC 28144 • Admissions: 704-637-4402

Survey Snapshot
Students are happy
Lab facilities are great
Everyone loves the Catawba Indians

RATINGS

Quality of Life	78
Fire Safety	89
Green	90
Academic	78
Profs Interesting	87
Profs Accessible	90
Admissions	83
Financial Aid	87

CAMPUS LIFE

Type of school	Private
Affiliation	United Church of Christ
Environment	Town

Students

Degree-seeking undergrad enrollment	1,261
% male/female/not reported	46/53/1
% from out of state	20
% First-year live on campus	78
% Ugrads live on campus	54
# of fraternities	0
# of sororities	0
% Asian	1
% Black or African American	20
% Hispanic	10
% Native American	<1
% Pacific Islander	<1
% Race and/or ethnicity unknown	3
% Two or more races	5
% White	52
% International	8
# of countries represented	37

CAMPUS MENTAL HEALTH SERVICES

Offers mental health/wellness program	Yes
Mental health training available to students	Yes
Employs Chief Wellness Officer	No
Peer-to-peer mental health offerings	Yes
Counseling center has guidelines or accreditation	Yes
Mental health/well-being courses	Yes, for-credit

ACADEMICS

% students returning for sophomore year	76
% students graduating within 4 years	36
% students graduating within 6 years	48
Calendar	Semester
Student/faculty ratio	11:1
Most common class size 10–19.	(48%)
Most common lab/discussion size 10–19.	(47%)

Most Popular Majors

Sport and Fitness Administration/Management; Business Administration and Management; Kindergarten/Preschool Education and Teaching

STUDENTS SAY "..."

Academics

Catawba College is a small private liberal arts school in North Carolina affiliated with the United Church of Christ. Catawba students most often describe their professors as the best aspect of their learning experience. "We have some of the most strong-minded, dedicated, and knowledgeable professors who want nothing more than their students to succeed." As another student explains, "Professors are engaging and made textbook material relatable and interesting." Many believe that it is the high quality of teaching coupled with small classes, enabled by a relatively low student to faculty ratio, that makes for a superior academic environment. "Every professor gets to essentially learn about us one on one instead of students just being a name on a paper." Students also praise the wide variety and availability of scholarships at Catawba, which are offered based on financial need, merit, and participation in various athletics, extracurricular clubs, or other programs. "Giving out plenty of scholarships makes college much more affordable and possible for so many kids and...gives them so many possibilities in their future." This variety is also reflected in Catawba's courses, which span more than 70 majors and minors. This allows students to choose between the traditional (like mathematics, psychology, and English) or to opt for innovative subjects like exercise science, sustainable planning and leadership, or music business. International study provides yet another layer, with programs available in places as different as Ireland, Madagascar, and Bonaire. Students appreciate the abundance of diversified opportunities available at Catawba to meet their academic needs.

Campus Life

Catawba is located in historic Salisbury, North Carolina (approximately forty miles north of Charlotte). "The campus is beautiful with many green spaces to sit outside and enjoy the outdoors...." There is a 189-acre ecological preserve adjacent to the campus, which hosts a diverse group of birds and animals, is a popular retreat for busy students. Environmentalism and sustainability are a big part of the Catawba ethos, as the college is the first institution of higher learning in the southeast to be deemed "fully carbon neutral" by the nonprofit Second Nature. Athletics also play a large role at Catawba, with 24 NCAA Division II teams. In addition to organized sports, "many people like to hang out outside and play sports with each other." The school also offers many clubs ranging from chemical science and chess to anime and poetry. As one student notes, "All the different types of clubs our school offers have brought so many different experiences that I never would've gotten if it weren't for these clubs."

Student Body

Catawba students describe a deep sense of camaraderie with their peers. Students are in favor of Catawba's "close-knit environment," saying that "it's easier to make friends and be part of the community since everyone kind of knows everyone." Consequently, students describe Catawba positively as the sort of place where "when you walk to class you have to stop at least three times to say 'hi' to a friend." Approximately forty percent of Catawba undergraduates play on a varsity sports team, while many others play informally or simply attend games to cheer for their classmates. Accordingly, the student body is invariably seen as "sports-oriented." While many at Catawba are active Christians, diversity of thought and belief are greatly valued among the student body. A strong international presence is felt at Catawba and students welcome this inclusivity. "I've met people from Spain, Poland, China, Brazil, South Africa, [and] England, and the culture among them varies greatly." Approximately twenty percent of undergraduates commute and therefore don't experience dormitory life, but resident students attempt to include them in campus activities as much as possible. As one student observes, "Catawba students are very accepting; we receive you as you are, and no one is afraid to be themselves here."

Catawba College

Financial Aid: 704-637-4416 • E-Mail: admission@catawba.edu • Website: www.catawba.edu

THE PRINCETON REVIEW SAYS

Admissions

The school reports that its standardized testing policy for use in admission for Fall 2026 is Test Optional. The Princeton Review suggests that interested applicants consult with the school for the most up-to-date standardized testing policies. *Very important factors considered include:* rigor of secondary school record, academic GPA. *Important factors considered include:* application essay, extracurricular activities, character/personal qualities, level of applicant's interest. *Other factors considered include:* class rank, standardized test scores, recommendation(s), interview, talent/ability, first generation, alumni/ae relation, volunteer work, work experience. High school diploma is required and GED is accepted. *Academic units recommended:* 4 English, 4 math, 3 science, 3 science labs, 2 language (other than English), 3 social studies.

Financial Aid

Students should submit: State aid form; FAFSA. Priority filing deadline is 2/15. The Princeton Review suggests that all financial aid forms be submitted as soon as possible. *Need-based scholarships/grants offered:* College/university scholarship or grant aid from institutional funds; Federal Pell; Federal SEOG; State scholarships/grants; Private scholarships. *Loan aid offered:* Federal Direct Subsidized Loans; Federal Direct Unsubsidized Loans; Direct PLUS loans; State Loans. Admitted students will be notified of awards on a rolling basis beginning 2/1. Federal Work-Study Program available. Institutional employment available.

The Inside Word

Students with a solid academic portfolio stand a good chance of gaining admission. That said, those with their hearts set on the Catawba way should make that abundantly clear in their application by including optional material, such as standardized test scores, letters of recommendation, and a résumé of extracurricular experience. Also, because Catawba College admits students on a rolling basis, the earlier the better prior to May 1!

THE SCHOOL SAYS

From the Admissions Office

"What happens when you start from a place of good? "Things change for the better. For you. For all of us. That is what begins at Catawba College.

"Founded in 1851, Catawba College is a private liberal arts institution known for academic rigor, dedicated faculty, and a longstanding commitment to sustainability. Catawba offers more than 70 academic programs taught in small classes by faculty who are experts in their fields. Every aspect of a Catawba education is designed to help students thrive. Students can choose from a wide range of majors and minors to create an academic path that reflects their individual goals and interests.

"Learning extends beyond the classroom through honors programs, internships, service learning, hands-on research, and study-away opportunities. Students may also compete on one of Catawba's 24 NCAA Division II athletic teams or take part in more than 40 student-led clubs and organizations.

"Career and vocational development are central to the student experience. The Catawba to Career (C2C) program provides career counseling, résumé development, and networking opportunities, while Catawba's three signature Centers, The Center for the Environment, The Lilly Center for Vocation and Values, and the North Carolina Center for Politics and Public Service, help students connect their career aspirations with their passions and sense of purpose. Together, these efforts contribute to a 99% success rate for graduates within one year.

"Opportunities continue beyond campus. From internships to professional sports in nearby Charlotte and Winston-Salem to world-class theatres and museums, Catawba's location enhances both the academic and social experience. Let's go make some good."

SELECTIVITY

# of total applicants	3,094
% of total applicants accepted	79
% of total acceptees attending	12
# of in-state applicants	2,253
% of in-state applicants accepted	85
# of out-of-state-applicants	595
% of applicants accepted from out of state	82
# of international applicants	246
% of international applicants accepted	13

First-Year Profile

Testing policy	Test Optional
Range SAT composite	1100–1250
Range SAT EBRW	550–640
Range SAT math	520–640
Range ACT composite	18–25
% submitting SAT scores	17
% submitting ACT scores	45
Average HS GPA	3.8
% submitting high school GPA	85
% graduated top 10% of class	11
% graduated top 25% of class	32
% graduated top 50% of class	60
% submitting high school rank	79

Important Dates

Early action	
Apply by	11/15
Notified by	12/15
Regular	
Apply by	8/15
Notified by	Rolling, 10/1
Nonfall registration?	Yes

FINANCIAL FACTS

Annual tuition	$35,990
Food and housing	$14,000
Books and supplies	$1,400
Average need-based scholarship (First-year)	$11,310 ($11,308)
% students with need rec. need-based scholarship or grant aid (First-year)	76 (77)
% students with need rec. non-need-based scholarship or grant aid (First-year)	96 (99)
% students with need rec. need-based self-help aid (First-year)	52 (49)
% students rec. any financial aid (First-year)	99 (99)
% UG borrow to pay for school	51
Average cumulative indebtedness	$24,650
% of students with need fully met (First-year)	27 (28)
Average % of student need met (First-year)	85 (87)

The Catholic University of America

620 Michigan Avenue, NE, Washington, DC 20064 • Admissions: 202-319-5305

Survey Snapshot
Easy to get around campus
Students are very religious
Students involved in community service

RATINGS

Quality of Life	**86**
Fire Safety	**89**
Green	**99**
Academic	**79**
Profs Interesting	**89**
Profs Accessible	**90**
Admissions	**86**
Financial Aid	**89**

CAMPUS LIFE

Type of school	Private
Affiliation	Roman Catholic
Environment	Metropolis

Students

Degree-seeking undergrad enrollment	3,219
% male/female/not reported	46/54/0
% from out of state	89
% First-year from public high school	52
% First-year live on campus	83
% Ugrads live on campus	61
# of fraternities (% join)	2 (NR)
# of sororities (% join)	1 (NR)
% Asian	3
% Black or African American	9
% Hispanic	23
% Native American	<1
% Pacific Islander	0
% Race and/or ethnicity unknown	7
% Two or more races	5
% White	50
% International	3
# of countries represented	32

CAMPUS MENTAL HEALTH SERVICES

Offers mental health/wellness program	Yes
Mental health training available to students	No
Employs Chief Wellness Officer	NR
Peer-to-peer mental health offerings	NR
Counseling center has guidelines or accreditation	No
Mental health/well-being courses	NR

ACADEMICS

% students returning for sophomore year	84
% students graduating within 4 years	69
% students graduating within 6 years	76
Calendar	Semester
Student/faculty ratio	12:1
Most common class size 20–29.	(32%)
Most common lab/discussion size 10–19.	(36%)

Most Popular Majors
Architecture; Political Science and Government; Registered Nursing/Registered Nurse

Applicants Often Prefer
Villanova University

Applicants Sometimes Prefer
American University, Fordham University, The George Washington University, Loyola University Maryland

Applicants Rarely Prefer
Saint Joseph's University (PA)

STUDENTS SAY "..."

Academics

The Catholic University of America offers "strong academics," with one student saying, "I have been able to balance my workload even though it is intense." Many students appreciate The First-Year Experience Learning Communities, which pair small groups of students with a team of teachers to complete a core, four-course sequence in philosophy, theology, and English; these communities "are a great way to expose students to subjects that [they] wouldn't usually take, while developing friendships." Study abroad is also popular, with many students spending a semester at the Rome campus, where "for my liberal arts curriculum requirements, we were able to go out into Rome weekly and use real-life examples for our courses." Depending on the class, teaching methods range from lectures to more hands-on approaches like "simulation-based learning, where students use realistic scenarios (such as clinical simulations, case studies, or role-playing exercises) to apply concepts." Professors are "very approachable and open to discussing any remaining questions on the content or taking a deeper dive into applications of content," and many actively "check in with their students to make sure the class is running smoothly." This engagement reinforces the sense that professors "are there because they desire to be," which in turn "imparts [a] lively and energetic atmosphere that encourages students to ask questions, make connections, and take their work seriously." As one student summarizes, "The greatest strengths of The Catholic University of America are its integration of faith and academics, its strong sense of community, and its location in Washington, DC."

Campus Life

The campus "is absolutely stunning and is well-taken care of," remaining "clean while still maintaining a 'lived-in' feel." Students highlight "the amount of green space the campus has," and many can be found "sitting outside on warm days, playing volleyball, throwing a football around, and [doing] other fun stuff." The library "has an amazing supply of areas to study," and students also "enjoy hanging out with friends in the student center." Its location, along with convenient access to a nearby metro stop, is another major advantage, allowing students to explore downtown "to see the museums, attractions, restaurants, and try to immerse themselves in the DC culture." There are "a lot of extracurriculars that are a great source of close friends," including campus ministry, Knights of Columbus, and the Cardinal Service Corps, which serves DC-area food kitchens and shelters. A large portion of the campus community "attends Daily Mass at some point throughout the day," reflecting how "Catholic offers a lot of opportunities for students to connect with others." As one student puts it, "Peers truly bond within clubs, classes, and organizations."

Student Body

This is "a diverse and content group of people" who "are genuinely interested in their fields of study and have clear aspirations for the future." While most students are Catholic, "the degree to which they practice their faith varies." This "kind and open" group "welcomes you with open arms. Everyone finds their people." Students are often described as "funny, caring, and hardworking, and they embrace being themselves." The school's size allows for "a tight-knit community feel without it being a repeat of high school, [with] plenty of new people and groups to meet through[out] all four years." Cardinals "are willing to help others out when needed," and there is a "strong sense of morality and social justice" here. Many students are "academically driven in and out of the classroom," with some "spending most of their time researching and debating academic topics for fun." At the same time, students "manage to balance education with socialization, and still have time to be introspective and learn about their own beliefs and grow as a person."

The Catholic University of America

Financial Aid: 202-319-5307 • E-Mail: cua-admissions@cua.edu • Website: www.catholic.edu

THE PRINCETON REVIEW SAYS

Admissions

The school reports that its standardized testing policy for use in admission for Fall 2026 is Test Optional. The Princeton Review suggests that interested applicants consult with the school for the most up-to-date standardized testing policies. *Very important factors considered include:* rigor of secondary school record, academic GPA, character/personal qualities. *Important factors considered include:* application essay, recommendation(s), extracurricular activities, first generation. *Other factors considered include:* class rank, standardized test scores, interview, talent/ability, geographical residence, volunteer work, work experience, level of applicant's interest. High school diploma is required and GED is accepted. *Academic units required:* 4 English, 4 math, 3 science, 2 science labs, 2 language (other than English), 4 social studies, 4 history, 2 academic electives. *Academic units recommended:* 4 English, 4 math, 4 science, 2 science labs, 3 language (other than English), 4 social studies, 4 history, 4 academic electives.

Financial Aid

Students should submit: FAFSA. Priority filing deadline is 2/1. The Princeton Review suggests that all financial aid forms be submitted as soon as possible. *Need-based scholarships/grants offered:* Federal Pell; Federal SEOG; State scholarships/grants; Private scholarships; College/university scholarship or grant aid from institutional funds; United Negro College Fund; Federal Nursing Scholarships. *Loan aid offered:* Federal Direct Subsidized Loans; Federal Direct Unsubsidized Loans; Direct PLUS loans; State Loans. Admitted students will be notified of awards on a rolling basis beginning 2/1. Federal Work-Study Program available. Institutional employment available.

The Inside Word

The Catholic University of America's admission committee carefully assesses your GPA and the rigor of your course load. And while Catholic is test optional, you must not slack on the other facets of your application as close attention is given to your personal statement and recommendations. Your extracurricular involvement is also vetted, and the university is especially on the lookout for candidates dedicated to community service.

THE SCHOOL SAYS

From the Admissions Office

"Students at The Catholic University of America have opportunities and advantages unlike anywhere else. Our remarkable combination of outstanding academics, a vibrant residential student life, opportunities for meaningful undergraduate research, competitive athletics, and a rich array of student clubs and organizations is made even more distinctive by our location in Washington, D.C.—a world center for "big ideas" in business, science, politics and government, public policy, health care, the arts, and more. By the time they graduate, more than 75 percent of our students complete internships (more than 60 percent complete two or more) on Capitol Hill, at the Smithsonian, with NASA, the National Institutes of Health, or any of the hundreds of leading corporations and nonprofit organizations with headquarters in D.C. And when not studying or working, they and their classmates also get to enjoy the scores of museums and galleries, theaters, restaurants, monuments, markets, parks, and historic sites that make the U.S. capital one of the most interesting, dynamic, and influential cities in the world.

"Add to all of this having the largest and greenest campus in the District, our own University center in Rome (among nearly 100 international study programs we offer), rich opportunities for student leadership and community service, and the Office of Academic and Career Success, where dedicated professionals are ready to help guide and support students from the moment they enroll right through graduation and beyond, and you start to realize why the educational experience at Catholic University is unparalleled.

SELECTIVITY

# of total applicants	7,121
% of total applicants accepted	73
% of total acceptees attending	16
# of in-state applicants	460
% of in-state applicants accepted	67
# of out-of-state-applicants	5,996
% of applicants accepted from out of state	77
# of international applicants	665
% of international applicants accepted	46

First-Year Profile

Testing policy	Test Optional
Range SAT EBRW	560–680
Range SAT math	540–670
Range ACT composite	23–30
% submitting SAT scores	12
% submitting ACT scores	3
Average HS GPA	3.5
% submitting high school GPA	97
% graduated top 10% of class	22
% graduated top 25% of class	54
% graduated top 50% of class	82
% submitting high school rank	20

Important Dates

Early decision	
Apply by	11/1
Notified by	1/1
Early action	
Apply by	11/1
Notified by	1/1
Regular	
Apply by	2/1
Notified by	3/20
Nonfall registration?	Yes

FINANCIAL FACTS

Annual tuition	$60,500
Food and housing	$20,940
Required fees	$1,286
Books and supplies	$1,286
Average need-based scholarship (First-year)	$41,780 ($40,393)
% students with need rec. need-based scholarship or grant aid (First-year)	100 (100)
% students with need rec. non-need-based scholarship or grant aid (First-year)	97 (98)
% students with need rec. need-based self-help aid (First-year)	53 (51)
% students rec. any financial aid (First-year)	93 (74)
% UG borrow to pay for school	59
Average cumulative indebtedness	$42,689
% of students with need fully met (First-year)	27 (29)
Average % of student need met (First-year)	78 (78)

Centre College

600 West Walnut Street, Danville, KY 40422-1394 • Admissions: 859-238-5350

Survey Snapshot
Recreation facilities are great
Intramural sports are popular
Easy to get around campus

RATINGS

Quality of Life	**85**
Fire Safety	**60***
Green	**60***
Academic	**89**
Profs Interesting	**91**
Profs Accessible	**93**
Admissions	**89**
Financial Aid	**90**

CAMPUS LIFE

Type of school	Private
Environment	Village

Students

Degree-seeking undergrad enrollment	1,401
% male/female/not reported	48/52/0
% from out of state	43
% First-year from public high school	66
% First-year live on campus	99
% Ugrads live on campus	99
# of fraternities (% join)	6 (37)
# of sororities (% join)	5 (42)
% Asian	4
% Black or African American	5
% Hispanic	6
% Native American	<1
% Pacific Islander	<1
% Race and/or ethnicity unknown	1
% Two or more races	4
% White	72
% International	6
# of countries represented	15

CAMPUS MENTAL HEALTH SERVICES

Offers mental health/wellness program	Yes
Mental health training available to students	Yes
Employs Chief Wellness Officer	NR
Peer-to-peer mental health offerings	NR
Counseling center has guidelines or accreditation	No
Mental health/well-being courses	NR

ACADEMICS

% students returning for sophomore year	90
% students graduating within 4 years	82
% students graduating within 6 years	84
Calendar	4-1-4
Student/faculty ratio	10:1
Most common class size 10–19.	(49%)
Most common lab/discussion size 10–19.	(69%)

Most Popular Majors
Economics; Biology/Biological Sciences; Economics, Other

Applicants Often Prefer
Vanderbilt University

Applicants Sometimes Prefer
Denison University, Furman University

Applicants Rarely Prefer
Miami University, The University of the South

STUDENTS SAY "..."

Academics

Centre College is a school that prides itself on fostering a "tight knit community," one in which "everyone genuinely cares." Undergrads appreciate the college's liberal arts education, which provides them with "substantial freedom to pursue whatever academic experience and career they wish." Additionally, "small class sizes" are the norm at Centre, leading to a very personalized classroom experience and education. "In every class I've ever taken in my four years, the professor has known my name and made an effort to get to know everyone." Of course, individualized attention also means that "you must work hard and you must be ready to learn!" A fellow classmate cautions that at Centre, "You cannot get by with not trying." But don't worry. The Centre faculty consists of "extremely knowledgeable" individuals who maintain "a vested interest in [their students'] success" and are there to support you on your academic journey. As this undergrad sums up, "Even professors that I've had in the past always have their door open, so to speak, to get questions answered or simply talk." Ultimately, students leave these courses well-equipped, quickly stressing that the "academic rigor is great preparation for graduate school and fellowships" along with "the real world." As one individual emphasizes, "I know that I'll have connections for internships and jobs for the remainder of my time here and after I graduate."

Campus Life

Given Centre's rigorous academics, a lot of "students' time is spent studying." But fear not, the college still manages to generate plenty of opportunities for fun. For starters, Greek life is quite popular. Indeed, Centre maintains a "healthy culture of fraternities and sororities," which many students engage in. Additionally, there are numerous career-focused organizations like the investment society that enables students to "manage over $200,000 in stocks [as well as] look for opportunities to grow [their] portfolio and teach others about investing." There are also more traditional clubs such as the college orchestra, garden club, intramural sports, and the Centre Environmental Association. Plus, "every weekend the campus center puts on an event from laser tag to mechanical bull riding." Students also simply "enjoy hanging out and watching shows or movies with friends" or "socializ[ing] during their meals." It is important to acknowledge hometown Danville is "a very small town." Because many feel "there's not much to do for fun" in the small town, most are content taking advantage of all of the built-in fun offered from their college.

Student Body

Centre College does a great job amassing a group of undergraduates who are "hard working, high achieving, and very involved on and off campus." Students here "are always happy to help in any way they can." And while they are undoubtedly "academically motivated," Centre students definitely "know how to have fun" as well. Most people "prioritize studying during the week and social life during the weekends, though the two are often combined."

In terms of diversity, undergrads recognize that the "student body is predominantly white." However, they rush to note that "Centre [is] certainly striv[ing] for a more diverse make up." And many also point out that you'll definitely meet "people from all over the country and the world" here. What's more, students report that their peers are "focus[ed] on [ensuring]...inclusion everywhere on campus in terms of sports, Greek life, academics, and extracurriculars." This undergrad agrees, adding, "Our community is very welcoming and warm to all student[s] whether you [are] international, American, Republican, Democrat, there is something and someone for everyone."

Centre College

Financial Aid: 800-423-6236 • E-Mail: admission@centre.edu • Website: www.centre.edu

THE PRINCETON REVIEW SAYS

Admissions

The school reports that its standardized testing policy for use in admission for Fall 2026 is Test Optional. The Princeton Review suggests that interested applicants consult with the school for the most up-to-date standardized testing policies. *Very important factors considered include:* rigor of secondary school record, academic GPA. *Important factors considered include:* class rank, standardized test scores, application essay, recommendation(s). *Other factors considered include:* interview, extracurricular activities, talent/ability, character/personal qualities, first generation, alumni/ae relation, geographical residence, volunteer work, work experience. High school diploma is required and GED is not accepted. *Academic units required:* 4 English, 3 math, 2 science, 2 science labs, 2 language (other than English), 2 history. *Academic units recommended:* 4 math, 4 science, 4 language (other than English), 2 social studies, 2 history, 1 visual/performing arts.

Financial Aid

Students should submit: FAFSA; Institution's own financial aid form. Priority filing deadline is By Admission Application Deadline. The Princeton Review suggests that all financial aid forms be submitted as soon as possible. *Need-based scholarships/grants offered:* Federal Pell; Federal SEOG; State scholarships/grants; Private scholarships; College/university scholarship or grant aid from institutional funds. *Loan aid offered:* Federal Direct Subsidized Loans; Federal Direct Unsubsidized Loans; Direct PLUS loans. Admitted students will be notified of awards on or about 12/23, 2/7, 3/15. Federal Work-Study Program available. Institutional employment available.

The Inside Word

Centre College evaluates applicants holistically. Students who have challenged themselves with high-level coursework, earned a solid GPA, and shown improvement throughout their high school career are strong candidates for admissions. Though the school is Test Optional, it still values those scores, and this is a good place for a driven student to get their attention. The college also gives appropriate weight to extracurriculars, letters of recommendations, and personal statements.

THE SCHOOL SAYS

From the Admissions Office

"Centre College students earn an extraordinary liberal arts and sciences education, put their education into practice in real-world settings, and explore their future in our Career Exploration Communities. The Centre Promise guarantees that the College will meet 100% of calculated financial need for incoming first-year students. We believe that a transformative education should be within reach for everyone. Centre is also proud to offer several competitive merit scholarship programs that cover the full cost of college as well as funds for enrichment experiences.

"The Centre Experience ensures opportunities for study abroad, participation in hands-on research, and internships, and purposeful networking with alumni and industry leaders. With our comprehensive support systems and focus on career readiness, you'll be equipped to make your mark on the world. At Centre you can build talents you might not even know you possess while making a positive difference in the world. With more than 70 majors and minors, from business to biology, engineering to history, and Chinese to data science, our exceptional faculty are dedicated to your success. Centre is a top institution for study abroad, with semester-long programs in thirteen countries, including Mexico, France, England, and Ghana, along with study away programs in Washington, D.C. and New York City. 84% of Centre students study abroad or away at least once, and our CentreTerm each January offers flexible opportunities to explore the world.

"On campus, there are more than 100 student clubs and activities, 42% of students participate in the arts, 40% of students belong to a fraternity or sorority, and nearly half participate in one of our 25 DIII varsity sports. There are dozens of campus performances each semester in the renowned Norton Center, including Broadway shows, concerts, and eminent guest speakers."

SELECTIVITY

# of total applicants	2,212
% of total applicants accepted	76
% of total acceptees attending	21
# of early decision applicants	73
% of early decision applicants accepted	88
# offered a place on the wait list	115
# admitted from wait list	17

First-Year Profile

Testing policy	Test Optional
Range SAT composite	1150–1380
Range SAT EBRW	570–650
Range SAT math	560–730
Range ACT composite	26–32
% submitting SAT scores	26
% submitting ACT scores	79
Average HS GPA	3.6
% submitting high school GPA	99
% graduated top 10% of class	52
% graduated top 25% of class	80
% graduated top 50% of class	97
% submitting high school rank	38

Important Dates

Early decision	
Apply by	11/15
Notified by	12/15
Early action	
Apply by	12/1
Notified by	1/15
Regular	
Apply by	1/15
Notified by	3/15
Nonfall registration?	No

FINANCIAL FACTS

Annual tuition	$43,000
Food and housing	$10,740
Books and supplies	$1,400
Average need-based scholarship (First-year)	$33,652 ($36,467)
% students with need rec. need-based scholarship or grant aid (First-year)	100 (100)
% students with need rec. non-need-based scholarship or grant aid (First-year)	0 (0)
% students with need rec. need-based self-help aid (First-year)	65 (62)
% students rec. any financial aid (First-year)	96 (97)
% UG borrow to pay for school	51
Average cumulative indebtedness	$27,418
% of students with need fully met (First-year)	32 (36)
Average % of student need met (First-year)	87 (90)

Champlain College

163 South Willard Street, Burlington, VT 05402 • Admissions: 802-860-2727

Survey Snapshot
Students environmentally aware
Students love Burlington, VT
Great off-campus food

RATINGS

Quality of Life	92
Fire Safety	99
Green	60*
Academic	84
Profs Interesting	94
Profs Accessible	93
Admissions	83
Financial Aid	87

CAMPUS LIFE

Type of school	Private
Environment	Town

Students

Degree-seeking undergrad enrollment	1,479
% male/female/not reported	62/38/<1
% from out of state	77
% First-year live on campus	93
% Ugrads live on campus	82
# of fraternities	0
# of sororities	0
% Asian	4
% Black or African American	3
% Hispanic	8
% Native American	<1
% Pacific Islander	<1
% Race and/or ethnicity unknown	5
% Two or more races	5
% White	75
% International	<1
# of countries represented	8

CAMPUS MENTAL HEALTH SERVICES

Offers mental health/wellness program	Yes
Mental health training available to students	Yes
Employs Chief Wellness Officer	Yes
Peer-to-peer mental health offerings	Yes
Counseling center has guidelines or accreditation	No
Mental health/well-being courses	Yes, for-credit

ACADEMICS

% students returning for sophomore year	75
% students graduating within 4 years	50
% students graduating within 6 years	60
Calendar	Semester
Student/faculty ratio	12:1
Most common class size 10–19.	(63%)

Most Popular Majors

Computer and Information Systems Security/Auditing/Information Assurance; Cyber/Computer Forensics and Counterterrorism; Game and Interactive Media Design

Applicants Also Look At

Clark University, Ithaca College, Plymouth State University, Quinnipiac University, Rochester Institute of Technology, Rutgers University–New Brunswick, Saint Michael's College, University of Connecticut, University of Massachusetts—Amherst, University of New Hampshire, University of Vermont, Worcester Polytechnic Institute

STUDENTS SAY "..."

Academics

Champlain College is a "career-focused school that gives students the tools to succeed in the professional world." As one student extols, "Networking and the emphasis on internships at Champlain lead to a great deal of job placements relevant to your chosen major after (or before!) graduation." Students love the "small class sizes," which "allow your professors and classmates to know, contribute, and follow your success." They're also wild about Champlain's UpsideDown Curriculum, which allows undergraduates to jump right into key classes: "I could begin major-related work on the first day." Game design, filmmaking, digital forensics, psychology, and marketing are all offered as majors, distinguishing Champlain's available courses of study to many applicants, with its "strong focus on major-specific skills, and field-applicable classwork." For the most part, students say the professors are "engaging, encouraging, and interesting" and "do all they can to help students understand the material and reach their full potential." This career-conscious education is animated by Champlain's "engaging, encouraging, and interesting" professors, who "know your name," are "enthusiastic about the students' education," and "come from extremely professional backgrounds and add personal touches to their discussions that make students want to participate." In addition to academic curricula, Champlain's InSight program "readies students for outside life," teaching life skills such as "financial sophistication" and fostering a "strong sense of community." With "excellent professors, innovative classes" and an "inviting small classroom environment," Champlain helps students keep the focus on their careers.

Campus Life

The small liberal arts college in cozy Burlington, Vermont, has a heavy academic focus on the video game industry, and skiing and gaming figure prominently into Champlain's social life. "There is a lot to do in town, and on campus there are often events put on by clubs or the SGA [Student Government Association]. Every Thursday, a bus also takes students from campus to free bowling or to see a free movie at the movie theater." Students love Burlington—"full of endless opportunities for both outside and indoor activities"—and enjoy the shops and nightlife of Church Street. Both Champlain and Burlington "heavily promote sustainable living," and as such, students learn "an incredible amount about how to help and be aware of my community and ecosystem." For the dedicated skier/student, Champlain IDs will nab you discounted ski passes in the area, and "snow dictates class attendance in the spring." Per its students, Champlain fulfills both those who would do "anything to be outside" and those who prefer a "laid back" social atmosphere or "an excellent music scene."

Student Body

"Champlain attracts a certain type: open, artistic, thoughtful, and intelligent." It's a self-selective, "open-minded" population that's passionately adored by those who know what to expect: students "fit in well if they have researched the college before coming, as it is a small community within a larger community." There is "literally a bit of everything. Nerds, partiers, skiers, snowboarders, skateboarders, and hippies." Another summarizes the Champlain student body as "everyone is incredibly friendly and supportive. I love that it's large enough not to know everyone but small enough that it still feels like family." As a whole, Champlain students are "motivated and engaged." They enjoy the social opportunities afforded by Burlington and Champlain, but "are also serious about doing big things and going far in life."

CHAMPLAIN COLLEGE

Financial Aid: 802-992-1474 • E-Mail: admission@champlain.edu • Website: www.champlain.edu

THE PRINCETON REVIEW SAYS

Admissions

The school reports that its standardized testing policy for use in admission for Fall 2026 is Test Optional. The Princeton Review suggests that interested applicants consult with the school for the most up-to-date standardized testing policies. *Very important factors considered include:* academic GPA. *Important factors considered include:* rigor of secondary school record. *Other factors considered include:* standardized test scores, application essay, recommendation(s), interview, extracurricular activities, character/personal qualities. High school diploma is required and GED is accepted. *Academic units required:* 4 English, 3 math, 3 science, 2 science labs, 3 history, 5 academic electives. *Academic units recommended:* 4 math, 4 science, 2 language (other than English), 4 history, 5 academic electives, 2 computer science, 2 visual/performing arts.

Financial Aid

Students should submit: FAFSA. The Princeton Review suggests that all financial aid forms be submitted as soon as possible. *Need-based scholarships/grants offered:* Federal Pell; Federal SEOG; State scholarships/grants. *Loan aid offered:* Federal Direct Subsidized Loans; Federal Direct Unsubsidized Loans; Direct PLUS loans. Admitted students will be notified of awards on a rolling basis beginning 12/15. Federal Work-Study Program available. Institutional employment available.

The Inside Word

For the BFA or BS programs in creative media, filmmaking, graphic design and digital media, game art and animation, and game design, prospective students must submit a portfolio of relevant creative work. Strong writing skills are important for all applicants.

THE SCHOOL SAYS

From the Admissions Office

"Nestled in vibrant Burlington, Vermont, Champlain College isn't just another four years of education—it's where careers begin. At Champlain, the revolutionary "Upside-Down Curriculum" flips traditional education on its head—allowing students to dive into their chosen fields from day one. With 31 professionally focused majors and nearly 100 specialized areas of study, students join a close-knit community of passionate, driven peers, faculty, and staff who collaborate on real-world projects while building impressive portfolios. Thanks to Champlain's extensive employer network, students secure meaningful internships as early as their first year—often leading to job offers before graduation. Learning from industry insiders who bring their expertise directly to the classroom, students develop the critical thinking that employers prize, resulting in 90% of 2023 graduates achieving career success within six months of graduation.

"Champlain's award-winning campus overlooks Lake Champlain. Life is different here: Our first-year students don't live in cookie-cutter "dorms," they live in Victorian-era mansions that feel like home. Whether they've mapped their career since middle school or they're still exploring options, Champlain students quickly find their people: creators, innovators, and future industry leaders who push each other to excellence. At Champlain, students build more than memories, they build the confidence that only comes from years of hands-on experiences and learning that builds on itself—and a community that supports them every step of the way. Champlain students aren't just prepared for their first jobs—they're ready to launch into lifetimes of success as part of a supportive alumni network that continues long after graduation."

SELECTIVITY

# of total applicants	2,386
% of total applicants accepted	87
% of total acceptees attending	13
# of in-state applicants	276
% of in-state applicants accepted	87
# of out-of-state-applicants	2,000
% of applicants accepted from out of state	91
# of international applicants	109
% of international applicants accepted	22
# of early decision applicants	147
% of early decision applicants accepted	94
# offered a place on the wait list	79
# admitted from wait list	0

First-Year Profile

Testing policy	Test Optional
Range SAT composite	1190–1340
Range SAT EBRW	610–700
Range SAT math	560–670
Range ACT composite	25–30
% submitting SAT scores	18
% submitting ACT scores	4
Average HS GPA	3.5
% submitting high school GPA	96

Important Dates

Early decision	
Apply by	11/15
Notified by	12/15
Early action	
Apply by	12/15
Notified by	1/3
Regular	
Notified by	Rolling, 12/15
Nonfall registration?	Yes

FINANCIAL FACTS

Annual tuition	$49,500
Food and housing	$18,500
Required fees (First-year)	$1,500 ($1,625)
Books and supplies	$1,000
Average need-based scholarship (First-year)	$31,875 ($33,423)
% students with need rec. need-based scholarship or grant aid (First-year)	100 (100)
% students with need rec. non-need-based scholarship or grant aid (First-year)	15 (11)
% students with need rec. need-based self-help aid (First-year)	76 (75)
% students rec. any financial aid (First-year)	97 (100)
% UG borrow to pay for school	65
Average cumulative indebtedness	$36,226
% of students with need fully met (First-year)	19 (17)
Average % of student need met (First-year)	73 (73)

CHAPMAN UNIVERSITY

One University Drive, Orange, CA 92866 • Admissions: 714-997-6711

Survey Snapshot
Easy to get around campus
Great off-campus food
Students love Orange, CA

RATINGS

Quality of Life	89
Fire Safety	94
Green	60*
Academic	80
Profs Interesting	89
Profs Accessible	92
Admissions	87
Financial Aid	86

CAMPUS LIFE

Type of school	Private
Affiliation	Disciples of Christ
Environment	Metropolis

Students

Degree-seeking undergrad enrollment	7,392
% male/female/not reported	38/62/<1
% from out of state	34
% First-year live on campus	86
% Ugrads live on campus	52
# of fraternities (% join)	9 (24)
# of sororities (% join)	10 (30)
% Asian	15
% Black or African American	2
% Hispanic	22
% Native American	<1
% Pacific Islander	<1
% Race and/or ethnicity unknown	3
% Two or more races	9
% White	46
% International	3
# of countries represented	57

CAMPUS MENTAL HEALTH SERVICES

Offers mental health/wellness program	Yes
Mental health training available to students	Yes
Employs Chief Wellness Officer	No
Peer-to-peer mental health offerings	Yes
Counseling center has guidelines or accreditation	No
Mental health/well-being courses	Yes, for-credit

ACADEMICS

% students returning for sophomore year	91
% students graduating within 4 years	70
% students graduating within 6 years	83
Calendar	4-1-4
Student/faculty ratio	12:1
Most common class size 10–19.	(37%)
Most common lab/discussion size 10–19.	(69%)

Most Popular Majors

Psychology; Cinematography and Film/ Video Production; Business Administration and Management

STUDENTS SAY "…"

Academics

Every student receives a customized education at Chapman University, a private institution known for its personalized approach to both academic and creative development. The university is home to eleven distinct colleges of study, allowing students to forge individualized, interdisciplinary paths—and, as students note, "each college excels at their own craft." Those who choose thoughtfully quickly recognize "the effort the school puts in to getting us involved and making sure we are having a good time," with many curricula emphasizing "a more active learning approach: group discussions, help from upperclassmen, and student-led presentations." Undergraduates appreciate that they "have choices on how we want to be creative on an assignment," an approach reinforced by "interactive and proactive lessons that thrive off of community input." Teaching methods often extend beyond the traditional classroom; one economics course, for example, asked students to hypothetically bid on "bags of Takis at varying prices to show how monopolies choose the sell prices they use." Professors "have a good concept of a comfortable workload for students, [and] most homework is purposeful and supports the exam content," contributing to a balanced academic environment. Furthermore, teachers "provide constant support and also recommend job/professional opportunities," and a student says that "with numerous opportunities nearby (such as in Hollywood and other businesses) my peers can take their passion to the professional level." At Chapman, support is readily available, and students consistently find "an open door, whether that is personally, academically, or culturally."

Campus Life

Chapman maintains a "very beautiful campus," reinforcing the feeling that "wherever you are is a wonderful place to be." The university offers "excellent social opportunities and campus life" in a sunny Southern California setting just fifteen miles from the beach and five miles from Disneyland. A majority of students live on campus during their first year, and "there are constantly events going on that help to bring the students together, whether it's orientation week with games and information sessions," or "campus events [with] free food in the piazza." Students emphasize that "if you want networking opportunities, they're there and very accessible." For example, the popular Dodge College of Film and Media Arts hosts regular Master Classes, "where they bring in actors, singers, directors, writers, etc. to come and speak to students as well as screen movies." The "small class sizes and small campus" make it easy "to build connections with peers," and many students "love to walk down the street to the Circle, where there are a bunch of cute local shops and restaurants." No matter the activity, students highlight the inclusive atmosphere: "People are always getting invited to things and trying to make sure you feel connected to the school."

Student Body

Chapman is home to a diverse mix of backgrounds and personalities, united by "lots of appreciation for the arts"—an ideal environment where "everyone seems like they have a story to tell." One student describes the impact of having such "incredibly welcoming and social" peers: "I'll lose an hour trying to walk from my class to my car." Rather than a drawback, this sense of connection is embraced, as "being busy is a great benefit of college." The campus culture is described as "collaborative over competitive, as well as friendly and welcoming," where "everyone is excited to share their knowledge to help others." With "countless clubs and organizations," there are "opportunities to get involved in [the] social scene at every corner," and students note that "people support each other's passions, collaborate across disciplines, and genuinely celebrate unconventional thinking." One student captures the spirit of the university, saying, "Chapman feels driven, close-knit, and welcoming. It's a place where you feel supported and encouraged to grow."

Chapman University

Financial Aid: 714-997-6741 • E-Mail: admit@chapman.edu • Website: www.chapman.edu

THE PRINCETON REVIEW SAYS

Admissions

The school reports that its standardized testing policy for use in admission for Fall 2026 is Test Optional. The Princeton Review suggests that interested applicants consult with the school for the most up-to-date standardized testing policies. *Very important factors considered include:* rigor of secondary school record, class rank, academic GPA, application essay, character/personal qualities. *Important factors considered include:* extracurricular activities, talent/ability. *Other factors considered include:* standardized test scores, recommendation(s), interview, first generation, geographical residence, state residency, volunteer work, work experience, level of applicant's interest. High school diploma is required and GED is accepted. *Academic units required:* 4 English, 3 math, 2 science, 1 science lab, 2 language (other than English), 2 social studies, 2 history. *Academic units recommended:* 4 English, 4 math, 4 science, 2 science labs, 4 language (other than English), 2 social studies, 2 history, 2 academic electives.

Financial Aid

Students should submit: FAFSA; State aid form. Priority filing deadline is 3/2. The Princeton Review suggests that all financial aid forms be submitted as soon as possible. *Need-based scholarships/grants offered:* Federal Pell; Federal SEOG; State scholarships/grants; Private scholarships; College/university scholarship or grant aid from institutional funds. *Loan aid offered:* Federal Direct Subsidized Loans; Federal Direct Unsubsidized Loans; Direct PLUS loans; College/university loans from institutional funds. Admitted students will be notified of awards on a rolling basis beginning 3/15. Federal Work-Study Program available. Institutional employment available.

The Inside Word

Admissions officers at Chapman take a more holistic approach when reviewing applications. The rigor of an academic curriculum, grade trends, letters of recommendation, extracurricular activities, and personal statements will all be closely evaluated. The deadlines and application requirements for programs in film and television production, dance, pre-pharmacy, screen acting, theatre performance, and writing for film and television may differ, so check the school's website.

THE SCHOOL SAYS

From the Admissions Office

"Chapman University provides a personalized and interdisciplinary educational experience to highly qualified students. We offer more than 120 areas of study—options for nearly every interest and passion. Not sure what you want to do? No problem. Entering Undeclared is also a popular option. Our academic plans encourage you to explore across subject areas—something that's supported in and out of class.

- Our average class size is 24; most of your classes will range from 10–19 students.
- There are more than 200 academic, professional, and special-interest clubs on campus.
- We offer 21 intercollegiate athletic teams (NCAA Division III) and 3 club teams.
- You can choose from over 100 semester and academic-year study abroad programs. (More than 40 percent of Chapman students study abroad.)

"With Chapman housing guaranteed for first-year students' first three years at the university (around 90 percent of first-years live on campus), our campus is a vibrant community located in the heart of Orange County. From campus you can walk to Old Town Orange, or drive to nearby attractions, including beaches, mountains, sporting venues, or Disneyland. We invite you to visit Chapman and see what's possible here. In the meantime, our website is a great resource to learn more about the university and schedule a campus tour."

SELECTIVITY

# of total applicants	14,769
% of total applicants accepted	72
% of total acceptees attending	16
# of early decision applicants	282
% of early decision applicants accepted	51
# offered a place on the wait list	1,726
# admitted from wait list	246

First-Year Profile

Testing policy	Test Optional
Range SAT composite	1260–1420
Range SAT EBRW	640–720
Range SAT math	590–710
Range ACT composite	28–32
% submitting SAT scores	16
% submitting ACT scores	6
% graduated top 10% of class	30
% graduated top 25% of class	64
% graduated top 50% of class	90
% submitting high school rank	25

Important Dates

Early decision	
Apply by	11/1
Notified by	12/20
Early action	
Apply by	11/1
Notified by	12/20
Regular	
Apply by	1/15
Notified by	4/1
Nonfall registration?	Yes

FINANCIAL FACTS

Annual tuition	$69,990
Food and housing	$18,900
Required fees	$404
Books and supplies	$1,600
Average need-based scholarship (First-year)	$25,365 ($26,718)
% students with need rec. need-based scholarship or grant aid (First-year)	89 (87)
% students with need rec. non-need-based scholarship or grant aid (First-year)	88 (97)
% students with need rec. need-based self-help aid (First-year)	87 (86)
% students rec. any financial aid (First-year)	86 (90)
% UG borrow to pay for school	41
Average cumulative indebtedness	$34,500
% of students with need fully met (First-year)	19 (29)
Average % of student need met (First-year)	75 (83)

Christopher Newport University

1 Avenue of the Arts, Newport News, VA 23606-3072 • Admissions: 757-594-7015

Survey Snapshot
Lots of conservative students
Students are happy
Classroom facilities are great

RATINGS

Quality of Life	87
Fire Safety	94
Green	60*
Academic	79
Profs Interesting	85
Profs Accessible	90
Admissions	83
Financial Aid	83

CAMPUS LIFE

Type of school	Public
Environment	City

Students

Degree-seeking undergrad enrollment	4,365
% male/female/not reported	48/52/0
% from out of state	7
% First-year from public high school	80
% First-year live on campus	94
% Ugrads live on campus	82
# of fraternities (% join)	11 (19)
# of sororities (% join)	10 (21)
% Asian	4
% Black or African American	9
% Hispanic	9
% Native American	<1
% Pacific Islander	<1
% Race and/or ethnicity unknown	3
% Two or more races	6
% White	68
% International	<1
# of countries represented	29

CAMPUS MENTAL HEALTH SERVICES

Offers mental health/wellness program	Yes
Mental health training available to students	Yes
Employs Chief Wellness Officer	No
Peer-to-peer mental health offerings	No
Counseling center has guidelines or accreditation	Yes
Mental health/well-being courses	No

ACADEMICS

% students returning for sophomore year	81
% students graduating within 4 years	64
% students graduating within 6 years	72
Calendar	Semester
Student/faculty ratio	13:1
Most common class size 20–29.	(45%)

Most Popular Majors
Speech Communication and Rhetoric; Computer Science; Psychology

Applicants Often Prefer
James Madison University, Virginia Tech

Applicants Sometimes Prefer
George Mason University, University of Virginia, Virginia Commonwealth University, William & Mary

Applicants Rarely Prefer
Longwood University, University of Mary Washington

STUDENTS SAY "..."

Academics

Christopher Newport University invites students to become part of a "vibrant community," one that's truly "invested in the well-being and growth" of all undergraduates who attend. Indeed, CNU students are privy to both "strong academics and [a] very strong support system." Many individuals here also appreciate that there's a "focus on undergraduate research," noting how easy it is "to ask a professor if you can join them." Additionally, they are quick to mention that "service...and study abroad opportunities" abound as well. And they certainly benefit from "small class sizes" too, which allows "for more personal attention from professors." The faculty here "make a strong effort to get to know you and create a relationship with you while [you're] in their class." In turn, "this... makes it easier to ask for help when you need it and/or gives you a faculty member you can always reach out to." It's also abundantly clear that "their passion is teaching students, and they are very good at it." As this grateful undergrad illustrates, "They get more excited about my accomplishment[s] than I do and are always an ear when needed." Some may even go as far as stating that "professors at CNU are the strongest asset of this university."

Campus Life

Christopher Newport's modest size belies a campus that's always abuzz with activity. "The fact that [it is] a smaller campus does not mean there are fewer opportunities to be involved." With "over 200 clubs and organizations at CNU" and "students are always going to events put on by their student organizations or to ones put on by our Campus Activities Board." Importantly, these clubs run the gamut; there's everything from "the student-run farmers market and sustainability commission" to "CNU Survivor...a club [that] mimic[s] the show Survivor on [CBS]." There are also many opportunities to "volunteer at local community sites." Moreover, it's common for students to "fill their days by working on campus." One undergrad explains, "CNU has a lot of job opportunities for students that allow us to study and work simultaneously."

Undergrads here love taking advantage of the nice weather as well. In the "warmer seasons a lot of students will fill the many lawns of the campus with Frisbees, lacrosse sticks, footballs, etc." Then again, it's easy to get a break from campus life if you need. In fact, it's part of a classic CNU tradition. "One signature activity here at CNU is watching the sunset at a location called Lions Bridge. It's roughly a 30-minute walk from campus and a 10-minute drive to watch the beautiful pinks and oranges set over the coast." No matter on campus or off, "there always seems to be fun things to do."

Student Body

Students at Christopher Newport speak highly of their "driven and friendly" peers. It's easy to understand why. The vast majority "are super optimistic and outgoing people who love to get involved in organizations both on and off campus." They also tend to be "overwhelmingly kind," but share "a strange unspoken expectation for all students to present themselves as more formal." You'll often see students "go out of their way to open doors and smile at strangers." But don't worry; their kindness is no less authentic! "While walking to class you quickly see friends or classmates, and nobody is afraid to wave or ask how your day is going." Although a few individuals do caution that the university is a "predominantly white institution," and it can feel as though "most students come from the Northern Virginia or Richmond area," rest assured, even if you don't fit that mold, you'll still find everyone is "very respectful" and "welcoming community." As this undergrad sums up, "The student body at Christopher Newport is the...most supportive network any student can ask for. It is truly a community."

Christopher Newport University

Financial Aid: 757-594-7170 • E-Mail: admit@cnu.edu • Website: www.cnu.edu

THE PRINCETON REVIEW SAYS

Admissions

The school reports that its standardized testing policy for use in admission for Fall 2026 is Test Optional. The Princeton Review suggests that interested applicants consult with the school for the most up-to-date standardized testing policies. *Very important factors considered include:* rigor of secondary school record, academic GPA. *Important factors considered include:* class rank, standardized test scores, application essay, recommendation(s), interview, extracurricular activities, talent/ability, character/personal qualities, volunteer work, work experience, level of applicant's interest. *Other factors considered include:* first generation, alumni/ae relation, geographical residence, state residency. High school diploma is required and GED is not accepted. *Academic units required:* 4 English, 4 math, 4 science, 4 science labs, 3 language (other than English), 4 social studies, 2 academic electives, 1 visual/performing arts. *Academic units recommended:* 4 English, 4 math, 4 science, 4 science labs, 3 language (other than English), 4 social studies, 2 academic electives, 1 visual/performing arts.

Financial Aid

Students should submit: FAFSA. Priority filing deadline is 3/1. The Princeton Review suggests that all financial aid forms be submitted as soon as possible. *Need-based scholarships/grants offered:* Federal Pell; Federal SEOG; State scholarships/grants; Private scholarships; College/university scholarship or grant aid from institutional funds. *Loan aid offered:* Federal Direct Subsidized Loans; Federal Direct Unsubsidized Loans; Direct PLUS loans. Admitted students will be notified of awards on a rolling basis beginning 3/1. Federal Work-Study Program available. Institutional employment available.

The Inside Word

Christopher Newport values strong academics as well as students whose character and goals are a good fit. Therefore, pay special attention to your application essay, choose your recommenders wisely, and highlight your extracurriculars strategically. That being said, the rigor of your high school curriculum will still take priority. If you're taking a few honors, AP, or IB courses, you will be in good shape. And even though they are Test Optional, a good SAT or ACT score won't hurt your chances!

THE SCHOOL SAYS

From the Admissions Office

"At Christopher Newport University, we cultivate future leaders—students who thrive academically and socially and graduate prepared to make meaningful contributions to the world. Our undergraduate experience blends engaging academics, cutting-edge research and technology, and real-world service-learning to empower students to become engaged citizens and visionary changemakers. CNU is grounded in the liberal arts and sciences, providing a strong intellectual foundation for lifelong learning and purposeful careers. Our values—honor, scholarship, service, and leadership—are woven into every aspect of campus life. Students benefit from guaranteed housing through their junior year in award-winning, state-of-the-art residential facilities that consistently earn rave reviews.

"What sets us apart is our unwavering commitment to undergraduate education. You'll be mentored by dedicated teacher-scholars (never graduate assistants) who are passionate about their fields and your success. From day one, students engage in research and land high-impact internships with powerhouse organizations near campus like NASA, Jefferson Lab, Ferguson Enterprises, and Canon Virginia. Outside the classroom, CNU offers pathways for personal and professional growth. Join the internationally-recognized President's Leadership Program, dive deep into the Honors Program, explore the world through study abroad, or share your talents in one of our 200+ student organizations. Our student-athletes compete at the highest levels of NCAA Division III, achieving excellence on the field and in the classroom.

"Come visit our breathtaking campus and discover a community that will champion your potential every step of the way. At Christopher Newport, you won't just earn a degree, you will begin a life of significance."

SELECTIVITY

# of total applicants	7,341
% of total applicants accepted	86
% of total acceptees attending	18
# of in-state applicants	6,030
% of in-state applicants accepted	86
# of out-of-state-applicants	1,293
% of applicants accepted from out of state	87
# of international applicants	18
% of international applicants accepted	56
# of early decision applicants	229
% of early decision applicants accepted	85
# offered a place on the wait list	378
# admitted from wait list	36

First-Year Profile

Testing policy	Test Optional
Range SAT composite	1050–1180
Range SAT EBRW	550–660
Range SAT math	510–630
Range ACT composite	25–30
% submitting SAT scores	38
% submitting ACT scores	3
Average HS GPA	3.7
% submitting high school GPA	100
% graduated top 10% of class	13
% graduated top 25% of class	39
% graduated top 50% of class	74
% submitting high school rank	58

Important Dates

Early decision	
Apply by	11/15
Notified by	12/15
Early action	
Apply by	12/1
Notified by	1/15
Regular	
Apply by	2/1
Notified by	3/15
Nonfall registration?	Yes

FINANCIAL FACTS

Annual in-state tuition	$10,417
Annual out-of-state tuition	$24,238
Food and housing	$12,460
Required fees	$6,540
Books and supplies	$1,564
Average need-based scholarship (First-year)	$11,586 ($13,326)
% students with need rec. need-based scholarship or grant aid (First-year)	77 (78)
% students with need rec. non-need-based scholarship or grant aid (First-year)	39 (57)
% students with need rec. need-based self-help aid (First-year)	80 (75)
% students rec. any financial aid (First-year)	75 (87)
% UG borrow to pay for school	49
Average cumulative indebtedness	$36,265
% of students with need fully met (First-year)	11 (19)
Average % of student need met (First-year)	69 (70)

City University of New York—Baruch College

55 Lexington Avenue, New York, NY 10010 • Admissions: 646-312-1400

Survey Snapshot
Great library
Career services are great
Students love New York, NY

RATINGS	
Quality of Life	87
Fire Safety	60*
Green	60*
Academic	80
Profs Interesting	89
Profs Accessible	90
Admissions	90
Financial Aid	83

CAMPUS LIFE

Type of school	Public
Environment	Metropolis

Students

Degree-seeking undergrad enrollment	16,359
% male/female/not reported	50/46/4
% from out of state	3
% First-year live on campus	1
% Ugrads live on campus	2
# of fraternities	0
# of sororities	0
% Asian	36
% Black or African American	9
% Hispanic	29
% Native American	<1
% Pacific Islander	<1
% Race and/or ethnicity unknown	0
% Two or more races	2
% White	17
% International	7

CAMPUS MENTAL HEALTH SERVICES

Offers mental health/wellness program	Yes
Mental health training available to students	No
Employs Chief Wellness Officer	NR
Peer-to-peer mental health offerings	NR
Counseling center has guidelines or accreditation	No
Mental health/well-being courses	NR

ACADEMICS

% students returning for sophomore year	89
% students graduating within 4 years	52
% students graduating within 6 years	72
Calendar	Semester
Student/faculty ratio	21:1
Most common class size 20–29.	(41%)
Most common lab/discussion size 20–29.	(52%)

Most Popular Majors
Accounting; Finance

Applicants Often Prefer
City University of New York—Brooklyn College, City University of New York—Hunter College, City University of New York—Queens College

Applicants Sometimes Prefer
St. John's University (NY), State University of New York—Stony Brook University

STUDENTS SAY "..."

Academics

One of the City University of New York's senior colleges, Baruch College's schools (Weissman School of Arts and Sciences, Marxe School of Public and International Affairs, and the Zicklin School of Business, which is the largest of the three) are located in Manhattan and take full advantage of being in "the greatest city of the world": students here have access to "internships, big companies, and...Wall Street." Low in-state (as well as reasonable out-of-state) tuition means that many here "go to school while already working in interesting and impressive positions," and have come to Baruch purely "to improve themselves," which increases the level of maturity in the classroom. There is a wide variety of courses ("especially [for] those interested in business"), and the school offers ad-hoc majors, which allows students to design programs that will support their career goals.

Though this is not a research university, there are a "vast amount of resources" that are available to the students here. The education system is "well organized and up to date with the current world," and Baruch is tied with many companies in New York, which "creates even more opportunities for internships as well as job opportunities." "Some of my business professors came from leading huge corporations, and their anecdotes about their prior work help students internalize the material," says one student. There is "an impressive number of career-developing programs on campus that are free of charge and readily available to all students," and "it is clear that the professors at Baruch have first-hand experience in the material they are teaching to students."

Campus Life

As a commuter school, most students go to classes and go home, but "there are great clubs and events always happening" for those that do hang around, and the "lounges are usually packed." "It is all about how much time and effort you put into finding things to do," says a student. Most students are working part-time or full-time while taking courses here, but find plenty to do in between classes, from "hanging out in the club area with the clubs, playing in the game room, working out in the gym, or taking classes in our trading floor." There is so much student activity around Baruch that it is often hard to contain, and "there is always something going on and always free food around campus."

Though most do not get the typical on-campus college experience, all agree that "for the price and the benefits associated with the school, the trade-off is worth it." This is New York City, which means "you can practically do ANYTHING with your day." Museums are free for students, and "of course the shopping and food are amazing." The school's Newman Vertical Campus on Lexington Ave is a hive of activity, and though elevator crowding is a problem, when a student's eyes look at the breathtaking view of the building, "It makes you feel proud to be a Baruchi!"

Student Body

Students come from all over the world and Baruch is "full of bright and ambitious minds"; being a student here "means you learn to interact with peers from all over the world." "My fellow peers have a good sense of where they want to steer their careers and exactly what they want to do after college," says one student. Baruch is "full of first-generation college graduates," and the school is a real microcosm of NYC: "the hustle and bustle, crowds, everyone has somewhere to go, and everyone has a dream they hope will one day be fulfilled." This is a very unique commuter school in that "it has such an involved student body" where "there is a sense of community through clubs and extracurriculars."

City University of New York—Baruch College

Financial Aid: 646-312-1390 • E-Mail: admissions@baruch.cuny.edu • Website: www.baruch.cuny.edu

THE PRINCETON REVIEW SAYS

Admissions

The school reports that its standardized testing policy for use in admission for Fall 2026 is Test Optional. The Princeton Review suggests that interested applicants consult with the school for the most up-to-date standardized testing policies. *Very important factors considered include:* rigor of secondary school record, academic GPA. *Important factors considered include:* application essay, recommendation(s). *Other factors considered include:* standardized test scores, interview, extracurricular activities, talent/ability, character/personal qualities, work experience. High school diploma is required and GED is accepted. *Academic units required:* 4 English, 3 math, 2 science, 2 science labs, 2 language (other than English), 3 social studies, 1 visual/performing arts. *Academic units recommended:* 4 English, 4 math, 3 science, 2 science labs, 2 language (other than English), 4 social studies, 1 academic elective, 1 visual/performing arts.

Financial Aid

Students should submit: FAFSA; State aid form. The Princeton Review suggests that all financial aid forms be submitted as soon as possible. *Need-based scholarships/grants offered:* Federal Pell; Federal SEOG; State scholarships/grants. *Loan aid offered:* Federal Direct Subsidized Loans; Federal Direct Unsubsidized Loans; Direct PLUS loans. Federal Work-Study Program available. Institutional employment available.

The Inside Word

Admissions have grown steadily more competitive in recent years, especially for students seeking undergraduate business degrees. Today, Baruch receives nearly 15 applications for every slot in its first-year class.

THE SCHOOL SAYS

From the Admissions Office

"As an undergraduate at Baruch College, you will join a vibrant learning community of students and scholars in the heart of exhilarating, possibility-filled New York City. Baruch is a place where theory meets practice. You can network with city leaders; secure business, cultural, and nonprofit internships; access the music, art, and business scene; and meet experts who visit our campus. You will take classes that bridge business, arts, science, government, political and international affairs, learning from professors who are among the best in their fields. One-third of our freshmen participate in learning communities, which offer incoming students small, interdisciplinary classes and an opportunity to get to know our faculty through classroom discussion and planned field trips throughout the city. Baruch offers 30 majors and 60 minors in three schools: the Marxe School of Public Affairs and International Affairs, the Weissman School of Arts and Science, and the Zicklin School of Business. Highly qualified undergraduates may apply to the Baruch College Honors program, which offers scholarships, small seminars and honors courses. Students may also study abroad through programs in more than 30 countries. Our 17-floor Newman Vertical Campus serves as the college's hub. Here you will find the atmosphere and resources of a traditional college campus, but in a lively urban setting. Our classrooms have state-of-the-art technology, and our library was named the top college library in the nation. Baruch also has a simulated trading floor for students who are interested in Wall Street. You can also enjoy a three-level athletics and recreation complex, which features a twenty-five-meter indoor pool as well as a performing arts complex. The state-of-the-art residences, blocks from Central Park on the Upper East Side, are equipped with a concierge, high tech gym, laundry facility that texts when your clothes are dry, and a very chill lounge to study or relax with your friends. Baruch's selective admission standards, strong academic programs, top national honors, as well as its internship and job-placement opportunities make it an exceptional educational value."

SELECTIVITY

# of total applicants	25,299
% of total applicants accepted	49
% of total acceptees attending	20
# offered a place on the wait list	1,309
# admitted from wait list	40

First-Year Profile

Testing policy	Test Optional
Range SAT EBRW	650–710
Range SAT math	660–740
% submitting SAT scores	3
Average HS GPA	3.7
% submitting high school GPA	98

Important Dates

Regular	
Apply by	Rolling
Notified by	Rolling, 12/15
Nonfall registration?	Yes

FINANCIAL FACTS

Annual in-state tuition	$6,930
Annual out-of-state tuition	$18,600
Food and housing	$18,600
Required fees	$530
Books and supplies	$1,364
Average need-based scholarship (First-year)	$8,847 ($7,248)
% students with need rec. need-based scholarship or grant aid (First-year)	93 (95)
% students with need rec. non-need-based scholarship or grant aid (First-year)	49 (83)
% students with need rec. need-based self-help aid (First-year)	18 (13)
% UG borrow to pay for school	15
Average cumulative indebtedness	$13,244
% of students with need fully met (First-year)	2 (2)
Average % of student need met (First-year)	47 (50)

City University of New York—Brooklyn College

2900 Bedford Avenue, Brooklyn, NY 11210 • Admissions: 718-951-5001

Survey Snapshot
Great library
Recreation facilities are great
Easy to get around campus

RATINGS

Quality of Life	79
Fire Safety	60*
Green	84
Academic	72
Profs Interesting	81
Profs Accessible	84
Admissions	76
Financial Aid	91

CAMPUS LIFE

Type of school	Public
Environment	Metropolis

Students

Degree-seeking undergrad enrollment	10,523
% male/female/not reported	46/54/<1
% from out of state	3
% First-year live on campus	0
% Ugrads live on campus	0
# of fraternities (% join)	7 (<1)
# of sororities (% join)	5 (<1)
% Asian	23
% Black or African American	22
% Hispanic	25
% Native American	<1
% Pacific Islander	<1
% Race and/or ethnicity unknown	0
% Two or more races	4
% White	24
% International	3

CAMPUS MENTAL HEALTH SERVICES

Offers mental health/wellness program	Yes
Mental health training available to students	No
Employs Chief Wellness Officer	NR
Peer-to-peer mental health offerings	NR
Counseling center has guidelines or accreditation	No
Mental health/well-being courses	NR

ACADEMICS

% students returning for sophomore year	81
% students graduating within 4 years	34
% students graduating within 6 years	53
Calendar	Semester
Student/faculty ratio	16:1
Most common class size 20–29.	(37%)

Most Popular Majors

Psychology; Accounting; Business Administration and Management

STUDENTS SAY "..."

Academics

At Brooklyn College, a key part of the City University of New York system, its more than 10,000 undergraduate "students receive a quality education for a fraction of the price," especially for in-state residents. Autonomy is woven throughout the curricula and activities; one class required students "to input topics we would like to see on the syllabus, creating a more engaged environment," and "there are so many different options of choosing your own schedule." Students can also take part in special programs such as First College Year, which is designed to help students transition to the social and academic aspects of higher education the summer before their first year, or can avail themselves of what one respondent considers "the greatest strength of my school...[the] tons of resources and help throughout the semester" provided by the Magner Career Center. The administration also makes sure that students "can find answers to possibly any and all questions you may have," and provides "resources I can't find anywhere else," such as "advisement, trainings/workshops, [and] work readiness workshops."

Classes are varied and may include fieldwork or interactive labs, which creates "an active learning environment and further learning about what is taught in lectures." An increase in online courses has been said to provide "an innovative way [of] learning without walls." These learning environments succeed in "encouraging students to speak freely and challenge ideas in a respectful way." In addition, "professors...push you in a good way" and are "very kind and understanding as well as extremely knowledgeable in their subjects" and "keep in touch regularly."

Campus Life

The Brooklyn "campus is beautiful [with] lots of space," and since it is located in a mass transit hub, there are "many ways of traveling easily" around New York City. One student says, "I took a class called Arts in NYC and we took many trips outside the classroom to the Metropolitan Opera, various museums, other plays/theater events." Though no dorms are available through the school itself, residences are available through an associated non-profit organization. The campus "closes late, [so] there's lots of access to buildings and rooms on site" for those that need a place (like the library) to study or meet, and there are also "many tables and benches around the campus so we have more than enough space [to] hang around." Activities give a further reason to linger, with plenty of "very diverse and fun" clubs, ranging from badminton to ASL. The student government "[holds] different events that help students communicate and connect with others," and the especially popular movie nights are "usually well-known movies so more students can participate and converse with other students or staff."

Student Body

Students here "come from all different countries, cultures and religions," and "everyone has a place to fit in...no matter what boxes you as a student may or may not tick off." This diversity helps create an environment where students are constantly "learning something new from everyone's own perspectives and shared experiences" and are "welcoming, kind, and always willing to get together to study." Brooklyn College is primarily a commuter school, and everyone "has a common goal and is serious about their future." Students "constantly want the best for each other while also pushing each other to discover their potentials," and "there's an effort to make everyone seen." The strong sense of community means "people aren't shy to help each other out, share views, and create safe spaces for everyone to thrive," and "you will be able to find friends and peers from cultures all over the world." There "are very close-knit relationships among the student body, whether it's between students or with professors as well." Ultimately "everybody gets very comfortable with one another and ends up getting...together at the food plaza right behind the library." One student confirms: "I never feel out of place when I am in school and whenever I need help, someone is always willing to assist me."

City University of New York—Brooklyn College

Financial Aid: 718-951-4195 • E-Mail: adminqry@brooklyn.cuny.edu • Website: www.brooklyn.cuny.edu

THE PRINCETON REVIEW SAYS

Admissions

The school reports that its standardized testing policy for use in admission for Fall 2026 is Test Optional. The Princeton Review suggests that interested applicants consult with the school for the most up-to-date standardized testing policies. *Very important factors considered include:* rigor of secondary school record, academic GPA. *Other factors considered include:* High school diploma is required and GED is accepted. *Academic units required:* 4 English, 3 math, 3 science, 3 language (other than English), 4 social studies, 2 visual/performing arts. *Academic units recommended:* 4 English, 3 math, 3 science, 3 language (other than English), 4 social studies, 2 visual/performing arts.

Financial Aid

Students should submit: FAFSA; State aid form. Priority filing deadline is 5/1. The Princeton Review suggests that all financial aid forms be submitted as soon as possible. *Need-based scholarships/grants offered:* Federal Pell; Federal SEOG; State scholarships/grants; Private scholarships; College/university scholarship or grant aid from institutional funds. *Loan aid offered:* Federal Direct Subsidized Loans; Federal Direct Unsubsidized Loans; Direct PLUS loans. Admitted students will be notified of awards on a rolling basis beginning 2/1. Federal Work-Study Program available. Institutional employment available.

The Inside Word

Students with strong applications (GPA and demonstrated academic rigor) have a decent shot at being accepted to Brooklyn College. While the most weight is given to your academic ability, Brooklyn also considers other factors, including the optional, but recommended, college essay. Standardized tests are optional, but if you feel they would be helpful, then go ahead and submit them.

THE SCHOOL SAYS

From the Admissions Office

"Known for its rigorous academics, enormous value, and ability to help students climb the socioeconomic ladder, Brooklyn College is a leading senior college within The City University of New York system that offers a vibrant and supportive student experience on a beautifully landscaped 35-acre campus. Offering more than 100 undergraduate and graduate degree programs in the arts, humanities, sciences, education, and business, the College is also renowned for its diversity, award-winning faculty, distinguished alumni, and community impact.

"The School of Education is ranked nationally in the top 20 for graduates who go on to become some of the top educators in New York City. The Murray Koppelman School of Business is the only program in Brooklyn that is accredited by the prestigious international Association to Advance Collegiate Schools of Business, and it regularly connects students with industry leaders and top-tier business internships.

"Brooklyn College's strong academic reputation has attracted faculty who have been awarded Pulitzer Prizes, Guggenheim Fellowships, Fulbright Awards, National Institutes of Health grants, and other awards. The student body consists of 15,938 students who have been awarded Fulbright, Truman, and Rhodes scholarships, among other awards.

"The College has been repeatedly recognized by The Princeton Review as one of America's Best Value Colleges (2019, 2020, 2021), as well as recently being ranked in the top 10 nationwide on the latest Social Mobility Index Report. It was also named the No. 1 College Among North Regional Universities for Campus Ethnic Diversity by U.S. News and World Report (2019).

"Recent additions to campus include the Feirstein Graduate School of Cinema—the only film school housed on a working lot—and the Leonard & Claire Tow Center for the Performing Arts."

SELECTIVITY

# of total applicants	29,760
% of total applicants accepted	58
% of total acceptees attending	9
# of in-state applicants	27,799
% of in-state applicants accepted	58
# of out-of-state-applicants	911
% of applicants accepted from out of state	67
# of international applicants	1,039
% of international applicants accepted	33

First-Year Profile

Testing policy	Test Optional
Average HS GPA	3.4
% submitting high school GPA	99

Important Dates

Regular	
Notified by	Rolling, 2/1
Nonfall registration?	Yes

FINANCIAL FACTS

Annual in-state tuition	$6,930
Annual out-of-state tuition	$18,600
Food and housing	$22,260
Required fees	$520
Books and supplies	$1,500
Average need-based scholarship (First-year)	$6,489 ($6,578)
% students with need rec. need-based scholarship or grant aid (First-year)	85 (78)
% students with need rec. non-need-based scholarship or grant aid (First-year)	12 (16)
% students with need rec. need-based self-help aid (First-year)	10 (6)
% UG borrow to pay for school	4
Average cumulative indebtedness	$1,000
% of students with need fully met (First-year)	92 (90)
Average % of student need met (First-year)	55 (55)

City University of New York—City College

160 Convent Avenue, New York, NY 10031 • Admissions: 212-650-6977

Survey Snapshot
Diverse student types interact on campus
Easy to get around campus
Internships are widely available

RATINGS

Quality of Life	82
Fire Safety	97
Green	80
Academic	73
Profs Interesting	84
Profs Accessible	85
Admissions	77
Financial Aid	82

CAMPUS LIFE

Type of school	Public
Environment	Metropolis

Students

Degree-seeking undergrad enrollment	13,047
% male/female/not reported	52/48/0
% from out of state	2
% First-year from public high school	81
# of fraternities (% join)	3 (NR)
# of sororities (% join)	3 (NR)
% Asian	25
% Black or African American	16
% Hispanic	41
% Native American	<1
% Pacific Islander	<1
% Race and/or ethnicity unknown	0
% Two or more races	3
% White	11
% International	4
# of countries represented	157

CAMPUS MENTAL HEALTH SERVICES

Offers mental health/wellness program	Yes
Mental health training available to students	No
Employs Chief Wellness Officer	No
Peer-to-peer mental health offerings	Yes
Counseling center has guidelines or accreditation	Yes
Mental health/well-being courses	Yes, for-credit

ACADEMICS

% students returning for sophomore year	83
% students graduating within 4 years	25
% students graduating within 6 years	50
Calendar	Semester
Student/faculty ratio	14:1
Most common class size 20–29.	(34%)
Most common lab/discussion size 20–29.	(52%)

Most Popular Majors

General Studies; Liberal Arts and Sciences, General Studies and Humanities; Psychology

Applicants Sometimes Prefer

City University of New York—Baruch College, City University of New York—Brooklyn College, City University of New York—Hunter College, City University of New York—John Jay College of Criminal Justice, City University of New York—Queens College

STUDENTS SAY "…"

Academics

The City College of New York—the founding institution of the City University of New York (CUNY)—provides its students with "strong STEM programs, diverse academic paths, and…access to research labs and professors." The college "makes students aware of the resources available to them," including "help at The Hub (for example, with class selection and major requirements) and tech loans." Students also value City College's connections with organizations and "the opportunity to network with professionals" through career development events, which open the door for "mentorships, volunteer work, or internships, so that students can gain experience and develop their skills." There are "many advisors that truly want to see students doing well," and this enthusiasm for education is spread across the board, as professors "truly make material accessible." The members of the faculty have "an extensive background or are currently practicing, [which] helps a lot with creating a realistic and driven academic experience." Professors are "engaging and effective," and students "like the balance between interactive classes and strong, clear lectures." Some professors also "incorporate case studies, peer teaching, and in-class problem-solving activities that make the material feel more practical and engaging." No matter where students were before City College or where they are looking to go, "professors meet students…where they are and…encourage them to be the best they can be."

Campus Life

Life at City College "is as dynamic as the city it sits in," and on a typical day, "you'll see students hanging out on the quad between lectures, grabbing empanadas from food trucks, or catching their breath in the [North Academic Center] rotunda," while some will "study together in the library, others hold club meetings, rehearse performances, or unwind in the student lounges." The school's uptown campus location "is great…[an] ideal combination of green space, tranquility, with easy access to all Harlem has to offer." Students say "everything is pretty accessible…nothing is too far, and you don't have to wander down streets to get anywhere." Many students like to "explore places around campus and try new restaurants together." This Division III school has more than 100 student clubs, and they are known for "offering multiple events during club hours where you can get free food, meet other students and learn." In addition, there are "tons of student showcases all the time." With its active clubs and frequent events, "for students who do desire a larger community on campus, there are plenty of opportunities if they seek them out."

Student Body

City College is a microcosm of its location, with a student body that is "constantly in motion" and "very much representative of New York City." To wit, students "are proud" of their backgrounds and appreciate that there are "many different clubs to find and connect with people [of the] same heritage." This rich tapestry of people is "a culturally diverse group of students who think differently but work well collaboratively." There is a "heavy emphasis on lending a helping hand and giving people the push they need to get to the destination they need to make." As one student explains, "We share ideas, help when someone doesn't understand something, and motivate each other to keep going. It feels like a community where everyone is trying to grow and move forward." The student body "includes everyone from young adults just beginning their academic journey to older students returning to school after time away, [and] each person brings a unique blend of life experience, ambition, and insight that feels both distinct and deeply connected."

City University of New York—City College

Financial Aid: 212-650-5824 • E-Mail: admissions@ccny.cuny.edu • Website: www.ccny.cuny.edu

THE PRINCETON REVIEW SAYS

Admissions

The school reports that its standardized testing policy for use in admission for Fall 2026 is Test Optional. The Princeton Review suggests that interested applicants consult with the school for the most up-to-date standardized testing policies. *Very important factors considered include:* academic GPA. *Important factors considered include:* rigor of secondary school record. *Other factors considered include:* standardized test scores. High school diploma is required and GED is accepted. *Academic units required:* 2 English, 2 math. *Academic units recommended:* 4 English, 3 math, 2 science, 3 language (other than English), 3 social studies, 3 history, 1 academic elective, 1 computer science, 1 visual/performing arts.

Financial Aid

Students should submit: FAFSA; State aid form. Priority filing deadline is 3/15. The Princeton Review suggests that all financial aid forms be submitted as soon as possible. *Need-based scholarships/grants offered:* Federal Pell; Federal SEOG. *Loan aid offered:* Federal Direct Subsidized Loans; Federal Direct Unsubsidized Loans; Direct PLUS loans. Admitted students will be notified of awards on a rolling basis beginning 3/1. Federal Work-Study Program available. Institutional employment available.

The Inside Word

The City College of New York has a fairly standard application process, with an emphasis on your academic transcript and GPA. Some majors have unique application requirements, such as an audition or degree-specific writing component. When applying, make sure to confirm your specific program's requirements.

THE SCHOOL SAYS

From the Admissions Office

"The City College of New York is the founding institution of the City University of New York and home to over 100 outstanding undergraduate and graduate programs, and eight schools and divisions, each dedicated to the advancement of research and knowledge. City College is the place where Albert Einstein first presented his theory of general relativity outside of Europe, and where our alumni discovered the polio vaccine, helped build the Internet, and designed the Panama Canal.

"Since 1847, CCNY has provided a high-quality and affordable education to generations of New Yorkers in a wide variety of disciplines. Embracing our position at the forefront of social change we serve more than 15,000 students, representing over 150 nationalities, pursuing undergraduate and graduate degrees driven by significant funded research, creativity, and scholarship. In fact, 2022 launched the most expansive fundraising campaign in CCNY history titled "Doing Remarkable Things Together" with a goal of raising more than $1 billion in total assets in support of the College mission.

"From architecture, engineering, education, medicine and liberal arts and sciences, CCNY offers programming in emerging fields, such as sonic arts and biomedical engineering.

"City College is located in Harlem. The 37-acre tree-lined campus boasts neo-Gothic architecture, complete with gargoyles and grotesques in the North Campus, while facilities, including the Spitzer School of Architecture and the Center for Discovery and Innovation occupy the South Campus. City College's downtown campus, the Center for Worker Education, is located in the Wall Street area in the iconic Cunard Building."

SELECTIVITY

# of total applicants	34,284
% of total applicants accepted	58
% of total acceptees attending	14
# of in-state applicants	31,076
% of in-state applicants accepted	59
# of out-of-state-applicants	2,038
% of applicants accepted from out of state	53
# of international applicants	1,170
% of international applicants accepted	27

First-Year Profile

Testing policy	Test Optional
Average HS GPA	3.1
% submitting high school GPA	92

Important Dates

Regular	
Notified by	Rolling, 12/15
Nonfall registration?	Yes

FINANCIAL FACTS

Annual in-state tuition	$6,930
Annual out-of-state tuition	$18,600
Food and housing	$19,552
Required fees	$410
Books and supplies	$1,500
Average need-based scholarship (First-year)	$9,976 ($10,131)
% students with need rec. need-based scholarship or grant aid (First-year)	94 (95)
% students with need rec. non-need-based scholarship or grant aid (First-year)	49 (70)
% students with need rec. need-based self-help aid (First-year)	17 (11)
% students rec. any financial aid (First-year)	82 (87)
% UG borrow to pay for school	14
Average cumulative indebtedness	$7,849
% of students with need fully met (First-year)	3 (3)
Average % of student need met (First-year)	52 (53)

City University of New York—Hunter College

695 Park Ave, New York, NY 10065 • Admissions: 212-772-4490

Survey Snapshot
Lots of liberal students
Students love New York, NY
College radio is popular

RATINGS	
Quality of Life	79
Fire Safety	90
Green	60*
Academic	76
Profs Interesting	84
Profs Accessible	85
Admissions	90
Financial Aid	92

CAMPUS LIFE

Type of school	Public
Environment	Metropolis

Students

Degree-seeking undergrad enrollment	17,736
% male/female/not reported	33/67/0
% from out of state	3
% First-year from public high school	80
# of fraternities (% join)	2 (NR)
# of sororities (% join)	2 (NR)
% Asian	32
% Black or African American	12
% Hispanic	23
% Native American	<1
% Pacific Islander	0
% Race and/or ethnicity unknown	0
% Two or more races	0
% White	29
% International	5
# of countries represented	158

CAMPUS MENTAL HEALTH SERVICES

Offers mental health/wellness program	Yes
Mental health training available to students	No
Employs Chief Wellness Officer	NR
Peer-to-peer mental health offerings	NR
Counseling center has guidelines or accreditation	No
Mental health/well-being courses	NR

ACADEMICS

% students returning for sophomore year	87
% students graduating within 4 years	25
% students graduating within 6 years	57
Calendar	Semester
Student/faculty ratio	13:1
Most common class size 30–39.	(30%)

Most Popular Majors

Computer Science; Human Biology; Psychology

STUDENTS SAY "..."

Academics

The crown jewel of the CUNY system, Hunter College is an institution teeming with "resources" and "endless...opportunities." Of course, many students are drawn to Hunter for its "very affordable" price tag and "prime location." Undergrads also love just how many "great" academic programs the college truly offers, including "nursing," "psychology," "political science," and "education." No matter what you want to study, you can rest assured Hunter will deliver. Students also benefit from the amazing "support systems" that Hunter maintains. Indeed, they can rely on the fact that numerous "advisors are always there to answer questions about careers, classes to take, and graduation needs." This care and concern can be found within the classroom as well. After all, Hunter professors tend to be "passionate about what they teach and prefer for students to be active in class." Moreover, "they are extremely willing to help outside the classroom" as well. And many undergrads simply find their instructors "very nice and knowledgeable." Finally, as this thrilled student boasts, "They keep challenging me to do better with my work and to never stop working at the idea that is in my head to make it a reality. They genuinely believe that the students at Hunter are above others, which gives me a confidence that I chose the right school."

Campus Life

Hunter College doesn't have a sprawling or self-contained campus. And, given that many undergrads here commute, it's quite common for people to pop in "just for classes and are running back to the train when classes are over." Of course, "if there's a break, people often join up with friends to eat, or study together in the library, by the halls, or the digital cafes." And, when time allows, "people often go to the gyms and workout downstairs." A large percentage of undergrads here hold "part-time jobs that offer flexible hours" as well. A decent number also carve out time to "volunteer." Additionally, the college itself "hosts many, many programs and activities all throughout the week." When the weather is nice, many students like to head to "nearby Central Park" to hang out and/or study. Students frequently "explore the city because there is always stuff to do in New York." For example, "there are tons of museums in the area that are free for Hunter students." And undergrads who are of age seem to love checking out the "bars and clubs" the city has to offer.

Student Body

Primarily a "commuter" school, Hunter's student body is dominated by New York City "locals who are trying to get their education in a cost-efficient manner." Fortunately, they are also an extremely "diverse" lot. You can find undergrads of "every culture, religion, race, etc." And since "everyone comes from different walks of life," you will "never feel like an outcast." Indeed, Hunter students are extraordinarily "accepting." Some individuals lament, however, that their peers do tend to "keep to themselves." Others argue that if you take the time to talk to people, you quickly discover that most students are "friendly" and "welcoming." They can also be "very supportive and caring." As one undergrad explains, "We make sure that we help each other out in our studies and teach each other when there is something we do not understand." Additionally, the vast majority of Hunter students are "driven to succeed." They are often "found vigorously studying for their classes and forming networks with people that have similar interests as them." It's quite evident that everyone here really "wants to achieve something in life." And, as this wise undergrad succinctly states, "Being around people with that general same motivation is really good."

City University of New York—Hunter College

Financial Aid: 212-772-4820 • E-Mail: admissions@hunter.cuny.edu • Website: www.hunter.cuny.edu/main/

THE PRINCETON REVIEW SAYS

Admissions

The school reports that its standardized testing policy for use in admission for Fall 2026 is Test Optional. The Princeton Review suggests that interested applicants consult with the school for the most up-to-date standardized testing policies. *Very important factors considered include:* rigor of secondary school record, academic GPA. *Other factors considered include:* standardized test scores, application essay, recommendation(s), extracurricular activities, talent/ability, character/personal qualities, geographical residence, state residency, volunteer work, work experience. High school diploma is required and GED is accepted. *Academic units required:* 2 English, 2 math, 1 science, 1 science lab. *Academic units recommended:* 4 English, 3 math, 2 science, 2 language (other than English), 4 social studies, 1 academic elective, 1 visual/performing arts.

Financial Aid

Students should submit: FAFSA; State aid form. Priority filing deadline is 5/1. The Princeton Review suggests that all financial aid forms be submitted as soon as possible. *Need-based scholarships/grants offered:* Federal Pell; State scholarships/grants; College/university scholarship or grant aid from institutional funds; Federal SEOG; Private scholarships. *Loan aid offered:* Federal Direct Subsidized Loans; Federal Direct Unsubsidized Loans; Direct PLUS loans. Admitted students will be notified of awards on a rolling basis beginning 5/15. Federal Work-Study Program available. Institutional employment available.

The Inside Word

The admissions process at Hunter College is rather straightforward. Admissions officers do their utmost to take a well-rounded approach, giving all application facets careful consideration. Of course, your high school transcript and GPA will hold the most weight, as Hunter wants evidence that you're prepared for college-level courses. And, finally, the admissions committee relies on supplemental essays to assess what kind of impact you might have on life at Hunter.

THE SCHOOL SAYS

From the Admissions Office

"Located in the heart of Manhattan, Hunter offers students the stimulating learning environment and career-building opportunities you might expect from a college that's been a part of the world's most exciting city since 1870. The largest senior college in the City University of New York, Hunter pulses with energy. Hunter's vitality stems from a large, highly diverse faculty and student body. Its schools—Arts and Sciences, Education, Nursing, Social Work and Public Health—provide an affordable first-rate education. Undergraduates have extraordinary opportunities to conduct high-level research with renowned faculty, and to participate in credit-bearing internships in media, the arts, government and many other fields. The college's high standards and special programs ensure a challenging education. Specialized programs for first-year students keep classmates together as they pursue courses in the liberal arts, pre-health science, pre-nursing, pre-med, or honors. A range of honors programs is available for students with strong academic records, including the highly competitive Macaulay Honors College for entering freshmen and the Thomas Hunter Honors Program for continuing students. There are also six different freshman scholar programs offered in the arts, sciences, humanities, computer science, public policy, and nursing. All honors programs are accompanied by significant merit scholarship opportunities and feature small classes with personalized mentoring by outstanding faculty members. Qualified students also benefit from Hunter's participation in minority science research and training programs, the prestigious Andrew W. Mellon Minority Undergraduate Program, and many other passports to professional success. Hunter College has four residence halls on Manhattan's east side, housing almost 1,000 students."

SELECTIVITY

# of total applicants	32,287
% of total applicants accepted	40
% of total acceptees attending	20

First-Year Profile

Testing policy	Test Optional
Range SAT EBRW	570–650
Range SAT math	580–690
% submitting SAT scores	96
Average HS GPA	3.5
% submitting high school GPA	99

Important Dates

Regular	
Notified by	Rolling, 1/15
Nonfall registration?	Yes

FINANCIAL FACTS

Annual in-state tuition	$6,930
Annual out-of-state tuition	$18,600
Food and housing	$16,067
Required fees	$450
Books and supplies	$1,364
Average need-based scholarship (First-year)	$8,142 ($8,892)
% students with need rec. need-based scholarship or grant aid (First-year)	88 (89)
% students with need rec. non-need-based scholarship or grant aid (First-year)	46 (76)
% students with need rec. need-based self-help aid (First-year)	11 (6)
% students rec. any financial aid (First-year)	92 (96)
% UG borrow to pay for school	15
Average cumulative indebtedness	$16,272
% of students with need fully met (First-year)	58 (41)
Average % of student need met (First-year)	82 (79)

City University of New York—Queens College

65-30 Kissena Blvd, Queens, NY 11367 • Admissions: 718-997-5614

Survey Snapshot
Students love Queens, NY
Diverse student types interact on campus
Great library

RATINGS

Quality of Life	80
Fire Safety	99
Green	60*
Academic	77
Profs Interesting	83
Profs Accessible	86
Admissions	88
Financial Aid	82

CAMPUS LIFE

Type of school	Public
Environment	Metropolis

Students

Degree-seeking undergrad enrollment	11,814
% male/female/not reported	47/50/3
% from out of state	1
% First-year from public high school	89
% First-year live on campus	7
% Ugrads live on campus	3
# of fraternities (% join)	2 (1)
# of sororities (% join)	4 (1)
% Asian	31
% Black or African American	10
% Hispanic	32
% Native American	<1
% Pacific Islander	<1
% Race and/or ethnicity unknown	0
% Two or more races	3
% White	16
% International	7
# of countries represented	143

CAMPUS MENTAL HEALTH SERVICES

Offers mental health/wellness program	Yes
Mental health training available to students	Yes
Employs Chief Wellness Officer	Yes
Peer-to-peer mental health offerings	No
Counseling center has guidelines or accreditation	No
Mental health/well-being courses	No

ACADEMICS

% students returning for sophomore year	79
% students graduating within 4 years	34
% students graduating within 6 years	53
Calendar	Semester
Student/faculty ratio	13:1
Most common class size 20–29.	(32%)

Most Popular Majors

Computer Science; Psychology; Accounting

Applicants Also Look At

Adelphi University, Columbia University, Hofstra University, New York University, Radford University, St. John's University (NY), State University of New York—Stony Brook University, State University of New York—University at Albany

STUDENTS SAY "..."

Academics

Located in New York's "most diverse borough," Queens College "offers high quality academics for a very reasonable price." As one student puts it, "Queens is about getting a valuable and quality education that does not drain you financially for the future." In keeping with the fact that the majority of QC students live off campus in a variety of nearby communities, one of the school's strengths is helping students become "the best you can be so you can give back to the community." One student even goes as far as to say that QC is "considered the Harvard of CUNY." The Macaulay Honors College and the Aaron Copeland School of Music both get high marks, with students saying that QC as a whole "provides a strong liberal arts education to give [students] well-rounded knowledge and skills." Professors generally "genuinely care about [students'] grades and well-being"; as one student puts it, "They won't let me fall behind." But while "most professors genuinely care for [students'] success," it's inevitable that they will "vary in terms of quality." As one student puts it, "Many of my professors just lecture and don't interact too much, however, some are very involved and passionate." Students appreciate the "challenging yet interesting courses" but some lament that for the coveted courses, "you have to really run and register for those classes like it's a competition."

Campus Life

Though the school opened the Summit Apartments, its first residence hall, in 2009, the majority of QC students still commute; as one student observes, "Even though the Summit Apartments can only house 500 students, it still remains pretty empty throughout the semesters." Since "most students come here to go to class and then head home or to their job afterwards," many QC students say that it's difficult to foster much sense of a school community—"the sense of community could use some work." But others counter, saying that, "I would not expect a school composed mostly of commuters to bond as much as we do." Outside of class, it's "very hard to be bored," especially "being so close to the city, there are a lot of activities to do around the area." Many students explore Queens, which is accessible via a free QC shuttle. For those who live on campus, or those commuters who stick around after class, as one student puts it, "We have clubs for everything, and if there isn't a club for something you like, you could always start [one] up." One thing that students agree helps unite QC as a community is student government: "Student government provides us with events and carnivals during both the fall and spring semesters. It brings people together."

Student Body

Diversity is key at Queens College, where, as one student puts it, "We have a very diverse campus, so no minority is really ever a minority." "If one were to ask me to name every ethnicity, nationality, and religious group on campus, I would not even know where to begin," says another. QC "has a very friendly student body" and some says that "the friendships and bonds you make from taking transit together, or sharing stories is special in [its] own way." Others note that "there is not much of an established social life" and that "if you want to make friends here you really have to work for it." Many students "have part-time jobs," some students "are parents, and have to take care of their children"—"Of course, many people are straight out of high school [too], but even these people usually spend a lot of time off campus." Students describe their peers as "career-minded and focused"; they "love to have fun, but they [are] still focused on their studies and their futures."

City University of New York—Queens College

Financial Aid: 718-997-5102 • E-Mail: admissions@qc.cuny.edu • Website: www.qc.cuny.edu

THE PRINCETON REVIEW SAYS

Admissions

The school reports that its standardized testing policy for use in admission for Fall 2026 is Test Optional. The Princeton Review suggests that interested applicants consult with the school for the most up-to-date standardized testing policies. *Very important factors considered include:* rigor of secondary school record, academic GPA. *Important factors considered include:* application essay. *Other factors considered include:* standardized test scores, recommendation(s), work experience. High school diploma is required and GED is accepted. *Academic units required:* 4 English, 3 math, 2 science, 2 science labs, 3 language (other than English), 4 social studies. *Academic units recommended:* 4 English, 3 math, 3 science, 3 science labs, 3 language (other than English), 4 social studies.

Financial Aid

Students should submit: FAFSA; State aid form. The Princeton Review suggests that all financial aid forms be submitted as soon as possible. *Need-based scholarships/grants offered:* Federal Pell; Federal SEOG; State scholarships/grants; Private scholarships; College/university scholarship or grant aid from institutional funds. *Loan aid offered:* Federal Direct Subsidized Loans; Federal Direct Unsubsidized Loans; Direct PLUS loans. Admitted students will be notified of awards on a rolling basis beginning 3/1. Federal Work-Study Program available. Institutional employment available.

The Inside Word

Queens College looks for students with a B average (or better) or a GED score of at least 350 to be a strong candidate for admission; the school encourages a high school education that includes a full range of language arts and science courses. Exceptional applicants should look into Macaulay Honors College, which provides free tuition and other benefits.

THE SCHOOL SAYS

From the Admissions Office

"Queens College prepares students to become the leaders of tomorrow by offering a rigorous education in the liberal arts, business, and sciences under the guidance of an outstanding faculty dedicated to teaching and scholarship.

"Queens College has over 170 programs and is recognized nationally for the excellence of its academic offerings. New this year, the Queens College School of Business and School of Arts offer the best of the liberal arts while building on emerging trends and our vast network of business partners and community organizations. These new schools combine coursework in areas such as fintech and studio art with interdisciplinary research and community collaboration, preparing our students to solve real-world problems.

"Our tuition won't break the bank, as it's among the most affordable in the nation. Over 85% of students who enter as freshmen and graduate within four years earn their degrees without taking federal student loans, and we are in the top 1% of colleges nationwide in helping students from lower-income families attain upward social and economic mobility. "Located in the world's most exciting city, QC provides a vibrant student life experience for students who live on or off campus. We have over 100 student clubs, 15 NCAA Division II teams, and numerous intramural and recreation programs. Our students represent 140 countries, creating an extraordinarily diverse and welcoming campus community. QC is home to the Kupferberg Center for the Arts, which presents a vast amount of programming, and the Godwin-Ternbach Museum, which holds thought-provoking exhibitions."

SELECTIVITY

# of total applicants	21,597
% of total applicants accepted	63
% of total acceptees attending	12
# of in-state applicants	19,287
% of in-state applicants accepted	66
# of out-of-state-applicants	465
% of applicants accepted from out of state	72
# of international applicants	1,845
% of international applicants accepted	24

First-Year Profile

Testing policy	Test Optional
Range SAT composite	1260–1450
Range SAT EBRW	590–740
Range SAT math	650–760
% submitting SAT scores	2
Average HS GPA	3.5
% submitting high school GPA	93

Important Dates

Regular	
Notified by	Rolling, 2/1
Nonfall registration?	Yes

FINANCIAL FACTS

Annual in-state tuition	$6,930
Annual out-of-state tuition	$18,600
Food and housing	$17,132
Required fees	$608
Books and supplies	$1,500
Average need-based scholarship (First-year)	$9,800 ($10,100)
% students with need rec. need-based scholarship or grant aid (First-year)	92 (93)
% students with need rec. non-need-based scholarship or grant aid (First-year)	67 (87)
% students with need rec. need-based self-help aid (First-year)	11 (7)
% students rec. any financial aid (First-year)	62 (70)
% UG borrow to pay for school	13
Average cumulative indebtedness	$13,868
% of students with need fully met (First-year)	3 (3)
Average % of student need met (First-year)	47 (48)

Claremont McKenna College

500 E 9th Street, Claremont, CA 91711 • Admissions: 909-621-8088

Survey Snapshot
Career services are great
Internships are widely available
Lab facilities are great

RATINGS	
Quality of Life	97
Fire Safety	89
Green	91
Academic	96
Profs Interesting	98
Profs Accessible	98
Admissions	98
Financial Aid	97

CAMPUS LIFE

Type of school	Private
Environment	Town

Students

Degree-seeking undergrad enrollment	1,371
% male/female/not reported	51/49/0
% from out of state	54
% First-year live on campus	100
% Ugrads live on campus	97
# of fraternities	0
# of sororities	0
% Asian	20
% Black or African American	4
% Hispanic	14
% Native American	0
% Pacific Islander	<1
% Race and/or ethnicity unknown	5
% Two or more races	10
% White	35
% International	14
# of countries represented	41

CAMPUS MENTAL HEALTH SERVICES

Offers mental health/wellness program	Yes
Mental health training available to students	Yes
Employs Chief Wellness Officer	NR
Peer-to-peer mental health offerings	Yes
Counseling center has guidelines or accreditation	NR
Mental health/well-being courses	NR

ACADEMICS

% students returning for sophomore year	98
% students graduating within 4 years	70
% students graduating within 6 years	90
Calendar	Semester
Student/faculty ratio	8:1
Most common class size 10–19.	(76%)

STUDENTS SAY "..."

Academics

Claremont McKenna College offers a "very challenging but rewarding" liberal arts education, leveraging its proximity to Los Angeles—just 30 miles away—and joint curriculars with the other four undergraduate member schools of The Claremont Colleges to ensure that students get large university resources but small school relationships with faculty. Experiential learning is a keystone of the curriculum, and "there are many opportunities for students to work with professors outside of class on research projects, or in campus research centers"; more than 90 percent of students also complete internships. The Athenaeum speaking series also offers students prominent guest speakers on a regular basis: "Oftentimes, someone who would be a commencement speaker somewhere else will be a speaker at the Athenaeum on a random Wednesday."

Professors "are very open to seeing us outside of class and facilitating the tough discussions in class that we need to have in order to grow," and "are flexible but also have high expectations that you get motivated to meet." Classes are designed with innovative pedagogy in mind: for example, the Philosophy, Politics, and Economics programs have "three courses dedicated to weekly one-on-one debates and paper exchanges in 'tutorials,'" and another class uses "a digital simulator where we can simulate economic concepts in class in a game-like interface." The administration is incredibly supportive, and there are "counseling, tutoring, career services, and many resources and locations for students to just go to whenever they need to talk about anything."

Campus Life

There "is a rich social life to be had on campus," and everyone is "very involved and engaged, so when students are not in classes, they're taking meetings for clubs or working at research institutes." CMC has a "very high caliber of student clubs and organizations"; for instance, the CMC Mock Trial and Model UN teams are nationally lauded, and there "is a dedicated group of welcoming students behind every club and sport." The school also knows how to make the most of its beautiful campus and weather that "is almost always sunny." There are "many free day trips and incredible opportunities to see sporting events, concerts, or just get into nature," and one student cites activities such as intramural sports, fitness classes, and painting before summing things up simply as "there's just so [much] offered here." There's also a variety of athletic offerings: "basically our entire campus shows up to big football/water polo games," and there are also intramural sports as well as the fact that "people love getting outside [and] playing casual sports."

Student Body

The "highly intelligent and supportive" students at CMC "are very driven and bring multiple different perspectives to the table," with a "critical thinking mindset and freedom of speech mentality." As one student says, "We pride ourselves on considering a wide variety of opinions as we develop solutions for the modern world." That means that while some think it's "kind of a preppy school," there are also "a lot of opportunities here for first generation or low-income students, and so there is quite a diverse population." Students suggest the overall attitude is "beyond humble" and this drives long-term support, as students "continue to receive good support from a strong alumni network after college."

Claremont McKenna College

Financial Aid: 909-621-8356 • E-Mail: admission@cmc.edu • Website: www.claremontmckenna.edu

THE PRINCETON REVIEW SAYS

Admissions

The school reports that its standardized testing policy for use in admission for Fall 2026 is Test Optional. The Princeton Review suggests that interested applicants consult with the school for the most up-to-date standardized testing policies. *Very important factors considered include:* rigor of secondary school record, academic GPA, application essay, recommendation(s), extracurricular activities, character/personal qualities. *Important factors considered include:* interview, talent/ability. *Other factors considered include:* class rank, standardized test scores, first generation, geographical residence, volunteer work, work experience. High school diploma is required and GED is accepted. *Academic units required:* 4 English, 3 math, 2 science, 2 science labs, 3 language (other than English), 1 social studies, 1 history. *Academic units recommended:* 4 English, 4 math, 3 science, 3 science labs, 3 language (other than English), 1 social studies, 2 history.

Financial Aid

Students should submit: FAFSA; CSS PROFILE; Business/Farm Supplement. Priority filing deadline is 1/17. The Princeton Review suggests that all financial aid forms be submitted as soon as possible. *Need-based scholarships/grants offered:* Federal Pell; Federal SEOG; State scholarships/grants; Private scholarships; College/university scholarship or grant aid from institutional funds. *Loan aid offered:* Federal Direct Subsidized Loans; Federal Direct Unsubsidized Loans; Direct PLUS loans; College/university loans from institutional funds. Admitted students will be notified of awards on a rolling basis beginning 3/22. Federal Work-Study Program available. Institutional employment available.

The Inside Word

In general, small and selective schools like CMC, which accepts only 10 percent of applicants, are more likely to look beyond your grades. As CMC is currently Test Optional, that's even truer. Claremont McKenna's policy of not considering financial need when making admission decisions means there are a lot of applicants, and you'll want to have an outstanding academic record to stand out from the crowd. Just be prepared to back that up with a demonstration of how well you'd fit the school.

THE SCHOOL SAYS

From the Admissions Office

"Since 1946, Claremont McKenna has been guided by a distinctive mission in higher education: to prepare students for thoughtful and productive lives, and responsible leadership in business, government, and the professions. CMC is committed to higher, deeper, and broader learning through the support of faculty and student scholarship that contributes to intellectual vitality and the understanding of public policy issues. Our students may choose from majors across 11 academic departments, including the social sciences, humanities, and innovative programs such as our new Kravis Department of Integrated Sciences and the Oxford-style Philosophy, Politics, and Economics (PPE) program. We prepare our students for leadership roles that address the world's challenges through our culture of individualized mentorship, coupled with robust access to research with faculty, most notably through 11 institutes and centers specializing in a range of interests, including finance and economics, human rights, local and state politics, and entrepreneurship. In tandem with academics, our students receive expert guidance to help them discover how their intellectual curiosity pairs with real-life experiences. With career readiness support from our Soll Center for Student Opportunity, 88% of our students participate in at least one internship by their senior year and 97% of our graduates have defined plans six months after graduation. A CMC hallmark is also our commitment to cultivating an inclusive community and fostering our Open Academy commitments to freedom of expression, viewpoint diversity, and constructive dialogue. Through The Open Academy—our nationally-recognized integration of these commitments through college-wide programs including new student orientation, faculty-led salons, and our CARE Center and signature Athenaeum speaker series—CMC students are given the tools to listen respectfully, ask incisive questions, engage with greater curiosity, and be open to differences of opinion. By blending the intellectual breadth of a liberal arts education with the practical concerns of public affairs, CMC students develop the vision, skills, and values necessary to become leaders in all sectors of society."

SELECTIVITY

# of total applicants	6,939
% of total applicants accepted	9
% of total acceptees attending	51
# of in-state applicants	2,599
% of in-state applicants accepted	10
# of out-of-state-applicants	1,996
% of applicants accepted from out of state	14
# of international applicants	2,344
% of international applicants accepted	5
# of early decision applicants	978
% of early decision applicants accepted	22
# offered a place on the wait list	711
# admitted from wait list	61

First-Year Profile

Testing policy	Test Optional
Range SAT composite	1480–1540
Range SAT EBRW	730–760
Range SAT math	740–790
Range ACT composite	33–35
% submitting SAT scores	34
% submitting ACT scores	14
% graduated top 10% of class	64
% graduated top 25% of class	94
% graduated top 50% of class	100
% submitting high school rank	15

Important Dates

Early decision	
Apply by	11/1
Notified by	12/15
Other ED apply by	1/10
Other ED notified by	2/15
Regular	
Apply by	1/10
Notified by	4/1
Nonfall registration?	Yes

FINANCIAL FACTS

Annual tuition	$75,300
Food and housing	$23,270
Required fees	$420
Average need-based scholarship (First-year)	$63,485 ($68,936)
% students with need rec. need-based scholarship or grant aid (First-year)	100 (100)
% students with need rec. non-need-based scholarship or grant aid (First-year)	50 (52)
% students with need rec. need-based self-help aid (First-year)	91 (86)
% students rec. any financial aid (First-year)	46 (46)
% UG borrow to pay for school	34
Average cumulative indebtedness	$27,023
% of students with need fully met (First-year)	98 (100)
Average % of student need met (First-year)	100 (100)

CLARK UNIVERSITY

950 Main Street, Worcester, MA 01610-1477 • Admissions: 508-793-7431

Survey Snapshot
Great off-campus food
Active minority support groups
Easy to get around campus

RATINGS

Quality of Life	**81**
Fire Safety	**97**
Green	**60***
Academic	**82**
Profs Interesting	**89**
Profs Accessible	**90**
Admissions	**91**
Financial Aid	**91**

CAMPUS LIFE

Type of school	Private
Environment	City

Students

Degree-seeking undergrad enrollment	2,077
% male/female/not reported	43/57/<1
% from out of state	59
% First-year from public high school	68
% First-year live on campus	96
% Ugrads live on campus	67
# of fraternities	0
# of sororities	0
% Asian	7
% Black or African American	7
% Hispanic	14
% Native American	0
% Pacific Islander	<1
% Race and/or ethnicity unknown	3
% Two or more races	5
% White	59
% International	6
# of countries represented	52

CAMPUS MENTAL HEALTH SERVICES

Offers mental health/wellness program	Yes
Mental health training available to students	Yes
Employs Chief Wellness Officer	Yes
Peer-to-peer mental health offerings	Yes
Counseling center has guidelines or accreditation	Yes
Mental health/well-being courses	Yes, for-credit

ACADEMICS

% students returning for sophomore year	84
% students graduating within 4 years	73
% students graduating within 6 years	77
Calendar	Semester
Student/faculty ratio	10:1
Most common class size 10–19.	(48%)
Most common lab/discussion size 10–19.	(52%)

Most Popular Majors
Psychology; Political Science and Government; Business Administration and Management

Applicants Often Prefer
Boston College, Boston University, Brandeis University

Applicants Sometimes Prefer
American University, Connecticut College, The George Washington University, Mount Holyoke College, Northeastern University, Skidmore College, Syracuse University, University of Massachusetts—Amherst

Applicants Rarely Prefer
Ithaca College, University of Vermont, Wheaton College (MA)

STUDENTS SAY "..."

Academics

The liberal arts curriculum at Clark University is often described as having "an incredible range and value of programs offered," including "interdisciplinary study, experiential learning, research opportunities, small close-knit campus, [and] abundant resources." The school "offers so much support, especially to first-years," and "from your first day on campus you have a peer mentor, a pre-major advisor, and a first-year success advisor to guide and help you." Furthermore, Clark Core courses, designed to develop critical thinking through real-world experiences and capstone projects, ensure that the school is full of "options for students who don't [yet] know what they want to study." Cross-disciplinary exploration is highly encouraged, and students appreciate "the flexibility of the courses you're able to take," though some caution that the beloved small class sizes can occasionally backfire, making it "hard to get into a course you need when there are only 10 seats." For those who have narrowed down their interests, the university is "excellent for outreach and field-specific career and experience opportunities." Although a few note that the "administration plays a minimal part in the welcoming environment," it's generally agreed that peers are supportive and faculty "bring a great deal of knowledge and experience that is worth the academic rigor." Many classes "utilize unorthodox methods of curriculum," as one student recounts: "I had a seminar class that was entirely student-run and took place at a kitchen table." Between the "ability to connect with your professors and the strong academics," students feel they "are able to really do what you are interested in."

Campus Life

For many undergrads, student clubs and organizations are "the basis for how people make friends and social groups are formed." While this can make the school "a little cliquey," it also serves to make "the student-run club scene…very popular since we don't have Greek life." The "emphasis on clubs [fosters] community and inclusivity on our campus," and "student organization events are well run and well executed," although there's a bit of concern about recent budget cutbacks, especially when it comes to the dining hall. The performing arts scene "is very big…,with all of the dance troupes, a cappella groups, and improv troupes" bringing people together for practices and performances. While students say there isn't that much to do in Worcester, the school makes up for that with a long menu of events, clubs, and activities. Schedules are packed with "consistent and easily available events such as karaoke nights, open mics, dances, shows, dinners, craft nights, and guest speakers," as well as campus traditions like Spree Day, when students blow off steam in a big outdoor party before finals and GALA, an international dance performance that some describe as "the biggest event on campus." And ultimately, "It's really just being around friends, whether it's grabbing food or studying in the library together; once you find your people at Clark, you're set."

Student Body

"For a school this size, it's genuinely impressive the breadth of backgrounds that are represented," says one student. There is "a large emphasis from the student body on arts," part of what a student calls "a nice blend of sports kids and non-sports kids." These "quirky multi-faceted students and people…value academics and extracurriculars," and many people "have very niche academic interests and use their majors to reflect interdisciplinary interests." There is a significant LGBTQ+ population, which "fosters a pretty open-minded and inclusive environment for students"—at least those who are likewise open—and "many…have the opportunity to express themselves and explore their identities alongside their supportive peers." This "very outspoken" crowd is "civically engaged and will be involved in political discussions through both direct action and passive resistance." Overall, Clark is a place with "a strong sense of camaraderie where everyone feels included and motivated to do their best."

Clark University

E-Mail: admissions@clarku.edu • Website: www.clarku.edu

THE PRINCETON REVIEW SAYS

Admissions

The school reports that its standardized testing policy for use in admission for Fall 2026 is Test Optional. The Princeton Review suggests that interested applicants consult with the school for the most up-to-date standardized testing policies. *Very important factors considered include:* rigor of secondary school record, academic GPA, recommendation(s). *Important factors considered include:* application essay, extracurricular activities, talent/ability, character/personal qualities, volunteer work. *Other factors considered include:* class rank, standardized test scores, interview, first generation, geographical residence, work experience, level of applicant's interest. High school diploma is required and GED is accepted. *Academic units recommended:* 4 English, 3 math, 3 science, 2 science labs, 2 language (other than English), 2 social studies, 2 history.

Financial Aid

Students should submit: FAFSA; CSS PROFILE; Institution's own financial aid form; State aid form; Business/Farm Supplement. Priority filing deadline is 1/15. The Princeton Review suggests that all financial aid forms be submitted as soon as possible. *Need-based scholarships/grants offered:* Federal Pell; Federal SEOG; State scholarships/grants; Private scholarships. *Loan aid offered:* Federal Direct Subsidized Loans; Federal Direct Unsubsidized Loans; Direct PLUS loans; State Loans; College/university loans from institutional funds. Admitted students will be notified of awards on or about 3/31. Federal Work-Study Program available. Institutional employment available.

The Inside Word

Admissions officers at Clark want students who want to challenge themselves both in and out of the classroom. Successful applicants tend to have achieved a strong A/B average in demanding honors, AP, or equivalent courses. However, the university also acknowledges and appreciates those candidates who have demonstrated a steady improvement throughout their high school tenure. Since admissions officers aim to take a holistic approach, they also closely assess essays, extracurricular involvement, and letters of recommendations. Clark is a Test Optional school, and that applies to merit aid as well.

THE SCHOOL SAYS

From the Admissions Office

"Clark University empowers students to drive meaningful change in a dynamic world. Founded in 1887 and located in the vibrant second-largest city in New England, we offer a hands-on, liberal arts-based research education that extends beyond traditional classrooms. Students engage in real-world projects, guided by dedicated faculty who are passionate about teaching and innovation. Within the School of Climate, Environment, and Society, students tackle pressing environmental challenges through research and fieldwork, collaborating on projects like climate change studies and sustainable urban planning. The Becker School of Design & Technology provides a cutting-edge environment for aspiring game designers and interactive media creators, fostering innovation in digital art and technology. Meanwhile, the School of Business equips future leaders with the skills and knowledge to navigate the complexities of the global marketplace, offering opportunities for internships and networking through the Stevenish Career Management Center. Undergraduates across all disciplines collaborate with award-winning researchers, developing solutions to pressing global challenges. Real-world examples include environmental science students contributing to climate research and art history students curating exhibits at the Worcester Art Museum. Our nationally recognized 4+1 Master's program provides a unique, tuition-free pathway to graduate studies. We selectively admit students who thrive in our collaborative environment and embody our motto: 'Challenge Convention. Change Our World.'"

SELECTIVITY

# of total applicants	10,936
% of total applicants accepted	40
% of total acceptees attending	10
# offered a place on the wait list	289
# admitted from wait list	57

First-Year Profile

Testing policy	Test Optional
Range SAT composite	1270–1410
Range SAT EBRW	650–730
Range SAT math	610–690
Range ACT composite	26–32
% submitting SAT scores	81
% submitting ACT scores	13
Average HS GPA	3.8
% submitting high school GPA	62
% graduated top 10% of class	29
% graduated top 25% of class	61
% graduated top 50% of class	90
% submitting high school rank	100

Important Dates

Early decision	
Apply by	11/1
Notified by	12/15
Other ED apply by	1/15
Other ED notified by	2/15
Early action	
Apply by	11/1
Notified by	1/15
Regular	
Notified by	4/1
Nonfall registration?	Yes

FINANCIAL FACTS

Annual tuition	$62,070
Food and housing	$14,360
Required fees (First-year)	$1,140 ($1,540)
Books and supplies	$900
Average need-based scholarship (First-year)	$43,797 ($44,164)
% students with need rec. need-based scholarship or grant aid (First-year)	99 (97)
% students with need rec. non-need-based scholarship or grant aid (First-year)	16 (24)
% students with need rec. need-based self-help aid (First-year)	70 (65)
% students rec. any financial aid (First-year)	97 (99)
% UG borrow to pay for school	53
Average cumulative indebtedness	$37,343
% of students with need fully met (First-year)	35 (52)
Average % of student need met (First-year)	90 (92)

CLARKSON UNIVERSITY

8 Clarkson Avenue, Potsdam, NY 13699 • Admissions: 315-268-6480

Survey Snapshot
Career services are great
Intramural sports are popular
Alumni active on campus

RATINGS	
Quality of Life	77
Fire Safety	94
Green	93
Academic	74
Profs Interesting	80
Profs Accessible	87
Admissions	88
Financial Aid	90

CAMPUS LIFE

Type of school	Private
Environment	Village

Students

Degree-seeking undergrad enrollment	2,066
% male/female/not reported	69/31/0
% from out of state	30
% First-year from public high school	84
% First-year live on campus	94
% Ugrads live on campus	94
# of fraternities (% join)	8 (9)
# of sororities (% join)	4 (7)
% Asian	2
% Black or African American	2
% Hispanic	13
% Native American	<1
% Pacific Islander	0
% Race and/or ethnicity unknown	<1
% Two or more races	4
% White	73
% International	5
# of countries represented	42

CAMPUS MENTAL HEALTH SERVICES

Offers mental health/wellness program	Yes
Mental health training available to students	Yes
Employs Chief Wellness Officer	No
Peer-to-peer mental health offerings	Yes
Counseling center has guidelines or accreditation	No
Mental health/well-being courses	Yes, non-credit

ACADEMICS

% students returning for sophomore year	88
% students graduating within 4 years	59
% students graduating within 6 years	72
Calendar	Semester
Student/faculty ratio	14:1
Most common class size 10–19.	(30%)
Most common lab/discussion size 10–19.	(45%)

Most Popular Majors
Aerospace, Aeronautical and Astronautical/Space Engineering; Civil Engineering; Mechanical Engineering

Applicants Often Prefer
Rensselaer Polytechnic Institute, Rochester Institute of Technology, Syracuse University

Applicants Sometimes Prefer
Le Moyne College, St. Lawrence University, Worcester Polytechnic Institute

Applicants Rarely Prefer
Embry—Riddle Aeronautical University (FL), Siena University, Union College (NY), University of Rochester

STUDENTS SAY "..."

Academics

Clarkson University is a private research university that makes the most of its scenic upstate New York location to make it "very easy to enter research as an undergraduate." Academics at Clarkson are "appropriately challenging" and one biologist notes that it "keeps you busy, but it is manageable." Students appreciate the variety of "project-based classes" and report that even lectures "often have a project component." Students also enjoy the internship opportunities and research labs; one student details spending a semester working for biologists in the Adirondack Park Forest. Students describe a supportive and engaging academic environment where "discussion is prioritized over lectures" and professors provide "strong academic support outside class time" and are "always ready to give a helping hand." While some students say that a few professors are "tough" or "seem as if they are here for their research and teaching is a side job," many others emphasize that their professors "are engaging, fun, and very knowledgeable in their curriculum" and that most "teach well and grade generously." One student adds, "I love my professors. They are very understanding and are always willing to help you."

Campus Life

Students report an academically focused culture where peers are often "studying during the day. It's not surprising that many of the popular extracurriculars at UofL tend to reflect the school's STEM focus, including a number of SPEED teams (Student Projects for Engineering Experience and Design) where students can build various vehicles (all-terrain to an open-wheel race car) or "team up with the local community to design and build mostly wooden bridges spanning from five to 75 feet." Of course, there's also a good mix of athletic options; as one student illustrates, "I play softball, and I also enjoy using the gym to lift weights, run, and play different sports like pickleball and basketball." Other popular activities include attending hockey games, playing rugby and golf, and horseback riding with the equestrian team. So far as purely social events go, students mention frat parties, although some find their way to "casual and calm" hangouts instead. Students say the location is one of the best things about the school, which tends to attract "people who like the mountains" and enjoy hiking, skiing, camping, and rock climbing. "The Clarkson Outing Club is absolutely phenomenal," says one student. Whatever type of activity you choose, students agree that it is "easy to get outdoors with groups of new people often."

Student Body

Clarkson is a "close-knit community" of people who are mostly "very open to conversation and friendly." As one student describes it, "By the end of your senior year you will know everyone if you are a social person." Clarkson "attracts outdoorsy engineers" and there is a "great emphasis on spending time outside and sustainability." Another student agrees, describing fellow classmates as "pretty down-to-earth people who are very nature-oriented." Given the school's niche—"a small technology-based school very far north in New York"—Clarkson has tended to have a large male population, hailing largely from New England and the Northeast. That said, "the amount of diversity on campus is increasing with more promotion of our international programs" and the students who attend are definitively "here because they want to be." Because of its size, "Everyone knows everyone. You get to have the same classes with the same people for a while," which is "a great opportunity to form close friendships." It's a very supportive environment where "you will find help everywhere you look for it," says one student, whether it's from fellow students or professors. Another student agrees, saying, "all of us help and push each other to perform the best we can as well. Overall, it is a great environment to be in for college."

CLARKSON UNIVERSITY

Financial Aid: 315-268-3707 • E-Mail: admissions@clarkson.edu • Website: www.clarkson.edu

THE PRINCETON REVIEW SAYS

Admissions

The school reports that its standardized testing policy for use in admission for Fall 2026 is Test Optional. The Princeton Review suggests that interested applicants consult with the school for the most up-to-date standardized testing policies. *Very important factors considered include:* rigor of secondary school record. *Important factors considered include:* academic GPA, application essay, recommendation(s), interview, extracurricular activities. *Other factors considered include:* class rank, standardized test scores, talent/ability, character/personal qualities, first generation, volunteer work, work experience, level of applicant's interest. High school diploma is required and GED is accepted. *Academic units required:* 4 English, 3 math, 3 science, 4 social studies. *Academic units recommended:* 4 English, 4 math, 4 science, 4 social studies.

Financial Aid

Students should submit: FAFSA. Priority filing deadline is 2/1. The Princeton Review suggests that all financial aid forms be submitted as soon as possible. *Need-based scholarships/grants offered:* Federal Pell; Federal SEOG; State scholarships/grants; Private scholarships; College/university scholarship or grant aid from institutional funds. *Loan aid offered:* Federal Direct Subsidized Loans; Federal Direct Unsubsidized Loans; Direct PLUS loans; College/university loans from institutional funds. Admitted students will be notified of awards on or about 2/15. Federal Work-Study Program available. Institutional employment available.

The Inside Word

Clarkson wants students with a strong background in science and math who exhibit a curiosity for applying technology and science in the real world. Also show them that you're interested in being involved outside the classroom. Students with solid transcripts will have a good shot at admission. Serious candidates should avail themselves of the interview, as well. If you have a strong application and strong desire to come here, the interview could help you get some scholarship money.

THE SCHOOL SAYS

From the Admissions Office

"Clarkson University is the institution of choice for more than 4,600 undergraduate and graduate students from diverse backgrounds who embrace challenge and thrive in a rigorous, highly collaborative learning environment. Our 640-wooded-acre main campus is adjacent to the six-million-acre Adirondack Park, which offers exceptional outdoor recreation and a living laboratory for field research and environmental studies.

"Clarkson's programs in engineering, business, the sciences, liberal arts, education, and the health professions emphasize team-based learning as well as immersion in sustainability principles, creative problem-solving and leadership skills. Clarkson is also on the leading edge of today's emerging technologies and fields of study offering innovative, boundary-spanning degree programs in engineering and management, digital arts and sciences, environmental science and policy, and the health professions among others.

"At Clarkson, students and faculty work closely together in a supportive and personalized environment. Students are encouraged to participate in faculty-mentored research projects from their first year, and to take advantage of co-ops and study abroad programs. Our collaborative and hands-on approach to education translates into remarkably successful careers and meaningful contributions to society; our placement rates into students' career choice are among the highest in the country. Alumni experience accelerated career growth. One in five alumni is already a CEO, president, or vice president of a company."

SELECTIVITY

# of total applicants	4,948
% of total applicants accepted	82
% of total acceptees attending	13
# of in-state applicants	2,312
% of in-state applicants accepted	85
# of out-of-state-applicants	1,493
% of applicants accepted from out of state	92
# of international applicants	1,143
% of international applicants accepted	65
# of early decision applicants	235
% of early decision applicants accepted	76
# offered a place on the wait list	44
# admitted from wait list	3

First-Year Profile

Testing policy	Test Optional
Range SAT composite	1190–1360
Range SAT EBRW	590–680
Range SAT math	590–690
Range ACT composite	26–31
% submitting SAT scores	49
% submitting ACT scores	7
Average HS GPA	3.7
% submitting high school GPA	95
% graduated top 10% of class	46
% graduated top 25% of class	75
% graduated top 50% of class	95
% submitting high school rank	48

Important Dates

Early decision	
Apply by	12/1
Regular	
Notified by	Rolling, 11/1
Nonfall registration?	Yes

FINANCIAL FACTS

Annual tuition	$61,594
Food and housing	$19,368
Required fees	$1,370
Books and supplies	$1,560
Average need-based scholarship (First-year)	$42,010 ($42,092)
% students with need rec. need-based scholarship or grant aid (First-year)	99 (99)
% students with need rec. non-need-based scholarship or grant aid (First-year)	31 (36)
% students with need rec. need-based self-help aid (First-year)	64 (58)
% students rec. any financial aid (First-year)	100 (94)
% UG borrow to pay for school	75
Average cumulative indebtedness	$27,000
% of students with need fully met (First-year)	37 (41)
Average % of student need met (First-year)	80 (83)

Clemson University

105 Sikes Hall, Clemson, SC 29634 • Admissions: 864-656-2287

Survey Snapshot
Recreation facilities are great
Frats and sororities are popular
Intramural sports are popular

RATINGS

Quality of Life	92
Fire Safety	95
Green	96
Academic	83
Profs Interesting	90
Profs Accessible	93
Admissions	93
Financial Aid	82

CAMPUS LIFE

Type of school	Public
Environment	Village

Students

Degree-seeking undergrad enrollment	23,300
% male/female/not reported	46/54/0
% from out of state	41
% First-year from public high school	89
% First-year live on campus	97
% Ugrads live on campus	8
# of fraternities (% join)	26 (19)
# of sororities (% join)	20 (38)
% Asian	3
% Black or African American	5
% Hispanic	9
% Native American	<1
% Pacific Islander	<1
% Race and/or ethnicity unknown	2
% Two or more races	4
% White	76
% International	1
# of countries represented	61

CAMPUS MENTAL HEALTH SERVICES

Offers mental health/wellness program	Yes
Mental health training available to students	Yes
Employs Chief Wellness Officer	Yes
Peer-to-peer mental health offerings	Yes
Counseling center has guidelines or accreditation	Yes
Mental health/well-being courses	Yes, for-credit

ACADEMICS

% students returning for sophomore year	94
% students graduating within 4 years	68
% students graduating within 6 years	87
Calendar	Semester
Student/faculty ratio	16:1
Most common class size 10–19.	(21%)

Most Popular Majors
Business/Commerce; Engineering; Biology/Biological Sciences

Applicants Also Look At
Auburn University, College of Charleston, Georgia Institute of Technology, North Carolina State University, University of Florida, University of Georgia, University of North Carolina at Chapel Hill, University of South Carolina—Columbia, University of Tennessee—Knoxville, Virginia Tech

STUDENTS SAY "..."

Academics

One of Clemson University's "greatest strengths is its ability to balance growth with tradition" to create "a campus that feels both forward-thinking and deeply rooted." Experiential learning and undergraduate research—the Clemson Elevate strategy—provide the support needed to take students "out of the classroom to gather data, conduct experiments, and test theories." Its innovative, cross-disciplinary Creative Inquiry approach offers nearly 400 multi-year projects, through which students can be "led in research and community projects by faculty mentors in small groups." Additionally, students note that "at least 100 hours of hands-on experience in the field" is a requirement for some of their degrees, and even when not, it's a great way to pick up "skills that help supplement your learning." To that end, the environment "is very open and encourages discourse from all viewpoints," led by faculty who "drive a challenging curriculum, and expect the best from their students." That said, professors are "willing to help students in any way they can" and "provide all the tools necessary to succeed in their class, future classes, and in life itself." As one student puts it: "Academic excellence here is not pursued in isolation; it is supported by a culture that values mentorship, collaboration, and personal growth."

Campus Life

Clemson is surrounded by numerous things to do, from local restaurants to three neighboring towns, with students noting that it's "easy to walk everywhere," including an Amtrak station: "I am easily able to travel despite not having a car." More importantly, Clemson itself is "active, social, and centered around a strong sense of community," with hundreds of student organizations, "decently big" Greek life, and "lots of events"—especially when it comes to sports: "Game days are a centerpiece of campus life, beginning early with tailgates and continuing through packed stadiums and celebrations afterward." Additionally, there's "such great nature and weather so students go on walks and runs outside," either through "the beautiful campus" or down to the beach at Lake Hartwell, South Carolina Botanical Gardens, or the mountain, meaning there's a nice mix of kayaking, paddleboarding, and hiking. Other highlights mentioned include "lounging by the reflection pond" or heading to the Fike Center, which "is like a gym/pool/yoga studio that is very nice." As one student puts it, "There really is always something to do and someone to do it with."

Student Body

Tigers are described as being "very driven for academic success, while balancing a healthy social life and strong school spirit." This bunch "[takes] pride in this school and it shows through the strong participation in campus traditions, athletics, and student organizations." Between projects, clubs, and athletic teams, Clemson "has countless communities" so "everyone can feel like they have somewhere to belong as long as they are willing to look for it." Students "come from many backgrounds, which makes campus lively and full of different perspectives," and most "have the Southern hospitality you want to see when making new friends, even if they aren't from the South." Most of this ambitious crew "have very different interests and hobbies that they pursue to a very high level," which contributes to a student body that "feels energetic, loud at games, and [is] very involved on campus, but also friendly and easy to talk to." At its heart, this "vibrant culture of tradition, from the sea of orange in Death Valley [the stadium] to the symbolic Clemson Ring, creates a unique, unified environment that motivates every Tiger to strive for the best in all they do."

CLEMSON UNIVERSITY

Financial Aid: 864-656-2280 • E-Mail: apply@clemson.edu • Website: www.clemson.edu

THE PRINCETON REVIEW SAYS

Admissions

The school reports that its standardized testing policy for use in admission for Fall 2026 is Test Optional. The Princeton Review suggests that interested applicants consult with the school for the most up-to-date standardized testing policies. *Very important factors considered include:* rigor of secondary school record, class rank, academic GPA, state residency. *Important factors considered include:* standardized test scores. *Other factors considered include:* recommendation(s), extracurricular activities, talent/ability, first generation, alumni/ae relation, geographical residence. High school diploma is required and GED is accepted. *Academic units required:* 4 English, 3 math, 3 science, 3 science labs, 2 language (other than English), 2 social studies, 1 history, 2 academic electives, 1 visual/performing arts. *Academic units recommended:* 3 language (other than English).

Financial Aid

Students should submit: FAFSA. Priority filing deadline is 1/2. The Princeton Review suggests that all financial aid forms be submitted as soon as possible. *Need-based scholarships/grants offered:* Federal Pell; Federal SEOG; State scholarships/grants; Private scholarships; College/university scholarship or grant aid from institutional funds. *Loan aid offered:* Federal Direct Subsidized Loans; Federal Direct Unsubsidized Loans; Direct PLUS loans. Admitted students will be notified of awards on a rolling basis beginning 3/1. Federal Work-Study Program available. Institutional employment available.

The Inside Word

Earning admission to Clemson is challenging and competitive, but not unattainable. Clemson's first and foremost priority is considering students' academic achievements. Candidates will significantly improve their chances of admission with a strong GPA, challenging coursework, and a high SAT or ACT score, if submitting. The university aims to build a diverse class every year, so they also pay attention to applicants' unique experiences, backgrounds, and community engagement. Therefore, demonstrated involvement in things like clubs, teams, community service, or part-time jobs will help you stand out from the crowd.

THE SCHOOL SAYS

From the Admissions Office

"Set in a college town with a beautiful backdrop of lakeshore and mountains, Clemson University attracts students looking for a rigorous academic experience, world-class research opportunities, strong sense of community, and vibrant school spirit.

"One of the country's most selective public research universities, Clemson was founded in 1889 with a mission to be a 'high seminary of learning' dedicated to teaching, research, and service. Today, these three concepts remain at the heart of the University and provide the framework for an exceptional educational experience. At Clemson, professors take the time to get to know students and explore innovative ways of teaching. Exceptional teaching is one reason our retention and graduation rates rank among the highest in the country for public universities and why Clemson continues to attract a talented student body.

"Clemson offers over 550 student clubs and organizations; the spirit that students show for this university is unparalleled.

"Midway between Charlotte, North Carolina, and Atlanta, Georgia, Clemson University is located on 1,400 acres of beautiful rolling hills within the foothills of the Blue Ridge Mountains and along the shores of Lake Hartwell.

"Test scores must be submitted electronically by the respective testing agency. Clemson does not require the SAT or ACT essay. Clemson University super-scores both the SAT and the ACT."

SELECTIVITY

# of total applicants	61,517
% of total applicants accepted	38
% of total acceptees attending	21
# of in-state applicants	9,902
% of in-state applicants accepted	56
# of out-of-state-applicants	50,273
% of applicants accepted from out of state	35
# of international applicants	1,342
% of international applicants accepted	36
# offered a place on the wait list	11,102
# admitted from wait list	112

First-Year Profile

Testing policy	Test Optional
Range SAT composite	1250–1320
Range SAT EBRW	620–700
Range SAT math	620–710
Range ACT composite	28–32
% submitting SAT scores	35
% submitting ACT scores	20
% submitting high school GPA	100
% graduated top 10% of class	55
% graduated top 25% of class	92
% graduated top 50% of class	100
% submitting high school rank	66

Important Dates

Early action	
Apply by	10/15
Notified by	12/15
Regular	
Apply by	5/1
Notified by	Rolling, 2/15
Nonfall registration?	Yes

FINANCIAL FACTS

Annual in-state tuition	$14,038
Annual out-of-state tuition	$39,350
Food and housing	$13,284
Required fees	$1,516
Books and supplies	$1,456
Average need-based scholarship (First-year)	$11,196 ($11,942)
% students with need rec. need-based scholarship or grant aid (First-year)	80 (85)
% students with need rec. non-need-based scholarship or grant aid (First-year)	69 (84)
% students with need rec. need-based self-help aid (First-year)	69 (63)
% students rec. any financial aid (First-year)	37 (45)
% UG borrow to pay for school	48
Average cumulative indebtedness	$32,934
% of students with need fully met (First-year)	13 (13)
Average % of student need met (First-year)	47 (48)

Coe College

1220 First Avenue NE, Cedar Rapids, IA 52402 • Admissions: 319-399-8500

Survey Snapshot
Great library
Internships are widely available
Students are friendly

RATINGS

Quality of Life	85
Fire Safety	88
Green	60*
Academic	85
Profs Interesting	91
Profs Accessible	95
Admissions	87
Financial Aid	90

CAMPUS LIFE

Type of school	Private
Affiliation	Presbyterian
Environment	City

Students

Degree-seeking undergrad enrollment	1,154
% male/female/not reported	55/45/0
% from out of state	46
% First-year live on campus	98
% Ugrads live on campus	89
# of fraternities (% join)	5 (21)
# of sororities (% join)	3 (21)
% Asian	2
% Black or African American	10
% Hispanic	15
% Native American	<1
% Pacific Islander	<1
% Race and/or ethnicity unknown	5
% Two or more races	1
% White	63
% International	4
# of countries represented	24

CAMPUS MENTAL HEALTH SERVICES

Offers mental health/wellness program	Yes
Mental health training available to students	Yes
Employs Chief Wellness Officer	NR
Peer-to-peer mental health offerings	NR
Counseling center has guidelines or accreditation	Yes
Mental health/well-being courses	NR

ACADEMICS

% students returning for sophomore year	76
% students graduating within 4 years	50
% students graduating within 6 years	60
Calendar	Semester
Student/faculty ratio	12:1
Most common class size 10–19.	(40%)
Most common lab/discussion size 10–19.	(57%)

Most Popular Majors

Biology/Biological Sciences; Psychology; Business Administration and Management

Applicants Also Look At

Carthage College, Iowa State University, Mount Mercy University, University of Iowa, University of Northern Iowa

STUDENTS SAY "..."

Academics

Coe College is a small private school that encourages its undergraduates to learn through experience, ensuring that every student takes part in at least one internship, research, or off-campus study opportunity. For the goal-driven population, wanting to make the most of one's time at school is a recurring theme, and students feel "if you put in the work, success is secure." That's at least in part due to "small class sizes, [which are] a HUGE plus in terms of building relationships with professors and other students." That connection with faculty goes a long way, with teachers described as "always here for the students whether it be as an educator or a support mechanism" and as having "the best interest of the students in mind." Many professors "prefer hands-on projects to test our learning or discussions with other students," such as a professional writing class in which "we practiced the skills we learned when we partnered with a local nonprofit and...helped them rework their website to make it more accessible and clear about their mission." Outside of the classroom, students find C3: Creativity, Careers, Community a "phenomenal" place to "build their résumés [and] gain an internship, job opportunities, work studies, graduate school applications, interview coaching, and other amazing opportunities you may need." One student attests: "I went to C3 this last semester and within three weeks, I already had a résumé built, connected with countless people in my area on LinkedIn, and interviewed and got an internship." This type of career support is just one of the reasons why Coe is approaching a decade of nearly 100 percent reported placement in jobs or grad school within nine months of graduation.

Campus Life

"When [the] weather is nice, a lot of people spend it outdoors," and "there is a diverse range of extracurriculars here that students can get involved in." Clubs and organizations "are run by students and bring new and unique events from cultural, educative, and environmental backgrounds," and more than 90 percent of students choose to join. Events are organized by the Student Activities Committee (SAC), which puts on "a lot of things on campus, from taking students to Scream Acres to having bingo nights with great prizes." One student shares that their favorite extracurricular activities are the "cultural clubs, which host many events throughout the year that provide a great learning experience." The school itself "provides a wide array of weekly activities": everything from career fairs and guest speakers to yoga and hot cocoa in the library. "We probably get 25 emails a day from Coe, [and] at least 3 of them are events that are going on that day and 5 others are upcoming events that anyone can attend."

Student Body

Students at Coe "come from a vast array of backgrounds, helping to give many diverse perspectives and ideas, leading [the] campus toward the future." They quickly find unity in this "very tight-knit" and village-like community and note that "It's very easy for all of us to come together under our pride for our school." Many "are involved in athletics on campus, working to balance both varsity athletics and a full courseload," and "you will see multiple people be involved in athletics, Greek life, work, and still maintain a good GPA." This "diverse, optimistic, positive, and determined" bunch "is very welcoming and willing to meet new people" and are willing to "work hard for what they want to achieve."

Coe College

Financial Aid: 319-399-8540 • E-Mail: admission@coe.edu • Website: www.coe.edu

THE PRINCETON REVIEW SAYS

Admissions

The school reports that its standardized testing policy for use in admission for Fall 2026 is Test Optional. The Princeton Review suggests that interested applicants consult with the school for the most up-to-date standardized testing policies. *Very important factors considered include:* academic GPA. *Other factors considered include:* rigor of secondary school record, class rank, standardized test scores, application essay, recommendation(s), interview, extracurricular activities, talent/ability, character/personal qualities, volunteer work, work experience, level of applicant's interest. High school diploma is required and GED is accepted. *Academic units recommended:* 4 English, 3 math, 3 science, 1 science lab, 2 language (other than English), 3 social studies.

Financial Aid

Students should submit: FAFSA. The Princeton Review suggests that all financial aid forms be submitted as soon as possible. *Need-based scholarships/grants offered:* Federal Pell; Federal SEOG; State scholarships/grants; Private scholarships; College/university scholarship or grant aid from institutional funds. *Loan aid offered:* Federal Direct Subsidized Loans; Federal Direct Unsubsidized Loans; Direct PLUS loans. Admitted students will be notified of awards on a rolling basis beginning 12/1. Federal Work-Study Program available. Institutional employment available.

The Inside Word

Students seeking to gain admission to Coe College should illustrate not only academic excellence with a high GPA and test scores (if submitted), but also be well-rounded, displaying interests and ambitions outside the classroom. Of course, academics comes first, so candidates that have completed challenging curriculum will fare best during the review process. For those of you with an aversion to standardized tests, you'll be happy to know that Coe is a Test Optional school. However, in order to qualify for this policy, you must have a minimum GPA of 3.0 or higher.

THE SCHOOL SAYS

From the Admissions Office

"At Coe, your success is our success, so we make sure we help you achieve the goals you have for your degree like starting your dream career or gaining acceptance into a prestigious graduate program. Our emphasis on hands-on instruction and out-of-class experience is one of the reasons a Coe education pays off and graduates find success so quickly. For over a decade, nearly 100% of reporting graduates have been either employed or in graduate school within nine months of graduation. On campus, C3: Creativity, Careers, Community center maintains connections with alumni and industry experts who inform C3 staff on the types of experience employers are looking for and directly assists students in getting that experience. In the classroom, our lower student-faculty ratio and average class size of 16 students means you'll receive personalized, one-on-one attention. Coe is one of the few liberal arts institutions in the country to require hands-on learning for graduation, and that can be satisfied through an internship, research, practicum or off-campus study. Many students complete more than one experience. Coe students have interned at places like the Chicago Board of Trade, Google, Mayo Clinic and NASA. Others have completed research on Coe's campus through the National Science Foundation's Research Experiences for Undergraduates program or the Stead Department of Business Administration & Economics' Spellman Summer Research Program. Still others have combined study abroad with an internship in Monaco or student teaching in Tanzania for an unforgettable offcampus experience. The flexibility in choosing classes and outside learning opportunities creates well-prepared critical thinkers who are adaptable to changing needs in their field."

SELECTIVITY

# of total applicants	4,810
% of total applicants accepted	55
% of total acceptees attending	8

First-Year Profile

Testing policy	Test Optional
Range SAT composite	1050–1250
Range SAT EBRW	560–640
Range SAT math	540–630
Range ACT composite	22–29
% submitting SAT scores	28
% submitting ACT scores	71
Average HS GPA	3.6
% submitting high school GPA	100
% graduated top 10% of class	21
% graduated top 25% of class	43
% graduated top 50% of class	79
% submitting high school rank	60

Important Dates

Early action	
Apply by	12/10
Notified by	1/20
Regular	
Apply by	3/1
Notified by	Rolling, 9/1
Nonfall registration?	Yes

FINANCIAL FACTS

Annual tuition	$58,780
Food and housing	$12,760
Required fees	$350
Books and supplies	$1,000
Average need-based scholarship (First-year)	$46,340 ($49,998)
% students with need rec. need-based scholarship or grant aid (First-year)	100 (100)
% students with need rec. non-need-based scholarship or grant aid (First-year)	24 (25)
% students with need rec. need-based self-help aid (First-year)	72 (71)
% students rec. any financial aid (First-year)	99 (99)
% UG borrow to pay for school	78
Average cumulative indebtedness	$39,399
% of students with need fully met (First-year)	27 (27)
Average % of student need met (First-year)	88 (93)

Colby College

4000 Mayflower Hill, Waterville, ME 04901 • Admissions: 207-859-4800

Survey Snapshot
Recreation facilities are great
Students take advantage of the outdoors
Easy to get around campus

RATINGS

Quality of Life	**84**
Fire Safety	**85**
Green	**93**
Academic	**92**
Profs Interesting	**95**
Profs Accessible	**96**
Admissions	**98**
Financial Aid	**99**

CAMPUS LIFE

Type of school	Private
Environment	Village

Students

Degree-seeking undergrad enrollment	2,354
% male/female/not reported	49/51/<1
% from out of state	91
% First-year live on campus	100
% Ugrads live on campus	97
# of fraternities	0
# of sororities	0
% Asian	8
% Black or African American	5
% Hispanic	9
% Native American	<1
% Pacific Islander	<1
% Race and/or ethnicity unknown	3
% Two or more races	7
% White	57
% International	11

CAMPUS MENTAL HEALTH SERVICES

Offers mental health/wellness program	Yes
Mental health training available to students	Yes
Employs Chief Wellness Officer	Yes
Peer-to-peer mental health offerings	Yes
Counseling center has guidelines or accreditation	Yes
Mental health/well-being courses	Yes, non-credit

ACADEMICS

% students returning for sophomore year	91
% students graduating within 4 years	78
% students graduating within 6 years	87
Calendar	4-1-4
Student/faculty ratio	10:1
Most common class size 10–19.	(100%)

Most Popular Majors

Computer Science; Econometrics and Quantitative Economics; Political Science and Government

Applicants Also Look At

Amherst College; Boston College; Bowdoin College; Brown University; Colgate University; Cornell University; Dartmouth College; Georgetown University; Harvard University; Middlebury College; Tufts University; University of Michigan

STUDENTS SAY "..."

Academics

Colby College is a liberal arts institution that places "an emphasis on active learning," delivering "strong academics [and] lots of resources and opportunities." That extends from student jobs "that often help students explore future career interests" to how funding "for academic or professional endeavors [is] great." Overall, there's the perception of "a strong 'yes' culture that supports students in their endeavors." One student received funding for "a group Spanish immersion in Salamanca, Spain; an internship in Washington, D.C.; and I'm currently…volunteering at a coffee farm in Monteverde, Costa Rica," and feels that "students can do anything they put their mind to and be backed by the College." Another instance of this is the Jan Plan, an immersive term where students explore their interests, choosing from hundreds of unique academic experiences, internships, and individual projects. Global impact is central to a Colby education, with one student sharing that there are "TONS of study abroad options—I'm writing these words from a hotel in Nepal, where I've been studying wildlife and conservation." On the whole, students say "professors are very responsive, passionate, and care deeply for the students," with one adding, "they're eager to share their knowledge with students." Many teachers "integrate research into their courses or experiential learning," like the student whose art history professor "had us deconstruct art takes from…AI, effectively debating (or building upon) it on topics we found interesting." In addition, students appreciate that they are given the opportunity to "learn so many different topics and skills at once that do not limit or pigeonhole [them] into a specific career." Another adds that Colby has "made me feel valued as a student, thinker, person, and global citizen."

Campus Life

"There are a ton of clubs and organizations" to join, and the Student Programming Board "does a great job making sure there is an activity every weekend and many during the week," including Big Prize Bingo, Potato Fest, and Fall Fest. Many students give back by volunteering with Colby Cares about Kids, a "peer mentorship program where you stay with the same kid at a local elementary or middle school year after year." On campus, "the small student population makes it really easy to make spontaneous plans as you run into people throughout the day," and when students want to leave campus, they "often go out to eat downtown or on Main Street." The school's Central Maine location is a veritable outdoor playground. The Outing Club leads weekly hiking trips, and students also enjoy "swimming at the Belgrade lakes (only 10 minutes from campus), watching the annual Colby-Bowdoin games, [and] skiing at Sugarloaf Mountain." Additionally, "the [Ski and Snowboard] club (probably the most popular club on campus) is great at organizing ski trips and helping students get discounts on ski passes." The abundance of social outlets is a great source of balance for Colby students, who say that while "academics are intense, the people are all very focused on living life outside of academics together."

Student Body

"Being surrounded by smart, engaged, and genuinely fun people makes [the] social scene very open," and people "want to continue to engage with big ideas outside of the classroom as well." This is a "warm and close-knit" group wherein many are "white New Englanders," and people "are first and foremost kind." There is "a large student-athlete population on campus" that creates "a strong culture of watching Colby sports," and "many students' schedules revolve around their sport." Most people at Colby "have some sort of academic niche and they love to engage with it," which "is very conducive to a well-rounded life and students can make great connections." A student neatly bundles up their college experience: "To choose Colby, you have to completely buy into your academics, buy into living in Central Maine, buy into the winter. In doing so, the community truly comes together around itself."

COLBY COLLEGE

Financial Aid: 207-859-4830 • E-Mail: admissions@colby.edu • Website: www.colby.edu

THE PRINCETON REVIEW SAYS

Admissions

The school reports that its standardized testing policy for use in admission for Fall 2026 is Test Optional. The Princeton Review suggests that interested applicants consult with the school for the most up-to-date standardized testing policies. *Very important factors considered include:* rigor of secondary school record, academic GPA, recommendation(s), character/personal qualities. *Important factors considered include:* class rank, application essay, extracurricular activities, talent/ability. *Other factors considered include:* standardized test scores, first generation, geographical residence, volunteer work, work experience, level of applicant's interest. High school diploma is required and GED is accepted. *Academic units recommended:* 4 English, 3 math, 2 science, 2 science labs, 3 language (other than English), 2 social studies.

Financial Aid

Students should submit: FAFSA; CSS PROFILE. The Princeton Review suggests that all financial aid forms be submitted as soon as possible. *Need-based scholarships/grants offered:* Federal Pell; Federal SEOG; State scholarships/grants; College/university scholarship or grant aid from institutional funds. *Loan aid offered:* Federal Direct Subsidized Loans; Federal Direct Unsubsidized Loans; Direct PLUS loans. Admitted students will be notified of awards on or about 4/1. Federal Work-Study Program available. Institutional employment available.

The Inside Word

Earning admission to Colby College is no small feat. Most admitted students here are at the top of their class and have equally impressive extracurriculars bolstering their applications. The college has been Test Optional since 2018, so applicants with a strong GPA, several high-level courses like honors, APs, or IBs, and demonstrated commitment to an afterschool activity or something similar that highlights their character are best positioned for acceptance.

THE SCHOOL SAYS

From the Admissions Office

"One of the nation's premier liberal arts colleges, Colby offers 46 majors and 38 minors, close interaction with faculty, and a rigorous academic experience connected to the world's most complex challenges. Founded in 2017, the College's DavisConnects program has invested more than $10 million to provide access for all students to research, internships, and global learning. Colby was the first liberal arts college in the United States to establish an institute for artificial intelligence, and is a leader in integrating AI into the curriculum, preparing students to be innovators in a rapidly changing world. Additionally, Colby offers cross-disciplinary initiatives focused in the arts and humanities, public policy and public affairs, biosciences innovation, the climate and environment, and entrepreneurship, which provide funding and resource opportunities for innovative exploration across the curriculum. Exceptional campus facilities, including one of the finest college art museums, state-of-the-art academic buildings, a 350,000-square-foot athletics and recreation facility, and a new creative and performing arts center, are enhanced by Maine's unique natural resources. Applying to Colby is straightforward: there are no fees, no extra essays, and test scores are optional. The College meets 100 percent of demonstrated financial need for all admitted students without loans. Families with a total household income of $75,000 or less with typical assets can expect a parent or guardian contribution of $0. Additionally, families earning a total income of up to $100,000, $150,000, or $200,000 with typical assets can expect a parent or guardian contribution of no more than $10,000, $15,000, or $20,000, respectively. These initiatives position Colby as one of the most affordable four-year colleges in the country."

SELECTIVITY

# of total applicants	20,144
% of total applicants accepted	8
% of total acceptees attending	39

First-Year Profile

Testing policy	Test Optional
Range SAT composite	1450–1530
Range SAT EBRW	720–770
Range SAT math	710–790
Range ACT composite	32–34
% submitting SAT scores	28
% submitting ACT scores	15
% graduated top 10% of class	78
% graduated top 25% of class	93
% graduated top 50% of class	99
% submitting high school rank	18

Important Dates

Early decision	
Apply by	11/15
Notified by	12/15
Other ED apply by	1/5
Other ED notified by	2/15
Regular	
Apply by	1/5
Notified by	4/1
Nonfall registration?	Yes

FINANCIAL FACTS

Annual tuition	$72,590
Food and housing	$19,480
Required fees	$3,200
Books and supplies	$850
Average need-based scholarship (First-year)	$74,164 ($75,967)
% students with need rec. need-based scholarship or grant aid (First-year)	100 (100)
% students with need rec. non-need-based scholarship or grant aid (First-year)	0 (0)
% students with need rec. need-based self-help aid (First-year)	78 (56)
% students rec. any financial aid (First-year)	47 (47)
% UG borrow to pay for school	18
Average cumulative indebtedness	$26,729
% of students with need fully met (First-year)	100 (100)
Average % of student need met (First-year)	100 (100)

Colgate University

13 Oak Drive, Hamilton, NY 13346 • Admissions: 315-228-7401

Survey Snapshot
Career services are great
Great financial aid
Recreation facilities are great

RATINGS	
Quality of Life	82
Fire Safety	97
Green	60*
Academic	94
Profs Interesting	94
Profs Accessible	97
Admissions	98
Financial Aid	97

CAMPUS LIFE

Type of school	Private
Environment	Rural

Students

Degree-seeking undergrad enrollment	3,050
% male/female/not reported	43/57/0
% from out of state	76
% First-year from public high school	54
% First-year live on campus	100
% Ugrads live on campus	91
# of fraternities (% join)	5 (NR)
# of sororities (% join)	3 (NR)
% Asian	6
% Black or African American	4
% Hispanic	10
% Native American	<1
% Pacific Islander	<1
% Race and/or ethnicity unknown	3
% Two or more races	6
% White	64
% International	7
# of countries represented	38

CAMPUS MENTAL HEALTH SERVICES

Offers mental health/wellness program	Yes
Mental health training available to students	No
Employs Chief Wellness Officer	NR
Peer-to-peer mental health offerings	NR
Counseling center has guidelines or accreditation	No
Mental health/well-being courses	NR

ACADEMICS

% students returning for sophomore year	92
% students graduating within 4 years	83
% students graduating within 6 years	89
Calendar	Semester
Student/faculty ratio	9:1
Most common class size 10–19.	(51%)

Most Popular Majors

Econometrics and Quantitative Economics; Political Science and Government; Research and Experimental Psychology

Applicants Also Look At

Boston College, Bowdoin College, Cornell University, Dartmouth College, Georgetown University, New York University, Tufts University, University of California—Berkeley, University of California—Los Angeles, University of Michigan—Ann Arbor, University of North Carolina at Chapel Hill, University of Pennsylvania, University of Southern California, University of Virginia, Washington University in St. Louis

STUDENTS SAY "..."

Academics

Nestled in the charming upstate New York village of Hamilton, Colgate University attracts students who have said they are seeking "a small liberal arts school that had the opportunities and resources of a larger institution." A Colgate bond is for life, and the university's "invaluable" professors are a driving factor in creating a loyal and "heavily involved alumni network" that "makes the Colgate connection a truly valuable resource." A senior recognizes the lasting impact of their choice before graduating: "Colgate allowed me to become the person I always wanted to be, but didn't know I was capable of being." That's due in part to a "very rigorous academic curriculum" that includes foundational experiences such as First-Year Seminars and Living and Learning Workshops; students find the tools imparted at the early stages of the college path make them feel they are "more than just a number" and that support can be found from any one of the "internationally influential" professors who "are the glue that hold the university together." A student says, "One of the wonderful things about Colgate is that...students do not have to wait until their senior year to build fantastic relationships with the faculty." While some say that "course selection is very stressful, and [first-years] often get slighted," students assure there are "caring professors that are meaningfully invested in your academic success." The school encourages students to supplement their classes with pre-professional programs and immersive learning experiences, and to work with faculty on graduate-level research and ensures "there are a plethora of resources available to students to succeed."

Campus Life

The Colgate bubble is a happy enclave in which "everything [revolves] around the campus," where housing is guaranteed for all four years. One student means it fully as a compliment when saying "I loved how Colgate was located in the middle of nowhere." That peaceful isolation and "intimate nature" means that "it is easy for students to contact the administration," and even the dean has drop-in office hours. The school also goes out of its way to "[bring] a lot of interesting speakers to the campus, which helps provide for a more rounded liberal arts experience," and students are also actively involved in Greek life and Division I athletics. "Colgate strives for the perfect combination of academics and extracurriculars," and students say the school "does a great job at helping us balance those and gives us opportunities to get involved in all the groups and events around campus." The Get Involved platform acts as an online hub for students wishing to join or administrate the hundreds of organizations and clubs, making it even easier for students to stay active and happy on this "amazing campus with people who work hard and have goals but also know how to have a really fun time." A student says, "Colgate is great because you can't walk 200 feet without a professor, student, or faculty member acknowledging you by name, yet you're constantly meeting new people and having new experiences. There is never a dull moment at Colgate."

Student Body

Colgate students are all about balance: they "enjoy having fun, but [spend] time in the library as well." Some depict this as a "country club atmosphere," at least so far as style goes, but the school has been prioritizing diversity and inclusion and has a "happy and enthusiastic student body." Students also explain that "when you're stranded in Hamilton, New York, for four years you'll inevitably end up fitting in...whether you are the typical student or not." That said, those who attend Colgate tend to be "athletic, smart, engaged, and down to earth." While "Greek life does have a huge presence in the social life at Colgate," students say "it is not exclusive to just those who are members," and the administration has undertaken "initiatives to expand the amount of alternatives to partying on weekends." At the end of the day, if a student is "not afraid to do what they love, they will find their niche and fit in."

Colgate University

Financial Aid: 315-228-7431 • E-Mail: admission@colgate.edu • Website: www.colgate.edu

THE PRINCETON REVIEW SAYS

Admissions

The school reports that its standardized testing policy for use in admission for Fall 2026 is Test Optional. The Princeton Review suggests that interested applicants consult with the school for the most up-to-date standardized testing policies. *Very important factors considered include:* rigor of secondary school record, class rank, academic GPA. *Important factors considered include:* standardized test scores, application essay, recommendation(s), extracurricular activities, talent/ability, character/personal qualities. *Other factors considered include:* first generation, alumni/ae relation, geographical residence, volunteer work, work experience. High school diploma is required and GED is accepted. *Academic units required:* 4 English, 3 math, 3 science, 2 science labs, 3 language (other than English), 3 social studies. *Academic units recommended:* 4 English, 4 math, 4 science, 4 science labs, 4 language (other than English), 4 social studies.

Financial Aid

Students should submit: FAFSA; CSS PROFILE. The Princeton Review suggests that all financial aid forms be submitted as soon as possible. *Need-based scholarships/grants offered:* Federal Pell; Federal SEOG; College/university scholarship or grant aid from institutional funds; State scholarships/grants; Private scholarships. *Loan aid offered:* Federal Direct Subsidized Loans; Federal Direct Unsubsidized Loans; Direct PLUS loans; College/university loans from institutional funds. Admitted students will be notified of awards on or about 3/21. Federal Work-Study Program available. Institutional employment available.

The Inside Word

Admission to this upstate New York gem is some of the most competitive around. You need to prepare yourself with excellent grades, scores, recommendations, and extracurricular activities. Colgate is also seeking that unique quality that may not be evident from the Common App alone, as the university aims to enhance diversity across the board. Colgate is Test Optional, but students who wish to submit SAT or ACT scores are welcome to do so, and these scores will be considered as part of the holistic review of the applicant.

THE SCHOOL SAYS

From the Admissions Office

"Colgate provides an intellectually rigorous academic environment on a beautiful 575-acre campus in rural upstate New York. Students and faculty alike are drawn to Colgate by the quality of its academic programs. Faculty initiative has given the university a broad mix of learning opportunities that includes a liberal arts core curriculum, 57 academic concentrations, and a wealth of chances for off-campus study abroad and within the United States, including Colgate faculty-led semester long and briefer programs, as well as approved programs offered by other institutions. The residential commons, Colgate's living and learning program, eases students' academic and social transition to college, and residential life in general includes an array of living options, on a campus described as one of the most beautiful in the country. The Trudy Fitness Center is a popular student destination, and the Shaw Wellness Institute fosters healthy, purposeful, and balanced lifestyles. The Max A. Shacknai Center for Outreach, Volunteerism, and Education builds upon the tradition of Colgate students interacting with the surrounding community in meaningful ways. Colgate students become extraordinarily devoted alumni, contributing significantly to career networking and exploration programs both on and off campus. These and many other points of distinction will be supported and expanded through the Third-Century Plan, a strategic framework designed to establish the University as one of the very finest undergraduate institutions in the nation and the world."

SELECTIVITY

# of total applicants	17,310
% of total applicants accepted	18
% of total acceptees attending	27
# of in-state applicants	2,975
% of in-state applicants accepted	22
# of out-of-state-applicants	7,380
% of applicants accepted from out of state	28
# of international applicants	6,955
% of international applicants accepted	4
# of early decision applicants	1,342
% of early decision applicants accepted	36
# offered a place on the wait list	2,381
# admitted from wait list	23

First-Year Profile

Testing policy	Test Optional
Range SAT composite	1450–1510
Range SAT EBRW	720–750
Range SAT math	710–770
Range ACT composite	33–35
% submitting SAT scores	23
% submitting ACT scores	16
Average HS GPA	3.9
% submitting high school GPA	100
% graduated top 10% of class	78
% graduated top 25% of class	96
% graduated top 50% of class	99
% submitting high school rank	17

Important Dates

Early decision	
Apply by	11/1
Notified by	12/15
Other ED apply by	1/15
Other ED notified by	3/1
Regular	
Apply by	1/15
Notified by	4/1
Nonfall registration?	No

FINANCIAL FACTS

Annual tuition	$76,828
Food and housing	$19,356
Required fees	$462
Books and supplies	$1,600
Average need-based scholarship (First-year)	$71,688 ($72,605)
% students with need rec. need-based scholarship or grant aid (First-year)	100 (100)
% students with need rec. non-need-based scholarship or grant aid (First-year)	26 (23)
% students with need rec. need-based self-help aid (First-year)	74 (73)
% students rec. any financial aid (First-year)	51 (50)
% UG borrow to pay for school	21
Average cumulative indebtedness	$21,643
% of students with need fully met (First-year)	80 (81)
Average % of student need met (First-year)	100 (100)

COLLEGE OF CHARLESTON

66 George Street, Charleston, SC 29424 • Admissions: 843-953-5670

Survey Snapshot
Great library
Students love Charleston, SC
Great off-campus food

RATINGS

Quality of Life	**86**
Fire Safety	**91**
Green	**90**
Academic	**79**
Profs Interesting	**88**
Profs Accessible	**91**
Admissions	**85**
Financial Aid	**82**

CAMPUS LIFE

Type of school	Public
Environment	City

Students

Degree-seeking undergrad enrollment	10,289
% male/female/not reported	32/68/0
% from out of state	49
% First-year from public high school	77
% First-year live on campus	91
% Ugrads live on campus	33
# of fraternities (% join)	12 (16)
# of sororities (% join)	12 (27)
% Asian	2
% Black or African American	6
% Hispanic	8
% Native American	<1
% Pacific Islander	<1
% Race and/or ethnicity unknown	1
% Two or more races	4
% White	77
% International	1
# of countries represented	69

CAMPUS MENTAL HEALTH SERVICES

Offers mental health/wellness program	Yes
Mental health training available to students	Yes
Employs Chief Wellness Officer	Yes
Peer-to-peer mental health offerings	Yes
Counseling center has guidelines or accreditation	Yes
Mental health/well-being courses	No

ACADEMICS

% students returning for sophomore year	82
% students graduating within 4 years	56
% students graduating within 6 years	65
Calendar	Semester
Student/faculty ratio	16:1
Most common class size 20–29.	(34%)
Most common lab/discussion size 20–29.	(48%)

Most Popular Majors

Biology/Biological Sciences; Psychology; Business Administration and Management

Applicants Also Look At

Clemson University, Coastal Carolina University, Elon University, Penn State University Park, University of South Carolina—Columbia, The University of Tampa, University of Tennessee—Knoxville

STUDENTS SAY "…"

Academics

Founded in 1770, the College of Charleston is a public liberal arts institution "focused on educating its students to be well-rounded intellectual citizens." With 150 undergraduate majors and minors offered, there are a "wide variety of classes and programs" available, ensuring that "there's something here for almost everyone." Historic, "beautiful" downtown Charleston doubles as "a unique experience to enjoy and learn from the outdoors while still in an academic setting" and comes with "lots of fieldwork." That is matched by the "incredible experience and education" professors offer, many of whom "have very interesting and unique backgrounds that help engage students and relate to the real world." Specifically, they "do a great job of helping students network and gain experience before graduation through internships and on-campus work." It's also well-received that "small class sizes make it easy to ask questions and participate in class," and there's the sense that faculty are "invested in each student's learning process, encouraging students to ask them for help if they need it, or to simply stop by during office hours if they want to discuss something." As one student puts it, Charleston helps "you to have a plan and be ready for anything the future can throw at you…and they have the resources to back up these goals."

Campus Life

Students at the College of Charleston "are extremely involved…and likely participate in multiple clubs," not to mention "volunteering events, jobs, internships, and study abroad trips." The school hosts "tons of talks and activities" and "constantly keeps us updated on events and opportunities." With more than 240 options, students say that "there are so many clubs to choose from," including the "Belly Dance club," the Esports club, and the Cheese Club (exactly what it sounds like). They also "love going to school sporting events (especially basketball)," and Greek life is singled out as being "really fun…because it is so low-key compared to other colleges." On the weekends, students might step off campus into the "vibrant city" of Charleston, where "there is always something happening, whether it be the Fall Arts Festival, an a cappella concert, or a concert." The college enjoys an excellent relationship with its community, and "many local coffee shops are also "frequented by students and provide a nice place to hang out with friends or study." Geographically speaking, proximity to the water "is icing on the cake," so students "do a lot of beach-going (Charleston is close to several beaches)," and one student's weekend rotation involves "Hitting the bars on Friday night, going to the farmer's market then beach on Saturdays, while still having energy to study hard [on] Sunday nights." Another student claims, "The great thing about our college is that there is so much going on around here on any given day."

Student Body

Cougars are known for being a "fun, outgoing, [and] involved community" where "everyone is really friendly." On campus, "camaraderie is evident, and morale is high." The "unique and thriving atmosphere that surrounds the college draws many different types of people." There is "a wide variety of backgrounds and personalities of students here," which many appreciate because it "allows students to gain perspective and insight as to how others think and feel." One student adds that "MOST students are respectful of others' opinions and beliefs." Students also engage across different majors: "We all mingle together and are friends with people in all different fields of study." And one student shares, "The one thing I love most about the College of Charleston is how we can all come together and co-exist." Another student agrees, "Anyone and everyone can find someone to be friends with and fit in with here."

College of Charleston

Financial Aid: 843-953-5540 • E-Mail: admissions@cofc.edu • Website: charleston.edu

THE PRINCETON REVIEW SAYS

Admissions

The school reports that its standardized testing policy for use in admission for Fall 2026 is Test Optional. The Princeton Review suggests that interested applicants consult with the school for the most up-to-date standardized testing policies. *Very important factors considered include:* rigor of secondary school record, academic GPA. *Important factors considered include:* class rank, geographical residence, state residency. *Other factors considered include:* standardized test scores, application essay, recommendation(s), extracurricular activities, talent/ability, character/personal qualities, first generation, alumni/ae relation, volunteer work, work experience, level of applicant's interest. High school diploma is required and GED is accepted. *Academic units required:* 4 English, 4 math, 3 science, 3 science labs, 2 language (other than English), 2 social studies, 1 history, 2 academic electives, 1 visual/performing arts. *Academic units recommended:* 4 English, 4 math, 3 science, 3 science labs, 3 language (other than English), 2 social studies, 2 history, 2 academic electives, 1 computer science, 1 visual/performing arts.

Financial Aid

Students should submit: FAFSA. Priority filing deadline is 3/1. The Princeton Review suggests that all financial aid forms be submitted as soon as possible. *Need-based scholarships/grants offered:* Federal Pell; Federal SEOG; State scholarships/grants; Private scholarships; College/university scholarship or grant aid from institutional funds. *Loan aid offered:* Federal Direct Subsidized Loans; Federal Direct Unsubsidized Loans; Direct PLUS loans. Admitted students will be notified of awards on a rolling basis beginning April 1st. Federal Work-Study Program available. Institutional employment available.

The Inside Word

The average admitted first-year students at the College of Charleston had consistent academic achievement in the A/B range in high school. The admissions committee takes a hard look at high school performance, including the rigor of the pre-college workload, when making their decisions.

THE SCHOOL SAYS

From the Admissions Office

"To succeed in our increasingly complex world, college graduates must be able to think creatively, explore new ideas, and meet the challenges of our global society. At the College of Charleston, located in coastal South Carolina, students find out about themselves and the lives of others. Through a robust, wide-ranging curriculum, they discover how to shape their futures.

"Founded in 1770, the College of Charleston's mission is to provide students with a world-class education in the arts and sciences, business and technology, engineering and health sciences. Students have more than 150 majors and minors from which to choose—and they often choose to combine several—and complement their academic courses with overseas study, undergraduate research and internships for a truly customized education.

"Nearly 12,000 students choose the college for its unique urban, mid-sized university feel. The College, home to undergraduates from across the country and around the globe, provides a creative and intellectually stimulating environment where students are challenged and guided by a committed and caring faculty of distinguished teacher-scholars. The city of Charleston serves as a living and learning laboratory for student experiences and opportunities for career development. The university bridges the old with the new in a setting that is truly extraordinary—where historic character and forward-looking innovation come together to shape a distinctive and inspiring environment for learning. A College of Charleston education focuses on discovery and personal growth, as well as preparation for life, work, and service to our society."

SELECTIVITY

# of total applicants	32,330
% of total applicants accepted	73
% of total acceptees attending	10
# of in-state applicants	7,648
% of in-state applicants accepted	73
# of out-of-state-applicants	24,315
% of applicants accepted from out of state	74
# of international applicants	367
% of international applicants accepted	48
# of early decision applicants	428
% of early decision applicants accepted	72
# offered a place on the wait list	2,819
# admitted from wait list	521

First-Year Profile

Testing policy	Test Optional
Range SAT composite	1160–1300
Range SAT EBRW	590–680
Range SAT math	550–640
Range ACT composite	23–29
% submitting SAT scores	19
% submitting ACT scores	9
Average HS GPA	4.0
% submitting high school GPA	100
% graduated top 10% of class	15
% graduated top 25% of class	43
% graduated top 50% of class	78
% submitting high school rank	53

Important Dates

Early decision	
Apply by	11/1
Notified by	12/1
Early action	
Apply by	11/1
Notified by	12/15
Regular	
Apply by	1/15
Nonfall registration?	Yes

FINANCIAL FACTS

Annual in-state tuition	$12,518
Annual out-of-state tuition	$38,384
Food and housing	$15,653
Required fees (First-year)	$460 ($320)
Books and supplies	$1,560
Average need-based scholarship (First-year)	$3,013 ($3,140)
% students with need rec. need-based scholarship or grant aid (First-year)	85 (89)
% students with need rec. non-need-based scholarship or grant aid (First-year)	45 (68)
% students with need rec. need-based self-help aid (First-year)	69 (69)
% UG borrow to pay for school	48.7
Average cumulative indebtedness	$33,803
% of students with need fully met (First-year)	14 (17)
Average % of student need met (First-year)	49 (54)

The College of New Jersey

2000 Pennington Road, Ewing, NJ 08628-0718 • Admissions: 609-771-2131

Survey Snapshot
Students are happy
Easy to get around campus
Frats and sororities are popular

RATINGS	
Quality of Life	87
Fire Safety	99
Green	60*
Academic	82
Profs Interesting	89
Profs Accessible	92
Admissions	88
Financial Aid	79

CAMPUS LIFE

Type of school	Public
Environment	Town

Students

Degree-seeking undergrad enrollment	7,223
% male/female/not reported	46/54/0
% from out of state	5
% First-year from public high school	93
% First-year live on campus	84
% Ugrads live on campus	44
# of fraternities (% join)	14 (16)
# of sororities (% join)	14 (19)
% Asian	10
% Black or African American	6
% Hispanic	18
% Native American	<1
% Pacific Islander	<1
% Race and/or ethnicity unknown	3
% Two or more races	3
% White	58
% International	1
# of countries represented	32

CAMPUS MENTAL HEALTH SERVICES

Offers mental health/wellness program	Yes
Mental health training available to students	Yes
Employs Chief Wellness Officer	NR
Peer-to-peer mental health offerings	Yes
Counseling center has guidelines or accreditation	No
Mental health/well-being courses	NR

ACADEMICS

% students returning for sophomore year	90
% students graduating within 4 years	74
% students graduating within 6 years	85
Calendar	Semester
Student/faculty ratio	15:1
Most common class size 20–29.	(39%)
Most common lab/discussion size 20–29.	(62%)

Most Popular Majors
Education; Psychology; Biology

Applicants Often Prefer
Rowan University, Rutgers University–New Brunswick, Stevens Institute of Technology, University of Delaware

Applicants Sometimes Prefer
New Jersey Institute of Technology, Penn State University Park, Seton Hall University, Temple University, Villanova University

STUDENTS SAY "..."

Academics

The College of New Jersey emphasizes collaborative academics, research and internship opportunities, and community-based learning, all of which provide "a great foundation for people who may look for jobs right out of college." While some students conclude that "networking is easy," they also acknowledge that it requires effort: "TCNJ is an extremely competitive institution and [it] forces students to rise to the challenge." Those who embrace the "academic rigor and opportunities" of the programs feel that they "prepare us very well for our careers" and provide numerous "opportunities to take part in multiple organizations, research, and to grow." In addition to all this, "professional development seminars are typically packed." Through it all, students "are always the top priority at the college," and "small class sizes foster close relationships between students and professors." Instructors are said to "maintain excellent academic relationships with their students and are always discussing research, internship, or other involvements." As a result, they get to know you "on a first-name basis and they know your strengths and weaknesses." So, if you are "relying on them for letters of recommendation, or having a professor update you on internship opportunities, the results are tangible" and seem to "have the student's best interest in mind." Multiple respondents acknowledge that "The College of New Jersey is an academically challenging institute that focuses on the preparation of its students for their entire life, not just their career."

Campus Life

Life at TCNJ is busy, but there is "a fair balance of academic life with socialness, athletics, or relaxing time." TCNJ is housed on a "very beautiful and very unified" campus "[where] everything is in walking distance," and "people are always out and about so you never feel alone." The "Office of Student [Life] has fun programs that focused on extra activities," and there "are a lot of concerts and guest speakers, as well." Greek life "is pretty strong on campus," and "there are always philanthropy events to go to." While TCNJ has multiple sports teams, some students suggest that regular games are "sparsely attended," That said, there "are many nearby off-campus activities or group bike rides that students participate in," and days can fill up with a wide variety of activities like "going to the gym, fishing, running, sleeping, watching a movie, ice cream party, [visiting] friends, [or] extra readings." Philadelphia is just a half hour away for those wanting to sample the city, and "we are close to malls, restaurants, and movie theaters, which are all easily accessible through the highway nearby." Overall, the school "provides a lot of ways for students to get involved on campus and makes them readily known," and students "tend to engage fully in supplementary programs (i.e., lecture, awareness, volunteer, celebratory, or other campus events) often affiliated with their major."

Student Body

Students at TCNJ "are a breed all of their own" with "a wide variety of interests and talents." These "well-rounded and extraordinary individuals" are "determined and full of energy," and "dedicated in what they are participating in, whether it be academics, extracurricular activities, or sports." Together, these qualities create "a strong sense of community around an academic hub." A "large percentage of the student body is constantly busy" and "heavily involved in extracurricular activities." There's "a real sense of school spirit and camaraderie," and "we don't have a cliquey feeling or vibe." In fact, it's just the opposite: "Everyone is generally very helpful, supportive, and engaging of one another."

THE COLLEGE OF NEW JERSEY

Financial Aid: 609-771-2211 • E-Mail: tcnjinfo@tcnj.edu • Website: www.tcnj.edu

THE PRINCETON REVIEW SAYS

Admissions

The school reports that its standardized testing policy for use in admission for Fall 2026 is Test Optional. The Princeton Review suggests that interested applicants consult with the school for the most up-to-date standardized testing policies. *Very important factors considered include:* rigor of secondary school record, class rank, extracurricular activities, volunteer work, level of applicant's interest. *Important factors considered include:* academic GPA, application essay, recommendation(s), talent/ability, character/personal qualities, geographical residence, state residency. *Other factors considered include:* standardized test scores, first generation, work experience. High school diploma is required and GED is accepted. *Academic units required:* 4 English, 4 math, 4 science, 2 science labs, 2 language (other than English), 2 social studies, 2 academic electives. *Academic units recommended:* 4 English, 4 math, 4 science, 2 science labs, 2 language (other than English), 2 social studies, 4 academic electives.

Financial Aid

Students should submit: FAFSA. Priority filing deadline is 3/1. The Princeton Review suggests that all financial aid forms be submitted as soon as possible. *Need-based scholarships/grants offered:* Federal Pell; Federal SEOG; State scholarships/grants; Private scholarships; College/university scholarship or grant aid from institutional funds. *Loan aid offered:* Federal Direct Subsidized Loans; Federal Direct Unsubsidized Loans; Direct PLUS loans; State Loans. Admitted students will be notified of awards on a rolling basis beginning 6/1. Federal Work-Study Program available. Institutional employment available.

The Inside Word

TCNJ accepts around 60 percent of its nearly 13,000 applicants, but that level of competition is what you might expect at a school that offers state residents a small-college experience and a highly respected degree at a good price. TCNJ's admissions staff examines every component of a student's application, but none more carefully than the high school transcript. Students should apply as soon as possible once the application becomes available.

THE SCHOOL SAYS

From the Admissions Office

"The College of New Jersey is one of the United States' great higher education success stories. With a long history as New Jersey's preeminent teacher of teachers, the college has grown into a new role as an educator of the nation's best students in a wide range of fields. The College of New Jersey has created a culture of constant questioning—a place where knowledge is not merely received but reconfigured. In small classes, students and faculty members collaborate in a rewarding process: As they seek to understand fundamental principles, apply key concepts, reveal new problems, and pursue new lines of inquiry, students gain a fluency of thought in their disciplines. The college's 289-acre tree-lined campus is a union of vision, engineering, beauty, and functionality. Neoclassical Georgian Colonial architecture, meticulous landscaping, and thoughtful design merge in a dynamic system, constantly evolving to meet the needs of TCNJ students. About half of TCNJ's entering class will be academic scholars. The College of New Jersey is bringing together the best ideas from around the nation and building a new model for public undergraduate education on one campus."

SELECTIVITY

# of total applicants	12,793
% of total applicants accepted	61
% of total acceptees attending	18
# of in-state applicants	11,232
% of in-state applicants accepted	63
# of out-of-state-applicants	1,304
% of applicants accepted from out of state	54
# of international applicants	257
% of international applicants accepted	18
# of early decision applicants	401
% of early decision applicants accepted	77
# offered a place on the wait list	543
# admitted from wait list	12

First-Year Profile

Testing policy	Test Optional
Range SAT composite	1140–1330
Range SAT EBRW	570–670
Range SAT math	560–670
Range ACT composite	25–30
% submitting SAT scores	50
% submitting ACT scores	3
% graduated top 10% of class	24
% graduated top 25% of class	52
% graduated top 50% of class	88
% submitting high school rank	43

Important Dates

Early decision	
Apply by	11/1
Notified by	12/1
Early action	
Apply by	11/1
Notified by	1/15
Regular	
Apply by	2/1
Notified by	4/1
Nonfall registration?	Yes

FINANCIAL FACTS

Annual in-state tuition	$15,906
Annual out-of-state tuition	$22,270
Food and housing	$17,292
Required fees	$4,492
Books and supplies	$1,200
Average need-based scholarship (First-year)	$14,054 ($15,917)
% students with need rec. need-based scholarship or grant aid (First-year)	62 (60)
% students with need rec. non-need-based scholarship or grant aid (First-year)	54 (52)
% students with need rec. need-based self-help aid (First-year)	65 (67)
% students rec. any financial aid (First-year)	49 (57)
% UG borrow to pay for school	51
Average cumulative indebtedness	$29,079
% of students with need fully met (First-year)	11 (11)
Average % of student need met (First-year)	43 (41)

College of Saint Benedict/Saint John's University

2850 Abbey Plaza, Collegeville, MN 56321 • Admissions: 320-363-3664

Survey Snapshot
Students are happy
Great library
Career services are great

RATINGS

Quality of Life	**89**
Fire Safety	**99**
Green	**60***
Academic	**86**
Profs Interesting	**91**
Profs Accessible	**95**
Admissions	**81**
Financial Aid	**91**

CAMPUS LIFE

Type of school	Private
Affiliation	Roman Catholic
Environment	Village

Students

Degree-seeking undergrad enrollment	2,659
% male/female/not reported	50/50/0
% from out of state	11
% First-year live on campus	100
% Ugrads live on campus	90
# of fraternities (% join)	1 (<1)
# of sororities (% join)	1 (<1)
% Asian	4
% Black or African American	3
% Hispanic	9
% Native American	1
% Pacific Islander	<1
% Race and/or ethnicity unknown	6
% Two or more races	<1
% White	73
% International	3
# of countries represented	21

CAMPUS MENTAL HEALTH SERVICES

Offers mental health/wellness program	Yes
Mental health training available to students	No
Employs Chief Wellness Officer	NR
Peer-to-peer mental health offerings	NR
Counseling center has guidelines or accreditation	No
Mental health/well-being courses	NR

ACADEMICS

% students returning for sophomore year	83
% students graduating within 4 years	72
% students graduating within 6 years	77
Calendar	Semester
Student/faculty ratio	12:1
Most common class size 20–29.	(40%)
Most common lab/discussion size 10–19.	(72%)

Applicants Also Look At

Gustavus Adolphus College, Saint Cloud State University, St. Catherine University, St. Olaf College, University of Minnesota Duluth, University of Minnesota—Twin Cities, University of St. Thomas (MN), University of Wisconsin—Eau Claire

STUDENTS SAY "…"

Academics

The partnership between College of Saint Benedict (for women) and Saint John's University (for men) is evident in the Benedictine values "upheld by every student in everyday life." For over 60 years, the two schools have shared both faith and curriculum, taking a free shuttle between classes on the two campuses while maintaining separate dorms and traditions. Part of the Integrations Curriculum includes two theology courses that are "all about service and making an impact in the world," as well as an experiential engagement component that includes service-learning opportunities or an "incredible" study abroad program utilized by more than half of all students. It is, claim attendees, "an education that is second to none," especially given the lecture series that bring scholars and experts to campus to share insights and global perspectives, helping students to forge "endless connections with not only other schools across the nation, but…across the world."

The "extremely dedicated and passionate" professors are at the heart of both liberal arts colleges, not just in their teaching but in their guidance toward intellectual discovery. They "are interested in us figuring things out for ourselves" and "big on [students] being prepared for class so more time can be spent discussing or practicing material instead of lecturing." One-quarter of all students complete research or a creative project each year, often under mentorship provided by faculty who "are willing to work…on projects outside of class even if it means extra work for them." With the resources of two colleges and 1,500 years of Benedictine values at their disposal, students come away with "a well-rounded education…ready to take on the world."

Campus Life

Though they maintain separate dorms and visiting hours, all other facilities (including dining, athletic complexes, and libraries) are shared between students at the two colleges, so they "have a lot of options for meeting new people." This includes over 100 clubs and organizations, an "inspired leaders series," and school-run "large campus events such as orientation and Thanksgiving dinners." The location in Minnesota provides "rich recreational abilities" and students often take adventure trips through the schools' Peer Resource Program. Even outside of sponsored activities, nearby natural resources include 3,000 acres of woods and lakes, where "ice fishing, fishing, hiking, and hanging out at the beach are popular." A student assures, "the warm months of the year are awesome with the lake/raft open. It feels like a summer camp." An abundance of school pride can be found during athletic events, "the high points for entertainment." Many here "do go out on the weekends" to hang out at bars or parties, but the "outstanding campus programming board" also plans weekend events for those that don't want to drink. A student vouches that with two schools, there is no shortage of ways to entertain yourself, and "as long as you can step out that door and make good use of your time, you'll have an amazing time."

Student Body

Many students at both CSB and SJU are Catholic and tend to come "from Minnesota or the surrounding states." Regardless of where you're from, you'll likely find your peers bringing "'Minnesota Nice' to a whole new level," which makes it relatively easy to befriend these "hard-working, fun-loving people," especially if you take some of "the many clubs and activities that are offered." Most of the caring "Johnnies" and "Bennies" here "commonly have social issues that they are passionate about, such as gender equality, sustainability, [or] health and wellness," and "believe in the importance of education." In a pleasant place where "everyone fits like a puzzle piece," one can always "expect to have doors open for you [and] people smile and greet you on occasion when you're passing by."

College of Saint Benedict/Saint John's University

Financial Aid: 320-363-5388 • E-Mail: admissions@csbsju.edu • Website: www.csbsju.edu

THE PRINCETON REVIEW SAYS

Admissions

The school reports that its standardized testing policy for use in admission for Fall 2026 is Test Optional. The Princeton Review suggests that interested applicants consult with the school for the most up-to-date standardized testing policies. *Very important factors considered include:* rigor of secondary school record, academic GPA, extracurricular activities. *Other factors considered include:* standardized test scores, application essay, recommendation(s), interview, talent/ability, character/personal qualities, volunteer work, work experience. High school diploma is required and GED is accepted. *Academic units required:* 4 English, 3 math, 2 science, 2 science labs, 2 social studies, 4 academic electives. *Academic units recommended:* 4 English, 3 math, 2 science, 2 science labs, 2 language (other than English), 2 social studies, 4 academic electives.

Financial Aid

Students should submit: FAFSA. Priority filing deadline is 3/15. The Princeton Review suggests that all financial aid forms be submitted as soon as possible. *Need-based scholarships/grants offered:* Federal Pell; Federal SEOG; State scholarships/grants; College/university scholarship or grant aid from institutional funds; Private scholarships. *Loan aid offered:* Federal Direct Subsidized Loans; Federal Direct Unsubsidized Loans; Direct PLUS loans; State Loans. Admitted students will be notified of awards on a rolling basis beginning 12/20. Federal Work-Study Program available. Institutional employment available.

The Inside Word

Students with decent grades and a few extracurricular activities that "show promise of community contribution" shouldn't have any problem getting into CSB and SJU. You may apply to CSB and SJU using the Common Application or by using the school's CSB+SJU Application—the school doesn't have a preference.

THE SCHOOL SAYS

From the Admissions Office

"The College of Saint Benedict, a residential college for women, and Saint John's University, a residential college for men, are two top-tier liberal arts schools joined in a uniquely integrated learning community with the limitless learning opportunities of TWO nationally ranked institutions. The students, known as Bennies and Johnnies, flourish at these two historic Catholic, Benedictine schools that blend 3,300 acres of Minnesota lakes, forests and college-town experiences. This integrated experience, with two stunning campuses and decades of traditions, offers exceptional academics, a commitment to experiential learning, a fun residential experience and an unparalleled network of alums blazing trails and opening doors."

SELECTIVITY

# of total applicants	3,934
% of total applicants accepted	91
% of total acceptees attending	20

First-Year Profile

Testing policy	Test Optional
Range SAT composite	970–1240
Range SAT EBRW	490–630
Range SAT math	450–620
Range ACT composite	22–28
% submitting SAT scores	4
% submitting ACT scores	41
Average HS GPA	3.6
% submitting high school GPA	98
% graduated top 10% of class	23
% graduated top 25% of class	46
% graduated top 50% of class	82
% submitting high school rank	46

Important Dates

Early action	
Apply by	12/1
Notified by	1/5
Regular	
Notified by	Rolling, 10/1
Nonfall registration?	Yes

FINANCIAL FACTS

Annual tuition	$58,430
Food and housing	$13,350
Required fees	$1,352
Books and supplies	$1,000
% students with need rec. need-based scholarship or grant aid (First-year)	100 (100)
% students with need rec. non-need-based scholarship or grant aid (First-year)	30 (33)
% students with need rec. need-based self-help aid (First-year)	69 (67)
% students rec. any financial aid (First-year)	100 (100)
% of students with need fully met (First-year)	45 (45)

College of the Atlantic

105 Eden Street, Bar Harbor, ME 04609 • Admissions: 207-288-5015

Survey Snapshot
Students get along with local community
Students involved in community service
Students love Bar Harbor, ME

RATINGS

Quality of Life	96
Fire Safety	91
Green	99
Academic	90
Profs Interesting	95
Profs Accessible	92
Admissions	90
Financial Aid	95

CAMPUS LIFE

Type of school	Private
Environment	Rural

Students

Degree-seeking undergrad enrollment	340
% male/female/not reported	28/71/1
% from out of state	80
% First-year from public high school	56
% First-year live on campus	100
% Ugrads live on campus	82
# of fraternities	0
# of sororities	0
% Asian	2
% Black or African American	1
% Hispanic	2
% Native American	0
% Pacific Islander	0
% Race and/or ethnicity unknown	2
% Two or more races	2
% White	71
% International	20
# of countries represented	43

CAMPUS MENTAL HEALTH SERVICES

Offers mental health/wellness program	Yes
Mental health training available to students	Yes
Employs Chief Wellness Officer	Yes
Peer-to-peer mental health offerings	Yes
Counseling center has guidelines or accreditation	No
Mental health/well-being courses	Yes, for-credit

ACADEMICS

% students returning for sophomore year	90
% students graduating within 4 years	55
% students graduating within 6 years	68
Calendar	Trimester
Student/faculty ratio	9:1
Most common class size 10–19.	(70%)
Most common lab/discussion size 10–19.	(50%)

Most Popular Majors
Liberal Arts and Sciences/Liberal Studies

Applicants Sometimes Prefer
Bennington College, Eckerd College, Hampshire College, University of Maine, University of New England, University of New Hampshire, University of Vermont, Warren Wilson College

Applicants Rarely Prefer
University of Southern Maine

STUDENTS SAY "..."

Academics

College of the Atlantic only admits a limited number of applicants each year, which allows it to focus on and fully serve the approximately 350 students enrolled. There's an "encouragement to pave our own paths and build our learning to suit ourselves," which can be seen in the way enrollees design their own major and course of study, a format that "attracts a self-selected group of passionate, driven, and deeply curious individuals who are committed to interdisciplinary learning and environmental and social justice." This "adaptability to allow for every student to have an experience that is meaningful to them" is aided by a system of three classes per trimester "so that work never becomes overbearing but gives us many opportunities." A student says: "You can choose to do whatever you want, and if the hyper-specific thing you want isn't offered yet, you can ask a teacher and they'll make it happen for you." The experiential nature of the curriculum means "classes are usually project-based, which allows students to delve into particular subjects of their interest within the topic and gain experience with such things as research design, field methods, analysis, artistic creation, and much more." Students appreciate the hands-on learning opportunities, with one student sharing, "I did my internship on one of our island research stations, monitoring copepod population health for 10 weeks while simultaneously contributing to the college's 40-year-old whale presence dataset."

Campus Life

The "campus is beautiful" and "in the fall and spring, there's constantly people hanging out outside, either playing instruments, reading, painting, playing soccer or Frisbee, or just enjoying the weather." Given the school's Maine location, many students also enjoy "the Outing Program (adventures like hiking, stargazing, boogie boarding, and polar plunging)" or activities in nearby Acadia National Park, which "provides endless exploration for both the Outing Program and individuals." You can find people participating "in just about every hobby under the sun. From tincture making to taxidermy, there is a place for all crafts and activities here." There are also plenty of "student activist clubs and college-sponsored outdoor recreation," as well as regularly scheduled activities like "Fireside Friday (crafting club held weekly), Mending Matters (clothing and gear repair club), and COAmmunity Dinner (weekly community dinner club)." The school's small size "means that academic and social life often blend together, with discussions continuing over meals in Take-A-Break [dining hall] or spontaneous gatherings in the library or on the pier." For the students wanting to "make change on campus and in local communities," there is the weekly All College Meeting, in which faculty, staff, and students come together to discuss and vote on large-scale decisions, policies, and community issues, fitting for a population that's "highly committed to curiosity and bettering the planet."

Student Body

While there are many different personalities at COA, "everyone holds the same inherent values of kindness, giving back through nature, curiosity, and exploration." Among this "very accepting and diverse, very LGBTQ-friendly" group, "activism and rhetoric [are] extremely well-intentioned among virtually all students, often translating to engaging conversations." On the whole, enrollees "are quite invested in change-making, both at the school and on a national and international scale." There also seems to be less of a digital focus, as students tend to "have very tangible hobbies...for example, lots of people knit, sew, carve wood, play instruments, make art, that sort of thing." One student describes the potpourri of their peers as a "perfect...mix of art/theater kids and science kids, both extroverted and introverted, down to go hunt for worms in the forest at 2 a.m. or make elaborate costumes for a one-off play written in 12 hours." As one student sums up: "COA students come here each looking for something different...[and] weave their own tapestry of campus culture, which includes a little bit of everything and everyone."

College of the Atlantic

Financial Aid: 207-801-5645 • E-Mail: inquiry@coa.edu • Website: www.coa.edu

THE PRINCETON REVIEW SAYS

Admissions

The school reports that its standardized testing policy for use in admission for Fall 2026 is Test Optional. The Princeton Review suggests that interested applicants consult with the school for the most up-to-date standardized testing policies. *Very important factors considered include:* rigor of secondary school record, application essay, recommendation(s). *Important factors considered include:* class rank, academic GPA, extracurricular activities, character/personal qualities. *Other factors considered include:* standardized test scores, interview, talent/ability, first generation, volunteer work, work experience, level of applicant's interest. High school diploma is required and GED is accepted.

Financial Aid

Students should submit: FAFSA; Institution's own financial aid form; Business/Farm Supplement. Priority filing deadline is 2/1. The Princeton Review suggests that all financial aid forms be submitted as soon as possible. *Need-based scholarships/grants offered:* Federal Pell; Federal SEOG; State scholarships/grants; Private scholarships; College/university scholarship or grant aid from institutional funds. *Loan aid offered:* Federal Direct Subsidized Loans; Federal Direct Unsubsidized Loans; Direct PLUS loans. Admitted students will be notified of awards on or about 4/1. Federal Work-Study Program available. Institutional employment available.

The Inside Word

College of the Atlantic is a very small, tight-knit community, and admissions officers here are incredibly focused on finding candidates who will be a great fit for the school. Successful applicants demonstrate a specific interest in the school and value independent learning, community building, and curiosity. Admission officers also look for students who thrive in self-directed settings. Given how important character is to the college, completing an interview is highly suggested.

THE SCHOOL SAYS

From the Admissions Office

"College of the Atlantic is a small, interdisciplinary college on Maine's Mount Desert Island. All students design their own course of study in human ecology—an educational approach that integrates knowledge from across academic disciplines and personal experience to investigate, and ultimately improve, the relationships between humans and our natural, social, and built environments. COA prepares students to become independent thinkers, challenge conventional wisdom, deal with pressing environmental and social issues, and engage passionately and thoughtfully to transform the world around them into a better place.

"Our campus is located on the shore of Frenchman Bay, a short walk from the mountains and trails of Acadia National Park—an ideal location for learning in the field. Many students spend time working or conducting research in the national park or on the college's two organic farms, forest protectorate, wilderness center, and offshore field research stations on Mount Desert Rock and Great Duck Island. In addition to having numerous opportunities for research and field study, all COA students complete an internship and a capstone senior project.

"We look for students seeking a rigorous, experiential, self-directed academic experience and meaningful engagement in a dynamic community of scholars. The best way to experience COA's unique approach to education, governance, and community life is to visit the campus. While you're here, make time to sit in on classes, explore the national park, connect with faculty and current students, and sample a homemade meal in the dining hall."

SELECTIVITY

# of total applicants	474
% of total applicants accepted	69
% of total acceptees attending	43
# of early decision applicants	23
% of early decision applicants accepted	74
# offered a place on the wait list	17
# admitted from wait list	6

First-Year Profile

Testing policy	Test Optional
Range SAT composite	1200–1340
Range SAT EBRW	660–750
Range SAT math	540–610
Range ACT composite	29–34
% submitting SAT scores	21
% submitting ACT scores	9
Average HS GPA	3.8
% submitting high school GPA	56
% graduated top 10% of class	40
% graduated top 25% of class	60
% graduated top 50% of class	93
% submitting high school rank	19

Important Dates

Early decision	
Apply by	11/15
Notified by	12/15
Other ED apply by	1/15
Other ED notified by	1/30
Early action	
Apply by	12/1
Notified by	1/31
Regular	
Apply by	2/1
Notified by	4/1
Nonfall registration?	Yes

FINANCIAL FACTS

Annual tuition	$50,895
Food and housing	$12,237
Required fees	$549
Books and supplies	$600
Average need-based scholarship (First-year)	$40,226 ($42,485)
% students with need rec. need-based scholarship or grant aid (First-year)	100 (100)
% students with need rec. non-need-based scholarship or grant aid (First-year)	9 (18)
% students with need rec. need-based self-help aid (First-year)	88 (87)
% students rec. any financial aid (First-year)	98 (100)
% UG borrow to pay for school	62
Average cumulative indebtedness	$26,413
% of students with need fully met (First-year)	70 (82)
Average % of student need met (First-year)	99 (99)

College of the Holy Cross

1 College Street, Worcester, MA 01610-2395 • Admissions: 508-793-2443

Survey Snapshot
Alumni active on campus
Students involved in community service
Students are very religious

RATINGS

Quality of Life	74
Fire Safety	96
Green	96
Academic	88
Profs Interesting	89
Profs Accessible	91
Admissions	95
Financial Aid	96

CAMPUS LIFE

Type of school	Private
Affiliation	Roman Catholic
Environment	City

Students

Degree-seeking undergrad enrollment	3,107
% male/female/not reported	46/54/<1
% First-year from public high school	49
% First-year live on campus	98
% Ugrads live on campus	88
# of fraternities	0
# of sororities	0
% Asian	3
% Black or African American	5
% Hispanic	13
% Native American	<1
% Pacific Islander	<1
% Race and/or ethnicity unknown	4
% Two or more races	4
% White	68
% International	3
# of countries represented	22

CAMPUS MENTAL HEALTH SERVICES

Offers mental health/wellness program	Yes
Mental health training available to students	Yes
Employs Chief Wellness Officer	Yes
Peer-to-peer mental health offerings	Yes
Counseling center has guidelines or accreditation	Yes
Mental health/well-being courses	No

ACADEMICS

% students returning for sophomore year	95
% students graduating within 4 years	85
% students graduating within 6 years	87
Calendar	Semester
Student/faculty ratio	9:1
Most common class size 10–19.	(55%)
Most common lab/discussion size 10–19.	(56%)

Most Popular Majors
Psychology; Economics; Political Science and Government

STUDENTS SAY "..."

Academics

College of the Holy Cross provides "an incredible learning environment for students" through a holistic and self-explorational combination of academics, "strong student life," and "small classes." As a Jesuit liberal arts school with the mission of "men and women for and with others," it sends students into the world with "a broad-based foundation to be successful in a variety of careers." The school encourages students "to reflect on their experiences and continue to better himself/herself as a whole person" and to this end is "dedicated to creating an exciting learning environment" and offering "endless opportunities." One such means to this end is the Montserrat program, which places first-years in one of six interdisciplinary "cluster," with whom they'll live and study, creating a personalized experience that blends classroom and life: where "you're more than just a number in the classroom and on the field." One student attests, "From the acceptance letter alone, I knew that my entire application was read thoroughly and that my character was closely examined." Each incoming class has a dedicated Class Dean that remains with them throughout graduation to provide mentorship and guidance, and additional support can be found in the "fantastic alumni network." Those undergoing the "rigorous" academics say the school equips them "with an intangible set of skills that not only prepares them for a job, but for life." Professors "get to know you on an individual and personal level" and are "always accessible and more than happy to help." As one student puts it, "It is a place where like in the parable of the mustard seed one can grow." One student, recognizing that their work will not go unrewarded, says that Holy Cross "demands enormous amounts of work from its students, but puts them in a great position to succeed."

Campus Life

Because each study cluster lives together, "many of the friends you make your first year will stay with you for years to come," and 88 percent of students remain on the "exceptionally beautiful" campus after their mandatory first year. All types of dietary needs are catered to (the college has previously been selected for a "healthiest dining halls" list), but students also point to "amazing" options in nearby Worcester or Boston, which is just a free 45-mile shuttle away. For those interested, there are "countless opportunities to learn through internships [and] speaker series." Additionally, there are "a multitude" of more than 100 student organizations ranging from academic to the arts, the largest being the Student Programs for Urban Development (SPUD), which organizes community service programs in the surrounding area and nationwide. While the library dominates the week, weekends are for letting loose, whether that's "riding the mechanical bull at a local bar" or events sponsored by the Student Government Association "such as karaoke or dances [that] are a blast."

Student Body

At College of the Holy Cross, "people take their work very seriously" and tend to be "studious with an activity or two that defines their interests and what they do during the weekend." They are also "very put together" and "generally articulate," with "a diverse set of interests" that range from ballroom dance to space exploration. It is rare "to find someone with no extracurricular responsibilities," according to one student. While most are from New England, the main commonality is that "all love being here" and "there is a tremendous sense of community." School pride is rampant among this "uncommonly friendly" group and everyone loves "going to sporting events, especially football and basketball." A student sums up, "If you want to do well academically, have fun on the weekend...study hard and play hard, then you will fit in at Holy Cross."

College of the Holy Cross

Financial Aid: 508-793-2265 • E-Mail: admissions@holycross.edu • Website: www.holycross.edu

THE PRINCETON REVIEW SAYS

Admissions

The school reports that its standardized testing policy for use in admission for Fall 2026 is Test Optional. The Princeton Review suggests that interested applicants consult with the school for the most up-to-date standardized testing policies. *Very important factors considered include:* rigor of secondary school record, academic GPA, application essay, recommendation(s), interview, character/personal qualities. *Important factors considered include:* extracurricular activities, talent/ability. *Other factors considered include:* class rank, standardized test scores, first generation, alumni/ae relation, geographical residence, state residency, religious affiliation/commitment, volunteer work, work experience, level of applicant's interest. High school diploma is required and GED is accepted. *Academic units recommended:* 4 English, 4 math, 4 science, 2 science labs, 4 language (other than English), 2 social studies.

Financial Aid

Students should submit: FAFSA; CSS PROFILE. Priority filing deadline is 1/15. The Princeton Review suggests that all financial aid forms be submitted as soon as possible. *Need-based scholarships/grants offered:* Federal Pell; Federal SEOG; State scholarships/grants; Private scholarships; College/university scholarship or grant aid from institutional funds. *Loan aid offered:* Federal Direct Subsidized Loans; Federal Direct Unsubsidized Loans; Direct PLUS loans; College/university loans from institutional funds. Admitted students will be notified of awards on or about Late March. Federal Work-Study Program available. Institutional employment available.

The Inside Word

Admission to Holy Cross is very competitive; therefore, a demanding high school course load is required to be a viable candidate. The college values effective communication skills—it thoroughly evaluates each applicant's personal statement and short essay responses. Interviews are important, especially for those applying early decision. Students who graduate from a Jesuit high school might find themselves at a slight advantage. Holy Cross meets 100 percent of an admitted student's demonstrated financial need.

THE SCHOOL SAYS

From the Admissions Office

"When applying to Holy Cross, two aspects of your application deserve particular attention. First, write your college essay with thought and care. This is your opportunity to share your unique story with the Admission Committee—to help us understand what matters to you, what you care about, and the experiences that have shaped you.

"Second, we want to get to know you, and we want you to get to know us, so demonstrating interest is also important. This includes visiting campus, attending Open Houses or virtual events like webinars, speaking with us at your high school or college fairs, or simply sending us an email. Interviews are highly recommended, as well, as they help us learn more about you while offering you the chance to ask questions about the College.

"Lastly, standardized test scores are optional. Students may submit their scores if they believe the results provide a more comprehensive picture of their achievements and potential, but students who don't submit scores will not be at a disadvantage in the admission process."

SELECTIVITY

# of total applicants	9,568
% of total applicants accepted	18
% of total acceptees attending	50
# of in-state applicants	2,951
% of in-state applicants accepted	19
# of out-of-state-applicants	5,701
% of applicants accepted from out of state	18
# of international applicants	916
% of international applicants accepted	9
# of early decision applicants	901
% of early decision applicants accepted	60
# offered a place on the wait list	4,186
# admitted from wait list	105

First-Year Profile

Testing policy	Test Optional
Range SAT composite	1250–1340
Range SAT EBRW	630–710
Range SAT math	610–700
Range ACT composite	27–32
% submitting SAT scores	30
% submitting ACT scores	15
% graduated top 10% of class	46
% graduated top 25% of class	78
% graduated top 50% of class	93
% submitting high school rank	21

Important Dates

Early decision	
Apply by	11/15
Notified by	12/15
Other ED apply by	1/15
Other ED notified by	2/15
Regular	
Apply by	1/15
Nonfall registration?	No

FINANCIAL FACTS

Annual tuition	$63,650
Food and housing	$18,820
Required fees	$850
Books and supplies	$1,000
Average need-based scholarship (First-year)	$49,643 ($50,427)
% students with need rec. need-based scholarship or grant aid (First-year)	88 (86)
% students with need rec. non-need-based scholarship or grant aid (First-year)	14 (15)
% students with need rec. need-based self-help aid (First-year)	59 (52)
% students rec. any financial aid (First-year)	61 (63)
% UG borrow to pay for school	41
Average cumulative indebtedness	$21,107
% of students with need fully met (First-year)	100 (100)
Average % of student need met (First-year)	100 (100)

College of the Ozarks

1 Opportunity Ave., Point Lookout, MO 65726 • Admissions: 417-690-2636

Survey Snapshot
Lots of conservative students
Great financial aid
Students are very religious

RATINGS

Quality of Life	**85**
Fire Safety	**60***
Green	**60***
Academic	**82**
Profs Interesting	**90**
Profs Accessible	**89**
Admissions	**97**
Financial Aid	**60***

CAMPUS LIFE

Type of school	Private
Affiliation	Evangelical Christian Interdenominational
Environment	Rural

Students

Degree-seeking undergrad enrollment	1,491
% male/female/not reported	45/55/0
% from out of state	24
% First-year from public high school	78
% First-year live on campus	93
% Ugrads live on campus	90
# of fraternities	0
# of sororities	0
% Asian	1
% Black or African American	1
% Hispanic	2
% Native American	<1
% Pacific Islander	<1
% Race and/or ethnicity unknown	2
% Two or more races	2
% White	90
% International	1
# of countries represented	17

CAMPUS MENTAL HEALTH SERVICES

Offers mental health/wellness program	Yes
Mental health training available to students	No
Employs Chief Wellness Officer	NR
Peer-to-peer mental health offerings	NR
Counseling center has guidelines or accreditation	No
Mental health/well-being courses	NR

ACADEMICS

% students returning for sophomore year	73
% students graduating within 4 years	55
Calendar	Semester
Student/faculty ratio	14:1
Most common class size 10–19.	(33%)
Most common lab/discussion size 10–19.	(77%)

Most Popular Majors

Elementary Education and Teaching; Business Administration and Management

Applicants Also Look At

Evangel University, Missouri State University, Southwest Baptist University, William Jewell College

STUDENTS SAY "..."

Academics

Students who attend the College of Ozarks leave feeling academically, spiritually, and monetarily richer, thanks to the solid scholastic programs, Christian beliefs, and "the biggest strength ... [getting] to graduate debt-free." Consensus is that having a combination of scholarships and a work program that requires all undergrads to hold a campus job is a "huge asset" because it fosters a "unique sense of community" and ensures that students have real-world experience: "I personally have jumped around and gained a variety of skills that I can add to my résumé." These benefits do come with a measure of strictness in terms of a dress code and curfew, but attendees largely agree that these make "the work ethic of the student body unbelievable. As a whole, we are unmatched." They're also balanced with the school's Christian background, which "does an amazing job at creating a wonderful environment to grow our relationship with God."

Undergrads are quick to praise their "extremely knowledgeable" professors, and the way in which they can bring "topics to life" and "easily connect with the students." Plus, "most professors have found a strong balance between discussion and lecture to create a positive environment and promote student interaction." Though some undergrads do caution that the "classes and academics are rigorous," they emphasize that "professors do everything they can to help students succeed." That interaction goes a long way: "They have prompted [me] to grow in my writing and analytical skills, and have enriched my understanding of the world."

Campus Life

College of the Ozarks certainly lives up to its nickname, "Hard Work U." Not only are students "very devoted to their studies," they also work "15 hours a week on campus" at one of over 80 work stations. Job placements are wide-ranging and include the Print Shop, the Power Plant, and the school radio station, KCOZ. Of course, these industrious undergrads still manage to make time for extracurriculars, from the "pretty popular" worship nights to intramurals that range from seasons of classic sports and tournaments "between dorm buildings" to "a disc golf team...with a huge course going throughout the campus." Additionally, the Student Union "does a great job of putting on different activities," including the highly anticipated Mudfest, an annual game of tug-of-war over a mud pit. For more relaxing fare, students flock to events where they can indulge in "free coffee, treats, and live music." It's also just as common to find undergrads taking advantage of their beautiful surroundings. This often entails "hammocking,...having picnics, [or simply] strolling around campus." Best of all, your walk can take you right to the school's dairy: "You can go there anytime to pet and feed the calves." One thing students feel worth emphasizing is that all of this is "good, clean, real fun," thanks to a "zero-tolerance policy for drugs and alcohol."

Student Body

A sense of community permeates the College of Ozarks' campus and it's easy to understand why. As one junior explains, "We definitely have a relatively small student body here, which makes everyone feel like family." This runs deeper than casual kindness: "People here are genuinely concerned about you; they take five minutes of their day to listen to you and give advice." One area that could stand a little improvement is diversity, with some undergrads acknowledging that the "student body is fairly homogeneous" and mainly hails from "in/around the Ozarks region." However, they also highlight the fact that the school "has its fair sprinkling of international, transfer, and non-traditional students." Of course, no matter where they're from, the vast majority are "Christians who... desire to grow in their knowledge and love of Jesus Christ." Most importantly, they tend to lead with kindness and are quick to "open doors, walk people back to dorms, and frequently donate time or money." As one senior sums up, "My peers are so life-giving. We laugh, cry, and learn to be better people together."

College of the Ozarks

Financial Aid: 417-690-3292 • E-Mail: admissions@cofo.edu • Website: www.cofo.edu

THE PRINCETON REVIEW SAYS

Admissions

The school reports that its standardized testing policy for use in admission for Fall 2026 will require applicants to submit either the SAT or ACT. The Princeton Review suggests that interested applicants consult with the school for the most up-to-date standardized testing policies. *Very important factors considered include:* rigor of secondary school record, class rank, interview, character/personal qualities. *Important factors considered include:* academic GPA, standardized test scores, recommendation(s), geographical residence, volunteer work, work experience, level of applicant's interest. *Other factors considered include:* extracurricular activities, talent/ability, first generation, alumni/ae relation, state residency, religious affiliation/commitment. High school diploma is required and GED is accepted. *Academic units required:* 4 English, 3 math, 2 science, 1 science lab, 3 history. *Academic units recommended:* 2 language (other than English), 3 social studies.

Financial Aid

Students should submit: FAFSA. Priority filing deadline is 11/15. The Princeton Review suggests that all financial aid forms be submitted as soon as possible. *Need-based scholarships/grants offered:* Federal Pell; Federal SEOG; State scholarships/grants; Private scholarships; College/university scholarship or grant aid from institutional funds. Admitted students will be notified of awards on or about 7/1. Federal Work-Study Program available. Institutional employment available.

The Inside Word

Admissions officers at College of the Ozarks are generally looking to serve students hailing from the Ozark region. Indeed, they're seeking local applicants in the top half of their class who lack the financial resources to pay for college. Applicants should also be individuals who are specifically looking for a Christian education.

THE SCHOOL SAYS

From the Admissions Office

"College of the Ozarks is unique because of its no-tuition, work-study program, but also because it strives to educate the head, the heart, and the hands. At C of O, there are high expectations of students—the college stresses character development as well as study and work. An education from 'Hard Work U.' offers many opportunities, not the least of which is the chance to graduate debt-free. Life at C of O isn't all hard work and no play, however. There are many opportunities for fun. The nearby resort town of Branson, Missouri, offers ample opportunities for recreation and summer employment, and Table Rock Lake, only a few miles away, is a terrific spot to swim, sun, and relax. Numerous on-campus activities such as Mudfest, Luau Night, dances, and holiday parties give students lots of chances for fun without leaving the college. At 'Hard Work U.,' we work hard, but we know how to have fun too."

SELECTIVITY

# of total applicants	2,879
% of total applicants accepted	16
% of total acceptees attending	84
# offered a place on the wait list	586
# admitted from wait list	24

First-Year Profile

Testing policy	SAT or ACT Required
Range SAT EBRW	560–630
Range SAT math	540–610
Range ACT composite	21–26
% submitting SAT scores	3
% submitting ACT scores	97
Average HS GPA	3.7
% submitting high school GPA	99
% graduated top 10% of class	25
% graduated top 25% of class	62
% graduated top 50% of class	96
% submitting high school rank	74

Important Dates

Regular	
Notified by	Rolling, 12/31
Nonfall registration?	Yes

FINANCIAL FACTS

Annual tuition	$25,095
Food and housing	$9,400
Required fees	$594
Books and supplies	$1,100
Average need-based scholarship (First-year)	$11,182 ($11,182)
% students with need rec. need-based scholarship or grant aid (First-year)	100 (100)
% students with need rec. non-need-based scholarship or grant aid (First-year)	94 (36)
% students with need rec. need-based self-help aid (First-year)	94 (64)
% students rec. any financial aid (First-year)	100 (100)
% of students with need fully met (First-year)	40 (18)
Average % of student need met (First-year)	81 (75)

The College of Wooster

1189 Beall Avenue, Wooster, OH 44691 • Admissions: 330-263-2322

Survey Snapshot
Great library
Lab facilities are great
Easy to get around campus

RATINGS

Quality of Life	85
Fire Safety	86
Green	85
Academic	88
Profs Interesting	92
Profs Accessible	95
Admissions	88
Financial Aid	94

CAMPUS LIFE

Type of school	Private
Affiliation	Presbyterian (historically affiliated)
Environment	Town

Students

Degree-seeking undergrad enrollment	1,507
% male/female/not reported	47/53/<1
% from out of state	58
% First-year from public high school	60
% First-year live on campus	98
% Ugrads live on campus	98
# of fraternities (% join)	3 (12)
# of sororities (% join)	6 (21)
% Asian	4
% Black or African American	10
% Hispanic	6
% Native American	<1
% Pacific Islander	<1
% Race and/or ethnicity unknown	2
% Two or more races	4
% White	61
% International	12

CAMPUS MENTAL HEALTH SERVICES

Offers mental health/wellness program	Yes
Mental health training available to students	Yes
Employs Chief Wellness Officer	No
Peer-to-peer mental health offerings	Yes
Counseling center has guidelines or accreditation	No
Mental health/well-being courses	No

ACADEMICS

% students returning for sophomore year	85
% students graduating within 4 years	59
% students graduating within 6 years	71
Calendar	Semester
Student/faculty ratio	9:1
Most common class size 10–19.	(41%)
Most common lab/discussion size 10–19.	(61%)

STUDENTS SAY "…"

Academics

At the College of Wooster, a "deeply rooted culture of mentorship" shapes the academic experience. Wooster students are designated a "faculty mentor throughout their time at the college, which is an excellent resource for planning courses and thinking about research topics." This becomes particularly useful during their third or fourth year when students begin Independent Study (IS), "a mentored research program where students pursue a topic of personal interest within their major. IS gives students the perfect balance of independence and guidance." Uniformly, instructors "are passionate about their subjects…and I feel incredibly supported across every department I've taken a class in." This can make for some creative classroom activities, as with one professor who went above-and-beyond to design a final exam consisting of a staged crime scene, "in which the class had to use analytical chemical techniques to analyze the planted evidence and hold a court trial to determine the perpetrator." Students, known as Fighting Scots, also appreciate "how intentional [professors] are about connecting course material to real-world applications, which makes even the more challenging concepts feel relevant and meaningful." Overwhelmingly, "the strong mentorship culture and the close relationships with professors truly define the academic experience here."

Campus Life

Life at Wooster "is busy, but in the best way." Given Wooster's rural Ohio locale, "most students seek out community through organizations on campus." Campus favorites include musical clubs, particularly the a cappella group's "very positive environment" and the Wooster Chorus's "amazing opportunities to perform with high-level groups such as the Cleveland Orchestra." Finance enthusiasts also enjoy the Jenny Investment Club, which offers "the space to learn about finance and the corporate and investment world from the ground up." Many Scots find their community through athletics, with one swimmer reporting having developed "a strong network of friends, who I know will be a part of my support network for years to come." Scots looking to unwind also "love going to school-led events—things like craft nights, movie screenings, cultural celebrations, and weekend programs. Wooster has a way of organizing events that makes even a random Tuesday feel exciting." Whether it's a club, a sporting event, or a campus social, one Scot sums up their extracurricular experience best: "It has taught me the importance of a work-life balance, made me a better person, and given me a community filled with amazing people I want to keep in contact [with] for years to come."

Student Body

"Wooster is exactly the kind of place that values curiosity, independence, and community." One student says, "We come from all different parts of the world,…and we find home in a small city in Ohio. It's a beautiful showing of community strength, action, and determination." As another Scot adds, "Our student body is made up of a lot of international individuals, and they really give our campus a lot of color and vibrancy." And "what stands out the most is how willing students are to show up for each other. Whether it is sharing notes after a tough class, forming spontaneous study groups in the library, or showing up to support someone's club event, there is this unspoken culture of community." Additionally, "there is strong support for the LGBTQIA+ community at Wooster, as well as a large community of students who openly identify as such." Scots also prioritize "making a positive impact on the community…Some examples of success can be preparing to be an influential educator, gathering peers on a Saturday to protest against certain policy stances, or striving to bring out the best in others day in and day out." In short, Wooster is an ideal college for those who "want to build a community rich in collaboration and research while enjoying the benefits of a liberal arts experience."

The College of Wooster

Financial Aid: 330-263-2317 • E-Mail: admissions@wooster.edu • Website: www.wooster.edu

THE PRINCETON REVIEW SAYS

Admissions

The school reports that its standardized testing policy for use in admission for Fall 2026 is Test Optional. The Princeton Review suggests that interested applicants consult with the school for the most up-to-date standardized testing policies. *Very important factors considered include:* rigor of secondary school record, academic GPA. *Important factors considered include:* class rank, application essay, recommendation(s), extracurricular activities, character/personal qualities. *Other factors considered include:* standardized test scores, interview, talent/ability, volunteer work, work experience, level of applicant's interest. High school diploma is required and GED is accepted. *Academic units required:* 4 English, 3 math, 3 science, 2 language (other than English), 3 social studies, 1 academic elective.

Financial Aid

Students should submit: FAFSA. Priority filing deadline is 1/1. The Princeton Review suggests that all financial aid forms be submitted as soon as possible. *Need-based scholarships/grants offered:* Federal Pell; Federal SEOG; State scholarships/grants; Private scholarships; College/university scholarship or grant aid from institutional funds. *Loan aid offered:* Federal Direct Subsidized Loans; Federal Direct Unsubsidized Loans; Direct PLUS loans. Admitted students will be notified of awards on a rolling basis beginning 1/15. Federal Work-Study Program available. Institutional employment available.

The Inside Word

The College of Wooster is focused on accessibility and finding a diverse student body. If you've got character and think you can add to this community's social, intellectual, and scholastic achievements, admissions officers will be interested in you. Don't be discouraged if your grades are a little below the accepted range—especially since standardized tests are optional—and check with the school if you've missed the application deadline, as they may still be able to consider you (with no penalty to potential scholarships and other aid).

THE SCHOOL SAYS

From the Admissions Office

"At The College of Wooster, curiosity is the core of our educational experience. Through rigorous academics and personalized faculty mentorship, students hone the skills to ask questions, solve problems, and tackle complex challenges with confidence. Wooster's approach leads to impressive outcomes: within six months of graduation, 96% of our graduates are employed in their field of choice, and 94% of those pursuing post-graduate studies are accepted into their top-choice programs.

"Wooster is nationally ranked for its accessible professors, exceptional classroom experience, top-tier internship opportunities, and much more. Our renowned Independent Study (I.S.) program allows every student to delve into a topic of their choice with individual guidance from a faculty mentor. Through I.S., our students not only develop new knowledge, they form a community of shared experience with their classmates and learn what they're truly capable of.

"Beyond academics, Wooster is also a vibrant and supportive community of Independent Minds, Working Together, with students from 76 countries and nearly every U.S. state. Our students develop confidence, skills and relationships that last a lifetime while playing on one of our 23 varsity athletic teams, performing in one of our seven music ensembles, participating in our 120 clubs, and enjoying campus festivals and off-campus experiences like study abroad, internships and volunteering.

"Discover why the world comes to Wooster. Step into the power of your curiosity, begin a lifelong journey of self-discovery, and graduate with the confidence and skills to make your mark in the world."

SELECTIVITY

# of total applicants	4,568
% of total applicants accepted	64
% of total acceptees attending	12
# of in-state applicants	1,075
% of in-state applicants accepted	89
# of out-of-state-applicants	1,679
% of applicants accepted from out of state	63
# of international applicants	1,814
% of international applicants accepted	26
# of early decision applicants	173
% of early decision applicants accepted	64
# offered a place on the wait list	179
# admitted from wait list	22

First-Year Profile

Testing policy	Test Optional
Range SAT composite	1250–1440
Range SAT EBRW	630–730
Range SAT math	590–720
Range ACT composite	27–32
% submitting SAT scores	20
% submitting ACT scores	23
Average HS GPA	3.6
% submitting high school GPA	100
% graduated top 10% of class	48
% graduated top 25% of class	66
% graduated top 50% of class	86
% submitting high school rank	44

Important Dates

Early decision	
Apply by	11/1
Notified by	11/15
Other ED apply by	1/15
Other ED notified by	2/1
Early action	
Apply by	11/15
Notified by	1/15
Regular	
Apply by	2/15
Notified by	4/1
Nonfall registration?	Yes

FINANCIAL FACTS

Annual tuition	$65,510
Food and housing	$16,050
Required fees	$780
Books and supplies	$2,250
Average need-based scholarship (First-year)	$48,870 ($50,920)
% students with need rec. need-based scholarship or grant aid (First-year)	99 (99)
% students with need rec. non-need-based scholarship or grant aid (First-year)	21 (24)
% students with need rec. need-based self-help aid (First-year)	66 (70)
% students rec. any financial aid (First-year)	100 (100)
% UG borrow to pay for school	51
Average cumulative indebtedness	$32,479
% of students with need fully met (First-year)	63 (77)
Average % of student need met (First-year)	94 (96)

Colorado College

14 East Cache la Poudre St., Colorado Springs, CO 80903 • Admissions: 719-389-6344

Survey Snapshot
Lots of liberal students
Students are happy
Class discussions encouraged

RATINGS

Quality of Life	88
Fire Safety	97
Green	97
Academic	92
Profs Interesting	94
Profs Accessible	96
Admissions	94
Financial Aid	98

CAMPUS LIFE

Type of school	Private
Environment	Metropolis

Students

Degree-seeking undergrad enrollment	1,873
% male/female/not reported	45/53/2
% from out of state	79
% First-year live on campus	100
% Ugrads live on campus	76
# of fraternities (% join)	2 (12)
# of sororities (% join)	2 (14)
% Asian	4
% Black or African American	3
% Hispanic	10
% Native American	<1
% Pacific Islander	<1
% Race and/or ethnicity unknown	2
% Two or more races	7
% White	69
% International	5
# of countries represented	47

CAMPUS MENTAL HEALTH SERVICES

Offers mental health/wellness program	Yes
Mental health training available to students	Yes
Employs Chief Wellness Officer	Yes
Peer-to-peer mental health offerings	Yes
Counseling center has guidelines or accreditation	Yes
Mental health/well-being courses	Yes, for-credit

ACADEMICS

% students returning for sophomore year	93
% students graduating within 4 years	74
% students graduating within 6 years	86
Calendar	Block Plan (eight 3.5-week blocks)
Student/faculty ratio	8:1
Most common class size 10–19.	(39%)

Most Popular Majors
Ecology; Political Science and Government; Business/Managerial Economics

STUDENTS SAY "..."

Academics

Under the "strongly immersive approach to education" at Colorado College, students take life 3.5 weeks at a time as part of a unique Block Plan. There's just one intensive class per block, followed by a 4.5 day break. Eight blocks later, students have an academic year under their belts, along with a slight feeling of invincibility: "The classes are very challenging, but after cramming in a semester's worth of calculus in four weeks, you basically feel like you can conquer anything." As an added benefit, professors are only teaching one class at a time, which "[does] away with student anonymity" and offers "more opportunities for growth." One student confides that "In my last block the professor was spending the whole morning [and] afternoon—and evening—with us!" Students appreciate the "immersion in a dynamic array of intellectual endeavors," which "[fosters] excellent discussion and intellectual growth." Whether learning a language on an "intense and exhausting" schedule or studying rock formations on a weeklong hiking trip, students "feel fully invested in each class I take here." Blocks also allow students to tailor their schedules to easily include hobbies, "internship opportunities," and rehearsals, with the college ensuring a "great support system and connections" to do so. In "pursuing excellence through diverse and rich viewpoints," students obtain excellent "preparation for post-graduation," aided by the "ability to study off campus or abroad." This is not to say that students roam completely wild; all must complete broad all-college requirements and take part in a First-Year Program, designed to show students how to explore different disciplines and find their focus (or focuses). "I have been amazed at the extent to which the block plan allows each student to delve into their course material," says one happy student.

Campus Life

The chunks of time afforded by the "focused study" at Colorado College has everyone "working diligently, so that free time can be appreciated to its fullest." Students say that nearby Pikes Peak is "a constant reminder about how beautiful of a state we are in" and note that "outdoor activities are a big thing here." That said, "people are pretty accepting [of] what you like doing for fun," (and note a lack of peer pressure) the range of which often includes "slacklining, doing homework in the sun, and playing guitar on the lawn all happen when it's nice out. Sledding and skiing down campus hills, snowball fights, and fire pits happen in the winter." With all of this going on right outside their doors (all are required to live on campus for their first three years), students say that "you really don't have to leave campus if you don't want to," but those that do want to get a little bit of city flavor can head to downtown Colorado Springs, which "is only about a 10-minute walk from campus, and there are many interesting restaurants to dine at for special occasions or a fun night out." As one student puts it, "The common slang is 'you do you.'"

Student Body

Colorado College's emphasis on curiosity and learning draws a smart crowd that is "largely involved with their community, environment and academics," so much so that it sometimes seems that "almost everyone was a valedictorian or salutatorian." Most agree that "everyone here is very intelligent" and "very vocal about their opinions"; these can surface at any time, such as during "intellectual discussion about our impact on nature while rock climbing." Students "are usually very accepting and friendly" and have the opportunity to have deeper discourse through the Breaking Bread program, wherein faculty or staff members invite students to their home or an off-site location to engage in conversation. Generally speaking, "CC students have passion for academic and outdoor pursuits," and "the typical student is well-traveled, intelligent...quirky, outdoorsy, and a bit of a hipster." Regardless of background or future path, students say that "the shared values of intellectual engagement, physical and mental health, passion, and a sense of adventure define Colorado College's spirit."

COLORADO COLLEGE

Financial Aid: 719-389-6762 • E-Mail: admission@coloradocollege.edu • Website: www.coloradocollege.edu

THE PRINCETON REVIEW SAYS

Admissions

The school reports that its standardized testing policy for use in admission for Fall 2026 is Test Optional. The Princeton Review suggests that interested applicants consult with the school for the most up-to-date standardized testing policies. *Important factors considered include:* rigor of secondary school record, academic GPA, application essay, recommendation(s), extracurricular activities. *Other factors considered include:* class rank, standardized test scores, interview, talent/ability, character/personal qualities, first generation, alumni/ae relation, geographical residence, state residency, religious affiliation/commitment, volunteer work, work experience, level of applicant's interest. High school diploma or equivalent is not required. *Academic units required:* 4 English.

Financial Aid

Students should submit: FAFSA; CSS PROFILE. Priority filing deadline is 11/1. The Princeton Review suggests that all financial aid forms be submitted as soon as possible. *Need-based scholarships/grants offered:* Federal Pell; Federal SEOG; State scholarships/grants; Private scholarships; College/university scholarship or grant aid from institutional funds. *Loan aid offered:* Federal Direct Subsidized Loans; Federal Direct Unsubsidized Loans; Direct PLUS loans. Admitted students will be notified of awards on or about 12/20. Federal Work-Study Program available. Institutional employment available.

The Inside Word

Admission at Colorado College is highly competitive, with almost 90 percent of the student body accepted last year coming from the top quarter of their high school class. The rigor of the block program requires students to demonstrate self-motivation and commitment to both academics and extracurriculars, and strong writing skills are considered essential to the application. Interviews and arts supplements are non-required application options; students who feel their strengths will be showcased by these options should carefully consider them.

THE SCHOOL SAYS

From the Admissions Office

"Students enter Colorado College for the opportunity to study intensely in small learning communities. Groups of students work closely with one another and faculty in discussion-based classes and hands-on labs. CC encourages a well-rounded education, combining the academic rigor of a traditional liberal arts college, with the focus and flexibility of the block plan. Rich programs in athletics, community service, student government, and the arts balance an engaged student life. The college encourages students to push themselves academically, and many continue their studies at the best graduate and professional schools in the nation. Because roughly 80 percent of students study abroad while at CC, the college has been recognized as a national leader in international education. The block plan allows classes to incorporate field study into the curriculum, whether studying winter field ecology at the CC Cabin or Dante and Michelangelo in Italy. Its location at the base of the Rockies makes CC a great choice for students who enjoy backpacking, hiking, climbing, and skiing."

SELECTIVITY

# of total applicants	8,822
% of total applicants accepted	22
% of total acceptees attending	26
# of in-state applicants	1,605
% of in-state applicants accepted	19
# of out-of-state-applicants	4,847
% of applicants accepted from out of state	31
# of international applicants	2,370
% of international applicants accepted	7
# of early decision applicants	773
% of early decision applicants accepted	35
# offered a place on the wait list	400
# admitted from wait list	20

First-Year Profile

Testing policy	Test Optional
Range SAT composite	1240–1430
Range SAT EBRW	640–740
Range SAT math	610–700
Range ACT composite	28–34
% submitting SAT scores	28
% submitting ACT scores	12
Average HS GPA	3.9
% submitting high school GPA	87
% graduated top 10% of class	58
% graduated top 25% of class	86
% graduated top 50% of class	97
% submitting high school rank	23

Important Dates

Early decision	
Apply by	11/1
Notified by	12/11
Other ED apply by	1/15
Other ED notified by	2/12
Early action	
Apply by	11/1
Notified by	1/8
Regular	
Apply by	1/15
Notified by	3/12
Nonfall registration?	Yes

FINANCIAL FACTS

Annual tuition	$75,702
Food and housing	$17,360
Required fees	$528
Books and supplies	$1,240
Average need-based scholarship (First-year)	$67,143 ($68,552)
% students with need rec. need-based scholarship or grant aid (First-year)	99 (99)
% students with need rec. non-need-based scholarship or grant aid (First-year)	13 (19)
% students with need rec. need-based self-help aid (First-year)	95 (96)
% students rec. any financial aid (First-year)	41 (49)
% UG borrow to pay for school	33
Average cumulative indebtedness	$23,140
% of students with need fully met (First-year)	100 (100)
Average % of student need met (First-year)	100 (100)

Colorado State University

711 Oval Drive, Fort Collins, CO 80523 • Admissions: 970-491-6909

Survey Snapshot

Students take advantage of the outdoors
Recreation facilities are great
Students love Fort Collins, CO

RATINGS

Quality of Life	92
Fire Safety	90
Green	99
Academic	77
Profs Interesting	86
Profs Accessible	88
Admissions	82
Financial Aid	81

CAMPUS LIFE

Type of school	Public
Environment	City

Students

Degree-seeking undergrad enrollment	25,676
% male/female/not reported	45/55/0
% from out of state	31
% First-year live on campus	93
% Ugrads live on campus	27
# of fraternities (% join)	31 (6)
# of sororities (% join)	20 (6)
% Asian	3
% Black or African American	3
% Hispanic	17
% Native American	1
% Pacific Islander	<1
% Race and/or ethnicity unknown	1
% Two or more races	5
% White	68
% International	2
# of countries represented	79

CAMPUS MENTAL HEALTH SERVICES

Offers mental health/wellness program	Yes
Mental health training available to students	Yes
Employs Chief Wellness Officer	Yes
Peer-to-peer mental health offerings	Yes
Counseling center has guidelines or accreditation	Yes
Mental health/well-being courses	Yes, for-credit

ACADEMICS

% students returning for sophomore year	88
% students graduating within 4 years	49
% students graduating within 6 years	68
Calendar	Semester
Student/faculty ratio	17:1
Most common class size 20–29.	(23%)
Most common lab/discussion size 20–29.	(43%)

Most Popular Majors

Psychology; Business Administration and Management; Mechanical Engineering

Applicants Also Look At

California Polytechnic State University—San Luis Obispo, Colorado School of Mines, University of Colorado at Denver, University of Colorado Boulder, University of Utah

STUDENTS SAY "…"

Academics

Colorado State University excels "at providing connection, support, and resources" to its students. CSU also supports "those who traditionally are underrepresented in educational settings," offering "resources for low-income and first-generation students" and a robust "transportation system for local and commuting students." Among CSU's academic strengths are its highly regarded College of Agricultural Sciences and its engineering school with "cutting-edge academic programs." First-year engineering students are organized into 30-person cohorts so they "share the same engineering classes for the first year, encouraging engagement and inducing familiarity between the students," building strong academic and social connections early. Experiential learning is a defining feature of many CSU programs. One student highlights opportunities to "walk through construction job sites, visit and explore how reservoirs work, along with going on field trips to see how steel is created." And one student in animal sciences recalls a lab where they "took care of calves and learned how to feed them and make sure they look healthy and are growing well." Students report that CSU offers students "plenty of support for career planning and job opportunities. They also have many programs to help those in need…whether that be financial, mental, or emotional support." As one student summarizes, "CSU is a fantastic school. I feel immensely supported and happy here."

Campus Life

"The campus is BEAUTIFUL, and there is no shortage of clubs and groups to participate in," says one enthusiastic Ram, as CSU students are known. Student organizations cover a wide range of interests and identities, like the "Asian Pacific American Cultural Center, which has given me a meaningful space to connect with others," and groups like Wildlife Society, Mountain Riders, Biology Collection, and Polo Club. Off campus, "a huge part of the culture here in Fort Collins is outdoor activities, so most students participate in skiing, biking, hiking, camping, climbing, and many other outdoor sports." Warmer seasons also see Rams fly fishing and swimming in Horsetooth Reservoir, and many like to "go to downtown Fort Collins and connect with the community." During the day, students "explore nearby cafés and shops," and those looking for nightlife enjoy "going to the bars in town." Overall, Rams enjoy a "life at school [that] is very busy and full of constant activities and opportunities to enjoy the outdoors, social life, and all the beauty Fort Collins has to offer."

Student Body

At CSU, students are supportive of each other and "very friendly." As one student explains, "There is a big focus on helping out the 'ramily,' aka the Ram family." Rams also value making friends with those who are different from themselves and appreciate that CSU "allows for free exploration of differing views and cultures." Students say there's "tons of diversity in the aspects of culture, race, religion, ethnicity, political views, etc.…CSU all comes together as one and cheers for each other and helps one another." Students describe their peers as "intelligent, motivated, and overall positive people." CSU "is totally an outdoorsy school located in a great area," and "it is quite rare to meet someone who doesn't enjoy being outside in some way." Rams are also united by the activities that comprise CSU's campus culture, such as "clubs, cultural organizations, or sports, which help build a sense of community." In short, "CSU has a community with an emphasis on supporting each other. 'Rams always take care of Rams,' is an important phrase, taken seriously."

Colorado State University

Financial Aid: 970-491-6321 • E-Mail: admissions@colostate.edu • Website: www.colostate.edu

THE PRINCETON REVIEW SAYS

Admissions

The school reports that its standardized testing policy for use in admission for Fall 2026 is Test Free. The Princeton Review suggests that interested applicants consult with the school for the most up-to-date standardized testing policies. *Very important factors considered include:* rigor of secondary school record, academic GPA. *Important factors considered include:* application essay. *Other factors considered include:* class rank, recommendation(s), extracurricular activities, talent/ability, character/personal qualities, first generation, geographical residence, state residency, volunteer work, work experience. High school diploma is required and GED is accepted. *Academic units required:* 4 English, 4 math, 3 science, 2 science labs, 1 language (other than English), 3 social studies, 1 history, 2 academic electives. *Academic units recommended:* 4 English, 4 math, 3 science, 2 science labs, 2 language (other than English), 3 social studies, 1 history, 2 academic electives.

Financial Aid

Students should submit: FAFSA. Priority filing deadline is 3/1. The Princeton Review suggests that all financial aid forms be submitted as soon as possible. *Need-based scholarships/grants offered:* Federal Pell; Federal SEOG; State scholarships/grants; Private scholarships; College/university scholarship or grant aid from institutional funds. *Loan aid offered:* Federal Direct Subsidized Loans; Federal Direct Unsubsidized Loans; Direct PLUS loans; College/university loans from institutional funds. Admitted students will be notified of awards on a rolling basis beginning 3/1. Federal Work-Study Program available. Institutional employment available.

The Inside Word

When building their incoming class, Colorado State University seeks out students who will be able to meet the school's high academic standards. To do so, they closely examine the rigor of your high school curriculum. Admissions officers want to see that you've been successful in challenging college prep courses. If submitted, your standardized test scores will also hold weight. The university looks at your extracurricular involvement as well. Finally, the admissions office considers circumstances that might have impacted your course selection or academic performance.

THE SCHOOL SAYS

From the Admissions Office

"As one of the nation's premier research universities, Colorado State University offers more than 150 undergraduate programs of study across eight colleges. Students from fifty states and eighty-five countries choose Colorado State for the quality and comprehensiveness of the University's academic offerings. As students discover, Colorado State is more than a college where they can elevate their scholarship to the highest level. It's also a place where they can gain essential experience in the fields of their choice, whether they're engaging in professional internships, studying on the other side of the globe, or collaborating with world-class faculty on groundbreaking research projects. In addition to being a part of an outstanding experiential learning environment, Colorado State students benefit from a sense of community that's unique for a large university. They develop meaningful relationships with faculty who inspire their best work, and they live and learn with diverse peers who value their ideas and expand their perspectives. These connections can lead to authentic opportunities for social networking and professional advancement. When Rams graduate from Colorado State, they possess the knowledge, practical experience, and interpersonal skills they need to help move their work and the world forward.

"Although academic performance is a primary factor in admissions decisions, Colorado State's holistic review process also recognizes personal qualities and experiences that have the potential to enrich the University and the Fort Collins community. Students must submit the Common Application for admission."

SELECTIVITY

# of total applicants	38,365
% of total applicants accepted	89
% of total acceptees attending	16

First-Year Profile

Testing policy	Test Free
Average HS GPA	3.7
% submitting high school GPA	100
% graduated top 10% of class	19
% graduated top 25% of class	45
% graduated top 50% of class	77
% submitting high school rank	60

Important Dates

Early action	
Apply by	11/15
Notified by	1/15
Regular	
Apply by	7/31
Notified by	Rolling, 10/1
Nonfall registration?	Yes

FINANCIAL FACTS

Annual in-state tuition	$11,093
Annual out-of-state tuition	$33,432
Food and housing	$17,508
Required fees	$2,681
Books and supplies	$1,200
Average need-based scholarship (First-year)	$12,367 ($12,658)
% students with need rec. need-based scholarship or grant aid (First-year)	75 (85)
% students with need rec. non-need-based scholarship or grant aid (First-year)	36 (62)
% students with need rec. need-based self-help aid (First-year)	55 (54)
% students rec. any financial aid (First-year)	72 (83)
% UG borrow to pay for school	45
Average cumulative indebtedness	$32,519
% of students with need fully met (First-year)	7 (9)
Average % of student need met (First-year)	68 (71)

COLUMBIA UNIVERSITY

535 W 116th Street, New York, NY 10027 • Admissions: 212-854-2522

Survey Snapshot
Students love New York, NY
Easy to get around campus
Great off-campus food

RATINGS

Quality of Life	89
Fire Safety	86
Green	60*
Academic	90
Profs Interesting	91
Profs Accessible	89
Admissions	99
Financial Aid	98

CAMPUS LIFE

Type of school	Private
Environment	Metropolis

Students

Degree-seeking undergrad enrollment	6,872
% male/female/not reported	50/50/0
% from out of state	80
% First-year from public high school	51
% First-year live on campus	99
% Ugrads live on campus	90
# of fraternities (% join)	7 (9)
# of sororities (% join)	10 (14)
% Asian	24
% Black or African American	7
% Hispanic	16
% Native American	<1
% Pacific Islander	<1
% Race and/or ethnicity unknown	4
% Two or more races	7
% White	24
% International	17
# of countries represented	118

CAMPUS MENTAL HEALTH SERVICES

Offers mental health/wellness program	Yes
Mental health training available to students	Yes
Employs Chief Wellness Officer	Yes
Peer-to-peer mental health offerings	Yes
Counseling center has guidelines or accreditation	Yes
Mental health/well-being courses	Yes, for-credit

ACADEMICS

% students returning for sophomore year	98
% students graduating within 4 years	84
% students graduating within 6 years	96
Calendar	Semester
Student/faculty ratio	11:1

Most Popular Majors

Computer Science; Mechanical Engineering; Economics

Applicants Also Look At

Harvard College, Massachusetts Institute of Technology, Princeton University, Stanford University, Yale University

STUDENTS SAY "..."

Academics

Columbia University, the Ivy League's "New York City office," has been around for more than 270 years, providing prestige, rigorous academics, a strong alumni network, and a multitude of opportunities to its students. As intimate spaces carved out of the larger university, Columbia College and The Fu Foundation School of Engineering and Applied Science throw a "vast amount of resources" at its students, with benefits that "extend from clubs to study abroad programs [to]...proximity to one of the greatest cities in the world." Columbia is "all about building intelligent [and] confident students who are ready for the workplace," and there are "many opportunities to satiate intellectual curiosity." The school's core curriculum ensures students leave with a breadth of knowledge, and "everyone is smart in some way."

Though some students have a bad teacher or two, Columbia professors are "fantastic in both their leadership in their field as well as in their interest in teaching students," and if "students carefully select which classes they will take they can find professors they like." The academics here "are truly great" and students "always know you're being taught by people at the forefront of their fields." Columbia attracts a very specific type of student "who is devoted to receiving a true liberal arts education in a variety of subjects," but those who go here shouldn't expect to have knowledge handed to them on a platter: "It is up to the student to get the most out of a class," says one.

Campus Life

When it comes to free time, there's no question as to where students turn: New York City, where there are "countless things to do for fun." The "clubs downtown are always a late-night option as are the Broadway shows and comedy clubs near Times Square" and "from shopping in Soho to visiting museums to trying out a new restaurant in Midtown, there's literally nothing you can't do here." That's not to say that students don't stay on campus; people often hang out in dorms and sometimes this turns into a social event itself. "I can walk into my floor lounge at any moment for homework help on anything from Chinese to econometrics, and upon doing so I inevitably wind up having a mind-blowing intellectual discussion of some sort," says a student. The "Monday to Thursday grind is usually pretty tough": people go to classes, do homework and readings, and "try to fit in time with friends in between all the chaos." Weekends are more fun, and Columbia has "a great arts initiative which is perfect for getting [tickets] cheaper" as well as a World Leaders Forum where speakers historically have included "presidents and prime ministers from countries far and wide."

Student Body

This collection of "very ambitious" students is "not only extremely intelligent, but also passionate about everything they do." This group is "diverse in every sense of the word," from race to sexuality to age, and everyone has "a high awareness of the connections between academic, personal, and social issues." People "aren't afraid to speak out against what they think is wrong"; activism is "essential to the Columbia experience," and in fact, "it is encouraged by the school itself." This go-getting crowd tries to do it all, "taking on 5 to 6 classes per semester and holding multiple jobs and internships and leadership positions"; as a result, Columbia does have a bit of a "stress culture," due to the fact that "everyone here really wants to succeed." While it "can be competitive for programs," most students find people here "to be more kind than shrewd."

Columbia University

Financial Aid: 212-854-3711 • E-Mail: ugrad-ask@columbia.edu • Website: www.columbia.edu

THE PRINCETON REVIEW SAYS

Admissions

The school reports that its standardized testing policy for use in admission for Fall 2026 is Test Optional. The Princeton Review suggests that interested applicants consult with the school for the most up-to-date standardized testing policies. *Very important factors considered include:* rigor of secondary school record, class rank, academic GPA, application essay, recommendation(s), extracurricular activities, character/personal qualities. *Important factors considered include:* talent/ability. *Other factors considered include:* standardized test scores, first generation, alumni/ae relation, geographical residence, volunteer work, work experience. High school diploma is required and GED is accepted. *Academic units required:* 4 English, 4 math, 3 science, 3 science labs, 3 language (other than English), 3 history, 3 academic electives. *Academic units recommended:* 4 English, 4 math, 4 science, 4 science labs, 4 language (other than English), 4 history, 4 academic electives.

Financial Aid

Students should submit: FAFSA; State aid form; CSS PROFILE. The Princeton Review suggests that all financial aid forms be submitted as soon as possible. *Need-based scholarships/grants offered:* Federal Pell; Federal SEOG; State scholarships/grants; Private scholarships; College/university scholarship or grant aid from institutional funds. *Loan aid offered:* Federal Direct Subsidized Loans; Federal Direct Unsubsidized Loans; Direct PLUS loans; College/university loans from institutional funds. Admitted students will be notified of awards on or about 4/1. Federal Work-Study Program available. Institutional employment available.

The Inside Word

There's no magic formula or pattern to guide students who are seeking admission to Columbia University. Excellent grades in rigorous classes may not be enough, and many great candidates are rejected each year. Admissions officers take a holistic approach to evaluating applications, and they pay extra attention to personal accomplishments in nonacademic activities as they look to build a diverse class that will greatly contribute to the university.

THE SCHOOL SAYS

From the Admissions Office

"Columbia maintains an intimate college campus within one of the world's most vibrant cities. After a day exploring New York City you come home to a traditional college campus within an intimate neighborhood. Nobel Prize-winning professors will challenge you in class discussions and meet one-on-one afterward. The Core Curriculum attracts intensely free-minded scholars, and connects all undergraduates. Science and engineering students pursue cutting-edge research in world-class laboratories with faculty members at the forefront of scientific discovery. Classroom discussions are only the beginning of your education. Ideas spill out from the classrooms, electrifying the campus and Morningside Heights. Friendships formed in the residence halls solidify during a game of Frisbee on the South Lawn or over bagels on the steps of Low Library. From your first day on campus, you will be part of our diverse community.

"Columbia offers extensive need-based financial aid and meets the full need of every student admitted as a first-year with grants instead of loans. Parents with calculated incomes below $66,000 are not expected to contribute any income or assets to the cost of attendance, and families with calculated incomes below $150,000 will have free tuition. Parents earning over $150,000 can still qualify for significant financial aid. To support students pursuing study abroad, research, internships and community service opportunities, Columbia offers the opportunity to apply for additional funding. A commitment to diversity—of every kind—is a long-standing Columbia hallmark. We believe cost should not be a barrier to pursuing your educational dreams."

SELECTIVITY

# of total applicants	59,611
% of total applicants accepted	5
% of total acceptees attending	61
# of in-state applicants	8,882
% of in-state applicants accepted	5
# of out-of-state-applicants	35,349
% of applicants accepted from out of state	6
# of international applicants	15,380
% of international applicants accepted	3
# of early decision applicants	5,868
% of early decision applicants accepted	14

First-Year Profile

Testing policy	Test Optional
Range SAT composite	1510–1560
Range SAT EBRW	740–780
Range SAT math	760–800
Range ACT composite	34–35
% submitting SAT scores	50
% submitting ACT scores	17
% graduated top 10% of class	94
% graduated top 25% of class	99
% graduated top 50% of class	100
% submitting high school rank	25

Important Dates

Early decision	
Apply by	11/1
Notified by	12/15
Regular	
Apply by	1/1
Notified by	4/1
Nonfall registration?	No

FINANCIAL FACTS*

Annual tuition	$70,170
Food and housing	$18,680
Required fees	$4,010
Books and supplies	$1,282
Average need-based scholarship (First-year)	$77,410 ($78,198)
% students with need rec. need-based scholarship or grant aid (First-year)	100 (100)
% students with need rec. non-need-based scholarship or grant aid (First-year)	6 (8)
% students with need rec. need-based self-help aid (First-year)	79 (71)
% students rec. any financial aid (First-year)	48 (48)
% UG borrow to pay for school	14
Average cumulative indebtedness	$37,357
% of students with need fully met (First-year)	100 (100)
Average % of student need met (First-year)	100 (100)

* Most recently reported data at time of printing. Scan the QR code to find the latest updates.

CONNECTICUT COLLEGE

270 Mohegan Avenue, New London, CT 06320 • Admissions: 860-439-2200

Survey Snapshot
Internships are widely available
Great financial aid
Career services are great

RATINGS

Quality of Life	79
Fire Safety	62
Green	92
Academic	88
Profs Interesting	93
Profs Accessible	94
Admissions	91
Financial Aid	98

CAMPUS LIFE

Type of school	Private
Environment	Town

Students

Degree-seeking undergrad enrollment	1,880
% male/female/not reported	38/61/<1
% from out of state	84
% First-year from public high school	50
% First-year live on campus	100
% Ugrads live on campus	99
# of fraternities	0
# of sororities	0
% Asian	4
% Black or African American	5
% Hispanic	12
% Native American	0
% Pacific Islander	<1
% Race and/or ethnicity unknown	2
% Two or more races	5
% White	66
% International	6
# of countries represented	50

CAMPUS MENTAL HEALTH SERVICES

Offers mental health/wellness program	Yes
Mental health training available to students	Yes
Employs Chief Wellness Officer	Yes
Peer-to-peer mental health offerings	Yes
Counseling center has guidelines or accreditation	Yes
Mental health/well-being courses	No

ACADEMICS

% students returning for sophomore year	91
% students graduating within 4 years	76
% students graduating within 6 years	82
Calendar	Semester
Student/faculty ratio	10:1
Most common class size 10–19.	(51%)
Most common lab/discussion size 10–19.	(92%)

Most Popular Majors

Psychology; Economics; Political Science and Government

STUDENTS SAY "..."

Academics

Located in eastern Connecticut, the picturesque Connecticut College is a classic private New England liberal arts school that shows a "great commitment to being sustainable, to promoting community service, and to learning." The college provides "great academic, extracurricular, and athletic opportunities to all students," and the "beloved" honor code makes for "a close-knit, supportive community." A strong focus on interdisciplinary education, small classes, and self-scheduled exams gives students the autonomy to truly tailor their learning around their interests. The academics are "rigorous but continuously relevant, interesting, and enlightening." Most classes are discussion-based, which "allows students to express their own opinions while hearing from their fellow students and professors." Though there are a few bad apples, most professors are always accessible ("especially outside of their office hours") and are "constantly bringing learning outside of the classroom, whether it be within a residence hall, a restaurant, museum, or gallery downtown, or within their own homes." "All of my professors are incredibly engaging and obviously here to excite students about their studies," says a student. Other high points include the "approachability of the staff," excellent career office and internship opportunities, and strong residential programs and academic centers that "help students with a myriad of topics." Connecticut College assures that no student will go through school with "your typical major/minor pairing"; with certificate programs, tons of research opportunities, independent studies and more, every student "has a completely unique and entirely interdisciplinary experience here."

Campus Life

Life as a student is all about balancing your school work with your extracurricular activities and choosing which events you want to attend, says one. The residential programs lay a great groundwork for student life, and much of the fun on campus "is through social events through the dorms." It helps that "everyone knows one another—between offices, custodial staff, campus safety, and students." There are a wide range of activities to get involved with (everything from athletics, to arts, to activism, to community service, etc.), as well as "numerous faculty-led discussions and speakers every week." Most activities that take place on campus make it "lively and interesting." The campus as a whole is "very friendly, and you are always surrounded by familiar faces," though the relationship with the town of New London is "something that can always be improved upon." For fun, students "attend each other's events, attend social functions in the student center, grab some coffee at one of our coffee shops, and generally hang out with each other." The library is "a very social place during the week," and though students work very hard, they "know how to have a good time on the weekends"—every weekend there is a variety of on-campus social events (concerts, dances, spoken-word performances) put on by the Student Activities Council. Day trips to Boston and New York are also common.

Student Body

Students note that Conn "embraces diversity," although that doesn't mean there isn't also a sizable population that some describe as "smart, probably upper-class, well-dressed, and white." The common theme among all Conn students is "their active involvement both on campus and off and their desire to be challenged in all aspects of their educations." Students fit in by "showing an interest in their studies, but also carrying on an active social life." It is fairly easy to find one's niche within the community, and "while it might take a semester to become adjusted, there are many groups, teams, and other resources...that help freshmen find a place here."

CONNECTICUT COLLEGE

Financial Aid: 860-439-2058 • E-Mail: admission@conncoll.edu • Website: www.conncoll.edu

THE PRINCETON REVIEW SAYS

Admissions

The school reports that its standardized testing policy for use in admission for Fall 2026 is Test Optional. The Princeton Review suggests that interested applicants consult with the school for the most up-to-date standardized testing policies. *Very important factors considered include:* rigor of secondary school record, academic GPA, character/personal qualities. *Important factors considered include:* application essay, recommendation(s), interview, extracurricular activities, talent/ability, volunteer work, work experience. *Other factors considered include:* standardized test scores, first generation, alumni/ae relation, geographical residence, state residency, religious affiliation/commitment, level of applicant's interest. High school diploma is required and GED is accepted.

Financial Aid

Students should submit: FAFSA; CSS PROFILE. Priority filing deadline is 1/15. The Princeton Review suggests that all financial aid forms be submitted as soon as possible. *Need-based scholarships/grants offered:* Federal Pell; Federal SEOG; State scholarships/grants; College/university scholarship or grant aid from institutional funds. *Loan aid offered:* Federal Direct Subsidized Loans; Federal Direct Unsubsidized Loans; Direct PLUS loans; College/university loans from institutional funds. Admitted students will be notified of awards on or about 4/1. Federal Work-Study Program available. Institutional employment available.

The Inside Word

Connecticut College is the archetypal selective New England college, and admissions officers are judicious in their decisions. Competitive applicants will have undertaken a demanding course load in high school. Admissions officers look for students who are curious and who thrive in challenging academic environments. Since Connecticut College has a close-knit community, personal qualities are also closely evaluated, and interviews are important.

THE SCHOOL SAYS

From the Admissions Office

"Connecticut College has all the hallmarks of the best liberal arts colleges: small classes, stellar teaching, close faculty-student relationships, a residential campus and plentiful cocurricular activities. But what sets this college apart is its active, outward-focused vision of 'the liberal arts in action.'

"A rigorous new curriculum, Connections, gives students a chance to tailor their academic experiences around a topic of interest to them, a problem they want to solve. It teaches complex thinking and real-world problem-solving, and ultimately ensures successful lives and careers for students beyond college. Students can choose from 9 Integrative Pathways or five centers for interdisciplinary scholarship (our version of an honors college), 42 majors and 47 minors. Students connect theory to the real world through community learning, student-faculty research, international experiences and campus leadership. Ninety-two percent of the Class of 2024 cited Connections as an important factor in why they chose to enroll at Conn.

"Liberal arts in action also means living under a 96-year-old Honor Code that provides for self-scheduled exams, a student-run Honor Council and a student voice in campus decision-making. Our four-year career program puts the liberal arts to work, with courses, programming and funding for career exploration and development, including internships. While at Conn, 95% of students work with the career office.

"More than half of students are athletes competing at the varsity level in the New England Small College Athletic Conference (NCAA Division III) or in club sports. The campus community is close and supportive; there is no Greek life."

SELECTIVITY

# of total applicants	7,338
% of total applicants accepted	39
% of total acceptees attending	16
# of in-state applicants	810
% of in-state applicants accepted	37
# of out-of-state-applicants	3,976
% of applicants accepted from out of state	62
# of international applicants	2,552
% of international applicants accepted	5
# of early decision applicants	546
% of early decision applicants accepted	41
# offered a place on the wait list	1,269
# admitted from wait list	5

First-Year Profile

Testing policy	Test Optional
Range SAT composite	1160–1370
Range SAT EBRW	610–710
Range SAT math	550–670
Range ACT composite	26–32
% submitting SAT scores	52
% submitting ACT scores	14

Important Dates

Early decision	
Apply by	11/15
Notified by	Mid-December
Other ED apply by	1/15
Other ED notified by	Mid-February
Regular	
Apply by	1/15
Notified by	3/31
Nonfall registration?	Yes

FINANCIAL FACTS

Comprehensive fee	$92,800
Books and supplies	$1,000
Average need-based scholarship (First-year)	$52,433 ($52,660)
% students with need rec. need-based scholarship or grant aid (First-year)	98 (98)
% students with need rec. non-need-based scholarship or grant aid (First-year)	24 (27)
% students with need rec. need-based self-help aid (First-year)	63 (56)
% students rec. any financial aid (First-year)	NR (97)
% UG borrow to pay for school	44
Average cumulative indebtedness	$36,950
% of students with need fully met (First-year)	100 (100)
Average % of student need met (First-year)	100 (100)

THE COOPER UNION FOR THE ADVANCEMENT OF SCIENCE AND ART

30 Cooper Square, New York, NY 10003 • Admissions: 212-353-4120

Survey Snapshot
Students love New York, NY
Easy to get around campus
Active student government

RATINGS

Quality of Life	**83**
Fire Safety	**93**
Green	**60***
Academic	**86**
Profs Interesting	**90**
Profs Accessible	**92**
Admissions	**98**
Financial Aid	**88**

CAMPUS LIFE

Type of school	Private
Environment	Metropolis

Students

Degree-seeking undergrad enrollment	869
% male/female/not reported	53/47/0
% from out of state	39
% First-year live on campus	80
% Ugrads live on campus	20
# of fraternities (% join)	1 (4)
# of sororities	0
% Asian	29
% Black or African American	5
% Hispanic	12
% Native American	0
% Pacific Islander	0
% Race and/or ethnicity unknown	6
% Two or more races	4
% White	30
% International	14

CAMPUS MENTAL HEALTH SERVICES

Offers mental health/wellness program	Yes
Mental health training available to students	No
Employs Chief Wellness Officer	NR
Peer-to-peer mental health offerings	NR
Counseling center has guidelines or accreditation	No
Mental health/well-being courses	NR

ACADEMICS

% students returning for sophomore year	91
% students graduating within 4 years	62
% students graduating within 6 years	83
Calendar	Semester
Student/faculty ratio	9:1
Most common class size 10–19.	(47%)
Most common lab/discussion size 10–19.	(83%)

Most Popular Majors
Electrical and Electronics Engineering; Mechanical Engineering

Applicants Often Prefer
California Institute of Technology, Carnegie Mellon University, Cornell University, Johns Hopkins University, Massachusetts Institute of Technology, New York University, Princeton University, University of California—Berkeley, University of Pennsylvania

Applicants Sometimes Prefer
Columbia University, Georgia Institute of Technology, Maryland Institute College of Art, Rensselaer Polytechnic Institute

Applicants Rarely Prefer
Pratt Institute, Rhode Island School of Design, State University of New York—Stony Brook University, State University of New York—University at Albany

STUDENTS SAY "..."

Academics

The Cooper Union for the Advancement of Science and Art is a renowned New York City institution that works "to create a rich environment for scholarly thinking, problem-solving, learning, and debate." It does so by serving an especially sharp cadre of students—under a thousand in all—degree programs in art, engineering, and architecture, all buttressed by required humanities courses. Students develop independence and autonomy through "major projects that offer them a great deal of academic freedom to create their own content." In turn, this environment encourages students to "achieve the most in a short amount of time." The "very focused" engineering program prepares students to be "a functioning member of the engineering community and workforce." Cooper Union offers academics that are "very rigorous, although consistent and achievable with the resources provided." As one student states, "Even as a sophomore, I have had the opportunity to take (and understand) graduate level material. Students benefit from a diverse array of instructors, so "you're not likely [to] have the same professor over and over again." Professors are "generally very knowledgeable in their subject area" with students noting that the "caliber of [the] art teachers is unbelievable." Some of the art instructors "have exhibited at the MOMA and Guggenheim," and other prestigious venues. Overall, students feel that Cooper Union combines a great education along with a good ROI when considering the "cost of tuition and good job placement after graduating."

Campus Life

Cooper Union is located in the heart of the East Village, a busy and buzzing metropolitan area that provides students "ample opportunity to explore New York City" and its "abundance of...places of interest." There are well-used meeting areas on campus "for both group study and recreational uses" and clubs and organizations offering a variety of events from "Paint and Chill Night" to runs around the city organized by the Cooper Union Track Club. In general, it's a small campus, which is great in that students are "always near each other, ready to chat and grab a coffee for a little break." On the other hand, limited on-campus food services push students to visit local city restaurants or to use residence hall stovetops "to cook their own food when time permits." This isn't a bother for students, who say that "life is packed" and say they often head to a bar on weekends, hit the gym, or play sports or video games as "stress-management mechanisms." And in a nod to the city's location, location, location, "as a means to decompress, a stroll through the streets of New York City is always beneficial—the city is our campus."

Student Body

Students at Cooper Union are dedicated, ambitious, and focused, as the school "requires a lot of time to study in order to pass the courses." They are often described as "generally stressed and hardworking, but high-spirited," as well as "highly intelligent...and helpful." Within this "small but complex community," many students work part-time while in school, and it is generally understood that "schoolwork is valued over social interaction." As one student describes, "The level students are at, and their work ethic makes you feel like the people here are destined for success." It's a community where "almost everyone is pretty friendly," and most students lean "socially and politically left." It's a place where niche interests thrive and "everyone has their own thing that makes them tick." Students at Cooper Union delve deeply into their interests and excel in their field by "doing extra activities that they don't need to" purely for their innate "curiosity and fun."

THE COOPER UNION FOR THE ADVANCEMENT OF SCIENCE AND ART

Financial Aid: 212-353-4113 • E-Mail: admissions@cooper.edu • Website: www.cooper.edu

THE PRINCETON REVIEW SAYS

Admissions

The school reports that its standardized testing policy for use in admission for Fall 2026 is Test Optional. The Princeton Review suggests that interested applicants consult with the school for the most up-to-date standardized testing policies. *Very important factors considered include:* academic GPA, talent/ability. *Important factors considered include:* rigor of secondary school record, application essay, recommendation(s), interview, character/personal qualities. *Other factors considered include:* class rank, standardized test scores, extracurricular activities, first generation, alumni/ae relation, volunteer work, work experience, level of applicant's interest. High school diploma is required and GED is accepted. *Academic units required:* 4 English, 1 math, 1 science, 1 social studies, 1 history, 8 academic electives. *Academic units recommended:* 4 English, 4 math, 3 science, 2 science labs, 4 language (other than English), 2 social studies, 2 history, 4 computer science, 4 visual/performing arts.

Financial Aid

Students should submit: FAFSA. Priority filing deadline is 3/31. The Princeton Review suggests that all financial aid forms be submitted as soon as possible. *Need-based scholarships/grants offered:* Federal Pell; Federal SEOG; State scholarships/grants; Private scholarships; College/university scholarship or grant aid from institutional funds. *Loan aid offered:* Federal Direct Subsidized Loans; Federal Direct Unsubsidized Loans; Direct PLUS loans. Admitted students will be notified of awards on a rolling basis beginning 1/5. Federal Work-Study Program available. Institutional employment available.

The Inside Word

The admission rate to Cooper Union is extremely competitive. All Cooper admits must be academically accomplished and top of their high school class. That said, specific admissions requirements and application deadlines vary based on major, be it engineering, art, or architecture. Since all enrolled undergraduate students receive a half-tuition scholarship each school year, with additional need-based financial aid available, and tuition is waived for the senior year, there's serious competition to obtain one of the coveted spots in the first-year class.

THE SCHOOL SAYS

From the Admissions Office

"The Cooper Union was founded in 1859 in the East Village of Manhattan by inventor, industrialist, and social reformer, Peter Cooper. The Cooper Union is a top-ranked, all-honors college committed to making education fair and accessible to all. Every admitted undergraduate student is granted a half-tuition scholarship as well as need-based aid.

"Comprised of three schools specializing in architecture, art, and engineering, The Cooper Union offers small, intimate classes organized around a culture of collaboration led by a faculty of teachers who are also leading practitioners in their fields. Throughout its history, Cooper has been a place where thinkers, builders, artists, activists, and dreamers have thrived and contributed to New York City and the world in large and small ways—being of this world and for this world. The Cooper Union also boasts its historic Great Hall; once the largest meeting space in New York City, the Great Hall has hosted 11 US presidents (from Abraham Lincoln to Barack Obama) as well as other national leaders and thinkers from Susan B. Anthony and Frederick Douglass to Congressman John Lewis, activist Gloria Steinem, and artist Ai Weiwei, among others."

SELECTIVITY

# of total applicants	2,678
% of total applicants accepted	15
% of total acceptees attending	53
# of early decision applicants	200
% of early decision applicants accepted	27
# offered a place on the wait list	147
# admitted from wait list	31

First-Year Profile

Testing policy	Test Optional
Range SAT composite	1390–1500
Range SAT EBRW	660–730
Range SAT math	730–790
Range ACT composite	31–34
% submitting SAT scores	47
% submitting ACT scores	14
Average HS GPA	3.7
% submitting high school GPA	91

Important Dates

Early decision	
Apply by	11/1
Notified by	12/15
Other ED apply by	12/1
Other ED notified by	12/1
Regular	
Apply by	1/5
Notified by	4/1
Nonfall registration?	No

FINANCIAL FACTS

Annual tuition	$44,550
Food and housing	$13,812
Required fees	$2,270
Books and supplies	$1,800
Average need-based scholarship (First-year)	$46,823 ($46,135)
% students with need rec. need-based scholarship or grant aid (First-year)	62 (100)
% students with need rec. non-need-based scholarship or grant aid (First-year)	62 (100)
% students with need rec. need-based self-help aid (First-year)	11 (19)
% students rec. any financial aid (First-year)	99 (100)
% UG borrow to pay for school	30
Average cumulative indebtedness	$11,840
% of students with need fully met (First-year)	39 (55)
Average % of student need met (First-year)	91 (90)

CORNELL COLLEGE

600 First Street SW, Mount Vernon, IA 52314 • Admissions: 319-895-4477

Survey Snapshot
Class discussions encouraged
Easy to get around campus
Great library

RATINGS

Quality of Life	**84**
Fire Safety	**85**
Green	**60***
Academic	**84**
Profs Interesting	**88**
Profs Accessible	**94**
Admissions	**83**
Financial Aid	**82**

CAMPUS LIFE

Type of school	Private
Affiliation	Methodist
Environment	Rural

Students

Degree-seeking undergrad enrollment	973
% male/female/not reported	49/43/8
% from out of state	64
% First-year from public high school	87
% First-year live on campus	97
% Ugrads live on campus	92
# of fraternities (% join)	5 (6)
# of sororities (% join)	6 (13)
% Asian	3
% Black or African American	9
% Hispanic	12
% Native American	3
% Pacific Islander	<1
% Race and/or ethnicity unknown	3
% Two or more races	1
% White	65
% International	3
# of countries represented	19

CAMPUS MENTAL HEALTH SERVICES

Offers mental health/wellness program	Yes
Mental health training available to students	No
Employs Chief Wellness Officer	NR
Peer-to-peer mental health offerings	NR
Counseling center has guidelines or accreditation	No
Mental health/well-being courses	NR

ACADEMICS

% students returning for sophomore year	73
% students graduating within 4 years	57
% students graduating within 6 years	60
Calendar	Block Plan (eight 3.5-week blocks)
Student/faculty ratio	12:1
Most common class size 10–19.	(52%)

Most Popular Majors
Engineering; Biochemistry; Computer Science

Applicants Also Look At
Arizona State University, Iowa State University, St. Olaf College, University of Colorado Boulder, University of Illinois at Chicago, University of Illinois at Urbana—Champaign, University of Iowa, University of Minnesota—Twin Cities

STUDENTS SAY "..."

Academics

Cornell College, a small liberal arts school in Iowa, employs a unique one-course-at-a-time program, allowing students to focus on just one course (or "block") each month, providing an "intense, thorough, and complete immersion." Though students agree that this "doesn't give you any time to think about anything but the class you're in right then," it allows for personalized curricula design, and areas like the humanities "work perfectly with the block plan." Students also "always know when to find people," which makes it easy to get together. Some classes may not be the most challenging, but "upper-level courses are very engaging and fulfilling." It's very varied, according to one student: "You could have hours and hours of homework one block and practically none the next." The block plan makes it very easy to gain off-campus field experience or do international study, and it's "easier to try off-campus opportunities." Administration is generally "excellent at taking a personal interest in each student," though some note, "There is not much transparency at the administrative level," which can be "out of touch" at times. On the classroom side, professors "know how to motivate and encourage their students," and though "you may get a bad apple maybe once a year," they're "not only knowledgeable but dedicated." As one student puts it, "The personal attention you can receive from any given professor, if you seek them out, is especially rewarding." All in all, students love the block structure and the sense of community it creates, as "no matter what it is you may want to do, you can find someone to do it with you." One student claims he "cannot imagine learning any other way."

Campus Life

Since Cornell is very campus-focused, the school makes sure there's a large variety of campus organizations and "many events going on almost every weekend." Though there's definitely a "small-town quiet," Cedar Rapids and Iowa City are both only a twenty minute drive away, and "ice climbing, rock-climbing, paddling, and hiking" are popular outdoor pastimes. It's also "fairly easy to start up a new club or group." In addition, the school provides fall, winter, and spring breaks as well as "block breaks," which last four and a half days and give students the opportunity to travel, go skiing or camping, and so on. The cold weather can cause problems here, in both a locked-in feel and the possibility for accidents, and students are encouraged to "bring snow boots!" Many here tend to have a love-hate relationship with sports; while athletics are a huge boon, "the athletes and the non-athletes are seldom friends." Much like the curriculum, lunchtimes are pretty unique, and students all eat in a common cafeteria, naturally falling into a somewhat "high school" habit of eating at the same tables every day. Most people stay on campus for entertainment and socializing, "creating a cohesive community." Parties do take place on weekends, and "drinking is popular on campus but never forced," but in general, "people are more interested in just having a good conversation with their peers."

Student Body

There's "a great diversity of interests" in people who attend Cornell, and the "super busy" students have a hard time defining a more common characteristic than the fact that almost all are driven and involved. Some division into typical groups does occur—"the cafeteria design and Greek life are very conducive to this problem"—but "even group to group there is always mingling because you never know who will be in your next class." Since the classes are so small and "you see the same people four hours a day for three and a half weeks," people are generally accepting, and "you have to be really, really strange here to stick out." As one first-year says, "The only intolerance I've seen is toward the consistently indolent."

CORNELL COLLEGE

Financial Aid: 319-895-4216 • E-Mail: admission@cornellcollege.edu • Website: www.cornellcollege.edu/index.shtml

THE PRINCETON REVIEW SAYS

Admissions

The school reports that its standardized testing policy for use in admission for Fall 2026 is Test Optional. The Princeton Review suggests that interested applicants consult with the school for the most up-to-date standardized testing policies. *Very important factors considered include:* academic GPA. *Important factors considered include:* application essay. *Other factors considered include:* rigor of secondary school record, class rank, recommendation(s), interview, extracurricular activities, character/personal qualities, first generation, alumni/ae relation, geographical residence, state residency, volunteer work, work experience, level of applicant's interest. High school diploma is required and GED is accepted. *Academic units recommended:* 4 English, 3 math, 3 science, 2 science labs, 2 language (other than English), 3 social studies.

Financial Aid

Students should submit: FAFSA. Priority filing deadline is 3/1. The Princeton Review suggests that all financial aid forms be submitted as soon as possible. *Need-based scholarships/grants offered:* Federal Pell; Federal SEOG; State scholarships/grants; College/university scholarship or grant aid from institutional funds. *Loan aid offered:* Federal Direct Subsidized Loans; Federal Direct Unsubsidized Loans; Direct PLUS loans; College/university loans from institutional funds. Admitted students will be notified of awards on a rolling basis beginning 12/15. Federal Work-Study Program available. Institutional employment available.

The Inside Word

Given Cornell's relatively unique approach to study, it's no surprise that the admissions committee here focuses attention on both academic and personal strengths. Cornell's small, highly self-selected applicant pool is chock-full of students with solid self-awareness, motivation, and discipline.

THE SCHOOL SAYS

From the Admissions Office

"Cornell College, a selective liberal arts college in Mount Vernon, Iowa, is one of the colleges featured in Colleges That Change Lives. Characterized by the life-changing academic immersion of its One Course At A Time curriculum, this distinctive approach allows students to focus on a single academic subject per eighteen-day block. It lays the foundation for a student's entire Cornell education through transformative intellectual partnerships and close-knit learning communities that bring out the best in our ambitious students. The One Course curriculum mirrors the pace of most working environments where employees are expected to handle tight deadlines and high expectations on every project, every day. Since there is never more than one course to focus on, faculty can take entire classes on field trips for a day or an entire block. Cornell's residential campus attracts a student body from 45 states and 16 foreign countries. Together, they experience a vast array of off-campus opportunities designed to take them into the world to fulfill their academic and personal goals, as well as a lineup of speakers and entertainment options that brings the world to them. Cornell College is frequently cited as a 'Best Buy.' Ninety-three percent of Cornell graduates complete their degrees in four years, and 55 percent go on to complete an advanced degree."

SELECTIVITY

# of total applicants	1,952
% of total applicants accepted	89
% of total acceptees attending	14
# of in-state applicants	299
% of in-state applicants accepted	92
# of out-of-state-applicants	1,591
% of applicants accepted from out of state	90
# of international applicants	62
% of international applicants accepted	68
# offered a place on the wait list	0

First-Year Profile

Testing policy	Test Optional
Range SAT composite	1040–1300
Range SAT EBRW	540–680
Range SAT math	500–620
Range ACT composite	23–30
% submitting SAT scores	10
% submitting ACT scores	15
Average HS GPA	3.6
% submitting high school GPA	86
% graduated top 10% of class	16
% graduated top 25% of class	44
% graduated top 50% of class	74
% submitting high school rank	48

Important Dates

Regular	
Apply by	8/23
Notified by	Rolling, 10/1
Nonfall registration?	Yes

FINANCIAL FACTS

Annual tuition	$55,950
Food and housing	$12,486
Required fees	$784
Books and supplies	$720
Average need-based scholarship (First-year)	$42,128 ($46,320)
% students with need rec. need-based scholarship or grant aid (First-year)	100 (100)
% students with need rec. non-need-based scholarship or grant aid (First-year)	21 (11)
% students with need rec. need-based self-help aid (First-year)	71 (69)
% students rec. any financial aid (First-year)	99 (100)
% UG borrow to pay for school	64
Average cumulative indebtedness	$33,666
% of students with need fully met (First-year)	28 (25)
Average % of student need met (First-year)	85 (87)

CORNELL UNIVERSITY

410 Thurston Avenue, Ithaca, NY 14850 • Admissions: 607-255-5241

Survey Snapshot
Students always studying
Students are happy
Classroom facilities are great

RATINGS

Quality of Life	**90**
Fire Safety	**92**
Green	**99**
Academic	**92**
Profs Interesting	**89**
Profs Accessible	**92**
Admissions	**99**
Financial Aid	**98**

CAMPUS LIFE

Type of school	Private
Environment	Town

Students

Degree-seeking undergrad enrollment	15,979
% male/female/not reported	46/54/<1
% from out of state	64
# of fraternities (% join)	34 (NR)
# of sororities (% join)	19 (NR)
% Asian	28
% Black or African American	6
% Hispanic	12
% Native American	<1
% Pacific Islander	<1
% Race and/or ethnicity unknown	7
% Two or more races	6
% White	31
% International	10
# of countries represented	90

CAMPUS MENTAL HEALTH SERVICES

Offers mental health/wellness program	Yes
Mental health training available to students	No
Employs Chief Wellness Officer	NR
Peer-to-peer mental health offerings	NR
Counseling center has guidelines or accreditation	No
Mental health/well-being courses	NR

ACADEMICS

% students returning for sophomore year	98
% students graduating within 4 years	86
% students graduating within 6 years	95
Calendar	Semester
Student/faculty ratio	9:1
Most common class size 10–19.	(41%)
Most common lab/discussion size 10–19.	(39%)

Most Popular Majors

Engineering; Liberal Arts and Sciences/Liberal Studies; Biology/Biological Sciences

STUDENTS SAY "..."

Academics

Cornell University more than earns its Ivy League stature with the prestigious education it provides. Students can choose from nearly 80 fields of study and they are encouraged to "break free from their comfort zones" and explore any interest they may have. As one student notes, there are endless opportunities to "pursue other topics, enhance your knowledge of things that you're already interested in and try completely random things that you'd never even heard of before." One of the more unusual fields of study includes a Viticulture and Enology program where students can learn the science and art of wine-making, including vineyard management and wine production. Information Science, an especially current focus in today's society, is where students study the relationships and impacts that technology has on people, and they can go on to shape tech policy and our future relationship with the digital world. At Cornell, professors are "experts in their field, almost always conducting their own research, and are enthusiastic about passing their knowledge on to their students," and "Cornell as an administration keeps the faculty, research, and access to the most recent information so up-to-date that this campus is as connected as any place in the world." The university has multiple satellite campuses—New York (Ithaca, Geneva, NYC), Qatar, Washington, D.C., and Rome, Italy—affording students superb opportunities to study, for example, ancient architecture in Rome, or experience a semester in the nation's capital with exposure to policymakers, think tanks, and more. Additionally, Cornell's "top notch faculty" and administration have "proven time and time again that they care, both on an individual and system-wide level." Cornell University is the very "definition of amazing" thanks to great internships, a strong alumni network, and "boundless opportunities after graduation" Says a junior, "I was intimidated to go here, but now I will say that I cannot imagine going anywhere else."

Campus Life

Upstate New York's Finger Lakes region is filled with natural beauty and students report that the saying about how "Ithaca is gorges" extends to Cornell University's "absolutely gorgeous campus." Students enthuse over the school's fresh-made ice cream and yogurt—"We have our own dairy [the Cornell Dairy] so that we can make our own milk, for goodness' sake!"—and note that "There's just so much going on at every moment [that] the hard part is choosing what it is you want to do." Students say they "truly, purely enjoy their time here," whether it's relating a quiet tale of ordering cookies for an in-dorm movie night or heading to "an awesome party in Collegetown." Celebratory traditions like Slope Day, Cornell's largest annual outdoor student gathering, and Fall Fest, also offer great opportunities for students to connect and let loose, but "it's definitely acceptable to turn down weekend plans because you have too much work to do."

Student Body

From farm kids and pre-med students to engineers and hoteliers, enrollees come to call Cornell University "home" for all sorts of reasons, and accordingly they come from all over. This "plethora of diverse students," almost half of whom identify as multicultural, arrive from all backgrounds and ethnicities and range from all 50 states, representing more than 120 nations. The integration of people with eclectic interests "[inspires] others to become active students," and this can be seen in their penchant to pick up research or volunteer work, sometimes through their service to Greek life, and others by joining one of the hundreds upon hundreds of student organizations. The vast number of opportunities to get involved also means that "a competitive environment isn't created," even among students united by "ambition and ability." Students also point out that despite the academic commitment—"everyone's smart"—Cornellians "know how to put books aside and relax."

Cornell University

Financial Aid: 607-255-5145 • E-Mail: admissions@cornell.edu • Website: www.cornell.edu

THE PRINCETON REVIEW SAYS

Admissions

The school reports that its standardized testing policy for use in admission for Fall 2026 will require applicants to submit either the SAT or ACT. The Princeton Review suggests that interested applicants consult with the school for the most up-to-date standardized testing policies. *Very important factors considered include:* rigor of secondary school record, application essay, recommendation(s), extracurricular activities, talent/ability, character/personal qualities. *Important factors considered include:* class rank, academic GPA. *Other factors considered include:* standardized test scores, interview, first generation, alumni/ae relation, geographical residence, state residency, volunteer work, work experience. High school diploma is required and GED is accepted.

Financial Aid

Students should submit: FAFSA; CSS PROFILE. Priority filing deadline is 2/15. The Princeton Review suggests that all financial aid forms be submitted as soon as possible. *Need-based scholarships/grants offered:* Federal Pell; Federal SEOG; State scholarships/grants; Private scholarships; College/university scholarship or grant aid from institutional funds. *Loan aid offered:* Federal Direct Subsidized Loans; Federal Direct Unsubsidized Loans; Direct PLUS loans; College/university loans from institutional funds. Admitted students will be notified of awards on or about 4/1. Federal Work-Study Program available. Institutional employment available.

The Inside Word

Gaining admission to Cornell is competitive regardless of your intended field of study, but some of the university's eight colleges are more competitive than others. If you're thinking of trying to "backdoor" your way into one of the most competitive schools—by gaining admission to a less competitive one, then transferring after one year—be aware that you will have to complete an internal transfer application and provide a statement outlining your academic plans. While internal transfer is possible, Cornell encourages students to put forth their strongest application with clearly defined academic and personal goals.

THE SCHOOL SAYS

From the Admissions Office

"Cornell University, an Ivy League school and land-grant university located in the scenic Finger Lakes region of central New York, provides an outstanding education to students in eight small to midsize undergraduate colleges: Agriculture and Life Sciences; Architecture, Art, and Planning; Arts and Sciences; The Cornell Jeb E. Brooks School of Public Policy; Engineering; Human Ecology; The Cornell SC Johnson College of Business; and Industrial and Labor Relations. Cornellians come from all fifty states and more than 130 countries, and they pursue their academic goals in more than 100 departments. The College of Arts and Sciences, one of the smallest liberal arts schools in the Ivy League, offers more than forty majors, most of which rank near the top nationwide. Applied programs in the other six colleges also rank among the best in the world. Other special features of the university include a world-renowned faculty; over 4,000 courses available to all students; an extensive undergraduate research program; superb research, teaching, and library facilities; a large, diverse study abroad program; and more than 1,000 student organizations and thirty-seven varsity sports. Cornell's campus is one of the most beautiful in the country; students pass streams, rocky gorges, and waterfalls on their way to class. First-year students make their home on North Campus, a living-learning community that features a special advising center, faculty-in-residence, a fitness center, and traditional residence halls as well as program houses such as Ecology House. Cornell University invites applications from all interested students and uses the Common Application with a required Cornell Supplement."

SELECTIVITY

# of total applicants	72,523
% of total applicants accepted	8
% of total acceptees attending	63
# of in-state applicants	12,978
% of in-state applicants accepted	13
# of out-of-state-applicants	40,975
% of applicants accepted from out of state	9
# of international applicants	18,566
% of international applicants accepted	3
# of early decision applicants	10,057
% of early decision applicants accepted	21
# offered a place on the wait list	9,720
# admitted from wait list	254

First-Year Profile

Testing policy	SAT or ACT Required
Range SAT EBRW	730–770
Range SAT math	770–800
Range ACT composite	33–35
% submitting SAT scores	11
% submitting ACT scores	0

Important Dates

Early decision	
Apply by	11/1
Notified by	Mid December
Regular	
Apply by	1/2
Notified by	4/1
Nonfall registration?	No

FINANCIAL FACTS

Annual tuition	$73,946
Food and housing	$21,348
Required fees	$1,024
Books and supplies	$1,234
Average need-based scholarship (First-year)	$63,827 ($63,023)
% students with need rec. need-based scholarship or grant aid (First-year)	96 (97)
% students with need rec. non-need-based scholarship or grant aid (First-year)	0 (0)
% students with need rec. need-based self-help aid (First-year)	63 (68)
% students rec. any financial aid (First-year)	48 (50)
% UG borrow to pay for school	33
Average cumulative indebtedness	$25,655
% of students with need fully met (First-year)	100 (100)
Average % of student need met (First-year)	100 (100)

Creighton University

2500 California Plaza, Omaha, NE 68178 • Admissions: 402-280-2703

Survey Snapshot
Students are very religious
Students involved in community service
Everyone loves the Bluejays

RATINGS

Quality of Life	83
Fire Safety	96
Green	83
Academic	84
Profs Interesting	90
Profs Accessible	93
Admissions	88
Financial Aid	88

CAMPUS LIFE

Type of school	Private
Affiliation	Roman Catholic
Environment	Metropolis

Students

Degree-seeking undergrad enrollment	4,544
% male/female/not reported	42/58/0
% from out of state	76
% First-year from public high school	53
% First-year live on campus	95
% Ugrads live on campus	52
# of fraternities (% join)	9 (23)
# of sororities (% join)	13 (33)
% Asian	8
% Black or African American	3
% Hispanic	11
% Native American	<1
% Pacific Islander	<1
% Race and/or ethnicity unknown	1
% Two or more races	6
% White	68
% International	2
# of countries represented	36

CAMPUS MENTAL HEALTH SERVICES

Offers mental health/wellness program	Yes
Mental health training available to students	No
Employs Chief Wellness Officer	NR
Peer-to-peer mental health offerings	NR
Counseling center has guidelines or accreditation	No
Mental health/well-being courses	NR

ACADEMICS

% students returning for sophomore year	92
% students graduating within 4 years	73
% students graduating within 6 years	83
Calendar	Semester
Student/faculty ratio	11:1
Most common class size 10–19.	(30%)
Most common lab/discussion size 10–19.	(39%)

Most Popular Majors
Registered Nursing/Registered Nurse; Biology/Biological Sciences; Psychology

Applicants Often Prefer
Baylor University, University of Kansas

Applicants Sometimes Prefer
Gonzaga University, Loyola University Chicago, Marquette University, Saint Louis University, University of Iowa, University of Minnesota—Twin Cities, University of Nebraska at Omaha, University of Nebraska—Lincoln

STUDENTS SAY "..."

Academics

Omaha's Creighton University is a Jesuit institution that prides itself on "shaping the whole person," which means that students find themselves "extremely involved in academic and extracurricular activities." As for the core class structure, all of its more than four thousand undergraduates must fulfill a set curriculum, with a variety of course options available for all requirements (other than a required one-hour oral communication course). By all accounts, this "sets you up very well for success," with students adding that the process "nearly holds your hand into your first job" and "prepares you for the next step, whether that is medical school, law school, or going out to work in the real world." Creighton "works so hard to make sure their students are successful learners and thinkers" by offering programs like EDGE, an all-inclusive tutoring, academic coaching, and academic counseling service that doubles as "a great platform for advisors to gear students to explore certain classes while remaining on track." All of this helps in "cultivating a safe community where we're encouraged to dive into what we believe, figure out what that is exactly, and serve others."

Creighton features an 11:1 student-faculty ratio, which leads to "really awesome relationships with faculty and many opportunities for things like undergraduate research." Professors go above and beyond in all ways, from doing their best "not to make lectures dry and boring" to being super receptive to students. Courses offered "are challenging to say the least," but because teachers are "willing to work on your terms and help at all hours of the day and night," both in and out of the classroom, it's a "very rewarding and manageable" process. Dialogue is also crucial: teachers "love when you ask questions" and many utilize a flipped classroom, where peers teach the rest of the class, which "provides a broken- down and simplified way of explaining difficult topics to provide clarification and insight." Adding to the variety and support offered, there are plenty of "field trips that [are] very interesting and insightful" and opportunities for "many upperclassmen [to] participate in research or internships."

Campus Life

The pace at Creighton tends to be a busy one, and not just because of academic or school-related activities: "A lot of students work." That said, things get a bit more relaxed on weekends, which "consist of sporting events, parties, fraternity events, and the like." Creighton students are "very supportive of one another and go to all the home soccer, basketball, baseball, and volleyball games for both men and women's teams," and "people often take part in sports or group exercise programs on campus." The city setting also means that the "campus is a few blocks away from Old Market and Midtown which are full of activities, shops, and restaurants," and there are "also gorgeous outdoor places to go running/walking near downtown when the weather is nice." Students "are encouraged to form clubs and join organizations," and "the resources available to students are absolutely endless."

Student Body

There's a sense of togetherness at Creighton, to the extent that, because there's an "expectation that you go to class every day and on time...if you don't, people will reach out." In short, the community is "very goal-oriented toward their careers," although not in an oppressive sense. If anything, students describe the atmosphere as "fun and light-hearted" and note that "wherever you go you will find a welcoming environment." (This applies across all grades, with students noting that senior students "work hard to make [first-years] feel at home during the first couple weeks at school.") Students are in it together, according to those who list "service and giving back" as a core value, and there's an eagerness described for all activities: "When it comes to getting involved with student organizations and other things on campus, students will jump at the chance to do so.

Creighton University

Financial Aid: 402-280-1110 • E-Mail: admissions@creighton.edu • Website: www.creighton.edu

THE PRINCETON REVIEW SAYS

Admissions

The school reports that its standardized testing policy for use in admission for Fall 2026 is Test Optional. The Princeton Review suggests that interested applicants consult with the school for the most up-to-date standardized testing policies. *Very important factors considered include:* rigor of secondary school record, academic GPA. *Important factors considered include:* standardized test scores, application essay. *Other factors considered include:* class rank, recommendation(s), extracurricular activities, talent/ability, character/personal qualities, first generation, volunteer work, level of applicant's interest. High school diploma is required and GED is accepted. *Academic units required:* 4 English, 3 math, 2 science, 1 science lab, 2 language (other than English), 2 social studies, 3 academic electives. *Academic units recommended:* 4 English, 4 math, 3 science, 2 science labs, 3 language (other than English), 4 social studies, 3 academic electives.

Financial Aid

Students should submit: FAFSA; Institution's own financial aid form. Priority filing deadline is 1/15. The Princeton Review suggests that all financial aid forms be submitted as soon as possible. *Need-based scholarships/grants offered:* Federal Pell; Federal SEOG; State scholarships/grants; Private scholarships; College/university scholarship or grant aid from institutional funds. *Loan aid offered:* Federal Direct Subsidized Loans; Federal Direct Unsubsidized Loans; Direct PLUS loans; College/university loans from institutional funds. Admitted students will be notified of awards on a rolling basis beginning 2/15. Federal Work-Study Program available. Institutional employment available.

The Inside Word

Creighton University proudly takes a holistic approach to the admissions process. The school doesn't maintain any strict standardized test score or GPA minimums. However, the committee does scour transcripts for evidence of academic rigor and intellectual curiosity. Applicants who have taken multiple AP, honors, or IB classes will have a leg up. Moreover, as a Jesuit university, Creighton is partial to students who are committed to making the world a better place. Candidates with a passion for social justice issues will be noted.

THE SCHOOL SAYS

From the Admissions Office

"Creighton University is a top-ranked Catholic, Jesuit institution in the heart of a thriving urban setting in Omaha, NE. Rooted in Jesuit values, Creighton inspires leadership, service and excellence through diverse undergraduate, graduate and professional programs.

"More than 8,500 students at our institution chose from over 60 undergraduate majors in arts and sciences, business and nursing, and programs across six graduate and professional schools, including medicine, law, dentistry and pharmacy. Small class sizes and experienced faculty mentors promote personal connections that yield academic excellence. Our walkable, 120-acre campus emphasizes interprofessional study across nine colleges and highlights leadership in the health sciences. More than half of the entering freshman class is interested in pursuing a pre-professional program at Creighton. This, coupled with abundant research opportunities in the first year and 83% of undergraduates participating in experiential learning (internships and research projects), signals a highly motivated and goal-driven student body. This leads to a 99% success rate, with graduates launching their careers, pursuing advanced degrees or engaging in volunteer work within six months. Creighton University prepares students for impactful and fulfilling futures. Rooted in Jesuit tradition, Creighton students receive more than just an education—they engage in transformative service and global learning opportunities that prepare them to lead with purpose. The school combines nationally renowned academics with NCAA Division I athletics to create an unparalleled college experience. We'd love it if you came to visit us."

SELECTIVITY

# of total applicants	6,389
% of total applicants accepted	92
% of total acceptees attending	21
# of in-state applicants	1,005
% of in-state applicants accepted	91
# of out-of-state-applicants	5,237
% of applicants accepted from out of state	93
# of international applicants	145
% of international applicants accepted	87
# offered a place on the wait list	53
# admitted from wait list	9

First-Year Profile

Testing policy	Test Optional
Range SAT composite	1280–1410
Range SAT EBRW	650–710
Range SAT math	620–710
Range ACT composite	26–31
% submitting SAT scores	8
% submitting ACT scores	40
Average HS GPA	3.9
% submitting high school GPA	100
% graduated top 10% of class	37
% graduated top 25% of class	70
% graduated top 50% of class	90
% submitting high school rank	30

Important Dates

Early action	
Apply by	11/1
Notified by	Rolling
Regular	
Notified by	Rolling, 11/1
Nonfall registration?	Yes

FINANCIAL FACTS

Annual tuition	$50,580
Food and housing	$14,930
Required fees	$2,322
Books and supplies	$1,200
Average need-based scholarship (First-year)	$37,128 ($29,500)
% students with need rec. need-based scholarship or grant aid (First-year)	91 (94)
% students with need rec. non-need-based scholarship or grant aid (First-year)	25 (31)
% students with need rec. need-based self-help aid (First-year)	6 (56)
% students rec. any financial aid (First-year)	96 (100)
% UG borrow to pay for school	55
Average cumulative indebtedness	$33,313
% of students with need fully met (First-year)	29 (35)
Average % of student need met (First-year)	79 (84)

DARTMOUTH COLLEGE

6016 McNutt Hall, Hanover, NH 03755 • Admissions: 603-646-2875

Survey Snapshot
Classroom facilities are great
Lab facilities are great
Great library

RATINGS

Quality of Life	84
Fire Safety	89
Green	60*
Academic	94
Profs Interesting	91
Profs Accessible	97
Admissions	99
Financial Aid	98

CAMPUS LIFE

Type of school	Private
Environment	Village

Students

Degree-seeking undergrad enrollment	4,464
% male/female/not reported	52/48/0
% from out of state	98
% First-year from public high school	54
% First-year live on campus	100
% Ugrads live on campus	85
# of fraternities (% join)	17 (33)
# of sororities (% join)	8 (33)
% Asian	13
% Black or African American	6
% Hispanic	10
% Native American	1
% Pacific Islander	0
% Race and/or ethnicity unknown	3
% Two or more races	8
% White	45
% International	15
# of countries represented	96

CAMPUS MENTAL HEALTH SERVICES

Offers mental health/wellness program	Yes
Mental health training available to students	Yes
Employs Chief Wellness Officer	Yes
Peer-to-peer mental health offerings	Yes
Counseling center has guidelines or accreditation	Yes
Mental health/well-being courses	Yes, for-credit

ACADEMICS

% students returning for sophomore year	98
% students graduating within 4 years	79
% students graduating within 6 years	95
Calendar	Quarter
Student/faculty ratio	7:1
Most common class size 10–19.	(41%)

Most Popular Majors
Engineering; Economics; Political Science and Government

Applicants Often Prefer
Harvard College, Princeton University, Stanford University, Yale University

Applicants Sometimes Prefer
Brown University, Columbia University, Massachusetts Institute of Technology, University of Pennsylvania

Applicants Rarely Prefer
Cornell University, Duke University, Johns Hopkins University, Northwestern University, The University of Chicago, Vanderbilt University

STUDENTS SAY "..."

Academics

Dartmouth College's scenic 269-acre campus is the perfect setting for an academic environment that puts an "emphasis on pursuing passions, and making the college experience your own." With over 40 academic departments and programs, undergraduates are encouraged to explore their interests before declaring or even designing a major. The academics are certainly competitive, but students report that "no one really talks about their grades openly" and it's "generally understood that everyone is smart." The professors at Dartmouth exceed student expectations both in the classroom and outside of it. As one student explains, "Dartmouth puts a huge focus on the undergraduate students, and I have found my professors to be available and engaging in nearly every instance." Another student agrees, saying, "I came to Dartmouth for the professors, [and] they were far beyond anything I could have hoped for. Not only are they great lecturers and accomplished scholars, [but] they go out of their way to be available outside of the classroom, and to forge relationships beyond what is expected or necessary." Classes are described as challenging— in a good way, with an emphasis on being "discussion based and...small." This is a school "known for its community and intelligent students and faculty, who are also personable and know how to have fun."

Campus Life

Dartmouth fosters a sense of community from the moment students arrive on campus. Undergraduates are randomly sorted into one of six houses, which they'll stick with for all four years of college. Each house has its own dormitories as well as House Centers, which are communal spaces to meet or study. Houses also host optional activities so that students can get to know each other. Dartmouth's natural surroundings make outdoor activities popular, too. "The Appalachian Trail literally runs right through our campus," says one student. "Many students (even students who never did so before college) get involved with hiking, canoeing, rock climbing, and so forth." And although students say that the "Greek system is the main source of social activity" they also note that because so many students participate, the chapters are "quite diverse and representative of the student body as a whole." Beyond Greek life, "there are so many options to do whatever you're interested in doing," enthuses one student. Students enjoy going to hockey games, skating on Occom Pond in the winter, going kayaking, apple picking, or catching the "early premiere of some cool new movie at the Hop[kins Center for the Arts]." Socializing with friends depends on what you're in the mood for, whether that's a dance party or having a quiet night in to "play cards or jam out on guitar."

Student Body

It can be "hard to define a typical student" because at Dartmouth "every type of person is represented." As one senior elaborates, "The common denominator is that Dartmouth students are very involved." This is underscored by others who report that, "whether it's with a club sports team, a cappella group, community service project, academic research, or a Greek house, Dartmouth students manage to do a lot of things in the course of the day." As one sophomore observes, students always seem to be "studying and participating in some extracurricular activity, ...[and] out at a frat too," and yet still able to "show up at class the next morning with all of the work completed." Students say their peers are very smart and the average student could be described as "academically goal oriented but also extremely social." For many, Dartmouth strikes the perfect balance. As one junior says, "It's a small enough school that there is a sense of community that's always present, but large enough that everyone can find their own niche and their own area of the school and the community that caters to them perfectly."

Dartmouth College

Financial Aid: 800-443-3605 • E-Mail: admissions.office@dartmouth.edu • Website: www.dartmouth.edu

THE PRINCETON REVIEW SAYS

Admissions

The school reports that its standardized testing policy for use in admission for Fall 2026 will require applicants to submit either the SAT or ACT. The Princeton Review suggests that interested applicants consult with the school for the most up-to-date standardized testing policies. *Very important factors considered include:* rigor of secondary school record, class rank, academic GPA, standardized test scores, application essay, recommendation(s), extracurricular activities, character/personal qualities. *Important factors considered include:* talent/ability. *Other factors considered include:* interview, first generation, alumni/ae relation, geographical residence, volunteer work, work experience, level of applicant's interest. High school diploma or equivalent is not required. *Academic units recommended:* 4 English, 4 math, 4 science, 4 language (other than English), 4 social studies.

Financial Aid

Students should submit: FAFSA; CSS PROFILE; Business/Farm Supplement. The Princeton Review suggests that all financial aid forms be submitted as soon as possible. *Need-based scholarships/grants offered:* Federal Pell; Federal SEOG; State scholarships/grants; Private scholarships; College/university scholarship or grant aid from institutional funds. *Loan aid offered:* Federal Direct Subsidized Loans; Federal Direct Unsubsidized Loans; Direct PLUS loans; College/university loans from institutional funds; State Loans. Admitted students will be notified of awards on or about 4/2. Federal Work-Study Program available. Institutional employment available.

The Inside Word

Competition to secure a coveted acceptance letter from Dartmouth is fierce. After all, the majority of admitted students are in the top of their respective high school classes. Therefore, academic success is mandatory for any serious contender as is a transcript chock full of honors, AP and/or IB courses. Of course, admissions officers are looking for well-rounded students so extracurricular activities, personal statements and recommendations will also be closely assessed. Finally, it's important to know that Dartmouth makes its admission decisions independent of a student's financial need.

THE SCHOOL SAYS

From the Admissions Office

"Dartmouth College is a fusion of a renowned liberal arts college and a robust research university. Framed by nature in the small college town of Hanover, New Hampshire, Dartmouth is a place where students partner with leading scholars to take on some of the biggest challenges facing our world. All classes are taught by professors who advance the frontiers of knowledge by teaching, mentoring, and collaborating with undergraduates in and out of class.

"Dartmouth's academic quarter system—the D-Plan—allows students the flexibility to pursue research, off-campus study, internships, volunteerism, and more year-round while staying on track with their academic aspirations. The adventuresome spirit of the College permeates its nearly 400 student groups, from the country's oldest outing club to 35 Division I athletic teams and a vibrant arts scene.

"Dartmouth students share a powerful sense of community developed over its 253-year history, thanks in part to many beloved traditions including Winter Carnival and the Homecoming Bonfire. Upon graduation, they join a global network of more than 80,000 alumni who remain deeply committed to the College.

"Dartmouth's holistic, need-blind admissions process is designed to identify students who will thrive in this intimate environment of curiosity and creativity. There is no 'typical' Dartmouth student, but most tend to share a passion for intellectual inquiry, a willingness to embrace adventure, and a desire to build a close-knit community."

SELECTIVITY

# of total applicants	31,655
% of total applicants accepted	5
% of total acceptees attending	69
# of in-state applicants	468
# of out-of-state-applicants	21,220
# of international applicants	9,968
# of early decision applicants	3,551
% of early decision applicants accepted	19
# offered a place on the wait list	2,589
# admitted from wait list	29

First-Year Profile

Testing policy	SAT or ACT Required
% graduated top 10% of class	93
% graduated top 25% of class	99
% graduated top 50% of class	100
% submitting high school rank	44

Important Dates

Early decision	
Apply by	11/1
Notified by	12/23
Regular	
Apply by	1/1
Notified by	4/1
Nonfall registration?	No

FINANCIAL FACTS

Annual tuition	$66,123
Food and housing	$19,999
Required fees (First-year)	$1,896 ($2,145)
Books and supplies	$1,005
Average need-based scholarship (First-year)	$69,595 ($69,466)
% students with need rec. need-based scholarship or grant aid (First-year)	99 (99)
% students with need rec. non-need-based scholarship or grant aid (First-year)	0 (0)
% students with need rec. need-based self-help aid (First-year)	86 (79)
% students rec. any financial aid (First-year)	NR (54)
% UG borrow to pay for school	33
Average cumulative indebtedness	$24,021
% of students with need fully met (First-year)	100 (100)
Average % of student need met (First-year)	100 (100)

DAVIDSON COLLEGE

209 Ridge Rd, Davidson, NC 28035 • Admissions: 704-894-2000

Survey Snapshot
Students always studying
Great financial aid
Alumni active on campus

RATINGS	
Quality of Life	85
Fire Safety	60*
Green	60*
Academic	84
Profs Interesting	85
Profs Accessible	89
Admissions	98
Financial Aid	98

CAMPUS LIFE

Type of school	Private
Affiliation	Presbyterian
Environment	Village

Students

Degree-seeking undergrad enrollment	1,878
% male/female/not reported	47/53/0
% from out of state	79
% First-year live on campus	100
% Ugrads live on campus	93
# of fraternities (% join)	8 (14)
# of sororities (% join)	6 (32)
% Asian	5
% Black or African American	7
% Hispanic	12
% Native American	<1
% Pacific Islander	0
% Race and/or ethnicity unknown	2
% Two or more races	5
% White	57
% International	11
# of countries represented	42

CAMPUS MENTAL HEALTH SERVICES

Offers mental health/wellness program	Yes
Mental health training available to students	No
Employs Chief Wellness Officer	NR
Peer-to-peer mental health offerings	NR
Counseling center has guidelines or accreditation	No
Mental health/well-being courses	NR

ACADEMICS

% students returning for sophomore year	96
% students graduating within 4 years	86
% students graduating within 6 years	90
Calendar	Semester
Student/faculty ratio	8:1
Most common class size 10–19.	(48%)
Most common lab/discussion size 1–9.	(100%)

Most Popular Majors
Biology/Biological Sciences; Political Science and Government; Psychology

Applicants Often Prefer
University of North Carolina at Chapel Hill

Applicants Sometimes Prefer
Duke University, University of Virginia, Wake Forest University

STUDENTS SAY "..."

Academics

Students proudly say of Davidson College that the goal isn't just to "come out smarter than they came in" but also to "be better people and make a difference in the world." Going that extra mile with a classic liberal arts education is hard work—"99 percent of us left our 4.0 GPAs back in high school," admits a student—but "though the work is rigorous, time spent in school never feels wasted." (It helps that the administration is "very open to change and improvement" and constantly seeking "to support and improve Davidson.") Integrity and creativity are at the forefront of a Davidson education, and the college's Honor Code speaks to the trust and freedom that is given to the community (including unproctored, self-scheduled finals). Likewise, the "fascinating and rewarding" classes often incorporate original research from professors, and the Experiential Learning Team helps guide hands-on experiences for both students and professors. There is no doubt that the workload is intense, but students say it is "is accompanied by even more resources with which it can be successfully managed," including study abroad advisers, career counselors, and peer tutors. As a student says, "I have never witnessed people so eager to come do their job every day." In fact, with an average class size of 14, faculty are waiting in the wings to offer their help, leading a student to vow, "If I could spend twenty years being educated by this administration and these professors, I would."

Campus Life

While academics are a priority at Davidson, it's not for the sake of grades: this place "possesses an intense study culture, and people hit the books regularly; it's cool to be smart." Even though the tough academics "can make it hard to stay up to date on current events... most students remain well-informed," and most here happily weave their classroom commitments with their social desires: "You see your friends because you are doing homework together or eating meals together, not because you're vegging out." As one student points out, "It's not uncommon to hear people discussing their current academic topics at lunch or in the gym." Athletics are actually a big meeting point for Davidson (basketball in particular), and more than a quarter of students are varsity scholar-athletes at this Division I school. "Everyone enjoys being a part of the underdog/Cinderella story," says a student of their book-heavy institution. The city of Charlotte is just under twenty miles away, but 90 percent of the school's 2,000 students live on campus, where they can join any of the 200 student organizations or the popular fraternities, sororities, or eating houses (Davidson's co-ed social organizations). Students stress that no matter your preference, "there really is no pressure to drink. You can go out and dance and have a great time or have movie nights with friends."

Student Body

One has to work quite hard in order to get into Davidson, so it makes sense that all who make it here are "united under the umbrella of intellectual curiosity." There's not a high turnover (Davidson has a 96 percent retention rate), and it doesn't go unnoticed that admissions "does a good job...so if you're in, you'll probably make the cut all the way through the four years." This level of academics fosters a real all-in-it-together mentality, and the entire student body is "eager to watch you succeed." It also means that "academics voluntarily leave the classroom," and a student says that "during the week we work hard. On the weekends we play hard. We don't do anything halfway." This is well-rounded group is "an amalgamation of all types of people, religiously, ethnically, politically, economically, etc.," and hits the size sweet spot where "there are enough people that one can find a similar group to connect with, and there are few enough people that one ends up connecting with dissimilar [people] anyway."

Davidson College

E-Mail: admission@davidson.edu • Website: www.davidson.edu

THE PRINCETON REVIEW SAYS

Admissions

The school reports that its standardized testing policy for use in admission for Fall 2026 is Test Optional. The Princeton Review suggests that interested applicants consult with the school for the most up-to-date standardized testing policies. *Very important factors considered include:* rigor of secondary school record, recommendation(s), character/personal qualities. *Important factors considered include:* application essay. *Other factors considered include:* class rank, academic GPA, standardized test scores, extracurricular activities, talent/ability, first generation, volunteer work, work experience, level of applicant's interest. High school diploma is required and GED is accepted. *Academic units required:* 4 English, 3 math, 2 science, 2 language (other than English), 2 social studies. *Academic units recommended:* 4 math, 4 science, 4 language (other than English), 4 social studies.

Financial Aid

Students should submit: FAFSA; CSS PROFILE. Priority filing deadline is 1/10. The Princeton Review suggests that all financial aid forms be submitted as soon as possible. *Need-based scholarships/grants offered:* Federal Pell; Federal SEOG; State scholarships/grants; Private scholarships; College/university scholarship or grant aid from institutional funds. *Loan aid offered:* Federal Direct Subsidized Loans; Federal Direct Unsubsidized Loans; Direct PLUS loans. Admitted students will be notified of awards on or about 4/1. Federal Work-Study Program available. Institutional employment available.

The Inside Word

Securing admission to Davidson is no easy feat. Admitted students typically rank at the top of their high school classes and, if submitted, have strong standardized test scores. Leadership experience is a plus, and character matters here too—Davidson takes its honor code seriously and actively looks for students who demonstrate integrity. If Davidson is your top choice, applying early decision may improve your chances, as it signals a strong commitment to the school.

THE SCHOOL SAYS

From the Admissions Office

"Davidson is a community of smart, driven and kind people. The relationships and experiences here develop the capacities needed in a society and in an economy where artificial intelligence is driving rapid change. Students graduate with the deep skills to navigate the gray and unfamiliar. They are encouraged to think critically, ask good questions and communicate with audiences from all backgrounds. Mentors push and counsel. They know their students and share their hopes and dreams. A strong honor code means doing right when no one is watching. Davidson keeps its costs accessible through a rare trio of: admitting students without regard for what they can pay, covering all costs beyond the calculated family contribution and covering those costs without loans. Students connect what they learn in the classroom with real world experience—research, internships, a campus-based innovation and entrepreneurship hub and international programs. The Davidson experience builds curiosity, empathy, integrity and courage. These qualities prepare students to serve as ethical leaders and citizens who will advance the public good."

SELECTIVITY

# of total applicants	8,932
% of total applicants accepted	12
% of total acceptees attending	48
# of early decision applicants	1,004
% of early decision applicants accepted	35
# offered a place on the wait list	1,856
# admitted from wait list	35

First-Year Profile

Testing policy	Test Optional
Range SAT composite	1410–1500
Range SAT EBRW	710–760
Range SAT math	700–760
Range ACT composite	32–34
% submitting SAT scores	25
% submitting ACT scores	24
Average HS GPA	3.9
% submitting high school GPA	100
% graduated top 10% of class	77
% graduated top 25% of class	13
% graduated top 50% of class	99
% submitting high school rank	22

Important Dates

Early decision	
Apply by	11/15
Notified by	12/15
Other ED apply by	1/5
Other ED notified by	2/7
Regular	
Apply by	1/10
Notified by	4/1
Nonfall registration?	No

FINANCIAL FACTS

Annual tuition	$73,090
Food and housing	$18,780
Required fees (First-year)	$650 ($900)
Books and supplies	$825
Average need-based scholarship (First-year)	$64,305 ($65,233)
% students with need rec. need-based scholarship or grant aid (First-year)	100 (100)
% students with need rec. non-need-based scholarship or grant aid (First-year)	26 (21)
% students with need rec. need-based self-help aid (First-year)	66 (61)
% students rec. any financial aid (First-year)	51 (49)
% UG borrow to pay for school	19
Average cumulative indebtedness	$29,410
% of students with need fully met (First-year)	100 (100)
Average % of student need met (First-year)	100 (100)

DENISON UNIVERSITY

100 West College Street, Granville, OH 43023 • Admissions: 740-587-6276

Survey Snapshot
Career services are great
Recreation facilities are great
Internships are widely available

RATINGS

Quality of Life	**96**
Fire Safety	**99**
Green	**60***
Academic	**94**
Profs Interesting	**95**
Profs Accessible	**97**
Admissions	**94**
Financial Aid	**98**

CAMPUS LIFE

Type of school	Private
Environment	Village

Students

Degree-seeking undergrad enrollment	2,442
% male/female/not reported	47/53/0
% from out of state	73
% First-year from public high school	58
% First-year live on campus	100
% Ugrads live on campus	99
# of fraternities (% join)	9 (19)
# of sororities (% join)	9 (28)
% Asian	4
% Black or African American	5
% Hispanic	7
% Native American	<1
% Pacific Islander	<1
% Race and/or ethnicity unknown	1
% Two or more races	4
% White	63
% International	16
# of countries represented	73

CAMPUS MENTAL HEALTH SERVICES

Offers mental health/wellness program	Yes
Mental health training available to students	Yes
Employs Chief Wellness Officer	No
Peer-to-peer mental health offerings	NR
Counseling center has guidelines or accreditation	No
Mental health/well-being courses	NR

ACADEMICS

% students returning for sophomore year	91
% students graduating within 4 years	74
% students graduating within 6 years	78
Calendar	Semester
Student/faculty ratio	9:1
Most common class size 10–19.	(45%)

Most Popular Majors

Data Analytics; Psychology; International Business/Trade/Commerce

Applicants Often Prefer

Carleton College, Davidson College, Hamilton College, University of Michigan—Ann Arbor, Vanderbilt University, Washington University in St. Louis

Applicants Sometimes Prefer

American University, Bates College, Boston College, Bucknell University, Case Western Reserve University, Colby College, Colgate University, Colorado College, Dickinson College, Franklin & Marshall College, Kenyon College, Lafayette College, Lehigh University, Macalester College, Skidmore College, Southern Methodist University, Texas Christian University, The Ohio State University—Columbus, Trinity College, Tufts University, University of North Carolina at Chapel Hill, University of Richmond, Wake Forest University, Washington & Lee University

STUDENTS SAY "..."

Academics

At Denison University, students are encouraged to explore their interests "in and out of the classroom." This is encouraged and enabled by a faculty full of "the most caring, supportive, and knowledgeable human beings" and students having "voting powers on many administrative councils, committees, and task forces," which allows them to help shape the school's decision-making. That cooperation may explain why, when it comes to academics, undergrads find the coursework "challenging but certainly worth it." It may also be from the presentation of the work itself: "classes are rarely taught in the form of lectures...rather they feel like focus groups dedicated to the pursuit of knowledge." The vast majority praise teachers as "enthusiastic about their area of study" and as "caring, thoughtful, and always [challenging] you without ever letting you fail." The consensus is that they're "truly focused on students' learning and development" and want "to see you succeed and become a better person." As one undergrad concludes, "I have built a team of faculty who I can lean on."

Campus Life

Life at Denison can be hectic. Thankfully, students maintain "a good balance of academics, extracurriculars, and fun." The university itself sponsors plenty of activities including "food trucks, movie nights, [and] trivia nights" along with "guest speakers and performances." You can also find numerous student-run clubs for a variety of interests. Groups range from "the Burpees Improv group, which does lots of great shows with high campus engagement," to Quidditch, ski club, and Habitat for Humanity. Students appreciate the way arts are handled: "unlike bigger schools, it's less competitive and just focused on fostering a community" and resources are generally open to students, like "music facilities that we can use at our own leisure." Those into sports appreciate the way that the school helps them juggle "a competitive, serious career in athletics and a rigorous, rewarding academic experience."

Outside of structured events, "hundreds of students...pass time lounging on the main academic quad between classes." And once the weekend rolls around, there tend to be apartment-based parties on Fridays and frat-based ones on Saturdays, though it's noted that while "students are typically social, [they are] not necessarily party animals." That said, those who want to hang together can do so "regardless of Greek life status, which is cool," and those who need a break from the hustle and bustle of college life can visit the quiet village of Granville or "drive to Columbus and explore the city."

Student Body

Denison students are "both ambitious and also open minded...curious, innovative thinkers that are motivated by making a wise impact." While you can still see "the remnants" of a "predominantly white" and "wealthy East-coaster" background, the overall consensus is that you can now meet "all types of students on campus." One undergrad elaborates further, "As an Ohioan, it is really special to go to an in-state school where I can have roommates, friends, and classmates from Britain, India, and China." Driven and diverse, students agree that it's "great to see people support each other in athletic events, theater performances, and even Bluegrass ensembles," all of which makes the school feel like a real community. Indeed, "it is the type of campus where...you keep your head up and say 'hi' to everyone that you pass." Adds another undergrad, "I feel really safe at Denison because I know that if something were to happen to me, students that I know and don't know would step up to help." Ultimately, when it comes down to it, "There is someone representing every personality, character, experience, and friendship style at Denison, so you are guaranteed to find a great group of friends."

DENISON UNIVERSITY

Financial Aid: 740-587-6279 • E-Mail: admission@denison.edu • Website: denison.edu

THE PRINCETON REVIEW SAYS

Admissions

The school reports that its standardized testing policy for use in admission for Fall 2026 is Test Optional. The Princeton Review suggests that interested applicants consult with the school for the most up-to-date standardized testing policies. *Very important factors considered include:* rigor of secondary school record, academic GPA, application essay, recommendation(s). *Important factors considered include:* interview, extracurricular activities, talent/ability. *Other factors considered include:* class rank, standardized test scores, character/personal qualities, first generation, alumni/ae relation, geographical residence, state residency, volunteer work, work experience, level of applicant's interest. High school diploma is required and GED is accepted. *Academic units recommended:* 4 English, 4 math, 4 science, 4 language (other than English), 4 social studies.

Financial Aid

Students should submit: FAFSA; CSS PROFILE. Priority filing deadline is 1/15. The Princeton Review suggests that all financial aid forms be submitted as soon as possible. *Need-based scholarships/grants offered:* Federal Pell; Federal SEOG; State scholarships/grants; Private scholarships; College/university scholarship or grant aid from institutional funds. *Loan aid offered:* Federal Direct Subsidized Loans; Federal Direct Unsubsidized Loans; Direct PLUS loans; College/university loans from institutional funds. Admitted students will be notified of awards on or about 4/1. Federal Work-Study Program available. Institutional employment available.

The Inside Word

Denison's admission process is relatively straightforward. The school strongly encourages an interview, and if you can do one, you should. It's a great way to demonstrate genuine interest, which can make a real difference if your grades, test scores, or overall profile put you on the cusp. Students may apply using either the Common Application or the Coalition Application.

THE SCHOOL SAYS

From the Admissions Office

"Recognized as one of America's best universities for career preparation and innovation, Denison University delivers a rigorous and pragmatic education that launches students quickly and successfully into their lives and careers. Located just 25 minutes from Ohio's bustling capital city of Columbus—a leading city in business, medicine, and technology—Denison's fully residential campus is uniquely balanced by Granville's charming downtown and picturesque rolling hills. Founded nearly 200 years ago, Denison's modern approach fuses academic discovery and practical workforce preparation to shape students into uniquely skilled, relationship-driven individuals. Students are challenged by a rigorous curriculum and taught by world-class faculty. In small classes, they're pushed to think critically and connect ideas across disciplines. These same faculty members become trusted mentors, guiding research, co-authoring publications, and—alongside Denison's best-in-class career preparation team—direct students toward sought-after internship, postgraduate, and career opportunities.

"Students learn in cutting-edge facilities like Knobel Hall, a first-of-its-kind hub for data integration across the curriculum, and choose from over 65 academically demanding areas of study, including in-demand programs such as data analytics, finance, and machine learning and AI. They're guided by 30+ career professionals, join career communities, and tap into hundreds of employer connections. They complete paid internships and real consulting projects with top brands. Students join 170+ student organizations, perform in conservatory-level music and theatre spaces, and compete on 27 varsity teams (including four national champion teams this past year). After four years, Denison graduates leave with résumés full of real experience, global connections, and the confidence, adaptability, and problem-solving skills employers and graduate schools demand."

SELECTIVITY

# of total applicants	12,202
% of total applicants accepted	20
% of total acceptees attending	26
# of early decision applicants	1,589
% of early decision applicants accepted	25
# offered a place on the wait list	1,376
# admitted from wait list	31

First-Year Profile

Testing policy	Test Optional
Range SAT composite	1270–1420
Range SAT EBRW	640–720
Range SAT math	630–710
Range ACT composite	28–33
% submitting SAT scores	27
% submitting ACT scores	19
% graduated top 10% of class	45
% graduated top 25% of class	78
% graduated top 50% of class	95

Important Dates

Early decision	
Apply by	11/15
Notified by	12/15
Other ED apply by	1/15
Other ED notified by	2/15
Regular	
Apply by	1/15
Notified by	4/1
Nonfall registration?	No

FINANCIAL FACTS

Annual tuition	$74,000
Food and housing	$18,400
Books and supplies	$1,000
Average need-based scholarship (First-year)	$57,569 ($58,935)
% students with need rec. need-based scholarship or grant aid (First-year)	99 (98)
% students with need rec. non-need-based scholarship or grant aid (First-year)	9 (8)
% students with need rec. need-based self-help aid (First-year)	100 (100)
% students rec. any financial aid (First-year)	93 (93)
% UG borrow to pay for school	36
Average cumulative indebtedness	$30,116
% of students with need fully met (First-year)	100 (100)
Average % of student need met (First-year)	100 (100)

DePaul University

1 East Jackson Boulevard, Chicago, IL 60604-2287 • Admissions: 312-362-8300

Survey Snapshot
Lots of conservative students
Students are happy
Classroom facilities are great

RATINGS

Quality of Life	**88**
Fire Safety	**96**
Green	**60***
Academic	**81**
Profs Interesting	**90**
Profs Accessible	**93**
Admissions	**84**
Financial Aid	**86**

CAMPUS LIFE

Type of school	Private
Affiliation	Roman Catholic
Environment	Metropolis

Students

Degree-seeking undergrad enrollment	14,253
% male/female/not reported	45/55/0
% from out of state	26
% First-year from public high school	81
% First-year live on campus	55
% Ugrads live on campus	18
# of fraternities (% join)	9 (3)
# of sororities (% join)	17 (7)
% Asian	13
% Black or African American	8
% Hispanic	26
% Native American	<1
% Pacific Islander	<1
% Race and/or ethnicity unknown	2
% Two or more races	5
% White	43
% International	4
# of countries represented	129

CAMPUS MENTAL HEALTH SERVICES

Offers mental health/wellness program	Yes
Mental health training available to students	No
Employs Chief Wellness Officer	NR
Peer-to-peer mental health offerings	NR
Counseling center has guidelines or accreditation	No
Mental health/well-being courses	NR

ACADEMICS

% students returning for sophomore year	86
% students graduating within 4 years	53
% students graduating within 6 years	67
Calendar	Differs By Program
Student/faculty ratio	17:1
Most common class size 20–29.	(36%)
Most common lab/discussion size 20–29.	(48%)

Most Popular Majors
Finance; Cinematography and Film/Video Production; Psychology

STUDENTS SAY "..."

Academics

DePaul University is the nation's largest Catholic university, offering its 14,000 undergraduate students over 130 majors across two campuses, including the option for combined Bachelor's and Master's degrees. These various programs are anchored by a core curriculum that features over 1,400 course options and a Focal Point Seminar, in which students must investigate a significant person, place, event, or idea. Further supplementing that core is an ever-expanding series of options, as "each year [DePaul] strives to improve and add new programs to suit different future career paths of its students." Such offerings are only enhanced by the school's heart-of-Chicago location, which puts it "close to so many educational and vocational opportunities." There are thousands of internships available, as well as "peer-to-peer study groups" and study abroad programs. The administration rises to the task of "keeping the school's environment safe, clean, and well-educated," and "there are plenty of resources specifically set up to help students with pretty much anything," including "tutoring sessions every day, a writing center to help improve papers, a counseling center, [and] financial aid advisers."

Ninety-eight percent of classes are taught by the "highly professional" faculty, so "instead of only learning from a textbook, I am able to gain real experience from professors who have worked in the field for decades at a time." There's a maximum to each class size as well, which guarantees that "teachers actually get to know the students that are in the class." This also lends itself to an accessibility "like no other and it really helps the students that need extra help outside of the classroom." All in all, professors have so "many years of experience behind them, they are able to transfer all their knowledge to students in an effective and fun way." There "are museums, parks, guest speakers in the city that professors will often take advantage of by taking the class to them allowing us to learn the subject from a real-world perspective."

Campus Life

DePaul has "lots of organizations that cater to different causes and a lot of extracurricular activities," as well as 15 Division I athletic teams that students enjoy watching. The Chicago-based campus also ensures that there's not only a lot to do, but plenty of opportunity to put what's being learned to the test. In particular, students complete "a lot of community service in the neighborhood as well as throughout the USA," but many also just "enjoy going out into the city and trying out new restaurants around the city." That doesn't mean DePaul skimps out on campus offerings! There are "always events happening to increase student interaction," and these are "really creative and interesting." And even though DePaul is spread across two campuses, students note that activities are always planned in such a way "that there is enough time to catch a train to get to the other campus."

Student Body

One in three people at DePaul is a first-generation college student, and the student body as a whole "is pretty diverse when it comes to race, gender, religion, and orientation of each student." Attendees find this to be a bonus, because not only are they learning from the professors, but they're also "gain[ing] considerable knowledge from [their] peers." This is especially true given the warm atmosphere, where it is both "easy to make friends and easy to get engaged with events going on around campus," regardless of socioeconomic background. "The campus is pretty liberal," students observe, but stress that everyone has "freedom and respect of choice for views [and] religion." This ultimately results in "a large sense of belonging in any classroom between all the students," and helps to ensure that everyone remains "very focused."

DePaul University

Financial Aid: 312-362-8610 • E-Mail: admission@depaul.edu • Website: www.depaul.edu

THE PRINCETON REVIEW SAYS

Admissions

The school reports that its standardized testing policy for use in admission for Fall 2026 is Test Optional. The Princeton Review suggests that interested applicants consult with the school for the most up-to-date standardized testing policies. *Very important factors considered include:* rigor of secondary school record, academic GPA, standardized test scores. *Important factors considered include:* class rank, recommendation(s), extracurricular activities, talent/ability, character/personal qualities, volunteer work, work experience, level of applicant's interest. *Other factors considered include:* application essay, interview, first generation, alumni/ae relation, geographical residence, state residency, religious affiliation/commitment. High school diploma is required and GED is accepted. *Academic units required:* 4 English, 3 math, 3 science, 2 science labs, 2 social studies. *Academic units recommended:* 4 English, 3 math, 3 science, 2 science labs, 2 language (other than English), 2 social studies.

Financial Aid

Students should submit: FAFSA. Priority filing deadline is 12/31. The Princeton Review suggests that all financial aid forms be submitted as soon as possible. *Need-based scholarships/grants offered:* Federal Pell; Federal SEOG; State scholarships/grants; Private scholarships; College/university scholarship or grant aid from institutional funds. *Loan aid offered:* Federal Direct Subsidized Loans; Federal Direct Unsubsidized Loans; Direct PLUS loans. Admitted students will be notified of awards on a rolling basis beginning 1/2. Federal Work-Study Program available. Institutional employment available.

The Inside Word

DePaul's reputation as one of the most diverse schools in the country is not mere hyperbole, it's a truth expressed by student after student, and by the actions of the administration itself. In an effort to surmount tuition-related obstacles, DePaul works with local community colleges so students can meet their requirements at a lower cost before transferring to DePaul. DePaul takes a holistic approach when reviewing applicants for admission.

THE SCHOOL SAYS

From the Admissions Office

"The nation's largest Catholic university, DePaul University is nationally recognized for its innovative academic programs that embrace a comprehensive learn-by-doing approach. DePaul has two residential locations. The Lincoln Park Campus is home to the College of Liberal Arts and Social Sciences, the College of Science and Health, the College of Education, the School of Music, The Theatre School and the extensive John T. Richardson Library. The Loop location, located in Chicago's downtown—a world-class center for business, government, law, and culture—is home to DePaul's Driehaus College of Business, College of Communication, College of Law, College of Computing and Digital Media, and School of Continuing & Professional Studies."

SELECTIVITY

# of total applicants	27,462
% of total applicants accepted	88
% of total acceptees attending	12
# offered a place on the wait list	658
# admitted from wait list	148

First-Year Profile

Testing policy	Test Optional
Range SAT composite	1150–1330
Range SAT EBRW	580–680
Range SAT math	550–660
Range ACT composite	26–31
% submitting SAT scores	30
% submitting ACT scores	11
Average HS GPA	3.8
% submitting high school GPA	94
% graduated top 10% of class	22
% graduated top 25% of class	51
% graduated top 50% of class	83
% submitting high school rank	30

Important Dates

Early action	
Apply by	11/15
Notified by	12/15
Regular	
Apply by	2/1
Notified by	3/15
Nonfall registration?	Yes

FINANCIAL FACTS

Annual tuition	$46,776
Food and housing	$19,896
Required fees	$900
Books and supplies	$1,104
Average need-based scholarship (First-year)	$30,014 ($32,136)
% students with need rec. need-based scholarship or grant aid (First-year)	98 (99)
% students with need rec. non-need-based scholarship or grant aid (First-year)	12 (14)
% students with need rec. need-based self-help aid (First-year)	59 (52)
% students rec. any financial aid (First-year)	91 (98)
% UG borrow to pay for school	58
Average cumulative indebtedness	$28,434
% of students with need fully met (First-year)	13 (15)
Average % of student need met (First-year)	70 (73)

DePauw University

313 S. Locust Street, Greencastle, IN 46135 • Admissions: 765-658-4006

Survey Snapshot
Internships are widely available
Class discussions encouraged
Alumni active on campus

RATINGS

Quality of Life	**78**
Fire Safety	**60***
Green	**60***
Academic	**85**
Profs Interesting	**86**
Profs Accessible	**89**
Admissions	**89**
Financial Aid	**91**

CAMPUS LIFE

Type of school	Private
Environment	Village

Students

Degree-seeking undergrad enrollment	1,847
% male/female/not reported	50/50/<1
% from out of state	49
% First-year live on campus	100
% Ugrads live on campus	97
# of fraternities (% join)	13 (47)
# of sororities (% join)	11 (44)
% Asian	2
% Black or African American	7
% Hispanic	9
% Native American	0
% Pacific Islander	0
% Race and/or ethnicity unknown	1
% Two or more races	3
% White	57
% International	21
# of countries represented	38

CAMPUS MENTAL HEALTH SERVICES

Offers mental health/wellness program	Yes
Mental health training available to students	No
Employs Chief Wellness Officer	NR
Peer-to-peer mental health offerings	NR
Counseling center has guidelines or accreditation	No
Mental health/well-being courses	NR

ACADEMICS

% students returning for sophomore year	89
% students graduating within 4 years	68
% students graduating within 6 years	78
Calendar	4-1-4
Student/faculty ratio	10:1
Most common class size 10–19.	(57%)
Most common lab/discussion size 10–19.	(50%)

Most Popular Majors

Speech Communication and Rhetoric; Economics

STUDENTS SAY "..."

Academics

DePauw University has done an incredible job of building a "collaborative community" that prioritizes the needs and desires of its undergraduates. Whether it's cultivating a "truly caring faculty," being wholly "receptive to student feedback" or developing "excellent study abroad options," students here are set up to thrive. Importantly, DePauw "emphasizes [a] well-rounded education" as undergrads are expected to "take classes in nearly all departments over their four years." Inevitably, this allows them to develop "both [a] depth and breadth of knowledge" and also helps ensure that there are "programs and courses for every student." Another great benefit of a DePauw education? The "classes are small so students are able to really engage in discussion." But perhaps the true highlight of studying here are the professors who tend to be "knowledgeable, interesting, empathetic and invested." As this undergrad explains, "My professors do a great job at making sure we don't grow tired of our material. They always switch things up to make sure we are learning and growing as individuals." They're also "eager to tell students about internships or job opportunities, and love connecting students with alumni." As another grateful undergrad simply concludes, "The professors at DePauw University are some of the most phenomenal people I have ever met."

Campus Life

Undergrads at DePauw are "very committed to their academics" and it's common for people to "spend much of the week studying." Nevertheless, there's plenty to enjoy when they want to take a break from their books. To begin with, DePauw maintains a fairly robust fraternity and sorority system. "Many students join Greek life at some point and are involved in [their] philanthropy, academic and social activities including partying. Even those not in the Greek system are likely to attend the Greek parties." Additionally, athletics are "very popular" as well and you'll often see "students [at] football games... during the fall semester, especially when they play our rival team during the Monon Bell game." Of course, the university itself also "hosts many fun events to bring students together, such as food truck Fridays." And there are numerous organizations and clubs to join ranging from the student newspaper and TV station to the future medical professionals club and sustainability leadership program. When wanting to get off outside for a bit, "many students go to the Nature Park (a DePauw owned nature preserve). It is very popular in the spring and fall and many students enjoy hiking, reading, or working on homework [there]."

And if you're venturing off campus, undergrads note that "Greencastle['s] downtown has grown tremendously these past few years, and there are many cute restaurants and bars to visit." Students also like to "go to dinner with friends and go see a movie or go bowling, which are free in the town if you are a student."

Student Body

At DePauw, you'll find "students from all over the world" and, accordingly, "open-minded individuals who are eager to learn about the world around them." At a glance, some students observe a "core group [of] Midwestern white students" and that there are "well-off" local attendees, but note that diversity can be found throughout this group, and the school "in lots of ways—in terms of ethnicity, sexuality, sexual orientation/identity, thoughts, political viewpoints, country of origin/nationality, etc." As one student puts it, "My peers are often unafraid to stand up for what they believe to be right, and actively work to better the DePauw community." Ultimately, when it comes down to it, "The university has a very social student base that acts as a very tight-knit community."

DePauw University

Financial Aid: 765-658-4191 • E-Mail: admission@depauw.edu • Website: www.depauw.edu

THE PRINCETON REVIEW SAYS

Admissions

The school reports that its standardized testing policy for use in admission for Fall 2026 is Test Optional. The Princeton Review suggests that interested applicants consult with the school for the most up-to-date standardized testing policies. *Very important factors considered include:* rigor of secondary school record, academic GPA. *Important factors considered include:* class rank, application essay, recommendation(s). *Other factors considered include:* standardized test scores, interview, extracurricular activities, talent/ability, character/personal qualities, first generation, alumni/ae relation, geographical residence, state residency, work experience, level of applicant's interest. High school diploma is required and GED is accepted. *Academic units required:* 4 English, 3 math, 2 science, 2 science labs, 2 language (other than English), 2 social studies. *Academic units recommended:* 4 English, 4 math, 3 science, 2 science labs, 2 language (other than English), 3 social studies, 3 history.

Financial Aid

Students should submit: FAFSA. Priority filing deadline is 11/1. The Princeton Review suggests that all financial aid forms be submitted as soon as possible. *Need-based scholarships/grants offered:* Federal Pell; Federal SEOG; State scholarships/grants; Private scholarships; College/university scholarship or grant aid from institutional funds. *Loan aid offered:* Federal Direct Subsidized Loans; Federal Direct Unsubsidized Loans; Direct PLUS loans; College/university loans from institutional funds. Admitted students will be notified of awards on a rolling basis beginning 1/15. Federal Work-Study Program available. Institutional employment available.

The Inside Word

Admissions officers at DePauw University consider both students' academic performance and involvement outside the classroom when determining whether or not a student will be admitted. They want candidates who will contribute positively to the campus as a whole. A strong application will demonstrate above average achievement, from high GPAs and challenging coursework to leadership roles in extracurriculars.

THE SCHOOL SAYS

From the Admissions Office

"DePauw University unites rigorous academics and immersive experiential learning across its three schools—the College of Liberal Arts and Sciences, the Creative School, and the School of Business and Leadership. Ranked among the nation's top liberal arts institutions with a 90% first-year retention rate, DePauw fosters a close-knit, fully residential community where small class sizes and collaborative faculty mentorship thrive.

"With a top 30 graduation rate among liberal arts colleges, DePauw students pursue their passions with confidence amongst 75+ areas of study. Alumni excel as leaders across diverse fields, from CEOs and Pulitzer Prize winners to influential scientists and civic innovators, attaining lifetime earnings in the top 7% nationally.

"DePauw students demonstrate intellectual curiosity, a drive to explore uncharted paths, and the courage to challenge assumptions. Over 90% study abroad, 84% complete internships, and 36% engage in research, while Winter Term and May Term programs deepen global perspectives. Ranked among the top universities for study abroad, DePauw ensures students connect with diverse communities and emerge ready to address complex challenges."

SELECTIVITY

# of total applicants	5,862
% of total applicants accepted	65
% of total acceptees attending	13

First-Year Profile

Testing policy	Test Optional
Range SAT composite	1170–1390
Range SAT EBRW	590–700
Range SAT math	570–690
Range ACT composite	26–32
% submitting SAT scores	53
% submitting ACT scores	19
Average HS GPA	3.9
% submitting high school GPA	100
% graduated top 10% of class	35
% graduated top 25% of class	69
% graduated top 50% of class	94
% submitting high school rank	37

Important Dates

Early decision	
Apply by	11/1
Notified by	12/15
Other ED apply by	12/15
Other ED notified by	2/15
Early action	
Apply by	11/1
Notified by	12/15
Regular	
Apply by	2/1
Nonfall registration?	Yes

FINANCIAL FACTS

Annual tuition	$62,710
Food and housing	$16,240
Required fees	$1,170
Books and supplies	$800
Average need-based scholarship (First-year)	$49,381 ($50,061)
% students with need rec. need-based scholarship or grant aid (First-year)	100 (100)
% students with need rec. non-need-based scholarship or grant aid (First-year)	29 (34)
% students with need rec. need-based self-help aid (First-year)	78 (73)
% students rec. any financial aid (First-year)	100 (100)
% UG borrow to pay for school	83
Average cumulative indebtedness	$25,565
% of students with need fully met (First-year)	35 (39)
Average % of student need met (First-year)	89 (91)

Dickinson College

P.O. Box 1773, Carlisle, PA 17013 • Admissions: 717-245-1231

Survey Snapshot
Great library
Students environmentally aware
Active student government

RATINGS

Quality of Life	87
Fire Safety	92
Green	95
Academic	88
Profs Interesting	93
Profs Accessible	95
Admissions	92
Financial Aid	96

CAMPUS LIFE

Type of school	Private
Environment	Town

Students

Degree-seeking undergrad enrollment	2,094
% male/female/not reported	41/59/0
% from out of state	71
% First-year from public high school	60
% First-year live on campus	100
% Ugrads live on campus	100
# of fraternities (% join)	3 (7)
# of sororities (% join)	6 (23)
% Asian	5
% Black or African American	4
% Hispanic	8
% Native American	<1
% Pacific Islander	<1
% Race and/or ethnicity unknown	1
% Two or more races	5
% White	66
% International	11
# of countries represented	47

CAMPUS MENTAL HEALTH SERVICES

Offers mental health/wellness program	Yes
Mental health training available to students	Yes
Employs Chief Wellness Officer	Yes
Peer-to-peer mental health offerings	Yes
Counseling center has guidelines or accreditation	Yes
Mental health/well-being courses	Yes, non-credit

ACADEMICS

% students returning for sophomore year	93
% students graduating within 4 years	62
% students graduating within 6 years	74
Calendar	Semester
Student/faculty ratio	8:1
Most common class size 10–19.	(46%)

Most Popular Majors
Psychology; Political Science and Government; International Business/ Trade/Commerce

Applicants Often Prefer
Bucknell University, Denison University, Lafayette College, Oberlin College, William & Mary

Applicants Sometimes Prefer
American University, Connecticut College, Franklin & Marshall College, Muhlenberg College, Skidmore College

Applicants Rarely Prefer
Gettysburg College, Penn State University Park, Union College (NY), University of Vermont, Ursinus College

STUDENTS SAY "..."

Academics

As a historic liberal arts college dating back to 1783, Dickinson College "does a great job at working to expose you to as much as possible" and helping students to "discover their interests." The "very interdisciplinary" environment challenges students to "think critically" and consider "alternative points of view," which, as one enrollee notes, has "been transformative in my worldview.... I feel like I've become a better writer, communicator, and person." The "very hands-on and interactive" curriculum means that most students complete either an internship or externship or take a research, service-learning, or field-experience class. One student describes their multi-year internship working with a psychology professor as the "highlight of my experience" at Dickinson. Dickinson also offers "extensive study abroad opportunities," which 63 percent of students participate in. In terms of classroom dynamics, students say Dickinson is a "very healthy environment with excellent professors" who "expect high-quality effort and everyday attendance and engagement." In return, students receive "actual helpful feedback" and feel challenged by "interesting topics that push us to think out of the box." Ultimately, students applaud the school's strong, "personalized approach to education."

Campus Life

Dickinson's campus features a number of unique facilities and resources, including a makerspace with craft supplies, and an outdoor-gear–loaning program. There's also the Dickinson farm, which supplies organic produce to the local community and dining hall, helping to provide a range of food options. (There's also a weekly farmer's market and "a lot of very good, student-affordable restaurants within walking distance.") There's "a big emphasis on school spirit," and students "are big on attending sports games." Another popular activity among this well-rounded student body is attending the Clarke Forum lectures, which host guest speakers, including renowned scholars and celebrated authors. While "some people party," it's overall "not a party school" and "drinking is not an expectation," especially with so many other on-campus activities, as well as shopping and movies in the town of Carlisle. Students appreciate the "lively and diverse" music scene that includes a cappella groups, the student-run radio station, and "band performances almost every weekend." And when it comes to keeping busy, they point to how "MOB—our student planning committee—often throws amazing concerts and events," including "a winter carnival with indoor obstacle courses."

Student Body

The "passionate, empathetic, and curious" students at Dickinson "care a lot about the world (globally and domestically) and are in large part motivated by...want[ing] to make the world a better place," which can be seen across a "campus that focuses on human rights and the environment." This also produces a driven population, as "it seems like everybody has something that makes them want to get out of bed in the morning." While some have noticed a "slight social divide" between athletes and non-athletes, others say "artistic individuals are friends with athletes on campus and vice versa." Overall, "You don't need to be a specific type of person to succeed here," and "everyone here encourages you to try again instead of putting you down." Moreover, "each person at this institution has their own unique perspective and is not afraid to share what it is." The school attracts "a lot of people who are bold [and] outspoken." In this overall positive and supportive environment, students "find ways to comfortably discuss uncomfortable topics" and "appreciate meaningful conversations with one another."

DICKINSON COLLEGE

Financial Aid: 717-245-1308 • E-Mail: admissions@dickinson.edu • Website: www.dickinson.edu

THE PRINCETON REVIEW SAYS

Admissions

The school reports that its standardized testing policy for use in admission for Fall 2026 is Test Optional. The Princeton Review suggests that interested applicants consult with the school for the most up-to-date standardized testing policies. *Very important factors considered include:* rigor of secondary school record, class rank, academic GPA, recommendation(s), talent/ability, character/personal qualities, level of applicant's interest. *Important factors considered include:* application essay, interview, extracurricular activities. *Other factors considered include:* standardized test scores, first generation, alumni/ae relation, geographical residence, volunteer work, work experience. High school diploma is required and GED is accepted. *Academic units required:* 4 English, 3 math, 3 science, 2 science labs, 2 language (other than English), 2 social studies. *Academic units recommended:* 3 language (other than English).

Financial Aid

Students should submit: FAFSA; CSS PROFILE; State aid form. Priority filing deadline is 11/15. The Princeton Review suggests that all financial aid forms be submitted as soon as possible. *Need-based scholarships/grants offered:* Federal Pell; Federal SEOG; State scholarships/grants; Private scholarships; College/university scholarship or grant aid from institutional funds. *Loan aid offered:* Federal Direct Subsidized Loans; Federal Direct Unsubsidized Loans; Direct PLUS loans; State Loans; College/university loans from institutional funds. Federal Work-Study Program available. Institutional employment available.

The Inside Word

The applicant pool for small liberal arts colleges has become increasingly competitive, and Dickinson is no exception. Successful applicants balance strong academics in challenging coursework with extracurricular, service, and/or work experience.

THE SCHOOL SAYS

From the Admissions Office

"Dickinson College is one of the nation's oldest institutions, founded in 1783 with a mission rooted in active citizenship, global awareness and intellectual inquiry. From its earliest years—shaped by signer of the Declaration of Independence Benjamin Rush—the college has emphasized educating students not only for successful careers but for lives of purpose and leadership.

"Dickinson's values center on engaged, experiential learning; ethical responsibility; and faculty mentorship. Small classes and a interdisciplinary curriculum encourage students to think critically, communicate clearly and apply knowledge beyond the classroom. This philosophy drives strong outcomes: graduates secure employment, fellowships and admission to selective graduate, law and medical schools, supported by advising, experience-based learning and an active alumni network.

"The college is widely known for global education, with one of the highest study-abroad participation rates among all colleges and universities. Programs in more than 60 locations worldwide are supported by exceptional language study, international internships and globally focused coursework. Dickinson is also a leader in sustainability, integrating environmental responsibility into academics, campus operations and community partnerships—reflecting its belief that stewardship and innovation are essential to modern leadership.

"High-impact practices define the Dickinson experience, including research, internships, service learning and senior capstones. Signature experiential programs like the Burgess Institute for the Global Economy prepare students for careers through analytics, internships and applied research, while Mosaics provide hands-on learning across the country and across the globe. Located in historic Carlisle, Pennsylvania, Dickinson offers a college-town setting near regional cities and opportunities on a global scale."

SELECTIVITY

# of total applicants	5,719
% of total applicants accepted	41
% of total acceptees attending	20
# of in-state applicants	1,068
% of in-state applicants accepted	50
# of out-of-state-applicants	3,102
% of applicants accepted from out of state	52
# of international applicants	1,549
% of international applicants accepted	13
# of early decision applicants	454
% of early decision applicants accepted	57
# offered a place on the wait list	335
# admitted from wait list	8

First-Year Profile

Testing policy	Test Optional
Range SAT composite	1340–1440
Range SAT EBRW	680–730
Range SAT math	660–710
Range ACT composite	29–32
% submitting SAT scores	13
% submitting ACT scores	4
% graduated top 10% of class	49
% graduated top 25% of class	81
% graduated top 50% of class	97
% submitting high school rank	28

Important Dates

Early decision	
Apply by	11/15
Notified by	Mid December
Other ED apply by	1/15
Other ED notified by	Mid February
Regular	
Apply by	1/15
Notified by	Late March
Nonfall registration?	No

FINANCIAL FACTS

Annual tuition	$71,100
Food and housing	$18,650
Required fees (First-year)	$550 ($575)
Books and supplies	$1,324
Average need-based scholarship (First-year)	$54,208 ($55,321)
% students with need rec. need-based scholarship or grant aid (First-year)	99 (98)
% students with need rec. non-need-based scholarship or grant aid (First-year)	17 (23)
% students with need rec. need-based self-help aid (First-year)	81 (74)
% students rec. any financial aid (First-year)	96 (99)
% UG borrow to pay for school	60
Average cumulative indebtedness	$33,289
% of students with need fully met (First-year)	80 (89)
Average % of student need met (First-year)	99 (99)

Drew University

36 Madison Avenue, Madison, NJ 07940 • Admissions: 973-408-2739

Survey Snapshot
Theater is popular
College radio is popular
Students are happy

Ratings

Quality of Life	**82**
Fire Safety	**92**
Green	**60***
Academic	**81**
Profs Interesting	**88**
Profs Accessible	**89**
Admissions	**86**
Financial Aid	**79**

Campus Life

Type of school	Private
Affiliation	Methodist
Environment	Village

Students

Degree-seeking undergrad enrollment	1,533
% male/female/not reported	44/56/0
% from out of state	27
% First-year from public high school	63
% First-year live on campus	78
% Ugrads live on campus	70
# of fraternities	0
# of sororities	0
% Asian	4
% Black or African American	11
% Hispanic	7
% Native American	<1
% Pacific Islander	<1
% Race and/or ethnicity unknown	7
% Two or more races	4
% White	56
% International	11
# of countries represented	52

Campus Mental Health Services

Offers mental health/wellness program	Yes
Mental health training available to students	No
Employs Chief Wellness Officer	Yes
Peer-to-peer mental health offerings	NR
Counseling center has guidelines or accreditation	No
Mental health/well-being courses	Yes, non-credit

Academics

% students returning for sophomore year	88
% students graduating within 4 years	63
% students graduating within 6 years	70
Calendar	Semester
Student/faculty ratio	12:1
Most common class size 10–19.	(48%)
Most common lab/discussion size 1–9.	(83%)

Most Popular Majors

Biology/Biological Sciences; Psychology; Business Administration and Management

Applicants Also Look At

The College of New Jersey, Drexel University, Ithaca College, Montclair State University, Muhlenberg College, New York University

Students Say "..."

Academics

Located in Madison, New Jersey, Drew University is just a hop-and-a-skip away from the New York City universe, and the school takes full advantage of its proximity to industry hubs. The 1,600 undergraduates have access to more than 60 majors, minors, and dual-degree programs, and thousands of related internships, as well as lots of study abroad options. Drew's seven unique New York Semesters allow students to do coursework with professors and then commute into New York City to learn in the field (for example, on Wall Street, at the United Nations, or in the art, communications, social entrepreneurship and theatre scene). The science departments are standouts—one of its fellows won the Nobel Prize for Medicine in 2015—and its top-ranked theatre program is "comprehensive in such a way that every graduate of the program will have at least tried every single part of the theatrical process."

The "incredibly engaging" professors go "above and beyond the role of just...teacher" and are "very much willing to assist in any way." They "facilitate conversations so that you learn in a way that's not just your average PowerPoint [presentation]" and "invest time in you academically and as a young adult looking for a career." The university does an excellent job of fostering undergraduate student research, and professors "require a level of accountability that motivates a student to perform" both in and out of the classroom. Far and away the things that students appreciate the most about Drew are its small class sizes, which bolster the personal attention from teachers, almost all of whom have PhDs. ("There are no classes taught by TAs, which makes for better quality learning.") This "mentorship with professors" is a lasting benefit to students, who say that "you really get to know your professors in an impactful way."

Campus Life

While the small, wooded town of Madison isn't exactly hopping, students make the most of the "gorgeous" campus (where housing is guaranteed all four years; currently 70 percent of the student body lives on campus) and "tend to be proactive in creating their own recreational experiences." People "are very involved in sports and activities, such as clubs and organizations," and many have jobs or internships. New York City is a short 50-minute train ride away, and nearby Morristown also provides some flavor. Academics "take up a good amount of daytime, but life at school is "always manageable"; "classes are challenging enough and the workload isn't overbearing," so "there is always time to relax if you're responsible and manage your time well." Tuesdays and Thursdays are dollar beer nights, so "many students take time out of studying to go out for a little," but "most free time is spent in friends' rooms, playing video games or watching shows." Though school events aren't terribly well-attended, from time to time there are things which students make sure to have fun at, "such as Bingo night, the holiday ball, and Drewchella (a live music festival)." All in all, "there is a good balance of leisure and education."

Student Body

While about half of the students are from New Jersey, the student body is diverse and includes a large international student population. As a small school, "Everyone at least knows of everyone else and is friendly with them." "Drew students are the type that see a $50 bill in the street and find the person who dropped it," says one student of this group that is "attractive inside and out." There's a large percentage of people actively involved in both the arts and sciences, and the regular cliques—"jocks, theatre kids, science nerds"—all "blend together and overlap so that there are no definite lines separating people." Drew is an eco-friendly campus, and "there is a fairly large number of gluten free/vegetarian students."

Drew University

Financial Aid: 973-408-3188 • E-Mail: admissions@drew.edu • Website: www.drew.edu

THE PRINCETON REVIEW SAYS

Admissions

The school reports that its standardized testing policy for use in admission for Fall 2026 is Test Optional. The Princeton Review suggests that interested applicants consult with the school for the most up-to-date standardized testing policies. *Very important factors considered include:* rigor of secondary school record, academic GPA, interview. *Important factors considered include:* application essay, recommendation(s), extracurricular activities, talent/ability, character/personal qualities. *Other factors considered include:* class rank, standardized test scores, first generation, alumni/ae relation, volunteer work, work experience, level of applicant's interest. High school diploma is required and GED is accepted.

Financial Aid

Students should submit: FAFSA. The Princeton Review suggests that all financial aid forms be submitted as soon as possible. *Need-based scholarships/grants offered:* Federal Pell; Federal SEOG; State scholarships/grants; Private scholarships; College/university scholarship or grant aid from institutional funds. *Loan aid offered:* Federal Direct Subsidized Loans; Federal Direct Unsubsidized Loans; Direct PLUS loans. Federal Work-Study Program available. Institutional employment available.

The Inside Word

Drew takes a holistic approach to evaluating applications, so you definitely want to showcase more than just your GPA (though that's also important). Drew's applicant pool has grown significantly in recent years, so presenting yourself as not only a great student but also a great fit with the school will help you stand out from the pack.

THE SCHOOL SAYS

From the Admissions Office

"Drew is so much more than a place to earn your degree. It's where you'll meet some of your closest friends. Get connected to life-changing mentors. Gain real-world experiences in our guaranteed immersive experiences like internships, community engagement, and high-level research. Everything we do is designed to prepare you for a lifetime of success.

"Drew's beautiful and vibrant campus in Madison, New Jersey—less than an hour from New York City—offers the comforts of small-town living in The Forest, the thrill of big city adventure, and easy access to transformative academic, social, and career-related experiences on campus and beyond.

"You'll choose from 60+ programs, including options to graduate in 3 years or complete an accelerated graduate program in just 5 years. And, you can take advantage of one of our seven New York City semesters on Wall Street, at the United Nations, or with grassroots organizers, media giants, or the theatre and art scenes.

"Drew is all about big experiences and bold futures. With 90+ clubs and organizations, 26 NCAA Division III athletic teams, and a thriving performing arts scene, Drew Rangers are never bored.

"This is where you'll find your purpose. make your plan, and propel yourself into a brilliant future."

SELECTIVITY

# of total applicants	5,021
% of total applicants accepted	68
% of total acceptees attending	11
# of in-state applicants	3,256
% of in-state applicants accepted	71
# of out-of-state-applicants	1,194
% of applicants accepted from out of state	73
# of international applicants	572
% of international applicants accepted	39
# offered a place on the wait list	129
# admitted from wait list	4

First-Year Profile

Testing policy	Test Optional
Range SAT composite	1120–1220
Range SAT EBRW	570–690
Range SAT math	530–650
Range ACT composite	24–30
% submitting SAT scores	23
% submitting ACT scores	2
Average HS GPA	3.5
% submitting high school GPA	86
% graduated top 10% of class	26
% graduated top 25% of class	57
% graduated top 50% of class	82
% submitting high school rank	25

Important Dates

Early decision	
Apply by	11/1
Notified by	12/15
Other ED apply by	1/15
Other ED notified by	1/31
Early action	
Apply by	12/1
Notified by	1/15
Regular	
Apply by	2/1
Notified by	3/6
Nonfall registration?	Yes

FINANCIAL FACTS

Annual tuition	$45,950
Food and housing	$17,640
Required fees	$1,150
Books and supplies	$2,035
% students rec. any financial aid (First-year)	97 (98)

DREXEL UNIVERSITY

3141 Chestnut Street, Philadelphia, PA 19104 • Admissions: 215-895-2400

Survey Snapshot
Career services are great
Internships are widely available
Students love Philadelphia, PA

RATINGS

Quality of Life	80
Fire Safety	60*
Green	91
Academic	80
Profs Interesting	82
Profs Accessible	85
Admissions	88
Financial Aid	87

CAMPUS LIFE

Type of school	Private
Environment	Metropolis

Students

Degree-seeking undergrad enrollment	12,287
% male/female/not reported	51/47/2
% from out of state	42
% First-year live on campus	75
% Ugrads live on campus	16
# of fraternities (% join)	20 (12)
# of sororities (% join)	11 (8)
% Asian	26
% Black or African American	10
% Hispanic	9
% Native American	<1
% Pacific Islander	<1
% Race and/or ethnicity unknown	2
% Two or more races	5
% White	38
% International	9
# of countries represented	115

CAMPUS MENTAL HEALTH SERVICES

Offers mental health/wellness program	Yes
Mental health training available to students	Yes
Employs Chief Wellness Officer	Yes
Peer-to-peer mental health offerings	Yes
Counseling center has guidelines or accreditation	Yes
Mental health/well-being courses	Yes, for-credit

ACADEMICS

% students returning for sophomore year	89
% students graduating within 6 years	78
Calendar	Quarter
Student/faculty ratio	9:1
Most common class size 10–19.	(36%)

Most Popular Majors

Business/Commerce; Registered Nursing/Registered Nurse; Mechanical Engineering

Applicants Also Look At

American University, Boston University, Case Western Reserve University, The College of New Jersey, Fordham University, Hofstra University, Lehigh University, New York University, Penn State University Park, Purdue University—Northwest, Rensselaer Polytechnic Institute, Rochester Institute of Technology, Saint Joseph's University (PA), St. John's University (NY), Syracuse University, Temple University, University of Connecticut, University of Delaware, University of Massachusetts—Amherst, University of Pittsburgh—Pittsburgh Campus, Villanova University, West Chester University of Pennsylvania

STUDENTS SAY "..."

Academics

Thanks to Drexel University's combination of a quarterly schedule and a built-in cooperative education plan, West Philadelphia is the place to be for "self-motivated, hard-working students," especially those with an interest in the sciences. Depending on whether students are on a four-year or five-year plan, students spend their first one or two years absorbed in major-oriented classes, and then immediately get "a hands-on look at what [they] can do with [their] degree as they alternate six months in school and six months at full-time employment. Students take pride knowing that "our work makes an impact in real companies" and one student on the five-year plan notes that you "can't beat 21 months' worth of full-time experiences."

Students acknowledge that this program is "very different compared to the normal college experience," as it is "a lot more challenging [and with] a lot less downtime." The quarter system may be new to some students but can "make the year go by faster." As one quarter system fan says, "I was skeptical at first, but it was worth it." Students mention that their "extremely intelligent" professors are "resourceful and ready to help solve a problem or redirect to someone who can." They also credit the staff, a good number of whom are Drexel alumni and who work in the industry they're teaching about, as being "beyond knowledgeable on [their] subject." Come here, suggest students, for "a rigorous, great education that almost guarantees a job or place in grad school."

Campus Life

Drexel University's urban, 74-acre campus brings "all the comforts of being on a college campus (security, familiarity)" along with "all the conveniences and exciting things about city life in your backyard." Center City is packed with history, culture, and entertainment, so whether you want to visit the Philadelphia Orchestra or hang at "a variety of clubs, theaters, and bars," it's within walking distance. (A short subway ride is also an option.) For those who feel the school's academic rigor means "there is never a time where students aren't hitting the library or studying with friends," the campus features multiple open areas to gather. While students tend to prioritize studying, they also make time for working out or playing intramural sports to let off some steam. There are various dining options available on campus and "Food Truck Alley" is a particularly popular and convenient place to sample a wide range of cuisines. Whatever you need, suggest students, you can find at Drexel.

Student Body

Drexel University is filled with "lots of colorful and unique characters on campus," most of whom are highly motivated individuals who "consistently challenge themselves and are willing to push themselves so that they can tap their full potential," often with the motivation of "looking for a good job." This focus can sometimes lead the community to feel "cliquey," but students note that the suite-style housing on campus "really helps with making friends." That goes a long way given a curriculum that can be "very stressful," with students often "in a state of caffeination or exhaustion (or both)." Students also note that the rigorous workload promotes a community atmosphere where they "rely on one another to ensure they understand and complete the tasks that are assigned."

DREXEL UNIVERSITY

Financial Aid: 215-895-2537 • E-Mail: enroll@drexel.edu • Website: www.drexel.edu

THE PRINCETON REVIEW SAYS

Admissions

The school reports that its standardized testing policy for use in admission for Fall 2026 is Test Optional. The Princeton Review suggests that interested applicants consult with the school for the most up-to-date standardized testing policies. *Very important factors considered include:* rigor of secondary school record, class rank, academic GPA, standardized test scores. *Important factors considered include:* application essay, recommendation(s), character/personal qualities. *Other factors considered include:* interview, extracurricular activities, talent/ability, first generation, alumni/ae relation, volunteer work, work experience, level of applicant's interest. High school diploma is required and GED is accepted. *Academic units required:* 3 math, 1 science, 1 science lab. *Academic units recommended:* 1 language (other than English).

Financial Aid

Students should submit: FAFSA; CSS PROFILE. Priority filing deadline is 2/1. The Princeton Review suggests that all financial aid forms be submitted as soon as possible. *Need-based scholarships/grants offered:* College/university scholarship or grant aid from institutional funds; Private scholarships; State scholarships/grants; Federal SEOG; Federal Pell. *Loan aid offered:* Federal Direct Subsidized Loans; Federal Direct Unsubsidized Loans; Direct PLUS loans; State Loans. Admitted students will be notified of awards on or about 4/1. Federal Work-Study Program available. Institutional employment available.

The Inside Word

Drexel University's nationally recognized co-op program provides unique hands-on experience for students with companies in and around Philadelphia to help them in their post-college employment. That's a huge draw for prospective applicants, especially in the engineering fields that Drexel still specializes in. Drexel accepts the Common Application for most programs, and takes into consideration a number of criteria when determining admission, including high school performance, letters of recommendation, standardized test scores (if submitted), and the essay.

THE SCHOOL SAYS

From the Admissions Office

"Drexel University has maintained a reputation for academic excellence since its founding in 1891. Through Drexel Co-op, students have the opportunity to test-drive their degree in paid full-time positions where they can earn up to 18 months of workplace experience before graduation with employers such as Fortune 500 companies, major pharmaceutical companies, and top design firms, as well as nonprofit agencies and government organizations. More than 1,600 employers in thirty-two states and forty-six international locations participate in the Drexel Co-op program. The average six-month paid co-op salary is more than $16,000.

"Drexel offers more than 80 undergraduate majors and over twenty accelerated degree programs. Accelerated degree options include the BA/BS/JD in law; BA/BS+MD in medicine; BS/DPT in physical therapy; BS/MS in computing and informatics; and BS/MBA in business.

"Qualified students can apply to the Honors program, which is open to students in every academic discipline. The Honors program offers special living communities designed for the exceptional student and opportunities for social activities, traveling, and independent projects. The STAR (Students Tackling Advanced Research) Scholars program invites qualified students to participate in faculty-mentored research projects in their chosen fields as early as the freshman year. Drexel also has an active Study Abroad program in more than two dozen countries around the world."

SELECTIVITY

# of total applicants	38,030
% of total applicants accepted	70
% of total acceptees attending	7
# of in-state applicants	10,005
% of in-state applicants accepted	69
# of out-of-state-applicants	19,173
% of applicants accepted from out of state	76
# of international applicants	8,852
% of international applicants accepted	57
# of early decision applicants	299
% of early decision applicants accepted	78

First-Year Profile

Testing policy	Test Optional
Range SAT composite	1260–1430
Range SAT EBRW	630–710
Range SAT math	630–730
Range ACT composite	28–33
% submitting SAT scores	35
% submitting ACT scores	4
Average HS GPA	3.8
% submitting high school GPA	94
% graduated top 10% of class	32
% graduated top 25% of class	63
% graduated top 50% of class	89
% submitting high school rank	27

Important Dates

Early decision	
Apply by	11/15
Notified by	12/15
Early action	
Apply by	11/15
Notified by	12/15
Regular	
Apply by	1/15
Notified by	4/1
Nonfall registration?	Yes

FINANCIAL FACTS

Annual tuition	$63,078
Food and housing	$19,398
Required fees	$2,370
Books and supplies	$1,200
Average need-based scholarship (First-year)	$35,138 ($42,870)
% students with need rec. need-based scholarship or grant aid (First-year)	98 (100)
% students with need rec. non-need-based scholarship or grant aid (First-year)	13 (21)
% students with need rec. need-based self-help aid (First-year)	66 (55)
% students rec. any financial aid (First-year)	94 (100)
% of students with need fully met (First-year)	21 (32)
Average % of student need met (First-year)	71 (82)

DRURY UNIVERSITY

900 North Benton Avenue, Springfield, MO 65802-3712 • Admissions: 417-873-7205

Survey Snapshot
Students are happy
Internships are widely available
Diverse student types interact on campus

RATINGS	
Quality of Life	88
Fire Safety	81
Green	60*
Academic	85
Profs Interesting	93
Profs Accessible	95
Admissions	88
Financial Aid	89

CAMPUS LIFE

Type of school	Private
Affiliation	UCC and Christian Church (Disciples of Christ)
Environment	Metropolis

Students

Degree-seeking undergrad enrollment	1,382
% male/female/not reported	49/51/0
% from out of state	31
% First-year live on campus	77
% Ugrads live on campus	67
# of fraternities (% join)	4 (16)
# of sororities (% join)	4 (17)
% Asian	2
% Black or African American	3
% Hispanic	4
% Native American	1
% Pacific Islander	0
% Race and/or ethnicity unknown	4
% Two or more races	4
% White	71
% International	9
# of countries represented	49

CAMPUS MENTAL HEALTH SERVICES

Offers mental health/wellness program	Yes
Mental health training available to students	Yes
Employs Chief Wellness Officer	No
Peer-to-peer mental health offerings	No
Counseling center has guidelines or accreditation	No
Mental health/well-being courses	No

ACADEMICS

% students returning for sophomore year	76
% students graduating within 4 years	44
% students graduating within 6 years	62
Calendar	Semester
Student/faculty ratio	14:1
Most common class size 10–19.	(38%)
Most common lab/discussion size 10–19.	(54%)

Most Popular Majors

Architectural and Building Sciences/Technology; Biology/Biological Sciences; Psychology

Applicants Also Look At

Creighton University, Hendrix College, Missouri State University, Truman State University, University of Missouri, The University of Tulsa

STUDENTS SAY "..."

Academics

Students at Drury University praise the school for its personalized and well-rounded educational experience. There are numerous opportunities to shape your academic path in this "welcoming and unique" environment. The school's curriculum, known as Drury Fusion, allows students to pursue their passions by combining coursework with hands-on experiences, such as service learning or internships. In addition to their major, students must choose at least one certificate to specialize in, with options ranging from Graphic Storytelling and Arts Administration to Ethical Leadership and Cybersecurity Fundamentals. All Drury students also have the opportunity to study abroad, and it is a degree requirement for students in the architecture and business schools. Students appreciate that the faculty "want to see you succeed." As one enrollee explains, professors "take an interest in their students and desire to see them achieve both inside the classroom and in the real world." For example, one student shares, "I've never had a professor nor heard of a professor turning down an independent study with a student." Professors here "expect the best out of you" and provide an education that's both "useful and valuable." The small classes "allow your professors to get to know you as an individual," and they appreciate that their instructors offer guidance with "career plans and paths, as well as provide mentorship" to their students.

Campus Life

At this "very social" school, students enjoy "friendly gatherings and discussions" around campus, especially "during the Fall semester," and casual hangouts in the dorms like movie nights and board game nights. Many students participate in intramural sports or are student- athletes. Overall, "athletics are pretty big" here, with some adding that Greek life is "also very fun." Drury "encourages students to be involved in the community" and has weekly opportunities to volunteer, including "at the local juvenile probation office, humane society, and elementary schools." There are numerous clubs available, and students tend to be involved "in at least one organization on campus." There are also campus-wide events hosted by the Student Union Board, such as Fall Fest, Homecoming, and Spring Fling. Students often venture off campus to explore Springfield, which has "so much to see and do," including movie theaters, a mall, restaurants, coffee shops, and music venues. Springfield also hosts cultural events like the First Friday Art Walk, where "various galleries (including Drury-owned and student-run ones) host different art shows all around town.... It's really an amazing night out on the town exploring different art and city life." Whether on or off-campus, hanging with the community, or checking things out solo, the consensus is that you will "have free time to pursue whatever it is that will fill your needs" and that you can find it at Drury.

Student Body

Students here are "inviting and willing to always let someone join in on the fun." As one student says, "I never imagined a college campus could feel so supportive and connected until I came to Drury." Classmates have "a lot of school spirit" and "are so nice and welcoming." There isn't "only a single type of person on campus;" instead, there's a "community for everyone, whether they are musicians, writers, athletes, artists, gamers, or anything in between." A common bond among students is "a strong desire to learn." Classmates here are "bright and ambitious" and "very studious." As one student describes, "It is a small campus with hardworking people." At the same time, this focused student body is "very personal and outgoing." The school's relatively small size creates "so much room for building friendships" and makes it possible to have "friends from across all the disciplines." As one student says, "You get to know everyone at such a personal level; it makes the school feel like a true community."

Drury University

Financial Aid: 417-873-7312 • E-Mail: druryad@drury.edu • Website: www.drury.edu

THE PRINCETON REVIEW SAYS

Admissions

The school reports that its standardized testing policy for use in admission for Fall 2026 is Test Optional. The Princeton Review suggests that interested applicants consult with the school for the most up-to-date standardized testing policies. *Very important factors considered include:* rigor of secondary school record, academic GPA. *Important factors considered include:* application essay. *Other factors considered include:* class rank, standardized test scores, recommendation(s), interview, extracurricular activities, talent/ability, character/personal qualities, first generation, alumni/ae relation, volunteer work, work experience, level of applicant's interest. High school diploma is required and GED is accepted. *Academic units required:* 4 English, 3 math, 3 science, 2 science labs, 2 language (other than English), 4 social studies, 2 history. *Academic units recommended:* 4 English, 4 math, 4 science, 3 science labs, 3 language (other than English), 4 social studies, 2 history, 1 computer science, 1 visual/performing arts.

Financial Aid

Students should submit: FAFSA. The Princeton Review suggests that all financial aid forms be submitted as soon as possible. *Need-based scholarships/grants offered:* Federal Pell; Federal SEOG; State scholarships/grants; Private scholarships; College/university scholarship or grant aid from institutional funds. *Loan aid offered:* Federal Direct Subsidized Loans; Federal Direct Unsubsidized Loans; Direct PLUS loans. Admitted students will be notified of awards on a rolling basis beginning 9/15. Federal Work-Study Program available. Institutional employment available.

The Inside Word

The admissions process at Drury is fairly selective. Admissions officers look for applicants who have taken a challenging college prep curriculum. They also closely evaluate personal statements and each student's extracurricular participation. Finally, Drury operates on a basis of rolling admission. If you're really interested in attending, consider submitting your application as early as possible.

THE SCHOOL SAYS

From the Admissions Office

"From day one, Drury students are engaged in real research and scholarship with faculty mentors. This is a rare advantage; one that speaks to Drury's singular approach to equipping students for leadership in the 21st century. Through its distinctive Your Drury Fusion program, the University provides students with an opportunity to blend career, calling, life, community, self and service to gain a broader perspective on the world. It also is a place where students get to really know their professors as well as their classmates, creating a strong sense of culture and community that transcends the classroom.

"Established in 1873, Drury University sits on 90 acres in the heart of Springfield, Missouri. A designated "Tree Campus" by the Arbor Day Foundation, it is an oasis within the city where students are engaged in highly interactive, intellectual exercises that teach them to be flexible, innovative and creative problem solvers.

"The university offers all of the majors you would expect from a top liberal arts university plus majors like architecture, music therapy, software engineering, computer game design and a pre-med program with five pre-acceptance partner medical schools.

"Your Drury Fusion provides all students multiple credentials, holistic advising which combines academic and career planning from day 1, and a minimum of three experiential projects over your four-year career. The Drury Difference leads to 97% of graduates employed or in professional or graduate school within six months of graduation."

SELECTIVITY

# of total applicants	2,659
% of total applicants accepted	58
% of total acceptees attending	22

First-Year Profile

Testing policy	Test Optional
Range SAT composite	1140–1210
Range SAT EBRW	570–670
Range SAT math	560–620
Range ACT composite	22–29
% submitting SAT scores	7
% submitting ACT scores	58
Average HS GPA	3.8
% submitting high school GPA	100
% graduated top 10% of class	28
% graduated top 25% of class	57
% graduated top 50% of class	88
% submitting high school rank	44

Important Dates

Regular	
Apply by	8/15
Notified by	Rolling, 9/1
Nonfall registration?	Yes

FINANCIAL FACTS

Annual tuition	$35,400
Food and housing	$11,690
Required fees	$1,555
Books and supplies	$1,250
Average need-based scholarship (First-year)	$26,701 ($27,066)
% students with need rec. need-based scholarship or grant aid (First-year)	100 (100)
% students with need rec. non-need-based scholarship or grant aid (First-year)	21 (21)
% students with need rec. need-based self-help aid (First-year)	62 (64)
% students rec. any financial aid (First-year)	98 (100)
% UG borrow to pay for school	63
Average cumulative indebtedness	$36,053
% of students with need fully met (First-year)	24 (24)
Average % of student need met (First-year)	76 (77)

Duke University

Chapel Drive, Durham, NC 27708 • Admissions: 919-684-3214

Survey Snapshot
Great library
Recreation facilities are great
Everyone loves the Blue Devils

RATINGS

Quality of Life	70
Fire Safety	60*
Green	60*
Academic	88
Profs Interesting	81
Profs Accessible	85
Admissions	99
Financial Aid	96

CAMPUS LIFE

Type of school	Private
Affiliation	Methodist
Environment	Metropolis

Students

Degree-seeking undergrad enrollment	6,442
% male/female/not reported	46/54/0
% from out of state	85
% First-year from public high school	65
% First-year live on campus	100
% Ugrads live on campus	84
# of fraternities (% join)	21 (30)
# of sororities (% join)	14 (42)
% Asian	22
% Black or African American	9
% Hispanic	11
% Native American	<1
% Pacific Islander	<1
% Race and/or ethnicity unknown	5
% Two or more races	7
% White	35
% International	11
# of countries represented	89

CAMPUS MENTAL HEALTH SERVICES

Offers mental health/wellness program	Yes
Mental health training available to students	No
Employs Chief Wellness Officer	NR
Peer-to-peer mental health offerings	NR
Counseling center has guidelines or accreditation	No
Mental health/well-being courses	NR

ACADEMICS

% students returning for sophomore year	98
% students graduating within 4 years	87
% students graduating within 6 years	97
Calendar	Semester
Student/faculty ratio	5:1
Most common class size 10–19.	(42%)
Most common lab/discussion size 10–19.	(49%)

Most Popular Majors
Public Policy Analysis; Economics; Psychology

STUDENTS SAY "..."

Academics

Duke University is a prestigious institution known for "academic excellence, complemented by highly competitive Division I sports and an enriching array of extracurricular activities." These things make it "an exciting, challenging, and enjoyable place to be." Duke takes pride in its "across-the-board excellence in all departments from humanities to engineering" and its "supportive environment in which the faculty, staff, and students are willing to look out for the other person and help them succeed." Students love that "the school has a lot of confidence in its students" and offers them "seemingly limitless opportunities" for personal and academic growth. As one student explains, "Duke is for the Ivy League candidate who is a little bit more laid-back about school and overachieving (but just a bit)." Classes at Duke are challenging, but "the review sessions, peer tutoring system, writing center, and academic support center are always helpful when students are struggling with anything from math homework to creating a résumé." Students say that Duke professors are likewise supportive and that their "number-one priority is teaching undergraduates." Professors foster independence and critical thinking by encouraging "students [to] lead the class as opposed to them leading the class." Professors are highly regarded, with one student remarking, "There are a few who make me want to stay at Duke forever." Overall, Duke University is an excellent choice for students who "are passionate about a wide range of things, including academics, sports, community service, research, and fun."

Campus Life

According to enrollees, the priority is "getting a ton of work done first," but after that, there's plenty of stuff to spend your time on. In fact, one student notes that "you can be so over-committed that it's not even funny." For one, "the student union and other organizations provide entertainment all the time, from movies to shows to campus-wide parties." School spirit for national award-winning Blue Devils sports, "especially basketball, are a huge deal here," and dedicated fans, known as the Cameron Crazies, "will paint themselves completely blue and wait in line on the sidewalk in K-Ville for three days." Greek life also "plays a big role in the social scene here," and "almost all the parties are open, so it definitely isn't hard to get into a party." There is "a wealth of fun opportunities within walking distance from campus" in Durham, and students say they "go out two to three times a week" to socialize and unwind.

Student Body

A typical Duke student is often described as "someone who cares a lot about his or her education but at the same time won't sacrifice a social life for it." However, many students stress that the workload at Duke is intense, and students are "incredibly focused" on their studies. The student body is known for its school spirit and numerous student-athletes, "not just varsity athletes...but athletes in high school or generally active people. Duke's athletic pride attracts this kind of person." Whether or not you are interested in athletics, "every type of person finds a welcoming group where he or she fits in."

DUKE UNIVERSITY

E-Mail: undergrad-admissions@duke.edu • Website: www.duke.edu

THE PRINCETON REVIEW SAYS

Admissions

The school reports that its standardized testing policy for use in admission for Fall 2026 is Test Optional. The Princeton Review suggests that interested applicants consult with the school for the most up-to-date standardized testing policies. *Very important factors considered include:* rigor of secondary school record, academic GPA, recommendation(s), extracurricular activities, talent/ability, character/personal qualities. *Important factors considered include:* class rank. *Other factors considered include:* standardized test scores, application essay, interview, first generation, alumni/ae relation, geographical residence, state residency, volunteer work, work experience, level of applicant's interest. High school diploma is required and GED is accepted. *Academic units recommended:* 4 English, 3 math, 3 science, 3 language (other than English), 3 social studies.

Financial Aid

Students should submit: FAFSA; CSS PROFILE; Business/Farm Supplement. The Princeton Review suggests that all financial aid forms be submitted as soon as possible. *Need-based scholarships/grants offered:* Federal Pell; Federal SEOG; State scholarships/grants; Private scholarships; College/university scholarship or grant aid from institutional funds; United Negro College Fund. *Loan aid offered:* Federal Direct Subsidized Loans; Federal Direct Unsubsidized Loans; Direct PLUS loans; College/university loans from institutional funds. Admitted students will be notified of awards on or about 4/1. Federal Work-Study Program available. Institutional employment available.

The Inside Word

Duke is an extremely selective undergraduate institution, which affords the school the luxury of rejecting many qualified applicants. You'll need to present an exceptional record just to be considered; to make yourself stand out from the crowd, you should demonstrate to the admissions office that you can contribute something unique and valuable to the incoming class. Being one of the best basketball players in the nation (male or female) helps a lot, but even athletes have to show academic excellence to get in the door here.

THE SCHOOL SAYS

From the Admissions Office

"Duke University offers a blend of tradition and innovation, undergraduate college and major research university, academic excellence and athletic achievement, and global presence and regional charm. Students come to Duke from all over the United States and the world and from a range of racial, ethnic, and socioeconomic backgrounds. They enjoy contact with a world-class faculty through small classes and independent study. More than forty majors are available in the arts and sciences and engineering; arts and sciences students may also design their own curriculum through Program II. Certificate programs are available in a number of interdisciplinary areas. Special academic opportunities include the Focus Program and seminars for first-year students DukeImmerse, study abroad, domestic study away programs in New York, Los Angeles, Washington, DC, Chicago, Silicon Valley, and Alaska, Bass Connections research programs, and DukeEngage summer service opportunities. While admission to Duke is highly selective, applications of U.S. citizens, permanent residents, and undocumented students are evaluated without regard to financial need and the university pledges to meet 100 percent of the demonstrated need of all admitted U.S. students and permanent residents. A limited amount of financial aid is also available for foreign citizens, and the university will meet the full demonstrated financial need for those admitted students as well."

SELECTIVITY

# of total applicants	51,795
% of total applicants accepted	6
% of total acceptees attending	59
# of early decision applicants	6,013
% of early decision applicants accepted	17

First-Year Profile

Testing policy	Test Optional
Range SAT EBRW	740–770
Range SAT math	760–800
Range ACT composite	34–35
% submitting SAT scores	48
% submitting ACT scores	30
% graduated top 10% of class	92
% graduated top 25% of class	98
% graduated top 50% of class	99
% submitting high school rank	25

Important Dates

Early decision	
Apply by	11/1
Notified by	12/15
Regular	
Apply by	1/2
Notified by	4/1
Nonfall registration?	No

FINANCIAL FACTS

Annual tuition	$70,265
Food and housing	$19,247
Required fees (First-year)	$2,530 ($2,907)
Books and supplies	$536
Average need-based scholarship (First-year)	$67,217 ($70,439)
% students with need rec. need-based scholarship or grant aid (First-year)	100 (99)
% students with need rec. non-need-based scholarship or grant aid (First-year)	10 (12)
% students with need rec. need-based self-help aid (First-year)	77 (72)
% UG borrow to pay for school	25
Average cumulative indebtedness	$27,515
% of students with need fully met (First-year)	92 (95)
Average % of student need met (First-year)	100 (100)

DUQUESNE UNIVERSITY

600 Forbes Avenue, Pittsburgh, PA 15282-0201 • Admissions: 412-396-6222

Survey Snapshot
Lots of conservative students
Students love Pittsburgh, PA
Frats and sororities are popular

RATINGS

Quality of Life	**82**
Fire Safety	**99**
Green	**90**
Academic	**78**
Profs Interesting	**85**
Profs Accessible	**88**
Admissions	**85**
Financial Aid	**86**

CAMPUS LIFE

Type of school	Private
Affiliation	Roman Catholic
Environment	Metropolis

Students

Degree-seeking undergrad enrollment	5,368
% male/female/not reported	38/62/0
% from out of state	25
% First-year from public high school	76
% First-year live on campus	89
% Ugrads live on campus	53
# of fraternities (% join)	9 (15)
# of sororities (% join)	11 (21)
% Asian	3
% Black or African American	6
% Hispanic	6
% Native American	<1
% Pacific Islander	<1
% Race and/or ethnicity unknown	1
% Two or more races	4
% White	77
% International	3
# of countries represented	65

CAMPUS MENTAL HEALTH SERVICES

Offers mental health/wellness program	Yes
Mental health training available to students	Yes
Employs Chief Wellness Officer	Yes
Peer-to-peer mental health offerings	Yes
Counseling center has guidelines or accreditation	Yes
Mental health/well-being courses	Yes, for-credit

ACADEMICS

% students returning for sophomore year	85
% students graduating within 4 years	68
% students graduating within 6 years	75
Calendar	Semester
Student/faculty ratio	13:1
Most common class size 10–19.	(30%)
Most common lab/discussion size 20–29.	(38%)

Most Popular Majors

Biology/Biological Sciences; Nursing Science; Finance

Applicants Often Prefer

Penn State University Park, Robert Morris University, University of Pittsburgh—Pittsburgh Campus, West Chester University of Pennsylvania, West Virginia University

Applicants Sometimes Prefer

Indiana University of Pennsylvania, Kent State University— Kent Campus, The Ohio State University—Columbus, Slippery Rock University of Pennsylvania, State University of New York—University at Buffalo, Temple University, University of Delaware

STUDENTS SAY "..."

Academics

Students describe their time at Duquesne University as "beyond satisfying.... I was able to discover new subjects that I love learning about and tailor my academic experience to those interests." In particular, students laud the nursing, education, business, and biomedical engineering fields. On the medical side, the "informative" and "hands-on" clinicals and lab simulation opportunities are seen as some of the campus' best and most "one-of-a-kind" academic features. Across the board, students highlight frequently updated technology and a variety of classroom types as benefits, such as the experience-based style: "We have to do whatever we are learning, and it vastly improves my learning." Enrollees also cite "a good number of guest speakers and experts," all of which "breaks up the heavy lectures."

Professors are passionate about what they teach and "want to see their students succeed in everything that they do later in life." They're described as being "always willing to meet," and are good for "possible research experience or anything that the student may need." Along those lines, they also practice a range of teaching methods, which some undergrads suggest offers "new ways [of] engaging us, involving us..., and treating us like adults." Another benefit comes in the small, focused class sizes "in which students can discuss specific topics in depth" and also have "better relationships with professors and classmates." For those looking to get out of the classroom, Duquesne's outdoor classes and study-abroad opportunities are much appreciated.

Campus Life

Either at Duquesne University itself, or from its bustling location in downtown Pittsburgh, "there is nearly always something to do," and students praise its "incredible night life." Most on-campus activities are "cost-free to students," which is a plus, and there are nearly 300 clubs and a thriving Greek Life system to choose from. "There are more than enough active and very involved clubs to keep one engaged for the entire day, every day of the week." Sports are also a healthy part of campus life, including organized team activities as well as "exercise classes that Duquesne offers for free to all students such as spin class [and] yoga." Pittsburgh itself has plenty to offer, especially if you're into sports; the stadium for the National Hockey League's Penguins is "a 45-second walk from campus and the tickets are discounted for students; this is my favorite thing to do for fun."

Student Body

Duquesne has a long history as a private Catholic research university, but while those traditions remain a part of the school, students emphasize that "this campus is a place for anyone" where "there are people of all religions and walks of life." Spirited discussions in "the welcoming nature of the Duquesne classroom" recognize that those "from different political, social, and financial backgrounds have unique experiences" and make for a more enriched learning experience: "Students enjoy sharing in class, and I love learning from them. My classes have been very supportive environments." Overall, attendees see themselves and their peers united as "dedicated individuals who wish to pursue careers after college while also trying to maintain a fun, involved environment at the school."

Duquesne University

Financial Aid: 412-396-6607 • E-Mail: admissions@duq.edu • Website: www.duq.edu

THE PRINCETON REVIEW SAYS

Admissions

The school reports that its standardized testing policy for use in admission for Fall 2026 is Test Optional. The Princeton Review suggests that interested applicants consult with the school for the most up-to-date standardized testing policies. *Very important factors considered include:* rigor of secondary school record, academic GPA, standardized test scores. *Important factors considered include:* class rank, extracurricular activities, talent/ability, character/personal qualities, volunteer work, work experience. *Other factors considered include:* application essay, recommendation(s), interview, first generation, alumni/ae relation, geographical residence, state residency, religious affiliation/commitment, level of applicant's interest. High school diploma is required and GED is accepted. *Academic units required:* 4 English, 2 math, 2 science, 2 language (other than English), 2 social studies, 4 academic electives.

Financial Aid

Students should submit: FAFSA; CSS PROFILE; Non Custodial Parent Profile. Priority filing deadline is 3/15. The Princeton Review suggests that all financial aid forms be submitted as soon as possible. *Need-based scholarships/grants offered:* Federal Pell; Federal SEOG; State scholarships/grants; Private scholarships; College/university scholarship or grant aid from institutional funds. *Loan aid offered:* Federal Direct Subsidized Loans; Federal Direct Unsubsidized Loans; Direct PLUS loans; Federal Nursing Loans; College/university loans from institutional funds. Admitted students will be notified of awards on a rolling basis beginning 11/1. Federal Work-Study Program available.

The Inside Word

Duquesne encourages you to submit SAT, ACT, or CLT scores, but if your scores don't reflect your abilities, you can apply test optional. A minimum 3.0 GPA is generally recommended for test-optional applicants. AP, IB, and CLEP exam scores may also be submitted to support your application and for college credit consideration.

THE SCHOOL SAYS

From the Admissions Office

"Duquesne's admissions team is excited to support your college search! Schedule a visit today to learn why students love Duquesne's secure, park-like campus next to downtown Pittsburgh with convenient access to the Cultural District, pro sports, entertainment, dining and parks.

"A *2026 Best Value University*, at Duquesne you'll gain the professional confidence, impressive experience and powerful networks to get a running start on a meaningful career or graduate school. When you apply, you're automatically considered for scholarships up to full tuition, based on your accomplishments. Choose from 85+ future-focused majors in business, education, engineering, health sciences, liberal arts, music, nursing, pharmacy and science, Discover/undecided, and direct entry/early assurance programs in medical and health professional programs. Optional opportunities include: Honors College, pre-med/pre-health, pre-law, 3+3 law program and 35+ study abroad programs.

"You'll develop friendships that last a lifetime, learning with students of diverse cultural, socioeconomic and religious backgrounds from every state and more than 85 countries. With an average student-faculty ratio of 13:1, your professors will walk alongside you to help reach your boldest goals. Duquesne's Pittsburgh location provides invaluable access to community engagement and hands-on experience through fieldwork, research projects and internships at corporations, health care systems, schools and other organizations.

"Choose from 300 student organizations, including academic, Greek, service, social, spiritual, sports and recreation. Duquesne has 19 NCAA Division I athletics teams plus club and intramural sports. Drawing on our 150-year Catholic Spiritan heritage, we'll help you discover what you're good at and why that's good for the world."

SELECTIVITY

# of total applicants	13,270
% of total applicants accepted	86
% of total acceptees attending	12
# of in-state applicants	7,381
% of in-state applicants accepted	90
# of out-of-state-applicants	4,752
% of applicants accepted from out of state	90
# of international applicants	1,117
% of international applicants accepted	45
# offered a place on the wait list	435
# admitted from wait list	77

First-Year Profile

Testing policy	Test Optional
Range SAT composite	1130–1330
Range SAT EBRW	580–680
Range SAT math	550–670
Range ACT composite	25–30
% submitting SAT scores	14
% submitting ACT scores	3
Average HS GPA	3.8
% submitting high school GPA	99
% graduated top 10% of class	28
% graduated top 25% of class	56
% graduated top 50% of class	83
% submitting high school rank	39

Important Dates

Early action	
Apply by	11/15
Notified by	12/15
Regular	
Apply by	8/28
Notified by	Rolling, 9/1
Nonfall registration?	Yes

FINANCIAL FACTS*

Annual tuition	$51,068
Food and housing	$17,070
Books and supplies	$1,440
Average need-based scholarship (First-year)	$28,661 ($33,963)
% students with need rec. need-based scholarship or grant aid (First-year)	100 (100)
% students with need rec. non-need-based scholarship or grant aid (First-year)	99 (100)
% students with need rec. need-based self-help aid (First-year)	63 (72)
% students rec. any financial aid (First-year)	98 (100)
% UG borrow to pay for school	72
Average cumulative indebtedness	$57,681
% of students with need fully met (First-year)	15 (19)
Average % of student need met (First-year)	70 (73)

* Most recently reported data at time of printing. Scan the QR code to find the latest updates.

EARLHAM COLLEGE

801 National Road West, Richmond, IN 47374 • Admissions: 765-983-1600

Survey Snapshot
Active minority support groups
Great library
Internships are widely available

RATINGS	
Quality of Life	**87**
Fire Safety	**60***
Green	**85**
Academic	**89**
Profs Interesting	**96**
Profs Accessible	**97**
Admissions	**85**
Financial Aid	**93**

CAMPUS LIFE

Type of school	Private
Affiliation	Quaker
Environment	Town

Students

Degree-seeking undergrad enrollment	656
% male/female/not reported	47/53/0
% from out of state	58
% First-year from public high school	73
% First-year live on campus	90
% Ugrads live on campus	88
# of fraternities	0
# of sororities	0
% Asian	3
% Black or African American	8
% Hispanic	7
% Native American	<1
% Pacific Islander	<1
% Race and/or ethnicity unknown	1
% Two or more races	5
% White	57
% International	18
# of countries represented	59

CAMPUS MENTAL HEALTH SERVICES

Offers mental health/wellness program	Yes
Mental health training available to students	Yes
Employs Chief Wellness Officer	Yes
Peer-to-peer mental health offerings	Yes
Counseling center has guidelines or accreditation	Yes
Mental health/well-being courses	Yes, for-credit

ACADEMICS

% students returning for sophomore year	82
% students graduating within 4 years	64
% students graduating within 6 years	75
Calendar	Semester
Student/faculty ratio	7:1
Most common class size 10–19.	(42%)
Most common lab/discussion size 10–19.	(58%)

Most Popular Majors

Biology/Biological Sciences; Research and Experimental Psychology; Business

Applicants Also Look At

Ball State University, DePauw University, Indiana University—Bloomington, Purdue University—West Lafayette, St. Olaf College, Oberlin College

STUDENTS SAY "..."

Academics

A small school with Quaker roots, Earlham College offers "small class sizes [that allow] faculty to easily connect with students." This is a result of a low student-faculty ratio which means students have plenty of opportunity to "have a strong and close connection with professors." Additionally, faculty are "extremely available and willing to connect" to help their students really understand the subjects they "are passionate in teaching." Those professors are "amazing to work with," says a student. Another gushes, "They are like incredibly knowledgeable friends who have [a] strong interest in your future and helping you succeed." Overall, their courses are described as "rigorous," "interesting," and "engaging," and students also find they can "get the help [they] need" without much trouble. Students here cite the unique academic programs which include Peace and Global Studies as well as a program called Epic Journey, "which [allots] students funds to...research [or intern] in any place or country of their liking." One student sums up the academic experience at Earlham: "Each professor...has made me care about the subject of their class in a way I never would have expected—whether that's opening up a field I already love or finding ways to connect new material to the subjects that are close to me."

Campus Life

Many undergrads proudly proclaim that the "possibilities are endless" at Earlham when it comes to campus activities. Indeed, it's "a wonderful environment for passionate and self-driven students" who thrive on having "back-to-back commitments." As one enthusiastic individual explains, "I run a club, direct and act in plays, sing in the choir, go to the gym, and still take nineteen credits." It's hard to resist the many school-sponsored activities "such as concerts, bowling, movie night, [and] roller skating." Another popular activity is Dance Alloy, which is a "bi-yearly student choreographed dance performance" that many students join and "spend multiple nights a week practicing and preparing" to get just right. Moreover, "every other Friday night there is an open mic event...[where] everyone is welcome to perform." And when the weekend fully rolls around, you can "usually [find some] house parties or people just [hanging] out with their friends." Those hang-out sessions can include "talking about literature, playing cards, [or having] occasional nights of drinking and video games." And a good number simply love exploring the "large chunk of undeveloped woods behind [the] campus."

Student Body

Despite being a small school, Earlham manages to yield a "diverse population." Indeed, you can find students "from all over the world" who enrich the campus with their "interesting stories and backgrounds." Undergrads seem to mesh well as everyone treats each other "with kindness and compassion." Moreover, many students here are "concerned about social issues and justice" and a large number "seem to be inclined to left-wing policies." Or, as another undergrad puts it, "Earlham is hippies. Earlham is bare feet and climbing trees. Earlhamites are activists. They are earth lovers, peace lovers, and lovers of learning." Therefore, it's not too shocking to learn that many students also describe their peers as "collaborative and encouraging" because of the "close-knit bonds [they have] to the people around them." They "care a lot about [their] community" and "make sure everyone feels welcomed." As one undergrad concludes, "After being on campus for so long, it is easy to realize that everyone here is weird in their own ways, and the great part is that the community is very accepting and less judgmental than most other places."

EARLHAM COLLEGE

Financial Aid: 765-983-1217 • E-Mail: admissions@earlham.edu • Website: www.earlham.edu

THE PRINCETON REVIEW SAYS

Admissions

The school reports that its standardized testing policy for use in admission for Fall 2026 is Test Optional. The Princeton Review suggests that interested applicants consult with the school for the most up-to-date standardized testing policies. *Very important factors considered include:* rigor of secondary school record, academic GPA. *Important factors considered include:* application essay, extracurricular activities, character/personal qualities. *Other factors considered include:* class rank, standardized test scores, recommendation(s), interview, talent/ability, volunteer work, work experience. High school diploma is required and GED is accepted. *Academic units recommended:* 4 English, 3 math, 2 science, 2 language (other than English), 2 social studies, 2 visual/performing arts.

Financial Aid

Students should submit: FAFSA. Priority filing deadline is 4/1. The Princeton Review suggests that all financial aid forms be submitted as soon as possible. *Need-based scholarships/grants offered:* Federal Pell; Federal SEOG; State scholarships/grants; Private scholarships; College/university scholarship or grant aid from institutional funds. *Loan aid offered:* Federal Direct Subsidized Loans; Federal Direct Unsubsidized Loans; Direct PLUS loans. Admitted students will be notified of awards on a rolling basis. Federal Work-Study Program available. Institutional employment available.

The Inside Word

The admissions team at Earlham notes that they've "always taken a holistic approach in its review of students' applicants for admission." That means that interested applicants should really work on crafting an essay that represents who they are, and finding ways to showcase their academic readiness, both in and out of the classroom. Remember that while standardized tests are not required, they can be considered, so if your scores are above the average composite, you should submit them.

THE SCHOOL SAYS

From the Admissions Office

"Earlham is an academically distinguished liberal arts college that uniquely equips students for the 21st century. In addition to its programs of study, the College emphasizes hands-on and collaborative learning through the Epic Advantage, a central feature of the Earlham experience. Thanks to a generous gift from an alumnus, the College funds high-impact, immersive experiences like internships and student-faculty research for all students, making these experiences possible to students regardless of family income. These powerful experiences take place across the United States and the world. The result is transformative and leads to compelling opportunities for graduates. Earlham ranks among the top percent of all colleges for graduates who earn a PhD, and acceptance rates to medical, law, and other professional schools are exceptionally high. Earlham has recently invested more than $60 million in academic facilities, and its professors are known for both their scholarship and innovative teaching. Earlham is renowned as a distinctively welcoming community, embracing both individual and cultural differences. Shaped by Quaker perspectives, Earlham prepares its students to be catalysts for good in a changing world. Earlham enrolls students from almost all fifty states and sixty nations. Students compete in seventeen intercollegiate sports and in an equestrian program. The College's diverse and multi-talented student body brings positive energy to campus life, community service, and a drive to make a difference."

SELECTIVITY

# of total applicants	2,128
% of total applicants accepted	79
% of total acceptees attending	10
# of in-state applicants	556
% of in-state applicants accepted	96
# of out-of-state-applicants	925
% of applicants accepted from out of state	96
# of international applicants	647
% of international applicants accepted	40
# of early decision applicants	1,036
% of early decision applicants accepted	84
# offered a place on the wait list	0

First-Year Profile

Testing policy	Test Optional
Range SAT composite	1080–1270
Range SAT EBRW	550–700
Range SAT math	530–640
Range ACT composite	24–30
% submitting SAT scores	30
% submitting ACT scores	20
Average HS GPA	3.6
% submitting high school GPA	100
% graduated top 10% of class	26
% graduated top 25% of class	55
% graduated top 50% of class	81
% submitting high school rank	46

Important Dates

Early decision	
Apply by	11/1
Notified by	12/1
Early action	
Apply by	11/1
Notified by	12/1
Regular	
Apply by	2/1
Notified by	2/15
Nonfall registration?	No

FINANCIAL FACTS

Annual tuition	$56,784
Food and housing	$15,762
Required fees	$980
Books and supplies	$1,000
Average need-based scholarship (First-year)	$44,827 ($46,707)
% students with need rec. need-based scholarship or grant aid (First-year)	100 (100)
% students with need rec. non-need-based scholarship or grant aid (First-year)	21 (15)
% students with need rec. need-based self-help aid (First-year)	81 (80)
% students rec. any financial aid (First-year)	96 (99)
% UG borrow to pay for school	47
Average cumulative indebtedness	$30,310
% of students with need fully met (First-year)	45 (42)
Average % of student need met (First-year)	90 (89)

East Carolina University

East 5th Street, Greenville, NC 27858-4353 • Admissions: 252-328-6640

Survey Snapshot
Great library
Recreation facilities are great
Intramural sports are popular

RATINGS

Quality of Life	81
Fire Safety	99
Green	88
Academic	75
Profs Interesting	84
Profs Accessible	88
Admissions	82
Financial Aid	82

CAMPUS LIFE

Type of school	Public
Environment	City

Students

Degree-seeking undergrad enrollment	19,896
% male/female/not reported	43/57/0
% from out of state	12
% First-year from public high school	91
% First-year live on campus	94
% Ugrads live on campus	29
# of fraternities (% join)	27 (NR)
# of sororities (% join)	16 (NR)
% Asian	3
% Black or African American	16
% Hispanic	10
% Native American	<1
% Pacific Islander	<1
% Race and/or ethnicity unknown	4
% Two or more races	4
% White	61
% International	1
# of countries represented	59

CAMPUS MENTAL HEALTH SERVICES

Offers mental health/wellness program	Yes
Mental health training available to students	No
Employs Chief Wellness Officer	NR
Peer-to-peer mental health offerings	NR
Counseling center has guidelines or accreditation	No
Mental health/well-being courses	NR

ACADEMICS

% students returning for sophomore year	83
% students graduating within 4 years	43
% students graduating within 6 years	63
Calendar	Semester
Student/faculty ratio	17:1
Most common class size 20–29.	(30%)
Most common lab/discussion size 10–19.	(43%)

Most Popular Majors
Speech Communication and Rhetoric; Psychology; Registered Nursing/Registered Nurse

Applicants Often Prefer
North Carolina State University, University of North Carolina at Chapel Hill, The University of North Carolina—Charlotte

Applicants Sometimes Prefer
Appalachian State University, The University of North Carolina—Wilmington, Western Carolina University

STUDENTS SAY "..."

Academics

Students don't have to look far to see how much East Carolina University is investing in their education. From infrastructure like the new Life Sciences and Biotechnology Building to development for the Research and Innovation Campus, to robust academic assistance through "the Writing Center, the Counseling Center, the Women and Gender Center," which students say, "everyone knows about them and how to access them." One student notes that their Senior Academic Support Specialist is also "a licensed clinical mental health counselor." Students may be known as Pirates, but they don't have to sail the seven seas to find a strong sense of community support: it's all freely provided. "The professors at ECU are exceptional," elaborates one student, with another going so far as to say, "I wouldn't have remained an engineering major without the support of my professors." In particular, students call out how "there's a lot of support for students going into healthcare, and professors and advisors genuinely want to see students succeed." Another student reports that health-related courses emphasize labs, simulations, and clinical-style experiences, "which helps connect material to real situations. Professors also encourage discussion and application rather than just reading off slides, making classes more engaging and interactive." Across majors, Pirates value that "ECU provides an encouraging, community-driven atmosphere with space for many interests and talents."

Campus Life

East Carolina offers "a great balance between working hard to get that degree...while also being able to have a good time with good friends." It is "a major frat and sorority school," and students speak highly of the opportunities that it provides, whether that's volunteering in the community or holding executive positions. Those within and without Greek life suggest that it's "super inclusive and feels like home," with one noting, "you don't have to be in it to enjoy it or go to events. Everyone is welcomed no matter what." Another big communal activity: "sports...especially football," but never at the expense of academic success. "Tailgating is something we are very good at, but so is research. The great spectrum between crazy party school and good education opportunities is amazing." Another student agrees, saying, "We love our football and bond over going out downtown! We also prioritize our school and strive to be able to make good grades while having fun!" All told, being involved socially on the campus lets students "meet people, build confidence, and feel more connected to ECU, beyond just academics."

Student Body

At ECU, "everyone loves being a Pirate." One student describes Pirate Nation: "The ECU student body is diverse, welcoming, and community-oriented. My peers come from many backgrounds, including a large number of first-generation and in-state students, which creates a supportive and down-to-earth environment." Students also share a "strong sense of school pride and collaboration. Students are driven, but they genuinely support one another and value service, leadership, and real-world impact." Another student concurs, highlighting "how supportive students are of each other, especially in health-related majors. People are willing to help, share advice, and lift each other up instead of competing." Similarly, another student describes their peers as "a giant body of spirited, social butterflies." Some credit the large student body with enhancing this effect, "because it seems that everyone here knows that there are so many different people that all have their own interests and accept that." As a result, the campus vibe is "very open and friendly...I can always find someone to hang out with, play games, go out to town, or just have a good time at the dorms," says one student. Overall, Pirates enjoy "awesome school spirit" in the form of "a collaborative environment where students genuinely want to help each other succeed."

East Carolina University

Financial Aid: 252-328-4347 • E-mail: admissions@ecu.edu • Website: www.ecu.edu

THE PRINCETON REVIEW SAYS

Admissions

While the school reports that its standardized testing policy for Fall 2026 is Test Optional, applicants with a weighted high school GPA below 2.8 must submit an ACT or SAT score. *Very important factors considered include:* rigor of secondary school record, academic GPA, application essay, recommendation(s), state residency. *Important factors considered include:* class rank, standardized test scores. *Other factors considered include:* extracurricular activities, talent/ability, character/personal qualities, first generation, alumni/ae relation, volunteer work, work experience, level of applicant's interest. High school diploma is required and GED is accepted. *Academic units required:* 4 English, 4 math, 3 science, 1 science lab, 2 language (other than English), 1 social studies, 1 history. *Academic units recommended:* 4 English, 4 math, 3 science, 1 science lab, 2 language (other than English), 2 social studies, 1 history, 1 visual/performing arts.

Financial Aid

Students should submit: FAFSA. Priority filing deadline is 3/1. The Princeton Review suggests that all financial aid forms be submitted as soon as possible. *Need-based scholarships/grants offered:* Federal Pell; Federal SEOG; State scholarships/grants; Private scholarships; College/university scholarship or grant aid from institutional funds; Federal Nursing Scholarships. *Loan aid offered:* Federal Direct Subsidized Loans; Federal Direct Unsubsidized Loans; Direct PLUS loans; State Loans. Admitted students will be notified of awards on a rolling basis beginning 5/1. Federal Work-Study Program available. Institutional employment available.

The Inside Word

Admissions shouldn't be a problem for B students who have taken a solid roster of college preparatory classes. Students with a weighted GPA of 2.8 or higher are not required to submit standardized test scores. If you are applying for in-state tuition, you must visit NCresidency.org and verify your residency first.

THE SCHOOL SAYS

From the Admissions Office

"East Carolina University is a nationally recognized R1 research institution where students benefit from the opportunities of a large university paired with the support of a student-centered community. With nearly 20,000 undergraduate students, ECU offers more than 100 areas of study across disciplines including health sciences, business, engineering, education, and the arts. Students engage in hands-on learning through research, internships, clinical experiences, and community-based projects that connect their academic experience to real-world outcomes.

"At ECU, student success is at the core of our mission. From the first year through graduation, students are supported by accessible faculty, dedicated advising, and a wide range of academic and wellness resources designed to help them thrive. ECU is committed to delivering a strong return on investment, preparing graduates with the knowledge, skills, and experiences needed for career success or continued education. Located in Greenville, North Carolina, ECU offers a vibrant college town experience and a welcoming campus environment where students quickly find their place and become part of Pirate Nation."

SELECTIVITY

# of total applicants	26,369
% of total applicants accepted	89
% of total acceptees attending	17
# of in-state applicants	17,413
% of in-state applicants accepted	94
# of out-of-state-applicants	8,643
% of applicants accepted from out of state	79
# of international applicants	313
% of international applicants accepted	93

First-Year Profile

Testing policy	Test Optional !
Range SAT composite	1060–1150
Range SAT EBRW	520–630
Range SAT math	520–600
Range ACT composite	19–25
% submitting SAT scores	10
% submitting ACT scores	23
Average HS GPA	3.3
% submitting high school GPA	100
% graduated top 10% of class	11
% graduated top 25% of class	31
% graduated top 50% of class	64
% submitting high school rank	37

Important Dates

Regular	
Apply by	4/1
Notified by	Rolling, 9/1
Nonfall registration?	Yes

FINANCIAL FACTS

Annual in-state tuition	$4,452
Annual out-of-state tuition	$20,729
Food and housing	$11,350
Required fees	$2,909
Books and supplies	$1,510
Average need-based scholarship (First-year)	$9,702 ($9,952)
% students with need rec. need-based scholarship or grant aid (First-year)	83 (82)
% students with need rec. non-need-based scholarship or grant aid (First-year)	7 (8)
% students with need rec. need-based self-help aid (First-year)	65 (67)
% UG borrow to pay for school	59
Average cumulative indebtedness	$25,617
% of students with need fully met (First-year)	7 (8)
Average % of student need met (First-year)	55 (56)

! Test Optional if you have a GPA of 2.8 or higher.

EASTERN MICHIGAN UNIVERSITY

900 Oakwood, Ypsilanti, MI 48197 • Admissions: 734-487-3060

Survey Snapshot
Students are happy
Great library
Lab facilities are great

RATINGS

Quality of Life	75
Fire Safety	60*
Green	80
Academic	74
Profs Interesting	82
Profs Accessible	84
Admissions	82
Financial Aid	80

CAMPUS LIFE

Type of school	Public
Environment	City

Students

Degree-seeking undergrad enrollment	9,573
% male/female/not reported	42/58/0
% from out of state	12
% First-year from public high school	85
% First-year live on campus	61
% Ugrads live on campus	24
# of fraternities (% join)	11 (NR)
# of sororities (% join)	13 (NR)
% Asian	3
% Black or African American	18
% Hispanic	10
% Native American	<1
% Pacific Islander	<1
% Race and/or ethnicity unknown	2
% Two or more races	5
% White	55
% International	6
# of countries represented	80

CAMPUS MENTAL HEALTH SERVICES

Offers mental health/wellness program	Yes
Mental health training available to students	No
Employs Chief Wellness Officer	NR
Peer-to-peer mental health offerings	NR
Counseling center has guidelines or accreditation	No
Mental health/well-being courses	NR

ACADEMICS

% students returning for sophomore year	72
% students graduating within 4 years	25
% students graduating within 6 years	46
Calendar	Semester
Student/faculty ratio	14:1
Most common class size 20–29.	(36%)
Most common lab/discussion size 10–19.	(41%)

STUDENTS SAY "..."

Academics

There are more than 300 majors, minors, and concentrations available to the undergraduates at Eastern Michigan University, representative of "the resources that [the school gives] to the students so that they have a chance to improve on themselves." Some students take note of "how passionate and dedicated the staff are to their students," and say that professors "are generally accessible and willing to go above and beyond to help you with any questions, projects, or future planning you might have." There is a feeling that the university values and promotes inclusivity and "is constantly creating opportunities for their students to grow, learn, and be integrated into the college lifestyle," and "they also do a good job of making sure students know about events that are available to them."

Classroom formats vary from projects to lectures to online components, as "instructors always make an effort to make class exciting and more than just a simple teaching course." For instance, "a class focused on disability accessibility had an activity where we tried to navigate the building in a wheelchair." There are also plenty of chances for "learning outside of the classroom through field trips, volunteer opportunities, and student organizations," including "going off site with place-based education directives within the local neighborhood." Students appreciate that many classes are taught by professors that "have gone out into the world and have held jobs instead of only doing research." Many also utilize active learning styles in which students "watch a video some time before the lecture to prepare ourselves for the lecture, and during the lecture we do a lot of group work and practice questions on the content." The university offers flexible learning options with "a good combination of online and in person instruction that allows for you to study at home to supplement the lecture material."

Campus Life

Students consider EMU's main campus in Ypsilanti small but active. Given that there are "a lot of events," such as "paint and pour (non-alcoholic) [or] a carving pumpkin contest," it is "easy to connect with people." Students enjoy the "different activities that the different clubs and organizations put on periodically." Additionally, students "[go] to the mini golf place Putterz that is near campus," and also "go to the gym [or] go to the student center with friends to study." Although many students are commuters, when not studying, they "like to hang out in the common room and the Eagles [Cafés] on the weekends and after class." The school is "far more affordable than many other options" and there "are many job opportunities in the surrounding area" for students looking to earn some extra money (or stay local after graduation). Students note that "the atmosphere on the campus is very laid back," and "it's very easy to get involved on-campus and to meet new friends."

Student Body

EMU has "a lot of representation in the student body," and this is "a very unique place in the sense that the student age range is large," with a mix of "traditional college students who have recently graduated high school and first-time college students in their middle adult years." Students "are active on campus and are diverse in their interests, pursuits, and backgrounds" and "thrive on teamwork and communication with each other." One student attests, "As a transgender student, I generally feel very welcomed and safe. The campus population is majority white in my experience, but there is a large POC population." Another agrees, saying that this "very diverse student body...has been an incredible experience and has helped further my understanding of other cultures as well as [making] me a more well-rounded individual." DEI is also a priority, and "there are many events about religion and/or culture that help [students and their] peers connect." All in all, the school provides an environment in which "students with a variety of backgrounds are coming together to graduate with a diploma, pursue a career, and become the greater adults of tomorrow."

EASTERN MICHIGAN UNIVERSITY

Financial Aid: 734-487-0455 • E-Mail: undergraduate_admissions@emich.edu • Website: www.emich.edu

THE PRINCETON REVIEW SAYS

Admissions

While the school reports that its standardized testing policy for Fall 2026 is Test Optional, applicants with a cumulative high school GPA below 2.5 must submit an ACT or SAT score. The Princeton Review suggests that interested applicants consult with the school for the most up-to-date standardized testing policies. *Very important factors considered include:* academic GPA. *Important factors considered include:* rigor of secondary school record. *Other factors considered include:* standardized test scores. High school diploma is required and GED is accepted. *Academic units recommended:* 4 English, 4 math, 3 science, 2 language (other than English), 3 social studies, 1 computer science, 1 visual/performing arts.

Financial Aid

Students should submit: FAFSA. The Princeton Review suggests that all financial aid forms be submitted as soon as possible. *Need-based scholarships/grants offered:* Federal Pell; Federal SEOG; State scholarships/grants; Private scholarships; College/university scholarship or grant aid from institutional funds; United Negro College Fund; Federal Nursing Scholarships. *Loan aid offered:* Federal Direct Subsidized Loans; Federal Direct Unsubsidized Loans; Direct PLUS loans. Admitted students will be notified of awards on a rolling basis beginning 12/15. Federal Work-Study Program available. Institutional employment available.

The Inside Word

Non-residents will appreciates EMU's tuition pricing policy, which keeps tuition the same for in-state, out-of-state, and international students. EMU also has block tuition pricing, which encourages students to take a full course load and graduate in four years. Students with a GPA of 2.75 or above are not required to submit test scores. Those with a GPA of 2.50–2.74 can apply test optional, but may be asked to provide test scores following a review of their application. Students with a GPA of 2.49 or below are required to submit standardized test scores.

THE SCHOOL SAYS

From the Admissions Office

"Located in the heart of Ypsilanti, Michigan, Eastern Michigan University (EMU) serves 13,000 students pursuing undergraduate, graduate, specialist, doctoral, and certificate degrees. As the second oldest public institution in the state of Michigan, EMU is proud to provide a personalized education to everyone as is evident by the 14.5:1 student-to-faculty ratio. EMU offers more than 200 majors and minors, providing students with a wealth of opportunities to pursue their passions and career goals through the University's College of Arts and Sciences, College of Business, College of Education, GameAbove College of Engineering and Technology, College of Health and Human Services, the Honors College, and its graduate school. Financial accessibility is also a cornerstone of EMU's mission, with 97% of first-year students receiving some form of financial aid. EMU's commitment to student success is also reflected in its outstanding employment rate, with the vast majority of graduates securing employment soon after graduation. Campus life is dynamic and engaging, featuring over 150 student organizations and Division I athletics, ensuring that every student can find their niche and thrive. EMU's serene campus atmosphere with the added benefit of proximity to the bustling cities of Ann Arbor and Detroit provides countless opportunities for internships, cultural experiences, and professional growth. Plus, a $200 million investment in student housing has created two new student apartment buildings and renovations to virtually every other residence hall on campus. At Eastern Michigan University, students forge lifelong friendships, develop critical skills, and start their lasting success in their future careers."

SELECTIVITY

# of total applicants	18,548
% of total applicants accepted	78
% of total acceptees attending	9
# of in-state applicants	11,086
% of in-state applicants accepted	93
# of out-of-state-applicants	2,707
% of applicants accepted from out of state	95
# of international applicants	4,755
% of international applicants accepted	31

First-Year Profile

Testing policy	Test Optional !
Range SAT composite	920–1160
Range SAT EBRW	480–610
Range SAT math	440–570
Range ACT composite	18–25
% submitting SAT scores	48
% submitting ACT scores	5
Average HS GPA	3.4
% submitting high school GPA	94
% graduated top 10% of class	12
% graduated top 25% of class	38
% graduated top 50% of class	69
% submitting high school rank	55

Important Dates

Regular	
Apply by	Rolling
Notified by	Rolling
Nonfall registration?	Yes

FINANCIAL FACTS

Annual tuition	$17,352
Food and housing	$14,748
Required fees	$120
Books and supplies	$1,000
Average need-based scholarship (First-year)	$9,123 ($10,740)
% students with need rec. need-based scholarship or grant aid (First-year)	73 (88)
% students with need rec. non-need-based scholarship or grant aid (First-year)	51 (65)
% students with need rec. need-based self-help aid (First-year)	61 (54)
% students rec. any financial aid (First-year)	NR (98)
% UG borrow to pay for school	60
Average cumulative indebtedness	$26,497
% of students with need fully met (First-year)	9 (15)
Average % of student need met (First-year)	46 (62)

! Test Optional if you have a GPA of 2.5 or higher.

ECKERD COLLEGE

4200 54th Avenue South, St. Petersburg, FL 33716 • Admissions: 727-864-8331

Survey Snapshot
Students take advantage of the outdoors
Great off-campus food
Students environmentally aware

RATINGS

Quality of Life	88
Fire Safety	90
Green	60*
Academic	83
Profs Interesting	93
Profs Accessible	92
Admissions	85
Financial Aid	85

CAMPUS LIFE

Type of school	Private
Affiliation	Presbyterian
Environment	City

Students

Degree-seeking undergrad enrollment	1,738
% male/female/not reported	30/70/0
% from out of state	79
% First-year live on campus	98
% Ugrads live on campus	87
# of fraternities	0
# of sororities	0
% Asian	2
% Black or African American	3
% Hispanic	10
% Native American	<1
% Pacific Islander	<1
% Race and/or ethnicity unknown	1
% Two or more races	6
% White	74
% International	3
# of countries represented	41

CAMPUS MENTAL HEALTH SERVICES

Offers mental health/wellness program	Yes
Mental health training available to students	No
Employs Chief Wellness Officer	NR
Peer-to-peer mental health offerings	NR
Counseling center has guidelines or accreditation	No
Mental health/well-being courses	NR

ACADEMICS

% students returning for sophomore year	77
% students graduating within 4 years	59
% students graduating within 6 years	67
Calendar	4-1-4
Student/faculty ratio	11:1
Most common class size 20–29.	(49%)
Most common lab/discussion size 20–29.	(48%)

Most Popular Majors
Environmental Studies; Biology/Biological Sciences; Animal Behavior and Ethology

STUDENTS SAY "..."

Academics

The waterfront view from Eckerd College's beach isn't the only thing that wows students—the "top notch academics" of this Gulf Coast college "continue to impress." In particular, some students appreciate the care that's gone into the liberal arts curriculum to "make the classes fun and interesting" and to ensure students "are not pigeonholed into the skills associated with their major." As enrollees put it, they expect to graduate with a "wide range of abilities, which make them attractive to employers."

Eckerd enrolls just under 2,000 undergraduates, and the school's small class sizes help "maximize learning and personal connections to professors." Professors at Eckerd show a "level of genuine care" and create "an environment where it is easy for everybody to openly express their opinions without judgment." Students describe professors who are "always approachable on an academic and personal level." In short: "If I have a question, it gets answered, simple as that." This supportive environment is underscored by Eckerd's Mentor program, which pairs students with professors in their area of study to "help guide the student through choosing classes and registration, or anything else."

Eckerd also has a standout study abroad program, in which over 500 students participate each year. In addition, as a member of the Peace Corps Prep undergraduate certificate program, over 150 Eckerd graduates have gone on to serve in (or in organizations like) the Peace Corps. Overall, Eckerd emphasizes an expansive education that creates "well-rounded, educated people [ready] for the 'real world,' rather than for just one job."

Campus Life

How can you beat a dorm that overlooks the bay? asks one student, confirming that the residence halls "are beautiful, so there is no need to live off campus." The result, which some call "summer camp with an enriching academic experience," tends to be a fairly active community, further encouraged by the Community Bike program, which lets students "just pick up the yellow bikes and ride wherever you need." Students also enjoy exploring off-campus, including dining out at one of the many restaurants in downtown St. Petersburg. And of course, the school's location is great for people who enjoy going out on the water.

The school has no Greek life, although students note there are still parties to be found ("pot and beer are not strangers"), which often take place outside. That said, the school has a "very 'free as a bird' mentality," meaning that "people rarely feel trapped," so when it comes to choosing activities, it's "a very no-pressure environment." To make sure there are plenty of evening events, the Campus Activities crew has a generous budget, which results in many "eclectic options" including "cookouts, dances, casino nights, and an actual carnival brought onto campus." When it comes to having fun, the hardest choice to make may be whether to go to the beach or go downtown to get "paddleboards/kayaks at the Waterfront."

Student Body

Students describe their peers as a "barefooted and brainy" community that's "very relaxed" and adopts a "laid-back Florida attitude." That's not to say everyone fits the same mold. Students say the college "has a wide variety of students who all fit different niches." As one student elaborates, "It isn't unheard of to see people in three-piece suits sitting with what we might call modern-day hippies." Students say their peers are "pretty liberal" and have "a strong interest in environmental sustainability"; notably, 71% of students are women. Overall, it's a friendly campus with a lot of school spirit, as most students have "a general positive attitude about being here at Eckerd."

Eckerd College

Financial Aid: 727-864-8854 • E-mail: admissions@eckerd.edu • Website: www.eckerd.edu

THE PRINCETON REVIEW SAYS

Admissions

The school reports that its standardized testing policy for use in admission for Fall 2026 is Test Optional. The Princeton Review suggests that interested applicants consult with the school for the most up-to-date standardized testing policies. *Very important factors considered include:* rigor of secondary school record, academic GPA. *Important factors considered include:* standardized test scores, application essay, recommendation(s), interview, extracurricular activities, talent/ability, character/personal qualities, volunteer work, work experience, level of applicant's interest. *Other factors considered include:* class rank, first generation, alumni/ae relation. High school diploma is required and GED is accepted. *Academic units recommended:* 4 English, 3 math, 3 science, 2 science labs, 2 language (other than English), 2 social studies, 1 history, 3 academic electives.

Financial Aid

Students should submit: FAFSA. Priority filing deadline is 2/1. The Princeton Review suggests that all financial aid forms be submitted as soon as possible. *Need-based scholarships/grants offered:* Federal Pell; Federal SEOG; State scholarships/grants; College/university scholarship or grant aid from institutional funds; Private scholarships. *Loan aid offered:* Federal Direct Subsidized Loans; Federal Direct Unsubsidized Loans; Direct PLUS loans. Federal Work-Study Program available. Institutional employment available.

The Inside Word

Eckerd is a relatively easy admit for B-plus students with a college prep curriculum. The admissions process offers Early Action and rolling admission options, meaning that applying early will help your chances. Eckerd can afford to be more selective later on in the admissions cycle, especially for candidates who profess an interest in its most esteemed programs (for example, marine science), so those with serious interest should consider Eckerd's early admission policy.

THE SCHOOL SAYS

From the Admissions Office

"Students from 48 states and territories and 39 countries take advantage of our spectacular mile of campus waterfront near the Gulf of Mexico for outdoor laboratories in biology, marine science and environmental studies along with an array of intramural, club and intercollegiate sports and water recreation. Offerings in the arts and humanities inspire creativity and foster critical thinking and self-awareness. Eckerd is dedicated to minimizing its operational footprint and maximizing sustainable practices, and our students are service-oriented—donating over 12,000 hours of service outside of graduation requirements annually. With 180 Eckerd grads having served in the Peace Corps, we're a top producer of volunteers among small colleges in the U.S. and recently joined the nationally recognized Peace Corps Prep undergraduate certificate program.

"Eckerd's innovative 4-1-4 calendar gives students the opportunity to study abroad during the January Winter Term or semester-long programs. Nearly 70 percent of our graduates have taken classes overseas, many at our London Study Centre.

"In addition to building the 55,000-square-foot James Center for Molecular and Life Sciences, which opened in 2013, the college significantly upgraded equipment, labs and classrooms for the environmental studies, math, physics, computer science and behavioral sciences departments and in 2018 opened the Nielsen Center for Visual Arts. This state-of-the-art facility provides space and equipment for studying, creating and exhibiting visual art—with student studios for ceramics and sculpture, printmaking, painting, drawing, digital arts, film production, and more.

"We venture together in the Eckerd experience to think beyond the conventional questions, methods and solutions. At Eckerd College, we ThinkOUTside."

SELECTIVITY

# of total applicants	5,250
% of total applicants accepted	70
% of total acceptees attending	13

First-Year Profile

Testing policy	Test Optional
Range SAT composite	1110–1300
Range SAT EBRW	570–680
Range SAT math	530–640
Range ACT composite	22–29
% submitting SAT scores	21
% submitting ACT scores	13
Average HS GPA	3.6
% submitting high school GPA	100

Important Dates

Early action	
Apply by	11/15
Notified by	12/15
Regular	
Apply by	7/25
Notified by	Rolling, 12/1
Nonfall registration?	Yes

FINANCIAL FACTS

Annual tuition	$52,690
Food and housing	$15,176
Required fees	$766
Books and supplies	$1,350
Average need-based scholarship (First-year)	$27,454 ($27,714)
% students with need rec. need-based scholarship or grant aid (First-year)	99 (99)
% students with need rec. non-need-based scholarship or grant aid (First-year)	13 (15)
% students with need rec. need-based self-help aid (First-year)	72 (69)
% of students with need fully met (First-year)	15 (15)
Average % of student need met (First-year)	56 (58)

ELMIRA COLLEGE

One Park Place, Elmira, NY 14901 • Admissions: 607-735-1724

Survey Snapshot
Everyone loves the Soaring Eagles
Intramural sports are popular
Easy to get around campus

RATINGS

Quality of Life	**76**
Fire Safety	**86**
Green	**60***
Academic	**81**
Profs Interesting	**83**
Profs Accessible	**88**
Admissions	**86**
Financial Aid	**87**

CAMPUS LIFE

Type of school	Private
Environment	Town

Students

Degree-seeking undergrad enrollment	762
% male/female/not reported	33/66/1
% from out of state	27
% First-year from public high school	98
% First-year live on campus	84
% Ugrads live on campus	76
# of fraternities	0
# of sororities	0
% Asian	6
% Black or African American	4
% Hispanic	9
% Native American	<1
% Pacific Islander	0
% Race and/or ethnicity unknown	6
% Two or more races	4
% White	67
% International	5
# of countries represented	12

CAMPUS MENTAL HEALTH SERVICES

Offers mental health/wellness program	Yes
Mental health training available to students	Yes
Employs Chief Wellness Officer	Yes
Peer-to-peer mental health offerings	No
Counseling center has guidelines or accreditation	No
Mental health/well-being courses	No

ACADEMICS

% students returning for sophomore year	75
% students graduating within 4 years	43
% students graduating within 6 years	48
Calendar (Two 12-wk terms followed by a 4-wk term)	4-4-1
Student/faculty ratio	12:1
Most common class size 1–9.	(47%)
Most common lab/discussion size 10–19.	(47%)

Most Popular Majors
Education; Psychology; Business Administration and Management

Applicants Often Prefer
Hartwick College, St. John Fisher University, State University of New York–Brockport

Applicants Sometimes Prefer
Ithaca College, Le Moyne College, State University of New York—Geneseo

Applicants Rarely Prefer
Alfred University, Houghton College

STUDENTS SAY "..."

Academics

Elmira College provides a "very student-led" education, which includes the opportunity for students to create their own major through the Individualized Studies program. Hands-on and immersive learning is a significant part of the academic experience. One example of this is Term III, a six-week period in the spring semester dedicated to off-campus immersive learning. This experience varies for each student: education majors might student-teach, while nursing students can participate in clinical work. Many others choose to study abroad or conduct field research during Term III. According to the school, Term III is an opportunity for "low-stakes exploration," allowing students to pursue their interests without the pressure of grades or evaluations. Another unique feature of the school is the service-learning requirement, which requires students to complete 60 hours of community engagement with a nearby nonprofit organization. A recent addition to Elmira is the Tommy Hilfiger Fashion Business School, offering a degree in business administration alongside minors and concentrations in fashion merchandising or fashion marketing. Elmira emphasizes career preparation, with 97 percent of students completing an internship before graduation. Classroom learning is characterized by healthy discussions, creating an environment where "your voice can always be heard and your opinion valued." Professors are "very involved" and genuinely "want to see their students succeed," often going out of their way to "give you more help outside of the classroom." Students also appreciate that most professors "have an abundance of real work experience" and find that "their passion for their field truly comes out when teaching and lecturing."

Campus Life

The cobblestone paths and Gothic Revival-style buildings bring "an air of elegance and beauty" to this intimate campus, where "everything is within 10 minutes of walking distance." The campus is home to the Center of Mark Twain Studies, which hosts literary events throughout the year. Mark Twain's own octagonal study, where he penned many of his most famous works, is also located here, and Elmira's connection to the famous author is a big draw for some students. On this historic campus that dates back to 1855, "there is always something going on." From poetry readings and sports games to a cappella performances and variety shows, Elmira students stay busy exploring their interests alongside their classmates. The school has over 50 clubs and organizations, including Competitive Dance, Hiking Club, and PRIDE club, along with 19 varsity athletics teams. The campus has several unique traditions, including some "events dating back 100+ years." This includes Mountain Day, which was started in 1918 and involves the entire campus gathering for a picnic lunch before enjoying games and outdoor activities in the fall weather. In addition to participating in clubs, attending games, and enjoying campus events, students often catch up with friends in the dorms or have movie nights. With so many options available, "students can partake in what they like best."

Student Body

The student body is very welcoming and aims to "always make sure everyone is comfortable." Elmira's small size "allows everyone to get to know each other," so it's "easy to make friends here." As one student describes the dynamic, "Though I do have a close-knit circle of who I see as my best friends… [in the dining hall] I see a sea of people that I would feel comfortable sitting with," adding, "I don't feel like just another number or a nameless student here." Students here are "encouraged to cultivate their interests and be as involved and outgoing as possible." It's a group that is "passionate about the clubs, activities, and athletic programs to which they belong," and these extracurricular activities "keep us intermingling." As one student sums up, people here "go out of their way to help one another," adding, "I love the care and support; it is a community that respects one another."

Elmira College

Financial Aid: 607-735-1734 • E-Mail: admissions@elmira.edu • Website: www.elmira.edu

THE PRINCETON REVIEW SAYS

Admissions

The school reports that its standardized testing policy for use in admission for Fall 2026 is Test Optional. The Princeton Review suggests that interested applicants consult with the school for the most up-to-date standardized testing policies. *Very important factors considered include:* rigor of secondary school record, academic GPA, application essay, interview, character/personal qualities. *Important factors considered include:* class rank, recommendation(s), extracurricular activities, level of applicant's interest. *Other factors considered include:* talent/ability, first generation, alumni/ae relation, geographical residence, state residency, volunteer work, work experience. High school diploma is required and GED is not accepted. *Academic units required:* 4 English, 3 math, 3 science, 2 science labs, 3 social studies, 1 history, 2 academic electives. *Academic units recommended:* 2 language (other than English).

Financial Aid

Students should submit: FAFSA; State aid form. The Princeton Review suggests that all financial aid forms be submitted as soon as possible. *Need-based scholarships/grants offered:* Federal Pell; Federal SEOG; State scholarships/grants; Private scholarships; College/university scholarship or grant aid from institutional funds. *Loan aid offered:* Federal Direct Subsidized Loans; Federal Direct Unsubsidized Loans; Direct PLUS loans; State Loans. Admitted students will be notified of awards on a rolling basis beginning 10/15. Federal Work-Study Program available. Institutional employment available.

The Inside Word

At Elmira, test scores and interviews are optional, but both are encouraged if the student believes it will improve their application. Test-optional applicants are encouraged to submit a personal statement, second letter of recommendation, and schedule an interview. With its fairly high acceptance rate, students without any major blemishes on their record have a good shot at admission.

THE SCHOOL SAYS

From the Admissions Office

"Founded in 1855, Elmira College is a private, residential, liberal arts college offering more than 30 majors and academic programs, an honors program, 17 academic societies, and 19 Division III varsity teams. Located in the Southern Finger Lakes Region of New York, Elmira's undergraduate and graduate student population hails from more than 40 states and 25 countries. Elmira is a Phi Beta Kappa College and has been ranked a top college, nationally, for student internships.

"Elmira College has a tradition of offering hands-on, immersive learning experiences with small classes. Alumni report the opportunity to complete research, the development of relationships with faculty, and the lifelong friendships with classmates among their most impactful experiences at Elmira.

"The College offers several opportunities for post-graduate work through partnerships with various graduate schools including Lake Erie College of Osteopathic Medicine. Elmira College students who meet the LECOM acceptance requirements, enjoy reserved, early acceptance spots at LECOM sites, including LECOM at Elmira. This provides a seamless transition from undergraduate coursework to medical school.

"The College is also home to the Center for Mark Twain Studies, one of four historically significant Twain heritage sites in the U.S., which attracts Twain scholars and educators from around the world. Proud of its history and tradition, the College is committed to the ideals of community service and intellectual growth."

SELECTIVITY

# of total applicants	2,436
% of total applicants accepted	81
% of total acceptees attending	12
# offered a place on the wait list	0
# admitted from wait list	0

First-Year Profile

Testing policy	Test Optional
Range SAT composite	1360–1500
Range SAT EBRW	640–730
Range SAT math	710–770
Range ACT composite	25–34
% submitting SAT scores	10
% submitting ACT scores	5
Average HS GPA	3.8
% submitting high school GPA	99
% graduated top 10% of class	6
% graduated top 25% of class	26
% graduated top 50% of class	49
% submitting high school rank	41

Important Dates

Early action	
Apply by	11/15
Notified by	12/1
Regular	
Notified by	Rolling, 11/1
Nonfall registration?	Yes

FINANCIAL FACTS

Annual tuition	$38,560
Food and housing	$14,970
Required fees	$2,000
Books and supplies	$600
Average need-based scholarship (First-year)	$29,112 ($30,832)
% students with need rec. need-based scholarship or grant aid (First-year)	100 (100)
% students with need rec. non-need-based scholarship or grant aid (First-year)	15 (15)
% students with need rec. need-based self-help aid (First-year)	79 (82)
% students rec. any financial aid (First-year)	98 (100)
% UG borrow to pay for school	75
Average cumulative indebtedness	$30,958
% of students with need fully met (First-year)	17 (17)
Average % of student need met (First-year)	75 (77)

ELON UNIVERSITY

100 Campus Drive, Elon, NC 27244-2010 • Admissions: 336-278-3566

Survey Snapshot
Intramural sports are popular
Internships are widely available
Students are happy

RATINGS

Quality of Life	92
Fire Safety	81
Green	91
Academic	85
Profs Interesting	95
Profs Accessible	95
Admissions	87
Financial Aid	86

CAMPUS LIFE

Type of school	Private
Environment	Town

Students

Degree-seeking undergrad enrollment	6,150
% male/female/not reported	41/59/0
% from out of state	76
% First-year from public high school	64
% First-year live on campus	99
% Ugrads live on campus	70
# of fraternities (% join)	14 (20)
# of sororities (% join)	16 (39)
% Asian	2
% Black or African American	6
% Hispanic	9
% Native American	<1
% Pacific Islander	<1
% Race and/or ethnicity unknown	3
% Two or more races	3
% White	74
% International	2
# of countries represented	52

CAMPUS MENTAL HEALTH SERVICES

Offers mental health/wellness program	Yes
Mental health training available to students	Yes
Employs Chief Wellness Officer	Yes
Peer-to-peer mental health offerings	Yes
Counseling center has guidelines or accreditation	No
Mental health/well-being courses	Yes, for-credit

ACADEMICS

% students returning for sophomore year	90
% students graduating within 4 years	78
% students graduating within 6 years	81
Calendar	4-1-4
Student/faculty ratio	11:1
Most common class size 10–19.	(38%)

Most Popular Majors

Communication; Psychology; Business Administration and Management

Applicants Often Prefer

Clemson University, Indiana University—Bloomington, James Madison University, North Carolina State University, Penn State University Park, Syracuse University, University of North Carolina at Chapel Hill, The University of North Carolina—Charlotte, University of South Carolina—Columbia, Virginia Tech

Applicants Sometimes Prefer

Appalachian State University, College of Charleston, High Point University, University of Delaware, The University of North Carolina—Wilmington, Wake Forest University

STUDENTS SAY "..."

Academics

Elon University is all about providing "meaningful access to professors, research opportunities, internships, and leadership roles early…which allows [students] to explore their interests in practical, hands-on ways." The community—"everyone from the most esteemed professors to our incredible dining hall workers, to the student life staff, to our groundskeepers"—is described as "the most incredible support system" and said to "want the best for all the students." In practice, this means that the "highly experienced and enthusiastic" professors do "constant check-ups and meetings with you. They want to make sure that you're not only succeeding in their class, but also having an amazing, enriching time in college." Additionally, the small class sizes allow for bonding "with both my professors and my peers, and it gives me more opportunities for success." There's also lots of experiential learning, where "students can use both classroom learning and real-world experience to understand the information being taught." For instance, one education student reports: "We can student teach and participate in practicum experiences as early as our first year." The J-term—an abbreviated semester in January—also gives students, even those with strict major requirements, the chance to apply what they've learned abroad. Case in point, one student took a course titled "Through the Lens of ESPN" that involved traveling to Brazil: "I can surely say it was one of the best experiences of my life." All told, students report that Elon provides the "kind of hands-on, inquiry-driven learning" that makes their college experience "feel deeply engaging, relevant, and transformative."

Campus Life

With its "mix of modernity and brick," sweeping lawns, and picturesque fountains, Elon is a "very beautiful campus." Students name Lake Mary Nell, the Historic Neighborhood on campus, and the Center for the Arts (CFA) as favorite places to find students "lounging around, chatting, or doing their work." The CFA is a particular hot spot, as it features a variety of theaters and studio spaces that house some of Elon's popular performing arts programs, including Elon Student Television, "a sketch comedy show similar to SNL." Student-run radio also "adds color" to campus life ("WSOE 89.3FM forever!") Students enthuse about "our amazing theater program and productions…We are definitely an arts school." Outside of creative endeavors, many students credit Greek life ("I wouldn't be the student I am without it," confesses one student) and athletics for opening doors to "incredibly strong" communities. One student sums up campus life best: "There's a strong culture of involvement here: students are constantly balancing academics with leadership roles, service organizations, research, athletics, and creative projects, and that energy creates an environment where it feels normal to want to do big things."

Student Body

"The student body at Elon University is most akin to a mosaic, where there are a wide variety of colors everywhere, but all together it's like you stepped into a rainbow." There's a broad range "of backgrounds and individuals from…all over the world, that bring a wide variety of perspectives to the learning experience." Another student agrees, explaining that the students at Elon are also "diverse when it comes to student interest and extracurricular involvement. I find a lot of athletes involved in art and music communities, and lots of cross-major friendship and interaction." Perhaps inspiring these cross-curricular interests is the fact that Elon students share "a specific drive, and everyone is able to be involved on campus in some way." As one student confesses, "I want to be as involved as I am because of those around me, and I am grateful for that every day." In short, "everyone here belongs to Elon. We have different backgrounds, majors, goals, etc., but deep down, we are here because we care about having a community. Elon students seek community and seek to make you a part of it."

ELON UNIVERSITY

Financial Aid: 336-278-7640 • E-Mail: admissions@elon.edu • Website: www.elon.edu

THE PRINCETON REVIEW SAYS

Admissions

The school reports that its standardized testing policy for use in admission for Fall 2026 is Test Optional. The Princeton Review suggests that interested applicants consult with the school for the most up-to-date standardized testing policies. *Very important factors considered include:* rigor of secondary school record, academic GPA, application essay, recommendation(s). *Important factors considered include:* extracurricular activities, talent/ability, alumni/ae relation, volunteer work, work experience, level of applicant's interest. *Other factors considered include:* class rank, character/personal qualities, first generation, geographical residence, state residency. High school diploma is required and GED is accepted. *Academic units required:* 4 English, 3 math, 3 science, 1 science lab, 2 language (other than English), 2 social studies, 1 history. *Academic units recommended:* 4 English, 4 math, 3 science, 1 science lab, 3 language (other than English), 2 social studies, 1 history.

Financial Aid

Students should submit: FAFSA; CSS PROFILE. Priority filing deadline is 3/15. The Princeton Review suggests that all financial aid forms be submitted as soon as possible. *Need-based scholarships/grants offered:* Federal Pell; Federal SEOG; State scholarships/grants; Private scholarships; College/university scholarship or grant aid from institutional funds; United Negro College Fund. *Loan aid offered:* Federal Direct Subsidized Loans; Federal Direct Unsubsidized Loans; Direct PLUS loans; College/university loans from institutional funds. Admitted students will be notified of awards on a rolling basis beginning 1/1. Federal Work-Study Program available. Institutional employment available.

The Inside Word

Admission to Elon University is a competitive process. In addition to a strong GPA, applicants should have accomplishments outside of the classroom, including participation in extracurricular activities and service. Your class ranking is of equal importance to your hours of volunteer work.

THE SCHOOL SAYS

From the Admissions Office

"At Elon University, students are engaged, immersed and empowered from day one. With more than 7,000 undergraduates and 80 majors, Elon combines academic rigor with a nationally recognized model of engaged learning that delivers tangible outcomes for students and confidence for families. Experiential, hands-on learning is central to an Elon education. The five Elon Experiences — study abroad, internships, service, leadership and undergraduate research—ensure that students apply what they learn in meaningful ways. Participation is widespread, as most students complete at least two of the experiences and many complete all five. Elon's global study participation ranks among the highest in the nation. These experiences build perspective, independence and career readiness. Elon's 4-1-4 academic calendar creates space to explore interests more deeply, especially during the January term, when students pursue immersive courses, internships, research or global study. Investment in facilities reinforces this hands-on approach. The Innovation Quad includes the new School of Engineering and Computing, where students access advanced labs for engineering, design, astrophysics, robotics, virtual reality and prototyping. The HealthEU Center, scheduled to open fall 2026, expands opportunities for collaboration and well-being, featuring research labs, a counseling center, gym, aquatics center with a competition pool, indoor track, climbing wall and outdoor fitness spaces. Equally important is Elon's culture of mentorship. Faculty know students personally and help connect their interests to meaningful outcomes. The result is clear: graduates leave Elon prepared, experienced and ready to lead with purpose."

SELECTIVITY

# of total applicants	18,557
% of total applicants accepted	63
% of total acceptees attending	11
# of in-state applicants	4,225
% of in-state applicants accepted	61
# of out-of-state-applicants	13,850
% of applicants accepted from out of state	64
# of international applicants	482
% of international applicants accepted	64
# of early decision applicants	353
% of early decision applicants accepted	86
# offered a place on the wait list	4,214
# admitted from wait list	98

First-Year Profile

Testing policy	Test Optional
Range SAT composite	1190–1340
Range SAT EBRW	590–690
Range SAT math	580–660
Range ACT composite	25–31
% submitting SAT scores	23
% submitting ACT scores	17
Average HS GPA	4.1
% submitting high school GPA	75
% graduated top 10% of class	20
% graduated top 25% of class	48
% graduated top 50% of class	81
% submitting high school rank	35

Important Dates

Early decision	
Apply by	11/1
Notified by	12/1
Early action	
Apply by	11/1
Notified by	12/20
Regular	
Apply by	1/10
Notified by	3/20
Nonfall registration?	Yes

FINANCIAL FACTS

Annual tuition	$50,386
Food and housing	$17,127
Required fees	$982
Books and supplies	$900
Average need-based scholarship (First-year)	$22,951 ($24,540)
% students with need rec. need-based scholarship or grant aid (First-year)	92 (91)
% students with need rec. non-need-based scholarship or grant aid (First-year)	80 (83)
% students with need rec. need-based self-help aid (First-year)	62 (65)
% students rec. any financial aid (First-year)	79 (71)
% UG borrow to pay for school	25
Average cumulative indebtedness	$22,650
% of students with need fully met (First-year)	30 (31)
Average % of student need met (First-year)	74 (72)

EMERSON COLLEGE

120 Boylston Street, Boston, MA 02116-4624 • Admissions: 617-824-8600

Survey Snapshot
Class discussions encouraged
Students aren't religious
Students love Boston, MA

RATINGS	
Quality of Life	**84**
Fire Safety	**89**
Green	**96**
Academic	**76**
Profs Interesting	**90**
Profs Accessible	**89**
Admissions	**82**
Financial Aid	**83**

CAMPUS LIFE

Type of school	Private
Environment	Metropolis

Students

Degree-seeking undergrad enrollment	4,148
% male/female/not reported	33/67/0
# of fraternities (% join)	NR (2)
# of sororities (% join)	NR (3)
% Asian	6
% Black or African American	5
% Hispanic	11
% Native American	<1
% Pacific Islander	<1
% Race and/or ethnicity unknown	2
% Two or more races	5
% White	55
% International	16
# of countries represented	60

CAMPUS MENTAL HEALTH SERVICES

Offers mental health/wellness program	Yes
Mental health training available to students	No
Employs Chief Wellness Officer	NR
Peer-to-peer mental health offerings	NR
Counseling center has guidelines or accreditation	No
Mental health/well-being courses	NR

ACADEMICS

% students returning for sophomore year	88
% students graduating within 4 years	73
% students graduating within 6 years	79
Calendar	Semester
Student/faculty ratio	14:1
Most common class size 10–19.	(57%)

Most Popular Majors
Theatre/Theater; Cinematography and Film/Video Production; Journalism

Applicants Often Prefer
Boston University, Chapman University, New York University, University of Southern California

Applicants Sometimes Prefer
American University, Fordham University, Ithaca College, Northeastern University, Syracuse University

Applicants Rarely Prefer
Pace University

STUDENTS SAY "..."

Academics

Emerson College boasts its "urban" Boston location as a solid locus for "networking and career-preparation," including the "amazing alumni network," lovingly referred to as the "Emerson Mafia." In particular, "journalism, writing, film, marketing, and theater programs" are especially "strong," and classes are "taught by industry professionals" who "never fail to enlighten." Most of the classes are focused on job readiness: "You do work with actual organizations rather than discuss theories." There are "impressive" facilities and resources, including "film and TV studio facilities and equipment" with broad "availability to students," and "small class sizes with easy-to-reach professors, specific course material, and no meaningless busy work," that "often work more like collaborations than lectures." "We aren't test takers at Emerson," one student says, "so we don't study. We create projects, videos, presentations, [and so on]." Professors are "passionate about the learning material," and "are in constant discourse with the class," "keen on showcasing global perspectives." Emerson stresses "hands on activities, volunteer opportunities, real-time demonstrations, and frequent class discussions," and classes "integrated with external organizations," means students are often out in the community, "working with local nonprofits," or navigating "creative opportunities through internships in the Boston area." Emerson offers a "wealth of resources" on campus, including the "ArtsEmerson productions," "Bright Lights Film series," "Emerson Channel," and the "EVVY Award" give "media creators" all the immersive experience they need to prepare for post-college professions. The study abroad trips are "phenomenal," with students raving about trips to Cuba, Colombia, and the Netherlands.

Campus Life

Students report that while Boston gives them everything they can hope for in terms of entertainment and culture, the on-campus extracurricular activities at Emerson "are innumerable and invaluable." Emerson provides "enough resources that you can do pretty much anything you want to do": clubs are "largely student run and provide a good amount of field experience for whatever it is you want to do." The campus is located "right on the Boston Common," so students enjoy "taking walks," visiting museums, many with "free entry," and trying out "lots of good food." Many students "work part-time" in the city, and otherwise students "hang out in the common rooms," "spend time working with a number of student organizations," exploring "wonderful Common Park," which is located close to campus. Other students like "watching NCAA games" or "attending interesting plays at the Emerson theatre." "Emerson students are known to overcommit themselves to activities," says one student. Another says, "It is not unusual to hear of students working on...several different shows and organizations while always taking challenging courses. Students, however, rarely complain that this affects the "quality of their lives or academic experience."

Student Body

The student body is described as "small, open-minded, artsy, but with a distinct student athlete crowd." Emerson students "usually enter the school with a career already in mind" with some having "prior experience." It is "rare to find people who are undeclared." Students describe Emerson as "an art school without the label," attracting "creative forces" who are "ambitious, driven, and self-starters." Students "can be a little pretentious and business oriented" and "casual conversations can sometimes feel like a networking event." Yet others stress that their "peers are collaborative and kind," with most "extremely kind and willing to work with each other." Everybody is generally "open to new ideas and perspectives, very accepting and friendly," and "all very committed to their art." One student comments on diversity: "It's a diverse campus in sexual and gender identity, however, racial diversity is limited. There's a range of interests, but the majority of students at Emerson are here to study some aspect of film, and so life is somewhat dominated by that." The campus tends to be "pro-social justice," with a "great activism community" that is "highly involved in Black Lives Matter," "climate change," and other hot-button political issues.

Emerson College

Financial Aid: 617-824-8655 • E-Mail: admission@emerson.edu • Website: www.emerson.edu

THE PRINCETON REVIEW SAYS

Admissions

The school reports that its standardized testing policy for use in admission for Fall 2026 is Test Optional. The Princeton Review suggests that interested applicants consult with the school for the most up-to-date standardized testing policies. *Very important factors considered include:* academic GPA, application essay. *Important factors considered include:* rigor of secondary school record, class rank, recommendation(s), extracurricular activities, talent/ability, character/personal qualities. *Other factors considered include:* standardized test scores, first generation, alumni/ae relation, geographical residence, volunteer work, work experience. High school diploma is required and GED is accepted. *Academic units required:* 4 English, 3 math, 3 science, 3 language (other than English), 3 social studies. *Academic units recommended:* 4 English, 3 math, 3 science, 3 language (other than English), 3 social studies, 4 academic electives.

Financial Aid

Students should submit: FAFSA; CSS PROFILE. Priority filing deadline is 11/15. The Princeton Review suggests that all financial aid forms be submitted as soon as possible. *Need-based scholarships/grants offered:* Federal Pell; Federal SEOG; State scholarships/grants; Private scholarships; College/university scholarship or grant aid from institutional funds. *Loan aid offered:* Federal Direct Subsidized Loans; Federal Direct Unsubsidized Loans; Direct PLUS loans. Admitted students will be notified of awards on or about 4/1. Federal Work-Study Program available. Institutional employment available.

The Inside Word

Emerson's theater-district location and large alumni network make it perfect for those interested in communications, theater, and television, as opportunities and internships abound in those fields. Applicants to the Honors Program must meet certain criteria, and those interested in the Comedic Arts, Media Production, and Performing Arts programs should note that they require the submission of creative samples.

THE SCHOOL SAYS

From the Admissions Office

"Emerson College is the nation's only four-year, liberal arts institution devoted exclusively to the study of communication and the arts. For over 140 years Emerson has educated the most innovative and creative minds in the fields of marketing, visual and media arts, entrepreneurship, publishing and writing, journalism, performing arts, and speech pathology and audiology. Guided by an award-winning faculty, Emerson students are provided with the real-world experience, professional-grade facilities, and foundational liberal arts knowledge they need to be at the cutting edge of their ever-changing industries. Located in the heart of Boston's Theatre District, Emerson's main campus is home to award-winning literary journals, sound treated television studios, and several digital editing and audio post-production suites. The Tufte Performance and Production Center houses a theater design/technology center, makeup lab, and costume shop. There are several programs to observe speech and hearing therapy, a professional marketing focus group room, digital newsroom, and the Paramount Center, which includes a sound stage, scene shop, rehearsal studios, black box theatre, and film screening room. Emerson has nearly eighty student organizations and performance groups as well as fourteen NCAA Division III teams. The college also sponsors programs in Los Angeles and Washington, D.C.; study abroad in the Netherlands, France, and Spain; and course cross-registration with the six-member Boston ProArts Consortium. The tightly-knit network of 51,000 alumni and the connections that Emerson students make on campus follow them into their post-graduate life, paving the way to collaborative projects, internships, and career opportunities across the globe."

SELECTIVITY

# of total applicants	11,092
% of total applicants accepted	48
% of total acceptees attending	19
# of in-state applicants	1,352
% of in-state applicants accepted	41
# of out-of-state-applicants	8,309
% of applicants accepted from out of state	49
# of international applicants	1,431
% of international applicants accepted	48
# offered a place on the wait list	1,537
# admitted from wait list	141

First-Year Profile

Testing policy	Test Optional

Important Dates

Early decision	
Apply by	11/1
Notified by	12/15
Early action	
Apply by	11/1
Notified by	12/15
Regular	
Apply by	1/15
Notified by	4/1
Nonfall registration?	Yes

FINANCIAL FACTS

Annual tuition	$54,400
Food and housing	$20,310
Required fees	$992
Books and supplies	$1,250
Average need-based scholarship (First-year)	$30,119 ($31,042)
% students with need rec. need-based scholarship or grant aid (First-year)	96 (97)
% students with need rec. non-need-based scholarship or grant aid (First-year)	14 (26)
% students with need rec. need-based self-help aid (First-year)	85 (86)
% of students with need fully met (First-year)	13 (23)
Average % of student need met (First-year)	60 (70)

Emory University

201 Dowman Drive, Atlanta, GA 30322 • Admissions: 404-727-6036

Survey Snapshot
School is well run
Great financial aid
Students are friendly

RATINGS

Quality of Life	94
Fire Safety	65
Green	98
Academic	92
Profs Interesting	95
Profs Accessible	94
Admissions	98
Financial Aid	97

CAMPUS LIFE

Type of school	Private
Affiliation	Methodist
Environment	City

Students

Degree-seeking undergrad enrollment	7,185
% male/female/not reported	44/56/0
% from out of state	81
% First-year from public high school	57
% First-year live on campus	98
% Ugrads live on campus	58
# of fraternities (% join)	NR (22)
# of sororities (% join)	NR (22)
% Asian	26
% Black or African American	10
% Hispanic	12
% Native American	<1
% Pacific Islander	<1
% Race and/or ethnicity unknown	3
% Two or more races	4
% White	28
% International	15
# of countries represented	70

CAMPUS MENTAL HEALTH SERVICES

Offers mental health/wellness program	Yes
Mental health training available to students	No
Employs Chief Wellness Officer	NR
Peer-to-peer mental health offerings	NR
Counseling center has guidelines or accreditation	No
Mental health/well-being courses	NR

ACADEMICS

% students returning for sophomore year	95
% students graduating within 4 years	82
% students graduating within 6 years	91
Calendar	Semester
Student/faculty ratio	8:1
Most common class size 10–19.	(44%)
Most common lab/discussion size 10–19.	(47%)

Most Popular Majors

Biology/Biological Sciences; Registered Nursing/Registered Nurse; Business Administration; Neuroscience and Behavioral Biology

STUDENTS SAY "..."

Academics

"Emory University has the beauty of being a liberal arts institute merged inside of a research institution." The academic experience at Emory is described as both "challenging and thought-provoking." The university encourages you to "get out of your comfort zone" and gives you "the tools to find out who you really are." With over 80 undergraduate majors available across nine colleges and schools, including a business school and a medical school, Emory offers a wide range of opportunities for academic exploration. Students are guided in their academic journey by professors who "made me passionate about fields I never thought I would be passionate about." Emory is home to "groundbreaking research" in numerous fields, and "research opportunities are available for [students in] "all majors and disciplines." Students note that professors "are very accessible and make the material interesting and relatable to the real world." Beyond the classroom, professors "want to know about your life, your drives, your ambitions." Emory encourages students to "become scholars and humanitarians," and over the past decade, 103 Emory alumni have been Fulbright scholars. Overall, students say Emory is "about pushing yourself beyond academics to understand how you can succeed in your career, your community, and the world." And one student says, "We have access to renowned faculty and speakers who inspire us every day not only to be our best but to leave the best impact on the world we can."

Campus Life

There is always something to do and so many activities to get involved in on this "gorgeous campus." As one student succinctly puts it, "My days are full, but I wouldn't want it any other way." A great way to discover everything happening on campus is to stop by Wonderful Wednesday, a weekly event where "student organizations set up tables around the circle and showcase their events happening, throw out free T-shirts, and even hand out food." Each week, there's a different theme, such as Sustainability or Women's History Month, and it's "a great time to really see everything that Emory offers us." Another favorite tradition is the annual Dooley's Week in the spring, which is filled with fun activities and culminates in a concert called Dooleypalooza. The campus has a strong sense of community that's "aided by Greek life and athletics but not dominated by them." There's "a ton of stuff to do on weekend nights," and popular activities include attending on-campus performances, hanging out with friends in the dorms, or exploring the vibrant city of Atlanta, where there is "always cool things going on."

Student Body

Students are driven and "determined to achieve their goals," but they "work together to do it rather than compete with each other." Emory is a "very diverse" campus with students from all over the world. Most students appreciate the opportunity to learn from their classmates, and many find it "truly a thrill" to be around so many people who "challenge you to think about what you know and reveal how much you don't." Students like that their peers "are serious in school but also find time to be involved." It's an environment where people "are extremely passionate about whatever their thing (or things!) is and tend to have very diverse interests, whether it's their Indian bhangra dance group, their research on Japanese literature, [or] their ultimate Frisbee team." Overall, it's a fun, supportive, and engaged community. Instead of getting "riled up about football games," students are more likely to "get riled up about elections and social issues and our weird unofficial skeleton mascot Dooley." As one student describes their peers, "They push me to be the best version of myself, help me with anything I need, are always there to talk, and constantly make me laugh."

EMORY UNIVERSITY

Financial Aid: 404-727-6039 • E-Mail: admiss@emory.edu • Website: www.emory.edu

THE PRINCETON REVIEW SAYS

Admissions

The school reports that its standardized testing policy for use in admission for Fall 2026 is Test Optional. The Princeton Review suggests that interested applicants consult with the school for the most up-to-date standardized testing policies. *Very important factors considered include:* rigor of secondary school record, academic GPA, recommendation(s), extracurricular activities, talent/ability, character/personal qualities. *Important factors considered include:* standardized test scores, application essay, volunteer work. *Other factors considered include:* class rank, interview, first generation, alumni/ae relation, geographical residence, state residency, work experience. High school diploma is required and GED is not accepted. *Academic units recommended:* 4 English, 4 math, 4 science, 2 science labs, 4 language (other than English), 2 social studies, 2 history, 1 computer science, 1 visual/performing arts.

Financial Aid

Students should submit: FAFSA; CSS PROFILE. Priority filing deadline is 2/15. The Princeton Review suggests that all financial aid forms be submitted as soon as possible. *Need-based scholarships/grants offered:* Federal Pell; Federal SEOG; Private scholarships; College/university scholarship or grant aid from institutional funds. *Loan aid offered:* Federal Direct Subsidized Loans; Federal Direct Unsubsidized Loans; Direct PLUS loans; State Loans; College/university loans from institutional funds. Admitted students will be notified of awards on or about 4/1. Federal Work-Study Program available. Institutional employment available.

The Inside Word

Applying to Emory means more than submitting a transcript and test scores. They evaluate each applicant in the context of their own high school, so strong grades in challenging courses carry real weight. Test scores are optional, but no score can compensate for a weak academic record. Choose recommenders who can speak to both your strengths and your ability to overcome challenges. Your essays should show a distinct voice, genuine curiosity, and real engagement with the world around you. Finally, Emory wants to know what you'll contribute. Whether through clubs, sports, work, research, or service, they're looking for students who make a difference and will continue to do so on campus and beyond.

THE SCHOOL SAYS

From the Admissions Office

"One of the most selective and diverse universities in the US, Emory offers a distinctive undergraduate education with programs in the humanities, sciences, business, and nursing on its two campuses. First-year students have the option to apply to either Emory College or Oxford College. Emory College, located in Atlanta and set among the energy and pace of the university's seven graduate and professional schools, offers a rigorous four-year liberal arts education at a research university in a thriving, global city. Students also can choose to spend the first two years of their Emory education at Oxford College, located on Emory's original campus, 38 miles (61 km) from Atlanta, in a close-knit, rigorous, small liberal arts college setting. At both campuses, students are taught by faculty who are experts in their fields and dedicated to creating an enriching academic environment.

"Emory's global community represents more than 100 countries. It is a community that comes together for a shared purpose: helping students to flourish and succeed. Faculty, staff, and alumni work together to support students' academic, personal, and professional development. There are abundant extracurricular activities that give students a chance to perform, lead, and interact meaningfully with one another and with the greater Emory and Atlanta communities. The city of Atlanta offers affordable cultural opportunities for students as well as a booming business climate with numerous opportunities for internships and jobs. Emory's dynamic community life inspires students to do more with what they learn."

SELECTIVITY

# of total applicants	37,561
% of total applicants accepted	10
% of total acceptees attending	37
# of in-state applicants	4,380
% of in-state applicants accepted	10
# of out-of-state-applicants	23,974
% of applicants accepted from out of state	12
# of international applicants	9,207
% of international applicants accepted	6
# of early decision applicants	4,725
% of early decision applicants accepted	22
# offered a place on the wait list	7,608
# admitted from wait list	274

First-Year Profile

Testing policy	Test Optional
Range SAT composite	1480–1540
Range SAT EBRW	720–760
Range SAT math	740–790
Range ACT composite	33–35
% submitting SAT scores	47
% submitting ACT scores	21
Average HS GPA	3.8
% submitting high school GPA	95
% graduated top 10% of class	76
% graduated top 25% of class	97
% graduated top 50% of class	99
% submitting high school rank	17

Important Dates

Early decision	
Apply by	11/1
Notified by	12/15
Other ED apply by	1/1
Other ED notified by	2/15
Regular	
Apply by	1/1
Notified by	4/1
Nonfall registration?	No

FINANCIAL FACTS*

Annual tuition	$70,300
Food and housing	$22,406
Required fees	$1,148
Books and supplies	$1,286
Average need-based scholarship (First-year)	$61,022 ($65,482)
% students with need rec. need-based scholarship or grant aid (First-year)	97 (98)
% students with need rec. non-need-based scholarship or grant aid (First-year)	26 (37)
% students with need rec. need-based self-help aid (First-year)	74 (70)
% students rec. any financial aid (First-year)	54 (54)
% UG borrow to pay for school	27
Average cumulative indebtedness	$24,562
% of students with need fully met (First-year)	98 (100)
Average % of student need met (First-year)	100 (100)

* Most recently reported data at time of printing. Scan the QR code to find the latest updates.

Eugene Lang College of Liberal Arts at The New School

The New School/66 West 12th Street, New York, NY 10011 • Admissions: 212-229-5150

Survey Snapshot
Lots of liberal students
Students aren't religious
Students love New York, NY

RATINGS

Quality of Life	80
Fire Safety	94
Green	87
Academic	78
Profs Interesting	91
Profs Accessible	87
Admissions	75
Financial Aid	81

CAMPUS LIFE

Type of school	Private
Environment	Metropolis

Students

Degree-seeking undergrad enrollment	1,213
% male/female/not reported	25/75/0
% from out of state	79
% First-year from public high school	52
% First-year live on campus	84
% Ugrads live on campus	30
# of fraternities	0
# of sororities	0
% Asian	7
% Black or African American	8
% Hispanic	17
% Native American	<1
% Pacific Islander	<1
% Race and/or ethnicity unknown	2
% Two or more races	9
% White	47
% International	10
# of countries represented	34

CAMPUS MENTAL HEALTH SERVICES

Offers mental health/wellness program	Yes
Mental health training available to students	Yes
Employs Chief Wellness Officer	No
Peer-to-peer mental health offerings	Yes
Counseling center has guidelines or accreditation	No
Mental health/well-being courses	Yes, for-credit

ACADEMICS

% students returning for sophomore year	71
% students graduating within 4 years	53
% students graduating within 6 years	77
Calendar	Semester
Student/faculty ratio	5:1
Most common class size 10–19.	(81%)
Most common lab/discussion size 10–19.	(81%)

Most Popular Majors

Culture & Media, Journalism + Design; Liberal Arts and Sciences/Liberal Studies; Psychology

Applicants Also Look At

New York University, Emerson College, Pratt Institute, Santa Monica College, Sarah Lawrence College

STUDENTS SAY "…"

Academics

Eugene Lang College is the liberal arts college of New York City's The New School, where students are allowed to customize their curriculum using resources throughout The New School, including Parsons School of Design, The College of Performing Arts, and a range of other colleges and schools. Classes at Lang itself are reading- and writing-intensive and typically conducted seminar-style, with the curriculum inherently cross-disciplinary (dual degrees and cross-university minors are readily available). All students complete a First Year Seminar and writing courses as well as some light general requirements (though "the bare credit minimum to graduate for each kind of course is flexible and forgiving"), and are encouraged to look into study abroad and internships as early as their sophomore year. The school understands that "not everyone learns the same way," and so the highly specific courses on offer "are all unique and crafted with care and deliberateness," and most take high advantage of the locale, with "field trips almost every class around New York City." Career Services also taps into the city to connect students with moments for growth: "internships and opportunities are truly out there."

Professors "put effort into creating comfortable atmospheres for student discussion" and "their knowledge comes from real world experience rather than pure theory." As one student says: "You can tell they always come to class ready and excited (in their own way) to discuss the topic they teach." Unique projects often replace exams and assignments, with students citing "graphic arts or musical pieces or performance art in lieu of written essays," or a class in which "we created a zine which was shared with the Lang community." There's "a level of freedom across all disciplines of study," and students appreciate that the texts used "discuss different perspectives on the topics" come from "authors of all different types of backgrounds, rather sticking to the traditional canon."

Campus Life

When your campus is New York City, the cultural world is your oyster: whether "seeing Broadway shows, visiting parks, going to food festivals," there is enough to do that "it often leads me to forget I am a student." That said, the campus is never overlooked: it has highly enjoyable workshops from people both within and without the campus and clubs often organize events to "bring awareness [to various causes]…or to spread positivity on campus." Upon arriving at Lang, people "throw themselves into the New York experience" and many occupy their time with "personal projects such as theater productions, student films, small businesses, [and] writing books." Nearby Washington Square Park and Union Square are common hangout spots, and many explore further and "find their favorite hole in the wall places and bring their friends with them to enjoy it."

Student Body

The New School offers "a highly creative environment" filled with "incredibly smart, driven and ambitious" people who "genuinely have an academic pursuit they care about strongly." To that, those specifically within the Lang college "usher in a new era of style, intelligence, and swagger," bringing a "progressive,… strong sense of urban sensibility" and enjoyment of "the finer things in life like art, music, and literature." While the student body does tend to skew wealthy, everyone "recognizes the privileges that come with attending a private institution" such as Lang. It is, overall, "a haven for [the] creative, opinionated, [and] LGBTQ," and students—many of whom are "international or have some connection to somewhere outside the United States" are "very open-minded and kind."

Eugene Lang College of Liberal Arts at The New School

Financial Aid: 212-229-8930 • E-Mail: lang@newschool.edu • Website: www.newschool.edu/lang

THE PRINCETON REVIEW SAYS

Admissions

The school reports that its standardized testing policy for use in admission for Fall 2026 is Test Free. The Princeton Review suggests that interested applicants consult with the school for the most up-to-date standardized testing policies. *Very important factors considered include:* academic GPA, application essay, extracurricular activities. *Important factors considered include:* rigor of secondary school record, recommendation(s), talent/ability, character/personal qualities. *Other factors considered include:* class rank, interview, first generation, volunteer work, work experience, level of applicant's interest. High school diploma is required and GED is accepted. *Academic units required:* 4 English. *Academic units recommended:* 4 math, 4 science, 4 language (other than English), 4 social studies, 4 history.

Financial Aid

Students should submit: FAFSA. Priority filing deadline is 3/1. The Princeton Review suggests that all financial aid forms be submitted as soon as possible. *Need-based scholarships/grants offered:* Federal Pell; Federal SEOG; State scholarships/grants; Private scholarships; College/university scholarship or grant aid from institutional funds; United Negro College Fund. *Loan aid offered:* Federal Direct Subsidized Loans; Federal Direct Unsubsidized Loans; Direct PLUS loans. Admitted students will be notified of awards on a rolling basis. Federal Work-Study Program available. Institutional employment available.

The Inside Word

Eugene Lang College of Liberal Arts is a test-free school, so SAT and ACT scores won't help your application. Focus instead on keeping up your academic record and getting glowing recommendation letters: those who apply early action may be shifted to regular decision if the school isn't suitably impressed by your grades or current extracurriculars. Know that the school looks for "commitment, independence, and passion," and you should make the most of both the New School's and the Common App's essay prompts to help convey that, or anything else the school should know about you, especially since interviews are not conducted. The school is pricey, especially when housing is factored in, but all students are automatically considered for merit scholarships.

THE SCHOOL SAYS

From the Admissions Office

"Eugene Lang College of Liberal Arts at The New School offers all the benefits of a small college experience plus the added opportunities created by its home within New York City and The New School, which includes a renowned design school, an outstanding performing arts college, and world-famous graduate schools. With roughly 1500 students and a faculty ratio of 9:1, Lang offers close relationships with faculty through its seminar-style classes. Lang also connects students to New York City and beyond through its close relationships with local activists, artists, policymakers, and community leaders.

"Academic and faculty advisors work closely with students to choose a course of study in any of Lang's 16 majors, including the self-designed Liberal Arts major. Majors can be paired with one of over 50 university-wide minors ranging from Fashion Studies to Law and Social Change. Lang students also have the option of enrolling in a five-year dual degree (BA/BFA) program with either The New School's Parsons School of Design or its School of Jazz and Contemporary Music, and many Lang students also take advantage of the five-year bachelors-master's program, which pairs Lang undergraduate degrees with masters programs such as Fashion Studies and Creative Publishing & Critical Journalism."

SELECTIVITY

# of total applicants	2,968
% of total applicants accepted	92
% of total acceptees attending	10
# offered a place on the wait list	45
# admitted from wait list	21

First-Year Profile

Testing policy	Test Free
Average HS GPA	3.5
% submitting high school GPA	96
% graduated top 10% of class	0
% graduated top 25% of class	33
% graduated top 50% of class	67
% submitting high school rank	6

Important Dates

Early action	
Apply by	11/11
Notified by	12/20
Regular	
Apply by	8/1
Notified by	Rolling, 3/16
Nonfall registration?	Yes

FINANCIAL FACTS

Annual tuition	$62,348
Food and housing	$27,400
Books and supplies	$1,450
Average need-based scholarship (First-year)	$15,287 ($17,386)
% students with need rec. need-based scholarship or grant aid (First-year)	86 (97)
% students with need rec. non-need-based scholarship or grant aid (First-year)	92 (99)
% students with need rec. need-based self-help aid (First-year)	63 (62)
% students rec. any financial aid (First-year)	96 (87)
% UG borrow to pay for school	41
Average cumulative indebtedness	$38,236
% of students with need fully met (First-year)	10 (7)
Average % of student need met (First-year)	58 (63)

FAIRFIELD UNIVERSITY

1073 North Benson Road, Fairfield, CT 06824 • Admissions: 203-254-4100

Survey Snapshot
Great off-campus food
Students love Fairfield, CT
Easy to get around campus

RATINGS

Quality of Life	91
Fire Safety	97
Green	60*
Academic	83
Profs Interesting	91
Profs Accessible	94
Admissions	94
Financial Aid	89

CAMPUS LIFE

Type of school	Private
Affiliation	Roman Catholic-Jesuit
Environment	Town

Students

Degree-seeking undergrad enrollment	5,664
% male/female/not reported	42/58/0
% from out of state	82
% First-year from public high school	55
% First-year live on campus	97
% Ugrads live on campus	74
# of fraternities	0
# of sororities	0
% Asian	2
% Black or African American	2
% Hispanic	10
% Native American	<1
% Pacific Islander	<1
% Race and/or ethnicity unknown	4
% Two or more races	2
% White	79
% International	2
# of countries represented	34

CAMPUS MENTAL HEALTH SERVICES

Offers mental health/wellness program	Yes
Mental health training available to students	Yes
Employs Chief Wellness Officer	Yes
Peer-to-peer mental health offerings	Yes
Counseling center has guidelines or accreditation	Yes
Mental health/well-being courses	Yes, for-credit

ACADEMICS

% students returning for sophomore year	91
% students graduating within 4 years	83
% students graduating within 6 years	85
Calendar	Semester
Student/faculty ratio	12:1
Most common class size 20–29.	(49%)
Most common lab/discussion size 1–9.	(51%)

Most Popular Majors

Registered Nursing/Registered Nurse; Finance; Marketing/Marketing Management

Applicants Often Prefer

Boston College, Wake Forest University

Applicants Sometimes Prefer

Bucknell University, Holy Cross College, Lehigh University, Northeastern University, Providence College, Syracuse University, Villanova University

Applicants Rarely Prefer

University of Connecticut

STUDENTS SAY "..."

Academics

Fairfield University is "rooted in real-world application" and career development. "Service learning is a big thing," with one student pointing to work in a computer science class for a local nonprofit's website: "Our group did everything from the ground up, developing and communicating with the clients." Some classes let students "go off campus to engage with the local community, and we bring what we learned back into the class curriculum.... They are always my favorite because they are engaging and get me out of my comfort zone." One student finds that their "academic experience has been both rigorous and deeply rewarding. My professors challenge me to master complex material while also... offering encouragement that reinforced my confidence and motivation." Across majors, students name "the faculty who care about student success" as one of Fairfield's greatest strengths. One student appreciates that professors go out "of their way to nourish my passions and help me go further with my academics." Students also note Fairfield's "incredible career development services." The Dolan School of Business "excels at preparing students for life beyond college. Networking events and career preparation activities occur daily," with some students reporting that they "have jobs lined up once they graduate." In short, "Fairfield allows for students to explore so many different options and has a great career center to help prepare students for life after graduation."

Campus Life

Stags, as Fairfield students are playfully known, note that "there are so many great student organizations that foster such amazing communities on campus," which "makes Fairfield feel like home." Students also speak highly of the "many facilities," from the residences to dining areas like Peet's, where they can "hang out with friends, socialize, or get work done together." The "great recreational facility" is also a social hub. "There's also always a lot of people at the gym, and we have a strong intramural sports program," which "provides the opportunity to meet lots of different people and have fun." During warmer weather, "everyone loves to use the grass spaces to hang out outside, doing work or playing games." Sunny weather also sees Stags heading "down to the beach area to relax with friends." Just a short walk from campus, the Long Island Sound "is a major selling point for the school, creating a large community of beach-house students." While at the shore, students can be found exercising—walking, running and paddleboarding are popular—and socializing, whether it's a casual hang or one of the daytime parties ("darties") that students say happen Thursdays through Saturdays. Students also point to the free programming of Fairfield at Night for its "very fun activities and ways to meet people." Whether it's sports, clubs, or beaches, "people tend to be active."

Student Body

Stags are "Fairfield-centric and beach-loving students" who prioritize "everyone helping each other." As Fairfield attracts "a large Catholic population and people interested in service who were drawn to a Jesuit school," students "value serving the community...[and have a] strong sense of compassion, initiative, and commitment to service." As one student describes it: "My peers look to help one another by...participating in class discussions, and supporting peers at club events and sporting events." As a result, the overall ethos is that of "one big friendly community of people all connected." Students also share that the student body, "while innovative, warm, and encouraging, is not the most diverse." According to some undergrads, "most students fall within the same demographic," of East Coast, "predominantly white, [and] from middle-upper class backgrounds." Within the campus community, Stags count on each other to "listen and support one another, and help each other along their journey of life."

FAIRFIELD UNIVERSITY

Financial Aid: 203-254-4125 • E-Mail: admis@fairfield.edu • Website: www.fairfield.edu

THE PRINCETON REVIEW SAYS

Admissions

The school reports that its standardized testing policy for use in admission for Fall 2026 is Test Optional. The Princeton Review suggests that interested applicants consult with the school for the most up-to-date standardized testing policies. *Very important factors considered include:* rigor of secondary school record, academic GPA, application essay, recommendation(s), level of applicant's interest. *Important factors considered include:* interview, extracurricular activities, talent/ability, character/personal qualities, volunteer work, work experience. *Other factors considered include:* class rank, standardized test scores, first generation, alumni/ae relation, geographical residence. High school diploma is required and GED is accepted. *Academic units required:* 4 English, 3 math, 3 science, 2 science labs, 2 language (other than English), 2 social studies, 2 history. *Academic units recommended:* 4 English, 4 math, 4 science, 2 science labs, 4 language (other than English), 2 social studies, 2 history.

Financial Aid

Students should submit: FAFSA; CSS PROFILE; Business/Farm Supplement; Non-Custodial Parent Profile. Priority filing deadline is 12/1. The Princeton Review suggests that all financial aid forms be submitted as soon as possible. *Need-based scholarships/grants offered:* Federal Pell; Federal SEOG; State scholarships/grants; College/university scholarship or grant aid from institutional funds; Private scholarships. *Loan aid offered:* Federal Direct Subsidized Loans; Federal Direct Unsubsidized Loans; Direct PLUS loans. Admitted students will be notified of awards on a rolling basis beginning 1/1. Federal Work-Study Program available. Institutional employment available.

The Inside Word

While all facets of the application are critical, there's no denying academic records will be of primary importance. Expect admissions officers to closely assess both grades and the rigor of your curriculum; they are also looking for students who will be successful and reflect their Jesuit ideals. And if you panic at the thought of standardized tests, you can breathe a sigh of relief: Fairfield is test optional. However, if you choose not to submit, it's highly recommended you sit for an interview.

THE SCHOOL SAYS

From the Admissions Office

"Fairfield University welcomes students into a living and learning community that will give them a solid intellectual foundation, the confidence they need to reach their individual goals, and six months after graduation, "99 percent of the Class of 2025 is employed full-time, in graduate school, or pursuing a service opportunity." Students at Fairfield benefit from the deep-rooted Jesuit commitment to education of the whole person—mind, body, and spirit—and our admission policies are consistent with that mission. When considering an applicant, Fairfield looks at measures of academic achievement, students' curricular and extracurricular activities, their life skills and accomplishments, and the degree to which they have an appreciation for Fairfield's mission and outlook. In keeping with its holistic review process, Fairfield is a Test Optional institution. Students choosing not to submit test scores do not have to submit any additional documents but are encouraged to schedule a campus interview. Fairfield University students are challenged to be creative and active members of a community in which diversity is encouraged and honored. The university community is committed to excellence in educating, serving, inspiring and training students in a wide variety of disciplines and fields. Students can complement their classroom performance with a rich array of study abroad, internship and research opportunities. Our location is ideal, offering a picturesque 2100-acre campus in the coastal community of Fairfield, Connecticut, just an hour away from the cultural, intellectual and economic opportunities of New York City. On campus, students participate in a vast array of activities, including varsity and intramural athletics, performing arts groups and an extremely active student government. All of this prepares our graduates for a rich and fulfilling future."

SELECTIVITY

# of total applicants	21,299
% of total applicants accepted	25
% of total acceptees attending	28
# of in-state applicants	3,411
% of in-state applicants accepted	20
# of out-of-state-applicants	17,156
% of applicants accepted from out of state	27
# of international applicants	732
% of international applicants accepted	5
# of early decision applicants	689
% of early decision applicants accepted	82
# offered a place on the wait list	10,741
# admitted from wait list	15

First-Year Profile

Testing policy	Test Optional
Range SAT composite	1280–1370
Range SAT EBRW	640–700
Range SAT math	630–690
Range ACT composite	29–32
% submitting SAT scores	17
% submitting ACT scores	4
Average HS GPA	3.7
% submitting high school GPA	99
% graduated top 10% of class	30
% graduated top 25% of class	64
% graduated top 50% of class	94
% submitting high school rank	18

Important Dates

Early decision	
Apply by	11/15
Notified by	12/15
Other ED apply by	1/15
Other ED notified by	2/15
Early action	
Apply by	11/1
Notified by	12/20
Regular	
Apply by	1/15
Notified by	4/1
Nonfall registration?	Yes

FINANCIAL FACTS

Annual tuition	$61,390
Food and housing	$21,564
Required fees	$1,025
Books and supplies	$1,175
Average need-based scholarship (First-year)	$31,744 ($32,045)
% students with need rec. need-based scholarship or grant aid (First-year)	97 (96)
% students with need rec. non-need-based scholarship or grant aid (First-year)	34 (43)
% students with need rec. need-based self-help aid (First-year)	55 (53)
% students rec. any financial aid (First-year)	93 (94)
% UG borrow to pay for school	64
Average cumulative indebtedness	$36,776
% of students with need fully met (First-year)	36 (43)
Average % of student need met (First-year)	68 (76)

Flagler College

74 King Street, St. Augustine, FL 32084 • Admissions: 904-819-6220

Survey Snapshot
Students are happy
Students love St. Augustine, FL
Easy to get around campus

RATINGS

Quality of Life	90
Fire Safety	77
Green	60*
Academic	77
Profs Interesting	92
Profs Accessible	94
Admissions	84
Financial Aid	83

CAMPUS LIFE

Type of school	Private
Environment	Village

Students

Degree-seeking undergrad enrollment	2,336
% male/female/not reported	32/68/<1
% from out of state	50
% First-year live on campus	96
% Ugrads live on campus	49
# of fraternities (% join)	1 (NR)
# of sororities (% join)	2 (NR)
% Asian	1
% Black or African American	3
% Hispanic	15
% Native American	<1
% Pacific Islander	<1
% Race and/or ethnicity unknown	5
% Two or more races	4
% White	69
% International	2
# of countries represented	28

CAMPUS MENTAL HEALTH SERVICES

Offers mental health/wellness program	Yes
Mental health training available to students	No
Employs Chief Wellness Officer	NR
Peer-to-peer mental health offerings	NR
Counseling center has guidelines or accreditation	No
Mental health/well-being courses	NR

ACADEMICS

% students returning for sophomore year	72
% students graduating within 4 years	43
% students graduating within 6 years	52
Calendar	Semester
Student/faculty ratio	13:1

Most Popular Majors

Environmental Science; Psychology; Business Administration and Management

STUDENTS SAY "..."

Academics

Flagler College, located just a few miles from the ocean, offers 44 majors and provides "an excellent education in a beautiful location." To help students broaden their horizons, the college has a required Core Experience. This begins with a one-semester class that introduces students to college life, covering everything from how to register for classes to familiarizing themselves with the city. Then, students select classes across nine required skill areas, which range from Academic Writing and Natural Scientific Inquiry to Oral Communication and Ethical Reasoning. In their sophomore year, students can choose to study abroad or get involved in a local service project. According to one student, the opportunity to learn outside the classroom "has been the most valuable aspect" of their education. Another big draw for students is the faculty, who are described as "very knowledgeable in their fields" and "extremely enthusiastic about their jobs." Students find it "pretty easy to get to know the professors within your major on a personal basis, [which] makes things a lot easier and comfortable." They appreciate the "ample help from teachers," noting that professors are "always willing to meet and discuss work outside of the classroom." Classes are seen as an "intellectual journey," with professors facilitating discussions that encourage exploration of various topics or questions. This approach "evokes curiosity from all students, leaving very little room for confusion." As a result, participants feel engaged and want "to share experiences and knowledge with the faculty and other students."

Campus Life

Flagler College offers an impressive array of opportunities for student involvement on its sunny and vibrant campus. Since "homework usually isn't too bad most of the time," students have ample time to engage in everything Flagler has available. There are numerous clubs and organizations for students, including academic clubs like the Student Accounting Society, advocacy organizations such as the Green Beans Environmental Club, which promotes sustainability on campus, the Black Student Union, and the Pride Alliance, as well as a few sororities and fraternities. Students love the proximity to the beach and all it offers, whether it's playing beach volleyball, walking along the sand dunes, or learning how to sail with the Sailing Club. First- and second-year students are required to live on campus, which creates a close-knit community. The campus "is beautiful, we sometimes even compare it to Hogwarts." Students report that when the weather is nice, "the pool and West lawn are the places to be." Within walking distance from campus is the "casual and quaint" town of St. Augustine, which "is an awesome place to spend your time, walking around, going out to eat, and doing a little bit of shopping." A little further away, students can "drive to Jacksonville and go out at night there."

Student Body

Students at Flagler College bond over their love for the ocean and credit the "easygoing and very laid-back" culture to its proximity to the beach. As one student notes, "The beach mentality triumphs, including surfer culture." Others agree, saying that life is "pretty chill at Flagler." Many students are surfers or artistic types, although any stereotypes about these groups don't apply. Rather, classmates are "very motivated and ready to broaden their education." Approximately 55 percent of students are from outside Florida, primarily from the Southeast and Northeast regions, with a few international students as well. Students appreciate the inclusive environment, saying, "There is a crowd for everybody, despite the small size of the student body," and their classmates "seem to be very respectful of others' views." Students here are "super nice and friendly," making it easy to break the ice and connect with others. All you need to do is "attend a few of the many social activities that Flagler College offers. It's really easy to make friends there!"

FLAGLER COLLEGE

Financial Aid: 904-819-6225 • E-Mail: admissions@flagler.edu • Website: www.flagler.edu

THE PRINCETON REVIEW SAYS

Admissions

The school reports that its standardized testing policy for use in admission for Fall 2026 is Test Optional. The Princeton Review suggests that interested applicants consult with the school for the most up-to-date standardized testing policies. *Very important factors considered include:* academic GPA. *Important factors considered include:* rigor of secondary school record, application essay, recommendation(s), first generation, geographical residence. *Other factors considered include:* standardized test scores, extracurricular activities, character/personal qualities, alumni/ae relation, volunteer work, work experience, level of applicant's interest. High school diploma is required and GED is accepted. *Academic units recommended:* 4 English, 4 math, 3 science, 1 science lab, 2 language (other than English), 1 social studies, 3 history.

Financial Aid

Students should submit: FAFSA; State aid form. Priority filing deadline is 3/1. The Princeton Review suggests that all financial aid forms be submitted as soon as possible. *Need-based scholarships/grants offered:* Federal Pell; Federal SEOG; State scholarships/grants; Private scholarships; College/university scholarship or grant aid from institutional funds. *Loan aid offered:* Federal Direct Subsidized Loans; Federal Direct Unsubsidized Loans; Direct PLUS loans. Admitted students will be notified of awards on a rolling basis beginning 10/25. Federal Work-Study Program available. Institutional employment available.

The Inside Word

Several high-profile programs and a desirable location make Flagler an appealing choice for many students. Strong candidates should meet little resistance from the admissions office. However, admission is not a given, so make sure you have a strong application with challenging courses and high grades.

THE SCHOOL SAYS

From the Admissions Office

"Flagler College is an independent, four-year, coeducational, residential institution located in picturesque St. Augustine. A famous historic tourist center in northeast Florida, it is located to the south of Jacksonville and north of Daytona Beach. Flagler students have ample opportunity to explore the rich cultural heritage and international flavor of St. Augustine, and there's always time for a relaxing day at the beach, about four miles from campus. The annual cost for tuition, room, and board at Flagler is typically less expensive than most comparable private schools in Florida. The small student body helps to keep one from becoming 'just a number.' Flagler serves a predominately full-time student body and seeks to enroll students who can benefit from the type of educational experience the college offers. Because of the college's mission and distinctive characteristics, some students may benefit more from an educational experience at Flagler than others. The college's admission standards and procedures are designed to select from among the applicants those students most likely to succeed academically, to contribute significantly to the student life program at Flagler, and to become graduates of the college. Flagler College provides an exceptional opportunity for a private education at an extremely affordable cost."

SELECTIVITY

# of total applicants	5,085
% of total applicants accepted	79
% of total acceptees attending	16
# of early decision applicants	277
% of early decision applicants accepted	68

First-Year Profile

Testing policy	Test Optional
Range SAT EBRW	560–650
Range SAT math	520–600
Range ACT composite	22–27
% submitting SAT scores	18
% submitting ACT scores	8

Important Dates

Early decision	
Apply by	11/1
Regular	
Apply by	3/1
Notified by	Rolling, 10/1
Nonfall registration?	Yes

FINANCIAL FACTS

Annual tuition	$36,120
Food and housing	$17,420
Required fees	$600
Books and supplies	$960

Florida International University

11200 SW 8 St., Miami, FL 33199 • Admissions: 305-348-7000

Survey Snapshot
Great off-campus food
Students love Miami, FL
Intramural sports are popular

RATINGS

Quality of Life	87
Fire Safety	97
Green	93
Academic	77
Profs Interesting	85
Profs Accessible	87
Admissions	87
Financial Aid	81

CAMPUS LIFE

Type of school	Public
Environment	Metropolis

Students

Degree-seeking undergrad enrollment	40,908
% male/female/not reported	45/55/0
% from out of state	4
% First-year live on campus	25
% Ugrads live on campus	7
# of fraternities (% join)	27 (NR)
# of sororities (% join)	15 (NR)
% Asian	3
% Black or African American	11
% Hispanic	68
% Native American	<1
% Pacific Islander	<1
% Race and/or ethnicity unknown	1
% Two or more races	2
% White	8
% International	7
# of countries represented	167

CAMPUS MENTAL HEALTH SERVICES

Offers mental health/wellness program	Yes
Mental health training available to students	No
Employs Chief Wellness Officer	NR
Peer-to-peer mental health offerings	NR
Counseling center has guidelines or accreditation	No
Mental health/well-being courses	NR

ACADEMICS

% students returning for sophomore year	92
% students graduating within 4 years	64
% students graduating within 6 years	78
Calendar	Semester
Student/faculty ratio	25:1
Most common class size 10–19.	(28%)
Most common lab/discussion size 20–29.	(51%)

Most Popular Majors
Biology/Biological Sciences; Business Administration and Management; Psychology

STUDENTS SAY "…"

Academics

Florida International University lives up to its name with "strong programs in business, engineering, and international relations, making it a great place for students pursuing global careers." Students appreciate the collaborative, interdisciplinary atmosphere on campus: "You'll see pre-health students exchanging study tips with engineering majors, business students teaming up with artists on creative projects, and social science students sharing ideas with future tech innovators." There's also a lauded flexibility, whether that's for studying in-person or online or as seen in the "great support system [for] physical, mental, or emotional needs." Additionally, a steady influx of emails helps to communicate opportunities like "internships or mentorships and career fairs." The school's location in Miami is advantageous for the professional connections—there are "tons of networking and job opportunities in a major global city"—and the academic experience. Instructors often integrate the city into their classes, whether that's "walking around a new part of South Florida every Wednesday for six hours, and learning about the history of Miami," getting "extra credit points for participating in community events," or having "a blast" learning about art directly from artists at local museums. Overall, students praise the "vast knowledge of the educators" here who "bring real-world experience into the classroom, which makes learning more engaging and applicable."

Campus Life

"The campus is buzzing with activity" and there's "something for everyone," whether that's tailgating during football season, building a race car with the Panther Motorsports club, or taking fitness classes like yoga, spin, and Zumba. Outdoor activities are plentiful and include surfing, kayaking at FIU's waterfront Biscayne Bay Campus, or volunteering for a beach clean-up. Students say that while "Greek life exists, the absence of a designated Greek row hinders its visibility," and some wish the scene were stronger. That doesn't mean that the energy on this campus is lacking. FIU offers "incredible school spirit," which is "on full display" during athletic games, and the on-campus concerts are "a great experience." Students often gather at the Graham Center, where there is "always music playing and there are restaurants and lounge areas." Many students enjoy exploring everything Miami has to offer, including museums, restaurants, parks, and nightlife. In short, "It's a fast-paced environment, but it has a laid-back, Miami vibe that makes it feel balanced."

Student Body

The student body is "extremely diverse," which students consistently cite as a top strength of the school. There's "a large representation of Hispanic and Latinx students" and students "from all different parts of the city, country, and world." One student shares, "I've been able to meet students from South Korea, Chile, Azerbaijan, and Sweden all within the Miami campus." Another student agrees, saying, "My peers at FIU are a vibrant mix of local commuters and international students, [which reflects] both our name, Florida International University, and the city of Miami itself." Students here "bring unique perspectives that make discussions engaging and thought-provoking," and classmates enjoy learning "not just from classes, but from the students and their culture." Students are "very enthusiastic" and have "a lot of school pride." It's an atmosphere where people are "spirited, welcoming, and passionate about learning and building a community." Fellow classmates can be found "studying when they have free time, but at the same time, they enjoy their time on campus." Overall, it's a place where it's "easy to connect with others and find great people" and "people go out of their way to be kind."

Florida International University

Financial Aid: 305-348-7272 • E-Mail: admiss@fiu.edu • Website: www.fiu.edu

THE PRINCETON REVIEW SAYS

Admissions

The school reports that its standardized testing policy for use in admission for Fall 2026 will require applicants to submit either the SAT or ACT. The Princeton Review suggests that interested applicants consult with the school for the most up-to-date standardized testing policies. *Very important factors considered include:* rigor of secondary school record, class rank, academic GPA, standardized test scores. *Other factors considered include:* application essay, recommendation(s), extracurricular activities, talent/ability, character/personal qualities, first generation, alumni/ae relation, geographical residence, state residency, volunteer work, work experience, level of applicant's interest. High school diploma is required and GED is accepted. *Academic units required:* 4 English, 4 math, 3 science, 2 science labs, 2 language (other than English), 3 social studies, 2 academic electives. *Academic units recommended:* 4 English, 4 math, 3 science, 2 science labs, 2 language (other than English), 3 social studies, 2 academic electives.

Financial Aid

Students should submit: FAFSA. Priority filing deadline is 3/1. The Princeton Review suggests that all financial aid forms be submitted as soon as possible. *Need-based scholarships/grants offered:* Federal Pell; Federal SEOG; State scholarships/grants; Private scholarships; College/university scholarship or grant aid from institutional funds. *Loan aid offered:* Federal Direct Subsidized Loans; Federal Direct Unsubsidized Loans; Direct PLUS loans. Admitted students will be notified of awards on a rolling basis beginning 2/1. Federal Work-Study Program available. Institutional employment available.

The Inside Word

Florida International University is a selective school, and admission officers want to be sure that accepted students have what it takes to handle FIU's academics rigors. You'll have a leg up with advanced courses on your high school transcript. FIU is seeking individuals who welcome challenges and strive for greatness when faced with adversity. In addition to an impressive course load, be sure to highlight extracurriculars and community involvement for a well-rounded application. Finally, it's important to know that certain degree programs (like architecture and nursing) maintain more stringent admissions requirements.

THE SCHOOL SAYS

From the Admissions Office

"Florida International University (FIU) is Miami's first and only public research university. With more than 200 bachelor's, master's and doctoral options (many available online) and South Florida's only public colleges of law and medicine, FIU offers a program to fit every passion. FIU is dedicated to enriching the lives of the local and global community. With a student body of nearly 55,000 students, FIU is among the top 10 largest universities in the nation and has graduated more than 300,000 alumni. Diversity and access are essential to FIU's mission. Over 80% of the student body is comprised of minorities and FIU ranks first among U.S. public institutions for granting bachelor's and graduate degrees to Hispanics and ranks in the top 5 for bachelor's and graduate degrees granted to Black/African American students. Additionally, more than 50% of FIU's undergraduates come from low-income households and more than 38% are the first in their family to attend college. Designated as a top-tier research institution, FIU also emphasizes research as a major component in the university's mission. FIU's exploration, research and community engagement is supported by more than 40 centers and institutes. From the sciences to socio-political studies, these centers and institutes serve to further student's pursuit of knowledge and understanding."

SELECTIVITY

# of total applicants	36,113
% of total applicants accepted	61
% of total acceptees attending	27
# of in-state applicants	20,734
% of in-state applicants accepted	80
# of out-of-state-applicants	8,882
% of applicants accepted from out of state	36
# of international applicants	6,487
% of international applicants accepted	34

First-Year Profile

Testing policy	SAT or ACT Required
Range SAT composite	1070–1260
Range SAT EBRW	560–650
Range SAT math	510–620
Range ACT composite	22–27
% submitting SAT scores	92
% submitting ACT scores	8
Average HS GPA	4.0
% submitting high school GPA	99
% graduated top 10% of class	23
% graduated top 25% of class	46
% graduated top 50% of class	55
% submitting high school rank	76

Important Dates

Early action	
Apply by	11/3
Notified by	12/11
Regular	
Apply by	3/2
Notified by	6/1
Nonfall registration?	Yes

FINANCIAL FACTS

Annual in-state tuition	$6,168
Annual out-of-state tuition	$19,806
Food and housing	$13,852
Required fees	$398
Books and supplies	$1,350
Average need-based scholarship (First-year)	$9,733 ($10,270)
% students with need rec. need-based scholarship or grant aid (First-year)	93 (92)
% students with need rec. non-need-based scholarship or grant aid (First-year)	40 (76)
% students with need rec. need-based self-help aid (First-year)	28 (18)
% students rec. any financial aid (First-year)	61 (75)
% UG borrow to pay for school	21
Average cumulative indebtedness	$18,003
% of students with need fully met (First-year)	10 (14)
Average % of student need met (First-year)	35 (49)

Florida Southern College

111 Lake Hollingsworth Drive, Lakeland, FL 33801-5698 • Admissions: 863-680-4131

Survey Snapshot
Lots of conservative students
Everyone loves the Moccasins
Intramural sports are popular

RATINGS

Quality of Life	86
Fire Safety	89
Green	60*
Academic	78
Profs Interesting	89
Profs Accessible	91
Admissions	87
Financial Aid	89

CAMPUS LIFE

Type of school	Private
Affiliation	United Methodist
Environment	City

Students

Degree-seeking undergrad enrollment	2,694
% male/female/not reported	34/66/0
% from out of state	38
% First-year from public high school	81
% First-year live on campus	85
% Ugrads live on campus	84
# of fraternities (% join)	6 (17)
# of sororities (% join)	6 (26)
% Asian	2
% Black or African American	7
% Hispanic	17
% Native American	0
% Pacific Islander	0
% Race and/or ethnicity unknown	11
% Two or more races	4
% White	56
% International	3
# of countries represented	36

CAMPUS MENTAL HEALTH SERVICES

Offers mental health/wellness program	Yes
Mental health training available to students	Yes
Employs Chief Wellness Officer	Yes
Peer-to-peer mental health offerings	No
Counseling center has guidelines or accreditation	Yes
Mental health/well-being courses	Yes

ACADEMICS

% students returning for sophomore year	77
% students graduating within 4 years	60
% students graduating within 6 years	68
Calendar	Semester
Student/faculty ratio	13:1
Most common class size 10–19.	(38%)
Most common lab/discussion size 10–19.	(73%)

Most Popular Majors
Business/Marketing; Biology/Biological Sciences; Nursing

Applicants Sometimes Prefer
Florida State University, University of Florida

Applicants Rarely Prefer
Rollins College, Stetson University, The University of Tampa

STUDENTS SAY "..."

Academics

Florida Southern College is a private university that "fosters collaboration, offers growth opportunities, and values inclusivity" among its 2,600 undergraduates. The school offers more than seventy programs and places an emphasis on "engaged learning," which includes "experiences relating to the lecture from professors and students, in-person games...to test our knowledge, and real-life simulation technology that helps us practice what we're learning." The school's smaller size facilitates engagement and provides "great one-on-one attention in the classroom." The school also gives teachers the flexibility to "hold classes in different spaces on and off campus," going wherever the lessons are best taught. As one student puts it, "Faculty doesn't just lecture us, they find ways to help us learn in exciting and interesting ways." FSC has "a very invested body of teachers," and "professors are incredibly engaging and accommodating to learning preferences and interests of students." Some students say that "internships [are] readily available and encouraged," and professors will even "implore you to branch out and participate in great opportunities." One student says the school is "very unbiased and accepts everyone...All majors and organizations are very equal and are all seen and appreciated." There are "new ideas and technologies being implemented into curriculum" on a regular basis, as well as "lots of project-based learning." Looking to the future, the school also "offers many career fairs which [are] very helpful for making connections," and there is even a "Shark Tank business class where you pitch a product in front of a large audience downtown."

Campus Life

Students speak to their peers' "positive attitude" and how that support works "to make the campus the best place it can be." From the look of it, "everyone knows quite a lot of people, so it's good to have that camaraderie and closeness to other students." That also means that "student involvement (clubs, organizations, events, etc.) is extremely important and taken seriously," and "there's always something happening—club meetings, cultural festivals, or intramural sports." There is also the "Association of Campus Entertainment (ACE), which organizes several large events throughout the school year, like concerts and brain breaks for students to enjoy." Nearby is "the beautiful Lake Hollingsworth where students walk/run/bike/picnic/rollerblade/drive around." For those looking for excuses to hang out, "coffee is definitely part of the culture here," as is SnakePit, "a gaming center where [students] are able to utilize gaming computers to play what they please." Within walking distance is downtown Lakeland, which "is very pretty and has a farmer's market every Saturday."

Student Body

Overall, students at Florida Southern College are described as "very personable and community-based" and very "close-knit," which is great for those who love "to be surrounded in each other's company" and "enjoy spending quality time with each other beyond small talk." The size of the campus plays a big role in bonding: "You can walk across campus and make a new friend every day but also see five friends on every outing." There is a powerful sense of community and students are "always welcome in interest groups, events, and in the classroom." One student notes that "athletes are a large portion of campus," but another assures that "People from all backgrounds, majors, and cultures play intramurals. You don't have to be good to play, either!" There are also plenty of opportunities to socialize "through campus-wide traditions, celebrations, Greek life, and festivals such as our end of the year carnival, the students spend lots of time coming together to celebrate college life."

FLORIDA SOUTHERN COLLEGE

Financial Aid: 863-680-4140 • E-Mail: fscadm@flsouthern.edu • Website: www.flsouthern.edu

THE PRINCETON REVIEW SAYS

Admissions

The school reports that its standardized testing policy for use in admission for Fall 2026 is Test Optional. The Princeton Review suggests that interested applicants consult with the school for the most up-to-date standardized testing policies. *Very important factors considered include:* rigor of secondary school record, academic GPA. *Important factors considered include:* application essay, recommendation(s), extracurricular activities, talent/ability, character/personal qualities, level of applicant's interest. *Other factors considered include:* class rank, standardized test scores, interview, first generation, alumni/ae relation, religious affiliation/commitment, volunteer work, work experience. High school diploma is required and GED is accepted. *Academic units required:* 4 English, 3 math, 2 science, 2 science labs, 3 social studies, 3 history, 1 academic elective. *Academic units recommended:* 4 English, 3 math, 2 science, 2 science labs, 2 language (other than English), 3 social studies, 3 history, 1 academic elective.

Financial Aid

Students should submit: FAFSA. Priority filing deadline is 3/1. The Princeton Review suggests that all financial aid forms be submitted as soon as possible. *Need-based scholarships/grants offered:* Federal Pell; Federal SEOG; State scholarships/grants; Private scholarships; College/university scholarship or grant aid from institutional funds; Federal Nursing Scholarships. *Loan aid offered:* Federal Direct Subsidized Loans; Federal Direct Unsubsidized Loans; Direct PLUS loans. Admitted students will be notified of awards on a rolling basis beginning 3/1. Federal Work-Study Program available. Institutional employment available.

The Inside Word

Florida Southern College admits students based on the usual mix of GPA, transcript, recommendations, and extracurriculars. Special attention is given to those whose accomplishments include peer-engagement and leadership roles.

THE SCHOOL SAYS

From the Admissions Office

"Florida Southern is a national leader in engaged learning, offering real-world, hands-on experiences that include internships, student-faculty collaborative research, performance, service opportunities, and study abroad. The Junior Journey is an innovative travel program that allows students to study overseas or domestically.

"FSC offers more than seventy majors, ranging from business, biology, and nursing to architecture, art and museum studies, music, and theatre performance. Students looking to enter highly specialized career fields can choose from a range of interdisciplinary minors like ethics and neuroscience; there are also 15+ pre-professional programs with outstanding placement rates in subjects like law and medicine. Students wanting to put their career on the fast track can take advantage of a range of 4+1 options allowing them to earn a master's degree, including an MBA, with an extra year of study. The College also offers doctoral programs in education, nursing, and physical therapy.

"The College is known for its friendly, vibrant, and energetic community. Our involved student body enjoys rich and varied campus activities and programming that includes 20 championship NCAA Division II athletic programs, four club sports (equestrian, esports, ice hockey, and water ski), intramurals, 100+ clubs and organizations, and 12 national fraternities and sororities. The College's popular lakefront allows for recreational activities like kayaking, canoeing, and paddle boarding. The College has a state-of-the-art technology center, as well as contemporary residence halls with scenic views of Lake Hollingsworth. FSC is home to the world's largest single-site collection of Frank Lloyd Wright structures, which provides a stunning setting for living and learning.

"Within a year of graduation, 99 percent of students report achieving their post-baccalaureate degree goals by securing employment or beginning an advanced degree program."

SELECTIVITY

# of total applicants	10,731
% of total applicants accepted	65
% of total acceptees attending	10
# of in-state applicants	5,403
% of in-state applicants accepted	69
# of out-of-state-applicants	4,238
% of applicants accepted from out of state	66
# of international applicants	1,034
% of international applicants accepted	44
# of early decision applicants	168
% of early decision applicants accepted	69

First-Year Profile

Testing policy	Test Optional
Range SAT composite	1150–1310
Range SAT EBRW	580–670
Range SAT math	540–640
Range ACT composite	25–29
% submitting SAT scores	22
% submitting ACT scores	16
Average HS GPA	3.8
% submitting high school GPA	100
% graduated top 10% of class	20
% graduated top 25% of class	50
% graduated top 50% of class	83
% submitting high school rank	60

Important Dates

Early decision	
Apply by	11/1
Notified by	12/15
Early action	
Apply by	11/1
Notified by	12/15
Regular	
Apply by	5/1
Notified by	Rolling, 8/1
Nonfall registration?	Yes

FINANCIAL FACTS*

Annual tuition	$46,350
Food and housing	$15,130
Required fees	$1,320
Books and supplies	$1,290
Average need-based scholarship (First-year)	$27,763 ($28,693)
% students with need rec. need-based scholarship or grant aid (First-year)	99 (100)
% students with need rec. non-need-based scholarship or grant aid (First-year)	67 (59)
% students with need rec. need-based self-help aid (First-year)	9 (2)
% students rec. any financial aid (First-year)	98 (100)
% UG borrow to pay for school	83
Average cumulative indebtedness	$27,170
% of students with need fully met (First-year)	28 (26)
Average % of student need met (First-year)	76 (74)

* Most recently reported data at time of printing. Scan the QR code to find the latest updates.

FLORIDA STATE UNIVERSITY

PO Box 3062400, Tallahassee, FL 32306 • Admissions: 850-644-6200

Survey Snapshot
Everyone loves the Seminoles
Intramural sports are popular
Frats and sororities are popular

RATINGS

Quality of Life	88
Fire Safety	60*
Green	95
Academic	83
Profs Interesting	89
Profs Accessible	92
Admissions	94
Financial Aid	86

CAMPUS LIFE

Type of school	Public
Environment	City

Students

Degree-seeking undergrad enrollment	32,921
% male/female/not reported	44/56/<1
% from out of state	14
% First-year from public high school	79
% First-year live on campus	75
% Ugrads live on campus	20
# of fraternities (% join)	27 (19)
# of sororities (% join)	24 (26)
% Asian	4
% Black or African American	7
% Hispanic	24
% Native American	<1
% Pacific Islander	<1
% Race and/or ethnicity unknown	2
% Two or more races	5
% White	56
% International	2
# of countries represented	109

CAMPUS MENTAL HEALTH SERVICES

Offers mental health/wellness program	NR
Mental health training available to students	Yes
Employs Chief Wellness Officer	Yes
Peer-to-peer mental health offerings	Yes
Counseling center has guidelines or accreditation	No
Mental health/well-being courses	NR

ACADEMICS

% students returning for sophomore year	97
% students graduating within 4 years	75
% students graduating within 6 years	86
Calendar	Semester
Student/faculty ratio	17:1
Most common class size 10–19.	(37%)
Most common lab/discussion size 20–29.	(56%)

Most Popular Majors

Psychology; Registered Nursing/Registered Nurse; Finance

STUDENTS SAY "..."

Academics

Research, service, scholarship, and extracurricular opportunities are abundant at the "large campus" of Florida State University in Tallahassee. It's rather easy to understand why students are drawn to Florida State. After all, the "campus is gorgeous," "the weather is always nice" and there are an abundance "of resources at your fingertips." What's more, "despite its large size...the community is welcoming and [undergrads] don't feel like an anonymous face in the student body." Incredibly, it's still "easy to feel at home." Much of that can be credited to faculty who "are very willing to help undergraduate students with classes, research, career prospects, and everything in between." Florida State professors also excel at bringing their "courses to life and mak[ing] them interesting enough that [students truly] want to learn." Many are also "experts in their field." And "they make it known that they want students to succeed." To that end, "in addition to making themselves available... for office hours, they [continually] offer to make time for students [beyond those hours]." Perhaps this grateful undergrad says it best, "Their advice has pushed me to be a better student and pushed me to find a great future."

Campus Life

Life at Florida State offers a great "mix of academics, socializing, [and] extracurricular [activities]." To begin with, athletics are fairly popular and you can frequently spot "basketball games and volleyball games" popping up around campus. And during the fall, weekends "are spent [at] football games and tailgates." Aside from sports, we've been informed that the "Student Life Cinema always has cool events going on" and "there are always free concerts at Club Down Under on campus" as well. FSU also has "many organizations that are focused on philanthropy." For example, "Dance Marathon is the largest student run organization on campus and we have one of the largest Dance Marathons in the entire country. We also have a large Relay for Life organization." Moreover, a number of undergrads enjoy FSU's reservation, an "off campus [spot] where students can go swimming, paddle boarding, relaxing, or even [try out a] ropes course." Of course, it's also important to mention that some students feel as though "Greek life dominates" the social scene, even though "less than 50% of the student population [participates]." Finally, undergrads greatly appreciate hometown Tallahassee. The city offers "endless" nightlife along with "many great clubs and places for social events as well as pretty landscapes and historical sites."

Student Body

Florida State manages to attract a student body that's a "unique mixture of south Floridians, crunchy granolas, Northern snowbirds, sorority girls, and good ole boys, with a nice international population mixed in there." Despite these diverse personalities, the university still seems to cultivate a "strong sense of community." Of course, it definitely helps that students are "very friendly and always willing to [strike] up conversation." Even better, "everyone you see seems genuinely happy" and everyone "is pushing for you." People here want to see their peers "succeed." As one impressed student shares, "Everyone is so kind. No one is afraid to ask for help, and if they do most would be more than willing to help you out." Undergrads also applaud FSU for doing "a great job in creating or allowing students to create spaces for all communities, particularly those that are historically marginalized/typically first gen students." And no matter what else, students here come together in their shared "love for FSU." As this satisfied student sums up, "I have never been on a campus with such school spirit, excitement, and motivation to improve."

FLORIDA STATE UNIVERSITY

Financial Aid: 850-644-5716 • E-Mail: admissions@fsu.edu • Website: www.fsu.edu

THE PRINCETON REVIEW SAYS

Admissions

The school reports that its standardized testing policy for use in admission for Fall 2026 will require applicants to submit either the SAT or ACT. The Princeton Review suggests that interested applicants consult with the school for the most up-to-date standardized testing policies. *Very important factors considered include:* rigor of secondary school record. *Important factors considered include:* class rank, academic GPA, standardized test scores, application essay, extracurricular activities, talent/ability, character/personal qualities, first generation, geographical residence, state residency, volunteer work, work experience. High school diploma is required and GED is accepted. *Academic units required:* 4 English, 4 math, 3 science, 2 science labs, 2 language (other than English), 1 social studies, 2 history, 3 academic electives. *Academic units recommended:* 4 English, 4 math, 4 science, 2 science labs, 4 language (other than English), 2 social studies, 2 history, 3 academic electives.

Financial Aid

Students should submit: FAFSA; State aid form. The Princeton Review suggests that all financial aid forms be submitted as soon as possible. *Need-based scholarships/grants offered:* Federal Pell; Federal SEOG; State scholarships/grants; Private scholarships; College/university scholarship or grant aid from institutional funds; United Negro College Fund. *Loan aid offered:* Federal Direct Subsidized Loans; Federal Direct Unsubsidized Loans; Direct PLUS loans. Admitted students will be notified of awards on a rolling basis. Federal Work-Study Program available. Institutional employment available.

The Inside Word

Aspiring FSU students should be forewarned that admission here is selective. Fortunately, the university does take a holistic approach to the process. And candidates should expect that all facets of their application will be thoroughly reviewed. Of course, admissions officers favor students who have taken a rigorous course load throughout high school. A solid GPA is also a must. Finally, the essay and résumé sections of the application allow you to showcase who you are.

THE SCHOOL SAYS

From the Admissions Office

"Florida State University is one of the top public universities in the world and is proud to be recognized as a Preeminent University by the State of Florida. Designated as a Carnegie Research University (with very high research activity), Florida State offers more than 320 undergraduate, graduate, and professional degree programs, including medicine and law. Our diverse and highly talented student body includes students from all fifty states and more than 130 countries. The university is committed to student success for all students as evidenced by impressive retention and graduation rates that place us at the highest levels nationally. World class faculty, including Nobel laureates, Pulitzer Prize winners, Guggenheim Fellows, members of the National Academy of Sciences and American Academy of Arts and Sciences, and other globally recognized teachers and researchers, are actively creating the knowledge you will be studying in class. You will be encouraged to become engaged in research, internships, entrepreneurial initiatives and other creative activities. You will be supported by comprehensive and innovative student services. And you will be enriched by the extensive variety of cultural, athletic, and recreational offerings available outside the classroom. Our singular goal is to make you better than when you arrived, so that you can make a difference in your community and the world."

SELECTIVITY

# of total applicants	83,469
% of total applicants accepted	24
% of total acceptees attending	32

First-Year Profile

Testing policy	SAT or ACT Required
Range SAT composite	1300–1410
Range SAT EBRW	650–720
Range SAT math	630–710
Range ACT composite	29–32
% submitting SAT scores	64
% submitting ACT scores	36
Average HS GPA	3.7
% submitting high school GPA	99
% graduated top 10% of class	78
% graduated top 25% of class	92
% graduated top 50% of class	98
% submitting high school rank	53

Important Dates

Early action	
Apply by	10/15
Notified by	12/11
Regular	
Apply by	3/1
Notified by	Rolling, April for applications received after 12/1/26
Nonfall registration?	Yes

FINANCIAL FACTS

Annual in-state tuition	$4,640
Annual out-of-state tuition	$19,806
Food and housing	$13,474
Required fees	$1,877
Books and supplies	$1,200
Average need-based scholarship (First-year)	$13,476 ($15,326)
% students with need rec. need-based scholarship or grant aid (First-year)	98 (99)
% students with need rec. non-need-based scholarship or grant aid (First-year)	10 (19)
% students with need rec. need-based self-help aid (First-year)	36 (28)
% students rec. any financial aid (First-year)	89 (95)
% UG borrow to pay for school	30
Average cumulative indebtedness	$20,800
% of students with need fully met (First-year)	11 (19)
Average % of student need met (First-year)	66 (75)

Fordham University

441 East Fordham Road, Bronx, NY 10458 • Admissions: 718-817-4000

Survey Snapshot
Students love Bronx, NY
Great off-campus food
Easy to get around campus

RATINGS

Quality of Life	87
Fire Safety	99
Green	93
Academic	80
Profs Interesting	86
Profs Accessible	89
Admissions	90
Financial Aid	85

CAMPUS LIFE

Type of school	Private
Affiliation	Roman Catholic
Environment	Metropolis

Students

Degree-seeking undergrad enrollment	10,313
% male/female/not reported	40/60/<1
% from out of state	42
% First-year from public high school	51
% First-year live on campus	75
% Ugrads live on campus	44
# of fraternities	0
# of sororities	0
% Asian	13
% Black or African American	7
% Hispanic	23
% Native American	<1
% Pacific Islander	<1
% Race and/or ethnicity unknown	3
% Two or more races	6
% White	41
% International	8
# of countries represented	99

CAMPUS MENTAL HEALTH SERVICES

Offers mental health/wellness program	Yes
Mental health training available to students	Yes
Employs Chief Wellness Officer	No
Peer-to-peer mental health offerings	Yes
Counseling center has guidelines or accreditation	Yes
Mental health/well-being courses	Yes, for-credit

ACADEMICS

% students returning for sophomore year	87
% students graduating within 4 years	75
% students graduating within 6 years	81
Calendar	Semester
Student/faculty ratio	14:1
Most common class size 10–19.	(42%)
Most common lab/discussion size 10–19.	(47%)

Most Popular Majors

Psychology; Political Science and Government; Finance

Applicants Often Prefer

Boston College, Boston University, City University of New York—Baruch College, City University of New York—Hunter College, The George Washington University, New York University, Northeastern University, Rutgers University–New Brunswick, State University of New York—Binghamton University, State University of New York—Stony Brook University

STUDENTS SAY "..."

Academics

Fordham University "[takes] pride in caring for the whole person" and reinforces the value of an education through its "dedication to making as many opportunities available to students as possible." Students appreciate that the curriculum helps them "think critically and sets up a good base for a liberal arts education," and many highlight how "required core classes such as theology and philosophy" mean that "students have to at least dip their toes in" a variety of disciplines. Professional development resources are plentiful, with "many opportunities for internships and mentorship," as well as "a great Career Center that helps students with résumés, provides free headshots, and oftentimes will include free professional clothing." It also helps that Fordham "has one of the strongest alumni networks, the connections made through this network are unmatched." Class formats vary across departments and professors, and "[include] several learning approaches that go beyond traditional lectures," such as "field trips meant to make us explore and respect [others]," like visiting a Buddhist temple. Many classes are "small and discussion-based, which creates an environment where students feel comfortable sharing ideas and engaging with different perspectives." Across disciplines, faculty consistently "bring insight from their career and own experience...and just want to see you succeed." One student concludes, "After four years I feel as though my education was as well-rounded as it could possibly be."

Campus Life

Days at Fordham "are busy but not frantic: classes, study groups, club meetings, part-time jobs, and practices for sports or intramurals." The two main campuses are located in Manhattan and the Bronx, which "makes for the perfect university setting since there are many 'third spaces' available for students." In addition, the Ram Van campus shuttle allows all to "really get the best of both worlds...there's always something new to explore either on or off campus." The Bronx campus is "located right by the NYBG [New York Botanical Garden] and Bronx Zoo." Given the ease of public transportation, people "spend a lot of free time exploring the city," including "shopping, visiting Central Park, going out to eat, going to Broadway shows or movies, and more." The school demonstrates a "commitment to generous funding for clubs and extracurriculars," and the Campus Activities Board "often has free, fun events to attend" like the popular monthly bingo game. Overall, campus life is "active, engaging, and career-focused," and "days bounce between classes, internships, and long library grinds, with coffee runs and campus hangs in between." One student sums up the overall Fordham experience: "Gated Gothic campus, familiar faces, traditions that repeat. That sense of intimacy is real and durable."

Student Body

The cosmopolitan campuses of Fordham house a "fashionable, fast-paced and focused" student body from all over the world, including "a mixture of resident and commuting students." There is "a strong intellectual community" to be found among this group, which is "hard-working and driven, striving to excel in [their] careers after graduation." This goal-minded set is also "open to collaboration and conversation." People "aren't here to just sit down and take classes, but to explore their future and push themselves," and "you'll see students who are focused on business or law alongside artists, activists, and people still figuring things out." Creativity is also prized and "people are allowed and encouraged to shine." While there is a wide range of backgrounds and interests, and the "population of students can be quite different between the two campuses," most agree that Fordham students are "welcoming and outgoing," and there's "a keen sense of wanting to be in New York City and [a] focus on getting the most out of lived experiences."

FORDHAM UNIVERSITY

Financial Aid: 718-817-3800 • E-Mail: enroll@fordham.edu • Website: www.fordham.edu

THE PRINCETON REVIEW SAYS

Admissions

The school reports that its standardized testing policy for use in admission for Fall 2026 is Test Optional. The Princeton Review suggests that interested applicants consult with the school for the most up-to-date standardized testing policies. *Very important factors considered include:* rigor of secondary school record, academic GPA. *Important factors considered include:* application essay, recommendation(s), extracurricular activities, talent/ability, character/personal qualities, volunteer work, work experience. *Other factors considered include:* class rank, standardized test scores, first generation, geographical residence, level of applicant's interest. High school diploma is required and GED is accepted. *Academic units required:* 4 English, 3 math, 3 science, 2 language (other than English), 3 social studies. *Academic units recommended:* 4 English, 4 math, 4 science, 4 language (other than English), 4 social studies.

Financial Aid

Students should submit: FAFSA; CSS PROFILE; State aid form; Business/Farm Supplement. Priority filing deadline is 11/15. The Princeton Review suggests that all financial aid forms be submitted as soon as possible. *Need-based scholarships/grants offered:* Federal Pell; Federal SEOG; State scholarships/grants; Private scholarships; College/university scholarship or grant aid from institutional funds. *Loan aid offered:* Federal Direct Subsidized Loans; Federal Direct Unsubsidized Loans; Direct PLUS loans. Admitted students will be notified of awards on or about 2/1. Federal Work-Study Program available. Institutional employment available.

The Inside Word

Admissions officers at Fordham are on the search for candidates who would be a good match for the school. And in order to find them, they closely consider all facets of student applications. Demonstrated interest such as online engagement or regional programming can help, but a student's inability to visit would never be a barrier to admission. The application review is holistic, and the university seeks evidence of leadership, integrity, and academic excellence. The strongest applicants will have taken a challenging course load in high school. You'll definitely want a transcript laden with honors and AP classes, if possible.

THE SCHOOL SAYS

From the Admissions Office

"Founded in 1841, Fordham is the Jesuit University of New York, committed to educating students in the Jesuit tradition to care for the whole person and address the world's most pressing challenges. With residential campuses in the Bronx and Manhattan, as well as campuses in Westchester and London, Fordham enrolls approximately 17,000 students across its eight undergraduate, graduate, and professional schools, preparing them with sound hearts and strong minds to become leaders who pursue excellence and make an impact in every field from Wall Street to Broadway, in media, law, social service, STEM, and beyond."

SELECTIVITY

# of total applicants	43,697
% of total applicants accepted	58
% of total acceptees attending	10
# of in-state applicants	12,384
% of in-state applicants accepted	58
# of out-of-state-applicants	25,649
% of applicants accepted from out of state	63
# of international applicants	5,664
% of international applicants accepted	35
# of early decision applicants	616
% of early decision applicants accepted	61
# offered a place on the wait list	9,376
# admitted from wait list	1,361

First-Year Profile

Testing policy	Test Optional
Range SAT composite	1350–1480
Range SAT EBRW	680–740
Range SAT math	660–750
Range ACT composite	30–34
% submitting SAT scores	20
% submitting ACT scores	6
Average HS GPA	3.6
% submitting high school GPA	99
% graduated top 10% of class	39
% graduated top 25% of class	76
% graduated top 50% of class	94
% submitting high school rank	20

Important Dates

Early decision	
Apply by	11/1
Notified by	12/20
Early action	
Apply by	11/1
Notified by	12/20
Regular	
Apply by	1/3
Notified by	4/1
Nonfall registration?	Yes

FINANCIAL FACTS*

Annual tuition	$65,920
Food and housing	$25,200
Required fees (First-year)	$1,532 ($1,977)
Books and supplies	$1,088
Average need-based scholarship (First-year)	$35,111 ($41,919)
% students with need rec. need-based scholarship or grant aid (First-year)	97 (97)
% students with need rec. non-need-based scholarship or grant aid (First-year)	13 (18)
% students with need rec. need-based self-help aid (First-year)	86 (82)
% students rec. any financial aid (First-year)	90 (96)
% UG borrow to pay for school	58
Average cumulative indebtedness	$37,868
% of students with need fully met (First-year)	20 (25)
Average % of student need met (First-year)	66 (76)

* Most recently reported data at time of printing. Scan the QR code to find the latest updates.

FRANKLIN & MARSHALL COLLEGE

College Ave, Lancaster, PA 17604 • Admissions: 717-358-3953

Survey Snapshot
Students always studying
Lab facilities are great
Great financial aid

RATINGS	
Quality of Life	86
Fire Safety	90
Green	60*
Academic	91
Profs Interesting	92
Profs Accessible	95
Admissions	92
Financial Aid	93

CAMPUS LIFE

Type of school	Private
Environment	Town

Students

Degree-seeking undergrad enrollment	1,773
% male/female/not reported	49/51/0
% from out of state	67
% First-year from public high school	65
% First-year live on campus	99
% Ugrads live on campus	97
# of fraternities (% join)	4 (9)
# of sororities (% join)	7 (21)
% Asian	6
% Black or African American	5
% Hispanic	10
% Native American	<1
% Pacific Islander	0
% Race and/or ethnicity unknown	1
% Two or more races	4
% White	55
% International	20
# of countries represented	50

CAMPUS MENTAL HEALTH SERVICES

Offers mental health/wellness program	Yes
Mental health training available to students	Yes
Employs Chief Wellness Officer	NR
Peer-to-peer mental health offerings	NR
Counseling center has guidelines or accreditation	No
Mental health/well-being courses	NR

ACADEMICS

% students returning for sophomore year	91
% students graduating within 4 years	72
% students graduating within 6 years	79
Calendar	Semester
Student/faculty ratio	9:1
Most common class size 10–19.	(45%)
Most common lab/discussion size 20–29.	(56%)

Most Popular Majors

Psychology; Political Science and Government; Business Administration, Management, and Operations

Applicants Also Look At

Bucknell University, Lafayette College, Penn State University Park, University of Delaware, University of Pittsburgh—Pittsburgh Campus

STUDENTS SAY "..."

Academics

At Franklin & Marshall, one of the oldest colleges in the country, "you'll work hard but you'll learn a lot." In large part, that's due to the private liberal arts college's standout professors, who make the most of smaller, focused classes, many of which "have round tables for close discussion," as well as off-hours, where one student says you're missing out "if you haven't been to a professor's office and discussed something other than class." Consensus is that there's a lot to be learned in and out of class from these "esteemed published scholars in their respective fields," and enrollees applaud their teachers for finding interesting ways "to get me engaged in areas that have always seemed like a bore to me."

About half of F&M students also seek out off-campus opportunities through the school, whether study abroad programs, research projects, or internships. The school offers support to help guide students through the process of finding a program that best fits their academic and professional goals. Overall, the school offers students "a great balance between a strong and competitive academic culture, talented and successful athletic teams, and a vibrant social life."

Campus Life

F&M has a lively, residential campus on which you can get anywhere in "about ten minutes no matter where you are." Students bond quickly in their assigned college houses, and receive a budget for special events, which can include anything from formal dances and theatrical productions to hosting visiting authors or throwing pizza parties. The campus is rife with further activities, which students "really get into." This is especially so with intramural and varsity athletics—around 32% of students are either Division III or Division II athletes—and so are "highly competitive and...very active in the local community." On the weekends, students can choose between frat parties and "alternative options" hosted by other school organizations. They can also head to downtown Lancaster for additional food and entertainment, including places like a famed 300-year-old farmer's market.

Student Body

The student body at F&M is made up of "people who are active both in school and extracurriculars, and who get excited about both." A typical student "is probably involved in three to five clubs and is trying out for theater, an a cappella group, or another organization." Many F&M students play a varsity sport or are a member of one of the seven sororities or four fraternities on campus. F&M students manage to strike a balance between studying with socializing, filling their "free time with fun and meaningful clubs and community service."

Fellow classmates are both studious and supportive, as students describe their peers as "smart overachievers who work hard" as well as "some of the nicest people you'll ever meet." Students say there is "amazing diversity" on campus and "very open minded" classmates, with nearly 20% of the population being first-generation college students and another 17% traveling from 50 different countries for a quality F&M education.

FRANKLIN & MARSHALL COLLEGE

Financial Aid: 717-358-3991 • E-Mail: admission@fandm.edu • Website: www.fandm.edu

THE PRINCETON REVIEW SAYS

Admissions

The school reports that its standardized testing policy for use in admission for Fall 2026 is Test Optional. The Princeton Review suggests that interested applicants consult with the school for the most up-to-date standardized testing policies. *Very important factors considered include:* rigor of secondary school record, class rank, academic GPA, character/personal qualities. *Important factors considered include:* application essay, recommendation(s), interview, extracurricular activities, talent/ability, volunteer work. *Other factors considered include:* standardized test scores, alumni/ae relation, geographical residence, work experience, level of applicant's interest. High school diploma is required and GED is accepted. *Academic units required:* 4 English, 3 math, 2 science, 2 science labs, 2 language (other than English), 1 social studies, 2 history, 1 visual/performing arts. *Academic units recommended:* 4 math, 3 science, 3 science labs, 4 language (other than English), 3 social studies, 3 history.

Financial Aid

Students should submit: FAFSA; CSS PROFILE. Priority filing deadline is 1/6. The Princeton Review suggests that all financial aid forms be submitted as soon as possible. *Need-based scholarships/grants offered:* Federal Pell; Federal SEOG; State scholarships/grants; Private scholarships; College/university scholarship or grant aid from institutional funds. *Loan aid offered:* Federal Direct Subsidized Loans; Federal Direct Unsubsidized Loans; Direct PLUS loans; State Loans. Admitted students will be notified of awards on or about 4/1. Federal Work-Study Program available.

The Inside Word

While admission at Franklin & Marshall College is very competitive, the admissions committee does show some flexibility. Applicants are encouraged to include nontraditional materials, such as art portfolios or recordings of musical performances, in their applications.

THE SCHOOL SAYS

From the Admissions Office

"The hallmarks of a Franklin & Marshall education are academic challenge, a connected and supportive community, and practical experiences on and off campus that enable you to shape the world as you prepare for your future. Our professors extend learning beyond classrooms and labs to the field, the local community, and abroad. On this campus full of bright, curious, interested students, you learn from everyone around you—in and outside of the classroom. Our College House system, which brings first-year students together into close-knit communities, are student-governed spaces where you socialize, learn, and belong with the support of both faculty and staff. In addition, our students find their 'homes' in a wide variety of clubs and activities, fraternities and sororities, athletic teams and the arts. Our Center for Career and Professional Development works with you from your first months on campus to help you plan and prepare for life after graduation and it shows in our graduates' success: ninety-two percent of 2025 graduates were employed or pursuing further education six months after graduating."

SELECTIVITY

# of total applicants	9,634
% of total applicants accepted	32
% of total acceptees attending	16
# of in-state applicants	1,309
% of in-state applicants accepted	52
# of out-of-state-applicants	3,667
% of applicants accepted from out of state	48
# of international applicants	4,658
% of international applicants accepted	13
# of early decision applicants	860
% of early decision applicants accepted	30

First-Year Profile

Testing policy	Test Optional
Range SAT composite	1310–1470
Range SAT EBRW	650–730
Range SAT math	650–760
Range ACT composite	29–32
% submitting SAT scores	31
% submitting ACT scores	7
% graduated top 10% of class	45
% graduated top 50% of class	88
% submitting high school rank	23

Important Dates

Early decision	
Apply by	11/15
Notified by	12/15
Other ED apply by	1/6
Other ED notified by	2/6
Regular	
Apply by	1/6
Notified by	4/1
Nonfall registration?	Yes

FINANCIAL FACTS

Annual tuition	$74,770
Food and housing	$17,330
Required fees (First-year)	$346 ($556)
Books and supplies	$800
% students with need rec. need-based scholarship or grant aid (First-year)	100 (100)
% UG borrow to pay for school	59
Average cumulative indebtedness	$36,010
% of students with need fully met (First-year)	100 (100)
Average % of student need met (First-year)	100 (100)

Franklin W. Olin College of Engineering

1000 Olin Way, Needham, MA 02492-1200 • Admissions: 781-292-2222

Survey Snapshot
Students always studying
Students are happy
Classroom facilities are great

RATINGS

Quality of Life	**86**
Fire Safety	**98**
Green	**60***
Academic	**93**
Profs Interesting	**99**
Profs Accessible	**96**
Admissions	**95**
Financial Aid	**96**

CAMPUS LIFE

Type of school	Private
Environment	Town

Students

Degree-seeking undergrad enrollment	378
% male/female/not reported	57/43/<1
% First-year from public high school	61
# of fraternities	0
# of sororities	0
% Asian	26
% Black or African American	2
% Hispanic	11
% Native American	0
% Pacific Islander	0
% Race and/or ethnicity unknown	4
% Two or more races	7
% White	40
% International	8
# of countries represented	15

CAMPUS MENTAL HEALTH SERVICES

Offers mental health/wellness program	Yes
Mental health training available to students	No
Employs Chief Wellness Officer	NR
Peer-to-peer mental health offerings	NR
Counseling center has guidelines or accreditation	No
Mental health/well-being courses	NR

ACADEMICS

% students returning for sophomore year	98
% students graduating within 4 years	63
% students graduating within 6 years	95
Calendar	Semester
Student/faculty ratio	10:1
Most common class size 20–29.	(41%)

Most Popular Majors

Engineering; Electrical and Electronics Engineering; Mechanical Engineering

STUDENTS SAY "..."

Academics

Franklin W. Olin College of Engineering's beloved project-based curriculum offers an engineering education rooted in "hands-on, team-based learning" with an emphasis on "learning the practical skills engineers actually need." Students appreciatively explain that the few lectures at the school are "short, concise, and interesting," and that "we have almost no tests." Instead, projects are "used to immediately apply things learned in class to real-world scenarios," whether that's programming robots or learning "how to build a facial recognition algorithm." This specialized approach carries the advantage of, as one student describes it, doing "one specific thing really, really well." That said, there are also opportunities for "independent study/research to learn more about specific topics that we're interested in." And while "there isn't a huge variety of classes" in non-engineering subjects, students can round out their options by cross-registering at Babson, Wellesley, and Brandeis. Students say that "academically, classes are challenging but there are many resources," including professors who are available to meet outside of class as well as tutors. The professors "are all passionate individuals that understand the content really well and are constantly adapting their courses to make it a better experience for students." Students feel "continually inspired," "listened to," and "really engaged." Ultimately, because so much work involves being "in pairs or groups," enrollees categorize Olin as "a very collaborative environment" where "everybody is willing to help out and bring each other up."

Campus Life

Students describe a lively campus where their enthusiastic peers pursue an eclectic array of interests. "It feels like everyone is always busy and running around," explains one student. Popular activities range from the fire arts club, where students "spin different items with fire on it for fun," to competitive sailing. As one student explains, "I didn't know how to sail before coming here but now during sailing season I sail at races most weekends, which is really fun." In addition to activities such as rock climbing, soccer, and ultimate Frisbee, there are also unusual activities like beekeeping and the Baja off-road race team. It's also "common to see people being active on the great lawn," says one student, and "there are a lot of social events too, from small hangouts in someone's room to larger parties in suites/wings." You'll even find students working on personal projects for fun in the available shop spaces. In fact, there are so many options that students actually use a public email list to "announce spontaneous events they're hosting. That's a good way to spice up the day."

Student Body

Olin is "filled to the brim with interesting and brilliant people who all want to do incredible things." Students describe the school as a "very close-knit community" where "everyone supports each other." As one student says, most people are "typically motivated in a collaborative way, not competitive" and students are often described as "hard working, kind, empathetic, smart and quirky." The student body is made up of "very different people" who are "able to meld well to be an entire school." In addition, "Olin is a gender-balanced institution, which is very refreshing" and "has a massive LGBTQ population." The small campus means "everyone knows everyone." It's a "very welcoming environment" where, as one student describes, "you can sit down at any table in the dining hall with any group of students and have a good conversation." Olin is a "school of nerds," which students embrace. It's a place where "everyone has something they're extremely excited about, which is inspiring to see." In addition to engineering, these interests "range from music to cooking to theater to writing and reading," explains one student. "I think that because we are all engineers and are so close, these interests are allowed to shine more than they would at a larger school."

Franklin W. Olin College of Engineering

Financial Aid: 781-292-2215 • E-Mail: info@olin.edu • Website: www.olin.edu

THE PRINCETON REVIEW SAYS

Admissions

The school reports that its standardized testing policy for use in admission for Fall 2026 is Test Optional. The Princeton Review suggests that interested applicants consult with the school for the most up-to-date standardized testing policies. *Very important factors considered include:* rigor of secondary school record, academic GPA, application essay, recommendation(s), interview, extracurricular activities, talent/ability, character/personal qualities, level of applicant's interest. *Important factors considered include:* class rank, volunteer work, work experience. *Other factors considered include:* standardized test scores, first generation, geographical residence, state residency. High school diploma is required and GED is accepted.

Financial Aid

The Princeton Review suggests that all financial aid forms be submitted as soon as possible. Federal Work-Study Program not available. Institutional employment available.

The Inside Word

Getting into Olin takes more than stellar academics. Social skills, depth, and the ability to communicate are weighed just as heavily as academic talent, which is why some students turn down offers from MIT and Caltech to come here. Olin seeks students with passion, creativity, and a genuine spirit of adventure.

THE SCHOOL SAYS

From the Admissions Office

"We are a vibrant community of talented, empathetic, energetic students and faculty and we are looking for students who are not only academically accomplished but also like adventure, thrive on creativity and use their engineering skills to make a positive impact on people and the world—and come from every kind of cultural, economic and geographic background imaginable. The Olin Tuition Scholarship, valued at more than $115,000, is awarded to every enrolled student to recognize their achievements and is complemented by our policy of meeting full demonstrated need—meaning finances should never stand in the way of an Olin education.

"Our admission process is, like Olin, unique. It's done in two stages; first students apply using the Common Application; then from our exceptionally talented and academically gifted applicant pool we invite between 225–250 students to attend one of three Candidates' Weekends. We seek to get to know our applicants' personal qualities (like risktaking, creativity, passion and team spirit) during these weekends of getting acquainted through group activities and interviews. Admission is then offered to candidates who possess the greatest promise of contributing to—and benefiting from—the Olin experience. Following the Candidates' Weekends admission is offered to approximately 125–135 students.

"Olin is not your typical engineering school. We are a creative, collaborative community of team players who want to work hard to solve problems and have some serious fun along the way!"

SELECTIVITY

# of total applicants	1,151
% of total applicants accepted	21
% of total acceptees attending	8
# of in-state applicants	199
% of in-state applicants accepted	19
# of out-of-state-applicants	726
% of applicants accepted from out of state	24
# of international applicants	220
% of international applicants accepted	14
# offered a place on the wait list	70
# admitted from wait list	12

First-Year Profile

Testing policy	Test Optional
Range SAT composite	1490–1540
Range SAT EBRW	730–770
Range SAT math	750–780
Range ACT composite	34–36
% submitting SAT scores	54
% submitting ACT scores	3
Average HS GPA	3.9
% submitting high school GPA	100

Important Dates

Regular	
Apply by	1/1
Notified by	4/1
Nonfall registration?	No

FINANCIAL FACTS

Annual tuition	$67,004
Food and housing	$22,682
Required fees (First-year)	$2,270 ($4,926)
% students rec. any financial aid (First-year)	100 (100)

FURMAN UNIVERSITY

3300 Poinsett Highway, Greenville, SC 29613 • Admissions: 864-294-2034

Survey Snapshot
Lots of conservative students
Students are happy
Classroom facilities are great

RATINGS

Quality of Life	87
Fire Safety	90
Green	90
Academic	87
Profs Interesting	95
Profs Accessible	96
Admissions	91
Financial Aid	82

CAMPUS LIFE

Type of school	Private
Environment	City

Students

Degree-seeking undergrad enrollment	2,378
% male/female/not reported	42/57/<1
% from out of state	64
% First-year from public high school	54
% First-year live on campus	99
% Ugrads live on campus	97
# of fraternities (% join)	5 (25)
# of sororities (% join)	7 (44)
% Asian	3
% Black or African American	6
% Hispanic	7
% Native American	<1
% Pacific Islander	<1
% Race and/or ethnicity unknown	1
% Two or more races	4
% White	73
% International	6
# of countries represented	28

CAMPUS MENTAL HEALTH SERVICES

Offers mental health/wellness program	Yes
Mental health training available to students	No
Employs Chief Wellness Officer	NR
Peer-to-peer mental health offerings	NR
Counseling center has guidelines or accreditation	No
Mental health/well-being courses	NR

ACADEMICS

% students returning for sophomore year	92
% students graduating within 4 years	73
% students graduating within 6 years	79
Calendar	Semester
Student/faculty ratio	10:1
Most common class size 10–19.	(55%)
Most common lab/discussion size 10–19.	(59%)

Most Popular Majors

Business/Commerce; Health Professions and Related Clinical Sciences; Political Science and Government

STUDENTS SAY "..."

Academics

Furman University is a school that helps its undergraduates "become the best version[s] of [themselves]." That potentially daunting task is made possible thanks to the school's ample resources ranging from "good study abroad [options]" and "experiential learning" to the "many opportunities for research and internships." One of Furman's top selling points is "the strength of its pre-professional curriculum." The university's "pre-health and pre-law advisors are exceptional, and they greatly help students get into graduate programs, regardless of major." Of course, prospective students should be aware that the academics here "are very difficult, particularly [the] science courses." It's important that you come prepared to study. Fortunately, the "overwhelming majority of professors at Furman are experts in their field and truly care about helping students succeed." They seem to excel at creating a classroom environment wherein undergrads "feel comfortable yet challenged at all times." And it's definitely evident that they "love teaching and instilling a passion for growth, inquiry, and engagement." We'll give the last word to this student who shares, "My professors have changed my life by supporting me and working with me from academic interests to personal crises. They are easily the best part of Furman."

Campus Life

If you've done enough to attend Furman, you can expect to maintain a pretty busy schedule. "It is very common for everyone to be involved with many clubs and organizations." After all, there's so much to discover and partake in outside of academics. To begin with, Furman undergrads are an athletic lot and you'll often find "people play[ing] pick-up games on the sports fields" or participating in intramurals and club sports. Plus, "athletic events are very accessible to students and are free." For individuals with an altruistic bent, there are a "variety of community service opportunities." Greek life is also fairly popular at Furman. However, students make a point of mentioning that "party culture isn't extremely prevalent on campus, and the Greek organizations are very welcoming and open to anyone, regardless of appearances, socioeconomic class, or affinity for partying." The university itself hosts numerous "cultural events" where undergrads "can go learn about something new or hear an engaging speaker." And, of course, people can easily join some of the many organizations like Residential Life Council, Eco Reps, and the student run musical theatre group, Pauper Players. Lastly, when undergrads want a respite from campus life, they head into "downtown Greenville and try new restaurants, go to concerts, bar hop and EXPLORE. You can often find students downtown at the various "cute coffee shops [and] farmers markets." Given its proximity to the outdoors, many also like to "get into nature and hike Paris Mountain" or "bik[e] the Swamp Rabbit Trail."

Student Body

Furman seems to attract students who "are very motivated and driven to perform well academically." Thankfully, though most everyone has "high aspirations," this isn't a very competitive student body. Instead, undergrads here simply "push...each other to be the best people possible." Students do readily admit that Furman "generally draws a Southern white demographic" with many kids hailing from "generally wealthy backgrounds." However, they note that the university "has expanded its recruitment initiatives and current on-campus opportunities to invite a greater diversity of individuals especially in regard to race." Students also stress that you'll find plenty of people with "unique talents" and "fairly diverse [interests] when it comes to hobbies, interests, majors, etc." And they certainly "know how to have a good time" and "enjoy stimulating discussions and new experiences." Best of all, they form a "community of open-minded people" who are "willing to help one another." As this student explains, "I transferred to Furman because of the student body. I was completely taken aback at how genuine and kind the people here are."

FURMAN UNIVERSITY

Financial Aid: 864-294-2030 • E-Mail: admissions@furman.edu • Website: www.furman.edu

THE PRINCETON REVIEW SAYS

Admissions

The school reports that its standardized testing policy for use in admission for Fall 2026 is Test Optional. The Princeton Review suggests that interested applicants consult with the school for the most up-to-date standardized testing policies. *Very important factors considered include:* rigor of secondary school record, academic GPA. *Important factors considered include:* application essay, extracurricular activities, character/personal qualities. *Other factors considered include:* class rank, standardized test scores, recommendation(s), talent/ability, volunteer work, work experience, level of applicant's interest. High school diploma is required and GED is accepted. *Academic units required:* 4 English, 3 math, 2 science, 2 science labs, 2 language (other than English), 3 social studies. *Academic units recommended:* 4 English, 4 math, 3 science, 2 science labs, 3 language (other than English), 4 social studies.

Financial Aid

The Princeton Review suggests that all financial aid forms be submitted as soon as possible. Federal Work-Study Program available. Institutional employment available.

The Inside Word

Furman University is best known for its outstanding academic program. With that in mind, applicants should present a well-rounded transcript complete with advanced courses to show they are used to a challenging academic environment. Though Furman is test optional, having strong standardized test scores will work in your favor. The university is looking for prospective students who thrive in the classroom and are not afraid to get involved in their community. We recommend using your personal statement to address issues that you are passionate about and shine a light on what differentiates you from the other applicants. If Furman is your top choice, we strongly suggest you consider applying early.

THE SCHOOL SAYS

From the Admissions Office

"At Furman, your experience is your education. Through stimulating coursework, combined with relevant, real-world experiences, you will explore your interests and passions to discover what drives you. Guaranteed for every Furman student are opportunities to get involved in internships, study away, research, and community-centered learning experiences that will empower you to apply your classroom learning in a variety of settings and prepare you for success. Furman's highly qualified faculty and dedicated mentors will provide the knowledge, skills, and support you need to achieve your personal and professional goals. Your experience will take place on a stunningly beautiful 940-acre, residential campus in the foothills of the Blue Ridge Mountains, in one of the country's fastest growing and most vibrant cities, Greenville, South Carolina. There will be endless opportunities for outdoor excursions and urban adventures. We strive to give you a well-rounded, once-in-a-lifetime college experience that will prepare you for anything. That's The Furman Advantage.

"Our holistic application review is based on an evaluation of your grades, rigor of curriculum, test scores (optional), essay, extracurricular involvement, and potential contribution to campus. Beyond your application, we value personally connecting with each applicant to learn more about you and your interest in Furman. We invite you to visit campus, connect with students and faculty, and learn more about The Furman Advantage that is awaiting you."

SELECTIVITY

# of total applicants	10,813
% of total applicants accepted	43
% of total acceptees attending	13

First-Year Profile

Testing policy	Test Optional
Range SAT composite	1280–1340
Range SAT EBRW	650–720
Range SAT math	610–710
Range ACT composite	28–32
% submitting SAT scores	27
% submitting ACT scores	22
Average HS GPA	3.7
% submitting high school GPA	100
% graduated top 10% of class	40
% graduated top 25% of class	73
% graduated top 50% of class	91
% submitting high school rank	50

Important Dates

Early decision	
Apply by	11/1
Notified by	11/15
Other ED apply by	1/15
Other ED notified by	2/1
Early action	
Apply by	11/1
Notified by	12/20
Regular	
Apply by	1/15
Notified by	2/15
Nonfall registration?	No

FINANCIAL FACTS

Annual tuition	$61,034
Food and housing	$17,164
Required fees	$410
Books and supplies	$1,250

George Mason University

4400 University Drive, Fairfax, VA 22030-4444 • Admissions: 703-993-4622

Survey Snapshot
Students love Fairfax, VA
Classroom facilities are great
Diverse student types interact on campus

RATINGS

Quality of Life	**83**
Fire Safety	**60***
Green	**94**
Academic	**76**
Profs Interesting	**84**
Profs Accessible	**88**
Admissions	**83**
Financial Aid	**82**

CAMPUS LIFE

Type of school	Public
Environment	City

Students

Degree-seeking undergrad enrollment	28,364
% male/female/not reported	51/49/<1
% from out of state	9
% First-year from public high school	72
% First-year live on campus	44
% Ugrads live on campus	18
# of fraternities (% join)	24 (3)
# of sororities (% join)	19 (3)
% Asian	23
% Black or African American	13
% Hispanic	19
% Native American	<1
% Pacific Islander	<1
% Race and/or ethnicity unknown	3
% Two or more races	6
% White	30
% International	6
# of countries represented	143

CAMPUS MENTAL HEALTH SERVICES

Offers mental health/wellness program	Yes
Mental health training available to students	No
Employs Chief Wellness Officer	NR
Peer-to-peer mental health offerings	NR
Counseling center has guidelines or accreditation	No
Mental health/well-being courses	NR

ACADEMICS

% students returning for sophomore year	86
% students graduating within 4 years	46
% students graduating within 6 years	66
Calendar	Semester
Student/faculty ratio	17:1
Most common class size 20–29.	(27%)
Most common lab/discussion size 20–29.	(50%)

Most Popular Majors

Information Technology; Computer Science; Biology/Biological Sciences

Applicants Sometimes Prefer

The George Washington University, James Madison University, Old Dominion University, Penn State University Park, University of Maryland, College Park, University of Virginia, Virginia Commonwealth University, Virginia Tech

STUDENTS SAY "…"

Academics

With the "nation's capital in its backyard," George Mason University in Fairfax, Virginia offers "strong academics" combined with proximity to a bustling center of industry and innovation. Mason prepares its students to enter by offering a "large variety of academic programs" and providing a solid infrastructure that is "constantly growing" and "providing many excellent opportunities for students," including research opportunities for undergraduates. The "humanities and economics draw on the local Washington D.C. talent" "and the engineering school has an "advanced" IT program that "Is developed with concentrations in information security, healthcare, networking, and more." Students note that "jobs in all the fields that Mason provides are just within a 10-mile radius of campus," including "top tech companies," which "come to Mason because there is a huge Mason alumni community in the Northern Virginia area." One grateful student notes "it was easy to transfer to with NOVA's Pathway Program" because they had an "easy outline of what classes I needed to take at NOVA to transfer over and pursue a certain degree."

Campus Life

With Washington, D.C. just "a metro ride away," "the majority of students at Mason are commuters," meaning "many of them are not very involved." Even in the "close-knit layout of the main campus," in fact, even for on-campus residents, most campus life happens off campus, including the partying, since fraternities are off-campus. There are many social clubs and organizations, however, with "most students taking part in several." Examples include the a cappella group and swing dancing. Many also "meet to practice for competitions, including the Indian dance troupe." Mason has a "free shuttle bus that takes students to the metro" for activities in D.C. The Johnson Center is another "major place that students spend time: there is a food court, a library, meeting rooms, kiosks, the cinema, and huge study areas." Students will also "go to one of the three gyms on campus and work out; a lot of people bike around campus."

Student Body

This is one school where "diversity" is truly an accurate term in all its breadth. Students choose Mason for this wide representation of culture and experience. "As a first-generation student of color," one student says, "I think representation is integral to creating a sense of belonging. Because I could see myself reflected in the students, I chose Mason because I knew that I wouldn't be bothered or feel like I was the minority." There is a "large population of immigrant-heritage students, international students, and students from almost every state in the United States," and the "littlest differences like different name spellings, accents, dress, and more importantly, different political ideas and perspectives are respected and acknowledged, and even more so, celebrated here at Mason." While there are "many students who entered straight from high school…there are also many students who are already working and are returning to school as well as many international students." The "campus keeps growing, housing over 6,000 residents,"—of the 38,000 or so total students. "Due to the enormous and intimidating physical size of GMU, the school offers many ways for students to feel included and engage themselves in extracurricular activities should they choose to do so," one student offers.

GEORGE MASON UNIVERSITY

Financial Aid: 703-993-2353 • E-Mail: admissions@gmu.edu • Website: www.gmu.edu

THE PRINCETON REVIEW SAYS

Admissions

The school reports that its standardized testing policy for use in admission for Fall 2026 is Test Optional. The Princeton Review suggests that interested applicants consult with the school for the most up-to-date standardized testing policies. *Very important factors considered include:* rigor of secondary school record, academic GPA. *Important factors considered include:* talent/ability. *Other factors considered include:* standardized test scores, application essay, recommendation(s), extracurricular activities, character/personal qualities, geographical residence, state residency, volunteer work, work experience. High school diploma is required and GED is accepted. *Academic units required:* 4 English, 3 math, 2 science, 2 science labs, 2 language (other than English), 3 social studies, 3 academic electives. *Academic units recommended:* 4 English, 4 math, 3 science, 3 science labs, 3 language (other than English), 4 social studies, 5 academic electives.

Financial Aid

Students should submit: FAFSA. Priority filing deadline is 3/1. The Princeton Review suggests that all financial aid forms be submitted as soon as possible. *Need-based scholarships/grants offered:* Federal Pell; Federal SEOG; State scholarships/grants; Private scholarships; College/university scholarship or grant aid from institutional funds. *Loan aid offered:* Federal Direct Subsidized Loans; Federal Direct Unsubsidized Loans; Direct PLUS loans. Admitted students will be notified of awards on a rolling basis beginning 2/15. Federal Work-Study Program available. Institutional employment available.

The Inside Word

GMU is a popular college choice for two key reasons: its proximity to Washington, D.C., and its more attainable admissions standards compared to other universities in the Virginia state system. GMU's quality faculty and impressive facilities make it worth consideration, especially if you're looking for a school in the D.C. area and affordability is a factor.

THE SCHOOL SAYS

From the Admissions Office

"George Mason University is the only public doctoral university in Virginia, and one of just five very large public universities in the nation, recognized in the highest tier of the Carnegie Foundation and the American Council on Education's Opportunity Colleges and Universities. This recognition reflects the university's commitment to expanding access while delivering strong student outcomes and upward mobility and welcoming all who are prepared for the academic rigor of a top R1 research university.

"Located just outside Washington, D.C., George Mason's beautiful 677-acre Fairfax Campus is home to nearly 6,000 students living in more than 40 residence halls. They're just a fraction of the student population of more than 40,000, hailing from all 50 states and 130 countries and enrolling in 211 degree programs at the undergraduate, master's, doctoral, and professional levels.

"Working at the crossroads of government, industry, and research, George Mason's physical presence extends across Virginia and beyond, with Mason Square in Arlington; the Science and Technology Campus in Manassas; the Smithsonian-Mason School of Conservation in Front Royal; and a campus in Songdo, South Korea.

"Eighty-five percent of new George Mason alumni report advancing their careers within six months of graduation, and the university delivers the best salary outcomes of a public university in Virginia, Maryland, and Washington, D.C. Graduates join the university's network of more than 250,000 alumni, two-thirds of whom continue working in the Washington metropolitan area, strengthening the region's leadership in key public and private companies."

SELECTIVITY

# of total applicants	26,014
% of total applicants accepted	86
% of total acceptees attending	19
# of in-state applicants	16,236
% of in-state applicants accepted	88
# of out-of-state-applicants	9,778
% of applicants accepted from out of state	85
# offered a place on the wait list	1,289
# admitted from wait list	415

First-Year Profile

Testing policy	Test Optional
Range SAT composite	1180–1360
Range SAT EBRW	590–690
Range SAT math	570–680
Range ACT composite	25–31
% submitting SAT scores	18
% submitting ACT scores	1
Average HS GPA	3.7
% submitting high school GPA	100
% graduated top 10% of class	23
% graduated top 25% of class	55
% graduated top 50% of class	89
% submitting high school rank	18

Important Dates

Early action	
Apply by	11/1
Notified by	12/16
Regular	
Apply by	8/24
Notified by	Rolling, late December
Nonfall registration?	Yes

FINANCIAL FACTS*

Annual in-state tuition	$14,316
Annual out-of-state tuition	$39,312
Food and housing	$16,156
Required fees	$3,924
Books and supplies	$1,290
Average need-based scholarship (First-year)	$12,717 ($12,032)
% students with need rec. need-based scholarship or grant aid (First-year)	45 (45)
% students with need rec. non-need-based scholarship or grant aid (First-year)	31 (44)
% students with need rec. need-based self-help aid (First-year)	48 (62)
% students rec. any financial aid (First-year)	71 (81)
% UG borrow to pay for school	45
Average cumulative indebtedness	$30,007
% of students with need fully met (First-year)	6 (8)
Average % of student need met (First-year)	58 (67)

* Most recently reported data at time of printing. Scan the QR code to find the latest updates.

Georgetown University

37th and O Streets, NW, Washington, DC 20057 • Admissions: 202-687-0100

Survey Snapshot
Great financial aid
Alumni active on campus
Students politically aware

RATINGS	
Quality of Life	**63**
Fire Safety	**85**
Green	**60***
Academic	**85**
Profs Interesting	**83**
Profs Accessible	**84**
Admissions	**98**
Financial Aid	**96**

CAMPUS LIFE

Type of school	Private
Affiliation	Roman Catholic
Environment	Metropolis

Students

Degree-seeking undergrad enrollment	7,718
% male/female/not reported	40/59/1
% from out of state	98
% First-year live on campus	100
% Ugrads live on campus	68
# of fraternities	0
# of sororities	0
% Asian	17
% Black or African American	5
% Hispanic	6
% Native American	<1
% Pacific Islander	<1
% Race and/or ethnicity unknown	8
% Two or more races	6
% White	44
% International	14
# of countries represented	138

CAMPUS MENTAL HEALTH SERVICES

Offers mental health/wellness program	Yes
Mental health training available to students	No
Employs Chief Wellness Officer	NR
Peer-to-peer mental health offerings	NR
Counseling center has guidelines or accreditation	No
Mental health/well-being courses	NR

ACADEMICS

% students returning for sophomore year	96
% students graduating within 4 years	86
% students graduating within 6 years	94
Calendar	Semester
Student/faculty ratio	11:1
Most common class size 10–19.	(43%)
Most common lab/discussion size 10–19.	(42%)

Most Popular Majors

English Language and Literature; International Relations and Affairs; Political Science and Government

STUDENTS SAY "..."

Academics

Georgetown University's Jesuit roots are reflected in its educational mission of "care for the whole person." This helps to foster a vibrant intellectual atmosphere, one where classroom learning is "balanced with extracurricular learning and development." The school is also rooted in a spirit of "restless inquiry," and students are encouraged to constantly question the world around them, whether—for example—in a robust study abroad program at Georgetown's villa outside of Florence, Italy, or an undergraduate course aimed at fighting wrongful convictions. Along with its many stellar academic programs, the university features the standout School of Foreign Service, which, thanks to its direct proximity to Washington D.C., offers key internships in government, "high-profile guest speakers," and one-of-a-kind networking opportunities, like the chance to discuss conflict resolution with ambassadors.

Regardless of major, all Hoyas have access to a "great selection of very knowledgeable professors, split with a good proportion of those who are experienced in realms outside of academia...and career academics." Undergrads also report that the faculty tend to be "fantastic scholars and teachers" and are "generally available to students." Even better, professors are typically "interested in getting to know you as a person (if you put forth the effort to talk to them and go to office hours)." Finally, while classes are rather rigorous, students emphasize that "Georgetown is...a place where people work very, very hard without feeling like they are in direct competition."

Campus Life

Georgetown pulses with an energy and activity that's to be expected from a school in the heart of America's capital. Students here are motivated and eager to participate in campus life, and "are always headed somewhere, it seems—to rehearsal, athletic practice, a guest speaker, [or] the gym." Indeed, from the university's six a cappella groups and the Guild of Bands (an organization for pop, jazz, and rock ensembles) to club rock climbing and the Georgetown FinTech Club, there's so much to take part in. Community service and political activism are especially popular, along with cheering on Georgetown's storied basketball team. One thing that students note is that many events, like parties, "tend to have a somewhat networking atmosphere; meeting people you don't know is a constant theme." Regardless of the activities, Hoyas pride themselves on always learning.

Student Body

Georgetown's global reach is certainly reflected in its student body. With undergraduates hailing from all 50 states and "a ton of international students" from over 130 countries, you'll find plenty of classmates from diverse, well-traveled, and well-educated backgrounds. Even better, students here actively want to learn about different people and experiences and benefit from the fact that roughly one-third of the student body is fluent in more than one language. Many undergrads are also very interested in the goings on of the government, so much so that they advise enrollees to "have at least some interest in politics or you will feel out-of-place." Overall, students tend to carry themselves with a professional polish that extends from attitudes and interests to wardrobes. To that end, preppy-casual is the fashion de rigueur. Nevertheless, with over 7,000 students, you can rest assured that there are "plenty of groups for everybody to fit into and find their niche" and even "much crossover between groups."

GEORGETOWN UNIVERSITY

Financial Aid: 202-687-4547 • E-Mail: guadmiss@georgetown.edu • Website: www.georgetown.edu

THE PRINCETON REVIEW SAYS

Admissions

The school reports that its standardized testing policy for use in admission for Fall 2026 will require applicants to submit either the SAT or ACT. The Princeton Review suggests that interested applicants consult with the school for the most up-to-date standardized testing policies. *Very important factors considered include:* rigor of secondary school record, class rank, academic GPA, standardized test scores, application essay, recommendation(s), talent/ability, character/personal qualities. *Important factors considered include:* interview, extracurricular activities. *Other factors considered include:* first generation, alumni/ae relation, geographical residence, state residency, volunteer work, work experience. High school diploma is required and GED is accepted. *Academic units required:* 4 English, 2 math, 1 science, 2 language (other than English), 2 social studies, 2 history.

Financial Aid

Students should submit: FAFSA; CSS PROFILE; Business/Farm Supplement. Priority filing deadline is 2/1. The Princeton Review suggests that all financial aid forms be submitted as soon as possible. *Need-based scholarships/grants offered:* Federal Pell; Federal SEOG; State scholarships/grants; Private scholarships; College/university scholarship or grant aid from institutional funds. *Loan aid offered:* Direct PLUS loans; Federal Direct Unsubsidized Loans; Federal Direct Subsidized Loans. Admitted students will be notified of awards on or about 4/1. Federal Work-Study Program available. Institutional employment available.

The Inside Word

Georgetown is highly selective, accepting just 13 percent of its applicants, so the academic strength of the applicant pool is impressive. Georgetown uses its own application to gain a more holistic view of applicants. Beyond a stellar academic record and test scores, admissions officers want to learn who you are as a person, as well as your talents, skills, and accomplishments. An interview is not required but is highly recommended.

THE SCHOOL SAYS

From the Admissions Office

"Georgetown was founded in 1789 by John Carroll, who concurred with his contemporaries Benjamin Franklin and Thomas Jefferson in believing that the success of the young democracy depended upon an educated and virtuous citizenry. Carroll founded the school with the dynamic Jesuit tradition of education, characterized by humanism and committed to the assumption of responsibility and action. Georgetown is a national and international university, enrolling students from all fifty states and over 100 foreign countries. Undergraduate students are enrolled in one of five undergraduate schools: the College of Arts and Sciences, School of Foreign Service, Georgetown School of Business, School of Nursing, and School of Health. All students share a common liberal arts core and have access to the entire university curriculum."

SELECTIVITY

# of total applicants	26,822
% of total applicants accepted	13
% of total acceptees attending	44
# of in-state applicants	243
% of in-state applicants accepted	20
# of out-of-state-applicants	22,653
% of applicants accepted from out of state	14
# of international applicants	3,926
% of international applicants accepted	8
# offered a place on the wait list	2,672
# admitted from wait list	356

First-Year Profile

Testing policy	SAT or ACT Required
Range SAT composite	1410–1530
Range SAT EBRW	710–760
Range SAT math	700–780
Range ACT composite	32–35
% submitting SAT scores	78
% submitting ACT scores	32
% graduated top 10% of class	87
% graduated top 25% of class	97
% graduated top 50% of class	100
% submitting high school rank	49

Important Dates

Early action	
Apply by	11/1
Notified by	12/15
Regular	
Apply by	1/10
Notified by	4/1
Nonfall registration?	No

FINANCIAL FACTS

Annual tuition	$74,520
Food and housing (First-year)	$23,004 ($22,180)
Required fees	$212
Average need-based scholarship (First-year)	$58,163 ($57,490)
% students with need rec. need-based scholarship or grant aid (First-year)	97 (97)
% students with need rec. non-need-based scholarship or grant aid (First-year)	34 (58)
% students with need rec. need-based self-help aid (First-year)	64 (62)
% UG borrow to pay for school	28
Average cumulative indebtedness	$33,272
% of students with need fully met (First-year)	100 (100)
Average % of student need met (First-year)	100 (100)

THE GEORGE WASHINGTON UNIVERSITY

1918 F Street, NW, Washington, DC 20052 • Admissions: 202-994-6040

Survey Snapshot
Students love Washington, DC
Easy to get around campus
Great off-campus food

RATINGS

Quality of Life	84
Fire Safety	60*
Green	94
Academic	80
Profs Interesting	88
Profs Accessible	89
Admissions	91
Financial Aid	93

CAMPUS LIFE

Type of school	Private
Environment	Metropolis

Students

Degree-seeking undergrad enrollment	10,929
% male/female/not reported	37/63/0
% from out of state	97
% First-year from public high school	70
% First-year live on campus	97
% Ugrads live on campus	58
# of fraternities (% join)	12 (5)
# of sororities (% join)	9 (9)
% Asian	12
% Black or African American	8
% Hispanic	13
% Native American	<1
% Pacific Islander	<1
% Race and/or ethnicity unknown	3
% Two or more races	5
% White	50
% International	9
# of countries represented	122

CAMPUS MENTAL HEALTH SERVICES

Offers mental health/wellness program	Yes
Mental health training available to students	No
Employs Chief Wellness Officer	NR
Peer-to-peer mental health offerings	NR
Counseling center has guidelines or accreditation	No
Mental health/well-being courses	NR

ACADEMICS

% students returning for sophomore year	91
% students graduating within 4 years	77
% students graduating within 6 years	84
Calendar	Semester
Student/faculty ratio	13:1
Most common class size 10–19.	(42%)
Most common lab/discussion size 20–29.	(54%)

Most Popular Majors

International Relations and Affairs; Business Administration and Management; Psychology

STUDENTS SAY "..."

Academics

Located in the heart of Washington, DC, George Washington University offers "unparalleled access to internships and jobs," and students appreciate the "ability to do internships during your academic year and not just the summer." Its downtown location affords students a "high frequency of accomplished guest speakers," meaning that "seeing everyone from senators to CEOs casually on campus is normal." Faculty also "genuinely do a great job encouraging students to take advantage of everything DC has to offer," and some even use the cultural resources nearby as classrooms: "I took a class called 'The Grateful and the Dead' where the class would go on field trips looking at lesser-known memorials and popular cemeteries," says one student. Another speaks of the incorporation of nearby Smithsonian resources into the curriculum: "I was required to visit the National Portrait Gallery for my Arts in America class, and the Natural History Museum for my Biological Anthropology class." Many professors are well-connected, "quite knowledgeable in their subjects, clearly care and are passionate, making it exciting to learn," and are "willing to connect students with their contacts." Classes "that lean into discussion during lectures are also very common," and teachers often encourage students to attend "tutoring groups and work on projects with other students to help us with collaboration skills." One of the highlights of GW is that "it really attracts so many different types of people, cultures, and viewpoints, and it makes learning so much more interesting and unique as we have all these different voices."

Campus Life

The pre-professional nature of GW means that "people take their classes very seriously [and] spend a lot of time studying," but as one says, "We still like to have fun." In-dorm socializing, like movie and crafts nights, are a classic, and "the student organizations are very active and great opportunities to make friends and build community." Since the campus is centrally located, "there is so much to do, from ice skating [in] Georgetown, going to the Wharf, [to] catching sports games like the Capitals or Nationals." There "is always some kind of event going on in the city—the list is truly endless, from festivals, museum parties, thrifting pop-ups, food markets, concerts, dance classes, and more." Many students make the most of DC's public transportation, "utilizing our student Metro passes and getting to know the city better." For those who prefer to travel on foot, "there are at least nine free major museums within walking distance as well as some of the best parks in the country." One appreciative student says, "Being in DC is a truly incredible experience, and I think many of us are incredibly grateful to be spending such pivotal years of our lives here."

Student Body

Many GW students "are very politically engaged and stay informed on current events." While many report that students are "more left-leaning," others say that they "range on the political spectrum." A large part of the student body is international, and "many are upper class, white, and from the Northeast." Most here "are extremely career and internship-oriented, for the best and worst," and "there is a very big LinkedIn culture here to take the most classes, get the best internships, double major, network, etc." Still, many find this creates a "healthy form of competition and self-motivation," and many are "hoping to make some large contribution beyond working in the private sector." This is a place where "it is easy to find academically and career-driven friends who will lift you up," and most are "welcoming and willing to understand others' perspectives on life." They also find time to stop and smell the roses, and one says, "It's a great place to be while you're young and looking for opportunities."

The George Washington University

E-Mail: gwadm@gwu.edu • Website: www.gwu.edu

THE PRINCETON REVIEW SAYS

Admissions

The school reports that its standardized testing policy for use in admission for Fall 2026 is Test Optional. The Princeton Review suggests that interested applicants consult with the school for the most up-to-date standardized testing policies. *Very important factors considered include:* rigor of secondary school record, academic GPA. *Important factors considered include:* application essay, recommendation(s), extracurricular activities, talent/ability, volunteer work. *Other factors considered include:* standardized test scores, character/personal qualities, first generation, alumni/ae relation, geographical residence, work experience, level of applicant's interest. High school diploma is required and GED is accepted. *Academic units required:* 4 English, 2 math, 2 science, 1 science lab, 2 language (other than English), 2 social studies. *Academic units recommended:* 4 English, 4 math, 4 science, 4 language (other than English), 4 social studies.

Financial Aid

Students should submit: FAFSA; CSS PROFILE. Priority filing deadline is 2/1. The Princeton Review suggests that all financial aid forms be submitted as soon as possible. *Need-based scholarships/grants offered:* Federal Pell; Federal SEOG; State scholarships/grants; College/university scholarship or grant aid from institutional funds. *Loan aid offered:* Federal Direct Subsidized Loans; Federal Direct Unsubsidized Loans; Direct PLUS loans. Admitted students will be notified of awards on a rolling basis beginning 3/24. Federal Work-Study Program available. Institutional employment available.

The Inside Word

GW knows that its location and academic offerings make it a highly sought-after institution—each year, more students apply, bringing the current number up to just over 27,000. As a result, it seeks to "enroll a bright, talented, and diverse body of students." GW's Test Optional policy allows it to look more broadly at each student's background and what they bring to the table. Demonstrate your interest by utilizing any of the school's resources that you're applicable for, like for first-generation students, or by appealing directly to special interest programs like the Cisneros Scholars, which supports the Latino community; don't miss an opportunity to tell your story.

THE SCHOOL SAYS

From the Admissions Office

"Located in the heart of Washington, DC, the George Washington University enrolls a diverse, motivated, and active student body from all 50 states and 122 countries. Our students study, learn, and grow on two fully integrated DC campuses—Foggy Bottom, blocks from the National Mall, and Mount Vernon, in a residential neighborhood.

"As a comprehensive global research university, GW offers more than 75 majors in the arts, business, engineering, international affairs, public health, and social and physical sciences—all taught mere blocks from the White House and amid DC's business and high-tech sectors. Students work closely with well-connected faculty to utilize the many academic and cultural resources of the District. Some classes take field trips to museums to study collections while others welcome guest speakers who are experts in their fields. In addition to dynamic classroom experiences, a GW education allows students the ability to put knowledge in action. Through research, internships, community service, and study abroad, GW students implement classroom learning to change the world and improve the human experience.

"We look for bright and diverse students who are ambitious, energetic, and self-motivated. As a Test Optional school, we believe that the best indicator of success at GW is a student's high school performance. Our holistic review takes all pieces of a student's admission application into consideration. We aim to make a GW education affordable to all admitted students, offering generous scholarships and financial aid."

SELECTIVITY

# of total applicants	27,236
% of total applicants accepted	50
% of total acceptees attending	19
# of early decision applicants	986
% of early decision applicants accepted	66
# offered a place on the wait list	6,187
# admitted from wait list	163

First-Year Profile

Testing policy	Test Optional
Range SAT composite	1320–1460
Range SAT EBRW	660–740
Range SAT math	650–750
Range ACT composite	30–34
% submitting SAT scores	29
% submitting ACT scores	18
% graduated top 10% of class	50
% graduated top 25% of class	83
% graduated top 50% of class	98
% submitting high school rank	26

Important Dates

Early decision	
Apply by	11/1
Notified by	12/20
Other ED apply by	1/5
Other ED notified by	2/28
Regular	
Apply by	1/5
Notified by	4/1
Nonfall registration?	Yes

FINANCIAL FACTS

Annual tuition	$59,780
Food and housing	$14,711
Required fees	$ 90
Books and supplies	$1,400
Average need-based scholarship (First-year)	$30,868 ($32,574)
% students with need rec. need-based scholarship or grant aid (First-year)	83 (89)
% students with need rec. non-need-based scholarship or grant aid (First-year)	50 (49)
% students with need rec. need-based self-help aid (First-year)	58 (58)
% UG borrow to pay for school	44
Average cumulative indebtedness	$36,731
% of students with need fully met (First-year)	74 (81)
Average % of student need met (First-year)	92 (93)

GEORGIA INSTITUTE OF TECHNOLOGY

North Avenue, Atlanta, GA 30332 • Admissions: 404-894-4154

Survey Snapshot
Students are happy
Lab facilities are great
Internships are widely available

RATINGS

Quality of Life	**88**
Fire Safety	**97**
Green	**88**
Academic	**85**
Profs Interesting	**87**
Profs Accessible	**90**
Admissions	**98**
Financial Aid	**85**

CAMPUS LIFE

Type of school	Public
Environment	Metropolis

Students

Degree-seeking undergrad enrollment	19,063
% male/female/not reported	60/40/0
% from out of state	31
% First-year live on campus	92
% Ugrads live on campus	30
# of fraternities (% join)	38 (20)
# of sororities (% join)	15 (23)
% Asian	35
% Black or African American	8
% Hispanic	9
% Native American	0
% Pacific Islander	<1
% Race and/or ethnicity unknown	1
% Two or more races	5
% White	33
% International	7
# of countries represented	122

CAMPUS MENTAL HEALTH SERVICES

Offers mental health/wellness program	Yes
Mental health training available to students	Yes
Employs Chief Wellness Officer	Yes
Peer-to-peer mental health offerings	Yes
Counseling center has guidelines or accreditation	Yes
Mental health/well-being courses	Yes, for-credit

ACADEMICS

% students returning for sophomore year	97
% students graduating within 4 years	66
% students graduating within 6 years	94
Calendar	Semester
Student/faculty ratio	20:1
Most common class size 10–19.	(22%)
Most common lab/discussion size 20–29.	(31%)

Most Popular Majors

Computer and Information Sciences; Mechanical Engineering; Business Administration and Management

Applicants Also Look At

Kennesaw State University, Purdue University—West Lafayette, University of Florida, University of Georgia, University of Illinois at Urbana—Champaign

STUDENTS SAY "..."

Academics

A world-renowned public research university, Georgia Institute of Technology has a reputations that "opens many doors" for its students. Undergrads here are quick to sing the praises of the university's "rigorous" and "challenging" engineering, science, and business programs. Students also love Georgia Tech's focus on "innovation and hands-on learning," which leaves them well prepared to face the job market come graduation. For example, "throughout the school year there are plenty of competitions to create startup companies, flesh out innovative ideas, and show off prototypes." As if that wasn't enough, many courses have "a project built-in to force you to apply the material you've been studying." Inside the classroom, undergrads are greeted by professors who are "truly passionate about what they are teaching." One student further explains, "Most of the professors do research and continue learning themselves. This is the sort of environment that they foster." Undergrads further appreciate that their instructors "try and stimulate thinking rather than just letting you regurgitate facts." Another undergrad concurs remarking that her professors "challenge me to grow as an intellectual." Best of all, they frequently demonstrate themselves to be "invested in your success and making their classes interesting and applicable to real life."

Campus Life

Given the academic rigors at Georgia Tech, many students will tell you that "studying" is the number one activity. However, even these hardworking undergrads need a break every now and then. And thankfully "there is almost always something going on somewhere on campus." For starters, "there are an abundance of clubs...covering a huge variety of interests, and the majority of students are involved in at least one." Additionally, "during the fall, large numbers of students spend their weekends tailgating and attending football games." Undergrads here also enjoy attending "plays and musical events at the arts center." Moreover, Greek life is extremely popular at Georgia Tech. Fortunately, if you choose not join a sorority or fraternity, your social life won't take a hit. After all, we've been informed that "fraternity parties are generally very welcome...even [to] students who choose not to drink" or "people who are not members." Finally, students also love the opportunities of Georgia Tech's prime Atlanta location. The city offers many things to do "from museums, to concerts, festivals, restaurants, clubs, and every other sort of attraction in between!"

Student Body

When asked about their peers, Georgia Tech students immediately describe them as "smart," "driven, and ambitious." Indeed, it's rare to find an undergrad here who is "slacking off." Fortunately, "there isn't a sense of cut-throat academic rivalry; everyone is much more helpful and supportive of one another." As one relieved student shares, "People will help you if you're struggling on a math problem, or if you can't get your program to function correctly, instead of letting you suffer so that they can get a better grade." Undergrads also report that their fellow students are often quite "passionate." Unsurprisingly, that passion is "usually [connected to something] in the technology field." Indeed, "You walk to campus and you hear kids debating which programming language is better." Another student agrees explaining, "Most of the jokes exchanged seem to be science-related, and every now and then you see remote-controlled drones flying in the air." Aside from the "nerd" exterior, you'll find undergrads that are "witty" and "quirky" as well as "sleep deprived." There's also "a very large foreign component to the student body," which many here appreciate. Finally, we'd be remiss if we didn't mention that Georgia Tech is "not just a bunch of computer geeks sitting in their room all day but a group of people who are out there making a difference."

GEORGIA INSTITUTE OF TECHNOLOGY

Financial Aid: 404-894-4160 • E-Mail: admission@gatech.edu • Website: www.gatech.edu

THE PRINCETON REVIEW SAYS

Admissions

The school reports that its standardized testing policy for use in admission for Fall 2026 will require applicants to submit either the SAT or ACT. The Princeton Review suggests that interested applicants consult with the school for the most up-to-date standardized testing policies. *Very important factors considered include:* rigor of secondary school record, academic GPA, character/personal qualities, state residency. *Important factors considered include:* application essay, extracurricular activities. *Other factors considered include:* standardized test scores, recommendation(s), talent/ability, geographical residence, volunteer work, work experience. High school diploma is required and GED is not accepted. *Academic units required:* 4 English, 4 math, 4 science, 2 science labs, 2 language (other than English), 3 social studies.

Financial Aid

Students should submit: FAFSA; Institution's own financial aid form; CSS PROFILE. Priority filing deadline is 1/31. The Princeton Review suggests that all financial aid forms be submitted as soon as possible. *Need-based scholarships/grants offered:* Federal Pell; Federal SEOG; State scholarships/grants; Private scholarships; College/university scholarship or grant aid from institutional funds. *Loan aid offered:* Federal Direct Subsidized Loans; Federal Direct Unsubsidized Loans; Direct PLUS loans; State Loans; College/university loans from institutional funds. Admitted students will be notified of awards on a rolling basis beginning 4/1. Federal Work-Study Program available. Institutional employment available.

The Inside Word

Gaining admission to Georgia Tech is extremely competitive. Admissions officers here are looking to see how much candidates have pushed and stretched themselves academically throughout high school. They want intellectually curious students who aren't afraid of a challenge. Where possible, take honors, AP, and IB classes, and be sure that you're involved in your community.

THE SCHOOL SAYS

From the Admissions Office

"Georgia Tech consistently ranks among the nation's top public universities producing leaders in engineering, computing, business, architecture, and the sciences while remaining one of the best college buys in the country. The 400-acre campus is nestled in the heart of the fun, dynamic and progressive city of Atlanta. Recent campus improvements yielded new state-of-the art academic and research buildings, apartment-style housing, phenomenal social and recreational facilities, and the most extensive fiber-optic cable system on any college campus.

"Georgia Tech has a great academic reputation, and our graduates are well-prepared to meet today's challenges. Georgia Tech places a strong emphasis on undergraduate students, with practical work experience offered through our co-op and internship programs, and research opportunities for freshmen. Students can also gain an international perspective through study abroad, work abroad, or the international plan. There's also the Clough Undergraduate Center, which includes forty-one classrooms, two 300-plus seat auditoriums, group study rooms, presentation rehearsal studios, a rooftop garden, and a Café.

"With a Division I ACC sports program and access to Atlanta's music, theater, and other cultural venues, Georgia Tech offers its diverse and passionate student body a unique combination of top academics in a thriving and vibrant setting. We encourage you to come visit campus and see why Georgia Tech continues to attract the nation's most motivated, interesting, and creative students."

SELECTIVITY

# of total applicants	66,881
% of total applicants accepted	13
% of total acceptees attending	46
# of in-state applicants	12,527
% of in-state applicants accepted	29
# of out-of-state-applicants	44,596
% of applicants accepted from out of state	10
# of international applicants	9,758
% of international applicants accepted	7
# offered a place on the wait list	7,651
# admitted from wait list	653

First-Year Profile

Testing policy	SAT or ACT Required
Range SAT composite	1370–1530
Range SAT EBRW	680–760
Range SAT math	700–790
Range ACT composite	31–35
% submitting SAT scores	78
% submitting ACT scores	33
Average HS GPA	4.2
% submitting high school GPA	95
% graduated top 10% of class	89
% graduated top 25% of class	98
% graduated top 50% of class	99
% submitting high school rank	40

Important Dates

Early action	
Apply by	11/1
Notified by	1/31
Regular	
Apply by	1/5
Notified by	3/31
Nonfall registration?	Yes

FINANCIAL FACTS

Annual in-state tuition	$10,512
Annual out-of-state tuition	$33,596
Food and housing	$13,996
Required fees	$1,496
Books and supplies	$800
Average need-based scholarship (First-year)	$16,851 ($18,131)
% students with need rec. need-based scholarship or grant aid (First-year)	93 (94)
% students with need rec. non-need-based scholarship or grant aid (First-year)	21 (27)
% students with need rec. need-based self-help aid (First-year)	40 (35)
% students rec. any financial aid (First-year)	76 (76)
% UG borrow to pay for school	27
Average cumulative indebtedness	$25,348
% of students with need fully met (First-year)	20 (25)
Average % of student need met (First-year)	55 (61)

GETTYSBURG COLLEGE

300 North Washington Street, Gettysburg, PA 17325 • Admissions: 717-337-6100

Survey Snapshot
Classroom facilities are great
Lab facilities are great
Great library

RATINGS

Quality of Life	86
Fire Safety	97
Green	60*
Academic	93
Profs Interesting	94
Profs Accessible	95
Admissions	91
Financial Aid	97

CAMPUS LIFE

Type of school	Private
Affiliation	Lutheran
Environment	Village

Students

Degree-seeking undergrad enrollment	2,081
% male/female/not reported	50/50/0
% from out of state	76
% First-year live on campus	99
% Ugrads live on campus	95
# of fraternities (% join)	9 (26)
# of sororities (% join)	9 (32)
% Asian	2
% Black or African American	4
% Hispanic	10
% Native American	<1
% Pacific Islander	<1
% Race and/or ethnicity unknown	3
% Two or more races	3
% White	61
% International	17
# of countries represented	62

CAMPUS MENTAL HEALTH SERVICES

Offers mental health/wellness program	Yes
Mental health training available to students	Yes
Employs Chief Wellness Officer	NR
Peer-to-peer mental health offerings	NR
Counseling center has guidelines or accreditation	No
Mental health/well-being courses	NR

ACADEMICS

% students returning for sophomore year	91
% students graduating within 4 years	79
% students graduating within 6 years	80
Calendar	Semester
Student/faculty ratio	10:1
Most common class size 10–19.	(48%)

Most Popular Majors
Business, Organizations, & Management; Psychology; Economics and Mathematical Economics

Applicants Also Look At
Bucknell University, Dickinson College, Franklin & Marshall College, Lafayette College, University of Richmond

STUDENTS SAY "..."

Academics

Established in 1832, Pennsylvania's Gettysburg College is a selective college of the liberal arts and sciences that focuses on interdisciplinary study and advanced scholarship. One such example is the school's Eisenhower Institute, which is dedicated to civic engagement and leadership. To "support intellectual curiosity" for the school's 2,200 students, Gettysburg also provides an individualized major option; for instance, the CrossDisciplinary Science Institute prepares students to answer big questions across subjects. Faculty mentors are also at the ready, and they collaborate with hundreds of students on projects each year. "There are a lot of research opportunities for us even though we are undergraduate students," says one. There are also tons of chances "to present research, field trips, hands-on learning experiences, [and] immersion trips."

Small class sizes—there's a 10:1 student-faculty ratio—provide students with further opportunities to "form close relationships with professors, which makes the education experience personalized and thorough." Professors also take point in encouraging "leadership and involvement in academics through research and presentations," and utilize "discussion- based classes [to] foster a greater sense of investment." In turn, the inquisitive minds at Gettysburg "feel comfortable sharing their perspectives and opinions, which makes classes and discussions on campus much more interesting and eye-opening." Experiential learning also keeps things fresh and active, like "community service, going to see movies pertinent to a course's topic, field trips" or, for example, a German class that "used the rock wall in our gym as a trust exercise and to practice giving commands in German." Whatever the situation, professors "are always willing to help and make time to meet outside of class."

Campus Life

The work week is, in fact, a work week here. "Almost everyone is studying or doing work at their favorite study space," says one student. But while there's a lot of agreement that "Mondays to Fridays are rigorous," there's also consensus that "then the weekend rolls around." With 95 percent of the student body living on campus, there are lots of ways to stay active, "whether it be in a Greek organization, clubs, athletics, or working on-campus." Sports and Greek life may "dominate the social scene," but there are plenty of other entertainment outlets, like "cool reenactment options." Gettysburg also boasts "all the advantages other more rural schools have, like plenty of space to run, bike, and walk, and a quaint town too."

Student Body

Students describe their "very interconnected" community as "unmatched," thanks largely to the smaller size and high levels of sociability. "Everybody knows most of the other students from a class taken together, or a club they both attend, or maybe they just go to the gym at the same time." Diversity is important to both students and the school, and there's a lot of appreciation voiced for how the community is "open to different opinions" and "able to have healthy conversations about hard topics." Perhaps that's because students are all "eager to learn about the world beyond their academic area" or because they're "diligent with work and extracurriculars." Whatever the case, "we all click very well."

Gettysburg College

Financial Aid: 717-337-6611 • E-Mail: admiss@gettysburg.edu • Website: www.gettysburg.edu

THE PRINCETON REVIEW SAYS

Admissions

The school reports that its standardized testing policy for use in admission for Fall 2026 is Test Optional. The Princeton Review suggests that interested applicants consult with the school for the most up-to-date standardized testing policies. *Very important factors considered include:* rigor of secondary school record, academic GPA, application essay, recommendation(s). *Important factors considered include:* class rank, standardized test scores, interview, extracurricular activities, talent/ability, character/personal qualities, volunteer work. *Other factors considered include:* first generation, geographical residence, work experience, level of applicant's interest. High school diploma is required and GED is accepted. *Academic units required:* 4 English, 3 math, 3 science, 3 science labs, 3 language (other than English), 3 social studies, 3 history, 3 academic electives, 2 computer science. *Academic units recommended:* 4 English, 4 math, 4 science, 4 science labs, 4 language (other than English), 4 social studies, 4 history, 4 academic electives.

Financial Aid

Students should submit: FAFSA; CSS PROFILE. Priority filing deadline is 1/15. The Princeton Review suggests that all financial aid forms be submitted as soon as possible. *Need-based scholarships/grants offered:* Federal Pell; Federal SEOG; State scholarships/grants; Private scholarships; College/university scholarship or grant aid from institutional funds. *Loan aid offered:* Federal Direct Subsidized Loans; Federal Direct Unsubsidized Loans; Direct PLUS loans; State Loans; College/university loans from institutional funds. Admitted students will be notified of awards on or about 3/15. Federal Work-Study Program available. Institutional employment available.

The Inside Word

To really get a feel for Gettysburg, many students say a campus visit is a must. Test scores are optional here, and the school strongly emphasizes its desire for extracurricular involvement and positive contributions to the community, as well as students who have made the most of the academic offerings of their high school.

THE SCHOOL SAYS

From the Admissions Office

"For almost 200 years, Gettysburg College has provided a consequential education to generations of innovative, driven students and encouraged them to Do Great Work in their communities and across the world. Gettysburg College provides students with a breadth and depth of knowledge through a rigorous and contemporary education in the liberal arts and sciences. Students choose from 65 majors, minors, and academic programs. Our world-class faculty brings to life the arts, humanities, social sciences, and natural sciences, ensuring that our students are exposed to viewpoints across the disciplines.

"Our students' intellectual growth extends beyond the classroom. Gettysburg is committed to high-impact experiential learning like student-faculty research, study abroad, civic engagement, and leadership development that translate to valuable outcomes and careers for our 2,250 undergraduate students. Mentorship is central to the Gettysburg experience. Every student is assigned a personal success team—comprised of a faculty advisor, co-curricular advisor, and career advisor. Our active global community of over 32,000 alumni provides students with a powerful network to tap into even before they graduate. We see the return on investment as 98 percent of our most recent alums are either employed or enrolled in graduate school one year after graduation.

"At Gettysburg, there are no bystanders. With more than 120 clubs and organizations offering a thousand leadership positions and sponsoring more than 800 events on campus each year, Gettysburg students have many avenues to get involved. As a result, our students are prepared to make a difference—here at Gettysburg and in the world after they graduate."

SELECTIVITY

# of total applicants	7,929
% of total applicants accepted	40
% of total acceptees attending	16
# of early decision applicants	774
% of early decision applicants accepted	38

First-Year Profile

Testing policy	Test Optional
Range SAT EBRW	640–710
Range SAT math	590–730
Range ACT composite	27–32
% graduated top 10% of class	42
% graduated top 25% of class	75
% graduated top 50% of class	95

Important Dates

Early decision	
Apply by	11/15
Notified by	12/15
Other ED apply by	1/15
Other ED notified by	2/1
Early action	
Apply by	12/1
Notified by	2/1
Nonfall registration?	No

FINANCIAL FACTS

Annual tuition	$71,730
Food and housing	$17,340
Books and supplies	$1,000
Average need-based scholarship (First-year)	$55,505 ($55,859)
% students with need rec. need-based scholarship or grant aid (First-year)	100 (100)
% students with need rec. non-need-based scholarship or grant aid (First-year)	74 (97)
% students with need rec. need-based self-help aid (First-year)	78 (73)
% students rec. any financial aid (First-year)	61 (60)
% UG borrow to pay for school	65
Average cumulative indebtedness	$36,569
% of students with need fully met (First-year)	90 (90)
Average % of student need met (First-year)	90 (90)

GONZAGA UNIVERSITY

502 E Boone Avenue, Spokane, WA 99258 • Admissions: 509-313-6572

Survey Snapshot
Frats and sororities are popular
Everyone loves the Bulldogs
Easy to get around campus

RATINGS

Quality of Life	90
Fire Safety	97
Green	90
Academic	84
Profs Interesting	93
Profs Accessible	95
Admissions	88
Financial Aid	93

CAMPUS LIFE

Type of school	Private
Affiliation	Roman Catholic
Environment	Metropolis

Students

Degree-seeking undergrad enrollment	4,962
% male/female/not reported	47/53/0
% from out of state	48
% First-year from public high school	64
% First-year live on campus	93
% Ugrads live on campus	52
# of fraternities	0
# of sororities	0
% Asian	6
% Black or African American	1
% Hispanic	15
% Native American	1
% Pacific Islander	<1
% Race and/or ethnicity unknown	2
% Two or more races	9
% White	62
% International	4
# of countries represented	31

CAMPUS MENTAL HEALTH SERVICES

Offers mental health/wellness program	Yes
Mental health training available to students	Yes
Employs Chief Wellness Officer	Yes
Peer-to-peer mental health offerings	Yes
Counseling center has guidelines or accreditation	No
Mental health/well-being courses	No

ACADEMICS

% students returning for sophomore year	90
% students graduating within 4 years	75
% students graduating within 6 years	86
Calendar	Semester
Student/faculty ratio	11:1
Most common class size 20–29.	(37%)
Most common lab/discussion size 10–19.	(83%)

Most Popular Majors
Business/Commerce; Psychology; Registered Nursing/Registered Nurse

Applicants Often Prefer
University of Washington

Applicants Sometimes Prefer
Santa Clara University, University of Oregon, University of Portland, Washington State University

STUDENTS SAY "..."

Academics

Holistic learning is a highlight of Gonzaga University: the school "focuses on preparing students spiritually, intellectually, physically, and emotionally" for their futures. For instance, the school "encourages students to take classes outside of their majors in order to broaden their learning experiences." It also takes an interdisciplinary approach to the core curriculum, with one student noting that "an advanced biochemistry course...also aimed to apply concepts learned in Communications 100." Together, these approaches help to "develop people as a whole, so they have the skills to live a full and impactful life." Gonzaga also fosters student growth through Community Engaged Learning courses that partner "with local organizations or university clubs to support the Spokane community through a variety of types of service." Even dorm life connects to academics through Living-Learning Communities (LLCs), where first- and second-year students can "live in a community surrounding a centralized topic," such as health professions, outdoor pursuits, or creative expression. This emphasis on personal growth, connection, and community carries over into the close, supportive relationships students build with professors. "I have professors from two years ago who still remember me by name and ask questions about my life when I see them on campus," shares one student, adding, "Our professors are unafraid to discuss challenging perspectives and implore us to consider numerous sides to an argument, which has really helped me grow as a critical thinker." As one undergrad sums it up: "Every part of this school helps shape students into individuals for and with others, who are ready to use their intellect and skills to do good in the world."

Campus Life

Gonzaga's "guiding theme" is *cura personalis*, or caring for the whole person, mind and body. For many Zags, this means balancing "academics with involvement in clubs, service, and social events." Gonzaga "has strong service and community engagement opportunities that I have loved and…continued involvement with all four years here. Our student clubs are also easy to get involved in and have helped me build friendships and feel connected to the campus community." One thing students don't seem to have trouble fitting into their busy schedule is intramural sports (which are "a HUGE thing"): "I love love love the basketball games here! Both men's and women's!" Beyond campus, GU Outdoors "encourages people to get outside" and stay active, offering opportunities for snowboarding as well as "great hiking, mountain biking, and skiing." Overall, students describe Gonzaga as a place where "there's a shared sense of energy and belonging that makes daily life feel both purposeful and connected."

Student Body

"Zags help Zags" is more than a campus motto: "It's the culture here. Community is a core value of all Gonzaga students, and it shows." Gonzaga's campus culture is such that "you will have the door held open for you, you will have people ask how you are doing, and you will be made to feel that you belong." One student adds, "I think Gonzaga does a great job fostering a community of learners and leaders that really support and care for each other. It's impossible to walk around campus and not see someone you've connected with through student clubs, classes, volunteering, or on-campus housing." These "involved, passionate, and welcoming" Zags are also "driven and ambitious," and love feeling "positively motivated" by their peers. As one undergrad explains, "I feel most proud to be a Zag when I'm supporting my peers at sports, performing arts, or academic presentation events, and I have a lot of confidence knowing my friends always have my back here too."

GONZAGA UNIVERSITY

Financial Aid: 509-313-6582 • E-Mail: admissions@gonzaga.edu • Website: www.gonzaga.edu

THE PRINCETON REVIEW SAYS

Admissions

The school reports that its standardized testing policy for use in admission for Fall 2026 is Test Optional. The Princeton Review suggests that interested applicants consult with the school for the most up-to-date standardized testing policies. *Very important factors considered include:* rigor of secondary school record, academic GPA. *Important factors considered include:* recommendation(s), extracurricular activities, level of applicant's interest. *Other factors considered include:* standardized test scores, application essay, interview, character/personal qualities, first generation, volunteer work, work experience. High school diploma is required and GED is not accepted. *Academic units required:* 4 English, 3 math, 3 science, 3 science labs, 2 language (other than English), 3 social studies, 3 history, 2 academic electives. *Academic units recommended:* 4 English, 4 math, 4 science, 4 science labs, 3 language (other than English), 3 social studies, 3 history, 3 academic electives.

Financial Aid

Students should submit: FAFSA. Priority filing deadline is 2/1. The Princeton Review suggests that all financial aid forms be submitted as soon as possible. *Need-based scholarships/grants offered:* Federal Pell; Federal SEOG; Private scholarships; State scholarships/grants; College/university scholarship or grant aid from institutional funds. *Loan aid offered:* Federal Direct Subsidized Loans; Federal Direct Unsubsidized Loans; Direct PLUS loans; College/university loans from institutional funds. Admitted students will be notified of awards on a rolling basis beginning 3/1. Federal Work-Study Program available. Institutional employment available.

The Inside Word

When applying to Gonzaga, prospective students should focus on more than just their GPA. Though admissions officers will be interested in seeing your strengths in the classroom, they are also looking for applicants interested and involved with the world around them. Extracurriculars such as volunteer work can only help you. Though Gonzaga has strong Catholic studies and theology programs, religious background is not a consideration in applications. Gonzaga's testing policy is test optional, which should alleviate some stress and allow you to focus more on community involvement, a topic that Gonzaga cares about deeply.

THE SCHOOL SAYS

From the Admissions Office

"Gonzaga educates students for lives of leadership and service for the common good. We seek motivated students who will benefit from the University's challenging academic programs and will positively contribute to our campus with extracurricular achievement, community involvement, unique experiences, and diverse personal interests. In the application, let us know about your experiences thus far and your goals and hopes for the future. Please note that we are Test Optional. Grades and grade trends, curriculum, and writing in the application will be weighted more heavily for students applying without a test score. If you want to discuss admission to Gonzaga, please contact your admission counselor at gonzaga.edu/mycounselor."

SELECTIVITY

# of total applicants	8,906
% of total applicants accepted	80
% of total acceptees attending	16
# of in-state applicants	3,342
% of in-state applicants accepted	78
# of out-of-state-applicants	5,301
% of applicants accepted from out of state	82
# of international applicants	263
% of international applicants accepted	52
# offered a place on the wait list	676
# admitted from wait list	66

First-Year Profile

Testing policy	Test Optional
Range SAT composite	1230–1380
Range SAT EBRW	630–710
Range SAT math	590–690
Range ACT composite	29–32
% submitting SAT scores	19
% submitting ACT scores	6
Average HS GPA	3.7
% submitting high school GPA	99
% graduated top 10% of class	36
% graduated top 25% of class	69
% graduated top 50% of class	90
% submitting high school rank	39

Important Dates

Early action	
Apply by	11/15
Notified by	12/31
Regular	
Apply by	2/1
Notified by	2/28
Nonfall registration?	Yes

FINANCIAL FACTS

Annual tuition	$58,390
Food and housing	$17,135
Required fees	$1,120
Books and supplies	$1,188
Average need-based scholarship (First-year)	$16,211 ($18,094)
% students with need rec. need-based scholarship or grant aid (First-year)	95 (98)
% students with need rec. non-need-based scholarship or grant aid (First-year)	99 (100)
% students with need rec. need-based self-help aid (First-year)	62 (58)
% students rec. any financial aid (First-year)	98 (99)
% UG borrow to pay for school	45
Average cumulative indebtedness	$30,333
% of students with need fully met (First-year)	55 (54)
Average % of student need met (First-year)	82 (86)

Gordon College

255 Grapevine Road, Wenham, MA 01984 • Admissions: 978-867-4218

Survey Snapshot
Lots of conservative students
Students are very religious
Students are friendly

RATINGS

Quality of Life	87
Fire Safety	97
Green	60*
Academic	86
Profs Interesting	92
Profs Accessible	93
Admissions	85
Financial Aid	88

CAMPUS LIFE

Type of school	Private
Affiliation	Multidenominational - Evangelical
Environment	Village

Students

Degree-seeking undergrad enrollment	1,208
% male/female/not reported	96/4/0
% from out of state	61
% First-year from public high school	51
% First-year live on campus	95
% Ugrads live on campus	88
# of fraternities	0
# of sororities	0
% Asian	3
% Black or African American	4
% Hispanic	11
% Native American	<1
% Pacific Islander	<1
% Race and/or ethnicity unknown	9
% Two or more races	3
% White	63
% International	7
# of countries represented	38

CAMPUS MENTAL HEALTH SERVICES

Offers mental health/wellness program	Yes
Mental health training available to students	Yes
Employs Chief Wellness Officer	Yes
Peer-to-peer mental health offerings	Yes
Counseling center has guidelines or accreditation	Yes
Mental health/well-being courses	Yes, non-credit

ACADEMICS

% students returning for sophomore year	81
% students graduating within 4 years	61
% students graduating within 6 years	71
Calendar	Semester
Student/faculty ratio	11:1
Most common class size 10–19.	(47%)
Most common lab/discussion size 10–19.	(50%)

Most Popular Majors

Exercise Physiology and Kinesiology; Experimental Psychology; Business Administration and Management

Applicants Also Look At

Liberty University, Merrimack College, Messiah University, University of Massachusetts—Amherst, University of Massachusetts—Boston, University of Massachusetts—Lowell, University of New Hampshire, Wheaton College (IL)

STUDENTS SAY "..."

Academics

Tucked away in beautiful, bucolic Massachusetts, Gordon College is a liberal-arts institution that's built on "Christian values without being unnecessarily strict." Here, students receive a "well-rounded education" that encourages them "to make interdisciplinary connections." There's also an appreciated "emphasis on servant leadership through opportunities like the outdoor education requirement." And while there's no denying that "the school is academically rigorous," students note that "there's so much here for support, so it's hard to do poorly in a course." The faculty is described both as "accomplished" and "extremely passionate about the subjects that they teach." and the majority are "very involved and want to know you personally." Students are proud to share their own relationships: "I'm actually friends with my English professor and I've only been in class with him for a semester so far." Another divulges, "I was struggling financially and had professors email me over the summer to help me find a way to get back." This isn't just an "enjoyable [academic] environment" either; there's a sense that "when people leave here, they are prepared to get a job and do well."

Campus Life

Gordon is a school that's always humming with some sort of activity, especially on Mondays, Wednesdays, and Fridays, where "you can find a good portion of [the] student body in chapel." Outside of that, the college sponsors numerous events like "waffle nights, student hosted dinners, coffeehouses, parties [and] game nights," and "sports are pretty popular on campus." (We've been told that "the quad is great for playing spikeball.") There's also a music department that "is very strong and holds a lot of performances," though it's not uncommon to stumble upon unofficial "chill house concerts or jam sessions." Of course, New England weather plays a fairly big role in dictating the activity schedule. "When it's warm everyone hammocks [and] when it snows everyone has snowball fights and builds snowmen." When the opportunity presents itself, undergrads enjoy exploring the "quaint New England coastal towns" that surround the campus, whether that's "to hike or spend a day at the beach," and of course nearby Boston makes for a good weekend getaway for those seeking out things like "museums or concerts." Overall, though, students note that campus life is "pretty tame": there are "some off-campus parties," but people "who drink [and] do drugs...are the exception and are in the minority."

Student Body

When asked about their peers, many individuals at Gordon gush that their classmates are "genuine and kind people" who really "care about how you are doing socially, academically, and spiritually." According to one undergrad, "I could pull aside any random person, tell them I'm having a bad day, and they would listen to me and care about me." Students also value that many of their peers "have a real, lived-out relationship with God." And though it frequently feels as though most students come from "Massachusetts or New England" and are "majority white, majority Christian," you'll also discover that "there are many countries and nationalities represented" among the student body as well. And while there's "not a lot of middle ground" between the very liberal and conservative points of view on campus, students take pride in everyone's ability to "enter into a curious and respectful conversation" when encountering someone who disagrees with them. Perhaps that's because at the end of the day, students find unity in being "committed to their education and goals" and gladly help "one another achieve academic success."

GORDON COLLEGE

Financial Aid: 978-867-4246 • E-Mail: admissions@gordon.edu • Website: www.gordon.edu

THE PRINCETON REVIEW SAYS

Admissions

The school reports that its standardized testing policy for use in admission for Fall 2026 is Test Optional. The Princeton Review suggests that interested applicants consult with the school for the most up-to-date standardized testing policies. *Very important factors considered include:* application essay, character/personal qualities, religious affiliation/commitment. *Important factors considered include:* rigor of secondary school record, class rank, academic GPA. *Other factors considered include:* standardized test scores, recommendation(s), interview, extracurricular activities, talent/ability. High school diploma is required and GED is accepted. *Academic units required:* 4 English, 2 math, 2 science, 1 science lab, 2 language (other than English), 2 social studies, 5 academic electives. *Academic units recommended:* 4 English, 3 math, 3 science, 1 science lab, 4 language (other than English), 2 social studies, 5 academic electives.

Financial Aid

Students should submit: FAFSA. The Princeton Review suggests that all financial aid forms be submitted as soon as possible. *Need-based scholarships/grants offered:* Federal Pell; Federal SEOG; State scholarships/grants; Private scholarships; College/university scholarship or grant aid from institutional funds. *Loan aid offered:* Federal Direct Subsidized Loans; Federal Direct Unsubsidized Loans; Direct PLUS loans; State Loans. Admitted students will be notified of awards on a rolling basis beginning 12/1. Federal Work-Study Program available. Institutional employment available.

The Inside Word

Gordon College seeks applicants who display an intellectual curiosity and excitement for learning. You'll need solid grades, a commitment to Christian values, and a readiness for college demonstrated through academic efforts and extracurricular activities. While an interview may not be required, visiting campus is highly encouraged.

THE SCHOOL SAYS

From the Admissions Office

"Gordon College is New England's top Christian college where students are equipped to flourish in a changing world. We blend career-focused academics with life-giving faith to prepare young Christians to make a difference with hope and confidence. With seven distinct schools, new academic programs, a vibrant campus experience on the North Shore of Boston and a host of experiential learning opportunities, students are known, grown and prepared.

"**Academics that build a career.** At Gordon a classroom could be an internship in downtown Boston, making art in the Italian countryside, working with a human rights organization in Croatia or conducting research with professors on Gordon's 485-acre wooded campus. With 93% of alumni in grad school or employed at companies like Disney, Salesforce and ESPN within a year of graduation, students join a powerful network when they become a Scot.

"**Experiences that build confidence.** Students grow in heart and mind by trekking through the Adirondacks on a La Vida expedition, exploring 55+ student-led clubs and organizations or joining Fighting Scots Nation as an athlete or superfan. A vibrant campus energy inspires lifelong bonds through student improv performances, worshiping in Chapel, snowball fights on the quad and beach campfires at Gull Pond.

"**Christian community that builds character.** The Gordon community is marked by caring individuals who want to help solve global challenges with a Christian voice during a critical time in history. At Gordon students deepen their relationships with Jesus and one another as they learn to thrive."

SELECTIVITY

# of total applicants	1,561
% of total applicants accepted	90
% of total acceptees attending	21
# of in-state applicants	490
% of in-state applicants accepted	93
# of out-of-state-applicants	951
% of applicants accepted from out of state	94
# of international applicants	118
% of international applicants accepted	47

First-Year Profile

Testing policy	Test Optional
Range SAT composite	1100–1300
Range SAT EBRW	550–690
Range SAT math	530–650
Range ACT composite	24–30
% submitting SAT scores	29
% submitting ACT scores	6
Average HS GPA	3.7
% submitting high school GPA	100
% graduated top 10% of class	28
% graduated top 25% of class	60
% graduated top 50% of class	74
% submitting high school rank	25

Important Dates

Early action	
Apply by	11/1
Notified by	11/15
Regular	
Apply by	8/28
Notified by	Rolling, 10/1
Nonfall registration?	Yes

FINANCIAL FACTS

Annual tuition	$34,980
Food and housing	$15,000
Required fees	$1,380
Books and supplies	$800
Average need-based scholarship (First-year)	$20,944 ($23,375)
% students with need rec. need-based scholarship or grant aid (First-year)	100 (100)
% students with need rec. non-need-based scholarship or grant aid (First-year)	19 (22)
% students with need rec. need-based self-help aid (First-year)	79 (74)
% students rec. any financial aid (First-year)	100 (99)
% UG borrow to pay for school	63
Average cumulative indebtedness	$34,094
% of students with need fully met (First-year)	22 (24)
Average % of student need met (First-year)	70 (74)

Goucher College

1021 Dulaney Valley Road, Baltimore, MD 21204-2794 • Admissions: 410-337-6100

Survey Snapshot
Lots of liberal students
Class discussions encouraged
Students environmentally aware

RATINGS

Quality of Life	**84**
Fire Safety	**94**
Green	**60***
Academic	**83**
Profs Interesting	**93**
Profs Accessible	**91**
Admissions	**85**
Financial Aid	**90**

CAMPUS LIFE

Type of school	Private
Environment	City

Students

Degree-seeking undergrad enrollment	1,055
% male/female/not reported	35/64/1
% from out of state	33
% First-year live on campus	88
% Ugrads live on campus	74
# of fraternities	0
# of sororities	0
% Asian	5
% Black or African American	33
% Hispanic	13
% Native American	<1
% Pacific Islander	0
% Race and/or ethnicity unknown	5
% Two or more races	<1
% White	36
% International	8
# of countries represented	51

CAMPUS MENTAL HEALTH SERVICES

Offers mental health/wellness program	Yes
Mental health training available to students	Yes
Employs Chief Wellness Officer	No
Peer-to-peer mental health offerings	Yes
Counseling center has guidelines or accreditation	No
Mental health/well-being courses	NR

ACADEMICS

% students returning for sophomore year	77
% students graduating within 4 years	43
% students graduating within 6 years	54
Calendar	Semester
Student/faculty ratio	10:1
Most common class size 10–19.	(53%)
Most common lab/discussion size 20–29.	(39%)

Applicants Sometimes Prefer

American University, McDaniel College, St. Mary's College of Maryland, Towson University, University of Maryland, Baltimore County, University of Maryland, College Park

STUDENTS SAY "..."

Academics

The small and innovative Goucher College, located just outside of Baltimore, boasts a welcoming, collaborative learning environment, a 100 percent study abroad rate/requirement, and a liberal arts curriculum that focuses on interdisciplinary complex-problem solving. The foundation for every major is the Goucher Commons Curriculum, which creates shared, problem-based learning experiences across disciplines. The school encourages its students to live outside of their comfort zones when it comes to being "mindful" of others "so as to learn from...diverse perspectives." Students here are "curious to learn" and "thrive on engaging in deep conversation, and are not afraid to speak their minds." Small class sizes and a low student-to-faculty ratio promote these conversations, and "discussion and critical thinking skills are built into every class so you learn or formulate an argument around a wide variety of issues."

As a way of easing the transition into college, Goucher's Commons Curriculum features a First Year Seminar that every first-year student is required to take. During the seminar, first-year students "meet with their mentor who was with them during orientation to talk about certain resources provided [at] Goucher for safety, and other subjects about racial identity and how we're getting acquainted with our new environment." As for regular classes, there are a ton of "very interesting" classes, and "it is easy to enroll in a class that is either full or that you don't have the prerequisites for." Professors receive high marks across the board; they get to know students on a personal level and are "invested in [their] unique reasoning for being a part of the department." They "want everyone to share their opinions and certain personal experiences that go along with the topic" at hand. "I know they see me first as a person, second as a student," says one happy student.

Campus Life

The Goucher campus is "beautiful." When it's sunny, "a lot of students are outside doing homework, socializing, playing Frisbee, or doing various other physical activities." During the week, most people work and study ("lots of people use the library as a common place"), so the weekend "is when people hang out." Not a lot of students go off campus, so a lot of small groups and open mics form. Parties "aren't all that common."

Students subscribe to the idea that "a rising tide lifts all boats." One student explains, "There is no internal competition at Goucher; we all work together." Sports are becoming more popular, and there are 20 Division III athletic teams and even an equestrian team. Activism is huge on campus, and if you are passionate about a cause with these seemingly "liberal, outspoken" students, "there is usually a club or student union that is already organized, or students who are more than willing to start a club."

Student Body

The Goucher student body comprises "a symposium [of students] to do Socrates proud." Goucher students are "engaged, trust each other, and are brave enough to dialogue in a way most campuses don't seem to be anymore." The degree of political openness here is "only left-looking," and this "delightfully weird" group tends to include "alternative, creative, artistic people who aren't afraid to express themselves." Students describe their peers as middle to upper-middle class and from the East Coast. Diversity and inclusivity are strong at Goucher, with nearly half of the student population consisting of people of color, and the Center for Race, Equity, and Identity supporting the sizable BIPOC and LGBTQ+ communities on campus. Keeping it in their own backyard, students love to help and "do their best to give back to their Baltimore and local community."

Goucher College

Financial Aid: 410-337-6141 • E-Mail: admissions@goucher.edu • Website: www.goucher.edu

THE PRINCETON REVIEW SAYS

Admissions

The school reports that its standardized testing policy for use in admission for Fall 2026 is Test Optional. The Princeton Review suggests that interested applicants consult with the school for the most up-to-date standardized testing policies. *Very important factors considered include:* rigor of secondary school record, academic GPA. *Important factors considered include:* application essay, recommendation(s), extracurricular activities, volunteer work. *Other factors considered include:* class rank, standardized test scores, interview, talent/ability, character/personal qualities, first generation, alumni/ae relation, geographical residence, state residency, work experience, level of applicant's interest. High school diploma is required and GED is accepted. *Academic units required:* 4 English, 4 math, 3 science, 2 science labs, 2 language (other than English), 3 social studies. *Academic units recommended:* 4 English, 4 math, 3 science, 3 science labs, 4 language (other than English), 3 social studies.

Financial Aid

Students should submit: FAFSA. Priority filing deadline is 11/5. The Princeton Review suggests that all financial aid forms be submitted as soon as possible. *Need-based scholarships/grants offered:* Federal Pell; Federal SEOG; State scholarships/grants; Private scholarships; College/university scholarship or grant aid from institutional funds. *Loan aid offered:* Federal Direct Subsidized Loans; Federal Direct Unsubsidized Loans; Direct PLUS loans. Admitted students will be notified of awards on a rolling basis beginning 11/1. Federal Work-Study Program available. Institutional employment available.

The Inside Word

At Goucher College, all students participate in a study abroad experience, so make sure you've factored that in before applying. Also note that while early decision is not an option here, early action is, and students who have their application materials ready are encouraged to submit.

THE SCHOOL SAYS

From the Admissions Office

"Goucher College is a private, liberal arts college dedicated to teaching students to be complex problem-solvers prepared for the jobs of the future. Goucher's emphasis on experiential learning takes shape through its 100 percent study abroad program, an innovative internship accelerator, and support from an individualized student success team.

"Every Goucher student is supported by their own Success Team. Students are assigned a Success Advisor who monitors a student's progress through graduation along with colleagues in Residential Life, Career Education, and Global Education among others.

"Through Goucher's general education requirement, the Commons, students master a range of skills—critical thinking, problem-solving, collaboration, and communication—the very skills being sought by today's employers. Goucher's more than 30 majors are rooted in the core principles of interdisciplinary study and range from the sciences, to the social sciences, humanities, education and the arts. The emphasis on global education provides 100% of our students the opportunity to study abroad at no additional charge. Further experiential learning opportunities exist through internships, research with faculty, and community-based learning. With career education integrated throughout the curriculum, Goucher's unique Internship Accelerator provides micro-internships to first year and sophomore students that lead to robust experiences as juniors and seniors. Within one year of graduation, 96% of recent graduates are employed or are enrolled in graduate/professional programs.

"Goucher is committed to creating a unique learning and living environment that exposes students to new experiences and is a proud member of the Colleges That Change Lives organization."

SELECTIVITY

# of total applicants	2,808
% of total applicants accepted	82
% of total acceptees attending	12

First-Year Profile

Testing policy	Test Optional
Range SAT composite	1100–1320
Range SAT EBRW	550–700
Range SAT math	510–640
Range ACT composite	26–32
% submitting SAT scores	23
% submitting ACT scores	3
Average HS GPA	3.2
% submitting high school GPA	100
% graduated top 10% of class	27
% graduated top 25% of class	53
% graduated top 50% of class	94
% submitting high school rank	38

Important Dates

Early action	
Apply by	11/15
Notified by	Rolling
Regular	
Apply by	1/15
Notified by	Rolling, 11/15
Nonfall registration?	Yes

FINANCIAL FACTS

Annual tuition	$57,500
Food and housing	$18,150
Required fees	$300
Books and supplies	$1,200
Average need-based scholarship (First-year)	$46,643 ($54,838)
% students with need rec. need-based scholarship or grant aid (First-year)	99 (100)
% students with need rec. non-need-based scholarship or grant aid (First-year)	16 (17)
% students with need rec. need-based self-help aid (First-year)	66 (66)
% students rec. any financial aid (First-year)	98 (100)
% UG borrow to pay for school	66
Average cumulative indebtedness	$29,090
% of students with need fully met (First-year)	23 (18)
Average % of student need met (First-year)	84 (89)

GRINNELL COLLEGE

1227 Park Street, 1st Floor, Grinnell, IA 50112 • Admissions: 641-269-3600

Survey Snapshot
Class discussions encouraged
Great financial aid
Dorms are like palaces

RATINGS	
Quality of Life	80
Fire Safety	92
Green	60*
Academic	92
Profs Interesting	94
Profs Accessible	95
Admissions	96
Financial Aid	99

CAMPUS LIFE

Type of school	Private
Environment	Village

Students

Degree-seeking undergrad enrollment	1,625
% male/female/not reported	46/54/0
% from out of state	90
% First-year live on campus	100
% Ugrads live on campus	80
# of fraternities	0
# of sororities	0
% Asian	10
% Black or African American	5
% Hispanic	10
% Native American	<1
% Pacific Islander	<1
% Race and/or ethnicity unknown	<1
% Two or more races	7
% White	48
% International	19
# of countries represented	60

CAMPUS MENTAL HEALTH SERVICES

Offers mental health/wellness program	Yes
Mental health training available to students	Yes
Employs Chief Wellness Officer	Yes
Peer-to-peer mental health offerings	No
Counseling center has guidelines or accreditation	No
Mental health/well-being courses	Yes, non-credit

ACADEMICS

% students returning for sophomore year	91
% students graduating within 4 years	69
% students graduating within 6 years	86
Calendar	Semester
Student/faculty ratio	8:1
Most common class size 10–19.	(47%)
Most common lab/discussion size 10–19.	(49%)

Most Popular Majors

Computer Science; Biology/Biological Sciences

Applicants Also Look At

Bowdoin College, Carleton College, Harvard College, Macalester College, Northwestern University, Pomona College, University of California—Berkeley, University of Southern California, Williams College, Yale University

STUDENTS SAY "..."

Academics

The unique appeal of Grinnell College, according to students, is that you'll get "elite academics in a small-town environment" and a "great educational experience" that many describe as "the best you can find in the Midwest." The overall sense is that "the students are smart, professors outstanding, and the administration does a good job of bringing the world to Grinnell." That plays out in the "depth at which courses are taught," with some proudly noting that there's an "emphasis on understanding rather than rote learning." Enrollees also benefit greatly from "small classes" and an "open curriculum" that enables students to pursue whatever interests them.

While there's "a lot of reading and assignment," students don't mind that rigor, saying that "it is genuinely enjoyable to learn here" and noting that "academics are intense at Grinnell, but as a result I've learned so much." Much of that can be attributed to professors who, by and large, "welcome questions and critique and genuinely care about learning." They also make it easy to foster "strong relationships" with them: "I've been to so many of their houses for meals with my classes." A classmate concurs, adding, "There are many departments here at the college that have great faculty, and they are usually quite willing to engage with students and help them when they need it."

Campus Life

Grinnell is "very academically oriented" and accordingly, undergrads dedicate a lot of time to schoolwork. But when they want to kick back and relax, the college sponsors numerous events ranging from "All-Campus Parties (which are hosted by the student government)" to bingo, dances, trivia, and more. Many students also participate in clubs and extracurricular activities, and the fact that "you only need five people to start a club" means that "it's very easy to make your own," which goes a long way to explain the range of niches filled by DAG, a club devoted to foam sword-fighting; the fiber arts club; a "low-stakes band class"; GORP (Grinnell Outdoor Recreation Program); mock trial; and so much more. Additionally, "intramural sports are slowly becoming popular again." The most commonly shared concept is that Grinnellians are quite adept at making their own fun, in ways that can be life-changing: "I watched a lunar eclipse with a group of people who I didn't know before 1:00am that night; I still keep up with them." And, of course, plenty of people choose to unwind by simply "watching bad movies on Saturday nights."

Student Body

From the moment you step foot on the campus of Grinnell College, you can sense that this is a "tight-knit community" where students are free "to be whoever [they] want... without judgment or reservation." This results in a lot of "passionate, quirky, [and] curious" individuals who tend to maintain "high standards for themselves." Peers are also described as "really smart and driven," so much so that "I feel like everyone I know is working to achieve some rather impressive goals and are actually making good progress." Students tend to identify as liberal and are "not afraid to challenge the status quo or how things are," especially when it comes to "social issues." Additionally, undergrads note that there's "a higher-than-average percentage of students in the LGBTQ+ community," though some also note that many peers seem to be "white, predominantly middle- and upper-class" kids who "went to quite well-funded high schools." Regardless of background, students mostly agree that on campus, everyone is "down to earth and friendly" or at the very least, benefiting from a "lack of pretentiousness" that fosters a sense of community. As this student concludes, "My favorite thing about the Grinnell student body is inclusivity. I never feel like I am not welcome at an event, and while social groups exist, nothing has ever been cliquey or exclusive to me."

Grinnell College

Financial Aid: 641-269-3250 • E-Mail: admission@grinnell.edu • Website: www.grinnell.edu

THE PRINCETON REVIEW SAYS

Admissions

The school reports that its standardized testing policy for use in admission for Fall 2026 is Test Optional. The Princeton Review suggests that interested applicants consult with the school for the most up-to-date standardized testing policies. *Very important factors considered include:* rigor of secondary school record, class rank, recommendation(s). *Important factors considered include:* academic GPA, standardized test scores, application essay, extracurricular activities, talent/ability. *Other factors considered include:* interview, character/personal qualities, first generation, alumni/ae relation, geographical residence, state residency, volunteer work, work experience, level of applicant's interest. High school diploma is required and GED is accepted. *Academic units recommended:* 4 English, 4 math, 3 science, 3 science labs, 3 language (other than English), 3 social studies, 3 history.

Financial Aid

Students should submit: FAFSA; CSS PROFILE. Priority filing deadline is 1/15. The Princeton Review suggests that all financial aid forms be submitted as soon as possible. *Need-based scholarships/grants offered:* Federal Pell; Federal SEOG; State scholarships/grants; Private scholarships; College/university scholarship or grant aid from institutional funds. *Loan aid offered:* Federal Direct Subsidized Loans; Federal Direct Unsubsidized Loans; Direct PLUS loans; College/university loans from institutional funds. Admitted students will be notified of awards on or about 4/1. Federal Work-Study Program available. Institutional employment available.

The Inside Word

Accepting just 15 percent of its applicants, if you're serious about becoming a Grinnellian, you'll want to take every opportunity to demonstrate that, especially since, according to the school, "no single factor guarantees admission." Take the school up on its preliminary application, request information about and attend any events it may host in your area, and make sure that you're challenging yourself with your high-school courses and scoring well on either the SAT or ACT if you are submitting your scores.

THE SCHOOL SAYS

From the Admissions Office

"Grinnell College is a place where independence of thought and social conscience are instilled. Grinnell is a college with the resources of a school ten times its size, a faculty that reads like a Who's Who of Teaching, and a learning environment where debate does not end in the classroom and often begins in the dining hall.

"Grinnellians are committed to learning, respect for themselves and others, contributing to global social good, willing collaboration, and the courage to try.

"We look for students who show strong potential, have the courage to try new things, demonstrate a willingness to speak out and share their opinions, and bring different perspectives to our international campus in the middle of Iowa. Grinnell College is filled with students who are serious about learning but are not always serious.

"Students applying for first-year admission are not required to submit an SAT and/or ACT test score. Applicants are required to inform us whether or not they will submit a test score by their respective application deadline. Students are not permitted to change their test score preference after their respective application deadline. Applicants who choose to apply with an SAT and/or ACT test score must submit official test scores to Grinnell College."

SELECTIVITY

# of total applicants	9,303
% of total applicants accepted	16
% of total acceptees attending	28
# of early decision applicants	865
% of early decision applicants accepted	35
# offered a place on the wait list	1,467
# admitted from wait list	21

First-Year Profile

Testing policy	Test Optional
Range SAT composite	1420–1530
Range SAT EBRW	710–760
Range SAT math	710–790
Range ACT composite	31–34
% submitting SAT scores	29
% submitting ACT scores	22
% graduated top 10% of class	71
% graduated top 25% of class	19
% graduated top 50% of class	11

Important Dates

Early decision	
Apply by	11/15
Notified by	12/15
Other ED apply by	1/5
Other ED notified by	1/31
Regular	
Apply by	1/15
Notified by	4/1
Nonfall registration?	No

FINANCIAL FACTS

Annual tuition	$73,582
Food and housing	$17,784
Required fees	$572
Average need-based scholarship (First-year)	$67,852 ($69,834)
% students with need rec. need-based scholarship or grant aid (First-year)	100 (100)
% students with need rec. non-need-based scholarship or grant aid (First-year)	14 (18)
% students with need rec. need-based self-help aid (First-year)	85 (80)
% students rec. any financial aid (First-year)	92 (93)
% UG borrow to pay for school	27
Average cumulative indebtedness	$16,787
% of students with need fully met (First-year)	100 (100)
Average % of student need met (First-year)	100 (100)

GROVE CITY COLLEGE

100 Campus Drive, Grove City, PA 16127-2104 • Admissions: 724-458-2100

Survey Snapshot
Lots of conservative students
Students are happy
Students take advantage of the outdoors

RATINGS

Quality of Life	94
Fire Safety	94
Green	60*
Academic	85
Profs Interesting	93
Profs Accessible	96
Admissions	88
Financial Aid	88

CAMPUS LIFE

Type of school	Private
Affiliation	Nondenominational
Environment	Village

Students

Degree-seeking undergrad enrollment	2,120
% male/female/not reported	53/47/0
% from out of state	48
% First-year from public high school	55
% First-year live on campus	98
% Ugrads live on campus	93
# of fraternities (% join)	10 (17)
# of sororities (% join)	8 (20)
% Asian	2
% Black or African American	<1
% Hispanic	1
% Native American	<1
% Pacific Islander	<1
% Race and/or ethnicity unknown	0
% Two or more races	6
% White	90
% International	1
# of countries represented	11

CAMPUS MENTAL HEALTH SERVICES

Offers mental health/wellness program	Yes
Mental health training available to students	Yes
Employs Chief Wellness Officer	Yes
Peer-to-peer mental health offerings	Yes
Counseling center has guidelines or accreditation	Yes
Mental health/well-being courses	Yes, for-credit

ACADEMICS

% students returning for sophomore year	83
% students graduating within 4 years	74
% students graduating within 6 years	80
Calendar	Semester
Student/faculty ratio	12:1
Most common class size 10–19.	(31%)
Most common lab/discussion size 20–29.	(40%)

Most Popular Majors

Mechanical Engineering; Kinesiology and Exercise Science; Health/Medical Preparatory Programs

Applicants Often Prefer

Calvin University, Cedarville University, Geneva College, Liberty University, Messiah University, Penn State University Park, Saint Vincent College, University of Pittsburgh—Pittsburgh Campus, Westminster College (PA)

Applicants Sometimes Prefer

Allegheny College, Covenant College, Duquesne University, Gordon College, Hillsdale College, Houghton College, John Carroll University, Robert Morris University, Slippery Rock University of Pennsylvania, Wheaton College (IL), Youngstown State University

STUDENTS SAY "..."

Academics

Grove City College draws "conscientious and hardworking" students who have "high standards for themselves and others in both academic and personal areas." Students appreciate the "Christ-centered learning" and find that the "rigorous coursework" creates an overall academic experience that "truly prepares people for the real world." The school offers 70 majors and every student takes the humanities core—a series of seven courses centered around analyzing Bible scriptures alongside significant events in Western civilization. Students appreciate that Grove City "makes their students branch out and learn a lot of different material so that they are well-rounded." For instance, there's an entrepreneurship class where teams of students create their own businesses, and education majors spend time each week at local schools. Among the greatest strengths of Grove City are the professors. In the classroom, students speak to how they're "very engaging" and "willing and eager to answer questions" as they "bring the material to life." Out of it, students appreciate that they "always make time for their students no matter what" and overall, instructors are "very caring, and they want us all to do well." Its professors "provide challenging, yet achievable expectations" and "always have connections that help a lot of students get jobs right out of college." Overall, the school provides "many options for students to get real world experience while still in school, which makes the transition from in school to post-graduation much easier."

Campus Life

Grove City is located about an hour outside Pittsburgh, PA, and when the weather is nice, students can be found on the quad playing games like spike ball or simply enjoying the sun. Intramural sports are popular, and there are "loads of different clubs on campus to fit any type of student's interests," whether that's swing dancing, fencing, or exploring the outdoors. According to students, Bible study and attending church are also popular. The school hosts many activities and "on weekend nights there are usually 3 or so big events going on that you have to choose between." There are also plenty of Greek life events and "movie nights are also a crowd favorite." The surrounding town is a "little quiet" and while there are things to do, "they can get repetitive." Consequently, there is "far more activity on-campus than off-campus." Many students enjoy attending sporting events, and Homecoming is "one of the best events that Grove City College has." Students also note that the RAs "strive to build a strong community on their halls." As one student explains, "I know my hall so well and we are comfortable with dropping into each other's dorm rooms or planning silly events together."

Student Body

Students at Grove City are "extremely friendly and academically driven." It's a "very social" campus and "no matter where you turn at Grove City, there is always someone who is excited to see you." There's a community feeling and students actively "seek out opportunities to connect with others and be involved in campus life." Being "passionate about pursuing a relationship with God" or having a shared belief in Christianity creates a quick bond between students and allows "for Christ-centered conversation to flow through all aspects of campus life." Another commonality among students is in their being "Groverachievers," which is to say, "hard workers who are passionate and respectful." However, as one student explains, they're "also quite capable of relaxing and having fun as a group." Classmates can count on their peers for support: "the schoolwork is hard, but the students are here to help each other." Another student agrees, saying, "[my peers] are so encouraging. From uplifting me in my academics to walking alongside me in my relationship with Jesus, I feel very supported here all around."

Grove City College

Financial Aid: 724-458-3300 • E-Mail: admissions@gcc.edu • Website: www.gcc.edu

THE PRINCETON REVIEW SAYS

Admissions

The school reports that its standardized testing policy for use in admission for Fall 2026 is Test Optional. The Princeton Review suggests that interested applicants consult with the school for the most up-to-date standardized testing policies. *Very important factors considered include:* rigor of secondary school record, academic GPA, application essay, interview, character/personal qualities, level of applicant's interest. *Important factors considered include:* recommendation(s), extracurricular activities. *Other factors considered include:* class rank, standardized test scores, talent/ability, first generation, alumni/ae relation, geographical residence, state residency, religious affiliation/commitment, volunteer work, work experience. High school diploma is required and GED is accepted. *Academic units required:* 4 English, 3 math, 3 science, 2 science labs, 3 language (other than English), 3 social studies, 2 history. *Academic units recommended:* 4 English, 3 math, 3 science, 2 science labs, 3 language (other than English), 3 social studies, 2 history.

Financial Aid

Students should submit: CSS PROFILE. The Princeton Review suggests that all financial aid forms be submitted as soon as possible. *Need-based scholarships/grants offered:* State scholarships/grants; Private scholarships; College/university scholarship or grant aid from institutional funds. Admitted students will be notified of awards on a rolling basis beginning 2/20. Federal Work-Study Program not available. Institutional employment available.

The Inside Word

Gaining entrance to Grove City College is competitive and students must have outstanding personal qualities and be prepared for a strenuous but workable course load. Christian values are of utmost importance at Grove City College, and the school values students who seek out surroundings based on those principles. Interviews and letters of recommendation are highly valued as components of the admission process.

THE SCHOOL SAYS

From the Admissions Office

"Students flourish at Grove City College because faith is its foundation. From the classroom to the practice fields, from the dining halls to the dormitories, students seek to understand how faith influences their daily activities and ultimately how they might use their abilities to serve others. The College equips students to discover and pursue their unique callings through an academically excellent and Christ-centered learning and living experience.

"The cornerstone of our excellent education is our incredible community of learners—students, faculty and staff who are committed to pursuing knowledge and truth for the advancement of the common good. Surrounded by peers and mentors who sharpen them, students develop into leaders of the highest proficiency guided by these core values: faithfulness, excellence, community, stewardship, and independence.

"We offer students and families an amazing value. Tuition and costs run about half the national average before scholarships and financial aid. Unlike the vast majority of colleges and universities, we do not practice tuition discounting—tuition price is the same for every student and no student unwittingly subsidizes another student's tuition through artificial scholarships.

"Our nationally ranked Career Services Office begins working with students before they arrive as freshmen, ensuring that by the time they graduate, they will be prepared not only to pursue a fulfilling career but for a lifetime of professional success."

SELECTIVITY

# of total applicants	2,225
% of total applicants accepted	67
% of total acceptees attending	38
# of in-state applicants	770
% of in-state applicants accepted	79
# of out-of-state-applicants	1,378
% of applicants accepted from out of state	63
# of international applicants	77
% of international applicants accepted	16
# of early decision applicants	328
% of early decision applicants accepted	90

First-Year Profile

Testing policy	Test Optional
Range SAT composite	1120–1370
Range SAT EBRW	570–700
Range SAT math	540–670
Range ACT composite	23–31
% submitting SAT scores	50
% submitting ACT scores	15
Average HS GPA	3.8
% submitting high school GPA	75

Important Dates

Early decision	
Apply by	11/1
Notified by	12/15
Regular	
Apply by	3/15
Notified by	Rolling, 12/15
Nonfall registration?	Yes

FINANCIAL FACTS

Annual tuition	$23,470
Food and housing	$13,230
Books and supplies	$1,000
Average need-based scholarship (First-year)	$13,125 ($14,672)
% students with need rec. need-based scholarship or grant aid (First-year)	99 (100)
% students with need rec. non-need-based scholarship or grant aid (First-year)	20 (29)
% students with need rec. need-based self-help aid (First-year)	40 (34)
% students rec. any financial aid (First-year)	77 (84)
% UG borrow to pay for school	41
Average cumulative indebtedness	$49,136
% of students with need fully met (First-year)	30 (36)
Average % of student need met (First-year)	74 (78)

HAMILTON COLLEGE

198 College Hill Road, Clinton, NY 13323 • Admissions: 315-859-4421

Survey Snapshot
Great library
Great financial aid
Campus newspaper is popular

RATINGS

Quality of Life	84
Fire Safety	91
Green	60*
Academic	91
Profs Interesting	93
Profs Accessible	94
Admissions	97
Financial Aid	98

CAMPUS LIFE

Type of school	Private
Environment	Rural

Students

Degree-seeking undergrad enrollment	1,976
% male/female/not reported	47/53/0
% from out of state	71
% First-year from public high school	72
% First-year live on campus	100
% Ugrads live on campus	100
# of fraternities (% join)	5 (11)
# of sororities (% join)	3 (14)
% Asian	9
% Black or African American	4
% Hispanic	10
% Native American	<1
% Pacific Islander	0
% Race and/or ethnicity unknown	2
% Two or more races	6
% White	61
% International	8
# of countries represented	57

CAMPUS MENTAL HEALTH SERVICES

Offers mental health/wellness program	Yes
Mental health training available to students	No
Employs Chief Wellness Officer	NR
Peer-to-peer mental health offerings	NR
Counseling center has guidelines or accreditation	No
Mental health/well-being courses	NR

ACADEMICS

% students returning for sophomore year	96
% students graduating within 4 years	82
% students graduating within 6 years	90
Calendar	Semester
Student/faculty ratio	9:1
Most common class size 10–19.	(41%)
Most common lab/discussion size 10–19.	(55%)

Most Popular Majors

Econometrics and Quantitative Economics; Mathematics; Political Science and Government

Applicants Often Prefer

Amherst College, Bowdoin College, Brown University; Dartmouth College, Williams College

Applicants Sometimes Prefer

Colgate University, Middlebury College, Tufts University, Vassar College, Wesleyan University

Applicants Rarely Prefer

Bates College, Colby College, Skidmore College

STUDENTS SAY "..."

Academics

At Hamilton College in upstate New York, students design their own academic paths through an open curriculum, selecting courses that reflect their interests with guidance from multiple advisors. Students enjoy the open curriculum, "as it allows for experimentation in different fields of study." As one student explains, "the open curriculum gives you freedom and responsibility over what and how you want to learn." Another undergrad notes that students "are very engaged [in their classes] since they chose to be there rather than doing it for a core requirement." The college is "a living and learning community where learning happens outside the classroom." Students relate that some of their most memorable educational experiences include visiting "the Glen for investigation for a bio class," taking "field trips to New York City and Utica, volunteering in [the] local Early Childhood Center," and even "making music with programming hardware components in the computer." Many consider small class sizes to be another benefit of attending Hamilton—"not only because your professors are available...but also because you get to know other students in your classes very well." Professors at Hamilton are "very engaged in the material and make class enjoyable." They also "make their expectations clear" and "will challenge students to produce reasonable yet impassioned results." Such "very accessible and kind" attention from the professors emphasizes the Hamilton experience: a place that takes an interest in how "students are doing both in and out of the classroom."

Campus Life

Set atop a hill and among corn fields, Hamilton has a "quintessential small, communal, and progressive liberal arts feel" that its students and staff love. Hamilton affords students endless opportunities to form friendships and try new things, thanks to the school's "incredible array of student clubs and organizations on campus," led by dedicated students. On weekends and evenings, "there are a lot of bingo, trivia, sports watch parties, and concerts" plus performances courtesy of the "student-choreographed dance troupes and a cappella groups." Students definitely enjoy a party, although attendance is "pretty optional." One student notes, "if you're an active student, Hamilton is a great place to be," as many students enjoy skiing, rock climbing, and "runs in our massive glen." It's not all go-go-go, though—self-care is crucial, and Hamilton has a Health & Wellness Center, which includes a Counseling Center. Says one student, "There are many resources on campus for mental wellness," and also "many initiatives for students to be aware of these resources." When the weather is favorable, students "read outside, or play spikeball on the quad," or gather with friends in the "Adirondack chairs scattered around campus." Students have the sense that "everyone really wants to be here, which is really valuable and contributes to the vibe on campus."

Student Body

Students describe their Hamilton peers in the highest of terms: "all active citizens" who are "intelligent, engaged, thoughtful, hard-working, community-oriented, capable, athletic, and charitable." Overall, students are "incredibly engaged in community events such as sports, fundraisers, workshops, and speaking engagements." There is a wide variety of students at Hamilton. Those who "balance Greek life and varsity sports teams" as well as "students who spend their Friday nights playing D&D (Dungeons and Dragons)." One trait they all seem to share is that they are hard workers who enjoy the "established academic culture," where it is "cool to be smart and care about the work you do." Hamilton students are described as "dedicated, hard-working, happy," and "genuinely curious people who listen." As one student sums it up: People here are "smart but not competitive."

Hamilton College

Financial Aid: 800-859-4413 • E-Mail: admission@hamilton.edu • Website: www.hamilton.edu

THE PRINCETON REVIEW SAYS

Admissions

The school reports that its standardized testing policy for use in admission for Fall 2026 is Test Optional. The Princeton Review suggests that interested applicants consult with the school for the most up-to-date standardized testing policies. *Very important factors considered include:* rigor of secondary school record, class rank, academic GPA. *Important factors considered include:* application essay, recommendation(s), character/personal qualities. *Other factors considered include:* standardized test scores, interview, extracurricular activities, talent/ability, first generation, alumni/ae relation, geographical residence, state residency, volunteer work, work experience, level of applicant's interest. High school diploma is required and GED is accepted. *Academic units recommended:* 4 English, 3 math, 3 science, 3 language (other than English), 3 social studies.

Financial Aid

Students should submit: FAFSA; CSS PROFILE; State aid form. Priority filing deadline is 1/15. The Princeton Review suggests that all financial aid forms be submitted as soon as possible. *Need-based scholarships/grants offered:* Federal Pell; Federal SEOG; State scholarships/grants; Private scholarships; College/university scholarship or grant aid from institutional funds. *Loan aid offered:* Federal Direct Subsidized Loans; Federal Direct Unsubsidized Loans; Direct PLUS loans. Admitted students will be notified of awards on or about 4/1. Federal Work-Study Program available. Institutional employment available.

The Inside Word

Hamilton looks for students who will engage deeply with campus life and contribute meaningfully to its community. A strong academic record is a must, but the admissions team takes a broad view of each application, drawing on essays, recommendation letters, an optional but encouraged interview, and other supplemental materials. When it comes to extracurricular involvement, genuine passion and commitment to a few meaningful pursuits will resonate more than a lengthy list of activities.

THE SCHOOL SAYS

From the Admissions Office

"There is no one Hamilton student, just as there is no one Hamilton experience, but the promise we make to our students is the same: at Hamilton, our open curriculum enables you to explore your passions, our welcoming student body from diverse backgrounds will expand your perspectives, and our value of writing and communicating well prepares you to express yourself no matter what path you choose after graduation. Our faculty will expect your full attention and participation academically, and you will embark on a lifelong journey to "Know Thyself" (the college's motto).

"We are also committed to ensuring that a Hamilton education is available to all deserving students. We will review your application without considering your financial circumstances (which is known as 'need-blind' admission) and then, once you are admitted, we will meet your full demonstrated need for all four years. Hamilton is one of the few colleges that pledges to do both. Application fees are waived for those who are from the first generation in their family to attend college.

"Hamilton operates like a small city, but has the feel of a close neighborhood. ALEX (Advise, Learn, EXperience—and named for our favorite founding father!) is Hamilton's coordinated network of on-campus academic centers, and advisors that work together to support students and offer guidance in areas such as off-campus study, experiential learning, and finding balance in their lives. The College's investment in state-of-the-art facilities, like the new digital makerspace (and an Innovation Center to open in 2027) ensures students get to research, collaborate, and learn using cutting-edge tools and technologies."

SELECTIVITY

# of total applicants	8,904
% of total applicants accepted	14
% of total acceptees attending	40
# of in-state applicants	1,611
% of in-state applicants accepted	21
# of out-of-state-applicants	3,707
% of applicants accepted from out of state	21
# of international applicants	3,586
% of international applicants accepted	3
# of early decision applicants	1,120
% of early decision applicants accepted	28
# offered a place on the wait list	2,032
# admitted from wait list	49

First-Year Profile

Testing policy	Test Optional
Range SAT composite	1440–1510
Range SAT EBRW	710–760
Range SAT math	710–770
Range ACT composite	33–35
% submitting SAT scores	35
% submitting ACT scores	13
% graduated top 10% of class	86
% graduated top 25% of class	98
% graduated top 50% of class	100
% submitting high school rank	18

Important Dates

Early decision	
Apply by	11/15
Notified by	12/15
Other ED apply by	1/6
Other ED notified by	2/10
Regular	
Apply by	1/6
Notified by	4/1
Nonfall registration?	Yes

FINANCIAL FACTS

Annual tuition	$75,210
Food and housing	$19,290
Required fees	$750
Books and supplies	$800
Average need-based scholarship (First-year)	$63,267 ($66,176)
% students with need rec. need-based scholarship or grant aid (First-year)	98 (100)
% students with need rec. non-need-based scholarship or grant aid (First-year)	0 (0)
% students with need rec. need-based self-help aid (First-year)	77 (80)
% students rec. any financial aid (First-year)	55 (58)
% UG borrow to pay for school	40
Average cumulative indebtedness	$17,971
% of students with need fully met (First-year)	100 (100)
Average % of student need met (First-year)	100 (100)

Hampden-Sydney College

172 Via Sacra, Hampden-Sydney, VA 23943-0067 • Admissions: 434-223-6120

Survey Snapshot
Students take advantage of the outdoors
Lots of conservative students
Students are happy

RATINGS

Quality of Life	87
Fire Safety	92
Green	60*
Academic	87
Profs Interesting	92
Profs Accessible	94
Admissions	91
Financial Aid	92

CAMPUS LIFE

Type of school	Private
Affiliation	No affiliation
Environment	Rural

Students

Degree-seeking undergrad enrollment	924
% male/female/not reported	100/0/0
% from out of state	38
% First-year live on campus	98
% Ugrads live on campus	98
# of fraternities (% join)	12 (29)
% Asian	1
% Black or African American	6
% Hispanic	6
% Native American	<1
% Pacific Islander	<1
% Race and/or ethnicity unknown	1
% Two or more races	4
% White	81
% International	1
# of countries represented	3

CAMPUS MENTAL HEALTH SERVICES

Offers mental health/wellness program	Yes
Mental health training available to students	Yes
Employs Chief Wellness Officer	Yes
Peer-to-peer mental health offerings	Yes
Counseling center has guidelines or accreditation	No
Mental health/well-being courses	No

ACADEMICS

% students returning for sophomore year	78
% students graduating within 4 years	61
% students graduating within 6 years	63
Calendar	Semester
Student/faculty ratio	9:1
Most common class size 10–19.	(48%)
Most common lab/discussion size 1–9.	(53%)

Most Popular Majors

Business/Managerial Economics, Social Sciences, History, Biology/Biological Sciences

Applicants Sometimes Prefer

James Madison University, Virginia Tech

Applicants Rarely Prefer

Appalachian State University, Christopher Newport University, The University of the South, Virginia Commonwealth University, Virginia Military Institute

STUDENTS SAY "..."

Academics

Hampden-Sydney College "provides young men with a liberal arts education steeped in brotherhood and tradition." Students are proud of the school's 250-year history and status as one of the oldest institutions of high learning in the nation. That status also affords them a staff of "very involved teachers, faculty, and alumni who care about your learning and future after college." Academics at H-SC center focus on communication—there's a studio dedicated to it—and all students take courses and an exam in rhetoric. Consequently, academic discourse is "stimulating" and "rewarding," and popular class projects involve creative twists on the subject: asking students to simulate high-intensity leadership scenarios, role-play as activists from the 1920s, and collaborate in collective oral chemistry quizzes. There are also plenty of experiential learning options, including bee-keeping and documentary filmmaking, and study abroad destinations, like Oxford University in England and Akita International University in Japan. The professors at H-SC are "brilliant, accomplished scholars" with whom students forge "phenomenal" relationships. Students also consider "excellent career preparation" and "huge alumni network" to be major perks of enrolling in H-SC. It's "hands down the best alumni network I could have imagined. I have one-on-one calls with alumni once a month to orient myself towards my career after graduation." As one student sums it up, H-SC is "a great place to become a man."

Campus Life

There are plenty of opportunities to connect with other students at Hampden-Sydney College. Academic clubs such as the Union-Philanthropic Literary Society are popular and host debates as well as social events, such as "an annual ball to which alumni are invited, weekly teas with cheese and meat spreads, and holiday parties." And with more than a third of students joining fraternities, "Greek life is huge" and one of the school's "greatest strengths," with events "generally open to the public, and everyone is on such friendly terms (and close by enough) that people generally mix around different fraternity houses." The Division III Tigers are a joy to watch (the "tailgates are unmatched") and there's a robust intramural program. Outdoor enthusiasts enjoy "a variety of trails and hiking paths" throughout their 1,400-acre campus, as well as "disc golf, lakes, and zip lines." One student's various favorites include "playing sports on campus with friends as a hobby, in addition to working as a firefighter for the town's volunteer fire and rescue service." With a population of around 7,500, "Farmville is a very nice and beautiful town," providing Tigers access to golf, food, and fishing. "The Tiger Inn serves as a secondary food facility," and students can venture to nearby Richmond for "plays [and] music productions." Students note that "homework can be hectic," so the overall goal for many students is "spending time with the boys" to relax in whichever of the many shapes that entertainment may take.

Student Body

The connection between students at Hampden-Sydney College meets the "true definition of brotherhood, united with an unbreakable bond." Students say, "the H-SC community is one that makes you feel at home," one that is "inclusive and collaborative" and which "upholds and uplifts." Students can be found "supporting each other, helping each other, and sometimes even stopping each other from doing something stupid." The school's honor code maintains that and sees to it that Tigers are generally "solid blokes. They value each other's well-being over themselves." Students enjoy "a lot of freedom to act how we please because we have respect for each other. You don't have to worry about someone stealing your things, [and] you sleep with the doors unlocked without worry." In short, Hampden-Sydney men are "kind, care about each other, and are seekers of knowledge in all that they do."

HAMPDEN-SYDNEY COLLEGE

Financial Aid: 434-223-6119 • E-Mail: admission@hsc.edu • Website: www.hsc.edu

THE PRINCETON REVIEW SAYS

Admissions

The school reports that its standardized testing policy for use in admission for Fall 2026 is Test Optional. The Princeton Review suggests that interested applicants consult with the school for the most up-to-date standardized testing policies. *Very important factors considered include:* rigor of secondary school record, class rank, academic GPA, application essay, recommendation(s), character/personal qualities. *Important factors considered include:* interview, extracurricular activities, first generation, alumni/ae relation. *Other factors considered include:* standardized test scores, talent/ability, volunteer work, work experience, level of applicant's interest. High school diploma is required and GED is accepted. *Academic units required:* 4 English, 3 math, 2 science, 1 science lab, 2 language (other than English), 1 social studies. *Academic units recommended:* 4 math, 3 language (other than English).

Financial Aid

Students should submit: FAFSA; State aid form. Priority filing deadline is 2/1. The Princeton Review suggests that all financial aid forms be submitted as soon as possible. *Need-based scholarships/grants offered:* Federal Pell; Federal SEOG; State scholarships/grants; Private scholarships; College/university scholarship or grant aid from institutional funds. *Loan aid offered:* Federal Direct Subsidized Loans; Federal Direct Unsubsidized Loans; Direct PLUS loans; College/university loans from institutional funds. Admitted students will be notified of awards on a rolling basis beginning 11/1. Federal Work-Study Program available. Institutional employment available.

The Inside Word

Heed the school's motto—"Forming good men and good citizens"—and make sure you can show yourself to be among that crowd. If you're interested in being a Tiger, consider scheduling a personal campus visit to help get the ball rolling, and if you're sure this is the school for you, make that commitment clear by applying early. The school is test optional (with a few exceptions for international and homeschooled students), but if you go that route, be sure you submit a powerful college essay and are well-prepared for a live interview.

THE SCHOOL SAYS

From the Admissions Office

"Hampden-Sydney believes the world needs good men and good citizens, and has been forming them since 1775.

"Scholars, leaders, athletes, creators, and outdoorsmen alike thrive in our highly personal educational experience that emphasizes both intellectual growth and character development. Students benefit from small classes, where they can develop impactful relationships with top-notch professors; a robust research program that rivals what large universities offer; and a renowned Rhetoric Program that develops first-rate communication skills that wow employers.

"With three lakes on campus; miles of woodland trails; a disc golf course; a high-ropes course; and a High Adventure program that sponsors kayaking, hiking, fishing, and skiing excursions, your time out of the classroom promises to be just as fulfilling.

"Our legendary brotherhood—ranked the nation's No. 2 Best Alumni Network by the Princeton Review—illustrates the lifelong bonds that students develop on our scenic 1,300-acre campus nestled in the heart of Virginia."

SELECTIVITY

# of total applicants	3,270
% of total applicants accepted	38
% of total acceptees attending	20
# of in-state applicants	973
% of in-state applicants accepted	55
# of out-of-state-applicants	2,123
% of applicants accepted from out of state	32
# of international applicants	172
% of international applicants accepted	3
# offered a place on the wait list	72
# admitted from wait list	4

First-Year Profile

Testing policy	Test Optional
Range SAT composite	1050–1310
Range SAT EBRW	540–660
Range SAT math	530–650
Range ACT composite	22–29
% submitting SAT scores	12
% submitting ACT scores	6
Average HS GPA	3.4
% submitting high school GPA	100
% graduated top 10% of class	12
% graduated top 25% of class	27
% graduated top 50% of class	70
% submitting high school rank	46

Important Dates

Early decision	
Apply by	11/1
Notified by	11/21
Early action	
Apply by	10/15
Notified by	45 days after closing date
Regular	
Apply by	2/1
Notified by	3/1
Nonfall registration?	Yes

FINANCIAL FACTS

Annual tuition	$55,981
Food and housing	$18,078
Required fees	$3,169
Books and supplies	$1,290
Average need-based scholarship (First-year)	$46,011 ($47,378)
% students with need rec. need-based scholarship or grant aid (First-year)	100 (100)
% students with need rec. non-need-based scholarship or grant aid (First-year)	36 (39)
% students with need rec. need-based self-help aid (First-year)	57 (55)
% students rec. any financial aid (First-year)	99 (100)
% UG borrow to pay for school	58
Average cumulative indebtedness	$33,000
% of students with need fully met (First-year)	42 (43)
Average % of student need met (First-year)	90 (92)

Hampton University

Hampton University, Hampton, VA 23668 • Admissions: 757-727-6238

Survey Snapshot
Lots of liberal students
Students are very religious
Campus newspaper is popular

RATINGS

Quality of Life	73
Fire Safety	60*
Green	60*
Academic	76
Profs Interesting	79
Profs Accessible	85
Admissions	84
Financial Aid	84

CAMPUS LIFE

Type of school	Private
Environment	City

Students

Degree-seeking undergrad enrollment	4,046
% male/female/not reported	33/67/<1
% from out of state	78
% First-year from public high school	90
% First-year live on campus	95
% Ugrads live on campus	71
# of fraternities (% join)	5 (NR)
# of sororities (% join)	4 (NR)
% Asian	<1
% Black or African American	84
% Hispanic	<1
% Native American	<1
% Pacific Islander	<1
% Race and/or ethnicity unknown	14
% Two or more races	0
% White	<1
% International	2
# of countries represented	22

CAMPUS MENTAL HEALTH SERVICES

Offers mental health/wellness program	Yes
Mental health training available to students	Yes
Employs Chief Wellness Officer	No
Peer-to-peer mental health offerings	Yes
Counseling center has guidelines or accreditation	Yes
Mental health/well-being courses	Yes, non-credit

ACADEMICS

% students returning for sophomore year	83
% students graduating within 4 years	43
% students graduating within 6 years	56
Calendar	Semester
Student/faculty ratio	17:1
Most common class size 1–9.	(29%)
Most common lab/discussion size 1–9.	(45%)

Most Popular Majors
Biology; Psychology; Business Administration, Management and Operations

Applicants Often Prefer
Howard University, North Carolina A&T State University, Radford University, University of Richmond

Applicants Sometimes Prefer
Old Dominion University, Virginia Commonwealth University, Virginia State University

STUDENTS SAY "…"

Academics

Hampton University is a historically Black research university located in Virginia along the Chesapeake Bay. The school offers 97 programs and 75 majors on its picturesque 314-acre campus that's right on the water. It is a "school of tradition, family values, and excellent education" that "exudes and strives for a standard of excellence in any and every aspect." There is "an immense amount of clout and history behind Hampton University's walls," and students say this "historically rich" institution supports "their professional and academic endeavors through all available resources." Hampton professors "are at the top of their field" and students appreciate the "one-to-one assistance" and support given to them during office hours. Undergraduates say professors go above and beyond to establish connections with students and help prepare them for life after graduation. One student shares, "My professors have not only been teachers in the classroom but in my personal life as well. I have been taught how to use the communication and research skills that I have obtained outside of the classroom." Beyond the classroom, Hampton provides students with a "plethora of outside resources," including paid internships, undergraduate research, and job shadowing opportunities. As a research university with a strong focus on STEM, Hampton offers numerous opportunities for students to gain hands-on learning experience. For example, biology is among the most popular majors at Hampton, and a long-standing project with NOAA provides stipends, travel, assistantships, and more for biology students to study coastal ecology along the Chesapeake Bay. In addition, the strong alumni network and "excellent career planning tools" expand the opportunities available to students both "during and after their tenure at Hampton."

Campus Life

On this beautiful campus with over 55 student organizations, there are an "unlimited [number] of activities for students to participate in." Students love that Hampton blends "past traditions with modern times" and two of its most popular events are Homecoming and Spring Fest. During the week, life on campus is "mostly academic and extracurricular," with students focusing on their coursework and attending meetings or events for various clubs. To unwind, students often catch a movie at the student center or hang out with friends in the glass-walled dining hall that overlooks the water. On the weekends, there are parties both on and off campus, along with "kickbacks," which are "a more low-key version of a party." Some students describe the town of Hampton as small and "not a college town," so they recommend having access to a car to get around, noting that students "often interact with the students from [nearby] NSU, ODU, and William & Mary."

Student Body

Students describe their peers as driven, hardworking, and ambitious. As one student explains, "Everyone on campus has the same mindset, a unanimous goal, and that's to graduate and strive for a successful life." Students are committed to personal and professional growth and "trying to make something of themselves." Peers say their classmates are "poised, considerate, and self-sufficient." As one student elaborates, "Hampton students have a certain attitude about themselves; you can always tell a Hamptonian. Once you have been Hamptonized, there is no going back." On this social and supportive campus, most students are "outgoing and involved in many organizations within the school and the community."

Hampton University

Financial Aid: 757-727-5332 • E-Mail: admit@hamptonu.edu • Website: www.hamptonu.edu

THE PRINCETON REVIEW SAYS

Admissions

The school reports that its standardized testing policy for use in admission for Fall 2026 is Test Optional. The Princeton Review suggests that interested applicants consult with the school for the most up-to-date standardized testing policies. *Very important factors considered include:* rigor of secondary school record, academic GPA, recommendation(s), character/personal qualities. *Important factors considered include:* class rank, standardized test scores. *Other factors considered include:* application essay, interview, extracurricular activities, talent/ability, volunteer work, work experience, level of applicant's interest. High school diploma is required and GED is accepted. *Academic units required:* 4 English, 3 math, 3 science, 2 science labs, 2 social studies, 2 history, 1 visual/performing arts. *Academic units recommended:* 2 language (other than English).

Financial Aid

Students should submit: FAFSA. Priority filing deadline is 2/15. The Princeton Review suggests that all financial aid forms be submitted as soon as possible. *Need-based scholarships/grants offered:* Federal Pell; Federal SEOG; State scholarships/grants; Private scholarships; College/university scholarship or grant aid from institutional funds; Federal Nursing Scholarships. *Loan aid offered:* Federal Direct Subsidized Loans; Federal Direct Unsubsidized Loans; Direct PLUS loans. Admitted students will be notified of awards on a rolling basis beginning 2/15. Federal Work-Study Program available.

The Inside Word

Hampton University allows for early action admissions, meaning that students can receive an early decision without having to commit to attending the school. Around one-quarter of HU's applicant pool pursues this option. You would be wise to follow suit; the school is bound to be more lenient early in the process than later, when it has already admitted many qualified students.

THE SCHOOL SAYS

From the Admissions Office

"Hampton attempts to provide the environment and structures most conducive to the intellectual, emotional, and aesthetic enlargement of the lives of its members. The university gives priority to effective teaching and scholarly research while placing the student at the center of its planning. Hampton will ask you to look inwardly at your own history and culture and examine your relationship to the aspirations and development of the world."

SELECTIVITY

# of total applicants	16,664
% of total applicants accepted	64
% of total acceptees attending	15
# of in-state applicants	1,699
% of in-state applicants accepted	100
# of out-of-state-applicants	8,881
% of applicants accepted from out of state	96
# of international applicants	6,084
% of international applicants accepted	6

First-Year Profile

Testing policy	Test Optional
Range SAT EBRW	450–570
Range SAT math	410–530
Range ACT composite	16–23
% submitting SAT scores	16
% submitting ACT scores	32
Average HS GPA	3.6
% submitting high school GPA	59
% graduated top 10% of class	17
% graduated top 25% of class	35
% graduated top 50% of class	40
% submitting high school rank	42

Important Dates

Early action	
Apply by	11/5
Notified by	12/31
Regular	
Apply by	3/1
Nonfall registration?	Yes

FINANCIAL FACTS

Annual tuition	$28,308
Food and housing	$14,988
Required fees	$3,204
Books and supplies	$1,100
Average need-based scholarship (First-year)	$10,991 ($11,158)
% students with need rec. need-based scholarship or grant aid (First-year)	96 (97)
% students with need rec. non-need-based scholarship or grant aid (First-year)	70 (75)
% students with need rec. need-based self-help aid (First-year)	75 (72)
% students rec. any financial aid (First-year)	44 (43)
% UG borrow to pay for school	74
Average cumulative indebtedness	$30,676
% of students with need fully met (First-year)	36 (33)
Average % of student need met (First-year)	37 (33)

HANOVER COLLEGE

517 Ball Drive, Hanover, IN 47243-0108 • Admissions: 800-213-2178

Survey Snapshot
Lab facilities are great
Class discussions encouraged
Frats and sororities are popular

RATINGS

Quality of Life	**84**
Fire Safety	**60***
Green	**60***
Academic	**88**
Profs Interesting	**92**
Profs Accessible	**96**
Admissions	**85**
Financial Aid	**92**

CAMPUS LIFE

Type of school	Private
Affiliation	Presbyterian
Environment	Rural

Students

Degree-seeking undergrad enrollment	1,001
% male/female/not reported	48/51/1
% from out of state	32
% First-year live on campus	92
% Ugrads live on campus	91
# of fraternities (% join)	4 (44)
# of sororities (% join)	4 (32)
% Asian	<1
% Black or African American	5
% Hispanic	4
% Native American	1
% Pacific Islander	<1
% Race and/or ethnicity unknown	1
% Two or more races	4
% White	81
% International	2
# of countries represented	17

CAMPUS MENTAL HEALTH SERVICES

Offers mental health/wellness program	Yes
Mental health training available to students	No
Employs Chief Wellness Officer	NR
Peer-to-peer mental health offerings	NR
Counseling center has guidelines or accreditation	No
Mental health/well-being courses	NR

ACADEMICS

% students returning for sophomore year	82
% students graduating within 4 years	65
% students graduating within 6 years	69
Calendar	4-4-1
Student/faculty ratio	12:1
Most common class size 10–19.	(45%)

Most Popular Majors

Economics; Psychology; Speech Communication and Rhetoric

STUDENTS SAY "..."

Academics

Hanover College is a school that is brimming with opportunity. And with its "beautiful" campus and emphasis on "gaining real-life skills and making lifelong connections," it's easy to understand why students are drawn here. The vast majority of classes at Hanover are "small and discussion based," and many also place "a heavy focus on writing." While the academics can be challenging, students eagerly report that "many of the harder classes have tutors for that specific class." Additionally, the Learning Center is always "willing to go over things with you, edit papers and more." Importantly, it's evident that Hanover professors "love what they teach...and that excitement often carries over to the student." Indeed, they excel at "bring[ing] the material to life...and easily keep the attention of the class." Just as essential, Hanover professors are also known to be "caring and down to earth" and "devoted to their students." And, as this ecstatic art history major concludes, "Most of the professors on staff are part of the best people you will ever meet in life."

Campus Life

While some undergrads grumble that "life at Hanover is pretty slow," others steadfastly argue that "there are SO many things [with which] to be involved." For starters, students can participate in "over sixty organizations" including "Adopt A Grandparent, Circle K Community Service, Best Buddies, and so many more." Additionally, individuals who enjoy the arts will be delighted to hear that both "the theater department and the improv group...never disappoint [and] the choir and band concerts [are] always very enjoyable [as well]." For those that are more athletically inclined, we're told that "when it's warm out, students go hiking, play wiffleball, or...sand volleyball." Many undergrads also gravitate to the Student Activities Center which offers "game tables, [a] theater room, televisions [and] study spots." And, in the evenings, "chances are some club always has something planned—be it a movie showing [or] a poetry night!" Hanover also has a relatively robust party scene. Indeed, undergrads inform us that "Greek life is big on...campus." And while there "are only four frats...they are a [major] part of [the] social life." Finally, when students are looking for a break from the campus routine, they often head to nearby Madison or Louisville, which is a mere "forty-minute drive [away]" and the closest major city.

Student Body

Hanover is home to a "small, pretty laid back and surprising[ly] interesting community." Indeed, while undergrads here admit that ethnic diversity "is still an issue," they happily point out that you'll find a wide array of personality types. Of course, the "majority of the students are committed to their academics and [strive to find] a balance between work and play." Many Hanover undergrads "are also extremely passionate about the things in which they invest their time, whatever that may be, and encourage that passion in others." It's important to note that the college's small size does make it "[easy] for cliques...to form." However, we're assured "it is also quite easy to break into the cliques if you are really interested in hanging out with certain groups of people." This social ease can be attributed to the fact that Hanover features some of the "friendliest individuals that Indiana has to offer." In fact, you are virtually guaranteed "to see a smiling face or to get a hello anywhere you walk on campus, whether it be from a fellow student or a faculty member." As one satisfied economics major sums up, "We are all about making everyone feel welcome and making Hanover College home."

Hanover College

Financial Aid: 812-866-7029 • E-Mail: admission@hanover.edu • Website: www.hanover.edu

THE PRINCETON REVIEW SAYS

Admissions

The school reports that its standardized testing policy for use in admission for Fall 2026 is Test Optional. *Very important factors considered include:* academic GPA, talent/ability, level of applicant's interest. *Important factors considered include:* extracurricular activities, character/personal qualities, first generation, alumni/ae relation. *Other factors considered include:* rigor of secondary school record, class rank, standardized test scores, application essay, recommendation(s), interview, geographical residence, volunteer work, work experience. High school diploma is required and GED is accepted. *Academic units required:* 4 English, 3 math, 2 science, 1 science lab, 2 language (other than English), 2 social studies.

Financial Aid

Students should submit: FAFSA. The Princeton Review suggests that all financial aid forms be submitted as soon as possible. *Need-based scholarships/grants offered:* Federal Pell; Federal SEOG; State scholarships/grants; Private scholarships; College/university scholarship or grant aid from institutional funds. *Loan aid offered:* Federal Direct Subsidized Loans; Federal Direct Unsubsidized Loans; Direct PLUS loans. Admitted students will be notified of awards on or about 3/1. Federal Work-Study Program available. Institutional employment available.

The Inside Word

Like many liberal arts colleges, Hanover takes a holistic approach to admissions, closely evaluating your high school curriculum, GPA, and the overall strength of your high school. Standardized test scores are considered if submitted, though they carry less weight than your transcript. Beyond academics, admissions officers also weigh extracurricular participation, community involvement, letters of recommendation, and a writing sample.

THE SCHOOL SAYS

From the Admissions Office

"When you're looking for your perfect fit, it's all about you. You're not looking to fit into a mold, to find that one-size-fits-all experience. At Hanover College, we couldn't agree more.

"Our students choose Hanover because it feels like a new home and a place to grow at the same time. A Hanover student doesn't box themselves in or limit their options to just one thing. Here, we challenge and encourage our students to explore all their potential on the path to becoming their greatest selves.

"For nearly 200 years, our graduates have discovered their passions through our wide variety of opportunities, from academics, athletics and the arts, to social life and study abroad. Experience and exploration are mandatory, and it sets our alumni apart."

SELECTIVITY

# of total applicants	2,712
% of total applicants accepted	82
% of total acceptees attending	13
# offered a place on the wait list	0
# admitted from wait list	0

First-Year Profile

Testing policy	Test Optional
Range SAT composite	1060–1260
Range SAT EBRW	540–640
Range SAT math	510–610
Range ACT composite	24–27
% submitting SAT scores	20
% submitting ACT scores	11
Average HS GPA	3.8
% submitting high school GPA	99
% graduated top 10% of class	27
% graduated top 25% of class	56
% graduated top 50% of class	84
% submitting high school rank	56

Important Dates

Early decision	
Apply by	11/1
Notified by	11/15
Other ED apply by	12/1
Other ED notified by	Rolling
Early action	
Apply by	11/1 or 12/11
Notified by	Rolling
Regular	
Apply by	2/1
Notified by	Rolling
Nonfall registration?	Yes

FINANCIAL FACTS

Annual tuition (First-year)	$43,457 ($46,232)
Food and housing	$14,503
Required fees	$1,720
Books and supplies	$1,000
Average need-based scholarship (First-year)	$34,624 ($35,445)
% students with need rec. need-based scholarship or grant aid (First-year)	100 (100)
% students with need rec. non-need-based scholarship or grant aid (First-year)	29 (33)
% students with need rec. need-based self-help aid (First-year)	69 (64)
% UG borrow to pay for school	95
Average cumulative indebtedness	$27,191
% of students with need fully met (First-year)	41 (46)
Average % of student need met (First-year)	88 (87)

HARVARD COLLEGE

86 Brattle Street, Cambridge, MA 02138 • Admissions: 617-495-1551

Survey Snapshot
Campus newspaper is popular
Students politically aware
Students love Cambridge, MA

RATINGS

Quality of Life	71
Fire Safety	60*
Green	60*
Academic	83
Profs Interesting	81
Profs Accessible	81
Admissions	99
Financial Aid	99

CAMPUS LIFE

Type of school	Private
Environment	City

Students

Degree-seeking undergrad enrollment	6,675
% male/female/not reported	46/54/0
% from out of state	85
% First-year from public high school	58
% First-year live on campus	100
% Ugrads live on campus	97
# of fraternities	0
# of sororities	0
% Asian	25
% Black or African American	8
% Hispanic	11
% Native American	<1
% Pacific Islander	<1
% Race and/or ethnicity unknown	3
% Two or more races	8
% White	29
% International	15
# of countries represented	120

CAMPUS MENTAL HEALTH SERVICES

Offers mental health/wellness program	Yes
Mental health training available to students	No
Employs Chief Wellness Officer	NR
Peer-to-peer mental health offerings	NR
Counseling center has guidelines or accreditation	No
Mental health/well-being courses	NR

ACADEMICS

% students returning for sophomore year	98
% students graduating within 4 years	61
% students graduating within 6 years	97
Calendar	Semester
Student/faculty ratio	11:1
Most common class size 1–9.	(45%)
Most common lab/discussion size 1–9.	(24%)

Most Popular Majors
Social Sciences; Economics; Computer Science

Applicants Also Look At
Duke University, Massachusetts Institute of Technology, Princeton University, Stanford University, Yale University

STUDENTS SAY "..."

Academics

Harvard College is a highly selective school for a reason: those who earn their way into this Ivy enter a "dynamic universe" that is "academically alive" and teeming with possibility, as well as top-tier internship and employment opportunities, a strong alumni network, and a crimson pedigree for your résumé. Perhaps this is why one undergrad refers to his experience as "rewarding beyond anything else I've ever done." Academically, the breadth of courses astounds, with everything from the rise of machines and implications of AI to the relationship of Taylor Swift's lyrics to Romantic-era poets. Even better, at least once you're through some of the larger, less personable lectures of your underclass years (or you "go to office hours to get to know your big lecture class professors on a personal level"), you'll find them to be taught by some of "the brightest minds in the world." Indeed, "the level of achievement [of the faculty] is unbelievable." Even when students butt heads with a "reticent to change" administration, they acknowledge that the school "does a good job of watching over its freshmen through extensive advising programs," and students trust that their best interests are being kept in mind. The only thing that's impossible here, apparently, is the idea of "getting the most out of Harvard"—and that's "because Harvard offers so much."

Campus Life

Simply put, "boredom does not exist" at Harvard. The school maintains "a vibrant social atmosphere," one that provides "endless opportunities" and plenty of "passionate people to [pursue] them with." As one undergrad explains, "Basically, if you want to do it, Harvard either has it or has the money to give to you so you can start it." Of course, with more than 450 student organizations already in existence, it's almost a given you'll find something that excites you. Undergrads also love partaking in Harvard traditions like Yardfest, a spring music festival and attending "The Game," the annual football match with Ivy rival Yale. By and large, drinking does not seem to dominate the social scene. "Partying in a more traditional setting is available at Harvard, but is not a prevalent aspect of the school's social life. There is a pub on campus that provides an excellent venue to hang out and play a game of pool or have a reasonably priced drink." And, of course, a handful of parties happen on weekends at Harvard's finals clubs. However, there's no real pressure for students to partake if they're not interested, and with Cambridge and Boston right there, it's no surprise that you can always find students hitting the city to "go see a play, a concert...go to the movies, or dine out."

Student Body

People find ways to make everything (especially clubs and even partying) competitive. Harvard students are, after all, high achievers oozing with talent and ambition. But this isn't a negative, and "Everyone is great for one reason or another." Certainly, most students are not afraid of a challenge and look to milk every opportunity presented to them. This sentiment is supported by another undergrad who notes that the average Harvard student "works really hard, doesn't sleep, [and is] involved in a million extracurriculars." Underneath this impressive drive, you're also likely to find compassionate individuals who enjoy interacting with and learning from their diverse peers. One undergrad elaborates, insisting that "there is a lot of tolerance and acceptance at Harvard for individuals of all races, religions, socioeconomic backgrounds, lifestyles, etc." And given that 156 nationalities are represented among the student body, it's fairly easy to interact with people across a spectrum of ideologies, religions, and backgrounds.

Harvard College

Financial Aid: 617-495-1581 • E-Mail: college@fas.harvard.edu • Website: www.college.harvard.edu

THE PRINCETON REVIEW SAYS

Admissions

The school reports that its standardized testing policy for use in admission for Fall 2026 will require applicants to submit either the SAT or ACT. The Princeton Review suggests that interested applicants consult with the school for the most up-to-date standardized testing policies. *Other factors considered include:* rigor of secondary school record, academic GPA, standardized test scores, application essay, recommendation(s), interview, extracurricular activities, talent/ability, character/personal qualities, first generation, alumni/ae relation. High school diploma or equivalent is not required. *Academic units recommended:* 4 English, 4 math, 4 science, 4 language (other than English), 3 social studies, 2 history.

Financial Aid

Students should submit: FAFSA; CSS PROFILE. Priority filing deadline is 2/1. The Princeton Review suggests that all financial aid forms be submitted as soon as possible. *Need-based scholarships/grants offered:* Federal Pell; Federal SEOG; State scholarships/grants; Private scholarships; College/university scholarship or grant aid from institutional funds. *Loan aid offered:* Federal Direct Subsidized Loans; Federal Direct Unsubsidized Loans; Direct PLUS loans; State Loans; College/university loans from institutional funds. Admitted students will be notified of awards on or about 4/1. Federal Work-Study Program available. Institutional employment available.

The Inside Word

It just doesn't get any tougher than this. Candidates to Harvard face dual obstacles—an awe-inspiring applicant pool and, as a result, admissions standards that defy explanation in quantifiable terms. Harvard denies admission to the vast majority, and virtually all of them are top students. (Also, as a result of switching to the Common App, it has never been easier to apply to Harvard, which keeps application numbers high.) It all boils down to splitting hairs, which is quite hard to explain and even harder for candidates to understand: for instance, it has been suggested that applicants from lesser-populated states like South Dakota may have an advantage, but Harvard will neither confirm nor deny their policies.

THE SCHOOL SAYS

From the Admissions Office

"The admissions committee looks for energy, ambition, and the capacity to make the most of opportunities. Academic ability and preparation are important, and so is intellectual curiosity—but many of the strongest applicants have significant, non-academic interests and accomplishments, as well. There is no formula for admission, and applicants are considered carefully, with attention to future promise."

SELECTIVITY

# of total applicants	47,893
% of total applicants accepted	4
% of total acceptees attending	84
# admitted from wait list	75

First-Year Profile

Testing policy	SAT or ACT Required
Range SAT EBRW	720–770
Range SAT math	730–790
Range ACT composite	33–36
% submitting SAT scores	79
% submitting ACT scores	27
Average HS GPA	4.2
% submitting high school GPA	99
% graduated top 10% of class	95
% graduated top 25% of class	99
% graduated top 50% of class	100
% submitting high school rank	25

Important Dates

Early action	
Apply by	11/1
Notified by	12/16
Regular	
Apply by	1/1
Notified by	3/31
Nonfall registration?	No

FINANCIAL FACTS

Annual tuition	$52,659
Food and housing	$19,502
Required fees	$4,602
Books and supplies	$800
Average need-based scholarship (First-year)	$71,448 ($72,749)
% students with need rec. need-based scholarship or grant aid (First-year)	100 (100)
% students with need rec. non-need-based scholarship or grant aid (First-year)	0 (0)
% students with need rec. need-based self-help aid (First-year)	85 (75)
% students rec. any financial aid (First-year)	64 (74)
% UG borrow to pay for school	16
Average cumulative indebtedness	$22,926
% of students with need fully met (First-year)	100 (100)
Average % of student need met (First-year)	100 (100)

HARVEY MUDD COLLEGE

301 Platt Boulevard, Claremont, CA 91711 • Admissions: 909-621-8011

Survey Snapshot
Lab facilities are great
Internships are widely available
School is well run

RATINGS

Quality of Life	**94**
Fire Safety	**60***
Green	**60***
Academic	**95**
Profs Interesting	**98**
Profs Accessible	**97**
Admissions	**98**
Financial Aid	**97**

CAMPUS LIFE

Type of school	Private
Environment	Town

Students

Degree-seeking undergrad enrollment	913
% male/female/not reported	49/51/<1
% from out of state	50
% First-year from public high school	60
% First-year live on campus	99
% Ugrads live on campus	97
# of fraternities	0
# of sororities	0
% Asian	22
% Black or African American	4
% Hispanic	20
% Native American	<1
% Pacific Islander	<1
% Race and/or ethnicity unknown	7
% Two or more races	11
% White	26
% International	11
# of countries represented	11

CAMPUS MENTAL HEALTH SERVICES

Offers mental health/wellness program	Yes
Mental health training available to students	Yes
Employs Chief Wellness Officer	NR
Peer-to-peer mental health offerings	NR
Counseling center has guidelines or accreditation	No
Mental health/well-being courses	NR

ACADEMICS

% students returning for sophomore year	95
% students graduating within 4 years	83
% students graduating within 6 years	93
Calendar	Semester
Student/faculty ratio	8:1
Most common class size 10–19.	(30%)
Most common lab/discussion size 10–19.	(33%)

Most Popular Majors
Engineering; Computer and Information Sciences; Mathematics

Applicants Often Prefer
California Institute of Technology, Massachusetts Institute of Technology, Stanford University

Applicants Sometimes Prefer
Carnegie Mellon University, University of California—Berkeley, University of Southern California

Applicants Rarely Prefer
Case Western Reserve University, Rose—Hulman Institute of Technology, University of California—Los Angeles

STUDENTS SAY "..."

Academics

Harvey Mudd College "does a great job at fulfilling its specific niche as a top-tier STEM college with all the support and benefits of a liberal arts college." In contrast to other competitive STEM schools, "students here can continue to pursue their passions in [the] arts and humanities." All students take core courses that combine "a solid foundation in each of the major STEM areas" with courses in the humanities, social sciences, and the arts (HSA). One student majoring in Computer Science appreciates being able to "easily register for classes like Quantum Physics, Music Theory III, and Abstract Algebra, despite them being unrelated to my major," the idea being that this helps them "understand the impact" of their work as scientists. As a student at Mudd, "you lead projects and follow your interests, and have a lot of freedom." But make no mistake, Mudd is a place for students who are very serious about science and engineering. Students say that "the course load is rigorous," but "comprehensive and rewarding," even though some "struggle with the intensity of classes." Mudders particularly value their professors—and their genuine friendships with them—noting that teachers "put in a lot of effort to make sure everyone has a strong understanding of everything we learn." Their accessibility and eagerness extend beyond the classroom: "They really care about [us] and that we are doing okay in life outside of our courses." No wonder, then, that students are left with the overall impression that "the workload is worth it simply because of what comes out of it; that is, the friends and the knowledge that you know will last forever."

Campus Life

While studying is "one of the primary social activities at Harvey Mudd College," students make time for "hanging out with friends or partying" on the weekends. As a part of the Claremont Consortium, students get "resources typical of a larger institution: solid party culture, athletics, [and] opportunities for research" and they find it "really refreshing to talk to people from other campuses." Highlights at Harvey Mudd itself focus on both tinkerers and gamers. "Being in the Makerspace [a student-run collective workshop open 24/7] is just awesome," and in the Machine Shop, you can "learn how to effectively design" with manufacturing in mind. "My favorite extracurricular activity is definitely MuddEscapes," a club where students create escape rooms. There are traditional intramural sports, clubs, and dorm events (like movie nights or mocktail mixers); students appreciate that there's always a way to get away.

Student Body

At Harvey Mudd, everyone is passionate about something, "whether it's their schoolwork, extracurriculars that vary from sports to music to LARP, or parties and pranks." The combination of engineering and humanities emphasized in the curriculum attracts a curious and engaged student body. "I love asking friends and classmates about their research interests and the humanities subject they are concentrating in…their enthusiasm is infectious." Another Mudder says, "My class is full of intelligent people who are interested in a wide variety of topics, such as robotics or social action." The school attracts "a healthy blend of personalities:" students who are "interested in intense and difficult STEM classes, …but who also care more about their impact on the world and having a strong humanities/ liberal arts background." Shared interests make it easy to make friends on campus. "When you're talking to a Mudder, you can assume a certain background knowledge in STEM fields, which lets us make niche math jokes and have all sorts of interesting conversations." A friendly atmosphere characterizes the Mudd experience: "There is always an upperclassman who will help you on your homework at odd hours in the night and another one who will remind you that sleep is more important than a perfect grade."

HARVEY MUDD COLLEGE

Financial Aid: 909-621-8055 • E-Mail: admission@hmc.edu • Website: www.hmc.edu

THE PRINCETON REVIEW SAYS

Admissions

The school reports that its standardized testing policy for use in admission for Fall 2026 is Test Optional. The Princeton Review suggests that interested applicants consult with the school for the most up-to-date standardized testing policies. *Very important factors considered include:* rigor of secondary school record, academic GPA, recommendation(s). *Important factors considered include:* application essay, extracurricular activities, character/personal qualities. *Other factors considered include:* class rank, standardized test scores, interview, talent/ability, first generation, geographical residence, state residency, volunteer work, work experience. High school diploma or equivalent is not required. *Academic units recommended:* 4 English, 4 math, 4 science, 2 science labs, 2 language (other than English), 2 social studies, 2 history, 2 academic electives.

Financial Aid

Students should submit: FAFSA; CSS PROFILE; State aid form; Business/Farm Supplement. The Princeton Review suggests that all financial aid forms be submitted as soon as possible. *Need-based scholarships/grants offered:* Federal Pell; Federal SEOG; State scholarships/grants; Private scholarships; College/university scholarship or grant aid from institutional funds. *Loan aid offered:* Federal Direct Subsidized Loans; Federal Direct Unsubsidized Loans; Direct PLUS loans; College/university loans from institutional funds. Admitted students will be notified of awards on or about 4/1. Federal Work-Study Program available. Institutional employment available.

The Inside Word

Harvey Mudd College is as rigorous in its admissions process as it is in its educational programs. Therefore, serious applicants should excel in their high school STEM courses while also engaging in humanities classes and extracurricular activities. It is important for applicants to review HMC's eligibility requirements regarding high school transcripts carefully. Keep in mind that the college is highly selective, and admission is not guaranteed even for those who are highly qualified.

THE SCHOOL SAYS

From the Admissions Office

"HMC is a liberal arts college and research institute with an emphasis on cooperation and collaboration. Our students, or Mudders, love math and science, thrive on innovation and discovery, and enjoy rigorous coursework in arts, humanities, and social sciences in addition to a technical, hands-on curriculum. One year of research is required (or guaranteed) via a senior thesis or the Clinic Program. The resources at HMC are accessible to all students: labs, shops, work areas, and most importantly, faculty. You'll find the professors and student body supportive and engaging. In fact, our faculty were ranked #1 for most accessible faculty in the country according to the Princeton Review, so rest assured they'll be available inside and outside of class. In addition, we benefit from the Claremont College consortium that pools resources together between five undergraduate colleges. Our students rave about the number of activities happening on and off campus.

"By graduation, our students can see relationships between disparate fields of study and investigation, are excellent team members and team leaders, and are able to articulate their ideas to anyone with clarity. A wide range of companies are eager to hire our seniors; the average starting salary for the Class of 2025 was $124,999. HMC also sends the second highest proportion of graduates to STEM PhD programs, relative to school size, of any undergraduate college in the country."

SELECTIVITY

# of total applicants	5,217
% of total applicants accepted	12
% of total acceptees attending	37
# of in-state applicants	2,291
% of in-state applicants accepted	12
# of out-of-state-applicants	1,631
% of applicants accepted from out of state	18
# of international applicants	1,295
% of international applicants accepted	5
# of early decision applicants	594
% of early decision applicants accepted	18
# offered a place on the wait list	685
# admitted from wait list	0

First-Year Profile

Testing policy	Test Optional
Range SAT composite	1500–1560
Range SAT EBRW	740–770
Range SAT math	760–800
Range ACT composite	35–36
% submitting SAT scores	55
% submitting ACT scores	21
% graduated top 10% of class	95
% graduated top 25% of class	100
% graduated top 50% of class	100
% submitting high school rank	18

Important Dates

Early decision	
Apply by	11/15
Notified by	12/15
Other ED apply by	1/5
Other ED notified by	2/15
Regular	
Apply by	1/5
Notified by	4/1
Nonfall registration?	No

FINANCIAL FACTS

Annual tuition	$76,879
Food and housing	$24,782
Required fees	$401
Books and supplies	$800
Average need-based scholarship (First-year)	$58,910 ($64,941)
% students with need rec. need-based scholarship or grant aid (First-year)	97 (98)
% students with need rec. non-need-based scholarship or grant aid (First-year)	49 (41)
% students with need rec. need-based self-help aid (First-year)	59 (52)
% students rec. any financial aid (First-year)	70 (68)
% UG borrow to pay for school	44
Average cumulative indebtedness	$30,350
% of students with need fully met (First-year)	100 (100)
Average % of student need met (First-year)	100 (100)

HAVERFORD COLLEGE

370 Lancaster Avenue, Haverford, PA 19041 • Admissions: 610-896-1350

Survey Snapshot
Diverse student types interact on campus
Recreation facilities are great
Active minority support groups

RATINGS

Quality of Life	83
Fire Safety	84
Green	92
Academic	96
Profs Interesting	94
Profs Accessible	98
Admissions	98
Financial Aid	98

CAMPUS LIFE

Type of school	Private
Environment	Town

Students

Degree-seeking undergrad enrollment	1,418
% male/female/not reported	43/57/0
% from out of state	84
% First-year live on campus	100
% Ugrads live on campus	96
# of fraternities	0
# of sororities	0
% Asian	14
% Black or African American	4
% Hispanic	13
% Native American	0
% Pacific Islander	<1
% Race and/or ethnicity unknown	1
% Two or more races	10
% White	48
% International	11
# of countries represented	52

CAMPUS MENTAL HEALTH SERVICES

Offers mental health/wellness program	Yes
Mental health training available to students	No
Employs Chief Wellness Officer	NR
Peer-to-peer mental health offerings	NR
Counseling center has guidelines or accreditation	No
Mental health/well-being courses	NR

ACADEMICS

% students returning for sophomore year	95
% students graduating within 4 years	79
% students graduating within 6 years	89
Calendar	Semester
Student/faculty ratio	9:1
Most common class size 10–19.	(38%)

Most Popular Majors
Biology/Biological Sciences; Chemistry; Econometrics and Quantitative Economics

STUDENTS SAY "..."

Academics

Haverford College's Quaker roots still reverberate through this nonsectarian academic powerhouse, bringing a strong focus on community and integrity. Haverford maintains one of the country's oldest honor codes, which fosters a "trust, concern, and respect" between students and professors. As one undergrad elaborates, "Being able to take an exam in your own room, sitting relaxed on your bed because your professor trusts you not to look at your books is one of the luxuries of being here." A classmate adds, "I love the amount of independence and autonomy [the school] gives to its students." Undergrads also "have a lot of power" when it comes to how the college is run. This ensures that Haverford has "a really conscientious student body invested in the school."

Enrollees note that Haverford's small size "allows for plenty of opportunities for collaborating with faculty and staff " and the college even grants "credit for research." Also, thanks to partnerships with nearby Swarthmore, Bryn Mawr, and the University of Pennsylvania, students have even more opportunities to cross-register, though one student suggests you won't want to leave Haverford's "exceptionally vibrant and engaging" campus or the "awesome, invested" professors that challenge you to think critically. Here, "you are more than just a face in a classroom...you are a unique person that has something to offer." This is underscored by another student who shares, "My 'big intro lecture course' has 41 students. My professor still knows me by name, and we have long conversations when we pass on Founder's Green." Ultimately, Haverford undergrads are privy to "a challenging, interesting environment with the best people I know."

Campus Life

Haverford has a sense of community that's fueled by its honor code and size. Sometimes that feels "like everyone knows your business," but undergrads emphasize that their peers are very nice and that "the social scene is great." In short, it's an "awesome...place where community thrives and cliques are very loose if existent at all." Though students are incredibly diligent about their coursework, they certainly carve out time for fun as well. The college maintains over 145 organizations including Brew Club (for home brewing enthusiasts), Haute (a fashion collective), and the Haverford Microfinance Consulting Club. Additionally, athletics are also "really important," with more than 50% of undergrads participating in a club or varsity sport. And while Haverford doesn't maintain any Greek life, some teams "function like fraternities." Finally, when people want a breather from campus life, there's plenty to enjoy and explore. After all, New York and Philadelphia are both easily accessible by train, and "Suburban Square (the local outdoor shopping center) is a great place to hang out, get coffee, or even go shopping."

Student Body

The "ridiculously friendly" undergrads at Haverford are united in their passion for learning. Indeed, many students are armed with an insatiable curiosity, which means that "people are always up for intellectual discussion." This also means that "everyone works very hard" to be educated, and for all the right reasons: they "want to succeed for themselves and not to appease others." Though many of your peers likely hail from the mid-Atlantic and New England, they come "from all different social circles" and the school is increasingly diverse—just over 50% of the student body now identifies as a person of color. Moreover, members of the overall population are perceived to have "hearts of gold and giant brains that they put to use to change the world for the better." As one undergrad explains, "I feel like I could potentially become friends with anyone on campus." As one student further explains, "It's a small school full of nice kids...just genuinely compassionate and interested in other people, whether or not that's 'cool.'"

Haverford College

Financial Aid: 610-896-1350 • E-Mail: admission@haverford.edu • Website: www.haverford.edu

THE PRINCETON REVIEW SAYS

Admissions

The school reports that its standardized testing policy for use in admission for Fall 2026 is Test Optional. The Princeton Review suggests that interested applicants consult with the school for the most up-to-date standardized testing policies. *Very important factors considered include:* rigor of secondary school record, academic GPA, application essay, recommendation(s), extracurricular activities, character/personal qualities. *Important factors considered include:* class rank, talent/ability, volunteer work, work experience. *Other factors considered include:* standardized test scores, interview, first generation, alumni/ae relation, geographical residence, level of applicant's interest. High school diploma is required and GED is accepted.

Financial Aid

Students should submit: FAFSA; CSS PROFILE. Priority filing deadline is 1/10. The Princeton Review suggests that all financial aid forms be submitted as soon as possible. *Need-based scholarships/grants offered:* Federal Pell; Federal SEOG; State scholarships/grants; College/university scholarship or grant aid from institutional funds; Private scholarships. *Loan aid offered:* Federal Direct Subsidized Loans; Federal Direct Unsubsidized Loans; Direct PLUS loans; College/university loans from institutional funds. Admitted students will be notified of awards on or about 3/15. Federal Work-Study Program available. Institutional employment available.

The Inside Word

Haverford's applicant pool is an impressive and competitive lot (only 13 percent of applicants get in). Intellectual curiosity is paramount, and applicants are expected to keep a demanding academic schedule in high school. Additionally, the college places a high value on ethics, as evidenced by its honor code. The admissions office seeks students who will reflect and promote Haverford's ideals.

THE SCHOOL SAYS

From the Admissions Office

"Haverford College offers one of the finest liberal arts educations in the world and attracts incredibly bright and dedicated students from nearly every state and 52 foreign countries. Haverford students reap the many benefits of attending an all-undergraduate institution, where all courses are taught by professors, and all resources and facilities are available to undergraduates. Haverford provides a rigorous and intensely personal undergraduate education inspired by intellectual depth, integrity, collaboration, and dedication to improving the human condition.

"Our campus culture engenders an immediate sense of colleagueship between students and faculty and creates a relaxed, personal atmosphere. A philosophy of trust, concern, and respect for every individual guides our community and serves as the basis of our completely student-governed honor code. In addition to governing the honor code, students serve on hiring committees, manage budgets, and run more than 145 clubs and organizations.

"Haverford College meets 100 percent of the demonstrated need of all admitted students and seeks to minimize debt for our graduates. Students with family income below $60,000 will not have any loans included in their financial aid package; students with family income above this level will have loans ranging from $1,500 to $3,000 per year. The Haverford Student Loan Debt Relief Fund, an innovative program to help students who do graduate from Haverford with debt, provides funds to young alumni who are employed in jobs of high social value with low remuneration or who are in transition at some point following graduation."

SELECTIVITY

# of total applicants	6,730
% of total applicants accepted	13
% of total acceptees attending	44
# of in-state applicants	626
% of in-state applicants accepted	17
# of out-of-state-applicants	2,850
% of applicants accepted from out of state	23
# of international applicants	3,254
% of international applicants accepted	4
# of early decision applicants	702
% of early decision applicants accepted	33
# offered a place on the wait list	1,342
# admitted from wait list	11

First-Year Profile

Testing policy	Test Optional
Range SAT composite	1460–1530
Range SAT EBRW	720–760
Range SAT math	720–780
Range ACT composite	33–35
% submitting SAT scores	40
% submitting ACT scores	14
% graduated top 10% of class	93
% graduated top 25% of class	100
% graduated top 50% of class	100
% submitting high school rank	19

Important Dates

Early decision	
Apply by	11/15
Notified by	12/15
Other ED apply by	1/5
Other ED notified by	2/15
Regular	
Apply by	1/10
Notified by	4/1
Nonfall registration?	No

FINANCIAL FACTS*

Annual tuition	$70,030
Food and housing	$20,426
Required fees (First-year)	$538 ($841)
Books and supplies	$1,290
Average need-based scholarship (First-year)	$70,718 ($70,214)
% students with need rec. need-based scholarship or grant aid (First-year)	93 (88)
% students with need rec. non-need-based scholarship or grant aid (First-year)	11 (18)
% students with need rec. need-based self-help aid (First-year)	82 (75)
% UG borrow to pay for school	16
Average cumulative indebtedness	$13,015
% of students with need fully met (First-year)	99 (97)
Average % of student need met (First-year)	100 (100)

* Most recently reported data at time of printing. Scan the QR code to find the latest updates.

HIGH POINT UNIVERSITY

One University Parkway, High Point, NC 27268 • Admissions: 336-841-9216

Survey Snapshot
Lots of conservative students
Dorms are like palaces
Students are happy

RATINGS

Quality of Life	**88**
Fire Safety	**85**
Green	**60***
Academic	**82**
Profs Interesting	**92**
Profs Accessible	**95**
Admissions	**84**
Financial Aid	**85**

CAMPUS LIFE

Type of school	Private
Affiliation	Methodist
Environment	City

Students

Degree-seeking undergrad enrollment	4,969
% male/female/not reported	45/55/0
% from out of state	74
% First-year live on campus	97
% Ugrads live on campus	93
# of fraternities (% join)	6 (11)
# of sororities (% join)	10 (26)
% Asian	2
% Black or African American	7
% Hispanic	8
% Native American	<1
% Pacific Islander	<1
% Race and/or ethnicity unknown	5
% Two or more races	1
% White	76
% International	<1
# of countries represented	30

CAMPUS MENTAL HEALTH SERVICES

Offers mental health/wellness program	Yes
Mental health training available to students	No
Employs Chief Wellness Officer	NR
Peer-to-peer mental health offerings	NR
Counseling center has guidelines or accreditation	No
Mental health/well-being courses	NR

ACADEMICS

% students returning for sophomore year	84
% students graduating within 4 years	67
% students graduating within 6 years	71
Calendar	Semester
Student/faculty ratio	17:1
Most common class size 20–29.	(42%)
Most common lab/discussion size 20–29.	(63%)

Most Popular Majors

Communication; Kinesiology and Exercise Science; Business Administration and Management

Applicants Also Look At

Appalachian State University, College of Charleston, East Carolina University, Elon University, North Carolina State University, Penn State University Park, University of North Carolina at Chapel Hill, The University of North Carolina—Charlotte

STUDENTS SAY "…"

Academics

High Point University is a school that undoubtedly "put[s] the academic and professional success of each of their students first." To that end, it offers "many resources" including counseling, library services, tutoring options, and "so many more [services] that are ready and willing to help students with their careers." Undergrads also highlight the university's emphasis on "career development," which really "prepares students to find a full-time job after graduation." As this undergrad explains, "They assist with your résumé, LinkedIn profile (even the ability to have professional photos taken), [and hold] seminars on everything from how to dress to how to prepare for an interview." Of course, much of this success can also be attributed to a great classroom experience. By and large, High Point students are greeted by professors who "are so passionate about what they do [that] it makes [their courses] much more meaningful and engaging." It's also quite evident that the faculty here want to "build true connections with students." They're also "truly knowledgeable and bring real-world experience to the classroom." In turn, this "makes it so much better to sit through their classes because you are able to really trust what they say." When it comes down to it, "HPU is an extraordinary campus with extraordinary professors [who] put the students first."

Campus Life

There's plenty of fun to be had when High Point students step away from their studies. The "Campus Activities Team puts on several events throughout the week and weekends" including "Food Truck Wednesdays, [which] is amazing." Undergrads can also participate in numerous organizations ranging from investment club and the studio art club to Genesis Gospel Choir and "Wishmakers Club, [a group] devoted to earning money to grant wishes for children with cancer." And prospective students with a hankering for outdoor adventure will be delighted to learn that High Point sponsors an "annual whitewater rafting and zipline trip in the fall [and an] annual ski trip in the spring." You can also rent bikes (free of charge!) from the rec center or indulge in the school's ice-skating rink, another very popular activity. Additionally, the university maintains "very nice gym facilities" and has "lots of club and intramural sports" including volleyball and rowing. "A large majority are involved in Greek life," which we're told is an "extremely inclusive" scene.

Student Body

Undergrads have seemingly built a "strong community" that's based upon "pride in being a High Point student." Of course, it also helps that most people here are "very welcoming and genuine." As this student demonstrates, "You always see people smiling, holding doors, or speaking when you walk by." Another common attribute of High Point undergrads? They're "hardworking and driven individuals" who are "very passionate about learning." Some students do point out that the university is a "predominantly white school" and one that some feel is "only for the rich kids." Nevertheless, "while there are definitely students who have got loads of money coming into the school, there are still plenty of down to earth individuals who just want the best education they can get." Moreover, students stress "most everyone is very inclusive" regardless of your background. "We are becoming more diverse every year. People from all majors are friends and there is no one that is alone if they do not want to be." As one satisfied student sums up, "My peers are collaborative, outgoing, and some of the most fun people I've met."

High Point University

Financial Aid: 336-841-9032 • E-Mail: admiss@highpoint.edu • Website: www.highpoint.edu

THE PRINCETON REVIEW SAYS

Admissions

The school reports that its standardized testing policy for use in admission for Fall 2026 is Test Optional. The Princeton Review suggests that interested applicants consult with the school for the most up-to-date standardized testing policies. *Very important factors considered include:* academic GPA. *Important factors considered include:* rigor of secondary school record, standardized test scores, application essay, recommendation(s), interview, extracurricular activities, talent/ability, character/personal qualities, volunteer work, work experience, level of applicant's interest. *Other factors considered include:* class rank, first generation, alumni/ae relation. High school diploma is required and GED is accepted. *Academic units required:* 4 English, 3 math, 3 science, 1 science lab, 2 language (other than English), 3 social studies. *Academic units recommended:* 4 English, 4 math, 3 science, 1 science lab, 3 language (other than English), 3 social studies.

Financial Aid

Students should submit: FAFSA; State aid form. Priority filing deadline is 3/1. The Princeton Review suggests that all financial aid forms be submitted as soon as possible. *Need-based scholarships/grants offered:* Federal Pell; Federal SEOG; State scholarships/grants; Private scholarships; College/university scholarship or grant aid from institutional funds. *Loan aid offered:* Federal Direct Subsidized Loans; Federal Direct Unsubsidized Loans; Direct PLUS loans. Admitted students will be notified of awards on a rolling basis beginning 4/1. Federal Work-Study Program available. Institutional employment available.

The Inside Word

High Point considers a variety of factors when it comes to granting students admission to their university. With that being said, your transcript and GPA will be their primary concern. To stand out, we suggest you focus on taking some advanced courses while in high school to prove you can handle a more rigorous course load. In addition to your grades, admissions officers will also be interested in your community involvement and any extracurriculars you participated in while in school. Interests outside of the classroom will prove that you can balance academic life and the more social aspects of student life, such as involvement in clubs or programs.

THE SCHOOL SAYS

From the Admissions Office

"High Point University is The Premier Life Skills University working to transform the lives of our students. HPU knows a thing or two about transformation because we've transformed our campus and our culture in a compressed amount of time that would usually take decades to achieve. HPU invests in educational opportunities that empower you to craft your character and your career in unison, ensuring you are prepared for the world as it is going to be. Through this journey, you'll develop the life skills needed to thrive in an ever-changing global marketplace. You will constantly be given the opportunity to combine classroom content with real-world context as experiential learning is woven into every major. You will have undergraduate research opportunities and a wide range of learning labs that extend well beyond traditional classroom walls. At HPU, you will receive an education that inspires greatness, instills purpose, fosters faith, family and patriotism, and stimulates the desire to live a life of both success and significance.

"Nationally recognized for innovation, HPU's academic model is based on four pillars: academic innovation, experiential learning, modeling values and building character, and the four-year development of each student's life skills. This educating of the entire person coupled with our four-year Career Development plan best positions our students for success. Ninety-eight percent of HPU graduates launch their careers or begin graduate school within 180 days of graduation. At High Point University, every student receives an extraordinary education in an inspiring environment with caring people."

SELECTIVITY

# of total applicants	15,243
% of total applicants accepted	77
% of total acceptees attending	12
# of in-state applicants	3,017
% of in-state applicants accepted	77
# of out-of-state-applicants	11,889
% of applicants accepted from out of state	78
# of international applicants	338
% of international applicants accepted	39
# of early decision applicants	782
% of early decision applicants accepted	87
# offered a place on the wait list	815
# admitted from wait list	19

First-Year Profile

Testing policy	Test Optional
Range SAT composite	1130–1210
Range SAT EBRW	560–650
Range SAT math	550–650
Range ACT composite	23–31
% submitting SAT scores	23
% submitting ACT scores	16
Average HS GPA	3.2
% submitting high school GPA	92
% graduated top 10% of class	19
% graduated top 25% of class	43
% graduated top 50% of class	75
% submitting high school rank	35

Important Dates

Early decision	
Apply by	11/1
Notified by	11/22
Other ED apply by	2/1
Other ED notified by	2/1
Early action	
Apply by	11/15
Notified by	12/16
Regular	
Apply by	3/1
Notified by	2/1
Nonfall registration?	Yes

FINANCIAL FACTS

Annual tuition	$38,748
Food and housing	$18,482
Required fees	$5,460
Books and supplies	$1,500
Average need-based scholarship (First-year)	$19,604 ($22,227)
% students with need rec. need-based scholarship or grant aid (First-year)	98 (100)
% students with need rec. non-need-based scholarship or grant aid (First-year)	89 (94)
% students with need rec. need-based self-help aid (First-year)	64 (53)
% students rec. any financial aid (First-year)	89 (95)
% UG borrow to pay for school	54
Average cumulative indebtedness	$47,721
% of students with need fully met (First-year)	17 (25)
Average % of student need met (First-year)	61 (69)

HILLSDALE COLLEGE

33 East College Street, Hillsdale, MI 49242 • Admissions: 517-607-2327

Survey Snapshot
Lots of conservative students
Students are very religious
Active student government

RATINGS

Quality of Life	**87**
Fire Safety	**91**
Green	**60***
Academic	**90**
Profs Interesting	**94**
Profs Accessible	**93**
Admissions	**97**
Financial Aid	**88**

CAMPUS LIFE

Type of school	Private
Affiliation	Christian (Nondenominational)
Environment	Village

Students

Degree-seeking undergrad enrollment	1,520
% male/female/not reported	49/51/0
% from out of state	78
% First-year from public high school	34
% First-year live on campus	99
% Ugrads live on campus	78
# of fraternities (% join)	4 (15)
# of sororities (% join)	3 (24)
% Asian	0
% Black or African American	0
% Hispanic	0
% Native American	0
% Pacific Islander	0
% Race and/or ethnicity unknown	100
% Two or more races	0
% White	0
# of countries represented	18

CAMPUS MENTAL HEALTH SERVICES

Offers mental health/wellness program	Yes
Mental health training available to students	No
Employs Chief Wellness Officer	NR
Peer-to-peer mental health offerings	NR
Counseling center has guidelines or accreditation	No
Mental health/well-being courses	NR

ACADEMICS

% students returning for sophomore year	94
% students graduating within 4 years	76
% students graduating within 6 years	89
Calendar	Semester
Student/faculty ratio	8:1
Most common class size 1–9.	(41%)
Most common lab/discussion size 10–19.	(50%)

Most Popular Majors

English Language and Literature; Economics; History

Applicants Also Look At

Albion College, Arizona State University, Baylor University, Calvin University, Eastern Michigan University, Gordon College, Grove City College, Harvard College, Michigan State University, Princeton University, Taylor University, Texas A&M University—College Station, United States Air Force Academy, United States Military Academy, United States Naval Academy, University of Dallas, University of Michigan—Ann Arbor, University of Notre Dame, Vanderbilt University, Wheaton College (IL), Yale University

STUDENTS SAY "..."

Academics

Taking pride in its status as a "small, Christian, classical liberal arts college," Hillsdale College "challenges its students to become confident and independent individuals." Students can earn a bachelor's degree in the arts or sciences while studying a core curriculum focused on "literature, philosophy, theology, history, the fine arts, and the natural sciences" that establishes "a common baseline for all." This sense of community drives "non-sectarian" classrooms where "open-minded and respectful discourse is promoted and encouraged." This applies equally to teachers who "are not only scholarly and professional, but also people that care about their students" and who "participate in the discussions as well, without stamping down our ideas. They have a heart to grow our minds and independence." Teaching is "an opportunity for mentorship and not just as a requirement for a research grant." Classes are "very discussion-focused and rooted in the large amounts of reading [we do]." One Museum Studies student loved the chance to "collaborate with other classmates to design and curate museum displays, work with the college archivist, and get to be hands-on with original artifacts." Overall, there's an appreciation for how academics lead to opportunities to "become more virtuous and faithful."

Campus Life

The average Hillsdalian is likely to "spend their mornings and afternoons going to and from classes and studying in between, as well as getting hours in their on-campus jobs." Outside of class, "thrifting and antique shopping around campus [are] popular...as well as going to local coffee shops and watching basketball and baseball games on campus." Students enjoy spending "a lot of time in the Student Union, playing ping pong, pool, and talking with each other," which carries over to the dining hall, a major location for socializing. "Students are very conscious of keeping their mealtime free to see their friends, and there is a vibrant culture of scheduling conversations and catch-up time over a meal in the dining hall." Other noted activities include various club- or intramural sports; a series of rotating, weekly events; clubs ranging from "swing dancing and sword fighting" to "religious associations and reading"; and Greek life, which includes a music-focused fraternity. Students say there's space both for those who enjoy solitude to "focus on my classes" and those happy that "there's always something to do or people to serve."

Student Body

Students at Hillsdale are "friendly and welcoming; you can have an engaging conversation with someone you've never met before in the cafeteria without feeling nervous to do so." It's a "very politically conservative school" where "most students on campus go to church weekly and participate in Bible studies. Students deeply value discussion and debate, finding that "disagreement...is a reason to improve a friendship, not to disintegrate it." This makes for a supportive, familiar group of peers who say, "I feel challenged to think deeply and aspire to ever improve myself in order to reach my fullest potential, but I also feel supported and encouraged when I fall short." As one student explains it: "I can't go anywhere on campus without seeing someone I know, whether they're from my dorm, a class or club we're both in, or we just met in the cafeteria one day through a mutual friend. And no matter how I met them or how long I've known them, we'll probably chat and be invested in each other's lives." In short, "Hillsdale students are dedicated to their schoolwork, but also constantly seeking to balance their spiritual, physical, and social lives."

Hillsdale College

Financial Aid: 517-607-2350 • E-Mail: admissions@hillsdale.edu • Website: www.hillsdale.edu

THE PRINCETON REVIEW SAYS

Admissions

The school reports that its standardized testing policy for use in admission for Fall 2026 is Test Optional. The Princeton Review suggests that interested applicants consult with the school for the most up-to-date standardized testing policies. *Very important factors considered include:* rigor of secondary school record, academic GPA, application essay, extracurricular activities, character/personal qualities. *Important factors considered include:* recommendation(s), interview, volunteer work, work experience, level of applicant's interest. *Other factors considered include:* standardized test scores, talent/ability. High school diploma is required and GED is accepted. *Academic units required:* 4 English. *Academic units recommended:* 4 math, 3 science, 2 science labs, 3 language (other than English), 3 social studies, 3 history.

Financial Aid

Students should submit: Institution's own financial aid form. The Princeton Review suggests that all financial aid forms be submitted as soon as possible. *Need-based scholarships/grants offered:* Private scholarships; College/university scholarship or grant aid from institutional funds. *Loan aid offered:* College/university loans from institutional funds. Admitted students will be notified of awards on a rolling basis beginning 12/1. Federal Work-Study Program not available. Institutional employment available.

The Inside Word

While the academic profile of incoming students is impressive, the college strongly considers a student's extracurricular activities, character, and ambition as well. For students submitting test scores, in addition to the SAT and ACT, Hillsdale also accepts the Classic Learning Test (CLT). Applicants are encouraged to submit a résumé of their extracurricular, leadership, and work experiences along with their applications. Interviews are highly recommended, especially for those seeking a scholarship.

THE SCHOOL SAYS

From the Admissions Office

"The College's strength is found in its mission and curriculum. The core curriculum at Hillsdale contains the essence of the classical liberal arts education. Through it, students are introduced to the history, the philosophical and theological ideas, the works of literature, and the scientific discoveries that set Western Civilization apart. As explained in its mission statement, 'the College also considers itself a trustee of our Western philosophical and theological inheritance tracing to Athens and Jerusalem, a heritage finding its clearest expression in the American experiment of self-government under law.'

"Personal attention is a hallmark at Hillsdale. Small classes are combined with teaching professors who make their students a priority. The academic environment at Hillsdale will actively engage you as a student. Extracurricular activities abound at Hillsdale with more than 100 clubs and organizations that offer excellent leadership opportunities. From athletics and the fine arts, to Greek life and community volunteer programs, you will find it difficult not to be involved in our thriving campus community. In addition, numerous study abroad programs, a 685-acre biological station in northern Michigan, and an internship program in Washington, D.C., are just a few of the unique off-campus opportunities available to students at Hillsdale.

"We seek students who are ambitious, intellectually active and who are ready to become leaders worthy of this heritage in their personal as well as professional lives.

"All students sign and abide by the Honor Code, which says: 'A Hillsdale College student is honorable in conduct, honest in word and deed, dutiful in study and service, and respectful of the rights of other. Through education, the student rises to self-government.'"

SELECTIVITY

# of total applicants	3,143
% of total applicants accepted	19
% of total acceptees attending	61
# of in-state applicants	575
% of in-state applicants accepted	18
# of out-of-state-applicants	2,174
% of applicants accepted from out of state	23
# of international applicants	394
% of international applicants accepted	3
# offered a place on the wait list	161
# admitted from wait list	6

First-Year Profile

Testing policy	Test Optional
Range SAT composite	1330–1470
Range SAT EBRW	680–750
Range SAT math	650–740
Range ACT composite	30–33
% submitting SAT scores	39
% submitting ACT scores	37
Average HS GPA	4.0
% submitting high school GPA	100

Important Dates

Early decision	
Apply by	11/1
Notified by	12/1
Regular	
Apply by	3/15
Nonfall registration?	Yes

FINANCIAL FACTS

Annual tuition	$32,730
Food and housing	$14,020
Required fees	$1,459
Books and supplies	$1,200
Average need-based scholarship (First-year)	$14,816 ($16,603)
% students with need rec. need-based scholarship or grant aid (First-year)	88 (89)
% students with need rec. non-need-based scholarship or grant aid (First-year)	98 (96)
% students with need rec. need-based self-help aid (First-year)	64 (80)
% students rec. any financial aid (First-year)	99 (99)
% UG borrow to pay for school	37
Average cumulative indebtedness	$32,705
% of students with need fully met (First-year)	31 (40)
Average % of student need met (First-year)	78 (78)

Hobart and William Smith Colleges

300 Pulteney Street, Geneva, NY 14456 • Admissions: 315-781-3622

Survey Snapshot
Internships are widely available
Students are happy
Easy to get around campus

RATINGS

Quality of Life	**89**
Fire Safety	**95**
Green	**87**
Academic	**88**
Profs Interesting	**93**
Profs Accessible	**97**
Admissions	**88**
Financial Aid	**92**

CAMPUS LIFE

Type of school	Private
Environment	Village

Students

Degree-seeking undergrad enrollment	1,848
% male/female/not reported	47/52/2
% from out of state	55
% First-year from public high school	58
% First-year live on campus	100
% Ugrads live on campus	85
# of fraternities (% join)	6 (8)
# of sororities (% join)	1 (1)
% Asian	2
% Black or African American	8
% Hispanic	12
% Native American	<1
% Pacific Islander	0
% Race and/or ethnicity unknown	3
% Two or more races	4
% White	66
% International	5
# of countries represented	39

CAMPUS MENTAL HEALTH SERVICES

Offers mental health/wellness program	Yes
Mental health training available to students	Yes
Employs Chief Wellness Officer	No
Peer-to-peer mental health offerings	No
Counseling center has guidelines or accreditation	Yes
Mental health/well-being courses	Yes, for-credit

ACADEMICS

% students returning for sophomore year	88
% students graduating within 4 years	62
% students graduating within 6 years	71
Calendar	Semester
Student/faculty ratio	11:1
Most common class size 1–9.	(41%)
Most common lab/discussion size 10–19.	(50%)

Most Popular Majors

Econometrics and Quantitative Economics; Mass Communication/Media Studies; Entrepreneurship/Entrepreneurial Studies

Applicants Often Prefer

Connecticut College, Skidmore College, St. Lawrence University, Syracuse University, University of Vermont, Hamilton College, Colgate University, Colby College, Bard College

Applicants Sometimes Prefer

Dickinson College, Fordham University, State University of New York—Binghamton University, Trinity College, Union College, Ithaca College, Franklin and Marshall College

Applicants Rarely Prefer

St. John Fisher University, SUNY Oswego

STUDENTS SAY "…"

Academics

Originally founded as separate schools, Hobart and William Smith is united with one campus, administration, and curriculum allowing students to take full advantage of the resources offered by HWS. Professors at Hobart and William Smith "not only care a great deal, but go out of their way to push students and individualize the experience for each person." One student enthuses that teachers are "more than instructors; they are mentors whose expertise and teaching methods have truly ignited my passion for my current studies." Small, discussion-based classes are a priority, explains another student. Perhaps as a result of this individual focus, "academic curiosity" among students "is truly remarkable." First-year students get to select from an array of unique seminars, with topics ranging from ghosts in Japan to social justice and service opportunities in the local community. In "my FSEM class we learned about the community and how we can make a difference...I was able to work...with kids while still implementing what I learned in class." Other unique experiences are available, including the opportunity for science students to conduct research aboard The William Scandling, HWS' own research vessel.

Campus Life

Much of life at HWS centers around the campus's idyllic setting. "My favorite thing to do for fun on campus is to go down to the docks and enjoy the beauty and waters of Seneca Lake with my friends," says one student. During warm weather, "you will see many students hanging out at our boat house and swimming whether it is the weekend or after class" or anywhere on campus "with a good view and a nice chair." The scenic environment inspires days of service at HWS, featuring "local cleanup initiatives [and] assisting in community centers, [where] each student contributes their time and energy to support the well-being of those around us." Clubs and sports provide other means for students to get involved on campus. Campus favorites include the Kinetic Dance Collective, the HWS Tutor Corps, and the String Ensemble. And athletes enjoy getting involved at all levels of competition: "We have so many opportunities to play sports, and many teams welcome walk-ons. We also have a strong recreational and club sport program, which allows students who may not want the full commitment of a varsity sport to have the option of being a part of an active team." Thanks to the school's size, "you are able to be a leader in the classroom and on the athletic field."

Student Body

The student body at HWS "is a vibrant tapestry of diversity and dynamism...that makes our campus life so distinctive." As one student notes, "I would describe my peers as motivated, engaged...as well as generally kind and inclusive." This makeup offers "the opportunity to have real conversations and debates rather than being in a political echo chamber." While celebrating a plurality of opinions, students say they are "liberal-arts-educated critical thinkers who understand their impact on the world and strive to leave it in a better place." Because most attendees remain on-campus throughout their enrollment, student interactions thrive in and out of class. As one student notes, "My housemates vary from individuals on the sailing team, to dancers, to student government members...yet everyone... still gets together to do house dinners and movie nights.... Our student body is engaged in campus life, but we are also committed to being involved with one another in rich relationships." One student explains that "from studying abroad in Rome, Italy to being a part of the William Smith Lacrosse team, my time at the colleges has provided me with opportunities to have peers from all different groups...I love that I can sit in the dining hall with all of my teammates after practice and have the opportunity to reconnect with the friends I made abroad."

Hobart and William Smith Colleges

Financial Aid: 315-781-3315 • E-Mail: admissions@hws.edu • Website: www.hws.edu

THE PRINCETON REVIEW SAYS

Admissions

The school reports that its standardized testing policy for use in admission for Fall 2026 is Test Optional. The Princeton Review suggests that interested applicants consult with the school for the most up-to-date standardized testing policies. *Very important factors considered include:* rigor of secondary school record, academic GPA. *Important factors considered include:* application essay, recommendation(s), extracurricular activities, character/personal qualities, volunteer work, work experience. *Other factors considered include:* class rank, standardized test scores, interview, talent/ability, first generation, alumni/ae relation, geographical residence, state residency, level of applicant's interest. High school diploma is required and GED is accepted. *Academic units required:* 4 English, 3 math, 3 science, 2 science labs, 2 language (other than English), 4 social studies, 2 academic electives. *Academic units recommended:* 4 English, 4 math, 4 science, 2 science labs, 3 language (other than English), 4 social studies, 4 academic electives.

Financial Aid

Students should submit: FAFSA; State aid form. Priority filing deadline is 11/15. The Princeton Review suggests that all financial aid forms be submitted as soon as possible. *Need-based scholarships/grants offered:* Federal Pell; Federal SEOG; State scholarships/grants; Private scholarships; College/university scholarship or grant aid from institutional funds. *Loan aid offered:* Federal Direct Subsidized Loans; Federal Direct Unsubsidized Loans; Direct PLUS loans. Admitted students will be notified of awards on a rolling basis beginning 12/15. Federal Work-Study Program available. Institutional employment available.

The Inside Word

Hobart and William Smith seeks applicants who want to be challenged both inside and outside the classroom. To find such students, the school takes a holistic approach to the admissions process. Therefore, you can expect that all facets of your application will be carefully assessed. And if you're truly seeking admittance, you'll want to make sure you've taken a rigorous curriculum throughout high school. HWS also typically favors students who have actively worked to better their community and demonstrate great character.

THE SCHOOL SAYS

From the Admissions Office

"Hobart and William Smith is known for consistent success in preparing students for meaningful lives and fulfilling careers through an outcomes-based focus on their futures. To best prepare students for impact and success in an ever-shifting world, HWS nurtures intellectual, professional and ethical development. Students benefit from an extraordinarily dedicated faculty who serve as teachers, mentors and guides. They complement broad, interdisciplinary study with hands-on learning experiences including study abroad (60+% participate) and community service. Preparation for a career or graduate school begins as early as the first semester through HWS' Pathways program. Students find friendship, discovery and belonging as valued members of a collaborative residential community that values the dignity and potential of each individual. At every step, they enjoy the benefits of life on the shores of a stunning lake that is a classroom, a destination and a constant reminder of their endless potential."

SELECTIVITY

# of total applicants	5,865
% of total applicants accepted	67
% of total acceptees attending	12
# of in-state applicants	1,976
% of in-state applicants accepted	77
# of out-of-state-applicants	2,421
% of applicants accepted from out of state	83
# of international applicants	1,464
% of international applicants accepted	27
# of early decision applicants	220
% of early decision applicants accepted	57

First-Year Profile

Testing policy	Test Optional
Range SAT composite	1190–1380
Range SAT EBRW	600–710
Range SAT math	580–680
Range ACT composite	27–32
% submitting SAT scores	23
% submitting ACT scores	6
Average HS GPA	3.8
% submitting high school GPA	98
% graduated top 10% of class	27
% graduated top 25% of class	62
% graduated top 50% of class	89
% submitting high school rank	21

Important Dates

Early decision	
Apply by	11/15
Notified by	12/15
Other ED apply by	1/15
Other ED notified by	1/25
Early action	
Apply by	11/15
Notified by	1/25
Regular	
Apply by	2/1
Notified by	3/1
Nonfall registration?	Yes

FINANCIAL FACTS*

Annual tuition	$64,988
Food and housing	$18,210
Required fees (First-year)	$1,574 ($1,854)
Books and supplies	$1,000
Average need-based scholarship (First-year)	$52,644 ($53,392)
% students with need rec. need-based scholarship or grant aid (First-year)	100 (100)
% students with need rec. non-need-based scholarship or grant aid (First-year)	29 (29)
% students with need rec. need-based self-help aid (First-year)	69 (69)
% students rec. any financial aid (First-year)	98 (98)
% UG borrow to pay for school	72
Average cumulative indebtedness	$31,392
% of students with need fully met (First-year)	37 (37)
Average % of student need met (First-year)	90 (90)

* Most recently reported data at time of printing. Scan the QR code to find the latest updates.

HOFSTRA UNIVERSITY

100 Hofstra University, Hempstead, NY 11549 • Admissions: 516-463-6700

Survey Snapshot
Intramural sports are popular
Students are happy
Theater is popular

RATINGS

Quality of Life	**82**
Fire Safety	**99**
Green	**60***
Academic	**78**
Profs Interesting	**85**
Profs Accessible	**87**
Admissions	**86**
Financial Aid	**86**

CAMPUS LIFE

Type of school	Private
Environment	City

Students

Degree-seeking undergrad enrollment	6,512
% male/female/not reported	43/57/<1
% from out of state	29
% First-year from public high school	82
% First-year live on campus	49
% Ugrads live on campus	36
# of fraternities (% join)	7 (2)
# of sororities (% join)	9 (5)
% Asian	17
% Black or African American	10
% Hispanic	20
% Native American	<1
% Pacific Islander	0
% Race and/or ethnicity unknown	2
% Two or more races	8
% White	41
% International	3
# of countries represented	61

CAMPUS MENTAL HEALTH SERVICES

Offers mental health/wellness program	Yes
Mental health training available to students	No
Employs Chief Wellness Officer	Yes
Peer-to-peer mental health offerings	Yes
Counseling center has guidelines or accreditation	Yes
Mental health/well-being courses	Yes

ACADEMICS

% students returning for sophomore year	85
% students graduating within 4 years	57
% students graduating within 6 years	66
Calendar	Semester
Student/faculty ratio	13:1
Most common class size 10–19.	(36%)
Most common lab/discussion size 10–19.	(41%)

Most Popular Majors

Biology/Biological Sciences; Psychology; Radio, Television, and Digital Communication

Applicants Often Prefer

Boston University, New York University, Northeastern University, Syracuse University

Applicants Sometimes Prefer

City University of New York—Hunter College, Drexel University, Fordham University, Penn State University Park, Rutgers University–New Brunswick, State University of New York—Binghamton University, State University of New York—Stony Brook University, University of Connecticut, University of Delaware

Applicants Rarely Prefer

Adelphi University, Quinnipiac University

STUDENTS SAY "..."

Academics

At Hofstra University, enrollees praise the "sheer variety of learning experiences" and subject matter that is "very unique and fleshed out" across 175 undergraduate programs, with specific callouts to "film, music business, and medical programs." One enthusiastic first-year student says, "As a biochemistry major I already got a research opportunity.... And I'm getting a stipend for it." Students also say that the school is supportive and offers many resources: "From tutoring to IT help to mental health help, they have it all!" Students appreciate that their professors foster "a very positive learning environment" and are "genuinely kind and clear." As one student says, "I often look forward to classes and feel comfortable asking questions." Another student agrees, describing how professors "make every class worth attending." Professors keep things engaging through interactive teaching styles, including "discussion-based courses, courses that revolve around guest lecturers, and field trips into the city!" In addition, "the small class sizes allow for personal relationship[s] with professors," with one student adding, "One reason I loved Hofstra and decided to go here is that I could build a connection with my teachers, which would help me in the future." And because it's so easy to get involved and supported, students suggest that the "opportunities that the school offers are amazing."

Campus Life

This "very walkable" campus offers "lots of activities" and "many areas to lounge," including the game room "where you can play pool and games with peers." One favorite activity is the annual Fall Festival, which features musical performances and carnival rides. Students here take the initiative with student-led events and activities, such as the weekly Hofstra Concerts Coffeehouse, where student bands perform, and the HEAT Network, a TV network that runs student-produced shows. Students are also very involved in clubs and one of the most popular is Danceworks, which puts on dance shows that are choreographed and performed by students. As one student shares, "the student body goes out of their way to host and organize events," and this wide range of events "allows for inclusivity on our campus." Students also support each other's work, with one student giving an example: "The end-of-year film festival is a great way to see people's work across the school." The school's proximity to New York City also makes it possible for students to take a day trip to see a concert, shop, or see a show on Broadway. Closer to campus, there are also "many shopping centers nearby, a nice mall, and a beautiful beach." Wherever students go, they find there is a "strong sense of community" that encourages them to get involved.

Student Body

Hofstra is made up of "a lot of really hardworking, interesting people." Students here are "generally friendly and intelligent with a wide variety of interests and passions" and come from a "good mix of student athletes as well as more creative arts lovers." These "very diverse" enrollees "express themselves in a variety of ways, which ensures that no one feels ostracized or judged." As one student describes it, "Overall the student body is very liberal and loves advocating for positive change in the community." It's a place where "it's easy to find someone to talk to" and people are "always willing to help." As one student illustrates, "I have yet to meet someone on campus who isn't down to help with an assignment, answer a question, or guide you in the right direction." Another student agrees, saying, "During finals week, it's common to see study groups sprawled out in Axinn Library, exchanging notes and encouraging each other through tough subjects." To put it another way, "Hofstra students are trailblazers, innovators, and team players—individuals who are unafraid to carve their own paths while lifting others along the way."

Hofstra University

Financial Aid: 516-463-8000 • E-Mail: admission@hofstra.edu • Website: www.hofstra.edu

THE PRINCETON REVIEW SAYS

Admissions

The school reports that its standardized testing policy for use in admission for Fall 2026 is Test Optional. The Princeton Review suggests that interested applicants consult with the school for the most up-to-date standardized testing policies. *Very important factors considered include:* rigor of secondary school record, class rank, academic GPA, application essay, recommendation(s). *Important factors considered include:* interview, extracurricular activities, talent/ability, character/personal qualities. *Other factors considered include:* standardized test scores, first generation, geographical residence, volunteer work, work experience, level of applicant's interest. High school diploma is required and GED is accepted. *Academic units required:* 4 English, 3 math, 3 science, 1 science lab, 2 language (other than English), 3 social studies. *Academic units recommended:* 4 English, 4 math, 4 science, 2 science labs, 3 language (other than English), 4 social studies.

Financial Aid

Students should submit: State aid form; FAFSA. Priority filing deadline is 11/15. The Princeton Review suggests that all financial aid forms be submitted as soon as possible. *Need-based scholarships/grants offered:* Federal Pell; Federal SEOG; State scholarships/grants; Private scholarships; College/university scholarship or grant aid from institutional funds; United Negro College Fund. *Loan aid offered:* Federal Direct Subsidized Loans; Federal Direct Unsubsidized Loans; Direct PLUS loans; State Loans. Admitted students will be notified of awards on a rolling basis beginning 1/15. Federal Work-Study Program available. Institutional employment available.

The Inside Word

At Hofstra, your high school transcript is usually the most important part of your application. While the school is test optional, submitting SAT or ACT scores can still help strengthen your application. About 30 percent of students choose to submit scores, so if yours fall within or above Hofstra's typical range for admission, it's a good idea to include them. The university operates on the basis of rolling admission, meaning the earlier you apply, the better.

THE SCHOOL SAYS

From the Admissions Office

"Hofstra is a dynamic private institution that is internationally recognized for academic excellence, civic engagement and community service. We provide you with the resources of a large university, but the personal attention of a small college. Students come from 50 U.S. states and territories and over 60 countries, and can choose from 180 program options. Hofstra is home to schools of engineering, business, communication, education, nursing, medicine and law, as well as 21 Division I sports and 35 residence halls. Our 244-acre suburban campus, which is a nationally recognized arboretum, is just 25 miles east of New York City, opening the door to prestigious internships at world-class corporations.

"You'll also benefit from experiential learning on campus in our state-of-the-art facilities, including an academic trading room with 34 Bloomberg terminals; advanced engineering labs; and a cutting-edge converged newsroom and multimedia classroom. More than 200 pre-professional, social and academic clubs provide leadership and community service opportunities. Hofstra also values bringing exclusive learning opportunities to campus, most notably by being the only school to ever host 3 consecutive presidential debates (2008, 2012, and 2016). Our faculty are entrepreneurs, scholars, artists, and scientists who are pioneers in their disciplines and mentors in the classroom. They'll invite you to collaborate on research projects and connect you with industry veterans.

"At Hofstra, you will pursue your passion and find your purpose."

SELECTIVITY

# of total applicants	21,771
% of total applicants accepted	73
% of total acceptees attending	10
# of in-state applicants	11,963
% of in-state applicants accepted	76
# of out-of-state-applicants	8,143
% of applicants accepted from out of state	82
# of international applicants	1,661
% of international applicants accepted	6
# offered a place on the wait list	190
# admitted from wait list	22

First-Year Profile

Testing policy	Test Optional
Range SAT composite	1260–1390
Range SAT EBRW	620–700
Range SAT math	620–700
Range ACT composite	28–32
% submitting SAT scores	25
% submitting ACT scores	4
Average HS GPA	3.8
% submitting high school GPA	100
% graduated top 10% of class	24
% graduated top 25% of class	55
% graduated top 50% of class	88
% submitting high school rank	21

Important Dates

Early action	
Apply by	12/15
Notified by	1/15
Regular	
Apply by	Rolling
Notified by	Rolling
Nonfall registration?	Yes

FINANCIAL FACTS

Annual tuition	$60,936
Food and housing	$20,850
Required fees	$1,174
Books and supplies	$1,000
Average need-based scholarship (First-year)	$31,570 ($34,745)
% students with need rec. need-based scholarship or grant aid (First-year)	98 (99)
% students with need rec. non-need-based scholarship or grant aid (First-year)	17 (20)
% students with need rec. need-based self-help aid (First-year)	81 (79)
% students rec. any financial aid (First-year)	96 (100)
% UG borrow to pay for school	61
Average cumulative indebtedness	$42,608
% of students with need fully met (First-year)	20 (21)
Average % of student need met (First-year)	69 (72)

HOLLINS UNIVERSITY

7916 Williamson Road, Roanoke, VA 24020 • Admissions: 540-362-6401

Survey Snapshot
Lots of liberal students
Internships are widely available
Class discussions encouraged

RATINGS

Quality of Life	81
Fire Safety	82
Green	60*
Academic	85
Profs Interesting	92
Profs Accessible	92
Admissions	86
Financial Aid	91

CAMPUS LIFE

Type of school	Private
Environment	City

Students

Degree-seeking undergrad enrollment	665
% male/female/not reported	0/100/0
% from out of state	37
% First-year from public high school	60
% First-year live on campus	84
% Ugrads live on campus	81
# of sororities	0
% Asian	2
% Black or African American	16
% Hispanic	12
% Native American	1
% Pacific Islander	<1
% Race and/or ethnicity unknown	<1
% Two or more races	3
% White	60
% International	6
# of countries represented	23

CAMPUS MENTAL HEALTH SERVICES

Offers mental health/wellness program	Yes
Mental health training available to students	No
Employs Chief Wellness Officer	NR
Peer-to-peer mental health offerings	NR
Counseling center has guidelines or accreditation	No
Mental health/well-being courses	NR

ACADEMICS

% students returning for sophomore year	74
% students graduating within 4 years	57
Calendar	Semester
Student/faculty ratio	8:1
Most common class size 10–19.	(44%)

Most Popular Majors

English Language and Literature; Psychology; Business/Commerce

Applicants Also Look At

George Mason University, James Madison University, John Tyler Community College, North Carolina State University, Northern Virginia Community College, Old Dominion University, Prince George's Community College—Andrews Air Force Base Degree Center, Tidewater Community College, Virginia Commonwealth University, Virginia Tech

STUDENTS SAY "..."

Academics

Hollins University is a private liberal arts college in Roanoke, Virginia, that heralds the unique benefits that come with being an all-women's college, which includes a student-to-faculty ratio of 8:1, a relatively low class size, and a global network of alums that connects students to mentors, jobs, and internships. "Our community and traditions help us create connections with students and alumnae that will last well into our adulthood," says a student. As for hands-on experiences, they are guaranteed for every eligible student, and three out of four students complete at least one: "I am currently doing an internship that is completely out of my field, but one class I took intrigued me to do so," reports a student, while another notes "I have done three internships through Hollins and it contributes a lot to my career." The so-called J-Term, or January Short Term, helps free up students to pursue such opportunities, as well as research and study abroad. Students also note that the school has made a serious "investment in the creative fields," with plenty of "readings and Q&A sessions by guest authors," and classes incorporate plenty of hands-on elements, such as a public health class where students had "to complete a field experience assignment where we study a disease, and then interview random students about [it] just as a real epidemiologist would."

The school is "academic and forward-thinking without putting a ton of pressure on students to maintain perfect grades," and creates "a positive intellectual standard that makes me and my peers want to really grow and push our education further." Faculty are "absolutely the backbone of this school and have such a passion to support their students in any way they can, both academically, emotionally, and just in life." They "are more than willing to work with you when life throws you curve balls" and are "very good about answering questions and making themselves available outside of class."

Campus Life

Hollins University is "a beautiful, optimistic place" where almost all first-years live, be that in one of the 10 home-style residences or seven special interest houses and halls, all located "right next to a huge natural preserve and reservoir." (That historical, picturesque quality does come with a bit of a price: several students report a desire for renovations—like air-conditioning—in the oldest dorms, and for a more varied menu in the dining hall.) Given the natural scenery, students appreciate the school's outdoor activities, like "hiking and trail walks they set up" to horseback riding and a climbing team (that can also make use of the gym's rock wall). The student government also works to organize "many great sponsored events that take us out of Hollins and into the city of Roanoke," like basketball games, and "lots of social events, ranging from the little hot chocolate buffet on the quad... to the semi-formal fall dance." (Hollins students do love "a party with a theme, any excuse to dress up.") Students also report a lot of activities ("everything from crafting club to anime club") and note that the school is "really great about making sure everyone can get involved."

Student Body

Despite being a historically women's college, "Hollins students represent a wide range of gender identities," including "AFAB, non-binary, trans-masculine, LGBTQIA+ students, as well as cis-gendered women." There is a "Culture of Care implemented on campus, which makes respect and empathy for one another a conscious mindset throughout all of campus." There are just seven hundred undergraduates, which "makes finding friends and familiar faces easy." As one student says: "I never see a face I've never seen before.... I find it comforting." This is "a safe place to express oneself " and "everyone is so open and accepting and the clubs, societies, and traditions give everyone a unique place in the school." Overall, this group of "kind, smart, funny, talented" individuals create "a warm and friendly environment where everyone feels like they belong."

HOLLINS UNIVERSITY

Financial Aid: 540-362-6332 • E-Mail: huadm@hollins.edu • Website: www.hollins.edu

THE PRINCETON REVIEW SAYS

Admissions

The school reports that its standardized testing policy for use in admission for Fall 2026 is Test Optional. The Princeton Review suggests that interested applicants consult with the school for the most up-to-date standardized testing policies. *Very important factors considered include:* academic GPA. *Important factors considered include:* rigor of secondary school record, application essay, recommendation(s). *Other factors considered include:* class rank, standardized test scores, interview, extracurricular activities, talent/ability, character/personal qualities, first generation, alumni/ae relation, geographical residence, state residency, volunteer work, work experience, level of applicant's interest. High school diploma is required and GED is accepted. *Academic units required:* 4 English, 3 math, 3 science, 3 social studies. *Academic units recommended:* 3 language (other than English).

Financial Aid

Students should submit: FAFSA; State aid form. Priority filing deadline is 2/1. The Princeton Review suggests that all financial aid forms be submitted as soon as possible. *Need-based scholarships/grants offered:* Federal Pell; Federal SEOG; State scholarships/grants; Private scholarships; College/university scholarship or grant aid from institutional funds. *Loan aid offered:* Federal Direct Subsidized Loans; Federal Direct Unsubsidized Loans; Direct PLUS loans; College/university loans from institutional funds. Admitted students will be notified of awards on or about 3/10. Federal Work-Study Program available. Institutional employment available.

The Inside Word

If you've got solid grades and—though submitting them is optional—good test scores, you stand a good chance of being in the 71% of students accepted to Hollins University each year. If you're from the Roanoke area, your chances may be even higher—12% of all students are local—and you may even qualify for a HOPE scholarship that fully covers tuition. If you can manage it, there's a grant provided to those who visit the school (and subsequently enroll), and since the school is looking for best-fit candidates, it's a good idea to take them up on this.

THE SCHOOL SAYS

From the Admissions Office

"Empowering women since 1842, Hollins University unites excellence in liberal arts education with experiential learning opportunities and career preparation to help our students lead lives of consequence.

"Our broad liberal arts curriculum offers strong academic programs and superior teaching that emphasize critical thinking, problem solving, creativity, and collaboration—skills that employers seek. Our top five majors (psychology, biology, English/creative writing, studio art, and business) underscore the breadth and scope of the Hollins experience in the physical sciences, social sciences, arts, and humanities. The university's athletic program is dedicated to the pursuit of academic achievement and athletic excellence, and is committed to the overall success of the student-athlete.

"Career mentorship; global learning opportunities; resources for low-income, first-generation, and BIPOC and international students; and academic support networks are all located in The Green, Hollins' new integrative learning commons.

"Career preparation is also a hallmark: three out of four Hollins graduates complete at least one internship during their undergraduate careers, and half of those participate in two or more internships. The university places students in companies, nonprofits, museums, law firms, and hospitals, both in the U.S. and abroad. One year after graduation, 95 percent of our students are employed or in graduate school."

SELECTIVITY

# of total applicants	2,827
% of total applicants accepted	68
% of total acceptees attending	10
# of in-state applicants	1,109
% of in-state applicants accepted	82
# of out-of-state-applicants	1,247
% of applicants accepted from out of state	77
# of international applicants	453
% of international applicants accepted	11
# of early decision applicants	12
% of early decision applicants accepted	92
# offered a place on the wait list	0
# admitted from wait list	0

First-Year Profile

Testing policy	Test Optional
Range SAT composite	1160–1360
Range SAT EBRW	610–730
Range SAT math	530–640
Range ACT composite	28–28
% submitting SAT scores	12
% submitting ACT scores	0
Average HS GPA	3.7
% submitting high school GPA	99

Important Dates

Early decision	
Apply by	11/1
Notified by	11/15
Early action	
Apply by	11/15
Notified by	12/1
Regular	
Apply by	7/1
Notified by	Rolling, 11/1
Nonfall registration?	Yes

FINANCIAL FACTS

Annual tuition	$43,650
Food and housing	$16,200
Required fees (First-year)	$1,260 ($1,585)
Books and supplies	$800
Average need-based scholarship (First-year)	$35,774 ($37,469)
% students with need rec. need-based scholarship or grant aid (First-year)	100 (100)
% students with need rec. non-need-based scholarship or grant aid (First-year)	33 (33)
% students with need rec. need-based self-help aid (First-year)	77 (74)
% students rec. any financial aid (First-year)	100 (100)
% UG borrow to pay for school	65
Average cumulative indebtedness	$30,142
% of students with need fully met (First-year)	38 (39)
Average % of student need met (First-year)	81 (81)

Howard University

2400 Sixth Street, NW, Washington, DC 20059 • Admissions: 202-806-2755

Survey Snapshot
Lots of liberal students
Frats and sororities are popular
College radio is popular

RATINGS

Quality of Life	**70**
Fire Safety	**74**
Green	**60***
Academic	**74**
Profs Interesting	**78**
Profs Accessible	**82**
Admissions	**90**
Financial Aid	**83**

CAMPUS LIFE

Type of school	Private
Environment	Metropolis

Students

Degree-seeking undergrad enrollment	11,084
% male/female/not reported	29/71/0
% from out of state	95
% First-year live on campus	100
% Ugrads live on campus	53
# of fraternities (% join)	5 (1)
# of sororities (% join)	4 (1)
% Asian	<1
% Black or African American	69
% Hispanic	6
% Native American	<1
% Pacific Islander	0
% Race and/or ethnicity unknown	14
% Two or more races	5
% White	<1
% International	4
# of countries represented	46

CAMPUS MENTAL HEALTH SERVICES

Offers mental health/wellness program	Yes
Mental health training available to students	No
Employs Chief Wellness Officer	NR
Peer-to-peer mental health offerings	NR
Counseling center has guidelines or accreditation	No
Mental health/well-being courses	NR

ACADEMICS

% students returning for sophomore year	88
% students graduating within 4 years	63
% students graduating within 6 years	74
Calendar	Semester
Student/faculty ratio	13:1
Most common class size 20–29.	(31%)
Most common lab/discussion size 20–29.	(51%)

Most Popular Majors
Biology/Biological Sciences

STUDENTS SAY "..."

Academics

Prospective students interested in attending a historically Black college would be hard-pressed to find a better option than Howard University. With the "outstanding...accomplishments of a great majority of its alumni," including notable figures like Thurgood Marshall, Elijah Cummings, Toni Morrison, and Kamala Harris, the university has certainly earned its reputation as a "formidable force in producing African American intellectuals." Howard University takes great care in preparing students "to compete on a local and global level," instilling in them a deep sense of "pride and excellence." As one student expresses, "Howard University is more than a place to get an education; it is a once-in-a-lifetime experience that not only strengthens your mind, but also your spirit and pride in who you are as a person and who you have the potential to become." As you stroll across the campus, you can't help but feel "the sense of being a part of such a tremendous legacy." Students benefit from an "inspiring faculty" that both "pushes you and teaches patience." In addition, professors effectively "bridge the gap between the real world and the textbook," by teaching students how to apply their classroom knowledge to future careers. The majority of the faculty are "supportive and helpful" and "have a genuine interest in their subject." At Howard, classroom discussions are lively and highly encouraged. This type of learning is appreciated, with one student explaining, "I am able to have a voice in the class and share my opinion." This inclusive environment underscores how a Howard education can serve as a robust foundation for professional success.

Campus Life

Life at Howard moves at a fast pace and these students wouldn't have it any other way. The campus crackles with energy, from the "lively" dorms to the well-attended school events, which are "a major part of the social calendar." In addition, undergrads enjoy taking full advantage of the opportunities available in Washington, D.C. and find the Metro station "very easily accessible." The campus hosts a wide range of engaging events, including cookie decorating competitions, Karaoke Night, Game Night Mixers, and Entrepreneurship Fest (a showdown where students pitch their business ideas to industry experts and potential investors). Additionally, students are encouraged "to be involved in campus organizations and student government," and with hundreds of clubs to choose from, there's something for everyone. Fraternities and sororities are also popular at Howard, although you should dispel ideas of raging keg parties. Indeed, "the main focus of our Greek life is community service. Any social event or gathering that is hosted by the Greeks normally has most or all of the proceeds going to a charity or community service project." There are also "student-run organizations that work in the community," providing "opportunities to be a part of something bigger than you."

Student Body

Given that Howard promotes a "culture of achievement and encouragement," it's not too surprising to learn that students here tend to be "very goal-oriented and driven." Indeed, it's common to find undergrads "taking a full course load, working, and interning," with many also participating in community service and extracurricular activities. However, undergrads aren't just high achievers; they're also "friendly, outgoing, stylish, and fashionable" as well. Many students are "very socially conscious" and often engage in "discussions surrounding social and political issues." This makes sense, considering that "Howard students are educated to think on a global scale." Howard fosters an "ever-changing, comprehensive, innovative, and supportive community" where "students are very accepting of each other." As this undergrad puts it, "Howard represents the best of the educated and progressive African American community."

Howard University

E-Mail: admission@howard.edu • Website: www.howard.edu

THE PRINCETON REVIEW SAYS

Admissions

The school reports that its standardized testing policy for use in admission for Fall 2026 will require applicants to submit either the SAT or ACT. The Princeton Review suggests that interested applicants consult with the school for the most up-to-date standardized testing policies. *Very important factors considered include:* rigor of secondary school record, academic GPA, standardized test scores. *Important factors considered include:* character/personal qualities. *Other factors considered include:* class rank, application essay, recommendation(s), extracurricular activities, talent/ability, first generation, alumni/ae relation, volunteer work, work experience, level of applicant's interest. High school diploma is required and GED is accepted. *Academic units required:* 4 English, 3 math, 2 science, 2 science labs, 2 language (other than English), 2 social studies, 4 academic electives. *Academic units recommended:* 4 English, 3 math, 2 science, 2 science labs, 2 language (other than English), 2 social studies, 4 academic electives.

Financial Aid

Students should submit: FAFSA. Priority filing deadline is 2/1. The Princeton Review suggests that all financial aid forms be submitted as soon as possible. *Need-based scholarships/grants offered:* Federal Pell; Federal SEOG; State scholarships/grants; Private scholarships; College/university scholarship or grant aid from institutional funds; Federal Nursing Scholarships; United Negro College Fund. *Loan aid offered:* Federal Direct Subsidized Loans; Federal Direct Unsubsidized Loans; Direct PLUS loans; College/university loans from institutional funds; State Loans. Admitted students will be notified of awards on a rolling basis beginning 2/1. Federal Work-Study Program available. Institutional employment available.

The Inside Word

Howard attracts quite a significant number of applicants, and the school maintains a high rate of graduation for those who do gain admittance. Howard places high value on each student's academic record, which is why you may want to consider submitting your standardized test scores, even though the university is Test Optional. The demonstrated capacity to handle higher learning in a diligent, responsible manner is also highly valued.

THE SCHOOL SAYS

From the Admissions Office

"Since its founding, Howard has stood among the few institutions of higher learning where Blacks and other minorities have participated freely in a truly comprehensive university experience. Thus, Howard has assumed a special responsibility in preparing its students to exercise leadership wherever their interests and commitments take them. Howard has issued over 100,000 degrees, diplomas, and certificates to men and women in the professions, the arts and sciences, and the humanities. The university has produced and continues to produce a high percentage of the nation's African American professionals in the fields of medicine, dentistry, pharmacy, engineering, nursing, architecture, religion, law, music, social work, education, and business. There are more than 14,000 students from across the nation and approximately forty-six countries and territories attending the university. Their varied customs, cultures, ideas, and interests contribute to Howard's international character and vitality. More than 1,500 faculty members represent the largest concentration of black scholars in any single institution of higher education."

SELECTIVITY

# of total applicants	37,270
% of total applicants accepted	42
% of total acceptees attending	16
# of early decision applicants	430
% of early decision applicants accepted	84
# offered a place on the wait list	1,310

First-Year Profile

Testing policy	SAT or ACT Required
Range SAT composite	1050–1270
Range SAT EBRW	540–660
Range SAT math	510–620
Range ACT composite	20–26
% submitting SAT scores	47
% submitting ACT scores	15
Average HS GPA	3.7
% submitting high school GPA	100

Important Dates

Early decision	
Apply by	11/15
Notified by	12/30
Early action	
Apply by	11/15
Notified by	12/30
Regular	
Apply by	2/1
Notified by	4/15
Nonfall registration?	No

FINANCIAL FACTS

Annual tuition	$37,996
Food and housing	$21,048
Required fees	$990
Books and supplies	$1,220
Average need-based scholarship (First-year)	$10,786 ($9,275)
% students with need rec. need-based scholarship or grant aid (First-year)	80 (80)
% students with need rec. non-need-based scholarship or grant aid (First-year)	92 (96)
% students with need rec. need-based self-help aid (First-year)	67 (61)
% students rec. any financial aid (First-year)	99 (100)
% UG borrow to pay for school	63
Average cumulative indebtedness	$34,465
% of students with need fully met (First-year)	10 (10)
Average % of student need met (First-year)	50 (59)

Illinois Institute of Technology

10 West 35th Street, Chicago, IL 60616 • Admissions: 312-567-3025

Survey Snapshot
Students love Chicago, IL
College radio is popular
Easy to get around campus

RATINGS

Quality of Life	79
Fire Safety	60*
Green	60*
Academic	75
Profs Interesting	82
Profs Accessible	88
Admissions	89
Financial Aid	90

CAMPUS LIFE

Type of school	Private
Environment	Metropolis

Students

Degree-seeking undergrad enrollment	2,828
% male/female/not reported	65/34/1
% from out of state	32
% First-year live on campus	62
% Ugrads live on campus	44
# of fraternities (% join)	7 (8)
# of sororities (% join)	3 (10)
% Asian	16
% Black or African American	6
% Hispanic	28
% Native American	<1
% Pacific Islander	0
% Race and/or ethnicity unknown	2
% Two or more races	4
% White	31
% International	14
# of countries represented	54

CAMPUS MENTAL HEALTH SERVICES

Offers mental health/wellness program	Yes
Mental health training available to students	No
Employs Chief Wellness Officer	NR
Peer-to-peer mental health offerings	NR
Counseling center has guidelines or accreditation	No
Mental health/well-being courses	NR

ACADEMICS

% students returning for sophomore year	86
% students graduating within 4 years	34
% students graduating within 6 years	75
Calendar	Semester
Most common class size 10–19.	(26%)
Most common lab/discussion size 1–9.	(63%)

Most Popular Majors

Architecture; Computer and Information Sciences; Mechanical Engineering

Applicants Also Look At

Bradley University, California Polytechnic State University—San Luis Obispo, Case Western Reserve University, DePaul University, Georgia Institute of Technology, Iowa State University, Loyola University Chicago, Marquette University, Milwaukee School of Engineering, Northwestern University, Purdue University—West Lafayette, Rensselaer Polytechnic Institute, Rochester Institute of Technology, Rose—Hulman Institute of Technology, University of Illinois at Chicago, University of Illinois at Urbana—Champaign, University of Michigan—Ann Arbor, University of Minnesota—Twin Cities, University of Wisconsin—Madison, Worcester Polytechnic Institute

STUDENTS SAY "..."

Academics

The Illinois Institute of Technology teaches students what "you really need to know…in the professional world." That means that coursework is "very challenging but rewarding," and that rigor is well-matched by "a lot of support available" from the faculty, the administration, and the "student culture of helping each other." This support is underpinned by the school's relatively small size, which allows for "lots of close peer interaction" and "a lot of attention from faculty." Incoming students can expect to jump right into hands-on learning. As one student says, "[In] my very first electrical engineering class, I got to build an autonomous robot car!" The opportunities for hands-on learning only increase during your time at Illinois Tech. For example, every student is required to complete the Interprofessional Projects (IPRO) Program. As the school explains, IPRO "joins students from various majors to work together to solve real-world problems, often on behalf of sponsor companies and nonprofits." Students say the IPRO courses "are a cool way to get involved in innovative projects" and they enjoy collaborating with their classmates. Students also praise Illinois Tech for its "great networking opportunities with great companies in Chicago" and the fact that just about "everyone gets scholarships." They feel confident stepping out into the job market knowing that "the curriculum is adapted to current technologies and is frequently updated to reflect what is necessary within the workforce."

Campus Life

This "compact but not cramped" walkable campus is "pretty convenient," and architecture majors especially appreciate studying on a "masterpiece campus" designed by the famous architect Mies Van der Rohe. When it comes to extracurriculars, students note that there's not that much variety—although students do have "freedom and autonomy" to pursue their passions, hence organizations like the comedy club, the community radio station, and the esports club. Just as students tend to be "academically driven," so too do most clubs represent professional interests, such as the Women in STEM group, the pre-med student organizations, and the chemistry club. Many students are involved in athletics and "intramural sports are always something to be excited about." Students note that "Greek Life here is very relaxed and feels more like a community." When students get a break from studying, they can hang out at the Bog, the on-campus "arcade/bowling alley/bar." The school's own train stop (and free transit pass for students) makes for easy public transit throughout Chicago, whether you want to eat, see a concert, or visit a museum. There's "also a beach a mile from campus, with bike/running trails to spend time on." Ultimately students acknowledge that "you get out what you put in" and for those who "make an effort to be social and take part in any of the many activities on campus, community is flourishing and welcoming."

Student Body

Illinois Tech draws a hardworking and collaborative crowd. It's a community where "everyone is willing to help each other" and "homework is often completed in groups." Incoming students can expect to join a group of "highly intelligent individuals who are passionate about school." In other words, "people study for fun." For this group, that's a feature, not a bug. As one student says, "I love how much all of my peers care about school. I also love that even though many of my friends are different majors, we are all still STEM majors." Illinois Tech has many international students and students from the Chicago area, as well as classmates who "come from all over the country." The result is a diverse group of people who all have unique interests. While the student body, as a whole, would not be called extroverted, classmates will come out of their shells "when prompted with conversation." As one student elaborates, "For the most part, [my peers] simply require an icebreaker to uncover everything." Once you get them talking, it's easy to be inspired by this "creative and innovative" group.

ILLINOIS INSTITUTE OF TECHNOLOGY

Financial Aid: 312-567-7219 • E-Mail: admission@iit.edu • Website: www.iit.edu

THE PRINCETON REVIEW SAYS

Admissions

The school reports that its standardized testing policy for use in admission for Fall 2026 is Test Optional. The Princeton Review suggests that interested applicants consult with the school for the most up-to-date standardized testing policies. *Very important factors considered include:* rigor of secondary school record, academic GPA. *Other factors considered include:* class rank, standardized test scores, application essay, recommendation(s), extracurricular activities, talent/ability, character/personal qualities, volunteer work, work experience. High school diploma is required and GED is accepted. *Academic units required:* 4 English, 4 math, 3 science, 2 social studies. *Academic units recommended:* 4 English, 4 math, 3 science, 2 science labs, 2 language (other than English), 2 social studies, 2 history, 1 computer science, 1 visual/performing arts.

Financial Aid

Students should submit: FAFSA. Priority filing deadline is 10/1. The Princeton Review suggests that all financial aid forms be submitted as soon as possible. *Need-based scholarships/grants offered:* Federal Pell; Federal SEOG; State scholarships/grants; Private scholarships; College/university scholarship or grant aid from institutional funds. *Loan aid offered:* Federal Direct Subsidized Loans; Federal Direct Unsubsidized Loans; Direct PLUS loans; College/university loans from institutional funds. Admitted students will be notified of awards on a rolling basis beginning 2/15. Federal Work-Study Program available. Institutional employment available.

The Inside Word

Admission is competitive, drawing students who may qualify for top tech schools like MIT and CalTech. So, while the acceptance rate seems promising, you are competing against some very high achievers. Accordingly, it would be smart to emphasize work ethic and career goals to win over admission officers at this academically demanding and career-driven school. Extracurriculars and leadership roles always look good, but you should especially highlight any STEM-based activities outside the classroom.

THE SCHOOL SAYS

From the Admissions Office

"As Chicago's leading tech university, Illinois Tech provides students with a distinctive and relevant education through hands-on learning, dedicated teachers, small class sizes, and research opportunities. From high-tech maker spaces to cutting-edge research, we prepare students to think big and lead big like no other university can. Classes are taught by senior faculty—not teaching assistants—who foster our culture of innovation with their own research experience. Our one-of-a-kind Elevate program ensures that our students develop the twenty-first century skills that employers seek and that they graduate with career readiness. Elevate guarantees our students access to hands-on experiences such as internships, research, study away, competitions, and short courses, while also providing them with academic and career mentorship.

"A thriving ecosystem for startups and for advancements in tech, Chicago is a living lab where Illinois Tech students apply what they learn in the classroom through real-world opportunities. Students also receive a multitude of opportunities for networking, internships, and mentorship, as well as opportunities for job placement. Illinois Tech's Accelerated Master's Program allows students to complete both a bachelor's and master's degree in as few as five years. Undergraduate scholarships apply to the fifth year of study, meaning students pay the lower undergraduate tuition rate for graduate courses. In our unique Discover+ degree program, students have the freedom to wait until year two to choose their majors—all while receiving guidance from experienced professional advisers.

"Illinois Tech strives to make higher education accessible for all. Ninety-eight percent of undergraduates receive some form of financial aid, including merit-based scholarships ranging from $20,000 to full tuition."

SELECTIVITY

# of total applicants	12,216
% of total applicants accepted	55
% of total acceptees attending	8
# of early decision applicants	146
% of early decision applicants accepted	36

First-Year Profile

Testing policy	Test Optional
Range SAT composite	1190–1300
Range SAT EBRW	590–680
Range SAT math	590–720
Range ACT composite	26–32
% submitting SAT scores	30
% submitting ACT scores	8
% graduated top 10% of class	45
% graduated top 25% of class	77
% graduated top 50% of class	94
% submitting high school rank	13

Important Dates

Early decision	
Apply by	11/1
Notified by	12/1
Other ED apply by	1/1
Other ED notified by	2/1
Early action	
Apply by	11/15
Notified by	1/3
Regular	
Apply by	8/1
Notified by	Rolling, 10/1
Nonfall registration?	Yes

FINANCIAL FACTS

Annual tuition	$50,636
Food and housing	$17,356
Required fees (First-year)	$1,750 ($2,100)
Books and supplies	$1,240
Average need-based scholarship (First-year)	$43,609 ($47,812)
% students with need rec. need-based scholarship or grant aid (First-year)	100 (100)
% students with need rec. non-need-based scholarship or grant aid (First-year)	15 (15)
% students with need rec. need-based self-help aid (First-year)	52 (53)
% UG borrow to pay for school	53
Average cumulative indebtedness	$30,454
% of students with need fully met (First-year)	16 (16)
Average % of student need met (First-year)	82 (87)

ILLINOIS WESLEYAN UNIVERSITY

1312 N. Park St., Bloomington, IL 61702-2900 • Admissions: 309-556-3031

Survey Snapshot
Students get along with local community
Easy to get around campus
Recreation facilities are great

RATINGS	
Quality of Life	81
Fire Safety	92
Green	60*
Academic	81
Profs Interesting	84
Profs Accessible	90
Admissions	89
Financial Aid	89

CAMPUS LIFE

Type of school	Private
Environment	City

Students

Degree-seeking undergrad enrollment	1,683
% male/female/not reported	47/52/1
% from out of state	15
% First-year from public high school	85
% First-year live on campus	97
% Ugrads live on campus	88
# of fraternities (% join)	4 (22)
# of sororities (% join)	4 (22)
% Asian	5
% Black or African American	9
% Hispanic	13
% Native American	<1
% Pacific Islander	0
% Race and/or ethnicity unknown	3
% Two or more races	4
% White	62
% International	4
# of countries represented	25

CAMPUS MENTAL HEALTH SERVICES

Offers mental health/wellness program	Yes
Mental health training available to students	Yes
Employs Chief Wellness Officer	Yes
Peer-to-peer mental health offerings	No
Counseling center has guidelines or accreditation	Yes
Mental health/well-being courses	Yes, for-credit

ACADEMICS

% students returning for sophomore year	82
% students graduating within 4 years	67
% students graduating within 6 years	73
Calendar	4-4-1
Student/faculty ratio	12:1
Most common class size 10–19.	(45%)
Most common lab/discussion size 10–19.	(48%)

Most Popular Majors

Registered Nursing/Registered Nurse; Business/Commerce; Accounting

Applicants Also Look At

Augustana College (IL), Bradley University, DePaul University, Illinois State University, Loyola University Chicago, Northern Illinois University, Northwestern University, The University of Chicago, University of Illinois at Chicago, University of Illinois at Urbana—Champaign

STUDENTS SAY "..."

Academics

Located in Bloomington, Illinois Wesleyan University is a community that "invites you to make the most of your education and is ready to bend over backwards to ensure you enjoy your experience." Though the school doesn't have that big of a reputation outside the Midwest "despite its excellent education," it is an underrated gem that is "always trying to give students opportunities that are beyond what most schools can give." It truly is "a small school that oozes big opportunities." Professors are "brilliant and accessible" "insightful" individuals who are "the best in their field." "The exuberance they have for their subject area and their students is very evident." Many of them are involved in research and "often include students in helping them," while others are involved in other ways; for example, "the [former] mayor of Bloomington is also a political science professor—how cool is that!" "There have been a few life-changing professors who I am so grateful to have taken their class," says a business administration major.

Facilities and the career center are excellent, there are numerous opportunities for community engagement and research, and "there are so many resources and programs that help students who are seeking any type of support, whether it be academic, moral, or health." Wesleyan also "does a great job getting students ready for graduate school," and faculty "put [a lot of] effort into the information being taught, and really try and relate it to real life." The school has a reputation for "overinvolved students who travel abroad, are the president of three clubs, and still maintain excellent grades." "IWU pushes us to excel academically while encouraging us to pursue our passions outside of our schoolwork," says a student. Overall, IWU is "a friendly community where your professors become mentors, your classmates become lifelong friends, and you graduate prepared to make a real difference in the world."

Campus Life

As with many colleges, there's a strong weekday-weekend divide: "There is a fair trade of work and play." Sunday through Wednesday nights, "people are studying, going to meetings for clubs, maybe going to an event or two," but come the weekend, students "will go to parties at fraternity houses or off-campus houses, or go to the bars." Bloomington—Normal also has a variety of "great restaurants" and shopping venues which "are fun places to go to on the weekends," and neighboring ISU offers "some of that big college town culture [that] can be found in the area."

The Office of Student Activities "does a great job having entertainment available for students" and almost every weekend a free event is held in the student center, "whether that be a concert, comedian, movie, or other entertainment." Because "people are very receptive to getting work done together," you can find a "plethora of study groups," as well as "great opportunities for intellectual discussions" at the coffee shop, and "students are always in food areas discussing, reading, or doing homework."

Student Body

The typical Wesleyan student "has a major that they take great pride in studying" and "often compare workloads to bond." Students here are "very academically focused" ("it's very rare to find students who don't try") but are also aware that "having a social life is important as well." Almost everyone is "very liberal and rather artistic" and "very involved with many different activities." While there are noticeable groups such as "athletes, Greek life, and theater kids" which mainly stick together, "everyone has friends in other departments and organizations." There is "lots of competition on campus for internships and research opportunities," but "everyone is very helpful when it comes to informing others of opportunities." A "large percentage" of the campus is Greek life-affiliated.

Illinois Wesleyan University

Financial Aid: 309-556-3096 • E-Mail: iwuadmit@iwu.edu • Website: www.iwu.edu

THE PRINCETON REVIEW SAYS

Admissions

The school reports that its standardized testing policy for use in admission for Fall 2026 is Test Optional. The Princeton Review suggests that interested applicants consult with the school for the most up-to-date standardized testing policies. *Very important factors considered include:* rigor of secondary school record, class rank, academic GPA. *Important factors considered include:* application essay, extracurricular activities. *Other factors considered include:* standardized test scores, recommendation(s), talent/ability, character/personal qualities, volunteer work, work experience, level of applicant's interest. High school diploma is required and GED is accepted. *Academic units recommended:* 4 English, 3 math, 3 science, 2 science labs, 3 language (other than English), 2 social studies.

Financial Aid

Students should submit: FAFSA. Priority filing deadline is 11/1. The Princeton Review suggests that all financial aid forms be submitted as soon as possible. *Need-based scholarships/grants offered:* Federal Pell; Federal SEOG; State scholarships/grants; College/university scholarship or grant aid from institutional funds; Private scholarships. *Loan aid offered:* Federal Direct Subsidized Loans; Federal Direct Unsubsidized Loans; Direct PLUS loans; College/university loans from institutional funds. Federal Work-Study Program available. Institutional employment available.

The Inside Word

There's no application fee at IWU, and the school accepts the Common Application, so there are few reasons not to apply to IWU if you're even slightly interested in attending. Don't expect to breeze through, though. You won't get into this selective college without a solid academic profile or a compelling story. Those applying to any of the creative arts schools may be required to submit additional materials such as a portfolio.

THE SCHOOL SAYS

From the Admissions Office

"Illinois Wesleyan University attracts a wide variety of students who are interested in pursuing diverse fields such as vocal performance, biology, psychology, political science, physics, or business administration. At IWU, students are not forced into either/or choices. Rather, they are encouraged to pursue multiple interests simultaneously—a philosophy that is in keeping with the spirit and value of a liberal arts education. The distinctive 4-4-1 calendar allows students to follow their interests each school year in two semesters followed by an optional month-long class in May. May Term opportunities include classes on campus; research collaboration with faculty; travel and study in such places as Australia, China, South Africa, and Europe; as well as local, national, and international internships. Study abroad is very popular, with one out of every two students enjoying a travel experience.

"The IWU mission statement reads in part: 'A liberal education at Illinois Wesleyan fosters creativity, critical thinking, effective communication, strength of character, and a spirit of inquiry; it deepens the specialized knowledge of a discipline with a comprehensive world view. It affords the greatest possibilities for realizing individual potential while preparing students for democratic citizenship and life in a global society....The university, through its policies, programs, and practices, is committed to diversity, social justice, and environmental sustainability. A tightly knit, supportive university community, together with a variety of opportunities for close interaction with excellent faculty, both challenges and supports students in their personal and intellectual development.'"

SELECTIVITY

# of total applicants	11,195
% of total applicants accepted	49
% of total acceptees attending	10
# offered a place on the wait list	0
# admitted from wait list	0

First-Year Profile

Testing policy	Test Optional
Range SAT composite	1110–1300
Range SAT EBRW	550–670
Range SAT math	530–630
Range ACT composite	26–31
% submitting SAT scores	26
% submitting ACT scores	8
Average HS GPA	3.8
% submitting high school GPA	99

Important Dates

Early action	
Apply by	11/15
Notified by	12/15
Regular	
Notified by	Rolling, 9/26
Nonfall registration?	Yes

FINANCIAL FACTS

Annual tuition	$61,004
Food and housing	$14,440
Required fees	$234
Books and supplies	$800
Average need-based scholarship (First-year)	$45,980 ($49,784)
% students with need rec. need-based scholarship or grant aid (First-year)	100 (100)
% students with need rec. non-need-based scholarship or grant aid (First-year)	17 (19)
% students with need rec. need-based self-help aid (First-year)	73 (75)
% students rec. any financial aid (First-year)	100 (100)
% UG borrow to pay for school	76
Average cumulative indebtedness	$32,218
% of students with need fully met (First-year)	22 (23)
Average % of student need met (First-year)	89 (92)

Indiana University—Bloomington

107 S. Indiana Avenue, Bloomington, IN 47405-7000 • Admissions: 812-855-0661

Survey Snapshot
Students love Bloomington, IN
Recreation facilities are great
Everyone loves the Hoosiers

RATINGS

Quality of Life	**83**
Fire Safety	**97**
Green	**90**
Academic	**83**
Profs Interesting	**89**
Profs Accessible	**94**
Admissions	**88**
Financial Aid	**85**

CAMPUS LIFE

Type of school	Public
Environment	City

Students

Degree-seeking undergrad enrollment	38,177
% male/female/not reported	50/50/<1
% from out of state	43
% First-year live on campus	97
% Ugrads live on campus	33
# of fraternities (% join)	37 (23)
# of sororities (% join)	33 (22)
% Asian	12
% Black or African American	5
% Hispanic	9
% Native American	<1
% Pacific Islander	<1
% Race and/or ethnicity unknown	1
% Two or more races	6
% White	63
% International	4
# of countries represented	135

CAMPUS MENTAL HEALTH SERVICES

Offers mental health/wellness program	Yes
Mental health training available to students	Yes
Employs Chief Wellness Officer	Yes
Peer-to-peer mental health offerings	No
Counseling center has guidelines or accreditation	Yes
Mental health/well-being courses	Yes, non-credit

ACADEMICS

% students returning for sophomore year	90
% students graduating within 4 years	70
% students graduating within 6 years	80
Calendar	Semester
Student/faculty ratio	17:1
Most common class size 20–29.	(25%)
Most common lab/discussion size 20–29.	(37%)

Most Popular Majors

Biology/Biological Sciences; Kinesiology and Exercise Science; Business/Commerce

Applicants Also Look At

The Ohio State University—Columbus, Purdue University—West Lafayette, University of Illinois at Urbana—Champaign, University of Michigan—Ann Arbor, University of Wisconsin—Milwaukee

STUDENTS SAY "..."

Academics

Indiana University Bloomington provides its Hoosier students "the knowledge to be successful in our futures through great faculty, facilities, and tradition." That translates to 16 separate colleges and "school systems [that] are great and easy to access," with enrollees noting that they can explore "anything we want, whenever," an ability that ultimately helps them find "the key thing we'll love through many opportunities and great programs." IU endeavors toward that discovery by proudly offering students access to courses outside of their designated field, allowing them to guide their own research, and providing the opportunity to personalize one's education through the Individualized Major Program. Other favorite academic features at IU are the "world-renowned business program" at the Kelley School of Business and the Jacobs School of Music, both of which attract students from around the globe. Courses across campus are known for being "rigorous," and students collaborate "academically and non-academically as one community." Guidance and support also come from "many excellent professors" on campus that "clearly want what's best for their students." One student points out that "communicating with students/professors is easy." Another student explains that their instructors "really care about what they do" and "bring their subjects to life." With that in mind, students feel equipped to get the most out of this "rigorous and competitive" education.

Campus Life

Indiana University Bloomington offers "the perfect combination of excellent undergraduate teaching, Division I athletic teams backed by a passionate sense of school spirit, and a lively social scene." One student reports that "academics and school spirit are [the] specialties," so when not studying, a weekend for Hoosier families in the fall features a tailgate party; basketball season kicks off with a rally known as Hoosier Hysteria; and IU hosts the Little 500 each year, a stadium-based bicycle race that's modeled after the Indianapolis 500. In their free time, Hoosiers can be found "working out" or "running" regularly. Students also like to unwind by the fire pit or watch free movies at the Indiana Memorial Union, or get involved in one of the many clubs on campus. Off campus, "the vibrant city of Bloomington" (or "B-town," as the students describe it) is "the best-kept secret of the Midwest." Food is a particular highlight, with "many options to choose from," all described as "amazing." The town also hosts the Lotus World Music and Arts Festival as well as Freezefest, an ice-sculpture competition. In warmer months, nearby Griffy Lake and Monroe Lake offer kayaking, canoeing, and boating. And for the Hoosiers in need of repose, like-minded peers can be found "lying outside on the grass and on benches snoozing." Thanks to student groups having "much freedom of planning," it seems there's "always something going on...that will fit the needs of any student."

Student Body

With more than 37,000 undergraduate students at IU, "you are destined to find someone whom you 'click' with." On campus and around Bloomington, "Hoosier Hospitality" is a huge perk for IU students, and students find their niche at one of the 750-plus student organizations on campus, athletic events, or just hanging out at Indiana Memorial Union on campus. One student emphasizes that students on campus are "very respectful of one another and ready to help out a fellow Hoosier." Generally, Hoosiers are known for finding "an equal balance of school and social life" and being "hard workers who also know how to have fun on the weekends." Between "popular" house parties and the 25% of undergrads who join one of the 60+ fraternities, there's "a strong social scene" at IU. But regardless of your scene, students find IU to be a "fun collegiate environment."

INDIANA UNIVERSITY—BLOOMINGTON

Financial Aid: 812-855-6500 • E-Mail: admissions@iu.edu • Website: www.indiana.edu

THE PRINCETON REVIEW SAYS

Admissions

The school reports that its standardized testing policy for use in admission for Fall 2026 is Test Optional. The Princeton Review suggests that interested applicants consult with the school for the most up-to-date standardized testing policies. *Very important factors considered include:* rigor of secondary school record, class rank, academic GPA. *Important factors considered include:* standardized test scores, application essay. *Other factors considered include:* recommendation(s), interview, extracurricular activities, talent/ability, character/personal qualities, first generation, geographical residence, state residency, volunteer work, work experience. High school diploma is required and GED is accepted. *Academic units required:* 8 English, 7 math, 6 science, 4 science labs, 4 language (other than English), 4 social studies, 2 history, 3 academic electives.

Financial Aid

Students should submit: FAFSA. Priority filing deadline is 4/15. The Princeton Review suggests that all financial aid forms be submitted as soon as possible. *Need-based scholarships/grants offered:* Federal Pell; Federal SEOG; State scholarships/grants; Private scholarships; College/university scholarship or grant aid from institutional funds. *Loan aid offered:* Federal Direct Subsidized Loans; Federal Direct Unsubsidized Loans; Direct PLUS loans; College/university loans from institutional funds. Admitted students will be notified of awards on a rolling basis beginning 2/15. Federal Work-Study Program available. Institutional employment available.

The Inside Word

Above-average high school performers (defined by grade point average and/or test scores) should meet little resistance from the IU admissions office. Students also have the opportunity to meet admissions representatives at numerous recruiting events held in many locations throughout the country or during a campus visit. IU's music program is highly competitive; admission hinges upon a successful audition.

THE SCHOOL SAYS

From the Admissions Office

"Indiana University Bloomington provides the ideal college experience that prepares students for a successful future. Students enjoy the advantages, opportunities, and resources of a large school while still receiving personal attention and support. Students come to IU from all fifty states and more than 110 countries, bringing their diverse backgrounds, experiences, and beliefs to provide opportunities to connect with and learn from each other. They converge on one of the most beautiful and inspiring campuses in the country. When visiting campus, students and parents often describe IU as 'what college should be like.' Outstanding academic and cultural resources combine to provide space to grow and a place to excel.

"Indiana University is a top teaching and research university that provides students with countless opportunities to expand knowledge and skills in and out of the classroom. Offering 200+ majors and more than 4,000 courses, students can study the arts, sciences, humanities, social sciences, languages, technology, and engineering to create the perfect academic path to reach their goals. Students engage in hands-on experiences to enhance learning and build marketable skills, including internships, research opportunities, mentorships, service-learning courses, and study abroad. Those experiences are valuable when students meet with the businesses, government agencies, and not-for-profit organizations that come to campus each year to recruit, with over 2,500 students participating in on-campus interviews each year.

"Applicants must submit a complete application for admission, including official transcripts, and SAT/ACT scores (if applicable) by November 1 to receive highest consideration for IU Academic Scholarships."

SELECTIVITY

# of total applicants	74,077
% of total applicants accepted	76
% of total acceptees attending	18
# of in-state applicants	17,458
% of in-state applicants accepted	72
# of out-of-state-applicants	50,700
% of applicants accepted from out of state	79
# of international applicants	5,919
% of international applicants accepted	64
# offered a place on the wait list	6,271
# admitted from wait list	97

First-Year Profile

Testing policy	Test Optional
Range SAT composite	1200–1410
Range SAT EBRW	610–700
Range SAT math	590–710
Range ACT composite	28–33
% submitting SAT scores	43
% submitting ACT scores	15
Average HS GPA	3.8
% submitting high school GPA	95
% graduated top 10% of class	31
% graduated top 25% of class	63
% graduated top 50% of class	93
% submitting high school rank	27

Important Dates

Early action	
Apply by	11/1
Notified by	1/15
Regular	
Notified by	1/15
Nonfall registration?	Yes

FINANCIAL FACTS

Annual in-state tuition	$10,622
Annual out-of-state tuition	$40,369
Food and housing	$14,160
Required fees	$1,522
Books and supplies	$1,290
Average need-based scholarship (First-year)	$15,861 ($15,719)
% students with need rec. need-based scholarship or grant aid (First-year)	87 (89)
% students with need rec. non-need-based scholarship or grant aid (First-year)	11 (12)
% students with need rec. need-based self-help aid (First-year)	45 (43)
% students rec. any financial aid (First-year)	79 (83)
% UG borrow to pay for school	40
Average cumulative indebtedness	$32,238
% of students with need fully met (First-year)	19 (21)
Average % of student need met (First-year)	66 (65)

Indiana University of Pennsylvania

1011 South Drive, Indiana, PA 15705-1085 • Admissions: 724-357-2230

Survey Snapshot
Frats and sororities are popular
Dorms are like palaces
Students are happy

RATINGS

Quality of Life	80
Fire Safety	97
Green	60*
Academic	73
Profs Interesting	83
Profs Accessible	87
Admissions	81
Financial Aid	84

CAMPUS LIFE

Type of school	Public
Environment	Village

Students

Degree-seeking undergrad enrollment	6,922
% male/female/not reported	38/62/0
% from out of state	4
% First-year live on campus	87
% Ugrads live on campus	43
# of fraternities (% join)	11 (9)
# of sororities (% join)	14 (8)
% Asian	1
% Black or African American	10
% Hispanic	6
% Native American	1
% Pacific Islander	<1
% Race and/or ethnicity unknown	2
% Two or more races	5
% White	75
% International	1
# of countries represented	35

CAMPUS MENTAL HEALTH SERVICES

Offers mental health/wellness program	Yes
Mental health training available to students	Yes
Employs Chief Wellness Officer	No
Peer-to-peer mental health offerings	Yes
Counseling center has guidelines or accreditation	Yes
Mental health/well-being courses	Yes, for-credit

ACADEMICS

% students returning for sophomore year	75
% students graduating within 4 years	38
% students graduating within 6 years	52
Calendar	Semester
Student/faculty ratio	18:1
Most common class size 20–29.	(32%)

Most Popular Majors

Psychology; Criminology; Registered Nursing/ Registered Nurse

Applicants Often Prefer

Bloomsburg University of Pennsylvania, Penn State University Park, Penn West—California, Robert Morris University, Shippensburg University of Pennsylvania, Slippery Rock University of Pennsylvania, University of Pittsburgh—Pittsburgh Campus

STUDENTS SAY "..."

Academics

From the first day a student sets foot on the Indiana University of Pennsylvania campus, they receive highly personalized attention and support. Each student is immediately assigned a professional mentor, and students say one of the school's greatest strengths are these "staff and faculty who aim to help the students academically, personally, or professionally." Affirms one student, "they want to ensure we all have a good and safe experience at IUP." Class sizes "are small, so there is more one-on-one time with professors," and "[there are] a lot of resources that you can use if you need help, whether it's with academics or [wellness]." Among students' most appreciated aspects of the school are the "variety of academic choices, the writing center, "and the "state-of-the-art labs with amazing resources." Also, "through the multicultural center there are a lot of programs that focus on leadership and all of the soft skills."

Professors "care a lot about the success of their students and go out of their way to help them to truly understand what is being taught." The amount of work a student puts in shapes the relationship with the teachers, and "you have to try in your classes and be present, [but] they will notice you if you do." Classes can be lecture-style or "very discussion-based, [which] it makes it interesting to know everyone's opinion on a topic," and some incorporate field trips or outdoor classrooms. "For my language development class, we had a project where we had to find a child and do a book reading activity with them in order to practice using book reading as a method of treatment for those with language impairments," says a student.

Campus Life

Students say that even though "most people are in a routine of going to classes, studying, and either balancing work, an extracurricular, or a varsity sport," the "workload [is] challenging but doable." Part of this credit goes to the school itself, which is "good at making sure everyone feels included with the various clubs and activities," features many "organizations to join that are both fun and helpful for jobs outside of school," and is "amazing at communicating these opportunities." Off-campus, the town of Indiana "is small so there is not much to do besides explore Main Street and outdoor hiking/ activities," but students agree "it's great to walk around during the fall and spring." All in all, the "opportunity that IUP provides students in terms of activities, networking, and future career guidance" is at a high level, especially for "great on-campus job[s]" and there are "a lot of resources around campus to help you with anything you could think of."

Student Body

The community found at IUP "is widely diverse, yet inclusive, [which] creates a wonderful environment to want to be a part of." Students here are "supportive, collaborative, and unique" and "provide a welcoming environment for [incoming] students" of all kinds, including the "very welcoming" LGBTQIA student body and international population. This is "a group of people that likes to try new things from cooking, workout, intense board games, or watching a sports game on campus," and "everyone has their own style and views," and "seems to be respectful of each other." People here are "very well-rounded along with committed to working together as a whole" and "are attentive in class, make smart [decisions], and are passionate about their futures." This bond transcends academic interests; as a student says, "It is so easy to make friends here, even in classes that don't pertain to your major."

INDIANA UNIVERSITY OF PENNSYLVANIA

Financial Aid: 724-357-2218 • E-Mail: admissions-inquiry@iup.edu • Website: www.iup.edu

THE PRINCETON REVIEW SAYS

Admissions

The school reports that its standardized testing policy for use in admission for Fall 2026 is Test Optional. The Princeton Review suggests that interested applicants consult with the school for the most up-to-date standardized testing policies. *Very important factors considered include:* academic GPA. *Important factors considered include:* rigor of secondary school record. *Other factors considered include:* standardized test scores, application essay, recommendation(s), interview, extracurricular activities, talent/ability, character/personal qualities, first generation. High school diploma is required and GED is accepted. *Academic units required:* 4 English, 3 math, 3 science, 2 science lab. *Academic units recommended:* 2 language (other than English), 3 social studies.

Financial Aid

Students should submit: FAFSA; State aid form. Priority filing deadline is 5/1. The Princeton Review suggests that all financial aid forms be submitted as soon as possible. *Need-based scholarships/grants offered:* Federal Pell; Federal SEOG; State scholarships/grants; Private scholarships; College/university scholarship or grant aid from institutional funds; United Negro College Fund. *Loan aid offered:* Federal Direct Subsidized Loans; Federal Direct Unsubsidized Loans; Direct PLUS loans. Admitted students will be notified of awards on a rolling basis beginning 11/20. Federal Work-Study Program available. Institutional employment available.

The Inside Word

Admissions officers at Indiana University of Pennsylvania pay closest attention to academic preparation and performance when considering applications. Officers typically only consider personal statements, recommendations, and extracurricular participation for applicants on the border of eligibility. Finally, IUP has rolling admissions, so it's to your benefit to apply as early as possible.

THE SCHOOL SAYS

From the Admissions Office

"At IUP, we look at each applicant as an individual, not as a number. That means we'll review your application materials very carefully. When reviewing applications, the admissions committee's primary focus is on the student's high school record. We're always happy to speak with prospective students. E-mail us at admissions-inquiry@iup.edu."

SELECTIVITY

# of total applicants	7,951
% of total applicants accepted	91
% of total acceptees attending	26
# of in-state applicants	7,397
% of in-state applicants accepted	91
# of out-of-state-applicants	441
% of applicants accepted from out of state	92
# of international applicants	113
% of international applicants accepted	98

First-Year Profile

Testing policy	Test Optional
Range SAT composite	970–1070
Range SAT EBRW	500–620
Range SAT math	450–570
Range ACT composite	16–28
% submitting SAT scores	28
% submitting ACT scores	2
Average HS GPA	3.3
% submitting high school GPA	98

Important Dates

Regular	
Notified by	Rolling, 9/1
Nonfall registration?	Yes

FINANCIAL FACTS

Annual in-state tuition	$8,090
Annual out-of-state tuition	$11,732
Food and housing	$12,008
Required fees (out-of-state)	$3,846 ($5,351)
Books and supplies	$1,100
Average need-based scholarship (First-year)	$9,029 ($9,437)
% students with need rec. need-based scholarship or grant aid (First-year)	74 (73)
% students with need rec. non-need-based scholarship or grant aid (First-year)	88 (98)
% students with need rec. need-based self-help aid (First-year)	80 (83)
% students rec. any financial aid (First-year)	75 (71)
% UG borrow to pay for school	79
Average cumulative indebtedness	$35,326
% of students with need fully met (First-year)	19 (19)
Average % of student need met (First-year)	75 (78)

IONA UNIVERSITY

715 North Avenue, New Rochelle, NY 10801-1890 • Admissions: 914-633-2502

Survey Snapshot
Easy to get around campus
Great off-campus food
Students are happy

RATINGS

Quality of Life	88
Fire Safety	92
Green	60*
Academic	75
Profs Interesting	87
Profs Accessible	88
Admissions	81
Financial Aid	88

CAMPUS LIFE

Type of school	Private
Affiliation	Roman Catholic
Environment	City

Students

Degree-seeking undergrad enrollment	2,933
% male/female/not reported	47/53/<1
% from out of state	19
% First-year from public high school	57
% First-year live on campus	52
% Ugrads live on campus	41
# of fraternities (% join)	4 (5)
# of sororities (% join)	7 (18)
% Asian	3
% Black or African American	9
% Hispanic	34
% Native American	<1
% Pacific Islander	<1
% Race and/or ethnicity unknown	3
% Two or more races	3
% White	46
% International	3
# of countries represented	32

CAMPUS MENTAL HEALTH SERVICES

Offers mental health/wellness program	Yes
Mental health training available to students	Yes
Employs Chief Wellness Officer	Yes
Peer-to-peer mental health offerings	Yes
Counseling center has guidelines or accreditation	Yes
Mental health/well-being courses	Yes, for-credit

ACADEMICS

% students returning for sophomore year	80
% students graduating within 4 years	53
% students graduating within 6 years	59
Calendar	Semester
Student/faculty ratio	15:1
Most common class size 20–29.	(55%)
Most common lab/discussion size 10–19.	(52%)

Most Popular Majors

Psychology; Registered Nursing/Registered Nurse; Marketing/Marketing Management; Mass Communication/Media Studies; Finance

Applicants Also Look At

Adelphi University, City University of New York—Hunter College, City University of New York—Lehman College, Fairfield University, Fordham University, Marist University, Mercy University, Pace University, Quinnipiac University, Sacred Heart University, St. John's University (NY), State University of New York—Stony Brook University, State University of New York—University at Albany, University of Connecticut

STUDENTS SAY "..."

Academics

Iona University is a New York City metropolitan area school that provides a "close-knit, student-centered learning environment and...career-focused academic programs." The school prides itself on sending career-ready students out into the world, and students note that the school is "very organized, which makes it helpful...to know when events are coming and what to look for on the website." Professional development is strongly emphasized; students meet with career services multiple times a year to work on résumés and interviews, optimizing their chances "to intern at some amazing organizations and businesses." Career-focused students appreciate the university's annual career fairs and reputation for having both a "great business school [and] great alumni network." Iona Gaels also have access to resources like the interdisciplinary Hynes Institute for Entrepreneurship & Innovation and the Kelly Center for Health Sciences, which includes an entire floor dedicated to a simulated hospital setting. Likewise, modern facilities incorporate the use of "updated technology in classrooms, like virtual simulations or digital lab tools," allowing for work that is "very hands-on and group-based." There are also "interactive speaker events" as well as off-campus "seminars and conferences to meet with successful people in various fields." All first-year students take part in the foundational Columba Cornerstone course during their first semester, which links to a different core curriculum course and "introduces people to subjects that they might never have tried otherwise" and opens up the idea of cross-disciplinary study. One student sums up: "My academic experience at Iona has shown me how strongly the university values collaboration, hands-on learning, and real-world engagement."

Campus Life

Students relay that Iona's "academics and extracurriculars are fantastic and offer a wide range of activities and topics," and people are "always finding more ways to get involved or create events or programs that are very diverse and engaging." There are multiple organizations to help fill that role, ranging from academically-focused clubs to special interest clubs like esports and fashion. "All of the extracurricular activities are great," says one student. The Division I school has 26 varsity athletic teams, including a men's basketball team that has made it to the NCAA Tournament 16 times. Another agrees that "the games and pre-game events are always so fun and great ways to socialize." Outside of sports, students point to the Center for Student Engagement as another place to find "events to get the student body involved," and for those who want a campus breather, they can "walk to the restaurants here to have a nice dinner or go shopping in Bronxville or White Plains, which have nice shopping centers." Between studying, clubs, and location, "there's a good balance of work and fun, and it's easy to find people to hang out with or things to do."

Student Body

Students appreciate that Iona is a "small school" where "you can find yourself and your friends really fast." This is a "tight-knit community where everyone pretty much knows everyone," and "you create really good connections." The student body is "very friendly," and "even in randomly assigned group work, it is very easy to chat with everyone." While "there are so many people with different backgrounds," they share similar "values which are based on service, integrity, and community." Overall, undergrads describe their peers as "very kind and open to all new kinds of things," and this "high energy student body" is "upbeat and motivated." There are also "a large portion of student athletes, which gives students the chance to bond over sports." The warmth felt at Iona even has its own motto, with one student saying, "We really take 'Gaels take care of Gaels' seriously." Another concurs: "We all look out for one another...I feel safe and a sense of belonging."

IONA UNIVERSITY

Financial Aid: 914-633-2497 • E-Mail: admissions@iona.edu • Website: www.iona.edu

THE PRINCETON REVIEW SAYS

Admissions

The school reports that its standardized testing policy for use in admission for Fall 2026 is Test Optional. The Princeton Review suggests that interested applicants consult with the school for the most up-to-date standardized testing policies. *Very important factors considered include:* rigor of secondary school record, academic GPA, extracurricular activities, character/personal qualities. *Important factors considered include:* application essay, recommendation(s), interview, talent/ability, level of applicant's interest. *Other factors considered include:* class rank, standardized test scores, first generation, alumni/ae relation, geographical residence, volunteer work, work experience. High school diploma is required and GED is accepted. *Academic units required:* 4 English, 3 math, 3 science, 2 science labs, 2 language (other than English), 2 social studies, 1 history, 1 academic elective. *Academic units recommended:* 4 math, 2 history, 3 academic electives.

Financial Aid

Students should submit: FAFSA; State aid form. Priority filing deadline is 2/15. The Princeton Review suggests that all financial aid forms be submitted as soon as possible. *Need-based scholarships/grants offered:* Federal Pell; Federal SEOG; State scholarships/grants; Private scholarships; College/university scholarship or grant aid from institutional funds. *Loan aid offered:* Federal Direct Subsidized Loans; Federal Direct Unsubsidized Loans; Direct PLUS loans. Admitted students will be notified of awards on a rolling basis beginning 2/1. Federal Work-Study Program available. Institutional employment available.

The Inside Word

Iona University has a high rate of acceptance, but admission can still be a competitive process. To put your best foot forward, find ways to demonstrate your personality, ethics, and drive for success—on top of having strong high school coursework, of course. Standardized tests are optional, but absolutely considered if submitted.

THE SCHOOL SAYS

From the Admissions Office

"Iona is where innovation meets opportunity. Here, students are encouraged to see beyond their horizons, find their passions and forge their own paths.

"Iona students enjoy small class sizes, engaged professors and a wide array of undergraduate and graduate programs.

"Iona's picturesque campuses in New Rochelle and Bronxville, N.Y., are both just 20 miles north of Midtown Manhattan. Iona also offers a diverse array of study abroad experiences, offering students an opportunity to immerse themselves in global learning.

"Outside of the classroom, meanwhile, Iona boasts 26 Division I varsity sports and over 100 student clubs and leadership organizations. Iona also has a robust club sports program, including a championship esports team, plus a thriving performing arts program and a wide range of community service opportunities both locally and around the world.

"Founded in 1940, Iona is a Catholic institution inspired by the legacy of Blessed Edmund Rice and the Congregation of Christian Brothers. Find your fit at Iona University today!"

SELECTIVITY

# of total applicants	9,476
% of total applicants accepted	87
% of total acceptees attending	10
# of in-state applicants	6,219
% of in-state applicants accepted	88
# of out-of-state-applicants	2,880
% of applicants accepted from out of state	88
# of international applicants	367
% of international applicants accepted	62
# of early decision applicants	83
% of early decision applicants accepted	100
# offered a place on the wait list	0
# admitted from wait list	0

First-Year Profile

Testing policy	Test Optional
Range SAT composite	1040–1260
Range SAT EBRW	520–650
Range SAT math	500–620
Range ACT composite	21–29
% submitting SAT scores	9
% submitting ACT scores	2
Average HS GPA	3.4
% submitting high school GPA	100
% graduated top 10% of class	8
% graduated top 25% of class	27
% graduated top 50% of class	58
% submitting high school rank	37

Important Dates

Early decision	
Apply by	12/1
Early action	
Apply by	12/15
Notified by	1/15
Regular	
Apply by	2/15
Notified by	Rolling, 1/15
Nonfall registration?	Yes

FINANCIAL FACTS

Annual tuition	$47,960
Food and housing	$19,996
Required fees	$2,210
Books and supplies	$1,000
Average need-based scholarship (First-year)	$29,676 ($31,026)
% students with need rec. need-based scholarship or grant aid (First-year)	97 (98)
% students with need rec. non-need-based scholarship or grant aid (First-year)	23 (24)
% students with need rec. need-based self-help aid (First-year)	53 (55)
% students rec. any financial aid (First-year)	98 (99)
% UG borrow to pay for school	65
Average cumulative indebtedness	$36,077
% of students with need fully met (First-year)	25 (26)
Average % of student need met (First-year)	71 (72)

Iowa State University

100 Enrollment Services Center, Ames, IA 50011 • Admissions: 515-294-5836

Survey Snapshot
Everyone loves the Cyclones
Intramural sports are popular
Frats and sororities are popular

RATINGS

Quality of Life	88
Fire Safety	89
Green	60*
Academic	78
Profs Interesting	85
Profs Accessible	90
Admissions	84
Financial Aid	88

CAMPUS LIFE

Type of school	Public
Environment	Town

Students

Degree-seeking undergrad enrollment	25,359
% male/female/not reported	55/45/<1
% from out of state	40
% First-year live on campus	89
% Ugrads live on campus	31
# of fraternities (% join)	36 (14)
# of sororities (% join)	25 (14)
% Asian	4
% Black or African American	2
% Hispanic	7
% Native American	<1
% Pacific Islander	<1
% Race and/or ethnicity unknown	4
% Two or more races	3
% White	75
% International	4
# of countries represented	91

CAMPUS MENTAL HEALTH SERVICES

Offers mental health/wellness program	Yes
Mental health training available to students	No
Employs Chief Wellness Officer	NR
Peer-to-peer mental health offerings	NR
Counseling center has guidelines or accreditation	No
Mental health/well-being courses	NR

ACADEMICS

% students returning for sophomore year	88
% students graduating within 4 years	57
% students graduating within 6 years	75
Calendar	Semester
Student/faculty ratio	18:1
Most common class size 20–29.	(25%)
Most common lab/discussion size 20–29.	(37%)

STUDENTS SAY "..."

Academics

Iowa State University is the state's largest research university, offering more than 100 majors, most notably in the science and technical fields, including an engineering program which is "practically unrivaled." Other standouts include the aerospace program and the journalism and design schools. The school is "quick to add new courses on developing technology" and even make some courses available online, and an excellent job placement rate means "if you're looking to not just get a job but build a career, you're in the right place." Due to the size of the university, there are a lot of opportunities (such as "getting to tour and even work at some of the cutting-edge research locations in the world"), and teachers will bring in people who work in the field "to talk to you about what their job is like so you can network and learn about your opportunities." In addition to all the classroom and professional resources, there is a largely popular campus lecture series on various topics, and the university is also currently building a student innovation center. "If you are willing to work hard, you can accomplish a lot."

The faculty at the school are "outstanding" and "represent some of the best instructors in the country." Professors "have so much knowledge to share" and include "innovative approaches" in which students "use technology and applications to do assignments." "Not only are they great teachers, but they're great people," says one student. Classes are hands-on and coursework is "challenging in a way that helps [students] know that [they] will be prepared to perform well" in their future careers, but for anyone struggling with their work, "there's a lot of help if you look for it." Overall, students find that Iowa State "offers everything a student needs to succeed" and strives to ensure that every student "succeeds and performs at a high level academically, professionally, and in their personal lives."

Campus Life

Ames is "the perfect college town." Since Iowa State is the main focus, "everyone that lives here cheers for the Cyclones." The school as a whole has "Midwest values," as well as "a plethora of extracurricular opportunities to be involved as a leader or for fun." All of the classes and buildings are located in the same area or near each other to help students avoid being late to class and "a walk across campus is usually only 10 minutes." The fun usually happens on the weekends, with students heading to parties, bars, or sporting events, and there are also "great places to go for dinner, movie theaters, and lots of volunteering opportunities" to keep busy. Clubs (over 800!) "are huge here" and "everyone has their niche." One student says, "Living in a dorm is the best choice" you can make as a first-year student. Dorms often host game tournaments, movie nights, and other events. There's a "state of the art" recreation center (and other facilities), and during nice times of the year, people around campus hammock in the trees and go hiking.

Student Body

According to some students, Iowa State University "lacks diversity as a student body." But students consistently feel that their peers are "very kind, hardworking, and smart," and tend to be "generally a mix of engineering, design, and agriculture students," all of whom comprise "a good mix of people having fun and studying." There is a sizable number of international students at Iowa State, and the entire student body "looks after one another and are always very helpful toward newcomers." The "Iowa Nice" idea is "clearly embodied by the students of Iowa State," and this is "a special breed of people displaying hospitality and kindness in any situation."

IOWA STATE UNIVERSITY

Financial Aid: 515-294-2223 • E-Mail: admissions@iastate.edu • Website: www.iastate.edu

THE PRINCETON REVIEW SAYS

Admissions

The school reports that its standardized testing policy for use in admission for Fall 2026 is Test Optional. The Princeton Review suggests that interested applicants consult with the school for the most up-to-date standardized testing policies. *Very important factors considered include:* rigor of secondary school record, academic GPA. *Important factors considered include:* standardized test scores. *Other factors considered include:* class rank, application essay, recommendation(s), interview, extracurricular activities, talent/ability, character/personal qualities, geographical residence, state residency, volunteer work, work experience. High school diploma is required and GED is accepted. *Academic units required:* 4 English, 3 math, 3 science, 2 science labs, 2 language (other than English), 2 social studies. *Academic units recommended:* 4 English, 4 math, 4 science, 3 science labs, 3 language (other than English), 4 social studies.

Financial Aid

Students should submit: FAFSA. Priority filing deadline is 1/3. The Princeton Review suggests that all financial aid forms be submitted as soon as possible. *Need-based scholarships/grants offered:* Federal Pell; Federal SEOG; College/university scholarship or grant aid from institutional funds; State scholarships/grants. *Loan aid offered:* Federal Direct Subsidized Loans; Federal Direct Unsubsidized Loans; Direct PLUS loans; State Loans; College/university loans from institutional funds. Admitted students will be notified of awards on a rolling basis beginning 1/30. Federal Work-Study Program available. Institutional employment available.

The Inside Word

Admission to Iowa State University is based on the Regent Admission Index (RAI) formula and anyone earning an RAI score of at least 245 is automatically admitted. The admissions office reviews applicants scoring below 245 individually to determine whom among them will also be admitted. For applicants choosing not to report an ACT or SAT score, admission will be based on high school grade point average and high school core course requirements.

THE SCHOOL SAYS

From the Admissions Office

"Iowa State University offers all the advantages of a major university along with the friendliness and warmth of a residential campus. There are more than 100 undergraduate programs of study in the Colleges of Agriculture and Life Sciences, Business, Design, Human Sciences, Engineering, Liberal Arts and Sciences, and Veterinary Medicine. Our 1,800 faculty members include Rhodes Scholars, Fulbright Scholars, and National Academy of Sciences and National Academy of Engineering members. Recognized for its high quality of life, Iowa State has taken practical steps to make the university a place where students feel like they belong. Iowa State has been recognized for the high quality of campus life and the exemplary out-of-class experiences offered to its students. Along with a strong academic experience, students also have opportunities for further developing their leadership skills and interpersonal relationships through any of the more than 800 student organizations, sixty intramural sports, and a multitude of arts and recreational activities."

SELECTIVITY

# of total applicants	23,095
% of total applicants accepted	89
% of total acceptees attending	29
# of in-state applicants	5,644
% of in-state applicants accepted	93
# of out-of-state-applicants	14,161
% of applicants accepted from out of state	91
# of international applicants	3,290
% of international applicants accepted	68

First-Year Profile

Testing policy	Test Optional
Range SAT composite	1130–1250
Range SAT EBRW	560–670
Range SAT math	560–690
Range ACT composite	21–28
% submitting SAT scores	13
% submitting ACT scores	46
Average HS GPA	3.8
% submitting high school GPA	99

Important Dates

Nonfall registration?	Yes

FINANCIAL FACTS

Annual in-state tuition	$9,252
Annual out-of-state tuition	$27,346
Food and housing	$10,808
Required fees	$1,535
Books and supplies	$700
Average need-based scholarship (First-year)	$11,488 ($11,951)
% students with need rec. need-based scholarship or grant aid (First-year)	97 (97)
% students with need rec. non-need-based scholarship or grant aid (First-year)	44 (46)
% students with need rec. need-based self-help aid (First-year)	62 (58)
% students rec. any financial aid (First-year)	78 (80)
% UG borrow to pay for school	55
Average cumulative indebtedness	$29,475
% of students with need fully met (First-year)	24 (23)
Average % of student need met (First-year)	78 (80)

Ithaca College

953 Danby Road, Ithaca, NY 14850-7002 • Admissions: 607-274-3124

Survey Snapshot
Students love Ithaca, NY
Theater is popular
College radio is popular

RATINGS

Quality of Life	**80**
Fire Safety	**99**
Green	**94**
Academic	**79**
Profs Interesting	**86**
Profs Accessible	**86**
Admissions	**86**
Financial Aid	**93**

CAMPUS LIFE

Type of school	Private
Environment	Town

Students

Degree-seeking undergrad enrollment	4,189
% male/female/not reported	46/54/0
% from out of state	60
% First-year from public high school	82
% First-year live on campus	98
% Ugrads live on campus	85
# of fraternities	NR
# of sororities	NR
% Asian	3
% Black or African American	5
% Hispanic	12
% Native American	<1
% Pacific Islander	<1
% Race and/or ethnicity unknown	3
% Two or more races	5
% White	71
% International	2
# of countries represented	45

CAMPUS MENTAL HEALTH SERVICES

Offers mental health/wellness program	Yes
Mental health training available to students	Yes
Employs Chief Wellness Officer	Yes
Peer-to-peer mental health offerings	No
Counseling center has guidelines or accreditation	Yes
Mental health/well-being courses	Yes, for-credit

ACADEMICS

% students returning for sophomore year	86
% students graduating within 4 years	62
% students graduating within 6 years	72
Calendar	Semester
Student/faculty ratio	11:1
Most common class size 10–19.	(41%)

Most Popular Majors

Radio and Television; Music; Physical Therapy/Therapist

Applicants Also Look At

Emerson College, Marist University, Penn State University Park, State University of New York—Binghamton University, State University of New York—University at Albany, State University of New York—University at Buffalo, Syracuse University, University of Delaware, University of Massachusetts—Amherst, University of Vermont

STUDENTS SAY "..."

Academics

Small class sizes that afford plenty of "personal attention," "outstanding" scholarships, and cross-registration with nearby Cornell University are a few great reasons to choose Ithaca College, a smallish school in central New York that offers many of the resources you would expect to find at a much larger university. "You are able to be a part of a community and get the chance to pursue interests that are not necessarily a part of your chosen course of study," relates an English major. "We have loads of opportunities to do and try a wide variety of things." The vast multitude of academic offerings includes "one of the best communication schools in the country." Also notable are "strong" majors in music, business, and drama; a "highly competitive" six-year doctorate program in physical therapy; and programs in television, photography, and digital media and in film. Professors are "really engaging and understand how to present the material so that it is relevant and meaningful." On the whole, faculty members are "really passionate about their fields and have a genuine interest in getting students excited about their passions." By far, the most common academic complaint about academics at Ithaca concerns registration, which can be trying. Some say, "the buildings—inside and out—are a bit outdated."

Campus Life

The number of extracurricular choices is "considerable" at Ithaca College. At the same time, "the school is small enough for anyone to get involved." There are "speakers and events offered on campus." There's also a nearly professional-quality college radio station. Many students "are part of an athletic team or participate in intramural athletics." For relaxation, students often "hang out on the quad," throwing Frisbees or "playing music on the lawns on tie-dye sheets." The social situation at Ithaca is "nothing like the party scene you'd find at a larger university," but "there are some good parties" now and then. While the campus is a little "isolated," students also frequently manage to attend frat parties at Cornell and generally "enjoy the social scene" the nearby Ivy offers. "The town of Ithaca is quaint but lively." There's "a good music scene and a lot of cool stores." When the weather is nice, "there's always some festival," or at least it seems that way. "If you're an outdoorsy person," the wooded and rocky surrounding area is a wonderland of activity. "The hiking here is unbelievable," and few other schools offer the opportunity to "go cliff jumping on a hot Saturday." On the negative side, winters are cold as a matter of course, and "the cold and rain do hinder activities." Students joke, be prepared to get your exercise walking between classes; "the hills here will kill you." That said, the walk is worth it, as the campus is known for its picturesque beauty. "People aren't kidding when they say 'Ithaca is Gorges (gorgeous),'" promises one student.

Student Body

The typical undergrad here is "genuine," "easygoing," "always busy," "well-dressed," and has a "sunny disposition despite the gray skies." Beyond those qualities, the population is "a wide mix of hipsters, jocks, theater kids, music students," and "crunchy granola hippies." Cliques are often based loosely on academics, but it's worth noting that "people of all kinds fit in here" and "everyone finds their niche," thanks in part to the way that "each school (music, communications, business, etc.) is its own community." Ethnic diversity and other kinds of diversity are "not entirely unheard of." However, people are "usually from the Northeast," and "the population of students that fit into the typical suburban, upper-middle-class family is definitely significant." Politically, "students at Ithaca tend to be liberal." Some students tell us that you'll find "a lot of people are environmentally and socially conscious" here who want "to change the world."

ITHACA COLLEGE

Financial Aid: 607-274-3131 • E-Mail: admission@ithaca.edu • Website: www.ithaca.edu

THE PRINCETON REVIEW SAYS

Admissions

The school reports that its standardized testing policy for use in admission for Fall 2026 is Test Optional. The Princeton Review suggests that interested applicants consult with the school for the most up-to-date standardized testing policies. *Very important factors considered include:* rigor of secondary school record, academic GPA. *Important factors considered include:* application essay, recommendation(s), extracurricular activities, talent/ability, character/personal qualities. *Other factors considered include:* class rank, standardized test scores, first generation, alumni/ae relation, volunteer work, work experience, level of applicant's interest. High school diploma is required and GED is accepted. *Academic units required:* 4 English, 3 math, 3 science, 2 language (other than English), 3 social studies, 1 academic elective. *Academic units recommended:* 4 English, 4 math, 4 science, 3 language (other than English), 4 social studies, 1 academic elective.

Financial Aid

Students should submit: FAFSA. Priority filing deadline is 1/15. The Princeton Review suggests that all financial aid forms be submitted as soon as possible. *Need-based scholarships/grants offered:* Federal Pell; Federal SEOG; State scholarships/grants; Private scholarships; College/university scholarship or grant aid from institutional funds. *Loan aid offered:* Federal Direct Subsidized Loans; Federal Direct Unsubsidized Loans; Direct PLUS loans. Admitted students will be notified of awards on a rolling basis beginning 2/15 regular admission and early action, 12/15 early decision. Federal Work-Study Program available. Institutional employment available.

The Inside Word

Ithaca's admissions profile continues to be on the rise with a good deal of highly competitive applicants. Programs requiring an audition (for example, music) are among Ithaca's most demanding for admission. If you want to pursue the six-year clinical doctorate in physical therapy, focus on completing substantial math and science coursework in high school.

THE SCHOOL SAYS

From the Admissions Office

"Ithaca College is a welcoming community where immersive learning experiences lead students to lifelong impact in their careers and beyond. IC graduates launch startups, win Pulitzers, forge health-care solutions, anchor national news, and lead global companies.

"Founded in 1892, IC offers students a unique combination of academic theory, applied practice, and performance. Small class sizes, close mentorship, and first-rate facilities more typical of large universities ensure that students receive personal attention and professional preparation. Students unlock their potential through rigorous study with faculty experts in over 70 majors and 70 minors offered by five schools: business; communications; health sciences and human performance; humanities and sciences; and music, theatre, and dance.

"Students who are "undecided" at other institutions find the academic path that's right for them in IC's distinctive Exploratory Program. With expert guidance, they can explore their academic interests across disciplines and still graduate on time.

"Life outside the classroom is an equally rich launchpad for growth and discovery. In themed living communities and through more than 200 clubs and organizations, students lead initiatives rooted in their passions. They also build resilient, engaged lives through internships, global study away opportunities and alumni mentorship. IC's 28 NCAA Division III teams demonstrate the drive, enthusiasm, and camaraderie that energize the campus culture.

"Located in New York's Finger Lakes region, Ithaca was named America's best town to visit by CNN in 2025. It is surrounded by 150 "gorges" waterfalls and features tech startups, a vibrant music scene, theatres, art galleries, and restaurants."

SELECTIVITY

# of total applicants	12,735
% of total applicants accepted	70
% of total acceptees attending	12
# of in-state applicants	4,451
% of in-state applicants accepted	82
# of out-of-state-applicants	6,973
% of applicants accepted from out of state	70
# of international applicants	1,311
% of international applicants accepted	30
# of early decision applicants	98
% of early decision applicants accepted	85
# offered a place on the wait list	203
# admitted from wait list	29

First-Year Profile

Testing policy	Test Optional
Range SAT composite	1240–1370
Range SAT EBRW	640–720
Range SAT math	590–680
Range ACT composite	29–32
% submitting SAT scores	22
% submitting ACT scores	5
% graduated top 10% of class	21
% graduated top 25% of class	55
% graduated top 50% of class	84
% submitting high school rank	26

Important Dates

Early decision	
Apply by	11/1
Notified by	12/15
Early action	
Apply by	12/1
Notified by	2/1
Regular	
Apply by	2/1
Notified by	Rolling, 11/15
Nonfall registration?	Yes

FINANCIAL FACTS

Annual tuition (First-year)	$57,392 ($59,440)
Food and housing	$16,520
Required fees (First-year)	$300 ($625)
Books and supplies	$850
Average need-based scholarship (First-year)	$28,725 ($30,204)
% students with need rec. need-based scholarship or grant aid (First-year)	98 (100)
% students with need rec. non-need-based scholarship or grant aid (First-year)	50 (54)
% students with need rec. need-based self-help aid (First-year)	72 (69)
% students rec. any financial aid (First-year)	98 (100)
% UG borrow to pay for school	65
Average cumulative indebtedness	$31,677
% of students with need fully met (First-year)	59 (62)
Average % of student need met (First-year)	89 (91)

JAMES MADISON UNIVERSITY

800 S. Main Street, Harrisonburg, VA 22807 • Admissions: 540-568-5681

Survey Snapshot
Recreation facilities are great
Intramural sports are popular
Students are happy

RATINGS

Quality of Life	91
Fire Safety	60*
Green	91
Academic	77
Profs Interesting	87
Profs Accessible	90
Admissions	86
Financial Aid	83

CAMPUS LIFE

Type of school	Public
Environment	Town

Students

Degree-seeking undergrad enrollment	20,840
% male/female/not reported	44/56/<1
% from out of state	21
% First-year from public high school	60
% First-year live on campus	99
% Ugrads live on campus	10
# of fraternities (% join)	15 (NR)
# of sororities (% join)	13 (NR)
% Asian	5
% Black or African American	5
% Hispanic	9
% Native American	<1
% Pacific Islander	<1
% Race and/or ethnicity unknown	2
% Two or more races	6
% White	72
% International	1
# of countries represented	70

CAMPUS MENTAL HEALTH SERVICES

Offers mental health/wellness program	Yes
Mental health training available to students	No
Employs Chief Wellness Officer	NR
Peer-to-peer mental health offerings	NR
Counseling center has guidelines or accreditation	No
Mental health/well-being courses	NR

ACADEMICS

% students returning for sophomore year	92
% students graduating within 4 years	66
% students graduating within 6 years	80
Calendar	Semester
Student/faculty ratio	17:1
Most common class size 20–29.	(29%)
Most common lab/discussion size 20–29.	(53%)

Most Popular Majors

Psychology; Community Health Services/Liaison/Counseling; Registered Nursing/Registered Nurse

Applicants Sometimes Prefer

George Mason University, Old Dominion University, University of Virginia, Virginia Commonwealth University, Virginia Tech

STUDENTS SAY "..."

Academics

With over 70 majors and 130 programs at James Madison University to choose from, students note that there are "many different paths you could take with your education." But what stands out to them is how the school provides "so many resources to help you with the switch from high school to college" (free tutoring, study sessions, a Student Success center), and how the university's core curriculum gives them "an innovative way to see other majors, such as [using] the planetarium and getting to look through the telescopes for scientific projects." Classes are peppered with hands-on learning opportunities like "undergraduate research, symposiums, poster presentations, [and] conferences." For instance, one management class features the Dukes Impact Challenge, where students "have to design and sell merchandise within six weeks, and all the money goes to a local non-profit." Professors are "very accessible," at least during office hours, and "always feel helpful and like they genuinely want to see you do your best." This approachability makes teachers feel "personable, and you can create strong relationships with them." One student adds, "They are extremely flexible (depending on situations) and understand life gets in the way sometimes." Many professors bring "their life experiences and implement them into the class to make the learning experience more enriching." This desire to engage students is one reason why, "for many people, JMU is the perfect college."

Campus Life

JMU gives students "so many ways to get involved and try new things," and in return, the "very passionate" students "don't just go to class then go home; they join clubs, show up to events, and make campus feel alive." That's perhaps because "with more than 400 clubs and organizations, it's easy to find your people." Greek life is popular, the recreation center (UREC) is a common destination, and you'll often see students "engage in Spikeball and lacrosse on the quad." This Division I school also has a strong athletic program, and "football games are extremely popular and definitely fun and worth going [to]." The "dining hall system is an incredible asset," and JMU has "great food for a university." Mainly, students simply enjoy being around each other, even if it's just to "watch a lot of shows and movies, or all lie on the ground and doomscroll together." Between the people and clubs, JMU "really [has] something for everyone and [wants] people to be involved." Consequently, as one student says, "Everyone has so much school spirit for JMU, it makes you feel like you belong no matter what you are involved in."

Student Body

A strong, shared identity is at the heart of the JMU experience. "Everyone's such a proud student/staff/alumni of JMU. It's so refreshing seeing such pride in the community." That's impressive with over 20,000 undergraduates, and some note that "while it is a larger school, it feels very well contained" and integrates seamlessly with the community, as students "are very connected to the people that live in Harrisonburg and to the natural surroundings." Dukes, the name for JMU students, are a social bunch, and students say that it is "very easy to get into a conversation with any person." And one student attests, "I have had lunch bought for me when my campus card didn't swipe." Balance is a key tenet of JMU life, and "mental health is extremely important to the staff and students." This is good for those who have "different aspirations and passions that they pursue in their own unique ways here," and everyone is "supportive of decisions but not afraid to speak up for what they believe." This group "[radiates] positivity and friendliness" and "shows compassion, reliability, and love for each other no matter the circumstances."

James Madison University

Financial Aid: 540-568-7820 • E-Mail: admissions@jmu.edu • Website: www.jmu.edu

THE PRINCETON REVIEW SAYS

Admissions

The school reports that its standardized testing policy for use in admission for Fall 2026 is Test Optional. The Princeton Review suggests that interested applicants consult with the school for the most up-to-date standardized testing policies. *Very important factors considered include:* rigor of secondary school record, academic GPA. *Important factors considered include:* first generation, state residency. *Other factors considered include:* standardized test scores, application essay, recommendation(s), extracurricular activities, talent/ability, character/personal qualities, geographical residence, volunteer work, work experience, level of applicant's interest. High school diploma is required and GED is accepted. *Academic units required:* 4 English, 4 math, 4 science, 3 language (other than English), 3 history.

Financial Aid

Students should submit: FAFSA. Priority filing deadline is 3/1. The Princeton Review suggests that all financial aid forms be submitted as soon as possible. *Need-based scholarships/grants offered:* Federal Pell; Federal SEOG; State scholarships/grants; Private scholarships. *Loan aid offered:* Federal Direct Subsidized Loans; Federal Direct Unsubsidized Loans; Direct PLUS loans. Admitted students will be notified of awards on a rolling basis beginning 4/1. Federal Work-Study Program available. Institutional employment available.

The Inside Word

At JMU, the admissions staff states that they're not searching for a "magic combination" of test scores and GPA. Admissions officers review each application individually and are most interested in the quality of an applicant's secondary school education, followed by performance and, optionally, test scores. The personal statement is a vehicle for conveying information an applicant deems important but doesn't appear elsewhere in the application; as such, it's optional.

THE SCHOOL SAYS

From the Admissions Office

"James Madison University's philosophy of inclusiveness—known as 'all together one'—means that students become a part of a real community that nurtures its own to learn, grow, and succeed. Our professors, many of whom have a wealth of real-world experience, pride themselves on making teaching their top priority. We take seriously the responsibility to maintain an environment that fosters learning and encourages students to excel in and out of the classroom. Our rich variety of educational, social, and extracurricular activities includes more than 100 innovative and traditional undergraduate majors and programs, a well-established study abroad program, a cutting-edge information security program, more than 350 student clubs and organizations, and an expanded 280,000-square-foot, state-of-the-art recreation center. The university's picturesque, self-contained campus is located in the heart of the Shenandoah Valley, a four-season area that's easy to call home. Great food, fun times, exciting intercollegiate athletics, and rigorous academics all combine to create the unique James Madison experience. From the library to the residence halls and from our outstanding Honors College to our highly successful career placement program, the university is committed to equipping our students with the tools they need to achieve their dreams."

SELECTIVITY

# of total applicants	38,423
% of total applicants accepted	72
% of total acceptees attending	18
# of in-state applicants	20,306
% of in-state applicants accepted	66
# of out-of-state-applicants	18,120
% of applicants accepted from out of state	78
# offered a place on the wait list	2,926
# admitted from wait list	41

First-Year Profile

Testing policy	Test Optional
Range SAT composite	1190–1330
Range SAT EBRW	600–680
Range SAT math	570–660
Range ACT composite	24–29
% submitting SAT scores	14
% submitting ACT scores	3
% graduated top 10% of class	19
% graduated top 25% of class	32
% graduated top 50% of class	37
% submitting high school rank	46

Important Dates

Early action	
Apply by	11/1
Notified by	Mid-Late January
Regular	
Apply by	1/15
Notified by	Mid-Late March
Nonfall registration?	Yes

FINANCIAL FACTS

Annual in-state tuition	$15,060
Annual out-of-state tuition	$32,876
Food and housing	$15,016
Books and supplies	$1,374
Average need-based scholarship (First-year)	$9,714 ($10,384)
% students with need rec. need-based scholarship or grant aid (First-year)	65 (55)
% students with need rec. non-need-based scholarship or grant aid (First-year)	12 (11)
% students with need rec. need-based self-help aid (First-year)	55 (54)
% students rec. any financial aid (First-year)	58 (62)
% UG borrow to pay for school	43
Average cumulative indebtedness	$31,357
% of students with need fully met (First-year)	30 (31)
Average % of student need met (First-year)	46 (42)

John Carroll University

1 John Carroll Boulevard, University Heights, OH 44118-4581 • Admissions: 216-397-4294

Survey Snapshot
Students involved in community service
Everyone loves the Blue Streaks
Intramural sports are popular

RATINGS

Quality of Life	87
Fire Safety	87
Green	78
Academic	81
Profs Interesting	88
Profs Accessible	92
Admissions	87
Financial Aid	90

CAMPUS LIFE

Type of school	Private
Affiliation	Roman Catholic
Environment	Metropolis

Students

Degree-seeking undergrad enrollment	2,408
% male/female/not reported	52/48/0
% from out of state	31
% First-year live on campus	83
% Ugrads live on campus	62
# of fraternities (% join)	2 (3)
# of sororities (% join)	4 (19)
% Asian	3
% Black or African American	6
% Hispanic	3
% Native American	<1
% Pacific Islander	0
% Race and/or ethnicity unknown	<1
% Two or more races	3
% White	81
% International	4
# of countries represented	15

CAMPUS MENTAL HEALTH SERVICES

Offers mental health/wellness program	Yes
Mental health training available to students	Yes
Employs Chief Wellness Officer	Yes
Peer-to-peer mental health offerings	Yes
Counseling center has guidelines or accreditation	Yes
Mental health/well-being courses	Yes, for-credit

ACADEMICS

% students returning for sophomore year	86
% students graduating within 4 years	68
% students graduating within 6 years	74
Calendar	Semester
Student/faculty ratio	15:1
Most common class size 20–29.	(49%)
Most common lab/discussion size 20–29.	(44%)

Most Popular Majors

Biology/Biological Sciences; Finance; Marketing/ Marketing Management

STUDENTS SAY "..."

Academics

John Carroll University is a Jesuit Catholic university that "challenge[s] students to advocate for justice and work toward being better people." The ethos of service and giving back influences the academic experience with many service-learning opportunities as well as internships focused on social justice. JCU "generally emphasizes critical thinking and active learning," and classes are "rigorous and rewarding." Some classes incorporate off-campus service, such as the Inside-Out Prison Exchange course, which brings together students from JCU with students incarcerated at a nearby women's prison. Another example is Carroll Reads, a tutoring program that matches JCU students with elementary school students for one-on-one reading support. JCU also offers over 45 study abroad programs, including some that involve interning abroad to help students gain experience working internationally. When it comes to on-campus learning, students describe professors as "approachable, supportive, and genuinely invested." Beyond the classroom, professors "give great advice" and "are more than willing to help in all areas of life." Students feel supported by the administration as well, noting that the school "makes an effort to provide students with networking opportunities" and "offers a lot of connections to internships and jobs."

Campus Life

JCU is a "supportive environment," and "this sense of belonging makes it easy to get involved, whether it's through clubs, volunteer opportunities, or student organizations." Students enjoy both letting off steam by playing intramural sports and socializing and networking through "clubs that help you advance towards your professional career." Greek life is fairly popular, alongside associations and faith-based activities such as Labre, a weekly outreach program where students provide meals to people experiencing homelessness in Cleveland. The University Club organizes campus-wide events such as bingo, movie nights, and outings to see the Guardians, Cleveland's baseball team, play. It's a lively campus and the "student center atrium is always buzzing with groups of people." There are many "great study spaces, from quiet corners in the library to group areas in the student center" and these are often "filled with students working on group projects or revising for exams." On the weekends, students frequently go off-campus to eat, shop, or spend time in the nearby parks, including "beach days at Lake Erie when it is nice out." One student neatly sums up the typical day as revolving "around classes, studying, and engaging with campus activities, but there's always time to unwind and explore interests beyond academics."

Student Body

JCU students are "very welcoming," making it "easy to find a group of people that you get along with." Students here are friendly and when you see someone, "you will be met with a smile." As one student observes, "Most people will want to get to know you and then say hi outside of class or work." Overall, there is a "sense of collaboration and support among peers, making it easy to form genuine connections." Students at JCU can also be described as determined, "very smart," and involved, and "it is great to see how hardworking everybody is!" As one student elaborates, "Everyone I know takes school seriously and tries their best." JCU's focus on service draws "pragmatic social justice-minded people," which fosters an environment where "everyone wants to succeed and help each other succeed for the greater good." While students are serious about school, they also know how to relax: "We are always planning events and coordinating fun things to do while still accomplishing our academic goals." Another student agrees, describing their peers as "kind, funny people that make school fun every day!"

John Carroll University

Financial Aid: 216-397-4248 • E-Mail: admission@jcu.edu • Website: jcu.edu

THE PRINCETON REVIEW SAYS

Admissions

The school reports that its standardized testing policy for use in admission for Fall 2026 is Test Optional. The Princeton Review suggests that interested applicants consult with the school for the most up-to-date standardized testing policies. *Very important factors considered include:* rigor of secondary school record, academic GPA. *Important factors considered include:* application essay, extracurricular activities, talent/ability, character/personal qualities, volunteer work. *Other factors considered include:* class rank, standardized test scores, recommendation(s), interview, alumni/ae relation, work experience, level of applicant's interest. High school diploma is required and GED is accepted. *Academic units required:* 4 English, 3 math, 2 science, 2 science labs, 2 language (other than English), 2 social studies, 3 academic electives. *Academic units recommended:* 4 English, 4 math, 3 science, 3 science labs, 3 language (other than English), 4 social studies, 3 academic electives.

Financial Aid

Students should submit: FAFSA. Priority filing deadline is 12/1. The Princeton Review suggests that all financial aid forms be submitted as soon as possible. *Need-based scholarships/grants offered:* Federal Pell; Federal SEOG; State scholarships/grants. Admitted students will be notified of awards on a rolling basis beginning 2/15. Federal Work-Study Program available. Institutional employment available.

The Inside Word

JCU's admission process takes a holistic approach, considering grades, the rigor of coursework, essays, recommendations, activities, and—if submitted—SAT or ACT scores. Students are encouraged to submit test scores if they reflect their strengths, but doing so is optional. Under JCU's "no harm" policy, scores that do not strengthen an application are simply not considered. For students not submitting test scores, additional emphasis is placed on academic performance—especially the rigor of high school coursework and grades in subjects like English and math. Test scores also do not impact merit scholarships or eligibility for specific majors or programs.

THE SCHOOL SAYS

From the Admissions Office

"Since 1886, John Carroll University has prepared students not just for what's next, but for lives of purpose. That approach comes to life through Onward, our signature student success program that connects every student with a personalized team, a tailored plan, real-world experience, and a confident launch into what comes next. Located in University Heights, Ohio, just minutes from Cleveland, John Carroll offers the best of a close-knit campus community with access to internships, research, and career opportunities in a major metropolitan area. With more than 70 majors, minors, concentrations, and graduate programs across the College of Arts & Sciences, the Boler College of Business, and the College of Health, students are challenged to think critically, lead with purpose, and prepare for meaningful careers. They come from across the country, drawn to our distinctive combination of academic rigor, personal support, and career-ready experiences.

"At John Carroll, your experience is guided by Onward. You won't have to figure things out on your own. Your team of advisors, faculty, alumni mentors, and career specialists works together on your behalf—so every step builds on the one before. You'll build a personalized plan, gain hands-on experience through internships and immersive learning, and graduate ready to take your next step with confidence. Rooted in the Jesuit tradition, John Carroll is committed to the development of the whole person. Here, you'll be known, supported, and inspired to make an impact in your community and around the world. Outside the classroom, more than 700 student-athletes compete in NCAA Division III's North Coast Athletic Conference, alongside a vibrant campus life that includes club sports, intramurals, and leadership opportunities."

SELECTIVITY

# of total applicants	4,745
% of total applicants accepted	77
% of total acceptees attending	18
# of in-state applicants	2,826
% of in-state applicants accepted	82
# of out-of-state-applicants	1,603
% of applicants accepted from out of state	81
# of international applicants	316
% of international applicants accepted	11

First-Year Profile

Testing policy	Test Optional
Range SAT composite	1220–1330
Range SAT EBRW	610–670
Range SAT math	590–680
Range ACT composite	25–30
% submitting SAT scores	15
% submitting ACT scores	14
Average HS GPA	3.8
% submitting high school GPA	100
% graduated top 10% of class	30
% graduated top 25% of class	60
% graduated top 50% of class	86
% submitting high school rank	31

Important Dates

Early action	
Apply by	11/1
Notified by	12/1
Regular	
Notified by	Rolling, 12/1
Nonfall registration?	Yes

FINANCIAL FACTS

Annual tuition	$51,650
Food and housing	$15,380
Required fees	$1,800
Books and supplies	$1,300
Average need-based scholarship (First-year)	$35,078 ($37,243)
% students with need rec. need-based scholarship or grant aid (First-year)	98 (99)
% students with need rec. non-need-based scholarship or grant aid (First-year)	98 (99)
% students with need rec. need-based self-help aid (First-year)	79 (84)
% students rec. any financial aid (First-year)	99 (99)
% UG borrow to pay for school	65
Average cumulative indebtedness	$34,684
% of students with need fully met (First-year)	30 (27)
Average % of student need met (First-year)	85 (85)

Johns Hopkins University

3400 North Charles Street, Baltimore, MD 21218 • Admissions: 410-516-8171

Survey Snapshot
Students always studying
Students are happy
Lab facilities are great

RATINGS

Quality of Life	84
Fire Safety	98
Green	60*
Academic	94
Profs Interesting	88
Profs Accessible	92
Admissions	99
Financial Aid	96

CAMPUS LIFE

Type of school	Private
Environment	Metropolis

Students

Degree-seeking undergrad enrollment	5,693
% male/female/not reported	45/55/<1
% from out of state	85
% First-year live on campus	91
% Ugrads live on campus	46
# of fraternities (% join)	12 (22)
# of sororities (% join)	13 (13)
% Asian	29
% Black or African American	8
% Hispanic	19
% Native American	<1
% Pacific Islander	<1
% Race and/or ethnicity unknown	2
% Two or more races	7
% White	19
% International	15
# of countries represented	110

CAMPUS MENTAL HEALTH SERVICES

Offers mental health/wellness program	Yes
Mental health training available to students	Yes
Employs Chief Wellness Officer	Yes
Peer-to-peer mental health offerings	Yes
Counseling center has guidelines or accreditation	Yes
Mental health/well-being courses	Yes, for-credit

ACADEMICS

% students returning for sophomore year	98
% students graduating within 4 years	87
% students graduating within 6 years	94
Calendar	4-1-4
Student/faculty ratio	6:1
Most common class size 10–19.	(100%)

STUDENTS SAY "..."

Academics

At Johns Hopkins University, students learn "how to approach any problem fearlessly." Academic programs on offer are "beyond compare" and provide the opportunity to "study anything and still be taught by the highest of experts." As a result, Hopkins attracts students who are "overwhelmingly passionate about what they do and aspire to make an impact in their field." Students also enroll for the "availability of resources, research, internship, and job opportunities [that] are unmatched." One Hopkins student offers an example: "One of my art history major friends curated his own exhibit in a gallery downtown (with work from several world-renowned artists) as his research project."

Professors "make themselves very accessible to their students for coffee chats, career advice or even just to give life advice." One student describes professors as "almost giddy even" to provide individualized guidance for students. And it's common for instructors to be "more than willing to push class topics beyond the confines of the textbook to expose us to the implications of the topics discussed in class." Thoughtful debate is made easier in Hopkins's "rigorous but very cooperative" environment as the community is "small enough for strong interactions among students." Overall, Hopkins provides "unparalleled opportunities to pursue research, form strong relationships with professors, and learn from an outstanding group of peers."

Campus Life

Experiencing life in Baltimore, Maryland, is intrinsic to the Hopkins experience. The affordable city offers a "great music and food scene," and nearby Mount Vernon has "fantastic food and culture." Neighborhoods such as Fells Point and Federal Hill offer nightlife attractions; Orioles and Ravens games are favorite student pastimes. That said, students are candid that only a fraction of the campus seems to engage in other social activities, like going "out to parties and bars," which creates the sensation that "it's always the same people you see out." Put frankly, "some of the students prefer to study all the time" or to stay among the campus's picturesque brick buildings. Of course, many students also find that their time "revolves around clubs and organizations." Hopkins has over 400 undergraduate student-run organizations. There are 24 varsity sports teams; most play Division III, but the Division I lacrosse teams are a student favorite. Fans are known to "get really involved in the season." Enrollees acknowledge that the school's reputation as one of America's first research universities is well-earned, such that "concerts [and] symposiums with famous guest speakers" are quite popular.

Student Body

Hopkins students are known for being "the type that thrive under pressure." Though they may "come from various backgrounds and have vastly different experiences," this batch of "very intellectually curious and smart" students are united as "ambitious workhorses" with a desire "to be on the forefront of innovation." In addition, there are "a lot of international people and people from various backgrounds" who are "invested in the livelihood of the Hopkins community." Some might find that there appear to be "a lot of introverts" around, though others point out that "people are very nice and helpful." And one student confesses that the average Hopkins student "works really hard, and knows how to cut loose as well." All in all, a Hopkins student "brings something unique to the school whether it is their love for art, school spirit at sporting events, or their desire to find a cure for cancer."

Johns Hopkins University

Financial Aid: 410-516-8028 • E-Mail: gotojhu@jhu.edu • Website: www.jhu.ed

THE PRINCETON REVIEW SAYS

Admissions

The school reports that its standardized testing policy for use in admission for Fall 2026 will require applicants to submit either the SAT or ACT. The Princeton Review suggests that interested applicants consult with the school for the most up-to-date standardized testing policies. *Very important factors considered include:* rigor of secondary school record, class rank, academic GPA, standardized test scores, application essay, recommendation(s). *Important factors considered include:* extracurricular activities, talent/ability, character/personal qualities, volunteer work, work experience. *Other factors considered include:* first generation, geographical residence. High school diploma is required and GED is accepted. *Academic units recommended:* 4 English, 4 math, 4 science, 4 language (other than English), 2 social studies, 2 history.

Financial Aid

Students should submit: FAFSA; CSS PROFILE. The Princeton Review suggests that all financial aid forms be submitted as soon as possible. *Need-based scholarships/grants offered:* Federal Pell; Federal SEOG; State scholarships/grants; Private scholarships; College/university scholarship or grant aid from institutional funds. *Loan aid offered:* Federal Direct Subsidized Loans; Federal Direct Unsubsidized Loans; Direct PLUS loans. Admitted students will be notified of awards in mid-March. Federal Work-Study Program available. Institutional employment available.

The Inside Word

Top schools like Hopkins receive more and more applications every year and, as a result, grow harder and harder to get into. With so many applicants, Hopkins can be highly selective and looks for individuals who will thrive in the Hopkins community. Admissions counselors utilize a holistic approach to admissions and in particular are looking for applicants who can demonstrate their academic character, their impact outside of the classroom, and how they engage with their communities. Hopkins does not consider financial need when making admission decisions, meets 100 percent of demonstrated need, and funds financial aid offers with need-based scholarships work opportunities.

THE SCHOOL SAYS

From the Admissions Office

"Located in Baltimore, Maryland, Johns Hopkins University is a global community of 5,600 undergraduate students from all 50 U.S. states and over 100 countries. The close-knit community offers deep friendships, small class sizes, and faculty mentorship alongside the resources of the nation's leading research university. Students are encouraged to explore widely, connect ideas across disciplines, and shape a path inside and outside the classroom that reflects their interests while developing key skills for success in any field.

"Discovery happens during everyday moments as a Hopkins student—asking a bold question in a First-Year Seminar, cheering on fellow Blue Jays on Homewood field, or making new friends through 430-plus student organizations. Students are active and engaged citizens of Baltimore, whether they are going to Orioles games, visiting the next-door Baltimore Museum of Art, or engaging with local organizations to learn from and contribute to the city we call home. Alumni paths span journalism and the arts, design and entrepreneurship, medicine and public health, engineering and innovation—careers shaped as much by curiosity and adaptability as by a declared major. Blue Jays are sought-after by graduate schools, with an 85% admit rate to medical school and 97% admit rate to law school.

"The university invests deeply in student success, so they can say yes to all the available opportunities. Hopkins offers free tuition for students from families earning up to $200,000, free tuition plus living expenses for families earning up to $100,000, and meets 100% of financial need, debt-free, for all students."

SELECTIVITY

# of total applicants	45,895
% of total applicants accepted	6
% of total acceptees attending	47
# of in-state applicants	3,851
% of in-state applicants accepted	6
# of out-of-state-applicants	31,318
% of applicants accepted from out of state	7
# of international applicants	10,726
% of international applicants accepted	5
# of early decision applicants	7,028
% of early decision applicants accepted	12
# offered a place on the wait list	2,374
# admitted from wait list	30

First-Year Profile

Testing policy	SAT or ACT Required
Range SAT composite	1530–1560
Range SAT EBRW	740–770
Range SAT math	780–800
Range ACT composite	34–36
% submitting SAT scores	50
% submitting ACT scores	18
Average HS GPA	3.9
% submitting high school GPA	93
% graduated top 10% of class	100
% graduated top 25% of class	100
% graduated top 50% of class	100
% submitting high school rank	23

Important Dates

Early decision	
Apply by	11/1
Notified by	Mid-December
Other ED apply by	1/2
Other ED notified by	Mid-February
Regular	
Apply by	1/2
Notified by	Mid-March
Nonfall registration?	No

FINANCIAL FACTS

Annual tuition	$68,670
Food and housing	$21,967
Required fees	$500
Books and supplies	$1,377
Average need-based scholarship (First-year)	$63,401 ($65,703)
% students with need rec. need-based scholarship or grant aid (First-year)	99 (100)
% students with need rec. non-need-based scholarship or grant aid (First-year)	8 (10)
% students with need rec. need-based self-help aid (First-year)	82 (77)
% students rec. any financial aid (First-year)	55 (56)
% UG borrow to pay for school	20
Average cumulative indebtedness	$30,803
% of students with need fully met (First-year)	96 (100)
Average % of student need met (First-year)	100 (100)

JUNIATA COLLEGE

1700 Moore Street, Huntingdon, PA 16652 • Admissions: 814-641-3420

Survey Snapshot
Lab facilities are great
Internships are widely available
Class discussions encouraged

RATINGS

Quality of Life	87
Fire Safety	86
Green	80
Academic	88
Profs Interesting	94
Profs Accessible	97
Admissions	85
Financial Aid	91

CAMPUS LIFE

Type of school	Private
Environment	Village

Students

Degree-seeking undergrad enrollment	1,238
% male/female/not reported	49/51/0
% from out of state	30
% First-year from public high school	63
% First-year live on campus	96
% Ugrads live on campus	95
# of fraternities	0
# of sororities	0
% Asian	2
% Black or African American	6
% Hispanic	9
% Native American	<1
% Pacific Islander	<1
% Race and/or ethnicity unknown	5
% Two or more races	3
% White	67
% International	8
# of countries represented	26

CAMPUS MENTAL HEALTH SERVICES

Offers mental health/wellness program	Yes
Mental health training available to students	Yes
Employs Chief Wellness Officer	Yes
Peer-to-peer mental health offerings	Yes
Counseling center has guidelines or accreditation	Yes
Mental health/well-being courses	Yes, for-credit

ACADEMICS

% students returning for sophomore year	83
% students graduating within 4 years	63
% students graduating within 6 years	69
Calendar	Semester
Student/faculty ratio	12:1
Most common class size 10–19.	(42%)

Most Popular Majors

Environmental Science; Biology/Biological Sciences; Teacher Education

Applicants Sometimes Prefer

Dickinson College, Elizabethtown College, Indiana University of Pennsylvania, Lycoming College, Penn State University Park, Saint Francis University (PA), Shippensburg University of Pennsylvania, Susquehanna University, Temple University, University of Pittsburgh—Pittsburgh Campus

STUDENTS SAY "…"

Academics

For incoming first-year students at Juniata College, the Inbound Retreats offered each August are a great way to meet other students and glimpse college life without attending classes. The school has "excellent science programs," and a few students say that there need to be "more resources [for] nonscience programs." However, even students not majoring in science get access to some great facilities, with theater students exclaiming, "The theater program is unlike any other in country" and praising their new Halbritter Center for the Performing Arts. At Juniata, students have the option to design their educational plan with the college's Program of Emphasis, while those interested in a specific established program—something like accounting or chemistry—can use an existing designated Program of Emphasis. All students have the option of working with two faculty advisors. The "outstanding education" is built on a bedrock of strong faculty members who offer "superior education through meaningful personal interaction." Most class sizes tend to be fairly small, and though some classes are "tough to get in to because there is only one professor for a certain subject," many agree that they love the attention that each professor gives and that the teachers "really go out of their way" to help students succeed and "value student success as much as the student does." Success, however, doesn't come without a price at Juniata, with a large amount of the students agreeing that their "good grades do not come without effort," but that the class load is "challenging, but not overwhelming."

Campus Life

Students seem to agree that there "isn't much to do in the town" of Huntingdon, but Juniata College makes up for it by making sure there is "always something to do" on campus. There are so many activities and groups on campus that some say, "It feels like you're missing out if you go home for the weekend." There are a "lot of traditions such as Storming of the Arch, Mountain Day, and Madrigal" that have been around the campus for decades and help bring students together. For instance, during Mountain Day, classes are canceled, and students and faculty are shuttled to a state park near the school where there are lunches, nature walks, and various games being played, and neither group knows when exactly it is going to be until the morning of the event. While there might be a lot of activities to do on campus, "if you want to party you can find one." If you want to just relax with your fellow students, "Raystown Lake is only twenty minutes away," where many students like to go and relax. Back on campus, many students seem to think that the "dorms and food" need improvement, but believe that the academic experience they receive outweighs those drawbacks.

Student Body

Students tend to describe themselves as "driven" and "passionately interested in their subjects," though they also take pride in their "laid-back" attitudes, saying they "know how to balance fun and work." During the week students "tend to buckle down and get their work done." A lot of "exchange students from around the world" come to Juniata College to pursue their education. Students agree that "everyone fits in somewhere" at Juniata College because "people are accepted not despite their differences, but because of them."

Juniata College

Financial Aid: 814-641-3142 • E-Mail: info@juniata.edu • Website: www.juniata.edu

THE PRINCETON REVIEW SAYS

Admissions

The school reports that its standardized testing policy for use in admission for Fall 2026 is Test Optional. The Princeton Review suggests that interested applicants consult with the school for the most up-to-date standardized testing policies. *Very important factors considered include:* academic GPA. *Important factors considered include:* rigor of secondary school record, application essay, recommendation(s), extracurricular activities, talent/ability, character/personal qualities. *Other factors considered include:* class rank, standardized test scores, interview, first generation, alumni/ae relation, geographical residence, state residency, volunteer work, work experience. High school diploma is required and GED is accepted. *Academic units required:* 4 English, 3 math, 3 science, 1 science lab, 3 social studies. *Academic units recommended:* 2 language (other than English), 3 academic electives.

Financial Aid

Students should submit: FAFSA. Priority filing deadline is 3/15. The Princeton Review suggests that all financial aid forms be submitted as soon as possible. *Need-based scholarships/grants offered:* Federal Pell; Federal SEOG; State scholarships/grants; Private scholarships; College/university scholarship or grant aid from institutional funds. *Loan aid offered:* Federal Direct Subsidized Loans; Federal Direct Unsubsidized Loans; Direct PLUS loans; College/university loans from institutional funds. Admitted students will be notified of awards on a rolling basis beginning 11/30. Federal Work-Study Program available. Institutional employment available.

The Inside Word

Juniata is test optional, so you only need to submit SAT or ACT scores if they showcase your strengths. Choosing not to submit scores won't affect your chances for merit scholarships. The only exception is the Nursing Program—applicants there must submit SAT, ACT, or TEAS scores. Plus, there's no application fee if you apply through Juniata's website.

THE SCHOOL SAYS

From the Admissions Office

"Surrounded by stunning natural beauty, Juniata College welcomes inquisitive, talented, and hardworking students who do the work of becoming broadly educated, effective citizens of the world. Students can write their own academic programs based on their interests, talents, and goals. They contribute to a close-knit community of people who support, celebrate, and enjoy one another. Highly focused scholars, Juniata students conduct research, engage in meaningful service, intern on or near campus and across the globe, compete as athletes, and collaborate as artists. All of this happens in a modern oasis seemingly reserved for the purpose of fostering exploration and reflection.

"We firmly believe college years are the time to contemplate individual goals and explore options while enjoying the journey. We encourage students to consider new ideas and perspectives, take risks, push themselves to new experiences. As a result, our students graduate in four years not only with a useful college degree, but also with self-reliance, intellectual dexterity, courage of heart, and a collaborative, compassionate spirit.

"In discussions with their advisers, students choose a single discipline POE or write one that is customized to their interests. Still others become the authors of a POE no student has done before. The POE system at Juniata helps students act upon their deepening understanding of themselves and complete an undergraduate education that prepares them for success as they choose to define it. The true power of the POE, however, is that it provides a foundation upon which layers of experiences and opportunities can be added. The result is meaningful outcomes for individuals of consequence."

SELECTIVITY

# of total applicants	3,177
% of total applicants accepted	79
% of total acceptees attending	14
# of in-state applicants	1,247
% of in-state applicants accepted	82
# of out-of-state-applicants	1,369
% of applicants accepted from out of state	83
# of international applicants	559
% of international applicants accepted	64
# of early decision applicants	84
% of early decision applicants accepted	82

First-Year Profile

Testing policy	Test Optional
Range SAT composite	1150–1320
Range SAT EBRW	590–700
Range SAT math	560–650
Range ACT composite	27–32
% submitting SAT scores	27
% submitting ACT scores	5
Average HS GPA	3.6
% submitting high school GPA	99
% graduated top 10% of class	31
% graduated top 25% of class	51
% graduated top 50% of class	82
% submitting high school rank	45

Important Dates

Early decision	
Apply by	11/15
Notified by	12/15
Early action	
Apply by	1/15
Notified by	2/15
Regular	
Apply by	3/15
Notified by	Rolling, 10/30
Nonfall registration?	Yes

FINANCIAL FACTS

Annual tuition	$61,600
Food and housing	$15,000
Required fees	$1,100
Books and supplies	$1,000
Average need-based scholarship (First-year)	$19,051 ($19,336)
% students with need rec. need-based scholarship or grant aid (First-year)	100 (100)
% students with need rec. non-need-based scholarship or grant aid (First-year)	100 (100)
% students with need rec. need-based self-help aid (First-year)	100 (100)
% students rec. any financial aid (First-year)	100 (100)
% UG borrow to pay for school	70
Average cumulative indebtedness	$41,995
% of students with need fully met (First-year)	24 (25)
Average % of student need met (First-year)	90 (90)

Kalamazoo College

1200 Academy Street, Kalamazoo, MI 49006 • Admissions: 800-253-3602

Survey Snapshot
Active minority support groups
Great library
Recreation facilities are great

RATINGS

Quality of Life	**84**
Fire Safety	**79**
Green	**60***
Academic	**88**
Profs Interesting	**93**
Profs Accessible	**95**
Admissions	**87**
Financial Aid	**93**

CAMPUS LIFE

Type of school	Private
Environment	City

Students

Degree-seeking undergrad enrollment	1,098
% male/female/not reported	47/53/0
% from out of state	32
% First-year live on campus	100
% Ugrads live on campus	64
# of fraternities	0
# of sororities	0
% Asian	3
% Black or African American	6
% Hispanic	17
% Native American	<1
% Pacific Islander	0
% Race and/or ethnicity unknown	3
% Two or more races	6
% White	61
% International	4
# of countries represented	26

CAMPUS MENTAL HEALTH SERVICES

Offers mental health/wellness program	Yes
Mental health training available to students	Yes
Employs Chief Wellness Officer	NR
Peer-to-peer mental health offerings	Yes
Counseling center has guidelines or accreditation	Yes
Mental health/well-being courses	NR

ACADEMICS

% students returning for sophomore year	86
% students graduating within 4 years	64
% students graduating within 6 years	74
Calendar	Quarter
Student/faculty ratio	10:1

Most Popular Majors
Business; Psychology; Biology

STUDENTS SAY "..."

Academics

Kalamazoo College, also more familiarly known as K, is a private liberal arts college in Michigan that brings a personalized approach to education through a flexible, open curriculum featuring real-world experience, service learning, study abroad, and an independent senior year project. This small, nationally-recognized institution "allows students to really develop personal relationships with their peers and professors" and is "a campus run by and for the students." The open curriculum means "students have more time to explore exactly what they want to learn, rather than being required to take classes in which they have no interest," and the school motto of "More in Four" not only describes how much students will learn in their time at K, but "also that this institution will try as hard as possible to get you to graduate in four years." As for post-graduate plans, alumni are "very easy to contact and willing to help." As one student puts it, "Through alumni interaction and my experiences at Kalamazoo, there is a huge culture of giving back to the school and being there for each other."

Full-time professors here, 96 percent of whom hold a PhD or the highest degree in their field, "present challenging information and generally work to achieve camaraderie with students." They "definitely understand that classes may be difficult and really, truly want to help students learn the best they can," and also view students "as equals and peers, and are open to listening to everyone's ideas in classes." Professors "demand quite a lot, but only from a desire to teach the material effectively"; they also "message their departments with internship opportunities quite regularly." Most students have only three classes at a time (the school is on a quarter system) "because each class here tends to be more intense."

Campus Life

Academics are a universal student priority at Kalamazoo College, and "missing classes or letting work slack for social lives and hangovers doesn't happen often." Many times residence halls will host community building events that provide "good food and fun activities," and the school puts on numerous events for the students such as Friday night movies and "Zoo After Dark," and offers a wide variety of programs and clubs to join, and "all are accessible to students who want to pursue them." There "isn't a lot to do" in the surrounding area, but those that are 21 can hit a few bars or clubs and those with access to a car can drive to nearby malls and cities. There "is not a lot of time to have fun on weekdays since things move quickly," but people make time for hanging out. Athletics are popular and "easy to get into"; some teams are more competitive than others, "but for the most part, if you played in high school, you can play in college." Most students study abroad at some point in their K career (typically junior year).

Student Body

Kalamazoo College students are generally "very open-minded, unique, liberal, and quirky," and "you will never find any two students that are the same here." This is mostly a campus of "socially conscious liberals who are predominantly white," though there are a fair number of people with conservative ideologies. While many admit Kalamazoo "needs more diversity in race," students say it is a "very open campus community for people of different gender identities and sexualities." Each student is able to find their niche quickly due to the small school environment, thus "everyone is always engaged in some kind of work they truly care about."

KALAMAZOO COLLEGE

Financial Aid: 269-337-7192 • E-Mail: admission@kzoo.edu • Website: www.kzoo.edu

THE PRINCETON REVIEW SAYS

Admissions

The school reports that its standardized testing policy for use in admission for Fall 2026 is Test Optional. The Princeton Review suggests that interested applicants consult with the school for the most up-to-date standardized testing policies. *Very important factors considered include:* rigor of secondary school record, extracurricular activities. *Important factors considered include:* application essay, recommendation(s). *Other factors considered include:* academic GPA, standardized test scores, talent/ability, character/personal qualities, first generation, alumni/ae relation, geographical residence, state residency, volunteer work, work experience, level of applicant's interest. High school diploma is required and GED is accepted. *Academic units required:* 4 English, 3 math, 3 science, 2 language (other than English), 2 social studies, 2 history. *Academic units recommended:* 4 English, 4 math, 4 science, 3 language (other than English), 2 social studies, 2 history.

Financial Aid

Students should submit: FAFSA. Priority filing deadline is 3/1. The Princeton Review suggests that all financial aid forms be submitted as soon as possible. *Need-based scholarships/grants offered:* Federal Pell; Federal SEOG; State scholarships/grants; Private scholarships; College/university scholarship or grant aid from institutional funds. *Loan aid offered:* Federal Direct Subsidized Loans; Federal Direct Unsubsidized Loans. Admitted students will be notified of awards on a rolling basis beginning 12/1. Federal Work-Study Program available. Institutional employment available.

The Inside Word

Whether you're focusing on liberal arts or sciences, much of Kalamazoo College revolves around its academic K-Plan, and admission officers are looking for students who show the intellectual curiosity, engagement, and motivation to make the most out of the school's experiential education. They also seek students who challenge themselves through a rigorous curriculum, co-curricular involvement, or independent pursuits and who demonstrate initiative and follow-through. Be sure to highlight activities that have taken you outside your comfort zone and have involved interactions with the world.

THE SCHOOL SAYS

From the Admissions Office

"At Kalamazoo College, faculty and staff embrace our motto—More in Four. More in a Lifetime.—by offering students more opportunities to explore, more mentorship and support, and more preparation for meaningful careers that make a positive impact on the world.

"The K-Plan provides an integrated, customizable, and experiential education. The majority of students participate in an immersive, academically focused study abroad program; most participate in career development through internships, career treks or an array of community partnerships and community-based courses; and 100 percent complete a senior project in an area of personal interest. Also, Kalamazoo College is one of the few selective liberal arts colleges to be found in a city—the Kalamazoo metro area has a population of over 260,000 with the advantage of being near a university of nearly 20,000 students. It is a diverse and vibrant community with wonderful access to the arts, athletics, service-learning, and social activism opportunities. K's campus is adjacent to downtown Kalamazoo, which offers shops, restaurants, art galleries, live music and more.

"Kalamazoo College uses a holistic review process to fully assess a student's candidacy for admission. Emphasis is placed on a student's high school experience, including GPA, course selection, application essay, and co-curricular involvement."

SELECTIVITY

# of total applicants	3,684
% of total applicants accepted	77
% of total acceptees attending	9
# of in-state applicants	1,756
% of in-state applicants accepted	82
# of out-of-state-applicants	1,279
% of applicants accepted from out of state	89
# of international applicants	648
% of international applicants accepted	39
# of early decision applicants	43
% of early decision applicants accepted	71
# offered a place on the wait list	0

First-Year Profile

Testing policy	Test Optional
Range SAT composite	1170–1370
Range SAT EBRW	580–710
Range SAT math	350–670
Range ACT composite	19–31
% submitting SAT scores	35
% submitting ACT scores	11
Average HS GPA	3.8
% submitting high school GPA	100
% graduated top 10% of class	32
% graduated top 25% of class	62
% graduated top 50% of class	90
% submitting high school rank	40

Important Dates

Early decision	
Apply by	11/1
Notified by	12/1
Early action	
Apply by	11/1
Notified by	12/20
Regular	
Apply by	1/15
Notified by	Rolling
Nonfall registration?	No

FINANCIAL FACTS

Annual tuition	$65,265
Food and housing	$13,803
Required fees	$693
Books and supplies	$1,020
Average need-based scholarship (First-year)	$51,900 ($55,951)
% students with need rec. need-based scholarship or grant aid (First-year)	98 (99)
% students with need rec. non-need-based scholarship or grant aid (First-year)	29 (28)
% students with need rec. need-based self-help aid (First-year)	72 (72)
% students rec. any financial aid (First-year)	97 (99)
% UG borrow to pay for school	54
Average cumulative indebtedness	$31,125
% of students with need fully met (First-year)	38 (35)
Average % of student need met (First-year)	93 (95)

KANSAS STATE UNIVERSITY

110 Anderson Hall, Manhattan, KS 66506 • Admissions: 785-532-6250

Survey Snapshot
Students are happy
Students get along with local community
Students love Manhattan, KS

RATINGS

Quality of Life	**95**
Fire Safety	**60***
Green	**60***
Academic	**81**
Profs Interesting	**91**
Profs Accessible	**94**
Admissions	**84**
Financial Aid	**84**

CAMPUS LIFE

Type of school	Public
Environment	Town

Students

Degree-seeking undergrad enrollment	15,919
% male/female/not reported	48/52/<1
% from out of state	26
% First-year from public high school	74
% First-year live on campus	81
% Ugrads live on campus	28
# of fraternities (% join)	28 (NR)
# of sororities (% join)	16 (NR)
% Asian	2
% Black or African American	3
% Hispanic	10
% Native American	<1
% Pacific Islander	<1
% Race and/or ethnicity unknown	1
% Two or more races	4
% White	78
% International	2
# of countries represented	78

CAMPUS MENTAL HEALTH SERVICES

Offers mental health/wellness program	Yes
Mental health training available to students	No
Employs Chief Wellness Officer	NR
Peer-to-peer mental health offerings	NR
Counseling center has guidelines or accreditation	No
Mental health/well-being courses	NR

ACADEMICS

% students returning for sophomore year	86
% students graduating within 4 years	51
% students graduating within 6 years	71
Calendar	Semester
Student/faculty ratio	19:1
Most common class size 10–19.	(29%)

Most Popular Majors

Business Administration and Management; Agriculture; Mechanical Engineering

STUDENTS SAY "..."

Academics

With more than 150 years of traditions and achievements on the record, Kansas State University is the nation's first operational land-grant university, offering more than 250 undergraduate majors and programs across three campuses, as well as various global online courses. The university's sprawling 2,300-acre main campus in Manhattan, Kansas (nicknamed "The Little Apple") includes comprehensive agricultural and research facilities, while the newest campus, Olathe, is located in the Kansas Biosciences Park and works to expand partnerships between students, researchers, and companies. "Leadership opportunities are always within an arm's length," says a student. On the administration's part, there is excellent "communication of resources available to students," and the school is "very conscious of showing students what they are paying for and listening to student feedback in what prices should be for fees/services." In demonstrating further commitment to quality, "professor performance grades are sent out to students at the end of every semester."

At this research powerhouse, faculty members not only conduct "amazing research that is being nationally recognized" but also strive to do in a way that lets them "pass on their knowledge to the students." Such efforts are also recognized in and out of the classroom, whether that's in the way teachers "are skilled at making classes interesting" or how they lead review sessions "to better help students focus on harder topics." (Students also mention how discussion boards are "largely utilized for engagement.) In general, professors are praised for responding "quickly and well to emails" and overall come across as "approachable and really want to see their students learn and succeed."

Campus Life

The college town of Manhattan "provides those from bigger cities with the pros of a small-town feel (community, laid-back style) while also giving students from rural areas a more city-like lifestyle." As one student puts it: "It is super easy to balance school and a social life here since the majority of the people who live here are students." The bars, restaurants, and shopping in the neighborhood of Aggieville make it "a vibrant hotspot for activity every weekend and even on weekdays." The "gym facilities and hiking trails nearby are beautiful and a great way to get moving," and "the city and university maintain public sidewalks and trails for those wishing to bike/run." All student amenities "are within walking distance," and for fun, "many people attend parties, hang out with friends, and attend events hosted in the student union." Intramurals are wildly popular, and Greek life "is fun but not too overpowering," ensuring that the overall vibe allows students to "focus on their studies and dedicate their daytime hours to ensuring they complete their coursework."

Student Body

K-State is composed of "many international students, first generation students, and students from virtually all race, religion, and age," as well as "many students who grew up on a farm or other rural areas," all of whom contribute to a "wonderful community mindset." Traditions abound here, and "the university instills this very real feeling of belonging and family" known as the Wildcat Way. "Purple pride is taken very seriously" here, so much so that one student notes how "We see that Wildcat, and know we're part of the same family." This is "a big school with a small-town feel," and everyone is "exceedingly friendly and proud of the university." The school itself provides plenty of ways for students to be involved, and there are "a multitude of opportunities for students to find their own space to grow and succeed in."

Kansas State University

Financial Aid: 785-532-6420 • E-Mail: apply@k-state.edu • Website: www.k-state.edu

THE PRINCETON REVIEW SAYS

Admissions

The school reports that its standardized testing policy for use in admission for Fall 2026 is Test Optional. The Princeton Review suggests that interested applicants consult with the school for the most up-to-date standardized testing policies. *Very important factors considered include:* academic GPA. *Important factors considered include:* standardized test scores. *Other factors considered include:* class rank, application essay, recommendation(s), work experience. High school diploma is required and GED is accepted. *Academic units required:* 4 English, 4 math, 3 science, 2 language (other than English), 3 social studies.

Financial Aid

Students should submit: FAFSA. Priority filing deadline is 12/1. The Princeton Review suggests that all financial aid forms be submitted as soon as possible. *Need-based scholarships/grants offered:* Federal Pell; Federal SEOG; State scholarships/grants; Private scholarships; College/university scholarship or grant aid from institutional funds. *Loan aid offered:* Federal Direct Subsidized Loans; Federal Direct Unsubsidized Loans; Direct PLUS loans. Admitted students will be notified of awards on a rolling basis beginning 4/1. Federal Work-Study Program available. Institutional employment available.

The Inside Word

Kansas State is pretty transparent about their admission requirements, and the school is Test Optional. So long as your cumulative high school GPA (weighted or unweighted) is above a 3.25, you should be fine; otherwise, you'll want to include an ACT composite of at least 21 or an SAT total of 1060 or higher. Students who don't meet these standards may appeal and have their application considered on a case-by-case basis, but be aware that this might entail sending in additional documentation or information.

THE SCHOOL SAYS

From the Admissions Office

"Kansas State University is synonymous with community, and its family-like environment is hailed by students past and present. The land-grant university also is home to some of the nation's top academic programs, world-renowned researchers, and unparalleled student support. K-State students have access to first-year programs, free tutoring, research opportunities, career exploration, and much more.

"K-State is rooted in diversity and inclusion with students from all 50 states and 100-plus countries. There are numerous opportunities to explore other cultures through student groups and events, and our Black Student Union has been named No. 1 in the Big 12 almost every year in the last decade. Academic experiences can easily be customized for individual goals with 250-plus majors and options alongside faculty who are committed to helping students find success. Our student experience is one of the best in the nation thanks to programs like K-State First, a first-year experience program helping freshmen connect with the university, and K-State Proud, a student-led philanthropy that has raised more than $1 million for fellow students in need.

"The university awards $38 million in scholarships each year, as well as $248 million in financial aid. Whatever it takes to help students succeed both today and in the future, the K-State family is committed to making it happen."

SELECTIVITY

# of total applicants	15,591
% of total applicants accepted	87
% of total acceptees attending	28
# of in-state applicants	7,088
% of in-state applicants accepted	94
# of out-of-state-applicants	7,102
% of applicants accepted from out of state	92
# of international applicants	1,401
% of international applicants accepted	33

First-Year Profile

Testing policy	Test Optional
Range SAT composite	1040–1260
Range SAT EBRW	520–660
Range SAT math	500–650
Range ACT composite	20–27
% submitting SAT scores	7
% submitting ACT scores	80
Average HS GPA	3.9
% submitting high school GPA	87
% graduated top 10% of class	29
% graduated top 25% of class	56
% graduated top 50% of class	84
% submitting high school rank	64

Important Dates

Regular	
Nonfall registration?	Yes

FINANCIAL FACTS*

Annual in-state tuition	$10,601
Annual out-of-state tuition	$28,555
Food and housing	$11,520
Required fees	$978
Books and supplies	$1,062
Average need-based scholarship (First-year)	$7,507 ($8,106)
% students with need rec. need-based scholarship or grant aid (First-year)	64 (61)
% students with need rec. non-need-based scholarship or grant aid (First-year)	71 (84)
% students with need rec. need-based self-help aid (First-year)	56 (57)
% students rec. any financial aid (First-year)	80 (94)
% UG borrow to pay for school	47
Average cumulative indebtedness	$25,718
% of students with need fully met (First-year)	27 (32)
Average % of student need met (First-year)	76 (79)

* Most recently reported data at time of printing. Scan the QR code to find the latest updates.

Kenyon College

103 Chase Ave, Gambier, OH 43022 • Admissions: 740-427-5776

Survey Snapshot
Lots of liberal students
Students always studying
Theater is popular

RATINGS

Quality of Life	**88**
Fire Safety	**91**
Green	**60***
Academic	**95**
Profs Interesting	**95**
Profs Accessible	**98**
Admissions	**93**
Financial Aid	**99**

CAMPUS LIFE

Type of school	Private
Affiliation	Episcopal (non-denominational in practice)
Environment	Rural

Students

Degree-seeking undergrad enrollment	1,589
% male/female/not reported	45/55/0
% from out of state	85
% First-year from public high school	50
% First-year live on campus	100
% Ugrads live on campus	100
# of fraternities (% join)	5 (14)
# of sororities (% join)	4 (20)
% Asian	4
% Black or African American	3
% Hispanic	8
% Native American	<1
% Pacific Islander	0
% Race and/or ethnicity unknown	1
% Two or more races	7
% White	65
% International	11
# of countries represented	53

CAMPUS MENTAL HEALTH SERVICES

Offers mental health/wellness program	Yes
Mental health training available to students	Yes
Employs Chief Wellness Officer	NR
Peer-to-peer mental health offerings	NR
Counseling center has guidelines or accreditation	NR
Mental health/well-being courses	NR

ACADEMICS

% students returning for sophomore year	91
% students graduating within 4 years	80
% students graduating within 6 years	85
Calendar	Semester
Student/faculty ratio	9:1
Most common class size 10–19.	(52%)

Most Popular Majors

English Language and Literature; Psychology; Economics

Applicants Also Look At

Bates College, Bowdoin College, Brown University, Carleton College, Denison University, Grinnell College, Hamilton College, Middlebury College, Oberlin College, The Ohio State University—Columbus, University of California—Berkeley, University of California—Los Angeles, University of Michigan—Ann Arbor, University of North Carolina at Chapel Hill, Vassar College, Washington University in St. Louis, Wesleyan University, William & Mary

STUDENTS SAY "…"

Academics

Kenyon College champions "academic vigor" and has earned its designation as "The Writers' College." Students value the school's focus on writing, with one student saying, "Even though I don't want to be an English major, I think any college that values writing as much as Kenyon does has its priorities straight." This private college provides a "well-rounded liberal arts education in which emphasis [is] placed on critical thinking and class discussion." Kenyon offers "small, individualized class sizes" with "terrifically interesting" courses. Faculty members are exceptionally supportive; one student recounts meeting with a professor "for an hour every day leading up to the final because I was so nervous about it, and he hardly batted an eye at taking that much time out of his day for only one student." Professors at Kenyon "love learning just as much as the students," and students say, "It is honestly hard to find a professor who is not thrilled by the content that they are teaching." The faculty creates an engaging environment where students are taught "to see, discuss, and connect the dots" and feel "your voice is valued in class discussion." Additionally, the school "really knows how to offer a huge diversity of programs and activities to a very small campus." There is "a wide variety of options available in terms of classes," and research opportunities are available to all students, including first-years. While Kenyon fosters a studious environment, overall, it's not a competitive place. Instead, the college encourages a "cooperative learning environment," making academics "less stressful." Students say that "out-of-class work is always meaningful" and while "you will spend the vast majority of your time studying...it is also extremely rewarding."

Campus Life

Kenyon is a "small campus with a big sense of community." The campus itself is "utterly pastoral," and students say, "It's like going to school in a Marlowe poem—and with all of the English majors running around, most people know who Marlowe is." As one student recalls, "I stepped on campus and noticed two things: everyone was happy and the campus was gorgeous." The trade-off for these "absolutely lovely" surroundings is that the town of Gambier is "in the middle of nowhere, so campus can get to be claustrophobic at times." However, students find plenty of ways to stay busy and connect with peers who share their passions. There are numerous clubs and organizations, as wells as "activist groups for everything from gender awareness to Palestine." Parties, including Greek life parties, are a "typical activity to unwind after a challenging week of academics." Students also let off steam through intramural sports, hiking on the nearby Kokosing Gap Trail, or working out in the gym.

Student Body

The student body is made up of "forward-thinking students who study hard but also understand the necessity of taking breaks and having a good time on weekends." Most students are heavily involved in both their studies and in extracurriculars. As one student observes, "You're either a jack of all trades here or a master of four." Students describe an environment that is very inclusive. For example, "someone on the football team could just as easily be in the community choir or quiz bowl club." These diverse interests paint a picture of a community that is eclectic and welcoming. As one student explains, "Even though I'm not a philosophy major, I feel just as at home in those conversations as I do when I discuss Mahler or the next big party." Another adds, "Most people [here] have a quirk or five." Overall, Kenyon is a social campus where people are engaged, passionate, and interested in the world around them. As one student sums up, everyone "tends to be extremely friendly, well-rounded, and smart."

KENYON COLLEGE

Financial Aid: 740-427-5430 • E-Mail: admissions@kenyon.edu • Website: www.kenyon.edu

THE PRINCETON REVIEW SAYS

Admissions

The school reports that its standardized testing policy for use in admission for Fall 2026 is Test Optional. The Princeton Review suggests that interested applicants consult with the school for the most up-to-date standardized testing policies. *Very important factors considered include:* rigor of secondary school record, academic GPA. *Important factors considered include:* application essay, recommendation(s), extracurricular activities, talent/ability, character/personal qualities, level of applicant's interest. *Other factors considered include:* class rank, standardized test scores, interview, first generation, alumni/ae relation, geographical residence, state residency, volunteer work, work experience. High school diploma is required and GED is accepted. *Academic units required:* 4 English, 4 math, 3 science, 3 science labs, 3 language (other than English), 3 social studies, 3 academic electives. *Academic units recommended:* 4 English, 4 math, 4 science, 3 science labs, 4 language (other than English), 3 social studies, 3 history.

Financial Aid

Students should submit: FAFSA; CSS PROFILE. Priority filing deadline is 1/15. The Princeton Review suggests that all financial aid forms be submitted as soon as possible. *Need-based scholarships/grants offered:* Federal Pell; Federal SEOG; State scholarships/grants; College/university scholarship or grant aid from institutional funds. *Loan aid offered:* Federal Direct Subsidized Loans; Federal Direct Unsubsidized Loans; Direct PLUS loans; College/university loans from institutional funds. Admitted students will be notified of awards on or about 3/15. Federal Work-Study Program available. Institutional employment available.

The Inside Word

In terms of admissions selectivity, Kenyon is of the first order of selective, small, Midwestern, liberal arts schools. Kenyon shares a lot of application and admit overlap with other schools in this niche, and the choice for many students comes down to "best fit." As Kenyon is a writing-intensive institution, applicants should expect that all written material submitted to the school in the admissions process will be scrutinized. Revise and proofread accordingly.

THE SCHOOL SAYS

From the Admissions Office

"Students and alumni alike think of Kenyon as a place that fosters 'learning in the company of friends.' While faculty expectations are rigorous and the work challenging, the academic atmosphere is cooperative, not competitive. Indications of intellectual curiosity and passion for learning, more than just high grades and test scores, are what we look for in applications. Important as well are demonstrated interests in non-academic pursuits, whether in athletics, the arts, writing, or another passion. Life in this small college community is fueled by the talents and enthusiasm of our students, so the admission staff seeks students who have a range of talents and interests.

"The high school transcript, recommendations, and the personal statement are of primary importance in reviewing preparedness and fit."

SELECTIVITY

# of total applicants	7,091
% of total applicants accepted	30
% of total acceptees attending	19
# of early decision applicants	663
% of early decision applicants accepted	35
# offered a place on the wait list	1,439
# admitted from wait list	63

First-Year Profile

Testing policy	Test Optional
Range SAT composite	1400–1500
Range SAT EBRW	700–740
Range SAT math	680–770
Range ACT composite	31–34
% submitting SAT scores	8
% submitting ACT scores	8
Average HS GPA	4.2
% submitting high school GPA	94
% graduated top 10% of class	53
% graduated top 25% of class	80
% graduated top 50% of class	100
% submitting high school rank	21

Important Dates

Early decision	
Apply by	11/15
Notified by	12/15
Other ED apply by	1/15
Other ED notified by	2/1
Regular	
Apply by	1/15
Notified by	3/23
Nonfall registration?	No

FINANCIAL FACTS

Annual tuition	$72,880
Food and housing	$19,860
Required fees	$350
Books and supplies	$1,900
Average need-based scholarship (First-year)	$61,668 ($59,495)
% students with need rec. need-based scholarship or grant aid (First-year)	100 (100)
% students with need rec. non-need-based scholarship or grant aid (First-year)	47 (73)
% students with need rec. need-based self-help aid (First-year)	81 (73)
% students rec. any financial aid (First-year)	83 (91)
% UG borrow to pay for school	41
Average cumulative indebtedness	$28,833
% of students with need fully met (First-year)	100 (100)
Average % of student need met (First-year)	100 (100)

KETTERING UNIVERSITY

1700 University Avenue, Flint, MI 48504 • Admissions: 810-762-9500

Survey Snapshot
Lots of conservative students
Frats and sororities are popular
Internships are widely available

RATINGS

Quality of Life	69
Fire Safety	85
Green	60*
Academic	75
Profs Interesting	77
Profs Accessible	86
Admissions	86
Financial Aid	89

CAMPUS LIFE

Type of school	Private
Environment	City

Students

Degree-seeking undergrad enrollment	1,261
% male/female/not reported	80/20/0
% from out of state	13
% First-year from public high school	86
% First-year live on campus	100
% Ugrads live on campus	35
# of fraternities (% join)	11 (32)
# of sororities (% join)	3 (5)
% Asian	7
% Black or African American	7
% Hispanic	5
% Native American	<1
% Pacific Islander	<1
% Race and/or ethnicity unknown	3
% Two or more races	5
% White	70
% International	3
# of countries represented	25

CAMPUS MENTAL HEALTH SERVICES

Offers mental health/wellness program	Yes
Mental health training available to students	Yes
Employs Chief Wellness Officer	No
Peer-to-peer mental health offerings	Yes
Counseling center has guidelines or accreditation	Yes
Mental health/well-being courses	No

ACADEMICS

% students returning for sophomore year	90
% students graduating within 4 years	46
% students graduating within 6 years	73
Calendar	Semester
Student/faculty ratio	12:1
Most common class size 10–19.	(28%)
Most common lab/discussion size 20–29.	(33%)

Most Popular Majors
Chemical Engineering; Electrical Engineering; Mechanical Engineering

Applicants Often Prefer
Michigan State University, Michigan Technological University, University of Michigan—Ann Arbor

Applicants Sometimes Prefer
Wayne State College

Applicants Rarely Prefer
Grand Valley State University, Lawrence Technological University, Oakland University, Purdue University—West Lafayette, University of Michigan—Dearborn, University of Michigan—Flint

STUDENTS SAY "…"

Academics

Students with an interest in business or STEM subjects will be pleased with the offerings of Kettering University, which has a focus not just on those disciplines, but in fostering the next generation of industry leaders. Students attribute some of their success to the institution's "awesome" Co-op program, which is "unparalleled in preparing students." The way Co-op works is by splitting the academic calendar into four approximately 11-week terms, two of which are for school, and two of which are for work. This means that from their first year on, undergrads "get to make money during school while also getting experience and making industry connections."

A word of warning from students, though: this type of scheduling is quite demanding. "Course loads are high and there is often a lot of homework." This can be compounded by what current enrollees feel is an all-or-nothing split between instructor styles: some "care deeply about the subject and the students" and others who are just plain prickly, or as one puts it, "I have had many professors gladly tell me how many students have failed their class." There are plenty of students who share happy stories of faculty members who are "available almost whenever you need them" or who are "very understanding" and "always willing to help," but "there isn't really an in-between."

Campus Life

Kettering may have an unconventional calendar, and some busy students may quip that "We're all engineers, so we're studying all the time," and yet we heard at length about all the fun activities that students found time to squeeze in. "There is a club for anything and everyone," shares one student, and that doesn't seem to be an exaggeration. In addition to the school's SAE teams, which are among "the best in the country," there are plenty of other interest-driven activities like the Financial Club and even a blacksmithing club. Students also list a variety of intramural sports like flag football and basketball as a great way to escape academic stress. "We may go out bowling, to play Topgolf, to catch a movie, [to go] skiing or off-roading." Nearby Detroit and Ann Arbor offer even more events, as does the university itself. Undergrads also share that "Greek life is very popular," although here, too, note that some describe the Greek scene as "completely different at Kettering than it is at other campuses."

Student Body

The "very bright" students at Kettering, despite sometimes feeling "overworked, stressed out, and sleep deprived," overall find themselves "bonded by our struggles in our rigorous coursework." Students stay in good humor and find the silver lining in every experience, or as one colorfully puts it, "We are all...caffeine-fueled sarcasm machines that pump out math and science equations at the drop of a hat." The "personable" atmosphere of this "relatively small" school may help to liven everyone's mood. "Even if you do not know someone's name, you recognize a face in the hallway or in a lecture that you can share a smile with." More importantly, students say that their classmates are "very helpful" and note that "it is easy to join a group who is studying and get to know them." Easy, at least, if you're male—the "vast majority is white male engineering students," and some find that to create "a culture of masculinity" that sometimes offers "very little support for the women." Then again, other enrollees dispute this, suggesting that Kettering is "a very inclusive school" where students "accept and accommodate each other's differences." At the end of the day, all undergrads are "technically minded people" who "want to push boundaries and go further than anyone else," and one notes that "if you love cars, engineering, and the automotive industry, there probably is no better school."

KETTERING UNIVERSITY

Financial Aid: 810-762-7859 • E-Mail: admissions@kettering.edu • Website: www.kettering.edu

THE PRINCETON REVIEW SAYS

Admissions

The school reports that its standardized testing policy for use in admission for Fall 2026 is Test Optional. The Princeton Review suggests that interested applicants consult with the school for the most up-to-date standardized testing policies. *Very important factors considered include:* rigor of secondary school record, academic GPA. *Other factors considered include:* class rank, standardized test scores, application essay, recommendation(s), extracurricular activities, character/personal qualities, volunteer work, work experience. High school diploma is required and GED is accepted. *Academic units required:* 3 English, 3.5 math, 1 science, 1 science lab. *Academic units recommended:* 4 English, 4 math, 3 science, 3 science labs, 2 social studies, 2 history, 1 computer science.

Financial Aid

Students should submit: FAFSA. The Princeton Review suggests that all financial aid forms be submitted as soon as possible. *Need-based scholarships/grants offered:* Federal Pell; Federal SEOG; State scholarships/grants; Private scholarships; College/university scholarship or grant aid from institutional funds. *Loan aid offered:* Federal Direct Subsidized Loans; Federal Direct Unsubsidized Loans; Direct PLUS loans. Federal Work-Study Program available. Institutional employment available.

The Inside Word

Kettering aims to find students who will be able to handle the university's demanding curriculum. Given that it's mainly a STEM school, the grades you earned in your math and science classes will need to be high. It's also strongly recommended that you take calculus and any computer programming or CAD courses available. If for any reason you think your GPA or test scores don't accurately reflect your abilities, you are invited to call the admissions office to discuss your application with one of the school's counselors.

THE SCHOOL SAYS

From the Admissions Office

"Kettering University began in 1919 as The School of Automobile Trades, a bold experiment in applied education created to serve the rapidly expanding automotive industry. With more than 570 employer partners across the U.S. and worldwide, Kettering's combination of rigorous academics and full-time, paid Co-op employment helps students graduate with 2.5 years of industry experience while typically earning $55,000 to $75,000, often offsetting a portion of their tuition. The model has earned recognition from The Wall Street Journal, placing Kettering among the top 10 universities for career preparation.

"From designing electric drivetrains and next-generation battery systems to building intelligent software and optimizing business logistics, Kettering students turn ideas into solutions. Through a robust merit scholarship program, the university recognizes academic achievement and future potential, helping high-performing students pursue the rigor and opportunity of the Kettering model.

"Kettering Bulldogs don't just innovate in the lab or the classroom. They bring that same drive to robotics arenas, racetracks, and gaming competitions. Many have competed with KUdos, the university's VEX U robotics team, applying CAD, 3D printing, and programming. Kettering is one of eight North American universities in the AutoDrive Challenge II, developing autonomous vehicles with General Motors and SAE International. Baja SAE teams design, build, and race off-road vehicles while competing in cost, design, and marketing events. Kettering's ESports program has also claimed national titles in Rainbow 6: Siege. Kettering students do not just meet challenges. They create them."

SELECTIVITY

# of total applicants	2,085
% of total applicants accepted	80
% of total acceptees attending	20
# of in-state applicants	1,540
% of in-state applicants accepted	83
# of out-of-state-applicants	447
% of applicants accepted from out of state	75
# of international applicants	91
% of international applicants accepted	45

First-Year Profile

Testing policy	Test Optional
Range SAT composite	1020–1570
Range SAT EBRW	450–780
Range SAT math	450–780
Range ACT composite	23–33
% submitting SAT scores	52
% submitting ACT scores	5
Average HS GPA	3.7
% submitting high school GPA	100
% graduated top 10% of class	27
% graduated top 25% of class	63
% graduated top 50% of class	90
% submitting high school rank	56

Important Dates

Early action	
Apply by	11/15
Notified by	Rolling
Regular	
Notified by	Rolling, 11/15
Nonfall registration?	Yes

FINANCIAL FACTS

Annual tuition	$50,650
Books and supplies	$800
Average need-based scholarship (First-year)	$29,665 ($34,788)
% students with need rec. need-based scholarship or grant aid (First-year)	100 (100)
% students with need rec. non-need-based scholarship or grant aid (First-year)	5 (9)
% students with need rec. need-based self-help aid (First-year)	70 (66)
% students rec. any financial aid (First-year)	99 (100)
% UG borrow to pay for school	65
Average cumulative indebtedness	$48,569
% of students with need fully met (First-year)	30 (38)
Average % of student need met (First-year)	89 (94)

KNOX COLLEGE

2 East South Street, Galesburg, IL 61401 • Admissions: 309-341-7100

Survey Snapshot
Lots of liberal students
Great library
Students environmentally aware

RATINGS

Quality of Life	**78**
Fire Safety	**96**
Green	**87**
Academic	**90**
Profs Interesting	**95**
Profs Accessible	**97**
Admissions	**86**
Financial Aid	**91**

CAMPUS LIFE

Type of school	Private
Environment	Town

Students

Degree-seeking undergrad enrollment	1,100
% male/female/not reported	51/48/<1
% from out of state	45
% First-year from public high school	56
% First-year live on campus	95
% Ugrads live on campus	98
# of fraternities (% join)	4 (6)
# of sororities (% join)	3 (3)
% Asian	3
% Black or African American	9
% Hispanic	14
% Native American	<1
% Pacific Islander	<1
% Race and/or ethnicity unknown	3
% Two or more races	3
% White	37
% International	29
# of countries represented	54

CAMPUS MENTAL HEALTH SERVICES

Offers mental health/wellness program	Yes
Mental health training available to students	Yes
Employs Chief Wellness Officer	Yes
Peer-to-peer mental health offerings	Yes
Counseling center has guidelines or accreditation	Yes
Mental health/well-being courses	Yes, non-credit

ACADEMICS

% students returning for sophomore year	81
% students graduating within 4 years	48
% students graduating within 6 years	73
Calendar	Quarter
Student/faculty ratio	11:1
Most common class size 10–19.	(45%)
Most common lab/discussion size 10–19.	(57%)

Most Popular Majors
Computer Science; Creative Writing; Business Administration and Management

Applicants Often Prefer
Augustana College (IL)

Applicants Sometimes Prefer
Beloit College, DePaul University, Grinnell College, Hope College, Illinois Wesleyan University, Kenyon College, Lake Forest College, Lawrence University, Loyola University Chicago, St. Olaf College, The University of Chicago, University of Illinois at Chicago, University of Illinois at Urbana—Champaign, University of Iowa

Applicants Rarely Prefer
Bradley University, The College of Wooster, Denison University, DePauw University, Illinois State University

STUDENTS SAY "..."

Academics

Knox College offers students a "well-rounded liberal arts program" with a "great academic reputation." Known for valuing "independent initiative," Knox students can be found "commonly studying two vastly different subjects and allowing them to merge into one interdisciplinary interest." One student chose to attend Knox because "I knew that I would be allowed to be myself, choose the classes that I felt would have the most influence on my education and prepare me for the future." To support student independence and depth of study, Knox has an academic calendar that allows for "a semester's worth of coursework in a ten-week period" as well as an extended break between the fall and winter terms in which students can engage in research or internships. Students report that this system also "promotes better study habits and more attention focused on each class."

Students appreciate that they are "academically challenged without fierce competition," though they admit that courses can be "tough and require a lot of time studying, reading, writing, and thinking." Don't plan to come to Knox "if you want to shy away from class discussion." Student opinions are taken seriously. Administration and faculty "not only encourage the students to take charge and make change, but they listen and act on the student body's opinions." In so doing, Knox succeeds in "staying in tune with its roots as a progressive and accessible institution."

Campus Life

Students share that "when we want to do something fun, we typically organize it ourselves." Students can join any of the over 80 student-led clubs and student organizations on campus, and they delight in "artistic expression, be it poetry, visual art, performance art, music." Students also enjoy Thursday night jazz on campus, as well as a lively athletics scene. Some 70% of students participate in a varsity, club, or intramural sport. Fun on campus also comes courtesy of the Union Board, which "brings films, entertainers, concerts, and other groups to campus, including Second City," and sponsors movie nights that feature a 24-foot inflatable screen. Knox does have a Greek scene with four sororities and five fraternities. Students "go to parties, play games, dance, etc., just like any other college campus. The difference is our fraternity parties are open to the entire campus and do not serve alcohol." Fraternity parties are known as "places where you generally know everyone there, you have a good time, and no one steals your coat or purse." Students agree that their favorite on-campus event is Flunk Day, a 100-year-old tradition that takes place on a secret date each year. Recent Flunk Days have included obstacle courses, carnival games, rides, and live performances. One student describes it as "a day every spring when classes are canceled, and the entire campus goes out on the lawn and plays games, eats great food, and enjoys free entertainment."

Student Body

Students have been known to thank the "college admission gods" for their good fortune in being part of the Knox community. Students are quick to assure that "you'll meet a lot of people very fast, and by the end of your first term, you'll already be good friends with a pretty big portion of the student body." Camaraderie also develops quickly as a result of the Pumphandle, an event prior to the start of fall courses where each student shakes hands with every other student. Students find that their peers are a "highly diverse combination of creative, intellectual minds." As one student says, "Everyone at Knox is a little eccentric; we embrace each other's differences." In fact, students take pride in their "Knoxwardness" and advise that the best way to "fit in [is] by being themselves."

Knox College

Financial Aid: 309-341-7149 • E-Mail: admission@knox.edu • Website: www.knox.edu

THE PRINCETON REVIEW SAYS

Admissions

The school reports that its standardized testing policy for use in admission for Fall 2026 is Test Optional. The Princeton Review suggests that interested applicants consult with the school for the most up-to-date standardized testing policies. *Very important factors considered include:* rigor of secondary school record, academic GPA. *Important factors considered include:* class rank, application essay. *Other factors considered include:* standardized test scores, recommendation(s), interview, extracurricular activities, talent/ability, character/personal qualities, first generation, alumni/ae relation, geographical residence, state residency, volunteer work, work experience, level of applicant's interest. High school diploma is required and GED is accepted. *Academic units recommended:* 4 English, 4 math, 3 science, 2 science labs, 3 language (other than English), 2 social studies, 1 history.

Financial Aid

Students should submit: FAFSA. The Princeton Review suggests that all financial aid forms be submitted as soon as possible. *Need-based scholarships/grants offered:* Federal Pell; Federal SEOG; State scholarships/grants; Private scholarships; College/university scholarship or grant aid from institutional funds. *Loan aid offered:* Federal Direct Subsidized Loans; Federal Direct Unsubsidized Loans; Direct PLUS loans; College/university loans from institutional funds. Admitted students will be notified of awards on a rolling basis beginning 12/1. Federal Work-Study Program available. Institutional employment available.

The Inside Word

Knox draws students from 54 countries and almost 50 states—with a student body of only 1,000 or so, diversity is hugely important here. Admission standards are high, and prospective students are viewed both qualitatively and quantitatively. More than half of all accepted students were ranked in the top quarter of their high school classes.

THE SCHOOL SAYS

From the Admissions Office

"We believe that every experience is an education and that everything you learn in the classroom gains value when you apply it. We also believe you learn the most from the people least like you. Knox is one of the most diverse campuses in America, with a campus community of 1000 students from nearly every state and 54 countries, including a wide array of races, ethnicities, ages, cultures, backgrounds, genders and gender identities, sexual orientations, and beliefs. A Knox education is not something you sit and watch—it's something you do. Our students test their knowledge by applying theory to practice both in and out of the classroom. That can take the form of advanced research and creative work, internships, off-campus (sometimes way off-campus) programs, community service, or some combination of your own devising. All students are guaranteed funding—at least $2,000—through Knox's innovative Power of Experience program to make these opportunities available to everyone, typically in the junior or senior year. These experiences, combined with opportunities to live and learn with students from different backgrounds and to develop leadership skills in clubs and organizations, empower graduates to find success after Knox. Our students become engaged, innovative, and productive global citizens, ready to lead lives of purpose and prepared to work in fields that don't even exist yet. They run Fortune 500 companies and grassroots nonprofits, they conduct major research at sites around the world, they found startups and music festivals, they see a need, and they meet it."

SELECTIVITY

# of total applicants	4,469
% of total applicants accepted	77
% of total acceptees attending	9
# of in-state applicants	1,503
% of in-state applicants accepted	92
# of out-of-state-applicants	1,614
% of applicants accepted from out of state	89
# of international applicants	1,351
% of international applicants accepted	46

First-Year Profile

Testing policy	Test Optional
Range SAT composite	1150–1410
Range SAT EBRW	580–700
Range SAT math	540–740
Range ACT composite	26–31
% submitting SAT scores	29
% submitting ACT scores	8
Average HS GPA	3.6
% submitting high school GPA	51
% graduated top 10% of class	33
% graduated top 25% of class	52
% graduated top 50% of class	86
% submitting high school rank	37

Important Dates

Early action	
Apply by	11/1
Notified by	12/15
Regular	
Notified by	Rolling, 1/15
Nonfall registration?	Yes

FINANCIAL FACTS

Annual tuition	$61,998
Food and housing	$11,862
Required fees	$897
Books and supplies	$1,200
Average need-based scholarship (First-year)	$48,350 ($50,234)
% students with need rec. need-based scholarship or grant aid (First-year)	100 (100)
% students with need rec. non-need-based scholarship or grant aid (First-year)	25 (35)
% students with need rec. need-based self-help aid (First-year)	53 (50)
% students rec. any financial aid (First-year)	99 (100)
% UG borrow to pay for school	65
Average cumulative indebtedness	$30,438
% of students with need fully met (First-year)	26 (37)
Average % of student need met (First-year)	92 (93)

LAFAYETTE COLLEGE

730 High Street, Easton, PA 18042 • Admissions: 610-330-5100

Survey Snapshot
Easy to get around campus
Career services are great
Students are happy

RATINGS

Quality of Life	89
Fire Safety	60*
Green	95
Academic	90
Profs Interesting	95
Profs Accessible	96
Admissions	94
Financial Aid	98

CAMPUS LIFE

Type of school	Private
Environment	City

Students

Degree-seeking undergrad enrollment	2,675
% male/female/not reported	50/50/0
% from out of state	83
% First-year from public high school	62
% First-year live on campus	99
% Ugrads live on campus	92
# of fraternities (% join)	3 (24)
# of sororities (% join)	6 (36)
% Asian	4
% Black or African American	6
% Hispanic	11
% Native American	<1
% Pacific Islander	0
% Race and/or ethnicity unknown	3
% Two or more races	5
% White	64
% International	7
# of countries represented	44

CAMPUS MENTAL HEALTH SERVICES

Offers mental health/wellness program	Yes
Mental health training available to students	Yes
Employs Chief Wellness Officer	No
Peer-to-peer mental health offerings	Yes
Counseling center has guidelines or accreditation	No
Mental health/well-being courses	Yes, non-credit

ACADEMICS

% students returning for sophomore year	90
% students graduating within 4 years	80
% students graduating within 6 years	85
Calendar	Semester
Student/faculty ratio	10:1
Most common class size 10–19.	(50%)
Most common lab/discussion size 10–19.	(74%)

Most Popular Majors
Engineering; Biology/Biological Sciences; Social Sciences

Applicants Often Prefer
Cornell College, Princeton University, Tufts University

Applicants Sometimes Prefer
Boston College, Brown University, Bucknell University, Colgate University, Dickinson College, Fordham University, Lehigh University, Northeastern University, Villanova University

STUDENTS SAY "..."

Academics

Many students are motivated by the active education opportunities at Lafayette College: "It's never a lecture alone, you always get to apply the learning you gained." Across many majors at this "small, prestigious liberal arts school," time is well-spent on "hands-on learning through field trips to relevant and interesting locations," such as a geology class using lab time to travel to state parks around the area and explore the natural geography and a "Women's Gender and Sexuality Studies class following the Inside-Out Program model of having class inside the local women's prison." Even when students don't leave the classroom, their work is described as "interpretive and creative." They also note that even "classes that are lecture-heavy will offer collaborative projects" and that labs are "attended by professors (and not graduate students or TAs)." Lafayette Leopards also celebrate the school's strong study abroad program, including about ten interim trips a year, "which are three-week trips to locations all over the world." The overall educational focus is fostered by the professors, who are "personable and intelligent" and "super accessible and accommodating." In addition, "there are resources for every class in addition to the professors, such as TAs, writing assistants, tutors, and supplemental instructors." Lafayette may be a "challenging academic institution," but it's one that impresses with its engagement and support: professors "all have good intentions and want to help."

Campus Life

"Students value the work hard, play hard mindset at Lafayette," noting that while they "study rigorously for assignments and exams," there are also those who "enjoy partying even on weekdays." This also results in college-led events being well attended, whether that's "food trucks on the quad" or "fun events" with the Lafayette Activities Forum, which run the gamut from "trivia nights to festivals on the quad." Reviews are mixed on the importance and popularity of Greek life, with one student saying, "Greek Life and athletics dominate the social scene" while another insists that whether the school "is leaning away from it" or making it "more pronounced, it just depends on the people you surround yourself with." Off campus is a draw, too, as downtown Easton boasts "dozens of consignment shops and small businesses that offer student discounts" and has a "vibrant food scene" that's "a gem for nightlife, restaurants, and walking around." Either way, "there is an opportunity to socialize in any shape or form if students get involved on campus."

Student Body

Lafayette students are typically "involved in many campus activities, clubs, and commitments" and "generally respectful and look out for each other, which establishes a sense of community and belonging on campus." While the student body seems to get along, there is some consternation with the administration, with one student sharing that "the student body and the administration are consistently at odds over decisions made with very little student input and which act against our own interests." The vibe among the student community is strong and positive, though, with one student describing Lafayette students as, "nerds who enjoy having fun," and "genuinely fun people to be around" who "also value interesting conversations about the college, academics, and the world around us."

LAFAYETTE COLLEGE

Financial Aid: 610-330-5055 • E-Mail: admissions@lafayette.edu • Website: www.lafayette.edu

THE PRINCETON REVIEW SAYS

Admissions

The school reports that its standardized testing policy for use in admission for Fall 2026 is Test Optional. The Princeton Review suggests that interested applicants consult with the school for the most up-to-date standardized testing policies. *Very important factors considered include:* rigor of secondary school record, academic GPA. *Important factors considered include:* class rank, standardized test scores, application essay, recommendation(s), interview, extracurricular activities, talent/ability, character/personal qualities. *Other factors considered include:* first generation, alumni/ae relation, geographical residence, volunteer work, work experience, level of applicant's interest. High school diploma is required and GED is accepted. *Academic units recommended:* 4 English, 3 math, 2 science, 2 science labs, 2 language (other than English), 5 academic electives.

Financial Aid

Students should submit: FAFSA; CSS PROFILE. The Princeton Review suggests that all financial aid forms be submitted as soon as possible. *Need-based scholarships/grants offered:* Federal Pell; Federal SEOG; State scholarships/grants; Private scholarships; College/university scholarship or grant aid from institutional funds. *Loan aid offered:* Federal Direct Subsidized Loans; Federal Direct Unsubsidized Loans; Direct PLUS loans; College/university loans from institutional funds. Admitted students will be notified of awards with admissions decision. Federal Work-Study Program available. Institutional employment available.

The Inside Word

Like all selective institutions, Lafayette College takes into account a variety of factors when evaluating prospective students. These factors include your high school record (GPA, rigor of courses, and honors classes) and test scores, if submitting. The admissions committee also values a commitment to social awareness and potential for leadership as exhibited through extracurricular activities such as community service. In fact, service is a big part of the Lafayette community.

THE SCHOOL SAYS

From the Admissions Office

"In the spirit of the Marquis de Lafayette, Lafayette College says "why not" to your biggest dreams.

"We're an undergraduate-only institution located in Easton, PA, where a liberal arts education meshes seamlessly with our nationally recognized engineering program. At Lafayette, students engage in cutting-edge research under the mentorship of professors, compete in Division I athletics, and discover their passions, both in and out of the classroom. Plus, we're just 90 minutes away from New York City and Philadelphia, providing you with additional opportunities for internships, recreation, and more.

"Easton is a small city with big charm. From food festivals and free live music events to bike races and dozens of foodie destinations, there's always something happening in this Lehigh Valley city.

"Will you find your people here?

"We know you will. Lafayette is the kind of place you can call home. But don't just take our word for it."

SELECTIVITY

# of total applicants	10,556
% of total applicants accepted	31
% of total acceptees attending	21
# of in-state applicants	1,233
% of in-state applicants accepted	34
# of out-of-state-applicants	5,410
% of applicants accepted from out of state	48
# of international applicants	3,913
% of international applicants accepted	7
# of early decision applicants	937
% of early decision applicants accepted	38
# offered a place on the wait list	2,660
# admitted from wait list	171

First-Year Profile

Testing policy	Test Optional
Range SAT composite	1370–1420
Range SAT EBRW	690–750
Range SAT math	690–760
Range ACT composite	32–34
% submitting SAT scores	27
% submitting ACT scores	9
Average HS GPA	3.6
% submitting high school GPA	99
% graduated top 10% of class	53
% graduated top 25% of class	81
% graduated top 50% of class	98
% submitting high school rank	22

Important Dates

Early decision	
Apply by	11/15
Notified by	12/15
Other ED apply by	2/1
Other ED notified by	2/15
Regular	
Apply by	1/15
Notified by	3/23
Nonfall registration?	No

FINANCIAL FACTS

Annual tuition	$70,486
Food and housing	$20,896
Required fees (First-year)	$360 ($1,110)
Books and supplies	$1,000
Average need-based scholarship (First-year)	$54,031 ($54,046)
% students with need rec. need-based scholarship or grant aid (First-year)	100 (100)
% students with need rec. non-need-based scholarship or grant aid (First-year)	23 (33)
% students with need rec. need-based self-help aid (First-year)	73 (67)
% students rec. any financial aid (First-year)	66 (79)
% UG borrow to pay for school	37
Average cumulative indebtedness	$28,840
% of students with need fully met (First-year)	100 (100)
Average % of student need met (First-year)	100 (100)

LAKE FOREST COLLEGE

555 North Sheridan Road, Lake Forest, IL 60045 • Admissions: 847-735-5000

Survey Snapshot
Recreation facilities are great
Everyone loves the Foresters
Students love Lake Forest, IL

RATINGS

Quality of Life	90
Fire Safety	89
Green	60*
Academic	89
Profs Interesting	92
Profs Accessible	97
Admissions	89
Financial Aid	93

CAMPUS LIFE

Type of school	Private
Environment	Village

Students

Degree-seeking undergrad enrollment	1,781
% male/female/not reported	42/58/<1
% from out of state	37
% First-year live on campus	83
% Ugrads live on campus	70
# of fraternities (% join)	3 (6)
# of sororities (% join)	4 (8)
% Asian	6
% Black or African American	3
% Hispanic	19
% Native American	<1
% Pacific Islander	0
% Race and/or ethnicity unknown	3
% Two or more races	4
% White	45
% International	20
# of countries represented	115

CAMPUS MENTAL HEALTH SERVICES

Offers mental health/wellness program	Yes
Mental health training available to students	No
Employs Chief Wellness Officer	NR
Peer-to-peer mental health offerings	NR
Counseling center has guidelines or accreditation	No
Mental health/well-being courses	NR

ACADEMICS

% students returning for sophomore year	89
% students graduating within 4 years	66
% students graduating within 6 years	73
Calendar	Semester
Student/faculty ratio	11:1
Most common class size 20–29.	(43%)
Most common lab/discussion size 10–19.	(89%)

Most Popular Majors

Research and Experimental Psychology; Business/Commerce; Finance

Applicants Also Look At

Augustana College (IL), Beloit College, Denison University, DePaul University, Hobart and William Smith Colleges, Illinois Wesleyan University, Kalamazoo College, Lawrence University, Loyola University Chicago, Macalester College, Marquette University, St. Olaf College, University of Illinois at Chicago, University of Illinois at Urbana—Champaign

STUDENTS SAY "..."

Academics

Nestled in the Northern suburbs of Chicago, students at Lake Forest College rave about the "excellent professors, small class sizes, and fantastic financial aid." Dedicated to their studies, students feed off of each other's successes. "Everyone wants to do as well as the next person and hearing that one person did well on a test pushes another person to do better going forward." Behind these driven students are a team of equally supportive professors. "One big strength of Lake Forest College is how accessible professors are even outside class hours." Students describe their instructors as "very easy to talk to and very helpful," and report that they are "challenging and professional, yet maintain a consistent amiability and approachable nature at the same time." As one undergrad elaborates, "The professors are teaching at Lake Forest because they want to teach small classes and connect with undergrad students." Truly, "They take the time to get to know you personally, and they are cheering you on every step of your college career." It's clear to those who attend Lake Forest that "staff work endlessly to develop relationships with students and make it hard for you not to succeed."

Lake Forest College offers 32 majors, and students insist "you will always find something you love" and ways to keep it interesting, even in your first year. For example, students have the opportunity to take field trips into Chicago, only an hour by train, through the "First Year Study Courses," which are "specifically designed to get students interested in Chicago, and show how different areas of study connect to Chicago and the surrounding areas." Such engaging classes are truly reflective of the "high quality" education you receive at Lake Forest.

Campus Life

The weekdays are mostly for study, and you find that many "people will spend time in the library." But in their downtime and on weekends, students love to "go to the beach, hang out in the quad area, take the train to Chicago, [and] attend school events" or go to "parties in dorms on weekend[s]." Greek life and "playing intramural sports or going to sports games" are popular pastimes, as are cultural clubs and service opportunities. "We all participate in a bunch of cultural and academic clubs that help us...establish a healthy relationship/friendship with each other," one student says. These healthy relationships also extend to those between student and staff when undergrads express interest in creating new programming or events for things undergrads are passionate about, like mental health. "We are always looking for new ways to express our interests to administration, and they always work with us to the best of their abilities."

Student Body

Lake Forest College has "a very diverse student body with a large number of international students mixed with students from all over the U.S." Students are "socioeconomically diverse, with many choosing Lake Forest because of the financial aid offer."

Many feel "the sense of community on our campus is extremely strong." Undergrads can be counted on to look out for each other, as Lake Forest College has "a lot [of] student leaders that help the incoming class [adjust to] the college as well as the workload." Indeed, many feel like their peers are "awesome, smart and talented," and "very supportive of each other." Students truly feel invested in their community. "Everyone is so willing to help out with anything, and I have felt so welcomed by my peers in class, intramural, social, and academic environments," one student says. At this small school, "everyone tends to know everyone" and "there's never a time where I don't see someone I know or someone I don't know greets me." It is this "really welcoming" environment and student population that make students feel right at home at Lake Forest.

LAKE FOREST COLLEGE

Financial Aid: 847-725-5103 • E-Mail: admissions@lakeforest.edu • Website: www.lakeforest.edu

THE PRINCETON REVIEW SAYS

Admissions

The school reports that its standardized testing policy for use in admission for Fall 2026 is Test Optional. The Princeton Review suggests that interested applicants consult with the school for the most up-to-date standardized testing policies. *Very important factors considered include:* academic GPA, application essay, interview, extracurricular activities, talent/ability, character/personal qualities. *Important factors considered include:* rigor of secondary school record. *Other factors considered include:* class rank, standardized test scores, recommendation(s), first generation, alumni/ae relation, volunteer work, work experience, level of applicant's interest. High school diploma is required and GED is accepted. *Academic units required:* 4 English, 3 math, 3 science, 3 science labs, 2 language (other than English), 2 social studies, 3 history, 3 academic electives. *Academic units recommended:* 4 English, 4 math, 4 science, 4 science labs, 2 language (other than English), 2 social studies, 3 history, 3 academic electives.

Financial Aid

Students should submit: FAFSA; CSS PROFILE. Priority filing deadline is 3/1. The Princeton Review suggests that all financial aid forms be submitted as soon as possible. *Need-based scholarships/grants offered:* Federal Pell; Federal SEOG; State scholarships/grants; Private scholarships; College/university scholarship or grant aid from institutional funds. *Loan aid offered:* Federal Direct Subsidized Loans; Federal Direct Unsubsidized Loans; Direct PLUS loans. Admitted students will be notified of awards on a rolling basis beginning December 1st. Federal Work-Study Program available. Institutional employment available.

The Inside Word

Given this diverse college's top-notch academic programming, Lake Forest aims to create a class of students with high GPAs, intellectual curiosity, and individuality and character who can have a positive impact on campus. Given that Lake Forest is Test Optional, applicants are reviewed holistically, with most emphasis placed on the rigor of your courses, extracurriculars, application essay, interview, and your personal qualities.

THE SCHOOL SAYS

From the Admissions Office

"Lake Forest College offers an unparalleled combination of an idyllic 107-acre campus near the shores of Lake Forest and a 10-minute walk to downtown Lake Forest. In town, students can catch the Metra train taking them into Chicago in less than an hour. Foresters benefit from a liberal arts education that integrates hands-on career preparation and pragmatic learning experiences. Students have direct access to superb faculty, excellent staff, and a powerful network of alumni all of whom are invested in each student's personal potential and future success. Our flexible curriculum supports double majors and minors, allows room for up to 3 internships for credit—including in nearby Chicago. On campus, students benefit from exceptional lab experiences, championship athletics, and a wide range of student clubs and organizations.

"Students learn in a rigorous academic environment in small class settings where professors do all of the teaching and advising. Study abroad is encouraged, and students can also spend a semester living and interning in Chicago. The student body comes from nearly every state and over 100 countries around the world, forming a diverse learning community that is prepared to succeed in today's global society.

"Developing career goals—and a plan of action to achieve them—is fundamental at Lake Forest College. Students have access to programs, resources, career advisors, and a powerful network of alumni throughout their four years.

"Our outcomes are hard to match: Ninety-seven percent of recent graduates had jobs, graduate school, or other opportunities secured within six to nine months of graduation, well above the national average."

SELECTIVITY

# of total applicants	5,411
% of total applicants accepted	54
% of total acceptees attending	13
# of early decision applicants	65
% of early decision applicants accepted	38
# offered a place on the wait list	48
# admitted from wait list	27

First-Year Profile

Testing policy	Test Optional
Range SAT composite	1200–1370
Range SAT EBRW	600–690
Range SAT math	590–690
Range ACT composite	27–30
% submitting SAT scores	11
% submitting ACT scores	8
Average HS GPA	3.7
% submitting high school GPA	100
% graduated top 10% of class	36
% graduated top 25% of class	66
% graduated top 50% of class	95
% submitting high school rank	19

Important Dates

Early decision	
Apply by	11/1
Notified by	12/15
Other ED apply by	1/15
Other ED notified by	2/15
Early action	
Apply by	11/1
Notified by	12/15
Regular	
Apply by	2/15
Notified by	Rolling, 11/1
Nonfall registration?	Yes

FINANCIAL FACTS

Annual tuition	$60,204
Food and housing	$13,546
Required fees	$952
Books and supplies	$1,340
Average need-based scholarship (First-year)	$53,800 ($56,750)
% students with need rec. need-based scholarship or grant aid (First-year)	100 (100)
% students with need rec. non-need-based scholarship or grant aid (First-year)	0 (0)
% students with need rec. need-based self-help aid (First-year)	81 (80)
% students rec. any financial aid (First-year)	100 (100)
% UG borrow to pay for school	46
Average cumulative indebtedness	$37,595
% of students with need fully met (First-year)	47 (44)
Average % of student need met (First-year)	90 (92)

LAWRENCE TECHNOLOGICAL UNIVERSITY

21000 West Ten Mile Rd., Southfield, MI 48075-1058 • Admissions: 248-204-3160

Survey Snapshot
Students are happy
Easy to get around campus
Students are friendly

RATINGS

Quality of Life	82
Fire Safety	95
Green	60*
Academic	79
Profs Interesting	85
Profs Accessible	88
Admissions	83
Financial Aid	89

CAMPUS LIFE

Type of school	Private
Environment	City

Students

Degree-seeking undergrad enrollment	1,606
% male/female/not reported	66/34/0
% from out of state	12
% First-year live on campus	69
% Ugrads live on campus	53
# of fraternities (% join)	6 (NR)
# of sororities (% join)	5 (NR)
% Asian	3
% Black or African American	12
% Hispanic	5
% Native American	<1
% Pacific Islander	<1
% Race and/or ethnicity unknown	2
% Two or more races	5
% White	63
% International	9
# of countries represented	50

CAMPUS MENTAL HEALTH SERVICES

Offers mental health/wellness program	Yes
Mental health training available to students	Yes
Employs Chief Wellness Officer	Yes
Peer-to-peer mental health offerings	No
Counseling center has guidelines or accreditation	Yes
Mental health/well-being courses	Yes, non-credit

ACADEMICS

% students returning for sophomore year	76
% students graduating within 4 years	26
Calendar	Semester
Student/faculty ratio	11:1
Most common class size 10–19.	(45%)
Most common lab/discussion size 10–19.	(45%)

Most Popular Majors
Mechanical Engineering; Business Administration and Management; Architecture

STUDENTS SAY "..."

Academics

Founded in 1932, Michigan's Lawrence Technological University is based on the simple notion of "Theory and Practice"—taking abstract ideas and applying them to real world problems. The university offers about 100 academic programs across its four colleges, as well as numerous mentorship, internship, and practical research opportunities via the Centrepolis Accelerator, the school's manufacturing business accelerator. Just 2,300 undergraduates means "small class sizes with one-on-one opportunities," and plenty of certification, coaching, and consulting support through "professional programs for helping with future careers." LTU has an excellent reputation with companies that recruit and hire students, and the "potential for high quality jobs after college is very helpful and exciting." Resources are readily available, and all undergraduates receive a laptop or tablet, with over 80 percent of students receiving some form of financial aid.

Professors at LTU "are extremely flexible and truly do want to help you and see you succeed," which can be seen in their willingness "to accommodate special situations." They are also "clearly knowledgeable in their fields and do their best to share that experience with students," running application-based courses with the most "up-to-date labs and tools" that are centered around "creating problems and processes to outline the ever-changing industry standards and practices." One student says: "In my computer networks class the professor brought in material to create our own Ethernet cords." Students feel they leave with a lot of experience, thanks to instructors frequently bringing in "guests from popular companies to explain how our work is tied to real life work scenarios" and working to show "the application of the theory you learned in class."

Campus Life

Most out-of-classroom socializing comes by way of clubs, intramural sports, and "a great array of organizations which allow for anyone to find their interest." At least once a week there is an activity hosted by a student organization "that is fun and interactive to attend," and for those who prefer to "often play games on our computers," the school also coaches across various esports. While there are also "some casual parties surrounding Greek life," on the whole, students here are busy with "lots of studying [and being] devoted to school and a career afterwards."

Student Body

With having a small campus comes having a close-knit student body, and there is "a strong sense of community" where "everyone really looks out for each other." As one student says: "If you ask for help from any of your peers, you'll receive it or you'll solve the problem together." Despite its small size, this is a "group of diverse students who come from different backgrounds, race, and countries." Students do say that there is "a large percentage of commuters," but the school is working on changing that into a more "typical college on campus student body." Around half of students are athletes and many are also "a part of Greek life or a part-time on-campus job."

Lawrence Technological University

Financial Aid: 248-204-3177 • E-Mail: admissions@ltu.edu • Website: www.ltu.edu

THE PRINCETON REVIEW SAYS

Admissions

The school reports that its standardized testing policy for use in admission for Fall 2026 is Test Optional. The Princeton Review suggests that interested applicants consult with the school for the most up-to-date standardized testing policies. *Very important factors considered include:* rigor of secondary school record, academic GPA. *Other factors considered include:* application essay. High school diploma is required and GED is accepted. *Academic units required:* 4 English, 3 math, 2 science, 3 social studies. *Academic units recommended:* 4 English, 4 math, 4 science, 2 science labs, 2 history.

Financial Aid

Students should submit: FAFSA. Priority filing deadline is 3/1. The Princeton Review suggests that all financial aid forms be submitted as soon as possible. *Need-based scholarships/grants offered:* Federal Pell; Federal SEOG; State scholarships/grants; Private scholarships; College/university scholarship or grant aid from institutional funds. *Loan aid offered:* Federal Direct Subsidized Loans; Federal Direct Unsubsidized Loans; Direct PLUS loans. Admitted students will be notified of awards on a rolling basis beginning 1/1. Federal Work-Study Program available. Institutional employment available.

The Inside Word

While Lawrence Tech values an applicant's academic transcript above all, the admissions office also takes into account all factors which demonstrate an aptitude for successful study. Solid B students who have taken a college preparatory curriculum and shown an interest in extracurriculars should have no problems getting in. There is no formal deadline for applications, but students are advised to apply as early as possible to maximize scholarships and financial aid.

THE SCHOOL SAYS

From the Admissions Office

"Lawrence Technological University is a private, nearly 3,000-student university that offers about 100 innovative programs in Colleges of Architecture and Design, Arts and Sciences, Business and Information Technology, and Engineering.

"Lawrence Technological University is one of only 13 private, technical, comprehensive doctoral universities in the U.S.

"At LTU, you will benefit from small class sizes, taught by faculty with industry savvy, and an exceptional focus on theory and practice, with a hands-on education that begins on day one in programs such as design, engineering, nursing, and business. You will also have access to LTU's well-connected career placement services on a high-tech, wireless 107-acre campus. Lawrence Tech produces leaders with an entrepreneurial spirit and global view—helping LTU grads earn some of the highest alumni salaries in the nation.

"Lawrence Tech's unique Southfield, Michigan location also provides you with opportunities for co-ops, internships, and professional development in a region with one of the largest concentrations of engineering, architecture, and technology jobs in the world. Not only that—you will gain exposure to architecture and design, the sciences, and engineering through interdisciplinary projects, giving you a distinct advantage in today's technologically driven global job market.

"You will also be provided with your own high-end laptop loaded with industry standard software—retailing on average over $75,000—a benefit you'll only get at LTU. And there are plenty of opportunities to get involved with on campus including fraternities, sororities, honor societies and student chapters of professional groups; NAIA men's and women's athletics; and residential living."

SELECTIVITY

# of total applicants	3,412
% of total applicants accepted	81
% of total acceptees attending	14
# offered a place on the wait list	0
# admitted from wait list	0

First-Year Profile

Testing policy	Test Optional
Range SAT composite	1030–1250
Range SAT EBRW	510–630
Range SAT math	510–630
Range ACT composite	22–28
% submitting SAT scores	45
% submitting ACT scores	4
Average HS GPA	3.5
% submitting high school GPA	99

Important Dates

Regular	
Notified by	Rolling
Nonfall registration?	Yes

FINANCIAL FACTS

Annual tuition	$43,440
Food and housing	$12,484
Required fees	$2,400
Books and supplies	$1,874
Average need-based scholarship (First-year)	$26,075 ($29,153)
% students with need rec. need-based scholarship or grant aid (First-year)	99 (99)
% students with need rec. non-need-based scholarship or grant aid (First-year)	95 (99)
% students with need rec. need-based self-help aid (First-year)	65 (65)
% students rec. any financial aid (First-year)	58 (97)
% UG borrow to pay for school	63
Average cumulative indebtedness	$52,525
% of students with need fully met (First-year)	30 (34)
Average % of student need met (First-year)	85 (87)

Lawrence University

711 East Boldt Way, Appleton, WI 54911-5626 • Admissions: 920-832-6500

Survey Snapshot
Lots of liberal students
Students aren't religious
Theater is popular

RATINGS	
Quality of Life	85
Fire Safety	89
Green	60*
Academic	89
Profs Interesting	93
Profs Accessible	96
Admissions	89
Financial Aid	94

CAMPUS LIFE

Type of school	Private
Environment	City

Students

Degree-seeking undergrad enrollment	1,396
% male/female/not reported	48/52/<1
% from out of state	71
% First-year live on campus	100
% Ugrads live on campus	94
# of fraternities (% join)	3 (4)
# of sororities (% join)	4 (3)
% Asian	4
% Black or African American	5
% Hispanic	12
% Native American	<1
% Pacific Islander	0
% Race and/or ethnicity unknown	3
% Two or more races	5
% White	60
% International	11
# of countries represented	39

CAMPUS MENTAL HEALTH SERVICES

Offers mental health/wellness program	Yes
Mental health training available to students	No
Employs Chief Wellness Officer	NR
Peer-to-peer mental health offerings	NR
Counseling center has guidelines or accreditation	No
Mental health/well-being courses	NR

ACADEMICS

% students returning for sophomore year	87
% students graduating within 4 years	57
% students graduating within 6 years	77
Calendar	Trimester
Student/faculty ratio	7:1
Most common class size 10–19.	(44%)

Most Popular Majors
Psychology; Music Performance; Biology/Biological Sciences

Applicants Sometimes Prefer
St. Olaf College, University of Wisconsin—Madison

Applicants Rarely Prefer
Denison University, Macalester College

STUDENTS SAY "..."

Academics

Lawrence University is a small liberal arts college in Appleton, Wisconsin, centered entirely around the ethos of Engaged Learning, in which students learn by doing. Beginning with the cornerstone Freshman Studies program, these "crazy smart" students are grouped into course sections of about 15 students, and commence the reading and discussion of great works. Exploration of the mind is stressed, and "even the smallest idea is considered on a grand scale." Tutoring is readily available, and the school "places an incredible focus on mental health issues and counseling." Professors "have great opportunities for help and discussion outside of class," and "there are many opportunities for experiential learning (off-campus study, visits, field trips, grants) that are available to those that work for them, without being too hard to get." Lawrence is especially good at "providing a creative and explorative atmosphere within the college," and structuring itself in a manner that allows for student flexibility, so students "are able to explore and study whatever we are interested in, and we are encouraged to do so." A stunning 7:1 student-to-faculty ratio means students have access to their professors at all times, all of whom "are excited to transfer their knowledge to us through various kind of ways." Professors are "upfront with us and treat us more like academic peers," and make time to help students outside of class and connect the course to larger ideas. "To the professors, you are a person, and they make sure that they know your name and what you're about," says a student.

Campus Life

One student sums up Lawrentian life: "cheese curds, high stress, ten weeks, snow, repeat." "Study takes big part of people's life," but most are also on many different clubs or committees "whether for the student government, toward our major, or just for fun like long boarding club or painting club." "People are always hoping for more time in a day here," says a student. Admittedly, "there isn't much to do in Appleton," so this entirely residential campus is able "to cultivate a fantastic atmosphere within the college," but "outside of the Lawrence bubble is a mystery to most of us." Many people engage with the school's dances, comedians, musicians, speakers who are brought to campus, and movies shown in the cinema, and every term has a big event, such as the Fall Festival, Trivia, Winter Carnival, Cabaret, and LU-aroo. On weekends, partying is a popular pastime; underclassmen spend their time at the cafe on campus while upperclassmen "flock to our on-campus bar, where we often see our professors during happy hour." As the university houses a popular music conservatory, "there is ALWAYS a type of concert going on (Monday jazz sessions are highlight)."

Student Body

There's a surprisingly large number of international students at Lawrence University, and people embrace the opportunity to learn about different cultures and topics in general: they are all "exceptionally curious and eager to explore fields outside their own major." "Not only do we yearn for experiences that take us outside what is comfortable and known, it is safe to do so," says one. Students here "are not afraid to show who they really are" and "truly just love expressing how every person is their own and that we all accept it." This "healthy and excellent" social atmosphere is due to the chemistry of the student body, which is a "combination of odd, quirky kids, who are dedicated to music or the arts, but also dedicated student athletes." More than anything, the students here "are kind, funny, intelligent and a little bit wacko—in the best way."

Lawrence University

Financial Aid: 920-832-6583 • E-Mail: admissions@lawrence.edu • Website: www.lawrence.edu

THE PRINCETON REVIEW SAYS

Admissions

The school reports that its standardized testing policy for use in admission for Fall 2026 is Test Optional. The Princeton Review suggests that interested applicants consult with the school for the most up-to-date standardized testing policies. *Very important factors considered include:* rigor of secondary school record, class rank, academic GPA, talent/ability, character/personal qualities. *Important factors considered include:* application essay, interview, extracurricular activities. *Other factors considered include:* standardized test scores, recommendation(s), first generation, geographical residence, volunteer work, work experience, level of applicant's interest. High school diploma is required and GED is accepted. *Academic units recommended:* 4 English, 3 math, 3 science, 2 language (other than English), 2 social studies, 2 history.

Financial Aid

Students should submit: FAFSA; CSS PROFILE; Institution's own financial aid form. Priority filing deadline is 12/1. The Princeton Review suggests that all financial aid forms be submitted as soon as possible. *Need-based scholarships/grants offered:* Federal Pell; Federal SEOG; State scholarships/grants; Private scholarships; College/university scholarship or grant aid from institutional funds. *Loan aid offered:* Federal Direct Subsidized Loans; Federal Direct Unsubsidized Loans; Direct PLUS loans. Admitted students will be notified of awards on or about 12/1. Federal Work-Study Program available. Institutional employment available.

The Inside Word

Lawrence University takes a holistic approach to the admissions game. The school does its best to look beyond numbers and get a full sense of each applicant. Admissions officers pay close attention to the types of classes candidates have taken and the activities pursued. They also consider a student's background. Interviews are highly important so it would behoove applicants to sit for one. Finally, those who are test-taking averse can breathe a sigh of relief; submitting SAT or ACT scores is optional.

THE SCHOOL SAYS

From the Admissions Office

"Lawrence believes college should not be a one-size-fits-all experience, and that you'll learn best when you're educated as a unique individual. Within our college of liberal arts and sciences and our conservatory of music—both devoted exclusively to undergraduate education—you'll have unparalleled opportunities to collaborate closely with your professors. With one of the smallest student-faculty ratios in the country (7:1) and an average class size of 15, Lawrence is built to deliver a highly individualized, interactive (and challenging) academic experience. Our 1,500 students come from nearly every state and about fifty countries to enjoy the distinctive benefits of this engaged—and engaging—community. It's a welcoming and supportive, residential, 24/7 campus filled with smart and talented people who are pursuing an astonishing variety of academic and extracurricular interests in a collaborative rather than competitive way. Our picturesque, residential campus is nestled on the banks of the Fox River in Appleton, Wisconsin, (metro population: 250,000), one of the fastest growing metropolitan areas in the Midwest. Björklunden, our 441-acre estate on more than one mile of pristine Lake Michigan shoreline (two hours north of campus), provides educational and recreational opportunities for students to enhance their on-campus learning experiences. Lawrentians enjoy 99 percent placement within six months of graduation (73 percent working; 23 percent in graduate/professional school; 4 percent traveling/volunteering)."

SELECTIVITY

# of total applicants	3,269
% of total applicants accepted	64
% of total acceptees attending	17
# of in-state applicants	461
% of in-state applicants accepted	83
# of out-of-state-applicants	1,796
% of applicants accepted from out of state	83
# of international applicants	1,013
% of international applicants accepted	21
# of early decision applicants	62
% of early decision applicants accepted	73
# offered a place on the wait list	2
# admitted from wait list	2

First-Year Profile

Testing policy	Test Optional
Range SAT composite	1240–1340
Range SAT EBRW	610–710
Range SAT math	590–710
Range ACT composite	24–31
% submitting SAT scores	21
% submitting ACT scores	33
Average HS GPA	3.5
% submitting high school GPA	99
% graduated top 10% of class	34
% graduated top 25% of class	58
% graduated top 50% of class	92
% submitting high school rank	38

Important Dates

Early decision	
Apply by	11/1
Notified by	12/1
Early action	
Apply by	11/1
Notified by	12/15
Regular	
Notified by	Rolling, 11/1

FINANCIAL FACTS

Annual tuition	$58,482
Food and housing	$12,972
Required fees	$312
Books and supplies	$750
Average need-based scholarship (First-year)	$44,104 ($47,410)
% students with need rec. need-based scholarship or grant aid (First-year)	100 (100)
% students with need rec. non-need-based scholarship or grant aid (First-year)	23 (18)
% students with need rec. need-based self-help aid (First-year)	65 (71)
% students rec. any financial aid (First-year)	99 (100)
% UG borrow to pay for school	53
Average cumulative indebtedness	$31,359
% of students with need fully met (First-year)	60 (55)
Average % of student need met (First-year)	93 (94)

LEHIGH UNIVERSITY

27 Memorial Drive West, Bethlehem, PA 18015 • Admissions: 610-758-3100

Survey Snapshot
Students are happy
Great library
Internships are widely available

RATINGS

Quality of Life	**87**
Fire Safety	**97**
Green	**99**
Academic	**86**
Profs Interesting	**88**
Profs Accessible	**91**
Admissions	**94**
Financial Aid	**94**

CAMPUS LIFE

Type of school	Private
Environment	City

Students

Degree-seeking undergrad enrollment	5,973
% male/female/not reported	51/49/0
% from out of state	74
% First-year live on campus	97
% Ugrads live on campus	60
# of fraternities (% join)	8 (18)
# of sororities (% join)	8 (25)
% Asian	11
% Black or African American	4
% Hispanic	12
% Native American	<1
% Pacific Islander	<1
% Race and/or ethnicity unknown	2
% Two or more races	5
% White	60
% International	6
# of countries represented	64

CAMPUS MENTAL HEALTH SERVICES

Offers mental health/wellness program	Yes
Mental health training available to students	Yes
Employs Chief Wellness Officer	No
Peer-to-peer mental health offerings	Yes
Counseling center has guidelines or accreditation	Yes
Mental health/well-being courses	Yes, for-credit

ACADEMICS

% students returning for sophomore year	94
% students graduating within 4 years	76
% students graduating within 6 years	85
Calendar	Semester
Student/faculty ratio	11:1
Most common class size 10–19.	(32%)
Most common lab/discussion size 20–29.	(38%)

Most Popular Majors

Computer Science; Mechanical Engineering; Finance

Applicants Often Prefer

Cornell University, Purdue University—West Lafayette, University of Maryland, College Park, University of Michigan—Engineering

Applicants Sometimes Prefer

Bucknell University, Drexel University, Northeastern University, Pittsburg State University, Rutgers University–New Brunswick, State University of New York—Binghamton University, Syracuse University, University of Connecticut, University of Delaware, Villanova University

STUDENTS SAY "…"

Academics

Lehigh University is an "academically rigorous school that challenges you to adapt to real world scenarios." Students appreciate the many resources and opportunities offered, including "extremely advanced and high-tech" lab facilities and equipment and numerous "research opportunities for undergrad students looking for field experience." There are many standout programs, including fully funded study abroad opportunities, Impact Fellowships that match students to sustainable development projects, and the United Nations Youth Representative Program, which allows students to work with NGOs and speak on the floor of the General Assembly. Professors here are "extremely helpful" and many "will allow you to get involved in their research, even as a first-year student." Professors also "try to incorporate their personal research or experiences into [the] lecture, which makes it extremely engaging." As one student elaborates, "There is nothing quite like seeing someone talk about something they are truly passionate about." Professors offer "lots of opportunities for students to get extra help," including "plenty of office hours and group study sessions." Some "will slow down or adjust their course plans to ensure students are learning." The school also offers an "incredibly strong" alumni network that "helps many current students prepare for and land career opportunities." All in all, the "academics are tough and definitely make you work hard, but they one hundred percent make you better."

Campus Life

Lehigh's "stunning and beautiful" campus offers students plenty of activities and a thriving social scene. There is "a club, organization, and society for just about every type of student." Some popular standouts include Cheese Club, where "all we do is eat cheese and learn about cheese," and the Outing Club, which offers "a lot of very cool off-campus trips, from camping to whitewater rafting." Many students also enjoy intramural sports, cultural clubs, and working out at the gym. While "Greek life is pretty popular" and some students "enjoy their weekends by partying," there are also plenty of substance-free events. For example, on the weekends, Lehigh After Dark hosts "fun events like carnivals, movie nights, trivia nights, and Wingo (wings and bingo)," which "often have a full house." Lehigh's "school spirit is high," and its athletic traditions bring students together, like "Rivalry Week" when the football team plays against their longstanding rival, Lafayette College, brings students together. The plethora of activities offered on campus allows "you to find your people easily."

Student Body

Students here are "incredibly academic and driven. but also love to have fun," with one student adding, "Students are just as passionate about having fun as they are about their grades." During the week, "the library is always packed," and on the weekends, students "tend to let off steam." Lehigh is "not huge, so you become quite close to your peers, especially in your class/major." Students note that many of their peers are from New Jersey, Pennsylvania, and New York but that the school is "becoming more diverse and every class [is] bigger than the [last]." Another student agrees, saying, "There is a growing presence of students internationally and from other states in the U.S." Students are "open to meeting new people and trying new experiences, which creates a great environment for personal growth." It's a place where "most people are welcoming and friendly, especially when you join a club that links you to people with shared interests." As one student sums up, "Whenever I am confused or need guidance, the person sitting next to me is always happy to help. Lehigh is very challenging academically but offers a very supportive and friendly environment for us to succeed."

LEHIGH UNIVERSITY

Financial Aid: 610-758-3181 • E-Mail: admissions@lehigh.edu • Website: www.lehigh.edu

THE PRINCETON REVIEW SAYS

Admissions

The school reports that its standardized testing policy for use in admission for Fall 2026 is Test Optional. The Princeton Review suggests that interested applicants consult with the school for the most up-to-date standardized testing policies. *Very important factors considered include:* rigor of secondary school record, academic GPA. *Important factors considered include:* class rank, standardized test scores, application essay, recommendation(s), extracurricular activities, talent/ability, character/personal qualities, volunteer work, level of applicant's interest. *Other factors considered include:* interview, first generation, alumni/ae relation, geographical residence, state residency, work experience. High school diploma is required and GED is accepted. *Academic units required:* 4 English, 3 math, 2 science, 2 science labs, 2 language (other than English), 2 social studies, 2 history, 2 academic electives, 1 computer science, 1 visual/performing arts. *Academic units recommended:* 4 English, 4 math, 4 science, 2 science labs, 2 language (other than English), 4 social studies, 2 history, 2 academic electives, 2 computer science, 1 visual/performing arts.

Financial Aid

Students should submit: FAFSA; CSS PROFILE; Business/Farm Supplement. The Princeton Review suggests that all financial aid forms be submitted as soon as possible. *Need-based scholarships/grants offered:* Federal Pell; State scholarships/grants; Private scholarships; College/university scholarship or grant aid from institutional funds. *Loan aid offered:* Federal Direct Subsidized Loans; Federal Direct Unsubsidized Loans; Direct PLUS loans. Admitted students will be notified of awards on or about 3/30.

The Inside Word

Competition for spots in Lehigh's first-year class is quite high. Students should be sure to start their applications early, be well prepared with scores and grades, as well as demonstrate their talents and passions through volunteer opportunities, work experience, or extracurricular activities. Prospective students are encouraged to visit the campus and make contact with the admissions staff. Interviews are recommended but not required.

THE SCHOOL SAYS

From the Admissions Office

"Lehigh is a premier residential research university that empowers pragmatic problem-solvers through collaborative research, faculty mentorship and a supportive community. The majority of our students—undergraduate and graduate—live on campus, allowing research, discovery and impact to happen almost anywhere.

"Here, you'll pursue your passions through a flexible curriculum and integrative programs that bridge disciplines. Whether you are studying in the College of Arts and Sciences, the College of Business, the P.C. Rossin College of Engineering and Applied Science or the College of Health, you will find a personalized environment backed by the resources of an internationally recognized institution. Our students lead through engaged research, entrepreneurship and global experiences, grounded by core values of integrity, equity and intellectual freedom.

"Approximately 92% of our graduates were employed, continuing education or engaged in other pursuits within six months of graduation, showcasing how hard work leads to proven outcomes. Joining Lehigh means joining a loyal global network of more than 89,000 alumni who are making their mark on the world.

"Our 2,358-acre campus on South Mountain offers the best of both worlds: a quintessential collegiate setting in the scenic Lehigh Valley with direct access to the professional hubs of New York City and Philadelphia. At Lehigh, a focus on real-world impact gives you the foundation to create meaningful change in your communities and the world."

SELECTIVITY

# of total applicants	19,342
% of total applicants accepted	29
% of total acceptees attending	27
# of in-state applicants	3,090
% of in-state applicants accepted	33
# of out-of-state-applicants	12,070
% of applicants accepted from out of state	37
# of international applicants	4,182
% of international applicants accepted	4
# of early decision applicants	2,040
% of early decision applicants accepted	47
# offered a place on the wait list	4,083
# admitted from wait list	80

First-Year Profile

Testing policy	Test Optional
Range SAT composite	1380–1480
Range SAT EBRW	680–740
Range SAT math	690–760
Range ACT composite	31–34
% submitting SAT scores	33
% submitting ACT scores	10
% graduated top 10% of class	60
% graduated top 25% of class	87
% graduated top 50% of class	98
% submitting high school rank	23

Important Dates

Early decision	
Apply by	11/1
Notified by	12/5
Other ED apply by	1/1
Other ED notified by	2/5
Regular	
Apply by	1/1
Notified by	3/20
Nonfall registration?	No

FINANCIAL FACTS

Annual tuition	$69,420
Food and housing	$19,230
Required fees	$1,170
Average need-based scholarship (First-year)	$56,368 ($56,575)
% students with need rec. need-based scholarship or grant aid (First-year)	99 (98)
% students with need rec. non-need-based scholarship or grant aid (First-year)	35 (37)
% students with need rec. need-based self-help aid (First-year)	91 (92)
% UG borrow to pay for school	48
Average cumulative indebtedness	$39,806
% of students with need fully met (First-year)	70 (66)
Average % of student need met (First-year)	97 (97)

LE MOYNE COLLEGE

1419 Salt Springs Rd., Syracuse, NY 13214-1301 • Admissions: 315-445-4300

Survey Snapshot
Lab facilities are great
Students are happy
Great library

RATINGS

Quality of Life	**85**
Fire Safety	**89**
Green	**60***
Academic	**79**
Profs Interesting	**88**
Profs Accessible	**91**
Admissions	**86**
Financial Aid	**89**

CAMPUS LIFE

Type of school	Private
Affiliation	Roman Catholic
Environment	City

Students

Degree-seeking undergrad enrollment	2,398
% male/female/not reported	40/60/0
% from out of state	9
% First-year from public high school	83
% First-year live on campus	76
% Ugrads live on campus	54
# of fraternities	0
# of sororities	0
% Asian	4
% Black or African American	8
% Hispanic	9
% Native American	<1
% Pacific Islander	<1
% Race and/or ethnicity unknown	1
% Two or more races	4
% White	71
% International	3
# of countries represented	18

CAMPUS MENTAL HEALTH SERVICES

Offers mental health/wellness program	Yes
Mental health training available to students	Yes
Employs Chief Wellness Officer	Yes
Peer-to-peer mental health offerings	Yes
Counseling center has guidelines or accreditation	Yes
Mental health/well-being courses	Yes, for-credit

ACADEMICS

% students returning for sophomore year	87
% students graduating within 4 years	65
% students graduating within 6 years	73
Calendar	Semester
Student/faculty ratio	12:1
Most common class size 20–29.	(44%)
Most common lab/discussion size 10–19.	(71%)

Most Popular Majors

Biology/Biological Sciences; Psychology; Registered Nursing/Registered Nurse

Applicants Sometimes Prefer

Ithaca College, Nazareth University, Siena University, St. John Fisher University, State University of New York—Binghamton University, State University of New York—Cortland, State University of New York—Geneseo, State University of New York—Oswego, State University of New York—University at Albany, State University of New York—University at Buffalo, Syracuse University

STUDENTS SAY "..."

Academics

Le Moyne College is a small private liberal arts college rooted in the Catholic and Jesuit tradition that seeks to provide a full education that will prepare students for a lifetime of leadership and service. Located in upstate New York, Le Moyne's undergraduates follow a core curriculum that introduces them to the knowledge and skills that will carry them through their time at the college and beyond, bookended by a first-year Transitions seminar and a senior Transformations capstone course or project. Interdisciplinary learning is encouraged, and most departments put on extra credit lectures with guest speakers that are "always educational but entertaining."

Professors at Le Moyne "ensure that you are actually learning and retaining information, [and] that their course has benefited you in every way." In the classroom, they make "use of real-life scenarios or hands-on examples" to demonstrate their lessons, and "frequently mention that they prefer to have a conversation about the material rather than simply talk at the students." Discussion-based exercises are preferred over straight lectures, and many classes incorporate "unique group projects." Faculty work to "establish incredibly close connections with students," which helps to "truly understand and accommodate" students. Smaller class sizes provide "a more personal experience with their professors and peers," and both teachers and staff are "always willing to meet with you and do their best to help you succeed."

Campus Life

Le Moyne is a relatively small school, "which allows for it to feel like home away from home." Around 60 percent of students live on the "very well kept" campus: students note the constant renovations (like that of the library and science buildings) that are "always happening to keep it feeling fresh." No matter where they live, students can be found "studying all over campus, from dorm rooms to the library to outside under the trees," and "when people aren't working they'll typically visit downtown Syracuse." A vehicle is highly recommended for such excursions, particular when it comes to taking advantage of "plenty of outdoor activities such as hiking in the local state park." That said, students say "there is always something to do" on campus, whether that's a club or a school-run event like trivia night, bingo, and Dolphy Day, where "students and faculty gather on the quad for a day of food, drinks, and music." Sports are popular both to play and to watch, and students also go up the road to nearby Syracuse University to attend larger athletic events.

Student Body

Given the school's Jesuit values, it makes sense that people are "committed to helping others and have a tremendous sense of empathy and desire to serve others. One student says, "I am proud of Le Moyne's commitment to promoting good character in addition to academics." Students are also "extremely well driven and dedicated toward their goals." Le Moyne is "really great with diversity and bringing in people from all over the world," forming a very inclusive bunch where "you make friends easy, and they're there for life." Many students come from New York State (especially nearby suburbs), and "it is common to share multiple classes with the same people."

LE MOYNE COLLEGE

Financial Aid: 315-445-4400 • E-Mail: admission@lemoyne.edu • Website: www.lemoyne.edu

THE PRINCETON REVIEW SAYS

Admissions

The school reports that its standardized testing policy for use in admission for Fall 2026 is Test Optional. The Princeton Review suggests that interested applicants consult with the school for the most up-to-date standardized testing policies. *Very important factors considered include:* rigor of secondary school record, academic GPA, work experience. *Important factors considered include:* class rank, application essay, recommendation(s), interview, extracurricular activities, talent/ability. *Other factors considered include:* standardized test scores, character/personal qualities, alumni/ae relation, volunteer work, level of applicant's interest. High school diploma is required and GED is accepted. *Academic units required:* 4 English, 3 math, 3 science, 4 social studies. *Academic units recommended:* 4 English, 3 math, 4 science, 3 science labs, 3 language (other than English), 4 social studies.

Financial Aid

Students should submit: FAFSA; State aid form. Priority filing deadline is 12/15. The Princeton Review suggests that all financial aid forms be submitted as soon as possible. *Need-based scholarships/grants offered:* Federal Pell; Federal SEOG; State scholarships/grants; Private scholarships; College/university scholarship or grant aid from institutional funds; United Negro College Fund. *Loan aid offered:* Federal Direct Subsidized Loans; Federal Direct Unsubsidized Loans; Direct PLUS loans. Admitted students will be notified of awards on or about 2/15. Federal Work-Study Program available. Institutional employment available.

The Inside Word

As a younger college, Le Moyne sees slightly lower application numbers than many other small private colleges in the Northeast. Those with a good academic record and a letter of recommendation from a guidance counselor or teacher (or three letters from clergy, coaches, employers, teachers, etc.) should have no trouble getting in, but a stronger college prep record and a good SAT or ACT score may help seal the deal.

THE SCHOOL SAYS

From the Admissions Office

"Learning, leadership and service are the hallmarks of a Le Moyne College education. Those values are evident in the College's Core Curriculum, a series of courses steeped in the Jesuit tradition and designed to develop intellectual skills critical for success in the 21st century. The intent of the Core Curriculum is to do more than provide knowledge in specific disciplines, though. It was created to stretch the minds of our students, to remove barriers to their ways of thinking, and to help them discover new approaches to life's challenges. At the center of the Le Moyne experience is a commitment to social justice and to providing students with the best possible preparation for life and work. A place where Greatness meets Goodness.

"Le Moyne students can choose from 100+ undergraduate majors, minors and special programs, as well as graduate programs in arts administration, business administration, education, nursing, occupational therapy, physician assistant studies, mental health counseling and executive leadership. Whatever field they choose to pursue, Le Moyne graduates are prepared to lead successful lives of leadership and service.

"Beyond academics, Le Moyne students have the opportunity to grow and explore on a campus with dynamic academic, athletic and social spaces at a cost that is remarkably affordable. (More than 95 percent of undergrads receive some form of financial aid). With over eighty clubs and organizations, students are sure to find an activity that interests them while forming life-long friendships. Our picturesque 160-acre campus in the heart of New York state enhances Le Moyne's outstanding programs."

SELECTIVITY

# of total applicants	8,411
% of total applicants accepted	68
% of total acceptees attending	10
# of in-state applicants	6,174
% of in-state applicants accepted	71
# of out-of-state-applicants	1,706
% of applicants accepted from out of state	66
# of international applicants	531
% of international applicants accepted	39
# offered a place on the wait list	258
# admitted from wait list	13

First-Year Profile

Testing policy	Test Optional
Range SAT composite	1190–1320
Range SAT EBRW	590–660
Range SAT math	570–660
Range ACT composite	25–29
% submitting SAT scores	12
% submitting ACT scores	3
Average HS GPA	3.7
% submitting high school GPA	100
% graduated top 10% of class	22
% graduated top 25% of class	34
% graduated top 50% of class	87
% submitting high school rank	48

Important Dates

Early action	
Apply by	11/1
Notified by	12/1
Regular	
Notified by	Rolling, 1/1
Nonfall registration?	Yes

FINANCIAL FACTS

Annual tuition	$42,080
Food and housing	$17,372
Required fees	$1,366
Books and supplies	$1,345
Average need-based scholarship (First-year)	$28,782 ($29,792)
% students with need rec. need-based scholarship or grant aid (First-year)	100 (100)
% students with need rec. non-need-based scholarship or grant aid (First-year)	22 (24)
% students with need rec. need-based self-help aid (First-year)	70 (68)
% students rec. any financial aid (First-year)	89 (100)
% UG borrow to pay for school	85
Average cumulative indebtedness	$32,509
% of students with need fully met (First-year)	25 (26)
Average % of student need met (First-year)	80 (81)

LEWIS & CLARK COLLEGE

615 S Palatine Hill Road, Portland, OR 97219-7899 • Admissions: 503-768-7040

Survey Snapshot
Lots of liberal students
Students aren't religious
Students environmentally aware

RATINGS	
Quality of Life	80
Fire Safety	88
Green	96
Academic	82
Profs Interesting	93
Profs Accessible	94
Admissions	80
Financial Aid	93

CAMPUS LIFE

Type of school	Private
Environment	Metropolis

Students

Degree-seeking undergrad enrollment	1,967
% male/female/not reported	37/63/1
% from out of state	82
% First-year from public high school	60
% First-year live on campus	95
% Ugrads live on campus	69
# of fraternities	0
# of sororities	0
% Asian	4
% Black or African American	3
% Hispanic	14
% Native American	<1
% Pacific Islander	<1
% Race and/or ethnicity unknown	2
% Two or more races	10
% White	60
% International	6
# of countries represented	70

CAMPUS MENTAL HEALTH SERVICES

Offers mental health/wellness program	Yes
Mental health training available to students	Yes
Employs Chief Wellness Officer	Yes
Peer-to-peer mental health offerings	Yes
Counseling center has guidelines or accreditation	Yes
Mental health/well-being courses	Yes, for-credit

ACADEMICS

% students returning for sophomore year	83
% students graduating within 4 years	60
% students graduating within 6 years	74
Calendar	Semester
Student/faculty ratio	12:1
Most common class size 10–19.	(38%)
Most common lab/discussion size 20–29.	(40%)

Most Popular Majors

Biology/Biological Sciences; Psychology; Sociology and Anthropology

Applicants Also Look At

Colorado College, Occidental College, Pitzer College, Reed College, University of California—Berkeley, University of California—Davis, University of California—Santa Cruz, University of Oregon, University of Puget Sound, University of Washington, Whitman College, Willamette University

STUDENTS SAY "..."

Academics

Lewis & Clark College offers students everything they could possibly want: a "sense of community, beautiful campus, great academics, and lots of opportunities to engage in extracurriculars." Indeed, "it is a very welcoming" school, one filled with people who "care about the classes they are taking and the work that they are doing." In particular, students shine a spotlight on the school's "amazing job of engaging students in experiential learning," which includes "service work to underserved communities as well as educational and mentorship opportunities at nearby schools." Undergrads praise being able to "work with incarcerated people to explore topics of historical injustices in the criminal justice system or write expert witness statements for immigrants seeking citizenship in the U.S."

Students note that lower-level classes tend to be "much more lecture based" than many of the seminar-style upper-level classes that feature active group discussion, but are described as "still fascinating," due in large part to the fact that "professors are sure to engage their students by asking questions and encouraging participation." On this, undergraduates are largely unanimous: their teachers "are one of the best things about Lewis & Clark...dedicated to teaching and exclusively focused on the undergraduate experience." As one enrollee puts it, "Not only do they provide great instruction in the classroom, but they are available outside of the classroom to talk about class, life, and your future after college." A classmate concurs, adding, "I have made close connections with professors here—they have me feel like I am valuable, that my voice is important. I am so grateful for this, and I think this is a rare thing."

Campus Life

Lewis & Clark is "a pretty lax place, so you can kind of socialize at your own pace," whether that means partaking in the countless school events or just chilling in one's dorm. It's "really easy to start a club, so there is also something that caters to everyone." This eclectic mix includes "a club dedicated to the art of fire dancing" and a "beekeeping and gardening club," as well as staples like cheer and step, speech and debate, and a radio station. Some students also highlight the international affairs symposium, noting that it's "one of the most special things we have. They bring speakers from all over the world to debate on controversial topics and they are very interdisciplinary." Crafty and creatively inclined undergrads can spend plenty of time in the Platteau, a "student-centered art center with free access to a ceramics studio, dance studio, darkroom, printing press, music studio, and general arts needs." Additionally, the school is a haven for outdoor enthusiasts, with the College Outdoors office providing "affordable weekend trips and free gear...for backpacking, white-water rafting, rock climbing, etc." As for Portland, it offers a nice respite from campus life. It's typical to see students sampling the "cafés, brunch places, and thrift shops, museums, [and] malls."

Student Body

Peers at Lewis & Clark are described as "overwhelmingly white, very liberal, and generally pretty well-off, financially," with many hailing from the Bay Area, Washington, and Oregon. Among this cohort, there is also a group of "tight-knit international students" and "a very large and welcoming queer community." Some of the population describes itself as politically "very radical...compared to other colleges," but the overall consensus is of a student body that is "pretty balanced," particularly when it comes to the partying culture, which "never feels unhealthy or unsafe." The atmosphere, in short, is "very warm, welcoming, and open-minded," the sort of place where "no matter where I go on campus, there is always someone to wave to or stop and chat with." Indeed, "it is a very accepting community where everyone can feel comfortable in being their true selves and it is a place where you'll find your people." In other words, as this classmate sums up, "We form such special bonds at this institution and I can't imagine going to school anywhere else."

LEWIS & CLARK COLLEGE

Financial Aid: 503-768-7090 • E-Mail: admissions@lclark.edu • Website: www.lclark.edu

THE PRINCETON REVIEW SAYS

Admissions

The school reports that its standardized testing policy for use in admission for Fall 2026 is Test Free. The Princeton Review suggests that interested applicants consult with the school for the most up-to-date standardized testing policies. *Very important factors considered include:* rigor of secondary school record, academic GPA. *Important factors considered include:* application essay, recommendation(s), extracurricular activities, talent/ability, character/personal qualities, volunteer work, work experience. *Other factors considered include:* class rank, interview, first generation, geographical residence, level of applicant's interest. High school diploma is required and GED is accepted. *Academic units recommended:* 4 English, 4 math, 3 science, 2 science labs, 2 language (other than English), 3 social studies, 1 visual/performing arts.

Financial Aid

Students should submit: FAFSA. Priority filing deadline is 1/15. The Princeton Review suggests that all financial aid forms be submitted as soon as possible. *Need-based scholarships/grants offered:* Federal Pell; Federal SEOG; State scholarships/grants; Private scholarships; College/university scholarship or grant aid from institutional funds. *Loan aid offered:* Federal Direct Subsidized Loans; Federal Direct Unsubsidized Loans; Direct PLUS loans. Admitted students will be notified of awards on a rolling basis beginning 3/1. Federal Work-Study Program available. Institutional employment available.

The Inside Word

If you have your heart set on Lewis & Clark, make sure you tell that to the admissions committee because the college is interested in students who will make the most of the school's unique philosophy and educational environment. So make sure your application essay and interview both emphasize why Lewis & Clark is the right fit for you.

THE SCHOOL SAYS

From the Admissions Office

"No matter which of our 29 majors and 34 minors you choose, the top-tier liberal arts education you receive at Lewis & Clark will give you the knowledge, skills, and confidence you need to lead with purpose and make an impact on your community. Our small, discussion-based classes; the mentorship you will receive from your professors; and culture of curiosity align perfectly with the skills you need to succeed in any career: communication, critical thinking, leadership, professionalism, teamwork, and technology. Our post-graduation success rate speaks for itself: 98% of our reporting graduates are working, pursuing graduate degrees, or engaged in meaningful volunteer experiences within six months of getting their degree. Our recent $5 million investment in our Career Accelerator, paves the way for you to align your curiosity and creativity with real-world skills, providing hands-on preparation for making change that matters. Entering first-year students benefit from our 4-5-6 Commitment, in which professors and professional academic advisors guide you to graduation in four years, or we pay for an additional semester. We offer a pathway to our Graduate School of Education and Counseling that will get you an MAT + licensure in five years, and an option to earn your BA + a JD from our School of Law in just six years. You'll be surrounded by our welcoming community, rooted in empathy, kindness, and understanding, and full of people who are rooting for you and your success. You'll graduate from Lewis & Clark ready to take on the world!"

SELECTIVITY

# of total applicants	5,804
% of total applicants accepted	71
% of total acceptees attending	13
# of early decision applicants	98
% of early decision applicants accepted	74
# offered a place on the wait list	140
# admitted from wait list	2

First-Year Profile

Testing policy	Test Free
Average HS GPA	3.7
% submitting high school GPA	98

Important Dates

Early decision	
Apply by	11/1
Notified by	12/5
Early action	
Apply by	11/1
Notified by	12/31
Regular	
Apply by	1/15
Notified by	4/1
Nonfall registration?	No

FINANCIAL FACTS

Annual tuition	$70,657
Food and housing	$16,892
Required fees	$434
Books and supplies	$800
Average need-based scholarship (First-year)	$57,170 ($57,147)
% students with need rec. need-based scholarship or grant aid (First-year)	99 (99)
% students with need rec. non-need-based scholarship or grant aid (First-year)	18 (24)
% students with need rec. need-based self-help aid (First-year)	77 (74)
% students rec. any financial aid (First-year)	99 (100)
% UG borrow to pay for school	45
Average cumulative indebtedness	$28,637
% of students with need fully met (First-year)	47 (43)
Average % of student need met (First-year)	92 (92)

LOUISIANA STATE UNIVERSITY—BATON ROUGE

Pleasant Hall, Baton Rouge, LA 70803 • Admissions: 225-578-1175

Survey Snapshot
Recreation facilities are great
College radio is popular
Everyone loves the Tigers

RATINGS

Quality of Life	79
Fire Safety	99
Green	60*
Academic	73
Profs Interesting	81
Profs Accessible	88
Admissions	86
Financial Aid	83

CAMPUS LIFE

Type of school	Public
Environment	City

Students

Degree-seeking undergrad enrollment	30,594
% male/female/not reported	43/57/0
% from out of state	34
% First-year from public high school	72
% First-year live on campus	83
% Ugrads live on campus	29
# of fraternities (% join)	18 (17)
# of sororities (% join)	22 (24)
% Asian	5
% Black or African American	21
% Hispanic	11
% Native American	<1
% Pacific Islander	<1
% Race and/or ethnicity unknown	1
% Two or more races	4
% White	57
% International	1
# of countries represented	103

CAMPUS MENTAL HEALTH SERVICES

Offers mental health/wellness program	Yes
Mental health training available to students	Yes
Employs Chief Wellness Officer	No
Peer-to-peer mental health offerings	Yes
Counseling center has guidelines or accreditation	Yes
Mental health/well-being courses	No

ACADEMICS

% students returning for sophomore year	85
% students graduating within 4 years	48
% students graduating within 6 years	68
Calendar	Semester
Student/faculty ratio	22:1
Most common class size 10–19.	(33%)
Most common lab/discussion size 20–29.	(32%)

Most Popular Majors

Kinesiology; Biology/Biological Sciences; Psychology

Applicants Also Look At

Texas A&M University—College Station, The University of Alabama—Tuscaloosa, University of Georgia, University of Louisiana at Lafayette, University of Mississippi, University of Tennessee—Knoxville

STUDENTS SAY "..."

Academics

Louisiana State University is heralded by its students for having "tons of different programs to choose from" and "stellar academics." A few that students mention are the strong engineering and mass communications programs. Students also appreciate that they're not just abandoned under a variety of classes and programs. "No matter what issue you're having, there is [someone] whose entire job is to help you deal with it," says a student. "The tutoring centers are beyond helpful," if you need assistance with your studies, and faculty is "always available to help students" outside of class. This extra scaffolding keeps the rigor of academic programs "challenging but not unbearable." Some students recall lectures that are "extremely boring," and cite language barriers they've encountered with a few professors. But undergrads are impressed overall, stating, "Professors at LSU...are passionate about their fields of study" and are "accessible, accommodating, and well-informed."

Campus Life

This "beautiful southern university" offers "the best of both worlds," combining its academics with "so many clubs and groups...for students to join." For fun and fitness, "the weather is beautiful here and [the] campus is located next to large lakes where a lot of people run or walk." If you want to take it indoors, the recreation center is an "amazing facility" that "is great for group classes and working out during the day or relaxing at the pool." Socially, "Greek life is prominent," but if that's not your thing, "there are so many different subgroups, and there's really a place for everyone." No matter where you fit in, "tailgating and football are central to the school." As one student says, "It is [an] absolutely amazing environment [in which] everyone comes together to support the teams." Another adds, "When 'Calling Baton Rouge' gets played at an event you end up singing it and dancing to it with someone new, whoever is next to you, no matter where they are from." That love for Baton Rouge extends off-campus as well, to the city itself, which students call "underrated [and] cool."

Student Body

Southern hospitality shines through in most here, as "many students are clearly Louisianans first and students second." While many may be state natives, students frequently comment that "the student body at LSU is very diverse." One adds, "I love being able to walk around campus and see people of all cultures speaking different languages and engaging with one another." Along with cultures, interests vary too: "You have people that are party animals, Christian loyalists, sports enthusiasts, [and] academic maniacs." While students appreciate the diversity, some note that the population "continues to be predominated by white, cisgender, and mostly heterosexual people." Nonetheless, a community atmosphere prevails, allowing students to "really feel like they are a part of something bigger." This camaraderie extends all across campus because "people here care about smiles and friendliness," giving it "a smaller and more intimate atmosphere." As one student puts it, as long as "you're a Tiger, then you're family." As another student observes, "When you mix Louisiana culture with 30,000 students who love their school, you get an amazing combination."

Louisiana State University—Baton Rouge

Financial Aid: 225-578-3103 • E-Mail: admissions@lsu.edu • Website: www.lsu.edu

THE PRINCETON REVIEW SAYS

Admissions

The school reports that its standardized testing policy for use in admission for Fall 2026 is Test Optional for applicants with a cumulative, weighted high school GPA of 3.5 or higher. Applicants with a GPA below 3.5 are required to submit standardized test scores. *Very important factors considered include:* rigor of secondary school record, academic GPA, standardized test scores, recommendation(s). *Important factors considered include:* class rank, talent/ability. *Other factors considered include:* application essay, interview, extracurricular activities, character/personal qualities, first generation, alumni/ae relation, volunteer work, work experience, level of applicant's interest. High school diploma is required and GED is accepted. *Academic units required:* 4 English, 4 math, 4 science, 2 language (other than English), 3 social studies, 1 history, 1 visual/performing arts.

Financial Aid

Students should submit: FAFSA. Priority filing deadline is 2/1. The Princeton Review suggests that all financial aid forms be submitted as soon as possible. *Need-based scholarships/grants offered:* Federal Pell; Federal SEOG; State scholarships/grants; Private scholarships; College/university scholarship or grant aid from institutional funds. *Loan aid offered:* Federal Direct Subsidized Loans; Federal Direct Unsubsidized Loans; Direct PLUS loans; College/university loans from institutional funds. Admitted students will be notified of awards on a rolling basis beginning 12/15. Federal Work-Study Program available. Institutional employment available.

The Inside Word

LSU takes a well-rounded look at each applicant's academic background rather than focusing on any single factor. LSU will look at your overall GPA, the difficulty of your coursework, how your grades have trended over time, and how you've done in classes related to your intended major. Be sure to highlight any other qualities that show you're ready to succeed at LSU.

THE SCHOOL SAYS

From the Admissions Office

"As one of the nation's most prestigious flagship institutions, Louisiana State University is a top-tier research powerhouse tackling some of the world's greatest challenges. LSU is also one of only a handful of universities in the nation with land-, sea-, and space-grant designations, which attracts world-renowned faculty who are invested in your success and committed to sharing their extensive knowledge and global network with you. Our students and faculty work together to generate innovative, groundbreaking solutions across more than 330 academic programs.

"Guiding you along your path to graduation is a top priority at LSU, and that support begins day 1. Every freshman at LSU is assigned a Student Success Team made up of five professional staff and a peer mentor on campus who are committed to personally assisting you throughout your academic journey. From national titles to Nobel Prizes, and Heisman winners to Rhodes scholars, success is tradition at LSU, and we build teams that win. In Louisiana. For the world."

SELECTIVITY

# of total applicants	47,063
% of total applicants accepted	73
% of total acceptees attending	23
# of in-state applicants	11,135
% of in-state applicants accepted	80
# of out-of-state-applicants	34,357
% of applicants accepted from out of state	72
# of international applicants	1,573
% of international applicants accepted	48

First-Year Profile

Testing policy	Test Optional !
Range SAT composite	1180–1320
Range SAT EBRW	600–680
Range SAT math	580–660
Range ACT composite	24–30
% submitting SAT scores	7
% submitting ACT scores	40
Average HS GPA	3.8
% submitting high school GPA	99
% graduated top 10% of class	26
% graduated top 25% of class	54
% graduated top 50% of class	83
% submitting high school rank	77

Important Dates

Regular	
Apply by	4/15
Notified by	Rolling, 10/15
Nonfall registration?	Yes

FINANCIAL FACTS

Annual in-state tuition	$8,278
Annual out-of-state tuition	$24,955
Food and housing	$15,686
Required fees	$4,273
Books and supplies	$1,084
Average need-based scholarship (First-year)	$14,276 ($14,981)
% students with need rec. need-based scholarship or grant aid (First-year)	91 (95)
% students with need rec. non-need-based scholarship or grant aid (First-year)	3 (4)
% students with need rec. need-based self-help aid (First-year)	58 (52)
% students rec. any financial aid (First-year)	77 (96)
% UG borrow to pay for school	43
Average cumulative indebtedness	$25,590
% of students with need fully met (First-year)	11 (12)
Average % of student need met (First-year)	55 (57)

! Test Optional if you have a GPA of 3.5 or higher.

LOYOLA MARYMOUNT UNIVERSITY

1 LMU Drive, Los Angeles, CA 90045 • Admissions: 310-338-2750

Survey Snapshot
Great library
Easy to get around campus
Students love Los Angeles, CA

RATINGS

Quality of Life	90
Fire Safety	91
Green	99
Academic	83
Profs Interesting	92
Profs Accessible	93
Admissions	90
Financial Aid	86

CAMPUS LIFE

Type of school	Private
Affiliation	Roman Catholic
Environment	Town

Students

Degree-seeking undergrad enrollment	7,020
% male/female/not reported	47/53/0
% from out of state	32
% First-year from public high school	51
% First-year live on campus	91
% Ugrads live on campus	48
# of fraternities (% join)	9 (14)
# of sororities (% join)	11 (26)
% Asian	11
% Black or African American	7
% Hispanic	25
% Native American	<1
% Pacific Islander	<1
% Race and/or ethnicity unknown	<1
% Two or more races	9
% White	38
% International	9
# of countries represented	81

CAMPUS MENTAL HEALTH SERVICES

Offers mental health/wellness program	Yes
Mental health training available to students	No
Employs Chief Wellness Officer	No
Peer-to-peer mental health offerings	Yes
Counseling center has guidelines or accreditation	Yes
Mental health/well-being courses	No

ACADEMICS

% students returning for sophomore year	89
% students graduating within 4 years	66
% students graduating within 6 years	79
Calendar	Semester
Student/faculty ratio	10:1
Most common class size 20–29.	(41%)
Most common lab/discussion size 10–19.	(64%)

Most Popular Majors
Psychology; Marketing/Marketing Management; Finance

Applicants Often Prefer
University of California—Berkeley, University of California—Los Angeles, University of Southern California

Applicants Sometimes Prefer
California Polytechnic State University—San Luis Obispo, New York University, Santa Clara University, University of California—Santa Barbara

Applicants Rarely Prefer
Chapman University, University of California—Irvine

STUDENTS SAY "..."

Academics

Loyola Marymount University is a Catholic university founded in the Jesuit tradition. These roots are reflected in the academics, which often incorporate "ethical views from the Jesuit practices." Students find the overall academic experience to be "challenging and fulfilling." As one student says, "LMU courses put you to work—not busy work, but meaningful work that you will learn from." Students describe an atmosphere where "everybody is willing to help each other" and fellow classmates are "open to collaboration on assignments and projects so that everyone can be successful." As one student puts it, "Never have I felt a sense of rivalry or competition amongst my peers." The faculty are described as being "more like mentors" who are "very friendly" and "attentive to students' questions and concerns." As one student puts it, "The professors at LMU want to see you succeed and will do anything to help you do that." This is good news for career-oriented students, as "professors will genuinely make an effort to connect students with internship[s]" and "lead you to many different opportunities on and off campus." Students appreciate the hands-on approach taken in many classes, whether it's film students getting experience "directing or using a camera," marketing students collaborating with "real businesses," or science classes traveling to "various field sites during lab time, such as the beach, hikes, parks, and Catalina Island."

Campus Life

The campus provides many opportunities to soak up the sunshine, including the lawns of the Sunken Gardens and the Bluff and "having views of both the ocean and LA never gets old." Students also enjoy using the gym and attending the workout classes, where instructors "foster a fun environment." Another favorite event is Wellness Wednesdays, a weekly market where "small businesses set up booths and showcase their items for sale." Students at LMU "fill their day with extracurricular activities." Outdoor recreation is popular, including surfing and hiking as well as intramural sports like beach volleyball and soccer. "Everyone is involved in something," explains one student. Whether it's rock climbing, open mic night, cultural clubs, Greek life, service organizations, or 3D printing, there is "something here for everyone." For getting off-campus, exploring Los Angeles is a frequent activity. LMU provides a shuttle to the nearby neighborhood of Playa Vista where students often shop at the farmer's market or see a movie. Students note that exploring beyond Playa Vista requires the use of a car, but for many, the proximity to all of what LA offers is a big perk. As one student who loves exploring the city says, "I've been here four years and I feel like I have barely scratched the surface of what is here."

Student Body

Students describe their peers as "creative, progressive, and passionate." Although some report that LMU doesn't have the stereotypical "school spirit because we are a smaller school with less of an emphasis on sports," overall LMU is "very social." One student emphasizes that it's "still surprising after three semesters how kind and friendly people are here." Many students describe "a very diverse student body," while others say LMU could improve on diversity. One common theme from students is that the campus is a place that's "composed of communities for all kinds of people to fit in" with programming that "caters to every student." Students say that LMU "feels like a small community where everyone know each other, which is very nice." As one person describes it, "You can make friends just by chatting with people in a line at a dining place on campus." Overall, students describe a community that is "tight knit and very supportive of each other." And as one student sums up, "You can always find your group of people where you fit in."

LOYOLA MARYMOUNT UNIVERSITY

Financial Aid: 310-338-2753 • E-Mail: admissions@lmu.edu • Website: www.lmu.edu

THE PRINCETON REVIEW SAYS

Admissions

The school reports that its standardized testing policy for use in admission for Fall 2026 is Test Optional. The Princeton Review suggests that interested applicants consult with the school for the most up-to-date standardized testing policies. *Very important factors considered include:* rigor of secondary school record, academic GPA, application essay. *Important factors considered include:* recommendation(s), talent/ability, character/personal qualities. *Other factors considered include:* class rank, standardized test scores, extracurricular activities, first generation, volunteer work, work experience. High school diploma is required and GED is not accepted. *Academic units recommended:* 4 English, 3 math, 2 science, 2 science labs, 3 language (other than English), 3 social studies, 1 academic elective.

Financial Aid

Students should submit: FAFSA. Priority filing deadline is 2/1. The Princeton Review suggests that all financial aid forms be submitted as soon as possible. *Need-based scholarships/grants offered:* Federal Pell; Federal SEOG; State scholarships/grants; Private scholarships; College/university scholarship or grant aid from institutional funds. *Loan aid offered:* Federal Direct Subsidized Loans; Federal Direct Unsubsidized Loans; Direct PLUS loans; College/university loans from institutional funds. Admitted students will be notified of awards on a rolling basis beginning 12/15. Federal Work-Study Program available. Institutional employment available.

The Inside Word

A selective institution, Loyola Marymount University takes a well-rounded approach to admissions. While each applicant's academic record is of primary importance, LMU also considers everything from writing ability and service-related endeavors to letters of recommendation, artistic and athletic prowess, and even an individual's relationship to the university. It should be noted that requirements can vary depending on the program. For example, business students must have taken elementary algebra, geometry, intermediate algebra/trigonometry, and precalculus. Arts applicants must audition or submit a portfolio.

THE SCHOOL SAYS

From the Admissions Office

"Loyola Marymount University (LMU) is a nationally ranked Catholic, Jesuit university where academic excellence, Los Angeles, and a deep focus on formation come together. LMU is committed to *cura personalis*—care for the whole person—helping students grow in intellect, character, creativity, and sense of purpose while they prepare for life after graduation. Curiosity and intellectual exploration are central to an LMU education. With more than 150 undergraduate programs, 4+1 master's options, and over 90 graduate programs, students pursue rigorous study in liberal arts, business, film and television, communication, fine arts, science and engineering, education, and more. Small classes taught by dedicated, award-winning faculty foster close mentoring relationships, undergraduate research, and collaborative creative work. Students connect learning to real-world experience early, often through internships, community-engaged projects, and one-on-one work with professors.

"Our location on a bluff in Los Angeles is a distinctive advantage. Adjacent to Silicon Beach and within easy reach of the region's media, arts, tech, healthcare, and nonprofit sectors, LMU students turn the city into their classroom, studio, and lab through internships, networking, and professional immersion. Within six months of graduation, the vast majority of LMU graduates are working, pursuing advanced study, or serving in programs such as service organizations and the military.

"Rooted in Jesuit and Marymount traditions, LMU challenges students to think critically, act with integrity, and ask how their talents can serve a world in need. Graduates leave with strong outcomes—and with the habits of mind, heart, and leadership that shape a meaningful life."

SELECTIVITY

# of total applicants	22,798
% of total applicants accepted	48
% of total acceptees attending	14
# of in-state applicants	12,133
% of in-state applicants accepted	55
# of out-of-state-applicants	7,958
% of applicants accepted from out of state	52
# of international applicants	2,707
% of international applicants accepted	6
# of early decision applicants	858
% of early decision applicants accepted	42
# offered a place on the wait list	6,148
# admitted from wait list	208

First-Year Profile

Testing policy	Test Optional
Range SAT composite	1270–1410
Range SAT EBRW	640–720
Range SAT math	610–700
Range ACT composite	28–33
% submitting SAT scores	20
% submitting ACT scores	7
Average HS GPA	3.98
% submitting high school GPA	100
% graduated top 10% of class	28
% graduated top 25% of class	67
% graduated top 50% of class	93
% submitting high school rank	23

Important Dates

Early decision	
Apply by	11/1
Notified by	12/17
Other ED apply by	1/8
Other ED notified by	2/17
Early action	
Apply by	11/1
Notified by	12/17
Regular	
Apply by	1/15
Nonfall registration?	Yes

FINANCIAL FACTS*

Annual tuition	$64,470
Food and housing	$20,628
Required fees (First-year)	$897 ($1,387)
Books and supplies	$1,089
Average need-based scholarship (First-year)	$34,639 ($39,722)
% students with need rec. need-based scholarship or grant aid (First-year)	98 (99)
% students with need rec. non-need-based scholarship or grant aid (First-year)	16 (15)
% students with need rec. need-based self-help aid (First-year)	68 (66)
% students rec. any financial aid (First-year)	90 (100)
% UG borrow to pay for school	39
Average cumulative indebtedness	$33,482
% of students with need fully met (First-year)	21 (19)
Average % of student need met (First-year)	68 (71)

* Most recently reported data at time of printing. Scan the QR code to find the latest updates.

LOYOLA UNIVERSITY CHICAGO

1032 W. Sheridan Rd, Chicago, IL 60660 • Admissions: 312-915-6500

Survey Snapshot
Students love Chicago, IL
Great off-campus food
Lab facilities are great

RATINGS

Quality of Life	78
Fire Safety	90
Green	99
Academic	82
Profs Interesting	86
Profs Accessible	90
Admissions	87
Financial Aid	87

CAMPUS LIFE

Type of school	Private
Affiliation	Roman Catholic-Jesuit
Environment	Metropolis

Students

Degree-seeking undergrad enrollment	11,585
% male/female/not reported	30/70/<1
% from out of state	42
% First-year from public high school	76
% First-year live on campus	82
% Ugrads live on campus	42
# of fraternities (% join)	2 (5)
# of sororities (% join)	5 (9)
% Asian	13
% Black or African American	9
% Hispanic	25
% Native American	<1
% Pacific Islander	<1
% Race and/or ethnicity unknown	1
% Two or more races	5
% White	45
% International	2

CAMPUS MENTAL HEALTH SERVICES

Offers mental health/wellness program	Yes
Mental health training available to students	Yes
Employs Chief Wellness Officer	Yes
Peer-to-peer mental health offerings	Yes
Counseling center has guidelines or accreditation	Yes
Mental health/well-being courses	Yes, non-credit

ACADEMICS

% students returning for sophomore year	85
% students graduating within 4 years	67
% students graduating within 6 years	74
Calendar	Semester
Student/faculty ratio	13:1
Most common class size 10–19.	(28%)
Most common lab/discussion size 20–29.	(36%)

Most Popular Majors
Biology/Biological Sciences; Psychology; Registered Nursing/Registered Nurse

Applicants Often Prefer
DePaul University, University of Illinois at Chicago, University of Illinois at Urbana—Champaign, University of Wisconsin—Madison

Applicants Sometimes Prefer
Indiana University—Bloomington, Marquette University, Michigan State University, Purdue University—West Lafayette, University of Michigan—Ann Arbor

Applicants Rarely Prefer
Dominican University, Northern Illinois University

STUDENTS SAY "..."

Academics

Students of all disciplines at Loyola University Chicago are given every opportunity to follow what interests them and to "build an education that will serve them well in the future." To that end, Loyola's Jesuit ideals yield "rigorous and fascinating" programs that are "developing intellectual and socially responsible students" and preparing them both for careers and "being aware of problems around us." The offering of "significant financial assistance and plenty of scholarships" helps, as do specializations like Loyola's intensive January term, where students have the freedom to do a deep dive into the subject of their choice.

The school's prime lakeside location, just eight miles north of downtown Chicago, "allows Loyola to attract top-notch faculty." Those professors then "find a good balance in their teaching methods that allows students to engage the material" utilizing "connections and opportunities," such as bringing in "business professionals to relate our classroom material to the real world." One student states: "The majority of the professors [are] excellent," while another confesses to having "several professors who I would go out of my way to take again." Coursework itself is "challenging, but not overbearing," keeping with the "well known academic integrity of the school."

Campus Life

Life at Loyola "provides the best of both worlds: an integrated campus and a taste of the city life." On campus, the vibe is "very relaxed, a sort of oasis in a bustling city." The classic brick buildings are "gorgeous," and the grounds boast a beach on Lake Michigan, so "clearly, it does not feel much like a city most of the time." There are over 250 student-run clubs and organizations on campus, and student athletes compete in 15 Division I sports. Informal coffee chats, chess workshops, and Latin music ensembles can all be found on campus throughout any given week. Off campus, central Chicago is "a gold mine," and for some "the biggest hobby around here is exploring Chicago. We go out every weekend, just looking for things to do and always finding them." Some describe Loyola's "social atmosphere" itself as a little "dull," though others rave about getting to "go on trips that involve doing out-of-the-ordinary activities." Overall, students appreciate the balance of fun and preparation that Loyola provides: "What's great about Loyola is that it is very future focused, but it never forgets about the present either."

Student Body

At Loyola University Chicago, "there is a real feel of family." One student describes the atmosphere as "very easy to fit in because of how accepting people are." In fact, over 80% of first-year students reported that helping others in need was an "essential" or "very important value." Generally, students are known to be "witty, hardworking, smart, and outgoing," and most likely "involved in some extracurricular or another." The average student seems to come "from an upper-middle class family, has some faith background, and balances school with social life well." Another student concurs, describing their peers as "studious and fairly involved, but able to have fun." Overall, most students "find a good core group of people that they work together with in classes, clubs, organizations, and/or athletics."

Loyola University Chicago

Financial Aid: 773-508-7704 • E-Mail: admission@luc.edu • Website: www.luc.edu

THE PRINCETON REVIEW SAYS

Admissions

The school reports that its standardized testing policy for use in admission for Fall 2026 is Test Optional. The Princeton Review suggests that interested applicants consult with the school for the most up-to-date standardized testing policies. *Very important factors considered include:* rigor of secondary school record, academic GPA. *Important factors considered include:* application essay, recommendation(s), extracurricular activities, character/personal qualities, volunteer work, work experience. *Other factors considered include:* class rank, standardized test scores, talent/ability, first generation, alumni/ae relation, level of applicant's interest. High school diploma is required and GED is accepted. *Academic units required:* 4 English, 3 math, 3 science, 2 language (other than English), 2 social studies, 1 history. *Academic units recommended:* 4 English, 4 math, 3 science, 2 language (other than English), 2 social studies, 2 history, 3 computer science.

Financial Aid

Students should submit: FAFSA. The Princeton Review suggests that all financial aid forms be submitted as soon as possible. *Need-based scholarships/grants offered:* Federal Pell; Federal SEOG; State scholarships/grants; Private scholarships; College/university scholarship or grant aid from institutional funds. *Loan aid offered:* Federal Direct Subsidized Loans; Federal Direct Unsubsidized Loans; Direct PLUS loans; College/university loans from institutional funds. Admitted students will be notified of awards on a rolling basis beginning 2/1. Federal Work-Study Program available. Institutional employment available.

The Inside Word

Loyola is fairly conventional when it comes to admissions policies. Successful candidates usually have a combination of strong grades, success in a tough college preparatory curriculum, and solid extracurricular activities. The school adheres to Jesuit teaching, so applicants with significant volunteer work should impress admissions officers.

THE SCHOOL SAYS

From the Admissions Office

"As a Jesuit, Catholic university, Loyola University Chicago provides a strong liberal arts education, one that stresses the importance of knowledge, curiosity, global perspectives, and *cura personalis*, which translates to "care for the whole person." Loyola offers more than 80 majors and minors, with extensive program options that allow students to explore and develop their unique talents in a vibrant, urban atmosphere. The Core Curriculum provides a rich selection of courses with a diverse focus, emphasizing lifelong skills and values. The University continues to enhance its undergraduate academic programming by modifying and adding majors in emerging fields.

"For example, Loyola's Parkinson School of Health Sciences and Public Health is dedicated to improving patient and population health and minimizing inequities—with degrees in exercise science, health systems management, and dietetics. Loyola's School of Environmental Sustainability offers degree program options in environmental studies, environmental policy, and environmental science with concentrations such as conservation and restoration. Housed in a state-of-the-art and LEED-certified facility, the institute features a greenhouse, a biodiesel lab, collaborative research labs, and one of the largest geothermal facilities in the Chicago region. Loyola continues to open new facilities and renovate existing buildings, including a new freshman residence hall, athletics facility, and engineering lab. Between Loyola's two lakeside campuses, students benefit from a traditional campus feel as well as a downtown that's home to Fortune 500 companies. For more information about undergraduate academics, housing, student life, financial aid, scholarship opportunities, and more, visit LUC.edu/undergrad."

SELECTIVITY

# of total applicants	43,954
% of total applicants accepted	75
% of total acceptees attending	8
# offered a place on the wait list	0
# admitted from wait list	0

First-Year Profile

Testing policy	Test Optional
Range SAT composite	1220–1390
Range SAT EBRW	580–690
Range SAT math	540–660
Range ACT composite	26–31
% submitting SAT scores	39
% submitting ACT scores	15
Average HS GPA	3.7
% submitting high school GPA	100
% graduated top 10% of class	37
% graduated top 25% of class	69
% graduated top 50% of class	92
% submitting high school rank	19

Important Dates

Regular	
Apply by	Rolling
Notified by	Rolling, 10/15
Nonfall registration?	Yes

FINANCIAL FACTS

Annual tuition	$56,930
Food and housing	$17,980
Required fees	$1,580
Books and supplies	$1,600
Average need-based scholarship (First-year)	$33,467 ($35,854)
% students with need rec. need-based scholarship or grant aid (First-year)	97 (99)
% students with need rec. non-need-based scholarship or grant aid (First-year)	13 (15)
% students with need rec. need-based self-help aid (First-year)	59 (79)
% students rec. any financial aid (First-year)	98 (100)
% UG borrow to pay for school	58
Average cumulative indebtedness	$42,570
% of students with need fully met (First-year)	17 (19)
Average % of student need met (First-year)	83 (84)

LOYOLA UNIVERSITY MARYLAND

4501 North Charles Street, Baltimore, MD 21210 • Admissions: 410-617-5012

Survey Snapshot
Lots of conservative students
Classroom facilities are great
Dorms are like palaces

RATINGS	
Quality of Life	86
Fire Safety	94
Green	86
Academic	84
Profs Interesting	89
Profs Accessible	94
Admissions	88
Financial Aid	88

CAMPUS LIFE

Type of school	Private
Affiliation	Roman Catholic
Environment	Metropolis

Students

Degree-seeking undergrad enrollment	3,996
% male/female/not reported	43/57/0
% from out of state	62
% First-year from public high school	60
% First-year live on campus	91
% Ugrads live on campus	77
# of fraternities	0
# of sororities	0
% Asian	4
% Black or African American	13
% Hispanic	16
% Native American	<1
% Pacific Islander	<1
% Race and/or ethnicity unknown	2
% Two or more races	5
% White	59
% International	2
# of countries represented	49

CAMPUS MENTAL HEALTH SERVICES

Offers mental health/wellness program	Yes
Mental health training available to students	Yes
Employs Chief Wellness Officer	Yes
Peer-to-peer mental health offerings	Yes
Counseling center has guidelines or accreditation	Yes
Mental health/well-being courses	Yes, for-credit

ACADEMICS

% students returning for sophomore year	86
% students graduating within 4 years	70
% students graduating within 6 years	75
Calendar	Semester
Student/faculty ratio	12:1
Most common class size 20–29.	(40%)
Most common lab/discussion size 10–19.	(49%)

Most Popular Majors

Biology/Biological Sciences; Psychology; Finance

Applicants Also Look At

The Catholic University of America, Fairfield University, Fordham University, Providence College, Towson University, University of Delaware, University of Maryland, Baltimore County, University of Maryland, College Park, Villanova University

STUDENTS SAY "..."

Academics

Students who earn the opportunity to study at Loyola University Maryland get to "take some awesome classes that will completely change your perspective on the world." As part of Loyola's "fantastic core curriculum," students get "a solid foundation in the natural sciences, English, history, philosophy, and theology." Students emphasize that the three distinct colleges devoted to arts and sciences, business, and education "are outstanding and the coursework is challenging." There's also robust academic support: the "career center is open for students starting at day one." The "excellent study abroad program" is particularly popular, with some 60% of students studying internationally over the course of their undergraduate career.

With a very manageable student-to-faculty ratio, professors "get to know you personally, take time out of their office hours to have intellectual discussions, show you how to learn and how to teach, and help you out when you are having difficulties." One student reports that their instructors "actually know each of their students by name." Moreover, instructional strategies consider "different learning techniques to cater to everyone's different learning styles." Students love that it's "fairly common for professors to give out their personal cell phone numbers or to even invite the class to their home for dinner."

Campus Life

Affectionately known as Greyhounds, Loyola students find the "right balance between religion, spirituality, and the everyday life of college students." True to its Jesuit legacy, Loyola offers "amazing opportunities to get involved in the Baltimore community through service," a learning experience that students positively describe as "an extension of the classroom." (Students also say they enjoy just "walking around the harbor.") With its primary undergraduate campus in northern Baltimore City, "most students live on campus" and those who move into suites and apartments can enjoy such amenities as "full kitchens in your dorm by sophomore year." Staying central to campus allows Greyhounds to easily attend the "numerous speakers, movies, events, [and] sporting events" available on campus. Student athletes compete in the Patriot League, and Loyola boasts eight men's and nine women's varsity sports teams. Don't expect any stereotypically wild parties, as "there is no Greek life" on campus and there are strict rules for 21-year-olds about where they can have alcohol; some students note that they instead "go out to bars on Fridays and Saturdays." However, late-night students swear by Midnight Breakfast at the Boulder Cafe, and come spring, students of all stripes can be found enjoying Loyolapalooza, a music festival for the entire student body to enjoy before finals. Like the Greyhounds they take their name from, students are "busy doing loads of homework, projects, reading, community service, clubs, lectures, [and] sports," and they're happy doing it.

Student Body

With a student body nearly 4,000 strong, Greyhounds value being able to "find their niche at Loyola very quickly." Loyola attracts students who "care about their academics and do well in school, but they also try to balance that with extracurriculars and their spiritual life." The vibe on campus is "really welcoming and trustworthy" and fosters a "great sense of community." Some students feel that "the student body may appear homogeneous," with a population where "many of the students are white" and often hail from the East Coast. A plurality also self-identify as Catholics. Beneath that surface, attendees explain that "everyone can fit in well," especially when you "immerse yourself in the opportunities Loyola has to offer." As one Greyhound puts it best, Loyola students "live out the core values of the university and enjoy being a contributing member of the school community."

LOYOLA UNIVERSITY MARYLAND

Financial Aid: 410-617-2576 • E-Mail: admission@loyola.edu • Website: www.loyola.edu

THE PRINCETON REVIEW SAYS

Admissions

The school reports that its standardized testing policy for use in admission for Fall 2026 is Test Optional. The Princeton Review suggests that interested applicants consult with the school for the most up-to-date standardized testing policies. *Very important factors considered include:* rigor of secondary school record, academic GPA, character/personal qualities. *Important factors considered include:* application essay, recommendation(s), extracurricular activities, talent/ability, volunteer work, work experience. *Other factors considered include:* standardized test scores, first generation, geographical residence. High school diploma is required and GED is accepted. *Academic units required:* 4 English, 3 math, 3 science, 3 language (other than English), 2 history. *Academic units recommended:* 4 English, 4 math, 4 science, 4 language (other than English), 3 history.

Financial Aid

Students should submit: FAFSA. Priority filing deadline is 12/1. The Princeton Review suggests that all financial aid forms be submitted as soon as possible. *Need-based scholarships/grants offered:* Federal Pell; Federal SEOG; State scholarships/grants; Private scholarships. *Loan aid offered:* Federal Direct Subsidized Loans; Federal Direct Unsubsidized Loans; Direct PLUS loans. Admitted students will be notified of awards on a rolling basis beginning 2/1. Federal Work-Study Program available. Institutional employment available.

The Inside Word

Loyola University Maryland considers a student's academic record to be among the most important factors in an admissions decision. Successful students usually rank in the top quarter of their classes. Although Loyola will consider standardized test scores if you submit them, the SAT or ACT are optional for all first-year applicants.

THE SCHOOL SAYS

From the Admissions Office

"Founded in 1852 in Baltimore, Maryland, Loyola University Maryland is a Jesuit, Catholic liberal arts university dedicated to the holistic education of mind, body, and spirit. Loyola welcomes just under 4,000 undergraduates and 2,200 graduate students across its three schools: Loyola College of Arts and Sciences, the Sellinger School of Business and Management, and the School of Education. The university offers 45+ undergraduate majors, 55+ minors, and 25 graduate programs. The most popular majors are biology, business, communication, computer science, engineering, political science, and psychology.

"Boasting a 12:1 student/faculty ratio and an average class size of 20, Loyola fosters close-knit learning communities and opportunities for faculty mentorship. Loyola's first-year living-learning program, Messina, establishes a solid foundation for success.

"Loyola's 81-acre campus, nestled in a residential neighborhood just north of downtown Baltimore, is also an accredited arboretum. More than 80% of undergraduates reside on campus, creating a vibrant student body from 40 states and 35 countries. Students engage in hundreds of clubs and organizations, participate in 18 NCAA Division I athletic programs, and enjoy numerous school traditions and events throughout the academic year.

"Recognized for its return on investment, Loyola reports that 99% of its alumni are employed, pursuing further education, or engaged in service within six to nine months post-graduation. The mid-career salary of Loyola graduates surpasses those from peer institutions by 30%, evidencing the lasting value of a Loyola education."

SELECTIVITY

# of total applicants	11,850
% of total applicants accepted	70
% of total acceptees attending	13
# of in-state applicants	4,019
% of in-state applicants accepted	65
# of out-of-state-applicants	6,664
% of applicants accepted from out of state	80
# of international applicants	1,143
% of international applicants accepted	27
# of early decision applicants	157
% of early decision applicants accepted	39
# offered a place on the wait list	1,770
# admitted from wait list	45

First-Year Profile

Testing policy	Test Optional
Range SAT composite	1250–1370
Range SAT EBRW	640–710
Range SAT math	600–670
Range ACT composite	29–33
% submitting SAT scores	13
% submitting ACT scores	2
Average HS GPA	3.7
% submitting high school GPA	100
% graduated top 10% of class	22
% graduated top 25% of class	57
% graduated top 50% of class	86
% submitting high school rank	27

Important Dates

Early decision	
Apply by	11/15
Notified by	12/31
Other ED apply by	1/15
Other ED notified by	3/1
Early action	
Apply by	11/15
Notified by	1/15
Regular	
Apply by	1/15
Nonfall registration?	Yes

FINANCIAL FACTS

Annual tuition	$61,810
Food and housing	$19,630
Books and supplies	$800
Average need-based scholarship (First-year)	$41,940 ($42,639)
% students with need rec. need-based scholarship or grant aid (First-year)	89 (86)
% students with need rec. non-need-based scholarship or grant aid (First-year)	93 (91)
% students with need rec. need-based self-help aid (First-year)	75 (75)
% students rec. any financial aid (First-year)	99 (99)
% UG borrow to pay for school	62
Average cumulative indebtedness	$39,399
% of students with need fully met (First-year)	20 (32)
Average % of student need met (First-year)	84 (84)

LOYOLA UNIVERSITY NEW ORLEANS

6363 St. Charles Avenue, New Orleans, LA 70118-6195 • Admissions: 504-865-3240

Survey Snapshot
Easy to get around campus
Great off-campus food
Students love New Orleans, LA

RATINGS

Quality of Life	**88**
Fire Safety	**99**
Green	**60***
Academic	**78**
Profs Interesting	**88**
Profs Accessible	**89**
Admissions	**81**
Financial Aid	**87**

CAMPUS LIFE

Type of school	Private
Affiliation	Roman Catholic-Jesuit
Environment	Metropolis

Students

Degree-seeking undergrad enrollment	2,724
% male/female/not reported	37/63/0
% from out of state	58
% First-year from public high school	65
% First-year live on campus	64
% Ugrads live on campus	41
# of fraternities (% join)	3 (1)
# of sororities (% join)	8 (6)
% Asian	3
% Black or African American	23
% Hispanic	22
% Native American	<1
% Pacific Islander	<1
% Race and/or ethnicity unknown	1
% Two or more races	6
% White	41
% International	4
# of countries represented	38

CAMPUS MENTAL HEALTH SERVICES

Offers mental health/wellness program	Yes
Mental health training available to students	Yes
Employs Chief Wellness Officer	No
Peer-to-peer mental health offerings	No
Counseling center has guidelines or accreditation	Yes
Mental health/well-being courses	No

ACADEMICS

% students returning for sophomore year	76
% students graduating within 4 years	50
% students graduating within 6 years	61
Calendar	Semester
Student/faculty ratio	12:1
Most common class size 10–19.	(42%)
Most common lab/discussion size 10–19.	(60%)

Most Popular Majors

Psychology; Biology/Biological Sciences; Criminology

Applicants Also Look At

Belmont University, College of Charleston, DePaul University, Florida International University, Florida State University, Howard University, Louisiana State University—Baton Rouge, Loyola University Chicago, Morehouse College, Saint Louis University, Southeastern Louisiana University, Tulane University, The University of Alabama—Tuscaloosa, University of Colorado Boulder, University of Florida, University of Louisiana at Lafayette, University of Miami, University of New Orleans, The University of Tampa, Xavier University of Louisiana

STUDENTS SAY "..."

Academics

Loyola University New Orleans goes above and beyond its academics, with students calling out how "the emphasis on social justice and community service really sets us apart...it's about using our knowledge to make a positive impact." That speaks to "the Jesuit values at the foundation of the school," which enrollees say produce "caring, compassionate, serving individuals who will make their communities better." To that end, there are "a lot of resources overall to make sure [you] as a whole person [are] taken care of," and students "feel supported to succeed by this school." Alumni in particular are "genuinely engaged and accessible," and there is "a strong culture of mentorship that encourages students to reach out, ask questions, and seek guidance."

Another place where the school excels is with an "exceptionally small cohort [that] allows for comprehensive, personalized support and an intimate learning environment." The accordingly small class sizes and the "deeply invested" professors ensure that "students are challenged intellectually while being supported academically and personally." Many are said to be "always looking for undergraduate researchers and promoting opportunities to their students," and faculty "really tries to integrate professionalism into the classrooms." Teaching techniques are up to the professor: some "bring guest stars into the lectures to shine a light on what they do," some incorporate "research, field trips, heavy discussion, [and] seminars," and some focus on "community engagement, social justice, and the New Orleans environment." A satisfied student says, "There is no uniform way a class is run at Loyola and that is how it should be."

Campus Life

The campus has "a great location in the city of New Orleans" and "the environment directly outside of the school is...very college student-friendly," with many taking time each week to "[go] to Audubon Park or enjoying the nightlife options." There are many different clubs and organizations for students, including Students for Environmental Action, the esports team, STEM clubs, Greek life, and intramural sports. There are also "a lot of fairs and events at school that are really fun to participate in." Here in the birthplace of jazz, "music is a very common passion," and one can find "so many opportunities...if you're interested in art, music, or dance." The arts "are well-supported" by the university—the Music & Media school is one of its largest—and "it's a very cultural place" overall. Student concerts have "proven to be a very popular place to get some homework done while supporting your peers," but even without a program, people cultivate a caring environment "by showing up for each other, whether it be for events or just personal things." Speaking for many of their peers, one student simply says, "It's impossible to not have fun in New Orleans."

Student Body

There are "lots of cultures within Loyola that mix and help each other grow," and the university "prides itself on celebrating those of all ethnicities, backgrounds, and religions." With a campus populated by individuals that are "curious, socially aware, and deeply engaged with the world around them," Loyola "always feels inclusive and welcoming to students no matter...their background" and various groups are further represented "through the many pop-up events the university has." The campus in general is said to be "a very judgement-free environment where you can really feel comfortable exploring your sense of style and new expressions of yourself." It also acts as a natural parade, and students "feel free to dress alternatively and express themselves through clothes, pronouns, and academic endeavors." One student philosophizes on the Loyola diversity: "To each [their] own—everyone is completely individual and different from another."

Loyola University New Orleans

Financial Aid: 504-865-3231 • E-Mail: admit@loyno.edu • Website: www.loyno.edu

THE PRINCETON REVIEW SAYS

Admissions

The school reports that its standardized testing policy for use in admission for Fall 2026 is Test Optional. The Princeton Review suggests that interested applicants consult with the school for the most up-to-date standardized testing policies. *Very important factors considered include:* rigor of secondary school record, academic GPA. *Important factors considered include:* extracurricular activities, talent/ability. *Other factors considered include:* class rank, standardized test scores, interview, character/personal qualities, alumni/ae relation, geographical residence, volunteer work, work experience, level of applicant's interest. High school diploma is required and GED is accepted. *Academic units required:* 4 English, 2 math, 2 science, 2 social studies. *Academic units recommended:* 4 English, 3 math, 3 science, 1 science lab, 2 language (other than English), 2 social studies, 2 history.

Financial Aid

Students should submit: FAFSA. Priority filing deadline is 2/15. The Princeton Review suggests that all financial aid forms be submitted as soon as possible. *Need-based scholarships/grants offered:* Federal Pell; Federal SEOG; State scholarships/grants; Private scholarships; College/university scholarship or grant aid from institutional funds; United Negro College Fund. *Loan aid offered:* Federal Direct Subsidized Loans; Federal Direct Unsubsidized Loans; Direct PLUS loans. Admitted students will be notified of awards on a rolling basis beginning 3/1. Federal Work-Study Program available. Institutional employment available.

The Inside Word

The admission process at Loyola University New Orleans focuses on understanding who each applicant is, not just how they score. Of course, your GPA and high school transcript will still carry weight, so we suggest taking advanced courses to help your transcript stand out. Loyola values community involvement, so be sure to include any community service participation in your application. Students who want to enroll in the theater or music program must also be prepared to audition.

THE SCHOOL SAYS

From the Admissions Office

"Nationally recognized for diversity and inclusion, Loyola University New Orleans celebrates the rich history of a Jesuit education, including the commitment to social justice and education of the whole person—body, mind, and spirit.

"Loyola is home to three undergraduate colleges, a College of Law, and a College of Nursing and Health, which offers a bachelor's degree. Home to aspiring journalists, filmmakers, musicians, designers, artists, producers and music industry executives, the College of Music and Media fosters cross-collaborative learning and innovative storytelling of all kinds. The College of Business capitalizes on New Orleans' entrepreneurial spirit and burgeoning tech and creativity hubs; its Center for Entrepreneurship provides vital links to the business community. The College of Arts and Sciences is home to the Center for Editing and Publishing, which provides opportunities for students to engage in the creation of books and articles. In 2020, the college created two exciting new programs in neuroscience and cybersecurity, and launched two public health majors and a minor in 2021.

"All first-year students at Loyola receive personalized student success coaching and enjoy a wealth of mentoring, advising and tutoring services in the Pan-American Student Success Center. In the last five years, Loyola New Orleans has twice been named a Top Producer of Fulbright Students and Scholars, as well as a Top Producer of Peace Corps Volunteers and Top Producer of Teach for America Volunteers, demonstrating the school's commitment to academic excellence and service. The Maroon, Loyola's 100-year-old student newspaper routinely wins top awards in the field."

SELECTIVITY

# of total applicants	6,073
% of total applicants accepted	91
% of total acceptees attending	14

First-Year Profile

Testing policy	Test Optional
Range SAT composite	1090–1290
Range SAT EBRW	560–660
Range SAT math	520–620
Range ACT composite	20–26
% submitting SAT scores	6
% submitting ACT scores	40
Average HS GPA	3.5
% submitting high school GPA	99

Important Dates

Early action	
Apply by	11/15
Notified by	12/1
Regular	
Notified by	Rolling, 12/1
Nonfall registration?	Yes

FINANCIAL FACTS

Annual tuition	$51,008
Food and housing	$16,180
Required fees (First-year)	$2,140 ($2,400)
Books and supplies	$1,394
Average need-based scholarship (First-year)	$39,876 ($45,688)
% students with need rec. need-based scholarship or grant aid (First-year)	99 (100)
% students with need rec. non-need-based scholarship or grant aid (First-year)	13 (12)
% students with need rec. need-based self-help aid (First-year)	73 (77)
% students rec. any financial aid (First-year)	91 (100)
% UG borrow to pay for school	65
Average cumulative indebtedness	$28,944
% of students with need fully met (First-year)	15 (15)
Average % of student need met (First-year)	74 (81)

LYCOMING COLLEGE

One College Place, Williamsport, PA 17701-5192 • Admissions: 570-321-4026

Survey Snapshot
Internships are widely available
Great library
Easy to get around campus

RATINGS	
Quality of Life	82
Fire Safety	60*
Green	60*
Academic	83
Profs Interesting	91
Profs Accessible	93
Admissions	85
Financial Aid	91

CAMPUS LIFE

Type of school	Private
Affiliation	Methodist
Environment	Town

Students

Degree-seeking undergrad enrollment	984
% male/female/not reported	49/51/0
% from out of state	40
% First-year from public high school	90
% First-year live on campus	89
% Ugrads live on campus	84
# of fraternities (% join)	3 (2)
# of sororities (% join)	5 (4)
% Asian	1
% Black or African American	12
% Hispanic	13
% Native American	<1
% Pacific Islander	<1
% Race and/or ethnicity unknown	4
% Two or more races	3
% White	64
% International	2
# of countries represented	13

CAMPUS MENTAL HEALTH SERVICES

Offers mental health/wellness program	Yes
Mental health training available to students	No
Employs Chief Wellness Officer	NR
Peer-to-peer mental health offerings	NR
Counseling center has guidelines or accreditation	No
Mental health/well-being courses	NR

ACADEMICS

% students returning for sophomore year	69
% students graduating within 4 years	47
% students graduating within 6 years	58
Calendar	Semester
Student/faculty ratio	10:1
Most common class size 10–19.	(50%)
Most common lab/discussion size 1–9.	(57%)

Most Popular Majors

Biology/Biological Sciences; Psychology; Business Administration and Management

STUDENTS SAY "..."

Academics

Lycoming College encourages students to incorporate real-world experiences into their liberal arts education. It does so by offering many experiential learning opportunities and outside-the-classroom activities, which help students "better understand and apply class material" and "make and build community relationships." For an art history class, this meant that "after learning about Ancient Japanese ceramics, we were able to go to the ceramic studio and make pots and bowls with terra cotta to understand the different tools and difficulty of the craft." Other real-world opportunities mentioned include criminal justice students touring the local corrections facility and visiting the courthouse, aspiring teachers assisting in nearby schools, and archeology students visiting museums. Students also appreciate the "colloquiums that bring guest speakers in, study abroad opportunities, research opportunities, and internships" that enhance their coursework. Of the many things students appreciate about the school, the faculty gets top marks. "They make an effort to get to know students outside the classroom and ensure that students are able to keep up with the material." As one undergrad shares, "The greatest thing about Lycoming is that if you start to slip, like failing your classes, then they help you…so that you don't slip through the cracks. Adds another undergraduate, "The close relationship between the faculty and the students is what makes Lycoming College stand out."

Campus Life

Across Lycoming's small campus, students typically "fill their days with sports, exercise, studying, and hanging out in each other's rooms." There's a lot of variety to be found in those areas, as athletes can make their mark in everything from intramural sports to the competitive NCAA D3 teams and even a popular esports club. The Keiper Recreation Center contains an indoor track, a lounge area, and a sauna, but also doubles as a bustling destination for students who want to stay active and socialize. Other hangs are an "activity center right in town" and "shopping center less than a 10-minute drive away," events through the Campus Activities Board, and the many student-driven groups from Sign Language Club to the Student Senate. "There's always something going on," notes one student, while another adds "The college does a great job of making students feel included and providing things to do."

Student Body

Lycoming students appreciate that "there is so much diversity on campus." While the student body is largely from Pennsylvania, "many different races, cultures, and ethnicities [are] represented." Likewise, there's an "accepting atmosphere" and "strong sense of community," and students note that Lycoming strives "to make all feel included and safe." In general, undergrads are "very tightly knit" because "the small student population makes the campus environment very personable and intimate and allows for very close bonds to be formed." Undergrads find their peers especially supportive: "There's a lot of students that want to be helpful." As one student puts it, "Whenever you need help or have a question about a class or an area on campus, people are willing to help," and work with "one another to accomplish whatever we set our minds to."

LYCOMING COLLEGE

Financial Aid: 570-321-4040 • E-Mail: admissions@lycoming.edu • Website: www.lycoming.edu

THE PRINCETON REVIEW SAYS

Admissions

The school reports that its standardized testing policy for use in admission for Fall 2026 is Test Optional. The Princeton Review suggests that interested applicants consult with the school for the most up-to-date standardized testing policies. *Very important factors considered include:* rigor of secondary school record, recommendation(s). *Important factors considered include:* class rank, academic GPA, standardized test scores, application essay, interview. *Other factors considered include:* extracurricular activities, talent/ability, character/personal qualities, first generation, geographical residence, state residency, volunteer work, work experience, level of applicant's interest. High school diploma is required and GED is accepted. *Academic units required:* 4 English, 3 math, 3 science, 2 language (other than English), 3 social studies, 2 academic electives. *Academic units recommended:* 4 English, 4 math, 3 science, 3 language (other than English), 4 social studies, 3 academic electives.

Financial Aid

Students should submit: FAFSA; State aid form. Priority filing deadline is 5/1. The Princeton Review suggests that all financial aid forms be submitted as soon as possible. *Need-based scholarships/grants offered:* Federal Pell; Federal SEOG; State scholarships/grants; Private scholarships; College/university scholarship or grant aid from institutional funds. *Loan aid offered:* Federal Direct Subsidized Loans; Federal Direct Unsubsidized Loans; Direct PLUS loans. Admitted students will be notified of awards on a rolling basis beginning 10/10. Federal Work-Study Program available. Institutional employment available.

The Inside Word

Admissions officers at Lycoming College take a holistic approach, closely evaluating everything from GPA and course rigor to recommendations and personal essays.

THE SCHOOL SAYS

From the Admissions Office

"Lycoming College takes traditional liberal arts to the next level with cutting-edge programs, experiential learning, and extracurriculars that let students think deeply and act boldly. Students are encouraged to craft customized, cross-disciplinary academic pathways tailored to their unique interests and career goals. Lycoming offers fifty-four majors and sixty-seven minors, with programs that seek to answer 21st-century questions, such as neuroscience, astrophysics, computer science, data science, environmental science, and entrepreneurship.

"As a solely undergraduate institution, Lycoming is able to give students access to advanced equipment, research opportunities, and fieldwork starting freshman year. Professors are both scholars in their field as well as mentors and regularly include students in their personal research projects. Small class sizes foster workshops, hands-on labs, and discussion-based learning. Professors know students by name and have even been known to invite students to their homes for dinner.

"Unique to Lycoming is the Center for Enhanced Academic Experiences, which offers internships, research, fellowships, and study abroad opportunities as well as subject-specific career advising and pre-professional/graduate school guidance. One-hundred percent of students participate in at least one enhanced academic experience before graduation, preparing them to pursue careers of significance and lives of meaning.

"Nestled in the Susquehanna River Valley, Williamsport offers: a vibrant entertainment, shopping, and arts scene and a rich, natural landscape that beckons outdoor adventure. On campus, the already tight-knit community is strengthened through clubs, organizations, and programming—including the Outdoor Leadership & Education program. It is often said that at Lycoming, it's not a matter of if you'll get involved, but how much."

SELECTIVITY

# of total applicants	3,429
% of total applicants accepted	77
% of total acceptees attending	11
# of in-state applicants	967
% of in-state applicants accepted	90
# of out-of-state-applicants	1,869
% of applicants accepted from out of state	84
# of international applicants	593
% of international applicants accepted	36

First-Year Profile

Testing policy	Test Optional
Range SAT composite	1070–1260
Range SAT EBRW	540–630
Range SAT math	510–620
% submitting SAT scores	18
% submitting ACT scores	1
Average HS GPA	3.5
% submitting high school GPA	95
% graduated top 10% of class	24
% graduated top 25% of class	44
% graduated top 50% of class	75
% submitting high school rank	54

Important Dates

Early decision	
Apply by	11/15
Notified by	12/1
Early action	
Apply by	12/1
Notified by	12/15
Regular	
Apply by	Rolling
Notified by	Rolling
Nonfall registration?	Yes

FINANCIAL FACTS

Annual tuition	$52,416
Food and housing	$14,890
Required fees (First-year)	$785 ($1,010)
Books and supplies	$1,200
Average need-based scholarship (First-year)	$43,284 ($46,079)
% students with need rec. need-based scholarship or grant aid (First-year)	100 (100)
% students with need rec. non-need-based scholarship or grant aid (First-year)	20 (22)
% students with need rec. need-based self-help aid (First-year)	67 (66)
% students rec. any financial aid (First-year)	100 (100)
% of students with need fully met (First-year)	31 (32)
Average % of student need met (First-year)	89 (90)

Macalester College

1600 Grand Avenue, St. Paul, MN 55105-1899 • Admissions: 651-696-6357

Survey Snapshot
Easy to get around campus
Students environmentally aware
Students love St. Paul, MN

RATINGS

Quality of Life	**90**
Fire Safety	**99**
Green	**97**
Academic	**89**
Profs Interesting	**96**
Profs Accessible	**95**
Admissions	**93**
Financial Aid	**95**

CAMPUS LIFE

Type of school	Private
Affiliation	Presbyterian
Environment	Metropolis

Students

Degree-seeking undergrad enrollment	2,061
% male/female/not reported	41/54/5
% from out of state	78
% First-year from public high school	60
% First-year live on campus	100
% Ugrads live on campus	59
# of fraternities	0
# of sororities	0
% Asian	8
% Black or African American	6
% Hispanic	11
% Native American	<1
% Pacific Islander	<1
% Race and/or ethnicity unknown	2
% Two or more races	9
% White	49
% International	16
# of countries represented	108

CAMPUS MENTAL HEALTH SERVICES

Offers mental health/wellness program	Yes
Mental health training available to students	Yes
Employs Chief Wellness Officer	No
Peer-to-peer mental health offerings	Yes
Counseling center has guidelines or accreditation	No
Mental health/well-being courses	Yes, non-credit

ACADEMICS

% students returning for sophomore year	92
% students graduating within 4 years	81
% students graduating within 6 years	91
Calendar	Semester
Student/faculty ratio	10:1
Most common class size 10–19.	(56%)
Most common lab/discussion size 10–19.	(43%)

Most Popular Majors

Biology/Biological Sciences; Econometrics and Quantitative Economics; Mathematics

Applicants Also Look At

Brown University, Carleton College, Grinnell College, New York University, Northwestern University, Oberlin College, Occidental College, St. Olaf College, Tufts University, University of California—Berkeley, University of California—Los Angeles, The University of Chicago, University of Michigan—Ann Arbor, University of Minnesota—Twin Cities, University of Wisconsin—Madison, Vassar College, Washington University in St. Louis, Wesleyan University

STUDENTS SAY "..."

Academics

An education at Macalester College emphasizes "scholarship, internationalism, multiculturalism, and service to society," as well as a mix of "rigorous academics with research, civic engagement, and creative work." For many students, "study-abroad programs are considered fundamental at Macalester in the learning process," and nearly 60 percent of undergrads participate in semester-long or short-term travel. Students also appreciate the flexible curriculum, which makes it "possible to combine different areas of interest in a very open way," and the workload itself is said to be "a perfect balance of self-initiated and given from the professor." The primary approach to learning is very discussion-oriented, and "priority is placed on students reading and taking notes on their own time to develop opinions and ideas." Specifically, "collaboration, critical thinking, and communication are the foundational aspects of all classes." Many courses also incorporate out-of-the-box projects, like the semester of computer science where one student's group "simulated a real-life software development project but with the support and feedback of our professor, preceptors, and peers." These unique academic elements are made possible by an "abundance of enthusiastic and understanding professors who are passionate about what they teach." They "are interested in students' process of learning and give feedback to improve their understanding on an individual level" and "go above and beyond to advise them and set them up for success." The Macalester vibe supports an "individualized form of teaching...[that] creates a great learning experience that nurtures creativity" wherever you go.

Campus Life

Generally speaking, Mac students "are pretty driven and involved in activities." There is "lots of studying," which often involves "hanging out around campus, studying in public spaces to be social and see people." Hitting the books is typically followed by attending "an event that is more social/extracurricular based," such as a sporting event, a club meeting, or a music event. Mac "has many work study opportunities available for students," and "most people work on campus or have jobs in the community." The sports clubs "are a lot of fun, forming a very friendly and light-hearted group," and students also enjoy topic-specific clubs like Game Devs at Mac, Birding Club, and Climbing Club. There isn't much of a party culture at Mac; instead, it is "very common for people to talk about having been at a protest, volunteering for charity, or other forms of involvement." The location in the city lets students "leave campus at any time and go explore the surrounding communities." While "winters are definitely cold," the other three seasons make up for it: "People are outside studying on the lawn, playing pickup sports, and spending weekends biking, going to lakes, or just enjoying how beautiful the city and campus are in the spring, summer, and fall."

Student Body

The student body is diverse, "with a well-established international student body." No one shies away from politics—this is a "very liberal campus" with students who "are very socially active." Even those who differ from the majority opinion find themselves among friends, as these are "very open-minded individuals who are very accepting of individuals different from themselves." People's hobbies run the gamut, with everyone having "passions that consume them, whether that be collective change or etymology." As one student puts it: "Every student has a secret superpower, skill, or interest you learn about once getting to know them that is really impressive." Make time for chit-chat, as Mac students "are extremely friendly and are always excited to talk about anything that might be on your mind." One says, "No one is shy to jump in on the learning and most people you come across are excited to have academic conversations." And another sums it up, saying, "My peers at Macalester are intellectually curious, collaborative, and genuinely engaged with the world around them."

MACALESTER COLLEGE

Financial Aid: 651-696-6214 • E-Mail: admissions@macalester.edu • Website: www.macalester.edu

THE PRINCETON REVIEW SAYS

Admissions

The school reports that its standardized testing policy for use in admission for Fall 2026 is Test Optional. The Princeton Review suggests that interested applicants consult with the school for the most up-to-date standardized testing policies. *Very important factors considered include:* rigor of secondary school record, academic GPA. *Important factors considered include:* application essay, recommendation(s), extracurricular activities, character/personal qualities. *Other factors considered include:* class rank, standardized test scores, interview, talent/ability, first generation, alumni/ae relation, geographical residence, state residency, volunteer work, work experience. High school diploma or equivalent is not required. *Academic units recommended:* 4 English, 3 math, 3 science, 3 science labs, 3 language (other than English), 3 social studies.

Financial Aid

Students should submit: FAFSA; CSS PROFILE. Priority filing deadline is 1/22. The Princeton Review suggests that all financial aid forms be submitted as soon as possible. *Need-based scholarships/grants offered:* Federal Pell; Federal SEOG; State scholarships/grants; Private scholarships; College/university scholarship or grant aid from institutional funds. *Loan aid offered:* Federal Direct Subsidized Loans; Federal Direct Unsubsidized Loans; Direct PLUS loans. Admitted students will be notified of awards on or about 3/15 Regular Decision. Federal Work-Study Program available. Institutional employment available.

The Inside Word

Admission is competitive, so standing out matters—whether through strong standardized test scores, a rigorous academic transcript, or impressive extracurriculars.

THE SCHOOL SAYS

From the Admissions Office

"Macalester College is one of few selective liberal arts colleges located in the heart of a major metropolitan area. Students who thrive at Macalester are curious, highly motivated, serious about their academic pursuits, and supportive of each other; choosing collective success over competition. The demanding academic program and commitments to internationalism, multiculturalism, and service to society are amplified by Macalester's location in the Twin Cities of Saint Paul and Minneapolis. Courses and internships partner with organizations including nonprofits, government agencies, and Fortune 500 companies. Small class sizes allow for a rich experience with strong faculty partnerships, individual attention, and meaningful connections with classmates from more than 100 countries and 49 US states. Professors are familiar with their students' names and interests, frequently guiding them toward internship, research, and grant opportunities that align with their goals. Many students consider this mentorship and collaboration a defining aspect of their Macalester journey. Macalester has 19 varsity athletic teams as well as club and intramural sports. More than 60% of students study abroad for 15 weeks or longer, immersing themselves in another culture and widening their global perspective. Macalester provides a financial aid package meeting 100% of demonstrated financial need for every admitted student, and offers a robust merit-based scholarship program. The United Nations flag has flown over campus since 1950, symbolizing Macalester's commitment to world peace and understanding. Macalester is consistently ranked a top producer of Fulbright Scholars. Campus Pride Index gives Macalester its highest rating (five out of five)."

SELECTIVITY

# of total applicants	8,819
% of total applicants accepted	28
% of total acceptees attending	22
# of early decision applicants	479
% of early decision applicants accepted	42
# offered a place on the wait list	765
# admitted from wait list	82

First-Year Profile

Testing policy	Test Optional
Range SAT composite	1350–1480
Range SAT EBRW	680–750
Range SAT math	650–750
Range ACT composite	30–33
% submitting SAT scores	35
% submitting ACT scores	24
% graduated top 10% of class	53
% graduated top 25% of class	89
% graduated top 50% of class	99
% submitting high school rank	26

Important Dates

Early decision	
Apply by	11/1
Notified by	12/7
Other ED apply by	1/1
Other ED notified by	1/25
Early action	
Apply by	11/1
Notified by	12/20
Regular	
Apply by	1/15
Notified by	3/15
Nonfall registration?	No

FINANCIAL FACTS

Annual tuition	$74,394
Food and housing	$17,464
Required fees	$330
Average need-based scholarship (First-year)	$60,079 ($62,134)
% students with need rec. need-based scholarship or grant aid (First-year)	99 (99)
% students with need rec. non-need-based scholarship or grant aid (First-year)	11 (15)
% students with need rec. need-based self-help aid (First-year)	87 (81)
% students rec. any financial aid (First-year)	91 (94)
% UG borrow to pay for school	52
Average cumulative indebtedness	$25,511
% of students with need fully met (First-year)	69 (77)
Average % of student need met (First-year)	100 (100)

MANHATTAN UNIVERSITY

Manhattan College Parkway, Riverdale, NY 10471 • Admissions: 718-862-7200

Survey Snapshot
Great library
Internships are widely available
Students are happy

RATINGS

Quality of Life	**85**
Fire Safety	**90**
Green	**60***
Academic	**79**
Profs Interesting	**85**
Profs Accessible	**90**
Admissions	**82**
Financial Aid	**84**

CAMPUS LIFE

Type of school	Private
Affiliation	Roman Catholic
Environment	Metropolis

Students

Degree-seeking undergrad enrollment	2,371
% male/female/not reported	61/39/0
% from out of state	25
% First-year live on campus	59
% Ugrads live on campus	31
# of fraternities (% join)	2 (NR)
# of sororities (% join)	2 (NR)
% Asian	6
% Black or African American	9
% Hispanic	34
% Native American	<1
% Pacific Islander	<1
% Race and/or ethnicity unknown	3
% Two or more races	4
% White	40
% International	4
# of countries represented	57

CAMPUS MENTAL HEALTH SERVICES

Offers mental health/wellness program	Yes
Mental health training available to students	Yes
Employs Chief Wellness Officer	Yes
Peer-to-peer mental health offerings	No
Counseling center has guidelines or accreditation	NR
Mental health/well-being courses	No

ACADEMICS

% students returning for sophomore year	78
% students graduating within 4 years	54
% students graduating within 6 years	69
Calendar	Semester
Student/faculty ratio	14:1
Most common class size 20–29.	(43%)
Most common lab/discussion size 10–19.	(46%)

Most Popular Majors

Civil Engineering; Mechanical Engineering; Management Science

Applicants Sometimes Prefer

Fordham University, Iona University, Pace University, St. John's University (NY)

STUDENTS SAY "..."

Academics

Manhattan University provides "an unbelievable community" where students are encouraged to "think critically, collaborate, and apply what they learn beyond the classroom." The school's location is another major draw: "Being in New York gives us access to real projects, internships, and connections with professionals." That industry experience often extends into the classroom. "For example, our jazz band director is a professional jazz musician in the city and is an incredible mentor for students," says one student. An engineering student similarly reports that instructors are "approachable and actually want you to succeed—they take time to explain things and push you to think like an engineer." Small "class sizes allow for meaningful interaction, feedback, and mentorship" from professors across majors. Beyond the classroom, Manhattan's alumni network also plays an important role in helping students prepare for their careers. "It is very easy to build alumni relationships. Alumni are generally very willing to meet virtually or in-person for discussions and advice, [and] provide referrals for internship or job opportunities." Together, these academic and professional connections shape the supportive environment students describe. As one student puts it: "My entire academic experience at Manhattan has been wonderful, and I can truly attribute that to the incredible staff and the caring nature of the community as a whole."

Campus Life

Student-run clubs are at the heart of the social scene at MU, and students love that many offer academic or pre-professional elements that complement coursework: "Many of the clubs at our school offer alumni presentations so that students may gain insight about where they could be headed once they graduate." For example, one student cites the investment club as "my true introduction to finance, and it set me up for success in my future classes." Other favorite clubs are based on culture or interests. The treasurer of the Asian Student Association says, "I love my culture..., so getting to interact with others through a club that makes Asian culture the centerpiece is great." In addition, many students report that their "favorite extracurricular activities include club/intramural sports," including volleyball, basketball, flag football, and soccer. Students also highlight the performing arts department. "We put out amazing performances each semester and there is such a lovely community within the performing arts." Off campus, many students make the most of "our location in NYC to engage with the city's culture and nightlife." Overall, students enjoy the balance between "the comfort and community of a college campus, while also being deeply connected to the 'real world' and the rest of NYC."

Student Body

Manhattan University students are "focused on building something for themselves and their families, which creates a strong sense of grit and community." Many "commute, work part-time, and still show up ready to contribute." Students are supportive and often "share notes, explain challenging concepts, and try to make sure everyone understands what's going on. It feels less like competition and more like a group of people all trying to make something out of their lives."

Overall, MU students are "creative, productive, passionate, and dedicated...and bring new ideas to the table," which may stem from the fact that students "come from a variety of cultural, socioeconomic, and academic backgrounds. For example, many students on campus are first-generation (like myself) or international students. Furthermore,...we have students from different states and areas of New York." Once on campus, "everyone is open to becoming friends with whomever they speak to." Another student likewise describes their peers as "hardworking, but also a bit delightful, people who can joke around, keep things light, and still take the work seriously when it matters." In short, "the student body at Manhattan University is AMAZING!"

MANHATTAN UNIVERSITY

Financial Aid: 718-862-7100 • E-Mail: admit@manhattan.edu • Website: www.manhattan.edu

THE PRINCETON REVIEW SAYS

Admissions

The school reports that its standardized testing policy for use in admission for Fall 2026 is Test Optional. The Princeton Review suggests that interested applicants consult with the school for the most up-to-date standardized testing policies. *Very important factors considered include:* rigor of secondary school record, academic GPA. *Important factors considered include:* application essay, recommendation(s). *Other factors considered include:* class rank, standardized test scores, interview, extracurricular activities, talent/ability, character/ personal qualities, alumni/ae relation, volunteer work, work experience, level of applicant's interest. High school diploma is required and GED is accepted. *Academic units required:* 4 English, 3 math, 2 science, 2 science labs, 2 language (other than English), 3 social studies. *Academic units recommended:* 4 English, 4 math, 4 science, 4 science labs, 3 language (other than English), 4 social studies.

Financial Aid

Students should submit: FAFSA. The Princeton Review suggests that all financial aid forms be submitted as soon as possible. *Need-based scholarships/grants offered:* Federal Pell; Federal SEOG; College/university scholarship or grant aid from institutional funds; State scholarships/grants; Private scholarships. *Loan aid offered:* Federal Direct Subsidized Loans; Federal Direct Unsubsidized Loans; Direct PLUS loans. Admitted students will be notified of awards on a rolling basis beginning 12/1. Federal Work-Study Program available. Institutional employment available.

The Inside Word

Manhattan University admission is done on a rolling basis, though priority is given to those who apply before March 1. With around three-quarters of applicants gaining admission, students with solid, rigorous academics should get in.

THE SCHOOL SAYS

From the Admissions Office

"We are a Lasallian Catholic college offering a transformative education that touches your mind and heart. We strive to promote faith, respect, education, community and social action. Manhattan University promises great value by consistently ranking among schools with the best return on investment and highest graduate salaries. In Riverdale, the greatest city in the world is at the doorstep of campus. In a quiet neighborhood in the Bronx, located ten miles from the bustling streets of midtown Manhattan, students enjoy a traditional college campus that's just a short subway ride from the endless opportunities available in NYC. Our professors often use the city as a classroom with field trips to Wall Street, museums and other world-famous locations.

"We have just under 3,500 students and a student-to-faculty ratio of 14:1, so our students enjoy the benefits of a small college with close faculty interaction. With more than forty majors and twenty graduate programs across six distinct schools, Manhattan University has big academic opportunities. Our students take what they learn in the classroom and apply it to the real world through internships, service-learning projects and study abroad.

"Founded on the principles of John Baptist de La Salle, patron saint of teachers, the College strives to promote faith, respect, quality education, community and social justice in all that we do. One example, The Lasallian Outreach Volunteer Experience (L.O.V.E.), provides service and social-justice travel experiences. Some offer immersion experiences: the chance to live in solidarity with the poor, experience an unfamiliar culture and learn about issues of social justice. Others involve more hands-on service work, such as helping rebuild in New Orleans post-Hurricane Katrina."

SELECTIVITY

# of total applicants	14,570
% of total applicants accepted	82
% of total acceptees attending	4
# of in-state applicants	7,023
% of in-state applicants accepted	83
# of out-of-state-applicants	7,088
% of applicants accepted from out of state	81
# of international applicants	451
% of international applicants accepted	90
# of early decision applicants	28
% of early decision applicants accepted	100
# offered a place on the wait list	0
# admitted from wait list	0

First-Year Profile

Testing policy	Test Optional
Range SAT composite	1010–1330
Range SAT EBRW	530–690
Range SAT math	470–670
Range ACT composite	23–28
% submitting SAT scores	9
% submitting ACT scores	2
Average HS GPA	3.6
% submitting high school GPA	100

Important Dates

Early decision	
Apply by	11/15
Notified by	12/1
Regular	
Apply by	8/1
Notified by	Rolling, 12/15
Nonfall registration?	Yes

FINANCIAL FACTS

Annual tuition	$50,000
Food and housing	$19,150
Required fees (First-year)	$2,533 ($5,075)
Books and supplies	$1,200
Average need-based scholarship (First-year)	$32,750 ($35,763)
% students with need rec. need-based scholarship or grant aid (First-year)	93 (99)
% students with need rec. non-need-based scholarship or grant aid (First-year)	17 (17)
% students with need rec. need-based self-help aid (First-year)	60 (58)
% UG borrow to pay for school	65
Average cumulative indebtedness	$21,261
% of students with need fully met (First-year)	17 (17)
Average % of student need met (First-year)	60 (66)

MANHATTANVILLE UNIVERSITY

2900 Purchase Street, Purchase, NY 10577 • Admissions: 914-694-2200

Survey Snapshot
College radio is popular
Students are happy
Theater is popular

RATINGS	
Quality of Life	81
Fire Safety	97
Green	60*
Academic	77
Profs Interesting	85
Profs Accessible	88
Admissions	81
Financial Aid	89

CAMPUS LIFE

Type of school	Private
Environment	Town
Students	
Degree-seeking undergrad enrollment	1,446
% male/female/not reported	37/63/<1
% from out of state	19
% First-year from public high school	78
% First-year live on campus	54
% Ugrads live on campus	45
# of fraternities	0
# of sororities	0
% Asian	3
% Black or African American	11
% Hispanic	39
% Native American	<1
% Pacific Islander	0
% Race and/or ethnicity unknown	1
% Two or more races	3
% White	40
% International	3
# of countries represented	19

CAMPUS MENTAL HEALTH SERVICES

Offers mental health/wellness program	Yes
Mental health training available to students	Yes
Employs Chief Wellness Officer	No
Peer-to-peer mental health offerings	No
Counseling center has guidelines or accreditation	No
Mental health/well-being courses	Yes, for-credit

ACADEMICS

% students returning for sophomore year	79
% students graduating within 4 years	53
Calendar	Semester
Student/faculty ratio	14:1
Most common class size 10–19.	(44%)
Most common lab/discussion size 1–9.	(70%)

Most Popular Majors

Psychology; Registered Nursing/Registered Nurse; Business Administration and Management

Applicants Sometimes Prefer

Iona University, Manhattan University, Marist University, Mercy University, Sacred Heart University, St. John's University (NY)

STUDENTS SAY "..."

Academics

For students who don't like to limit themselves, Manhattanville University provides "endless opportunities to find your passion and get involved." Undergraduates take comfort from the institution's carefully fostered "communal environment" and the "close-knit relationships" this leads to. They also freely capitalize on the university's "diverse course selection," and the way both the academics and school provide "many connections for internships and jobs" while also serving to "help you build your portfolio as a young professional." Students are fairly quick to give credit where it's due, praising professors who often act as "amazing resources" and generally "bring a lot of expertise into their classrooms." In particular, those at Manhattanville appreciate that professors strive to "teach in a way that makes learning interesting and fun." It's no wonder, then, that students actually seem eager to take difficult courses, knowing they'll be backed up by a faculty member who is "very personable and clearly communicates that they are here to help their students and facilitate their success." Based on the feedback we've seen, it's clear that "no matter what the students need, there is always an office, a person, or department ready, willing, and able to help out." Considering all that, it's no wonder that one undergrad describes time spent at Manhattanville as a "challenging but stressless experience."

Campus Life

At Manhattanville, there's tons of fun to be had both in and out of the classroom. To begin with, sports are certainly very popular, and you'll find that the "majority of students attend athletic events to support their fellow Valiants." Many people also participate in intramurals for rugby, volleyball and dodgeball (among others). But don't fret if you're not particularly sporty; there are plenty of other ways to get involved, whether that's participating in the active student government, joining the Finance Society, working on the Manhattanville Video Project, or joining a cultural institution like the Latin American Student Association. One particular highlight is the Sister Mary T. Clark Center for Religion and Social Justice, "where students often will go just to be around the positive energy." Additionally, "a cappella and performance opportunities [abound]" and the university sponsors numerous events such as Fall Fest, a family weekend "with rides, food, and plenty of entertainment" as well as Quad Jam, a music festival with "food trucks, student performances, and a headliner performance such as We The Kings and Lupe Fiasco." Once the weekend rolls around, it's fairly common for undergrads to head off campus-free transportation both to White Plains and New York City doesn't hurt. "There's something for everyone; you just have to be ambitious enough to find exactly what it is you like to do."

Student Body

Manhattanville undergrads seem to pride themselves on the school's "very diverse" community. As one student immediately explains, "I have made friends from all different backgrounds, states, and countries." Just as critically, people here are "willing to embrace different cultures, ethnicities, sexualities and personality types." While a few individuals do note that the "student body is somewhat divided into athletes and non-athletes," others insist that "it's easy to meet people and make friends." By and large, students say their classmates "genuinely care about everyone's well-being" and are "willing to help you when you need." And it's certainly common to encounter a "friendly face" as you walk across campus. The vast majority of students are also "very hardworking" and extremely "passionate about their education and extracurriculars." Indeed, "they know the fields they want to be in and strive to achieve their goals." One individual further elaborates, "I also describe them as warriors who don't give up once they reach a failure; they keep on going no matter the road ahead." As this undergrad concludes, "Everyone I've met is so kind and passionate and talented; it's a great environment to be in."

Manhattanville University

Financial Aid: 914-323-5357 • E-Mail: admissions@mville.edu • Website: www.mville.edu

THE PRINCETON REVIEW SAYS

Admissions

The school reports that its standardized testing policy for use in admission for Fall 2026 is Test Free. The Princeton Review suggests that interested applicants consult with the school for the most up-to-date standardized testing policies. *Very important factors considered include:* rigor of secondary school record, academic GPA, application essay, recommendation(s), extracurricular activities, talent/ability, volunteer work, level of applicant's interest. *Important factors considered include:* geographical residence. *Other factors considered include:* class rank, interview, character/personal qualities, state residency, work experience. High school diploma is required and GED is accepted. *Academic units required:* 4 English, 3 math, 2 science, 2 social studies, 5 academic electives.

Financial Aid

Students should submit: FAFSA; State aid form. Priority filing deadline is 3/1. The Princeton Review suggests that all financial aid forms be submitted as soon as possible. *Need-based scholarships/grants offered:* Federal Pell; Federal SEOG; State scholarships/grants; Private scholarships; College/university scholarship or grant aid from institutional funds; United Negro College Fund. *Loan aid offered:* Federal Direct Subsidized Loans; Federal Direct Unsubsidized Loans; Direct PLUS loans. Admitted students will be notified of awards on a rolling basis beginning 10/1. Federal Work-Study Program available. Institutional employment available.

The Inside Word

Manhattanville takes a straightforward approach when assessing applicants. You can expect your high school transcripts will be carefully considered along with your personal statement and letters of recommendation. While you are not required to sit for an interview, it is strongly recommended. It's also important to note that Manhattanville operates on the basis of rolling admissions. Therefore, the earlier you apply the better your chances.

THE SCHOOL SAYS

From the Admissions Office

"At Manhattanville University, we believe higher education elevates students' knowledge both academically and practically. That's why we offer more than 55 undergraduate areas of study in three academic schools; Arts and Sciences, Education, and Nursing and Health Sciences, wherein all undergraduate students complete a required internship or experiential learning experience prior to completing their undergraduate degree. We call it outcome-based learning. Popular majors at Manhattanville include education, business, sport studies, Nursing, psychology, and fine and performing arts. Our Accelerated Bachelor's-Master's degree options in the sciences, education, and business programs have become a popular choice for students, allowing them to complete both a bachelor's and master's degree in 5 years. 84 percent of our full-time faculty hold the highest degree in their field. There are ample opportunities to participate in community service on campus and outside in the community through the Sister Mary T. Clark Center for Religion and Social Justice, the Center for Inclusion, and the more than 70 student clubs and organizations on campus. There are more than 200 outlets for community service available on and off campus and more than 1,000 Manhattanville University students give their time to service projects. With a wide range of academic programs, diverse student population, and community service found at Manhattanville University, we are committed to fulfilling our mission to educate students to be ethical and socially responsible leaders in a global community."

SELECTIVITY

# of total applicants	5,944
% of total applicants accepted	87
% of total acceptees attending	8

First-Year Profile

Testing policy	Test Free
Average HS GPA	3.3
% submitting high school GPA	100

Important Dates

Early action	
Apply by	12/1
Notified by	1/1
Regular	
Notified by	Rolling, 12/1
Nonfall registration?	Yes

FINANCIAL FACTS

Annual tuition	$45,940
Food and housing	$17,100
Required fees (First-year)	$2,240 ($2,465)
Books and supplies	$1,000
Average need-based scholarship (First-year)	$8,981 ($12,340)
% students with need rec. need-based scholarship or grant aid (First-year)	94 (99)
% students with need rec. non-need-based scholarship or grant aid (First-year)	95 (60)
% students with need rec. need-based self-help aid (First-year)	7 (9)
% students rec. any financial aid (First-year)	97 (100)
% UG borrow to pay for school	64
Average cumulative indebtedness	$51,963
% of students with need fully met (First-year)	41 (39)
Average % of student need met (First-year)	77 (83)

MARIST UNIVERSITY

3399 North Road, Poughkeepsie, NY 12601-1387 • Admissions: 845-575-3226

Survey Snapshot
Students are happy
Great library
Internships are widely available

RATINGS

Quality of Life	83
Fire Safety	64
Green	60*
Academic	82
Profs Interesting	91
Profs Accessible	91
Admissions	89
Financial Aid	88

CAMPUS LIFE

Type of school	Private
Environment	Town

Students

Degree-seeking undergrad enrollment	5,125
% male/female/not reported	41/59/0
% from out of state	46
% First-year from public high school	77
% First-year live on campus	93
% Ugrads live on campus	60
# of fraternities (% join)	3 (NR)
# of sororities (% join)	4 (NR)
% Asian	4
% Black or African American	4
% Hispanic	15
% Native American	<1
% Pacific Islander	0
% Race and/or ethnicity unknown	1
% Two or more races	4
% White	70
% International	2
# of countries represented	59

CAMPUS MENTAL HEALTH SERVICES

Offers mental health/wellness program	Yes
Mental health training available to students	Yes
Employs Chief Wellness Officer	No
Peer-to-peer mental health offerings	Yes
Counseling center has guidelines or accreditation	Yes
Mental health/well-being courses	Yes, non-credit

ACADEMICS

% students returning for sophomore year	89
% students graduating within 4 years	70
% students graduating within 6 years	81
Calendar	Semester
Student/faculty ratio	15:1
Most common class size 20–29.	(47%)
Most common lab/discussion size 10–19.	(68%)

Most Popular Majors
Communication and Media Studies; Psychology; Business Administration and Management

Applicants Often Prefer
Fairfield University, Quinnipiac University, Sacred Heart University, State University of New York—Binghamton University, Syracuse University, University of Connecticut, University of Delaware

Applicants Sometimes Prefer
University of Massachusetts—Amherst, University of Rhode Island

STUDENTS SAY "..."

Academics

At Marist University, faculty "like to make classes interactive yet challenging in a positive aspect." They also value real-life experience and connections in their classrooms. "I have had faculty...[in contact with] a finance firm...within minutes of me mentioning interest in working there," says a student. Professors are "highly qualified," "diverse in the way they teach," and "always willing to help," both in and out of class. "The academics are the best thing about Marist," says another student. Support staff and advisors are also highly praised for being "some of the most supportive people."

The Honors program at Marist is "a huge strength because it unlocks many advantages" by "[exploring] unique perspectives on topics related to all sorts of majors." Honors courses include "a class on the ethical implications of emerging technology [and] an economics course focused on why nations fail." One course even involves "riding a boat up and down the Hudson River" in order to examine the environment of the area.

Campus Life

Marist is near the Hudson River, so students often "fill their days by walking along and laying out...when [the weather] is nice." In the winter, "students may be sledding on snow days or getting together with friends" elsewhere. "A big tradition is jumping into the Hudson River before you graduate," says a student. Indeed, Marist's beauty, which "never fails to amaze" students, offers nearby Rhinebeck and New Paltz for hiking and access to the Walkway Over the Hudson, as well as the chance to just walk around the "rich community."

For study time, there are campus Cafés, and "there are a lot of cute [off-campus Cafés] around Poughkeepsie" too. The library "is a very popular hub for studying, group work, or just [hanging] out." Clubs and intramurals "[give] the campus life after dark." Students also mention that "the student center often holds events like bingo nights, stand-up [comedy nights], and more." Outside of participating either in sports or clubs, many students "intern in NYC several times a week while also maintaining a social life."

Student Body

Students identify the community at Marist as "incredibly friendly," and they point out that students have an unspoken "policy to hold the door open for people," "no matter the weather condition." One student commented: "I've never met so many friendly strangers in New York in my life." Another observes that "nearly everyone...is Catholic, but the majority are not religious."

While many students herald Marist for its diversity, others claim that appears more "on paper" than on campus. The dominant groups on campus appear to be "athletes," "in the fashion department," or those "studying computers/ technology." "I find that students are very hungry for knowledge," says a student. A large portion of the student body also likes to give back: it's common for students to "participate in two hours of weekly community service...[or] help with one-time community-service events."

Marist University

Financial Aid: 845-575-3230 • E-Mail: admission@marist.edu • Website: www.marist.edu

THE PRINCETON REVIEW SAYS

Admissions

The school reports that its standardized testing policy for use in admission for Fall 2026 is Test Optional. The Princeton Review suggests that interested applicants consult with the school for the most up-to-date standardized testing policies. *Very important factors considered include:* rigor of secondary school record, academic GPA. *Important factors considered include:* character/personal qualities. *Other factors considered include:* class rank, standardized test scores, application essay, extracurricular activities, talent/ability, first generation, geographical residence, volunteer work, work experience, level of applicant's interest. High school diploma is required and GED is accepted. *Academic units required:* 4 English, 3 math, 3 science, 2 language (other than English), 3 social studies, 3 history, 1 computer science. *Academic units recommended:* 4 English, 3 math, 3 science, 3 language (other than English), 3 social studies, 3 history, 1 computer science.

Financial Aid

Students should submit: FAFSA; CSS PROFILE. Priority filing deadline is 11/15. The Princeton Review suggests that all financial aid forms be submitted as soon as possible. *Need-based scholarships/grants offered:* Federal Pell; Federal SEOG; State scholarships/grants; Private scholarships; College/university scholarship or grant aid from institutional funds. *Loan aid offered:* Federal Direct Subsidized Loans; Federal Direct Unsubsidized Loans; Direct PLUS loans. Admitted students will be notified of awards on a rolling basis beginning 1/15. Federal Work-Study Program available. Institutional employment available.

The Inside Word

Applicants with strong academic records are well-positioned for admission to Marist. For standardized tests, submitting scores in the average admitted range or higher can strengthen an application. That said, a compelling essay, meaningful extracurriculars, leadership accomplishments, and strong recommendation letters remain important to the overall application.

THE SCHOOL SAYS

From the Admissions Office

"The number of seats available for the first-year class remains at about 1,275, making for a competitive admission process. Our recommendations: keep your grades up, participate in community service, and exercise leadership in the classroom, extracurricular endeavors, and your community. We encourage a campus visit. It's the best way to experience Marist firsthand: our Hudson River setting, top-tier facilities, and close student-faculty relationships. What begins as something you see, quickly becomes something you feel—a community rooted in care, kindness, and connection.

"We'll help you in the transition to college through an innovative first-year program that provides mentors for every student. Here, learning pairs theory with real-world application through leadership development, faculty-mentored research, and countless student-run experiences like managing a café, boutique, or credit union.

"Marist invests in the student experience. New academic buildings (business, social and health sciences, and fashion) and top-ranked residence halls have dramatically improved both academic and social space. Students call the dining hall "Hogwarts on the Hudson."

"Marist's core priorities are student success and advancing the social good—equipping students to solve real challenges and make a global impact. The University is home to the nationally recognized Marist Poll, which employs hundreds of students each year, offering valuable experience in polling, politics, journalism, and data-based research.

"At Marist, you'll get a premium education, develop skills, have fun and make lifelong friends, and gain valuable experience through internship and study abroad programs, including at our branch campus in Florence, Italy, so you can be ahead of the competition for graduate school or a career."

SELECTIVITY

# of total applicants	11,248
% of total applicants accepted	56
% of total acceptees attending	19
# of in-state applicants	5,312
% of in-state applicants accepted	50
# of out-of-state-applicants	5,425
% of applicants accepted from out of state	63
# of international applicants	511
% of international applicants accepted	49
# of early decision applicants	236
% of early decision applicants accepted	73
# offered a place on the wait list	3,798
# admitted from wait list	207

First-Year Profile

Testing policy	Test Optional
Range SAT composite	1200–1330
Range SAT EBRW	600–680
Range SAT math	580–670
Range ACT composite	27–31
% submitting SAT scores	12
% submitting ACT scores	3
Average HS GPA	3.6
% submitting high school GPA	100
% graduated top 10% of class	18
% graduated top 25% of class	5
% graduated top 50% of class	82
% submitting high school rank	100

Important Dates

Early decision	
Apply by	11/15
Notified by	12/15
Other ED apply by	2/15
Other ED notified by	3/15
Early action	
Apply by	11/15
Notified by	1/15
Regular	
Apply by	2/15
Notified by	3/15
Nonfall registration?	Yes

FINANCIAL FACTS

Annual tuition	$50,760
Food and housing	$20,130
Required fees (First-year)	$940 ($1,140)
Books and supplies	$2,425
Average need-based scholarship (First-year)	$27,943 ($28,586)
% students with need rec. need-based scholarship or grant aid (First-year)	98 (99)
% students with need rec. non-need-based scholarship or grant aid (First-year)	21 (30)
% students with need rec. need-based self-help aid (First-year)	71 (66)
% students rec. any financial aid (First-year)	94 (98)
% UG borrow to pay for school	63
Average cumulative indebtedness	$41,395
% of students with need fully met (First-year)	26 (35)
Average % of student need met (First-year)	76 (80)

Marquette University

1250 W. Wisconsin Ave., Milwaukee, WI 53233 • Admissions: 414-288-7302

Survey Snapshot
Recreation facilities are great
Easy to get around campus
Students involved in community service

RATINGS

Quality of Life	**87**
Fire Safety	**99**
Green	**60***
Academic	**81**
Profs Interesting	**88**
Profs Accessible	**93**
Admissions	**87**
Financial Aid	**91**

CAMPUS LIFE

Type of school	Private
Affiliation	Roman Catholic-Jesuit
Environment	Metropolis

Students

Degree-seeking undergrad enrollment	7,903
% male/female/not reported	44/56/0
% from out of state	64
% First-year from public high school	63
% First-year live on campus	89
% Ugrads live on campus	57
# of fraternities (% join)	10 (NR)
# of sororities (% join)	14 (NR)
% Asian	6
% Black or African American	5
% Hispanic	16
% Native American	<1
% Pacific Islander	<1
% Race and/or ethnicity unknown	1
% Two or more races	4
% White	66
% International	1
# of countries represented	53

CAMPUS MENTAL HEALTH SERVICES

Offers mental health/wellness program	Yes
Mental health training available to students	Yes
Employs Chief Wellness Officer	Yes
Peer-to-peer mental health offerings	Yes
Counseling center has guidelines or accreditation	Yes
Mental health/well-being courses	Yes, for-credit

ACADEMICS

% students returning for sophomore year	93
% students graduating within 4 years	68
% students graduating within 6 years	79
Calendar	Semester
Student/faculty ratio	14:1
Most common class size 20–29.	(30%)
Most common lab/discussion size 10–19.	(41%)

Most Popular Majors

Biomedical Sciences; Registered Nursing/Registered Nurse; Finance

Applicants Also Look At

DePaul University, Indiana University—Bloomington, Loyola University Chicago, Purdue University—West Lafayette, Saint Louis University, University of Illinois at Chicago, University of Illinois at Urbana—Champaign, University of Iowa, University of Minnesota—Twin Cities, University of Wisconsin—Madison, University of Wisconsin—Milwaukee

STUDENTS SAY "..."

Academics

Marquette University is all about education in and out of the classroom. That means there's a lot of "learning through service and community engagement," and there's good use of the central Milwaukee location as an extended classroom. Students might visit the Haggerty Museum of Art for inspiration on their essays, and lessons meant to ensure "social justice [is] strongly integrated into the curriculum" might take place at the Milwaukee County Courthouse. Students in specialized programs also get out in the community. Education students can "volunteer in a school once a week…to meet and interact with Milwaukee community members, while also seeing the things I was learning in class in the students I was working with." One nursing student adds: "Clinical opportunities, interprofessional days for collaboration between different health professionals, mentorship opportunities, and connections to Milwaukee make the Marquette experience." On campus, academic work is likewise impactful. Computer science students appreciate that "at an undergraduate level, we are taught how to customize, utilize, and implement AI systems into business, particularly accounting and finance," and engineering students look forward to the Marmon Holdings Innovation Challenge, where they are given ten hours to solve a real-world problem. Overall, "professors are very knowledgeable in what they teach, most have had careers in it, and they provide real-world examples to help engage students." Marquette further connects students with industry professionals outside of the faculty via one-credit seminars and the Marquette Mentors Program, which partners students with "accomplished alumni and friends of the university for one-on-one guidance, career exploration and growth." In prioritizing service and community involvement throughout its coursework, Marquette is "very much oriented towards how we can apply what we are learning in a real-life situation."

Campus Life

Students love the "city-life feel" they get at Marquette: "I often go downtown by the waterfront and run, go to the coffee shops, and attend the many festivals that happen downtown." One student found the Coffee Club was a great introduction to Milwaukee life: "Every month, a group of about 15…get on the bus and try a new cafe. As an avid coffee drinker, this was right up my alley and allowed me to explore the Milwaukee area and meet new people as a freshman coming in from out of state." In addition to exploring Milwaukee, many students cite sports as a favorite extracurricular activity, and sharing a basketball stadium with the professional Milwaukee Bucks brings "big school spirit" when it comes to Marquette basketball games. "Thousands of students, alumni, and community members come together to celebrate and cheer on our basketball team. It is a surreal feeling to have so many people together for the same reason on a regular basis." Whether it's finding the perfect farmer's market or study spot, watching a basketball game, or enjoying the lake on a warm day, "Milwaukee has so much to offer the students of Marquette."

Student Body

Marquette students feel that "you will never have a hard time finding someone who is friendly." Another student agrees, describing their peers as "friendly, optimistic, typical Midwestern nice. Everyone looks out for each other and treats classmates like family." For many, "the tight-knit community feels special…For 8,000 students, it feels much smaller when it comes to campus community, but much bigger when it comes to large campus events, as everyone shows up." Marquette students also appreciate the balance between honoring "the Jesuit values of the university" while also maintaining a welcoming atmosphere that "creates spaces for all religions." One student describes their peers as "inclusive and welcoming…Everyone is always so willing to learn about new cultures and activities around campus, which makes it joyous to be here." In short, Marquette "students hope to make a difference in the world and are excited to do so together."

MARQUETTE UNIVERSITY

Financial Aid: 414-288-4000 • E-Mail: admissions@marquette.edu • Website: www.marquette.edu

THE PRINCETON REVIEW SAYS

Admissions

The school reports that its standardized testing policy for use in admission for Fall 2026 is Test Optional. The Princeton Review suggests that interested applicants consult with the school for the most up-to-date standardized testing policies. *Very important factors considered include:* rigor of secondary school record, academic GPA. *Important factors considered include:* standardized test scores, application essay, extracurricular activities, volunteer work. *Other factors considered include:* class rank, recommendation(s), interview, talent/ability, character/personal qualities, first generation, work experience. High school diploma is required and GED is accepted. *Academic units required:* 4 English, 3 math, 2 science, 2 social studies. *Academic units recommended:* 4 English, 4 math, 3 science, 2 science labs, 2 language (other than English), 3 social studies, 2 history.

Financial Aid

Students should submit: FAFSA. The Princeton Review suggests that all financial aid forms be submitted as soon as possible. *Need-based scholarships/grants offered:* Federal Pell; Federal SEOG; State scholarships/grants; Private scholarships; College/university scholarship or grant aid from institutional funds; Federal Nursing Scholarships. *Loan aid offered:* Federal Direct Subsidized Loans; Federal Direct Unsubsidized Loans; Direct PLUS loans; State Loans; College/university loans from institutional funds. Admitted students will be notified of awards on a rolling basis beginning 2/7. Federal Work-Study Program available. Institutional employment available.

The Inside Word

Marquette's admissions officers do not take their job lightly. Each application is read by an admissions counselor, and most files are read by a second counselor before any decisions are made. When evaluating a candidate, officers first look to assess the high school transcript. They make a note of grade trends and pay close attention to how challenging an applicant's course load was. Students not submitting a test score will not be penalized for making this choice. However, if a student chooses to submit an ACT or SAT score, the counselor will consider it as part of the review. Next, they take into account an applicant's personal statement along with their extracurricular activities. Finally, the school weighs the evaluation submitted by the guidance counselor.

THE SCHOOL SAYS

From the Admissions Office

"Marquette University is a Catholic, Jesuit university located near the heart of downtown Milwaukee, Wisconsin. Our student population consists of nearly 8,000 undergraduate students and 3,500 graduate and professional students seeking degrees across seven academic colleges, a law school, and dental school. Marquette consistently ranks near the top in the country in job placement, undergraduate teaching, innovation, commitment to service, and school spirit. Additionally, Marquette students are incredibly active, participating in over 275 student clubs and organizations, undergraduate research, internships and co-ops, community service, study abroad experiences and much more.

"Students come here to cultivate the knowledge, skills and sense of community they need to build meaningful careers, lead purposeful lives and reshape the world around them. At Marquette, you'll be surrounded by a supportive, diverse community. You'll thrive in our faith-based, respectful, and caring environment. Ultimately, you'll have an experience that will transform you into the truest version of yourself, ready to go out into the world and Be The Difference."

SELECTIVITY

# of total applicants	20,002
% of total applicants accepted	78
% of total acceptees attending	12
# of in-state applicants	4,282
% of in-state applicants accepted	77
# of out-of-state-applicants	14,157
% of applicants accepted from out of state	80
# of international applicants	1,563
% of international applicants accepted	65
# offered a place on the wait list	1,397
# admitted from wait list	183

First-Year Profile

Testing policy	Test Optional
Range SAT composite	1230–1360
Range SAT EBRW	610–700
Range SAT math	600–680
Range ACT composite	26–30
% submitting SAT scores	15
% submitting ACT scores	26
Average HS GPA	3.6
% submitting high school GPA	100
% graduated top 10% of class	28
% graduated top 25% of class	64
% graduated top 50% of class	95
% submitting high school rank	24

Important Dates

Early action	
Apply by	11/15
Notified by	12/20
Regular	
Apply by	8/10
Notified by	Rolling, 12/20
Nonfall registration?	Yes

FINANCIAL FACTS

Annual tuition	$53,890
Food and housing	$17,480
Required fees	$1,200
Books and supplies	$720
Average need-based scholarship (First-year)	$34,999 ($37,500)
% students with need rec. need-based scholarship or grant aid (First-year)	98 (99)
% students with need rec. non-need-based scholarship or grant aid (First-year)	23 (24)
% students with need rec. need-based self-help aid (First-year)	65 (64)
% students rec. any financial aid (First-year)	99 (100)
% UG borrow to pay for school	60
Average cumulative indebtedness	$34,571
% of students with need fully met (First-year)	38 (37)
Average % of student need met (First-year)	85 (86)

MASSACHUSETTS INSTITUTE OF TECHNOLOGY

77 Massachusetts Avenue, Cambridge, MA 02139 • Admissions: 617-253-3400

Survey Snapshot
Students always studying
Classroom facilities are great
Lab facilities are great

RATINGS

Quality of Life	83
Fire Safety	85
Green	60*
Academic	94
Profs Interesting	88
Profs Accessible	93
Admissions	99
Financial Aid	98

CAMPUS LIFE

Type of school	Private
Environment	City

Students

Degree-seeking undergrad enrollment	4,561
% male/female/not reported	52/48/0
% from out of state	90
% First-year from public high school	68
% First-year live on campus	100
% Ugrads live on campus	93
# of fraternities (% join)	42 (48)
# of sororities (% join)	26 (33)
% Asian	36
% Black or African American	7
% Hispanic	14
% Native American	<1
% Pacific Islander	<1
% Race and/or ethnicity unknown	4
% Two or more races	7
% White	22
% International	12
# of countries represented	109

CAMPUS MENTAL HEALTH SERVICES

Offers mental health/wellness program	Yes
Mental health training available to students	Yes
Employs Chief Wellness Officer	Yes
Peer-to-peer mental health offerings	Yes
Counseling center has guidelines or accreditation	Yes
Mental health/well-being courses	Yes, for-credit

ACADEMICS

% students returning for sophomore year	99
% students graduating within 4 years	86
% students graduating within 6 years	96
Calendar	4-1-4
Student/faculty ratio	3:1
Most common class size 1–9.	(44%)
Most common lab/discussion size 10–19.	(38%)

Most Popular Majors
Computer Science; Mechanical Engineering; Artificial Intelligence

Applicants Sometimes Prefer
Harvard College, Princeton University, Stanford University, Yale University

Applicants Rarely Prefer
California Institute of Technology, Columbia University, Cornell University, Duke University, University of Pennsylvania

STUDENTS SAY "..."

Academics

The Massachusetts Institute of Technology is renowned for its engineering, science, and Mathematics departments. Academic programs at MIT feature 65 unique research centers, and faculty and students currently collaborate with around 700 companies on projects ranging from computational science to gender studies. "The administration's attitude toward students is one of respect. As soon as you come on campus, you are bombarded with choices," including "research opportunities for undergrads with some of the nation's leading professors." MIT's "amazing collection of creative minds" encourages students to problem-solve and think critically. A chemical engineering major elaborates: "MIT is different from many schools in that its goal is not to teach you specific facts in each subject. MIT teaches you how to think, not about opinions but about problem-solving. Facts and memorization are useless unless you know how to approach a tough problem." As expected, MIT has "excellent teachers who make lectures fun and exciting." One student says that professors "make a serious effort to make the material they teach interesting by throwing in jokes and cool demonstrations." While the academic challenges students face "definitely push [you] beyond your comfort level," students laud MIT as "the ultimate place for information overload, endless possibilities, and expanding your horizons."

Campus Life

MIT students have "access to an amazing number of resources, both academic and recreational." Students also report that "there's always time for extracurricular activities or just relaxing. And students occasionally find time to "pull a hack," or an elaborate practical joke—presumably to counteract academic stress. One such hack featured "the life-size Wright brothers' plane that appeared on top of the Great Dome for the one-hundredth anniversary of flight." Undergrads say that "MIT has great parties—a lot of Wellesley, Harvard, and BU students come to them" but also that "there are tons of things to do other than party" here. That includes "enjoying the largest collection of science fiction novels in the United States at the MIT Science Fiction Library" as well as "movies, shopping, museums, and plays...[and] great restaurants only [blocks] away from campus, too." On campus and off, the MIT experience builds a strong sense of unity. Ask any "MIT alumni where they went to college, most will immediately stick out their hand and show you their 'brass rat' (the MIT ring)."

Student Body

"Contrary to MIT's stereotype, most MIT students are not geeks who study all the time and have no social skills," explains one student. "The majority of the students here are actually quite 'normal.'" Many fellow students agree: "Most students do have some form of 'nerdiness'" (like telling nerdy jokes, being an avid fan of Star Wars, etc.)," but the "stereotypical student [who] looks techy...only represents about 25 percent of the school." Others concur, saying that "there actually isn't one typical student at MIT." As one student elaborates, MIT has all types: "multiple-sport standouts, political activists, fraternity and sorority members, hippies, clean-cut business types, LARPers, hackers, musicians, and artisans." Adding that "not everyone relates to everyone else, but most people get along, and it's almost a guarantee that you'll fit in somewhere." As one undergrad sums up, "The one thing students all have in common is that they are insanely smart and love to learn. Pretty much anyone can find the perfect group of friends to hang out with at MIT."

MASSACHUSETTS INSTITUTE OF TECHNOLOGY

Financial Aid: 617-258-8600 • E-Mail: admissions@mit.edu • Website: web.mit.edu

THE PRINCETON REVIEW SAYS

Admissions

The school reports that its standardized testing policy for use in admission for Fall 2026 will require applicants to submit either the SAT or ACT. The Princeton Review suggests that interested applicants consult with the school for the most up-to-date standardized testing policies. *Very important factors considered include:* character/personal qualities. *Important factors considered include:* rigor of secondary school record, academic GPA, standardized test scores, application essay, recommendation(s), interview, extracurricular activities, talent/ability. *Other factors considered include:* class rank, first generation, geographical residence, volunteer work, work experience. High school diploma or equivalent is not required. *Academic units recommended:* 4 English, 4 math, 4 science, 2 language (other than English), 2 social studies.

Financial Aid

Students should submit: FAFSA; CSS PROFILE. Priority filing deadline is 2/15. The Princeton Review suggests that all financial aid forms be submitted as soon as possible. *Need-based scholarships/grants offered:* Federal Pell; Federal SEOG; State scholarships/grants; Private scholarships; College/university scholarship or grant aid from institutional funds; United Negro College Fund. *Loan aid offered:* Federal Direct Subsidized Loans; Federal Direct Unsubsidized Loans; Direct PLUS loans. Admitted students will be notified of awards on a rolling basis beginning 3/17. Federal Work-Study Program available. Institutional employment available.

The Inside Word

MIT has one of the nation's most competitive admissions processes. The school's applicant pool is so rich it turns away numerous qualified candidates each year. Put your best foot forward and take consolation in the fact that rejection doesn't necessarily mean that you don't belong at MIT, but only that there wasn't enough room for you the year you applied. Your best chance to get an edge: find ways to stress your creativity.

THE SCHOOL SAYS

From the Admissions Office

"The students who come to the Massachusetts Institute of Technology are some of America's—and the world's—best and most creative. As graduates, they leave here to make real contributions—in science, technology, business, education, politics, architecture, and the arts. From any class, many will go on to do work that is historically significant. These young men and women are leaders, achievers, and producers. Helping such students make the most of their talents and dreams would challenge any educational institution. MIT gives them its best advantages: a world-class faculty, unparalleled facilities, and remarkable opportunities. In turn, these students help to make the institute the vital place it is. They bring fresh viewpoints to faculty research: More than three-quarters participate in the Undergraduate Research Opportunities Program, developing solutions for the world's problems in areas such as energy, the environment, cancer, and poverty. They play on MIT's thirty-three intercollegiate teams as well as in its fifty-plus music, theater, and dance groups. To their classes and to their out-of-class activities, they bring enthusiasm, energy, and individual style."

SELECTIVITY

# of total applicants	29,281
% of total applicants accepted	5
% of total acceptees attending	86
# offered a place on the wait list	561
# admitted from wait list	10

First-Year Profile

Testing policy	SAT or ACT Required
Range SAT composite	1520–1570
Range SAT EBRW	740–780
Range SAT math	780–800
Range ACT composite	34–35
% submitting SAT scores	83
% submitting ACT scores	31
% graduated top 10% of class	97
% graduated top 25% of class	100
% graduated top 50% of class	100
% submitting high school rank	31

Important Dates

Early action	
Apply by	11/1
Notified by	12/20
Regular	
Apply by	1/1
Notified by	3/20
Nonfall registration?	No

FINANCIAL FACTS

Annual tuition	$64,310
Food and housing	$21,264
Required fees	$420
Books and supplies	$910
Average need-based scholarship (First-year)	$71,120 ($73,398)
% students with need rec. need-based scholarship or grant aid (First-year)	99 (99)
% students with need rec. non-need-based scholarship or grant aid (First-year)	2 (2)
% students with need rec. need-based self-help aid (First-year)	61 (51)
% students rec. any financial aid (First-year)	69 (79)
% UG borrow to pay for school	13
Average cumulative indebtedness	$41,297
% of students with need fully met (First-year)	100 (100)
Average % of student need met (First-year)	100 (100)

McDaniel College

2 College Hill, Westminster, MD 21157 • Admissions: 410-857-2230

Survey Snapshot
Great off-campus food
Internships are widely available
Frats and sororities are popular

RATINGS

Quality of Life	**84**
Fire Safety	**61**
Green	**60***
Academic	**78**
Profs Interesting	**86**
Profs Accessible	**88**
Admissions	**77**
Financial Aid	**89**

CAMPUS LIFE

Type of school	Private
Environment	Town

Students

Degree-seeking undergrad enrollment	1,619
% male/female/not reported	44/56/0
% from out of state	25
% First-year live on campus	95
% Ugrads live on campus	80
# of fraternities (% join)	5 (15)
# of sororities (% join)	6 (37)
% Asian	2
% Black or African American	22
% Hispanic	11
% Native American	<1
% Pacific Islander	<1
% Race and/or ethnicity unknown	2
% Two or more races	8
% White	53
% International	1
# of countries represented	30

CAMPUS MENTAL HEALTH SERVICES

Offers mental health/wellness program	Yes
Mental health training available to students	No
Employs Chief Wellness Officer	NR
Peer-to-peer mental health offerings	Yes
Counseling center has guidelines or accreditation	No
Mental health/well-being courses	Yes

ACADEMICS

% students returning for sophomore year	81
% students graduating within 4 years	47
% students graduating within 6 years	56
Calendar	4-1-4
Student/faculty ratio	13:1
Most common class size 10–19.	(45%)

Most Popular Majors
Health and Physical Education/Fitness; Psychology; Business Administration and Management

STUDENTS SAY "..."

Academics

Maryland's McDaniel College is a small, private college that takes pride in making its standards for academic excellence achievable to all via an administration and staff that "go above and beyond to accommodate the needs of all the students." Everyone is guaranteed at least two experiential learning opportunities during their time at the college, and students are encouraged to assemble their own platter of courses (from the 650 offered annually) in order to design a fully customizable degree. Additionally, the faculty "will work alongside the students to plan out a custom major or minor that fits their education layout the best." This is exemplified by a January Term course called My Design, where first-year students identify their strengths, interests, and goals. Students also point to the availability of "great academic support," with a Student Outreach Network designed to help at-risk students by connecting them early with the various centers for writing or STEM. That support extends, students note, to students with accessibility needs, and degree offerings include "a powerful and well led ASL program." On a class-by-class basis, professors "know their subjects and they are willing to help with anything you might struggle with." To keep students interested, they ensure that the curriculum "[includes] a diverse array of different teaching methods, such as discussions, lectures, and in-class activities," or "having a backwards-taught class where you learn the material before class then do practice problems in the class." It seems clear to students that McDaniel College is dedicated to student success.

Campus Life

Students find McDaniel College's campus to be so beautiful that they'll find any reason to be outside, whether it's setting up hammocks, socializing, studying, or simply "walking around campus, [which] is very enjoyable because of how nice it is." Many "that go to McDaniel are athletes, and...if you aren't on a sports team you are most likely in some type of club that takes up your time"; there is also "the option where if you don't see a club you can always start it." The school offers a full lineup of programming through its various offices and organizations, "including weekend blitzes once per month where people go out to a sports game or a theme park or an endless amount of places," and after classes are done, "many people participate in small events on campus," which are sponsored by the CEO (Center for Experience & Opportunity), Office of Student Engagement, and student-led clubs.

Student Body

McDaniel "is a small, tight-knit community, where peers become close both in and out of the classroom" and most everyone seems "to have a clear goal of what they want to do here and how." Agrees one student, "They are very supportive and understanding." Students are also bonded by the fact that around 80 percent of students live on campus, and "are involved not just with the college community but with the broader community." This is all the more impressive given that there are "a multitude of students with their own identities," with one student pointing to "the cinema program and interesting clubs like a witchcraft club, photography, our own chapter of the American Marketing Association, and a lot more." Students are simultaneously "very diverse in personality and very inclusive," and one proudly says that "We are not all interested in the same subjects but [we] support each other in our individual pursuits."

McDaniel College

Financial Aid: 410-857-2233 • E-Mail: admissions@mcdaniel.edu • Website: www.mcdaniel.edu

THE PRINCETON REVIEW SAYS

Admissions

The school reports that its standardized testing policy for use in admission for Fall 2026 is Test Optional. The Princeton Review suggests that interested applicants consult with the school for the most up-to-date standardized testing policies. *Very important factors considered include:* rigor of secondary school record, academic GPA. *Important factors considered include:* application essay, recommendation(s). *Other factors considered include:* class rank, interview, extracurricular activities, talent/ability, character/personal qualities, first generation, alumni/ae relation, volunteer work, work experience. High school diploma is required and GED is accepted. *Academic units required:* 4 English, 3 math, 3 science, 3 science labs, 3 language (other than English), 3 social studies. *Academic units recommended:* 4 English, 4 math, 4 science, 4 language (other than English), 3 social studies.

Financial Aid

Students should submit: FAFSA. Priority filing deadline is 3/1. The Princeton Review suggests that all financial aid forms be submitted as soon as possible. *Need-based scholarships/grants offered:* Federal Pell; Federal SEOG; State scholarships/grants; Private scholarships; College/university scholarship or grant aid from institutional funds. *Loan aid offered:* Federal Direct Subsidized Loans; Federal Direct Unsubsidized Loans; Direct PLUS loans. Admitted students will be notified of awards on a rolling basis beginning 1/2. Federal Work-Study Program available. Institutional employment available.

The Inside Word

This small liberal arts college is seeking students who challenge themselves academically and personally. McDaniel College values individuality, so we suggest you use your student essay as an opportunity to shine a spotlight on your interests that set you apart from the other applicants. McDaniel is looking for creative individuals who will thrive at a university that allows you to customize your degree while preparing you for life beyond the classroom.

THE SCHOOL SAYS

From the Admissions Office

"McDaniel College is a nationally recognized four-year, independent college of the liberal arts and sciences. Founded in 1867 as one of the first coeducational colleges in the nation, McDaniel is a diverse, student-centered community of 1,600 undergraduates and 1,400 graduate students. One of the original "Colleges That Change Lives," McDaniel is committed to access and affordability with over 90% of students receiving some type of financial assistance. McDaniel offers over 100 undergraduate and graduate programs with academics centered on the McDaniel Plan, a customized, interdisciplinary curriculum that emphasizes experiential learning and student-faculty collaboration to develop the unique potential in every student. The signature McDaniel Commitment also guarantees every student is prepared for personal and professional success. Students enroll in first-year seminars, complete senior capstone projects, and have the opportunity to participate in faculty-led study trips during McDaniel's three-week January Term. Special opportunities abound through McDaniel's Center for Experience and Opportunity, Program in Innovation & Entrepreneurship, Lumen Scholars Program, Green Terror Army ROTC Battalion, National Security Fellows, and Global Fellows. Student Accessibility and Support Services (SASS) is available to assist all students with documented disabilities and works with each student on a case-by-case basis. Represented by the Green Terror, over 20 athletic teams compete in the NCAA Division III Centennial Conference. Additionally, students are involved in almost 100 student organizations, including intramural sports, fraternities, and sororities. McDaniel offers access to Baltimore and Washington, D.C., plus a European campus in Budapest, Hungary."

SELECTIVITY

# of total applicants	4,765
% of total applicants accepted	78
% of total acceptees attending	9
# of in-state applicants	3,354
% of in-state applicants accepted	77
# of out-of-state-applicants	1,351
% of applicants accepted from out of state	83
# of international applicants	60
% of international applicants accepted	12
# of early decision applicants	51
% of early decision applicants accepted	98

First-Year Profile

Testing policy	Test Optional
% submitting SAT scores	9
% submitting ACT scores	5
Average HS GPA	3.8
% submitting high school GPA	100
% graduated top 10% of class	14
% graduated top 25% of class	49
% graduated top 50% of class	81
% submitting high school rank	40

Important Dates

Early decision	
Apply by	11/1
Notified by	12/1
Early action	
Apply by	12/15
Notified by	1/15
Regular	
Apply by	2/1
Notified by	Rolling, 3/1
Nonfall registration?	Yes

FINANCIAL FACTS

Annual tuition	$54,745
Food and housing	$14,723
Required fees	$975
Books and supplies	$1,612
Average need-based scholarship (First-year)	$41,106 ($43,609)
% students with need rec. need-based scholarship or grant aid (First-year)	99 (100)
% students with need rec. non-need-based scholarship or grant aid (First-year)	22 (21)
% students with need rec. need-based self-help aid (First-year)	77 (78)
% UG borrow to pay for school	71
Average cumulative indebtedness	$29,323
% of students with need fully met (First-year)	25 (23)
Average % of student need met (First-year)	86 (88)

MERCER UNIVERSITY

1501 Mercer University Drive, Macon, GA 31207-0001 • Admissions: 478-301-2650

Survey Snapshot
Intramural sports are popular
Everyone loves the Bears
Students involved in community service

RATINGS

Quality of Life	83
Fire Safety	88
Green	60*
Academic	81
Profs Interesting	88
Profs Accessible	91
Admissions	88
Financial Aid	87

CAMPUS LIFE

Type of school	Private
Environment	City

Students

Degree-seeking undergrad enrollment	4,514
% male/female/not reported	36/64/0
% from out of state	11
% First-year from public high school	78
% First-year live on campus	86
% Ugrads live on campus	42
# of fraternities (% join)	9 (18)
# of sororities (% join)	8 (14)
% Asian	9
% Black or African American	33
% Hispanic	9
% Native American	<1
% Pacific Islander	<1
% Race and/or ethnicity unknown	3
% Two or more races	4
% White	38
% International	3
# of countries represented	36

CAMPUS MENTAL HEALTH SERVICES

Offers mental health/wellness program	Yes
Mental health training available to students	Yes
Employs Chief Wellness Officer	Yes
Peer-to-peer mental health offerings	Yes
Counseling center has guidelines or accreditation	Yes
Mental health/well-being courses	Yes, for-credit

ACADEMICS

% students returning for sophomore year	82
% students graduating within 4 years	59
% students graduating within 6 years	72
Calendar	Semester
Student/faculty ratio	10:1
Most common class size 10–19.	(39%)
Most common lab/discussion size 2–9.	(61%)

Most Popular Majors

Engineering; Biological And Biomedical Sciences; Business, Management, Marketing, And Related Support Services

Applicants Also Look At

Auburn University, Clemson University, Emory University, Furman University, Georgia Institute of Technology, Samford University, University of Georgia

STUDENTS SAY "..."

Academics

Many students cite the quality of Mercer University's education as a high point, applauding a curriculum that provides "a lot of versatile exposure to different subjects." This can be seen especially in study abroad options that are available to every major and which range from semester and year-long programs to shorter, faculty-led trips or service-learning experiences. Even at home, there are "plenty of ways to gain leadership and research experience"—Mercer is known for its research opportunities. As one student explains, "Research and liberal arts go hand in hand here." Another student describes the school as "well-rounded in its academic offerings and quality" and emphasizes that "students of all intended majors should feel welcomed." It's an academically rigorous environment and professors "expect you to put in the work." As one student explains, "There is no such thing as an 'easy A.' However, [the professors] are there to help if you ask" and "There's help for anyone for anything." The school's "small class size allows you to connect with faculty"—you "feel like a person rather than just a number at Mercer." As one student describes, "Professors are willing to put in the extra effort to help students with their needs and/or direct them to those that can best help them." In short, Mercer "challenges you to learn and do better, and has a great amount of opportunities to enrich your learning."

Campus Life

Mercer has a beautiful campus and students enjoy "reading on the benches [and] doing work outside in good weather." On the weekends, many students enjoy tailgating and attending sporting events and can also head into nearby Macon. Many students spend time at the gym and join the group fitness classes, which range from spin to yoga. The school also collaborates with the local climbing gym, allowing students to rock climb for free, and many students participate in the "massive intramural sports program." One favorite Mercer tradition is BearStock, a music festival that takes place during the spring semester. While Greek life is popular, there is also a "ginormous selection of clubs" and students can easily get involved in something that interests them, whether it's astronomy, D&D, volunteer work, theater, or ballroom dance. It's a studious environment, so much so that the "open and accessible" library keeps some floors open 24 hours a day and sometimes provides "little goodies to give us motivation to get through the week." All these offerings lead students to conclude "the community is truly unmatched if you reach out and get involved."

Student Body

"Even though this is a small school in Georgia, there are people from all over who attend Mercer." What unites them is that they're "full of school spirit" and "highly engaged on campus and in our community." It's "easy to find a group that you fit in with," and "everyone always finds their niche and their people," the result of which is that "there is always going to be someone there when you need support." Overall, people are "very friendly and outgoing" and "easy to talk to and work with." Students are "very smart and dedicated" and there is "lots of studying and importance put on academics," though they're also described as "deeply committed to extracurriculars," whether it's clubs, intramurals, or student government. From participating in research to leading an organization, Mercerians "are highly motivated and have ambitious goals." However, it's far from being overly competitive. Rather, students feel supported by their peers, who "are not just people you see in passing, they are people who will uplift you and inspire you to continue to do your best."

Mercer University

Financial Aid: 478-301-2670 • E-Mail: admissions@mercer.edu • Website: www.mercer.edu

THE PRINCETON REVIEW SAYS

Admissions

The school reports that its standardized testing policy for use in admission for Fall 2026 will require applicants to submit either the SAT or ACT. The Princeton Review suggests that interested applicants consult with the school for the most up-to-date standardized testing policies. *Very important factors considered include:* rigor of secondary school record, academic GPA, level of applicant's interest. *Important factors considered include:* application essay, recommendation(s), extracurricular activities, talent/ability, character/personal qualities, volunteer work. *Other factors considered include:* class rank, standardized test scores, interview, work experience. High school diploma is required and GED is accepted. *Academic units required:* 4 English, 4 math, 4 science, 3 science labs, 2 language (other than English), 1 social studies, 2 history.

Financial Aid

Students should submit: FAFSA; State aid form. Priority filing deadline is 2/2. The Princeton Review suggests that all financial aid forms be submitted as soon as possible. *Need-based scholarships/grants offered:* Federal Pell; Federal SEOG; State scholarships/grants; College/university scholarship or grant aid from institutional funds; Private scholarships. *Loan aid offered:* Federal Direct Subsidized Loans; Federal Direct Unsubsidized Loans; Direct PLUS loans; State Loans; College/university loans from institutional funds. Admitted students will be notified of awards on a rolling basis. Federal Work-Study Program available. Institutional employment available.

The Inside Word

Admissions officers at Mercer seek individuals who will both add to the university's vibrant campus life as well as benefit from the myriad academic opportunities provided. To that end, they carefully consider the rigor of each applicant's high school curriculum and GPA. Standardized test scores (if submitted), personal statements and teacher recommendations are also heavily weighed. Lastly, officers evaluate extracurricular involvement, paying close attention to any leadership roles attained.

THE SCHOOL SAYS

From the Admissions Office

"Mercer University is one of America's most distinctive and most impactful private research universities, offering academic programs that span the undergraduate liberal arts and sciences to doctoral-level degrees. Since its founding in 1833, Mercer has impacted tens of thousands of graduates who, in turn, are making impactful contributions to their professions and communities throughout the world.

"With nearly 9,000 students enrolled across 12 schools and colleges, Mercer uniquely and purposefully fuses the intimate, student-focused culture characteristic of a small liberal arts college with the expansive academic resources and opportunities of a major research university.

"Mercer University offers two ways to apply for admission to the residential undergraduate program on its historic Macon, Georgia, campus: The Common Application or the Mercer Application. First-year applicants may choose to apply for Early Action—a non-binding admission process that gives students priority scholarship consideration—or via Regular Decision. All first-year applicants are considered for University merit scholarship eligibility. Transfer applicants may apply for fall, spring, or summer admission and are considered for University merit scholarships at the point of admission. All applicants are encouraged to submit the Free Application for Federal Student Aid (FAFSA) as early as possible to be considered for every type of financial aid available.

"The best way to see what Mercer has to offer is to visit in person. Visit opportunities range from campus tours to immersive, full-day experiences. Schedule a visit to Mercer or explore campus virtually at visit.mercer.edu."

SELECTIVITY

# of total applicants	10,839
% of total applicants accepted	64
% of total acceptees attending	15
# of in-state applicants	8,538
% of in-state applicants accepted	67
# of out-of-state-applicants	1,685
% of applicants accepted from out of state	63
# of international applicants	614
% of international applicants accepted	34
# offered a place on the wait list	682
# admitted from wait list	120

First-Year Profile

Testing policy	SAT or ACT Required
Range SAT composite	1160–1320
Range SAT EBRW	590–680
Range SAT math	560–660
Range ACT composite	25–31
% submitting SAT scores	47
% submitting ACT scores	17
Average HS GPA	3.9
% submitting high school GPA	100
% graduated top 10% of class	32
% graduated top 25% of class	63
% graduated top 50% of class	90
% submitting high school rank	63

Important Dates

Early action	
Apply by	11/1
Notified by	11/15
Regular	
Apply by	2/1
Notified by	Rolling, 2/15
Nonfall registration?	Yes

FINANCIAL FACTS

Annual tuition	$44,784
Food and housing	$15,912
Required fees	$500
Books and supplies	$1,200
Average need-based scholarship (First-year)	$31,478 ($37,684)
% students with need rec. need-based scholarship or grant aid (First-year)	99 (100)
% students with need rec. non-need-based scholarship or grant aid (First-year)	19 (30)
% students with need rec. need-based self-help aid (First-year)	75 (63)
% students rec. any financial aid (First-year)	99 (100)
% UG borrow to pay for school	60
Average cumulative indebtedness	$33,713
% of students with need fully met (First-year)	22 (31)
Average % of student need met (First-year)	72 (85)

Miami University

501 E. High Street, Oxford, OH 45056 • Admissions: 513-529-2531

Survey Snapshot
Classroom facilities are great
Great library
Career services are great

RATINGS

Quality of Life	**83**
Fire Safety	**86**
Green	**94**
Academic	**82**
Profs Interesting	**92**
Profs Accessible	**96**
Admissions	**86**
Financial Aid	**86**

CAMPUS LIFE

Type of school	Public
Environment	Village

Students

Degree-seeking undergrad enrollment	16,301
% male/female/not reported	47/53/0
% from out of state	34
% First-year from public high school	75
% First-year live on campus	95
% Ugrads live on campus	47
# of fraternities (% join)	25 (23)
# of sororities (% join)	22 (32)
% Asian	2
% Black or African American	3
% Hispanic	5
% Native American	<1
% Pacific Islander	<1
% Race and/or ethnicity unknown	1
% Two or more races	4
% White	83
% International	2
# of countries represented	68

CAMPUS MENTAL HEALTH SERVICES

Offers mental health/wellness program	Yes
Mental health training available to students	No
Employs Chief Wellness Officer	NR
Peer-to-peer mental health offerings	NR
Counseling center has guidelines or accreditation	No
Mental health/well-being courses	NR

ACADEMICS

% students returning for sophomore year	90
% students graduating within 4 years	73
% students graduating within 6 years	81
Calendar	Semester
Student/faculty ratio	15:1

Most Popular Majors
Finance; Marketing; Biology; Psychology

Applicants Often Prefer
Case Western Reserve University, Northwestern University, University of Illinois at Urbana—Champaign, University of Michigan—Ann Arbor, Vanderbilt University, Washington University in St. Louis

Applicants Sometimes Prefer
Indiana University—Bloomington, The Ohio State University—Columbus, Penn State University Park, Purdue University—West Lafayette, Southern Methodist University, University of Wisconsin—Madison

Applicants Rarely Prefer
Michigan State University, Ohio University—Athens, Syracuse University, University of Cincinnati, University of Connecticut, University of Dayton

STUDENTS SAY "..."

Academics

In keeping with its "rich tradition and history," Miami University delivers "the iconic college experience" while maintaining its "devotion to excellent undergraduate instruction." The academic experience at Miami University begins with "an extremely strong orientation program, a dedicated student affairs department, and an overwhelming amount of student involvement in co-curricular activities." Regardless of major, undergraduates experience the Miami Plan, which provides a specific liberal arts framework for exploring academic, social, and professional opportunities. The Honors Program is "phenomenal. It offers the ability to grow as a student and person through both in and out of class experiences." Students may have "a challenging academic workload" but say that courses are "engaging" and getting the right professors "makes all the difference."

All students complete their Miami experience with a capstone experience, resulting in an individual or group project. This structure "prepares students for the workplace after graduation while also giving them the opportunity to thrive while on campus." As a result, "Miami University students are recruited by companies, and that provides great leverage when looking for internships and jobs." Many students report that "Miami really prepares students for the real world after college." Another student agrees: "A degree from Miami is worth a lot to many employers." Students appreciate that Miami "is committed to its image as a premier undergraduate institution."

Campus Life

Students agree: Miami University is "astoundingly beautiful." In "a quaint college town" with a "beautiful red brick campus," Miami students enjoy "a vibrant social atmosphere" that offers a "plethora of student activities." On campus, "Miami makes it possible to find groups or organizations that can fit any student's interest, and many tend to help in propelling graduates into jobs or programs once they leave the campus." With more than 600 student-run clubs and organizations on campus, students have many opportunities to find their niche. While one student remarks that "it often seems as though everyone is [Greek affiliated] because of how visible they are on campus," others point out that two-thirds of students are not affiliated with a fraternity or sorority. On the weekends, "Miami students can find a wealth of great bars and clubs uptown—many of which are eighteen—plus, allowing freshmen and sophomores to enjoy the dance floors and bars that makeup almost all of the nightlife." However, other students point out that Miami "offers a lot of alternative programs for students who wish to avoid alcohol." There is "late night programming... offered through Miami, as well as athletic events and other cultural events." On any given day, "there is a ton to do on and off campus. The town is quaint, but it is mainly a college town, so it's like an extension of the school. Nightlife is pretty big here, but so are academics and activities. Students definitely are actively thinking about their futures, and they take academics seriously."

Student Body

With just over 16,000 undergrads, Miami University is "the perfect size," where you "can see everyone...but still meet many new people." The average Miami student is "very involved on campus, is concerned about his or her academics, and wants to make a good impression on others. We care about how we present ourselves, but in a good way." One student observes that their peers often seem to be "white, upper-middle-class, and Christian....; however, the student body is generally accepting of all students no matter the background." Regardless of appearances, "the typical student is very academically focused, challenge-driven, competitive, [and] extraverted." Feeling at home at Miami University is "all about finding your niche on campus, which is generally done through people in your major, and especially student organizations."

Miami University

Financial Aid: 513-529-8558 • E-Mail: admission@miamioh.edu • Website: www.miamioh.edu

THE PRINCETON REVIEW SAYS

Admissions

The school reports that its standardized testing policy for use in admission for Fall 2026 is Test Optional. The Princeton Review suggests that interested applicants consult with the school for the most up-to-date standardized testing policies. *Very important factors considered include:* rigor of secondary school record, class rank, academic GPA, standardized test scores, application essay, recommendation(s), talent/ability, character/personal qualities. *Other factors considered include:* extracurricular activities, first generation, alumni/ae relation, geographical residence, state residency, volunteer work, work experience, level of applicant's interest. High school diploma is required and GED is accepted. *Academic units recommended:* 4 English, 4 math, 3 science, 2 language (other than English), 2 social studies, 1 history, 1 visual/performing arts.

Financial Aid

Students should submit: FAFSA. Priority filing deadline is 2/15. The Princeton Review suggests that all financial aid forms be submitted as soon as possible. *Need-based scholarships/grants offered:* Federal Pell; Federal SEOG; State scholarships/grants; Private scholarships; College/university scholarship or grant aid from institutional funds. *Loan aid offered:* Federal Direct Subsidized Loans; Federal Direct Unsubsidized Loans; Direct PLUS loans; College/university loans from institutional funds. Admitted students will be notified of awards on a rolling basis. Federal Work-Study Program available. Institutional employment available.

The Inside Word

Getting into Miami University isn't a given. High grades and test scores are a good start, but there is more you can do to better your odds. Admissions officers favor students who have challenged themselves academically, are active in their schools, lead student organizations or other activities, and volunteer in their community.

THE SCHOOL SAYS

From the Admissions Office

"At Miami, you'll find a level of involvement—in your classes, in your research, in your extracurricular activities—that you won't find at other schools. What sets Miami apart as a Public Ivy is the ability to give students a personalized small-college experience within the reputation, experiences, and opportunities of a large research university, all at a public school cost. With more than 100 majors to choose from, and a liberal arts foundation that allows students to explore different areas of interest, finding your true passion—in and out of the classroom—is at the heart of what the Miami University experience is all about. This deep level of engagement is reflected in the 89 percent freshman to sophomore retention rate and Miami's 73 percent four-year graduation rate, which is among the top for public universities across the country. Miami's reputation for producing outstanding leaders with real-world experience makes us a target school for top global firms, leads to acceptance rates into law and medical school which far exceed the national averages, and result in impressive placement rates for graduates. Students also benefit from small class sizes—most undergraduate classes have fewer than thirty students—and personal attention from faculty members in the classroom, through research opportunities, and through faculty mentoring programs. Outside of the classroom, students can participate in over 500 student organizations, attend social and cultural events, or get involved with one of the most extensive intramural and club sports program in the country."

SELECTIVITY

# of total applicants	40,782
% of total applicants accepted	74
% of total acceptees attending	14
# of in-state applicants	19,386
% of in-state applicants accepted	76
# of out-of-state-applicants	18,639
% of applicants accepted from out of state	78
# of international applicants	2,757
% of international applicants accepted	38
# of early decision applicants	520
% of early decision applicants accepted	74
# offered a place on the wait list	7,060
# admitted from wait list	147

First-Year Profile

Testing policy	Test Optional
Range SAT composite	1250–1350
Range SAT EBRW	620–690
Range SAT math	610–680
Range ACT composite	24–30
% submitting SAT scores	8
% submitting ACT scores	21
Average HS GPA	3.9
% submitting high school GPA	100

Important Dates

Early decision	
Apply by	11/15
Notified by	12/15
Early action	
Apply by	12/1
Notified by	2/1
Regular	
Apply by	2/1
Notified by	3/15
Nonfall registration?	Yes

FINANCIAL FACTS*

Annual in-state tuition	$15,616
Annual out-of-state tuition	$39,844
Food and housing	$17,832
Required fees	$3,254
Books and supplies	$1,330
Average need-based scholarship (First-year)	$14,857 ($14,797)
% students with need rec. need-based scholarship or grant aid (First-year)	95 (95)
% students with need rec. non-need-based scholarship or grant aid (First-year)	18 (18)
% students with need rec. need-based self-help aid (First-year)	65 (61)
% UG borrow to pay for school	43
Average cumulative indebtedness	$30,757
% of students with need fully met (First-year)	22 (20)
Average % of student need met (First-year)	62 (56)

* Most recently reported data at time of printing. Scan the QR code to find the latest updates.

MICHIGAN STATE UNIVERSITY

426 Auditorium Rd, East Lansing, MI 48824 • Admissions: 517-355-8332

Survey Snapshot
Great library
Frats and sororities are popular
Intramural sports are popular

RATINGS

Quality of Life	**84**
Fire Safety	**60***
Green	**60***
Academic	**72**
Profs Interesting	**83**
Profs Accessible	**87**
Admissions	**84**
Financial Aid	**81**

CAMPUS LIFE

Type of school	Public
Environment	City

Students

Degree-seeking undergrad enrollment	41,197
% male/female/not reported	48/52/0
% from out of state	17
% First-year live on campus	95
% Ugrads live on campus	40
# of fraternities (% join)	38 (12)
# of sororities (% join)	23 (13)
% Asian	8
% Black or African American	7
% Hispanic	7
% Native American	<1
% Pacific Islander	<1
% Race and/or ethnicity unknown	1
% Two or more races	5
% White	67
% International	5
# of countries represented	118

CAMPUS MENTAL HEALTH SERVICES

Offers mental health/wellness program	Yes
Mental health training available to students	Yes
Employs Chief Wellness Officer	Yes
Peer-to-peer mental health offerings	Yes
Counseling center has guidelines or accreditation	Yes
Mental health/well-being courses	Yes, non-credit

ACADEMICS

% students returning for sophomore year	91
% students graduating within 4 years	62
% students graduating within 6 years	81
Calendar	Semester
Student/faculty ratio	17:1

STUDENTS SAY "..."

Academics

Michigan State University makes the most of its size, with students impressed by the "amount of resources available," including "great…women's student services," and the "variety of courses…there's something for everyone here" with more than 400 academic programs and 300 study abroad options. MSU may be big, but students feel seen, citing challenging and "creative and hands-on" classes in which "curiosity is encouraged, ideas are valued, and learning feels connected to something bigger." In the classroom, teachers use a wide range of pedagogical methods to keep students engaged, including "fieldwork, peer presentations, and discussions that connect what we learn to current events," and "many courses have a 'flipped format,' allowing more opportunities for students to ask questions in class." Classes also incorporate modern technology like "online learning platforms, adaptive testing tools, and virtual tutoring systems that personalize instruction for students." According to one biochemistry major, "MSU's emphasis on active learning and real-world application makes the academic experience feel dynamic and meaningful." Students largely attribute this to how "professors and TAs put so much effort into making the learning experience enjoyable and worthwhile." They are "very helpful, especially with office hours and help room, always doing their best to make you succeed." Spartans generally concur that the staff is the heart of the school, as they "genuinely care and want to see you succeed. They do their best to send various opportunities and foster connections with important figures in your field." Small surprise, then, that some students describe their time at MSU as "not just about earning a degree, but about discovering what I'm passionate about and how I want to make an impact after graduation."

Campus Life

MSU's verdant 5,200-acre campus has "great accessibility with sidewalks and walking paths," and "a lot of people run or just go for walks." Students "really appreciate the effort MSU puts into making sure students stay safe and healthy." For instance, one student remarks that the "food in the dining halls is exceptional." Another adds, "We have so many places, including the arboretum, that are amazing spaces to get outside and just breathe." As a Division I school with 23 varsity teams, "sports are a big part of the culture here." Students say that "going out to tailgates with friends beforehand is a great experience," and "team spirit is very present, with people yelling 'Go Green' and 'Go White.'" Students say they've "learned so much from other perspectives" at Round Table discussions offered by the Mutual Respect, Understanding, Learning, & Empathy program, they've "had the opportunity to experience new things while on campus for free" through the University Activities Board, and have found "different ways to grow and make an impact" through work on the President's Advisory Council. In short, "There is always something happening on campus, and those moments remind me of the pride and energy that come with being a Spartan."

Student Body

With so many students, MSU's East Lansing campus "is pretty diverse, with people from all of Michigan and around the world," and the variety of backgrounds creates a "very inclusive environment that supports getting a hard-earned education." This student body potpourri "makes campus life vibrant and eye-opening," populated by individuals who "are passionate not only about academics but also about making a difference through research, leadership, creative expression, and community involvement." While the size of the school can be daunting at first, most say that "no matter where you came from, what you believe in, or what your hobbies are, there is a group that feels the same." Another reinforces that "it can take time to find your place, but once you do, those smaller communities feel supportive and connected, and you still get that shared Spartan pride."

MICHIGAN STATE UNIVERSITY

Financial Aid: 517-353-5940 • E-Mail: admis@msu.edu • Website: www.msu.edu

THE PRINCETON REVIEW SAYS

Admissions

The school reports that its standardized testing policy for use in admission for Fall 2026 is Test Optional. The Princeton Review suggests that interested applicants consult with the school for the most up-to-date standardized testing policies. *Very important factors considered include:* academic GPA. *Important factors considered include:* rigor of secondary school record, application essay, extracurricular activities. *Other factors considered include:* standardized test scores, interview, talent/ability, character/personal qualities, first generation, volunteer work, work experience, level of applicant's interest. High school diploma is required and GED is accepted. *Academic units required:* 4 English, 3 math, 3 science, 1 science lab, 1 language (other than English), 3 social studies.

Financial Aid

Students should submit: FAFSA. The Princeton Review suggests that all financial aid forms be submitted as soon as possible. *Need-based scholarships/grants offered:* Federal Pell; Federal SEOG; State scholarships/grants; Private scholarships; College/university scholarship or grant aid from institutional funds; United Negro College Fund; Federal Nursing Scholarships. *Loan aid offered:* Federal Direct Subsidized Loans; Federal Direct Unsubsidized Loans; Direct PLUS loans; College/university loans from institutional funds. Admitted students will be notified of awards on a rolling basis beginning 1/1. Federal Work-Study Program available. Institutional employment available.

The Inside Word

Michigan State takes a traditional approach to evaluation: your academic performance in high school, strength and quality of your curriculum, recent trends in your academic performance, class rank, and your leadership, talents, conduct, and diversity of experience are all factors in admission.

THE SCHOOL SAYS

From the Admissions Office

"At Michigan State University, we believe in the power of uncommon will.

"It's the will to think bigger, work harder and never give up. We are united in our drive to achieve our personal best while together pushing the limits of what's possible to make a better world for all.

"MSU was founded more than 170 years ago on the idea that education should open doors and serve the greater good. That spirit still defines us. Today, we're one of the world's top 100 and a leading U.S. public research university—home to nationally ranked programs, more than 400 areas of study, and world-class academic and research facilities.

"Here, students access opportunities that set them apart. Students collaborate with faculty on groundbreaking research, gain experience through internships with industry leaders, and make a difference in communities on and off campus. With more than 1,000 student organizations, every Spartan finds where they belong.

"Graduates move forward with the skills and perspective to adapt, lead, and keep learning. That's why MSU is among the top 10 public universities for graduate employability and why more than half a million Spartan alumni are found solving problems and leading change in critical industries around the globe.

"At MSU, you'll find your path, your people, and your purpose. And you'll leave ready to take on whatever comes next with confidence and uncommon will."

SELECTIVITY

# of total applicants	62,965
% of total applicants accepted	83
% of total acceptees attending	18
# of in-state applicants	25,102
% of in-state applicants accepted	84
# of out-of-state-applicants	30,768
% of applicants accepted from out of state	82
# of international applicants	7,095
% of international applicants accepted	88
# offered a place on the wait list	4,241
# admitted from wait list	2,254

First-Year Profile

Testing policy	Test Optional
Range SAT composite	1100–1310
Range SAT EBRW	550–660
Range SAT math	530–660
Range ACT composite	25–31
% submitting SAT scores	52
% submitting ACT scores	7
Average HS GPA	3.7
% submitting high school GPA	92
% graduated top 10% of class	20
% graduated top 25% of class	53
% graduated top 50% of class	90
% submitting high school rank	32

Important Dates

Early action	
Apply by	11/1
Notified by	1/15
Regular	
Apply by	4/1
Notified by	Rolling, 10/15
Nonfall registration?	Yes

FINANCIAL FACTS*

Annual in-state tuition (First-year)	$19,284 ($16,916)
Annual out-of-state tuition (First-year)	$45,636 ($44,300)
Food and housing	$12,928
Required fees	$340
Books and supplies	$1,420
Average need-based scholarship (First-year)	$13,954 ($13,950)
% students with need rec. need-based scholarship or grant aid (First-year)	80 (79)
% students with need rec. non-need-based scholarship or grant aid (First-year)	61 (51)
% students with need rec. need-based self-help aid (First-year)	56 (52)
% UG borrow to pay for school	45
Average cumulative indebtedness	$31,468
% of students with need fully met (First-year)	12 (13)
Average % of student need met (First-year)	60 (61)

* Most recently reported data at time of printing. Scan the QR code to find the latest updates.

Michigan Technological University

1400 Townsend Drive, Houghton, MI 49931 • Admissions: 888-688-1885

Survey Snapshot
Lots of conservative students
Career services are great
Internships are widely available

RATINGS	
Quality of Life	86
Fire Safety	96
Green	88
Academic	82
Profs Interesting	90
Profs Accessible	93
Admissions	86
Financial Aid	89

CAMPUS LIFE

Type of school	Public
Environment	Village

Students

Degree-seeking undergrad enrollment	5,936
% male/female/not reported	71/29/0
% from out of state	24
% First-year live on campus	96
% Ugrads live on campus	47
# of fraternities (% join)	13 (11)
# of sororities (% join)	7 (12)
% Asian	2
% Black or African American	1
% Hispanic	3
% Native American	<1
% Pacific Islander	<1
% Race and/or ethnicity unknown	7
% Two or more races	3
% White	82
% International	1
# of countries represented	20

CAMPUS MENTAL HEALTH SERVICES

Offers mental health/wellness program	Yes
Mental health training available to students	Yes
Employs Chief Wellness Officer	No
Peer-to-peer mental health offerings	Yes
Counseling center has guidelines or accreditation	Yes
Mental health/well-being courses	Yes, for-credit

ACADEMICS

% students returning for sophomore year	89
% students graduating within 4 years	42
% students graduating within 6 years	70
Calendar	Semester
Student/faculty ratio	15:1
Most common class size 10–19.	(26%)
Most common lab/discussion size 10–19.	(49%)

Most Popular Majors

Computer Science; Mechanical Engineering; Electrical and Electronics Engineering

Applicants Sometimes Prefer

Grand Valley State University, Michigan State University, Milwaukee School of Engineering, Northern Michigan University, Purdue University—West Lafayette, University of Illinois at Urbana—Champaign, University of Michigan—Ann Arbor, University of Minnesota—Twin Cities, University of Wisconsin—Madison, Western Michigan University

STUDENTS SAY "..."

Academics

At Michigan Technological University, "engineering is a part of everybody's life" and students take pride in having a "really good reputation" and "very high standards" in that field. And while students, also known as Huskies, take the time to mention the "beautiful (often snowy) environment," they emphasize that the school's 160 undergraduate programs are "serious study," with everything from STEM-focused subjects in polymer science, wildlife ecology and conservation, and cybersecurity, to jazz studies and writing. These "challenging" courses bring with them a strong emphasis on "pathways for career development and professional advancement," and popular class activities include things like building nanosatellites and making prosthetic limbs. Moreover, in addition to "lots of internship and co-op opportunities," Huskies have clocked more than 132,000 paid undergraduate research hours in recent years. Many students say that the "concentrated courses are great," though some say that general education courses can be "huge" and "impersonal." That said, students feel that "the more time you put into your program, the professors become more interactive, and the experience becomes more meaningful." And throughout, "the administration in every department works hard to answer questions and help out as much as possible." Ultimately, across all subjects, students feel that, "Michigan Tech provides an atmosphere that nurtures learning" and "pushes students to excel academically."

Campus Life

Nestled "in a small town in the middle of the deep North woods," Michigan Tech attracts students who love the winter. "Winters are long and cold up here," explains one student, and there are plenty of "winter activities to be a part of." Students enjoy access to Mont Ripley, home of "hiking, biking, four-wheeling, skiing, [and] snowmobiling" and Husky pride is on display during Winter Carnival, "a long weekend off from classes where students build giant, impressive snow sculptures, play broomball, [and] stay out all night." Students also mention "house parties and moderate drinking/merrymaking [to] warm up the cold winters." Many stay warm by keeping active, and with "over 200 clubs," students say "there are a lot of opportunities to get involved." Student athletes compete across 14 NCAA sports, including seven men's teams and seven women's teams. The campus itself is "incredibly safe" and supports a "strong student community." With students who are both "outdoorsy" and like to "stay in and play video games," Huskies generally "work hard during the week and look forward to relaxing and having fun on the weekends."

Student Body

By and large, Huskies are "down-to-earth, friendly people," who "are looking to get a good education and are fairly laid-back." Students are up in the air about which takes precedence some suggest that "most people think about classes first, hanging out second," while others find them to be "great at balancing school and hanging out." Students do note that the student "ratio is a little guy-heavy," but overall, "the sense of community is remarkable," with one student noting that though there are nearly 6,000 undergraduates on campus, "you start to see people you know everywhere....It is really easy to find a friend and talk to someone." That happens more often than not, as the typical Husky "is smart and a little more introspective than average." Above all, even when it's cold outside, it's warm among peers: "the atmosphere is very friendly."

MICHIGAN TECHNOLOGICAL UNIVERSITY

Financial Aid: 906-487-2622 • E-Mail: mtu4u@mtu.edu • Website: www.mtu.edu

THE PRINCETON REVIEW SAYS

Admissions

The school reports that its standardized testing policy for use in admission for Fall 2026 is Test Optional. The Princeton Review suggests that interested applicants consult with the school for the most up-to-date standardized testing policies. *Very important factors considered include:* academic GPA. *Important factors considered include:* rigor of secondary school record, standardized test scores. *Other factors considered include:* application essay, recommendation(s), extracurricular activities, talent/ability, character/personal qualities. High school diploma is required and GED is accepted. *Academic units required:* 3 English, 3 math, 2 science. *Academic units recommended:* 4 English, 4 math, 3 science, 2 language (other than English), 3 social studies, 2 academic electives, 1 computer science.

Financial Aid

Students should submit: FAFSA. Priority filing deadline is 3/1. The Princeton Review suggests that all financial aid forms be submitted as soon as possible. *Need-based scholarships/grants offered:* Federal Pell; Federal SEOG; State scholarships/grants; Private scholarships; College/university scholarship or grant aid from institutional funds. *Loan aid offered:* Federal Direct Subsidized Loans; Federal Direct Unsubsidized Loans; Direct PLUS loans; College/university loans from institutional funds. Admitted students will be notified of awards on a rolling basis beginning 1/1. Federal Work-Study Program available. Institutional employment available.

The Inside Word

Michigan Tech strives to enroll bright, adventurous students. Students aren't required to submit recommendations from teachers, although they may submit a "High School Counselor Information Page" if they would like their counselor to share information regarding their high school performance. Applicants to the Visual and Performing Arts Department degree programs may be required to submit supplemental materials, including an essay.

THE SCHOOL SAYS

From the Admissions Office

"The world is changing. Fast. Tomorrow needs talented visionaries and new solutions. At Michigan Tech, an R1 public research university founded in 1885 in Houghton, you'll design, build, code, and lead. You'll work and play on the shores of Lake Superior, with 5,000+ acres of research forests and limitless opportunities for outdoor adventure. Our unique Enterprise Program lets you work on real industry projects, from building and launching spacecraft for NASA to designing advanced robotics systems. We're ready for tomorrow. Are you?

"Students can choose from more than 160 undergraduate programs in engineering; forest resources; technology; business and economics; mathematics; natural, physical and environmental sciences; arts; humanities; health professions and pre-health preparation; and social sciences. We offer degree opportunities in growing fields such as biomedical engineering and wildlife ecology and management, as well as cybersecurity and mechatronics in our College of Computing, the first college of its kind in the state of Michigan.

"Outside of classrooms and labs, students enjoy our golf course, ski hill, recreational trails, and University forests, along with a safe, friendly, small-town atmosphere in beautiful Upper Michigan. Situated on the Keweenaw Waterway, the campus is minutes from Lake Superior. During Winter Carnival, students build huge snow statues and play broomball, the most popular of many intramural sports on campus. The varsity sports line-up includes the first varsity-level esports team at a public university in Michigan, along with football, men's and women's basketball, tennis, cross-country, Nordic skiing, track and field, soccer, volleyball, and NCAA Division I hockey."

SELECTIVITY

# of total applicants	10,359
% of total applicants accepted	85
% of total acceptees attending	16
# of in-state applicants	6,047
% of in-state applicants accepted	86
# of out-of-state-applicants	3,428
% of applicants accepted from out of state	82
# of international applicants	884
% of international applicants accepted	96

First-Year Profile

Testing policy	Test Optional
Range SAT composite	1120–1330
Range SAT EBRW	560–670
Range SAT math	560–670
Range ACT composite	25–32
% submitting SAT scores	66
% submitting ACT scores	18
Average HS GPA	3.9
% submitting high school GPA	94
% graduated top 10% of class	34
% graduated top 25% of class	64
% graduated top 50% of class	91
% submitting high school rank	53

Important Dates

Regular	
Notified by	Rolling, 6/15
Nonfall registration?	Yes

FINANCIAL FACTS

Annual in-state tuition	$19,608
Annual out-of-state tuition	$44,504
Food and housing	$14,142
Required fees	$374
Books and supplies	$1,200
Average need-based scholarship (First-year)	$12,253 ($13,933)
% students with need rec. need-based scholarship or grant aid (First-year)	84 (89)
% students with need rec. non-need-based scholarship or grant aid (First-year)	92 (98)
% students with need rec. need-based self-help aid (First-year)	63 (50)
% students rec. any financial aid (First-year)	94 (100)
% UG borrow to pay for school	59
Average cumulative indebtedness	$35,920
% of students with need fully met (First-year)	36 (52)
Average % of student need met (First-year)	83 (92)

MIDDLEBURY COLLEGE

The Emma Willard House, Middlebury, VT 05753 • Admissions: 802-443-3000

Survey Snapshot
Easy to get around campus
Students take advantage of the outdoors
Recreation facilities are great

RATINGS

Quality of Life	88
Fire Safety	61
Green	60*
Academic	97
Profs Interesting	98
Profs Accessible	99
Admissions	98
Financial Aid	92

CAMPUS LIFE

Type of school	Private
Environment	Village

Students

Degree-seeking undergrad enrollment	2,738
% male/female/not reported	46/53/<1
% from out of state	94
% First-year live on campus	100
% Ugrads live on campus	95
# of fraternities	0
# of sororities	0
% Asian	7
% Black or African American	5
% Hispanic	12
% Native American	<1
% Pacific Islander	0
% Race and/or ethnicity unknown	1
% Two or more races	7
% White	54
% International	12
# of countries represented	66

CAMPUS MENTAL HEALTH SERVICES

Offers mental health/wellness program	Yes
Mental health training available to students	No
Employs Chief Wellness Officer	NR
Peer-to-peer mental health offerings	NR
Counseling center has guidelines or accreditation	No
Mental health/well-being courses	NR

ACADEMICS

% students returning for sophomore year	94
% students graduating within 4 years	66
% students graduating within 6 years	91
Calendar	4-1-4
Student/faculty ratio	8:1
Most common class size 10–19.	(43%)

Most Popular Majors

Economics; Computer Science; Neuroscience

STUDENTS SAY "…"

Academics

Middlebury College ensures that its students are "both socially and intellectually prepared for the world" by providing a first-class education and "the encouragement to make sure students succeed." Most known for its programs in environmental science, English, and international studies, Middlebury encourages "global thinking" and touts academic programs with an "emerging focus on creativity and entrepreneurship." For instance, Middlebury's Bread Loaf School of English hosts summer intensives that attract international educators, writers, and translators. Students appreciate that the winter term in January provides a month-long opportunity for students and professors to focus on just one subject. Such programming "allows you to develop" communication, writing, creativity, and critical thinking skills "in whatever subject or subjects that one is most passionate about." The "truly top-notch" professors are "brilliant academics, but they are also adept teachers and classroom leaders." While professors care about research, they prioritize teaching—"Middlebury expects both; most professors deliver." Students note that the "academics are reputed to be "very intense" ("If you haven't done the reading, prepare to be called out for it") but also that "students reliably enjoy their classes." Middlebury also encourages creative thinking regarding academics by providing "institutional support for whatever...idea might strike you."

Campus Life

Located between the Green Mountains and the Adirondacks, Middlebury College has a vibrant social scene. "Most people actually choose not to go into cities on weekends because they would hate to miss what's going on on-campus." It's also fair to say that the social scene is "very centered around athletic teams." Middlebury boasts 31 NCAA varsity teams and reports that 28% of students participate in varsity sports. The Vermont location is a plus: Twelve miles east of Middlebury's main campus, the Bread Loaf campus features 30,000 acres of forest and is a base camp for students interested in skiing, snowshoeing, and fatbiking. "At the end of the day, we all just like to get together and hit up the Snow Bowl to go skiing," shares one Middlebury student. Overall, it's hard to overstate "how important the outdoor experience is for the school."

Indoors, students rave about dorms that are "gorgeous." There is even one called the Chateau, modeled after the largest chateau in Fontainebleau, France. There are no traditional fraternities or sororities on campus, but students connect through Middlebury's more than 200 student organizations, student government, on-campus newspaper, and Middlebury Outdoor Programs, which provides students gear and support for enjoying the local environs. As one student says: "If you've got free time in your day at Middlebury, you're doing something wrong."

Student Body

With just under 3,000 undergraduates, the Middlebury student body is "a perfect blend of intellectual curiosity, responsible living, and fun." Known as Midd Kids, students are apt to be "well-read, outgoing," and "engaged, active." They often pursue "at least one major, a minor, and [are] the star of at least one sports team or special interest group, but usually more." In joking agreement, another student describes their peers as "bright kids doing too many things—all of them good, none related to sleep." Midd Kids don't "take themselves too seriously, but do take serious initiative." While driven, Middlebury students cultivate a "super-friendly and caring" atmosphere and "compete with themselves, not their classmates." Undergrads here tend to be "well-rounded students from stable backgrounds" who "know how to hold a conversation and [are] open to new experiences." So sociable is the scene on campus; one student confesses that "with all the different friends you will make," it's hard to find time for everything.

Middlebury College

Financial Aid: 802-443-5158 • E-Mail: admissions@middlebury.edu • Website: www.middlebury.edu

THE PRINCETON REVIEW SAYS

Admissions

The school reports that its standardized testing policy for use in admission for Fall 2026 is Test Optional. The Princeton Review suggests that interested applicants consult with the school for the most up-to-date standardized testing policies. *Very important factors considered include:* rigor of secondary school record, class rank, academic GPA, extracurricular activities, talent/ability, character/personal qualities. *Important factors considered include:* standardized test scores, application essay, recommendation(s). *Other factors considered include:* first generation, alumni/ae relation, geographical residence, volunteer work, work experience, level of applicant's interest. High school diploma or equivalent is not required. *Academic units recommended:* 4 English, 4 math, 3 science, 3 science labs, 4 language (other than English), 3 social studies.

Financial Aid

Students should submit: FAFSA; CSS PROFILE. Priority filing deadline is 11/15. The Princeton Review suggests that all financial aid forms be submitted as soon as possible. *Need-based scholarships/grants offered:* Federal Pell; Federal SEOG; State scholarships/grants; Private scholarships; College/university scholarship or grant aid from institutional funds. *Loan aid offered:* Federal Direct Subsidized Loans; Federal Direct Unsubsidized Loans; Direct PLUS loans. Admitted students will be notified of awards on or about 4/1. Federal Work-Study Program available. Institutional employment available.

The Inside Word

Middlebury is extremely competitive; improve your chances of admission by submitting materials that paint you in the best possible light. If Middlebury is your top choice, you can increase your chances by applying early decision to let the school know the level of your commitment.

THE SCHOOL SAYS

From the Admissions Office

"The successful Middlebury candidate excels in a variety of areas including academics, athletics, the arts, leadership, and service to others. These strengths and interests permit students to grow beyond their traditional 'comfort zones' and conventional limits. Our classrooms are as varied as the Green Mountains, the Metropolitan Museum of Art, or the great cities of Russia and Japan. Outside the classroom, students informally interact with professors in activities such as intramural basketball games and community service. At Middlebury, students develop critical-thinking skills, enduring bonds of friendship, and the ability to challenge themselves.

"Middlebury has more than 60 on-campus buildings for student housing. First-year students are housed within designated first-year communities. Sophomores have the opportunity to select housing with friends in sophomore residential communities. Juniors and seniors live together with friends and can choose from a wide variety of Junior/Senior housing options available across campus.

"Middlebury offers majors and programs in forty-six different fields, with particular strengths in languages, international studies, environmental studies, literature and creative writing, and the sciences. Opportunities for engaging in individual research with faculty abound at Middlebury."

SELECTIVITY

# of total applicants	12,540
% of total applicants accepted	11
% of total acceptees attending	44
# of early decision applicants	1,341
% of early decision applicants accepted	30
# offered a place on the wait list	2,285
# admitted from wait list	45

First-Year Profile

Testing policy	Test Optional
Range SAT composite	1450–1530
Range SAT EBRW	720–760
Range SAT math	730–790
Range ACT composite	33–35
% submitting SAT scores	28
% submitting ACT scores	18

Important Dates

Early decision	
Apply by	11/1
Notified by	Mid December
Other ED apply by	1/1
Other ED notified by	2/1
Regular	
Apply by	1/1
Notified by	Late March
Nonfall registration?	Yes

FINANCIAL FACTS

Annual tuition	$72,924
Food and housing	$20,920
Required fees	$542
Average need-based scholarship (First-year)	$64,631 ($62,768)
% students with need rec. need-based scholarship or grant aid (First-year)	100 (100)
% students with need rec. non-need-based scholarship or grant aid (First-year)	0 (0)
% students with need rec. need-based self-help aid (First-year)	87 (88)
% UG borrow to pay for school	41
Average cumulative indebtedness	$25,225
% of students with need fully met (First-year)	100 (100)
Average % of student need met (First-year)	100 (100)

Middle Tennessee State University

1301 East Main Street, Murfreesboro, TN 37132 • Admissions: 615-898-2233

Survey Snapshot
Active student government
Recreation facilities are great
Active minority support groups

RATINGS

Quality of Life	86
Fire Safety	91
Green	60*
Academic	84
Profs Interesting	95
Profs Accessible	92
Admissions	86
Financial Aid	81

CAMPUS LIFE

Type of school	Public
Environment	City

Students

Degree-seeking undergrad enrollment	16,301
% male/female/not reported	48/52/0
% from out of state	8
% First-year live on campus	30
% Ugrads live on campus	17
# of fraternities (% join)	15 (5)
# of sororities (% join)	10 (6)
% Asian	4
% Black or African American	14
% Hispanic	11
% Native American	<1
% Pacific Islander	<1
% Race and/or ethnicity unknown	2
% Two or more races	4
% White	63
% International	2
# of countries represented	52

CAMPUS MENTAL HEALTH SERVICES

Offers mental health/wellness program	Yes
Mental health training available to students	No
Employs Chief Wellness Officer	NR
Peer-to-peer mental health offerings	NR
Counseling center has guidelines or accreditation	No
Mental health/well-being courses	NR

ACADEMICS

% students returning for sophomore year	79
% students graduating within 4 years	36
% students graduating within 6 years	54
Calendar	Semester
Student/faculty ratio	17:1
Most common class size 10–19.	(37%)
Most common lab/discussion size 20–29.	(32%)

Most Popular Majors

Biology/Biological Sciences; Psychology; Aeronautics/Aviation/Aerospace Science and Technology

Applicants Also Look At

Austin Peay State University, Motlow State Community College, Tennessee State University, Tennessee Technological University, University of Memphis, University of Tennessee—Chattanooga, University of Tennessee—Knoxville

STUDENTS SAY "..."

Academics

Middle Tennessee State University has become a go-to choice for those wishing to receive a quality and affordable education close to home. The school offers more than 140 degree programs for undergraduates—some "that are not seen in other universities, like animation." One student says, "You can literally major in fermentation and learn about the process of brewing beer." Students find these "highly specialized programs are closely tied to their industry, which means really good job placement." The on-campus growth doesn't stop there: "A staggering amount of resources [are] available to students, [ranging] from research programs to counseling services to 3D printing." Furthermore, students cite "pretty good technology [being] available for students to use or borrow, with updated versions of most programs."

As far as professors go, they "like to be on a first name basis" with students and often "make it a point to get to know you." Students call faculty "very helpful and fair" and "thorough in every aspect of the subject matter." One student shares, "A professor of mine teaches by walking around to every individual student and making sure they understand the subject matter." They're also "willing to circle back around if anyone in the class gets off track." Students who do find themselves needing extra assistance with coursework or concepts can rest easy: "There are a lot of programs in place to help you, such as free tutoring," and students also have "plenty of opportunities to gain a mentor" for more focused guidance during their college careers. Many say this "advising is top notch," and that MTSU takes the time to "foster an environment of care for each and every student." Overall, students agree: "This school is amazing, and it is such a hidden gem."

Campus Life

The campus is big but feels like a "comfortable and home-like school" environment where people "sit on the quad by the library and talk with their friends, play music, and skateboard." This type of campus takes advantage of the other outdoor areas of campus too, and students like to "hang hammocks on trees to sit and read and study." One student comments, "There are also many different parks and greenways that we enjoy visiting." For on-campus events, the school is always offering things "like art classes, study groups, or simply a movie showing." Those looking to spend a little time elsewhere, though, will turn to nearby Murfreesboro, where they can hang out at the "plethora of restaurants and bars." Nashville isn't far, either, and students will often "go out to...clubs or arcades" there on weekends. Overall, students find themselves to be quite busy, but the good kind of busy—as one student puts it: "Despite how busy I am, I am happy doing it."

Student Body

At a school as large as MTSU, you see all types [of students] from different ends of the spectrum as everyone "is very open to whoever comes into the school." Here you'll find "a mixed bag of fresh-out-of-high-school students,...parents,...returning military veterans, and foreign students." No matter who they are, people at Middle Tennessee are "extremely friendly and inclusive," "pretty laid back," and "nice, courteous and really helpful." "Though everyone is different here, it is still easy to find people like yourself [who are] studying the same things or taking similar classes," says a student.

MIDDLE TENNESSEE STATE UNIVERSITY

Financial Aid: 615-898-2111 • E-Mail: admissions@mtsu.edu • Website: www.mtsu.edu

THE PRINCETON REVIEW SAYS

Admissions

The school reports that its standardized testing policy for use in admission for Fall 2026 will require applicants to submit either the SAT or ACT. The Princeton Review suggests that interested applicants consult with the school for the most up-to-date standardized testing policies. *Very important factors considered include:* academic GPA, standardized test scores. *Other factors considered include:* rigor of secondary school record, application essay, recommendation(s). High school diploma is required and GED is accepted. *Academic units required:* 4 English, 4 math, 3 science, 1 science lab, 2 language (other than English), 1 social studies, 1 history, 1 visual/performing arts.

Financial Aid

The Princeton Review suggests that all financial aid forms be submitted as soon as possible. *Need-based scholarships/grants offered:* Federal Pell; Federal SEOG; State scholarships/grants; Private scholarships. *Loan aid offered:* Federal Direct Subsidized Loans; Federal Direct Unsubsidized Loans; Direct PLUS loans. Admitted students will be notified of awards on a rolling basis beginning 3/1. Federal Work-Study Program available. Institutional employment available.

The Inside Word

Middle Tennessee State University is very transparent about what guarantees admission for first-year students: Anyone who has completed the recommended college prep classes with a 3.0 GPA will be admitted, as will anyone with a minimum total SAT of 1100 or a composite ACT score of 22. Those with lower scores will need to submit both a GPA of at least 2.7 and either an SAT of 990+ or ACT of 19+. Students who do not meet any of these requirements can still be considered for conditional admission, but they must submit a personal statement and are subjected to an individual review process.

THE SCHOOL SAYS

From the Admissions Office

"One of MTSU's biggest selling points is the sense of community that stems from its roots as a small, regional college. Although MTSU has grown over the years, it maintains a commitment to students, seeking to provide a supportive learning environment, the finest faculty, quality programs, and a learning experience as remarkable and diverse as its students.

"Hands-on learning is a focus, and undergraduates can pursue research experience that other colleges may offer only to graduate students.

"MTSU offers students every opportunity to succeed, with guidance from highly qualified advisors and resources that range from free tutoring and writing help to a Makerspace (with 3D printing!) and even a Career Closet with professional attire."

SELECTIVITY

# of total applicants	14,989
% of total applicants accepted	69
% of total acceptees attending	30
# of in-state applicants	11,516
% of in-state applicants accepted	74
# of out-of-state-applicants	2,691
% of applicants accepted from out of state	53
# of international applicants	782
% of international applicants accepted	56

First-Year Profile

Testing policy	SAT or ACT Required
Range SAT composite	1010–1220
Range SAT EBRW	520–630
Range SAT math	490–600
Range ACT composite	20–26
% submitting SAT scores	6
% submitting ACT scores	93
Average HS GPA	3.7
% submitting high school GPA	100

Important Dates

Regular	
Apply by	8/15
Notified by	Rolling, 8/1
Nonfall registration?	Yes

FINANCIAL FACTS

Annual in-state tuition	$11,186
Annual out-of-state tuition	$34,154
Food and housing	$12,550
Books and supplies	$1,260
Average need-based scholarship (First-year)	$7,355 ($7,862)
% students with need rec. need-based scholarship or grant aid (First-year)	60 (60)
% students with need rec. non-need-based scholarship or grant aid (First-year)	73 (91)
% students with need rec. need-based self-help aid (First-year)	39 (32)
% students rec. any financial aid (First-year)	86 (97)
% UG borrow to pay for school	45
Average cumulative indebtedness	$23,748
% of students with need fully met (First-year)	13 (15)
Average % of student need met (First-year)	62 (66)

Missouri University of Science and Technology

1870 Miner Circle, Rolla, MO 65409-0910 • Admissions: 573-341-6731

Survey Snapshot
Lab facilities are great
Career services are great
Internships are widely available

RATINGS

Quality of Life	**79**
Fire Safety	**62**
Green	**60***
Academic	**82**
Profs Interesting	**88**
Profs Accessible	**91**
Admissions	**86**
Financial Aid	**88**

CAMPUS LIFE

Type of school	Public
Environment	Village

Students

Degree-seeking undergrad enrollment	5,659
% male/female/not reported	77/23/0
% from out of state	18
% First-year from public high school	85
% First-year live on campus	94
% Ugrads live on campus	80
# of fraternities (% join)	20 (25)
# of sororities (% join)	6 (24)
% Asian	4
% Black or African American	4
% Hispanic	5
% Native American	1
% Pacific Islander	<1
% Race and/or ethnicity unknown	7
% Two or more races	3
% White	73
% International	4
# of countries represented	60

CAMPUS MENTAL HEALTH SERVICES

Offers mental health/wellness program	Yes
Mental health training available to students	No
Employs Chief Wellness Officer	NR
Peer-to-peer mental health offerings	NR
Counseling center has guidelines or accreditation	No
Mental health/well-being courses	NR

ACADEMICS

% students returning for sophomore year	88
% students graduating within 4 years	33
% students graduating within 6 years	67
Calendar	Semester
Student/faculty ratio	17:1
Most common class size 10–19.	(30%)
Most common lab/discussion size 30–39.	(32%)

Most Popular Majors

Civil Engineering; Electrical and Electronics Engineering; Mechanical Engineering

STUDENTS SAY "..."

Academics

STEM standouts and rigorous academics will fit right in at Missouri University of Science and Technology. Aspiring engineers "are exposed to just about every different type of engineering"—including aerospace, metallurgical and mechanical—making it "one of the best universities that prepares engineers for industry." Students acknowledge that courses are "very tough and intimidating," to the point at which "it's not uncommon to have a 55 percent or less average on a test." That said, the purpose isn't to deflate GPAs; it's to "prepare students to find a job in the real world and help us to get the experience to succeed in it," and graduates claim "the quality of education and availability of resources here is second to none." Undergraduates master material via "hands-on learning, small class sizes, and caring professors" who are "some of the smartest professors in the world." And though "the professors are there to challenge you" and matriculants caution that you should "not expect to be babied at all," enrollees make clear that "all of the professors have office hours, whether open or by appointment" and they consider "the accessibility of instructors and other faculty/staff " one of the school's strengths. Plus, all that time spent puzzling over problem sets typically pays off; Missouri S&T "comes in the top ten schools in average starting salary for graduates and won't guarantee a huge debt burden."

Campus Life

Missouri S&T may be "a small school in the middle of Missouri," but its "range of student organizations is mind-boggling." Besides joining such groups, students can participate in Greek life and partake in school-sponsored recreation like "scavenger hunts, video game nights, cooking classes, viewing parties, dance lessons, and much more." That said, at a place where "all of the students are always worrying about that next exam in calculus," it isn't surprising that undergrads spend a lot of their free time studying. Here, "academics are everyone's top priority." But students say that when they're not hitting the books, "drinking is pretty big on weekends" and also cite athletics and fitness as popular pastimes. Those who need to get off-campus note that "there's not so much to do in the town" of Rolla but say that St. Louis is accessible for day trips. Most enrollees busy themselves on campus with extracurriculars or further exploration of their academic interests. "Virtually every student is either heavily involved in a diverse group of these student organizations or devotes much of their time to design teams or research."

Student Body

The Missouri S&T campus is a safe place to be smart and draws an accordingly bookish student body. As students put it, those who were "a little nerdy" and out of place, "now can be themselves" as proud S&T Miners. And while they "came here primarily to learn," they're not opposed to socializing or making new friends—in fact, that commonality makes it "really easy to just to strike up a conversation with someone." The "very friendly" folks on campus "live together in harmony" and with over 200 student organizations, "everyone can find a place to fit in." While the majority of the students enrolled are from Missouri, the others hail "from the edges of the nation and even some foreign countries, which is astounding considering our small enrollment size." Regardless of their origins, students say they "adapt to the social environment" fairly quickly and then, for the most part, coexist happily as like-minded, hardworking peers.

Missouri University of Science and Technology

Financial Aid: 573-341-4282 • E-Mail: admissions@mst.edu • Website: www.mst.edu

THE PRINCETON REVIEW SAYS

Admissions

The school reports that its standardized testing policy for use in admission for Fall 2026 is Test Optional. The Princeton Review suggests that interested applicants consult with the school for the most up-to-date standardized testing policies. *Very important factors considered include:* rigor of secondary school record, academic GPA, standardized test scores. *Other factors considered include:* class rank, application essay, recommendation(s), interview, extracurricular activities, talent/ability, character/personal qualities, volunteer work, work experience, level of applicant's interest. High school diploma is required and GED is accepted. *Academic units required:* 4 English, 4 math, 3 science, 1 science lab, 2 language (other than English), 3 social studies, 1 visual/performing arts.

Financial Aid

Priority filing deadline is 2/1. The Princeton Review suggests that all financial aid forms be submitted as soon as possible. *Need-based scholarships/grants offered:* Federal Pell; Federal SEOG; State scholarships/grants; Private scholarships; College/university scholarship or grant aid from institutional funds. *Loan aid offered:* Federal Direct Subsidized Loans; Federal Direct Unsubsidized Loans; Direct PLUS loans; College/university loans from institutional funds. Admitted students will be notified of awards on a rolling basis beginning 2/1. Federal Work-Study Program available. Institutional employment available.

The Inside Word

Winning admission to Missouri University of Science and Technology is largely a numbers game, as it often is with other leading public universities. Expect to have to meet class rank and standardized test cutoffs, along with general education requirements, in order to be granted admission. And apply early if possible. The pool of applicants is competitive, and is made up of students of similar caliber. Get off to an early start and you'll have an advantage.

THE SCHOOL SAYS

From the Admissions Office

"Missouri University of Science and Technology is one of the nation's top technological universities and offers strong academics in humanities, social sciences, education, business and other degree programs. Our fifteen engineering programs and computing and science programs are nationally and internationally renowned. With 7,645 students from the U.S. and around the globe, Missouri S&T provides a 'big campus' feel of diversity and student engagement on a medium-sized campus.

"S&T offers rigorous academics, exceptional graduation and placement rates, excellent access to co-ops and internships, experiential learning for all undergraduates, affordable tuition combined with generous scholarship programs, and a 3.4 percent loan default rate as a result of superior career outcomes for our students. The average starting salary for S&T graduates in 2022 was $69,033.

"S&T students are successful due to a combination of outstanding academics and easy access to personal and professional growth. The vast majority of courses are taught by tenured professors engaged in relevant research and scholarship, in a faculty culture that values undergraduate education and hands-on learning and personal attention, which extends back to our founding in 1870. S&T sponsors over 250 student clubs, and students enjoy outdoor activities among the area's scenic parks, lakes and riverways.

"Widely recognized as one of the nation's best universities, Missouri S&T provides an outstanding education, at an affordable cost with exceptional student outcomes."

SELECTIVITY

# of total applicants	8,330
% of total applicants accepted	79
% of total acceptees attending	19
# of in-state applicants	2,966
% of in-state applicants accepted	87
# of out-of-state-applicants	3,373
% of applicants accepted from out of state	84
# of international applicants	1,986
% of international applicants accepted	56

First-Year Profile

Testing policy	Test Optional
Range SAT composite	1220–1380
Range SAT EBRW	600–700
Range SAT math	610–720
Range ACT composite	25–31
% submitting SAT scores	12
% submitting ACT scores	68
Average HS GPA	3.8
% submitting high school GPA	98
% graduated top 10% of class	44
% graduated top 25% of class	71
% graduated top 50% of class	93
% submitting high school rank	51

Important Dates

Regular	
Apply by	7/1
Notified by	Rolling, 7/1
Nonfall registration?	Yes

FINANCIAL FACTS

Annual in-state tuition	$14,328
Annual out-of-state tuition	$33,516
Food and housing	$13,422
Required fees	$1,636
Books and supplies	$720
Average need-based scholarship (First-year)	$13,066 ($15,780)
% students with need rec. need-based scholarship or grant aid (First-year)	95 (99)
% students with need rec. non-need-based scholarship or grant aid (First-year)	31 (60)
% students with need rec. need-based self-help aid (First-year)	88 (82)
% students rec. any financial aid (First-year)	88 (95)
% UG borrow to pay for school	55
Average cumulative indebtedness	$27,461
% of students with need fully met (First-year)	33 (60)
Average % of student need met (First-year)	71 (83)

MONMOUTH UNIVERSITY (NJ)

400 Cedar Avenue, West Long Branch, NJ 07764-1898 • Admissions: 732-571-3456

Survey Snapshot
Frats and sororities are popular
Great off-campus food
Great library

RATINGS

Quality of Life	83
Fire Safety	99
Green	60*
Academic	76
Profs Interesting	85
Profs Accessible	88
Admissions	83
Financial Aid	84

CAMPUS LIFE

Type of school	Private
Environment	Village

Students

Degree-seeking undergrad enrollment	3,636
% male/female/not reported	36/64/<1
% from out of state	22
% First-year from public high school	80
% First-year live on campus	77
% Ugrads live on campus	43
# of fraternities (% join)	9 (15)
# of sororities (% join)	9 (22)
% Asian	3
% Black or African American	6
% Hispanic	19
% Native American	<1
% Pacific Islander	<1
% Race and/or ethnicity unknown	2
% Two or more races	3
% White	65
% International	2
# of countries represented	28

CAMPUS MENTAL HEALTH SERVICES

Offers mental health/wellness program	Yes
Mental health training available to students	Yes
Employs Chief Wellness Officer	Yes
Peer-to-peer mental health offerings	No
Counseling center has guidelines or accreditation	Yes
Mental health/well-being courses	Yes, for-credit

ACADEMICS

% students returning for sophomore year	83
% students graduating within 4 years	64
% students graduating within 6 years	72
Calendar	Semester
Student/faculty ratio	11:1
Most common class size 20–29.	(40%)
Most common lab/discussion size 10–19.	(68%)

Most Popular Majors
Health Services/Allied Health/Health Sciences; Business Administration and Management; Speech Communication and Rhetoric

STUDENTS SAY "..."

Academics

Monmouth University's core principles outline an experience of transformative learning that "truly provides ample opportunities to prepare [students] for their careers." There is an "endless amount of opportunities to gain help in any given circumstance," such as "free tutoring for the majority of classes," and career support is readily available. There's also an Experiential Education requirement that gets students into internships, service learning, and study abroad, as well as seven centers and institutes (including the Institute for Global Understanding and The Bruce Springsteen Archives and Center for American Music) that offer students the chance to gain experience beyond the classroom. Numerous conferences and panels hosted by the school "provide opportunities for students to engage with experts in their field, explore cutting-edge research and ideas, and network with professionals and peers." There are also ample chances to work with faculty, thanks to "a wonderful student-to-teacher ratio that allows for students to actually create a relationship with the professors rather than just being a face in a lecture." Faculty "are very accommodating and make themselves available for students when needed" and "are open to office hours and out-of-the-classroom help for the students that need it." A student confirms: "My professors have allowed me to flourish....What I once thought was a dream career is within reach because of their efforts and encouragement."

Campus Life

Students describe Monmouth University's setting as being the "best of two worlds," as it's only an hour from either New York City or Philadelphia, and "the beach [is] only a mile away." The campus "is beautiful and the facilities are updated," and its proximity to the shore means "it is very popular here to go to Pier Village and go shopping and out to dinner with friends by the beach if you are done with classes for the day." Those who remain on campus will find plenty of common spaces, and the Student Center is a popular spot to "get food, chat with friends, learn more about clubs, [and] play pool." The "Student Activities Board is the best at events" and regularly puts on "fairs, movie nights, bingo nights, breakfast for dinner, homecoming, and Springfest." Rounding out the activities, Division I athletics "are always fun and usually have a good turnout of students" and "Greek life in general is a very key part of the social culture at Monmouth." All in all, students declare "it is very easy to fill your days."

Student Body

Monmouth University is an "extremely diverse and integrated campus and everyone is very polite and has manners." That respect is for the best, as "many look to get involved, be a part of the student body, and find ways to encourage each other." It may also be an effect of a smaller campus, such that "you get to see the same people quite often either around campus or in your classes," This also means "you can easily make connections by networking with people." While some find enrollees to be "mostly from the Tri-State area," it's a welcoming environment where "if you make an effort to be nice to people and start a friendship they won't turn you down." Overall, Hawks are "small but interconnected and they frequently help each other through academic and social problems." A student says, "I feel like I've never experienced a place where the staff and the student body were so overwhelmingly positive, cheerful, and helpful."

Monmouth University (NJ)

Financial Aid: 732-571-3463 • E-Mail: admission@monmouth.edu • Website: www.monmouth.edu

THE PRINCETON REVIEW SAYS

Admissions

The school reports that its standardized testing policy for use in admission for Fall 2026 is Test Optional. The Princeton Review suggests that interested applicants consult with the school for the most up-to-date standardized testing policies. *Very important factors considered include:* rigor of secondary school record, academic GPA. *Important factors considered include:* application essay, recommendation(s). *Other factors considered include:* standardized test scores, extracurricular activities, character/personal qualities, alumni/ae relation, volunteer work, work experience. High school diploma is required and GED is accepted. *Academic units required:* 4 English, 3 math, 2 science, 1 science lab, 2 history, 5 academic electives. *Academic units recommended:* 2 language (other than English), 2 social studies.

Financial Aid

Students should submit: FAFSA. The Princeton Review suggests that all financial aid forms be submitted as soon as possible. *Need-based scholarships/grants offered:* Federal Pell; Federal SEOG; State scholarships/grants; Private scholarships; College/university scholarship or grant aid from institutional funds. *Loan aid offered:* Federal Direct Subsidized Loans; Federal Direct Unsubsidized Loans; Direct PLUS loans; State Loans. Admitted students will be notified of awards on a rolling basis beginning 12/15. Federal Work-Study Program available. Institutional employment available.

The Inside Word

Monmouth University takes a fairly standard approach to the admissions process: your cumulative GPA is the most critical factor. Letters of recommendation and extracurricular activities will be of secondary importance, and although the school is Test Optional, they will review your SAT and ACT scores if provided. Undergrads interested in transferring to Monmouth can utilize Personalized Transfer Appointments wherein they meet with an admissions counselor to discuss enrollment potential, the university experience, and scholarship opportunities.

THE SCHOOL SAYS

From the Admissions Office

"As one of the nation's top universities integrating access and excellence, Monmouth University attracts students looking for a personalized learning environment that will ignite their curiosity and prepare them for life after graduation.

"Students benefit from an intellectually challenging academic experience built on a strong liberal arts foundation and learning experiences that are both high impact and immersive, extending beyond the classroom. Small class sizes foster collaborative learning and research opportunities with faculty and peers who know you by name. Our breathtaking coastal campus provides a safe, suburban setting in one of the world's largest metropolitan regions, ideally positioned to help our students develop and pursue their career interests while enjoying rich cultural opportunities.

"Monmouth's student life features more than 100 active student clubs and organizations, nine sororities and eight fraternities, and dozens of academic/leadership honor societies. Monmouth's 24 Division I athletic teams attract lively support from students and other members of the campus and local communities while instilling university pride. "There is a real spirit of entrepreneurship on campus that comes to life through activities like Blue Hawk Records, our student-run record label, and the student-managed investment fund, Hawk Capital. For those adventurers interested in extending their experiences beyond campus, Monmouth encourages students to take part in service projects, study abroad programs, and community-building activities in locales around the globe. Monmouth University is committed to graduating people of purpose with the critical thinking skills required for global relevance and impact."

SELECTIVITY

# of total applicants	9,040
% of total applicants accepted	87
% of total acceptees attending	11
# of in-state applicants	6,801
% of in-state applicants accepted	88
# of out-of-state-applicants	2,112
% of applicants accepted from out of state	86
# of international applicants	127
% of international applicants accepted	90
# of early decision applicants	58
% of early decision applicants accepted	81

First-Year Profile

Testing policy	Test Optional
Range SAT composite	1150–1280
Range SAT EBRW	580–660
Range SAT math	550–640
Range ACT composite	22–28
% submitting SAT scores	19
% submitting ACT scores	2
Average HS GPA	3.7
% submitting high school GPA	100
% graduated top 10% of class	20
% graduated top 25% of class	47
% graduated top 50% of class	81
% submitting high school rank	36

Important Dates

Early decision	
Apply by	11/15
Notified by	12/15
Early action	
Apply by	12/1
Notified by	1/15
Regular	
Notified by	4/1
Nonfall registration?	Yes

FINANCIAL FACTS

Annual tuition	$48,894
Food and housing	$19,668
Required fees	$900
Books and supplies	$1,000
Average need-based scholarship (First-year)	$16,390 ($21,564)
% students with need rec. need-based scholarship or grant aid (First-year)	75 (81)
% students with need rec. non-need-based scholarship or grant aid (First-year)	100 (98)
% students with need rec. need-based self-help aid (First-year)	77 (75)
% students rec. any financial aid (First-year)	95 (100)
% UG borrow to pay for school	71
Average cumulative indebtedness	$28,021
% of students with need fully met (First-year)	20 (23)
Average % of student need met (First-year)	74 (81)

MONTANA TECHNOLOGICAL UNIVERSITY

1300 West Park Street, Butte, MT 59701 • Admissions: 406-496-4791

Survey Snapshot
Lots of conservative students
Frats and sororities are popular
Internships are widely available

RATINGS

Quality of Life	80
Fire Safety	83
Green	60*
Academic	79
Profs Interesting	86
Profs Accessible	89
Admissions	82
Financial Aid	83

CAMPUS LIFE

Type of school	Public
Environment	Town

Students

Degree-seeking undergrad enrollment	1,822
% male/female/not reported	62/38/0
% from out of state	21
% First-year live on campus	69
% Ugrads live on campus	26
# of fraternities	0
# of sororities	0
% Asian	1
% Black or African American	2
% Hispanic	5
% Native American	2
% Pacific Islander	0
% Race and/or ethnicity unknown	7
% Two or more races	6
% White	77
% International	1
# of countries represented	10

CAMPUS MENTAL HEALTH SERVICES

Offers mental health/wellness program	Yes
Mental health training available to students	No
Employs Chief Wellness Officer	NR
Peer-to-peer mental health offerings	NR
Counseling center has guidelines or accreditation	No
Mental health/well-being courses	NR

ACADEMICS

% students returning for sophomore year	76
% students graduating within 4 years	34
% students graduating within 6 years	58
Calendar	Semester
Student/faculty ratio	14:1
Most common class size 1–9.	(33%)
Most common lab/discussion size 1–9.	(32%)

Most Popular Majors

Mechanical Engineering; Registered Nursing/Registered Nurse; Management Information Systems and Services

Applicants Also Look At

Carroll College (MT), Colorado School of Mines, Montana State University, New Mexico Institute of Mining and Technology, South Dakota School of Mines and Technology, The University of Montana—Missoula, The University of Montana—Western

STUDENTS SAY "..."

Academics

Students choose Montana Technological University for its "quality of instruction," "small class sizes," and "practical learning." Montana Tech "challenges students to work hard" and is dedicated to "preparing you to be the best in your field and getting you ready for the world." The school is known for its "strong STEM programs" and its focus on research in areas such as advanced materials and manufacturing, environmental remediation, mining engineering, and biomedical science. Montana Tech's School of Nursing is academically challenging, but its "rigorous workload" pays off; according to the school, graduates pass the licensing exam at rates that exceed both the state and national averages. Regardless of their chosen major, Montana Tech provides students with "a great experience on your path to a successful career." This career readiness is supported by professors who "teach real-life scenarios" and "bring their industry experience to the classroom." Students see the benefits of this hands-on education almost immediately. As one student says, "What I have learned in some of my classes directly affected my work during my internship last summer." In addition to their effective teaching methods, professors here are also "easy to approach," always willing to help, and committed to ensuring that students "learn, not fail." The small class sizes ensure students "plenty of one-on-one opportunity if we need it." Another advantage of Montana Tech is its alumni network, which is "extremely supportive of the school." Many alumni "work in some of the highest positions in our fields," creating avenues for "applicable internships, networking opportunities, and jobs."

Campus Life

When not studying, students take full advantage of the school's location in the foothills of the Rocky Mountains, with outdoor activities such as skiing, hunting, fishing, biking, and camping. The area also features numerous hiking trails and "lots of rivers for floating." In addition to outdoor recreation, students find common ground in sports; games here are "well attended" and the crowds are enthusiastic. Students enjoy letting off steam and staying active through any of the various intramural sports offered. Most students prioritize "academics above partying," although some enjoy visiting local bars or attending house parties on the weekends. Undergraduates enjoy grabbing a bite to eat with friends off campus, but overall, the town of Butte "isn't a city with a lot to do." Consequently, students make their own fun on campus, whether it's a low-key night playing video games with friends or getting involved in an extracurricular like Powerlifting Club, Engineers Without Borders, or the Mining Team that competes worldwide.

Student Body

Students here are "down to earth" and "know how to get the job done well while still knowing how to let loose and have fun doing it." There is plenty of school spirit here: "We are loud and proud of our school, unafraid to yell at the top of our lungs for everything from the Mining Team to the football field to our hockey team. Go Orediggers!" Given the beautiful location, it's not surprising that there are "a lot of outdoorsy people" here. While there is no one type of student, most agree that "When doing homework or studying for exams, everyone takes it seriously and attempts to do the best they can." Another student adds that their peers "truly wish to better themselves as they are extremely dedicated to the craft they are trying to pursue." The school has a strong sense of community, and "you end up knowing a lot of people and making a lot of friends throughout your classes." On this tight-knit campus, students are quick to support one another. It's an environment where "you can literally ask anyone for help and they will help you in an instant."

MONTANA TECHNOLOGICAL UNIVERSITY

Financial Aid: 406-496-4223 • E-Mail: admissions@mtech.edu • Website: www.mtech.edu

THE PRINCETON REVIEW SAYS

Admissions

The school reports that its standardized testing policy for use in admission for Fall 2026 is Test Optional. The Princeton Review suggests that interested applicants consult with the school for the most up-to-date standardized testing policies. *Very important factors considered include:* class rank, academic GPA. High school diploma is required and GED is accepted. *Academic units required:* 4 English, 3 math, 2 science, 2 science labs, 3 social studies. *Academic units recommended:* 4 math.

Financial Aid

Students should submit: FAFSA. Priority filing deadline is 12/1. The Princeton Review suggests that all financial aid forms be submitted as soon as possible. *Need-based scholarships/grants offered:* Federal Pell; Federal SEOG; State scholarships/grants; Private scholarships; College/university scholarship or grant aid from institutional funds. *Loan aid offered:* Federal Direct Subsidized Loans; Federal Direct Unsubsidized Loans; Direct PLUS loans. Admitted students will be notified of awards on a rolling basis beginning 2/1. Federal Work-Study Program available. Institutional employment available.

The Inside Word

For those leaning toward a technical career, Montana Tech is the place to go. Strong academics are important, but the school can be a great choice for students that may not be offered a spot at one of the country's larger tech schools. The acceptance rate is high, and admitted students generally have a high school GPA around 3.6. Transcripts are important as well as high school class rank. Though the school is Test Optional, standardized test scores can still be useful if trying to impress the admission team. There are a variety of math and writing proficiency requirements students must meet and the school looks for a high school course load that includes a full range of college prep classes.

THE SCHOOL SAYS

From the Admissions Office

"Montana Technological University is a place of purpose, home to uncommon thinking, research, innovation, and ideas. The university embraces Montana as its living laboratory and emphasizes experiential learning in and outside the classroom and a sense of belonging among our tight-knit community of determined doers. As Montana's special focus university, Montana Tech offers a world-class education in the science, technology, engineering, math, and healthcare disciplines, offering certificates, associate, bachelor's, master's, and doctoral degrees. Learning occurs in personalized environments in the heart of the Rocky Mountains. Outdoor recreation provides a balance to the rigors of the coursework at Montana Tech. The university is perched high on the hillside above Butte, Montana, offering access to the local trail system and mountain bike skills course, and is located in a recreational paradise with snow-capped mountains, blue-ribbon rivers, and millions of acres of public lands in every direction. The university's high-demand degrees prepare students for careers in various settings. The main campus blends historic architecture with state-of-the-art facilities, including the Lesar Family Nursing Simulation Center, SAP Next-Gen Lab, and an on-campus Underground Mine Education Center. The university's Highlands College is home to career-ready trades, technology, and transfer programs that develop the workforce needed to better lives in our community, state, and beyond. Test scores are optional for an admission decision but are used to determine course placement and scholarship eligibility. Our personal atmosphere, internship opportunities, and an outcomes rate of 90% for over a decade make Montana Tech a smart investment for your future."

SELECTIVITY

# of total applicants	2,466
% of total applicants accepted	90
% of total acceptees attending	23
# of in-state applicants	1,823
% of in-state applicants accepted	94
# of out-of-state-applicants	529
% of applicants accepted from out of state	89
# of international applicants	109
% of international applicants accepted	35

First-Year Profile

Testing policy	Test Optional
Range SAT EBRW	510–630
Range SAT math	530–630
Range ACT composite	19–25
% submitting SAT scores	13
% submitting ACT scores	82
Average HS GPA	3.6
% submitting high school GPA	99
% graduated top 10% of class	23
% graduated top 25% of class	50
% graduated top 50% of class	83
% submitting high school rank	81

Important Dates

Nonfall registration?	Yes

FINANCIAL FACTS

Annual in-state tuition	$6,358
Annual out-of-state tuition	$24,163
Food and housing	$11,696
Required fees	$1,984
Books and supplies	$1,240
Average need-based scholarship (First-year)	$7,224 ($7,381)
% students with need rec. need-based scholarship or grant aid (First-year)	84 (88)
% students with need rec. non-need-based scholarship or grant aid (First-year)	6 (11)
% students with need rec. need-based self-help aid (First-year)	71 (65)
% students rec. any financial aid (First-year)	73 (91)
% UG borrow to pay for school	50
Average cumulative indebtedness	$21,413
% of students with need fully met (First-year)	10 (14)
Average % of student need met (First-year)	58 (60)

Montclair State University

1 Normal Avenue, Montclair, NJ 07043 • Admissions: 973-655-4444

Survey Snapshot
Great library
Students love Montclair, NJ
Diverse student types interact on campus

RATINGS

Quality of Life	84
Fire Safety	97
Green	93
Academic	75
Profs Interesting	85
Profs Accessible	86
Admissions	80
Financial Aid	79

CAMPUS LIFE

Type of school	Public
Environment	Town

Students

Degree-seeking undergrad enrollment	18,703
% male/female/not reported	43/57/0
% from out of state	4
% First-year live on campus	37
% Ugrads live on campus	26
# of fraternities (% join)	14 (3)
# of sororities (% join)	18 (3)
% Asian	6
% Black or African American	14
% Hispanic	42
% Native American	<1
% Pacific Islander	<1
% Race and/or ethnicity unknown	3
% Two or more races	3
% White	31
% International	2
# of countries represented	106

CAMPUS MENTAL HEALTH SERVICES

Offers mental health/wellness program	Yes
Mental health training available to students	Yes
Employs Chief Wellness Officer	Yes
Peer-to-peer mental health offerings	Yes
Counseling center has guidelines or accreditation	Yes
Mental health/well-being courses	Yes, for-credit

ACADEMICS

% students returning for sophomore year	79
% students graduating within 4 years	49
% students graduating within 6 years	66
Calendar	Semester
Student/faculty ratio	17:1
Most common class size 20–29.	(32%)

Applicants Sometimes Prefer

Kean University, Rowan University, Rutgers University–New Brunswick, Rutgers University—Newark

Applicants Rarely Prefer

The College of New Jersey, Ramapo College of New Jersey, Seton Hall University, William Paterson University

STUDENTS SAY "..."

Academics

Montclair State University provides "diverse programs/curriculum, and [a] focus on student success and career readiness." The school "does an amazing job creating opportunities for students to gain hands-on experience—from internships and media projects to programs that help us build professional networks before graduation." Montclair also offers a "strong support system for students" and "the resources you need to succeed." As one student explains, "Having multiple communications that can help me with a problem from financial aid, classes, etc., is super helpful and puts a lot less stress on me." Among the many types of resources for students are classrooms with "interactive platforms, live coding sessions, and simulations to make lessons more engaging and practical." And one student reports, "In my History of the Spanish Inquisition class, we're doing a unit on using AI to build databases." Professors are "passionate about what they teach and truly invested in their students' growth, often going out of their way to provide guidance, opportunities, and real-world insight." In the classroom, they also "make the material engaging by connecting lessons to real-world situations and encouraging open discussion in class." This eye toward practicality and future application does not go unnoticed by students, one of whom says, "I feel like I am learning critical information pertaining to my future career path."

Campus Life

The school "is always pushing student involvement and for students to put themselves out there and go out of [their] comfort [zones]," and "it is very fun to try new things...and [see] what becomes of an event and what you as a student gain from it." As one student explains, "I never thought I would be doing Brazilian jiu-jitsu in my free time, but turns out I am." There are numerous clubs and organizations, and "you're sure to find something you like no matter how specific your interest," whether it's photography, anime, sports, or music. The Student Center often plays host to activities, "like cultural nights and volunteer drives," as well as "awesome affordable off-campus activities like trips to [New York City], hikes, and local outdoor venues." For unstructured fun, "a lot of people hang out in the quad, go to the gym, or use the dorm lounges to play pool or just spend time with other people in the building." A large portion of students are commuters, and the university "has a lot of events and things and spaces for commuters to go and stay while waiting for classes." Life at Montclair State "moves at a fast but exciting pace," and students say that on most days the "campus buzzes with classes, club meetings, and study sessions in every corner of the library."

Student Body

Students appreciate that Montclair State is "an incredibly diverse school with people from all over the world." Students "vary in age, culture, and experiences" and "everyone is extremely accepting." Wandering the campus, one can "see all kinds of expression here, from the way people dress to the way they speak up for what they believe in." Red Hawks, as students are called, "are nice, very respectful, and helpful throughout campus, [and] the friendly nature of the students makes for a lively atmosphere." At Montclair, "you'll meet people who are career focused, others who are passionate about activism, and some who are still figuring things out, and that mix creates a really dynamic environment." The mix of goals and backgrounds culminates in a harmonious thrum to daily living: "There's this incredible energy on campus; everyone's always juggling classes, jobs, and internships, yet still finding time to support one another and get involved."

MONTCLAIR STATE UNIVERSITY

Financial Aid: 973-655-7600 • E-Mail: msuadm@montclair.edu • Website: www.montclair.edu

THE PRINCETON REVIEW SAYS

Admissions

The school reports that its standardized testing policy for use in admission for Fall 2026 is Test Optional. The Princeton Review suggests that interested applicants consult with the school for the most up-to-date standardized testing policies. *Very important factors considered include:* academic GPA. *Important factors considered include:* rigor of secondary school record, application essay, recommendation(s). *Other factors considered include:* class rank, extracurricular activities, talent/ability, character/personal qualities, volunteer work, work experience. High school diploma is required and GED is accepted. *Academic units required:* 4 English, 3 math, 2 science, 2 science labs, 2 language (other than English), 2 social studies, 2 history. *Academic units recommended:* 4 English, 4 math, 3 science, 3 science labs, 2 language (other than English), 2 social studies, 2 history.

Financial Aid

Students should submit: FAFSA. Priority filing deadline is 3/1. The Princeton Review suggests that all financial aid forms be submitted as soon as possible. *Need-based scholarships/grants offered:* Federal Pell; Federal SEOG; State scholarships/grants; Private scholarships; College/university scholarship or grant aid from institutional funds. *Loan aid offered:* Federal Direct Subsidized Loans; Federal Direct Unsubsidized Loans; Direct PLUS loans; State Loans. Admitted students will be notified of awards on a rolling basis beginning 5/1. Federal Work-Study Program available. Institutional employment available.

The Inside Word

Montclair State University reviews admissions applications holistically, taking a number of factors into account. The most important of these is academic performance, including high school GPA and the rigor of coursework completed. The review process also considers letters of recommendation from teachers and/or counselors, a thoughtful personal essay, extracurricular involvement (such as community service, leadership roles, athletics, artistic or performance activities, and part-time work), and standardized test scores, if submitted. Students applying to select College of the Arts programs may also need to complete an interview, audition, or portfolio.

SELECTIVITY

# of total applicants	26,224
% of total applicants accepted	89
% of total acceptees attending	17
# of in-state applicants	21,206
% of in-state applicants accepted	90
# of out-of-state-applicants	3,559
% of applicants accepted from out of state	87
# of international applicants	1,459
% of international applicants accepted	84
# offered a place on the wait list	2,187
# admitted from wait list	1,129

First-Year Profile

Testing policy	Test Optional
Range SAT composite	850–1160
Range SAT EBRW	430–600
Range SAT math	420–560
% submitting SAT scores	10
Average HS GPA	3.4
% submitting high school GPA	94
% graduated top 10% of class	8
% graduated top 25% of class	28
% graduated top 50% of class	62
% submitting high school rank	35

Important Dates

Early action	
Apply by	12/1
Notified by	12/23
Regular	
Apply by	3/1
Notified by	Rolling, 10/15
Nonfall registration?	Yes

FINANCIAL FACTS

Annual in-state tuition	$15,678
Annual out-of-state tuition	$26,394
Food and housing	$16,862
Required fees	$1,176
Books and supplies	$1,340
Average need-based scholarship (First-year)	$13,819 ($14,599)
% students with need rec. need-based scholarship or grant aid (First-year)	77 (78)
% students with need rec. non-need-based scholarship or grant aid (First-year)	53 (62)
% students with need rec. need-based self-help aid (First-year)	47 (42)
% students rec. any financial aid (First-year)	82 (89)
% UG borrow to pay for school	58
Average cumulative indebtedness	$39,728
% of students with need fully met (First-year)	1 (1)
Average % of student need met (First-year)	44 (45)

MORAVIAN UNIVERSITY

1200 Main Street, Bethlehem, PA 18018 • Admissions: 610-861-1320

Survey Snapshot
Students love Bethlehem, PA
Career services are great
Easy to get around campus

RATINGS	
Quality of Life	90
Fire Safety	99
Green	60*
Academic	82
Profs Interesting	89
Profs Accessible	92
Admissions	86
Financial Aid	87

CAMPUS LIFE

Type of school	Private
Affiliation	Moravian
Environment	City

Students

Degree-seeking undergrad enrollment	2,093
% male/female/not reported	38/61/<1
% from out of state	28
% First-year from public high school	89
% First-year live on campus	68
% Ugrads live on campus	53
# of fraternities (% join)	4 (6)
# of sororities (% join)	5 (10)
% Asian	3
% Black or African American	7
% Hispanic	18
% Native American	<1
% Pacific Islander	<1
% Race and/or ethnicity unknown	5
% Two or more races	3
% White	63
% International	1
# of countries represented	8

CAMPUS MENTAL HEALTH SERVICES

Offers mental health/wellness program	Yes
Mental health training available to students	Yes
Employs Chief Wellness Officer	Yes
Peer-to-peer mental health offerings	Yes
Counseling center has guidelines or accreditation	No
Mental health/well-being courses	No

ACADEMICS

% students returning for sophomore year	79
% students graduating within 4 years	71
% students graduating within 6 years	74
Calendar	Semester
Student/faculty ratio	10:1
Most common class size 20–29.	(35%)
Most common lab/discussion size 10–19.	(34%)

Most Popular Majors
Registered Nursing/Registered Nurse; Health Services/Allied Health/Health Sciences, General; Business Administration and Management

Applicants Often Prefer
Lehigh University, Penn State University Park, Temple University

Applicants Sometimes Prefer
The College of New Jersey, Kutztown University of Pennsylvania, The University of Scranton

Applicants Rarely Prefer
Albright College, Misericordia University

STUDENTS SAY "..."

Academics

Moravian University offers students a lot of support and opportunities to keep them career-ready. To begin with, "up-front technology" is provided to students for free through the school's partnership with Apple, and there's also ample "opportunity to pursue research with my professors" as an undergraduate. There's also the unique Elevate Career Promise, which provides specific scaffolding to develop "career-oriented leader[ship]" skills and guarantees students financial support if they're not employed or enrolled in graduate school within a year of graduation. Moravian earns students' accolades with an "innovative approach" to academics that incorporates "project-based classes where we work with local businesses, and collaborative courses that mix students from different majors." To highlight the school's fostering of "hands-on learning, independent inquiry, and meaningful engagement with the community," undergrads point to "requirements for study abroad and internships," "the ability to self-design a major," and opportunities to "practice skills in a realistic, controlled environment." Moravian's professors are almost universally acclaimed for being "approachable, genuinely invested in students, and willing to offer extra help when needed." Students recognize the faculty's "real-world experience from the field... [which] helps me feel prepared for when I graduate and enter the workforce." As one student gushed, "I find myself chatting with professors often, not only for academic purposes, but to further discuss interesting class topics or related topics." In short, "our staff is amazing."

Campus Life

Moravian students assert that they have a "sense of belonging" and "feel part of a community" on a campus that is "welcoming and academically focused at the same time." In the center of campus is Moravian's brand-new student union building, the HUB, which opened in October 2025 and, among a variety of "area[s] for students to gather and study," houses the highly lauded Center for Career and Civic Engagement, "mindfulness spaces," and a dedicated home for the popular Moravian Activities Council (MAC), which hosts events like "wing-o in which wings are offered whilst playing bingo," giving students a way to "branch out and connect." In general, undergraduates enjoy "many opportunities for all types of students to be involved on campus," emphasize a focus on "community service," and observe that they "have an entire community of wonderful people to spend [their] time with." Many students appreciate the school's location in the heart of a small city, and it is a common pastime to wander "through the Bethlehem area...to shop or just walk around," and check out the "nice parks and interesting scenery in the older parts of Bethlehem, as well as historical factors related to the steel industry." All in all, life on the Moravian campus "feels relaxed and easy to navigate, with plenty of chances to get involved or just unwind with friends."

Student Body

Students at Moravian describe a "powerful community" of "incredibly welcoming," "friendly, hardworking, and career-oriented leaders." Undergraduates consistently proclaim a "warm, close-knit vibe" among "focused individuals," saying that "Students here value collaboration over competition" and are "interesting and kindhearted people." Moravian "feels like a place where people are encouraged to be themselves, and everyone's individuality adds something valuable to the campus atmosphere. You'll meet students who are passionate about the arts, dedicated athletes, first-generation scholars, future scientists, international students, and so many others, all contributing their own strengths." A shared ethos of service and community engagement permeates the student commentary, evident in remarks like "I have a handful of projects that are focused on serving the community," "I love the leadership and service opportunities offered," and "Everyone works together to create a loving environment." Overall, at Moravian University the overwhelming sentiment is that "people know each other, professors are accessible, and the campus has a close-knit feel."

Moravian University

Financial Aid: 610-861-1330 • E-Mail: admission@moravian.edu • Website: www.moravian.edu

THE PRINCETON REVIEW SAYS

Admissions

The school reports that its standardized testing policy for use in admission for Fall 2026 is Test Optional. The Princeton Review suggests that interested applicants consult with the school for the most up-to-date standardized testing policies. *Very important factors considered include:* rigor of secondary school record, extracurricular activities, character/personal qualities. *Important factors considered include:* class rank, academic GPA, application essay, recommendation(s), interview, talent/ability, volunteer work, level of applicant's interest. *Other factors considered include:* standardized test scores, first generation, alumni/ae relation, work experience. High school diploma is required and GED is accepted. *Academic units required:* 4 English, 3 math, 3 science, 2 science labs, 2 language (other than English), 4 social studies. *Academic units recommended:* 4 math.

Financial Aid

Students should submit: FAFSA. The Princeton Review suggests that all financial aid forms be submitted as soon as possible. *Need-based scholarships/grants offered:* Federal Pell; Federal SEOG; State scholarships/grants; Private scholarships; College/university scholarship or grant aid from institutional funds. *Loan aid offered:* Federal Direct Subsidized Loans; Federal Direct Unsubsidized Loans; Direct PLUS loans. Admitted students will be notified of awards on a rolling basis beginning 11/15. Federal Work-Study Program available. Institutional employment available.

The Inside Word

Admissions officers seek applicants who will best complement life at Moravian. The school is looking for students who have taken a challenging college prep curriculum and have demonstrated that they're ready for collegiate level coursework. Importantly, Moravian is Test Optional and you will not be at a disadvantage if you choose not to submit scores. However, it is highly recommended that you schedule an interview with an admissions counselor if at all possible.

THE SCHOOL SAYS

From the Admissions Office

"Moravian University emphasizes hands-on learning to prepare students for successful careers rather than just their first jobs. We excel at transforming students into highly competent graduates ready for the workplace or advanced degree programs. Students benefit from robust academic majors, undergraduate research, internships, and a campus culture that fosters a deeper enjoyment of life. Located in historic Bethlehem, PA, Moravian was founded in 1742 and is the 6th oldest college in the U.S.

"In the fall of 2025, Moravian opened the HUB, a state-of-the-art student center designed with wellness at the forefront, including resources for mental and physical health, as well as career services. With a 10:1 student-faculty ratio, students receive personalized attention from world-class professors. Moravian has been an Apple Distinguished School since 2018 and all incoming first-year students receive a MacBook Pro laptop, an iPad, and an Apple Watch to ensure an accessible, engaging, and digitally integrated educational experience.

"Moravian offers 70+ programs of study, with business, education, and health professions among the most popular. Adult students can also enroll in industry-relevant graduate, certificate and professional development programs through the School of Professional Studies and Innovation.

"As only the second university in the U.S. that is part of a UNESCO World Heritage site, Moravian University has a storied history of developing leaders. Today, 98% of our graduates are employed or in graduate school within 10 months of graduation."

SELECTIVITY

# of total applicants	5,679
% of total applicants accepted	74
% of total acceptees attending	12
# of in-state applicants	2,682
% of in-state applicants accepted	83
# of out-of-state-applicants	2,631
% of applicants accepted from out of state	72
# of international applicants	366
% of international applicants accepted	18
# offered a place on the wait list	0

First-Year Profile

Testing policy	Test Optional
Range SAT composite	1030–1240
Range SAT EBRW	530–640
Range SAT math	480–600
Range ACT composite	25–28
% submitting SAT scores	18
% submitting ACT scores	1
Average HS GPA	3.6
% submitting high school GPA	99
% graduated top 10% of class	30
% graduated top 25% of class	62
% graduated top 50% of class	91
% submitting high school rank	32

Important Dates

Early action	
Apply by	11/15
Notified by	5/1
Regular	
Apply by	Rolling
Notified by	Rolling, 10/10
Nonfall registration?	Yes

FINANCIAL FACTS

Annual tuition	$54,180
Food and housing	$16,776
Required fees	$2,440
Books and supplies	$1,200
Average need-based scholarship (First-year)	$35,900 ($41,698)
% students with need rec. need-based scholarship or grant aid (First-year)	99 (100)
% students with need rec. non-need-based scholarship or grant aid (First-year)	16 (16)
% students with need rec. need-based self-help aid (First-year)	84 (84)
% students rec. any financial aid (First-year)	99 (100)
% UG borrow to pay for school	87
Average cumulative indebtedness	$51,940
% of students with need fully met (First-year)	19 (16)
Average % of student need met (First-year)	73 (77)

MOUNT HOLYOKE COLLEGE

50 College Street, South Hadley, MA 01075 • Admissions: 413-538-2023

Survey Snapshot
Active minority support groups
Great library
Easy to get around campus

RATINGS

Quality of Life	**91**
Fire Safety	**91**
Green	**60***
Academic	**91**
Profs Interesting	**95**
Profs Accessible	**96**
Admissions	**93**
Financial Aid	**99**

CAMPUS LIFE

Type of school	Private
Environment	Town

Students

Degree-seeking undergrad enrollment	2,126
% male/female/not reported	0/100/0
% from out of state	77
% First-year from public high school	74
% First-year live on campus	100
% Ugrads live on campus	97
# of sororities	0
% Asian	6
% Black or African American	5
% Hispanic	12
% Native American	<1
% Pacific Islander	0
% Race and/or ethnicity unknown	1
% Two or more races	6
% White	51
% International	20
# of countries represented	75

CAMPUS MENTAL HEALTH SERVICES

Offers mental health/wellness program	Yes
Mental health training available to students	No
Employs Chief Wellness Officer	NR
Peer-to-peer mental health offerings	NR
Counseling center has guidelines or accreditation	No
Mental health/well-being courses	NR

ACADEMICS

% students returning for sophomore year	92
% students graduating within 4 years	69
% students graduating within 6 years	82
Calendar	Semester
Student/faculty ratio	9:1
Most common class size 10–19.	(61%)
Most common lab/discussion size 10–19.	(76%)

Most Popular Majors
Computer Science; English Language and Literature; Psychology

Applicants Often Prefer
Bryn Mawr College, Smith College, University of Massachusetts—Amherst, Wellesley College

Applicants Sometimes Prefer
Brandeis University, Connecticut College, New York University, Northeastern University, Oberlin College, Scripps College, Simmons University, Skidmore College, University of California—Berkeley, University of Connecticut, University of Vermont, University of Washington, Vassar College, Wesleyan University

STUDENTS SAY "..."

Academics

Mount Holyoke College delivers "endless chances for students to get involved in both the school and the outer community, while learning from top professors who genuinely care about their students." Students appreciate the "motivated and motivating faculty" that provide self-directed, interdisciplinary experiences. One student explains: "Classes often allow you to use your creativity with projects…I wrote a paper about Mattel's Monster High generations and how it reflects the intersections between capitalism, children's media, and moral panics." One environmental science student appreciates that "the last month of the course was dedicated to our own independent research project" in the community. Students further highlight instructors that "are always open for personal connections and incredibly supportive" of individualized projects. "I have created zines, podcasts, and video interviews for final projects before," explains one Mount Holyoke attendee. Students agree that one of Mount Holyoke's strengths is the support given to students, whether for academics, mental health, or accommodations. Mount Holyoke is "genuinely very caring of student success." Such accommodations may include self-scheduled exams, which are "innovative because they are also student-run and give the students taking finals freedom" to determine their study needs and the best time and setting for testing. Another student also points to Mount Holyoke's "devotion to gender minorities, especially in STEM" as one of the school's distinguishing characteristics. In short, "Mount Holyoke's greatest strengths lie in its inclusive and supportive community, rigorous academics, and strong commitment to student care."

Campus Life

Warmer months see students "spending time on the green in the sun," while winters find students "down by the lake. It's really pretty when it snows." Students also love the "very welcoming and very homey" vibe they find indoors. "The amount of students who live in single rooms is astounding!" says one student. Dining options are "also phenomenal" and "very accommodating to all diets." Students particularly enjoy that the library "on campus is absolutely beautiful," and "there are often local vendors or college-sponsored events on the green." Popular events include "film screenings, workshops, craft nights, guest lectures, concerts, plays, and celebrations." There are numerous clubs to join for just about any interest you have, from knitting to Model UN, and "the sports clubs (in my case, soccer and volleyball) are a lot of fun." Musical clubs and campus radio are other favorite pastimes. "Hosting a show and listening to others is a great way to connect with others around campus," says one Mount Holyoke student. "The school holds events on weekends till midnight that are alcohol free that are also very popular." Parties occur, but mostly "on the weekends and they aren't huge. But the school for sure has a strong social atmosphere."

Student Body

As a gender-diverse women's college, Mount Holyoke "welcomes applications from female, transgender, and non-binary students." Many students feel that "this creates an empowering and inclusive environment." This means students feel comfortable sharing "a LOT of personality. There is no 'one' Mount Holyoke student; there is so much acceptance and inclusivity that there is no leaning into stereotypes/norms; everyone is free to do and be (express) who they want to be." Mount Holyoke students also value that "there are many students of differing genders, and along with that, different presentations of gender." One student jokes, "Everybody is some form of queer, and it's great." Others further appreciate that diversity at Mount Holyoke features students who "come from many states, countries, economic backgrounds, home lives, and academic interests. In class, students are engaged in course content and establish strong connections with their professors. Outside of class, they are engaged in clubs and extracurricular activities." One student sums up Mount Holyoke students best, saying: "My peers are thoughtful, open-minded, and respectful of different identities, backgrounds, and lived experiences, which creates a campus environment where students feel safe being themselves."

Mount Holyoke College

Financial Aid: 413-538-2291 • E-Mail: admission@mtholyoke.edu • Website: www.mtholyoke.edu

THE PRINCETON REVIEW SAYS

Admissions

The school reports that its standardized testing policy for use in admission for Fall 2026 is Test Optional. The Princeton Review suggests that interested applicants consult with the school for the most up-to-date standardized testing policies. *Very important factors considered include:* rigor of secondary school record, academic GPA, application essay, recommendation(s). *Important factors considered include:* class rank, interview, extracurricular activities, talent/ability, character/personal qualities, volunteer work, work experience. *Other factors considered include:* standardized test scores, first generation, alumni/ae relation, geographical residence, level of applicant's interest. High school diploma is required and GED is accepted. *Academic units recommended:* 4 English, 3 math, 3 science, 3 science labs, 3 language (other than English), 3 history, 1 academic elective.

Financial Aid

Students should submit: FAFSA; CSS PROFILE. Priority filing deadline is 2/1. The Princeton Review suggests that all financial aid forms be submitted as soon as possible. *Need-based scholarships/grants offered:* Federal Pell; Federal SEOG; State scholarships/grants; Private scholarships; College/university scholarship or grant aid from institutional funds. *Loan aid offered:* Federal Direct Subsidized Loans; Federal Direct Unsubsidized Loans; State Loans; College/university loans from institutional funds. Admitted students will be notified of awards on or about 4/1. Federal Work-Study Program available. Institutional employment available.

The Inside Word

Competition to gain admission to Mount Holyoke is tight but there are no defined cutoffs or scores; therefore, a strong academic record is a must. Transcripts are evaluated first for performance over time, and candidates should have taken a rigorous course load, complete with honors, AP, and/or IB classes. The college also values strong writing skills, so expect essays/personal statements and short answers to be closely assessed. While interviews are not required they are strongly recommended. Standardized tests are optional, but home-schooled and other students who feel that their application may need more traditional measurements are encouraged to submit scores.

THE SCHOOL SAYS

From the Admissions Office

"The majority of students who choose Mount Holyoke do so because it is an outstanding research liberal arts college. After a semester or two, they start to appreciate the distinctive advantages of a women's college, even though most never thought they'd attend a women's college when they started their college search. They appreciate the remarkable array of opportunities that are available—for academic achievement, career exploration, internships, study abroad, and leadership—and the impressive, creative accomplishments of their peers. If you're looking for a college that will challenge you to be your best, most powerful self and to fulfill your potential, Mount Holyoke should be at the top of your list.

"Submission of standardized test scores is optional for most applicants to Mount Holyoke College. However, the TOEFL is required of students whose primary language is not English."

SELECTIVITY

# of total applicants	4,619
% of total applicants accepted	38
% of total acceptees attending	30
# of in-state applicants	519
% of in-state applicants accepted	48
# of out-of-state-applicants	2,346
% of applicants accepted from out of state	50
# of international applicants	1,749
% of international applicants accepted	20
# of early decision applicants	411
% of early decision applicants accepted	51
# offered a place on the wait list	474
# admitted from wait list	9

First-Year Profile

Testing policy	Test Optional
Range SAT composite	1370–1490
Range SAT EBRW	700–760
Range SAT math	640–760
Range ACT composite	30–32
% submitting SAT scores	15
% submitting ACT scores	2
Average HS GPA	3.9
% submitting high school GPA	85
% graduated top 10% of class	49
% graduated top 25% of class	79
% graduated top 50% of class	98
% submitting high school rank	33

Important Dates

Early decision	
Apply by	11/15
Notified by	1/1
Other ED apply by	1/5
Other ED notified by	2/1
Regular	
Apply by	1/15
Notified by	4/1
Nonfall registration?	Yes

FINANCIAL FACTS

Annual tuition	$71,178
Food and housing	$21,596
Required fees	$272
Books and supplies	$1,000
Average need-based scholarship (First-year)	$58,046 ($60,742)
% students with need rec. need-based scholarship or grant aid (First-year)	100 (100)
% students with need rec. non-need-based scholarship or grant aid (First-year)	14 (21)
% students with need rec. need-based self-help aid (First-year)	92 (89)
% UG borrow to pay for school	64
Average cumulative indebtedness	$24,305
% of students with need fully met (First-year)	100 (100)
Average % of student need met (First-year)	100 (100)

Muhlenberg College

2400 West Chew Street, Allentown, PA 18104-5596 • Admissions: 484-664-3200

Survey Snapshot
Class discussions encouraged
Students are friendly
Theater is popular

RATINGS	
Quality of Life	81
Fire Safety	99
Green	95
Academic	84
Profs Interesting	90
Profs Accessible	92
Admissions	88
Financial Aid	89

CAMPUS LIFE

Type of school	Private
Affiliation	Lutheran
Environment	City

Students

Degree-seeking undergrad enrollment	1,648
% male/female/not reported	42/58/0
% from out of state	67
% First-year from public high school	71
% First-year live on campus	96
% Ugrads live on campus	84
# of fraternities (% join)	3 (19)
# of sororities (% join)	5 (25)
% Asian	4
% Black or African American	8
% Hispanic	14
% Native American	0
% Pacific Islander	0
% Race and/or ethnicity unknown	3
% Two or more races	4
% White	66
% International	1
# of countries represented	20

CAMPUS MENTAL HEALTH SERVICES

Offers mental health/wellness program	Yes
Mental health training available to students	Yes
Employs Chief Wellness Officer	Yes
Peer-to-peer mental health offerings	Yes
Counseling center has guidelines or accreditation	Yes
Mental health/well-being courses	Yes

ACADEMICS

% students returning for sophomore year	90
% students graduating within 4 years	68
% students graduating within 6 years	83
Calendar	Semester
Student/faculty ratio	8:1
Most common class size 10–19.	(55%)
Most common lab/discussion size 10–19.	(69%)

Most Popular Majors

Psychology; Drama and Dramatics/Theatre Arts; Finance

Applicants Often Prefer

Dickinson College, Ithaca College, New York University, Skidmore College

Applicants Sometimes Prefer

Franklin & Marshall College, Gettysburg College, Lafayette College, State University of New York—Binghamton University, Syracuse University

Applicants Rarely Prefer

Brandeis University, The College of New Jersey, Lehigh University, Rutgers University–New Brunswick

STUDENTS SAY "..."

Academics

Students who attend Muhlenberg College in Allentown, Pennsylvania are welcomed into a "close-knit" community and are privy to "a well-rounded liberal arts education." And while the academics are certainly "rigorous," undergraduates here love the fact it's "[not] a cutthroat atmosphere." Importantly, students have their pick of many terrific disciplines, from the "amazing theater department" to the "extremely strong" business and science programs. Undergrads are also happy to champion their "dedicated" professors who understand how to create and foster "engaging courses." They also value the fact that Muhlenberg instructors "really take the time to get to know you and answer your questions." As one satisfied student says, "My professors so far have all been amazing and truly want me to succeed." Finally, as an international studies and Spanish double major sums up, "Muhlenberg is a place where someone can pursue theater AND chemistry, play a varsity sport, AND lead a volunteer organization, work individually with a professor, AND befriend a dining services worker."

Campus Life

It's quite easy to lead a full and fulfilling life at Muhlenberg. To begin with, the "school offers tons of free activities over the weekends," from movie showings to bingo and game night. Undergrads here also love the college's strong performing arts scene. Indeed, "a cappella groups are very popular at Muhlenberg." Additionally, given "the large theater department," it's virtually guaranteed that "there's always a show in production." Sports are equally popular: "football and basketball games have good attendance records." While there's a modest amount of drinking, the college doesn't have a crazy party scene. As a biology major shares, "There's a few bars and clubs in the area that offer college nights on Thursdays, which is fun." Lastly, undergrads enjoy Allentown's public parks which provide "great areas to hike, explore, bird-watch, read or take a jog." And they periodically capitalize on Muhlenberg's relatively close proximity to both Philadelphia and New York.

Student Body

Students at Muhlenberg College are described as extremely "hardworking" and "friendly." A French and education double-major explains, "Most people are involved with many different aspects of campus life, and these aspects tend not to be 'cliquey' because of the crossover. For example, there are...football players who are members of a cappella groups or who take dance." Importantly, we're also told that "being nice is kind of important" at Muhlenberg. An English major somewhat sarcastically qualifies, "If someone doesn't hold the door open for the person behind them, they're basically made to wear a scarlet letter and deemed a pariah." The overall demographics have been changing over the last several years, but some students still describe a number of their peers as "white, upper-middle class, [and] from New Jersey." That said, students agree that there's no one fixed type; in fact: "There is a place for everyone on campus. We have a huge theater program, yet almost 30 percent of our school participates in athletics, so you can see there are all extremes and everything in between."

MUHLENBERG COLLEGE

Financial Aid: 484-664-3175 • E-Mail: admissions@muhlenberg.edu • Website: www.muhlenberg.edu

THE PRINCETON REVIEW SAYS

Admissions

The school reports that its standardized testing policy for use in admission for Fall 2026 is Test Optional. The Princeton Review suggests that interested applicants consult with the school for the most up-to-date standardized testing policies. *Very important factors considered include:* rigor of secondary school record, academic GPA, character/personal qualities. *Important factors considered include:* application essay, recommendation(s), interview, extracurricular activities, talent/ability, volunteer work, work experience. *Other factors considered include:* class rank, standardized test scores, first generation, alumni/ae relation, geographical residence, level of applicant's interest. High school diploma is required and GED is accepted. *Academic units required:* 4 English, 3 math, 2 science, 2 science labs, 2 language (other than English), 2 history, 1 academic elective. *Academic units recommended:* 4 English, 4 math, 3 science, 3 science labs, 4 language (other than English), 2 social studies, 2 history, 1 academic elective.

Financial Aid

Students should submit: FAFSA. Priority filing deadline is 2/1. The Princeton Review suggests that all financial aid forms be submitted as soon as possible. *Need-based scholarships/grants offered:* Federal Pell; Federal SEOG; State scholarships/grants; Private scholarships; College/university scholarship or grant aid from institutional funds. *Loan aid offered:* Federal Direct Subsidized Loans; Federal Direct Unsubsidized Loans; Direct PLUS loans. Admitted students will be notified of awards when they receive their admission decision. Federal Work-Study Program available. Institutional employment available.

The Inside Word

Muhlenberg's admissions officers take a holistic approach to evaluating each candidate, seeking students who will both thrive at the college and enrich its community. While a strong academic record remains the top priority, particularly rigorous performance in college preparatory coursework, the process extends well beyond grades and transcripts. Personal interviews are required for applicants to the academic partnership program with UPenn Dental, but Muhlenberg strongly encourages all prospective students to interview, viewing it as a valuable opportunity to connect with and get a better sense of the applicant.

THE SCHOOL SAYS

From the Admissions Office

"Listening to our own students, we've learned that many picked Muhlenberg for its unique combination of academic challenge and deep, individualized support. We expect a lot from our students, and we also expect a lot from ourselves. This ethos is embodied in several signature and graduate degree options, including an MBA. Muhlenberg's academic program emphasizes exploration and discovery, requires hands-on learning, and empowers students to make an immediate impact. The college's 360-degree coaching model offers personalized support. Every student works with three coaches—their academic advisor, a college life coach and a career coach—who help them understand and maximize their potential and navigate challenges. Professors are very accessible to students and encourage them to reach out with questions. "We really know about collegiality here," says an alumna who now works at Muhlenberg. "It's that kind of place." The supportive atmosphere and students' strong work ethic produce lots of successes. The pre-med and pre-law programs are very strong, with over 90% acceptance rates to medical, dental, and law school, as are programs in media and communications, theatre, psychology, the sciences, business, and accounting."

SELECTIVITY

# of total applicants	4,662
% of total applicants accepted	75
% of total acceptees attending	12
# of in-state applicants	1,039
% of in-state applicants accepted	77
# of out-of-state-applicants	3,235
% of applicants accepted from out of state	80
# of international applicants	379
% of international applicants accepted	24
# of early decision applicants	220
% of early decision applicants accepted	77
# offered a place on the wait list	0
# admitted from wait list	0

First-Year Profile

Testing policy	Test Optional
Range SAT composite	1260–1330
Range SAT EBRW	640–710
Range SAT math	610–700
Range ACT composite	29–33
% submitting SAT scores	16
% submitting ACT scores	6
Average HS GPA	3.5
% submitting high school GPA	100
% graduated top 10% of class	31
% graduated top 25% of class	58
% graduated top 50% of class	90
% submitting high school rank	31

Important Dates

Early decision	
Apply by	11/15
Notified by	12/15
Other ED apply by	2/1
Other ED notified by	2/15
Early action	
Apply by	12/1
Notified by	2/1
Regular	
Apply by	2/1
Notified by	3/15
Nonfall registration?	No

FINANCIAL FACTS

Annual tuition	$66,930
Food and housing	$15,758
Required fees	$830
Books and supplies	$1,600
Average need-based scholarship (First-year)	$49,220 ($49,143)
% students with need rec. need-based scholarship or grant aid (First-year)	98 (100)
% students with need rec. non-need-based scholarship or grant aid (First-year)	53 (33)
% students with need rec. need-based self-help aid (First-year)	91 (87)
% students rec. any financial aid (First-year)	100 (100)
% UG borrow to pay for school	68
Average cumulative indebtedness	$32,499
% of students with need fully met (First-year)	20 (18)
Average % of student need met (First-year)	86 (88)

Nazareth University

4245 East Avenue, Rochester, NY 14618-3790 • Admissions: 585-389-2860

Survey Snapshot
Easy to get around campus
Students love Rochester, NY
Internships are widely available

RATINGS

Quality of Life	87
Fire Safety	93
Green	60*
Academic	81
Profs Interesting	87
Profs Accessible	90
Admissions	86
Financial Aid	91

CAMPUS LIFE

Type of school	Private
Environment	Village

Students

Degree-seeking undergrad enrollment	1,852
% male/female/not reported	29/71/<1
% from out of state	15
% First-year from public high school	90
% First-year live on campus	86
% Ugrads live on campus	60
# of fraternities	0
# of sororities	0
% Asian	3
% Black or African American	6
% Hispanic	8
% Native American	<1
% Pacific Islander	0
% Race and/or ethnicity unknown	1
% Two or more races	4
% White	77
% International	1
# of countries represented	12

CAMPUS MENTAL HEALTH SERVICES

Offers mental health/wellness program	Yes
Mental health training available to students	Yes
Employs Chief Wellness Officer	Yes
Peer-to-peer mental health offerings	Yes
Counseling center has guidelines or accreditation	Yes
Mental health/well-being courses	Yes, for-credit

ACADEMICS

% students returning for sophomore year	85
% students graduating within 4 years	64
% students graduating within 6 years	73
Calendar	Semester
Student/faculty ratio	8:1
Most common class size 10–19.	(44%)
Most common lab/discussion size 1–9.	(45%)

Most Popular Majors

Education; Physical Therapy/Therapist; Business Administration, Management and Operations

Applicants Sometimes Prefer

Daemen College, Duquesne University, D'Youville College, Ithaca College, Keuka College, Rider University, St. Bonaventure University, St. John Fisher University, State University of New York–Brockport, State University of New York—Geneseo

STUDENTS SAY "..."

Academics

Nazareth University describes itself as "a learning community that purposefully integrates liberal arts and professional programs," one that offers a small student–faculty ratio and a commitment to shaping its undergraduate students through impactful learning and experiences. Students note that programs feel tailored to them, and that "Everything is meant to boost us." For instance, the school's therapy programs (occupational, physical, and speech) run clinics on campus, "where students provide therapy to community members under supervision." There are also "several places to receive tutoring," and students can avail themselves of the school's unique SPARK Grants, which award $1,500 to all qualified students to use for unpaid internships, research, and study abroad experiences. There's even an Alternative Breaks program, through which students can make the most of their time off with global and local projects that allow them to "live, learn, and serve alongside peers and community members." As a relatively small school, "the teacher-student relationships are very strong," and "office hours tend not to be super crowded...so one-on-one help is there." And because "classes are excellent," this makes them "extremely fruitful for students who engage with them deeply." Faculty members "are very understanding of circumstances that might come up,...are accessible outside of classroom instruction,...[and] provide a safe space for discussion and new questions." Nazareth helps students grow in and out of the classroom, no matter the topic; as one student puts it, "I don't think there have been any classes where we did not ever speak with the professor about life in general."

Campus Life

"It's always so gorgeous" at Nazareth, particularly for "walking in the beautiful trails on campus," which speaks to why, of the more than 50 student organizations, "clubs and events, specifically arts- and hiking-oriented, are very popular." This is also true for athletics, "with about 1/3 of the population being on a sports team" and engaging in "recreational athletics with friends," including basketball, pickleball, and volleyball. Students also point to the "many on-campus free events to attend," which include things like "grocery bingo, midnight breakfast, [and] relaxation night." In fact, the student government puts on so many "fun activities such as Springfest, Fun Fridays, and Wellness Wednesdays that help [students] feel more welcome and at home" that one student says the school never fails to keep students busy and entertained." Where students quibble is with the dining hall options, which with few exceptions are said to be "the same thing day in and day out, just prepared slightly different." That said, some areas like the school's café, Millie's, are praised as a "great comfortable area to relax and study," and there's nearby shopping and restaurants. All in all, Nazareth "offers a good number of things to do to make new friends along the way while keeping up with schoolwork."

Student Body

This "very welcoming and inclusive" community fosters a general sense of Naz nice, wherein "if you need help, it's almost guaranteed that it will [be] noticed and someone will help you." A student assures: "It is incredibly easy to make friends at Nazareth University," especially if you're artistic or athletic, which are two of the main categories that come up when describing the population, along with being academically strong. There's also a sense that "my peers believe in human rights and equality and stand with diversity." Many here "have jobs on campus, or off campus," and "many people are on sports teams." People "tend to be part of many different circles and know a wide variety of people," perhaps due to the "campus-wide events that make everyone at Naz feel like one big family." A student sums up, "Our campus is inclusive, welcoming, and provides support in so many ways."

Nazareth University

Financial Aid: 585-389-2310 • E-Mail: admissions@naz.edu • Website: www.naz.edu

THE PRINCETON REVIEW SAYS

Admissions

The school reports that its standardized testing policy for use in admission for Fall 2026 is Test Optional. The Princeton Review suggests that interested applicants consult with the school for the most up-to-date standardized testing policies. *Very important factors considered include:* rigor of secondary school record, academic GPA, recommendation(s). *Important factors considered include:* extracurricular activities, talent/ability, character/personal qualities, geographical residence, state residency, volunteer work, work experience, level of applicant's interest. *Other factors considered include:* class rank, standardized test scores, application essay, interview, first generation, alumni/ae relation. High school diploma is required and GED is accepted. *Academic units required:* 3 English, 3 math, 3 science, 1 science lab, 3 language (other than English), 3 social studies. *Academic units recommended:* 4 English, 4 math, 4 science, 4 language (other than English), 4 social studies.

Financial Aid

Students should submit: FAFSA; State aid form. Priority filing deadline is 2/15. The Princeton Review suggests that all financial aid forms be submitted as soon as possible. *Need-based scholarships/grants offered:* Federal Pell; Federal SEOG; State scholarships/grants; Private scholarships; College/university scholarship or grant aid from institutional funds. *Loan aid offered:* Federal Direct Subsidized Loans; Federal Direct Unsubsidized Loans; Direct PLUS loans. Admitted students will be notified of awards on a rolling basis beginning 2/1. Federal Work-Study Program available. Institutional employment available.

The Inside Word

Applicants to Nazareth are evaluated on a holistic model. Working hard to earn good grades and participating in extracurriculars or being involved with your community will help you stand out and move your application toward the "accepted" pile. The college has been Test Optional since 2008, but submitted scores will be considered alongside other components if you choose to send them along. They may also be used for scholarship opportunities.

THE SCHOOL SAYS

From the Admissions Office

"Nazareth University is the place to become a brave, bold changemaker, committed to progress and growth—within ourselves, within our professions, and for the good of our world. That is why our collective community is known for its strength of impact.

"Located on 150 wooded acres in the village of Pittsford, just outside Rochester, New York, we offer 60 programs of study in sought-after fields, including health professions, business, and the performing arts. We're proud to have 25 Division III athletic teams, over 400 student activities and events yearly, more than 50 student organizations, a 10:1 student-to-faculty ratio, and 39,000 vibrant alumni making a difference across the globe.

"Nazareth Golden Flyers believe in possibility and hope in their studies. It is the pursuit of ideas that propels our students forward, ever learning, ever innovating, until the passion behind those ideas makes us all feel unstoppable.

"Then, as our graduates charge into the world, there's a new and larger community where they will make a mark and give their all, with a confidence that can only come from clarity of task and superb preparation. We encourage everyone on campus to listen, learn, advocate, and innovate to create action constantly. Our students will actively bridge the world's differences and fractures and lead progress by inspiring people's life's work, no matter where it takes them.

"This is Nazareth University. Where changemakers learn to evolve and thrive."

SELECTIVITY

# of total applicants	5,947
% of total applicants accepted	74
% of total acceptees attending	15
# of in-state applicants	3,887
% of in-state applicants accepted	78
# of out-of-state-applicants	2,055
% of applicants accepted from out of state	66
# of international applicants	5
% of international applicants accepted	100
# of early decision applicants	68
% of early decision applicants accepted	75
# offered a place on the wait list	368
# admitted from wait list	5

First-Year Profile

Testing policy	Test Optional
Range SAT composite	1210–1340
Range SAT EBRW	620–680
Range SAT math	580–660
Range ACT composite	26–29
% submitting SAT scores	8
% submitting ACT scores	2
Average HS GPA	3.6
% submitting high school GPA	99
% graduated top 10% of class	24
% graduated top 25% of class	68
% graduated top 50% of class	87
% submitting high school rank	33

Important Dates

Early decision	
Apply by	11/1
Notified by	12/15
Early action	
Apply by	12/1
Notified by	1/1
Regular	
Apply by	2/1
Notified by	Rolling, 1/1
Nonfall registration?	Yes

FINANCIAL FACTS

Annual tuition	$43,630
Food and housing	$17,440
Required fees	$2,050
Books and supplies	$1,226
Average need-based scholarship (First-year)	$27,312 ($36,552)
% students with need rec. need-based scholarship or grant aid (First-year)	99 (99)
% students with need rec. non-need-based scholarship or grant aid (First-year)	16 (21)
% students with need rec. need-based self-help aid (First-year)	79 (77)
% students rec. any financial aid (First-year)	100 (100)
% UG borrow to pay for school	80
Average cumulative indebtedness	$50,473
% of students with need fully met (First-year)	26 (28)
Average % of student need met (First-year)	77 (81)

NEW COLLEGE OF FLORIDA

5800 Bay Shore Rd, Sarasota, FL 34243-2109 • Admissions: 941-487-5000

Survey Snapshot
Class discussions encouraged
Alumni active on campus
Active student government

RATINGS	
Quality of Life	76
Fire Safety	73
Green	60*
Academic	88
Profs Interesting	95
Profs Accessible	95
Admissions	87
Financial Aid	92

CAMPUS LIFE

Type of school	Public
Environment	Town

Students

Degree-seeking undergrad enrollment	856
% male/female/not reported	46/54/0
% from out of state	16
% First-year from public high school	62
% First-year live on campus	83
% Ugrads live on campus	72
# of fraternities	0
# of sororities	0
% Asian	2
% Black or African American	5
% Hispanic	18
% Native American	<1
% Pacific Islander	0
% Race and/or ethnicity unknown	<1
% Two or more races	5
% White	53
% International	16
# of countries represented	34

CAMPUS MENTAL HEALTH SERVICES

Offers mental health/wellness program	Yes
Mental health training available to students	Yes
Employs Chief Wellness Officer	No
Peer-to-peer mental health offerings	No
Counseling center has guidelines or accreditation	No
Mental health/well-being courses	Yes, for-credit

ACADEMICS

% students returning for sophomore year	79
% students graduating within 4 years	53
% students graduating within 6 years	62
Calendar	4-1-4
Student/faculty ratio	8:1
Most common class size 10–19.	(43%)

Most Popular Majors
Computer Science; Psychology; Economics

Applicants Often Prefer
Florida International University, University of Central Florida, University of Florida, University of South Florida

Applicants Sometimes Prefer
Florida Atlantic University, Florida Gulf Coast University, Florida State University

Applicants Rarely Prefer
Eckerd College, Mount Holyoke College, Rollins College, St. John's College (NM)

STUDENTS SAY "..."

Academics

New College of Florida is the state's public honors college, and students appreciate the school's signature, personalized curriculum. This begins with the Chart Your Course (CYC) curriculum, which pairs a student's academic interests with practical skillsets like teamwork and problem solving, and continues with a January Independent Study Period (ISP) on a topic of their choosing where they can research, create, or intern in a way that gives them the highly appreciated "opportunity to engage with community members and the endless possibilities of scholarships for internships and study abroad courses." The academic process culminates with a capstone project that "allows students an opportunity to focus on an area of academic growth and discipline that they can apply later in life (especially in graduate school)." As one student reports, "I've started my own business and so many of my peers have also done so for academic credit." This method, which provides "narrative evaluations instead of grades," helps engage students, as do the professors. "The research opportunities here are great because of how much professors involve undergraduate students in their research." This demonstration of "the respect the professors have for students and their opinions" is just another example of these "incredible professors who pour everything into their teaching and care a lot about the well-being of students." Those seeking "a massive amount of freedom" in their education are likely to have that wish granted.

Campus Life

With a prime waterfront location in the Sarasota area, "people use outdoor spaces a lot, including the bayfront or reading under the Banyan tree"; kayaking is also popular, as "it is always nice to go take a break from classes and connect with nature." The college is "a very small campus with a big sense community...[where] most students live on campus," and there are "multiple events throughout the year" to help students connect. On weekends there are "parties on campus, which are a wonderful and safe way to have fun," and there are "three large parties, typically referred to as 'Center of the Universe Parties' or COUPs...held annually, [where] students get to vote on the themes." There are also "a lot of sports/active clubs," to get involved in with students mentioning the "biggest ones" as rock climbing, court soccer, dance collective, and sailing. As befits the school's academic freedom, most "students are involved in many things at once."

Student Body

This honors college attracts "high-achieving, liberal leaning students that are very focused on academics and making an impact on the world around them." While students say that interest-wise, the school is "extremely diverse...we currently have it all," some students share their concerns regarding the recent ending of diversity, equity and inclusion programs in Florida. Still changes can be made: Every New College student is a senator in the student government, which means they "are able to join discussions on academic subjects, educational policy, and be elected as representatives to speak on behalf of student voices in those meetings." Students note that the school is "currently undergoing some changes to incorporate athletes, which has made things interesting," but one student seems confident that those changes won't affect "the integrity and reputation of our institution." Overall, this group is "open-minded and friendly, [and] always willing to say 'hi' or wave in the hallway."

NEW COLLEGE OF FLORIDA

Financial Aid: 941-487-5000 • E-Mail: admissions@ncf.edu • Website: www.ncf.edu

THE PRINCETON REVIEW SAYS

Admissions

The school reports that its standardized testing policy for use in admission for Fall 2026 will require applicants to submit either the SAT or ACT. The Princeton Review suggests that interested applicants consult with the school for the most up-to-date standardized testing policies. *Very important factors considered include:* rigor of secondary school record, academic GPA. *Important factors considered include:* standardized test scores, extracurricular activities, character/personal qualities. *Other factors considered include:* class rank, application essay, recommendation(s), talent/ability, first generation, geographical residence, state residency, volunteer work, work experience, level of applicant's interest. High school diploma is required and GED is accepted. *Academic units required:* 4 English, 4 math, 3 science, 2 science labs, 2 language (other than English), 3 social studies, 2 academic electives. *Academic units recommended:* 4 English, 4 math, 3 science, 2 science labs, 2 language (other than English), 3 social studies, 4 academic electives.

Financial Aid

Students should submit: FAFSA. Priority filing deadline is 2/1. The Princeton Review suggests that all financial aid forms be submitted as soon as possible. *Need-based scholarships/grants offered:* Federal Pell; Federal SEOG; State scholarships/grants; Private scholarships; College/university scholarship or grant aid from institutional funds. *Loan aid offered:* Federal Direct Subsidized Loans; Federal Direct Unsubsidized Loans; Direct PLUS loans. Admitted students will be notified of awards on a rolling basis beginning 3/15. Federal Work-Study Program available. Institutional employment available.

The Inside Word

New College isn't your typical public school. Freethinking students tend to thrive here, and the admissions staff knows that. Don't be afraid to showcase your individuality; it won't get you in here if your academics aren't top flight, but it certainly won't hurt you either.

THE SCHOOL SAYS

From the Admissions Office

"New College of Florida provides a unique, high-quality liberal arts education preparing graduates for an unpredictable world ahead. With over 50 academic concentrations, students choose from a wide variety of course work in the natural and social sciences and humanities. Our beautiful campus is located on Sarasota Bay, where students can take advantage of all that Florida's gulf coast has to offer.

"As a student at New College, you will work with your faculty advisor to design an individualized academic plan that includes both our broad core curriculum and challenging courses toward your specific degree. You will build an academic contract each semester with your faculty advisor and experience hands-on learning through mentorships, internships, and research projects—the kind of learning students don't typically experience until graduate school. Along with traditional courses, you'll explore new subjects through labs, tutorials, and Independent Study Projects (ISPs). Every New College degree culminates in a senior capstone project or thesis, which may be a research paper, film, or art exhibit that you design as your own grand finale.

"As in the real world, where performance evaluations are the norm, your professors will give you in-depth narrative evaluations on your performance in each class. Your coursework review highlights your success, shows your promise, and offers constructive critique on your opportunities to improve.

"We offer many of the benefits of a small, private liberal arts college experience: personalized curriculum, small classes, close student faculty relationships, individualized career planning, and graduate-level research opportunities. But, as one of Florida's affordable public schools, and offering generous scholarships—this is all available at a much lower cost."

SELECTIVITY

# of total applicants	1,674
% of total applicants accepted	64
% of total acceptees attending	17
# of in-state applicants	1,235
% of in-state applicants accepted	65
# of out-of-state-applicants	388
% of applicants accepted from out of state	58
# of international applicants	51
% of international applicants accepted	82
# offered a place on the wait list	6
# admitted from wait list	4

First-Year Profile

Testing policy	SAT or ACT Required
Range SAT composite	1120–1280
Range SAT EBRW	570–660
Range SAT math	540–640
Range ACT composite	22–27
% submitting SAT scores	74
% submitting ACT scores	38
Average HS GPA	4.0
% submitting high school GPA	100
% graduated top 10% of class	27
% graduated top 25% of class	60
% graduated top 50% of class	90
% submitting high school rank	56

Important Dates

Early action	
Apply by	12/1
Notified by	12/15
Regular	
Apply by	7/1
Notified by	11/1
Nonfall registration?	Yes

FINANCIAL FACTS

Annual in-state tuition	$6,724
Annual out-of-state tuition	$32,471
Food and housing	$14,534
Books and supplies	$1,200
Average need-based scholarship (First-year)	$16,640 ($15,116)
% students with need rec. need-based scholarship or grant aid (First-year)	97 (100)
% students with need rec. non-need-based scholarship or grant aid (First-year)	25 (30)
% students with need rec. need-based self-help aid (First-year)	61 (54)
% students rec. any financial aid (First-year)	97 (100)
% UG borrow to pay for school	33
Average cumulative indebtedness	$19,558
% of students with need fully met (First-year)	27 (34)
Average % of student need met (First-year)	100 (100)

NEW JERSEY INSTITUTE OF TECHNOLOGY

University Heights, Newark, NJ 07102 • Admissions: 973-596-3300

Survey Snapshot
Easy to get around campus
Recreation facilities are great
Diverse student types interact on campus

RATINGS

Quality of Life	**79**
Fire Safety	**95**
Green	**89**
Academic	**74**
Profs Interesting	**78**
Profs Accessible	**85**
Admissions	**89**
Financial Aid	**84**

CAMPUS LIFE

Type of school	Public
Environment	Metropolis

Students

Degree-seeking undergrad enrollment	9,209
% male/female/not reported	72/28/0
% from out of state	12
% First-year from public high school	90
% First-year live on campus	38
% Ugrads live on campus	25
# of fraternities (% join)	22 (5)
# of sororities (% join)	8 (4)
% Asian	20
% Black or African American	10
% Hispanic	29
% Native American	<1
% Pacific Islander	<1
% Race and/or ethnicity unknown	2
% Two or more races	3
% White	29
% International	6
# of countries represented	105

CAMPUS MENTAL HEALTH SERVICES

Offers mental health/wellness program	Yes
Mental health training available to students	Yes
Employs Chief Wellness Officer	NR
Peer-to-peer mental health offerings	No
Counseling center has guidelines or accreditation	Yes
Mental health/well-being courses	Yes, non-credit

ACADEMICS

% students returning for sophomore year	90
% students graduating within 4 years	49
% students graduating within 6 years	73
Calendar	Semester
Student/faculty ratio	16:1
Most common class size 20–29.	(37%)

Most Popular Majors

Computer and Information Sciences; Computer Engineering; Engineering Technologies/Technicians

Applicants Sometimes Prefer

Drexel University, Rutgers University–New Brunswick, Rutgers University—Newark, Stevens Institute of Technology

STUDENTS SAY "..."

Academics

Students at New Jersey Institute of Technology say "the classes and academic resources are great" and are overall pleased with "excellent academics for a low price" and its "reputation to connect me to a job and related career opportunities." There's a bit of a nuance among respondents, however: those who actively "work hard with the opportunities they find here so that they can pursue better careers and better lives" tend to have a better outlook than those who get stuck with a rough schedule or an unhelpful professor. All told, with more than 175 research institutes, centers, and specialized labs, most find NJIT to be "a great opportunity," particularly for those in tech or who "want to expand their horizons as a scientist, graduate student, or full-time researcher." The school's location and industry connections allow for "a lot of...internships and co-op experiences," and "many research positions [are] open to even first-year students." And "in terms of doing projects, this school is amazing: the makerspace is fantastic." Many students also "participate in undergraduate research opportunities and are working toward innovative, positively impactful, and/or sellable ideas." Most of the faculty at NJIT "are passionate about their subject [and] are extremely amazing," and "have years of industry experience and can convert that into useful real-world lessons." Courses emphasize practical application with "testing materials, designing systems, and analyzing real data rather than only learning theory," and "labs often involve using industry standard equipment." Overall, "the challenging curriculum, combined with motivated peers and hands-on learning, prepares students well for real-world engineering careers and professional success after graduation."

Campus Life

Academics are king, and "most days revolve around classes, labs, group projects, and studying." The campus is small enough that students "can walk from back-to-back classes and have time to spare to grab a coffee from the campus center in between." Students also "use recreational facilities like the gym for physical activities," as well as "a local climbing gym that's popular," although a few share frustration that because the school is commuter-driven, facilities like the library, dining hall, and dorms don't always get as much attention as they should. Students say the downtown Newark location is relatively safe—"I walk back from studio at 3 AM almost every day during finals and midterms and have never felt threatened"—although one student reports the occasional presence in the evening of "individuals who are not affiliated with the university lingering on campus and actively soliciting money." None of this gets in the way of campus events, whether that's Greek life—"[I] enjoyed both the social and philanthropic events"—or Student Common Hour, which is "a time during the week where students get together to participate [in] extracurricular activities" like Anime Club, Dice and Decks, and intramural sports. The school succeeds at finding ways "to bring students together from various departments under one activity they share in common."

Student Body

The makeup of NJIT "is very ethnically diverse; there are a lot of different backgrounds and lots of international students." This is "a great community of smart, intellectual, and driven students" that keeps busy but takes the time to "have fun... and intellectual conversations." The majority live off-campus, and several say they wish more could be done in terms of scheduling so commuters don't "get stuck on campus for hours [while] people who live on campus can return to their dorm and rest." People tend to be "very technical-minded and detail-oriented," but those who look can find a "group of like-minded people who strive for the best." A student says optimistically, "There is opportunity to take your life in any direction you please, both social and professionally, at this school as long as you take the steps to pursue it."

NEW JERSEY INSTITUTE OF TECHNOLOGY

Financial Aid: 973-596-3479 • E-Mail: admissions@njit.edu • Website: www.njit.edu

THE PRINCETON REVIEW SAYS

Admissions

The school reports that its standardized testing policy for use in admission for Fall 2026 is Test Optional. The Princeton Review suggests that interested applicants consult with the school for the most up-to-date standardized testing policies. *Very important factors considered include:* rigor of secondary school record, academic GPA. *Important factors considered include:* class rank. *Other factors considered include:* standardized test scores, application essay, recommendation(s), extracurricular activities, talent/ability, character/personal qualities, alumni/ae relation, geographical residence, state residency, level of applicant's interest. High school diploma is required and GED is accepted. *Academic units required:* 4 English, 4 math, 2 science, 2 science lab. *Academic units recommended:* 2 language (other than English), 1 social studies, 1 history, 2 academic electives.

Financial Aid

Students should submit: FAFSA. Priority filing deadline is 2/15. The Princeton Review suggests that all financial aid forms be submitted as soon as possible. *Need-based scholarships/grants offered:* Federal Pell; Federal SEOG; State scholarships/grants; Private scholarships; College/university scholarship or grant aid from institutional funds. *Loan aid offered:* Federal Direct Subsidized Loans; Federal Direct Unsubsidized Loans; Direct PLUS loans; State Loans. Admitted students will be notified of awards on a rolling basis. Federal Work-Study Program available. Institutional employment available.

The Inside Word

Admission officers at NJIT look for innovative applicants who are committed to their academic success and have dreams of a compelling future career. A solid GPA, improved grade trends, and advanced coursework will help make your case. Additionally, while the school remains Test Optional, good test scores can also assist you on your road to acceptance. Equally important are your extracurriculars. Those who also pursue their passions, illustrate a go-getter attitude, and get involved stand the best chance of admission.

THE SCHOOL SAYS

From the Admissions Office

"Talented high school graduates from across the nation come to NJIT to prepare for leadership roles in architecture, business, engineering, medical, legal, science, and technological fields. Students experience a public research university conducting over $160 million in research that maintains a small-college atmosphere at a modest cost. Our attractive forty-five-acre campus is just minutes from New York City and less than an hour from the Jersey shore. Students find an outstanding faculty and a safe, diverse, and caring learning and residential community. NJIT's academic environment challenges and prepares students for rewarding careers and full-time advanced study after graduation. The campus is computing-intensive."

SELECTIVITY

# of total applicants	15,607
% of total applicants accepted	65
% of total acceptees attending	34
# of in-state applicants	9,984
% of in-state applicants accepted	69
# of out-of-state-applicants	4,030
% of applicants accepted from out of state	64
# of international applicants	1,593
% of international applicants accepted	45
# offered a place on the wait list	3,621
# admitted from wait list	827

First-Year Profile

Testing policy	Test Optional
Range SAT composite	1240–1340
Range SAT EBRW	610–710
Range SAT math	630–760
Range ACT composite	28–31
% submitting SAT scores	40
% submitting ACT scores	3
Average HS GPA	3.7
% submitting high school GPA	85
% graduated top 10% of class	30
% graduated top 25% of class	57
% graduated top 50% of class	89
% submitting high school rank	37

Important Dates

Early action	
Apply by	11/15
Notified by	12/15
Regular	
Apply by	3/1
Notified by	Rolling, 11/15
Nonfall registration?	Yes

FINANCIAL FACTS

Annual in-state tuition	$17,312
Annual out-of-state tuition	$36,062
Food and housing	$16,450
Required fees	$3,850
Books and supplies	$2,900
Average need-based scholarship (First-year)	$16,885 ($17,780)
% students with need rec. need-based scholarship or grant aid (First-year)	97 (98)
% students with need rec. non-need-based scholarship or grant aid (First-year)	5 (8)
% students with need rec. need-based self-help aid (First-year)	48 (37)
% students rec. any financial aid (First-year)	69 (89)
% UG borrow to pay for school	50
Average cumulative indebtedness	$32,459
% of students with need fully met (First-year)	9 (10)
Average % of student need met (First-year)	57 (58)

New York University

70 Washington Square South, New York, NY 10012 • Admissions: 212-998-4500

Survey Snapshot
Students love New York, NY
Great off-campus food
Great library

RATINGS

Quality of Life	84
Fire Safety	99
Green	97
Academic	84
Profs Interesting	87
Profs Accessible	87
Admissions	98
Financial Aid	85

CAMPUS LIFE

Type of school	Private
Environment	Metropolis

Students

Degree-seeking undergrad enrollment	29,046
% male/female/not reported	42/58/0
% from out of state	65
% First-year live on campus	82
% Ugrads live on campus	38
# of fraternities (% join)	19 (2)
# of sororities (% join)	11 (6)
% Asian	25
% Black or African American	6
% Hispanic	11
% Native American	<1
% Pacific Islander	<1
% Race and/or ethnicity unknown	4
% Two or more races	5
% White	23
% International	26
# of countries represented	128

CAMPUS MENTAL HEALTH SERVICES

Offers mental health/wellness program	Yes
Mental health training available to students	Yes
Employs Chief Wellness Officer	Yes
Peer-to-peer mental health offerings	Yes
Counseling center has guidelines or accreditation	Yes
Mental health/well-being courses	Yes, for-credit

ACADEMICS

% students returning for sophomore year	96
% students graduating within 4 years	74
% students graduating within 6 years	88
Calendar	Semester
Student/faculty ratio	8:1
Most common class size 10–19.	(43%)
Most common lab/discussion size 10–19.	(36%)

Most Popular Majors

Liberal Arts and Sciences/Liberal Studies; Drama and Dramatics/Theatre Arts; Business/Commerce

STUDENTS SAY "..."

Academics

Regardless of which of the prestigious schools under the New York University banner students attend, the consensus is that there's "unparalleled access to global industries, cultural experiences, internships, and networking opportunities. Whether you're into finance, arts, media, or tech, being in NYC puts you right in the action." Students note an accordingly high academic rigor that requires "you to spend extra study time on your own or even require outside resources like the University Learning center," but that while hard, the classes are fair: "I am able to score well and learn as long as I attend class and study for exams." The school's "huge scale and diversity" lets it offer everything from "pre-professional pursuits at hospitals or investment firms," and "the ability to take courses at the other colleges [within the university]," to "multidisciplinary projects that emphasize innovative and research-active education." It's a huge benefit to have "very intelligent, professional leaders as professors. It encourages me to engage with the material and is an opportunity to connect with the field." This is also true of "NYU's vast network and strong industry ties" with faculty that "are all experts in their fields," which make it "a great place to launch a career in various fields." Students also point to the benefit of being "able to visit the museums and exhibitions that hold the very things we are studying in class." Many courses "have integrated field trips within them, such as a class that I am currently taking which is called urban waterfront development," and a "sophomore year Environmental Science class [that] went kayaking on the Hudson piers, we went to a cemetery, we went to a recycling/landfill center, and to the Brooklyn botanical garden." NYU offers a broad, concurrent professional experience that provides students with direct access to working television show creators, ground-breaking environmental scientists, business leaders, and more.

Campus Life

New York University students consider New York City an extension of the university: "A buzzing city as our campus." Going to school in NYC "allows you to leave the bubble of wherever you came from" gain independence and provide "opportunities and resources that can help us to explore ourselves and succeed beyond academic goals," which may make housing that some consider to be "excessively expensive" easier to bear. It helps that "the night-life in NYC is unbeatable" and there are infinite things to do in the city, "whatever you're interested in, it is available." And while the school's sprawl can sometimes make it "hard to feel like a community," students note that there are a "plethora of clubs"—American Sign Language (ASL), philosophy, investment, music, fashion, cheese, entrepreneurship, intramural sports, volunteer work, and so many more—to actively connect students and build community.

Student Body

"Intelligent and motivated students of many different backgrounds" gather at NYU to study, and multiculturalism is an often-repeated theme. "The peers I have at NYU are probably the most diverse group of friends I have ever had in my life.... I feel that in NYU people are more open in making friends outside of their comfort zone." Students learn from their differences and relish their commonalities, sharing that their peers are "ambitious and creative," "motivated and hardworking,...very passionate about what they study and competitive in classes," and "very studious." While some respondents expressed concern that the student body is "super polarized," and that wealth disparities and privilege play a role in that, most saw their contrasts in culture and background as inherent growth opportunities and felt fundamentally "comfortable and respected" by their peers.

NEW YORK UNIVERSITY

E-Mail: admissions@nyu.edu • Website: www.nyu.edu

THE PRINCETON REVIEW SAYS

Admissions

The school reports that its standardized testing policy for use in admission for Fall 2026 is Test Optional. The Princeton Review suggests that interested applicants consult with the school for the most up-to-date standardized testing policies. *Very important factors considered include:* rigor of secondary school record, academic GPA, application essay, recommendation(s), character/personal qualities. *Important factors considered include:* standardized test scores. *Other factors considered include:* extracurricular activities, talent/ability, first generation, geographical residence, volunteer work, work experience, level of applicant's interest. High school diploma is required and GED is accepted. *Academic units required:* 4 English, 3 math, 3 science, 3 science labs, 3 language (other than English), 3 social studies. *Academic units recommended:* 4 English, 4 math, 4 science, 4 science labs, 4 language (other than English), 4 social studies.

Financial Aid

The Princeton Review suggests that all financial aid forms be submitted as soon as possible. Federal Work-Study Program available. Institutional employment available.

The Inside Word

Undergraduates can apply to more than one of NYU's degree-granting campuses. If you are interested in the New York campus, you must also apply to one of NYU's undergraduate schools and colleges: the College of Arts and Science; the Tandon School of Engineering; the Liberal Studies Program; the Stern School of Business; Meyers College of Nursing; the Gallatin School of Individualized Study; the Silver School of Social Work; the Steinhardt School of Culture, Education, and Human Development; the Tisch School of the Arts; or the School of Professional Studies. This is different from the application process at some universities and obviously requires some forethought. Remember that this is a highly competitive university; if your application doesn't reflect a serious interest in your intended area of study, your chances of gaining admission will be diminished. NYU's Test Optional policy is more flexible than most. If you choose to submit test scores, NYU accepts SAT, ACT, IB, AP, GCE, and many international exams.

THE SCHOOL SAYS

From the Admissions Office

"NYU is about connections. We connect your classroom to the real world and connect our students to limitless opportunities. That's why NYU has become one of the most influential universities in the world with degree-granting campuses in New York, Abu Dhabi, and Shanghai along with 12 global academic centers and research programs in more than 25 countries. Our expansive global network directly serves our students by allowing a uniquely rich academic experience led by renowned faculty with accolades ranging from the Nobel Prize and MacArthur Genius Grant to Emmy, Oscar, and Grammy Awards. But our community is more than a list of cities and fancy awards. Since our beginning in 1831, we've been champions of diversity, access, and inclusion, creating one of the most diverse student bodies on Earth with no single ethnic majority and students from over 150 countries. NYU is for bridge builders; for the bold, the curious, the innovative, for those that feel compelled to bridge divides and find common ground because no one is better positioned to do so. For more than 190 years, we have produced some of the brightest minds, ground-breaking research, and most influential people capable of being comfortable anywhere and effective everywhere."

SELECTIVITY

# of total applicants	114,125
% of total applicants accepted	9
% of total acceptees attending	55

First-Year Profile

Testing policy	Test Optional
Range SAT composite	1480–1550
Range SAT EBRW	730–770
Range SAT math	750–790
Range ACT composite	34–35
% submitting SAT scores	27
% submitting ACT scores	10
Average HS GPA	3.8
% submitting high school GPA	100

Important Dates

Early decision	
Apply by	11/1
Notified by	12/15
Other ED apply by	1/1
Other ED notified by	2/15
Regular	
Apply by	1/5
Notified by	4/1
Nonfall registration?	Yes

FINANCIAL FACTS

Annual tuition	$65,622
Food and housing	$24,376
Books and supplies	$1,470
% students rec. any financial aid (First-year)	30 (29)

North Carolina State University

1210 Varsity Drive, Raleigh, NC 27695 • Admissions: 919-515-2434

Survey Snapshot
Recreation facilities are great
Great library
Frats and sororities are popular

RATINGS	
Quality of Life	84
Fire Safety	99
Green	98
Academic	81
Profs Interesting	82
Profs Accessible	91
Admissions	92
Financial Aid	87

CAMPUS LIFE

Type of school	Public
Environment	Metropolis

Students

Degree-seeking undergrad enrollment	28,344
% male/female/not reported	51/49/0
% from out of state	11
% First-year from public high school	85
% First-year live on campus	97
% Ugrads live on campus	36
# of fraternities (% join)	29 (11)
# of sororities (% join)	22 (15)
% Asian	10
% Black or African American	6
% Hispanic	10
% Native American	<1
% Pacific Islander	<1
% Race and/or ethnicity unknown	1
% Two or more races	5
% White	65
% International	2
# of countries represented	100

CAMPUS MENTAL HEALTH SERVICES

Offers mental health/wellness program	Yes
Mental health training available to students	Yes
Employs Chief Wellness Officer	Yes
Peer-to-peer mental health offerings	Yes
Counseling center has guidelines or accreditation	Yes
Mental health/well-being courses	Yes, for-credit

ACADEMICS

% students returning for sophomore year	94
% students graduating within 4 years	65
% students graduating within 6 years	85
Calendar	Semester
Student/faculty ratio	16:1
Most common class size 20–29.	(28%)
Most common lab/discussion size 20–29.	(38%)

Most Popular Majors

Engineering; Biology/Biological Sciences; Business Administration and Management

Applicants Also Look At

Clemson University, University of Florida, University of North Carolina at Chapel Hill, University of South Carolina—Columbia, Virginia Tech

STUDENTS SAY "..."

Academics

Students who pursue their education at North Carolina State University will find a "very welcoming" environment, one filled with a variety of "programs to help you succeed." The university offers "strong academics" across a wide range of disciplines, "from the highly ranked engineering school to the textiles school to the life sciences school." Undergrads also benefit from coursework that emphasizes "research opportunities," "creative projects," and "real life applications." For example, "the NC State civil engineering department has a cool driving simulator that they use to test out new interchange designs." And the business school offers "entrepreneurship initiatives...that help students turn ideas into real startups." By and large, undergrads also give their professors high marks, noting that they typically "prioritize communication with students and are easily accessible outside of class." Students also emphasize that it's easy to find help should you need it. As this undergrad elaborates, "We have a free tutoring program...free therapy, and there [are] so many different places to study and decompress!" Overall, "the academic experience feels challenging but super rewarding."

Campus Life

Life at North Carolina State is "a good mix of busy and fun" where "people spend a lot of time studying or working on projects during the week, but there's always something social happening too." Just strolling around, you're likely to see "skateboarders practicing tricks [or] people making art on the free expression tunnel." That's why some students have expressed concern about current construction, which has made the campus "difficult to navigate." Importantly, athletics are quite big, and you'll frequently find students heading "to Carmichael gym, playing intramural sports, [or] attending NCSU athletic events." One undergrad explains, "Everyone tries to get student tickets to football and men's basketball games, and our women's basketball team and our men's soccer teams are also very popular." Additionally, students highlight the wonderful Wellness and Recreation Department, which "organizes all sorts of things, including backpacking trips and spring break trips." Of course, you don't need to be sporty or outdoorsy to get involved; the university offers a range of clubs catering to a wide variety of interests: "We have a great many, from Ballroom Dancing, to Beekeeping, to App Development...and political clubs. [There's even a] club dedicated to giving out flowers to student passersby." When the weekend rolls around, lots of "people go to the frats or bars, or to different schools to see their friends." Rest assured that "there's always something going on, so it's easy to find stuff that fits your vibe."

Student Body

Undergraduates at NC State have high esteem for their peers who, in addition to being "really friendly and [having] great school spirit," are described as "good people [who] make you feel right at home." Students also appreciate that, along with "a ton of hometown North Carolinians," you can meet classmates "from all corners of the planet." As this impressed undergrad shares, "My closest friend my [first] year was from Kazakhstan, my coworker at my student job is from Iraq, I know several people from India, China, Korea, and Malaysia." Students welcome this diversity, noting that "everyone brings their own vibe, and it makes campus feel welcoming and full of personality." They also note that you'll find that "queer orgs thrive right alongside religious organizations of all denominations and faiths." In short, NCSU has "very supportive" students who are "easy to talk to and fun to be around" and who tend to "treat those around them with great kindness." It's a school where "everyone is smart, but the atmosphere doesn't feel competitive, everyone collaborates and wants to help each other."

North Carolina State University

Financial Aid: 919-515-2421 • E-Mail: undergrad-admissions@ncsu.edu • Website: www.ncsu.edu

THE PRINCETON REVIEW SAYS

Admissions

While the school reports that its standardized testing policy for Fall 2026 is Test Optional, applicants with a weighted high school GPA below 2.8 must submit an ACT or SAT score. *Very important factors considered include:* rigor of secondary school record, academic GPA. *Important factors considered include:* class rank. *Other factors considered include:* standardized test scores, application essay, recommendation(s), extracurricular activities, talent/ability, character/personal qualities, first generation, geographical residence, state residency, volunteer work, work experience. High school diploma is required and GED is accepted. *Academic units required:* 4 English, 4 math, 3 science, 1 science lab, 1 social studies, 1 history, 2 academic electives.

Financial Aid

Students should submit: FAFSA. Priority filing deadline is 3/1. The Princeton Review suggests that all financial aid forms be submitted as soon as possible. *Need-based scholarships/grants offered:* Federal Pell; Federal SEOG; State scholarships/grants; Private scholarships; College/university scholarship or grant aid from institutional funds; United Negro College Fund. *Loan aid offered:* Federal Direct Subsidized Loans; Federal Direct Unsubsidized Loans; Direct PLUS loans; State Loans; College/university loans from institutional funds. Admitted students will be notified of awards on a rolling basis beginning 4/1. Federal Work-Study Program available. Institutional employment available.

The Inside Word

As one of the nation's top research universities, NC State maintains a competitive admissions process. Successful applicants take a rigorous course load and often have a B-plus average or better. Admissions officers also closely weigh GPA, class rank and rigor of secondary school record. Extracurricular activities, while helpful, factor less heavily into admission decisions.

THE SCHOOL SAYS

From the Admissions Office

"Students choose NC State University for its strong and varied academic programs, national reputation for excellence, and friendly atmosphere. The university is consistently rated as a best value in North Carolina. NC State is in Raleigh, the capital of the state, and is minutes away from the nationally known Research Triangle Park which provides access to unlimited internships and co-op opportunities. NC State degrees earn the top return on student investment among North Carolina's public universities, and job recruiters rate our alumni among the top 20 most attractive job candidates in the country. Our students thrive with the benefits of a large school but love the tight-knit feel of our community. NC State offers more than 100 majors and 120 minors, over 600 clubs and organizations, and the opportunity to study abroad and engage in research so students have the opportunity to explore all their interests. Members of the Wolfpack aren't only successful—they're passionate. With 21 Division I sports and lifelong traditions, NC State students feel the power of the Pack from the roaring stadiums to the support on campus to the strong network of alumni. Once you're part of the Pack, you're a member for life."

SELECTIVITY

# of total applicants	49,351
% of total applicants accepted	40
% of total acceptees attending	30
# of in-state applicants	24,140
% of in-state applicants accepted	46
# of out-of-state-applicants	21,853
% of applicants accepted from out of state	25
# of international applicants	3,358
% of international applicants accepted	34
# offered a place on the wait list	10,710
# admitted from wait list	476

First-Year Profile

Testing policy	Test Optional !
Range SAT composite	1310–1440
Range SAT EBRW	650–720
Range SAT math	660–730
Range ACT composite	28–32
% submitting SAT scores	11
% submitting ACT scores	29
Average HS GPA	3.8
% submitting high school GPA	98
% graduated top 10% of class	40
% graduated top 25% of class	77
% graduated top 50% of class	96
% submitting high school rank	75

Important Dates

Early action	
Apply by	11/1
Notified by	1/30
Regular	
Apply by	6/1
Notified by	3/30
Nonfall registration?	Yes

FINANCIAL FACTS*

Annual in-state tuition	$6,535
Annual out-of-state tuition	$31,500
Food and housing	$14,741
Required fees	$2,493
Books and supplies	$624
Average need-based scholarship (First-year)	$14,743 ($14,983)
% students with need rec. need-based scholarship or grant aid (First-year)	98 (99)
% students with need rec. non-need-based scholarship or grant aid (First-year)	9 (10)
% students with need rec. need-based self-help aid (First-year)	55 (56)
% students rec. any financial aid (First-year)	59 (67)
% UG borrow to pay for school	44
Average cumulative indebtedness	$25,393
% of students with need fully met (First-year)	16 (16)
Average % of student need met (First-year)	75 (75)

! Test Optional if you have a GPA of 2.8 or higher.
* Most recently reported data at time of printing. Scan the QR code to find the latest updates.

Northeastern University

360 Huntington Avenue, Boston, MA 02115 • Admissions: 617-373-8780

Survey Snapshot
Career services are great
Internships are widely available
Students love Boston, MA

RATINGS

Quality of Life	85
Fire Safety	91
Green	96
Academic	83
Profs Interesting	85
Profs Accessible	88
Admissions	98
Financial Aid	89

CAMPUS LIFE

Type of school	Private
Environment	Metropolis

Students

Degree-seeking undergrad enrollment	22,386
% male/female/not reported	44/56/<1
% from out of state	70
% First-year live on campus	98
% Ugrads live on campus	45
# of fraternities (% join)	NR (12)
# of sororities (% join)	NR (20)
% Asian	25
% Black or African American	4
% Hispanic	10
% Native American	<1
% Pacific Islander	<1
% Race and/or ethnicity unknown	2
% Two or more races	7
% White	39
% International	13
# of countries represented	107

CAMPUS MENTAL HEALTH SERVICES

Offers mental health/wellness program	Yes
Mental health training available to students	Yes
Employs Chief Wellness Officer	NR
Peer-to-peer mental health offerings	NR
Counseling center has guidelines or accreditation	No
Mental health/well-being courses	NR

ACADEMICS

% students returning for sophomore year	97
% students graduating within 6 years	91
Calendar	Semester
Student/faculty ratio	15:1
Most common class size 10–19.	(38%)
Most common lab/discussion size 30–39.	(60%)

Most Popular Majors

Engineering; Health Professions and Related Programs; Business Administration, Management and Operations

STUDENTS SAY "…"

Academics

Founded in 1898, Northeastern University is an old Boston stalwart, but its "globally-minded and career-focused" approach to education is as current as ever. The school's focus on experiential learning is never more apparent than in the co-op programs, which have been around for more than 100 years. In these, students alternate rigorous classes with full-time work in career-related jobs for six months (during which they do not pay tuition and are often paid), providing "an open-minded, explorative environment where real-life work experience...combined with top-level academics to provide the best preparation possible for students post-college." Often, students receive job offers from previous co-op employers upon graduation. "My overall academic experience has been pretty grueling but completely worth it," says one satisfied student of the "strong academics in conjunction with a reasonable and healthy atmosphere."

On top of the "strong academic pipeline to university-cultivated co-ops and jobs," students benefit from professors who are "passionate about the subject and about you learning the subject." While students admit that there are a handful of "not-so-great professors," they say "the ones that are great, however, are fabulous," elaborating that "they always offer help or ways to give you experience, are there for you in and outside the classroom, and are extremely intelligent." Students love how encouraging both the university and the faculty are, pushing students to study abroad, do a dialogue (a Northeastern global/international summer program that focuses on critical current issues), or complete an international co-op—"anything to experience another culture and be fully emerged in it," one student notes. Different majors benefit from unique integration of their programs with co-op learning, and the way that Northeastern "[marries] theory with practicality," no matter the course of study, is a huge benefit to students throughout their post-graduate lives.

Campus Life

There is certainly no lack of activities in which to participate in nearby Boston (there are four T stops on campus), from movie theaters, museums, restaurants, and shopping malls to the Prudential Center and the Charles River, which "provides opportunities for running, walking, biking, [and] kayaking." One student happily notes that "our location means that I can get dumplings in Chinatown, see a show, or attend the Christmas tree lighting without much effort to get off campus." Weekends are traditionally for city exploring, and weekdays usually are filled with people participating in one of the many clubs the school offers. Plus, Northeastern has "a ton of amazing events and programs on campus that make the campus feel like a community." Students on co-op "tend to have a lot more free time at night and on the weekends, allowing them to get more involved and spend more time with friends." Still, life outside of school is "pretty substantial" for this "extremely social" crowd: Mission Hill is a popular spot for a Friday and Saturday night activities. Greek life is small but "becoming more popular" on campus.

Student Body

Northeastern is "both incredibly diverse as well as being a quintessential New England school." This environment is filled with many people from different backgrounds (including a sizable international population), and "it's not unusual to hear ten languages in ten minutes walking across campus." People are "motivated and passionate about the issues or projects they care about" and "are implementing and rolling with those ideas." No one here is cookie-cutter in any way, as "everyone has their quirks and qualities that shine through." All are "very supportive and seem to genuinely care about each other," which is useful since the nature of the school requires quite a few independent student decisions and those who go here "quickly have to become an adult and take charge of [their] life."

Northeastern University

Financial Aid: 617-373-3190 • E-Mail: admissions@northeastern.edu • Website: www.northeastern.edu

THE PRINCETON REVIEW SAYS

Admissions

The school reports that its standardized testing policy for use in admission for Fall 2026 is Test Optional. The Princeton Review suggests that interested applicants consult with the school for the most up-to-date standardized testing policies. *Very important factors considered include:* rigor of secondary school record, academic GPA, standardized test scores, recommendation(s). *Important factors considered include:* extracurricular activities, talent/ability, character/personal qualities, volunteer work, work experience. *Other factors considered include:* class rank, application essay, first generation, geographical residence, level of applicant's interest. High school diploma is required and GED is accepted. *Academic units required:* 4 English, 3 math, 3 science, 2 science labs, 2 language (other than English), 3 social studies, 2 history. *Academic units recommended:* 4 math, 4 science, 4 science labs, 4 language (other than English), 4 social studies.

Financial Aid

Students should submit: FAFSA; CSS PROFILE. Priority filing deadline is 2/15. The Princeton Review suggests that all financial aid forms be submitted as soon as possible. *Need-based scholarships/grants offered:* Federal Pell; Federal SEOG; State scholarships/grants; Private scholarships; College/university scholarship or grant aid from institutional funds. *Loan aid offered:* Federal Direct Subsidized Loans; Federal Direct Unsubsidized Loans; Direct PLUS loans; State Loans. Admitted students will be notified of awards on or about 4/1. Federal Work-Study Program available. Institutional employment available.

The Inside Word

Due to the huge number of applicants, Northeastern has an acceptance rate of only 5 percent. Therefore, your application needs to stand out from the crowd. Top grades are important and emphasis is given to the difficulty of courses you pursued—you should go beyond minimum high school graduation requirements to show broad intellectual curiosity. The admission committee recommends having strong standardized test scores, if submitting. Both the Common Application and the Coalition Application are accepted.

THE SCHOOL SAYS

From the Admissions Office

"There's a certain energy about Northeastern University. It comes from our bright, ambitious students, exhibiting a strong sense of purpose in the classroom and while working or studying abroad. In the heart of Boston—the ultimate college city—and across the globe, Northeastern students challenge themselves intellectually, investigate career options, participate in community service, and graduate both personally and professionally prepared for their future careers and graduate school. A Northeastern education is like no other, integrating rigorous classroom learning with real-world experiences—through opportunities to study, work, research, and serve on seven continents. Our students learn how to apply their knowledge, to solve problems, and to make a difference in the world—before they graduate."

SELECTIVITY

# of total applicants	105,257
% of total applicants accepted	6
% of total acceptees attending	46
# of early decision applicants	5,404
% of early decision applicants accepted	35

First-Year Profile

Testing policy	Test Optional
Range SAT composite	1440–1510
Range SAT EBRW	710–750
Range SAT math	720–780
Range ACT composite	33–34
% submitting SAT scores	22
% submitting ACT scores	8
Average HS GPA	4.2
% submitting high school GPA	100
% graduated top 10% of class	40
% graduated top 25% of class	70
% graduated top 50% of class	98
% submitting high school rank	7

Important Dates

Early decision	
Apply by	11/1
Notified by	1/1
Other ED apply by	1/1
Other ED notified by	3/1
Early action	
Apply by	11/1
Notified by	2/15
Regular	
Apply by	1/1
Notified by	4/1
Nonfall registration?	Yes

FINANCIAL FACTS

Annual tuition	$67,990
Food and housing	$22,048
Required fees	$1,299
Books and supplies	$1,000
Average need-based scholarship (First-year)	$44,807 ($58,707)
% students with need rec. need-based scholarship or grant aid (First-year)	96 (99)
% students with need rec. non-need-based scholarship or grant aid (First-year)	19 (32)
% students with need rec. need-based self-help aid (First-year)	70 (75)
% UG borrow to pay for school	44
Average cumulative indebtedness	$32,461
% of students with need fully met (First-year)	24 (100)
Average % of student need met (First-year)	87 (100)

Northwestern University

633 Clark Street, Evanston, IL 60208 • Admissions: 847-491-7271

Survey Snapshot
Great financial aid
Theater is popular
Campus newspaper is popular

RATINGS

Quality of Life	78
Fire Safety	81
Green	60*
Academic	89
Profs Interesting	88
Profs Accessible	92
Admissions	99
Financial Aid	96

CAMPUS LIFE

Type of school	Private
Environment	City

Students

Degree-seeking undergrad enrollment	8,811
% male/female/not reported	46/54/<1
% from out of state	73
% First-year from public high school	65
% First-year live on campus	99
% Ugrads live on campus	95
# of fraternities (% join)	NR
# of sororities (% join)	NR
% Asian	22
% Black or African American	7
% Hispanic	15
% Native American	<1
% Pacific Islander	<1
% Race and/or ethnicity unknown	4
% Two or more races	8
% White	34
% International	11
# of countries represented	105

CAMPUS MENTAL HEALTH SERVICES

Offers mental health/wellness program	Yes
Mental health training available to students	No
Employs Chief Wellness Officer	NR
Peer-to-peer mental health offerings	NR
Counseling center has guidelines or accreditation	No
Mental health/well-being courses	NR

ACADEMICS

% students returning for sophomore year	99
% students graduating within 4 years	86
% students graduating within 6 years	95
Calendar	Quarter
Student/faculty ratio	6:1
Most common class size 1–9.	(39%)
Most common lab/discussion size 10–19.	(50%)

Most Popular Majors
Engineering; Economics; Journalism

STUDENTS SAY "..."

Academics

Students enthuse that Northwestern University "has everything," including "nationally acclaimed programs for almost anything anyone could be interested in, from engineering to theater to journalism to music." With such a diverse array of academic options, students appreciate that "everything is given fairly equal weight. Northwestern students and faculty do not show a considerable bias" toward specific fields. One student adds, "The strength of the school is its range." Northwestern encourages students to pursue multidisciplinary paths, with approximately 74% of undergraduates choosing to combine two or more areas of study. For instance, one student on campus is successfully pursuing a dual degree in trumpet performance as well as engineering. Additionally, Northwestern features "all the perks" of a big school, including "many opportunities" for research and internships. The university provides undergraduate support in applying for grants and fellowships, as well as for presenting and publishing findings. That said, "Northwestern is not an easy school. It takes hard work to be average here." Northwestern attracts students who "learn from [their] failures quickly and love to learn for the sake of learning rather than the grade." In addition to receiving an outstanding education, students appreciate the "many connections and opportunities [available to them] during and after graduation."

Campus Life

With a sprawling campus in Evanston and a smaller campus in Chicago proper, Northwestern offers students the traditional college experiences such as "great extracurriculars and good parties," as well as big-city fun. The Evanston campus is informally divided into north and south, each with its own distinct character. In North Evanston, "you can find a party every night of the week," and "the Greek scene is strong." Meanwhile, the "South Campus is nice and quiet in its own way. I enjoy reading and watching movies here, and the quietude is appreciated when study time rolls around." The South Campus is also closer to town, so "it is easy" to "buy dinner, see a show at the movies, and go shopping." Overall, the South Campus is "more artsy and has minimal partying on weeknights." The convenient on-campus shuttle allows for easy travel to the Chicago campus and the city, which students love visiting. Chicago "is a wonderful resource. People go into the city for a wide variety of things—daily excursions, jobs, internships, nights out, parties, etc." Athletics are a big deal at Northwestern, and as a founding member of the Big Ten, students "attend some of the best sporting events in the country." In addition to sports, the extracurriculars are "incredible here. There is a group for every interest, and the groups are amazingly well-managed by students." Many students "are involved in plays, a cappella groups, comedy troupes, and other organizations geared toward the performing arts. Activism is also very popular, with many involved in political groups, human-rights activism, and volunteering."

Student Body

Known for being engaged in and out of the classroom, the typical Northwestern undergrad "is an excellent student who works hard" and is "intelligent but laid-back." It's quite common to make a new friend who "was high school class president with a 4.0, swim team captain, and on the chess team." If students offer a critique of the culture at Northwestern, it's that "there's [a] great separation between North Campus (think: fraternities, engineering, state school mentality) and South Campus (think: closer to Chicago and its culture, arts and letters, liberal arts school mentality). Students segregate themselves depending on background and interests, and it's rare for these two groups to interact beyond a superficial level." Regardless of which side of campus they live on, most "students at Northwestern are [passionate] about what they love," which fosters a dynamic and engaged community for everyone.

NORTHWESTERN UNIVERSITY

Financial Aid: 847-491-7400 • E-Mail: ug-admission@northwestern.edu • Website: www.northwestern.edu

THE PRINCETON REVIEW SAYS

Admissions

The school reports that its standardized testing policy for use in admission for Fall 2026 is Test Optional. The Princeton Review suggests that interested applicants consult with the school for the most up-to-date standardized testing policies. *Very important factors considered include:* rigor of secondary school record, class rank, academic GPA, application essay, recommendation(s), extracurricular activities, talent/ability, character/personal qualities. *Other factors considered include:* standardized test scores, interview, first generation, alumni/ae relation, volunteer work, work experience, level of applicant's interest. High school diploma is required and GED is accepted. *Academic units recommended:* 4 English, 3 math, 2 science, 2 science labs, 2 language (other than English), 2 social studies, 2 history, 1 academic elective.

Financial Aid

Students should submit: FAFSA; CSS PROFILE. Priority filing deadline is 2/1. The Princeton Review suggests that all financial aid forms be submitted as soon as possible. *Need-based scholarships/grants offered:* Federal Pell; Federal SEOG; State scholarships/grants; College/university scholarship or grant aid from institutional funds. *Loan aid offered:* Federal Direct Subsidized Loans; Federal Direct Unsubsidized Loans; Direct PLUS loans. Admitted students will be notified of awards on or about 3/15. Federal Work-Study Program available. Institutional employment available.

The Inside Word

Northwestern is among the nation's most expensive undergraduate institutions, a fact that dissuades some qualified students from applying. The school is working to attract more low-income applicants by increasing the number of full scholarships available for students. Low-income students who score well on the ACT may receive a letter from the school encouraging them to apply. Even if you don't receive this letter, you should consider applying if you've got the goods—you may be pleasantly surprised by the offer you receive from the financial aid office.

THE SCHOOL SAYS

From the Admissions Office

"Consistent with its dedication to excellence, Northwestern provides both an educational and an extracurricular environment that enables its undergraduate students to become accomplished individuals and informed and responsible citizens. To the students in all its undergraduate schools, Northwestern offers liberal learning and professional education to help them gain the depth of knowledge that will empower them to become leaders in their professions and communities. Furthermore, Northwestern fosters in its students a broad understanding of the world in which we live as well as excellence in the competencies that transcend any particular field of study: writing and oral communication, analytical and creative thinking and expression, and quantitative and qualitative methods of thinking."

SELECTIVITY

# of total applicants	51,769
% of total applicants accepted	7
% of total acceptees attending	56
# of early decision applicants	5,207
% of early decision applicants accepted	23
# admitted from wait list	55

First-Year Profile

Testing policy	Test Optional
Range SAT composite	1500–1530
Range SAT EBRW	730–770
Range SAT math	760–790
Range ACT composite	33–35
% submitting SAT scores	50
% submitting ACT scores	29
% graduated top 10% of class	96
% graduated top 25% of class	100
% graduated top 50% of class	100

Important Dates

Early decision	
Apply by	11/1
Notified by	Mid December
Regular	
Apply by	1/2
Notified by	4/1
Nonfall registration?	No

FINANCIAL FACTS

Annual tuition	$69,375
Food and housing	$21,975
Required fees	$1,214
Books and supplies	$1,539
Average need-based scholarship (First-year)	$60,889 ($62,898)
% students with need rec. need-based scholarship or grant aid (First-year)	97 (97)
% students with need rec. non-need-based scholarship or grant aid (First-year)	0 (0)
% students with need rec. need-based self-help aid (First-year)	67 (69)
% UG borrow to pay for school	29
Average cumulative indebtedness	$34,309
% of students with need fully met (First-year)	100 (100)
Average % of student need met (First-year)	100 (100)

OBERLIN COLLEGE

173 West Lorain Street, Oberlin, OH 44074 • Admissions: 440-775-8411

Survey Snapshot
Easy to get around campus
Students environmentally aware
Great library

RATINGS

Quality of Life	**85**
Fire Safety	**91**
Green	**95**
Academic	**88**
Profs Interesting	**94**
Profs Accessible	**94**
Admissions	**92**
Financial Aid	**99**

CAMPUS LIFE

Type of school	Private
Environment	Village

Students

Degree-seeking undergrad enrollment	2,987
% male/female/not reported	42/58/<1
% from out of state	92
% First-year from public high school	66
% First-year live on campus	100
% Ugrads live on campus	93
# of fraternities	0
# of sororities	0
% Asian	5
% Black or African American	5
% Hispanic	8
% Native American	0
% Pacific Islander	0
% Race and/or ethnicity unknown	1
% Two or more races	10
% White	61
% International	10
# of countries represented	58

CAMPUS MENTAL HEALTH SERVICES

Offers mental health/wellness program	Yes
Mental health training available to students	Yes
Employs Chief Wellness Officer	Yes
Peer-to-peer mental health offerings	Yes
Counseling center has guidelines or accreditation	Yes
Mental health/well-being courses	Yes, for-credit

ACADEMICS

% students returning for sophomore year	92
% students graduating within 4 years	63
% students graduating within 6 years	80
Calendar	4-1-4
Student/faculty ratio	9:1
Most common class size 1–9.	(38%)
Most common lab/discussion size 1–9.	(65%)

Most Popular Majors

Visual and Performing Arts; Psychology; Biology

Applicants Also Look At

Brown University, Denison University, Kenyon College, Smith College, Tufts University, University of California-Berkeley, University of California-Los Angeles, University of Michigan-Ann Arbor, William & Mary, Yale University

STUDENTS SAY "..."

Academics

The "rich academic courses and extensive resources" at Oberlin College, as well as its prestigious conservatory of music, make it "the ideal place to be passionate about a subject." The school's liberal arts curriculum and interdisciplinary emphasis give students maximum flexibility, and many "pick up double majors and multiple minors just by taking classes they enjoy." With this support, there are "so many different paths students can follow to pursue one or more degrees, and [the school is] fully prepared to help you meet your academic goals." Furthermore, the college has a roster of established programs like the Experimental College (ExCo), "an accredited organization in which students can teach for-credit classes to students, faculty, and community members," and Winter Term, when students can "pursue short-term internships, intensive classes, individual projects, or study abroad programs." Professors "are active contributors to their fields and are eager to engage with the student body." Many classes set aside time for discussion, which helps "solidify learning and understanding over simply memorization." Others incorporate community-based learning elements or innovative approaches to the specific material, such as an archaeology class where students recall "using traditional carving techniques to create real bone tools." With the backing of a school that "supports you as you discover your place in the world," it's said that "you can become a big fish in a small pond, if you wish." One student says, "There's a general understanding that although it will be difficult, anyone can do well here. There's like one million student resources to back that up."

Campus Life

The cooperative association at Oberlin "holds together a strong community," providing at-cost dining and housing to student members who put in hours to keep the co-op running. Those who participate tout the affordability and community offered, with one saying it "has allowed me to build relationships with my peers, learn new skills, and eat nutritious meals." Another adds, "Joining OSCA [Oberlin Student Cooperative Association] is the best decision I made at Oberlin, and it has taught me so much about democracy, working with people, cooking, and nonprofits." Even with academic credit in play, the ExCos become pastimes unto themselves, and help "build third-space communities around students' hobbies, interests, and passions." There are "so many opportunities to get involved with the arts" at this creative college, which means "lots of musical performances for free all the time," and "there is always a lunchtime talk or lecture by a visiting alum or lecturer." There are also "a lot of volunteering opportunities and natural resources, like the Arboretum and bike trail." One student puts it simply: "Folks here are always busy."

Student Body

Oberlin is "a unique space where people regularly have multiple interests simultaneously," and "it is very common to see people double majoring in very distinct fields." Obies tend to be "expressive, quirky, and unapologetically themselves," and with everyone putting it all out in the open, "you can definitely find people who share your...niche interests." Each student "shows up to do the best they can, and the atmosphere...is not one of competition but of collaboration," as people see one another as "a resource for everyone else to learn from and work with on interesting projects." Most here are "generally very creative and artistic," as well as being "curious and over-booked" with activities stemming from their many interests. They "are super into the things that they are into and really driven by innate interest in the topics they study, not by academic competition or prestige." "Kindness and understanding [are] above all else at Oberlin," and people are "grateful for a student body that never wanes in its desire to explore ideas and talk about them deeply."

Oberlin College

Financial Aid: 440-775-8142 • E-Mail: college.admissions@oberlin.edu • Website: www.oberlin.edu

THE PRINCETON REVIEW SAYS

Admissions

The school reports that its standardized testing policy for use in admission for Fall 2026 is Test Optional. The Princeton Review suggests that interested applicants consult with the school for the most up-to-date standardized testing policies. *Very important factors considered include:* rigor of secondary school record, class rank, academic GPA. *Important factors considered include:* application essay, recommendation(s), extracurricular activities, talent/ability, character/personal qualities. *Other factors considered include:* standardized test scores, interview, first generation, alumni/ae relation, volunteer work, work experience, level of applicant's interest. High school diploma is required and GED is accepted. *Academic units recommended:* 4 English, 4 math, 3 science, 3 science labs, 3 language (other than English), 3 social studies.

Financial Aid

Students should submit: FAFSA; CSS PROFILE; Business/Farm Supplement. Priority filing deadline is 1/15. The Princeton Review suggests that all financial aid forms be submitted as soon as possible. *Need-based scholarships/grants offered:* Federal Pell; Federal SEOG; State scholarships/grants; Private scholarships; College/university scholarship or grant aid from institutional funds. *Loan aid offered:* Federal Direct Subsidized Loans; Federal Direct Unsubsidized Loans; Direct PLUS loans. Admitted students will be notified of awards at the time of admission. Federal Work-Study Program available. Institutional employment available.

The Inside Word

Oberlin's conservatory of music is one of the most elite programs in the nation. Aspiring music students should expect stiff competition for one of the available slots. Applicants to Oberlin's College of Arts and Sciences won't have a much easier time of it. Oberlin is a selective institution that attracts a highly competitive applicant pool.

THE SCHOOL SAYS

From the Admissions Office

"Located in Oberlin, Ohio, about 40 minutes from Cleveland, Oberlin offers one of the world's great undergraduate educations. Ranked among the nation's top liberal arts institutions, Oberlin College and Conservatory is known for its exemplary academic and musical pedagogy and its commitment to social justice, sustainability, and creative entrepreneurship. Founded in 1833, it holds a distinguished place among American colleges and universities as the first to grant bachelor's degrees to women in a coeducational environment and the first to adopt a policy to admit African Americans. Its 2900 students pursue multiple passions and interests within a supportive, collaborative community. The College of Arts and Sciences focuses on undergraduate teaching, hands-on research, culturally immersive study away experiences, and world-class performing arts opportunities. The innovative Conservatory of Music, a recipient of the National Medal of Arts, was founded in 1865, making it the oldest continuously operating conservatory in the United States. In the last century, Oberlin alumni have gone on to earn more PhDs than graduates of any other liberal arts institution. In nearly every career field, Oberlin graduates are making an impact and improving our world."

SELECTIVITY

# of total applicants	11,723
% of total applicants accepted	33
% of total acceptees attending	20
# of in-state applicants	801
% of in-state applicants accepted	36
# of out-of-state-applicants	6,914
% of applicants accepted from out of state	45
# of international applicants	4,013
% of international applicants accepted	11
# of early decision applicants	635
% of early decision applicants accepted	39
# offered a place on the wait list	879
# admitted from wait list	26

First-Year Profile

Testing policy	Test Optional
Range SAT composite	1370–1480
Range SAT EBRW	690–760
Range SAT math	660–740
Range ACT composite	30–33
% submitting SAT scores	31
% submitting ACT scores	13
Average HS GPA	3.6
% submitting high school GPA	86
% graduated top 10% of class	43
% graduated top 25% of class	69
% graduated top 50% of class	96
% submitting high school rank	26

Important Dates

Early decision	
Apply by	11/1
Notified by	12/15
Other ED apply by	1/5
Other ED notified by	2/1
Early action	
Apply by	11/1
Notified by	1/15
Regular	
Apply by	1/15
Notified by	4/1
Nonfall registration?	No

FINANCIAL FACTS*

Annual tuition	$68,340
Food and housing	$20,096
Required fees	$1,142
Books and supplies	$930
Average need-based scholarship (First-year)	$56,848 ($59,480)
% students with need rec. need-based scholarship or grant aid (First-year)	100 (100)
% students with need rec. non-need-based scholarship or grant aid (First-year)	100 (100)
% students with need rec. need-based self-help aid (First-year)	82 (79)
% students rec. any financial aid (First-year)	100 (100)
% UG borrow to pay for school	43
Average cumulative indebtedness	$28,452
% of students with need fully met (First-year)	100 (100)
Average % of student need met (First-year)	100 (100)

* Most recently reported data at time of printing. Scan the QR code to find the latest updates.

OCCIDENTAL COLLEGE

1600 Campus Road, Los Angeles, CA 90041-3314 • Admissions: 800-825-5262

Survey Snapshot
Lots of liberal students
Students are friendly
Diverse student types interact on campus

RATINGS

Quality of Life	89
Fire Safety	65
Green	89
Academic	90
Profs Interesting	93
Profs Accessible	96
Admissions	92
Financial Aid	95

CAMPUS LIFE

Type of school	Private
Environment	Metropolis

Students

Degree-seeking undergrad enrollment	1,815
% male/female/not reported	41/59/0
% from out of state	55
% First-year live on campus	100
% Ugrads live on campus	82
# of fraternities (% join)	NR
# of sororities (% join)	NR
% Asian	16
% Black or African American	4
% Hispanic	18
% Native American	<1
% Pacific Islander	<1
% Race and/or ethnicity unknown	1
% Two or more races	12
% White	46
% International	5
# of countries represented	32

CAMPUS MENTAL HEALTH SERVICES

Offers mental health/wellness program	Yes
Mental health training available to students	No
Employs Chief Wellness Officer	NR
Peer-to-peer mental health offerings	NR
Counseling center has guidelines or accreditation	No
Mental health/well-being courses	NR

ACADEMICS

% students returning for sophomore year	91
% students graduating within 4 years	55
% students graduating within 6 years	79
Calendar	Semester
Student/faculty ratio	8:1
Most common class size 10–19.	(53%)
Most common lab/discussion size 10–19.	(67%)

Most Popular Majors

Biology/Biological Sciences; Econometrics and Quantitative Economics; International Relations and Affairs

Applicants Often Prefer

New York University, Pitzer College, Pomona College, Santa Clara University, Scripps College, University of California—Berkeley, University of California—Los Angeles, University of California—San Diego, University of California—Santa Barbara, University of Southern California, University of Washington

Applicants Sometimes Prefer

American University, Claremont McKenna College, The George Washington University, Macalester College

STUDENTS SAY "..."

Academics

Occidental College, in northeast Los Angeles, offers undergrads an "intellectually stimulating" environment, one that "really encourages [them] to take a proactive role in their education" and "experiment with a wide range of courses." As this student shares, "I love the interdisciplinary aspect of academics. I can really tailor my coursework to what I am interested in." Undergrads also appreciate that Oxy emphasizes a global perspective. Beyond traditional study abroad programs, students can enroll in courses that include an international field trip. For example, they might travel with faculty to study marine biology in Costa Rica or music history in Austria. Students can also apply to spend a semester at the U.N., completing internships with country missions or various NGOs. Back at home, undergrads have classes with professors who "encourage critical analysis, ask interesting questions, and allow students to create informed opinions about the subject." They also do a great job of "finding ways to connect [their] lectures to the real world." Perhaps more importantly, Oxy professors are "very willing to have students help them with their research." And while they work hard to ensure their "courses are challenging," it's clear the faculty "want to see you succeed." Undergrads report that instructors often "go the extra mile to make themselves available" and that "there are plenty of opportunities to get extra help on the tough material." Best of all, it's evident that professors "are invested in cultivating real relationships with students."

Campus Life

As you stroll around the campus, it's not hard to see that students are "excited to be at Occidental" and "people are really passionate about their extracurricular activities and internships." Undergrads can join a wide range of groups, including a sketch comedy troupe, a fiber arts club, and a food justice organization. Sports are also a popular social outlet. In fact, 45% of the student body is involved in athletics, be it a varsity, club, or intramural team. Additionally, school-sponsored events are typically well attended. Students often flock to hear "guest speakers [or participate in] dialogues and workshops." They also love going to the "dances, trivia nights, movie screenings, fashion shows, concerts, and food tastings" that Oxy organizes. And of course, off-campus "house parties are a huge source of fun on the weekends." And speaking of off-campus, undergrads appreciate that they have "Los Angeles as [their] backyard," especially since the school is "not isolated from the surrounding community like many other college campuses." It's common to see students hitting up "music shows, bars, and clubs" or heading out to "go to the beach, go shopping in L.A., go out to eat in Eagle Rock, and go hiking."

Student Body

One of the many reasons students love Occidental is because it's really easy to find "a good niche of close friends at Oxy." As one undergrad notes, "If you're involved on campus, expect your friend group to continually grow." This welcoming and supportive nature even extends into the classroom, where "there is a communal desire to help each other succeed." Undergrads assert that their peers are "socially and politically conscious" and care deeply about issues affecting the world at large. Although some do acknowledge that it can feel as though the school maintains an "overwhelmingly left-wing atmosphere," they also insist that "every student at Oxy treats all persons equally, regardless of sexual orientation, gender identity, or religious views," and most are readily "accepting of different opinions." Indeed, there's an emphasis on inclusion and visibility that is evident from groups like the First Gen Coalition and Chinese Culture Club, as well as themed housing like Women in Wellness and The Latinx Culture Collective. These all make it easy for students to foster a strong sense of community at Occidental.

OCCIDENTAL COLLEGE

Financial Aid: 323-259-2548 • E-Mail: admission@oxy.edu • Website: www.oxy.edu

THE PRINCETON REVIEW SAYS

Admissions

The school reports that its standardized testing policy for use in admission for Fall 2026 is Test Optional. The Princeton Review suggests that interested applicants consult with the school for the most up-to-date standardized testing policies. *Very important factors considered include:* rigor of secondary school record, academic GPA, application essay. *Important factors considered include:* class rank, recommendation(s), extracurricular activities, character/personal qualities, volunteer work, work experience. *Other factors considered include:* standardized test scores, interview, talent/ability, first generation, geographical residence, level of applicant's interest. High school diploma is required and GED is accepted. *Academic units recommended:* 4 English, 4 math, 3 science, 3 language (other than English), 3 social studies.

Financial Aid

Students should submit: FAFSA; CSS PROFILE; State aid form. Priority filing deadline is 1/10. The Princeton Review suggests that all financial aid forms be submitted as soon as possible. *Need-based scholarships/grants offered:* Federal Pell; Federal SEOG; State scholarships/grants; Private scholarships; College/university scholarship or grant aid from institutional funds. *Loan aid offered:* Federal Direct Subsidized Loans; Federal Direct Unsubsidized Loans; Direct PLUS loans. Admitted students will be notified of awards on or about 3/20. Federal Work-Study Program available. Institutional employment available.

The Inside Word

The admissions team at Occidental does not use any minimums or formulas when evaluating an applicant's eligibility for the incoming class. In addition to academic achievement, they place a lot of weight on essays and recommendations in their mission to create a diverse incoming class. A demanding course load in high school is essential for competitive candidates, but successful applicants will also show what makes them distinct, from volunteer experiences to artistic talent.

THE SCHOOL SAYS

From the Admissions Office

"Here's what our students tell us:

'The professors have all been just amazing. They're all very willing to coordinate times to meet and discuss how you feel about a class and what you want to get out of it.'

'I realize the caliber of discussion that occurs at Oxy is not easily matched. I've developed very strong relationships with many professors, and that's something I believe is unique to Oxy.'

'The program has been awesome. Whether you want to go to med school or grad school, it's a great experience. The professors really want you to succeed.'

'I've been working with postdoctoral researchers as an undergraduate. It's very rewarding. Oxy challenges me both inside and outside the classroom.'

'Occidental opened my eyes to different beliefs, values, and ideas. Discussions in class are much more interesting, because you consider things you might not have thought about before.'

'Oxy's close-knit community and its size make me feel this is a place I can call home.'

'Oxy instills curiosity and makes students want to go out and learn a subject on their own. I've gotten a broader sense of self and have been able to fulfill my learning goals.'"

SELECTIVITY

# of total applicants	7,490
% of total applicants accepted	45
% of total acceptees attending	13

First-Year Profile

Testing policy	Test Optional
Range SAT composite	1400–1510
Range SAT EBRW	700–760
Range SAT math	670–760
Range ACT composite	31–34
% submitting SAT scores	25
% submitting ACT scores	8
Average HS GPA	3.6
% submitting high school GPA	97

Important Dates

Early decision	
Apply by	11/1
Notified by	Mid December
Other ED apply by	1/10
Other ED notified by	Mid February
Early action	
Apply by	11/1
Notified by	Mid January
Regular	
Apply by	1/10
Nonfall registration?	No

FINANCIAL FACTS

Annual tuition	$68,108
Food and housing	$20,321
Required fees	$596
Books and supplies	$1,290
Average need-based scholarship (First-year)	$55,380 ($56,023)
% students with need rec. need-based scholarship or grant aid (First-year)	99 (98)
% students with need rec. non-need-based scholarship or grant aid (First-year)	73 (84)
% students with need rec. need-based self-help aid (First-year)	94 (91)
% students rec. any financial aid (First-year)	77 (80)
% UG borrow to pay for school	50
Average cumulative indebtedness	$32,170
% of students with need fully met (First-year)	73 (84)
Average % of student need met (First-year)	100 (100)

Ohio Northern University

525 South Main Street, Ada, OH 45810 • Admissions: 419-772-2260

Survey Snapshot
Students are happy
Internships are widely available
Theater is popular

RATINGS

Quality of Life	85
Fire Safety	60*
Green	60*
Academic	83
Profs Interesting	89
Profs Accessible	95
Admissions	86
Financial Aid	91

CAMPUS LIFE

Type of school	Private
Affiliation	Methodist
Environment	Village

Students

Degree-seeking undergrad enrollment	2,516
% male/female/not reported	56/44/0
% from out of state	13
% First-year live on campus	90
% Ugrads live on campus	72
# of fraternities (% join)	6 (11)
# of sororities (% join)	4 (17)
% Asian	2
% Black or African American	3
% Hispanic	4
% Native American	<1
% Pacific Islander	0
% Race and/or ethnicity unknown	4
% Two or more races	5
% White	81
% International	2
# of countries represented	17

CAMPUS MENTAL HEALTH SERVICES

Offers mental health/wellness program	Yes
Mental health training available to students	No
Employs Chief Wellness Officer	NR
Peer-to-peer mental health offerings	NR
Counseling center has guidelines or accreditation	No
Mental health/well-being courses	NR

ACADEMICS

% students returning for sophomore year	85
% students graduating within 4 years	61
% students graduating within 6 years	71
Calendar	Semester
Student/faculty ratio	14:1
Most common class size 10–19.	(35%)

Most Popular Majors

Registered Nursing/Registered Nurse; Biology/Biological Sciences; Mechanical Engineering

STUDENTS SAY "..."

Academics

At Ohio Northern University, incoming undergraduates benefit from the school's first-year curriculum seminars. Available in most areas of study, the program offers regular one-on-one time with professors and encourages opportunities for collaborative education while even presenting some of the faculty's own research in the field. The seminars help forge a bond between the students and the "renowned faculty" at ONU, who are "always available to help," "very friendly and down to earth," and "are outstanding and all influential in their field." ONU offers five colleges with a variety of programs, including "a great political science program [that] has sent many students to graduate school and politics," with 95% finding placement within six months of graduation. Students also point out that the "accounting program is highly ranked" and "the engineering college is great." One of the biggest draws is the university's Raabe College of Pharmacy, a "prestigious" educational track that "is focused on developing the next generation of clinical pharmacists who are well-rounded leaders, clinicians, and members of society." It offers direct entry into pharmaceutical careers with patient experiences available in the first year of study. The programs and opportunities offered at ONU add up to "a top-notch education." As one student remarks, ONU's "classes are tough, no doubt about it," but "my overall academic experience has been above and beyond anything I could've expected."

Campus Life

Ohio Northern University believes finding a good balance is the key to a great student experience. So, while there are "students who spend all of their time focused on school," there's also a "good number of students who enjoy having a good time and hanging out with friends." ONU's 200 student-led organizations plus programs in music, athletics, and Greek life provide ample opportunities to help undergrads and graduates help discover and develop personal interests. In fact, 82% of enrollees take part in student organizations, and 22% are involved in sports. As one undergrad explains, "Most students are friends with other people in the same activities that they're involved in, so join something you're interested in and don't be shy!"

The campus, located in the town of Ada, provides "a family-like atmosphere" and a more communal feel. "Because we are in a small town, the students bond together to find fun things to do," such as "pick-up sports games," "fraternity house parties and local bars (The Cask Room)," as well as "several university-sponsored events throughout the year." Students like to combine socializing and working: "People love hanging out with each other, especially when they are trying to get things done."

Student Body

One of the great attributes of being an ONU Polar Bear is that "everyone is very caring toward each other," and their fellow undergrads are "always willing to help [out] or mentor younger students." The typical ONU student "is committed to academics, to service, and has leadership potential," students appreciate that "everyone here finds a supportive group of friends." Many students are Midwestern and "some denomination of Christian," with a majority of ONU's population hailing from "in-state, some surrounding states, and internationals." The general vibe at ONU is: "People here are very relaxed—you do what you want, and everyone is fine with you being who you are."

Ohio Northern University

Financial Aid: 419-772-2272 • E-Mail: admissions-ug@onu.edu • Website: www.onu.edu

THE PRINCETON REVIEW SAYS

Admissions

The school reports that its standardized testing policy for use in admission for Fall 2026 is Test Optional. The Princeton Review suggests that interested applicants consult with the school for the most up-to-date standardized testing policies. *Very important factors considered include:* rigor of secondary school record, academic GPA, standardized test scores. *Important factors considered include:* interview, extracurricular activities. *Other factors considered include:* application essay, recommendation(s), talent/ability, character/personal qualities, first generation, alumni/ae relation, volunteer work, level of applicant's interest. High school diploma is required and GED is accepted. *Academic units required:* 4 English, 2 math, 2 science, 2 science labs, 2 social studies, 2 history, 4 academic electives. *Academic units recommended:* 4 English, 4 math, 3 science, 2 science labs, 2 language (other than English), 3 social studies, 2 history, 4 academic electives, 1 computer science, 1 visual/performing arts.

Financial Aid

Students should submit: FAFSA. The Princeton Review suggests that all financial aid forms be submitted as soon as possible. Federal Work-Study Program available. Institutional employment available.

The Inside Word

Admissions are holistic, meaning your academic transcript matters, but so do leadership roles and community service. Since applications are reviewed on a rolling basis, submitting early works in your favor. While strong high school transcripts and standardized test scores will assist any application, particularly those seeking merit-based financial aid, applicants are eligible for academic scholarships without test scores. ONU's well-regarded pharmacy school has its own specific requirements, so be sure to check with the school directly if that's your area of interest.

THE SCHOOL SAYS

From the Admissions Office

"The purpose of Ohio Northern is to help students develop into self-reliant, mature men and women capable of clear and logical thinking and sensitive to the higher values of truth, beauty, and goodness. ONU selects its student body from among those students possessing characteristics congruent with the institution's objectives. Generally, a student must be prepared to use the resources of the institution to achieve personal and educational goals.

"The Office of Admissions highly encourages a campus visit. To schedule a visit, please go to www.onu.edu/visit or call 888-408-4668."

SELECTIVITY

# of total applicants	5,226
% of total applicants accepted	71
% of total acceptees attending	20
# of in-state applicants	3,724
% of in-state applicants accepted	79
# of out-of-state-applicants	1,083
% of applicants accepted from out of state	69
# of international applicants	404
% of international applicants accepted	4

First-Year Profile

Testing policy	Test Optional
Range SAT composite	1180–1290
Range SAT EBRW	600–640
Range SAT math	590–640
Range ACT composite	25–29
% submitting SAT scores	11
% submitting ACT scores	34
Average HS GPA	3.9
% submitting high school GPA	100

Important Dates

Regular	
Apply by	Rolling
Notified by	Rolling
Nonfall registration?	Yes

FINANCIAL FACTS

Annual tuition	$41,720
Food and housing	$14,100
Required fees (First-year)	$1,650 ($1,860)
Books and supplies	$1,200
Average need-based scholarship (First-year)	$33,473 ($35,587)
% students with need rec. need-based scholarship or grant aid (First-year)	100 (100)
% students with need rec. non-need-based scholarship or grant aid (First-year)	0 (0)
% students with need rec. need-based self-help aid (First-year)	51 (43)
% UG borrow to pay for school	69
Average cumulative indebtedness	$42,798
% of students with need fully met (First-year)	38 (42)
Average % of student need met (First-year)	81 (83)

THE OHIO STATE UNIVERSITY—COLUMBUS

Student Academic Services Building, Columbus, OH 43210 • Admissions: 614-292-3980

Survey Snapshot
Students love Columbus, OH
Recreation facilities are great
Everyone loves the Buckeyes

RATINGS

Quality of Life	88
Fire Safety	86
Green	97
Academic	81
Profs Interesting	86
Profs Accessible	89
Admissions	90
Financial Aid	86

CAMPUS LIFE

Type of school	Public
Environment	Metropolis

Students

Degree-seeking undergrad enrollment	45,433
% male/female/not reported	50/50/0
% from out of state	22
% First-year from public high school	84
% First-year live on campus	92
% Ugrads live on campus	33
# of fraternities (% join)	37 (9)
# of sororities (% join)	27 (13)
% Asian	11
% Black or African American	8
% Hispanic	6
% Native American	<1
% Pacific Islander	<1
% Race and/or ethnicity unknown	3
% Two or more races	5
% White	58
% International	7
# of countries represented	75

CAMPUS MENTAL HEALTH SERVICES

Offers mental health/wellness program	Yes
Mental health training available to students	Yes
Employs Chief Wellness Officer	Yes
Peer-to-peer mental health offerings	Yes
Counseling center has guidelines or accreditation	No
Mental health/well-being courses	NR

ACADEMICS

% students returning for sophomore year	93
% students graduating within 4 years	71
% students graduating within 6 years	87
Calendar	Semester
Student/faculty ratio	13:1
Most common class size 10–19.	(26%)
Most common lab/discussion size 20–29.	(48%)

Most Popular Majors
Psychology; Finance

Applicants Often Prefer
University of Michigan—Ann Arbor, University of Wisconsin—Madison

Applicants Sometimes Prefer
Case Western Reserve University, Indiana University—Bloomington, Penn State University Park, Purdue University—West Lafayette, University of Cincinnati

Applicants Rarely Prefer
Miami University, Ohio University—Athens

STUDENTS SAY "..."

Academics

Ohio State, one of the Midwest's premier universities, is a school with "strong name-brand recognition." Of course, it also has a massive student population, which makes the "campus feel like its own city." Nevertheless, OSU does an admirable job of "handling the large number of students that attend and creating opportunities for over 40,000 undergraduates." As one impressed student explains, "Every single student feels personally attended to and not [like] a number in the crowd of Buckeyes." Many undergrads here also appreciate that "the college is very research-based, which allows students to fully discover what exactly they want to do, and to also build connections with faculty." And while there are many great academic programs, a number of undergrads specifically highlight the "very strong business school, medical program, and engineering school." Moreover, students generally give high marks to their "friendly and approachable" professors. Though you might encounter a "couple of duds...depend[ing] on the department," OSU's faculty are usually "very passionate about the material they teach," which even makes for "very interesting general education classes." They're also "more than willing to meet outside of their designated office hours to help a student struggling with course materials or even just to get coffee and chat." Best of all, "they truly seem to have a genuine interest in the students' academic and career success."

Campus Life

OSU students boast that "it's impossible to be bored here" given that the university provides "thousands of opportunities" for extracurricular involvement. For starters, undergrads can participate in "countless intramural or club sport[s]," including volleyball, basketball and rock climbing. "When it's football season, game days are always the best," says a student. They go on to add, "Experiencing the atmosphere of the entire Ohio State campus in one stadium is amazing." Aside from athletics, students can join a number of clubs like "Dungeons and Dragons...student leadership, [and even] small [music] ensembles that don't require auditions." Buckeyes also quickly find that "going out on Thursdays, Fridays, and Saturdays is extremely popular, whether [to] the bars or frat parties." Nevertheless, one student assures that "although partying is common, there is absolutely no pressure to partake in any of it." In fact, "there are an abundance of [alternative] options [like] weekly karaoke and trivia." Finally, should you need a breather from all that campus excitement, downtown Columbus is a "great place...[filled with] art galleries, coffee shops," and "top-notch" restaurants.

Student Body

Undergrads at Ohio State love that their peers come "from quite a range of backgrounds." Indeed, you can just as easily "find yourself meeting an individual from a very remote city in the state...[as you can] an out of state or international student from places...you'd think [the school] wouldn't have a reach." Thankfully, no matter where they grew up, these Buckeyes are typically "down-to-earth and have a strong desire to succeed." They also comprise "some of the most spirited fans" you'll ever meet. And while students here "take their academics quite seriously," there's still "a very friendly [and] cooperative atmosphere." As one undergrad shares, "I've never encountered anybody that didn't want to work on... homework or [study] for an exam due to selfish competitive reasons." Students also greatly appreciate the fact that "there are so many people here that every social group is well represented." For example, "there's a party scene, a big Esports scene, a lot of gym rats," and representatives from many religious groups. In other words, rest assured that "there's a place for everyone" at Ohio State.

The Ohio State University—Columbus

Financial Aid: 614-292-0300 • E-Mail: askabuckeye@osu.edu • Website: www.osu.edu

THE PRINCETON REVIEW SAYS

Admissions

The school reports that its standardized testing policy for use in admission for Fall 2026 will require applicants to submit either the SAT or ACT. The Princeton Review suggests that interested applicants consult with the school for the most up-to-date standardized testing policies. *Very important factors considered include:* rigor of secondary school record, class rank, academic GPA, standardized test scores. *Important factors considered include:* application essay, recommendation(s), extracurricular activities, talent/ability, first generation, volunteer work, work experience. *Other factors considered include:* character/personal qualities, geographical residence, state residency. High school diploma is required and GED is accepted. *Academic units required:* 4 English, 3 math, 3 science, 3 science labs, 2 language (other than English), 2 social studies, 1 academic elective, 1 visual/performing arts. *Academic units recommended:* 4 English, 4 math, 3 science, 3 science labs, 3 language (other than English), 3 social studies, 1 academic elective, 1 visual/performing arts.

Financial Aid

Students should submit: FAFSA. Priority filing deadline is 2/1. The Princeton Review suggests that all financial aid forms be submitted as soon as possible. *Need-based scholarships/grants offered:* Federal Pell; Federal SEOG; State scholarships/grants; Private scholarships; College/university scholarship or grant aid from institutional funds. *Loan aid offered:* Federal Direct Subsidized Loans; Federal Direct Unsubsidized Loans; Direct PLUS loans; State Loans; College/university loans from institutional funds. Admitted students will be notified of awards on or about 3/6. Federal Work-Study Program available. Institutional employment available.

The Inside Word

Despite being a huge state university, OSU truly strives to evaluate applications holistically. The school endeavors to build an incoming class filled with intellectually curious individuals who have proven leadership skills. To that end, admissions officers review all academic achievement, paying close attention to whether applicants have challenged themselves with honors, AP, or IB courses. They also consider level of extracurricular involvement, outstanding talent in a particular area, desire to engage with a diverse campus community, and whether a candidate is a first-generation college student.

THE SCHOOL SAYS

From the Admissions Office

"We understand you don't want just any university. You want THE university that's right for you. There's a reason why Ohio State is a leading university and the #1 university in Ohio. Here you can achieve your goals doing what you love. You'll have THE opportunities to get involved in what matters most to you. You'll have THE support you need, when you need it. And you'll have THE experiences that enable you to stand out, build a network of mentors and gain real-world experience. Apply today!"

SELECTIVITY

# of total applicants	81,392
% of total applicants accepted	49
% of total acceptees attending	21
# of in-state applicants	25,273
% of in-state applicants accepted	45
# of out-of-state-applicants	42,898
% of applicants accepted from out of state	46
# of international applicants	13,221
% of international applicants accepted	66
# offered a place on the wait list	5,358
# admitted from wait list	2,049

First-Year Profile

Testing policy	SAT or ACT Required
Range SAT composite	1300–1440
Range SAT EBRW	640–720
Range SAT math	650–740
Range ACT composite	27–32
% submitting SAT scores	25
% submitting ACT scores	42
% graduated top 10% of class	3
% graduated top 25% of class	96
% graduated top 50% of class	99
% submitting high school rank	27

Important Dates

Early action	
Apply by	11/1
Notified by	1/31
Regular	
Apply by	1/15
Notified by	3/31
Nonfall registration?	Yes

FINANCIAL FACTS

Annual in-state tuition	$12,545
Annual out-of-state tuition	$41,327
Food and housing	$16,222
Required fees	$1,096
Books and supplies	$1,020
Average need-based scholarship (First-year)	$17,614 ($17,907)
% students with need rec. need-based scholarship or grant aid (First-year)	90 (93)
% students with need rec. non-need-based scholarship or grant aid (First-year)	4 (7)
% students with need rec. need-based self-help aid (First-year)	74 (67)
% students rec. any financial aid (First-year)	75 (83)
% UG borrow to pay for school	42
Average cumulative indebtedness	$26,869
% of students with need fully met (First-year)	15 (20)
Average % of student need met (First-year)	72 (73)

Ohio University—Athens

1 Ohio University, Athens, OH 45701 • Admissions: 740-593-4100

Survey Snapshot
Students are friendly
Students are happy
Students politically aware

RATINGS

Quality of Life	84
Fire Safety	65
Green	60*
Academic	74
Profs Interesting	84
Profs Accessible	88
Admissions	83
Financial Aid	84

CAMPUS LIFE

Type of school	Public
Environment	Town

Students

Degree-seeking undergrad enrollment	20,421
% male/female/not reported	39/61/0
% from out of state	16
% First-year live on campus	95
% Ugrads live on campus	38
# of fraternities (% join)	17 (6)
# of sororities (% join)	14 (4)
% Asian	2
% Black or African American	5
% Hispanic	5
% Native American	<1
% Pacific Islander	<1
% Race and/or ethnicity unknown	1
% Two or more races	4
% White	81
% International	1
# of countries represented	55

CAMPUS MENTAL HEALTH SERVICES

Offers mental health/wellness program	Yes
Mental health training available to students	No
Employs Chief Wellness Officer	NR
Peer-to-peer mental health offerings	NR
Counseling center has guidelines or accreditation	No
Mental health/well-being courses	NR

ACADEMICS

% students returning for sophomore year	85
% students graduating within 4 years	51
% students graduating within 6 years	65
Calendar	Semester
Student/faculty ratio	19:1
Most common class size 20–29.	(29%)
Most common lab/discussion size 10–19.	(44%)

Most Popular Majors
Zoology/Animal Biology; Psychology; Marketing/Marketing Management

Applicants Often Prefer
The Ohio State University—Columbus, University of Cincinnati

Applicants Sometimes Prefer
Bowling Green State University, Kent State University—Kent Campus, Miami University, University of Dayton

STUDENTS SAY "..."

Academics

Students at Ohio University—Athens can't get enough of its "great research opportunities, a wide array of majors, [a] beautiful campus and installations, and friendly professors." The security of the OHIO Guarantee+ which states that "scholarships and tuition price will not change [during] your four years here" helps to ensure they can remain enrolled. Students also benefit from the school's excellent reputation, which "creates great connections for the job world post college." One business student points to how their school "focuses a lot on experiential learning so we do a lot of roleplays, simulations, and interact with professionals in industry as part of our classwork." Students of other majors share similar experiences with classes that do "an amazing job at correlating new and innovative approaches" and also point to how the school "offers a lot of resources to its students, staff, and the local Athens residents, whether it's counseling, study abroad, academic guidance, and so much more." Professors are "very open with office hours and are more than happy to work with you outside of class, [and] there are also many tutoring opportunities and [Supplemental Instruction] sessions that are available." These teachers "encourage learning outside the classroom by promoting arts, activities, and other opportunities on and off campus" and "You can tell they want to be here, want to be teaching and imparting their knowledge." Many classes "utilize a lot of discussion so that everyone can hear each other's opinions and feel heard, and it allows for great ideas to be spread." Across the board, OU excels at "making everyone feel like they are a part of something."

Campus Life

There are a lot of events to keep the student body involved, which is good, because students are said to "heavily look forward to the weekend." Athletics (particularly football and hockey) are popular, and "OU makes it easy for everyone to be able to do something fun [that includes] sports, whether or not you are on a team or not." School spirit flows throughout the campus, "whether that be attending sports games, or wearing university merchandise daily" and everyone "genuinely seems to like being Bobcats and...[is] proud of our university." And with more than 550 student organizations (and the university's encouragement to start new ones), "many students are involved in clubs." Students also "spend as much time outside being social as they can" thanks to a campus that features "lots of historic buildings as well as beautiful nature and scenery" to say nothing of proximity to the Southeast Ohio foothills, where "hiking, camping, fishing, [and] hunting opportunities abound." Add in the way in which students say that "Uptown is integrated with campus and many students go shopping or hang out in the cafes there" and Athens is the quintessential college town with "a great live music scene and outdoor recreation scene all stemming from the student population."

Student Body

Ohio University has "a very diverse campus and the individuals here are very friendly and involved," with "many opportunities to learn from classmates from all over America and the world." Ohio "is a very liberal school," and most students "tend to be very engaging in class and open to sharing and hearing each other's ideas and opinions." Students feel that "you can approach anyone on the street and be able to have a conversation with them," and "if you get down and start to doubt yourself, they are always there to help you get your head back up and back in the game." In addition, "the students and faculty have created a closely connected community that feels judgment free." A student sums up their peers with the statement, "Whether you are a jock, in Greek life, into volunteering, very school focused, or just looking to hang out there really is someone for everyone."

Ohio University—Athens

Financial Aid: 740-593-4141 • E-Mail: admissions@ohio.edu • Website: www.ohio.edu

THE PRINCETON REVIEW SAYS

Admissions

The school reports that its standardized testing policy for use in admission for Fall 2026 is Test Optional. The Princeton Review suggests that interested applicants consult with the school for the most up-to-date standardized testing policies. *Very important factors considered include:* rigor of secondary school record, academic GPA. *Important factors considered include:* class rank. *Other factors considered include:* standardized test scores, application essay, recommendation(s), extracurricular activities, talent/ability, character/personal qualities, first generation, alumni/ae relation, geographical residence, state residency, volunteer work, work experience. High school diploma is required and GED is accepted. *Academic units required:* 4 English, 4 math, 3 science, 3 social studies, 5 academic electives. *Academic units recommended:* 2 language (other than English), 1 visual/performing arts.

Financial Aid

Students should submit: FAFSA. The Princeton Review suggests that all financial aid forms be submitted as soon as possible. *Need-based scholarships/grants offered:* Federal Pell; Federal SEOG; State scholarships/grants; Private scholarships; College/university scholarship or grant aid from institutional funds. *Loan aid offered:* Federal Direct Subsidized Loans; Federal Direct Unsubsidized Loans; Direct PLUS loans. Admitted students will be notified of awards on a rolling basis beginning 2/1.

The Inside Word

Admissions requirements vary from school to school at Ohio University. The Honors Tutorial College is most selective (top 10 percent of your graduating class), followed by the journalism school (top 15 percent), the business college (top 20 percent), media arts and studies, engineering, and visual communication. Admissions decisions are made through holistic review; those on the cusp should get in if they've demonstrated academic improvement during their junior and senior years and show evidence of academic preparation.

THE SCHOOL SAYS

From the Admissions Office

"Ohio University offers a welcoming campus and more than 240 outstanding academic programs. Our dedicated professors do more than just teach—they serve as mentors and advisors who prepare students for success. Ohio University's recently launched initiative, The OHIO Guarantee, may be of particular interest to families facing budgetary challenges: It enables undergraduate students to pay a single fixed" rate that covers tuition, room and meal plan, and most fees for four years. In addition, Ohio University is home to an Honors Tutorial College that offers high-ability students distinctive, tutorial-based learning opportunities that mirror the instructional model used for centuries at British universities such as Cambridge and Oxford. Students can enhance their educational experiences with adventures beyond the classroom. Opportunities can range from studying the plays of Shakespeare in London to retail merchandising in China. Students also can participate in meaningful research and internships, community service, and 530 student organizations. OHIO's picturesque campus—among the most beautiful in the nation—features learning communities that create a welcoming environment for first-year students. Friendships are forged as students with diverse backgrounds study, learn, and socialize together. Many students proudly cheer on Ohio University's athletics teams. The Bobcats have garnered consistent national attention in recent years, with the football team earning multiple bowl game experiences and the men's and women's basketball teams excelling in the Mid-American Conference and playing in post-season tournaments. All told, OHIO sponsors 16 varsity sports. Many nonvarsity students participate in club and intramural sports or learn to rappel, kayak, or canoe through OHIO's Outdoor Pursuits Program."

SELECTIVITY

# of total applicants	25,126
% of total applicants accepted	87
% of total acceptees attending	21
# of in-state applicants	18,562
% of in-state applicants accepted	89
# of out-of-state-applicants	5,349
% of applicants accepted from out of state	99
# of international applicants	1,215
% of international applicants accepted	63

First-Year Profile

Testing policy	Test Optional
Range SAT composite	1130–1300
Range SAT EBRW	570–670
Range SAT math	550–640
Range ACT composite	23–28
% submitting SAT scores	11
% submitting ACT scores	28
Average HS GPA	3.7
% submitting high school GPA	100
% graduated top 10% of class	27
% graduated top 25% of class	55
% graduated top 50% of class	85
% submitting high school rank	53

Important Dates

Early action	
Apply by	11/15
Notified by	9/15
Regular	
Apply by	2/1
Notified by	Rolling, 9/15
Nonfall registration?	Yes

FINANCIAL FACTS

Annual in-state tuition	$15,018
Annual out-of-state tuition	$26,792
Food and housing	$15,320
Books and supplies	$918
Average need-based scholarship (First-year)	$9,699 ($10,400)
% students with need rec. need-based scholarship or grant aid (First-year)	87 (97)
% students with need rec. non-need-based scholarship or grant aid (First-year)	13 (16)
% students with need rec. need-based self-help aid (First-year)	75 (74)
% UG borrow to pay for school	61
Average cumulative indebtedness	$26,968
% of students with need fully met (First-year)	16 (20)
Average % of student need met (First-year)	63 (71)

Ohio Wesleyan University

61 South Sandusky Street, Delaware, OH 43015 • Admissions: 740-368-3020

Survey Snapshot
Students are happy
Internships are widely available
Frats and sororities are popular

RATINGS

Quality of Life	**81**
Fire Safety	**99**
Green	**60***
Academic	**78**
Profs Interesting	**87**
Profs Accessible	**90**
Admissions	**77**
Financial Aid	**91**

CAMPUS LIFE

Type of school	Private
Affiliation	Methodist
Environment	Town

Students

Degree-seeking undergrad enrollment	1,649
% male/female/not reported	44/55/1
% from out of state	23
% First-year from public high school	80
% First-year live on campus	88
% Ugrads live on campus	82
# of fraternities (% join)	7 (34)
# of sororities (% join)	5 (22)
% Asian	2
% Black or African American	11
% Hispanic	7
% Native American	<1
% Pacific Islander	<1
% Race and/or ethnicity unknown	1
% Two or more races	4
% White	69
% International	5
# of countries represented	29

CAMPUS MENTAL HEALTH SERVICES

Offers mental health/wellness program	Yes
Mental health training available to students	Yes
Employs Chief Wellness Officer	No
Peer-to-peer mental health offerings	Yes
Counseling center has guidelines or accreditation	No
Mental health/well-being courses	Yes, non-credit

ACADEMICS

% students returning for sophomore year	84
% students graduating within 4 years	59
% students graduating within 6 years	64
Calendar	Semester
Student/faculty ratio	12:1
Most common class size 20–29.	(39%)
Most common lab/discussion size 10–19.	(70%)

Most Popular Majors

Zoology/Animal Biology; Economics; Psychology

STUDENTS SAY "…"

Academics

To some, Ohio Wesleyan University offers the best of both worlds: the "smaller school" experience of a "liberal arts education" along with the "fantastic financial aid," "scholarship money," and "opportunity to play a collegiate sport" available at a "global" university. OWU offers pre-professional majors in areas like pre-medicine, pre-engineering, and pre-law, along with "enriching" programs called out by students in "psychology," "economics," "Black World Studies," and others. In addition, the university facilitates special programs like "the undergraduate research program, SSRP, which allows only Ohio Wesleyan students to work with a professor over the summer," and which entrusts undergrads with "a rare opportunity to get paid to do research almost always one-on-one with a PhD, where at any other school you'll be working with lab techs and graduate students." Connection Grants challenge students to design their own project applications "for grants through the school that allow you to do your own research [and] travel to gain new experience." Similarly, OWU's "Travel-Learning Courses" create "many opportunities to go abroad" for students with intellectual wanderlust, and with such a global focus, OWU also attracts "many international students" to its Ohio campus. The faculty participates in this global citizenship as well: "The professors are very diverse, like the students here, bringing different perspectives and knowledge to campus." They're also committed to their students, who find that professors are "good at engaging the student in classroom discussions" and "will go out of their way to help you. I have had numerous professors support me in applying for grants, applying for research experiences at other universities, as well as jobs." Students report that "a major benefit of going to a smaller school is that I am on a first-name basis with multiple professors, and even text them if I need help with something," and that they've "had professors stay until 6pm just to make sure I understood a concept." An OWU education also builds a foundation for the future: the university boasts "strong career services," and "OWU alums are very dedicated to helping provide employment to students post-graduation."

Campus Life

OWU's "close knit community" is forged through common-interest bonds: "Most students are nerds/passionate about something. They usually fit in by finding people interested in the same things they are." The prototypical OWU student is "extremely involved in clubs/organizations," but has lots of choices of what to join: there's an "amazing club and Greek life," "varsity sports," "jobs on campus," and "SLUs (small living units)," described as "intentional communities centered around various mission statements." All of this adds up to a robust "overall community" and "great campus culture" that "make OWU an even better school to attend. The majority of students stay on campus because of the community and friendships that they have formed." That said, a lot of students "go to class and study during the week like its [their] job," "and every night do homework followed by Netflix." "In general, everyone is in study groups during the week and watching movies with friends when free"; then "weekends are spent with friends at a frat, sorority, or sport house." "Drinking does occur, as does drug usage," but "it's not a huge party school," and "many people are devoted strongly to their academics."

Student Body

OWU is populated by enthusiastic joiners of all different stripes, and students love the "very culturally diverse" atmosphere of the school. "I've never met so many people that are religiously and culturally different in a single place. It's amazing!" Because "students and faculty alike push for acceptance of everyone," it's "very easy to make friends in this type of environment." Students extol each other as "friendly and smart," as well as "outgoing, overcommitted in student organizations, and driven," and love that "it is impossible to judge or peg people" because "everyone here is from all over with different backgrounds." At OWU, "everyone fits in somewhere."

Ohio Wesleyan University

Financial Aid: 740-368-3050 • E-Mail: owuadmit@owu.edu • Website: www.owu.edu

THE PRINCETON REVIEW SAYS

Admissions

The school reports that its standardized testing policy for use in admission for Fall 2026 is Test Optional. The Princeton Review suggests that interested applicants consult with the school for the most up-to-date standardized testing policies. *Very important factors considered include:* rigor of secondary school record, academic GPA. *Important factors considered include:* application essay, recommendation(s), character/personal qualities. *Other factors considered include:* class rank, interview, extracurricular activities, talent/ability, first generation, alumni/ae relation, geographical residence, state residency, religious affiliation/commitment, volunteer work, work experience, level of applicant's interest. High school diploma is required and GED is accepted. *Academic units required:* 4 English, 3 math, 3 science, 2 science labs, 3 social studies. *Academic units recommended:* 4 English, 3 math, 3 science, 2 science labs, 2 language (other than English), 3 social studies.

Financial Aid

Students should submit: FAFSA. Priority filing deadline is 2/15. The Princeton Review suggests that all financial aid forms be submitted as soon as possible. *Need-based scholarships/grants offered:* Federal Pell; Federal SEOG; State scholarships/grants; Private scholarships; College/university scholarship or grant aid from institutional funds. *Loan aid offered:* Federal Direct Subsidized Loans; Federal Direct Unsubsidized Loans; Direct PLUS loans. Admitted students will be notified of awards on a rolling basis beginning 12/15. Federal Work-Study Program available. Institutional employment available.

The Inside Word

OWU is Test Optional, but as the university states, "While you are welcome to send your test scores, OWU does not use them for admission or scholarship consideration. Therefore, they will not help or hinder your application." Well-roundedness is a must for any serious applicant, so use the application process to let admission officers know who you are.

THE SCHOOL SAYS

From the Admissions Office

"Ohio Wesleyan offers a dynamic residential experience just minutes from Columbus, placing students in the heart of Ohio's fastest growing region with access to internships, research, and career opportunities. Academically, OWU offers more than 70 majors, allowing students to explore a wide variety of courses to discover who they want to become and how they want to impact the world. The university is especially strong in the health professions and STEM fields, and the recent addition of Engineering expands pathways for hands-on, career-focused learning. OWU's Career Connection office begins working with students during their first year, helping them to find meaningful internships, build job-ready skills, and create resumes that will help them achieve their career goals. On campus, students engage in more than 100 clubs and organizations, a vibrant arts scene, and 24 Division III NCAA varsity women's and men's athletic teams. Students are admitted free to nearly every campus event, encouraging them to explore every aspect of being a Bishop. With a range of housing options, most newly built or renovated in the past decade, students find a true sense of community from their first year through graduation. That connection continues after graduation, with strong alumni networks filled with mentors and friends."

SELECTIVITY

# of total applicants	5,706
% of total applicants accepted	64
% of total acceptees attending	14
# of in-state applicants	2,560
% of in-state applicants accepted	87
# of out-of-state-applicants	1,147
% of applicants accepted from out of state	88
# of international applicants	1,999
% of international applicants accepted	23
# of early decision applicants	155
% of early decision applicants accepted	41

First-Year Profile

Testing policy	Test Optional
Average HS GPA	3.7
% submitting high school GPA	100
% graduated top 10% of class	26
% graduated top 25% of class	52
% graduated top 50% of class	87
% submitting high school rank	47

Important Dates

Early decision	
Apply by	10/15
Notified by	12/1
Early action	
Apply by	12/1
Notified by	12/15
Regular	
Apply by	3/1
Notified by	Rolling, 8/15
Nonfall registration?	Yes

FINANCIAL FACTS

Annual tuition	$55,416
Food and housing	$15,882
Required fees	$624
Books and supplies	$1,150
Average need-based scholarship (First-year)	$48,338 ($49,099)
% students with need rec. need-based scholarship or grant aid (First-year)	100 (100)
% students with need rec. non-need-based scholarship or grant aid (First-year)	27 (27)
% students with need rec. need-based self-help aid (First-year)	65 (67)
% students rec. any financial aid (First-year)	98 (99)
% UG borrow to pay for school	64
Average cumulative indebtedness	$32,684
% of students with need fully met (First-year)	35 (32)
Average % of student need met (First-year)	91 (90)

Oregon State University

1500 SW Jefferson Ave., Corvallis, OR 97331 • Admissions: 541-737-4411

Survey Snapshot
Frats and sororities are popular
Recreation facilities are great
Students aren't religious

RATINGS

Quality of Life	**83**
Fire Safety	**92**
Green	**92**
Academic	**78**
Profs Interesting	**84**
Profs Accessible	**87**
Admissions	**87**
Financial Aid	**83**

CAMPUS LIFE

Type of school	Public
Environment	Town

Students

Degree-seeking undergrad enrollment	30,641
% male/female/not reported	51/49/0
% from out of state	46
% First-year live on campus	87
% Ugrads live on campus	17
# of fraternities (% join)	27 (14)
# of sororities (% join)	22 (15)
% Asian	8
% Black or African American	2
% Hispanic	13
% Native American	1
% Pacific Islander	<1
% Race and/or ethnicity unknown	2
% Two or more races	7
% White	63
% International	3
# of countries represented	81

CAMPUS MENTAL HEALTH SERVICES

Offers mental health/wellness program	Yes
Mental health training available to students	Yes
Employs Chief Wellness Officer	Yes
Peer-to-peer mental health offerings	Yes
Counseling center has guidelines or accreditation	No
Mental health/well-being courses	NR

ACADEMICS

% students returning for sophomore year	88
% students graduating within 4 years	47
% students graduating within 6 years	70
Calendar	Quarter
Student/faculty ratio	17:1
Most common class size 20–29.	(31%)
Most common lab/discussion size 20–29.	(41%)

Most Popular Majors
Computer Science; Mechanical Engineering; Business Administration and Management

Applicants Often Prefer
University of California—Davis, University of Washington

Applicants Sometimes Prefer
University of Oregon, Washington State University, Willamette University

Applicants Rarely Prefer
Portland State University, Western Oregon University

STUDENTS SAY "..."

Academics

It's not just that Oregon State University seems to have it all, from "amazing research programs" to an "incredibly beautiful" campus and "inviting community." It's also that the administration does its utmost to ensure undergrads feel supported from the moment their first semester begins. This includes sending "frequent emails to check in on students' progress" and weekly "updates on career development, research, and community building" initiatives. Students praise many of OSU's offerings, from technology—and specifically engineering, given that the school has "an on-campus nuclear reactor"—to "excellent wildlife, ecology, and natural resources" programs. The hands-on nature of business classes also stood out to this first-year student: "We had to create microbusinesses with teams and sell products we made. It gave me a lot of insight and experience." No matter the course of study, undergrads generally receive a nice balance between "discussion-based classes and experiential learning." Moreover, "there are so many innovative peer education programs that supplement traditional lecture classes and give students another way to learn."

Though "experience varies quite drastically from professor to professor," students say that most of their instructors are "accessible, knowledgeable, and engaging." Indeed, "it's pretty rare that I have a class that feels like a drag." Overall, professors seem to be "very understanding of personal issues and are willing to be flexible and work with individual students to be sure that they succeed." As one enrollee concludes, "I have been blessed with some fantastic professors who have gone above and beyond in the time they put into me and my learning goals."

Campus Life

For the hardworking students of Oregon State who need a break from their studies, "the massive amount of extracurricular clubs and activities is amazing. Anyone can find a group of people with...similar interests." That's great, whether you're into formula racing, bouldering, or drag; there's even stuff like "Concrete Canoe (the civil engineering club where we build a canoe out of concrete, then race it against other school's concrete canoe teams)." There are even non-credited courses like a "bushcraft class." As this individual boasts, "I slept out in the woods for two nights in a tarp shelter using my skills!" For more traditional entertainments, students can "enjoy the active Greek life surrounding the campus." Students also note that because "the beach and mountains are both only an hour away... outdoor recreation is abundant."

Student Body

If Oregon State University were "the set of a movie, then it is very fair to say that we have a very diverse cast that come from all kinds of ethnic backgrounds." A wide variety of personality types as well, united by being "very smart and having fun quirks" from magnetics to country dancing. Students suggest that "the majority are very welcoming and nice and helpful" and that "I never had trouble starting conversations with anyone." Students note that while their classmates are "driven" they also manage to give off a "relaxed" vibe. Case in point: "You'll see multiple people wearing pajamas to class." This all makes it easy to recognize that most "everyone is down to have a really good time." Indeed, "I believe that everyone feels a sense of belonging here because of that."

OREGON STATE UNIVERSITY

Financial Aid: 541-737-2241 • E-Mail: osuadmit@oregonstate.edu • Website: oregonstate.edu

THE PRINCETON REVIEW SAYS

Admissions

The school reports that its standardized testing policy for use in admission for Fall 2026 is Test Optional. The Princeton Review suggests that interested applicants consult with the school for the most up-to-date standardized testing policies. *Very important factors considered include:* academic GPA. *Important factors considered include:* rigor of secondary school record, application essay, character/personal qualities. *Other factors considered include:* class rank, standardized test scores, recommendation(s), extracurricular activities, talent/ability, volunteer work, work experience, level of applicant's interest. High school diploma is required and GED is accepted. *Academic units required:* 4 English, 3 math, 3 science, 2 science labs, 2 language (other than English), 3 social studies.

Financial Aid

The Princeton Review suggests that all financial aid forms be submitted as soon as possible. *Need-based scholarships/grants offered:* Federal Pell; Federal SEOG; State scholarships/grants; Private scholarships; College/university scholarship or grant aid from institutional funds. *Loan aid offered:* Federal Direct Subsidized Loans; Federal Direct Unsubsidized Loans; Direct PLUS loans. Federal Work-Study Program available. Institutional employment available.

The Inside Word

Oregon State University duly notes that academic performance and test scores are not the only criteria for admission. A broad range of characteristics and perspectives are taken into consideration during the university's admissions process to determine if prospective students are able to succeed here. OSU wants to understand you as a unique, contributing individual.

THE SCHOOL SAYS

From the Admissions Office

"Since 1868, Oregon State University's mission has been to conduct world-leading research and provide a high-quality, relevant, and affordable education for the people of Oregon and beyond.

"We are Oregon's leading public research university with two welcoming campuses, 11 colleges, 200 academic programs, and excellent and inspiring faculty committed to the success of each student.

"Oregon State is one of only two universities in the U.S. to have land, sea, space and sun grant designations, and we take seriously our responsibility to serve the people of Oregon, the nation and the world. Our impact resounds around the globe because we are out there, addressing the most pressing challenges and providing discoveries that improve the health and prosperity of society, the economy and our planet.

"We are known for offering some of the top programs in the world, including forestry (No. 2), oceanography (No. 3) and agriculture (No. 13). Nationally, Oregon State is among the nation's academic leaders in robotics, creative writing and innovative on-line learning. In the classroom, in laboratories and in the community, we provide students the opportunities and the tools necessary to succeed, including exposure to innovations in educational technology and access to opportunities for experiential learning and discovery.

"Our students learn by doing. And what students experience at Oregon State University not only shapes their own lives, it prepares them to transform a future that is smarter, healthier, more prosperous and just."

SELECTIVITY

# of total applicants	30,246
% of total applicants accepted	77
% of total acceptees attending	20
# offered a place on the wait list	1,013
# admitted from wait list	84

First-Year Profile

Testing policy	Test Optional
Range SAT composite	1160–1390
Range SAT EBRW	580–700
Range SAT math	560–700
Range ACT composite	24–31
% submitting SAT scores	10
% submitting ACT scores	4
Average HS GPA	3.7
% submitting high school GPA	98
% graduated top 10% of class	29
% graduated top 25% of class	58
% graduated top 50% of class	88
% submitting high school rank	51

Important Dates

Early action	
Apply by	11/1
Notified by	12/15
Regular	
Apply by	8/25
Notified by	Rolling, 10/15
Nonfall registration?	Yes

FINANCIAL FACTS

Annual in-state tuition	$9,390
Annual out-of-state tuition	$28,365
Food and housing	$12,855
Required fees	$1,776
Books and supplies	$1,200
Average need-based scholarship (First-year)	$13,650 ($16,173)
% students with need rec. need-based scholarship or grant aid (First-year)	91 (97)
% students with need rec. non-need-based scholarship or grant aid (First-year)	43 (49)
% students with need rec. need-based self-help aid (First-year)	57 (56)
% students rec. any financial aid (First-year)	69 (76)
% UG borrow to pay for school	43
Average cumulative indebtedness	$26,345
% of students with need fully met (First-year)	12 (21)
Average % of student need met (First-year)	54 (66)

Pace University

One Pace Plaza, New York, NY 10038 • Admissions: 212-346-1950

Survey Snapshot
Easy to get around campus
Diverse student types interact on campus
Students love New York, NY

RATINGS

Quality of Life	85
Fire Safety	97
Green	89
Academic	78
Profs Interesting	84
Profs Accessible	84
Admissions	85
Financial Aid	87

CAMPUS LIFE

Type of school	Private
Environment	Metropolis

Students

Degree-seeking undergrad enrollment	7,675
% male/female/not reported	36/64/<1
% from out of state	48
% First-year live on campus	69
% Ugrads live on campus	59
# of fraternities (% join)	5 (3)
# of sororities (% join)	8 (4)
% Asian	7
% Black or African American	12
% Hispanic	28
% Native American	<1
% Pacific Islander	<1
% Race and/or ethnicity unknown	<1
% Two or more races	5
% White	42
% International	6
# of countries represented	32

CAMPUS MENTAL HEALTH SERVICES

Offers mental health/wellness program	Yes
Mental health training available to students	Yes
Employs Chief Wellness Officer	Yes
Peer-to-peer mental health offerings	Yes
Counseling center has guidelines or accreditation	Yes
Mental health/well-being courses	Yes, for-credit

ACADEMICS

% students returning for sophomore year	78
% students graduating within 4 years	43
% students graduating within 6 years	56
Calendar	Semester
Student/faculty ratio	14:1
Most common class size 10–19.	(40%)
Most common lab/discussion size 20–29.	(49%)

Most Popular Majors

General Studies; Research and Experimental Psychology; Registered Nursing/Registered Nurse

Applicants Also Look At

City University of New York—Baruch College, City University of New York—Hunter College, Fordham University, Iona University, Mercy University, New York University, Sacred Heart University

STUDENTS SAY "..."

Academics

Students at Pace University follow the Pace Path, a personalized approach to education designed around each individual's goals, with immersive learning at its core and opportunities that offer "a little bit of everything for students, allowing us to gain enough experiences, recognizing our own selves as students and individuals." Leveraging its strong industry connections and New York location, the university excels at "providing a working environment for students to thrive," while academic programs consistently "focus on how [the] university can help you get a job." This emphasis on real-world readiness is reflected in the more than 9,000 experiential learning opportunities, including internships, co-ops, and clinicals, completed by students in the past year through more than 1,000 employers. In the classroom, "very well-versed and experienced" faculty lead "fast but interesting" courses, sometimes taking innovative approaches like "[requiring] major projects over exams for knowledge of material to be shown," all within modern learning environments that include simulation labs, VR classrooms, and Bloomberg Terminals. Beyond coursework, students can pursue their interests through more than 50 centers dedicated to research, training, and professional development, while also benefiting from experiences like "[field] trips where we learn more about the lectures," along with access to some of the nation's top museums. As one student puts it, "Pace University's greatest strength is its strong focus on career readiness. With personalized support, industry connections, and practical learning opportunities, it equips students with the skills, experience, and networks needed to succeed in their chosen fields."

Campus Life

Pace students "balance heavy workloads but still help each other, creating a friendly and collaborative campus environment," fostering a strong sense of community both on and off campus. With its NYC location, students note that "there is always something to do outside of school, whether that be for food, shopping, or anything [else]," and many cite "exploring the city with friends" as a favorite pastime. The university enhances student life with special events like "visiting JPMorgan Chase Headquarters and seeing alumni in the workforce," alongside "a lot of interactive clubs" such as the Criminal Justice Club, intramural sports, and "Pace Film Club, where we not only create our own films, but we discuss the history of other directors and cinematographers." Across these experiences, students share a common focus on "getting involved in activities that help build community on campus," which gives them "a chance to meet new people, de-stress, and feel more connected to the school."

Student Body

Pace attracts a wide range of students who "bring global perspectives, work hard toward their goals, and create a collaborative, career-focused community." On this urban campus, this "very diverse" student body is "from all different states and countries, with a wide variety of side hustles and activities outside of school," contributing to an environment that "feel[s] very international and dynamic." The student population skews female, is "accepting of queer community," and is "expressive and independent." It is composed of "self-determined students, focusing on their studies and school while also having friends and collaborating with one another." As one student notes, "You can find just about any kind of person and all different kinds of career goals; it's really refreshing and comforting." At the same time, it's not all business; most undergrads are "fun and relatable" and "always there when needed," with classmates described as "very sweet and respectful...[and who] help each other when needed." This "very hardworking" community is driven to succeed, and "they know how to advocate, explore, and have fun." One grateful student says, "My peers push me to be the best version of myself. They inspire me to reach my goals and enact change within my community."

PACE UNIVERSITY

Financial Aid: 212-346-1309 • E-Mail: undergradadmission@pace.edu • Website: www.pace.edu

THE PRINCETON REVIEW SAYS

Admissions

The school reports that its standardized testing policy for use in admission for Fall 2026 is Test Optional. The Princeton Review suggests that interested applicants consult with the school for the most up-to-date standardized testing policies. *Very important factors considered include:* rigor of secondary school record, application essay. *Important factors considered include:* class rank, academic GPA, recommendation(s). *Other factors considered include:* standardized test scores, interview, extracurricular activities, talent/ability, character/personal qualities, alumni/ae relation, volunteer work, work experience. High school diploma is required and GED is accepted. *Academic units required:* 4 English, 3 math, 2 science, 2 science labs, 2 language (other than English), 3 social studies, 2 history. *Academic units recommended:* 4 math, 4 social studies, 3 history.

Financial Aid

Students should submit: FAFSA; State aid form. Priority filing deadline is 11/15. The Princeton Review suggests that all financial aid forms be submitted as soon as possible. *Need-based scholarships/grants offered:* Federal Pell; Federal SEOG; State scholarships/grants; Private scholarships; College/university scholarship or grant aid from institutional funds; Federal Nursing Scholarships. *Loan aid offered:* Federal Direct Unsubsidized Loans; Direct PLUS loans; Federal Direct Subsidized Loans. Admitted students will be notified of awards on a rolling basis beginning 12/1. Federal Work-Study Program available. Institutional employment available.

The Inside Word

Pace takes a holistic approach when reviewing candidates. Therefore, it's important not to slack on any facet of your application. When choosing teachers and mentors for your letters of recommendation, make sure they can really speak to your character and academic potential. Also, taking an official campus tour not only shows your interest, but will net you a yearly, renewable $2,000 Pace Visit Grant. Finally, we should note that auditions and/or interviews are required for any student who wants to enroll in the School of Performing Arts.

THE SCHOOL SAYS

From the Admissions Office

"Through the convergence of strong academics, real-world learning, and dedicated advising, we empower our students and positively impact our communities. Programs are relevant, focused, and forward-looking to meet the needs of the workforce of the future. We harness the world-class energy and talent of New York City and Westchester County and leverage the unparalleled access to internship and job opportunities. We champion diversity, equity, and inclusion and celebrate the innate potential of learners of all ages to achieve success.

"Currently, Pace University enrolls more than 13,000 diverse individuals (both undergraduate and graduate). Pace combines the benefits and resources of a large university with the personalized attention and focus associated with a small college. Dedicated full-time and adjunct faculty members balance academic preparation with professional experience, bringing a unique dynamic to the classroom. They are practitioners, consultants, advisors, and mentors to our students.

"Pace's signature program, the Pace Path, empowers students to succeed in their fields by combining powerful academics, dedicated mentoring, and immersive experiences including research, clinicals, civic engagement, study abroad, and internships. Pace University has one of the largest internship programs of any college in the New York metropolitan area. Last year, Pace students engaged in more than 9,000 internships, co-ops, field experiences, and clinicals with more than 1,200 different employers. That's why within one year of graduation, Pace students are employed at a rate almost 10% ahead of the national average."

SELECTIVITY

# of total applicants	31,753
% of total applicants accepted	78
% of total acceptees attending	8
# of in-state applicants	13,888
% of in-state applicants accepted	79
# of out-of-state-applicants	15,070
% of applicants accepted from out of state	81
# of international applicants	2,795
% of international applicants accepted	62
# of early decision applicants	221
% of early decision applicants accepted	44
# offered a place on the wait list	156
# admitted from wait list	0

First-Year Profile

Testing policy	Test Optional
Range SAT composite	1200–1350
Range SAT EBRW	610–700
Range SAT math	570–660
Range ACT composite	25–30
% submitting SAT scores	15
% submitting ACT scores	3
% submitting high school GPA	100
% graduated top 10% of class	20
% graduated top 25% of class	45
% graduated top 50% of class	78
% submitting high school rank	27

Important Dates

Early decision	
Apply by	11/1
Notified by	12/1
Early action	
Apply by	11/15
Notified by	1/2
Regular	
Apply by	2/15
Notified by	Rolling, 11/20
Nonfall registration?	Yes

FINANCIAL FACTS

Annual tuition	$55,040
Food and housing	$24,048
Required fees (First-year)	$1,536 ($1,968)
Books and supplies	$980
Average need-based scholarship (First-year)	$37,601 ($41,637)
% students with need rec. need-based scholarship or grant aid (First-year)	99 (100)
% students with need rec. non-need-based scholarship or grant aid (First-year)	16 (18)
% students with need rec. need-based self-help aid (First-year)	73 (73)
% students rec. any financial aid (First-year)	97 (100)
% UG borrow to pay for school	64
Average cumulative indebtedness	$40,544
% of students with need fully met (First-year)	19 (21)
Average % of student need met (First-year)	74 (78)

PENN STATE UNIVERSITY PARK

201 Old Main, University Park, PA 16802 • Admissions: 814-865-5471

Survey Snapshot
Students are happy
Students get along with local community
Everyone loves the Nittany Lions

RATINGS

Quality of Life	86
Fire Safety	95
Green	98
Academic	83
Profs Interesting	88
Profs Accessible	92
Admissions	90
Financial Aid	82

CAMPUS LIFE

Type of school	Public
Environment	Town

Students

Degree-seeking undergrad enrollment	42,260
% male/female/not reported	52/47/1
% from out of state	38
% First-year live on campus	96
% Ugrads live on campus	35
# of fraternities (% join)	45 (NR)
# of sororities (% join)	26 (NR)
% Asian	8
% Black or African American	5
% Hispanic	9
% Native American	<1
% Pacific Islander	<1
% Race and/or ethnicity unknown	2
% Two or more races	4
% White	63
% International	9
# of countries represented	124

CAMPUS MENTAL HEALTH SERVICES

Offers mental health/wellness program	Yes
Mental health training available to students	No
Employs Chief Wellness Officer	NR
Peer-to-peer mental health offerings	NR
Counseling center has guidelines or accreditation	No
Mental health/well-being courses	NR

ACADEMICS

% students returning for sophomore year	93
% students graduating within 4 years	71
% students graduating within 6 years	86
Calendar	Semester
Student/faculty ratio	15:1
Most common class size 20–29.	(29%)
Most common lab/discussion size 20–29.	(35%)

Applicants Also Look At

Rutgers University—Camden, Temple University, University of Delaware, University of Maryland, College Park, University of Pittsburgh—Pittsburgh Campus

STUDENTS SAY "..."

Academics

Penn State University Park provides students with a "quality education" through "highly regarded programs across a wide range of academic colleges." These programs include the "prestigious undergrad business school" Smeal, standout engineering and education majors, and Schreyer Honors College, which participants call "the finest honors program in the nation." Undergraduates note that due to Penn State's size, "classes freshman year are mostly lectures," which new students may find intimidating. But "even in lectures with hundreds of students, many professors still make an effort to get to know their class and have plenty of office hours to make themselves more accessible." As students advance in their studies and complete more General Education and major requirements, they find that their academic experience becomes more individualized. One student shares, "As I have gotten into my majors, my classes are down to about 15 to 40 people and there are a lot more discussions. I know all of my professors personally now." Students often describe the academics as "rigorous" and "competitive" but not overwhelming. Here, "professors will challenge you, but it's nothing that a hard-working student can't handle." The school's career services and strong alumni network help many graduating seniors find jobs, with one student exclaiming, "The Penn State networking web is incredible!" Additionally, its prime "location, within driving distance to Philadelphia, Washington, and New York," provides valuable opportunities for internships and employment.

Campus Life

At Penn State, students can immerse themselves in the "full college experience," which has "the perfect mix of great academics, social life, and sports." Football dominates campus throughout fall semester; "game days are super exciting and unifying for the student population," who turn out in large, spirited numbers to tailgate and root for the Nittany Lions. In addition to sports, Greek life has a strong presence on campus, and students enjoy patronizing the many bars of State College's downtown on weekends. Those seeking alternative pursuits won't have trouble finding "on-campus concerts, stand-up comedians, craft nights, sporting events, and other ways of having fun without drugs or alcohol." Many students opt to "go out to the local avenue and try new eateries and walk around campus and enjoy the scenery." Besides these activities, there are over 1,000 recognized student organizations to join, and Penn Staters have "a great enthusiasm for extracurricular and philanthropic involvement." One particularly popular event is THON, "a 46-hour, no-sitting, no-sleeping dance marathon" that "raises money for children with pediatric cancer." No matter your interests or hobbies, "between football games, Late Nights in the HUB, festivities downtown, movies, shows at Eisenhower Auditorium or the Penn State Theatre, concerts at the BJC [Bryce Jordan Center]...there is something for everyone."

Student Body

Though students hail from all 50 states and over 140 foreign countries, Penn State draws heavily from the Northeast, with "lots of kids from the tristate area" who are mostly "athletic, suburban, and friendly middle-class." Penn State offers various orientation and transition programs to help new students make social connections and build relationships on campus. "There are many opportunities to meet new people," especially throughout the first year, and students say that "everyone is friendly." Students claim that the best way to meet like-minded people is to "try different clubs and find your niche" among the many options available, from fraternities and sororities to sports teams and student-organized groups. With such a wide array of opportunities and the sheer number of students and personalities, "pretty much every student will find somewhere to fit in." There is "a sense of community" and "school spirit" among students: "Penn State is the passion and pride of a large and diverse student body."

PENN STATE UNIVERSITY PARK

Financial Aid: 814-865-6301 • E-Mail: admissions@psu.edu • Website: www.psu.edu

THE PRINCETON REVIEW SAYS

Admissions

The school reports that its standardized testing policy for use in admission for Fall 2026 is Test Optional. The Princeton Review suggests that interested applicants consult with the school for the most up-to-date standardized testing policies. *Very important factors considered include:* academic GPA. *Important factors considered include:* rigor of secondary school record. *Other factors considered include:* standardized test scores, talent/ability, geographical residence, state residency. High school diploma is required and GED is accepted. *Academic units required:* 4 English, 3 math, 3 science, 2 language (other than English), 3 social studies. *Academic units recommended:* 3 language (other than English).

Financial Aid

Students should submit: FAFSA. Priority filing deadline is 2/15. The Princeton Review suggests that all financial aid forms be submitted as soon as possible. *Need-based scholarships/grants offered:* Federal Pell; Federal SEOG; State scholarships/grants; Private scholarships; College/university scholarship or grant aid from institutional funds; United Negro College Fund. *Loan aid offered:* Federal Direct Subsidized Loans; Federal Direct Unsubsidized Loans; Direct PLUS loans; College/university loans from institutional funds. Admitted students will be notified of awards on a rolling basis beginning March. Federal Work-Study Program available. Institutional employment available.

The Inside Word

Though the school does not have any minimum requirements for an incoming student's GPA or standardized test scores, high school GPA is by far the most important factor in PSU admissions. In the absence of a test score, Penn State will continue to look at all factors of a student's application, including grades earned in academic coursework; performance in honors, IB, and AP courses; a student's essay/personal statement; involvement in activities; and other achievements. PSU is a popular choice for Pennsylvania residents and admits on a rolling basis; prospective students should submit their applications as early as possible.

THE SCHOOL SAYS

From the Admissions Office

"Founded in 1855, Penn State is a world-class public research university with a broad mission of teaching, research and public service. Ranked as one of the world's top universities, Penn State serves a total of nearly 100,000 students through its 24 campuses, which include a medical college, two law schools, an online World Campus and a school of graduate professional studies. As Pennsylvania's sole land-grant institution, Penn State educates nearly 100,000 students each year in more than 160 undergraduate and more than 160 graduate degree programs.

"Ranging in size from 600 to 4,000 students, most of Penn State's residential and commuter locations offer the first two years of baccalaureate instruction as well as a limited number of two- and four-year degree programs. These small-college settings focus on the needs of new students by offering smaller classes and close interaction with faculty. More than half of the undergraduates who complete their studies at University Park start at another Penn State campus.

"Applicants are qualified for review for any of Penn State's campuses, with preferences considered in the order requested. Choice of location and entrance difficulty are based, in part, on demand. Due to its popularity, the University Park campus is the most competitive for admission. Freshman applicants may submit the results from the SAT or the ACT with the writing component.

"Visit www.psu.edu for more information."

SELECTIVITY

# of total applicants	88,397
% of total applicants accepted	61
% of total acceptees attending	17
# offered a place on the wait list	1,818
# admitted from wait list	654

First-Year Profile

Testing policy	Test Optional
Range SAT composite	1250–1410
Range SAT EBRW	620–700
Range SAT math	620–720
Range ACT composite	27–32
% submitting SAT scores	31
% submitting ACT scores	5
Average HS GPA	3.8
% submitting high school GPA	95
% graduated top 10% of class	37
% graduated top 25% of class	72
% graduated top 50% of class	95
% submitting high school rank	33

Important Dates

Early action	
Apply by	11/1
Notified by	12/24
Regular	
Notified by	Rolling, 10/1
Nonfall registration?	Yes

FINANCIAL FACTS

Annual in-state tuition	$20,066
Annual out-of-state tuition	$41,212
Food and housing	$15,044
Required fees	$578
Books and supplies	$1,200
Average need-based scholarship (First-year)	$8,335 ($7,016)
% students with need rec. need-based scholarship or grant aid (First-year)	52 (45)
% students with need rec. non-need-based scholarship or grant aid (First-year)	62 (53)
% students with need rec. need-based self-help aid (First-year)	71 (67)
% students rec. any financial aid (First-year)	65 (64)
% UG borrow to pay for school	52
Average cumulative indebtedness	$48,037
% of students with need fully met (First-year)	36 (37)
Average % of student need met (First-year)	67 (66)

PEPPERDINE UNIVERSITY

24255 Pacific Coast Highway, Malibu, CA 90263 • Admissions: 310-506-4392

Survey Snapshot
Students are happy
Students love Malibu, CA
Students take advantage of the outdoors

RATINGS

Quality of Life	87
Fire Safety	60*
Green	60*
Academic	81
Profs Interesting	90
Profs Accessible	93
Admissions	87
Financial Aid	88

CAMPUS LIFE

Type of school	Private
Affiliation	Church of Christ
Environment	City

Students

Degree-seeking undergrad enrollment	3,457
% male/female/not reported	38/62/0
% from out of state	37
% First-year live on campus	98
% Ugrads live on campus	65
# of fraternities (% join)	6 (22)
# of sororities (% join)	9 (33)
% Asian	13
% Black or African American	4
% Hispanic	22
% Native American	<1
% Pacific Islander	<1
% Race and/or ethnicity unknown	4
% Two or more races	7
% White	41
% International	8
# of countries represented	78

CAMPUS MENTAL HEALTH SERVICES

Offers mental health/wellness program	Yes
Mental health training available to students	No
Employs Chief Wellness Officer	NR
Peer-to-peer mental health offerings	NR
Counseling center has guidelines or accreditation	No
Mental health/well-being courses	NR

ACADEMICS

% students returning for sophomore year	83
% students graduating within 4 years	67
% students graduating within 6 years	78
Calendar	Semester
Student/faculty ratio	12:1
Most common class size 10–19.	(46%)
Most common lab/discussion size 10–19.	(56%)

Most Popular Majors

Biology/Biological Sciences; Psychology; Business Administration and Management

Applicants Also Look At

Loyola Marymount University, University of California—Los Angeles, University of California—San Diego, University of California—Santa Barbara, University of Southern California

STUDENTS SAY "..."

Academics

Pepperdine University is a Christian liberal arts school situated in picturesque Malibu, California. Many students say the "professors are the greatest strength of Pepperdine," citing "mentorship [and] research collaboration" opportunities thanks to the small classes. Faculty "genuinely care about your individual success, both personally and academically." One student says that it's normal for "them to invite students to their homes for dinner or to host a Bible study group." Professors are lauded as "very passionate" and "successful in their field." Many professors utilize Pepperdine's location to take "field trips to the beach, lagoon, waste treatment plant, museums, and organizations in Los Angeles." The great scenery doesn't just include California: Pepperdine's "absolutely fantastic" international programs are a draw for many, sending students to destinations like Argentina, Italy, Germany, Switzerland, and England. "The Church of Christ mission is prevalent," as all undergrads are required to take three religion courses.

Campus Life

Students take pride in their "academically rigorous and beautiful school." They find Pepperdine's campus to be "drop dead gorgeous" with an "amazing ocean view." Its prime location in Southern California means there are plenty of options for activities outside of the classroom: students "surf, hike, [and visit] museums." Of course, church is prominent here too. "We are...allowed to freely incorporate our faith into our education," one student says. The school also features a Convocation Series, although some express concerns about that since it "is required [and] factors into [students'] GPA." They still find other ways to connect with religious communities, though, often "doing [community] service in an off-campus location" with a religious affiliation. Evenings bring "a lot of events on campus either sponsored by clubs, athletics, [or] the student programming board," but one thing undergrads would like to see more of is "school spirit at the athletic games." Pepperdine has a dry campus, so students looking for that kind of nightlife spend "weekends...[taking] trips into L.A. [or attending] parties off campus."

Student Body

Pepperdine students rave about their "welcoming," "caring," and "tight-knit" community. "Everyone is genuinely interested in how to make the world better and people take up a real interest in each other," says a student. "Everyone always has a smile on their face" and "in times of crisis the support system is tremendously helpful." "Even though there is a large group of both the left and right," one student says this is "the most open-minded student body." Students find "diverse...personalities and ideas" but say the school would benefit from attracting more students who don't exactly fit the "Christian, white, conservative," and affluent background. Students are "taught to live life with purpose, service, and leadership." Overall there's a "mix of driven entrepreneurs and chill surfers," and "you have your partiers and then you have the very religious" students.

PEPPERDINE UNIVERSITY

Financial Aid: 310-506-4301 • E-Mail: admission-seaver@pepperdine.edu • Website: www.pepperdine.edu

THE PRINCETON REVIEW SAYS

Admissions

The school reports that its standardized testing policy for use in admission for Fall 2026 is Test Optional. The Princeton Review suggests that interested applicants consult with the school for the most up-to-date standardized testing policies. *Very important factors considered include:* rigor of secondary school record, academic GPA, application essay, extracurricular activities, talent/ability, character/personal qualities, religious affiliation/commitment. *Important factors considered include:* recommendation(s), volunteer work. *Other factors considered include:* standardized test scores, interview, first generation, work experience. High school diploma is required and GED is accepted.

Financial Aid

Students should submit: FAFSA. Priority filing deadline is 2/15. The Princeton Review suggests that all financial aid forms be submitted as soon as possible. *Need-based scholarships/grants offered:* Federal Pell; Federal SEOG; State scholarships/grants; Private scholarships; College/university scholarship or grant aid from institutional funds; United Negro College Fund. *Loan aid offered:* Federal Direct Subsidized Loans; Federal Direct Unsubsidized Loans; Direct PLUS loans; College/university loans from institutional funds. Admitted students will be notified of awards on or about 4/5. Federal Work-Study Program available. Institutional employment available.

The Inside Word

Pepperdine cares about the whole student, so they look at everything from academic record and GPA to one's "background of service and leadership," so applicants should be sure to get good recommendations and reflect these qualities in their personal statement. The school will consider submitted standardized test scores, and you MUST submit them if you're angling for a Regents Scholars Program scholarship. Students affiliated with the Church of Christ are eligible for special $5,000 Church of Christ scholarships; to be considered, applicants must submit a letter of recommendation from a church leader.

THE SCHOOL SAYS

From the Admissions Office

"Pepperdine's curriculum emphasizes the broad discovery of all disciplines and is at the forefront of holistically developing the next generation of global leaders through rigorous curriculum, faculty mentorship, internship experiences, and tailored research opportunities. With its renowned Malibu campus, facilities throughout California and in Washington, D.C., and five international campuses in South America and Europe, the University is a point of convergence for scholars, believers, artists, athletes, and innovators. We seek students who show promise of academic achievement at the collegiate level. We also look for students who are committed to serving others and demonstrate the potential of emerging as a leader in our community."

SELECTIVITY

# of total applicants	13,445
% of total applicants accepted	69
% of total acceptees attending	11
# offered a place on the wait list	1,303
# admitted from wait list	670

First-Year Profile

Testing policy	Test Optional
Range SAT composite	1240–1410
Range SAT EBRW	640–720
Range SAT math	600–710
Range ACT composite	28–32
% submitting SAT scores	17
% submitting ACT scores	8
Average HS GPA	3.6
% submitting high school GPA	100

Important Dates

Early decision	
Apply by	11/1
Notified by	1/10
Early action	
Apply by	11/1
Notified by	1/10
Regular	
Apply by	1/15
Notified by	4/1
Nonfall registration?	Yes

FINANCIAL FACTS

Annual tuition	$74,370
Food and housing	$20,490
Required fees	$832
Books and supplies	$1,000
Average need-based scholarship (First-year)	$43,070 ($41,568)
% students with need rec. need-based scholarship or grant aid (First-year)	97 (96)
% students with need rec. non-need-based scholarship or grant aid (First-year)	90 (96)
% students with need rec. need-based self-help aid (First-year)	66 (66)
% students rec. any financial aid (First-year)	92 (93)
% UG borrow to pay for school	43
Average cumulative indebtedness	$32,826
% of students with need fully met (First-year)	21 (19)
Average % of student need met (First-year)	73 (76)

Pitzer College

1050 North Mills Avenue, Claremont, CA 91711-6101 • Admissions: 909-621-8129

Survey Snapshot
Active minority support groups
Students take advantage of the outdoors
Students environmentally aware

RATINGS	
Quality of Life	91
Fire Safety	95
Green	98
Academic	88
Profs Interesting	92
Profs Accessible	94
Admissions	93
Financial Aid	97

CAMPUS LIFE

Type of school	Private
Environment	Town

Students

Degree-seeking undergrad enrollment	1,175
% male/female/not reported	42/58/0
% from out of state	50
% First-year from public high school	46
% First-year live on campus	100
% Ugrads live on campus	80
# of fraternities	0
# of sororities	0
% Asian	15
% Black or African American	4
% Hispanic	14
% Native American	0
% Pacific Islander	1
% Race and/or ethnicity unknown	4
% Two or more races	10
% White	44
% International	9
# of countries represented	37

CAMPUS MENTAL HEALTH SERVICES

Offers mental health/wellness program	Yes
Mental health training available to students	Yes
Employs Chief Wellness Officer	Yes
Peer-to-peer mental health offerings	Yes
Counseling center has guidelines or accreditation	Yes
Mental health/well-being courses	Yes, for-credit

ACADEMICS

% students returning for sophomore year	90
% students graduating within 4 years	58
% students graduating within 6 years	83
Calendar	Semester
Student/faculty ratio	9:1
Most common class size 10–19.	(65%)

Most Popular Majors

Biological and Physical Sciences; Psychology; Political Science and Government

Applicants Also Look At

The George Washington University, Loyola Marymount University, Northeastern Illinois University, Occidental College, Pomona College, Santa Clara University, Scripps College, Tufts University, University of California—Berkeley, University of California—Davis, University of California—Los Angeles, University of California—San Diego, University of California—Santa Barbara, University of California—Santa Cruz, University of Southern California, University of Washington

STUDENTS SAY "..."

Academics

Just outside of Los Angeles, Pitzer College is a "socially responsible and progressive" liberal arts and sciences college with "great academics" and "active students" and that "feels like a second home." Students highlight "the ability to create your own major," and "the options and resources offered throughout the Claremont Consortium," which includes the ability to take classes at any of the other four Claremont Colleges. Because the school is so small, with an enrollment of around 1,200 undergrads, students feel they belong to a close and caring community: a place where "people go to grow as individuals through liberal arts studies and through relationships that they build." Current students praise the school's "interdisciplinary focus and non-Western centric studies." Furthermore, students say they "love the academic support" they receive at Pitzer, especially the professors, who are "well connected but incredibly caring." As one student puts it, "All my professors know me by name, even in introductory courses. [Instructors] all have PhDs from prestigious universities and demonstrate love for teaching." Experiential learning opportunities "[extend] far beyond the classroom to community service projects, the dorms, and abroad," and, because of the school's size, students often get the chance to conduct research with their professors as well. "By my second semester of my first year a professor offered me a research position," one student tells us, which "is typical for many students since class sizes are small, so we get to create intimate relationships and have direct discussions with professors."

Campus Life

Because of the mild southern California climate, Pitzer students can be found "around the pool or in the Grove House" (a student center), as well as enjoying other idyllic locations. "I manage the school garden and care for chickens," one student tells us. "I spend a lot of afternoons just hanging out in the garden doing homework or talking to friends." Weekends are spent taking advantage of the surrounding landscapes by "hiking in the mountains by the school or [driving] into L.A. to shop or go to the beach." Students here are serious about their academics, but they do "study together and mix chatting in with homework." They also take a lot of ownership over how the campus is run: "Students are directly involved with college governance. [The] administration is always open to hearing student input and working together to get it done." There's also talk of the school's "collaborative atmosphere," which can be seen in "strong student organizations." And while this isn't a school for Greek life, students note that on weekends, themed "parties are usually hosted by the school." Students "love that Pitzer provides a super progressive environment."

Student Body

While Pitzer's student body contains diverse personalities and backgrounds, in one respect these Sagehens are the same: "Everyone is passionate about something. You won't find a single student who isn't somehow involved on campus outside of the classroom." At Pitzer, "most students tend to lean far left in ideology," and they are generally "outspoken about their views...but open-minded students of any political ideology should not fear the liberal environment." "I cannot count the number of nights I have stayed up until 2:00 a.m. discussing issues ranging from Middle Eastern politics to growing up in the inner-cities," one student tells us. Students speak highly of one another and judge that their peers "are sincerely pursuing passions that they believe are reflective of themselves, as opposed to doing things for jobs/other forms of external validation." Many students are focused on "social justice" and environmental issues, though some reject the "Pitzer hippy stereotype." More than anything, they seem to agree that Pitzer students are "intellectual, and seeking to use that intellect to do good in the world."

PITZER COLLEGE

Financial Aid: 909-621-8208 • E-Mail: admission@pitzer.edu • Website: www.pitzer.edu

THE PRINCETON REVIEW SAYS

Admissions

The school reports that its standardized testing policy for use in admission for Fall 2026 is Test Free. The Princeton Review suggests that interested applicants consult with the school for the most up-to-date standardized testing policies. *Very important factors considered include:* rigor of secondary school record, academic GPA, application essay, character/personal qualities, level of applicant's interest. *Important factors considered include:* recommendation(s), extracurricular activities. *Other factors considered include:* class rank, interview, talent/ability, first generation, geographical residence, state residency, volunteer work, work experience. High school diploma is required and GED is accepted. *Academic units recommended:* 4 English, 3 math, 3 science, 3.0 language (other than English), 3 social studies.

Financial Aid

Students should submit: FAFSA; CSS PROFILE. The Princeton Review suggests that all financial aid forms be submitted as soon as possible. *Need-based scholarships/grants offered:* Federal Pell; Federal SEOG; State scholarships/grants; Private scholarships; College/university scholarship or grant aid from institutional funds. *Loan aid offered:* Federal Direct Subsidized Loans; Federal Direct Unsubsidized Loans; Direct PLUS loans. Admitted students will be notified of awards on or about 4/1. Federal Work-Study Program available. Institutional employment available.

The Inside Word

Because Pitzer will not consider test scores and is somewhat selective, make sure you have solid recommendations along with extracurriculars that demonstrate a care for Pitzer's values (social responsibility, intercultural understanding, interdisciplinary learning, engagement, and environmental sustainability). A particularly good opportunity to stand out is with the writing supplement they require as part of the Common Application. Use it to demonstrate your passion, creativity, and overall fit for the campus.

THE SCHOOL SAYS

From the Admissions Office

"Pitzer is about opportunities. It's about possibilities. The students who come here are looking for something different from the usual 'take two courses from column A, two courses from column B, and two courses from column C.' That kind of arbitrary selection doesn't make a satisfying education at Pitzer. So we look for students who want to have an impact on their own education, who want the chief responsibility—with help from their faculty advisors—in designing their own futures."

SELECTIVITY

# of total applicants	3,683
% of total applicants accepted	27
% of total acceptees attending	29
# of in-state applicants	1,420
% of in-state applicants accepted	35
# of out-of-state-applicants	980
% of applicants accepted from out of state	42
# of international applicants	1,348
% of international applicants accepted	5
# of early decision applicants	385
% of early decision applicants accepted	43
# offered a place on the wait list	578
# admitted from wait list	57

First-Year Profile

Testing policy	Test Free
Average HS GPA	4.0
% submitting high school GPA	97

Important Dates

Early decision	
Apply by	11/15
Notified by	12/13
Other ED apply by	1/6
Other ED notified by	2/13
Regular	
Apply by	1/6
Notified by	4/1
Nonfall registration?	No

FINANCIAL FACTS

Annual tuition	$70,184
Food and housing	$23,760
Required fees	$312
Books and supplies	$1,100
Average need-based scholarship (First-year)	$58,302 ($56,715)
% students with need rec. need-based scholarship or grant aid (First-year)	98 (98)
% students with need rec. non-need-based scholarship or grant aid (First-year)	2 (4)
% students with need rec. need-based self-help aid (First-year)	75 (68)
% students rec. any financial aid (First-year)	34 (33)
% UG borrow to pay for school	24
Average cumulative indebtedness	$23,350
% of students with need fully met (First-year)	98 (98)
Average % of student need met (First-year)	100 (100)

POMONA COLLEGE

333 N. College Way, Claremont, CA 91711 • Admissions: 909-621-8134

Survey Snapshot
Lots of liberal students
Diverse student types interact on campus
Students aren't religious

RATINGS

Quality of Life	85
Fire Safety	60*
Green	98
Academic	95
Profs Interesting	95
Profs Accessible	95
Admissions	98
Financial Aid	99

CAMPUS LIFE

Type of school	Private
Environment	Town

Students

Degree-seeking undergrad enrollment	1,690
% male/female/not reported	45/55/0
% from out of state	68
% First-year from public high school	68
% First-year live on campus	100
# of fraternities (% join)	3 (NR)
# of sororities	0
% Asian	19
% Black or African American	9
% Hispanic	19
% Native American	<1
% Pacific Islander	<1
% Race and/or ethnicity unknown	4
% Two or more races	9
% White	27
% International	13
# of countries represented	65

CAMPUS MENTAL HEALTH SERVICES

Offers mental health/wellness program	Yes
Mental health training available to students	No
Employs Chief Wellness Officer	NR
Peer-to-peer mental health offerings	NR
Counseling center has guidelines or accreditation	No
Mental health/well-being courses	NR

ACADEMICS

% students returning for sophomore year	95
% students graduating within 4 years	92
% students graduating within 6 years	92
Calendar	Semester
Student/faculty ratio	7:1
Most common class size 10–19.	(58%)

STUDENTS SAY "..."

Academics

Pomona College provides students with an unbeatable combination: "an academically rigorous education" in a "low-stress California atmosphere." Students note that the administration is "very good at responding to what students want" and highly "efficient in taking care of administrative tasks such as financial aid and registration." While Pomona is a relatively small school, it "offers the resources of a large university." As part of The Claremont Colleges, Pomona students can cross-register and attend events at the institutions that comprise the consortium, including Harvey Mudd, Pitzer, Scripps, and Claremont-McKenna. The average class size at Pomona is only 13 students, and "all classes are taught by professors, not grad students or TAs." As one undergrad shares, "Today, I had a class with seven people in it, then lunch with a physics professor, and then a personal tutorial with a philosophy professor." Indeed, undergrads are able to forge close bonds with the faculty. It's extremely easy to "get to know professors outside the classroom, in any setting, from office hours to Thanksgiving dinner at their homes." Another student elaborates, "Between department barbecues, parties, and weekend retreats, by the time you're an upperclassman, you will know most of the professors in your major department quite well." This helps explain how over half of Pomona students end up conducting research with faculty. It also doesn't hurt that instructors "are, for the most part, fantastic—engaging, creative, and sharp." They're also "great discussion leaders and really motivate students to get involved in class."

Campus Life

Life at Pomona is pretty grand. After all, there are "amazing academics, brilliant opportunities to get involved in, and enough sunshine to make anyone happy to be alive." Students certainly love to soak up SoCal's awesome weather; on nice days, you'll find most "everyone heads outside in shorts and T-shirts to do their class work." Beyond academics, students can participate in over 200 clubs and activities. These range from hosting a radio show to tending their own plot at the school's organic farm. Additionally, "many people are involved in intramural sports." Pomona also sponsors plenty of events. For example, students can hear live bands at Art After Hours, attend lectures on the sociology of monogamy, or take contra dancing lessons. On any given day, you might "see people setting up telescopes outside the dorms to get a glimpse of the stars...people practicing ukulele on our quad...[or] students filming a project in the dining halls." There's also plenty of opportunity to socialize with students enrolled in the other Claremont consortium schools, including at the "large 5C-sponsored parties." Pomona's location also allows for some great off-campus fun. Students love "hiking, skiing, and going to the beach year-round."

Student Body

Pomona undergrads seem to reflect Southern California's laid-back vibes. Students here are typically pretty casual, and most sport "flip-flops, polo, or tank tops and shorts" as their unofficial uniform. At first glance, many also give the appearance of a "liberal, upper-middle class, hipster athlete." But take a minute to look beneath that facade and you'll "meet the football player who got a perfect score on his SAT or the dreadlocked hippie who took multivariable calculus when he was 16." Additionally, undergrads appreciate the breadth of people they can meet. Students note that the college has a "decent level of diversity and a strong international community." This is certainly evident in their stats; the student body hails from all 50 states and several territories, as well as over 60 different countries. Further, more than half identify as a person of color, and over 23% are first-generation college students. It's fair to say that Pomona undergrads are "intelligent, engaging, and open individuals" who "excel in the classroom and usually have some sort of passion that they pursue outside of the classroom."

Pomona College

Financial Aid: 909-621-8205 • E-Mail: admissions@pomona.edu • Website: www.pomona.edu

THE PRINCETON REVIEW SAYS

Admissions

The school reports that its standardized testing policy for use in admission for Fall 2026 is Test Optional. The Princeton Review suggests that interested applicants consult with the school for the most up-to-date standardized testing policies. *Very important factors considered include:* rigor of secondary school record, class rank, academic GPA, application essay, recommendation(s), extracurricular activities, talent/ability, character/personal qualities. *Other factors considered include:* standardized test scores, first generation, geographical residence, volunteer work, work experience. High school diploma or equivalent is not required. *Academic units required:* 4 English, 3 math, 2 science, 2 science labs, 3 language (other than English), 2 social studies. *Academic units recommended:* 4 English, 4 math, 4 science, 3 science labs, 3 language (other than English), 3 social studies.

Financial Aid

Students should submit: FAFSA; CSS PROFILE; State aid form. The Princeton Review suggests that all financial aid forms be submitted as soon as possible. *Need-based scholarships/grants offered:* Federal Pell; Federal SEOG; State scholarships/grants; Private scholarships; College/university scholarship or grant aid from institutional funds. *Loan aid offered:* Federal Direct Subsidized Loans; Federal Direct Unsubsidized Loans; Direct PLUS loans; College/university loans from institutional funds. Admitted students will be notified of awards on or about 4/1. Federal Work-Study Program available. Institutional employment available.

The Inside Word

For first-year applicants, Pomona College offers regular decision admissions, as well as two binding early decision programs. Admissions officials evaluate a student's academic record carefully, examining the rigor of high school coursework, class rank, and grade point average. Students are encouraged to visit campus and meet with admissions staff, though it's not required.

THE SCHOOL SAYS

From the Admissions Office

"Pomona College is a place for ambitious, creative students who are prepared to dream big, who value diverse learning environments, and who are eager to collaborate across differences as they seek to make an impact on the world. Students enjoy a broad, liberal arts curriculum and ultimately choose among 48 majors.

"At Pomona, professors teach every class (with an average class size of 13). Yet, students enjoy the opportunities and resources of a larger university, with more than 6,300 undergraduates at The Claremont Colleges consortium.

"As the founding member of The Claremont Colleges, Pomona is one of five adjacent undergraduate colleges and two graduate institutions that make up this unique consortium. Students may take classes at any of the other Claremont Colleges, each no more than a few minutes' walk away. Athletics, clubs and organizations, dining and social opportunities are all 5-college strong.

"Located in Southern California, near Los Angeles, Pomona provides students with opportunities for scientific and community-based research, internships with major global companies and local start-ups, countless options to engage with diverse urban communities and natural environments, as well as a stellar range of arts and entertainment options."

SELECTIVITY

# of total applicants	12,470
% of total applicants accepted	7
% of total acceptees attending	47
# of early decision applicants	1,656
% of early decision applicants accepted	14
# offered a place on the wait list	1,017
# admitted from wait list	31

First-Year Profile

Testing policy	Test Optional
Range SAT composite	1490–1550
Range SAT EBRW	740–770
Range SAT math	730–790
Range ACT composite	32–34
% submitting SAT scores	37
% submitting ACT scores	12
% submitting high school rank	32

Important Dates

Early decision	
Apply by	11/8
Notified by	12/15
Other ED apply by	1/8
Other ED notified by	2/15
Regular	
Apply by	1/8
Notified by	4/1
Nonfall registration?	No

FINANCIAL FACTS

Annual tuition	$71,660
Food and housing	$23,590
Required fees	$420
Average need-based scholarship (First-year)	$70,652 ($69,920)
% students with need rec. need-based scholarship or grant aid (First-year)	100 (100)
% students with need rec. non-need-based scholarship or grant aid (First-year)	0 (0)
% students with need rec. need-based self-help aid (First-year)	100 (100)
% students rec. any financial aid (First-year)	55 (55)
% UG borrow to pay for school	18
Average cumulative indebtedness	$22,838
% of students with need fully met (First-year)	100 (100)
Average % of student need met (First-year)	100 (100)

PORTLAND STATE UNIVERSITY

1825 SW Broadway, Portland, OR 97201 • Admissions: 503-725-3511

Survey Snapshot
Lots of liberal students
Students environmentally aware
Recreation facilities are great

RATINGS

Quality of Life	77
Fire Safety	89
Green	97
Academic	77
Profs Interesting	86
Profs Accessible	86
Admissions	81
Financial Aid	82

CAMPUS LIFE

Type of school	Public
Environment	Metropolis

Students

Degree-seeking undergrad enrollment	13,182
% male/female/not reported	42/55/3
% from out of state	13
% First-year live on campus	41
% Ugrads live on campus	10
# of fraternities (% join)	1 (<1)
# of sororities (% join)	2 (<1)
% Asian	10
% Black or African American	6
% Hispanic	23
% Native American	<1
% Pacific Islander	1
% Race and/or ethnicity unknown	2
% Two or more races	8
% White	47
% International	3
# of countries represented	53

CAMPUS MENTAL HEALTH SERVICES

Offers mental health/wellness program	Yes
Mental health training available to students	Yes
Employs Chief Wellness Officer	Yes
Peer-to-peer mental health offerings	Yes
Counseling center has guidelines or accreditation	Yes
Mental health/well-being courses	Yes, non-credit

ACADEMICS

% students returning for sophomore year	76
% students graduating within 4 years	34
% students graduating within 6 years	47
Calendar	Quarter
Student/faculty ratio	17:1
Most common class size 10–19.	(33%)
Most common lab/discussion size 10–19.	(55%)

Most Popular Majors
Psychology; Computer Science; Accounting

Applicants Also Look At
Oregon State University, University of Oregon

STUDENTS SAY "..."

Academics

Portland State University encourages its students to think bigger and bolder during the course of their studies. PSU offers 200 varied degree programs in art and design, public policy, education, technology, and writing, among other tracks, and the opportunities to learn extend well beyond the campus walls. Portland State adheres to its motto to "let knowledge serve the city," with a unique four-year university studies program that allows participants the chance to self-guide their educational journey by honing in on a real-world issue and tackling it through a multidisciplinary approach that combines historical knowledge, science applications, and research. The program has helped foster PSU's reputation as a university that "has a strong focus on civic engagement and sustainability" as well as "a green-minded urban school" that's "training students to be good community members." Another advantage of a PSU education is that "classes are usually pretty small," which "promotes lots of in-class discussion." Students also mention that "Most professors are engaging and truly want to challenge you and help you succeed." Another student concurs, saying that professors "really care about the student's success, and they really help broaden our scope of learning and thinking critically."

Campus Life

The campus is extraordinarily beautiful and ideally located, so say students at PSU. While the majority of students live off campus, the school encourages a feeling of community and inclusivity. Students note that "there are a lot of things to do on campus" and "PSU has tons of programs/clubs/groups that help make you feel more involved with your school," including an Anime and Manga Club, Las Mujeres PSU, and a Self-Care Sanctuary, among a plethora of other options. The Portland State Vikings athletics program is also robust, with football, basketball, golf, tennis, and track and field being just some of the team sports offered. Students report that the school is supportive of its "really diverse" student body with various resources such as the Native American Student and Community Center and the Queer Resource Center. Students proudly share that "there are lots of activist and awareness-raising events going on all the time, and lots of students are involved in volunteering (on and off campus)."

Its Portland location is another huge draw of PSU, with "public transportation [that] is outstanding," making it easy to explore the city. Not only does "the downtown area [have] plenty of microbrew pubs, nightlife, eateries, and theaters," but the outdoor recreation options in Oregon are numerous: "There's skiing, hiking, camping, [and] fishing." Plus, "you can go to the beach or to the mountain in about two hours, and...there are great parks throughout the city."

Student Body

It is difficult to define the typical PSU student because there are so many of us from so many different backgrounds, one student remarks. That is because there is a large number of nontraditional undergraduates at PSU. Students tend to be "either typical college-age... or people in their thirties and forties with kids and a full-time job trying to juggle everything." Regardless of the differences in background and age, students describe themselves as "environmentally aware, hip," and "very liberal." Most Vikings are also "invested in their education and are friendly," and before long, "everyone finds a niche pretty quickly." As one student elaborates, "It's easy to find people you get along with, but it's also easy to find people who are completely different from you, which makes school a lot more interesting."

PORTLAND STATE UNIVERSITY

Financial Aid: 503-725-3461 • E-Mail: admissions@pdx.edu • Website: www.pdx.edu

THE PRINCETON REVIEW SAYS

Admissions

The school reports that its standardized testing policy for use in admission for Fall 2026 is Test Optional. The Princeton Review suggests that interested applicants consult with the school for the most up-to-date standardized testing policies. *Very important factors considered include:* academic GPA. *Other factors considered include:* recommendation(s). High school diploma is required and GED is accepted. *Academic units required:* 4 English, 3 math, 3 science, 2 language (other than English), 3 social studies. *Academic units recommended:* 4 math, 1 science lab.

Financial Aid

Students should submit: FAFSA. Priority filing deadline is 8/1. The Princeton Review suggests that all financial aid forms be submitted as soon as possible. *Need-based scholarships/grants offered:* Federal Pell; Federal SEOG; State scholarships/grants; Private scholarships; College/university scholarship or grant aid from institutional funds. *Loan aid offered:* Federal Direct Subsidized Loans; Federal Direct Unsubsidized Loans; Direct PLUS loans. Admitted students will be notified of awards on a rolling basis. Federal Work-Study Program available. Institutional employment available.

The Inside Word

PSU offers a range of admission options for new first-years, transfers, students enrolled at local community colleges, continuing students, and those with nontraditional high school backgrounds. GPA matters a lot here: those above a 3.0 are automatically admitted (assuming the required academic units were fulfilled). Those between a 2.5 and 3.0 must participate in the Portland Scholars program, and anyone with a GPA below 2.5 will not be considered for admission.

THE SCHOOL SAYS

From the Admissions Office

"Portland State University is Oregon's most diverse public university located in the heart of one of America's most progressive cities. It offers more than sixty undergraduate and forty graduate programs in fine and performing arts, liberal arts and sciences, business administration, education, urban and public affairs, social work, engineering, and computer science. PSU offers more than 120 bachelor's, master's, and doctoral degrees.

"The forty-nine-acre downtown campus—whose motto is 'Let Knowledge Serve the City'—places students in a vibrant center of culture, business, and technology. Portland State's urban mission offers opportunities for every student to participate in internships and community-based projects in business, education, social services, government, technology, and the arts and sciences.

"The award-winning University Studies curriculum provides small class sizes and mentoring for undergraduates and culminates in Senior Capstone, which takes students out of the classroom and into the field, where they utilize their knowledge and skills to develop community projects.

"Portland State has taken aggressive steps to enhance the student experience and campus life, with new student housing and a comprehensive recreation complex and remodeled science and performing arts facilities. The university also has hired more academic and career advisers and created new programs to support students. Sustainability—initiatives that balance environmental, economic, and social concerns—is incorporated throughout the curriculum and across the campus."

SELECTIVITY

# of total applicants	9,071
% of total applicants accepted	91
% of total acceptees attending	18
# of in-state applicants	4,280
% of in-state applicants accepted	91
# of out-of-state-applicants	4,505
% of applicants accepted from out of state	91
# of international applicants	292
% of international applicants accepted	94

First-Year Profile

Testing policy	Test Optional
Range SAT composite	930–1090
Range SAT EBRW	500–640
Range SAT math	450–630
Range ACT composite	17–28
% submitting SAT scores	4
% submitting ACT scores	3
Average HS GPA	3.4
% submitting high school GPA	97
% graduated top 10% of class	8
% graduated top 25% of class	26
% graduated top 50% of class	66
% submitting high school rank	6

Important Dates

Regular	
Apply by	8/1
Nonfall registration?	Yes

FINANCIAL FACTS

Annual in-state tuition	$12,999
Annual out-of-state tuition	$34,599
Food and housing	$15,783
Books and supplies	$750
Average need-based scholarship (First-year)	$12,189 ($12,922)
% students with need rec. need-based scholarship or grant aid (First-year)	84 (84)
% students with need rec. non-need-based scholarship or grant aid (First-year)	2 (4)
% students with need rec. need-based self-help aid (First-year)	45 (36)
% students rec. any financial aid (First-year)	74 (89)
% UG borrow to pay for school	46
Average cumulative indebtedness	$23,107
% of students with need fully met (First-year)	3 (6)
Average % of student need met (First-year)	57 (62)

PRINCETON UNIVERSITY

PO Box 430, Princeton, NJ 08544 • Admissions: 609-258-3060

Survey Snapshot
Students always studying
Great library
Great financial aid

RATINGS

Quality of Life	**83**
Fire Safety	**95**
Green	**91**
Academic	**88**
Profs Interesting	**85**
Profs Accessible	**84**
Admissions	**99**
Financial Aid	**99**

CAMPUS LIFE

Type of school	Private
Environment	Town

Students

Degree-seeking undergrad enrollment	5,899
% male/female/not reported	50/50/<1
% from out of state	82
% First-year live on campus	100
% Ugrads live on campus	94
# of fraternities	0
# of sororities	0
% Asian	25
% Black or African American	8
% Hispanic	10
% Native American	<1
% Pacific Islander	<1
% Race and/or ethnicity unknown	5
% Two or more races	7
% White	31
% International	13
# of countries represented	115

CAMPUS MENTAL HEALTH SERVICES

Offers mental health/wellness program	Yes
Mental health training available to students	Yes
Employs Chief Wellness Officer	Yes
Peer-to-peer mental health offerings	Yes
Counseling center has guidelines or accreditation	Yes
Mental health/well-being courses	Yes, for-credit

ACADEMICS

% students returning for sophomore year	99
% students graduating within 4 years	73
% students graduating within 6 years	97
Calendar	Semester
Student/faculty ratio	8:1
Most common class size 10–19.	(38%)
Most common lab/discussion size 10–19.	(56%)

STUDENTS SAY "..."

Academics

As a member of the grand old Ivy League, Princeton University has long maintained a "sterling reputation" for quality academics; however, students say Princeton's "unique focus on the undergraduate experience" is what makes their school stand out among institutions. It attracts "really experienced and big-name professors, who actually want to teach undergraduates." Introductory lecture classes can be rather large, but "once you take upper-level courses, you'll have a lot of chances to work closely with professors and study what you are most interested in." A current undergrad enthuses, "The discussions I have in seminar are the reason I get out of bed in the morning; after a great class, I feel incredibly invigorated." Though all Princeton professors are "leading scholars in their field," students admit that some classes can be "dry." Fortunately, "the overwhelming majority of professors are wonderful, captivating lecturers" who are "dedicated to their students." While you may be taking a class from a Nobel laureate, "the humility and accessibility of world-famous researchers and public figures is always remarkable." At Princeton, "there are so many chances to meet writers, performers, and professionals you admire." A student details, "The two years I've been here, I've been in discussions with Frank Gehry, David Sedaris, Peter Hessler, John McPhee, Jeff Koons, Chang-rae Lee, Joyce Carol Oates, W.S. Merwin, and on and on." No matter what you study, Princeton is an "intellectually challenging place," and the student experience is "intense in almost every way." Hard work pays off, though "the academic caliber of the school is unparalleled," and a Princeton education is "magnificently rewarding."

Campus Life

Princeton students "tend to participate in a lot of different activities, from varsity sports (recruits), intramural sports (high school athletes), and more academically restricted activities like autonomous vehicle design club, Engineers Without Borders, and the literary magazine." In and out of the classroom, there are a "billion opportunities to do what you know you love" on the Princeton campus, from performance to sports to research. "Princeton offers a lot of different opportunities to relax and de-stress," including "sporting events, concerts, recreational facilities," "a movie theater that frequently screens current films for free," and "arts and crafts at the student center." For some, social life is centered along Prospect Avenue, where "Princeton's eating clubs are lined up like ten...ducklings in a row." These eating clubs—private houses that serve as social clubs and cafeterias for upperclassmen—"play a large role in the social scene at the university." On the weekends, "the eating clubs are extremely popular for partying, chatting, drinking, and dancing"—not to mention, "free beer." Though students gush that "the campus is gorgeous year round," when students need a break from the college atmosphere, "there's NJ Transit if you want to go to New York, Philly, or even just the local mall."

Student Body

It's not surprising that most undergraduates are "driven, competitive, and obsessed with perfection." That's because Princeton students emphasize that "Academics come first," which is typified by "a tendency to overwork" and dedication to studying. "Almost everyone at Princeton is involved with something other than school about which they are extremely passionate," and most have "at least one distinct, remarkable talent." This variety means that it's actually "fairly easy for most people to find a good group of friends with whom they have something in common," and many students get involved in one of the "infinite number of clubs" on campus. Superficially, "the preppy Ivy League stereotype" is reflected in the student population, and many students are "well-spoken," "dress nicely," and stay in shape. A student jokes, "Going to Princeton is like being in a contest to see who can be the biggest nerd while simultaneously appearing least nerdy."

Princeton University

Financial Aid: 609-258-3330 • E-Mail: uaoffice@princeton.edu • Website: www.princeton.edu

THE PRINCETON REVIEW SAYS

Admissions

The school reports that its standardized testing policy for use in admission for Fall 2026 is Test Optional. The Princeton Review suggests that interested applicants consult with the school for the most up-to-date standardized testing policies. *Very important factors considered include:* rigor of secondary school record, class rank, academic GPA, standardized test scores, application essay, recommendation(s), extracurricular activities, talent/ability, character/personal qualities. *Other factors considered include:* interview, first generation, alumni/ae relation, geographical residence, volunteer work, work experience. High school diploma is required and GED is accepted. *Academic units recommended:* 4 English, 4 math, 4 science, 2 science labs, 4 language (other than English), 2 social studies, 2 history, 1 visual/performing arts.

Financial Aid

Students should submit: FAFSA; Institution's own financial aid form. Priority filing deadline is 2/1. The Princeton Review suggests that all financial aid forms be submitted as soon as possible. *Need-based scholarships/grants offered:* College/university scholarship or grant aid from institutional funds; Private scholarships; State scholarships/grants; Federal SEOG; Federal Pell. *Loan aid offered:* Federal Direct Subsidized Loans; Federal Direct Unsubsidized Loans; Direct PLUS loans; College/university loans from institutional funds; State Loans. Admitted students will be notified of awards on or about 4/1. Federal Work-Study Program available. Institutional employment available.

The Inside Word

Getting into Princeton is tough—only a small percentage of applicants are accepted, usually those at the top of their class. To be competitive, focus on excelling in honors, AP, and other advanced courses throughout high school. Involvement in clubs, sports, community service, or other leadership activities show your passions and impact. Your application and personal essays are carefully read, so give yourself plenty of time to prepare them thoughtfully and highlight what makes you unique.

THE SCHOOL SAYS

From the Admissions Office

"Methods of instruction at Princeton vary widely, but common to all areas is a strong emphasis on individual responsibility and the free interchange of ideas. This is displayed most notably in the wide use of preceptorials and seminars, in the provision of independent study for all upperclass students, and in the availability of a series of special programs to meet a range of individual interests. The undergraduate college encourages the student to be an independent seeker of information and to assume responsibility for gaining both knowledge and judgment that will strengthen later contributions to society. Two hallmarks of the academic experience are the junior paper and senior thesis, which allow students the opportunity to pursue original research and scholarship in a field of their choosing. Princeton offers a distinctive financial aid program that provides grants, which do not have to be repaid. Princeton meets the full demonstrated financial need of all students offered admission, including international students. Most families earning up to $100,000 a year will pay nothing."

SELECTIVITY

# of total applicants	42,303
% of total applicants accepted	4
% of total acceptees attending	75
# of in-state applicants	4,602
% of in-state applicants accepted	5
# of out-of-state-applicants	27,134
% of applicants accepted from out of state	5
# of international applicants	10,567
% of international applicants accepted	2
# offered a place on the wait list	1,370
# admitted from wait list	36

First-Year Profile

Testing policy	Test Optional
Range SAT composite	1490–1560
Range SAT EBRW	740–780
Range SAT math	760–800
Range ACT composite	34–35
% submitting SAT scores	60
% submitting ACT scores	20
Average HS GPA	4.0
% submitting high school GPA	99

Important Dates

Early action	
Apply by	11/1
Notified by	Mid December
Regular	
Apply by	1/1
Notified by	4/1
Nonfall registration?	No

FINANCIAL FACTS

Annual tuition	$68,140
Food and housing	$22,120
Required fees	$314
Books and supplies	$1,050
Average need-based scholarship (First-year)	$80,837 ($79,320)
% students with need rec. need-based scholarship or grant aid (First-year)	100 (100)
% students with need rec. non-need-based scholarship or grant aid (First-year)	0 (0)
% students with need rec. need-based self-help aid (First-year)	7 (8)
% students rec. any financial aid (First-year)	67 (74)
% UG borrow to pay for school	11
Average cumulative indebtedness	$21,251
% of students with need fully met (First-year)	100 (100)
Average % of student need met (First-year)	100 (100)

PROVIDENCE COLLEGE

1 Cunningham Square, Providence, RI 02918 • Admissions: 401-865-2535

Survey Snapshot
Everyone loves the Friars
Intramural sports are popular
College radio is popular

RATINGS	
Quality of Life	81
Fire Safety	60*
Green	60*
Academic	84
Profs Interesting	89
Profs Accessible	93
Admissions	91
Financial Aid	90

CAMPUS LIFE

Type of school	Private
Affiliation	Roman Catholic
Environment	City

Students

Degree-seeking undergrad enrollment	4,670
% male/female/not reported	45/55/0
% from out of state	91
% First-year from public high school	57
% First-year live on campus	98
% Ugrads live on campus	69
# of fraternities	0
# of sororities	0
% Asian	1
% Black or African American	2
% Hispanic	9
% Native American	<1
% Pacific Islander	<1
% Race and/or ethnicity unknown	4
% Two or more races	3
% White	80
% International	2
# of countries represented	25

CAMPUS MENTAL HEALTH SERVICES

Offers mental health/wellness program	Yes
Mental health training available to students	No
Employs Chief Wellness Officer	NR
Peer-to-peer mental health offerings	NR
Counseling center has guidelines or accreditation	No
Mental health/well-being courses	NR

ACADEMICS

% students returning for sophomore year	93
% students graduating within 4 years	82
% students graduating within 6 years	86
Calendar	Semester
Student/faculty ratio	11:1
Most common class size 20–29.	(44%)
Most common lab/discussion size 10–19.	(62%)

Most Popular Majors
Biology/Biological Sciences; Finance; Marketing/Marketing Management

Applicants Often Prefer
Boston College, College of the Holy Cross

Applicants Sometimes Prefer
Villanova University

Applicants Rarely Prefer
Fairfield University, Loyola University Maryland

STUDENTS SAY "..."

Academics

A "small" Catholic college in Rhode Island, Providence College offers students a "strong" liberal arts curriculum and a "fun and flourishing social environment." Academically, many undergrads point to Providence's "Western Civilization program" as a highlight of their collegiate experience. This interdisciplinary series exposes students to art, literature, philosophy, and theology and shapes undergrads into "well-rounded and deep thinkers." Students are also quick to highlight Providence's "strong business school" as well. And they certainly appreciate that they are "taught to think on our feet and to apply what we have learned in the classroom to real life situations." "Small classes" are another hallmark of a Providence education. In turn, this enables students to develop "great relationships" with their professors. And speaking of professors, undergrads here happily report that their teachers are "phenomenal." Not only are they "extremely knowledgeable," they also "have a real passion for teaching." As one thankful student boasts, "My professors have met with me on the weekends, over the summer, and responded to text messages/emails/phone calls. We have gone off campus just to chat and keep up to date on how things are going." Indeed, these professors might just be Providence's "biggest asset."

Campus Life

Life at Providence can aptly be described as a "whirlwind." This is due to the myriad of "recreational activities," "school sponsored trips," and "programmed nights" the college offers. Additionally, school spirit abounds and students are "very enthusiastic" about attending sporting events, "especially men's basketball and hockey." Students do admit that "partying is a pretty large part of the social life." And on the weekends you'll find that lots of people "go out, either to bars/clubs or senior off-campus housing." One student shares, "People will sit out on the quad on nice sunny days and play catch. We have many activities such as dances and cookouts that the school holds year round." Moreover, there are "two concerts each year where [basically] the entire school attends." Many individuals are also "highly involved in intramural sports" as well as clubs "aligning with social, political and relig[ious] interests." Of course, students here love exploring the city of Providence too, "which is a short car ride or public bus trip [away]." And undergrads "can [check out] activities around Brown University/Thayer Street, as well as DownCity where there are many shops and a large artistic influence."

Student Body

Students at Providence attest that the college is "very homogenous in regard to race and socioeconomic status," noting that most undergrads are "white" and come from "upper middle class families." Additionally, a large percentage hail from "New England, New York, [or] New Jersey." And many don "preppy" clothing; you frequently "see backwards hats, Vineyard Vines, Patagonia, and bean boots or boat shoes." Thankfully, Providence has grown "increasingly diverse" in the last few years. On top of that, undergrads gush that their peers are "genuinely nice" and quite "inclusive" regardless of background. Students are also quite impressed with how "polite" everyone seems to be. As one undergrad explains, "Doors are held, everyone thanks the professor after class, people say hello as you walk by—it's phenomenal!" Moreover, as a Catholic institution, you do find "kids who take their faith seriously." However, "you do not need to be religious to feel welcomed here." Indeed, "the college preaches about the Friar Family which the students are supposed to embody. When I first started here, I thought that this motto was quite ludicrous, but it honestly seems as though it is true. The way everyone acts is just so kind toward one another. The students here really do treat everyone like family."

PROVIDENCE COLLEGE

Financial Aid: 401-865-2286 • E-Mail: pcadmiss@providence.edu • Website: www.providence.edu

THE PRINCETON REVIEW SAYS

Admissions

The school reports that its standardized testing policy for use in admission for Fall 2026 is Test Optional. The Princeton Review suggests that interested applicants consult with the school for the most up-to-date standardized testing policies. *Very important factors considered include:* rigor of secondary school record, academic GPA, application essay. *Important factors considered include:* recommendation(s), extracurricular activities, character/personal qualities. *Other factors considered include:* class rank, standardized test scores, talent/ability, first generation, alumni/ae relation, geographical residence, volunteer work, work experience, level of applicant's interest. High school diploma is required and GED is not accepted. *Academic units required:* 4 English, 4 math, 3 science, 2 science labs, 2 social studies, 2 history. *Academic units recommended:* 4 English, 4 math, 4 science, 2 science labs, 4 language (other than English), 2 social studies, 2 history.

Financial Aid

Students should submit: FAFSA; CSS PROFILE. The Princeton Review suggests that all financial aid forms be submitted as soon as possible. *Need-based scholarships/grants offered:* Federal Pell; Federal SEOG; State scholarships/grants; Private scholarships; College/university scholarship or grant aid from institutional funds; United Negro College Fund. *Loan aid offered:* Federal Direct Subsidized Loans; Federal Direct Unsubsidized Loans; Direct PLUS loans; State Loans. Admitted students will be notified of awards on a rolling basis beginning 12/1. Federal Work-Study Program available. Institutional employment available.

The Inside Word

Applicants to Providence College can feel confident that the school takes a holistic approach to admissions. While your high school transcript remains the most important factor, the strongest candidates typically have taken multiple honors or AP classes. Beyond academics, the college carefully considers personal statements, recommendations, and extracurricular involvement, giving you multiple ways to stand out.

THE SCHOOL SAYS

From the Admissions Office

"A Providence College education is defined by a shared commitment to intellectual rigor that invites students to seek meaning, purpose, and perspective. It is fueled by a supportive community of thinkers and problem solvers who are open to exploring diverse ideas to gain a broader understanding of the world and their place in it.

"Rooted in the Catholic and Dominican tradition, Providence College offers a liberal arts education that challenges students to think deeply, ask difficult questions, and seek truth (Veritas) with open-minded curiosity. Through the Core Curriculum and the distinctive Development of Western Civilization Program, all students gain a common academic foundation that encourages dialogue across disciplines and viewpoints.

"Students are encouraged to grow academically, personally, and spiritually, while learning to reflect, make ethical decisions, and act with intention in their studies, campus life, and future work. Providence College emphasizes applying learning beyond the classroom. Research opportunities, study abroad programs, and internships allow students to connect theory to practice, build skills, and explore career paths that match their interests.

"Within a close-knit community that values respect and mutual care, students are supported by faculty, staff, and peers who inspire each other. A vibrant campus life offering more than 120 clubs and organizations and energized by NCAA Division I athletics brings students together and helps them discover what excites them and how to turn passion into action.

"Graduates leave with a strong academic foundation, a clear sense of direction, and the preparation to contribute meaningfully to their professions and communities."

SELECTIVITY

# of total applicants	13,232
% of total applicants accepted	50
% of total acceptees attending	18
# of in-state applicants	969
% of in-state applicants accepted	41
# of out-of-state-applicants	11,858
% of applicants accepted from out of state	52
# of international applicants	405
% of international applicants accepted	16
# of early decision applicants	569
% of early decision applicants accepted	81
# offered a place on the wait list	3,319
# admitted from wait list	275

First-Year Profile

Testing policy	Test Optional
Range SAT composite	1290–1380
Range SAT EBRW	640–710
Range SAT math	620–690
Range ACT composite	29–32
% submitting SAT scores	17
% submitting ACT scores	5
Average HS GPA	3.5
% submitting high school GPA	100
% graduated top 10% of class	37
% graduated top 25% of class	69
% graduated top 50% of class	95
% submitting high school rank	14

Important Dates

Early decision	
Apply by	11/1
Notified by	12/1
Other ED apply by	1/15
Other ED notified by	3/1
Early action	
Apply by	11/1
Notified by	1/1
Regular	
Apply by	1/15
Notified by	4/1
Nonfall registration?	Yes

FINANCIAL FACTS

Annual tuition	$68,630
Food and housing	$19,690
Books and supplies	$450
Average need-based scholarship (First-year)	$42,288 ($43,126)
% students with need rec. need-based scholarship or grant aid (First-year)	99 (99)
% students with need rec. non-need-based scholarship or grant aid (First-year)	8 (12)
% students with need rec. need-based self-help aid (First-year)	75 (69)
% students rec. any financial aid (First-year)	75 (79)
% UG borrow to pay for school	87
Average cumulative indebtedness	$40,138
% of students with need fully met (First-year)	30 (40)
Average % of student need met (First-year)	88 (90)

PURDUE UNIVERSITY—WEST LAFAYETTE

475 Stadium Mall Drive, West Lafayette, IN 47907-2050 • Admissions: 765-494-1776

Survey Snapshot
Students are friendly
Students are very religious
Great food on campus

RATINGS

Quality of Life	90
Fire Safety	60*
Green	91
Academic	85
Profs Interesting	84
Profs Accessible	94
Admissions	91
Financial Aid	87

CAMPUS LIFE

Type of school	Public
Environment	Town

Students

Degree-seeking undergrad enrollment	39,017
% male/female/not reported	57/43/0
% from out of state	48
% First-year live on campus	95
% Ugrads live on campus	41
# of fraternities (% join)	30 (16)
# of sororities (% join)	25 (18)
% Asian	14
% Black or African American	3
% Hispanic	7
% Native American	<1
% Pacific Islander	<1
% Race and/or ethnicity unknown	2
% Two or more races	5
% White	59
% International	10
# of countries represented	123

CAMPUS MENTAL HEALTH SERVICES

Offers mental health/wellness program	Yes
Mental health training available to students	No
Employs Chief Wellness Officer	NR
Peer-to-peer mental health offerings	NR
Counseling center has guidelines or accreditation	No
Mental health/well-being courses	NR

ACADEMICS

% students returning for sophomore year	92
% students graduating within 4 years	65
% students graduating within 6 years	84
Calendar	Semester
Student/faculty ratio	14:1
Most common class size 10–19.	(21%)
Most common lab/discussion size 20–29.	(44%)

Most Popular Majors

Mechanical/Mechanical Engineering Technology/Technician; Computer Science; Mechanical Engineering

Applicants Often Prefer

Indiana University—Bloomington, University of Illinois at Urbana—Champaign

Applicants Sometimes Prefer

Georgia Institute of Technology, The Ohio State University—Columbus, Penn State University Park, University of California—Berkeley, University of California—Davis, University of California—San Diego, University of Michigan—Ann Arbor, University of Texas at Austin, University of Wisconsin—Madison

STUDENTS SAY "..."

Academics

Purdue University—West Lafayette is a public research university that has a "big campus atmosphere" while maintaining a "small school feel within [the] individual colleges." Though students say to expect a "difficult and rigorous curriculum," it's all in the service of obtaining "a world-class education" from a globally recognized university. With over 400 research labs throughout the system, Purdue is noted for its strong reputation in the STEM fields. In particular, it is "known for being a great engineering school," with about 30 percent of students majoring in engineering. Additionally, the university offers a range of other excellent majors and programs, including "a great pharmacy program," "a great nursing program," and a "speech pathology program [that] is one of the best." Classes across the more than 200 programs offered are described as "excellent and stimulating," with professors who "expect the most out of you." They come to class "very excited about…teaching" and encourage students to share a similar enthusiasm for learning. Many instructors are seasoned educators, often having "at least ten years under their belts with PhDs." Students who commit to working hard, collaborating with their peers, and fully immersing themselves in university life will find that Purdue provides "everything a college kid could want: sports, academics, clubs, and delicious food."

Campus Life

There are numerous opportunities to get involved on campus, along with plenty of ways to "unwind and have fun by joining a club or organization." With over 1,000 options, there is something for everyone, everything from The Art of the Bonsai Club to Act Natural, Purdue's own sketch comedy group. Students can also kick back at the Union Rack and Roll, which features bowling lanes, billiard tables, and arcade games. As a Big Ten school with "great school spirit," Purdue boasts more than 30 varsity teams to root for. Cheering for these teams can feel like a sport in itself: "We have Ross-Ade Brigade and Paint Crew, student clubs for cheering on the athletic teams, and they're fairly large." For those who want to participate at a more casual level, there are three dozen intramural sports; students can obtain an Intramural Sports Pass to play as many as they like. There are also plenty of school-sponsored events for students, including the Grand Prix during Gala Week, a 160-lap go-kart race known as "The Greatest Spectacle in College Racing," and Spring Fest, which offers a ton of activities and attractions. While "there is always something fun to do on campus," students can also explore nearby Indianapolis or Chicago for a taste of city life. With so many clubs, sports, and activities available, a "typical student has a hard time completing all three S's (sleep, study, socialize) but has fun trying."

Student Body

While it can seem like most of the students at Purdue are "white and from the Midwest" (almost half of all first-year students are Indiana residents), the student body includes individuals from more than 100 countries and represents a wide array of personalities, backgrounds, and ethnicities. Many students socialize and make friends "within their majors," which "helps create a small-school feel within a huge university." People say it's not hard to make friends in a place where "most students are really down to earth." Even those who are initially more reserved can "find their niche here and get along well," as the welcoming "atmosphere on campus coaxes most out of their shell sooner or later." And once you become a Boilermaker, you are one for life, with the benefit and support of a strong alumni network of over 600,000 individuals spanning the globe.

Purdue University—West Lafayette

Financial Aid: 765-494-0998 • E-Mail: admissions@purdue.edu • Website: www.purdue.edu

THE PRINCETON REVIEW SAYS

Admissions

The school reports that its standardized testing policy for use in admission for Fall 2026 will require applicants to submit either the SAT or ACT. The Princeton Review suggests that interested applicants consult with the school for the most up-to-date standardized testing policies. *Very important factors considered include:* rigor of secondary school record, academic GPA, standardized test scores. *Important factors considered include:* application essay, recommendation(s), extracurricular activities, character/personal qualities, first generation. *Other factors considered include:* class rank, talent/ability, geographical residence, state residency, volunteer work, work experience, level of applicant's interest. High school diploma is required and GED is accepted. *Academic units required:* 4 English, 4 math, 3 science, 3 science labs, 2 language (other than English), 3 social studies.

Financial Aid

Students should submit: FAFSA. Priority filing deadline is 4/15. The Princeton Review suggests that all financial aid forms be submitted as soon as possible. *Need-based scholarships/grants offered:* Federal Pell; Federal SEOG; State scholarships/grants; Private scholarships; College/university scholarship or grant aid from institutional funds. *Loan aid offered:* Federal Direct Subsidized Loans; Federal Direct Unsubsidized Loans; Direct PLUS loans. Admitted students will be notified of awards on or about 3/15. Federal Work-Study Program available. Institutional employment available.

The Inside Word

Purdue reviews applications holistically, weighing more than just academic performance. That said, the university does have minimum high school course requirements, so be sure you've met or exceeded all of them before applying. To become a strong candidate, take the most rigorous college prep classes your school offers, including AP, IB, or dual enrollment courses. Interested in technical programs like engineering, science, health science, technology, or agriculture? Plan to take as many advanced math and science courses as you can.

THE SCHOOL SAYS

From the Admissions Office

"Although it is one of America's largest universities, Purdue does not 'feel' big to its students. The campus is very compact when compared to universities with similar enrollment. Purdue is a comprehensive university with an international reputation in a wide range of academic fields. A strong work ethic prevails at Purdue. As a member of the Big Ten, Purdue has a strong and diverse athletic program. Purdue offers more than 1,000 clubs and organizations. The residence halls and Greek community offer many participatory activities for students. Numerous convocations and lectures are presented each year. Purdue is all about people, and allowing students to grow academically as well as socially, preparing them for the real world.

"To be considered for the full range of merit-based scholarships, students must complete their admission application by November 1.

"Purdue is a member of the Common Application."

SELECTIVITY

# of total applicants	72,800
% of total applicants accepted	50
% of total acceptees attending	25
# of in-state applicants	12,038
% of in-state applicants accepted	74
# of out-of-state-applicants	46,929
% of applicants accepted from out of state	50
# of international applicants	13,833
% of international applicants accepted	30
# offered a place on the wait list	14,184
# admitted from wait list	466

First-Year Profile

Testing policy	SAT or ACT Required
Range SAT composite	1210–1330
Range SAT EBRW	590–710
Range SAT math	600–760
Range ACT composite	27–34
% submitting SAT scores	73
% submitting ACT scores	24
Average HS GPA	3.8
% submitting high school GPA	96
% graduated top 10% of class	47
% graduated top 25% of class	78
% graduated top 50% of class	96
% submitting high school rank	36

Important Dates

Early action	
Apply by	11/1
Notified by	1/15
Nonfall registration?	Yes

FINANCIAL FACTS

Annual in-state tuition	$9,208
Annual out-of-state tuition	$28,010
Food and housing	$10,030
Required fees	$784
Books and supplies	$1,160
Average need-based scholarship (First-year)	$12,580 ($12,587)
% students with need rec. need-based scholarship or grant aid (First-year)	82 (80)
% students with need rec. non-need-based scholarship or grant aid (First-year)	13 (17)
% students with need rec. need-based self-help aid (First-year)	51 (51)
% students rec. any financial aid (First-year)	77 (74)
% UG borrow to pay for school	36
Average cumulative indebtedness	$30,075
% of students with need fully met (First-year)	23 (24)
Average % of student need met (First-year)	81 (79)

Quinnipiac University

275 Mount Carmel Avenue, Hamden, CT 06518-1940 • Admissions: 203-582-8600

Survey Snapshot
Recreation facilities are great
Frats and sororities are popular
Great library

RATINGS

Quality of Life	84
Fire Safety	99
Green	85
Academic	80
Profs Interesting	87
Profs Accessible	90
Admissions	86
Financial Aid	87

CAMPUS LIFE

Type of school	Private
Environment	Town

Students

Degree-seeking undergrad enrollment	6,575
% male/female/not reported	40/60/0
% from out of state	65
% First-year from public high school	87
% First-year live on campus	92
% Ugrads live on campus	75
# of fraternities (% join)	12 (17)
# of sororities (% join)	18 (22)
% Asian	3
% Black or African American	4
% Hispanic	12
% Native American	<1
% Pacific Islander	<1
% Race and/or ethnicity unknown	6
% Two or more races	2
% White	71
% International	2
# of countries represented	52

CAMPUS MENTAL HEALTH SERVICES

Offers mental health/wellness program	Yes
Mental health training available to students	Yes
Employs Chief Wellness Officer	Yes
Peer-to-peer mental health offerings	Yes
Counseling center has guidelines or accreditation	No
Mental health/well-being courses	Yes, non-credit

ACADEMICS

% students returning for sophomore year	89
% students graduating within 4 years	75
% students graduating within 6 years	79
Calendar	Semester
Student/faculty ratio	15:1
Most common class size 10–19.	(33%)
Most common lab/discussion size 10–19.	(76%)

Most Popular Majors

Registered Nursing/Registered Nurse; Health Professions and Related Clinical Sciences; Finance

Applicants Also Look At

Bryant University, Fairfield University, Sacred Heart University, University of Connecticut

STUDENTS SAY "..."

Academics

Quinnipiac University equips undergraduates with the knowledge and skills needed for a thriving career. Students say "the ability to achieve a master's degree in almost any subject in a shortened amount of time" through a range of accelerated dual-degree programs (like a 3+1 BS/MBA) is one of the QU's greatest strengths. They appreciate that the school is "not just focused on theoretical knowledge but also on applying their skills" and highlight the "valuable experiential learning opportunities," like a cadaver lab to study anatomy or a student-managed investment fund. Professors at QU are supportive, and "mostly all know my name and care about my learning process. They are understanding, and I am able to reach most of them outside of class hours." Many enrollees choose QU for its strong career preparation; one student says a "top benefit" of the school is "its ability to help students get employed." Ambitious undergrads can attend "bi-term career fairs" and register for "multiple classes which are specific to career readiness." They also benefit from resources like "an amazing alumni connection network and career development programs." One enthusiastic student attests, "Career services are amazing. I got an internship after freshman year and so did many of my peers." According to one enrollee, this "challenging, engaging, and supportive" setting makes QU "a great choice for students looking for an academic environment that prepares them for real-world challenges."

Campus Life

At Quinnipiac, students like to get "heavily involved on campus": "Everyone that I know is involved in at least 2–3 different clubs, holds some sort of leadership position, or works for the school." The Student Programming Board (SPB) "hosts multiple events weekly" that draw many attendees, including trivia, bingo, and "stuffed night," where students create their own stuffed animals. QU's Division 1 athletics are another popular attraction: "Personally, I love the hockey and basketball games. They are always loud, engaging, and filled with school spirit!" Undergrads can explore their academic and extracurricular interests through over 140 student-run organizations ranging from Mock Trial to Q30 Television, the university's student-managed TV station. On weekends, Bobcats enjoy venturing off campus through the Hamden area or driving down to New Haven, which has "restaurants and fun places to visit." (Try the pizza, says one student.) Students stay active by visiting the "brand new, state of the art fitness facility" RecWell, where they can take free fitness classes and use the rock-climbing wall, though "when the weather is warm," they can just as easily "hike the Sleeping Giant trail right across from campus."

Student Body

Though Quinnipiac attracts ambitious, professionally oriented students, the prevailing vibe is not one of competition: "[Students are] focused on their academic and career goals but also maintain a friendly, collaborative atmosphere on campus. Whether through involvement in clubs, sports, or volunteer work, students are well-rounded and dedicated to both personal growth and helping others succeed." Another QU matriculant agrees, describing undergraduates as "respectful and intelligent. Whenever I'm confused on the coursework, I can reach out to my peers for help; they help and go one more step by providing resources I can use." With the majority of Bobcats hailing "from the Northeast," some note that the university could work on "diversifying the student body." But many students are just as quick to cite the school's strong sense of acceptance: "After transferring here...I've noticed the community at Quinnipiac and how welcoming it is. Everyone is very open and kind, and I haven't had any bad experiences with students." Despite differing backgrounds and academic interests, QU undergrads share a common bond as "dedicated self-starters who strive to make the most out of their education...the work ethic and pure determination that is demonstrated by our students is what sets us apart from other schools."

QUINNIPIAC UNIVERSITY

Financial Aid: 203-582-8750 • E-Mail: admissions@qu.edu • Website: www.qu.edu

THE PRINCETON REVIEW SAYS

Admissions

The school reports that its standardized testing policy for use in admission for Fall 2026 is Test Optional. The Princeton Review suggests that interested applicants consult with the school for the most up-to-date standardized testing policies. *Very important factors considered include:* rigor of secondary school record, academic GPA, character/personal qualities, level of applicant's interest. *Important factors considered include:* application essay, recommendation(s), interview, extracurricular activities, volunteer work. *Other factors considered include:* standardized test scores, talent/ability, first generation, geographical residence, work experience. High school diploma is required and GED is accepted. *Academic units required:* 4 English, 3 math, 3 science, 2 language (other than English), 2 social studies, 4 academic electives.

Financial Aid

Students should submit: FAFSA. Priority filing deadline is 3/1. The Princeton Review suggests that all financial aid forms be submitted as soon as possible. *Need-based scholarships/grants offered:* Federal Pell; Federal SEOG; State scholarships/grants; Private scholarships; College/university scholarship or grant aid from institutional funds. *Loan aid offered:* Federal Direct Subsidized Loans; Federal Direct Unsubsidized Loans; Direct PLUS loans; State Loans. Admitted students will be notified of awards on a rolling basis beginning 12/3. Federal Work-Study Program available. Institutional employment available.

The Inside Word

Quinnipiac University offers a variety of admissions options, and students are encouraged to choose the one they feel will best serve their interests. Early Action is strongly recommended for those applying to competitive programs such as physical therapy, nursing, occupational therapy, and the physician assistant program. The school advises students to file their applications early in the fall of their senior year and to provide supporting transcripts and test scores (as applicable) when available.

THE SCHOOL SAYS

From the Admissions Office

"You bring the passion. Together, we'll unleash it. An education at Quinnipiac embodies the university's commitment to deliver innovative programming that anticipates the future, while developing enlightened global citizens eager to make an impact in their communities and the world.

"Quinnipiac's mission is to fuel the ambition that moves the world forward. The university provides a supportive and stimulating environment for the intellectual and personal growth of its approximately 6,800 undergraduate and 3,000 graduate, law, and medical students.

"The university offers a welcoming community where everyone can thrive—individually and together. The Mount Carmel Campus is the academic home to all undergraduates with traditional, suite, and apartment housing for first-year and sophomore students located on 250 picturesque acres adjacent to Sleeping Giant State Park. The nearby 250-acre York Hill Campus is home to juniors and seniors in apartment-style residences with panoramic views, a lodge-style student center, pub and grill, and the M&T Bank Arena with twin arenas for hockey and basketball. The 100-acre North Haven Campus, just five miles away, is home to graduate programs in Health Sciences, Nursing, Education, Law, Social Work, and Medicine.

"Immersive learning experiences both inside and outside the classroom help prepare students for the evolving careers of the 21st century. Academic initiatives such as the honors program, QU seminar series, extensive internship experiences, study abroad and other experiential learning opportunities, and leadership opportunities through academic clubs and student organizations form the foundation for excellence in business, communications, health sciences, nursing, computing and engineering, education, liberal arts, law, and medicine."

SELECTIVITY

# of total applicants	25,202
% of total applicants accepted	70
% of total acceptees attending	10
# of in-state applicants	5,933
% of in-state applicants accepted	74
# of out-of-state-applicants	17,635
% of applicants accepted from out of state	74
# of international applicants	1,625
% of international applicants accepted	15
# of early decision applicants	181
% of early decision applicants accepted	80
# offered a place on the wait list	3,711
# admitted from wait list	1,104

First-Year Profile

Testing policy	Test Optional
Range SAT composite	1170–1300
Range SAT EBRW	590–670
Range SAT math	570–650
Range ACT composite	25–30
% submitting SAT scores	23
% submitting ACT scores	3
Average HS GPA	3.7
% submitting high school GPA	100
% graduated top 10% of class	21
% graduated top 25% of class	55
% graduated top 50% of class	87
% submitting high school rank	32

Important Dates

Early decision	
Apply by	11/1
Notified by	11/15
Early action	
Apply by	11/15
Notified by	12/1
Regular	
Apply by	2/1
Notified by	Rolling, 12/1
Nonfall registration?	Yes

FINANCIAL FACTS

Annual tuition	$56,430
Food and housing	$19,120
Required fees	$3,000
Books and supplies	$1,100
Average need-based scholarship (First-year)	$32,522 ($34,100)
% students with need rec. need-based scholarship or grant aid (First-year)	99 (99)
% students with need rec. non-need-based scholarship or grant aid (First-year)	98 (98)
% students with need rec. need-based self-help aid (First-year)	66 (61)
% students rec. any financial aid (First-year)	92 (96)
% of students with need fully met (First-year)	24 (30)
Average % of student need met (First-year)	70 (75)

RANDOLPH COLLEGE

2500 Rivermont Avenue, Lynchburg, VA 24503-1555 • Admissions: 434-947-8100

Survey Snapshot
Students are happy
Great library
Internships are widely available

RATINGS

Quality of Life	80
Fire Safety	93
Green	99
Academic	78
Profs Interesting	84
Profs Accessible	91
Admissions	82
Financial Aid	87

CAMPUS LIFE

Type of school	Private
Environment	City

Students

Degree-seeking undergrad enrollment	749
% male/female/not reported	46/54/<1
% from out of state	24
% First-year from public high school	88
% First-year live on campus	73
% Ugrads live on campus	76
# of fraternities	0
# of sororities	0
% Asian	3
% Black or African American	23
% Hispanic	10
% Native American	1
% Pacific Islander	0
% Race and/or ethnicity unknown	2
% Two or more races	3
% White	56
% International	2
# of countries represented	20

CAMPUS MENTAL HEALTH SERVICES

Offers mental health/wellness program	Yes
Mental health training available to students	Yes
Employs Chief Wellness Officer	Yes
Peer-to-peer mental health offerings	No
Counseling center has guidelines or accreditation	Yes
Mental health/well-being courses	Yes, non-credit

ACADEMICS

% students returning for sophomore year	70
% students graduating within 4 years	48
% students graduating within 6 years	54
Calendar	Semester
Student/faculty ratio	9:1
Most common class size 10–19.	(42%)

Most Popular Majors

Biology/Biological Sciences; Psychology

Applicants Sometimes Prefer

George Mason University, James Madison University, Randolph—Macon College, University of Virginia, Virginia Commonwealth University, Virginia Tech

STUDENTS SAY "..."

Academics

Rest assured, at Randolph College, "You're not just a number; you matter as an individual." Indeed, this "small, tight-knit community" instantly "makes you feel welcome." Additionally, students at Randolph are grateful they attend a college that "promotes self-discovery, personal growth, and individuality." Further, "small class sizes" allow for an "emphasis on student-professor relationships," a hallmark of a Randolph education. One undergrad happily confirms, "My academic experience has been challenging, there's no doubt, but the professor support has made that challenge enjoyable and exciting." A fellow student agrees, sharing, "My professors are excellent. Everyone I have had here has been supremely knowledgeable, understanding, and helpful to students. The number one goal is always to make students better thinkers." Finally, as this student gushes, "My professors are amazing! Their passion for the subject matter and course content is infectious. I look forward to each class each day and feel confident in my education. Learning is interesting and fun here, and professors are eager to answer questions and provide resources to supplement lectures and experiments. Often professors list their home phone numbers on syllabi to allow students to contact them outside of office hours. Every professor replies to email quickly, and professors are all very easy to communicate with in the classroom and one-on-one."

Campus Life

According to many undergrads, "life at Randolph is always busy and exciting." As one ecstatic student quickly asserts, "I don't think I have [been] bored [since] the day I stepped foot on this campus." And why would you be? Indeed, there are "a wide variety of clubs and organizations [in which] to become involved." Moreover, there are "many sports teams and exciting competitions to watch" as well as intramurals, which "offer a chance for non-athletes to" participate. In addition, there are a myriad of "parties and dances...sponsored by various organizations." These events are typically well-attended by students, as "they never disappoint." And for those undergrads looking for an activity a little more out of the box, there's "even a game called Humans vs. Zombies where students dress up and try to 'turn people into zombies' with Nerf guns. It's a lot of fun." Randolph is also home to many proud traditions and students love to partake. An insider reveals, "The even-odd class rivalry is definitely one popular school tradition. Skeller Sings are one of the events where the even spirit society (ETAs) and odd spirit society (Gammas) will sing (read: shout) songs at each other and try to create distractions while the other group sings." Finally, when students want to look beyond the campus for fun, they can "go hiking, swimming, and boating at all the lakes, rivers, and trails. [Indeed] there is a lot of nature and history surrounding the Lynchburg area."

Student Body

Undergrads at Randolph emphatically state that there's no typical student to be found wandering around campus. As one knowing undergrad shares, "Students vary widely in background and personality, preferences, [and] habits." Additionally, a "considerable percentage of the student body is comprised of international students," which certainly adds to the diversity of the school. Of course, if pressed to throw out some adjectives, Randolph undergrads will likely say that their peers are "hardworking, artistic, and caring." They are also "intelligent," "unafraid to speak their minds," and "committed to doing excellent work." Fortunately, "being such a small campus, it is hard not [to] develop lots of friends from several different social groups," and certainly, "campus traditions help form a very strong sense of community here." Or, as one content undergrad simply states, "Everyone gets along fairly well and it's not too hard to fit in when there aren't really any labels for people."

RANDOLPH COLLEGE

Financial Aid: 434-947-8128 • E-Mail: admissions@randolphcollege.edu • Website: www.randolphcollege.com

THE PRINCETON REVIEW SAYS

Admissions

The school reports that its standardized testing policy for use in admission for Fall 2026 is Test Optional. The Princeton Review suggests that interested applicants consult with the school for the most up-to-date standardized testing policies. *Very important factors considered include:* academic GPA. *Important factors considered include:* rigor of secondary school record, level of applicant's interest. *Other factors considered include:* class rank, standardized test scores, application essay, recommendation(s), volunteer work, work experience. High school diploma is required and GED is accepted. *Academic units required:* 4 English, 3 math, 3 science, 2 science labs, 2 history, 1 academic elective. *Academic units recommended:* 4 math, 3 language (other than English), 3 academic electives.

Financial Aid

Students should submit: FAFSA; State aid form. The Princeton Review suggests that all financial aid forms be submitted as soon as possible. *Need-based scholarships/grants offered:* Federal Pell; Federal SEOG; State scholarships/grants; Private scholarships; College/university scholarship or grant aid from institutional funds. *Loan aid offered:* Federal Direct Subsidized Loans; Federal Direct Unsubsidized Loans; Direct PLUS loans; College/university loans from institutional funds. Admitted students will be notified of awards on a rolling basis beginning 10/15. Federal Work-Study Program available. Institutional employment available.

The Inside Word

At Randolph College, your transcript traditionally carries the most weight. That said, given that the school's slogan is to "Be an original," expect that your specific recommendations, personal essays, and extracurricular activities will be important factors in the admissions process.

THE SCHOOL SAYS

From the Admissions Office

"Known for its academic programs and affordability, Randolph College offers students the best features of breadth—including a comprehensive general education curriculum and a wide range of majors—as well as specialization. Embedded within a liberal arts framework are ample opportunities for study abroad, leadership roles, research partnerships with faculty, and practical experience through internships and service learning. Students are encouraged to pursue academic goals that are personalized and meaningful to them.

"In Fall 2021, Randolph College launched its "TAKE2" curriculum. This unique curricular model splits the semester into two seven-week sessions. During each one, students concentrate on two courses at a time. TAKE2 was designed by faculty to enable a more successful, enjoyable, and rewarding academic experience. Students focus on two courses, rather than several, at a time, in extended class sessions that allow for more applied activities and group interaction. No classes are held on Wednesdays, allowing for a cognitive break to study and prepare for classes, as well as extracurricular activities, community engagement, field trips, and internships.

"A graduate of Randolph College understands the intellectual foundations of the arts, sciences, and humanities while developing critical skills to learn, adapt, and succeed in a rapidly changing global environment. The college's strong emphasis on writing enables students to communicate clearly and persuasively, and the diverse student population and study abroad programs enable students to expand their horizons. The distinctive student-led honor system has long been a central part of daily life at Randolph and adds to the cohesive community feel. A member of the Old Dominion Athletic Conference, Randolph's holistic approach to student development enables scholar-athletes to excel in a variety of sports while focusing on academic excellence. Located in the heart of Virginia near the Blue Ridge Mountains, Randolph College's campus is part of the multi-college town of Lynchburg, with abundant cultural, entertainment, and recreational opportunities."

SELECTIVITY

# of total applicants	2,590
% of total applicants accepted	90
% of total acceptees attending	12

First-Year Profile

Testing policy	Test Optional
Range SAT composite	1040–1090
Range SAT EBRW	520–580
Range SAT math	440–630
Range ACT composite	20–24
% submitting SAT scores	4
% submitting ACT scores	6
Average HS GPA	3.5
% submitting high school GPA	100
% graduated top 10% of class	16
% graduated top 25% of class	54
% graduated top 50% of class	79
% submitting high school rank	25

Important Dates

Early action	
Apply by	11/15
Notified by	Rolling
Regular	
Apply by	3/1 then Rolling
Notified by	Rolling, 9/1
Nonfall registration?	Yes

FINANCIAL FACTS

Annual tuition	$32,300
Food and housing	$13,250
Required fees (First-year)	$1,050 ($1,250)
Books and supplies	$1,340
Average need-based scholarship (First-year)	$24,897 ($25,478)
% students with need rec. need-based scholarship or grant aid (First-year)	100 (100)
% students with need rec. non-need-based scholarship or grant aid (First-year)	17 (20)
% students with need rec. need-based self-help aid (First-year)	67 (60)
% students rec. any financial aid (First-year)	100 (100)
% UG borrow to pay for school	80
Average cumulative indebtedness	$34,909
% of students with need fully met (First-year)	18 (22)
Average % of student need met (First-year)	70 (72)

RANDOLPH-MACON COLLEGE

202 Henry Street, Ashland, VA 23005-5505 • Admissions: 804-752-7305

Survey Snapshot
Easy to get around campus
Everyone loves the Yellow Jackets
Career services are great

RATINGS

Quality of Life	**89**
Fire Safety	**94**
Green	**60***
Academic	**82**
Profs Interesting	**88**
Profs Accessible	**91**
Admissions	**83**
Financial Aid	**93**

CAMPUS LIFE

Type of school	Private
Affiliation	Methodist
Environment	Village

Students

Degree-seeking undergrad enrollment	1,789
% male/female/not reported	46/54/0
% from out of state	18
% First-year from public high school	82
% First-year live on campus	85
% Ugrads live on campus	74
# of fraternities (% join)	6 (14)
# of sororities (% join)	5 (22)
% Asian	3
% Black or African American	9
% Hispanic	7
% Native American	<1
% Pacific Islander	0
% Race and/or ethnicity unknown	2
% Two or more races	6
% White	71
% International	1
# of countries represented	25

CAMPUS MENTAL HEALTH SERVICES

Offers mental health/wellness program	Yes
Mental health training available to students	Yes
Employs Chief Wellness Officer	Yes
Peer-to-peer mental health offerings	Yes
Counseling center has guidelines or accreditation	Yes
Mental health/well-being courses	No

ACADEMICS

% students returning for sophomore year	79
% students graduating within 4 years	63
% students graduating within 6 years	74
Calendar	4-1-4
Student/faculty ratio	12:1
Most common class size 10–19.	(41%)

Most Popular Majors

Communication; Biology/Biological Sciences; Business/Commerce

Applicants Also Look At

Bridgewater College, Christopher Newport University, East Carolina University, George Mason University, Hampden—Sydney College, James Madison University, Longwood University, Old Dominion University, Roanoke College, Shenandoah University, University of Mary Washington, University of Virginia, Virginia Commonwealth University, Virginia Tech, William & Mary

STUDENTS SAY "..."

Academics

Randolph-Macon College, a historic Virginia institution, offers a rigorous liberal arts education distinguished by its commitment to a "focus on well-rounded individuals." Its thoughtfully designed core curriculum incorporates experiential learning—such as field study or service learning—alongside a capstone experience, while also providing students with "many outside-of-class opportunities to interact with their departments, including workshops, guest lectures, and other educational events." The college's "mini-mester" January Term (J-Term) is often devoted to study abroad programs or internships, and as one student notes, "being able to travel with your professors during J-term to explore a country that they know well is an experience that most don't get." Students also benefit from accessible professional development resources like the Edge Boot Camp and leadership training, where many find that "the resources, connections, workshops, and staff are incredible [and] truly help in all aspects of getting you ready for the real world." Strong career outcomes are further supported by "a powerful alumni connection," through which students "get great support in terms of looking for internships and jobs for after graduation." Faculty emphasize applied learning, integrating opportunities such as "labs that are specifically designed for students to gain a hands-on experience," and even immersive classroom simulations, including a political science course where students "roleplay as members of Congress to make and pass bills!" The college's small class sizes foster the "ability to have personal relationships with professors," and it is "extremely easy to get in touch with most professors, and to talk to them about things, whether it be about classwork or the course itself...or just general things." As one student reflects, "Because of some of my professors, I have been able to discover some passions which I would have never had without them."

Campus Life

Students say that RMC fosters a close-knit environment "with a big emphasis on campus life," where "there is always something to do on campus to make sure you don't feel alone." There "are a lot of clubs [and] events on campus that [help students] to socialize beyond the classroom," including a semiannual campus-wide community service day during which students "go around our college town and do jobs for local residents, such as yard work and housework." The recreation center serves as a lively hub and "is always packed with people playing basketball, volleyball, or working out," and intramurals are a favorite among students seeking both competition and camaraderie. Many also embrace the outdoor opportunities offered by the school, "where students can go on hikes, go rock climbing...and more." Students at RMC "have a lot of pride in their school; it's impossible to go a single day on campus without seeing at least three people wearing RMC merch." Overall, the atmosphere is vibrant and social: "People connect with each other often, and there are always groups of people walking around campus or doing something fun together."

Student Body

RMC students "are well-rounded individuals who are taught to think for themselves." The mix of students includes "in-state and out-of-state students, people of all races, and people from different walks of life," as well as a good number of athletes and "a substantial commuter, transfer, and neurodivergent student population." There is also "a vibrant queer community here," and students "put a huge emphasis on involvement and belonging." One vouches, "Students are allowed to be themselves and explore all of their interests." Most "are welcoming, incredibly friendly, and skilled at their passions," and find that "everyone on campus is very nice and understanding." Since RMC is a smaller campus, "once you see one person, you see them everywhere for the rest of your time on campus," which provides more of a chance to "collaborate and work with them," as well as build friendships.

Randolph-Macon College

Financial Aid: 804-752-7259 • E-Mail: admissions@rmc.edu • Website: www.rmc.edu

THE PRINCETON REVIEW SAYS

Admissions

The school reports that its standardized testing policy for use in admission for Fall 2026 is Test Optional. The Princeton Review suggests that interested applicants consult with the school for the most up-to-date standardized testing policies. *Very important factors considered include:* rigor of secondary school record, academic GPA. *Important factors considered include:* application essay. *Other factors considered include:* class rank, standardized test scores, recommendation(s), interview, extracurricular activities, talent/ability, character/personal qualities, first generation, alumni/ae relation, geographical residence, volunteer work, work experience, level of applicant's interest. High school diploma is required and GED is accepted. *Academic units required:* 4 English, 3 math, 2 science, 2 science labs, 2 language (other than English), 2 social studies, 3 academic electives. *Academic units recommended:* 4 English, 4 math, 4 science, 4 science labs, 3 language (other than English), 3 social studies, 5 academic electives.

Financial Aid

Students should submit: FAFSA. Priority filing deadline is 2/1. The Princeton Review suggests that all financial aid forms be submitted as soon as possible. *Need-based scholarships/grants offered:* Federal Pell; Federal SEOG; State scholarships/grants; Private scholarships; College/university scholarship or grant aid from institutional funds. *Loan aid offered:* Federal Direct Subsidized Loans; Federal Direct Unsubsidized Loans; Direct PLUS loans. Federal Work-Study Program available. Institutional employment available.

The Inside Word

Randolph-Macon College takes a holistic approach to reviewing applications, considering your experiences, talents, and activities alongside traditional measures like grades and test scores. The school is test-optional, so submit scores only if they reflect your academic abilities. Letters of recommendation can help the school gain a better sense of you, though only Nursing Program applicants must submit one. Completion and passing of Algebra II or a higher-level math is required before enrollment. Demonstrated interest can also strengthen your application.

THE SCHOOL SAYS

From the Admissions Office

"A Randolph-Macon College education begins with your future in mind. RMC integrates an extraordinary education and pairs it with faculty, staff, coaches and alumni that provide you with a campus-wide support system to help you make the most of your RMC experience. Campus life offers over one hundred organizations, including eSports, an equestrian program, and 18 varsity sports, to provide a dynamic event schedule that enriches your experience. Our challenging curriculum, national and global opportunities through internships and study abroad programs, which include our unique January Term experience, make Randolph-Macon students competitive for any career or academic pursuit post-graduation. This, paired with Randolph-Macon's four-year career preparation program, The Edge, gives students a distinct, competitive advantage after graduation in reaching their career or graduate school goals. Ideally located just outside of Richmond, Virginia and 90 miles from Washington, D.C., RMC offers a wide range of educational and career possibilities, partnerships with prestigious medical institutions, including guaranteed admissions to qualified students to medical or nursing school. The college also offers a Bachelor of Science in Nursing with a direct entry option for qualified students. Our Four-Year Degree Guarantee program promises that freshmen who meet the necessary requirements will graduate within four years, which ninety-five percent of Randolph- Macon College students achieve. RMC's loyal alumni rank in the top 30 in the nation for alumni giving, a true testament to their love of, and gratitude for, their Randolph-Macon experience. Randolph-Macon gets you up close and future ready."

SELECTIVITY

# of total applicants	3,138
% of total applicants accepted	91
% of total acceptees attending	19
# of in-state applicants	2,406
% of in-state applicants accepted	91
# of out-of-state-applicants	630
% of applicants accepted from out of state	94
# of international applicants	79
% of international applicants accepted	65
# of early decision applicants	80
% of early decision applicants accepted	93
# offered a place on the wait list	0
# admitted from wait list	0

First-Year Profile

Testing policy	Test Optional
Range SAT composite	1000–1220
Range SAT EBRW	510–640
Range SAT math	480–610
Range ACT composite	21–27
% submitting SAT scores	22
% submitting ACT scores	2
Average HS GPA	3.7
% submitting high school GPA	100
% graduated top 10% of class	14
% graduated top 25% of class	39
% graduated top 50% of class	80
% submitting high school rank	60

Important Dates

Early decision	
Apply by	11/15
Notified by	Rolling
Early action	
Apply by	10/17
Notified by	Rolling
Regular	
Apply by	Last week of August
Notified by	Rolling, Late September
Nonfall registration?	Yes

FINANCIAL FACTS

Annual tuition	$50,574
Food and housing	$15,432
Required fees	$1,918
Books and supplies	$1,000
Average need-based scholarship (First-year)	$43,080 ($44,456)
% students with need rec. need-based scholarship or grant aid (First-year)	100 (100)
% students with need rec. non-need-based scholarship or grant aid (First-year)	48 (44)
% students with need rec. need-based self-help aid (First-year)	83 (80)
% students rec. any financial aid (First-year)	99 (100)
% UG borrow to pay for school	62
Average cumulative indebtedness	$49,546
% of students with need fully met (First-year)	48 (44)
Average % of student need met (First-year)	87 (86)

REED COLLEGE

3203 SE Woodstock Boulevard, Portland, OR 97202-8199 • Admissions: 503-777-7511

Survey Snapshot
Easy to get around campus
Great library
Great off-campus food

RATINGS

Quality of Life	**91**
Fire Safety	**97**
Green	**60***
Academic	**96**
Profs Interesting	**99**
Profs Accessible	**96**
Admissions	**94**
Financial Aid	**99**

CAMPUS LIFE

Type of school	Private
Environment	Metropolis

Students

Degree-seeking undergrad enrollment	1,278
% male/female/not reported	34/44/22
% First-year from public high school	55
% First-year live on campus	100
% Ugrads live on campus	76
# of fraternities	0
# of sororities	0
% Asian	8
% Black or African American	2
% Hispanic	13
% Native American	<1
% Pacific Islander	<1
% Race and/or ethnicity unknown	<1
% Two or more races	12
% White	54
% International	11
# of countries represented	28

CAMPUS MENTAL HEALTH SERVICES

Offers mental health/wellness program	Yes
Mental health training available to students	Yes
Employs Chief Wellness Officer	Yes
Peer-to-peer mental health offerings	Yes
Counseling center has guidelines or accreditation	Yes
Mental health/well-being courses	Yes

ACADEMICS

% students returning for sophomore year	90
% students graduating within 4 years	59
% students graduating within 6 years	73
Calendar	Semester
Student/faculty ratio	9:1
Most common class size 10–19.	(50%)
Most common lab/discussion size 10–19.	(67%)

Most Popular Majors

Computer Science; Psychology; Political Science and Government

STUDENTS SAY "..."

Academics

Reed College in Portland, Oregon, is a private liberal arts institution known for its devotion to intellectual inquiry and critical thought. Academics are "quite challenging and rigorous," and "there can be heavy reading assignments, lengthy lab reports, and exams all in the same week." That said, none of this is seen as "busy work," but rather as an integral part of the community, which "is generally centered around the passion to learn and gain more knowledge." Reed's structure is designed to focus "on learning significantly more than grades," so much so that unless directly requested, students don't see their grades; they learn about their performance through specific feedback and evaluations from faculty. To assist students, there are "many networks of support" available, including a peer tutoring program used by more than half of all students.

Unsurprisingly, the faculty-student bond is the foundation of a Reed education, and most classes are conference style, "meaning the students all read the material before the class and come to class to ask questions and discuss with the professor." This interruptible format "pushes us to use our brains and think critically about the readings we have done" and "places responsibility on the individual to do their work." Professors "have such a mastery of their material that they're able to let discussions go and let students explore material on their own," and they will "excitedly jump in the conversation just like a peer and make wonderful co-learners." And one student "finds it awesome" that the school invites them to attend lectures by potential professors: "In this way, I have learned a lot about topics related to my major."

Campus Life

If "you are looking to party or become enthralled in a sports culture" or Greek life, Reed is not the school for you, as students here "pride themselves on the amount of work they have to do." That said, "Reedies are also very laid-back, making sure that time for work has corresponding times for play." That's how you wind up with traditions like the Thesis Parade and Renn Fayre, in which seniors burn their notes and thesis drafts in a bonfire, or "themed dances where you get to dress up, dance, and let loose." The college has "a program called 'The Gray Fund' which helps fund all types of activities that are completely outside of academics," and these "can be as extensive as weeklong trips, or as simple as visits to the local cat Café." The pool hall is a massively popular meeting space, and there are weekly events "where students gather for pool tournaments and hanging out." Since this bunch is generally creative, many here "play a lot of board games, have radio shows at the station, knit or crochet, or play musical instruments." Downtown Portland "is very easily accessed by bus" and students also "take day trips to the Oregon coast and go into the mountains near the city."

Student Body

First and foremost, "Reedies are invested in the learning process," so be prepared to meet plenty of students who "are often taking very niche classes that don't pertain to their own major" and who subsequently have "something they could talk your ear off about." This is a group of "academically driven, extremely progressive, friendly, inclusive, and uniquely talented" individuals. Gender minorities and LGBTQIA+ students find that the school "feels incredibly welcoming and nurturing." As one student puts it: "Our motley of student-run clubs and work activities and school-supported extracurriculars end up forming hundreds of mini- communities across campus that give many a chance to be a part of something."

Reed College

Financial Aid: 800-547-4750 • E-Mail: admission@reed.edu • Website: www.reed.edu

THE PRINCETON REVIEW SAYS

Admissions

The school reports that its standardized testing policy for use in admission for Fall 2026 is Test Free. The Princeton Review suggests that interested applicants consult with the school for the most up-to-date standardized testing policies. *Very important factors considered include:* rigor of secondary school record, academic GPA, application essay. *Important factors considered include:* class rank, recommendation(s), interview, character/personal qualities. *Other factors considered include:* extracurricular activities, talent/ability, first generation, alumni/ae relation, geographical residence, volunteer work, work experience, level of applicant's interest. High school diploma is required and GED is accepted. *Academic units recommended:* 4 English, 4 math, 4 science, 3.5 language (other than English), 4 social studies.

Financial Aid

Students should submit: FAFSA; CSS PROFILE. Priority filing deadline is 1/15. The Princeton Review suggests that all financial aid forms be submitted as soon as possible. *Need-based scholarships/grants offered:* Federal Pell; Federal SEOG; State scholarships/grants; Private scholarships; College/university scholarship or grant aid from institutional funds. *Loan aid offered:* Federal Direct Subsidized Loans; Federal Direct Unsubsidized Loans; Direct PLUS loans; College/university loans from institutional funds. Admitted students will be notified of awards on a rolling basis two weeks after an admission decision. Federal Work-Study Program available. Institutional employment available.

The Inside Word

Reed College values students who are authentic and intellectually curious. Its academics are rigorous, and admission is highly competitive, though early decision applicants may have a stronger chance of acceptance. Reed does not require or consider SAT or ACT scores in its review, so you can focus on showcasing your strengths in other ways. Scores from AP or IB exams can be submitted upon enrollment for credit.

THE SCHOOL SAYS

From the Admissions Office

"One of the most distinctive colleges in the nation, Reed provides a singular example of the liberal arts experience: a structured curriculum with an emphasis on personal inquiry; extensive written and in-person feedback from professors on assignments; and a deeply collaborative academic environment. Classes are small, faculty members are highly accessible, and students are active participants in the production of new knowledge.

"The Reed community is guided by the Honor Principle. The commitment to the independence of thought and mutual trust and respect helps to create an environment in which students feel connected, challenged, and fulfilled. Reed students are culturally diverse and hail from 48 states. In fact, Reedies travel the farthest to attend Reed out of any school in the nation. The student body is also composed of 9 percent international students.

"The breadth, depth, and rigor of the curriculum provide excellent preparation for nearly any career. Reed is ranked second in the nation in the percentage of graduates who earn PhDs in the humanities, third in the nation in the percentage who earn PhDs in the physical sciences, and fourth across all disciplines. Many Reed alumni win major graduate fellowships, found or lead companies and organizations, and earn medical, business, or law degrees."

SELECTIVITY

# of total applicants	9,606
% of total applicants accepted	29
% of total acceptees attending	12
# of in-state applicants	610
% of in-state applicants accepted	36
# of out-of-state-applicants	4,511
% of applicants accepted from out of state	51
# of international applicants	4,485
% of international applicants accepted	7
# offered a place on the wait list	5,305
# admitted from wait list	110

First-Year Profile

Testing policy	Test Free
Average HS GPA	4.0
% submitting high school GPA	87
% graduated top 10% of class	51
% graduated top 25% of class	83
% graduated top 50% of class	97
% submitting high school rank	30

Important Dates

Early decision	
Apply by	11/1
Notified by	12/20
Other ED apply by	1/15
Other ED notified by	3/1
Early action	
Apply by	11/1
Notified by	2/15
Regular	
Apply by	1/15
Notified by	4/1
Nonfall registration?	No

FINANCIAL FACTS

Annual tuition	$71,460
Food and housing	$18,228
Required fees	$310
Books and supplies	$1,050
Average need-based scholarship (First-year)	$55,923 ($57,550)
% students with need rec. need-based scholarship or grant aid (First-year)	100 (100)
% students with need rec. non-need-based scholarship or grant aid (First-year)	0 (0)
% students with need rec. need-based self-help aid (First-year)	75 (81)
% students rec. any financial aid (First-year)	59 (53)
% UG borrow to pay for school	50
Average cumulative indebtedness	$26,598
% of students with need fully met (First-year)	100 (100)
Average % of student need met (First-year)	100 (100)

RENSSELAER POLYTECHNIC INSTITUTE

110 8th Street, Troy, NY 12180-3590 • Admissions: 518-276-6216

Survey Snapshot
Internships are widely available
Alumni active on campus
Students aren't religious

RATINGS

Quality of Life	**80**
Fire Safety	**89**
Green	**60***
Academic	**81**
Profs Interesting	**86**
Profs Accessible	**89**
Admissions	**91**
Financial Aid	**88**

CAMPUS LIFE

Type of school	Private
Environment	City

Students

Degree-seeking undergrad enrollment	5,779
% male/female/not reported	68/32/0
% from out of state	60
% First-year from public high school	70
% First-year live on campus	100
% Ugrads live on campus	54
# of fraternities (% join)	29 (17)
# of sororities (% join)	5 (12)
% Asian	22
% Black or African American	5
% Hispanic	11
% Native American	<1
% Pacific Islander	<1
% Race and/or ethnicity unknown	5
% Two or more races	6
% White	47
% International	4
# of countries represented	51

CAMPUS MENTAL HEALTH SERVICES

Offers mental health/wellness program	Yes
Mental health training available to students	No
Employs Chief Wellness Officer	NR
Peer-to-peer mental health offerings	NR
Counseling center has guidelines or accreditation	No
Mental health/well-being courses	NR

ACADEMICS

% students returning for sophomore year	91
% students graduating within 4 years	68
% students graduating within 6 years	80
Calendar	Semester
Student/faculty ratio	15:1
Most common class size 10–19.	(26%)
Most common lab/discussion size 30–39.	(38%)

Most Popular Majors

Business/Commerce; Computer Engineering; Electrical and Electronics Engineering

Applicants Also Look At

Carnegie Mellon University, Cornell University, Georgia Institute of Technology, Massachusetts Institute of Technology, Worcester Polytechnic Institute

STUDENTS SAY "..."

Academics

Students name Rensselaer Polytechnic Institute's academic rigor as one if its greatest strength, saying that they both "want to be challenged" and desire the "many cutting-edge research opportunities." For example: "I can help run a fully functioning critical nuclear reactor, use one of the strongest linear particle accelerators in the nation, and so much more as an undergraduate." The trade-off is a tricky school-life balance, with one enrollee describing time spent studying as "almost the equivalent of a full-time job." That said, "there are many supports for students who may need extra help," and the school "will not let you fall behind." There are "very strong" tutoring services available and "the counseling center is great." Students appreciate the chance to learn from professors with "real-world experiences." Many of the professors are at the top of their field, and students have the opportunity to work with them on "amazing research projects." This prepares RPI graduates "to exceed expectations [in] any opportunities we may pursue." As one student sums up, "Everyone here makes you work hard, but that pushes you to definite success."

Campus Life

One student captures the campus vibe, saying, "I wish I could clone myself just so I can partake in a fraction of the amount of things the school has to offer." There is plenty to do on this "very beautiful and very walkable" campus. Many students enjoy STEM-focused clubs, such as the Flying Club for aviation enthusiasts, Rensselaer Rocketry for building rockets, and Engineers Without Borders, which "focuses on sustainable engineering projects to help underdeveloped communities (locally and internationally)." There are many activities for outdoorsy students, such as wilderness excursions, birdwatching, and skiing. The campus also boasts a thriving college radio station, providing "free self-expression" through "less conventional" content. Each week, weather permitting, you might witness a lively game of Humans Versus Zombies, similar to tag, that's "very fun" and brings students together. Students also enjoy crafting at The Forge, a makerspace equipped with tools like a 3D printer, laser cutter, and sticker maker. On the weekends, students can head to downtown Troy for the farmer's market, which features "a lot of well-made items and delicious food." Whether you're an "incessant party animal" or someone who is "passionate about their work," there's plenty to do.

Student Body

This school is "truly brewing with amazing people." Many students affectionately describe their peers as nerds—not in a negative sense, "but more toward the sheer dedication they put towards what matters to them." That means that "there is a niche for everyone to find" where "you can be yourself and people won't judge." As one undergrad puts it, "[We] are unapologetically ourselves in every aspect of our lives, from the way we dress to the way we speak." It's an environment where "nearly everybody has their own special interests and an avenue to pursue them." Given the challenging academics, it's understandable that students here "take a great deal of pride in their work" and "spend countless hours studying and refining [their] study habits." There is "no sense of cutthroat competitiveness;" overall, it's a "very collaborative and supportive" group. There is a wide "variety of personalities," and students find their peers to be "very sociable," even though many define themselves as introverts. RPI has "a really nice sense of community" full of people who "are kind, funny, and motivated."

Rensselaer Polytechnic Institute

Financial Aid: 518-276-6813 • E-Mail: Admissions@rpi.edu • Website: www.rpi.edu

THE PRINCETON REVIEW SAYS

Admissions

The school reports that its standardized testing policy for use in admission for Fall 2026 is Test Optional. The Princeton Review suggests that interested applicants consult with the school for the most up-to-date standardized testing policies. *Very important factors considered include:* rigor of secondary school record, class rank, academic GPA. *Important factors considered include:* application essay, recommendation(s), extracurricular activities, character/personal qualities. *Other factors considered include:* standardized test scores, talent/ability, first generation, alumni/ae relation, volunteer work, work experience, level of applicant's interest. High school diploma is required and GED is accepted. *Academic units required:* 4 English, 4 math, 3 science, 3 social studies. *Academic units recommended:* 4 science.

Financial Aid

Students should submit: FAFSA; CSS PROFILE. Priority filing deadline is 12/1. The Princeton Review suggests that all financial aid forms be submitted as soon as possible. *Need-based scholarships/grants offered:* Federal Pell; Federal SEOG; State scholarships/grants; Private scholarships; College/university scholarship or grant aid from institutional funds; United Negro College Fund. *Loan aid offered:* Federal Direct Subsidized Loans; Federal Direct Unsubsidized Loans; Direct PLUS loans; State Loans. Admitted students will be notified of awards on or about 3/6. Federal Work-Study Program available. Institutional employment available.

The Inside Word

Strong grades and test scores, if you choose to submit them, are important for applicants hoping to stand out to the RPI admissions committee. A letter of recommendation is best coming from a math or science teacher. Also, you'll want to know what major you're declaring—you can change it down the road. Even better, apply directly to the program in which you're interested.

THE SCHOOL SAYS

From the Admissions Office

"The oldest degree-granting technological research university in the U.S., RPI was founded in 1824 to instruct students to apply 'science to the common purposes of life.' Students immerse themselves in course work that combines theory with learning by experience in unparalleled facilities, using advanced technology. RPI offers more than 140 programs and 1,000 courses leading to bachelor's, master's, and doctoral degrees. Undergraduates pursue studies in architecture; engineering; humanities, arts, and social sciences; business; science; and information technology (web science). A pioneer in interactive learning, RPI provides real-world, hands-on educational opportunities that cut across academic disciplines. The RPI student experience, or CLASS (Clustered Learning, Advocacy, and Support for Students) provides programs and support for students that begins even before they arrive on campus. Students have ready access to laboratories and classes involving lively discussion, problem solving, and faculty mentoring. Students are able to take full advantage of RPI's unique research platforms: the Center for Biotechnology and Interdisciplinary Studies; one of the world's most powerful academic supercomputers, the Center for Computational Innovations; and the Experimental Media and Performing Arts Center, which encourages students to explore the intersection of science, technology, and the arts. All students have access to RPI's IBM Quantum System One, the first at a university in the world. Newly renovated residence halls, wireless computing network, and studio classrooms create a fertile environment for study and learning. RPI offers recreational and fitness facilities plus numerous student-run organizations and activities, including fraternities and sororities, newspaper, television and radio station, drama and musical groups, and more than 200 clubs. In addition to intramural sports, NCAA varsity sports include Division I men's and women's ice hockey teams and twenty-one Division III men's and women's teams in thirteen sports. The East Campus Athletic Village raises the bar for student athletic facilities for varsity and non-varsity athletes alike, and includes a football arena, basketball stadium, and sports medicine and training complex."

SELECTIVITY

# of total applicants	14,356
% of total applicants accepted	67
% of total acceptees attending	14
# of in-state applicants	4,319
% of in-state applicants accepted	68
# of out-of-state-applicants	8,947
% of applicants accepted from out of state	68
# of international applicants	1,090
% of international applicants accepted	56
# of early decision applicants	317
% of early decision applicants accepted	69
# offered a place on the wait list	1,008
# admitted from wait list	6

First-Year Profile

Testing policy	Test Optional
Range SAT composite	1380–1500
Range SAT EBRW	680–750
Range SAT math	690–770
Range ACT composite	31–34
% submitting SAT scores	53
% submitting ACT scores	13
Average HS GPA	3.9
% submitting high school GPA	96
% graduated top 10% of class	63
% graduated top 25% of class	90
% graduated top 50% of class	99
% submitting high school rank	28

Important Dates

Early decision	
Apply by	11/1
Notified by	12/14
Other ED apply by	1/3
Other ED notified by	1/15
Early action	
Apply by	12/1
Notified by	1/29
Regular	
Apply by	1/15
Notified by	3/11
Nonfall registration?	Yes

FINANCIAL FACTS

Annual tuition	$66,300
Food and housing	$18,870
Required fees	$1,676
Books and supplies	$1,410
Average need-based scholarship (First-year)	$11,143 ($9,303)
% students with need rec. need-based scholarship or grant aid (First-year)	100 (100)
% students with need rec. non-need-based scholarship or grant aid (First-year)	99 (99)
% students with need rec. need-based self-help aid (First-year)	80 (79)
% students rec. any financial aid (First-year)	98 (77)
% UG borrow to pay for school	55
Average cumulative indebtedness	$39,539
% of students with need fully met (First-year)	27 (32)
Average % of student need met (First-year)	66 (63)

RHODES COLLEGE

2000 North Parkway, Memphis, TN 38112 • Admissions: 901-843-3700

Survey Snapshot
Easy to get around campus
Great library
Active minority support groups

RATINGS

Quality of Life	88
Fire Safety	80
Green	60*
Academic	89
Profs Interesting	93
Profs Accessible	95
Admissions	91
Financial Aid	92

CAMPUS LIFE

Type of school	Private
Affiliation	Presbyterian
Environment	Metropolis

Students

Degree-seeking undergrad enrollment	1,715
% male/female/not reported	43/57/0
% from out of state	62
% First-year from public high school	62
% First-year live on campus	95
% Ugrads live on campus	80
# of fraternities (% join)	9 (26)
# of sororities (% join)	9 (32)
% Asian	9
% Black or African American	11
% Hispanic	8
% Native American	<1
% Pacific Islander	0
% Race and/or ethnicity unknown	5
% Two or more races	5
% White	52
% International	9
# of countries represented	63

CAMPUS MENTAL HEALTH SERVICES

Offers mental health/wellness program	Yes
Mental health training available to students	Yes
Employs Chief Wellness Officer	No
Peer-to-peer mental health offerings	No
Counseling center has guidelines or accreditation	Yes
Mental health/well-being courses	Yes, non-credit

ACADEMICS

% students returning for sophomore year	91
% students graduating within 4 years	76
% students graduating within 6 years	81
Calendar	Semester
Student/faculty ratio	9:1
Most common class size 10–19.	(61%)
Most common lab/discussion size 10–19.	(75%)

Most Popular Majors
Business Administration and Management; Biology/Biological Sciences; Psychology

Applicants Often Prefer
Tulane University, University of Tennessee—Knoxville

Applicants Sometimes Prefer
Emory University, Trinity University, The University of the South, University of Texas at Austin, Vanderbilt University, Washington University in St. Louis

Applicants Rarely Prefer
Elon University, Florida State University, Furman University, New York University, University of North Carolina at Chapel Hill, University of Richmond

STUDENTS SAY "…"

Academics

Rhodes College centers its academics around the Foundations Curriculum, which "truly rounds out an individual's education…[and] forces students out of their comfort zone and exposes them to different topics, cultures, and subjects." Classes are largely discussion-driven and are "really fun despite the workload," with one student sharing, "One of my favorite classes I've taken was called 'Weapons of Mass Deception,' in which we as a class watched propaganda films together, then spent time discussing them with the professor." Other classes incorporate unique experiences like "field trips…, research opportunities, class research projects, [and] academic internships." Students emphasize the advantage of location, noting that "being in Memphis gives us amazing opportunities to intern and places like FedEx, AutoZone, etc.," alongside abundant "professional development opportunities…[and] the networking opportunities available during both undergraduate and graduate studies." Offering further guidance, the faculty "also give extensive, specific feedback…, which is very helpful," while fostering an environment of "participation and collaboration." Professors "are really interested in teaching first," and many "want to help you and get you involved in their research, no matter your year." The low student-to-faculty ratio means faculty are accessible to students and "able to truly invest in students and help us out without being overburdened." Classes "are academically rigorous, but not enough to cause intense struggle," and many courses "ask students to apply the content to the real world outside of the classroom" in preparation for life after college.

Campus Life

The Rhodes environment naturally encourages an active and engaged lifestyle, where "a big percentage of our students work out, eat healthy, and [are] mentally open and healthy." The striking surroundings also provide a lift, and people "often fill their time here at the library [or] café because both are so beautiful it motivates you to go and stay on top of your work." Beyond campus, Memphis adds to the student experience, offering "large botanic gardens and a myriad of parks, …dozens of artsy thrift stores" and "constant festivals and events to visit," creating a vibrant backdrop for exploration and recreation. On campus, more than 150 student organizations span a wide range of interests—from gardening and beekeeping to outdoor adventure groups—and most "show up to events hosted by [these groups], as well as attend on-campus parties hosted by the different Greek life organizations," fostering a socially active community. Students consistently point to the abundance of opportunities, with one noting, "I love how many clubs and student organizations there are. There is always an event happening," and many emphasize that with such variety, "all you need to do is step outside of the group you've gotten comfortable with to see how much Rhodes has to offer."

Student Body

A strong sense of pride and connection is a unifying thread across campus, where "everyone is so ambitious and excited to be learning" and "every class is filled with people who want to be there and participate." The student body "is both diverse and deeply supportive," and the school's intimate size fosters a comfortable familiarity in which students feel that "we all know each other or know someone that knows them." This sense of community is reflected in "lots of small groups and clubs with differing opinions" where interactions remain respectful and civil, reinforcing the impression that "Rhodes is very dedicated to creating an inclusive, enriching, and welcoming environment, and they've succeeded in every possible way." Academic commitment and school pride go hand-in-hand, and most students are "very driven regarding their education and are very proud of our school." Many are inspired by their peers, with one reflecting, "I am in constant awe of how much people put on their plates here, and are able to balance."

RHODES COLLEGE

Financial Aid: 901-843-3808 • E-Mail: adminfo@rhodes.edu • Website: www.rhodes.edu

THE PRINCETON REVIEW SAYS

Admissions

The school reports that its standardized testing policy for use in admission for Fall 2026 is Test Optional. The Princeton Review suggests that interested applicants consult with the school for the most up-to-date standardized testing policies. *Very important factors considered include:* rigor of secondary school record, class rank, academic GPA. *Important factors considered include:* standardized test scores, application essay, recommendation(s), character/personal qualities. *Other factors considered include:* interview, extracurricular activities, talent/ability, first generation, alumni/ae relation, geographical residence, state residency, volunteer work, work experience, level of applicant's interest. High school diploma is required and GED is accepted. *Academic units required:* 4 English, 3 math, 2 science, 2 science labs, 2 language (other than English), 2 social studies, 3 academic electives.

Financial Aid

Students should submit: FAFSA; CSS PROFILE. Priority filing deadline is 11/15. The Princeton Review suggests that all financial aid forms be submitted as soon as possible. *Need-based scholarships/grants offered:* Federal Pell; Federal SEOG; State scholarships/grants; Private scholarships; College/university scholarship or grant aid from institutional funds. *Loan aid offered:* Federal Direct Subsidized Loans; Federal Direct Unsubsidized Loans; Direct PLUS loans. Admitted students will be notified of awards on a rolling basis beginning 11/15. Federal Work-Study Program available. Institutional employment available.

The Inside Word

Admissions officers at Rhodes make it their mission to find candidates who will be a great fit for the school. This means that you can expect all facets of your application to be carefully considered: from your GPA to your letters of recommendation and extracurricular involvement. And if you're confident Rhodes is your top choice, we recommend applying early decision. Not only will you get priority consideration for admission and aid, but there's currently a renewable, yearly $3,000 Early Decision grant.

THE SCHOOL SAYS

From the Admissions Office

"Rhodes is a residential college committed to liberal arts and sciences. Our highest priorities are intellectual engagement, service to others, and honor among ourselves. We live this life on one of the country's most beautiful campuses in the heart of Memphis, Tennessee, an economic, political, and cultural center, making Rhodes one of a handful of top-tier, liberal arts colleges in a major metropolitan area.

"Rhodes has the soul of a liberal arts college coupled with a real-world mindset. Our students put their liberal arts knowledge to work in the world starting their first year. You'll be encouraged to engage in research, leadership and service opportunities—and to take responsibility for shaping your educational experience to meet your personal interests and goals. Memphis is a thriving city right on Rhodes' doorstep, with spectacular resources for students, and the college has pioneered the establishment of programs with world-class institutions and companies, including St. Jude Children's Research Hospital, FedEx and the Memphis Zoo, which take advantage of the college's metropolitan location and provide students with real-world opportunities for academic and personal growth."

SELECTIVITY

# of total applicants	5,682
% of total applicants accepted	52
% of total acceptees attending	17
# of in-state applicants	936
% of in-state applicants accepted	68
# of out-of-state-applicants	2,500
% of applicants accepted from out of state	75
# of international applicants	2,239
% of international applicants accepted	19
# of early decision applicants	357
% of early decision applicants accepted	55
# offered a place on the wait list	893
# admitted from wait list	0

First-Year Profile

Testing policy	Test Optional
Range SAT composite	1360–1470
Range SAT EBRW	670–740
Range SAT math	660–770
Range ACT composite	28–32
% submitting SAT scores	20
% submitting ACT scores	35
Average HS GPA	3.8
% submitting high school GPA	85
% graduated top 10% of class	44
% graduated top 25% of class	79
% graduated top 50% of class	93
% submitting high school rank	27

Important Dates

Early decision	
Apply by	11/1
Notified by	11/15
Other ED apply by	1/15
Other ED notified by	2/1
Early action	
Apply by	11/15
Notified by	1/15
Regular	
Apply by	1/15
Notified by	3/15
Nonfall registration?	No

FINANCIAL FACTS

Annual tuition	$58,272
Food and housing	$14,336
Required fees	$810
Books and supplies	$1,200
Average need-based scholarship (First-year)	$46,458 ($47,154)
% students with need rec. need-based scholarship or grant aid (First-year)	100 (100)
% students with need rec. non-need-based scholarship or grant aid (First-year)	34 (37)
% students with need rec. need-based self-help aid (First-year)	61 (59)
% students rec. any financial aid (First-year)	95 (100)
% UG borrow to pay for school	39
Average cumulative indebtedness	$37,203
% of students with need fully met (First-year)	39 (39)
Average % of student need met (First-year)	87 (89)

Rice University

6100 Main Street, Houston, TX 77005 • Admissions: 713-348-7423

Survey Snapshot
Students are happy
Easy to get around campus
Active minority support groups

RATINGS

Quality of Life	95
Fire Safety	95
Green	60*
Academic	88
Profs Interesting	90
Profs Accessible	92
Admissions	98
Financial Aid	98

CAMPUS LIFE

Type of school	Private
Environment	Metropolis

Students

Degree-seeking undergrad enrollment	4,793
% male/female/not reported	50/50/<1
% from out of state	57
% First-year live on campus	99
% Ugrads live on campus	59
# of fraternities	0
# of sororities	0
% Asian	30
% Black or African American	8
% Hispanic	16
% Native American	<1
% Pacific Islander	<1
% Race and/or ethnicity unknown	3
% Two or more races	5
% White	24
% International	13
# of countries represented	93

CAMPUS MENTAL HEALTH SERVICES

Offers mental health/wellness program	Yes
Mental health training available to students	Yes
Employs Chief Wellness Officer	Yes
Peer-to-peer mental health offerings	Yes
Counseling center has guidelines or accreditation	Yes
Mental health/well-being courses	Yes, for-credit

ACADEMICS

% students returning for sophomore year	97
% students graduating within 4 years	88
% students graduating within 6 years	95
Calendar	Semester
Student/faculty ratio	6:1
Most common class size 10–19.	(48%)

Most Popular Majors

Computer Science; Bioscience; Business; Mechanical Engineering; Psychology

Applicants Also Look At

Harvard College, Stanford University, University of Pennsylvania, University of Texas at Austin, Yale University

STUDENTS SAY "..."

Academics

Rice University stands out as a leading research university where academic diversity and a wide array of interdisciplinary institutes and centers make it easy for students to explore multiple areas of interest. At Rice, "knowledge isn't siloed—students are constantly crossing disciplines and interests in ways that feel natural rather than exceptional." Another hallmark of Rice is that many departments offer a research-for-credit model, which lets undergraduates "contribute meaningfully to faculty-led studies from day one—turning classrooms into launchpads." Students also consistently cite experiential learning as a highlight, from a "data science capstone project with real data and a sponsor to directly work with" to an education class in which they attended "multiple school board meetings in Houston...to experience firsthand what the experience of governing a school district looks like." The academic environment is further "defined by highly approachable professors and consistently small, discussion-based classes," where many courses "function as seminars rather than lectures." Innovative teaching techniques and academic support extend beyond the classroom: "from student-run societies, bootcamps, and clubs that supplement academics in very practical ways," to "peer tutor opportunities every day at nearly every hour for specific courses." With "an abundance of supportive events on campus and opportunities to grow" both academically and socially, one finds that "the resources available to assist students are plentiful and always there."

Campus Life

Rice's wooded campus "is absolutely gorgeous," and students embrace the many opportunities to connect and unwind, from "college parties, themed events, intramural sports, and traditions like Beer Bike that bring the entire community together" to exploring the shops and restaurants in nearby Rice Village. First-year students are assigned to one of eleven residential colleges where they remain throughout their time on campus, a system that "provides a welcoming community to new students that lasts all the way to graduation." These colleges also provide much of the day-to-day structure, including shared meals and close-knit social networks. Involvement is the norm at Rice, with most students participating in "some intramural sport, a club related to their major, or research." Students also engage in "the many internships, jobs, and volunteer opportunities available in the surrounding area." One student adds, "I think it's impossible to find someone who is doing academics only." This level of engagement is supported by "a strong culture of doing things together," which means that "studying often turns into group work, late-night snack runs, or just hanging out and talking." With so many academic and social opportunities available, students ultimately "try to find the ambitious people's version of work-life balance."

Student Body

Students widely agree that their peers are "incredibly collaborative and supportive in every sense of the word." This description reflects an often-cited "culture of care" at Rice that fosters "a 'pact' between all the student and faculty community to [keep] each other safe." Many attribute this environment in part to the residential college system, which helps them connect with a wide range of people and build friendships across disciplines, noting that having "friends from diverse backgrounds and different majors makes it very supportive and less competitive." The structure also creates "a lot of pockets of people with different interests and habits," ensuring that "everyone is able to settle with a group that matches their interests." And one student shares, "You'll meet people who are grinding through problem sets and then immediately switching to band practice, club meetings, or just hanging out at the colleges." This "sneaky smart and extremely motivated" student body is broadly regarded as "extremely passionate, intelligent, and hardworking," as well as "very outgoing and compassionate." As another student puts it neatly: "Although we are competitive in academics, this is very much outweighed by the amount of encouragement received by everyone. We all push each other to be better."

Rice University

Financial Aid: 713-348-4958 • E-Mail: admission@rice.edu • Website: www.rice.edu

THE PRINCETON REVIEW SAYS

Admissions

The school reports that its standardized testing policy for use in admission for Fall 2026 is Test Optional. The Princeton Review suggests that interested applicants consult with the school for the most up-to-date standardized testing policies. *Very important factors considered include:* rigor of secondary school record, class rank, academic GPA, standardized test scores, application essay, recommendation(s), extracurricular activities, talent/ability, character/personal qualities. *Other factors considered include:* interview, first generation, alumni/ae relation, geographical residence, state residency, volunteer work, work experience, level of applicant's interest. High school diploma is required and GED is accepted. *Academic units required:* 4 English, 3 math, 2 science, 2 language (other than English), 2 social studies, 3 academic electives.

Financial Aid

Students should submit: FAFSA; CSS PROFILE; Income Documents (IDOC). Priority filing deadline is 2/1. The Princeton Review suggests that all financial aid forms be submitted as soon as possible. *Need-based scholarships/grants offered:* Federal Pell; Federal SEOG; State scholarships/grants; Private scholarships; College/university scholarship or grant aid from institutional funds. *Loan aid offered:* Federal Direct Subsidized Loans; Federal Direct Unsubsidized Loans; Direct PLUS loans; Private Loans. Admitted students will be notified of awards on or about 4/1. Federal Work-Study Program available. Institutional employment available.

The Inside Word

Rice University is highly competitive, and while submitting SAT or ACT scores is strongly recommended for admission, students who choose not to submit them will still receive full consideration. Applicants can also showcase their academic strengths through AP, IB, or other relevant test scores. The university evaluates a range of factors, from academic ability and special talents to creativity, life experiences, and leadership. Additionally, Rice participates in QuestBridge, offering comprehensive support for high-achieving, low-income students, including assistance with tuition, housing, books, and other essential expenses.

THE SCHOOL SAYS

From the Admissions Office

"What if your next four years exceeded all expectations? Rice University sits in the heart of Houston on a 300-acre, tree-lined campus next to the Texas Medical Center and the Houston Museum District. As a top-tier research institution, we offer more than 50 majors across seven schools of study where students have the freedom and ability to choose their own path. From your first semester on campus, no matter your major, you'll have the opportunity to conduct research alongside experts. You'll be able to apply your skills, gain valuable professional experience, and interact with industry leaders as you address real-world issues. Bright, curious, and diverse, our students have a thirst for knowledge and a desire to shape the world around them.

"Our student life begins with our residential colleges, where we randomly sort new students and where they stay throughout their time at Rice. Because each student is randomly assigned and stays in the same college throughout their undergraduate years, the diversity of our student body creates a rich tapestry of traditions, culture, and, most importantly, community. And by focusing on a culture of care, students find support from their peers resulting in an environment of collaboration over competition.

"This combination of excellence in academics, a vibrant and caring student life and our commitment to access and affordability forms the heart of Rice University."

SELECTIVITY

# of total applicants	36,791
% of total applicants accepted	8
% of total acceptees attending	43
# of in-state applicants	10,610
# of out-of-state-applicants	17,388
# of international applicants	8,793
# of early decision applicants	5,748
% of early decision applicants accepted	11
# offered a place on the wait list	3,196
# admitted from wait list	66

First-Year Profile

Testing policy	Test Optional
Range SAT composite	1510–1560
Range SAT EBRW	740–770
Range SAT math	760–800
Range ACT composite	34–36
% submitting SAT scores	59
% submitting ACT scores	24
% graduated top 10% of class	90
% graduated top 25% of class	97
% graduated top 50% of class	100
% submitting high school rank	40

Important Dates

Early decision	
Apply by	11/1
Notified by	12/15
Other ED apply by	1/4
Other ED notified by	2/5
Regular	
Apply by	1/4
Notified by	4/1
Nonfall registration?	No

FINANCIAL FACTS

Annual tuition (First-year)	$65,280 ($71,140)
Food and housing	$20,530
Required fees	$984
Books and supplies	$1,540
Average need-based scholarship (First-year)	$69,521 ($73,663)
% students with need rec. need-based scholarship or grant aid (First-year)	99 (98)
% students with need rec. non-need-based scholarship or grant aid (First-year)	10 (12)
% students with need rec. need-based self-help aid (First-year)	59 (48)
% students rec. any financial aid (First-year)	54 (54)
% UG borrow to pay for school	12
Average cumulative indebtedness	$26,491
% of students with need fully met (First-year)	99 (100)
Average % of student need met (First-year)	100 (100)

Rider University

2083 Lawrenceville Road, Lawrenceville, NJ 08648-3099 • Admissions: 609-896-5042

Survey Snapshot
Theater is popular
Students are friendly
College radio is popular

RATINGS

Quality of Life	81
Fire Safety	91
Green	60*
Academic	79
Profs Interesting	87
Profs Accessible	90
Admissions	84
Financial Aid	89

CAMPUS LIFE

Type of school	Private
Environment	Village

Students

Degree-seeking undergrad enrollment	3,097
% male/female/not reported	44/56/0
% from out of state	24
% First-year from public high school	88
% First-year live on campus	77
% Ugrads live on campus	53
# of fraternities (% join)	6 (8)
# of sororities (% join)	8 (10)
% Asian	5
% Black or African American	14
% Hispanic	20
% Native American	<1
% Pacific Islander	<1
% Race and/or ethnicity unknown	1
% Two or more races	3
% White	52
% International	3
# of countries represented	63

CAMPUS MENTAL HEALTH SERVICES

Offers mental health/wellness program	Yes
Mental health training available to students	Yes
Employs Chief Wellness Officer	No
Peer-to-peer mental health offerings	Yes
Counseling center has guidelines or accreditation	Yes
Mental health/well-being courses	No

ACADEMICS

% students returning for sophomore year	78
% students graduating within 4 years	54
% students graduating within 6 years	61
Calendar	Semester
Student/faculty ratio	13:1
Most common class size 10–19.	(49%)
Most common lab/discussion size 10–19.	(82%)

Most Popular Majors

Psychology; Business Administration, Management and Operations; Accounting

Applicants Sometimes Prefer

The College of New Jersey, Kean University, Monmouth University (NJ), Montclair State University, New Jersey Institute of Technology, Ramapo College of New Jersey, Rowan University, Rutgers University–New Brunswick, Seton Hall University, Stockton University

STUDENTS SAY "..."

Academics

Rider University is dedicated to the success of its undergraduates and "has made strong strides in recent years to improve facilities and provide new opportunities." From the get-go, students have access to accessibility and support services, including the career center's help with résumés and interview skills. Enrollees also mention how "the Engaged Learning Program is a great part of Rider's commitment" in that it makes clear to students not just how they're doing academically but in skills translatable to a real-world setting. This, in turn, is backed up by the Cranberry Investment, which "guarantees a job, internship, or graduate program acceptance within 1 year of graduation...[or post-graduate] assistance and courses to help you attain this goal."

Students note that this isn't just scaffolding—classes offer unique learning opportunities that go beyond textbooks and lectures, like the Business in Action Program: "I was placed in a group of four of my peers and we were tasked with creating a business idea and executing it from start to finish." Another undergrad adds that they were "able to go out on campus and film things for an assignment" and really enjoyed "being given creative freedom to complete projects." The focused class sizes come in handy here, as they "allow for a more personal connection with professors." And speaking of the faculty, they are typically "very engaged in the class material and willing to help students, inside and outside of the classroom." They also "really do seem to love their job and motivate kids to actually learn to expand their knowledge, not just do the work for a grade." Indeed, they understand how to foster "a safe learning space for students."

Campus Life

At first glance, Rider's campus may appear quiet, given that "a decent portion of the student body commutes." But students list countless "amazing extracurriculars like a tabletop club, a dance ensemble, a student-directed theatre company, and more. There is truly something for everyone!" Additionally, students say that intramurals are "a lot of fun" and that "Greek life is a big way for students to become more involved and engaged." The school also hosts "many events that bring students together," including their twist on the X Factor television show, R Factor, and sometimes works with clubs to expand offerings like a beach cleanup. Students note that you can participate at your own pace, and appreciate that they can "easily get together to hang out or work on projects, go to the SRC to attend a fitness class, [or head] to our on-campus pub to watch sports games."

Student Body

Rider University's student body "is very small, yet welcoming." Many undergrads say it's "so easy to make connections with people," noting that everyone is "friendly and willing to help you with anything...academic or personal." That doesn't mean the school is without cliques that "tend to stick together as they share most of their classes," but it's not seen as a negative. Rider is also seen as a haven for "many different people here who didn't know if they would be able to go to college," and it shows—individuals work to make the most of this opportunity. "I haven't met one person at this school who hasn't been hardworking or determined with a set of goals in mind." A classmate adds, "I have had an amazing experience with everyone that I have met here at Rider and am really looking forward to seeing where life takes me."

RIDER UNIVERSITY

Financial Aid: 609-896-5360 • E-Mail: admissions@rider.edu • Website: www.rider.edu

THE PRINCETON REVIEW SAYS

Admissions

The school reports that its standardized testing policy for use in admission for Fall 2026 is Test Optional. The Princeton Review suggests that interested applicants consult with the school for the most up-to-date standardized testing policies. *Very important factors considered include:* rigor of secondary school record, academic GPA, application essay, recommendation(s). *Other factors considered include:* standardized test scores, interview, extracurricular activities, talent/ability, character/personal qualities, geographical residence, state residency, volunteer work, work experience, level of applicant's interest. High school diploma is required and GED is accepted. *Academic units required:* 4 English, 3 math. *Academic units recommended:* 4 math, 4 science, 4 science labs, 2 language (other than English), 2 social studies, 2 history, 1 academic elective.

Financial Aid

Students should submit: FAFSA. Priority filing deadline is 3/1. The Princeton Review suggests that all financial aid forms be submitted as soon as possible. *Need-based scholarships/grants offered:* Federal Pell; Federal SEOG; State scholarships/grants; Private scholarships; College/university scholarship or grant aid from institutional funds. *Loan aid offered:* Federal Direct Subsidized Loans; Federal Direct Unsubsidized Loans; State Loans; Direct PLUS loans. Admitted students will be notified of awards on a rolling basis beginning 12/20. Federal Work-Study Program available. Institutional employment available.

The Inside Word

To prepare for college, Rider University suggests that high school students follow a rigorous curriculum of college prep courses, including AP and honors classes. Although most students major in the liberal arts and sciences, a significant percentage of undergraduates are enrolled in the business school. Rider University accepts applications on a rolling basis.

THE SCHOOL SAYS

From the Admissions Office

"Career preparation is central to the Rider experience. Whether you know exactly what you want to do or are still figuring it out, Rider University helps you turn your goals into a plan—and that plan into a future.

"With 60+ undergraduate majors to choose from, Rider offers the flexibility to explore your interests and the support to sharpen your focus. Our expert faculty are committed mentors who bring real-world insight into the classroom and invest in your success.

"At the core of a Rider education is our Engaged Learning Program, which connects what you learn with how you'll use it—through internships, research, study abroad, community service and more. These experiences build your résumé and your confidence, giving you a competitive edge in the job market.

"Rider's value is more than academic. It's personal. You'll be supported by a tight-knit community that puts students first, with a strong emphasis on safety, well-being and belonging. We offer generous scholarships and financial aid, making a high-quality private education accessible and affordable.

"We're so confident in the outcomes of a Rider education, we back it with the Cranberry Investment—our promise that you'll land a job in your field or gain acceptance into graduate/professional school within six months of graduation, or you can receive additional support at no cost.

"The best way to understand what makes Rider different is to experience it in person. Visit our beautiful Lawrenceville campus and discover how we prepare you to turn your goals into achievements."

SELECTIVITY

# of total applicants	10,070
% of total applicants accepted	79
% of total acceptees attending	9
# of in-state applicants	7,073
% of in-state applicants accepted	87
# of out-of-state-applicants	2,505
% of applicants accepted from out of state	61
# of international applicants	484
% of international applicants accepted	50
# offered a place on the wait list	108
# admitted from wait list	23

First-Year Profile

Testing policy	Test Optional
Range SAT composite	1110–1190
Range SAT EBRW	550–670
Range SAT math	550–650
Range ACT composite	27–31
% submitting SAT scores	12
% submitting ACT scores	2
Average HS GPA	3.5
% submitting high school GPA	100
% graduated top 10% of class	19
% graduated top 25% of class	45
% graduated top 50% of class	80
% submitting high school rank	27

Important Dates

Early action	
Apply by	11/15
Notified by	12/20
Regular	
Notified by	Rolling, 12/15
Nonfall registration?	Yes

FINANCIAL FACTS

Annual tuition	$39,700
Food and housing	$17,230
Required fees (First-year)	$1,420 ($1,695)
Books and supplies	$900
Average need-based scholarship (First-year)	$29,080 ($31,840)
% students with need rec. need-based scholarship or grant aid (First-year)	99 (100)
% students with need rec. non-need-based scholarship or grant aid (First-year)	23 (24)
% students with need rec. need-based self-help aid (First-year)	72 (70)
% students rec. any financial aid (First-year)	95 (99)
% UG borrow to pay for school	73
Average cumulative indebtedness	$40,410
% of students with need fully met (First-year)	20 (20)
Average % of student need met (First-year)	83 (84)

Ripon College

300 W. Seward St., Ripon, WI 54971 • Admissions: 920-748-8337

Survey Snapshot
Lab facilities are great
Recreation facilities are great
Frats and sororities are popular

RATINGS	
Quality of Life	83
Fire Safety	73
Green	60*
Academic	82
Profs Interesting	87
Profs Accessible	92
Admissions	82
Financial Aid	91

CAMPUS LIFE

Type of school	Private
Environment	Village

Students

Degree-seeking undergrad enrollment	649
% male/female/not reported	57/43/0
% from out of state	32
% First-year from public high school	75
% First-year live on campus	98
% Ugrads live on campus	98
# of fraternities (% join)	4 (10)
# of sororities (% join)	3 (10)
% Asian	1
% Black or African American	6
% Hispanic	11
% Native American	0
% Pacific Islander	0
% Race and/or ethnicity unknown	4
% Two or more races	1
% White	77
% International	2
# of countries represented	11

CAMPUS MENTAL HEALTH SERVICES

Offers mental health/wellness program	Yes
Mental health training available to students	No
Employs Chief Wellness Officer	NR
Peer-to-peer mental health offerings	NR
Counseling center has guidelines or accreditation	No
Mental health/well-being courses	NR

ACADEMICS

% students returning for sophomore year	77
% students graduating within 4 years	44
% students graduating within 6 years	59
Calendar	Semester
Student/faculty ratio	10:1
Most common class size 1–9.	(34%)
Most common lab/discussion size 10–19.	(75%)

Most Popular Majors
Psychology; Biology; Exercise Science-Human Performance

STUDENTS SAY "..."

Academics

Ripon College offers streamlined academic pathways and strong interpersonal support, helping students achieve their goals "without overwhelming us with general education requirements." Instead of traditional gen ed requirements, Ripon features the Catalyst Curriculum, a series of courses that "promote innovation through real-world problem-solving and interdisciplinary thinking." These courses emphasize "public speaking, writing, critical thinking, quantitative reasoning, information literacy, intercultural competence, and group collaboration," while allowing students to explore "different cultures and issues" and begin major requirements as early as their first year. In their third year, students "partake in a collaborative capstone, where [they] develop solutions to real-world problems. They prepare all semester to perfect their solution and present them on a dedicated day known as 'Catalyst Day.'" Small classes create "super effective and efficient class time," where "professors are able to have one-on-one interactions with students, allowing for strong student-professor relationships." As one student explains, "Professors genuinely care about their students and take the time to get to know us." Students also highlight their academic advisors, who "show great care about the future of their students," as well as alumni who demonstrate "engagement and eagerness to see the institution prosper for future generations." From its efficient curriculum to its engaged instructors, advisors, and alumni, "Ripon College's biggest strength is how much they care about their students."

Campus Life

Ripon students widely report that their "favorite extracurricular activities are the sports teams," with over 35% competing on one of 18 Division III varsity teams, and "sports are consistently going on" around campus. The Wilmore Center, described as "super nice and truly amazing for athletes and the public," serves as a hub for those who work out and "have classes down there." One student lauds the equestrian team for combining their "passion for horseback riding [and] the opportunity for growth in the organization." Beyond athletics, "there are many clubs, organizations, and groups on campus to be involved in," including academic and pre-professional clubs, diversity and inclusion organizations, and special interest clubs. One student adds, "I partake in the Paranormal Investigators Club, the Queer-Straight Alliance, and the College Days newspaper." Students also enjoy the nearby Ceresco Prairie Conservancy: "I also love walking through the prairie—it's peaceful and beautiful, especially when I need a break from classes." Greater Ripon "offers free music in the park" and opportunities for "going fishing or hunting in the public lands near the town." Altogether, "life at Ripon College feels full and connected, both on campus and in the surrounding town."

Student Body

Ripon College attracts "incredibly kindhearted and genuine people," who are often united by a shared enthusiasm for athletics, with participation in intramural and intercollegiate sports making the student body feel like "a majority of athletes." The combination of having a shared interest and being a "smaller school" lends a strong sense of camaraderie to the campus: "Everyone knows everyone! As I walk to my class, half of it is spent waving to my peers!" At the same time, students appreciate the "diversity in childhood experiences...I have found a wide range of experiences, some being similar to my own and many being far different." Another student agrees: "At Ripon, there is a very diverse community...Everyone gets to know each other through clubs, Greek life, classes, etc. While many of us differ from each other, we also are able to provide each other support in many different ways." Many also find their "peers are welcoming," noting that "it has been surprisingly easy to make friends with people that I didn't initially realize I had much in common with," contributing to a campus where students are "kind and generous. They're quick to offer a smile, hold a door, or share a laugh between classes," creating an overall "campus atmosphere that feels welcoming and inclusive."

RIPON COLLEGE

Financial Aid: 920-748-8301 • E-Mail: adminfo@ripon.edu • Website: www.ripon.edu

THE PRINCETON REVIEW SAYS

Admissions

The school reports that its standardized testing policy for use in admission for Fall 2026 is Test Optional. The Princeton Review suggests that interested applicants consult with the school for the most up-to-date standardized testing policies. *Very important factors considered include:* rigor of secondary school record, interview. *Important factors considered include:* class rank, academic GPA, extracurricular activities, character/personal qualities. *Other factors considered include:* standardized test scores, application essay, recommendation(s), talent/ability, volunteer work. High school diploma is required and GED is accepted. *Academic units required:* 4 English, 2 math, 2 science, 2 social studies. *Academic units recommended:* 4 math, 4 science, 2 language (other than English), 4 social studies.

Financial Aid

Students should submit: FAFSA. Priority filing deadline is 3/1. The Princeton Review suggests that all financial aid forms be submitted as soon as possible. *Need-based scholarships/grants offered:* Federal Pell; Federal SEOG; State scholarships/grants; Private scholarships; College/university scholarship or grant aid from institutional funds. *Loan aid offered:* Federal Direct Subsidized Loans; Federal Direct Unsubsidized Loans; Direct PLUS loans. Admitted students will be notified of awards on a rolling basis beginning 1/1. Federal Work-Study Program available. Institutional employment available.

The Inside Word

Ripon seeks high school students who challenge themselves academically and beyond. Students with a 3.4 GPA or higher in a college-prep curriculum are well positioned, although the school also considers extracurriculars and a candidate's likelihood of thriving in a small-school environment. Most AP exams with scores of 3 or higher earn credits toward graduation. Tuition and fees are free for Wisconsin residents with a household AGI of $75,000 or less, and residents of WI, IL, IA, MI, and MN pay no more than the in-state tuition and fees at UW-Madison.

THE SCHOOL SAYS

From the Admissions Office

"Since its founding in 1851, Ripon College has adhered to the philosophy that the liberal arts offer the richest foundation for intellectual, cultural, social, and spiritual growth. Academic strength is a 175-year tradition at Ripon. We attract excellent professors who are dedicated to their disciplines; they in turn attract bright, committed students. Together with the other members of our tightly knit learning community, students at Ripon learn more deeply, live more fully, and achieve more success. Students are surprised to discover that here there are more opportunities—to be involved, to lead, to speak out, to make a difference, to explore new interests—than at a college ten times our size. Through collaborative learning, group living, teamwork, and networking, students tap into the power of a community where we all work together to ensure success—at Ripon and beyond.

"All of the best residential liberal arts colleges strive to be true learning communities like Ripon. We succeed better than most because our enrollment of about 700 students is perfect for fostering connections inside and outside the classroom. Our students flourish in this environment of mutual respect, where shared values are elevated and diverse ideas are valued. If you are seeking academic challenge and want to benefit from an environment of personal attention and support—then you should take a closer look at Ripon."

SELECTIVITY

# of total applicants	2,040
% of total applicants accepted	81
% of total acceptees attending	13

First-Year Profile

Testing policy	Test Optional
Range SAT EBRW	510–600
Range SAT math	490–590
Range ACT composite	20–27
% submitting SAT scores	13
% submitting ACT scores	41
Average HS GPA	3.4
% submitting high school GPA	100
% graduated top 10% of class	21
% graduated top 25% of class	43
% graduated top 50% of class	78
% submitting high school rank	63

Important Dates

Regular	
Notified by	Rolling, 9/15
Nonfall registration?	Yes

FINANCIAL FACTS

Annual tuition	$52,900
Food and housing	$11,100
Required fees	$350
Books and supplies	$750
Average need-based scholarship (First-year)	$43,196 ($46,139)
% students with need rec. need-based scholarship or grant aid (First-year)	100 (100)
% students with need rec. non-need-based scholarship or grant aid (First-year)	97 (99)
% students with need rec. need-based self-help aid (First-year)	61 (73)
% students rec. any financial aid (First-year)	61 (72)
% UG borrow to pay for school	82
Average cumulative indebtedness	$35,375
% of students with need fully met (First-year)	32 (28)
Average % of student need met (First-year)	87 (89)

ROANOKE COLLEGE

221 College Lane, Salem, VA 24153-3794 • Admissions: 540-375-2270

Survey Snapshot
Students are happy
Internships are widely available
College radio is popular

RATINGS

Quality of Life	87
Fire Safety	86
Green	60*
Academic	85
Profs Interesting	93
Profs Accessible	95
Admissions	83
Financial Aid	89

CAMPUS LIFE

Type of school	Private
Affiliation	Lutheran
Environment	City

Students

Degree-seeking undergrad enrollment	1,736
% male/female/not reported	49/51/0
% from out of state	36
% First-year from public high school	83
% First-year live on campus	87
% Ugrads live on campus	81
# of fraternities (% join)	5 (16)
# of sororities (% join)	4 (12)
% Asian	1
% Black or African American	8
% Hispanic	7
% Native American	<1
% Pacific Islander	<1
% Race and/or ethnicity unknown	0
% Two or more races	5
% White	75
% International	3
# of countries represented	26

CAMPUS MENTAL HEALTH SERVICES

Offers mental health/wellness program	Yes
Mental health training available to students	No
Employs Chief Wellness Officer	NR
Peer-to-peer mental health offerings	NR
Counseling center has guidelines or accreditation	No
Mental health/well-being courses	NR

ACADEMICS

% students returning for sophomore year	81
% students graduating within 4 years	58
% students graduating within 6 years	64
Calendar	Semester
Student/faculty ratio	12:1
Most common class size 10–19.	(42%)
Most common lab/discussion size 10–19.	(48%)

Most Popular Majors
Psychology; Business Administration and Management; Health and Exercise Science

Applicants Often Prefer
James Madison University, University of Virginia, William & Mary

Applicants Sometimes Prefer
Christopher Newport University, University of Lynchburg, University of Richmond, Virginia Tech

Applicants Rarely Prefer
Bridgewater College, Radford University

STUDENTS SAY "..."

Academics

Founded in 1842, Roanoke College is a private Lutheran school that wants students to leverage all of the academic, cultural, and practical resources the school has to offer. Real-world experiences such as "field trips, service components, [and interacting with guest] speakers" are encouraged, and there are also study abroad opportunities available in 50 different countries. Students value the flexibility and range of the Intellectual Inquiry curriculum, as well as a three-week Intensive Learning Program in which students focus on a single topic through a variety of activities. These help students "find their purpose on campus and explore several different fields of interest at once."

On the whole, "many classes are discussion-based," and professors strive to engage their students and focus on critical thinking. "Some [professors] even encourage respectful arguments to show different views to get students thinking about [what] they are learning." Many students relate that the professors are what they like most about the college. As one student puts it, "I always feel welcomed and listened to by my professors." Another says, "I think it's rare to have this many professors that truly care about your success and well-being."

Campus Life

There is a "strong community both within and outside of the campus," and the school does "an amazing job of emphasizing the 'family' aspect of what it means to be a Maroon." Typical days involve some combination of the following: going to class, working out, eating with friends, doing homework, and hanging out on the Quad. Many students remark that they would like more on-campus dining options but note that there is a coffee shop just off campus that many students frequent. Athletic games (especially basketball) are highly attended, and students enjoy spending time outside playing games like spikeball or relaxing in hammocks. On Mondays, "most students go to Theology on Tap, which provides free food and is hosted by the chaplain." Roanoke is located "in a beautiful area filled with hiking and kayaking nearby," and "there are lots of hiking trips on the weekends." In any time not spent studying, there "are always people hosting hangouts from Greek life" and people going into the towns of Salem and Roanoke to "take advantage of the things like outdoor gear rentals and movie ticket discounts." In general, people "like to participate in many clubs."

Student Body

This "smaller, community-like college" has nearly 1,900 undergraduates, which "allows for relationships between students and faculty," but it's still large enough that "you can walk across campus and say 'hi' to five people you know and still see five people you don't." Though most here are "white and come from [an] affluent background," the school is "steadily working toward a reflection of the diverse population of Virginia," and students themselves strive "toward building a diverse, welcoming community for fellow peers on campus." And as another student says, "Everybody is unique in their own way and makes you feel welcome." Roanoke attracts "smart, kind people who are genuine and excited to get to know each other," and even in class, students "are very open in sharing their opinion and personal life when it is relevant to the lecture." The overall sentiment is that "the students are caring, determined, and outgoing."

Roanoke College

Financial Aid: 540-375-2235 • E-Mail: admissions@roanoke.edu • Website: www.roanoke.edu

THE PRINCETON REVIEW SAYS

Admissions

The school reports that its standardized testing policy for use in admission for Fall 2026 is Test Optional. The Princeton Review suggests that interested applicants consult with the school for the most up-to-date standardized testing policies. *Very important factors considered include:* rigor of secondary school record, academic GPA, character/personal qualities. *Important factors considered include:* class rank, interview, extracurricular activities, level of applicant's interest. *Other factors considered include:* standardized test scores, application essay, recommendation(s), talent/ability, alumni/ae relation, volunteer work, work experience. High school diploma is required and GED is accepted. *Academic units required:* 4 English, 3 math, 2 science, 2 science labs, 2 language (other than English), 2 social studies, 5 academic electives. *Academic units recommended:* 2 language (other than English).

Financial Aid

Students should submit: FAFSA; State aid form. The Princeton Review suggests that all financial aid forms be submitted as soon as possible. *Need-based scholarships/grants offered:* Federal Pell; Federal SEOG; State scholarships/grants; Private scholarships; College/university scholarship or grant aid from institutional funds. *Loan aid offered:* Federal Direct Subsidized Loans; Federal Direct Unsubsidized Loans; Direct PLUS loans. Admitted students will be notified of awards on a rolling basis beginning 11/15. Federal Work-Study Program available. Institutional employment available.

The Inside Word

Roanoke evaluates each application holistically, looking at the whole student—not just grades or test scores. That said, the average admitted student has a high school GPA of 3.6, giving a sense of the academic preparation typically expected.

THE SCHOOL SAYS

From the Admissions Office

"Roanoke College, located in Salem, Virginia—just minutes from the city of Roanoke in the scenic Blue Ridge Mountains—delivers a small-school experience with big-school opportunities. Here, students are known by name, mentored closely by faculty, and supported by a community invested in their success—while still accessing research, internships, leadership roles and global experiences typically found at larger universities.

"Our campus features state-of-the-art facilities, including a new Science Center opening this fall, an Athletic Center that's earned national recognition, and academic programs recognized by the Princeton Review for academic excellence and student experience. From high-tech labs to our nationally ranked Cregger Center and Athletic Performance Center, students have resources to thrive both in and outside the classroom.

"From day one, students aren't just preparing for their first job—they're building the skills to adapt, grow, and change careers over time. Roanoke emphasizes critical thinking, communication and real-world learning, so graduates are ready for whatever comes next.

"With more than 91 percent of graduates employed or in graduate school within six months, Roanoke combines strong outcomes with a vibrant campus experience. With its location in a safe, welcoming college town with access to outdoor recreation, cultural attractions and career opportunities, students enjoy a supportive community and a holistic college experience."

SELECTIVITY

# of total applicants	4,230
% of total applicants accepted	84
% of total acceptees attending	12
# of early decision applicants	162
% of early decision applicants accepted	77
# offered a place on the wait list	167
# admitted from wait list	15

First-Year Profile

Testing policy	Test Optional
Range SAT composite	1120–1290
Range SAT EBRW	550–660
Range SAT math	540–640
Range ACT composite	23–28
% submitting SAT scores	22
% submitting ACT scores	8
Average HS GPA	3.6
% submitting high school GPA	99
% graduated top 10% of class	21
% graduated top 25% of class	46
% graduated top 50% of class	77
% submitting high school rank	48

Important Dates

Early decision	
Apply by	11/15
Notified by	11/5
Early action	
Apply by	10/18
Notified by	11/5
Regular	
Apply by	3/15
Notified by	Rolling, 11/5
Nonfall registration?	Yes

FINANCIAL FACTS

Annual tuition	$37,120
Food and housing	$15,828
Required fees	$2,088
Books and supplies	$1,000
Average need-based scholarship (First-year)	$36,129 ($36,780)
% students with need rec. need-based scholarship or grant aid (First-year)	99 (99)
% students with need rec. non-need-based scholarship or grant aid (First-year)	98 (99)
% students with need rec. need-based self-help aid (First-year)	68 (68)
% students rec. any financial aid (First-year)	97 (100)
% UG borrow to pay for school	68
Average cumulative indebtedness	$39,576
% of students with need fully met (First-year)	19 (18)
Average % of student need met (First-year)	84 (84)

Rochester Institute of Technology

One Lomb Memorial Drive, Rochester, NY 14623 • Admissions: 585-475-6631

Survey Snapshot
Students are happy
Lab facilities are great
Recreation facilities are great

RATINGS

Quality of Life	**77**
Fire Safety	**90**
Green	**60***
Academic	**76**
Profs Interesting	**80**
Profs Accessible	**88**
Admissions	**90**
Financial Aid	**90**

CAMPUS LIFE

Type of school	Private
Environment	City

Students

Degree-seeking undergrad enrollment	13,194
% male/female/not reported	65/35/0
% from out of state	52
% First-year from public high school	80
% First-year live on campus	95
% Ugrads live on campus	49
# of fraternities (% join)	19 (3)
# of sororities (% join)	10 (2)
% Asian	12
% Black or African American	6
% Hispanic	10
% Native American	<1
% Pacific Islander	<1
% Race and/or ethnicity unknown	2
% Two or more races	6
% White	60
% International	4
# of countries represented	71

CAMPUS MENTAL HEALTH SERVICES

Offers mental health/wellness program	Yes
Mental health training available to students	No
Employs Chief Wellness Officer	NR
Peer-to-peer mental health offerings	NR
Counseling center has guidelines or accreditation	No
Mental health/well-being courses	NR

ACADEMICS

% students returning for sophomore year	89
% students graduating within 4 years	28
% students graduating within 6 years	72
Calendar	Semester
Student/faculty ratio	13:1
Most common class size 10–19.	(34%)
Most common lab/discussion size 10–19.	(53%)

Most Popular Majors

Modeling, Virtual Environments and Simulation; Computer Science; Mechanical Engineering

Applicants Often Prefer

Penn State University Park, Purdue University—West Lafayette, Rensselaer Polytechnic Institute, State University of New York—Binghamton University, State University of New York—Buffalo State University

Applicants Sometimes Prefer

Carnegie Mellon University, Cornell University, Syracuse University, Worcester Polytechnic Institute

Applicants Rarely Prefer

Clarkson University, Drexel University

STUDENTS SAY "..."

Academics

This western New York academic stalwart boasts one of the country's oldest (and largest) co-op programs and regularly turns out job-ready students from its business, computing, and engineering programs alike. Rochester Institute of Technology is laser-focused on "creating students that are more than prepared to enter the job force," and faculty "bring the material to life" by keeping lectures work-related and placing emphasis on "how you would use what we are learning on the job site." "Professors work with the students and see them as equals," says one mechanical engineering major. "When I'm in the classroom, I feel like I'm learning and that I have a voice."

The workload is legendarily daunting and "you will have to reach out and form study groups and pull all-nighters," but professors are "more than happy to help their students" and "truly take pride in helping their students become successful." While the material may be difficult, faculty "are willing to stay after hours, meet with the student, and hold group study/review sessions to help their students understand the material." The easy A is "not very common, especially in engineering classes," but "if you work hard, you will be recognized and grades will reflect that."

The opportunity for students to dip their toes into real-world experience abounds throughout the college, and the paid co-op program (mandatory for most majors) is considered by many to be "the best thing anyone could ever choose to go through if you are a career-driven individual." Additionally, there are "plenty of materials and machines students can use for free where in other schools you still have to pay."

Campus Life

While schoolwork takes up the majority of students' time, outside the classroom they "are constantly doing something to keep busy," whether that's joining one of the 300-plus clubs or chilling at the lab. "RIT has a culture for everybody," so if you are interested in a broad topic like computing, "there are a dozen different clubs/societies that you can join to learn more about whatever niche topic interests you."

Students cop to their being "a large gamer population" at RIT, and both electronic and tabletop gaming clubs and tournaments are wildly popular, as is anime. Hockey is a huge part of RIT and "it is very common to see a large number of students at the games." People also "go to the free on-campus movies, see guest speakers, listen to comedians, and attend events hosted by the College Activities Board."

The atmosphere and layout of the campus are beautifully balanced in that "it is not very spread out but not very small at the same time." More than half of the growing population of students live on campus, meaning housing "is not always available for everyone who applies" and dorms can be crowded. While one student notes that "the existing infrastructure is okay at best," the school recently added a new 120,000-square-foot maker space, a performing arts center, and is upgrading its athletic facilities.

Student Body

RIT is a place "where diversity is highlighted [and] academics are prominent," and the population is "as unique and diverse as they come." This environment "allows for a good [facsimile] of the real world." The school's internationally recognized National Technical Institute for the Deaf means there are "amazing accommodations for deaf and hard of hearing students that attend the university," including "note-taking, interpreters, [and C Print(r) technology]," and a vibrant LGBT+ community also exists on campus. "Video games are a way of life" and students tend to have a nerdy streak ("We are geeky and we love it"). Large groups and clubs for "anime, World of Warcraft, [and] chain mail" happily thrive among students that are all "very accepting of each other's interests." "This is where students are able to create what their minds generate. It's like teenager's dream," says one.

Rochester Institute of Technology

Financial Aid: 585-475-2186 • E-Mail: admissions@rit.edu • Website: www.rit.edu

THE PRINCETON REVIEW SAYS

Admissions

The school reports that its standardized testing policy for use in admission for Fall 2026 is Test Optional. The Princeton Review suggests that interested applicants consult with the school for the most up-to-date standardized testing policies. *Very important factors considered include:* rigor of secondary school record, academic GPA. *Important factors considered include:* class rank, standardized test scores, application essay, recommendation(s), character/personal qualities, level of applicant's interest. *Other factors considered include:* interview, extracurricular activities, talent/ability, first generation, alumni/ae relation, volunteer work, work experience. High school diploma is required and GED is accepted. *Academic units required:* 4 English, 3 math, 2 science, 2 science labs, 1 social studies, 3 history. *Academic units recommended:* 4 English, 3 math, 3 science, 3 science labs, 1 language (other than English), 1 social studies, 3 history, 3 academic electives.

Financial Aid

Students should submit: FAFSA; State aid form. Priority filing deadline is 1/15. The Princeton Review suggests that all financial aid forms be submitted as soon as possible. *Need-based scholarships/grants offered:* Federal Pell; Federal SEOG; State scholarships/grants; Private scholarships; College/university scholarship or grant aid from institutional funds. *Loan aid offered:* Federal Direct Subsidized Loans; Federal Direct Unsubsidized Loans; Direct PLUS loans. Admitted students will be notified of awards on a rolling basis beginning 3/2. Federal Work-Study Program available. Institutional employment available.

The Inside Word

The admissions committee is on the lookout for bright, highly motivated students who will make the most out of the university's experiential learning opportunities, and the majority of students must choose their intended course of study during the admissions process. You'll also need a transcript that reflects a rigorous high school curriculum (including APs and honors classes) to have a shot at admission here. RIT uses a 100-point scale for the average high school GPA for admitted students.

THE SCHOOL SAYS

From the Admissions Office

"Rochester Institute of Technology (RIT) is a launchpad for ambitious, curious students who want to combine creativity with real-world impact. At RIT, students go beyond theory—they live it through hands-on, immersive experiences that prepare them for meaningful careers and bold futures. RIT offers a powerful blend of technology, science, business, the arts, and innovation. With more than 90 undergraduate majors and over 80 minors across engineering and engineering technology, science and mathematics, art and design, health science technology, and business students can build a customized academic path that aligns their passions with professional goals.

"At RIT, experiential learning is a key aspect of your education. As a national leader in cooperative education—paid, career-focused work experiences that build résumés, confidence, and professional networks at globally recognized companies—co-op is a corner stone for RIT. Students can refine their experiential learning by taking advantage of internships, research opportunities, entrepreneurship programs, and study abroad. Campus life is packed with clubs, events, festivals, and traditions further customizing your experience. Each opportunity shapes your career design.

"You'll be part of a vibrant and inclusive community with students from all 50 states and over 100 countries. RIT is also home to the National Technical Institute for the Deaf (NTID) adding to richly diverse and accessible campus. At RIT, students push boundaries, explore boldly, and graduate ready to lead. If you're looking for a university where you can design your future, do what you love, and make an impact—this is your place."

SELECTIVITY

# of total applicants	27,881
% of total applicants accepted	67
% of total acceptees attending	16
# of in-state applicants	10,281
% of in-state applicants accepted	63
# of out-of-state-applicants	14,442
% of applicants accepted from out of state	76
# of international applicants	3,169
% of international applicants accepted	37
# of early decision applicants	2,090
% of early decision applicants accepted	72
# offered a place on the wait list	2,556
# admitted from wait list	100

First-Year Profile

Testing policy	Test Optional
Range SAT composite	1300–1440
Range SAT EBRW	640–720
Range SAT math	640–740
Range ACT composite	27–33
% submitting SAT scores	43
% submitting ACT scores	11
Average HS GPA	93.8
% submitting high school GPA	96
% graduated top 10% of class	45
% graduated top 25% of class	65
% graduated top 50% of class	94
% submitting high school rank	38

Important Dates

Early decision	
Apply by	11/1
Notified by	12/1
Other ED apply by	1/1
Other ED notified by	1/15
Early action	
Apply by	11/1
Notified by	1/31
Nonfall registration?	Yes

FINANCIAL FACTS

Annual tuition	$60,774
Food and housing	$16,750
Required fees	$1,030
Books and supplies	$1,100
Average need-based scholarship (First-year)	$39,904 ($44,179)
% students with need rec. need-based scholarship or grant aid (First-year)	100 (100)
% students with need rec. non-need-based scholarship or grant aid (First-year)	18 (16)
% students with need rec. need-based self-help aid (First-year)	95 (94)
% students rec. any financial aid (First-year)	98 (100)
% UG borrow to pay for school	70
Average cumulative indebtedness	$40,336
% of students with need fully met (First-year)	21 (19)
Average % of student need met (First-year)	89 (91)

Rollins College

1000 Holt Avenue, Winter Park, FL 32789-4499 • Admissions: 407-646-2161

Survey Snapshot
Easy to get around campus
Students love Winter Park, FL
Great off-campus food

RATINGS

Quality of Life	93
Fire Safety	97
Green	88
Academic	87
Profs Interesting	91
Profs Accessible	92
Admissions	89
Financial Aid	91

CAMPUS LIFE

Type of school	Private
Environment	Town

Students

Degree-seeking undergrad enrollment	2,630
% male/female/not reported	39/61/0
% from out of state	40
% First-year from public high school	56
% First-year live on campus	81
% Ugrads live on campus	58
# of fraternities (% join)	4 (7)
# of sororities (% join)	8 (15)
% Asian	3
% Black or African American	6
% Hispanic	20
% Native American	<1
% Pacific Islander	<1
% Race and/or ethnicity unknown	3
% Two or more races	5
% White	54
% International	9
# of countries represented	69

CAMPUS MENTAL HEALTH SERVICES

Offers mental health/wellness program	Yes
Mental health training available to students	Yes
Employs Chief Wellness Officer	Yes
Peer-to-peer mental health offerings	Yes
Counseling center has guidelines or accreditation	Yes
Mental health/well-being courses	Yes, for-credit

ACADEMICS

% students returning for sophomore year	81
% students graduating within 4 years	68
% students graduating within 6 years	77
Calendar	Semester
Student/faculty ratio	12:1
Most common class size 10–19.	(49%)
Most common lab/discussion size 10–19.	(72%)

Most Popular Majors

Communication and Media Studies; Business Administration and Management; Psychology

Applicants Also Look At

College of Charleston, Elon University, Florida Southern College, Florida State University, Stetson University, University of Central Florida, University of Florida, University of Miami, University of South Florida, The University of Tampa

STUDENTS SAY "..."

Academics

Rollins College emphasizes "community engagement" and "hands-on experience," giving students the chance to apply what they learn in the classroom. In particular, one student reports "tackling real-world projects" in their human resources course: "We provided evidence-based solutions...to the company's HR for a chance for our recommendations to be implemented state and nationwide." Similarly, one student studying business had the chance "to do real PR work" for a local nonprofit. Weekend and Spring Break Community Engagement trips are free or heavily subsidized, and offer immersive experiences, such as "a service-based learning experience in Tampa focused on the shelter system." Students also have ample opportunities to study abroad. One student reports that it's "cost-effective to study abroad because your scholarships travel with you and there are lots of options for long and short-term programs." Both on- and off-campus, professors at Rollins "are absolutely life-changing." One student recounts: "My professors are incredible and truly aim to have their students succeed and actually take something away from the lecture that can be applicable to their day-to-day lives." The small class sizes "feel more personal, and you're able to connect to the professor." Another student agrees: "My favorite professors are those who don't just teach us facts. I have found the most joy from the professors who teach me about life!" Overall, Rollins' community-engaged coursework and vibrant instructors motivate students to complete their education "with determination and pride."

Campus Life

When Rollins students aren't in class, they can be found "out and about on campus." Mills Lawn is a popular spot for studying, picnics, and playing games, while "the lake on campus is a place you can go paddleboarding or kayaking." With its beautiful campus and sunny weather, Rollins students like to "spend time outside, whether it be playing sports or just chilling by the lake." One treasured campus tradition is Fox Day, a surprise in the spring when the president decides it is "too pretty for class" and cancels classes for undergraduates, providing the perfect opportunity to "play games on our lawn" or go "to the pool." Tars, as Rollins students are affectionately known, looking for community can find it in recreational fitness classes ("barre, yoga, bodyworks, pilates, Zumba") or performing arts spaces. One student explains that "Whenever I need a laugh, a cry, or just to escape for a little bit, I know the improv team is going to give me that." The "Greek community is flourishing" as well, shares one student: "I've not only enjoyed the experience as a member of my chapter, but I've also made many friends in other chapters along the way." Whether Tars connect through classes, Greek life, or extracurriculars, they love "hanging out with friends around the beautiful campus."

Student Body

Students are impressed by the "drive and determination" of their peers, describing them as "motivated, ambitious, and focused on success, not just academically, but in everything they do." The school's small size makes "the creation of lasting relationships" easy. "You will always see a familiar face or two when walking to class." Across the board, "people are genuinely nice...I'm not sure if it is the beautiful campus or just the people a small liberal arts college attracts, but it definitely feels like a community." The student body particularly values the school's "commitment to progressive ideals." Tars note that the student population is "mostly women, [and] mostly white," while at the same time a "melting pot of cultures." Shares one Tar: "You meet a lot of international people, which is quite cool since you get a lot of different insights." In general, everyone wants "to push themselves and grow. Being surrounded by students who care that much about their goals is inspiring. It creates an environment where we support each other while also challenging one another to be our very best."

ROLLINS COLLEGE

Financial Aid: 407-646-2395 • E-Mail: admission@rollins.edu • Website: www.rollins.edu

THE PRINCETON REVIEW SAYS

Admissions

The school reports that its standardized testing policy for use in admission for Fall 2026 is Test Optional. The Princeton Review suggests that interested applicants consult with the school for the most up-to-date standardized testing policies. *Very important factors considered include:* academic GPA. *Important factors considered include:* rigor of secondary school record, standardized test scores, application essay, recommendation(s), extracurricular activities, talent/ability, level of applicant's interest. *Other factors considered include:* class rank, character/personal qualities, volunteer work, work experience. High school diploma is required and GED is accepted. *Academic units required:* 4 English, 3 math, 2 science, 2 language (other than English), 2 social studies, 2 history, 2 academic electives. *Academic units recommended:* 4 English, 4 math, 4 science, 3-4 language (other than English), 4 social studies, 3 history, 3 academic electives.

Financial Aid

Students should submit: FAFSA. The Princeton Review suggests that all financial aid forms be submitted as soon as possible. *Need-based scholarships/grants offered:* Federal Pell; Federal SEOG; State scholarships/grants; Private scholarships; College/university scholarship or grant aid from institutional funds. *Loan aid offered:* Federal Direct Subsidized Loans; Federal Direct Unsubsidized Loans; Direct PLUS loans. Admitted students will be notified of awards on a rolling basis beginning 12/15. Federal Work-Study Program available. Institutional employment available.

The Inside Word

Academic and need-based scholarships are available to all students, including those who do not submit standardized test scores. It's the school's way of creating another opportunity for students whose test results do not match their overall academic performance, and it's characteristic of the individualized approach taken here. Each applicant is assigned an admissions officer who acts as their liaison, ensuring a personalized admissions experience. Early decision applicants are given priority consideration for school scholarships and grants, and receive early notification for admission and financial aid decisions.

THE SCHOOL SAYS

From the Admissions Office

"Rollins' mission is to nurture global citizens and responsible leaders as they chart their own course to a meaningful life and productive career. We believe an education is about more than a degree or that first job after graduation. It's about empowering students to discover what they truly care about and preparing them to pursue that passion with all their might. As you begin the college selection process, remember that you are in control of your destiny. Your academic record—course load, grades earned, test scores—is the most important part of your application credentials. But Rollins also pays close attention to your personal dimension—interests, strengths, values, and potential to contribute to college life. Don't sell yourself short in the application process. Be proud of what you've accomplished and who you are, and be honest when you describe yourself. Finally, the admission committee always likes to see candidates who express interest in Rollins. If we're your first choice, apply early decision because doing so comes with a range of benefits. Each year we admit approximately one-third of the entering class through the early decision process. We encourage you to visit us here on America's most beautiful campus, meet with an admission counselor, and sit in on a class so you can see for yourself what Rollins is all about."

SELECTIVITY

# of total applicants	8,460
% of total applicants accepted	53
% of total acceptees attending	13
# of in-state applicants	3,732
% of in-state applicants accepted	58
# of out-of-state-applicants	2,742
% of applicants accepted from out of state	70
# of international applicants	1,980
% of international applicants accepted	21
# of early decision applicants	384
% of early decision applicants accepted	38
# offered a place on the wait list	328
# admitted from wait list	6

First-Year Profile

Testing policy	Test Optional
Range SAT composite	1210–1340
Range SAT EBRW	620–700
Range SAT math	560–660
Range ACT composite	26–30
% submitting SAT scores	66
% submitting ACT scores	34
Average HS GPA	3.4
% submitting high school GPA	88
% graduated top 10% of class	23
% graduated top 25% of class	52
% graduated top 50% of class	82
% submitting high school rank	35

Important Dates

Early decision	
Apply by	11/15
Notified by	12/15
Other ED apply by	1/5
Other ED notified by	2/1
Early action	
Apply by	11/15
Notified by	1/15
Regular	
Apply by	2/1
Notified by	Rolling, 11/15
Nonfall registration?	Yes

FINANCIAL FACTS

Annual tuition	$65,410
Food and housing	$19,770
Books and supplies	$960
Average need-based scholarship (First-year)	$39,371 ($42,475)
% students with need rec. need-based scholarship or grant aid (First-year)	98 (97)
% students with need rec. non-need-based scholarship or grant aid (First-year)	17 (17)
% students with need rec. need-based self-help aid (First-year)	75 (75)
% students rec. any financial aid (First-year)	90 (94)
% UG borrow to pay for school	48
Average cumulative indebtedness	$34,729
% of students with need fully met (First-year)	37 (38)
Average % of student need met (First-year)	84 (87)

ROSE-HULMAN INSTITUTE OF TECHNOLOGY

5500 Wabash Avenue, Terre Haute, IN 47803-3999 • Admissions: 812-877-8213

Survey Snapshot
Career services are great
Easy to get around campus
Internships are widely available

RATINGS

Quality of Life	89
Fire Safety	96
Green	60*
Academic	87
Profs Interesting	92
Profs Accessible	94
Admissions	90
Financial Aid	88

CAMPUS LIFE

Type of school	Private
Environment	Town

Students

Degree-seeking undergrad enrollment	2,153
% male/female/not reported	76/24/0
% from out of state	67
% First-year live on campus	97
% Ugrads live on campus	55
# of fraternities (% join)	8 (37)
# of sororities (% join)	3 (33)
% Asian	8
% Black or African American	2
% Hispanic	5
% Native American	<1
% Pacific Islander	<1
% Race and/or ethnicity unknown	1
% Two or more races	6
% White	68
% International	9
# of countries represented	35

CAMPUS MENTAL HEALTH SERVICES

Offers mental health/wellness program	Yes
Mental health training available to students	Yes
Employs Chief Wellness Officer	No
Peer-to-peer mental health offerings	Yes
Counseling center has guidelines or accreditation	Yes
Mental health/well-being courses	Yes, non-credit

ACADEMICS

% students returning for sophomore year	92
% students graduating within 4 years	59
% students graduating within 6 years	74
Calendar	Quarter
Student/faculty ratio	11:1
Most common class size 20–29.	(47%)
Most common lab/discussion size 20–29.	(49%)

Most Popular Majors

Mechanical Engineering; Computer Science; Chemical Engineering

Applicants Sometimes Prefer

Colorado School of Mines, Purdue University—West Lafayette

Applicants Rarely Prefer

Carnegie Mellon University, Illinois Institute of Technology, Rochester Institute of Technology

STUDENTS SAY "..."

Academics

Rose-Hulman Institute of Technology delivers a top-notch STEM education that is driven by a "strong hands-on, project-based learning environment" and "dedicated professors who prioritize mentorship and student success." Practical experience is a key component of the curriculum, and students "do interesting labs in most classes to support what we learn in lecture." One elaborates: "For my concrete class, we got to actually tie and pour concrete for a beam. A month later, we got to test it in a barn to see at what force it cracks." As a relatively small school, the "one-on-one connections you can build with the professors [are] a huge benefit," and they "make themselves very available through office hours, drop-ins, and appointments." There is a constant flow of information, and faculty members "have so much industry experience and share that knowledge at every opportunity...to make sure that we are set up the absolute best that we can be for our careers." Students also note that most teachers are flexible in their styles, and "genuinely [take] feedback from students and [are] willing to adapt on the fly to each individual student." The school also offers "extensive academic support and resources," with one student suggesting that "Whether you struggle academically, personally, with health, or with something else, if you can ask, there are always resources available." This "focus on the undergraduate experience along with a fantastic Career Services" yields "one of the most challenging and rewarding educational experiences."

Campus Life

Rose-Hulman is a homework-intensive school, so much of campus life is built around having fun while working: "Being able to get your friends together and interact, have fun, [and] make jokes [is] a core part of the experience." All first-years are required to live on campus, which makes for "a super close-knit community," and events like "Greatest Floor and Hallympics" are common. As one student confidently puts it, "On our floors, I know almost everyone." For a tech school, "the arts are VERY popular...and they provide an amazing outlet away from engineering and science." Intramurals are also beloved: "It's a big deal here and the different residence halls each have their own team." Additionally, the "Student Activities and Student Affairs offices do a great job with planning fun events and social opportunities," including comedy nights, bonfires, and dance lessons. Rose students "like to keep themselves busy, so almost everyone is in a sport or multiple clubs," and there are more than 90 clubs, teams, and organizations to choose from. There is "always something happening on campus, as long as you read the bulletin boards and just show up." As another student puts it, "The grind never stops, but it's a part of what makes Rose so much fun and challenging!"

Student Body

"Everyone here is an engineer, which allows for a very unique student body makeup," and one that lends itself to "a collaborative focus with many group projects that require cooperation." To put it another way, "If you love STEM, you will be in your happy place." These "extremely hard-working, motivated, and caring" students are "technically-oriented with multitudes of close-knit circles usually bonded based on majors." Between majors and the residence hall system, "there is a very strong community built up starting [the first year] and it carries throughout your whole time here." Everyone is here "to get a top-tier STEM education and we are all in this together, so they are willing to help." A student says, "I feel surrounded by 'my people' while at the same time standing out for my own unique solutions to problems."

Rose-Hulman Institute of Technology

Financial Aid: 812-877-8259 • E-Mail: admissions@rose-hulman.edu • Website: www.rose-hulman.edu

THE PRINCETON REVIEW SAYS

Admissions

The school reports that its standardized testing policy for use in admission for Fall 2026 is Test Optional. The Princeton Review suggests that interested applicants consult with the school for the most up-to-date standardized testing policies. *Very important factors considered include:* rigor of secondary school record, academic GPA, extracurricular activities, character/personal qualities. *Important factors considered include:* application essay, recommendation(s). *Other factors considered include:* class rank, standardized test scores, interview, talent/ability, geographical residence, volunteer work, work experience. High school diploma is required and GED is not accepted. *Academic units required:* 4 English, 4 math, 3 science, 3 science labs, 2 social studies. *Academic units recommended:* 5 math, 4 science, 4 academic electives.

Financial Aid

Students should submit: FAFSA. Priority filing deadline is 3/10. The Princeton Review suggests that all financial aid forms be submitted as soon as possible. *Need-based scholarships/grants offered:* Federal Pell; Federal SEOG; State scholarships/grants; College/university scholarship or grant aid from institutional funds; Private scholarships. *Loan aid offered:* Federal Direct Subsidized Loans; Federal Direct Unsubsidized Loans; Direct PLUS loans. Admitted students will be notified of awards on or about 1/15 (early action) 3/15 (regular decision). Federal Work-Study Program available. Institutional employment available.

The Inside Word

The admissions committee at Rose-Hulman is clear about its commitment to selecting top-tier students. While they look for candidates who are in the top 25 percent of their graduating class, they also consider other factors—such as the rigor of your coursework—if your high school does not provide rankings. Applying early is a smart move: Rose-Hulman's Early Action is non-binding, meaning you'll receive your admission decision sooner without any obligation to commit.

THE SCHOOL SAYS

From the Admissions Office

"Imagine a college where your classes are taught by professors who know you by name and who also happen to be among the best in the world; a place with a rigorous curriculum that prepares you for today's jobs and for careers that don't yet exist; a place where you have access to state-of-the-art labs, equipment, and research opportunities that are off-limits to undergrads at most schools; a friendly, safe, and collaborative place where you're surrounded by people who love science, engineering, and math as much as you do; and a place where everyone on campus, from your residence hall housekeeper to your academic adviser, will take the time to help you when needed.

"That place is Rose-Hulman, and our culture is the secret to our success.

"Here, your STEM education isn't just about getting a degree, or even a job. It's about taking what you learn and applying it to match your passions. You'll be the center of your experience; not stuck with a one-size-fits-all college career.

"Rose-Hulman has been recognized for more than two decades as the best undergraduate engineering school in the U.S., and we have a track record of excelling at career placement rate consistently between 95–99 percent, with the average starting salary over $82,000—with some of the best-known companies in the world seeking out our students for paid internships and full-time employment.

"There are many more accomplishments we're proud of, but we're prouder of why we're so highly regarded. To fully appreciate that, schedule a visit and come see for yourself."

SELECTIVITY

# of total applicants	5,991
% of total applicants accepted	81
% of total acceptees attending	10
# of in-state applicants	1,341
% of in-state applicants accepted	72
# of out-of-state-applicants	3,614
% of applicants accepted from out of state	85
# of international applicants	1,036
% of international applicants accepted	78
# offered a place on the wait list	272
# admitted from wait list	1

First-Year Profile

Testing policy	Test Optional
Range SAT composite	1270–1450
Range SAT EBRW	620–750
Range SAT math	650–750
Range ACT composite	28–34
% submitting SAT scores	36
% submitting ACT scores	17
Average HS GPA	3.9
% submitting high school GPA	98
% graduated top 10% of class	59
% graduated top 25% of class	86
% graduated top 50% of class	98
% submitting high school rank	38

Important Dates

Early action	
Apply by	11/1
Notified by	12/15
Regular	
Apply by	2/1
Notified by	12/15
Nonfall registration?	Yes

FINANCIAL FACTS

Annual tuition	$58,200
Food and housing (First-year)	$19,281 ($17,727)
Books and supplies	$1,500
Average need-based scholarship (First-year)	$39,009 ($40,728)
% students with need rec. need-based scholarship or grant aid (First-year)	91 (87)
% students with need rec. non-need-based scholarship or grant aid (First-year)	98 (79)
% students with need rec. need-based self-help aid (First-year)	67 (64)
% students rec. any financial aid (First-year)	100 (100)
% UG borrow to pay for school	48
Average cumulative indebtedness	$46,909
% of students with need fully met (First-year)	26 (28)
Average % of student need met (First-year)	69 (69)

Rowan University

201 Mullica Hill Road, Glassboro, NJ 08028-1701 • Admissions: 856-256-4200

Survey Snapshot
Great library
Students are happy
Intramural sports are popular

RATINGS

Quality of Life	79
Fire Safety	91
Green	81
Academic	77
Profs Interesting	86
Profs Accessible	88
Admissions	85
Financial Aid	81

CAMPUS LIFE

Type of school	Public
Environment	Town

Students

Degree-seeking undergrad enrollment	16,852
% male/female/not reported	50/50/0
% from out of state	5
% First-year from public high school	83
% First-year live on campus	64
% Ugrads live on campus	34
# of fraternities (% join)	20 (4)
# of sororities (% join)	14 (5)
% Asian	6
% Black or African American	12
% Hispanic	17
% Native American	<1
% Pacific Islander	<1
% Race and/or ethnicity unknown	1
% Two or more races	4
% White	56
% International	3
# of countries represented	53

CAMPUS MENTAL HEALTH SERVICES

Offers mental health/wellness program	Yes
Mental health training available to students	Yes
Employs Chief Wellness Officer	Yes
Peer-to-peer mental health offerings	Yes
Counseling center has guidelines or accreditation	Yes
Mental health/well-being courses	Yes, for-credit

ACADEMICS

% students returning for sophomore year	83
% students graduating within 4 years	53
% students graduating within 6 years	69
Calendar	Semester
Student/faculty ratio	17:1
Most common class size 20–29.	(39%)
Most common lab/discussion size 20–29.	(87%)

Most Popular Majors

Biology/Biological Sciences; Psychology; Business Administration and Management

STUDENTS SAY "..."

Academics

Rowan University is a large and prominent public research university located in the heart of South Jersey. Students emphatically cite quality teaching, made possible by the ardent dedication of an accomplished faculty, as Rowan's greatest strength. "The professors absolutely make Rowan. Every single one genuinely cares about his or her students and has a passion to teach." That extra mile of interest does not go unnoticed: "I love the way my... professors supported me through this journey." Rowan offers over 120 majors, not just in the traditional areas of study, but also innovative fields such as bioinformatics, supply chain and logistics systems, jazz studies, inclusive education, and exercise science. For those still undecided, the Exploratory Studies Program offers personalized attention, advice, and assistance from faculty and staff as students explore their academic and career options. Rowan prides itself on such support, which also ranges from tutoring to success coaching to the ASCEND program, which supports students who are challenged by educational, cultural, or economic circumstances. "Being an international student sometimes can be difficult, but having the confidence that your school has your back and understands you is the best feeling and helps you to keep going and give your best."

Campus Life

Students describe the large suburban Rowan campus as "always buzzing with events" and full of people who like to have fun. There are innumerable student resources and activities, clubs and organizations, and opportunities to socialize: "There is a club out there for every student on campus," with examples ranging from E-sports to Parkour and a thriving Greek life scene. On- and off-campus students alike love to engage with the cultural benefits of being between three major cities—20 minutes from Philadelphia and two hours from both New York City and Washington, D.C.

Student Body

At Rowan University, "Everywhere you look, there is an interesting person with a different story," and these backgrounds are found to enhance the overall educational experience without hindering school unity. "My peers vary in age, gender and demographics, yet through our courses we find commonality." The university greatly values inclusivity and the ideal of providing a welcoming environment for all. "Rowan really has striven to accomplish such a harmonious atmosphere here, and they've done a good job." As another student observes, "It is truly a comfortable campus to be on and everyone is genuine and welcoming." Students speak glowingly of their peers and note a work ethic that creates a supportive and collaborative sentiment on campus. "All students that I have come to meet in my years at Rowan University are friendly, have a passion for learning, and are always willing to help other students as needed."

Rowan University

Financial Aid: 856-256-4250 • E-Mail: admissions@rowan.edu • Website: www.rowan.edu

THE PRINCETON REVIEW SAYS

Admissions

The school reports that its standardized testing policy for use in admission for Fall 2026 is Test Optional. The Princeton Review suggests that interested applicants consult with the school for the most up-to-date standardized testing policies. *Very important factors considered include:* academic GPA. *Important factors considered include:* rigor of secondary school record. *Other factors considered include:* standardized test scores, application essay, recommendation(s), talent/ability. High school diploma is required and GED is accepted. *Academic units required:* 4 English, 3 math, 2 science, 2 science labs, 2 language (other than English), 2 social studies, 1 history, 2 academic electives. *Academic units recommended:* 4 math, 3 science, 3 science lab.

Financial Aid

Students should submit: FAFSA. The Princeton Review suggests that all financial aid forms be submitted as soon as possible. *Need-based scholarships/grants offered:* Federal Pell; Federal SEOG; State scholarships/grants; Private scholarships; College/university scholarship or grant aid from institutional funds; United Negro College Fund. *Loan aid offered:* Federal Direct Subsidized Loans; Federal Direct Unsubsidized Loans; Direct PLUS loans; State Loans. Admitted students will be notified of awards on a rolling basis beginning December/January. Federal Work-Study Program available. Institutional employment available.

The Inside Word

This quality New Jersey state school gets a solid number of applicants each year, especially from residents who would pay a reduced in-state tuition. A good percentage of them are accepted and those with the best shot come from the top 25 percent of their class. While standardized test scores are optional, it's a good idea to submit your scores if they are on the higher end or if you're seeking some form of scholarship.

THE SCHOOL SAYS

From the Admissions Office

"Since its founding in 1923, Rowan University has evolved from a teacher preparation college to a public research institution ranked among the top 100 in the nation by U.S. News & World Report. Rowan University offers bachelor's through doctoral degrees and professional certificates in person and online to nearly 25,000 students through its main campus in Glassboro and its eight other locations in southern New Jersey.

"Rowan focuses on practical research at the intersection of health care, engineering, science and business, while ensuring excellence in undergraduate education. The University has earned national recognition for innovation; commitment to high-quality, affordable education; and the development of public-private partnerships.

"A Carnegie-classified R2 (high research activity) institution, Rowan is the fastest-growing public research university in the Northeast and among the nation's top 10 fastest-growing, as reported by The Chronicle of Higher Education.

"In 2025, Rowan opened New Jersey's only veterinary school and is one of only two universities in the nation to offer M.D., D.O. and D.V.M. medical degrees."

SELECTIVITY

# of total applicants	22,410
% of total applicants accepted	77
% of total acceptees attending	20
# of in-state applicants	17,318
% of in-state applicants accepted	78
# of out-of-state-applicants	2,831
% of applicants accepted from out of state	71
# of international applicants	2,261
% of international applicants accepted	71

First-Year Profile

Testing policy	Test Optional
Range SAT composite	1100–1300
Range SAT EBRW	560–660
Range SAT math	530–640
Range ACT composite	23–30
% submitting SAT scores	26
% submitting ACT scores	1
Average HS GPA	3.4
% submitting high school GPA	100
% graduated top 10% of class	16
% graduated top 25% of class	40
% graduated top 50% of class	72
% submitting high school rank	47

Important Dates

Regular	
Apply by	7/15
Notified by	Rolling, 10/15
Nonfall registration?	Yes

FINANCIAL FACTS*

Annual in-state tuition	$12,344
Annual out-of-state tuition	$23,168
Food and housing	$15,354
Required fees	$5,084
Books and supplies	$1,330
Average need-based scholarship (First-year)	$14,944 ($18,510)
% students with need rec. need-based scholarship or grant aid (First-year)	92 (96)
% students with need rec. non-need-based scholarship or grant aid (First-year)	0 (0)
% students with need rec. need-based self-help aid (First-year)	66 (63)
% students rec. any financial aid (First-year)	63 (66)
% UG borrow to pay for school	58
Average cumulative indebtedness	$34,439
% of students with need fully met (First-year)	9 (13)
Average % of student need met (First-year)	47 (56)

* Most recently reported data at time of printing. Scan the QR code to find the latest updates.

RUTGERS UNIVERSITY—NEW BRUNSWICK

65 Davidson Road, Room #202, Piscataway, NJ 08854-8097 • Admissions: 848-445-4636

Survey Snapshot
Campus newspaper is popular
Students are happy
Great library

RATINGS

Quality of Life	74
Fire Safety	84
Green	88
Academic	76
Profs Interesting	82
Profs Accessible	90
Admissions	92
Financial Aid	79

CAMPUS LIFE

Type of school	Public
Environment	Town

Students

Degree-seeking undergrad enrollment	37,751
% male/female/not reported	50/50/0
% from out of state	8
% First-year live on campus	77
% Ugrads live on campus	40
# of fraternities (% join)	45 (NR)
# of sororities (% join)	30 (NR)
% Asian	34
% Black or African American	7
% Hispanic	16
% Native American	<1
% Pacific Islander	<1
% Race and/or ethnicity unknown	2
% Two or more races	4
% White	30
% International	7
# of countries represented	87

CAMPUS MENTAL HEALTH SERVICES

Offers mental health/wellness program	Yes
Mental health training available to students	No
Employs Chief Wellness Officer	NR
Peer-to-peer mental health offerings	NR
Counseling center has guidelines or accreditation	No
Mental health/well-being courses	NR

ACADEMICS

% students returning for sophomore year	93
% students graduating within 4 years	69
% students graduating within 6 years	84
Calendar	Semester
Student/faculty ratio	15:1

Most Popular Majors
Computer and Information Sciences; Business Administration and Management; Finance

Applicants Often Prefer
Cornell University, Princeton University, University of Pennsylvania

Applicants Sometimes Prefer
Boston University, New York University, Penn State University Park, University of Maryland, College Park

STUDENTS SAY "..."

Academics

A Rutgers education delivers "opportunities around every corner." After all, it's a "diverse university in all aspects of the word—academically, culturally, politically, ethnically, linguistically, and socially." And from the School of Engineering to the Mason Gross School of the Arts, undergraduates have the ability to "pursue anything they're interested in." Since it is known as a research university, it's quite common for undergraduates "to conduct research and work with professors in any number of fields." They even have opportunities to present their work, like at the annual Aresty Undergraduate Research Symposium.

When it comes to the classroom, most courses are taught in a lecture format. However, electives tend to be "much smaller and thus much more open to discussion and student presentation." As at most schools, you'll find a mix of "great professors, average professors, and bad professors." However, most students insist that the vast majority of professors are "intelligent people who have a lot of information to share and a lot of experience that allows them to elaborate on many topics." And the best of these instructors are "experienced, intelligent, and helpful," as well as "diverse, accessible, proactive...and interested in students who take initiative." These educators know how to make learning "enjoyable and informative."

Campus Life

Rutgers students report that "there's rarely a dull moment" on campus. Indeed, you can "always [find] something going on," whether it's "movie screenings, arcade games at the RutgersZone, performing arts, local theaters, university-sponsored concerts, free food events, community service days, [or] Greek life." The university offers more than 500 academic, service, social, and athletic clubs, so you're bound to find an organization that strikes your fancy. There's even an annual Involvement Fair every fall, making it easy to meet student leaders and explore what's available. Undergrads also enjoy Late Knights, twice monthly late-night programming that ranges from trivia to open mics. Additionally, they love to support their more athletically inclined classmates. As one undergrad shares, "During football season...everyone can be found cheering in the student section at the games." When the weekend rolls around, it's not uncommon to find students socializing, whether on campus or at the local bars. Undergrads report that they generally feel safe, highlighting the fact that the school "sends out (campus) police to patrol around the campus twenty-four hours to ensure student safety." Finally, for those who want to explore life beyond campus, New York City and Philadelphia are both an easy bus or train ride away.

Student Body

Sure, at first glance it might seem like the average Rutgers student hails from New Jersey. It is a state school after all. And while you will meet plenty of Jersey locals, undergrads offer assurances that "Rutgers is truly a melting pot of people from all over the world, of all different backgrounds with different interests." Given that the student body includes people from over 130 countries and more than 60% of students identify as a person of color, that sentiment seems to bear out. Students share that "no matter what you're interested in, there is a group of students here who share the same exact interests. It's really easy to find your own niche." While Rutgers students are united in their "dedication to academics and community service" and "are serious about their work and studying," students stress that their peers also "know how to party and have fun." Moreover, they're quick to note that their classmates are "very friendly, funny, and nice." Perhaps best of all, with a campus of over 40,000 students, "It is not uncommon to meet someone new weekly... With so many students here, everyone is able to find someone to befriend and interact with."

Rutgers University–New Brunswick

Financial Aid: 848-932-7385 • E-Mail: admissions@ugadm.rutgers.edu • Website: www.newbrunswick.rutgers.edu

THE PRINCETON REVIEW SAYS

Admissions

The school reports that its standardized testing policy for use in admission for Fall 2026 is Test Optional. The Princeton Review suggests that interested applicants consult with the school for the most up-to-date standardized testing policies. *Very important factors considered include:* rigor of secondary school record, academic GPA. *Important factors considered include:* application essay, extracurricular activities, character/personal qualities. *Other factors considered include:* class rank, standardized test scores, interview, talent/ability, first generation, geographical residence, state residency, volunteer work, work experience. High school diploma is required and GED is accepted. *Academic units required:* 4 English, 3 math, 2 science, 2 language (other than English), 5 academic electives.

Financial Aid

Students should submit: FAFSA. Priority filing deadline is 12/1. The Princeton Review suggests that all financial aid forms be submitted as soon as possible. *Need-based scholarships/grants offered:* Federal Pell; Federal SEOG; College/university scholarship or grant aid from institutional funds; State scholarships/grants; Federal Nursing Scholarships. *Loan aid offered:* Federal Direct Subsidized Loans; Federal Direct Unsubsidized Loans; Direct PLUS loans. Admitted students will be notified of awards on a rolling basis beginning 2/15. Federal Work-Study Program available. Institutional employment available.

The Inside Word

Due to the vast number of applications the university gets each year, applicants will be reviewed based on the standard criteria—grades, the quality of your high school curriculum, standardized test scores (if submitted), and your student essay. To maximize your chances of admission, aim for scores and class standing above the typical range for accepted students.

THE SCHOOL SAYS

From the Admissions Office

"Standing as one of the nation's leading research universities, Rutgers University–New Brunswick is acclaimed for the excellent achievements of our people and for their contributions to society in the pursuit of education, research, and health care.

"With a diverse student body, prestigious faculty, vast resources, the champion Scarlet Knights, and a national rank among the top 20 public schools, Rutgers is the ideal destination for your curiosity and perseverance.

"Take a closer look:

- At the doorsteps of New York City and Philadelphia, Rutgers–New Brunswick is the flagship location with 2,600+ acres-spanning five campuses that together form a single community.
- With 120+ undergraduate majors, 19 schools and colleges, and a 15:1 student-to-faculty ratio to deliver a more personalized learning experience, your Rutgers education transcends the theoretical and puts your coursework into practice.
- 89% of students report positive career outcomes within six months of graduation with top employers including Amazon, RWJ Barnabas Health, Lockheed Martin, and JPMorgan Chase & Co.
- With a global reach, 1000+ students participate annually in study and service-learning abroad programs with access to 120+ programs in 50+ countries.
- Whether you're cheering on our beloved Scarlet Knights at a Big Ten football game or joining one of the 750+ student organizations, there are endless opportunities.
- #1 in diversity among Big Ten schools, with students from 50+ states and territories and 100+ countries.

"From rich academic offerings to a vibrant community and a robust range of global opportunities, Rutgers–New Brunswick ignites purpose and is the ultimate beginning to a remarkable future."

SELECTIVITY

# of total applicants	68,614
% of total applicants accepted	41
% of total acceptees attending	29
# of in-state applicants	35,993
% of in-state applicants accepted	51
# of out-of-state-applicants	22,421
% of applicants accepted from out of state	66
# of international applicants	10,200
% of international applicants accepted	67

First-Year Profile

Testing policy	Test Optional
Range SAT EBRW	650–730
Range SAT math	660–770
Range ACT composite	28–33
% submitting SAT scores	50
% submitting ACT scores	5
% graduated top 10% of class	34
% graduated top 25% of class	69
% graduated top 50% of class	92
% submitting high school rank	13

Important Dates

Early action	
Apply by	11/1
Notified by	1/31
Regular	
Apply by	Varies by year
Nonfall registration?	Yes

FINANCIAL FACTS

Annual in-state tuition	$14,933
Annual out-of-state tuition	$35,758
Food and housing	$15,332
Books and supplies	$3,891
Average need-based scholarship (First-year)	$13,516 ($14,849)
% students with need rec. need-based scholarship or grant aid (First-year)	70 (68)
% students with need rec. non-need-based scholarship or grant aid (First-year)	53 (50)
% students with need rec. need-based self-help aid (First-year)	65 (73)
% students rec. any financial aid (First-year)	59 (67)
% UG borrow to pay for school	49
Average cumulative indebtedness	$28,227
% of students with need fully met (First-year)	18 (23)
Average % of student need met (First-year)	14 (12)

Sacred Heart University

5151 Park Avenue, Fairfield, CT 06825 • Admissions: 203-371-7880

Survey Snapshot
Theater is popular
Intramural sports are popular
Frats and sororities are popular

RATINGS	
Quality of Life	92
Fire Safety	94
Green	60*
Academic	83
Profs Interesting	90
Profs Accessible	91
Admissions	87
Financial Aid	86

CAMPUS LIFE

Type of school	Private
Affiliation	Roman Catholic
Environment	Town

Students

Degree-seeking undergrad enrollment	7,148
% male/female/not reported	37/63/0
% from out of state	72
% First-year from public high school	66
% First-year live on campus	91
% Ugrads live on campus	51
# of fraternities (% join)	6 (22)
# of sororities (% join)	10 (34)
% Asian	1
% Black or African American	3
% Hispanic	16
% Native American	<1
% Pacific Islander	<1
% Race and/or ethnicity unknown	5
% Two or more races	3
% White	71
% International	1
# of countries represented	37

CAMPUS MENTAL HEALTH SERVICES

Offers mental health/wellness program	Yes
Mental health training available to students	Yes
Employs Chief Wellness Officer	Yes
Peer-to-peer mental health offerings	Yes
Counseling center has guidelines or accreditation	NR
Mental health/well-being courses	NR

ACADEMICS

% students returning for sophomore year	86
% students graduating within 4 years	72
% students graduating within 6 years	77
Calendar	Differs By Program
Student/faculty ratio	15:1
Most common class size 20–29.	(40%)

Most Popular Majors
Nursing; Finance; Psychology; Exercise Science; Marketing

Applicants Sometimes Prefer
Delaware State University, Fairfield University, Providence College, Quinnipiac University, University of Connecticut

STUDENTS SAY "…"

Academics

Sacred Heart University (SHU) is a private Catholic liberal arts institution committed to "caring about the needs of every student and providing them the resources to reach their goals." In addition to New Student Orientation, SHU offers the First-Year Experience, a 10-week course designed to help students transition successfully to college life. Classes at SHU extend beyond traditional lectures, using "interactive platforms, project-based learning, and service-learning projects," enabling students "to engage with the material in new and exciting ways." For instance, the Catholic Intellectual Tradition (CIT) seminar series encourages students to lead class for a day, a "very fun and interesting" experience. Multiple students point to the "endless opportunities" of a robust performing arts department, from writing a script to learning from a Broadway producer to working on a premiere. That "real-world experience" is what many suggest the "passionate" faculty bring to the table, along with being "available for extra help and [making] time for their students." All said, the "comprehensive learning experience" professors offer flows naturally from the sense that most are "very active in their respective fields" and can offer "up-to-date information and advice about the field and jobs for us post-graduation." The faculty inspires and challenges students: "They also push us to do things that we didn't know we could accomplish."

Campus Life

Sacred Heart "does a very good job in giving all students experiences to meet new people" and to "unwind and meet people" through activities like the First 50 Days program, which "offers fun events for first-years and current students." There are also "many different activities and clubs, which gives the student body a chance to really immerse themselves in," everything from club sports and academic clubs to more casual groups like the crochet club. Students enjoy activities and events like "make your own bracelet or stuffed animal, as well as the Fall Fest and Spring Carnival," and "bingo night is so much fun." Students are quick to note that the "performing arts programs are a big part of campus life" and help "bring us together." The only quibble is that a few feel the school "could expand on the dining hall options," though the larger takeaway is that the provided options for "food on campus [are] delicious." Mainly, though, the "university is filled with school spirit," especially evident at sporting events. SHU has more than 30 Division I teams, with hockey games being particularly popular. The campus is within "walking distance to a golf course" and students "like to play pickleball whenever the temperature is nice outside." Greek life offers "a supportive and engaging community" and "a lot of opportunities to give back." As one enrollee summarizes, "We have a good balance of academics and having fun on campus."

Student Body

SHU is described as a "hold-the-door-open community" characterized by "small acts of kindness wherever you go." The university's Catholic affiliation "really speaks to the values of the overall student population," and students "seem to be very dedicated to working hard to receive good grades." Most students at SHU are "enthusiastic and excited to be at the campus." They're also characterized as "supportive, uplifting, driven, kind, and passionate about their respective clubs and organizations." Regardless of their backgrounds or demographics, students say that the school offers an "environment where everyone feels like they belong." As one student put it, "I really feel like I've found my family here."

Sacred Heart University

Financial Aid: 203-371-7980 • E-Mail: enroll@sacredheart.edu • Website: www.sacredheart.edu

THE PRINCETON REVIEW SAYS

Admissions

The school reports that its standardized testing policy for use in admission for Fall 2026 is Test Optional. The Princeton Review suggests that interested applicants consult with the school for the most up-to-date standardized testing policies. *Very important factors considered include:* rigor of secondary school record, academic GPA, volunteer work, work experience, level of applicant's interest. *Important factors considered include:* class rank, application essay, recommendation(s), interview, extracurricular activities, talent/ability, character/personal qualities. *Other factors considered include:* standardized test scores. High school diploma is required and GED is accepted. *Academic units required:* 4 English, 3 math, 3 science, 1 science lab, 2 language (other than English), 3 social studies, 3 history, 3 academic electives. *Academic units recommended:* 4 English, 4 math, 4 science, 2 science labs, 4 language (other than English), 4 social studies, 4 history, 4 academic electives.

Financial Aid

Students should submit: FAFSA; CSS PROFILE. The Princeton Review suggests that all financial aid forms be submitted as soon as possible. *Need-based scholarships/grants offered:* Federal Pell; Federal SEOG; State scholarships/grants; Private scholarships; College/university scholarship or grant aid from institutional funds. *Loan aid offered:* Federal Direct Subsidized Loans; Federal Direct Unsubsidized Loans; Direct PLUS loans; State Loans. Admitted students will be notified of awards on a rolling basis beginning 3/1. Federal Work-Study Program available. Institutional employment available.

The Inside Word

Sacred Heart takes a holistic approach to the admissions process and the school aims to get a sense of every candidate beyond their quantitative metrics. Nevertheless, while recommendation letters and extracurricular participation are important, academic achievement still carries the most weight. To be seen as a competitive candidate, you should take several honors or AP courses during high school.

THE SCHOOL SAYS

From the Admissions Office

"At Sacred Heart University, education is personal and purposeful. Rooted in a Catholic tradition that values the whole person, SHU empowers students to grow intellectually, professionally and ethically. With more than 100 undergraduate, graduate and doctoral programs across five colleges and three schools, students are prepared to lead and make an impact—both locally and globally.

"Innovation meets opportunity on SHU's campus. Students collaborate with expert faculty in cutting-edge labs, simulation centers and creative studios—from finance and AI to health care and cybersecurity. SHU's West Campus, formerly GE's global headquarters, and international sites in Ireland and Italy offer immersive, hands-on learning experiences that prepare students for the future.

"A vibrant campus life fuels connection and growth. With 34 Division I teams, 100+ clubs, performing arts led by industry professionals and a strong culture of service and inclusion, students find their place and purpose. Located just an hour from NYC and close to Boston, SHU offers unmatched access to internships, clinical placements, and career opportunities—contributing to a 99% placement rate within a year of graduation."

SELECTIVITY

# of total applicants	16,608
% of total applicants accepted	64
% of total acceptees attending	18
# of in-state applicants	4,196
% of in-state applicants accepted	65
# of out-of-state-applicants	11,836
% of applicants accepted from out of state	64
# of international applicants	576
% of international applicants accepted	44
# of early decision applicants	203
% of early decision applicants accepted	94

First-Year Profile

Testing policy	Test Optional
Range SAT composite	1200–1330
Range SAT EBRW	600–680
Range SAT math	580–650
Range ACT composite	27–29
% submitting SAT scores	11
% submitting ACT scores	2
Average HS GPA	3.6
% submitting high school GPA	100
% graduated top 10% of class	16
% graduated top 25% of class	45
% graduated top 50% of class	83
% submitting high school rank	43

Important Dates

Early decision	
Apply by	11/15
Notified by	12/1
Early action	
Apply by	12/1
Notified by	1/15
Regular	
Notified by	4/1
Nonfall registration?	Yes

FINANCIAL FACTS

Annual tuition	$54,520
Food and housing	$20,700
Books and supplies	$1,200
Average need-based scholarship (First-year)	$23,785 ($29,631)
% students with need rec. need-based scholarship or grant aid (First-year)	99 (100)
% students with need rec. non-need-based scholarship or grant aid (First-year)	19 (24)
% students with need rec. need-based self-help aid (First-year)	76 (72)
% students rec. any financial aid (First-year)	98 (100)
% UG borrow to pay for school	67
Average cumulative indebtedness	$53,809
% of students with need fully met (First-year)	22 (25)
Average % of student need met (First-year)	59 (62)

SAINT ANSELM COLLEGE

100 Saint Anselm Drive, Manchester, NH 03102-1310 • Admissions: 603-641-7500

Survey Snapshot
Students are happy
Alumni active on campus
Active student-run political groups

RATINGS

Quality of Life	**86**
Fire Safety	**84**
Green	**60***
Academic	**87**
Profs Interesting	**91**
Profs Accessible	**95**
Admissions	**86**
Financial Aid	**91**

CAMPUS LIFE

Type of school	Private
Affiliation	Roman Catholic
Environment	City

Students

Degree-seeking undergrad enrollment	2,229
% male/female/not reported	41/59/<1
% from out of state	73
% First-year live on campus	93
% Ugrads live on campus	90
# of fraternities	0
# of sororities	0
% Asian	1
% Black or African American	2
% Hispanic	6
% Native American	<1
% Pacific Islander	<1
% Race and/or ethnicity unknown	5
% Two or more races	2
% White	84
% International	1
# of countries represented	10

CAMPUS MENTAL HEALTH SERVICES

Offers mental health/wellness program	Yes
Mental health training available to students	No
Employs Chief Wellness Officer	NR
Peer-to-peer mental health offerings	NR
Counseling center has guidelines or accreditation	No
Mental health/well-being courses	NR

ACADEMICS

% students returning for sophomore year	90
% students graduating within 4 years	72
% students graduating within 6 years	80
Calendar	Semester
Student/faculty ratio	13:1
Most common class size 10–19.	(38%)
Most common lab/discussion size 1–9.	(58%)

Most Popular Majors

Business Administration and Management; Nursing; Political Science and Government

Applicants Often Prefer

Boston College, Colby College, College of the Holy Cross, Villanova University

Applicants Sometimes Prefer

Fairfield University, Fordham University, Merrimack College, Providence College, Quinnipiac University, Sacred Heart University, Saint Michael's College, Salve Regina University, Simmons University, Stonehill College, University of New Hampshire, Wheaton College (MA)

Applicants Rarely Prefer

Assumption University, Emmanuel College, Regis College, Saint Joseph's College of Maine, Siena University, University of Massachusetts—Amherst

STUDENTS SAY "..."

Academics

Saint Anselm College is a Benedictine Catholic liberal arts school, a "welcoming, safe place where students can receive an amazing education" within the surroundings of a quintessential New England setting. Adhering to the school's service roots, the monks "are a huge part of life on campus, and even teach some classes" and "any courses that fulfill your civic requirement have an aspect called Community Engaged Learning where you volunteer in the surrounding towns as a part of your grade." To help bridge its 2,000 students into the discussion-based, inquisitive learning of its core curriculum, all first-year students take the two-part Conversatio class, where students "explore the connection between ourselves, the world, and the divine through many pieces of historical literature" and "spend most of the time outside lecture talking to classmates and leading discussions on the literature we study."

The smaller class sizes make it easier to form personal relationships with the "very caring and knowledgeable" professors, who "are always willing to meet with students to help them." There's also an Academic Resource Center that offers further workshops, writing assistance, and peer tutoring. And while some classes may lean heavily on lectures, teachers are praised for bringing in guests who are professionals in their fields to help illustrate the concepts being taught, and the school has a popular study abroad program that seeks to give students first-hand research opportunities. Ultimately, students applaud the Saint Anselm experience, as "no matter what your major is, you will experience a little bit of everything."

Campus Life

The average Saint Anselm enrollee is constantly on the move, "going from meeting to meeting, class to class, club to club." Still, "while everyone is busy, no one is overwhelmed," and students can slow down to enjoy the simple pleasures of "spending time with friends at the dining hall and taking long walks throughout campus." During the day, it tends to be all business: "you will often see people working on their laptops in common areas, the student center, library, even at the dining hall." However, after the books are closed, "people love to spend time outside, whether it's sledding, playing KanJam, cornhole, [or] hiking." Almost all students live on campus for their four years, and "the campus events clubs try to have events or food trucks as much as possible to make an average day just a little more special."

Student Body

People at Saint Anselm are "easy to get to know," with "a large student athlete population and campus ministry/service population," and everyone tries to "embrace the community as much as we can, and cherish all of the time that we have here." As one student says, "The people who go to Saint Anselm College genuinely love the school and want to be at 'the Hilltop' [the affectionate name for the school campus] as much as possible." While "ethnic and racial diversity is not entirely large" here, this group of "warm-hearted welcoming individuals" say that "no matter your background, you'll find your niche here." To better understand the vibe, know that students commonly say things like "That was [or wasn't] very Anselmian of you," as they expect their peers to be "kind, respectful, and compassionate."

SAINT ANSELM COLLEGE

Financial Aid: 603-641-7110 • E-Mail: admission@anselm.edu • Website: www.anselm.edu

THE PRINCETON REVIEW SAYS

Admissions

The school reports that its standardized testing policy for use in admission for Fall 2026 is Test Optional. The Princeton Review suggests that interested applicants consult with the school for the most up-to-date standardized testing policies. *Very important factors considered include:* academic GPA. *Other factors considered include:* rigor of secondary school record, standardized test scores, application essay, recommendation(s), interview, extracurricular activities, talent/ability, character/personal qualities, first generation, alumni/ae relation, geographical residence, volunteer work, work experience, level of applicant's interest. High school diploma is required and GED is accepted. *Academic units required:* 4 English, 3 math, 3 science, 2 science labs, 2 language (other than English), 2 social studies. *Academic units recommended:* 4 English, 4 math, 4 science, 2 science labs, 4 language (other than English), 4 social studies.

Financial Aid

Students should submit: FAFSA. Priority filing deadline is 2/15. The Princeton Review suggests that all financial aid forms be submitted as soon as possible. *Need-based scholarships/grants offered:* Federal Pell; Federal SEOG; State scholarships/grants; Private scholarships; College/university scholarship or grant aid from institutional funds. *Loan aid offered:* Federal Direct Subsidized Loans; Federal Direct Unsubsidized Loans; Direct PLUS loans. Admitted students will be notified of awards on a rolling basis beginning 11/1. Federal Work-Study Program available. Institutional employment available.

The Inside Word

Students can submit the Common Application or the Saint Anselm Application, but on either form, you'll want to highlight personal character and community service. Applicants who feel their grades are not as high as they'd like should make sure to emphasize their out-of-class skills and experiences in their application. Note that nursing applicants must apply early action or early decision.

THE SCHOOL SAYS

From the Admissions Office

"Saint Anselm is New England's only Benedictine College, a place where a time-honored tradition that values a love of learning and a balanced life is coupled with a contemporary liberal arts education. The College offers over 100 academic programs and is particularly well-known for nursing, politics, business, criminal justice, psychology, and health sciences. Located in the first-in-the-nation primary state, Saint Anselm is the home of the New Hampshire Institute of Politics, which hosts national debates and provides opportunities for students of any major to engage with world leaders. The Jean School of Nursing and Health Sciences at Saint Anselm offers state-of-the-art resources for students interested in nursing, health sciences, and community and public health. The Gregory J. Grappone Humanities Institute serves as a home on campus for humanitarian discussion. The Dana Center for the Performing Arts and Aaron Tolson Institute of Dance provide unique opportunities for students interested in dance, music, theater, visual arts, and more. Saint Anselm has recently been nationally recognized as a top college for liberal arts, value, service, and first-generation student-support by organizations like The Princeton Review, U.S. News & World Report, the Carnegie Foundation, and more. Saint Anselm students should expect to keep busy both inside and outside of the classroom: over 85% of students participate in at least one club, organization, committee, or athletic program. The College offers a wide variety of student organizations, study abroad options, and community engagement opportunities."

SELECTIVITY

# of total applicants	4,422
% of total applicants accepted	71
% of total acceptees attending	21
# of in-state applicants	1,207
% of in-state applicants accepted	75
# of out-of-state-applicants	3,132
% of applicants accepted from out of state	71
# of international applicants	83
% of international applicants accepted	8
# of early decision applicants	34
% of early decision applicants accepted	88
# offered a place on the wait list	237
# admitted from wait list	1

First-Year Profile

Testing policy	Test Optional
Range SAT composite	1100–1300
Range SAT EBRW	560–670
Range SAT math	530–640
Range ACT composite	25–30
% submitting SAT scores	21
% submitting ACT scores	1
Average HS GPA	3.5
% submitting high school GPA	100
% graduated top 10% of class	25
% graduated top 25% of class	56
% graduated top 50% of class	86
% submitting high school rank	35

Important Dates

Early decision	
Apply by	12/1
Notified by	1/1
Early action	
Apply by	11/15
Notified by	1/15
Regular	
Apply by	2/1
Notified by	3/15
Nonfall registration?	Yes

FINANCIAL FACTS

Annual tuition	$49,000
Food and housing	$17,630
Required fees	$1,580
Books and supplies	$3,142
Average need-based scholarship (First-year)	$32,305 ($33,862)
% students with need rec. need-based scholarship or grant aid (First-year)	100 (100)
% students with need rec. non-need-based scholarship or grant aid (First-year)	34 (34)
% students with need rec. need-based self-help aid (First-year)	64 (65)
% students rec. any financial aid (First-year)	100 (100)
% UG borrow to pay for school	73
Average cumulative indebtedness	$48,201
% of students with need fully met (First-year)	40 (36)
Average % of student need met (First-year)	84 (84)

St. Bonaventure University

3261 West State Road, St. Bonaventure, NY 14778 • Admissions: 716-375-2400

Survey Snapshot
Students are happy
Students are friendly
College radio is popular

RATINGS

Quality of Life	**86**
Fire Safety	**87**
Green	**60***
Academic	**80**
Profs Interesting	**90**
Profs Accessible	**95**
Admissions	**83**
Financial Aid	**89**

CAMPUS LIFE

Type of school	Private
Affiliation	Roman Catholic
Environment	Village

Students

Degree-seeking undergrad enrollment	2,087
% male/female/not reported	50/50/0
% from out of state	17
% First-year from public high school	82
% First-year live on campus	96
% Ugrads live on campus	80
# of fraternities	0
# of sororities	0
% Asian	2
% Black or African American	4
% Hispanic	6
% Native American	1
% Pacific Islander	<1
% Race and/or ethnicity unknown	1
% Two or more races	4
% White	79
% International	5
# of countries represented	33

CAMPUS MENTAL HEALTH SERVICES

Offers mental health/wellness program	Yes
Mental health training available to students	Yes
Employs Chief Wellness Officer	Yes
Peer-to-peer mental health offerings	Yes
Counseling center has guidelines or accreditation	No
Mental health/well-being courses	NR

ACADEMICS

% students returning for sophomore year	83
% students graduating within 4 years	62
% students graduating within 6 years	69
Calendar	Semester
Student/faculty ratio	14:1
Most common class size 20–29.	(49%)
Most common lab/discussion size 10–19.	(73%)

Most Popular Majors

Finance; Marketing/Marketing Management; Health Services/Allied Health/Health Sciences

Applicants Sometimes Prefer

Niagara University, St. John Fisher University, State University of New York—Buffalo State University, State University of New York—Geneseo

STUDENTS SAY "…"

Academics

St. Bonaventure University, located in Western New York, is a "Catholic university in the Franciscan tradition." The university's "greatest strengths include its qualified staff, welcoming student body, and opportunities for service and extracurricular activities," all contributing to "a well-rounded college experience." Most students agree that "the professors are the backbone of this university." The faculty "is genuinely engaged with the students, their education, and their lives." One student says the professors are "amazing; easy to work with, helpful with all questions, and [they] make class as interesting as possible." Professors "are always willing to spend extra time with you when needed," understanding "the value of one-on-one conversation and availability outside of the classroom." Students are encouraged to provide feedback to the faculty, noting that professors "really take our teacher evaluations to heart." The intimate size of the university ensures that every student has "the opportunity to tutor, teach, do research, and lead during their undergrad" career. The school "fosters social, academic, and spiritual growth for students of all backgrounds," which "prepares students for the professional world." This holistic approach may explain why 99 percent of graduates are employed or enter graduate school within six months of graduation. As one student says, "It's a small school with great programs and an enormously huge heart."

Campus Life

"SBU is filled with students who are passionate in the classroom, in the line of volunteer service, and in school spirit," and "getting involved is a huge part of the culture here." The school "holds a ton of events on campus, which are extremely fun and entertaining. Clubs are big at Bonas, too." When students are not studying or in class, they often spend time with friends, going to the gym, playing sports, and participating in club meetings and school events. Students also enjoy walking on the "beautiful trail" around campus and "exploring the nearby national forest." As one student remarks, "There is always something fun to do." The sense of school spirit is palpable, especially during basketball games, which "are a lot of fun." One student concurs, "You can always tell when game day is for the men's basketball team just by walking through campus; it gets pretty crazy." During the week, "students are very focused on studies," but "on weekends, there are a ton of fun parties off campus," and "the 'Skeller' (campus bar) is also popular." And one student thoughtfully adds, "Weekends for Bona's students are fun because everyone knows each other."

Student Body

SBU is "all about Franciscan values and learning how to be successful yet ethical," resulting in a "very open and accepting community." The school's size allows students to "all share the same teachers, dining hall, and sports teams," creating an atmosphere where "everyone is like family." Students are described as "young professionals with open minds and a drive to change the world. They are creative, thoughtful, respectful of others, and well-informed." One undergrad observes that the student body is "Unfailingly kind to one another. There is a true sense of comradery and support." Another student shares, "We affectionately call our student body the Bona Bubble because of how inclusive and loving it is." It's a place where "everyone knows each other and looks out for one another." Students "at Bonaventure come from all different walks of life, but friendships are formed that last a lifetime, no matter the differences in backgrounds." As one student states, "I would not change my experience at Bona's for the world."

St. Bonaventure University

Financial Aid: 716-375-2020 • E-Mail: admissions@sbu.edu • Website: www.sbu.edu

THE PRINCETON REVIEW SAYS

Admissions

The school reports that its standardized testing policy for use in admission for Fall 2026 is Test Optional. The Princeton Review suggests that interested applicants consult with the school for the most up-to-date standardized testing policies. *Very important factors considered include:* rigor of secondary school record, academic GPA, recommendation(s), character/personal qualities. *Important factors considered include:* application essay, extracurricular activities, talent/ability, volunteer work. *Other factors considered include:* class rank, standardized test scores, interview, first generation, alumni/ae relation, geographical residence, state residency, work experience, level of applicant's interest. High school diploma is required and GED is accepted. *Academic units recommended:* 4 English, 3 math, 3 science, 3 science labs, 2 language (other than English), 4 social studies.

Financial Aid

Students should submit: FAFSA; State aid form. Priority filing deadline is 2/1. The Princeton Review suggests that all financial aid forms be submitted as soon as possible. *Need-based scholarships/grants offered:* Federal Pell; Federal SEOG; State scholarships/grants; Private scholarships; College/university scholarship or grant aid from institutional funds. *Loan aid offered:* Federal Direct Subsidized Loans; Federal Direct Unsubsidized Loans; Direct PLUS loans; College/university loans from institutional funds. Admitted students will be notified of awards on a rolling basis beginning 1/1. Federal Work-Study Program available. Institutional employment available.

The Inside Word

Prospective students at Bonaventure are evaluated individually and accepted based on their capacity for success in college. St. Bonaventure recommends that applicants submit academic transcripts, standardized test scores, recommendations, and a personal essay, and the admissions committee will consider any other supporting materials that prove a student's overall eligibility for admission. St. Bonaventure has a rolling admissions program, so applications are reviewed as soon as they arrive at the admissions office, and encouraged to apply early in the admission cycle.

THE SCHOOL SAYS

From the Admissions Office

"For more than 160 years, St. Bonaventure University has been dedicated to education excellence as informed by our Franciscan and liberal arts traditions. We seek to transform the lives of our students, inspiring in them a lifelong commitment to service and citizenship.

"The charm of our campus and the inspirational beauty of the surrounding hills provide a special place where growth in learning and living is abundantly realized. St. Bonaventure establishes pathways to internships, graduate schools and careers through its innovate Career and Professional Readiness Center, which engages students from the time they step onto campus. The Richter Recreation Center provides all students with state-of-the-art facilities for athletics and wellness. As a student at one of the smallest Division I schools in the country, you get the benefits of big-time sports along with those of a small, student-centered university. St. Bonaventure is a member of the Atlantic 10.

"Academics at St. Bonaventure are challenging. Small classes and personalized attention encourage individual growth and development. St. Bonaventure's schools of Arts and Sciences, Business, (Jandoli School of) Communications, Education and Health Professions offer fifty majors. The School of Graduate Studies also offers several programs— on-ground, on-line and hybrid formats—leading to the master's degree.

"While St. Bonaventure has adopted a Test Optional policy for standardized tests (ACT and SAT), such scores will still be required for some specific majors, and to be eligible for the university's top three scholarship levels."

SELECTIVITY

# of total applicants	3,654
% of total applicants accepted	85
% of total acceptees attending	18
# of in-state applicants	2,825
% of in-state applicants accepted	87
# of out-of-state-applicants	658
% of applicants accepted from out of state	90
# of international applicants	159
% of international applicants accepted	43

First-Year Profile

Testing policy	Test Optional
Range SAT composite	1070–1240
Range SAT EBRW	530–640
Range SAT math	530–610
Range ACT composite	21–29
% submitting SAT scores	16
% submitting ACT scores	2
Average HS GPA	3.7
% submitting high school GPA	100
% graduated top 10% of class	18
% graduated top 25% of class	26
% graduated top 50% of class	78
% submitting high school rank	53

Important Dates

Regular	
Apply by	7/28
Notified by	Rolling, 10/1
Nonfall registration?	Yes

FINANCIAL FACTS

Annual tuition	$42,220
Food and housing	$16,210
Required fees	$1,285
Books and supplies	$800
Average need-based scholarship (First-year)	$24,965 ($24,825)
% students with need rec. need-based scholarship or grant aid (First-year)	98 (99)
% students with need rec. non-need-based scholarship or grant aid (First-year)	98 (99)
% students with need rec. need-based self-help aid (First-year)	90 (95)
% students rec. any financial aid (First-year)	97 (99)
% UG borrow to pay for school	88
Average cumulative indebtedness	$28,408
% of students with need fully met (First-year)	34 (23)
Average % of student need met (First-year)	66 (71)

St. John's College (MD)

60 College Avenue, Annapolis, MD 21401 • Admissions: 410-626-2522

Survey Snapshot
Class discussions encouraged
Students are happy
Theater is popular

RATINGS

Quality of Life	**92**
Fire Safety	**70**
Green	**60***
Academic	**96**
Profs Interesting	**97**
Profs Accessible	**98**
Admissions	**90**
Financial Aid	**89**

CAMPUS LIFE

Type of school	Private
Environment	Town

Students

Degree-seeking undergrad enrollment	471
% male/female/not reported	51/49/0
% from out of state	84
% First-year from public high school	49
% First-year live on campus	97
% Ugrads live on campus	75
# of fraternities	0
# of sororities	0
% Asian	3
% Black or African American	1
% Hispanic	9
% Native American	0
% Pacific Islander	0
% Race and/or ethnicity unknown	4
% Two or more races	6
% White	63
% International	14
# of countries represented	30

CAMPUS MENTAL HEALTH SERVICES

Offers mental health/wellness program	Yes
Mental health training available to students	Yes
Employs Chief Wellness Officer	Yes
Peer-to-peer mental health offerings	Yes
Counseling center has guidelines or accreditation	No
Mental health/well-being courses	No

ACADEMICS

% students returning for sophomore year	82
% students graduating within 4 years	51
% students graduating within 6 years	60
Calendar	Semester
Student/faculty ratio	8:1
Most common class size 10–19.	(96%)

Most Popular Majors
Liberal Arts and Sciences/Liberal Studies

Applicants Often Prefer
Brown University, Harvard College, The University of Chicago

Applicants Sometimes Prefer
Bard College, Reed College, William & Mary

Applicants Rarely Prefer
University of Maryland, College Park

STUDENTS SAY "..."

Academics

At St. John's College in Maryland, the "great books," or texts commonly viewed as the most important books in history, form the backbone of the unique curriculum. St. John's is a liberal arts college with two campuses that encourages exploration and dissection of original, foundational texts so that students may develop critical analysis skills within a "safe and prosperous learning environment." "The teaching of St. John's College is all about allowing individuals to collectively discover the essence of being a human being," sums up one student. Classes are pretty straightforward: "We read, and we talk about what we read." The curriculum includes obscure texts as well as the major classic players, and one of the greatest things about studying here is "engaging with difficult and renowned texts without worrying about impressing others or having to show off."

The "largely brilliant and caring" faculty members at St. John's are "some of the most wonderful and interesting people," and are "willing to meet for coffee or lunch to discuss essays, questions from class, concerns, and even non-program texts." They are "engaged and enthralled by the learning process at St. John's, just as the students are." The college has a unique evaluation system in place, so students at St. John's "are faced with reports not just on their academic success, but also on the way that they treat and interact with their peers, via classroom dynamic." The college has made academic rigor an "overwhelmingly social issue," and the "'too cool for school' attitude is not socially rewarded" here. Not only do students discuss the same works and questions, "they do so in a respectful, tactful manner." In any classroom "you get the sense of togetherness" where everyone listens and "no one's points are any more or less important to the discussion than any other's."

Campus Life

There are "no two Johnnies that are alike" and students at St. John's display a wide range of interests. Most participate in "a study group of some sort, at least one artistic extracurricular, and an intramural sport." St. John's "robust intramural program" is a major component of campus social life, and creates a "fantastic" community in which students are alphabetically sorted onto teams "where anyone can participate in various seasonal sports." "Although I have never been athletic, this is a very welcoming group regardless of ability, and playing intramural sports here has given me a lot of confidence," says one student. A large amount of extracurricular time is spent studying and reading, but there are also "very many popular club options," including "swing dance lessons, fencing, the croquet team, student play productions, orchestra, various choral groups, community service, [and the] environmental club." St. John's also offers students spots in classes run by non-faculty members of the Annapolis community, including "writing classes, poetry, watercolor, and sculpture." Off campus, people often go out to eat at many of the great restaurants in Annapolis, or head to the museums and monuments in Washington, D.C., which is "just a short train ride away." Students can also transfer between the Annapolis or the Santa Fe campuses, and many in Maryland spend a year studying in New Mexico.

Student Body

The student body at St. John's is "intellectual, but far from pretentious," and given that all students go through the same academic program "there is a strong and warm sense of camaraderie." Upper-level students "couldn't care less that you're a freshmen," and people "who would have never become friends anywhere else are able to come together here and form bonds that start in the classroom but continue into life outside the academics." The curiosity students develop here extends to outside the program as well, so while the program at St. John's is classically oriented, students at the college "are aware of pop culture, current events, and politics." The bubble at St. John's is "real, but in no way impenetrable."

St. John's College (MD)

Financial Aid: 410-626-2502 • E-Mail: Annapolis.Admissions@sjc.edu • Website: www.sjc.edu

THE PRINCETON REVIEW SAYS

Admissions

The school reports that its standardized testing policy for use in admission for Fall 2026 is Test Optional. The Princeton Review suggests that interested applicants consult with the school for the most up-to-date standardized testing policies. *Very important factors considered include:* application essay. *Important factors considered include:* rigor of secondary school record, character/personal qualities, level of applicant's interest. *Other factors considered include:* class rank, academic GPA, standardized test scores, recommendation(s), interview, extracurricular activities, talent/ability, first generation, geographical residence, volunteer work, work experience. *Academic units recommended:* 4 English, 4 math, 4 science, 4 language (other than English), 4 history.

Financial Aid

Students should submit: FAFSA. Priority filing deadline is 2/1. The Princeton Review suggests that all financial aid forms be submitted as soon as possible. *Need-based scholarships/grants offered:* Federal Pell; Federal SEOG; State scholarships/grants; Private scholarships; College/university scholarship or grant aid from institutional funds. *Loan aid offered:* Federal Direct Subsidized Loans; Federal Direct Unsubsidized Loans; Direct PLUS loans; College/university loans from institutional funds. Admitted students will be notified of awards on a rolling basis beginning 12/1. Federal Work-Study Program available. Institutional employment available.

The Inside Word

St. John's is a unique environment, best suited to students of a quirky yet serious intellectual predilection. To test the waters before you jump in, consider taking a campus tour or even sitting in on an active tutorial session with students. You can also send your questions about academics and life on campus to a current student through the St. John website. Each applicant is evaluated individually for potential success in the program, and submitting standardized test scores is optional.

THE SCHOOL SAYS

From the Admissions Office

"St. John's College is centered on reading and discussing the greatest books in history. With teachers such as Plato, Shakespeare, Euclid, Nietzsche, Einstein, Austen, and Du Bois, students at St. John's are original and unconventional, love big questions and discussion, and are excited to join an intellectual community of thinkers and seekers.

"All students at St. John's explore our great books curriculum in interdisciplinary classes focused on philosophy, classics, literature, politics, religion, biology, chemistry, physics, mathematics, music, history, language, and more. With a 8:1 student to faculty ratio, every class is a discussion led by one or two faculty members. If the degree were categorized by conventional college credits, each student would earn a triple major in philosophy, literature, and the natural sciences. The college regularly ranks among the best for undergraduate teaching and student-faculty relationships.

"Over 70% of Johnnies attend graduate school, particularly in law, business, and journalism, and the college is among the best for students receiving PhDs in the humanities and sciences. Students are free to transfer between the campuses in Annapolis, MD, and Santa Fe, NM.

"On the Annapolis campus, 500 students experience an idyllic college town along the Chesapeake Bay. Annapolis is close to Washington, DC, with dozens of nearby museums and cultural offerings. The college was founded here in 1696, and students embrace long-held traditions such as waltz parties, intramural sports, and the annual croquet match against the Naval Academy. Popular student groups include musical ensembles, community service organizations, and the college's theatrical troupe, King Williams Players."

SELECTIVITY

# of total applicants	836
% of total applicants accepted	55
% of total acceptees attending	25
# of in-state applicants	165
% of in-state applicants accepted	46
# of out-of-state-applicants	399
% of applicants accepted from out of state	80
# of international applicants	282
% of international applicants accepted	26
# of early decision applicants	61
% of early decision applicants accepted	70
# offered a place on the wait list	26
# admitted from wait list	0

First-Year Profile

Testing policy	Test Optional
Range SAT composite	1290–1360
Range SAT EBRW	680–750
Range SAT math	590–690
Range ACT composite	27–32
% submitting SAT scores	38
% submitting ACT scores	12
Average HS GPA	3.7
% submitting high school GPA	89
% graduated top 10% of class	29
% graduated top 25% of class	60
% graduated top 50% of class	79
% submitting high school rank	36

Important Dates

Early decision	
Apply by	11/1
Notified by	12/5
Other ED apply by	1/15
Other ED notified by	2/6
Early action	
Apply by	11/15
Notified by	12/19
Regular	
Notified by	Rolling, 2/20
Nonfall registration?	No

FINANCIAL FACTS

Annual tuition	$40,936
Food and housing	$16,428
Required fees (First-year)	$1,381 ($1,581)
Books and supplies	$680
Average need-based scholarship (First-year)	$31,423 ($31,496)
% students with need rec. need-based scholarship or grant aid (First-year)	100 (100)
% students with need rec. non-need-based scholarship or grant aid (First-year)	18 (23)
% students with need rec. need-based self-help aid (First-year)	70 (63)
% students rec. any financial aid (First-year)	96 (99)
% UG borrow to pay for school	64
Average cumulative indebtedness	$29,354
% of students with need fully met (First-year)	22 (27)
Average % of student need met (First-year)	80 (80)

ST. JOHN'S COLLEGE (NM)

1160 Camino Cruz Blanca, Santa Fe, NM 87505 • Admissions: 505-984-6060

Survey Snapshot
Diverse student types interact on campus
Class discussions encouraged
Great library

RATINGS

Quality of Life	90
Fire Safety	69
Green	60*
Academic	94
Profs Interesting	97
Profs Accessible	94
Admissions	91
Financial Aid	89

CAMPUS LIFE

Type of school	Private
Environment	Town

Students

Degree-seeking undergrad enrollment	368
% male/female/not reported	50/50/0
% from out of state	87
% First-year from public high school	57
% First-year live on campus	94
% Ugrads live on campus	93
# of fraternities	0
# of sororities	0
% Asian	1
% Black or African American	1
% Hispanic	11
% Native American	0
% Pacific Islander	1
% Race and/or ethnicity unknown	2
% Two or more races	7
% White	64
% International	12
# of countries represented	28

CAMPUS MENTAL HEALTH SERVICES

Offers mental health/wellness program	Yes
Mental health training available to students	Yes
Employs Chief Wellness Officer	Yes
Peer-to-peer mental health offerings	Yes
Counseling center has guidelines or accreditation	No
Mental health/well-being courses	No

ACADEMICS

% students returning for sophomore year	81
% students graduating within 4 years	39
% students graduating within 6 years	55
Calendar	Semester
Student/faculty ratio	8:1
Most common class size 10–19.	(96%)

Most Popular Majors
Liberal Arts and Sciences/Liberal Studies

Applicants Often Prefer
Colorado College, Reed College, University of California—Berkeley

Applicants Sometimes Prefer
Kenyon College, Thomas Aquinas College (CA), Whitman College

Applicants Rarely Prefer
University of New Mexico

STUDENTS SAY "..."

Academics

The mountains of Santa Fe provide a fertile setting for intellectual exploration at St. John's College, a liberal arts institution defined by a distinctive curriculum centered on the reading and discussion of the Great Books in literature, history, religion, and more. Johnnies—as students are known—say the "integration between the student body and the curriculum is so beautiful," giving them "the space to think and to grow through the texts that are read." Every student participates in seminar twice a week, gathering on Monday and Thursday evenings to discuss one of the texts, while classes more broadly promote "personal growth" by "teaching us how to have good conversations with each other." This ethos extends to the faculty—called tutors—who must "teach everything from Ancient Greek for translation to Einstein's theory of relativity, regardless of their specialty," making them "incredibly committed to learning and unusually curious, open, and full of intellectual humility." Within this shared academic structure, tutors "have great freedom to ask innovative questions, pursue surprising ways of thinking, and take the class on productive tangents." Students emphasize that this approach not only makes tutors "a great joy to be around," but also fosters strong "potential for intensive learning," along with a "[high] degree of academic intimacy." In short, it's a great fit for a "like-minded group of ambitious individuals that have learning and insight as a top priority."

Campus Life

By academic design—all students share the same classes and texts with those in their year—Johnnies "interact so heavily with the curriculum outside of class." The result is a campus environment filled "with the wilder, funkier ideas that constantly spill out from classroom rigor," where "just as many students spend their Friday nights studying Aristotle or field theory or law (for fun!) as they do going to parties." Although most students "spend a lot of time studying and preparing for class," leaving relatively limited free time, they make the most of it on this "absolutely breathtakingly beautiful" campus. Outdoor recreation is a key feature of student life: "Camping trips with friends are a popular weekend activity," supported by the Outdoor Program, "which frequently holds camping, climbing, skiing, etc., trips that are very affordable and easy to get into." Students also point to "many reading groups on campus" and note that "intramural sports are also excellent." Between lively discussions among peers, reading outdoors, and the lure of the mountains, one student observes that there is "so much variety of interest and extracurricular activity and social activity that the environment is almost frantic, constantly productive and interesting, and meaningful."

Student Body

Students who choose St. John's "are seeking out knowledge and wisdom beyond just the academics," and readily embrace the rigor of the program. The college's size fosters close relationships—"it is a small school, so everyone knows each other"—and contributes to "a strong level of respect between peers." The student body is described as "an eclectic group of students, all of whom have interesting personalities and immense passion," united by a shared love of reading and inquiry. As one student puts it, "I will say that I am surrounded by the most honestly curious oddities to walk on two legs," capturing both the individuality and intellectual intensity of the community. Indeed, this lot of "community-driven and academically minded individuals" has "diverse interests but are usually targeted toward a specific area." Summing up the experience, one student explains: "We're fitting 3,000 years of thought in philosophy, mathematics, science, language, and more into just four years of schooling. If we weren't so supportive and intelligent, we would never make it to the end."

ST. JOHN'S COLLEGE (NM)

Financial Aid: 505-984-6058 • E-Mail: Admissions@sjc.edu • Website: www.sjc.edu

THE PRINCETON REVIEW SAYS

Admissions

The school reports that its standardized testing policy for use in admission for Fall 2026 is Test Optional. The Princeton Review suggests that interested applicants consult with the school for the most up-to-date standardized testing policies. *Very important factors considered include:* application essay. *Important factors considered include:* rigor of secondary school record, character/personal qualities, level of applicant's interest. *Other factors considered include:* class rank, academic GPA, standardized test scores, recommendation(s), interview, extracurricular activities, talent/ability, first generation, geographical residence, volunteer work, work experience. High school diploma is required and GED is accepted. *Academic units recommended:* 4 English, 4 math, 4 science, 4 language (other than English), 4 history.

Financial Aid

Students should submit: FAFSA. The Princeton Review suggests that all financial aid forms be submitted as soon as possible. *Need-based scholarships/grants offered:* Federal Pell; Federal SEOG; State scholarships/grants; Private scholarships; College/university scholarship or grant aid from institutional funds; United Negro College Fund. *Loan aid offered:* Federal Direct Subsidized Loans; Federal Direct Unsubsidized Loans; Direct PLUS loans. Admitted students will be notified of awards on a rolling basis beginning 12/1. Federal Work-Study Program available. Institutional employment available.

The Inside Word

St. John's College has been test optional for decades and has a no "harm policy" as well, so you might as well submit scores, since they will never be used against you. Interviews are optional, but strongly recommended, especially if you're concerned about your essay or application not properly summing you up.

THE SCHOOL SAYS

From the Admissions Office

"St. John's College is centered on reading and discussing the greatest books in history. With teachers such as Plato, Shakespeare, Euclid, Nietzsche, Einstein, Austen, and Du Bois, students at St. John's are original and unconventional, love big questions and discussion, and are excited to join an intellectual community of thinkers and seekers.

"All students at St. John's explore our great books curriculum in interdisciplinary classes focused on philosophy, classics, literature, politics, religion, biology, chemistry, physics, mathematics, music, history, language, and more. With a 8:1 student to faculty ratio, every class is a discussion led by one or two faculty members. If the degree were categorized by conventional college credits, each student would earn a triple major in philosophy, literature, and the natural sciences. The college regularly ranks among the best for undergraduate teaching and student-faculty relationships.

"Over 70% of Johnnies attend graduate school, particularly in law, business, and journalism, and the college is among the best for students receiving PhDs in the humanities and sciences. Students are free to transfer between the campuses in Annapolis, MD, and Santa Fe, NM.

"The Santa Fe campus, in the foothills of the Rocky Mountains, is a one-minute walk to the best hiking, biking, and skiing in the southwest. Santa Fe is also home to more than 250 art galleries, great food, and live music. Nearly 400 Johnnies embrace the stunning natural environment and rich cultural heritage of New Mexico while reading great books on the placita, hiking 12,000-foot mountains, sculpting in the pottery studio, or socializing in the student-run coffee shop."

SELECTIVITY

# of total applicants	394
% of total applicants accepted	53
% of total acceptees attending	37
# of in-state applicants	9
% of in-state applicants accepted	67
# of out-of-state-applicants	252
% of applicants accepted from out of state	70
# of international applicants	135
% of international applicants accepted	21
# of early decision applicants	37
% of early decision applicants accepted	70
# offered a place on the wait list	1
# admitted from wait list	0

First-Year Profile

Testing policy	Test Optional
Range SAT composite	1290–1400
Range SAT EBRW	680–750
Range SAT math	610–710
Range ACT composite	28–34
% submitting SAT scores	35
% submitting ACT scores	14
Average HS GPA	3.7
% submitting high school GPA	91
% graduated top 10% of class	44
% graduated top 25% of class	69
% graduated top 50% of class	78
% submitting high school rank	46

Important Dates

Early decision	
Apply by	11/1
Notified by	12/5
Other ED apply by	1/15
Other ED notified by	2/6
Early action	
Apply by	11/15
Notified by	12/19
Regular	
Notified by	Rolling, 2/20
Nonfall registration?	Yes

FINANCIAL FACTS

Annual tuition	$40,936
Food and housing	$16,462
Required fees	$1,638
Books and supplies	$444
Average need-based scholarship (First-year)	$37,393 ($35,427)
% students with need rec. need-based scholarship or grant aid (First-year)	99 (100)
% students with need rec. non-need-based scholarship or grant aid (First-year)	16 (17)
% students with need rec. need-based self-help aid (First-year)	83 (90)
% students rec. any financial aid (First-year)	96 (99)
% UG borrow to pay for school	55
Average cumulative indebtedness	$21,964
% of students with need fully met (First-year)	19 (20)
Average % of student need met (First-year)	84 (86)

St. John's University (NY)

8000 Utopia Parkway, Queens, NY 11439 • Admissions: 718-990-2000

Survey Snapshot

Everyone loves the Red Storm
Students love Queens, NY
Students are happy

RATINGS

Quality of Life	85
Fire Safety	99
Green	92
Academic	75
Profs Interesting	83
Profs Accessible	87
Admissions	83
Financial Aid	82

CAMPUS LIFE

Type of school	Private
Affiliation	Roman Catholic
Environment	Metropolis

Students

Degree-seeking undergrad enrollment	9,384
% male/female/not reported	44/56/0
% from out of state	16
% First-year live on campus	39
% Ugrads live on campus	25
# of fraternities (% join)	10 (5)
# of sororities (% join)	12 (9)
% Asian	16
% Black or African American	17
% Hispanic	27
% Native American	<1
% Pacific Islander	<1
% Race and/or ethnicity unknown	1
% Two or more races	5
% White	32
% International	3
# of countries represented	41

CAMPUS MENTAL HEALTH SERVICES

Offers mental health/wellness program	Yes
Mental health training available to students	Yes
Employs Chief Wellness Officer	Yes
Peer-to-peer mental health offerings	Yes
Counseling center has guidelines or accreditation	Yes
Mental health/well-being courses	Yes, non-credit

ACADEMICS

% students returning for sophomore year	79
% students graduating within 4 years	52
% students graduating within 6 years	69
Calendar	Semester
Student/faculty ratio	16:1
Most common class size 20–29.	(44%)
Most common lab/discussion size 20–29.	(47%)

Most Popular Majors

Biology/Biological Sciences; Psychology; Pharmacy

Applicants Also Look At

Fordham University, Hofstra University, New York University, State University of New York—Stony Brook University

STUDENTS SAY "..."

Academics

St. John's University upholds the Catholic and Vincentian traditions set forth at its founding in 1870. At the residential Queens, New York, campus, located in a suburban area (as well as at the additional New York City campus found in Manhattan), students receive "a well-nurtured education that can help one turn into a specialist in whatever field they desire." A wide range of support systems, such as career services, campus ministry, the writing center, and a focus on mentoring ensure that "every student has a safe, healthy, and challenging academic career" while at St. John's.

Most professors are generous "when it comes to providing help and any aids for you to succeed" and "are here to help you and prepare you for the rest of your life." "Almost all my experiences with professors have been positive. If you are willing to put in the work they are willing to work with you," says one actuarial science major. They are very helpful "in making sure you actually understand the information rather than memorize it and not use it outside the classroom," and "provide guidance with classwork, finding jobs and internships, and more." On top of faculty help, the career services office is "amazing." "They help you with your résumé, cover letter, [telling] you when there are career fairs, picking graduate schools, [and] finding internships."

Classes are "easy to follow and there are never any surprises from the professors," and most are discussion-based. Students in all majors find that "the workload is not overwhelming and the assignments are helpful and relevant to the subjects." For commuter and noncommuter students alike, the Monday and Thursday afternoon common hour provides a universal time for most social and academic clubs to meet.

Campus Life

From athletics to coffeehouse shows and cultural events, there are "multiple things to do on campus every day." Many people swear by the gym and the classes it offers, or "hang out on the Great Lawn and play Frisbee and other similar games." Students "sometimes have to wait a long time for their next class" so the school provides "too many extracurricular activities to count" to help time pass. There are clubs to represent "almost every racial, religious and interest group" and "there's never a day where there isn't anything to do." Basketball season is a huge rally booster (the men's team plays some games at Madison Square Garden), and St. John's also hosts "many great events on off days such as family day, picnics, barbecues, and more." There are a fair number of commuters, and those who live on campus often venture into the city to "enjoy the fast pace and vibrant life of New York City." Between "the spring carnival, the free commuter breakfasts, and reduced prices on movie tickets, [and] Broadway shows, St. John's wants their students' experience to be unforgettable."

Student Body

This "very diverse" group has students from all over the country and world (it "falls perfectly into place with the diversity of the New York City area as a whole"), which "exposes everyone to new ideas and helps us better define where we stand on our own views." "There's an atmosphere of the core staples of the University: Catholic, Vincentian, and metropolitan," says a student. People speak of the sense of unity that comes from everyone being "more than happy to be here, excited to learn, and [willing to] participate in campus activities." There is a lot of collaboration when it comes to student organizations, and students also "have great initiative when it comes to getting their voice heard."

St. John's University (NY)

Financial Aid: 718-990-2000 • E-Mail: admhelp@stjohns.edu • Website: www.stjohns.edu

THE PRINCETON REVIEW SAYS

Admissions

The school reports that its standardized testing policy for use in admission for Fall 2026 is Test Optional. The Princeton Review suggests that interested applicants consult with the school for the most up-to-date standardized testing policies. *Very important factors considered include:* academic GPA. *Important factors considered include:* rigor of secondary school record, standardized test scores. *Other factors considered include:* class rank, application essay, recommendation(s), extracurricular activities, volunteer work, work experience, level of applicant's interest. High school diploma is required and GED is accepted. *Academic units recommended:* 4 English, 3 math, 3 science, 2 language (other than English), 2 social studies, 2 history.

Financial Aid

Students should submit: FAFSA. The Princeton Review suggests that all financial aid forms be submitted as soon as possible. *Need-based scholarships/grants offered:* Federal Pell; Federal SEOG; State scholarships/grants; College/university scholarship or grant aid from institutional funds; Private scholarships. *Loan aid offered:* Federal Direct Subsidized Loans; Federal Direct Unsubsidized Loans; Direct PLUS loans. Admitted students will be notified of awards on a rolling basis beginning 2/15. Federal Work-Study Program available. Institutional employment available.

The Inside Word

The admissions process at St. John's is quite straightforward. High school grades are undoubtedly the most important factors, though volunteer work and extracurricular activities are also highly regarded. The university doesn't consider religious affiliation at all when making admissions decisions; there are students of every religious stripe here.

THE SCHOOL SAYS

From the Admissions Office

"Founded in 1870, St. John's is a Catholic and Vincentian University that prepares students for personal and professional success—and emphasizes academic excellence without bounds—by providing talented students with an outstanding education that builds upon their abilities and aspirations. On the playing courts and athletic fields, St. John's is New York City's team, with 17 NCAA Division I men's and women's athletic teams.

"St. John's offers more than 100 associate, bachelor's, master's, and doctoral degrees in areas including the arts, business, communication arts, education, law, nursing, pharmacy, and the natural and applied sciences. More than 94 percent of our full-time professors hold a PhD or comparable terminal degree in their field. Our 16:1 student/faculty ratio ensures personal attention.

"Faith, service, and student success are central to a St. John's education. Each year, students perform more than 100,000 service hours. With world-class academics, renowned professors, outstanding resources, and a storied tradition of academic excellence and service, St. John's prepares you to change the world for the better.

"Our students enjoy both a metropolitan and global experience that starts at our two New York City campuses—in Queens and in Manhattan; an international campus in Rome, Italy; and study abroad locations in Paris, France, and Limerick, Ireland, and around the world. Enhancing the University's cosmopolitan character, students come from nearly 50 states and 118 foreign countries—all of them benefiting from the University's network of more than 198,000 alumni."

SELECTIVITY

# of total applicants	24,208
% of total applicants accepted	83
% of total acceptees attending	12
# offered a place on the wait list	1,167
# admitted from wait list	617

First-Year Profile

Testing policy	Test Optional
Range SAT composite	1150–1240
Range SAT EBRW	580–670
Range SAT math	570–670
Range ACT composite	24–29
% submitting SAT scores	23
% submitting ACT scores	2
Average HS GPA	3.5
% submitting high school GPA	100
% graduated top 10% of class	21
% graduated top 25% of class	46
% graduated top 50% of class	75
% submitting high school rank	25

Important Dates

Early action	
Apply by	12/1
Notified by	1/1
Regular	
Notified by	Rolling, 12/1
Nonfall registration?	Yes

FINANCIAL FACTS

Annual tuition	$53,980
Food and housing	$21,710
Required fees (First-year)	$1,410 ($1,660)
Books and supplies	$820
Average need-based scholarship (First-year)	$8,132 ($8,388)
% students with need rec. need-based scholarship or grant aid (First-year)	63 (75)
% students with need rec. non-need-based scholarship or grant aid (First-year)	91 (100)
% students with need rec. need-based self-help aid (First-year)	51 (45)
% students rec. any financial aid (First-year)	99 (99)
% UG borrow to pay for school	53
Average cumulative indebtedness	$26,890
% of students with need fully met (First-year)	15 (17)
Average % of student need met (First-year)	68 (73)

Saint Joseph's University (PA)

5600 City Avenue, Philadelphia, PA 19131 • Admissions: 610-660-1300

Survey Snapshot
Recreation facilities are great
Great library
Frats and sororities are popular

RATINGS

Quality of Life	79
Fire Safety	90
Green	60*
Academic	75
Profs Interesting	84
Profs Accessible	88
Admissions	82
Financial Aid	89

CAMPUS LIFE

Type of school	Private
Affiliation	Roman Catholic-Jesuit
Environment	Metropolis

Students

Degree-seeking undergrad enrollment	4,918
% male/female/not reported	45/55/0
% from out of state	42
% First-year from public high school	56
% First-year live on campus	90
% Ugrads live on campus	49
# of fraternities (% join)	2 (10)
# of sororities (% join)	5 (26)
% Asian	8
% Black or African American	7
% Hispanic	10
% Native American	<1
% Pacific Islander	<1
% Race and/or ethnicity unknown	1
% Two or more races	4
% White	69
% International	2
# of countries represented	30

CAMPUS MENTAL HEALTH SERVICES

Offers mental health/wellness program	Yes
Mental health training available to students	No
Employs Chief Wellness Officer	NR
Peer-to-peer mental health offerings	NR
Counseling center has guidelines or accreditation	No
Mental health/well-being courses	NR

ACADEMICS

% students returning for sophomore year	87
% students graduating within 4 years	77
% students graduating within 6 years	81
Calendar	Semester
Student/faculty ratio	12:1
Most common class size 20–29.	(31%)
Most common lab/discussion size 10–19.	(54%)

Most Popular Majors

Finance; Health Professions and Related Clinical Sciences; Pharmacy, Pharmaceutical Sciences, and Administration

Applicants Often Prefer

Drexel University, Penn State University Park, Temple University, University of Delaware

Applicants Sometimes Prefer

Boston College, The Catholic University of America, The College of New Jersey, Fairfield University, Fordham University, James Madison University, La Salle University, Loyola University Maryland, Marist University, Providence College, Rutgers University—Newark, University of Pittsburgh—Pittsburgh Campus, The University of Scranton, Villanova University, West Chester University of Pennsylvania

STUDENTS SAY "..."

Academics

One of the best parts about Saint Joseph's University is "the dedication to service and experiential learning." This is baked into the requirements for many majors, and the Service-Learning program incorporates weekly volunteering opportunities into the coursework. Says one student: "The entire year I was at the same service site, allowing me to build genuine relationships with the people at my site who I'd see every week." Students also value "many opportunities to learn off-campus, such as the Inside-Out program" where students "visit local prisons" and build empathy by learning alongside the incarcerated population. The SJU Study Tours program helps students extend their classroom learning: "[I] went to Northern Ireland, and it was so enlightening and really reinforced what we learned in class." On-campus programs are known for being likewise interactive and engaging, and students report that the business and health science programs are standouts. The Haub Innovative Speaker Series invites professionals "to come to campus and offer insights to students," and one nursing student appreciates being able to "jump into clinicals our second year of school, which is great." In the classroom, students report that the "student-to-teacher ratio is really amazing. It allows you to build a close connection to your teachers and feel like you could ask them for help." SJU students point to their professors as the "best parts of my academic experience…The classes can be challenging, but you feel like you're learning things that actually matter for your future career." Students enjoy a "good balance between lectures, labs, and real application" and describe their academic experience as "demanding but supportive."

Campus Life

At SJU, "almost everyone is in some sort of extracurricular." For many, spending time with friends means joining in "activities that involve community outreach," and service is "a huge part of a lot of students' lives on campus." As one Hawk explains it: "We have a large amount of clubs and programs dedicated to service, since we are a Jesuit school. I am personally part of a club that advocates for refugees and migrants around the world." Spending time with friends on campus can also involve sports. With a robust intramural program and D1 collegiate teams, athletics at SJU are "really great, they always try to get everyone involved, and the games are always super fun to attend." Student football fans are particularly enthused about a recent partnership with the Philadelphia Eagles, featuring "defined internships, associate roles, and game-day positions." Beyond campus, students "go into Manayunk for nightlife…Philly is also nearby, and it is easy to take the train there to grab something to eat, go shopping, or see a sporting event." Overall, service clubs and sports "are a great way to get involved and are really how students will have the best time here at Saint Joe's."

Student Body

"My peers at Saint Joseph's are a mix of hardworking, supportive, and down-to-earth students," says one Hawk. "Most people are really focused on their majors…What stands out is how willing students are to help each other, whether it's sharing notes, forming study groups, or explaining a tough topic after class." While it feels like many students are from the greater "Philadelphia and New Jersey suburbs," students report that "there is a large amount of variety here at SJU, with different people having different goals and aspirations in life…Students are kind and helpful if you don't know how something works." As one Hawk sums it up: "Our community is our strength by FAR. It is lovely to see such a great community where we all have several ties to each other and care for each other's needs and concerns."

SAINT JOSEPH'S UNIVERSITY (PA)

Financial Aid: 610-660-2500 • E-Mail: admit@sju.edu • Website: www.sju.edu

THE PRINCETON REVIEW SAYS

Admissions

The school reports that its standardized testing policy for use in admission for Fall 2026 is Test Optional. The Princeton Review suggests that interested applicants consult with the school for the most up-to-date standardized testing policies. *Very important factors considered include:* rigor of secondary school record, class rank, academic GPA. *Important factors considered include:* application essay, recommendation(s). *Other factors considered include:* standardized test scores, interview, extracurricular activities, talent/ability, character/personal qualities, first generation, alumni/ae relation, volunteer work, work experience, level of applicant's interest. High school diploma is required and GED is accepted. *Academic units required:* 4 English, 3 math, 2 science, 2 science labs, 2 language (other than English), 2 history. *Academic units recommended:* 4 English, 4 math, 4 science, 4 science labs, 4 language (other than English), 4 history.

Financial Aid

Students should submit: FAFSA; State aid form. Priority filing deadline is 12/1. The Princeton Review suggests that all financial aid forms be submitted as soon as possible. *Need-based scholarships/grants offered:* Federal Pell; Federal SEOG; State scholarships/grants; Private scholarships; College/university scholarship or grant aid from institutional funds. *Loan aid offered:* Federal Direct Subsidized Loans; Federal Direct Unsubsidized Loans; Direct PLUS loans. Admitted students will be notified of awards on or about 12/20 for Early Action and Early Decision 1, 2/15 for Early Decision 2, and 3/15 for Regular Decision. Federal Work-Study Program available. Institutional employment available.

The Inside Word

Students at Saint Joseph's University tend to be high achievers. Expect the school to focus on your academic rigor and work in the community, so use the optional test scores and interviews (remote or in-person) to help emphasize those areas.

THE SCHOOL SAYS

From the Admissions Office

"Founded in 1851 as Philadelphia's Jesuit university, Saint Joseph's University prepares students for a rapidly changing world by focusing on academic excellence and courageous exploration. With an intellectual tradition distinguished by a foundational liberal arts core and diversified by strong professional programs in business, nursing, health and science, and education, Saint Joseph's students are empowered, challenged and supported by high-quality faculty members to follow their own path. As a comprehensive university with locations in Philadelphia and Lancaster, Pennsylvania, undergraduate and graduate students study in the University's five schools and colleges—the College of Arts and Sciences, the Erivan K. Haub School of Business, the School of Education and Human Development, the School of Health Professions and the School of Nursing and Allied Health. With academic offerings in the most sought-after majors, including leading programs in the first-in-the-nation Philadelphia College of Pharmacy, a Saint Joseph's education is enriched through the University's network of cooperative education employers, clinical placements and professional internships. Outside of the classroom, the University's Division I student-athletes compete at the highest levels in 21 different sports. Upon graduation, nearly 100% of students are employed, pursuing advanced degrees or volunteering in prestigious service programs. The University's network of more than 110,000 proud alumni keep alive the rallying cry—The Hawk Will Never Die."

SELECTIVITY

# of total applicants	11,442
% of total applicants accepted	93
% of total acceptees attending	13
# of early decision applicants	87
% of early decision applicants accepted	94
# offered a place on the wait list	250
# admitted from wait list	86

First-Year Profile

Testing policy	Test Optional
Range SAT composite	1180–1340
Range SAT EBRW	590–680
Range SAT math	560–670
Range ACT composite	26–32
% submitting SAT scores	21
% submitting ACT scores	2
Average HS GPA	3.7
% submitting high school GPA	100
% graduated top 10% of class	23
% graduated top 25% of class	53
% graduated top 50% of class	81
% submitting high school rank	26

Important Dates

Early decision	
Apply by	11/15
Notified by	12/15
Other ED apply by	1/15
Other ED notified by	2/15
Early action	
Apply by	11/15
Notified by	12/15
Regular	
Apply by	2/1
Notified by	Rolling, 12/15
Nonfall registration?	Yes

FINANCIAL FACTS

Annual tuition	$57,940
Food and housing	$17,942
Required fees	$250
Books and supplies	$1,160
Average need-based scholarship (First-year)	$32,517 ($35,117)
% students with need rec. need-based scholarship or grant aid (First-year)	98 (99)
% students with need rec. non-need-based scholarship or grant aid (First-year)	24 (24)
% students with need rec. need-based self-help aid (First-year)	69 (68)
% students rec. any financial aid (First-year)	95 (100)
% UG borrow to pay for school	69
Average cumulative indebtedness	$39,480
% of students with need fully met (First-year)	30 (30)
Average % of student need met (First-year)	80 (83)

St. Lawrence University

23 Romoda Drive, Canton, NY 13617 • Admissions: 315-229-5261

Survey Snapshot
Students take advantage of the outdoors
Career services are great
Easy to get around campus

RATINGS

Quality of Life	**92**
Fire Safety	**78**
Green	**60***
Academic	**86**
Profs Interesting	**94**
Profs Accessible	**96**
Admissions	**90**
Financial Aid	**92**

CAMPUS LIFE

Type of school	Private
Environment	Village

Students

Degree-seeking undergrad enrollment	1,759
% male/female/not reported	49/51/0
% from out of state	60
% First-year from public high school	63
% First-year live on campus	100
% Ugrads live on campus	99
# of fraternities (% join)	2 (11)
# of sororities (% join)	4 (24)
% Asian	2
% Black or African American	2
% Hispanic	6
% Native American	1
% Pacific Islander	<1
% Race and/or ethnicity unknown	1
% Two or more races	2
% White	75
% International	11
# of countries represented	70

CAMPUS MENTAL HEALTH SERVICES

Offers mental health/wellness program	Yes
Mental health training available to students	Yes
Employs Chief Wellness Officer	Yes
Peer-to-peer mental health offerings	Yes
Counseling center has guidelines or accreditation	No
Mental health/well-being courses	Yes, non-credit

ACADEMICS

% students returning for sophomore year	90
% students graduating within 4 years	69
% students graduating within 6 years	79
Calendar	Semester
Student/faculty ratio	11:1
Most common class size 10–19.	(56%)
Most common lab/discussion size 10–19.	(66%)

Most Popular Majors

Biology/Biological Sciences; Psychology; Economics

Applicants Also Look At

Colby College, Hamilton College, Hobart and William Smith Colleges, Union College (NY), University of Vermont

STUDENTS SAY "…"

Academics

St. Lawrence University is a vibrant liberal arts institution of around 1,800 undergraduates and a very long reach. The "alumni network is super active," students have "lots of opportunities for hands-on research" and nearly two-thirds of SLU undergrads study abroad. With 47 majors and 41 minors to choose from, and the option to design one's own course of study in the multifield major program, there are "a plethora of options for one's academic path." Small class sizes—an average of 16 students in each—further focus those options, as enrollees note that they "feel more comfortable asking questions and having conversation," which "fosters learning." Adding to that comfort is a First-Year Program that helps with the transition to college and which is described as "a great way to bond" through living-learning communities in the dorms. The school also offers Community-Based Learning (CBL) courses that immerse students in the real world.

As for the staff, "I've never felt so supported and believed in." Students specifically note that the "compassion professors have for individual success is incredible," particularly in the way that they "know people have different styles of learning" and so "are responsive to questions and always try to make the class [as] interactive as possible." Their classes work "to deliver a well-rounded education and develop our interpersonal skills," and "a lot of the intro classes are very reasonable and give you the right amount of work." And for those interested, you can dive into research from your very first year: "I was offered an opportunity to study and train wildlife detection dogs with a focus on locating amphibians, all thanks to my professors." Overall, students suggest that "St. Lawrence is a place for students to explore past thinkers and ideas while also conversing with their peers to help them establish their own thoughts and views."

Campus Life

Ninety-nine percent of students live on this "walking campus" and "have the opportunity to live in theme houses or Greek houses, which support high-quality residential communities." There are over 150 clubs and organizations, and "skiing, hiking, rock climbing, and other outdoor activities are popular" among this nature-loving group. "The incredible outdoors that SLU has around us is [wonderful]," says a student. And while Canton "is a small and rural town" where "there is not a hopping night scene," students actually appreciate knowing "where everyone is going to be on a Saturday night." This means that "sports events are popular," as is "spend[ing] time in the student center to talk and grab coffee, go outside and sit in hammocks if the weather is permitting, and do homework in the library."

Student Body

St. Lawrence students "wear many different hats and are involved in almost all aspects of the school community and culture," including the "large student-athlete population." Undergrads describe this society as "tight knit," such that "even if you don't know someone, you treat them as if you do," and they speak warmly of the "extremely positive and loving" atmosphere this creates. Peers are seen as "a welcoming family in which everybody can find friends," something that's only enhanced by "very low-key people who work very hard in the classroom as well as [at] athletics, but [who] treat it like it is no big deal." One student posits that it might be the cold of being so close to Canada, which "brings a level of closeness and different atmosphere," but based on responses, we think SLU just chooses warm students.

St. Lawrence University

Financial Aid: 315-229-5266 • E-Mail: admissions@stlawu.edu • Website: www.stlawu.edu

THE PRINCETON REVIEW SAYS

Admissions

The school reports that its standardized testing policy for use in admission for Fall 2026 is Test Optional. The Princeton Review suggests that interested applicants consult with the school for the most up-to-date standardized testing policies. *Very important factors considered include:* rigor of secondary school record, academic GPA, application essay, recommendation(s), character/personal qualities. *Important factors considered include:* class rank, interview, extracurricular activities. *Other factors considered include:* standardized test scores, talent/ability, first generation, geographical residence, volunteer work, work experience. High school diploma is required and GED is accepted. *Academic units recommended:* 4 English, 3 math, 3 science, 3 language (other than English), 3 social studies, 2 history.

Financial Aid

Students should submit: FAFSA; CSS PROFILE. Priority filing deadline is 2/1. The Princeton Review suggests that all financial aid forms be submitted as soon as possible. *Need-based scholarships/grants offered:* Federal Pell; Federal SEOG; State scholarships/grants; Private scholarships; College/university scholarship or grant aid from institutional funds. *Loan aid offered:* Federal Direct Subsidized Loans; Federal Direct Unsubsidized Loans; Direct PLUS loans; College/university loans from institutional funds. Admitted students will be notified of awards on a rolling basis beginning 11/21. Federal Work-Study Program available. Institutional employment available.

The Inside Word

At St. Lawrence, you're not required to submit scores from the SAT or the ACT, but that means your high school transcript and teacher recommendations are that much more important during the application review. Merit scholarships selection is based on your overall academic profile.

THE SCHOOL SAYS

From the Admissions Office

"Nestled in the heart of New York's scenic North Country region, St. Lawrence University is a close-knit liberal arts learning community of talented students and inspiring faculty. We're proud of the traditions that bring us together and are guided by our enduring spirit of collaboration and curiosity as we focus on the future. At St. Lawrence, you'll tap into your full potential as you learn by doing, engage with global challenges, engage with global challenges, and leverage your liberal arts education to tackle the issues that you care about. Whether you're designing your own research project with your faculty mentor, studying in places like London or Kenya, or joining one of more than 150 campus organizations, you'll find countless ways to pursue your interests and contribute to a community that celebrates creativity and innovation.

"Our faculty has chosen St. Lawrence intentionally for the chance to work closely with students of all class years. They're always looking out for opportunities to connect classroom theory to hands-on, real-world experience through internships, volunteer efforts, co-curricular involvement, and off-campus study. Over 50% of our student body study off campus at least once. Just like our 1,000 acre campus, our curriculum is boundless, and our students customize their education to reflect their unique aspirations and career goals. Our seven new majors—cybersecurity, data science, finance, public health, digital media and film, pre-health chemistry, and biomedical sciences—represent cutting-edge fields where recent grads are in high demand. We've also invested in state-of-the-art spaces so students can do their best work with professional tools. These include our Bloomberg Finance Lab, Digital Scholarship Studio, and our Makerspace. Our graduates make up one of the strongest alumni networks in the country. They're ready, willing, and excited to connect with you to show you how your liberal arts education can make an impact. Personalized degree paths and comprehensive career preparation programs—including alumni mentoring, career courses, one-on-one coaching, individualized planning, networking trips, and internship opportunities—allow students to discover their passions and turn them into meaningful careers."

SELECTIVITY

# of total applicants	5,229
% of total applicants accepted	56
% of total acceptees attending	14
# of early decision applicants	276
% of early decision applicants accepted	50
# offered a place on the wait list	101
# admitted from wait list	3

First-Year Profile

Testing policy	Test Optional
Range SAT composite	1270–1380
Range SAT EBRW	630–730
Range SAT math	620–690
Range ACT composite	27–32
% submitting SAT scores	14
% submitting ACT scores	3
Average HS GPA	3.6
% submitting high school GPA	100
% graduated top 10% of class	33
% graduated top 25% of class	65
% graduated top 50% of class	91
% submitting high school rank	28

Important Dates

Early decision	
Apply by	11/2
Notified by	Rolling
Other ED apply by	2/1
Other ED notified by	Rolling
Early action	
Apply by	12/1
Notified by	1/16
Regular	
Apply by	2/1
Notified by	Rolling, 1/1
Nonfall registration?	Yes

FINANCIAL FACTS

Annual tuition	$69,460
Food and housing	$18,030
Required fees	$475
Books and supplies	$750
Average need-based scholarship (First-year)	$50,777 ($55,572)
% students with need rec. need-based scholarship or grant aid (First-year)	100 (100)
% students with need rec. non-need-based scholarship or grant aid (First-year)	39 (37)
% students with need rec. need-based self-help aid (First-year)	65 (65)
% students rec. any financial aid (First-year)	97 (98)
% UG borrow to pay for school	58
Average cumulative indebtedness	$36,426
% of students with need fully met (First-year)	34 (24)
Average % of student need met (First-year)	90 (91)

Saint Louis University

One N. Grand Boulevard, Saint Louis, MO 63103 • Admissions: 314-977-2500

Survey Snapshot
Students involved in community service
Active student government
Active minority support groups

RATINGS

Quality of Life	**83**
Fire Safety	**60***
Green	**60***
Academic	**83**
Profs Interesting	**89**
Profs Accessible	**91**
Admissions	**87**
Financial Aid	**89**

CAMPUS LIFE

Type of school	Private
Affiliation	Roman Catholic-Jesuit
Environment	Metropolis

Students

Degree-seeking undergrad enrollment	6,695
% male/female/not reported	41/59/<1
% from out of state	50
% First-year live on campus	75
% Ugrads live on campus	46
# of fraternities (% join)	NR
# of sororities (% join)	NR
% Asian	15
% Black or African American	11
% Hispanic	9
% Native American	<1
% Pacific Islander	<1
% Race and/or ethnicity unknown	2
% Two or more races	6
% White	52
% International	5

CAMPUS MENTAL HEALTH SERVICES

Offers mental health/wellness program	Yes
Mental health training available to students	No
Employs Chief Wellness Officer	NR
Peer-to-peer mental health offerings	NR
Counseling center has guidelines or accreditation	No
Mental health/well-being courses	NR

ACADEMICS

% students returning for sophomore year	86
% students graduating within 4 years	72
% students graduating within 6 years	79
Calendar	Semester
Student/faculty ratio	9:1
Most common class size 20–29.	(37%)
Most common lab/discussion size 20–29.	(42%)

Most Popular Majors
Biology/Biological Sciences; Psychology; Registered Nursing/Registered Nurse

STUDENTS SAY "..."

Academics

As one of the first institutions of higher learning west of the Mississippi River, Saint Louis University lives up to its over 200-year academic legacy: "At SLU, there is a lot of emphasis on academic success, and the very rigorous classes make it imperative that you focus." This mid-sized university offers a whopping 97 bachelor degree programs, each featuring a variety of large-lecture and small-discussion based formats, and even hybrids of the two. Impressively, students suggest that even in large courses, they were "able to connect with not only other classmates and teaching assistants, but...with my professors." Other students revel in the way programs make learning concrete, whether that's from a nursing student getting "so many clinical hours in very diverse fields" or "lots of opportunities to perform independent guided research as an undergraduate." The list goes on, citing classes that utilize "flight simulators" and backing up the study of world religions by visiting "a Hindu temple, Muslim mosque, and Buddhist meditation center."

Courses may be challenging, but students point to the personal support they receive from their instructors: "I truly believe that the professors I've encountered at Saint Louis University want their students to succeed. The Dean of Students is a wonderful individual and a great resource, and SLU's President is incredible," raves one second-year student. "I have never felt more supported by academic staff ever," adds another. "I have always felt like a student AND a person in my classrooms, and teachers are always one email or text away." As one third-year puts it, "SLU actively does its best to ensure that students succeed academically, professionally, and personally." This extends not just to the academics to but also to "generous financial aid" and professional resources in tutoring, time-management, and career: "With these, I could handle anything that college would throw at me."

Campus Life

Saint Louis University looks for well-rounded students, and to that end offers a robust suite of extracurricular activities and opportunities for service. Among student favorites are the theater program, music program, mock trial, sporting events, and student government. One student enjoys the Micah Program "where we serve [the] community as tutors for elementary-aged kids," and the Billiken Success Program "where we help with new-student events." Warm weather brings even more opportunities for students to come together, "When the weather is nice students will hang hammocks from the trees on campus... They'll play frisbee on the quad or sit with friends and talk in the shade. Our campus comes alive when the weather is warm." Students also remind us that "Saint Louis University is known not only for its large STEM programs, but for having...great soccer and basketball teams."

Student Body

The SLU community hails from 87 different countries, and many students take pride in the diversity celebrated on the SLU campus: "We host a lot of international students as well as students from different socioeconomic, cultural, and geographical backgrounds. I love getting to learn about other students' experiences and how they differ from mine." Even with so many different backgrounds, a shared passion for enriching the "mind, body, heart, and spirit" unites the student body. "I've found that the overwhelming majority of my peers are supportive of me as an academic and as a whole person, emotionally and spiritually." One first-year student explains, "My peers are helpful, friendly, positive, happy, and ignited with a passion for social justice." Overall, these ambitious students "are here to create a better future."

Saint Louis University

Financial Aid: 314-977-2350 • E-Mail: admission@slu.edu • Website: www.slu.edu

THE PRINCETON REVIEW SAYS

Admissions

The school reports that its standardized testing policy for use in admission for Fall 2026 is Test Optional. The Princeton Review suggests that interested applicants consult with the school for the most up-to-date standardized testing policies. *Very important factors considered include:* academic GPA. *Important factors considered include:* rigor of secondary school record, application essay, extracurricular activities, talent/ability, character/personal qualities, volunteer work. *Other factors considered include:* standardized test scores, recommendation(s), interview, work experience. High school diploma is required and GED is accepted. *Academic units required:* 4 English, 4 math, 3 science, 3 language (other than English), 3 social studies, 3 academic electives. *Academic units recommended:* 4 English, 4 math, 3 science, 3 language (other than English), 3 social studies, 3 academic electives.

Financial Aid

Students should submit: FAFSA. Priority filing deadline is 7/10. The Princeton Review suggests that all financial aid forms be submitted as soon as possible. *Need-based scholarships/grants offered:* Federal Pell; Federal SEOG; State scholarships/grants; Private scholarships; College/university scholarship or grant aid from institutional funds; Federal Nursing Scholarships. *Loan aid offered:* Federal Direct Subsidized Loans; Federal Direct Unsubsidized Loans; Direct PLUS loans. Admitted students will be notified of awards on a rolling basis. Federal Work-Study Program available. Institutional employment available.

The Inside Word

Despite being known for mostly drawing its students from the immediate region, SLU continues to expand its range and now half of students are from out of state. While your academic transcript is very important, the university also weighs each applicant's commitment to the Jesuit ideals of service to the community, so volunteering for Habitat for Humanity can be just as important as scoring off the charts.

THE SCHOOL SAYS

From the Admissions Office

"Saint Louis University gives students the knowledge, skills, and values to build a successful career and make a difference in the lives of those around them. Students live and learn in a safe and attractive campus environment. The beautiful urban residential campus offers many internship, outreach, and recreational opportunities. Ranked as one of the best educational values in the country, the university welcomes students—from all 50 states and 82 foreign countries—who pursue rigorous majors that invite individualization. Accessible faculty, study abroad opportunities, and many small, interactive classes make SLU a great place to learn.

"Founded in 1818, Saint Louis University is one of the nation's oldest and most prestigious Catholic institutions. Rooted in Jesuit values and its pioneering history as the first university west of the Mississippi River, SLU offers nearly 13,000 students a rigorous, transformative education of the whole person. At the core of the University's diverse community of scholars is SLU's service-focused mission, which challenges and prepares students to make the world a better, more just place. Saint Louis University's admission process is standardized-Test Optional for all undergraduate programs. Applicants may submit ACT or SAT test scores, but those who choose not to will not be disadvantaged in the admission process."

SELECTIVITY

# of total applicants	14,759
% of total applicants accepted	75
% of total acceptees attending	12
# of in-state applicants	2,883
% of in-state applicants accepted	87
# of out-of-state-applicants	6,745
% of applicants accepted from out of state	87
# of international applicants	1,792
% of international applicants accepted	67
# of early decision applicants	270
% of early decision applicants accepted	46

First-Year Profile

Testing policy	Test Optional
Range SAT composite	1120–1370
Range SAT EBRW	560–680
Range SAT math	540–690
Range ACT composite	23–30
% submitting SAT scores	11
% submitting ACT scores	44
Average HS GPA	3.8
% submitting high school GPA	100
% graduated top 10% of class	33
% graduated top 25% of class	63
% graduated top 50% of class	88
% submitting high school rank	31

Important Dates

Early decision	
Apply by	11/1
Notified by	12/1
Other ED apply by	1/13
Other ED notified by	2/1
Early action	
Apply by	12/1
Notified by	2/1
Regular	
Apply by	Rolling
Notified by	Rolling, 12/1
Nonfall registration?	Yes

FINANCIAL FACTS

Annual tuition	$58,960
Food and housing	$16,360
Required fees	$1,000
Books and supplies	$1,290
Average need-based scholarship (First-year)	$40,276 ($39,759)
% students with need rec. need-based scholarship or grant aid (First-year)	98 (98)
% students with need rec. non-need-based scholarship or grant aid (First-year)	24 (27)
% students with need rec. need-based self-help aid (First-year)	53 (49)
% UG borrow to pay for school	59
Average cumulative indebtedness	$30,184
% of students with need fully met (First-year)	26 (29)
Average % of student need met (First-year)	79 (81)

Saint Mary's College of California

1928 St. Mary's Road, PMB 4433, Moraga, CA 94575 • Admissions: 925-631-4224

Survey Snapshot
Career services are great
Class discussions encouraged
Everyone loves the Gaels

RATINGS

Quality of Life	**81**
Fire Safety	**93**
Green	**93**
Academic	**76**
Profs Interesting	**87**
Profs Accessible	**89**
Admissions	**71**
Financial Aid	**87**

CAMPUS LIFE

Type of school	Private
Affiliation	Roman Catholic
Environment	Village

Students

Degree-seeking undergrad enrollment	1,898
% male/female/not reported	45/55/0
% from out of state	13
% First-year from public high school	59
% First-year live on campus	99
% Ugrads live on campus	79
# of fraternities	0
# of sororities	0
% Asian	9
% Black or African American	4
% Hispanic	35
% Native American	<1
% Pacific Islander	2
% Race and/or ethnicity unknown	2
% Two or more races	9
% White	36
% International	3
# of countries represented	39

CAMPUS MENTAL HEALTH SERVICES

Offers mental health/wellness program	Yes
Mental health training available to students	Yes
Employs Chief Wellness Officer	Yes
Peer-to-peer mental health offerings	Yes
Counseling center has guidelines or accreditation	No
Mental health/well-being courses	Yes, non-credit

ACADEMICS

% students returning for sophomore year	83
% students graduating within 4 years	61
% students graduating within 6 years	69
Calendar	4-1-4
Student/faculty ratio	11:1
Most common class size 10–19.	(44%)

Most Popular Majors

Communication and Media Studies; Liberal Arts and Sciences, General Studies and Humanities; Clinical, Counseling and Applied Psychology

Applicants Often Prefer

California Polytechnic State University—San Luis Obispo, University of California—Davis, University of California—Santa Cruz

Applicants Sometimes Prefer

San Jose State University, Santa Clara University, University of California—Berkeley, University of California—Santa Barbara, University of San Francisco

Applicants Rarely Prefer

Chapman University, San Diego State University, University of California—Irvine

STUDENTS SAY "..."

Academics

Saint Mary's College of California takes a Lasallian approach to service and learning, using the study of the liberal arts to produce students who are both passionate learners and committed citizens. The diverse core curriculum is centered around the Collegiate Seminar, a series of courses in which undergrads read, dissect, discuss, and live the ideas behind major works of Western civilization. This foundation of "interesting texts...allows for students to bring in real world experiences," and encourages the "student-based discussions rather than professor lectures" that are a key aspect of a SMC education. The academic calendar also includes January Term, a month-long course in which enrollees deep dive into one single topic, which many agree is "a fun and exciting way to keep students engaged." Undergrads can choose from one of the many robust study-abroad programs to gain valuable experience (and college credit) while immersed in a different culture. Students also have access to a plethora of academic support services, including tutoring, mental health counseling, and the Center for Writing Across the Curriculum. And if there's anything that attendees need, the administration is committed to listening to student needs: "The staff have been here for all of us students every step of the way."

There are 44 majors offered across four schools, and a student-to-faculty ratio that allows "amazing relationships with professors thanks to the small classroom sizes." Faculty "makes sure that you know everything that you need to prepare you for life," and are "always accessible for meetings and office hours because they want their students to succeed." Additionally, teachers are "an incredible resource for internships, grad school, [and] jobs," and "are always trying to get us involved in outside events."

Campus Life

According to students, this is most definitely "a calm campus," one that goes hand-in-hand with the chill vibe of the San Francisco Bay and the student population, most of which leads a laid-back life when not engrossed in studying: "People walk around campus, occasionally work out, and get food from local places." Cooking and watching Netflix are classic pastimes, and "people spend a lot of time exploring the Bay Area," as the campus is close to Walnut Creek, Oakland, and San Francisco, where the weather is reportedly "beautiful no matter [the] time of year." In fact, the Campus Activities Board "frequently gives BART tickets for students to take public transportation to go to events." Game days are some of the biggest of the year, and "basketball is huge here."

First-year students are required to live on campus, but they may choose to live off-campus their sophomore year. The tight-knit nature of the school creates a "communal, friendly, and intimate" sense of familiarity, as does its modest population of under 2,500 undergraduates: "I enjoy walking to class and knowing eighty percent of the people I pass on the way there."

Student Body

There is "diversity both ethnically and intellectually," and since one-third of Saint Mary's College's students are the first in their families to attend college, there is a "great alumni network" that understands the remarkability of what many students have achieved in order to attend SMC, as well as the school's "ability to produce well-rounded students through a well-designed curriculum." There's also a strong "emphasis on culture and ethic identities" throughout every aspect of the school, which students find desirable on account of the way it "fosters a sense of community." This isn't a gradual effect, either—students agree with the idea that "From the first day of orientation I knew that the student body was very accepting."

Saint Mary's College of California

Financial Aid: 925-631-4370 • E-Mail: smcadmit@stmarys-ca.edu • Website: www.stmarys-ca.edu

THE PRINCETON REVIEW SAYS

Admissions

The school reports that its standardized testing policy for use in admission for Fall 2026 is Test Free. The Princeton Review suggests that interested applicants consult with the school for the most up-to-date standardized testing policies. *Very important factors considered include:* rigor of secondary school record, academic GPA. *Important factors considered include:* first generation. *Other factors considered include:* class rank, application essay, recommendation(s), interview, extracurricular activities, talent/ability, character/personal qualities, alumni/ae relation, geographical residence, volunteer work, work experience, level of applicant's interest. High school diploma is required and GED is accepted. *Academic units required:* 4 English, 3 math, 2 science, 1 science lab, 2 language (other than English), 2 social studies, 1 history. *Academic units recommended:* 4 English, 4 math, 2 science, 1 science lab, 3 language (other than English), 2 social studies, 1 history.

Financial Aid

Students should submit: FAFSA. The Princeton Review suggests that all financial aid forms be submitted as soon as possible. *Need-based scholarships/grants offered:* Federal Pell; Federal SEOG; State scholarships/grants; Private scholarships; College/university scholarship or grant aid from institutional funds. *Loan aid offered:* Federal Direct Subsidized Loans; Federal Direct Unsubsidized Loans; Direct PLUS loans. Admitted students will be notified of awards on a rolling basis beginning 10/1. Federal Work-Study Program available. Institutional employment available.

The Inside Word

Saint Mary's has a holistic admissions process, but academics are the driving force behind it. Those looking to major in math or science should be sure their grades are outstanding in that area. Because letters of recommendation are optional, including one can help to push your application over the edge.

THE SCHOOL SAYS

From the Admissions Office

"At Saint Mary's College of California, we inspire minds, engage the world, and transform lives. With small class sizes and professors who know you by name, the Saint Mary's experience enables students to thrive—in the classroom, in careers, and beyond.

"From a stunning campus in the San Francisco Bay Area, Saint Mary's offers boundless opportunities in California and around the globe. That includes careers and internships in Silicon Valley and a unique Jan Term program through which students work with faculty in dozens of locations locally, regionally, and internationally. And with knowledge and skills, confidence and support from the Gael community, you'll imagine, discover, and make a lasting impact...Wherever you're at...Whatever you set your heart to become.

"Founded in 1863 with a commitment to making an exemplary education accessible to all, Saint Mary's lives out its Catholic, Lasallian values that embody compassion, dignity, and social justice. We are a community of scholars committed to cultivating leaders who are eager to be agents of change in business, politics, the arts, science, and more.

"Undergraduate research programs provide students a rare opportunity to do hands-on work with real-world applications. Collegiate Seminar brings a rigorous approach to asking big questions—and to understanding diverse perspectives. The High Potential program ensures first-generation and low-income college students have the support they need to succeed.

"At Saint Mary's, our students break the mold by expanding their intellect, fostering innovation, growing their spirit, and embracing the 'Gael Force' attributes of enthusiasm, diversity, belonging, service, passion, and pride."

SELECTIVITY

# of total applicants	6,865
% of total applicants accepted	89
% of total acceptees attending	7
# of in-state applicants	3,874
% of in-state applicants accepted	94
# of out-of-state-applicants	2,762
% of applicants accepted from out of state	85
# of international applicants	232
% of international applicants accepted	66

First-Year Profile

Testing policy	Test Free
Average HS GPA	3.7
% submitting high school GPA	96

Important Dates

Early action	
Apply by	11/11
Notified by	12/1
Regular	
Apply by	1/15
Notified by	Rolling, 1/15
Nonfall registration?	Yes

FINANCIAL FACTS

Annual tuition	$61,416
Food and housing	$18,900
Required fees	$636
Books and supplies	$1,304
Average need-based scholarship (First-year)	$18,328 ($18,388)
% students with need rec. need-based scholarship or grant aid (First-year)	85 (92)
% students with need rec. non-need-based scholarship or grant aid (First-year)	94 (98)
% students with need rec. need-based self-help aid (First-year)	80 (75)
% students rec. any financial aid (First-year)	95 (100)
% UG borrow to pay for school	58
Average cumulative indebtedness	$35,593
% of students with need fully met (First-year)	27 (32)
Average % of student need met (First-year)	75 (85)

St. Mary's College of Maryland

18952 E. Fisher Road, St. Mary's City, MD 20686 • Admissions: 240-895-5000

Survey Snapshot
Lots of liberal students
Students are happy
Theater is popular

RATINGS

Quality of Life	80
Fire Safety	88
Green	60*
Academic	84
Profs Interesting	93
Profs Accessible	93
Admissions	86
Financial Aid	87

CAMPUS LIFE

Type of school	Public
Environment	Rural

Students

Degree-seeking undergrad enrollment	1,609
% male/female/not reported	39/61/0
% from out of state	11
% First-year from public high school	79
% First-year live on campus	93
% Ugrads live on campus	82
# of fraternities	0
# of sororities	0
% Asian	3
% Black or African American	11
% Hispanic	12
% Native American	<1
% Pacific Islander	0
% Race and/or ethnicity unknown	1
% Two or more races	6
% White	66
% International	<1
# of countries represented	1

CAMPUS MENTAL HEALTH SERVICES

Offers mental health/wellness program	Yes
Mental health training available to students	Yes
Employs Chief Wellness Officer	No
Peer-to-peer mental health offerings	Yes
Counseling center has guidelines or accreditation	Yes
Mental health/well-being courses	Yes, for-credit

ACADEMICS

% students returning for sophomore year	82
% students graduating within 4 years	56
% students graduating within 6 years	65
Calendar	Semester
Student/faculty ratio	10:1
Most common class size 10–19.	(56%)
Most common lab/discussion size 10–19.	(62%)

Most Popular Majors
Environmental Studies; Biology/Biological Sciences; Psychology

Applicants Sometimes Prefer
Loyola University Maryland, McDaniel College, Salisbury University, Towson University, University of Maryland, Baltimore County, University of Maryland, College Park

STUDENTS SAY "..."

Academics

Students fortunate enough to attend St. Mary's College of Maryland receive a "top-tier education" wherein they have ample "opportunity to try new things and explore their interests." That extends beyond the applauded "research-based curriculum" to the environment—" the campus is absolutely gorgeous"—and even the food in the "great dining hall." Where St. Mary's shines most, however, is in its academic offerings, which "reflect the challenges that [students] will face in the workplace," particularly for those in the STEM field who "can really get a leg up by doing publishable work even prior to grad school." In this, the faculty are routinely praised for "always [being] super helpful," noting that they "care about your experience and want you to understand the material" and "genuinely try to engage students during lectures." Enrollees feel they're able to properly assess their teachers because of the "small class sizes," which means "you get to know your professors really well, and build relationships and networks with them." This sort of backing makes the rigor tolerable, at least according to those who say "I've...definitely had to work hard but also had the support of professors when I needed it" and note that "They are willing to work with you, to enable and encourage you to have the best academic experience possible!"

Campus Life

There's never a dull moment at St. Mary's thanks to an "extremely active" campus life (and the potential for getaways to nearby DC). Undergrads have the opportunity to participate in "a wide range of clubs from windsurfing to student government to theater and sword fighting." Moreover, "there are multiple events on campus each week including guest magicians, comedians, and musicians," as well as "a murder mystery." The quality of those events has recently improved, as well, with the addition of "a brand-new stadium" which has led to an increasing number of students attending sporting events. And those looking to see a sillier side of their faculty appreciate the various "social events where you can play a game of Cornhole with your professors and get to know them more." St. Mary's gorgeous waterfront location also gets a lot of love: "During the warmer months the river center has free kayak and boat and paddleboard rentals for students and many students go swimming in the river or just sit on the docks." As for weekend-specific activities, it's not only common to find "parties [happening] all over campus," but "most of the time you can just walk [in]...and join...without an invitation."

Student Body

Though the St. Mary's community isn't the most diverse campus around, students emphasize that they are very proud of the diversity they do have, describing their "very creative" and "unique" peers as "extremely accepting." Undergrads are quick to note that "minority communities [are] visible and present" and that the school is "super inclusive [with regards to] LGBT+ students." This applies to personal opinions as well; while many individuals identify as "fairly liberal," classmates are described as "very open to different cultural viewpoints." In fact, some even refer to the friendliness as "quite bold" in that "I've never been at a place where more people will randomly walk up to you and just start a conversation." Indeed, "You can't walk for five minutes in any direction without getting a friendly greeting from someone." Of course, you'll definitely find a range of personality types, "from the athletes to dancers to light-saber fighters" as well as "hippie/hipsters, and nerdy academic students." Ultimately, when it comes down to it, there "seems to be a place for everyone to fit into at St. Mary's."

St. Mary's College of Maryland

Financial Aid: 240-895-3000 • E-Mail: admissions@smcm.edu • Website: www.smcm.edu

THE PRINCETON REVIEW SAYS

Admissions

The school reports that its standardized testing policy for use in admission for Fall 2026 is Test Optional. The Princeton Review suggests that interested applicants consult with the school for the most up-to-date standardized testing policies. *Very important factors considered include:* rigor of secondary school record, academic GPA, application essay, recommendation(s). *Important factors considered include:* class rank, extracurricular activities, talent/ability, character/personal qualities, volunteer work. *Other factors considered include:* standardized test scores, interview, first generation, geographical residence, state residency, work experience, level of applicant's interest. High school diploma is required and GED is accepted. *Academic units required:* 4 English, 3 math, 3 science, 2 science labs, 2 social studies, 1 history. *Academic units recommended:* 4 language (other than English), 3 social studies.

Financial Aid

Students should submit: FAFSA. Priority filing deadline is 2/28. The Princeton Review suggests that all financial aid forms be submitted as soon as possible. *Need-based scholarships/grants offered:* Federal Pell; Federal SEOG; State scholarships/grants; Private scholarships; College/university scholarship or grant aid from institutional funds. *Loan aid offered:* Federal Direct Subsidized Loans; Federal Direct Unsubsidized Loans; Direct PLUS loans. Admitted students will be notified of awards on a rolling basis beginning 12/1. Federal Work-Study Program available. Institutional employment available.

The Inside Word

St. Mary's is a public honors college that is looking for intellectually curious students who will be thoroughly engaged in the classroom as well as campus life. Top candidates tend to have taken a rigorous course-load in high school, so you'll want to load up on honors and AP classes. And if you're test averse, you'll be delighted to hear that St. Mary's is a Test Optional school (with the exception of home-school applicants and students who must demonstrate proficiency with English).

THE SCHOOL SAYS

From the Admissions Office

"St. Mary's College of Maryland, The National Public Honors College, features a stunning, waterfront campus adjacent to historic St. Mary's City, located about 90 minutes from Washington, D.C. As the designated public honors college for the state of Maryland, we offer a prestigious and affordable honors-level liberal arts and sciences education for every member of our diverse community. You will be encouraged to strive higher as you motivate others to set their own bar. Along the way we'll support you on your journey, because to us, honors is about where you are going, not where you are from.

"Our award-winning Learning through Experiential and Applied Discovery (LEAD) curriculum blends rigorous academics with professional skill development, in which you will learn how disciplines connect, the power of collaboration, critical thinking skills, multiple ways to approach problems, and so much more. We believe that the best learning springs from the rich human exchange that takes place in our challenging and engaging small classes, in one-on-one interactions, and even on the walking paths that cross campus. This promotes learning on a personalized level as our faculty, coaches, advisors, and staff play a role in your college career. Through the Honors College Promise, you are guaranteed the opportunity to apply your learning through internships, faculty-guided research, or international experiences. You'll be prepared for a world of possibilities.

"It is this mix of academic excellence, experiential learning, campus environment, and affordability that makes St. Mary's College an education that is uncommonly worth it."

SELECTIVITY

# of total applicants	3,504
% of total applicants accepted	73
% of total acceptees attending	16
# of in-state applicants	2,681
% of in-state applicants accepted	75
# of out-of-state-applicants	699
% of applicants accepted from out of state	74
# of international applicants	124
% of international applicants accepted	11
# of early decision applicants	101
% of early decision applicants accepted	77
# offered a place on the wait list	364
# admitted from wait list	13

First-Year Profile

Testing policy	Test Optional
Range SAT composite	1110–1320
Range SAT EBRW	590–700
Range SAT math	520–630
Range ACT composite	23–31
% submitting SAT scores	22
% submitting ACT scores	4
Average HS GPA	3.5
% submitting high school GPA	100
% graduated top 10% of class	15
% graduated top 25% of class	45
% graduated top 50% of class	88
% submitting high school rank	41

Important Dates

Early decision	
Apply by	11/1
Notified by	12/1
Other ED apply by	1/15
Other ED notified by	2/15
Early action	
Apply by	11/1
Notified by	1/1
Regular	
Apply by	1/15
Notified by	4/1
Nonfall registration?	Yes

FINANCIAL FACTS*

Annual in-state tuition	$12,480
Annual out-of-state tuition	$29,038
Food and housing	$16,256
Required fees	$3,206
Books and supplies	$1,000
Average need-based scholarship (First-year)	$12,358 ($13,277)
% students with need rec. need-based scholarship or grant aid (First-year)	85 (83)
% students with need rec. non-need-based scholarship or grant aid (First-year)	81 (77)
% students with need rec. need-based self-help aid (First-year)	55 (50)
% students rec. any financial aid (First-year)	93 (97)
% UG borrow to pay for school	59
Average cumulative indebtedness	$22,422
% of students with need fully met (First-year)	22 (24)
Average % of student need met (First-year)	80 (88)

* Most recently reported data at time of printing. Scan the QR code to find the latest updates.

Saint Michael's College

One Winooski Park, Colchester, VT 05439 • Admissions: 802-654-3000

Survey Snapshot
Students are happy
Great library
College radio is popular

RATINGS

Quality of Life	86
Fire Safety	87
Green	60*
Academic	86
Profs Interesting	92
Profs Accessible	95
Admissions	83
Financial Aid	91

CAMPUS LIFE

Type of school	Private
Affiliation	Roman Catholic
Environment	City

Students

Degree-seeking undergrad enrollment	1,019
% male/female/not reported	45/55/0
% from out of state	71
% First-year from public high school	69
% First-year live on campus	95
% Ugrads live on campus	93
# of fraternities	0
# of sororities	0
% Asian	1
% Black or African American	5
% Hispanic	6
% Native American	<1
% Pacific Islander	0
% Race and/or ethnicity unknown	<1
% Two or more races	3
% White	80
% International	4
# of countries represented	13

CAMPUS MENTAL HEALTH SERVICES

Offers mental health/wellness program	Yes
Mental health training available to students	Yes
Employs Chief Wellness Officer	Yes
Peer-to-peer mental health offerings	Yes
Counseling center has guidelines or accreditation	Yes
Mental health/well-being courses	Yes, for-credit

ACADEMICS

% students returning for sophomore year	78
% students graduating within 4 years	64
% students graduating within 6 years	71
Calendar	Semester
Student/faculty ratio	9:1
Most common class size 10–19.	(48%)
Most common lab/discussion size 1–9.	(44%)

Most Popular Majors

Health Science; Psychology; Business Administration and Management

Applicants Often Prefer

Saint Anselm College, Stonehill College, University of Massachusetts—Amherst, University of New Hampshire, University of Vermont

Applicants Sometimes Prefer

College of the Holy Cross, Fairfield University, Providence College, St. Lawrence University, University of Connecticut, University of Maine, University of Rhode Island, Wheaton College (MA)

Applicants Rarely Prefer

Assumption University, Salve Regina University

STUDENTS SAY "..."

Academics

Purposeful learning is the hallmark of the educational experience at Saint Michael's College. Here, students are encouraged to "discover passions, develop skills, and find meaning and connection in and out of the classroom," much, in the same way, students are encouraged to engage with their religious beliefs at the predominately Catholic school (though undergrads of all denominations and cultural backgrounds are welcome). Saint Michael's has a "faith in action" foundation where many enrollees participate in faith-based services in addition to their core academic curriculum "to help students realize their full potential." Of the more than 40 major and minor programs offered, students have highly touted the schools of education, biology, and religion; criminology, environmental science, and journalism are additional tracks, while pre-law, ROTC, and pre-medical professional programs prepare undergrads for specialized fields. Saint Michael's also offers 100-plus study abroad programs with opportunities in Argentina, China, and England, among others. Further setting the college apart is the fact that Saint Michael's has a chapter of the academic honor society Phi Beta Kappa; it's one of just four Northeast Catholic colleges with this distinction.

Professors are highly regarded by students, who say, "Regardless of which class you're in, you can tell that each professor's #1 priority is that the students succeed." The small, "discussion-based" class structure on campus also guarantees that "you are not just another number in a lecture hall." Faculty are praised for "really helping me in beginning my career-setting up research studies in my field of interest, writing incredible letters of recommendation for grad school, or networking to get me internships."

Campus Life

Saint Michael's College is distinct for being a fully residential campus where students live on-site for all four years of their undergrad experience. As such, the Vermont-based college has taken great strides to ensure activities and community fill everyday life for the students who call Saint Michael's home. The Bergeron Wellness Center and Edmundite Campus Ministry are two facilities that help nourish undergrad's minds, bodies, and souls. Forty-plus student-led organizations and an athletic program—including an Alpine Racing Club—add to the variety of options available. The school's 480 acres of "indoor-outdoor learning" terrain, located between Lake Champlain and the Green Mountains, is attractive to students, especially those who love to ski, hike, and snowboard. "Saint Michael's provides amazing ski pass deals and transportation to amazing ski resorts in the area." Located just a 10-minute bus ride away, the main hub of Burlington, Vermont, is another big draw, offering "so much to do in such a small, convenient area." In particular, many students love the sprawling Church Street district that's "crowded with unique shops, fantastic restaurants, and interesting people." The fact that the campus is also concentrated in a small radius is an advantage, particularly "in the cold months of winter [when] five-minute walks to class are a godsend."

Student Body

While some students self-identify as "upper-middle class, and environmentally and politically aware," others are quick to note that students "are all different in regard to religions, races, sexual orientations, and genders." Saint Michael's is a sustainable campus that encourages eco-friendly behaviors through the use of natural resources and supplemental educational programs for students. "Most [students] are concerned about the environment and social justice." Community engagement is another tenet adopted by the student body where "meaningful activity" is a shared experience and "nearly all students participate in at least one service project during their four years here." As one student shares, "If you're genuine and true to who you are, you're bound to do well at St. Mike's."

SAINT MICHAEL'S COLLEGE

Financial Aid: 802-654-3243 • E-Mail: admission@smcvt.edu • Website: www.smcvt.edu

THE PRINCETON REVIEW SAYS

Admissions

The school reports that its standardized testing policy for use in admission for Fall 2026 is Test Optional. The Princeton Review suggests that interested applicants consult with the school for the most up-to-date standardized testing policies. *Very important factors considered include:* rigor of secondary school record, class rank, academic GPA, application essay. *Important factors considered include:* recommendation(s), extracurricular activities, talent/ability, character/personal qualities, volunteer work, work experience. *Other factors considered include:* standardized test scores, first generation, level of applicant's interest. High school diploma is required and GED is accepted. *Academic units required:* 4 English, 3 math, 3 science, 2 science labs, 3 language (other than English), 3 social studies, 3 history. *Academic units recommended:* 4 English, 4 math, 4 science, 3 science labs, 4 language (other than English), 4 social studies, 4 history.

Financial Aid

Students should submit: FAFSA; State aid form. The Princeton Review suggests that all financial aid forms be submitted as soon as possible. *Need-based scholarships/grants offered:* Federal Pell; Federal SEOG; State scholarships/grants; Private scholarships; College/university scholarship or grant aid from institutional funds. *Loan aid offered:* Federal Direct Subsidized Loans; Federal Direct Unsubsidized Loans; Direct PLUS loans. Admitted students will be notified of awards on a rolling basis beginning December. Federal Work-Study Program available. Institutional employment available.

The Inside Word

Applicants to St. Mike's are more than just a number, and admissions officers do their utmost to consider candidates in their entirety. Officers consider everything from essays to extracurricular activities, though most weight is given to academic record. The college has been standardized Test Optional for over a decade, and applicants are not penalized in the admission or scholarship process if they choose not to submit their scores.

THE SCHOOL SAYS

From the Admissions Office

"A residential Catholic college welcoming to all, Saint Michael's is steeped in the spirit of our founders, the Society of Saint Edmund. Their example inspires our community to embrace the values of intellectual inquiry, peace, justice, and service to others. Students at St. Mike's are challenged to do well and driven to do good.

"Choosing a major is not always easy. At St. Mike's, students can take advantage of the flexible structure of their majors and our liberal arts core to explore then pursue more than one academic interest. In fact, over 80 percent of our students complete more than just their major, with over 40 percent completing at least a double major or double minor. We help students find and follow their passions and excel at them.

"Outside the classroom, students grow into impressive leaders through their experiences with the Adventure Sports Center, Fire & Rescue, our MOVE service work program, varsity and club athletics, a uniquely active student government, our student run radio station WWPV, the student paper, the College farm, the Center for the Environment, and numerous other opportunities.

"Named among the 'best college towns' in the country, nearby Burlington is a vibrant city with a wealth of professional experiences, arts, and culture. Campus is also located just ninety minutes from the multicultural center of Montreal, Canada. Students enjoy a deeply discounted season's pass to Sugarbush, access to our campus and 440-acre Natural Area for research and recreation, and meaningful internships at top companies.

"St. Mike's will take you wherever you want to go."

SELECTIVITY

# of total applicants	1,748
% of total applicants accepted	90
% of total acceptees attending	16
# of in-state applicants	367
% of in-state applicants accepted	92
# of out-of-state-applicants	1,200
% of applicants accepted from out of state	95
# of international applicants	181
% of international applicants accepted	47

First-Year Profile

Testing policy	Test Optional
Range SAT composite	1240–1290
Range SAT EBRW	640–700
Range SAT math	570–620
% submitting SAT scores	8
% submitting ACT scores	2
% graduated top 10% of class	21
% graduated top 25% of class	51
% graduated top 50% of class	81
% submitting high school rank	22

Important Dates

Nonfall registration?	Yes

FINANCIAL FACTS

Annual tuition	$49,950
Food and housing	$19,550
Required fees	$2,950
Books and supplies	$1,000
Average need-based scholarship (First-year)	$41,668 ($43,619)
% students with need rec. need-based scholarship or grant aid (First-year)	100 (100)
% students with need rec. non-need-based scholarship or grant aid (First-year)	26 (25)
% students with need rec. need-based self-help aid (First-year)	66 (63)
% students rec. any financial aid (First-year)	98 (99)
% UG borrow to pay for school	69
Average cumulative indebtedness	$38,130
% of students with need fully met (First-year)	32 (33)
Average % of student need met (First-year)	87 (87)

St. Olaf College

1520 St. Olaf Avenue, Northfield, MN 55057 • Admissions: 507-786-3025

Survey Snapshot
Students get along with local community
Students environmentally aware
Active student-run political groups

RATINGS

Quality of Life	89
Fire Safety	92
Green	60*
Academic	90
Profs Interesting	93
Profs Accessible	95
Admissions	91
Financial Aid	98

CAMPUS LIFE

Type of school	Private
Affiliation	Lutheran
Environment	Village

Students

Degree-seeking undergrad enrollment	3,105
% male/female/not reported	40/57/3
% from out of state	48
% First-year from public high school	73
% First-year live on campus	100
% Ugrads live on campus	97
# of fraternities	0
# of sororities	0
% Asian	4
% Black or African American	3
% Hispanic	10
% Native American	<1
% Pacific Islander	<1
% Race and/or ethnicity unknown	<1
% Two or more races	5
% White	66
% International	11
# of countries represented	100

CAMPUS MENTAL HEALTH SERVICES

Offers mental health/wellness program	Yes
Mental health training available to students	Yes
Employs Chief Wellness Officer	Yes
Peer-to-peer mental health offerings	Yes
Counseling center has guidelines or accreditation	Yes
Mental health/well-being courses	Yes, non-credit

ACADEMICS

% students returning for sophomore year	94
% students graduating within 4 years	77
% students graduating within 6 years	83
Calendar	4-1-4
Student/faculty ratio	11:1
Most common class size 20–29.	(45%)
Most common lab/discussion size 10–19.	(57%)

Most Popular Majors
Biology/Biological Sciences; Mathematics; Research and Experimental Psychology

Applicants Often Prefer
Carleton College, Oberlin College

Applicants Sometimes Prefer
Grinnell College, Lawrence University, Macalester College, University of Minnesota—Twin Cities, University of Wisconsin—Madison

Applicants Rarely Prefer
Gustavus Adolphus College, Luther College

STUDENTS SAY "…"

Academics

Founded in 1874, St. Olaf College is a liberal arts college that views the entire undergraduate experience as an education. The Piper Center for Vocation and Career "constantly has new opportunities available for students in any field of study," science classes offer students the chance "to dip their toes in research," and approximately 70% of students participate in the "second to none" study abroad programs. There are endless resources in support of students, and "if you need something, St. Olaf will do everything in their power to accommodate."

Professors at St. Olaf are universally beloved, helping with "everything from a mistake on a homework assignment, a course concept that is confusing, writing a thesis for a paper, planning course schedules, and advising students on how to reach their long-term goals." The best classes "tend to include a lot of discussion and focus on the process of learning rather than the graded outcome"; indeed, academic innovation thrives at St. Olaf, with courses featuring "conversation dinners for language classes, exploratory field trips, exhibition tours for art courses, guest speakers, and interactive seminars." Professors also organize "panels of people to share their expertise and perspectives (such as a panel of local farmers when studying environmental science)." Academics are "challenging with enough resources that they're manageable," and the school "gets students ready to apply to jobs, internships, and graduate school all over the course of four years."

Campus Life

Though St. Olaf is located only 45 minutes from the bustling Twin Cities, nearly all students live on the beautiful campus. The college provides "social activities which do not rely on alcohol" and, consequently, there's "a lot of school programming with relatively high attendance." This is especially true of extracurriculars: students describe being "very involved at high levels" in things like music ensembles and sports. Academics are equally taken seriously, such that "studying is also a form of hanging out for many people." That said, students do find time for relaxing, especially on weekends, which are filled with seasonal activities like "going to the pumpkin patch or apple orchard ten minutes from campus," and a main student pastime is simply "going to dinner and seeing all of their friends and then going to each other's rooms afterwards." Oles are an outdoorsy bunch, and students "have access to hundreds of acres of forest and prairie on campus to run, bike, and cross-country ski," and "the natural lands and hiking trails are often used."

Student Body

St. Olaf College is entirely welcome to all students and faiths: "the chapel and college pastors, rabbi, [and] Muslim chaplain are very inclusive." Students feel that they are all united by "an interest and desire to learn" that often manifests itself "in deep discussions in and out of the classroom." Moreover, because the school is interdisciplinary, you're likely to get exposure to a wider variety of perspectives, as "it is not uncommon to be in a philosophy class full of biology and music majors." On the whole, Oles are "generally kind and cheerful, and with an unmatched respect for others and their property."

St. Olaf College

Financial Aid: 507-786-3019 • E-Mail: admissions@stolaf.edu • Website: wp.stolaf.edu

THE PRINCETON REVIEW SAYS

Admissions

The school reports that its standardized testing policy for use in admission for Fall 2026 is Test Optional. The Princeton Review suggests that interested applicants consult with the school for the most up-to-date standardized testing policies. *Very important factors considered include:* rigor of secondary school record, academic GPA, application essay. *Important factors considered include:* class rank, recommendation(s), interview, extracurricular activities, talent/ability, character/personal qualities, level of applicant's interest. *Other factors considered include:* standardized test scores, first generation, geographical residence, state residency, religious affiliation/commitment, volunteer work, work experience. High school diploma is required and GED is accepted. *Academic units recommended:* 4 English, 4 math, 4 science, 2 science labs, 4 language (other than English), 4 social studies.

Financial Aid

Students should submit: FAFSA; CSS PROFILE. Priority filing deadline is 11/1. The Princeton Review suggests that all financial aid forms be submitted as soon as possible. *Need-based scholarships/grants offered:* Federal Pell; Federal SEOG; State scholarships/grants; Private scholarships; College/university scholarship or grant aid from institutional funds. *Loan aid offered:* Federal Direct Subsidized Loans; Federal Direct Unsubsidized Loans; Direct PLUS loans; State Loans; College/university loans from institutional funds. Federal Work-Study Program available. Institutional employment available.

The Inside Word

St. Olaf's gets a little more competitive each year, so aim for the upper boundaries of the first-year profile. Also consider that, admissions officers here assess the rigor of each applicant's course load (and subsequent success in the classroom), though there is no minimum GPA threshold and test scores are optional. Of course, as a tight-knit community, the college also looks to admit students who will complement St. Olaf 's ethos. To that end, admissions officers also closely analyze personal essays, recommendations, and participation in extracurricular activities.

THE SCHOOL SAYS

From the Admissions Office

"St. Olaf's goal is to develop individuals of action and substance who will shape the world. St. Olaf aims to help students discover their strengths, explore their passions, and launch their futures. St. Olaf College is a residential liberal arts institution with an enrollment of more than 3,000 students offering over 85 undergraduate majors, concentrations, and pre-professional tracks. The college's goal is to develop individuals of action and substance who will shape the world. St. Olaf aims to help students discover their strengths, explore their passions, and launch their futures. More than 5,000 experiential learning opportunities are available each year for students to test out opportunities and learn new skills to be prepared for life after graduation.All students are able to participate in a semester-long study-abroad program for the same cost as attending class on campus, and over 70% of recent graduates studied abroad or away at least once. All students are able to participate in a semester-long study-abroad program for the same cost as attending class on campus. St. Olaf is enriched by a strong community of civically engaged students, faculty, and staff—hosting community work projects, thoughtful events, and strong academic rigor. 95 percent of recent graduates are employed, in graduate school, or engaged in full-time service work. St. Olaf is committed to meeting the demonstrated financial need of every student with 99 percent of students receiving scholarships or grants.

"Visit stolaf.edu."

SELECTIVITY

# of total applicants	7,310
% of total applicants accepted	43
% of total acceptees attending	25
# of in-state applicants	1,861
% of in-state applicants accepted	64
# of out-of-state-applicants	2,877
% of applicants accepted from out of state	52
# of international applicants	2,569
% of international applicants accepted	19
# of early decision applicants	504
% of early decision applicants accepted	55
# offered a place on the wait list	1,696
# admitted from wait list	23

First-Year Profile

Testing policy	Test Optional
Range SAT composite	1320–1440
Range SAT EBRW	670–740
Range SAT math	640–720
Range ACT composite	28–32
% submitting SAT scores	13
% submitting ACT scores	30
Average HS GPA	3.8
% submitting high school GPA	88
% graduated top 10% of class	40
% graduated top 25% of class	73
% graduated top 50% of class	94
% submitting high school rank	33

Important Dates

Early decision	
Apply by	11/1
Notified by	12/10
Other ED apply by	1/15
Other ED notified by	2/10
Early action	
Apply by	11/1
Notified by	12/23
Regular	
Apply by	1/15
Notified by	3/10
Nonfall registration?	No

FINANCIAL FACTS

Annual tuition	$65,700
Food and housing	$15,000
Required fees	$500
Books and supplies	$1,000
Average need-based scholarship (First-year)	$55,146 ($56,959)
% students with need rec. need-based scholarship or grant aid (First-year)	100 (100)
% students with need rec. non-need-based scholarship or grant aid (First-year)	0 (0)
% students with need rec. need-based self-help aid (First-year)	99 (99)
% students rec. any financial aid (First-year)	99 (99)
% UG borrow to pay for school	57
Average cumulative indebtedness	$26,863
% of students with need fully met (First-year)	98 (100)
Average % of student need met (First-year)	99 (100)

SALISBURY UNIVERSITY

1101 Camden Avenue, Salisbury, MD 21801 • Admissions: 410-543-6161

Survey Snapshot
Great library
Intramural sports are popular
Frats and sororities are popular

RATINGS

Quality of Life	80
Fire Safety	96
Green	95
Academic	78
Profs Interesting	84
Profs Accessible	86
Admissions	83
Financial Aid	83

CAMPUS LIFE

Type of school	Public
Environment	Town

Students

Degree-seeking undergrad enrollment	6,211
% male/female/not reported	44/56/0
% from out of state	17
% First-year from public high school	85
% First-year live on campus	87
% Ugrads live on campus	51
# of fraternities (% join)	9 (7)
# of sororities (% join)	7 (7)
% Asian	2
% Black or African American	14
% Hispanic	9
% Native American	<1
% Pacific Islander	<1
% Race and/or ethnicity unknown	1
% Two or more races	5
% White	67
% International	1
# of countries represented	30

CAMPUS MENTAL HEALTH SERVICES

Offers mental health/wellness program	Yes
Mental health training available to students	Yes
Employs Chief Wellness Officer	Yes
Peer-to-peer mental health offerings	No
Counseling center has guidelines or accreditation	Yes
Mental health/well-being courses	Yes, for-credit

ACADEMICS

% students returning for sophomore year	79
% students graduating within 4 years	45
% students graduating within 6 years	61
Calendar	4-1-4
Student/faculty ratio	15:1
Most common class size 10–19.	(35%)
Most common lab/discussion size 20–29.	(45%)

Most Popular Majors

Kinesiology and Exercise Science; Psychology; Registered Nursing/Registered Nurse

Applicants Also Look At

Coastal Carolina University, James Madison University, Stevenson University, Towson University, University of Delaware, University of Maryland, Baltimore County, University of Maryland, College Park

STUDENTS SAY "..."

Academics

Salisbury University is packed with academic features that thrill its enrollees. From the "good nursing program" to a biology department that is "quite extensive in...labs and research studies" to an education program that offers opportunities to engage "with the local community schools," students are thrilled. Atop that, there's also the Clarke Honors College, which "gave me opportunities to be more personal with what I study and write about," and of course the Perdue School of Business, which they find to be "one of the best in the state." Students also rave about support services: the library "services are amazing" and there's a robust network of academic encouragement from groups like Women in STEM. One student with a learning difference also notes that "teachers are very respectful of my disorder and provide me [with] what I need to succeed." Though Salisbury offers all of this and more to its attendees, it also gives students "a lot of freedom to work things out" independently. Students enthuse about outdoor classes, "team-based learning," the ability to use "augmented reality to give a presentation virtually," and "really strong study abroad [programs] for lots of different majors." One art student sums up Salisbury by saying: "The opportunities provided, especially in the art department, are absolutely fantastic."

Campus Life

Students gush about the food at Salisbury: "I'm in love with the variety of healthy options and vegetarian accommodations!" says one student; "I love food truck night!" announces another; "I love the poke bowls when they are available in the Bistro," agrees another student. Lobster nights, and the convenience of "being able to stop and get food at the many places on campus in between classes," are also among students' favorite aspects of Salisbury living. Additionally, Salisbury has a thriving athletic community with lots of options for students to enjoy varsity, club, and intramural sports. One student explains that "people are always playing outside or going to the gym." On the weekends, students can be found cheering on the football, softball, basketball, and rugby teams, and enjoying the local food scene afterwards. For those not interested in athletics, "there is a club or group for everyone and anyone. It is very inclusive" and as one student notes, "I strongly enjoy the many events programs and clubs available on campus." Another student offered a final assessment of life at Salisbury: "I rate this campus 100/100. Everything is excellent."

Student Body

If you want the support of peers who "push me to work hard every day and do not let me procrastinate," Salisbury University's a great choice. Students have warm words for their fellows, saying that they're "open to help and make connections," as well as "welcoming and supportive," and, in short, among "the best people I have met." That community praise is well-earned by "a super diverse and awesome student body with people from all walks of life. We've got artists, musicians, and more." If anything, students say they'll "be sad to leave" the school when they graduate: "I have made lifelong friends and had a ton of fun."

SALISBURY UNIVERSITY

Financial Aid: 410-543-6165 • E-Mail: admissions@salisbury.edu • Website: www.salisbury.edu

THE PRINCETON REVIEW SAYS

Admissions

The school reports that its standardized testing policy for use in admission for Fall 2026 is Test Optional. The Princeton Review suggests that interested applicants consult with the school for the most up-to-date standardized testing policies. *Very important factors considered include:* rigor of secondary school record, academic GPA. *Important factors considered include:* standardized test scores. *Other factors considered include:* application essay, recommendation(s), interview, extracurricular activities, talent/ability, character/personal qualities, geographical residence, state residency, volunteer work, work experience, level of applicant's interest. High school diploma is required and GED is accepted. *Academic units required:* 4 English, 4 math, 3 science, 2 science labs, 2 language (other than English), 3 social studies. *Academic units recommended:* 4 English, 4 math, 4 science, 3 science labs, 3 language (other than English), 3 social studies, 3 academic electives.

Financial Aid

Students should submit: FAFSA. Priority filing deadline is 3/1. The Princeton Review suggests that all financial aid forms be submitted as soon as possible. *Need-based scholarships/grants offered:* Federal Pell; Federal SEOG; State scholarships/grants; Private scholarships; College/university scholarship or grant aid from institutional funds. *Loan aid offered:* Federal Direct Subsidized Loans; Federal Direct Unsubsidized Loans; Direct PLUS loans. Admitted students will be notified of awards on a rolling basis beginning 2/15. Federal Work-Study Program available. Institutional employment available.

The Inside Word

The SU Admissions Office takes a comprehensive view of a student's application and puts top priority on the academic record, including curriculum and performance. Preference is for a college preparatory curriculum and a strong history of leadership experience and community service. Students must submit recommendations and a personal essay with their application, and a portfolio is required for Bachelor of Fine Arts applicants.

THE SCHOOL SAYS

From the Admissions Office

"Salisbury University sets success in motion with a welcoming, "just right" size campus and a culture where students are seen, heard, supported, and challenged. The University is a must-see, with flowering trees, green spaces, and traditional red brick echoing the natural beauty of Maryland's Eastern Shore. The City of Salisbury offers restaurants, shops and a re-energized downtown area, with the lively atmosphere of the region's popular beaches nearby. SU's high-impact, student-focused academic programs, taught by world-class educators, provide the perfect environment for students to develop a liberal arts foundation, hone their communication and business skills, engage in public service, especially education and health care, and explore the sciences, including coastal engineering. A top producer of student and faculty Fulbright awards, SU offers access to research in the first semester. Faculty mentors coach students toward opportunities for study abroad, experiential learning (required for all students), and national fellowships. Expansive facilities include the Guerrieri Academic Commons—a state-of-the-art 'library of the future' and the hub of academic life. With strong job and graduate school placements, SU offers students a return on investment that pays back a lifetime of possibilities. Academic success is matched by a spirit of community involvement through over 100 student clubs and service projects; a continual commitment to inclusion, diversity, opportunity and equity; and the cultivation of a sense of belonging. Students cheer on SU's Division III athletic programs (with 47 team and individual national championships) in new facilities. The campus also is known nationally for sustainability. SU seeks students who want to shape tomorrow."

SELECTIVITY

# of total applicants	8,793
% of total applicants accepted	88
% of total acceptees attending	19
# of in-state applicants	6,840
% of in-state applicants accepted	89
# of out-of-state-applicants	1,666
% of applicants accepted from out of state	86
# of international applicants	287
% of international applicants accepted	72
# of early decision applicants	302
% of early decision applicants accepted	83

First-Year Profile

Testing policy	Test Optional
Range SAT composite	1190–1300
Range SAT EBRW	600–670
Range SAT math	570–650
% submitting SAT scores	10
% submitting ACT scores	2
Average HS GPA	3.7
% submitting high school GPA	100

Important Dates

Early decision	
Apply by	11/15
Notified by	12/15
Early action	
Apply by	12/1
Notified by	1/15
Regular	
Notified by	Rolling, 10/15
Nonfall registration?	Yes

FINANCIAL FACTS*

Annual in-state tuition	$8,016
Annual out-of-state tuition	$19,520
Food and housing	$14,190
Required fees	$3,290
Books and supplies	$1,300
Average need-based scholarship (First-year)	$11,739 ($12,762)
% students with need rec. need-based scholarship or grant aid (First-year)	94 (98)
% students with need rec. non-need-based scholarship or grant aid (First-year)	0 (0)
% students with need rec. need-based self-help aid (First-year)	54 (46)
% students rec. any financial aid (First-year)	95 (98)
% UG borrow to pay for school	52
Average cumulative indebtedness	$29,070
% of students with need fully met (First-year)	15 (20)
Average % of student need met (First-year)	59 (61)

* Most recently reported data at time of printing. Scan the QR code to find the latest updates.

SALVE REGINA UNIVERSITY

100 Ochre Point Avenue, Newport, RI 02840-4192 • Admissions: 401-341-2908

Survey Snapshot
Students love Newport, RI
Great off-campus food
Easy to get around campus

RATINGS

Quality of Life	**91**
Fire Safety	**94**
Green	**81**
Academic	**82**
Profs Interesting	**90**
Profs Accessible	**91**
Admissions	**86**
Financial Aid	**89**

CAMPUS LIFE

Type of school	Private
Affiliation	Roman Catholic
Environment	Town

Students

Degree-seeking undergrad enrollment	2,116
% male/female/not reported	28/72/0
% from out of state	86
% First-year from public high school	73
% First-year live on campus	98
% Ugrads live on campus	59
# of fraternities	0
# of sororities	0
% Asian	2
% Black or African American	2
% Hispanic	13
% Native American	<1
% Pacific Islander	<1
% Race and/or ethnicity unknown	4
% Two or more races	4
% White	72
% International	2
# of countries represented	15

CAMPUS MENTAL HEALTH SERVICES

Offers mental health/wellness program	Yes
Mental health training available to students	No
Employs Chief Wellness Officer	NR
Peer-to-peer mental health offerings	NR
Counseling center has guidelines or accreditation	No
Mental health/well-being courses	NR

ACADEMICS

% students returning for sophomore year	82
% students graduating within 4 years	67
% students graduating within 6 years	73
Calendar	Semester
Student/faculty ratio	13:1
Most common class size 20–29.	(45%)
Most common lab/discussion size 10–19.	(50%)

Most Popular Majors

Psychology; Registered Nursing/Registered Nurse; Business Administration and Management

Applicants Also Look At

Assumption University, Bryant University, College of Charleston, Endicott College, Fairfield University, Fordham University, Loyola University Maryland, Marist University, Providence College, Quinnipiac University, Roger Williams University, Sacred Heart University, Saint Anselm College, Stonehill College, University of Connecticut, University of Massachusetts—Amherst, University of New Hampshire, University of Rhode Island, The University of Tampa, Wheaton College (MA)

STUDENTS SAY "..."

Academics

Rooted in the values of the Catholic Sisters of Mercy who founded it, students at Salve Regina University are "drawn here...because they want to make a positive impact in the world." An ethos of service and community involvement shapes the Salve experience, with classes that often "involve volunteering or working on projects in the community, which makes learning feel more meaningful." Every undergraduate participates in the Salve Compass program, which integrates mentorship, advising, and real-world experiences into the curriculum through opportunities like "field placement...for education majors [which] gives us valuable hands-on experience," lab research that "gives you many opportunities to interact with local non-profits and organizations," and "in-person clinical rotations for nursing majors." Undergrads cite the "supportive resources [and] strong academic programs" as well as the "tight-knit community" as the greatest assets of attending Salve. While some students aren't fans of the "lecture-heavy" teaching structure, they appreciate the "small class sizes [in which] professors learn your name and you develop a relationship with them," which "really makes a difference in learning." Students describe their "really down-to-earth professors who...encourage curiosity and character" as "top-tier" and "absolutely fabulous...[and] so passionate about what they do [that] it makes me excited to attend class and learn." In short, "The community and the professors are amazing, and it feels like a family."

Campus Life

"Newport, RI, is one of the most beautiful coastal towns in the country!"—a sentiment echoed by the vast majority of students at Salve, who "love spending time at the beach, outside and in nature" and "going downtown or taking a walk on the cliff walk." In town, undergrads enjoy "visiting the historical places," "trying new places to eat," and just "experiencing the city of Newport [and] the nature of our island." Life at this "welcoming college" includes abundant "community service opportunities" and "Mercy-based initiatives," along with "great and extremely diverse" clubs representing an array of interests, including intramural sports, activities such as yoga and dance, the "Outdoor Adventure Club," and academic groups like the Student Nursing Organization (SNO) and the Campus Activities Board (CAB), which sponsors social events throughout the year. Additionally, Salve has a competitive Division III varsity sports program, and "going to our school's sports games" is a very popular pastime. While several students noted that the number of "events sponsored by the university [has] decreased in the past year," the prevailing sentiment is that "there is a wide range of interests and passions on campus, and a club or activity that caters to almost all of them."

Student Body

Salve Regina undergrads see themselves as "friendly and always willing to help." The campus is a "close-knit community" of "kind and good-natured people who are hardworking and encouraging." While some students note that "a few groups...[to] be very cliquey," the overall environment is one where their peers "exhibit acts of respect every day." While the school is based on a foundation of Catholicism and the Sisters of Mercy, students affirm that "it's not expected [that] you be Catholic or believe in God." Students relish the intimacy of their smaller campus, deeming the size fundamental to their ability to "connect with my professors and get to know them, making it easier for me to approach them if/when I need help," and asserting that "I feel like I found more people just by socializing in class." The smaller population can have drawbacks; as one student noted, "Social life can be limited at times, but if you try to get involved, it works out." Most students note that they "prioritize studying first," leading to classrooms where "discussions are lively because the students genuinely care" and where "students are treated with respect."

Salve Regina University

Financial Aid: 401-341-2901 • E-Mail: admissions@salve.edu • Website: www.salve.edu

THE PRINCETON REVIEW SAYS

Admissions

The school reports that its standardized testing policy for use in admission for Fall 2026 is Test Optional. The Princeton Review suggests that interested applicants consult with the school for the most up-to-date standardized testing policies. *Very important factors considered include:* rigor of secondary school record, academic GPA. *Important factors considered include:* application essay, recommendation(s). *Other factors considered include:* class rank, standardized test scores, extracurricular activities, talent/ability, character/personal qualities, first generation, alumni/ae relation, volunteer work, work experience, level of applicant's interest. High school diploma is required and GED is accepted. *Academic units required:* 4 English, 3 math, 2 science, 2 science labs, 2 language (other than English), 1 social studies, 4 academic electives.

Financial Aid

Students should submit: FAFSA. Priority filing deadline is 3/1. The Princeton Review suggests that all financial aid forms be submitted as soon as possible. *Need-based scholarships/grants offered:* Federal Pell; Federal SEOG; State scholarships/grants; Private scholarships; College/university scholarship or grant aid from institutional funds. *Loan aid offered:* Federal Direct Subsidized Loans; Federal Direct Unsubsidized Loans; Direct PLUS loans. Admitted students will be notified of awards on a rolling basis. Federal Work-Study Program available. Institutional employment available.

The Inside Word

Ideal candidates, per the school, "will contribute to our campus community, grow as compassionate individuals, and embrace the mission of the university." Admission is lightly competitive—roughly 4,400 applicants were accepted out of the approximately 6,600 total—and because the school assesses each student holistically, being able to demonstrate extracurricular interests that coincide with its goals will help, especially since SAT/ACT scores are optional. Note that your GPA is recalculated by the admissions team to more heavily weigh rigorous honors and AP courses and core academic subjects.

THE SCHOOL SAYS

From the Admissions Office

"Salve Regina University offers students the opportunity to experience a transformative educational experience through a rigorous curriculum and supportive mentorship from dedicated faculty. It also allows them to discover their place in today's complicated world and work to make a positive contribution to improving society. The small, close-knit campus community encourages the development of close relationships amongst students as they work together to come to a greater understanding of how the world works and how they may impact it, as informed by our Mercy mission imparted from the founding order, the Sisters of Mercy.

"Students benefit from Salve's unique, historic campus, which overlooks the ocean on the famed Cliff Walk of Newport, Rhode Island. Through the Salve Compass—a bold, bright thread running through every undergraduate student's Salve education—theory and practice are integrated to connect curriculum to career through experiences like Compass Summer in the sophomore year where students experience Newport through an engagement that highlights professional competency development. They also participate in a robust offering of student organizations, activities, sports, and enrichment opportunities including speakers sponsored by Salve's Pell Center for International Relations and Public Policy, the on campus 'think tank.' The measure of Salve's strength is the success of students who graduate at rates far exceeding national averages, complete their degrees on time in four years, and demonstrate lifetime ROI as measured by earnings that put Salve in the top 6% of all colleges and universities in the U.S., per a study by the Georgetown Center on Education and the Workforce."

SELECTIVITY

# of total applicants	6,588
% of total applicants accepted	66
% of total acceptees attending	13
# of in-state applicants	763
% of in-state applicants accepted	53
# of out-of-state-applicants	5,667
% of applicants accepted from out of state	68
# of international applicants	158
% of international applicants accepted	59
# of early decision applicants	56
% of early decision applicants accepted	86
# offered a place on the wait list	509
# admitted from wait list	28

First-Year Profile

Testing policy	Test Optional
Range SAT composite	1200–1320
Range SAT EBRW	610–690
Range SAT math	560–640
Range ACT composite	26–30
% submitting SAT scores	17
% submitting ACT scores	1
Average HS GPA	3.6
% submitting high school GPA	100
% graduated top 10% of class	19
% graduated top 25% of class	54
% graduated top 50% of class	89
% submitting high school rank	29

Important Dates

Early decision	
Apply by	11/1
Notified by	12/15
Early action	
Apply by	11/1
Notified by	12/25
Regular	
Notified by	4/1
Nonfall registration?	Yes

FINANCIAL FACTS

Annual tuition	$53,600
Food and housing	$20,300
Required fees	$1,000
Books and supplies	$2,000
Average need-based scholarship (First-year)	$31,339 ($34,256)
% students with need rec. need-based scholarship or grant aid (First-year)	100 (100)
% students with need rec. non-need-based scholarship or grant aid (First-year)	27 (30)
% students with need rec. need-based self-help aid (First-year)	70 (67)
% students rec. any financial aid (First-year)	99 (100)
% UG borrow to pay for school	80
Average cumulative indebtedness	$50,982
% of students with need fully met (First-year)	30 (32)
Average % of student need met (First-year)	73 (76)

San Diego State University

5500 Campanile Drive, San Diego, CA 92182-7455 • Admissions: 619-594-6336

Survey Snapshot
Students are happy
Students love San Diego, CA
Recreation facilities are great

RATINGS

Quality of Life	87
Fire Safety	96
Green	97
Academic	76
Profs Interesting	86
Profs Accessible	90
Admissions	85
Financial Aid	86

CAMPUS LIFE

Type of school	Public
Environment	Metropolis

Students

Degree-seeking undergrad enrollment	36,196
% male/female/not reported	42/56/3
% from out of state	15
% First-year from public high school	92
% First-year live on campus	71
% Ugrads live on campus	25
# of fraternities (% join)	19 (11)
# of sororities (% join)	21 (12)
% Asian	13
% Black or African American	3
% Hispanic	37
% Native American	<1
% Pacific Islander	<1
% Race and/or ethnicity unknown	3
% Two or more races	8
% White	33
% International	2
# of countries represented	120

CAMPUS MENTAL HEALTH SERVICES

Offers mental health/wellness program	Yes
Mental health training available to students	Yes
Employs Chief Wellness Officer	Yes
Peer-to-peer mental health offerings	Yes
Counseling center has guidelines or accreditation	Yes
Mental health/well-being courses	Yes, for-credit

ACADEMICS

% students returning for sophomore year	91
% students graduating within 4 years	58
% students graduating within 6 years	78
Calendar	Semester
Student/faculty ratio	24:1
Most common class size 20–29.	(31%)
Most common lab/discussion size 20–29.	(52%)

Most Popular Majors

Computer Science; Business Administration and Management; Finance

Applicants Also Look At

California Polytechnic State University—San Luis Obispo, University of California—Los Angeles, University of California—San Diego, University of California—Santa Barbara

STUDENTS SAY "..."

Academics

San Diego State University is a top research university that offers "a unique and full college experience to every student while...preparing them for a future in the workforce." Many professors have successful backgrounds in their respective fields, allowing them to share "credible and valuable learning experiences" with their students. In addition, the faculty designs classes that "are project-based so we have real work to show after graduation." Students also appreciate the "plethora of programs offered to students and the hundreds of resources available," with one student adding, "Everything is here for you to succeed, you only have to grab it." Professors "make learning the material easy and fun" and "classrooms are conducted with enthusiasm and passion for both educating and the subjects themselves." They "actively engage the students in meaningful conversations about the topic discussed and create a welcoming learning environment." This environment fosters a sense of community, "where professors have an open-door policy and are truly invested in our success." One student adds, "I feel that I learn a lot of important and interesting information on a daily basis that benefits me in my everyday life." Overall, students feel the university provides "an excellent learning environment...[and] supplies an endless amount of activities and opportunities that allow its students to have fun and enjoy their time at San Diego State."

Campus Life

SDSU is a "very social and outgoing campus," and students agree that "it's hard not to be happy when living in beautiful San Diego." Being located in San Diego "means that flip flops are appropriate attire year-round, and you can see students skateboarding, longboarding, penny-boarding, you-name-it-boarding down the bike paths on campus." With over four hundred student organizations, "involvement in school clubs is common," and "there are tight communities focused on extracurricular activities." The school also has "amazing athletics" programs, drawing enthusiastic crowds for "football, basketball, and other sporting events." Many students agree that "the best part of going to school here is the beach," which they visit "almost year-round, and water sports are very popular." Students love living in San Diego because it "is a great hybrid between an active city life and a laid-back beach town." The "campus is located ten minutes from Fashion Valley or Balboa Park, and there are tons of good restaurants around. It is also very close to the Mexican border for easy day trips." Students also like to "go on hikes at Cowles Mountain or Potato Chip Rock, have dinner and drinks downtown or in Pacific Beach, hang out with each other, and go to many different types of parties." Greek life "is very active on campus, which makes it very fun," and the nightlife "is second to none when it comes to how fun all the parties are."

Student Body

Aztecs are described as "intelligent, very diverse, [and] amazing people" who are generally "very friendly and accepting." One student says, "It's a very social school that knows how to have fun and study very hard to make room for all the opportunities the school has to offer." Overall, "the community here is very friendly, smart, and laid back" and has "an overall good energy." As one student explains, "You feel comfortable talking to people since everyone is so outgoing." Another undergrad notes that "nearly all the students here have side hobbies or pastimes, as a break from the books." This is truly southern California, and many students here "have a physical fitness mindset," and "try to get some exercise each day." Much of the student body "is involved in clubs, athletics, or other school-run organizations," providing "endless opportunities to meet new people because the campus is swarming with students."

San Diego State University

E-Mail: admissions@sdsu.edu • Website: www.sdsu.edu

THE PRINCETON REVIEW SAYS

Admissions

The school reports that its standardized testing policy for use in admission for Fall 2026 is Test Free. The Princeton Review suggests that interested applicants consult with the school for the most up-to-date standardized testing policies. *Very important factors considered include:* rigor of secondary school record, academic GPA. *Important factors considered include:* geographical residence, state residency. High school diploma is required and GED is accepted. *Academic units required:* 4 English, 3 math, 2 science, 2 science labs, 2 language (other than English), 1 social studies, 1 history, 1 academic elective, 1 visual/performing arts. *Academic units recommended:* 4 math, 3 science, 3 science lab.

Financial Aid

Students should submit: FAFSA; State aid form. Priority filing deadline is 4/1. The Princeton Review suggests that all financial aid forms be submitted as soon as possible. *Need-based scholarships/grants offered:* Federal Pell; Federal SEOG; State scholarships/grants; Private scholarships; College/university scholarship or grant aid from institutional funds. *Loan aid offered:* Federal Direct Subsidized Loans; Federal Direct Unsubsidized Loans; Direct PLUS loans; State Loans; College/university loans from institutional funds. Admitted students will be notified of awards on a rolling basis beginning 3/15. Federal Work-Study Program available. Institutional employment available.

The Inside Word

The admissions process at San Diego State is very by the book. Similar to other universities within the California State system, San Diego relies on the eligibility index as the crux of their decision making. Hence, your GPA will be critical. Moreover, the application is major specific; candidates will be ranked against all other individuals applying to that particular major. You will not be able to change your major during this process (though, aside from nursing, you will once you arrive on campus). Finally, all music, dance, and/or theater candidates will have to audition as well.

THE SCHOOL SAYS

From the Admissions Office

"San Diego State University is a major public research institution and an R1, as designated by Carnegie. SDSU provides transformative experiences for more than 43,000 students, at multiple campus locations spanning the U.S. Mexico international border. SDSU offers bachelor's degrees in 97 areas, master's degrees in 88 fields and 29 doctoral programs, with SDSU Global Campus offering additional online training, certificates and degrees. On campus, students participate in robust research, entrepreneurship initiatives, internships, and mentoring. SDSU is nationally recognized for its study abroad initiatives and global footprint, its veterans' programs, LGBTQIA+ student support, and its powerhouse Division I athletics program. SDSU is a Hispanic-Serving Institution and an Asian American Native American Pacific Islander-Serving Institution (AANAPISI), and boasts more than a half million living alumni."

SELECTIVITY

# of total applicants	95,444
% of total applicants accepted	37
% of total acceptees attending	19
# of in-state applicants	84,805
% of in-state applicants accepted	31
# of out-of-state-applicants	9,043
% of applicants accepted from out of state	91
# of international applicants	1,596
% of international applicants accepted	59
# offered a place on the wait list	11,627
# admitted from wait list	962

First-Year Profile

Testing policy	Test Free
Average HS GPA	3.8
% submitting high school GPA	100
% graduated top 10% of class	25
% graduated top 25% of class	66
% graduated top 50% of class	95
% submitting high school rank	29

Important Dates

Regular	
Apply by	11/30
Notified by	3/1
Nonfall registration?	No

FINANCIAL FACTS

Annual in-state tuition	$6,838
Annual out-of-state tuition	$20,968
Food and housing	$21,856
Required fees	$2,824
Books and supplies	$1,014
Average need-based scholarship (First-year)	$13,254 ($12,330)
% students with need rec. need-based scholarship or grant aid (First-year)	90 (85)
% students with need rec. non-need-based scholarship or grant aid (First-year)	72 (83)
% students with need rec. need-based self-help aid (First-year)	68 (66)
% students rec. any financial aid (First-year)	64 (63)
% UG borrow to pay for school	31
Average cumulative indebtedness	$19,993
% of students with need fully met (First-year)	16 (32)
Average % of student need met (First-year)	74 (73)

SANTA CLARA UNIVERSITY

500 El Camino Real, Santa Clara, CA 95053 • Admissions: 408-554-4700

Survey Snapshot
Great library
Lab facilities are great
Easy to get around campus

RATINGS

Quality of Life	**83**
Fire Safety	**96**
Green	**96**
Academic	**83**
Profs Interesting	**86**
Profs Accessible	**92**
Admissions	**90**
Financial Aid	**90**

CAMPUS LIFE

Type of school	Private
Affiliation	Roman Catholic-Jesuit
Environment	City

Students

Degree-seeking undergrad enrollment	6,686
% male/female/not reported	50/50/0
% from out of state	40
% First-year from public high school	49
% First-year live on campus	94
% Ugrads live on campus	51
# of fraternities	0
# of sororities	0
% Asian	22
% Black or African American	3
% Hispanic	21
% Native American	<1
% Pacific Islander	<1
% Race and/or ethnicity unknown	2
% Two or more races	9
% White	36
% International	7
# of countries represented	40

CAMPUS MENTAL HEALTH SERVICES

Offers mental health/wellness program	Yes
Mental health training available to students	Yes
Employs Chief Wellness Officer	Yes
Peer-to-peer mental health offerings	Yes
Counseling center has guidelines or accreditation	Yes
Mental health/well-being courses	Yes, non-credit

ACADEMICS

% students returning for sophomore year	93
% students graduating within 4 years	81
% students graduating within 6 years	87
Calendar	Differs By Program
Student/faculty ratio	11:1
Most common class size 20–29.	(33%)
Most common lab/discussion size 10–19.	(62%)

Most Popular Majors

Speech Communication and Rhetoric; Psychology; Finance

Applicants Also Look At

Boston College, California Polytechnic State University—San Luis Obispo, Chapman University, Loyola Marymount University, New York University, Northeastern University, University of California—Berkeley, University of California—Davis, University of California—Los Angeles, University of California—Santa Barbara, University of San Diego, University of Southern California

STUDENTS SAY "..."

Academics

Situated "at the heart of Silicon Valley," Santa Clara University is a Jesuit school with "rigorous but rewarding [courses]," a place where "you'll never meet more passionate, more intelligent, and often down-to-earth professors." Thanks to small class sizes, professors remain "accessible"; as one student puts it: "I have had a real relationship with every one of my professors at SCU." Meanwhile, the school administration is "great at listening to and implementing student feedback" and "welcomes students to talk with people in high positions of power." There's also an appreciated "openness of the students and faculty to consider new possibilities in academia" and one student notes being "challenged to extend my thinking in every class."

Of the various majors, students speak fondly of the "massive array of classes and professors" in the business school, and the many connections offered from faculty "[that] are CEOs and founders that relate the material we learn to their experiences." Other programs students spoke affectionately of are those for "top-tier" accounting, "amazing" public health, and both computer and environmental science. Enrollees appreciate that the school is keeping with the times—one science building is described as having "awesome, state-of-the-art equipment"—and overall sum up their experience as "perfect, I love it."

Campus Life

On evenings and weekends, "Santa Clara students can be seen at local restaurants, bars, parties, golfing, or just having fun with friends." Fraternities and sororities are independent from the university, but are "huge" and "everywhere," perhaps contributing to the "big party culture at SCU." Additionally, "there are multiple social activities and events hosted by clubs and other organizations on campus almost every day of the week, and clubs do their best to be readily accessible to nonmembers." One student particularly loves the Investment Fund, "a student-led club that invests a portion of the university's endowment." There's also plenty to do even from the comfort of a residence hall, from pool to ping pong and foosball.

Students rave about the intramural sports available on SCU's "gorgeous" campus, including soccer, volleyball, flag football, and water polo. Though some admit it can be challenging to explore neighboring areas without a car, many value both the urban and wilderness adventures SCU's Northern California location provides. "I love the hiking and backpacking club called 'Into the Wild,' which takes students to local scenery," says one student. Others share that weekend adventures to the beach in Santa Cruz or enjoying the nightlife in San Francisco make for excellent SCU memories.

Student Body

Santa Clara University attracts students that are "smart, dedicated, funny, committed, [and] intelligent." While students are "focused on academics"—as one puts it, "People like to have fun, but only after the work is finished"—they "definitely prioritize having a good time." There is a "good sense of community" on campus, but also "enough harmless shenanigans (lightsaber fights in the cafeteria, Shakespeare flash mobs, etc.)" to ensure you're "having a really fun college experience."

"Everyone here is quite relaxed and happy," explains one student. It's not that people aren't academically focused, "they just know how to balance work and school well." The school is fairly diverse in ethnicity, but some students note an "overwhelmingly upper-middle class" vibe. This may just be part of the easy-going atmosphere, however, given that 75% of students are reported to receive aid. At any rate, these "hardworking [students are] always open to help someone," so much so that a first-year "automatically felt at home at Santa Clara because of the warm and welcoming community."

SANTA CLARA UNIVERSITY

Financial Aid: 408-551-1000 • E-Mail: Admission@scu.edu • Website: www.scu.edu

THE PRINCETON REVIEW SAYS

Admissions

The school reports that its standardized testing policy for use in admission for Fall 2026 is Test Optional. The Princeton Review suggests that interested applicants consult with the school for the most up-to-date standardized testing policies. *Very important factors considered include:* rigor of secondary school record, academic GPA, application essay, extracurricular activities, talent/ability, character/personal qualities, volunteer work, work experience. *Important factors considered include:* class rank, recommendation(s), level of applicant's interest. *Other factors considered include:* standardized test scores, first generation, alumni/ae relation, geographical residence, state residency, religious affiliation/commitment. High school diploma is required and GED is accepted. *Academic units required:* 4 English, 3 math, 2 science, 2 science labs, 2 language (other than English), 3 social studies. *Academic units recommended:* 4 English, 4 math, 3 science, 3 science labs, 3 language (other than English), 3 social studies, 1 visual/performing arts.

Financial Aid

Students should submit: FAFSA; CSS PROFILE. Priority filing deadline is 1/15. The Princeton Review suggests that all financial aid forms be submitted as soon as possible. *Need-based scholarships/grants offered:* Federal Pell; Federal SEOG; State scholarships/grants; Private scholarships; College/university scholarship or grant aid from institutional funds. *Loan aid offered:* Federal Direct Subsidized Loans; Federal Direct Unsubsidized Loans; College/university loans from institutional funds. Admitted students will be notified of awards on a rolling basis beginning 12/21. Federal Work-Study Program available. Institutional employment available.

The Inside Word

The admission criteria for Santa Clara University is stringent and growing tougher. The number of applications has been increasing over the last few years, and the university's Silicon Valley address ensures even more attention is coming the school's way. Applicants apply to one of SCU's three schools and colleges: Arts and Sciences, School of Business, or School of Engineering. School visits are available. There are no admissions interviews offered.

THE SCHOOL SAYS

From the Admissions Office

"Founded in 1851, Santa Clara University sits in the heart of Silicon Valley—the world's most innovative and entrepreneurial region. The University's stunningly landscaped 106-acre campus is home to the historic Mission Santa Clara de Asís. Ranked among the top 15 percent of national universities by U.S. News & World Report, SCU has among the best four-year graduation rates in the nation and is rated by PayScale in the top 1 percent of universities with the highest-paid graduates. SCU has produced elite levels of Fulbright Scholars as well as four Rhodes Scholars. With undergraduate programs in arts and sciences, business, and engineering, and graduate programs in six disciplines, the curriculum blends high-tech innovation with social consciousness grounded in the tradition of Jesuit, Catholic education. For more information see www.scu.edu."

SELECTIVITY

# of total applicants	20,032
% of total applicants accepted	48
% of total acceptees attending	17
# of in-state applicants	10,205
% of in-state applicants accepted	48
# of out-of-state-applicants	7,213
% of applicants accepted from out of state	54
# of international applicants	2,604
% of international applicants accepted	29
# of early decision applicants	611
% of early decision applicants accepted	76
# offered a place on the wait list	405
# admitted from wait list	263

First-Year Profile

Testing policy	Test Optional
Range SAT composite	1330–1470
Range SAT EBRW	660–730
Range SAT math	660–750
Range ACT composite	29–33
% submitting SAT scores	29
% submitting ACT scores	9
Average HS GPA	3.7
% submitting high school GPA	100
% graduated top 10% of class	47
% graduated top 25% of class	74
% graduated top 50% of class	91
% submitting high school rank	3

Important Dates

Early decision	
Apply by	11/1
Notified by	12/31
Other ED apply by	1/7
Other ED notified by	2/15
Early action	
Apply by	11/1
Notified by	12/31
Regular	
Apply by	1/7
Notified by	Late March
Nonfall registration?	Yes

FINANCIAL FACTS

Annual tuition	$64,956
Food and housing	$21,234
Required fees	$780
Books and supplies	$1,305
Average need-based scholarship (First-year)	$46,540 ($50,851)
% students with need rec. need-based scholarship or grant aid (First-year)	98 (98)
% students with need rec. non-need-based scholarship or grant aid (First-year)	15 (16)
% students with need rec. need-based self-help aid (First-year)	81 (79)
% students rec. any financial aid (First-year)	76 (76)
% UG borrow to pay for school	33
Average cumulative indebtedness	$28,838
% of students with need fully met (First-year)	41 (57)
Average % of student need met (First-year)	77 (87)

SARAH LAWRENCE COLLEGE

1 Mead Way, Bronxville, NY 10708-5999 • Admissions: 914-395-2510

Survey Snapshot
Theater is popular
Active student-run political groups
Class discussions encouraged

RATINGS	
Quality of Life	80
Fire Safety	95
Green	60*
Academic	84
Profs Interesting	98
Profs Accessible	92
Admissions	88
Financial Aid	88

CAMPUS LIFE

Type of school	Private
Environment	Metropolis

Students

Degree-seeking undergrad enrollment	1,390
% male/female/not reported	20/80/0
% from out of state	78
% First-year from public high school	65
% First-year live on campus	98
% Ugrads live on campus	85
# of fraternities	0
# of sororities	0
% Asian	5
% Black or African American	5
% Hispanic	15
% Native American	<1
% Pacific Islander	<1
% Race and/or ethnicity unknown	2
% Two or more races	5
% White	62
% International	5
# of countries represented	39

CAMPUS MENTAL HEALTH SERVICES

Offers mental health/wellness program	Yes
Mental health training available to students	Yes
Employs Chief Wellness Officer	Yes
Peer-to-peer mental health offerings	Yes
Counseling center has guidelines or accreditation	Yes
Mental health/well-being courses	Yes, non-credit

ACADEMICS

% students returning for sophomore year	81
% students graduating within 4 years	52
% students graduating within 6 years	66
Calendar	Semester
Student/faculty ratio	10:1
Most common class size 10–19.	(62%)

Most Popular Majors

Liberal Arts and Sciences/Liberal Studies

Applicants Also Look At

Bard College, Barnard College, Boston University, Emerson College, Eugene Lang College of Liberal Arts at The New School, Fordham University, New York University, Reed College, Skidmore College, Smith College, Vassar College, Wesleyan University

STUDENTS SAY "..."

Academics

Students at Sarah Lawrence College are deeply passionate about having a "multidisciplinary liberal arts curriculum" that allows them to "carve their own path and find an educational niche that excites them." The college's "choose-your-own-adventure experience" is the cornerstone of an SLC education, grounded in the "freedom to learn and explore" by rejecting the "restriction of typical majors." Accordingly, students are empowered to "closely curate [their] projects to [their] particular interests." The two key components of SLC's open curriculum are the donning system, which doubles professors as "personal advisor[s]" who work to support each student's academic journey, and the rigorous conference courses that provide semester-long opportunities for students to work "more independently with [their] professors" to develop a "cross examination between subjects to create unique courses and new research ideas." As one student describes the experience: "I've really pushed myself with these long, academic projects." Fundamental to the success of the program are the "truly exceptional" relationships between the undergrads and their professors, which are bolstered by a "one-on-one conference system [that] allows us to individually connect with professors in an extremely rewarding and enlightening way." Students also credit the "absolutely fantastic" small class format, and the "super unique and interesting classes," summing up the experience as a "rich intellectual environment" in which creative students can connect niche studies or "multiple concentrations."

Campus Life

Sarah Lawrence is in Bronxville, NY, just 30 minutes by train from Manhattan, and this proximity gives students the opportunity to "spend time in New York City at museums, shows, stores, and to explore" as well as "see work our professors are involved in for free or reduced cost." That said, students also enjoy a robust array of on-campus choices: "Every weekend, there are multiple options for student art performances to attend… [and] there are also lots of for-fun club meetings... I always have trouble choosing what to do because there's so many great options!" In particular, the "student theater scene is vibrant and joyful, open to all…and full of opportunity for exploration and experimentation." The Sarah Lawrence Activities Council (SLAC) frequently hosts popular events "such as fairs, movie screenings, and game nights," and there are plenty of "on-campus live music events" and other entertainment. Students also mention the "culture of athletics" as one of the best parts of student life on campus. Undergrads note, positively, that "protests are common, and political discussion is fiery and often encouraged." All of this makes extracurriculars a place where "personal expression is not only accepted but expected."

Student Body

Students at Sarah Lawrence see themselves as "passionate, creative people…[who] are politically and socially conscious." This vibrant campus of "intellectual, ambitious, and often self-interested" students does, according to some respondents, occasionally fall prey to "rumors and gossip… [and the student-run] groups can also become cliquey," but this is softened by the widely-asserted observation that SLC is a "small and tight-knit" community of people who are "generally passionate about their interests, outspoken about their opinions, and willing to dive headfirst into creative projects." Students are "politically driven with an extreme liberal mindset" and affirm that SLC has "a lot of diversity," not just "in terms of the LGBTQIA+ community" but also so far as "interests and [an] interdisciplinary approach to study." That said, numerous students underscored that their school "is very white," despite programs like the THRIVE Mentorship Program for Students of Color. Some report that SLC has made notable outreach, and attendees say that "students of color/affinity groups still have a very active place on campus." Overall, students agree that their peers have "a unique passion that drives them," and express gratitude that "we have athletes who are gifted in violin, drum players who excel in physics, and English literature students deeply devoted to social justice issues."

SARAH LAWRENCE COLLEGE

Financial Aid: 914-395-2570 • E-Mail: slcadmit@sarahlawrence.edu • Website: www.sarahlawrence.edu

THE PRINCETON REVIEW SAYS

Admissions

The school reports that its standardized testing policy for use in admission for Fall 2026 is Test Optional. The Princeton Review suggests that interested applicants consult with the school for the most up-to-date standardized testing policies. *Very important factors considered include:* application essay, recommendation(s). *Important factors considered include:* rigor of secondary school record, academic GPA, extracurricular activities, talent/ability, character/personal qualities. *Other factors considered include:* class rank, standardized test scores, interview, first generation, geographical residence, volunteer work, work experience, level of applicant's interest. High school diploma is required and GED is accepted. *Academic units required:* 2 English, 2 math, 2 science, 2 language (other than English), 2 social studies, 2 history. *Academic units recommended:* 4 English, 4 math, 4 science, 4 language (other than English), 4 social studies, 4 history.

Financial Aid

Students should submit: FAFSA; State aid form. Priority filing deadline is 1/15. The Princeton Review suggests that all financial aid forms be submitted as soon as possible. *Need-based scholarships/grants offered:* Federal Pell; Federal SEOG; State scholarships/grants; Private scholarships; College/university scholarship or grant aid from institutional funds. *Loan aid offered:* Federal Direct Subsidized Loans; Federal Direct Unsubsidized Loans; Direct PLUS loans. Admitted students will be notified of awards on or about 4/1. Federal Work-Study Program available. Institutional employment available.

The Inside Word

To gain admission to Sarah Lawrence, a strong college prep curriculum and solid GPA are of utmost importance, though submitting standardized test scores is optional. Candidates are encouraged to submit scores only if it will enhance their application. Additionally, interviews are optional, but may offer an opportunity to demonstrate what you can bring to this unique community.

THE SCHOOL SAYS

From the Admissions Office

"Students who come to Sarah Lawrence are curious about the world, and they have an ardent desire to satisfy that curiosity. Sarah Lawrence offers such students two innovative academic structures: the seminar/conference system and the arts components. Courses in the humanities, social sciences, natural sciences, and mathematics are taught in the seminar/conference style. The seminars enroll an average of eleven students and consist of lecture, discussion, readings, and assigned papers. For each seminar, students also meet one-on-one in biweekly conferences, for which they conceive of individualized projects and shape them under the direction of professors. Arts components let students combine history and theory with practice. Painters, printmakers, photographers, sculptors, filmmakers, composers, musicians, choreographers, dancers, actors, and directors work in readily available studios, editing facilities, and darkrooms, guided by accomplished professionals. The suburban, wooded campus is thirty minutes from midtown Manhattan, and the diversity of people and ideas at Sarah Lawrence make it an extraordinary educational environment.

"Sarah Lawrence College is Test Optional, accepting and reviewing standardized test scores if they are submitted; however, they are not required as part of the admission application."

SELECTIVITY

# of total applicants	4,085
% of total applicants accepted	66
% of total acceptees attending	26
# of in-state applicants	761
% of in-state applicants accepted	61
# of out-of-state-applicants	2,656
% of applicants accepted from out of state	75
# of international applicants	668
% of international applicants accepted	36
# of early decision applicants	117
% of early decision applicants accepted	50
# offered a place on the wait list	890
# admitted from wait list	169

First-Year Profile

Testing policy	Test Optional
Range SAT composite	1240–1380
Range SAT EBRW	630–740
Range SAT math	610–670
Range ACT composite	28–32
% submitting SAT scores	9
% submitting ACT scores	3
Average HS GPA	3.8
% submitting high school GPA	88
% graduated top 10% of class	18
% graduated top 25% of class	32
% graduated top 50% of class	78
% submitting high school rank	21

Important Dates

Early decision	
Apply by	11/1
Notified by	12/15
Other ED apply by	1/15
Early action	
Apply by	11/1
Notified by	12/15
Regular	
Apply by	1/15
Nonfall registration?	No

FINANCIAL FACTS

Annual tuition	$73,088
Food and housing	$20,316
Required fees	$612
Books and supplies	$600
Average need-based scholarship (First-year)	$45,667 ($48,948)
% students with need rec. need-based scholarship or grant aid (First-year)	97 (99)
% students with need rec. non-need-based scholarship or grant aid (First-year)	20 (21)
% students with need rec. need-based self-help aid (First-year)	76 (76)
% students rec. any financial aid (First-year)	89 (73)
% UG borrow to pay for school	58
Average cumulative indebtedness	$33,471
% of students with need fully met (First-year)	21 (24)
Average % of student need met (First-year)	76 (77)

Scripps College

1030 Columbia Avenue, Claremont, CA 91711-3948 • Admissions: 909-621-8149

Survey Snapshot
Career services are great
Class discussions encouraged
Students love Claremont, CA

RATINGS

Quality of Life	**92**
Fire Safety	**96**
Green	**60***
Academic	**88**
Profs Interesting	**95**
Profs Accessible	**95**
Admissions	**93**
Financial Aid	**98**

CAMPUS LIFE

Type of school	Private
Environment	Town

Students

Degree-seeking undergrad enrollment	1,098
% male/female/not reported	0/100/0
% from out of state	58
% First-year from public high school	55
% First-year live on campus	100
% Ugrads live on campus	97
# of sororities	0
% Asian	13
% Black or African American	4
% Hispanic	12
% Native American	0
% Pacific Islander	0
% Race and/or ethnicity unknown	2
% Two or more races	11
% White	54
% International	5
# of countries represented	25

CAMPUS MENTAL HEALTH SERVICES

Offers mental health/wellness program	Yes
Mental health training available to students	No
Employs Chief Wellness Officer	NR
Peer-to-peer mental health offerings	NR
Counseling center has guidelines or accreditation	No
Mental health/well-being courses	NR

ACADEMICS

% students returning for sophomore year	92
% students graduating within 4 years	64
% students graduating within 6 years	85
Calendar	Semester
Most common class size 10–19.	(64%)

Most Popular Majors

Research and Experimental Psychology; Political Science and Government

STUDENTS SAY "..."

Academics

Scripps College has an "absolutely gorgeous" campus and terrific Southern California vibes, but the reason applicants clamor to attend is because of its "dedication to empowering female voices and education." The focus may be on its "supportive, small community of women who want to fight to make the world a better place," but students won't have to worry about missing out on the resources often attributed to larger institutions, as Scripps is part of The Claremont Colleges, a consortium that grants undergraduates access "to all of the benefits and resources within [four] other colleges."

Access is key across the "challenging and engaging" academic offerings at Scripps, whether that's one-on-one time with professors or simply having opportunity for undergraduate research. This extends to "discussion-based [classes], which allows students to raise questions..., [gain] a better understanding of the course, and connect to the subject more intimately." It helps, too, that professors "are very good at creating interesting courses," and are "generally accepting of a wide range of student opinions," though students should be aware that these freedoms come with "high expectations." Ultimately, what undergrads appreciate the most is that it's "very easy to form close connections with professors both in class and out of class."

Campus Life

Scripps students are fairly studious, and during the week you'll often find them congregating in one of the "many outdoor study spaces, such as courtyards, lawns, or the lounge chairs by the pool." Of course, there's lots of fun to be had beyond academics. For example, undergrads can participate in "a ton of free fitness courses on campus like CrossFit, yoga, and Zumba" as well as unique "intramural sports like inner-tube water polo." Additionally, "there are hundreds of clubs to join that are both specific to Scripps and also across all The Claremont Colleges" as well as school-sponsored "speakers, screenings, presentations, workshops, [and] de-stress activities." Should you need a respite from that overflowing campus life, the surrounding area provides many options. "The train to downtown Los Angeles is about a 10-minute walk away, Mt. Baldy is about a 20-minute drive, and the village in Claremont is filled with shops and eateries."

Student Body

When asked to describe their peers, Scripps undergrads are prone to using effusive adjectives such as "passionate, driven, [and] creative." Many students also "identify as liberal, feminist, [and] social-justice oriented." As one individual explains, "From reproductive rights, prison abolition, racial justice, everyone you talk to has the desire to change the world." Indeed, they are certainly "not afraid to let their voices be heard." A number of undergrads appreciate that the college attracts "many transgender and non-binary students, which creates a very open and safe environment." However, a few do caution that there is a little "tension between white feminism and intersectionality" on campus. Fortunately, most everyone enjoys the fact their classmates are often "intelligent and ready to have in-depth conversations about topics from politics to The Bachelor to data on climate change." Undergrads here also tend to be "very supportive of one another" and "very accepting" as well. In fact, when strolling through campus, it's even common to "receive smiles from students [you] don't know." All in all, the Scripps student body offers the "type of community that will cheer with and for you when you succeed and be a shoulder to cry on when needed."

Scripps College

Financial Aid: 909-621-8275 • E-Mail: admission@scrippscollege.edu • Website: www.scrippscollege.edu

THE PRINCETON REVIEW SAYS

Admissions

The school reports that its standardized testing policy for use in admission for Fall 2026 is Test Optional. The Princeton Review suggests that interested applicants consult with the school for the most up-to-date standardized testing policies. *Very important factors considered include:* rigor of secondary school record, academic GPA, application essay, character/personal qualities. *Important factors considered include:* recommendation(s). *Other factors considered include:* class rank, standardized test scores, interview, extracurricular activities, talent/ability, first generation, geographical residence, volunteer work, work experience. High school diploma is required and GED is accepted. *Academic units recommended:* 4 English, 3 math, 3 science, 3 language (other than English), 3 social studies.

Financial Aid

Students should submit: FAFSA; CSS PROFILE; State aid form. Priority filing deadline is 2/1. The Princeton Review suggests that all financial aid forms be submitted as soon as possible. *Need-based scholarships/grants offered:* Federal Pell; Federal SEOG; State scholarships/grants; Private scholarships; College/university scholarship or grant aid from institutional funds. *Loan aid offered:* Federal Direct Subsidized Loans; Federal Direct Unsubsidized Loans; Direct PLUS loans; College/university loans from institutional funds. Admitted students will be notified of awards on or about 3/20. Federal Work-Study Program available. Institutional employment available.

The Inside Word

Admission officers at Scripps truly strive to get to know each applicant. After all, they are looking for the students who will best complement the college and go furthest with the opportunities offered. Therefore, expect every part of your application to be carefully vetted. Your academic achievements will still hold the most weight, but your recommendations, personal statement, and extracurriculars are of great importance.

THE SCHOOL SAYS

From the Admissions Office

"Scripps College is a top liberal arts women's college, where academic rigor and collaboration go hand-in-hand. With small class sizes (averaging 15 students), students engage in undergraduate research, critical thinking, and exploration, all while being mentored by distinguished faculty experts. Scripps' two-semester Core Curriculum introduces interdisciplinary inquiry and equips students with essential skills in research, information literacy, and academic discourse, culminating in a final project. Every Scripps student also completes a semester- or year-long senior thesis project.

"Sixty percent of students study abroad, over 87% complete at least one internship, and students can participate in eleven NCAA Division III sports teams. As part of The Claremont Colleges, a consortium of five prestigious undergraduate institutions within walking distance, Scripps students have access to over 65 majors (including joint and intercollegiate programs), along with shared clubs, organizations, and resources. The college meets 100% of institutionally determined financial need for admitted students who submit the FAFSA and CSS/Profile, and all first-year applicants are considered for scholarships ranging from $15,000 to $30,000 annually."

SELECTIVITY

# of total applicants	3,230
% of total applicants accepted	40
% of total acceptees attending	23
# of in-state applicants	1,477
% of in-state applicants accepted	44
# of out-of-state-applicants	1,304
% of applicants accepted from out of state	43
# of international applicants	449
% of international applicants accepted	18
# of early decision applicants	275
% of early decision applicants accepted	51
# offered a place on the wait list	537
# admitted from wait list	70

First-Year Profile

Testing policy	Test Optional
Range SAT composite	1430–1500
Range SAT EBRW	730–770
Range SAT math	690–750
Range ACT composite	32–34
% submitting SAT scores	19
% submitting ACT scores	12
% graduated top 10% of class	63
% graduated top 25% of class	90
% graduated top 50% of class	100
% submitting high school rank	13

Important Dates

Early decision	
Apply by	11/15
Notified by	12/15
Other ED apply by	1/8
Other ED notified by	2/15
Regular	
Apply by	1/8
Notified by	4/1
Nonfall registration?	No

FINANCIAL FACTS

Annual tuition	$70,600
Food and housing	$23,472
Required fees	$326
Books and supplies	$800
Average need-based scholarship (First-year)	$56,301 ($55,673)
% students with need rec. need-based scholarship or grant aid (First-year)	100 (99)
% students with need rec. non-need-based scholarship or grant aid (First-year)	0 (0)
% students with need rec. need-based self-help aid (First-year)	76 (75)
% UG borrow to pay for school	25
Average cumulative indebtedness	$25,027
% of students with need fully met (First-year)	100 (100)
Average % of student need met (First-year)	100 (100)

Seattle University

901 12th Ave, Seattle, WA 98122-1090 • Admissions: 206-220-8040

Survey Snapshot
Lots of liberal students
Students love Seattle, WA
Great off-campus food

RATINGS

Quality of Life	**81**
Fire Safety	**97**
Green	**92**
Academic	**81**
Profs Interesting	**85**
Profs Accessible	**89**
Admissions	**86**
Financial Aid	**88**

CAMPUS LIFE

Type of school	Private
Affiliation	Roman Catholic-Jesuit
Environment	Metropolis

Students

Degree-seeking undergrad enrollment	4,350
% male/female/not reported	39/61/<1
% from out of state	44
% First-year from public high school	62
% First-year live on campus	86
% Ugrads live on campus	52
# of fraternities	0
# of sororities	0
% Asian	26
% Black or African American	8
% Hispanic	16
% Native American	<1
% Pacific Islander	1
% Race and/or ethnicity unknown	2
% Two or more races	11
% White	30
% International	6
# of countries represented	81

CAMPUS MENTAL HEALTH SERVICES

Offers mental health/wellness program	Yes
Mental health training available to students	No
Employs Chief Wellness Officer	NR
Peer-to-peer mental health offerings	NR
Counseling center has guidelines or accreditation	No
Mental health/well-being courses	NR

ACADEMICS

% students returning for sophomore year	85
% students graduating within 4 years	59
% students graduating within 6 years	71
Calendar	Differs By Program
Student/faculty ratio	12:1
Most common class size 10–19.	(35%)
Most common lab/discussion size 10–19.	(42%)

Most Popular Majors

Liberal Arts and Sciences, General Studies and Humanities; Business/Commerce; Registered Nursing/Registered Nurse

STUDENTS SAY "..."

Academics

Students attribute Seattle University with having "really expanded my thinking," thanks in part to its 12 Core courses, taught in the Jesuit tradition, that are designed to teach "the whole person" and help them think critically and act ethically. But it's not only this—what some consider the school's greatest strength—that students admire and value. They also note that there are over 65 majors to choose from (including many other minors and specializations), and that active learning is a boon: "There are lots of hands-on activities and practice problems in class; I have never sat through an entire class of just lecturing." It's here that being a city school is most beneficial, as it leads to many praise-worthy opportunities for real-world experiences, such as the computer science capstone program in which local industries sponsor student projects. Students also appreciate that professors "don't shy away from rough topics, which is important." Students speak about their professors affectionately, and the caliber of the instructors is frequently listed as one of the university's best assets. As one student notes, "I haven't had one professor that I didn't enjoy," and another adds that these teachers provide "absolutely amazing support for students academically."

Campus Life

It's impossible to experience Seattle University without factoring in the city itself—the two are interwoven, and students note that its central location leads them to "take advantage of all the city has to offer" while another notes that the city's ubiquitous drink of choice makes "off-campus coffee shops...the study spots." That said, the majority of first-year students live on campus, which provides another common location for activities. Students describe informal movie nights, cooking parties, or simply "hanging out" with their classmates as experiences that lead to camaraderie and a pleasant atmosphere. "It's a very friendly environment where students work together instead of competing against each other." That camaraderie carries over to the numerous and diverse on-campus activities as a major benefit of the school. From a club centered on Japanese food to an aerospace group to a club that explores the ethics of artificial intelligence, students appreciate the wide range of choices and feel that, in general, the school "encourages...students to excel at what they like."

Student Body

The university reflects the spirit and culture of Seattle, leading one satisfied student with an interest in social justice to observe, "I think there are a lot more liberal students than the average college campus." This serves to unite the many students who are "passionate about social justice" and politically active for causes such as sustainability. Students also point to the school's demographics when saying that "inclusion and diversity is a big part of what makes Seattle U a great university." Students also point to how the school's "values of being a Jesuit university are shining through each student as they move forward with their academics, careers, and personal lives." One student simply sums up Seattle University undergraduates as "all from different backgrounds, but fun to be around, and we get along."

SEATTLE UNIVERSITY

Financial Aid: 206-296-8020 • E-Mail: admissions@seattleu.edu • Website: www.seattleu.edu

THE PRINCETON REVIEW SAYS

Admissions

The school reports that its standardized testing policy for use in admission for Fall 2026 is Test Optional. The Princeton Review suggests that interested applicants consult with the school for the most up-to-date standardized testing policies. *Very important factors considered include:* rigor of secondary school record, academic GPA, character/personal qualities. *Important factors considered include:* application essay, recommendation(s), extracurricular activities, level of applicant's interest. *Other factors considered include:* class rank, standardized test scores, interview, talent/ability, first generation, alumni/ae relation, geographical residence, state residency, religious affiliation/commitment, volunteer work, work experience. High school diploma is required and GED is accepted. *Academic units required:* 4 English, 3 math, 2 science, 2 science labs, 2 language (other than English), 3 social studies, 1 history, 2 academic electives. *Academic units recommended:* 4 English, 3 math, 2 science, 2 science labs, 2 language (other than English), 3 social studies, 1 history, 2 academic electives.

Financial Aid

Students should submit: FAFSA. Priority filing deadline is 2/1. The Princeton Review suggests that all financial aid forms be submitted as soon as possible. *Need-based scholarships/grants offered:* Federal Pell; Federal SEOG; State scholarships/grants; Private scholarships; College/university scholarship or grant aid from institutional funds; Federal Nursing Scholarships. *Loan aid offered:* Federal Direct Subsidized Loans; Federal Direct Unsubsidized Loans; Direct PLUS loans. Federal Work-Study Program available. Institutional employment available.

The Inside Word

At this Jesuit, Catholic school, in addition to strong academics, admission officers tend to value community service as well as overall "life experience." Those who demonstrate a significant commitment to volunteerism will find themselves at an advantage, as will those who convey a clear sense of their academic and career goals. Applicants should keep in mind that Seattle University has more stringent course work requirements for certain majors.

THE SCHOOL SAYS

From the Admissions Office

"Seattle University is a place 'where innovation meets humanity.' Students who are adventurous, forward-thinking, creative and have an interest in social justice are drawn to Seattle University, located in the heart of a city with unparalleled access to innovation, technology, the arts and culture. Personalized learning—with a 12:1 student-faculty ratio—provides opportunities for research alongside accomplished faculty. Internships and community engagement give students relevant experience for their résumés and the chance to be noticed by some of the world's most influential nonprofits and companies that call the Seattle area home, such as Microsoft, the Gates Foundation, Starbucks, Amazon, Boeing and Costco. Seattle University is a school of action with an ever-growing impact on the city, the region and throughout the world. In Washington state, where dozens of different languages are spoken and every race, religion and perspective is represented, Seattle University nearly 4,400 undergraduate students from 53 states and territories and 70 nations fit right in. Service is a cornerstone of the SU experience with the majority of students participating in some form of community-engaged learning. That spirit is especially visible in the Seattle University Youth Initiative. As the university's largest-ever community engagement project, the Youth Initiative is transforming lives of Seattle's underserved children while becoming a model of service.

"Discover Seattle University's sustainable campus, which is pesticide-free and wins top awards for its environmental leadership and energy conservation. The urban campus is woven into Seattle's thriving Capitol Hill and First Hill neighborhoods, which abound with culture and entertainment options."

SELECTIVITY

# of total applicants	11,600
% of total applicants accepted	73
% of total acceptees attending	11
# of in-state applicants	4,296
% of in-state applicants accepted	76
# of out-of-state-applicants	6,172
% of applicants accepted from out of state	75
# of international applicants	1,020
% of international applicants accepted	48
# offered a place on the wait list	294
# admitted from wait list	50

First-Year Profile

Testing policy	Test Optional
Range SAT composite	1230–1380
Range SAT EBRW	620–710
Range SAT math	580–700
Range ACT composite	24–30
% submitting SAT scores	15
% submitting ACT scores	4
Average HS GPA	3.6
% submitting high school GPA	100
% graduated top 10% of class	28
% graduated top 25% of class	58
% graduated top 50% of class	86
% submitting high school rank	33

Important Dates

Early action	
Apply by	11/15
Notified by	12/23
Regular	
Apply by	7/31
Notified by	Rolling, 3/1
Nonfall registration?	Yes

FINANCIAL FACTS

Annual tuition	$59,400
Food and housing	$17,628
Required fees	$1,356
Books and supplies	$594
Average need-based scholarship (First-year)	$40,009 ($45,644)
% students with need rec. need-based scholarship or grant aid (First-year)	93 (93)
% students with need rec. non-need-based scholarship or grant aid (First-year)	88 (91)
% students with need rec. need-based self-help aid (First-year)	72 (72)
% UG borrow to pay for school	69
Average cumulative indebtedness	$26,772
% of students with need fully met (First-year)	36 (38)
Average % of student need met (First-year)	83 (87)

SETON HALL UNIVERSITY

400 South Orange Avenue, South Orange, NJ 07079 • Admissions: 973-313-6146

Survey Snapshot
Easy to get around campus
College radio is popular
Everyone loves the Pirates

RATINGS

Quality of Life	88
Fire Safety	91
Green	60*
Academic	80
Profs Interesting	87
Profs Accessible	90
Admissions	88
Financial Aid	78

CAMPUS LIFE

Type of school	Private
Affiliation	Roman Catholic
Environment	Village

Students

Degree-seeking undergrad enrollment	6,066
% male/female/not reported	43/57/0
% from out of state	23
% First-year live on campus	54
% Ugrads live on campus	34
# of fraternities (% join)	20 (4)
# of sororities (% join)	15 (7)
% Asian	9
% Black or African American	12
% Hispanic	31
% Native American	<1
% Pacific Islander	<1
% Race and/or ethnicity unknown	3
% Two or more races	4
% White	39
% International	2
# of countries represented	63

CAMPUS MENTAL HEALTH SERVICES

Offers mental health/wellness program	Yes
Mental health training available to students	Yes
Employs Chief Wellness Officer	Yes
Peer-to-peer mental health offerings	Yes
Counseling center has guidelines or accreditation	No
Mental health/well-being courses	NR

ACADEMICS

% students returning for sophomore year	83
% students graduating within 4 years	64
% students graduating within 6 years	70
Calendar	Semester
Student/faculty ratio	14:1
Most common class size 10–19.	(34%)
Most common lab/discussion size 10–19.	(97%)

Most Popular Majors

Biology/Biological Sciences; Registered Nursing/Registered Nurse; Finance

Applicants Often Prefer

The College of New Jersey, Kean University, Montclair State University, Rowan University, Rutgers University–New Brunswick

Applicants Sometimes Prefer

Fordham University, Monmouth University (NJ), New York University, Ramapo College of New Jersey, William Paterson University

Applicants Rarely Prefer

Felician University, The George Washington University, Saint Joseph's University (PA)

STUDENTS SAY "..."

Academics

Seton Hall University is a Catholic liberal arts college providing its students with "tremendous professional and recreational opportunities," including "amazing, accelerated programs and certificate programs that are easy to do with any major. They also make it easy to double or even triple major across two or three different colleges." The Honors Program "is very thorough and well-put together," and students enjoy the interactive format of the "colloquium- style classes." The Buccino Leadership Institute "focuses on tangible, group style projects" and experiential learning, and the university offers "lots of opportunities for undergraduate research in the hard sciences." The university is "small enough where you are not lost in the crowd" or feel like just a number. Additionally, there are "very strong support systems for all students to make sure they are successful inside as well as outside of the classroom." One student finds that the school's size and options for specialization "attracts very passionate and dedicated professors and students, which have made my class experiences entertaining, educational, and captivating." Faculty "are all very committed to their work" and "make themselves accessible outside of class and by email easily." Whether they're "agreeing to be project advisors or providing career-oriented help, they're always quick to step in and give students the best experiences they can." Professors make classes interesting and relevant with guest speakers, hosting field "trips relevant to the class, [and] incorporating recent events and news into discussions." Seton Hall graduates have "a very high employment rate," perhaps due in part to the school's "excellent career center" and proximity to New York. Students appreciate the "great connections and job events," as well as "the opportunity to network with Seton Hall alumni [who] are now business professionals."

Campus Life

Seton Hall's "beautiful and clean campus" is "located in a suburban and green environment," just "a 10-minute walk to the train station," making it "super easy to go to New York City." The university "wants to make their students happy by organizing events for us and entertaining us," and the events "are always fun with DJs, free food, and tons of merch or handouts to go around." In addition, many people "are involved in clubs and sports and use that to fill their time," and "enjoy going to the gym, tabling/relaxing on the Green," or simply "hanging out in the University Center that has pool tables, air hockey, and foosball." There are also "various social activities exclusive to Greek life, trips hosted by the Student Activities Board into New York City, as well as club events hosted on campus." With "so many different clubs or organizations that allow each student to find their place on campus," students say, "there is never a dull moment at Seton Hall."

Student Body

Seton Hall students are "high achievers," and this "incredibly driven and career-focused" group tends to "spend the days doing schoolwork in the university center or library between classes and work." The atmosphere on campus is supportive, and students are "generally eager to collaborate and succeed both academically and personally." While this Catholic university has "a great campus ministry community," there "are many other religions practiced on campus." Overall, the student body is "fairly diverse in regard to race" with "a wide range of students all from different backgrounds and identities," as well as "a heavy commuter population." In this "very welcoming community" it's "very easy to build relationships and make connections with people outside your particular field of study," and there are "many opportunities for team building and making friends" for first-years. As one student says, "There's never a time I'm on campus where I don't see a friendly face."

Seton Hall University

Financial Aid: 973-761-9332 • E-Mail: thehall@shu.edu • Website: admissions.shu.edu

THE PRINCETON REVIEW SAYS

Admissions

The school reports that its standardized testing policy for use in admission for Fall 2026 is Test Optional. The Princeton Review suggests that interested applicants consult with the school for the most up-to-date standardized testing policies. *Very important factors considered include:* rigor of secondary school record, academic GPA, application essay, recommendation(s), level of applicant's interest. *Important factors considered include:* extracurricular activities. *Other factors considered include:* class rank, standardized test scores, interview, talent/ability, character/personal qualities, alumni/ae relation. High school diploma is required and GED is accepted. *Academic units required:* 4 English, 3 math, 1 science, 1 science lab, 2 language (other than English), 2 social studies, 4 academic electives.

Financial Aid

Students should submit: FAFSA. The Princeton Review suggests that all financial aid forms be submitted as soon as possible. Admitted students will be notified of awards on a rolling basis. Federal Work-Study Program available. Institutional employment available.

The Inside Word

Seton Hall accepts both its own online application and the Common Application. Students with reasonably solid high school transcripts and strong recommendations won't have trouble getting in, and Seton Hall makes an effort to sweeten the deal financially for standout students: generally, the higher a student's academic standing, the higher the scholarship award.

THE SCHOOL SAYS

From the Admissions Office

"A top 20 Catholic university since 1856, Seton Hall educates great minds like in a challenging, supportive and rigorous environment. With approximately 6,000 undergraduate students and a 14:1 student to faculty ratio, students develop a mentoring relationship with faculty. At Seton Hall, students have unprecedented access to research, conferences, clinicals, corporate mentors, internships, study abroad and many other hands-on learning opportunities as early as freshman year. Located just 14 miles from New York City in suburban South Orange, New Jersey, Seton Hall benefits from all the opportunities the Big Apple has to offer. Graduates also have 50 percent higher mid-career earnings than the national average. Seton Hall offers over 17,000 internships. Students have found internships or employment upon graduation at Goldman Sachs, CNN, Pfizer, Google, the United Nations, ABC, NBC, CBS, Lockheed Martin, Morgan Stanley, The Wall Street Journal, HBO, Amazon, Prudential, Lincoln Center, Standard and Poor's, The State Department and The New York Times, as well as acclaimed hospitals, schools and nonprofit organizations. Seton Hall has been rated in the top 10% nationally for a return on investment and for having the highest paid graduates, who also boast 97% employment rate. Seton Hall also provides more than $170 million dollars a year in scholarships and grants to students; 98 percent of students receive some form of financial assistance from the University."

SELECTIVITY

# of total applicants	26,562
% of total applicants accepted	69
% of total acceptees attending	9
# of in-state applicants	14,873
% of in-state applicants accepted	71
# of out-of-state-applicants	11,157
% of applicants accepted from out of state	67
# of international applicants	432
% of international applicants accepted	58
# offered a place on the wait list	5,650
# admitted from wait list	1,686

First-Year Profile

Testing policy	Test Optional
Range SAT composite	1240–1390
Range SAT EBRW	630–710
Range SAT math	610–700
Range ACT composite	27–31
% submitting SAT scores	25
% submitting ACT scores	5
Average HS GPA	3.6
% submitting high school GPA	100
% graduated top 10% of class	39
% graduated top 25% of class	61
% graduated top 50% of class	85
% submitting high school rank	23

Important Dates

Early action	
Apply by	12/15
Notified by	1/31
Regular	
Apply by	2/15
Nonfall registration?	Yes

FINANCIAL FACTS

Annual tuition	$53,840
Food and housing	$20,290
Required fees (First-year)	$2,960 ($3,340)
Books and supplies	$1,000

SIENA UNIVERSITY

515 Loudon Road, Loudonville, NY 12211-1462 • Admissions: 518-783-2423

Survey Snapshot
Great off-campus food
Easy to get around campus
Intramural sports are popular

RATINGS

Quality of Life	**84**
Fire Safety	**91**
Green	**60***
Academic	**79**
Profs Interesting	**87**
Profs Accessible	**89**
Admissions	**85**
Financial Aid	**89**

CAMPUS LIFE

Type of school	Private
Affiliation	Roman Catholic
Environment	City

Students

Degree-seeking undergrad enrollment	3,100
% male/female/not reported	45/55/<1
% from out of state	15
% First-year live on campus	81
% Ugrads live on campus	69
# of fraternities	0
# of sororities	0
% Asian	6
% Black or African American	4
% Hispanic	11
% Native American	<1
% Pacific Islander	<1
% Race and/or ethnicity unknown	1
% Two or more races	4
% White	72
% International	3
# of countries represented	29

CAMPUS MENTAL HEALTH SERVICES

Offers mental health/wellness program	Yes
Mental health training available to students	Yes
Employs Chief Wellness Officer	Yes
Peer-to-peer mental health offerings	Yes
Counseling center has guidelines or accreditation	No
Mental health/well-being courses	Yes, for-credit

ACADEMICS

% students returning for sophomore year	83
% students graduating within 4 years	69
% students graduating within 6 years	75
Calendar	Semester
Student/faculty ratio	11:1
Most common class size 20–29.	(46%)
Most common lab/discussion size 10–19.	(77%)

Most Popular Majors

Psychology; Business/Commerce; Accounting

Applicants Often Prefer

Marist University, Sacred Heart University, State University of New York College at Oneonta, State University of New York—Binghamton University, State University of New York—Cortland, State University of New York—University at Albany, State University of New York—University at Buffalo, University of Connecticut

Applicants Rarely Prefer

Quinnipiac University, St. John's University (NY)

STUDENTS SAY "..."

Academics

Siena University offers a "welcoming environment, nice walkable campus, [and is] very generous in scholarships." Students are afforded the opportunity to "work on in-depth projects that require research, problem-solving, and collaboration." For example, "Siena has built a growing ecosystem of entrepreneurship resources, including programs that help students launch start-ups, develop prototypes, and work with local businesses." Undergrads also have access to "innovative classroom setups providing more of a seminar setting rather than a lecture setting." Additionally, "the labs are a great opportunity for hands-on learning with new technology such as advanced microscopes." Most professors manage to find a nice "balance between rigor and encouragement," though a few can be "painfully boring." However, "many of them make an effort to get to know us individually, asking about our goals, encouraging our interests, and checking in when they know we're juggling a lot." Another student chimes in, "They also create a very hospitable and safe environment where I feel comfortable talking to them about anything." Simply put, professors here "want to see you excel and if you work hard in class, they will recommend you for tons of opportunities, both within and outside of the university." But perhaps best of all, as graduation nears, students "are able to find help from alumni and the administration to obtain a job after Siena."

Campus Life

Students appreciate the "huge number of clubs to choose from" at Siena. These range from "mock trial team and Lost in Sound" (an a cappella group) to "intramural football and softball." The university also sponsors "events every week, whether that be food trucks on campus, therapy dogs, free giveaways, or even just giving out Boba." Additionally, students enjoy "club-sponsored movie nights, student government activities, improv shows, or late-night runs to the dining hall with friends." Nevertheless, a few undergrads lament that "on the weekends there's not much to do." Some attribute this to the fact that "the majority of the residential student body live in-state, so a lot of people go home very often." Others counter that there are still activities happening. For example, "Saturdays are spent at the rugby field where the berm gets packed and...[there's] a real community spirit." When it comes down to it, "spending time with friends is a big part of college...whether it's study sessions with them or just dinner in the hall." Another student sums up, "One of my favorite parts of campus life is how easy it is to run into people you know...It makes school feel close-knit in a way that's comforting."

Student Body

Overall, students at Siena think highly of their classmates, insisting they're "some of the most welcoming people [you'll] ever meet." As one individual explains, "My peers take their academics seriously, but they're equally committed to supporting one another, whether that's sharing study guides, saving a seat in the library or showing up to cheer on a friend at a performance or game." Some do caution that Siena can seem "not very... diverse," noting that "most students are white, straight, and some form of Christian." However, you'll certainly find peers who fall outside of those demographics. One student explains, "While the population is predominantly Christian and Catholic, as it is a Catholic university, I feel comfortable as a Jewish student and as a queer woman." But what undergrads say "stands out most is how genuinely curious everyone is, not just about their majors, but about the world, ideas, and each other. I'm surrounded by students who ask thoughtful questions, challenge assumptions, and care deeply about learning for its own sake." In turn, these individuals help foster "an environment that is non-competitive, and one where you build confidence in each other inside and outside of the classroom."

SIENA UNIVERSITY

Financial Aid: 518-783-2427 • E-Mail: admissions@siena.edu • Website: www.siena.edu

THE PRINCETON REVIEW SAYS

Admissions

The school reports that its standardized testing policy for use in admission for Fall 2026 is Test Optional. The Princeton Review suggests that interested applicants consult with the school for the most up-to-date standardized testing policies. *Very important factors considered include:* rigor of secondary school record, academic GPA. *Important factors considered include:* recommendation(s), interview. *Other factors considered include:* class rank, standardized test scores, application essay, extracurricular activities, talent/ability, character/personal qualities, first generation, alumni/ae relation, geographical residence, volunteer work, work experience, level of applicant's interest. High school diploma is required and GED is accepted. *Academic units required:* 4 English, 3 math, 3 science, 3 science labs, 2 language (other than English), 2 social studies, 2 history. *Academic units recommended:* 4 English, 4 math, 4 science, 4 science labs, 3 language (other than English), 2 social studies, 2 history.

Financial Aid

Students should submit: FAFSA; State aid form. Priority filing deadline is 11/15. The Princeton Review suggests that all financial aid forms be submitted as soon as possible. *Need-based scholarships/grants offered:* Federal Pell; Federal SEOG; State scholarships/grants; Private scholarships; College/university scholarship or grant aid from institutional funds. *Loan aid offered:* Federal Direct Subsidized Loans; Federal Direct Unsubsidized Loans; Direct PLUS loans. Admitted students will be notified of awards on or about 12/1. Federal Work-Study Program available. Institutional employment available.

The Inside Word

For incoming first-years, admissions officers look for a strong academic record. Academic interests and extracurricular activities also play a role. Prior to applying, a campus tour or participation in an admissions program is strongly encouraged.

THE SCHOOL SAYS

From the Admissions Office

"Located in Loudonville, New York—just 10 minutes from the state capital of Albany—the Siena experience is built for a new generation of leaders. The College offers a wide range of scholarship and financial aid opportunities, as well as customized internships. After all, a Siena education isn't something you get, it's something you get to do. Our 3,500 Saints have endless ways to reach their personal and professional goals and engage personally with top professors in a dynamic, customized learning environment. From internships to research to service, they get real world experience now, not later. The result: sought-after graduates prepared to succeed in an ever-changing global society. Hundreds of student life options ranging from Red Cross to rugby join with Siena's Division I athletic program to provide students the opportunity to get in the game, whatever their interests may be. Extensive study abroad programs and immersive service programs allow for discovery and reflection. Saints learn to lead by putting others first, thinking creatively, and developing innovative solutions in pursuit of the greater good. And it's what connects them to Siena, and each other, forever."

SELECTIVITY

# of total applicants	8,048
% of total applicants accepted	85
% of total acceptees attending	11
# of in-state applicants	7,100
% of in-state applicants accepted	85
# of out-of-state-applicants	921
% of applicants accepted from out of state	84
# of international applicants	25
% of international applicants accepted	88
# offered a place on the wait list	187
# admitted from wait list	7

First-Year Profile

Testing policy	Test Optional
Range SAT composite	1140–1430
Range SAT EBRW	580–710
Range SAT math	590–720
Range ACT composite	29–34
% submitting SAT scores	6
% submitting ACT scores	1
Average HS GPA	3.5
% submitting high school GPA	100
% graduated top 10% of class	22
% graduated top 25% of class	48
% graduated top 50% of class	86
% submitting high school rank	20

Important Dates

Early decision	
Apply by	11/15
Notified by	1/1
Early action	
Apply by	12/15
Notified by	Within one week of completion
Regular	
Apply by	2/15
Notified by	3/15
Nonfall registration?	Yes

FINANCIAL FACTS

Annual tuition	$48,300
Food and housing	$17,745
Required fees (First-year)	$1,400 ($2,253)
Books and supplies	$1,388
Average need-based scholarship (First-year)	$28,314 ($28,937)
% students with need rec. need-based scholarship or grant aid (First-year)	99 (100)
% students with need rec. non-need-based scholarship or grant aid (First-year)	93 (94)
% students with need rec. need-based self-help aid (First-year)	63 (56)
% students rec. any financial aid (First-year)	99 (93)
% UG borrow to pay for school	78
Average cumulative indebtedness	$43,859
% of students with need fully met (First-year)	39 (46)
Average % of student need met (First-year)	74 (76)

Simmons University

300 The Fenway, Boston, MA 02115 • Admissions: 617-521-2051

Survey Snapshot
Students aren't religious
Students love Boston, MA
Great off-campus food

RATINGS	
Quality of Life	79
Fire Safety	83
Green	60*
Academic	81
Profs Interesting	87
Profs Accessible	89
Admissions	87
Financial Aid	89

CAMPUS LIFE

Type of school	Private
Environment	Metropolis

Students

Degree-seeking undergrad enrollment	1,563
% male/female/not reported	0/81/19
% from out of state	31
% First-year live on campus	84
% Ugrads live on campus	59
# of fraternities	0
# of sororities	0
% Asian	11
% Black or African American	13
% Hispanic	17
% Native American	<1
% Pacific Islander	0
% Race and/or ethnicity unknown	4
% Two or more races	4
% White	45
% International	6
# of countries represented	6

CAMPUS MENTAL HEALTH SERVICES

Offers mental health/wellness program	Yes
Mental health training available to students	Yes
Employs Chief Wellness Officer	Yes
Peer-to-peer mental health offerings	No
Counseling center has guidelines or accreditation	No
Mental health/well-being courses	Yes, non-credit

ACADEMICS

% students returning for sophomore year	88
% students graduating within 4 years	72
% students graduating within 6 years	79
Calendar	Semester
Student/faculty ratio	8:1
Most common class size 10–19.	(47%)
Most common lab/discussion size 1–9.	(79%)

Most Popular Majors
Nursing Practice

Applicants Often Prefer
Boston University, Mount Holyoke College, Northeastern University

Applicants Sometimes Prefer
Regis College, Stonehill College, University of Massachusetts—Boston, Wheaton College (MA)

STUDENTS SAY "..."

Academics

Located in the middle of Boston, the women's-centered Simmons University is a liberal arts center, offering its undergraduates more than sixty majors and programs, including a well-known nursing school. Some courses require field trips and city exploration or internships relevant to the course, while others involve projects that "place students in volunteering jobs to work with the surrounding communities." "Classes involve significant amounts of discussions and presentations," and with small class sizes, students generally get to know all of their peers. Similarly, students enjoy "the ability to create strong personal relationships with professors and advisors" and say that teachers "truly are there for you as human beings, not just professors."

The workload is "heavy, but always doable" at Simmons, and clinicals tend to let students in earlier than many other schools would. "Labs go above and beyond" here, and the school incorporates video lectures into its courses "so that class periods can be more discussion- based." One student says, "Even as a first-year I have already been given multiple research opportunities that amaze and excite me." There are many accelerated programs to which undergraduate students can apply in order to achieve a graduate degree at a faster rate (many at Simmons go on to graduate school), and employers are well-aware of the school's curriculum, which requires every student to partake in "at least one internship, clinical, research [project], or other type of real-world learning." "When I say I attend Simmons, people know I have received a quality education," says a student.

Campus Life

There are two campuses at Simmons: academic and residential. The academic campus has "lots of places to study," such as the library, multicultural center, and cafés, but most students stay on the residential campus when classes aren't going on, and more than half live there. Most in this "nomadic bunch" like to use their free time to explore Boston and surrounding neighborhoods, including nearby Fenway Park. "I spend my days living my best city life," says a student. There are no parties on this "very academics-oriented" campus, especially given the "strict drug and alcohol policy." This is a campus of "all-around intellectuals who are serious about their careers after university [who] will more likely be found studying than partying." A lot of students work "either on campus or in hospitals or restaurants." Boston sporting events are popular pastimes, as is going to the gym, and "there is always something to do off campus." Almost all students go out into the city only on weekends, as "there usually isn't anything going on on-campus," and they get discounts or free admission to many events or institutions, like the Museum of Fine Arts and the Isabella Stewart Gardener Museum, "both of which are right down the street from campus."

Student Body

The women here are "generally highly liberal and outspoken," and "you have to find your niche." Students at Simmons are typically "advocates for a number of causes" and are extremely political. A huge number are healthcare majors, and everyone is "incredibly passionate and intelligent [and] invested in the community." This group is "very centered around acceptance of various identities as well as female empowerment," and "there is a theme of personal growth reflected in the gender identity."

Simmons University

Financial Aid: 617-521-2037 • E-Mail: ugadm@simmons.edu • Website: www.simmons.edu

THE PRINCETON REVIEW SAYS

Admissions

The school reports that its standardized testing policy for use in admission for Fall 2026 is Test Optional. The Princeton Review suggests that interested applicants consult with the school for the most up-to-date standardized testing policies. *Very important factors considered include:* rigor of secondary school record, academic GPA, application essay, recommendation(s). *Other factors considered include:* class rank, standardized test scores, interview, extracurricular activities, volunteer work, work experience. High school diploma is required and GED is accepted. *Academic units required:* 4 English, 4 math, 3 science, 3 language (other than English), 3 social studies, 3 history.

Financial Aid

Students should submit: FAFSA. The Princeton Review suggests that all financial aid forms be submitted as soon as possible. *Need-based scholarships/grants offered:* Federal Pell; Federal SEOG; State scholarships/grants; Private scholarships; College/university scholarship or grant aid from institutional funds. *Loan aid offered:* Federal Direct Subsidized Loans; Federal Direct Unsubsidized Loans; Direct PLUS loans; College/university loans from institutional funds. Admitted students will be notified of awards on a rolling basis beginning 1/20. Federal Work-Study Program available. Institutional employment available.

The Inside Word

Simmons evaluates prospective students on both academic strength and personal qualities, including community involvement or leadership. Applicants to Simmons should use their personal essays, letters of recommendation, and applications to show the admissions committee who they are as a person. Although a personal interview isn't required, it can be a great way to augment your application, as well as a chance to experience the unique environment at Simmons.

THE SCHOOL SAYS

From the Admissions Office

"Simmons University offers a transformative education that combines liberal arts, science, and the professions. We empower students who are intellectually curious, ambitious, and socially conscious to become everyday leaders in their careers, communities, and beyond.

"Located in the heart of Boston, Simmons is best known for its small classes, access to faculty, and internship and research opportunities. Students say that Simmons's location offers the best of both worlds—an intimate college experience in the heart of a vibrant city. Simmons's nearly 2,000 undergraduates love the fact that they can easily access the city's rich social and cultural resources but also come home to a safe, friendly campus.

"Simmons offers a learning experience that is highly collaborative and much more personal than that of large universities. Simmons professors include distinguished researchers, published authors, Fulbright scholars, health professionals, and community leaders. Seventy percent of faculty are women, and nearly 100 percent hold a terminal degree. They advise numerous government, nonprofit, and corporate organizations in the United States and in the world.

"To help students succeed, career support starts as soon as students step on campus and continues as an ongoing, lifelong service. Ninety-one percent of Simmons graduates are employed or in graduate school within six months of graduation. As the only women's university in Boston, employers see Simmons as a beacon of leadership with a reputation for professionalism and well-prepared graduates."

SELECTIVITY

# of total applicants	4,322
% of total applicants accepted	73
% of total acceptees attending	11
# of in-state applicants	2,135
% of in-state applicants accepted	78
# of out-of-state-applicants	1,329
% of applicants accepted from out of state	85
# of international applicants	858
% of international applicants accepted	42

First-Year Profile

Testing policy	Test Optional
Range SAT composite	1230–1360
Range SAT EBRW	620–730
Range SAT math	580–670
Range ACT composite	25–31
% submitting SAT scores	17
% submitting ACT scores	2
Average HS GPA	3.8
% submitting high school GPA	100
% graduated top 10% of class	31
% graduated top 25% of class	66
% graduated top 50% of class	92
% submitting high school rank	35

Important Dates

Early action	
Apply by	11/1
Notified by	12/15
Regular	
Notified by	Rolling, 12/15
Nonfall registration?	Yes

FINANCIAL FACTS

Annual tuition	$48,308
Food and housing	$18,960
Required fees	$1,340
Books and supplies	$1,280
Average need-based scholarship (First-year)	$38,303 ($40,403)
% students with need rec. need-based scholarship or grant aid (First-year)	99 (100)
% students with need rec. non-need-based scholarship or grant aid (First-year)	16 (15)
% students with need rec. need-based self-help aid (First-year)	82 (81)
% students rec. any financial aid (First-year)	95 (99)
% UG borrow to pay for school	79
Average cumulative indebtedness	$30,674
% of students with need fully met (First-year)	22 (20)
Average % of student need met (First-year)	85 (84)

Skidmore College

815 North Broadway, Saratoga Springs, NY 12866-1632 • Admissions: 518-580-5570

Survey Snapshot
Recreation facilities are great
Easy to get around campus
Lab facilities are great

RATINGS

Quality of Life	92
Fire Safety	99
Green	94
Academic	88
Profs Interesting	93
Profs Accessible	93
Admissions	94
Financial Aid	96

CAMPUS LIFE

Type of school	Private
Environment	Town

Students

Degree-seeking undergrad enrollment	2,709
% male/female/not reported	38/62/<1
% from out of state	66
% First-year from public high school	63
% First-year live on campus	99
% Ugrads live on campus	83
# of fraternities	0
# of sororities	0
% Asian	6
% Black or African American	4
% Hispanic	11
% Native American	<1
% Pacific Islander	<1
% Race and/or ethnicity unknown	2
% Two or more races	6
% White	64
% International	7
# of countries represented	60

CAMPUS MENTAL HEALTH SERVICES

Offers mental health/wellness program	Yes
Mental health training available to students	Yes
Employs Chief Wellness Officer	Yes
Peer-to-peer mental health offerings	Yes
Counseling center has guidelines or accreditation	Yes
Mental health/well-being courses	Yes, for-credit

ACADEMICS

% students returning for sophomore year	94
% students graduating within 4 years	74
% students graduating within 6 years	82
Calendar	Semester
Student/faculty ratio	8:1
Most common class size 10–19.	(53%)
Most common lab/discussion size 10–19.	(82%)

Most Popular Majors
Business/Commerce; Experimental Psychology; English Language and Literature

Applicants Often Prefer
Bowdoin College, Colby College, Connecticut College, Vassar College, Wesleyan College

Applicants Sometimes Prefer
Colgate University, Hamilton College, Middlebury College, New York University, Northeastern University, Oberlin College, Tufts University, University of Vermont

STUDENTS SAY "..."

Academics

Skidmore College "offers a strong liberal arts curriculum with abundant opportunities to engage professionally with coursework and fields of study." Students appreciate that creativity seems to be a foundation of academics, "with the arts being well mixed into all areas of study," and a "mind and hand" integration of classroom and experiential learning that offers a flexible curriculum. As a result, there are "many interdisciplinary experiences and projects" that students can use in plotting their educational path, along with "individualized support and care to their students" to get them there and a "very big emphasis on mental health awareness and advocacy."

Professors are "incredibly engaged in the material they are teaching" and succeed in "bringing it to life and encouraging passion for the subjects." Faculty "are very supportive and engaging" and "willing to support student learning outside the classroom." The school also taps the outside world for resources, and "does a great job bringing in visiting professionals to teach classes, lead workshops, and give lectures on campus that expand the learning goals in the classroom." There's also access to practical career training, as one student illustrates: "I trained in wilderness first aid, and they're offering an EMT course in the spring." Altogether, students receive "a foundation to understand the basics but most importantly…how to apply what [you] learn to real-world situations."

Campus Life

Skidmore students are "invested in extracurriculars" and are "enjoyers of the outdoors." They appreciate that "there are plenty of on-campus events run by cultural clubs or others" with "free food and free entertainment." There's also an Outing Club that offers structured events for the many students who "go hiking, skiing, [and take] day trips to [New York City]." Students also feel encouraged to get active because there are "really nice athletic facilities for athletes and non-athletes," with "plenty of opportunities to play pickup basketball or pretty much any sport casually." A student mentions that "[we] don't have a football team, but the ultimate Frisbee team functions like that socially." Everything "is so close together" on this cozy campus, which is "beautiful, especially in the fall," and students can easily "walk around in clothes they handmade in the Idea Lab and host celebratory events for the different cultures with which they identify." One student says, "There are so many things to do, and most students take those opportunities."

Student Body

Students here "are driven and tend to put schoolwork first," and are "highly motivated and care deeply about their academic performance." Most are also "involved with [the arts] in some way, even if it is not their primary area of study," and many "have two majors that don't seem to correlate thematically but end up tying together through creativity in unexpected ways." It follows that friend groups tend to be "very diverse here—less so based on interests, more so based on personalities," but "it's easy to strike up a conversation with someone new." That being said, the school is still intimate enough that "everyone knows everyone, and after four years here it's strange to be in a room where you don't know anybody." Everyone "comes from somewhere different and interesting and those attributes are reflected" in the student body, and "you can expect to meet a lot of people with diverse interests that bring them here." At Skidmore, "emphasis is placed on creative thought… and students are quick to deviate from popular trends," making for a crowd of "open-minded individuals with a good sense of individuality." Curiosity is an overarching theme, and those "who are not locked into a specific field tend to think very outside of the box and want to try new things." Overall, students "are incredibly proud of their backgrounds and their interests…[and] there is a great feeling of school spirit and pride."

Skidmore College

Financial Aid: 518-580-5750 • E-Mail: admissions@skidmore.edu • Website: www.skidmore.edu

THE PRINCETON REVIEW SAYS

Admissions

The school reports that its standardized testing policy for use in admission for Fall 2026 is Test Optional. The Princeton Review suggests that interested applicants consult with the school for the most up-to-date standardized testing policies. *Very important factors considered include:* rigor of secondary school record, academic GPA, character/personal qualities. *Important factors considered include:* class rank, application essay, recommendation(s), extracurricular activities, talent/ability, volunteer work, work experience. *Other factors considered include:* standardized test scores, first generation, geographical residence, level of applicant's interest. High school diploma is required and GED is accepted. *Academic units recommended:* 4 English, 4 math, 4 science, 3 science labs, 4 language (other than English), 4 social studies.

Financial Aid

Students should submit: CSS PROFILE. The Princeton Review suggests that all financial aid forms be submitted as soon as possible. *Need-based scholarships/grants offered:* Federal Pell; Federal SEOG; State scholarships/grants; Private scholarships; College/university scholarship or grant aid from institutional funds. *Loan aid offered:* Federal Direct Subsidized Loans; Federal Direct Unsubsidized Loans; Direct PLUS loans; State Loans. Admitted students will be notified of awards on or about 3/15. Federal Work-Study Program available. Institutional employment available.

The Inside Word

Admission to Skidmore is highly competitive, and the admissions staff carefully considers each applicant's academic background. Consistent with their motto ("Creative Thought Matters"), Skidmore carefully reviews a student's extracurricular talents, achievements, and passions when making decisions. Standardized tests are optional in most cases, and students should check with the school for exceptions. While admissions interviews aren't a requirement for Skidmore applicants, students may request a personal interview on campus or with an alum in their area.

THE SCHOOL SAYS

From the Admissions Office

"At Skidmore, we believe a great education is about putting academic theory and creative expression into practice; hence, our belief that creative thought matters. It's a place where faculty and students work together, then figure out how to use what they've learned to make a difference. This often leads to multidisciplinary approaches, where students carry more than one major, student-faculty research is common, most students study abroad, and service-learning courses, internships and community service are standard. Skidmore students develop into independent, creative problem-solvers who aren't restricted to looking at things in traditional ways. This personal journey starts with the First-Year Experience-forty seminars from which to choose, faculty and peer mentors and planned gatherings beyond the classroom. It's meant to ensure that first-year students hit the ground running on day one, connected and involved. When it comes to your major, you can choose from 44 offerings in the sciences, social sciences, arts and humanities, as well as pre-professional fields like management and business. Since we have no fraternities or sororities, student life centers on the 120 student clubs and organizations, which range from the Environmental Action Club to a cappella groups to snowboarding. Add to this the prominence of the arts, which has long set Skidmore apart. When they're not doing lab work in our new Center for Integrated Sciences, science classes can be found collaborating on exhibits at the Tang Museum. Hundreds of students perform, often in the Zankel Music Center. Enroll in dance courses. Participate in theater performances. Most are not even arts majors. Saratoga Springs offers a downtown brimming with shops, galleries, coffeehouses, and great restaurants. Boston, New York City, and Montreal are a three-hour car ride from campus. The Adirondacks, Berkshires, and Green Mountains provide opportunities for skiing, mountain biking, hiking, rockclimbing, and kayaking."

SELECTIVITY

# of total applicants	12,273
% of total applicants accepted	24
% of total acceptees attending	24
# of in-state applicants	2,636
% of in-state applicants accepted	28
# of out-of-state-applicants	4,872
% of applicants accepted from out of state	39
# of international applicants	4,765
% of international applicants accepted	6
# of early decision applicants	847
% of early decision applicants accepted	42
# offered a place on the wait list	2,360
# admitted from wait list	35

First-Year Profile

Testing policy	Test Optional
Range SAT composite	1360–1460
Range SAT EBRW	690–740
Range SAT math	650–730
Range ACT composite	31–34
% submitting SAT scores	25
% submitting ACT scores	8
% graduated top 10% of class	45
% graduated top 25% of class	70
% graduated top 50% of class	97
% submitting high school rank	17

Important Dates

Early decision	
Apply by	11/1
Notified by	Mid December
Other ED apply by	1/8
Other ED notified by	Mid February
Regular	
Apply by	1/8
Notified by	4/1
Nonfall registration?	No

FINANCIAL FACTS

Annual tuition	$69,210
Food and housing	$18,820
Required fees (First-year)	$1,220 ($1,370)
Books and supplies	$1,300
Average need-based scholarship (First-year)	$57,050 ($58,100)
% students with need rec. need-based scholarship or grant aid (First-year)	100 (100)
% students with need rec. non-need-based scholarship or grant aid (First-year)	4 (3)
% students with need rec. need-based self-help aid (First-year)	87 (87)
% students rec. any financial aid (First-year)	57 (64)
% UG borrow to pay for school	44
Average cumulative indebtedness	$29,458
% of students with need fully met (First-year)	86 (100)
Average % of student need met (First-year)	98 (100)

Smith College

Elm St., Northampton, MA 01063 • Admissions: 413-585-2500

Survey Snapshot
Lots of liberal students
Career services are great
Active student-run political groups

RATINGS

Quality of Life	92
Fire Safety	60*
Green	60*
Academic	87
Profs Interesting	95
Profs Accessible	89
Admissions	96
Financial Aid	97

CAMPUS LIFE

Type of school	Private
Environment	Town

Students

Degree-seeking undergrad enrollment	2,574
% male/female/not reported	0/100/0
% from out of state	82
% First-year from public high school	62
% First-year live on campus	100
% Ugrads live on campus	98
# of sororities	0
% Asian	10
% Black or African American	6
% Hispanic	14
% Native American	<1
% Pacific Islander	<1
% Race and/or ethnicity unknown	3
% Two or more races	7
% White	49
% International	13
# of countries represented	65

CAMPUS MENTAL HEALTH SERVICES

Offers mental health/wellness program	Yes
Mental health training available to students	No
Employs Chief Wellness Officer	NR
Peer-to-peer mental health offerings	NR
Counseling center has guidelines or accreditation	No
Mental health/well-being courses	NR

ACADEMICS

% students returning for sophomore year	95
% students graduating within 4 years	66
% students graduating within 6 years	86
Calendar	Semester
Student/faculty ratio	8:1
Most common class size 10–19.	(48%)

Most Popular Majors

Economics; Political Science and Government; Psychology

STUDENTS SAY "..."

Academics

Smith College is "an incredibly prestigious...and socially liberal" institution that places a premium on "academic freedom." Students here are encouraged to explore, "find and pursue [their] passions." To that end, there are no course requirements beyond a writing-intensive for first-years (and your major credits). This sense of autonomy even extends to the "self-scheduled finals" that allow students to take exam week at their own pace. Undergraduates are also quick to note that Smith is "one of the most prominent women's colleges in the country." They applaud the school's efforts in "build[ing] the self confidence of smart women" and note that "most classes, even in math and sciences, are very interdisciplinary and often have a feminist" slant. Additionally, students heap praise on their "inspiring, dynamic, accessible, and brilliant" professors. It's evident that Smith's faculty really "care deeply about students" and "take the time to get to know you on a first-name basis." They also excel at fostering "engaging [classes that] promote critical thought." Of course, learning goes on far beyond the college's hallowed academic halls. Smith maintains a "wonderful study abroad department" where students can choose from over 100 different programs on six continents. Students also benefit from the ability to "take classes at the other four schools nearby (UMass Amherst, Amherst College, Hampshire College, and Mount Holyoke College)" through the Five College Consortium. Perhaps most importantly, as graduation nears, undergrads can rely on an "excellent alumnae network" as well as a Career Development Office that does "everything in its power to help you get a job."

Campus Life

It's easy to understand why Smith students declare that their "quality of life is outstanding." After all, the college's "dorms are...beautiful houses" and the dining halls are a cut above, serving up delectable dishes like custard French toast and spicy chorizo shakshuka. Of course, there's far more to the Smith experience than this. Academics take precedence here and Smithies "strive to succeed in [their] classes." This means that they spend a lot of time "study[ing], writing papers, rehearsing, or practicing," along with attending various "lectures and symposiums." Outside of coursework, many of these idealistic students are involved with "community service and activism for global issues, women's rights, LGBTQ rights, the environment, and pretty much anything that fights oppression." When they need a break from studying, undergrads can enjoy "free movies and concerts, plays, speakers, sports events, and dances," ...and can register small house parties or attend "other college parties at surrounding campuses." They can also look forward to school traditions like Mountain Day, when the college president randomly cancels classes on a beautiful fall day.

Student Body

Undergrads at Smith don't deny that they prioritize their academics. Students arrive here ready to "study hard." And many admit that they've been known to get "ridiculously stressed" about their courses from time to time. As one student explains, "It's the nature of Smithies to be driven, but we all want to see our friends and housemates succeed as well." Of course, this go-getter attitude extends far beyond classwork; students "are passionate about everything they do." Undergrads also applaud the college's ability to attract a diverse student body, both in background and personality. At Smith, you'll find "a great mix of nerdy, edgy, and traditional" students with approximately one-third of undergrads identifying as a person of color and 67 different nationalities represented on campus. Students eagerly embrace this diversity noting that there's a "strong sense of community" and everyone "fits in easily." Additionally, "one thing all students have in common here is the will for women's empowerment and acceptance of any gender or sexual preference." Finally, while you can find students across the political spectrum, most Smithies hold "very liberal views," and many are "very conscious and aware, not only of their community but the world in general."

Smith College

Financial Aid: 413-585-2530 • E-Mail: admission@smith.edu • Website: www.smith.edu

THE PRINCETON REVIEW SAYS

Admissions

The school reports that its standardized testing policy for use in admission for Fall 2026 is Test Optional. The Princeton Review suggests that interested applicants consult with the school for the most up-to-date standardized testing policies. *Very important factors considered include:* rigor of secondary school record, academic GPA, application essay, recommendation(s), character/personal qualities. *Important factors considered include:* class rank, interview, extracurricular activities, talent/ability. *Other factors considered include:* standardized test scores, first generation, alumni/ae relation, volunteer work, work experience. High school diploma or equivalent is not required. *Academic units recommended:* 4 English, 3 math, 3 science, 3 science labs, 3 language (other than English), 2 history, 1 academic elective.

Financial Aid

Students should submit: FAFSA; Institution's own financial aid form; CSS PROFILE. Priority filing deadline is 1/25. The Princeton Review suggests that all financial aid forms be submitted as soon as possible. *Need-based scholarships/grants offered:* Federal Pell; Federal SEOG; State scholarships/grants; Private scholarships; College/university scholarship or grant aid from institutional funds. *Loan aid offered:* Federal Direct Subsidized Loans; Federal Direct Unsubsidized Loans; Direct PLUS loans. Admitted students will be notified of awards on or about 3/19. Federal Work-Study Program available. Institutional employment available.

The Inside Word

The type of application you provide to Smith doesn't matter—Common or Coalition—but the school's high levels of freedom mean that it does look closely at those submissions to ensure that it admits only those students it feels best have a chance to succeed. This means that you should be preparing for admission throughout your high school years, as your performance both in and out of school will be evaluated. You'll also have a slightly better chance of getting in if you're prepared to submit and commit to early decision. Make a point of highlighting your extracurriculars, either in your essay or the optional interview.

THE SCHOOL SAYS

From the Admissions Office

"Smith is a world-class, women's liberal arts and sciences college. For 150 years, we have been a force for change, transforming our society, our history, and the lives and leadership of women. We offer over 1000 courses in 83 areas of study. Our open curriculum gives you the freedom to discover your passion and purpose. A partner in the Five College Consortium, Smithies can also take advantage of four other nearby institutions: Amherst, Mount Holyoke, Hampshire, and the University of Massachusetts Amherst.

"Smith offers what you need to achieve your most ambitious goals—cutting-edge STEM facilities, high-end digital media studios, first-class performance spaces, a world-renowned art museum and women's history archive, and a remarkable library filled with flexible spaces and technology to bring scholarship to life. All students have access to guaranteed internship funding and can engage with research starting their first year at the Smith.

"Our vibrant student life helps Smithies form lasting friendships with each other, while our small class sizes encourage close connections and offer ample academic opportunities. With over 50,000 alums around the world, our students are supported and celebrated long after they graduate.

"Who you are and what you bring to our campus is really important. We're an institution founded on a mission of access and diversity for women who weren't allowed to attend elite institutions of higher education. That's still the heart of who we are at Smith."

SELECTIVITY

# of total applicants	8,102
% of total applicants accepted	22
% of total acceptees attending	38
# of in-state applicants	716
% of in-state applicants accepted	28
# of out-of-state-applicants	4,399
% of applicants accepted from out of state	33
# of international applicants	2,987
% of international applicants accepted	5
# of early decision applicants	1,107
% of early decision applicants accepted	34
# offered a place on the wait list	1,440
# admitted from wait list	0

First-Year Profile

Testing policy	Test Optional
Range SAT composite	1420–1520
Range SAT EBRW	720–760
Range SAT math	690–760
Range ACT composite	32–34
% submitting SAT scores	30
% submitting ACT scores	15
Average HS GPA	4.0
% submitting high school GPA	67
% graduated top 10% of class	74
% graduated top 25% of class	96
% graduated top 50% of class	100
% submitting high school rank	29

Important Dates

Early decision	
Apply by	11/15
Notified by	Mid December
Other ED apply by	1/5
Other ED notified by	Late January
Regular	
Apply by	1/15
Notified by	4/1
Nonfall registration?	Yes

FINANCIAL FACTS

Annual tuition	$70,460
Food and housing	$24,520
Required fees	$308
Books and supplies	$800
Average need-based scholarship (First-year)	$70,643 ($73,031)
% students with need rec. need-based scholarship or grant aid (First-year)	99 (99)
% students with need rec. non-need-based scholarship or grant aid (First-year)	12 (7)
% students with need rec. need-based self-help aid (First-year)	84 (79)
% students rec. any financial aid (First-year)	71 (70)
% UG borrow to pay for school	57
Average cumulative indebtedness	$14,383
% of students with need fully met (First-year)	100 (100)
Average % of student need met (First-year)	100 (100)

SOUTHERN METHODIST UNIVERSITY

6425 Boaz Lane, Dallas, TX 75205 • Admissions: 214-768-2058

Survey Snapshot
Students get along with local community
Students love Dallas, TX
Frats and sororities are popular

RATINGS

Quality of Life	87
Fire Safety	90
Green	60*
Academic	87
Profs Interesting	92
Profs Accessible	96
Admissions	91
Financial Aid	93

CAMPUS LIFE

Type of school	Private
Affiliation	Methodist
Environment	Metropolis

Students

Degree-seeking undergrad enrollment	7,530
% male/female/not reported	49/51/0
% from out of state	53
% First-year from public high school	43
% First-year live on campus	96
% Ugrads live on campus	45
# of fraternities (% join)	15 (36)
# of sororities (% join)	13 (45)
% Asian	8
% Black or African American	5
% Hispanic	20
% Native American	<1
% Pacific Islander	<1
% Race and/or ethnicity unknown	4
% Two or more races	5
% White	54
% International	4
# of countries represented	62

CAMPUS MENTAL HEALTH SERVICES

Offers mental health/wellness program	Yes
Mental health training available to students	Yes
Employs Chief Wellness Officer	No
Peer-to-peer mental health offerings	No
Counseling center has guidelines or accreditation	Yes
Mental health/well-being courses	NR

ACADEMICS

% students returning for sophomore year	91
% students graduating within 4 years	76
% students graduating within 6 years	83
Calendar	Semester
Student/faculty ratio	11:1
Most common class size 10–19.	(37%)
Most common lab/discussion size 20–29.	(31%)

Most Popular Majors
Finance; Psychology; Economics

Applicants Often Prefer
Duke University, University of Southern California, Vanderbilt University

Applicants Sometimes Prefer
Tulane University, Boston College, University of Miami

Applicants Rarely Prefer
Baylor University, Texas Christian University

STUDENTS SAY "..."

Academics

Thanks to the "strong traditions" and "top academics" of Southern Methodist University, graduates—especially those from the "phenomenal business school"—are well-prepared to make a positive impact on the world. Students praise the academic process, which is filled with "fun and interesting courses," and which places students in "a close-knit community of the intellectually elite." This mid-size private university provides "a wealth of academic resources...[and] a flood of opportunities for those who want them," allowing SMU to lead the way for the Dallas-Fort Worth area in developing innovative industries and initiatives in semiconductors, biotechnology, clean energy, precision medicine, and AI. Students find their coursework to be synced "to what you'll face in the real world," aided no doubt by the fact that many professors are "incredibly gifted in their fields" and have real-world experience in the subjects they teach. They're also described as "exceptional communicators" who "love interacting with students," all of which allows them to better "offer real-life connections to the material we learn." As one enrollee puts it, professors "are willing to put in extra time to convey the material" and "will change their schedule to accommodate people." The "incredible alumni support" at SMU provides excellent connections into the business world (among others), and three "dedicated career services centers" help students find a job to further their career path. Since many attend the university for the Cox School of Business, internship seekers and graduating students who want to stay in Dallas will appreciate that the school is ideally located "to secure great jobs with Fortune 500 companies right here in Dallas." The school's administration also "understands that studying abroad, internships, extracurriculars, etc., also play a crucial role in developing students into the adults and professionals they want to become."

Campus Life

There's no shortage of things to do at and around SMU. Students will find everything from foosball matches in Klyde Warren Park, SMU football games, and "boulevarding" ("basically tailgating but on steroids") to the "amazing arts and restaurant scene around campus," the "fine dining and dancing" in uptown Dallas, and the museums in the Dallas Arts District, which are common destinations for walking tours. A large portion of every SMU student's time is devoted to their studies (and preparing for their careers) and many are "definitely wanting to become leaders in their field or profession." Students take their academics seriously, but they also value socializing and have a "vibrant social life." One student notes that "There is always a social event every weekend night to blow off steam." And although some students describe wanting "less emphasis on Greek life," they do acknowledge there are plenty of extracurricular organizations at SMU and that students "are involved...and have fun a lot."

Student Body

On the whole, the student body is "happy and leads a balanced life." Some students at SMU "tend to be a bit preppy," polite, and come from "influential backgrounds," although plenty of students "work a lot for pay or do internships." SMU students "are very busy people, and they prefer it that way," says one student. These "motivated, outgoing," people "thrive on leadership" and are "dedicated to academics and involvement, both at SMU and in the greater community."

SOUTHERN METHODIST UNIVERSITY

Financial Aid: 214-768-5555 • E-Mail: ugadmission@smu.edu • Website: www.smu.edu

THE PRINCETON REVIEW SAYS

Admissions

The school reports that its standardized testing policy for use in admission for Fall 2026 is Test Optional. The Princeton Review suggests that interested applicants consult with the school for the most up-to-date standardized testing policies. *Very important factors considered include:* rigor of secondary school record, academic GPA, application essay, recommendation(s). *Important factors considered include:* class rank, standardized test scores, extracurricular activities, talent/ability, character/personal qualities. *Other factors considered include:* first generation, alumni/ae relation, volunteer work, work experience, level of applicant's interest. High school diploma is required and GED is not accepted. *Academic units required:* 4 English, 3 math, 3 science, 2 science labs, 2 language (other than English), 3 social studies. *Academic units recommended:* 4 English, 4 math, 3 science, 2 science labs, 3 language (other than English), 3 history, 3 academic electives.

Financial Aid

Students should submit: FAFSA; CSS PROFILE. The Princeton Review suggests that all financial aid forms be submitted as soon as possible. *Need-based scholarships/grants offered:* Federal Pell; Federal SEOG; State scholarships/grants; Private scholarships; College/university scholarship or grant aid from institutional funds. *Loan aid offered:* Federal Direct Subsidized Loans; Federal Direct Unsubsidized Loans; Direct PLUS loans; State Loans. Admitted students will be notified of awards on a rolling basis beginning 12/15. Federal Work-Study Program available. Institutional employment available.

The Inside Word

SMU boasts a potent combination: high-caliber academics, a desirable location, and a beautiful campus. No surprise then that gaining admission is challenging, and growing more so all the time. Solid high school grades and a compelling list of extracurricular activities will usually do the trick. "Special talent" students—artists and athletes in particular—can make up for academic deficiencies; those in the arts must undergo an audition/portfolio review, while promising athletes are scouted.

THE SCHOOL SAYS

From the Admissions Office

"At Southern Methodist University, we define excellence through student impact. Guided by a bold vision and enterprising spirit, SMU brings together hardworking students, distinguished faculty and strong institutional partnerships to create a university meaningfully connected to the world beyond campus. Our academic approach is grounded in rigor, interdisciplinary exploration and a clear commitment to what matters most: academic excellence, career preparedness, principled leadership and lifelong community. From the admission process onward, SMU is dedicated to expanding access through generous, merit-based scholarships and financial resources that make a nationally recognized education attainable. Situated in one of the nation's fastest-growing metropolitan areas, Dallas offers SMU students exceptional access to internships, research initiatives, entrepreneurship and cross-sector collaboration. Our liberal arts foundation fosters intellectual engagement, enabling the opportunity to pursue multiple academic interests and graduate with the adaptability employers seek. Small classes and close faculty mentorship place students at the center of discovery, with opportunities to engage in research and applied learning as early as the first year. Innovation and entrepreneurship are integral to our culture, supported by resources such as the SMU Incubator and experiential learning opportunities across campus. Through distinctive collaborations including the George W. Bush Presidential Center and the Tate Lecture Series, students engage with global leaders and diverse perspectives. SMU graduates emerge prepared not only for professional success, but to lead with integrity, creativity and purpose in a rapidly changing world."

SELECTIVITY

# of total applicants	24,053
% of total applicants accepted	48
% of total acceptees attending	15
# of in-state applicants	12,254
% of in-state applicants accepted	41
# of out-of-state-applicants	9,805
% of applicants accepted from out of state	60
# of international applicants	1,994
% of international applicants accepted	27
# of early decision applicants	528
% of early decision applicants accepted	80
# offered a place on the wait list	4,249
# admitted from wait list	243

First-Year Profile

Testing policy	Test Optional
Range SAT composite	1360–1470
Range SAT EBRW	670–730
Range SAT math	670–750
Range ACT composite	31–34
% submitting SAT scores	9
% submitting ACT scores	9
Average HS GPA	3.7
% submitting high school GPA	100
% graduated top 10% of class	49
% graduated top 25% of class	79
% graduated top 50% of class	94
% submitting high school rank	24

Important Dates

Early decision	
Apply by	11/1
Notified by	12/31
Other ED apply by	1/15
Other ED notified by	3/1
Early action	
Apply by	11/1
Notified by	12/31
Regular	
Apply by	7/31
Notified by	4/1
Nonfall registration?	Yes

FINANCIAL FACTS

Annual tuition	$63,736
Food and housing	$20,834
Required fees	$8,080
Books and supplies	$888
Average need-based scholarship (First-year)	$52,260 ($56,396)
% students with need rec. need-based scholarship or grant aid (First-year)	98 (98)
% students with need rec. non-need-based scholarship or grant aid (First-year)	29 (33)
% students with need rec. need-based self-help aid (First-year)	74 (71)
% students rec. any financial aid (First-year)	70 (72)
% UG borrow to pay for school	30
Average cumulative indebtedness	$41,290
% of students with need fully met (First-year)	48 (59)
Average % of student need met (First-year)	88 (90)

SOUTHWESTERN UNIVERSITY

1001 East University Avenue, Georgetown, TX 78627-0770 • Admissions: 512-863-1200

Survey Snapshot
Students are happy
Internships are widely available
Class discussions encouraged

RATINGS

Quality of Life	86
Fire Safety	97
Green	60*
Academic	86
Profs Interesting	98
Profs Accessible	95
Admissions	90
Financial Aid	90

CAMPUS LIFE

Type of school	Private
Affiliation	Methodist
Environment	Town

Students

Degree-seeking undergrad enrollment	1,430
% male/female/not reported	45/55/0
% from out of state	11
% First-year from public high school	75
% First-year live on campus	97
% Ugrads live on campus	67
# of fraternities (% join)	4 (32)
# of sororities (% join)	6 (34)
% Asian	3
% Black or African American	7
% Hispanic	30
% Native American	<1
% Pacific Islander	<1
% Race and/or ethnicity unknown	6
% Two or more races	4
% White	47
% International	2
# of countries represented	20

CAMPUS MENTAL HEALTH SERVICES

Offers mental health/wellness program	Yes
Mental health training available to students	Yes
Employs Chief Wellness Officer	No
Peer-to-peer mental health offerings	No
Counseling center has guidelines or accreditation	Yes
Mental health/well-being courses	No

ACADEMICS

% students returning for sophomore year	83
% students graduating within 4 years	66
% students graduating within 6 years	74
Calendar	Semester
Student/faculty ratio	11:1
Most common class size 10–19.	(49%)
Most common lab/discussion size 10–19.	(54%)

Most Popular Majors
Kinesiology and Exercise Science; Psychology; Business/Commerce

Applicants Often Prefer
Texas A&M University—College Station, Trinity University, University of Texas at Austin

Applicants Sometimes Prefer
Austin College, Baylor University

STUDENTS SAY "..."

Academics

Southwestern University is "academically driven to produce not just educated people to work in various fields, but future academics." Its flexible curriculum promotes intellectual exploration rather than only knowledge accumulation. The school's interdisciplinary Paideia approach emphasizes "finding all sorts of connections with everything you learn" across the liberal arts, linking real-world experiences, research, and communities. "I have been able to connect so much of my knowledge in fairly different classes," says one student. Students are encouraged to "think and develop a stance every chance they get." Classrooms foster creative pedagogy, as demonstrated by a student who enjoyed "doing math in a group and not in a lecture." Nearly three-quarters of students engage in experiential learning or clinical placements, and the Center for Career & Professional Development "is very helpful for student internships, networking, and jobs post-graduation." Faculty members often go beyond "the teaching norm to engage students, from having classes outside to creating activities and assignments...[enabling] students to have a more hands-on and memorable experience." Students say this is "a very tight-knit community, meaning you can talk with your professors very easily," class discussions "both engage students' opinions of the material with the professor and foster unique and important dialogue." One of Southwestern's greatest strengths is its professors. As one student says, "Their commitment to fostering curiosity and critical thinking is evident in how they challenge students to engage with complex ideas and push the boundaries of their understanding."

Campus Life

Students say, "There is never a dull moment" at SU, highlighting the "abundance of amenities and events" available on campus. Since "academics are the top priority of most individuals at SU" and "studying takes center stage," many students "try to get their social time while being productive (studying at the same time, club activities)." So, while "the days are very busy," students use the weekends as a "time for exploring the town and doing outdoor activities for fun." For instance, "lots of kids like to play pickleball," other popular activities include volleyball, a garden club, horseback riding, and rock climbing. There are numerous student organizations and clubs for almost every interest. One student notes, "I appreciate the organizations that offer opportunities for community service, as well as the social-justice-oriented groups that help make campus better for marginalized groups." While there is plenty to do on campus, students also add, "We're not that far from Austin, so if you have transportation, you have a lot of options."

Student Body

Southwestern students are "a dynamic and eclectic mix of individuals united by a shared passion for learning and personal growth." There is "a large queer community as well as a strong sense of social justice throughout the school," fostering an inclusive environment where "everyone is their own true person." At SU, "you'll find students from diverse backgrounds,...bringing their cultures, perspectives, and ideas into every conversation," almost everyone is "very kind and respectful" of other viewpoints. At Southwestern, every student is "seen and heard, and resources can be devoted to every student in need." The smaller student population creates "a unique sense of community at Southwestern," as students "all know each other from class/events, and are very friendly with everyone we come across." Overall, students find this to be a "vibrant and supportive community" of "involved, communicative, productive, and supportive" students. And while no place is perfect, the "majority of the people here are absolutely lovely."

SOUTHWESTERN UNIVERSITY

Financial Aid: 512-863-1259 • E-Mail: admission@southwestern.edu • Website: www.southwestern.edu

THE PRINCETON REVIEW SAYS

Admissions

The school reports that its standardized testing policy for use in admission for Fall 2026 is Test Optional. The Princeton Review suggests that interested applicants consult with the school for the most up-to-date standardized testing policies. *Very important factors considered include:* rigor of secondary school record, class rank, academic GPA, standardized test scores, application essay, recommendation(s). *Important factors considered include:* interview, extracurricular activities, talent/ability, character/personal qualities, first generation, alumni/ae relation, geographical residence, state residency, volunteer work, level of applicant's interest. *Other factors considered include:* religious affiliation/commitment, work experience. High school diploma is required and GED is accepted. *Academic units required:* 4 English, 4 math, 3 science, 2 science labs, 2 language (other than English), 2 social studies, 1 history, 1 academic elective. *Academic units recommended:* 4 English, 4 math, 4 science, 3 science labs, 3 language (other than English), 3 social studies, 1 history, 1 academic elective.

Financial Aid

Students should submit: FAFSA. Priority filing deadline is 3/1. The Princeton Review suggests that all financial aid forms be submitted as soon as possible. *Need-based scholarships/grants offered:* Federal Pell; Federal SEOG; State scholarships/grants; Private scholarships; College/university scholarship or grant aid from institutional funds. *Loan aid offered:* Federal Direct Subsidized Loans; Federal Direct Unsubsidized Loans; Direct PLUS loans; State Loans; College/university loans from institutional funds. Admitted students will be notified of awards on a rolling basis beginning 12/2. Federal Work-Study Program available. Institutional employment available.

The Inside Word

Successful applicants to Southwestern University demonstrate intellectual curiosity and a strong desire to participate in an active collegiate community. Students need to be well-rounded and highly motivated. The vast majority of those who are accepted are in the top quarter of their class and have above-average standardized test scores.

THE SCHOOL SAYS

From the Admissions Office

"For nearly two centuries Southwestern University has stood proudly as one of the nation's oldest and finest liberal arts institutions. Our beautiful, tree-lined residential campus encompasses more than 700 acres featuring spacious sports and recreational facilities, multiple research laboratories, two live-performance theaters, and countless outdoor places to study, relax or socialize. Recognized for our commitment to sustainable, eco-friendly practices, our campus was one of the first in the nation to meet 100 percent of its electric needs from renewable wind power, and since 1972 we've nourished our landscapes and athletic fields with recycled water.

"Throughout campus and in the world beyond our students make meaningful connections across disciplines, cultures, and experiences through our unique Paideia approach—a curriculum that allows to students to chart a course that best suits their passions and life goals as they develop creative, critical thinking skills that make them adaptable to any challenge or opportunity. The results are impressive: less than a year after graduation, 98 percent of Southwestern students are either employed, attending a professional school or pursuing advanced studies. But while you're at Southwestern you should also know you have the best of all worlds for some good times, whether it's a relaxing stroll through Georgetown's historic town square, spending a day on the crystal-clear San Gabriel River, or enjoying an evening reveling in Austin's live music scene. A bright future begins here, right in the heart of Texas."

SELECTIVITY

# of total applicants	5,879
% of total applicants accepted	43
% of total acceptees attending	14
# of in-state applicants	4,388
% of in-state applicants accepted	51
# of out-of-state-applicants	640
% of applicants accepted from out of state	44
# of international applicants	851
% of international applicants accepted	6
# of early decision applicants	29
% of early decision applicants accepted	76
# offered a place on the wait list	65
# admitted from wait list	14

First-Year Profile

Testing policy	Test Optional
Range SAT composite	1170–1340
Range SAT EBRW	590–690
Range SAT math	560–670
Range ACT composite	24–30
% submitting SAT scores	46
% submitting ACT scores	13
Average HS GPA	3.5
% submitting high school GPA	100
% graduated top 10% of class	35
% graduated top 25% of class	61
% graduated top 50% of class	90
% submitting high school rank	54

Important Dates

Early decision	
Apply by	11/1
Notified by	12/1
Early action	
Apply by	12/1
Notified by	3/1
Regular	
Apply by	2/1
Notified by	4/1
Nonfall registration?	No

FINANCIAL FACTS

Annual tuition	$59,648
Food and housing	$17,432
Required fees (First-year)	$550 ($750)
Books and supplies	$1,250
Average need-based scholarship (First-year)	$46,570 ($48,531)
% students with need rec. need-based scholarship or grant aid (First-year)	99 (98)
% students with need rec. non-need-based scholarship or grant aid (First-year)	60 (96)
% students with need rec. need-based self-help aid (First-year)	81 (76)
% students rec. any financial aid (First-year)	97 (98)
% UG borrow to pay for school	56
Average cumulative indebtedness	$29,241
% of students with need fully met (First-year)	27 (32)
Average % of student need met (First-year)	87 (93)

SPELMAN COLLEGE

350 Spelman Lane, Atlanta, GA 30314 • Admissions: 404-270-5193

Survey Snapshot
Lots of liberal students
Lab facilities are great
Students are very religious

RATINGS

Quality of Life	78
Fire Safety	75
Green	60*
Academic	81
Profs Interesting	83
Profs Accessible	84
Admissions	92
Financial Aid	79

CAMPUS LIFE

Type of school	Private
Environment	Metropolis

Students

Degree-seeking undergrad enrollment	2,708
% male/female/not reported	0/100/0
% from out of state	75
% First-year live on campus	99
% Ugrads live on campus	54
# of sororities (% join)	4 (5)
% Asian	1
% Black or African American	97
% Hispanic	0
% Native American	1
% Pacific Islander	<1
% Race and/or ethnicity unknown	0
% Two or more races	0
% White	<1
% International	<1
# of countries represented	8

CAMPUS MENTAL HEALTH SERVICES

Offers mental health/wellness program	Yes
Mental health training available to students	No
Employs Chief Wellness Officer	NR
Peer-to-peer mental health offerings	NR
Counseling center has guidelines or accreditation	No
Mental health/well-being courses	NR

ACADEMICS

% students returning for sophomore year	94
% students graduating within 4 years	70
% students graduating within 6 years	78
Calendar	Semester
Student/faculty ratio	11:1
Most common class size 10–19.	(36%)
Most common lab/discussion size 10–19.	(60%)

Most Popular Majors
Psychology; Health Services/Allied Health/Health Sciences; Biology/Biological Sciences

Applicants Often Prefer
Clark Atlanta University, Georgia State University, Howard University, North Carolina A&T State University, Xavier University of Louisiana

Applicants Sometimes Prefer
Kennesaw State University, Louisiana State University—Baton Rouge, Temple University, Tennessee State University, University of Illinois at Urbana—Champaign

STUDENTS SAY "..."

Academics

A historically Black women's institution, Spelman College has built a strong reputation for "molding intelligent, goal-oriented young ladies into determined, successful, free-thinking women." Many prospective students are attracted to the school's "powerful history," including the "long list of successful, educated, strong Black women who have attended Spelman College" during the century since its founding. Once on campus, students are happy to report that Spelman's "professors are committed to the mission of the school," and they really "bring out the best" in their students. In the classroom, students are "encouraged to state our opinions," and professors "allow room for us to challenge and discuss what they present." You'll definitely work hard in this "challenging academic environment," because professors "do not allow for even a minute amount of slacking when it comes to completing assignments and being on time for class." Fortunately, there are "many academic resources available to help us, such as tutoring services and a writing center." Plus, the majority of Spelman professors "take additional time outside of instructional time to assist their students" with course work. Of particular note, Spelman is "very focused on the sciences and improving the number of African American women in this field, and they offer many facilities, faculty, and opportunities" for advanced study. As graduation approaches, the "Career Counseling Center is extremely strong and has helped numerous students find employment and graduate school placements." While the future looks bright for Spelman grads, many say this private institution could better serve its students by providing "more money for scholarships and financial aid."

Campus Life

There's a "strong sense of tradition and loyalty" on the Spelman campus, and most students are deeply involved in the community. From service groups to sororities, "there are so many organizations and clubs that you're bound to find one that fits you." There are tons of "opportunities to obtain leadership positions" outside the classroom, and many students are "very involved in campus life." A first-year student details, "In my freshman year already, I've walked in a fashion show, I was crowned Miss Glee Club, I write for the campus newspaper." There's a constant buzz of activity on campus, and "informational forums, career fairs, college fairs, performances, and sporting events are at the forefront of everyone's campus life." Socially, "Greek life is quite important at Spelman College, but isn't a must." Even if you don't join a sorority, "there are a lot of social events on campus," and two other historically Black colleges, Clark Atlanta and Morehouse, "are only inches away." Spelman undergrads say, "The camaraderie between the schools is great," and "joint homecoming with Morehouse is the highlight of the entire year." Off campus, students "go skating, bowling, and to Six Flags Over Georgia, as well as to Atlanta Falcons, Hawks, and Braves [games]." Nearby, Atlantic Station is home to "a major movie theater, shopping, [and] restaurants."

Student Body

Spelman College is "full of warm, welcoming, sisterly, and highly educated African American women." A unique environment, "Spelman College offers a chance for African American women to be the majority," and students appreciate being "surrounded and empowered by other young, intelligent, and goal-oriented women like myself." At the same time, "the institution promotes diversity within the student body," and Spelman women "come in all shapes and sizes and from all walks of life, though linked by our African descent. Anyone can find their place here." Confidence and individuality are prized at Spelman, and the typical undergraduate "speaks her mind, wears what she wants, [and] is comfortable in her own skin, yet she has empathy and a strong sense of social justice." Many students "love to do service for the community" and are involved in philanthropic projects around Atlanta. Spelman women are "hardworking and focused on academics." However, most are "excellent at balancing a full course load and an active social life."

SPELMAN COLLEGE

Financial Aid: 404-270-5212 • E-Mail: admiss@spelman.edu • Website: www.spelman.edu

THE PRINCETON REVIEW SAYS

Admissions

The school reports that its standardized testing policy for use in admission for Fall 2026 is Test Optional. The Princeton Review suggests that interested applicants consult with the school for the most up-to-date standardized testing policies. *Very important factors considered include:* rigor of secondary school record, academic GPA, application essay, extracurricular activities. *Important factors considered include:* recommendation(s), character/personal qualities, volunteer work, work experience. *Other factors considered include:* class rank, standardized test scores, talent/ability, first generation, alumni/ae relation, geographical residence, state residency, level of applicant's interest. High school diploma is required and GED is accepted. *Academic units required:* 4 English, 2 math, 3 science, 1 science lab, 2 language (other than English), 2 social studies, 2 history. *Academic units recommended:* 4 English, 4 math, 4 science, 1 science lab, 2 language (other than English), 3 social studies, 2 history, 7 computer science.

Financial Aid

Students should submit: FAFSA. Priority filing deadline is 3/1. The Princeton Review suggests that all financial aid forms be submitted as soon as possible. *Need-based scholarships/grants offered:* Federal SEOG; State scholarships/grants; College/university scholarship or grant aid from institutional funds; United Negro College Fund; Federal Pell; Private scholarships. *Loan aid offered:* Federal Direct Subsidized Loans; Federal Direct Unsubsidized Loans; Direct PLUS loans. Admitted students will be notified of awards on a rolling basis beginning 3/15. Federal Work-Study Program available. Institutional employment available.

The Inside Word

The best way to prepare for admission to Spelman is to pursue a strong, precollege academic curriculum during high school, as the average high school GPA for admission is around 3.9. Students who are particularly interested in Spelman have two early application options: early decision, which is binding, and early action, which is nonbinding, but allows students to receive a response more quickly.

THE SCHOOL SAYS

From the Admissions Office

"As an outstanding Historically Black College for women, Spelman strives for academic excellence in liberal arts education. This predominantly residential private college provides students with an academic climate conducive to the full development of their intellectual and leadership potential. The college is a member of the Atlanta University Center Consortium, and Spelman students enjoy the benefits of a small college while having access to the resources of the other three participating institutions. The purpose extends beyond intellectual development and professional career preparation of students. It seeks to develop the total person. The college provides an academic and social environment that strengthens those qualities that enable women to be self-confident as well as culturally and spiritually enriched. This environment attempts to instill in students both an appreciation for the multicultural communities of the world and a sense of responsibility for bringing about positive change in those communities."

SELECTIVITY

# of total applicants	12,023
% of total applicants accepted	25
% of total acceptees attending	24
# of early decision applicants	439
% of early decision applicants accepted	29
# offered a place on the wait list	1,140
# admitted from wait list	0

First-Year Profile

Testing policy	Test Optional
Range SAT composite	1130–1240
Range SAT EBRW	590–680
Range SAT math	520–640
Range ACT composite	22–29
% submitting SAT scores	23
% submitting ACT scores	16
Average HS GPA	3.9
% submitting high school GPA	98
% graduated top 10% of class	35
% graduated top 25% of class	69
% graduated top 50% of class	92
% submitting high school rank	25

Important Dates

Early decision	
Apply by	11/1
Early action	
Apply by	11/1
Regular	
Apply by	2/1
Notified by	4/1
Nonfall registration?	Yes

FINANCIAL FACTS

Annual tuition	$28,207
Food and housing	$18,091
Required fees	$3,349
Books and supplies	$1,500
Average need-based scholarship (First-year)	$18,643 ($16,508)
% students with need rec. need-based scholarship or grant aid (First-year)	57 (62)
% students with need rec. non-need-based scholarship or grant aid (First-year)	10 (6)
% students with need rec. need-based self-help aid (First-year)	14 (18)
% students rec. any financial aid (First-year)	63 (96)
% UG borrow to pay for school	48
Average cumulative indebtedness	$42,568
% of students with need fully met (First-year)	11 (11)
Average % of student need met (First-year)	35 (26)

Stanford University

450 Jane Stanford Way, Stanford, CA 94305 • Admissions: 650-723-6050

Survey Snapshot
Classroom facilities are great
Great financial aid
Diverse student types interact on campus

RATINGS

Quality of Life	93
Fire Safety	86
Green	99
Academic	92
Profs Interesting	90
Profs Accessible	94
Admissions	99
Financial Aid	98

CAMPUS LIFE

Type of school	Private
Environment	City

Students

Degree-seeking undergrad enrollment	7,289
% male/female/not reported	49/51/0
% from out of state	56
% First-year from public high school	58
% First-year live on campus	100
% Ugrads live on campus	93
# of fraternities (% join)	15 (22)
# of sororities (% join)	10 (28)
% Asian	31
% Black or African American	6
% Hispanic	16
% Native American	1
% Pacific Islander	<1
% Race and/or ethnicity unknown	<1
% Two or more races	9
% White	24
% International	13
# of countries represented	104

CAMPUS MENTAL HEALTH SERVICES

Offers mental health/wellness program	Yes
Mental health training available to students	No
Employs Chief Wellness Officer	NR
Peer-to-peer mental health offerings	NR
Counseling center has guidelines or accreditation	No
Mental health/well-being courses	NR

ACADEMICS

% students returning for sophomore year	97
% students graduating within 4 years	45
% students graduating within 6 years	92
Calendar	Quarter
Student/faculty ratio	10:1
Most common class size 10–19.	(36%)
Most common lab/discussion size 1–9.	(54%)

Most Popular Majors

Computer Science; Economics; Human Biology; Symbolic Systems; Mathematics

Applicants Also Look At

Brown University, California Institute of Technology, Columbia University, Duke University, Harvard College, Massachusetts Institute of Technology, Princeton University, University of California—Los Angeles, University of Southern California, Yale University

STUDENTS SAY "..."

Academics

As one of the preeminent institutions of higher education and research on the West Coast, Stanford University is a magnet for both aspiring and established scholars looking to learn in a place where "the support for students (residential, emotional, academic) is unrivaled." Research opportunities abound for Stanford students. As one student says, "At Stanford, anything is possible; I've lived on a schooner with faculty studying sharks, snorkeled on the Great Barrier Reef, hiked in the Australian rainforest, studied Antarctic phytoplankton with world-class scientists, and spent countless nights discussing philosophy, politics, film, and art until sunrise." The location in the Bay Area also puts the school in a prime location for access to Silicon Valley, which is highly populated with Stanford alumni.

The school's reputation for being at "the forefront of [nearly] every field of study" draws talented faculty that are "at the top of their respective fields." And with an extremely low 6:1 student-to-faculty ratio, students have the ability to forge close relationships with their professors. Even though Nobel Prize winners walk the halls, faculty remain undaunting to students, who find them "engaging and approachable" and "so excited to share their passion for the subject." In giving students access to every resource they need to become lifelong learners and societal contributors, Stanford seeks to "expand your creativity, challenge and deepen your world view, and make you a passionate and informed citizen of the world."

Campus Life

With the vast majority of students living on campus, there is a wide variety of activities to keep students engaged and entertained—"there's always so much going on on-campus that sometimes it's hard to leave!" The social scene is California relaxed, and students say "you can find as much or as little of a party culture here as you're looking for. There's always a frat party to attend on the weekends, and there's always people to just hang out with at the dorm." In addition, there are university-hosted "Cardinal Nights," including "trips to Great America, a local amusement park, a movie pre-screening, and Stanford's Got Talent. All of the events are either free or extremely cheap for students." Academics take priority here and students "work insanely hard during the week," but recognize the importance of balance and "also make it a priority to have a great time." Although students say "it's pretty much impossible to be bored" at Stanford, the siren song of San Francisco does occasionally call, and "a trip to the city is a short train ride or car ride away, so going to concerts and events in the city is always a fun option. Same goes for the nearby beaches."

Student Body

While students are adamant that "there really is no typical Stanford student," it is generally agreed that they are all "very driven, independently motivated and willing to seek out opportunities," making for an ambitious environment that is "without the competitive edge that many top-tier institutions are known for." One common thread does emerge in that "everyone here is smart and has some story that will blow you out of the water if you ask." One student reiterates: "Everyone fits in because we're united by a fire that drives us all to be excited about what we do. The trends you'll see will be along the lines of leadership and crazy intellect." All say it's easy to find your niche, as everyone here is "ridiculously friendly and you can meet new people all over campus at almost every type of event."

STANFORD UNIVERSITY

Financial Aid: 650-723-3058 • E-Mail: admission@stanford.edu • Website: www.stanford.edu

THE PRINCETON REVIEW SAYS

Admissions

The school reports that its standardized testing policy for use in admission for Fall 2026 will require applicants to submit either the SAT or ACT. The Princeton Review suggests that interested applicants consult with the school for the most up-to-date standardized testing policies. *Very important factors considered include:* rigor of secondary school record, class rank, academic GPA, application essay, recommendation(s), extracurricular activities, talent/ability, character/personal qualities. *Other factors considered include:* standardized test scores, interview, first generation, alumni/ae relation, geographical residence, volunteer work, work experience. High school diploma is required and GED is accepted. *Academic units recommended:* 4 English, 4 math, 3 science, 3 science labs, 3 language (other than English), 3 social studies.

Financial Aid

Students should submit: FAFSA; CSS PROFILE. The Princeton Review suggests that all financial aid forms be submitted as soon as possible. *Need-based scholarships/grants offered:* Federal Pell; Federal SEOG; State scholarships/grants; Private scholarships; College/university scholarship or grant aid from institutional funds. *Loan aid offered:* Federal Direct Subsidized Loans; Federal Direct Unsubsidized Loans; Direct PLUS loans. Admitted students will be notified of award with their admissions decision. Federal Work-Study Program available. Institutional employment available.

The Inside Word

Receiving a highly coveted acceptance letter from Stanford is no easy feat! Indeed, competition to gain admission is fierce. There is no magic formula, although a stellar academic record is a must. Beyond strong transcripts and test scores, successful applicants readily display intellectual curiosity and vigor, commitment to the topics and activities they are passionate about, and initiative in seeking out opportunity.

THE SCHOOL SAYS

From the Admissions Office

"Stanford looks for distinctive students who exhibit energy, personality, a sense of intellectual vitality and extraordinary impact outside the classroom. While there is no minimum grade point average, class rank, or test score one needs to be admitted to Stanford, the vast majority of successful applicants will be among the strongest students (academically) in their secondary schools. We want to understand the impact you have had at your job, in your family, in a club, in your school, or in the larger community, and we want to learn of the impact that experience has had on you. By focusing on your achievements in context, we evaluate how you have excelled in your school environment and how you have taken advantage of what is available to you in your school and community.

"The Common Application and Stanford Questions are both required and must be submitted online. In the Stanford Questions, accessed at www.commonapp.org, candidates write about an idea or experience that makes them genuinely excited about learning, as well as a note to their future roommate. In the final essay, candidates are asked to describe what aspects of their life experiences, interests, and character would help them make a distinctive contribution as an undergraduate to Stanford University.

"Need-based financial aid is determined by each family's financial circumstances. To provide some benchmarks for undergraduates: Stanford covers at least the cost of tuition for families whose annual incomes are below $150,000. No expected parent contribution for families whose annual incomes are below $100,000."

SELECTIVITY

# of total applicants	60,646
% of total applicants accepted	4
% of total acceptees attending	80
# offered a place on the wait list	669
# admitted from wait list	57

First-Year Profile

Testing policy	SAT or ACT Required
Range SAT composite	1520–1570
Range SAT EBRW	750–780
Range SAT math	770–800
Range ACT composite	34–36
% submitting SAT scores	56
% submitting ACT scores	21
Average HS GPA	3.9
% submitting high school GPA	70
% graduated top 10% of class	97
% graduated top 25% of class	100
% graduated top 50% of class	100
% submitting high school rank	23

Important Dates

Early action	
Apply by	11/1
Notified by	12/15
Regular	
Apply by	1/5
Notified by	4/1
Nonfall registration?	No

FINANCIAL FACTS

Annual tuition	$67,731
Food and housing	$22,944
Required fees	$843
Books and supplies	$855
Average need-based scholarship (First-year)	$71,440 ($72,166)
% students with need rec. need-based scholarship or grant aid (First-year)	99 (99)
% students with need rec. non-need-based scholarship or grant aid (First-year)	3 (7)
% students with need rec. need-based self-help aid (First-year)	71 (59)
% students rec. any financial aid (First-year)	100 (100)
% UG borrow to pay for school	14
Average cumulative indebtedness	$28,507
% of students with need fully met (First-year)	88 (98)
Average % of student need met (First-year)	100 (100)

STATE UNIVERSITY OF NEW YORK—UNIVERSITY AT ALBANY

1400 Washington Avenue, Albany, NY 12222 • Admissions: 518-442-5435

Survey Snapshot
Great library
Frats and sororities are popular
Internships are widely available

RATINGS

Quality of Life	78
Fire Safety	90
Green	94
Academic	75
Profs Interesting	82
Profs Accessible	87
Admissions	84
Financial Aid	80

CAMPUS LIFE

Type of school	Public
Environment	City

Students

Degree-seeking undergrad enrollment	12,768
% male/female/not reported	45/55/<1
% from out of state	5
% First-year live on campus	88
% Ugrads live on campus	54
# of fraternities (% join)	12 (1)
# of sororities (% join)	13 (1)
% Asian	10
% Black or African American	25
% Hispanic	21
% Native American	<1
% Pacific Islander	<1
% Race and/or ethnicity unknown	2
% Two or more races	4
% White	35
% International	3
# of countries represented	84

CAMPUS MENTAL HEALTH SERVICES

Offers mental health/wellness program	Yes
Mental health training available to students	Yes
Employs Chief Wellness Officer	Yes
Peer-to-peer mental health offerings	Yes
Counseling center has guidelines or accreditation	Yes
Mental health/well-being courses	Yes, non-credit

ACADEMICS

% students returning for sophomore year	85
% students graduating within 4 years	58
Calendar	Semester
Student/faculty ratio	15:1
Most common class size 10–19.	(26%)
Most common lab/discussion size 10–19.	(42%)

Most Popular Majors

Psychology; Business Administration and Management; Social Sciences

Applicants Also Look At

City University of New York—Brooklyn College, City University of New York—Hunter College, Hudson Valley Community College, State University of New York—Binghamton University, State University of New York—Stony Brook University, State University of New York—University at Buffalo, SUNY Schenectady County Community College

STUDENTS SAY "..."

Academics

Students at the State University of New York—University at Albany have access to what they consider an "unmatched lineup of degree programs, world-class faculty, and amazing support." Of particular note is how well UAlbany communicates with students, from advisors who "are on top of students about registering and obtaining classes" to the "many different groups and support systems for all types of students." All of these teams—of both students and staff—"are dedicated to making sure everyone feels like they belong and has something to do or someplace to go that they enjoy."

Faculty use "methods that cause us to think outside the box" and offer up "personal stories and experiences [they] themselves have had, showing real time research they are working on and how it has made an impact, and what future careers you can hold with your interests." They offer "quick responses to issues regarding work, but a kind and empathetic approach during bad times." According to one student, they are "so passionate about their course material, which made learning exciting and interactive." The school's reputation and location and "the incredible networking and relations UAlbany has with hiring businesses... makes it relatively easy to get an internship or job after graduation." From start to finish, enrollees admire that "the school is about being there for the students."

Campus Life

One of the best things about this "very social school" is that "there is always something to do and truly never a dull moment." The "beautiful campus that's easy to get around" is great, as it gives individuals or the many people with "big friend groups they spend their time with" (or the organizations they're involved with) plenty of places to work or hang, or to "go to the gym or sporting events, play volleyball, basketball, or soccer at the outdoor courts." Over the weekend, students add that "nightlife is a very big thing at the school," as are visits to the state capital of Albany, which "is huge and there are so many different places to go and explore (coffee shops, tons of street festivals and flea markets, art shows, lots of food options)." Explorative students also call out "all the historical places nearby," not to mention opportunities for winter skiing and snowboarding in the Adirondacks.

Student Body

Diversity is not just respected but it is honored and appreciated among the "inquisitive and hard-working" population of UAlbany, who find that it "enriches academic discourse, fosters cultural understanding, and prepares students for a globalized world." There are multiple resources for various student groups on campus, "like the women's resource center, the interfaith center, the multicultural resource center, and the gender and sexuality resource center," furthering an environment where "every individual has a safe space to truly express themselves to their fullest extent." If there's one understandably typical trait, it's that there are "a lot of people from all over the state of New York." Students are highly active and "spend time outside of class studying but always leave room for some fun"; you can "always see other students participating in bake sales, fundraisers, events, and displaying school spirit at sports games or in everyday campus life." On the whole, students present "a strong welcoming ambiance" and "there are always events going on hosted by students to engage with peers."

State University of New York—University at Albany

Financial Aid: 518-442-8037 • E-Mail: ugadmissions@albany.edu • Website: www.albany.edu

THE PRINCETON REVIEW SAYS

Admissions

The school reports that its standardized testing policy for use in admission for Fall 2026 is Test Optional. The Princeton Review suggests that interested applicants consult with the school for the most up-to-date standardized testing policies. *Very important factors considered include:* rigor of secondary school record, academic GPA, character/personal qualities. *Other factors considered include:* class rank, standardized test scores, application essay, recommendation(s), interview, extracurricular activities, talent/ability, first generation, alumni/ae relation, geographical residence, volunteer work, work experience, level of applicant's interest. High school diploma is required and GED is accepted. *Academic units required:* 4 English, 3 math, 2 science, 2 science labs, 1 language (other than English), 3 social studies, 2 history, 4 academic electives. *Academic units recommended:* 4 math, 3 science, 3 science labs, 3 language (other than English).

Financial Aid

Students should submit: FAFSA. Priority filing deadline is 1/29. The Princeton Review suggests that all financial aid forms be submitted as soon as possible. *Need-based scholarships/grants offered:* Federal Pell; Federal SEOG; State scholarships/grants; Private scholarships; College/university scholarship or grant aid from institutional funds; United Negro College Fund. *Loan aid offered:* Federal Direct Subsidized Loans; Federal Direct Unsubsidized Loans; Direct PLUS loans. Admitted students will be notified of awards on a rolling basis beginning 2/12. Federal Work-Study Program available. Institutional employment available.

The Inside Word

Students can apply to UAlbany with either the Common Application or the SUNY application. In addition to a strong academic record, admission officers at UAlbany are looking for well-rounded individuals interested in attending the school. UAlbany uses a 100-point scale for the average high school GPA for admitted students. Personal interviews are not required as part of the admissions process.

THE SCHOOL SAYS

From the Admissions Office

"The University at Albany, located in the heart of New York State's capital, offers students unparalleled access to a vibrant business environment, the center of state government and a diverse cultural landscape. Often referred to as "Tech Valley," the region is home to major employers such as GE, Regeneron, Tokyo Electron and GlobalFoundries, providing students with valuable internship and career opportunities.

"As a top-tier R1 research institution, UAlbany ensures that all students—across more than 55 majors—can engage in innovative research and hands-on learning experiences. The University is committed to affordability, offering an average financial aid package of $12,541 and extending flagship scholarship opportunities to students from all states.

"UAlbany's student body represents communities from across New York, more than 40 states and around the world, fostering a dynamic and inclusive campus environment. With over 150 student organizations, students can easily find ways to connect, lead and grow. Academic success is supported through dedicated faculty researchers, personalized advising and comprehensive services such as CAPS and Middle Earth peer counseling.

"A hallmark of the UAlbany experience is the annual campus-wide Showcase, where students present their work across disciplines—from nanotechnology to the performing arts. With 94% of graduates employed or enrolled in graduate school within six months, UAlbany prepares students to become leaders and changemakers. Backed by a network of over 200,000 alumni and innovative initiatives like AI+, the University continues its 180-year legacy of empowering students for the future."

SELECTIVITY

# of total applicants	35,664
% of total applicants accepted	70
% of total acceptees attending	11
# of in-state applicants	31,503
% of in-state applicants accepted	70
# of out-of-state-applicants	2,664
% of applicants accepted from out of state	83
# of international applicants	1,497
% of international applicants accepted	8

First-Year Profile

Testing policy	Test Optional
Average HS GPA	90
% submitting high school GPA	100
% graduated top 10% of class	17
% graduated top 25% of class	45
% graduated top 50% of class	83
% submitting high school rank	39

Important Dates

Early action	
Apply by	11/15
Notified by	1/15
Regular	
Apply by	7/1
Nonfall registration?	Yes

FINANCIAL FACTS*

Annual in-state tuition	$7,070
Annual out-of-state tuition	$28,280
Food and housing	$16,752
Required fees	$4,071
Books and supplies	$1,000
Average need-based scholarship (First-year)	$9,690 ($10,783)
% students with need rec. need-based scholarship or grant aid (First-year)	76 (97)
% students with need rec. non-need-based scholarship or grant aid (First-year)	4 (6)
% students with need rec. need-based self-help aid (First-year)	52 (64)
% students rec. any financial aid (First-year)	57 (70)
% UG borrow to pay for school	66
Average cumulative indebtedness	$26,652
% of students with need fully met (First-year)	7 (9)
Average % of student need met (First-year)	55 (57)

* Most recently reported data at time of printing. Scan the QR code to find the latest updates.

STATE UNIVERSITY OF NEW YORK—BINGHAMTON UNIVERSITY

4400 Vestal Parkway East, Binghamton, NY 13902-6000 • Admissions: 607-777-2171

Survey Snapshot
Diverse student types interact on campus
Great library
Students are happy

RATINGS

Quality of Life	**83**
Fire Safety	**92**
Green	**95**
Academic	**81**
Profs Interesting	**85**
Profs Accessible	**89**
Admissions	**92**
Financial Aid	**85**

CAMPUS LIFE

Type of school	Public
Environment	City

Students

Degree-seeking undergrad enrollment	14,655
% male/female/not reported	48/52/<1
% from out of state	10
% First-year from public high school	90
% First-year live on campus	97
% Ugrads live on campus	43
# of fraternities (% join)	36 (16)
# of sororities (% join)	17 (16)
% Asian	19
% Black or African American	5
% Hispanic	13
% Native American	<1
% Pacific Islander	<1
% Race and/or ethnicity unknown	3
% Two or more races	4
% White	51
% International	4
# of countries represented	91

CAMPUS MENTAL HEALTH SERVICES

Offers mental health/wellness program	Yes
Mental health training available to students	No
Employs Chief Wellness Officer	NR
Peer-to-peer mental health offerings	NR
Counseling center has guidelines or accreditation	No
Mental health/well-being courses	NR

ACADEMICS

% students returning for sophomore year	90
% students graduating within 4 years	75
% students graduating within 6 years	82
Calendar	Semester
Student/faculty ratio	17:1
Most common class size 10–19.	(31%)
Most common lab/discussion size 20–29.	(49%)

Most Popular Majors
Psychology; Business Administration and Management

Applicants Often Prefer
Cornell University

Applicants Sometimes Prefer
Boston University, New York University

Applicants Rarely Prefer
Rutgers University—Newark, State University of New York—Stony Brook University

STUDENTS SAY "…"

Academics

As one of the central institutions in one of the country's strongest public university systems, Binghamton University upholds rigorous academic, cultural, and engagement standards. The research university's six schools are spread across 930 acres of the beautiful upstate Susquehanna Valley. The nursing, business, and engineering schools are three standouts, but no matter what course a student chooses to study, you're sure to get the "best bang for your buck." Binghamton's multidisciplinary education "prepares you not only for your career, but for the rest of your life," by instilling students with leadership, academic and social skills, and "employers rave about the school, especially if you are applying to jobs in New York City or on Long Island." In essence, "Binghamton is all about giving students many options to do what they want," and the career services office is an excellent complement to that; fellow students and alums are also "very willing to give out information that will benefit others, such as an internship or winter program."

Faculty members here are "dedicated and willing to invest in the university," and hold regular office hours, though students "have so many places to go if they are not available." As students get into their major-specific courses, "there is more discussion and less lecturing." Professors are "supportive, reasonable, accessible, clear and fair," and "as long as you are genuinely interested in the subject and willing to put in the work, you will succeed." High-quality research endeavors are available to all (especially those in the sciences), through programs like First-year Research Immersion, which provides first-year students with a three semester-long research experience in sciences, engineering, and public health. The Source Project provides similar research experiences for students in the humanities and social sciences.

Campus Life

The "excellent student board" organizes tons of events throughout the week and is "keen on getting the students…involved and [making] a difference." The university's 450+ organizations carry various roles "from community service to professionalism," and it has "almost any kind of club out there," from club sports to the hula hoop club to L.O.C.K.S. (Ladies Owning their Curls Kinks and Straights). The school's residential college system is modeled after the one at Oxford University, with students living in six different communities, each with its own personality. The living communities "really help break it up and make it feel smaller," and "there are a lot of study spaces and a lot of places to spend time." Though academics take priority, when students do leave their books, "Binghamton offers so many activities to do on campus that it is hard to ever be bored."

The town of Vestal is small and quiet, and there is a 190-acre nature preserve on campus that is frequently hiked by students. The nearby city and communities of greater Binghamton are constantly improving: "Change happens all of the time and the students are getting ready for it." People here do like to party on the weekends, and "going out into downtown Binghamton on Friday and Saturday nights to hit up the bars is popular." For those who prefer to keep it more low-key, the University Union always has "games, arts and crafts, free bowling (with free shoe rentals), ping pong (you do have to rent the paddles if you don't bring your own), billiards, and movie rentals," and there are often performances or movies shown on campus.

Student Body

A high proportion of students are from Long Island or Westchester, but they do report "a surprising amount of diversity" on campus, and students are "happy to step outside of their comfort zones and learn about different cultures." The majority of students "worked hard to afford school and to get into a school as intense as Binghamton" and there is "a very friendly and homey atmosphere at the school." This "extremely loving and generous" group is "multi-disciplined" and "involved in many organizations, leadership roles, jobs, internships, or research."

State University of New York—Binghamton University

Financial Aid: 607-777-2428 • E-Mail: admit@binghamton.edu • Website: www.binghamton.edu

THE PRINCETON REVIEW SAYS

Admissions

The school reports that its standardized testing policy for use in admission for Fall 2026 is Test Optional. The Princeton Review suggests that interested applicants consult with the school for the most up-to-date standardized testing policies. *Very important factors considered include:* rigor of secondary school record, academic GPA. *Important factors considered include:* class rank, application essay. *Other factors considered include:* standardized test scores, recommendation(s), extracurricular activities, talent/ability, character/personal qualities, first generation, volunteer work, work experience. High school diploma is required and GED is accepted. *Academic units required:* 4 English, 3 math, 2 science, 3 language (other than English), 2 social studies. *Academic units recommended:* 4 math, 4 science, 4 social studies, 4 history.

Financial Aid

Students should submit: FAFSA; State aid form. Priority filing deadline is 1/15. The Princeton Review suggests that all financial aid forms be submitted as soon as possible. *Need-based scholarships/grants offered:* Federal Pell; Federal SEOG; State scholarships/grants; Private scholarships; College/university scholarship or grant aid from institutional funds. *Loan aid offered:* Federal Direct Subsidized Loans; Federal Direct Unsubsidized Loans; Direct PLUS loans. Admitted students will be notified of awards on a rolling basis beginning 1/31. Federal Work-Study Program available. Institutional employment available.

The Inside Word

Like the vast majority of New York state schools, Binghamton accepts the single-apply SUNY application. Binghamton also accepts the Common Application, making it easy to apply to Binghamton University and other schools at the same time. Binghamton is one of the top public universities in the country—it's often referred to as a "public Ivy"—so expect competition to be stiff.

THE SCHOOL SAYS

From the Admissions Office

"Binghamton has established itself as the premier public university in the Northeast, because of our outstanding undergraduate programs, vibrant campus culture, and committed faculty. Students are academically motivated, but there is a great deal of mutual help as they compete against the standard of a class rather than each other. Faculty and students work side by side in research labs or on artistic pursuits. Achievement, exploration, and leadership are hallmarks of a Binghamton education. Add to that a campus-wide commitment to internationalization that includes a robust education abroad program, cultural offerings, languages and international studies, and you have a place where graduates leave prepared for success. Binghamton University graduates lead the nation in top starting salaries among public universities, demonstrating that our students are recognized by employers and recruiters for having strong abilities to be leaders, critical thinkers, decision makers, analysts, and researchers in many fields and industries."

SELECTIVITY

# of total applicants	53,007
% of total applicants accepted	39
% of total acceptees attending	16
# offered a place on the wait list	13,341
# admitted from wait list	842

First-Year Profile

Testing policy	Test Optional
Range SAT composite	1360–1480
Range SAT EBRW	660–730
Range SAT math	680–760
Range ACT composite	31–34
% submitting SAT scores	44
% submitting ACT scores	9
Average HS GPA	3.9
% submitting high school GPA	100
% graduated top 10% of class	52
% graduated top 25% of class	83
% graduated top 50% of class	98
% submitting high school rank	25

Important Dates

Early action	
Apply by	11/1
Notified by	1/15
Regular	
Apply by	4/1

FINANCIAL FACTS

Annual in-state tuition	$7,070
Annual out-of-state tuition	$26,950
Food and housing	$17,556
Required fees	$3,497
Books and supplies	$1,000
Average need-based scholarship (First-year)	$12,253 ($12,943)
% students with need rec. need-based scholarship or grant aid (First-year)	91 (92)
% students with need rec. non-need-based scholarship or grant aid (First-year)	10 (22)
% students with need rec. need-based self-help aid (First-year)	96 (94)
% students rec. any financial aid (First-year)	77 (94)
% UG borrow to pay for school	52
Average cumulative indebtedness	$27,208
% of students with need fully met (First-year)	17 (21)
Average % of student need met (First-year)	74 (76)

State University of New York—College of Environmental Science and Forestry

1 Forestry Drive, Syracuse, NY 13210-2779 • Admissions: 315-470-6600

Survey Snapshot
Students environmentally aware
Students take advantage of the outdoors
Active student government

RATINGS

Quality of Life	85
Fire Safety	99
Green	99
Academic	79
Profs Interesting	91
Profs Accessible	90
Admissions	81
Financial Aid	86

CAMPUS LIFE

Type of school	Public
Environment	City

Students

Degree-seeking undergrad enrollment	1,839
% male/female/not reported	47/47/6
% from out of state	21
% First-year from public high school	92
% First-year live on campus	96
% Ugrads live on campus	32
# of fraternities	NR
# of sororities	NR
% Asian	3
% Black or African American	3
% Hispanic	11
% Native American	<1
% Pacific Islander	<1
% Race and/or ethnicity unknown	2
% Two or more races	4
% White	75
% International	2
# of countries represented	10

CAMPUS MENTAL HEALTH SERVICES

Offers mental health/wellness program	Yes
Mental health training available to students	Yes
Employs Chief Wellness Officer	No
Peer-to-peer mental health offerings	Yes
Counseling center has guidelines or accreditation	Yes
Mental health/well-being courses	Yes, non-credit

ACADEMICS

% students returning for sophomore year	87
% students graduating within 4 years	56
% students graduating within 6 years	66
Calendar	Semester
Student/faculty ratio	14:1
Most common class size 10–19.	(30%)
Most common lab/discussion size 20–29.	(42%)

Most Popular Majors

Environmental Biology; Landscape Architecture; Environmental Science

Applicants Sometimes Prefer

Cornell University, State University of New York—Binghamton University, State University of New York—Stony Brook University, State University of New York—University at Buffalo, University of Vermont

STUDENTS SAY "…"

Academics

"If you want to save the world, there's no better place" than State University of New York, College of Environmental Science and Forestry, where "the forest is the classroom." With "outdoor facilities and multiple campuses in working forests," ESF's greatest strength is its "emphasis on field experience." One student shares, "For my work-study, I built, maintained, and collected data from eddy covariance flux towers in wetlands around NY state." Another proudly points to their practical opportunities: "At the ESF Ranger School, there would be days where we would spend from 8 am to 5 pm doing fieldwork." The popular Cranberry Lake Biological Station also offers "a ton of field courses and unique course offerings that allow students to get hands-on experience in forestry, field techniques, and all sorts of environmental knowledge that is better taught in the field itself." Across its 25,000 acres of field stations, students revel in exploring "niche interests from tiny fungi, finding alternative fuels, to creating sustainable energy, studying animal diversity, and paper engineering." Students value that ESF caters to a "very specific career path" that supports "making connections in the field." That's driven from the top down as "from running labs to organizing national conferences, there is not a single professor who hasn't had an impact in the fight to create a sustainable future." For those passionate about environment science and forestry, SUNY ESF provides singular field experiences and instructors who students feel "are genuinely looking out for me and providing opportunities to support my professional development."

Campus Life

With buildings adorned with landscape murals and wildlife photographs, the "passion for sustainability and positive change is one that can be recognized instantly when you're on our campus." For example, "we have a single-use plastic ban and make sure all the products we use are recyclable or compostable." Student groups have the same focus, with popular groups including the Plant Propagation Club, which runs a greenhouse, and the Urban Food Forest Project, where students plant "edible trees/bushes in underserved communities in the town." Each April, students across campus unite for Earth Week, culminating in Quadstock, a lively concert of student bands that draws the whole school together for "a good time." There's also "a contract we have with Syracuse University, [where] we are allowed to use their clubs and recreational facilities," which expands the options students already have at ESF. Activities at ESF give students the chance to connect and celebrate their "community of people who are all dedicated to protecting the environment."

Student Body

At SUNY ESF, students agree that "everyone is like-minded in the sense that we are environmentally focused, but there are diverse perspectives of solutions, motivations, and values informing our mindsets." As one student jokes, "The typical ESF student is very passionate about the environment, or a specific species of insect, or at least going fishing." Politically, some describe their peers as "left-leaning environmentalists (makes sense, as it IS an environmental science college)." Others contend that "SUNY ESF has a blend of two broad categories: liberal, somewhat hippie, and preservationist biology students, and Republican, often hunters and fishers, conservationist management students. What unites us all is our dear love for the environment." Regardless of their political views, "students here are empowered to take up space. We organize, speak, and make ourselves known. The campus is by us, for us." The cooperative vibe crosses through to academics, too. "The student body is just so chill, non-competitive, and supportive…It makes you want to be there and succeed," says one student. Composed of future "environmentalists, leaders, managers, idealists, [and] scientists," the SUNY ESF student body is singular in its shared "goal of being a steward of the natural world and the resources it provides."

State University of New York—College of Environmental Science and Forestry

Financial Aid: 315-470-6706 • E-Mail: esfinfo@esf.edu • Website: www.esf.edu

THE PRINCETON REVIEW SAYS

Admissions

The school reports that its standardized testing policy for use in admission for Fall 2026 is Test Optional. The Princeton Review suggests that interested applicants consult with the school for the most up-to-date standardized testing policies. *Very important factors considered include:* rigor of secondary school record, academic GPA, application essay, level of applicant's interest. *Important factors considered include:* class rank, recommendation(s), extracurricular activities, talent/ability. *Other factors considered include:* standardized test scores, interview, character/personal qualities, first generation, alumni/ae relation, geographical residence, state residency, volunteer work, work experience. High school diploma is required and GED is accepted. *Academic units required:* 4 English, 3 math, 3 science, 3 social studies, 1 history. *Academic units recommended:* 4 math, 4 science, 3 science labs, 3 language (other than English).

Financial Aid

Students should submit: FAFSA; State aid form. Priority filing deadline is 2/1. The Princeton Review suggests that all financial aid forms be submitted as soon as possible. *Need-based scholarships/grants offered:* Federal Pell; Federal SEOG; State scholarships/grants; Private scholarships; College/university scholarship or grant aid from institutional funds; United Negro College Fund. *Loan aid offered:* Federal Direct Subsidized Loans; Federal Direct Unsubsidized Loans; Direct PLUS loans. Admitted students will be notified of awards on a rolling basis beginning 3/15. Federal Work-Study Program available. Institutional employment available.

The Inside Word

ESF is an excellent value even for students hailing from outside the Empire State. While there are many specialized bachelor of science degrees, there are also coordinated programs between the college and the Upstate Medical University, as well as a host of pre-professional programs. GPA is an important factor in ESF's admission calculus, but level of demonstrated interest, particularly when it comes to the ways in which you want to study the environment to improve the world, carries as much weight as statistical information. Aspiring Mighty Oaks should make their interest known early and often.

THE SCHOOL SAYS

From the Admissions Office

"ESF is a small college with big ideas. We make a global impact improving and sustaining the environment. We offer a world-class education among a close-knit community of scholars with common values and a shared sense of purpose.

"ESF offers a variety of academic programs leading to Associate, Bachelor's, Master's, and Doctorate degrees, for students interested in sustainability and the science, engineering, design, and management of natural resources and the environment.

"At ESF, students are part of one of the world's largest college campuses which spans from Syracuse, New York, across more than 25,000 acres of forests and wetlands at our field stations throughout Central New York and in the Adirondack Park.

"ESF is a small, specialized college community. Through our long-standing partnership with Syracuse University (SU), which is located right next door, students have access to big university benefits—including classes, student activities and organizations, and recreational facilities.

"Students leave ESF well-trained to execute on improving the world—and their expertise has never been more in demand."

SELECTIVITY

# of total applicants	3,745
% of total applicants accepted	63
% of total acceptees attending	18
# of in-state applicants	2,378
% of in-state applicants accepted	63
# of out-of-state-applicants	1,253
% of applicants accepted from out of state	63
# of international applicants	89
% of international applicants accepted	66
# offered a place on the wait list	142
# admitted from wait list	101

First-Year Profile

Testing policy	Test Optional
% submitting ACT scores	8
Average HS GPA	3.7
% submitting high school GPA	100
% graduated top 10% of class	21
% graduated top 25% of class	58
% graduated top 50% of class	93
% submitting high school rank	38

Important Dates

Early action	
Apply by	11/15
Notified by	1/15
Regular	
Apply by	3/1
Notified by	Rolling, 12/1
Nonfall registration?	Yes

FINANCIAL FACTS

Annual in-state tuition	$7,070
Annual out-of-state tuition	$20,034
Food and housing	$14,140
Required fees	$2,136
Books and supplies	$1,260
Average need-based scholarship (First-year)	$7,716 ($8,488)
% students with need rec. need-based scholarship or grant aid (First-year)	90 (99)
% students with need rec. non-need-based scholarship or grant aid (First-year)	46 (58)
% students with need rec. need-based self-help aid (First-year)	76 (78)
% students rec. any financial aid (First-year)	86 (97)
% UG borrow to pay for school	63
Average cumulative indebtedness	$22,622
% of students with need fully met (First-year)	21 (22)
Average % of student need met (First-year)	69 (69)

State University of New York at Geneseo

1 College Circle, Geneseo, NY 14454 • Admissions: 585-245-5571

Survey Snapshot
Great library
Intramural sports are popular
Frats and sororities are popular

RATINGS

Quality of Life	**82**
Fire Safety	**99**
Green	**60***
Academic	**81**
Profs Interesting	**88**
Profs Accessible	**91**
Admissions	**89**
Financial Aid	**86**

CAMPUS LIFE

Type of school	Public
Environment	Village

Students

Degree-seeking undergrad enrollment	3,909
% male/female/not reported	36/64/0
% from out of state	1
% First-year live on campus	97
% Ugrads live on campus	59
# of fraternities (% join)	10 (13)
# of sororities (% join)	14 (21)
% Asian	4
% Black or African American	4
% Hispanic	9
% Native American	1
% Pacific Islander	<1
% Race and/or ethnicity unknown	4
% Two or more races	<1
% White	77
% International	1
# of countries represented	19

CAMPUS MENTAL HEALTH SERVICES

Offers mental health/wellness program	Yes
Mental health training available to students	Yes
Employs Chief Wellness Officer	Yes
Peer-to-peer mental health offerings	Yes
Counseling center has guidelines or accreditation	Yes
Mental health/well-being courses	Yes, for-credit

ACADEMICS

% students returning for sophomore year	86
% students graduating within 4 years	61
% students graduating within 6 years	70
Calendar	Semester
Student/faculty ratio	15:1
Most common class size 20–29.	(29%)
Most common lab/discussion size 10–19.	(52%)

Most Popular Majors

Biology/Biological Sciences; Psychology; Business Administration and Management

Applicants Sometimes Prefer

City University of New York—Baruch College, City University of New York—Hunter College, State University of New York College at Oneonta, State University of New York—Binghamton University, State University of New York—Cortland, State University of New York—New Paltz, State University of New York—Oswego, State University of New York—Stony Brook University, State University of New York—University at Albany, State University of New York—University at Buffalo

STUDENTS SAY "..."

Academics

State University of New York at Geneseo is a public honors college with a commitment to equity and access that attracts students searching for a "quality education at an affordable price." Undergrads say this academics-focused college provides "challenging but rewarding" courses taught by faculty who are "here to teach and prepare students for the real world." Students find professors to be "fair in terms of tests and expectations," and note that they "really push the students." While most professors use traditional teaching methods, "giving very interesting lectures or leading good group discussions," other notable forms of learning include "live experiments in class," labs that "develop skills necessary for future studies...as well as for general team work," and "counseling services for local businesses." Some classes seem needlessly difficult to students, with the sole purpose of "weeding people out" of competitive majors, but thankfully there are "great resources available to anyone who needs help regardless of the subject matter." Professors provide generous office hours and are mostly "accommodating as long as you reach out to them" and students can "seek help and work with peers" at the tutoring centers. Students seeking a rigorous liberal arts college environment with a state school price are pleased with the choice to attend Geneseo.

Campus Life

At Geneseo, which sits on a "gorgeous campus [with] beautiful sunsets," students "focus on their academics," but they also make time for clubs or athletics-hockey games in particular bring out school spirit. In addition to team sports, undergrads stay active by "going to the gym or various classes offered by [the] school such as spin, yoga, or Zumba." On warm days, students love to "hang out and do work on the quad, put up a hammock between two trees, or throw a Frisbee around...with friends." Fraternity/sorority life is a big part of the Geneseo experience for some students, as are college sponsored events by the organization Geneseo Late Knight, which "puts on events every single weekend that are free for students." The weekends are also when "students definitely like to party," and they spend time at nearby bars. For those looking to get outside, the "scenery of the Geneseo area" has much more to offer: Students mention it's also great for hiking. Despite this, they note that "the town around us is small so there's not a lot to do," which makes trips to Rochester popular: "it's a short drive away" and reachable via a bus shuttle on the weekends.

Student Body

With its small campus, Geneseo is a "tightly knit community" of "intelligent and kind individuals" where "all members support each other." Students value the "strong sense of community" and say all types of people can be found at Geneseo, although some do claim that their peers are "mostly white," however, students come from "very different upbringings and are from different social classes." One student describes her friends as a mix of "some quiet, some outgoing, some party-animals, and some bookworms." Regardless of this broad range, almost everyone is there to "receive a higher education and be successful." Campus culture is generally liberal, featuring "inclusivity involving ethnicity, religion, and sexuality," but some describe social life as cliquey, noting "it is much harder to make friends if you are not in Greek life." On a final note, one student reassures us, "once you find your people, you will feel right at home."

State University of New York at Geneseo

Financial Aid: 585-245-5731 • E-Mail: admissions@geneseo.edu • Website: www.geneseo.edu

THE PRINCETON REVIEW SAYS

Admissions

The school reports that its standardized testing policy for use in admission for Fall 2026 is Test Optional. The Princeton Review suggests that interested applicants consult with the school for the most up-to-date standardized testing policies. *Very important factors considered include:* rigor of secondary school record, academic GPA, recommendation(s), interview, level of applicant's interest. *Important factors considered include:* application essay, extracurricular activities. *Other factors considered include:* standardized test scores, talent/ability, character/personal qualities, volunteer work, work experience. High school diploma is required and GED is accepted. *Academic units required:* 2 English, 2 math, 2 science, 2 language (other than English), 2 social studies, 2 history. *Academic units recommended:* 4 English, 4 math, 4 science, 1 science lab, 4 language (other than English), 4 social studies, 4 history, 2 academic electives, 1 computer science, 1 visual/performing arts.

Financial Aid

Students should submit: FAFSA; State aid form. Priority filing deadline is 2/1. The Princeton Review suggests that all financial aid forms be submitted as soon as possible. *Need-based scholarships/grants offered:* Federal Pell; Federal SEOG; State scholarships/grants; College/university scholarship or grant aid from institutional funds. *Loan aid offered:* Federal Direct Subsidized Loans; Federal Direct Unsubsidized Loans; Direct PLUS loans. Admitted students will be notified of awards on a rolling basis beginning 1/1. Federal Work-Study Program available. Institutional employment available.

The Inside Word

The acceptance rate at SUNY Geneseo has been steadily decreasing, which means that the applicant pool for SUNY Geneseo grows increasingly competitive each year. Grades and rigor of study carry the most weight with the admissions committee here, followed by the rigor of an applicant's high school classes. The personal essay, résumé of cocurricular activities, and recommendations round out the holistic application review.

THE SCHOOL SAYS

From the Admissions Office

"SUNY Geneseo fills a distinct niche among the nation's premier public honors colleges, allowing it to attract highly motivated and talented students from diverse backgrounds. Its highly regarded professional programs, and its cultural, social, recreational, and volunteer opportunities, and its commitment to equity and access provide Geneseo's students with the opportunity and tools to become service-minded global citizens. Geneseo is the only SUNY undergraduate college with a chapter of Phi Beta Kappa, the nation's most prestigious academic honor society, further solidifying the college's reputation as a community of outstanding scholars. Inspired by a transformative core curriculum and extraordinary active learning opportunities, Geneseo students can pursue independent study, take advantage of global experiences and get involved in undergraduate research with faculty who value close working relationships with exceptional students. And for savvy students who recognize Geneseo's value and the financial advantage it affords, the College is a smart investment. Founded in 1871, the College occupies a beautiful 220-acre campus in the historic Village of Geneseo, contributing to its inclusive sense of community. This intellectual and supportive environment is a hallmark of the Geneseo honors college experience that successfully inspires students to pursue life and career goals. Over 40 percent of students pursue graduate study immediately upon graduation, making Geneseo among the country's top 10 master's-awarding colleges for the number of doctorates earned, and in the top seven for those who earn doctorates in STEM fields."

SELECTIVITY

# of total applicants	17,033
% of total applicants accepted	54
% of total acceptees attending	11
# of in-state applicants	15,898
% of in-state applicants accepted	54
# of out-of-state-applicants	685
% of applicants accepted from out of state	67
# of international applicants	434
% of international applicants accepted	43
# offered a place on the wait list	2,414
# admitted from wait list	97

First-Year Profile

Testing policy	Test Optional
Range SAT composite	1210–1330
Range SAT EBRW	610–680
Range SAT math	590–670
Range ACT composite	26–28
% submitting SAT scores	11
% submitting ACT scores	0
Average HS GPA	3.7
% submitting high school GPA	100
% graduated top 10% of class	32
% graduated top 25% of class	71
% graduated top 50% of class	93
% submitting high school rank	33

Important Dates

Early action	
Apply by	11/15
Notified by	12/15
Regular	
Apply by	7/31
Notified by	Rolling, 12/15
Nonfall registration?	Yes

FINANCIAL FACTS*

Annual in-state tuition	$7,070
Annual out-of-state tuition	$17,970
Food and housing	$16,408
Required fees (First-year)	$1,965 ($2,145)
Books and supplies	$1,290
Average need-based scholarship (First-year)	$10,200 ($12,352)
% students with need rec. need-based scholarship or grant aid (First-year)	98 (100)
% students with need rec. non-need-based scholarship or grant aid (First-year)	10 (13)
% students with need rec. need-based self-help aid (First-year)	84 (84)
% students rec. any financial aid (First-year)	92 (100)
% UG borrow to pay for school	63
Average cumulative indebtedness	$27,217
% of students with need fully met (First-year)	20 (21)
Average % of student need met (First-year)	62 (66)

* Most recently reported data at time of printing. Scan the QR code to find the latest updates.

STATE UNIVERSITY OF NEW YORK—PURCHASE COLLEGE

735 Anderson Hill Road, Purchase, NY 10577 • Admissions: 914-251-6300

Survey Snapshot
Lots of liberal students
Theater is popular
Active student government

RATINGS

Quality of Life	77
Fire Safety	93
Green	93
Academic	77
Profs Interesting	88
Profs Accessible	88
Admissions	86
Financial Aid	82

CAMPUS LIFE

Type of school	Public
Environment	Town

Students

Degree-seeking undergrad enrollment	3,202
% male/female/not reported	42/58/0
% from out of state	16
% First-year live on campus	86
% Ugrads live on campus	73
# of fraternities (% join)	NR
# of sororities (% join)	NR
% Asian	4
% Black or African American	12
% Hispanic	29
% Native American	<1
% Pacific Islander	<1
% Race and/or ethnicity unknown	<1
% Two or more races	6
% White	47
% International	2
# of countries represented	54

CAMPUS MENTAL HEALTH SERVICES

Offers mental health/wellness program	Yes
Mental health training available to students	No
Employs Chief Wellness Officer	NR
Peer-to-peer mental health offerings	NR
Counseling center has guidelines or accreditation	No
Mental health/well-being courses	NR

ACADEMICS

% students returning for sophomore year	80
% students graduating within 4 years	52
% students graduating within 6 years	62
Calendar	Semester
Student/faculty ratio	11:1
Most common class size 10–19.	(45%)
Most common lab/discussion size 10–19.	(44%)

Most Popular Majors
Psychology; Communication, Journalism, And Related Programs; Playwriting and Screenwriting

STUDENTS SAY "..."

Academics

Its motto "Think Wide Open" perfectly sums up Purchase College, SUNY, long the artsy lodestone in the SUNY system: the conservatory here "deserves and receives the highest respect." Between the School of the Arts and the School of Liberal Arts & Sciences, there are over 40 majors to choose (and, if those don't suit you, a rarely chosen option to design your own). Nearly all bachelor's students must complete a senior project in which they devote two semesters to in-depth, original, and creative study, and students welcome the chance to explore. "We're all about finding new ways to think about things, from science to art to management," says one.

Classes tend to be about "learning through discussion" rather than lecture, and professors "go out of their way to make sure that everyone is on the same page, and don't leave anyone behind." They often actively work in the field in which they teach, and therefore "bring the material life and take learning outside the classroom." Classes in both the creative arts and general education are "rich and exciting," such as the professor who "teaches classes about Jack Kerouac on a train and walks the path of On the Road." Students benefit from the school's proximity to New York City (less than an hour away), where auditions, showcases, and a fertile alumni network thrive, and "some of the best artists in the NY area become adjunct faculty at this school at some point."

Campus Life

For fun, there's "a TON of things going on": weekly dance parties and concerts, student clubs, lectures, an on-campus museum, free yoga classes, Cheese Club, and tons of festivals. People "pay a lot of money to see bands and they support music and musicians here," and theatre is also "very, very big and popular." Though there are 17 Division III athletics teams, students feel that they get less emphasis, and Greek life is non-existent. Students receive email digests of all the events on campus, and for those who want to get off campus, it's easy to take a bus into White Plains or take the train into Manhattan. "The question isn't 'What to do for fun?' but rather 'Where do you even start?'" Professors usually "know a lot about what's going on" and will often get free tickets to performances for students. While the Student Center (Stood) and library facilities are admittedly great ("there are different levels, so students never have to be isolated in one spot"), many dorms are still on the older side and "need to be updated badly." To its credit, Purchase has been making yearly renovations, including the Wayback residence hall for upper-level students.

Student Body

Students at Purchase describe the school as a place for everyone, particularly the "artsy, unique, passionate, [and] intelligent." The overall "sense of unity and acceptance" means that students are free to be themselves and can "walk around confident in who they are, and they aren't afraid to show their unique styles and personalities." There are a lot of "free spirits" and the atmosphere is "filled with liberal ideologies," and the high concentration of visual/multi-media artists, musicians, and dancers means that "creativity and the arts flourish." The decent number of commuters don't have any real problem integrating with the resident population, and "you can always incorporate your craft into whatever you create at Purchase."

State University of New York—Purchase College

E-Mail: admissions@purchase.edu • Website: www.purchase.edu

THE PRINCETON REVIEW SAYS

Admissions

The school reports that its standardized testing policy for use in admission for Fall 2026 is Test Optional. The Princeton Review suggests that interested applicants consult with the school for the most up-to-date standardized testing policies. *Very important factors considered include:* academic GPA, application essay, talent/ability. *Important factors considered include:* rigor of secondary school record, class rank, character/personal qualities. *Other factors considered include:* standardized test scores, recommendation(s), interview, extracurricular activities, first generation, alumni/ae relation, geographical residence, state residency, volunteer work, work experience, level of applicant's interest. High school diploma is required and GED is accepted. *Academic units required:* 4 English, 4 math, 3 science, 1 science lab, 3 language (other than English), 4 social studies, 2 academic electives.

Financial Aid

Students should submit: FAFSA; State aid form. Priority filing deadline is 2/1. The Princeton Review suggests that all financial aid forms be submitted as soon as possible. *Need-based scholarships/grants offered:* Federal Pell; Federal SEOG; State scholarships/grants; Private scholarships; College/university scholarship or grant aid from institutional funds. *Loan aid offered:* Federal Direct Subsidized Loans; Federal Direct Unsubsidized Loans; Direct PLUS loans. Admitted students will be notified of awards on a rolling basis beginning 3/1. Federal Work-Study Program available. Institutional employment available.

The Inside Word

While the application deadline is July 1, it is recommended that you get your application in by April 1. The application requirements and deadlines for students applying to acting, art+design, creative writing, dance, film, music, and theatre design/tech programs differ, so check on the school's website.

THE SCHOOL SAYS

From the Admissions Office

"Whether for our top-ranked and innovative liberal arts majors or our world-class arts programs, Purchase attracts students from around the globe seeking to cultivate their intellectual identity, develop their talents, expand their minds and transform their passions into action. By choosing Purchase, students make a conscious decision to join an intense community with a deep respect for individuality and diversity and an unparalleled environment of creativity and innovation.

"Our dynamic faculty are not only among the most accomplished in their fields but also partner with students on research projects and work tirelessly to ensure students succeed in their chosen fields of study or career. The intimate classroom setting and engaged faculty inspire lively classroom discussion and debate, critical thinking, originality, and discovery and invention.

"Purchase students represent a broad spectrum of familial, social, ethnic, economic, and geographical backgrounds. The student body is also diverse in terms of gender identity and sexual orientation. Highly talented, motivated, and entrepreneurial, Purchase students strive to impact our society through civic and cultural engagement.

"Still a relatively young college, Purchase offers students an opportunity to build upon established campus traditions as well as create new ones. Our proximity to New York City provides students access to outstanding cultural and career-related opportunities. On campus, students can see world-class performances at the Performing Arts Center (PAC) and notable exhibitions at the Neuberger Museum.

"We seek to enroll highly motivated, hard-working and academically strong students with a consistent record of achievement in a challenging high school curriculum. Admission criteria vary amongst programs."

SELECTIVITY

# of total applicants	7,845
% of total applicants accepted	74
% of total acceptees attending	13

First-Year Profile

Testing policy	Test Optional
Range SAT composite	1200–1300
Range SAT EBRW	620–710
Range SAT math	570–670
Range ACT composite	27–30
% submitting SAT scores	6
% submitting ACT scores	2
Average HS GPA	3.4
% submitting high school GPA	99

Important Dates

Early action	
Apply by	11/15
Notified by	1/1
Regular	
Apply by	7/1
Notified by	Rolling, 7/1
Nonfall registration?	Yes

FINANCIAL FACTS

Annual in-state tuition	$7,070
Annual out-of-state tuition	$17,320
Food and housing	$17,940
Required fees	$1,946
Books and supplies	$1,240
Average need-based scholarship (First-year)	$12,890 ($12,532)
% students with need rec. need-based scholarship or grant aid (First-year)	98 (98)
% students with need rec. non-need-based scholarship or grant aid (First-year)	8 (5)
% students with need rec. need-based self-help aid (First-year)	85 (85)
% of students with need fully met (First-year)	3 (3)
Average % of student need met (First-year)	54 (53)

State University of New York—Stony Brook University

Office of Admissions, Stony Brook, NY 11794-1901 • Admissions: 631-632-6868

Survey Snapshot
Great library
Recreation facilities are great
Active minority support groups

RATINGS	
Quality of Life	81
Fire Safety	90
Green	93
Academic	77
Profs Interesting	81
Profs Accessible	86
Admissions	91
Financial Aid	83

CAMPUS LIFE

Type of school	Public
Environment	Town

Students

Degree-seeking undergrad enrollment	18,444
% male/female/not reported	49/51/0
% from out of state	8
% First-year from public high school	90
% First-year live on campus	71
% Ugrads live on campus	52
# of fraternities (% join)	14 (2)
# of sororities (% join)	15 (3)
% Asian	36
% Black or African American	6
% Hispanic	16
% Native American	<1
% Pacific Islander	<1
% Race and/or ethnicity unknown	5
% Two or more races	3
% White	23
% International	10
# of countries represented	105

CAMPUS MENTAL HEALTH SERVICES

Offers mental health/wellness program	Yes
Mental health training available to students	Yes
Employs Chief Wellness Officer	Yes
Peer-to-peer mental health offerings	Yes
Counseling center has guidelines or accreditation	Yes
Mental health/well-being courses	Yes, for-credit

ACADEMICS

% students returning for sophomore year	89
% students graduating within 4 years	64
% students graduating within 6 years	77
Calendar	Semester
Student/faculty ratio	19:1
Most common class size 10–19.	(31%)
Most common lab/discussion size 20–29.	(30%)

Most Popular Majors
Biology/Biological Sciences; Health Services/Allied Health/Health Sciences; Business Administration and Management

Applicants Often Prefer
Cornell University, New York University, Rensselaer Polytechnic Institute, State University of New York—Binghamton University

Applicants Sometimes Prefer
Penn State University Park, Rutgers University–New Brunswick, State University of New York—Geneseo, State University of New York—University at Buffalo, University of Connecticut

Applicants Rarely Prefer
Adelphi University, Hofstra University, Pace University

STUDENTS SAY "…"

Academics

Students at the State University of New York at Stony Brook take on demanding coursework and benefit from abundant research opportunities, especially in the sciences. Many highlight "an amazing STEM program for anyone wanting to pursue any field of STEM, whether health, engineering, [or] policy." Even in introductory classes, students note having the chance to design "a fully operational customized robot" and others happily spend their time hanging out in labs "to explore the different tools available to students." Those in popular majors (Biology, Psychology, Health Science, Applied Mathematics and Statistics) say their "academics are rigorous and prepare [them] well for the future," with "lots of great classes and professors." Beyond the classroom, students cite the abundant "research opportunities offered to undergraduates" as one of Stony Brook's greatest strengths. Designated as an R1 research institution, projects on campus can be as local as cleaning up the waterways around Long Island or as far-reaching as building the "nation's largest quantum network" to advance internet safety and speed for all. One professor's hands-on lesson captures the school's ethos: "[It's] the difference between playing baseball and doing baseball, the latter being our participation in the camaraderie, thrill, teamwork, and more that comes with baseball as a sport, activity, and life." Stony Brook is a place for *doing* things, led by professors who "care about their students and…aim to help [them] all."

Campus Life

"I love the clubs that are offered here," enthuses one of many undergrads who look to student groups to provide "a small community on campus to interact with and have fun events." Students note they "can find a club for any of their interests," including performance groups, identity-based organizations, and leisure clubs. As many groups meet weekly, it's "simple to be consistent and show up." One student cites the "radio station and the SBU Pocket Theatre" as personal favorites, providing the "best outlet here in order to explore and pursue the arts as a secondary to academics." Others find clubs an effective way to reinforce their academics. For instance, the robotics team does "an internal competition to engage the general campus on robotics," and many groups invite guest speakers, which is a "cool [way] to get to meet more people." Outside of clubs, the recreation center is a major student hub that is "very nice, clean, and well-maintained." Intramural basketball, volleyball, and badminton are favorite pastimes. Overall, students value that with "countless opportunities" to get involved, "there is quite literally an activity for everyone."

Student Body

SUNY Stony Brook attracts "people who are focused on academics but enjoy maintaining worthwhile social connections." As one student explains, "They're definitely more driven toward studies and school. However, my peers are from all kinds of different backgrounds and come from all over." Another student emphasizes the "rich blend of international students" at Stony Brook. With such diversity, academic enthusiasm is a uniting factor across campus. "The student body is very supportive and always willing to help each other out. Everyone is hard-working and high-achieving, but the environment never feels competitive or uncomfortable." This balance between academics and social activities creates a welcoming atmosphere. "Our student body always makes events inclusive to everyone whether it be the theme or holiday or something else. Everyone has something they can do here." Another student elaborates, describing Stony Brook students as "the most genuine and down-to-earth people…[which is] exceptionally inspiring, and each peer that I come into contact with pushes me to my fullest potential." Stony Brook, as one student puts it best, "fosters so many connections from various perspectives of life and allows for connection whether it be through arts, sports, or academics."

State University of New York—Stony Brook University

Financial Aid: 631-632-6840 • E-Mail: enroll@stonybrook.edu • Website: www.stonybrook.edu

THE PRINCETON REVIEW SAYS

Admissions

The school reports that its standardized testing policy for use in admission for Fall 2026 is Test Optional. The Princeton Review suggests that interested applicants consult with the school for the most up-to-date standardized testing policies. *Very important factors considered include:* rigor of secondary school record, academic GPA, standardized test scores, application essay. *Important factors considered include:* recommendation(s). *Other factors considered include:* class rank, interview, extracurricular activities, talent/ability, character/personal qualities, first generation, alumni/ae relation, geographical residence, state residency, volunteer work, work experience, level of applicant's interest. High school diploma is required and GED is accepted. *Academic units required:* 4 English, 3 math, 3 science, 4 social studies. *Academic units recommended:* 4 English, 4 math, 4 science, 3 language (other than English), 4 social studies.

Financial Aid

Students should submit: FAFSA; State aid form. The Princeton Review suggests that all financial aid forms be submitted as soon as possible. *Need-based scholarships/grants offered:* Federal Pell; Federal SEOG; State scholarships/grants; Private scholarships; College/university scholarship or grant aid from institutional funds. *Loan aid offered:* Federal Direct Subsidized Loans; Federal Direct Unsubsidized Loans; Direct PLUS loans. Admitted students will be notified of awards on a rolling basis beginning 4/1. Federal Work-Study Program available. Institutional employment available.

The Inside Word

Successful applicants have typically taken a rigorous college prep curriculum in high school; the university gives special consideration to leadership experience, talents demonstrated through extracurricular activities, or volunteer work. Stony Brook uses a 100-point scale for the average high school GPA for admitted students. Students with a strong academic record may be considered for the university's special programs, including the Honors College, University Scholars program, and Women in Science and Engineering.

THE SCHOOL SAYS

From the Admissions Office

"Stony Brook's designation as a flagship of the State University of New York (SUNY) system reflects the preeminent role that the university plays statewide, nationally, and internationally as a model of research and academic excellence. With more than 200 majors, minors, and combined-degree programs, Stony Brook offers students an elite education with an outstanding return on investment. Among our innovative programs are an accelerated MBA program and the award-winning Undergraduate Research and Creative Activities (URECA) program. Unique research opportunities abound at our medical center, in our marine sciences program, and at nearby Brookhaven National Laboratory, which Stony Brook has a role in running.

"Admission to Stony Brook University is competitive. Successful applicants will have typically followed a rigorous college prep curriculum in high school, and we also consider leadership experience or talents demonstrated through extracurricular activities or volunteer work. We offer a variety of honors programs—such as University Scholars, Honors College, and WISE, as well as honors tracks in Computer Science and Nursing—to challenge and inspire our students. Faculty include Nobel laureates, MacArthur grant recipients, Fields medalists and Pulitzer Prize winners. Stony Brook offers unique study abroad programs on six continents in nearly 30 different countries. Students enjoy a dynamic first-year experience in one of three small undergraduate communities, reside in comfortable campus housing, and have access to outstanding recreational facilities, including a 12,300-seat stadium, a sports complex housing a 4,000-seat arena, and a state-of-the art campus recreation center devoted entirely to the health and well-being of the campus community."

SELECTIVITY

# of total applicants	64,197
% of total applicants accepted	48
% of total acceptees attending	13
# of in-state applicants	42,719
% of in-state applicants accepted	40
# of out-of-state-applicants	13,031
% of applicants accepted from out of state	63
# of international applicants	8,447
% of international applicants accepted	67
# offered a place on the wait list	10,563
# admitted from wait list	3,462

First-Year Profile

Testing policy	Test Optional
Range SAT composite	1350–1470
Range SAT EBRW	650–730
Range SAT math	680–760
Range ACT composite	30–34
% submitting SAT scores	38
% submitting ACT scores	4
Average HS GPA	94.5
% submitting high school GPA	100
% graduated top 10% of class	59
% graduated top 25% of class	86
% graduated top 50% of class	98
% submitting high school rank	31

Important Dates

Early action	
Apply by	11/1
Notified by	1/31
Regular	
Apply by	1/15
Notified by	3/31
Nonfall registration?	Yes

FINANCIAL FACTS*

Annual in-state tuition	$7,070
Annual out-of-state tuition	$31,050
Food and housing	$18,478
Required fees	$3,861
Books and supplies	$900
Average need-based scholarship (First-year)	$11,785 ($12,997)
% students with need rec. need-based scholarship or grant aid (First-year)	94 (99)
% students with need rec. non-need-based scholarship or grant aid (First-year)	4 (6)
% students with need rec. need-based self-help aid (First-year)	90 (91)
% students rec. any financial aid (First-year)	81 (99)
% UG borrow to pay for school	46
Average cumulative indebtedness	$25,283
% of students with need fully met (First-year)	9 (8)
Average % of student need met (First-year)	58 (59)

* Most recently reported data at time of printing. Scan the QR code to find the latest updates.

STETSON UNIVERSITY

421 N. Woodland Boulevard, DeLand, FL 32723 • Admissions: 386-822-7100

Survey Snapshot
Students are happy
Great library
Intramural sports are popular

RATINGS

Quality of Life	84
Fire Safety	90
Green	75
Academic	83
Profs Interesting	90
Profs Accessible	92
Admissions	85
Financial Aid	88

CAMPUS LIFE

Type of school	Private
Environment	Town

Students

Degree-seeking undergrad enrollment	2,359
% male/female/not reported	43/57/0
% from out of state	25
% First-year from public high school	80
% First-year live on campus	84
% Ugrads live on campus	70
# of fraternities (% join)	8 (23)
# of sororities (% join)	8 (18)
% Asian	2
% Black or African American	13
% Hispanic	22
% Native American	<1
% Pacific Islander	<1
% Race and/or ethnicity unknown	1
% Two or more races	7
% White	47
% International	8
# of countries represented	54

CAMPUS MENTAL HEALTH SERVICES

Offers mental health/wellness program	Yes
Mental health training available to students	Yes
Employs Chief Wellness Officer	Yes
Peer-to-peer mental health offerings	Yes
Counseling center has guidelines or accreditation	Yes
Mental health/well-being courses	Yes, for-credit

ACADEMICS

% students returning for sophomore year	73
% students graduating within 4 years	56
% students graduating within 6 years	60
Calendar	Semester
Student/faculty ratio	11:1
Most common class size 10–19.	(43%)
Most common lab/discussion size 10–19.	(46%)

Most Popular Majors

Psychology; Health Services/Allied Health/ Health Sciences; Business Administration and Management

Applicants Also Look At

Daytona State College, Florida Atlantic University, Florida Gulf Coast University, Florida International University, Florida State University, Miami Dade College, University of Central Florida, University of Florida, University of South Florida, The University of Tampa

STUDENTS SAY "..."

Academics

Stetson University is a private university that offers "great resources for students" among the palm trees of central Florida. The small size allows for flexibility in the curriculum and teaching styles aimed at making classes "the best success for the students as possible." One student enthuses about how a finance class discusses real-world impact: "we look at stock market trends daily, discuss governments around the world, and even watch some Federal Reserve press conferences." In other classes, professors who work in the industry "bring people from the government, school districts, and scientists" in for discussions. In almost every major, students point to "labs available for real life experiences" and "plenty of hands-on activities and work done in groups," noting that this practical focus extends to faculty who "help me find resources and opportunities that empower my academic capacity, and they provide me with concrete options for after I complete my undergraduate degree." The university focuses on supporting its students and "makes available as best they can solutions to any problem you might encounter on campus, from academics to social life." As one student says, "The university's commitment to interactive technologies, collaborative projects, and experiential learning creates a vibrant educational environment."

Campus Life

While students take their academics seriously, the overall environment at Stetson is "very pleasant and relaxing" and "our campus and town are so beautiful." The main campus in the college town of Deland includes an expansive green where students can often be found "studying and hammocking," and "the beach is an essential part of the Stetson experience." On the weekends, the school is "filled with events, parties, or supporting the athletes" of the school's 19 Division I sports teams, and there's a big downtown scene for those looking to get away. Not that you need to, note students of the "vibrant and close-knit community," given that "there are so many [student organizations] to choose from," and that they're "lively and very inclusive." Meanwhile, the programming board "always hosts fun events [from laser tag to arcade night to concerts] for students to attend." As for the school itself, students appreciate that "Stetson constantly brings in guest speakers which allows us to...become connected to the outside world." The opportunity of such events "provides great connections for your future."

Student Body

Students are at Stetson because they are high achievers and want to make real change, say students. "My peers...show genuine interest in a wide variety of social justice issues and express concern for the wellbeing of others" and "are always willing to go the extra mile in and out of the classroom." Within this "goal-oriented and charismatic" group of Hatters, there is "a strong international presence in a small college community" and there are "many cultural organizations that support the many international students that come from all over the world." Students say, "it's easy to get to know people and create wonderful friendships" and one of the school's big strengths "is the sense of vibrancy, warmth, and relaxation the environment has overall." Students agree that it's good to have "a diverse and well-rounded group of individuals from all backgrounds" because given the small campus, people "are found everywhere on campus in small groups and you'll likely see your friends walking past you throughout the day." The overall impression is "that everyone is happy and taken care of here."

Stetson University

Financial Aid: 386-822-7100 • E-Mail: admissions@stetson.edu • Website: www.stetson.edu

THE PRINCETON REVIEW SAYS

Admissions

The school reports that its standardized testing policy for use in admission for Fall 2026 is Test Optional. The Princeton Review suggests that interested applicants consult with the school for the most up-to-date standardized testing policies. *Very important factors considered include:* rigor of secondary school record, academic GPA. *Important factors considered include:* class rank, application essay, recommendation(s), interview, extracurricular activities, talent/ability, character/personal qualities, volunteer work, work experience. *Other factors considered include:* standardized test scores, first generation, alumni/ae relation, geographical residence, state residency, level of applicant's interest. High school diploma is required and GED is accepted. *Academic units required:* 4 English, 3 math, 3 science, 2 language (other than English), 2 social studies. *Academic units recommended:* 4 English, 4 math, 4 science, 2 language (other than English), 4 social studies.

Financial Aid

Students should submit: FAFSA; State aid form. Priority filing deadline is 11/1. The Princeton Review suggests that all financial aid forms be submitted as soon as possible. *Need-based scholarships/grants offered:* Federal Pell; Federal SEOG; State scholarships/grants; Private scholarships; College/university scholarship or grant aid from institutional funds. *Loan aid offered:* Federal Direct Subsidized Loans; Federal Direct Unsubsidized Loans; Direct PLUS loans. Admitted students will be notified of awards on a rolling basis beginning 12/15. Federal Work-Study Program available. Institutional employment available.

The Inside Word

Stetson University operates with several application deadlines. Applicants are required to submit an official transcript, while a letter of recommendation and a writing sample are highly recommended. Standardized test scores are optional but considered if submitted. Stetson's acceptance rate is deceptively high: this school attracts go-getters, and each year's first-year class profile is more impressive than the last.

THE SCHOOL SAYS

From the Admissions Office

"Stetson University offers top academic programs, small class sizes and world-class faculty who provide the individual attention and mentoring that set students up for success. Outside of class, the Hatter Ready program immerses students in hands-on learning through internships, research and study abroad. We believe in lived experience, leadership and learning that goes way beyond standard course material. Stetson students gain the skills that life requires and success demands.

"Named one of the most beautiful college campuses in the South, Stetson is located near beaches and theme parks in Florida. Students come from across America and 56 countries worldwide. They enjoy a vibrant community with over 100 clubs and organizations, Greek life, and robust NCAA Division I athletics.

"Since 1883, Stetson has built a reputation for academic excellence and is recognized as one of the Best Colleges in America by The Princeton Review, Wall Street Journal and others. U.S. News & World Report ranks Stetson among the South's top universities and Best Value schools. Stetson offers 115 areas of study, including business, finance, cybersecurity, music and psychology. The Pre-Law program offers direct admission and an accelerated track to earn a law degree from Stetson College of Law, ranked No. 1 in the nation for both Trial Advocacy and Legal Writing by U.S. News & World Report.

"For financial aid, Stetson invests in its students, helping make a top-ranked private education more affordable. For 2025–2026, the average undergraduate financial aid package was $57,841, with 99% of students receiving assistance."

SELECTIVITY

# of total applicants	11,957
% of total applicants accepted	72
% of total acceptees attending	8
# of in-state applicants	7,381
% of in-state applicants accepted	80
# of out-of-state-applicants	2,622
% of applicants accepted from out of state	81
# of international applicants	1,953
% of international applicants accepted	29
# of early decision applicants	155
% of early decision applicants accepted	81
# offered a place on the wait list	32
# admitted from wait list	2

First-Year Profile

Testing policy	Test Optional
Range SAT composite	950–1190
Range SAT EBRW	500–620
Range SAT math	450–580
Range ACT composite	18–27
% submitting SAT scores	33
% submitting ACT scores	12
Average HS GPA	3.7
% submitting high school GPA	100
% graduated top 10% of class	32
% graduated top 25% of class	51
% graduated top 50% of class	75
% submitting high school rank	84

Important Dates

Early decision	
Apply by	11/1
Notified by	12/7
Early action	
Apply by	11/15
Notified by	12/15
Nonfall registration?	Yes

FINANCIAL FACTS

Annual tuition	$61,660
Food and housing	$19,853
Required fees	$400
Books and supplies	$850
Average need-based scholarship (First-year)	$50,400 ($51,478)
% students with need rec. need-based scholarship or grant aid (First-year)	99 (99)
% students with need rec. non-need-based scholarship or grant aid (First-year)	20 (22)
% students with need rec. need-based self-help aid (First-year)	60 (65)
% students rec. any financial aid (First-year)	99 (100)
% UG borrow to pay for school	61
Average cumulative indebtedness	$35,543
% of students with need fully met (First-year)	15 (25)
Average % of student need met (First-year)	81 (90)

STEVENS INSTITUTE OF TECHNOLOGY

1 Castle Point Terrace, Hoboken, NJ 07030 • Admissions: 201-216-5194

Survey Snapshot
Students love Hoboken, NJ
Great off-campus food
Easy to get around campus

RATINGS

Quality of Life	**93**
Fire Safety	**60***
Green	**99**
Academic	**78**
Profs Interesting	**83**
Profs Accessible	**90**
Admissions	**91**
Financial Aid	**86**

CAMPUS LIFE

Type of school	Private
Environment	Town

Students

Degree-seeking undergrad enrollment	4,192
% male/female/not reported	66/33/1
% from out of state	33
% First-year live on campus	81
% Ugrads live on campus	47
# of fraternities (% join)	13 (13)
# of sororities (% join)	8 (16)
% Asian	21
% Black or African American	3
% Hispanic	18
% Native American	<1
% Pacific Islander	<1
% Race and/or ethnicity unknown	6
% Two or more races	5
% White	44
% International	4
# of countries represented	44

CAMPUS MENTAL HEALTH SERVICES

Offers mental health/wellness program	Yes
Mental health training available to students	Yes
Employs Chief Wellness Officer	Yes
Peer-to-peer mental health offerings	Yes
Counseling center has guidelines or accreditation	Yes
Mental health/well-being courses	Yes, for-credit

ACADEMICS

% students returning for sophomore year	94
% students graduating within 4 years	75
% students graduating within 6 years	89
Calendar	Semester
Student/faculty ratio	11:1
Most common class size 20–29.	(27%)
Most common lab/discussion size 30–39.	(40%)

Most Popular Majors

Computer Science; Mechanical Engineering; Business and Technology

Applicants Also Look At

New Jersey Institute of Technology, Northeastern University, Rensselaer Polytechnic Institute, Rochester Institute of Technology, Rutgers University–New Brunswick

STUDENTS SAY "..."

Academics

Stevens Institute of Technology is a private research university that stands out for its research opportunities and hands-on curriculum. One student describes how the school's research focus "gave me the opportunity to publish papers and get 1-on-1 mentoring to expand my knowledge of certain topics." Another calls out the engineering school's "Design Spine": a focus on collaborative design challenges and project-based learning that, for one student, involved "creating air testers, robots, [and] speakers from the ground up using skills that I have been taught strictly at Stevens." For those interested, there's also a co-op program that allows students to alternate between academic study and full-time, paid work experience. Classes at Stevens are "often very small," which is great for instructors "accomplished in their respective fields" who "like to engage with every student in their class." One student finds it to be a Goldilocks school: "just the right size—large enough to have lots of peers and not see the same people every day, but small enough to build close relationships with professors." Among Stevens' other strengths are its "post-graduate connections," which help students get jobs and internships, and an "easy access to New York City [that] is hard to match." The "really rigorous" coursework helps in that regard as it "prepares you well" for future careers, and the school's reputation offers a good return on investment. As one student explains, "Many students graduate with a job offer since Stevens is very well known among tech companies in the area."

Campus Life

Stevens offers "plenty of opportunities to meet people and go to events," and as a result, many students are involved in extracurriculars, including academic clubs like the American Society of Mechanical Engineers, interest-based activities like rock climbing, chess club, and photography, and service organizations like Alpha Phi Omega. Greek life provides "a lot of opportunity for fun," and "cultural organizations are huge." Fall Fest and Winter Wonderland are campus-wide events offering seasonal activities like carnivals and barbecues in the fall and ice skating in the winter. Hoboken is "a vibrant city...that is super safe and cozy but still has a lot going on," and students often use their free time to try "all of the different food spots" and walk along the waterfront. In addition, New York City is a short trip away and the school's entertainment committee helps make it more accessible by offering discounted tickets to see certain Broadway shows, concerts, and games. "There's something for everyone," whether you're on campus or enjoying the city.

Student Body

Students here are "curious and welcoming" individuals. The campus is "very work-centered," and fellow classmates are "very smart and focused on learning and getting a great job afterward." While everyone is "super determined to achieve their goals," it's an environment that's more collaborative than competitive. Students are "willing to help others reach their goals as well." As one student describes it, while their peers tend to be quieter and more focused on school, there's "a deep sense of camaraderie that emerges when we come together for shared academic interests or special events." Another student agrees, saying, "I've never been to a place where I've met so many genuinely nice and easy to talk to people." Stevens is a close-knit community, and students say the school's smaller size means they're able to "truly make change on campus." The size also means that "you see the same people more often and feel less alone." Students here "are often passionate about one particular thing," and "it's clear that every single student is inspired to strive as high as possible." As one student says, "I find it refreshing to be able to meet so many ambitious people every day."

Stevens Institute of Technology

Financial Aid: 201-216-3400 • E-Mail: admissions@stevens.edu • Website: www.stevens.edu

THE PRINCETON REVIEW SAYS

Admissions

The school reports that its standardized testing policy for use in admission for Fall 2026 is Test Optional. The Princeton Review suggests that interested applicants consult with the school for the most up-to-date standardized testing policies. *Very important factors considered include:* academic GPA. *Important factors considered include:* rigor of secondary school record, application essay, recommendation(s). *Other factors considered include:* class rank, standardized test scores, interview, extracurricular activities, talent/ability, character/personal qualities, first generation, geographical residence, state residency, volunteer work, level of applicant's interest. High school diploma is required and GED is accepted. *Academic units required:* 4 English, 4 math, 3 science, 3 science lab.

Financial Aid

Students should submit: FAFSA; CSS PROFILE. Priority filing deadline is 2/15. The Princeton Review suggests that all financial aid forms be submitted as soon as possible. *Need-based scholarships/grants offered:* Federal Pell; Federal SEOG; State scholarships/grants; Private scholarships; College/university scholarship or grant aid from institutional funds; United Negro College Fund. *Loan aid offered:* Federal Direct Subsidized Loans; Federal Direct Unsubsidized Loans; Direct PLUS loans. Federal Work-Study Program available. Institutional employment available.

The Inside Word

The admissions process at Stevens Institute of Technology is definitely competitive. To be a serious contender, you will need a strong GPA and solid standardized test scores if you submit them. Most highly qualified applicants also have plenty of honors, AP, or IB classes on their transcript. And given that Stevens is a tech school, your science and math courses will be closely evaluated. Finally, if Stevens is a top choice, consider applying early decision to push the scales a bit further in your favor.

THE SCHOOL SAYS

From the Admissions Office

"Whether they're designing an autonomous robot to detect hazards in real time, launching the next great technology startup or performing innovative research, Stevens Institute of Technology students and faculty collaborate in an interdisciplinary, student-centric, entrepreneurial environment to confront global challenges. Leading-edge programs in 34 undergraduate majors in business, computer science, arts, humanities, engineering, systems and the sciences teach students how to create and leverage technology in ways that matter to today's society. Tying education to a career path is a long-standing tradition at Stevens, which is why the university is consistently ranked among the nation's elite for student ROI, career services and mid-career salaries of alumni. Stevens' location in Hoboken, New Jersey, minutes from New York City and the surrounding metro area, cultivates unmatched internship, cooperative education and other real-world and hands-on work and research experiences so that when students graduate from Stevens, they are ready to hit the ground running. Stevens' Class of 2025 is the most recent proof, as 93.4% achieved their desired outcome—employment or graduate school—within six months of graduation and had an average salary of $86,900.

"Entrepreneurship programs encourage students to think creatively and to pursue big ideas. The annual Innovation Expo is a celebration of interdisciplinary senior capstone projects, mentored by faculty and sponsored by industry partners. A robust student life, a diverse and supportive community, an exciting college town, and more than 130 student organizations and 23 NCAA Division III athletics teams add to an enriching student experience."

SELECTIVITY

# of total applicants	10,499
% of total applicants accepted	51
% of total acceptees attending	21
# of in-state applicants	5,234
% of in-state applicants accepted	53
# of out-of-state-applicants	3,881
% of applicants accepted from out of state	52
# of international applicants	1,371
% of international applicants accepted	38
# of early decision applicants	407
% of early decision applicants accepted	284
# offered a place on the wait list	2,565
# admitted from wait list	517

First-Year Profile

Testing policy	Test Optional
Range SAT composite	1370–1470
Range SAT EBRW	670–730
Range SAT math	690–760
Range ACT composite	32–34
% submitting SAT scores	36
% submitting ACT scores	4
Average HS GPA	3.8
% submitting high school GPA	98
% graduated top 10% of class	48
% graduated top 25% of class	79
% graduated top 50% of class	96
% submitting high school rank	25

Important Dates

Early decision	
Apply by	11/15
Notified by	12/15
Other ED apply by	1/5
Other ED notified by	2/15
Early action	
Apply by	12/1
Notified by	2/1
Regular	
Apply by	1/5
Notified by	4/1
Nonfall registration?	No

FINANCIAL FACTS

Annual tuition	$65,530
Food and housing	$20,744
Required fees	$2,700
Books and supplies	$1,200
Average need-based scholarship (First-year)	$37,333 ($41,788)
% students with need rec. need-based scholarship or grant aid (First-year)	100 (100)
% students with need rec. non-need-based scholarship or grant aid (First-year)	18 (19)
% students with need rec. need-based self-help aid (First-year)	66 (59)
% UG borrow to pay for school	63
Average cumulative indebtedness	$44,816
% of students with need fully met (First-year)	20 (22)
Average % of student need met (First-year)	69 (74)

STONEHILL COLLEGE

320 Washington Street, Easton, MA 02357 • Admissions: 508-565-1373

Survey Snapshot
Students are happy
Lab facilities are great
Active student government

RATINGS

Quality of Life	90
Fire Safety	90
Green	87
Academic	87
Profs Interesting	93
Profs Accessible	96
Admissions	78
Financial Aid	91

CAMPUS LIFE

Type of school	Private
Affiliation	Roman Catholic
Environment	Village

Students

Degree-seeking undergrad enrollment	2,481
% male/female/not reported	44/56/0
% from out of state	36
% First-year from public high school	62
% First-year live on campus	94
% Ugrads live on campus	86
# of fraternities	0
# of sororities	0
% Asian	3
% Black or African American	5
% Hispanic	9
% Native American	0
% Pacific Islander	0
% Race and/or ethnicity unknown	2
% Two or more races	3
% White	75
% International	2
# of countries represented	26

CAMPUS MENTAL HEALTH SERVICES

Offers mental health/wellness program	Yes
Mental health training available to students	No
Employs Chief Wellness Officer	NR
Peer-to-peer mental health offerings	NR
Counseling center has guidelines or accreditation	No
Mental health/well-being courses	NR

ACADEMICS

% students returning for sophomore year	86
% students graduating within 4 years	69
% students graduating within 6 years	74
Calendar	Semester
Student/faculty ratio	12:1
Most common class size 20–29.	(42%)
Most common lab/discussion size 10–19.	(56%)

Most Popular Majors
Psychology; Criminology; Finance

Applicants Often Prefer
Boston College, College of the Holy Cross

Applicants Sometimes Prefer
Assumption University, Bentley University, Boston University, Bryant University, Fairfield University, Fordham University, Loyola University Maryland, Merrimack College, Northeastern University, Providence College, Quinnipiac University, Saint Anselm College, Saint Michael's College, University of Connecticut, University of Massachusetts—Amherst, University of New Hampshire

STUDENTS SAY "..."

Academics

Founded in 1948, Stonehill College is located an hour's drive south of Boston and prides itself on a fresh approach to the intersection of education and faith. Offering programs that span everything from Arts to Business to STEM, the Roman Catholic Liberal Arts school is known for its "strong academics" and tailored approach to education. Students have the opportunity to complete an independent major or minor "where you can create your own degree from scratch," as well as participate in IDEAS (Integrating Democratic Education at Stonehill). This "experience central and only available at Stonehill" is "a program through which students can apply to design their own 1-credit, multimodal, discussion-based courses, and then teach them to their peers." Indeed, Stonehill's "academics are challenging but those who work hard are successful," and the institution is known for "helping students reach their full potential academically and guiding [them] toward what [they] might want in [their] future."

When it comes to the professors, students "cannot speak highly enough about the faculty," with many seeing the academic instruction as "the most compelling strength at Stonehill." Professors are "passionate about their subject matter" and "make learning interesting and engaging," which helps to "transfer that passion to their students." Some undergrads note the use of adjunct professors for smaller majors, with one student expressing, "As an education major, I have only had two professors over the course of three years that have been full time." In spite of this, students report building strong relationships with faculty members, using these connections "as a resource as well as a way to make learning better and more meaningful." As one enrollee puts it, "I feel like I have learned the most in my entire life in my four years at Stonehill."

Campus Life

Outside of the classroom, students love "enjoy[ing] the beautiful campus." Staying active is a priority, with "a lot of athletes that dominant most of the social life on campus." Many undergrads devote time to working out at the gym, and "a majority of people are involved" with a team. "The intramural sports and club sports are also awesome to play in," one student notes. For those who prefer less formal activity, "many go to socialize and play catch on the quad" when the weather is nice.

But there's more to Stonehill activities beyond athletics. Undergrads can choose from a "wide variety of clubs and societies to join." Clubs like the school newspaper are "wonderful and very informative" and groups like "physics and engineering club [do] a lot of really fun events like building solar panels from scratch." There are also "a lot of programs out of the Office of Student Engagement, so there is always something to do on weekends and weekdays!" Word is, their "food truck days on the quad with corn hole and other cookout games are awesome." In general, people love "just walking around campus" or "hanging out with friends outside." By the time the weekend rolls around, "if partying is your thing, then there's definitely a party culture on campus." If not, there's always a group that's down to "go off campus for food" or and "go for hikes on the weekends."

Student Body

The students on campus are by far the friendliest, most welcoming, kind, and caring people I know, says one enrollee. Many agree, describing their peers as "respectful of each other" and the thing that "truly [makes] Stonehill a great place to be." United in their values, the student body is "built on a structure of community rather than looking out for yourself." Just walking around, you're "constantly seeing friendly faces around the close-knit campus," and it's clear that people are "have a sense of curiosity that sets them apart." While some report that "the school significantly lacks diversity," others feel that the community is "heading in a more diverse direction." Regardless of your background, rest assured that "a large portion of the student body...works to foster inclusive environments."

Stonehill College

Financial Aid: 508-565-1088 • E-Mail: admission@stonehill.edu • Website: www.stonehill.edu

THE PRINCETON REVIEW SAYS

Admissions

The school reports that its standardized testing policy for use in admission for Fall 2026 is Test Free. The Princeton Review suggests that interested applicants consult with the school for the most up-to-date standardized testing policies. *Very important factors considered include:* rigor of secondary school record, academic GPA, talent/ability. *Important factors considered include:* class rank, application essay, recommendation(s), extracurricular activities. *Other factors considered include:* character/personal qualities, first generation, alumni/ae relation, geographical residence, religious affiliation/commitment, volunteer work, work experience, level of applicant's interest. High school diploma is required and GED is accepted. *Academic units required:* 4 English, 3 math, 3 science, 3 science labs, 3 language (other than English), 3 history. *Academic units recommended:* 4 English, 4 math, 4 science, 3 science labs, 4 language (other than English), 4 history.

Financial Aid

Students should submit: FAFSA. Priority filing deadline is 1/15. The Princeton Review suggests that all financial aid forms be submitted as soon as possible. *Need-based scholarships/grants offered:* Federal Pell; Federal SEOG; State scholarships/grants; Private scholarships; College/university scholarship or grant aid from institutional funds. *Loan aid offered:* Federal Direct Subsidized Loans; Federal Direct Unsubsidized Loans; Direct PLUS loans; State Loans. Admitted students will be notified of awards on or about 3/31. Federal Work-Study Program available. Institutional employment available.

The Inside Word

Stonehill's admissions team takes GPA and academic record into consideration while evaluating applicants, but demonstrated interest, student activities, and the application essay are also weighted heavily, perhaps even more so because the school is Test Free and will not accept standardized test scores. Applicants eager for admission should consider a virtual or in-person campus visit or informational sessions when possible.

THE SCHOOL SAYS

From the Admissions Office

"Founded by the Congregation of Holy Cross, Stonehill is a Catholic college that values integrity, tradition, diversity, and the rewards that come when you pair rigorous academics with committed, world-class faculty. Our distinctive approach to liberal arts education melds challenging courses, nationally recognized experiential learning, and life-changing service opportunities to shape compassionate leaders and global thinkers.

"Stonehill is on a beautiful 384-acre campus with architecture ranging from traditional brick-and-ivy academic buildings to our new May School of Arts & Sciences and Meehan School of Business. With its ideal location between Boston and Providence, Stonehill is perfectly situated for internships, professional networking, cultural experiences, pro sports and countless entertainment options.

"More than 90 percent of our students study abroad, complete an internship or perform field research before graduation. Such experiences along with 49 majors and 54 minors in the liberal arts, sciences and business prepare them for productive careers or lives of leadership and service. Our students are also active outside of class. Whether it is Ultimate Disc, dance or one of our Division II varsity teams, most participate in some form of athletics. With a student/ faculty ratio of 12:1 and an average class size of nineteen, individual attention is a Stonehill hallmark. Whether collaborating on research or mentoring students on careers and graduate school, our faculty puts students first: 94 percent of alumni respondents report being in careers, top graduate programs, or volunteer positions within six months of graduation."

SELECTIVITY

# of total applicants	7,106
% of total applicants accepted	71
% of total acceptees attending	12
# of in-state applicants	4,042
% of in-state applicants accepted	73
# of out-of-state-applicants	2,802
% of applicants accepted from out of state	71
# of international applicants	262
% of international applicants accepted	32
# offered a place on the wait list	1,038
# admitted from wait list	32

First-Year Profile

Testing policy	Test Free
Average HS GPA	3.4
% submitting high school GPA	100
% graduated top 10% of class	16
% graduated top 25% of class	45
% graduated top 50% of class	80
% submitting high school rank	38

Important Dates

Early decision	
Apply by	12/1
Notified by	12/31
Other ED apply by	2/1
Other ED notified by	2/28
Early action	
Apply by	11/1
Notified by	1/1
Regular	
Apply by	2/15
Notified by	3/15
Nonfall registration?	Yes

FINANCIAL FACTS

Annual tuition	$58,000
Food and housing	$16,850
Required fees	$1,300
Books and supplies	$893
Average need-based scholarship (First-year)	$39,141 ($40,078)
% students with need rec. need-based scholarship or grant aid (First-year)	98 (99)
% students with need rec. non-need-based scholarship or grant aid (First-year)	29 (34)
% students with need rec. need-based self-help aid (First-year)	64 (59)
% students rec. any financial aid (First-year)	100 (100)
% UG borrow to pay for school	72
Average cumulative indebtedness	$41,707
% of students with need fully met (First-year)	40 (44)
Average % of student need met (First-year)	86 (86)

SUFFOLK UNIVERSITY

8 Ashburton Place, Boston, MA 02108 • Admissions: 617-573-8460

Survey Snapshot
Great library
Students love Boston, MA
Great off-campus food

RATINGS

Quality of Life	83
Fire Safety	97
Green	60*
Academic	76
Profs Interesting	87
Profs Accessible	87
Admissions	83
Financial Aid	86

CAMPUS LIFE

Type of school	Private
Environment	Metropolis

Students

Degree-seeking undergrad enrollment	4,199
% male/female/not reported	34/65/<1
% from out of state	31
% First-year from public high school	75
% First-year live on campus	70
% Ugrads live on campus	48
# of fraternities (% join)	1 (NR)
# of sororities (% join)	2 (NR)
% Asian	8
% Black or African American	10
% Hispanic	20
% Native American	<1
% Pacific Islander	<1
% Race and/or ethnicity unknown	2
% Two or more races	3
% White	47
% International	10
# of countries represented	79

CAMPUS MENTAL HEALTH SERVICES

Offers mental health/wellness program	Yes
Mental health training available to students	Yes
Employs Chief Wellness Officer	Yes
Peer-to-peer mental health offerings	Yes
Counseling center has guidelines or accreditation	Yes
Mental health/well-being courses	Yes, non-credit

ACADEMICS

% students returning for sophomore year	78
% students graduating within 4 years	42
% students graduating within 6 years	59
Calendar	Semester
Most common class size 20–29.	(42%)
Most common lab/discussion size 20–29.	(43%)

Most Popular Majors

Psychology; Marketing/Marketing Management

Applicants Also Look At

Boston College, Boston University, Bridgewater State University, Emerson College, Hofstra University, Merrimack College, New York University, Northeastern University, Quinnipiac University, Roger Williams University, Stonehill College, Syracuse University, University of Connecticut, University of Massachusetts Dartmouth, University of Massachusetts—Amherst, University of Massachusetts—Boston, University of Massachusetts—Lowell, University of New Hampshire, University of Rhode Island, Wheaton College (MA)

STUDENTS SAY "..."

Academics

One of the many assets of Suffolk University is its strong emphasis on the connection between academic work and "experiential learning." For example, the Sawyer Business School, described as one of Suffolk's "greatest strengths," offers in-class IP and pitch competitions and opportunities to work with "the Boston Celtics and the Boston Bruins [that] have been incorporated as an interactive way of learning outside of the classroom." One biology student's favorite class takes place "at the New England Aquarium, where I have the opportunity every week to learn about the fishes...and get taught by the personnel there." Similarly, a playwriting class features "multiple writers and actors from around the Boston area [that] come in to speak." In addition, many of the courses give students the opportunity to go "all over the city on tours of different places," which makes them very popular with the students. One student fondly recalls "a few field trips...where we visited museums, walked around the city to view historical sites, and I even did a presentation in a historical building." One business student cites their "on-campus job as a Sawyer Business School ambassador" as one of their most valued college experiences, and others point to clubs such as Women in Business, Sports and Business, and Latinas in Law as valuable extensions to their in-class learning. Across subjects, favorite campus professors are those "who work directly in the field they teach." One student studying English reports "great professional relationships" with instructors who "have supported me, challenged me, and pushed me towards great successes." Overall, "professors at Suffolk are engaged, responsive, and [students] are able to make meaningful connections with them...and they are genuinely invested in your success."

Campus Life

Students report that "There are plenty of clubs and organizations on campus"; everything from video gaming clubs and the Taylor Swift Society to professional organizations (i.e., Latinas in Law), numerous cultural clubs, and performing arts groups. And while there is Greek life on campus, it's reputed to be "very lowkey and a welcoming environment." As one student notes, "Everyone can find their people through clubs and organizations, and Suffolk prides itself on that." Suffolk has students from all different backgrounds, including a fair number of commuter students who appreciate the commuter lounge as a place for socializing and hanging out, and as one student recalls, "I made a lot of friends there and I'm super grateful that Suffolk created that community for me." Students also appreciate the school's location. "Exploring Boston is full of endless opportunities," enthuses one student, "and it's always an amazing experience." When not on campus, Suffolk students can be found hanging out at Boston Common, the Seaport District, Chinatown, and the North End. Its Boston location is also advantageous for jobs and networking. "Suffolk University has an amazing civic engagement program which lends itself to many connections throughout the city. It is very common for students to get internships at the State House if they want them."

Student Body

The student body "is one of a diverse group of people who come from a multitude of backgrounds and walks of life. People at Suffolk are welcoming of those of every background and cultivate a welcoming environment for those around them." As one student recalls, "Upon entering the school,...I was greeted by upperclassmen who welcomed me to the Suffolk community with open arms," adding, "Now that I have begun my second semester, I have learned that this embrace was not just a welcoming gesture, but also the continuous environment in which the school thrives." Another student concurs, saying that campus is "a friendly place that is abuzz with conversation and debate." Suffolk students are known for being "very inclusive, and they always try to make sure nobody is left behind...they will make sure everyone's voice is heard no matter what."

SUFFOLK UNIVERSITY

Financial Aid: 617-573-8470 • E-Mail: admission@suffolk.edu • Website: www.suffolk.edu

THE PRINCETON REVIEW SAYS

Admissions

The school reports that its standardized testing policy for use in admission for Fall 2026 is Test Optional. The Princeton Review suggests that interested applicants consult with the school for the most up-to-date standardized testing policies. *Very important factors considered include:* rigor of secondary school record, academic GPA. *Important factors considered include:* application essay, recommendation(s), extracurricular activities, character/personal qualities. *Other factors considered include:* class rank, standardized test scores, interview, talent/ability, volunteer work, work experience, level of applicant's interest. High school diploma is required and GED is accepted. *Academic units required:* 4 English, 3 math, 2 science, 1 science lab, 2 language (other than English), 1 history, 4 academic electives. *Academic units recommended:* 4 English, 4 math, 3 science, 1 science lab, 2 language (other than English), 1 social studies, 2 history, 4 academic electives.

Financial Aid

Students should submit: FAFSA. Priority filing deadline is 3/1. The Princeton Review suggests that all financial aid forms be submitted as soon as possible. *Need-based scholarships/grants offered:* Federal Pell; Federal SEOG; State scholarships/grants; Private scholarships; College/university scholarship or grant aid from institutional funds. *Loan aid offered:* Federal Direct Subsidized Loans; Federal Direct Unsubsidized Loans; Direct PLUS loans. Admitted students will be notified of awards on a rolling basis beginning 1/15. Federal Work-Study Program available. Institutional employment available.

The Inside Word

The admissions team at Suffolk is looking for applicants who are ambitious, motivated, and passionate. The institution takes a comprehensive look at potential undergrads, evaluating everything from their academic history and GPA to their out-of-classroom experiences. The school's emphasis on overall uniqueness over a single test score led them to adopt a Test Optional policy for students. Applicants will have the choice to submit their SAT or ACT score if they feel it will enhance their application.

THE SCHOOL SAYS

From the Admissions Office

"Located in the heart of downtown Boston, Suffolk University gives students unparalleled access to this dynamic city and transforms their lives. Suffolk offers more than 60 undergraduate programs and over 50 graduate degree programs, including our doctoral program in clinical psychology and numerous certificate options. Students in our College of Arts & Sciences, Sawyer Business School, and Law School come to Suffolk to gain the knowledge and hands-on experiential learning they need to become leaders in their chosen fields. We take pride in being a personal, student-centered university, where faculty members lead small classes and nurture their students' success. Suffolk offers a 13:1 student-faculty ratio and the average undergraduate class size is 23 students. Undergraduates may study at both our flagship Boston campus and our campus in Madrid, Spain. We are steps—or a short T ride—away from Boston's top employers, and we prepare students for professional success from day one. Our partnerships with myriad institutions in Boston, across Massachusetts, and around the world grant Suffolk students a wealth of choices when it comes to internships and co-op experiences. Indeed, 98 percent of recent graduates are employed or enrolled in graduate school."

SELECTIVITY

# of total applicants	9,551
% of total applicants accepted	82
% of total acceptees attending	13
# offered a place on the wait list	109
# admitted from wait list	2

First-Year Profile

Testing policy	Test Optional
Range SAT composite	1100–1270
Range SAT EBRW	570–660
Range SAT math	510–620
Range ACT composite	24–31
% submitting SAT scores	19
% submitting ACT scores	2
Average HS GPA	3.7
% submitting high school GPA	81

Important Dates

Early action	
Apply by	11/15
Notified by	12/20
Regular	
Apply by	8/31
Notified by	Rolling, 1/15
Nonfall registration?	Yes

FINANCIAL FACTS

Annual tuition	$51,530
Food and housing	$25,862
Required fees (First-year)	$656 ($939)
Books and supplies	$1,200
Average need-based scholarship (First-year)	$34,201 ($37,150)
% students with need rec. need-based scholarship or grant aid (First-year)	98 (98)
% students with need rec. non-need-based scholarship or grant aid (First-year)	16 (13)
% students with need rec. need-based self-help aid (First-year)	94 (94)
% UG borrow to pay for school	65
Average cumulative indebtedness	$60,804
% of students with need fully met (First-year)	14 (11)
Average % of student need met (First-year)	73 (76)

Susquehanna University

514 University Avenue, Selinsgrove, PA 17870 • Admissions: 570-372-4260

Survey Snapshot
Lab facilities are great
Career services are great
Easy to get around campus

RATINGS

Quality of Life	86
Fire Safety	93
Green	60*
Academic	84
Profs Interesting	88
Profs Accessible	94
Admissions	83
Financial Aid	90

CAMPUS LIFE

Type of school	Private
Affiliation	Lutheran
Environment	Town

Students

Degree-seeking undergrad enrollment	2,112
% male/female/not reported	44/56/0
% from out of state	35
% First-year from public high school	85
% First-year live on campus	97
% Ugrads live on campus	89
# of fraternities (% join)	6 (19)
# of sororities (% join)	5 (17)
% Asian	2
% Black or African American	6
% Hispanic	7
% Native American	<1
% Pacific Islander	<1
% Race and/or ethnicity unknown	2
% Two or more races	3
% White	79
% International	1
# of countries represented	21

CAMPUS MENTAL HEALTH SERVICES

Offers mental health/wellness program	Yes
Mental health training available to students	No
Employs Chief Wellness Officer	NR
Peer-to-peer mental health offerings	NR
Counseling center has guidelines or accreditation	No
Mental health/well-being courses	NR

ACADEMICS

% students returning for sophomore year	88
% students graduating within 4 years	66
% students graduating within 6 years	71
Calendar	Semester
Student/faculty ratio	13:1
Most common class size 10–19.	(42%)
Most common lab/discussion size 10–19.	(73%)

Most Popular Majors

Communication; Business/Commerce; Creative Writing

Applicants Also Look At

Dickinson College, Elizabethtown College, Gettysburg College, Ithaca College, Juniata College, Penn State University Park

STUDENTS SAY "..."

Academics

Susquehanna University is an institution that "thrives on building strong leaders and independent thinkers." The school's small size means undergrads are joining a "close-knit community" replete with a "strong alumni network." Perhaps more importantly, it's evident that the school "is invested...in the success of their students." While Susquehanna offers a variety of great majors, students are prone to highlight the "top-notch creative writing program," "outstanding music education program," and "strong" science departments. Undergrads also praise a more unique aspect of a Susquehanna education-mandatory study off campus in a culture different from one's own (95 percent of students choose to go abroad). One senior elated about this requirement shares, "I believe that every young adult should have access to a cross-cultural experience and I value Susquehanna for making such an experience a priority for its students." Thankfully, for the most part, undergrads enjoy their on-campus education as well. By and large, this can be attributed to "fantastic" professors who "take a personal interest in their students." Indeed, the "friendly" teachers here really strive to make themselves "accessible." And, as one impressed creative writing major adds, a handful "often invite [students] up to their houses for dinner and discussion." However, one neuroscience major does caution that "you usually have to fight to get into a class with a 'good' professor and the registration process is always a hassle."

Campus Life

There is always something exciting to seek out at Susquehanna! To begin with, "there are over [120] clubs and organizations (academic, cultural, religious, arts, service, special interest, etc.)" in which students can participate. Additionally, "the Student Activities Committee [sponsors] a lot of free events—including the occasional trapeze and gyroscope!" Many undergrads also enjoy the "on-campus nightclub [which] hosts free dances on the weekends." Moreover, Susquehanna is a fairly athletic school. Indeed, "varsity sports are huge on campus; we have a large number of athletic teams for such a small school. Students love "tailgating [at] sporting events" as well. Undergrads also flock to "Charlie's Coffeehouse to watch movies or hang out with friends during the week." And, for students looking to unwind, "every Wednesday, Friday, and Saturday night there is usually off campus partying happening." If students are itching to escape for a bit, there are several "recreational places off campus (Bounce Plex, bowling alley, racetrack, rock climbing, hiking, etc.)." And though Selinsgrove "is a small town, it's got everything you need." A senior confidently proclaims that "there are plenty of places to eat and shop!"

Student Body

It can easily feel as though most Susquehanna students hail from "upper-middle class" homes located in either the "Mid-Atlantic [region or] New England." Fortunately, to the delight of many students, the "campus has been steadily diversifying over the years." And besides, these "outgoing" undergrads are able to forge bonds that go well beyond geography. After all, this is the type of student body that "will hold the door for you, even if you are 100 feet away." However, there are a handful of students who feel that, to fully fit in, you have to be "part of either Greek life or a sport." Naturally, other undergrads vehemently disagree, emphatically stating that "students find their niche quickly and make friends easily." A history major helps clarify by relaying that "roughly 25 percent of students are athletes and 17 percent are involved in Greek life. However, for the most part students from every range of the spectrum interact and support each other." As one immensely proud student triumphantly sums up, "We are all awesome. There's no other way to describe it besides awesomeness."

Susquehanna University

Financial Aid: 570-372-4450 • E-Mail: suadmiss@susqu.edu • Website: www.susqu.edu

THE PRINCETON REVIEW SAYS

Admissions

The school reports that its standardized testing policy for use in admission for Fall 2026 is Test Optional. The Princeton Review suggests that interested applicants consult with the school for the most up-to-date standardized testing policies. *Very important factors considered include:* rigor of secondary school record, academic GPA. *Important factors considered include:* class rank, standardized test scores, application essay, recommendation(s), interview, extracurricular activities, talent/ability, character/personal qualities, alumni/ae relation, volunteer work, work experience, level of applicant's interest. *Other factors considered include:* first generation, geographical residence, state residency. High school diploma is required and GED is accepted. *Academic units recommended:* 4 English, 4 math, 4 science, 2 science labs, 2 social studies, 1 history, 3 academic electives.

Financial Aid

Students should submit: FAFSA; State aid form. Priority filing deadline is 12/1. The Princeton Review suggests that all financial aid forms be submitted as soon as possible. *Need-based scholarships/grants offered:* Federal Pell; Federal SEOG; State scholarships/grants; Private scholarships; College/university scholarship or grant aid from institutional funds. *Loan aid offered:* Federal Direct Subsidized Loans; Federal Direct Unsubsidized Loans; Direct PLUS loans. Admitted students will be notified of awards on a rolling basis. Federal Work-Study Program available. Institutional employment available.

The Inside Word

Admissions officers at Susquehanna aim to understand the candidate behind the numbers. They want students who demonstrate intellect, creativity, and leadership. The university also realizes that standardized test scores aren't always representative of a student's abilities. That's why the school is Test Optional.

THE SCHOOL SAYS

From the Admissions Office

"As a graduate from Susquehanna your career will ascend from your broad academic foundation, intercultural competence and other skills that you'll gain—critical thinking, writing, teamwork and communication. The median of our grads' earnings six years after graduation is $54,100—that's 64% higher than the national figure.

"Susquehanna faculty members care about your success. Ninety percent of our students participate in internships, hands-on practicum and/or undergraduate research and alumni go on to rank in the top 11% nationally for graduate earnings (Georgetown University Center on Education and the Workforce, 2022). Faculty will advise you about career strategies and support you with letters of recommendation. Many professors stay connected and follow their students' careers after graduation.

"Choose from more than 100 majors and minors in arts, humanities and sciences, or our pre-professional and engineering programs. Our business school guarantees international internships and is AACSB accredited—placing it among the top 5% worldwide.

"By completing a cross-cultural experience for at least two weeks in the U.S. or abroad through our nationally recognized Global Opportunities program, you'll broaden your perspective and professional options.

"You will enjoy exceptional learning, living, and health facilities on our beautiful 297-acre residential campus, much of it run on solar power. Make friends through 120+ student organizations, 23 NCAA Division III intercollegiate sports, fraternities, sororities, and affinity and service groups. Easy access to metropolitan hubs allows you to network with alumni, engage in professional development, and explore infinite options!"

SELECTIVITY

# of total applicants	4,594
% of total applicants accepted	87
% of total acceptees attending	14
# of early decision applicants	61
% of early decision applicants accepted	82
# offered a place on the wait list	0
# admitted from wait list	0

First-Year Profile

Testing policy	Test Optional
Range SAT composite	1170–1230
Range SAT EBRW	540–630
Range SAT math	530–610
Range ACT composite	22–28
% submitting SAT scores	83
% submitting ACT scores	15
Average HS GPA	3.6
% submitting high school GPA	99
% graduated top 10% of class	23
% graduated top 25% of class	53
% graduated top 50% of class	84
% submitting high school rank	64

Important Dates

Early decision	
Apply by	11/15
Notified by	12/1
Early action	
Apply by	11/1
Notified by	12/1
Regular	
Notified by	Rolling, 10/1
Nonfall registration?	Yes

FINANCIAL FACTS

Annual tuition	$52,380
Food and housing	$14,350
Required fees	$680
Books and supplies	$1,200
Average need-based scholarship (First-year)	$36,533 ($36,416)
% students with need rec. need-based scholarship or grant aid (First-year)	100 (100)
% students with need rec. non-need-based scholarship or grant aid (First-year)	23 (32)
% students with need rec. need-based self-help aid (First-year)	75 (67)
% students rec. any financial aid (First-year)	100 (99)
% UG borrow to pay for school	86
Average cumulative indebtedness	$43,366
% of students with need fully met (First-year)	27 (36)
Average % of student need met (First-year)	85 (86)

SWARTHMORE COLLEGE

500 College Avenue, Swarthmore, PA 19081 • Admissions: 610-328-8300

Survey Snapshot
Lots of liberal students
Class discussions encouraged
Great financial aid

RATINGS

Quality of Life	**71**
Fire Safety	**95**
Green	**92**
Academic	**82**
Profs Interesting	**85**
Profs Accessible	**83**
Admissions	**98**
Financial Aid	**99**

CAMPUS LIFE

Type of school	Private
Environment	Village

Students

Degree-seeking undergrad enrollment	1,623
% male/female/not reported	47/53/0
% from out of state	87
% First-year live on campus	100
% Ugrads live on campus	94
# of fraternities	0
# of sororities	0
% Asian	17
% Black or African American	8
% Hispanic	16
% Native American	<1
% Pacific Islander	<1
% Race and/or ethnicity unknown	3
% Two or more races	11
% White	31
% International	14
# of countries represented	60

CAMPUS MENTAL HEALTH SERVICES

Offers mental health/wellness program	Yes
Mental health training available to students	Yes
Employs Chief Wellness Officer	NR
Peer-to-peer mental health offerings	NR
Counseling center has guidelines or accreditation	Yes
Mental health/well-being courses	NR

ACADEMICS

% students returning for sophomore year	98
% students graduating within 4 years	80
% students graduating within 6 years	93
Calendar	Semester
Student/faculty ratio	7:1
Most common class size 10–19.	(38%)
Most common lab/discussion size 10–19.	(46%)

Most Popular Majors

Economics; Computer and Information Sciences; Mathematics

STUDENTS SAY "..."

Academics

Pennsylvania's Swarthmore College is a hidden gem that encourages self-discovery through a liberal arts curriculum that is "not only about classes, but about life." Students agree that it's academically rigorous, but also that "it's totally worth it," and that "although it's not one of the most well-known schools, those who do know of it also know of its wonderful reputation." Everyone's first semester is pass-fail to reinforce the fact that learning is the ultimate goal, but this doesn't mean that anyone slacks off at this open, thriving campus—in fact, one in three graduates goes on to pursue or earn a doctoral degree. Rather, students understand that Swarthmore is "where to go for a real education—for learning for the sake of truly learning, rather than just for grades." Students also appreciate that "Swarthmore is amazingly flexible. The requirements are very limited, allowing you to explore whatever you are interested in and change your mind millions of times about your major and career path. If they don't offer a major you want, you can design your own with ease." While some do admit that constant intellectual examination can be "stressful," they say that "there are tons of resources to help you— professors, academic mentors, writing associates (who are really helpful to talk to when you have major papers), residential assistants, psychological counseling, multicultural support groups, queer/trans support groups—basically, whenever you need help with something, there's someone you can talk to." One satisfied student ties a neat bow around the present that is Swarthmore: "[It] has a lovely campus, the people are almost unbelievably friendly, it's a safe environment, and it's really, really challenging academically."

Campus Life

Around 94 percent of Swarthmore's students live on the school's beautiful arboretum campus and they appreciate its feeling of community. Students say they are "a family... who are engaged in academics, learning, politics, activism, and civic responsibility, with a work hard, play hard, intense mentality, who don't get enough sleep because they're too busy doing all they want to do in their time here." One student says of the small school's impressive array of extracurriculars: "There are so many organizations and clubs on campus that you'd be pressed to find none of the activities interesting" and another adds, "there is almost always something to do." In addition, there are "several parties every weekend," as well as "student musical performances, drama performances, movies, speakers, and comedy shows." Students shake their heads at the "misconception that Swarthmore students do nothing but study...while we certainly do a lot of it, we still find many ways to have fun."

Student Body

While some students say they are "not sure if there is a typical [Swarthmore student]," many agree that all "are really just smart students who care about the world and want to make it better." Students report that the campus "is very diverse racially...[and] multicultural and queer issues are big here." Another undergrad adds that their peers are often "involved in some kind of activism group or multicultural group, talks about classes all the time, was labeled a nerd by people in high school, and is really smart." Above all else, there's one thing all enrollees have in common, which is that "each person here has at least one thing that [they do] extraordinarily well."

Swarthmore College

Financial Aid: 610-328-8358 • E-Mail: admissions@swarthmore.edu • Website: www.swarthmore.edu

THE PRINCETON REVIEW SAYS

Admissions

The school reports that its standardized testing policy for use in admission for Fall 2026 is Test Optional. The Princeton Review suggests that interested applicants consult with the school for the most up-to-date standardized testing policies. *Very important factors considered include:* rigor of secondary school record, class rank, academic GPA, application essay, recommendation(s), character/personal qualities. *Other factors considered include:* standardized test scores, interview, extracurricular activities, talent/ability, first generation, alumni/ae relation, geographical residence, state residency, religious affiliation/commitment, volunteer work, work experience. High school diploma or equivalent is not required. *Academic units recommended:* 4 English, 3 math, 3 science, 3 language (other than English), 3 social studies, 3 history.

Financial Aid

Students should submit: FAFSA; CSS PROFILE; State aid form. Priority filing deadline is 1/4. The Princeton Review suggests that all financial aid forms be submitted as soon as possible. *Need-based scholarships/grants offered:* Federal Pell; Federal SEOG; State scholarships/grants; Private scholarships; College/university scholarship or grant aid from institutional funds. *Loan aid offered:* Federal Direct Subsidized Loans; Federal Direct Unsubsidized Loans; Direct PLUS loans; State Loans. Admitted students will be notified of awards on or about 4/1. Federal Work-Study Program available. Institutional employment available.

The Inside Word

Competition for admission to Swarthmore remains fierce, as the school consistently receives applications from top students across the country. The SAT and ACT are optional, and note that the school will not consider the essay portion of either test. Admissions officers comb applications carefully for evidence of intellectually curious, highly motivated, and creative-minded candidates.

THE SCHOOL SAYS

From the Admissions Office

"Swarthmore College is a highly selective college of liberal arts and engineering located twenty-five minutes outside of Philadelphia. The College provides a transformative education that empowers individuals to contribute to a better world. The campus community fully supports this mission, from world-class professors who engage directly with students in meaningful ways, to staff in the dining hall and libraries who can come to feel like friends. Close relationships fuel life at Swarthmore. Many students collaborate with professors on joint research projects, and the exchange of intellectual ideas is facilitated by small class sizes. The Honors Program extends the depth of free and critical discussion of ideas via small-group seminars. One trademark of a "Swattie" is the passion they devote to their many interests. Swatties can be astrophysicists who write poetry, economists who love to code, and athletes with a passion for choreography. Almost half of students enjoy playing sports, at the Division III level or in club and intramural teams. The College's Quaker roots emphasize the concept of access regardless of income; nearly everything is included in the annual activity fee, so things like movie nights, laundry, printing, and athletic events are free to all students. Students also receive a free transit pass allowing them to take trains and buses into Philadelphia and around the region. Additionally, as part of the Textbook Affordability Program, each student receives an annual $800 credit at the Swarthmore Campus and Community Store (the bookstore) for required course materials. Swarthmore's financial aid program ensures affordability—without loans. Fifty-six percent of Swarthmore's student body received aid in 2025–26, with an average aid award of $69,022. Swarthmore makes admissions decisions for U.S. citizens, permanent residents, and undocumented or DACA-eligible students graduating from U.S. high schools without considering a family's ability to pay. International applicants are admitted on a need-aware basis and are eligible for financial aid."

SELECTIVITY

# of total applicants	12,995
% of total applicants accepted	8
% of total acceptees attending	44
# of early decision applicants	1,281
% of early decision applicants accepted	18
# admitted from wait list	14

First-Year Profile

Testing policy	Test Optional
Range SAT composite	1480–1550
Range SAT EBRW	740–770
Range SAT math	740–790
Range ACT composite	33–35
% submitting SAT scores	40
% submitting ACT scores	15
% graduated top 10% of class	87
% graduated top 25% of class	98
% graduated top 50% of class	100
% submitting high school rank	30

Important Dates

Early decision	
Apply by	11/15
Notified by	12/15
Other ED apply by	1/4
Other ED notified by	2/15
Regular	
Apply by	1/4
Notified by	4/1
Nonfall registration?	No

FINANCIAL FACTS

Annual tuition	$72,722
Food and housing	$22,566
Required fees	$482
Books and supplies	$760
Average need-based scholarship (First-year)	$73,786 ($74,043)
% students with need rec. need-based scholarship or grant aid (First-year)	100 (100)
% students with need rec. non-need-based scholarship or grant aid (First-year)	0 (0)
% students with need rec. need-based self-help aid (First-year)	98 (100)
% UG borrow to pay for school	18
Average cumulative indebtedness	$22,817
% of students with need fully met (First-year)	100 (100)
Average % of student need met (First-year)	100 (100)

SYRACUSE UNIVERSITY

900 South Crouse Ave., Syracuse, NY 13244 • Admissions: 315-443-3611

Survey Snapshot
Great library
Everyone loves the Orange
Campus newspaper is popular

RATINGS

Quality of Life	**82**
Fire Safety	**95**
Green	**91**
Academic	**81**
Profs Interesting	**87**
Profs Accessible	**89**
Admissions	**90**
Financial Aid	**93**

CAMPUS LIFE

Type of school	Private
Environment	City

Students*

Degree-seeking undergrad enrollment	15,645
% male/female/not reported	44/56/<1
% from out of state	64
% First-year from public high school	68
% First-year live on campus	98
% Ugrads live on campus	51
# of fraternities (% join)	36 (25)
# of sororities (% join)	28 (42)
% Asian	7
% Black or African American	8
% Hispanic	12
% Native American	1
% Pacific Islander	<1
% Race and/or ethnicity unknown	2
% Two or more races	4
% White	57
% International	9
# of countries represented	98

CAMPUS MENTAL HEALTH SERVICES

Offers mental health/wellness program	Yes
Mental health training available to students	Yes
Employs Chief Wellness Officer	Yes
Peer-to-peer mental health offerings	Yes
Counseling center has guidelines or accreditation	Yes
Mental health/well-being courses	Yes, for-credit

ACADEMICS

% students returning for sophomore year	92
% students graduating within 4 years	69
% students graduating within 6 years	81
Calendar	Semester
Student/faculty ratio	14:1
Most common class size 10–19.	(40%)
Most common lab/discussion size 20–29.	(55%)

Most Popular Majors
Architectural and Building Sciences/Technology; Liberal Arts and Sciences/Liberal Studies; Psychology

* Most recently reported data at time of printing. Scan the QR code to find the latest updates.

STUDENTS SAY "..."

Academics

The Orange of Syracuse University love their school and want the world to know it. Those who brave the northern winters are rewarded with a choice of around 200 majors and 100 minors, and "the distinct tracks students can take within each of the professional schools" is one of the university's greatest strengths. "There is so much to do with your education and it can be as specific or broad as you would like," says one student. "If you put in the work...it can make a world of a difference to your college experience." The school does a good job of being cohesive for its size, and "there is a sense of connection between all years of study." Alumni form an "everlasting network between Syracuse students" and the school has a "big reach" for a relatively tucked away school: "There is somebody from Syracuse everywhere you look." On top of the alumni, the school provides "ample amounts of resources in regard to finding jobs or applying to graduate programs," which "makes looking for that next step easy and not so intimidating."

Professors are "very intelligent and qualified individuals who have a strong base in what they teach," and are here "as a tool to enhance your knowledge and to help in any way possible." In general education classes, professors are "attentive and aware that students of varying interests and backgrounds are enrolled in the 101-level class and adjust teaching strategies accordingly." They are "quick to respond to emails," and "always open to meeting with you if you need help with anything, academic or personal." Professors typically "do justice to both sides of various arguments" and classroom discussions don't feel biased.

Campus Life

The atmosphere of Syracuse is "always electric, with something going on at all times." Student life can revolve around athletics, and campus is "the most fun place on the planet when the basketball team is doing well, but could be very dreary if they're not and the weather is bad." Students are especially eager to don their orange apparel and "tailgate until the wee hours," but they "always get studying done first." Greek life is popular for many students and "once the sun goes down, you will find a lot of the students all gathering at the fraternities and the bars on Marshall street," though 'Cuse still offers alternative activities, including the Orange After Dark program, "bowling, shopping, whitewater rafting, day trips to NYC, [and] movie nights" for students who have no interest in parties. The gym is always thumping: "it's a social thing here."

As this is Central NY, life takes a little hit when winter comes, and indoor socializing is more prominent. "Floors become close" and "movies and video games" are popular distractions. Syracuse has been quick to respond to student feedback about food, and has renovated to offer more dining options and a more flexible meal plan. That said, students note that off-campus has plenty of dining options at Destiny USA (one of the country's largest malls) and Armory Square.

Student Body

School spirit "runs rampant" here, and this "energized" group can be found "seeking the fun out of every opportunity thrown at them." Syracuse is "not as diverse as a city school but still pretty diverse nonetheless," with most students hailing from the northeast. No matter their background, students "very quickly find a home" whether it's with a sports team, club, organization, or Greek life, and everyone is active in the community. There is "very little competition" among this "practical student body...that doesn't take flack or do unnecessary work," and if there is any divide, it is between the driven students and those just here for a degree. Students "love to party, especially on game days, but also understand that they are here for academics."

Syracuse University

Financial Aid: 315-443-1513 • E-Mail: orange@syr.edu • Website: www.syracuse.edu

THE PRINCETON REVIEW SAYS

Admissions

The school reports that its standardized testing policy for use in admission for Fall 2026 is Test Optional. The Princeton Review suggests that interested applicants consult with the school for the most up-to-date standardized testing policies. *Very important factors considered include:* rigor of secondary school record, academic GPA, application essay, recommendation(s), extracurricular activities, talent/ability, character/personal qualities. *Important factors considered include:* class rank, standardized test scores, first generation, volunteer work, work experience, level of applicant's interest. *Other factors considered include:* interview, geographical residence, state residency. High school diploma is required and GED is accepted. *Academic units recommended:* 4 English, 4 math, 4 science, 4 science labs, 3 language (other than English), 4 social studies, 4 history.

Financial Aid

Students should submit: FAFSA; CSS PROFILE. Priority filing deadline is 1/5. The Princeton Review suggests that all financial aid forms be submitted as soon as possible. *Need-based scholarships/grants offered:* Federal Pell; Federal SEOG; State scholarships/grants; Private scholarships; College/university scholarship or grant aid from institutional funds. *Loan aid offered:* Federal Direct Subsidized Loans; Federal Direct Unsubsidized Loans; Direct PLUS loans. Admitted students will be notified of awards on or about 4/1. Federal Work-Study Program available. Institutional employment available.

The Inside Word

Syracuse's admissions process is competitive. Successful candidates will have strong GPAs and solid test scores, if submitting. It's also important to note that students interested in applying to any fine or performing arts or architecture programs will need to audition and/or submit a portfolio. Finally, applicants who strongly feel that Syracuse is their first choice are highly encouraged to apply early decision.

THE SCHOOL SAYS

From the Admissions Office

"In a world undergoing extraordinary transformation, leadership and innovation are more critical than ever. As a Carnegie classification Research 1 university, our students work alongside leading scholars and have access to hands-on research and learning opportunities —all of which prepare them to shape their communities and become the changemakers of tomorrow. From a rich array of degree programs and extracurricular activities that ignite their passions, to integrated health and wellness offerings that empower them to embrace the college experience with a sense of well-being—Syracuse University goes beyond the classroom to fuel discovery and drive positive impact.

"With 13 schools and colleges, 200 customizable majors and 100 minors, and online degrees and certificates, Syracuse University provides limitless educational pathways. New interdisciplinary areas ranging from social justice and artificial intelligence to energy and environment provide hands-on research experiences that broaden perspectives and prepare students for the careers of tomorrow. Syracuse University has five award-winning study abroad centers and international programs in 60 countries, where our students gain global perspectives that last a lifetime.

"The university is dedicated to being the best university for veterans and military-connected students, who make up more than five percent of the student body. The National Veterans Resource Center is located in the Daniel and Gayle D'Aniello Building. This state-of-the-art, fully-accessible facility is home to Syracuse University's innovative academic, government and community collaborations positioned to empower those who have or will serve in defense of the nation."

SELECTIVITY

# of total applicants	46,645
% of total applicants accepted	49
% of total acceptees attending	17
# of in-state applicants	13,154
% of in-state applicants accepted	46
# of out-of-state-applicants	29,307
% of applicants accepted from out of state	52
# of international applicants	4,184
% of international applicants accepted	33
# of early decision applicants	2,654
% of early decision applicants accepted	56
# offered a place on the wait list	14,242
# admitted from wait list	2,039

First-Year Profile

Testing policy	Test Optional
Range SAT composite	1300–1410
Range SAT EBRW	650–720
Range SAT math	640–710
Range ACT composite	29–33
% submitting SAT scores	23
% submitting ACT scores	8
Average HS GPA	3.7
% submitting high school GPA	100
% graduated top 10% of class	36
% graduated top 25% of class	69
% graduated top 50% of class	92
% submitting high school rank	20

Important Dates

Early decision	
Apply by	11/15
Notified by	1/1
Other ED apply by	1/5
Other ED notified by	2/1
Regular	
Apply by	1/5
Nonfall registration?	Yes

FINANCIAL FACTS

Annual tuition	$63,710
Food and housing	$19,188
Required fees	$1,818
Books and supplies	$1,753
Average need-based scholarship (First-year)	$47,607 ($48,257)
% students with need rec. need-based scholarship or grant aid (First-year)	98 (97)
% students with need rec. non-need-based scholarship or grant aid (First-year)	24 (30)
% students with need rec. need-based self-help aid (First-year)	75 (72)
% students rec. any financial aid (First-year)	82 (84)
% UG borrow to pay for school	47
Average cumulative indebtedness	$39,532
% of students with need fully met (First-year)	59 (60)
Average % of student need met (First-year)	95 (96)

TAYLOR UNIVERSITY

1846 Main Street, Upland, IN 46989-1001 • Admissions: 765-998-5134

Survey Snapshot
Lots of conservative students
Students are happy
Internships are widely available

RATINGS	
Quality of Life	95
Fire Safety	97
Green	60*
Academic	82
Profs Interesting	92
Profs Accessible	92
Admissions	86
Financial Aid	91

CAMPUS LIFE

Type of school	Private
Affiliation	Christian (Nondenominational)
Environment	Rural

Students

Degree-seeking undergrad enrollment	2,333
% male/female/not reported	46/54/0
% from out of state	55
% First-year from public high school	52
% First-year live on campus	99
% Ugrads live on campus	93
# of fraternities	0
# of sororities	0
% Asian	6
% Black or African American	3
% Hispanic	5
% Native American	0
% Pacific Islander	<1
% Race and/or ethnicity unknown	2
% Two or more races	3
% White	81
% International	6
# of countries represented	46

CAMPUS MENTAL HEALTH SERVICES

Offers mental health/wellness program	Yes
Mental health training available to students	No
Employs Chief Wellness Officer	NR
Peer-to-peer mental health offerings	NR
Counseling center has guidelines or accreditation	No
Mental health/well-being courses	NR

ACADEMICS

% students returning for sophomore year	94
% students graduating within 4 years	74
% students graduating within 6 years	78
Calendar	4-1-4
Student/faculty ratio	15:1
Most common class size 10–19.	(37%)
Most common lab/discussion size 10–19.	(58%)

Most Popular Majors
Finance, Management; Elementary Education; Psychology

Applicants Often Prefer
Cedarville University, Grace College and Seminary, Indiana Wesleyan University, Purdue University—West Lafayette, Wheaton College (IL)

Applicants Sometimes Prefer
Ball State University, Calvin University, Liberty University

Applicants Rarely Prefer
Indiana University—Bloomington, Olivet Nazarene University

STUDENTS SAY "..."

Academics

Taylor University offers a "strong [Christian] faith-based curriculum" that includes a minor in Scripture Engagement and the backing of a supportive community in which "servant leadership is very apparent." Within that comes a "focus on developing well-rounded students" that's considered "one of the best things" about Taylor. The school maintains "academically high standards," and students appreciate that their "Christian faith is integrated into the classes." They're also fond of the interactive curriculum, where "project-based learning takes a front seat in most classrooms." Examples include a history class where students act out Bible stories and physical therapy classes where students "get to help assess, diagnose, and treat patients." Through it all, faculty are considered "more than teachers. They are mentors for our faith and our lives." As one student shares, "I feel like I can talk with many of them as friends but also experts in their field." Professors here are "always so welcoming and supportive," and students appreciate the quality education they receive. As one student remarks, "My academic experience has prepared me well for graduate school."

Campus Life

Taylor is a vibrant campus filled with traditions and student-led activities. The dorms serve as a central hub for community building, fostering an "awesome resident life culture." As one student describes, "In my dorm, we all leave our doors open and share our rooms. It's very much a community that we're all involved in." This community feeling is enhanced by fun competitions between the dorms, including Airband, a lip-syncing and choreography contest, and Nostalgia Night, where students perform covers of songs released before the senior class was born. A favorite tradition is the annual Silent Night, where students wear costumes and remain silent until the basketball team scores its 10th point, at which point they erupt with cheers. Beyond these traditions, students fill their days with extracurricular activities, such as sports, clubs, and "pick-a-dates," where a group of students who live on a floor or a wing together "invite a friend of the opposite sex and go bowling, canoeing, or roller-skating." Many students also attend Bible study and chapel services. As one student explains, chapels "are optional, but you have to go early if you want a seat. This shows the electric energy at Taylor." Another student adds, "My peers at Taylor have a unique fire and energy. Every chapel is filled with energetic students excited to worship the Lord."

Student Body

The student body is described as "very inclusive and communal." It's a group of "happy and energetic" people who are "very friendly and welcoming." Students are thoughtful and look out for one another: "When you have a bad day they notice and ask you how you're doing." Students are "typically very responsible" and "hold each other accountable in academics and faith." One of the school's greatest strengths is the "unity of the students because of [their] shared values." Students "love the Lord and show the love of Jesus to all those around them." Taylor stands out for "the strength of [its] community" and the "genuine care students have for each other." And one student describes their peers as "excited and happy to be here." The community is "active and inviting," and "making friends is easy." As one student illustrates, "My friends visiting from other schools for only the weekend notice the difference in the community here," adding, "I am surrounded by the best people I've ever known, and it's a whole school full of them! I am very thankful."

TAYLOR UNIVERSITY

Financial Aid: 765-998-5358 • E-Mail: admissions@taylor.edu • Website: www.taylor.edu

THE PRINCETON REVIEW SAYS

Admissions

The school reports that its standardized testing policy for use in admission for Fall 2026 is Test Optional. The Princeton Review suggests that interested applicants consult with the school for the most up-to-date standardized testing policies. *Very important factors considered include:* rigor of secondary school record, academic GPA, standardized test scores, application essay, recommendation(s), character/personal qualities, religious affiliation/commitment. *Important factors considered include:* class rank, interview, extracurricular activities, volunteer work. *Other factors considered include:* talent/ability, first generation, geographical residence, state residency, work experience. High school diploma is required and GED is accepted. *Academic units required:* 4 English, 3 math, 3 science, 3 science labs, 2 social studies. *Academic units recommended:* 4 math, 4 science, 4 science labs, 4 language (other than English), 3 social studies, 1 computer science, 1 visual/performing arts.

Financial Aid

Students should submit: FAFSA. Priority filing deadline is 2/1. The Princeton Review suggests that all financial aid forms be submitted as soon as possible. *Need-based scholarships/grants offered:* Federal Pell; Federal SEOG; State scholarships/grants; Private scholarships; College/university scholarship or grant aid from institutional funds. *Loan aid offered:* Federal Direct Subsidized Loans; Federal Direct Unsubsidized Loans; Direct PLUS loans; College/university loans from institutional funds. Admitted students will be notified of awards on a rolling basis beginning 11/1. Federal Work-Study Program available. Institutional employment available.

The Inside Word

Taylor University takes a well-rounded approach to the application process. Hence, they thoroughly evaluate all aspects of a candidate's application, from academic achievements to personal statements and recommendations. Admission officers also look for students who demonstrate leadership and community engagement.

THE SCHOOL SAYS

From the Admissions Office

"Pursue Life to the Full at Taylor! Taylor University has provided outstanding Christ-centered education since 1846. We offer 120+ areas of study, and our graduates are prepared for impactful careers through challenging curriculum, hands-on learning, internships, and research alongside our distinguished faculty. Taylor students are known personally by their professors and inspired by rich class discussions. A Taylor liberal arts education prepares you to thrive in a fast-changing world.

"All Taylor's students, faculty, and staff profess a personal relationship with Christ, and we pursue our faith with passion and purpose. We gather together three times a week to worship and hear God's Word, and we are inspired to live out our calling with an unwavering commitment to God and His word, which drives us to serve and lead with excellence for His glory.

"Relationships are the foundation of the Taylor experience and contribute to the energy, joy, and hospitality our community is known for. At Taylor, every student is drawn into a vibrant community of people who deeply know them, actively encourage them, gracefully hold them accountable, point them to Jesus, and help them to thrive. Our residential campus is alive (even on weekends!) with fun gatherings, athletic events, intramural sports, and campus-wide traditions—along with creatively themed residence hall open houses, brother-sister wing worship nights, and midnight runs to get donuts. These are the experiences you'll remember and the friendships you'll maintain for years to come."

SELECTIVITY

# of total applicants	2,658
% of total applicants accepted	99
% of total acceptees attending	33
# of in-state applicants	1,162
% of in-state applicants accepted	99
# of out-of-state-applicants	1,252
% of applicants accepted from out of state	82
# of international applicants	244
% of international applicants accepted	97

First-Year Profile

Testing policy	Test Optional
Range SAT composite	1070–1320
Range SAT EBRW	540–680
Range SAT math	530–650
Range ACT composite	24–31
% submitting SAT scores	66
% submitting ACT scores	28
Average HS GPA	3.8
% submitting high school GPA	100
% graduated top 10% of class	39
% graduated top 25% of class	67
% graduated top 50% of class	90
% submitting high school rank	33

Important Dates

Regular	
Apply by	8/1
Notified by	Rolling, 8/1
Nonfall registration?	Yes

FINANCIAL FACTS

Annual tuition	$41,300
Food and housing	$12,660
Required fees	$1,100
Books and supplies	$1,240
Average need-based scholarship (First-year)	$29,822 ($29,234)
% students with need rec. need-based scholarship or grant aid (First-year)	100 (100)
% students with need rec. non-need-based scholarship or grant aid (First-year)	26 (31)
% students with need rec. need-based self-help aid (First-year)	65 (63)
% students rec. any financial aid (First-year)	98 (100)
% UG borrow to pay for school	50
Average cumulative indebtedness	$26,185
% of students with need fully met (First-year)	31 (35)
Average % of student need met (First-year)	83 (84)

Temple University

1801 North Broad Street, Philadelphia, PA 19122 • Admissions: 215-204-7200

Survey Snapshot
Lots of liberal students
Students love Philadelphia, PA
Everyone loves the Owls

RATINGS

Quality of Life	**82**
Fire Safety	**91**
Green	**92**
Academic	**77**
Profs Interesting	**86**
Profs Accessible	**87**
Admissions	**82**
Financial Aid	**83**

CAMPUS LIFE

Type of school	Public
Environment	Metropolis

Students

Degree-seeking undergrad enrollment	20,636
% male/female/not reported	44/55/<1
% from out of state	31
% First-year live on campus	64
% Ugrads live on campus	22
# of fraternities (% join)	15 (3)
# of sororities (% join)	16 (5)
% Asian	16
% Black or African American	24
% Hispanic	12
% Native American	<1
% Pacific Islander	<1
% Race and/or ethnicity unknown	6
% Two or more races	4
% White	34
% International	4
# of countries represented	118

CAMPUS MENTAL HEALTH SERVICES

Offers mental health/wellness program	Yes
Mental health training available to students	Yes
Employs Chief Wellness Officer	Yes
Peer-to-peer mental health offerings	Yes
Counseling center has guidelines or accreditation	Yes
Mental health/well-being courses	Yes, for-credit

ACADEMICS

% students returning for sophomore year	82
% students graduating within 4 years	58
% students graduating within 6 years	73
Calendar	Semester
Student/faculty ratio	15:1
Most common class size 10–19.	(31%)
Most common lab/discussion size 20–29.	(29%)

Most Popular Majors
Biology/Biological Sciences; Psychology; Finance

Applicants Often Prefer
Penn State University Park, Rutgers University–New Brunswick, University of Pittsburgh—Pittsburgh Campus

Applicants Sometimes Prefer
Drexel University, Thomas Jefferson University, University of Delaware, University of Maryland, College Park

Applicants Rarely Prefer
Rowan University, Saint Joseph's University (PA), West Chester University of Pennsylvania

STUDENTS SAY "..."

Academics

Philadelphia's Temple University is a large public university that offers "strong academic programs, vibrant student life, [and a] prime location in Philadelphia...that collectively contribute to a rich and fulfilling educational experience for its students." Students also report that "the research and job opportunities are one of the best things here at Temple," and they laud the robust Honors Program and the benefits of "the professional connections [from] having such a big alumni community." Additionally, with offerings across 17 schools and colleges, there are "amazing mentorship/internship opportunities," with even more focused growth coming from Student Professional Organizations (SPOs), which are "like a club for your specific major." All told, "the sheer range of major-minor combinations and skill sets...creates a very unique collaborative environment."

Students say of the faculty that "it's evident that they genuinely love what they do, and this enthusiasm is contagious." They "show...pride in their specialties" and "have a ton of work experience and most still work in their field so they can give you up-to-date information on what's going on." A student testifies, "They are all extremely well-credited and amazing teachers." The flipped classroom approach is often used "to provide more time for questions and participation in lecture," and the curriculum includes the "teaching of modern technologies important for the job market." There are also "frequent guest lectures at multiple academic departments that give students opportunities to connect and network... and learn from their paths." Whatever path a student chooses to lay, students say the bricks are there: "If a student is hardworking and highly motivated, it is possible to make a name for yourself both within [and without] the university."

Campus Life

Temple is a large commuter school, but whether enrollees live on-campus or not, they acknowledge "the housing is beautiful and all spaces around campus are structurally comfortable." Students also note that "dining options are fantastic" thanks to the inclusion of "many food trucks around campus with many good foods to choose from after or before class." Those looking for activities should know that the pace of life is heavily reliant not just on workload but on temperature. When it's warm outside, students are everywhere, the campus is alive and vibrant, and people are happy. When it's cold,...everyone hunkers down." This Division I school "has great sport teams and great recreation facilities and learning halls," and students pride themselves on a number of "on-campus clubs that emphasize community service." The university also "has a lot of easily accessible public transport (subway station, train station, multiple bus stations, bike rentals) and is very close to Center City and other popular areas," which serves the needs of "people [who] like to explore the city aspect of Philadelphia."

Student Body

At Temple "everyone has their own style," with one student proudly believing this makes them "one of the most unique student bodies I've seen on a college campus." The school is described as having "lots of diversity in things like gender, race, and sexuality," but everyone is linked by being "extremely hard-working students...who all care about their academic career however are all still fun and outgoing." Another student says, "Everyone at Temple truly wants the best for themselves and others, and that is very clear." A rising tide lifts all boats, and there are "a ton of groups dedicated to helping fellow students. There are always class group chats and study sessions, and a lot of peer tutoring" which is why attendees note that "Temple is great with providing an inclusive environment." Those thinking of attending ought to know that even though "a lot of people work part time at Temple and are very busy," they're all still "very friendly, open minded, free spirited, and devoted."

Temple University

Financial Aid: 215-204-2244 • E-Mail: askanowl@temple.edu • Website: www.temple.edu

THE PRINCETON REVIEW SAYS

Admissions

The school reports that its standardized testing policy for use in admission for Fall 2026 is Test Optional. The Princeton Review suggests that interested applicants consult with the school for the most up-to-date standardized testing policies. *Very important factors considered include:* rigor of secondary school record, academic GPA. *Other factors considered include:* standardized test scores, application essay, recommendation(s), extracurricular activities, talent/ability, character/personal qualities, first generation, alumni/ae relation, geographical residence, state residency, volunteer work, work experience, level of applicant's interest. High school diploma is required and GED is accepted. *Academic units required:* 4 English, 3 math, 2 science, 1 science lab, 2 language (other than English), 2 social studies, 1 history, 1 academic elective, 1 visual/performing arts. *Academic units recommended:* 4 English, 4 math, 3 science, 2 science labs, 2 language (other than English), 2 social studies, 1 history, 3 academic electives, 1 visual/performing arts.

Financial Aid

Students should submit: FAFSA; State aid form. Priority filing deadline is 2/1. The Princeton Review suggests that all financial aid forms be submitted as soon as possible. *Need-based scholarships/grants offered:* Federal Pell; Federal SEOG; State scholarships/grants; Private scholarships; College/university scholarship or grant aid from institutional funds; Federal Nursing Scholarships; United Negro College Fund. *Loan aid offered:* Federal Direct Subsidized Loans; Federal Direct Unsubsidized Loans; Federal Direct PLUS Loans; Federal Nursing Loans; State Loans. Admitted students will be notified of awards on a rolling basis beginning October. Federal Work-Study Program available. Institutional employment available.

The Inside Word

Gaining admission to Temple is competitive and a solid academic record is a must. Temple University is looking for students who are serious about academics, with at least a B average in high school classes and in the 3.0 GPA range for college-prep courses, and should demonstrate a well-rounded academic background and course distribution.

THE SCHOOL SAYS

From the Admissions Office

"As Philadelphia's public research institution, Temple University attracts some of the most diverse, driven and motivated minds from across the nation and around the world. These students and faculty bring the university to life and move Temple forward and upward in academics, teaching, research, athletics, and the arts. The Carnegie Classification of Institutions of Higher Education designates Temple as "Research 1: Very High Research Spending and Doctorate Production." Temple is home to more than 30,000 students and offers more than 650 academic programs in 17 schools and colleges, on eight campuses, including locations in Japan and Italy. More than 3,400 distinguished faculty members, five professional schools and dozens of renowned programs make Temple an academic powerhouse. Students enjoy the advantages and atmosphere of a large urban, public research university with the individualized attention that comes from a 15-1 student-faculty ratio. The majority of first-year students live on campus, where they are steps away from classes; the state-of-the-art Charles Library; the TECH Center; fitness and recreation facilities; dining options; and the many arts, cultural, sports and scholarly events that happen daily at Temple and throughout the city. By living and learning in an urban environment, Temple students are well-prepared for the world. Employers laud Owls for their tenacity, teamwork and talent. Students also have access to an immense alumni network more than 380,000 strong for guidance, job opportunities and mentoring."

SELECTIVITY

# of total applicants	42,824
% of total applicants accepted	86
% of total acceptees attending	14
# of in-state applicants	14,512
% of in-state applicants accepted	87
# of out-of-state-applicants	24,878
% of applicants accepted from out of state	88
# of international applicants	3,434
% of international applicants accepted	72

First-Year Profile

Testing policy	Test Optional
Range SAT composite	1030–1310
Range SAT EBRW	530–670
Range SAT math	490–650
Range ACT composite	23–30
% submitting SAT scores	19
% submitting ACT scores	1

Important Dates

Early action	
Apply by	11/1
Notified by	1/10
Regular	
Apply by	2/1
Notified by	Rolling
Nonfall registration?	Yes

FINANCIAL FACTS*

Annual in-state tuition	$22,667
Annual out-of-state tuition	$39,088
Food and housing	$15,280
Required fees	$1,056
Books and supplies	$1,290
Average need-based scholarship (First-year)	$15,475 ($19,252)
% students with need rec. need-based scholarship or grant aid (First-year)	96 (99)
% students with need rec. non-need-based scholarship or grant aid (First-year)	81 (94)
% students with need rec. need-based self-help aid (First-year)	70 (61)
% students rec. any financial aid (First-year)	86 (97)
% UG borrow to pay for school	69
Average cumulative indebtedness	$42,571
% of students with need fully met (First-year)	6 (7)
Average % of student need met (First-year)	61 (64)

* Most recently reported data at time of printing. Scan the QR code to find the latest updates.

Texas A&M University—College Station

400 Bizzell Street, College Station, TX 77843 • Admissions: 979-845-1060

Survey Snapshot
Students are very religious
Students get along with local community
Recreation facilities are great

RATINGS

Quality of Life	81
Fire Safety	96
Green	95
Academic	79
Profs Interesting	86
Profs Accessible	91
Admissions	91
Financial Aid	86

CAMPUS LIFE

Type of school	Public
Environment	City

Students

Degree-seeking undergrad enrollment	60,765
% male/female/not reported	53/47/0
% from out of state	4
% First-year from public high school	84
% First-year live on campus	55
% Ugrads live on campus	20
# of fraternities (% join)	30 (NR)
# of sororities (% join)	29 (NR)
% Asian	15
% Black or African American	3
% Hispanic	26
% Native American	<1
% Pacific Islander	<1
% Race and/or ethnicity unknown	1
% Two or more races	4
% White	50
% International	1
# of countries represented	72

CAMPUS MENTAL HEALTH SERVICES

Offers mental health/wellness program	Yes
Mental health training available to students	Yes
Employs Chief Wellness Officer	No
Peer-to-peer mental health offerings	Yes
Counseling center has guidelines or accreditation	Yes
Mental health/well-being courses	Yes, non-credit

ACADEMICS

% students returning for sophomore year	95
% students graduating within 4 years	63
% students graduating within 6 years	85
Calendar	Semester
Student/faculty ratio	20:1
Most common class size 20–29.	(25%)
Most common lab/discussion size 20–29.	(41%)

Most Popular Majors

Communication; Mechanical Engineering; Biomedical Sciences; Psychology

Applicants Also Look At

Baylor University, Purdue University—West Lafayette, Rice University, Texas Christian University, Texas Tech University, University of Houston, University of North Texas UNT, University of Texas at Austin, The University of Texas at Dallas

STUDENTS SAY "…"

Academics

Texas A&M University—College Station is more than just the massive 60,000+ undergraduate centerpiece of the Texas A&M system with "top-notch professors" and "world-changing research": it's a place where "you learn to be a well-rounded, moral, and ethical person." As you'd expect of a premiere institution—one of just 24 to be a land-grant, sea-grant, and space-grant university—the academics can be challenging, but that's in service of setting students "apart from the rest, so we can excel." Moreover, the size of the school results in students feeling "part of something bigger than themselves" with professors that "effectively prepare students for world-class challenges." And don't let the size of the school fool you: according to students, at Texas A&M's heart lie "deep-rooted values" and traditions that make it an "open, friendly place to learn and grow" that "runs as a tight-knit family." Students are guided by professors who "all have life experiences working with the topics that they teach, making them the perfect resource for information." These teachers "love the atmosphere and the students," and vice versa: "I have never skipped a class because I thoroughly enjoy going." That goodwill creates students who are "loyal to their school forever," which means that there's a vast "Aggie network" of alumni that is "good for getting jobs after graduation," especially if you're into the sciences.

Campus Life

Texas A&M is a big school with even bigger spirit: When the football team is "belting the war hymn and linking arms, I feel like I am part of a huge family." Students point to many such instances of community and traditions. The Corps of Cadets, a leadership program of over 2,000 uniformed students, plays a key part of many activities, like the famed Fightin' Texas Aggie Band that puts on football half-time spectacles. There are also over 60 fraternities and sororities and a student government with over 1,400 active participants. As one student puts it, "There's a club for just about everything." Service also unites many students, so much so that the Big Event is the largest one-day, student-led service project in the country, with tens of thousands of students thanking the residents of the surrounding community by doing yard work, window washing, and house painting. During the week, students tend to work hard "so we can party hard on the weekends." This usually takes place off-campus at Northgate, known as the "bar street." Other off-campus activities include seeing movies, going to dance halls and restaurants, and shopping at the mall. There is also "an ice-skating rink, bowling alley, and miniature golf place." Whether on campus or off-campus, students say it's not hard to "get involved in something you're passionate about."

Student Body

The school brings a distinctly Texan flair to the college experience, and the typical Aggie is "involved in at least one club, spends a fair amount of time studying, and learns to two-step for Thursday nights." You can also expect some peers to "wear cowboy boots, a flannel shirt, a cowboy hat/baseball cap, and jeans." Thousands of students attend a weekly non-denominational Bible study in the arena, and much of the population leans conservative, but students emphasize—most importantly—that regardless of their beliefs, they're "loyal to one another and are always willing to support their fellow Aggies." It's a large campus, but students note "a lot of classes are pretty small, so it's easy to make friends in class." Students add that there are "no pretenses" among their fellows and "everyone shows who they are." As one student elaborates, "Most of the people I have met here are truly genuine individuals."

Texas A&M University—College Station

Financial Aid: 979-847-1787 • E-Mail: admissions@tamu.edu • Website: www.tamu.edu

THE PRINCETON REVIEW SAYS

Admissions

The school reports that its standardized testing policy for use in admission for Fall 2026 is Test Optional. The Princeton Review suggests that interested applicants consult with the school for the most up-to-date standardized testing policies. *Very important factors considered include:* rigor of secondary school record, class rank, academic GPA, extracurricular activities, talent/ability. *Important factors considered include:* application essay, first generation, geographical residence, state residency. *Other factors considered include:* standardized test scores, recommendation(s), character/personal qualities. High school diploma is required and GED is accepted. *Academic units required:* 4 English, 3 math, 3 science, 2 language (other than English), 3 social studies, 5 academic electives, 1 visual/performing arts. *Academic units recommended:* 4 English, 4 math, 4 science, 2 language (other than English), 4 social studies, 6 academic electives, 1 visual/performing arts.

Financial Aid

Students should submit: FAFSA. Priority filing deadline is 1/15. The Princeton Review suggests that all financial aid forms be submitted as soon as possible. *Need-based scholarships/grants offered:* Federal Pell; Federal SEOG; State scholarships/grants; Private scholarships; College/university scholarship or grant aid from institutional funds. *Loan aid offered:* Federal Direct Subsidized Loans; Federal Direct Unsubsidized Loans; Direct PLUS loans; State Loans; College/university loans from institutional funds. Admitted students will be notified of awards on a rolling basis beginning 2/1. Federal Work-Study Program available. Institutional employment available.

The Inside Word

Texas A&M's admissions process for Texas residents is more straightforward than most: students who graduate in the top 10% of any recognized public or private high school in the state earn automatic acceptance—just meet the application deadline and you're in. For those who fall outside that top 10% threshold but still meet the State of Texas Uniform Admission Policy, the university takes a broader look at the full application, weighing multiple factors before making a decision. For non-Texas residents, their application will be reviewed holistically.

THE SCHOOL SAYS

From the Admissions Office

"Established in 1876 as the first public college in the state, Texas A&M University has become a world leader in teaching, research, and public service. Located in College Station in the heart of Texas, it is centrally situated among three of the country's ten largest cities: Dallas, Houston, and San Antonio. Texas A&M is ranked nationally in these four areas: enrollment, enrollment of top students, value of research, and endowment."

SELECTIVITY

# of total applicants	62,967
% of total applicants accepted	52
% of total acceptees attending	38
# of in-state applicants	49,156
% of in-state applicants accepted	54
# of out-of-state-applicants	10,882
% of applicants accepted from out of state	41
# of international applicants	2,929
% of international applicants accepted	49

First-Year Profile

Testing policy	Test Optional
Range SAT composite	1160–1390
Range SAT EBRW	580–690
Range SAT math	570–710
Range ACT composite	24–32
% submitting SAT scores	77
% submitting ACT scores	19
% graduated top 10% of class	72
% graduated top 25% of class	93
% graduated top 50% of class	99
% submitting high school rank	72

Important Dates

Regular	
Apply by	12/1
Notified by	Rolling, 12/15

FINANCIAL FACTS

Annual in-state tuition	$8,958
Annual out-of-state tuition	$36,187
Food and housing	$13,008
Required fees	$3,970
Books and supplies	$1,104
Average need-based scholarship (First-year)	$14,086 ($14,880)
% students with need rec. need-based scholarship or grant aid (First-year)	92 (93)
% students with need rec. non-need-based scholarship or grant aid (First-year)	7 (11)
% students with need rec. need-based self-help aid (First-year)	47 (42)
% students rec. any financial aid (First-year)	68 (73)
% UG borrow to pay for school	36
Average cumulative indebtedness	$27,831
% of students with need fully met (First-year)	19 (22)
Average % of student need met (First-year)	70 (71)

Texas Christian University

2800 South University Drive, Fort Worth, TX 76109 • Admissions: 817-257-7490

Survey Snapshot
Intramural sports are popular
Recreation facilities are great
Great library

RATINGS	
Quality of Life	97
Fire Safety	93
Green	60*
Academic	83
Profs Interesting	93
Profs Accessible	94
Admissions	90
Financial Aid	88

CAMPUS LIFE

Type of school	Private
Affiliation	Disciples of Christ
Environment	Metropolis

Students

Degree-seeking undergrad enrollment	11,126
% male/female/not reported	38/62/0
% from out of state	48
% First-year from public high school	63
% First-year live on campus	96
% Ugrads live on campus	51
# of fraternities (% join)	18 (48)
# of sororities (% join)	23 (59)
% Asian	3
% Black or African American	4
% Hispanic	21
% Native American	<1
% Pacific Islander	<1
% Race and/or ethnicity unknown	5
% Two or more races	4
% White	59
% International	4
# of countries represented	73

CAMPUS MENTAL HEALTH SERVICES

Offers mental health/wellness program	Yes
Mental health training available to students	Yes
Employs Chief Wellness Officer	Yes
Peer-to-peer mental health offerings	Yes
Counseling center has guidelines or accreditation	Yes
Mental health/well-being courses	Yes, for-credit

ACADEMICS

% students returning for sophomore year	93
% students graduating within 4 years	75
% students graduating within 6 years	86
Calendar	Semester
Student/faculty ratio	13:1
Most common class size 20–29.	(30%)
Most common lab/discussion size 20–29.	(48%)

Most Popular Majors
Business; Nursing; Biology

Applicants Often Prefer
University of Southern California, Vanderbilt University

Applicants Sometimes Prefer
Baylor University, Clemson University, Gonzaga University, Miami University, Santa Clara University, Southern Methodist University, Texas A&M University—College Station, Trinity University, The University of Alabama—Tuscaloosa, University of Miami, University of Texas at Austin

Applicants Rarely Prefer
Texas Tech University, University of Arizona, University of Arkansas—Little Rock, University of Colorado Boulder, University of Mississippi

STUDENTS SAY "…"

Academics

Texas Christian University is a private institution that "provides more than enough resources to help each and every student." Interdisciplinary study is encouraged, and there are "plenty of research opportunities to get involved in knowledge outside of the strict curriculum." Leadership and experiential learning opportunities can be found throughout a student's college career, with "a great network of connections within each major" that includes—even as an undergraduate—"access to helping professors with research and actual, practical community projects." Adaptation is an important facet of a TCU education, and one student says that "academics are always improving with a great Honors program, new research opportunities, and new technology/class options every year." One student appreciates having such "a deep dive of unheard topics, such as a class I took last semester on public apologies." Students appreciate that their professors have plenty of "background experiences outside their academic career" in addition to "extensive knowledge on the subjects they teach," and students note that these "unique" perspectives really "add to the classes you are in." These willing mentors are also described as "very dedicated to their students" and "excited to interact with students in a positive, constructive manner." At TCU, "the professors are rooting for our well-being and accomplishment of our goals."

Campus Life

"Life at TCU is busy in the best way," with most days being "a mix of classes, meetings, and being constantly on the move across campus." The school "does a great job of making their students feel comfortable and at home on campus," and there are "a lot of organizations and ways to get plugged in." While this is a Big 12 school for varsity teams with "incredible to watch" sports, there is also a wide variety of intramural sports "ranging from video game tournaments, ping pong tournaments, all the way to outdoor soccer, indoor soccer, flag football, and the list goes on." The school's location also provides access to big sports teams and "a bunch of concerts in the [Dallas-Fort Worth] area that a lot of students go to." Come springtime, "the campus comes alive and most people during their free time spend it outside on campus having a lot of fun and playing games." Friendly faces are the norm, and it's "common to see classmates supporting each other at athletic events, service projects, or student organization meetings." Whatever you end up doing, "there is so much opportunity for students to interact with others."

Student Body

This is "a diverse, kind, and welcoming community" wherein "there are so many groups to get involved in and it's heavily encouraged to do so." Campus is said to feel more like a "collection of overlapping communities" and "there is a strong sense that students here are involved in more than one world at once." Horned Frogs are "very driven and motivated to succeed in their classes but also manage their time well to have a balanced life outside of classes." A "lot of folks [are] involved in Greek life or an organization on campus," and "everyone seems to have a good friend group and people they do things with." One says, "Everyone is so happy and nice. Just walking around, you feel better instantly because [of] the community." While these friends are often made within classes, "it doesn't matter what degree you're pursuing, you can always meet other people who you can share talks, moments, and memories with." As one student puts it, "Many students hold leadership roles, work jobs, participate in service, or compete in athletics, yet still make time to build genuine relationships."

TEXAS CHRISTIAN UNIVERSITY

Financial Aid: 817-257-7858 • E-Mail: frogmail@tcu.edu • Website: www.tcu.edu

THE PRINCETON REVIEW SAYS

Admissions

The school reports that its standardized testing policy for use in admission for Fall is Test Optional. The Princeton Review suggests that interested applicants consult with the school for the most up-to-date standardized testing policies. *Very important factors considered include:* rigor of secondary school record, academic GPA. *Important factors considered include:* application essay, extracurricular activities, character/personal qualities, first generation, volunteer work, work experience. *Other factors considered include:* standardized test scores, recommendation(s), talent/ability, alumni/ae relation, geographical residence, state residency, religious affiliation/commitment, level of applicant's interest. High school diploma is required and GED is accepted. *Academic units required:* 4 English, 3 math, 3 science, 1 science lab, 2 language (other than English), 3 social studies, 2 academic electives. *Academic units recommended:* 4 English, 4 math, 4 science, 1 science lab, 4 language (other than English), 4 social studies.

Financial Aid

Students should submit: FAFSA; CSS PROFILE. Priority filing deadline is 2/1. The Princeton Review suggests that all financial aid forms be submitted as soon as possible. *Need-based scholarships/grants offered:* Federal Pell; Federal SEOG; State scholarships/grants; Private scholarships; College/university scholarship or grant aid from institutional funds. *Loan aid offered:* Federal Direct Subsidized Loans; Federal Direct Unsubsidized Loans; Direct PLUS loans; State Loans; College/university loans from institutional funds. Admitted students will be notified of awards on a rolling basis beginning in December. Federal Work-Study Program available. Institutional employment available.

The Inside Word

Admissions officers at Texas Christian University make it a priority to find applicants who will enrich the TCU community. The school does not maintain strict minimums for GPA or test scores. Admitted applicants are typically in the top 13 percent of their graduating class, with a roster of challenging courses behind them. Evaluations, essays, and activities will all be closely evaluated.

THE SCHOOL SAYS

From the Admissions Office

"TCU is a major teaching and research university with the feel of a small college. The TCU academic experience includes small classes with top faculty; cutting-edge technology; a liberal arts and sciences core curriculum; and real-life application through faculty-directed research, group projects, and internships. While TCU faculty members are recognized for research, their main focus is on teaching and mentoring students. The friendly campus community welcomes new students at Frog Camp before classes begin, where students find three days of fun meeting new friends, learning campus traditions, and serving the community. Campus life includes 275 clubs and organizations and a spirited NCAA Division I athletics program in the Big 12 Conference. More than half of the students participate in a wide array of intramural sports, and about 40 percent are involved in Greek organizations, including ones emphasizing ethnic diversity as well as the Christian faith. The historic relationship to the Christian Church (Disciples of Christ) encourages a balance of faith and reason and a spirit for social justice and inclusiveness that's rooted in respect for one another. The university's mission—to educate individuals to think and act as ethical leaders and responsible citizens in a global community—influences everything from course work to study abroad to the way Horned Frogs act and interact. TCU attracts and serves students who are learning to change the world.

"TCU is Test Optional through 2027 and will accept either the SAT or the ACT (with or without the writing component) in admission and scholarship processes."

SELECTIVITY

# of total applicants	22,680
% of total applicants accepted	48
% of total acceptees attending	25
# of in-state applicants	10,757
% of in-state applicants accepted	43
# of out-of-state-applicants	10,483
% of applicants accepted from out of state	55
# of international applicants	1,277
% of international applicants accepted	26
# of early decision applicants	1,373
% of early decision applicants accepted	68
# offered a place on the wait list	3,676
# admitted from wait list	396

First-Year Profile

Testing policy	Test Optional
Range SAT composite	1110–1330
Range SAT EBRW	560–680
Range SAT math	540–660
Range ACT composite	26–31
% submitting SAT scores	27
% submitting ACT scores	21
% graduated top 10% of class	46
% graduated top 25% of class	78
% graduated top 50% of class	95
% submitting high school rank	37

Important Dates

Early decision	
Apply by	11/1
Notified by	1/1
Other ED apply by	2/1
Other ED notified by	3/15
Early action	
Apply by	11/1
Notified by	1/1
Regular	
Apply by	2/1
Notified by	4/1
Nonfall registration?	Yes

FINANCIAL FACTS

Annual tuition	$66,520
Food and housing	$18,780
Required fees	$ 90
Books and supplies	$700
Average need-based scholarship (First-year)	$50,820 ($50,804)
% students with need rec. need-based scholarship or grant aid (First-year)	97 (98)
% students with need rec. non-need-based scholarship or grant aid (First-year)	92 (92)
% students with need rec. need-based self-help aid (First-year)	67 (68)
% UG borrow to pay for school	34
Average cumulative indebtedness	$46,027
% of students with need fully met (First-year)	25 (30)
Average % of student need met (First-year)	75 (79)

TEXAS STATE UNIVERSITY

601 University Drive, San Marcos, TX 78666 • Admissions: 512-245-2364

Survey Snapshot
Students love San Marcos, TX
Students are happy
Great library

RATINGS

Quality of Life	**84**
Fire Safety	**99**
Green	**60***
Academic	**74**
Profs Interesting	**87**
Profs Accessible	**89**
Admissions	**81**
Financial Aid	**84**

CAMPUS LIFE

Type of school	Public
Environment	Town

Students

Degree-seeking undergrad enrollment	39,290
% male/female/not reported	41/59/0
% from out of state	3
% First-year from public high school	98
% First-year live on campus	84
% Ugrads live on campus	25
# of fraternities (% join)	21 (5)
# of sororities (% join)	14 (5)
% Asian	3
% Black or African American	11
% Hispanic	39
% Native American	<1
% Pacific Islander	<1
% Race and/or ethnicity unknown	6
% Two or more races	3
% White	35
% International	3
# of countries represented	72

CAMPUS MENTAL HEALTH SERVICES

Offers mental health/wellness program	Yes
Mental health training available to students	Yes
Employs Chief Wellness Officer	Yes
Peer-to-peer mental health offerings	No
Counseling center has guidelines or accreditation	Yes
Mental health/well-being courses	Yes, for-credit

ACADEMICS

% students returning for sophomore year	80
% students graduating within 4 years	36
% students graduating within 6 years	55
Calendar	Semester
Student/faculty ratio	22:1
Most common class size 20–29.	(30%)
Most common lab/discussion size 10–19.	(50%)

Most Popular Majors
Exercise Science and Kinesiology; Psychology; Health Services/Allied Health/Health Sciences

Applicants Often Prefer
University of Texas at Austin

Applicants Sometimes Prefer
Texas A&M University—College Station

Applicants Rarely Prefer
Texas Tech University, University of Houston, University of Texas—San Antonio

STUDENTS SAY "..."

Academics

Students are drawn to Texas State University based on the quality and opportunity of its many offerings, in particular the "very strong STEM program," the "top of the line" education program, and for those studying chemistry, biology, and human health, "exceptional" research programs. Faculty are also admired on a personal level as they're "not only skilled, but care deeply about their students' success." One student enthuses: "I can't emphasize how much I love my professors and coursework. Honestly, school has felt like a hobby these past years that I have thoroughly enjoyed." Given that Texas State caters to over 33,000 undergraduates and offers more than 200 degree programs, students admit that there are a number of large-class lectures. But the general high satisfaction of students speaks to the quality of classes, and the "wonderful professors that ignite [their] academic passions." There's talk of a science course that had students "playing with Play-Doh to learn structures of meiosis" and taking a "New York fashion trip to learn about popular businesses." Marketing students enthusiastically speak of the actual campaigns they had to put together for class: "We actually demonstrated our knowledge when we implemented it in our project." As one student puts it: "I have loved all of my professors so far, they really are passionate about their work and their research, and they are also wonderful people to talk to. My overall experience has been amazing."

Campus Life

Texas State is an "absolutely beautiful" campus that is "surrounded by trees and wildlife" and marked by the "gorgeous river that runs through it." It's no surprise that river-based activities such as tubing, kayaking, and "the moonlight paddle board" are extremely popular. It's also fitting that students also make the most of opportunities to preserve that beauty "in the community, helping to conserve the San Marcos river and organize clean ups for the area." Other "outdoor opportunities," such as hiking, camping, or hanging out nearby Sewell Park, are favorite ways for Bobcats to "ease their worries." As one fourth-year student puts it, "you won't be bored." Some undergraduates "come to Texas State thinking it's party hard, which it can be and is, but you also have to work hard." It's an all-in sort of attitude, one that's best evoked by sports, shows, and Greek life: "I believe my school's spirit is our biggest trait."

Student Body

"The community of peers I have built at Texas State University is something I have always dreamed of," confides one senior. That's a common refrain, given there are over 350 student groups to choose from: "I am involved with TXST Trainwreck (ultimate frisbee) which has let me meet my closest friends on campus and future roommates!" Academically, "students at Texas State actively seek support through one another during class and outside." Students describe their peers as "knowledgeable and passionate for their studies," and given the school's demographics, are appreciative of the "strong female presence overall."

With a majority of students hailing originally from the Lone Star State, the vibe on campus is "very homey and welcoming." But don't be fooled, as "Texas State is a really diverse school in many aspects (race, national origin, gender/sexuality, etc.)." Moreover, "the curriculum is oriented toward inclusivity." The result, say students, is "a welcoming environment where the student body feels that they can be their true selves here without any judgment." All in all, "there's a place for everyone here."

TEXAS STATE UNIVERSITY

Financial Aid: 512-245-2315 • E-Mail: admissions@txstate.edu • Website: www.txst.edu

THE PRINCETON REVIEW SAYS

Admissions

The school reports that its standardized testing policy for use in admission for Fall 2026 is Test Optional for students ranked in the top 75% of their high school class. *Very important factors considered include:* class rank, standardized test scores. *Other factors considered include:* rigor of secondary school record, application essay, extracurricular activities, talent/ability, first generation, volunteer work. High school diploma is required and GED is accepted. *Academic units required:* 4 English, 4 math, 4 science, 2 science labs, 2 language (other than English), 2 social studies, 2 history, 6 academic electives, 1 visual/performing arts. *Academic units recommended:* 4 English, 4 math, 4 science, 2 science labs, 2 language (other than English), 2 social studies, 2 history, 6 academic electives, 1 visual/performing arts.

Financial Aid

Students should submit: FAFSA. Priority filing deadline is 1/15. The Princeton Review suggests that all financial aid forms be submitted as soon as possible. *Need-based scholarships/grants offered:* Federal Pell; Federal SEOG; State scholarships/grants; Private scholarships; College/university scholarship or grant aid from institutional funds. *Loan aid offered:* Federal Direct Subsidized Loans; Federal Direct Unsubsidized Loans; Direct PLUS loans; State Loans; College/university loans from institutional funds. Admitted students will be notified of awards on a rolling basis beginning 9/24. Federal Work-Study Program available. Institutional employment available.

The Inside Word

The state of Texas requires that all students meet specific college readiness standards, and assured admission is granted to all students with certain diploma types who meet specific test score and class ranking standards—students should visit the school's website in order to see if they qualify. Even if a student does not meet assured admission requirements, their application will be holistically reviewed by the school.

THE SCHOOL SAYS

From the Admissions Office

"Texas State University is nestled in the heart of central Texas and close to some of the most vibrant cities in the nation—Austin to the north, San Antonio to the south, and Houston to the east. No other university in Texas can rival the natural beauty and opportunities to live, learn, work, and excel found at Texas State!

"For 125 years, our university has been united by the belief that we can do great things through our love of learning and our hard work. We're innovators and artists, investigators and inventors, entrepreneurs and idealists, all united by one shared purpose: to make a positive impact on our world. More than 40,000 undergraduate and graduate students are pursuing degrees from 200+ bachelor's, master's, and doctoral programs—including distinguished and innovative programs in business, education, theatre and the arts, nursing, geography, engineering, and more. Texas State can help you achieve your academic and career goals through access to the personalized support and opportunities you need to succeed in and beyond the classroom.

"At TXST, we believe in connecting what you learn here to the world beyond graduation with degree programs that can prepare you for hundreds of exciting career paths. Our dedicated faculty will help you gain the experience you need to apply classroom discoveries as you meet real-world challenges.

"Are you ready to... ...reveal your full potential? ...explore possibilities? ...have an impact on the world? ...open your mind to the future?

"If so, Texas State University is ready for you!"

SELECTIVITY

# of total applicants	44,436
% of total applicants accepted	91
% of total acceptees attending	23
# of in-state applicants	36,941
% of in-state applicants accepted	92
# of out-of-state-applicants	5,351
% of applicants accepted from out of state	82
# of international applicants	2,144
% of international applicants accepted	96

First-Year Profile

Testing policy	Test Optional !
Range SAT composite	960–1180
Range SAT EBRW	490–610
Range SAT math	460–580
Range ACT composite	19–25
% submitting SAT scores	40
% submitting ACT scores	6
% graduated top 10% of class	12
% graduated top 25% of class	42
% graduated top 50% of class	76
% submitting high school rank	100

Important Dates

Regular	
Apply by	7/15
Notified by	Rolling, 9/1
Nonfall registration?	Yes

FINANCIAL FACTS

Annual in-state tuition	$9,221
Annual out-of-state tuition	$21,521
Food and housing	$11,762
Required fees	$3,019
Books and supplies	$780
Average need-based scholarship (First-year)	$11,412 ($12,425)
% students with need rec. need-based scholarship or grant aid (First-year)	86 (86)
% students with need rec. non-need-based scholarship or grant aid (First-year)	14 (19)
% students with need rec. need-based self-help aid (First-year)	50 (50)
% students rec. any financial aid (First-year)	77 (91)
% UG borrow to pay for school	55
Average cumulative indebtedness	$23,498
% of students with need fully met (First-year)	20 (23)
Average % of student need met (First-year)	64 (67)

! Test Optional if ranked in top 75% of your class.

THOMAS AQUINAS COLLEGE (CA)

10,000 Ojai Road, Santa Paula, CA 93060 • Admissions: 805-525-4417

Survey Snapshot
Lots of conservative students
Students are happy
Classroom facilities are great

RATINGS

Quality of Life	**94**
Fire Safety	**97**
Green	**60***
Academic	**92**
Profs Interesting	**97**
Profs Accessible	**98**
Admissions	**88**
Financial Aid	**95**

CAMPUS LIFE

Type of school	Private
Affiliation	Roman Catholic
Environment	Town

Students

Degree-seeking undergrad enrollment	369
% male/female/not reported	50/50/0
% from out of state	56
% First-year from public high school	33
% First-year live on campus	100
% Ugrads live on campus	100
# of fraternities	0
# of sororities	0
% Asian	2
% Black or African American	0
% Hispanic	19
% Native American	0
% Pacific Islander	0
% Race and/or ethnicity unknown	4
% Two or more races	7
% White	64
% International	4
# of countries represented	10

CAMPUS MENTAL HEALTH SERVICES

Offers mental health/wellness program	Yes
Mental health training available to students	No
Employs Chief Wellness Officer	NR
Peer-to-peer mental health offerings	NR
Counseling center has guidelines or accreditation	No
Mental health/well-being courses	NR

ACADEMICS

% students returning for sophomore year	94
% students graduating within 4 years	77
% students graduating within 6 years	84
Calendar	Semester
Student/faculty ratio	10:1
Most common class size 10–19.	(100%)

Most Popular Majors
Liberal Arts and Sciences/Liberal Studies

Applicants Also Look At
Benedictine College, Christendom College, Franciscan University of Steubenville, Thomas More College of Liberal Arts, University of Dallas

STUDENTS SAY "..."

Academics

Thomas Aquinas College is a private Catholic college known for its dedication to the Socratic method style of teaching, so much so that the "brilliant, yet down to earth" professors are called tutors. Students appreciate these touches, explaining that "all our lessons, other than the monthly lectures, are in-classroom discussions in which tutors lead with a question and guide the conversation." This also provides much appreciated freedom through which "students can direct the path of learning each day," though "some tutors have a more hands-on style" while others "give the students more of a free rein in discussions." Given the small student-to-faculty ratio tutors are described as "part of the community" and "are always available to talk, whether during meals in our cafeteria or if I need to ask them something in their office. They look out for me if I am struggling in a class and are open to any and all questions I may have." Students describe an environment that challenges them and supports their growth. As one student puts it, "You have to show up every day prepared and ready to engage constructively and kindly with your peers, and that takes some serious discipline."

Campus Life

The California campus is located in Santa Paula near the Topatopa mountain range and is within driving distance of Los Angeles. Outdoor recreation is popular, as students enjoy the school's proximity to "extremely beautiful" hiking trails as well as the nearby beaches that are frequent weekend destinations. Many students play intramural sports or join in as spectators to support their classmates. As one student describes it, intramural sports "bring the entire college community together and provide a healthy outlet for energy and stress." There are plenty of activities on campus, including a "lively drama department that does a show each semester," open mic nights, and chess, pool, and video game tournaments throughout the year. Choir is another popular activity, and there are "many different choirs, some for religious purposes, and some for entertainment." Students note that religion plays a big role on campus, and most students "go to one of the daily Masses."

Students describe off-campus parties—TAC is a dry campus—as "usually pretty lowkey; it's overall not at all a party school." This isn't seen as a loss by attendees; many spend their evenings instead reading for school or for fun, listening to music, baking, or socializing with friends in the dorm. As one student enthuses, "Dorm life is fantastic: people hang out in common areas and stop by for a fun conversation."

Student Body

Overall, the student body is "really friendly and wholesome." Many students are "animated by a definitively Catholic spirit" and are "trying to grow in their faith and relationship with God." Students describe their classmates as "studious and with a strong desire to do good and help others." There is "no label [that] will accurately describe everyone, but for the most part, these are students who care about learning." TAC "has a strong sense of community and mutual support. You can walk into any building on campus and find students helping each other with homework and engaged in conversation." Students form "really deep friendships based on the things that really matter" and describe their peers as "some of the happiest, funniest, and smartest people I've ever known." As one enthusiastic student elaborates, "There are simply too many fantastic people here. I would love to become close friends with everyone but there is simply not enough time! Everyone is very kind, fun and hard-working."

THOMAS AQUINAS COLLEGE (CA)

Financial Aid: 800-634-9797 • E-Mail: admissions@thomasaquinas.edu • Website: www.thomasaquinas.edu

THE PRINCETON REVIEW SAYS

Admissions

The school reports that its standardized testing policy for use in admission for Fall 2026 will require applicants to submit either the SAT or ACT. The Princeton Review suggests that interested applicants consult with the school for the most up-to-date standardized testing policies. *Very important factors considered include:* rigor of secondary school record, standardized test scores, application essay, recommendation(s), character/personal qualities, level of applicant's interest. *Important factors considered include:* academic GPA. *Other factors considered include:* class rank, interview, extracurricular activities, talent/ability, religious affiliation/commitment, volunteer work, work experience. High school diploma is required and GED is accepted. *Academic units required:* 4 English, 3 math, 2 science, 2 language (other than English), 2 history. *Academic units recommended:* 4 English, 4 math, 3 science, 2 science labs, 2 history, 3 academic electives.

Financial Aid

Students should submit: FAFSA; State aid form; Institution's own financial aid form. The Princeton Review suggests that all financial aid forms be submitted as soon as possible. *Need-based scholarships/grants offered:* Federal Pell; State scholarships/grants; Private scholarships; College/university scholarship or grant aid from institutional funds. *Loan aid offered:* Federal Direct Subsidized Loans; Federal Direct Unsubsidized Loans; Direct PLUS loans. Admitted students will be notified of awards on a rolling basis beginning 3/15. Federal Work-Study Program not available. Institutional employment available.

The Inside Word

A unique academic institution, Thomas Aquinas College thoroughly analyzes applicants to ensure accepted students will be a good fit on campus. Therefore, academic prowess is a must, and candidates should also demonstrate intellectual curiosity. Because of their holistic approach, admissions officers pay close attention to the application essays. The college operates on a rolling admissions schedule and, if interested, you should apply as early as possible. If you're thinking about attending the new western Massachusetts campus, note that you can only apply for admission at one location.

THE SCHOOL SAYS

From the Admissions Office

"In 2019 Thomas Aquinas College launched a second campus on the beautiful former site of a preparatory school in Northfield, Massachusetts. Students can now choose between two locations to pursue the College's unique program of Catholic liberal education. California boasts year-round sunshine, mission architecture, and nearby beaches; New England claims four seasons, historic colonial buildings, and the majestic Connecticut River Valley. But both campuses offer the same comprehensive and unified academic program, taught under the light of faith.

"The College's curriculum includes no textbooks or lecture classes. In every subject—from philosophy, theology, mathematics, and science to language, music, literature, and history—students read the greatest written works in those disciplines, both ancient and modern: Homer, Plato, Aristotle, Augustine, Aquinas, Newton, Maxwell, Einstein, the Founding Fathers of the American Republic, Shakespeare, and T. S. Eliot, to name just a few. Instead of attending lecture classes, students gather in small tutorials, seminars, and laboratories for Socratic-style discussions. One mark of the program's success is the variety of professions and careers that graduates enter. Many attend graduate and professional schools in a wide array of disciplines; among them, theology, law, business, literature, medicine, and the sciences are most often chosen.

"High school juniors who are interested in learning more about the academic, spiritual, and social life of Thomas Aquinas College are strongly encouraged to participate in TAC's two-week Great Books Summer Program, offered both in California and New England. See thomasaquinas.edu/summer."

SELECTIVITY

# of total applicants	185
% of total applicants accepted	80
% of total acceptees attending	59
# of in-state applicants	57
% of in-state applicants accepted	81
# of out-of-state-applicants	92
% of applicants accepted from out of state	86
# of international applicants	17
% of international applicants accepted	41

First-Year Profile

Testing policy	SAT or ACT Required
Range SAT composite	1160–1340
Range SAT EBRW	620–690
Range SAT math	550–660
Range ACT composite	25–30
% submitting SAT scores	46
% submitting ACT scores	13
Average HS GPA	3.7
% submitting high school GPA	82

Important Dates

Regular	
Notified by	Rolling, 10/1
Nonfall registration?	No

FINANCIAL FACTS

Annual tuition	$31,900
Food and housing	$11,800
Required fees	$0
Books and supplies	$0
Average need-based scholarship (First-year)	$17,189 ($17,945)
% students with need rec. need-based scholarship or grant aid (First-year)	77 (84)
% students with need rec. non-need-based scholarship or grant aid (First-year)	5 (13)
% students with need rec. need-based self-help aid (First-year)	88 (95)
% students rec. any financial aid (First-year)	78 (78)
% UG borrow to pay for school	70
Average cumulative indebtedness	$18,642
% of students with need fully met (First-year)	90 (100)
Average % of student need met (First-year)	100 (100)

Transylvania University

300 North Broadway, Lexington, KY 40508-1797 • Admissions: 859-233-8242

Survey Snapshot
Students love Lexington, KY
Recreation facilities are great
Frats and sororities are popular

RATINGS

Quality of Life	85
Fire Safety	92
Green	60*
Academic	87
Profs Interesting	94
Profs Accessible	95
Admissions	85
Financial Aid	90

CAMPUS LIFE

Type of school	Private
Affiliation	Disciples of Christ
Environment	Metropolis

Students

Degree-seeking undergrad enrollment	950
% male/female/not reported	43/57/<1
% from out of state	17
% First-year from public high school	78
% First-year live on campus	85
% Ugrads live on campus	47
# of fraternities (% join)	5 (49)
# of sororities (% join)	5 (44)
% Asian	2
% Black or African American	5
% Hispanic	5
% Native American	0
% Pacific Islander	0
% Race and/or ethnicity unknown	1
% Two or more races	6
% White	80
% International	<1
# of countries represented	8

CAMPUS MENTAL HEALTH SERVICES

Offers mental health/wellness program	Yes
Mental health training available to students	No
Employs Chief Wellness Officer	NR
Peer-to-peer mental health offerings	NR
Counseling center has guidelines or accreditation	No
Mental health/well-being courses	NR

ACADEMICS

% students returning for sophomore year	86
% students graduating within 4 years	56
% students graduating within 6 years	71
Calendar	4-4-1
Student/faculty ratio	11:1
Most common class size 10–19.	(53%)
Most common lab/discussion size 20–29.	(71%)

Most Popular Majors

Psychology; Business/Commerce; Accounting

Applicants Often Prefer

Centre College, University of Kentucky

Applicants Sometimes Prefer

Bellarmine University, Eastern Kentucky University, Georgetown College, Hanover College, University of Louisville, Western Kentucky University

Applicants Rarely Prefer

Morehead State University, Northern Kentucky University, University of Cincinnati

STUDENTS SAY "…"

Academics

For many thrilled students, Transylvania University in Lexington, Kentucky feels "like home" from the minute they set foot on campus. This is due in large part to its "small size," which allows "Transy" to maintain a very "supportive" environment. When it comes to academics, undergrads at Transylvania savor the breadth of courses that are available. And they rush to highlight the "inclusive fine arts program," which lets non-majors still actively participate in "music or theatre." Many also note student success with graduate school, boasting of a "95 percent" acceptance rate to medical school and a whopping "100 percent" acceptance rate to law school. Much of this can be attributed to "rigorous" classes that "require you to think deeply and critically." Transy's "brilliant faculty" is owed some credit as well. They are "highly dedicated" instructors who continually demonstrate "interest…in [their] students' lives and ambitions." Even better, "they all have open office hours multiple days a week and often will meet with students other times as well." And one incredulous student interjects, "I am close enough with my professors to join them for department dinners or [non-alcoholic] drinks with guest lecturers. It is a one-of-a-kind situation that I wouldn't trade for the world."

Campus Life

It is pretty easy to lead a fun and robust life at Transylvania. While academics take top priority, there are also "many opportunities to get involved on campus." For example, "there are frequently guest speakers and movie nights that students can attend for fun and for class credit." The university hosts "a lot of theater productions and music concerts" as well. Most "people are involved with school-affiliated organizations, like the school's "environmental conservation group" and the "Student Activities Board." Athletics are a big draw too and you can often find undergrads playing "volleyball, basketball, soccer," and "intramurals." Those looking for instant community will be happy to hear that "Greek life is extremely popular." When students are itching to get a break from campus life, downtown Lexington offers a plethora of great options including "a ton of neat places within walking distance, such as…the Central Bank Center, Triangle Park, the Mary Todd Lincoln House, and the Lexington Opera House." All in all, there's "so much to do, and there's always something new to discover."

Student Body

Transylvania manages to foster a "very safe and accepting" atmosphere. Much of that can be attributed to the "incredibly welcoming and friendly" student body. And though the university is set in Kentucky, we're told you find a nice "mix of classic south[ern] and northern attitudes." You're also likely to discover both "liberal" and "conservative" students. Unfortunately, some undergrads do caution that Transylvania is "not very diverse." But many people insist that their peers "seem willing and curious to learn about different cultures and perspectives." As one undergrad shares, "The majority of students on campus are open-minded, creative people, and incredibly accepting of others no matter their gender, race, sexual/gender orientation, or socioeconomic status. They do not hesitate to band together to aid another student in need." Students also love that their peers are "goal oriented" and "take their education seriously." They "push to excel academically, socially, and athletically." And they all enjoy being "extremely involved on campus." Of course, the best aspect of Transy's student body is the fact that "anywhere you go you can always find a friend or at least some people that are easy to talk to."

TRANSYLVANIA UNIVERSITY

Financial Aid: 859-233-8239 • E-Mail: admissions@transy.edu • Website: www.transy.edu

THE PRINCETON REVIEW SAYS

Admissions

The school reports that its standardized testing policy for use in admission for Fall 2026 is Test Optional. The Princeton Review suggests that interested applicants consult with the school for the most up-to-date standardized testing policies. *Very important factors considered include:* rigor of secondary school record, academic GPA, standardized test scores, application essay. *Important factors considered include:* recommendation(s), extracurricular activities, talent/ability, character/personal qualities. *Other factors considered include:* class rank, interview, first generation, alumni/ae relation, geographical residence, volunteer work, work experience. High school diploma is required and GED is accepted. *Academic units required:* 4 English, 3 math, 3 science, 2 science labs, 2 language (other than English), 2 social studies, 2 academic electives. *Academic units recommended:* 4 English, 4 math, 4 science, 3 science labs, 2 language (other than English), 2 social studies, 1 history, 2 academic electives.

Financial Aid

Students should submit: FAFSA. Priority filing deadline is 10/15. The Princeton Review suggests that all financial aid forms be submitted as soon as possible. *Need-based scholarships/grants offered:* Federal Pell; Federal SEOG; State scholarships/grants; Private scholarships; College/university scholarship or grant aid from institutional funds. *Loan aid offered:* Federal Direct Subsidized Loans; Federal Direct Unsubsidized Loans; Direct PLUS loans. Admitted students will be notified of awards on a rolling basis. Federal Work-Study Program available. Institutional employment available.

The Inside Word

Admissions officers at Transylvania realize that students are more than the mere sum of their GPA and test scores and strive to get a clear picture of the entire applicant. Therefore, while high school transcripts hold the most weight, the committee also closely considers your personal statement, extracurricular activities, and recommendations. And applicants wary of the SATs and ACTs can breathe a sigh of relief; Transylvania is a Test Optional school. You will not be at a disadvantage if you choose not to submit your scores.

THE SCHOOL SAYS

From the Admissions Office

"At Transylvania, the 16th-oldest college in the U.S., students receive the skills they need to pursue bold paths toward personal fulfillment and professional success in any field. Professors get to know their students personally, helping them find opportunities to reach their academic and career goals. There are no teaching assistants—just expert faculty who include students in research, help them find jobs and internships and work with them on an academic plan that may even include designing their own major. The liberal arts curriculum gives students broad experience and deep subject training, while developing their skills in communication, problem-solving and adaptability, which is why nearly all of them find a job or graduate school placement within six months of graduation. A testoptional institution, Transylvania is also surprisingly affordable, with a below-average tuition for national liberal arts colleges. In fact, 99 percent of students receive financial aid. Additionally, students benefit from being in downtown Lexington, Kentucky—a thriving city of 320,000 people offering plenty of opportunities for community engagement and career training.

"It's small enough for them to stand out, but with the amenities of one of the best college cities in America. On campus, they can access modern facilities and comprehensive student services, with more than 50 clubs and organizations that let them pursue their interests and develop leadership skills. Transy also has 27 NCAA Division III men's and women's intercollegiate athletic teams."

SELECTIVITY

# of total applicants	2,259
% of total applicants accepted	66
% of total acceptees attending	13
# of in-state applicants	1,273
% of in-state applicants accepted	92
# of out-of-state-applicants	381
% of applicants accepted from out of state	91
# of international applicants	197
% of international applicants accepted	44

First-Year Profile

Testing policy	Test Optional
Range SAT composite	1120–1250
Range SAT EBRW	580–690
Range SAT math	540–690
Range ACT composite	24–30
% submitting SAT scores	5
% submitting ACT scores	67
Average HS GPA	3.8
% submitting high school GPA	98
% graduated top 10% of class	26
% graduated top 25% of class	52
% graduated top 50% of class	84
% submitting high school rank	53

Important Dates

Regular	
Apply by	Rolling
Notified by	Rolling, 11/1
Nonfall registration?	Yes

FINANCIAL FACTS

Annual tuition	$48,380
Food and housing	$15,010
Required fees	$2,260
Books and supplies	$1,000
Average need-based scholarship	$39,844
% students with need rec. need-based scholarship or grant aid	100
% students with need rec. non-need-based scholarship or grant aid	21
% students with need rec. need-based self-help aid	70
% students rec. any financial aid	99
% UG borrow to pay for school	58
Average cumulative indebtedness	$34,124
% of students with need fully met	24
Average % of student need met	84

TRINITY COLLEGE (CT)

300 Summit Street, Hartford, CT 06106 • Admissions: 860-297-2180

Survey Snapshot
Easy to get around campus
Intramural sports are popular
Great library

RATINGS

Quality of Life	**78**
Fire Safety	**85**
Green	**84**
Academic	**86**
Profs Interesting	**91**
Profs Accessible	**93**
Admissions	**93**
Financial Aid	**98**

CAMPUS LIFE

Type of school	Private
Environment	City

Students

Degree-seeking undergrad enrollment	2,071
% male/female/not reported	46/54/0
% from out of state	83
% First-year from public high school	47
% First-year live on campus	100
% Ugrads live on campus	82
# of fraternities (% join)	6 (NR)
# of sororities (% join)	6 (NR)
% Asian	4
% Black or African American	6
% Hispanic	11
% Native American	<1
% Pacific Islander	0
% Race and/or ethnicity unknown	2
% Two or more races	5
% White	59
% International	12
# of countries represented	80

CAMPUS MENTAL HEALTH SERVICES

Offers mental health/wellness program	Yes
Mental health training available to students	Yes
Employs Chief Wellness Officer	Yes
Peer-to-peer mental health offerings	NR
Counseling center has guidelines or accreditation	No
Mental health/well-being courses	Yes, for-credit

ACADEMICS

% students returning for sophomore year	90
% students graduating within 4 years	76
% students graduating within 6 years	83
Calendar	Semester
Student/faculty ratio	8:1
Most common class size 10–19.	(48%)
Most common lab/discussion size 10–19.	(52%)

Most Popular Majors
English Language and Literature; Economics; Political Science and Government

Applicants Also Look At
Boston College, Colby College, College of the Holy Cross, Connecticut College, Fairfield University, Lafayette College, Skidmore College, Tufts University, University of Connecticut, Wesleyan University

STUDENTS SAY "..."

Academics

Trinity College "offers a good balance" of academic rigor and social engagement. It's a place where "you can truly craft your experience" through opportunities such as creating a student-designed interdisciplinary major or minor, studying abroad, or completing a self-directed capstone project. The curriculum encourages "individuals to be multifaceted, [and] students are encouraged to double major" in order to explore other interests and not limit themselves to one particular field. Further, "student research is profound and heavily funded," with one student noting that "financial aid, research opportunities, [and] study abroad programs with transferable financial aid" are readily accessible. Faculty earn high marks, with one student sharing, "The professors are a huge asset, [and] Trinity's humanities professors especially are very good at what they do." In particular, they "really make you question your perceptions on reality, rather than strengthening already established notions." Another student adds, "I love…how they help me find new ways to think," and model how to disagree "in a calm and respectful manner." Students also appreciate that when they run into challenges, "there is acknowledgment of the difficulty in our course load and content, followed by an outreach of extra support or point of contact throughout the semester." And students widely report feeling that professors care about "the education of their students above and beyond all." Alumni are also supportive and are "willing to help current undergrads with their career search." Overall, Trinity students agree that "the biggest strength of our school is the sense of community."

Campus Life

For many students, days in the Coop, as students playfully refer to the Trinity campus, are enjoyable and busy. "There are opportunities to have fun in planned activities on campus almost every day." For many Bantams, as students are known, Greek life offers an outlet for "partying on the weekend if that's your thing," while others describe it as "an oasis from the rest of campus and provides relief from difficult classes or trying social circumstances." Another student adds that Greek life provides "opportunities to do community outreach in both my positions in philanthropy and as treasurer." Athletics are very popular and come in many forms at the Coop. Bantams enthuse about club and intramural sports, and varsity teams compete in the Division III NESCAC. Hikers, rock climbers, and backpackers love Quest, an outdoor education program focused on "leadership development and community building." Combined with a wide range of clubs and organizations for just about every interest, these offerings help ensure that "there is a place for everyone" at Trinity.

Student Body

With just over 2,000 students, Trinity is a close-knit community where "it feels like you know everyone, and at the same time, there are always people you are meeting." Students often connect through the interdisciplinary nature of their studies. As one student shares, "We are all different, but at the same time everyone has many interests, [such as a] STEM major with minors in all different areas of humanities, and the other way around." Echoing that sentiment, another student describes their peers as having "areas of interest that spread from the arts, sciences, to community outreach." While some students acknowledge socioeconomic differences on campus, noting that "the wealth gap is real, and often very easy to identify," they also value the college's "wide range of geographical and cultural backgrounds, with a high percent of international students." One student sums up their social experience at Trinity: "I have met some of the kindest people, many of whom will continue to be part of my life, and I can proudly say I have a home in many different countries around the world thanks to the diverse friendships I've developed."

Trinity College (CT)

Financial Aid: 860-297-2046 • E-Mail: admissions.office@trincoll.edu • Website: www.trincoll.edu

THE PRINCETON REVIEW SAYS

Admissions

The school reports that its standardized testing policy for use in admission for Fall 2026 is Test Optional. The Princeton Review suggests that interested applicants consult with the school for the most up-to-date standardized testing policies. *Very important factors considered include:* rigor of secondary school record, academic GPA, character/personal qualities. *Important factors considered include:* application essay, recommendation(s), extracurricular activities, talent/ability, level of applicant's interest. *Other factors considered include:* class rank, standardized test scores, interview, first generation, alumni/ae relation, geographical residence, state residency, volunteer work, work experience. High school diploma is required and GED is accepted. *Academic units recommended:* 4 English, 3 math, 2 science, 2 science labs, 3 language (other than English), 2 history.

Financial Aid

Students should submit: FAFSA; CSS PROFILE. Priority filing deadline is 1/15. The Princeton Review suggests that all financial aid forms be submitted as soon as possible. *Need-based scholarships/grants offered:* Federal Pell; Federal SEOG; State scholarships/grants; Private scholarships; College/university scholarship or grant aid from institutional funds. *Loan aid offered:* Federal Direct Subsidized Loans; Federal Direct Unsubsidized Loans; Direct PLUS loans; State Loans; College/university loans from institutional funds. Admitted students will be notified of awards on or about 4/1. Federal Work-Study Program available. Institutional employment available.

The Inside Word

Trinity College is seeking a wide range of individuals, and as such, there are many avenues for applicants to consider. Admission is competitive, so finding ways to distinguish yourself, either by submitting optional standardized test scores or with an accomplished, rigorous academic transcript can take you far.

THE SCHOOL SAYS

From the Admissions Office

"At Trinity College, we're known for getting things done—and for doing them in a way that creates lasting meaning. Students come to Trinity to engage in a challenging liberal arts education, live as part of a tenacious community, explore what's possible, and find answers to the challenges of tomorrow. When you become a Trinity Bantam, you will build a foundation of critical thinking that will prepare you to ask the right questions and seek the best solutions. Our small classes and 8:1 student-faculty ratio mean that professors will know you and take a personal interest in your success.

"On our 100-acre campus, you will join a vibrant community of peers from all over the world, engage with like-minded students in over 150 student clubs and organizations, and compete in the storied New England Small College Athletic Conference (NESCAC).

"Living in the heart of Connecticut's state capital, you can take advantage of all that Hartford has to offer, including diverse perspectives, experiential learning, and an energetic cultural life. You will gain experience in our thriving city through academic internships, including our Legislative Internship and Health Fellows programs, and a variety of community service and civic engagement opportunities.

"After graduating, you will join a distinguished, 200-year-old alumni network, including Fulbright and Watson scholars, MacArthur Fellows, and five Pulitzer Prize winners.

"At Trinity College, we are committed to making higher education accessible to more students and families. We offer generous financial aid and grant packages and meet the full calculated need for admitted students. Please visit us in Hartford to learn more about the Trinity experience."

SELECTIVITY

# of total applicants	7,273
% of total applicants accepted	30
% of total acceptees attending	22
# of in-state applicants	663
% of in-state applicants accepted	36
# of out-of-state-applicants	3,262
% of applicants accepted from out of state	53
# of international applicants	3,348
% of international applicants accepted	5
# of early decision applicants	643
% of early decision applicants accepted	41
# offered a place on the wait list	2,468
# admitted from wait list	19

First-Year Profile

Testing policy	Test Optional
Range SAT composite	1350–1460
Range SAT EBRW	670–740
Range SAT math	660–730
Range ACT composite	31–33
% submitting SAT scores	9
% submitting ACT scores	4
% graduated top 10% of class	57
% graduated top 25% of class	82
% graduated top 50% of class	96
% submitting high school rank	14

Important Dates

Early decision	
Apply by	11/15
Notified by	12/15
Other ED apply by	1/12
Other ED notified by	2/10
Regular	
Apply by	1/15
Notified by	4/1
Nonfall registration?	No

FINANCIAL FACTS

Annual tuition	$72,820
Food and housing	$20,330
Required fees	$3,330
Books and supplies	$1,000
Average need-based scholarship (First-year)	$60,186 ($62,221)
% students with need rec. need-based scholarship or grant aid (First-year)	97 (98)
% students with need rec. non-need-based scholarship or grant aid (First-year)	22 (31)
% students with need rec. need-based self-help aid (First-year)	56 (40)
% UG borrow to pay for school	53
Average cumulative indebtedness	$47,068
% of students with need fully met (First-year)	99 (100)
Average % of student need met (First-year)	100 (100)

TRINITY UNIVERSITY

One Trinity Place, San Antonio, TX 78212-7200 • Admissions: 210-999-7207

Survey Snapshot
Internships are widely available
Diverse student types interact on campus
Dorms are like palaces

RATINGS

Quality of Life	86
Fire Safety	60*
Green	60*
Academic	88
Profs Interesting	92
Profs Accessible	94
Admissions	94
Financial Aid	98

CAMPUS LIFE

Type of school	Private
Affiliation	Presbyterian
Environment	Metropolis

Students

Degree-seeking undergrad enrollment	2,415
% male/female/not reported	45/55/0
% from out of state	21
% First-year from public high school	68
% First-year live on campus	100
% Ugrads live on campus	80
# of fraternities (% join)	7 (22)
# of sororities (% join)	7 (32)
% Asian	9
% Black or African American	4
% Hispanic	26
% Native American	<1
% Pacific Islander	<1
% Race and/or ethnicity unknown	1
% Two or more races	7
% White	48
% International	5
# of countries represented	53

CAMPUS MENTAL HEALTH SERVICES

Offers mental health/wellness program	Yes
Mental health training available to students	No
Employs Chief Wellness Officer	NR
Peer-to-peer mental health offerings	NR
Counseling center has guidelines or accreditation	No
Mental health/well-being courses	NR

ACADEMICS

% students returning for sophomore year	92
% students graduating within 4 years	77
% students graduating within 6 years	82
Calendar	Semester
Student/faculty ratio	8:1
Most common class size 10–19.	(45%)
Most common lab/discussion size 10–19.	(46%)

Most Popular Majors

Business Administration and Management; Finance; Mass Communication/Media Studies

Applicants Also Look At

Baylor University, Southern Methodist University, Southwestern University, Texas A&M University—College Station, Texas Christian University, University of Texas at Austin, The University of Texas at Dallas

STUDENTS SAY "..."

Academics

Trinity University's alumni employment rate is ranked number one in Texas. Students appreciate this San Antonio-based university's hands-on academic programming, which they describe as an "excellent pipeline into getting a good job [that's] almost guaranteed for some majors." This success is credited in part to "faculty members [that] are highly knowledgeable and experienced in their respective fields." In fact, 97% of Trinity professors hold a doctorate or the highest degree available in their field. Smaller class sizes offer the chance for "a lot of interaction" between professors and undergrads and helps create "classes that are challenging and enjoyable." Students also note that Trinity's career focus doesn't come at the cost of expansive education opportunities. The school offers almost 60 majors that range from the arts and humanities to the social sciences, along with special interests like pre-law that are supported by real-world experiences, special programming like "regular entrepreneurship competitions," and motivational "high profile speakers such as Venus Williams." Trinity's interdisciplinary approach is another benefit that "encourages students to take a wide range of courses and develop many skills." Students also say the university "makes it very easy to change majors, pick up a second one, or [add a] minor." In addition to robust higher ed courses, "great academic facilities" are part of the appeal of Trinity, with many of its buildings included on the National Registry of Historic Places. Coates Library is a prime example, offering more than 1 million research sources, and adding to the campus' reputation as a living library.

Campus Life

While academics are a large focal point of the Trinity University experience, the campus promotes a "work hard/play hard dynamic." In addition to a large focus on studies, there are also ample opportunities for recreation through numerous student-led organizations. Greek life, intramural sports, an on-site fitness center, theater and film clubs, and mock trials are some of the most popular activities and "rec sports are top notch." There are also more niche interests such as a "knitting club...and Taylor Swift club [that help students] find people with similar interests." Many student organizations are connected with the larger San Antonio community and offer ways to "engage with volunteering"; a popular pick among students is the Cats Alliance that "feeds, spays/neuters, [and] vaccinates" any stray cats on campus, and "has a great group of people involved in taking care of them." Students attest to how well these activities add to Trinity's "well-rounded experience, both academically and socially," by allowing them to "explore interests and develop new skills."

Student Body

Trinity University has a varied demographic, which creates a "rich tapestry of experiences." More importantly to students, this "abundant diversity of personalities, races, identities... interests and passions," which includes "a strong LGBTQ+ community," comes together in a "very family-like atmosphere." The university is credited with fostering how "students interact, really bringing out a certain unity." Within the student body there are also "student leaders who have great pride for their cultures," which makes it "extremely enjoyable to join culture clubs around campus to celebrate different ethnic groups." The breadth of diversity on campus also is evident "in relation to character and ideas. The campus is filled with unique individuals who each bring something different to the table." Students also share a common goal of "being interested in learning and [being] hardworking" and many "take on multiple disciplines of education and are involved in an array of campus organizations." There's a reason students are known as Trinity Tigers: they are "helpful, collaborative, and rarely competitive," say enrollees, and are "cultivating life-long relationships."

Trinity University

Financial Aid: 210-999-8898 • E-Mail: admissions@trinity.edu • Website: www.trinity.edu

THE PRINCETON REVIEW SAYS

Admissions

The school reports that its standardized testing policy for use in admission for Fall 2026 is Test Optional. The Princeton Review suggests that interested applicants consult with the school for the most up-to-date standardized testing policies. *Very important factors considered include:* rigor of secondary school record, class rank, academic GPA. *Important factors considered include:* application essay, recommendation(s), interview, extracurricular activities, talent/ability, character/personal qualities. *Other factors considered include:* standardized test scores, first generation, alumni/ae relation, geographical residence, volunteer work, work experience, level of applicant's interest. High school diploma is required and GED is accepted. *Academic units required:* 4 English, 3 math, 3 science, 2 science labs, 2 language (other than English), 3 social studies. *Academic units recommended:* 4 English, 3 math, 3 science, 2 science labs, 2 language (other than English), 3 social studies.

Financial Aid

Students should submit: FAFSA; CSS PROFILE. Priority filing deadline is 3/1. The Princeton Review suggests that all financial aid forms be submitted as soon as possible. *Need-based scholarships/grants offered:* Federal Pell; Federal SEOG; State scholarships/grants; Private scholarships; College/university scholarship or grant aid from institutional funds. *Loan aid offered:* Federal Direct Subsidized Loans; Federal Direct Unsubsidized Loans; Direct PLUS loans; State Loans; College/university loans from institutional funds. Admitted students will be notified of awards on or about 3/15. Federal Work-Study Program available. Institutional employment available.

The Inside Word

As Trinity embraces a small, close-knit community of students, admission officers are looking for the complete package: bright, capable, motivated students who are ready to make the most of all the school has to offer. While academic performance is the factor considered most heavily on each application, recommendations, extracurricular activities, and standardized test scores, if submitting, should all be very strong as well.

THE SCHOOL SAYS

From the Admissions Office

"Trinity University is one of the nation's leading private liberal arts and sciences universities, distinguished by its academic excellence, innovative programs, and commitment to student success. Located in San Antonio—America's seventh-largest and one of its fastest-growing cities—Trinity offers students a dynamic learning environment enriched by cultural diversity, professional opportunities, and a thriving urban landscape.

"At Trinity, education extends beyond the classroom. The University fosters intellectual curiosity, holistic well-being, and a lifelong passion for discovery. With a student-centered approach, Trinity provides the personalized experience of a small college while leveraging the expansive and powerful resources, networks, and opportunities typically found at larger institutions. Students can choose from more than 100 majors and minors, including dedicated pre-law and health professions advising (such as pre-medical). Trinity's unique interdisciplinary second major allows students to customize their academic journey, fostering a broad and flexible skill set. More than 70% of students engage in internships or undergraduate research, while over 70 student-led entrepreneurial ventures have launched from campus. Trinity is also home to 18 NCAA Division III varsity athletics teams, where student-athletes excel both on and off the field.

"A hallmark of Trinity's experience is its emphasis on connection—between students, faculty, alumni, and professional networks. This supportive and engaged community empowers students to thrive academically, explore their passions, and prepare for meaningful careers and lives of purpose."

SELECTIVITY

# of total applicants	11,927
% of total applicants accepted	25
% of total acceptees attending	20
# of in-state applicants	6,892
% of in-state applicants accepted	29
# of out-of-state-applicants	1,762
% of applicants accepted from out of state	41
# of international applicants	3,273
% of international applicants accepted	8
# of early decision applicants	399
% of early decision applicants accepted	53
# offered a place on the wait list	2,244
# admitted from wait list	51

First-Year Profile

Testing policy	Test Optional
Range SAT composite	1330–1460
Range SAT EBRW	670–740
Range SAT math	650–740
Range ACT composite	30–34
% submitting SAT scores	39
% submitting ACT scores	14
Average HS GPA	3.7
% submitting high school GPA	100
% graduated top 10% of class	55
% graduated top 25% of class	31
% graduated top 50% of class	98
% submitting high school rank	43

Important Dates

Early decision	
Apply by	11/1
Notified by	12/1
Other ED apply by	2/1
Other ED notified by	3/1
Early action	
Apply by	11/1
Notified by	12/5
Regular	
Apply by	2/1
Notified by	3/15
Nonfall registration?	Yes

FINANCIAL FACTS

Annual tuition	$59,280
Food and housing	$16,166
Required fees	$0
Books and supplies	$1,000
Average need-based scholarship (First-year)	$43,485 ($40,942)
% students with need rec. need-based scholarship or grant aid (First-year)	97 (95)
% students with need rec. non-need-based scholarship or grant aid (First-year)	43 (57)
% students with need rec. need-based self-help aid (First-year)	70 (55)
% students rec. any financial aid (First-year)	97 (99)
% UG borrow to pay for school	44
Average cumulative indebtedness	$44,451
% of students with need fully met (First-year)	100 (100)
Average % of student need met (First-year)	95 (98)

TRUMAN STATE UNIVERSITY

100 E. Normal Ave., Kirksville, MO 63501 • Admissions: 660-785-4114

Survey Snapshot
Students are friendly
Frats and sororities are popular
College radio is popular

RATINGS

Quality of Life	80
Fire Safety	99
Green	60*
Academic	81
Profs Interesting	85
Profs Accessible	90
Admissions	84
Financial Aid	91

CAMPUS LIFE

Type of school	Public
Environment	Village

Students

Degree-seeking undergrad enrollment	2,549
% male/female/not reported	40/60/0
% from out of state	16
% First-year from public high school	78
% First-year live on campus	95
% Ugrads live on campus	47
# of fraternities (% join)	10 (21)
# of sororities (% join)	7 (17)
% Asian	2
% Black or African American	3
% Hispanic	5
% Native American	<1
% Pacific Islander	<1
% Race and/or ethnicity unknown	1
% Two or more races	3
% White	76
% International	9
# of countries represented	46

CAMPUS MENTAL HEALTH SERVICES

Offers mental health/wellness program	Yes
Mental health training available to students	Yes
Employs Chief Wellness Officer	No
Peer-to-peer mental health offerings	Yes
Counseling center has guidelines or accreditation	Yes
Mental health/well-being courses	Yes, for-credit

ACADEMICS

% students returning for sophomore year	87
% students graduating within 4 years	58
% students graduating within 6 years	69
Calendar	Semester
Student/faculty ratio	13:1
Most common class size 10–19.	(33%)
Most common lab/discussion size 1–9.	(54%)

Most Popular Majors
Biology/Biological Sciences; Exercise Science and Kinesiology; Business Administration and Management

Applicants Often Prefer
Missouri State University, Saint Louis University, University of Missouri

Applicants Sometimes Prefer
Washington University in St. Louis

STUDENTS SAY "..."

Academics

Located in northeast Missouri, Truman State University is a public university that combines the fundamentals of a liberal arts education with specialized programming and hands-on learning, offering "an amazing education at a great price." There are 52 majors available, with all students completing a core curriculum (called the Dialogues) that ensures they develop proficiencies in areas such as writing, speaking, and social perspectives. Truman undergrads also take part in the Truman Symposium, an educational endeavor in which they participate in projects and shared experiences that benefit the students, the university, and the Kirksville community.

This is "a very academically rigorous and challenging school" with "interesting classes galore," and "if you plan to attend any form of graduate school, this school definitely prepares you."

Every student "has to actually attend classes in order to get something out of the experience," but "the workload is manageable." To keep students involved and engaged, many classes are discussion-based and include projects called Facilitations, where students lead the class in a discussion related to a specific topic. Students appreciate the just-right size of the university and say "student-professor relationships are great for mentoring purposes and for future networking opportunities." Many professors have daily office hours "and even more answer emails outside of normal hours or even give students their personal contact info"; they "truly care about individual students, but in a tough love sort of way."

Campus Life

Making your own fun is a real thing in the small town of Kirksville, but "students here know how to make the most out of it." And because "Truman offers so many clubs and activities, that between those and classes and homework, you'll probably never get truly bored." In fact, Truman has well over 230 clubs and organizations, so it makes sense that "student organizations are the main source of socialization here." The Student Activities Board also provides events and entertainment for the students, including a Mario Kart tournament, entertainers like Josh Peck, and even bringing hot air balloons on campus. The university promotes school spirit with weekly events like Purple Friday, where faculty, students, and staff are encouraged to wear school colors, and there are activities and events in the student union and on the Mall. Not all entertainment is school-related; students also note that there is a "great Greek life" for those that want to partake.

When students need some downtime, there is "a state park close to Kirksville where you can go hiking and go to the lake," and "when the weather is nice it's such a mental health support being able to just sit on the Quad." There are various housing options for students, including the Living Learning Communities for students that want to share living space with others with similar academic interests. Kirksville is a college town, so every year the school has a community service day called The Big Event, and students show their appreciation of the surrounding community by performing volunteer services such as cleanup and maintenance tasks.

Student Body

Motivated students will do well here as Truman is "a collective place for ambitious individuals." The "majority of students here are focused on their academic studies" and are "driven, smart individuals who also value community." Although the school "is not racially diverse," there are "quite a few international students," as the overall population comes from a variety of socioeconomic backgrounds. "Many work a required campus job necessary for scholarships, along with taking heavy class loads, and being involved in multiple extracurriculars." Whether or not you're one of the "mainly liberal students" the atmosphere seems to be one where we are "all in this together."

Truman State University

Financial Aid: 660-785-4130 • E-Mail: admissions@truman.edu • Website: www.truman.edu

THE PRINCETON REVIEW SAYS

Admissions

The school reports that its standardized testing policy for use in admission for Fall 2026 is Test Optional. The Princeton Review suggests that interested applicants consult with the school for the most up-to-date standardized testing policies. *Very important factors considered include:* rigor of secondary school record, class rank, academic GPA. *Important factors considered include:* application essay. *Other factors considered include:* standardized test scores, recommendation(s), extracurricular activities, talent/ability, character/personal qualities, first generation, alumni/ae relation, geographical residence, state residency, volunteer work, work experience, level of applicant's interest. High school diploma is required and GED is accepted. *Academic units required:* 4 English, 3 math, 3 science, 2 science labs, 2 language (other than English), 2 social studies, 1 history, 5 academic electives, 1 visual/performing arts. *Academic units recommended:* 4 English, 3 math, 3 science, 2 science labs, 2 language (other than English), 2 social studies, 1 history, 5 academic electives, 1 visual/performing arts.

Financial Aid

Students should submit: FAFSA. Priority filing deadline is 2/1. The Princeton Review suggests that all financial aid forms be submitted as soon as possible. *Need-based scholarships/grants offered:* Federal Pell; Federal SEOG; State scholarships/grants; Private scholarships; College/university scholarship or grant aid from institutional funds. *Loan aid offered:* Federal Direct Subsidized Loans; Federal Direct Unsubsidized Loans; Direct PLUS loans; College/university loans from institutional funds. Admitted students will be notified of awards on a rolling basis beginning 1/1. Federal Work-Study Program available. Institutional employment available.

The Inside Word

Truman State prides itself on taking a well-rounded approach to the admissions process. The university truly believes that students are more than just the sum of their grades and test scores. Therefore, expect that all application facets, from transcripts to extracurricular participation, will be heavily scrutinized. You should note that intended music majors will have to sit for an audition in addition to the regular application. And nursing candidates will need to be admitted to both the university overall as well as the specific nursing program.

THE SCHOOL SAYS

From the Admissions Office

"Truman's talented student body enjoys small classes where undergraduate research and personal interaction with professors are the norm. Our outstanding internship and study abroad opportunities allow students to attend top graduate schools and graduate with strong job prospects. We are recognized consistently as one of the nation's 'Best Values' in higher education. Because we offer a variety of competitive scholarships but not a separate application for them, students are strongly encouraged to apply for admission by December 1st and submit an activities list or résumé along with an essay for best consideration. Students applying to Truman State University can submit scores from both the ACT and the SAT. Their superscore from either test will be considered in admission and scholarship selection along with the student's weighted GPA. The ACT's writing section is not required. We believe a quality college experience starts in the classroom and travels with you past its doors. A sense of scholarship and discovery permeates our campus, offering opportunities that entertain, pique students' interest, and invite them deeper into their learning with practical experiences. Your time in college is about making great friends, getting involved in one of over 230 student organizations, exploring the areas you can influence in our world, and creating memories that will last a lifetime. Ours is a university that transforms lives. As one of the nation's premier public liberal arts and sciences institutions, our successes can be traced to one guiding principle: an unwavering devotion to the pursuit of knowledge, wherever your journey leads you."

SELECTIVITY

# of total applicants	4,661
% of total applicants accepted	85
% of total acceptees attending	16
# of in-state applicants	2,201
% of in-state applicants accepted	85
# of out-of-state-applicants	2,319
% of applicants accepted from out of state	85
# of international applicants	141
% of international applicants accepted	72

First-Year Profile

Testing policy	Test Optional
Range SAT composite	1250–1310
Range SAT EBRW	600–700
Range SAT math	570–670
Range ACT composite	25–31
% submitting SAT scores	5
% submitting ACT scores	43
Average HS GPA	3.8
% submitting high school GPA	93
% graduated top 10% of class	31
% graduated top 25% of class	36
% graduated top 50% of class	27
% submitting high school rank	41

Important Dates

Regular	
Notified by	Rolling, 9/1
Nonfall registration?	Yes

FINANCIAL FACTS

Annual in-state tuition	$10,658
Annual out-of-state tuition	$20,297
Food and housing	$13,034
Required fees	$1,170
Books and supplies	$1,000
Average need-based scholarship (First-year)	$12,658 ($14,208)
% students with need rec. need-based scholarship or grant aid (First-year)	98 (100)
% students with need rec. non-need-based scholarship or grant aid (First-year)	93 (100)
% students with need rec. need-based self-help aid (First-year)	69 (59)
% students rec. any financial aid (First-year)	75 (100)
% UG borrow to pay for school	45
Average cumulative indebtedness	$24,778
% of students with need fully met (First-year)	35 (44)
Average % of student need met (First-year)	87 (91)

TUFTS UNIVERSITY

2 The Green, Medford, MA 02155 • Admissions: 617-627-3170

Survey Snapshot
Lots of liberal students
Diverse student types interact on campus
Active student-run political groups

RATINGS

Quality of Life	**91**
Fire Safety	**97**
Green	**60***
Academic	**90**
Profs Interesting	**92**
Profs Accessible	**94**
Admissions	**97**
Financial Aid	**97**

CAMPUS LIFE

Type of school	Private
Environment	Metropolis

Students

Degree-seeking undergrad enrollment	6,945
% male/female/not reported	44/56/0
% from out of state	71
% First-year live on campus	100
% Ugrads live on campus	60
# of fraternities (% join)	5 (12)
# of sororities (% join)	2 (15)
% Asian	17
% Black or African American	6
% Hispanic	10
% Native American	<1
% Pacific Islander	<1
% Race and/or ethnicity unknown	7
% Two or more races	8
% White	40
% International	13

CAMPUS MENTAL HEALTH SERVICES

Offers mental health/wellness program	Yes
Mental health training available to students	No
Employs Chief Wellness Officer	NR
Peer-to-peer mental health offerings	NR
Counseling center has guidelines or accreditation	No
Mental health/well-being courses	NR

ACADEMICS

% students returning for sophomore year	95
% students graduating within 4 years	83
% students graduating within 6 years	94
Calendar	Semester
Student/faculty ratio	10:1
Most common class size 10–19.	(47%)
Most common lab/discussion size 10–19.	(47%)

Most Popular Majors
International Relations and Affairs; Economics; Computer Science

Applicants Often Prefer
Brown University, Georgetown University, Harvard College, University of Pennsylvania

Applicants Sometimes Prefer
Cornell University, Dartmouth College, Johns Hopkins University, Northwestern University, The University of Chicago, Washington University in St. Louis

Applicants Rarely Prefer
Boston College, Boston University, Carnegie Mellon University, New York University

STUDENTS SAY "..."

Academics

Tufts University offers more than 90 undergraduate academic programs and over 400 student organizations, making it the "perfect mix of liberal arts and university." Tufts students are encouraged to pursue both their academic and social interests "in a passionate way." One student reflects, "I have had the opportunity to explore a huge amount of academic subjects and really challenge myself." The classroom environment promotes dynamic discussions and intellectual curiosity, fostering "a better learning experience and with incomparable relationships with brilliant (yet down to earth) professors." One student shares, "I've literally been offered a research position by asking questions multiple times." The "knowledgeable and interesting professors" are known for being "highly accessible" and responsive to students' academic needs. "It is far easier to succeed here than to fail," relates one student, "as long as you are committed to getting as strong an education as possible." In general, administrators and instructors are receptive to student feedback. As one student notes, "Change is easily made here," and "if you have a problem with something, you can easily address it." Tufts is committed to providing "a world of opportunities" for its students as they prepare for life after graduation.

Campus Life

Student participation and school spirit foster Tufts' "thriving and alive" campus culture. "Almost everything here is run by clubs and student organizations." On offer are fraternities and sororities, if you decide to go Greek, as well as community service organizations, student government, and performance groups. Students rave about the wide variety of activities available, from "dancing and singing to teaching and tutoring to international community service." Tufts Dance Collective, Quadball clubs, and a cappella groups are also campus favorites. Tufts undergrads primarily spend their time on two of Tufts' four campuses: the suburban Medford/Somerville campus and the urban Fenway campus. The campus shuttle system and public transportation "make everything accessible," enabling students to explore Boston as though it is their own personal playground. As one student enthusiastically remarks, "There is more to do in this city than anyone can possibly do in four years." Davis Square is very popular due to its close proximity to campus and its reputation as a great place to shop, dine, and hang out. Students report that "there are usually good parties to go to" and there are "always a lot of events going on around campus that attract students every weekend."

Student Body

The typical Tufts student "is engaged in so many activities on campus," making them "stunningly busy and happy to be so." One student says, "It's really nice to walk around campus knowing that you're in a place where almost everyone is excited to be there." This positive atmosphere encourages meaningful discussions, particularly interdisciplinary conversations. "This is a great place to share knowledge you have because everyone wants to hear it and share their own experiences and thoughts." And one student humorously adds, "It's like a competition to be the 'most interesting [person] in the world.'" Along with lively and passionate discussions, students appreciate individuality. "The true beauty of the school is in the unique and quirky nature of its student body." As one student puts it: "We here embrace weirdness." Eclectic or not, the student body at Tufts is "global minded, ambitious," and has a "passion for excellence." This is a group of "young adults with not only big dreams for the world, but with [the] dedication and motivation to complete them."

TUFTS UNIVERSITY

Financial Aid: 617-627-2000 • E-Mail: undergraduate.admissions@tufts.edu • Website: www.tufts.edu

THE PRINCETON REVIEW SAYS

Admissions

The school reports that its standardized testing policy for use in admission for Fall 2026 is Test Optional. The Princeton Review suggests that interested applicants consult with the school for the most up-to-date standardized testing policies. *Very important factors considered include:* rigor of secondary school record, class rank, academic GPA, application essay, recommendation(s), character/personal qualities. *Important factors considered include:* extracurricular activities, talent/ability. *Other factors considered include:* standardized test scores, interview, first generation, alumni/ae relation, geographical residence, volunteer work, work experience, level of applicant's interest. High school diploma is required and GED is accepted. *Academic units required:* 4 English, 3 math, 3 science, 3 language (other than English), 3 social studies. *Academic units recommended:* 4 math, 4 science, 4 language (other than English), 4 social studies.

Financial Aid

Students should submit: FAFSA; CSS PROFILE. The Princeton Review suggests that all financial aid forms be submitted as soon as possible. *Need-based scholarships/grants offered:* Federal Pell; Federal SEOG; State scholarships/grants; College/university scholarship or grant aid from institutional funds; Private scholarships. *Loan aid offered:* Federal Direct Subsidized Loans; Federal Direct Unsubsidized Loans; Direct PLUS loans. Admitted students will be notified of awards on or about 4/1. Federal Work-Study Program available. Institutional employment available.

The Inside Word

Admission to Tufts is very competitive. You'll need a stellar transcript to get accepted here, rounded out with strong recommendations and extracurriculars that reflect substantive engagement with your school or community. The Common App with Tufts' own writing supplement is required.

THE SCHOOL SAYS

From the Admissions Office

"Tufts is a medium-sized liberal arts university with a focus on faculty relationships, research, and celebrating diverse experiences. Our 6,000+ undergraduate students pursue majors in one of three schools: the School of Arts and Sciences, the School of Engineering, or the School of the Museum of Fine Arts (SMFA). As part of a tier one research university, our students delve into world-class research easily and early, exploring fields from soft-bodied robotics to the rebirth of urban democracy, microbial communities to musical theater. Tufts offers the chance to join a close-knit community that supports intellectual risk-taking and a global outlook, all in a beautiful campus setting just five miles from downtown Boston.

"You can't fit Tufts students into a box. They are intellectually powerful, down-to-earth, driven, and civic-minded. At Tufts, they learn how to make a measurable difference and then start making it—even as undergraduates. On campus, the Tisch College of Civic Life leads the way, allowing students to take curricular courses in social change or even enroll in the Tufts Civic Semester. Whether they are engineers, studio artists, environment advocates, or poets, our students graduate from Tufts ready to enact positive change in the communities they join."

SELECTIVITY

# of total applicants	33,415
% of total applicants accepted	11
% of total acceptees attending	49
# of in-state applicants	4,733
# of out-of-state-applicants	19,414
# of international applicants	9,260
# of early decision applicants	3,344
# offered a place on the wait list	3,061
# admitted from wait list	71

First-Year Profile

Testing policy	Test Optional
Range SAT composite	1460–1520
Range SAT EBRW	720–760
Range SAT math	730–780
Range ACT composite	33–35
% submitting SAT scores	42
% submitting ACT scores	16
% graduated top 10% of class	87
% graduated top 25% of class	96
% graduated top 50% of class	97
% submitting high school rank	21

Important Dates

Early decision	
Apply by	11/3
Notified by	12/15
Other ED apply by	1/5
Other ED notified by	2/15
Regular	
Apply by	1/5
Notified by	4/1
Nonfall registration?	No

FINANCIAL FACTS*

Annual tuition	$69,146
Food and housing	$18,588
Required fees	$1,558
Books and supplies	$1,000
Average need-based scholarship (First-year)	$56,241 ($55,617)
% students with need rec. need-based scholarship or grant aid (First-year)	94 (94)
% students with need rec. non-need-based scholarship or grant aid (First-year)	89 (2)
% students with need rec. need-based self-help aid (First-year)	89 (87)
% students rec. any financial aid (First-year)	35 (39)
% UG borrow to pay for school	27
Average cumulative indebtedness	$27,162
% of students with need fully met (First-year)	99 (98)
Average % of student need met (First-year)	100 (100)

* Most recently reported data at time of printing. Scan the QR code to find the latest updates.

TULANE UNIVERSITY

6823 St. Charles Avenue, New Orleans, LA 70118 • Admissions: 504-865-5731

Survey Snapshot
Great off-campus food
Students love New Orleans, LA
Easy to get around campus

RATINGS

Quality of Life	**90**
Fire Safety	**96**
Green	**92**
Academic	**87**
Profs Interesting	**90**
Profs Accessible	**93**
Admissions	**97**
Financial Aid	**91**

CAMPUS LIFE

Type of school	Private
Environment	Metropolis

Students

Degree-seeking undergrad enrollment	6,839
% male/female/not reported	39/61/<1
% from out of state	86
% First-year from public high school	50
% First-year live on campus	97
% Ugrads live on campus	57
# of fraternities (% join)	9 (32)
# of sororities (% join)	14 (53)
% Asian	6
% Black or African American	6
% Hispanic	13
% Native American	<1
% Pacific Islander	<1
% Race and/or ethnicity unknown	2
% Two or more races	5
% White	63
% International	5
# of countries represented	71

CAMPUS MENTAL HEALTH SERVICES

Offers mental health/wellness program	Yes
Mental health training available to students	Yes
Employs Chief Wellness Officer	Yes
Peer-to-peer mental health offerings	Yes
Counseling center has guidelines or accreditation	Yes
Mental health/well-being courses	NR

ACADEMICS

% students returning for sophomore year	93
% students graduating within 4 years	79
% students graduating within 6 years	87
Calendar	Semester
Student/faculty ratio	7:1
Most common class size 10–19.	(39%)
Most common lab/discussion size 10–19.	(52%)

Most Popular Majors
Business; Finance; Psychology

Applicants Sometimes Prefer
Louisiana State University—Baton Rouge, University of Michigan—Ann Arbor, University of Southern California, University of Texas at Austin, University of Wisconsin—Madison

STUDENTS SAY "..."

Academics

Tulane University's core curriculum blends disciplines in a way that feels both expansive and grounded, offering students access to "endless resources, from career advising to school-sanctioned excursions to the city." That support network is palpable; as one student shares, "There are so many support systems I honestly feel like it's impossible to fail sometimes." First-years take part in TIDES (Tulane Interdisciplinary Experience Seminar), where all students complete at least two service-learning experiences, designed to offer "alternative learning methods and get us involved with the greater New Orleans community." Study abroad is a priority for many—about a third of students participate—and "the programs are well-structured, accessible, and integrated into almost every major." Tulane is responsive to its students, as it "emphasizes student feedback and adapts to those critiques," with support from "a great group of academic advisors and career counselors as well who help with anything you need." Many courses incorporate experiential learning, such as "working with local businesses and non-profits, case studies and real-world applications, research opportunities, [and] presentations," while professors "[make] a strong effort to connect us with people in the real world and bring interesting guest speakers." As another student notes, "They do an amazing job working to support students, pushing them academically while encouraging and guiding them through challenging content or work." By combining challenging academics with real-world opportunities, Tulane fosters students who are prepared and ready to make an impact on the world.

Campus Life

Tulane students are eager to learn, but they also want "to have fun while we do it." With the city itself serving as an extension of campus, students note that "the exposure to New Orleans culture, from the music and food to the parades and energy, is amazing and really shapes the college experience here." Warm weather and green campus spaces make it easy to spend time in the open air, whether "studying outside in the outdoors classrooms or [enjoying] recreational activities." Early in the week, students "attend campus events (comedy shows, movie nights, dorm bonding activities, sports games, trivia nights)" with the social scene shifting toward exploring music venues and bars as the weekend approaches. Community events "such as festivals surrounding the campus," are popular pastimes, alongside "trying new restaurants and coffee shops," while trips to the waterfront or "Audubon Park every Friday for a picnic with many other students" offer relaxed ways to connect. The Big Easy is undeniably a draw, but Tulane students "are very involved on campus" and strike a "balance between having fun and academic rigor." Classes may be challenging, yet one student emphasizes, "I don't think this prevents people from partying, going to athletic events, involving themselves in clubs or Greek life, or engaging with the New Orleans community."

Student Body

The collaborative environment at Tulane "allows the students to feel comfortable branching out, trying new things, and fostering positive relationships." Students are inclusive and welcoming, and "everyone goes above and beyond to make plans and include whoever wants to come." Students aren't afraid to make their voices heard: Tulane students "speak out about what they are passionate about and believe in" and "love collaborating to turn many small ideas into a great one." While the school may be predominantly white, it is "geographically diverse, bringing together people from every corner of the country and many different backgrounds," creating a community connected through shared experiences and mutual support. As one student explains, "Everyone loves this school so much, and I think a large part of that love comes from such an uplifting and positive community of both students and faculty alike."

TULANE UNIVERSITY

Financial Aid: 504-865-5723 • E-Mail: undergrad.admission@tulane.edu • Website: www.tulane.edu

THE PRINCETON REVIEW SAYS

Admissions

The school reports that its standardized testing policy for use in admission for Fall 2026 is Test Optional but testing is preferred for students who want to be competitive for academic merit scholarships. The Princeton Review suggests that interested applicants consult with the school for the most up-to-date standardized testing policies. *Very important factors considered include:* rigor of secondary school record, class rank, academic GPA, extracurricular activities, volunteer work. *Important factors considered include:* standardized test scores, application essay, recommendation(s), character/personal qualities, first generation, level of applicant's interest. *Other factors considered include:* talent/ability, alumni/ae relation, geographical residence, state residency, work experience. High school diploma is required and GED is accepted.

Financial Aid

Students should submit: FAFSA; CSS PROFILE. Priority filing deadline is 2/15. The Princeton Review suggests that all financial aid forms be submitted as soon as possible. *Need-based scholarships/grants offered:* Federal Pell; Federal SEOG; State scholarships/grants; Private scholarships; College/university scholarship or grant aid from institutional funds. *Loan aid offered:* Federal Direct Subsidized Loans; Federal Direct Unsubsidized Loans; Direct PLUS loans. Admitted students will be notified of awards on a rolling basis beginning 2/15. Federal Work-Study Program available. Institutional employment available.

The Inside Word

Tulane is a highly competitive school, and admissions reflect that. The university places significant weight on your high school transcript and standardized test scores, though the latter are optional. That said, submitting scores is strongly encouraged for students who want to be competitive for academic merit scholarships. The most successful applicants tend to have challenged themselves with a rigorous course load, so honors and AP classes can strengthen your application. Extracurricular activities are considered, but carry less weight than academic factors. Prospective architecture students should also note that submitting a portfolio is highly recommended.

THE SCHOOL SAYS

From the Admissions Office

"Tulane is one of the very few universities where students do not apply directly to a school or college and instead have immediate access to all academic programs upon admission. In addition, as the only major research university in America with a public service requirement for graduation, Tulane students are wholly committed to giving back to their communities. The opportunities for students to use their knowledge to improve life in the historic city of New Orleans offer an experience unavailable at any other place, at any other time.

"Tulane is committed to undergraduate education. Senior faculty members teach most introductory and lower-level courses, and most classes have twenty-five or fewer students. The close student-teacher relationship pays off. Tulane graduates are among the most likely to be selected for several prestigious fellowships that support graduate study abroad. Founded in 1834 and reorganized as Tulane University in 1884, Tulane is one of the major private research universities in the South.

"As previously mentioned, Tulane students highly value balance, and most of all they're happy with their choice and love the school."

SELECTIVITY

# of total applicants	32,942
% of total applicants accepted	14
% of total acceptees attending	39
# of in-state applicants	2,676
% of in-state applicants accepted	22
# of out-of-state-applicants	25,512
% of applicants accepted from out of state	14
# of international applicants	4,754
% of international applicants accepted	12
# of early decision applicants	2,077
% of early decision applicants accepted	58
# offered a place on the wait list	5,842
# admitted from wait list	64

First-Year Profile

Testing policy	Test Optional
Range SAT composite	1430–1500
Range SAT EBRW	710–750
Range SAT math	710–760
Range ACT composite	32–34
% submitting SAT scores	11
% submitting ACT scores	27
Average HS GPA	3.7
% submitting high school GPA	100
% graduated top 10% of class	53
% graduated top 25% of class	80
% graduated top 50% of class	95
% submitting high school rank	20

Important Dates

Early decision	
Apply by	11/1
Notified by	12/15
Other ED apply by	1/15
Other ED notified by	2/15
Early action	
Apply by	11/10
Notified by	1/10
Regular	
Apply by	1/15
Notified by	4/1
Nonfall registration?	Yes

FINANCIAL FACTS

Annual tuition	$67,592
Food and housing	$19,630
Required fees	$4,406
Books and supplies	$1,200
Average need-based scholarship (First-year)	$60,630 ($64,125)
% students with need rec. need-based scholarship or grant aid (First-year)	94 (92)
% students with need rec. non-need-based scholarship or grant aid (First-year)	31 (47)
% students with need rec. need-based self-help aid (First-year)	53 (51)
% students rec. any financial aid (First-year)	64 (72)
% UG borrow to pay for school	26
Average cumulative indebtedness	$38,066
% of students with need fully met (First-year)	50 (73)
Average % of student need met (First-year)	90 (94)

UNION COLLEGE (NY)

807 Union Street, Schenectady, NY 12308 • Admissions: 518-388-6112

Survey Snapshot
Lab facilities are great
Easy to get around campus
Great library

RATINGS

Quality of Life	83
Fire Safety	92
Green	83
Academic	88
Profs Interesting	93
Profs Accessible	95
Admissions	92
Financial Aid	99

CAMPUS LIFE

Type of school	Private
Environment	Town

Students

Degree-seeking undergrad enrollment	1,939
% male/female/not reported	53/47/0
% from out of state	68
% First-year live on campus	98
% Ugrads live on campus	91
# of fraternities (% join)	9 (20)
# of sororities (% join)	3 (29)
% Asian	8
% Black or African American	6
% Hispanic	12
% Native American	0
% Pacific Islander	<1
% Race and/or ethnicity unknown	<1
% Two or more races	5
% White	60
% International	10
# of countries represented	48

CAMPUS MENTAL HEALTH SERVICES

Offers mental health/wellness program	Yes
Mental health training available to students	Yes
Employs Chief Wellness Officer	No
Peer-to-peer mental health offerings	No
Counseling center has guidelines or accreditation	No
Mental health/well-being courses	Yes, for-credit

ACADEMICS

% students returning for sophomore year	89
% students graduating within 4 years	67
% students graduating within 6 years	81
Calendar	Trimester
Student/faculty ratio	9:1
Most common class size 10–19.	(44%)

Most Popular Majors
Mechanical Engineering; Psychology; Biology/Biological Sciences

Applicants Often Prefer
Colgate University, Cornell University, Tufts University

Applicants Sometimes Prefer
Hamilton College, Lafayette College, University of Rochester

Applicants Rarely Prefer
University of Vermont

STUDENTS SAY "…"

Academics

Union College puts an interdisciplinary lens on the liberal arts, giving students the freedom to combine majors and minors across multiple departments, both in STEM and the humanities. "Union has so many opportunities, and many pathways to access them," says one student. Take, for instance, the trimester structure, where some students suggest that because they take three courses every ten weeks, they can "be more nimble and pivot majors more quickly." The majority of students complete an internship and/or faculty-mentored research, and "professors emphasize teaching quality equally to research at Union, which makes for a great classroom environment." Overall, smaller class sizes "make it so that actual conversations can be had…that are beneficial for the whole class." Informed critical thinking is an end goal, beginning with the way faculty are "really engaged in the academic discourse and work to bring the classroom up to speed," through the way in which they "give us the resources to keep on learning the subject outside the classroom." This explains the popularity of Steinmetz Day, an all-campus event in which students showcase their work: "everyone watches their peers' research presentations and talks." This commitment and follow-through with the liberal arts "not only prepares you professionally,…but gives you a well-rounded understanding of the real world and how to identify patterns, understand them, and how that applies in all disciplines of life."

Campus Life

A few exceptions and exemptions aside, students live on campus for their entire time at Union. Accordingly, there is a focus on the residential experience, with "very good housing selections," all of which are "within walking distance and close to your classes." Every student also belongs to one of seven Minerva Houses, which act as academic and social centers for their members; one student says that "being involved in my Minerva or attending other Minerva events" is a highlight of their time at Union. Greek life is popular, and while some people "do party on the weekends," there are "a lot of people [who] find other ways to have fun with their friends," such as reserving common spaces for movie or game nights. As for activities, "There are so many clubs to be involved in it is hard to keep count, as one student adds, "we get a daily email and everything." Many also make the most of the location, like how the Outing Club "runs near-weekly hikes to the wonderful natural areas within a few hours of our campus, such as the Catskills and Adirondacks." Finally, student organizations have an "all-comers" policy that allows everyone to participate. These options work hand-in-hand to ensure there are "constant activities running to support the student body's interest."

Student Body

Union College is home to a group of people who are "super enthusiastic and motivated scholastically." They are a "thoughtful and welcoming" crowd that is "encouraged to develop their leadership skills while diving into what they are passionate about." There is "a wide variety of interests and it's fairly easy to find people who share your niche." Due to the size, some say "it's a rare moment when you walk into a room and see someone you don't recognize," but the proximity "allows for plenty of interaction during the academic week and the weekends." One student adds, "I'm always able to spot a friendly face on campus and it's a really pleasant environment." There are sizable international and athlete contingents, and students enjoy "having friends from all groups because it is such a small school." Overall, students keep coming back to the sense of "union" itself, finding that their school is indeed a place for "constantly supporting each other to do better and still [having] the most fun while making meaningful change."

UNION COLLEGE (NY)

Financial Aid: 518-388-6123 • E-Mail: admissions@union.edu • Website: www.union.edu

THE PRINCETON REVIEW SAYS

Admissions

The school reports that its standardized testing policy for use in admission for Fall 2026 is Test Optional. The Princeton Review suggests that interested applicants consult with the school for the most up-to-date standardized testing policies. *Very important factors considered include:* rigor of secondary school record, class rank, academic GPA. *Important factors considered include:* standardized test scores, application essay, recommendation(s), extracurricular activities, talent/ability, character/personal qualities, volunteer work, work experience. *Other factors considered include:* interview, first generation, geographical residence, state residency, level of applicant's interest. High school diploma is required and GED is not accepted. *Academic units required:* 4 English, 3 math, 2 science, 2 language (other than English), 2 social studies. *Academic units recommended:* 4 English, 4 math, 3 science, 3 language (other than English), 2 social studies, 2 history, 1 visual/performing arts.

Financial Aid

Students should submit: FAFSA; CSS PROFILE; State aid form. Priority filing deadline is 1/15. The Princeton Review suggests that all financial aid forms be submitted as soon as possible. *Need-based scholarships/grants offered:* Federal Pell; Federal SEOG; State scholarships/grants; Private scholarships; College/university scholarship or grant aid from institutional funds. *Loan aid offered:* Federal Direct Subsidized Loans; Federal Direct Unsubsidized Loans; Direct PLUS loans. Admitted students will be notified of awards on or about 3/25. Federal Work-Study Program available. Institutional employment available.

The Inside Word

While Union College is Test Optional, applicants to the Leadership in Medicine Program (an eight-year MD/MBA program with Albany Medical College and Clarkson University Capital Region Campus), the Law and Public Policy program (a combined BA and JD with Albany Law School), and homeschooled students must submit test scores for consideration. For students who know that Union is their first choice, the school offers two early decision deadlines.

THE SCHOOL SAYS

From the Admissions Office

"The Union academic program is characterized by breadth and flexibility across a range of disciplines and interdisciplinary programs in the liberal arts, sciences, and engineering. With nearly 1,000 courses to choose from, Union students may major in a single field, combine work in two or more departments, or create their own major. Opportunities for research are robust and give students a chance to work closely with professors year-round, take part in conferences, and use sophisticated scientific equipment. More than half of Union's students take advantage of the college's extensive international study program, and the College places students in internships with more than 500 companies and organizations. A rich array of service-learning programs and strong athletic, cultural, and social activities also enhance the overall Union experience. Union's Scholars Program is a rigorous academic program offered to a select group of approximately 60 incoming students each year. Union's seven student-run Minerva Houses are lively hubs for intellectual and social activities. They bring together students, faculty and staff for hundreds of events, from lectures to live bands.

"The Union community welcomes talented and diverse students, and we work closely with each one to help identify and cultivate their passions. Admission to the college is based on excellent academic credentials (transcript, courses, recommendations) and essays. Personal interviews are recommended. All candidates who apply to Union receive a thorough and thoughtful review of their application. Submission of SAT and ACT scores is optional except for the law and medicine programs. Union College is one of the very few colleges and universities in the country (fewer than 5%) that commits to meeting 100% of demonstrated financial need of all admitted students."

SELECTIVITY

# of total applicants	9,246
% of total applicants accepted	43
% of total acceptees attending	12
# of in-state applicants	1,811
% of in-state applicants accepted	60
# of out-of-state-applicants	3,327
% of applicants accepted from out of state	71
# of international applicants	4,108
% of international applicants accepted	14
# of early decision applicants	370
% of early decision applicants accepted	45
# offered a place on the wait list	322
# admitted from wait list	106

First-Year Profile

Testing policy	Test Optional
Range SAT composite	1320–1470
Range SAT EBRW	660–730
Range SAT math	660–740
Range ACT composite	30–34
% submitting SAT scores	33
% submitting ACT scores	8
Average HS GPA	3.7
% submitting high school GPA	100
% graduated top 10% of class	59
% graduated top 25% of class	79
% graduated top 50% of class	95
% submitting high school rank	28

Important Dates

Early decision	
Apply by	11/1
Notified by	12/15
Other ED apply by	1/15
Other ED notified by	2/8
Early action	
Apply by	11/1
Notified by	12/21
Regular	
Apply by	1/15
Notified by	4/1
Nonfall registration?	Yes

FINANCIAL FACTS

Annual tuition	$73,863
Food and housing	$18,297
Required fees	$450
Books and supplies	$1,500
Average need-based scholarship (First-year)	$57,713 ($59,792)
% students with need rec. need-based scholarship or grant aid (First-year)	100 (100)
% students with need rec. non-need-based scholarship or grant aid (First-year)	0 (0)
% students with need rec. need-based self-help aid (First-year)	88 (85)
% students rec. any financial aid (First-year)	92 (96)
% UG borrow to pay for school	57
Average cumulative indebtedness	$34,282
% of students with need fully met (First-year)	100 (100)
Average % of student need met (First-year)	100 (100)

United States Air Force Academy

2304 Cadet Drive, USAF Academy, CO 80840 • Admissions: 719-333-3070

Survey Snapshot
Lots of conservative students
Students get along with local community
Students involved in community service

RATINGS

Quality of Life	88
Fire Safety	99
Green	60*
Academic	90
Profs Interesting	90
Profs Accessible	97
Admissions	98
Financial Aid	60*

CAMPUS LIFE

Type of school	Public
Environment	Metropolis

Students

Degree-seeking undergrad enrollment	4,142
% male/female/not reported	72/28/0
% from out of state	94
% First-year from public high school	76
% First-year live on campus	100
% Ugrads live on campus	100
# of fraternities	0
# of sororities	0
% Asian	9
% Black or African American	5
% Hispanic	12
% Native American	<1
% Pacific Islander	<1
% Race and/or ethnicity unknown	1
% Two or more races	10
% White	62
% International	1
# of countries represented	30

CAMPUS MENTAL HEALTH SERVICES

Offers mental health/wellness program	Yes
Mental health training available to students	Yes
Employs Chief Wellness Officer	Yes
Peer-to-peer mental health offerings	Yes
Counseling center has guidelines or accreditation	No
Mental health/well-being courses	No

ACADEMICS

% students returning for sophomore year	94
% students graduating within 4 years	81
% students graduating within 6 years	84
Calendar	Semester
Student/faculty ratio	8:1
Most common class size 10–19.	(50%)

Most Popular Majors

Aerospace, Aeronautical, and Astronautical/Space Engineering; Business, Management, Marketing, And Related Support Services; Biology/Biological Sciences

Applicants Rarely Prefer

United States Coast Guard Academy, United States Merchant Marine Academy, United States Military Academy, United States Naval Academy

STUDENTS SAY "..."

Academics

Students who seek out a United States Air Force Academy education note their satisfaction in how "values of integrity, service, and excellence...are actually the norm." This esteemed institution not only promotes a "culture of excellence" that molds students into "leaders of character," but also offers "prestige in both the military and private sector." It does so, incidentally, while offering free tuition and a "guaranteed job" following graduation. Of course, if you decide to attend, be prepared to "be challenged physically and mentally" and held "to a higher standard" than at your average college. In return, however, students suggest you'll also get "incredible opportunities" not found elsewhere. These opportunities can range from taking "trips around the world" or "operating a real DoD satellite" to "jumping out of planes [and] getting a secret clearance." Additionally, undergrads benefit from "extremely small" class sizes. As one cadet shares, "the biggest class I've had in four years was 24 students." The faculty itself is a nice "mix of military and civilian" instructors who "tend to make class interesting" and often excel at "bring[ing] their life experiences into the classroom." The majority also do their utmost to ensure that they are "accessible for extra instruction, exam review, etc." Many students also feel that their professors "really seem to care about your performance and work with you on a one-on-one basis." As one cadet frames it, "Their only focus is supporting us."

Campus Life

As you might have suspected, life at the Air Force Academy is rather regimented and cadets "don't have much free time." Students "go to class from 0730 to 1530 [and] freshmen have physical training multiple times a week after[wards]." Additionally, everyone "participate[s] in an athletic activity [whether] it be NCAA athletics, club sports, or intramurals." And on the weekends it's quite common to "have the Cadet Wing marching" or to have to perform "other military duties." Students also make a point of mentioning that "once every semester we have mandatory fitness tests, and throughout the semester [there are] random mandatory military briefs in the evenings." Even with a schedule packed with academic obligations and military training, one individual notes that there are "various clubs and activities for different interests, as well as religious services, all [of] which take [place] intermittently throughout the week." And if they do have a moment to relax, cadets will typically kick back with "Netflix or video games." Of course, when students really want to have fun, they generally leave "USAFA and [go] out into CO Springs or Denver" or they will "take advantage of outdoor areas for hiking, fishing, etc."

Student Body

Air Force Academy cadets seem to agree that the school attracts a number of "type A personalities" and "hard working" individuals who are "much more motivated than many other normal college students." They are also united in their deep desire "to serve [the] country" and are often "team oriented" as well. Further, cadets pride themselves on being "more fit than the general population," and cadets at USAFA "come from all over the nation, territories included, and from allied partner nations." While there may be a "healthy diversity of thought" at the academy, students do acknowledge a disparity in gender. A few individuals also grumble that some of their peers can be "very cynical." Thankfully, students view themselves as "one brotherhood and sisterhood looking out for each other." One cadet delves deeper adding, "We hold each other to an honor code the best we can and feel very close as a student body because we all live on campus and spend a majority of our time together." All in all, "there is a definite culture of helping out fellow cadets and of striving to bring peers up that helps people to perform at their best."

UNITED STATES AIR FORCE ACADEMY

E-Mail: rr_admissions@usafa.edu • Website: www.usafa.edu

THE PRINCETON REVIEW SAYS

Admissions

The school reports that its standardized testing policy for use in admission for Fall 2026 will require applicants to submit either the SAT or ACT. The Princeton Review suggests that interested applicants consult with the school for the most up-to-date standardized testing policies. *Very important factors considered include:* rigor of secondary school record, academic GPA, standardized test scores, application essay, recommendation(s), interview, extracurricular activities, character/personal qualities, geographical residence. *Important factors considered include:* class rank, talent/ability, volunteer work, work experience. *Other factors considered include:* first generation, level of applicant's interest. High school diploma is required and GED is accepted. *Academic units required:* 4 English, 3 math, 3 science, 3 social studies, 1 history. *Academic units recommended:* 4 English, 4 math, 4 science, 3 science labs, 2 language (other than English), 3 social studies, 2 history, 1 academic elective, 1 computer science.

Financial Aid

Aside from receiving a fully funded education—including tuition, room, board, and medical care—cadets at the United States Air Force Academy receive a monthly stipend (which increases over time but is partially offset by required expenses in the early years). Upon graduation, cadets are commissioned as second lieutenants in the U.S. Air Force or Space Force and incur a minimum of five years of active-duty service. Certain career paths, such as pilot training or advanced education, require additional service commitments.

The Inside Word

Earning admission to the United States Air Force Academy is no easy feat. The process is extraordinarily competitive, and you'll need a very high GPA and class rank to be in contention. Beyond strong academics, your teacher evaluations and letters of recommendation will be extremely important. The school uses them to assess your moral character and leadership capabilities. Additionally, cadet life is physically demanding, and you'll have to meet specific fitness requirements. Finally, you must be a U.S. citizen in order to apply.

THE SCHOOL SAYS

From the Admissions Office

"The United States Air Force Academy offers one of the most prestigious and respected undergraduate programs available. With twenty-seven majors and four minors offered at the Academy, there are programs of study for every interest. The academic challenges and expectations are high—but so are the rewards. You will emerge from the Academy with a well-rounded knowledge in many fields, an intimate knowledge in your major area of study, and the ability to serve our nation as a Second Lieutenant in the world's greatest air, space, and cyberspace force.

"At the United States Air Force Academy, every cadet is an athlete. Our extensive athletic program includes twenty-nine men's and women's NCAA Division I intercollegiate teams, intramural sports, physical education courses, and physical fitness tests tailored to prepare you for Air Force leadership by building confidence, physical courage, and the ability to perform under pressure.

"The Academy experience requires cadets to become active participants in leadership roles and opportunities that give a sense of honor and duty. The Air Force Academy's mission is to educate, train, and inspire men and women to become officers of character motivated to lead the United States Air Force in service to our nation. If you choose to accept the challenges, you will be rewarded with unique experiences and opportunities incomparable to any other college experience and the honor of serving your country in the United States Air Force."

SELECTIVITY

# of total applicants	9,682
% of total applicants accepted	15
% of total acceptees attending	78
# of in-state applicants	499
% of in-state applicants accepted	17
# of out-of-state-applicants	9,124
% of applicants accepted from out of state	15
# of international applicants	59
% of international applicants accepted	25

First-Year Profile

Testing policy	SAT or ACT Required
Range SAT composite	1240–1430
Range SAT EBRW	620–710
Range SAT math	610–730
Range ACT composite	26–33
% submitting SAT scores	60
% submitting ACT scores	40
Average HS GPA	3.9
% submitting high school GPA	99
% graduated top 10% of class	55
% graduated top 25% of class	83
% graduated top 50% of class	98
% submitting high school rank	48

Important Dates

Regular	
Apply by	12/31
Notified by	10/15
Nonfall registration?	No

FINANCIAL FACTS

Annual tuition	$0

UNITED STATES COAST GUARD ACADEMY

15 Mohegan Avenue, New London, CT 06320-8103 • Admissions: 800-883-8724

Survey Snapshot
Students always studying
Students involved in community service
Diverse student types interact on campus

RATINGS

Quality of Life	83
Fire Safety	71
Green	60*
Academic	87
Profs Interesting	88
Profs Accessible	96
Admissions	96
Financial Aid	60*

CAMPUS LIFE

Type of school	Public
Environment	City

Students

Degree-seeking undergrad enrollment	1,063
% male/female/not reported	63/37/0
% from out of state	95
% First-year from public high school	79
% First-year live on campus	100
% Ugrads live on campus	100
# of fraternities	0
# of sororities	0
% Asian	5
% Black or African American	3
% Hispanic	13
% Native American	0
% Pacific Islander	1
% Race and/or ethnicity unknown	2
% Two or more races	8
% White	65
% International	3
# of countries represented	13

CAMPUS MENTAL HEALTH SERVICES

Offers mental health/wellness program	Yes
Mental health training available to students	No
Employs Chief Wellness Officer	NR
Peer-to-peer mental health offerings	NR
Counseling center has guidelines or accreditation	No
Mental health/well-being courses	NR

ACADEMICS

% students returning for sophomore year	97
% students graduating within 4 years	89
% students graduating within 6 years	95
Calendar	Semester
Student/faculty ratio	7:1
Most common class size 20–29.	(39%)
Most common lab/discussion size 10–19.	(44%)

STUDENTS SAY "..."

Academics

Cadets at the highly selective United States Coast Guard Academy take pride in being "pushed to [the] limits" to "reach farther, expand their horizons, and to develop outside the classroom as much as inside of it." With a specific mission to prepare future leaders of the U.S. Coast Guard, attending the academy is more than just an education; it's a lifestyle choice. The academy's "regimented environment" is "highly demanding, immensely rewarding, professionally oriented, and the best choice to make the best friends you are ever going to have." One cadet reports that the USCGA provides "a standard to live up to and hold myself to, even when I am away from here." Cadets agree that the academy is "academically, emotionally, and physically" challenging. While USCGA is best known for its robust engineering and maritime sciences programs, there are nine majors to choose from, and all students take liberal arts classes as part of the "challenging but rewarding" core curriculum. An electrical engineering student particularly appreciates the dedicated instructors: "The most surprising and excellent trait that all teachers have is that they are always willing to help outside of the classrooms. Always." Another cadet says, "The best part about my school is the summer training programs." Summer adventures include sailing "across the Atlantic Ocean," stopping "in London, Iceland, and Nova Scotia," which are "absolutely amazing." Upon graduation, cadets enjoy one of the truly unique perks of USCGA: a "guaranteed job upon graduation."

Campus Life

"Life at USCGA is unique." Cadets are expected to participate in intercollegiate or intramural sports, as "physical fitness, teamwork, and competition" are highly valued. Among these sports offerings are men's and women's rugby, rifle and pistol clubs, archery, scuba diving, fencing, and ice hockey. In addition to sports, there are various activities available for cadets, including cheer squad, dance and drill teams, yearbook, and a blog club. Students describe life at USCGA as "orderly and predictable," but it can be challenging to find time for activities "outside of their military, athletic, and academic obligations." While "students aren't allowed off campus during the week," except for academy-sanctioned activities, "most try and get away for the weekend" to "explore New England, New York City, and the downtown New London area." One cadet notes that "underage students tend to go to the movies or the local mall. Of-age students usually spend their time off drinking at the bars downtown." Outdoor enthusiasts "go to the beach, [or] head up to Vermont for some hiking or skiing...There is a lot to do if you look for it." Life at USCGA can be "very challenging and demanding at times, but the goal of becoming an officer makes it worth it."

Student Body

Simply put, USCGA attracts "highly motivated" young adults "with a strong desire to serve in the Coast Guard." Cadets can rely on their shipmates to be "hardworking, smart, motivated, and in great shape." Cadets are "very close with each other" because they share similar career goals and "all wear the same uniforms, take the same classes, and are going through the same experiences," and "for the most part, everyone has a group of friends that they fit in quite well with." One student adds, "The academy fosters camaraderie amongst the Corps of Cadets that can't be found anywhere else...The Coast Guard Academy is truly unique in its ability to provide an environment where classmates become shipmates, friends, and eventually family." As one cadet humorously explains, "A typical student here is just like a typical student anywhere else but works harder, follows stricter rules, is in better shape, and is owned by the federal government."

UNITED STATES COAST GUARD ACADEMY

E-Mail: admissions@uscga.edu • Website: www.uscga.edu

THE PRINCETON REVIEW SAYS

Admissions

The school reports that its standardized testing policy for use in admission for Fall 2026 will require applicants to submit either the SAT or ACT. The Princeton Review suggests that interested applicants consult with the school for the most up-to-date standardized testing policies. *Very important factors considered include:* rigor of secondary school record, academic GPA, application essay, extracurricular activities, talent/ability, character/personal qualities. *Important factors considered include:* class rank, standardized test scores, recommendation(s), level of applicant's interest. *Other factors considered include:* interview, first generation, alumni/ae relation, geographical residence, state residency, volunteer work, work experience. High school diploma is required and GED is accepted. *Academic units required:* 4 English, 4 math, 4 science, 3 science labs, 5 academic electives. *Academic units recommended:* 4 English, 4 math, 4 science, 3 science labs, 2 language (other than English), 2 social studies, 2 history, 3 academic electives.

Financial Aid

At the United States Coast Guard Academy, there is no cost for tuition, room, or board. This fully funded education—valued at over $280,000—is paid for by the federal government. In addition, cadets receive a monthly stipend and, upon graduation, are commissioned as officers in the U.S. Coast Guard with a minimum active-duty service commitment.

The Inside Word

Gaining acceptance into the Coast Guard Academy is a highly competitive process. The admissions committee is looking not only for outstanding academic achievement but also for applicants who demonstrate leadership ability and strong moral character. In addition, unlike other colleges, you'll also need a physical fitness examination and evaluation.

THE SCHOOL SAYS

From the Admissions Office

"Established in 1876, the Coast Guard Academy educates, trains, and inspires Cadets to serve their country and humanity. Leadership and character development are emphasized in academic life, athletic pursuits, and military training. Commitment to helping those in need is a personal quality shared by every student selected to attend the Coast Guard Academy. High levels of personal accountability are expected of Cadets and graduates.

"Fourth Class (freshmen) arrive in June to begin a strenuous seven-week training program (Swab Summer) that prepares them to join the Corps of Cadets in August. Swab Summer culminates with a week at sea aboard America's only active tall ship, the EAGLE.

"The Corps of Cadets is comprised of talented Cadets from all fifty states and about twenty other nations, which affords the Academy the opportunity to leverage a diverse range of backgrounds, experiences, and perspectives that contribute to the overall success of the Corps. Most Cadets are athletes—over 60 percent play on at least one NCAA Division III team. The opportunity to play is nearly unmatched in college athletics.

"The Academy's value proposition is also tough to beat. This is the only small, highly selective four-year college in the U.S. that is free of charge to attend. This is possible because Academy grads go straight to a position of responsibility as a commissioned officer in the Coast Guard. All are obligated to serve for five years, and most make it a career. Aside from the satisfaction of saving lives and protecting others, the opportunity to fly is exceptional. And, about 85 percent of officers also earn a graduate degree at Coast Guard expense.

"If you are smart, adventuresome, physically fit, and want to achieve a higher purpose in your life, the U.S. Coast Guard Academy may be for you!"

SELECTIVITY

# of total applicants	1,825
% of total applicants accepted	21
% of total acceptees attending	67
# of in-state applicants	69
% of in-state applicants accepted	26
# of out-of-state-applicants	1,724
% of applicants accepted from out of state	20
# of international applicants	32
% of international applicants accepted	22
# offered a place on the wait list	482
# admitted from wait list	49

First-Year Profile

Testing policy	SAT or ACT Required
Range SAT composite	1240–1390
Range SAT EBRW	618–700
Range SAT math	620–700
Range ACT composite	26–31
% submitting SAT scores	68
% submitting ACT scores	28
Average HS GPA	3.8
% submitting high school GPA	100
% graduated top 10% of class	50
% graduated top 25% of class	84
% graduated top 50% of class	99
% submitting high school rank	100

Important Dates

Early action	
Apply by	10/15
Notified by	12/23
Regular	
Apply by	1/15
Notified by	Rolling, 9/1
Nonfall registration?	No

FINANCIAL FACTS

Annual tuition	$0

United States Military Academy

646 Swift Road, West Point, NY 10996-1905 • Admissions: 845-938-4041

Survey Snapshot
Students always studying
Classroom facilities are great
Great library

RATINGS

Quality of Life	85
Fire Safety	79
Green	60*
Academic	99
Profs Interesting	95
Profs Accessible	96
Admissions	98
Financial Aid	60*

CAMPUS LIFE

Type of school	Public
Environment	Village

Students

Degree-seeking undergrad enrollment	4,439
% male/female/not reported	79/21/0
% from out of state	93
% First-year live on campus	100
% Ugrads live on campus	100
# of fraternities	0
# of sororities	0
% Asian	13
% Black or African American	8
% Hispanic	12
% Native American	1
% Pacific Islander	1
% Race and/or ethnicity unknown	<1
% Two or more races	1
% White	64
% International	1
# of countries represented	29

CAMPUS MENTAL HEALTH SERVICES

Offers mental health/wellness program	Yes
Mental health training available to students	No
Employs Chief Wellness Officer	NR
Peer-to-peer mental health offerings	NR
Counseling center has guidelines or accreditation	No
Mental health/well-being courses	NR

ACADEMICS

% students returning for sophomore year	95
% students graduating within 4 years	79
% students graduating within 6 years	85
Calendar	Semester
Student/faculty ratio	6:1
Most common class size 10–19.	(81%)
Most common lab/discussion size 10–19.	(88%)

Applicants Sometimes Prefer

United States Air Force Academy, United States Coast Guard Academy, United States Naval Academy

STUDENTS SAY "..."

Academics

The United States Military Academy at West Point, the nation's first military academy, prepares students to serve as officers in the U.S. Army. Cadets who successfully complete the rigorous academic, military, and physical programs earn a bachelor's degree and are commissioned as second lieutenants. Students attend USMA to "receive the best leadership training" possible and laud the institution for "[striving] to develop cadets' leadership and character, which sets it apart from most...universities." Enrollees are given "opportunities to challenge yourself " through opportunities like training at the Airborne School and AirAssault, where cadets learn how to parachute out of planes and rappel from helicopters. Additionally, they benefit from "countless academic enrichment activities," including study abroad programs, internships, and the Service Academy Exchange Program (SAEP), where participants spend a semester at one of USMA's sister federal service agencies: the U.S. Naval Academy, U.S. Air Force Academy, or the U.S. Coast Guard Academy. While "freshman and sophomore classes are already picked for you," upper-level students can choose courses based on their major. "This is nice because...you don't have to worry about a class filling up." Professors receive almost unanimous praise for their accessibility and devotion to students: "I've had teachers give me their cellphone numbers on the first day and actually help at all hours of the night. I've had teachers reply to emails at 4 a.m. about a problem." The "academics at USMA are very challenging," but professors "bend over backwards to accommodate" cadets' busy schedules and "always will go the extra mile to help you succeed if you're willing to ask." In addition to receiving a prestigious education, students resoundingly agree that one of the best things about attending USMA is the "guaranteed job after graduation (commissioning as a 2LT in the US Army)."

Campus Life

"Life is extremely busy" at West Point. "School and athletics take up most of the time." On weekdays, "classes start at 7:30 a.m. and continue until the last class concludes at 4 p.m." After classes, "everyone participates in some kind of physical training or event. Athletics go "until around 6:00 p.m." Then, "the evenings are taken up by dinner or studying" or commitments like club meetings and religious gatherings. Everyone agrees: "We are very busy here, all day, every day." When cadets need a break, they often lift weights, run, or rock climb; working out "is a huge part of West Point culture." On weekends, there are many options for fun, "everything from trips for clubs and sports to inspections, parades, and football games." Cadets of legal age "enjoy frequenting the on-campus bar in the evening and taking [a] pass on the weekends to study outside of the school or visit with friends in the city." While cadets acknowledge that maintaining such a hectic schedule "is challenging," it "teaches you the valuable life skills of time management and work ethic."

Student Body

The student body at USMA is "geographically unique." In order to gain admission, applicants "must be nominated by a congressman or senator, resulting in cadets from all across America as well as a small number of international cadets." Cadets express great admiration for their peers, with one praising their "integrity, smarts, athleticism, and drive to succeed." Another says, "I am surrounded by a large number of motivated, caring, capable, and skilled friends. People here care about the academics...but more importantly, care about each other and the real reason we are here at West Point." One cadet claims that USMA attracts "some of the best, most intelligent, and uniquely remarkable students America has to offer." Additionally, cadets "form special bonds with their peers as they go through rigorous military training with their units...the camaraderie is unparalleled at other institutions."

UNITED STATES MILITARY ACADEMY

E-Mail: admissions@westpoint.edu • Website: www.westpoint.edu

THE PRINCETON REVIEW SAYS

Admissions

The school reports that its standardized testing policy for use in admission for Fall 2026 will require applicants to submit either the SAT or ACT. The Princeton Review suggests that interested applicants consult with the school for the most up-to-date standardized testing policies. *Very important factors considered include:* rigor of secondary school record, academic GPA, standardized test scores, interview, character/personal qualities. *Important factors considered include:* application essay, recommendation(s), extracurricular activities, talent/ability, level of applicant's interest. *Other factors considered include:* class rank, volunteer work, work experience. High school diploma is required and GED is accepted. *Academic units recommended:* 4 English, 4 math, 2 science, 2 science labs, 1 language (other than English), 1 social studies, 2 history.

Financial Aid

There is no tuition or financial aid at the United States Military Academy. The U.S. Army covers 100 percent of the cost of tuition, room, board, and medical and dental care for all cadets. As a result, all West Point cadets attend on a full scholarship in exchange for a service commitment upon graduation (currently five years of active duty and three years in the inactive reserve). In addition, cadets receive a monthly stipend to help cover the cost of uniforms, books, and other required supplies.

The Inside Word

The fact that you must request to be nominated in order to apply to West Point tells you all you need to know about the school's selectivity. Successful candidates must demonstrate excellence in academics, physical conditioning, extracurricular involvement, and leadership. They must also be willing to commit to five years of active duty and three years of reserve duty upon graduation. The rigorous requirements and demanding commitments of a West Point education hardly dissuade applicants.

THE SCHOOL SAYS

From the Admissions Office

"West Point is searching for applicants who possess the leadership skills, cultural sensibilities, and the moral fiber to handle the volatile, uncertain, complex, and ambiguous contemporary operating environment of today's world as a future U.S. Army Officer. As the preeminent leader development institute, we are looking for critical thinkers who have the sound judgment and drive to become leaders of character upon graduation.

"To assess your ability and preparation, admissions looks at more than your GPA or standardized test scores. The applications of almost 13,000 students are evaluated based on academic, physical, and leadership potential to find approximately 1,150 candidates who are ready to overcome the challenges they will face as members of the Corps of Cadets. With an amazingly high offer—acceptance rate, only the most dedicated, enthusiastic applicants make it to the finish line and report for duty each June.

"If you accept the challenge, you will be immersed in a military training program that ranges from marksmanship to orienteering, an academic program that offers over 36 majors ranging from electrical engineering to philosophy, and a physical program that finds every cadet participating in an intercollegiate, club, or intramural-level sport. The fully funded, four-year college education includes tuition, room, board, full medical and dental care, and a stipend for personal expenses. In return, you will graduate with a Bachelor of Science degree and be commissioned as a U.S. Army Officer with an active-duty service obligation of five years active and three years reserve. Complete admissions guidance found online."

SELECTIVITY

# of total applicants	13,780
% of total applicants accepted	12
% of total acceptees attending	75
# of in-state applicants	867
% of in-state applicants accepted	11
# of out-of-state-applicants	12,122
% of applicants accepted from out of state	12
# of international applicants	792
% of international applicants accepted	3

First-Year Profile

Testing policy	SAT or ACT Required
Range SAT composite	1220–1430
Range SAT EBRW	610–710
Range SAT math	600–730
Range ACT composite	28–33
% submitting SAT scores	71
% submitting ACT scores	29
Average HS GPA	3.8
% submitting high school GPA	78
% graduated top 10% of class	47
% graduated top 25% of class	78
% graduated top 50% of class	95
% submitting high school rank	41

Important Dates

Regular	
Apply by	1/31
Notified by	Rolling, 11/1
Nonfall registration?	No

FINANCIAL FACTS

Annual tuition	$0

United States Naval Academy

121 Blake Road, Annapolis, MD 21402 • Admissions: 410-293-1858

Survey Snapshot
Diverse student types interact on campus
Students get along with local community
Students love Annapolis, MD

RATINGS

Quality of Life	**94**
Fire Safety	**73**
Green	**60***
Academic	**90**
Profs Interesting	**94**
Profs Accessible	**98**
Admissions	**98**
Financial Aid	**60***

CAMPUS LIFE

Type of school	Public
Environment	Town

Students

Degree-seeking undergrad enrollment	4,474
% male/female/not reported	70/30/0
% from out of state	68
% First-year from public high school	60
% First-year live on campus	100
% Ugrads live on campus	100
# of fraternities	0
# of sororities	0
% Asian	10
% Black or African American	7
% Hispanic	15
% Native American	<1
% Pacific Islander	<1
% Race and/or ethnicity unknown	1
% Two or more races	9
% White	56
% International	1
# of countries represented	29

CAMPUS MENTAL HEALTH SERVICES

Offers mental health/wellness program	Yes
Mental health training available to students	Yes
Employs Chief Wellness Officer	Yes
Peer-to-peer mental health offerings	Yes
Counseling center has guidelines or accreditation	Yes
Mental health/well-being courses	Yes, for-credit

ACADEMICS

% students returning for sophomore year	97
% students graduating within 4 years	92
% students graduating within 6 years	93
Calendar	Semester
Student/faculty ratio	8:1
Most common class size 10–19.	(63%)
Most common lab/discussion size 10–19.	(48%)

Most Popular Majors
Econometrics and Quantitative Economics; Political Science and Government; Mechatronics, Robotics, and Automation Engineering

Applicants Also Look At
United States Air Force Academy, United States Military Academy

STUDENTS SAY "..."

Academics

Students at the United States Naval Academy aren't just students; "they are future Naval and Marine Corps officers being trained under constant pressure, responsibility, and accountability." The USNA offers "elite education [and] training opportunities" that are "completely free" to students. Upon graduation, midshipmen, as all USNA students are called, earn a Bachelor of Science and will "commission into either the US Navy or Marine Corps" as officers. Coursework leans toward STEM subjects but also includes "a wide variety of classes, ranging from Arabic to aeronautics." Students note that "every class is tied to real-world application. Even math-heavy courses are centered around military systems that are used." Classes are taught by a "mix of military and civilian professors, leading to a wide range of experience." One midshipman recalls: "I took a course on ethics that was instructed by a retired Navy SEAL, who really invested in the class....It's enlightening to learn valuable skills from those who have had such unique and difficult experiences." Midshipmen regularly take over 17 units per semester alongside "graded leadership responsibilities, inspections, and professional training," and rely on supportive academic staff who "ensure you can succeed." Overall, students agree that "the workload is extremely high, but the call to serve demands the best, and the tough work-life balance prepares you to lead in times of trial."

Campus Life

"Life at the United States Naval Academy is structured, demanding, and very full—but also uniquely rewarding." As one student explains, "Every Midshipman has mandatory breakfast and lunch, wears a Navy uniform to school every day, and is expected to be clean-shaven with cut hair and clean rooms at all times throughout the week." Balancing everything can be challenging. "Sometimes I neglect studying for a quiz so I can go on a run. Sometimes I submit a homework late because I need to discuss a subordinate's recent problematic behavior," admits one student. At USNA, "time management isn't optional—it's a survival skill." Yet the Academy offers unique opportunities that make the demands worthwhile. Clubs include the Combat Arms Team, the Drum and Bugle Corps, and the Naval Academy Wargaming Society, which enjoys "touring the Pentagon and other intelligence community facilities." The Glee Club performs at presidential inaugurations and funerals and has "performances with world-renowned symphonies." Local families volunteer to sponsor midshipmen; "having a home-cooked meal and a couch to relax on provides a much-needed mental break," says one. In short, "every person here balances a full academic load with military duties, physical training, and leadership roles, which creates a culture where discipline, teamwork, and resilience are not buzzwords, but daily expectations."

Student Body

The Naval Academy attracts "people who want to serve a greater purpose than themselves." One midshipman says, "We all go through basic training together, which is an incredible bonding experience. I am an only child, and a lot of my friends here are like my brothers and sisters." And "because everyone comes from different congressional districts due to the nominations process, we have people from everywhere around the country, from all walks of life. Whether you're a big athlete or big into books, you will find your group of people here." One student adds, "I know world record holders, rodeo stars, incredible athletes, and Rhodes Scholars. I know people who want to be snake-eaters, jet pilots, divers, lawyers, and president." Across all pursuits, "midshipmen go above and beyond in every aspect of their lives." One student captures the ethos best, saying, "My peers are [among] the smartest, fittest, and most caring people that I know, and I am so glad to be surrounded with them each day."

United States Naval Academy

E-Mail: inquire@usna.edu • Website: www.usna.edu

THE PRINCETON REVIEW SAYS

Admissions

The school reports that its standardized testing policy for use in admission for Fall 2026 is Test Optional. The Princeton Review suggests that interested applicants consult with the school for the most up-to-date standardized testing policies. *Very important factors considered include:* rigor of secondary school record, class rank, academic GPA, application essay, recommendation(s), interview, extracurricular activities, talent/ability, work experience, level of applicant's interest. *Important factors considered include:* standardized test scores. *Other factors considered include:* character/personal qualities, first generation, alumni/ae relation, geographical residence, religious affiliation/commitment, volunteer work. High school diploma or equivalent is not required. *Academic units recommended:* 4 English, 4 math, 2 science, 1 science lab, 2 language (other than English), 2 history, 2 computer science.

Financial Aid

The U.S. Navy covers 100 percent of the cost of tuition, room, board, and medical and dental care for all Naval Academy midshipmen. As a result, all students attend on a full scholarship in exchange for a service commitment upon graduation (currently five years of active-duty service). In addition, midshipmen receive a monthly stipend to help cover the cost of uniforms, books, and other required supplies.

The Inside Word

Securing admission to the Naval Academy is no easy feat. To begin with, a top-notch academic record is a must. In addition to strong GPA and test scores, applicants also have to secure an official nomination (typically granted by a U.S. representative, U.S. senator, or the Vice President). Further, candidates need to prove physical fitness, be an unmarried U.S. citizen between the ages of seventeen and twenty-three with no dependents. And, perhaps most importantly, applicants should also demonstrate strong moral character. Finally, the earlier you apply the better.

THE SCHOOL SAYS

From the Admissions Office

"The finest young men and women in the country come to the Naval Academy to develop into leaders to serve the nation; USNA is the school of admirals, presidents, Nobel Prize winners, astronauts, jet pilots and CEOs. At USNA, you will have the opportunity to pursue a four-year degree program that develops you mentally, morally, and physically as no civilian college can. As you might expect, this program is demanding, but the opportunities are limitless and more than worth the effort.

"Upon throwing the iconic Midshipmen hat into the air at graduation, you will serve your country in one of dozens of professional fields—primarily aviation, submarines, ships, or the Marine Corps, but with additional limited options for the SEALs, medical, and other communities."

SELECTIVITY

# of total applicants	15,149
% of total applicants accepted	9
% of total acceptees attending	84
# offered a place on the wait list	238
# admitted from wait list	70

First-Year Profile

Testing policy	Test Optional
Range SAT composite	1210–1300
Range SAT EBRW	610–700
Range SAT math	600–710
Range ACT composite	25–31
% submitting SAT scores	74
% submitting ACT scores	44
% graduated top 10% of class	63
% graduated top 25% of class	86
% graduated top 50% of class	97
% submitting high school rank	45

Important Dates

Regular	
Apply by	1/31
Notified by	4/15
Nonfall registration?	No

FINANCIAL FACTS

Annual tuition	$0

The University of Alabama at Birmingham

1720 2nd Avenue South, Birmingham, AL 35294 • Admissions: 205-934-8221

Survey Snapshot
Diverse student types interact on campus
Students are very religious
Alumni active on campus

RATINGS

Quality of Life	**83**
Fire Safety	**93**
Green	**60***
Academic	**81**
Profs Interesting	**89**
Profs Accessible	**93**
Admissions	**84**
Financial Aid	**81**

CAMPUS LIFE

Type of school	Public
Environment	Metropolis

Students

Degree-seeking undergrad enrollment	11,824
% male/female/not reported	36/64/<1
% from out of state	14
% First-year live on campus	81
% Ugrads live on campus	28
# of fraternities (% join)	13 (NR)
# of sororities (% join)	13 (NR)
% Asian	9
% Black or African American	29
% Hispanic	9
% Native American	<1
% Pacific Islander	<1
% Race and/or ethnicity unknown	1
% Two or more races	5
% White	44
% International	3
# of countries represented	60

CAMPUS MENTAL HEALTH SERVICES

Offers mental health/wellness program	Yes
Mental health training available to students	No
Employs Chief Wellness Officer	NR
Peer-to-peer mental health offerings	NR
Counseling center has guidelines or accreditation	No
Mental health/well-being courses	NR

ACADEMICS

% students returning for sophomore year	80
% students graduating within 4 years	49
% students graduating within 6 years	66
Calendar	Semester
Student/faculty ratio	18:1
Most common class size 10–19.	(29%)

Most Popular Majors
Biology/Biological Sciences; Psychology; Biomedical Sciences

STUDENTS SAY "..."

Academics

The University of Alabama at Birmingham is committed to the education and growth of its students and encourages them to become "a better person for having experienced the challenge of UAB." With a wide array of impressive programs, UAB is particularly noted for housing one of the largest schools of health professions in the country. Undergrads appreciate that the university offers "small class sizes in even the 100-level classes," which allows for a more personalized learning experience. They also note that the faculty are passionate "experts in their fields" who "care about teaching their subjects to the students." They describe professors as "accessible and exciting" and "down-to-earth enough to give students a real view of what it's like to enter the world of academia." As one student elaborates, "For many of the professors, it's not just about a grade in a class that you are taking…it's an experience and preparation for any of our further endeavors." Students specifically call out the professors in the science departments, who "do a great job with interactive learning" and "really put forth every effort to make sure that those who want help get it." Students may find the academic workload demanding, but most agree it is "certainly worth the challenge." They describe an environment where professors and administrators "care about you" and demonstrate a genuine commitment to student welfare. This is evidenced by initiatives like the biannual student forum, where departments share updates on efforts to improve student life and address student questions. As one student says, "The faculty and administration are very close with students and actively look to pursuing perfection and improving the collegiate experience."

Campus Life

This "vibrant and exciting" campus feels "like a small town in a big city." Students are encouraged "to get involved on campus in some shape or form." With about 380 student organizations available, there is "something for everyone to get involved in." As one student puts it, "the problem [is] having to narrow down opportunities." The "widely used Campus Recreation Center" offers free workout classes, including "kickboxing, krunk/ hip-hop class, yoga, [and] spin," as well as amenities like a wave pool and a rock wall. Additionally, students can participate in intramural sports such as "flag football, dodgeball, soccer, volleyball, [and] slow pitch softball." When students have the time, some like to "dine or shop at the many malls" in Birmingham, which also has a wide variety of attractions, including "many museums, art shows, concerts, dance clubs, [and] movie theaters to choose from." In addition to the activities on campus and the attractions of Birmingham, students love life at UAB because it's "large enough that [you] meet and see new faces daily, but small enough to where [you] have personal relationships with teachers and the administration."

Student Body

The student body at UAB is often described as "down to earth," where "no one looks down on anyone," making it "easy to find a place where you fit in." Many students note that there is "no typical student" at UAB and that "everyone is so diverse" in their thoughts, opinions, and personalities. Overall, this is a supportive community and "there is a genuine interest among students in learning about the other cultures and religions represented on campus and in other cultures around the world." While students come from a range of backgrounds, many share the experience of coming "from modest households." The UAB community is made up of "hardworking and serious" people who still find time to "enjoy weekend fun with friends."

The University of Alabama at Birmingham

Financial Aid: 205-934-8223 • E-Mail: chooseuab@uab.edu • Website: www.uab.edu

THE PRINCETON REVIEW SAYS

Admissions

The school reports that its standardized testing policy for use in admission for Fall 2026 is Test Optional. The Princeton Review suggests that interested applicants consult with the school for the most up-to-date standardized testing policies. *Very important factors considered include:* rigor of secondary school record, academic GPA. *Other factors considered include:* standardized test scores. High school diploma is required and GED is accepted. *Academic units required:* 4 English, 3 math, 3 science, 2 science labs, 3 social studies. *Academic units recommended:* 4 English, 4 math, 4 science, 2 science labs, 4 social studies.

Financial Aid

Students should submit: FAFSA. Priority filing deadline is 12/1. The Princeton Review suggests that all financial aid forms be submitted as soon as possible. *Need-based scholarships/grants offered:* Federal Pell; Federal SEOG; State scholarships/grants; Private scholarships; College/university scholarship or grant aid from institutional funds; United Negro College Fund. *Loan aid offered:* Federal Direct Subsidized Loans; Federal Direct Unsubsidized Loans; Direct PLUS loans. Admitted students will be notified of awards on a rolling basis beginning 12/1. Federal Work-Study Program available. Institutional employment available.

The Inside Word

UAB's incoming class tends to have an average GPA of 3.8, and that's the most important factor for admission. Administrators here are looking to admit a student body that's friendly, diverse, and intelligent with students who strive to be active in the community.

THE SCHOOL SAYS

From the Admissions Office

"The University of Alabama at Birmingham (UAB) is a young, dynamic teaching and research university that has—in just four decades—won international renown for our collaborative and interdisciplinary culture. Our academic programs afford students unrivaled, hands-on experience in research and scholarship as UAB is first in the nation among public universities of federal research dollars per freshman. With over 120 areas of study, UAB attracts the best and brightest students from Alabama, the nation, and 109 countries around the globe.

"UAB students learn from—and work alongside—some of the world's top researchers, scholars, performers, and experts. Programs from the sciences and engineering to the arts and humanities give students the benefit of globally recognized faculty, exciting academic challenges, and experiences that will prepare them for a future in the job market.

"At UAB, we understand that having a fulfilling student life experience is as important as having a fulfilling academic experience. UAB has a rich mix of academic organizations, honor clubs, social fraternities and sororities, volunteer groups, and activities ranging from intramural sports and SGA to program-related clubs and supporting Blazer athletics. With 250 campus organizations to keep students involved, UAB offers the chance to make lifelong friendships while assisting in the development of skills essential to leadership and teamwork."

SELECTIVITY

# of total applicants	11,119
% of total applicants accepted	94
% of total acceptees attending	23
# of in-state applicants	7,028
% of in-state applicants accepted	94
# of out-of-state-applicants	4,091
% of applicants accepted from out of state	94
# of international applicants	1,016
% of international applicants accepted	94

First-Year Profile

Testing policy	Test Optional
Range SAT composite	1250–1420
Range SAT EBRW	620–720
Range SAT math	600–730
Range ACT composite	23–30
% submitting SAT scores	5
% submitting ACT scores	47
Average HS GPA	3.8
% submitting high school GPA	100
% graduated top 10% of class	6
% graduated top 25% of class	16
% graduated top 50% of class	55
% submitting high school rank	1

Important Dates

Regular	
Notified by	Rolling, 8/1
Nonfall registration?	Yes

FINANCIAL FACTS*

Annual in-state tuition	$11,640
Annual out-of-state tuition	$28,980
Food and housing	$13,690
Required fees	$1,200
Books and supplies	$1,200
Average need-based scholarship (First-year)	$6,808 ($6,726)
% students with need rec. need-based scholarship or grant aid (First-year)	76 (75)
% students with need rec. non-need-based scholarship or grant aid (First-year)	61 (73)
% students with need rec. need-based self-help aid (First-year)	61 (64)
% UG borrow to pay for school	50
Average cumulative indebtedness	$26,074
% of students with need fully met (First-year)	7 (10)
Average % of student need met (First-year)	37 (40)

* Most recently reported data at time of printing. Scan the QR code to find the latest updates.

THE UNIVERSITY OF ALABAMA—TUSCALOOSA

Box 870100, Tuscaloosa, AL 35487-0100 • Admissions: 205-348-5666

Survey Snapshot
Lots of conservative students
Students are happy
Students are friendly

RATINGS

Quality of Life	**88**
Fire Safety	**85**
Green	**85**
Academic	**79**
Profs Interesting	**87**
Profs Accessible	**91**
Admissions	**86**
Financial Aid	**86**

CAMPUS LIFE

Type of school	Public
Environment	City

Students

Degree-seeking undergrad enrollment	33,989
% male/female/not reported	44/56/0
% from out of state	58
% First-year live on campus	95
% Ugrads live on campus	26
# of fraternities (% join)	46 (30)
# of sororities (% join)	29 (44)
% Asian	1
% Black or African American	13
% Hispanic	8
% Native American	<1
% Pacific Islander	<1
% Race and/or ethnicity unknown	3
% Two or more races	4
% White	69
% International	1
# of countries represented	76

CAMPUS MENTAL HEALTH SERVICES

Offers mental health/wellness program	Yes
Mental health training available to students	Yes
Employs Chief Wellness Officer	Yes
Peer-to-peer mental health offerings	Yes
Counseling center has guidelines or accreditation	Yes
Mental health/well-being courses	No

ACADEMICS

% students returning for sophomore year	88
% students graduating within 4 years	58
% students graduating within 6 years	74
Calendar	Semester
Student/faculty ratio	19:1
Most common class size 10–19.	(28%)
Most common lab/discussion size 20–29.	(54%)

Most Popular Majors

Finance; Psychology; Marketing/Marketing Management

Applicants Often Prefer

Florida State University, University of Georgia, University of Tennessee—Knoxville

Applicants Sometimes Prefer

Auburn University, The University of Alabama at Birmingham, University of Florida

STUDENTS SAY "..."

Academics

Founded in 1831, University of Alabama—Tuscaloosa offers an educational experience ripe with "significant academic resources and infrastructure." Students can enroll in "strong academic programs that rank highly," and while there is a range of difficulty across different fields of study, many classes "provide the opportunities for deep, sustained, and interesting engagement with the course material." The undergrad experience is elevated by "many outstanding, passionate, and brilliant professors" who "teach from a real-world perspective" and provide "extensive research opportunities." Instructors are known for putting "a ton of strategy and preparation into their lectures," and many faculty members are "amazing and care deeply about teaching." There are "opportunities to be challenged academically through honors classes and higher-level courses," which can mean everything from "[interviewing] prominent people from the Civil Rights Movement" to studying "the science of baking." Non-traditional subjects are popular, and "Many students take a class that allows you to make a book from the paper to the binding."

Campus Life

Outside the classroom, "There is so much to get involved in" at the University of Alabama. UA's Crimson Tide athletics give the school "a well-known name" and "are such a fun part" of undergrad culture. As one student puts it, "Saturdays in the fall are 100% dedicated to game day." This strong sense of school spirit also allows individuals "to unite with students of varying backgrounds on game day." Greek life is a major part of Alabama life, with organizations "unlike anywhere else in the country" that create connections across the entire student body: "Even those not involved still support [Greek life's] philanthropy and service events."

Tuscaloosa's warm climate provides plenty of opportunity for getting outdoors, and "There is a strong campus culture of keeping active and enjoying time outside." Exploring nature tops the list of students' favorite activities, with many taking advantage of the "good hiking spots near campus" and "adventuring through the surrounding wilderness of Alabama." On campus, students "[play] sports on the quad or sand volleyball at the courts," and "The club sports have lots of funding," making them as accessible as they are enjoyable.

Student Body

Most students are here to have fun and learn at the same time and have "no shortage of enthusiasm for the school." Undergrads agree that "One of the greatest strengths of UA is the strong community," as demonstrated by the way enrollees are known to "stand up for things they believe in." They truly create an atmosphere where "everyone is willing to help everyone." The University of Alabama campus is full of "smiling faces" and students "eager to learn from one another." It's an environment where "People always ask how you are doing even if you've never seen them before." With "such a large student body, there are so many different skills and talents present," providing undergrads the opportunity to make "friends of all sorts of ethnicities, backgrounds, and personalities." Students come from all around the world and "The out-of-state population brings different perspectives and backgrounds to the school."

THE UNIVERSITY OF ALABAMA—TUSCALOOSA

Financial Aid: 205-348-7949 • E-Mail: admissions@ua.edu • Website: www.ua.edu

THE PRINCETON REVIEW SAYS

Admissions

The school reports that its standardized testing policy for use in admission for Fall 2026 is Test Optional. The Princeton Review suggests that interested applicants consult with the school for the most up-to-date standardized testing policies. *Very important factors considered include:* rigor of secondary school record, academic GPA, standardized test scores. *Important factors considered include:* extracurricular activities, volunteer work. *Other factors considered include:* class rank, application essay, recommendation(s), interview, talent/ability, character/personal qualities, first generation, alumni/ae relation, geographical residence, state residency, work experience. High school diploma is required and GED is accepted. *Academic units required:* 4 English, 3 math, 3 science, 2 science labs, 1 language (other than English), 4 social studies, 5 academic electives. *Academic units recommended:* 4 English, 3 math, 3 science, 2 science labs, 2 language (other than English), 4 social studies, 5 academic electives.

Financial Aid

Students should submit: FAFSA. Priority filing deadline is 12/1. The Princeton Review suggests that all financial aid forms be submitted as soon as possible. *Need-based scholarships/grants offered:* Federal Pell; Federal SEOG; State scholarships/grants; Private scholarships; College/university scholarship or grant aid from institutional funds; Federal Nursing Scholarships. *Loan aid offered:* Federal Direct Subsidized Loans; Federal Direct Unsubsidized Loans; Direct PLUS loans; College/university loans from institutional funds. Admitted students will be notified of awards on a rolling basis beginning 1/1. Federal Work-Study Program available. Institutional employment available.

The Inside Word

The best candidates for admission at Alabama are successful students who have big ambitions and the drive to make their dreams a reality. Students should possess a good GPA, impressive coursework, and solid test scores. Additionally, Alabama also takes your after-school activities, like employment, volunteer work, and clubs into consideration. Applicants who want priority consideration for competitive scholarships should make sure to apply early to make the cut off deadline.

THE SCHOOL SAYS

From the Admissions Office

"Since its founding in 1831 as the first public university in the state, the University of Alabama has been committed to providing the best, most complete education possible for its students. Our commitment to that goal means that as times change, we sharpen our focus and methods to keep our graduates competitive in their fields. By offering outstanding teaching in a solid core curriculum enhanced by multimedia classrooms and campus-wide computer labs, the University of Alabama keeps its focus on the future while maintaining a traditional college atmosphere. Extensive international study opportunities, internship programs, and cooperative education placements help our students prepare for successful futures. Consisting of twelve colleges and schools offering over 200 majors and degrees in more than 100 fields of study, the university gives its students a wide range of choices and offers courses of study at the bachelor's, master's, specialist, and doctoral levels. The university emphasizes quality and breadth of academic opportunities and challenging programs for well-prepared students through its Honors College, including the University Honors Program, Randall Research Scholars Program, and Blount Scholars Program. Sixty percent of undergraduates are from out of state, providing an enriching social and cultural environment."

SELECTIVITY

# of total applicants	61,994
% of total applicants accepted	71
% of total acceptees attending	18

First-Year Profile

Testing policy	Test Optional
Range SAT composite	1100–1360
Range SAT EBRW	560–680
Range SAT math	530–680
Range ACT composite	22–31
% submitting SAT scores	19
% submitting ACT scores	53
Average HS GPA	3.9
% submitting high school GPA	99
% graduated top 10% of class	23
% graduated top 25% of class	48
% graduated top 50% of class	79
% submitting high school rank	38

Important Dates

Regular	
Notified by	Rolling, Mid July
Nonfall registration?	Yes

FINANCIAL FACTS

Annual in-state tuition	$11,684
Annual out-of-state tuition	$34,542
Food and housing	$13,616
Required fees	$800
Books and supplies	$700
Average need-based scholarship (First-year)	$16,124 ($17,406)
% students with need rec. need-based scholarship or grant aid (First-year)	88 (92)
% students with need rec. non-need-based scholarship or grant aid (First-year)	72 (84)
% students with need rec. need-based self-help aid (First-year)	63 (57)
% students rec. any financial aid (First-year)	83 (91)
% UG borrow to pay for school	42
Average cumulative indebtedness	$39,767
% of students with need fully met (First-year)	20 (27)
Average % of student need met (First-year)	57 (63)

University of Arizona

1401 E University Blvd, Tucson, AZ 85721-0066 • Admissions: 520-621-3237

Survey Snapshot
Recreation facilities are great
Everyone loves the Wildcats
Frats and sororities are popular

RATINGS

Quality of Life	84
Fire Safety	99
Green	94
Academic	77
Profs Interesting	84
Profs Accessible	88
Admissions	84
Financial Aid	86

CAMPUS LIFE

Type of school	Public
Environment	Metropolis

Students

Degree-seeking undergrad enrollment	42,776
% male/female/not reported	44/56/0
% from out of state	48
% First-year live on campus	62
% Ugrads live on campus	5
# of fraternities (% join)	26 (NR)
# of sororities (% join)	23 (NR)
% Asian	5
% Black or African American	4
% Hispanic	28
% Native American	2
% Pacific Islander	<1
% Race and/or ethnicity unknown	6
% Two or more races	5
% White	46
% International	4
# of countries represented	138

CAMPUS MENTAL HEALTH SERVICES

Offers mental health/wellness program	Yes
Mental health training available to students	Yes
Employs Chief Wellness Officer	Yes
Peer-to-peer mental health offerings	Yes
Counseling center has guidelines or accreditation	Yes
Mental health/well-being courses	Yes, non-credit

ACADEMICS

% students returning for sophomore year	83
% students graduating within 4 years	50
% students graduating within 6 years	68
Calendar	Semester
Student/faculty ratio	20:1
Most common class size 20–29.	(37%)
Most common lab/discussion size 20–29.	(40%)

Most Popular Majors

Legal Professions and Studies; Psychology; Physiology

Applicants Also Look At

Arizona State University, University of Colorado Boulder, University of Oregon

STUDENTS SAY "..."

Academics

The University of Arizona is a public university that blends a deep history with innovative, cutting-edge research. The school offers its 40,000 undergraduates more than 150 majors spread across 20 colleges (and even more specialized schools within), and students "can choose from a variety of majors and minors and structure your own studies" in any way they see fit. The school highly emphasizes "communicating with its students and keeping up to date with student life," a service that extends to graduates as well, thanks to a "supportive and large alumni network." Current enrollees looking for additional support will find tons of resources, whether that's free tutoring in most introductory level subjects or "Supplemental Instruction sessions, which are like bonus discussion sections if you want more practice."

Professors here run the gamut in terms of passion and presentation, but for the most part, they "really [care] about the material; [have] funny, interesting, or engaging lectures; and [are] extremely willing to meet outside class." Some professors use a "flipped classroom" approach, "which really [helps] create an active learning environment," and the sciences offer lab-based classes with "many hands-on activities that teach what presentations [alone] could not." Many professors "bring in guest lectors or have guest presentations," and "classrooms are often set up in a manner in which group discussion is encouraged."

Campus Life

Amazing weather and a beautiful campus make for a happy, sunny time that is "full of life and fun." This is "a very active community [that uses] the gyms regularly," though there's plenty of exercise simply in traversing the sprawling campus via bike or foot. Arizona is "full of spirit" and sporting events (especially football and basketball) are popular; students describe hanging out in the raucous "ZonaZoo" to show support for their teams. Thanks to the centralized Mall, it's easy to find people to hang out with during the day, and clearly posted events speak to all types of nighttime entertainment, since "Some people love to party, some people love to study." The campus "has an extremely open, comfortable atmosphere," and because "some dorms cater to a certain audience with the in-hall communities," it's remarkably easy to find your niche. The community feel is a real bonus for students, who love that "it's a massive university, yet everyone knows everyone."

Student Body

Around 60 percent of students hail from Arizona in this diverse population that is "very passionate about what it means to [be a] Wildcat and [the] excessive amounts of school pride" that come with it. The university's sheer size means there are "people from all over the world studying hundreds of different things" and hence "there is a club, frat, sorority, [or] group to join for everyone to feel a part of something greater and get encouragement." An Arizona student "knows the importance of both studies and life experiences for a well-rounded college experience" and takes studying as seriously as the relaxing: "We all know that at the end of the day we're all here to get that degree, despite the fun we all have."

UNIVERSITY OF ARIZONA

Financial Aid: 520-621-1858 • E-Mail: admissions@arizona.edu • Website: www.arizona.edu

THE PRINCETON REVIEW SAYS

Admissions

The school reports that its standardized testing policy for use in admission for Fall 2026 is Test Optional. The Princeton Review suggests that interested applicants consult with the school for the most up-to-date standardized testing policies. *Very important factors considered include:* rigor of secondary school record, academic GPA. *Important factors considered include:* extracurricular activities, talent/ability, character/personal qualities, level of applicant's interest. *Other factors considered include:* class rank, standardized test scores, application essay, recommendation(s), volunteer work, work experience. High school diploma is required and GED is accepted. *Academic units required:* 4 English, 4 math, 3 science, 3 science labs, 2 language (other than English), 2 social studies. *Academic units recommended:* 4 English, 4 math, 3 science, 3 science labs, 2 language (other than English), 2 social studies.

Financial Aid

Students should submit: FAFSA. Priority filing deadline is 4/1. The Princeton Review suggests that all financial aid forms be submitted as soon as possible. *Need-based scholarships/grants offered:* Federal Pell; Federal SEOG; State scholarships/grants; Private scholarships; College/university scholarship or grant aid from institutional funds. *Loan aid offered:* Federal Direct Subsidized Loans; Federal Direct Unsubsidized Loans; Direct PLUS loans; State Loans; College/university loans from institutional funds. Admitted students will be notified of awards on a rolling basis beginning 2/1. Federal Work-Study Program available. Institutional employment available.

The Inside Word

Admission to the University of Arizona is competitive, and you'll need to demonstrate achievement in college prep courses. Candidates who meet certain requirements, such as graduating in the top 25 percent of a regionally accredited high school, are automatically accepted, so check to see if you qualify. Applicants should also recognize that some programs, such as the College of Engineering, College of Nursing, College of Fine Arts, and the W.A. Franke Honors College, mandate additional materials and requirements.

THE SCHOOL SAYS

From the Admissions Office

"From day one, University of Arizona students step into an unrivaled mix of academics, student life, and experiential learning enhanced with opportunities that only a top research institution can offer. A sunny campus, welcoming atmosphere, and diverse student body offer a place for everyone to pursue their passions. Students spend their days learning from a world-class faculty, participating in countless recreation activities, and being valued members of a close-knit, active community. Through services like Student Engagement and Career Development, the university connects students with education-enhancing experiences like internships, research, or volunteering. The innovative Student Success District in the heart of campus tremendously elevates student support in areas like academics, career, and health and wellness. Thanks to the knowledge and experience they gain here, Wildcats are often sought after by top employers because they graduate with a diverse set of knowledge and skills that can apply to the workplace. As the network of more than 300,000 global alumni can attest to, an Arizona education pays you back for a lifetime—one of the many reasons why Arizona is repeatedly recognized for its outstanding academics and exceptional value. From groundbreaking research to a bustling student life with 400+ student clubs, cultural centers, and unrivaled school spirit with winning athletics programs, the University of Arizona offers an ideal college experience."

SELECTIVITY

# of total applicants	58,339
% of total applicants accepted	86
% of total acceptees attending	18
# of in-state applicants	15,064
% of in-state applicants accepted	90
# of out-of-state-applicants	34,044
% of applicants accepted from out of state	92
# of international applicants	9,231
% of international applicants accepted	58

First-Year Profile

Testing policy	Test Optional
Range SAT composite	1130–1240
Range SAT EBRW	560–670
Range SAT math	560–680
Range ACT composite	21–28
% submitting SAT scores	11
% submitting ACT scores	18
Average HS GPA	3.5
% submitting high school GPA	98
% graduated top 10% of class	33
% graduated top 25% of class	62
% graduated top 50% of class	87
% submitting high school rank	35

Important Dates

Early action	
Apply by	11/1
Notified by	1/15
Regular	
Apply by	4/1
Notified by	Rolling
Nonfall registration?	Yes

FINANCIAL FACTS

Annual in-state tuition	$13,900
Annual out-of-state tuition	$43,100
Food and housing	$17,770
Required fees (First-year)	$1,738 ($1,758)
Books and supplies	$600
Average need-based scholarship (First-year)	$15,837 ($16,342)
% students with need rec. need-based scholarship or grant aid (First-year)	95 (99)
% students with need rec. non-need-based scholarship or grant aid (First-year)	15 (16)
% students with need rec. need-based self-help aid (First-year)	45 (40)
% students rec. any financial aid (First-year)	79 (95)
% UG borrow to pay for school	35
Average cumulative indebtedness	$25,000
% of students with need fully met (First-year)	18 (20)
Average % of student need met (First-year)	63 (61)

UNIVERSITY OF ARKANSAS—FAYETTEVILLE

232 Silas H. Hunt Hall, Fayetteville, AR 72701 • Admissions: 479-575-5346

Survey Snapshot
Students are happy
Students love Fayetteville, AR
Active student government

RATINGS

Quality of Life	**89**
Fire Safety	**93**
Green	**60***
Academic	**79**
Profs Interesting	**85**
Profs Accessible	**89**
Admissions	**86**
Financial Aid	**84**

CAMPUS LIFE

Type of school	Public
Environment	City

Students

Degree-seeking undergrad enrollment	29,039
% male/female/not reported	45/55/<1
% from out of state	54
% First-year from public high school	82
% First-year live on campus	92
# of fraternities (% join)	19 (24)
# of sororities (% join)	17 (47)
% Asian	3
% Black or African American	4
% Hispanic	13
% Native American	1
% Pacific Islander	<1
% Race and/or ethnicity unknown	1
% Two or more races	5
% White	73
% International	1
# of countries represented	68

CAMPUS MENTAL HEALTH SERVICES

Offers mental health/wellness program	Yes
Mental health training available to students	No
Employs Chief Wellness Officer	NR
Peer-to-peer mental health offerings	NR
Counseling center has guidelines or accreditation	No
Mental health/well-being courses	NR

ACADEMICS

% students returning for sophomore year	86
% students graduating within 4 years	55
% students graduating within 6 years	71
Calendar	Semester
Student/faculty ratio	20:1
Most common class size 10–19.	(25%)
Most common lab/discussion size 20–29.	(68%)

Most Popular Majors

Registered Nursing/Registered Nurse; Finance; Marketing/Marketing Management

Applicants Also Look At

Baylor University, Oklahoma State University, Texas A&M University—College Station, Texas Christian University, Texas State University, Texas Tech University, University of Oklahoma, University of Texas at Austin

STUDENTS SAY "..."

Academics

The University of Arkansas—Fayetteville "is a large university with a community feel. It's big enough to have a lot of great opportunities, but small enough you see people you know on campus." With Fayetteville's outdoorsy culture, some students "would describe [the school] as a weird cross between Southern and hippie." Research opportunities abound, and prospective students are drawn to both the Honors College and the Sam Walton School of Business. Students also single out U of A's "strong engineering program, with the depth and diversity in every discipline from mechanical to computer science [and] biomedical." Even with the relaxed atmosphere—one student coins it as "Fayettechill"—students say that there are "tough programs that really make you work for your grade so you can be sure you are worth your degree." Professors are hit or miss; while some students say, "Most of my professors are extremely helpful," others lament that while "I enjoy most of my professors, but I do sometimes get the impression that they don't care about my individual success." Students in the larger majors say they often lack individualized attention. As one student points out: "My major is located in a smaller department, so I know my professors very well. However, in larger classes and departments it is easy to 'get lost' or go unnoticed."

Campus Life

Football (this is Razorback country) and Greek activities are prevalent on campus, though some students say, "The school is very centered around Greek life, so for some students it is harder for them to find their place outside of Greek life." The school's location in the Ozark Mountains gives students ample opportunities for "hiking, kayaking, [and] rock climbing" on the weekends. Popular destinations "nearby to take daytrips with your friends [include] Devil's Den or Crystal Bridges." Students say, "The pace of life is comfortably slow, but still full of fun opportunities," and Fayetteville "is an incredibly vibrant city because it is a refreshing combination of elements of the old South and collegiate culture." One popular destination is Dickson Street, "home to a plethora of bars and restaurants." On campus, when the Razorbacks are playing, "The whole state turns up to 'Call the Hogs' on to victory." For those who aren't as interested in athletics, luckily, a "school this big has enough people of diverse interests to create a club or event almost incredibly tailored to you."

Student Body

Students describe their peers as "friendly" and living "relaxed lifestyles" but are quick to point out that this doesn't mean "they are not high-achieving students." In general, students say they're an "adventurous, fun loving, welcoming, genuine, [and] creative" bunch. While some say the school is "very diverse for a Southern university," others lament the lack of diversity and say that the campus is "very much white, upper-middle class" students from Arkansas and the surrounding states, noting that more could be done in "advocating for marginalized groups." But despite the lack of diversity, students say that their peers are "accepting" and "kind," and that "the campus has a very warm feeling to it."

University of Arkansas—Fayetteville

Financial Aid: 479-575-3806 • E-Mail: uofa@uark.edu • Website: www.uark.edu

THE PRINCETON REVIEW SAYS

Admissions

The school reports that its standardized testing policy for use in admission for Fall 2026 is Test Optional. The Princeton Review suggests that interested applicants consult with the school for the most up-to-date standardized testing policies. *Very important factors considered include:* academic GPA. *Important factors considered include:* standardized test scores. *Other factors considered include:* rigor of secondary school record, class rank, application essay, recommendation(s), extracurricular activities, talent/ability, character/personal qualities, first generation, alumni/ae relation, geographical residence, state residency, volunteer work, wo High school diploma is required and GED is accepted. *Academic units required:* 4 English, 4 math, 3 science, 1 science lab, 1 social studies, 2 history, 2 academic electives. *Academic units recommended:* 4 English, 4 math, 3 science, 1 science lab, 2 language (other than English), 1 social studies, 2 history, 2 academic electives.

Financial Aid

Students should submit: FAFSA. Priority filing deadline is 3/15. The Princeton Review suggests that all financial aid forms be submitted as soon as possible. *Need-based scholarships/grants offered:* Federal Pell; Federal SEOG; State scholarships/grants; Private scholarships; College/university scholarship or grant aid from institutional funds. *Loan aid offered:* Federal Direct Subsidized Loans; Federal Direct Unsubsidized Loans; Direct PLUS loans. Admitted students will be notified of awards on a rolling basis beginning 4/1. Federal Work-Study Program available. Institutional employment available.

The Inside Word

A student's GPA and rigor of their high school courses is important, but so are grade trends and the student's demonstrated academic improvement. The admissions office also considers skills, talents, or achievements, as well as work experience, military service, and a commitment to the community. University of Arkansas has a rolling admissions policy, but it's always in a prospective student's best interest to apply as early as possible.

THE SCHOOL SAYS

From the Admissions Office

"The University of Arkansas is located in Fayetteville, a town consistently listed among the nation's top five best places to live. The university promotes undergraduate research in nearly every discipline and provides affordable higher education with competitively priced tuition and generous financial aid. Founded in 1871 as a land-grant institution, the U of A is the flagship campus of the UA System, home to 10 colleges and schools offering nearly 270 academic programs, the most in the state. Though more than 30,000 enroll at the U of A, students benefit from a low student-to-faculty ratio-currently 20:1—that prioritizes personal attention and guidance from professors who are passionate about teaching. Likewise, the Carnegie Foundation recognizes the U of A among the top U.S. universities with the highest levels of research activity, and undergraduates regularly win national honors, including some of the nation's top scholarships. The U of A has produced 11 Rhodes Scholars; 60 Goldwater Scholars; 155 National Science Foundation Graduate Research Fellows; 8 Marshall Scholars; 25 Truman Scholars; and 99 Fulbright Students, among others. Students have access to opportunities and amenities throughout Northwest Arkansas, a hub for business and research innovation and home to multiple Fortune 500 companies—including Walmart, Tyson Foods, and J.B. Hunt Transport Services—and a thriving art scene that are all steps away from outdoor adventure in one of the most beautiful areas in the country."

SELECTIVITY

# of total applicants	32,928
% of total applicants accepted	74
% of total acceptees attending	29
# offered a place on the wait list	389
# admitted from wait list	32

First-Year Profile

Testing policy	Test Optional
Range SAT composite	1020–1210
Range SAT EBRW	520–620
Range SAT math	500–620
Range ACT composite	21–28
% submitting SAT scores	31
% submitting ACT scores	72
Average HS GPA	3.8
% submitting high school GPA	100
% graduated top 10% of class	26
% graduated top 25% of class	53
% graduated top 50% of class	85
% submitting high school rank	58

Important Dates

Early action	
Apply by	11/1
Notified by	12/15
Regular	
Apply by	8/1
Notified by	Rolling, 10/15
Nonfall registration?	Yes

FINANCIAL FACTS

Annual in-state tuition	$8,092
Annual out-of-state tuition	$29,146
Food and housing	$14,968
Required fees	$2,404
Books and supplies	$1,216
Average need-based scholarship (First-year)	$10,478 ($10,544)
% students with need rec. need-based scholarship or grant aid (First-year)	82 (85)
% students with need rec. non-need-based scholarship or grant aid (First-year)	7 (9)
% students with need rec. need-based self-help aid (First-year)	61 (62)
% students rec. any financial aid (First-year)	69 (76)
% UG borrow to pay for school	45
Average cumulative indebtedness	$29,394
% of students with need fully met (First-year)	11 (12)
Average % of student need met (First-year)	54 (55)

UNIVERSITY OF CALIFORNIA—BERKELEY

110 Sproul Hall, Berkeley, CA 94720-5800 • Admissions: 510-642-3175

Survey Snapshot
Lots of liberal students
Great library
Students politically aware

RATINGS

Quality of Life	81
Fire Safety	91
Green	99
Academic	81
Profs Interesting	86
Profs Accessible	87
Admissions	87
Financial Aid	89

CAMPUS LIFE

Type of school	Public
Environment	City

Students

Degree-seeking undergrad enrollment	32,725
% male/female/not reported	43/55/2
% from out of state	14
% First-year live on campus	93
% Ugrads live on campus	28
# of fraternities (% join)	38 (3)
# of sororities (% join)	19 (5)
% Asian	35
% Black or African American	2
% Hispanic	22
% Native American	<1
% Pacific Islander	<1
% Race and/or ethnicity unknown	4
% Two or more races	7
% White	20
% International	10

CAMPUS MENTAL HEALTH SERVICES

Offers mental health/wellness program	Yes
Mental health training available to students	No
Employs Chief Wellness Officer	NR
Peer-to-peer mental health offerings	NR
Counseling center has guidelines or accreditation	No
Mental health/well-being courses	NR

ACADEMICS

% students returning for sophomore year	97
% students graduating within 4 years	80
% students graduating within 6 years	93
Calendar	Semester
Student/faculty ratio	18:1
Most common class size 10–19.	(28%)
Most common lab/discussion size 20–29.	(52%)

Most Popular Majors
English Language and Literature; Computer Engineering; Political Science and Government

STUDENTS SAY "..."

Academics

University of California—Berkeley is renowned for its "great faculty, great research, [and] great classes," as well as its "open, liberal education and culture." The school is dedicated to providing students with "a well-rounded, diverse education," and many students suggest that it's the "best location in the country for entrepreneurship and innovation." UC Berkeley's business and computer science programs are highly regarded, and it is home to "some of the best engineering programs across the board among colleges." The abundance of "top-notch" research taking place on and off-campus creates "plenty of opportunities for undergrads to engage in it," such as the Undergraduate Research Apprentice Program (URAP) and Summer Undergraduate Research Fellowships (SURF). One of the distinct advantages of attending UC Berkeley is the expertise of its faculty, who are described by students as "fantastic" and among "the best in their fields." Professors "have full command of their subjects and are determined to find an answer to anything they don't know, within their discipline," while students describe their graduate instructors as "very accessible and helpful." Students also appreciate the school's culture, which fosters "independent and collaborative thinking across all fields." One student shares that the school "really encourages us to go out and learn, both inside and outside the classroom." Another student summarizes their academic journey by saying, "Berkeley will offer you all the opportunity you can handle; it's up to you to take hold of it."

Campus Life

Berkeley is "a great choice for students who want the feeling of a big state school but want to also be pushed to their limits." Although "academics are a priority," there's "a constant buzz of student activity that drives everyday life" on campus. There is an "amazing community" of student-run organizations, "clubs, sports, student-run classes, seminars, [and] research opportunities" that provides "many different venues for people to find their passion." On campus, there are plenty of things to occupy one's time, everything "from frat houses to coffee shop discussions, hiking the fire trails to studying for finals." Off-campus, there's lots to explore in the downtown Berkeley area, and students use the "really convenient and time-saving" Bay Area Rapid Transit (BART) to visit San Francisco. In true undergraduate fashion, lots of folks socialize by attending football games, going to restaurants, or party hopping. While some students enjoy partying and drinking, there's no pressure to do so and "if that's not your style, there are plenty of others to spend time with." One of the things that makes this campus so special is that "every single person has something that they are very passionate about." This diverse mix of interests really contributes to the school's vibrant and creative community.

Student Body

With an undergraduate enrollment of over 30,000, Berkeley is a bustling and welcoming community where all types "mix among each other easily" and friendships often form around majors or dorms. Says one junior, "From clubs to DeCal courses, there is no way a student will not make a group of friends while here at Cal." Berkeley undergrads are often described as "politically liberal, nonreligious, and pretty independent." In addition, they are known for their "ability to hold high-level conversation[s] about basically anything." And students' enthusiasm for their academic pursuits is inspiring; in fact, just "talking to them for five minutes about it makes you wonder if you should change your major." Berkeley attracts students from all over the United States and many other countries, including a high percentage of students from Asia. This rich diversity fosters an environment of inclusivity, where everyone can find their place, "regardless of their sexual orientation, religion, or political beliefs," thanks to the many opportunities for undergraduates to connect over shared interests.

UNIVERSITY OF CALIFORNIA—BERKELEY

Website: www.berkeley.edu

THE PRINCETON REVIEW SAYS

Admissions

The school reports that its standardized testing policy for use in admission for Fall 2026 is Test Free. The Princeton Review suggests that interested applicants consult with the school for the most up-to-date standardized testing policies. *Very important factors considered include:* rigor of secondary school record, academic GPA, application essay. *Important factors considered include:* extracurricular activities, character/personal qualities, volunteer work, work experience. *Other factors considered include:* standardized test scores, recommendation(s), talent/ability, first generation, state residency. High school diploma is required and GED is accepted. *Academic units required:* 4 English, 3 math, 2 science, 2 science labs, 2 language (other than English), 2 history, 1 academic elective, 1 visual/performing arts. *Academic units recommended:* 4 English, 4 math, 3 science, 3 science labs, 3 language (other than English), 2 history, 1 academic elective, 1 visual/performing arts.

Financial Aid

Students should submit: FAFSA; State aid form. Priority filing deadline is 3/2. The Princeton Review suggests that all financial aid forms be submitted as soon as possible. *Need-based scholarships/grants offered:* Federal Pell; Federal SEOG; State scholarships/grants; Private scholarships; College/university scholarship or grant aid from institutional funds. *Loan aid offered:* Federal Direct Subsidized Loans; Federal Direct Unsubsidized Loans; Direct PLUS loans; State Loans; College/university loans from institutional funds. Admitted students will be notified of awards on a rolling basis beginning 3/31. Federal Work-Study Program available. Institutional employment available.

The Inside Word

UC Berkeley is a top-notch public university that is highly selective. Importance is placed on the totality of a student's application with a joint focus on the personal statement and academic excellence as noted by a student's GPA. Class rank isn't considered. The school is home to an incredible amount of students with as wide a range of interests. Successful applicants here are generally stellar both academically and personally. Applications, especially the personal statement, should create a picture of a unique candidate with a diversity of skills to offer this active community.

THE SCHOOL SAYS

From the Admissions Office

"The University of California, Berkeley, is the world's premier public university, renowned for its academic excellence, groundbreaking research, and commitment to public service. Founded in 1868 as the flagship campus of the UC system. Berkeley offers more than 400 degree programs and 10,000 courses, attracting more than 45,000 undergraduate and graduate students and 2,000 faculty members. Consistently ranked among the top universities globally, it is a hub for innovation and intellectual exploration, with 26 Nobel Prizes awarded to faculty and 35 to alumni and fellows. As a powerhouse of discovery and progress, Berkeley continues to shape the future through cutting-edge research, technological advancements, and a dedication to social change, preparing students to lead and make a lasting impact on the world."

SELECTIVITY

# of total applicants	119,759
% of total applicants accepted	11
% of total acceptees attending	48
# offered a place on the wait list	10,894
# admitted from wait list	26

First-Year Profile

Testing policy	Test Free
Average HS GPA	3.9
% submitting high school GPA	100

Important Dates

Regular	
Apply by	11/30
Notified by	3/31
Nonfall registration?	Yes

FINANCIAL FACTS

Annual in-state tuition	$18,134
Annual out-of-state tuition	$57,204
Food and housing	$23,640
Books and supplies	$1,442
Average need-based scholarship (First-year)	$31,583 ($33,723)
% students with need rec. need-based scholarship or grant aid (First-year)	97 (96)
% students with need rec. non-need-based scholarship or grant aid (First-year)	4 (6)
% students with need rec. need-based self-help aid (First-year)	59 (59)
% UG borrow to pay for school	25
Average cumulative indebtedness	$18,728
% of students with need fully met (First-year)	32 (41)
Average % of student need met (First-year)	88 (90)

UNIVERSITY OF CALIFORNIA—DAVIS

One Shields Ave, Davis, CA 95616 • Admissions: 530-752-2971

Survey Snapshot
Students are happy
Students environmentally aware
Students love Davis, CA

RATINGS

Quality of Life	**91**
Fire Safety	**96**
Green	**97**
Academic	**78**
Profs Interesting	**86**
Profs Accessible	**89**
Admissions	**90**
Financial Aid	**86**

CAMPUS LIFE

Type of school	Public
Environment	Town

Students

Degree-seeking undergrad enrollment	31,162
% male/female/not reported	39/61/0
% from out of state	5
% First-year from public high school	84
% First-year live on campus	28
% Ugrads live on campus	15
# of fraternities (% join)	28 (5)
# of sororities (% join)	21 (7)
% Asian	28
% Black or African American	2
% Hispanic	24
% Native American	<1
% Pacific Islander	<1
% Race and/or ethnicity unknown	2
% Two or more races	6
% White	21
% International	16
# of countries represented	121

CAMPUS MENTAL HEALTH SERVICES

Offers mental health/wellness program	Yes
Mental health training available to students	No
Employs Chief Wellness Officer	NR
Peer-to-peer mental health offerings	NR
Counseling center has guidelines or accreditation	No
Mental health/well-being courses	NR

ACADEMICS

% students returning for sophomore year	92
% students graduating within 4 years	63
% students graduating within 6 years	87
Calendar	Quarter
Student/faculty ratio	20:1
Most common class size 20–29.	(25%)
Most common lab/discussion size 20–29.	(45%)

Most Popular Majors
Economics; Biology/Biological Sciences; Psychology

STUDENTS SAY "..."

Academics

The University of California—Davis is "a prestigious research university with great professors and brilliant students." With a longtime "focus on agriculture and biological science," Davis has cultivated a "strong science-based education." Students also praise its "other great programs such as engineering and political science," as well as the "large variety of majors" offered. "Davis does have a fast-paced quarter system," but the "resources available to assist students" help them "feel at ease." Beyond the "abundant research, internship, and job opportunities," Davis students rave about the support they receive from "tutoring and advising resources, opportunities to have a focus within each major, study abroad opportunities," and "all the counselors who can answer every question." As for professors, these "true experts" and "top researchers" lead classes that "are full of challenging, hands-on experiences." Students benefit from these "passionate and devoted" scholars who "have their own research projects going on, and apply what they are teaching to their work," though some point out that "research skills do not translate into teaching skills." But even when professors "seem to be more focused on research," students say that the teaching assistants "are also really great and amazing people" who "have a HUGE impact on classes." Overall, UC Davis students agree that most professors care "very deeply about teaching" and provide a "challenging but rewarding and successful academic experience."

Campus Life

UC Davis students boast about belonging to a "green school" that "promotes sustainability." Many students gravitate toward "outdoor activities to fill their time," like "pick-up soccer," visiting the local farmers market or "reading at the arboretum." Students report that "even if you don't have a car," the "bike paths make it really easy to get around the city and campus" and the "free convenient bus systems" ensure there are "plenty of transportation options" available to students. And with "700+ clubs on campus including [many] Greek organizations," and a variety of identity and cultural-based centers and programming, students have many opportunities to connect. The downtown Davis nightlife is "mostly low-key," but students can enjoy "good food, open mic night, trivia night," "local shows, line dancing, and just about everything in between." And because it is near "Tahoe, San Francisco, [and] Napa," Davis is "a great location for day trips or weekend trips." Students say they maintain a good "balance between school life and their social life because of all the opportunities and activities."

Student Body

Davis is a "pretty diverse community" where most students are "very friendly and thoughtful" and "few are quick to judge." As one undergrad notes, "Most students spend their days biking furiously from class to class," but "everyone is very nice and welcoming." "Anyone can ask any student for directions and the student will gladly stop biking to help out." While Davis "is a top university, you don't feel like everyone is competing against you" and "help from your peers" is easy to find. And while Davis students "are academically rigorous," they are "quirky and [creative]" too, creating "the perfect mixture of serious about studying and down to earth and fun." In general, "most are also very open to making new friends or trying something new."

UNIVERSITY OF CALIFORNIA—DAVIS

Financial Aid: 530-752-2396 • E-Mail: undergraduateadmissions@ucdavis.edu • Website: www.ucdavis.edu

THE PRINCETON REVIEW SAYS

Admissions

The school reports that its standardized testing policy for use in admission for Fall 2026 is Test Free. The Princeton Review suggests that interested applicants consult with the school for the most up-to-date standardized testing policies. *Very important factors considered include:* rigor of secondary school record, academic GPA, application essay. *Important factors considered include:* extracurricular activities, talent/ability, character/personal qualities, volunteer work. *Other factors considered include:* first generation, state residency, work experience. High school diploma is required and GED is accepted. *Academic units required:* 4 English, 3 math, 2 science, 2 science labs, 2 language (other than English), 1 social studies, 1 history, 1 academic elective, 1 visual/performing arts. *Academic units recommended:* 4 English, 4 math, 3 science, 3 science labs, 3 language (other than English), 1 social studies, 1 history, 1 academic elective, 1 visual/performing arts.

Financial Aid

Students should submit: FAFSA; State aid form. Priority filing deadline is 3/2. The Princeton Review suggests that all financial aid forms be submitted as soon as possible. *Need-based scholarships/grants offered:* Federal Pell; Federal SEOG; State scholarships/grants; Private scholarships; College/university scholarship or grant aid from institutional funds. *Loan aid offered:* Federal Direct Subsidized Loans; Federal Direct Unsubsidized Loans; Direct PLUS loans. Admitted students will be notified of awards on a rolling basis beginning 3/12. Federal Work-Study Program available. Institutional employment available.

The Inside Word

Admission to UC Davis is not as competitive as, say, admission to Berkeley. Nevertheless, every school in the UC system is world-class, and the UC system in general is geared toward the best and brightest of not only California's high school and community college students but the nation and the globe.

THE SCHOOL SAYS

From the Admissions Office

"UC Davis is one of the world's leading public research universities, providing undergraduates with a wealth of research opportunities and challenging academics in more than 100 majors. Collegiality is a hallmark of the UC Davis experience, encouraging students to ask questions, explore new avenues of study, and work alongside faculty members engaged in solving the critical issues facing society today. UC Davis Aggies embrace a culture where what's considered different is the norm, challenging expectations and putting those ideas to the test through capstone projects, internships, studying abroad, and volunteering in programs like our student-run community clinics.

"UC Davis students are part of an active, diverse student community immersed in the arts and sciences. Aggies enjoy world-class cultural programs at the Robert and Margrit Mondavi Center for the Performing Arts, cheer on our 25 NCAA Division I sports teams, ride at the only Equestrian Center in the UC system and stay fit at the Activities and Recreation Center. The friendly, supportive nature of our campus and California's College Town of Davis welcomes exploration of all kinds: learning about new cultures at a cultural celebration, connecting with students at a residence hall living-learning community, meeting new friends through more than 800 student-run organizations, or building a career network through internships and research opportunities.

"UC Davis is a place for students who seek to outgrow the expected and thrive when challenged. This spirit is reflected in the income potential and career successes of our graduates. Grow with us and apply this fall."

SELECTIVITY

# of total applicants	76,225
% of total applicants accepted	46
% of total acceptees attending	17
# offered a place on the wait list	13,092
# admitted from wait list	3,919

First-Year Profile

Testing policy	Test Free
Average HS GPA	4.0
% submitting high school GPA	100

Important Dates

Regular	
Apply by	11/30
Notified by	3/31
Nonfall registration?	No

FINANCIAL FACTS

Annual in-state tuition	$11,442
Annual out-of-state tuition	$41,196
Food and housing	$16,480
Required fees	$3,212
Books and supplies	$1,197
Average need-based scholarship (First-year)	$19,383 ($19,830)
% students with need rec. need-based scholarship or grant aid (First-year)	97 (96)
% students with need rec. non-need-based scholarship or grant aid (First-year)	2 (3)
% students with need rec. need-based self-help aid (First-year)	41 (42)
% students rec. any financial aid (First-year)	71 (67)
% UG borrow to pay for school	45
Average cumulative indebtedness	$17,736
% of students with need fully met (First-year)	19 (20)
Average % of student need met (First-year)	79 (80)

University of California—Irvine

Office of Admissions and Relations with Schools, Irvine, CA 92697 • Admissions: 949-824-6703

Survey Snapshot
Students love Irvine, CA
Great off-campus food
Great library

RATINGS

Quality of Life	**83**
Fire Safety	**62**
Green	**95**
Academic	**77**
Profs Interesting	**82**
Profs Accessible	**85**
Admissions	**85**
Financial Aid	**86**

CAMPUS LIFE

Type of school	Public
Environment	City

Students

Degree-seeking undergrad enrollment	30,260
% male/female/not reported	45/55/0
% from out of state	6
% First-year from public high school	69
% First-year live on campus	83
% Ugrads live on campus	47
# of fraternities (% join)	21 (NR)
# of sororities (% join)	22 (NR)
% Asian	38
% Black or African American	2
% Hispanic	26
% Native American	<1
% Pacific Islander	<1
% Race and/or ethnicity unknown	2
% Two or more races	7
% White	13
% International	12
# of countries represented	82

CAMPUS MENTAL HEALTH SERVICES

Offers mental health/wellness program	Yes
Mental health training available to students	No
Employs Chief Wellness Officer	NR
Peer-to-peer mental health offerings	NR
Counseling center has guidelines or accreditation	No
Mental health/well-being courses	NR

ACADEMICS

% students returning for sophomore year	93
% students graduating within 4 years	75
% students graduating within 6 years	87
Calendar	Quarter
Student/faculty ratio	19:1
Most common class size 1–9.	(26%)
Most common lab/discussion size 40–49.	(22%)

Most Popular Majors

Computer Science; Biology/Biological Sciences; Research and Experimental Psychology

STUDENTS SAY "..."

Academics

With its "abundance of opportunities," the University of California—Irvine delivers "a quality education" and the "critical thinking skills needed for life." In addition to career-building fairs and visiting speakers, the school also has "lots of resources if you are struggling," and students note that because the Orange County location is "becoming a hotspot for companies," there are an increasing number of options for "research, volunteer opportunities, and internships on and off-campus." All of this means that students "are encouraged to explore different paths" while also being supported with "the counseling and information resources necessary so that informed decisions are the only kind of decisions we ever make." While teachers can be "hit or miss," most are described as "great professors that make the class fun and enjoyable." These standout professors are "very informed and knowledgeable about what they're teaching," and try to draw from their "experience outside the classroom researching and practicing their profession." There's no one teaching style, so it really comes down to finding what works for you: "each lesson plan is specific to the professor's personal strengths and beliefs, as well [as] what the class needs." Regardless of the approach or the topic, professors are said to try and make the content "appealing and are available outside of class during office hours or open to making appointments." Taken together, the combination of knowledgeable professors and "wide range of resources" is "making our lives very rich and colorful."

Campus Life

"A diverse selection of clubs and inclusive campus-wide activities cater to individual interests" at Irvine, including Greek life and "a vast dance community." On busy weekdays, students "spend time at the library or other spots on campus and hang out and/or study between classes or other obligations." At the same time, students highlight strong involvement in professional clubs, noting that "many have participation from a variety of... majors." Other popular spots include the Esports lounge, the Anteater Recreation Center (ARC), "outdoors/hiking clubs and social events such as dog therapy," as well as the campus's Aldrich Park, where "the landscaping and greenery are very beautiful" and many "have picnics, read, spend time with others, play instruments, or do sports." The university has a sizable commuter population, and "there isn't much to do around UC Irvine if you don't have a car" so it can be "rather quiet on the weekends." However, others point out that there are "nice shuttle options" and "a lot of options for beaches to go to," as well as the University Town Center (UTC), "a great place near campus for clubs, organizations, or friends to spend quality time together." Students "all do various things," making the most of the vibrant and inclusive campus life that UC Irvine offers.

Student Body

UC Irvine "is very ethnically, religiously, and culturally diverse, and there is a large LGBTQ+ community," although students also say that it's a very local school, where "many students are from Orange County and knew each other prior to university." Either way, the "many different backgrounds and perspectives come together on one campus, which makes conversations and group work more interesting." Students emphasize that though there's a "mix of both extroverted and introverted" personalities, they're overall "kind and respectful people." While some students put in more time than others, most are "able to keep up with their assignments and take on a wide variety of activities," and some "even take it upon themselves to create groups to share reminders and helpful tips, [and] host study sessions." As one student describes the academic focus, "it feels like more of a 'we want to succeed and we want you to succeed' kind of way." That balance makes for a group of peers who are "overall laid-back and able to balance school with fun."

University of California—Irvine

Financial Aid: 949-824-5337 • E-Mail: admissions@uci.edu • Website: www.uci.edu

THE PRINCETON REVIEW SAYS

Admissions

The school reports that its standardized testing policy for use in admission for Fall 2026 is Test Free. The Princeton Review suggests that interested applicants consult with the school for the most up-to-date standardized testing policies. *Very important factors considered include:* rigor of secondary school record, academic GPA, application essay, extracurricular activities, talent/ability, volunteer work, work experience. *Important factors considered include:* character/personal qualities. *Other factors considered include:* first generation, geographical residence, state residency. High school diploma is required and GED is accepted. *Academic units required:* 4 English, 3 math, 2 science, 2 science labs, 2 language (other than English), 2 history, 1 academic elective, 1 visual/performing arts. *Academic units recommended:* 4 English, 4 math, 3 science, 3 science labs, 3 language (other than English), 2 history, 1 academic elective, 1 visual/performing arts.

Financial Aid

Students should submit: FAFSA; State aid form. Priority filing deadline is 3/2. The Princeton Review suggests that all financial aid forms be submitted as soon as possible. *Need-based scholarships/grants offered:* Federal Pell; State scholarships/grants; Federal SEOG; Private scholarships; College/university scholarship or grant aid from institutional funds. *Loan aid offered:* Federal Direct Subsidized Loans; Federal Direct Unsubsidized Loans; Direct PLUS loans; College/university loans from institutional funds. Admitted students will be notified of awards on a rolling basis beginning 4/1. Federal Work-Study Program available. Institutional employment available.

The Inside Word

University of California—Irvine is considered one of the top public universities in the country, and application numbers are expectedly high. Over 120,000 vie for a position here, so while the school is large, fewer than 30% of those are accepted. As a part of the University of California system, UCI is Test Free, meaning that standardized tests won't be reviewed, and letters of recommendation are not accepted. It's no surprise, then, that the majority of those accepted are in at least the top 10% of their class; if you think you're on the bubble, review the California system's method of evaluating your GPA.

THE SCHOOL SAYS

From the Admissions Office

"We like that you do things differently. So do we.

"At UCI, we believe in the infinitely curious. Our students are the tinkerers, the dreamers, and the courageous of thought. They are inspiring, motivated, and they care about the world around them. And they aren't afraid to go where others won't.

"No other college or university nurtures fearless, independent thought like UCI. We take you beyond the classroom to see possibility where others only see the impossible.

"One of the top public universities in the country, UCI offers more than 85 undergraduate degree programs and the opportunity to work alongside internationally renowned faculty producing groundbreaking work. In fact, by the time you are a senior, 73 percent of your graduating class will have participated in undergraduate research.

"Once you become an Anteater, you become part of a supportive, tight-knit family for the rest of your life. And it begins as soon as you step on campus."

SELECTIVITY

# of total applicants	124,231
% of total applicants accepted	29
% of total acceptees attending	18
# of in-state applicants	86,230
% of in-state applicants accepted	22
# of out-of-state-applicants	16,381
% of applicants accepted from out of state	48
# of international applicants	21,620
% of international applicants accepted	43
# offered a place on the wait list	12,967
# admitted from wait list	5,737

First-Year Profile

Testing policy	Test Free

Important Dates

Regular	
Apply by	11/30
Nonfall registration?	No

FINANCIAL FACTS

Annual in-state tuition	$13,602
Annual out-of-state tuition	$51,204
Food and housing	$20,416
Required fees	$3,056
Books and supplies	$1,750
Average need-based scholarship (First-year)	$24,200 ($25,236)
% students with need rec. need-based scholarship or grant aid (First-year)	95 (98)
% students with need rec. non-need-based scholarship or grant aid (First-year)	3 (5)
% students with need rec. need-based self-help aid (First-year)	52 (80)
% UG borrow to pay for school	32
Average cumulative indebtedness	$17,374
% of students with need fully met (First-year)	15 (26)
Average % of student need met (First-year)	78 (86)

UNIVERSITY OF CALIFORNIA—LOS ANGELES

405 Hilgard Avenue, Los Angeles, CA 90090 • Admissions: 310-825-3101

Survey Snapshot
Great library
Recreation facilities are great
Campus newspaper is popular

RATINGS

Quality of Life	**79**
Fire Safety	**91**
Green	**97**
Academic	**80**
Profs Interesting	**82**
Profs Accessible	**86**
Admissions	**89**
Financial Aid	**78**

CAMPUS LIFE

Type of school	Public
Environment	Metropolis

Students

Degree-seeking undergrad enrollment	33,471
% male/female/not reported	39/60/1
% from out of state	12
% First-year from public high school	77
% First-year live on campus	96
% Ugrads live on campus	60
# of fraternities (% join)	35 (NR)
# of sororities (% join)	35 (NR)
% Asian	29
% Black or African American	3
% Hispanic	24
% Native American	<1
% Pacific Islander	<1
% Race and/or ethnicity unknown	3
% Two or more races	8
% White	25
% International	8
# of countries represented	116

CAMPUS MENTAL HEALTH SERVICES

Offers mental health/wellness program	Yes
Mental health training available to students	No
Employs Chief Wellness Officer	NR
Peer-to-peer mental health offerings	NR
Counseling center has guidelines or accreditation	No
Mental health/well-being courses	NR

ACADEMICS

% students returning for sophomore year	97
% students graduating within 4 years	85
% students graduating within 6 years	93
Calendar	Quarter
Student/faculty ratio	20:1
Most common class size 1–9.	(25%)
Most common lab/discussion size 20–29.	(45%)

Most Popular Majors
Psychology; Political Science; Business Economics

STUDENTS SAY "..."

Academics

The University of California—Los Angeles is recognized as one of the top schools in the University of California system. UCLA "is the kind of school that pushes you to work hard academically but reminds you that interaction with people outside of the classroom is just as important." One geography and environmental science double major declares, "There's nothing that can't be accomplished at UCLA. The possibilities are endless, and the resources are unparalleled." One of UCLA's biggest draws is its faculty, who are often recognized as prominent "leaders in their field." While most consider it "a privilege to study under them," some undergrads note that at a large research university like UCLA, it's possible to encounter some instructors purely "in it for the research." Nevertheless, other students affirm that "most professors care about their students" and "are willing to work extra hours with students and help us with anything we need." An English major agrees, saying, "I have never had a professor that I did not feel comfortable approaching, which has made my academic experience incredibly more beneficial." In addition to the great faculty, students have many reasons for choosing to become a Bruin. One student enthusiastically explains their reasons: "The people, the weather, the academics, the sports; it has absolutely everything I could ever want."

Campus Life

Students praise UCLA's "ideal" location in West Los Angeles, appreciating its close proximity to local attractions. One enthusiastic undergraduate explains, "You can take a five minute drive, and you'll be soaking in the Pacific Ocean, or take an hour drive where you can be hitting the slopes in Big Bear. You can walk down to the theater and run into Jennifer Lopez. The possibilities are endless here." The campus itself is home to so much "hustle and bustle" that it's virtually "impossible to [be] bored." While nearly everyone's "main focus is on school," students also find time to embrace the college experience. "Whether it be in Greek life, a club, or [an] organization, everybody has somewhere they can go to relax and have some fun." Students also like that "the apartments are close to campus, so nearly everybody lives in a small area with close proximity," which adds to the sense of community. Sports also unify the community and "are extremely popular here, and conversations about the Bruins are common," The "pride of going to a Division I school with more NCAA championships than (almost) any other college/university" is palpable, adding to the overall spirit of the campus. In addition to sports, students have access to a wide range of recreational options, including "tons of movie showings on campus, recreation centers, pools, activities, [and] events." There are numerous opportunities for campus involvement; it often "seems like everyone is in at least one club or organization." The sheer variety of students and the over 1,200 clubs and student organizations on campus make it much easier to find new friends.

Student Body

Undergrads call the Bruin community "vibrant" and claim "there is no 'typical' student" here and "the only common denominator is truly an appetite for excellence." That said, most UCLA students are "very hardworking and ambitious" folks who "strive for success and to do their absolute best." While they take their academic pursuits seriously, students also describe their peers as "laid-back" and "not outright competitive with other students," which fosters a more supportive environment. With undergraduates hailing from all over the world, "everyone comes from different backgrounds with varied interests," which enriches the community. This "unmatched diversity" broadens students' horizons both culturally and socially. Overall, Bruins are open and inclusive, and most students find that "it is very easy to talk to and meet new people and make new friends."

UNIVERSITY OF CALIFORNIA—LOS ANGELES

Financial Aid: 310-206-0400 • Website: www.ucla.edu

THE PRINCETON REVIEW SAYS

Admissions

The school reports that its standardized testing policy for use in admission for Fall 2026 is Test Free. The Princeton Review suggests that interested applicants consult with the school for the most up-to-date standardized testing policies. *Very important factors considered include:* rigor of secondary school record, academic GPA, application essay. *Important factors considered include:* extracurricular activities, talent/ability, character/personal qualities, volunteer work, work experience. *Other factors considered include:* first generation, geographical residence, state residency. High school diploma is required and GED is accepted. *Academic units required:* 4 English, 3 math, 2 science, 2 science labs, 2 language (other than English), 2 history, 1 academic elective, 1 visual/performing arts. *Academic units recommended:* 4 English, 4 math, 3 science, 3 science labs, 3 language (other than English), 2 history, 1 academic elective, 1 visual/performing arts.

Financial Aid

The Princeton Review suggests that all financial aid forms be submitted as soon as possible. Federal Work-Study Program available. Institutional employment available.

The Inside Word

Competition is fierce to secure admittance to one of the nation's top public universities. Academic success is paramount, and your GPA factors heavily into admissions decisions. You'll want to load up on challenging courses in high school. Indeed, taking advanced placement, IB, or honors classes (if offered) is highly recommended. Of course, UCLA also wants students who will actively contribute to their community, and it's also important to demonstrate commitment to extracurricular activities.

THE SCHOOL SAYS

From the Admissions Office

"Undergraduates arrive at UCLA from throughout California and around the world with exceptional levels of academic preparation. They are attracted by our acclaimed degree programs, distinguished faculty, and the beauty of a park-like campus set amid the dynamism of the nation's second-largest city. UCLA's highly ranked undergraduate programs incorporate cutting-edge technology and teaching techniques that hone the critical-thinking skills and the global perspectives necessary for success in our rapidly changing world. The diversity of these programs draws strength from a student body that mirrors the cultural and ethnic vibrancy of Los Angeles. Generally ranked among the nation's top half-dozen universities, UCLA is at once distinguished and dynamic, academically rigorous, and responsive."

SELECTIVITY

# of total applicants	146,276
% of total applicants accepted	9
% of total acceptees attending	50
# offered a place on the wait list	15,023
# admitted from wait list	1,211

First-Year Profile

Testing policy	Test Free
Average HS GPA	3.9
% submitting high school GPA	100

Important Dates

Regular	
Apply by	11/30
Notified by	3/31
Nonfall registration?	No

FINANCIAL FACTS

Annual in-state tuition (First-year)	NR ($13,602)
Annual out-of-state tuition	$51,204
Food and housing	$18,960
Required fees	$2,099
Books and supplies	$1,680
Average need-based scholarship (First-year)	NR ($28,279)
% students with need rec. need-based scholarship or grant aid (First-year)	NR (98)
% students with need rec. non-need-based scholarship or grant aid (First-year)	NR (7)
% students with need rec. need-based self-help aid (First-year)	NR (35)
% students rec. any financial aid (First-year)	48 (45)
% UG borrow to pay for school	25
Average cumulative indebtedness	$19,209
% of students with need fully met (First-year)	NR (24)
Average % of student need met (First-year)	NR (85)

University of California—Merced

5200 North Lake Road, Merced, CA 95343 • Admissions: 209-228-7178

Survey Snapshot
Lab facilities are great
Great library
Diverse student types interact on campus

RATINGS	
Quality of Life	80
Fire Safety	97
Green	60*
Academic	73
Profs Interesting	83
Profs Accessible	88
Admissions	74
Financial Aid	89

CAMPUS LIFE

Type of school	Public
Environment	City

Students

Degree-seeking undergrad enrollment	8,135
% male/female/not reported	55/42/3
% from out of state	1
% First-year live on campus	75
% Ugrads live on campus	48
# of fraternities (% join)	3 (NR)
# of sororities (% join)	5 (NR)
% Asian	23
% Black or African American	5
% Hispanic	56
% Native American	<1
% Pacific Islander	<1
% Race and/or ethnicity unknown	1
% Two or more races	5
% White	9
% International	1
# of countries represented	9

CAMPUS MENTAL HEALTH SERVICES

Offers mental health/wellness program	Yes
Mental health training available to students	No
Employs Chief Wellness Officer	No
Peer-to-peer mental health offerings	No
Counseling center has guidelines or accreditation	No
Mental health/well-being courses	No

ACADEMICS

% students returning for sophomore year	85
% students graduating within 4 years	51
% students graduating within 6 years	68
Calendar	Semester
Student/faculty ratio	22:1
Most common class size 20–29.	(25%)
Most common lab/discussion size 20–29.	(43%)

Most Popular Majors

Psychology; Biology/Biological Sciences; Computer Engineering

Applicants Often Prefer

University of California—Berkeley, University of California—Davis, University of California—Irvine, University of California—Los Angeles, University of California—Riverside, University of California—San Diego, University of California—Santa Barbara, University of California—Santa Cruz

STUDENTS SAY "…"

Academics

The University of California—Merced, which opened in 2005, may be the most recent addition to the University of California system, but it has quickly positioned itself as a notable center for "cutting-edge research." The university features several research institutes and centers with "state-of-the-art lab and research facilities," and students appreciate the "abundance of opportunities" offered "in whatever field interests you." In particular, the Health Science Institute sees a lot of use in connecting undergrads to research, and the Sierra Nevada Research Institute helps students use their environment as an outdoor laboratory. The curriculum offers "hands-on experience and community engagement" that "goes beyond traditional lectures and allows students to apply what they've learned in a meaningful way." UC Merced's tight-knit and collaborative community fosters "numerous opportunities for mentorship, undergraduate research, and leadership development." Professors here are "very interactive" and "very knowledgeable in their fields." The classes tend to be small, so "students can actually have a relationship with their professors," which can be instrumental in creating future opportunities. As one student explains, "I was able to get into research my first year of college and make great connections with many of my professors." And notably, students say the experiential learning is "exciting and valuable," as it helps make to make one's "academic experience feel more connected to current trends in education."

Campus Life

While the school's "smaller, more quiet environment" makes it easier to focus on coursework or professional development, it also boasts a vibrant social scene with "many opportunities to find community on campus or give back to the community around the school." Students here are "deeply involved in shaping the campus culture" and there are "a lot of events, clubs, and activities to keep you busy." Extracurricular offerings encompass a wide range of options, from intramural sports and Greek life to crochet club and archery, as well as cultural organizations like the Philipinex American Alliance and Ballet Folklorico, "a club dedicated to teaching and performing traditional Mexican dance." The campus is easy to navigate and its smaller size "makes travel times between classes a lot shorter." For outdoor recreation, the school has a program that takes students to Yosemite and other nearby places for hiking and rock climbing. Additionally, a lake located just a ten-minute walk away is a popular spot for students looking to swim or kayak. As one student says, "Life at UC Merced is dynamic, with students balancing academics, extracurricular activities, and social experiences."

Student Body

UC Merced stands out for "how friendly it is." It's a place where the students are "kind, hardworking, and committed," the "support for one another is strong," and "everyone is willing to help." The student body is "very diverse," and many are first-generation college students. Students say inclusivity is among the school's greatest strengths and cite programs like Services for Undocumented Students and the Bobcat Underground, a group that supports justice-impacted students. Students who commute say they feel connected to the campus community, and all the campus events give "lots of chances to meet people that you can make friends with." The school attracts many students who "chose Merced for the peace and focus it allows." Everyone is "very focused on their work," as one student puts it, "We're not a loud crowd." It's a "relatively studious," open-minded, and helpful group of students who want to see their peers succeed. UC Merced fosters a "welcoming and warm environment" where students are "encouraged to think critically and make a difference in the world."

University of California—Merced

Financial Aid: 209-228-7178 • E-Mail: admissions@ucmerced.edu • Website: www.ucmerced.edu

THE PRINCETON REVIEW SAYS

Admissions

The school reports that its standardized testing policy for use in admission for Fall 2026 is Test Free. The Princeton Review suggests that interested applicants consult with the school for the most up-to-date standardized testing policies. *Very important factors considered include:* rigor of secondary school record, academic GPA, application essay. *Important factors considered include:* extracurricular activities, talent/ability. *Other factors considered include:* recommendation(s), character/personal qualities, first generation, geographical residence, state residency, volunteer work, work experience. High school diploma is required and GED is accepted. *Academic units required:* 4 English, 3 math, 2 science, 2 science labs, 2 language (other than English), 2 history, 1 academic elective, 1 visual/performing arts. *Academic units recommended:* 4 math, 3 science, 3 science labs, 3 language (other than English).

Financial Aid

Students should submit: FAFSA; CSS PROFILE; State aid form. The Princeton Review suggests that all financial aid forms be submitted as soon as possible. *Need-based scholarships/grants offered:* Federal Pell; Federal SEOG; State scholarships/grants; College/university scholarship or grant aid from institutional funds. *Loan aid offered:* Federal Direct Subsidized Loans; Federal Direct Unsubsidized Loans; Direct PLUS loans. Admitted students will be notified of awards on a rolling basis beginning 3/20. Federal Work-Study Program available. Institutional employment available.

The Inside Word

Perhaps because it's a relatively newer school, Merced isn't quite as competitive as some of the other UC schools—more than 90 percent of applicants get in. That said, the school's emphasis on research and sustainability may create a more self-selecting group, so make sure you make the most out of your application to demonstrate Bobcat pride for peers and the world. It also helps your chances if you're coming from in-state—your GPA doesn't need to be quite as high as a 3.6 in that case, and your tuition will be substantially less as well.

THE SCHOOL SAYS

From the Admissions Office

"UC Merced has earned widespread acclaim for building social mobility among first-generation and historically underrepresented groups, while advancing a research agenda that is creating new knowledge in sustainability, engineering, the sciences, humanities and more. The campus location provides a unique opportunity for research and stewardship crucial to the Central Valley and the state of California. The youngest research facility ever to earn Carnegie R2 research classification, UC Merced has R1 squarely within its sights.

"Sustainability is in UC Merced's DNA. It's the only U.S. campus with every building LEED-certified and has received a platinum rating—the highest rating possible—by the Association for the Advancement of Sustainability in Higher Education and the first public research university in the country to achieve carbon neutrality—two years ahead of its goal. Proximity to Yosemite National Park enables important studies in climate change, water and biological diversity at longtime field stations, while also educating the park leaders of the future.

"UC Merced is experiencing growth at a breakneck pace on multiple fronts. The campus recently doubled in size with a first-of-its-kind $1.2 billion public-private partnership (P3) project that features state-of-the-art facilities for students and faculty. Plans for new majors and emphases are being fast-tracked and the university's nascent medical education program—a partnership with UCSF and UCSF Fresno aimed at training local physicians committed to serving in the region—had its first cohort of students enroll in Fall '23. UC Merced Athletics is also on the precipice of transitioning to NCAA Division II."

SELECTIVITY

# of total applicants	47,985
% of total applicants accepted	97
% of total acceptees attending	4

First-Year Profile

Testing policy	Test Free
Average HS GPA	3.6
% submitting high school GPA	100

Important Dates

Regular	
Apply by	11/30
Notified by	Rolling, 3/1
Nonfall registration?	Yes

FINANCIAL FACTS

Annual in-state tuition (First-year)	$13,368 ($14,202)
Annual out-of-state tuition (First-year)	$49,280 ($53,472)
Food and housing	$23,126
Required fees (First-year)	$2,647 ($2,723)
Books and supplies	$1,073
Average need-based scholarship (First-year)	$29,363 ($32,435)
% students with need rec. need-based scholarship or grant aid (First-year)	100 (99)
% students with need rec. non-need-based scholarship or grant aid (First-year)	2 (2)
% students with need rec. need-based self-help aid (First-year)	42 (48)
% students rec. any financial aid (First-year)	78 (78)
% UG borrow to pay for school	45
Average cumulative indebtedness	$14,978
% of students with need fully met (First-year)	20 (24)
Average % of student need met (First-year)	83 (87)

UNIVERSITY OF CALIFORNIA—RIVERSIDE

900 University Ave., Riverside, CA 92521 • Admissions: 951-827-3411

Survey Snapshot
Recreation facilities are great
Diverse student types interact on campus
Campus newspaper is popular

RATINGS

Quality of Life	84
Fire Safety	86
Green	96
Academic	76
Profs Interesting	86
Profs Accessible	89
Admissions	76
Financial Aid	88

CAMPUS LIFE

Type of school	Public
Environment	City

Students

Degree-seeking undergrad enrollment	24,029
% male/female/not reported	47/50/3
% from out of state	1
% First-year from public high school	90
% First-year live on campus	69
% Ugrads live on campus	38
# of fraternities (% join)	6 (2)
# of sororities (% join)	17 (4)
% Asian	34
% Black or African American	4
% Hispanic	42
% Native American	<1
% Pacific Islander	<1
% Race and/or ethnicity unknown	1
% Two or more races	5
% White	10
% International	3
# of countries represented	91

CAMPUS MENTAL HEALTH SERVICES

Offers mental health/wellness program	Yes
Mental health training available to students	No
Employs Chief Wellness Officer	NR
Peer-to-peer mental health offerings	NR
Counseling center has guidelines or accreditation	No
Mental health/well-being courses	NR

ACADEMICS

% students returning for sophomore year	88
% students graduating within 4 years	64
% students graduating within 6 years	76
Calendar	Quarter
Student/faculty ratio	24:1
Most common class size 20–29.	(29%)
Most common lab/discussion size 20–29.	(57%)

Most Popular Majors
Psychology; Business Administration and Management; Biology/Biological Sciences

STUDENTS SAY "..."

Academics

Undergraduates at the University of California—Riverside have the opportunity to get "a great education while also having fun." The university goes to great lengths to ensure that "everyone feels welcome and wanted on campus" and that's palpable to the students. Undergrads here also greatly benefit from all the research being conducted at Riverside. As one giddy student explains, "There are so many different projects happening in [a variety of] fields" and the opportunities to participate are quite "generous." Additionally, UCR undergrads appreciate that "there are so many programs to help student[s] stay on track academically and even more to help student[s] in academic recovery." Students have an abundance of courses and majors from which to choose; highlights include the "very prestigious entomology and agriculture departments." In general, students report that professors are "very helpful and friendly." They tend to be "passionate and engaged" as well as "knowledgeable." And they make it abundantly clear that "they love their field, their job, and their students." As one amazed student reveals, "I have not yet met a professor that wasn't happy to rearrange their plans, so they could help a student in need."

Campus Life

Boredom is virtually non-existent at UC Riverside. After all, "there is always something to do on campus throughout the day." For example, "Every week there is a mini-concert in the middle of campus to showcase a local group (small band or DJ)." There are also a number of "career workshops, movie screenings, [and] cultural events" of which to take advantage. Additionally, students have the opportunity to participate in "over 400 clubs on campus, many of which organize their own activities and will often go on excursions or trips." A number of undergrads also report that the "party scene is decent," though it's often relegated to the weekend. Outdoor enthusiasts love that UCR is adjacent to the Box Spring Mountains. Hence, there are "a plethora of trails for hiking." Plenty of students can also be found hanging at the Hub which has "a game room where you can play pool, board games or watch TV." Even more enticing, "the recreation center has a hot tub and a recreational pool with vortex current as well as lap pool. It's also possible to play volleyball, basketball, badminton, racquetball, and other games [as well as use] the rock-climbing wall." But the best aspect of the rec center? It "provides free massages twice a week."

Student Body

Individuals greatly interested in UC Riverside will be delighted to learn that the school maintains a "very diverse" student body. In turn, this allows all undergrads to truly "feel welcome." Of course, the fact that most students here are "extremely friendly and supportive" also helps. One proud undergrad agrees sharing, "It is easy to approach most people and start a conversation." Beyond their general openness, Riverside students also describe their classmates as "liberal and politically-engaged." Additionally, the vast majority seem to have "an appetite to learn and discover." Perhaps more importantly, undergrads readily assert that their fellow students "are committed to the success of the [Riverside] community as a whole." Indeed, they empathize "with those who are struggling and they seek to be involved both on and off campus." And while they are certainly "passionate about what they believe in," they're also "respectful of...[the] opinions [of others]." Overall, as this grateful undergrad explains, "My peers at the University of California, Riverside make my college experience a great one. They make college feel safe, fun, and exciting." And this fellow student wholeheartedly agrees exclaiming, "College life is stressful but it is easier with the right people surrounding you. And that's what I have here at UCR."

University of California—Riverside

Financial Aid: 951-827-3878 • E-Mail: admissions@ucr.edu • Website: www.ucr.edu

THE PRINCETON REVIEW SAYS

Admissions

The school reports that its standardized testing policy for use in admission for Fall 2026 is Test Free. The Princeton Review suggests that interested applicants consult with the school for the most up-to-date standardized testing policies. *Very important factors considered include:* academic GPA, application essay. *Important factors considered include:* rigor of secondary school record. *Other factors considered include:* talent/ability, first generation, state residency. High school diploma is required and GED is accepted. *Academic units required:* 4 English, 3 math, 2 science, 2 science labs, 2 language (other than English), 2 history, 1 academic elective, 1 visual/performing arts. *Academic units recommended:* 4 English, 4 math, 3 science, 3 science labs, 3 language (other than English), 2 history, 1 academic elective, 1 visual/performing arts.

Financial Aid

Students should submit: FAFSA; State aid form. Priority filing deadline is 3/2. The Princeton Review suggests that all financial aid forms be submitted as soon as possible. *Need-based scholarships/grants offered:* Federal Pell; Federal SEOG; State scholarships/grants; Private scholarships; College/university scholarship or grant aid from institutional funds; United Negro College Fund. *Loan aid offered:* Federal Direct Subsidized Loans; Federal Direct Unsubsidized Loans; Direct PLUS loans; State Loans; College/university loans from institutional funds. Admitted students will be notified of awards on a rolling basis beginning 3/1. Federal Work-Study Program available. Institutional employment available.

The Inside Word

As one of the top-ranking universities within the California system, the admissions process at UC Riverside is competitive. To determine who earns a coveted acceptance letter, the school closely evaluates each student's GPA. Admissions officers are also on the lookout for students who have earned a C or higher in AP/IB courses. Lastly, extra consideration is given to both first-generation and low-income applicants.

THE SCHOOL SAYS

From the Admissions Office

"The University of California Riverside offers the quality, rigor, and facilities of a world class research institution, while assuring its undergraduates personal attention and a welcoming campus community. Academic programs, teaching, advising and student services all reflect the supportive attitudes that characterize the campus. Exceptional opportunities include undergraduate research, University Honors, and the Thomas Haider Program (up to 24 spots to the UCR School of Medicine are guaranteed to UCR undergraduates each year). UCR's largest undergraduate program is biology, and it offers the only Bachelor of Arts in Creative Writing in the UC system.

"Students are actively involved in campus life, thanks to a variety of athletic and cultural events, ethnic and gender programs, community service opportunities, and more than 450 student organizations."

SELECTIVITY

# of total applicants	61,184
% of total applicants accepted	86
% of total acceptees attending	13
# of in-state applicants	51,828
% of in-state applicants accepted	86
# of out-of-state-applicants	3,137
% of applicants accepted from out of state	90
# of international applicants	6,219
% of international applicants accepted	83
# offered a place on the wait list	3,783
# admitted from wait list	0

First-Year Profile

Testing policy	Test Free
Average HS GPA	3.8
% submitting high school GPA	100

Important Dates

Regular	
Apply by	12/2
Notified by	3/31
Nonfall registration?	No

FINANCIAL FACTS

Annual in-state tuition	$15,588
Annual out-of-state tuition	$54,858
Food and housing	$21,075
Required fees	$1,170
Books and supplies	$1,750
Average need-based scholarship (First-year)	$26,593 ($28,704)
% students with need rec. need-based scholarship or grant aid (First-year)	97 (98)
% students with need rec. non-need-based scholarship or grant aid (First-year)	4 (4)
% students with need rec. need-based self-help aid (First-year)	63 (74)
% students rec. any financial aid (First-year)	81 (88)
% UG borrow to pay for school	43
Average cumulative indebtedness	$18,621
% of students with need fully met (First-year)	13 (15)
Average % of student need met (First-year)	83 (87)

UNIVERSITY OF CALIFORNIA—SAN DIEGO

9500 Gilman Drive, La Jolla, CA 92093 • Admissions: 858-534-4831

Survey Snapshot
Students are happy
Great library
Recreation facilities are great

RATINGS	
Quality of Life	**75**
Fire Safety	**84**
Green	**97**
Academic	**78**
Profs Interesting	**81**
Profs Accessible	**86**
Admissions	**93**
Financial Aid	**87**

CAMPUS LIFE

Type of school	Public
Environment	Metropolis

Students

Degree-seeking undergrad enrollment	35,442
% male/female/not reported	44/53/2
% from out of state	9
% First-year live on campus	86
% Ugrads live on campus	54
# of fraternities (% join)	22 (8)
# of sororities (% join)	24 (7)
% Asian	35
% Black or African American	2
% Hispanic	27
% Native American	<1
% Pacific Islander	<1
% Race and/or ethnicity unknown	2
% Two or more races	6
% White	16
% International	12
# of countries represented	127

CAMPUS MENTAL HEALTH SERVICES

Offers mental health/wellness program	Yes
Mental health training available to students	Yes
Employs Chief Wellness Officer	Yes
Peer-to-peer mental health offerings	Yes
Counseling center has guidelines or accreditation	Yes
Mental health/well-being courses	Yes, for-credit

ACADEMICS

% students returning for sophomore year	95
% students graduating within 4 years	78
% students graduating within 6 years	86
Calendar	Quarter
Student/faculty ratio	19:1
Most common class size 10–19.	(22%)

Applicants Often Prefer
Stanford University, University of California—Berkeley, University of California—Los Angeles

Applicants Sometimes Prefer
University of California—Irvine, University of California—Santa Barbara, University of Southern California

STUDENTS SAY "..."

Academics

University of California—San Diego is widely recognized as "one of the top science universities in the United States." In addition to its strong STEM programs, UC San Diego offers students more than 100 degrees and programs across various disciplines. Many students choose UC San Diego for its "access to cutting-edge technology and theories" and the "great opportunities for undergraduates to do research." Professors here "are incredibly knowledgeable about their material, and many of them are actively doing research in their field." Students find the faculty "very helpful and willing to take extra time to help students understand material," and some professors will "mentor students if you seek them out." The university is organized into eight colleges, which help students navigate the complexities of a large institution, allowing them to feel less "like a small fish in a huge ocean." This system fosters a sense of belonging and ensures individual attention while still giving students all of the benefits of a large institution: "a lot of resources," along with supportive organizations and faculty "that will help you achieve what you want." If UC San Diego sounds like an ideal school, its students agree that "this university will undoubtedly set the new standard of what it means to be an elite public university in the years to come."

Campus Life

UC San Diego students have plenty of options for staying busy, engaged, and entertained. "There is always an event going on and so many clubs to be involved in." Students also love UC San Diego's "unbeatable location," which is just 10 minutes from the beach. It's easy to enjoy "all the nature around the campus by hiking, biking, [or] camping," and students can even take surf lessons "for a modest fee." On campus, students are provided with "tons of resources and ways to get involved," and many "play sports or participate in clubs." The campus boasts a state-of-the-art athletic training center, 10 different athletic venues, gardens where students can grow their own vegetables and herbs, and many other attractions. Each spring, the Sun God Festival, a music and arts celebration put on by students, is "always a popular event." In addition to on-campus activities and events, students appreciate the close proximity to downtown, noting that it's "super easy to get to San Diego proper for a fun night out." For many students, the academic rigor of the school keeps social activities in check. "Lots of people enjoy...small parties, but the party scene isn't too big here." One student happily observes: "From the Greek life to the intramural sports to the variety of clubs, there is literally a place for everyone."

Student Body

At UC San Diego, the student body "has such a diverse range of personalities" that it's easy for newcomers to find their niche. While many people might picture a typical UC San Diego student as someone who "studies a lot," there are "plenty of students who balance academics with other things, like sports or clubs." However, "doing well academically at UC San Diego is an extreme priority, even to students who are not good students," and "most of the students are geared toward extended education or professional school." Regardless of your career trajectory, almost anyone "can fit in here because it's such a big school, and there are so many different organizations and places where you can find people that enjoy the same things as you."

UNIVERSITY OF CALIFORNIA—SAN DIEGO

Financial Aid: 858-534-3800 • E-Mail: admissionsinfo@ucsd.edu • Website: www.ucsd.edu

THE PRINCETON REVIEW SAYS

Admissions

The school reports that its standardized testing policy for use in admission for Fall 2026 is Test Free. The Princeton Review suggests that interested applicants consult with the school for the most up-to-date standardized testing policies. *Very important factors considered include:* rigor of secondary school record, academic GPA, application essay. *Important factors considered include:* extracurricular activities, talent/ability, character/personal qualities, state residency, volunteer work. *Other factors considered include:* class rank, first generation, geographical residence, work experience. High school diploma is required and GED is accepted. *Academic units required:* 4 English, 3 math, 2 science, 2 science labs, 2 language (other than English), 2 history, 1 academic elective, 1 visual/performing arts. *Academic units recommended:* 4 English, 4 math, 3 science, 3 science labs, 3 language (other than English), 2 history, 1 academic elective, 1 visual/performing arts.

Financial Aid

Students should submit: FAFSA; State aid form. Priority filing deadline is 3/2. The Princeton Review suggests that all financial aid forms be submitted as soon as possible. *Need-based scholarships/grants offered:* Federal Pell; Federal SEOG; State scholarships/grants; Private scholarships; College/university scholarship or grant aid from institutional funds. *Loan aid offered:* Federal Direct Subsidized Loans; Federal Direct Unsubsidized Loans; Direct PLUS loans; State Loans; College/university loans from institutional funds. Admitted students will be notified of awards on a rolling basis beginning 8/2. Federal Work-Study Program available. Institutional employment available.

The Inside Word

UC San Diego is one of the gems of the UC system, and admission is very competitive. Applications are reviewed thoroughly by at least two readers. Applicants will need excellent grades in the rigorous college preparatory courses offered at their institution, and demonstrate personal qualities like leadership, tenacity, compassion, and independence.

THE SCHOOL SAYS

From the Admissions Office

"UC San Diego is recognized for the exceptional quality of its academic programs in the arts, humanities, social sciences, biological and physical sciences, and engineering. With annual research funding topping $1.64 billion, UC San Diego is the top undergraduate campus in the University of California system for research spending and sixth in the nation for research and development expenditures. UC San Diego also offers a unique college system, which assigns undergraduates to one of the university's colleges, each with its own residential neighborhood, general education curriculum, support services, and distinctive traditions. This system allows students to thrive in a smaller neighborhood setting and enjoy a more personalized experience in utilizing college resources.

"UC San Diego's interdisciplinary approach to learning allows students to push the boundaries of their chosen fields of study. Students in any major can explore artistic ventures at the Craft Center or through the on-campus theater district, develop groundbreaking projects and inventions in the EnVision Arts and Engineering Maker Studio, or even gain hands-on experience as student researchers in their first year on campus. The campus also helps to connect students to real-world job and internship opportunities in the greater San Diego area, with trolley stops right on campus making such opportunities more accessible than ever."

SELECTIVITY

# of total applicants	136,750
% of total applicants accepted	29
% of total acceptees attending	20
# of in-state applicants	87,584
% of in-state applicants accepted	25
# of out-of-state-applicants	24,912
% of applicants accepted from out of state	40
# of international applicants	24,254
% of international applicants accepted	31
# offered a place on the wait list	36,709
# admitted from wait list	5,284

First-Year Profile

Testing policy	Test Free
Average HS GPA	3.9
% submitting high school GPA	94
% graduated top 10% of class	100
% graduated top 25% of class	100
% graduated top 50% of class	100
% submitting high school rank	96

Important Dates

Regular	
Apply by	11/30
Notified by	Rolling, 3/15
Nonfall registration?	No

FINANCIAL FACTS

Annual in-state tuition	$14,934
Annual out-of-state tuition	$52,536
Food and housing	$20,445
Required fees (First-year)	$5,793 ($5,958)
Books and supplies	$1,203
Average need-based scholarship (First-year)	$27,393 ($27,749)
% students with need rec. need-based scholarship or grant aid (First-year)	97 (96)
% students with need rec. non-need-based scholarship or grant aid (First-year)	4 (6)
% students with need rec. need-based self-help aid (First-year)	58 (59)
% students rec. any financial aid (First-year)	78 (67)
% UG borrow to pay for school	31
Average cumulative indebtedness	$18,825
% of students with need fully met (First-year)	11 (14)
Average % of student need met (First-year)	81 (82)

UNIVERSITY OF CALIFORNIA—SANTA BARBARA

552 University Road, Santa Barbara, CA 93106 • Admissions: 805-893-2881

Survey Snapshot
Lab facilities are great
Students are friendly
Recreation facilities are great

RATINGS

Quality of Life	85
Fire Safety	93
Green	99
Academic	82
Profs Interesting	89
Profs Accessible	93
Admissions	85
Financial Aid	80

CAMPUS LIFE

Type of school	Public
Environment	City

Students

Degree-seeking undergrad enrollment	23,091
% male/female/not reported	42/57/1
% from out of state	9
% First-year from public high school	79
% First-year live on campus	94
% Ugrads live on campus	37
# of fraternities (% join)	41 (NR)
# of sororities (% join)	41 (NR)
% Asian	19
% Black or African American	2
% Hispanic	29
% Native American	<1
% Pacific Islander	<1
% Race and/or ethnicity unknown	3
% Two or more races	8
% White	31
% International	9
# of countries represented	82

CAMPUS MENTAL HEALTH SERVICES

Offers mental health/wellness program	Yes
Mental health training available to students	No
Employs Chief Wellness Officer	NR
Peer-to-peer mental health offerings	NR
Counseling center has guidelines or accreditation	No
Mental health/well-being courses	NR

ACADEMICS

% students returning for sophomore year	93
% students graduating within 4 years	71
% students graduating within 6 years	84
Calendar	Quarter
Student/faculty ratio	18:1
Most common class size 1–9.	(35%)
Most common lab/discussion size 20–29.	(57%)

Most Popular Majors
Biology/Biological Sciences; Psychology; Economics

Applicants Often Prefer
University of California—Berkeley, University of California—Los Angeles

Applicants Sometimes Prefer
University of California—Davis, University of California—Irvine

Applicants Rarely Prefer
California Polytechnic State University—San Luis Obispo, University of California—Santa Cruz

STUDENTS SAY "..."

Academics

University of California—Santa Barbara is a great choice for students who are serious about their studies but also want a fun and fulfilling college experience. As one student notes, "UCSB is the perfect blend of academics and social life. I get to study at a renowned research university and work closely with professors while living on the beach and making lifelong friendships." Indeed, while the school's "incredible location" and "safe and beautiful campus" are major attractions, so is the wide variety of academic programs offered—everything from actuarial science to zoology, according to the university. UCSB is known for being "strong in the sciences," especially its "highly ranked" mechanical and chemical engineering programs. If you're a self-directed learner, you may be interested in UCSB's highly selective College of Creative Studies, which one student says "allows me to pursue my academic interests with maximum freedom." While students appreciate the "laid-back" atmosphere at UCSB, they are quick to mention that the coursework can be "academically challenging." Fortunately, classes are taught by "outstanding professors" who, as one student declares, "I would challenge any Ivy school to match." While "many of [the] professors are Nobel Prize winners or well-known in their field," students say they are approachable and always available to help, rating "accessibility and knowledge of the professors" as one of the university's main strengths.

Campus Life

At USCB, there's a vibrant community with around 500 student organizations that make it easy for students to dive into enjoyable activities once they've put down their books. One undergrad estimates that "85 percent of our student body is in at least one extracurricular activity." Another student notes, "Whether it be with sports, or in a community service or environmental club, rock climbing, politics, the list goes on. Students fit in by finding a good group of friends in the dorms and by getting involved in extracurricular activities." Beyond school activities, one student points out that "People think of UCSB exclusively as a party school, but it's what you make of it." Another student adds, "A lot of people party at UCSB...But don't be fooled. I've met some of the smartest, most hard-working people [here]." The "down to earth" atmosphere on campus sets UCBS apart from many other schools. As one student shares, "Every other college on my list seemed locked in an ivory tower. UCSB was the exception with both the warm, sun-kissed charm of a beach town and excellent academics."

Student Body

UCSB students are often described as "laid-back but hard-working," with one student adding, "I've met the smartest people of my life here." There is not just one type of student here. People are "extremely diverse, personality-wise" and come from "all sorts of socioeconomic backgrounds." This variety helps everyone find their own group and "feel at home here." As one student puts it, "Everyone finds their niche here." Overall, UCSB undergrads are "intelligent, sociable, [and] engaging," and "there is a great sense of community among the students." At a school where students are "very motivated and driven to succeed academically," the vibe stays upbeat, with one student cheekily adding that "the sunny weather keeps people happy."

UNIVERSITY OF CALIFORNIA—SANTA BARBARA

Financial Aid: 805-893-2432 • E-Mail: admissions@sa.ucsb.edu • Website: www.ucsb.edu

THE PRINCETON REVIEW SAYS

Admissions

The school reports that its standardized testing policy for use in admission for Fall 2026 is Test Free. The Princeton Review suggests that interested applicants consult with the school for the most up-to-date standardized testing policies. *Very important factors considered include:* academic GPA, application essay. *Important factors considered include:* rigor of secondary school record. *Other factors considered include:* extracurricular activities, talent/ability, character/personal qualities, first generation, geographical residence, state residency, volunteer work, work experience. High school diploma is required and GED is accepted. *Academic units required:* 4 English, 3 math, 2 science, 2 science labs, 2 language (other than English), 2 history, 1 academic elective, 1 visual/performing arts. *Academic units recommended:* 4 English, 4 math, 3 science, 3 science labs, 3 language (other than English), 2 history, 1 academic elective, 1 visual/performing arts.

Financial Aid

The Princeton Review suggests that all financial aid forms be submitted as soon as possible. Federal Work-Study Program available. Institutional employment available.

The Inside Word

UCSB uses a "minimum eligibility" index as a formula to calculate a student's viability for admission; other standards, including high school course load, are synthesized with a 3.0 minimum GPA for California students and a 3.4 for out-of-state applicants. Weakness in one area may be balanced out by strength in another, but don't be fooled by the fact that it's a state school: UCSB is competitive.

THE SCHOOL SAYS

From the Admissions Office

"The University of California, Santa Barbara, is a leading research institution that also provides a comprehensive liberal arts learning experience. Teaching and research go hand-in-hand at UC Santa Barbara, and a majority of students are involved in the research process during their undergraduate studies. UCSB's academic community of faculty, students, and staff is characterized by a collaborative, dynamic atmosphere. Students at UCSB can choose from 90 majors, 40 minors, and honors programs for top students across three undergraduate colleges. Located on the edge of the Pacific Ocean, students have access to a stunning living-learning environment with excellent weather and outdoor recreation. The local Santa Barbara community enhances the on-campus experience by offering cultural outlets and access to a variety of job and internship opportunities in local schools, law offices, hospitals and clinics, and more.

"All applicants must complete the University of California application. UCSB uses eligibility requirements and selection criteria to admit its next class of first-time freshmen and junior-level transfers each year. UCSB does not use SAT/ACT scores in the admission decision or scholarship selection process."

SELECTIVITY

# of total applicants	110,187
% of total applicants accepted	38
% of total acceptees attending	12
# of in-state applicants	74,486
% of in-state applicants accepted	32
# of out-of-state-applicants	17,067
% of applicants accepted from out of state	55
# of international applicants	18,634
% of international applicants accepted	48
# offered a place on the wait list	25,713
# admitted from wait list	9,603

First-Year Profile

Testing policy	Test Free
Average HS GPA	4.3
% submitting high school GPA	97

Important Dates

Regular	
Apply by	11/30
Notified by	3/31
Nonfall registration?	Yes

FINANCIAL FACTS

Annual in-state tuition	\$15,588
Annual out-of-state tuition	\$54,858
Food and housing	\$23,646
Required fees	\$2,055
Books and supplies	\$1,479
% students rec. any financial aid (First-year)	59 (61)

UNIVERSITY OF CALIFORNIA—SANTA CRUZ

1156 High Street, Santa Cruz, CA 95064 • Admissions: 831-459-4008

Survey Snapshot
Students are happy
Students are friendly
Students aren't religious

RATINGS

Quality of Life	76
Fire Safety	62
Green	99
Academic	73
Profs Interesting	83
Profs Accessible	85
Admissions	78
Financial Aid	86

CAMPUS LIFE

Type of school	Public
Environment	City

Students

Degree-seeking undergrad enrollment	18,194
% male/female/not reported	47/53/0
% from out of state	4
% First-year from public high school	89
% First-year live on campus	98
% Ugrads live on campus	50
# of fraternities (% join)	NR (3)
# of sororities (% join)	NR (6)
% Asian	24
% Black or African American	2
% Hispanic	29
% Native American	<1
% Pacific Islander	<1
% Race and/or ethnicity unknown	2
% Two or more races	9
% White	30
% International	3
# of countries represented	47

CAMPUS MENTAL HEALTH SERVICES

Offers mental health/wellness program	Yes
Mental health training available to students	No
Employs Chief Wellness Officer	NR
Peer-to-peer mental health offerings	NR
Counseling center has guidelines or accreditation	No
Mental health/well-being courses	NR

ACADEMICS

% students returning for sophomore year	90
% students graduating within 4 years	60
% students graduating within 6 years	74
Calendar	Quarter
Student/faculty ratio	22:1
Most common class size 20–29.	(34%)
Most common lab/discussion size 20–29.	(41%)

STUDENTS SAY "..."

Academics

Nestled among California's coastal redwoods, UC Santa Cruz's campus "is one of the most unique, beautiful ecosystems I've ever seen," beams an environmental science major, noting that it's "a great resource for internship and job opportunities." It's also a boon for professors, who can "take time to teach students the importance of being outside and how it can impact their learning." It's not unusual for courses to include "taking class hikes and nature journaling trips," while also offering "extensive labs" and "rich discussions." Whether outdoors or in, UCSC presents "guest lectures and activities that allow for further engagement in many different areas of learning." As for academic support, "tutoring is widely available on campus no matter the class, and there are online tutoring options available that make it very accessible to those that may live off-campus or with transportation issues."

For all the support systems, as well as a number of professors who offer a much-appreciated series of "low stakes tests and essays instead of a big final and midterm," students emphasize that "UCSC is a very academically competitive school," particularly in the prized technical fields. Students who actively pursue and value STEM research enjoy "internships that I can do hands-on work with and earn credit for." Interdisciplinary teaching is also enjoyed, like the "amazing" resources of the Coastal Science Campus and the agroecology department's farm.

Campus Life

My college experience in the redwoods is magical, marvels one student. "The school is gorgeous and the coastline that surrounds us is second to none." This "beautiful forest setting," ideally located "between the mountains and the beach" means that many students "are active in outdoor hobbies including surfing, rock climbing, backpacking, and mountain biking." Students are equally interested in preserving the environment they so enjoy: "Everyone here cares about nature and the environment," and the UCSC Climate Coalition is "amazing." Others appreciate culturally based organizations such as Hillel and the Chinese Student Association. "It can be difficult to meet people without joining a club or group simply due to the nature of being a larger school."

Like many in California, UCSC has been affected by a housing shortage, and students wish for "more affordable and guaranteed student housing." Nevertheless, the school grounds provide "the perfect getaway when things get stressful" as well as the setting for plenty of college fun. "I enjoy the forest raves as well as the arts and crafts activities," says one student. "The Adventure Rec provides amazing programs for students to gain outdoor skills and experiences." As for off-campus experiences, students "love to go downtown and hang around, go to the beach at Sunny Cove or the boardwalk. They love to just bask in the California sun."

Student Body

The University of California—Santa Cruz isn't defined by any one thing, except for perhaps the way it's "extremely open and welcoming" such that there's the freedom to be anything." (Okay, and maybe an environment that is "perfect for outdoorsy folk.") You can see this uniqueness in the way students "express themselves through clothes, gender, hairstyle, [and] speech. There is a very laid-back and accepting mentality that all of us share." And yet, for all the different communities on campus, there's a sense that those at UCSC "help each other and stand with each other in times of need." That extends to the body's activism "in social justice and climate change cause" and "student clubs and organizations that promote social justice as well as inclusivity." As one student jokingly puts it, UCSC feels like "leftist Twitter, but real," a group of "very carefree, very creative, and very caring people with an anti-establishment lean and strong sustainability goals."

UNIVERSITY OF CALIFORNIA—SANTA CRUZ

E-Mail: admissions@ucsc.edu • Website: www.ucsc.edu

THE PRINCETON REVIEW SAYS

Admissions

The school reports that its standardized testing policy for use in admission for Fall 2026 is Test Free. The Princeton Review suggests that interested applicants consult with the school for the most up-to-date standardized testing policies. *Very important factors considered include:* rigor of secondary school record, academic GPA, application essay, state residency. *Important factors considered include:* extracurricular activities, talent/ability, character/personal qualities, first generation, geographical residence. *Other factors considered include:* volunteer work, work experience. High school diploma is required and GED is accepted. *Academic units required:* 4 English, 3 math, 2 science, 2 science labs, 2 language (other than English), 1 social studies, 1 history, 1 academic elective, 1 visual/performing arts. *Academic units recommended:* 4 English, 4 math, 3 science, 3 science labs, 3 language (other than English), 1 social studies, 1 history, 1 academic elective, 1 visual/performing arts.

Financial Aid

Students should submit: FAFSA; State aid form. The Princeton Review suggests that all financial aid forms be submitted as soon as possible. *Need-based scholarships/grants offered:* Federal Pell; Federal SEOG; State scholarships/grants; Private scholarships; College/university scholarship or grant aid from institutional funds. *Loan aid offered:* Federal Direct Subsidized Loans; Federal Direct Unsubsidized Loans; Direct PLUS loans. Admitted students will be notified of awards on a rolling basis beginning 4/1. Federal Work-Study Program available. Institutional employment available.

The Inside Word

UC Santa Cruz takes a comprehensive approach to admissions, evaluating your academic and personal achievements in the context of the opportunities available to you, as well as your potential to contribute to the intellectual and cultural life of the campus. The applicant pool is consistently strong, so a competitive application matters. At a minimum, applicants should have a GPA of 3.0 or higher (3.4 or higher for out-of-state students).

THE SCHOOL SAYS

From the Admissions Office

"UC—Santa Cruz students, faculty, and researchers are working together to make a world of difference. Within our extraordinary educational community, students participate in the creation of new knowledge, new technologies, and new forms of expressing and understanding cultures. From helping teachers improve their skills to building more efficient solar cells and working to save endangered sea turtles, our focus is on improving our planet and the lives of all its inhabitants. The academic programs at UCSC are challenging and rigorous, and many of them are in newer fields that focus on interdisciplinary thinking. At UCSC, undergraduates conduct and publish research, working closely with faculty on leading-edge projects. Taking advantage of the campus' proximity to centers of industry and innovation such as the Monterey Bay National Marine Sanctuary and Silicon Valley, many students at UC—Santa Cruz take part in fieldwork and internships that complement their studies and provide practical experience in their fields."

SELECTIVITY

# of total applicants	66,374
% of total applicants accepted	73
% of total acceptees attending	10
# of in-state applicants	52,573
% of in-state applicants accepted	71
# of out-of-state-applicants	7,248
% of applicants accepted from out of state	84
# of international applicants	6,554
% of international applicants accepted	72
# offered a place on the wait list	9,881
# admitted from wait list	2,648

First-Year Profile

Testing policy	Test Free
Average HS GPA	3.9
% submitting high school GPA	99

Important Dates

Regular	
Apply by	12/1
Notified by	3/31

FINANCIAL FACTS*

Annual in-state tuition (First-year)	$12,800 ($13,602)
Annual out-of-state tuition (First-year)	$46,650 ($51,204)
Food and housing	$20,929
Required fees (First-year)	$2,826 ($2,901)
Books and supplies	$1,256
Average need-based scholarship (First-year)	$20,744 ($19,899)
% students with need rec. need-based scholarship or grant aid (First-year)	94 (94)
% students with need rec. non-need-based scholarship or grant aid (First-year)	2 (2)
% students with need rec. need-based self-help aid (First-year)	50 (51)
% UG borrow to pay for school	53
Average cumulative indebtedness	$21,189
% of students with need fully met (First-year)	16 (12)
Average % of student need met (First-year)	78 (75)

* Most recently reported data at time of printing. Scan the QR code to find the latest updates.

University of Central Florida

4000 Central Florida Blvd., Orlando, FL 32816 • Admissions: 407-823-3000

Survey Snapshot
Everyone loves the Knights
Active student government
Students are happy

RATINGS

Quality of Life	85
Fire Safety	96
Green	95
Academic	76
Profs Interesting	82
Profs Accessible	86
Admissions	91
Financial Aid	83

CAMPUS LIFE

Type of school	Public
Environment	City

Students

Degree-seeking undergrad enrollment	59,608
% male/female/not reported	47/53/0
% from out of state	7
% First-year live on campus	69
% Ugrads live on campus	12
# of fraternities (% join)	23 (4)
# of sororities (% join)	23 (6)
% Asian	8
% Black or African American	9
% Hispanic	33
% Native American	<1
% Pacific Islander	<1
% Race and/or ethnicity unknown	1
% Two or more races	5
% White	41
% International	3
# of countries represented	135

CAMPUS MENTAL HEALTH SERVICES

Offers mental health/wellness program	NR
Mental health training available to students	NR
Employs Chief Wellness Officer	NR
Peer-to-peer mental health offerings	NR
Counseling center has guidelines or accreditation	NR
Mental health/well-being courses	NR

ACADEMICS

% students returning for sophomore year	93
% students graduating within 4 years	54
% students graduating within 6 years	78
Calendar	Semester
Student/faculty ratio	26:1
Most common class size 20–29.	(22%)
Most common lab/discussion size 30–39.	(36%)

Most Popular Majors

Aerospace, Aeronautical and Astronautical/Space Engineering; Biomedical Sciences; Finance

STUDENTS SAY "..."

Academics

To match "having one of the largest student bodies in the country," the University of Central Florida features "nearly every class or degree imaginable." Students speak fondly of that size, especially when it comes to registration, where they say "it's easy to get the classes you want." They also appreciate the location, as "there are many opportunities with big companies and corporations for...jobs and internships." Examples in action include the Aerospace Engineering department partnering "with NASA on new space-projects" and courses in 3D design that have led students "to start directly working with Universal Studios." One of the ways in which UCF accommodates so many students is with a mix of in-person and remote learning options. Some obvious favorites, like Wines of the World and a scuba class, require a physical presence for wine tastings and diving, but for most classes, students note "the experience online is just as robust" and the "classes are structured in a way that keeps students engaged." Regardless of how the class is organized, "most professors are interested and dedicated to their craft, and it shows in their teaching." As one student tells us: "If you need help, just ask and someone will jump through hoops to make sure you get what you need to succeed."

Campus Life

If there's any doubt about school spirit for the University of Central Florida's Knights, just look "all around campus at all events...[for] the massive amounts of crowds (students and non-students) that come together." It helps that "athletics tickets are free for students" and "it's very popular to tailgate in Memory Mall before football games." Other popular hangout highlights are the on-campus arcade and the "rock climbing wall in the gym." UCF also features "a huge arboretum with trails; I am able to go for a short hike between my classes." Students are even enthusiastic about the parking garages, one of which is praised for allowing band practices that can be enjoyed across campus. "My favorite memory here is going to a rooftop rock concert, the crowd was amazing, everyone participated and would help anyone that fell in the mosh pit."

With 650 student clubs and a thriving Greek scene, there are plenty of on-campus social events at any given time. Orlando itself also provides "big city energy" and is a great option for those who want to go "exploring new places" or visiting the familiar attractions of nearby Disney World and Universal. Those wanting a less-structured outdoors experience appreciate that "beaches and wildlife habitats" are just a 30-minute drive away.

Student Body

My university is one of the largest in the nation and with that comes...a mix of cultures, personalities, and traditions that allow for everyone at UCF to feel at home. Benefits of this "vast and diverse" student body extend throughout campus life, so you'll hear "many different ideas in the classroom." The only drawback for some is that the school's size "makes it difficult to make connections on a deeper level. You will see thousands of different faces every day." That's why students swear by the importance of clubs in forming relationships: "I was part of a club specifically for Latinos in the medical field, which made me feel included and seen on campus." While Knights hail from "all ethnic, religious, and social backgrounds," one student describes the "students at UCF" as "young and full of energy." Another student agrees: "Mostly everyone I've met since coming to UCF has been warm and welcoming." One student sums up their experience by saying, "I have studied with some of the brightest and best."

University of Central Florida

Financial Aid: 407-823-2827 • E-Mail: admission@ucf.edu • Website: www.ucf.edu

THE PRINCETON REVIEW SAYS

Admissions

The school reports that its standardized testing policy for use in admission for Fall 2026 will require applicants to submit either the SAT, ACT, or CLT. The Princeton Review suggests that interested applicants consult with the school for the most up-to-date standardized testing policies. *Very important factors considered include:* rigor of secondary school record, academic GPA, standardized test scores. *Important factors considered include:* application essay. *Other factors considered include:* class rank, extracurricular activities, talent/ability, character/personal qualities, first generation, geographical residence, state residency, volunteer work, work experience, level of applicant's interest. High school diploma is required and GED is accepted. *Academic units required:* 4 English, 4 math, 2 science, 2 language (other than English), 2 academic electives.

Financial Aid

Students should submit: FAFSA. Priority filing deadline is 12/1. The Princeton Review suggests that all financial aid forms be submitted as soon as possible. *Need-based scholarships/grants offered:* Federal Pell; Federal SEOG; State scholarships/grants; Private scholarships; College/university scholarship or grant aid from institutional funds. *Loan aid offered:* Federal Direct Subsidized Loans; Direct PLUS loans; Federal Direct Unsubsidized Loans. Admitted students will be notified of awards on a rolling basis beginning 3/1. Federal Work-Study Program available. Institutional employment available.

The Inside Word

Like many state schools, earning admission to UCF is primarily a numbers game, meaning that the college largely considers your GPA and standardized test scores (SAT, ACT, or CLT). We should also mention that grades earned in honors, IB, AP, AICE and/or dual enrollment classes will be given greater weight. UCF does not require applicants to submit a personal statement, however, you are likely to give your candidacy a modest boost if you include one.

THE SCHOOL SAYS

From the Admissions Office

"The University of Central Florida offers competitive advantages to its student body. We're committed to teaching, advising and coaching, academic support, and comprehensive care and well-being services for all students. Our undergraduates have access to state-of-the-art wireless buildings, high-tech classrooms, research labs, web-based and hybrid classes, undergraduate research and mentoring programs, and a university-wide honors college.

"Our Career Services professionals help students gain practical experiences at employer partners like NASA and Lockheed Martin, schools, hospitals, high-tech companies, local municipalities, and the entertainment industry. With an international focus on our curricula and research programs, we enroll international students from 135 nations. Our study abroad programs and other study and research opportunities include agreements with ninety-eight institutions and thirty-six countries.

"UCF's 1,420-acre campus provides a safe and serene setting for learning, with natural lakes and woodlands. The bustle of Orlando lies a short distance away: the pro sport teams, the Kennedy Space Center, film studios, Walt Disney World, Universal Orlando, Sea World, and sandy beaches are all nearby.

"UCF is proud to be designated as a Hispanic Serving Institution (HSI) with a 32 percent Hispanic population (54 percent are students of color)."

SELECTIVITY

# of total applicants	59,629
% of total applicants accepted	43
% of total acceptees attending	32
# of in-state applicants	46,049
% of in-state applicants accepted	47
# of out-of-state-applicants	11,215
% of applicants accepted from out of state	28
# of international applicants	2,365
% of international applicants accepted	24
# offered a place on the wait list	2,966
# admitted from wait list	343

First-Year Profile

Testing policy	SAT, ACT, or CLT Required
Range SAT composite	1220–1350
Range SAT EBRW	620–690
Range SAT math	590–680
Range ACT composite	25–30
% submitting SAT scores	74
% submitting ACT scores	26
Average HS GPA	4.2
% submitting high school GPA	100
% graduated top 10% of class	33
% graduated top 25% of class	68
% graduated top 50% of class	94
% submitting high school rank	76

Important Dates

Early action	
Apply by	10/15
Notified by	12/4
Regular	
Apply by	5/1
Notified by	Rolling, 1/15
Nonfall registration?	Yes

FINANCIAL FACTS*

Annual in-state tuition	$6,368
Annual out-of-state tuition	$24,076
Food and housing	$11,532
Books and supplies	$1,200
Average need-based scholarship (First-year)	$9,186 ($9,235)
% students with need rec. need-based scholarship or grant aid (First-year)	81 (74)
% students with need rec. non-need-based scholarship or grant aid (First-year)	54 (88)
% students with need rec. need-based self-help aid (First-year)	32 (22)
% students rec. any financial aid (First-year)	81 (85)
% UG borrow to pay for school	30
Average cumulative indebtedness	$21,003
% of students with need fully met (First-year)	10 (19)
Average % of student need met (First-year)	62 (72)

* Most recently reported data at time of printing. Scan the QR code to find the latest updates.

The University of Chicago

5801 South Ellis Avenue, Chicago, IL 60637 • Admissions: 773-702-8650

Survey Snapshot
Great library
Internships are widely available
Students love Chicago, IL

RATINGS

Quality of Life	**91**
Fire Safety	**97**
Green	**60***
Academic	**96**
Profs Interesting	**93**
Profs Accessible	**93**
Admissions	**99**
Financial Aid	**99**

CAMPUS LIFE

Type of school	Private
Environment	Metropolis

Students

Degree-seeking undergrad enrollment	7,438
% male/female/not reported	56/44/0
% from out of state	85
% First-year live on campus	100
% Ugrads live on campus	60
# of fraternities (% join)	NR
# of sororities (% join)	NR
% Asian	17
% Black or African American	6
% Hispanic	15
% Native American	<1
% Pacific Islander	<1
% Race and/or ethnicity unknown	12
% Two or more races	6
% White	25
% International	19
# of countries represented	130

CAMPUS MENTAL HEALTH SERVICES

Offers mental health/wellness program	Yes
Mental health training available to students	No
Employs Chief Wellness Officer	NR
Peer-to-peer mental health offerings	NR
Counseling center has guidelines or accreditation	No
Mental health/well-being courses	NR

ACADEMICS

% students returning for sophomore year	99
% students graduating within 4 years	85
% students graduating within 6 years	95
Calendar	Quarter
Student/faculty ratio	7:1
Most common class size 1–9.	(47%)
Most common lab/discussion size 10–19.	(51%)

Most Popular Majors
Biology/Biological Sciences; Mathematics; Econometrics and Quantitative Economics

Applicants Also Look At
Columbia University, Harvard College, Northwestern University, Stanford University, University of Pennsylvania, Yale University

STUDENTS SAY "..."

Academics

A "commitment to the liberal arts research institution model shapes the student experience" at The University of Chicago, which values intellectual discourse, thorough inquiry, and free thought in its efforts to be "a true place of learning and scholarship." The curriculum works on a 9-week quarter system, which provides an "ease with which we can double major and take lots of electives." Since all undergraduate classes run through one institution, students say there is "an amazing opportunity to gain exposure to different schools of thought and intellectual frameworks." Additionally, the curriculum is supplemented by "tons of university-organized events, debates, conferences, competitions, etc. that supercharge learning," ranging "from hackathons to startup accelerator programs to book clubs." Academics are "challenging but fulfilling, and the school provides more than adequate resources to navigate," as well as a faculty that are "experts in their respective fields [and] have a ton of freedom in their course material and leading of discussions." Utilizing these assets, professors "consistently challenge students to think critically, question assumptions, and articulate ideas clearly, skills that extend far beyond any single discipline." Small "classes emphasize discussion and debate," and it is "common for ideas from class to carry over into conversations well beyond the classroom." One student explains what sets the university apart: "The dedication by the administration, students, and professors to academics [makes] it one of the best environments to study."

Campus Life

At this academically demanding school, life "involves a lot of studying, doing homework, and going to classes, [and] discussion sections" before free time begins. "Research opportunities are a big extracurricular activity," and "fun often looks like late-night study sessions that turn into long conversations." Even within the "vibrant student organization scene," it's said that "many of the clubs on campus offer invaluable career training and mentorship." That said, it's not all academic: "sports and intramurals are big here," and "people play soccer on the quad, read in hammocks, and play other games" as well. "As the evening approaches, social life does as well," and "a lot of people hang out in each other's dorms or apartments and even in the fraternity houses." Dorms are divided under the House System, each of which has its own culture and traditions and hosts fun activities like "food tours, musicals, and board game nights." Chicago itself "has endless activities to offer," and "people go downtown to clubs, restaurants, museums, and beaches in the spring." As one student sums up, "Life is stressful, but rewarding."

Student Body

With a long and storied history of open discourse and intellectual freedom, the university "attracts the type of person that wants to excel in all fields and gain knowledge." To wit, the campus is "full of students who are dedicated to their passions and love supporting their friends with their own passions." They are "intellectually rigorous, deeply curious, and sometimes even a little quirky," to the point of being "unapologetically invested in niche interests, and that shows up everywhere on campus." One student says, "People are open to lend a helping hand because knowledge is non-rivalrous, [and] your peers know that you being smarter will make the conversation just much more interesting." Another finds that "the common thread around UChicago students is that they take a 'K+1' approach to everything—a second layer of thought." Students say that "everyone is their own person, each with their own style," and "has their own unique stories, passions, and motivations." Most here are "extremely intellectually curious about how the world works and thinks," and "everyone is undeniably very smart." These qualities lead some to call the University of Chicago a "bastion for intellectual curiosity."

THE UNIVERSITY OF CHICAGO

Financial Aid: 773-702-8666 • E-Mail: collegeadmissions@uchicago.edu • Website: uchicago.edu

THE PRINCETON REVIEW SAYS

Admissions

The school reports that its standardized testing policy for use in admission for Fall 2026 is Test Optional. The Princeton Review suggests that interested applicants consult with the school for the most up-to-date standardized testing policies. *Very important factors considered include:* rigor of secondary school record, application essay, recommendation(s), extracurricular activities, talent/ability, character/personal qualities. *Other factors considered include:* class rank, academic GPA, standardized test scores, first generation, alumni/ae relation, geographical residence, state residency, religious affiliation/commitment, volunteer work, work experience. High school diploma is required and GED is accepted.

Financial Aid

Students should submit: FAFSA; Institution's own financial aid form. Priority filing deadline is 2/15. The Princeton Review suggests that all financial aid forms be submitted as soon as possible. *Need-based scholarships/grants offered:* Federal Pell; Federal SEOG; State scholarships/grants; Private scholarships; College/university scholarship or grant aid from institutional funds. *Loan aid offered:* Federal Direct Subsidized Loans; Federal Direct Unsubsidized Loans; Direct PLUS loans. Admitted students will be notified of awards on or about 3/15. Federal Work-Study Program available. Institutional employment available.

The Inside Word

Students at the University of Chicago dwell on deep thoughts and big ideas. In your application, you'll need to demonstrate outstanding grades in tough courses and that you will fit in with a bunch of big thinkers. Although the University of Chicago uses the Common Application, essay topics remain "uncommon" and thought-provoking.

THE SCHOOL SAYS

From the Admissions Office

"Chartered in 1890, the University of Chicago is universally recognized for its devotion to open and rigorous inquiry. The University has over 7,000 undergraduates from 50 states and 100+ countries that comprise a community of exceptional student scholars who chose UChicago for its rigorous liberal arts curriculum, small discussion-style seminars, and 7:1 student-faculty ratio. UChicago also prepares students for challenging careers and competitive graduate schools through professional and recreational opportunities on campus and in Chicago.

"Focused on careful reading, analytical writing, and critical thinking, UChicago's Core Curriculum is the perfect foundation for any major—and for all future endeavors. With over 50 majors and minors, students can double-major, create their own major, or explore interdisciplinary opportunities. Our newest interdisciplinary majors include Urban Environmental Studies, Data Science, and Media Arts & Design. Undergraduates choose electives from the 3,000+ courses offered each year and more than 40% of our students study abroad through 60 faculty-designed and taught programs.

"UChicago sponsors a wealth of undergraduate research opportunities in programs ranging from Economics and Cinema Studies to Astrophysics and Sociology. More than 160 institutes and centers provide sites for groundbreaking research. UChicago's Pritzker School of Molecular Engineering offers a unique opportunity to pursue molecular-level science in both an academic and research context.

"Undergraduates actively participate in 450+ student organizations encompassing athletics, the arts, community service, and Greek life. Varsity teams compete at the NCAA Division III level, and more than 70% of the student body participates in UChicago's extensive intramural and club sports programs."

SELECTIVITY

# of total applicants	45,533
% of total applicants accepted	4
% of total acceptees attending	88

First-Year Profile

Testing policy	Test Optional
Range SAT composite	1500–1560
Range SAT EBRW	740–770
Range SAT math	760–790
Range ACT composite	34–35
% submitting SAT scores	57
% submitting ACT scores	25
Average HS GPA	4.5
% submitting high school GPA	62
% graduated top 10% of class	97
% graduated top 25% of class	100
% graduated top 50% of class	100
% submitting high school rank	32

Important Dates

Nonfall registration?	No

FINANCIAL FACTS

Annual tuition	$67,446
Food and housing	$20,109
Required fees (First-year)	$1,878 ($3,216)
Books and supplies	$1,800
Average need-based scholarship (First-year)	$77,445 ($78,651)
% students with need rec. need-based scholarship or grant aid (First-year)	100 (100)
% students with need rec. need-based self-help aid (First-year)	45 (49)
% students rec. any financial aid (First-year)	39 (40)
% UG borrow to pay for school	11
Average cumulative indebtedness	$35,364
% of students with need fully met (First-year)	100 (100)
Average % of student need met (First-year)	100 (100)

University of Cincinnati

2600 Clifton Avenue, Cincinnati, OH 45221-0063 • Admissions: 513-556-1100

Survey Snapshot
Internships are widely available
Great off-campus food
Recreation facilities are great

RATINGS

Quality of Life	85
Fire Safety	89
Green	98
Academic	74
Profs Interesting	83
Profs Accessible	86
Admissions	84
Financial Aid	79

CAMPUS LIFE

Type of school	Public
Environment	Metropolis

Students

Degree-seeking undergrad enrollment	30,963
% male/female/not reported	49/51/<1
% from out of state	22
% First-year from public high school	81
% First-year live on campus	77
% Ugrads live on campus	21
# of fraternities (% join)	21 (7)
# of sororities (% join)	17 (9)
% Asian	5
% Black or African American	10
% Hispanic	6
% Native American	<1
% Pacific Islander	<1
% Race and/or ethnicity unknown	1
% Two or more races	5
% White	67
% International	5
# of countries represented	102

CAMPUS MENTAL HEALTH SERVICES

Offers mental health/wellness program	Yes
Mental health training available to students	No
Employs Chief Wellness Officer	NR
Peer-to-peer mental health offerings	NR
Counseling center has guidelines or accreditation	NR
Mental health/well-being courses	NR

ACADEMICS

% students returning for sophomore year	86
% students graduating within 4 years	43
% students graduating within 6 years	75
Calendar	Semester
Student/faculty ratio	19:1
Most common class size 20–29.	(27%)
Most common lab/discussion size 10–19.	(31%)

Most Popular Majors
Mechanical Engineering; Multi-/Interdisciplinary Studies; Marketing

STUDENTS SAY "..."

Academics

At the University of Cincinnati, "students graduate with real work experience, strong professional skills, and clear direction for their future." Many students are drawn to Cincy for its education culture, "where students bring insights from internships back into academic settings." In short, these Bearcats—as students are known—"alternate between academic semesters [and] working paid, full-time positions in their industry," and the school "really helps students obtain these co-ops and internships." In turn, that work reaps immediate benefits in class: "I'm surrounded by individuals who think in terms of systems, data, and real-world impact. Classroom discussions are shaped by hands-on experience." Students particularly appreciate these career-oriented opportunities and feel "the faculty truly want us to succeed." One nursing student speaks to "the opportunity to have one-to-one clinical [experiences] with a nurse" at renowned institutions like UC Health and Cincinnati Children's. Similarly, the College of Design, Architecture, Art, and Planning (DAAP) keeps the focus on real-world application. Fine arts students rotate through different media modules, which "gets you into the studio to learn the basics of artistic creation, so you can learn early on if you want to pursue a specific form of art or not." One design student says, "The one-of-a-kind co-op program has allowed me to step outside of my comfort zone and to experience my career firsthand while building my portfolio." Overall, Bearcats really love that "the co-op program prepares students to apply classroom knowledge in professional settings, giving them a clear advantage in career readiness."

Campus Life

"UC is a place where people want to stay on campus even when they don't have classes. Just to walk around, find friends, get their work done, just overall be in the environment." This welcoming vibe stems from the school's design, "in that it is compact and walkable. You can go from one side of campus to the other at a leisurely stroll." Walks, "especially in the evenings…[provide] a great, stunning view of the city." Students also love to stay fit in the rec center, which features "six basketball courts, two floors worth of workout equipment, a pool, hot tub, and much more." Tennis, football, and soccer are student favorites; rock climbing, slacklining, and mountaineering are also popular. During the day, the student-run Program and Activities Council puts on events that are "so fun. They do build-a-bear, pumpkin painting, tote bags, coffee, it's the best." Students enjoy the fact that "UC has a great music scene, and there are shows most nights of the week." Overall, the "social life at UC is very much alive!"

Student Body

The UC student body is a "vibrant community of the Midwest." One Bearcat explains: "There truly is not a 'typical' University of Cincinnati student, and I find that beautiful. This makes it so easy to find yourself a home no matter who you are, what your background is, or what you look like." Another student shares, "I have been given the privilege of meeting so many people from all around the world, in so many different walks of life… and have been able to grow and expand my horizons here through those connections." Put another way, "I have found it really easy to open up to my peers and find friends in every single class that I've been in." This seems true from biomedical to fine-arts majors: "students are incredibly hardworking and have so much grit. Students will tackle any barrier to make a better life for themselves and their community." As one student puts it best: "I haven't doubted for a second that UC was the right school for me, and I am so grateful to call this place my second home."

UNIVERSITY OF CINCINNATI

Financial Aid: 513-556-1000 • E-Mail: admissions@uc.edu • Website: www.uc.edu

THE PRINCETON REVIEW SAYS

Admissions

The school reports that its standardized testing policy for use in admission for Fall 2026 is Test Optional. The Princeton Review suggests that interested applicants consult with the school for the most up-to-date standardized testing policies. *Very important factors considered include:* academic GPA, talent/ability. *Important factors considered include:* rigor of secondary school record. *Other factors considered include:* class rank, standardized test scores, application essay, recommendation(s), extracurricular activities, character/personal qualities, volunteer work, work experience, level of applicant's interest. High school diploma is required and GED is not accepted. *Academic units required:* 4 English, 4 math, 3 science, 3 social studies, 6 academic electives. *Academic units recommended:* 4 English, 4 math, 3 science, 3 social studies, 6 academic electives.

Financial Aid

Students should submit: FAFSA. Priority filing deadline is 12/1. The Princeton Review suggests that all financial aid forms be submitted as soon as possible. *Need-based scholarships/grants offered:* Federal Pell; Federal SEOG; State scholarships/grants; Private scholarships; College/university scholarship or grant aid from institutional funds; United Negro College Fund; Federal Nursing Scholarships. *Loan aid offered:* Federal Direct Subsidized Loans; Federal Direct Unsubsidized Loans; Direct PLUS loans; State Loans; College/university loans from institutional funds. Admitted students will be notified of awards on a rolling basis beginning 2/15. Federal Work-Study Program available. Institutional employment available.

The Inside Word

The University of Cincinnati wants students who are academically strong, show drive and challenge themselves, and are passionate about leaving a positive mark on the world. Essay prompts should be chosen with the goal of showing your authentic self in order to reveal something that wouldn't otherwise be apparent from other application material. All aspects of each student's application—from GPA to personal statements—are considered when making an admission decision. A letter of recommendation is optional for first-year applicants, although one is highly encouraged.

THE SCHOOL SAYS

From the Admissions Office

"The University of Cincinnati provides a unique learning experience to students from around the globe. All students hone their skills outside the classroom through the university's nationally top-ranked co-op and internship program where students collectively earn $75 million annually. Other experiential-learning options include clinicals, undergraduate research, study abroad, service-learning, performances, or other approved activities. This focus on experience-based learning not only builds a student's résumé, but allows students to network and build confidence within their chosen field. When combined with top academic programs, location, diversity, scope of majors and programs, and campus setting, the University of Cincinnati stands out among the top research universities in the country. Students and counselors agree:

"Heidi Clark-Smitley, the Director of Guidance and College Counseling at Catholic Central High School (Grand Rapids, MI) writes, 'I fell in love with the University of Cincinnati during an afternoon visit a few years ago. Cincinnati is one of the few out-of-state institutions I STRONGLY recommend for our students to consider.'

"Hannah, an architecture major, writes 'I knew the co-op program would allow me to have numerous professional experiences working in the design field and the university setting appealed to me more than a small art school. I am involved in several organizations and attend sporting events—which are both possible because DAAP is part of a larger university.'

"Come visit and find out how Cincinnati can benefit you both inside and outside the classroom: admissions.uc.edu/visit."

SELECTIVITY

# of total applicants	33,750
% of total applicants accepted	88
% of total acceptees attending	22
# of in-state applicants	19,700
% of in-state applicants accepted	90
# of out-of-state-applicants	11,319
% of applicants accepted from out of state	85
# of international applicants	2,731
% of international applicants accepted	83

First-Year Profile

Testing policy	Test Optional
Range SAT composite	1160–1340
Range SAT EBRW	580–680
Range SAT math	580–680
Range ACT composite	24–30
% submitting SAT scores	9
% submitting ACT scores	25
Average HS GPA	3.7
% submitting high school GPA	100
% graduated top 10% of class	22
% graduated top 25% of class	47
% graduated top 50% of class	81
% submitting high school rank	44

Important Dates

Regular	
Apply by	3/1
Notified by	Late December
Nonfall registration?	Yes

FINANCIAL FACTS

Annual in-state tuition	$14,394
Annual out-of-state tuition	$29,728
Food and housing	$16,511
Books and supplies	$1,300
Average need-based scholarship (First-year)	$8,877 ($9,106)
% students with need rec. need-based scholarship or grant aid (First-year)	74 (82)
% students with need rec. non-need-based scholarship or grant aid (First-year)	4 (5)
% students with need rec. need-based self-help aid (First-year)	65 (63)
% students rec. any financial aid (First-year)	79 (85)
% UG borrow to pay for school	53
Average cumulative indebtedness	$27,571
% of students with need fully met (First-year)	5 (7)
Average % of student need met (First-year)	37 (39)

University of Colorado Boulder

Office of Admissions, Boulder, CO 80309-0552 • Admissions: 303-492-6301

Survey Snapshot
Students environmentally aware
Students love Boulder, CO
Everyone loves the Buffalo

RATINGS

Quality of Life	**91**
Fire Safety	**91**
Green	**98**
Academic	**84**
Profs Interesting	**88**
Profs Accessible	**92**
Admissions	**87**
Financial Aid	**86**

CAMPUS LIFE

Type of school	Public
Environment	City

Students

Degree-seeking undergrad enrollment	33,675
% male/female/not reported	52/48/0
% from out of state	42
% First-year from public high school	95
% First-year live on campus	95
% Ugrads live on campus	26
# of fraternities (% join)	16 (9)
# of sororities (% join)	14 (22)
% Asian	6
% Black or African American	2
% Hispanic	14
% Native American	<1
% Pacific Islander	<1
% Race and/or ethnicity unknown	1
% Two or more races	7
% White	66
% International	2
# of countries represented	82

CAMPUS MENTAL HEALTH SERVICES

Offers mental health/wellness program	Yes
Mental health training available to students	Yes
Employs Chief Wellness Officer	Yes
Peer-to-peer mental health offerings	NR
Counseling center has guidelines or accreditation	No
Mental health/well-being courses	NR

ACADEMICS

% students returning for sophomore year	91
% students graduating within 4 years	57
% students graduating within 6 years	74
Calendar	Semester
Student/faculty ratio	20:1
Most common class size 10–19.	(33%)
Most common lab/discussion size 20–29.	(48%)

Most Popular Majors
Psychology; Finance; Physiology

Applicants Also Look At
California Polytechnic State University—San Luis Obispo, Colorado Mesa University, Colorado School of Mines, Colorado State University, Metropolitan State University of Denver, University of Colorado at Colorado Springs, University of Colorado at Denver, University of Denver, University of Northern Colorado, University of Utah

STUDENTS SAY "..."

Academics

Students praise the University of Colorado Boulder from the strength of its academics (particularly its "strong physics reputation" and business and environmental offerings) to "all the perks of a big state university," while maintaining the much-desired atmosphere of a "college town" filled with "young intellectuals." In-state students add that "the price for an education of this caliber is phenomenal," with one student adding that they found CU Boulder's education to be "significantly better" than that of the private school they'd transferred from. The school's "top-notch leadership program" facilitates teamwork, problem solving, and communication in a hands-on, challenging setting through the Mountain Research Station (MRS), the Outdoor Pursuits Challenge Course, and Peak to Peak Leadership. CU Boulder's "amazing" and "approachable" faculty lists five Nobel laureates and nine MacArthur 'genius grant' recipients among its ranks, but there's no need to worry about any big heads in the hallways or classrooms, as professors are "interested in students personally" and "will treat you as an adult." One student assures that professors are "consistently excellent across the wide variety of subjects I have taken courses in, from geography to astronomy and economics to literature." CU Boulder "provides a modern, research-based education that focuses on creating aware citizens [who] go on to change the world (while having fun)." Students agree, with one adding that the school has "excellent diversity in subjects and courses, [lots of] school spirit, [and] packed sports games." And one environmental studies major shares, "In my four years as an undergrad, I have traveled places and learned things that I never imagined I would or could experience." Life Nestled in the foothills of the Rocky Mountains, students appreciate nature and the great outdoors and sing the praises of their "fun, beautiful college town." Many students "go skiing in the mountains on days that [they] don't have classes," join in the "extremely popular" campus pastime of snowboarding, or "go hiking when the weather is nice." As one student states, "Being active and outdoors is a staple for students." One doesn't necessarily need to climb a mountain to have fun, though, and at the center of campus, "Farrand Field is always busy on nice days with students playing Frisbee, football, soccer [or] tanning." Students also consider themselves fortunate to live in "the best college town in the U.S.," citing Boulder's "diverse and active" music scene and a "prominent nightlife at the bars." Although "partying is big," students are devoted to their classes, and "most take school very seriously and are irritated by [its] depiction as a 'party school.'" While some students do "[like] to go out and party on the weekends," others prefer to "go shopping and eat out on Pearl Street," and "regardless of the time of day, students can be seen outside relaxing, exercising, or just hanging out with friends."

Campus Life

Nestled in the foothills of the Rocky Mountains, students appreciate nature and the great outdoors and sing the praises of their "fun, beautiful college town." Many students "go skiing in the mountains on days that [they] don't have classes," join in the "extremely popular" campus pastime of snowboarding, or "go hiking when the weather is nice." As one student states, "Being active and outdoors is a staple for students." One doesn't necessarily need to climb a mountain to have fun, though, and at the center of campus, "Farrand Field is always busy on nice days with students playing Frisbee, football, soccer [or] tanning." Students also consider themselves fortunate to live in "the best college town in the U.S.," citing Boulder's "diverse and active" music scene and a "prominent nightlife at the bars." Although "partying is big," students are devoted to their classes, and "most take school very seriously and are irritated by [its] depiction as a 'party school.'" While some students do "[like] to go out and party on the weekends," others prefer to "go shopping and eat out on Pearl Street," and "regardless of the time of day, students can be seen outside relaxing, exercising, or just hanging out with friends."

Student Body

Given how they spend their time, it should be unsurprising that CU Boulder students are often described as "outdoorsy, outgoing, and always up for anything." They "love to be outside and often will spend their weekends in the mountains." Students at CU Boulder have "diverse passions" and "diverse backgrounds" and are described as "kind," "genuine," "smart," and "athletic." In addition, many agree that "there isn't really a typical student, which is awesome." An additional benefit of CU Boulder is that "the school is so large everyone fits into a group, no matter what your interests are," with one student noting that those "who make an effort to meet new people and try new things will be very happy and have a great time at CU Boulder." Another student raves: "When I stepped foot on CU's campus, I immediately felt at home... Everyone is so friendly and welcoming. It's such a community atmosphere. Everyone watches out for each other and has each other's backs."

UNIVERSITY OF COLORADO BOULDER

Financial Aid: 303-492-5091 • E-Mail: admissions@colorado.edu • Website: www.colorado.edu

THE PRINCETON REVIEW SAYS

Admissions

The school reports that its standardized testing policy for use in admission for Fall 2026 is Test Optional. The Princeton Review suggests that interested applicants consult with the school for the most up-to-date standardized testing policies. *Very important factors considered include:* rigor of secondary school record, academic GPA. *Important factors considered include:* application essay, recommendation(s), extracurricular activities, talent/ability, character/personal qualities. *Other factors considered include:* class rank, standardized test scores, first generation, geographical residence, state residency, volunteer work, work experience. High school diploma is required and GED is accepted. *Academic units recommended:* 4 English, 4 math, 3 science, 2 science labs, 1 language (other than English), 3 social studies, 2 academic electives.

Financial Aid

Students should submit: FAFSA. Priority filing deadline is 3/1. The Princeton Review suggests that all financial aid forms be submitted as soon as possible. *Need-based scholarships/grants offered:* Federal Pell; Federal SEOG; State scholarships/grants; Private scholarships; College/university scholarship or grant aid from institutional funds. *Loan aid offered:* Federal Direct Subsidized Loans; Federal Direct Unsubsidized Loans; Direct PLUS loans. Admitted students will be notified of awards on a rolling basis beginning 2/15. Federal Work-Study Program available. Institutional employment available.

The Inside Word

Students must apply to a specific school within CU Boulder on their application. Some programs are more competitive than others, with Engineering and Applied Science and the Leeds School of Business being the most competitive. Those who apply to a competitive school within CU Boulder and are not selected will be automatically entered into consideration for admission to the College of Arts and Sciences.

THE SCHOOL SAYS

From the Admissions Office

"Located at the foot of the Rocky Mountains, the University of Colorado Boulder has a breathtaking view from campus. But don't just come for the view. CU Boulder and its nationally and internationally ranked faculty have built a global reputation for outstanding teaching, research and creative work across more than 150 academic fields. Our innovative academic programs, hands-on opportunities, and rigorous coursework will prepare you for a complex global society. While working with faculty, you'll develop a broad understanding of the world, strong leadership skills and an enhanced ability to think critically.

"Within CU Boulder's inclusive community, you'll find many ways to get involved and make lifelong friends. We have one of the most active college campuses in the nation, where recreation, sports and student groups play a key role in the unique CU Boulder experience. We don't claim that we can change the world. Instead, we teach, inspire and encourage our students, faculty and researchers. So they can change the world. Live in spectacular surroundings and learn in a campus environment of extraordinary opportunities.

"Come to CU Boulder and discover what you can be.

"To find out if CU Boulder is the place for you, we encourage you to learn more. Check out our website, visit campus or take a virtual tour online.

"Be inspired. Be unique. Be driven.

"Be Boulder."

SELECTIVITY

# of total applicants	73,180
% of total applicants accepted	71
% of total acceptees attending	14
# offered a place on the wait list	6,367
# admitted from wait list	92

First-Year Profile

Testing policy	Test Optional
Range SAT composite	1130–1370
Range SAT EBRW	570–700
Range SAT math	560–690
Range ACT composite	27–32
% submitting SAT scores	27
% submitting ACT scores	6
Average HS GPA	3.8
% submitting high school GPA	100
% graduated top 10% of class	26
% graduated top 25% of class	58
% graduated top 50% of class	88
% submitting high school rank	41

Important Dates

Early action	
Apply by	11/15
Notified by	2/1
Regular	
Apply by	1/15
Notified by	4/1
Nonfall registration?	Yes

FINANCIAL FACTS

Annual in-state tuition (First-year)	\$11,976 (\$12,312)
Annual out-of-state tuition (First-year)	\$40,320 (\$41,932)
Food and housing	\$17,794
Required fees (First-year)	\$1,646 (\$1,690)
Books and supplies	\$1,200
Average need-based scholarship (First-year)	\$17,613 (\$17,729)
% students with need rec. need-based scholarship or grant aid (First-year)	84 (82)
% students with need rec. non-need-based scholarship or grant aid (First-year)	5 (6)
% students with need rec. need-based self-help aid (First-year)	73 (74)
% students rec. any financial aid (First-year)	68 (79)
% UG borrow to pay for school	34
Average cumulative indebtedness	\$29,123
% of students with need fully met (First-year)	25 (29)
Average % of student need met (First-year)	72 (72)

University of Connecticut

2131 Hillside Road, Storrs, CT 06269 • Admissions: 860-486-3137

Survey Snapshot
Everyone loves the Huskies
Students are happy
Great off-campus food

RATINGS	
Quality of Life	84
Fire Safety	60*
Green	96
Academic	79
Profs Interesting	84
Profs Accessible	88
Admissions	90
Financial Aid	81

CAMPUS LIFE

Type of school	Public
Environment	Town

Students

Degree-seeking undergrad enrollment	19,030
% male/female/not reported	50/50/0
% from out of state	22
% First-year from public high school	88
% First-year live on campus	97
% Ugrads live on campus	67
# of fraternities (% join)	23 (12)
# of sororities (% join)	13 (17)
% Asian	11
% Black or African American	6
% Hispanic	10
% Native American	<1
% Pacific Islander	<1
% Race and/or ethnicity unknown	5
% Two or more races	3
% White	60
% International	6
# of countries represented	71

CAMPUS MENTAL HEALTH SERVICES

Offers mental health/wellness program	Yes
Mental health training available to students	No
Employs Chief Wellness Officer	NR
Peer-to-peer mental health offerings	NR
Counseling center has guidelines or accreditation	No
Mental health/well-being courses	NR

ACADEMICS

% students returning for sophomore year	92
% students graduating within 4 years	70
% students graduating within 6 years	82
Calendar	Semester
Student/faculty ratio	16:1
Most common class size 10–19.	(33%)
Most common lab/discussion size 10–19.	(48%)

Most Popular Majors
Economics; Communication; Psychology

STUDENTS SAY "..."

Academics

The University of Connecticut may be "known for our amazing athletics," but it's also "one of the top research universities and state schools," a "university [that] truly cares about their students." As one political science major puts it, UConn is "unique because it is comprised of all different types of students both in backgrounds and ethnicities. What makes us different than other universities is our cohesiveness despite these differences. We all go to one school, we all cheer on the same team, and we all bleed blue." While "basketball games are like religion," students say that, "UConn is focused on academic achievement." For one student, the school's main appeal is that it is a "large, public university [with] a variety of programs and diversity on campus." As the "flagship state school," UConn provides "research opportunities for undergrads" and "every student is supported in order to be the most successful student possible; UConn cares." When it comes to professors, the "performance level [varies], more so during the first couple years when the students are required to take general education requirements." Students say that in more advanced, major-specific courses, "the professors tend to be more interested in the topics of the course and thus more engaging." Those professors are "truly amazing, inspiring, and add so much to my academics," but the general consensus is that "UConn is a really big university, so professors can be hit or miss."

Campus Life

Since it's a big school, there is always something going on on-campus, whether it's free movies, lectures, concerts, food, or more. For students who want to experience nature, "There's always the opportunity to go outdoors and walk to Horsebarn Hill, go on runs around campus or go on hikes in the UConn forest." Even though the campus a little off the beaten path—one transfer student laments "the nickname for Storrs is Snores"—students say "the downtown area has developed into its own mini city" with restaurants and Cafés. As one student puts it, "I am never bored on the weekend between the many shows and concerts, movies and other activities offered by the university." Greek life plays a significant role on campus—some say that "Greek life dominates many aspects of social scene," while others say only that there are "frat parties if you're into that kind of scene." The school's reputation for top notch athletics is legendary; as one student puts it, "the celebrations after victories are unlike anything I've ever experienced elsewhere." Some students are frustrated that "athletics sometimes overshadows academic achievements in funding," but others underscore the rigorousness of UConn's academics, saying "UConn is a research school so classes are difficult, and professors will not go out of their way to ensure you get a good grade." When it comes to kicking back after a long week, one student succinctly sums up the alcohol culture at the school: "UConn doesn't seem to be a party school, it is a drinking school—there is a difference."

Student Body

UConn students are typically "very diverse due to the large student body"—you can find "students who love to go out every weekend at the bar [and] you can find students whose hobby is knitting or [to] go to ComiCONN...there really is a peer group for everyone." The students, "the majority of which are from Connecticut," are "uniquely passionate and spirited." As one student puts it, the school is composed of "many small communities based on academics, sports, clubs, and interests, that come together to form a large community connected by a mutual love of UConn." Some pinpoint the average student as "white, upper middle class and wears L.L. Bean boots, North Face coats," but others stress that "it's a big school, so there is no one word to describe my peers." With "more happening on campus than you expect," there are "athletic teams and Greek life" but also "human rights organizations, activists, and volunteers."

University of Connecticut

Financial Aid: 860-486-2819 • E-Mail: beahusky@uconn.edu • Website: www.uconn.edu

THE PRINCETON REVIEW SAYS

Admissions

The school reports that its standardized testing policy for use in admission for Fall 2026 is Test Optional. The Princeton Review suggests that interested applicants consult with the school for the most up-to-date standardized testing policies. *Very important factors considered include:* rigor of secondary school record, class rank, academic GPA, standardized test scores. *Important factors considered include:* application essay, recommendation(s), extracurricular activities, talent/ability, character/personal qualities, first generation, volunteer work. *Other factors considered include:* alumni/ae relation, geographical residence, state residency, work experience, level of applicant's interest. High school diploma is required and GED is accepted. *Academic units required:* 4 English, 3 math, 2 science, 2 science labs, 2 language (other than English), 2 social studies, 3 academic electives. *Academic units recommended:* 3 language (other than English).

Financial Aid

Students should submit: FAFSA. Priority filing deadline is 3/1. The Princeton Review suggests that all financial aid forms be submitted as soon as possible. *Need-based scholarships/grants offered:* Federal Pell; Federal SEOG; State scholarships/grants; Private scholarships; College/university scholarship or grant aid from institutional funds. *Loan aid offered:* Federal Direct Subsidized Loans; Federal Direct Unsubsidized Loans; Direct PLUS loans. Admitted students will be notified of awards on a rolling basis beginning 3/1. Federal Work-Study Program available. Institutional employment available.

The Inside Word

The UConn admissions committee looks at every aspect of a prospective first year's application, taking everything from GPA, class rank, extracurricular activities, standardized test scores (if submitted), a required essay, and two letters of recommendation into consideration. The university is a competitive school—college preparatory coursework in high school is required, with additional requirements for School of Engineering and School of Nursing applicants.

THE SCHOOL SAYS

From the Admissions Office

"Founded in 1881, the University of Connecticut is ranked as one of the best public universities in the United States. With a combination of dynamic faculty, strong athletic pride and an extraordinary sense of community, UConn is a university like no other. Offering over 110 majors and the ability to create a major of your own, a broad range of academic choices is provided. Faculty members are top experts in their fields, and serve as mentors and advisors to students. Distinctive research opportunities pair undergraduate students with faculty in every academic discipline offered. The main campus in Storrs is located in a safe New England town midway between New York City and Boston. With one of the highest percentages of students living on campus of any public university in the United States, UConn is its own community within a thriving rural town. With on-campus museums and performances, and newly released movies right inside the Student Union's theater, UConn students work hard and play hard. Over 650 student clubs and organizations allow students to pursue their passions outside the classroom. School spirit permeates the campus. Students can cheer on one of our twenty-four Division I teams, or join one of our intramural or club sports teams. No matter how students are involved, they exemplify the Husky Spirit.

"Interested in learning more about what UConn can offer you? For details on the admissions process or to schedule a campus tour, visit admissions.uconn.edu."

SELECTIVITY

# of total applicants	35,980
% of total applicants accepted	49
% of total acceptees attending	22
# offered a place on the wait list	3,386
# admitted from wait list	148

First-Year Profile

Testing policy	Test Optional
Range SAT EBRW	600–680
Range SAT math	610–710
Range ACT composite	26–31
% submitting SAT scores	82
% submitting ACT scores	33
% submitting high school GPA	89
% graduated top 10% of class	51
% graduated top 25% of class	84
% graduated top 50% of class	98
% submitting high school rank	41

Important Dates

Regular	
Apply by	1/15
Notified by	Rolling, 3/1
Nonfall registration?	Yes

FINANCIAL FACTS

Annual in-state tuition	$13,798
Annual out-of-state tuition	$36,466
Food and housing	$13,258
Required fees	$3,428
Books and supplies	$950
Average need-based scholarship (First-year)	$13,049 ($14,041)
% students with need rec. need-based scholarship or grant aid (First-year)	71 (67)
% students with need rec. non-need-based scholarship or grant aid (First-year)	33 (40)
% students with need rec. need-based self-help aid (First-year)	72 (62)
% students rec. any financial aid (First-year)	48 (49)
% UG borrow to pay for school	59
Average cumulative indebtedness	$28,028
% of students with need fully met (First-year)	12 (15)
Average % of student need met (First-year)	57 (58)

UNIVERSITY OF DALLAS

1845 East Northgate Drive, Irving, TX 75062 • Admissions: 972-721-5266

Survey Snapshot
Lots of conservative students
Students are very religious
Theater is popular

RATINGS

Quality of Life	**83**
Fire Safety	**93**
Green	**60***
Academic	**87**
Profs Interesting	**97**
Profs Accessible	**95**
Admissions	**89**
Financial Aid	**88**

CAMPUS LIFE

Type of school	Private
Affiliation	Roman Catholic
Environment	City

Students

Degree-seeking undergrad enrollment	1,403
% male/female/not reported	45/55/0
% from out of state	46
% First-year from public high school	52
% First-year live on campus	85
% Ugrads live on campus	57
# of fraternities	0
# of sororities	0
% Asian	7
% Black or African American	3
% Hispanic	28
% Native American	<1
% Pacific Islander	<1
% Race and/or ethnicity unknown	1
% Two or more races	2
% White	56
% International	2
# of countries represented	7

CAMPUS MENTAL HEALTH SERVICES

Offers mental health/wellness program	Yes
Mental health training available to students	No
Employs Chief Wellness Officer	NR
Peer-to-peer mental health offerings	NR
Counseling center has guidelines or accreditation	No
Mental health/well-being courses	NR

ACADEMICS

% students returning for sophomore year	80
% students graduating within 4 years	59
% students graduating within 6 years	67
Calendar	Semester
Student/faculty ratio	11:1
Most common class size 10–19.	(40%)
Most common lab/discussion size 10–19.	(51%)

Most Popular Majors

English Language and Literature; Biology/Biological Sciences

Applicants Also Look At

Baylor University, Benedictine College, The Catholic University of America, Franciscan University of Steubenville, Hillsdale College, Texas A&M University—College Station, Texas Tech University, Trinity University, University of Houston, University of North Texas UNT

STUDENTS SAY "..."

Academics

The University of Dallas is a great option for students looking to join a deeply intellectual and spiritual community. After all, the school "offers an incredible liberal arts education, an authentically Catholic community, an active and lively campus atmosphere, and a fantastic Rome study abroad program." UD prides itself on a core curriculum that introduces undergrads to "the great works of Western Civilization" and "gives all the students on campus a shared experience and a wide variety of subjects in which they have a foundational understanding." According to enrollees, this coursework is "good at making the students think independently." Students also appreciate that it is "rigorous but thorough,...[preparing] students to succeed after graduation." And while classes tend to be traditional, students emphasize that they're "done to the point of excellence." For example, a history discussion that weaves together "art, politics, music, literature, and philosophy."

That excellence may stem from the professors, described as "not only great teachers but great role models." They continually demonstrate that they "care about educating the entire person and are often willing to talk with students about broader life questions as well as course specific questions." And while they "expect students to work hard and grade accordingly," they're also "more than fair, and are always willing to go above and beyond to help any student who desires it." Even better, UD professors "truly engage the class and inspire learning through their own joy in the subject." Indeed, "they do everything in their power to bring to life the content and help each student grow."

Campus Life

There are so many things to do that I often find myself struggling to decide how to fit them all in! That's a great "problem" to have, and one that showcases that "while students spend substantial time during the week on coursework, they are also quite creative when it comes to relaxing and having fun." All interests are on the table, whether that's fencing, knitting, or "societies dedicated to Tocqueville and Alexander Hamilton." For those seeking additional intellectual stimulation, there are "many lectures, debates, and discussions given by our professors throughout the year." For those wanting something different, there are activities like "bonfires, musical jam sessions, intramural sports, events in Dallas and Fort Worth, road trips, camping, hiking, etc."

Student Body

The University of Dallas has cultivated a "very lively and friendly" student body that's "bright and highly driven." They're "always asking the deeper questions and very passionate about the truth." Indeed, undergrads here love to "engage in spontaneous conversation" and it's quite common to "find students in and out of class discussing the classics as if they were common knowledge to everyone." UD students also "tend to value tradition, family, and faith." This isn't too surprising given that "a majority of the students are Christian, and of those, most are Catholic." Another undergrad elaborates, "More than anywhere else I've been, my peers also have a genuine interest in being faithful people and growing in their spiritual lives." A few individuals caution that the university's culture is "catered to very conservative white Catholics," but the majority assert that "the small student body allows for genuine connections and positive interactions to take place daily—at the campus cappuccino bar, school events, and even walking down the mall between classes." As one contented undergrad shares, "I haven't walked away from a conversation without smiling."

UNIVERSITY OF DALLAS

Financial Aid: 972-721-5266 • E-Mail: admissions@udallas.edu • Website: www.udallas.edu

THE PRINCETON REVIEW SAYS

Admissions

The school reports that its standardized testing policy for use in admission for Fall 2026 will require applicants to submit either the SAT or ACT. The Princeton Review suggests that interested applicants consult with the school for the most up-to-date standardized testing policies. *Very important factors considered include:* rigor of secondary school record, academic GPA, standardized test scores, application essay, recommendation(s), character/personal qualities. *Important factors considered include:* class rank, talent/ability. *Other factors considered include:* interview, extracurricular activities, first generation, alumni/ae relation, volunteer work, work experience, level of applicant's interest. High school diploma is required and GED is accepted. *Academic units required:* 4 English, 3 math, 3 science, 2 language (other than English), 3 social studies, 3 history, 3 academic electives, 1 visual/performing arts. *Academic units recommended:* 4 English, 4 math, 3 science, 3 science labs, 3 language (other than English), 4 social studies, 4 history, 4 academic electives, 2 visual/performing arts.

Financial Aid

Students should submit: FAFSA. Priority filing deadline is 1/15. The Princeton Review suggests that all financial aid forms be submitted as soon as possible. *Need-based scholarships/grants offered:* Federal Pell; Federal SEOG; State scholarships/grants; Private scholarships; College/university scholarship or grant aid from institutional funds. *Loan aid offered:* Federal Direct Subsidized Loans; Federal Direct Unsubsidized Loans; Direct PLUS loans. Admitted students will be notified of awards on a rolling basis beginning 12/1. Federal Work-Study Program available. Institutional employment available.

The Inside Word

Because of University of Dallas' distinction as a Catholic liberal arts school, its applicant pool is frequently small but self-selective. Strong academic performance and test scores are closely considered, as are students who demonstrate moral and ethical commitment in addition to intellectual curiosity.

THE SCHOOL SAYS

From the Admissions Office

"Located in one of the fastest-growing metropolitan areas of the U.S., the University of Dallas is the premier Catholic liberal arts university in the nation, with campuses in Irving, Texas, and Rome, Italy. Nationally known for its undergraduate Core Curriculum, the University of Dallas fosters friendship, thrives on conversation, and prepares students for a life well-lived. UD's top-rated undergraduate Core Curriculum takes students on a quest to explore eternal questions by studying the great works of Western civilization and the Catholic intellectual tradition. During their first two years, students take common courses in literature, philosophy, theology, and science, fueling robust conversations inside and outside of the classroom. After completing the core, students choose from one of 27 academic major areas of study in the liberal arts, sciences, or business.

"Nearly 90% of students experience UD's signature Rome Program. Students live together with faculty in a rural Italian villa and study art and architecture, history, literature, theology and philosophy with travel through Europe to the places where Western civilization was born and where the Catholic tradition continues to flourish.

"Additionally, flexible graduate degrees and professional programs are offered in multiple disciplines, taught by exceptional faculty in small classes. The Gupta College of Business offers flexible MBA, MS, DBA, and professional programs, including accelerated "4+1" degrees for undergraduates. The Braniff Graduate School seeks to renew the Western heritage and the Christian intellectual tradition, offering master's programs in a broad cross section of the humanities, and doctoral degrees in literature, philosophy or politics."

SELECTIVITY

# of total applicants	4,179
% of total applicants accepted	54
% of total acceptees attending	15
# of in-state applicants	2,722
% of in-state applicants accepted	53
# of out-of-state-applicants	1,079
% of applicants accepted from out of state	71
# of international applicants	378
% of international applicants accepted	16

First-Year Profile

Testing policy	SAT or ACT Required
Range SAT composite	1180–1260
Range SAT EBRW	600–710
Range SAT math	570–660
Range ACT composite	25–32
% submitting SAT scores	30
% submitting ACT scores	13
Average HS GPA	3.9
% submitting high school GPA	100
% graduated top 10% of class	19
% graduated top 25% of class	40
% graduated top 50% of class	57
% submitting high school rank	17

Important Dates

Early action	
Apply by	12/1
Notified by	1/15
Regular	
Apply by	8/1
Notified by	Rolling, 9/15
Nonfall registration?	Yes

FINANCIAL FACTS

Annual tuition	$50,140
Food and housing	$15,010
Required fees	$3,790
Books and supplies	$1,000
Average need-based scholarship (First-year)	$37,423 ($36,959)
% students with need rec. need-based scholarship or grant aid (First-year)	98 (98)
% students with need rec. non-need-based scholarship or grant aid (First-year)	15 (17)
% students with need rec. need-based self-help aid (First-year)	64 (63)
% students rec. any financial aid (First-year)	99 (100)
% UG borrow to pay for school	60
Average cumulative indebtedness	$33,231
% of students with need fully met (First-year)	20 (20)
Average % of student need met (First-year)	81 (82)

UNIVERSITY OF DAYTON

300 College Park, Dayton, OH 45469 • Admissions: 800-837-7433

Survey Snapshot
Lots of conservative students
Internships are widely available
Great financial aid

RATINGS

Quality of Life	86
Fire Safety	90
Green	89
Academic	78
Profs Interesting	86
Profs Accessible	91
Admissions	87
Financial Aid	92

CAMPUS LIFE

Type of school	Private
Affiliation	Roman Catholic
Environment	City

Students

Degree-seeking undergrad enrollment	7,179
% male/female/not reported	53/47/<1
% from out of state	44
% First-year live on campus	92
% Ugrads live on campus	68
# of fraternities (% join)	9 (8)
# of sororities (% join)	12 (20)
% Asian	2
% Black or African American	5
% Hispanic	7
% Native American	<1
% Pacific Islander	<1
% Race and/or ethnicity unknown	1
% Two or more races	4
% White	79
% International	3
# of countries represented	33

CAMPUS MENTAL HEALTH SERVICES

Offers mental health/wellness program	Yes
Mental health training available to students	Yes
Employs Chief Wellness Officer	Yes
Peer-to-peer mental health offerings	Yes
Counseling center has guidelines or accreditation	Yes
Mental health/well-being courses	Yes, for-credit

ACADEMICS

% students returning for sophomore year	90
% students graduating within 4 years	65
% students graduating within 6 years	80
Calendar	Semester
Student/faculty ratio	15:1
Most common class size 20–29.	(34%)
Most common lab/discussion size 10–19.	(66%)

Most Popular Majors

Computer Engineering; Finance; Marketing/Marketing Management

Applicants Also Look At

Miami University, The Ohio State University—Columbus, University of Cincinnati

STUDENTS SAY "..."

Academics

There are many reasons to attend the University of Dayton, but the one mentioned above all is its experiential learning. "We have opportunities for real world experience in every major" (and sometimes even further independent expertises by department), like "the Sophomore Experience Entrepreneurship Program that gives students a $5,000 grant to run their own microbusiness." Engineers have space, time, and resources to build rigs and run experiments, "the music program is phenomenal," and minicourses in subjects like microeconomics utilize the Dayton area to show "the interaction between economics and the environment through outdoor excursions that were often very informative." All of this is backstopped by the professors, to whom students give high marks. "Most of my professors have been extremely nice, approachable, and engaging." They "challenge you but also really want you to succeed, especially if you participate in discussions and provide quality work on assignments and exams." Indeed, "they want to show each student that they have potential to be great, but they have to unlock it."

Campus Life

At the University of Dayton, learning and excitement extend far beyond the classroom: "there are activities going on everywhere, on-campus jobs to partake in, as well as a variety of organizations and clubs." As one undergrad elaborates, "I've been in Bella Voce (the women's choral ensembles), Opera Workshop (a musical theater class)...and Javanese Gamelan ensemble (a percussion tradition from Indonesia)." Additionally, "intramural sports are very active on campus...[along with] professional organizations that align with your major, ethnicity, or gender." Of course, there's plenty of casual fun to be had as well; students mention sledding in winter, hanging out at Kennedy Union and "[playing] pool or [going] bowling at the Hangar." And eating is a serious activity at Dayton, given that "the food is awesome." Some students describe "a lot of partying" on the weekends, but also suggest that "people do not pressure you into drinking if you don't want to."

Student Body

Undergrads at the University of Dayton overwhelmingly agree that their peers are "very sweet," and "super welcoming and approachable" people who foster a strong sense of community and school spirit. Given the "relatively small class sizes, it's easy to get to know a lot of people in your major" and others more simply describe it as common to see "strangers quickly become friends and friends become like family." As for finding a balance between school work and social lives: "we aren't just book worms, and we are not just party animals. We are both." The student body remains "predominantly white," though "there are [now] more POC and LGBTQ+ students than there have ever been before." Moreover, students feel strongly about inclusion, noting that "students never need to be told to work together to create a safe and inclusive campus, they just do."

UNIVERSITY OF DAYTON

Financial Aid: 800-837-7433 • E-Mail: admission@udayton.edu • Website: www.udayton.edu

THE PRINCETON REVIEW SAYS

Admissions

The school reports that its standardized testing policy for use in admission for Fall 2026 is Test Optional. The Princeton Review suggests that interested applicants consult with the school for the most up-to-date standardized testing policies. *Very important factors considered include:* rigor of secondary school record, academic GPA, application essay. *Important factors considered include:* recommendation(s), extracurricular activities, character/personal qualities, level of applicant's interest. *Other factors considered include:* class rank, standardized test scores, talent/ability, first generation, alumni/ae relation, volunteer work, work experience. High school diploma is required and GED is accepted. *Academic units recommended:* 4 English, 4 math, 4 science, 1 science lab, 2 language (other than English), 4 social studies, 4 history, 4 computer science, 4 visual/performing arts.

Financial Aid

Students should submit: FAFSA. Priority filing deadline is 2/1. The Princeton Review suggests that all financial aid forms be submitted as soon as possible. *Need-based scholarships/grants offered:* Federal Pell; State scholarships/grants; Private scholarships; Federal SEOG; College/university scholarship or grant aid from institutional funds. *Loan aid offered:* Federal Direct Subsidized Loans; Federal Direct Unsubsidized Loans; Direct PLUS loans; College/university loans from institutional funds. Admitted students will be notified of awards on a rolling basis. Federal Work-Study Program available. Institutional employment available.

The Inside Word

When it comes to the admissions process at the University of Dayton, academics take top priority. Indeed, the committee pays close attention to both your GPA and grade pattern throughout your high school tenure, course selection, and class rank. To a lesser extent, the university considers factors such as letters of recommendation. Demonstrating genuine, strong interest in the university helps.

THE SCHOOL SAYS

From the Admissions Office

"As a top-tier Catholic research university, the University of Dayton is committed to holistic support for every student, linking learning and scholarship through transformative leadership, experiential learning and service opportunities.

"We offer more than 80 undergraduate and nearly 50 graduate and doctoral programs, as well as 20+ graduate pathways. We provide credit for college-credit courses and exams and students can use our online transfer credit evaluation tool for an instant degree audit. Classes are small, which is one reason nearly all students find success within six months of graduation. UD is also a strong research institution; performing nearly $278 million in sponsored research last year, our faculty are committed to involving students in research projects.

"Dedicated to transparent affordability, UD provides undergraduates a four-year overview of costs upfront—including guaranteed net tuition—so students don't have to worry about unexpected tuition increases. Estimates for housing, meals, health and wellbeing and textbooks are provided for all four years, allowing students to understand their full investment. Since launching this plan, our students are more successful at paying student loans and have achieved record graduation rates of 80%, compared to a national average of 68% for private universities.

"A strong sense of community is core to the UD experience; 80% of our students live on campus in residence halls, apartments and our unique porch-clad student neighborhood. Through organizations like Multi-Ethnic Education and Engagement Center and Brook Center, we build community spirit that celebrates inclusivity and helps every student reach incredible heights."

SELECTIVITY

# of total applicants	22,247
% of total applicants accepted	67
% of total acceptees attending	11

First-Year Profile

Testing policy	Test Optional
Range SAT composite	1200–1290
Range SAT EBRW	590–690
Range SAT math	590–690
Range ACT composite	24–31
% submitting SAT scores	12
% submitting ACT scores	37
Average HS GPA	3.8
% submitting high school GPA	100
% graduated top 10% of class	27
% graduated top 25% of class	57
% graduated top 50% of class	85
% submitting high school rank	25

Important Dates

Early action	
Apply by	11/1
Notified by	Rolling
Regular	
Apply by	2/1
Notified by	Rolling
Nonfall registration?	Yes

FINANCIAL FACTS

Annual tuition (First-year)	NR ($51,910)
Food and housing	$17,190
Required fees	$600
Books and supplies	$1,000
Average need-based scholarship (First-year)	$41,066 ($39,393)
% students with need rec. need-based scholarship or grant aid (First-year)	99 (99)
% students with need rec. non-need-based scholarship or grant aid (First-year)	13 (12)
% students with need rec. need-based self-help aid (First-year)	76 (70)
% students rec. any financial aid (First-year)	97 (98)
% UG borrow to pay for school	58
Average cumulative indebtedness	$26,189
% of students with need fully met (First-year)	39 (33)
Average % of student need met (First-year)	88 (87)

UNIVERSITY OF DELAWARE

Undergraduate Admissions, Newark, DE 19716 • Admissions: 302-831-2126

Survey Snapshot
Intramural sports are popular
Great off-campus food
Great library

RATINGS

Quality of Life	86
Fire Safety	60*
Green	88
Academic	79
Profs Interesting	86
Profs Accessible	89
Admissions	88
Financial Aid	83

CAMPUS LIFE

Type of school	Public
Environment	Town

Students

Degree-seeking undergrad enrollment	18,592
% male/female/not reported	39/61/0
% from out of state	65
% First-year from public high school	80
% First-year live on campus	90
% Ugrads live on campus	38
# of fraternities (% join)	26 (22)
# of sororities (% join)	21 (27)
% Asian	6
% Black or African American	6
% Hispanic	10
% Native American	<1
% Pacific Islander	<1
% Race and/or ethnicity unknown	2
% Two or more races	5
% White	67
% International	3
# of countries represented	77

CAMPUS MENTAL HEALTH SERVICES

Offers mental health/wellness program	Yes
Mental health training available to students	Yes
Employs Chief Wellness Officer	Yes
Peer-to-peer mental health offerings	Yes
Counseling center has guidelines or accreditation	Yes
Mental health/well-being courses	Yes

ACADEMICS

% students returning for sophomore year	92
% students graduating within 4 years	72
% students graduating within 6 years	81
Calendar	4-1-4
Student/faculty ratio	13:1
Most common class size 20–29.	(24%)
Most common lab/discussion size 20–29.	(40%)

Most Popular Majors

Finance; Psychology; Communication

Applicants Often Prefer

Penn State University Park, University of Maryland, College Park

Applicants Sometimes Prefer

Rutgers University New Brunswick, Temple University

STUDENTS SAY "..."

Academics

The University of Delaware provides "strong academic programs, particularly in STEM, and the accessibility of hands-on research opportunities for undergraduates." With the only R1 designation in the state, students enjoy "many opportunities for undergraduate research and paid summer internships." For instance, those studying astronomy can visit the Mount Cuba Astronomical Observatory and utilize the computer lab, telescopes, and "go onto the roof of the building and use handmade astrolabes to track the movement of stars." Similarly, students studying information systems have the opportunity to "use simulations and work with real data to solve business problems, and some professors encourage group projects that mimic professional work environments." Students find it gratifying to take on community-improvement projects, such as addressing Heat Awareness Week: "It helped me step outside of my comfort zone [and] actively participate in discussions." Lively classroom environments are a common motif campus-wide, and students value that "professors are knowledgeable, approachable, and invested in student success, offering support both academically and professionally." Not only are professors said to have "helped me transition from high school to college easily," but the "wonderful and amazing staff" also "do their best to work with my schedule and treat me like an honorary member of the university!" One UD student summed it up best, saying: "Overall, my academic experience has been challenging but very rewarding, with strong support from faculty and ample opportunities for hands-on learning, collaboration, and intellectual growth."

Campus Life

Routines at UD are "fast-paced and collaborative, with students spending their days in classes, labs, research, and club activities, and their free time studying with friends, attending campus events, going to the gym, or exploring Main Street." For many, clubs anchor their busy day, giving students a chance to expand on their academic interests and socialize, as with "the University of Delaware's Sustainability Committee, where I engage with faculty and graduate students and construct plans to improve campus sustainability practices" or Caesura, UD'S literary magazine, where one can "connect with other students inside and outside of the English department." Sports also give UD students the chance to mingle, and "Spikeball, volleyball (on the sand courts), soccer, [and] football" are popular intramurals. Esports are also on the rise: "It is such an up-and-coming 'sport,' and I'm glad to see UD encouraging students to play." Students looking to cut loose love the "extremely strong Greek life presence" on campus and say the campus feels like "a mix of intellectually well-behaved students, and a mix of energetic 'party animals.'" Overall, students agree: "There is no shortage of fun here."

Student Body

Students say there's a wide variety of students here, united by how they're "both driven and grounded. Many students balance full course loads with jobs, research, internships, athletics, or family responsibilities, which creates a culture of accountability and resilience." In the classroom, students value UD's "diversity of backgrounds, perspectives, and ambitions. You can sit next to someone who is the first in their family to attend college, someone preparing for medical or law school, and someone building a startup, all in the same lecture." Specifically, one student values friends who encourage "asking questions and helping me understand topics I'm confused about." In agreement, another student describes peers that are "supportive and collaborative rather than overly competitive, which makes it easier to build connections both inside and outside the classroom." Many do so by striking a "good balance between working hard and having fun." Whether it's on campus or part of Greek life, "there's a large emphasis on getting involved because you will 100% meet your people if you try something out." All in all, "it feels like a campus full of people who are ambitious, but also real and down-to-earth."

UNIVERSITY OF DELAWARE

Financial Aid: 302-831-0520 • E-Mail: admissions@udel.edu • Website: udel.edu

THE PRINCETON REVIEW SAYS

Admissions

The school reports that its standardized testing policy for use in admission for Fall 2026 is Test Optional. The Princeton Review suggests that interested applicants consult with the school for the most up-to-date standardized testing policies. *Very important factors considered include:* rigor of secondary school record, academic GPA, state residency. *Important factors considered include:* application essay, recommendation(s), extracurricular activities, talent/ability, character/personal qualities, volunteer work, work experience. *Other factors considered include:* class rank, standardized test scores, interview, first generation, geographical residence, level of applicant's interest. High school diploma is required and GED is accepted. *Academic units required:* 4 English, 3 math, 3 science, 2 science labs, 2 language (other than English), 4 history/social studies, 2 academic electives. *Academic units recommended:* 4 English, 4 math, 4 science, 3 science labs, 4 language (other than English), 4 history/social studies, 2 academic electives.

Financial Aid

Students should submit: FAFSA. Priority filing deadline is 1/15. The Princeton Review suggests that all financial aid forms be submitted as soon as possible. *Need-based scholarships/grants offered:* Federal Pell; Federal SEOG; State scholarships/grants; Private scholarships; College/university scholarship or grant aid from institutional funds. *Loan aid offered:* Federal Direct Subsidized Loans; Federal Direct Unsubsidized Loans; Direct PLUS loans. Federal Work-Study Program available. Institutional employment available.

The Inside Word

UD is state assisted but privately governed, and the school is expressly committed to supporting Delawarean students, who compose about 30 percent of each incoming class. More details and samples of qualifying high school curricula are available on the admissions department website. In all admissions decisions, UD considers the entirety of a student's application; there are no minimum test scores or GPAs.

THE SCHOOL SAYS

From the Admissions Office

"The University of Delaware was chartered in 1743 and is located in Newark, DE, a vibrant college town midway between New York City and Washington, D.C. At UD, you can go from a concert in our music halls to a lecture on bioengineering to a tour of the ancient world in our study abroad program. For each of our 18,000+ undergraduate students, we foster connections: connections to ideas, to professors and to alumni, connections that can be cultivated into assets for the future. In each of our 150+ majors, our broad academic selections and our priority for hands-on research is designed to stimulate a passion for learning, curiosity and a connection with the larger world.

"Our distinguished faculty includes internationally known authors, scientists, business professionals and artists. State-of-the-art facilities support UD's academic, research and service activities. You'll find campus life is welcoming, enriched by distinguished speakers from various fields, NCAA Division I intercollegiate athletics, 400-plus student organizations, and a host of cultural activities."

SELECTIVITY

# of total applicants	40,943
% of total applicants accepted	73
% of total acceptees attending	15
# of in-state applicants	4,036
% of in-state applicants accepted	69
# of out-of-state-applicants	34,751
% of applicants accepted from out of state	74
# of international applicants	2,156
% of international applicants accepted	58
# offered a place on the wait list	2,584
# admitted from wait list	711

First-Year Profile

Testing policy	Test Optional
Range SAT composite	1240–1390
Range SAT EBRW	620–710
Range SAT math	610–690
Range ACT composite	27–32
% submitting SAT scores	23
% submitting ACT scores	3
Average HS GPA	3.9
% submitting high school GPA	98
% graduated top 10% of class	27
% graduated top 25% of class	60
% graduated top 50% of class	92
% submitting high school rank	32

Important Dates

Early action	
Apply by	11/1
Notified by	1/31
Regular	
Apply by	1/15
Notified by	Rolling, 11/1
Nonfall registration?	Yes

FINANCIAL FACTS*

Annual in-state tuition	$15,280
Annual out-of-state tuition	$40,840
Food and housing	$15,974
Required fees	$2,380
Books and supplies	$1,250
Average need-based scholarship (First-year)	$14,836 ($15,929)
% students with need rec. need-based scholarship or grant aid (First-year)	92 (98)
% students with need rec. non-need-based scholarship or grant aid (First-year)	10 (12)
% students with need rec. need-based self-help aid (First-year)	76 (71)
% students rec. any financial aid (First-year)	76 (83)
% UG borrow to pay for school	59
Average cumulative indebtedness	$38,652
% of students with need fully met (First-year)	14 (16)
Average % of student need met (First-year)	61 (64)

* Most recently reported data at time of printing. Scan the QR code to find the latest updates.

University of Denver

2199 South University Boulevard, Denver, CO 80208 • Admissions: 303-871-2036

Survey Snapshot
Lots of conservative students
Students are happy
Classroom facilities are great

RATINGS

Quality of Life	89
Fire Safety	90
Green	93
Academic	85
Profs Interesting	92
Profs Accessible	94
Admissions	87
Financial Aid	91

CAMPUS LIFE

Type of school	Private
Environment	Metropolis

Students

Degree-seeking undergrad enrollment	5,660
% male/female/not reported	46/54/0
% from out of state	67
% First-year live on campus	89
% Ugrads live on campus	45
# of fraternities (% join)	12 (24)
# of sororities (% join)	11 (21)
% Asian	4
% Black or African American	3
% Hispanic	16
% Native American	<1
% Pacific Islander	<1
% Race and/or ethnicity unknown	2
% Two or more races	7
% White	64
% International	3
# of countries represented	80

CAMPUS MENTAL HEALTH SERVICES

Offers mental health/wellness program	Yes
Mental health training available to students	Yes
Employs Chief Wellness Officer	Yes
Peer-to-peer mental health offerings	Yes
Counseling center has guidelines or accreditation	Yes
Mental health/well-being courses	Yes, for-credit

ACADEMICS

% students returning for sophomore year	89
% students graduating within 4 years	65
% students graduating within 6 years	74
Calendar	Quarter
Student/faculty ratio	10:1
Most common class size 10–19.	(43%)
Most common lab/discussion size 10–19.	(55%)

Most Popular Majors

Psychology; International Relations and Affairs; Business Statistics

Applicants Often Prefer

Colorado College, Colorado State University, University of Colorado Boulder

Applicants Sometimes Prefer

Boston University, The George Washington University, Santa Clara University, Southern Methodist University, University of Puget Sound, University of Southern California, University of Vermont

STUDENTS SAY "..."

Academics

My overall experience has been amazing, say students at the University of Denver. Given that they also describe the school as "extremely academically rigorous," that happiness can be partly credited to the professors, who students say are "helpful, interesting, informed, enthusiastic, resourceful, and truly [caring]." As one student elaborates, "For an institution that is highly focused on research, I've been so impressed with how invested my professors are in teaching. The majority of the professors I've had have been active researchers but still give their all to the class." Students also enjoy the wide range of classes available, like those that are service-learning and "allow for time to be spent outside the classroom applying what is learned on lecture days." Other specific examples include "a class in game design" that involved building "our own board games" and an anthropology class called "Museums and Public Culture that featured several trips to museums around Denver." Many students cite the James C. Kennedy Mountain Campus, the 724-acre campus near Roosevelt National Forest, as a positive and engaging part of their academic experience, with one business student spending a weekend there for "team-building activities and other workshops." Students appreciate their DU experience: "I am always learning something new and interesting, whether from class, guest lectures, clubs, events, or my friends."

Campus Life

Students enjoy "the natural beauty surrounding our campus" and swear by the location's scenery. Skiing and snowboarding are popular activities during the winter, and the Kennedy Mountain Campus "allows students to spend time hiking and rock climbing during the weekends." Beyond outdoor recreation, a wide array of extracurriculars reflect the varied interests of the student body, including the student newspaper and the undergraduate research journal as well as organizations like the Society of Physics Students and Divest DU, a "student organization dedicated to pushing the board to divest from fossil fuels." For a lot of students, athletics is a big part of daily life, whether it's playing sports or attending events. "Rugby is super popular and club sports are huge." And, as one student emphatically responds, "Don't forget our love of hockey!" Greek life is also popular, but students say, "it definitely does not dominate social life." As one student explains, "Everyone has their own interests, and they can usually find someone else who shares it with them, so community is built around that. We are all unique!"

Student Body

DU offers "a really strong sense of community and lots of incredible academic talent." One student describes the community as the "perfect size in my opinion—small enough to see familiar faces, but large enough to meet new ones." It's a "very outdoorsy" and social environment where students "love to interact, whether that's through clubs and organizations, on-campus jobs, or just hanging out at coffee shops." Many students note that a typical student at DU "tends to be from a wealthier background than most people." The student body is "predominately white, but there are students of color and LGBTQIA+ students as well," says one student, adding that there "are also plenty of POC, WOC, and LGBT groups, resources, and support on campus." Another student adds, "I feel free to be myself and express myself here, which I wouldn't at other schools." Peers tend to be "driven academically" and "committed, engaged, and caring." It's a place with students who are "all very opinionated and fight for a lot of things, which is nice to see," says one student. Another adds that the students share a "dedication to environmental initiatives, and social justice in general."

Financial Aid: 303-871-4020 • E-Mail: admission@du.edu • Website: www.du.edu

THE PRINCETON REVIEW SAYS

Admissions

The school reports that its standardized testing policy for use in admission for Fall 2026 is Test Optional. The Princeton Review suggests that interested applicants consult with the school for the most up-to-date standardized testing policies. *Very important factors considered include:* rigor of secondary school record, academic GPA. *Important factors considered include:* application essay, recommendation(s). *Other factors considered include:* class rank, standardized test scores, extracurricular activities, talent/ability, character/personal qualities, first generation, alumni/ae relation, geographical residence, state residency, volunteer work, work experience, level of applicant's interest. High school diploma is required and GED is accepted. *Academic units recommended:* 4 English, 3 math, 3 science, 2 science labs, 2 language (other than English), 3 social studies.

Financial Aid

Students should submit: FAFSA; CSS PROFILE. Priority filing deadline is 2/15. The Princeton Review suggests that all financial aid forms be submitted as soon as possible. *Need-based scholarships/grants offered:* Federal Pell; Federal SEOG; State scholarships/grants; Private scholarships; College/university scholarship or grant aid from institutional funds. *Loan aid offered:* Federal Direct Subsidized Loans; Federal Direct Unsubsidized Loans; Direct PLUS loans; College/university loans from institutional funds. Admitted students will be notified of awards on or about 3/1. Federal Work-Study Program available. Institutional employment available.

The Inside Word

Admission officers at University of Denver take a holistic approach to the application process. Therefore, they strive to look beyond quantitative factors and will also review your essay, recommendations, and extracurricular activities. The average high school GPA has been steadily rising each year, and is now up to a 3.8, so stay on top of your classes.

THE SCHOOL SAYS

From the Admissions Office

"At the University of Denver—in our setting of great natural beauty, cultural richness, and intellectual energy—you'll experience meaningful interaction with professors who set you on paths toward personal discovery, paths that can change the course of your future. Our diverse student body, engaged faculty, and prime location provide a culture of opportunity that is unique and unrivaled. DU is continually developing educational initiatives that help students prepare for an ever-changing world. Our Living and Learning Communities and Pioneer Leadership Program provide extracurricular and co-curricular programming in specialized areas; the Partners in Scholarship (PinS) program funds undergraduate research for students wishing to pursue a topic of personal interest in greater depth; and nearly 80 percent of our students are taking advantage of invaluable internship opportunities in laboratories, corporate offices, government agencies, and cultural settings. One of the university's signature offerings is the Cherrington Global Scholars program, which allows students to study abroad at the same cost of a quarter spent on campus at DU. Undergraduate students can choose from over 100 programs in over 40 countries; we have partner institutions on every continent except Antarctica! Outside the classroom, DU students put ideas and ideals into action. They are active members of our community and they take advantage of the numerous recreational opportunities available to them, including club, intramural, and 17 Division I sports. Whatever their majors and interests, DU students are inspired by Denver's Rocky Mountain spirit of exploration and openness, and are encouraged to engage in and personalize their educational journey."

SELECTIVITY

# of total applicants	16,637
% of total applicants accepted	85
% of total acceptees attending	8
# of in-state applicants	5,623
% of in-state applicants accepted	85
# of out-of-state-applicants	10,033
% of applicants accepted from out of state	88
# of international applicants	981
% of international applicants accepted	63
# of early decision applicants	273
% of early decision applicants accepted	85
# offered a place on the wait list	22
# admitted from wait list	0

First-Year Profile

Testing policy	Test Optional
Range SAT composite	1160–1360
Range SAT EBRW	600–700
Range SAT math	560–670
Range ACT composite	27–32
% submitting SAT scores	25
% submitting ACT scores	11
Average HS GPA	3.7
% submitting high school GPA	99
% graduated top 10% of class	34
% graduated top 25% of class	65
% graduated top 50% of class	93
% submitting high school rank	22

Important Dates

Early decision	
Apply by	11/1
Notified by	12/15
Other ED Apply by	1/15
Other ED Notified by	2/20
Early action	
Apply by	11/1
Notified by	1/15
Regular	
Apply by	1/15
Notified by	3/15
Nonfall registration?	Yes

FINANCIAL FACTS

Annual tuition	$63,720
Food and housing	$18,815
Required fees	$1,584
Books and supplies	$1,000
Average need-based scholarship (First-year)	$44,171 ($48,039)
% students with need rec. need-based scholarship or grant aid (First-year)	100 (100)
% students with need rec. non-need-based scholarship or grant aid (First-year)	29 (27)
% students with need rec. need-based self-help aid (First-year)	57 (64)
% students rec. any financial aid (First-year)	99 (100)
% UG borrow to pay for school	41
Average cumulative indebtedness	$30,116
% of students with need fully met (First-year)	35 (35)
Average % of student need met (First-year)	86 (88)

UNIVERSITY OF FLORIDA

201 Criser Hall, Gainesville, FL 32611 • Admissions: 352-392-1365

Survey Snapshot
Great library
Career services are great
Alumni active on campus

RATINGS	
Quality of Life	85
Fire Safety	90
Green	60*
Academic	77
Profs Interesting	83
Profs Accessible	90
Admissions	96
Financial Aid	94

CAMPUS LIFE

Type of school	Public
Environment	City

Students

Degree-seeking undergrad enrollment	36,625
% male/female/not reported	46/54/0
% from out of state	14
% First-year from public high school	82
% First-year live on campus	68
% Ugrads live on campus	23
# of fraternities (% join)	26 (17)
# of sororities (% join)	26 (26)
% Asian	13
% Black or African American	5
% Hispanic	25
% Native American	<1
% Pacific Islander	<1
% Race and/or ethnicity unknown	2
% Two or more races	5
% White	48
% International	3
# of countries represented	122

CAMPUS MENTAL HEALTH SERVICES

Offers mental health/wellness program	Yes
Mental health training available to students	Yes
Employs Chief Wellness Officer	Yes
Peer-to-peer mental health offerings	Yes
Counseling center has guidelines or accreditation	Yes
Mental health/well-being courses	No

ACADEMICS

% students returning for sophomore year	97
% students graduating within 4 years	77
% students graduating within 6 years	92
Calendar	Semester
Student/faculty ratio	17:1

Most Popular Majors

Computer and Information Sciences; Biology/Biological Sciences; Finance

Applicants Also Look At

Florida Atlantic University, Florida Gulf Coast University, Florida International University, Florida State University, University of Central Florida, University of Georgia, University of Miami, University of North Florida, University of South Florida, University of Texas at Austin

STUDENTS SAY "..."

Academics

Located in the heart of the "Gator Nation," the University of Florida offers "one of the best educations in the nation." Students are proud that UF is "the best state school in Florida" and "one of the top public universities in the nation"; they also love that it's "a great school with a large alumni network," that there's plenty of "intellectual stimulation" to be found there, and that UF's "research opportunities are abundant." Though the school has "strong academic standards" across the board, programs in Business and Journalism are particularly "highly ranked." Students say that the university's size doesn't sacrifice individuals' ability to focus on their course of study: "Classes for your major are hard, but they prepare you for more than easier classes would. They better prepare you for your career." Moreover, "as a research university with nearly every graduate program imaginable, the opportunities are endless." Students praise the "truly incredible faculty and staff" and appreciate that "one of the greatest strengths of UF is the fact there is always someone to turn to for help." Class structure is still impacted by the school's size in that "lectures are 80–90 percent of class activities," but conversely, students love "having experts in my field teaching all of my classes for my major." If "breadth of opportunities" for a value price is a priority for you, "The Gator Nation is one where anyone can build a future for themselves."

Campus Life

Students with "tons of school spirit" will fit right in at the University of Florida, as "a lot of UF culture is based around sports." There's also a healthy share of party culture, with students stating that "bars are the big scene" in town and that "there is a really intense nightlife," and noting that Greek life "is a big deal in both the social and extracurricular scene." Those seeking other options will find them, however, as "There is literally a club for everyone at UF" as well as volunteer opportunities, like "at the hospital located on campus." Ultimately, you "make it what you want. You can party every day or you can study every day."

Student Body

While "everyone is different," "fraternity and sorority participation...dominates the student culture." Students are "hardworking and interested in getting ahead," and "even though UF is considered a party school, it is full of people who put their future careers first." "Students fit in by taking part in and participating in the various things our campus offers" and are often "busy and focused usually on one subject matter or area of interest to be involved in through extracurricular activities." Even though it's a large campus, one student remarks on the sense of community: "We're students? I thought we were all part of one big family!" They find each other "mostly accepting and friendly," but as a whole "hard to define. Gators are religious and non-religious, Greek and non-Greek, obsessed with athletics and some couldn't care less." Overall, the typical UF student "knows how to balance their school work and still have a good time."

University of Florida

Financial Aid: 352-294-2244 • E-Mail: admissions@ufl.edu • Website: www.ufl.edu

THE PRINCETON REVIEW SAYS

Admissions

The school reports that its standardized testing policy for use in admission for Fall 2026 will require applicants to submit either the SAT, ACT, or CLT. The Princeton Review suggests that interested applicants consult with the school for the most up-to-date standardized testing policies. *Very important factors considered include:* rigor of secondary school record, academic GPA, extracurricular activities, talent/ability. *Important factors considered include:* standardized test scores, application essay, character/personal qualities, volunteer work, work experience. *Other factors considered include:* first generation, geographical residence, state residency. High school diploma is required and GED is accepted. *Academic units required:* 4 English, 4 math, 3 science, 2 science labs, 2 language (other than English). *Academic units recommended:* 4 English, 4 math, 4 science, 4 language (other than English).

Financial Aid

Students should submit: FAFSA. Priority filing deadline is 5/1. The Princeton Review suggests that all financial aid forms be submitted as soon as possible. *Need-based scholarships/grants offered:* Federal Pell; Federal SEOG; State scholarships/grants; Private scholarships; College/university scholarship or grant aid from institutional funds. *Loan aid offered:* Federal Direct Subsidized Loans; Federal Direct Unsubsidized Loans; Direct PLUS loans. Admitted students will be notified of awards on a rolling basis beginning 2/22. Federal Work-Study Program available. Institutional employment available.

The Inside Word

Unlike many state universities, UF doesn't publish an admissions formula, saying rather that they use a "holistic review" process to determine candidates' eligibility. Their application's short-answer and essay questions are emphasized in factors considered, and first-generation college students from low-income backgrounds should take note of the Florida Opportunity Scholars program, which covers four years of tuition in full.

THE SCHOOL SAYS

From the Admissions Office

"Thirty-six percent of the student body is composed of graduate students. Within the undergraduate population, approximately 1,733 African-American students, 8,268 Hispanic students, and 4,073 Asian-American students attend UF. Ninety percent of the entering freshmen rank above the national mean of scores on standard entrance exams. UF consistently ranks near the top among public universities in the number of new National Merit and Achievement scholars in attendance.

"Students must submit the SAT or the ACT with or without the writing section. UF considers your highest section scores across all SAT test dates."

SELECTIVITY

# of total applicants	90,523
% of total applicants accepted	20
% of total acceptees attending	41
# of in-state applicants	42,172
% of in-state applicants accepted	22
# of out-of-state-applicants	39,420
% of applicants accepted from out of state	21
# of international applicants	8,931
% of international applicants accepted	10

First-Year Profile

Testing policy	SAT, ACT, or CLT Required
Range SAT composite	1340–1470
Range SAT EBRW	670–740
Range SAT math	660–750
Range ACT composite	29–33
% submitting SAT scores	78
% submitting ACT scores	39
Average HS GPA	3.9
% submitting high school GPA	97
% graduated top 10% of class	84
% graduated top 25% of class	98
% graduated top 50% of class	100
% submitting high school rank	87

Important Dates

Early action	
Apply by	11/1
Notified by	1/24
Regular	
Apply by	1/15
Notified by	3/13
Nonfall registration?	Yes

FINANCIAL FACTS*

Annual in-state tuition	$6,380
Annual out-of-state tuition	$30,900
Food and housing	$14,190
Books and supplies	$1,220
Average need-based scholarship (First-year)	$11,590 ($11,236)
% students with need rec. need-based scholarship or grant aid (First-year)	92 (95)
% students with need rec. non-need-based scholarship or grant aid (First-year)	38 (54)
% students with need rec. need-based self-help aid (First-year)	62 (50)
% students rec. any financial aid (First-year)	85 (91)
% UG borrow to pay for school	17
Average cumulative indebtedness	$18,706
% of students with need fully met (First-year)	70 (80)
Average % of student need met (First-year)	98 (99)

* Most recently reported data at time of printing. Scan the QR code to find the latest updates.

UNIVERSITY OF GEORGIA

Administration Building, Athens, GA 30602 • Admissions: 706-542-8776

Survey Snapshot
Great food on campus
Recreation facilities are great
Everyone loves the Bulldogs

RATINGS

Quality of Life	83
Fire Safety	89
Green	60*
Academic	81
Profs Interesting	88
Profs Accessible	90
Admissions	93
Financial Aid	88

CAMPUS LIFE

Type of school	Public
Environment	City

Students

Degree-seeking undergrad enrollment	32,115
% male/female/not reported	43/57/0
% from out of state	15
% First-year from public high school	74
% First-year live on campus	98
% Ugrads live on campus	66
# of fraternities (% join)	38 (23)
# of sororities (% join)	30 (34)
% Asian	13
% Black or African American	6
% Hispanic	8
% Native American	<1
% Pacific Islander	<1
% Race and/or ethnicity unknown	1
% Two or more races	4
% White	66
% International	1
# of countries represented	84

CAMPUS MENTAL HEALTH SERVICES

Offers mental health/wellness program	Yes
Mental health training available to students	Yes
Employs Chief Wellness Officer	Yes
Peer-to-peer mental health offerings	Yes
Counseling center has guidelines or accreditation	Yes
Mental health/well-being courses	Yes, for-credit

ACADEMICS

% students returning for sophomore year	94
% students graduating within 4 years	76
% students graduating within 6 years	90
Calendar	Semester
Student/faculty ratio	17:1
Most common class size 10–19.	(34%)

Most Popular Majors
Biology/Biological Sciences; Psychology; Finance

STUDENTS SAY "..."

Academics

The University of Georgia is the flagship school in the state's university system, offering 142 majors across 17 colleges and schools. Students can also earn a bachelor's degree on an accelerated timeline through the Double Dawgs program. The well-regarded Honors Program is a big draw, incorporating experiential learning, travel, research opportunities, and a summer internship program in New York, Washington D.C., or Savannah. One student says, "Many of my best classes and favorite teachers have come from the Honors program." Although the number of students in some lectures can be large, UGA has increased the availability of in-demand classes and reduced class sizes in others through the Small Class Initiative. Most students say that there are "more good teachers" than bad and that "once [you're] in your particular program, the teachers are outstanding and easy to reach." Another student agrees, stating, "My major-related classes are very small, and each student receives individual attention." It's clear that the faculty is supportive: "The professors really do want to see you at office hours if you have questions," and they "want to share their love of learning with you." The university strives to create an environment that fosters success, and students appreciate that "the study spaces are well-equipped and quiet." At UGA, the commitment to academic excellence is evident, as shown by the impressive 95 percent placement rate for employment or graduate school within 6 months of graduation.

Campus Life

To be a Dawg is to love UGA's hometown of Athens, which is full of coffee shops, restaurants, music venues, and a lively bar scene. As one student declares, "Downtown Athens is fabulous!" A love for football is almost a requirement at UGA, with students noting that "on Saturday afternoons in the fall, nearly everyone on campus is at the football game. It's a way of life here." One student happily agrees, "Everybody really gets behind the team, and Saturdays in Athens feel like mini vacations." Even after football season, the town still hums with activity. One student says, "The Athens music and art scene is very inspiring, and there are tons of opportunities for creativity here." The campus offers just as much enjoyment: "Fun is a part of daily life...with a dozen intramural sports each semester...and many community activities (multiple movie theaters, bowling allies, golf course)." As one student says, "There are so many organizations that everyone can find a place that will feel like home or find a place to meet new people." And while "it's no secret that UGA knows how to party"—fraternities and sororities are very popular at UGA—many students insist that "there is definitely plenty to do, even if you don't go Greek." As one student says, "Ultimate Frisbee, walks around the multiple parks, days lounging on North Campus, and spending lots of time downtown are a couple ways I like to have fun at school."

Student Body

"The typical student at UGA is one who knows how and when to study but allows himself or herself to have a very active social life," claims one student. Another adds that Dawgs are generally "smart, involved, and have a good time." While some students say that their peers "seem to be predominantly conservative," others note that "there are a great number of atypical students in the liberal arts," which "creates a unique and exciting student body with greatly contrasting opinions." Students say that "there is a social scene for everyone in Athens" because there are so many opportunities to meet people. It helps that most students "are usually involved in at least one organization, whether it be Greek, a club, or sports."

University of Georgia

Financial Aid: 706-542-6147 • E-Mail: adm-info@uga.edu • Website: www.uga.edu

THE PRINCETON REVIEW SAYS

Admissions

The school reports that its standardized testing policy for use in admission for Fall 2026 will require applicants to submit either the SAT or ACT. The Princeton Review suggests that interested applicants consult with the school for the most up-to-date standardized testing policies. *Very important factors considered include:* rigor of secondary school record, academic GPA. *Important factors considered include:* standardized test scores. *Other factors considered include:* application essay, recommendation(s), extracurricular activities, talent/ability, character/personal qualities, first generation, volunteer work, work experience. High school diploma is required and GED is accepted. *Academic units required:* 4 English, 4 math, 4 science, 2 science labs, 2 language (other than English), 3 social studies. *Academic units recommended:* 4 English, 4 math, 4 science, 2 science labs, 3 language (other than English), 3 social studies, 1 academic elective.

Financial Aid

Students should submit: FAFSA. Priority filing deadline is 12/15. The Princeton Review suggests that all financial aid forms be submitted as soon as possible. *Need-based scholarships/grants offered:* Federal Pell; Federal SEOG; State scholarships/grants; Private scholarships. *Loan aid offered:* Federal Direct Subsidized Loans; Federal Direct Unsubsidized Loans; Direct PLUS loans; State Loans; College/university loans from institutional funds. Federal Work-Study Program available. Institutional employment available.

The Inside Word

UGA is competitive, and if you fail to meet certain baseline curricular, GPA, and standardized- test-score floors, only exceptional talent elsewhere (a gift for the arts or, better still, throwing a football) will get you past the first cut. The HOPE and the Zell Miller Scholarships, which cover tuition and most school-related fees, are available to qualifying Georgia residents who demonstrate strong academic achievement. Check out the school's website for details and requirements. Georgia state residents who earn at least a 3.0 in high school will also have a large portion of their tuition paid.

THE SCHOOL SAYS

From the Admissions Office

"The University of Georgia offers students the advantages and resources of a top public research university, including a wide range of majors and exceptional academic facilities such as the 260,000 square-foot Miller Learning Center. At the same time, UGA provides opportunities more common to smaller, private schools, such as first-year seminars led by distinguished faculty and learning communities that connect students with similar academic interests. The university is committed to challenging its academically superior students in the classroom and beyond, with increased emphasis on undergraduate research, service-learning, and study abroad. UGA students taking advantage of such offerings find themselves well positioned to compete with the best undergraduates in the country, as evidenced by their recent string of successes in winning Rhodes, Marshall, Truman, and other major scholarships. The UGA campus, considered one of the most beautiful in the nation, adjoins vibrant downtown Athens. While Athens is renowned for its local music scene, UGA also houses the Performing Arts Center, the Hugh Hodgson School of Music, the Lamar Dodd School of Art, and the Georgia Museum of Art. Sports—from football to gymnastics—are also a major attraction, with UGA teams perennially ranked among the best in the country. To experience the excitement of UGA, most prospective students visit campus, a ninety-minute drive northeast of the Atlanta airport. See the admissions website to sign up for a tour with the Visitors Center, view the weekday schedule of admissions information sessions, and find application details. Applicants for first-year admission will be required to submit either the SAT or ACT. Students submitting only the ACT must also submit the optional ACT Writing Test."

SELECTIVITY

# of total applicants	42,430
% of total applicants accepted	38
% of total acceptees attending	38
# of in-state applicants	19,041
% of in-state applicants accepted	47
# of out-of-state-applicants	22,113
% of applicants accepted from out of state	31
# of international applicants	1,282
% of international applicants accepted	21
# offered a place on the wait list	3,620
# admitted from wait list	157

First-Year Profile

Testing policy	SAT or ACT Required
Range SAT composite	1220–1400
Range SAT EBRW	620–710
Range SAT math	600–710
Range ACT composite	26–32
% submitting SAT scores	70
% submitting ACT scores	46
Average HS GPA	4.2
% submitting high school GPA	100

Important Dates

Early action	
Apply by	10/15
Notified by	12/1
Regular	
Apply by	1/1
Nonfall registration?	Yes

FINANCIAL FACTS

Annual in-state tuition	$10,134
Annual out-of-state tuition	$31,804
Food and housing	$12,440
Required fees	$1,494
Books and supplies	$978
Average need-based scholarship (First-year)	$12,568 ($13,372)
% students with need rec. need-based scholarship or grant aid (First-year)	95 (96)
% students with need rec. non-need-based scholarship or grant aid (First-year)	18 (24)
% students with need rec. need-based self-help aid (First-year)	34 (30)
% students rec. any financial aid (First-year)	89 (91)
% UG borrow to pay for school	32
Average cumulative indebtedness	$20,890
% of students with need fully met (First-year)	22 (28)
Average % of student need met (First-year)	73 (78)

UNIVERSITY OF HAWAI'I—MĀNOA

2500 Campus Road, Honolulu, HI 96822-2301 • Admissions: 808-956-8975

Survey Snapshot
Students love Honolulu, HI
Recreation facilities are great
Students are happy

RATINGS

Quality of Life	85
Fire Safety	88
Green	96
Academic	75
Profs Interesting	82
Profs Accessible	87
Admissions	77
Financial Aid	88

CAMPUS LIFE

Type of school	Public
Environment	Metropolis

Students

Degree-seeking undergrad enrollment	15,341
% male/female/not reported	42/57/1
% from out of state	36
% First-year from public high school	80
% First-year live on campus	50
% Ugrads live on campus	19
# of fraternities (% join)	2 (NR)
# of sororities (% join)	3 (NR)
% Asian	34
% Black or African American	2
% Hispanic	2
% Native American	1
% Pacific Islander	17
% Race and/or ethnicity unknown	<1
% Two or more races	16
% White	25
% International	3
# of countries represented	62

CAMPUS MENTAL HEALTH SERVICES

Offers mental health/wellness program	Yes
Mental health training available to students	No
Employs Chief Wellness Officer	NR
Peer-to-peer mental health offerings	NR
Counseling center has guidelines or accreditation	No
Mental health/well-being courses	NR

ACADEMICS

% students returning for sophomore year	80
% students graduating within 4 years	40
Calendar	Semester
Student/faculty ratio	14:1
Most common class size 10–19.	(29%)
Most common lab/discussion size 10–19.	(45%)

Most Popular Majors

Computer Science; Biology/Biological Sciences; Marine Biology and Biological Oceanography

STUDENTS SAY "..."

Academics

This flagship school of the University of Hawai'i system offers more than 100 bachelor's programs to the 14,000 or so students who call the O'ahu campus home during the school year. Nearly 250 degree programs across 15 schools are available to students, but no matter the course of study, Hawai'i plays TA. "When someone goes to UH Manoa, they aren't expecting to receive an education grounded in a Native Hawaiian place of learning but that is exactly what they get. Whether they are learning the Hawaiian language, Hawaiian culture, or about the Hawaiian ecosystem, there is a lot for everyone that goes along with their major," says a student. "UH really incorporates how important Hawai'i really is."

Sciences are particularly strong here, and the language offerings are incredibly diverse (think Ilocano and Samoan). Teachers are "always willing to go the extra mile to help students by offering office hours" and many professors challenge students while simultaneously "letting us know what content will be useful in our future careers and/or graduate-level exams." However, the real gold here is in the added resources for extra help in classes. There is "free one-on-one tutoring" and review sessions through the learning center, a writing center, a learning emporium for certain subjects, and "[you] can even walk into the library where librarians will help to find sources for papers and guide students in a great direction."

Campus Life

UH Manoa is on an island that offers a bit of everything. Here you can find "the city, the country, the surf, the mountains, the malls, and so on and so on. Oahu has something to fit my every mood and need," says a student. There are always cultural festivals and activities, and Hawai'i is made for active people who "like to get lost in nature's beauty." Whether you're "running up Koko Head, swimming with dolphins on the west side, catching some rays between classes on the Waikiki strip, or jumping off rocks on the north shore, there's no way to escape the beauty that is Hawai'i." On the weekend, many local students travel home so the campus can get very quiet, but students do use their IDs for free bus transportation to explore the relatively small island and student services and student affairs are "excellent." As is common with college students, "many of us do not have enough money to enjoy the nightlife; therefore we enjoy our free time at the beach." Still, students "have work that we can't just blow off for a swim or something." People like to use the grill that the school has set up, and there are "always people walking from place to place until late at night, hanging out with friends in the courtyards, skateboarding, or cooking out."

Student Body

This group—mainly from the Asia-Pacific region and mainland USA, with the occasional European or South American throw in—is a "huge melting pot" that is just "filled with Aloha." An "incredible amount of culture is exhibited here," most of all the Hawaiian cool: "I have never been on another college campus where it is completely normal to ride your skateboard barefoot or walk around with your surfboard." This is good news for the plenty of exchange students from Asia are here "trying to have an American campus experience"; ROTC also has a "very large" presence. On the whole, this is a "very relaxed and cool" bunch of students with whom "you can strike up friendly conversations with strangers in the cafeteria, or while waiting to cross the street, or while ordering food."

University of Hawai'i—Mānoa

Financial Aid: 808-956-7251 • E-Mail: manoa.admissions@hawaii.edu • Website: manoa.hawaii.edu

THE PRINCETON REVIEW SAYS

Admissions

The school reports that its standardized testing policy for use in admission for Fall 2026 is Test Optional. The Princeton Review suggests that interested applicants consult with the school for the most up-to-date standardized testing policies. *Very important factors considered include:* rigor of secondary school record, academic GPA. *Important factors considered include:* state residency. *Other factors considered include:* class rank, standardized test scores, application essay, recommendation(s), extracurricular activities, talent/ability, geographical residence. High school diploma is required and GED is accepted. *Academic units required:* 4 English, 3 math, 3 science, 3 social studies, 5 academic electives.

Financial Aid

Students should submit: FAFSA. Priority filing deadline is 2/1. The Princeton Review suggests that all financial aid forms be submitted as soon as possible. *Need-based scholarships/grants offered:* Federal Pell; Federal SEOG; State scholarships/grants; Private scholarships; College/university scholarship or grant aid from institutional funds. *Loan aid offered:* Federal Direct Subsidized Loans; Federal Direct Unsubsidized Loans; Direct PLUS loans. Admitted students will be notified of awards on a rolling basis beginning 3/1. Federal Work-Study Program available. Institutional employment available.

The Inside Word

All students must have a minimum GPA of 2.8 and be in the top 40 percent of their high school class. All applicants are encouraged to apply by the priority consideration deadline of January 5, as this deadline increases your chance of receiving financial aid and student housing. Certain programs (nursing, social work, education, and others) may have earlier admission deadlines.

THE SCHOOL SAYS

From the Admissions Office

"Aloha and welcome to UH Manoa, the largest campus in the University of Hawai'i System. We are located on the island of O'ahu, in Honolulu's lush Manoa valley. With over 100 undergraduate majors, over 200 student organizations, and a variety of Division I and intramural sports to choose from, you will agree that UH Manoa is a great place for you to realize your academic, professional, and personal dreams.

"UH Manoa is one of only a handful of institutions to hold the distinction of being a land-, sea-, sun-, and space-grant research institution. Classified by the Carnegie Foundation as having 'very high research activity,' UH Manoa is known for its pioneering research in such fields as oceanography, astronomy, Pacific Islands and Asian area studies, linguistics, cancer research, and genetics.

"Applicants to UH Manoa are expected to have completed a college preparatory high school curriculum. All applicants are encouraged to apply for priority consideration. Applying by this deadline (January 5 for fall admission, September 1 for spring) increases your chance of receiving financial aid and student housing.

"Experience the University of Hawai'i at Manoa first hand. We welcome you to tour our Manoa campus guided by our very own Rainbow Warrior students."

SELECTIVITY

# of total applicants	17,389
% of total applicants accepted	88
% of total acceptees attending	22
# of in-state applicants	5,335
% of in-state applicants accepted	90
# of out-of-state-applicants	11,485
% of applicants accepted from out of state	88
# of international applicants	569
% of international applicants accepted	76

First-Year Profile

Testing policy	Test Optional
Average HS GPA	3.7
% submitting high school GPA	84
% graduated top 10% of class	28
% graduated top 25% of class	49
% graduated top 50% of class	82
% submitting high school rank	51

Important Dates

Regular	
Apply by	3/1
Notified by	Rolling, 9/1
Nonfall registration?	Yes

FINANCIAL FACTS

Annual in-state tuition	$11,760
Annual out-of-state tuition	$33,792
Food and housing	$15,690
Required fees	$882
Books and supplies	$1,330
Average need-based scholarship (First-year)	$12,102 ($12,425)
% students with need rec. need-based scholarship or grant aid (First-year)	97 (99)
% students with need rec. non-need-based scholarship or grant aid (First-year)	27 (30)
% students with need rec. need-based self-help aid (First-year)	47 (43)
% students rec. any financial aid (First-year)	67 (72)
% UG borrow to pay for school	40
Average cumulative indebtedness	$23,479
% of students with need fully met (First-year)	35 (38)
Average % of student need met (First-year)	75 (77)

UNIVERSITY OF HOUSTON

4302 University Drive, Houston, TX 77204 • Admissions: 713-743-1010

Survey Snapshot
Students love Houston, TX
Diverse student types interact on campus
Students get along with local community

RATINGS

Quality of Life	77
Fire Safety	94
Green	87
Academic	75
Profs Interesting	82
Profs Accessible	86
Admissions	85
Financial Aid	83

CAMPUS LIFE

Type of school	Public
Environment	Metropolis

Students

Degree-seeking undergrad enrollment	40,366
% male/female/not reported	49/51/0
% from out of state	2
% First-year from public high school	95
% First-year live on campus	36
% Ugrads live on campus	16
# of fraternities (% join)	16 (3)
# of sororities (% join)	17 (4)
% Asian	22
% Black or African American	13
% Hispanic	38
% Native American	<1
% Pacific Islander	<1
% Race and/or ethnicity unknown	2
% Two or more races	3
% White	16
% International	6
# of countries represented	119

CAMPUS MENTAL HEALTH SERVICES

Offers mental health/wellness program	Yes
Mental health training available to students	Yes
Employs Chief Wellness Officer	Yes
Peer-to-peer mental health offerings	Yes
Counseling center has guidelines or accreditation	Yes
Mental health/well-being courses	Yes, non-credit

ACADEMICS

% students returning for sophomore year	86
% students graduating within 4 years	43
% students graduating within 6 years	66
Calendar	Semester
Student/faculty ratio	23:1
Most common class size 10–19.	(24%)
Most common lab/discussion size 20–29.	(43%)

Most Popular Majors

Business Administration and Management; Psychology; Computer and Information Sciences

Applicants Also Look At

Texas A&M University—College Station, University of Texas at Austin

STUDENTS SAY "..."

Academics

As a large public research school, The University of Houston is able to offer more than 100 undergraduate degree programs. Whether you're in- or out-of-state, students consider their school to be "not very expensive for the quality of education you're getting," and the constant improvements help "you feel like your degree is appreciating in value over time along with the school itself." Students confirm that "the research and other academic opportunities... are very accessible to students who seek it out." This includes taking advantage of UH's vast alumni network (more than 325,000 and counting), not to mention its location in the corporate center of Houston, where "the opportunities that are provided are immense."

Faculty have "all taken a keen interest in student success and are very available outside the classroom." They are said to "do a good job of bringing the material to life and explaining it well," which students also attribute to the variety of classes, from the discussion-based to those with innovative methods and projects. There are also "case competitions...sponsored by real local communities, and there is a chance to win money prizes if we advance to first place." This built-in real-world experience is buoyed by "the dedication and expertise of the career advisors at this institution, [who] have significantly contributed to students' success in navigating their professional paths." A student says that "Overall, the academic experience at the University of Houston is marked by quality instruction and a strong focus on preparing students for success beyond the classroom."

Campus Life

A majority of the student body are commuters, and one notes that "between classes, we love to visit the coffee spots on campus and work/talk." While some do think the school "could be more commuter friendly," they describe "lots of clubs and activities...and places and events to meet new people and make new friends." With 37,000 undergraduates, there are "so many people and possibilities for experiences and connections": you can "cheer on the [Division I] Coogs!" or visit "markets, booths and other activities that happen a couple times a month." Students also mention an active student body with "events that are accessible to anyone who wishes to join," and "a lot of clubs to join that are relevant to your major." University of Houston's overall vibe might be best summed up by its walkability: "The campus is beautiful and the nature is amazing, it makes the walks to class so peaceful." There's always something to see and do, and it's "all very well designed and enjoyable to be in."

Student Body

Students are "very accepting" and match "the diversity one sees across the city of Houston" and are "ambitious people who are aiming to get their dream job after [completing] college." They appreciate that the school "enables you to work and get an education, without having to sacrifice one for the other," and this eye towards the future means "the vibe is less party-focused, with students caring about getting through and moving into career opportunities." That said, whether coming from the "large number of commuter students" or not, those wishing to partake in the social aspects of UH find themselves in "a tight-knit community with many events and social spaces to commune and get to know each other." As one student says of their peers, "I know I can rely on them," and indeed, suggests that you can rely on finding "people with forward-thinking ideas and a passion for learning."

UNIVERSITY OF HOUSTON

Financial Aid: 713-743-1010 • E-Mail: admissions@uh.edu • Website: www.uh.edu

THE PRINCETON REVIEW SAYS

Admissions

The school reports that its standardized testing policy for use in admission for Fall 2026 is Test Optional. The Princeton Review suggests that interested applicants consult with the school for the most up-to-date standardized testing policies. *Important factors considered include:* academic GPA, standardized test scores. *Other factors considered include:* rigor of secondary school record, class rank, application essay, extracurricular activities, talent/ability, volunteer work, work experience. High school diploma is required and GED is accepted. *Academic units required:* 4 English, 4 math, 3 science, 3 social studies.

Financial Aid

Students should submit: FAFSA; State aid form. Priority filing deadline is 1/15. The Princeton Review suggests that all financial aid forms be submitted as soon as possible. *Need-based scholarships/grants offered:* Federal Pell; Federal SEOG; State scholarships/grants; Private scholarships; College/university scholarship or grant aid from institutional funds; United Negro College Fund. *Loan aid offered:* Federal Direct Subsidized Loans; Federal Direct Unsubsidized Loans; Direct PLUS loans; State Loans. Admitted students will be notified of awards on a rolling basis. Federal Work-Study Program available. Institutional employment available.

The Inside Word

Students who meet the State of Texas Uniform Admissions Policy and satisfy a certain scale of requirements are assured admission. But even if your grades aren't seemingly up to par, the admissions committee will consider students individually based on a holistic review of certain aspects, such as first-generation, socioeconomic background, rigor of high school curriculum, family responsibilities, special talents, public service, and strong letters of recommendation or a persuasive statement explaining your special circumstances.

THE SCHOOL SAYS

From the Admissions Office

"The University of Houston is a public research university recognized throughout the world as a leader in energy and health research, law, business, and environmental education. Located in America's fourth-largest city, the University of Houston is one of the most ethnically diverse metropolitan research universities in the United States. Its 47,000 students hail from 111 countries.

"In addition to preparing its students to succeed in today's global economy, the University of Houston also is a catalyst within its own community-changing lives through health, education, and outreach projects that help build a future for children in Houston, in Texas, and in the world.

"Other distinctive merits of the University of Houston include the establishment of a Phi Beta Kappa chapter, which indicates a strong foundation for undergraduate education and academic achievement, a historic Division I athletic program, with premier facilities, top-level arts programs, and an internationally recognized faculty including winners of the National Medal of Science, Pulitzer, and Tony awards; and members of prestigious National Academies. The Princeton Review has chosen the University of Houston for inclusion in its guidebook of the nation's best colleges.

"Discover the greatness of the University of Houston's dynamic campus of more than 895 acres—nestled just minutes from Houston's bustling theater and museum districts—where innovative teaching, revolutionary research, and nationally recognized and motivated students work together to create a globally competitive educational environment."

SELECTIVITY

# of total applicants	34,738
% of total applicants accepted	76
% of total acceptees attending	25
# of in-state applicants	28,049
% of in-state applicants accepted	77
# of out-of-state-applicants	4,940
% of applicants accepted from out of state	63
# of international applicants	1,750
% of international applicants accepted	85

First-Year Profile

Testing policy	Test Optional
Range SAT composite	1140–1310
Range SAT EBRW	570–660
Range SAT math	560–660
Range ACT composite	22–28
% submitting SAT scores	55
% submitting ACT scores	7
Average HS GPA	3.5
% submitting high school GPA	98
% graduated top 10% of class	25
% graduated top 25% of class	59
% graduated top 50% of class	90
% submitting high school rank	72

Important Dates

Regular	
Apply by	6/1
Nonfall registration?	Yes

FINANCIAL FACTS

Annual in-state tuition	$10,856
Annual out-of-state tuition	$26,744
Food and housing	$11,286
Required fees	$1,032
Books and supplies	$1,430
Average need-based scholarship (First-year)	$11,895 ($12,066)
% students with need rec. need-based scholarship or grant aid (First-year)	90 (92)
% students with need rec. non-need-based scholarship or grant aid (First-year)	2 (3)
% students with need rec. need-based self-help aid (First-year)	70 (66)
% students rec. any financial aid (First-year)	77 (84)
% UG borrow to pay for school	43
Average cumulative indebtedness	$22,495
% of students with need fully met (First-year)	10 (10)
Average % of student need met (First-year)	59 (57)

University of Idaho

875 Perimeter Drive MS 2282, Moscow, ID 83844-2282 • Admissions: 208-885-6326

Survey Snapshot
Students are happy
Great library
Students love Moscow, ID

RATINGS

Quality of Life	87
Fire Safety	88
Green	98
Academic	80
Profs Interesting	86
Profs Accessible	90
Admissions	84
Financial Aid	78

CAMPUS LIFE

Type of school	Public
Environment	Town

Students

Degree-seeking undergrad enrollment	7,978
% male/female/not reported	51/49/0
% from out of state	30
% First-year live on campus	82
% Ugrads live on campus	39
# of fraternities (% join)	19 (22)
# of sororities (% join)	10 (22)
% Asian	1
% Black or African American	1
% Hispanic	10
% Native American	1
% Pacific Islander	<1
% Race and/or ethnicity unknown	3
% Two or more races	5
% White	74
% International	5
# of countries represented	46

CAMPUS MENTAL HEALTH SERVICES

Offers mental health/wellness program	Yes
Mental health training available to students	Yes
Employs Chief Wellness Officer	No
Peer-to-peer mental health offerings	NR
Counseling center has guidelines or accreditation	No
Mental health/well-being courses	Yes, non-credit

ACADEMICS

% students returning for sophomore year	77
% students graduating within 4 years	43
% students graduating within 6 years	59
Calendar	Semester
Student/faculty ratio	18:1
Most common class size 1–9.	(32%)
Most common lab/discussion size 10–19.	(53%)

Most Popular Majors
Mechanical Engineering; Psychology; Marketing/Marketing Management

STUDENTS SAY "..."

Academics

University of Idaho is truly a school that invests in its students. Despite its large size, the university manages to create a "personalized learning experience" for all undergrads. Idaho also provides numerous "networking opportunities" for their students. One student explains, "Being here at UI, I've had the chance to meet many people in industry, which helped me land an internship at NASA JPL this past summer." Academically, Idaho offers students a wide range of stellar departments. However, undergrads especially like to tout the fantastic "engineering, agriculture, business, and law programs." Fortunately, no matter what you choose to study, the university is "incredible at creating an environment [in which] to build great relationships between professors and students." Though it's certainly helped by the fact that "the faculty here really cares about the students and genuinely wants to see them succeed." Undergrads appreciate that their professors help them become "well-educated students with the ability to think." Faculty are also happy to "host study sessions [in preparation] for exams and quizzes, and they are willing to answer all of your questions." And, best of all, Idaho professors "are very interesting and really bring their lectures to life."

Campus Life

Undergrads at Idaho happily report that "there are always a lot of activities going on around campus." For starters, the student recreation center is often a big draw where students can "work out, play a variety of indoor sports, take classes, climb the rock wall, or just hang out." Students also love to explore the "two arboretums on campus." Idaho also has "a very involved Greek system that is always holding a philanthropic event somewhere on campus or in the community." The university sponsors a number of great cultural affairs including "an amazing Jazz Festival, Native American celebrations, African American celebrations, and many many more throughout the year." In fact, "on the weekends there is almost always [an] event to attend that is hosted by an organization at the university, whether it is just for fun or to raise money for a cause." Finally, students also love taking advantage of everything hometown Moscow has to offer. As one pleased Vandal elaborates, "There is usually something going on every night, be it trivia nights at local restaurants, local musicians playing at a coffee shop, or a book signing at Book People."

Student Body

On the surface, the student body at University of Idaho might appear a bit homogenous; "most people are white," and it often feels like the vast majority hail from "Idaho, Washington, or Oregon." Nevertheless, the "population is slowly becoming more and more diverse." This is partially thanks to a "surprising number of international students." In turn, "this creates a unique opportunity to learn from people of different cultures." Undergrads also take great solace in the fact that their peers are "all very, very friendly" and united in their "kindness." Simply stroll across campus and you'll notice that "everyone smiles and says hi." An ecstatic student rushes to add, "My peers are the most supportive and uplifting people I've ever been surrounded by.... It's not uncommon to see students giving directions to lost tours or inviting perfect strangers to something like the farmers market or a film downtown." A lot of these Idaho Vandals also find common ground in their love of the outdoors, with many students looking to "take advantage of Moscow Mountain nearby for hiking, mountain biking, or snowshoeing." Finally, when it comes to political leanings, we're told that Idaho has an "unusually large number of libertarian-minded students here." Thankfully, most undergrads "are very respectful, even when they strongly disagree." As one contemplative student states, "We rarely talk about tolerance here, but we act on it daily."

University of Idaho

Financial Aid: 208-885-6312 • E-Mail: admissions@uidaho.edu • Website: www.uidaho.edu

THE PRINCETON REVIEW SAYS

Admissions

The school reports that its standardized testing policy for use in admission for Fall 2026 is Test Optional. The Princeton Review suggests that interested applicants consult with the school for the most up-to-date standardized testing policies. *Very important factors considered include:* academic GPA, standardized test scores. High school diploma is required and GED is accepted. *Academic units required:* 4 English, 3 math, 3 science, 1 science lab, 2.5 social studies, 1 history, 2 visual/performing arts.

Financial Aid

The Princeton Review suggests that all financial aid forms be submitted as soon as possible. *Need-based scholarships/grants offered:* Federal Pell; Federal SEOG; State scholarships/grants; Private scholarships; College/university scholarship or grant aid from institutional funds. *Loan aid offered:* Federal Direct Subsidized Loans; Federal Direct Unsubsidized Loans; Direct PLUS loans; College/university loans from institutional funds. Admitted students will be notified of awards on a rolling basis beginning 2/1. Federal Work-Study Program available. Institutional employment available.

The Inside Word

The admissions process at University of Idaho is fairly by the book. Indeed, officers closely consider each applicant's GPA and make sure that every candidate has completed their core requirements. Both homeschooled and GED students will have to submit three letters of recommendation attesting to their academic abilities. They'll also be expected to draft a written statement that discusses their educational goals and professional objectives.

THE SCHOOL SAYS

From the Admissions Office

"A leading public research university in the West, the University of Idaho offers a traditional residential campus experience in a spectacular natural setting. It provides more than 100 undergraduate degree options and graduate degrees in 65 discipline areas, which helps provide unprecedented undergraduate research opportunities. Idaho has become known for its academic excellence, student-centered, experiential learning, and an exceptional student living environment that coupled with dedicated faculty, world-class facilities, and renowned research has produced a proven track record of high-achieving graduates. The student population of 13,000 includes first-generation college students and ethnically diverse scholars, who select from hands-on learning experiences in the colleges of Agricultural and Life Sciences; Art and Architecture; Business and Economics; Education; Engineering; Law; Letters, Arts, and Social Sciences; Natural Resources; and Science. The university also provides medical education for the state through the WWAMI program. Increasingly its interdisciplinary teams involved in environmental, sustainability, engagement, and resource management have gained national recognition. Idaho combines the strength of a large, land grant university with the intimacy of a small learning community to help students succeed and become leaders. It is home to the Vandals and competes in the Big Sky Conference."

SELECTIVITY

# of total applicants	13,126
% of total applicants accepted	75
% of total acceptees attending	20
# of in-state applicants	6,937
% of in-state applicants accepted	87
# of out-of-state-applicants	3,588
% of applicants accepted from out of state	81
# of international applicants	2,601
% of international applicants accepted	33

First-Year Profile

Testing policy	Test Optional
Range SAT composite	990–1200
Range SAT EBRW	500–620
Range SAT math	470–600
Range ACT composite	21–28
% submitting SAT scores	53
% submitting ACT scores	5
Average HS GPA	3.5
% submitting high school GPA	97
% graduated top 10% of class	18
% graduated top 25% of class	42
% graduated top 50% of class	71
% submitting high school rank	56

Important Dates

Nonfall registration?	Yes

FINANCIAL FACTS

Annual in-state tuition	$9,824
Annual out-of-state tuition	$29,300
Food and housing	$12,995
Books and supplies	$1,227
% UG borrow to pay for school	45
Average cumulative indebtedness	$21,018

University of Illinois at Urbana-Champaign

601 E. John St., Champaign, IL 61820-5711 • Admissions: 217-333-0302

Survey Snapshot
Great library
Recreation facilities are great
Frats and sororities are popular

RATINGS

Quality of Life	77
Fire Safety	60*
Green	96
Academic	83
Profs Interesting	84
Profs Accessible	90
Admissions	93
Financial Aid	86

CAMPUS LIFE

Type of school	Public
Environment	City

Students

Degree-seeking undergrad enrollment	37,562
% male/female/not reported	51/49/<1
% from out of state	17
% First-year live on campus	99
% Ugrads live on campus	37
# of fraternities (% join)	NR (15)
# of sororities (% join)	NR (21)
% Asian	22
% Black or African American	5
% Hispanic	15
% Native American	<1
% Pacific Islander	<1
% Race and/or ethnicity unknown	2
% Two or more races	4
% White	37
% International	14
# of countries represented	90

CAMPUS MENTAL HEALTH SERVICES

Offers mental health/wellness program	Yes
Mental health training available to students	Yes
Employs Chief Wellness Officer	NR
Peer-to-peer mental health offerings	NR
Counseling center has guidelines or accreditation	No
Mental health/well-being courses	NR

ACADEMICS

% students returning for sophomore year	95
% students graduating within 4 years	74
% students graduating within 6 years	86
Calendar	Semester
Student/faculty ratio	20:1
Most common class size 10–19.	(24%)
Most common lab/discussion size 20–29.	(34%)

Applicants Also Look At

Georgia Institute of Technology, Indiana University—Bloomington, Loyola University Chicago, New York University, Northwestern University, Purdue University—West Lafayette, University of California—Berkeley, University of California—Davis, University of California—Los Angeles, University of Michigan—Ann Arbor, University of Wisconsin—Madison

STUDENTS SAY "..."

Academics

University of Illinois at Urbana-Champaign has "an amazing reputation and strong programs in many different majors," including notable programs in business and engineering. One student chose U of I for "the breadth of the engineering program and the opportunities associated with it." Students appreciate the variety and quality of academic programs available, with one student saying, "[I knew] that if I needed to change majors (which I ended up doing), I would still be getting a great degree." No matter your major, there are "a lot of resources to supplement your studies." These include a "fantastic library system," "phenomenal advisors," and "countless on-campus resources such as the Career Center, Writers Workshop, Office of Minority Student Affairs, free tutoring services, and the Study Abroad Office." Moreover, the university boasts more than 175 research centers and institutes, which are "such a benefit for research projects" and one reason why "the research support is phenomenal on campus." The "very approachable" faculty emphasizes hands-on experience and applied learning in their classes. One student shares, "The fieldwork (tons of fieldwork) that they make us do really helped in getting used to the field." These "wonderful" professors are "not just good at research but also instructing and mentoring." As one student points out, "As an underclassman, many classes I've taken have been with very large classes," but "the professors are engaging and know how to keep a class of 700-plus entertained." Getting admitted to U of I is no small feat; as one student says, "It obviously takes a lot to get into this school." However, the hard work pays off, as the university reports that 90 percent of graduates are employed or continuing their education within six months of graduation.

Campus Life

U of I has an "incredibly lively" campus with "thousands of clubs, two gyms and several sports facilities, and [an] array of establishments to explore on Green Street." The university also has "one of the largest Greek communities in the country," with more than 60 residential Greek houses. Students note that while "people here like to party…there are a lot of other fun things to do." According to some students, "the bars in downtown Champaign are great and super relaxed, plus there is an awesome music scene that most people don't expect from a college town." Arts and culture thrive here, and many enjoy "going to the Krannert Center to see plays or concerts" at one of the center's four theaters or even just going to "movie theater and mall...on Saturday afternoons. Champaign-Urbana seems small to city kids, but to me, it's the land of opportunity." Life at U of I "is busy, but rewarding," and these students wouldn't have it any other way.

Student Body

While the size of the university can seem daunting at first, "there are so many opportunities to get involved on the floor of your residence hall, in organizations, [and] in your classes, that it's hard not to make friends and close relationships." The reasonable in-state tuition attracts a lot of students from Illinois, so "a majority of the students that you meet here will be from the Chicago suburbs." However, you'll also find "a wide variety of students from all across the world." One student says, "University of Illinois houses so many different types of students that the only way we are alike is our dedication to getting an education and our loyalty to UIUC." Most students value these differences: "The diversity of the students here is astounding. Race, religion, major, you've got it all."

University of Illinois at Urbana-Champaign

Financial Aid: 217-333-0100 • E-Mail: admissions@illinois.edu • Website: illinois.edu

THE PRINCETON REVIEW SAYS

Admissions

The school reports that its standardized testing policy for use in admission for Fall 2026 is Test Optional. The Princeton Review suggests that interested applicants consult with the school for the most up-to-date standardized testing policies. *Very important factors considered include:* rigor of secondary school record, academic GPA, extracurricular activities, talent/ability, character/personal qualities, first generation. *Important factors considered include:* application essay. *Other factors considered include:* standardized test scores, geographical residence, state residency, volunteer work, work experience. High school diploma is required and GED is accepted. *Academic units required:* 4 English, 3 math, 2 science, 2 science labs, 2 language (other than English), 2 social studies, 2 academic electives. *Academic units recommended:* 4 English, 4 math, 4 science, 4 science labs, 4 language (other than English), 4 social studies, 4 academic electives.

Financial Aid

Students should submit: FAFSA. Priority filing deadline is 3/15. The Princeton Review suggests that all financial aid forms be submitted as soon as possible. *Need-based scholarships/grants offered:* Federal Pell; Federal SEOG; State scholarships/grants; Private scholarships; College/university scholarship or grant aid from institutional funds; United Negro College Fund. *Loan aid offered:* Federal Direct Subsidized Loans; Federal Direct Unsubsidized Loans; Direct PLUS loans; College/university loans from institutional funds. Admitted students will be notified of awards on a rolling basis beginning 2/15. Federal Work-Study Program available. Institutional employment available.

The Inside Word

The University of Illinois' application review process distinguishes itself from that of many state schools in that every application is considered individually—no small feat for a campus of over 30,000 students. U of I's applicant pool tends to be self-selective, and those without sufficient qualifications won't make the cut.

THE SCHOOL SAYS

From the Admissions Office

"The University of Illinois Urbana-Champaign offers multiple pathways for students to join our community, including first-year and transfer admission options. No matter the path, our goal is to understand each applicant as a whole person. We use a holistic review process that considers academic achievement, course rigor, extracurricular involvement, personal experiences, and context. This allows us to recognize the unique strengths and perspectives each student brings.

"Illinois is test-optional, meaning students can choose whether to include ACT or SAT scores as part of their application. Students who feel their scores reflect their academic ability are encouraged to submit them, while those who do not may still present a strong application through other components.

"One important aspect of applying to Illinois is that students apply directly to a major. This means you should carefully explore your academic interests and select a first-choice major that aligns with your goals. You may also select a second-choice major, which can provide an additional opportunity for admission consideration. Because some programs are more competitive than others, we encourage students to be thoughtful and intentional in their selections.

"We are committed to expanding access and supporting student success from application through graduation. Whether you are applying as a first-year or transfer student, Illinois provides a rigorous, supportive environment where students can grow academically, personally, and professionally."

SELECTIVITY

# of total applicants	83,045
% of total applicants accepted	37
% of total acceptees attending	30
# of in-state applicants	29,419
% of in-state applicants accepted	49
# of out-of-state-applicants	32,702
% of applicants accepted from out of state	29
# of international applicants	20,924
% of international applicants accepted	30
# offered a place on the wait list	6,826
# admitted from wait list	1

First-Year Profile

Testing policy	Test Optional
Range SAT composite	1390–1520
Range SAT EBRW	690–750
Range SAT math	700–790
Range ACT composite	31–34
% submitting SAT scores	43
% submitting ACT scores	14
% graduated top 10% of class	62
% graduated top 25% of class	89
% graduated top 50% of class	99
% submitting high school rank	22

Important Dates

Early action	
Apply by	11/1
Notified by	1/30
Regular	
Apply by	1/5
Notified by	3/6
Nonfall registration?	No

FINANCIAL FACTS

Annual in-state tuition	$12,992
Annual out-of-state tuition	$33,344
Food and housing	$15,184
Required fees	$5,054
Books and supplies	$1,200
Average need-based scholarship (First-year)	$24,235 ($25,878)
% students with need rec. need-based scholarship or grant aid (First-year)	91 (89)
% students with need rec. non-need-based scholarship or grant aid (First-year)	23 (35)
% students with need rec. need-based self-help aid (First-year)	60 (59)
% UG borrow to pay for school	38
Average cumulative indebtedness	$22,040
% of students with need fully met (First-year)	22 (33)
Average % of student need met (First-year)	79 (82)

UNIVERSITY OF IOWA

101 Jessup Hall, Iowa City, IA 52242-1396 • Admissions: 319-335-3847

Survey Snapshot
Classroom facilities are great
Lab facilities are great
Internships are widely available

RATINGS

Quality of Life	**80**
Fire Safety	**89**
Green	**98**
Academic	**86**
Profs Interesting	**91**
Profs Accessible	**95**
Admissions	**86**
Financial Aid	**88**

CAMPUS LIFE

Type of school	Public
Environment	City

Students

Degree-seeking undergrad enrollment	22,965
% male/female/not reported	42/57/1
% from out of state	43
% First-year from public high school	90
% First-year live on campus	92
% Ugrads live on campus	28
# of fraternities (% join)	27 (15)
# of sororities (% join)	23 (17)
% Asian	4
% Black or African American	3
% Hispanic	9
% Native American	<1
% Pacific Islander	<1
% Race and/or ethnicity unknown	5
% Two or more races	4
% White	74
% International	1
# of countries represented	56

CAMPUS MENTAL HEALTH SERVICES

Offers mental health/wellness program	Yes
Mental health training available to students	Yes
Employs Chief Wellness Officer	NR
Peer-to-peer mental health offerings	NR
Counseling center has guidelines or accreditation	No
Mental health/well-being courses	NR

ACADEMICS

% students returning for sophomore year	91
% students graduating within 4 years	61
% students graduating within 6 years	76
Calendar	Semester
Student/faculty ratio	17:1
Most common class size 10–19.	(29%)
Most common lab/discussion size 20–29.	(50%)

Most Popular Majors

Exercise Science and Kinesiology; Psychology; Business/Commerce

Applicants Also Look At

Illinois State University, Indiana University—Bloomington, Iowa State University, Loyola University Chicago, Marquette University, Miami University, Michigan State University, The Ohio State University—Columbus, Purdue University—West Lafayette, University of Illinois at Chicago, University of Illinois at Urbana—Champaign, University of Minnesota—Twin Cities, University of Missouri, University of Northern Iowa

STUDENTS SAY "..."

Academics

As the oldest institution of higher education in the state, the University of Iowa takes pride in its long history of educating Hawkeyes. Among the "[wide] range of degree programs," undergrads single out particularly strong offerings in pre-med, nursing, writing, journalism, and engineering. Many students appreciate that core curriculum "requirements are minimal," and the school's emphasis on interdisciplinary study gives students the flexibility to "make [their] education [their] own." Students say that one of the best things about attending the university is getting a "great education" at a "reasonable price." As one satisfied student says, "The University of Iowa is a platform to launch yourself to the top of your field at an affordable price." The University of Iowa (aka Iowa) is a "Big Ten university full of exciting opportunities." One of the engines behind those opportunities is the Iowa faculty, who are "very engaged with students and are always helpful to any student looking to push their learning beyond the classroom." Professors also try to bring their own experience into the classroom, with students saying they "do a nice job of balancing lectures with real-world applications of the material." Career preparation is a key pillar of an Iowa education, as evidenced by the impressive 96 percent employment and graduate school placement rate. All in all, Hawkeyes value the opportunities they're afforded by the school and its faculty, who are "passionate, encouraging, and invested in the success of their students both inside and outside of academia."

Campus Life

At this sports-loving Division I school, you'll feel the full force of Hawkeye spirit in the fall; students say that "during football season, Saturdays get crazy. There is just a sea of black and gold swarming toward the stadium. Nothing can really compare to 70,000 Hawkeye fans in one place." But even if football isn't your thing or if it's the off-season, the university provides plenty of events for students. "There are always concerts and comedians on campus, many are even free to students. There are also free movies shown at the Iowa Memorial Union." With more than 600 student clubs and organizations to choose from, you can find anything from professional groups to social clubs to intramural sports that match your interests. For a more "small-college feel," students can choose to reside in one of 10 living-learning communities, connecting with others who share their major or interests. Students report that "there is always a party going on here at Iowa," but there are also plenty of other options for fun. The recreation center frequently organizes trips "to go rock-climbing, camping, hiking, or kayaking." For those who want to do something a little less strenuous, the "vibrant downtown" of Iowa City is "literally across the street from campus" and is a popular destination with "unique places to eat, shop, or go out." All in all, students agree that "life is pretty fun at The University of Iowa."

Student Body

On the whole, Hawkeyes are "laid-back," "friendly, hardworking, and studious." The size and reputation of the school contribute to a diverse environment, including "a strong LGBTQA presence on campus, [and] different religious places near campus." This "very social" and inclusive community has "many different organizations for minorities, religions, and everything else here on campus. I couldn't imagine someone coming here and not being able to find a student organization that is for them." As one student puts it, "Everyone is unique and has a different story, but that's one thing that makes life here so great. You have the ability to meet people from around the country and around the world, and we all get to share the experience of college together."

UNIVERSITY OF IOWA

Financial Aid: 319-335-1450 • E-Mail: admissions@uiowa.edu • Website: www.uiowa.edu

THE PRINCETON REVIEW SAYS

Admissions

The school reports that its standardized testing policy for use in admission for Fall 2026 is Test Optional. The Princeton Review suggests that interested applicants consult with the school for the most up-to-date standardized testing policies. *Very important factors considered include:* rigor of secondary school record, academic GPA, standardized test scores. *Other factors considered include:* class rank, recommendation(s), talent/ability, character/personal qualities, state residency. High school diploma is required and GED is accepted. *Academic units required:* 4 English, 3 math, 3 science, 2 language (other than English), 3 social studies. *Academic units recommended:* 4 math.

Financial Aid

Students should submit: FAFSA. Priority filing deadline is 12/1. The Princeton Review suggests that all financial aid forms be submitted as soon as possible. *Need-based scholarships/grants offered:* Federal Pell; Federal SEOG; State scholarships/grants; Private scholarships; College/university scholarship or grant aid from institutional funds. *Loan aid offered:* Federal Direct Subsidized Loans; Federal Direct Unsubsidized Loans; Direct PLUS loans; College/university loans from institutional funds; State Loans. Admitted students will be notified of awards on a rolling basis. Federal Work-Study Program available. Institutional employment available.

The Inside Word

Like many large public universities, admission officers at the University of Iowa rely heavily on quantitative factors when determining an applicant's status. Therefore, GPA and standardized test scores (if submitted) will likely hold the most weight. The university's "no harm" test-optional policy means submitted ACT/SAT scores are considered only if they strengthen your application. It should also be noted that due to space concerns and the high volume of applications in recent years, students who met the admission requirements but submitted their applications after March 1 were placed on a waitlist. This may or may not happen again, but to be on the safe side, you may want to submit your application by March 1.

THE SCHOOL SAYS

From the Admissions Office

"The University of Iowa offers all of the opportunities and resources of a large, research university, while putting a strong emphasis on the undergraduate student experience. As the first public university to enroll men and women on an equal basis, Iowa is proud of its history in providing a world-class education to students from all backgrounds. Today, the University of Iowa offers nationally ranked academic programs, strong pre-professional programs in the health sciences and law, and access to world-renowned faculty. With an emphasis on small class sizes, students interact with faculty both inside and outside the classroom. Located in one of the top college towns in America, Iowa City's vibrant downtown seamlessly blends with the heart of campus, making it easy to access academic resources and belong to a larger, welcoming community."

SELECTIVITY

# of total applicants	31,454
% of total applicants accepted	80
% of total acceptees attending	22
# of in-state applicants	5,892
% of in-state applicants accepted	85
# of out-of-state-applicants	24,060
% of applicants accepted from out of state	81
# of international applicants	1,502
% of international applicants accepted	42
# offered a place on the wait list	12
# admitted from wait list	1

First-Year Profile

Testing policy	Test Optional
Range SAT composite	1130–1320
Range SAT EBRW	560–670
Range SAT math	550–660
Range ACT composite	21–28
% submitting SAT scores	22
% submitting ACT scores	60
Average HS GPA	3.9
% submitting high school GPA	99
% graduated top 10% of class	33
% graduated top 25% of class	68
% graduated top 50% of class	92
% submitting high school rank	34

Important Dates

Regular	
Apply by	5/1
Notified by	Rolling, 8/1
Nonfall registration?	Yes

FINANCIAL FACTS*

Annual in-state tuition	$11,622
Annual out-of-state tuition	$33,710
Food and housing	$14,022
Books and supplies	$950
Average need-based scholarship (First-year)	$11,802 ($11,938)
% students with need rec. need-based scholarship or grant aid (First-year)	89 (91)
% students with need rec. non-need-based scholarship or grant aid (First-year)	11 (13)
% students with need rec. need-based self-help aid (First-year)	66 (68)
% students rec. any financial aid (First-year)	69 (76)
% UG borrow to pay for school	51
Average cumulative indebtedness	$32,536
% of students with need fully met (First-year)	13 (14)
Average % of student need met (First-year)	51 (53)

* Most recently reported data at time of printing. Scan the QR code to find the latest updates.

University of Kansas

1450 Jayhawk Blvd., Lawrence, KS 66045 • Admissions: 785-864-3911

Survey Snapshot
Students love Lawrence, KS
Everyone loves the Jayhawks
Campus newspaper is popular

RATINGS	
Quality of Life	**92**
Fire Safety	**96**
Green	**60***
Academic	**79**
Profs Interesting	**86**
Profs Accessible	**93**
Admissions	**82**
Financial Aid	**89**

CAMPUS LIFE

Type of school	Public
Environment	City

Students

Degree-seeking undergrad enrollment	21,880
% male/female/not reported	46/54/0
% from out of state	35
% First-year live on campus	71
% Ugrads live on campus	25
# of fraternities (% join)	23 (14)
# of sororities (% join)	19 (28)
% Asian	6
% Black or African American	4
% Hispanic	12
% Native American	<1
% Pacific Islander	<1
% Race and/or ethnicity unknown	1
% Two or more races	6
% White	68
% International	3
# of countries represented	88

CAMPUS MENTAL HEALTH SERVICES

Offers mental health/wellness program	Yes
Mental health training available to students	Yes
Employs Chief Wellness Officer	Yes
Peer-to-peer mental health offerings	Yes
Counseling center has guidelines or accreditation	Yes
Mental health/well-being courses	No

ACADEMICS

% students returning for sophomore year	87
% students graduating within 4 years	56
% students graduating within 6 years	70
Calendar	Semester
Student/faculty ratio	18:1
Most common class size 10–19.	(29%)
Most common lab/discussion size 10–19.	(69%)

Most Popular Majors
Journalism; Psychology; Finance

Applicants Also Look At
Johnson County Community College, Kansas State University, University of Missouri, University of Nebraska—Lincoln, Wichita State University

STUDENTS SAY "..."

Academics

The University of Kansas provides "stimulating academics" and "a community that is passionate about the school." With an impressive array of over 400 degree and certificate programs, students can pursue their interests across a wide range of fields. The university has "abundant resources" available to undergrads, including the Center for Undergraduate Research & Fellowships, where students can explore "research opportunities" in nearly all disciplines. The faculty is another excellent resource; many professors are "actively engaged in research in their particular field." Students can also enhance their academic experience through "one of the best study abroad programs in the nation," with over 165 programs in more than 70 countries. Students recognize the value of these opportunities, with one emphasizing, "The experience outside of the classroom is what sets you up for success after college." Students also appreciate the faculty at KU. As one student explains, "The personalities and teaching styles of KU's professors vary widely, but all of the instructors I have had are fully engaged in teaching and truly enjoy helping students learn." Another students shares that "Teachers are always urging students to contact them with questions or visit their office hours." Overall, students agree that "the faculty is obviously willing to do what it takes to help" you succeed. This dedication to student success extends beyond graduation, as KU's "career center is committed to getting students hired."

Campus Life

Lawrence, Kansas, is often referred to as "the perfect college town." This lively campus has plenty of activities to keep students engaged. With over 500 student organizations to explore—everything from Greek life to chess clubs and intramural sports—there's something for everyone. In addition, KU's "Student Union Activities brings in comedians, authors, and movies on a regular basis," so there is "never a dull night" on campus. Sports are a big deal here, especially during the winter, when "KU basketball is our religion, and Allen Fieldhouse is our church." As one devoted Jayhawk explains, "I schedule everything in my life around the KU men's basketball schedule, as does much of the student population." But don't worry if sports aren't your thing; there are countless other ways to get involved and make the most of your time here. In addition to joining clubs or participating in sports, "the typical student probably volunteers in the community, has a part-time job, [and] has some special hobby (from rock climbing to tightrope walking)." Many students are also "very outdoorsy" and make the most of the nearby hills and lakes. When the weather is nice, "you can rent camping equipment from the rec for a weekend out at the lake" or "go rock climbing." Students also appreciate Lawrence's "great live music scene, cool coffee shops, and eclectic stores," as well as the popular bars and nightclubs. With such an array of entertainment and opportunities available, most students agree that KU provides an "incredible college experience."

Student Body

Students at KU are from "every county in Kansas, every state, and over 100 countries," reflecting many "different values and backgrounds" and a diverse array of personalities. As one student explains, "You have your 'here for a good time' types, absolutely rock-star scholars, and dedicated students who balance their GPA and their social calendar." Some students note that "there is definitely a big Greek life presence" on campus, and one student adds, "The Greek community does intermingle frequently with non-Greeks. I'm not Greek, but I see it a lot and have a lot of Greek friends." When it comes to making friends and fitting in, students agree that getting involved on campus is key. As one student illustrates, "There are so many opportunities at KU that it can seem a bit overwhelming, but students really find their niche and run with it."

University of Kansas

Financial Aid: 785-864-4700 • E-Mail: adm@ku.edu • Website: www.ku.edu

THE PRINCETON REVIEW SAYS

Admissions

The school reports that its standardized testing policy for use in admission for Fall 2026 is Test Optional. The Princeton Review suggests that interested applicants consult with the school for the most up-to-date standardized testing policies. *Very important factors considered include:* academic GPA. *Other factors considered include:* standardized test scores. High school diploma is required and GED is accepted. *Academic units recommended:* 4 English, 4 math, 3 science, 2 language (other than English), 2 social studies, 1 history.

Financial Aid

Students should submit: FAFSA. Priority filing deadline is 2/1. The Princeton Review suggests that all financial aid forms be submitted as soon as possible. *Need-based scholarships/grants offered:* Federal Pell; Federal SEOG; State scholarships/grants; Private scholarships; College/university scholarship or grant aid from institutional funds; Federal Nursing Scholarships. *Loan aid offered:* Federal Direct Subsidized Loans; Federal Direct Unsubsidized Loans; Direct PLUS loans; College/university loans from institutional funds. Admitted students will be notified of awards on a rolling basis beginning mid-February. Federal Work-Study Program available. Institutional employment available.

The Inside Word

KU has a great program for assured admission to the College of Liberal Arts and Sciences, the School of Education and Human Sciences, and the School of Social Welfare, so check the school's website for details and requirements to see if you qualify. Professional schools have different standards. The University of Kansas is Test Optional for both admissions and scholarships.

THE SCHOOL SAYS

From the Admissions Office

"The University of Kansas has a tradition of academic excellence. The mission of KU is to lift students and society by educating leaders, building healthy communities, and making discoveries that will change the world. Outstanding students from around the world attend KU for its outstanding academics, challenging opportunities, the Jayhawk community, and incredible value including four-year renewable scholarships. KU provides students exceptional opportunities in the University Honors Program, experiential learning, undergraduate research, internships, study abroad, and more than 500 clubs and organizations. The university is located in Lawrence (forty minutes from Kansas City), a vibrant community of 93,000 consistently recognized as one of the nation's top ten college towns.

"All students are encouraged to apply. KU does an individual review of each application. We consider many factors that are provided on the application such as cumulative high school GPA, ACT or SAT scores, GPA in the core curriculum, and strength of courses. We may also ask you to respond to short essay questions that will provide additional information to support your application."

SELECTIVITY

# of total applicants	22,187
% of total applicants accepted	93
% of total acceptees attending	25
# of in-state applicants	7,479
% of in-state applicants accepted	94
# of out-of-state-applicants	14,011
% of applicants accepted from out of state	92
# of international applicants	697
% of international applicants accepted	94

First-Year Profile

Testing policy	Test Optional
Range SAT composite	1080–1280
Range SAT EBRW	550–650
Range SAT math	520–640
Range ACT composite	20–28
% submitting SAT scores	7
% submitting ACT scores	51
Average HS GPA	3.7
% submitting high school GPA	98
% graduated top 10% of class	26
% graduated top 25% of class	53
% graduated top 50% of class	84
% submitting high school rank	53

Important Dates

Regular	
Apply by	One week before classes start
Notified by	Rolling, 7/1
Nonfall registration?	Yes

FINANCIAL FACTS

Annual in-state tuition	$11,298
Annual out-of-state tuition	$30,177
Food and housing	$11,798
Required fees	$1,155
Books and supplies	$1,224
Average need-based scholarship (First-year)	$11,972 ($12,980)
% students with need rec. need-based scholarship or grant aid (First-year)	87 (95)
% students with need rec. non-need-based scholarship or grant aid (First-year)	13 (15)
% students with need rec. need-based self-help aid (First-year)	54 (59)
% students rec. any financial aid (First-year)	83 (92)
% UG borrow to pay for school	47
Average cumulative indebtedness	$27,051
% of students with need fully met (First-year)	37 (40)
Average % of student need met (First-year)	77 (78)

University of Kentucky

101 Main Building, Lexington, KY 40506 • Admissions: 859-257-2000

Survey Snapshot
Dorms are like palaces
Everyone loves the Wildcats
Frats and sororities are popular

RATINGS

Quality of Life	85
Fire Safety	85
Green	88
Academic	76
Profs Interesting	83
Profs Accessible	88
Admissions	84
Financial Aid	80

CAMPUS LIFE

Type of school	Public
Environment	City

Students

Degree-seeking undergrad enrollment	26,479
% male/female/not reported	41/59/0
% from out of state	35
% First-year live on campus	85
% Ugrads live on campus	31
# of fraternities (% join)	17 (17)
# of sororities (% join)	14 (28)
% Asian	3
% Black or African American	6
% Hispanic	7
% Native American	<1
% Pacific Islander	<1
% Race and/or ethnicity unknown	1
% Two or more races	5
% White	76
% International	1
# of countries represented	82

CAMPUS MENTAL HEALTH SERVICES

Offers mental health/wellness program	Yes
Mental health training available to students	No
Employs Chief Wellness Officer	NR
Peer-to-peer mental health offerings	NR
Counseling center has guidelines or accreditation	No
Mental health/well-being courses	NR

ACADEMICS

% students returning for sophomore year	85
% students graduating within 4 years	58
% students graduating within 6 years	72
Calendar	Semester
Student/faculty ratio	18:1
Most common class size 20–29.	(32%)

Most Popular Majors

Marketing/Marketing Management; Finance; Registered Nursing/Registered Nurse

STUDENTS SAY "..."

Academics

Founded in 1865, the University of Kentucky in Lexington offers more than 200 academic programs to its undergraduate students. It is one of only eight institutions in the country with the full set of liberal arts, engineering, professional, agricultural and medical colleges. With a "great variety in majors and classes" available, many undergraduates find UK has "available opportunities for students in all fields of study." Enrollees find support outside their standard classroom work with "so many study abroad options" and the chance to "become involved in undergraduate research." Many courses also incorporate "active technology learning classrooms," and some degree programs have hybrid classes. From classroom to campus, Kentucky makes sure that "everything is there to help the students—all of the resources you could need."

Undergrads say the faculty is "passionate about giving us more than just degrees" and most have "a great base of knowledge, enthusiasm, and accessibility." Students enthusiastically recommend registering for courses with seasoned teachers who have industry experience because they "are the best at their job," and "are able to answer questions from personal experience more so than just textbook knowledge." But regardless of if you're learning from a TA or a tenured faculty member, undergrads appreciate the fact that their instructors "do their best to make the material interesting and engaging." Many enrollees also value "the availability of professors and their willingness to help" after class and during offices hours. "They are more than professors; they are mentors for me and networking connections for the field," says a student.

Campus Life

The University of Kentucky has made great efforts at "transforming itself into a more modern and thriving university city." "There is so much to do" at UK, and the "campus is close to downtown, so people will go out to eat or attend events happening there." The university is also located in "horse country and in a wonderful proximity to good hiking, so a lot of time is spent outdoors." During the week, you'll find students "[sitting] in common areas around campus to hang out and relax before the next class." After class, they will "usually study at the library or go to work" (UK has "a lot of opportunities for student employment"), but weekends are a time to let loose. "Sporting events are always popular," and students are "filled to the brim with pride." Home to a multitude of active Greek chapters, "Sorority/fraternity life is huge," as "Greek life is really important on campus." Beyond the Greek scene, "there are a lot of clubs that are very diverse and a lot of intramural sports," as well as opportunities to volunteer in Lexington and on campus.

Student Body

Many students express "a love for [their] school" and the "very friendly" community that comes with it. As one undergrad notes, "Big Blue Nation makes everyone feel a part of the school pride here at the University of Kentucky." The culture of being a Kentucky Wildcat unifies enrollees in many aspects of their college career. "Students of every major and discipline find commonality in a variety of things," including "great pride about the state of Kentucky and its values." And while the student body is diverse with "a healthy number of in-state and out-of-state students," as well as "many international students and nontraditional students," walking around campus, "there is a comfortable atmosphere," which "helps each student to learn how to communicate with people from many different backgrounds." "There isn't a sense of elitism here," but "students still value academia." In the end, "all of UK's students contribute to a very diverse atmosphere that creates its unique environment." As one student explains, "It's one big community, and people are so happy to engage in it."

UNIVERSITY OF KENTUCKY

Financial Aid: 859-257-3172 • E-Mail: admissions@uky.edu • Website: www.uky.edu

THE PRINCETON REVIEW SAYS

Admissions

The school reports that its standardized testing policy for use in admission for Fall 2026 is Test Optional. The Princeton Review suggests that interested applicants consult with the school for the most up-to-date standardized testing policies. *Very important factors considered include:* rigor of secondary school record, academic GPA, application essay. *Other factors considered include:* standardized test scores, recommendation(s), extracurricular activities, talent/ability, character/personal qualities, first generation, geographical residence, state residency, volunteer work, work experience. High school diploma is required and GED is accepted. *Academic units required:* 4 English, 3 math, 3 science, 1 science lab, 2 language (other than English), 3 social studies, 7 academic electives, 1 visual/performing arts. *Academic units recommended:* 1 computer science.

Financial Aid

Students should submit: FAFSA. The Princeton Review suggests that all financial aid forms be submitted as soon as possible. *Need-based scholarships/grants offered:* Federal Pell; Federal SEOG; State scholarships/grants; Private scholarships; College/university scholarship or grant aid from institutional funds. *Loan aid offered:* Federal Direct Subsidized Loans; Federal Direct Unsubsidized Loans; Direct PLUS loans; State Loans; College/university loans from institutional funds. Admitted students will be notified of awards on a rolling basis beginning 4/1. Federal Work-Study Program available.

The Inside Word

The University of Kentucky's admissions team is about as objective as they come. If you have the GPA, class rank, and test scores, you'll likely be welcomed into the Wildcat community. The university is continually looking to improve its selectivity, so hitting the books is a must if you want to be a serious contender. First-year applicants who have completed the pre-college curriculum, but do not have the requisite GPA, may be placed on a waitlist.

THE SCHOOL SAYS

From the Admissions Office

"The University of Kentucky has 16 degree-granting colleges, including the Lewis Honors College and the Graduate School. Only two percent of all colleges and universities in the country are comprehensive research-intensive institutions like UK.

"At UK, we don't just say we put students first in everything we do—we put our words into action. In the last 13 years alone, we've spent $6.5 billion transforming our campus. When you walk in your residence hall and first meet your roommate or meet up with your study group at the Gatton Student Center, you're walking into spaces that have been carefully designed with your success in mind. The heart of our campus—the academic core—is being revitalized. Just beyond beautiful Alumni Commons, new homes for the College of Communication and Information and the Martin School of Public Policy and Administration, along with the modernization of the White Hall Classroom Building, highlight the center of a campus built for collaboration.

"And in 2026, we'll open the largest academic building in the university's history, the 500,000 square feet Rankin Health Education Building. This state-of-the-art facility will house programs in the colleges of Medicine, Public Health, Health Sciences and Nursing, educating students for a new health care future. In Fall 2022, the university launched UK Invests, a first-of-its-kind holistic wellness program anchored in financial education and aimed at helping students secure a strong financial future.

"The university has a close connection with the city of Lexington, a vibrant, growing community with a culture students describe as close-knit, opportunity-rich and supportive of all things local. Students get the best of both worlds—urban bustle adjacent to campus and beautiful rolling hills, immaculate horse farms and outdoor adventures just a short drive out of town."

SELECTIVITY

# of total applicants	33,387
% of total applicants accepted	94
% of total acceptees attending	22
# of in-state applicants	9,087
% of in-state applicants accepted	95
# of out-of-state-applicants	23,214
% of applicants accepted from out of state	93
# of international applicants	1,086
% of international applicants accepted	90

First-Year Profile

Testing policy	Test Optional
Range SAT composite	1058–1270
Range SAT EBRW	540–650
Range SAT math	510–630
Range ACT composite	21–28
% submitting SAT scores	9
% submitting ACT scores	48
Average HS GPA	3.6
% submitting high school GPA	100
% graduated top 10% of class	28
% graduated top 25% of class	56
% graduated top 50% of class	84
% submitting high school rank	26

Important Dates

Early action	
Apply by	12/1
Regular	
Apply by	2/15
Notified by	Rolling, 8/1
Nonfall registration?	Yes

FINANCIAL FACTS*

Annual in-state tuition	$13,908
Annual out-of-state tuition	$35,164
Food and housing	$16,696
Books and supplies	$1,200
Average need-based scholarship (First-year)	$9,932 ($9,921)
% students with need rec. need-based scholarship or grant aid (First-year)	54 (52)
% students with need rec. non-need-based scholarship or grant aid (First-year)	88 (95)
% students with need rec. need-based self-help aid (First-year)	50 (50)
% UG borrow to pay for school	49
Average cumulative indebtedness	$34,922
% of students with need fully met (First-year)	11 (12)
Average % of student need met (First-year)	55 (57)

* Most recently reported data at time of printing. Scan the QR code to find the latest updates.

UNIVERSITY OF LOUISVILLE

2301 South Third Street, Louisville, KY 40292-0001 • Admissions: 502-852-6531

Survey Snapshot
Recreation facilities are great
Everyone loves the Cardinals
Students love Louisville, KY

RATINGS

Quality of Life	**78**
Fire Safety	**93**
Green	**95**
Academic	**75**
Profs Interesting	**82**
Profs Accessible	**88**
Admissions	**84**
Financial Aid	**85**

CAMPUS LIFE

Type of school	Public
Environment	Metropolis

Students

Degree-seeking undergrad enrollment	14,727
% male/female/not reported	44/56/0
% from out of state	24
% First-year from public high school	89
% First-year live on campus	64
% Ugrads live on campus	26
# of fraternities (% join)	14 (14)
# of sororities (% join)	19 (10)
% Asian	6
% Black or African American	16
% Hispanic	9
% Native American	<1
% Pacific Islander	<1
% Race and/or ethnicity unknown	<1
% Two or more races	6
% White	61
% International	2
# of countries represented	53

CAMPUS MENTAL HEALTH SERVICES

Offers mental health/wellness program	Yes
Mental health training available to students	Yes
Employs Chief Wellness Officer	Yes
Peer-to-peer mental health offerings	Yes
Counseling center has guidelines or accreditation	Yes
Mental health/well-being courses	Yes, for-credit

ACADEMICS

% students returning for sophomore year	82
% students graduating within 4 years	44
% students graduating within 6 years	61
Calendar	Semester
Student/faculty ratio	14:1
Most common class size 20–29.	(31%)

Most Popular Majors

Psychology; Registered Nursing/Registered Nurse; Biology/Biological Sciences

Applicants Also Look At

University of Kentucky

STUDENTS SAY "..."

Academics

The University of Louisville is a large research university that is part of the Kentucky state university system. The school provides "great STEM research" opportunities, and popular programs include the School of Medicine and the Speed School of Engineering. The academic experience is "very good" and many students also appreciate the classes that use a flipped classroom model, where more of class time is devoted to discussion or hands-on activities rather than lecture. Such learning experiences include field trips and opportunities to engage with the local community. One engineering student recounts working on a water filtration system that the class presented to the city's water utility, saying, "To be able to do something like that as [first years] was pretty cool." Professors at UofL are "passionate about the subject matter, knowledgeable, and care about their students" and overall, most students report positive experiences. As one student emphasizes, "Every professor I've had has been personable and understanding." The school's internship and research opportunities are also lauded, especially by engineering students who mention paid Co-op work with a variety of employers including NASA, GE, and Ford. For many enrollees, this "dedication to making students enter the workforce with applicable skills outside a degree" makes UofL stand out.

Campus Life

Students report spending a lot of their free time studying in the library or other academic buildings, but when students get a break from studying, they describe University of Louisville as a "beautiful campus" where, in warm weather, people flock to the "lawns to play sports games and/or have picnics." The school's activities also cater to a wide range of interests, with a special nod during the fall football season where "tailgates are the biggest events to go to." Intramural sports are also popular among many students, as well as working out in the recreation center. For those with a green thumb, UofL has a Garden Commons where volunteers help grow "free-to-pick, fresh, organic produce." One excited student explains, "I love gardening, so it's awesome we have this resource on campus." There are also "many creative events such as art galleries and poetry readings" happening on-campus, as well as clubs including the LGBT+ club, the commuter student club, the pre-pharmacy club, and the horseback riding club. As one student elaborates, "There are organizations ranging from helping people with their mental health to pickling different types of vegetables to research organizations for the STEM fields." Students note that Greek life is "pretty prominent but does not overrun the school"; it's possible to not participate and "still have a social life." For venturing off-campus, "People like to go to bars or find local restaurants to visit since there are so many," explains one student. Just as "lots of people gravitate towards Louisville's music scene," so too is there a scene for everyone at UofL.

Student Body

The overall atmosphere at University of Louisville is "supportive" and "feels like a family once you're there." As one student elaborates, "The community of this school is so embracing and kind." UofL is "a very diverse institution with students truly from every walk of life." The student body is "very inclusive" and "there is a large queer population." Students advocate for each other and are "quick to take action towards a better campus community." Undergraduates describe their peers as "academically driven," and "some of the smartest people I know." Many students also work while in school, balancing their classes with participating in programs such as the partnership between UPS and UofL, which pays tuition for students working the overnight shift at UPS. Many students agree the best thing about UofL is "the student body and how easy it is to find friends and a sense of belonging." As one student sums up, "If you ever need help with anything, there's always someone there to help you."

UNIVERSITY OF LOUISVILLE

Financial Aid: 502-852-5511 • E-Mail: admitme@louisville.edu • Website: www.louisville.edu

THE PRINCETON REVIEW SAYS

Admissions

The school reports that its standardized testing policy for use in admission for Fall 2026 is Test Optional. The Princeton Review suggests that interested applicants consult with the school for the most up-to-date standardized testing policies. *Very important factors considered include:* rigor of secondary school record, academic GPA. *Important factors considered include:* standardized test scores. *Other factors considered include:* class rank, application essay, recommendation(s), extracurricular activities, talent/ability, state residency, volunteer work, work experience. High school diploma is required and GED is accepted. *Academic units required:* 4 English, 3 math, 3 science, 1 science lab, 2 language (other than English), 3 social studies, 5 academic electives, 1 visual/performing arts. *Academic units recommended:* 4 math, 4 science, 3 language (other than English).

Financial Aid

Students should submit: FAFSA. The Princeton Review suggests that all financial aid forms be submitted as soon as possible. *Need-based scholarships/grants offered:* Federal Pell; Federal SEOG; State scholarships/grants; Private scholarships; College/university scholarship or grant aid from institutional funds. *Loan aid offered:* Federal Direct Subsidized Loans; Federal Direct Unsubsidized Loans; Direct PLUS loans. Admitted students will be notified of awards on a rolling basis. Federal Work-Study Program available. Institutional employment available.

The Inside Word

By and large, admission decisions at University of Louisville are highly dependent on quantitative data. This means that each applicant's class rank, GPA and standardized test scores (if submitted) will be of utmost importance. Attention will also be paid to course selection; a strong college prep curriculum should be a given. Requirements will vary depending on the specific school to which a candidate is applying. For example, the School of Music and the School of Nursing, to name a few, have additional requirements.

THE SCHOOL SAYS

From the Admissions Office

"The University of Louisville (UofL) has transformed into a premier metropolitan research university—and it keeps getting better. It is a tight knit community with the feel of a small college where you can walk anywhere on campus in only 10 minutes. Over the past ten years, it has dramatically improved its on-campus environment with the addition of new residence halls, new apartments near campus, a new state-of-the-art student recreation center, and restaurants and shopping near campus with the right mix of local flavor. Located in a vibrant city that is known worldwide for the Kentucky Derby, students quickly learn to navigate its great parks, discover local restaurants and explore a revitalized downtown and neighborhoods with an eclectic environment.

"With over 50 percent of our entering freshmen beginning their studies with college credit, UofL is a strong academic environment with opportunities inside and outside the classroom to prepare you for professional school or your first job. The city and UofL are closely linked, providing opportunities for internships, coops, part-time jobs and service-learning experiences. Our commitment to diversity has created a culture with support for LGBTQ+ students and students of all socioeconomic and ethnic backgrounds.

"Although widely known for our engineering, business and medical programs, we offer over 200 academic programs and in recent years have added undergraduate programs in Public Health, Social Work, Asian Studies and Latin American and Latino Studies, demonstrating a desire to prepare students for the 21st-century needs of our city, region and beyond."

SELECTIVITY

# of total applicants	15,668
% of total applicants accepted	79
% of total acceptees attending	25
# of in-state applicants	8,756
% of in-state applicants accepted	80
# of out-of-state-applicants	6,474
% of applicants accepted from out of state	82
# of international applicants	438
% of international applicants accepted	40

First-Year Profile

Testing policy	Test Optional
Range SAT composite	1010–1120
Range SAT EBRW	530–640
Range SAT math	510–630
Range ACT composite	19–27
% submitting SAT scores	18
% submitting ACT scores	85
Average HS GPA	3.6
% submitting high school GPA	100
% graduated top 10% of class	25
% graduated top 25% of class	52
% graduated top 50% of class	84
% submitting high school rank	33

Important Dates

Regular	
Apply by	8/1
Notified by	Rolling, 8/1
Nonfall registration?	Yes

FINANCIAL FACTS

Annual in-state tuition	$12,940
Annual out-of-state tuition	$28,978
Food and housing	$12,576
Required fees	$196
Books and supplies	$1,270
Average need-based scholarship (First-year)	$14,706 ($16,423)
% students with need rec. need-based scholarship or grant aid (First-year)	95 (99)
% students with need rec. non-need-based scholarship or grant aid (First-year)	10 (15)
% students with need rec. need-based self-help aid (First-year)	46 (41)
% students rec. any financial aid (First-year)	90 (92)
% UG borrow to pay for school	47
Average cumulative indebtedness	$25,854
% of students with need fully met (First-year)	15 (20)
Average % of student need met (First-year)	61 (65)

UNIVERSITY OF LYNCHBURG

1501 Lakeside Drive, Lynchburg, VA 24501 • Admissions: 434-544-8300

Survey Snapshot
Easy to get around campus
Intramural sports are popular
Theater is popular

RATINGS

Quality of Life	89
Fire Safety	85
Green	60*
Academic	85
Profs Interesting	92
Profs Accessible	94
Admissions	89
Financial Aid	88

CAMPUS LIFE

Type of school	Private
Affiliation	Disciples of Christ
Environment	City

Students

Degree-seeking undergrad enrollment	1,414
% male/female/not reported	43/57/0
% from out of state	24
% First-year from public high school	86
% First-year live on campus	85
% Ugrads live on campus	74
# of fraternities (% join)	3 (2)
# of sororities (% join)	5 (6)
% Asian	2
% Black or African American	8
% Hispanic	7
% Native American	<1
% Pacific Islander	<1
% Race and/or ethnicity unknown	7
% Two or more races	5
% White	58
% International	12
# of countries represented	32

CAMPUS MENTAL HEALTH SERVICES

Offers mental health/wellness program	Yes
Mental health training available to students	Yes
Employs Chief Wellness Officer	Yes
Peer-to-peer mental health offerings	No
Counseling center has guidelines or accreditation	Yes
Mental health/well-being courses	No

ACADEMICS

% students returning for sophomore year	59
% students graduating within 4 years	51
% students graduating within 6 years	59
Calendar	Semester
Student/faculty ratio	13:1
Most common class size 10–19.	(45%)
Most common lab/discussion size 10–19.	(67%)

Most Popular Majors

Exercise Physiology and Kinesiology; Registered Nursing/Registered Nurse; Business Administration and Management

Applicants Also Look At

George Mason University, James Madison University, Liberty University, Longwood University, Randolph College, Randolph-Macon College, Roanoke College, Virginia Commonwealth University, Virginia Tech, William & Mary

STUDENTS SAY "..."

Academics

Beneath the Blue Ridge Mountains in Lynchburg, Virginia, the University of Lynchburg students experience an "academic environment [that] is the perfect level of challenge and excitement." Lynchburg is "huge on community service" and opportunities on and around campus make it easy for students to "get out there and get involved in the local community." Students enjoy a "friendly environment" among peers who are "willing to help you out when needed." Students say that the academic environment is convivial, classes are "very discussion based and allow for conversation." Students appreciate that "class sizes are so small" and explain that this means "participation is necessary" from everyone. A low student-to-faculty ratio also means that it is "very easy to ask questions during class and meet with your professors" outside of class hours. One student in Lynchburg's well-regarded nursing program tells us "we have incredible faculty members who are caring, compassionate, and experienced. They go above and beyond for us each day to make us the best nurses possible." Lynchburg boasts "other amazing programs such as Exercise Physiology, Biology, Teaching, [and] Business," all of which "are backed by the liberal arts education that allows us to expand our thinking and look at the world in a broader view." "I have been given nothing but support and encouragement throughout my time in the program," one student tells us. This nurturing atmosphere helps students become "the best version of ourselves." It isn't uncommon to hear students say, "I wasn't very successful academically in high school but I have done extremely well in college. I would attribute that to the professors" who offer plenty of office hours to get in contact with them, as well as most classes having a class tutor with weekly study sessions to help you along with the class."

Campus Life

There is plenty going on around the University of Lynchburg campus to keep students busy. During the week "most people go to class and then have meetings for clubs," which are well attended at Lynchburg. "Very often, students are involved in at least two campus organizations," and it is a great way for them to get involved in the community: "Students spend a great deal of their out-of-class time working on planning events, service, and projects for these organizations." Athletics are popular on campus and "nearly 1 in 5 students is involved in Greek life." Students say they can "always fill any free time...exploring the city of Lynchburg," where they can check out "a movie, trampoline parks, skating rinks" or catch a bite downtown where "the restaurants and bars...are absolutely amazing." Outside the city, students can explore the foothills of the Blue Ridge Mountains where there are "lots of opportunities for hiking, cave diving, and rafting."

Student Body

Students at Lynchburg are described as "friendly and willing to work together and help each other out." Students agree that "the majority of students are from Virginia or neighboring states" and tend to be "primarily Caucasian," but observe that the university is "beginning to have more cultural diversity" and the overall number of international students has increased. Lynchburg students are "open to ideas and accepting to others" while extending their welcoming Southern hospitality. Students will "hold the door for you and give you a sincere smile as you walk by them on the way to class." As one student puts it, "Everyone is very helping. If someone is not able to help you with a homework question or a project, then they will find you someone that can. It does feel like one giant family here."

UNIVERSITY OF LYNCHBURG

Financial Aid: 434-544-8210 • E-mail: admissions@lynchburg.edu • Website: www.lynchburg.edu

THE PRINCETON REVIEW SAYS

Admissions

The school reports that its standardized testing policy for use in admission for Fall 2026 is Test Optional. The Princeton Review suggests that interested applicants consult with the school for the most up-to-date standardized testing policies. *Very important factors considered include:* rigor of secondary school record, academic GPA. *Important factors considered include:* interview. *Other factors considered include:* standardized test scores, application essay, recommendation(s), extracurricular activities, talent/ability, character/personal qualities, work experience, level of applicant's interest. High school diploma is required and GED is accepted. *Academic units required:* 4 English, 3 math, 3 science, 2 science labs, 2 language (other than English), 2 social studies, 2 history. *Academic units recommended:* 4 English, 4 math, 4 science, 2 science labs, 3 language (other than English), 2 social studies, 2 history, 1 academic elective.

Financial Aid

Students should submit: FAFSA; State aid form. Priority filing deadline is 11/1. The Princeton Review suggests that all financial aid forms be submitted as soon as possible. *Need-based scholarships/grants offered:* Federal Pell; Federal SEOG; College/university scholarship or grant aid from institutional funds. *Loan aid offered:* Federal Direct Subsidized Loans; Federal Direct Unsubsidized Loans; Direct PLUS loans. Admitted students will be notified of awards on a rolling basis beginning 12/1. Federal Work-Study Program available. Institutional employment available.

The Inside Word

Lynchburg uses rolling admission, as well as Early Decision, so you can apply any time after your junior year of high school, and they recommend that you apply by the fall of their senior year. You only need to submit transcripts, but they highly recommend including a letter of recommendation from a teacher or counselor and a writing sample. The writing sample can be an essay on a topic of your choice or a graded essay from a class. Accepted students are automatically considered for academic scholarship based on their application materials.

THE SCHOOL SAYS

From the Admissions Office

"The University of Lynchburg offers over 100 academic programs and offers degrees at the undergraduate, masters, and doctoral levels. Throughout their years at Lynchburg, students discover new things about themselves and their interests. Lynchburg provides an engaging and challenging curriculum of liberal arts, sciences, and professional programs that develops broad-based understanding and specialized knowledge, leading to fulfilling careers.

"Lynchburg students make many new connections starting with their first days on campus. They benefit from personal interaction with expert faculty. A vibrant campus life helps students forge meaningful connections with each other and with alumni who have excelled in countless career paths. Lynchburg students and alumni achieve excellence in the classroom, where they consistently earn places in competitive graduate programs; athletics, including multiple national and conference championships; and in the global workforce. Lynchburg students express high satisfaction with their school, giving it high marks in all five benchmarks of the National Survey of Student Engagement, which measures how colleges engage their students in activities related to learning and personal development. These areas include student-faculty interaction, supportive campus environment, level of academic challenge, active and collaborative learning, and enriching education experiences.

"From the moment prospective students step onto this beautiful campus, they begin to appreciate the Lynchburg experience. Students and families are invited to attend one of the many visit events throughout the year."

SELECTIVITY

# of total applicants	5,339
% of total applicants accepted	61
% of total acceptees attending	12
# of in-state applicants	2,785
% of in-state applicants accepted	83
# of out-of-state-applicants	1,068
% of applicants accepted from out of state	78
# of international applicants	1,483
% of international applicants accepted	8
# of early decision applicants	230
% of early decision applicants accepted	74

First-Year Profile

Testing policy	Test Optional
Range SAT composite	1000–1200
Range SAT EBRW	500–630
Range SAT math	480–590
Range ACT composite	17–24
% submitting SAT scores	15
% submitting ACT scores	3
Average HS GPA	3.5
% submitting high school GPA	92
% graduated top 10% of class	12
% graduated top 25% of class	34
% graduated top 50% of class	66
% submitting high school rank	51

Important Dates

Early decision	
Apply by	12/15
Notified by	12/31
Regular	
Apply by	7/31
Notified by	Rolling, 9/1
Nonfall registration?	Yes

FINANCIAL FACTS

Annual tuition	$38,990
Food and housing	$14,300
Required fees (First-year)	$300 ($700)
Books and supplies	$1,000
Average need-based scholarship (First-year)	$25,407 ($26,846)
% students with need rec. need-based scholarship or grant aid (First-year)	99 (100)
% students with need rec. non-need-based scholarship or grant aid (First-year)	76 (83)
% students with need rec. need-based self-help aid (First-year)	63 (60)
% students rec. any financial aid (First-year)	99 (98)
% UG borrow to pay for school	70
Average cumulative indebtedness	$35,090
% of students with need fully met (First-year)	26 (29)
Average % of student need met (First-year)	77 (81)

UNIVERSITY OF MAINE

168 College Ave, Orono, ME 04469 • Admissions: 207-581-1561

Survey Snapshot
Intramural sports are popular
Recreation facilities are great
Great library

RATINGS

Quality of Life	80
Fire Safety	99
Green	60*
Academic	77
Profs Interesting	83
Profs Accessible	88
Admissions	82
Financial Aid	87

CAMPUS LIFE

Type of school	Public
Environment	Village

Students

Degree-seeking undergrad enrollment	8,334
% male/female/not reported	53/47/1
% from out of state	33
% First-year live on campus	90
% Ugrads live on campus	43
# of fraternities (% join)	13 (NR)
# of sororities (% join)	6 (NR)
% Asian	2
% Black or African American	2
% Hispanic	5
% Native American	1
% Pacific Islander	<1
% Race and/or ethnicity unknown	3
% Two or more races	4
% White	81
% International	2
# of countries represented	45

CAMPUS MENTAL HEALTH SERVICES

Offers mental health/wellness program	Yes
Mental health training available to students	Yes
Employs Chief Wellness Officer	No
Peer-to-peer mental health offerings	No
Counseling center has guidelines or accreditation	Yes
Mental health/well-being courses	No

ACADEMICS

% students returning for sophomore year	79
% students graduating within 4 years	43
% students graduating within 6 years	57
Calendar	Semester
Student/faculty ratio	15:1
Most common class size 10–19.	(34%)
Most common lab/discussion size 10–19.	(46%)

Most Popular Majors
Mechanical Engineering; Psychology; Business Administration and Management

Applicants Often Prefer
University of Massachusetts—Amherst, University of New Hampshire, University of Rhode Island, University of Vermont

Applicants Sometimes Prefer
Husson University, Southern Maine Community College, University of Connecticut, University of Southern Maine

Applicants Rarely Prefer
Plymouth State University, University of New England

STUDENTS SAY "…"

Academics

Up in the Northeast corner of the United States, the University of Maine is a public research university with "all the opportunities of a large state school, while having the atmosphere of a small school." Students majoring in Business, Engineering, Marine Sciences, Forestry, Animal Science, Music, and Education majors all rave about their departments, but they also say that with nearly 100 majors, minors and degree programs, "the class choices are amazing." The great value is another draw: "UMaine provides one of the most affordable university educations in the area" with "great scholarships if you have decent high school grades." As for the classes themselves, undergrads caution that "the courses are rather challenging," but there's a sense of "camaraderie and willingness to… help—not just in professors but in your peers as well." Professors are generally "passionate, helpful, and actually want to see you at their office hours," and also bring "real-world experience into their classrooms." Juniors and seniors advise that "building a relationship with faculty is key" to success both at UMaine and beyond as they "are eager to recruit students to help with their [own] research" and provide connections to outside jobs and research positions in their fields. Other hands-on learning opportunities abound at UMaine, with some examples including "drilling through the ice to collect sediment samples" on a frozen lake and caring for "horses and dairy cows" on the university farm. Students also find "well-established connections outside of college" in the form of hospital internships to placements at local primary schools. Because of this, students seeking "opportunity and a sense of community" find this campus to "feel like home."

Campus Life

UMaine Black Bears are a very active bunch, and "sports, especially hockey, [are] a huge part of the…culture." At games, "the student section goes crazy (in the best way)" and "the school spirit is…incredible." Additionally, the school is situated in "such a unique place" that is "super green in the summer and pure white in the winter," providing this outdoorsy student body with miles of "trails for running and biking and a river [where] people often go paddling, kayaking, swimming, and fishing." (Yes, there's an on-campus canoe rental.) Both coastal Arcadia National Park and remote Baxter State Park, where "the Appalachian Trail ends…[atop] pristine Mount Katahdin," are just an hour's drive away. The winter season is popular for cross-country and alpine skiing, snowboarding, and other sports. Other forms of physical activity are available in UMaine's recreation center, which students boast is the "best in New England" and features "tons of equipment and…classes for people of all experience levels." For those who would rather stay inside during the winter, the campus puts on free movies, "drag shows, trivia nights, [and] amazing Collins Center performances." As for nightlife, while there are plenty of parties and drinking at downtown bars on weekends, there is little pressure to partake—students say their peers are "chill and accepting of whatever you do and do not do." While the school may be in a rural environment, that doesn't mean the students are bored or lonely. As one undergrad puts it: "When everyone's in the middle of nowhere, no one is."

Student Body

UMaine's "campus is filled with very welcoming people" who are "down to earth," "helpful," "hardworking," and, as one undergrad phrases it, "wicked friendly." The student body hails "mostly from the state of Maine or the surrounding New England area" and is predominantly white. Yet students emphasize that the campus is diverse, maintaining a "significant LGBT+ presence on campus" and a mix of social classes, religions, and political affiliations. Whatever the background, most students "share the love and passion of the outdoors." Additionally, one student tells us, "Everyone has their own different quirks and no one is judged for that." That acceptance also goes for nontraditional students. For example, the "veteran community is fantastic" and there are "many people with military partners [or] family members." Another student sums it up: "There is a unique sense of Maine here, and we are quite united under the Black Bear banner."

UNIVERSITY OF MAINE

Financial Aid: 207-581-1324 • E-Mail: umaineadmissions@maine.edu • Website: www.umaine.edu

THE PRINCETON REVIEW SAYS

Admissions

The school reports that its standardized testing policy for use in admission for Fall 2026 is Test Free. The Princeton Review suggests that interested applicants consult with the school for the most up-to-date standardized testing policies. *Very important factors considered include:* rigor of secondary school record, class rank, academic GPA. *Important factors considered include:* application essay, recommendation(s). *Other factors considered include:* interview, extracurricular activities, talent/ability, character/personal qualities, volunteer work, work experience. High school diploma is required and GED is accepted. *Academic units required:* 4 English, 3 math, 2 science, 2 science labs, 2 social studies, 4 academic electives. *Academic units recommended:* 4 English, 4 math, 4 science, 3 science labs, 2 language (other than English), 2 social studies, 1 history, 4 academic electives.

Financial Aid

Students should submit: FAFSA. Priority filing deadline is 3/1. The Princeton Review suggests that all financial aid forms be submitted as soon as possible. *Need-based scholarships/grants offered:* Federal Pell; Federal SEOG; State scholarships/grants; Private scholarships; College/university scholarship or grant aid from institutional funds. *Loan aid offered:* Federal Direct Subsidized Loans; Federal Direct Unsubsidized Loans; Direct PLUS loans; College/university loans from institutional funds; State Loans. Admitted students will be notified of awards on a rolling basis beginning 1/1. Federal Work-Study Program available. Institutional employment available.

The Inside Word

Find ways—like campus visits—to stand out among local UMaine applicants. Admission is rolling, but apply earlier to optimize housing and financial aid prospects.

THE SCHOOL SAYS

From the Admissions Office

"Maine's Flagship and Public Research University is at the forefront of national and international research, student engagement, innovation and collaboration. With experiential learning at its core, UMaine offers celebrated academics, student research opportunities and a close-knit community that strives for diversity, inclusion and excellence. UMaine offers more than one hundred undergraduate programs, and more than 140 programs through which students can earn graduate certificates, master's, C.A.S., Ed.S., and doctoral degrees. Top students are invited to join UMaine's Honors College, one of the country's oldest and most accomplished. The National Science Foundation ranks UMaine among the top third of public institutions engaged in research. Classified as a 'High Research Activity Institution' by the Carnegie Foundation for the Advancement of Teaching, its sixteen major research centers include The Laboratory for Surface Science and Technology, a hub for cutting-edge sensor and nanotechnology research, and the Advanced Structures and Composites Center, a global leader in deep water offshore wind energy development.

"Maine boasts a 15:1 student-to-faculty ratio, where faculty and administration members are known for having an open-door policy. Our students work alongside some of the most renowned scholars and scientists in their fields, whether they're talking civil engineering over lunch or traversing an Antarctic ice sheet with climate researchers.

"UMaine students gain real-world experience to prepare them for their professional careers after college. SPIFFY, our student investment club, manages a $3.2 million real-money portfolio. Wildlife ecology majors learn about bear behavior by going out and tagging cubs. Engineering majors take advantage of internships that often lead to employment after graduation. Marine science undergrads spend a semester by the sea at our internationally renowned Darling Marine Center."

SELECTIVITY

# of total applicants	13,828
% of total applicants accepted	96
% of total acceptees attending	15
# of in-state applicants	4,047
% of in-state applicants accepted	97
# of out-of-state-applicants	9,248
% of applicants accepted from out of state	95
# of international applicants	533
% of international applicants accepted	88

First-Year Profile

Testing policy	Test Free
Average HS GPA	3.5
% submitting high school GPA	98
% graduated top 10% of class	19
% graduated top 25% of class	46
% graduated top 50% of class	75
% submitting high school rank	50

Important Dates

Early action	
Apply by	12/1
Notified by	1/15
Regular	
Notified by	Rolling, 10/1
Nonfall registration?	Yes

FINANCIAL FACTS

Annual in-state tuition	$13,230
Annual out-of-state tuition	$38,340
Food and housing	$14,666
Required fees	$1,070
Books and supplies	$1,000
Average need-based scholarship (First-year)	$12,470 ($13,747)
% students with need rec. need-based scholarship or grant aid (First-year)	95 (99)
% students with need rec. non-need-based scholarship or grant aid (First-year)	14 (19)
% students with need rec. need-based self-help aid (First-year)	72 (69)
% students rec. any financial aid (First-year)	91 (99)
% UG borrow to pay for school	65
Average cumulative indebtedness	$34,033
% of students with need fully met (First-year)	25 (30)
Average % of student need met (First-year)	72 (75)

University of Mary Washington

1301 College Avenue, Fredericksburg, VA 22401 • Admissions: 540-654-2000

Survey Snapshot
Great library
Theater is popular
Students love Fredericksburg, VA

RATINGS	
Quality of Life	89
Fire Safety	89
Green	81
Academic	82
Profs Interesting	92
Profs Accessible	92
Admissions	85
Financial Aid	80

CAMPUS LIFE

Type of school	Public
Environment	City

Students

Degree-seeking undergrad enrollment	3,514
% male/female/not reported	37/63/<1
% from out of state	7
% First-year from public high school	86
% First-year live on campus	82
% Ugrads live on campus	58
# of fraternities	0
# of sororities	0
% Asian	4
% Black or African American	9
% Hispanic	13
% Native American	<1
% Pacific Islander	<1
% Race and/or ethnicity unknown	5
% Two or more races	7
% White	59
% International	3
# of countries represented	27

CAMPUS MENTAL HEALTH SERVICES

Offers mental health/wellness program	Yes
Mental health training available to students	Yes
Employs Chief Wellness Officer	Yes
Peer-to-peer mental health offerings	Yes
Counseling center has guidelines or accreditation	Yes
Mental health/well-being courses	Yes, for-credit

ACADEMICS

% students returning for sophomore year	84
% students graduating within 4 years	52
% students graduating within 6 years	66
Calendar	Semester
Student/faculty ratio	13:1
Most common class size 10–19.	(46%)
Most common lab/discussion size 10–19.	(49%)

Most Popular Majors
Biology/Biological Sciences; Psychology; Business Administration and Management; Communication & Digital Studies

Applicants Often Prefer
University of Virginia, William & Mary

Applicants Sometimes Prefer
Christopher Newport University, George Mason University, James Madison University, Virginia Commonwealth University, Virginia Tech

Applicants Rarely Prefer
Longwood University, Radford University

STUDENTS SAY "..."

Academics

University of Mary Washington students receive "an extremely thorough and well-rounded education." Classes at UMW take many different forms, from discussion-based seminars to collaborative learning. Moreover, the university provides opportunities for experiential learning beyond the classroom. For instance, a class called Alleviating Food Waste allows students to participate in volunteer initiatives and "make real change." First-year students can enroll in the Impact Program, which combines a one-credit course called "Doing the Work Together" with hands-on community service opportunities. Among the many programs the university offers, the Historic Preservation major is mentioned as "one of the best." As one student notes, "When speaking to alumni and professors at other institutions, they have likened my experience here to that of a graduate program." Professors are "typically very personable and understanding" and take the time to connect with students. One student shares, "As someone who has struggled with mental health in college, my professors have been very understanding and worked with me so I could be successful while taking care of myself." Another student sums it up by saying that when it comes to the professors, "We are a first priority to them and it shows."

Campus Life

This 234-acre campus, filled with trees and abundant green space, offers plenty of activities "that cater to so many different interests and types of people," whether that's hanging out to watch films at the Hurley Convergence Center or partaking in popular weekly activities like trivia, karaoke, and bingo. The school boasts a "strong athletics" program, and students enjoy both playing and watching sports. "Clubs are a huge part of campus life." There's a good mix of interest-based groups like the improv club and Yarnworks—a club for all things yarn—as well as service-based opportunities, such as COAR: SPCA, where students "volunteer at a local humane society and help dogs in need of homes." Creative expression is encouraged at UMW, with students showcasing their talents through art shows, music showcases, dramatic readings, and theater productions. With so much happening daily, students appreciate the school's website and app that curates "all of the events and when they're happening!" Some events are not to be missed, including the popular campus tradition known as "Devil-Goat Day," in which "devils" (students graduating in odd years) and "goats" (students graduating in even years) engage in friendly competitions, like jousting and tug-of-war. When not attending classes or participating in extracurricular activities, students often hang out by the river or visit "incredibly popular" and commercial downtown Fredericksburg. In all, "there's always some type of event going on."

Student Body

It's "very easy to feel part of the community" here. This welcoming environment is supported by initiatives that help students get to know each other when they first arrive on campus: "I was able to make some of my closest friends" in the first-year seminar. Students note that the school is making an effort "to be inclusive and diverse," and the student body reflects "a wide range of political leanings." One student shares, "As someone who falls under multiple marginalized groups and has moved a lot, this is the most comfortable I have felt in a school environment." UMW is supportive and "very open for those in the LGBTQ+ community." According to another student, "People can feel safe being themselves here and not be judged for who they are." There are many international students as well as older students at UMW. Students here are supportive and friendly, "always willing to lend a helping hand." As one student puts it, UMW "is a place where I can never fail to find friends."

UNIVERSITY OF MARY WASHINGTON

Financial Aid: 540-654-2468 • E-Mail: admit@umw.edu • Website: www.umw.edu

THE PRINCETON REVIEW SAYS

Admissions

The school reports that its standardized testing policy for use in admission for Fall 2026 is Test Optional. The Princeton Review suggests that interested applicants consult with the school for the most up-to-date standardized testing policies. *Very important factors considered include:* rigor of secondary school record, academic GPA. *Important factors considered include:* class rank, application essay, recommendation(s). *Other factors considered include:* standardized test scores, interview, extracurricular activities, talent/ability, character/ personal qualities, first generation, geographical residence, state residency, volunteer work, work experience, level of applicant's interest. High school diploma is required and GED is accepted. *Academic units required:* 4 English, 3 math, 3 science, 3 science labs, 3 language (other than English), 3 social studies. *Academic units recommended:* 4 English, 4 math, 4 science, 4 science labs, 4 language (other than English), 4 social studies.

Financial Aid

Students should submit: FAFSA. Priority filing deadline is 2/1. The Princeton Review suggests that all financial aid forms be submitted as soon as possible. *Need-based scholarships/ grants offered:* Federal Pell; Federal SEOG; State scholarships/grants; Private scholarships; College/university scholarship or grant aid from institutional funds. *Loan aid offered:* Federal Direct Subsidized Loans; Federal Direct Unsubsidized Loans; Direct PLUS loans; College/university loans from institutional funds. Admitted students will be notified of awards on a rolling basis beginning 12/1. Federal Work-Study Program available. Institutional employment available.

The Inside Word

When considering candidates for admissions, University of Mary Washington does not subscribe to any particular formula. Indeed, the committee simply strives to create a diverse and well-rounded incoming class. Therefore, all aspects of your application will hold some weight. Of course, strong emphasis is placed on the quality and rigor of your high school curriculum: successful applicants tend to have a handful of honors, AP, and/or IB classes.

THE SCHOOL SAYS

From the Admissions Office

"The University of Mary Washington is for students who are serious about academics, committed to an inclusive community, and eager to contribute to the greater good. At UMW, we focus on what matters. We are here to create meaningful connections and powerful experiences. As a public liberal arts and sciences university, we stand for bold knowledge-building. Our three colleges approach learning by giving your mind room to roam, go on adventures, take risks, seek out intersections, chase answers, and create fresh insight. We prepare students to think around corners and solve problems they've never imagined, let alone studied. Our small classes buzz with inquiry and exploration. Deep thinking and doing happen daily here. We go for collaboration over competition. Students work with professors who double as mentors. They'll help tap into students' strengths and talents.

"Distinctive to UMW is one of the nation's leading historic preservation programs, as well as a strong creative writing program. Other top majors include political science and international affairs, computer science and cybersecurity, communication and digital studies, English, biology, psychology, earth and environmental science, visual and performing arts, theatre, economics and business.

"We see students—their potential, their purpose, their future. Conveniently located between Washington, D.C. and Richmond, VA and with over 100+ majors, minors, and programs, UMW is committed to connecting students to internships, study abroad, over 150 student organizations and clubs, NCAA Division III Athletics, research projects, community service, and job opportunities—the experiences that will take you to the next level."

SELECTIVITY

# of total applicants	5,670
% of total applicants accepted	74
% of total acceptees attending	17
# of in-state applicants	4,147
% of in-state applicants accepted	83
# of out-of-state-applicants	750
% of applicants accepted from out of state	78
# of international applicants	768
% of international applicants accepted	19
# of early decision applicants	106
% of early decision applicants accepted	85
# offered a place on the wait list	338
# admitted from wait list	13

First-Year Profile

Testing policy	Test Optional
Range SAT composite	1180–1340
Range SAT EBRW	610–710
Range SAT math	560–650
Range ACT composite	27–30
% submitting SAT scores	27
% submitting ACT scores	3
Average HS GPA	3.8
% submitting high school GPA	78
% graduated top 10% of class	16
% graduated top 25% of class	30
% graduated top 50% of class	83
% submitting high school rank	42

Important Dates

Early decision	
Apply by	11/1
Notified by	12/10
Early action	
Apply by	11/15
Notified by	1/31
Regular	
Notified by	4/1
Nonfall registration?	Yes

FINANCIAL FACTS

Annual in-state tuition	$9,772
Annual out-of-state tuition	$23,884
Food and housing	$15,756
Required fees	$6,196
Books and supplies	$1,200
Average need-based scholarship (First-year)	$5,948 ($6,389)
% students with need rec. need-based scholarship or grant aid (First-year)	73 (72)
% students with need rec. non-need-based scholarship or grant aid (First-year)	54 (90)
% students with need rec. need-based self-help aid (First-year)	51 (46)
% students rec. any financial aid (First-year)	79 (100)
% UG borrow to pay for school	46
Average cumulative indebtedness	$33,039
% of students with need fully met (First-year)	7 (12)
Average % of student need met (First-year)	51 (54)

University of Maryland, Baltimore County

1000 Hilltop Circle, Baltimore, MD 21250 • Admissions: 410-455-2292

Survey Snapshot
School is well run
Students are happy
Career services are great

RATINGS

Quality of Life	81
Fire Safety	99
Green	94
Academic	79
Profs Interesting	85
Profs Accessible	87
Admissions	87
Financial Aid	82

CAMPUS LIFE

Type of school	Public
Environment	Metropolis

Students

Degree-seeking undergrad enrollment	11,009
% male/female/not reported	54/46/0
% from out of state	4
% First-year from public high school	89
% First-year live on campus	58
% Ugrads live on campus	35
# of fraternities (% join)	7 (2)
# of sororities (% join)	9 (4)
% Asian	24
% Black or African American	25
% Hispanic	11
% Native American	<1
% Pacific Islander	<1
% Race and/or ethnicity unknown	2
% Two or more races	6
% White	27
% International	5
# of countries represented	83

CAMPUS MENTAL HEALTH SERVICES

Offers mental health/wellness program	Yes
Mental health training available to students	No
Employs Chief Wellness Officer	NR
Peer-to-peer mental health offerings	NR
Counseling center has guidelines or accreditation	No
Mental health/well-being courses	NR

ACADEMICS

% students returning for sophomore year	86
% students graduating within 4 years	47
% students graduating within 6 years	68
Calendar	4-1-4
Student/faculty ratio	16:1
Most common class size 20–29.	(26%)
Most common lab/discussion size 20–29.	(28%)

Most Popular Majors
Biology/Biological Sciences; Psychology

Applicants Also Look At
Delaware State University, Johns Hopkins University, Towson University, University of Maryland, College Park, Virginia Tech

STUDENTS SAY "..."

Academics

The University of Maryland, Baltimore County, is a fitting choice for students who "want some research opportunities, but may also want more personal attention from professors. At this top-tier public research university, the STEM programs get a significant amount of the glory—the science labs are "gorgeous, state-of-the-art facilities," and many students "come out of school working for Boeing and the NSA" or, in the case of one scientist, developing the Moderna COVID-19 vaccine. But UMBC has strengths outside of science. As one student says, "I have had superb instruction in modern languages...including fantastic German translation and modern French literature courses." In fact, UMBC "has greatly expanded its support to the fine arts"—one can earn a Bachelor of Fine Arts in Acting and Studio Art, and one student describes a "really close-knit Arts department that feels like a second family." Overall, the feeling toward the faculty is very positive, and students feel that "professors are able to gain a better and closer professor-student relationship than those at large academic institutions." One student remarks, "They helped me see my true potential as a student, and also helped me find my passions," and another insists, "They really make the school shine."

Campus Life

Life at UMBC is never dull, and the "small and cozy" campus feels like a connected community: "Most people gather with their friends in the library to study together, then...grab food together in [the] Commons." It takes no time to get from the pond outside the library to the "highly impressive" lab facilities: "Anything is within a 10–15 [minute] walk. It's quite convenient," especially since there are "ample opportunities for students to engage on campus." For instance, students enjoy competition with tournaments of paintball or ping-pong, as well as putting their mental acuity to the test: "We do also have a thriving intellectual sports scene including chess, mock trial, and ethics bowl." Clubs range from cultural to sports to career-building: "My favorite one is the video game development club, as it combines my interests of programming and video games into an opportunity to showcase my work in a way that could lead to a future career." Students also delight in events hosted by the University, "like Homecoming...[where it is] so much fun to watch the Bonfire, attend the Carnival and even see the puppy parade!"

Student Body

The abundance of "cultures and backgrounds are celebrated," as is evidenced by the dozens of student-run cultural organizations and the echoed sentiment: "That's what makes UMBC so unique: the students are diverse and are not restricted by their appearances, personalities, religions, cultures, identities, etc. whatsoever." One student finds that the freedom to be oneself lays the foundation to thrive: "I feel as though it's a safe space and judgment-free zone. I've never been in an environment where people are themselves out loud the way they are at UMBC."

UNIVERSITY OF MARYLAND, BALTIMORE COUNTY

Financial Aid: 410-455-1517 • E-Mail: admissions@umbc.edu • Website: www.umbc.edu

THE PRINCETON REVIEW SAYS

Admissions

The school reports that its standardized testing policy for use in admission for Fall 2026 is Test Optional. The Princeton Review suggests that interested applicants consult with the school for the most up-to-date standardized testing policies. *Very important factors considered include:* rigor of secondary school record, academic GPA, application essay. *Important factors considered include:* class rank, talent/ability. *Other factors considered include:* standardized test scores, recommendation(s), extracurricular activities, character/personal qualities, first generation, volunteer work, work experience. High school diploma is required and GED is accepted. *Academic units required:* 4 English, 4 math, 3 science, 2 language (other than English), 3 social studies, 3 history. *Academic units recommended:* 3 social studies, 3 history.

Financial Aid

Students should submit: FAFSA. Priority filing deadline is 3/1. The Princeton Review suggests that all financial aid forms be submitted as soon as possible. *Need-based scholarships/grants offered:* Federal Pell; Federal SEOG; State scholarships/grants; Private scholarships; College/university scholarship or grant aid from institutional funds; United Negro College Fund. *Loan aid offered:* Federal Direct Subsidized Loans; Federal Direct Unsubsidized Loans; Direct PLUS loans. Admitted students will be notified of awards on a rolling basis beginning 3/25. Federal Work-Study Program available. Institutional employment available.

The Inside Word

UMBC offers a large number of admissions events, online chats, tours, and other opportunities for prospective students to connect with the admissions team. The admissions committee considers the strength of your secondary school curriculum and class rank in combination with traditional factors, such as GPA, test scores (if submitted), and essay when making an acceptance decision. Additionally, it's suggested that at least one letter of recommendation be written by a teacher.

THE SCHOOL SAYS

From the Admissions Office

"UMBC is a university where highly motivated students are taught and mentored by faculty who have been consistently recognized for their commitment to undergraduate teaching. Innovative approaches to learning take place in world-class facilities—such as the Howard Hughes Medical Institute at UMBC and the world-class Performing Arts and Humanities building. UMBC celebrates undergraduate research and creative achievement, which means even first-year students are involved in research with their classmates and professors. The location of UMBC is just right—nestled just outside of Baltimore, in a quiet, green setting. UMBC is also a short commute to D.C., an advantage for jobs, internships, and networking opportunities. About 82 percent of the UMBC class of 2020 are in prestigious graduate programs and careers within six months of graduation. Student life is abundant at UMBC. With more students living on campus each year (over 70 percent of freshman), Division 1 sports, the Chesapeake Employers Insurance Arena, and more than 200 student organizations, students are creating experiences and friendships that will last a lifetime."

SELECTIVITY

# of total applicants	14,802
% of total applicants accepted	74
% of total acceptees attending	21
# of in-state applicants	11,675
% of in-state applicants accepted	76
# of out-of-state-applicants	1,886
% of applicants accepted from out of state	61
# of international applicants	1,241
% of international applicants accepted	74
# offered a place on the wait list	1,680
# admitted from wait list	758

First-Year Profile

Testing policy	Test Optional
Range SAT composite	1250–1400
Range SAT EBRW	620–710
Range SAT math	610–710
Range ACT composite	26–31
% submitting SAT scores	33
% submitting ACT scores	3
Average HS GPA	4.1
% submitting high school GPA	99
% graduated top 10% of class	25
% graduated top 25% of class	58
% graduated top 50% of class	88
% submitting high school rank	18

Important Dates

Early action	
Apply by	11/1
Notified by	12/15
Regular	
Apply by	2/1
Notified by	Rolling, 2/1
Nonfall registration?	Yes

FINANCIAL FACTS

Annual in-state tuition	$9,706
Annual out-of-state tuition	$28,762
Food and housing	$15,336
Required fees	$3,973
Books and supplies	$1,600
Average need-based scholarship (First-year)	$13,352 ($13,899)
% students with need rec. need-based scholarship or grant aid (First-year)	89 (97)
% students with need rec. non-need-based scholarship or grant aid (First-year)	27 (49)
% students with need rec. need-based self-help aid (First-year)	43 (36)
% students rec. any financial aid (First-year)	80 (97)
% UG borrow to pay for school	84
Average cumulative indebtedness	$22,547
% of students with need fully met (First-year)	10 (12)
Average % of student need met (First-year)	56 (57)

University of Maryland, College Park

College Park, College Park, MD 20742 • Admissions: 301-314-8377

Survey Snapshot
Theater is popular
Campus newspaper is popular
Students are happy

RATINGS	
Quality of Life	63
Fire Safety	90
Green	98
Academic	75
Profs Interesting	76
Profs Accessible	81
Admissions	92
Financial Aid	85

CAMPUS LIFE

Type of school	Public
Environment	Metropolis

Students

Degree-seeking undergrad enrollment	31,482
% male/female/not reported	51/49/0
% from out of state	23
% First-year live on campus	88
% Ugrads live on campus	39
# of fraternities (% join)	28 (9)
# of sororities (% join)	29 (12)
% Asian	23
% Black or African American	14
% Hispanic	12
% Native American	<1
% Pacific Islander	<1
% Race and/or ethnicity unknown	5
% Two or more races	5
% White	37
% International	3
# of countries represented	78

CAMPUS MENTAL HEALTH SERVICES

Offers mental health/wellness program	Yes
Mental health training available to students	Yes
Employs Chief Wellness Officer	Yes
Peer-to-peer mental health offerings	Yes
Counseling center has guidelines or accreditation	Yes
Mental health/well-being courses	Yes, for-credit

ACADEMICS

% students returning for sophomore year	97
% students graduating within 4 years	78
% students graduating within 6 years	88
Calendar	Semester
Student/faculty ratio	17:1
Most common class size 10–19.	(32%)
Most common lab/discussion size 20–29.	(38%)

Most Popular Majors

Information Science/Studies; Computer Science; Criminology

STUDENTS SAY "…"

Academics

The University of Maryland, College Park, is a vibrant public research university located just a short drive from Washington, D.C. Here, undergraduates can explore over 100 majors or create their own through the Individual Studies Program. Many choose UMD for its "top-notch honors program," impressive engineering school, "nationally recognized business program," political science department, and "top-ranked criminology program." They also appreciate the numerous "high-level courses taught by the nation's top researchers." For students looking to broaden their horizons, UMD offers nearly 300 study abroad programs. In these inclusive programs, Education Abroad Advisors offer resources and support for all students, including LGBTQ+ students, first-generation college students, students with disabilities, and students of color. The campus is continually improving, and as one student says, "The administration shows a desire to always upgrade facilities." This includes improvements to the "tremendous business school" as well as the engineering building that opened in 2022. Overall, students find that the University of Maryland, College Park, offers "a great experience with a variety of opportunities that are what you make of them." As one student sums it up, "This school gives you a great education for a really cheap price."

Campus Life

"Life at UMD is awesome," and students love living on "one of the country's most beautiful campuses." Many choose to live in the optional living-learning communities, which are organized around different academic interests. This setup allows students to live and attend classes together, which helps "make the gigantic campus [feel] much smaller" and fosters a great sense of community. When students want to venture off campus, "the proximity to D.C. makes clubbing, nights out on the town, and general visits to D.C. frequent." Not having a car is not an obstacle because the "bus transportation around campus provided by the university is great." On campus, there are plenty of exciting activities, from "school-sponsored parties [and] games" to over 800 student clubs to join. The student union is "loaded with fun places like the arcade area [and] bowling alley," as well as "tons of places to eat." For those interested in staying active, there's a "campus recreation center that has virtually everything you could wish for, including pools, an extensive gym, a rock wall, squash courts, [and] an indoor track." The Division 1 men's and women's basketball teams are especially popular, and "there are always open games of soccer, football, or ultimate Frisbee being played on the mall and elsewhere." As one student says, "You can never get bored because there is always something to do" at UMD! With all of these activities available, it's no wonder that students say, "The social life at UMD is unsurpassed."

Student Body

Students describe the UMD as "an especially diverse school," noting that this diversity encourages their peers to be "more tolerant and accepting of people from different backgrounds and cultures." One student shares, "Coming from a very diverse area, I thought it was going to be hard to find a school that had that same representation of minority and atypical students until I found Maryland. I don't think I have ever learned so much about different religions, cultures, orientations, or lifestyles. All of them are accepted and even celebrated." Students also highlight that "there is no 'typical' student here. Everyone will find that they can fit in somewhere." The community is inclusive, as one student explains, "The different groups are very accepting of other groups. Students in Greek life are just as accepting of students in non-Greek life. Athletes blend in with non-athletes," adding, "UMD provides a great environment for students to meet people they would normally not know and helps to provide great connections with these people."

University of Maryland, College Park

Financial Aid: 888-313-2404 • E-Mail: ApplyMaryland@umd.edu • Website: www.umd.edu

THE PRINCETON REVIEW SAYS

Admissions

The school reports that its standardized testing policy for use in admission for Fall 2026 is Test Optional. The Princeton Review suggests that interested applicants consult with the school for the most up-to-date standardized testing policies. *Very important factors considered include:* rigor of secondary school record. *Important factors considered include:* academic GPA, application essay, recommendation(s), extracurricular activities, talent/ability, character/personal qualities. *Other factors considered include:* class rank, standardized test scores, first generation, geographical residence, state residency, volunteer work, work experience. High school diploma is required and GED is accepted. *Academic units required:* 4 English, 4 math, 3 science, 2 science labs, 2 language (other than English), 3 social studies, 3 history.

Financial Aid

Students should submit: FAFSA. Priority filing deadline is 1/1. The Princeton Review suggests that all financial aid forms be submitted as soon as possible. *Need-based scholarships/grants offered:* Federal Pell; Federal SEOG; State scholarships/grants; Private scholarships; College/university scholarship or grant aid from institutional funds. *Loan aid offered:* Federal Direct Subsidized Loans; Federal Direct Unsubsidized Loans; Direct PLUS loans. Admitted students will be notified of awards on a rolling basis. Federal Work-Study Program available. Institutional employment available.

The Inside Word

Maryland admissions officers don't simply crunch numbers and apply a formula. The school considers no fewer than 25 factors when determining who's in and who's out. Essays, recommendations, extracurricular activities, talents and skills, and demographic factors all figure into the mix along with high school transcript and GPA. Give all aspects of your application your utmost attention; admission is competitive.

THE SCHOOL SAYS

From the Admissions Office

"The University of Maryland (UMD) is a top-ranked flagship public research university, located within minutes from Washington, D.C. Students have opportunities to learn, explore and succeed through interaction with outstanding faculty that include Nobel Prize, Pulitzer Prize, Emmy and Tony winners. The beautifully landscaped 1,335-acre campus's proximity to major East Coast cities allows students to extend their education beyond the classroom through education abroad programs, and internships at U.S. federal agencies, research labs, global think tanks, major media outlets, world-class museums, and thriving companies. The university strongly encourages innovation, entrepreneurship and creativity by assisting students to launch startups, and serves as a model of cultural excellence through its arts programming. The University of Maryland also thrives on diversity, inclusion and engagement to prepare graduates to become excellent leaders in their communities and careers."

SELECTIVITY

# of total applicants	67,101
% of total applicants accepted	45
% of total acceptees attending	22
# of in-state applicants	18,487
% of in-state applicants accepted	44
# of out-of-state-applicants	48,614
% of applicants accepted from out of state	46
# offered a place on the wait list	247
# admitted from wait list	0

First-Year Profile

Testing policy	Test Optional
Range SAT composite	1410–1520
Range SAT EBRW	690–750
Range SAT math	700–780
Range ACT composite	32–35
% submitting SAT scores	37
% submitting ACT scores	7
Average HS GPA	4.4
% submitting high school GPA	95
% graduated top 10% of class	76
% graduated top 25% of class	90
% graduated top 50% of class	98
% submitting high school rank	25

Important Dates

Early action	
Apply by	11/1
Notified by	2/1
Regular	
Apply by	1/20
Notified by	4/1
Nonfall registration?	Yes

FINANCIAL FACTS

Annual in-state tuition	$10,490
Annual out-of-state tuition	$40,253
Food and housing	$16,747
Required fees	$1,800
Books and supplies	$1,250
Average need-based scholarship (First-year)	$18,070 ($18,332)
% students with need rec. need-based scholarship or grant aid (First-year)	86 (85)
% students with need rec. non-need-based scholarship or grant aid (First-year)	7 (11)
% students with need rec. need-based self-help aid (First-year)	82 (73)
% students rec. any financial aid (First-year)	69 (85)
% UG borrow to pay for school	31
Average cumulative indebtedness	$31,672
% of students with need fully met (First-year)	24 (27)
Average % of student need met (First-year)	75 (74)

UNIVERSITY OF MASSACHUSETTS—AMHERST

181 Presidents Dr, Amherst, MA 01003 • Admissions: 413-545-0222

Survey Snapshot
Great food on campus
Students are happy
Students take advantage of the outdoors

RATINGS

Quality of Life	83
Fire Safety	92
Green	96
Academic	78
Profs Interesting	83
Profs Accessible	84
Admissions	90
Financial Aid	88

CAMPUS LIFE

Type of school	Public
Environment	Town

Students

Degree-seeking undergrad enrollment	23,750
% male/female/not reported	48/52/0
% from out of state	23
% First-year live on campus	97
% Ugrads live on campus	58
# of fraternities (% join)	20 (8)
# of sororities (% join)	16 (7)
% Asian	14
% Black or African American	5
% Hispanic	10
% Native American	<1
% Pacific Islander	<1
% Race and/or ethnicity unknown	3
% Two or more races	5
% White	56
% International	8
# of countries represented	99

CAMPUS MENTAL HEALTH SERVICES

Offers mental health/wellness program	Yes
Mental health training available to students	Yes
Employs Chief Wellness Officer	Yes
Peer-to-peer mental health offerings	Yes
Counseling center has guidelines or accreditation	Yes
Mental health/well-being courses	Yes, for-credit

ACADEMICS

% students returning for sophomore year	92
% students graduating within 4 years	73
% students graduating within 6 years	81
Calendar	Semester
Student/faculty ratio	17:1
Most common class size 10–19.	(36%)
Most common lab/discussion size 20–29.	(47%)

Most Popular Majors
Computer Science; Psychology; Finance

Applicants Often Prefer
Northeastern University, Penn State University Park, University of Connecticut

Applicants Sometimes Prefer
Boston University, Purdue University—West Lafayette, University of Maryland, College Park

Applicants Rarely Prefer
Bentley University, Clark University, Suffolk University, University of Maine

STUDENTS SAY "..."

Academics

Pioneering research and "readily available internships" are just a few of the offerings at the University of Massachusetts—Amherst, where students have access to "many different degrees and routes to further education." There are "lots of resources for just about anything," including "access to networking opportunities and professional events." As a member of the Five College Consortium, the university allows students to take courses at nearby institutions, and one student notes that this "is really cool when looking for a specific class." Many local students appreciate the affordability, with one commenting that "it is not too expensive for in-state tuition, and it offers a huge variety of classes." The courses themselves offer a range of formats, including those that feature "open conversations during class," fostering an environment where students can "come together, see different ideas, and create a better environment." Other courses incorporate "field trips, engaging lectures, group activities," or "peer-led team learning where one person who took the class leads a discussion of current students working through a problem set." One student in an electrical engineering course (designed for non-engineers) describes its innovative approach: "Instead of traditional lectures, we learn by doing through building and programming a functional robot over the semester." No matter the format, professors are widely regarded as "unique individuals" who "really bring classes to life with their own teaching styles," with one undergrad sharing, "I love my professors and they make me eager to learn."

Campus Life

Amherst offers a wealth of activities, and "there are many options available to you on campus, [so] it's easy to get your schedule filled." A booked calendar suits many students, who "balance classes with club meetings, campus events, and time spent at the Rec Center or hanging out in the dining halls." Meals are events unto themselves since the "food here is really awesome," and "four dining halls help reduce the crowd size at each one." The student-run University Programming Council organizes popular events such as game nights, movie nights, and "UMass comedy nights," while hockey games draw large crowds. Students appreciate the scenic 1,450-acre campus and find that "sunset yoga and walking around the pond and seeing the ducks is very relaxing." The climbing gym and Outing Club are common ways for students to get active, while over 400 student clubs—ranging from the Robotics Club and Fiber Arts Club to the Investment Club—help forge both personal and professional connections. As one student says, "This school has done a really good job making this place a community."

Student Body

The student body at UMass is made up of "a true variety" of "fun, energetic, [and] motivated" individuals who are typically "open and expressive about their orientations" and place an "emphasis on diversity and belonging." As one of the largest schools in the state, it attracts "a lot of people from different areas and backgrounds into one place, which is really interesting and exciting." One student shares, "I feel like we get a little bit of everyone here, and that's what makes it unique. There's someone for everyone." Students note that UMass has "a strong campus culture that makes it so that you can easily connect with most people," so it's "really easy to make friends." One student adds, "Anyone can find a great community here with a lot of support." While "most are from Massachusetts," the different backgrounds and experiences create a "welcoming and enthusiastic mixing pot of communities representing [different] cultures…identities, and interests." Most here are "academically motivated" but "also like to have fun on the weekends," and the overall student dynamic "is very social." One student notes that one of the best things about UMass is that it's "very diverse and gives me a very well-rounded social experience."

University of Massachusetts—Amherst

Financial Aid: 413-545-0801 • E-Mail: mail@admissions.umass.edu • Website: www.umass.edu

THE PRINCETON REVIEW SAYS

Admissions

The school reports that its standardized testing policy for use in admission for Fall 2026 is Test Optional. The Princeton Review suggests that interested applicants consult with the school for the most up-to-date standardized testing policies. *Very important factors considered include:* rigor of secondary school record, academic GPA. *Important factors considered include:* class rank, application essay, recommendation(s), extracurricular activities, talent/ability, character/personal qualities, work experience. *Other factors considered include:* standardized test scores, first generation, volunteer work. High school diploma is required and GED is accepted. *Academic units required:* 4 English, 4 math, 3 science, 3 science labs, 2 language (other than English), 1 social studies, 1 history, 2 academic electives.

Financial Aid

Students should submit: FAFSA. Priority filing deadline is 3/1. The Princeton Review suggests that all financial aid forms be submitted as soon as possible. *Need-based scholarships/grants offered:* Federal Pell; Federal SEOG; State scholarships/grants; Private scholarships; College/university scholarship or grant aid from institutional funds. *Loan aid offered:* Federal Direct Subsidized Loans; Federal Direct Unsubsidized Loans; Direct PLUS loans. Admitted students will be notified of awards on a rolling basis beginning 1/1. Federal Work-Study Program available. Institutional employment available.

The Inside Word

UMass Amherst uses a holistic review process to carefully consider applicants in an individualized context. In addition to academic achievements (grade trends, course selection, major-related grades), the school is interested in a student's behavior and attitude. Applicants to the Architecture, Art, Dance, and Music majors are encouraged to contact the appropriate department and apply as early as possible to allow enough time for an audition or portfolio review. For all applicants, a rigorous senior year schedule is also strongly considered. The university is forward-thinking and socially conscious and therefore invites applications from and encourages the enrollment of undocumented students and students granted Deferred Action for Childhood Arrivals (DACA).

THE SCHOOL SAYS

From the Admissions Office

"The University of Massachusetts Amherst is the flagship campus of the commonwealth and one of the top public universities in the nation. The university offers 111 undergraduate degree programs, including a unique major called Bachelor's Degree with Individual Concentration (BDIC) in which students create their own program of study. There are opportunities for research and scholarship in any field of interest. The Commonwealth Honors College is a national model and welcomes students who seek additional academic challenge and meet the requirements for acceptance. The university uses a holistic review process of the student's application package. Standardized test scores (SAT or ACT) are optional, with a greater weight placed on the student's performance in a rigorous curriculum. Increased applications in recent years have made admission more selective. First-year students participate in the Residential First-Year Experience with opportunities to explore every possible interest through residential life. Its extensive library system is the largest state-supported academic library system in New England. Massachusetts athletics competes in NCAA Division I sports for men and women and will join the MAC conference in July 2025. Its hockey team competes in the Hockey East Association. Approximately 650 student-athletes participate in the athletics program. The town of Amherst is consistently ranked one of the top college towns in the country. Through the Five College Consortium, students have opportunities to enroll in classes at nearby Amherst, Hampshire, Mount Holyoke, and Smith Colleges at no extra charge. A free bus system connects these five campuses, allowing students to participate in a wide array of social and cultural events."

SELECTIVITY

# of total applicants	53,117
% of total applicants accepted	60
% of total acceptees attending	17
# of in-state applicants	22,603
% of in-state applicants accepted	58
# of out-of-state-applicants	23,800
% of applicants accepted from out of state	64
# of international applicants	6,714
% of international applicants accepted	54
# offered a place on the wait list	11,100
# admitted from wait list	2,349

First-Year Profile

Testing policy	Test Optional
Range SAT composite	1330–1480
Range SAT EBRW	660–740
Range SAT math	660–760
Range ACT composite	30–34
% submitting SAT scores	25
% submitting ACT scores	0
Average HS GPA	4.0
% submitting high school GPA	99
% graduated top 10% of class	34
% graduated top 25% of class	71
% graduated top 50% of class	95
% submitting high school rank	28

Important Dates

Early action	
Apply by	11/5
Notified by	1/25
Regular	
Apply by	1/15
Nonfall registration?	Yes

FINANCIAL FACTS

Annual in-state tuition	$17,601
Annual out-of-state tuition	$40,873
Food and housing	$16,726
Required fees (First-year)	$886 ($1,386)
Books and supplies	$1,200
Average need-based scholarship (First-year)	$19,013 ($18,559)
% students with need rec. need-based scholarship or grant aid (First-year)	93 (95)
% students with need rec. non-need-based scholarship or grant aid (First-year)	12 (13)
% students with need rec. need-based self-help aid (First-year)	84 (83)
% students rec. any financial aid (First-year)	88 (89)
% UG borrow to pay for school	58
Average cumulative indebtedness	$33,146
% of students with need fully met (First-year)	22 (20)
Average % of student need met (First-year)	88 (86)

UNIVERSITY OF MIAMI

P.O. Box 248025, Coral Gables, FL 33124 • Admissions: 305-284-6000

Survey Snapshot
Students are happy
Students love Miami, FL
Recreation facilities are great

RATINGS

Quality of Life	**87**
Fire Safety	**75**
Green	**99**
Academic	**82**
Profs Interesting	**87**
Profs Accessible	**91**
Admissions	**94**
Financial Aid	**95**

CAMPUS LIFE

Type of school	Private
Environment	Town

Students

Degree-seeking undergrad enrollment	12,836
% male/female/not reported	44/55/<1
% from out of state	61
% First-year live on campus	88
% Ugrads live on campus	36
# of fraternities (% join)	20 (11)
# of sororities (% join)	13 (14)
% Asian	5
% Black or African American	6
% Hispanic	26
% Native American	<1
% Pacific Islander	<1
% Race and/or ethnicity unknown	3
% Two or more races	5
% White	47
% International	7
# of countries represented	100

CAMPUS MENTAL HEALTH SERVICES

Offers mental health/wellness program	Yes
Mental health training available to students	Yes
Employs Chief Wellness Officer	Yes
Peer-to-peer mental health offerings	Yes
Counseling center has guidelines or accreditation	Yes
Mental health/well-being courses	Yes, for-credit

ACADEMICS

% students returning for sophomore year	93
% students graduating within 4 years	71
% students graduating within 6 years	84
Calendar	Semester
Student/faculty ratio	11:1
Most common class size 10–19.	(31%)
Most common lab/discussion size 1–9.	(35%)

Most Popular Majors

Biology/Biological Sciences; Psychology; Finance

Applicants Also Look At

Boston University, Cornell University, Drexel University, Duke University, Florida International University, Florida State University, Fordham University, New York University, Northeastern University, Penn State University Park, Syracuse University, Tulane University, University of California—Los Angeles, University of Central Florida, University of Florida, University of Maryland, College Park, University of Michigan—Ann Arbor, University of North Carolina at Chapel Hill, University of South Florida, University of Southern California

STUDENTS SAY "…"

Academics

Gorgeous University of Miami offers an "incredible range" of courses of study, chief among them "great programs in the sciences, engineering [and] music." Class sizes are small and internship opportunities are plentiful. Students here feel that they're getting a "well-rounded education," and "making connections" that they can capitalize on in the future. Though many undergrads report that their "courses are difficult," they also find them incredibly "rewarding." Inside the classroom, Miami students are delighted to find the majority of their professors are "easily approachable" and "incredibly knowledgeable." They clearly want "their students to learn and succeed." Indeed, "they are always there for you and open to helping in any way they can." Moreover, professors here are "well informed on the topic and are [typically] accessible after class." As one grateful student sums up, "I have had great academic success at UM largely because of my supportive and helpful professors. They deserve a lot more credit than they receive."

Campus Life

There is always something going on at the University of Miami. The campus is frequently abuzz with a multitude of fun events like the "farmers market, patio jams...and random activities [such as] laser tag, cornhole, food trucks [and] Frisbee game[s]." "The majority of students are involved in more than one campus club or activity" and a number of undergrads seek out volunteer opportunities. As one student explains, "We also have special service days that get good turnouts including Gandhi Day, Orientation Outreach, and MLK Day of Service." And plenty of undergrads spend their time "poolside, beachside, tailgating, anything they can find to have a good time." University of Miami also has a "very active/sporty population" with many students participating in both "club sports [and] intramural sports." Additionally, "Greek life is relatively popular, though the community is very welcoming and non-exclusive." And students also love "Canes After Dark [which often sponsors] cool activities like movies by the pool or snowball fights." Finally, nearby Miami "provides a lot of opportunity for adventure." Indeed, it has a "vibrant night life," a "wide array of cuisine," world-class museums, and beautiful beaches. You couldn't ask for anything more!

Student Body

Many undergrads at University of Miami proudly report that their peers are "very diverse." Indeed, you'll find that "there are people here from all over the world with different cultures, different experiences, and different likes and dislikes." As one amazed student shares, "You can hear so many different languages being spoken on campus." Nevertheless, while you might encounter people from around the country and the globe, a handful of undergrads insist that a number of their fellow students are "frat bros and girls that [simply] want to have fun." Additionally, a lot of students appear to come from "very affluent" families, and "luxury cars and going out to clubs on South Beach aren't out of the ordinary." However, others are quick to describe the culture as "very inclusive and understanding." And many assert that University of Miami students are "always willing to help out and assist you in finding your way." Another undergrad bolsters this claim by sharing, "I was lost on the first day of my first semester and an upperclassman pointed me in the direction of my class without being asked! It really made my day." Perhaps most importantly, we've been assured that "everyone can find their own social group here."

UNIVERSITY OF MIAMI

Financial Aid: 305-284-2270 • E-Mail: admission@miami.edu • Website: www.miami.edu

THE PRINCETON REVIEW SAYS

Admissions

The school reports that its standardized testing policy for use in admission for Fall 2026 will require applicants to submit either the SAT or ACT. The Princeton Review suggests that interested applicants consult with the school for the most up-to-date standardized testing policies. *Very important factors considered include:* rigor of secondary school record, class rank, academic GPA, standardized test scores, application essay, extracurricular activities. *Important factors considered include:* talent/ability, character/personal qualities, volunteer work, work experience. *Other factors considered include:* recommendation(s), first generation, geographical residence, state residency, level of applicant's interest. High school diploma is required and GED is accepted. *Academic units recommended:* 4 English, 4 math, 4 science, 2 science labs, 4 language (other than English), 4 social studies.

Financial Aid

Students should submit: FAFSA; CSS PROFILE; Business/Farm Supplement. Priority filing deadline is 1/6. The Princeton Review suggests that all financial aid forms be submitted as soon as possible. *Need-based scholarships/grants offered:* Federal Pell; Federal SEOG; State scholarships/grants; Private scholarships; College/university scholarship or grant aid from institutional funds. *Loan aid offered:* Federal Direct Subsidized Loans; Federal Direct Unsubsidized Loans; Direct PLUS loans. Admitted students will be notified of awards on a rolling basis beginning 12/13. Federal Work-Study Program available. Institutional employment available.

The Inside Word

Interested candidates should be aware that the admissions process at University of Miami is competitive. Fortunately, the committee does its utmost to consider the whole candidate. Therefore, everything from your academic GPA and the strength of your high school curriculum and standardized test scores (if submitted) to extracurricular activities and awards earned will be reviewed thoroughly. Ultimately, the university is looking for intellectually curious students who will be leaders both inside and outside the classroom.

THE SCHOOL SAYS

From the Admissions Office

"At the University of Miami, we educate leaders, problem solvers, and change makers. With the flexibility to choose from more than 180 majors and programs across 11 schools and colleges, students design their education based on the topics that excite them most. Here, coursework integrates academic rigor and theory with hands-on experience so students are able to convert knowledge into fulfilling achievements. As early as the first year of undergrad, students collaborate with award-winning faculty on projects that make meaningful contributions beyond the classroom. Projects range from volunteer experiences to cutting-edge research in topics such as climate change, public health, and privacy in the age of social media.

"With 10,000 undergraduate students, our close-knit campus combines the personal attention of a small college with the academic opportunity of a large research university. Our international location, just seven miles from downtown Miami, provides students with meaningful opportunities for experiential learning locally and in countries around the world. On campus, we are united in our diversity and working to cultivate a culture of belonging.

"Our students are passionate about learning, driven to contribute to their community, and encouraged to innovate. Whether you seek to make your mark in science, service, or the arts, the University of Miami will help you develop the skills needed to carve your own path to success."

SELECTIVITY

# of total applicants	58,167
% of total applicants accepted	18
% of total acceptees attending	26
# of in-state applicants	13,608
% of in-state applicants accepted	23
# of out-of-state-applicants	36,007
% of applicants accepted from out of state	17
# of international applicants	8,552
% of international applicants accepted	9
# of early decision applicants	2,395
% of early decision applicants accepted	44
# offered a place on the wait list	22,147
# admitted from wait list	703

First-Year Profile

Testing policy	SAT or ACT Required
Range SAT composite	1350–1450
Range SAT EBRW	670–730
Range SAT math	660–740
Range ACT composite	30–33
% submitting SAT scores	34
% submitting ACT scores	17
Average HS GPA	3.8
% submitting high school GPA	100
% graduated top 10% of class	55
% graduated top 25% of class	85
% graduated top 50% of class	97
% submitting high school rank	22

Important Dates

Early decision	
Apply by	11/1
Notified by	12/15
Other ED Apply by	1/5
Other ED Notified by	2/28
Early action	
Apply by	11/1
Notified by	1/31
Regular	
Apply by	1/5
Notified by	4/1
Nonfall registration?	Yes

FINANCIAL FACTS

Annual tuition	$60,720
Food and housing	$23,790
Required fees	$1,896
Books and supplies	$1,266
Average need-based scholarship (First-year)	$47,989 ($55,665)
% students with need rec. need-based scholarship or grant aid (First-year)	85 (90)
% students with need rec. non-need-based scholarship or grant aid (First-year)	29 (39)
% students with need rec. need-based self-help aid (First-year)	76 (72)
% students rec. any financial aid (First-year)	77 (82)
% UG borrow to pay for school	39
Average cumulative indebtedness	$25,250
% of students with need fully met (First-year)	100 (99)
Average % of student need met (First-year)	92 (100)

UNIVERSITY OF MICHIGAN—ANN ARBOR

500 S. State St., Ann Arbor, MI 48109 • Admissions: 734-764-7433

Survey Snapshot
Students love Ann Arbor, MI
Recreation facilities are great
Everyone loves the Wolverines

RATINGS	
Quality of Life	83
Fire Safety	85
Green	92
Academic	87
Profs Interesting	86
Profs Accessible	91
Admissions	97
Financial Aid	93

CAMPUS LIFE

Type of school	Public
Environment	City

Students

Degree-seeking undergrad enrollment	35,078
% male/female/not reported	46/54/0
% from out of state	43
% First-year live on campus	96
% Ugrads live on campus	26
# of fraternities (% join)	28 (11)
# of sororities (% join)	27 (16)
% Asian	18
% Black or African American	6
% Hispanic	13
% Native American	<1
% Pacific Islander	<1
% Race and/or ethnicity unknown	5
% Two or more races	6
% White	45
% International	7
# of countries represented	82

CAMPUS MENTAL HEALTH SERVICES

Offers mental health/wellness program	Yes
Mental health training available to students	No
Employs Chief Wellness Officer	NR
Peer-to-peer mental health offerings	NR
Counseling center has guidelines or accreditation	No
Mental health/well-being courses	NR

ACADEMICS

% students returning for sophomore year	97
% students graduating within 4 years	82
% students graduating within 6 years	93
Calendar	Trimester
Student/faculty ratio	15:1
Most common class size 10–19.	(35%)
Most common lab/discussion size 20–29.	(55%)

Most Popular Majors

Computer and Information Sciences; Business Administration and Management; Economics

STUDENTS SAY "..."

Academics

The University of Michigan—Ann Arbor is home to 19 schools and colleges, offers 250 degree programs, and "provides every kind of opportunity at all times to all people." Academically, Michigan "is very competitive, and the professors have high academic standards for all the students." The university has "an amazing honors program," some students say that "Michigan is as good as Ivy League schools in many disciplines." They particularly cite the "great engineering program" and report that the business program provides "access to some of the brightest leaders" in the business world. If you're considering medical school, Michigan has a "good undergraduate program for medical school preparation" that includes summer research opportunities. In addition, students appreciate that the school offers "a wide range of travel-abroad opportunities" in over 100 countries, numerous research opportunities, and excellent academics "at a low cost." The university also provides its students with "a vast amount of resources. Internships, career opportunities, tutoring, community service projects, a plethora of student organizations, and a wealth of other resources" are all available, but "you need to make the first move" because no one "will seek you out," explains one proactive student. Overall, students find Michigan to be "a great environment, both academically and socially." As one student says, "It has the social, fun atmosphere of any Big Ten university, but most people are still incredibly focused on their studies. It's great to be at a place where there is always something to do, but your friends completely understand when you have to stay in and get work done."

Campus Life

On this bustling campus, there are over 1,600 student organizations to get involved in. As one student says, "If you seek it out, you can find organizations for any interest. There are always people out there who share your interests. That's part of the benefit of [so many]... students!" Students say there is an active party scene, and "most students go to house parties [or] hit the bars" on weekends. However, there are plenty of opportunities to socialize outside the party scene. For example, on Friday nights, students can attend UMix, a free late-night campus tradition that features crafts, inflatables, games, and food. There are also "phenomenal cultural opportunities in Ann Arbor, especially music and movies." The university also proudly supports 29 NCAA Division 1 teams. "The hugely popular football Saturdays" bring everyone together to cheer on the Michigan Wolverines, and students say the "school spirit here is impressive." Overall, Michigan is a social campus filled with students who take academics seriously, and students appreciate this sense of balance. As one student puts it, "You can have a stimulating conversation with someone one day, and, the next day, be watching a silly movie or playing video games with this person."

Student Body

At Michigan, there's a place for everyone, with "hundreds of mini-communities within the campus, made [up] of everything from service fraternities to political organizations to dance groups." The student body is described as "hugely diverse," and is "one of the things Michigan prides itself on." As one student notes, "If you participate in extracurricular activities and make an effort to get to know other students in class and elsewhere, you'll definitely end up with a pretty diverse group of friends." Most students are considered "social but very academically driven." They are also recognized for being "on the cutting edge of both research and progressive thinking." Between the school's size and overall engaged student body, you can be sure that "if you have an interest, you can find a group of people who enjoy the same thing."

University of Michigan—Ann Arbor

Financial Aid: 734-763-6600 • E-Mail: oua-questions@umich.edu • Website: umich.edu

THE PRINCETON REVIEW SAYS

Admissions

The school reports that its standardized testing policy for use in admission for Fall 2026 is Test Optional. The Princeton Review suggests that interested applicants consult with the school for the most up-to-date standardized testing policies. *Very important factors considered include:* rigor of secondary school record, academic GPA. *Important factors considered include:* standardized test scores, application essay, recommendation(s), character/personal qualities, first generation. *Other factors considered include:* extracurricular activities, talent/ability, geographical residence, state residency, volunteer work, work experience, level of applicant's interest. High school diploma is required and GED is accepted. *Academic units required:* 4 English, 3 math, 3 science, 1 science lab, 2 language (other than English), 1 social studies, 3 history. *Academic units recommended:* 4 English, 4 math, 4 science, 1 science lab, 4 language (other than English), 1 social studies, 3 history, 1 computer science, 2 visual/performing arts.

Financial Aid

Students should submit: FAFSA; CSS PROFILE. Priority filing deadline is 12/15. The Princeton Review suggests that all financial aid forms be submitted as soon as possible. *Need-based scholarships/grants offered:* Federal Pell; Federal SEOG; State scholarships/grants; Private scholarships; College/university scholarship or grant aid from institutional funds. *Loan aid offered:* Federal Direct Subsidized Loans; Federal Direct Unsubsidized Loans; Direct PLUS loans; College/university loans from institutional funds. Admitted students will be notified of awards on a rolling basis beginning 1/1. Federal Work-Study Program available. Institutional employment available.

The Inside Word

Michigan admissions are extremely competitive, so you will need high test scores (if submitting), exemplary grades in challenging courses, and strong teacher recommendations to make the cut here. Though Michigan receives over 95,000 applications, each one is read at least twice. Use your extracurricular activities to demonstrate leadership and originality to stand out from the crowd.

THE SCHOOL SAYS

From the Admissions Office

"The University of Michigan is one of the great public research universities in the U.S. and the world, located in vibrant Ann Arbor. Since 1817, U-M has been a global model of a diverse, comprehensive academic institution committed to the public good. Nineteen schools and colleges offer over 260 degree programs, featuring tremendous academic breadth and opportunity for discovery. Our thriving innovation ecosystem cultivates the ingenuity and entrepreneurial spirit of students across campus. Students study in an immersive, cross-disciplinary environment that encourages inquiry in the classroom and in undergraduate research, with a 15:1 student/faculty ratio and more than 1,300 students participating in undergraduate research partnerships with more than 800 research advisors. Students cultivate new interests and learn from peers with differing backgrounds in more than 1,700 registered student organizations. Numerous service-learning programs link academics with volunteerism, such as Semester in Detroit. U-M is the fourth-largest all-time producer of Peace Corps volunteers. First-year students can find a sense of community and belonging in on-campus housing, which offers Living-Learning Programs for those interested in getting to know others with similar interests. With access to top-ranked programs and distinguished faculty, students have the resources and support they need to reach their full potential, to find their true voice, and to make a positive impact on the world. And with more than 668,000 living alumni around the world, new graduates can easily make personal and professional connections to other Michigan grads."

SELECTIVITY

# of total applicants	109,112
% of total applicants accepted	16
% of total acceptees attending	46
# offered a place on the wait list	24,447
# admitted from wait list	1,663

First-Year Profile

Testing policy	Test Optional
Range SAT composite	1370–1530
Range SAT EBRW	690–750
Range SAT math	680–780
Range ACT composite	32–34
% submitting SAT scores	55
% submitting ACT scores	18
Average HS GPA	3.9
% submitting high school GPA	98

Important Dates

Early action	
Apply by	11/1
Notified by	1/31
Regular	
Apply by	2/1
Notified by	1/31
Nonfall registration?	Yes

FINANCIAL FACTS

Annual in-state tuition (First-year)	$19,015 ($17,864)
Annual out-of-state tuition (First-year)	$65,721 ($63,480)
Food and housing	$16,246
Required fees	$482
Books and supplies	$1,184
Average need-based scholarship (First-year)	$30,693 ($30,307)
% students with need rec. need-based scholarship or grant aid (First-year)	94 (94)
% students with need rec. non-need-based scholarship or grant aid (First-year)	65 (66)
% students with need rec. need-based self-help aid (First-year)	43 (39)
% students rec. any financial aid (First-year)	63 (75)
% UG borrow to pay for school	31
Average cumulative indebtedness	$29,244
% of students with need fully met (First-year)	72 (67)
Average % of student need met (First-year)	92 (91)

University of Minnesota—Twin Cities

100 Church St. S.E., Minneapolis, MN 55455-0213 • Admissions: 612-625-2008

Survey Snapshot
Students are happy
Students love Minneapolis, MN
Everyone loves the Golden Gophers

RATINGS

Quality of Life	88
Fire Safety	89
Green	97
Academic	82
Profs Interesting	86
Profs Accessible	89
Admissions	87
Financial Aid	84

CAMPUS LIFE

Type of school	Public
Environment	Metropolis

Students

Degree-seeking undergrad enrollment	32,632
% male/female/not reported	46/53/1
% from out of state	25
% First-year live on campus	75
% Ugrads live on campus	20
# of fraternities (% join)	NR
# of sororities (% join)	NR
% Asian	13
% Black or African American	11
% Hispanic	7
% Native American	<1
% Pacific Islander	<1
% Race and/or ethnicity unknown	2
% Two or more races	6
% White	54
% International	7
# of countries represented	148

CAMPUS MENTAL HEALTH SERVICES

Offers mental health/wellness program	Yes
Mental health training available to students	Yes
Employs Chief Wellness Officer	Yes
Peer-to-peer mental health offerings	Yes
Counseling center has guidelines or accreditation	Yes
Mental health/well-being courses	Yes, for-credit

ACADEMICS

% students returning for sophomore year	91
% students graduating within 4 years	74
% students graduating within 6 years	85
Calendar	Semester
Student/faculty ratio	17:1
Most common class size 10–19.	(25%)
Most common lab/discussion size 10–19.	(35%)

Most Popular Majors
Computer Science; Psychology

STUDENTS SAY "..."

Academics

The University of Minnesota—Twin Cities is "a top-ranked university in a beautiful city that has a lot of great job opportunities," making it a place where "anyone can find what they want to do." This "Big Ten research university" offers over 150 undergraduate majors to "help students discover themselves" and their interests. As one student explains, "Our school pushes us to expand our horizons, to go outside of our comfort zones, and to try things that we never would have considered trying before." Many students are attracted to UMN for its "great research opportunities" and excellent academic programs, including the "phenomenal engineering programs," which include an earthquake simulation center, a nanotechnology lab, and a fluid mechanics lab on an island in the Mississippi River. Regarding classes, students report that most professors are "approachable and are more than willing to take time out of their day to ensure you understand the material." Overall, students say their professors are "very knowledgeable" and "strive to make [the subject matter] exciting." Students appreciate that the university fosters "a small school feeling" in "an urban setting," and describe it as "a place with endless opportunity for those willing to discover their passions."

Campus Life

Life at UMN is busy and "full of variety." Students fill their free time with a range of activities, including participating in intramural sports, attending sporting events, or joining any of the more than 1,000 student organizations on campus. For students in search of less active activities, UMN also "hosts a lot of lectures and discussions with prominent figures." In addition, "the Coffman Student Union always has something going on—movies, book signings—and there are a ton of student groups to join, no experience necessary." The school is also a member of the Big Ten conference of Division I teams, and "sporting events are widely popular, even if we aren't doing very well." The Greek life scene on campus is "thriving," and over 3,000 students participate. For those interested in a social scene with "alcohol and lots of dancing," there are often "house parties" on the weekends. Exploring the Twin Cities of Minneapolis and Saint Paul is a favorite pastime because there is "a lot going on!" Both the campus and surrounding cities are bike-friendly, and getting around is easy with the free university shuttle and public transportation options like buses and the light rail. Many students enjoy spending time outdoors, and popular activities include everything from "biking [and] outdoor games [to] reading in the park [and] going to the farmers market." Life at UMN is "full of variety" and undergraduates "can get involved in almost anything." In short, "If you're bored on a weekend, then you're not looking hard enough."

Student Body

Most students find UMN to be a friendly and supportive environment. They describe their peers as "generally quite friendly and outgoing," and everyone is "pretty willing to go out of their way for others, we are Minnesota nice, after all." While the school has a large Midwestern population, with "most likely hailing from Minnesota, Wisconsin, or the Dakotas," it attracts a broad mix of people and personalities. making it impossible to put everyone "into one category." As one student says, "We have so much diversity here, that it is hard to pinpoint a general student type" or slot everyone "into one category," and because of this, "everyone can find their niche and be free to express who they are." One topic that brings the campus together is the weather, and undergraduates can "fit in by bonding over how much [they] hate winter." Overall, this ambitious student body is filled with people who "are driven to succeed and to make the most of the vast opportunities offered by the UMN."

UNIVERSITY OF MINNESOTA—TWIN CITIES

Financial Aid: 612-624-1111 • E-Mail: admissions@umn.edu • Website: twin-cities.umn.edu

THE PRINCETON REVIEW SAYS

Admissions

The school reports that its standardized testing policy for use in admission for Fall 2026 is Test Optional. The Princeton Review suggests that interested applicants consult with the school for the most up-to-date standardized testing policies. *Very important factors considered include:* rigor of secondary school record, class rank, academic GPA. *Other factors considered include:* standardized test scores, application essay, recommendation(s), extracurricular activities, talent/ability, character/personal qualities, first generation, geographical residence, state residency, volunteer work, work experience. High school diploma is required and GED is accepted. *Academic units required:* 4 English, 4 math, 3 science, 1 science lab, 2 language (other than English), 3 social studies, 1 visual/performing arts. *Academic units recommended:* 4 English, 4 math, 4 science, 1 science lab, 2 language (other than English), 3 social studies, 1 visual/performing arts.

Financial Aid

Students should submit: FAFSA; Institution's own financial aid form. Priority filing deadline is 3/1. The Princeton Review suggests that all financial aid forms be submitted as soon as possible. *Need-based scholarships/grants offered:* Federal Pell; Federal SEOG; State scholarships/grants; Private scholarships; College/university scholarship or grant aid from institutional funds; Federal Nursing Scholarships. *Loan aid offered:* Federal Direct Subsidized Loans; Federal Direct Unsubsidized Loans; Direct PLUS loans; State Loans; College/university loans from institutional funds. Admitted students will be notified of awards on a rolling basis beginning 3/1. Federal Work-Study Program available. Institutional employment available.

The Inside Word

University of Minnesota, Twin Cities is a well-regarded institution and gaining admission is no easy feat. Academic preparation and performance are of primary concern. Therefore, course selection, GPA, and class rank will hold the most weight.

THE SCHOOL SAYS

From the Admissions Office

"The University of Minnesota is one of the nation's top public research universities. That means your college experience will be enhanced by world-renowned faculty, state-of-the-art learning facilities, and an unprecedented variety of options (such as 150 majors). Eighty-one percent of our classes have fewer than fifty students, and our caring advisers will help you find opportunities that are right for you. Hands-on courses, volunteer opportunities, internships, study abroad, and undergraduate research are part of the U of M experience. Students benefit from programs and traditions designed to support their success, like Welcome Week, where freshmen explore campus, meet their classmates, and connect with faculty and staff before the school year begins. Our classic Big Ten campus is located in the heart of the vibrant Twin Cities. Just minutes away, intern at a Fortune 500 company, volunteer at a major hospital, or relax at the beautiful Chain of Lakes. With a wealth of cultural, career, and recreational opportunities, there's no better place to earn your degree. Last year, we awarded over $50 million in four-year scholarship packages. Residents of Minnesota benefit from in-state tuition and income-based benefits: those under $50,000 may qualify for a new Promise Plus tuition guarantee program, while those under $120,000 may get tuition aid through the U Promise Scholarship. Residents of North Dakota, Wisconsin, or Manitoba qualify for special reciprocity tuition rates.

"The University of Minnesota has been named a 'Best Value in Public Colleges' by multiple ranking organizations. As a UMN student, you will experience this value first-hand: you will step into a thriving academic community with some of the world's most renowned researchers. With direct access to these incredible resources, you will get a great education and a prestigious degree that helps you achieve your dreams."

SELECTIVITY

# of total applicants	43,929
% of total applicants accepted	79
% of total acceptees attending	21

First-Year Profile

Testing policy	Test Optional
Range SAT composite	1310–1460
Range SAT EBRW	640–740
Range SAT math	650–750
Range ACT composite	26–32
% submitting SAT scores	7
% submitting ACT scores	34
% graduated top 10% of class	38
% graduated top 25% of class	71
% graduated top 50% of class	97
% submitting high school rank	40

Important Dates

Early action	
Apply by	11/1
Notified by	1/31
Regular	
Apply by	1/1
Nonfall registration?	Yes

FINANCIAL FACTS*

Annual in-state tuition	$16,132
Annual out-of-state tuition	$39,018
Food and housing	$14,822
Required fees	$2,350
Books and supplies	$1,000

* Most recently reported data at time of printing. Scan the QR code to find the latest updates.

University of Mississippi

PO Box 1848, University, MS 38677 • Admissions: 662-915-7226

Survey Snapshot
Students are very religious
Everyone loves the Ole Miss Rebels
Frats and sororities are popular

RATINGS	
Quality of Life	**85**
Fire Safety	**93**
Green	**60***
Academic	**80**
Profs Interesting	**89**
Profs Accessible	**94**
Admissions	**81**
Financial Aid	**87**

CAMPUS LIFE

Type of school	Public
Environment	Town

Students

Degree-seeking undergrad enrollment	21,473
% male/female/not reported	43/57/0
% from out of state	56
% First-year live on campus	98
% Ugrads live on campus	31
# of fraternities (% join)	20 (37)
# of sororities (% join)	15 (54)
% Asian	2
% Black or African American	10
% Hispanic	6
% Native American	<1
% Pacific Islander	<1
% Race and/or ethnicity unknown	1
% Two or more races	3
% White	78
% International	1
# of countries represented	66

CAMPUS MENTAL HEALTH SERVICES

Offers mental health/wellness program	Yes
Mental health training available to students	No
Employs Chief Wellness Officer	NR
Peer-to-peer mental health offerings	NR
Counseling center has guidelines or accreditation	No
Mental health/well-being courses	NR

ACADEMICS

% students returning for sophomore year	87
% students graduating within 4 years	57
% students graduating within 6 years	72
Calendar	Semester
Student/faculty ratio	18:1
Most common class size 10–19.	(28%)
Most common lab/discussion size 20–29.	(56%)

Most Popular Majors

Accounting; Marketing/Marketing Management

STUDENTS SAY "…"

Academics

The University of Mississippi offers "world-class programs and faculty," along with "'big-time' SEC athletics in the safe, quaint, and picturesque town of Oxford." It's a community that values traditions and fosters school spirit, making students "proud to have graduated from Ole Miss." There is "a highly academic side to Ole Miss that many outsiders do not see." The Honors College provides "unparalleled academic opportunities, such as beginning research as a freshman." In addition, many students cite the business and international studies programs as standouts. With over 100 majors available, "there is something for a person with any interest here." Classes at Ole Miss are "informative but also engaging and dynamic," attending classes is critical because professors "add much more than the textbook has to offer." Students appreciate how professors go above and beyond, both in the classroom and outside of it. Whether it's being available for office hours or helping connect students with internships, most of the professors here "hit the ball out of the park." In addition, some professors organize discussion groups, dinners, and other events to help "develop our ability to speak academically in a non-academic setting." At Ole Miss, you'll find a supportive environment where many services "are cheap if not free," the school "puts on many programs that bring together lots of different people of different backgrounds." As one student sums up, "The teachers care, the university cares, [and] the students all care about the school and what it stands for."

Campus Life

Life at Ole Miss "is always super busy" on this lively campus. While "school and grades are a very important aspect of life" and there is "a lot of work," the university also provides numerous extracurricular activities and "a lot of opportunities for fun." Sports are a big part of campus life: "During football season, the Grove consumes our weekends. It's an amazing experience!" While "known for its Greek life" and "great parties," the school has a wide variety of extracurriculars to get involved in. Students say it's a common misconception that "most people's minds revolve around drinking, college football, and church on Sunday." For example, students love events like the "Thacker Mountain Radio on Thursdays and poetry readings monthly at Proud Larry's," as well as live music. Students enjoy Oxford's "small, hometown feel" and frequently spend time in the Square, which offers restaurants, shopping, bars, and live music. With all the fun campus events and exploring the local scene, "there is never a dull moment, especially on the weekends."

Student Body

Ole Miss is "a blend of Southern charm and laid-back manners" in "a small-town" setting, where "studying for your next exam over a glass of sweet tea is a common practice." And students say their peers are good at balancing "decent grades and an extravagant social life." While students some note a divide between undergraduates who participate in Greek life and those who don't, others point out the wide range of personalities on campus, assuring that "you can find a group of friends without much effort. As one student elaborates, "You'll hear the term the 'Ole Miss family,' and it won't seem forced or strange." Overall, Ole Miss is a close community of students with "open minds" who "really want to be active in making changes in the world."

UNIVERSITY OF MISSISSIPPI

Financial Aid: 800-891-4596 • E-Mail: admissions@olemiss.edu • Website: www.olemiss.edu

THE PRINCETON REVIEW SAYS

Admissions

The school reports that its standardized testing policy for use in admission for Fall 2026 is Test Optional. The Princeton Review suggests that interested applicants consult with the school for the most up-to-date standardized testing policies. *Important factors considered include:* academic GPA, standardized test scores. *Other factors considered include:* rigor of secondary school record, class rank. High school diploma is required and GED is accepted. *Academic units required:* 4 English, 4 math, 3 science, 2 science labs, 3 social studies, 1 computer science, 1 visual/performing arts. *Academic units recommended:* 4 English, 4 math, 4 science, 3 science labs, 4 social studies, 1 computer science, 1 visual/performing arts.

Financial Aid

Priority filing deadline is 3/1. The Princeton Review suggests that all financial aid forms be submitted as soon as possible. *Need-based scholarships/grants offered:* Federal Pell; Federal SEOG; State scholarships/grants; Private scholarships; College/university scholarship or grant aid from institutional funds. *Loan aid offered:* Federal Direct Subsidized Loans; Federal Direct Unsubsidized Loans; Direct PLUS loans; College/university loans from institutional funds. Admitted students will be notified of awards on a rolling basis beginning 3/15. Federal Work-Study Program available. Institutional employment available.

The Inside Word

Ole Miss offers students tremendous educational opportunities and its admissions policies are designed to help in-state students attain a college degree. In-state applicants are admitted as long as they meet certain criteria, so check the school's website for exact details.

THE SCHOOL SAYS

From the Admissions Office

"The state's flagship university, affectionately known as Ole Miss, offers extraordinary opportunities through more than 120 areas of study from medicine and law to creative writing and accountancy. Its acclaimed offerings include the Sally McDonnell Barksdale Honors College, the Croft Institute for International Studies and the Center for Manufacturing Excellence, which incorporates coursework from schools of engineering, accountancy and business into its curriculum. Ole Miss is among a few universities nationally to house language flagship programs in both Chinese and Arabic. Its Patterson School of Accountancy is nationally ranked for undergraduate and graduate education, the School of Law is a national leader in the fields of air and space law and sports law. It was the state's first public university to shelter a chapter of the nation's oldest and most prestigious honor society, Phi Beta Kappa. Strong academic programs and a rich and varied campus life have helped Ole Miss produce 27 Rhodes Scholars, 26 Goldwater Scholars, 19 Truman Scholars, 55 Fulbright Scholars and 44 Boren Scholars.

"The campuses are diverse; 48 percent come from out of state, with all fifty states and ninety-six foreign countries represented, and 11 percent are Black. Recent significant campus improvements include several new residence halls and a totally renovated and expanded dining facility. Ole Miss is home to twenty research and education centers, including the National Center for Physical Acoustics, which is helping to quiet jet engines and use infrasound to detect tornadoes; and the National Center for Natural Products Research, where scientists are working to find new drugs to treat cancer, AIDS, fungal infections, and more.

"Students submitting the ACT are not required to take the writing section."

SELECTIVITY

# of total applicants	33,363
% of total applicants accepted	97
% of total acceptees attending	19
# of in-state applicants	4,820
% of in-state applicants accepted	93
# of out-of-state-applicants	28,168
% of applicants accepted from out of state	97
# of international applicants	375
% of international applicants accepted	100

First-Year Profile

Testing policy	Test Optional
Range SAT composite	1000–1090
Range SAT EBRW	510–610
Range SAT math	490–590
Range ACT composite	21–29
% submitting SAT scores	23
% submitting ACT scores	60
Average HS GPA	3.5
% submitting high school GPA	100
% graduated top 10% of class	22
% graduated top 25% of class	44
% graduated top 50% of class	71
% submitting high school rank	35

Important Dates

Regular	
Notified by	Rolling, 8/1
Nonfall registration?	Yes

FINANCIAL FACTS

Annual in-state tuition	$9,612
Annual out-of-state tuition	$28,440
Food and housing	$12,600
Required fees	$160
Books and supplies	$1,200
Average need-based scholarship (First-year)	$12,519 ($12,564)
% students with need rec. need-based scholarship or grant aid (First-year)	87 (85)
% students with need rec. non-need-based scholarship or grant aid (First-year)	15 (15)
% students with need rec. need-based self-help aid (First-year)	60 (64)
% UG borrow to pay for school	44
Average cumulative indebtedness	$34,596
% of students with need fully met (First-year)	17 (18)
Average % of student need met (First-year)	75 (78)

University of Missouri

230 Jesse Hall, Columbia, MO 65211 • Admissions: 573-882-7786

Survey Snapshot
Recreation facilities are great
Everyone loves the Tigers
Alumni active on campus

RATINGS

Quality of Life	79
Fire Safety	77
Green	60*
Academic	78
Profs Interesting	84
Profs Accessible	89
Admissions	86
Financial Aid	85

CAMPUS LIFE

Type of school	Public
Environment	City

Students

Degree-seeking undergrad enrollment	24,726
% male/female/not reported	45/55/0
% from out of state	23
% First-year from public high school	81
% First-year live on campus	94
% Ugrads live on campus	27
# of fraternities (% join)	34 (28)
# of sororities (% join)	20 (35)
% Asian	3
% Black or African American	5
% Hispanic	6
% Native American	<1
% Pacific Islander	<1
% Race and/or ethnicity unknown	1
% Two or more races	5
% White	79
% International	1
# of countries represented	50

CAMPUS MENTAL HEALTH SERVICES

Offers mental health/wellness program	Yes
Mental health training available to students	Yes
Employs Chief Wellness Officer	Yes
Peer-to-peer mental health offerings	No
Counseling center has guidelines or accreditation	Yes
Mental health/well-being courses	Yes

ACADEMICS

% students returning for sophomore year	90
% students graduating within 4 years	58
% students graduating within 6 years	77
Calendar	Semester
Student/faculty ratio	17:1
Most common class size 10–19.	(28%)
Most common lab/discussion size 20–29.	(36%)

Most Popular Majors
Health Services/Allied Health/Health Sciences; Business/Commerce; Biology/Biological Sciences

STUDENTS SAY "..."

Academics

Founded in 1839 as the first public university west of the Mississippi River, the University of Missouri is described as "a campus full of pride and spirit" featuring "top-of-the-line facilities" and "quality" academics. Numerous Pulitzer Prize winners have attended MU's renowned and "intense" journalism school, and the nursing and animal science programs also receive high praise. Students appreciate that they are given the freedom to explore different academic paths. "I came into college undecided and wanted to have plenty of options and opportunities to decide on a major," says one student. The advising system at MU is "great," and entrepreneurship is actively encouraged. Students have access to coaching and funding opportunities through the Center for Entrepreneurship and Innovation or the Entrepreneur Quest Student Accelerator. Additionally, they can even launch their own business in the MU Student Center through the Griggs Innovators Nexus. Classes at MU are comprised of "a diverse group of students who are eager to learn and a staff that is eager to teach them." The curriculum is made up of "comprehensive courses" that can be difficult, but students say that with hard work, "good grades are attainable." Student success is encouraged by professors who "are always available to answer a question," and "even with large classes…[they] are very attentive to individuals." One student shares, "I've always had professors who have had a million ways to explain any given theory, problem, or question." The administration also provides support, listening to students' concerns and acting: "When we say there is a problem, it gets fixed," says one student. MU "is always striving to achieve better, and not in just one specific category or area, but all around." There is a strong emphasis on "learning while networking," and with nearly 200,000 alumni just in Missouri alone, MU's extensive network helps students with internships and job opportunities. The university reports that thousands of employers recruit Mizzou graduates each year.

Campus Life

Mizzou features a "gorgeous campus" that is filled with school spirit, especially during football and basketball games, which are "heavily attended." This incredible school spirit helps bring people together, creating "a pretty close community." There are plenty of opportunities to have a good time here. As one undergrad notes, "A lot of students spend their time in class, but every night of the week there is a party to go to." While some students mention that there is "a huge Greek life" at MU, there are also plenty of social opportunities for everyone, noting that many "students enjoy going to off-campus parties or the bars downtown." Speaking of downtown, whether walking or biking, Columbia is easily navigable "because it's such a pedestrian-friendly place." Students also say Columbia is "the perfect mixture of small town and big city," and "there are plenty of opportunities to chill out" here. Plus, being located right between Kansas City and St. Louis means you get "the best of both worlds." As one student happily says of life at Mizzou, "There is never a dull moment to be had."

Student Body

Students at MU are described as "friendly, outgoing, social, [and] very involved." Most students find their friends "by joining one of our million organizations," or through academics, as "classes have always felt like big families." Since everyone is "pretty easygoing and easy to get along with," this "on-the-go" group says that "fitting in is easy; you just act like yourself!" There's every type of background and personality here, and because "everyone is different; anyone could fit in and find a group here." At the end of the day, everyone is "proud to be [a] Tiger," with one student adding, "We all fit in because we have this in common." To sum up the student body, Tigers are "pretty great company."

University of Missouri

Financial Aid: 573-882-7506 • E-Mail: MU4U@missouri.edu • Website: www.missouri.edu

THE PRINCETON REVIEW SAYS

Admissions

The school reports that its standardized testing policy for use in admission for Fall 2026 is Test Optional. The Princeton Review suggests that interested applicants consult with the school for the most up-to-date standardized testing policies. *Very important factors considered include:* class rank, academic GPA, standardized test scores. *Other factors considered include:* rigor of secondary school record, application essay, recommendation(s), talent/ability. High school diploma is required and GED is accepted. *Academic units required:* 4 English, 4 math, 3 science, 1 science lab, 2 language (other than English), 3 social studies, 1 academic elective.

Financial Aid

Students should submit: FAFSA. The Princeton Review suggests that all financial aid forms be submitted as soon as possible. *Need-based scholarships/grants offered:* Federal Pell; Federal SEOG; State scholarships/grants; Private scholarships; College/university scholarship or grant aid from institutional funds; Federal Nursing Scholarships. *Loan aid offered:* Federal Direct Subsidized Loans; Federal Direct Unsubsidized Loans; Direct PLUS loans; College/university loans from institutional funds. Admitted students will be notified of awards on a rolling basis beginning 3/1. Federal Work-Study Program available. Institutional employment available.

The Inside Word

If your application suggests that you can handle the workload here, i.e., a college-prep high school curriculum and a good GPA, the school will find a place for you. Even those who don't meet these criteria have a chance; admissions officers consider essays, recommendations, and special talents in the cases of borderline candidates.

THE SCHOOL SAYS

From the Admissions Office

"Founded in 1839 as the first public university west of the Mississippi River, Mizzou is a member of the Association of American Universities, the nation's most prestigious group of research institutions. Mizzou is one of only thirty-eight public universities in the AAU. The National Science Foundation has recognized Mizzou as one of the top ten universities in the country for integrating research into undergraduate education, and Mizzou offers twelve major undergraduate research programs, some with freshmen participants.

"Mizzou is nestled in the heart of downtown Columbia, Missouri. Galleries, concert halls, theaters, shops, festivals, and restaurants are all just steps from campus, making it hard to tell where campus ends and downtown begins.

"Students get right into the mix at Mizzou with the Missouri Method. This hands-on learning methodology is central to students' learning experiences. They'll be reporting news live on the local NBC TV station, working alongside researchers to advance health care, healing animals, trading stocks, and teaching kindergartners.

"Mizzou's Freshman Interest Groups (FIGs) program places freshmen in residence halls alongside students with similar interests. Freshmen take courses and participate in activities with the fellow FIG members, creating a sense of community and leading to academic success.

"There are more than 650 student organizations to belong to, and more than 300 degree programs for students to choose from. If a degree program doesn't quite meet a student's needs, they have the option of creating their own.

"Students can find admissions requirements at admissions.missouri.edu. The application takes about fifteen minutes to complete."

SELECTIVITY

# of total applicants	27,286
% of total applicants accepted	76
% of total acceptees attending	29
# of in-state applicants	10,576
% of in-state applicants accepted	80
# of out-of-state-applicants	15,471
% of applicants accepted from out of state	76
# of international applicants	1,239
% of international applicants accepted	46

First-Year Profile

Testing policy	Test Optional
Range SAT EBRW	590–680
Range SAT math	580–670
Range ACT composite	23–30
% submitting SAT scores	9
% submitting ACT scores	59
% graduated top 10% of class	34
% graduated top 25% of class	66
% graduated top 50% of class	93
% submitting high school rank	39

Important Dates

Regular	
Apply by	7/1
Notified by	Rolling, 10/1
Nonfall registration?	Yes

FINANCIAL FACTS

Annual in-state tuition	$14,334
Annual out-of-state tuition	$36,606
Food and housing	$15,008
Required fees	$1,214
Books and supplies	$918
Average need-based scholarship (First-year)	$15,051 ($16,583)
% students with need rec. need-based scholarship or grant aid (First-year)	95 (98)
% students with need rec. non-need-based scholarship or grant aid (First-year)	13 (16)
% students with need rec. need-based self-help aid (First-year)	56 (64)
% students rec. any financial aid (First-year)	NR (93)
% UG borrow to pay for school	47
Average cumulative indebtedness	$27,725
% of students with need fully met (First-year)	18 (21)
Average % of student need met (First-year)	66 (71)

THE UNIVERSITY OF MONTANA—MISSOULA

32 Campus Drive, Missoula, MT 59812 • Admissions: 406-243-6266

Survey Snapshot
Recreation facilities are great
Everyone loves the Grizzlies
Students love Missoula, MT

RATINGS

Quality of Life	**79**
Fire Safety	**84**
Green	**97**
Academic	**77**
Profs Interesting	**87**
Profs Accessible	**89**
Admissions	**82**
Financial Aid	**80**

CAMPUS LIFE

Type of school	Public
Environment	City

Students

Degree-seeking undergrad enrollment	7,515
% male/female/not reported	44/56/0
% from out of state	30
% First-year live on campus	76
% Ugrads live on campus	37
# of fraternities (% join)	6 (6)
# of sororities (% join)	4 (6)
% Asian	1
% Black or African American	1
% Hispanic	5
% Native American	3
% Pacific Islander	<1
% Race and/or ethnicity unknown	5
% Two or more races	5
% White	78
% International	1
# of countries represented	43

CAMPUS MENTAL HEALTH SERVICES

Offers mental health/wellness program	Yes
Mental health training available to students	No
Employs Chief Wellness Officer	NR
Peer-to-peer mental health offerings	NR
Counseling center has guidelines or accreditation	No
Mental health/well-being courses	NR

ACADEMICS

% students returning for sophomore year	71
% students graduating within 4 years	30
% students graduating within 6 years	49
Calendar	Semester
Student/faculty ratio	16:1
Most common class size 10–19.	(36%)
Most common lab/discussion size 10–19.	(38%)

Most Popular Majors

Business Administration and Management; Forest Management/Forest Resources Management; Psychology

STUDENTS SAY "..."

Academics

At the base of Mount Sentinel and along the banks of the Clark Fork River, the natural setting of the University of Montana—Missoula reflects its commitment to "environmental sustainability...and social justice." With over 175 academic programs to choose from, students rave about standout departments like wildlife biology, forestry, physical therapy, and forensic anthropology. The beautiful campus, wide range of academic offerings, and surrounding city of Missoula combine to make the University of Montana "a great place to live, work, and study." Professors at this public research university are described as "helpful, engaging, and accessible" and "very knowledgeable about what they are teaching." This fosters a learning environment that is "always interesting and inviting." As one student shares, "Math and science has never come easy for me, and my professors have taught in a way I completely understand the material." Students appreciate that they are never treated like "just a number" and are encouraged to be "creative thinkers and engaged citizens." As one student elaborates, "I truly appreciate all the effort that is put forward to help students succeed and prepare for the next steps in their life."

Campus Life

Students who love the great outdoors will appreciate the University of Montana's amazing location. One undergrad says, "Western Montana is a divine place for hiking, hunting, fishing, camping, snowshoeing, swimming, huckleberry picking, going to hot springs, mushroom picking, antler collecting, and just being immersed in nature." For those looking for an even greater adrenaline rush, there's also "skiing and skydiving, hang gliding and parasailing, mountain climbing and repelling, [and] caving and biking." On campus, "when it's not snowing in the fall or spring, you can find people playing Frisbee, walking their dogs, catching footballs, and even playing with lightsabers." When hunger strikes, U of M has 21 dining venues to choose from. They even have their own garden where they grow thousands of pounds of fresh produce each year and maintain an apiary for honeybees, underscoring U of M's focus on sustainability. The campus boasts great facilities, including a 25-yard competition pool, a golf course, and a fitness and recreation center with a climbing wall. Students report that "football is really big here," and during the season, the games are always packed with excited fans. Additionally, there are "many music concerts and dance parties" to attend. Missoula is known for its outdoor recreation, but students also enjoy exploring the city for its shopping, dining, outdoor food trucks, and theater. One student says that one of the best things about U of M is "there is always something to do no matter what your interests are and great people to do them with."

Student Body

In general, students who attend the University of Montana are "pretty laid-back and easygoing." They are also very supportive of one another. As one student notes, "If you're lost or need to ask a question, you can ask anyone, and they're willing to [help]." Although many students hail from Montana, students note that the school's "increasing diversity efforts have begun to show" within recent years. Most people at U of M are "accepting, friendly, and very involved in college and community life." In addition, the university's strong focus on the environment attracts many "outdoorsy" types and "future biologists" who want to make a difference. Overall, students say the U of M community is welcoming and accepting. As one student put it, "People here do not seem to judge others or hold stereotypes against each other." Another student adds, "I feel like I've stepped into a melting pot of all beliefs and ideals. You can be yourself and never be looked down on for that at this school."

THE UNIVERSITY OF MONTANA—MISSOULA

Financial Aid: 406-243-5373 • E-Mail: admiss@umontana.edu • Website: www.umt.edu

THE PRINCETON REVIEW SAYS

Admissions

The school reports that its standardized testing policy for use in admission for Fall 2026 is Test Optional. The Princeton Review suggests that interested applicants consult with the school for the most up-to-date standardized testing policies. *Very important factors considered include:* rigor of secondary school record, class rank, academic GPA, standardized test scores. *Important factors considered include:* extracurricular activities, talent/ability. High school diploma is required and GED is accepted. *Academic units required:* 4 English, 3 math, 2 science, 2 science labs, 3 social studies, 2 history. *Academic units recommended:* 2 language (other than English), 2 computer science, 2 visual/performing arts.

Financial Aid

Students should submit: FAFSA. Priority filing deadline is 12/1. The Princeton Review suggests that all financial aid forms be submitted as soon as possible. *Need-based scholarships/grants offered:* Federal Pell; Federal SEOG; State scholarships/grants; Private scholarships; College/university scholarship or grant aid from institutional funds. *Loan aid offered:* Federal Direct Subsidized Loans; Federal Direct Unsubsidized Loans; Direct PLUS loans. Admitted students will be notified of awards on a rolling basis beginning 3/16. Federal Work-Study Program available. Institutional employment available.

The Inside Word

The admissions process at the University of Montana is fairly straightforward. Officers here rely heavily on quantitative data. Applicants who meet GPA minimums and are in the top half of their graduating class generally receive an acceptance letter. Those who did not meet the minimum requirements can often enroll on a conditional basis.

THE SCHOOL SAYS

From the Admissions Office

"There's something special about this place. It's something different for each person. For some, it's the blend of academic quality and outdoor recreation. The University of Montana ranks fifth in the nation among public institutions for producing Rhodes scholars, and Outside Magazine lists Missoula in its 'Top Ten Amazing Places for Outdoor Recreation.' For others, it's size—not too big, not too small. The University of Montana is a midsized university in the heart of the Rocky Mountains—accessible in both admission and tuition bills—that produces graduates considered among the best and brightest in the world. It is located in a community that could pass for a cozy college town or a bustling big city, depending on your point of view. There's a lot happening, but you won't get lost. People are friendly and diverse. They come from all over the world to study and learn and to live a good life. They come to a place to be inspired, a place where they feel comfortable yet challenged. Some never leave. Most never want to."

SELECTIVITY

# of total applicants	4,910
% of total applicants accepted	94
% of total acceptees attending	32

First-Year Profile

Testing policy	Test Optional
Range SAT EBRW	540–640
Range SAT math	520–610
Range ACT composite	20–26
% submitting SAT scores	39
% submitting ACT scores	71
Average HS GPA	3.4
% submitting high school GPA	97
% graduated top 10% of class	16
% graduated top 25% of class	40
% graduated top 50% of class	73
% submitting high school rank	65

Important Dates

Regular	
Notified by	Rolling, 6/15
Nonfall registration?	Yes

FINANCIAL FACTS

Annual in-state tuition	$5,352
Annual out-of-state tuition	$24,144
Food and housing	$9,966
Required fees	$2,002
Books and supplies	$1,100
Average need-based scholarship (First-year)	$4,991 ($5,168)
% students with need rec. need-based scholarship or grant aid (First-year)	61 (56)
% students with need rec. non-need-based scholarship or grant aid (First-year)	52 (80)
% students with need rec. need-based self-help aid (First-year)	91 (95)
% students rec. any financial aid (First-year)	63 (74)
% UG borrow to pay for school	58
Average cumulative indebtedness	$27,132
% of students with need fully met (First-year)	11 (12)
Average % of student need met (First-year)	61 (69)

UNIVERSITY OF NEBRASKA—LINCOLN

1410 R St, Lincoln, NE 68588-0419 • Admissions: 402-472-2023

Survey Snapshot
Students are happy
Students love Lincoln, NE
Frats and sororities are popular

RATINGS	
Quality of Life	89
Fire Safety	86
Green	96
Academic	78
Profs Interesting	85
Profs Accessible	90
Admissions	84
Financial Aid	86

CAMPUS LIFE

Type of school	Public
Environment	City

Students

Degree-seeking undergrad enrollment	19,230
% male/female/not reported	51/49/0
% from out of state	23
% First-year live on campus	91
% Ugrads live on campus	52
# of fraternities (% join)	29 (30)
# of sororities (% join)	25 (37)
% Asian	4
% Black or African American	3
% Hispanic	10
% Native American	<1
% Pacific Islander	<1
% Race and/or ethnicity unknown	1
% Two or more races	4
% White	75
% International	2
# of countries represented	77

CAMPUS MENTAL HEALTH SERVICES

Offers mental health/wellness program	Yes
Mental health training available to students	Yes
Employs Chief Wellness Officer	Yes
Peer-to-peer mental health offerings	Yes
Counseling center has guidelines or accreditation	Yes
Mental health/well-being courses	Yes, for-credit

ACADEMICS

% students returning for sophomore year	86
% students graduating within 4 years	54
% students graduating within 6 years	69
Calendar	Semester
Student/faculty ratio	17:1
Most common class size 20–29.	(28%)
Most common lab/discussion size 20–29.	(47%)

Most Popular Majors
Psychology; Business Administration and Management; Finance

Applicants Often Prefer
University of Nebraska at Kearney, University of Nebraska at Omaha

Applicants Sometimes Prefer
Creighton University, Nebraska Wesleyan University, University of Kansas, Wayne State College

Applicants Rarely Prefer
Iowa State University, Kansas State University, Metropolitan Community College—Metropolitan Community College, Northeast Community College South Dakota State University

STUDENTS SAY "..."

Academics

The University of Nebraska–Lincoln is situated in a great spot—Nebraska's capital city—to make "connections with companies in Lincoln, Omaha, and surrounding areas," and provides "tons of undergraduate research opportunities," "amazing internships," and "leadership opportunities." Students find the university to pair this practical focus on "job placement," which is aided by "career coaches and employer-in residences, and partnerships with "local businesses," with the recognition and prestige of a Big Ten, "rigorous" research institution. Students also praise "phenomenal advisors," especially for pre-health students, "great study abroad programs," and other specific schools and programs such as the business school, the honors program, and Raikes School of Computer Science and Management. Because the school is a research institution, students in their second year onward benefit from "project-based courses where you…are paired with a company" and are taught from "real world examples" instead of just doing homework from textbooks. Faculty are known to be accessible and generous with students, offering "personal advice," orienting students and "introducing campus resources," and sometimes even "welcoming [students] to their home." Nebraska is also known to have a "fantastic financial aid and scholarship program that makes it very affordable to attend," offering "great scholarships, especially to out-of-state students" who would have a higher tuition bill.

Campus Life

Nebraska is the "smallest Big Ten public school," so students say their "beautiful campus" is "great if you're looking for a prestigious school, but a bit smaller." Students overwhelmingly name the Division I football team ("Go Big Red!") as being a generator of school spirit that spreads into the "incredible college town." "Since this is the only football team here in Nebraska, many people are very excited for game days here in Lincoln," one student reports. Intramural sports are also popular: "there are always pick-up games of soccer, ultimate Frisbee, football" and so on "on the outdoor artificial turf fields, as well as the indoor practice facilities," which includes an "indoor football field for students."

About "20 percent of students are in Greek life," and "the whole campus is always attending their philanthropy events." And with over 500 clubs, students need not leave campus to pack their schedules with activities outside of studying. However, campus is right next to downtown, so the campus isn't isolated; students are "part of the Lincoln community," which offers a "small town feel with big town amenities." In the city, students "catch a movie at the downtown movie theater," go "ice skating," and "jogging" or "shop in the Haymarket area."

Student Body

University of Nebraska–Lincoln's student body is made up of an "array of students from small town Nebraska, the big cities of Lincoln and Omaha" as well as a number of "out-of-state and international students." "Kindness permeates interactions across campus," and the "passion that the students have for their institution is palpable." Students are by and large "friendly but conservative," a "mixture of rural and city kids." "The mix of cultures works really well" reflecting "Midwestern manners of kind, friendly people." Students are studious but interconnected, especially through their identification with "Husker power." "Sports aren't my main concern," says another, "but it is super awesome attending a Big Ten university" because of the "pride" and "positive and outgoing" Lincoln community.

University of Nebraska—Lincoln

Financial Aid: 402-472-2030 • E-Mail: admissions@unl.edu • Website: www.unl.edu

THE PRINCETON REVIEW SAYS

Admissions

The school reports that its standardized testing policy for use in admission for Fall 2026 is Test Optional. The Princeton Review suggests that interested applicants consult with the school for the most up-to-date standardized testing policies. *Important factors considered include:* rigor of secondary school record, class rank, academic GPA, standardized test scores. High school diploma is required and GED is accepted. *Academic units required:* 4 English, 4 math, 3 science, 1 science lab, 2 language (other than English), 1 social studies, 2 history.

Financial Aid

Students should submit: FAFSA. The Princeton Review suggests that all financial aid forms be submitted as soon as possible. *Need-based scholarships/grants offered:* Federal Pell; Federal SEOG; State scholarships/grants; Private scholarships. *Loan aid offered:* Federal Direct Subsidized Loans; Federal Direct Unsubsidized Loans; Direct PLUS loans. Admitted students will be notified of awards on a rolling basis beginning 2/1. Federal Work-Study Program available. Institutional employment available.

The Inside Word

All applications will be weighed on the combined strength of course work, GPAs, and test scores (if submitted). Applicants interested in applying to a specific school within the university should take into account those school's specialized requirements as they may include additional high school coursework than what is required by the university's general studies program. To be considered for departmental scholarships as well as leadership and service scholarships, submit a supplemental scholarship application and include a narrative that focuses on leadership, community service, career goals and other experiences.

THE SCHOOL SAYS

From the Admissions Office

"We are Nebraska. We believe in the power of every person. We don't rest on our strengths—we stretch them. Sweat them. Combine them. Growing flexible, nimble, and strong minds. That's how we do big things. Our faculty and researchers work hard to help students succeed and to solve real-world issues. Students can quickly access the programs they desire, get involved in the university community and build their skills—all elements that will help them create the future they want. Nebraska has a low student-to-faculty ratio, a substantial out-of-state scholarship program and one of the nation's leading undergraduate research programs.

"The university is the heart of Lincoln, a growing, thriving contemporary city. Tech startups are flocking to Lincoln to recruit talent from the university and get involved with our cutting-edge Innovation Campus. The city's downtown is steps away from campus and home to a rich arts and music scene. Campus upgrades to the student union and rec centers, plus several building projects, contribute to a vibrant and dynamic culture. More than 200,000 alumni from the University of Nebraska–Lincoln's 150-year history have made a difference in the world and opened doors for those who've followed."

SELECTIVITY

# of total applicants	18,648
% of total applicants accepted	88
% of total acceptees attending	29
# of in-state applicants	9,229
% of in-state applicants accepted	89
# of out-of-state-applicants	8,413
% of applicants accepted from out of state	91
# of international applicants	1,006
% of international applicants accepted	43

First-Year Profile

Testing policy	Test Optional
Range SAT composite	1070–1310
Range SAT EBRW	540–670
Range SAT math	520–650
Range ACT composite	21–28
% submitting SAT scores	7
% submitting ACT scores	81
Average HS GPA	3.5
% submitting high school GPA	91
% graduated top 10% of class	30
% graduated top 25% of class	56
% graduated top 50% of class	85
% submitting high school rank	41

Important Dates

Regular	
Apply by	5/1
Notified by	Rolling, 8/1
Nonfall registration?	Yes

FINANCIAL FACTS

Annual in-state tuition	$11,382
Annual out-of-state tuition	$31,182
Food and housing	$13,950
Books and supplies	$1,128
Average need-based scholarship (First-year)	$11,627 ($11,938)
% students with need rec. need-based scholarship or grant aid (First-year)	97 (98)
% students with need rec. non-need-based scholarship or grant aid (First-year)	10 (12)
% students with need rec. need-based self-help aid (First-year)	51 (57)
% students rec. any financial aid (First-year)	92 (90)
% UG borrow to pay for school	46
Average cumulative indebtedness	$23,870
% of students with need fully met (First-year)	18 (20)
Average % of student need met (First-year)	73 (79)

University of New England

11 Hills Beach Road, Biddeford, ME 04005-9599 • Admissions: 207-602-2847

Survey Snapshot
Frats and sororities are popular
Everyone loves the Nor'Easters
Intramural sports are popular

RATINGS

Quality of Life	83
Fire Safety	95
Green	98
Academic	77
Profs Interesting	89
Profs Accessible	91
Admissions	72
Financial Aid	91

CAMPUS LIFE

Type of school	Private
Environment	Town

Students

Degree-seeking undergrad enrollment	2,106
% male/female/not reported	31/69/0
% from out of state	74
% First-year live on campus	95
% Ugrads live on campus	67
# of fraternities	0
# of sororities	0
% Asian	2
% Black or African American	2
% Hispanic	6
% Native American	<1
% Pacific Islander	0
% Race and/or ethnicity unknown	3
% Two or more races	3
% White	84
% International	<1
# of countries represented	4

CAMPUS MENTAL HEALTH SERVICES

Offers mental health/wellness program	Yes
Mental health training available to students	Yes
Employs Chief Wellness Officer	Yes
Peer-to-peer mental health offerings	No
Counseling center has guidelines or accreditation	Yes
Mental health/well-being courses	Yes, non-credit

ACADEMICS

% students returning for sophomore year	77
% students graduating within 4 years	55
% students graduating within 6 years	62
Calendar	Semester
Student/faculty ratio	11:1
Most common class size 10–19.	(40%)
Most common lab/discussion size 10–19.	(55%)

Most Popular Majors

Biomedical Sciences; Marine Biology and Biological Oceanography; Registered Nursing/Registered Nurse

Applicants Also Look At

University of Maine, University of New Hampshire, University of Rhode Island, University of Southern Maine, University of Vermont

STUDENTS SAY "..."

Academics

At the University of New England, students appreciate the "amazing and smart professors," the "great facilities for learning," and the "many resources that help people succeed." The marine and environmental programs are popular and utilize UNE's 363-acre forest, the Marine Science Center, and Ram Island (UNE's research ecosystem) to inspire students to "come up with our own ideas to help the planet!" There are "so many interesting classes offered," and the curriculum prioritizes hands-on learning experiences. For example, students describe tagging birds to gather data, taking boats out to sample water, and even training a rat for an animal learning class. Students can also participate in projects such as the Living Shoreline project, which is helping restore parts of UNE's shoreline that have been eroded through climate change. The opportunity to study abroad at UNE's campus in Morocco is another highlight, accessible to students from all majors. Resources such as academic tutoring and free counseling services help students feel supported during their time at UNE. Perhaps the biggest draw for many students are the professors, who possess "deep knowledge about the subjects they teach, are "easily accessible outside the classroom," and are "so passionate about their work." Most students agree that "the professors here truly love what they do and want to make classes worth coming to."

Campus Life

A major draw for many students is the school's scenic campus, which is surrounded by forests, fields, and a private beach. Plenty is happening on this active campus, including "tons of activities to attend and clubs to join." As one student emphasizes, "This place is truly amazing when it comes to extracurricular activities," which include an eclectic array of options, ranging from trivia and game nights to the fishing club, surf club, and Storm Surge, "a fun place for students who enjoy playing an instrument." Another favorite is the Outing Club, with its "trips to many different places like hiking trails, backpacking trips, rock climbing excursions, and so many more awesome opportunities," though it's easy for students to make their own plans: "You can always see students biking around [and] going for walks around campus, whether it's on trails or heading to the beach." Students also participate in intramural sports and make use of the gym, which features a pool and sauna. Students note that "school spirit is very high here" and "sports such as hockey and football always bring a large crowd!" One tradition that brings the campus together is the Teddy Bear Toss, where students throw teddy bears onto the ice after the first goal scored by UNE's hockey team. The bears are then donated, along with a financial donation, to local organizations. "School spirit is very high here, which I think is an important [part] of loving where you go."

Student Body

UNE students are "academically focused and engaged with their career paths." The school attracts "very unique and inspiring" individuals who "care about the well-being of others and the planet." It's a place where "just stepping on campus makes you feel a part of a loving community!" As one student describes it, "We are all very close and everyone is friendly with everyone," adding, "UNE is pretty small, so you really make friends everywhere you go." Another student agrees, explaining that "[My peers] help me when I need [it] and lift me up when I'm down. This school feels like home." Overall, "the student body encompasses a variety of personalities, [so] there's sure to be someone who shares the same interests as you." As one student says, "The UNE community is very accepting and supportive. Making friends was easy...There's always something to do and new people to meet."

University of New England

Financial Aid: 207-602-2342 • E-Mail: admissions@une.edu • Website: www.une.edu

THE PRINCETON REVIEW SAYS

Admissions

The school reports that its standardized testing policy for use in admission for Fall 2026 is Test Free. The Princeton Review suggests that interested applicants consult with the school for the most up-to-date standardized testing policies. *Very important factors considered include:* rigor of secondary school record, academic GPA. *Important factors considered include:* application essay, extracurricular activities. *Other factors considered include:* class rank, recommendation(s), talent/ability, character/personal qualities, first generation, alumni/ae relation, volunteer work, work experience. High school diploma is required and GED is accepted. *Academic units recommended:* 4 English, 3 math, 2 science, 2 science labs, 2 social studies.

Financial Aid

Students should submit: FAFSA. The Princeton Review suggests that all financial aid forms be submitted as soon as possible. *Need-based scholarships/grants offered:* Federal Pell; Federal SEOG; State scholarships/grants; Private scholarships; College/university scholarship or grant aid from institutional funds. *Loan aid offered:* Federal Direct Subsidized Loans; Federal Direct Unsubsidized Loans; Direct PLUS loans. Admitted students will be notified of awards on a rolling basis beginning 12/15. Federal Work-Study Program available. Institutional employment available.

The Inside Word

A strong high school transcript is the best way to get the attention of the admissions department at University of New England. The average high school GPA for admitted students is 3.5. Since the school is so heavily focused in the sciences, students with a rigorous math and science course load in high school will likely do well. For those students who apply with set career aspirations, the GradVantage program is intended to allow talented undergraduate applicants the opportunity to combine their UNE undergraduate admission with a potential track into one of the school's graduate programs. Any student who wants an admissions answer sooner rather than later should consider applying early action—it's non-binding.

THE SCHOOL SAYS

From the Admissions Office

"The University of New England (UNE) is a top-ranked private university on a stunning seaside campus in Biddeford, Maine. UNE offers over 60 undergraduate majors, including flagship programs in marine and environmental science with hands-on research along Maine's coastline, and health and life sciences with clear pathways into its health and medical graduate programs. The University also offers degrees in business, education, social sciences, and arts and humanities.

"In addition to its coastal undergraduate campus, UNE's Portland, Maine, campus is home to the University's graduate health profession programs, including the only medical school in the state. A third campus in Tangier, Morocco, serves as an international gateway to Africa and Europe. All UNE campuses foster close-knit student communities engaged in rigorous academic, professional, and extracurricular experiences. Outside the classroom, students enjoy a wide range of cultural and social events and participate in clubs, activities, and an NCAA Division III varsity athletics program.

"Students benefit from extensive opportunities for fieldwork, clinical experiences, research, internships, and global education. Interdisciplinary learning allows students to collaborate across majors and understand how their area of specialization functions within real-world professional settings. Eligible students can prepare for graduate study through programs such as Pre-Health Advising and GradVantage, an academic distinction that simplifies the path to advanced health degrees. UNE is committed to making students *Future Ready* by offering distinctive experiences and industry connections. Graduates build strong professional networks through the Nor'easter Global Network and gain practical insight into how emerging technologies will shape their fields."

SELECTIVITY

# of total applicants	4,666
% of total applicants accepted	92
% of total acceptees attending	12

First-Year Profile

Testing policy	Test Free
Average HS GPA	3.5
% submitting high school GPA	100

Important Dates

Early action	
Apply by	11/15
Notified by	varies
Regular	
Apply by	2/15
Nonfall registration?	Yes

FINANCIAL FACTS

Annual tuition	$44,280
Food and housing	$18,690
Required fees	$1,620
Books and supplies	$1,200
Average need-based scholarship (First-year)	$9,522 ($7,433)
% students with need rec. need-based scholarship or grant aid (First-year)	72 (NR)
% students with need rec. non-need-based scholarship or grant aid (First-year)	94 (91)
% students with need rec. need-based self-help aid (First-year)	84 (91)
% students rec. any financial aid (First-year)	98 (100)
% UG borrow to pay for school	83
Average cumulative indebtedness	$56,025
% of students with need fully met (First-year)	88 (84)
Average % of student need met (First-year)	75 (68)

UNIVERSITY OF NEW HAMPSHIRE

1 Garrison Avenue, Durham, NH 03824 • Admissions: 603-862-1360

Survey Snapshot
Great library
Students aren't religious
Everyone loves the Wildcats

RATINGS

Quality of Life	84
Fire Safety	99
Green	96
Academic	76
Profs Interesting	85
Profs Accessible	88
Admissions	82
Financial Aid	85

CAMPUS LIFE

Type of school	Public
Environment	Village

Students

Degree-seeking undergrad enrollment	10,809
% male/female/not reported	45/55/<1
% from out of state	51
% First-year live on campus	96
% Ugrads live on campus	59
# of fraternities (% join)	11 (19)
# of sororities (% join)	8 (16)
% Asian	3
% Black or African American	1
% Hispanic	5
% Native American	<1
% Pacific Islander	<1
% Race and/or ethnicity unknown	3
% Two or more races	3
% White	84
% International	1
# of countries represented	37

CAMPUS MENTAL HEALTH SERVICES

Offers mental health/wellness program	Yes
Mental health training available to students	Yes
Employs Chief Wellness Officer	Yes
Peer-to-peer mental health offerings	Yes
Counseling center has guidelines or accreditation	Yes
Mental health/well-being courses	Yes, for-credit

ACADEMICS

% students returning for sophomore year	88
% students graduating within 4 years	68
% students graduating within 6 years	77
Calendar	Semester
Student/faculty ratio	17:1
Most common class size 20–29.	(31%)
Most common lab/discussion size 20–29.	(40%)

Most Popular Majors

Psychology; Business Administration and Management; Registered Nursing/Registered Nurse

Applicants Also Look At

University of Connecticut, University of Maine, University of Massachusetts—Amherst, University of Rhode Island, University of Vermont

STUDENTS SAY "..."

Academics

The University of New Hampshire is about connections, whether that's what a "state school offers...to local community" or the way in which it "makes use of their outdoors... and gets students involved in hands-on services and experiences." The students of its 100+ majors (and eleven schools and colleges) get lifelong support from the office of Career and Professional Success, which leaves students feeling that they can "learn whatever you want." It helps that UNH "is especially good at providing information and resources. There are millions of flyers all around campus, including in lecture halls and dorms, informing you of what is going on on-campus and where you can go or who you can contact if you need help."

Professors are commended not just for being "very good lecturers" but for the way they are "happy to help in their area of expertise and genuinely interested in doing so." This may involve allowing students to "separate themselves in order to learn when necessary" during class and being "willing to spend time individually to explain material and offer learning resources outside of the classroom." Students also list a variety of teaching methods, including "small groups, large groups, class conversations, personal work, and all other manner of work in class, as well as a flipped classroom." Now add in "a constantly improving curriculum," "plenty of internships," "a plethora of research opportunities," and science labs that "have really taken the material to a whole other level of learning." As one student notes, "there is so much to do which prepares students for life after graduation that it's hard to list it all."

Campus Life

A student's standard routine is to "attend their classes, do work for a few hours, and hang out a lot with each other at night." Students do mention "a very active night life with dorm competitions and socials, countless intramural sports teams, and welcoming parties across the campus," as well as events like trivia and concerts. They also refer to the campus itself being "very pretty and easy to walk, making it have a more calming environment overall," and with a great location in Durham that provides "a safe rural environment while still being close to the ocean, activities, and cities like Boston." The winter gets a particular shout out because students can (and do) "go skiing or even just sledding around campus and there are always great trails to go hiking." Ultimately, with more than two hundred student clubs and organizations, including "student-run groups for various backgrounds, lifestyles and viewpoints, from political groups to hobby groups," students feel confident that there's something for everyone.

Student Body

Many students love the school's size of 11,000 students, which "is big enough to get lost in and small enough to find people who will become forever friends." People "tend to be very social" and many "are active and value physical activities, part of why the campus is so pristinely kept." Most students "are from New England in New Hampshire and Massachusetts," and although the school is "not very diverse, we have a lot of programs and are very accepting for our minority communities." Those who attend UNH are "generally driven, with a good sense of community and collaboration among the more difficult classes and majors," and "each student has a passion or goal that they want to achieve in life," so the university "is a great place to really expand your horizons and become who you've always wanted to be." There is "lots of pride in the school and events going on, so a lot of people are excited and energetic," and a student says that "whether it is presenting my research at our undergraduate research conference, or simply talking to somebody in the Dunkin' line in the MUB [student center], the student body at UNH is overall friendly and approachable."

University of New Hampshire

Financial Aid: 603-862-3600 • E-Mail: admissions@unh.edu • Website: www.unh.edu

THE PRINCETON REVIEW SAYS

Admissions

The school reports that its standardized testing policy for use in admission for Fall 2026 is Test Optional. The Princeton Review suggests that interested applicants consult with the school for the most up-to-date standardized testing policies. *Very important factors considered include:* rigor of secondary school record, academic GPA. *Important factors considered include:* recommendation(s). *Other factors considered include:* class rank, standardized test scores, application essay, extracurricular activities, talent/ability, character/personal qualities, first generation, volunteer work, work experience. High school diploma is required and GED is accepted. *Academic units required:* 4 English, 3 math, 2 science, 2 science labs, 2 social studies, 4 academic electives. *Academic units recommended:* 4 English, 4 math, 4 science, 3 science labs, 2 language (other than English), 3 social studies, 4 academic electives.

Financial Aid

Students should submit: FAFSA. Priority filing deadline is 3/1. The Princeton Review suggests that all financial aid forms be submitted as soon as possible. *Need-based scholarships/grants offered:* Federal Pell; Federal SEOG; State scholarships/grants; Private scholarships; College/university scholarship or grant aid from institutional funds. *Loan aid offered:* Federal Direct Subsidized Loans; Federal Direct Unsubsidized Loans; Direct PLUS loans. Admitted students will be notified of awards on a rolling basis beginning 1/15. Federal Work-Study Program available. Institutional employment available.

The Inside Word

UNH's emphasis on academic accomplishment in the admissions process makes it clear that the admissions committee is looking for students who have taken high school seriously. Standardized tests take as much of a backseat here as is possible at a large, public university.

THE SCHOOL SAYS

From the Admissions Office

"The University of New Hampshire is proud to be consistently recognized as one of the best-value public universities in the nation. As an R1 Carnegie research institution, we are a vibrant community of innovators and pioneers, tackling urgent global challenges and driving positive change through groundbreaking research and a strong commitment to sustainability. Nestled in the picturesque town of Durham, NH, our beautiful and safe campus offers an ideal setting for academic and personal growth. Surrounded by the White Mountains, the Atlantic Ocean, and just 60 miles from Boston, UNH provides endless opportunities for exploration and adventure. No matter which of our 100+ majors you choose, you'll have the chance to take your learning beyond the classroom. Three out of four of our undergraduate students engage in high-impact experiences such as internships, research, and study abroad. With over 200 student clubs, there's always a way to connect, grow, and make an impact. The Wildcat spirit goes beyond just cheering for the home team; it's about being part of an empowering community where students of all backgrounds and journeys come together to grow, explore, and succeed."

SELECTIVITY

# of total applicants	21,567
% of total applicants accepted	89
% of total acceptees attending	12
# of in-state applicants	4,548
% of in-state applicants accepted	87
# of out-of-state-applicants	16,521
% of applicants accepted from out of state	90
# of international applicants	498
% of international applicants accepted	85

First-Year Profile

Testing policy	Test Optional
Range SAT composite	1120–1310
Range SAT EBRW	560–680
Range SAT math	540–650
Range ACT composite	26–30
% submitting SAT scores	19
% submitting ACT scores	1
Average HS GPA	3.6
% submitting high school GPA	100

Important Dates

Early action	
Apply by	11/15
Notified by	1/30
Regular	
Apply by	2/1
Notified by	12/31
Nonfall registration?	Yes

FINANCIAL FACTS

Annual in-state tuition	$16,304
Annual out-of-state tuition	$37,996
Food and housing	$15,584
Required fees	$3,868
Books and supplies	$1,000
Average need-based scholarship (First-year)	$8,947 ($8,391)
% students with need rec. need-based scholarship or grant aid (First-year)	86 (80)
% students with need rec. non-need-based scholarship or grant aid (First-year)	37 (55)
% students with need rec. need-based self-help aid (First-year)	89 (86)
% students rec. any financial aid (First-year)	92 (97)
% UG borrow to pay for school	67
Average cumulative indebtedness	$45,196
% of students with need fully met (First-year)	15 (17)
Average % of student need met (First-year)	68 (68)

UNIVERSITY OF NEW HAVEN

300 Boston Post Road, West Haven, CT 06516 • Admissions: 203-932-7319

Survey Snapshot
Recreation facilities are great
Students are happy
Great library

RATINGS

Quality of Life	76
Fire Safety	60*
Green	60*
Academic	77
Profs Interesting	85
Profs Accessible	86
Admissions	87
Financial Aid	86

CAMPUS LIFE

Type of school	Private
Environment	Town

Students

Degree-seeking undergrad enrollment	4,969
% male/female/not reported	40/60/0
% from out of state	52
% First-year live on campus	76
% Ugrads live on campus	50
# of fraternities (% join)	7 (NR)
# of sororities (% join)	8 (NR)
% Asian	3
% Black or African American	12
% Hispanic	22
% Native American	<1
% Pacific Islander	<1
% Race and/or ethnicity unknown	3
% Two or more races	6
% White	50
% International	4
# of countries represented	29

CAMPUS MENTAL HEALTH SERVICES

Offers mental health/wellness program	Yes
Mental health training available to students	No
Employs Chief Wellness Officer	NR
Peer-to-peer mental health offerings	NR
Counseling center has guidelines or accreditation	No
Mental health/well-being courses	NR

ACADEMICS

% students returning for sophomore year	77
% students graduating within 4 years	55
% students graduating within 6 years	63
Calendar	Semester
Student/faculty ratio	16:1
Most common class size 20–29.	(45%)
Most common lab/discussion size 10–19.	(86%)

Most Popular Majors
Psychology; Criminal Justice/Law Enforcement Administration

Applicants Often Prefer
Central Connecticut State University, Southern Connecticut State University, University of Connecticut

Applicants Sometimes Prefer
City University of New York—John Jay College of Criminal Justice, Sacred Heart University, University of Hartford, University of Rhode Island

STUDENTS SAY "..."

Academics

Interdisciplinary study is the highlight of an education from the University of New Haven, where students take courses from across the five colleges and schools and engage in project-based learning to build out a practical, personalized degree. The lauded criminal justice program, for instance, has "a lot of opportunities...and different pathways offered for those going into law," and "academics, especially the legal studies department, are out of this world." Because at least one component of experiential education is required for graduation, the school works to ensure that students get internships or service learning, whether that's in a booming field like cybersecurity or international business, or an up-and-coming degree in Fire Science or Esports and Gaming. "Most students choose this school due to their specific major," notes one student, and another points out that New Haven "has a lot of amazing programs you cannot attend anywhere else." Several students point to the renowned Henry C. Lee Institute of Forensic Science, "a great strength in this school."

Faculty "have résumés that are incredibly proficient, in some cases to the point where they are overqualified to teach," and bring this experience to the classroom via case studies, examples, and "real world stories as well as hands-on events and exercises." Also, because "class sizes tend to stay small [we can form] better relationships with our professors." Those seeking further support outside class will find "flexible office hours for professors," a "writing center [that] helps with papers," and Centers for Academic Success and Advising. Overall, "the learning style here feels very hands-on," with burn rooms and a crime scene house that students can investigate and "unique equipment, materials, and procedures." As one student puts it, "I've taken a number of labs and field trips in my classes that have really prepared me to use equipment and methods I'll need in my field."

Campus Life

Slightly more than half of the students live on campus, enjoying the "wonderful facilities for a school of our size" and because first-years can choose their Enhanced Learning Community by interest, things like "watching movies in the lounges and playing poker, dominoes, or cards are always fun every night." The weekdays, however, are "usually packed with school time" and activities with the 150 clubs and organizations (like Greek life), many of which support the different majors, like the Forensic Science club, or which set about "taking part in public service opportunities." As for the weekends, athletics are a big part of this Division II school, and both intramurals and intercollegiate games "always can bring out a good crowd," while New Haven itself features plenty of "cool places and restaurants" to explore.

Student Body

At New Haven you'll find "a large number of like-minded people who are motivated by the course work and offered programs." There are "people of different race, religion, and all other kinds of backgrounds" here, and "it is easy to find people you fit in with because the campus is so diverse." Students and faculty "are very protective over making sure everyone gets along and doesn't feel out of place," and people here are "very welcoming, always open to helping one another and supportive of people who want to learn more" regardless of their major, as well as "caring and considerate." Students say that "even though it's a small campus, there are still tons of people to meet," and "you don't have to run into or see anyone you don't want to see, unless they live on your floor."

University of New Haven

Financial Aid: 203-479-4520 • E-Mail: admissions@newhaven.edu • Website: www.newhaven.edu

THE PRINCETON REVIEW SAYS

Admissions

The school reports that its standardized testing policy for use in admission for Fall 2026 is Test Optional. The Princeton Review suggests that interested applicants consult with the school for the most up-to-date standardized testing policies. *Very important factors considered include:* academic GPA. *Other factors considered include:* rigor of secondary school record, class rank, standardized test scores, application essay, recommendation(s), interview, extracurricular activities, character/personal qualities, volunteer work, work experience, level of applicant's interest. High school diploma is required and GED is accepted. *Academic units recommended:* 4 English, 3 math, 3 science, 2 science labs, 2 language (other than English).

Financial Aid

Students should submit: FAFSA. Priority filing deadline is 3/1. The Princeton Review suggests that all financial aid forms be submitted as soon as possible. *Need-based scholarships/grants offered:* Federal Pell; State scholarships/grants; Private scholarships; College/university scholarship or grant aid from institutional funds. *Loan aid offered:* Federal Direct Subsidized Loans; Federal Direct Unsubsidized Loans; Direct PLUS loans. Admitted students will be notified of awards on a rolling basis beginning 11/1. Federal Work-Study Program available. Institutional employment available.

The Inside Word

The University of New Haven is a welcoming institution, so don't feel rushed to apply for early decision (unless you want to have a personal interview). Although, it wouldn't hurt to demonstrate your interest or have a few AP-level courses to help you stand out.

THE SCHOOL SAYS

From the Admissions Office

"The University of New Haven is a leader in career-focused education, offering innovative majors in engineering, health sciences and healthcare, business, law enforcement and public service, liberal arts and sciences, and fine arts. In the last decade, the University has completed more than $300 million in major capital projects. Exciting facilities on campus include the Bergami Center for Science, Technology and Innovation (including a state-of-the-art communication studio), the Peterson Performance Center for student-athletes, the Henry C. Lee Institute of Forensic Science (featuring a crime-scene simulation center), a waterfront Marine Science Center, and various labs and clinical spaces for School of Health Sciences programs. Upcoming additions include a space to foster research, innovation, corporate partnerships, and applied technology called the Elevation Center as well as a new, on-campus building for the Pompea College of Business. Students engage in hands-on, resume-building experiences through faculty-mentored research, internships, service learning, and study abroad. While UNewHaven students partake in study abroad programs worldwide, the University's satellite campus in Prato, Italy, offers exclusive opportunities. Newer academic offerings include undergraduate degrees in Artificial Intelligence, Business Analytics, Cybersecurity, Game Design and Interactive Media, Health Sciences (including Occupational Therapy and Speech-Language Pathology), Homeland Security, Intelligence Analysis and Medical Laboratory Sciences. NCAA Division I athletics, a 260-member marching band, Greek life, Army ROTC, a student-run radio station, a showstopping theater production company, Model United Nations, and 150+ recognized student organizations are just a few of the great things students can get involved with at the University of New Haven."

SELECTIVITY

# of total applicants	22,529
% of total applicants accepted	60
% of total acceptees attending	9
# of in-state applicants	5,557
% of in-state applicants accepted	79
# of out-of-state-applicants	13,769
% of applicants accepted from out of state	61
# of international applicants	3,203
% of international applicants accepted	21
# of early decision applicants	122
% of early decision applicants accepted	50
# offered a place on the wait list	396
# admitted from wait list	45

First-Year Profile

Testing policy	Test Optional
Range SAT composite	1110–1300
Range SAT EBRW	580–670
Range SAT math	530–640
Range ACT composite	24–29
% submitting SAT scores	19
% submitting ACT scores	3
Average HS GPA	3.4
% submitting high school GPA	78
% graduated top 10% of class	14
% graduated top 25% of class	35
% graduated top 50% of class	75
% submitting high school rank	33

Important Dates

Early decision	
Apply by	12/1
Notified by	12/15
Early action	
Apply by	12/15
Notified by	1/15
Regular	
Notified by	Rolling, 9/1
Nonfall registration?	Yes

FINANCIAL FACTS

Annual tuition	$49,340
Food and housing	$20,998
Required fees	$1,930
Books and supplies	$1,324
Average need-based scholarship (First-year)	$31,004 ($32,696)
% students with need rec. need-based scholarship or grant aid (First-year)	99 (100)
% students with need rec. non-need-based scholarship or grant aid (First-year)	18 (19)
% students with need rec. need-based self-help aid (First-year)	72 (71)
% students rec. any financial aid (First-year)	99 (97)
% UG borrow to pay for school	80
Average cumulative indebtedness	$52,780
% of students with need fully met (First-year)	21 (21)
Average % of student need met (First-year)	67 (67)

UNIVERSITY OF NEW MEXICO

1 University of New Mexico, Albuquerque, NM 87131 • Admissions: 505-277-2446

Survey Snapshot
Diverse student types interact on campus
Students get along with local community
Great off-campus food

RATINGS

Quality of Life	**63**
Fire Safety	**60***
Green	**79**
Academic	**69**
Profs Interesting	**77**
Profs Accessible	**78**
Admissions	**84**
Financial Aid	**79**

CAMPUS LIFE

Type of school	Public
Environment	Metropolis

Students

Degree-seeking undergrad enrollment	17,562
% male/female/not reported	42/56/2
% from out of state	15
% First-year live on campus	49
% Ugrads live on campus	24
# of fraternities (% join)	10 (3)
# of sororities (% join)	10 (3)
% Asian	4
% Black or African American	3
% Hispanic	51
% Native American	6
% Pacific Islander	<1
% Race and/or ethnicity unknown	2
% Two or more races	4
% White	28
% International	2
# of countries represented	92

CAMPUS MENTAL HEALTH SERVICES

Offers mental health/wellness program	Yes
Mental health training available to students	No
Employs Chief Wellness Officer	NR
Peer-to-peer mental health offerings	NR
Counseling center has guidelines or accreditation	No
Mental health/well-being courses	NR

ACADEMICS

% students returning for sophomore year	75
% students graduating within 4 years	37
% students graduating within 6 years	46
Calendar	Semester
Student/faculty ratio	15:1
Most common class size 20–29.	(31%)
Most common lab/discussion size 20–29.	(42%)

Most Popular Majors

Biology/Biological Sciences; Business Administration and Management; Psychology

STUDENTS SAY "..."

Academics

The University of New Mexico, located in Albuquerque, is the state's flagship university. It offers students "academic excellence" at an affordable price, especially for in-state residents who qualify for the NM Lottery Scholarship, which covers seven semesters of tuition. UNM is an R1 research university, and some cite the numerous "research opportunities available" at UNM as one of its greatest strengths. Students can garner real-world experience since "oftentimes the research can be done with top-of-the-line equipment" at nearby Sandia National Labs, Los Alamos National Labs, or the Air Force Research Lab. Many students choose UNM for the quality and variety of its science programs, including Earth and planetary sciences, biology, and the premed and nursing programs. The university emphasizes that "there is something here for everyone" and offers "amazing opportunities to travel abroad" for those who want to expand their horizons. Regarding academics, students in the education and science programs praise UNM for providing "some of the best teachers" along with "tough classes." They also appreciate the academic support offered to them through "tutoring, study groups, and supplemental instruction for most courses." In class, students appreciate having "teachers who care" and are willing and able to "talk to and with you and not just at you." Students say that "it's very easy to come to instructors outside of class with questions." Overall, UNM prepares students for success with its strong academic programs and "very knowledgeable" professors who are "helpful [and] genuinely interested in your personal success."

Campus Life

At UNM, many students agree that "college is more than going to class." The school embraces this idea by offering "hundreds of great student organizations." And with so many groups and clubs to choose from, students are sure to find something "that will fit." The Student Union Building is the heart of campus life, where "there is always something going on." From weekly movies to "opportunities for fun events" and meetings in the workspaces of the Lobo Lair, there's plenty to keep you entertained. The Greek community is active on campus and "makes up a lot of the senate and other extracurricular activities," with one student noting that any Greek-sponsored "activity has fun attached." Although UNM has a dry-campus policy, students say that "a lot of people drink, just like at any college," and there's "excellent nightlife" available off campus. Plus, being in the city means students have easy access to great bars, dining, theaters, live music, and eclectic shops along Central Avenue and downtown. Students also say that "hanging out at the Duck Pond is a great way to pass time between classes in warmer months," and in colder months, the lure of the mountains draws people off campus, as "during the winter season, there are numerous ski resorts and places to go snowboarding that are not far away." Athletics are another of the many "ways for everyone to get involved," and many say that "attending games is a must." With so many activities and events to choose from, it's no wonder "everyone seems to find their niche."

Student Body

There are all types of students at UNM, and as one undergrad notes, "You meet someone different every day." The community is very diverse and welcoming; as one student observes, "No one will ever feel ethnically alone since there are so many different kinds of people." Just "like any school, there are cliques...but that does not mean they do not interact with each other," and most "people get along regardless of origin." Overall, students appreciate that the university is "sensitive and very engaged with its diverse population of students." In fact, most students agree that "everyone brings something to the table" at UNM, which makes for a vibrant and interesting environment.

University of New Mexico

Financial Aid: 505-277-8900 • E-Mail: apply@unm.edu • Website: www.unm.edu

THE PRINCETON REVIEW SAYS

Admissions

The school reports that its standardized testing policy for use in admission for Fall 2026 is Test Optional. The Princeton Review suggests that interested applicants consult with the school for the most up-to-date standardized testing policies.

Financial Aid

The Princeton Review suggests that all financial aid forms be submitted as soon as possible. Federal Work-Study Program available.

The Inside Word

UNM offers online applications through its website, and you will also find specific scholastic standards for traditional and nontraditional students interested in applying to UNM. Traditional applicants should have completed core coursework and have an average or above-average GPA if they would like to be considered for admission at UNM.

THE SCHOOL SAYS

From the Admissions Office

"The University of New Mexico is a major research institution nestled in the heart of multicultural Albuquerque on one of the nation's most beautiful and unique campuses. Students learn in an environment graced by distinctive Southwestern architecture, beautiful plazas and fountains, spectacular art and a national arboretum...all within view of the 10,000-foot Sandia Mountains. At UNM, diversity is a way of learning with education enriched by a lively mix of students being taught by a world-class research faculty that includes a Nobel laureate, a MacArthur Fellow, and members of several national academies. UNM offers more than 200 degree programs and majors and has earned national recognition in dozens of disciplines, ranging from primary care medicine and clinical law to engineering, photography, Latin American history, and intercultural communications. Research and the quest for new knowledge fuels the university's commitment to an undergraduate education where students work side-by-side with many of the finest scholars in their fields."

SELECTIVITY

# of total applicants	13,025
% of total applicants accepted	79
% of total acceptees attending	35

First-Year Profile

Testing policy	Test Optional
Range SAT composite	900–1160
Range SAT EBRW	460–600
Range SAT math	430–570
Range ACT composite	19–26
% submitting SAT scores	48
% submitting ACT scores	8
Average HS GPA	3.4
% submitting high school GPA	79

Important Dates

Regular	
Notified by	Rolling, 12/1
Nonfall registration?	Yes

FINANCIAL FACTS

Annual in-state tuition	$11,445
Annual out-of-state tuition	$34,594
Food and housing	$11,993
Books and supplies	$1,815
Average need-based scholarship (First-year)	$15,036 ($14,837)
% students with need rec. need-based scholarship or grant aid (First-year)	97 (100)
% students with need rec. non-need-based scholarship or grant aid (First-year)	2 (1)
% students with need rec. need-based self-help aid (First-year)	28 (19)
% UG borrow to pay for school	36
Average cumulative indebtedness	$22,587
% of students with need fully met (First-year)	23 (22)

UNIVERSITY OF NORTH CAROLINA ASHEVILLE

One University Heights, Asheville, NC 28804-8510 • Admissions: 828-251-6481

Survey Snapshot
Students environmentally aware
Students love Asheville, NC
Great off-campus food

RATINGS

Quality of Life	89
Fire Safety	97
Green	98
Academic	82
Profs Interesting	93
Profs Accessible	91
Admissions	81
Financial Aid	83

CAMPUS LIFE

Type of school	Public
Environment	City

Students

Degree-seeking undergrad enrollment	2,708
% male/female/not reported	42/58/0
% from out of state	13
% First-year from public high school	88
% First-year live on campus	90
% Ugrads live on campus	53
# of fraternities (% join)	2 (2)
# of sororities (% join)	1 (2)
% Asian	2
% Black or African American	7
% Hispanic	11
% Native American	<1
% Pacific Islander	<1
% Race and/or ethnicity unknown	2
% Two or more races	5
% White	70
% International	2
# of countries represented	24

CAMPUS MENTAL HEALTH SERVICES

Offers mental health/wellness program	Yes
Mental health training available to students	Yes
Employs Chief Wellness Officer	Yes
Peer-to-peer mental health offerings	No
Counseling center has guidelines or accreditation	Yes
Mental health/well-being courses	Yes, for-credit

ACADEMICS

% students returning for sophomore year	75
% students graduating within 4 years	40
% students graduating within 6 years	52
Calendar	Semester
Student/faculty ratio	13:1
Most common class size 10–19.	(42%)
Most common lab/discussion size 10–19.	(58%)

Most Popular Majors

Psychology; Art; Biology

Applicants Also Look At

Appalachian State University, Asheville-Buncombe Technical Community College, Central Piedmont Community College, East Carolina University, North Carolina A&T State University, North Carolina State University, University of North Carolina Chapel Hill, University of North Carolina Charlotte, University of North Carolina Greensboro, University of North Carolina Wilmington, Wake Technical Community College, Western Carolina University

STUDENTS SAY "..."

Academics

Students applaud the way the University of North Carolina—Asheville works to "provide and promote many opportunities for professional development, unique ways of learning, scholarships, programs, and further education for students." The curriculum offers numerous hands-on learning opportunities such as "outdoor labs, field trips, off-campus experiences, [and] paid trips to conferences." There's an "enthusiasm for undergraduate research," and the opportunity to "present results to my peers and other interested people has been an incredible experience." As a result, students feel they can "go out to the job market or on to grad school with robust experience." Students also point to the "constant availability and flexibility provided by professors and staff," and small class sizes that mean "each student gets individual attention, which makes it easier to succeed," especially as the teachers are "really good at cultivating relationships with students." Courses are far from cookie-cutter, as faculty members have "their own way of going about things," and "classes feel fun because you can tell they really enjoy sharing their love for their subject with others." UNCA's professors are widely adored and have been called "wonderful forces of good" who "are kind, understanding, and incredibly qualified." One student reflects on the direction faculty provide: "Many of my friends who came in not knowing what they wanted to do have been guided by our professors…and have even gained significant relevant experience."

Campus Life

Nestled in the Blue Ridge Mountains, the University of North Carolina—Asheville is "surrounded by beautiful trees all around," so time outdoors is practically a given. One student says, "It's normal to hike after class, drive a few minutes to a trailhead, or sit somewhere quiet with friends," and there are "hammock set-ups throughout campus that students will often be working, reading, or napping in." The Student Environmental Center often runs events, and they sometimes "have a free store or get local environmental-focused orgs to partner with them" to disperse goods. Dabbling is easy at UNCA, aided by "fun clubs that encourage students to engage in hobbies like gaming, crafting, [and] Dungeons & Dragons," and many also attend campus-wide events such as RockyPalooza, Syllabi and Spaghetti, and Late Night Breakfast. The entire community "is very connected to the arts," and downtown Asheville is an easy city bus ride away, where students can enjoy "the closeness to the city without feeling the hustle and bustle of the city." The "River Arts District is great," and students can also find an "inviting art scene, culture for foodies, boutique shopping, and lots of group activities/festivals in the area." There's a reinvigoration that comes from knowing "each day has opportunities to…have fun or try something new!"

Student Body

UNCA's size makes it "pretty tight-knit and allows for a lot of great relationships between both students and staff/faculty," and "people are very willing to chat." Many students "balance coursework with research, community work, or creative projects," and there is "a strong culture of showing up, whether that means late nights in a lab, student-led discussions in class, or public outreach events around Asheville." One student fondly describes their peers as "a mass of unique styles and personalities" who are "boldly themselves and amazing at expressing who they are." There "is a large LGBT community within the student body," and everyone here "expresses themselves in very outward ways (hair color, piercings, tattoos, clothing, etc.)." This is "a cool crowd of people who value art, friends, [and] the wilderness," as well as a liberal student body "who attempt to be as politically active as possible…[and are] defined by an effort to improve and a willingness to stand for what they believe."

University of North Carolina Asheville

Financial Aid: 828-251-6535 • E-Mail: admissions@unca.edu • Website: www.unca.edu

THE PRINCETON REVIEW SAYS

Admissions

While the school reports that its standardized testing policy for Fall 2026 is Test Optional, applicants with a weighted high school GPA below 2.8 must submit an ACT or SAT score. *Very important factors considered include:* rigor of secondary school record, class rank, academic GPA, standardized test scores, application essay, recommendation(s). *Important factors considered include:* extracurricular activities, talent/ability, character/personal qualities. *Other factors considered include:* first generation, alumni/ae relation, geographical residence, state residency, volunteer work, work experience, level of applicant's interest. High school diploma is required and GED is accepted. *Academic units required:* 4 English, 4 math, 3 science, 1 science lab, 2 social studies, 2 academic electives. *Academic units recommended:* 2 language (other than English).

Financial Aid

Students should submit: FAFSA. Priority filing deadline is 3/1. The Princeton Review suggests that all financial aid forms be submitted as soon as possible. *Need-based scholarships/grants offered:* Federal Pell; Federal SEOG; State scholarships/grants; Private scholarships; College/university scholarship or grant aid from institutional funds. *Loan aid offered:* Federal Direct Subsidized Loans; Federal Direct Unsubsidized Loans; Direct PLUS loans. Admitted students will be notified of awards on a rolling basis beginning 2/15. Federal Work-Study Program available. Institutional employment available.

The Inside Word

The admissions team at UNC Asheville seeks applicants who are open to new experiences, have original ideas, and want to embrace the opportunities before them. While high school classes, academic performance, and test scores (if submitting), are important, UNC Asheville uses a holistic model to determine a student's acceptance status. Applicants should carefully review their application essay and make sure to showcase their activities, leadership roles, and other talents as well.

THE SCHOOL SAYS

From the Admissions Office

"With a focus on collaborative, interdisciplinary education, UNC Asheville prepares students to be innovative critical thinkers, giving them the career-ready tools they need to thrive as experts in their area of study and beyond. More than 65 academic programs—including majors, minors, concentrations, and certificate programs—prepare students to understand and define their place in our ever-changing and increasingly complex world. UNC Asheville students ask important questions and pursue answers across disciplines with a commitment to making an impact and building community. The result is a competitive advantage, not only for graduates but also for the organizations they work for, where the convergence of art and science leads the way in today's dynamic economy.

"UNC Asheville offers both Early Action and Regular Decision plans."

SELECTIVITY

# of total applicants	14,499
% of total applicants accepted	86
% of total acceptees attending	4
# of in-state applicants	6,700
% of in-state applicants accepted	95
# of out-of-state-applicants	7,789
% of applicants accepted from out of state	79
# of international applicants	10
% of international applicants accepted	100

First-Year Profile

Testing policy	Test Optional !
Range SAT composite	1020–1270
Range SAT EBRW	550–670
Range SAT math	510–630
Range ACT composite	19–27
% submitting SAT scores	7
% submitting ACT scores	17
Average HS GPA	3.3
% submitting high school GPA	91
% graduated top 10% of class	7
% graduated top 25% of class	26
% graduated top 50% of class	62
% submitting high school rank	82

Important Dates

Early action	
Apply by	11/1
Notified by	Rolling
Regular	
Apply by	8/1
Notified by	Rolling, 12/15
Nonfall registration?	Yes

FINANCIAL FACTS

Annual in-state tuition	$4,184
Annual out-of-state tuition	$21,470
Food and housing	$14,460
Required fees	$3,444
Books and supplies	$1,000
Average need-based scholarship (First-year)	$11,539 ($11,433)
% students with need rec. need-based scholarship or grant aid (First-year)	100 (100)
% students with need rec. non-need-based scholarship or grant aid (First-year)	5 (6)
% students with need rec. need-based self-help aid (First-year)	61 (63)
% students rec. any financial aid (First-year)	97 (98)
% UG borrow to pay for school	54
Average cumulative indebtedness	$24,555
% of students with need fully met (First-year)	6 (6)
Average % of student need met (First-year)	56 (57)

! Test Optional if you have a GPA of 2.8 or higher.

University of North Carolina at Chapel Hill

Jackson Hall, Chapel Hill, NC 27599-9100 • Admissions: 919-962-2211

Survey Snapshot
Students love Chapel Hill, NC
Everyone loves the Tar Heels
Campus newspaper is popular

RATINGS	
Quality of Life	89
Fire Safety	99
Green	98
Academic	86
Profs Interesting	89
Profs Accessible	91
Admissions	97
Financial Aid	95

CAMPUS LIFE

Type of school	Public
Environment	Town

Students

Degree-seeking undergrad enrollment	21,338
% male/female/not reported	39/61/0
% from out of state	15
% First-year from public high school	83
% First-year live on campus	99
% Ugrads live on campus	42
# of fraternities (% join)	75 (6)
# of sororities (% join)	56 (9)
% Asian	17
% Black or African American	7
% Hispanic	10
% Native American	<1
% Pacific Islander	<1
% Race and/or ethnicity unknown	3
% Two or more races	5
% White	52
% International	6
# of countries represented	112

CAMPUS MENTAL HEALTH SERVICES

Offers mental health/wellness program	Yes
Mental health training available to students	Yes
Employs Chief Wellness Officer	No
Peer-to-peer mental health offerings	Yes
Counseling center has guidelines or accreditation	Yes
Mental health/well-being courses	Yes, for-credit

ACADEMICS

% students returning for sophomore year	97
% students graduating within 4 years	83
% students graduating within 6 years	91
Calendar	Semester
Student/faculty ratio	15:1
Most common class size 20–29.	(30%)
Most common lab/discussion size 20–29.	(41%)

Most Popular Majors
Computer Science; Biology/Biological Sciences; Behavioral Sciences

Applicants Sometimes Prefer
Duke University, North Carolina State University, University of Pennsylvania, University of Virginia, Vanderbilt University

Applicants Rarely Prefer
Appalachian State University, East Carolina University, The University of North Carolina—Charlotte

STUDENTS SAY "..."

Academics

Citing "academic prestige" and "affordability," the "beautiful," "historic" setting, and "world-renowned" faculty, students take pride in "being a Tar Heel" at the University of North Carolina at Chapel Hill. The professors at UNC-Chapel Hill are "top-notch, many of them being academic celebrities," but "like the students, are never flashy" and remain "humble." Students find that their professors frequently stress that they are here to "learn from you all as much as you are here to learn from me." UNC offers undergrads "bountiful resources" as "one of the top public research universities in the nation," and students have the opportunity to participate in this research by applying for "generous academic grants." Academics are "rigorous," but the "quality of teaching makes the material intellectually stimulating." The college is fairly large, so students will likely attend "large lecture-hall style classes," yet students stress that as they advance, "class sizes are smaller," and this leads to "the opportunity to build more personal relationships with professors." UNC's "reputation and ranking in STEM programs," along with its well-regarded business school, are among its greatest strengths. Said one transfer student, "I visited countless top universities," but UNC was the only one that had a "population...both economically and ethnically diverse."

Campus Life

UNC offers its "more than 20,000 undergrads" a host of opportunities to socialize, relax, and pack themselves all together at the Dean E. Smith Center to cheer on the men's basketball team. Carolina has strong athletics, including opportunities for "potential student athletes." For non-athletes, it's a great school to be a fan, "as basketball games especially create a special campus atmosphere that nothing can recreate." Despite the university's size, life on campus generally moves at a "slow pace"—in a good way. The campus is full of "gorgeous old buildings, towering oak trees, and ubiquitous birds, squirrels, and chipmunks," and students "love walking through the upper quad," a "beautiful green area with lots of old trees." Raleigh is "only 30 minutes away" and "Durham only 15," so students will head out there on weekends, and if they need to unwind during the week, they go "out to bars on Franklin Street." There's "always a party going on at UNC," but there are also "plenty of ways to have fun if you're not into the party scene." There are several "day hikes somewhat close to campus," and Carrboro is "within walking distance," providing a "hip space for social life including a farmers market, concert venue[s], and many bars and restaurants."

Student Body

The student body is "as helpful as it is inquisitive, and as creative as it is caring." Students are always "happy to direct you to your classes." Everyone at Carolina is "fun, energetic, and passionate about something." The students "are smart, but they aren't haughty and ostentatious about it." Students are "generally liberal, but there is a vocal religious/conservative presence on campus as well." Ultimately, UNC is "unified unlike any other school I have encountered," says one student, "whether it's in the common support of a sports team, music group, or simply the pride in saying you are a Tar Heel." Another student agrees, "Donning Carolina blue almost constantly, we all just really love our school!"

UNIVERSITY OF NORTH CAROLINA AT CHAPEL HILL

Financial Aid: 919-962-8396 • E-Mail: unchelp@admissions.unc.edu • Website: www.unc.edu

THE PRINCETON REVIEW SAYS

Admissions

While the school reports that its standardized testing policy for Fall 2026 is Test Optional, applicants with a weighted high school GPA below 2.8 must submit an ACT or SAT score. *Very important factors considered include:* rigor of secondary school record, application essay, recommendation(s), extracurricular activities, talent/ability, character/personal qualities, state residency. *Important factors considered include:* class rank, academic GPA, volunteer work, work experience. *Other factors considered include:* standardized test scores, first generation, alumni/ae relation. High school diploma is required and GED is not accepted. *Academic units required:* 4 English, 4 math, 3 science, 1 science lab, 2 social studies, 2 computer science.

Financial Aid

Students should submit: FAFSA; CSS PROFILE. Priority filing deadline is 3/1. The Princeton Review suggests that all financial aid forms be submitted as soon as possible. *Need-based scholarships/grants offered:* Federal Pell; Federal SEOG; State scholarships/grants; Private scholarships; College/university scholarship or grant aid from institutional funds. *Loan aid offered:* Federal Direct Subsidized Loans; Federal Direct Unsubsidized Loans; Direct PLUS loans; State Loans; College/university loans from institutional funds. Admitted students will be notified of awards on a rolling basis beginning 1/31. Federal Work-Study Program available. Institutional employment available.

The Inside Word

UNC's admissions process is highly selective. State residents will find the admissions standards high, and out-of-state applicants will find that it's one of the hardest offers of admission to come by in the country. While there's no formula, a fact UNC is proud of, students should expect to offer a compelling portrait to the admissions committee of their talents and achievements.

THE SCHOOL SAYS

From the Admissions Office

"Carolina is proudly public and has earned a reputation as one of the best universities in the world, preparing its students for a lifetime of leadership and service. Carolina is best known for having one of the strongest and most diverse student bodies in the nation. Carolina's most recently admitted class includes students who will be the first in their families to graduate from college (18 percent of the class), are high school valedictorians or salutatorians (14 percent of the class), and are committed to serving their communities (76 percent volunteered during high school). Carolina offers academic opportunities that prepare students to empower themselves and their communities; even during the pandemic, 95 percent of graduates earned jobs, entered graduate school, joined the military, or committed to volunteering within six months of graduation.

"Admission to Carolina is competitive, but we are dedicated to making it fair and considerate. We don't use formulas or cutoffs; instead, we know that students travel many roads to Carolina, and we celebrate the variety of interests, backgrounds, and aspirations they bring. We actively seek excellence in academics, arts, athletics, leadership, service, citizenship, and character. This list isn't exhaustive or prescriptive. When we read an application, we're interested in what a student has done, what they care about, and the difference they will make as a member of Carolina's community. We're committed to ensuring that every student who earns a place at Carolina can afford to attend, and our financial aid program meets full need and enables qualified low-income students to graduate debt-free through the Carolina Covenant."

SELECTIVITY

# of total applicants	76,247
% of total applicants accepted	17
% of total acceptees attending	40
# of in-state applicants	17,846
% of in-state applicants accepted	37
# of out-of-state-applicants	48,645
% of applicants accepted from out of state	10
# of international applicants	9,753
% of international applicants accepted	15
# offered a place on the wait list	7,355
# admitted from wait list	2,099

First-Year Profile

Testing policy	Test Optional !
Range SAT composite	1400–1530
Range SAT EBRW	690–750
Range SAT math	700–780
Range ACT composite	29–34
% submitting SAT scores	28
% submitting ACT scores	41
Average HS GPA	4.5
% submitting high school GPA	90
% graduated top 10% of class	76
% graduated top 25% of class	97
% graduated top 50% of class	100
% submitting high school rank	66

Important Dates

Early action	
Apply by	10/15
Notified by	1/31
Regular	
Apply by	1/15
Notified by	Jan 31 for priority; Mar 31 for regular
Nonfall registration?	No

FINANCIAL FACTS

Annual in-state tuition	$7,230
Annual out-of-state tuition	$47,472
Food and housing	$15,870
Required fees	$2,129
Books and supplies	$638
Average need-based scholarship (First-year)	$23,464 ($20,939)
% students with need rec. need-based scholarship or grant aid (First-year)	96 (95)
% students with need rec. non-need-based scholarship or grant aid (First-year)	14 (14)
% students with need rec. need-based self-help aid (First-year)	31 (28)
% students rec. any financial aid (First-year)	58 (56)
% UG borrow to pay for school	26
Average cumulative indebtedness	$22,675
% of students with need fully met (First-year)	68 (73)
Average % of student need met (First-year)	100 (100)

! Test Optional if you have a GPA of 2.8 or higher.

University of North Carolina at Charlotte

9201 University City Boulevard, Charlotte, NC 28223 • Admissions: 704-687-5507

Survey Snapshot
Great library
Recreation facilities are great
Diverse student types interact on campus

RATINGS	
Quality of Life	**85**
Fire Safety	**99**
Green	**89**
Academic	**73**
Profs Interesting	**84**
Profs Accessible	**87**
Admissions	**85**
Financial Aid	**81**

CAMPUS LIFE

Type of school	Public
Environment	Metropolis

Students

Degree-seeking undergrad enrollment	25,767
% male/female/not reported	51/49/0
% from out of state	7
% First-year live on campus	81
% Ugrads live on campus	23
# of fraternities (% join)	23 (6)
# of sororities (% join)	19 (8)
% Asian	11
% Black or African American	20
% Hispanic	16
% Native American	<1
% Pacific Islander	<1
% Race and/or ethnicity unknown	2
% Two or more races	5
% White	44
% International	3
# of countries represented	84

CAMPUS MENTAL HEALTH SERVICES

Offers mental health/wellness program	Yes
Mental health training available to students	Yes
Employs Chief Wellness Officer	Yes
Peer-to-peer mental health offerings	Yes
Counseling center has guidelines or accreditation	Yes
Mental health/well-being courses	Yes, for-credit

ACADEMICS

% students returning for sophomore year	86
% students graduating within 4 years	50
% students graduating within 6 years	68
Calendar	Semester
Student/faculty ratio	20:1
Most common class size 50–59.	(24%)
Most common lab/discussion size 20–29.	(31%)

Most Popular Majors

Computer Science; Business Administration and Management; Biology/Biological Sciences

Applicants Also Look At

Appalachian State University, Campbell University, Clemson University, Duke University, Elon University, High Point University, North Carolina State University, University of North Carolina Asheville, University of North Carolina at Chapel Hill, University of North Carolina at Greensboro, The University of North Carolina—Wilmington, University of South Carolina—Columbia

STUDENTS SAY "..."

Academics

The University of North Carolina at Charlotte's "flexible education...does stand out as a strength," backed up by a research-forward environment and a variety of traditional, hybrid, and online programs. In majors like health and medical humanities, "much of the class is discussion and diving deep into the material" through collaborative, hands-on engagement. Regardless of the course format, Charlotte students can count on their professors for support: "Every staff member I've reached out to regarding my intellectual interests has enthusiastically provided me with resources and encouragement to pursue both my academic and career goals." Students also highlight the school's major 2025 milestone in achieving R1 research status. They appreciate the "state-of-the-art research" facilities and "good student-employer connections" available. "I love how UNC Charlotte places a lot of emphasis on providing research opportunities for undergraduate students." For example, "in psychology and pre-health related classes, assignments often involve analyzing real research studies, designing mock experiments, or applying theoretical concepts to clinical or social scenarios." Another student notes: "I love being an undergraduate researcher. I get paid to do it and I get to interact with many professors and learn from them one-on-one." Students also appreciate the numerous opportunities available to them, whether it's a club to support them getting into a PhD program "immediately after graduation" or "a startup accelerator that helps students ideate and launch business endeavors." Altogether, Charlotte's blend of academic flexibility, faculty mentorship, and amazing research opportunities allows UNC Charlotte students "to feel secure in [their] future success and career."

Campus Life

Though UNC Charlotte is predominantly a commuter school, dorm life is growing, and students highlight the "many different ways people fill their days here at UNC Charlotte." As the day begins, "the campus is full of students rushing to class," but afterward, Niners, as students are called, are busy with "extracurricular activities, grabbing lunch, and catching up with friends. There are also sports games," like football, soccer, baseball, and basketball. Niners also enjoy downtime in "the botanical gardens, the hammocks, the nap pods, and the library." Students love being part of a campus that is "modern, growing quickly," and reflective of the larger city around it, with convenient light rail access from campus to downtown. Niner Engage, an online platform, helps students find clubs and events that match their interests, whether that's "a community tea group" or Late Night Breakfast—a pre-finals tradition where university administrators and staff serve students a free meal to kickstart studying for final exams. Niners can trust that "there is always an event or group of people who you'll find friends among." Admittedly, on weekends, the campus can feel "very quiet" without as many students around, but the Greek scene helps with that. Says one engineering student: "I love hanging out with my fraternity brothers. It doesn't matter what the event is...whether Intramurals, social events, or even just hanging out at the house." Students note that Charlotte and the school share a similar trajectory: both started off small, and now "the city and university are both booming."

Student Body

"The greatest strength is the sheer number of people around campus," explains one student. The "student body includes first-generation students, commuters, transfer and international students, which creates a campus culture rich in perspectives and experiences." As one student describes it: "You meet someone new every day, and there's such a diverse student population that you will never truly be alone in your interests." All in all, "the wide range of backgrounds, traditions, and perspectives creates an environment that feels vibrant and alive. You are constantly exposed to new ideas, new stories, and new ways of seeing the world, which makes learning extend far beyond the classroom."

UNIVERSITY OF NORTH CAROLINA AT CHARLOTTE

Financial Aid: 704-687-8622 • E-Mail: admissions@charlotte.edu • Website: www.charlotte.edu

THE PRINCETON REVIEW SAYS

Admissions

While the school reports that its standardized testing policy for Fall 2026 is Test Optional, applicants with a weighted high school GPA below 2.8 must submit an ACT or SAT score. *Very important factors considered include:* rigor of secondary school record, academic GPA, standardized test scores. *Other factors considered include:* application essay, recommendation(s), extracurricular activities, talent/ability, character/personal qualities, geographical residence, state residency, work experience, level of applicant's interest. High school diploma is required and GED is accepted. *Academic units required:* 4 English, 4 math, 3 science, 1 science lab, 2 language (other than English), 1 social studies, 1 history. *Academic units recommended:* 3 language (other than English).

Financial Aid

Students should submit: FAFSA. Priority filing deadline is 1/1. The Princeton Review suggests that all financial aid forms be submitted as soon as possible. *Need-based scholarships/grants offered:* Federal Pell; Federal SEOG; State scholarships/grants; Private scholarships. *Loan aid offered:* Federal Direct Subsidized Loans; Federal Direct Unsubsidized Loans; Direct PLUS loans; State Loans; College/university loans from institutional funds. Admitted students will be notified of awards on a rolling basis beginning 3/31. Federal Work-Study Program available. Institutional employment available.

The Inside Word

UNC Charlotte's admission requirements are straightforward: all applicants must submit an application, a high school transcript, and one essay. While these are the only required materials, submitting additional supporting documents—such as letters of recommendation or a personal statement—can strengthen your application and help you stand out. The admissions team takes a holistic approach, evaluating your academic background, opportunities, accomplishments, and extracurricular activities, drawn primarily from your application, transcript, and essay(s). If your GPA is 2.8 or higher, standardized test scores are optional—submit them if you believe they support your application, or leave them out to keep the focus on your high school record and other materials.

THE SCHOOL SAYS

From the Admissions Office

"UNC Charlotte is North Carolina's urban research university, located in one of the nation's largest and fastest-growing cities. As the only Carnegie R1 institution in the Charlotte region, the university offers students access to the resources of a major research university alongside the opportunities of a dynamic metropolitan environment. Undergraduate education is closely connected to the region's economy, with strong ties to industries including finance, energy, health care, manufacturing, technology, and motorsports. Students benefit from internships, applied research, and project-based learning experiences that are integrated into academic programs. All students who seek an internship are able to access one through coordinated employer partnerships and career support.

"Academic offerings reflect areas of workforce demand and institutional strength. UNC Charlotte is home to the largest business school in North Carolina and the first School of Data Science in the Carolinas. Additional areas of focus include engineering, cybersecurity, artificial intelligence, and health-related fields. The university also offers the only Bachelor of Science in Sports Analytics in North Carolina. Career development is integrated throughout the student experience, with support beginning early and continuing through graduation. Students graduate with academic preparation, professional experience, and connections to employers across the region."

SELECTIVITY

# of total applicants	27,218
% of total applicants accepted	78
% of total acceptees attending	23
# of in-state applicants	18,398
% of in-state applicants accepted	83
# of out-of-state-applicants	8,106
% of applicants accepted from out of state	67
# of international applicants	714
% of international applicants accepted	77

First-Year Profile

Testing policy	Test Optional !
Range SAT composite	1150–1340
Range SAT EBRW	570–670
Range SAT math	570–680
Range ACT composite	21–27
% submitting SAT scores	16
% submitting ACT scores	27
Average HS GPA	3.6
% submitting high school GPA	94
% graduated top 10% of class	19
% graduated top 25% of class	47
% graduated top 50% of class	83
% submitting high school rank	55

Important Dates

Early action	
Apply by	11/1
Notified by	1/30
Regular	
Apply by	6/1
Notified by	Rolling, 11/1
Nonfall registration?	Yes

FINANCIAL FACTS

Annual in-state tuition	$3,926
Annual out-of-state tuition	$20,018
Food and housing	$12,390
Required fees	$3,505
Books and supplies	$600
Average need-based scholarship (First-year)	$10,525 ($10,898)
% students with need rec. need-based scholarship or grant aid (First-year)	86 (87)
% students with need rec. non-need-based scholarship or grant aid (First-year)	3 (6)
% students with need rec. need-based self-help aid (First-year)	57 (57)
% students rec. any financial aid (First-year)	64 (72)
% UG borrow to pay for school	54
Average cumulative indebtedness	$25,688
% of students with need fully met (First-year)	4 (7)
Average % of student need met (First-year)	54 (57)

! Test Optional if you have a GPA of 2.8 or higher.

University of North Carolina at Greensboro

1400 Spring Garden St, Greensboro, NC 27402 • Admissions: 336-334-5243

Survey Snapshot
Recreation facilities are great
Easy to get around campus
Diverse student types interact on campus

RATINGS

Quality of Life	**84**
Fire Safety	**99**
Green	**94**
Academic	**76**
Profs Interesting	**84**
Profs Accessible	**87**
Admissions	**82**
Financial Aid	**83**

CAMPUS LIFE

Type of school	Public
Environment	Metropolis

Students

Degree-seeking undergrad enrollment	14,554
% male/female/not reported	34/66/0
% from out of state	4
% First-year from public high school	90
% First-year live on campus	77
% Ugrads live on campus	38
# of fraternities (% join)	19 (<1)
# of sororities (% join)	21 (<1)
% Asian	6
% Black or African American	32
% Hispanic	19
% Native American	<1
% Pacific Islander	<1
% Race and/or ethnicity unknown	1
% Two or more races	6
% White	36
% International	1
# of countries represented	86

CAMPUS MENTAL HEALTH SERVICES

Offers mental health/wellness program	Yes
Mental health training available to students	Yes
Employs Chief Wellness Officer	Yes
Peer-to-peer mental health offerings	Yes
Counseling center has guidelines or accreditation	Yes
Mental health/well-being courses	Yes, for-credit

ACADEMICS

% students returning for sophomore year	81
% students graduating within 4 years	40
% students graduating within 6 years	58
Calendar	Semester
Student/faculty ratio	18:1
Most common class size 20–29.	(33%)
Most common lab/discussion size 20–29.	(35%)

Most Popular Majors

Biology/Biological Sciences; Psychology; Business Administration and Management

STUDENTS SAY "..."

Academics

The University of North Carolina, Greensboro, "is an amazing place for creatives to come and further themselves personally and professionally." Students highlight hands-on opportunities such as "hosting my own musical live shows, performing at the NC Music Educators conference, [and an] internship with a prestigious music non-profit." Students also say that "the arts, 100 percent," are a major draw at UNCG. To enhance its fine-arts reputation, the university is building a new center for creative practice, featuring "a flexible performance space, gallery, instructional and studio rooms, [and] a digital lab" that will be "a hive of creativity and academic innovation." In addition to the arts, the business school is very popular, and one student says, "The amount of different classes and majors you can have are definitely a plus. I chose this school specifically for its genetic counseling program; something that's pretty unique to the school." And regardless of one's major, students can count on their professors to be "friendly, inclusive, welcoming, and diligent about teaching well." In addition, "there's always a resource or person who's ready to help you—whether that's the Office of Intercultural Engagement, your academic advisor, or even a professor who you connected with and genuinely cares about your growth," as well as "a plethora of opportunities for those who are first-generation or transfer students." All in all, students love that UNCG "truly encourages students to find their home, their people, and their community."

Campus Life

UNCG is a campus "alive with activity," with students pointing to the Elliott University Center as a place where "there's always something happening—from community service drives where I can write cards to veterans, to learning about new clubs or causes that I can share with my friends." Other Spartans, as students are known, agree: "UNCG always has something happening, whether it's table talks, guest speakers, or pop-up events," such as "fried chicken Wednesdays," which became so popular that "now we have a DJ that plays music during that time." Other spirited events include renaissance fair theme days, silent discos, and intramural sports. "Playing club basketball lets me stay active, meet new people, and take a break from classes while still doing something I love," says one Spartan, and that extends to everything from gaming (the Esports Arena) and swimming (the recreation center) to theater (Taylor Theater). Spartans also love to hang on College Avenue, "where there's often even more going on—fraternities hosting fundraisers, food trucks handing out free samples, or student groups promoting upcoming events." In short, "life at UNCG is always full of energy and connection."

Student Body

When it comes to representation at UNCG, students agree: "It's not just about seeing diversity; it's about experiencing it." Walking around campus, one notices all the "unique hair, makeup, and overall fashion choices." Moreover, Spartans value that their peers come "from all kinds of cultural backgrounds....Every day, I'm surrounded by people who not only look like me but also people who come from completely different experiences and walks of life." In fact, UNCG takes pride in being a "minority serving institution," featuring a "large population of students of color, women, and LGBTQIA+ students." Because Spartans particularly welcome "everyone's perspectives" there's also "a good amount of progressive political discussion." And "there are a lot of niche groups, so everyone can find somewhere to fit in." Students also value that the plurality among their peers brings them together: "What makes UNCG special is how welcoming and supportive the community is. Students help each other succeed instead of competing." One student sums up the vibe on campus best, saying: "Overall, the student body is creative, caring, and proud to be Spartans. It's a place where you can be yourself and still feel part of something bigger."

UNIVERSITY OF NORTH CAROLINA AT GREENSBORO

Financial Aid: 336-334-5702 • E-Mail: admissions@uncg.edu • Website: www.uncg.edu

THE PRINCETON REVIEW SAYS

Admissions

While the school reports that its standardized testing policy for Fall 2026 is Test Optional, applicants with a weighted high school GPA below 2.8 must submit an ACT or SAT score. *Very important factors considered include:* rigor of secondary school record, academic GPA. *Important factors considered include:* standardized test scores. *Other factors considered include:* class rank, application essay, recommendation(s), extracurricular activities, volunteer work. High school diploma is required and GED is accepted. *Academic units required:* 4 English, 4 math, 3 science, 1 science lab, 2 language (other than English), 2 social studies.

Financial Aid

Students should submit: FAFSA. Priority filing deadline is 3/1. The Princeton Review suggests that all financial aid forms be submitted as soon as possible. *Need-based scholarships/grants offered:* Federal Pell; Federal SEOG; State scholarships/grants; Private scholarships; College/university scholarship or grant aid from institutional funds. *Loan aid offered:* Federal Direct Subsidized Loans; Federal Direct Unsubsidized Loans; Direct PLUS loans; State Loans; College/university loans from institutional funds. Admitted students will be notified of awards on a rolling basis. Federal Work-Study Program available. Institutional employment available.

The Inside Word

UNCG emphasizes GPA and test scores (if submitting) in the admissions process. However, they also consider high school course selection and progression, senior class schedule, all test scores (where submitted), and community standards concerns. First-year applicants are encouraged to apply by the Early Action I deadline of November 1 to receive a decision in December.

THE SCHOOL SAYS

From the Admissions Office

"Located in North Carolina's third largest city, UNC Greensboro is among the most diverse, learner-centered public research universities in the state, with over 18,000 students in 8 colleges and schools pursuing more than 150 areas of undergraduate and over 200 areas of graduate study. UNCG continues to be recognized nationally for academic excellence, access, and affordability. UNCG is ranked No. 1 most affordable institution in North Carolina for net cost by the N.Y. Times and No. 1 in North Carolina for social mobility by The Wall Street Journal, helping first-generation and lower-income students find paths to prosperity. Designated an Innovation and Economic Prosperity University by the Association of Public and Land-grant Universities, UNCG is a community-engaged research institution with a portfolio of over $67M in research and creative activity. The University's 1,100 faculty and over 2,000 staff help create an annual economic impact for the Piedmont Triad region over $1B."

SELECTIVITY

# of total applicants	18,683
% of total applicants accepted	91
% of total acceptees attending	15
# of in-state applicants	11,760
% of in-state applicants accepted	92
# of out-of-state-applicants	6,506
% of applicants accepted from out of state	89
# of international applicants	417
% of international applicants accepted	89

First-Year Profile

Testing policy	Test Optional !
Range SAT composite	1130–1310
Range SAT EBRW	580–680
Range SAT math	530–630
Range ACT composite	21–26
% submitting SAT scores	2
% submitting ACT scores	9
Average HS GPA	3.7
% submitting high school GPA	100
% graduated top 10% of class	11
% graduated top 25% of class	34
% graduated top 50% of class	70
% submitting high school rank	89

Important Dates

Early action	
Apply by	11/1
Notified by	1/1
Regular	
Apply by	3/1
Notified by	4/1
Nonfall registration?	Yes

FINANCIAL FACTS

Annual in-state tuition	$4,422
Annual out-of-state tuition	$21,396
Food and housing	$11,642
Required fees	$3,309
Books and supplies	$676
Average need-based scholarship (First-year)	$11,043 ($11,783)
% students with need rec. need-based scholarship or grant aid (First-year)	94 (96)
% students with need rec. non-need-based scholarship or grant aid (First-year)	5 (8)
% students with need rec. need-based self-help aid (First-year)	57 (58)
% students rec. any financial aid (First-year)	81 (86)
% UG borrow to pay for school	61
Average cumulative indebtedness	$23,779
% of students with need fully met (First-year)	5 (8)
Average % of student need met (First-year)	57 (64)

! Test Optional if you have a GPA of 2.8 or higher.

UNIVERSITY OF NORTH DAKOTA

3501 University Avenue Stop 8357, Grand Forks, ND 58202 • Admissions: 701-777-3000

Survey Snapshot
Recreation facilities are great
Everyone loves the Fighting Hawks
Intramural sports are popular

RATINGS	
Quality of Life	83
Fire Safety	83
Green	60*
Academic	77
Profs Interesting	84
Profs Accessible	88
Admissions	85
Financial Aid	84

CAMPUS LIFE

Type of school	Public
Environment	Town

Students

Degree-seeking undergrad enrollment	10,641
% male/female/not reported	55/45/0
% from out of state	60
% First-year from public high school	97
% First-year live on campus	91
% Ugrads live on campus	25
# of fraternities (% join)	13 (12)
# of sororities (% join)	7 (9)
% Asian	2
% Black or African American	3
% Hispanic	6
% Native American	1
% Pacific Islander	<1
% Race and/or ethnicity unknown	2
% Two or more races	5
% White	78
% International	3
# of countries represented	97

CAMPUS MENTAL HEALTH SERVICES

Offers mental health/wellness program	Yes
Mental health training available to students	Yes
Employs Chief Wellness Officer	Yes
Peer-to-peer mental health offerings	Yes
Counseling center has guidelines or accreditation	Yes
Mental health/well-being courses	Yes, non-credit

ACADEMICS

% students returning for sophomore year	83
% students graduating within 4 years	39
% students graduating within 6 years	61
Calendar	Semester
Student/faculty ratio	18:1
Most common class size 20–29.	(23%)
Most common lab/discussion size 10–19.	(30%)

Most Popular Majors
Psychology; Aviation/Airway Management and Operations; Registered Nursing/Registered Nurse

Applicants Often Prefer
North Dakota State University, University of Minnesota Duluth

Applicants Sometimes Prefer
Concordia College (Moorhead, MN), Minnesota State University, Moorhead, South Dakota School of Mines and Technology, University of Minnesota—Twin Cities, The University of South Dakota

STUDENTS SAY "..."

Academics

If you love hockey, want to study at the nation's foremost aerospace and aviation school, and you're not afraid of the cold temperatures, the University of North Dakota in Grand Forks wants you on their team. The largest university in the state, UND is internationally recognized in the aviation industry for its aerospace program, which offers "the highest level of flight training," thanks to "incredible professors" who "know the industry." Other schools including the college of business and public administration, the college of engineering and mines, and the school of medicine and health sciences are praised for their "innovation and intelligence." UND also benefits from its "strong and active alumni network." Students have mixed experiences with the quality of advisement and experiences with faculty seeming to vary depending on the students' interests. "General education teachers are very hit or miss," one student says. But another offers, "Every single professor that I've had has been engaging, [and] interested in my learning...and have also given me opportunities for success by introducing me to internships or jobs that I should apply for, as well as being willing to write recommendation letters or talk during their office hours whenever possible." UND offers "great on-campus resources for its students, including "counseling, student health, LGBTQ+ office, International Center, Student Government, and The Dakota Student, the student newspaper." Small class sizes "make for a more personalized learning experience," and "tuition costs are still reasonable compared to other schools and states," proving "bang for your buck." And there are "numerous resources and organizations available for students on campus to help them succeed...academically, socially, and mentally"—including a "strategic plan recently implemented that focuses more on the student experience and being a leader in action."

Campus Life

Students love the "tight-knit community support," and say "everyone in Grand Forks wants the students at UND to succeed." School spirit "is very strong...which makes it extremely fun to attend basketball, football, volleyball, or hockey games." Emphasis on the hockey games: "There is nothing that brings us together more than hockey." The Ralph Engelstad Arena "nearly sells out at any home game" and "many people begin lining up in the cold as early as 8:00 a.m. on some game days." The city has a lot of outdoor skating rinks. The "greenway is great in the warmer months." The "beautiful campus" is "relatively compact in size," so traveling to and from classes is easy and "convenient." There is "support for Greek organizations and other organizations that support leadership opportunities," and the "attitude of all people, staff, and workers is always uplifting." Most students' days are "filled with studying and homework," but in between classes students visit the "local coffee shop, Archives," or visit the Wellness Center, which "is always busy, either with individual workouts, group exercise classes, intramural or pick-up games, or cooking classes."

Student Body

The "conservative" student body "is mostly comprised of Midwestern students," a "large majority from Minnesota and North Dakota," with the aviation program bringing in "a decent amount of diversity from around the U.S. and the world." Students also note the quality of their classmates: "It takes a special kind of person to be able to suffer through the long, dark, and extremely cold winters." Those who land on campus are more than "willing to lend a helping hand" and that's true "not only for the campus but for the community as well."

University of North Dakota

Financial Aid: 701-777-1234 • E-Mail: admissions@UND.edu • Website: und.edu

THE PRINCETON REVIEW SAYS

Admissions

The school reports that its standardized testing policy for use in admission for Fall 2026 is Test Optional. The Princeton Review suggests that interested applicants consult with the school for the most up-to-date standardized testing policies. *Very important factors considered include:* academic GPA. *Other factors considered include:* rigor of secondary school record. High school diploma is required and GED is accepted. *Academic units required:* 4 English, 3 math, 3 science, 3 science labs, 3 social studies.

Financial Aid

The Princeton Review suggests that all financial aid forms be submitted as soon as possible. *Need-based scholarships/grants offered:* Federal Pell; Federal SEOG; State scholarships/grants; Private scholarships; College/university scholarship or grant aid from institutional funds. *Loan aid offered:* Federal Direct Subsidized Loans; Federal Direct Unsubsidized Loans; Direct PLUS loans; State Loans. Admitted students will be notified of awards on a rolling basis beginning 12/15. Federal Work-Study Program available. Institutional employment available.

The Inside Word

As a potential incoming student, you will find that the University of North Dakota is ready and willing to help you apply. The website has applications broken down by student type, and you'll also find admission guidelines to help you see if you would be accepted. However, the school says that everyone should apply for admission, even if you don't meet these standards, since your application will be reviewed by a committee that may make the decision based on other factors or recommend you for its LAUNCH program. If you've taken the ACT or SAT, it's highly recommended that you submit your official scores to UND for proper placement into English and math courses, as well as for scholarship purposes.

THE SCHOOL SAYS

From the Admissions Office

"Founded in 1883, UND offers more than 225 fields of study, including aerospace, nursing, education, engineering, business, medicine, law, the arts and more. With so many options, you can explore all of your interests to discover your passion. You'll get the experience you need to succeed through internships, hands-on learning and real-world projects, such as building a hydrogen-powered car, writing and producing a magazine, running a capitalist venture fund, or simulating a mission to Mars. And you'll graduate with the skills that will get you hired by today's employers.

"Nestled in a classic college town of 65,000, UND offers the atmosphere of a small college campus while giving you opportunities found only at large universities. You can do what you love by joining one of 250+ student organizations—ranging from Swing Dance Club to Robotics Club to the Photography Society. And, if you're up for an adventure, you can study abroad in more than 40 countries around the world.

"Like to work out? You'll be at home in one of the best campus Wellness Centers in the nation. Love sports? Whether you're an athlete or a fan, you can get in the game with our Fighting Hawks NCAA Division I athletic teams and 20+ intramural and club sports. And did we mention that our 8-time national men's hockey champions play in the finest collegiate hockey venue in the world? After all, there's a reason Grand Forks has been named as America's Best Hockey Town—five years in a row!"

SELECTIVITY

# of total applicants	8,715
% of total applicants accepted	82
% of total acceptees attending	35

First-Year Profile

Testing policy	Test Optional
Range SAT composite	1140–1310
Range SAT EBRW	560–670
Range SAT math	550–660
Range ACT composite	21–27
% submitting SAT scores	15
% submitting ACT scores	85
Average HS GPA	3.6
% submitting high school GPA	99
% graduated top 10% of class	22
% graduated top 25% of class	48
% graduated top 50% of class	82
% submitting high school rank	29

Important Dates

Regular	
Apply by	8/15
Notified by	Rolling, 8/1
Nonfall registration?	Yes

FINANCIAL FACTS

Annual in-state tuition	$11,646
Annual out-of-state tuition	$16,542
Food and housing	$12,026
Required fees	$927
Books and supplies	$800
Average need-based scholarship (First-year)	$8,539 ($8,666)
% students with need rec. need-based scholarship or grant aid (First-year)	88 (93)
% students with need rec. non-need-based scholarship or grant aid (First-year)	11 (16)
% students with need rec. need-based self-help aid (First-year)	70 (69)
% UG borrow to pay for school	68
Average cumulative indebtedness	$39,631
% of students with need fully met (First-year)	33 (44)
Average % of student need met (First-year)	44 (53)

UNIVERSITY OF NOTRE DAME

McKenna Hall, Notre Dame, IN 46556 • Admissions: 574-631-7505

Survey Snapshot
Lots of conservative students
Students are very religious
Students involved in community service

RATINGS

Quality of Life	83
Fire Safety	91
Green	89
Academic	84
Profs Interesting	84
Profs Accessible	88
Admissions	98
Financial Aid	98

CAMPUS LIFE

Type of school	Private
Affiliation	Roman Catholic
Environment	City

Students

Degree-seeking undergrad enrollment	8,901
% male/female/not reported	52/48/0
% from out of state	92
% First-year from public high school	42
% First-year live on campus	100
% Ugrads live on campus	81
# of fraternities	0
# of sororities	0
% Asian	6
% Black or African American	5
% Hispanic	16
% Native American	<1
% Pacific Islander	<1
% Race and/or ethnicity unknown	3
% Two or more races	5
% White	58
% International	7
# of countries represented	68

CAMPUS MENTAL HEALTH SERVICES

Offers mental health/wellness program	Yes
Mental health training available to students	No
Employs Chief Wellness Officer	NR
Peer-to-peer mental health offerings	NR
Counseling center has guidelines or accreditation	No
Mental health/well-being courses	NR

ACADEMICS

% students returning for sophomore year	98
% students graduating within 4 years	90
% students graduating within 6 years	95
Calendar	Semester
Student/faculty ratio	8:1
Most common class size 10–19.	(44%)

Most Popular Majors
Psychology; Political Science and Government; Finance

Applicants Also Look At
Duke University, Harvard College, Northwestern University, Princeton University, University of Pennsylvania

STUDENTS SAY "…"

Academics

The University of Notre Dame focuses on both educating students and helping them achieve their goals. This commitment is reflected in the administration, which "tries its best to stay on top of the students' wants and needs." One student says, "Our president (a priest), as well as both of our presidents emeritus, make it a point to interact with the students in a variety of ways—teaching a class, saying mass in the dorms, etc." Notre Dame has many strong academic programs, with theology and philosophy as particular standouts. Notre Dame also focuses heavily on research as part of its "devotion to undergraduate education," and students have opportunities to work alongside experts in the school's research facilities. "While classes are difficult," the "wonderful" faculty are extremely supportive and "always willing to meet outside of class to give extra help." As one student says, "Not only are they invested in their students," professors are "genuinely passionate about their fields of study," as well as being "enthusiastic and animated in lectures." Professors even go the extra mile and make sure that "large lectures are broken down into smaller discussion groups once a week to help with class material and...give the class a personal touch." Academics at Notre Dame are demanding, but while "it's necessary to study hard and often, there's also time to do other things."

Campus Life

At Notre Dame, students "study a lot, but on the weekends, everyone seems to make up for the lack of partying during the week." With over 500 student clubs and organizations, there's something for everyone. Sports "are huge" on campus, and "everybody goes to the football games, and it's common to see 1,000 students at a home soccer game." One student playfully warns, "If someone is not interested in sports upon arrival, he or she will be by the time he or she leaves." That's partly due to the Interhall Sport System; "virtually every student plays some kind of sport [in] his/her residence hall"—students can still compete for a former residence even if they live off campus. "Dorms on campus provide the social structure," which many students appreciate. The dorms also act as an alternative to bars and house parties, as the administration reportedly tries "to keep the parties on campus due to the fact that campus is such a safe place, and they truly do care about our safety." One student explains that Notre Dame "does not have any fraternities or sororities, but campus is not dry, and drinking/partying is permitted within the residence halls." Beyond sports and dorm life, students say "religious activities," volunteering, "campus publications, student government, and academic clubs round out the rest of ND life."

Student Body

The typical Notre Dame student is "very smart" and exemplifies what one student describes as "a type-A personality that studies a lot, yet is athletic and involved in the community. They are usually the outstanding seniors in their high schools." Also, given the athletic environment, it follows that something like "85 percent of Notre Dame students earned a varsity letter in high school." While many, but not all, students are Catholic, most seem to "have some sort of spirituality present in their daily lives." Although some students note that there are many "white kids from upper- to middle-class backgrounds from all over the country, especially the Midwest and Northeast," others point out that the school is making efforts to improve diversity when it comes to "economic backgrounds, with the university's policy to meet all demonstrated financial need." No matter their background, Notre Dame students are always interesting. As one student says, they are the "sort of people who can talk about the BCS rankings and Derrida in the same breath."

UNIVERSITY OF NOTRE DAME

Financial Aid: 574-631-6436 • E-Mail: admissions@nd.edu • Website: www.nd.edu

THE PRINCETON REVIEW SAYS

Admissions

The school reports that its standardized testing policy for use in admission for Fall 2026 is Test Optional. The Princeton Review suggests that interested applicants consult with the school for the most up-to-date standardized testing policies. *Very important factors considered include:* rigor of secondary school record, class rank, academic GPA, application essay, recommendation(s), extracurricular activities, talent/ability, character/personal qualities, volunteer work. *Important factors considered include:* standardized test scores, first generation, religious affiliation/commitment. *Other factors considered include:* alumni/ae relation, geographical residence, state residency, work experience. High school diploma is required and GED is accepted. *Academic units required:* 4 English, 3 math, 2 science, 2 language (other than English), 2 history, 3 academic electives. *Academic units recommended:* 4 English, 4 math, 4 science, 2 science labs, 4 language (other than English), 4 history.

Financial Aid

Students should submit: FAFSA; CSS PROFILE. Priority filing deadline is 11/15. The Princeton Review suggests that all financial aid forms be submitted as soon as possible. *Need-based scholarships/grants offered:* Federal Pell; Federal SEOG; State scholarships/grants; Private scholarships; College/university scholarship or grant aid from institutional funds. *Loan aid offered:* Federal Direct Subsidized Loans; Federal Direct Unsubsidized Loans; Direct PLUS loans. Admitted students will be notified of awards on a rolling basis beginning 12/17 restrictive early action; 3/15 regular decision. Federal Work-Study Program available. Institutional employment available.

The Inside Word

Notre Dame is one of the most selective colleges in the country, so academic excellence alone isn't enough to secure admission. The university values well-rounded individuals with unique talents, often showing a preference for athletic achievement. While legacy applicants may have an advantage, admission is never guaranteed.

THE SCHOOL SAYS

From the Admissions Office

"Notre Dame is a Catholic university, which means it offers unique opportunities for academic, ethical, spiritual, and social service development. The First Year of Studies program provides special assistance to our students as they make the adjustment from high school to college. The first-year curriculum includes many core requirements, while allowing students to explore several areas of possible future study. Each residence hall is home to students from all classes; most will live in the same hall for all their years on campus. An average of 93 percent of entering students will graduate within five years."

SELECTIVITY

# of total applicants	35,401
% of total applicants accepted	9
% of total acceptees attending	64
# of in-state applicants	2,069
% of in-state applicants accepted	11
# of out-of-state-applicants	26,548
% of applicants accepted from out of state	11
# of international applicants	6,784
% of international applicants accepted	4
# offered a place on the wait list	2,186
# admitted from wait list	54

First-Year Profile

Testing policy	Test Optional
Range SAT composite	1460–1540
Range SAT EBRW	720–760
Range SAT math	730–780
Range ACT composite	33–35
% graduated top 10% of class	92
% graduated top 25% of class	100
% graduated top 50% of class	100

Important Dates

Early action	
Apply by	11/1
Notified by	12/16
Regular	
Apply by	1/2
Notified by	Rolling, 4/1
Nonfall registration?	Yes

FINANCIAL FACTS

Annual tuition	$69,280
Food and housing	$18,992
Required fees	$514
Books and supplies	$1,250
Average need-based scholarship (First-year)	$62,619 ($60,952)
% students with need rec. need-based scholarship or grant aid (First-year)	100 (100)
% students with need rec. non-need-based scholarship or grant aid (First-year)	31 (27)
% students with need rec. need-based self-help aid (First-year)	54 (46)
% students rec. any financial aid (First-year)	75 (63)
% UG borrow to pay for school	32
Average cumulative indebtedness	$27,861
% of students with need fully met (First-year)	100 (100)
Average % of student need met (First-year)	100 (100)

University of Oklahoma

660 Parrington Oval, Norman, OK 73019-0390 • Admissions: 405-325-2151

Survey Snapshot
School is well run
Students are friendly
Students are very religious

RATINGS

Quality of Life	**84**
Fire Safety	**97**
Green	**87**
Academic	**83**
Profs Interesting	**89**
Profs Accessible	**94**
Admissions	**86**
Financial Aid	**89**

CAMPUS LIFE

Type of school	Public
Environment	City

Students

Degree-seeking undergrad enrollment	24,425
% male/female/not reported	47/53/0
% from out of state	45
% First-year live on campus	90
% Ugrads live on campus	29
# of fraternities (% join)	27 (26)
# of sororities (% join)	25 (33)
% Asian	7
% Black or African American	5
% Hispanic	15
% Native American	3
% Pacific Islander	<1
% Race and/or ethnicity unknown	2
% Two or more races	10
% White	54
% International	2
# of countries represented	137

CAMPUS MENTAL HEALTH SERVICES

Offers mental health/wellness program	Yes
Mental health training available to students	No
Employs Chief Wellness Officer	NR
Peer-to-peer mental health offerings	NR
Counseling center has guidelines or accreditation	No
Mental health/well-being courses	NR

ACADEMICS

% students returning for sophomore year	89
% students graduating within 4 years	58
% students graduating within 6 years	75
Calendar	Semester
Student/faculty ratio	19:1
Most common class size 10–19.	(27%)
Most common lab/discussion size 20–29.	(46%)

Most Popular Majors

Zoology/Animal Biology; Psychology; Finance

Applicants Also Look At

Baylor University, Oklahoma State University, Southern Methodist University, Texas A&M University—College Station, Texas Christian University, Texas Tech University, The University of Alabama—Tuscaloosa, University of Arkansas—Fayetteville, University of Kansas, University of Missouri, University of Texas at Austin

STUDENTS SAY "..."

Academics

Founded in 1890, the University of Oklahoma predates the state itself, reflecting its long history as an "intellectually fertile, opportunity-laden public research institution." The university combines "tradition with advancement to encourage you to become the best version of yourself possible." Students from all 50 states come here to choose from more than 170 programs (Aviation and Atmospheric Science and Meteorology are particular standouts) and receive what one student calls "an Ivy League quality education within a public university." While OU "might be known for its athletic program" (NCAA Division I), the "academics don't suffer from it." In fact, students value OU as a place to "receive a quality education from challenging courses" and explore "tons of opportunities," including "jobs, networking, [and] study abroad" programs. What sets OU apart is its "fantastic," "engaging," and "encouraging" faculty. They are "exceptional instructors who relate [to you] on a personal basis and actually help you comprehend the material." One student notes, "The professors here don't feel like your average teachers." They "truly care for the well-being of the students" and contribute to the "very comfortable and welcoming" atmosphere. As Sooners say, this is "not just a school," but a "rich tradition of community."

Campus Life

"Life is great" here on the OU campus, where the "social atmosphere is very alive." That energy really shines during the fall when "most students attend at least one football game." Beyond attending "football games and other athletic events for fun," there's always "something going on, and whether it be a sports event or a fine arts event, the quality is always excellent." On campus, students can see world-renowned art in the Fred Jones Jr. Museum of Art, check out the Harry Potter-like Great Reading Room in the Bizzell Memorial Library, or marvel at the 26-foot-tall dinosaur at OU's Sam Noble Museum of Natural History. They can also visit "Campus Corner," which has "restaurants, bars and boutiques," or take "an easy drive to the movies, a nice restaurant, or nightlife." While "Greek life" is "very important" here, "there are many opportunities to be involved on campus"—everything from "free movie nights and pool" to "all kinds of volunteering opportunities." There is a strong sense of community on campus, and it extends to the local area as well: "Every year, everyone on campus drops what they're doing for one weekend to spend all day volunteering in the local Norman and Oklahoma City communities." These concentrated efforts by the university help foster a spirit of "tradition, unity, and togetherness. One satisfied Sooner says, "I cannot imagine there being a happier campus than OU anywhere in the country."

Student Body

At OU, students know how to find a "nice balance" between their "academic and social lives." This "friendly" and "down-to-earth" group is made up of "motivated" individuals who are always looking out for one another. While many students seem to be "white, upper-middle class, and Christian," there is also "a broad mix of international and minority students" and students of other religions. Overall, students feel supported and say that "people are very considerate of one another and make efforts to support each other during rough times." Most students at OU find that the best way to "fit in" is by "being involved on campus" and joining "lots of organizations," or taking part in the popular Sooner pastimes of "volunteering," "sports," and "Greek life." One undergrad sums up the student body: "We genuinely care for one another and are very passionate about the university."

University of Oklahoma

Financial Aid: 405-325-5505 • E-Mail: admissions@ou.edu • Website: www.ou.edu

THE PRINCETON REVIEW SAYS

Admissions

The school reports that its standardized testing policy for use in admission for Fall 2026 is Test Optional. The Princeton Review suggests that interested applicants consult with the school for the most up-to-date standardized testing policies. *Very important factors considered include:* rigor of secondary school record, academic GPA, standardized test scores. *Important factors considered include:* class rank, application essay, recommendation(s). *Other factors considered include:* interview, extracurricular activities, talent/ability, character/personal qualities, first generation, alumni/ae relation, geographical residence, state residency, volunteer work, work experience, level of applicant's interest. High school diploma is required and GED is accepted. *Academic units required:* 4 English, 3 math, 3 science, 3 science labs, 1 social studies, 2 history, 2 academic electives. *Academic units recommended:* 4 math, 4 science, 2 language (other than English), 1 computer science.

Financial Aid

Students should submit: FAFSA. Priority filing deadline is 3/1. The Princeton Review suggests that all financial aid forms be submitted as soon as possible. *Need-based scholarships/grants offered:* Federal Pell; Federal SEOG; State scholarships/grants; Private scholarships; College/university scholarship or grant aid from institutional funds; United Negro College Fund. *Loan aid offered:* Federal Direct Subsidized Loans; Federal Direct Unsubsidized Loans; Direct PLUS loans. Admitted students will be notified of awards on a rolling basis beginning 12/15. Federal Work-Study Program available. Institutional employment available.

The Inside Word

With one of the lowest in-state tuition rates in the country, the University of Oklahoma is a great value. Accepted students at OU graduated from high school with an average GPA of 3.6. But while academic grades and standardized test scores (if submitted) are very important to the admissions process at OU, they also place importance on community service, leadership, and extracurricular activities. In fact, the applicant's "engagement" accounts for one-quarter of their decision.

THE SCHOOL SAYS

From the Admissions Office

"Ask yourself some significant questions. What are your ambitions, goals, and dreams? Do you desire opportunity, and are you ready to accept challenge? What do you hope to gain from your educational experience? Are you looking for a university that will provide you with the tools, resources, and motivation to convert ambitions, opportunities, and challenges into meaningful achievement? To effectively answer these questions you must carefully seek out your options, look for direction, and make the right choice. The University of Oklahoma combines a unique mixture of academic excellence, varied social cultures, and a variety of campus activities to make your educational experience complete. At OU, comprehensive learning is our goal for your life. Not only do you receive a valuable classroom learning experience, but OU is also one of the finest research institutions in the United States. This allows OU students the opportunity to be a part of technology in progress. It's not just learning, it's discovery, invention, and dynamic creativity, a hands-on experience that allows you to be on the cutting edge of knowledge. Make the right choice and consider the University of Oklahoma!"

SELECTIVITY

# of total applicants	29,195
% of total applicants accepted	78
% of total acceptees attending	27
# of in-state applicants	6,694
% of in-state applicants accepted	76
# of out-of-state-applicants	20,948
% of applicants accepted from out of state	80
# of international applicants	1,553
% of international applicants accepted	48
# offered a place on the wait list	3,117
# admitted from wait list	133

First-Year Profile

Testing policy	Test Optional
Range SAT composite	1160–1310
Range SAT EBRW	570–660
Range SAT math	570–650
Range ACT composite	23–28
% submitting SAT scores	22
% submitting ACT scores	43
Average HS GPA	3.6
% submitting high school GPA	100
% graduated top 10% of class	30
% graduated top 25% of class	58
% graduated top 50% of class	89
% submitting high school rank	54

Important Dates

Early action	
Apply by	11/1
Notified by	Rolling
Regular	
Apply by	2/1
Notified by	Rolling, 9/1
Nonfall registration?	Yes

FINANCIAL FACTS

Annual in-state tuition	$5,370
Annual out-of-state tuition	$23,490
Food and housing	$15,798
Required fees	$4,811
Books and supplies	$800
Average need-based scholarship (First-year)	$7,955 ($8,222)
% students with need rec. need-based scholarship or grant aid (First-year)	61 (51)
% students with need rec. non-need-based scholarship or grant aid (First-year)	56 (70)
% students with need rec. need-based self-help aid (First-year)	55 (48)
% students rec. any financial aid (First-year)	94 (99)
% UG borrow to pay for school	44
Average cumulative indebtedness	$32,351
% of students with need fully met (First-year)	15 (18)
Average % of student need met (First-year)	62 (66)

University of Oregon

1226 University of Oregon, Eugene, OR 97403-1226 • Admissions: 541-346-3201

Survey Snapshot
Recreation facilities are great
Frats and sororities are popular
Easy to get around campus

RATINGS

Quality of Life	**86**
Fire Safety	**94**
Green	**97**
Academic	**77**
Profs Interesting	**86**
Profs Accessible	**89**
Admissions	**82**
Financial Aid	**82**

CAMPUS LIFE

Type of school	Public
Environment	City

Students

Degree-seeking undergrad enrollment	20,605
% male/female/not reported	44/56/<1
% from out of state	48
% First-year live on campus	94
% Ugrads live on campus	27
# of fraternities (% join)	20 (19)
# of sororities (% join)	16 (18)
% Asian	7
% Black or African American	3
% Hispanic	17
% Native American	1
% Pacific Islander	<1
% Race and/or ethnicity unknown	1
% Two or more races	10
% White	60
% International	1
# of countries represented	60

CAMPUS MENTAL HEALTH SERVICES

Offers mental health/wellness program	Yes
Mental health training available to students	Yes
Employs Chief Wellness Officer	Yes
Peer-to-peer mental health offerings	Yes
Counseling center has guidelines or accreditation	Yes
Mental health/well-being courses	Yes, for-credit

ACADEMICS

% students returning for sophomore year	86
% students graduating within 4 years	57
% students graduating within 6 years	71
Calendar	Quarter
Student/faculty ratio	19:1
Most common class size 20–29.	(29%)
Most common lab/discussion size 20–29.	(59%)

Most Popular Majors
Physiology; Psychology; Business/Commerce

STUDENTS SAY "..."

Academics

The University of Oregon provides "a wide variety of opportunities for students," a sentiment echoed by many, including one Duck who shares: "My school does a great job of allowing students to navigate different academic paths by not pressuring them into declaring a major or minor immediately," and encouraging them to take "a variety of diverse classes and explore different interests." For example, one Duck enjoys "being a research assistant in labs, working as an editor at multiple student journals, completing an independent thesis project, studying abroad, and conducting experiments in class." As an R1 research university, "there are so many opportunities to get involved in hands-on research." Pre-health programs, particularly in human physiology, are known for "pushing the boundary of undergraduate research and sports health," while the Warsaw Sports Business Center helps cultivate the "next generation of sports business leaders." Alumni connections also enhance student experiences, as demonstrated by the Ducks Shadow Ducks Program, which lets students "shadow alumni in their desired field and make connections at large companies such as Visa, Edelman, Washington Times, and the SF Giants!" With a vibrant academic community and diverse learning experiences, one Duck feels well-prepared to graduate "with projects I can talk about on my résumé and examples of my work to show employers."

Campus Life

"Nothing beats walking to Autzen Stadium for a football game," says one Duck, a feeling shared by many students at UO. As an unabashedly "sports-centric" school, Ducks take pride in "being a part of a Big 10 school," offering students the chance to experience top-tier college athletes in a variety of sports. Many students enjoy "working out at the student recreation center" or playing intramural flag football, basketball, and volleyball, while others combine fitness with outdoor adventure, as "it is easy to find clubs dedicated to hiking, running, camping, and more." Beyond athletics, the university thrives on its vibrant social scene: "There are so many lively clubs and organizations that are welcoming to everyone....It doesn't feel like a big university when you can make small communities inside of it." One of those communities is Greek life, which, as one student says, "has been a big part of my life and has truly given me my best friends." Ducks enjoy Oregon's natural beauty, and "if the weather is nice, students will be outside studying, lying in hammocks, and playing spike ball." For those over 21, "the three bars near campus are packed and very fun." One Duck sums up campus life at UO best: "The campus is beautiful, the football team is great, and the student body is lively."

Student Body

"Welcoming, with a sense of family," is how one Duck describes the vibe on campus, a sentiment shared by many at the university. Given the large size of the student body, students find that "there is a crowd for everyone at UO—athletes, sorority girls, frat bros, skaters, artists, outdoorsy, and more." One student reports: "A lot of people are experimenting with their style, their ideas, and their interests, so it results in a lot of fun sights and experiences." Another Duck agrees, describing their peers as "creative, eclectic, interesting, friendly, driven." The strong athletic culture at UO contributes to "a sense of community and a collective identity of being Ducks," while students also rally around "the outdoors and environmental activism." One student adds, "The campus is very politically active and left-leaning." Another proudly adds, "If there is something [Ducks] see wrong with the world, institution, etc., they will do something to try and change it." For many, the highlight of their UO experience is captured in this sentiment: "My favorite part of being at UO is the people I have met and the community I've built."

University of Oregon

Financial Aid: 541-346-3221 • E-Mail: admissions@uoregon.edu • Website: www.uoregon.edu

THE PRINCETON REVIEW SAYS

Admissions

The school reports that its standardized testing policy for use in admission for Fall 2026 is Test Optional. The Princeton Review suggests that interested applicants consult with the school for the most up-to-date standardized testing policies. *Very important factors considered include:* rigor of secondary school record, academic GPA. *Important factors considered include:* application essay. *Other factors considered include:* class rank, standardized test scores, recommendation(s), extracurricular activities, talent/ability, character/personal qualities, first generation, geographical residence, state residency, volunteer work, work experience. High school diploma is required and GED is accepted. *Academic units required:* 4 English, 3 math, 3 science, 2 language (other than English), 3 social studies. *Academic units recommended:* 1 science lab.

Financial Aid

Students should submit: FAFSA. Priority filing deadline is 3/1. The Princeton Review suggests that all financial aid forms be submitted as soon as possible. *Need-based scholarships/grants offered:* Federal Pell; Federal SEOG; State scholarships/grants; Private scholarships; College/university scholarship or grant aid from institutional funds. *Loan aid offered:* Federal Direct Subsidized Loans; Federal Direct Unsubsidized Loans; Direct PLUS loans. Admitted students will be notified of awards on a rolling basis beginning 4/1. Federal Work-Study Program available. Institutional employment available.

The Inside Word

Your ticket to UO is a strong GPA in challenging college prep courses, although you may consider optionally submitting your standardized test scores if they're particularly good. If your high school grades dropped due to personal circumstances, or indicate an upward trajectory due to personal growth, consider addressing that in your personal statement.

THE SCHOOL SAYS

From the Admissions Office

"At the University of Oregon, bold ideas move beyond the classroom to become breakthroughs that shape industries, communities, and lives. Known as the birthplace of Nike, UO blends entrepreneurial energy with the academic strength of a leading public research university.

"UO includes eight colleges and schools across two campuses—Eugene, the center of undergraduate life, and Portland, a growing hub for professional and graduate education—along with two nationally distinctive areas: the Phil and Penny Knight Campus for Accelerating Scientific Impact and the Ballmer Institute for Children's Behavioral Health. Together, they power interdisciplinary learning and real-world problem solving.

"Undergraduates choose from nearly 200 academic programs across nine areas of interest, including business, communications and media; climate, sustainability, and the built environment; the creative and performing arts; education and human services; global studies and history; literature and languages; health, medicine, and sports; science, technology, and mathematics; and social policy, justice, and economic systems—giving students flexibility to align learning with purpose and career goals.

"UO's academic rigor is reinforced by national recognition, including the 2026 Barry Goldwater Scholar, one of the most prestigious undergraduate STEM awards. High-achieving students can further elevate their experience through the Robert D. Clark Honors College, featuring small, discussion-based classes, close faculty mentorship, a senior thesis, and its own residence hall.

"Graduates launch impactful careers at organizations such as Nike, Intel, Microsoft, Deloitte, and the CDC. All of this is shaped by the UO vibe—creative, collaborative, sustainability-minded, and deeply connected to the Pacific Northwest."

SELECTIVITY

# of total applicants	41,368
% of total applicants accepted	87
% of total acceptees attending	14
# offered a place on the wait list	1,941
# admitted from wait list	422

First-Year Profile

Testing policy	Test Optional
Range SAT composite	1050–1320
Range SAT EBRW	540–680
Range SAT math	500–650
Range ACT composite	22–29
% submitting SAT scores	11
% submitting ACT scores	4
Average HS GPA	3.7
% submitting high school GPA	100

Important Dates

Early action	
Apply by	11/1
Notified by	12/15
Regular	
Apply by	1/15
Notified by	4/1
Nonfall registration?	Yes

FINANCIAL FACTS

Annual in-state tuition (First-year)	$13,714 ($14,532)
Annual out-of-state tuition (First-year)	$42,566 ($44,523)
Food and housing	$18,183
Required fees (First-year)	$2,795 ($2,943)
Books and supplies	$1,434
Average need-based scholarship (First-year)	$14,198 ($14,857)
% students with need rec. need-based scholarship or grant aid (First-year)	88 (92)
% students with need rec. non-need-based scholarship or grant aid (First-year)	42 (59)
% students with need rec. need-based self-help aid (First-year)	81 (83)
% students rec. any financial aid (First-year)	72 (76)
% UG borrow to pay for school	41
Average cumulative indebtedness	$26,691
% of students with need fully met (First-year)	8 (9)
Average % of student need met (First-year)	55 (54)

UNIVERSITY OF PENNSYLVANIA

1 College Hall, Room 100, Philadelphia, PA 19104-6228 • Admissions: 215-898-7507

Survey Snapshot
Internships are widely available
Campus newspaper is popular
Alumni active on campus

RATINGS

Quality of Life	**80**
Fire Safety	**60***
Green	**94**
Academic	**86**
Profs Interesting	**85**
Profs Accessible	**90**
Admissions	**99**
Financial Aid	**98**

CAMPUS LIFE

Type of school	Private
Environment	Metropolis

Students

Degree-seeking undergrad enrollment	9,989
% male/female/not reported	46/54/0
% from out of state	82
% First-year from public high school	60
% First-year live on campus	100
% Ugrads live on campus	56
# of fraternities (% join)	25 (19)
# of sororities (% join)	14 (17)
% Asian	30
% Black or African American	9
% Hispanic	11
% Native American	<1
% Pacific Islander	<1
% Race and/or ethnicity unknown	6
% Two or more races	5
% White	24
% International	13
# of countries represented	123

CAMPUS MENTAL HEALTH SERVICES

Offers mental health/wellness program	Yes
Mental health training available to students	No
Employs Chief Wellness Officer	NR
Peer-to-peer mental health offerings	NR
Counseling center has guidelines or accreditation	No
Mental health/well-being courses	NR

ACADEMICS

% students returning for sophomore year	99
% students graduating within 4 years	86
% students graduating within 6 years	97
Calendar	Semester
Student/faculty ratio	10:1
Most common class size 10–19.	(33%)

Most Popular Majors

Economics; Registered Nursing/Registered Nurse; Finance

STUDENTS SAY "..."

Academics

At the University of Pennsylvania, there are "more than enough" resources, funding, and opportunities, and students are constantly encouraged "to truly take advantage of it all!" There are four undergraduate colleges—the College of Arts and Sciences, the Wharton School of Business, the School of Engineering and Applied Science, and the School of Nursing—and students appreciate the range: "I can take a course in old Icelandic and even another one about the politics of food." That said, note that this prestigious Ivy League school is "very challenging," perhaps even more so at Wharton, which carries a "strenuous course load" for its "highly competitive" and "career-oriented" enrollees. Those interested in dual-degree and specialized programs can tack on interdisciplinary studies, with access to "courses in any of the schools, including graduate level courses." While "course and exam materials are difficult," professors balance that out and are described as being "down-to-earth and approachable in general.... The academic support is great." Between being "very passionate about what they do outside the classroom" and "incredibly well-versed in their subject (as well as their audience)," faculty are "always willing to offer their more-than-relevant life experience in class discussion." Students appreciate the student-to-faculty ratio, and report that when they "reach out," professors are "happy to reciprocate." This personal touch even extends to the application process, with one undergrad having enrolled because the campus outreach team "made me feel like I wasn't just another set of applications; instead, I was an actual human being—one that they valued and wanted."

Campus Life

The 64-acre campus at UPenn offers "the perfect mix between an urban setting and a traditional college campus." Located in West Philadelphia, students need only cross the Schuylkill River to access all of the City of Brotherly Love's delights. There's also easy transportation to other East Coast cities, and the weekend buses to/from New York and D.C. "are always packed." Not that there isn't plenty to do at UPenn: there are lots of guest speakers, cultural events, clubs, and organizations for the "mighty Quaker" students to channel. Conversations vary: "politics and religion come up often, but so do baseball, types of wine, and restaurants." Overall, "people are constantly trying to think about how they can balance getting good grades academically and their weekend plans." Some report that "partying is a much higher priority here than it is at other Ivy League schools." Students looking for a night out might find themselves "split between the downtown club scene and the frat/bar scene, depending on your preference." But make no mistake, when it's time to focus, "people get really serious and...buckle down and study."

Student Body

The UPenn student body is comprised of "people from all over the world, of all kinds of experiences, [and] of all perspectives. Students describe their peers as "determined" and "either focused on one specific interest or very well-rounded." Some find the academic atmosphere at UPenn to be competitive, though one student points out that "hyper-competitive" peers can be "helpful." It also makes overachievers feel right at home, and it says a lot that some describe their peers as "off-the-charts brilliant." Given each student's "strong sense of personal style and his or her own credo," the net result for many is a feeling of being "fascinated by everyone else."

UNIVERSITY OF PENNSYLVANIA

Financial Aid: 215-898-1988 • E-Mail: info@admissions.upenn.edu • Website: www.upenn.edu

THE PRINCETON REVIEW SAYS

Admissions

The school reports that its standardized testing policy for use in admission for Fall 2026 will require applicants to submit either the SAT or ACT. The Princeton Review suggests that interested applicants consult with the school for the most up-to-date standardized testing policies. *Very important factors considered include:* rigor of secondary school record, academic GPA, application essay, recommendation(s), character/personal qualities. *Important factors considered include:* class rank, extracurricular activities, talent/ability, volunteer work, work experience. *Other factors considered include:* standardized test scores, first generation, alumni/ae relation, geographical residence, state residency. High school diploma is required and GED is accepted. *Academic units recommended:* 4 English, 4 math, 4 science, 3 science labs, 4 language (other than English), 2 social studies, 2 history.

Financial Aid

Students should submit: FAFSA; CSS PROFILE; Business/Farm Supplement. Priority filing deadline is 2/1. The Princeton Review suggests that all financial aid forms be submitted as soon as possible. *Need-based scholarships/grants offered:* Federal Pell; Federal SEOG; State scholarships/grants; Private scholarships; College/university scholarship or grant aid from institutional funds. *Loan aid offered:* Federal Direct Subsidized Loans; Federal Direct Unsubsidized Loans; Direct PLUS loans; College/university loans from institutional funds. Admitted students will be notified of awards on or about 3/31. Federal Work-Study Program available. Institutional employment available.

The Inside Word

With an acceptance rate of just 5 percent, the competition in the applicant pool is formidable. Applicants can safely assume that they need to be one of the strongest students in their graduating class in order to be successful. The school is Test Optional, but submitting stellar test scores may help you stand out from the crowd.

THE SCHOOL SAYS

From the Admissions Office

"Founded by Benjamin Franklin in 1740 to push the frontiers of knowledge and to benefit society, Penn continues to nurture a sense of public mindedness in its students, inspiring them to make vital contributions as they become engaged citizens in an evolving world. Penn's students and faculty work toward the shared goal of enacting change by questioning, thinking, and doing—often across traditional academic disciplines. The integration of knowledge and learning spans four undergraduate schools: the College of Arts & Sciences, the School of Engineering & Applied Science, the Wharton School of Business, and the School of Nursing. Penn offers more than ninety majors, eighty minors, and the ability to earn more than one degree in four years.

"The Penn community thrives on the open exchange of ideas and shared learning experiences, made possible by the faculty and students of all four undergraduate and twelve graduate schools who coexist and collaborate on one beautiful 300 acre campus in Philadelphia. Students regularly conduct research with faculty and actively participate in over 500 clubs and organizations. Education through engagement is made possible by Penn's extensive partnerships around the world and close to our Philadelphia campus, ranging from over 150 Academically-Based Community Service courses to internships in twenty-two foreign countries.

"Penn understands that the best minds should have access to the finest education, regardless of their families' ability to pay. To achieve this, Penn practices need-blind admissions for applicants who are citizens and permanent residents of the United States, Canada, and Mexico, meets 100 percent of demonstrated financial need, and provides an all-grant aid package for all undergraduates receiving financial aid. Our goal is to allow students to pursue their aspirations without assuming a burden of debt."

SELECTIVITY

# of total applicants	72,544
% of total applicants accepted	5
% of total acceptees attending	68
# of in-state applicants	5,411
% of in-state applicants accepted	8
# of out-of-state-applicants	49,251
% of applicants accepted from out of state	5
# of international applicants	17,882
% of international applicants accepted	2
# of early decision applicants	9,503
% of early decision applicants accepted	13
# offered a place on the wait list	3,252
# admitted from wait list	60

First-Year Profile

Testing policy	SAT or ACT Required
Range SAT EBRW	740–770
Range SAT math	770–800
Range ACT composite	34–35
% submitting SAT scores	52
% submitting ACT scores	18
Average HS GPA	3.9
% submitting high school GPA	98
% graduated top 10% of class	92
% graduated top 25% of class	99
% graduated top 50% of class	100
% submitting high school rank	23

Important Dates

Early decision	
Apply by	11/1
Notified by	12/15
Regular	
Apply by	1/5
Notified by	Late March
Nonfall registration?	No

FINANCIAL FACTS

Annual tuition	$65,670
Food and housing	$20,604
Required fees	$8,308
Average need-based scholarship (First-year)	$70,215 ($70,867)
% students with need rec. need-based scholarship or grant aid (First-year)	100 (98)
% students with need rec. need-based self-help aid (First-year)	100 (100)
% students rec. any financial aid (First-year)	46 (47)
% UG borrow to pay for school	16
Average cumulative indebtedness	$33,655
% of students with need fully met (First-year)	100 (100)
Average % of student need met (First-year)	100 (100)

University of Pittsburgh—Pittsburgh Campus

4200 Fifth Avenue, Pittsburgh, PA 15260 • Admissions: 412-624-7488

Survey Snapshot
Recreation facilities are great
Great library
Frats and sororities are popular

RATINGS

Quality of Life	**83**
Fire Safety	**92**
Green	**93**
Academic	**79**
Profs Interesting	**85**
Profs Accessible	**88**
Admissions	**89**
Financial Aid	**82**

CAMPUS LIFE

Type of school	Public
Environment	Metropolis

Students

Degree-seeking undergrad enrollment	21,222
% male/female/not reported	42/58/0
% First-year live on campus	95
% Ugrads live on campus	44
# of fraternities (% join)	24 (9)
# of sororities (% join)	17 (12)
% Asian	15
% Black or African American	5
% Hispanic	7
% Native American	<1
% Pacific Islander	<1
% Race and/or ethnicity unknown	3
% Two or more races	5
% White	60
% International	4
# of countries represented	72

CAMPUS MENTAL HEALTH SERVICES

Offers mental health/wellness program	Yes
Mental health training available to students	Yes
Employs Chief Wellness Officer	Yes
Peer-to-peer mental health offerings	Yes
Counseling center has guidelines or accreditation	Yes
Mental health/well-being courses	Yes, for-credit

ACADEMICS

% students returning for sophomore year	93
% students graduating within 4 years	72
% students graduating within 6 years	86
Calendar	Semester
Student/faculty ratio	14:1
Most common class size 10–19.	(28%)
Most common lab/discussion size 20–29.	(53%)

Most Popular Majors

Biology/Biological Sciences; Research and Experimental Psychology; Finance

Applicants Often Prefer

Boston University, Carnegie Mellon University, New York University, University of Michigan—Ann Arbor, University of Pennsylvania, University of Virginia

Applicants Sometimes Prefer

Case Western Reserve University, Northeastern University, The Ohio State University—Columbus, Penn State University Park, Rochester Institute of Technology, Rutgers University—Camden, Syracuse University, Temple University, University of Delaware, University of Maryland, College Park

Applicants Rarely Prefer

Drexel University

STUDENTS SAY "..."

Academics

There are "a lot of students determined for success" at the Pittsburgh campus of the University of Pittsburgh, where the rigorous academics and urban opportunities allow them "to discover themselves and how they can impact the future of the world." The university "offers so many resources to help achieve the greatest understanding of material," and "there are a lot of opportunities to get out and learn in the field." Undergrads also have access to "very good research opportunities," and "study abroad is accessible in a variety of forms, with numerous full-semester programs, summer programs, and short-term experiences led by faculty members." Many students report that the "academics are very strong here," especially the STEM programs. Professors are "not only knowledgeable but also fairly accessible outside of lecture halls," and "most are skilled at conveying that knowledge in a digestible way." Many professors "provide supplemental information and resources to enhance the classwork and encourage students to do independent exploration of the class subject matter outside of the class materials." The combination of "amazing professors, so many academic resources, incredible health and wellness programs, and one-on-one support in every area" leads one student to say, "This is a universally loved school, and you can tell many students enjoy being here."

Campus Life

Pitt is a "combination of city campus and neighborhood, blending urban hustle and the chaotic fun of a college town." The city is full of opportunities for exploration, and people enjoy "trying new restaurants and cafes, going to Schenley Park, [and] events downtown." While a variety of dorms and campus-owned apartment buildings are available, "lots of people live off campus and host events," but it's still "easy to get around efficiently," thanks to free public transportation for Pitt students. There are "always a lot of activities and events going on throughout the week," and with more than 700 student organizations, there "are groups here for basically any interest or personality type, and it makes it easy to find friends." Weekdays are typically spent studying, and many students "do work in public spaces or at the library," and "also have on-campus or off-campus jobs to help pay their way through college." Sporting events are popular, and "everyone always puts their best into all of the games here." Reflecting on their experience, one student says, "Getting to attend a public university with strong academic and sports culture in the heart of an amazing city is such a wonderful opportunity."

Student Body

Pitt is home to "a very diverse group of students—ethnically, racially, socio-economically, religiously and academically," and most students are academically driven, "supportive, and have a lot of pride in their school." Students also mention that many come here with "a distinct goal in mind in terms of their careers and personal development." Overall, the university "does a very good job of having a wide range of programs, which helps attract that wide range of students" with diverse "interests, focuses, and subcultures." As one student puts it, "It feels like an equal mix of different personalities. You have artsy kids, STEM kids, athletics, Greek life, and just a ton of other 'troupes,' which I think overall add so much character to the school and student body." Some students find their peers warm and friendly, while others feel it can take some effort to connect, though one student explains, "I just think you have to take it upon yourself to make the first move to make friends here." All in all, one student notes that Pitt "establishes a healthy connection for students between academic work, cultural awareness of Pittsburgh itself, and extracurriculars that I feel builds a cohesive student body."

UNIVERSITY OF PITTSBURGH—PITTSBURGH CAMPUS

Financial Aid: 412-624-7488 • E-Mail: pitt.admissions@pitt.edu • Website: www.pitt.edu

THE PRINCETON REVIEW SAYS

Admissions

The school reports that its standardized testing policy for use in admission for Fall 2026 is Test Optional. The Princeton Review suggests that interested applicants consult with the school for the most up-to-date standardized testing policies. *Very important factors considered include:* rigor of secondary school record, academic GPA, application essay. *Important factors considered include:* talent/ability, character/personal qualities, volunteer work, work experience, level of applicant's interest. *Other factors considered include:* class rank, standardized test scores, recommendation(s), extracurricular activities, first generation, geographical residence, state residency. High school diploma is required and GED is accepted. *Academic units required:* 4 English, 3 math, 3 science, 2 language (other than English), 3 academic electives. *Academic units recommended:* 4 English, 4 math, 4 science, 3 language (other than English), 5 academic electives.

Financial Aid

Students should submit: FAFSA; State aid form. The Princeton Review suggests that all financial aid forms be submitted as soon as possible. *Need-based scholarships/grants offered:* Federal Pell; Federal SEOG; State scholarships/grants; Private scholarships; College/university scholarship or grant aid from institutional funds. *Loan aid offered:* Federal Direct Subsidized Loans; Federal Direct Unsubsidized Loans; Direct PLUS loans; College/university loans from institutional funds. Admitted students will be notified of awards on a rolling basis beginning 3/3. Federal Work-Study Program available. Institutional employment available.

The Inside Word

University of Pittsburgh operates on a rolling admission policy but your chances are better if you apply on the earlier side. Pitt reviews applications for the School of Medicine Guaranteed Admissions Application through November 1, and the Academic Scholarships Priority Review Application through October 15. Pitt offers extensive need- and merit-based financial aid, including the prestigious Chancellor's Scholarship. While SAT/ACT scores and the Short Answer Questions section of the Pitt application are optional, both are highly recommended.

THE SCHOOL SAYS

From the Admissions Office

"The University of Pittsburgh, a public research university, is a member of the Association of American Universities. Home to sixteen undergraduate, graduate, and professional schools, including an internationally renowned health sciences educational and research complex, Pitt is also affiliated with the University of Pittsburgh Medical Center. Its five-campus system offers more than 600 degree programs, and awards academic merit scholarships and guaranteed admission to graduate and professional programs. Pitt faculty have pioneered major medical advances including the Salk polio vaccine, multiple-organ transplantation, and CPR. Pitt alumni have won the Nobel Peace prize, the Nobel Prize in Medicine, the Pulitzer Prize, the National Medal of Science, Olympic gold medals, Academy Awards, and Super Bowl championships. University Honors College students have a proven track record of earning prestigious honors including Rhodes, Marshall, Goldwater, Truman, Udall Scholarships, Humanity in Action Scholarship, as well as a Gates Cambridge Scholarship; Pitt educates the whole student through a unique Outside the Classroom Curriculum program that helps students develop holistically; University Center for International Studies certificate programs; and Engineering Co-Op program; study abroad just about anywhere in the world; and more. There are 831 student organizations and student-athletes participate in Division I college athletics, supported by one of the most recognizable student-led fan bases in the nation. Encouraging students to take advantage of the city as their campus, Pitt grants fare-free access to city buses and discounted tickets to cultural events, opening them to the full experiences of a city that has been cited as the most livable in the U.S."

SELECTIVITY

# of total applicants	64,724
% of total applicants accepted	59
% of total acceptees attending	15
# offered a place on the wait list	6,245
# admitted from wait list	84

First-Year Profile

Testing policy	Test Optional
Range SAT EBRW	650–720
Range SAT math	630–730
Range ACT composite	29–33
% submitting SAT scores	40
% submitting ACT scores	8
Average HS GPA	4.1
% submitting high school GPA	99
% graduated top 10% of class	40
% graduated top 25% of class	73
% graduated top 50% of class	96
% submitting high school rank	29

Important Dates

Regular	
Apply by	7/30
Notified by	5/1
Nonfall registration?	Yes

FINANCIAL FACTS*

Annual in-state tuition	$20,966
Annual out-of-state tuition	$41,662
Food and housing	$14,720
Required fees	$1,770
Books and supplies	$576
Average need-based scholarship (First-year)	$17,819 ($19,110)
% students with need rec. need-based scholarship or grant aid (First-year)	88 (83)
% students with need rec. non-need-based scholarship or grant aid (First-year)	7 (6)
% students with need rec. need-based self-help aid (First-year)	70 (70)
% students rec. any financial aid (First-year)	52 (56)
% UG borrow to pay for school	57
Average cumulative indebtedness	$40,791
% of students with need fully met (First-year)	12 (10)
Average % of student need met (First-year)	60 (58)

* Most recently reported data at time of printing. Scan the QR code to find the latest updates.

UNIVERSITY OF PORTLAND

5000 N. Willamette Boulevard, Portland, OR 97203 • Admissions: 503-943-7147

Survey Snapshot
Students take advantage of the outdoors
Easy to get around campus
Student love Portland, OR

RATINGS

Quality of Life	**85**
Fire Safety	**60***
Green	**60***
Academic	**84**
Profs Interesting	**91**
Profs Accessible	**94**
Admissions	**83**
Financial Aid	**84**

CAMPUS LIFE

Type of school	Private
Affiliation	Roman Catholic
Environment	Metropolis

Students

Degree-seeking undergrad enrollment	2,785
% male/female/not reported	33/67/<1
% from out of state	59
% First-year live on campus	80
% Ugrads live on campus	55
# of fraternities	0
# of sororities	0
% Asian	21
% Black or African American	3
% Hispanic	24
% Native American	<1
% Pacific Islander	1
% Race and/or ethnicity unknown	1
% Two or more races	10
% White	35
% International	3
# of countries represented	29

CAMPUS MENTAL HEALTH SERVICES

Offers mental health/wellness program	Yes
Mental health training available to students	Yes
Employs Chief Wellness Officer	No
Peer-to-peer mental health offerings	Yes
Counseling center has guidelines or accreditation	No
Mental health/well-being courses	NR

ACADEMICS

% students returning for sophomore year	86
% students graduating within 4 years	67
% students graduating within 6 years	80
Calendar	Semester
Student/faculty ratio	10:1
Most common class size 10–19.	(35%)
Most common lab/discussion size 10–19.	(57%)

Most Popular Majors

Registered Nursing; Business Administration and Management; Biology/Biological Sciences; Psychology

Applicants Also Look At

Gonzaga University, Oregon State University, Seattle University, University of Oregon, University of Washington

STUDENTS SAY "..."

Academics

Students can't stop raving about the quality of professors at the University of Portland: "phenomenal—no question about it," puts one, while another elaborates that students are "always able to get something out of every lecture" because of how "clear, brilliant, and genuinely enjoyable" the teachers are. This boils down to two things: First, the smaller class sizes mean students establish a "super strong community" in which "the professors get the chance to get to know each and every one of their students personally and are able to help them in a way that is customized to them." Second, the faculty "are all incredibly knowledgeable and interested in both the course content and their students." As an education major puts it about their department, having professors who "were teachers themselves" is a huge perk that makes this undergrad "feel very confident about my ability to find a teaching job and thrive in my own classroom." Instructors also don't hesitate to take learning off campus. One senior boasts that as part of their capstone class they are "part of a racing team where we are developing an electric go-kart to race in an upcoming collegiate competition."

It seems that at UP, students do indeed go up, up, and away, with business students emphasizing the school's "connections at Nike, Adidas, Intel, and most companies based in Portland." The University of Portland also boasts a highly valued nursing program. "I'm very thankful and grateful for the professors I've had during my college experience," says one nursing student, "I feel better prepared for the beginning of my post-grad life working as an RN thanks to them."

Campus Life

Affectionately known as "The Bluff," the UP campus offers a lifestyle "like no other." Dorms offer a strong "'lobby culture' so there's always people in the lobby doing homework, or playing a game with a friend, or just relaxing." There's an equally strong culture of spirituality—true to the school's Holy Cross roots—in that each dorm has its own chapel. "There is always a way to grow stronger in your faith here." And while students emphasize all the fun there is to be had with sports and dances and the weekly Pilots After Dark pub-style event ("Sometimes there is trivia, drag performances, [or] seasonal activities"), UP is "overall not a party school." Instead of discussing drinking, students speak of how "The Bluff is a beautiful place, and just walking around campus is so relaxing," and revel in the "outdoor opportunities available in the Pacific Northwest," like kayaking, camping, and skiing. There's an Outdoor Pursuits Program that "offers students the ability to learn the basics and exposes people to the outdoors."

Student Body

The sense of community here is unmatched, enthuses one student—as long as you're willing to get involved. In short, "while students are focused on their academics...there is still a social scene and atmosphere if you want it." To put it another way: "Almost everyone I know is involved in a club or organization, and it is where I have met almost all of my friends." The student body includes "students with different identities, cultures, [and] passions." One student describes their peers as "mostly PNW-style, [and] outdoorsy...either nonreligious or progressive religious," and others value the "diverse set of minds" and "very unique people" they're surrounded by on campus. Students also note that "the University of Portland has been growing with more diverse students, but more importantly more diverse professors." The University of Portland also has "a large amount of students from other nations, which really enriches the culture and connectedness between one another." Students are "very outspoken, they are not scared to speak up," and are known for their willingness to "uplift each student's uniqueness."

UNIVERSITY OF PORTLAND

Financial Aid: 503-943-7311 • E-Mail: admissions@up.edu • Website: www.up.edu

THE PRINCETON REVIEW SAYS

Admissions

The school reports that its standardized testing policy for use in admission for Fall 2026 is Test Optional. The Princeton Review suggests that interested applicants consult with the school for the most up-to-date standardized testing policies. *Very important factors considered include:* rigor of secondary school record, academic GPA. *Important factors considered include:* class rank, application essay, extracurricular activities, talent/ability, volunteer work, work experience. *Other factors considered include:* standardized test scores, recommendation(s), interview, character/personal qualities, first generation, geographical residence, religious affiliation/commitment, level of applicant's interest. High school diploma is required and GED is accepted. *Academic units required:* 4 English, 3 math, 3 science, 2 language (other than English), 3 social studies, 2 history, 7 academic electives. *Academic units recommended:* 4 English, 4 math, 4 science, 3 language (other than English), 4 social studies, 4 history, 7 academic electives.

Financial Aid

Students should submit: FAFSA. Priority filing deadline is 2/15. The Princeton Review suggests that all financial aid forms be submitted as soon as possible. *Need-based scholarships/grants offered:* Federal Pell; Federal SEOG; State scholarships/grants; Private scholarships; College/university scholarship or grant aid from institutional funds; Federal Nursing Scholarships. *Loan aid offered:* Federal Direct Subsidized Loans; Federal Direct Unsubsidized Loans; Direct PLUS loans; College/university loans from institutional funds. Admitted students will be notified of awards on a rolling basis beginning 11/20. Federal Work-Study Program available. Institutional employment available.

The Inside Word

The University of Portland is a well-rounded college that welcomes all students. To make applying easier for students, standardized testing is optional, and they're equally accepting of both their own application and the Common App. That said, this means the admissions committee will be carefully looking at whatever you choose to submit, so it behooves you to have things like a thoughtful letter of recommendation and a solid transcript. Note that admission to the Honors Program is considered separately, so complete your general forms early if you're going this route.

THE SCHOOL SAYS

From the Admissions Office

"At University of Portland, a comprehensive, Catholic, Holy Cross university, there's no place for the status quo. We're always dreaming bigger, reaching higher, and going further than ever before. Why? Because we're always asking that too. As a Fulbright Top Producing Institution with the highest graduation rate in the state, we're a community of big thinkers and purpose-driven doers who are unafraid to ask tough questions, work together to find the answers, and keep pushing for progress with purpose.

"From our residential campus in Portland, Oregon, you'll have countless opportunities for internships, practicums, service work, and groundbreaking research with faculty. And with direct entry to our College of Arts and Sciences and four professional schools focused on business, engineering, health care, and education, you can start your major area of study right away. But no matter what major you choose, you will benefit from a core curriculum in the humanities and sciences that fosters critical thinking and problem-solving while providing a foundation in ethical decision making. You may not know exactly what you want to do, but one thing is certain: with an education at UP, you'll get your hands dirty, your heart connected, and your mind expanded in ways you never thought possible."

SELECTIVITY

# of total applicants	7,686
% of total applicants accepted	92
% of total acceptees attending	10
# offered a place on the wait list	202
# admitted from wait list	85

First-Year Profile

Testing policy	Test Optional
Range SAT composite	1210–1330
Range SAT EBRW	600–680
Range SAT math	570–680
Range ACT composite	28–33
% submitting SAT scores	4
% submitting ACT scores	1
Average HS GPA	3.7
% submitting high school GPA	100

Important Dates

Early action	
Apply by	12/1
Notified by	12/1
Regular	
Apply by	2/15
Notified by	Rolling, 10/1
Nonfall registration?	Yes

FINANCIAL FACTS

Annual tuition	$61,000
Food and housing	$18,650
Required fees (First-year)	$1,350 ($1,625)
Books and supplies	$1,140
Average need-based scholarship (First-year)	$44,681 ($46,235)
% students with need rec. need-based scholarship or grant aid (First-year)	79 (80)
% students with need rec. non-need-based scholarship or grant aid (First-year)	97 (99)
% students with need rec. need-based self-help aid (First-year)	68 (62)
% students rec. any financial aid (First-year)	99 (99)
% UG borrow to pay for school	54
Average cumulative indebtedness	$30,014
% of students with need fully met (First-year)	6 (7)
Average % of student need met (First-year)	79 (80)

UNIVERSITY OF PUGET SOUND

1500 North Warner Street, Tacoma, WA 98416-1062 • Admissions: 253-879-3211

Survey Snapshot
Lots of liberal students
Lab facilities are great
Active minority support groups

RATINGS

Quality of Life	89
Fire Safety	91
Green	87
Academic	89
Profs Interesting	93
Profs Accessible	95
Admissions	88
Financial Aid	89

CAMPUS LIFE

Type of school	Private
Environment	City

Students

Degree-seeking undergrad enrollment	1,619
% male/female/not reported	42/58/0
% from out of state	68
% First-year from public high school	76
% First-year live on campus	97
% Ugrads live on campus	68
# of fraternities (% join)	3 (27)
# of sororities (% join)	4 (17)
% Asian	6
% Black or African American	4
% Hispanic	12
% Native American	1
% Pacific Islander	1
% Race and/or ethnicity unknown	2
% Two or more races	9
% White	65
% International	<1
# of countries represented	6

CAMPUS MENTAL HEALTH SERVICES

Offers mental health/wellness program	Yes
Mental health training available to students	Yes
Employs Chief Wellness Officer	No
Peer-to-peer mental health offerings	Yes
Counseling center has guidelines or accreditation	No
Mental health/well-being courses	No

ACADEMICS

% students returning for sophomore year	88
% students graduating within 4 years	54
% students graduating within 6 years	69
Calendar	Semester
Student/faculty ratio	10:1
Most common class size 10–19.	(46%)
Most common lab/discussion size 10–19.	(58%)

Most Popular Majors

Biology/Biological Sciences; Psychology; Business Administration and Management

Applicants Also Look At

Gonzaga University, Lewis & Clark College, Pacific Lutheran University, Seattle University, University of California—Davis, University of Oregon, University of Portland, University of Washington, Western Washington University, Whitman College, Willamette University

STUDENTS SAY "..."

Academics

Featuring a "beautiful campus" and "excellent academics," the University of Puget Sound is a great option for anyone hoping to study in the Pacific Northwest. The school provides students with "an amazing support system" and truly strives to "help them [meet] their goal[s] in whatever capacity necessary." Academically, undergrads here are especially quick to highlight Puget Sound's "great arts programs, whether [in] English, music, or theater." They also applaud the fact that there are ample "project-based learning opportunities such as relevant work study [and] summer research for all majors and interests." Additionally, students benefit from small class sizes, which lead to plenty of "open discussion and interactive engagement with the course material." This also allows undergrads to develop "close student-professor relationships." And speaking of professors, they work hard to ensure their classes are "challenging" yet "accessible." Importantly, "they have open office hours that all students are encouraged to attend, and there is no shame in [doing so]." As one grateful student sums up, "Professors are genuinely excited to make time for students in their schedule for advice, homework help, or even just sharing a coffee. The level of concern of the professors for undergraduate education is almost unmatched."

Campus Life

It's no secret that undergrads at Puget Sound are "very dedicated to their studies." In fact, "most students have a fun time studying in [the] three different Cafés on campus." Of course, even these dedicated scholars need to kick back, so they frequently attend the various "performances, talks, or events going on almost every week." Additionally, many students flock to "the athletic center to get in a workout, attend a dance class, or rock climb." A good number also participate in "at least one club or are [involved] in Greek life." Puget Sound undergrads report that "on any given Friday night you can find a party" to attend. No need to worry if that's not your scene. Students here are an "outdoorsy" lot, and when the weekend rolls around, many of them can be found "hiking, skiing, kayaking" or "[taking] camping trips to the Olympic Peninsula or out to Eastern Washington." People are also just as happy to stay local and explore all that the surrounding area has to offer including "the Bridge of Glass, Point Defiance park, and the Puget Sound waterfront."

Student Body

At first glance, the University of Puget Sound's student body appears "fairly homogenous." After all, most undergrads come from "white middle-class families along the West Coast." However, the school is making strides to become "more diverse," especially "in terms of gender expression and sexuality." What's more, Puget Sound students are "not afraid to voice their [opinions or] their views [on] everything from political to social issues." In turn, students also caution that "more conservative views can [either] fall on deaf ears [or] can be met with a strong argument." However, others quickly assert that no matter your background or leanings, Puget Sound students are "open and welcoming to all." As one undergrad shares, "[Students are] not just nice in passing, but they have depth and consideration; when you run into someone in a Café and [make] small talk, it doesn't feel surface level." This makes for a "general vibe...[that is] laid back." Students also tend to describe their classmates as "unique," "adventurous," and "passionate" people who maintain a strong "desire for new experiences." Of course, if you're looking to easily pinpoint these undergrads, you'd simply say that the "typical [Puget Sound] student loves the outdoors, is a critical thinker, and knows what makes a good raincoat."

University of Puget Sound

Financial Aid: 253-879-3214 • E-Mail: admission@pugetsound.edu • Website: www.pugetsound.edu

THE PRINCETON REVIEW SAYS

Admissions

The school reports that its standardized testing policy for use in admission for Fall 2026 is Test Optional. The Princeton Review suggests that interested applicants consult with the school for the most up-to-date standardized testing policies. *Very important factors considered include:* rigor of secondary school record, academic GPA, application essay, character/personal qualities. *Important factors considered include:* recommendation(s), extracurricular activities, talent/ability, alumni/ae relation, volunteer work, work experience. *Other factors considered include:* class rank, standardized test scores, interview, first generation, level of applicant's interest. High school diploma is required and GED is accepted. *Academic units recommended:* 4 English, 3 math, 3 science, 3 science labs, 2 language (other than English), 3 social studies, 3 history, 1 visual/performing arts.

Financial Aid

Students should submit: FAFSA. Priority filing deadline is 11/1. The Princeton Review suggests that all financial aid forms be submitted as soon as possible. *Need-based scholarships/grants offered:* Federal Pell; Federal SEOG; State scholarships/grants; Private scholarships; College/university scholarship or grant aid from institutional funds. *Loan aid offered:* Federal Direct Subsidized Loans; Federal Direct Unsubsidized Loans; Direct PLUS loans. Admitted students will be notified of awards on or about 3/1. Federal Work-Study Program available. Institutional employment available.

The Inside Word

University of Puget Sound is a fairly selective school, so gaining admission is competitive. The college is eager to build a diverse student body that actively contributes to campus life. Thus, you can expect the admissions committee to take a holistic approach; everything from GPA to personal statements to extracurricular involvement will be closely considered. Nevertheless, the rigor of your high school curriculum will be of the utmost importance. It is also highly recommended that you sit for an interview, although it is not required.

THE SCHOOL SAYS

From the Admissions Office

"Located in the vibrant Pacific Northwest city of Tacoma, University of Puget Sound is a leading national liberal arts and sciences university. Tucked between mountain, sea, and forest, Puget Sound is ideal for students interested in a rigorous education rooted in hands-on learning. Puget Sound's liberal arts curriculum is flexible enough for students to pursue their passions and make unexpected connections. The university offers over 50 traditional and interdisciplinary programs, from bioethics to sociology, alongside unique offerings like the Business Leadership Program and the School of Music. Twenty percent of students participate in music. Popular majors include business, psychology, exercise science, and communication studies.

"The average class size is 17, and the average student-to-faculty ratio 10:1, so students benefit from 1:1 mentorship by professors who are leaders in their fields. Every student is guaranteed to complete at least one form of experiential learning—study abroad, research, internships, and/or community-based learning—with the majority supported by fellowships and grants. The University's support systems center academic excellence and include academic advisors, career counselors, subject-specific tutors, and student success coaches. The tailored Health Professions Advising program results in outstanding acceptance rates: 100% for 2025 graduates pursuing nursing, occupational therapy, physical therapy, athletic training, and veterinary medicine, and 89% for medical school.

"This focus on academic excellence is complemented by a close-knit community with 75 student-run clubs and 23 NCAA Division III teams. One-third of students are scholar-athletes, and outdoor recreation is made accessible via dedicated programming and Tacoma's central location."

SELECTIVITY

# of total applicants	4,711
% of total applicants accepted	72
% of total acceptees attending	11
# of in-state applicants	1,247
% of in-state applicants accepted	65
# of out-of-state-applicants	3,295
% of applicants accepted from out of state	78
# of international applicants	164
% of international applicants accepted	16
# of early decision applicants	157
% of early decision applicants accepted	58
# offered a place on the wait list	43
# admitted from wait list	1

First-Year Profile

Testing policy	Test Optional
Range SAT composite	1200–1370
Range SAT EBRW	620–720
Range SAT math	570–670
Range ACT composite	27–32
% submitting SAT scores	30
% submitting ACT scores	13
Average HS GPA	3.7
% submitting high school GPA	100
% graduated top 10% of class	33
% graduated top 25% of class	60
% graduated top 50% of class	93
% submitting high school rank	43

Important Dates

Early decision	
Apply by	11/1
Notified by	12/15
Early action	
Apply by	11/1
Notified by	1/31
Regular	
Notified by	4/1
Nonfall registration?	Yes

FINANCIAL FACTS

Annual tuition	$67,550
Food and housing	$17,140
Required fees	$638
Books and supplies	$1,000
Average need-based scholarship (First-year)	$53,274 ($58,426)
% students with need rec. need-based scholarship or grant aid (First-year)	99 (99)
% students with need rec. non-need-based scholarship or grant aid (First-year)	15 (17)
% students with need rec. need-based self-help aid (First-year)	65 (72)
% students rec. any financial aid (First-year)	98 (100)
% UG borrow to pay for school	51
Average cumulative indebtedness	$29,835
% of students with need fully met (First-year)	19 (21)
Average % of student need met (First-year)	87 (90)

University of Redlands

1200 East Colton Avenue, Redlands, CA 92373-0999 • Admissions: 909-748-8074

Survey Snapshot
Frats and sororities are popular
Students politically aware
Students are happy

RATINGS

Quality of Life	83
Fire Safety	60*
Green	60*
Academic	80
Profs Interesting	88
Profs Accessible	90
Admissions	83
Financial Aid	94

CAMPUS LIFE

Type of school	Private
Environment	Town

Students

Degree-seeking undergrad enrollment	1,912
% male/female/not reported	43/57/0
% from out of state	17
% First-year from public high school	45
% First-year live on campus	71
% Ugrads live on campus	60
# of fraternities (% join)	5 (7)
# of sororities (% join)	5 (13)
% Asian	4
% Black or African American	6
% Hispanic	47
% Native American	1
% Pacific Islander	<1
% Race and/or ethnicity unknown	1
% Two or more races	7
% White	33
% International	1
# of countries represented	11

CAMPUS MENTAL HEALTH SERVICES

Offers mental health/wellness program	Yes
Mental health training available to students	No
Employs Chief Wellness Officer	NR
Peer-to-peer mental health offerings	NR
Counseling center has guidelines or accreditation	No
Mental health/well-being courses	NR

ACADEMICS

% students returning for sophomore year	80
% students graduating within 4 years	56
% students graduating within 6 years	65
Calendar	4-4-1 Fall, Spring, and optional one-month May term
Student/faculty ratio	12:1
Most common class size 10–19.	(45%)
Most common lab/discussion size 10–19.	(79%)

Most Popular Majors

Liberal Arts and Sciences/Liberal Studies; Psychology; Business/Commerce

Applicants Also Look At

Azusa Pacific University, California Baptist University, California Lutheran University, Lewis & Clark College, Pacific Lutheran University, Saint Mary's College of California, Seattle Pacific University, University of San Francisco, Whittier College, Willamette University

STUDENTS SAY "..."

Academics

The principle of personal discovery and student-led learning is deeply ingrained in The University of Redlands. A prime example of this ethos is how the Johnston Center allows students to design unique multidisciplinary majors that combine their various interests. The university also shines in its experiential learning, which, as one student explains, "has allowed me to find out more about my interests inside and out of the classroom." For instance, students taking an environmental nonfiction course participated in local service activities, and there is a program that brings together students and faculty from Redlands to work with and learn from students currently in juvenile detention. When back in the classroom, students say that they "love the small class sizes and the community you build within classrooms" and "the opportunity to know your professors and peers on a personal level," The professors are "incredibly interactive and encourage discussion," and it's clear that they "put a lot of effort into their classes making sure students are really understanding the course material." Students say the instructors "make class so engaging" and appreciate that they "come to a lot of the events on campus, so students have pretty close bonds with them." As one student says, what makes Redlands special is "the social environment created between students and faculty. I will always treasure all the support that professors and others have given me."

Campus Life

There is a lot to love about this beautiful campus, including its convenient proximity to Los Angeles. Several of the most popular extracurricular activities revolve around staying active, playing sports, and attending games. Although sports are big here, they're by no means the extent of what the campus has to offer. There are "so many clubs you can join on campus, and if there isn't a club for you, you can always create your own." For those interested in activism, there are social justice-oriented clubs such as Students for Environmental Action and the Redlands chapter of Planned Parenthood Generation, which advocates for reproductive rights and sexual health. Identity-based organizations like the Latin American Student Alumni Association and First Gen Fam provide support and community by bringing together students with events and shared experiences. And when it comes to campus-wide activities, Doing Activities With Great Spirit—or DAWGS—organizes fun events like bingo games and movie nights. For off-campus adventuring, students can easily reach downtown Redlands in about five minutes on the metro, which also "lets students take trips down to LA or the beach." On the weekends, some students attend campus or Greek parties to socialize and let off steam. Whether you spend the night studying or partying, students agree that "the brunch here on the weekends is baller."

Student Body

For many, the school's community is "its biggest selling point." On this small, connected campus, "it feels like everybody knows everybody, which is so fun." As one student says, "There isn't a day that I walk to class without seeing a friend or someone I know." Students describe their peers as family, forming close friendships and establishing "a strong support group" of people you can "always rely on." The school is "super diverse" and "very LGBTQ+ inclusive," with students emphasizing that the atmosphere is nonjudgmental: "It's a community of different people who welcome others." Incoming students at Redlands can expect to find a nurturing environment where "everyone is willing to help you navigate college life." As one student shares, "The first time I stepped on campus, everyone was waving, smiling, and asking if I had any questions about the school." Overall, it's an "extremely kind" and "very hardworking" group of people with a common goal. As one student puts it, "We're all climbing the ladder, trying to reach our goals, and congratulating each other on the way there."

UNIVERSITY OF REDLANDS

Financial Aid: 909-748-8047 • E-Mail: admissions@redlands.edu • Website: www.redlands.edu

THE PRINCETON REVIEW SAYS

Admissions

The school reports that its standardized testing policy for use in admission for Fall 2026 is Test Optional. The Princeton Review suggests that interested applicants consult with the school for the most up-to-date standardized testing policies. *Very important factors considered include:* rigor of secondary school record, academic GPA. *Other factors considered include:* class rank, standardized test scores, application essay, recommendation(s), interview, extracurricular activities, talent/ability, character/personal qualities, first generation, alumni/ae relation, geographical residence, volunteer work, work experience, High school diploma is required and GED is accepted. *Academic units recommended:* 4 English, 3 math, 3 science, 3 science labs, 3 language (other than English), 3 social studies.

Financial Aid

Students should submit: FAFSA. Priority filing deadline is 3/2. The Princeton Review suggests that all financial aid forms be submitted as soon as possible. *Need-based scholarships/grants offered:* Federal Pell; Federal SEOG; State scholarships/grants; Private scholarships; College/university scholarship or grant aid from institutional funds. *Loan aid offered:* Federal Direct Subsidized Loans; Federal Direct Unsubsidized Loans; Direct PLUS loans; College/university loans from institutional funds. Admitted students will be notified of awards on a rolling basis beginning 12/10. Federal Work-Study Program available.

The Inside Word

The admit rate at the University of Redlands is 81 percent, and students with above average high school records are likely to be accepted. Candidates who are interested in pursuing the self-designed programs available through the Johnston Center for Integrative Studies will find the admissions process to be distinctly more personal. Note, though, that you have to be admitted as a regular student in the College of Arts and Sciences first.

THE SCHOOL SAYS

From the Admissions Office

"We've created an unusually blended curriculum of the liberal arts and pre-professional programs because we think education is about learning how to think and learning how to do. "Centrally located between the beaches, desert, and mountains in the heart of sunny Southern California, the Redlands education takes students beyond classroom walls to develop personally and professionally through experiential learning—an outdoor journey with peers, fieldwork, internships, research, and study abroad. All students commit to completing at least one community service internship before they graduate. "We are proud to be a connected, inclusive community where students feel they belong. We educate managers, poets, environmental scientists, teachers, musicians, and speech therapists to be reflective about culture and society so that they can better understand and improve the world they'll enter upon graduation. "Home of the Bulldogs, we love to cheer on our 21 men's and women's NCAA Bulldog athletic teams. Our students also spend their time as part of more than 70 clubs and organizations, enjoying theatre and musical performances on campus, or in enjoying the culture, arts, entertainment, and great restaurants the city of Redlands offers. "International students for whom English is not their first language may meet our English proficiency requirement through the SAT, ACT, Duolingo, TOEFL, or IELTS. Please check our website for score requirements. "More than 90% of our students receive some form of financial assistance."

SELECTIVITY

# of total applicants	3,322
% of total applicants accepted	83
% of total acceptees attending	15
# of in-state applicants	2,246
% of in-state applicants accepted	88
# of out-of-state-applicants	828
% of applicants accepted from out of state	86
# of international applicants	248
% of international applicants accepted	24

First-Year Profile

Testing policy	Test Optional
Range SAT composite	1130–1310
Range SAT EBRW	570–690
Range SAT math	550–640
Range ACT composite	25–30
% submitting SAT scores	14
% submitting ACT scores	2
Average HS GPA	3.7
% submitting high school GPA	100

Important Dates

Early action	
Apply by	11/1
Notified by	1/15
Regular	
Apply by	1/15
Notified by	Rolling, 1/15
Nonfall registration?	Yes

FINANCIAL FACTS

Annual tuition	$63,790
Food and housing	$19,410
Required fees	$750
Books and supplies	$1,700
Average need-based scholarship (First-year)	$47,523 ($52,244)
% students with need rec. need-based scholarship or grant aid (First-year)	99 (100)
% students with need rec. non-need-based scholarship or grant aid (First-year)	2 (0)
% students with need rec. need-based self-help aid (First-year)	84 (79)
% students rec. any financial aid (First-year)	94 (94)
% UG borrow to pay for school	89
Average cumulative indebtedness	$21,948
% of students with need fully met (First-year)	74 (71)
Average % of student need met (First-year)	97 (98)

University of Rhode Island

Undergraduate Admission, Kingston, RI 02881 • Admissions: 401-874-7100

Survey Snapshot
Students are happy
Frats and sororities are popular
Alumni active on campus

RATINGS

Quality of Life	81
Fire Safety	84
Green	60*
Academic	78
Profs Interesting	83
Profs Accessible	89
Admissions	85
Financial Aid	85

CAMPUS LIFE

Type of school	Public
Environment	Village

Students

Degree-seeking undergrad enrollment	13,436
% male/female/not reported	41/59/<1
% from out of state	52
% First-year live on campus	93
% Ugrads live on campus	46
# of fraternities (% join)	20 (24)
# of sororities (% join)	12 (30)
% Asian	3
% Black or African American	5
% Hispanic	13
% Native American	<1
% Pacific Islander	<1
% Race and/or ethnicity unknown	2
% Two or more races	4
% White	71
% International	1
# of countries represented	41

CAMPUS MENTAL HEALTH SERVICES

Offers mental health/wellness program	Yes
Mental health training available to students	No
Employs Chief Wellness Officer	NR
Peer-to-peer mental health offerings	NR
Counseling center has guidelines or accreditation	No
Mental health/well-being courses	NR

ACADEMICS

% students returning for sophomore year	85
% students graduating within 4 years	57
% students graduating within 6 years	71
Calendar	Semester
Student/faculty ratio	17:1
Most common class size 20–29.	(28%)
Most common lab/discussion size 10–19.	(48%)

Most Popular Majors
Psychology; Nursing; Kinesiology

Applicants Also Look At
Boston University, Northeastern University, University of Connecticut, University of Massachusetts—Boston, University of New Hampshire, University of Vermont

STUDENTS SAY "..."

Academics

Located in the village of Kingston in the southern part of the state, The University of Rhode Island is a public research institution known for having "excellent science programs," including a "marine biology program [that] is one of the best in the Northeast." URI is a school that challenges me to think big and outside the box," says one student. Other stand-out majors include "nursing, pharmacy," which students feel is "excellent—one of the top in the country," and engineering." Students feel that "all professors have a unique style of teaching. Most are very willing to adapt their style to fit students' needs though" and many "are able to share stories from their experiences that make the material more accessible and interesting." Another student observes that the staff is also "great at helping freshmen transferring from home to college, and there are lots of different programs offered to help students excel academically." Overall, URI is known to have a solid liberal ideology with "openness to creative and critical exploration." This engineering major finds the environment to be rather "forward-thinking [with an] emphasis on today's global workforce."

Campus Life

The school's proximity to the beach and to other major cities like Providence and Boston make it appealing to students from all over the Northeast. One student reports that "driving to one of the nearby beaches to just clear your mind and relax is one of the many benefits of URI's location." Students are said to have a "two brain track" in terms of serious attention to study followed by equal attention to "relaxing and having a good time." If fine dining is meaningful to your quality of life, it's worth noting that URI's dining hall has "won a national award the past two years in a row." And, while there are complaints about the dry campus, one senior notes that this is a surmountable obstacle, in that "people usually live in the surrounding neighborhoods, so you can travel to your friends' houses and party." Others say that students who live nearby still choose to stay on campus during weekends, since this is where their social life is centered. Life isn't all about "getting wasted," chides one sophomore. "Sometimes we get together [to] make dinner and just have a movie night inside our apartment."

Student Body

URI, as an affordable state school, naturally attracts a large percentage of Rhode Islanders. Rumor has it that this group "sticks to their friends from high school," yet one undergrad observes, "Rhody-borns are so afraid of college turning into another four years of high school that we go searching for new people to meet." The typical URI student "is involved in at least one student organization, but many are involved in more than one. They usually go out about once a week on average and study about an hour a day." There are "many students...involved in at least one type of extracurricular activity," "then there are students who are not involved at all." Campus diversity is strong, and most groups intermingle without issue.

UNIVERSITY OF RHODE ISLAND

Financial Aid: 401-874-7530 • E-Mail: admission@uri.edu • Website: www.uri.edu

THE PRINCETON REVIEW SAYS

Admissions

The school reports that its standardized testing policy for use in admission for Fall 2026 is Test Optional. The Princeton Review suggests that interested applicants consult with the school for the most up-to-date standardized testing policies. *Very important factors considered include:* rigor of secondary school record, academic GPA, application essay, recommendation(s). *Important factors considered include:* extracurricular activities, volunteer work, work experience. *Other factors considered include:* class rank, standardized test scores, talent/ability, character/personal qualities, first generation, geographical residence, state residency, level of applicant's interest. High school diploma is required and GED is accepted. *Academic units required:* 4 English, 3 math, 2 science, 1 science lab, 2 language (other than English), 2 social studies, 5 academic electives.

Financial Aid

Students should submit: FAFSA. Priority filing deadline is 3/1. The Princeton Review suggests that all financial aid forms be submitted as soon as possible. *Need-based scholarships/grants offered:* Federal Pell; Federal SEOG; State scholarships/grants; Private scholarships; College/university scholarship or grant aid from institutional funds. *Loan aid offered:* Federal Direct Subsidized Loans; Federal Direct Unsubsidized Loans; Direct PLUS loans; College/university loans from institutional funds. Admitted students will be notified of awards on a rolling basis beginning 3/1. Federal Work-Study Program available. Institutional employment available.

The Inside Word

Applications here are evaluated on the basis of course selection, academic performance, standardized test scores (if submitted), and unique talents. Don't forget to apply for URI's merit-based scholarships, which are open to international students as well. Remember if you're a resident of another New England state (besides Rhode Island) you may be eligible, depending on your major, for discounted tuition.

THE SCHOOL SAYS

From the Admissions Office

"One only needs to visit this beautiful coastal school to know that URI is a university on the move. In the past dozen years, URI has invested over $900 million in new facilities and improvements. The most recent two are the new $150 million engineering complex and a new 500-bed residence hall (and up next is a new Fine Arts Center). Students are excited about the many 4+1 accelerated bachelor's to master's programs, and families appreciate the overall value and the fact that 10% of students can graduate early thanks to the school's credit-friendly AP/IB and Early Enrollment policies. Global travel experiences all year long, including during the popular Winter J Term, are of interest to many. Student success support and wellness programs are campus-wide and support students inside and outside of the classroom.

"The University of Rhode Island is competitively priced, especially for out-of-state students, with a great range of merit scholarships to students who have demonstrated academic success in a challenging college preparatory curriculum with leadership and community involvement. Impressive full-ride scholarships are available through the prestigious Ryan and Verrecchia Scholar programs. All applicants are considered for these scholarships by submitting a complete application by February 1. There is no separate scholarship application. To be considered for the highest scholarships, we recommend applying by our December 1 Early Action deadline. We also strongly recommend that students interested in engineering, nursing, and the doctorate in pharmacy Apply by December 1 as spaces are limited in these programs."

SELECTIVITY

# of total applicants	28,021
% of total applicants accepted	73
% of total acceptees attending	17
# of in-state applicants	4,368
% of in-state applicants accepted	72
# of out-of-state-applicants	23,100
% of applicants accepted from out of state	73
# of international applicants	553
% of international applicants accepted	74
# offered a place on the wait list	1,430
# admitted from wait list	9

First-Year Profile

Testing policy	Test Optional
Range SAT composite	1090–1310
Range SAT EBRW	550–670
Range SAT math	520–650
Range ACT composite	25–31
% submitting SAT scores	23
% submitting ACT scores	2
Average HS GPA	3.7
% submitting high school GPA	100
% graduated top 10% of class	19
% graduated top 25% of class	48
% graduated top 50% of class	86
% submitting high school rank	42

Important Dates

Early decision	
Apply by	11/1
Notified by	Early December
Early action	
Apply by	12/1
Notified by	12/15
Regular	
Apply by	2/1
Notified by	Rolling, 1/31
Nonfall registration?	Yes

FINANCIAL FACTS

Annual in-state tuition	$15,684
Annual out-of-state tuition	$37,350
Food and housing	$16,704
Required fees	$2,396
Books and supplies	$1,330
Average need-based scholarship (First-year)	$11,857 ($13,313)
% students with need rec. need-based scholarship or grant aid (First-year)	94 (97)
% students with need rec. non-need-based scholarship or grant aid (First-year)	6 (8)
% students with need rec. need-based self-help aid (First-year)	49 (62)
% students rec. any financial aid (First-year)	90 (91)
% UG borrow to pay for school	70
Average cumulative indebtedness	$50,635
% of students with need fully met (First-year)	26 (32)
Average % of student need met (First-year)	55 (60)

UNIVERSITY OF RICHMOND

410 Westhampton Way, University of Richmond, VA 23173 • Admissions: 804-289-8640

Survey Snapshot
Students love Richmond, VA
Easy to get around campus
Recreation facilities are great

RATINGS

Quality of Life	95
Fire Safety	96
Green	95
Academic	90
Profs Interesting	94
Profs Accessible	96
Admissions	96
Financial Aid	97

CAMPUS LIFE

Type of school	Private
Environment	City

Students

Degree-seeking undergrad enrollment	2,974
% male/female/not reported	46/54/<1
% from out of state	81
% First-year from public high school	54
% First-year live on campus	99
% Ugrads live on campus	76
# of fraternities (% join)	7 (12)
# of sororities (% join)	7 (17)
% Asian	5
% Black or African American	6
% Hispanic	9
% Native American	<1
% Pacific Islander	<1
% Race and/or ethnicity unknown	2
% Two or more races	5
% White	63
% International	10
# of countries represented	71

CAMPUS MENTAL HEALTH SERVICES

Offers mental health/wellness program	Yes
Mental health training available to students	Yes
Employs Chief Wellness Officer	Yes
Peer-to-peer mental health offerings	Yes
Counseling center has guidelines or accreditation	Yes
Mental health/well-being courses	Yes, for-credit

ACADEMICS

% students returning for sophomore year	92
% students graduating within 4 years	81
% students graduating within 6 years	87
Calendar	Semester
Student/faculty ratio	7:1
Most common class size 10–19.	(53%)
Most common lab/discussion size 10–19.	(49%)

Most Popular Majors

Biology/Biological Sciences; Business Administration and Management; Organizational Behavior Studies

Applicants Often Prefer

Boston College, Georgetown University, University of Virginia, William & Mary

Applicants Sometimes Prefer

Emory University, University of North Carolina at Chapel Hill, University of Southern California, Wake Forest University, Washington University in St. Louis

STUDENTS SAY "..."

Academics

It pays to go to Richmond University—literally. Students speak highly of the way the school combines academic and real-world opportunities, whether that's "grant money to do summer internships" to getting paid "to do research...on a topic of my choice." These are great ways to explore career options, say students, like a sophomore program that pays "for you to go to a hotel over the weekend to learn business networking skills." Another student mentions the school covering travel to New Orleans for a week "as part of my class to learn about environmental racism," and one fondly cites their "international work experience, fully funded by the university." Locally, there are opportunities to "work with Richmond-based companies to implement skills and theories we have learned in class. For example, in Principles of Marketing, we worked with Capital One." Students also praise "a class called Benchmark where you create a product and start an actual business and have to have talks with suppliers, marketing teams, and try to truly manage a startup." Across academic programs, Students agree that professors comprise one of the school's greatest assets. As one student explains: "I love my professors and have developed close relationships with many of them. They genuinely care about me, my interests, and my career path. My professors have given me a wonderful academic experience." Between the top-notch professors and the travel and research opportunities, "the resources Richmond has are unparalleled."

Campus Life

Students agree that the Richmond "campus is gorgeous," with Gothic brick architecture and "unbeatable facilities" that are kept in "tip-top shape," and students accordingly find it to be "a blessing" that they have "housing available on campus all four years." Recreationally, students often enjoy grabbing "food or coffee with friends and walking around the lake" and have "dinner together at the dining hall, which is really good and family style." Students bond over "big events, such as concerts, basketball games, and the spring dance" as well as club sports, which are "extremely well-funded." Student athletes "have access to great facilities...the smaller student population makes these teams more attainable to get a spot on." Outside of sports, Greek life plays a strong role in the school's social scene, whether social or professional chapters. One student describes being "in a business fraternity and social sorority. I like these extracurriculars because they give me something to do on a small campus...joining has enriched my college experience, especially as an introvert." That said, students note that you are free to partake without joining, and that they are perfectly happy "to go downtown to bars or to eat at many of the great restaurants."

Student Body

Students at the University of Richmond are hard-working, athletic, friendly, engaged, and have many interests that connect us to many people and places on campus. Furthermore, Richmond students aren't "afraid to try something out or take risks to pursue what they love." One student explains: "You can find people here interested in every field and many have already made significant strides in their careers like starting businesses, filming documentaries, or producing music." Another student reports that their classmates are "motivated leaders," who are "socially aware," "future focused, and career oriented." By and large, students are "very diligent and hardworking individuals, who take their classes and extracurriculars seriously." They are also thoughtful, with one student elaborating, "The discussions in my classes, sometimes on pretty contentious topics, are generally well thought out and informed." One Richmond student summarizes their peers as "social, outgoing, and adventurous," with most "willing to help others in and outside of class, and although students like to...have fun, we also are devoted to our studies and enjoy learning at Richmond."

University of Richmond

Financial Aid: 804-289-8438 • E-Mail: admission@richmond.edu • Website: www.richmond.edu

THE PRINCETON REVIEW SAYS

Admissions

The school reports that its standardized testing policy for use in admission for Fall 2026 is Test Optional. The Princeton Review suggests that interested applicants consult with the school for the most up-to-date standardized testing policies. *Very important factors considered include:* rigor of secondary school record, academic GPA. *Important factors considered include:* class rank, standardized test scores, application essay, recommendation(s), extracurricular activities, talent/ability, character/personal qualities. *Other factors considered include:* first generation, alumni/ae relation, geographical residence, state residency, volunteer work, work experience. High school diploma is required and GED is accepted. *Academic units required:* 4 English, 3 math, 2 science, 2 science labs, 2 language (other than English), 2 history. *Academic units recommended:* 4 English, 4 math, 4 science, 4 science labs, 4 language (other than English), 4 history.

Financial Aid

Students should submit: FAFSA; CSS PROFILE. The Princeton Review suggests that all financial aid forms be submitted as soon as possible. *Need-based scholarships/grants offered:* Federal Pell; Federal SEOG; State scholarships/grants; Private scholarships; College/university scholarship or grant aid from institutional funds. *Loan aid offered:* Federal Direct Subsidized Loans; Federal Direct Unsubsidized Loans; Direct PLUS loans. Admitted students will be notified of awards on or about 4/1. Federal Work-Study Program available. Institutional employment available.

The Inside Word

The University of Richmond's admissions office takes a holistic view of applications, and the demonstration of character, leadership, and independence is evaluated alongside your academic record. That said, applicants will need strong transcripts and high test scores (if submitting) to compete in this applicant pool. The school provides aid to meet demonstrated need and generous merit-based scholarships to those who demonstrate exemplary academic achievement.

THE SCHOOL SAYS

From the Admissions Office

"University of Richmond is one of very few colleges that is need blind in admission and meets 100 percent of demonstrated financial need for all undergraduate students. University of Richmond combines the characteristics of a well-resourced college with the dynamics environment and resources of a large university to provide extraordinary opportunities. Our unique size, beautiful suburban campus in a capital city and outstanding facilities offer students opportunities for intellectual achievement and personal growth. While faculty student interaction and dialogue are at the forefront of the academic experience, research, internships and international experiences are important components of students' lives. Richmond is committed to providing students with rigorous academics and experiential learning. The university offers guarantees up to $5,000 to support summer research or an unpaid or underpaid internship. Our global approach to education shines through our many study-abroad programs. We are committed to well-being, diversity and belonging, and believe in leveraging its benefits in all aspects of college life. The student body is composed of scholars from a variety of backgrounds. More than one in four undergraduates is a domestic student of color; one in seven is the first in his or her family to attend college; one in eleven is an international student; and 77 percent are from outside of Virginia."

SELECTIVITY

# of total applicants	16,560
% of total applicants accepted	22
% of total acceptees attending	23
# of in-state applicants	2,273
% of in-state applicants accepted	22
# of out-of-state-applicants	10,183
% of applicants accepted from out of state	29
# of international applicants	4,104
% of international applicants accepted	7
# of early decision applicants	1,154
% of early decision applicants accepted	36
# offered a place on the wait list	3,634
# admitted from wait list	102

First-Year Profile

Testing policy	Test Optional
Range SAT composite	1420–1490
Range SAT EBRW	700–750
Range SAT math	700–770
Range ACT composite	33–34
% submitting SAT scores	19
% submitting ACT scores	15
Average HS GPA	3.8
% submitting high school GPA	100
% graduated top 10% of class	63
% graduated top 25% of class	89
% graduated top 50% of class	99
% submitting high school rank	20

Important Dates

Early decision	
Apply by	11/1
Notified by	12/15
Other ED Apply by	1/1
Other ED Notified by	2/15
Early action	
Apply by	11/1
Notified by	1/20
Regular	
Apply by	1/1
Notified by	4/1
Nonfall registration?	No

FINANCIAL FACTS

Annual tuition	$67,840
Food and housing	$18,010
Books and supplies	$1,000
Average need-based scholarship (First-year)	$58,477 ($56,400)
% students with need rec. need-based scholarship or grant aid (First-year)	99 (99)
% students with need rec. non-need-based scholarship or grant aid (First-year)	34 (37)
% students with need rec. need-based self-help aid (First-year)	61 (58)
% students rec. any financial aid (First-year)	70 (60)
% UG borrow to pay for school	36
Average cumulative indebtedness	$31,351
% of students with need fully met (First-year)	93 (94)
Average % of student need met (First-year)	100 (100)

University of Rochester

300 Wilson Boulevard, Rochester, NY 14627-0251 • Admissions: 585-275-3221

Survey Snapshot
Great library
Great financial aid
Recreation facilities are great

RATINGS	
Quality of Life	**84**
Fire Safety	**95**
Green	**90**
Academic	**85**
Profs Interesting	**87**
Profs Accessible	**89**
Admissions	**93**
Financial Aid	**96**

CAMPUS LIFE

Type of school	Private
Environment	City

Students

Degree-seeking undergrad enrollment	5,882
% male/female/not reported	47/52/1
% from out of state	54
% First-year from public high school	71
% First-year live on campus	98
% Ugrads live on campus	71
# of fraternities (% join)	9 (8)
# of sororities (% join)	6 (11)
% Asian	18
% Black or African American	6
% Hispanic	9
% Native American	<1
% Pacific Islander	<1
% Race and/or ethnicity unknown	2
% Two or more races	5
% White	38
% International	21
# of countries represented	95

CAMPUS MENTAL HEALTH SERVICES

Offers mental health/wellness program	Yes
Mental health training available to students	Yes
Employs Chief Wellness Officer	Yes
Peer-to-peer mental health offerings	No
Counseling center has guidelines or accreditation	Yes
Mental health/well-being courses	Yes, non-credit

ACADEMICS

% students returning for sophomore year	91
% students graduating within 4 years	75
% students graduating within 6 years	83
Calendar	Semester
Student/faculty ratio	10:1
Most common class size 10–19.	(37%)
Most common lab/discussion size 10–19.	(53%)

Most Popular Majors

Biology/Biological Sciences; Mechanical Engineering; Psychology

Applicants Also Look At

Boston University, Brown University, Case Western Reserve University, Columbia University, Cornell University, Johns Hopkins University, New York University, Northeastern University, Rochester Institute of Technology, State University of New York—Binghamton University, State University of New York—Stony Brook University, State University of New York—University at Buffalo, Syracuse University, Tufts University, University of California—Berkeley, University of California—Los Angeles, University of Michigan—Ann Arbor, University of Pittsburgh—Pittsburgh Campus

STUDENTS SAY "..."

Academics

The University of Rochester is a private research university in western New York. The school's programs are rigorous, but students appreciate the freedom to create their own paths. URochester "does not require general education classes, but instead encourages students to pursue their passions through the cluster system," which groups classes together in divisions of Humanities, Social Sciences, and Natural Sciences and Engineering. While the programs offer flexibility, the academic requirements are demanding, but regardless of field of study, "tutoring services, [the] University Counseling Center, and staff [who] focus on creating a supportive environment" are always available. "Most people...spend all of their time studying," says one student. But the intellectual efforts come with benefits: the combination of motivated peers and academics "makes...a better student and learner." Faculty also play an important role here with professors who are "really knowledgeable and passionate" about what they're teaching. One student comments that professors "keep material interesting, [are] approachable, and [are] very fair." And class structures are varied so as to "incorporate design thinking" or to feature "more interactive problems." Added benefits to that structure include "small class sizes and individual attention," and "so many opportunities...[are] offered to students both inside and outside of class."

Campus Life

University of Rochester is "very much an academically driven institution," and course work is the top priority. But as one student says, "The weekend [is] when most people fill their days with different activities." One such activity that many students rave about is movie night: "School movie nights are [the] best school-provided weekend activity." Athletics are, of course, present, but as one student notes, "Rochester varsity sports are not very competitive, [however]...a lot of people...do club sports." Other students mention weekend hikes, dance groups, plays and recitals. One thing to contend with at URochester is the long winter; as some students put it, it's "winter 90 percent of the time." Both the school and students have adapted, and one student offers assurances that URochester has "established a tunnel system which provides convenience." Dining halls on campus also provide comfort, and anyone looking for a tasty bite to eat can rest easy: "There are a bunch of places to eat on campus." Another way to socialize on campus is through Greek life, but even that is "not as fratty" as you'd expect. As for parties? "There is not a huge party scene on campus, but it's there if you want it," claims one Yellowjacket. Off-campus activities are plentiful, "if you have a car." Otherwise, students rely on the shuttle system. Overall, "there is always something to do on the weekend for entertainment" if students need a study break.

Student Body

Diversity is key at University of Rochester, "both [in] background and academic interests." As one student states, "In my class alone, 46 percent of us are international students." Those different backgrounds branch into an even wider range of activities. "Some [students] are filmmakers, some are dancers, some love sailing, some love art. Everyone has their own passions," another student describes. The variety is a benefit, with students claiming "the best thing about the UR community is that nobody can be put into a box." Undergrads describe their peers as "charmingly nerdy" or "chill nerds" who are "very down to have interesting and academic conversations." While most students are "academically focused" and "really care about what they do here," they are for the most part "more collaborative than competitive." "People range from passionate to apathetic, party animals to total nerds." However, amidst all the diversity is a strong sense of camaraderie, and "everyone holds each other accountable in terms of pursuing their absolute best."

UNIVERSITY OF ROCHESTER

Financial Aid: 585-275-3226 • E-Mail: admit@admissions.rochester.edu • Website: www.rochester.edu

THE PRINCETON REVIEW SAYS

Admissions

The school reports that its standardized testing policy for use in admission for Fall 2026 is Test Optional. The Princeton Review suggests that interested applicants consult with the school for the most up-to-date standardized testing policies. *Very important factors considered include:* rigor of secondary school record, academic GPA, application essay, extracurricular activities, character/personal qualities. *Important factors considered include:* recommendation(s), interview, level of applicant's interest. *Other factors considered include:* class rank, standardized test scores, talent/ability, first generation, geographical residence, volunteer work, work experience. High school diploma is required and GED is accepted.

Financial Aid

Students should submit: FAFSA; CSS PROFILE; State aid form. Priority filing deadline is 2/15. The Princeton Review suggests that all financial aid forms be submitted as soon as possible. *Need-based scholarships/grants offered:* Federal Pell; Federal SEOG; State scholarships/grants; Private scholarships; College/university scholarship or grant aid from institutional funds. *Loan aid offered:* Federal Direct Subsidized Loans; Federal Direct Unsubsidized Loans; Direct PLUS loans. Admitted students will be notified of awards on or about 3/15. Federal Work-Study Program available. Institutional employment available.

The Inside Word

The University of Rochester's academic reputation is supported by its competitive 40 percent acceptance rate. URochester is Test Optional, it considers a variety of academic records, including honors, AP, and/or IB courses and many international exams. Currently, admissions officers take a holistic approach, seeking applicants from around the world who have demonstrated intellectual curiosity, extracurricular engagement, and ethical character.

THE SCHOOL SAYS

From the Admissions Office

"A leading independent research institution, the University of Rochester is where boundless curiosity and creativity connect to ignite wonder in us all. At URochester, ideas and impact intersect as students pursue discoveries that make our world ever better and customize their academic experience from the outset. With no general education requirements, every student in every class wants to be there and is highly engaged. From day one, students explore specific academic areas and begin an intellectual journey with the support of advisors and faculty. Many pursue interdisciplinary studies or carry multiple majors.

"URochester is a research and creative powerhouse. Most research is student-driven, multidisciplinary, and collaborative. Students are highly motivated and supportive of one another.

"Learning takes place on a personal scale, through small classes and meaningful faculty collaboration—combined with the resources of a top research university. Students engage in research, internships, and shadowing experiences across URochester's nationally ranked schools of engineering, medicine, nursing, music, education, and business.

"URochester faculty are world-renowned experts who attract significant research funding and achieve breakthroughs across disciplines.

"Students live up to Meliora (ever better), preparing to lead the future of industry, education, and culture.

"The University of Rochester offers academic merit scholarships and meets 100% of demonstrated need for admitted students. Its holistic, test-optional admissions process considers academic excellence but also asks: What are your values? How have you made yourself and your community better? How will you make the world better?"

SELECTIVITY

# of total applicants	21,609
% of total applicants accepted	42
% of total acceptees attending	14
# of in-state applicants	4,551
% of in-state applicants accepted	50
# of out-of-state-applicants	9,060
% of applicants accepted from out of state	59
# of international applicants	7,998
% of international applicants accepted	18
# of early decision applicants	1,129
% of early decision applicants accepted	42
# offered a place on the wait list	1,197
# admitted from wait list	262

First-Year Profile

Testing policy	Test Optional
Range SAT composite	1400–1510
Range SAT EBRW	680–750
Range SAT math	700–780
Range ACT composite	31–34
% submitting SAT scores	16
% submitting ACT scores	6
Average HS GPA	3.7
% submitting high school GPA	100
% graduated top 10% of class	85
% graduated top 25% of class	95
% graduated top 50% of class	99
% submitting high school rank	32

Important Dates

Early decision	
Apply by	11/1
Notified by	12/15
Other ED Apply by	1/5
Other ED Notified by	2/7
Regular	
Apply by	1/5
Notified by	4/1
Nonfall registration?	Yes

FINANCIAL FACTS

Annual tuition	$71,750
Food and housing	$21,572
Required fees	$1,622
Books and supplies	$0
Average need-based scholarship (First-year)	$59,392 ($67,488)
% students with need rec. need-based scholarship or grant aid (First-year)	99 (99)
% students with need rec. non-need-based scholarship or grant aid (First-year)	13 (11)
% students with need rec. need-based self-help aid (First-year)	81 (80)
% students rec. any financial aid (First-year)	82 (77)
% UG borrow to pay for school	41
Average cumulative indebtedness	$30,785
% of students with need fully met (First-year)	90 (92)
Average % of student need met (First-year)	96 (97)

University of St. Francis (IL)

500 Wilcox Street, Joliet, IL 60435 • Admissions: 800-735-7500

Survey Snapshot
Students are happy
Lab facilities are great
Easy to get around campus

RATINGS

Quality of Life	83
Fire Safety	99
Green	60*
Academic	84
Profs Interesting	89
Profs Accessible	93
Admissions	85
Financial Aid	90

CAMPUS LIFE

Type of school	Private
Affiliation	Roman Catholic
Environment	City

Students

Degree-seeking undergrad enrollment	1,295
% male/female/not reported	35/65/0
% from out of state	7
% First-year from public high school	90
% First-year live on campus	36
% Ugrads live on campus	21
# of fraternities (% join)	1 (NR)
# of sororities (% join)	1 (4)
% Asian	3
% Black or African American	9
% Hispanic	37
% Native American	<1
% Pacific Islander	<1
% Race and/or ethnicity unknown	1
% Two or more races	2
% White	44
% International	2
# of countries represented	25

CAMPUS MENTAL HEALTH SERVICES

Offers mental health/wellness program	Yes
Mental health training available to students	Yes
Employs Chief Wellness Officer	No
Peer-to-peer mental health offerings	Yes
Counseling center has guidelines or accreditation	Yes
Mental health/well-being courses	Yes, non-credit

ACADEMICS

% students returning for sophomore year	78
% students graduating within 4 years	53
% students graduating within 6 years	64
Calendar	Semester
Student/faculty ratio	13:1
Most common class size 10–19.	(43%)
Most common lab/discussion size 10–19.	(84%)

Most Popular Majors

Registered Nursing/Registered Nurse; Business/Commerce

Applicants Sometimes Prefer

Aurora University, Benedictine University, DePaul University, Dominican University, Elmhurst University, Lewis University, Loyola University Chicago, North Central College, Saint Xavier University

STUDENTS SAY "..."

Academics

Education at the University of St. Francis centers on "lab-based and research-based assignments" and within this environment, "hands-on learning" opportunities abound. Ask a student from any department how they feel about it, and they'll probably be enthusiastic, like a science student who calls their department "one of the greatest strengths of the school" and values the emphasis on "research rather than lecture." You'll also hear about the advantages of "Business Research classes where we deal directly with clients," how the "robust nursing program" offers labs that are "quite exciting...learning how to truly care for someone is something St. Francis does well," or how the College of Education has "very vigorous and quality programs for undergrads." Another education student agrees, saying "There are no free grades, [and] each semester has challenged me academically and will make me a better person and future educator." Look to the professors for some credit in that regard: "Every teacher I have had has made themselves available to students, placing a high priority on their success, trust, and mental and physical health. The instructors are committed to getting to know the student on a personal level and supporting them to challenge themselves socially as well as academically."

Campus Life

The quad is beautiful and has many shady and sunny spots for relaxing and taking time in nature and it's also common "to see people in lounge areas enjoying meals, conversing with friends, working on homework, or playing games such as table tennis or billiards." Motherhouse is a favorite on-campus hang out, featuring a "fully functional fireplace to keep students warm in the cold...of a Chicagoland winter." Students point to "intramurals, athletic events, social activities organized by the clubs on campus, music concerts, [and] coffee talks" as favorite social activities. One student notes that their preferred organizations include the "Recreation Club, Student Activities Board, Scientific Research Club, Latino Honors Society, Asian American Student Association, and Unidos Vamos Alcanzar." The Duns SCOTUS Honors Program is known to host "bonfires and trivia nights" and the History Club offers "opportunities to serve the community, learn about local and state history, and get to know other history buffs." All told, students describe enjoying a multitude of academic and social clubs available on campus.

Student Body

The community at the University of St. Francis provides a "welcoming and friendly environment. The people who are here, from students to staff and faculty, all work to ensure everyone feels safe and accepted." One student describes their peers as "truly made of a different caliber than the rest. We care about helping our community and motivating those around us to achieve their full potential." Another student points out that "the student body at the University of St. Francis is very diverse and supportive of one another. There are many events for students to meet people....It is easy to get close to people." Nervous first-year students can rest easy knowing that "literally any student will be able to find their niche here with other students," says a self-described "former social outcast." Says one student: "If you want an intimate learning experience, this is the place."

UNIVERSITY OF ST. FRANCIS (IL)

Financial Aid: 866-890-8331 • E-Mail: admissions@stfrancis.edu • Website: www.stfrancis.edu

THE PRINCETON REVIEW SAYS

Admissions

The school reports that its standardized testing policy for use in admission for Fall 2026 is Test Optional. The Princeton Review suggests that interested applicants consult with the school for the most up-to-date standardized testing policies. *Very important factors considered include:* rigor of secondary school record, academic GPA. *Other factors considered include:* standardized test scores. High school diploma is required and GED is accepted. *Academic units required:* 4 English, 3 math, 2 science, 1 science lab, 2 social studies, 3 academic electives.

Financial Aid

Students should submit: FAFSA; Institution's own financial aid form. Priority filing deadline is 2/15. The Princeton Review suggests that all financial aid forms be submitted as soon as possible. *Need-based scholarships/grants offered:* Federal Pell; Federal SEOG; State scholarships/grants; College/university scholarship or grant aid from institutional funds; United Negro College Fund. *Loan aid offered:* Federal Direct Subsidized Loans; Federal Direct Unsubsidized Loans; Direct PLUS loans. Admitted students will be notified of awards on a rolling basis beginning 9/1. Federal Work-Study Program available. Institutional employment available.

The Inside Word

The application process for the University of St. Francis is made easier with the help of a personal admission counselor from the school. You can reach a counselor through their website or by calling the university. While a good GPA and challenging academic courses are paramount, the admissions team will also consider your recommendations, extracurricular activities, and essay when making their decision.

SELECTIVITY

# of total applicants	2,189
% of total applicants accepted	65
% of total acceptees attending	17

First-Year Profile

Testing policy	Test Optional
Range SAT composite	910–1020
Range SAT EBRW	460–580
Range SAT math	440–560
Range ACT composite	21–28
% submitting SAT scores	43
% submitting ACT scores	2
Average HS GPA	3.6
% submitting high school GPA	100

Important Dates

Regular	
Notified by	Rolling, 6/1
Nonfall registration?	Yes

FINANCIAL FACTS

Annual tuition	$38,110
Food and housing	$11,980
Books and supplies	$800
Average need-based scholarship (First-year)	$27,343 ($33,047)
% students with need rec. need-based scholarship or grant aid (First-year)	98 (100)
% students with need rec. non-need-based scholarship or grant aid (First-year)	16 (8)
% students with need rec. need-based self-help aid (First-year)	85 (85)
% students rec. any financial aid (First-year)	93 (99)
% UG borrow to pay for school	75
Average cumulative indebtedness	$28,546
% of students with need fully met (First-year)	32 (37)
Average % of student need met (First-year)	78 (85)

UNIVERSITY OF ST. THOMAS (MN)

2115 Summit Avenue, St. Paul, MN 55113 • Admissions: 651-962-6150

Survey Snapshot
Students are happy
Classroom facilities are great
Recreation facilities are great
Students environmentally aware

RATINGS

Quality of Life	87
Fire Safety	60*
Green	97
Academic	83
Profs Interesting	91
Profs Accessible	92
Admissions	84
Financial Aid	89

CAMPUS LIFE

Type of school	Private
Affiliation	Roman Catholic
Environment	Metropolis

Students

Degree-seeking undergrad enrollment	6,150
% male/female/not reported	51/49/0
% from out of state	18
% First-year from public high school	78
% First-year live on campus	91
% Ugrads live on campus	49
# of fraternities	0
# of sororities	0
% Asian	6
% Black or African American	9
% Hispanic	11
% Native American	<1
% Pacific Islander	<1
% Race and/or ethnicity unknown	3
% Two or more races	5
% White	63
% International	4
# of countries represented	85

CAMPUS MENTAL HEALTH SERVICES

Offers mental health/wellness program	Yes
Mental health training available to students	No
Employs Chief Wellness Officer	NR
Peer-to-peer mental health offerings	NR
Counseling center has guidelines or accreditation	No
Mental health/well-being courses	NR

ACADEMICS

% students returning for sophomore year	86
% students graduating within 4 years	67
% students graduating within 6 years	77
Calendar	4-1-4
Student/faculty ratio	13:1
Most common class size 20–29.	(43%)
Most common lab/discussion size 10–19.	(50%)

STUDENTS SAY "..."

Academics

University of St. Thomas is Minnesota's largest private university. The Catholic institution "[holds] a high standard of academic excellence," and in turn, "[offers a] myriad of resources for each student to take advantage of." Students have the opportunity to participate in honors classes that are "more discussion-based." Many students appreciate the chances to participate in non-traditional learning, citing activities such as "going" down to the Mississippi River to do research for geology class" or "attending the Nobel Peace Prize Conference," and "listening in on court cases."

Professors have the ability to "make or break the experience," and many faculty members prioritize "intellectual curiosity" and "get excited when you want to dive deeper into course material outside of the classroom." The modest student-to-faculty ratio makes it "easy to connect in the classroom, which then makes it easier to succeed in a class." Plus, many love that there are "professors who actively help find internships and jobs that expand learning and experience." And the relationships go beyond just the academic: "The faculty at St. Thomas [serves] as teachers, guidance counselors, career advisors, and even friends."

Campus Life

The greatest strengths of St. Thomas would be [its] dedication to making students feel at home through an "impactful focus on building community" among undergrads. As one transfer student puts it, "As soon as I moved in I felt like I found my home." In their free time, St. Thomas enrollees—affectionately known as "Tommies"—can be found working out at the gym, exploring "neighborhood bars and restaurants" and "[taking] advantage of our numerous coffee shops on campus and off." The school "offers free transportation to locations all around the Twin Cities," making it easy to get off campus even without access to a car. In the warmer months, people leverage the "many open grassy areas that allow students to hang out, hammock, play causal games, and even study," and they're "able to rent out yard games and other activity supplies either at a low cost or for free." If organized fun is more your style, "There are a lot of school-sponsored events" featuring "free goodies around campus (such as crafts, T-shirts, [and] food)." Truly, "You'd have to be actively trying to be bored" at St. Thomas.

Student Body

People at University of St. Thomas are first and foremost "friendly and nice" and "very respectful of each other." Here, your peers want you to succeed and are "eager to help each other out." In fact, some even say their student body is one of their "biggest motiving factors." For many, the student body "energy is very supportive and comforting."

Despite a lack of diversity on campus, students are focused on "always making connections." Most feel "there are lots of opportunities...for supporting underrepresented identities and magnifying those voices." Many students are "passionate advocates for inclusivity and representation," and in recent years, "creating a culture of love and kindness toward one another has been effective at changing the culture on campus and helping everyone feel more included." Even with the current advancements, some students would like to see further improvement in "diversity and outreach to underrepresented populations," but still acknowledge that it "is getting better."

UNIVERSITY OF ST. THOMAS (MN)

Financial Aid: 651-962-6550 • E-Mail: admissions@stthomas.edu • Website: www.stthomas.edu

THE PRINCETON REVIEW SAYS

Admissions

The school reports that its standardized testing policy for use in admission for Fall 2026 is Test Optional. The Princeton Review suggests that interested applicants consult with the school for the most up-to-date standardized testing policies. *Very important factors considered include:* rigor of secondary school record, academic GPA. *Important factors considered include:* application essay. *Other factors considered include:* class rank, standardized test scores, recommendation(s), extracurricular activities, talent/ability, character/personal qualities, volunteer work, work experience. High school diploma is required and GED is accepted. *Academic units required:* 3 math. *Academic units recommended:* 4 English, 4 math, 3 science, 4 language (other than English).

Financial Aid

Students should submit: FAFSA. Priority filing deadline is 4/1. The Princeton Review suggests that all financial aid forms be submitted as soon as possible. *Need-based scholarships/grants offered:* Federal Pell; Federal SEOG; State scholarships/grants; Private scholarships; College/university scholarship or grant aid from institutional funds. *Loan aid offered:* Federal Direct Subsidized Loans; Federal Direct Unsubsidized Loans; Direct PLUS loans; State Loans. Admitted students will be notified of awards on a rolling basis beginning January. Federal Work-Study Program available. Institutional employment available.

The Inside Word

It is easy to apply to St. Thomas since the application form is short and there's no fee to apply. The school evaluates each application holistically, and consideration is given both to academic performance and accomplishments outside the classroom. However, students should note the average GPA of admitted students is 3.7. Applicants should make sure their transcripts demonstrate diverse and challenging academics, good GPA trends, and a solid class rank.

THE SCHOOL SAYS

From the Admissions Office

"Nationally recognized as a top 20 Catholic university, the University of St. Thomas educates students to be morally responsible leaders who think critically, act wisely and work skillfully to advance the common good. St. Thomas is big enough to offer more than 150 undergraduate majors and minors, yet small enough for professors to know every student's name. We emphasize practical skills and hands-on experience that prepare students for today's workplace, while also preparing them for long-term success by building timeless qualities including leadership, creativity and ethical decision-making. Students have opportunities to conduct research alongside faculty in fields ranging from engineering and environmental science to English. The university's partnerships (with Fortune 500 companies and its 120,000+ alumni) connect students to internships and job opportunities—81 percent of undergraduates complete at least one internship. Ninety-seven percent of students are employed or enrolled in graduate school within one year of graduation. Campus life means getting involved. Now NCAA Division I athletics, St. Thomas has plenty of varsity sports to play or cheer on. Students widely participate in the 100+ academic and recreational clubs, and can live in learning communities with students who share their affinities."

SELECTIVITY

# of total applicants	9,269
% of total applicants accepted	86
% of total acceptees attending	20

First-Year Profile

Testing policy	Test Optional
Range SAT composite	1170–1280
Range SAT EBRW	580–680
Range SAT math	570–700
Range ACT composite	23–29
% submitting SAT scores	4
% submitting ACT scores	35
Average HS GPA	3.7
% submitting high school GPA	97
% graduated top 10% of class	22
% graduated top 25% of class	48
% graduated top 50% of class	83
% submitting high school rank	38

Important Dates

Early action	
Apply by	11/1
Notified by	12/15
Regular	
Notified by	2/15
Nonfall registration?	Yes

FINANCIAL FACTS

Annual tuition	$52,820
Food and housing	$14,969
Required fees	$1,578
Average need-based scholarship (First-year)	$32,999 ($33,217)
% students with need rec. need-based scholarship or grant aid (First-year)	97 (97)
% students with need rec. non-need-based scholarship or grant aid (First-year)	92 (88)
% students with need rec. need-based self-help aid (First-year)	71 (69)
% students rec. any financial aid (First-year)	94 (96)
% UG borrow to pay for school	58
Average cumulative indebtedness	$38,382
% of students with need fully met (First-year)	32 (32)
Average % of student need met (First-year)	75 (77)

UNIVERSITY OF SAN DIEGO

5998 Alcala Park, San Diego, CA 92110-2492 • Admissions: 619-260-4506

Survey Snapshot
Students love San Diego, CA
Students are happy
Easy to get around campus

RATINGS

Quality of Life	99
Fire Safety	92
Green	93
Academic	85
Profs Interesting	97
Profs Accessible	96
Admissions	84
Financial Aid	88

CAMPUS LIFE

Type of school	Private
Affiliation	Roman Catholic
Environment	Metropolis

Students

Degree-seeking undergrad enrollment	5,950
% male/female/not reported	43/57/0
% from out of state	40
% First-year from public high school	52
% First-year live on campus	94
% Ugrads live on campus	50
# of fraternities (% join)	9 (13)
# of sororities (% join)	9 (21)
% Asian	7
% Black or African American	4
% Hispanic	31
% Native American	<1
% Pacific Islander	<1
% Race and/or ethnicity unknown	3
% Two or more races	8
% White	41
% International	6
# of countries represented	52

CAMPUS MENTAL HEALTH SERVICES

Offers mental health/wellness program	Yes
Mental health training available to students	Yes
Employs Chief Wellness Officer	Yes
Peer-to-peer mental health offerings	Yes
Counseling center has guidelines or accreditation	Yes
Mental health/well-being courses	Yes, for-credit

ACADEMICS

% students returning for sophomore year	92
% students graduating within 4 years	70
% students graduating within 6 years	81
Calendar	4-1-4
Student/faculty ratio	14:1
Most common class size 20–29.	(34%)
Most common lab/discussion size 10–19.	(49%)

Most Popular Majors
Business Administration and Management; Finance; Real Estate

Applicants Often Prefer
University of California—San Diego

Applicants Sometimes Prefer
Loyola Marymount University, San Diego State University, Santa Clara University, University of California—Los Angeles, University of California—Santa Barbara, University of Southern California

Applicants Rarely Prefer
California Polytechnic State University—San Luis Obispo, Gonzaga University, Pepperdine University, University of California—Berkeley

STUDENTS SAY "..."

Academics

The University of San Diego is a private Catholic institution that prides itself on its status as a "Changemaker," which represents its dedication to creating sustainable solutions locally and afar. In fact, 50 percent of students find great opportunities through the school's vast study abroad network, which includes programs and internships in 44 countries. "USD encourages its students to apply what they learn in the world to make positive, impactful, sustainable change," says one. Strong curricula and academic advising help students construct four-year plans and create enjoyable schedules, and "projects, seminars, field trips, study abroad programs, and team-taught courses are some of the ways the university gets students engaged."

Professors "are eager to share" their passion for their subject with students and offer "personalized one-on-one learning through office hours." They "communicate directly with the students on what material they find to be important." Most "adapt to the new research that has come out on how students learn best" and "bring in speakers to show how [students] can implement Changemaking into...future classrooms." That also extends into "many informative meetings about research opportunities and internships." Speaking of which, the "Career Center [is] very helpful with landing students jobs."

Campus Life

The "weather is so perfect and the campus so beautiful [that] most students spend time outside" at USD, which is "ten minutes away from both the beach and city." Here it's easy for students to take their pick of a litany of activities—they can "lay out on the lawn, take in the sun, skateboard, surf, [or] go out in the town or beach." "San Diego [is] such a large city that there is so much to do and see," and weekends tend to be devoted to exploring; however, there are plenty of social activities and clubs to join on campus. The "Torero Program Board makes sure there is always something for the students to do." One student comments on the "very accepting Greek life system," citing their motto: "These hands don't haze." Of all first-year students, 95 percent live on campus, and all first years (and transfers) participate in a Living Learning Community, which "puts people from the same general living area in a class together focused on a general theme" such as innovation or advocacy. USD is a place where students "can thrive because [their] physical and mental wellness is cared for alongside [their] education."

Student Body

This is "truly...a campus of Changemakers" and "people passionate about causes [where] everyone is hard working yet still socially engaged." USD "does a great job of making sure that students feel like they have a home," and the school has worked to make common areas where students feel comfortable and seen. Because of the "sunny, more relaxed environment" students enjoy on this California campus, they lean "toward casual" in their attire—"balanced and stylish," as one student describes. Many here come from a "strong religious background and greatly utilize the ministry services on campus," and everyone is "welcoming and enjoyable to be around."

University of San Diego

Financial Aid: 619-260-2700 • E-Mail: admissions@sandiego.edu • Website: www.sandiego.edu

THE PRINCETON REVIEW SAYS

Admissions

The school reports that its standardized testing policy for use in admission for Fall 2026 is Test Free. The Princeton Review suggests that interested applicants consult with the school for the most up-to-date standardized testing policies. *Very important factors considered include:* rigor of secondary school record, academic GPA. *Important factors considered include:* class rank, application essay, recommendation(s), extracurricular activities, talent/ability, character/personal qualities, volunteer work. *Other factors considered include:* interview, first generation, geographical residence, religious affiliation/commitment, work experience, level of applicant's interest. High school diploma is required and GED is accepted. *Academic units required:* 4 English, 3 math, 3 science, 2 science labs, 3 language (other than English), 2 social studies. *Academic units recommended:* 4 English, 4 math, 4 science, 3 science labs, 4 language (other than English), 3 social studies.

Financial Aid

Students should submit: FAFSA. The Princeton Review suggests that all financial aid forms be submitted as soon as possible. *Need-based scholarships/grants offered:* Federal Pell; Federal SEOG; State scholarships/grants; Private scholarships; College/university scholarship or grant aid from institutional funds. *Loan aid offered:* Federal Direct Subsidized Loans; Federal Direct Unsubsidized Loans; Direct PLUS loans; College/university loans from institutional funds. Admitted students will be notified of awards on a rolling basis beginning 3/1. Federal Work-Study Program available. Institutional employment available.

The Inside Word

Admissions officers at University of San Diego aim to take a well-rounded approach to the application process. Hence, they thoroughly evaluate all aspects of a candidate's application, from academic achievements to personal statements and recommendations. Of course, since gaining admission to the university is moderately competitive (each year USD admits around half of those who apply), a strong academic showing is a must, and the school calculates a weighted GPA that awards credit for any honors, AP, or IB classes that have been completed. Admissions officers keep an eye out for students who demonstrate leadership and community engagement or who show genuine interest in sustainability and global perspective.

THE SCHOOL SAYS

From the Admissions Office

"For more than 75 years, the University of San Diego has been lighting the way forward, preparing students to take on complex challenges with purpose and compassion. As a contemporary Catholic university grounded in the liberal arts and uniquely situated along an international border, USD advances academic excellence while shaping a more inclusive, sustainable, and hopeful world.

"With an undergraduate population of 6,048 students, USD is intentionally designed for connection and access. Average class sizes are 21 students, creating a highly personalized academic experience where meaningful collaboration with faculty is part of everyday learning. Students are encouraged to explore across disciplines, participate in research, connect ideas, and pursue what drives them. In business, engineering, the sciences, humanities, or the arts, students build critical thinking and adaptability to lead in a rapidly changing world.

"That same spirit of exploration extends beyond campus. Nearly 90% of students study abroad, gaining global perspective through programs around the world, including USD's own center in Madrid, Spain. These experiences deepen students' understanding of different cultures and prepare them to make a meaningful impact.

"Located in San Diego, California—the eighth-largest city in the U.S.—USD's beautiful campus offers direct access to thriving industries, internships, and career opportunities across sectors. Ranked among the top 10 schools for making an impact, USD reflects its changemaker values through hands-on learning and community engagement."

SELECTIVITY

# of total applicants	17,468
% of total applicants accepted	54
% of total acceptees attending	14
# of in-state applicants	9,397
% of in-state applicants accepted	55
# of out-of-state-applicants	7,125
% of applicants accepted from out of state	52
# of international applicants	946
% of international applicants accepted	49

First-Year Profile

Testing policy	Test Free
Average HS GPA	4.0
% submitting high school GPA	100
% graduated top 10% of class	35
% graduated top 25% of class	76
% graduated top 50% of class	96
% submitting high school rank	30

Important Dates

Early decision	
Apply by	11/1
Notified by	12/15
Early action	
Apply by	11/1
Notified by	12/15
Regular	
Apply by	1/15
Notified by	Rolling, 3/1
Nonfall registration?	Yes

FINANCIAL FACTS

Annual tuition	$64,100
Food and housing	$19,200
Required fees	$1,099
Books and supplies	$1,320
Average need-based scholarship (First-year)	$49,166 ($54,059)
% students with need rec. need-based scholarship or grant aid (First-year)	98 (98)
% students with need rec. non-need-based scholarship or grant aid (First-year)	56 (57)
% students with need rec. need-based self-help aid (First-year)	64 (59)
% students rec. any financial aid (First-year)	81 (83)
% UG borrow to pay for school	46
Average cumulative indebtedness	$27,308
% of students with need fully met (First-year)	14 (15)
Average % of student need met (First-year)	79 (85)

UNIVERSITY OF SAN FRANCISCO

2130 Fulton Street, San Francisco, CA 94117-1080 • Admissions: 415-422-6563

Survey Snapshot
Lots of liberal students
Lab facilities are great
Students love San Francisco, CA

RATINGS

Quality of Life	89
Fire Safety	88
Green	60*
Academic	85
Profs Interesting	91
Profs Accessible	93
Admissions	87
Financial Aid	86

CAMPUS LIFE

Type of school	Private
Affiliation	Roman Catholic
Environment	Metropolis

Students

Degree-seeking undergrad enrollment	5,095
% male/female/not reported	34/66/0
% from out of state	24
% First-year from public high school	60
% First-year live on campus	82
% Ugrads live on campus	73
# of fraternities (% join)	4 (5)
# of sororities (% join)	6 (9)
% Asian	26
% Black or African American	8
% Hispanic	26
% Native American	<1
% Pacific Islander	<1
% Race and/or ethnicity unknown	1
% Two or more races	11
% White	21
% International	8
# of countries represented	85

CAMPUS MENTAL HEALTH SERVICES

Offers mental health/wellness program	Yes
Mental health training available to students	No
Employs Chief Wellness Officer	NR
Peer-to-peer mental health offerings	NR
Counseling center has guidelines or accreditation	No
Mental health/well-being courses	NR

ACADEMICS

% students returning for sophomore year	81
% students graduating within 4 years	57
% students graduating within 6 years	66
Calendar	Semester
Student/faculty ratio	11:1
Most common class size 10–19.	(35%)
Most common lab/discussion size 10–19.	(52%)

Most Popular Majors

Biology/Biological Sciences; Psychology; Registered Nursing/Registered Nurse

Applicants Also Look At

University of California—Berkeley, University of California—Davis, University of California—Irvine, University of California—Los Angeles, University of California—Santa Barbara

STUDENTS SAY "..."

Academics

The University of San Francisco "is outstanding for students who care about their community and the world beyond themselves." USF is a "small-ish private liberal arts college" known for providing a "diverse education in an even more diverse setting." The "comprehensive core curriculum" at USF spans six thematic areas: foundations of communication; math and the sciences; humanities; philosophy, theology, and religious studies; social sciences; and visual and performing arts. Students must also fulfill requirements related to foreign languages, service to the community, and cultural diversity, all of which are in line with USF "developing the individual into a strong leader with a particular emphasis on the forces of self-reflection and self-awareness." Classrooms reflect this, with students noting that they should expect "to discuss, to ask questions, and to give feedback" and that the intellectual atmosphere "emphasizes acceptance, diversity, and critical thinking." As one student puts it, "It was not the professor's classroom...it was our classroom, all of us together." Accordingly, there is praise for "interesting, engaging classes that are small" and the "extremely talented, well-educated, hard-working, and passionate" professors who enable them. Across academic programs, students are supported by professionals who "deeply care for education." In short, USF "is outstanding for students who care about their community and the world beyond themselves" and, in line with the school's Jesuit roots and motto, want to "change the world from here."

Campus Life

Anchored by the elegant St. Ignatius Church, the USF campus is a "welcoming, second home for all of its students." Known as Dons, attendees love "getting to know each other academically, socially, and morally while allowing ourselves to get distracted by the city of San Francisco." Located "in a beautiful location" just one block from San Francisco's geographical center, Dons can use "the Muni bus pass that USF gives you" to explore "the ultimate city to be in as a young person." Campus "is located near the Haight, which means that there's always something to do." Dons can pop over to the latest exhibits at the De Young or the Legion of Honor, soak in a view of the San Francisco Bay during a Giants game, and then head to the Mission for world-class cuisine followed by artisanal ice cream. As one student describes it: "Students very often go off-campus on weekends to visit tourist attractions, go hiking, explore new food places, go shopping." One Don likes to "hit the nightclubs and bars around the city." Students can be so busy with "concerts and trips to various museums, shows, and performances" that on "weekends campus is barren because everyone is out exploring." As one student puts it best: "San Francisco is a global city with a wealth of opportunity."

Student Body

San Francisco Dons "care about the community and believe in taking action to demonstrate their beliefs." Students are "artistic, smart, morally sound," and "committed to their education." Many are attracted to USF because it's "in one of the best cities in the world" and they enjoy getting involved in the community. "The average student may be working for an NGO or volunteering regularly at one of the many non-profits in San Francisco." Hailing "from all over the world," Dons are "quirky and interesting" and celebrate their many "different cultural backgrounds and hobbies and interests." The school also provides a "very LGBT-friendly environment" where diversity is celebrated. As one student observes: "Everyone gets along very well." Overall, USF is "a culturally diverse community that teaches respect, dignity, and honor for all individuals."

University of San Francisco

Financial Aid: 415-422-3387 • E-Mail: admission@usfca.edu • Website: www.usfca.edu

THE PRINCETON REVIEW SAYS

Admissions

The school reports that its standardized testing policy for use in admission for Fall 2026 is Test Optional. The Princeton Review suggests that interested applicants consult with the school for the most up-to-date standardized testing policies. *Very important factors considered include:* rigor of secondary school record, academic GPA. *Important factors considered include:* application essay, character/personal qualities, volunteer work. *Other factors considered include:* class rank, standardized test scores, recommendation(s), interview, extracurricular activities, talent/ability, first generation, work experience, level of applicant's interest. High school diploma is required and GED is accepted. *Academic units required:* 4 English, 3 math, 2 science, 2 science labs, 2 language (other than English), 3 social studies, 6 academic electives.

Financial Aid

Students should submit: FAFSA; State aid form. Priority filing deadline is 1/15. The Princeton Review suggests that all financial aid forms be submitted as soon as possible. *Need-based scholarships/grants offered:* Federal Pell; Federal SEOG; State scholarships/grants; Private scholarships; College/university scholarship or grant aid from institutional funds. *Loan aid offered:* Federal Direct Subsidized Loans; Federal Direct Unsubsidized Loans; Direct PLUS loans; State Loans. Admitted students will be notified of awards on a rolling basis beginning 12/23. Federal Work-Study Program available. Institutional employment available.

The Inside Word

USF offers attractive financial aid packages in a gorgeous city, but getting in isn't purely a competitive numbers game; successful applications show genuine intellectual and moral curiosity. Make sure there's real heart in your essay and recommendations. Also, interested students are encouraged to check out USF's early action and decision options and their multicultural recruitment.

THE SCHOOL SAYS

From the Admissions Office

"The University of San Francisco is a private university located on a 55-acre residential campus adjacent to Golden Gate Park. At USF, students enjoy a traditional college campus (grassy quads and residence halls) alongside immediate access to one of the world's most innovative cities for careers in technology, healthcare, finance, and the social sector.

"USF offers 42 majors and 70+ minors across five schools, with particular strengths in nursing, biology, computer science, psychology, and business. Students looking for an accelerated path should apply for a 4+1 program—bachelor's and master's degrees completed in five years. High-achieving students are encouraged to explore the Honors College, which offers smaller seminars, independent research opportunities, and a close-knit intellectual community within the larger university. The Horizon Collective, USF's signature cohort program, brings together students from 17 disciplines to pursue applied work in AI and technology, health and well-being, and climate solutions—with renewable scholarships, a dedicated professional coach, and direct connections to internship and research opportunities built in.

"91% of USF graduates from the Class of 2024 are employed or in grad school, and 79% of USF undergrads complete at least two internships while they're here.

"In reviewing applications, we look for students who have challenged themselves academically and who can speak to how their values align with USF's commitment to using education as a force for social good. A campus visit is the single best way to understand whether USF is the right fit."

SELECTIVITY

# of total applicants	18,299
% of total applicants accepted	72
% of total acceptees attending	9
# of in-state applicants	8,480
% of in-state applicants accepted	81
# of out-of-state-applicants	7,108
% of applicants accepted from out of state	73
# of international applicants	2,708
% of international applicants accepted	41
# of early decision applicants	262
% of early decision applicants accepted	42
# offered a place on the wait list	405
# admitted from wait list	12

First-Year Profile

Testing policy	Test Optional
Range SAT composite	1260–1410
Range SAT EBRW	630–730
Range SAT math	600–710
Range ACT composite	26–31
% submitting SAT scores	9
% submitting ACT scores	2
Average HS GPA	3.7
% submitting high school GPA	100
% graduated top 10% of class	45
% graduated top 25% of class	68
% graduated top 50% of class	93
% submitting high school rank	26

Important Dates

Early decision	
Apply by	11/1
Notified by	12/1
Early action	
Apply by	11/1
Notified by	12/14
Regular	
Apply by	1/15
Notified by	Rolling, 3/15
Nonfall registration?	Yes

FINANCIAL FACTS

Annual tuition	$63,880
Food and housing	$19,150
Required fees	$612
Books and supplies	$1,306
Average need-based scholarship (First-year)	$39,238 ($46,259)
% students with need rec. need-based scholarship or grant aid (First-year)	98 (99)
% students with need rec. non-need-based scholarship or grant aid (First-year)	9 (11)
% students with need rec. need-based self-help aid (First-year)	64 (59)
% students rec. any financial aid (First-year)	92 (93)
% UG borrow to pay for school	55
Average cumulative indebtedness	$40,972
% of students with need fully met (First-year)	11 (13)
Average % of student need met (First-year)	66 (74)

The University of Scranton

800 Linden Street, Scranton, PA 18510 • Admissions: 570-941-7540

Survey Snapshot
Students are happy
Classroom facilities are great
Intramural sports are popular

RATINGS

Quality of Life	85
Fire Safety	95
Green	60*
Academic	82
Profs Interesting	86
Profs Accessible	90
Admissions	86
Financial Aid	85

CAMPUS LIFE

Type of school	Private
Affiliation	Roman Catholic-Jesuit
Environment	City

Students

Degree-seeking undergrad enrollment	3,634
% male/female/not reported	45/55/0
% from out of state	52
% First-year live on campus	78
% Ugrads live on campus	59
# of fraternities	0
# of sororities	0
% Asian	3
% Black or African American	3
% Hispanic	14
% Native American	<1
% Pacific Islander	<1
% Race and/or ethnicity unknown	3
% Two or more races	3
% White	73
% International	<1
# of countries represented	12

CAMPUS MENTAL HEALTH SERVICES

Offers mental health/wellness program	Yes
Mental health training available to students	No
Employs Chief Wellness Officer	NR
Peer-to-peer mental health offerings	NR
Counseling center has guidelines or accreditation	No
Mental health/well-being courses	NR

ACADEMICS

% students returning for sophomore year	87
% students graduating within 4 years	77
% students graduating within 6 years	82
Calendar	Semester
Student/faculty ratio	11:1
Most common class size 10–19.	(41%)
Most common lab/discussion size 10–19.	(58%)

Applicants Often Prefer

Fairfield University, Penn State University Park, Sacred Heart University, Saint Joseph's University (PA), Temple University, University of Delaware, West Chester University of Pennsylvania

Applicants Sometimes Prefer

The College of New Jersey, Loyola University Maryland, Marist University, Quinnipiac University, Rutgers University–New Brunswick, Seton Hall University, State University of New York—Binghamton University, University of Pittsburgh—Pittsburgh Campus, University of Rhode Island

Applicants Rarely Prefer

Marywood University, State University of New York—University at Buffalo, Villanova University

STUDENTS SAY "…"

Academics

The University of Scranton is a Jesuit university that emphasizes "a well-rounded education" both in its "engaging and diverse" general education offerings and its methods, which include "discussions, hands-on learning with simulation laboratories, and outdoor classes." These approaches, along with varied classroom setups, allow professors "creative freedom and encourage discussions between students." This fits with the overall impression of teachers as being "at Scranton because they want to teach and forge relationships with students," and they "are very determined to see you succeed." They want to make sure "we complete our assignments and, most importantly, understand them." In fact, the whole school is said to "genuinely care about students and will do their best to accommodate you," whether that's peer-to-peer services in the Writing Center or Counseling and Human Services, which one student calls "the best out of anywhere in the world." In all, "The amount of resources available to students is outstanding. From physical and mental health to career opportunities and advancement, everything is [available]."

Campus Life

The atmosphere on campus at Scranton "is typically rather lively," and students "fill their days with schoolwork [and] socializing with other students." The campus is "pretty walkable," and there are many "comfortable and beautiful places to study and do work, or you'll see people on the green playing games." Recreational sports "are generally well run and pretty fun," and one student finds them to be a good way to "keep me active and allow me to connect with others." There are "plenty of events [to attend]" and numerous clubs and organizations to join, including the Cyber Investigation Club, Liva Arts Company, and Student Occupational Therapy Association. Students enjoy the unique activities they sponsor, "such as the art exhibition, the dog day where people bring their dogs in so you can pet them and sit with them, and random activities like giving out Dunkin' coffee to students." There are also a number of service-oriented clubs, and "activities like volunteering at food pantries or helping with educational programs for underserved communities [are] especially meaningful." Many students appreciate that at Scranton, housing is guaranteed for all four years, and "having so many students live on campus helps it stay alive and vibrant year-round."

Student Body

The "diverse student body" is full of people who are "friendly, kind, and warm." This "environment creates a cozy atmosphere where it's easy to make friends and share small talk," and students say their peers "have made this school…a comforting community." As one student shares, "Our school has always been described as extremely welcoming and friendly, which is one of the reasons why I chose it nearly four years ago." Students at Scranton "embody a unique combination of academic ambition and a strong sense of social responsibility, [and] tend to be actively involved in service projects, campus organizations, and outreach programs." The student body is "close-knit, supportive, and grounded in Jesuit values like service and reflection" and "always willing to lend a helping hand when in need."

The University of Scranton

Financial Aid: 570-941-7701 • E-Mail: admissions@scranton.edu • Website: www.scranton.edu

THE PRINCETON REVIEW SAYS

Admissions

The school reports that its standardized testing policy for use in admission for Fall 2026 is Test Optional. The Princeton Review suggests that interested applicants consult with the school for the most up-to-date standardized testing policies. *Very important factors considered include:* rigor of secondary school record, class rank, academic GPA, standardized test scores. *Important factors considered include:* extracurricular activities. *Other factors considered include:* application essay, recommendation(s), interview, talent/ability, character/personal qualities, alumni/ae relation, volunteer work, work experience, level of applicant's interest. High school diploma or equivalent is not required. *Academic units recommended:* 4 English, 4 math, 2 science, 2 language (other than English), 3 history, 4 visual/performing arts.

Financial Aid

The Princeton Review suggests that all financial aid forms be submitted as soon as possible. Federal Work-Study Program available. Institutional employment available.

The Inside Word

The University of Scranton claims to have "the keys to your success," and that much is certainly true for its easily unlocked Common Application process. That said, the school holistically reviews candidates, so they will consider whatever you include. Note that while the school's overall acceptance numbers are high—more than 80% of those who apply get in—certain programs are highly competitive, and the school encourages you to apply as early as possible for them.

THE SCHOOL SAYS

From the Admissions Office

"The University of Scranton is a premier Catholic and Jesuit university that provides rigorous academics grounded in the liberal arts. Our 58-acre campus offers the best of both worlds—the city and the mountains. We are in the heart of the city of Scranton, in Pennsylvania's Pocono Northeast, just two hours from New York City and Philadelphia. In recent years, we have invested more than $302 million in campus improvements, including new residence halls, an athletics campus, a science center and the state-of-the-art Leahy Hall, which houses our physical therapy, occupational therapy and health and human performance departments.

"The word most often used to distinguish Scranton from other universities is "community." At Scranton, we share a dedication to the values of a Jesuit education, and that propels all of our students as they advance in their lives and careers.

"We offer 69 majors, more than 90 clubs and organizations, and 23 Division III athletic teams to the 3,500 undergraduate students in attendance.

"Scranton develops leaders through rigorous preparation in students' chosen fields coupled with a commitment to educating the whole person. Students extend their academic experience through honors programs, internships, faculty-student research and study abroad, and the university provides excellent preparation for medical and other health professions doctoral programs, law school, graduate school, and post-graduate fellowships and scholarships. Our AACSB-accredited Kania School of Management has received national recognition for our business programs.

"Students can apply online for free at scranton.edu/apply. Students can schedule a visit either online at scranton.edu/visit or by calling us at 1-888-SCRANTON."

SELECTIVITY

# of total applicants	9,575
% of total applicants accepted	80
% of total acceptees attending	12
# of in-state applicants	3,521
% of in-state applicants accepted	81
# of out-of-state-applicants	5,866
% of applicants accepted from out of state	81
# of international applicants	188
% of international applicants accepted	26
# offered a place on the wait list	698
# admitted from wait list	7

First-Year Profile

Testing policy	Test Optional
Range SAT composite	1160–1300
Range SAT EBRW	580–670
Range SAT math	560–650
Range ACT composite	27–31
% submitting SAT scores	29
% submitting ACT scores	4
Average HS GPA	3.6
% submitting high school GPA	100
% graduated top 10% of class	26
% graduated top 25% of class	55
% graduated top 50% of class	89

Important Dates

Early action	
Apply by	11/15
Notified by	12/15
Regular	
Apply by	8/1
Notified by	Rolling, 12/15
Nonfall registration?	Yes

FINANCIAL FACTS

Annual tuition	$56,860
Food and housing	$17,858
Required fees	$500
Books and supplies	$1,300
Average need-based scholarship (First-year)	$18,151 ($16,119)
% students with need rec. need-based scholarship or grant aid (First-year)	86 (85)
% students with need rec. non-need-based scholarship or grant aid (First-year)	92 (96)
% students with need rec. need-based self-help aid (First-year)	65 (68)
% UG borrow to pay for school	71
Average cumulative indebtedness	$59,942
% of students with need fully met (First-year)	30 (27)
Average % of student need met (First-year)	69 (70)

The University of the South

735 University Avenue, Sewanee, TN 37383-1000 • Admissions: 931-598-1238

Survey Snapshot
Students take advantage of the outdoors
Intramural sports are popular
Students environmentally aware

RATINGS

Quality of Life	88
Fire Safety	97
Green	88
Academic	88
Profs Interesting	96
Profs Accessible	96
Admissions	89
Financial Aid	92

CAMPUS LIFE

Type of school	Private
Affiliation	Episcopal
Environment	Rural

Students

Degree-seeking undergrad enrollment	1,566
% male/female/not reported	46/54/0
% from out of state	76
% First-year from public high school	48
% First-year live on campus	100
% Ugrads live on campus	97
# of fraternities (% join)	10 (54)
# of sororities (% join)	9 (65)
% Asian	1
% Black or African American	4
% Hispanic	6
% Native American	<1
% Pacific Islander	0
% Race and/or ethnicity unknown	1
% Two or more races	3
% White	81
% International	4
# of countries represented	28

CAMPUS MENTAL HEALTH SERVICES

Offers mental health/wellness program	Yes
Mental health training available to students	Yes
Employs Chief Wellness Officer	Yes
Peer-to-peer mental health offerings	Yes
Counseling center has guidelines or accreditation	Yes
Mental health/well-being courses	Yes

ACADEMICS

% students returning for sophomore year	88
% students graduating within 4 years	72
% students graduating within 6 years	79
Calendar	Semester
Student/faculty ratio	9:1
Most common class size 10–19.	(48%)
Most common lab/discussion size 10–19.	(55%)

Most Popular Majors

Biology/Biological Sciences; Econometrics and Quantitative Economics; Political Science and Government

STUDENTS SAY "..."

Academics

The University of the South (known as Sewanee) emphasizes the "practical applications of learning instead of traditional final exams," offering "ample group projects which give [students] a chance to work collaboratively with classmates while learning to innovate and think critically." Through the Sewanee Pledge, all students receive funding for a summer internship or research fellowship, along with a semester-long study abroad experience at no additional cost. In the natural sciences, Sewanee "puts a huge emphasis on experiential learning, made possible through our access to the [Domain]"—13,000 acres of forests, bluffs, meadows, lakes, and caves. Courses also "prioritize engaging with members of organizations outside of the school in the surrounding counties," and many assignments "challenge what you have learned and allow for creative expression." This ability "to interact thoroughly with the content of the courses" is a highlight for many students. Faculty serve as the "biggest support pillars," and all "have a strong desire to connect with their students and aid in their overall academic journey," fostering an environment where discussion is encouraged both in traditional classrooms and in outdoor settings where many classes are held. One student recalls a course where "it felt as if the professors were our peers and wanted to learn from us and our perspectives in the same way we learn from them." Long-standing traditions such as the Honor Code "help create a strong sense of identity and community" and shape "a culture of trust, integrity, and mutual respect," leading one to say, "I love knowing everyone loves Sewanee as much as I do."

Campus Life

Sewanee's campus, known as the Domain, is widely celebrated for its natural surroundings, with students noting that "the beauty…is unmatched." One student adds, "It takes about two minutes to step into the woods and immerse yourself in the wilderness." The school "encourages students to lead an active, outdoors lifestyle and to engage with the surrounding community," and does so in part through the Sewanee Outing Program (SOP), which "leads a lot of hiking, caving, [and] canoeing…trips." The campus fosters a close-knit environment where everyone "is somehow connected to everyone else because it is a smaller campus," and nearly all students live on campus. Housing options include theme houses that group together students with similar identities and interests. Because "the school IS the town, on weekends the whole campus parties together," Greek life "is inclusive and social events include all members and non-members." Campus traditions such as the Order of the Gown are important to the Sewanee experience, reinforcing a strong sense of community. Another student adds, "The unique aspect of being on our own little mountain facilitates such a wonderful environment for everyone to thrive in."

Student Body

Many students here "have extremely specific interests," with the groups "that stand out as Sewanee-specific [being] nature lovers and civic service lovers," and the university supports this by providing "so many opportunities for students to find their place and try new things." A strong sense of camaraderie connects people across campus: "Everyone who goes to Sewanee or went to Sewanee swears by the university as a fundamental part of their lives." There is "abundant Southern charm," and "you can walk up to anybody on campus and strike up a conversation." One student describes their peers as "extremely smart and extremely nice," noting that students "value good grades and spend a lot of their nights focusing on schoolwork or even broadening their horizons themselves." Students also say that everyone "treats each other with an immense amount of respect." As one student says, "We are a collective, small enough for us to have friendships wherever we go, and big enough to still have the joy of meeting new people."

THE UNIVERSITY OF THE SOUTH

Financial Aid: 931-598-1312 • E-Mail: admiss@sewanee.edu • Website: www.sewanee.edu

THE PRINCETON REVIEW SAYS

Admissions

The school reports that its standardized testing policy for use in admission for Fall 2026 is Test Optional. The Princeton Review suggests that interested applicants consult with the school for the most up-to-date standardized testing policies. *Very important factors considered include:* rigor of secondary school record, academic GPA, recommendation(s). *Important factors considered include:* application essay, extracurricular activities, character/personal qualities, volunteer work, work experience. *Other factors considered include:* class rank, standardized test scores, interview, talent/ability, first generation, alumni/ae relation, geographical residence, level of applicant's interest. High school diploma is required and GED is not accepted. *Academic units required:* 4 English, 3 math, 2 science, 2 science labs, 2 language (other than English), 1 social studies, 1 history. *Academic units recommended:* 4 English, 4 math, 4 science, 3 science labs, 4 language (other than English), 2 social studies, 2 history.

Financial Aid

Students should submit: FAFSA; CSS PROFILE. Priority filing deadline is 1/1. The Princeton Review suggests that all financial aid forms be submitted as soon as possible. *Need-based scholarships/grants offered:* Federal Pell; Federal SEOG; State scholarships/grants; Private scholarships; College/university scholarship or grant aid from institutional funds. *Loan aid offered:* Federal Direct Subsidized Loans; Federal Direct Unsubsidized Loans; Direct PLUS loans. Admitted students will be notified of awards on a rolling basis beginning 2/14. Federal Work-Study Program available. Institutional employment available.

The Inside Word

The admissions office at University of the South is very accessible to students. Its staff includes some of the most well-respected admissions professionals in the South, and that shows in the way they work with students. Despite an acceptance rate of just over half, candidates who take the admissions process here lightly may find themselves disappointed. Applicant evaluation is too personal for a lackadaisical approach to yield success. A demonstrated interest in attending, such as campus visits or reaching out to the admissions office, is advised.

THE SCHOOL SAYS

From the Admissions Office

"The University of the South is consistently ranked among the top tier of national liberal arts universities. Sewanee is committed to a rigorous academic curriculum that focuses on the liberal arts as the most valuable form of undergraduate education. It offers a wide range of majors, minors, and pre-professional programs including business, medicine and health, law, and engineering. Sewanee is a small residential college located on a 13,000-acre campus atop Tennessee's Cumberland Plateau between Chattanooga and Nashville. Largely forested and rich in biodiversity, the campus is a distinctive asset offering an unparalleled outdoor laboratory and boundless recreational opportunities. The University has an impressive record of academic achievement—28 Rhodes Scholars and 35 NCAA postgraduate scholarship recipients have graduated from Sewanee. Professors are leading scholars and researchers with a commitment to teaching, and in Sewanee's close community they develop rich and lasting relationships with their students. Prospective students have had the option of choosing whether or not to submit standardized test scores. Test scores are considered to be purely supplementary in the admission process and students who choose not to submit them will be given equal consideration to those who do. To ensure that students get the most value out of their time at Sewanee, we make the Sewanee Pledge: we will help students secure good jobs or spots in graduate programs by providing funding for a summer internship or research opportunity; we will provide students with access to a semester-long study abroad program at no additional tuition cost; and we guarantee that you will graduate (with one major) in four consecutive years or the fifth is on us."

SELECTIVITY

# of total applicants	4,555
% of total applicants accepted	56
% of total acceptees attending	18
# of in-state applicants	687
% of in-state applicants accepted	82
# of out-of-state-applicants	2,287
% of applicants accepted from out of state	82
# of international applicants	1,581
% of international applicants accepted	8
# of early decision applicants	248
% of early decision applicants accepted	71
# offered a place on the wait list	229
# admitted from wait list	5

First-Year Profile

Testing policy	Test Optional
Range SAT composite	1210–1360
Range SAT EBRW	620–700
Range SAT math	580–690
Range ACT composite	27–31
% submitting SAT scores	24
% submitting ACT scores	36
% graduated top 10% of class	27
% graduated top 25% of class	69
% graduated top 50% of class	90
% submitting high school rank	26

Important Dates

Early decision	
Apply by	11/15
Notified by	Mid December
Other ED Apply by	1/15
Other ED Notified by	Late January
Early action	
Apply by	12/1
Notified by	Late January
Regular	
Apply by	2/1
Notified by	3/1
Nonfall registration?	Yes

FINANCIAL FACTS

Annual tuition	$60,088
Food and housing	$17,272
Required fees	$320
Books and supplies	$800
Average need-based scholarship (First-year)	$45,842 ($41,774)
% students with need rec. need-based scholarship or grant aid (First-year)	99 (99)
% students with need rec. non-need-based scholarship or grant aid (First-year)	23 (30)
% students with need rec. need-based self-help aid (First-year)	66 (66)
% students rec. any financial aid (First-year)	98 (98)
% UG borrow to pay for school	39
Average cumulative indebtedness	$30,254
% of students with need fully met (First-year)	38 (38)
Average % of student need met (First-year)	93 (89)

UNIVERSITY OF SOUTH CAROLINA—COLUMBIA

Office of Undergraduate Admissions, Columbia, SC 29208 • Admissions: 803-777-7700

Survey Snapshot
Lots of conservative students
Frats and sororities are popular
Campus newspaper is popular

RATINGS

Quality of Life	86
Fire Safety	60*
Green	60*
Academic	78
Profs Interesting	87
Profs Accessible	90
Admissions	88
Financial Aid	84

CAMPUS LIFE

Type of school	Public
Environment	City

Students

Degree-seeking undergrad enrollment	29,820
% male/female/not reported	41/59/0
% from out of state	40
% First-year live on campus	96
% Ugrads live on campus	29
# of fraternities (% join)	22 (30)
# of sororities (% join)	16 (36)
% Asian	4
% Black or African American	10
% Hispanic	7
% Native American	<1
% Pacific Islander	<1
% Race and/or ethnicity unknown	1
% Two or more races	4
% White	72
% International	1
# of countries represented	115

CAMPUS MENTAL HEALTH SERVICES

Offers mental health/wellness program	Yes
Mental health training available to students	No
Employs Chief Wellness Officer	NR
Peer-to-peer mental health offerings	NR
Counseling center has guidelines or accreditation	No
Mental health/well-being courses	NR

ACADEMICS

% students returning for sophomore year	92
% students graduating within 4 years	70
% students graduating within 6 years	79
Calendar	Semester
Student/faculty ratio	19:1
Most common class size 20–29.	(35%)
Most common lab/discussion size 20–29.	(40%)

Most Popular Majors

Criminal Justice/Law Enforcement Administration; Experimental Psychology; Registered Nursing, Nursing Administration, Nursing Research and Clinical Nursing

STUDENTS SAY "..."

Academics

The University of South Carolina—Columbia is a historic public research university built on 200 years of proud tradition and academic excellence. Those who enroll say the "school is always improving" right along with the students who are "learning and striving to be the best person you can be (academically and otherwise)." To that end, the university offers "students the resources they need to succeed through workshops...service opportunities, student organizations and various academic endeavors" and provides a strong support system for its "challenging courses" in "multiple success coaches, countless tutors, and advisors and professors who will get to know you outside of the basic classroom." That means that instructors "care about [your] success inside and outside of the classroom," and make a corresponding effort "to relate their in-class lectures to the real world." They're "also willing to give advice about...research, job, and internship opportunities," which can help students develop into "very employable prospect[s] upon graduation." Just be ready to "participate in class," as faculty are said to "foster an environment of respect and thoughtful discourse." Ultimately, U of SC "is about opportunity"—and making the most of it "really depends on what YOU are all about."

Campus Life

"It is quite normal for students to be involved in a variety of activities" at U of SC, ranging from "awesome" tailgates to Greek life and intramural sports. "Football games are the biggest social event of the fall" and constitute an important Gamecock tradition; "traffic patterns are altered because it is such a huge deal." Student spirit thrives in longstanding events like Tiger Burn and Homecoming, both fixtures of the academic year. More frequently, "there is almost always an event happening on Greene Street," like Hip Hop Wednesday or a farmers' market. "The weather makes it really easy to do things outside" and students are often found "scattered around sitting and playing on the Horseshoe" or participating in the many "outdoor recreation activities run through the university." The school's location gives the variety of "shorter distances to the beach as well as the mountains," and the "very artsy" city is easily navigable on foot. That's especially great on weekends, and older students can be found frequenting the "multitude of bars" in the Five Points neighborhood of downtown Columbia. Those who remain on campus say "there is an organization for everything," so undergraduates can explore options from "skydiving to Latin dance to language." Also, community service is "very common here" and on "Service Saturdays, hundreds of students are assigned to a community service site in the Columbia area." Finally, students also benefit from "phenomenal" amenities, from "free athletic tickets to twelve free counseling sessions a year."

Student Body

This historic Southern institution of U of SC is all "about everyone coming together and being one giant Gamecock family, whether in academics, sports, or anything else." Students suggest that "many different types of people" are drawn here and tend to be "incredibly friendly and filled with Southern charm." The "large Greek population" also results in "a lot of the student body [being] relatively laid back in dress and attitude," and one student notes that "I've never felt judged...and I feel a sense of camaraderie amongst my peers." Essentially, U of SC is a big school that "does an amazing job of making sure you don't get lost in the crowd."

University of South Carolina—Columbia

Financial Aid: 803-777-8134 • E-Mail: admissions-ugrad@sc.edu • Website: www.sc.edu

THE PRINCETON REVIEW SAYS

Admissions

The school reports that its standardized testing policy for use in admission for Fall 2026 is Test Optional. The Princeton Review suggests that interested applicants consult with the school for the most up-to-date standardized testing policies. *Very important factors considered include:* academic GPA. *Important factors considered include:* rigor of secondary school record, class rank, standardized test scores. *Other factors considered include:* application essay, recommendation(s), extracurricular activities, talent/ability, state residency, volunteer work, work experience. High school diploma is required and GED is accepted. *Academic units required:* 4 English, 4 math, 3 science, 3 science labs, 2 language (other than English), 2 social studies, 1 history, 2 academic electives, 1 visual/performing arts.

Financial Aid

Students should submit: FAFSA. Priority filing deadline is 4/1. The Princeton Review suggests that all financial aid forms be submitted as soon as possible. *Need-based scholarships/grants offered:* Federal Pell; Federal SEOG; State scholarships/grants; Private scholarships; College/university scholarship or grant aid from institutional funds; United Negro College Fund; Federal Nursing Scholarships. *Loan aid offered:* Federal Direct Subsidized Loans; Federal Direct Unsubsidized Loans; Direct PLUS loans; State Loans. Admitted students will be notified of awards on a rolling basis beginning 4/1. Federal Work-Study Program available. Institutional employment available.

The Inside Word

At University of South Carolina, as at most large schools, admissions decisions are based almost entirely on a prospective student's grades, test scores (if submitted), and high school curriculum. A personal statement is required. Good grades matter, but higher standardized test scores can offset a lower GPA.

THE SCHOOL SAYS

From the Admissions Office

"The University of South Carolina is a destination of choice for students from all fifty states and more than 100 countries. UofSC is one of only forty public research institutions to earn both the top-tier research classification and the community service classification from the Carnegie Foundation. As early as their freshman year, undergraduates are encouraged to compete for research grants. As South Carolina's flagship institution, UofSC offers more than 300 degree programs. More than 35,000 students seek baccalaureate, masters, or doctoral degrees. UofSC is known for its top-ranked academic programs, including its international business and exercise science programs—both rated number one nationally. Other notable programs include chemical and nuclear engineering; health education; hotel, restaurant, and tourism; marine science; law; medicine; nursing; and psychology, among others. UofSC is recognized for its pioneering efforts in freshman outreach, and the South Carolina Honors College is ranked number one in the country compared to all other honors colleges in public university settings. UofSC offers student support in such areas as career development, leadership training, research grants, pre-professional planning, and study abroad. On campus, students enjoy a state-of-the-art fitness center, an 18,000-seat arena, an 80,000-seat stadium, and more than 400 student organizations. Off campus, South Carolina's world-famous beaches and the Blue Ridge Mountains are each less than a three-hour drive away. The University of South Carolina is located in the state's capital city, making it a great place for internships and job opportunities."

SELECTIVITY

# of total applicants	52,703
% of total applicants accepted	60
% of total acceptees attending	23
# of in-state applicants	13,042
% of in-state applicants accepted	76
# of out-of-state-applicants	39,067
% of applicants accepted from out of state	55
# of international applicants	594
% of international applicants accepted	65
# offered a place on the wait list	7,332
# admitted from wait list	500

First-Year Profile

Testing policy	Test Optional
Range SAT composite	1190–1270
Range SAT EBRW	600–680
Range SAT math	580–680
Range ACT composite	26–32
% submitting SAT scores	29
% submitting ACT scores	15
Average HS GPA	3.7
% submitting high school GPA	98
% graduated top 10% of class	29
% graduated top 25% of class	63
% graduated top 50% of class	93
% submitting high school rank	62

Important Dates

Early action	
Apply by	10/15
Notified by	12/15
Regular	
Apply by	12/1
Notified by	3/15
Nonfall registration?	Yes

FINANCIAL FACTS

Annual in-state tuition	$12,288
Annual out-of-state tuition	$35,572
Food and housing	$15,708
Required fees	$400
Average need-based scholarship (First-year)	$14,049 ($14,644)
% students with need rec. need-based scholarship or grant aid (First-year)	84 (87)
% students with need rec. non-need-based scholarship or grant aid (First-year)	26 (30)
% students with need rec. need-based self-help aid (First-year)	71 (69)
% students rec. any financial aid (First-year)	87 (96)
% UG borrow to pay for school	53
Average cumulative indebtedness	$31,501
% of students with need fully met (First-year)	15 (15)
Average % of student need met (First-year)	59 (60)

THE UNIVERSITY OF SOUTH DAKOTA

414 East Clark St., Vermillion, SD 57069 • Admissions: 877-269-6837

Survey Snapshot
Campus newspaper is popular
Great library
Students are friendly

RATINGS

Quality of Life	74
Fire Safety	60*
Green	60*
Academic	78
Profs Interesting	85
Profs Accessible	88
Admissions	82
Financial Aid	82

CAMPUS LIFE

Type of school	Public
Environment	Village

Students

Degree-seeking undergrad enrollment	5,320
% male/female/not reported	36/64/0
% from out of state	38
% First-year live on campus	82
% Ugrads live on campus	37
# of fraternities (% join)	NR (20)
# of sororities (% join)	NR (12)
% Asian	2
% Black or African American	4
% Hispanic	6
% Native American	3
% Pacific Islander	<1
% Race and/or ethnicity unknown	1
% Two or more races	3
% White	76
% International	6

CAMPUS MENTAL HEALTH SERVICES

Offers mental health/wellness program	Yes
Mental health training available to students	No
Employs Chief Wellness Officer	NR
Peer-to-peer mental health offerings	NR
Counseling center has guidelines or accreditation	No
Mental health/well-being courses	NR

ACADEMICS

% students returning for sophomore year	77
% students graduating within 4 years	50
% students graduating within 6 years	61
Calendar	Semester
Student/faculty ratio	16:1
Most common class size 10–19.	(34%)
Most common lab/discussion size 10–19.	(42%)

STUDENTS SAY "..."

Academics

Students love the "many options as far as majors go" at The University of South Dakota, spotlighting the nursing school as well as labeling business, biology, premed, law, and psychology courses as "very solid." There's a lot of praise for the school's Honors Program, which offers smaller class sizes and discussion-based courses to qualifying students, and students call it the "best-kept secret in the country." Factor in the numerous winners of "big scholarships like the Goldwater and Truman" and it's clear why some students feel the school offers "a reasonable price"—especially for out-of-state students. So far as faculty go, there seem to be winners in every department, with "some of the best" music professors, according to one respondent, and more generally, staff who are "nearly always willing to go the extra mile for students."

Campus Life

The University of South Dakota has over 200 student organizations and offers everything from Greek life and club sports to drag shows, Zumba classes, and Bible study. Students feel that "since it is a smaller campus, [there are] more opportunities to be involved in internships and various other activities," though others suggest that they "have to make their own fun, which often involves partying or taking small road trips to other cities in the area." For that group, which describes a "lot of partying," Yankton, Sioux City, and Sioux Falls are "all within an hour" and "offer everything a person would want to do." Students also suggest that while only 34% of undergraduates remain on campus (84% of first-years do so), the nearby town of Vermillion is close enough that "no one is more than a 10-minute walk/bike ride away!" Regardless of where they live, the sense is that they "keep themselves occupied with schoolwork, intramural sports, and hanging out with their friends."

Student Body

Students at USD tend to be active and involved: it seems like "every person on campus is part of at least one" student organization, which is "a great way to meet new people and [to participate in] activities." Many enrollees appear to fit the bill of a "conservative Midwesterner," and the school is 80% Caucasian, but their interests vary. Some describe the campus as a place where "partying is a definite part of the culture," whereas others note that "many people join a Greek system or are athletes or musicians" and that those outside those roles "seem to focus on their academics." The big takeaway is that regardless of background or interests, you're likely to fit right in, thanks to "the open mindedness of most students."

THE UNIVERSITY OF SOUTH DAKOTA

E-Mail: admissions@usd.edu • Website: www.usd.edu

THE PRINCETON REVIEW SAYS

Admissions

The school reports that its standardized testing policy for use in admission for Fall 2026 is Test Optional. The Princeton Review suggests that interested applicants consult with the school for the most up-to-date standardized testing policies. *Very important factors considered include:* rigor of secondary school record, class rank, academic GPA, standardized test scores. *Other factors considered include:* application essay, recommendation(s). High school diploma is required and GED is accepted. *Academic units required:* 4 English, 3 math, 3 science, 3 science labs, 3 social studies, 1 visual/performing arts. *Academic units recommended:* 4 English, 4 math, 4 science, 3 science labs, 2 language (other than English), 3 social studies, 1 visual/performing arts.

Financial Aid

Students should submit: FAFSA. Priority filing deadline is 4/1. The Princeton Review suggests that all financial aid forms be submitted as soon as possible. *Need-based scholarships/grants offered:* Federal Pell; Federal SEOG; Private scholarships; College/university scholarship or grant aid from institutional funds; United Negro College Fund; State scholarships/grants. *Loan aid offered:* Federal Direct Subsidized Loans; Federal Direct Unsubsidized Loans; Direct PLUS loans. Admitted students will be notified of awards on a rolling basis beginning 5/1.

The Inside Word

Admission to The University of South Dakota is almost guaranteed, but you still must meet certain academic and high school curricula requirements before you are accepted to the school. Check on the school's website for the exact requirements to make sure you qualify.

THE SCHOOL SAYS

From the Admissions Office

"The University of South Dakota is the perfect fit for students looking for a smart educational investment. USD is South Dakota's only designated liberal arts university and is consistently rated among the top doctoral institutions in the country. Annually, USD awards $7.2 million in scholarships. More than 80 percent of USD students receive financial aid through grants, loans and work-study jobs.

"USD students earn the nation's most prestigious scholarships. Our quality of teaching and research prepares students to pursue their passions all over the world, at institutions such as Columbia, Princeton, John Hopkins, Harvard Medical School, Massachusetts Institute of Technology, The University of Chicago and beyond. One hundred and three students have been awarded prestigious Fulbright, Rhodes, National Science Foundation, Boren, Truman, Udall, Gilman and Goldwater scholarships and grants for graduate study. Personal attention from our award-winning faculty and our welcoming environment makes students feel right at home.

"As the flagship liberal arts institution in South Dakota, USD—founded in 1862—has long been regarded as a leader in the state and the region. Notable undergraduate and postgraduate alumni include author and former news anchor Tom Brokaw, U.S. Senator Tim Johnson, U.S. Representative Kevin Brady, USA Today founder Al Neuharth and U.S. Senator John Thune.

"Though it is currently optional, USD recommends taking the ACT over the SAT. Students who wish to send their SAT scores will have their scores converted to ACT scores for placement and scholarship consideration."

SELECTIVITY

# of total applicants	6,380
% of total applicants accepted	99
% of total acceptees attending	19
# of in-state applicants	2,241
% of in-state applicants accepted	100
# of out-of-state-applicants	2,115
% of applicants accepted from out of state	99
# of international applicants	2,024
% of international applicants accepted	98

First-Year Profile

Testing policy	Test Optional
Range SAT composite	1120–1290
Range SAT EBRW	500–630
Range SAT math	600–690
Range ACT composite	19–25
% submitting SAT scores	2
% submitting ACT scores	58
Average HS GPA	3.5
% submitting high school GPA	97
% graduated top 10% of class	18
% graduated top 25% of class	39
% graduated top 50% of class	70
% submitting high school rank	76

Important Dates

Regular	
Apply by	8/30
Notified by	Rolling, 8/1
Nonfall registration?	Yes

FINANCIAL FACTS

Annual in-state tuition	$7,998
Annual out-of-state tuition	$11,610
Food and housing	$9,794
Required fees	$1,689
Books and supplies	$800
Average need-based scholarship (First-year)	$7,311 ($7,259)
% students with need rec. need-based scholarship or grant aid (First-year)	67 (66)
% students with need rec. non-need-based scholarship or grant aid (First-year)	66 (85)
% students with need rec. need-based self-help aid (First-year)	88 (85)
% UG borrow to pay for school	65
Average cumulative indebtedness	$27,794
% of students with need fully met (First-year)	17 (19)
Average % of student need met (First-year)	62 (62)

UNIVERSITY OF SOUTH FLORIDA

4202 East Fowler Avenue, Tampa, FL 33620-9951 • Admissions: 813-974-3350

Survey Snapshot
Students are happy
Great library
Diverse student types interact on campus

RATINGS

Quality of Life	85
Fire Safety	99
Green	97
Academic	77
Profs Interesting	84
Profs Accessible	87
Admissions	90
Financial Aid	84

CAMPUS LIFE

Type of school	Public
Environment	Metropolis

Students

Degree-seeking undergrad enrollment	37,473
% male/female/not reported	43/57/<1
% from out of state	12
% First-year live on campus	56
% Ugrads live on campus	19
# of fraternities (% join)	34 (2)
# of sororities (% join)	29 (4)
% Asian	9
% Black or African American	8
% Hispanic	25
% Native American	<1
% Pacific Islander	<1
% Race and/or ethnicity unknown	3
% Two or more races	5
% White	42
% International	8
# of countries represented	132

CAMPUS MENTAL HEALTH SERVICES

Offers mental health/wellness program	NR
Mental health training available to students	NR
Employs Chief Wellness Officer	NR
Peer-to-peer mental health offerings	NR
Counseling center has guidelines or accreditation	NR
Mental health/well-being courses	NR

ACADEMICS

% students returning for sophomore year	91
% students graduating within 4 years	66
% students graduating within 6 years	78
Calendar	Semester
Student/faculty ratio	22:1
Most common class size 10–19.	(28%)

Most Popular Majors

Biomedical Sciences; Health Services/Allied Health/Health Sciences; Psychology

Applicants Also Look At

Florida International University, Florida State University, University of Central Florida, University of Florida, The University of Tampa

STUDENTS SAY "..."

Academics

The University of South Florida is a public research university offering its students a "strong research environment, diverse and inclusive campus community, and strategic location in a rapidly growing metropolitan area." The school has three campuses across Florida, with the main one in Tampa, and popular programs in nursing, public health, and engineering. Students highlight the "job fairs, study abroad opportunities, on-campus internships, and an abundant supply of resources for almost any situation you can imagine," including "free resources [for] students, whether it be related to academia, mental health, or physical health." Administrative processes are similarly streamlined, as "the general processes of creating schedules, paying fees, and other primary obligations are made easy," and "staff respond quickly to questions." Technology-enhanced learning is highly prevalent, and "many professors use interactive platforms, simulations, and digital tools that make the material more engaging," and implement tools like "virtual labs, online practice modules, [and] collaborative digital projects" outside the classroom. USF has "impressive teachers who know how to approach a subject well," and faculty "try to get people to take an experience-based education route whenever they can,"—as illustrated by one sustainable tourism class that "made [students] be a tourist for a day and see where sustainability could be viewed." This commitment to hands-on learning extends to research as well, and USF's "collaborative, forward-thinking atmosphere where students... are encouraged to innovate, research, and solve real-world problems" reflects an institution that takes both academic rigor and student support seriously.

Campus Life

USF "has a lot of pride in their sports culture," and games "are a great environment and way to meet new people as well as feel a sense of school spirit"—there is even a new 35,000-seat stadium on the way. That energy carries over into everyday life, as "the on-campus recreation center is very popular," and many students "use the gym or intramural sports as their main break from everything else." Beyond athletics, there is "an insane amount of clubs and social events that are provided through the school itself, along with those that are student-formed and led," with enough variety to "cater to everyone's interests and make everyone feel included and at home." Meals are not hard to find, as these clubs often organize "events sharing useful information and usually providing food," and the university also throws "a lot of events hosted on campus like Bulls Nite Out, or Patio Tuesday, where students can connect and do crafts while having free food." Taken together, "life at USF feels like this mix of being busy but also finding little moments to enjoy the campus."

Student Body

The "genuinely diverse and welcoming" student body fuels an environment where students are "constantly surrounded by people with different backgrounds, perspectives, and experiences, and that makes campus life feel open and dynamic." A strong international student contingent "contributes to the richness of culture and language on campus," and students note "there are always events to celebrate each country, and a lot of inclusion and help from the university." The sizable number of STEM and pre-health students leads one student to remark that "there's a strong, focused energy of ambition as people prepare for medical school, research, and engineering careers." Yet this "super diverse, hardworking, and always on-the-go" group still takes the time to be "welcoming and inviting," with one student adding, "The campus culture itself is calm—group projects rarely turn into drama, and most people default to cooperation instead of conflict." It is a dynamic that one student captures well: "What makes USF unique is how collaborative and down-to-earth everyone is. Students genuinely want to help each other succeed."

University of South Florida

Financial Aid: 813-974-4700 • E-Mail: admissions@usf.edu • Website: www.usf.edu

THE PRINCETON REVIEW SAYS

Admissions

The school reports that its standardized testing policy for use in admission for Fall 2026 will require applicants to submit either the SAT or ACT. The Princeton Review suggests that interested applicants consult with the school for the most up-to-date standardized testing policies. *Very important factors considered include:* rigor of secondary school record, academic GPA, standardized test scores. *Other factors considered include:* class rank. High school diploma is required and GED is accepted. *Academic units required:* 4 English, 4 math, 3 science, 2 science labs, 2 language (other than English), 3 social studies, 2 academic electives. *Academic units recommended:* 4 English, 4 math, 4 science, 2 science labs, 2 language (other than English), 2 social studies, 2 academic electives.

Financial Aid

Students should submit: FAFSA. Priority filing deadline is 1/1. The Princeton Review suggests that all financial aid forms be submitted as soon as possible. *Need-based scholarships/grants offered:* Federal Pell; Federal SEOG; State scholarships/grants; Private scholarships; College/university scholarship or grant aid from institutional funds; United Negro College Fund. *Loan aid offered:* Federal Direct Subsidized Loans; Federal Direct Unsubsidized Loans; Direct PLUS loans; College/university loans from institutional funds. Admitted students will be notified of awards on a rolling basis beginning 1/6. Federal Work-Study Program available. Institutional employment available.

The Inside Word

USF keeps the admissions process streamlined and simplified. In other words, the university takes a fairly quantitative and objective approach, so expect that your GPA and standardized test scores will hold the most weight. The admissions committee will also consider the rigor of your coursework, which means applicants who have taken multiple AP, IB, honors, or AICE courses are at a definite advantage. Finally, grade trends also matter; don't panic if your high school career began inauspiciously as long as your grades steadily improved. If they declined over time, you may have to make up for that elsewhere in your application.

THE SCHOOL SAYS

From the Admissions Office

"Located in the Tampa Bay metropolitan area, USF is recognized as a top-fifty public research university. USF takes great pride in its global faculty. Professors in all academic areas are responsible for discovering new solutions to existing and emerging problems. As an undergraduate at USF, you can participate actively in the creation of the knowledge that will be taught on other college campuses for decades to come. The faculty at USF is diverse as well.

"As students begin the application process, they should become familiar with USF's admission requirements. USF used extensive institutional research to validate that the high school GPA coupled with grade trends and the rigor of student's curriculum in high school are the most critical factors in student academic success at USF. Preference in admission, therefore, is given to students who complete at least three AP or IB courses, at least two college-level courses through dual enrollment, and additional coursework in math, science or foreign language beyond minimum requirements. SAT and ACT scores, while important, are less critical in USF's admission decisions when the high school GPA and rigor of curriculum are both strong. USF does use the ACT English/writing components to make decisions, as a score of 24 is an additional indicator of potential for academic success. USF also takes into account special talents in and outside of the classroom as well as whether a student would be in the first generation of the family to attend college. With some of the best weather in the country, it's always a great time to visit USF. Campus tours, information sessions and tours of the residence halls are offered on weekdays throughout the year and on most Saturday mornings from September through April. Reservations are strongly encouraged."

SELECTIVITY

# of total applicants	71,722
% of total applicants accepted	41
% of total acceptees attending	23
# of in-state applicants	7,283
% of in-state applicants accepted	76
# of out-of-state-applicants	63,880
% of applicants accepted from out of state	36
# of international applicants	559
% of international applicants accepted	88

First-Year Profile

Testing policy	SAT or ACT Required
Range SAT composite	1160–1340
Range SAT EBRW	590–670
Range SAT math	560–670
Range ACT composite	25–29
% submitting SAT scores	78
% submitting ACT scores	22
Average HS GPA	4.1
% submitting high school GPA	100
% graduated top 10% of class	29
% graduated top 25% of class	63
% graduated top 50% of class	89
% submitting high school rank	72

Important Dates

Regular	
Apply by	5/1
Notified by	Rolling, 11/15
Nonfall registration?	Yes

FINANCIAL FACTS

Annual in-state tuition	$5,988
Annual out-of-state tuition	$18,874
Food and housing	$15,408
Books and supplies	$728
Average need-based scholarship (First-year)	$12,688 ($14,244)
% students with need rec. need-based scholarship or grant aid (First-year)	90 (93)
% students with need rec. non-need-based scholarship or grant aid (First-year)	6 (9)
% students with need rec. need-based self-help aid (First-year)	37 (32)
% UG borrow to pay for school	32
Average cumulative indebtedness	$20,774
% of students with need fully met (First-year)	15 (11)
Average % of student need met (First-year)	64 (70)

University of Southern California

University Park, Los Angeles, CA 90089 • Admissions: 213-740-1111

Survey Snapshot
Everyone loves the Trojans
Theater is popular
Alumni active on campus

RATINGS	
Quality of Life	74
Fire Safety	60*
Green	96
Academic	82
Profs Interesting	83
Profs Accessible	88
Admissions	98
Financial Aid	94

CAMPUS LIFE

Type of school	Private
Environment	Metropolis

Students

Degree-seeking undergrad enrollment	20,817
% male/female/not reported	48/51/1
% from out of state	40
% First-year from public high school	54
% First-year live on campus	97
% Ugrads live on campus	36
# of fraternities (% join)	32 (2)
# of sororities (% join)	26 (12)
% Asian	25
% Black or African American	7
% Hispanic	18
% Native American	<1
% Pacific Islander	<1
% Race and/or ethnicity unknown	2
% Two or more races	6
% White	28
% International	14
# of countries represented	114

CAMPUS MENTAL HEALTH SERVICES

Offers mental health/wellness program	Yes
Mental health training available to students	No
Employs Chief Wellness Officer	NR
Peer-to-peer mental health offerings	NR
Counseling center has guidelines or accreditation	No
Mental health/well-being courses	NR

ACADEMICS

% students returning for sophomore year	96
% students graduating within 4 years	79
Calendar	Semester
Student/faculty ratio	9:1
Most common class size 10–19.	(44%)
Most common lab/discussion size 10–19.	(40%)

Most Popular Majors
Visual and Performing Arts; Business Administration and Management; Social Sciences

STUDENTS SAY "..."

Academics

The University of Southern California boasts "a dynamic and culturally diverse campus located in a world-class city which is equally dynamic and culturally diverse." Everything related to cinema is "top notch." Among the other 150 or so majors here, programs in journalism, business, engineering, and architecture are particularly notable. The honors programs are "very good" too. One of the best perks about USC is its "large and enthusiastic alumni network." Becoming "part of the Trojan Family" is a great way to jump-start your career because USC graduates love to hire other USC graduates. "Almost everyone talks about getting job offers based solely on going to USC." "The school seems to run very smoothly, with few administrative issues ever being problematic enough to reach the awareness of the USC student community," says an international relations major. The top brass "is a bit mysterious and heavy handed," though. Also, "they milk every dime they can get from you." Academically, some students call the general education courses "a complete waste of time" and note that some professors "seem to just be there because they want to do research." Overall, though, students report professors "make the subject matter come alive" and make themselves "very available" outside the classroom. "My academic experience at USC is fabulous," gushes an aerospace engineering major. "I would not choose any other school."

Campus Life

On campus, life is "vibrant." There are more than 850 student organizations. Theatrical and musical productions are "excellent." School spirit is "extreme" and "infectious." "Football games are huge." "There is absolutely nothing that can top watching our unbelievable football team throttle the competition," says a merciless sophomore. "Drinking is a big part of the social scene" as well. "We definitely have some of the sickest parties ever," claims an impressed first-year. "Greek life is very big" and, on the weekends, a strong contingent of students "religiously" visits "The Row, the street lined with all the fraternity and sorority houses." Students also have "the sprawling city of Los Angeles as their playground." It's an "eclectic place with both high and low culture and some of the best shopping in the world." "Hollywood clubs and downtown bars" are popular destinations. Art exhibits, concerts, and "hip restaurants" are everywhere. However, "you need a car." Los Angeles traffic may be "a buzz kill," but students report that it's considerably preferable to the "absolutely terrible" public transportation system.

Student Body

USC students are "intensely ambitious," and while there are some "complete slackers," many students hit the books "harder than they let on." While some say that "the stereotypical USC student is a surfer fraternity bro or a tan, trendy sorority girl from the O.C." and note that there are "prissy Los Angeles types" and "spoiled" kids who are "extremely good looking," many insist that, "contrary to popular belief, USC has immense diversity." One first-year adds, "No one cares what your orientation is."

In some circles, "family income and the brands of clothes you wear definitely matter." And while "there are quite a few who come from mega-wealth, there are also many who are here on a great deal of financial aid." And there are "lots of nerds," too, along with a smattering of "band geeks and film freaks." Whatever your background, the one thing that unites everyone here is "tons of Trojan pride."

University of Southern California

Financial Aid: 213-740-4444 • E-Mail: admitusc@usc.edu • Website: www.usc.edu

THE PRINCETON REVIEW SAYS

Admissions

The school reports that its standardized testing policy for use in admission for Fall 2026 will require applicants to submit either the SAT or ACT. The Princeton Review suggests that interested applicants consult with the school for the most up-to-date standardized testing policies. *Very important factors considered include:* rigor of secondary school record, academic GPA, application essay, recommendation(s). *Important factors considered include:* standardized test scores, extracurricular activities, talent/ability, character/personal qualities. *Other factors considered include:* class rank, first generation, alumni/ae relation, volunteer work, work experience. High school diploma is required and GED is not accepted. *Academic units required:* 4 English, 3 math, 2 science, 2 science labs, 2 language (other than English), 2 social studies, 3 academic electives. *Academic units recommended:* 4 English, 4 math, 3 science, 3 science labs, 3 language (other than English), 3 social studies, 3 academic electives.

Financial Aid

Students should submit: FAFSA; CSS PROFILE; Business/Farm Supplement. Priority filing deadline is 2/17. The Princeton Review suggests that all financial aid forms be submitted as soon as possible. *Need-based scholarships/grants offered:* Federal Pell; Federal SEOG; State scholarships/grants; Private scholarships; College/university scholarship or grant aid from institutional funds. *Loan aid offered:* Federal Direct Subsidized Loans; Federal Direct Unsubsidized Loans; Direct PLUS loans. Admitted students will be notified of awards on or about 4/1. Federal Work-Study Program available. Institutional employment available.

The Inside Word

USC doesn't have the toughest admissions standards in California, but it's right up there. Your grades and test scores (if submitted) need to be outstanding to compete. Even if you are a borderline candidate, though, USC is certainly worth a shot. Few schools have a better alumni network and the "Trojan Family" really does create all kinds of opportunities for its members upon graduation.

THE SCHOOL SAYS

From the Admissions Office

"One of the best ways to discover if USC is right for you is to walk around campus, talk to students, and get a feel for the area both as a place to study and a place to live. If you can't visit, we hold admission information programs around the country. Watch your mailbox for an invitation, or send us an e-mail if you're interested."

SELECTIVITY

# of total applicants	80,808
% of total applicants accepted	10
% of total acceptees attending	45
# of in-state applicants	31,120
% of in-state applicants accepted	10
# of out-of-state-applicants	35,378
% of applicants accepted from out of state	10
# of international applicants	14,310
% of international applicants accepted	10

First-Year Profile

Testing policy	SAT or ACT Required
Range SAT composite	1450–1490
Range SAT EBRW	700–760
Range SAT math	740–790
Range ACT composite	32–35
% submitting SAT scores	32
% submitting ACT scores	14
Average HS GPA	3.9
% submitting high school GPA	100
% graduated top 10% of class	67
% graduated top 25% of class	91
% graduated top 50% of class	98
% submitting high school rank	30

Important Dates

Early action	
Apply by	11/1
Notified by	1/19
Regular	
Apply by	1/15
Notified by	4/1
Nonfall registration?	Yes

FINANCIAL FACTS

Annual tuition (First-year)	$60,446 ($63,468)
Food and housing	$17,434
Required fees (First-year)	$1,057 ($1,258)
Books and supplies	$1,200
Average need-based scholarship (First-year)	$48,429 ($50,322)
% students with need rec. need-based scholarship or grant aid (First-year)	90 (89)
% students with need rec. non-need-based scholarship or grant aid (First-year)	63 (81)
% students with need rec. need-based self-help aid (First-year)	92 (88)
% students rec. any financial aid (First-year)	65 (68)
% UG borrow to pay for school	62
Average cumulative indebtedness	$24,404
% of students with need fully met (First-year)	91 (88)
Average % of student need met (First-year)	92 (100)

THE UNIVERSITY OF TAMPA

401 West Kennedy Boulevard, Tampa, FL 33606-1490 • Admissions: 813-253-6211

Survey Snapshot
Students love Tampa, FL
Easy to get around campus
Recreation facilities are great

RATINGS

Quality of Life	85
Fire Safety	91
Green	60*
Academic	79
Profs Interesting	87
Profs Accessible	90
Admissions	90
Financial Aid	86

CAMPUS LIFE

Type of school	Private
Environment	Metropolis

Students

Degree-seeking undergrad enrollment	10,683
% male/female/not reported	43/57/0
% from out of state	74
% First-year live on campus	96
% Ugrads live on campus	47
# of fraternities (% join)	13 (22)
# of sororities (% join)	13 (31)
% Asian	2
% Black or African American	3
% Hispanic	15
% Native American	<1
% Pacific Islander	<1
% Race and/or ethnicity unknown	3
% Two or more races	4
% White	68
% International	5
# of countries represented	96

CAMPUS MENTAL HEALTH SERVICES

Offers mental health/wellness program	Yes
Mental health training available to students	Yes
Employs Chief Wellness Officer	Yes
Peer-to-peer mental health offerings	Yes
Counseling center has guidelines or accreditation	NR
Mental health/well-being courses	Yes, for-credit

ACADEMICS

% students returning for sophomore year	85
% students graduating within 4 years	61
% students graduating within 6 years	70
Calendar	Semester
Student/faculty ratio	17:1
Most common class size 20–29.	(46%)
Most common lab/discussion size 10–19.	(85%)

Most Popular Majors
Finance; Marketing/Marketing Management; International Business/Trade/Commerce

STUDENTS SAY "…"

Academics

The University of Tampa is a sunny, growing, global university that affords its undergraduates the choice of more than 200 areas of study, as well as "many resources and opportunities...[that provide] hands-on and experiential learning." Students rarely feel overwhelmed, and they find they "have a lot of support from staff and peers." Everyone is "eager to help and provide opportunities to make up any missed work or [to] obtain extra credit." The business and the science programs here are "amazing and what UT's forefront is about," and the campus location near downtown means "job opportunities are everywhere." The school hosts "seminars going on all the time about...jobs, social skills, law school, [and] medical school."

"Professors are very personal with students" and "are very much available for extra help or extra explanations both during and outside of class." Faculty members are often also researchers, which gives students "the opportunity to create and carry out experiments," and additionally, there are "many internship and career opportunities that are available while you are still in college." Classes often take on a non-traditional format, featuring guest lectures from professionals or graduate professors. The experiential learning offered at UT means that "undergraduate time is not wasted and is truly going to prepare students for post-graduate [life]."

Campus Life

A typical day for students "is always planned around knowing it's going to be a sunny day." The university's campus "feels like summer every day," and it's within walking distance of downtown as well as "within a five-minute drive from Hyde Park, Ybor, and Soho, which all offer a wide variety of activities." The nearby theme parks are also a fun getaway. "A lot of students come [to UT] for the warm weather, the nice campus, and the city life," says one. Many students study by the river or walk around campus with others; "hammocks are super popular" (there's even a Hammock Club), and "renting bikes and biking the Riverwalk is also a fun way to pass time." Although students typically start partying on Thursday nights, some point out that "nothing is crazy" in that regard. "Many people are involved in Greek life," and others enjoy extracurricular clubs. Of course, students are always happy to head to the beach. "There is just so much to do so that every day is not exactly the same," one student says.

Student Body

The University of Tampa is "very diverse in that people from all different cultures make up the community." There is a large international student population and the majority of students are from out of state, and "many are very outgoing and will go out of their way to be there for other students." "I've met people from Sweden, Bermuda, Nigeria, and many other nations....The diversity among the...cultures [at] UT is something," says a student. There is much promotion of diversity among students, so they are introduced to "a large variety of beliefs, backgrounds, ethnicities, and ideologies." Many who go here "are in athletics or just use the gym regularly," but they are "motivated to do well in their field of study" at the same time.

The University of Tampa

Financial Aid: 813-253-6219 • E-Mail: admissions@ut.edu • Website: www.ut.edu

THE PRINCETON REVIEW SAYS

Admissions

The school reports that its standardized testing policy for use in admission for Fall 2026 is Test Optional. The Princeton Review suggests that interested applicants consult with the school for the most up-to-date standardized testing policies. *Very important factors considered include:* rigor of secondary school record, academic GPA. *Important factors considered include:* application essay, recommendation(s), talent/ability. *Other factors considered include:* class rank, interview, extracurricular activities, character/personal qualities, first generation, alumni/ae relation, volunteer work, work experience, level of applicant's interest. High school diploma is required and GED is accepted. *Academic units required:* 4 English, 3 math, 3 science, 2 science labs, 2 language (other than English), 3 social studies, 3 academic electives.

Financial Aid

Students should submit: FAFSA. Priority filing deadline is 11/1. The Princeton Review suggests that all financial aid forms be submitted as soon as possible. *Need-based scholarships/grants offered:* Federal Pell; Federal SEOG; State scholarships/grants; Private scholarships; College/university scholarship or grant aid from institutional funds. *Loan aid offered:* Federal Direct Subsidized Loans; Federal Direct Unsubsidized Loans; Direct PLUS loans. Admitted students will be notified of awards on a rolling basis beginning 12/15. Federal Work-Study Program available. Institutional employment available.

The Inside Word

The University of Tampa accepts either the Common Application, Coalition Application, or its own application, and admissions officers look for applicants with high standardized test scores, if submitted, and an average high school GPA of 3.6. A rigorous high school course load is encouraged, as are extracurricular activities such as participation in sports, internship experience, and volunteer work.

THE SCHOOL SAYS

From the Admissions Office

"The University of Tampa is a diverse and dynamic community of students from all 50 states and most of the world's countries. Situated on a beautiful 110-acre campus along the Hillsborough River, the University's location within downtown Tampa is unmatched, providing students walking access to hundreds of internships, jobs, and research opportunities. UTampa's enrollment (11,400), coupled with its small average class size (21), provides a unique balance for students looking to have the best of both worlds professionally, socially, and academically.

"Admission is competitive, and students are encouraged to apply early. Completed applications must include a student's official high school transcript and personal essay. A letter of recommendation is not required, but strongly encouraged. A college preparatory curriculum is required, including a minimum of eighteen academic units: four English courses, three sciences (two must be laboratory sciences), three mathematics, three social studies, two foreign languages and three academic electives. Certain majors require separate departmental applications and/or requirements. Applications are reviewed holistically, examining the entire student application file, the whole person, and the context of the student's environment. While academic accomplishment plays a strong role in evaluation, we are particularly interested in student character, leadership, and community service.

"Applicants are automatically considered for invitation to the University's Honors Program, as well as merit-based scholarships. Academic challenge (number of AP, IB, AICE, or dual enrollment courses attempted) and leadership are considered in these reviews. Admitted students are eligible to apply for additional departmental and specialized scholarships after receiving their acceptance notice."

SELECTIVITY

# of total applicants	39,743
% of total applicants accepted	44
% of total acceptees attending	16
# of in-state applicants	9,899
% of in-state applicants accepted	41
# of out-of-state-applicants	27,815
% of applicants accepted from out of state	46
# of international applicants	2,029
% of international applicants accepted	32
# of early decision applicants	635
% of early decision applicants accepted	53
# offered a place on the wait list	14,200
# admitted from wait list	389

First-Year Profile

Testing policy	Test Optional
Range SAT composite	1180–1300
Range SAT EBRW	590–660
Range SAT math	570–650
Range ACT composite	25–29
% submitting SAT scores	19
% submitting ACT scores	10
Average HS GPA	3.6
% submitting high school GPA	100
% graduated top 10% of class	19
% graduated top 25% of class	50
% graduated top 50% of class	86
% submitting high school rank	29

Important Dates

Early decision	
Apply by	11/1
Notified by	12/31
Early action	
Apply by	11/15
Notified by	2/28
Regular	
Notified by	Rolling, 3/1
Nonfall registration?	Yes

FINANCIAL FACTS

Annual tuition	$34,716
Food and housing	$15,572
Required fees	$2,544
Books and supplies	$1,500
Average need-based scholarship (First-year)	$18,207 ($23,648)
% students with need rec. need-based scholarship or grant aid (First-year)	98 (98)
% students with need rec. non-need-based scholarship or grant aid (First-year)	12 (13)
% students with need rec. need-based self-help aid (First-year)	83 (83)
% students rec. any financial aid (First-year)	91 (95)
% UG borrow to pay for school	83
Average cumulative indebtedness	$33,478
% of students with need fully met (First-year)	16 (17)
Average % of student need met (First-year)	65 (75)

UNIVERSITY OF TENNESSEE—KNOXVILLE

527 Andy Holt Tower, Knoxville, TN 37996-0230 • Admissions: 865-974-1111

Survey Snapshot
Everyone loves the Volunteers
Recreation facilities are great
Students love Knoxville, TN

RATINGS

Quality of Life	81
Fire Safety	95
Green	88
Academic	79
Profs Interesting	84
Profs Accessible	89
Admissions	91
Financial Aid	82

CAMPUS LIFE

Type of school	Public
Environment	City

Students

Degree-seeking undergrad enrollment	31,923
% male/female/not reported	47/53/0
% from out of state	37
% First-year from public high school	76
% First-year live on campus	90
% Ugrads live on campus	27
# of fraternities (% join)	28 (19)
# of sororities (% join)	21 (36)
% Asian	4
% Black or African American	4
% Hispanic	7
% Native American	<1
% Pacific Islander	0
% Race and/or ethnicity unknown	1
% Two or more races	5
% White	77
% International	1
# of countries represented	61

CAMPUS MENTAL HEALTH SERVICES

Offers mental health/wellness program	Yes
Mental health training available to students	Yes
Employs Chief Wellness Officer	Yes
Peer-to-peer mental health offerings	Yes
Counseling center has guidelines or accreditation	Yes
Mental health/well-being courses	Yes, for-credit

ACADEMICS

% students returning for sophomore year	92
% students graduating within 4 years	58
% students graduating within 6 years	75
Calendar	Semester
Student/faculty ratio	18:1
Most common class size 20–29.	(34%)

Most Popular Majors

Biology/Biological Sciences; Finance; Logistics, Materials, and Supply Chain Management

Applicants Also Look At

Middle Tennessee State University, The University of Alabama—Tuscaloosa, University of Georgia, University of South Carolina—Columbia, University of Tennessee—Chattanooga

STUDENTS SAY "..."

Academics

At the flagship University of Tennessee—Knoxville, students can test the variables of their education and explore the unknowns. Local affiliations, as with the Oak Ridge National Laboratory, are just one example of the "extensive opportunities for undergraduate research" that let students—especially those in engineering and life sciences—actively experiment with "really cool resources" and this availability is UTK's "biggest hidden treasure." Students also appreciate how UTK helps them zero in on their interests; though it's a moderately large school, "it is easy to make it a small school by focusing on a certain field" in which they can get all the attention they crave.

These strong academics owe a lot to the "outstanding, passionate, intelligent" professors, who are "compelling and excited to teach," though a few students note this depends on your department and recommend the school's honors program. Ultimately, students describe how professors " have helped me get published, navigate my academic program, and get experiences that I otherwise may not have had." As a backstop, there are also "countless centers to help students succeed and feel at home," like the Academic Success Center, which provides coaching and leadership workshops, academic strategies, and "true feedback" that "made me want to broaden my education." Whether inspiration is found in the woods, lab, or seminar, students know their "creativity is encouraged and rewarded."

Campus Life

UTK students contend that their "school spirit is unmatched." Decked in orange, they cheer with pride for their football team on game day: "The energy the stadiums and teams bring to campus is unparalleled," and the prestigious Pride of the Southland Marching Band dazzles fans at half-time. Even those that are "not a huge fan of sports" find, "You can truly feel the energy not just in the stadiums but also just walking through campus on a normal day."

Participation is high in clubs and intramural sports, and there are "constantly free events for students that exceed expectations," like shows and guest lectures. The campus is "quite walkable," so there's no reason not to partake in the various activities, whether that's hanging on the lawns, heading to the Student Union, or utilizing the rock climbing, tennis, and yoga of the athletic facilities. Those willing to go a bit further can sign up for the Outdoor Pursuits program or venture across the Tennessee river to hike the many trails at Urban Wilderness. Despite being a dry campus, students do note that there is a "Knoxville party scene" and Greek life, as well as a contingent of those who like "exploring downtown or having a nice night in."

Student Body

The UTK student body is a diverse group of people waiting to be friends with you. Self-described as outgoing and "remarkably kind," students seek out "stimulating conversations" with peers whose backgrounds contrast in culture, birthplace, sexual orientation and religious beliefs. While a number of students find pride in being a "progressive" University—asserting that "UTK is one of the most liberal schools in the South"—a few find things "very Southern, Christian, and conservative." Still, the spirit of UTK is strong; Vols take seriously their commitment to improving their community—volunteering for local organizations like Habitat for Humanity—and working actively to understand and support their classmates: "I feel it is vital to learn the perspectives of my peers," and to "always [be] willing to lend a helping hand." Above all, students describe the importance of safe spaces in queer, cultural, and religious organizations: "We look out for each other." With over 30,000 undergraduates, students can find the company that "does their best to make you feel like you belong."

University of Tennessee—Knoxville

Financial Aid: 865-974-1111 • E-Mail: admissions@utk.edu • Website: www.utk.edu

THE PRINCETON REVIEW SAYS

Admissions

The school reports that its standardized testing policy for use in admission for Fall 2026 will require applicants to submit either the SAT or ACT. The Princeton Review suggests that interested applicants consult with the school for the most up-to-date standardized testing policies. *Very important factors considered include:* rigor of secondary school record, academic GPA, standardized test scores, application essay, state residency. *Important factors considered include:* extracurricular activities, talent/ability, character/personal qualities, volunteer work, work experience. *Other factors considered include:* class rank, recommendation(s). High school diploma is required and GED is accepted. *Academic units recommended:* 4 English, 4 math, 3 science, 3 science labs, 2 language (other than English), 1 social studies, 1 history, 1 visual/performing arts.

Financial Aid

Students should submit: FAFSA. The Princeton Review suggests that all financial aid forms be submitted as soon as possible. *Need-based scholarships/grants offered:* Federal Pell; Federal SEOG; State scholarships/grants; Private scholarships; College/university scholarship or grant aid from institutional funds. *Loan aid offered:* Federal Direct Subsidized Loans; Federal Direct Unsubsidized Loans; Direct PLUS loans; State Loans; College/university loans from institutional funds. Admitted students will be notified of awards on a rolling basis. Federal Work-Study Program available.

The Inside Word

The University of Tennessee—Knoxville is looking for bright, competitive students to join the school's ranks. To find them, the school takes a holistic approach to the admissions process. UT considers everything from standardized test scores, rigor of high school curriculum, and overall GPA to personal statements and community engagement and leadership. Finally, certain colleges within the university have specific requirements. For example, applicants must audition for the Natalie L. Haslam College of Music and applicants to the Tickle College of Engineering must meet minimum academic requirements in math and science either through coursework or standardized test scores.

THE SCHOOL SAYS

From the Admissions Office

"The University of Tennessee, Knoxville, offers students the great program diversity of a major university, opportunities for research or original creative work in every degree program, and a welcoming campus environment. Twelve colleges offer more than 360 undergraduate programs of study to students from all fifty states and 59 foreign countries, Honors and Scholars Programs provide students with dynamic experiences through unique academic opportunities, interactive and interdisciplinary seminars, and hands-on activities. Students from all majors enjoy an intimate college experience that integrates academic achievement and student life within a culture of intellectual and civic engagement. More than 400 clubs and organizations on campus allow students to further individualize their college experience in service, recreation, academics, and professional development. UT blends more than 225 years of history, tradition, and 'Volunteer Spirit' with the latest technology and innovation."

SELECTIVITY

# of total applicants	53,841
% of total applicants accepted	44
% of total acceptees attending	30
# of in-state applicants	11,980
% of in-state applicants accepted	73
# of out-of-state-applicants	41,408
% of applicants accepted from out of state	35
# of international applicants	452
% of international applicants accepted	47
# offered a place on the wait list	11,980
# admitted from wait list	134

First-Year Profile

Testing policy	SAT or ACT Required
Range SAT composite	1280–1380
Range SAT EBRW	640–700
Range SAT math	630–700
Range ACT composite	26–31
% submitting SAT scores	25
% submitting ACT scores	80
Average HS GPA	4.3
% submitting high school GPA	100
% graduated top 10% of class	40
% graduated top 25% of class	70
% graduated top 50% of class	93
% submitting high school rank	25

Important Dates

Early action	
Apply by	11/1
Notified by	12/15
Regular	
Apply by	12/15
Notified by	3/9
Nonfall registration?	Yes

FINANCIAL FACTS

Annual in-state tuition	$11,560
Annual out-of-state tuition	$30,704
Food and housing	$13,594
Required fees	$2,252
Books and supplies	$1,598
Average need-based scholarship (First-year)	$13,396 ($15,874)
% students with need rec. need-based scholarship or grant aid (First-year)	91 (98)
% students with need rec. non-need-based scholarship or grant aid (First-year)	15 (19)
% students with need rec. need-based self-help aid (First-year)	38 (34)
% students rec. any financial aid (First-year)	91 (83)
% UG borrow to pay for school	40
Average cumulative indebtedness	$34,133
% of students with need fully met (First-year)	15 (18)
Average % of student need met (First-year)	50 (59)

UNIVERSITY OF TEXAS AT AUSTIN

110 Inner Campus Dr, Austin, TX 78705 • Admissions: 512-475-7399

Survey Snapshot
Students love Austin, TX
Everyone loves the Longhorns
Alumni active on campus

RATINGS

Quality of Life	**81**
Fire Safety	**84**
Green	**95**
Academic	**78**
Profs Interesting	**87**
Profs Accessible	**88**
Admissions	**85**
Financial Aid	**84**

CAMPUS LIFE

Type of school	Public
Environment	Metropolis

Students

Degree-seeking undergrad enrollment	43,778
% male/female/not reported	42/58/<1
% from out of state	6
% First-year live on campus	61
% Ugrads live on campus	17
# of fraternities (% join)	32 (13)
# of sororities (% join)	30 (17)
% Asian	26
% Black or African American	5
% Hispanic	29
% Native American	<1
% Pacific Islander	<1
% Race and/or ethnicity unknown	3
% Two or more races	4
% White	29
% International	4
# of countries represented	99

CAMPUS MENTAL HEALTH SERVICES

Offers mental health/wellness program	NR
Mental health training available to students	NR
Employs Chief Wellness Officer	NR
Peer-to-peer mental health offerings	NR
Counseling center has guidelines or accreditation	NR
Mental health/well-being courses	NR

ACADEMICS

% students returning for sophomore year	97
% students graduating within 4 years	74
% students graduating within 6 years	89
Calendar	Semester
Student/faculty ratio	18:1
Most common class size 10–19.	(28%)
Most common lab/discussion size 10–19.	(44%)

Most Popular Majors

Biology/Biological Sciences; Business Administration and Management

STUDENTS SAY "…"

Academics

Students at the University of Texas at Austin, often referred to as the "Harvard of the South," proudly say that the school offers them "an infinite number of possibilities." Known as Longhorns, these students highlight the extensive resources available through the university's 16 career centers. One astonished student lists their discoveries: "There is free tutoring, gym membership, professional counseling, doctor visits, legal help, career advising, and many distinguished outside speakers." On top of that, students in the College of Natural Sciences can utilize the Freshman Research Initiative to fund and promote their projects, and thousands of Longhorns make the most of study, intern, and research abroad opportunities each year. With over 40,000 undergrads on campus, UT Austin is "a huge school and has a lot to offer," including "experts in every field you can imagine"—to be precise, over 3,000 faculty and 156 degree programs. One student mentions that they had worried that the school's size would make it hard to connect with faculty, only to meet "professors who want to know you and [who] provide opportunities to get to know them." A few students acknowledge the quality of their instructors "can vary greatly," but the overall consensus is that "the class offerings at UT are generally vast and diverse." By and large, UT Austin offers "everything you want in a college: academics, athletics, social life, location."

Campus Life

Life at UT Austin is "very relaxed" and "students and faculty frequently picnic all over campus." As one student puts it, "It's truly what you see in one of those cheesy brochures with everyone studying and smiling." (During finals, students acknowledge there's more of a "an over-caffeinated, glazed-eye look.") Longhorns love that there are "festivals or fairs of some kind going on downtown all the time," such as South by Southwest and the Austin City Limits Music Festival. On a regular basis, socially minded Longhorns enjoy "the infamous 6th Street with nightlife that dies down only after the bars close." Students enthuse about the "many hike-and-bike trails and fitness organizations" on and near campus. "It's possible for students to train for marathons, half marathons, and triathlons while in school." Students also rave about Barton Springs, "a natural spring that is very popular year-round." One student explains what they like about UT Austin: "On any given Saturday you will find students throwing a football, going for a run, biking through the hills, kayaking in the river, having a late lunch at one of Austin's great restaurants, or just sleeping in."

Student Body

Students note that there are so many students at UT Austin that there's no typical Longhorn: "Everyone at Texas is different! When you walk across campus, you see every type of ethnicity." While there is a "huge Greek life at UT," they are "hardly the majority, since UT is actually made [up] of more 'atypical' people than most other schools." According to some, it's a positive, to "see someone dressed in a way you've never seen before….That's Austin!" As one student says, "Everyone here has their own niche, and I could not think of any type of individual who would not be able to find one of their own." Another student concurs, saying, "Everyone seems to get along. The different types of students just blend in together."

University of Texas at Austin

Financial Aid: 512-232-6988 • E-Mail: admissions@austin.utexas.edu • Website: www.utexas.edu

THE PRINCETON REVIEW SAYS

Admissions

The school reports that its standardized testing policy for use in admission for Fall 2026 will require applicants to submit either the SAT or ACT. The Princeton Review suggests that interested applicants consult with the school for the most up-to-date standardized testing policies. *Other factors considered include:* rigor of secondary school record, class rank, academic GPA, standardized test scores, application essay, recommendation(s), extracurricular activities, talent/ability, character/personal qualities, first generation, geographical residence, state residency. High school diploma is required and GED is accepted. *Academic units required:* 3 math, 2 science, 2 language (other than English), 3 social studies. *Academic units recommended:* 4 math, 4 science, 4 social studies, 6 academic electives, 1 visual/performing arts.

Financial Aid

Students should submit: FAFSA; Institution's own financial aid form. The Princeton Review suggests that all financial aid forms be submitted as soon as possible. *Need-based scholarships/grants offered:* Federal Pell; Federal SEOG; State scholarships/grants; Private scholarships; College/university scholarship or grant aid from institutional funds. *Loan aid offered:* Federal Direct Subsidized Loans; Federal Direct Unsubsidized Loans; Direct PLUS loans; State Loans. Admitted students will be notified of awards on a rolling basis beginning 3/15. Federal Work-Study Program available. Institutional employment available.

The Inside Word

The university is required to automatically admit enough Texas applicants to fill 75 percent of available spaces set aside for students from Texas. As a result, Texan students in the top 5 percent of their high school class are guaranteed admission. Applicants who have completed a non-traditional secondary education who submit an SAT composite score of 1570 or higher or an ACT composite score of 36 or higher will also receive automatic admission. All students, including those eligible for automatic admission, should submit the strongest possible application to increase the likelihood of admission to the university and to their requested major. Admission is competitive, and space for out-of-state students is limited, meaning they'll have even higher hurdles to clear.

THE SCHOOL SAYS

From the Admissions Office

"Like the state it calls home, The University of Texas at Austin is a bold, ambitious leader committed to innovative learning and research, and encourages creativity, analysis, and critical thinking. Ranked among the top research universities in the country, UT Austin is home to over 53,000 students and more than 3,800 teaching faculty. Through more than 170 undergraduate fields of study across 19 colleges and schools (and hundreds of study abroad programs, comprehensive student services, exceptional cultural centers, and more than 1,000 student organizations), you will find an engaging, diverse, multi-dimensional experience that will unlock your future potential and prepare you to make an impact on the world. Our students enjoy a vibrant college experience on our urban campus in the heart of the city of Austin—consistently recognized as the nation's best place to live—and an HQ for creatives and entrepreneurs. Longhorns are part of a strong community, and inherit a storied history and rich tradition of success that's as evident in our SEC athletics as it is in the classroom or laboratory. Almost half a million alumni lead worldwide industries from technology to politics to entertainment, and provide a robust network of UT connections around the world and in every field. Together, we're working to make the world a better place, united by the belief that creating and sharing knowledge can transform society. It's why we say 'What starts here changes the world.'"

SELECTIVITY

# of total applicants	90,690
% of total applicants accepted	22
% of total acceptees attending	49
# of in-state applicants	46,879
% of in-state applicants accepted	36
# of out-of-state-applicants	35,268
% of applicants accepted from out of state	8
# of international applicants	8,543
% of international applicants accepted	8

First-Year Profile

Testing policy	SAT or ACT Required

Important Dates

Early action	
Apply by	10/15
Notified by	1/15
Regular	
Apply by	12/1
Notified by	2/15
Nonfall registration?	Yes

FINANCIAL FACTS

Annual in-state tuition	$11,656
Annual out-of-state tuition	$44,816
Food and housing	$15,420
Books and supplies	$720
Average need-based scholarship (First-year)	$16,710 ($20,052)
% students with need rec. need-based scholarship or grant aid (First-year)	92 (92)
% students with need rec. non-need-based scholarship or grant aid (First-year)	<1 (<1)
% students with need rec. need-based self-help aid (First-year)	50 (43)
% students rec. any financial aid (First-year)	41 (43)
% UG borrow to pay for school	36
Average cumulative indebtedness	$20,429
% of students with need fully met (First-year)	7 (9)
Average % of student need met (First-year)	65 (71)

THE UNIVERSITY OF TEXAS AT DALLAS

800 West Campbell Road, Richardson, TX 75080 • Admissions: 972-883-2270

Survey Snapshot
Classroom facilities are great
Lab facilities are great
Career services are great

RATINGS

Quality of Life	82
Fire Safety	89
Green	91
Academic	77
Profs Interesting	88
Profs Accessible	89
Admissions	87
Financial Aid	84

CAMPUS LIFE

Type of school	Public
Environment	Metropolis

Students

Degree-seeking undergrad enrollment	22,869
% male/female/not reported	56/44/0
% from out of state	5
% First-year from public high school	92
% First-year live on campus	43
% Ugrads live on campus	22
# of fraternities (% join)	12 (3)
# of sororities (% join)	12 (3)
% Asian	42
% Black or African American	7
% Hispanic	19
% Native American	<1
% Pacific Islander	<1
% Race and/or ethnicity unknown	4
% Two or more races	4
% White	20
% International	5
# of countries represented	61

CAMPUS MENTAL HEALTH SERVICES

Offers mental health/wellness program	Yes
Mental health training available to students	No
Employs Chief Wellness Officer	NR
Peer-to-peer mental health offerings	NR
Counseling center has guidelines or accreditation	No
Mental health/well-being courses	NR

ACADEMICS

% students returning for sophomore year	90
% students graduating within 4 years	63
% students graduating within 6 years	79
Calendar	Semester
Student/faculty ratio	23:1
Most common class size 50–59.	(26%)
Most common lab/discussion size 20–29.	(62%)

Most Popular Majors

Computer and Information Sciences; Biology/Biological Sciences; Information Technology

Applicants Often Prefer

Texas A&M University—College Station, University of Texas at Austin

Applicants Sometimes Prefer

Texas Tech University, Texas Woman's University, University of Houston, University of North Texas UNT, University of Oklahoma, The University of Texas at Arlington

Applicants Rarely Prefer

Baylor University, University of Arkansas—Fayetteville

STUDENTS SAY "..."

Academics

The University of Texas at Dallas "is excellent at preparing students for their future careers," especially in any of the many degree programs that are related to technology: "Our school is very tech-savvy." Students appreciate that "there's always a research team, project, or development happening in [one of] the departments," which helps to maintain a "diverse learning culture." There's also "great guidance surrounding pre-professional careers," with professors praised as "great and well-respected" and able to "give all required resources to students in order to excel." Academics are by and large "very rigorous" and students should expect to "spend many hours on their lectures or doing homework" but are backed up by "very helpful" assistance in finding tutors. The administration also takes "great measures to make sure that students know that they are supported academically, emotionally, and mentally," and the campus itself provides "so much space to study or do whatever you need to." Overall, students love attending a school that offers "great academics and amazingly qualified professors and research opportunities."

Campus Life

When students aren't hard at work, they've got the choice of over 400 on-campus organizations, from 26 fraternities and sororities to "career-focused and community service clubs." Gaming is an emergent area of campus life, and esports enthusiasts are celebrated alongside other intercollegiate athletes. The Student Services Building features a gaming wall that's popular with Xbox players on campus, and there's an orchestra ensemble dedicated to playing anime scores. Students looking for fresh air enjoy the hammocks and disc golf course available through University Recreation. Other favorite activities include "sand volleyball, walks around campus with friends, [and] basketball." Because the UTD campus is connected to the greater Dallas area by rapid transit, students can also spend their free time following one of the seven professional local sports teams or enjoying the Dallas World Aquarium and Dallas Zoo at discounted prices. One key to understanding UTD life is that there's "no judgment" on how you spend your time "because there is every type of group of people at UTD."

Student Body

UTD students, affectionately referred to as Comets, hail from over 130 countries around the globe and all over the United States. This is seen as an asset, as it unites all those "very studious" and "academically focused" students and helps them "come together in a great way when it comes to research and developing new tech." As one student puts it, there's a "rich cultural diversity and academics that foster[s] a love for innovation through empathy," though others note that some peers "tend to be career and academic focused over being caring about campus social life." Respondents suggest that there's perhaps a "limited amount of 'jock culture' and traditional sports on campus," and that it's not uncommon to find that a new friend "probably enjoys games and anime." Overall, these students are "meme-heavy, but striving for good grades" and "you can really find or make your group here; you just have to seek it out."

THE UNIVERSITY OF TEXAS AT DALLAS

Financial Aid: 972-883-2941 • E-Mail: admission@utdallas.edu • Website: www.utdallas.edu

THE PRINCETON REVIEW SAYS

Admissions

The school reports that its standardized testing policy for use in admission for Fall 2026 is Test Optional. The Princeton Review suggests that interested applicants consult with the school for the most up-to-date standardized testing policies. *Very important factors considered include:* rigor of secondary school record, academic GPA. *Important factors considered include:* standardized test scores, application essay, recommendation(s), extracurricular activities, character/personal qualities, volunteer work, work experience. *Other factors considered include:* class rank, talent/ability, level of applicant's interest. High school diploma is required and GED is accepted. *Academic units required:* 4 English, 4 math, 4 science, 3 science labs, 2 language (other than English), 3 social studies, 1 visual/performing arts. *Academic units recommended:* 4 English, 4 math, 4 science, 3 science labs, 3 language (other than English), 4 social studies, 1 visual/performing arts.

Financial Aid

Students should submit: FAFSA. Priority filing deadline is 3/15. The Princeton Review suggests that all financial aid forms be submitted as soon as possible. *Need-based scholarships/grants offered:* Federal Pell; Federal SEOG; State scholarships/grants; Private scholarships; College/university scholarship or grant aid from institutional funds. *Loan aid offered:* Federal Direct Subsidized Loans; Federal Direct Unsubsidized Loans; Direct PLUS loans; State Loans; College/university loans from institutional funds. Admitted students will be notified of awards on a rolling basis. Federal Work-Study Program available. Institutional employment available.

The Inside Word

UT Dallas is a by-the-numbers school for the majority of its admitted students. Texas law requires that prospective students are automatically admitted to the university as first-years if they graduate in the top 10% of their class from an accredited Texas high school and successfully earn the Distinguished Level of Achievement. Students outside of the top 10 percent are subject to a more holistic review based on individual strengths.

THE SCHOOL SAYS

From the Admissions Office

"The University of Texas at Dallas is a leading research institution in Texas. It provides some of the state's most-lauded business, engineering and science programs, as well as innovative and traditional programs in the liberal arts, and offers diverse educational paths through 152 academic programs across seven schools.

"UTD's trajectory as one of the fastest-growing public universities in the U.S. is fueled by its bright students, faculty, staff, alumni and the stature of its programs. Designated as an "R1" institution—a classification reserved for doctoral universities with "very high research activity" by the Carnegie Commission on Higher Education, UTD is part of The University of Texas System and is aligned strategically with other institutions, corporations and nonprofits, including UT Southwestern Medical Center and prestigious universities worldwide. UTD is home to nearly 30,000 students, including more than 5,500 international students from 94 countries. This diverse student body benefits from a residential campus known for academic rigor, career focus and social opportunities.

"In addition to an array of nationally ranked programs, UTD is a campus enriched by prestigious art collections, service-learning opportunities, and NCAA Division II athletics. Its students have access to over 400 student organizations, various intramural sports, and nearly 30 club sports. At graduation, UTD students walk the stage ready for the next phase of life. Programs like UTDesign, UTDsolv, UTDiscovery, UTeach Dallas, and the Teacher Development Center provide students with the opportunity to stretch their creativity and work on projects with companies and other organizations before they leave the university."

SELECTIVITY

# of total applicants	36,353
% of total applicants accepted	69
% of total acceptees attending	20
# of in-state applicants	28,758
% of in-state applicants accepted	71
# of out-of-state-applicants	3,760
% of applicants accepted from out of state	68
# of international applicants	3,835
% of international applicants accepted	54

First-Year Profile

Testing policy	Test Optional
Range SAT composite	1170–1390
Range SAT EBRW	580–690
Range SAT math	580–710
Range ACT composite	24–32
% submitting SAT scores	79
% submitting ACT scores	12
% graduated top 10% of class	38
% graduated top 25% of class	70
% graduated top 50% of class	94
% submitting high school rank	57

Important Dates

Regular	
Apply by	6/1
Nonfall registration?	Yes

FINANCIAL FACTS*

Annual in-state tuition	$10,640
Annual out-of-state tuition	$36,140
Food and housing	$15,125
Required fees	$4,024
Books and supplies	$1,200
Average need-based scholarship (First-year)	$12,144 ($13,523)
% students with need rec. need-based scholarship or grant aid (First-year)	86 (85)
% students with need rec. non-need-based scholarship or grant aid (First-year)	4 (8)
% students with need rec. need-based self-help aid (First-year)	90 (88)
% students rec. any financial aid (First-year)	65 (73)
% UG borrow to pay for school	31
Average cumulative indebtedness	$24,908
% of students with need fully met (First-year)	12 (19)
Average % of student need met (First-year)	64 (69)

* Most recently reported data at time of printing. Scan the QR code to find the latest updates.

The University of Tulsa

800 South Tucker Drive, Tulsa, OK 74104 • Admissions: 918-631-2307

Survey Snapshot
Students are happy
Intramural sports are popular
Great library

RATINGS

Quality of Life	88
Fire Safety	89
Green	60*
Academic	82
Profs Interesting	88
Profs Accessible	92
Admissions	90
Financial Aid	89

CAMPUS LIFE

Type of school	Private
Affiliation	Presbyterian
Environment	Metropolis

Students

Degree-seeking undergrad enrollment	2,986
% male/female/not reported	48/52/0
% from out of state	41
% First-year live on campus	78
% Ugrads live on campus	63
# of fraternities (% join)	7 (22)
# of sororities (% join)	9 (19)
% Asian	8
% Black or African American	7
% Hispanic	12
% Native American	3
% Pacific Islander	<1
% Race and/or ethnicity unknown	4
% Two or more races	10
% White	50
% International	5
# of countries represented	44

CAMPUS MENTAL HEALTH SERVICES

Offers mental health/wellness program	Yes
Mental health training available to students	No
Employs Chief Wellness Officer	NR
Peer-to-peer mental health offerings	NR
Counseling center has guidelines or accreditation	No
Mental health/well-being courses	NR

ACADEMICS

% students returning for sophomore year	91
% students graduating within 4 years	56
% students graduating within 6 years	69
Calendar	Semester
Student/faculty ratio	11:1
Most common class size 20–29.	(31%)
Most common lab/discussion size 20–29.	(38%)

Most Popular Majors
Computer Science; Psychology; Business Statistics

Applicants Often Prefer
Rice University, Texas A&M University—College Station, University of Texas at Austin, Washington University in St. Louis

Applicants Sometimes Prefer
Baylor University, Colorado School of Mines, Oklahoma State University, Southern Methodist University, Texas Christian University, Trinity University, University of Arkansas—Fayetteville, University of Oklahoma

Applicants Rarely Prefer
Creighton University, University of Kansas, University of Missouri

STUDENTS SAY "…"

Academics

The many students at The University of Tulsa, a small private research university, find it to be the total package. After all, it combines "the friendly environment of a smaller university and the academic, employment, extracurricular, and service opportunities of a larger university." It also does a tremendous job of fostering an atmosphere that's "conducive to collaboration and growth." In general, students describe the academics as "challenging." And a number of undergrads emphasize TU's "strong engineering school," which thoroughly prepares students for "work[ing] in the industry, especially [within the] energy [sector]." All undergraduates, no matter their major, benefit from "small class sizes." In turn, this affords students the opportunity to build "close relationships...with [the] faculty," full of professors who "are great resources for [both] internships and real-world advice." Aside from being great contacts, Tulsa professors are "very knowledgeable and passionate about their subjects." They also "make their students a priority" and they're "very accessible outside of class." As one student expounds, "Many of my professors frequently invite students to their office hours and remind us of their availability.... [It's clear they] care about my academic experience, career readiness, and about me as a person."

Campus Life

While University of Tulsa undergrads say that "a good portion of [their] time is...spent studying," there's still plenty of fun to be had outside the confines of the library and/or classroom. For example, "there are a ton of active student organizations" and you can always find "an event to attend or free food to eat." Popular options include "homecoming... dog petting days, bowling, [and] carnivals." One excited student adds, "TU is good about providing events bi-weekly, like s'mores at the Student Union, an outdoor movie, or a play." If the Greek scene interests you, you'll be happy to learn that "the fraternities on campus...usually [host] events Thursday through Saturday." A number of undergrads also love to relax on the "many [beautiful] lawns" on the TU campus. And you're sure to find a handful of students playing any number of games, from "baseball [and] football [to] Capture the Flag." If you prefer your athletics to be a little more structured, there's also a "very popular...intramural sports [program]." As for hometown Tulsa, "there's a great food, music, and art culture in downtown Tulsa so you can always find something to do." And we're told that "the restaurants here are awesome, small and large concert venues attract all types of artists, and there all festivals of all types throughout the year."

Student Body

The student body at The University of Tulsa is comprised of "friendly" and "inclusive" individuals. Of course, it probably helps that the school is home to "a diverse group of students from various economic, academic, religious, political, and ethnic backgrounds." Indeed, "Division I athletes, international students, military veterans, sorority sisters, petroleum engineering majors, and piano performance majors represent a few of the many groups woven together on TU's campus." Undergrads are "committed to doing well in school." As one student explains, "We are all here to do well, but we are here to do well together." Undergrads also describe their classmates as "smart," "engaging," and "extremely focused on their studies." And most "are incredibly involved at TU, whether it be in Greek life, athletics, music, [or] research." Additionally, a lot of "TU students look for opportunities to challenge themselves and impact their community." One thrilled undergrad sums up the campus experience: "TU honestly feels like a small-town community. Everyone is so friendly and kind, and it's like having one giant family."

THE UNIVERSITY OF TULSA

Financial Aid: 918-631-2526 • E-Mail: admission@utulsa.edu • Website: utulsa.edu

THE PRINCETON REVIEW SAYS

Admissions

The school reports that its standardized testing policy for use in admission for Fall 2026 is Test Optional. The Princeton Review suggests that interested applicants consult with the school for the most up-to-date standardized testing policies. *Very important factors considered include:* rigor of secondary school record, academic GPA, standardized test scores, interview, talent/ability, level of applicant's interest. *Important factors considered include:* application essay, recommendation(s), extracurricular activities, character/personal qualities. *Other factors considered include:* class rank, first generation, alumni/ae relation, geographical residence, state residency, volunteer work, work experience. High school diploma is required and GED is accepted. *Academic units recommended:* 4 English, 4 math, 3 science, 3 science labs, 2 language (other than English), 3 social studies.

Financial Aid

Priority filing deadline is 2/1. The Princeton Review suggests that all financial aid forms be submitted as soon as possible. *Need-based scholarships/grants offered:* Federal Pell; Federal SEOG; State scholarships/grants; Private scholarships; College/university scholarship or grant aid from institutional funds. *Loan aid offered:* Federal Direct Subsidized Loans; Federal Direct Unsubsidized Loans; Direct PLUS loans. Admitted students will be notified of awards on a rolling basis beginning 2/1. Federal Work-Study Program available. Institutional employment available.

The Inside Word

The admissions process at TU is fairly straightforward. For starters, the school closely evaluates high school transcripts and standardized test scores (if submitted). Candidates are strongly encouraged to sit for an admissions interview, as well. It's also important to note that The University of Tulsa evaluates applications on a rolling basis. The earlier you apply, the more slots will be available. In fact, it's recommended that students submit their applications by January 15 for full consideration for scholarships.

THE SCHOOL SAYS

From the Admissions Office

"The University of Tulsa is a private university with a comprehensive scope. Students choose from more than fifty majors offered through four undergraduate colleges—Kendall College of Arts and Sciences, Collins College of Business, Oxley College of Health and Natural Sciences, and the College of Engineering and Computer Science. Curricula can be customized with collaborative and interdisciplinary research, joint undergraduate and graduate programs, the Global Scholars program and an honors program. Professors are equally committed to teaching undergraduates and to scholarly research. This results in extraordinary individual achievement, resulting in the nationally competitive scholarships students have won since 1995: sixty-five Goldwaters, seventy National Science Foundation scholars, twelve Trumans, nine Department of Defense scholars, twenty-two Fulbrights, eleven Phi Kappa Phi, nine Udalls, five British Marshalls, and three Rhodes Scholars, including one in 2017. In the past decade, over 1,000,000 square feet of facilities have been added. These include athletic venues, additional apartments, fitness center, Legal Information Center, library expansion and renovation, two new engineering buildings and a new performing arts center. Over 200 registered clubs and interest groups, including intramural and recreational sports teams exist along with seven fraternities and nine sororities. The 8,300 seat Reynolds Center is home to the men's and women's basketball teams, campus events, and concerts. A forty-acre sports complex includes the fitness center and indoor tennis center. An outdoor freshman orientation program launches an entire first-year experience dedicated to developing students' full potential."

SELECTIVITY

# of total applicants	3,517
% of total applicants accepted	75
% of total acceptees attending	25
# of in-state applicants	1,332
% of in-state applicants accepted	76
# of out-of-state-applicants	1,898
% of applicants accepted from out of state	73
# of international applicants	286
% of international applicants accepted	78

First-Year Profile

Testing policy	Test Optional
Range SAT composite	1250–1490
Range SAT EBRW	650–750
Range SAT math	620–750
Range ACT composite	25–33
% submitting SAT scores	17
% submitting ACT scores	56
Average HS GPA	3.7
% submitting high school GPA	97
% graduated top 10% of class	57
% graduated top 25% of class	80
% graduated top 50% of class	95
% submitting high school rank	49

Important Dates

Early action	
Apply by	2/1
Notified by	2/15
Regular	
Apply by	8/15
Notified by	Rolling, 12/15
Nonfall registration?	Yes

FINANCIAL FACTS

Annual tuition	$52,790
Food and housing	$15,458
Required fees (First-year)	$1,320 ($1,882)
Books and supplies	$600
Average need-based scholarship (First-year)	$31,600 ($32,503)
% students with need rec. need-based scholarship or grant aid (First-year)	87 (94)
% students with need rec. non-need-based scholarship or grant aid (First-year)	73 (77)
% students with need rec. need-based self-help aid (First-year)	49 (42)
% students rec. any financial aid (First-year)	54 (63)
% UG borrow to pay for school	49
Average cumulative indebtedness	$28,438
% of students with need fully met (First-year)	32 (44)
Average % of student need met (First-year)	77 (84)

University of Utah

201 Presidents Circle, Salt Lake City, UT 84112 • Admissions: 801-581-8761

Survey Snapshot
Students take advantage of the outdoors
Great library
Students love Salt Lake City, UT

RATINGS	
Quality of Life	**88**
Fire Safety	**96**
Green	**93**
Academic	**80**
Profs Interesting	**90**
Profs Accessible	**87**
Admissions	**85**
Financial Aid	**82**

CAMPUS LIFE

Type of school	Public
Environment	Metropolis

Students

Degree-seeking undergrad enrollment	28,418
% male/female/not reported	53/47/0
% from out of state	39
% First-year from public high school	91
% First-year live on campus	65
% Ugrads live on campus	17
# of fraternities (% join)	12 (8)
# of sororities (% join)	7 (14)
% Asian	6
% Black or African American	1
% Hispanic	14
% Native American	<1
% Pacific Islander	<1
% Race and/or ethnicity unknown	2
% Two or more races	6
% White	64
% International	6
# of countries represented	84

CAMPUS MENTAL HEALTH SERVICES

Offers mental health/wellness program	Yes
Mental health training available to students	Yes
Employs Chief Wellness Officer	Yes
Peer-to-peer mental health offerings	Yes
Counseling center has guidelines or accreditation	Yes
Mental health/well-being courses	No

ACADEMICS

% students returning for sophomore year	86
% students graduating within 4 years	39
% students graduating within 6 years	66
Calendar	Semester
Student/faculty ratio	19:1
Most common class size 10–19.	(25%)
Most common lab/discussion size 20–29.	(47%)

Applicants Often Prefer
Brigham Young University (UT), Salt Lake Community College, University of Colorado Boulder

Applicants Sometimes Prefer
University of Oregon, Utah State University, Utah Valley University

Applicants Rarely Prefer
California Polytechnic State University—San Luis Obispo, San Diego State University

STUDENTS SAY "..."

Academics

Nestled amid Salt Lake City's snowcapped mountains, the University of Utah is a large public school that offers extensive academic programs, ample research opportunities, and a surprisingly student-friendly atmosphere. No matter what your interests, you'll find like minds at The U. "I have studied everything from [the] Tai Chi/Yoga movement and stage combat to differential equations and linear algebra," says a junior. "The one thing that has remained consistent throughout is the appreciation and dedication the people have for the topic they are involved in." The U is a research university that actually takes teaching seriously, and "every teacher...shows incredible knowledge in their area, as well as personality and wit." "Classes are informative, challenging, and genuinely enjoyable." As is the case in many larger universities, students note that many "general education courses are taught by grad students," whose teaching abilities can range from great to below average. "Ninety percent of my professors are fantastic; the ones that aren't are usually grad students," explains a junior. On this large campus, students have little contact with the school's administration and "there's definitely no hand-holding at The U. If you're unsure of your major or career plans, it's easy to slip through the cracks." However, students assure us, "The administration puts student interests first whenever possible with a focus on keeping tuition low, creating a diverse environment, and providing opportunities and experience in order to prepare students to be productive citizens."

Campus Life

While a large percentage of the undergraduate community at the University of Utah commutes to campus, there are still plenty of activities for the school's 4,000 resident students. There are many people "active in politics, environmental issues, and international issues," and, after hours, "the school holds different events throughout the year, such as Crimson Nights that feature activities such as bowling, crafts, games, food, and music." Socially, "Greek life is not as large as at other schools but is definitely a lot of fun and the best way to get to know more people your age." In addition, "during football season there are great tailgate parties with friends, drinks, and food." Right off campus, there are a range of great restaurants, and "the nightlife is hard to keep up with." There's always something good going on—whether it's at the bars and clubs downtown, or at small music venues." For outdoorsy types, The U is a paradise. "We have all four seasons and some of the best outdoors in the nation," explains one student. "Killer snow, amazing hills, mountains, lakes, and streams." In this natural wonderland, "hiking, biking, boating, snow-skiing, and snowboarding are just a few of the hundreds of activities available to students."

Student Body

Located in Salt Lake City, The U has "plenty of social niches to fall into, and none of them are rigidly exclusive." One student notes that part of the student body is "the typical Utah Mormon, and [the rest] is a mix of everything. The two [groups] usually stay separate but they get along." University of Utah students agree that "there is more diversity here than in any other part of the state." However, out-of-state students are not as common, and "those of us not from Utah are definitely in the minority." While there are a number of residential students, a very large percentage of students also choose to commute to school while living with their parents or family. In addition, "there are a lot of older students and a lot of married students." Academically, however, U undergraduates are "independent, smart, and come to class ready to discuss ideas."

UNIVERSITY OF UTAH

Financial Aid: 801-581-6211 • E-Mail: admissions@utah.edu • Website: www.utah.edu

THE PRINCETON REVIEW SAYS

Admissions

The school reports that its standardized testing policy for use in admission for Fall 2026 is Test Optional. The Princeton Review suggests that interested applicants consult with the school for the most up-to-date standardized testing policies. *Very important factors considered include:* rigor of secondary school record, academic GPA. *Other factors considered include:* standardized test scores, application essay, recommendation(s), extracurricular activities, talent/ability, character/personal qualities, first generation, state residency, volunteer work, work experience. High school diploma is required and GED is accepted.

Financial Aid

Students should submit: FAFSA. Priority filing deadline is 2/1. The Princeton Review suggests that all financial aid forms be submitted as soon as possible. *Need-based scholarships/grants offered:* Federal Pell; Federal SEOG; State scholarships/grants; Private scholarships; College/university scholarship or grant aid from institutional funds; Federal Nursing Scholarships. *Loan aid offered:* Federal Direct Subsidized Loans; Federal Direct Unsubsidized Loans; Direct PLUS loans. Admitted students will be notified of awards on a rolling basis beginning 3/1. Federal Work-Study Program available. Institutional employment available.

The Inside Word

Admission is based primarily on course selection, grades, and test scores, if you choose to submit them. If you have a 3.0 GPA or better and average test scores (if submitting), you're close to a sure bet for admission.

THE SCHOOL SAYS

From the Admissions Office

"The university is uniquely situated to offer both unmatched outdoor and urban experiences. While mountain vistas are just steps away and vast red-rock desert landscapes are within a scenic afternoon's drive, the campus is also located in Salt Lake City—one of the most dynamic and fastest-growing economic and cultural centers in the U.S. With access to world-class skiing, mountain biking, and hiking, along with a vibrant array of cultural, culinary, and entertainment options, there is much to experience beyond campus.

"Within the university's 1,535-acre hillside campus, you'll find world-class research, education, and clinical care, complemented by a lively social, cultural, and athletic environment. A strong work ethic and a spirit of entrepreneurship, collaboration, and community service have enabled the U to innovate across disciplines, pioneer impactful programs, generate groundbreaking discoveries, and inspire new approaches to education.

"The U strives to be a model public university by delivering exceptional value in higher education and health care, while contributing socially, economically, and culturally to improve quality of life locally, nationally, and globally. Its reputation for excellence attracts top-tier faculty and motivated students from around the world. Students bring diverse perspectives and experiences—both traditional and nontraditional—enhancing the rich educational environment the U provides."

SELECTIVITY

# of total applicants	30,036
% of total applicants accepted	90
% of total acceptees attending	24
# of in-state applicants	10,063
% of in-state applicants accepted	90
# of out-of-state-applicants	18,977
% of applicants accepted from out of state	90
# of international applicants	996
% of international applicants accepted	90

First-Year Profile

Testing policy	Test Optional
Range SAT composite	1120–1320
Range SAT EBRW	560–670
Range SAT math	550–660
Range ACT composite	22–29
% submitting SAT scores	14
% submitting ACT scores	36
Average HS GPA	3.6
% submitting high school GPA	98

Important Dates

Early action	
Apply by	12/1
Notified by	1/15
Regular	
Apply by	4/1
Nonfall registration?	Yes

FINANCIAL FACTS

Annual in-state tuition	$9,739
Annual out-of-state tuition	$34,089
Food and housing	$14,637
Required fees	$1,109
Books and supplies	$1,300
Average need-based scholarship (First-year)	$10,501 ($10,870)
% students with need rec. need-based scholarship or grant aid (First-year)	79 (82)
% students with need rec. non-need-based scholarship or grant aid (First-year)	47 (61)
% students with need rec. need-based self-help aid (First-year)	54 (69)
% students rec. any financial aid (First-year)	73 (87)
% UG borrow to pay for school	31
Average cumulative indebtedness	$24,197
% of students with need fully met (First-year)	6 (12)
Average % of student need met (First-year)	37 (45)

University of Vermont

South Prospect Street, Burlington, VT 05405-0160 • Admissions: 802-656-3370

Survey Snapshot
Students take advantage of the outdoors
Lots of liberal students
Students environmentally aware

RATINGS

Quality of Life	86
Fire Safety	99
Green	96
Academic	78
Profs Interesting	88
Profs Accessible	90
Admissions	87
Financial Aid	89

CAMPUS LIFE

Type of school	Public
Environment	Town

Students

Degree-seeking undergrad enrollment	11,595
% male/female/not reported	38/62/0
% from out of state	77
% First-year from public high school	70
% First-year live on campus	98
% Ugrads live on campus	35
# of fraternities (% join)	7 (7)
# of sororities (% join)	6 (3)
% Asian	3
% Black or African American	1
% Hispanic	6
% Native American	<1
% Pacific Islander	<1
% Race and/or ethnicity unknown	3
% Two or more races	5
% White	81
% International	1
# of countries represented	44

CAMPUS MENTAL HEALTH SERVICES

Offers mental health/wellness program	Yes
Mental health training available to students	No
Employs Chief Wellness Officer	Yes
Peer-to-peer mental health offerings	Yes
Counseling center has guidelines or accreditation	Yes
Mental health/well-being courses	Yes, for-credit

ACADEMICS

% students returning for sophomore year	89
% students graduating within 4 years	72
% students graduating within 6 years	81
Calendar	Semester
Student/faculty ratio	17:1
Most common class size 10–19.	(25%)
Most common lab/discussion size 10–19.	(38%)

Most Popular Majors

Environmental Science; Psychology; Business Administration and Management

Applicants Also Look At

St. Lawrence University, State University of New York—Binghamton University, Syracuse University, University of Colorado Boulder, University of Connecticut, University of Massachusetts—Amherst, University of New Hampshire

STUDENTS SAY "..."

Academics

The University of Vermont is a public research university offering more than 100 majors and a "wide variety of courses that are all highly regarded," as well as numerous research opportunities, even for first-years. In addition, "the school does a wonderful job of supporting their students" in a variety of ways, including mental health and wellbeing, with "a wellness center and counseling available to everyone." Faculty members "really ensure a positive and curious environment" and they "make it a point to learn students' names and get to know them." The professors are "all highly qualified and are leaders of their field" and they "have flexibility with how they design curriculums," which means they "tend to teach in a style and format they enjoy" and are more willing to "meet outside of class and ensure you're on the correct path for success." The faculty are genuinely invested in their subjects "and make their lectures engaging and interesting," often employing unique pedagogical techniques. For example, one course "featured independent equity research and a school-sponsored trip to NYC to present a stock pitch to professionals." Another student adds, "One day, my English professor gave us a walking tour of campus to explain postmodernism through the architecture of [the] campus." Put simply: "I love my program!"

Campus Life

The student body is "a tight-knit community" where "you can always find another student doing similar interests." Community building is encouraged with "frequent postings on social media of students looking to meet up with people who want to go backcountry skiing, create an intramural sports team, or who need a ride to an East Coast city during school break." Students enjoy spending time in the great outdoors: whether that's snowboarding in the winter or, "during warmer weather, campus is jovial and students are all over playing Spikeball and other games outside." The campus "is beautiful and very active, [and] there is always something to keep you from being bored." Although classes take up a good chunk of time, students say, "a way to break up the week is [by] working out, doing intramurals [and] clubs," and on the weekends, going downtown to check out the "great bar scene." Downtown Burlington "is a hotspot for food and shopping," and many students simply "enjoy [being with] each other, spending time in residential areas or going out downtown." One student shares, "Between resident hall communities, professors who care about each and every one of their students, and the many clubs on campus, students are constantly forming connections with others."

Student Body

Among this "stylish… [and] academically driven" crowd, many "are focused on social activism, specifically environmental" and are "very passionate about politics, human rights, and social justice and equality." The students "project a creative and welcoming energy…wanting to learn and absorb all life has to offer." People tend to be "on the left side politically," but the "student community is a very inclusive and diverse group." Generally, "students tend to enjoy outdoor activities such as hiking and skiing, as well as music," and they are sometimes characterized as "outdoorsy." The school "is large enough to support a diverse community, but not overwhelmingly large," and Catamounts are "very strong in their pride and spirit of representing their school." A student assures that "while Vermont can feel small, there is truly so much to do, and UVM does a great job of cultivating meeting spaces and allowing you to find your people."

University of Vermont

Financial Aid: 802-656-5700 • E-Mail: admissions@uvm.edu • Website: www.uvm.edu

THE PRINCETON REVIEW SAYS

Admissions

The school reports that its standardized testing policy for use in admission for Fall 2026 is Test Optional. The Princeton Review suggests that interested applicants consult with the school for the most up-to-date standardized testing policies. *Very important factors considered include:* rigor of secondary school record. *Important factors considered include:* academic GPA, application essay, character/personal qualities, state residency. *Other factors considered include:* standardized test scores, recommendation(s), extracurricular activities, talent/ability, first generation, alumni/ae relation, geographical residence, volunteer work, work experience, level of applicant's interest. High school diploma is required and GED is accepted. *Academic units required:* 4 English, 3 math, 3 science, 1 science lab, 2 language (other than English), 3 social studies.

Financial Aid

Students should submit: FAFSA. Priority filing deadline is 2/1. The Princeton Review suggests that all financial aid forms be submitted as soon as possible. *Need-based scholarships/grants offered:* Federal Pell; Federal SEOG; State scholarships/grants; Private scholarships; College/university scholarship or grant aid from institutional funds. *Loan aid offered:* Federal Direct Subsidized Loans; Federal Direct Unsubsidized Loans; Direct PLUS loans; College/university loans from institutional funds. Admitted students will be notified of awards on a rolling basis beginning 3/1. Federal Work-Study Program available. Institutional employment available.

The Inside Word

Admissions officers take a broad view of an applicant's academic program, class standing, grades, standardized test results, and trends in performance. Though test scores are optional, they're still a good metric by which to assess your chances. Applicants must select one of seven undergraduate schools based on their desired major. Be aware of deadline variations for first-year, transfer, and international applicants.

THE SCHOOL SAYS

From the Admissions Office

"UVM is an R1 institution that champions sustainable, hopeful, and bold futures—strengthening Vermont and the world. Here, deep and broad thinking becomes action and advances personal and societal health and well-being, civic discourse, and new ways of thinking about and seeing the world. All members of our community are empowered to forge purposeful paths into work and life. In cooperation and partnership with the communities we touch, we engage as scholars, researchers, leaders, learners, and problem-solvers who seek to make an impact locally and globally.

"UVM's location enriches the student experience. National rankings praise Burlington for its livability, safety, recreation, and identity as a top college town, and tech hub. Experiential learning drives success, with 92% of students participating in internships, research, and other opportunities. Graduates thrive, with 94% employed or pursuing education within six months of graduation.

"UVM is ranked #1 among public schools on the Princeton Review's 2025 list of Best Schools for Making an Impact. Guided by Our Common Ground values of respect, integrity, innovation, openness, justice, and responsibility, UVM creates, shares, and applies knowledge to serve humanity. With optimism and purpose, the UVM community leads boldly to solve complex challenges, improve and sustain life and the planet, further meaningful inquiry, and advance the well-being of democracy in our state and the nation.

"This unique combination of academic excellence, offering over 100 undergraduate degree programs, experiential learning, and a vibrant community prepares graduates to succeed, and to lead with purpose and shape the future."

SELECTIVITY

# of total applicants	25,434
% of total applicants accepted	73
% of total acceptees attending	15
# of in-state applicants	1,948
% of in-state applicants accepted	77
# of out-of-state-applicants	22,205
% of applicants accepted from out of state	75
# of international applicants	1,281
% of international applicants accepted	30
# of early decision applicants	396
% of early decision applicants accepted	92
# offered a place on the wait list	2,752
# admitted from wait list	142

First-Year Profile

Testing policy	Test Optional
Range SAT composite	1300–1430
Range SAT EBRW	660–740
Range SAT math	630–700
Range ACT composite	29–33
% submitting SAT scores	32
% submitting ACT scores	8
% graduated top 10% of class	35
% graduated top 25% of class	68
% graduated top 50% of class	94
% submitting high school rank	18

Important Dates

Early decision	
Apply by	11/1
Notified by	12/1
Early action	
Apply by	11/1
Notified by	12/16
Regular	
Apply by	1/15
Notified by	3/31
Nonfall registration?	Yes

FINANCIAL FACTS

Annual in-state tuition	$16,606
Annual out-of-state tuition	$44,646
Food and housing	$14,226
Required fees	$2,908
Books and supplies	$1,320
Average need-based scholarship (First-year)	$21,567 ($24,421)
% students with need rec. need-based scholarship or grant aid (First-year)	100 (100)
% students with need rec. non-need-based scholarship or grant aid (First-year)	16 (21)
% students with need rec. need-based self-help aid (First-year)	60 (59)
% students rec. any financial aid (First-year)	92 (95)
% UG borrow to pay for school	54
Average cumulative indebtedness	$34,870
% of students with need fully met (First-year)	32 (36)
Average % of student need met (First-year)	77 (83)

University of Virginia

Office of Admission, Charlottesville, VA 22904 • Admissions: 434-982-3200

Survey Snapshot
Great library
Great financial aid
Students love Charlottesville, VA

RATINGS

Quality of Life	84
Fire Safety	89
Green	93
Academic	84
Profs Interesting	88
Profs Accessible	90
Admissions	97
Financial Aid	97

CAMPUS LIFE

Type of school	Public
Environment	City

Students

Degree-seeking undergrad enrollment	17,603
% male/female/not reported	44/56/<1
% from out of state	30
% First-year from public high school	70
% First-year live on campus	99
% Ugrads live on campus	41
# of fraternities (% join)	40 (17)
# of sororities (% join)	22 (24)
% Asian	20
% Black or African American	7
% Hispanic	9
% Native American	<1
% Pacific Islander	<1
% Race and/or ethnicity unknown	5
% Two or more races	6
% White	48
% International	5
# of countries represented	133

CAMPUS MENTAL HEALTH SERVICES

Offers mental health/wellness program	Yes
Mental health training available to students	No
Employs Chief Wellness Officer	NR
Peer-to-peer mental health offerings	NR
Counseling center has guidelines or accreditation	No
Mental health/well-being courses	NR

ACADEMICS

% students returning for sophomore year	97
% students graduating within 4 years	91
% students graduating within 6 years	94
Calendar	Semester
Student/faculty ratio	14:1
Most common class size 10–19.	(32%)
Most common lab/discussion size 20–29.	(53%)

Most Popular Majors

Business/Commerce; Economics; Biology/Biological Sciences

Applicants Also Look At

Brown University, Cornell University, Dartmouth College, Duke University, Emory University, Georgetown University, Georgia Institute Of Technology, Harvard University, Johns Hopkins University, New York University, Northwestern University, Princeton University, University Of Chicago, University Of Michigan, University Of North Carolina-Chapel Hill, University Of Notre Dame, University Of Pennsylvania, Vanderbilt University, Virginia Tech, Washington University, William & Mary, Yale University

STUDENTS SAY "..."

Academics

For over 200 years, the University of Virginia has been an anchor of the state, now serving 17,000 undergraduates and with almost 10,000 full-time faculty and staff. One of many "rigorous but rewarding" academic experience is the J term, a set of January classes based around field experiences and unusual topics such as "impact investing in Appalachia... which involves visiting various local businesses and VC firms." Other approaches lauded for "allow[ing] us to collaborate and think creatively" include active-learning classes, where students work and "the professor only teaches when the whole class gets stuck," and "class discussions, where material is studied beforehand, and learning mostly done in classroom through talking." These courses "are difficult, but in a way that will ensure a bright future for all students and helps guarantee careers upon graduation."

Overall, students are left happily fascinated by the available courses and the "highly encouraged" study abroad opportunities. They also find professors to be helpful in all regards: "very accessible outside of class and want[ing] their students to thrive; grading is fair; the workload is appropriate." There are "a lot of support resources for all areas of growth," and students say they "[have] never met someone unwilling to share their expertise with students." When it comes to crunch time, faculty "are also great about making sure you can succeed if you don't come to class all the time by posting their lectures."

Campus Life

UVA has "beautiful and historic grounds, which add to the unique character of the university." It's the sort of picturesque college setting wherein "the libraries are always full, the lawn and rotunda are frequently filled with friends hanging out," and "many students go to fitness centers often to fill their days and remain active." As you might expect from that setting, "during the week, UVA students can often be found studying with their friends, meeting with peers for group projects, and studying alone in the many quiet spaces grounds has to offer," like how "dorms and living spaces are used quite frequently for relaxing nights and study sessions." As for downtime and weekends, peers "are very engaged with social events that are hosted by the college or student organizations where there may be food or activities to do with friends."

Student Body

Students at the University of Virginia describe themselves and their peers as "kind and compassionate," the sort of "driven, empathetic, action-orientated, proactive leaders who know how to work across lines of difference and create a diverse yet cohesive community." This is due in part to trickle-down support, as the "environment here for learning and growing connections is exceptionally strong due to the eagerness of upperclassmen to help their younger peers." As one undergrad puts it, "there seems to be every kind of person here," and that's supported by an inclusive attitude that makes room for them. That said, the average student is a self-starter, in short the type "who want to be here, want to learn, and want to have a rounded college experience." According to one undergrad, "you won't find anyone who's not involved in at least one club or group outside of their classes, and it's more common to find people who fill their schedules with 4–5 groups and clubs." Posting extracurricular numbers like those means many are "involved in a really unexpected cross section of interests," and "there is a very strong esprit de corps." It also means that UVA is "a well-sized school where it feels like you can find anything you may be looking for, but also not so big you get overwhelmed."

UNIVERSITY OF VIRGINIA

Financial Aid: 434-982-6000 • E-Mail: undergradadmission@virginia.edu • Website: www.virginia.edu

THE PRINCETON REVIEW SAYS

Admissions

The school reports that its standardized testing policy for use in admission for Fall 2026 is Test Optional. The Princeton Review suggests that interested applicants consult with the school for the most up-to-date standardized testing policies. *Very important factors considered include:* rigor of secondary school record, class rank, academic GPA, character/personal qualities, state residency. *Important factors considered include:* application essay, recommendation(s), extracurricular activities, talent/ability. *Other factors considered include:* standardized test scores, first generation, alumni/ae relation, geographical residence, volunteer work, work experience. High school diploma is required and GED is accepted. *Academic units required:* 4 English, 4 math, 2 science, 2 language (other than English), 1 social studies. *Academic units recommended:* 4 English, 4 math, 4 science, 4 language (other than English), 3 social studies.

Financial Aid

Students should submit: FAFSA; CSS PROFILE. Priority filing deadline is 3/1. The Princeton Review suggests that all financial aid forms be submitted as soon as possible. *Need-based scholarships/grants offered:* Federal Pell; Federal SEOG; State scholarships/grants; Private scholarships; College/university scholarship or grant aid from institutional funds. *Loan aid offered:* Federal Direct Subsidized Loans; Federal Direct Unsubsidized Loans; Direct PLUS loans; State Loans. Admitted students will be notified of awards on or about 4/1. Federal Work-Study Program available. Institutional employment available.

The Inside Word

UVA is an extremely competitive public university, so applicants must have stellar academic records and demonstrate willingness to rise to the school's academic challenges. The most important parts of the application are academic performance, rigor of high school curriculum, and recommendations. Admission is even more competitive for students from out of state.

THE SCHOOL SAYS

From the Admissions Office

"UVA aspires to cultivate a vibrant, welcoming, and innovative community that prepares students to be servant-leaders in a diverse, globally connected world. We welcome talented students from all walks of life who are interested in the power of ideas and who thrive when working together. As a public university, we are dedicated to serving the Commonwealth, and outstanding Virginians who take at least five challenging academic courses each year and earn excellent grades are generally strong candidates for admission. Because we also aspire to serve the nation and the world, we welcome applications from candidates beyond Virginia who excel academically and will contribute as caring and engaged members of the UVA community.

"UVA is currently test-optional. If you're applying for Fall 2027 admission, you may choose whether or not you'll share results from the SAT and ACT. Whichever path you choose, we'll consider your application with care and respect, and you won't be disadvantaged because of your choice. Regardless of whether you think you'll share your scores, we encourage you to take either or both exams. Although you're more than any one test can ever say, these tests may help you identify strengths you can build on as you get ready for college. And whether you choose UVA or another school, we want you to be ready for the challenges and the opportunities that await you."

SELECTIVITY

# of total applicants	64,457
% of total applicants accepted	16
% of total acceptees attending	39
# of in-state applicants	17,370
% of in-state applicants accepted	24
# of out-of-state-applicants	39,271
% of applicants accepted from out of state	13
# of international applicants	7,816
% of international applicants accepted	12
# of early decision applicants	4,969
% of early decision applicants accepted	28
# offered a place on the wait list	8,398
# admitted from wait list	125

First-Year Profile

Testing policy	Test Optional
Range SAT composite	1410–1510
Range SAT EBRW	700–760
Range SAT math	710–780
Range ACT composite	32–34
% submitting SAT scores	49
% submitting ACT scores	15
% graduated top 10% of class	90
% graduated top 25% of class	98
% graduated top 50% of class	100
% submitting high school rank	30

Important Dates

Early decision	
Apply by	11/1
Notified by	12/15
Early action	
Apply by	11/1
Notified by	2/15
Regular	
Apply by	1/5
Notified by	4/1
Nonfall registration?	No

FINANCIAL FACTS

Annual in-state tuition (First-year)	$20,101 ($18,613)
Annual out-of-state tuition (First-year)	$59,127 ($56,994)
Food and housing	$16,416
Required fees (First-year)	$3,796 ($3,793)
Books and supplies	$1,520
Average need-based scholarship (First-year)	$37,354 ($35,691)
% students with need rec. need-based scholarship or grant aid (First-year)	99 (99)
% students with need rec. non-need-based scholarship or grant aid (First-year)	11 (15)
% students with need rec. need-based self-help aid (First-year)	42 (41)
% UG borrow to pay for school	28
Average cumulative indebtedness	$28,111
% of students with need fully met (First-year)	100 (100)
Average % of student need met (First-year)	100 (100)

UNIVERSITY OF WASHINGTON

Box 355852, Seattle, WA 98195-5852 • Admissions: 206-543-9686

Survey Snapshot
Great library
Internships are widely available
Recreation facilities are great

RATINGS

Quality of Life	**80**
Fire Safety	**88**
Green	**97**
Academic	**82**
Profs Interesting	**86**
Profs Accessible	**90**
Admissions	**91**
Financial Aid	**85**

CAMPUS LIFE

Type of school	Public
Environment	Metropolis

Students

Degree-seeking undergrad enrollment	32,140
% male/female/not reported	44/55/<1
% from out of state	23
% First-year live on campus	70
% Ugrads live on campus	24
# of fraternities (% join)	35 (7)
# of sororities (% join)	29 (9)
% Asian	27
% Black or African American	4
% Hispanic	11
% Native American	<1
% Pacific Islander	<1
% Race and/or ethnicity unknown	6
% Two or more races	8
% White	32
% International	11
# of countries represented	75

CAMPUS MENTAL HEALTH SERVICES

Offers mental health/wellness program	Yes
Mental health training available to students	Yes
Employs Chief Wellness Officer	Yes
Peer-to-peer mental health offerings	Yes
Counseling center has guidelines or accreditation	Yes
Mental health/well-being courses	Yes, for-credit

ACADEMICS

% students returning for sophomore year	95
% students graduating within 4 years	75
% students graduating within 6 years	85
Calendar	Quarter
Student/faculty ratio	21:1
Most common class size 20–29.	(24%)
Most common lab/discussion size 20–29.	(43%)

Applicants Also Look At

New York University, University of California—Berkeley, University of California—Davis, University of California—San Diego, University of Illinois at Urbana—Champaign, University of Oregon

STUDENTS SAY "..."

Academics

Students find "a great combination of high-powered academics, an excellent social life, and a wide variety of courses, all in the midst of the exciting Seattle life" at the University of Washington, the state's flagship institution of higher learning. UW offers "a lot of really stellar programs and the best bang for the buck, especially for in-state students or those in the sciences." Indeed, science programs "are incredible. The research going on here is cutting-edge and the leaders of biomedical sciences, stem cell research, etc. are accessible to students." Undergrads warn, however, that science programs are extremely competitive, "high pressure," and "challenging," with "core classes taught in lectures that seat more than 500 people," creating the sense that "professors don't seem to care too much whether you succeed." Pre-professional programs in business, law, nursing, medicine, and engineering all earn high marks, although again with the caveat that the workload is tough and the hand-holding nominal. As one student puts it, "The University of Washington provides every resource and opportunity for its students to succeed. You just have to take advantage of them. No one will do it for you." For those fortunate enough to get in, the Honors Program "creates a smaller community of highly motivated students.... It puts this school on top."

Campus Life

UW students typically "have a good balance in their lives of education and fun." They "generally study hard and work in the libraries, but once the nighttime hits, they look forward to enjoying the night with their friends." Between the large university community and the surrounding city of Seattle, undergrads have a near-limitless selection of extracurricular choices. As one student explains, "There are tons of options for fun in Seattle. Going down to Pike's Market on a Saturday and eating your way through is always popular. There are tons of places to eat on 'The Ave,'" the shopping district that abuts campus, "and the UVillage shopping mall is a five-minute walk from campus with chain-store comfort available. Intramural sports are big for activities, and going to undergraduate theater productions is never a disappointing experience. During autumn or spring, renting a canoe and paddling around lake Washington down by the stadium is fun." Husky football games "are amazing," and the Greek community "is very big" without dominating campus social life. In short, "UW has anything you could want to do in your free time."

Student Body

At such a large university, there is no 'typical' student, undergrads tell us, observing "one can find just about any demographic here and there is a huge variety in personalities." There "are quite a lot [of hipsters], but then again, it's Seattle," and by and large "the campus is ultraliberal. Most students care about the environment, are not religious, and are generally accepting of other diverse individuals." Otherwise, "you've got your stereotypes: the Greeks, the street fashion pioneers, the various ethnic communities, the Oxford-looking grad students, etc." In terms of demographics, "the typical student at UW is white, middle-class, and is from the Seattle area," but "there are a lot of African American students and a very large number of Asian students." All groups "seem to socialize with each other."

UNIVERSITY OF WASHINGTON

Financial Aid: 206-543-6101 • E-Mail: askuwadm@uw.edu • Website: www.washington.edu

THE PRINCETON REVIEW SAYS

Admissions

The school reports that its standardized testing policy for use in admission for Fall 2026 is Test Free. The Princeton Review suggests that interested applicants consult with the school for the most up-to-date standardized testing policies. *Very important factors considered include:* rigor of secondary school record, academic GPA, application essay, state residency. *Important factors considered include:* extracurricular activities, talent/ability, first generation, volunteer work, work experience. *Other factors considered include:* character/personal qualities. High school diploma or equivalent is not required. *Academic units required:* 4 English, 3 math, 3 science, 2 science labs, 2 language (other than English), 3 social studies, 1 visual/performing arts.

Financial Aid

Students should submit: FAFSA. Priority filing deadline is 2/28. The Princeton Review suggests that all financial aid forms be submitted as soon as possible. *Need-based scholarships/grants offered:* Federal Pell; Federal SEOG; State scholarships/grants; Private scholarships; College/university scholarship or grant aid from institutional funds. *Loan aid offered:* Federal Direct Subsidized Loans; Federal Direct Unsubsidized Loans; Direct PLUS loans; College/university loans from institutional funds. Admitted students will be notified of awards on or about 4/1. Federal Work-Study Program available. Institutional employment available.

The Inside Word

UW performs a thorough review of all first-year applications. Its holistic approach allows admissions officers to take into account a student's background, the degree to which you have overcome personal adversity, and such intangibles as leadership quality and special skills.

THE SCHOOL SAYS

From the Admissions Office

"Do you want to be an artist, adventurer, entrepreneur—or all the above? The University of Washington in Seattle can help make it happen. Nestled among two mountain ranges, old-growth forests, Lake Washington and the Pacific Ocean, Seattle is a vibrant, multicultural city with career, arts, sports, and outdoor opportunities for everyone.

"The UW offers a breadth of academic programs with more than 180 majors, many of which are ranked among the best in the country. With top-rated faculty and endless ways to feed your interests outside the classroom, no matter which challenges and curiosities you want to pursue, the UW will help you find them.

"Our graduates can start their careers anywhere, but many begin at well-known institutions right here in the Pacific Northwest. Rich in talent and capital, Seattle is a hotbed for innovators and entrepreneurs. Huskies can get hands-on experience through research, mentorships, and internships with some of the most groundbreaking visionaries in the world.

"At the UW, we aim to be the greatest public university in the world—as measured by our impact. That's why we're devoted to advancing a culture of belonging. We honor the relationships between people and our planet. We strive to create a just and sustainable future.

"Beyond grades, we consider an applicant's academic achievements (rigor of curriculum, academic preparation) and personal history, including community service, leadership, and accomplishments. We do this because we believe that what you care about can change the world. Are you ready?"

SELECTIVITY

# of total applicants	72,933
% of total applicants accepted	42
% of total acceptees attending	23
# of in-state applicants	15,260
% of in-state applicants accepted	46
# of out-of-state-applicants	44,619
% of applicants accepted from out of state	42
# of international applicants	13,054
% of international applicants accepted	36
# offered a place on the wait list	15,363
# admitted from wait list	2,252

First-Year Profile

Testing policy	Test Free
Average HS GPA	3.8
% submitting high school GPA	100

Important Dates

Regular	
Apply by	11/15
Notified by	3/15
Nonfall registration?	No

FINANCIAL FACTS

Annual in-state tuition	$12,664
Annual out-of-state tuition	$44,580
Food and housing	$18,858
Required fees	$1,209
Books and supplies	$900
Average need-based scholarship (First-year)	$22,054 ($21,532)
% students with need rec. need-based scholarship or grant aid (First-year)	90 (88)
% students with need rec. non-need-based scholarship or grant aid (First-year)	2 (3)
% students with need rec. need-based self-help aid (First-year)	38 (36)
% students rec. any financial aid (First-year)	38 (35)
% UG borrow to pay for school	26
Average cumulative indebtedness	$19,384
% of students with need fully met (First-year)	19 (20)
Average % of student need met (First-year)	74 (74)

UNIVERSITY OF WISCONSIN—MADISON

161 Bascom Hall, Madison, WI 53706 • Admissions: 608-262-3961

Survey Snapshot
Students are happy
Great library
Students love Madison, WI

RATINGS

Quality of Life	88
Fire Safety	88
Green	93
Academic	84
Profs Interesting	89
Profs Accessible	92
Admissions	92
Financial Aid	93

CAMPUS LIFE

Type of school	Public
Environment	City

Students

Degree-seeking undergrad enrollment	37,198
% male/female/not reported	46/54/<1
% from out of state	47
% First-year live on campus	94
% Ugrads live on campus	25
# of fraternities (% join)	26 (9)
# of sororities (% join)	11 (8)
% Asian	11
% Black or African American	3
% Hispanic	9
% Native American	<1
% Pacific Islander	<1
% Race and/or ethnicity unknown	4
% Two or more races	5
% White	58
% International	10
# of countries represented	111

CAMPUS MENTAL HEALTH SERVICES

Offers mental health/wellness program	Yes
Mental health training available to students	Yes
Employs Chief Wellness Officer	Yes
Peer-to-peer mental health offerings	Yes
Counseling center has guidelines or accreditation	Yes
Mental health/well-being courses	Yes, non-credit

ACADEMICS

% students returning for sophomore year	96
% students graduating within 4 years	76
% students graduating within 6 years	90
Calendar	Semester
Student/faculty ratio	18:1
Most common class size 10–19.	(31%)
Most common lab/discussion size 20–29.	(50%)

Most Popular Majors

Computer and Information Sciences; Psychology; Economics

Applicants Also Look At

Indiana University—Bloomington, Purdue University—West Lafayette, University of Illinois at Urbana—Champaign, University of Michigan—Ann Arbor, University of Minnesota—Twin Cities

STUDENTS SAY "..."

Academics

The University of Wisconsin—Madison's "great reputation" and "huge variety of programs" draw "enthusiastic students" who want to make a positive impact "through research and service." This large research university has over 321 undergraduate majors and the wide range of options makes it easy to "find one that you will enjoy." As one student describes, "I'm only taking one major, but I am pursuing three certificates (minors) because there are so many interesting options on campus." The academics "challenge you to your full potential," and if you work hard, you'll "be rewarded with amazing opportunities." The school puts a "huge emphasis on gaining research experience" and provides "wonderful facilities" where research is conducted on topics "ranging from environmental to sociological to biomedical and everything in between." This also means that classes are taught by "leading researchers in their fields" who are overall "great and passionate instructors." The majority are "so enthusiastic" and "very knowledgeable, interesting, and happy to help." Students recommend attending office hours "to get the most out of their expertise" and say some professors go above and beyond "to give students extra study tips and extra office hours before the exam." From the one-on-one support to the engaging classes, it's clear that professors here "care about their students and their success." As one student says, "I have learned more at this school than I ever knew was possible."

Campus Life

UWN delivers a neat blend of city and nature, as well as a mix of outdoor activities, whether it's warm or cold. The many trails and paths are "usually busy during the weekends with joggers and bikers" and there's also windsurfing, paddle boarding, sailing or ice fishing, and cross-country skiing. Students are said to "attend Badgers games sun or snow," and though "winters are brutal" according to some, they also provide great opportunities for school spirit, like "a massive campus-wide snowball fight." There are many indoor activities to be found as well, including "free movies, art workshops, concerts, open mic nights, guest lecture series, and performances from other student organizations." And "right off campus," there are "lots of options for shopping and really amazing restaurants." Students say that it can be "a bit of a party school," particularly on weekends and game days, though "it's easy to find other things to do to have fun." There are over 900 student organizations, and students say their peers are "extremely involved in diverse organizations and extracurriculars." Essentially, "people can always find something to fit their idea of fun."

Student Body

There is "great school camaraderie" thanks to a "well-rounded atmosphere" at Wisconsin—Madison where students bond over academics, sports, and having fun. Whether it's studying, cheering on the football team, or joining an extracurricular, students here "go all out at everything we do." There are students from all 50 states as well as 123 countries, and about half of the student body hails from Wisconsin. It's a "very lively" campus where students enjoy getting involved on campus. People here are "very self-driven" and UW's "large variety of clubs and organizations" speaks to the students' desire to pursue their interests "with everything they have." Overall, students are "able to find a good balance between work and fun." As one enrollee puts it, "When it is time to buckle down and study, we get the job done." While classmates are "working hard in classes," they're equally "willing to get involved with fun activities and meet new people." UW's large size means there are "many different individuals on campus, so there is really a fit for everyone." Overall, people are friendly and approachable. As one student explains, "People always talk to each other" in classes and labs," and, "[I] always end the semester with a couple new friends."

UNIVERSITY OF WISCONSIN—MADISON

Financial Aid: 608-262-3060 • E-Mail: onwisconsin@admissions.wisc.edu • Website: www.wisc.edu

THE PRINCETON REVIEW SAYS

Admissions

The school reports that its standardized testing policy for use in admission for Fall 2026 is Test Optional. The Princeton Review suggests that interested applicants consult with the school for the most up-to-date standardized testing policies. *Very important factors considered include:* rigor of secondary school record, academic GPA. *Important factors considered include:* application essay, recommendation(s), extracurricular activities, character/personal qualities, state residency. *Other factors considered include:* class rank, standardized test scores, talent/ability, first generation, geographical residence, volunteer work, work experience. High school diploma is required and GED is accepted. *Academic units required:* 4 English, 3 math, 3 science, 2 language (other than English), 3 social studies. *Academic units recommended:* 4 English, 4 math, 4 science, 2 science labs, 2 language (other than English), 4 social studies.

Financial Aid

Students should submit: FAFSA; CSS PROFILE. Priority filing deadline is 12/1. The Princeton Review suggests that all financial aid forms be submitted as soon as possible. *Need-based scholarships/grants offered:* Federal Pell; Federal SEOG; State scholarships/grants; Private scholarships; College/university scholarship or grant aid from institutional funds. *Loan aid offered:* Federal Direct Subsidized Loans; Federal Direct Unsubsidized Loans; Direct PLUS loans. Admitted students will be notified of awards on a rolling basis. Federal Work-Study Program available. Institutional employment available.

The Inside Word

Though UW—Madison is a large state school, it still manages to take a holistic approach to the admissions game. Indeed, there are no minimum GPAs, class ranks, or test scores required. That said, a strong academic record is paramount. Looking beyond your transcript, the school looks at your background and personal experience and whether you will actively contribute to campus life. Finally, students who intend to major in either dance or music must schedule an audition as well as submit a regular application.

THE SCHOOL SAYS

From the Admissions Office

"UW—Madison is the university of choice for some of the best students from around the world. First-year students have high GPAs and are ranked toward the top of their high school classes.

"These factors combine to make admission to UW—Madison both competitive and selective. We consider academic record, strength of curriculum (honors, AP, IB, etc.), grade trend, class rank, results of the ACT/SAT (when submitted), and non-academic factors. There is no prescribed minimum GPA or class rank criteria. Rather, we admit the best and most well-prepared students—students who have challenged themselves and who will contribute to Wisconsin's strength and diversity—for the limited space available.

"Each application is personally reviewed by our admission counselors. All freshman applications completed by February 1 receive full and equal consideration. We offer two decision plans for freshman applicants. To receive a decision during the Early Action period, you must complete the application by November 1 and submit all required materials (application fee, official transcript(s), personal essays, and one required academic letter of recommendation) by our materials deadline. Early Action period applicants will receive a decision by the end of January. All students who complete their application during the Regular Decision period (after November 1 but before the February 1 deadline) will receive a decision by the end of March. UW—Madison has a commitment to a holistic, competitive, and selective admission process for all applicants."

SELECTIVITY

# of total applicants	69,642
% of total applicants accepted	43
% of total acceptees attending	28
# offered a place on the wait list	6,476
# admitted from wait list	1,088

First-Year Profile

Testing policy	Test Optional
Range SAT composite	1400–1490
Range SAT EBRW	680–740
Range SAT math	700–780
Range ACT composite	29–33
% submitting SAT scores	12
% submitting ACT scores	29
Average HS GPA	3.9
% submitting high school GPA	94
% graduated top 10% of class	58
% graduated top 25% of class	91
% graduated top 50% of class	99
% submitting high school rank	36

Important Dates

Early action	
Apply by	11/1
Notified by	1/31
Regular	
Apply by	1/15
Notified by	3/31
Nonfall registration?	Yes

FINANCIAL FACTS

Annual in-state tuition	$10,506
Annual out-of-state tuition	$42,530
Food and housing	$14,520
Required fees	$1,660
Books and supplies	$700
Average need-based scholarship (First-year)	$28,321 ($34,869)
% students with need rec. need-based scholarship or grant aid (First-year)	86 (87)
% students with need rec. non-need-based scholarship or grant aid (First-year)	7 (7)
% students with need rec. need-based self-help aid (First-year)	72 (74)
% UG borrow to pay for school	33
Average cumulative indebtedness	$28,927
% of students with need fully met (First-year)	67 (77)
Average % of student need met (First-year)	88 (91)

University of Wyoming

1000 E. University Ave, Laramie, WY 82071 • Admissions: 307-766-5160

Survey Snapshot
Lots of conservative students
Recreation facilities are great
Students are happy

RATINGS

Quality of Life	**84**
Fire Safety	**71**
Green	**60***
Academic	**78**
Profs Interesting	**84**
Profs Accessible	**89**
Admissions	**80**
Financial Aid	**82**

CAMPUS LIFE

Type of school	Public
Environment	Town

Students

Degree-seeking undergrad enrollment	7,895
% male/female/not reported	46/53/2
% from out of state	28
% First-year live on campus	84
% Ugrads live on campus	26
# of fraternities (% join)	10 (7)
# of sororities (% join)	6 (5)
% Asian	1
% Black or African American	1
% Hispanic	11
% Native American	1
% Pacific Islander	<1
% Race and/or ethnicity unknown	8
% Two or more races	4
% White	73
% International	2
# of countries represented	48

CAMPUS MENTAL HEALTH SERVICES

Offers mental health/wellness program	Yes
Mental health training available to students	Yes
Employs Chief Wellness Officer	Yes
Peer-to-peer mental health offerings	Yes
Counseling center has guidelines or accreditation	No
Mental health/well-being courses	Yes, non-credit

ACADEMICS

% students returning for sophomore year	79
% students graduating within 4 years	43
% students graduating within 6 years	61
Calendar	Semester
Student/faculty ratio	13:1
Most common class size 10–19.	(35%)
Most common lab/discussion size 20–29.	(45%)

Most Popular Majors

Management Science; Experimental Psychology; Pre-Nursing Studies

Applicants Also Look At

Colorado Mesa University, Colorado State University, Laramie County Community College, Montana State University, University of Colorado Boulder, University of Utah

STUDENTS SAY "..."

Academics

At the University of Wyoming, students have access to "a great education for a low, affordable cost." Many students say the school's size is perfect: it's big enough to have over 80 majors and "high-grade faculty" to back them up, but still "small enough to be able to build meaningful relationships with other students and professors." UW "works hard to provide as many resources as possible," which can be seen in the "many undergraduate research opportunities" as well as "great scholarships for studying abroad." Between "good academic advisors" and "always [available] tutoring help," there's an appreciable feeling "that students come first." This means that teachers are "willing to help you in any way you need," and so while they "demand excellence," the overall learning environment is "pleasant as well as challenging." Students "actually look forward" to attending class and say that instructors are "very knowledgeable" and lead "meaningful discussions." Overall, professors do a good job "presenting the material clearly" and making it "really interesting." If students need extra support, the professors are "available for any questions" and "always happy to talk to you."

Campus Life

Students describe the school's scenic location poetically, pointing to the "vivid colors of the clear sky" and noting that "so much time is spent outside exploring" through activities like hiking, mountain biking, skiing, camping, hunting, and fishing. As one student puts it, "If it can be done outside, there are people here that will do it." Sports is also big, with games described as "always enjoyable to watch," so much so that it seems "everyone in the state comes to support our teams." The school is "constantly bringing in musicians, comedians, magicians, and other performers." Students say the "gym and recreational center is top-notch," and the library is a popular spot where people work well into the night (as one student explains, "Food and drinks are allowed in so people can get quite comfortable"). When students have some downtime, they can go into Laramie, which offers an "adorable downtown life" alongside staples like theaters, "a wide variety of restaurants," and "bars and [clubs] for the occasional night out." As one student puts it, "There is always something going on, whether on campus or off campus, as long as you're willing to find it."

Student Body

Most students at the University of Wyoming are active and share a love for the outdoors. It's a love that's about both "having fun and enjoying the natural beauty of Wyoming" and "also caring for and helping preserve the serene landscape." Nearly 60% of undergraduates are from Wyoming and many are from Colorado (though there are students from all 50 states and many countries), and their school pride unites them; everyone "loves wearing their brown and gold." Under that banner is a "wide variety of students," from those with a "deeply ingrained love for cowboy culture" to those who ride unicycles and play bagpipes. On the whole, people are "warm-hearted individuals" who are "very open-minded" and "non-judgmental," which means it's "easy to make friends" and "a safe zone where students are able to express their thoughts and ideas." It's a place where you can spot "the passion that accompanies each major." Walking around campus, you'll see "students stop and gather leaves on their walk to class, watch the wildlife, ... or skip, sing and act on their way to class."

University of Wyoming

Financial Aid: 307-766-2116 • E-Mail: admissions@uwyo.edu • Website: www.uwyo.edu

THE PRINCETON REVIEW SAYS

Admissions

The school reports that its standardized testing policy for use in admission for Fall 2026 is Test Optional. The Princeton Review suggests that interested applicants consult with the school for the most up-to-date standardized testing policies. *Very important factors considered include:* rigor of secondary school record, academic GPA. *Other factors considered include:* application essay. High school diploma is required and GED is accepted. *Academic units required:* 4 English, 4 math, 4 science, 3 science labs, 3 social studies. *Academic units recommended:* 4 English, 4 math, 4 science, 3 science labs, 3 social studies.

Financial Aid

Priority filing deadline is 2/1. The Princeton Review suggests that all financial aid forms be submitted as soon as possible. *Need-based scholarships/grants offered:* Federal Pell; Federal SEOG; State scholarships/grants; Private scholarships; College/university scholarship or grant aid from institutional funds. *Loan aid offered:* Federal Direct Subsidized Loans; Federal Direct Unsubsidized Loans; Direct PLUS loans; State Loans; College/university loans from institutional funds. Admitted students will be notified of awards on a rolling basis beginning 4/15. Federal Work-Study Program available. Institutional employment available.

The Inside Word

The admissions process at University of Wyoming is formula-driven. For assured admission, you must have a minimum cumulative GPA of 3.0 and have met the high school curriculum requirements.

THE SCHOOL SAYS

From the Admissions Office

"The University of Wyoming offers a personalized education for a fraction of the cost of other public universities. Located in Laramie, UW is regularly recognized as one of the nation's best college values. This comes as no surprise, as UW is a national research university offering countless academic opportunities.

"The University of Wyoming has earned its Research Level 1 (R1) status from the Carnegie Classification of Institutions of Higher Education, placing Wyoming's only four-year university with the top research universities in the United States.

"Explore 200+ programs of study through seven colleges and three specialized schools. From Engineering to Business, Performing Arts to Geology and Agricultural Economics to Nursing, we are sure you will find your program at UW.

"Students have a new place to live and eat on campus. UW built two new Residence Halls which are state-of-the-art along with a two-story dining center. The $285.5 million project is the largest construction project on the UW Campus. The new halls are located next to the Wyoming Union and Half Acre Recreation and Wellness Center. In addition to fantastic residence halls, undergraduate students have access to excellent facilities for instruction, internships, research and living opportunities.

"Set at 7,200 feet above sea level, UW and Laramie are in a pristine location to attend school and enjoy the outdoors. UW was recently recognized by Outside magazine as the fifteenth best college campus in the country for outdoor adventure. Just thirty miles from campus is over two million acres of national forest with peaks climbing over 12,000 feet. Campus life is exciting with 200+ student clubs and organizations as well as NCAA Division I-A sports in the Mountain West conference."

SELECTIVITY

# of total applicants	6,167
% of total applicants accepted	97
% of total acceptees attending	24
# of in-state applicants	1,710
% of in-state applicants accepted	97
# of out-of-state-applicants	4,360
% of applicants accepted from out of state	97
# of international applicants	96
% of international applicants accepted	91

First-Year Profile

Testing policy	Test Optional
Range SAT composite	1040–1280
Range SAT EBRW	520–660
Range SAT math	500–630
Range ACT composite	20–27
% submitting SAT scores	15
% submitting ACT scores	67
Average HS GPA	3.5
% submitting high school GPA	99
% graduated top 10% of class	21
% graduated top 25% of class	47
% graduated top 50% of class	77
% submitting high school rank	53

Important Dates

Regular	
Apply by	8/10
Notified by	Rolling
Nonfall registration?	Yes

FINANCIAL FACTS

Annual in-state tuition	$5,610
Annual out-of-state tuition	$22,470
Food and housing	$13,986
Required fees (First-year)	$2,920 ($3,070)
Books and supplies	$1,300
Average need-based scholarship (First-year)	$7,906 ($7,997)
% students with need rec. need-based scholarship or grant aid (First-year)	81 (81)
% students with need rec. non-need-based scholarship or grant aid (First-year)	77 (89)
% students with need rec. need-based self-help aid (First-year)	42 (43)
% students rec. any financial aid (First-year)	88 (94)
% UG borrow to pay for school	34
Average cumulative indebtedness	$24,313
% of students with need fully met (First-year)	14 (20)
Average % of student need met (First-year)	59 (63)

URSINUS COLLEGE

601 East Main St., Collegeville, PA 19426 • Admissions: 610-409-3200

Survey Snapshot
Easy to get around campus
Theater is popular
Students are happy

RATINGS

Quality of Life	83
Fire Safety	97
Green	82
Academic	86
Profs Interesting	91
Profs Accessible	95
Admissions	83
Financial Aid	90

CAMPUS LIFE

Type of school	Private
Environment	Town

Students

Degree-seeking undergrad enrollment	1,363
% male/female/not reported	52/48/0
% from out of state	38
% First-year from public high school	74
% First-year live on campus	93
% Ugrads live on campus	90
# of fraternities (% join)	8 (3)
# of sororities (% join)	5 (11)
% Asian	3
% Black or African American	9
% Hispanic	9
% Native American	<1
% Pacific Islander	<1
% Race and/or ethnicity unknown	3
% Two or more races	5
% White	69
% International	<1
# of countries represented	8

CAMPUS MENTAL HEALTH SERVICES

Offers mental health/wellness program	Yes
Mental health training available to students	Yes
Employs Chief Wellness Officer	Yes
Peer-to-peer mental health offerings	Yes
Counseling center has guidelines or accreditation	No
Mental health/well-being courses	Yes, for-credit

ACADEMICS

% students returning for sophomore year	77
% students graduating within 4 years	67
% students graduating within 6 years	73
Calendar	Semester
Student/faculty ratio	9:1
Most common class size 10–19.	(54%)
Most common lab/discussion size 10–19.	(84%)

Most Popular Majors
Biology/Biological Sciences; Finance; Psychology

Applicants Also Look At
Penn State University Park, Saint Joseph's University (PA), Temple University, University of Pittsburgh—Pittsburgh Campus, West Chester University of Pennsylvania

STUDENTS SAY "..."

Academics

Located just outside of Philadelphia, Ursinus College has done a remarkable job of building a "close-knit community" dedicated to helping students succeed with strong academics and "plenty of opportunities for leadership involvement through clubs, student jobs, and internships." The "liberal arts curricula [encourages undergrads] to explore different fields" and potentially uncover new academic areas of interest. Even better, there's a tremendous "focus on research." Students also rush to highlight the "science and pre-health prep program[s]," duly noting Ursinus's "high medical school acceptance rate." Some of that success can likely be attributed to "small" classes, which are a staple here. As one first-year student brags, "My smallest class size is seven and my largest is twenty-one." She continues, "I receive...[so much] attention that [it] makes it feel as though I have a seal team of PhDs looking out for me, and that is truly amazing." Indeed, professors here are "very supportive, intelligent, and passionate about the subjects they are teaching." And they work hard to make sure they're accessible. As one student shares, "Their office hours are incredibly flexible (at certain times and by appointment as well). I've gone into some professors' office hours three times a week for the entirety of the semester, I've had professors come in on Sundays to help, and I've been to their houses for dinner...I've grown substantially...with their help."

Campus Life

We've been assured that "there's never a dull moment" at Ursinus. After all, the college "offer[s] so many activities [with which] to get involved." Extracurricular clubs range from a "pre-medicine help group...to a nerf club where [members] battle on the weekends in academic buildings." Community service is also pretty popular here too. For example, "on Saturdays, groups of people will generally wake up and volunteer at the soup kitchen or go to the local nursing home and either visit or sing songs to them." Once the weekend rolls around, you can certainly find "a lot of parties." Then again, that's probably a given considering that "many students are [involved] in Greek life." However, if you aren't down for drinking, it's not a problem. There "are always people who will just hang out and watch movies or play silly board games." Students who love to laugh will be delighted to learn that Ursinus sponsors a number of "comedy events," either "hosted by the UC improv club or...a guest comedian [brought in by the school.]" Finally, the "Campus Activities Board also puts on events multiple times a month that can be anything from trivia to Pinterest nights." It's virtually impossible not to have fun here!

Student Body

Students at Ursinus speak enthusiastically about their classmates. Of course, it's difficult to say something negative about people who "are always smiling" and "very welcoming." Undergrads do admit that the majority of their peers are "white [and] middle class": "While the college is homogeneous...in ethnic terms, it is ideologically very heterogeneous." As one undergrad explains, "I have encountered many ideas and beliefs that have challenged my own...[which] I very much appreciate." Students also stress that their classmates are "hardworking" and "down to earth." Moreover, as you might expect with college students, these undergrads also "tend to be curious." Indeed, "Everyone has something they really want to know more about." Interests and passions seem to run the gamut at Ursinus; you'll find everyone from "athletes [and] bio nerds [to] theatre kids" along with "prep[s and] hipsters." You "truly get a bit of everything here." Another happy student concludes, "Ursinus is a school where everyone fits in and you are encouraged to be yourself no matter how weird you may be. [It's a place that] appreciates people with different backgrounds, interests, and abilities."

URSINUS COLLEGE

Financial Aid: 610-409-3600 • E-Mail: admission@ursinus.edu • Website: www.ursinus.edu

THE PRINCETON REVIEW SAYS

Admissions

The school reports that its standardized testing policy for use in admission for Fall 2026 is Test Optional. The Princeton Review suggests that interested applicants consult with the school for the most up-to-date standardized testing policies. *Very important factors considered include:* rigor of secondary school record, academic GPA, character/personal qualities. *Important factors considered include:* class rank, application essay, recommendation(s), extracurricular activities, talent/ability. *Other factors considered include:* standardized test scores, interview, first generation, alumni/ae relation, geographical residence, state residency, volunteer work, work experience, level of applicant's interest. High school diploma is required and GED is accepted. *Academic units required:* 4 English, 3 math, 1 science, 1 science lab, 2 language (other than English), 1 social studies, 5 academic electives. *Academic units recommended:* 4 English, 4 math, 4 science, 3 science labs, 3 language (other than English), 4 social studies, 5 academic electives.

Financial Aid

Students should submit: FAFSA; State aid form. Priority filing deadline is 2/1. The Princeton Review suggests that all financial aid forms be submitted as soon as possible. *Need-based scholarships/grants offered:* Federal Pell; Federal SEOG; State scholarships/grants; Private scholarships; College/university scholarship or grant aid from institutional funds. *Loan aid offered:* Federal Direct Subsidized Loans; Federal Direct Unsubsidized Loans; Direct PLUS loans. Admitted students will be notified of awards on a rolling basis beginning 11/11. Federal Work-Study Program available. Institutional employment available.

The Inside Word

Admissions officers at Ursinus are looking for motivated students who demonstrate intellectual curiosity. They want applicants who have pushed themselves academically in high school, beyond basic college prep courses. Students who have filled their schedules with some AP or IB classes might find they have a leg up. Finally, to be considered for all possible scholarships, it's best to apply either early action or early decision.

THE SCHOOL SAYS

From the Admissions Office

"Located in suburban Philadelphia, the college boasts a beautiful 170-acre campus that features a highly individualized academic experience; the nationally recognized Common Intellectual Experience first-year seminar, which is a component of the Quest: Open Questions Open Minds core curriculum; residential village housing for students; the Floy Lewis Bakes Athletic Center with an indoor track-and-field-house; the Berman Museum of Art; The Kaleidoscope performing arts center; the state-of-the-art interdisciplinary Innovation and Discovery Center; and the new Schellhase Commons, a student hub and admission welcome center. Ursinus is a member of the Centennial Conference along with Dickinson, Franklin & Marshall, Gettysburg, Muhlenberg, and Swarthmore. The academic environment is enhanced by a chapter of Phi Beta Kappa; a direct admission partnership with Saint Joseph's University (MBA program); dual-degree engineering agreements with Columbia University and Case Western Reserve; an affiliation agreement with the Villanova University M. Louise Fitzpatrick College of Nursing (accelerated BSN); international study abroad; and three centers: the Center for Science and the Common Good, the U-Imagine Center for Integrative and Entrepreneurial Studies, and the Melrose Center for Global Civic Engagement. The college offers student research carried out with one-on-one faculty attention and extensive internship opportunities. Financial aid and scholarships are generous with special awards for outstanding academics; distinguished creative writing; music, dance and theater auditions; and Bonner leadership in service. Intercollegiate and intramural sports are very popular on campus. The Ursinus admission application requires strong and consistent performance in a college preparatory curriculum. Submission of standardized test scores is optional."

SELECTIVITY

# of total applicants	2,867
% of total applicants accepted	93
% of total acceptees attending	13
# of in-state applicants	1,503
% of in-state applicants accepted	95
# of out-of-state-applicants	1,215
% of applicants accepted from out of state	97
# of international applicants	149
% of international applicants accepted	39
# of early decision applicants	40
% of early decision applicants accepted	95
# offered a place on the wait list	0
# admitted from wait list	0

First-Year Profile

Testing policy	Test Optional
Range SAT composite	1230–1390
Range SAT EBRW	620–710
Range SAT math	590–680
Range ACT composite	27–29
% submitting SAT scores	20
% submitting ACT scores	1
Average HS GPA	3.5
% submitting high school GPA	100
% graduated top 10% of class	24
% graduated top 25% of class	46
% graduated top 50% of class	72
% submitting high school rank	36

Important Dates

Early decision	
Apply by	12/1
Notified by	11/22
Other ED Apply by	2/1
Other ED Notified by	1/23
Early action	
Apply by	11/1
Notified by	11/22
Regular	
Apply by	5/1
Notified by	Rolling, 11/22
Nonfall registration?	Yes

FINANCIAL FACTS

Annual tuition	$61,500
Food and housing	$17,928
Required fees (First-year)	$750 ($960)
Books and supplies	$1,000
Average need-based scholarship (First-year)	$44,910 ($46,172)
% students with need rec. need-based scholarship or grant aid (First-year)	99 (98)
% students with need rec. non-need-based scholarship or grant aid (First-year)	27 (28)
% students with need rec. need-based self-help aid (First-year)	69 (67)
% students rec. any financial aid (First-year)	99 (100)
% UG borrow to pay for school	71
Average cumulative indebtedness	$49,728
% of students with need fully met (First-year)	33 (35)
Average % of student need met (First-year)	83 (84)

VANDERBILT UNIVERSITY

2301 Vanderbilt Place, Nashville, TN 37235 • Admissions: 615-322-2561

Survey Snapshot
Students are happy
Students love Nashville, TN
Great off-campus food

RATINGS

Quality of Life	**98**
Fire Safety	**60***
Green	**60***
Academic	**90**
Profs Interesting	**95**
Profs Accessible	**97**
Admissions	**99**
Financial Aid	**98**

CAMPUS LIFE

Type of school	Private
Environment	Metropolis

Students

Degree-seeking undergrad enrollment	7,208
% male/female/not reported	48/52/0
% from out of state	88
% First-year from public high school	64
% First-year live on campus	100
% Ugrads live on campus	84
# of fraternities (% join)	17 (24)
# of sororities (% join)	15 (28)
% Asian	19
% Black or African American	9
% Hispanic	11
% Native American	<1
% Pacific Islander	<1
% Race and/or ethnicity unknown	4
% Two or more races	6
% White	39
% International	11
# of countries represented	51

CAMPUS MENTAL HEALTH SERVICES

Offers mental health/wellness program	Yes
Mental health training available to students	No
Employs Chief Wellness Officer	No
Peer-to-peer mental health offerings	NR
Counseling center has guidelines or accreditation	No
Mental health/well-being courses	NR

ACADEMICS

% students returning for sophomore year	96
% students graduating within 4 years	90
% students graduating within 6 years	94
Calendar	Semester
Student/faculty ratio	8:1
Most common class size 10–19.	(33%)
Most common lab/discussion size 10–19.	(61%)

Most Popular Majors

Engineering Science; Multi-/Interdisciplinary Studies; Social Sciences

Applicants Also Look At

Brown University, Columbia University, Cornell University, Dartmouth College, Duke University, Harvard College, Johns Hopkins University, Northwestern University, Princeton University, Rice University, Stanford University, The University of Chicago, University of Pennsylvania, Washington University in St. Louis, Yale University

STUDENTS SAY "..."

Academics

Vanderbilt University is "an academically rigorous and vibrant school" where professors bring "diverse work experiences outside of Vanderbilt" into the classroom while remaining deeply invested in student success. One student explains that professors "will reach out personally to help students, hold extra office hours, and meet with students for things unrelated to class, such as interview prep or career advising." That accessibility extends into the curriculum itself: "you can take courses in a variety of subject areas, even if they are not within your major or minor requirements." One student notes getting to "frequently create scientific models, converse in foreign languages, and debate during classes." Another student shares, "As a first-year engineering student, I took three six-week engineering modules in three different engineering disciplines. For my first module, I got to build a ukulele from scratch using CAD programs, 3D printing, and laser cutting. It was amazing to be able to use so many tools that I did not believe I would have access to until I was an upperclassman." Students love that Vanderbilt provides "the resources and support they need to succeed, including access to world-class libraries, technology, and career services."

Campus Life

Commodores, as students are affectionately known across campus, enjoy being in "Nashville with SEC athletics"—and that school spirit is palpable. "Football has become a focal point. We have really embraced the 'football school' title, and people carve out the time from their studies to make sure to cheer on the team each weekend." The "amazing sports teams with free admission" further encourage "students to show up for one another." Beyond athletics, campus administration plays a meaningful role in the overall experience; "whether it's a football game or a religious celebration, each event is well thought-out, and the school always adds small details that push the experience over the edge in terms of satisfaction." That attention to detail contributes to the "balance and quality of life" students cite as one of their favorite parts of being a Commodore. "Vanderbilt effectively does double-duty as both a small-campus school and one in a large metropolitan city with plenty of opportunity," and students delight in "being in the heart of Nashville," a "booming city with so much to explore," including a thriving food scene. Students appreciate that Vanderbilt's Taste of Nashville Program allows them to "use our meal plan at certain restaurants off campus." Altogether, Vanderbilt offers "top-tier academics, athletics, and social life, all while being located in one of the fastest-growing cities in the country."

Student Body

"There is no single 'Vanderbilt student archetype'"; rather, Commodores are "diverse in background in all aspects (socio-economic, political, religious, etc.), yet we all are looking to strive toward excellence together." Another student describes their peers as "genuinely kind and deeply excited about their school," adding that "They're not only driven and passionate but also sincerely interested in getting to know everyone around them, creating a community that feels welcoming, supportive, and truly authentic." As one student simply puts it, "You'll find your community, whoever that may be." That spirit extends into everyday life, where "everyone studies outside, collaborates, and overall has an open mindset to learning that [develops] an exceptionally strong community for the whole school," and students can count on each other to "feel valued and are there for days when I have three exams, or when I want to hang out, they are there for it all." Ultimately, "the community culture here rests on the shoulders of the students and faculty that go out of their way to help out a fellow Commodore, build personal relationships, collaborate, foster dialogue about difficult topics, and generally support each other in every way possible."

Vanderbilt University

Financial Aid: 800-288-0204 • E-Mail: admissions@vanderbilt.edu • Website: www.vanderbilt.edu

THE PRINCETON REVIEW SAYS

Admissions

The school reports that its standardized testing policy for use in admission for Fall 2026 is Test Optional. The Princeton Review suggests that interested applicants consult with the school for the most up-to-date standardized testing policies. *Very important factors considered include:* rigor of secondary school record, class rank, academic GPA, application essay, extracurricular activities, character/personal qualities. *Important factors considered include:* standardized test scores, recommendation(s), talent/ability. *Other factors considered include:* first generation, alumni/ae relation, geographical residence, state residency, volunteer work, work experience. High school diploma is required and GED is accepted. *Academic units required:* 4 English, 3 math, 3 science, 2 science labs, 2 language (other than English), 2 social studies, 1 history, 3 academic electives. *Academic units recommended:* 4 English, 4 math, 4 science, 3 science labs, 2 language (other than English), 3 social studies, 1 history, 3 academic electives.

Financial Aid

Students should submit: FAFSA; CSS PROFILE. Priority filing deadline is 2/1. The Princeton Review suggests that all financial aid forms be submitted as soon as possible. *Need-based scholarships/grants offered:* Federal Pell; Federal SEOG; State scholarships/grants; Private scholarships; College/university scholarship or grant aid from institutional funds; United Negro College Fund. *Loan aid offered:* Federal Direct Subsidized Loans; Federal Direct Unsubsidized Loans; Direct PLUS loans; State Loans. Admitted students will be notified of awards on or about 4/1. Federal Work-Study Program available. Institutional employment available.

The Inside Word

Vanderbilt deliberately keeps its incoming first-year class small, and admission to this Nashville institution continues to be highly selective. With the admission committee's holistic approach to reviewing candidates, interested students should take stock of more than just their GPAs. Many students take the early decision route—Vanderbilt has two early decision deadlines. A final note: Most successful candidates take 5 core academic courses per year throughout all four years of high school.

THE SCHOOL SAYS

From the Admissions Office

"The Vanderbilt undergraduate experience is often described as uniquely balanced. Within the context of an outstanding academic landscape, students are encouraged to participate in a broad spectrum of campus organizations among a highly diverse population. Many students take classes in all five undergraduate schools, stretching their intellectual experience far beyond that of their declared major. Students typically live on campus all four years, beginning at The Martha Rivers Ingram College, a living and learning residential community for first-year students. In recent years, new residential colleges have expanded living-learning opportunities for upper-division students. Students take full advantage of Nashville, participating in internships and cultural offerings from a city that Travel + Leisure ranked as one of the 15 Best Cities in the United States.

"The university believes that cost should never be a barrier to a world-class education and makes three commitments as part of its Opportunity Vanderbilt financial aid program: (1) to be need-blind for all U.S. citizens and eligible non-citizens, (2) to meet 100 percent of a family's demonstrated financial need, (3) to avoid loans, instead providing grant assistance and reasonable work-study.

"The admissions process is holistic—Vanderbilt does not employ cutoffs for standardized testing or grade point averages. Students admitted to Vanderbilt typically show exceptional academic accomplishment and are highly engaged in their communities, often serving in leadership roles. The prescreening video and audition are of primary importance for students applying to the Blair School of Music."

SELECTIVITY

# of total applicants	45,404
% of total applicants accepted	6
% of total acceptees attending	61
# of in-state applicants	2,463
% of in-state applicants accepted	11
# of out-of-state-applicants	34,605
% of applicants accepted from out of state	6
# of international applicants	8,341
% of international applicants accepted	4
# of early decision applicants	5,363
% of early decision applicants accepted	15
# admitted from wait list	279

First-Year Profile

Testing policy	Test Optional
Range SAT composite	1510–1560
Range SAT EBRW	730–770
Range SAT math	770–800
Range ACT composite	34–35
% submitting SAT scores	27
% submitting ACT scores	25
Average HS GPA	3.9
% submitting high school GPA	100
% graduated top 10% of class	90
% graduated top 25% of class	94
% graduated top 50% of class	99
% submitting high school rank	23

Important Dates

Early decision	
Apply by	11/1
Notified by	12/15
Other ED Apply by	1/1
Regular	
Apply by	1/1
Notified by	4/1
Nonfall registration?	No

FINANCIAL FACTS*

Annual tuition	$67,934
Food and housing	$23,048
Required fees	$3,292
Books and supplies	$1,100
Average need-based scholarship (First-year)	$73,698 ($75,271)
% students with need rec. need-based scholarship or grant aid (First-year)	100 (100)
% students with need rec. non-need-based scholarship or grant aid (First-year)	7 (11)
% students with need rec. need-based self-help aid (First-year)	72 (64)
% students rec. any financial aid (First-year)	65 (70)
% UG borrow to pay for school	17
Average cumulative indebtedness	$27,795
% of students with need fully met (First-year)	100 (100)
Average % of student need met (First-year)	100 (100)

* Most recently reported data at time of printing. Scan the QR code to find the latest updates.

VASSAR COLLEGE

124 Raymond Avenue, Poughkeepsie, NY 12604 • Admissions: 845-437-7300

Survey Snapshot
Lots of liberal students
Class discussions encouraged
Theater is popular

RATINGS

Quality of Life	88
Fire Safety	63
Green	60*
Academic	93
Profs Interesting	95
Profs Accessible	95
Admissions	95
Financial Aid	99

CAMPUS LIFE

Type of school	Private
Environment	Town

Students

Degree-seeking undergrad enrollment	2,485
% male/female/not reported	39/61/<1
% from out of state	32
% First-year live on campus	100
% Ugrads live on campus	97
# of fraternities	0
# of sororities	0
% Asian	10
% Black or African American	3
% Hispanic	13
% Native American	<1
% Pacific Islander	0
% Race and/or ethnicity unknown	4
% Two or more races	8
% White	54
% International	6
# of countries represented	50

CAMPUS MENTAL HEALTH SERVICES

Offers mental health/wellness program	Yes
Mental health training available to students	No
Employs Chief Wellness Officer	NR
Peer-to-peer mental health offerings	NR
Counseling center has guidelines or accreditation	No
Mental health/well-being courses	NR

ACADEMICS

% students returning for sophomore year	95
% students graduating within 4 years	81
% students graduating within 6 years	88
Calendar	Semester
Student/faculty ratio	7:1
Most common class size 10–19.	(46%)
Most common lab/discussion size 10–19.	(60%)

Most Popular Majors

Mathematics; Research and Experimental Psychology; Economics

Applicants Sometimes Prefer

Amherst College, Bowdoin College, Brown University, Cornell University, Swarthmore College, Tufts University, University of California—Berkeley, Wesleyan University

STUDENTS SAY "..."

Academics

Vassar College, a small, "academically challenging" school, offers a "perfect liberal arts feel," blending intellectual rigor with a collaborative, creative spirit. Known for its multidisciplinary learning, Vassar encourages students to expand traditional academic boundaries and connect ideas across fields—a hallmark of its open curriculum. With no core requirements, students have the freedom to forge their own educational paths: "A great opportunity for students to explore anything they want before settling into a major," attests one student. The college excels in the humanities, sciences, and arts, with particularly strong programs in Art History, English, Drama, and Biology. Students describe classes as "very discussion-based," and that extends to the campus, where it's said "no problem goes undiscussed." The "amazing" and "super accessible" professors help to model this idea, by being "fully engaged in the total Vassar community" and "spectacular at illuminating difficult material," as well as "willing to meet you outside their office hours." Another distinguishing feature is that classes are taught exclusively by professors. This creates a much-appreciated mix of "high academics" and "a more relaxed environment."

Campus Life

Students find Vassar's accredited arboretum campus to be "stunning," and note that its mix of Gothic and futurist buildings starts to feel like home very quickly. The school is filled with magnificent sights, like a multifloor stained glass window in the library, but also accessible: "The vibe of the whole school is so chill," and there's a "vibrant extracurricular scene." Vassar is "bursting at the seams with orgs": intramural sports, a cappella, comedy, ice skating, ceramics, performing arts, politics, and "basically anything else you can think of." The "close-knit dormitory communities" and an emphasis on being "hyper-socially aware" shape a student body that is "excited to be with each other, which creates this school spirit that isn't necessarily based on sports." Although there is no Greek life, "there are always parties you can go to if you want," and with New York City just a train ride away, students enjoy easy access to world-class exhibitions, performances, and nightlife. Intellectual conversations abound at all hours, and students spend "significant time thinking about the state of the world and what's going on within the campus community."

Student Body

Vassar College is characterized by many degrees of freedom, not just its open curriculum. Students describe a freedom of expression that's "all about being unique and letting your quirky characteristics shine." They also speak to an intellectual freedom filled with thriving "open-minded" individuals. There's also a degree of financial freedom, as 100 percent of demonstrated financial need is met, which leads to "wide socioeconomic diversity" on campus. These freedoms mean that "you can definitely find at least one other student for every obscure interest you have." Whether it's in an inclusive first-year orientation that's "a great way for people to make friends" or the ways the school fosters community and connection, the "left-wing, artsy, intelligent" students feel genuinely supported.

Vassar College

Financial Aid: 845-437-5320 • E-Mail: admission@vassar.edu • Website: www.vassar.edu

THE PRINCETON REVIEW SAYS

Admissions

The school reports that its standardized testing policy for use in admission for Fall 2026 is Test Optional. The Princeton Review suggests that interested applicants consult with the school for the most up-to-date standardized testing policies. *Very important factors considered include:* rigor of secondary school record, academic GPA, application essay, recommendation(s), extracurricular activities, talent/ability, character/personal qualities. *Important factors considered include:* class rank, volunteer work, work experience. *Other factors considered include:* standardized test scores, interview, first generation, alumni/ae relation, geographical residence, religious affiliation/commitment. High school diploma is required and GED is accepted. *Academic units recommended:* 4 English, 4 math, 4 science, 4 language (other than English), 4 social studies.

Financial Aid

Students should submit: FAFSA; CSS PROFILE; State aid form; Business/Farm Supplement. Priority filing deadline is 2/1. The Princeton Review suggests that all financial aid forms be submitted as soon as possible. *Need-based scholarships/grants offered:* Federal Pell; Federal SEOG; State scholarships/grants; Private scholarships; College/university scholarship or grant aid from institutional funds; United Negro College Fund. *Loan aid offered:* Federal Direct Subsidized Loans; Federal Direct Unsubsidized Loans; Direct PLUS loans; College/university loans from institutional funds. Admitted students will be notified of awards on or about 3/25. Federal Work-Study Program available. Institutional employment available.

The Inside Word

With a low acceptance rate, stellar academic credentials are a must for any serious Vassar candidate. Once admissions officers see you meet their rigorous scholastic standards, they'll closely assess your personal essay, recommendations, and extracurricular activities. The college prides itself on selecting students who will add to the vitality of the campus. Demonstrating an intellectual curiosity that extends outside the classroom is as important as success within it.

THE SCHOOL SAYS

From the Admissions Office

"Vassar presents a rich variety of social and cultural activities, clubs, living arrangements, and regional attractions. Vassar also fields 25 Varsity sports plus 4 intercollegiate club teams, and more than 20 percent of students participate. Vassar is a vital, residential college community recognized for its respect for the rights and individuality of others."

SELECTIVITY

# of total applicants	11,118
% of total applicants accepted	21
% of total acceptees attending	30
# of in-state applicants	2,194
% of in-state applicants accepted	28
# of out-of-state-applicants	5,219
% of applicants accepted from out of state	29
# of international applicants	3,705
% of international applicants accepted	5
# of early decision applicants	1,046
% of early decision applicants accepted	38
# offered a place on the wait list	918
# admitted from wait list	30

First-Year Profile

Testing policy	Test Optional
Range SAT composite	1460–1520
Range SAT EBRW	730–770
Range SAT math	710–770
Range ACT composite	33–34
% submitting SAT scores	32
% submitting ACT scores	14
% graduated top 10% of class	79
% graduated top 25% of class	97
% graduated top 50% of class	100
% submitting high school rank	29

Important Dates

Early decision	
Apply by	11/15
Notified by	12/15
Other ED Apply by	1/1
Other ED Notified by	2/1
Regular	
Apply by	1/1
Notified by	4/1
Nonfall registration?	No

FINANCIAL FACTS

Annual tuition	$70,050
Food and housing	$18,240
Required fees	$980
Books and supplies	$2,250
Average need-based scholarship (First-year)	$65,876 ($67,214)
% students with need rec. need-based scholarship or grant aid (First-year)	100 (100)
% students with need rec. non-need-based scholarship or grant aid (First-year)	0 (0)
% students with need rec. need-based self-help aid (First-year)	92 (88)
% students rec. any financial aid (First-year)	53 (52)
% UG borrow to pay for school	45
Average cumulative indebtedness	$28,375
% of students with need fully met (First-year)	100 (100)
Average % of student need met (First-year)	100 (100)

VILLANOVA UNIVERSITY

800 E. Lancaster Avenue, Villanova, PA 19085 • Admissions: 610-519-6450

Survey Snapshot
Career services are great
School is well run
Students are very religious

RATINGS

Quality of Life	82
Fire Safety	60*
Green	60*
Academic	85
Profs Interesting	93
Profs Accessible	95
Admissions	94
Financial Aid	86

CAMPUS LIFE

Type of school	Private
Affiliation	Roman Catholic
Environment	Village

Students

Degree-seeking undergrad enrollment	6,860
% male/female/not reported	47/53/<1
% from out of state	76
% First-year live on campus	99
% Ugrads live on campus	82
# of fraternities (% join)	12 (18)
# of sororities (% join)	12 (16)
% Asian	6
% Black or African American	6
% Hispanic	12
% Native American	0
% Pacific Islander	<1
% Race and/or ethnicity unknown	2
% Two or more races	4
% White	68
% International	2

CAMPUS MENTAL HEALTH SERVICES

Offers mental health/wellness program	Yes
Mental health training available to students	Yes
Employs Chief Wellness Officer	No
Peer-to-peer mental health offerings	Yes
Counseling center has guidelines or accreditation	Yes
Mental health/well-being courses	Yes, for-credit

ACADEMICS

% students returning for sophomore year	95
% students graduating within 4 years	89
% students graduating within 6 years	93
Calendar	Semester
Student/faculty ratio	9:1

Applicants Also Look At

Boston College, University of Michigan—Ann Arbor, University of Notre Dame, University of Pennsylvania, University of Virginia

STUDENTS SAY "…"

Academics

Villanova University puts an "emphasis on service" and sets students up for success by providing numerous resources, not just for current enrollees but for graduates as well. The school's track record bears that out, with 95 percent of the graduating class of 2024 securing opportunities after graduation. To help students achieve their goals, classrooms tend to mix things up across lectures, discussions, field trips, and projects, the latter of which are specifically praised for having "real-world applications" and being "designed to help students in the long run." Along with that, students point to how "opportunities outside of the classroom really complement your education." For example, Nova offers service-learning courses where students work directly with partners in the local community, including volunteering with nonprofits focused on adult literacy, working with athletes in the Special Olympics, and tutoring in local prisons. Moreover, in addition to a wide variety of tutoring services, there are need-based initiatives like The Sunshine Fund, which helps to pay for things like attending conference or club fees. No matter what form the classes take, students can expect to find passionate professors who get "fired up about what they teach" and are "true teachers and scholars." Professors are "easily accessible" and "go above and beyond their office hours" to offer support, though students recommend being proactive: "It is mostly up to you to take advantage of them as a resource." Between the hands-on professors and the school's numerous resources, Nova is a place where "If you want to succeed, the community will do everything in its power to make sure you can do so."

Campus Life

On the busy Villanova campus, most people are involved in one of the 300 student organizations and "a ton of students get involved with intramurals or club sports teams, as well." There are opportunities to volunteer, such as "week-long service break experiences all over the world" or "driving into Philly to play with kids and help them with their studies." Events, like formals, are "a big deal," and at Fall Festival, the world's largest student-run Special Olympics event, students enjoy "cheering on the athletes." The same goes for basketball season, where "people get their work done early to flock to the [Pavilion] for games." Throughout the year, there are weekend activities hosted by the Campus Activity Team and students can hang out at the Connelly Center, which has lounges, meeting rooms, a coffee shop, an ice cream shop, and "a cinema that is always showing a movie." The majority of students live on campus and "most residence halls are really impressive and kept up very well." Philadelphia is "an easy short train ride" away and the school also offers a free weekend shuttle to the King of Prussia Mall, one of the largest in the country. On average, the campus "has a focused atmosphere" and as the weekend approaches, "you can feel [the] campus relax and people are more likely to go out."

Student Body

"We are the Nova Nation, built upon an unbreakable foundation of community." This sense of community stems "from service, school spirit around the basketball team, and everyone actively pursuing their own area of academic interest." Students balance their academics, extracurriculars, and volunteer work alongside having fun: they "party on the weekends and show up ready to all of their classes." Overall, the "well-rounded" and typical classmate is "extremely affable, professional, and an achiever," or to put it another way, "a school full of all the high school superstars." Overall, this crowd gets along well with each other, coming together to create an "outstanding community" that's built on "a lot of mutual respect."

VILLANOVA UNIVERSITY

Financial Aid: 610-519-4010 • E-Mail: gotovu@villanova.edu • Website: www.villanova.edu

THE PRINCETON REVIEW SAYS

Admissions

The school reports that its standardized testing policy for use in admission for Fall 2026 is Test Optional. The Princeton Review suggests that interested applicants consult with the school for the most up-to-date standardized testing policies. *Very important factors considered include:* rigor of secondary school record, academic GPA, application essay. *Important factors considered include:* recommendation(s), extracurricular activities, talent/ability, character/personal qualities, volunteer work. *Other factors considered include:* class rank, standardized test scores, first generation, alumni/ae relation, geographical residence, state residency, level of applicant's interest. High school diploma is required and GED is accepted. *Academic units required:* 4 English, 4 math, 4 science, 2 science labs, 3 language (other than English), 4 social studies, 2 academic electives. *Academic units recommended:* 4 English, 4 math, 4 science, 3 science labs, 4 language (other than English), 4 social studies, 2 academic electives.

Financial Aid

Students should submit: CSS PROFILE; FAFSA. Priority filing deadline is 1/15. The Princeton Review suggests that all financial aid forms be submitted as soon as possible. *Need-based scholarships/grants offered:* Federal Pell; Federal SEOG; State scholarships/grants; Private scholarships; College/university scholarship or grant aid from institutional funds. *Loan aid offered:* Federal Direct Subsidized Loans; Federal Direct Unsubsidized Loans; Direct PLUS loans. Federal Work-Study Program available. Institutional employment available.

The Inside Word

Villanova's growing academic reputation means its application process is growing more competitive: 84 percent of the most recent admitted first-year class ranked in the top 10 percent of their high school graduating class. Although academic achievement is important, the university looks at the whole package when considering applicants and expects candidates to be well rounded. As a private university, Villanova is not exactly cheap, but the school offers a wide variety of scholarships and aid to qualifying students.

THE SCHOOL SAYS

From the Admissions Office

"Villanova is the oldest and largest Catholic university in Pennsylvania, founded in 1842 by the Order of Saint Augustine. Students of all faiths are welcome. The university tends to attract students who are interested in volunteerism. Villanovans provide more than 249,000 hours of service annually and host the largest student-run Special Olympics in the nation. Villanova's scenic campus is located twelve miles west of Philadelphia. The university offers programs through four undergraduate colleges: the College of Liberal Arts and Sciences, the College of Engineering, the M. Louise Fitzpatrick College of Nursing, and the Villanova School of Business. There are 265 student organizations and thirty-six National Honor Societies at Villanova. Incoming freshmen can opt to be part of a Learning Community, through which student groups live together in specially-designated residence halls and learn together in courses and co-curricular programs. The university offers Naval and Marine Reserve Officers Training Corps (ROTC) programs and hundreds of options for studying abroad. Nova's alumni body is comprised of more than 135,000 people. Some prominent grads include: Bert Jacobs, co-founder, Life Is Good Co.; Dr. Jill Biden, First Lady of the United States of America; and James C. Davis, chairman, Allegis Group.

"If you're looking to join Nova Nation, be prepared: The competition for admission is getting tougher every year."

SELECTIVITY

# of total applicants	25,841
% of total applicants accepted	28
% of total acceptees attending	25
# of in-state applicants	522
% of in-state applicants accepted	41
# of out-of-state-applicants	23,777
% of applicants accepted from out of state	29
# of international applicants	1,542
% of international applicants accepted	11
# of early decision applicants	1,680
% of early decision applicants accepted	60

First-Year Profile

Testing policy	Test Optional
Range SAT EBRW	700–750
Range SAT math	710–770
Range ACT composite	32–34
% submitting SAT scores	19
% submitting ACT scores	9

Important Dates

Early decision	
Apply by	11/1
Notified by	12/15
Other ED Apply by	1/15
Other ED Notified by	3/1
Early action	
Apply by	11/1
Notified by	1/20
Regular	
Apply by	1/15
Notified by	4/1

FINANCIAL FACTS*

Annual tuition	$72,990
Food and housing	$19,354
Required fees	$1,024
Books and supplies	$1,160
Average need-based scholarship (First-year)	$40,453 ($40,829)
% students with need rec. need-based scholarship or grant aid (First-year)	89 (87)
% students with need rec. non-need-based scholarship or grant aid (First-year)	38 (28)
% students with need rec. need-based self-help aid (First-year)	92 (93)
% UG borrow to pay for school	37
Average cumulative indebtedness	$38,870
% of students with need fully met (First-year)	19 (19)
Average % of student need met (First-year)	80 (80)

* Most recently reported data at time of printing. Scan the QR code to find the latest updates.

Virginia Tech

800 Drillfield Drive, Blacksburg, VA 24061 • Admissions: 540-231-6267

Survey Snapshot
School is well run
Diverse student types interact on campus
Students get along with local community

RATINGS	
Quality of Life	82
Fire Safety	79
Green	99
Academic	83
Profs Interesting	88
Profs Accessible	94
Admissions	90
Financial Aid	83

CAMPUS LIFE

Type of school	Public
Environment	Town

Students

Degree-seeking undergrad enrollment	31,434
% male/female/not reported	56/44/<1
% from out of state	31
% First-year live on campus	99
% Ugrads live on campus	33
# of fraternities (% join)	27 (NR)
# of sororities (% join)	20 (NR)
% Asian	14
% Black or African American	6
% Hispanic	10
% Native American	<1
% Pacific Islander	<1
% Race and/or ethnicity unknown	3
% Two or more races	6
% White	55
% International	5
# of countries represented	116

CAMPUS MENTAL HEALTH SERVICES

Offers mental health/wellness program	Yes
Mental health training available to students	No
Employs Chief Wellness Officer	NR
Peer-to-peer mental health offerings	NR
Counseling center has guidelines or accreditation	No
Mental health/well-being courses	NR

ACADEMICS

% students returning for sophomore year	95
% students graduating within 4 years	69
% students graduating within 6 years	86
Calendar	Semester
Student/faculty ratio	17:1
Most common class size 20–29.	(21%)
Most common lab/discussion size 20–29.	(61%)

Most Popular Majors
Mechanical Engineering; Biology/Biological Sciences; Management Science

STUDENTS SAY "…"

Academics

Virginia Tech is a school with a reputation as big as its campus. Known for its "beautiful campus, amazing community feel, top-notch engineering field," and as a "good value"—not to mention its renowned athletics—Virginia Tech offers "a perfect blend of challenging and fun, encompassed in an unparalleled community feel." That community feel is a big part of the attraction to this top-ranked school, with students saying they feel "more comfortable here than anywhere in the world." Students are here, of course, for an education at a well-respected research university. At Virginia Tech, that education is provided by "passionate professors who bring real-life examples and cases into their teachings." The school's size and correspondingly large teaching staff mean that at times "professors are hit-or-miss," with "a few who just see it as another job." Most, however, "are really there to help you know as much as you can," a group who are "are extremely helpful and devoted to their students." The best of this school's professors "really makes students eager to learn." One student enthuses, "My professors here have changed the way I look at the world and have become some of my biggest heroes." But maybe another student sums it up best: "I would definitely say that my academic experience has been outstanding and that it has opened my eyes to even more possibilities.

Campus Life

Living "in the middle of nowhere" may seem like a recipe for boredom, but members of VT's Hokie Nation make the most of this "perfect college town." After all, when "there are 30,000 people around you that are the same age as you, you find stuff to do." When not consumed with Virginia Tech football—you'll see more maroon and orange in a single day here than most people will see in a lifetime—students here do, well, a little bit of everything. "School-related and Greek-life functions are the main sources of weekend activities," students say, but deceptively quiet Blacksburg and the surrounding area offer plenty of other options. On weekends, students "go out to parties or downtown with friends, we go out to eat, we play tennis, lay out on the Drillfield, play in the snow when we have some, go on hikes, and go to the river." That's just a start. Students find "there is always something fun going on to do with your friends," including "bowling, movies, club sports, video games," and more. If you can't find it in Blacksburg, it's ten minutes away in Christiansburg. Students enjoy relaxing, getting into discussions, or having outdoor adventures in a pastoral setting. When autumn arrives, "football games dominate the social scene."

Student Body

Better be ready to be part of the Hokie Nation, because the "typical student is someone who has a love for all things Virginia Tech." Those who attend VT "are proud of our school," and "A typical student here wears Virginia Tech clothes practically every day." Indeed, "you will find them at every VT football game." But the student body is about more than cheering for the maroon and orange. These "middle-class" students study hard "but play harder." Education matters here, but maybe not as much as living life. "The typical student is serious about schoolwork," students say, "but also knows how to have a good time." A majority of students are "white and from Virginia or North Carolina," but students prefer to describe their peers as "smart, approachable, and kind" and note that "we have every personality type and quirk you could ever imagine." If you are "well-rounded, involved, and [have] lots of school spirit," you are likely to fit in at VT.

Financial Aid: 540-231-5179 • E-Mail: admissions@vt.edu • Website: www.vt.edu

THE PRINCETON REVIEW SAYS

Admissions

The school reports that its standardized testing policy for use in admission for Fall 2026 is Test Optional. The Princeton Review suggests that interested applicants consult with the school for the most up-to-date standardized testing policies. *Very important factors considered include:* rigor of secondary school record, academic GPA, application essay, first generation, geographical residence, state residency. *Other factors considered include:* standardized test scores, extracurricular activities, talent/ability, character/personal qualities, volunteer work, work experience. High school diploma is required and GED is not accepted. *Academic units required:* 4 English, 3 math, 2 science, 2 science labs, 1 social studies, 1 history, 4 academic electives. *Academic units recommended:* 4 math, 3 science, 3 science labs, 3 language (other than English).

Financial Aid

Students should submit: FAFSA. Priority filing deadline is 3/1. The Princeton Review suggests that all financial aid forms be submitted as soon as possible. *Need-based scholarships/grants offered:* Federal Pell; Federal SEOG; State scholarships/grants; Private scholarships; College/university scholarship or grant aid from institutional funds; United Negro College Fund. *Loan aid offered:* Federal Direct Subsidized Loans; Federal Direct Unsubsidized Loans; Direct PLUS loans. Admitted students will be notified of awards on or about 3/5. Federal Work-Study Program available. Institutional employment available.

The Inside Word

With such a vast number of applications pouring into the admissions office each year, it's no wonder that it is all about numbers, numbers, numbers. Your high school grades will be top priority, so maintain strong grades. Most solid performers will find that acceptance comes with few problems, though the school's competitive disciplines— engineering and architecture, for example—will demand a higher caliber of student.

THE SCHOOL SAYS

From the Admissions Office

"Virginia Tech offers the best of both worlds—everything a large university can provide and a small-town atmosphere. Undergraduates choose from more than 150 majors in eight colleges, including nationally ranked architecture, business, forestry, and engineering schools, as well as excellent computer science, biology, and communication studies. Technology is a key focus, both in classes and in general. Faculty incorporate a wide variety of technology into class, utilizing chat rooms, online lecture notes, and multimedia presentations. The university offers cutting-edge facilities for classes and research, abundant opportunities for advanced study in the Honors College, undergraduate research opportunities, study abroad, internships, and cooperative education. Students enjoy nearly 800 organizations which offer something for everyone. Students living on campus can join one of the more than 20 living-learning communities that allow them to live among students with similar interests, areas of study, or population groups such as first-generation students."

SELECTIVITY

# of total applicants	57,755
% of total applicants accepted	55
% of total acceptees attending	23
# of in-state applicants	20,900
% of in-state applicants accepted	47
# of out-of-state-applicants	31,104
% of applicants accepted from out of state	59
# of international applicants	5,751
% of international applicants accepted	58
# offered a place on the wait list	22,526
# admitted from wait list	4,295

First-Year Profile

Testing policy	Test Optional
Range SAT EBRW	640–720
Range SAT math	640–730
Range ACT composite	28–32
% submitting SAT scores	42
% submitting ACT scores	8
Average HS GPA	4.1
% submitting high school GPA	97

Important Dates

Early action	
Apply by	11/15
Notified by	2/22
Regular	
Apply by	1/15
Notified by	3/15
Nonfall registration?	Yes

FINANCIAL FACTS

Annual in-state tuition	$13,938
Annual out-of-state tuition	$36,428
Food and housing	$17,220
Required fees	$3,150
Books and supplies	$1,120
Average need-based scholarship (First-year)	$11,597 ($11,119)
% students with need rec. need-based scholarship or grant aid (First-year)	81 (82)
% students with need rec. non-need-based scholarship or grant aid (First-year)	46 (51)
% students with need rec. need-based self-help aid (First-year)	58 (58)
% UG borrow to pay for school	46
Average cumulative indebtedness	$36,320
% of students with need fully met (First-year)	15 (14)
Average % of student need met (First-year)	64 (60)

WABASH COLLEGE

301 West Wabash Avenue, Crawfordsville, IN 47933 • Admissions: 765-361-6225

Survey Snapshot
Easy to get around campus
Intramural sports are popular
Alumni active on campus

RATINGS

Quality of Life	90
Fire Safety	95
Green	60*
Academic	89
Profs Interesting	94
Profs Accessible	97
Admissions	89
Financial Aid	93

CAMPUS LIFE

Type of school	Private
Environment	Village

Students

Degree-seeking undergrad enrollment	897
% male/female/not reported	100/0/0
% from out of state	23
% First-year from public high school	81
% First-year live on campus	100
% Ugrads live on campus	99
# of fraternities (% join)	10 (59)
% Asian	1
% Black or African American	6
% Hispanic	13
% Native American	0
% Pacific Islander	<1
% Race and/or ethnicity unknown	2
% Two or more races	3
% White	67
% International	7
# of countries represented	28

CAMPUS MENTAL HEALTH SERVICES

Offers mental health/wellness program	Yes
Mental health training available to students	Yes
Employs Chief Wellness Officer	No
Peer-to-peer mental health offerings	Yes
Counseling center has guidelines or accreditation	Yes
Mental health/well-being courses	Yes, non-credit

ACADEMICS

% students returning for sophomore year	84
% students graduating within 4 years	67
% students graduating within 6 years	73
Calendar	Semester
Student/faculty ratio	10:1
Most common class size 10–19.	(40%)
Most common lab/discussion size 1–9.	(61%)

Most Popular Majors
Biology/Biological Sciences; Philosophy, Politics, and Economics; Economics

Applicants Sometimes Prefer
DePauw University, Indiana University—Bloomington, Purdue University—West Lafayette

STUDENTS SAY "..."

Academics

The students at Wabash College, an all-male institution, feel it excels at "preparing young men for life, whether it is post-grad…[or] being a good person and man in society;" the school "is truly a place that is going to take you and turn you into the best version of yourself." The coursework here is "very hard but rewarding," and buoyed by small class sizes, which allow for maximum engagement. Students are pushed "out of [their] comfort zone through presentations, speeches, teaching [their] own class/peers, and reading challenging literature." Indeed, professors are almost "more of a facilitator…rather than a lecturer." They're also "very passionate and helpful" and clearly "invested in the education and the overall success of the students, no matter the circumstances." Additionally, undergrads rush to highlight Wabash's numerous immersion opportunities "that take you traveling to other parts of the world." As one student enthuses about an immersion trip in Costa Rica, "I was exposed to aspects of their culture and language, truly an experience I will never forget." And, when it comes time to consider their post-collegiate life, undergrads can easily tap into an extensive alumni network. "Any Wabash alum will drop what they're doing professionally to have a conversation with you, whether that's over the phone, in person, or on campus. The brotherhood is never-ending."

Campus Life

Undergrads at Wabash are "extremely involved and busy;" you'll find the campus "bustling from morning to night." Given Wabash's academic rigor, "students spend a lot of time working on their schoolwork." But there's plenty to enjoy beyond classes. For starters, "There is a visiting speaker at least twice a week, and we have a special speaker every Thursday give an impactful speech for Chapel Talks." Additionally, "sporting events are very well attended, and that doesn't just include football, basketball, and baseball. Every sport draws a crowd." Plus, "our intramural teams go above and beyond. They have all-star games, all-pro teams, and many unique ways to keep guys involved." Greek life is also very popular and the "inter-fraternity council does a great job of hosting Greek-life oriented events and functions." Students also have lots of arts and culture at their fingertips. As one undergrad shares, "I am thrilled to attend all of the fine-arts performances that the college hosts. They are a great way to sit back and relax from studying, while also supporting… friends." Moreover, the student senate works "very hard throughout the year to manage a $300,000+ budget, including bringing in major performers to campus such as BigXthaPlug." Ultimately, whether it's "tabletop games [or] ultimate Frisbee, [Wabash offers] something for everyone."

Student Body

When asked to describe their classmates, many undergrads emphasize that "Wabash is a brotherhood." It's evident that there's "a strong bond between those who go to the college, and everyone pushes each other to be better." Students also uphold "the gentleman's rule," wherein "we all conduct ourselves as gentlemen on and off campus in all respects, no matter what." In fact, they point to the college's all-male environment as a benefit, noting that it enables them to "feel more comfortable expressing their emotions and vulnerabilities without fear of judgment." Additionally, many view their peers as "hardworking, disciplined, focused, and driven." They're also quite friendly. As one undergrad shares, "Whether it is at the library, a fraternity, a team meeting, somebody checks up on you and asks how you are doing, and they genuinely care to know." Of course, it also helps that classmates are "easy to talk to, fun to hang around with, and are always happy to lend a hand wherever it is needed." Ultimately, students "take great pride in being among the community of Wabash men as we seek to honor the legacy of those who came before us and establish our own."

Wabash College

Financial Aid: 765-361-6083 • E-Mail: admissions@wabash.edu • Website: www.wabash.edu

THE PRINCETON REVIEW SAYS

Admissions

The school reports that its standardized testing policy for use in admission for Fall 2026 is Test Optional. The Princeton Review suggests that interested applicants consult with the school for the most up-to-date standardized testing policies. *Very important factors considered include:* rigor of secondary school record, class rank, academic GPA, level of applicant's interest. *Important factors considered include:* recommendation(s), interview, extracurricular activities, talent/ability. *Other factors considered include:* standardized test scores, application essay, character/personal qualities, first generation, alumni/ae relation, geographical residence, volunteer work, work experience. High school diploma is required and GED is accepted. *Academic units recommended:* 4 English, 4 math, 2 science, 2 science labs, 2 language (other than English), 2 social studies, 2 history, 2 academic electives.

Financial Aid

Students should submit: FAFSA. Priority filing deadline is 2/1. The Princeton Review suggests that all financial aid forms be submitted as soon as possible. *Need-based scholarships/grants offered:* Federal Pell; Federal SEOG; State scholarships/grants; Private scholarships; College/university scholarship or grant aid from institutional funds; United Negro College Fund. *Loan aid offered:* Federal Direct Subsidized Loans; Federal Direct Unsubsidized Loans; Direct PLUS loans. Admitted students will be notified of awards on a rolling basis beginning 12/15. Federal Work-Study Program available. Institutional employment available.

The Inside Word

Because Wabash is so specific and unique, it self-selects a small but strong applicant pool. Those who are admitted should come prepared for a rigorous academic experience that will require serious intellectual commitment and work ethic throughout their four years. Although not a requirement, an applicant may also submit their SAT/ACT scores and/or a written statement to include additional details about himself for consideration during the application review.

THE SCHOOL SAYS

From the Admissions Office

"Wabash College is different—and distinctive—from other liberal arts colleges. Different in that Wabash is an outstanding college for men only. Distinctive in the quality and character of the faculty, in the demanding nature of the academic program, in the seriousness and maturity of the men who enroll, and in the richness of the traditions that have evolved throughout its 194 years. Wabash is preeminently a teaching institution and The Princeton Review annually lauds the accessibility of the faculty and the classroom experience. Faculty and students talk to each other with mutual respect for the expression of informed opinion. Students who collaborate with faculty on research projects are considered their peers in the research—an esteem not usually extended to undergraduates—and are honored annually in a celebration of undergraduate research. Wabash also earns national recognition for its alumni network, internship program, and career services, all of which are critical to our graduates' success in every walk of life. But perhaps the single most striking aspect of student life at Wabash is personal freedom. The College has only one rule: 'The student is expected to conduct himself at all times, both on and off the campus, as a gentleman and a responsible citizen.' Wabash College treats students as adults, and such treatment attracts responsible freshmen and fosters their independence and maturity. For students seeking admission, Wabash places emphasis on high school GPA and difficulty of subjects, and is currently Test Optional."

SELECTIVITY

# of total applicants	2,496
% of total applicants accepted	57
% of total acceptees attending	19
# of in-state applicants	911
% of in-state applicants accepted	72
# of out-of-state-applicants	741
% of applicants accepted from out of state	70
# of international applicants	844
% of international applicants accepted	29
# of early decision applicants	108
% of early decision applicants accepted	90
# offered a place on the wait list	3
# admitted from wait list	0

First-Year Profile

Testing policy	Test Optional
Range SAT composite	1130–1340
Range SAT EBRW	560–670
Range SAT math	570–680
Range ACT composite	24–30
% submitting SAT scores	41
% submitting ACT scores	10
Average HS GPA	3.5
% submitting high school GPA	91
% graduated top 10% of class	16
% graduated top 25% of class	50
% graduated top 50% of class	84
% submitting high school rank	39

Important Dates

Early decision	
Apply by	11/15
Notified by	12/5
Early action	
Apply by	12/1
Notified by	12/31
Regular	
Notified by	Rolling, 1/18
Nonfall registration?	Yes

FINANCIAL FACTS

Annual tuition	$52,900
Food and housing	$16,000
Required fees	$1,200
Books and supplies	$1,300
Average need-based scholarship (First-year)	$43,409 ($47,705)
% students with need rec. need-based scholarship or grant aid (First-year)	99 (99)
% students with need rec. non-need-based scholarship or grant aid (First-year)	23 (24)
% students with need rec. need-based self-help aid (First-year)	76 (77)
% students rec. any financial aid (First-year)	100 (100)
% UG borrow to pay for school	66
Average cumulative indebtedness	$35,843
% of students with need fully met (First-year)	59 (63)
Average % of student need met (First-year)	92 (94)

Wagner College

One Campus Road, Staten Island, NY 10301 • Admissions: 718-390-3411

Survey Snapshot
Class discussions encouraged
Theater is popular
Everyone loves the Seahawks

RATINGS	
Quality of Life	81
Fire Safety	99
Green	60*
Academic	78
Profs Interesting	84
Profs Accessible	85
Admissions	84
Financial Aid	89

CAMPUS LIFE

Type of school	Private
Environment	Metropolis

Students

Degree-seeking undergrad enrollment	1,656
% male/female/not reported	39/61/0
% from out of state	40
% First-year from public high school	67
% First-year live on campus	59
% Ugrads live on campus	49
# of fraternities (% join)	2 (5)
# of sororities (% join)	4 (13)
% Asian	5
% Black or African American	7
% Hispanic	15
% Native American	<1
% Pacific Islander	<1
% Race and/or ethnicity unknown	4
% Two or more races	4
% White	56
% International	8
# of countries represented	47

CAMPUS MENTAL HEALTH SERVICES

Offers mental health/wellness program	Yes
Mental health training available to students	No
Employs Chief Wellness Officer	NR
Peer-to-peer mental health offerings	NR
Counseling center has guidelines or accreditation	No
Mental health/well-being courses	NR

ACADEMICS

% students returning for sophomore year	84
% students graduating within 4 years	56
% students graduating within 6 years	65
Calendar	Semester
Student/faculty ratio	9:1
Most common class size 10–19.	(38%)
Most common lab/discussion size 1–9.	(43%)

Most Popular Majors
Visual and Performing Arts; Nursing Science; Business/Commerce

Applicants Often Prefer
New York University

Applicants Sometimes Prefer
Long Island University, Pace University, Sacred Heart University

Applicants Rarely Prefer
Drew University, Manhattan University, Marist University

STUDENTS SAY "…"

Academics

Students at Wagner College receive a practical education with an eye toward professional development and hands-on learning, with every student completing an internship or practicum before they graduate. As an added bonus, the school's Staten Island location means there are "many different majors with connections to Manhattan for job opportunities post-graduation." Moreover, the school's curriculum is described as "a welcome departure from traditional graduation requirement systems," in that it features "experiential learning and community building" via three separate, small cross-disciplinary communities spread across a student's four years, "using what has been already taught to us and expanding it into subjects that we individually are curious about. Standard lectures are not a given here, with students instead doing "dissections in lab and using our virtual cadaver to learn about anatomy" or "[taking] on a role of a major player in the American Revolution and acting out our roles while learning, which has been an amazing experience so far." Professors "are super caring and generous with their time...and bring loads of real-world knowledge into the classroom. They can also connect us to people who currently work in the industry." With 92 percent of classes having fewer than 30 students, it's easy to get to know your professors and "you may maintain a relationship with some of your professors for the rest of your life." Students also report that you'll "get to actually experience what we were being taught and get feedback from professors who are active in the field."

Campus Life

At Wagner, "everyone has a willingness to participate at school activities and events," and the school accordingly "encourages students to go out of their way to apply what they have learned during lecture to [their] extracurricular activities." The Center for Intercultural Advancement and International Cultural Advancement offices are said to be doing a "great job" in engaging students, and there are plenty of organizations to join. Several students say that "the theatre department here is by far one of the best, sweetest, and strongest bodies," hosting "a variety of...parties that are open to all." The library "is a haven for students looking for some peace when studying, and with nice weather, most students sit on the great lawn and have picnics." Nearby Manhattan is also "really easy to get to because of the free Wagner shuttle" to and from the free ferry to the city. That said, students note there isn't always a need to do so, as they have the best possible problem: they "are heavily involved in extracurricular activities, so schedules are often pretty full."

Student Body

Wagner College a small school that is "the type of place where one makes long-lasting connections." That "close-knit community" is described as "very dedicated and newcomers are always made to feel welcome." Wagner students are "diverse and unique" and because they "come from all different areas and study all different areas," this creates an "amazing opportunity [for] meeting people." And whether you're one of the fair number of commuters or not, all "take advantage of the many outdoor spaces to either study or socialize." A student sings the praises of their "creative, helpful, smart" peers: "Imagine walking into a room and everybody is capable of some kind of insane artistic capability." Many feel that "there are so many events weekly to bring the community together," and cherish that "from student organizations to departmental events each student brings a unique and vibrant element to the table."

Wagner College

Financial Aid: 718-390-3183 • E-Mail: admissions@wagner.edu • Website: www.wagner.edu

THE PRINCETON REVIEW SAYS

Admissions

The school reports that its standardized testing policy for use in admission for Fall 2026 is Test Optional. The Princeton Review suggests that interested applicants consult with the school for the most up-to-date standardized testing policies. *Very important factors considered include:* rigor of secondary school record. *Important factors considered include:* academic GPA, application essay, recommendation(s), interview, extracurricular activities, talent/ability, character/personal qualities. *Other factors considered include:* class rank, standardized test scores, volunteer work, work experience, level of applicant's interest. High school diploma is required and GED is accepted. *Academic units required:* 4 English, 3 math, 2 science, 1 science lab, 2 language (other than English), 3 history, 7 academic electives.

Financial Aid

Students should submit: FAFSA. Priority filing deadline is 1/15. The Princeton Review suggests that all financial aid forms be submitted as soon as possible. *Need-based scholarships/grants offered:* Federal Pell; Federal SEOG; State scholarships/grants; Private scholarships; College/university scholarship or grant aid from institutional funds. *Loan aid offered:* Federal Direct Subsidized Loans; Federal Direct Unsubsidized Loans; Direct PLUS loans. Admitted students will be notified of awards on a rolling basis. Federal Work-Study Program available. Institutional employment available.

The Inside Word

As far as grades and test scores are concerned, the profile of the average first-year class at Wagner is solid. Standardized tests are optional, and there is more value placed on the rigor of your course load and your grades in those classes. Wagner uses a 100-point scale for the average high school GPA for admitted students. Wagner is looking for students who like to be involved in community events, so make sure your application reflects your extracurriculars. An interview bodes well for serious applicants.

THE SCHOOL SAYS

From the Admissions Office

"Wagner College, founded in 1883, seamlessly blends exceptional professional programs with a traditional academic ethos for a comprehensive, experiential-forward education that fosters well-rounded, adaptable graduates. Located on a scenic hilltop campus on New York City's Staten Island, the College provides a classic residential experience with sweeping views of Manhattan, Brooklyn, and the Atlantic. Just a short ferry ride from Manhattan, Wagner students benefit from direct access to internships, cultural institutions, and career opportunities in one of the world's most influential cities—all while enjoying a close-knit campus community.

"Wagner is committed to student success through personalized academic advising, comprehensive career development services, and a wide range of wellness and support programs. We believe that every student's journey is unique, and we're committed to guiding them from their first steps on our Oval to the moment they cross the graduation stage. Our support doesn't just prepare students for success—we ensure it. Faculty mentorship is central to the student experience, fostering intellectual growth, leadership, and a commitment to civic engagement. Wagner graduates are well-prepared to excel in competitive professional environments and pursue purposeful, impactful careers across sectors such as healthcare, business, education and entertainment.

"A Division I Athletics institution, Wagner enrolls 2,000 undergraduate and graduate students from 43 states and 49 countries. With a dynamic campus community, strong academic foundation, and unparalleled access to New York City, Wagner College equips students with the knowledge, experience, and professional networks needed to thrive in an ever-evolving global landscape."

SELECTIVITY

# of total applicants	2,566
% of total applicants accepted	88
% of total acceptees attending	20
# of in-state applicants	1,412
% of in-state applicants accepted	88
# of out-of-state-applicants	983
% of applicants accepted from out of state	88
# of international applicants	171
% of international applicants accepted	88
# offered a place on the wait list	52
# admitted from wait list	20

First-Year Profile

Testing policy	Test Optional
Range SAT composite	1190–1240
Range SAT EBRW	600–660
Range SAT math	590–630
Range ACT composite	23–28
% submitting SAT scores	14
% submitting ACT scores	6
Average HS GPA	91.0
% submitting high school GPA	100
% graduated top 10% of class	17
% graduated top 25% of class	42
% graduated top 50% of class	73
% submitting high school rank	31

Important Dates

Early action	
Apply by	11/15
Notified by	12/20
Regular	
Apply by	6/15
Notified by	Rolling, 1/5
Nonfall registration?	Yes

FINANCIAL FACTS

Annual tuition	$50,200
Food and housing	$16,012
Required fees	$2,000
Books and supplies	$1,034
Average need-based scholarship (First-year)	$31,798 ($23,560)
% students with need rec. need-based scholarship or grant aid (First-year)	100 (100)
% students with need rec. need-based self-help aid (First-year)	68 (64)
% students rec. any financial aid (First-year)	93 (99)
% of students with need fully met (First-year)	31 (33)
Average % of student need met (First-year)	80 (82)

WAKE FOREST UNIVERSITY

1834 Wake Forest Road, Winston Salem, NC 27109 • Admissions: 336-758-5201

Survey Snapshot
Students are happy
Classroom facilities are great
Intramural sports are popular

RATINGS

Quality of Life	**82**
Fire Safety	**60***
Green	**60***
Academic	**94**
Profs Interesting	**95**
Profs Accessible	**98**
Admissions	**95**
Financial Aid	**92**

CAMPUS LIFE

Type of school	Private
Environment	City

Students

Degree-seeking undergrad enrollment	5,592
% male/female/not reported	45/55/0
% from out of state	85
% First-year from public high school	65
% First-year live on campus	99
% Ugrads live on campus	78
# of fraternities (% join)	14 (28)
# of sororities (% join)	9 (65)
% Asian	5
% Black or African American	6
% Hispanic	8
% Native American	<1
% Pacific Islander	<1
% Race and/or ethnicity unknown	5
% Two or more races	5
% White	67
% International	4
# of countries represented	27

CAMPUS MENTAL HEALTH SERVICES

Offers mental health/wellness program	Yes
Mental health training available to students	No
Employs Chief Wellness Officer	NR
Peer-to-peer mental health offerings	NR
Counseling center has guidelines or accreditation	No
Mental health/well-being courses	NR

ACADEMICS

% students returning for sophomore year	92
% students graduating within 4 years	86
% students graduating within 6 years	90
Calendar	Semester
Student/faculty ratio	10:1
Most common class size 10–19.	(43%)

Most Popular Majors
Business/Commerce; Political Science and Government; Psychology

STUDENTS SAY "…"

Academics

Wake Forest University embodies its motto Pro Humanitate (For Humanity) by emphasizing "opportunities to serve, to become a leader, and to become part of initiatives that are larger than you." The Wake Forest experience is about becoming a well-rounded individual, and the school "practices intentional interactions between professors and students, students with each other, and students and their larger community." With over fifty majors across 29 academic departments and 16 interdisciplinary programs, there are many opportunities for undergraduate research, as seen during the annual URECA Day (or Undergraduate Research Day) when students showcase their work. Students say there's a "strong vision and support" from the administration and the alumni network, and per the school, 65% of 2023 undergraduates secured employment and 32% pursued higher education. That support isn't just for graduates: "I feel that I could ask any professor I've had at Wake for a letter of recommendation, and they would know me personally enough to do so." Students "feel comfortable" talking to their professors, who are "all unique and bring something new to the classroom." They "demand a lot of work," and classes "are not easy and good grades are tough to come by." While instructors "hold us to the highest standards," they are also "extremely helpful" as well as "encouraging and empathetic." It's clear they "love teaching" and they work to "ensure that students are comfortable with voicing their opinions." As one student says, "Overall I've had a fantastic academic experience with professors that have helped me discover my intellectual passions and have had a vested interest in my success."

Campus Life

The campus at Wake Forest is "always bustling with extracurricular activities," especially for active students with a taste for intramural sports. As a Division I school, there's a "big-school sports feel at a small school," and there's an ongoing tradition of celebrating by "rolling the quad after a big athletic win." Greek life is a big part of student life, as are "parties, going to bars downtown, concerts, game nights, and chill hangouts at friends' houses." The Student Union puts on over 200 programs each year, from big events like Homecoming to movie nights and trivia games. There are "lots of great traditions at Wake Forest, like our annual Shag on the Mag dance in the spring" and the Moravian Lovefeast, a candlelight service in December. Philanthropy is another "HUGE part of the WFU experience" and there are many annual events like Wake 'N Shake, a dance marathon fundraiser, and Hit the Bricks, a relay race, which both support cancer research. Through it all, academics come first, but students acknowledge that those weekday hours in the library give way to a "vibrant social scene" and that they "absolutely let loose on weekends."

Student Body

The idea of Southern hospitality can be felt among this student body, where people tend to be friendly and accepting. Greek life makes up a fairly significant part of the student body—just under 50% of students are part of a fraternity or sorority. Students emphasize that Wake Forest is a place where classmates "can usually easily find groups of people who share their interests." The school is home to "students from around the country and the world," and there are students from all 50 states and 39 countries in this "tight-knit, supportive community." Students describe a welcoming environment where "people generally don't have any trouble fitting in," and classmates overall are "intelligent, ambitious, [and] highly involved."

Wake Forest University

Financial Aid: 336-758-5154 • E-Mail: admissions@wfu.edu • Website: www.wfu.edu

THE PRINCETON REVIEW SAYS

Admissions

The school reports that its standardized testing policy for use in admission for Fall 2026 is Test Optional. The Princeton Review suggests that interested applicants consult with the school for the most up-to-date standardized testing policies. *Very important factors considered include:* rigor of secondary school record, class rank, academic GPA, application essay, character/personal qualities. *Important factors considered include:* recommendation(s), interview, extracurricular activities, talent/ability. *Other factors considered include:* standardized test scores, first generation, alumni/ae relation, geographical residence, state residency, religious affiliation/commitment, volunteer work, work experience, level of applicant's interest. High school diploma or equivalent is not required. *Academic units required:* 4 English, 3 math, 1 science, 2 language (other than English), 2 social studies. *Academic units recommended:* 4 English, 4 math, 4 science, 4 language (other than English), 4 social studies.

Financial Aid

The Princeton Review suggests that all financial aid forms be submitted as soon as possible. Federal Work-Study Program available. Institutional employment available.

The Inside Word

Wake Forest's considerable application numbers afford admissions officers the opportunity to be rather selective. In particular, admissions officers remain diligent in their matchmaking efforts—finding students who are good fits for the school—and their hard work is rewarded by a high graduation rate. Candidates will need to be impressive in all areas to gain admission, since all areas of their applications are considered carefully. A relatively large number of qualified students find themselves on Wake Forest's wait list.

THE SCHOOL SAYS

From the Admissions Office

"Wake Forest University has been dedicated to the liberal arts for over a century and a half; this means education in the fundamental fields of human knowledge and achievement. It seeks to encourage habits of mind that ask why, that evaluate evidence, that are open to new ideas, that attempt to understand and appreciate the perspective of others, that accept complexity and grapple with it, that admit error, and that pursue truth. Wake Forest is among a small, elite group of American colleges and universities recognized for their outstanding academic quality. It offers small classes taught by full-time faculty—not graduate assistants—and a commitment to student interaction with those professors. Wake Forest balances the personal attention of a liberal arts college with the academic vitality and broad opportunities of a research university. Students are admitted based on the unique qualities they bring to our community. Wake Forest's generous financial aid program allows deserving students to enroll regardless of their financial circumstances.

"Wake Forest is the first top thirty national university in the United States to make standardized tests such as the SAT and ACT with writing optional in the admissions process. If applicants feel that their SAT or ACT with writing scores are a good indicator of their abilities, they may submit them, and they will be considered in the admissions decision. If, however, a prospective student does not feel that their scores accurately represent their academic abilities, they do not need to submit them until after they have been accepted and choose to enroll. Wake Forest takes a holistic look at each applicant."

SELECTIVITY

# of total applicants	19,600
% of total applicants accepted	21
% of total acceptees attending	38

First-Year Profile

Testing policy	Test Optional
Range SAT composite	1420–1490
Range SAT EBRW	700–750
Range SAT math	700–760
Range ACT composite	32–34
% submitting SAT scores	24
% submitting ACT scores	22
% graduated top 10% of class	61
% graduated top 25% of class	90
% graduated top 50% of class	98
% submitting high school rank	17

Important Dates

Early decision	
Apply by	11/15
Notified by	Rolling
Other ED Apply by	1/1
Other ED Notified by	Rolling
Regular	
Apply by	1/1
Notified by	4/1

FINANCIAL FACTS

Annual tuition	$71,894
Food and housing	$23,430
Required fees	$1,276
Books and supplies	$1,720
Average need-based scholarship (First-year)	$69,008 ($71,567)
% students with need rec. need-based scholarship or grant aid (First-year)	99 (99)
% students with need rec. non-need-based scholarship or grant aid (First-year)	74 (78)
% students with need rec. need-based self-help aid (First-year)	62 (59)
% UG borrow to pay for school	21
Average cumulative indebtedness	$36,431
% student need fully met (First-year)	89 (95)
Average % of student need met (First-year)	99 (99)

WARREN WILSON COLLEGE

701 Warren Wilson College Road, Asheville, NC 28815-9000 • Admissions: 828-771-2000

Survey Snapshot
Students environmentally aware
Students take advantage of the outdoors
Students involved in community service

RATINGS

Quality of Life	**79**
Fire Safety	**67**
Green	**87**
Academic	**81**
Profs Interesting	**91**
Profs Accessible	**93**
Admissions	**85**
Financial Aid	**88**

CAMPUS LIFE

Type of school	Private
Environment	City

Students

Degree-seeking undergrad enrollment	707
% male/female/not reported	32/64/4
% from out of state	62
% First-year from public high school	71
% First-year live on campus	100
% Ugrads live on campus	89
# of fraternities	0
# of sororities	0
% Asian	1
% Black or African American	5
% Hispanic	9
% Native American	1
% Pacific Islander	0
% Race and/or ethnicity unknown	1
% Two or more races	4
% White	77
% International	3
# of countries represented	18

CAMPUS MENTAL HEALTH SERVICES

Offers mental health/wellness program	Yes
Mental health training available to students	Yes
Employs Chief Wellness Officer	Yes
Peer-to-peer mental health offerings	Yes
Counseling center has guidelines or accreditation	No
Mental health/well-being courses	Yes, for-credit

ACADEMICS

% students returning for sophomore year	71
% students graduating within 4 years	40
% students graduating within 6 years	42
Calendar	Semester
Student/faculty ratio	12:1
Most common class size 10–19.	(55%)

Most Popular Majors
Environmental Studies; Biology/Biological Sciences; Visual and Performing Arts

STUDENTS SAY "..."

Academics

Everything at Warren Wilson College, a small liberal arts school outside Asheville, North Carolina, can be attributed to its unique approach to learning, where academics are combined with "work and service." As one student describes the College, it's "work for the hands, service for the heart, learning for the mind." The "work program at Warren Wilson is one of the main reasons I chose the school," says one environmental science major, and another student adds that the "work program is [what's] truly interesting about this school. We run our own little country here basically." That doesn't mean academics take a backseat—as one history major points out, "We take as many credits as other college students and we work 8–16 hours a week." Professors at Warren Wilson earn mostly high praise from students: "They are great at both lectures and discussion, and are able to teach nuanced, complex ideas and concepts in interesting and concise ways." With the small size and strong sense of community, the faculty here is very involved and very accessible. With their help, and the experiences that come from service and internships, students say "you get a broad taste of a lot of different areas of work, hobbies, and future jobs."

Campus Life

With classwork, community service, and time spent on one of the numerous campus work crews, students say "days are easily filled" and "weekdays tend to be very busy." When it's time to relax, "plenty of students spend as much time outside as possible hiking, swimming, skating, exploring the city of Asheville, and partying." "It's a very outdoorsy campus environment because we are in the middle of Appalachia" and "we have miles and miles of hiking trails that are campus property." Beyond the outdoors, "creative writing and coffee culture are a big part of Warren Wilson's culture," along with live music and "contra dancing on Thursdays." Some students say that the work crews are the closest thing the school has to fraternities and some of the more popular pastimes are "activities related to the crews—like blacksmithing workshops, beekeeping workshops, fabric workshops." With the school's appreciation of music, the "cafe is usually hosting shows that are a huge draw." In one student's estimation, "Everyone at the school loves the outdoors and has a healthy appreciation for taking an afternoon off to explore the river or trails." Warren Wilson is a place where politically-, socially-, and environmentally-focused "discussions are ubiquitous in and out of the classroom."

Student Body

The student body at [Warren Wilson] is sustainable, eclectic, earthy, hard-working, and very community oriented. As one photography major puts it, "If you're looking for someplace different, this is it." The school's former motto was "We're not for everyone, but maybe you're not everyone," and some students find that still holds true, though others note that "limited racial diversity" "does not create a welcoming environment to racial and ethnic minorities on the campus." At the same time, vocal students stress the school's accepting nature, underscoring that Warren Wilson "has a strong LGBTQ community." As an environmental science major puts it, "The environment and proximity to Asheville attract the typical tree-hugging hippie crowd, but there's really a place for everyone at the college" and nearly everyone is "actively engaged in issues of social justice." In short, Warren Wilson students are "fantastically talented, hardworking, and willing to think outside the box."

Warren Wilson College

Financial Aid: 828-771-2081 • E-Mail: admit@warren-wilson.edu • Website: www.warren-wilson.edu

THE PRINCETON REVIEW SAYS

Admissions

The school reports that its standardized testing policy for use in admission for Fall 2026 is Test Optional. The Princeton Review suggests that interested applicants consult with the school for the most up-to-date standardized testing policies. *Very important factors considered include:* rigor of secondary school record, academic GPA. *Important factors considered include:* class rank, application essay, recommendation(s). *Other factors considered include:* standardized test scores, interview, extracurricular activities, talent/ability, character/personal qualities, first generation, volunteer work, work experience. High school diploma is required and GED is accepted. *Academic units required:* 4 English, 3 math, 2 science, 1 social studies, 2 history. *Academic units recommended:* 2 language (other than English), 2 academic electives.

Financial Aid

Students should submit: FAFSA. The Princeton Review suggests that all financial aid forms be submitted as soon as possible. *Need-based scholarships/grants offered:* Federal Pell; Federal SEOG; State scholarships/grants; Private scholarships; College/university scholarship or grant aid from institutional funds. *Loan aid offered:* Federal Direct Subsidized Loans; Federal Direct Unsubsidized Loans; Direct PLUS loans. Admitted students will be notified of awards on a rolling basis. Federal Work-Study Program available. Institutional employment available.

The Inside Word

In keeping with Warren Wilson College's mission of combining academics, work, and community service, prospective students should be aware that their efforts outside the classroom are as important as their performance in it. The admissions committee looks for signs of maturity, integrity, and a commitment to the mission of the college in each applicant. Warren Wilson accepts the Common Application, with their own writing supplement (not required, but strongly recommended), and standardized test scores are optional.

THE SCHOOL SAYS

From the Admissions Office

"Warren Wilson College is for people who want an active educational and intellectual experience. And with our deep, proven commitment to a just, equitable, and sustainable world, we're for people who see learning as a way to be a better human being.

"Our experiential academic program gives you breadth through a time-honored liberal arts core and depth through specialization. And with over a thousand acres of farm, forests, mountains, and streams right here on campus, your classrooms, studios, and laboratories are not limited to those with walls.

"As one of only nine Work Colleges nationally and as a top-ranked service-learning college, Warren Wilson College builds on academic experiences by fully integrating on-campus work, community engagement, and an internship into every student's learning. Your work and internship experiences set you apart when you're applying for jobs—you'll already have a résumé full of accomplishments. And community engagement gives you more than just marketable skills—you are empowered to advocate for causes you care about and improve your community.

"Our students can and do change the world. When you graduate, you won't say you learned how to do it. You will say you've done it.

"Warren Wilson College is committed to affordability, and beginning in fall 2025 we have lowered our tuition by 40%. Every student receives financial aid, including over $6,000 per year in work scholarships and grants, and our two free tuition programs provide even greater access for students who qualify. Our Financial Aid Office works with you to ensure that a Warren Wilson education is accessible."

SELECTIVITY

# of total applicants	1,361
% of total applicants accepted	71
% of total acceptees attending	18
# offered a place on the wait list	0
# admitted from wait list	0

First-Year Profile

Testing policy	Test Optional
Range ACT composite	25–29
% submitting ACT scores	6
Average HS GPA	3.7
% submitting high school GPA	79

Important Dates

Early decision	
Apply by	11/1
Notified by	12/1
Early action	
Apply by	11/15
Notified by	12/15
Regular	
Apply by	7/1
Notified by	Rolling, 12/1
Nonfall registration?	Yes

FINANCIAL FACTS

Annual tuition	$25,500
Food and housing	$13,450
Required fees (First-year)	$1,040 ($1,440)
Books and supplies	$1,000
Average need-based scholarship (First-year)	$28,934 ($28,934)
% students with need rec. need-based scholarship or grant aid (First-year)	100 (100)
% students with need rec. non-need-based scholarship or grant aid (First-year)	20 (20)
% students with need rec. need-based self-help aid (First-year)	80 (79)
% students rec. any financial aid (First-year)	99 (99)
% of students with need fully met (First-year)	22 (23)
Average % of student need met (First-year)	81 (80)

WASHINGTON COLLEGE

300 Washington Avenue, Chestertown, MD 21620 • Admissions: 410-778-2800

Survey Snapshot
Easy to get around campus
Internships are widely available
Students environmentally aware

RATINGS

Quality of Life	85
Fire Safety	99
Green	60*
Academic	83
Profs Interesting	92
Profs Accessible	93
Admissions	83
Financial Aid	86

CAMPUS LIFE

Type of school	Private
Environment	Village

Students

Degree-seeking undergrad enrollment	908
% male/female/not reported	42/58/1
% from out of state	51
% First-year live on campus	95
% Ugrads live on campus	83
# of fraternities (% join)	2 (13)
# of sororities (% join)	2 (9)
% Asian	2
% Black or African American	9
% Hispanic	10
% Native American	1
% Pacific Islander	<1
% Race and/or ethnicity unknown	6
% Two or more races	3
% White	66
% International	3
# of countries represented	26

CAMPUS MENTAL HEALTH SERVICES

Offers mental health/wellness program	Yes
Mental health training available to students	Yes
Employs Chief Wellness Officer	Yes
Peer-to-peer mental health offerings	Yes
Counseling center has guidelines or accreditation	Yes
Mental health/well-being courses	Yes, non-credit

ACADEMICS

% students returning for sophomore year	88
% students graduating within 4 years	58
% students graduating within 6 years	66
Calendar	Semester
Student/faculty ratio	9:1
Most common class size 10–19.	(45%)
Most common lab/discussion size 10–19.	(68%)

Most Popular Majors

Environmental Science; Biology/Biological Sciences; Business Administration and Management

Applicants Also Look At

Gettysburg College, Goucher College, McDaniel College, Pennsylvania State University, Salisbury University, Saint Mary's College of Maryland, Towson University, University of Delaware, University of Maryland—Baltimore County, University of Maryland—College Park

STUDENTS SAY "..."

Academics

Washington College in Chestertown, Maryland is "a really beautiful environment to learn in." The academic experience is "rigorous and rewarding," with small class sizes that allow students to "feel incredibly connected to your professors." The faculty is "incredibly kind, empathetic, and passionate" and "challenge students and push them to give their best work." Many say "The professors are the greatest strength" of Washington College. "They are always accessible, very understanding, and happy to help in pursuing your goals outside of class through letters of recommendations, internship searches, and graduate school research." Students feel "the courses are always engaging," noting specifically that the "English program is impeccable," with "many academic resources and opportunities for professional development," such as "field work, faculty-assisted studies, publication opportunities," and access to the renowned Rose O'Neill Literary House.

Campus Life

Some may worry that living in a small town while attending Washington College might be difficult, but rest assured "if you make friends and get involved, it's engaging and fun." The Student Events Board "does a lot of work to give everyone options and fun things to do," and offer involvement opportunities like "varsity sports, intramurals, [and] Greek life." Intramural sports, like dodgeball and ultimate Frisbee, are fun ways "to compete and make new friends," and for those in Greek life, "there's no competition or animosity between chapters." Organized events are plentiful, where "Theatre productions are somewhat significant events," as are "poetry readings and author discussions" at the Literary House. On evenings and weekends, "There's a party culture," one student admits, but it's "pretty safe and tame."

Students trying to get off-campus enjoy visiting the boathouse on the nearby Chester River, where they can kayak and paddleboard for free, or simply "take a step back from [their] busy life around school and enjoy the scenery on the water." Nearby Chestertown "is a really lovable town and the surrounding area is also incredibly pretty." Many feel that "The town is a great place for a walk," and "going to the farmer's market on Saturday mornings is popular." Beyond Chestertown, "going to Annapolis, MD or Middletown, DE [a]re the two major outings students take."

Student Body

At Washington College, "there is a connected feel throughout the student body," which is a product of the small campus size. "Everyone knows each other in some sort of fashion," and "it's quite the treat to walk around and only see familiar faces." Even though "everyone tends to stay in their groups," most "belong to multiple categories of social life," and "there is no animosity between any of the groups." As one undergrad notes, "By and at large, students are respectful and caring toward each other, and there's a broad friendliness to the community." Students describe their peers as "diverse, opinionated, and intelligent" people who "want to be actively involved in their institution and have their voices heard."

At Washington College, "there is a wide range of intellect, ability, and personality that come together to make an interesting campus atmosphere." Although there's "a diverse political background" among its student body, "it's still a predominantly white institution." Students say "addressing racial bias on campus is an ongoing process," but that the school and community have "taken ample steps" in addressing this. "For example, in my Human Right and Social Justice class, my group and I are working within the town and the college to create a plan of racial reconciliation that includes meetings with advocacy groups and the local community as well as with those from our institution," one student says. All in all, undergrads can confidently say that there are "plenty of nice and accepting students."

WASHINGTON COLLEGE

Financial Aid: 410-778-7214 • E-Mail: admissions@washcoll.edu • Website: www.washcoll.edu

THE PRINCETON REVIEW SAYS

Admissions

The school reports that its standardized testing policy for use in admission for Fall 2026 is Test Optional. The Princeton Review suggests that interested applicants consult with the school for the most up-to-date standardized testing policies. *Very important factors considered include:* rigor of secondary school record, academic GPA. *Important factors considered include:* application essay, recommendation(s), interview, level of applicant's interest. *Other factors considered include:* class rank, standardized test scores, extracurricular activities, talent/ability, character/personal qualities, first generation, volunteer work, work experience. High school diploma is required and GED is accepted. *Academic units required:* 4 English, 3 math, 3 science, 2 science labs, 2 language (other than English), 2 social studies, 2 history. *Academic units recommended:* 4 English, 4 math, 4 science, 3 science labs, 4 language (other than English), 2 social studies, 2 history.

Financial Aid

Students should submit: FAFSA. Priority filing deadline is 3/1. The Princeton Review suggests that all financial aid forms be submitted as soon as possible. *Need-based scholarships/grants offered:* Federal Pell; Federal SEOG; State scholarships/grants; Private scholarships; College/university scholarship or grant aid from institutional funds. *Loan aid offered:* Federal Direct Subsidized Loans; Federal Direct Unsubsidized Loans; Direct PLUS loans. Admitted students will be notified of awards on a rolling basis beginning 10/1. Federal Work-Study Program available. Institutional employment available.

The Inside Word

Washington College is interested in student potential inside the classroom and beyond, and therefore evaluates applicants based on a series of factors including academic performance, character, and extracurricular involvement. The most promising candidates possess high GPAs and have challenged themselves with APs, honors, or IB courses, but also perform well during their interview and in their essay by illustrating ways in which they've been involved with their school or community and steps they've taken to pursue their passions and goals.

THE SCHOOL SAYS

From the Admissions Office

"At Washington College, one of the nation's top liberal arts institutions, you work closely with remarkable professors who are experts in their fields and serve as mentors and advisors, providing a challenging but supportive academic environment. Beyond the classroom Washington provides an incredible range of experiential learning opportunities that empower you to create the future you want. From research, field work, and study abroad to internships and civic engagement: these unique opportunities combine with the classroom experience to prepare you for success. On average, 94% of Washington graduates are employed, pursuing an advanced degree, or in a full-time volunteer position within 9 months of graduation.

"Located on the Eastern Shore of Maryland in historic Chestertown, Washington College truly is a place like no other. Combining the best of small-town life, outdoor activities, and access to energetic urban hubs, Washington affords you unique opportunities. Sitting within 90 miles of Washington, D.C., Baltimore, and Philadelphia, you benefit from the cultural and professional offerings of some of the most dynamic cities on the East Coast. Our unique location complements Washington's focus on providing an experience that cares for both mind and body. With more than 80 student clubs and organizations, as well as varsity, club, and intramural sports, there are lots of ways to get involved. Through athletics, service clubs, and activities ranging from student publications to dance clubs, we forge leaders beyond the classroom.

"Admission to Washington College is selective; decisions are based primarily on a student's record of academic achievement. We strongly recommend visiting campus."

SELECTIVITY

# of total applicants	3,512
% of total applicants accepted	94
% of total acceptees attending	8
# of in-state applicants	1,251
% of in-state applicants accepted	93
# of out-of-state-applicants	1,852
% of applicants accepted from out of state	96
# of international applicants	409
% of international applicants accepted	86
# of early decision applicants	42
% of early decision applicants accepted	95
# offered a place on the wait list	0

First-Year Profile

Testing policy	Test Optional
Range SAT composite	1080–1310
Range SAT EBRW	560–690
Range SAT math	530–640
Range ACT composite	22–30
% submitting SAT scores	24
% submitting ACT scores	3
Average HS GPA	3.6
% submitting high school GPA	100
% graduated top 10% of class	25
% graduated top 25% of class	48
% graduated top 50% of class	83
% submitting high school rank	39

Important Dates

Early decision	
Apply by	11/15
Notified by	12/15
Early action	
Apply by	12/1
Notified by	1/15
Regular	
Apply by	2/15
Notified by	Rolling, 4/1
Nonfall registration?	Yes

FINANCIAL FACTS*

Annual tuition	$56,430
Food and housing	$18,582
Required fees (First-year)	$1,751 ($2,274)
Books and supplies	$938
Average need-based scholarship (First-year)	$7,280 ($13,772)
% students with need rec. need-based scholarship or grant aid (First-year)	69 (73)
% students with need rec. non-need-based scholarship or grant aid (First-year)	97 (100)
% students with need rec. need-based self-help aid (First-year)	47 (44)
% students rec. any financial aid (First-year)	98 (100)
% UG borrow to pay for school	58
Average cumulative indebtedness	$78,169
% of students with need fully met (First-year)	33 (93)
Average % of student need met (First-year)	77 (84)

* Most recently reported data at time of printing. Scan the QR code to find the latest updates.

WASHINGTON & JEFFERSON COLLEGE

60 South Lincoln Street, Washington, PA 15301 • Admissions: 724-223-6025

Survey Snapshot
Lab facilities are great
Frats and sororities are popular
Everyone loves the Presidents

RATINGS

Quality of Life	74
Fire Safety	97
Green	60*
Academic	81
Profs Interesting	88
Profs Accessible	93
Admissions	83
Financial Aid	88

CAMPUS LIFE

Type of school	Private
Environment	Village

Students

Degree-seeking undergrad enrollment	1,508
% male/female/not reported	53/47/0
% from out of state	26
% First-year from public high school	72
% First-year live on campus	88
% Ugrads live on campus	86
# of fraternities (% join)	4 (20)
# of sororities (% join)	4 (32)
% Asian	2
% Black or African American	5
% Hispanic	5
% Native American	<1
% Pacific Islander	<1
% Race and/or ethnicity unknown	<1
% Two or more races	6
% White	80
% International	1
# of countries represented	10

CAMPUS MENTAL HEALTH SERVICES

Offers mental health/wellness program	Yes
Mental health training available to students	No
Employs Chief Wellness Officer	NR
Peer-to-peer mental health offerings	NR
Counseling center has guidelines or accreditation	No
Mental health/well-being courses	NR

ACADEMICS

% students returning for sophomore year	79
% students graduating within 4 years	64
% students graduating within 6 years	69
Calendar	Semester
Student/faculty ratio	11:1
Most common class size 10–19.	(42%)
Most common lab/discussion size 10–19.	(77%)

Most Popular Majors

Psychology; Business Administration and Management; Biology/Biological Sciences

Applicants Often Prefer

Penn State University Park, University of Pittsburgh—Pittsburgh Campus

Applicants Sometimes Prefer

Duquesne University, Pennsylvania Western University, Slippery Rock University of Pennsylvania

STUDENTS SAY "..."

Academics

Founded in 1781, Washington & Jefferson College is a top-notch liberal arts college that offers an integrative education to 1,200 students, preparing students "for life after graduation, whether that be continuing education or getting a job." There is "a long and deep history that involves a lot of traditions," such as the college's signature Magellan Project, which provides funding for students to pursue internships and research to open their eyes to the possibilities that lie beyond the classroom, or the MayTerm that "allows students to take a class abroad with a professor." "First-Year Seminars also include trips off campus" such as "attending a concert by the Pittsburgh Symphony Orchestra," and "many professors are willing to hold class outside." There is "a lot of potential for opportunities and employment networking," and "small class sizes and activities outside of the classroom [allow students] to create trusting and productive networks with the faculty at the college."

Students say the student-to-faculty ratio "is just right and most professors are eager to interact with their students on a one-on-one basis," creating an environment where they "walk the line of friend and professor...in the best ways possible." It's not unusual that "each [professor] knows your name and little details about you," or comes to "support [you] at sporting events," and that connection helps to enhance the discussion-based classes, in that there's "a space where we can share our ideas without feeling insecure about it." Of course, that's also due to professors being "passionate about what they teach," that each class "is designed remarkably well and prepares each student for their respective majors and future careers," and that instructors "make sure that all the students understand the concepts and are thoroughly set for the exams."

Campus Life

Most students are constantly doing work for school or a job, but on weekends they "spend time on and off campus, hanging with friends or doing events." Foodies will rejoice to know there "are a high number of chain restaurants and local restaurants" within a five minute drive, and for those who want to explore, Pittsburgh is only 30 minutes away. "Leadership on campus is really strong among student organizations" and there's "a weekly calendar of different events that are happening, ranging from concerts to escape rooms." Everyone "is very involved on campus" and there is "a lot of school spirit [so] you'll always see people in the student section supporting their classmates at sports games." Students "fill their free time with studying, athletic practices, and club meetings in the evening," and "volunteering with professors for service activities like creek clean-ups."

Student Body

Washington & Jefferson College is "a positive environment that draws in students from all over the nation and world." The majority of the student body "is white, but our school is trying to grow and focus on diversity," and students often challenge each other "to have productive conversations" about their differences. Everyone "knows everyone because of how small our student body is," forming a "tight-knit community of people with a lot of different interests, whether that be primarily in academics, arts, sports, or other extracurriculars." While everyone is motivated, there "is a mixture of people who are more driven and people who are more laid-back."

WASHINGTON & JEFFERSON COLLEGE

Financial Aid: 724-503-1001 x3353 • E-Mail: admission@washjeff.edu • Website: www.washjeff.edu

THE PRINCETON REVIEW SAYS

Admissions

The school reports that its standardized testing policy for use in admission for Fall 2026 is Test Free. The Princeton Review suggests that interested applicants consult with the school for the most up-to-date standardized testing policies. *Very important factors considered include:* academic GPA. *Other factors considered include:* rigor of secondary school record, class rank, application essay, recommendation(s), interview, extracurricular activities, talent/ability, character/personal qualities, volunteer work, work experience, level of applicant's interest. High school diploma is required and GED is accepted. *Academic units required:* 4 English, 3 math, 1 science, 1 science lab, 2 language (other than English), 1 social studies, 4 academic electives.

Financial Aid

Students should submit: FAFSA; Institution's own financial aid form; State aid form. The Princeton Review suggests that all financial aid forms be submitted as soon as possible. *Need-based scholarships/grants offered:* Federal Pell; Federal SEOG; State scholarships/grants; Private scholarships; College/university scholarship or grant aid from institutional funds. *Loan aid offered:* Federal Direct Subsidized Loans; Federal Direct Unsubsidized Loans; Direct PLUS loans. Admitted students will be notified of awards on a rolling basis. Federal Work-Study Program available. Institutional employment available.

The Inside Word

While Washington & Jefferson College has a fairly high admittance rate, don't assume that acceptance here is a sure thing. A good GPA and challenging academic courses are the most considered factors, but the admissions team will also consider your recommendations, extracurricular activities, and your character (as shown by your essay, work experience, and extracurriculars) when making their decision.

THE SCHOOL SAYS

From the Admissions Office

"Washington & Jefferson College is one of America's most historic and distinguished private liberal arts colleges. Students at W&J receive a first-rate education that is both practical and liberating, preparing them to be ethical leaders poised for professional success. Located just south of Pittsburgh, Pennsylvania, W&J is proud to foster an environment where students engage their intellectual capabilities, allowing them to find their voice and pursue their passions.

"Professional Readiness Professional readiness is a key component of the W&J advantage and begins with the selection of two areas of study. The combination of majors and minors allows students to broaden their skills, experience a diverse curriculum and build a marketable pre-professional résumé. With more than 90 study areas, students can discover majors and minors that match their interests and passions.

"Professional Pathways W&J offers every student a personalized path to success for their next journey after graduation. The Center for Professional Pathways helps students discern interests, sharpen skills and pursue long-term goals.

"Student Life Belonging and engagement are central to the student life experience at W&J. Whether through participation in a club, organization, athletic team or intramural sport, students can enjoy endless opportunities to connect and engage with peers who share their passions and interests.

"Unsurpassed Value Another component of the W&J advantage is unsurpassed value, providing students with a quality education at an affordable price. Our simplified pricing structure ensures a W&J education is affordable and accessible to all students and their families."

SELECTIVITY

# of total applicants	3,947
% of total applicants accepted	81
% of total acceptees attending	13
# of in-state applicants	1,752
% of in-state applicants accepted	88
# of out-of-state-applicants	1,766
% of applicants accepted from out of state	89
# of international applicants	422
% of international applicants accepted	16
# of early decision applicants	55
% of early decision applicants accepted	55

First-Year Profile

Testing policy	Test Free
Average HS GPA	3.6
% submitting high school GPA	98
% graduated top 10% of class	22
% graduated top 25% of class	46
% graduated top 50% of class	79
% submitting high school rank	55

Important Dates

Early decision	
Apply by	12/1
Early action	
Apply by	1/15
Notified by	2/15
Regular	
Notified by	Rolling, 8/15
Nonfall registration?	Yes

FINANCIAL FACTS

Annual tuition	$29,430
Food and housing	$15,151
Required fees (First-year)	$750 ($850)
Books and supplies	$1,000
Average need-based scholarship (First-year)	$22,617 ($24,617)
% students with need rec. need-based scholarship or grant aid (First-year)	100 (100)
% students with need rec. non-need-based scholarship or grant aid (First-year)	85 (71)
% students with need rec. need-based self-help aid (First-year)	80 (79)
% students rec. any financial aid (First-year)	99 (100)
% UG borrow to pay for school	77
Average cumulative indebtedness	$34,731
% of students with need fully met (First-year)	16 (44)
Average % of student need met (First-year)	76 (76)

WASHINGTON AND LEE UNIVERSITY

204 W. Washington Street, Lexington, VA 24450-0303 • Admissions: 540-458-8710

Survey Snapshot
Internships are widely available
Career services are great
Students take advantage of the outdoors

RATINGS

Quality of Life	**96**
Fire Safety	**88**
Green	**89**
Academic	**92**
Profs Interesting	**95**
Profs Accessible	**97**
Admissions	**97**
Financial Aid	**99**

CAMPUS LIFE

Type of school	Private
Environment	Village

Students

Degree-seeking undergrad enrollment	1,912
% male/female/not reported	48/52/0
% from out of state	80
% First-year from public high school	52
% First-year live on campus	100
% Ugrads live on campus	74
# of fraternities (% join)	11 (71)
# of sororities (% join)	8 (73)
% Asian	5
% Black or African American	5
% Hispanic	9
% Native American	<1
% Pacific Islander	<1
% Race and/or ethnicity unknown	2
% Two or more races	4
% White	67
% International	9
# of countries represented	62

CAMPUS MENTAL HEALTH SERVICES

Offers mental health/wellness program	Yes
Mental health training available to students	No
Employs Chief Wellness Officer	No
Peer-to-peer mental health offerings	No
Counseling center has guidelines or accreditation	Yes
Mental health/well-being courses	No

ACADEMICS

% students returning for sophomore year	97
% students graduating within 4 years	91
% students graduating within 6 years	96
Calendar	4-4-1
Student/faculty ratio	7:1
Most common class size 10–19.	(65%)
Most common lab/discussion size 10–19.	(78%)

Most Popular Majors

Political Science and Government; Business Administration and Management; Accounting

Applicants Rarely Prefer

Duke University, University of North Carolina at Chapel Hill, University of Richmond, University of Virginia, Wake Forest University

STUDENTS SAY "..."

Academics

Washington and Lee University, one of the oldest colleges in the country, has a longstanding tradition of giving students the "unique opportunity to customize my academic path," which one student declares "a perfect example of how the school encourages an individualized and dynamic learning experience." W&L not only offers "some of the best educational opportunities," but it also provides ample "resources when it comes to studying abroad, conducting research, finding internships, and personal projects." The "career center is one of [the school's] strongest resources," along with the "elaborate alumni network of successful professionals that are enthusiastic to advise, recommend, and offer opportunities to current students." That support extends into the classroom with a student- to-faculty ratio that "is awesome. You get the chance to understand the concepts taught in class way better than in a huge lecture hall." It helps, too, that professors "are so helpful and want to build genuine connections with their students," which also means that they "like to see students succeed and push them academically." Many courses have a flipped classroom model: "Readings and assignments are completed before class so that class time is dedicated to peer discussions and clarification from the professor." In the much-loved four-week Spring Term, students take only one deep-dive course that affords students various opportunities as "often these courses involve travel, either domestically or abroad, and almost always include unique experimental opportunities." All this makes for a "very positive" overall academic experience, driven by "broad and interesting" class selections and professors who are "all very smart and interested in their subjects."

Campus Life

The community and traditions at W&L "[make] our students eager to come back in the fall." These traditions include Mock Convention (a simulated presidential nomination every four years) and Fancy Dress Ball as particular highlights. "You can usually find [at least] three club-hosted events such as dances, dinners, university guests talks every month to attend," and "everything is open to everyone…you can walk into a room not knowing anyone, and know that someone is going to come introduce themselves and start a conversation." Many students "are greatly invested in Greek life," which "is so much more than a social sphere; rather, many people contribute to the philanthropy of their fraternity/sorority and support their peers." The Outing Club is also popular, "they take you on hikes and backpacking to explore the beauty of the area." The region is known for its "beautiful mountains and trails" and "people love to get outside" and explore. Students also "like to spend time in the small town of Lexington, VA, and the cute local coffee shops or bookstores." As one student puts it, the school is "full of opportunities to get involved and stay busy, no matter what you're into."

Student Body

W&L is home to "a really talented group of friendly and respectful students." The university "has a way of making students come out of their shells," and "most people are very interested in specific topics, but end up well-rounded because of our liberal arts philosophy." As one student notes, "Many of my peers are creating combinations of majors I would never have thought of and pursuing careers that fit [a blend] of their interests, not just one." The honor system "is prevalent and impactful every day:" Students are responsible and "the school fosters a community of trust." Students at W&L "come from various socioeconomic backgrounds" and "are friendly and polite in a way that uniquely reflects Southern hospitality." The "say hey" tradition "is a vow we take to acknowledge the value in each and every person we see on and around campus," and most are "always excited to introduce you to whatever activities or events they are involved in." As one student sums up, "Everyone here is brilliant, and you'll likely never be the most intelligent person in any given class, which I think is a good thing."

WASHINGTON AND LEE UNIVERSITY

Financial Aid: 540-458-8720 • E-Mail: admissions@wlu.edu • Website: www.wlu.edu

THE PRINCETON REVIEW SAYS

Admissions

The school reports that its standardized testing policy for use in admission for Fall 2026 is Test Optional. The Princeton Review suggests that interested applicants consult with the school for the most up-to-date standardized testing policies. *Very important factors considered include:* rigor of secondary school record, recommendation(s), extracurricular activities, character/personal qualities. *Other factors considered include:* class rank, academic GPA, standardized test scores, application essay, interview, talent/ability, first generation, alumni/ae relation, geographical residence, state residency, volunteer work, work experience, level of applicant's interest. High school diploma is required and GED is accepted. *Academic units required:* 4 English, 3 math, 1 science, 1 science lab, 2 language (other than English), 1 social studies, 1 history, 4 academic electives. *Academic units recommended:* 4 English, 4 math, 4 science, 3 language (other than English), 2 social studies, 2 history, 4 academic electives.

Financial Aid

Students should submit: CSS PROFILE; FAFSA; Federal Tax Returns; Noncustodial Profile. The Princeton Review suggests that all financial aid forms be submitted as soon as possible. *Need-based scholarships/grants offered:* Federal Pell; Federal SEOG; State scholarships/grants; Private scholarships; College/university scholarship or grant aid from institutional funds. *Loan aid offered:* Federal Direct Subsidized Loans; Federal Direct Unsubsidized Loans; Direct PLUS loans; College/university loans from institutional funds. Admitted students will be notified of awards on or about 4/1. Federal Work-Study Program available. Institutional employment available.

The Inside Word

Admission to Washington and Lee University is very competitive, so students should have a strong academic record, including a rigorous course load with honors, AP, and/or IB classes.

THE SCHOOL SAYS

From the Admissions Office

"Washington and Lee University stands out for its academic excellence, commitment to affordability, and distinctive student experience. Our retention and four-year graduation rates are among the highest in the nation and our students graduate fully prepared for professional success and lifelong intellectual and civic engagement.

"W&L provides a dynamic and interdisciplinary education, and our students benefit from well-established programs in business, economics, politics, entrepreneurship, journalism, strategic communication, and engineering, as well as shared classes with a graduate law school. The university's culture is deeply rooted in student self-governance, as evidenced by our renowned Honor System, while the campus-wide Speaking Tradition and intentional efforts to foster free expression and civil discourse aid in creating a trusting, welcoming community that shapes every aspect of campus life.

"We are dedicated to making a W&L education accessible through generous need-based financial aid. We follow a need-blind admissions policy for all undergraduate applicants and guarantee to meet 100% of demonstrated financial need—without loans. Through the W&L Promise, students from families with annual incomes under $150,000 pay no tuition, while those with incomes under $75,000 receive full coverage for tuition, housing, and meals.

"Beyond need-based aid, the university awards the prestigious Johnson Scholarship to approximately 10% of each incoming class. This merit-based scholarship covers full tuition, housing, and meals while providing an additional $10,000 for summer experiences. Recipients are selected based on academic excellence, leadership, integrity, and their potential to contribute to the intellectual and civic life of the university and beyond."

SELECTIVITY

# of total applicants	8,963
% of total applicants accepted	14
% of total acceptees attending	41
# of in-state applicants	923
% of in-state applicants accepted	23
# of out-of-state-applicants	3,568
% of applicants accepted from out of state	26
# of international applicants	4,472
% of international applicants accepted	2
# of early decision applicants	1,048
% of early decision applicants accepted	28
# offered a place on the wait list	1,274
# admitted from wait list	2

First-Year Profile

Testing policy	Test Optional
Range SAT composite	1430–1530
Range SAT EBRW	710–750
Range SAT math	720–780
Range ACT composite	33–34
% submitting SAT scores	30
% submitting ACT scores	22
% graduated top 10% of class	85
% graduated top 25% of class	99
% graduated top 50% of class	100
% submitting high school rank	31

Important Dates

Early decision	
Apply by	11/1
Notified by	12/20
Other ED Apply by	1/5
Other ED Notified by	2/1
Regular	
Apply by	1/5
Notified by	4/1
Nonfall registration?	No

FINANCIAL FACTS

Annual tuition	$73,575
Food and housing	$20,575
Required fees	$1,285
Books and supplies	$1,900
Average need-based scholarship (First-year)	$71,291 ($71,985)
% students with need rec. need-based scholarship or grant aid (First-year)	100 (100)
% students with need rec. non-need-based scholarship or grant aid (First-year)	27 (30)
% students with need rec. need-based self-help aid (First-year)	56 (47)
% students rec. any financial aid (First-year)	71 (73)
% UG borrow to pay for school	25
Average cumulative indebtedness	$28,708
% of students with need fully met (First-year)	100 (100)
Average % of student need met (First-year)	100 (100)

WASHINGTON STATE UNIVERSITY

PO Box 645910, Pullman, WA 99164-5910 • Admissions: 509-553-5450

Survey Snapshot
Internships are widely available
Recreation facilities are great
Everyone loves the Cougars

RATINGS

Quality of Life	92
Fire Safety	92
Green	60*
Academic	80
Profs Interesting	86
Profs Accessible	92
Admissions	81
Financial Aid	84

CAMPUS LIFE

Type of school	Public
Environment	Town

Students

Degree-seeking undergrad enrollment	21,037
% male/female/not reported	47/53/0
% from out of state	12
% First-year live on campus	79
% Ugrads live on campus	26
# of fraternities (% join)	24 (18)
# of sororities (% join)	14 (19)
% Asian	6
% Black or African American	3
% Hispanic	20
% Native American	1
% Pacific Islander	1
% Race and/or ethnicity unknown	2
% Two or more races	9
% White	56
% International	2
# of countries represented	88

CAMPUS MENTAL HEALTH SERVICES

Offers mental health/wellness program	Yes
Mental health training available to students	Yes
Employs Chief Wellness Officer	Yes
Peer-to-peer mental health offerings	Yes
Counseling center has guidelines or accreditation	Yes
Mental health/well-being courses	Yes, for-credit

ACADEMICS

% students returning for sophomore year	80
% students graduating within 4 years	44
% students graduating within 6 years	63
Calendar	Semester
Student/faculty ratio	14:1
Most common class size 20–29.	(25%)

Applicants Often Prefer
Central Washington University, Eastern Washington University, University of Washington

Applicants Sometimes Prefer
Gonzaga University, Oregon State University, Seattle University, University of Idaho, University of Oregon, University of Portland

Applicants Rarely Prefer
Arizona State University, Pacific Lutheran University, Seattle Pacific University

STUDENTS SAY "..."

Academics

With six campuses across the state and $403 million in annual research expenditures, Washington State University is a public-school powerhouse, offering 95 majors and study abroad opportunities in 70 countries, and a library that's one of the largest in the entire Pacific Northwest. Here, there are "ample opportunities to explore interests" and research opportunities and associated funding are available at all levels. The state-of-the-art classrooms have "all-inclusive presentation screens for everyone to see," and The Spark (on the main Pullman campus) is an "academic innovation hub" that uses formal and informal learning to encourage collaboration between faculty and students. The administration also "provides some amazing resources and prioritizes mental health," and "makes students feel included and provide a great education."

The school's creativity and compassion extend to the professors, who provide ways to "learn in different forms" and bring in "guest speakers from the industry" to shake things up. Moreover, the "smaller student-to-faculty ratio has increased the amount of in-class discussion we do rather than sitting and listening." It also yields professors who are "extremely approachable and...always trying to help [us] find research opportunities." Those extra steps of encouragement, of teachers "eager to help students participate and build their résumé" are what lead students to declare things like "More than a university, WSU is a community," says a student.

Campus Life

There is never a day that an event is not happening at WSU, and "people find things to do on campus constantly." Whether students have a good old-fashioned "hang with friends" or get involved with the 350 clubs and student organizations, "there are so many ways to explore interests and find opportunities." The Student Entertainment Board is always putting on "up-all-night events or concerts," and "skiing, backpacking, [and] hiking" are common activities here, as are the wildly popular intramural programs ("The gym is also very accessible"). Greek life and multicultural organizations are big on campus, and students also enjoy taking part in "local community projects" and completing meaningful work.

Student Body

Students at WSU "come from everywhere," are "intelligent and creative," and "ask inquisitive questions and engage in class." The school's numerous extracurriculars give this "wide variety of students from various backgrounds" ample opportunity to show off their "many unique hobbies and values," and ultimately, "everyone is able to find a place where they feel they belong." An oft-spoken motto at WSU is "Cougs help Cougs," meaning "the student body supports and uplifts each other both academically and socially." As one student says: "Whenever I wear my WSU gear in public, whether at the airport or even at a beach in Hawaii, people will say 'Go Cougs.'" This is a group that is "like-minded in pursuing success and professional and academic development" all "with the desire to connect with others and learn from each other."

WASHINGTON STATE UNIVERSITY

Financial Aid: 509-335-9711 • E-Mail: future.coug@wsu.edu • Website: www.wsu.edu

THE PRINCETON REVIEW SAYS

Admissions

The school reports that its standardized testing policy for use in admission for Fall 2026 is Test Free. The Princeton Review suggests that interested applicants consult with the school for the most up-to-date standardized testing policies. *Very important factors considered include:* rigor of secondary school record, academic GPA. *Other factors considered include:* application essay, extracurricular activities, talent/ability, character/personal qualities, volunteer work, work experience. High school diploma is required and GED is accepted. *Academic units required:* 4 English, 3 math, 3 science, 2 language (other than English), 3 social studies, 1 visual/performing arts. *Academic units recommended:* 4 English, 4 math, 3 science, 2 language (other than English), 3 social studies, 1 visual/performing arts.

Financial Aid

Students should submit: FAFSA; State aid form. Priority filing deadline is 1/31. The Princeton Review suggests that all financial aid forms be submitted as soon as possible. *Need-based scholarships/grants offered:* Federal Pell; Federal SEOG; State scholarships/grants; Private scholarships; College/university scholarship or grant aid from institutional funds. *Loan aid offered:* Direct PLUS loans; Federal Direct Subsidized Loans; Federal Direct Unsubsidized Loans. Admitted students will be notified of awards on a rolling basis. Federal Work-Study Program available. Institutional employment available.

The Inside Word

Washington State's offerings are appealing enough to draw students from all fifty states, so applicants should have a competitive résumé if they want to attend. Washington applicants are eligible through the Washington Guaranteed Admissions Program (WAGAP) for automatic admission if they meet certain GPA and coursework requirements. Since WSU is Test Free, it won't look at your SAT or ACT scores, so you'll have to find other highlights with which to make a case for admission.

THE SCHOOL SAYS

From the Admissions Office

"One of America's leading public research institutions, Washington State University unlocks possibilities for eager minds to make an impact on the world. Graduates benefit from an outstanding education, delivered affordably, with exceptionally high return on investment.

"As a student, you'll explore your interests with guidance from nationally recognized faculty. Academic programs are so strong that graduates become a top pick for employers in every sector: high-tech, healthcare, news media, energy, finance, and more. A worldwide network of alumni supports your transition to a career.

"For more than 130 years, WSU has championed the greater good. Its research targets critical challenges: resource sustainability, human/animal health, opportunity and equity, smart systems, and national security. WSU Health Sciences colleges educate healthcare professionals to serve communities where they are needed most.

"WSU locations make degree programs accessible to all. Campuses in Pullman, Spokane, the Tri-Cities, Vancouver, Everett, and online (Global Campus) enroll undergraduate, graduate, and professional students from every state and 94 countries.

"The Global Campus shares its vast expertise in online teaching methods with faculty university-wide to deliver compelling academic experiences.

"To be considered for admission, complete the high school core curriculum. For priority dates and deadlines for admission, financial aid, and scholarship applications, check admission.wsu.edu."

SELECTIVITY

# of total applicants	26,403
% of total applicants accepted	86
% of total acceptees attending	19
# of in-state applicants	15,845
% of in-state applicants accepted	85
# of out-of-state-applicants	9,902
% of applicants accepted from out of state	88
# of international applicants	656
% of international applicants accepted	90
# offered a place on the wait list	0
# admitted from wait list	0

First-Year Profile

Testing policy	Test Free
Average HS GPA	3.5
% submitting high school GPA	99

Important Dates

Regular	
Notified by	Rolling, 11/1
Nonfall registration?	Yes

FINANCIAL FACTS

Annual in-state tuition	$12,063
Annual out-of-state tuition	$29,734
Food and housing	$15,245
Required fees	$2,298
Books and supplies	$900
Average need-based scholarship (First-year)	$15,980 ($16,069)
% students with need rec. need-based scholarship or grant aid (First-year)	93 (95)
% students with need rec. non-need-based scholarship or grant aid (First-year)	4 (8)
% students with need rec. need-based self-help aid (First-year)	49 (50)
% students rec. any financial aid (First-year)	77 (90)
% UG borrow to pay for school	44
Average cumulative indebtedness	$24,924
% of students with need fully met (First-year)	8 (12)
Average % of student need met (First-year)	62 (62)

WASHINGTON UNIVERSITY IN ST. LOUIS

1 Brookings Drive, St. Louis, MO 63130-4899 • Admissions: 314-935-6000

Survey Snapshot
Dorms are like palaces
Easy to get around campus
Lab facilities are great

RATINGS

Quality of Life	97
Fire Safety	97
Green	93
Academic	89
Profs Interesting	90
Profs Accessible	91
Admissions	99
Financial Aid	98

CAMPUS LIFE

Type of school	Private
Environment	City

Students

Degree-seeking undergrad enrollment	7,870
% male/female/not reported	45/55/<1
% from out of state	85
% First-year from public high school	58
% First-year live on campus	100
% Ugrads live on campus	71
# of fraternities (% join)	16 (17)
# of sororities (% join)	9 (21)
% Asian	22
% Black or African American	8
% Hispanic	12
% Native American	<1
% Pacific Islander	<1
% Race and/or ethnicity unknown	2
% Two or more races	6
% White	39
% International	10
# of countries represented	45

CAMPUS MENTAL HEALTH SERVICES

Offers mental health/wellness program	Yes
Mental health training available to students	Yes
Employs Chief Wellness Officer	Yes
Peer-to-peer mental health offerings	Yes
Counseling center has guidelines or accreditation	Yes
Mental health/well-being courses	No

ACADEMICS

% students returning for sophomore year	95
% students graduating within 4 years	85
% students graduating within 6 years	93
Calendar	Semester
Student/faculty ratio	10:1
Most common class size 10–19.	(39%)
Most common lab/discussion size 10–19.	(38%)

Most Popular Majors

Computer Science; Mechanical Engineering; Experimental Psychology

Applicants Often Prefer

Brown University, Columbia University, Harvard College, Princeton University, Stanford University, Yale University

Applicants Sometimes Prefer

Cornell University, Duke University, Johns Hopkins University, Northwestern University, University of California—Berkeley, University of California—Los Angeles, University of Pennsylvania

Applicants Rarely Prefer

Emory University, University of Michigan—Ann Arbor

STUDENTS SAY "..."

Academics

Washington University in St. Louis is "great at...teaching students what they need to know to thrive in their careers." The university is "a major research powerhouse [that] maintains a tight-knit atmosphere that allows for undergraduate participation," and encourages "delving into difficult questions." The academic experience is highly "interactive and consists of discussing questions in groups, then discussing it as a class." First-year Arts & Sciences students can participate in Ampersand Programs, which combine group and experiential learning across multiple semesters. In addition, several classes involve unique, first-hand opportunities—such as one class about aging where "each week we would do a different innovative activity like wearing suits that simulated disabilities or going to the art museum to learn about art from older artists." Professors are described as "highly qualified and involved in student success," as well as "incredibly personable" and genuinely invested in their students. One student humorously comments on the dedication of senior lecturers, noting that "the amount of work they put into meeting with students and holding office hours is kind of insane." WashU also "excels in their accessible student resources, which range from academic and social [support] to mental health support," as well as professional development services such as "résumé workshops and mentorship opportunities." According to one student, "The advising options, both academically and socially, make a huge difference in feeling valued and motivated to keep working." Another adds, "It's easy to find help with anything in any class or for applying for jobs, everyone tends to lend a hand." With its strong academic foundation and extensive support, "the motivation and hunger for success vibrates through the air at WashU."

Campus Life

All first-year students at Washington University live on campus in one of the ten residential communities located in the "South 40," which refers to the 40 acres dedicated to housing first- and second-year students. This area provides both social and physical infrastructure, including fitness centers, recreation and game rooms, and dining facilities. In terms of daily life, students note that there is "lots and lots of studying during the week and weekend," and that "any time that is free is spent...with friends or doing club activities." Fortunately, the university provides a wide variety of clubs, and almost "any organization you could be interested in is offered and supported." These clubs are described as "very open and welcoming, friendly, and well-led and organized [in] bringing together a community." In addition to club activities, many students at WashU "really like to exercise—the rec center is popular, and people enjoy running/biking, especially in Forest Park." Beyond campus, St. Louis "is a good food city, and students enjoy trying new restaurants." One student sums up the overall experience: "The campus is breathtaking, the dorms are great, the food is good, the area surrounding WashU is very nice, and the people are amazing."

Student Body

The Wash U student body is "an incredibly friendly group of people eager to learn," and while most "are very career-focused, the academic environment is collaborative and welcoming." One student adds, "Outside of class, people are passionate and invested in what they do, whether research in professors' labs, building rockets in design teams, or performing in a band." Another shares, "Nowhere else I've ever been has had this density of people who are actively working to push themselves in all directions at all times." Each person here possesses "their own individual opinions and styles, which allows for the growth and formation of new ideas," with one adding that "people really look at their personal holistic development." Another concludes, "The moment you step on campus, you can feel the friendly and welcoming atmosphere by students [and] staff...at WashU, people achieve their goals while supporting and helping others."

WASHINGTON UNIVERSITY IN ST. LOUIS

Financial Aid: 888-547-6670 • E-Mail: admissions@wustl.edu • Website: washu.edu

THE PRINCETON REVIEW SAYS

Admissions

The school reports that its standardized testing policy for use in admission for Fall 2026 is Test Optional. The Princeton Review suggests that interested applicants consult with the school for the most up-to-date standardized testing policies. *Very important factors considered include:* rigor of secondary school record, class rank, academic GPA, standardized test scores, application essay, recommendation(s), talent/ability, character/personal qualities. *Important factors considered include:* extracurricular activities, first generation. *Other factors considered include:* alumni/ae relation, geographical residence, state residency, volunteer work, work experience, level of applicant's interest. High school diploma is required and GED is accepted. *Academic units required:* 4 English, 3 math, 3 science, 2 science labs, 2 language (other than English), 2 social studies, 2 history. *Academic units recommended:* 4 English, 4 math, 4 science, 4 science labs, 4 language (other than English), 4 social studies, 4 history.

Financial Aid

Students should submit: FAFSA; CSS PROFILE. The Princeton Review suggests that all financial aid forms be submitted as soon as possible. *Need-based scholarships/grants offered:* Federal Pell; Federal SEOG; State scholarships/grants; Private scholarships; College/university scholarship or grant aid from institutional funds. *Loan aid offered:* Federal Direct Subsidized Loans; Federal Direct Unsubsidized Loans; Direct PLUS loans; State Loans; College/university loans from institutional funds. Admitted students will be notified simultaneously with their offer of admission on or about 4/1. Federal Work-Study Program available. Institutional employment available.

The Inside Word

Washington University is highly selective, and competition for admission is fierce. A strong transcript and course selection will also be important. For example, it's highly recommended that business candidates take calculus, and all STEM candidates take calculus, chemistry, and physics. Finally, portfolios are required for applicants to the College of Art and students applying to the College of Architecture are highly encouraged to submit a portfolio.

THE SCHOOL SAYS

From the Admissions Office

"Nestled in the heart of St. Louis, Washington University offers a nurturing, yet intellectually rigorous, environment where students from all identities and backgrounds thrive. WashU's state-of-the-art buildings, laboratories, classrooms, and libraries foster a sense of community, creativity, and collaboration. On campus and across the world, you'll find talented, inspiring students and faculty developing big ideas and tackling challenging problems.

"WashU's undergraduate program is comprised of four undergraduate schools: the Sam Fox School of Design & Visual Arts, which houses both the College of Architecture and College of Art, College of Arts & Sciences, Olin Business School, and McKelvey School of Engineering. Offering more than 100 areas of study and nearly 2,000 courses, students have the flexibility to explore multiple interests.

"Students can choose to join one of WashU's roughly 400 clubs and organizations, get involved in the St. Louis community, and have the opportunity to participate in cutting-edge research alongside professors who are leaders in their fields.

"WashU accepts Common and Coalition Applications in Early Decision I, Early Decision II, Early Action, and Regular Decision rounds. In an effort to make WashU accessible to every qualified student, each applicant is reviewed individually and with a holistic perspective. WashU doesn't consider the financial situation or ability to pay when making admissions decisions for first-year, domestic applicants. Additionally, we commit to meeting 100 percent of demonstrated financial need without any loans, and financial assistance counselors work with each family individually to provide the necessary assistance for an exceptional education and a successful future."

SELECTIVITY

# of total applicants	33,283
% of total applicants accepted	12
% of total acceptees attending	49
# of in-state applicants	2,017
% of in-state applicants accepted	19
# of out-of-state-applicants	23,436
% of applicants accepted from out of state	13
# of international applicants	7,830
% of international applicants accepted	7
# of early decision applicants	4,934
% of early decision applicants accepted	27
# admitted from wait list	327

First-Year Profile

Testing policy	Test Optional
Range SAT composite	1500–1550
Range SAT EBRW	730–760
Range SAT math	760–790
Range ACT composite	33–35
% submitting SAT scores	32
% submitting ACT scores	29
% submitting high school GPA	93
% graduated top 10% of class	86
% graduated top 25% of class	98
% graduated top 50% of class	100
% submitting high school rank	27

Important Dates

Early decision	
Apply by	11/2
Notified by	12/11
Other ED Apply by	1/4
Other ED Notified by	2/12
Early action	
Apply by	11/2
Notified by	12/23
Regular	
Apply by	1/4
Notified by	4/1
Nonfall registration?	No

FINANCIAL FACTS

Annual tuition	$71,310
Food and housing	$24,272
Required fees	$1,412
Books and supplies	$1,412
Average need-based scholarship (First-year)	$73,547 ($75,880)
% students with need rec. need-based scholarship or grant aid (First-year)	99 (99)
% students with need rec. non-need-based scholarship or grant aid (First-year)	24 (30)
% students with need rec. need-based self-help aid (First-year)	66 (65)
% students rec. any financial aid (First-year)	48 (45)
% UG borrow to pay for school	18
Average cumulative indebtedness	$22,127
% of students with need fully met (First-year)	100 (100)
Average % of student need met (First-year)	100 (100)

Webb Institute

298 Crescent Beach Road, Glen Cove, NY 11542-1398 • Admissions: 516-671-8355

Survey Snapshot
Students always studying
Internships are widely available
Students are friendly

RATINGS

Quality of Life	83
Fire Safety	99
Green	60*
Academic	93
Profs Interesting	95
Profs Accessible	96
Admissions	99
Financial Aid	60*

CAMPUS LIFE

Type of school	Private
Environment	Village

Students

Degree-seeking undergrad enrollment	106
% male/female/not reported	75/25/0
% from out of state	77
% First-year from public high school	88
% First-year live on campus	100
% Ugrads live on campus	100
# of fraternities	0
# of sororities	0
% Asian	2
% Black or African American	0
% Hispanic	8
% Native American	1
% Pacific Islander	0
% Race and/or ethnicity unknown	7
% Two or more races	6
% White	76
% International	0
# of countries represented	NR

CAMPUS MENTAL HEALTH SERVICES

Offers mental health/wellness program	Yes
Mental health training available to students	Yes
Employs Chief Wellness Officer	Yes
Peer-to-peer mental health offerings	Yes
Counseling center has guidelines or accreditation	Yes
Mental health/well-being courses	Yes, non-credit

ACADEMICS

% students returning for sophomore year	93
% students graduating within 4 years	88
% students graduating within 6 years	88
Calendar	Semester
Student/faculty ratio	11:1
Most common class size 30–39.	(100%)
Most common lab/discussion size 30–39.	(100%)

Applicants Sometimes Prefer

Massachusetts Institute of Technology, United States Naval Academy, University of Michigan—Ann Arbor

STUDENTS SAY "..."

Academics

All 100 students at Webb Institute are driven by two loves: engineering and ships. That's to be expected of this Long Island institution, the oldest school devoted to naval architecture and marine engineering in the United States. It's "a very niche school [that] is very good at what it does," and each student graduates with a dual degree in the school's two subjects. The academic calendar runs on semesters, and also adds a highly unique Winter Work Term, which takes place during Winter break and "tremendously augments learning and professional development" by letting students complete a paid internship in the maritime industry, whether that's yacht design or time on a cruise ship or Antarctic icebreaker. Needless to say, the hands-on learning opportunities are extremely interesting, and include "assembling and disassembling engines, visiting the Merchant Marine Academy's lab spaces, attending boat shows, [and] going on board ships for field trips." All students also attend a Monday Lecture Series, "where industry leaders come to campus and give lectures on leading-edge topics like environmental science and new technologies."

The two subjects taught at Webb have been "honed to excellence through the exhaustive course of study" and the invested professors "seek to support students both academically and personally." (Says one student, "it is normal to see several students talking with professors while waiting in line for lunch.") The small student body also naturally lends itself to close-knit bonds, both in terms of the present ("so many people collaborate on homework") and the future (warm relations with alumni "results in donations and job opportunities for Webb"). Brought and bonded together by their academic focus from the start of the first year, and students "know exactly what [they] are going to accomplish from the outset." In order "to cope with the stress students normally feel, Webb employs a psychologist," and there is a remediation program so that students can still get credit for a class if they do other work over the Winter Work or summer break.

Campus Life

Time has to be utilized very effectively at Webb to keep stress levels down, and if students work diligently, they "typically can have a day off on the weekend." All students live on campus, and since Webb is so small, there's opportunity to jump in on any activity, even sports. "Anyone can play anything even if they are not athletic or have never played the sport in their life." New York is only about 45 minutes away, and when the weather is nice, students "often take study breaks after class to go swimming or boating from the beach." There is a student-run pub on campus for those over 21, and "for the outdoorsy types, there's always sailing, hiking, kayaking, wakeboarding," and the nature preserve next door.

Student Body

At Webb, you are one percent of the school, which means "everyone goes through so much together" and it follows that everyone is "very independent and trustworthy." The student body "relies heavily on having each other around, both socially and academically," and there is "an environment of accountability and responsibility" that extends beyond the classroom and the school's respected Honor Code. There are "many musical members... many Eagle scouts, and fishing enthusiasts," and "water sports, disk golf, music, and video games" are some of the most popular hobbies. The "diversity itself at Webb is not the greatest" (approximately 80 percent of the student body is white), but at least "everyone has their own specific interests such as cruise ships, submarines, tankers, and private yachts," and everyone is accepting of absolutely everything: "We love our school and each other."

WEBB INSTITUTE

Financial Aid: 516-403-5926 • E-Mail: admissions@webb.edu • Website: www.webb.edu

THE PRINCETON REVIEW SAYS

Admissions

The school reports that its standardized testing policy for use in admission for Fall 2026 will require applicants to submit either the SAT or ACT. The Princeton Review suggests that interested applicants consult with the school for the most up-to-date standardized testing policies. *Very important factors considered include:* rigor of secondary school record, class rank, academic GPA, recommendation(s), interview, level of applicant's interest. *Important factors considered include:* standardized test scores, application essay, extracurricular activities. *Other factors considered include:* talent/ability, character/personal qualities, volunteer work, work experience. High school diploma is required and GED is not accepted. *Academic units required:* 4 English, 4 math, 2 science, 2 science labs, 2 social studies, 4 academic electives.

Financial Aid

Students should submit: FAFSA. Priority filing deadline is 12/1. The Princeton Review suggests that all financial aid forms be submitted as soon as possible. *Need-based scholarships/grants offered:* Federal Pell; State scholarships/grants; Private scholarships; College/university scholarship or grant aid from institutional funds; Federal SEOG. *Loan aid offered:* Federal Direct Subsidized Loans; Federal Direct Unsubsidized Loans; Direct PLUS loans. Admitted students will be notified of awards on or about 7/1. Federal Work-Study Program not available. Institutional employment not available.

The Inside Word

Although the applicant pool is highly self-selecting, admission to Webb is ultra-tough. (The fact that every enrolled student who is a U.S. citizen or permanent resident gets a full-tuition scholarship also draws a fair share of applicants.) The admissions committee is dedicated to finding students who will excel in the school's rigorous program. To apply, prospective students must submit high-school transcripts indicating rank in class, and two letters of recommendation.

THE SCHOOL SAYS

From the Admissions Office

"Webb, the only college in the country that specializes in the engineering field of naval architecture and marine engineering, seeks young men and women of all races from all over the country who are interested in receiving an excellent engineering education with a full-tuition scholarship. Students don't have to know anything about ships, they just have to be motivated to study how mechanical, civil, structural, and electrical engineering come together with the design elements that make up a ship and all its systems. Being small and private has its major advantages. Every applicant is special and the President as well as a faculty member will interview all entering students personally. The student/faculty ratio is eleven to one, and since there are no teaching assistants, interaction with the faculty occurs daily in class and labs at a level not found at most other colleges. The entire campus operates under the Student Organization's honor system that allows unsupervised exams and twenty-four-hour access to the library, every classroom and laboratory, and the shop and gymnasium. Despite a total enrollment of approximately one hundred students and a demanding workload, Webb manages to field five intercollegiate teams. Currently more than 60 percent of the members of the student body play on one or more intercollegiate teams. Work hard, play hard and the payoff is a job for every student upon graduation. The placement record of the college is 100 percent every year."

SELECTIVITY

# of total applicants	235
% of total applicants accepted	14
% of total acceptees attending	76
# of in-state applicants	59
% of in-state applicants accepted	12
# of out-of-state-applicants	127
% of applicants accepted from out of state	20
# of international applicants	49
% of international applicants accepted	0
# of early decision applicants	45
% of early decision applicants accepted	18
# offered a place on the wait list	14
# admitted from wait list	4

First-Year Profile

Testing policy	SAT or ACT Required
Range SAT composite	1430–1470
Range SAT EBRW	710–750
Range SAT math	720–780
Range ACT composite	32–34
% submitting SAT scores	80
% submitting ACT scores	20
Average HS GPA	3.9
% submitting high school GPA	100
% graduated top 10% of class	86
% graduated top 25% of class	100
% graduated top 50% of class	100
% submitting high school rank	28

Important Dates

Early decision	
Apply by	10/15
Notified by	12/15
Regular	
Apply by	1/15
Notified by	3/31
Nonfall registration?	No

FINANCIAL FACTS

Annual tuition	$61,650
Food and housing	$15,965
Required fees (First-year)	$3,655 ($7,565)
Books and supplies	$800
Average need-based scholarship (First-year)	$11,158 ($11,231)
% students with need rec. need-based scholarship or grant aid (First-year)	39 (26)
% students with need rec. non-need-based scholarship or grant aid (First-year)	100 (100)
% students with need rec. need-based self-help aid (First-year)	18 (21)
% students rec. any financial aid (First-year)	100 (100)
% UG borrow to pay for school	19
Average cumulative indebtedness	$13,925
% of students with need fully met (First-year)	100 (100)
Average % of student need met (First-year)	100 (100)

WELLESLEY COLLEGE

106 Central Street, Wellesley, MA 02481 • Admissions: 781-283-2270

Survey Snapshot
Class discussions encouraged
College radio is popular
Diverse student types interact on campus

RATINGS

Quality of Life	84
Fire Safety	84
Green	60*
Academic	95
Profs Interesting	96
Profs Accessible	95
Admissions	98
Financial Aid	95

CAMPUS LIFE

Type of school	Private
Environment	Town

Students

Degree-seeking undergrad enrollment	2,285
% male/female/not reported	0/100/<1
% from out of state	86
% First-year from public high school	62
% First-year live on campus	100
% Ugrads live on campus	92
# of sororities	0
% Asian	28
% Black or African American	7
% Hispanic	13
% Native American	<1
% Pacific Islander	<1
% Race and/or ethnicity unknown	<1
% Two or more races	8
% White	30
% International	13

CAMPUS MENTAL HEALTH SERVICES

Offers mental health/wellness program	Yes
Mental health training available to students	No
Employs Chief Wellness Officer	NR
Peer-to-peer mental health offerings	NR
Counseling center has guidelines or accreditation	No
Mental health/well-being courses	NR

ACADEMICS

% students returning for sophomore year	95
% students graduating within 4 years	79
% students graduating within 6 years	91
Calendar	Semester
Student/faculty ratio	8:1
Most common class size 10–19.	(52%)
Most common lab/discussion size 10–19.	(60%)

Most Popular Majors
Computer Science; Biological And Biomedical Sciences; Economics

Applicants Also Look At
Barnard College, Brown University, Cornell University, Harvard College, Princeton University, Smith College, University of California—Berkeley, University of California—Los Angeles, Yale University

STUDENTS SAY "..."

Academics

For more than 150 years, Wellesley College has given ambitious young women an education in the liberal arts with a global perspective by offering more than 50 majors and hundreds of funded internships around the world. The school's financial support allows "students to pursue internships and research [opportunities] that they would otherwise not take because they are unpaid." The school stresses leadership, service, and the idea of Wellesley students contributing to the world both now and after graduation. To enhance that education even further, enrollees are able to cross-register (or even dual degree) with other nearby colleges. Students are "pushed to explore different departments through the distribution requirements, providing them with a liberal arts education that shapes their personhood and education." And each department is "provided with ample resources and handpicked professors" who "truly value building relationships with their students." It's not uncommon for faculty "to take their class out to a restaurant, or even invite students to their home for a meal." The First-Year Experience at Wellesley further helps ease students into college, including mentor groups, a required writing class, and First-Year Seminars where new students "have the chance to dive deep into a specific topic without feeling the pressure of having [senior students] dominate the conversation."

Academic opportunities extend beyond the classroom: the school's reputation and alumnae network "open so many doors for you in the future," and students can "take part from the moment [they] accept the enrollment offer, and for as long afterwards as [they] wish." Wellesley works to create an environment "where students can naturally progress through leadership positions on campus, whether that be through research, residential life, or student-run organizations." There are also "vast opportunities [for] study abroad programs in so many locations."

Campus Life

While the average Wellesley "workload is not for the faint of heart," students find balance "with extracurricular activities, social life, and self-care." One student explains, "Even when classes are stressful, there is a beautiful campus that sparks happiness at random moments." That joy is apparent because almost everyone here is passionate about their extracurriculars, and "each organization at Wellesley is full of members who intensely love what they do." Outside of clubs or organizations, tons of students engage in "the weekly Thursday pub night" on campus, and Wellesley "usually has some cultural shows or lectures going on in the afternoon" which are well-attended. When they need a change of scenery, people often head to "neighboring universities to have fun on weekends" and "there is a bus that provides easy transportation" into Boston; many also "take advantage of [the] proximity to other east coast cities and states and take weekend trips." One student sums up the campus life at Wellesley: "Going to a party is just as acceptable as staying in and watching a movie or playing board games," and the school is "very much a choose your own adventure" environment.

Student Body

Among this "study-focused group of diverse people who hail from many countries and backgrounds," students "can be who [they] want and explore different identities." Thanks to that aspect of the student body, everyone is "exposed to countless cultures and viewpoints." These "intellectual, driven, [and] inclusive scholars" are "uplifting and kind to each other both in class and outside of class," and part of the campus culture "is the 'Why not?' attitude that we all share." There's also a "large feminist culture and LGBT population" on campus and overall, students suggest that their peers are "nonjudgmental." Another student sums up the campus environment, saying Wellesley makes a huge effort "to cultivate and facilitate a strong support network for all."

Wellesley College

Financial Aid: 781-283-2360 • E-Mail: admission@wellesley.edu • Website: www.wellesley.edu

THE PRINCETON REVIEW SAYS

Admissions

The school reports that its standardized testing policy for use in admission for Fall 2026 is Test Optional. The Princeton Review suggests that interested applicants consult with the school for the most up-to-date standardized testing policies. *Very important factors considered include:* rigor of secondary school record, academic GPA, recommendation(s), character/personal qualities. *Important factors considered include:* class rank, application essay, extracurricular activities, talent/ability. *Other factors considered include:* standardized test scores, first generation, alumni/ae relation, geographical residence, state residency, volunteer work, work experience, level of applicant's interest. High school diploma is required and GED is accepted. *Academic units recommended:* 4 English, 4 math, 3 science, 2 science labs, 4 language (other than English), 4 social studies.

Financial Aid

Students should submit: FAFSA; CSS PROFILE. Priority filing deadline is 1/15. The Princeton Review suggests that all financial aid forms be submitted as soon as possible. *Need-based scholarships/grants offered:* Federal Pell; Federal SEOG; State scholarships/grants; Private scholarships; College/university scholarship or grant aid from institutional funds. *Loan aid offered:* Federal Direct Subsidized Loans; Federal Direct Unsubsidized Loans; Direct PLUS loans; College/university loans from institutional funds. Admitted students will be notified of awards on or about 4/1. Federal Work-Study Program available. Institutional employment available.

The Inside Word

With an acceptance rate of just 15 percent, Wellesley College is highly selective. When making an admissions decision, Wellesley considers a broad range of factors, including a student's academic record, the difficulty of high school curriculum, participation in extracurricular activities, class rank, recommendations, personal essay, standardized test scores when submitted, leadership, and special talents (students may submit an art, music, or theater supplements along with their applications if they have a special talent in those areas).

THE SCHOOL SAYS

From the Admissions Office

"Wellesley is where students learn how to (and do!) change the world. Wellesley students fully immerse themselves in the tight-knit liberal arts community; taking full advantage of the over 50 academic departments, 1,000 courses, and 180 student organizations. It is a place grounded in inclusive excellence where support and celebration is the norm.

"There's no typical Wellesley student (we know: every college says that; and yet!), but they tend to be people who know that they don't know everything; who have a strong voice but listen to other voices; who have big plans but are totally open to changing them; who have taken risks, failed, and figured out a better way. They believe in connection. The College is easily accessible to Boston, a great city in which to meet other college students and to experience theater, art, sports, and entertainment. Considered one of the most diverse colleges in the nation, Wellesley students hail from over fifty countries and nearly all fifty states.

"As a community, we are looking for students who possess intellectual curiosity: the ability to think independently, ask challenging questions, and grapple with answers. Strong candidates demonstrate both academic achievement and an excitement for learning. They also display leadership, an appreciation for diverse perspectives, and an understanding of the College's mission to educate women who will make a difference in the world."

SELECTIVITY

# of total applicants	8,506
% of total applicants accepted	15
% of total acceptees attending	46
# of in-state applicants	698
% of in-state applicants accepted	22
# of out-of-state-applicants	4,676
% of applicants accepted from out of state	21
# of international applicants	3,132
% of international applicants accepted	3
# of early decision applicants	1,023
% of early decision applicants accepted	29
# offered a place on the wait list	2,214
# admitted from wait list	59

First-Year Profile

Testing policy	Test Optional
Range SAT composite	1460–1540
Range SAT EBRW	730–760
Range SAT math	720–790
Range ACT composite	33–35
% submitting SAT scores	44
% submitting ACT scores	18
% graduated top 10% of class	88
% graduated top 25% of class	99
% graduated top 50% of class	100
% submitting high school rank	25

Important Dates

Early decision	
Apply by	11/1
Notified by	Mid December
Other ED Apply by	1/5
Other ED Notified by	Mid February
Regular	
Apply by	1/8
Notified by	Late March
Nonfall registration?	No

FINANCIAL FACTS

Annual tuition	$72,570
Food and housing	$23,206
Required fees	$360
Books and supplies	$800
Average need-based scholarship (First-year)	$70,519 ($71,018)
% students with need rec. need-based scholarship or grant aid (First-year)	98 (98)
% students with need rec. non-need-based scholarship or grant aid (First-year)	1 (1)
% students with need rec. need-based self-help aid (First-year)	96 (98)
% students rec. any financial aid (First-year)	52 (55)
% UG borrow to pay for school	37
Average cumulative indebtedness	$12,364
% of students with need fully met (First-year)	69 (67)
Average % of student need met (First-year)	100 (100)

WESLEYAN UNIVERSITY

45 Wyllys Avenue, Middletown, CT 06459 • Admissions: 860-685-3000

Survey Snapshot
Lots of liberal students
Students politically aware
Great library

RATINGS

Quality of Life	87
Fire Safety	93
Green	96
Academic	90
Profs Interesting	99
Profs Accessible	95
Admissions	96
Financial Aid	99

CAMPUS LIFE

Type of school	Private
Environment	Town

Students

Degree-seeking undergrad enrollment	2,979
% male/female/not reported	48/52/<1
% from out of state	91
% First-year from public high school	57
% First-year live on campus	100
% Ugrads live on campus	94
# of fraternities (% join)	1 (4)
# of sororities	0
% Asian	9
% Black or African American	6
% Hispanic	10
% Native American	<1
% Pacific Islander	0
% Race and/or ethnicity unknown	6
% Two or more races	9
% White	50
% International	10
# of countries represented	61

CAMPUS MENTAL HEALTH SERVICES

Offers mental health/wellness program	Yes
Mental health training available to students	Yes
Employs Chief Wellness Officer	No
Peer-to-peer mental health offerings	No
Counseling center has guidelines or accreditation	No
Mental health/well-being courses	Yes, for-credit

ACADEMICS

% students returning for sophomore year	95
% students graduating within 4 years	81
% students graduating within 6 years	90
Calendar	Semester
Student/faculty ratio	7:1
Most common class size 10–19.	(46%)
Most common lab/discussion size 10–19.	(45%)

Most Popular Majors

Psychology; Political Science and Government; Econometrics and Quantitative Economics

Applicants Also Look At

Brown University, Columbia University, Cornell University, Georgetown University, Harvard College, Tufts University, University of California—Berkeley, University of Southern California, Williams College, Yale University

STUDENTS SAY "..."

Academics

Wesleyan University is committed to helping students discover their passions with an interdisciplinary, open curriculum that "allows students to explore their actual interests rather than being tied down by tedious general education requirements." Students "truly love that there are no required courses outside of our chosen majors/minors/concentrations. It really emphasizes that Wesleyan is a place to discover what we love." It also yields professors who "teach fascinating classes to medium and small groups of excited, passionate students" and facilitate "vibrant discussions on the course material." Professors are known for being "extremely creative and detailed with their course focuses, which makes for some amazing classes," like "civics classes that force you to dialogue with strangers in an effort to create connections and practice good conversation." Students also value the "many research opportunities and multiple ongoing research organizations headed by professors that include undergraduates." There are plenty of resources for students: "TA sessions, office hours, therapy, tutoring, are all readily available if you have a problem at school." One student concurs, saying, "When I have needed help navigating institutional challenges like declaring majors, transferring credits, and meeting language requirements for studying abroad, [my professors] have been enormously helpful." In all, Wesleyan is said to be "Inspiring students to expand their interests and cultivating a culture of support not competition."

Campus Life

Students are required to live on campus for all four years, and as a result, "people rarely go off campus on weekends because there's so much going on." Weekly events include everything "from group workout classes to painting workshops" and The Wes Film Series, "a wonderful group that plays four movies every week for free at Wesleyan's theater." Wesleyan offers over 250 clubs and groups that cater to a diverse range of interests, such as the Prometheus Fire Arts Club and the crafting club Threads and Thingamabobs. There is also "a "big [arts] scene on campus (visual arts, studio arts, performing arts, theater, music, dance)," along with "a large a cappella presence." Overall, "students are very involved in the school—having on-campus jobs, being a part of a club, running a social justice campaign, etc." In addition, "a lot of people are involved in intramural sports," such as soccer, rugby, and Ultimate Frisbee which "has an active community." Students say the "food is good, meals are very social, and our dining halls are always bustling." One of the benefits of "being at a small school means knowing everyone and running into them all the time" around campus.

Student Body

While "everyone is super smart and leans artsy,...you can also find all kinds of people" with a variety of personalities and interests. As one student happily notes, "Honestly, no two people are the same in expression." Many students "are strongly committed to social justice" and "engaged in the community and in broader social issues," while others "have niche interests in subjects that would be nearly impossible to study at universities not offering an open curriculum." A student says of the school's interdisciplinary environment: "This is a great place for people who love art and sports and science and mixing all of those things together." Students frequently "double major and often they major in two pretty unrelated fields." Wesleyan students "are constantly looking to better themselves," and no matter the subject, "people commit to their interests." Students are described as "social, passionate, and highly engaged," Wesleyan is a place where "you can absolutely find your people no matter who you are or what you are into."

Wesleyan University

Financial Aid: 860-685-2800 • E-Mail: admission@wesleyan.edu • Website: www.wesleyan.edu

THE PRINCETON REVIEW SAYS

Admissions

The school reports that its standardized testing policy for use in admission for Fall 2026 is Test Optional. The Princeton Review suggests that interested applicants consult with the school for the most up-to-date standardized testing policies. *Very important factors considered include:* rigor of secondary school record. *Important factors considered include:* class rank, academic GPA, application essay, recommendation(s), talent/ability, character/personal qualities, first generation. *Other factors considered include:* standardized test scores, extracurricular activities, geographical residence, state residency, volunteer work, work experience. High school diploma is required and GED is accepted. *Academic units recommended:* 4 English, 4 math, 4 science, 3 science labs, 4 language (other than English), 4 social studies, 4 history.

Financial Aid

Students should submit: FAFSA; CSS PROFILE. Priority filing deadline is 1/15. The Princeton Review suggests that all financial aid forms be submitted as soon as possible. *Need-based scholarships/grants offered:* Federal Pell; Federal SEOG; State scholarships/grants; Private scholarships; College/university scholarship or grant aid from institutional funds. *Loan aid offered:* Federal Direct Subsidized Loans; Federal Direct Unsubsidized Loans; Direct PLUS loans; College/university loans from institutional funds. Admitted students will be notified of awards on or about 4/1. Federal Work-Study Program available. Institutional employment available.

The Inside Word

Wesleyan meets 100 percent of demonstrated need, and the university provides aid offers with no loans for all students qualifying for need-based institutional aid. A three-year curriculum is offered for students who opt to also take summer courses, which saves about 20 percent of the total cost of a Wesleyan education.

THE SCHOOL SAYS

From the Admissions Office

"Wesleyan faculty believe in an education that is flexible and affords individual freedom and that a strong liberal arts education is the best foundation for success in any endeavor. The broad curriculum provides a rigorous education that values putting ideas into practice. Students have the opportunity to discover what they love to do, work at the highest level, and apply their knowledge in meaningful ways. As a result, Wesleyan students achieve a very personalized but broad education. Wesleyan's Vice President and Dean of Admission and Financial Aid, Amin Abdul-Malik Gonzalez, describes the qualities Wesleyan seeks in its students: 'Our holistic process, which carefully considers candidates in their respective contexts, aims to select high-achieving, intellectually engaged, broadly talented, and socially conscious students who will thrive in Wesleyan's vibrant academic environment. At Wesleyan, we value character and personal promise as much as impressive credentials and accomplishments. We seek students who will leverage our outstanding resources, realize their personal potentials, and make meaningful contributions to both our dynamically diverse community and wider world.'"

SELECTIVITY

# of total applicants	14,973
% of total applicants accepted	16
% of total acceptees attending	34
# of early decision applicants	1,220
% of early decision applicants accepted	43
# offered a place on the wait list	2,224
# admitted from wait list	54

First-Year Profile

Testing policy	Test Optional
Range SAT composite	1350–1510
Range SAT EBRW	690–750
Range SAT math	660–770
Range ACT composite	32–35
% submitting SAT scores	44
% submitting ACT scores	15
% graduated top 10% of class	73
% graduated top 25% of class	95
% graduated top 50% of class	100
% submitting high school rank	18

Important Dates

Early decision	
Apply by	11/15
Notified by	12/15
Other ED Apply by	1/1
Other ED Notified by	2/15
Regular	
Apply by	1/1
Notified by	4/1
Nonfall registration?	No

FINANCIAL FACTS

Annual tuition	$75,916
Food and housing	$21,660
Required fees (First-year)	$390 ($690)
Books and supplies	$1,200
Average need-based scholarship (First-year)	$72,372 ($71,740)
% students with need rec. need-based scholarship or grant aid (First-year)	100 (100)
% students with need rec. non-need-based scholarship or grant aid (First-year)	3 (2)
% students with need rec. need-based self-help aid (First-year)	95 (97)
% students rec. any financial aid (First-year)	46 (52)
% UG borrow to pay for school	28
Average cumulative indebtedness	$30,378
% of students with need fully met (First-year)	100 (100)
Average % of student need met (First-year)	100 (100)

WEST VIRGINIA UNIVERSITY

Admissions Office, Morgantown, WV 26506-6201 • Admissions: 304-293-2121

Survey Snapshot
Great library
Recreation facilities are great
Everyone loves the Mountaineers

RATINGS

Quality of Life	78
Fire Safety	60*
Green	60*
Academic	78
Profs Interesting	86
Profs Accessible	91
Admissions	84
Financial Aid	79

CAMPUS LIFE

Type of school	Public
Environment	Town

Students

Degree-seeking undergrad enrollment	20,499
% male/female/not reported	52/48/0
% from out of state	48
% First-year live on campus	92
% Ugrads live on campus	22
# of fraternities (% join)	9 (NR)
# of sororities (% join)	8 (NR)
% Asian	2
% Black or African American	4
% Hispanic	4
% Native American	<1
% Pacific Islander	<1
% Race and/or ethnicity unknown	<1
% Two or more races	4
% White	80
% International	6
# of countries represented	75

CAMPUS MENTAL HEALTH SERVICES

Offers mental health/wellness program	Yes
Mental health training available to students	No
Employs Chief Wellness Officer	NR
Peer-to-peer mental health offerings	NR
Counseling center has guidelines or accreditation	No
Mental health/well-being courses	NR

ACADEMICS

% students returning for sophomore year	76
% students graduating within 4 years	35
% students graduating within 6 years	58
Calendar	Semester
Student/faculty ratio	18:1
Most common class size 20–29.	(25%)
Most common lab/discussion size 20–29.	(48%)

Most Popular Majors
Engineering; Business Administration and Management; Journalism

Applicants Often Prefer
Penn State University Park, University of Maryland, College Park, Virginia Tech

Applicants Sometimes Prefer
James Madison University, Towson University, University of Pittsburgh—Pittsburgh Campus

Applicants Rarely Prefer
Pierpont Community and Technical College

STUDENTS SAY "..."

Academics

West Virginia University is a large research university known for providing a "great academic experience wrapped up in a fun college atmosphere." WVU offers a "diversity of programs" and academic experiences that "challenge students in the classroom" and prepare them "to be successful in the next step of life after college." The engineering program, in particular, receives high praise for offering "many opportunities for seniors looking for jobs." Courses at WVU are taught by a distinguished faculty "who bring a wide range of knowledge and experiences" to the classroom. In addition to the university's "high academic standards," in-state undergraduates cite affordability as a big reason for choosing WVU. While many students love attending the largest university in West Virginia, some suggest that "the large classes make it difficult to form solid teacher-student relationships." Others feel that while "you can sit in the back and go unnoticed…that's a personal choice" and "If you put forth any type of effort, you'll get to know your professors at WVU." Students appreciate the academic resources and support "outside the classroom with learning centers, free tutors, [and] group work areas." Overall, most students fondly recall their time at WVU as "a wonderful experience with a good balance of academics and fun opportunities."

Campus Life

A common refrain from students at WVU is that they're "born to be a Mountaineer," and their school spirit sings: "Mountaineer pride [is] only something you can feel at a football game singing 'Country Roads' with 50,000 of your closest friends." Unsurprisingly, there is "incredible enthusiasm for school activities," whether that's participating in clubs, playing in the marching band, or supporting the football and basketball teams. Although one student reports, "A lot of people here drink quite often," students also underscore that there is plenty to do on campus that doesn't involve alcohol. Highlights of campus life include the "amazing student recreational center," which is "complete with weight room, indoor swimming pool, hot tubs, indoor track, indoor basketball and racquetball courts, ping-pong tables, and boxing equipment." Another popular spot is the Mountainlair student union, affectionately known as "the Lair," where students enjoy watching free movies and grabbing a bite at the food court. To make getting around easier, the Personal Rapid Transit (PRT) system, Morgantown's free-to-students "electric people mover," seamlessly connects the three areas of the campus: Evansdale, Health Sciences, and Downtown. The latter of these spills into the town's High Street, described as "one of the best things about Morgantown," thanks to a wide selection of bars, clubs, lounges, and restaurants. Many students "like the fact that it is a big university, but being in Morgantown gives it a homey feel."

Student Body

WVU students see themselves as "relaxed and social" as well as full of school spirit; "the typical student always has some piece of WVU apparel on, and that's usually sweatpants." As far as engagement and community are concerned, "Students are very involved on campus with academics and various clubs and organizations. It is a very lively campus and there is always something going on."

WEST VIRGINIA UNIVERSITY

Financial Aid: 304-293-5242 • E-Mail: go2wvu@mail.wvu.edu • Website: www.wvu.edu

THE PRINCETON REVIEW SAYS

Admissions

The school reports that its standardized testing policy for use in admission for Fall 2026 will require applicants to submit either the SAT or ACT. The Princeton Review suggests that interested applicants consult with the school for the most up-to-date standardized testing policies. *Very important factors considered include:* academic GPA, standardized test scores. *Important factors considered include:* rigor of secondary school record, state residency. *Other factors considered include:* extracurricular activities, talent/ability. High school diploma is required and GED is accepted. *Academic units required:* 4 English, 4 math, 3 science, 3 science labs, 2 language (other than English), 3 social studies, 1 visual/performing arts.

Financial Aid

Students should submit: FAFSA. Priority filing deadline is 3/1. The Princeton Review suggests that all financial aid forms be submitted as soon as possible. *Need-based scholarships/grants offered:* Federal Pell; Federal SEOG; Private scholarships; College/university scholarship or grant aid from institutional funds; Federal Nursing Scholarships. *Loan aid offered:* Federal Direct Subsidized Loans; Federal Direct Unsubsidized Loans; Direct PLUS loans. Admitted students will be notified of awards on a rolling basis beginning 12/1. Federal Work-Study Program available. Institutional employment available.

The Inside Word

While standards for general admission to WVU aren't overly rigorous, you'll find admission to its premier programs to be quite competitive. Some of the school's programs, such as engineering and forensics, have certain GPA requirements for admission if you choose to apply test optional, so be sure and check their website. If you're not admitted to the program of your choice, you may be able to transfer to it later if your grades are good enough.

THE SCHOOL SAYS

From the Admissions Office

"From quality academic programs and outstanding, caring faculty, to incredible new facilities and a campus environment that focuses on students' needs, WVU is a place where dreams can come true. Our tradition of academic excellence attracts some of the region's best high school seniors. WVU has produced twenty-four Rhodes Scholars, thirty-five Goldwater Scholars, twenty-two Truman Scholars, six members of the USA Today's All-USA College Academic First Team, and two Udall Scholarship winners. Whether your goal is to be an aerospace engineer, reporter, physicist, athletic trainer, opera singer, forensic investigator, pharmacist, or CEO, WVU's 191 degree choices can make it happen. Unique student-centered initiatives help students experience true education beyond the classroom. The Mountaineer parents club connects more than 20,000 families, and a parents' helpline (800-WVU-0096) leads to a full-time parent advocate. A Student Recreation Center includes athletic courts, pools, weight/fitness equipment, and a fifty-foot indoor climbing wall. A major building program is creating new classrooms, labs, health-care facilities, an art museum, and a student wellness center. With programs for studying abroad, a Center from Black Culture and Research, and Office of Disability Services, and a student body that comes from every WV county, fifty states, and 108 different countries, WVU encourages diversity. WVU research funding has topped $174 million for the second consecutive year, making WVU a major research institution where undergraduates can participate."

SELECTIVITY

# of total applicants	18,639
% of total applicants accepted	82
% of total acceptees attending	31

First-Year Profile

Testing policy	SAT or ACT Required
Range SAT EBRW	530–620
Range SAT math	520–620
Range ACT composite	21–27
% submitting SAT scores	57
% submitting ACT scores	65
Average HS GPA	3.5
% submitting high school GPA	100
% graduated top 10% of class	23
% graduated top 25% of class	48
% graduated top 50% of class	78
% submitting high school rank	61

Important Dates

Regular	
Apply by	8/1
Notified by	Rolling, 9/15
Nonfall registration?	Yes

FINANCIAL FACTS

Annual in-state tuition	$8,976
Annual out-of-state tuition	$25,320
Food and housing	$10,918
Books and supplies	$950
Average need-based scholarship (First-year)	$5,812 ($6,190)
% students with need rec. need-based scholarship or grant aid (First-year)	74 (81)
% students with need rec. non-need-based scholarship or grant aid (First-year)	39 (46)
% students with need rec. need-based self-help aid (First-year)	77 (69)
% students rec. any financial aid (First-year)	75 (72)
% UG borrow to pay for school	61
Average cumulative indebtedness	$32,541
% of students with need fully met (First-year)	11 (13)

Westminster University

1840 South 1300 East, Salt Lake City, UT 84105 • Admissions: 801-832-2200

Survey Snapshot
Class discussions encouraged
Students environmentally aware
Students love Salt Lake City, UT

RATINGS	
Quality of Life	87
Fire Safety	94
Green	60*
Academic	88
Profs Interesting	91
Profs Accessible	93
Admissions	86
Financial Aid	91

CAMPUS LIFE

Type of school	Private
Environment	Metropolis

Students

Degree-seeking undergrad enrollment	818
% male/female/not reported	42/58/0
% from out of state	41
% First-year live on campus	83
% Ugrads live on campus	46
# of fraternities	0
# of sororities	0
% Asian	4
% Black or African American	2
% Hispanic	14
% Native American	<1
% Pacific Islander	2
% Race and/or ethnicity unknown	2
% Two or more races	6
% White	66
% International	4
# of countries represented	26

CAMPUS MENTAL HEALTH SERVICES

Offers mental health/wellness program	Yes
Mental health training available to students	No
Employs Chief Wellness Officer	NR
Peer-to-peer mental health offerings	NR
Counseling center has guidelines or accreditation	No
Mental health/well-being courses	NR

ACADEMICS

% students returning for sophomore year	76
% students graduating within 4 years	52
% students graduating within 6 years	64
Calendar	4-4-1
Student/faculty ratio	8:1
Most common class size 1–9.	(46%)
Most common lab/discussion size 10–19.	(67%)

Applicants Often Prefer
University of Utah, Utah State University

Applicants Sometimes Prefer
Brigham Young University (UT), Southern Utah University, Weber State University

Applicants Rarely Prefer
Boise State University, Idaho State University, Montana State University, Northern Arizona University, University of Portland

STUDENTS SAY "..."

Academics

Set amidst the spectacular peaks of the Wasatch Mountains, Westminster University is a quaint liberal arts college in a small neighborhood of Salt Lake City. Undergrads praise "a very rigorous academic load" and "a community that doesn't center around academic competition, but academic empowerment." This collaborative culture includes faculty that is "attentive and understanding." One undergrad says, "Professors are very accessible,... [and] if office hours don't work for you, they will make other times to meet." Students generally agree that professors are "experts in their fields [and] extremely knowledgeable." There are complaints, however, about adjunct professors who "seem to be less committed." The small campus and class sizes allow students "to communicate one-on-one with professors [and give students] the opportunity to get to know...classmates better." Despite the size of Westminster, "resources are abundant at the college," and students have access to hands-on research opportunities, internships, study abroad programs, and conferences. Frequently mentioned majors include "a great nursing program," biology, and theater.

Campus Life

Outdoor activities are a big draw to students at Westminster. And with six ski resorts within a half-hour drive, "a lot of people look forward to snowboarding and skiing." In fact, one student says that "Westminster has a core of people who like to ski and that is often all they do"—Griffins love their slopes! Others clarify that "there is more [to] Westminster than just skiing and snowboarding." Sure, "winter sports are popular here, but most of us are more concerned with our academics than the ski hill." A happy medium would be the on-campus clubs available to students, which "always try to provide activities or events." Something students are unanimous on is the food options, from on-campus student centers that "are great stops for a quick meal or coffee to recharge" to the restaurants in Salt Lake City, which has the added benefit of being "a very cool city."

Student Body

The culture is welcoming and socially relaxed at Westminster University. "There is a general mix of artistic and intellectual students who are driven by learning." Additionally, there is also an awareness of social issues, and "it's easy to strike up a conversation about gender bias or cultural inequality because our students are well educated and always up for challenging their thought process to make positive change happen," one undergrad reports. That said, some take issue with the common "liberal ideology." Moreover, while students may have a "diversity of interests," some find that "there is not much diversity in terms of race, gender, sexual orientation, and ability." The student body is predominantly "white and at least upper middle class." But while it might seem like a fairly uniform campus, "everyone you meet is open to every walk of life [and] accepting of differences."

WESTMINSTER UNIVERSITY

Financial Aid: 801-832-2502 • E-Mail: admission@westminsteru.edu • Website: www.westminstercollege.edu

THE PRINCETON REVIEW SAYS

Admissions

The school reports that its standardized testing policy for use in admission for Fall 2026 is Test Optional. The Princeton Review suggests that interested applicants consult with the school for the most up-to-date standardized testing policies. *Very important factors considered include:* rigor of secondary school record. *Important factors considered include:* class rank, academic GPA, extracurricular activities, talent/ability, character/personal qualities, first generation, volunteer work, work experience. *Other factors considered include:* standardized test scores, application essay, recommendation(s), interview, alumni/ae relation, religious affiliation/commitment, level of applicant's interest. High school diploma is required and GED is accepted. *Academic units recommended:* 4 English, 4 math, 3 science, 2 language (other than English), 3 social studies, 1 visual/performing arts.

Financial Aid

Students should submit: FAFSA. Priority filing deadline is 3/1. The Princeton Review suggests that all financial aid forms be submitted as soon as possible. *Need-based scholarships/grants offered:* Federal Pell; Federal SEOG; Private scholarships; College/university scholarship or grant aid from institutional funds; State scholarships/grants. *Loan aid offered:* Federal Direct Subsidized Loans; Federal Direct Unsubsidized Loans; Direct PLUS loans. Admitted students will be notified of awards on a rolling basis beginning 12/1. Federal Work-Study Program available. Institutional employment available.

The Inside Word

Westminster looks for a strong academic record and rigorous courses, but test scores will also be considered if submitted. A strong personal statement plays an important role in the admission decision and gives admissions officers an opportunity to get to know the person behind the transcript. A campus interview is encouraged, but not required.

THE SCHOOL SAYS

From the Admissions Office

"At Westminster, you'll spend less time with your nose in a textbook and more time engaged in lively discussion with your classmates. You'll be challenged to apply your knowledge in interesting, innovative ways, while learning from professors who are passionate about what they do. And with an average class size of 17, your teachers won't just know you by name, they'll know what drives you.

"Our new general education program, WCore, gives you the opportunity to explore new subjects through small, interdisciplinary courses, where you'll spend time engaging in and challenging ideas, rather than just memorizing facts. With specialized offerings like our Honors College, dedicated faculty mentors, and internship and professional connections throughout the community, you'll graduate prepared to take on whatever's next.

"Each application is read and reviewed individually by an admission committee that takes into account both level of challenge in coursework and grades received. Either the SAT or ACT is accepted. Westminster University has a rolling application deadline and will accept applications until the class is filled. To be eligible for the widest array of financial aid—more than 98 percent of first-year students receive scholarship or financial aid—April 15 is the priority consideration deadline for fall semester, and May 15 is the priority deadline for on-campus housing applications."

SELECTIVITY

# of total applicants	2,964
% of total applicants accepted	67
% of total acceptees attending	10
# of in-state applicants	1,521
% of in-state applicants accepted	76
# of out-of-state-applicants	1,039
% of applicants accepted from out of state	77
# of international applicants	405
% of international applicants accepted	6
# offered a place on the wait list	0
# admitted from wait list	0

First-Year Profile

Testing policy	Test Optional
Range SAT composite	1080–1200
Range SAT EBRW	540–670
Range SAT math	530–640
Range ACT composite	23–29
% submitting SAT scores	9
% submitting ACT scores	35
Average HS GPA	3.7
% submitting high school GPA	100
% graduated top 10% of class	18
% graduated top 25% of class	45
% graduated top 50% of class	77

Important Dates

Early action	
Apply by	12/1
Notified by	12/1
Regular	
Apply by	7/31
Notified by	Rolling, 12/1
Nonfall registration?	Yes

FINANCIAL FACTS

Annual tuition	$44,728
Food and housing	$15,080
Required fees	$252
Books and supplies	$1,000
Average need-based scholarship (First-year)	$36,911 ($38,390)
% students with need rec. need-based scholarship or grant aid (First-year)	100 (100)
% students with need rec. non-need-based scholarship or grant aid (First-year)	23 (34)
% students with need rec. need-based self-help aid (First-year)	79 (68)
% students rec. any financial aid (First-year)	99 (100)
% UG borrow to pay for school	48
Average cumulative indebtedness	$28,346
% of students with need fully met (First-year)	35 (46)
Average % of student need met (First-year)	87 (91)

WHEATON COLLEGE (IL)

501 College Avenue, Wheaton, IL 60187 • Admissions: 630-752-5011

Survey Snapshot
Lots of conservative students
Students are happy
Active minority support groups

RATINGS	
Quality of Life	89
Fire Safety	92
Green	60*
Academic	87
Profs Interesting	95
Profs Accessible	95
Admissions	86
Financial Aid	87

CAMPUS LIFE

Type of school	Private
Affiliation	Christian non-denominational
Environment	Town

Students

Degree-seeking undergrad enrollment	2,121
% male/female/not reported	46/54/0
% from out of state	73
% First-year from public high school	46
% First-year live on campus	97
% Ugrads live on campus	91
# of fraternities	0
# of sororities	0
% Asian	9
% Black or African American	3
% Hispanic	9
% Native American	<1
% Pacific Islander	<1
% Race and/or ethnicity unknown	2
% Two or more races	6
% White	67
% International	4
# of countries represented	25

CAMPUS MENTAL HEALTH SERVICES

Offers mental health/wellness program	Yes
Mental health training available to students	No
Employs Chief Wellness Officer	NR
Peer-to-peer mental health offerings	NR
Counseling center has guidelines or accreditation	No
Mental health/well-being courses	NR

ACADEMICS

% students returning for sophomore year	93
% students graduating within 4 years	76
% students graduating within 6 years	85
Calendar	Semester
Student/faculty ratio	10:1
Most common class size 10–19.	(36%)
Most common lab/discussion size 1–9.	(33%)

Applicants Sometimes Prefer
Calvin University, Taylor University

Applicants Rarely Prefer
Baylor University, Biola University, Covenant College, Gordon College, Grove City College, Hope College

STUDENTS SAY "…"

Academics

Wheaton College, located just outside of Chicago, Illinois, is a great option for students who want a school with a "phenomenal" sense of community and "exceptional liberal arts program." It's also an evangelical institution and undergrads here value "the college's commitment to providing a rigorous academic experience through a Christian worldview." As one undergrad explains, "I wanted to come to a school where my faith would be challenged and grown by those around me." Beyond religion, students love that class sizes are "relatively small," which "make it easier to develop relationships with professors and peers." The classroom experience consists of "uniformly fantastic" professors who care deeply and "genuinely want to know about their students' lives." Another incredulous undergrad shares, "They invest time and energy into their students and all are always available for office hours or meals." Wheaton professors also actively look to "involve students in research or mentoring." Just as crucial, they are "super knowledgeable and enthusiastic about the subject they teach." And they're "always open to questions/challenges and at the same time are willing to challenge and encourage students in a way that maximizes learning." It is truly evident that Wheaton professors "want their students to succeed."

Campus Life

It's rather easy to lead a fun and fulfilling life at Wheaton. For starters, students have "chapel services every other day during the week, with worship and guest speakers who are simply amazing." Many people also "like to attend events put on by Wheaton's music conservatory." Additionally, the majority of students are rather "active" and a large number "participat[e] in intramural sports." Even if sports aren't your strong suit, the athletic program "encourages non-athletic people to get involved." Wheaton students are also quite adept at finding "creative ways to have fun." For example, "geocaching" is pretty popular. Once the weekend rolls around, lots of undergrads participate in "game night," "movie night," or "college events such as lip-syncing competitions or an interactive art festival." It's also rather common for people to attend both "church and brunch." Of course, when students want a break from campus life, they can easily "take the train to Chicago to enjoy the sights and the lights." A student concludes, "There is never a dull moment here on campus, whether I'm studying or having fun with friends or attending special lectures, concerts, services, or just class. I love life at Wheaton!"

Student Body

Unsurprisingly, undergrads at Wheaton are "uniformly Christian" and "devoted to serving Christ and His Kingdom." The student body is also "predominantly white" though many individuals insist, "diversity is a big part of the campus conversation." And you will find a variety of "background[s], opinion[s], and interests around Wheaton." As one student interjects, "Wheaton gets a bad rap for being really conservative, but that doesn't mean there's not a diversity of political and theological thought." What's more, students say that their peers comprise of a "caring group of individuals who have fun while living an upright lifestyle." The vast majority are also "hardworking" and "very, very driven." And they're fairly worldly since a good number "have traveled to participate in some type of missions or humanitarian work." Wheaton undergrads are impressed by their fellow students' intellect as well, reporting that they "are exceptionally versatile, excelling in music, art, athletics, and oftentimes speaking multiple languages." Finally, another student praises, "I am consistently blown away by the high intellectual capacity the students of Wheaton College possess, as well as their resolve to live selflessly, and use their education to create a better world."

WHEATON COLLEGE (IL)

Financial Aid: 630-752-5021 • E-Mail: admissions@wheaton.edu • Website: www.wheaton.edu

THE PRINCETON REVIEW SAYS

Admissions

The school reports that its standardized testing policy for use in admission for Fall 2026 is Test Optional. The Princeton Review suggests that interested applicants consult with the school for the most up-to-date standardized testing policies. *Very important factors considered include:* rigor of secondary school record, academic GPA, application essay, recommendation(s), character/personal qualities, religious affiliation/commitment. *Important factors considered include:* interview, extracurricular activities, talent/ability, volunteer work. *Other factors considered include:* class rank, standardized test scores, first generation, alumni/ae relation, geographical residence, state residency, work experience, level of applicant's interest. High school diploma is required and GED is accepted. *Academic units required:* 4 English, 3 math, 3 science, 2 language (other than English), 3 social studies. *Academic units recommended:* 4 English, 4 math, 3 science, 3 language (other than English), 4 social studies.

Financial Aid

Students should submit: FAFSA. Priority filing deadline is 11/10. The Princeton Review suggests that all financial aid forms be submitted as soon as possible. *Need-based scholarships/grants offered:* Federal Pell; Federal SEOG; State scholarships/grants; Private scholarships; College/university scholarship or grant aid from institutional funds. *Loan aid offered:* Federal Direct Subsidized Loans; Federal Direct Unsubsidized Loans; Direct PLUS loans; College/university loans from institutional funds. Admitted students will be notified of awards on a rolling basis beginning 12/15. Federal Work-Study Program available. Institutional employment available.

The Inside Word

Wheaton College is looking for applicants who display a thirst for knowledge. Therefore, admissions officers tend to favor students who have taken at least a handful of honors, AP, or IB classes. Given the school's evangelical association, students must also demonstrate a commitment to their faith. To that end, all applicants are required to submit a Christian faith reference in the form of an interview or a Christian mentor recommendation letter. It's also important to note that candidates can apply to either the College of Arts and Sciences or the Conservatory of Music, but not both.

THE SCHOOL SAYS

From the Admissions Office

"Founded in 1860 and located just outside Chicago, Wheaton is a top-ranked Christian liberal arts college where rigorous academics and Christ-centered community come together. We offer 150+ majors, minors, and certificates—each designed to cultivate your God-given gifts through collaborative, hands-on learning. From Business and Psychology to Music and the Humanities, Wheaton prepares students for meaningful careers, service, and graduate study. Wheaton is the home of integrated faith and learning—a place of curiosity and conviction, wisdom and growth, beauty and belonging, grace and truth. You won't have to choose between academic challenge and deep faith centered on Jesus. With a 10:1 student-to-faculty ratio and emphasis on whole-person development, Wheaton offers an intellectually rich, spiritually grounded, and truly transformative education.

"We're also committed to affordability. Over 90% of Wheaton students receive scholarships or grants. Every applicant is considered holistically for academic scholarships ranging from $8,000–$24,000 (2025). Wheaton's vibrant campus life, global programs, and strong alumni network enhance your college experience. From residence hall traditions to small groups, chapel services, and student-led events, you'll find countless ways to connect and grow. Many students form lifelong friendships here—rooted in faith, deep conversations, and doing life together. The Wheaton community is one of encouragement, challenge, and purpose—walking with you long after graduation.

"Come find your place in a community that lasts a lifetime."

SELECTIVITY

# of total applicants	2,040
% of total applicants accepted	87
% of total acceptees attending	30

First-Year Profile

Testing policy	Test Optional
Range SAT composite	1260–1380
Range SAT EBRW	650–740
Range SAT math	610–730
Range ACT composite	28–32
% submitting SAT scores	35
% submitting ACT scores	20
Average HS GPA	3.8
% submitting high school GPA	54

Important Dates

Early action	
Apply by	11/15
Notified by	12/31
Regular	
Apply by	8/1
Notified by	4/1
Nonfall registration?	Yes

FINANCIAL FACTS

Annual tuition	$47,240
Food and housing	$13,660
Books and supplies	$840
Average need-based scholarship (First-year)	$17,805 ($18,193)
% students with need rec. need-based scholarship or grant aid (First-year)	100 (100)
% students with need rec. non-need-based scholarship or grant aid (First-year)	90 (96)
% students with need rec. need-based self-help aid (First-year)	62 (63)
% students rec. any financial aid (First-year)	88 (97)
% UG borrow to pay for school	61
Average cumulative indebtedness	$28,807
% of students with need fully met (First-year)	19 (20)
Average % of student need met (First-year)	74 (76)

Wheaton College (MA)

26 East Main Street, Norton, MA 02766 • Admissions: 508-286-8251

Survey Snapshot
Students are happy
Lab facilities are great
Students are friendly

RATINGS

Quality of Life	**78**
Fire Safety	**60***
Green	**60***
Academic	**88**
Profs Interesting	**92**
Profs Accessible	**93**
Admissions	**87**
Financial Aid	**89**

CAMPUS LIFE

Type of school	Private
Environment	Village

Students

Degree-seeking undergrad enrollment	1,767
% male/female/not reported	35/64/1
% from out of state	58
% First-year live on campus	94
% Ugrads live on campus	89
# of fraternities	0
# of sororities	0
% Asian	3
% Black or African American	6
% Hispanic	9
% Native American	0
% Pacific Islander	<1
% Race and/or ethnicity unknown	4
% Two or more races	5
% White	69
% International	4
# of countries represented	37

CAMPUS MENTAL HEALTH SERVICES

Offers mental health/wellness program	Yes
Mental health training available to students	No
Employs Chief Wellness Officer	NR
Peer-to-peer mental health offerings	NR
Counseling center has guidelines or accreditation	No
Mental health/well-being courses	NR

ACADEMICS

% students returning for sophomore year	82
% students graduating within 4 years	68
% students graduating within 6 years	73
Calendar	Semester
Student/faculty ratio	11:1
Most common class size 10–19.	(44%)

Most Popular Majors

Psychology; Business Administration and Management; Film/Cinema/Media Studies

STUDENTS SAY "…"

Academics

Set at a "gorgeous" campus in Norton, Massachusetts, that boasts a "community" feel, Wheaton College aims to provide an "interdisciplinary" liberal arts education that "fosters appreciation for critical thinking, diversity, and civic engagement." Undergrads here particularly love that their school champions "diversity and multiculturalism." And, in doing so, Wheaton has created a "very progressive and forward-thinking environment." Students also greatly appreciate that their classes are chock full of "active learning." Indeed, professors "encourage you to ask questions instead of quietly sitting in the back of the classroom." It also helps that instructors are "incredibly knowledgeable in their fields." More importantly, it's quite evident that professors "work really hard to put the student interests first." For example, "they love to discuss their areas of study with students and are accessible outside of class time." A junior explains, "I have made extremely close ties to many professors here at Wheaton. My art history professors have helped me get internships over the summer, given me research opportunities, and helped me with my transition to college. I honestly couldn't ask for a better support system." All in all, it is "obvious that everyone who works at Wheaton is passionate about the institution and care[s] about the student body."

Campus Life

There's no denying that Wheaton undergrads love to stay busy. As such, they are "very committed to extracurricular activities." To begin with, "student musical groups are big on campus as well as other performing arts groups." Many Wheaton undergraduates are "involved in community service" as well. People frequently gather at the Lyons Den, a student-run coffee shop that's "open late and hosts open mics on Wednesdays." Once the weekend rolls around, you'll discover that "there are numerous events scheduled. Anything from a movie in one of the auditoriums to food trucks to dance and music performances." Wheaton also sponsors "special treats from time to time." During a recent exam week, students were able to enjoy and de-stress with "a little animal petting farm." As if that wasn't enough, "cupcakes were brought in [too]!" Additionally, plenty of students can also be found attending parties on "Thursday, Friday, and Saturday" at different theme houses, though there "is a definite sober population on campus." Unfortunately, there "is not much to do in Norton." But if students are looking for off-campus excitement, they can easily head into Providence or Boston (20 minutes and 40 minutes away, respectively).

Student Body

Undergraduates at Wheaton seem to agree that their peers are "creative, energetic, and have a love for academics." They also continually prove themselves to be "kind," "respectful," and "interested in being...genuinely good [people]." Moreover, students here do an admirable job of making sure they're conscious about what's happening "outside the Wheaton bubble." To that end, many are "very liberally minded and outspoken with those views." Undergrads also applaud the fact that their college "is home to a wide array of culturally-diverse and open-minded individuals." Indeed, "everybody is very welcoming and very willing to learn about new cultures and experiences." That's probably due in large part to the fact that Wheaton has "students from all over the country as well as the world, a prominent LGBTQ community, [and] students from all walks of life." Further, since the college "is able to offer financial aid to many [individuals], Wheaton students are not all just upper-class suburban kids like at other private colleges around the country." All of this helps to foster a "sense of community [that] runs deep throughout the student body." As one thankful student summarizes, "Unity is a trait that shines here...[and] something that we are all extremely proud of."

WHEATON COLLEGE (MA)

Financial Aid: 508-286-8232 • E-Mail: admission@wheatoncollege.edu • Website: www.wheatoncollege.edu

THE PRINCETON REVIEW SAYS

Admissions

The school reports that its standardized testing policy for use in admission for Fall 2026 is Test Optional. The Princeton Review suggests that interested applicants consult with the school for the most up-to-date standardized testing policies. *Very important factors considered include:* rigor of secondary school record, academic GPA, application essay, recommendation(s), character/personal qualities. *Other factors considered include:* standardized test scores, interview, extracurricular activities, talent/ability, volunteer work, work experience, level of applicant's interest. High school diploma is required and GED is accepted. *Academic units required:* 4 English, 4 science, 2 science lab. *Academic units recommended:* 4 math, 4 science, 4 language (other than English), 4 social studies, 4 history.

Financial Aid

The Princeton Review suggests that all financial aid forms be submitted as soon as possible. *Need-based scholarships/grants offered:* Federal Pell; Federal SEOG; State scholarships/ grants; Private scholarships; College/university scholarship or grant aid from institutional funds. *Loan aid offered:* Federal Direct Subsidized Loans; Federal Direct Unsubsidized Loans; Direct PLUS loans. Admitted students will be notified of awards on or about 3/15. Federal Work-Study Program available. Institutional employment available.

The Inside Word

Wheaton College takes a holistic approach when evaluating applicants, meaning that everything from the difficulty of your high school curriculum to your writing ability and extracurricular involvement will be considered. And if you're standardized test-averse, take heart; Wheaton is Test Optional. Finally, if you're confident that Wheaton is your first choice, the college highly recommends that you apply early decision.

THE SCHOOL SAYS

From the Admissions Office

"Wheaton College is a nationally recognized liberal arts and sciences institution in Massachusetts that seamlessly combines academic rigor with experiential learning and 1:1 career mentorship.

"Through the flexible Compass Curriculum, students are encouraged to explore diverse interests across the arts, humanities, natural sciences, and social sciences. This empowers students to pursue interdisciplinary pathways, double majors, or self-designed programs tailored to their unique goals. Small classes, averaging 15 to 20 students, are taught exclusively by faculty with PhDs or terminal degrees and expertise in their fields. They provide numerous opportunities for in-depth discussions, individualized feedback and meaningful collaboration on research, scholarship and creative works. Experiential learning remains a hallmark of the Wheaton experience. Students enrich their learning through funded internships, faculty-led research, community-based projects and global study.

"Starting first semester through graduation, students partner with a Career Navigator in the Life and Career Design Institute. Through intentional planning and ongoing reflection, students align their academic choices, internships and co-curricular experiences with their personal and professional goals. Along the way, they cultivate the professional soft skills and workplace competencies needed not only to compete—but to excel—in an ever-changing global workforce.

"Renowned for excellence, Wheaton's prestige is reflected in its outcomes. Since 2000, Wheaton students have earned nearly 300 prestigious honors, including Rhodes, Marshall, and Truman Scholarships. The college also regularly ranks among the nation's top producers of Fulbright scholars. Within six months of graduation, 92% of students successfully launch their careers or pursue advanced studies. Learn more at wheatoncollege.edu."

SELECTIVITY

# of total applicants	6,014
% of total applicants accepted	63
% of total acceptees attending	12
# of in-state applicants	1,693
% of in-state applicants accepted	82
# of out-of-state-applicants	2,515
% of applicants accepted from out of state	82
# of international applicants	1,806
% of international applicants accepted	17
# of early decision applicants	209
% of early decision applicants accepted	37
# offered a place on the wait list	153
# admitted from wait list	1

First-Year Profile

Testing policy	Test Optional
Range SAT composite	1220–1370
Range SAT EBRW	630–720
Range SAT math	580–670
Range ACT composite	27–32
% submitting SAT scores	16
% submitting ACT scores	<1
Average HS GPA	3.6
% submitting high school GPA	100

Important Dates

Early decision	
Apply by	11/15
Notified by	12/15
Other ED Apply by	1/15
Other ED Notified by	2/1
Early action	
Apply by	11/15
Notified by	1/15
Regular	
Apply by	1/15
Notified by	3/31
Nonfall registration?	Yes

FINANCIAL FACTS

Annual tuition	$67,000
Food and housing	$17,800
Required fees	$800
Books and supplies	$940
Average need-based scholarship (First-year)	NR ($51,179)
% students with need rec. need-based scholarship or grant aid (First-year)	NR (73)
% students with need rec. non-need-based scholarship or grant aid (First-year)	NR (26)
% students with need rec. need-based self-help aid (First-year)	NR (72)
% students rec. any financial aid (First-year)	NR (97)
% UG borrow to pay for school	71
Average cumulative indebtedness	$35,386
% of students with need fully met (First-year)	NR (33)
Average % of student need met (First-year)	NR (91)

WHITMAN COLLEGE

345 Boyer Avenue, Walla Walla, WA 99362 • Admissions: 509-527-5176

Survey Snapshot
Easy to get around campus
Students take advantage of the outdoors
Great library

RATINGS

Quality of Life	88
Fire Safety	95
Green	96
Academic	90
Profs Interesting	91
Profs Accessible	95
Admissions	92
Financial Aid	91

CAMPUS LIFE

Type of school	Private
Environment	Town

Students

Degree-seeking undergrad enrollment	1,444
% male/female/not reported	40/60/<1
% from out of state	63
% First-year from public high school	68
% First-year live on campus	99
% Ugrads live on campus	75
# of fraternities (% join)	4 (16)
# of sororities (% join)	4 (20)
% Asian	5
% Black or African American	3
% Hispanic	14
% Native American	1
% Pacific Islander	<1
% Race and/or ethnicity unknown	1
% Two or more races	7
% White	55
% International	15
# of countries represented	68

CAMPUS MENTAL HEALTH SERVICES

Offers mental health/wellness program	Yes
Mental health training available to students	Yes
Employs Chief Wellness Officer	Yes
Peer-to-peer mental health offerings	No
Counseling center has guidelines or accreditation	Yes
Mental health/well-being courses	Yes, for-credit

ACADEMICS

% students returning for sophomore year	89
% students graduating within 4 years	56
% students graduating within 6 years	75
Calendar	Semester
Student/faculty ratio	10:1
Most common class size 10–19.	(45%)
Most common lab/discussion size 10–19.	(49%)

Most Popular Majors

Biology/Biological Sciences; Research and Experimental Psychology; Economics

Applicants Also Look At

California Polytechnic State University—San Luis Obispo, Colorado College, Gonzaga University, Lewis & Clark College, Oregon State University, Reed College, Scripps College, St. Olaf College, University of California—Berkeley, University of California—Davis, University of Oregon, University of Puget Sound, University of Washington, Western Washington University, Willamette University

STUDENTS SAY "..."

Academics

Whitman College offers a "genuine connection" between students and faculty, along with an education that is very strong across the board." In part, that's because it is said to be very "easy to take classes in lots of different areas," with an emphasis on there being "good research opportunities (especially in sciences like chemistry, biology, [and] physics)." It's also reported that coursework is "more focused on theory than practical application," which is generally considered a positive. Perhaps that's because the school offers "so much support academically, socially, [and] financially." A big part of that support stems from how "professors are always there for you and show that they care and want to help you succeed." Teachers are described as "incredibly accessible and happy to work with students on an individual level. I've had professors who let me add texts to their syllabuses, let me interpret assignment descriptions generously, and I even know students who have designed entire courses as part of an independent study." The takeaway is "positively challenging," with one student observing that thanks to the school's urging, "I've accomplished things I never knew I could have."

Campus Life

Whitman students prioritize their academics, but when they're ready to close their books, there's plenty to enjoy: "People really like on-campus events. Winter balls, film screenings, contra dances, crafts fairs; there's a lot to do." Students also eagerly participate in the college's 100+ clubs. For example, "the radio station is fairly popular, a lot of people do rec sports (ultimate frisbee [and] frolf [frisbee golf] especially)." More importantly, "clubs are not super competitive to get into, which leaves willing students a lot more opportunities to get involved outside the classroom," regardless of the topic, such as one student who volunteers that, "My friend and I founded the Whitman Students Dracula Club." For those seeking to give back to the community, strong volunteering opportunities are mentioned at local elementary schools, food distribution networks, and the nearby OddFellows elderly care facility. It's also easy for students to enjoy the surrounding area. Another undergrad explains, "In my free time, I love to bike, walk around Pioneer Park and Mill Creek and the surrounding neighborhoods. The downtown is really cute and I will go walk around the shops." In general, "outdoor activities are super popular," but the consensus is that "if you like it, there is a place for you at Whitman for it."

Student Body

Whitman undergrads appreciate that they're part of a "tight-knit" student body, one that tends to be more "collaborative than competitive." Many attribute this to the "small campus size," which certainly encourages students "to be very close" and only very occasionally "cliquey, for lack of a better term." Students bond over being "intellectual and able to have deep conversations" and appreciate that their peers are "interested in learning both in and out of the classroom," or as one puts it: "not just in college for the degree." Demographically, students suggest that it's "not super diverse racially or politically," but while it leans toward a mix of "liberal," "very white," and "wealthy," students acknowledge there's been a larger range "over the years in terms of racial diversity" and has a "large international student body." Students quickly strike up commonalities over a love of the outdoors or their creative efforts: "My peers are very friendly and warm. We usually see each other on campus and say hello and chat for a couple of minutes." When it comes down to it, "there is a specific kind of kid that chooses Whitman. One that uses what they know for good."

WHITMAN COLLEGE

Financial Aid: 509-527-5178 • E-Mail: admission@whitman.edu • Website: www.whitman.edu

THE PRINCETON REVIEW SAYS

Admissions

The school reports that its standardized testing policy for use in admission for Fall 2026 is Test Optional. The Princeton Review suggests that interested applicants consult with the school for the most up-to-date standardized testing policies. *Very important factors considered include:* rigor of secondary school record, academic GPA. *Important factors considered include:* application essay, recommendation(s), extracurricular activities, talent/ability, character/personal qualities. *Other factors considered include:* class rank, standardized test scores, interview, first generation, alumni/ae relation, geographical residence, state residency, religious affiliation/commitment, volunteer work, work experience, level of applicant's interest. High school diploma is required and GED is accepted. *Academic units recommended:* 4 English, 4 math, 3 science, 2 language (other than English), 2 social studies, 1 visual/performing arts.

Financial Aid

Students should submit: FAFSA; CSS PROFILE. Priority filing deadline is 11/15. The Princeton Review suggests that all financial aid forms be submitted as soon as possible. *Need-based scholarships/grants offered:* Federal Pell; Federal SEOG; State scholarships/grants; Private scholarships; College/university scholarship or grant aid from institutional funds. *Loan aid offered:* Federal Direct Subsidized Loans; Federal Direct Unsubsidized Loans; Direct PLUS loans. Federal Work-Study Program available. Institutional employment available.

The Inside Word

Whitman's admissions committee emphasizes essays and extracurriculars more than standardized test scores, which are optional here. The college cares much more about who you are and what you have to offer than it does about what your numbers will do for the firstyear academic profile. Educators all over the country know Whitman is an excellent institution, and the college's alums support it at one of the highest rates of giving at any college in the nation. Students seeking a top-quality liberal arts college owe it to themselves to take a look.

THE SCHOOL SAYS

From the Admissions Office

"Whitman College offers a rigorous but collaborative academic environment, a down-to-earth Northwest culture, and a vibrant campus life. Whitman is also distinguished by the following:

- Capstone written and oral assessments in one's major field of study
- Numerous winners of Fulbright, Watson, Goldwater, National Science Foundation, Projects for Peace, Rhodes, Truman, Beinecke, and Udall fellowships and scholarships
- A Career and Community Engagement Center which oversees internship and community service opportunities as well as graduate school and employment planning
- Science departments that have been recognized by the National Science Foundation as among the top fifty colleges per capita producing graduates who earn PhD's in science and engineering
- Eighty-eight off-campus study opportunities
- State of the art facilities including a library, computer labs and a health center
- The Harper Joy Theatre, which hosts 8 productions a year open to all students
- An annual undergraduate research conference with over 200 students presenting their original research to the Whitman community
- Strong intramural, club and NCAA Division III sports programs
- A nationally renowned Outdoor Program
- Semester in the West, an experiential, on-the-road study of economic, cultural and environmental issues
- A 94 percent retention rate, 87 percent graduation rate, and a 70 percent graduate school rate."

SELECTIVITY

# of total applicants	6,950
% of total applicants accepted	40
% of total acceptees attending	13
# of early decision applicants	542
% of early decision applicants accepted	21
# offered a place on the wait list	863
# admitted from wait list	33

First-Year Profile

Testing policy	Test Optional
Range SAT composite	1190–1420
Range SAT EBRW	650–740
Range SAT math	660–770
Range ACT composite	29–33
% submitting SAT scores	25
% submitting ACT scores	9
Average HS GPA	3.9
% submitting high school GPA	96
% graduated top 10% of class	52
% graduated top 25% of class	83
% graduated top 50% of class	95
% submitting high school rank	32

Important Dates

Early decision	
Apply by	11/15
Notified by	12/20
Other ED Apply by	1/10
Other ED Notified by	2/1
Regular	
Apply by	1/15
Notified by	3/1
Nonfall registration?	No

FINANCIAL FACTS

Annual tuition	$68,692
Food and housing	$15,952
Required fees	$576
Books and supplies	$1,332
Average need-based scholarship (First-year)	$59,565 ($60,770)
% students with need rec. need-based scholarship or grant aid (First-year)	85 (100)
% students with need rec. non-need-based scholarship or grant aid (First-year)	33 (44)
% students with need rec. need-based self-help aid (First-year)	85 (68)
% students rec. any financial aid (First-year)	92 (97)
% UG borrow to pay for school	37
Average cumulative indebtedness	$29,538
% of students with need fully met (First-year)	34 (46)
Average % of student need met (First-year)	97 (97)

WHITTIER COLLEGE

13406 Philadelphia Street, Whittier, CA 90608-0634 • Admissions: 562-907-4238

Survey Snapshot
Great library
Class discussions encouraged
Students are happy

RATINGS

Quality of Life	83
Fire Safety	87
Green	60*
Academic	84
Profs Interesting	93
Profs Accessible	95
Admissions	77
Financial Aid	89

CAMPUS LIFE

Type of school	Private
Environment	City

Students

Degree-seeking undergrad enrollment	801
% male/female/not reported	45/55/0
% from out of state	16
% First-year live on campus	67
% Ugrads live on campus	54
# of fraternities (% join)	4 (NR)
# of sororities (% join)	5 (NR)
% Asian	5
% Black or African American	5
% Hispanic	53
% Native American	1
% Pacific Islander	1
% Race and/or ethnicity unknown	1
% Two or more races	6
% White	19
% International	11
# of countries represented	33

CAMPUS MENTAL HEALTH SERVICES

Offers mental health/wellness program	Yes
Mental health training available to students	Yes
Employs Chief Wellness Officer	Yes
Peer-to-peer mental health offerings	Yes
Counseling center has guidelines or accreditation	Yes
Mental health/well-being courses	Yes, non-credit

ACADEMICS

% students returning for sophomore year	68
% students graduating within 4 years	43
% students graduating within 6 years	55
Calendar	Semester
Student/faculty ratio	9:1
Most common class size 20–29.	(37%)
Most common lab/discussion size 1–9.	(44%)

Most Popular Majors
Liberal Arts and Sciences/Liberal Studies; Exercise Science and Kinesiology; Business Administration and Management

Applicants Sometimes Prefer
Loyola Marymount University, Occidental College, Pitzer College, University of Redlands

Applicants Rarely Prefer
Chapman University, Claremont McKenna College

STUDENTS SAY "..."

Academics

This tiny pearl of a liberal arts school is home to around 1,600 undergrads and focuses on an interdisciplinary education for all. Considering the small population, Whittier offers a relatively good breadth in classes and "is a great school for those who are trying to figure out what they want to do or those who want to create their own major." One-on-one interaction is quite prevalent among teachers and students, and everyone here is "passionate about the subject that they teach." It should be unsurprising that a school whose mascot is Johnny Poet provides "a nuanced literary foundation" for all students.

The faculty brings real-world and work experience to their various courses: "they're not just lifelong academics; most of them have had successful professional careers outside of teaching" and they "really make [Whittier] worthwhile." These professors are "engaged, love what they do," and "truly care about the success of their students, both academically and personally." Discussions are highly encouraged and interesting debates fostered, and assigned papers "always force you to stretch your knowledge." Teachers sometimes challenge the class's knowledge by "presenting a topic that can have pros and cons and by asking to prove where the idea came from." Classes are small, so professors "know your strengths and weaknesses and try their best to help you out."

Campus Life

The campus is small, so "it's easy to make friends" and there are typically "lots of events (academic or recreational) to go to." Different clubs run the gamut from Anime Club to Fun Night Club to a larping group, but marauders beware: "RAs are required to put on events such as Assassins." "There was once a Beowulf reading at night where you got a free dinner in addition," says a student. Whittier's version of Greek life comes in the form of the school's 11 "societies," and a majority of students have some form of involvement in a society or a sport. The school's size naturally leaves enough time to for extracurriculars and outside interests, as "it is difficult not to get involved when everyone is."

Whitter is relatively close to LA and the beach, so the weather is "mostly very nice" and students often "lounge around outside under trees and on the grass to do homework and socialize," "play Frisbee, walk on slack lines, and play soccer for fun in the courtyards." The pool facility is brand new and many "hang out on the decks to tan and cool off in the heat," and there are hills behind the campus that are good for hiking or running. There "is always something going on on-campus and that makes students even more involved."

Student Body

This is a "diverse community" that includes a sizable number of non-Californians, and most people are "very friendly, respectful of others' different identities, and comfortable with people of different backgrounds." There is "a good meshing" of all the students regardless of what their involvements are, and a real "community-based feeling" abounds. Whittier sees a higher transfer rate than many similar schools, so "it is very easy to know at least ten or more students who transfer after a year or two." The majority of people here are involved in some form of sport, but are not looking to go beyond the collegiate or intramural level.

Whittier College

Financial Aid: 562-907-4285 • E-Mail: admissions@whittier.edu • Website: www.whittier.edu

THE PRINCETON REVIEW SAYS

Admissions

The school reports that its standardized testing policy for use in admission for Fall 2026 is Test Free. The Princeton Review suggests that interested applicants consult with the school for the most up-to-date standardized testing policies. *Other factors considered include:* academic GPA, application essay, recommendation(s), extracurricular activities, volunteer work, work experience. High school diploma is required and GED is accepted. *Academic units recommended:* 4 English, 3 math, 2 science, 1 science lab, 3 language (other than English), 2 social studies, 1 visual/performing arts.

Financial Aid

Students should submit: FAFSA. Priority filing deadline is 3/1. The Princeton Review suggests that all financial aid forms be submitted as soon as possible. *Need-based scholarships/grants offered:* Federal Pell; Federal SEOG; State scholarships/grants; Private scholarships; College/university scholarship or grant aid from institutional funds. *Loan aid offered:* Federal Direct Subsidized Loans; Federal Direct Unsubsidized Loans; Direct PLUS loans; College/university loans from institutional funds. Admitted students will be notified of awards on a rolling basis beginning 2/15. Federal Work-Study Program available.

The Inside Word

Whittier is looking for well-rounded students, and so activities and recommendations are just as important as scores and grades—the admissions office focuses on more than numbers. Though approximately 65 percent of students hail from California, no preference is given to state of origin. Through the Whittier Scholars program, students may construct a personalized major that fits academic and career goals.

THE SCHOOL SAYS

From the Admissions Office

"Faculty and students at Whittier share a love of learning and delight in the life of the mind. They join in understanding the value of the intellectual quest, the use of reason, and a respect for values. They seek knowledge of their own culture and the informed appreciation of other traditions, and they explore the interrelatedness of knowledge and the connections among disciplines. An extraordinary community emerges from teachers and students representing a variety of academic pursuits, individuals who have come together at Whittier in the belief that study within the liberal arts forms the best foundation for rewarding endeavor throughout a lifetime.

"Whittier College is a vibrant, residential, four-year liberal arts institution where intellectual inquiry and experiential learning are fostered in a community that promotes respect for diversity of thought and culture. A Whittier College education produces enthusiastic, independent thinkers who flourish in graduate studies, the evolving global workplace, and life."

SELECTIVITY

# of total applicants	5,928
% of total applicants accepted	83
% of total acceptees attending	11

First-Year Profile

Testing policy	Test Free
Average HS GPA	3.4
% submitting high school GPA	100

Important Dates

Early action	
Apply by	11/15
Regular	
Apply by	7/28
Notified by	Rolling, 12/1
Nonfall registration?	Yes

FINANCIAL FACTS

Annual tuition	$53,464
Food and housing	$18,530
Required fees (First-year)	$790 ($990)
Books and supplies	$1,000
Average need-based scholarship (First-year)	$53,866 ($56,060)
% students with need rec. need-based scholarship or grant aid (First-year)	100 (100)
% students with need rec. non-need-based scholarship or grant aid (First-year)	43 (37)
% students with need rec. need-based self-help aid (First-year)	41 (69)
% students rec. any financial aid (First-year)	96 (100)
% UG borrow to pay for school	100
Average cumulative indebtedness	$29,547
% of students with need fully met (First-year)	10 (12)
Average % of student need met (First-year)	86 (88)

WILLIAM & MARY

116 Jamestown Road, Williamsburg, VA 23187-8795 • Admissions: 757-221-4223

Survey Snapshot
Great library
Students are happy
Students are friendly

RATINGS

Quality of Life	90
Fire Safety	93
Green	96
Academic	86
Profs Interesting	93
Profs Accessible	93
Admissions	94
Financial Aid	87

CAMPUS LIFE

Type of school	Public
Environment	Town

Students

Degree-seeking undergrad enrollment	6,941
% male/female/not reported	40/59/<1
% from out of state	35
% First-year from public high school	72
% First-year live on campus	99
% Ugrads live on campus	65
# of fraternities (% join)	18 (NR)
# of sororities (% join)	16 (NR)
% Asian	11
% Black or African American	5
% Hispanic	9
% Native American	<1
% Pacific Islander	<1
% Race and/or ethnicity unknown	1
% Two or more races	8
% White	63
% International	3
# of countries represented	54

CAMPUS MENTAL HEALTH SERVICES

Offers mental health/wellness program	Yes
Mental health training available to students	Yes
Employs Chief Wellness Officer	Yes
Peer-to-peer mental health offerings	Yes
Counseling center has guidelines or accreditation	Yes
Mental health/well-being courses	Yes, for-credit

ACADEMICS

% students returning for sophomore year	95
% students graduating within 4 years	82
% students graduating within 6 years	88
Calendar	Semester
Student/faculty ratio	11:1
Most common class size 10–19.	(33%)
Most common lab/discussion size 10–19.	(52%)

Most Popular Majors
Biology; Economics; Psychology

Applicants Also Look At
Boston College, Brown University, Cornell University, Duke University, Georgetown University, University of Michigan—Ann Arbor, University of North Carolina at Chapel Hill, University of Richmond, University of Virginia, Virginia Tech, Wake Forest University

STUDENTS SAY "..."

Academics

William & Mary is an institution teeming with resources and opportunity. Undergrads here benefit from a curriculum that allows students to "step outside of my major and explore different fields, which broadens my perspective." Students note that this "truly well-rounded education" applies to courses from philosophy to art to business: there's a "wide variety of classes that encourage them to think critically about the world." And while the "academic rigor of the school is challenging…it cannot be overemphasized how well it prepares students for continuing education at medical school, graduate school, etc." Of course, it also helps that the majority of professors "are deeply passionate about their fields and actively seek to work with undergraduates and support them throughout their college career." They "push you to do your best, while also being very understanding about any outside factors that might be happening in your life." A number also take a creative approach to teaching. For example, one student shares, "In my Egyptology class, we went to the VMFA to do a competition: whichever team could translate the hieroglyphs on various artifacts first would win a prize." Outside the classroom, "opportunities for meaningful undergraduate research abound, and faculty are eager to get students involved throughout every step of the research journey." As another undergrad chimes in, "They truly are mentors academically, professionally, and in life." Ultimately, students appreciate W&M's "emphasis on being engaged and curious…and the [incredible] resources and faculty available."

Campus Life

Students might be a bit hyperbolic in exclaiming, "There are a billion and one things to do on campus," but there certainly seems to be a lot to enjoy at William & Mary. They can participate in everything from "the radio club (WCWM) and the outdoor recreation program (Tribe Adventure Program)" to "dance, multicultural orgs, advocacy groups, veggie society, [and even a] fermentation club." Additionally, "a cappella is another unusually popular activity for W&M students, with many teams performing regularly." There's also "a student org (AMP) that puts on a lot of fun events [including] English country dancing for Jane Austen's birthday, carnivals, [and] scare houses." When it comes to partying, some students insist the "scene isn't big, but you can find them if you look hard enough." Others report that there are "a considerable amount of people who participate in Greek Life and go to larger parties/event[s] pretty frequently." Off campus, "people spend lots of time in Colonial Williamsburg, [at] farmer's markets, art festivals, coffee shops, etc." All in all, W&M "has a wide variety of intellectual, creative, and personal opportunities for each and every student" to pursue.

Student Body

William & Mary "has a rep for being community-oriented," and undergrads say it's clear "that many people choose W&M because that is something they prioritize in a college." Indeed, "it's a place where you can feel welcome, find meaningful friendships, and share laughter with people who genuinely care." Students say their classmates are "curious and love learning but also have a healthy perspective…understanding that there is more to life than the classroom." Moreover, "everyone here is interested in very niche topics, but are also interested in getting to know what their peers are interested in," a trait that students feel "makes us a little nerdy but lovable." Students also value the fact that people are "internally competitive but not with one another—most people are hard on themselves but encouraging and collaborative with their peers." Finally, "there is such a diverse student body and so many different student organizations at this school that [it] is difficult for someone to feel left out at this college." As one undergrad proclaims, "Everywhere you go, you can find a friendly face, and developing interpersonal relationships is easy when everyone is a friend of a friend."

William & Mary

Financial Aid: 757-221-2420 • E-Mail: admission@wm.edu • Website: www.wm.edu

THE PRINCETON REVIEW SAYS

Admissions

The school reports that its standardized testing policy for use in admission for Fall 2026 is Test Optional. The Princeton Review suggests that interested applicants consult with the school for the most up-to-date standardized testing policies. *Very important factors considered include:* rigor of secondary school record, academic GPA, application essay, recommendation(s), extracurricular activities, talent/ability, character/personal qualities, state residency, volunteer work, work experience. *Other factors considered include:* standardized test scores, interview, first generation, geographical residence, level of applicant's interest. High school diploma is required and GED is accepted. *Academic units recommended:* 4 English, 4 math, 4 science, 3 science labs, 4 language (other than English), 4 social studies.

Financial Aid

Students should submit: FAFSA; CSS PROFILE. Priority filing deadline is 2/1. The Princeton Review suggests that all financial aid forms be submitted as soon as possible. *Need-based scholarships/grants offered:* Federal Pell; Federal SEOG; State scholarships/grants; Private scholarships; College/university scholarship or grant aid from institutional funds. *Loan aid offered:* Federal Direct Subsidized Loans; Federal Direct Unsubsidized Loans; Direct PLUS loans. Federal Work-Study Program available. Institutional employment available.

The Inside Word

The volume of applications at William & Mary is very high; thus, admission is competitive. The large applicant pool necessitates a labor-intensive evaluation process; each application is read twice, and each admissions officer reads roughly 150 application folders per week during the peak review season. But this is one admissions committee that moves fast without sacrificing a thorough holistic review.

THE SCHOOL SAYS

From the Admissions Office

"At William & Mary, you get the best of both worlds: the global reach of a public research university and the personal, close-knit feel of a liberal arts and sciences college—backed by more than 330 years of experience.

"W&M offers more than 115 majors, minors and pre-professional programs, with 45% of students majoring in STEM. With 475+ campus clubs and a Division I athletics program, students find countless ways to explore their passions and have fun.

"Forbes included W&M on its 2026 list of "The New Ivies" that are "attracting the best and the brightest and graduating students that are outpacing most Ivy Leaguers in the eyes of employers." Ninety-two percent of the Class of 2024 reported being employed or in graduate/professional school within six months of graduation, and 100% said they were working in jobs that align with their career interests. Underlying this is our commitment to guaranteed internship funding—ensuring every student has access to meaningful experiences.

"Our graduates include U.S. presidents, executives and innovators at Hulu, Netflix and Apple, Super Bowl head coaches, Oscar-winning actors, leaders of the FBI and CIA, NASA's chief scientist and groundbreaking producers in gaming.

"In short, W&M provides a top-rated educational experience while being consistently recognized as one of the best values in the nation. If you're an intellectually curious, community-minded student—come see what sets W&M apart."

SELECTIVITY

# of total applicants	16,895
% of total applicants accepted	37
% of total acceptees attending	26
# of early decision applicants	1,477
% of early decision applicants accepted	49
# offered a place on the wait list	4,085
# admitted from wait list	103

First-Year Profile

Testing policy	Test Optional
Range SAT composite	1390–1520
Range SAT EBRW	710–760
Range SAT math	680–760
Range ACT composite	32–34
% submitting SAT scores	48
% submitting ACT scores	14
Average HS GPA	4.3
% submitting high school GPA	88
% graduated top 10% of class	79
% graduated top 25% of class	95
% graduated top 50% of class	99
% submitting high school rank	30

Important Dates

Early decision	
Apply by	11/1
Notified by	Mid December
Other ED Apply by	1/5
Other ED Notified by	2/1
Regular	
Apply by	1/5
Nonfall registration?	No

FINANCIAL FACTS

Annual in-state tuition	$19,734
Annual out-of-state tuition	$46,177
Food and housing	$17,646
Required fees	$7,501
Books and supplies	$900
Average need-based scholarship (First-year)	$24,371 ($22,933)
% students with need rec. need-based scholarship or grant aid (First-year)	92 (90)
% students with need rec. non-need-based scholarship or grant aid (First-year)	44 (51)
% students with need rec. need-based self-help aid (First-year)	46 (37)
% students rec. any financial aid (First-year)	56 (55)
% UG borrow to pay for school	33
Average cumulative indebtedness	$28,934
% of students with need fully met (First-year)	27 (31)
Average % of student need met (First-year)	82 (82)

WILLIAM JEWELL COLLEGE

500 College Hill, Liberty, MO 64068 • Admissions: 816-415-7511

Survey Snapshot
Students are happy
Internships are widely available
Students get along with local community

RATINGS

Quality of Life	88
Fire Safety	88
Green	60*
Academic	91
Profs Interesting	94
Profs Accessible	97
Admissions	91
Financial Aid	86

CAMPUS LIFE

Type of school	Private
Environment	Town

Students

Degree-seeking undergrad enrollment	969
% male/female/not reported	49/51/0
% from out of state	42
% First-year from public high school	82
% First-year live on campus	83
% Ugrads live on campus	84
# of fraternities (% join)	3 (25)
# of sororities (% join)	3 (37)
% Asian	1
% Black or African American	7
% Hispanic	12
% Native American	1
% Pacific Islander	<1
% Race and/or ethnicity unknown	12
% Two or more races	6
% White	54
% International	5
# of countries represented	33

CAMPUS MENTAL HEALTH SERVICES

Offers mental health/wellness program	Yes
Mental health training available to students	Yes
Employs Chief Wellness Officer	Yes
Peer-to-peer mental health offerings	No
Counseling center has guidelines or accreditation	No
Mental health/well-being courses	Yes, non-credit

ACADEMICS

% students returning for sophomore year	74
% students graduating within 4 years	59
% students graduating within 6 years	61
Calendar	Semester
Student/faculty ratio	10:1
Most common class size 1–9.	(41%)
Most common lab/discussion size 10–19.	(62%)

Most Popular Majors
Registered Nursing/Registered Nurse; Business Administration and Management; Psychology

Applicants Often Prefer
Rockhurst University

Applicants Sometimes Prefer
Missouri State University, University of Kansas, University of Missouri, University of Missouri—Kansas City

Applicants Rarely Prefer
Truman State University

STUDENTS SAY "..."

Academics

William Jewel College's "rigorous set of programs that push you to the limits of your ability" and "top-notch academics" are considered by some enrollees to be "unmatched in the Midwest." Academics revolves around a core curriculum that transforms undergraduates into "critical thinkers" who can "step outside their own perspectives." The school requires every student to take courses in four areas: culture and traditions; science, technology, and the human experience; power and justice; and the sacred and secular. When it comes to specific majors, students are quick to applaud "the strong science and pre-med program," and also note that the nursing program has a "great reputation." Luckily, no matter your course of study, professors tend to be "great lecturers" and "amazingly dedicated." As one impressed student concludes, "The professors at William Jewell are very personable and willing to go the extra step to build a connection with each and every student. They are always finding the best way to reach out to their students and provide each student with the best chance of success."

Campus Life

Just as William Jewell's classes are filled with vigorous discussion, so too is the campus usually buzzing with activity, from "sporting events [to] resident hall gatherings [to] the occasional fraternity/sorority party." Additionally, undergrads can join numerous clubs, including the esports team, intramurals, and concert choir. Students also enjoy participating in Greek life and school traditions like homecoming, sledding down Browning Bowl, and the annual Billy J Day, when classes are canceled, and there are lawn games, live music, and free food. When students want a break from campus life, they can easily take the "twenty-minute drive" into downtown Kansas City, which features (just to name a few highlights) "the Power & Light District with the T-Mobile Center, the Kauffman Center, and just a few miles south you get into Westport where you can find numerous college/young adult students at any given time." All of these options mean—in the best possible way—that "life at Jewell is a busy one."

Student Body

Regardless of their path to William Jewell, undergraduates describe their "intelligent" and "laid back but focused" peers as "pretty open and accepting of just about anyone." This "amazing community," filled with "some of the most genuine people you will ever meet," enables students to "fit in very easily." The school's "white, Protestant, [and] upper-middle class" contingent has become more diverse over time—30% of the student body now identifies as a minority. In short, "No one really is ever left out of anything as long as they're putting the effort in to have friends and be a part of an organization as well as the Jewell community as a whole." The rich commonality shared by students is that they're "committed to their education and community."

William Jewell College

Financial Aid: 816-415-5973 • E-Mail: admission@william.jewell.edu • Website: www.jewell.edu

THE PRINCETON REVIEW SAYS

Admissions

The school reports that its standardized testing policy for use in admission for Fall 2026 is Test Optional. The Princeton Review suggests that interested applicants consult with the school for the most up-to-date standardized testing policies. *Very important factors considered include:* rigor of secondary school record, academic GPA. *Important factors considered include:* class rank, recommendation(s), extracurricular activities, talent/ability, character/personal qualities, level of applicant's interest. *Other factors considered include:* standardized test scores, application essay, interview, first generation, alumni/ae relation, volunteer work, work experience. High school diploma is required and GED is accepted. *Academic units required:* 4 English, 3 math, 3 science, 1 science lab, 2 language (other than English), 3 social studies. *Academic units recommended:* 4 math, 3 language (other than English), 2 academic electives.

Financial Aid

Students should submit: FAFSA. Priority filing deadline is 2/1. The Princeton Review suggests that all financial aid forms be submitted as soon as possible. *Need-based scholarships/grants offered:* Federal Pell; Federal SEOG; State scholarships/grants; Private scholarships; College/university scholarship or grant aid from institutional funds; Federal Nursing Scholarships. *Loan aid offered:* Federal Direct Subsidized Loans; Federal Direct Unsubsidized Loans; Direct PLUS loans. Admitted students will be notified of awards on a rolling basis beginning 11/1. Federal Work-Study Program available. Institutional employment available.

The Inside Word

Competition for admission is strong and candidates must demonstrate success with a rigorous course load. Of course, similar to most small colleges, Jewell is also looking for applicants who will complement the campus. Therefore, you can be assured that personal statements and recommendations will be closely assessed.

THE SCHOOL SAYS

From the Admissions Office

"William Jewell College is a four-year, private liberal arts college in Liberty, Missouri. Jewell's commitment to cultivating critical thinkers in pursuit of meaningful lives is woven into the living and learning community and is the basis of the Critical Thought and Inquiry Core Curriculum. Our 30-plus majors include nursing, civil engineering, data science, business, music, psychological science, cybersecurity and exercise science, with 98.8% of students employed or in graduate school within six months of graduation. Jewell's one to ten faculty-student ratio allows a personalized experience through numerous distinctive programs. Jewell's national award-winning Concert Choir has produced two CDs, and members go on a triennial concert tour in England and Scotland. A national champion debate team, the Harriman-Jewell premier performing arts series and the Mathes Innovation Center also demonstrate the depth of opportunities available to students."

SELECTIVITY

# of total applicants	1,929
% of total applicants accepted	38
% of total acceptees attending	33
# of in-state applicants	989
% of in-state applicants accepted	42
# of out-of-state-applicants	612
% of applicants accepted from out of state	42
# of international applicants	328
% of international applicants accepted	20

First-Year Profile

Testing policy	Test Optional
Range SAT composite	1030–1170
Range SAT EBRW	540–630
Range SAT math	540–640
Range ACT composite	18–24
% submitting SAT scores	5
% submitting ACT scores	53
Average HS GPA	3.6
% submitting high school GPA	100
% graduated top 10% of class	27
% graduated top 25% of class	54
% graduated top 50% of class	83
% submitting high school rank	68

Important Dates

Early action	
Apply by	Rolling
Regular	
Notified by	Rolling, 9/15
Nonfall registration?	Yes

FINANCIAL FACTS

Annual tuition	$22,160
Food and housing	$13,332
Required fees	$1,490
Books and supplies	$840
Average need-based scholarship (First-year)	$6,135 ($6,135)
% students with need rec. need-based scholarship or grant aid (First-year)	100 (100)
% students with need rec. non-need-based scholarship or grant aid (First-year)	76 (54)
% students with need rec. need-based self-help aid (First-year)	100 (100)
% students rec. any financial aid (First-year)	99 (99)
% UG borrow to pay for school	65
Average cumulative indebtedness	$36,045
% of students with need fully met (First-year)	16 (16)
Average % of student need met (First-year)	60 (85)

WILLIAMS COLLEGE

880 Main St., Williamstown, MA 01267 • Admissions: 413-597-2211

Survey Snapshot
Students always studying
Students are happy
Great financial aid

RATINGS

Quality of Life	89
Fire Safety	60*
Green	97
Academic	98
Profs Interesting	95
Profs Accessible	96
Admissions	98
Financial Aid	99

CAMPUS LIFE

Type of school	Private
Environment	Village

Students

Degree-seeking undergrad enrollment	2,067
% male/female/not reported	48/50/2
% from out of state	86
% First-year from public high school	51
% First-year live on campus	100
% Ugrads live on campus	93
# of fraternities	0
# of sororities	0
% Asian	13
% Black or African American	6
% Hispanic	15
% Native American	<1
% Pacific Islander	0
% Race and/or ethnicity unknown	5
% Two or more races	7
% White	43
% International	9
# of countries represented	56

CAMPUS MENTAL HEALTH SERVICES

Offers mental health/wellness program	Yes
Mental health training available to students	Yes
Employs Chief Wellness Officer	No
Peer-to-peer mental health offerings	No
Counseling center has guidelines or accreditation	No
Mental health/well-being courses	No

ACADEMICS

% students returning for sophomore year	97
% students graduating within 4 years	79
% students graduating within 6 years	95
Calendar	4-1-4
Student/faculty ratio	7:1
Most common class size 10–19.	(38%)
Most common lab/discussion size 10–19.	(54%)

Most Popular Majors
Biology/Biological Sciences; Mathematics; Econometrics and Quantitative Economics

Applicants Often Prefer
Brown University, Columbia University, Harvard College, Princeton University, Stanford University, University of Pennsylvania, Yale University

Applicants Sometimes Prefer
Cornell University, Dartmouth College, Northwestern University, The University of Chicago

Applicants Rarely Prefer
Amherst College, Bowdoin College, Middlebury College, Swarthmore College, Vanderbilt University

STUDENTS SAY "..."

Academics

Tucked away in western Massachusetts, Williams College is a "top-notch" liberal arts college that is "committed to making all students' dreams a reality." Indeed, this highly selective institution is an ideal place for people "who truly love to learn and explore new academic passions." And it offers the "perfect combination of...liberal arts and research opportunities; neither one has to be sacrificed here." Moreover, undergrads report that "the courses offered are diverse and interesting, while the divisional requirements mean that classes are more open to non-majors than at other schools." Of course, no matter what classes they take, students can rest assured that they'll be taught "how to think critically." Further, Williams' small size, with an enrollment of just over 2,000, also allows for "individualized attention." Undergrads also proudly proclaim that their professors are "the best in the nation, if not the world." Not only is each instructor "an expert in his or her field" but the vast majority have proven themselves to be "gifted teacher[s] as well." Even better, "they all make sure to be readily accessible and try to get to know every single student, even in a larger lecture class." And while they maintain "high expectations," courses are often "highly rewarding." What more could you hope for?

Campus Life

Undergrads at Williams are "always busy, always a little bit stressed." This comes as no surprise given that there are so many activities hosted on campus. To begin with, "the college makes sure to offer a ton of lectures, performances, art exhibits, movie screenings, fun activities, etc. so that people feel fulfilled staying on campus." There are also numerous "student-led events." As one content undergrad explains, "On Wednesday nights, my friends and I [go] to Stressbusters where you get free treats and the student-run coffee bar has an open tab." Additionally, Williams undergrads are always game for sporting events. After all, "35 percent of the school are varsity athletes [and] almost everyone else either is on a club sport, plays intramural, or goes to the gym regularly." There are also plenty of "opportunities to explore the outdoors [including] hiking, skiing, running, biking, [and] swimming." And once the weekend hits, you can find "lots of different kinds of parties... all-campus parties that the college puts on, big parties sponsored by different clubs, smaller parties, and people just hanging out in dorms." Lastly, though Williamstown is pretty "rural" and "remote," there are "amazing art offerings in the area at the Clark Art Institute, Massachusetts Museum of Contemporary Art, and the Williams College Museum of Art." Overall, you're bound to find something that will pique your interest and keep you entertained at Williams.

Student Body

The student body at Williams College is comprised of "driven," "quirky," and "mostly type-A" individuals. Across the board, undergrads here stress that their peers are incredibly "intelligent." As one impressed student shares, "Williams is great because you never feel like the smartest one in the room, and you genuinely feel as though your classmates have valuable input in all scenarios." In addition, Williams students are "dedicated to pursuing their passions, which cover a diverse spectrum and often fall outside of what is typical." Indeed, "it's not unusual to find a football player who is deeply interested in experimental theatre or a computer science major who is also one of the friendliest people you know." While some Williams students categorize each other as "white, athletic, [and] preppy," lots of undergrads assure us that "so many people fall outside of [these boxes]" as well. However, some do caution that "the average student is very socially and politically liberal, and conservative ideas (particularly socially conservative ideas) aren't welcome on campus." Nevertheless, most agree that the "sense of community is overwhelmingly strong and welcoming." After all, the students here "want to be surrounded by each other and learn from each other—otherwise they wouldn't have chosen to go to a school together in the middle of nowhere!"

WILLIAMS COLLEGE

Financial Aid: 413-597-4181 • E-Mail: admission@williams.edu • Website: www.williams.edu

THE PRINCETON REVIEW SAYS

Admissions

The school reports that its standardized testing policy for use in admission for Fall 2026 is Test Optional. The Princeton Review suggests that interested applicants consult with the school for the most up-to-date standardized testing policies. *Very important factors considered include:* rigor of secondary school record, academic GPA, recommendation(s), character/personal qualities. *Important factors considered include:* application essay, extracurricular activities, talent/ability, first generation, volunteer work, work experience. *Other factors considered include:* standardized test scores, alumni/ae relation, geographical residence, religious affiliation/commitment. High school diploma is required and GED is accepted. *Academic units recommended:* 4 English, 4 math, 4 science, 3 science labs, 4 language (other than English), 4 social studies.

Financial Aid

Students should submit: CSS PROFILE. The Princeton Review suggests that all financial aid forms be submitted as soon as possible. *Need-based scholarships/grants offered:* Federal Pell; Federal SEOG; State scholarships/grants; College/university scholarship or grant aid from institutional funds. *Loan aid offered:* Direct PLUS loans; Federal Direct Subsidized Loans; Federal Direct Unsubsidized Loans; College/university loans from institutional funds. Admitted students will be notified of awards on or about 4/1. Federal Work-Study Program available. Institutional employment available.

The Inside Word

Williams College is incredibly selective and earning a coveted spot will not be easy. Certainly, applicants will need to have earned top grades in a rigorous high school curriculum; honors, AP, and/or IB courses are a must. Beyond academic accolades, admissions officers are looking for students who demonstrate themselves to be creative thinkers and individuals who will bring diverse perspectives to campus life. To that end, personal statements, extracurricular involvement, and letters of recommendation also hold substantial weight.

THE SCHOOL SAYS

From the Admissions Office

"In addition to all the things that make liberal arts colleges the gold standard—small classes, attentive faculty, close-knit community—Williams offers unique opportunities like the renowned tutorial program, where students (in pairs) research and defend ideas and engage in weekly discussion with a professor. Half of Williams' students study abroad, with 26 juniors spending a year at Oxford annually. Four weeks of Winter Study each January provide time for individualized projects, research, and novel fields of study. The college receives several million dollars annually for undergraduate science research and is a leader in preparing students for graduate study. Students compete on 34 Division III athletic teams, perform in 25 musical groups, stage 10 theatrical productions, and volunteer in 300+ local organizations. The local community offers three distinguished art museums, the Williams College Museum of Art (new museum slated to open in 2027), the Clark Art Institute, the Massachusetts Museum of Contemporary Art, and 2,200 forest acres—complete with a treetop canopy walkway—for environmental research and recreation.

"All applications are reviewed in a student-centered, holistic admission process. As announced in Spring 2022, Williams is the first college in the nation to eliminate loans, as well as required campus and summer jobs from its financial aid packages. The components will be replaced with equivalent grant funds, dollar for dollar. Additionally, Williams guarantees free textbooks, health insurance, summer storage, optional funding for travel courses and internships, and more, for aid recipients."

SELECTIVITY

# of total applicants	15,520
% of total applicants accepted	9
% of total acceptees attending	42
# of early decision applicants	964
% of early decision applicants accepted	27
# offered a place on the wait list	2,193
# admitted from wait list	25

First-Year Profile

Testing policy	Test Optional
Range SAT composite	1490–1550
Range SAT EBRW	740–770
Range SAT math	740–790
Range ACT composite	33–35
% submitting SAT scores	43
% submitting ACT scores	18
% submitting high school GPA	74
% graduated top 10% of class	88
% graduated top 25% of class	97
% graduated top 50% of class	99
% submitting high school rank	17

Important Dates

Early decision	
Apply by	11/15
Notified by	12/15
Regular	
Apply by	1/6
Notified by	4/1
Nonfall registration?	No

FINANCIAL FACTS

Annual tuition	$76,300
Food and housing	$19,320
Required fees	$340
Books and supplies	$1,000
Average need-based scholarship (First-year)	$79,700 ($80,302)
% students with need rec. need-based scholarship or grant aid (First-year)	100 (100)
% students with need rec. non-need-based scholarship or grant aid (First-year)	0 (0)
% students with need rec. need-based self-help aid (First-year)	0 (0)
% students rec. any financial aid (First-year)	57 (57)
% UG borrow to pay for school	20
Average cumulative indebtedness	$18,266
% of students with need fully met (First-year)	100 (100)
Average % of student need met (First-year)	100 (100)

WITTENBERG UNIVERSITY

P.O. Box 720, Springfield, OH 45501 • Admissions: 937-327-6314

Survey Snapshot
Students are happy
Lab facilities are great
Students are friendly

RATINGS

Quality of Life	**79**
Fire Safety	**89**
Green	**60***
Academic	**87**
Profs Interesting	**94**
Profs Accessible	**97**
Admissions	**83**
Financial Aid	**86**

CAMPUS LIFE

Type of school	Private
Affiliation	Lutheran
Environment	Town

Students

Degree-seeking undergrad enrollment	1,007
% male/female/not reported	56/44/0
% from out of state	24
% First-year live on campus	91
% Ugrads live on campus	81
# of fraternities (% join)	5 (8)
# of sororities (% join)	6 (12)
% Asian	2
% Black or African American	16
% Hispanic	6
% Native American	<1
% Pacific Islander	0
% Race and/or ethnicity unknown	8
% Two or more races	4
% White	62
% International	1
# of countries represented	8

CAMPUS MENTAL HEALTH SERVICES

Offers mental health/wellness program	Yes
Mental health training available to students	Yes
Employs Chief Wellness Officer	Yes
Peer-to-peer mental health offerings	Yes
Counseling center has guidelines or accreditation	NR
Mental health/well-being courses	Yes, non-credit

ACADEMICS

% students returning for sophomore year	64
% students graduating within 4 years	54
% students graduating within 6 years	61
Calendar	Semester
Student/faculty ratio	13:1
Most common class size 10–19.	(37%)
Most common lab/discussion size 20–29.	(57%)

Most Popular Majors

Biology/Biological Sciences; Business/Commerce

Applicants Sometimes Prefer

Capital University, Miami University, The Ohio State University—Columbus, Ohio University—Athens, Ohio Wesleyan University, Otterbein University, University of Cincinnati, University of Dayton, Wright State University, Xavier University (OH)

STUDENTS SAY "..."

Academics

At Wittenberg University, "high academic standards and a dedication to research" are the norm and there's "high morale among the students." Unique opportunities like Witt in Washington and Witt in Poland immerse students in regions, whether that's a semester spent interning at embassies, museums, or government organizations like the FBI, or 24 days exploring the cultural and political ideology of the Polish people. Back on the "gorgeous campus," small classes yield "excellent attention [being] paid to students," and the "extremely engaging professors" are "committed to helping students both in and out of the classroom." As one student notes, "I feel like I am learning from my best friends." The low student-teacher ratio "really elevates the learning environment and makes classes far more interesting than large schools." It also encourages "students to build our own ideas and projects." Perhaps this is why one undergrad concludes, "Wittenberg is a place where students can develop themselves as a whole person—academically, professionally, and socially."

Campus Life

Life at this "beautiful school" is very busy. After all, the typical student is often "involved and overcommitted in at least two clubs and a sport or Greek life." In other words, these undergrads really embody the "work hard and play hard" mentality as they join groups ranging from Club Hockey and Kayak Club to the Anime Club and multiple a cappella groups. Some do caution that it can feel as though people "party every day," and it can be hard to fit in with that crowd. However, students also describe how they like to "just hang out and spend time with each other," going to see "comedians or musicians [who] come to entertain," or partaking in Witt Late Night activities like escape rooms, curling, and glow raves. For the outdoor enthusiasts itching to get off campus, there are plenty of options available, including "a reservoir to swim in, two playgrounds/parks, and three national parks for hiking." Ask one student jovially asks about all their offerings, "What don't we do?"

Student Body

The student body is "engaged, curious, and eager to learn" and sees itself as a "tight-knit community." The overall population tends to be perceived as "white, from Ohio, [and] middle class," but undergrads suggest that "Wittenberg has a wonderful variety of students" in terms of demographics (29% identifying as people of color), region (from the South, New England, and abroad), and generation (12% of attendees being first-generation collegiates). More importantly, attendees report that all "students here are welcomed in with ease." So, while some say "it is hard to describe a typical student," they agree that the atmosphere is uniformly "friendly" and "outgoing," making it easy to find your own group. In all, Wittenberg is a place where all you have to do to make a friend is "step out and say hello!"

WITTENBERG UNIVERSITY

Financial Aid: 937-327-7323 • E-Mail: admission@wittenberg.edu • Website: www.wittenberg.edu

THE PRINCETON REVIEW SAYS

Admissions

The school reports that its standardized testing policy for use in admission for Fall 2026 is Test Optional. The Princeton Review suggests that interested applicants consult with the school for the most up-to-date standardized testing policies. *Very important factors considered include:* rigor of secondary school record, academic GPA. *Important factors considered include:* class rank, application essay, recommendation(s), extracurricular activities, talent/ability, character/personal qualities, volunteer work. *Other factors considered include:* standardized test scores, interview, first generation, alumni/ae relation, work experience, level of applicant's interest. High school diploma is required and GED is accepted. *Academic units required:* 4 English, 3 math, 3 science, 2 science labs, 2 language (other than English), 2 history. *Academic units recommended:* 4 English, 4 math, 5 science, 2 science labs, 3 language (other than English), 3 history.

Financial Aid

Students should submit: FAFSA. Priority filing deadline is 2/15. The Princeton Review suggests that all financial aid forms be submitted as soon as possible. *Need-based scholarships/grants offered:* Federal Pell; Federal SEOG; State scholarships/grants; Private scholarships; College/university scholarship or grant aid from institutional funds; United Negro College Fund. *Loan aid offered:* Federal Direct Subsidized Loans; Federal Direct Unsubsidized Loans; Direct PLUS loans; College/university loans from institutional funds. Admitted students will be notified of awards on a rolling basis. Federal Work-Study Program available. Institutional employment available.

The Inside Word

Wittenberg accepts both its own application and the Common Application, and the application fee is waived if you apply online. The university only requires a short personal statement instead of the traditional formal essay. Wittenberg has a fairly high acceptance rate, but students will still want to make sure all parts of their application are the best they can be.

THE SCHOOL SAYS

From the Admissions Office

"Grounded in the liberal arts, Wittenberg fosters a culture where curiosity sparks questions and students explore across disciplines, test assumptions, and grow through dialogue. Rooted in a tradition that values reflection, purpose, and open inquiry, this approach—known as the Wittenberg Way—equips students to think critically, act ethically, and communicate meaningfully in the world.

"Here, students are shaped through active participation, where ideas are shared, challenged, and refined in community. Small classes ensure students are seen and heard. Professors know when to challenge and when to listen, helping students develop clarity, confidence, and direction. Signature experiences such as FIRE Week immerse students in focused, hands-on learning that brings ideas to life and deepens understanding.

"Intentionally sized to foster connection and collaboration, Wittenberg offers over 50 student organizations, NCAA Division III athletics, and opportunities to lead and serve. Located in Springfield, Ohio, with access to Columbus, Cincinnati, and Dayton, students engage in community service projects, internships, and professional networks. Wittenberg's test-optional admission policy allows applicants to decide whether ACT or SAT scores best reflect their potential.

"Graduates leave prepared to navigate complexity and contribute with purpose—bringing insight, integrity, and light to their communities and careers."

SELECTIVITY

# of total applicants	2,830
% of total applicants accepted	80
% of total acceptees attending	11
# of in-state applicants	1,747
% of in-state applicants accepted	90
# of out-of-state-applicants	750
% of applicants accepted from out of state	90
# of international applicants	333
% of international applicants accepted	11
# of early decision applicants	43
% of early decision applicants accepted	16

First-Year Profile

Testing policy	Test Optional
Range SAT composite	1080–1270
Range SAT EBRW	540–640
Range SAT math	540–650
Range ACT composite	21–27
% submitting SAT scores	8
% submitting ACT scores	15
Average HS GPA	3.4
% submitting high school GPA	94
% graduated top 10% of class	16
% graduated top 25% of class	36
% graduated top 50% of class	67
% submitting high school rank	49

Important Dates

Early decision	
Apply by	11/1
Notified by	12/1
Other ED Apply by	12/1
Other ED Notified by	1/1
Early action	
Apply by	12/1
Notified by	1/1
Nonfall registration?	Yes

FINANCIAL FACTS

Annual tuition	$47,000
Food and housing	$12,800
Required fees	$998
Books and supplies	$1,000
Average need-based scholarship (First-year)	$14,231 ($16,894)
% students with need rec. need-based scholarship or grant aid (First-year)	71 (92)
% students with need rec. non-need-based scholarship or grant aid (First-year)	100 (100)
% students with need rec. need-based self-help aid (First-year)	58 (64)
% students rec. any financial aid (First-year)	100 (100)
% UG borrow to pay for school	83
Average cumulative indebtedness	$8,500
% of students with need fully met (First-year)	1 (1)
Average % of student need met (First-year)	69 (80)

Wofford College

429 North Church Street, Spartanburg, SC 29303-3663 • Admissions: 864-597-4130

Survey Snapshot
Lots of conservative students
Classroom facilities are great
Lab facilities are great

RATINGS

Quality of Life	83
Fire Safety	93
Green	60*
Academic	87
Profs Interesting	92
Profs Accessible	94
Admissions	90
Financial Aid	93

CAMPUS LIFE

Type of school	Private
Affiliation	Methodist
Environment	City

Students

Degree-seeking undergrad enrollment	1,778
% male/female/not reported	48/52/<1
% from out of state	45
% First-year live on campus	97
% Ugrads live on campus	91
# of fraternities (% join)	6 (36)
# of sororities (% join)	4 (43)
% Asian	2
% Black or African American	7
% Hispanic	6
% Native American	<1
% Pacific Islander	<1
% Race and/or ethnicity unknown	<1
% Two or more races	4
% White	79
% International	2
# of countries represented	21

CAMPUS MENTAL HEALTH SERVICES

Offers mental health/wellness program	Yes
Mental health training available to students	No
Employs Chief Wellness Officer	NR
Peer-to-peer mental health offerings	NR
Counseling center has guidelines or accreditation	No
Mental health/well-being courses	NR

ACADEMICS

% students returning for sophomore year	90
% students graduating within 4 years	77
% students graduating within 6 years	80
Calendar	4-1-4
Student/faculty ratio	11:1
Most common class size 20–29.	(45%)
Most common lab/discussion size 10–19.	(35%)

Most Popular Majors
Biology/Biological Sciences; Finance; Psychology

Applicants Sometimes Prefer
Furman University

STUDENTS SAY "..."

Academics

With a "family atmosphere and close-knit community," Wofford College in Spartanburg, South Carolina, is a fantastic option for students seeking a "rigorous" liberal arts experience. It also helps that the "campus is beautiful" and "the facilities are clean and up to date." More impressively, undergrads here have the opportunity to "network with highly influential people" and participate in "an outstanding study abroad program." And thanks to Wofford's "small" size, students are truly able to receive "an individualized education and personal attention." While coursework is "challenging," undergrads are appreciative, noting that their college "specializes in preparing students for graduate or professional school." For the most part, they also give their professors high marks. After all, Wofford instructors tend to be "extremely passionate about their fields and are very well educated." And they "frequently hold review sessions and are always available by email if they are not in their offices." Best of all, "each person, whether in the dining hall or the classroom, is there for your success. Knowing that we have these amazing adults there for us no matter what is something that allows us to thrive and become the best personal versions of ourselves."

Campus Life

At Wofford College, dull moments are few and far between. Sure, students "work hard during the week," but they also manage to carve out time for some fun. For example, many undergrads "spend a lot of time at the gym, either working out, playing games, or participating in classes such as yoga or Afro beat." Students also "love to hang out at Burwell, our main cafeteria, and grab a bite to eat." Once the weekend hits, you will find lots of undergrads "playing sand volleyball and dancing at the Greek Village with their friends to the live bands." Indeed, the college maintains six fraternities, four sororities, two historically Black fraternities, and a multicultural house at the Greek Village and much of the social life revolves around them. However, there's still plenty to enjoy if Greek life isn't your scene. After all, Wofford sponsors a number of great events like "trivia nights," "cultural events" and concerts. Further, outdoor enthusiasts will be thrilled to learn that there are "countless hiking trails near campus, including those at Glendale Shoals," where Wofford's Goodall Environmental Studies Center with its vineyard garden and amphitheater is located. Lastly, though some individuals complain that the city of Spartanburg doesn't offer much to do for fun, heading "off-campus" for activities like "bowling, shopping, or movies are common."

Student Body

Wofford undergrads are "kind," "friendly" and often embody "Southern hospitality." They tend to view their peers as "family" rather than simply fellow students. And while people certainly "have friend groups that they commonly hang out with, [there are} no strict cliques like in high school." Just as critical, Wofford students are "hardworking" and "driven" and they "all take pride in their academic success." Undergrads do acknowledge, however, that the college is "predominantly white." Though they also insist "diversity has increased." And a handful of individuals argue that Wofford yields "many international students from various countries as well as American students from all across the country from all financial backgrounds." Regardless of where they come from, undergrads say it is very "easy to connect with most other students" and that everyone is "respectful and kind toward one another." After all, it is "a very open school and everyone says 'Hi' because you've most likely had a class with them before." One student points out, "you may not know everyone's name, but everyone has some common ground...no one feels left out."

Wofford College

Financial Aid: 864-597-4160 • E-Mail: admission@wofford.edu • Website: www.wofford.edu

THE PRINCETON REVIEW SAYS

Admissions

The school reports that its standardized testing policy for use in admission for Fall 2026 is Test Optional. The Princeton Review suggests that interested applicants consult with the school for the most up-to-date standardized testing policies. *Very important factors considered include:* rigor of secondary school record, academic GPA. *Important factors considered include:* class rank, application essay, extracurricular activities, talent/ability, character/personal qualities. *Other factors considered include:* standardized test scores, recommendation(s), interview, first generation, alumni/ae relation, geographical residence, state residency, religious affiliation/commitment, volunteer work, work experience, level of applicant's interest. High school diploma is required and GED is accepted. *Academic units required:* 4 English, 4 math, 3 science, 3 science labs, 3 language (other than English), 3 social studies. *Academic units recommended:* 4 English, 4 math, 3 science, 3 science labs, 3 language (other than English), 3 social studies, 1 history, 1 academic elective, 1 computer science, 1 visual/performing arts.

Financial Aid

Students should submit: FAFSA. Priority filing deadline is 1/15. The Princeton Review suggests that all financial aid forms be submitted as soon as possible. *Need-based scholarships/grants offered:* Federal Pell; Federal SEOG; State scholarships/grants; Private scholarships; College/university scholarship or grant aid from institutional funds. *Loan aid offered:* Federal Direct Subsidized Loans; Federal Direct Unsubsidized Loans; Direct PLUS loans. Admitted students will be notified of awards on or about 2/1. Federal Work-Study Program available. Institutional employment available.

The Inside Word

Wofford College aims to take a holistic approach to the admissions process. Therefore, students can expect all facets of their application will be closely scrutinized. Successful candidates typically have completed a rigorous high school curriculum, replete with a few honors or AP courses. They also present thoughtful personal statements and are active in their school and community. Students should only submit their standardized test scores if they feel that they adequately represent their academic abilities.

THE SCHOOL SAYS

From the Admissions Office

"When the first students began classes at Wofford College in 1854, Main Building—fondly called "Old Main"—was the college. Every Wofford student since then has taken classes in Main. Wofford College specializes in high-impact, experiential learning for the college's 1,781 undergraduates, including opportunities for study abroad, research, internships and community-based learning. The college is also nationally ranked for its outstanding faculty, successful and supportive graduates, and commitment to making college affordable and accessible; 99% of students receive some form of financial assistance. The college's residential, living and learning environment is based on a stunning 180-acre campus within walking distance of Spartanburg's thriving downtown and includes NCAA Division I athletics, fraternity and sorority life, offerings in the arts and career preparation. Student success is a priority at Wofford, and students graduate—most within four years—prepared for what's next and with a support network that lasts a lifetime."

SELECTIVITY

# of total applicants	4,516
% of total applicants accepted	55
% of total acceptees attending	18
# of early decision applicants	271
% of early decision applicants accepted	71
# offered a place on the wait list	827
# admitted from wait list	50

First-Year Profile

Testing policy	Test Optional
Range SAT composite	1200–1320
Range SAT EBRW	610–690
Range SAT math	570–660
Range ACT composite	28–31
% submitting SAT scores	23
% submitting ACT scores	19
Average HS GPA	3.6
% submitting high school GPA	100
% graduated top 10% of class	32
% graduated top 25% of class	61
% graduated top 50% of class	86
% submitting high school rank	57

Important Dates

Early decision	
Apply by	11/1
Notified by	12/1
Early action	
Apply by	11/15
Notified by	2/1
Regular	
Apply by	1/15
Notified by	3/15
Nonfall registration?	Yes

FINANCIAL FACTS

Annual tuition	$58,495
Food and housing	$17,545
Required fees	$2,085
Books and supplies	$1,307
Average need-based scholarship (First-year)	$46,468 ($44,811)
% students with need rec. need-based scholarship or grant aid (First-year)	100 (100)
% students with need rec. non-need-based scholarship or grant aid (First-year)	43 (47)
% students with need rec. need-based self-help aid (First-year)	46 (44)
% UG borrow to pay for school	52
Average cumulative indebtedness	$36,521
% of students with need fully met (First-year)	49 (52)
Average % of student need met (First-year)	89 (91)

Worcester Polytechnic Institute

100 Institute Road, Worcester, MA 01609 • Admissions: 508-831-5286

Survey Snapshot
Intramural sports are popular
Easy to get around campus
Active minority support groups

RATINGS

Quality of Life	85
Fire Safety	84
Green	60*
Academic	81
Profs Interesting	85
Profs Accessible	91
Admissions	84
Financial Aid	88

CAMPUS LIFE

Type of school	Private
Environment	City

Students

Degree-seeking undergrad enrollment	5,353
% male/female/not reported	71/29/0
% from out of state	50
% First-year live on campus	96
% Ugrads live on campus	44
# of fraternities (% join)	13 (21)
# of sororities (% join)	6 (31)
% Asian	13
% Black or African American	3
% Hispanic	8
% Native American	<1
% Pacific Islander	<1
% Race and/or ethnicity unknown	2
% Two or more races	4
% White	63
% International	6
# of countries represented	72

CAMPUS MENTAL HEALTH SERVICES

Offers mental health/wellness program	Yes
Mental health training available to students	Yes
Employs Chief Wellness Officer	Yes
Peer-to-peer mental health offerings	Yes
Counseling center has guidelines or accreditation	Yes
Mental health/well-being courses	Yes, for-credit

ACADEMICS

% students returning for sophomore year	95
% students graduating within 4 years	83
% students graduating within 6 years	90
Calendar	Four seven-week terms (two per semester)
Student/faculty ratio	13:1
Most common class size 1–9.	(52%)
Most common lab/discussion size 20–29.	(29%)

Most Popular Majors

Computer Science; Bioengineering and Biomedical Engineering; Mechanical Engineering

Applicants Also Look At

Boston University, Carnegie Mellon University, Case Western Reserve University, Georgia Institute of Technology, Massachusetts Institute of Technology, Northeastern University, Penn State University Park, Purdue University—West Lafayette, Rensselaer Polytechnic Institute, Rochester Institute of Technology, Stevens Institute of Technology, Tufts University, University of Connecticut, University of Massachusetts—Amherst, University of Massachusetts—Lowell, University of New Hampshire, University of Rhode Island, University of Vermont, Virginia Tech, Wentworth Institute of Technology

STUDENTS SAY "..."

Academics

Worcester Polytechnic Institute brings an international lens to its project-based STEM curriculum, beginning with first-year students in the Great Problems Seminar (GPS), where they are challenged to think "outside their disciplines to solve problems focused on themes of global importance" and present research-based solutions to an issue of their choice. One student enthuses about a "project I did for seven weeks in Istanbul studying impacts of earthquakes and possible search and rescue solutions," while another loved working with their GPS group to explore "how transportation of donor organs can be improved to increase the number of organs that are transplanted into patients." Because the "entire curriculum is built around projects, students naturally share ideas, test things out together, and turn class concepts into something tangible." Every student completes two signature projects during their time at WPI: an interactive qualifying project (IQP) and a major qualifying project (MQP). Both provide "an incredible depth and breadth to the learning experience at WPI. With the IQP, students gain a global perspective of how technical skills can make a difference solving real social issues...The MQP is a major-specific qualifying project that gives students the opportunity to innovate new solutions in their field of study." One student shares, "I have been able to work on projects from chemical engineering to machine learning, in both Worcester and Italy, and with people of all different backgrounds and perspectives." Ultimately, students are drawn to WPI so they can "innovate, push boundaries, and constantly improve themselves and the world around them."

Campus Life

WPI's campus offers a dynamic mix of personalities and passions, with students generally falling into two broad groups: "those focused purely on school and those who balance it with the large, Greek life scene." One student adds, "There's a pretty big chunk of students that are very homebody/introverted, but there are also plenty of people that are super involved in clubs and campus life, especially those in Greek life." For many, Greek life plays a prominent role in shaping social connections, providing "an amazing way to find a great group of people with similar values and then to be able to network with other Greek-like organizations." At the same time, outside of the Greek scene, "most students have real hobbies and real interests, and there are a multitude of student clubs and organizations where students find their niche." Another student emphasizes, "Most of our campus is...involved in many different organizations," highlighting a community where students can pursue academics, hobbies, and social life in ways that suit them best.

Student Body

Without a doubt, WPI attracts "engineering students who are passionate about learning," as well as individuals who are "vibrant, entertaining, intelligent, and kind." One student explains, "Almost everyone at WPI is unapologetically nerdy, in the best way. We embrace each other's quirks and celebrate them." Academics are important, but students are also supportive, sure "to help build each other up rather than compete to be the best." Students appreciate not having "to fit in just one box, there are so many opportunities to try everything possible," with one adding, "[We] have a large portion of students who are dedicated to sports and other activities." Another student shares, "Many of us are very social and like to join clubs or party. And that's not something I fully expected from this school," adding, "We have a really well-rounded group of individuals who all like different things." As one student observes, "Everyone is always busy, but it's an active and happy campus," while another states, "At WPI, my peers are some of the most collaborative and curious people I've ever met."

Worcester Polytechnic Institute

Financial Aid: 508-831-5469 • E-Mail: admissions@wpi.edu • Website: www.wpi.edu

THE PRINCETON REVIEW SAYS

Admissions

The school reports that its standardized testing policy for use in admission for Fall 2026 is Test Optional. The Princeton Review suggests that interested applicants consult with the school for the most up-to-date standardized testing policies. *Very important factors considered include:* rigor of secondary school record, academic GPA. *Important factors considered include:* class rank, recommendation(s), extracurricular activities, character/personal qualities. *Other factors considered include:* standardized test scores, application essay, talent/ability, first generation, alumni/ae relation, geographical residence, volunteer work, work experience, level of applicant's interest. High school diploma is required and GED is accepted. *Academic units required:* 4 English, 4 math, 2 science, 2 science lab. *Academic units recommended:* 4 science, 2 language (other than English), 2 social studies, 1 history, 1 computer science.

Financial Aid

Students should submit: FAFSA; CSS PROFILE. Priority filing deadline is 3/1. The Princeton Review suggests that all financial aid forms be submitted as soon as possible. *Need-based scholarships/grants offered:* Federal Pell; Federal SEOG; State scholarships/grants; Private scholarships; College/university scholarship or grant aid from institutional funds. *Loan aid offered:* Federal Direct Subsidized Loans; Federal Direct Unsubsidized Loans; Direct PLUS loans; College/university loans from institutional funds; State Loans. Admitted students will be notified of awards on a rolling basis beginning 12/15. Federal Work-Study Program available. Institutional employment available.

The Inside Word

The WPI applicant pool is both self-selective and competitive, due to its focused curriculum and solid reputation. Admissions officers tend to prioritize those interested in STEM fields and who show a fit with the campus vibe, but they are also looking for students who have interests that go beyond science and math. Consequently, it would be wise to emphasize your extracurricular passions on your applications along with your academic record.

THE SCHOOL SAYS

From the Admissions Office

"WPI is a research university distinguished by an innovative project-based curriculum converting classroom concepts to real-world impact, empowering students to pursue their passions in solving critical problems and developing skills employers seek. By pairing together theory and practice, students receive a high-caliber education fused with hands-on solving of issues in the world.

"WPI's return on investment enables students to receive a strong starting salary and to ascend to high-income brackets over their lives. Students call WPI's project-based, global approach "life-changing." WPI works with more than 400 companies, government agencies, and private organizations each year, providing opportunities to work in real, professional settings. WPI also receives acclaim for professors who engage their students in research.

"WPI consistently achieves high rankings for academic reputation and student satisfaction. A majority of students travel to over 50 global project centers as part of their project work, leading to ranking No. 1 for the best study-abroad program in the nation (Princeton Review). WPI offers every student a Global Scholarship of up to $5,000 to help with travel costs."

SELECTIVITY

# of total applicants	12,355
% of total applicants accepted	62
% of total acceptees attending	17
# of in-state applicants	3,920
% of in-state applicants accepted	66
# of out-of-state-applicants	6,735
% of applicants accepted from out of state	66
# of international applicants	1,700
% of international applicants accepted	39
# of early decision applicants	397
% of early decision applicants accepted	78
# offered a place on the wait list	2,293
# admitted from wait list	460

First-Year Profile

Testing policy	Test Optional
Average HS GPA	3.9
% submitting high school GPA	88
% graduated top 10% of class	51
% graduated top 25% of class	83
% graduated top 50% of class	98
% submitting high school rank	33

Important Dates

Early decision	
Apply by	11/1
Notified by	12/15
Other ED Apply by	1/5
Other ED Notified by	2/15
Early action	
Apply by	11/1
Notified by	2/1
Regular	
Apply by	2/1
Notified by	4/1
Nonfall registration?	No

FINANCIAL FACTS

Annual tuition	$63,936
Food and housing	$19,732
Required fees (First-year)	$1,302 ($1,502)
Books and supplies	$1,200
Average need-based scholarship (First-year)	$36,485 ($36,963)
% students with need rec. need-based scholarship or grant aid (First-year)	100 (100)
% students with need rec. non-need-based scholarship or grant aid (First-year)	23 (29)
% students with need rec. need-based self-help aid (First-year)	74 (72)
% students rec. any financial aid (First-year)	98 (99)
% of students with need fully met (First-year)	25 (29)
Average % of student need met (First-year)	74 (81)

XAVIER UNIVERSITY OF LOUISIANA

1 Drexel Drive, New Orleans, LA 70125 • Admissions: 504-520-7388

Survey Snapshot
Lots of liberal students
Campus newspaper is popular
Active minority support groups

RATINGS

Quality of Life	77
Fire Safety	99
Green	60*
Academic	81
Profs Interesting	83
Profs Accessible	88
Admissions	86
Financial Aid	85

CAMPUS LIFE

Type of school	Private
Affiliation	Roman Catholic
Environment	Metropolis

Students

Degree-seeking undergrad enrollment	2,546
% male/female/not reported	25/75/0
% from out of state	72
% First-year live on campus	87
% Ugrads live on campus	49
# of fraternities (% join)	4 (1)
# of sororities (% join)	4 (3)
% Asian	2
% Black or African American	86
% Hispanic	5
% Native American	0
% Pacific Islander	0
% Race and/or ethnicity unknown	<1
% Two or more races	3
% White	1
% International	3
# of countries represented	23

CAMPUS MENTAL HEALTH SERVICES

Offers mental health/wellness program	Yes
Mental health training available to students	No
Employs Chief Wellness Officer	Yes
Peer-to-peer mental health offerings	Yes
Counseling center has guidelines or accreditation	No
Mental health/well-being courses	NR

ACADEMICS

% students returning for sophomore year	69
% students graduating within 4 years	42
% students graduating within 6 years	53
Calendar	Semester
Student/faculty ratio	10:1
Most common class size 10–19.	(35%)
Most common lab/discussion size 20–29.	(48%)

Most Popular Majors

Psychology; Pre-Medicine/Pre-Medical Studies; Pre-Pharmacy Studies

STUDENTS SAY "..."

Academics

Recognized for its "challenging classes" and "academic resources," Xavier University of Louisiana is a Catholic and historically Black university that stresses a well-rounded curriculum within a nurturing learning environment. Students here can "be whoever they want to be," which is why the school's support extends beyond programs in STEM and health sciences to a required 40-hour credit core curriculum that focuses on Catholic tradition and contemporary learning. For many students, attending this "extremely academically focused" university pays off. Several undergrads cite that the university is "known for having successful graduates go on to complete medical and graduate school."

But don't let Xavier's strenuous curriculum intimidate you. Many students agree, "[Our] school's greatest strength is our sense of togetherness. We all want to see each other succeed and are willing to help each other along the way," professors included. Most students describe their professors as "kind, understanding and always willing to work with you to achieve a goal." Faculty at the university "value [their students'] education," as observed by students who find that their instructors go above and beyond conventional teaching methods and try to incorporate pedagogical innovation into classes: "Instead of a final exam, my professor is making us do a podcast project in the style of a Vanderbilt professor." Additionally, as a school that challenges its students to be their best, "there is always a resource center or a teacher offering their services" to offer additional guidance. Overall, students agree that Xavier "truly prepares students for experiences after they graduate."

Campus Life

It's a life of books at this rigorously academic university, so "literally most of us are in the library most of the day if not in class," though you will find that "students congregate in their dorm rooms or in the lobby area of the cafeteria." A life of books, at least, until the weekend, at which point the bustle of the nearby city calls out: "There's always something to do in New Orleans." As far as clubs and organizations go, there is "something for everyone, and you even have the opportunity to start clubs of your own." Many enrollees enjoy the Peer Dean Association, which has select members "provide a family space for incoming students" and help them acclimate to life on campus." Student ambassadors "are seen as the faces of Xavier" and offer tours and host events for prospective undergrads. Additionally, basketball games are wildly popular, and there are some events thrown on campus, such as "live music [on] Fridays," which "includes free food, dancing, and fun."

Student Body

Though Xavier University of Louisiana is a historically Black university, the student body is very diverse, with notably "well-rounded" and "community-minded" individuals. Several students note that "even though this is a small campus, the people can be so different." Since Xavierites come from so many different backgrounds and regions, "they bring unique elements such as regional dances, phrases, mannerisms, and recipes." Though some might worry about feeling isolated, Xavier is "one big family" where "no one feels unreachable or untouchable." Additionally, it's clear that Xavier students recognize how hard their classmates work and make the effort to lift one another up. As one student puts it best, "No one will allow you to fail," but they will "[give] you challenges to push yourself forward."

Xavier University of Louisiana

Financial Aid: 504-520-7835 • E-Mail: apply@xula.edu • Website: www.xula.edu

THE PRINCETON REVIEW SAYS

Admissions

The school reports that its standardized testing policy for use in admission for Fall 2026 is Test Optional. The Princeton Review suggests that interested applicants consult with the school for the most up-to-date standardized testing policies. *Important factors considered include:* academic GPA, standardized test scores. *Other factors considered include:* rigor of secondary school record, class rank, application essay, recommendation(s), extracurricular activities, volunteer work. High school diploma is required and GED is accepted. *Academic units required:* 4 English, 2 math, 2 science, 2 social studies, 8 academic electives. *Academic units recommended:* 4 math, 3 science, 2 language (other than English), 1 history.

Financial Aid

Students should submit: FAFSA. Priority filing deadline is 1/1. The Princeton Review suggests that all financial aid forms be submitted as soon as possible. *Need-based scholarships/grants offered:* Federal Pell; Federal SEOG; State scholarships/grants; Private scholarships; College/university scholarship or grant aid from institutional funds; United Negro College Fund. *Loan aid offered:* Federal Direct Subsidized Loans; Federal Direct Unsubsidized Loans; Direct PLUS loans. Admitted students will be notified of awards on a rolling basis beginning 4/1. Federal Work-Study Program available. Institutional employment available.

The Inside Word

Gaining admission to Xavier University of Louisiana is competitive. Fortunately, admissions officers make every effort to take a holistic approach and strive to get to know each candidate as best as possible. To that end, the university considers everything from high school transcripts and standardized test scores (if submitted) to recommendations and extracurricular involvement. Xavier also makes a point of noting that it does not consider gender, race, religion, creed, color, national origin, or handicap when deciding who to admit.

THE SCHOOL SAYS

From the Admissions Office

"You have made a great decision in planning to go to college. You will make another important decision when you select Xavier University of Louisiana for your college education. For over 100 years, Xavier has continued to create enriching experiences and foster relationships between faculty and students who go on to make a global impact. With a mission to 'seek a more just and humane society,' Xavier attracts students from all over the world who desire to be change agents. Xavier has recently been noted as a top HBCU for return on investment for Black students, and Xavier's impressive alumni network lends credence to how Xavierites fulfill the university's mission every day. Known for its strength in STEM, Xavier offers numerous research opportunities through our Center for Undergraduate Research and Graduate Opportunity (CURGO). In the health professions, Xavier is a national leader in providing graduates for schools of medicine and dentistry. Xavier's renowned College of Pharmacy continues to excel, with its graduates serving widely in the pharmaceutical industry, hospitals, and in neighborhoods often located in or central to underserved communities. Students studying the humanities receive one-on-one contact with professors as they strengthen their skill set, stretching their reach across various art performance stages, community-based organizations, national publications, network television and more. Xavier graduates have heeded the call to provide enlightened leadership in city government, and many alumni have and do serve as mayors, lead municipal agencies, don judicial robes and serve in state and national legislatures. Xavier-taught educators teach the next generation of changemakers at all academic levels, with other graduates acting as system presidents, superintendents, and principals. Business graduates from Xavier rise quickly in all industries, with a litany of Xavierites who are successful entrepreneurs. Students who leave Xavier leave ready. We stand prepared to motivate scholars through activism, elevate minds via a rigorous curriculum and educate students on how to merge their passion to influence the greater good. You can join the ranks of our notable alumni by joining the Xavier family today."

SELECTIVITY

# of total applicants	11,210
% of total applicants accepted	67
% of total acceptees attending	8
# of in-state applicants	2,523
% of in-state applicants accepted	68
# of out-of-state-applicants	8,014
% of applicants accepted from out of state	72
# of international applicants	671
% of international applicants accepted	11

First-Year Profile

Testing policy	Test Optional
Range SAT composite	950–1150
Range SAT EBRW	550–580
Range SAT math	460–560
Range ACT composite	18–24
% submitting SAT scores	36
% submitting ACT scores	44
Average HS GPA	3.6
% submitting high school GPA	99
% graduated top 10% of class	29
% graduated top 25% of class	61
% graduated top 50% of class	89
% submitting high school rank	17

Important Dates

Regular	
Notified by	10/1
Nonfall registration?	Yes

FINANCIAL FACTS

Annual tuition	$27,670
Food and housing	$11,129
Required fees	$3,564
Books and supplies	$1,385
Average need-based scholarship (First-year)	$12,033 ($12,874)
% students with need rec. need-based scholarship or grant aid (First-year)	100 (100)
% students with need rec. non-need-based scholarship or grant aid (First-year)	<1 (<1)
% students with need rec. need-based self-help aid (First-year)	95 (98)
% students rec. any financial aid (First-year)	99 (100)
% UG borrow to pay for school	98
Average cumulative indebtedness	$18,887
% of students with need fully met (First-year)	24 (20)
Average % of student need met (First-year)	55 (60)

XAVIER UNIVERSITY (OH)

3800 Victory Parkway, Cincinnati, OH 45207-5311 • Admissions: 513-745-3301

Survey Snapshot
Easy to get around campus
Recreation facilities are great
Everyone loves the Musketeers

RATINGS

Quality of Life	85
Fire Safety	89
Green	89
Academic	80
Profs Interesting	91
Profs Accessible	93
Admissions	85
Financial Aid	85

CAMPUS LIFE

Type of school	Private
Affiliation	Roman Catholic-Jesuit
Environment	Metropolis

Students

Degree-seeking undergrad enrollment	3,708
% male/female/not reported	44/56/0
% from out of state	51
% First-year from public high school	49
% First-year live on campus	83
% Ugrads live on campus	46
# of fraternities	0
# of sororities	0
% Asian	2
% Black or African American	12
% Hispanic	7
% Native American	<1
% Pacific Islander	<1
% Race and/or ethnicity unknown	1
% Two or more races	4
% White	72
% International	2
# of countries represented	32

CAMPUS MENTAL HEALTH SERVICES

Offers mental health/wellness program	Yes
Mental health training available to students	No
Employs Chief Wellness Officer	NR
Peer-to-peer mental health offerings	NR
Counseling center has guidelines or accreditation	No
Mental health/well-being courses	NR

ACADEMICS

% students returning for sophomore year	83
% students graduating within 4 years	63
% students graduating within 6 years	74
Calendar	Semester
Student/faculty ratio	10:1
Most common class size 20–29.	(53%)
Most common lab/discussion size 10–19.	(73%)

Most Popular Majors

Computer Science; Registered Nursing/Registered Nurse; Marketing/Marketing Management

Applicants Also Look At

Indiana University—Bloomington, Marquette University, Miami University, Miami University—Hamilton Campus, Miami University—Middletown Campus, The Ohio State University—Columbus, Ohio University—Athens, Purdue University—West Lafayette, Saint Louis University, University of Cincinnati, University of Dayton, University of Kentucky

STUDENTS SAY "..."

Academics

In addition to academics, students point to the professors at Xavier University as one of its "greatest strengths," noting that they're "always available and very accessible" and "actively interested in the learning, engagement, and success of their students." In particular, students value professors that "ask me what I want to do post-grad and ask how they can help me get there, whether it be looking at my résumé, giving me a recommendation, or letting me know about job opportunities from their own network!" Xavier supports a "holistic approach to learning" through foundational courses that focus on religion, liberal arts, rhetorical and quantitative reasoning, as well as cultural understanding. In addition, "Xavier's proximity to the city of Cincinnati is a huge perk, especially for those looking to enter in the sports industry, medical field, or corporate world." This access opens doors to real-world opportunities, with students completing "clinicals at some world-renowned hospitals like Cincinnati Medical Center and Cincinnati Children's" and doing "real and meaningful work, like the marketing research courses that collaborate with the Cincinnati Reds." The business school's highlights include networking events that encourage students to get "out there and talk to people," club events with company visits, and "in-class opportunities to work with businesses and clients." This all deepens the "community between students, staff, and faculty allowing for connection, networking, and a sense of belonging."

Campus Life

"Basketball season is king" at XU. Musketeers, as students are known, love going to "games at the Cintas Center. They are so fun and make you feel connected to the student body." A favorite student pastime is cheering "in the comfort of a packed stadium with ten thousand fans that all feel like friends." Off the court, "there is tons to do on campus and in Cincinnati," and students enjoy putting their Jesuit values into play by being of service to those around them. "Xavier is very intentional about providing service opportunities for their students to make a positive impact on their community, and most students are super into this." One Musketeer says, "I love the service club called X-Change. It is a weekly commitment, and I have made many friends through it." Similarly, one member of a healthcare club enjoys it "because many students are motivated not only by career goals... but also by a desire to make a meaningful impact beyond themselves." Summing up the extracurriculars on offer, one student says: "All these experiences brought me joy, taught me important life lessons, or increased my knowledge of the campus and community."

Student Body

As you might expect of those known as Musketeers, "We all connect very strongly with our faith, and I think that really brings us together as a giant family." In general, Musketeers are "driven, community-minded, and deeply purposeful. The student body is united by a shared belief that education is not just about personal success, but about service." Students are also "outgoing, loving," and "know how to have fun and do college, while being ethical and uplifting." As a result, students say things like "I have loved all the peers I have met through Xavier" and "I would consider myself an introvert but quickly realized that there is someone here for everyone. The student body is absolutely wonderful and so uplifting to each other." Another student explains: "I feel like since it's a smaller university and because it's a Jesuit institution, people here have a better sense of belonging and community." Even as they celebrate Xavier's Jesuit background, Musketeers are quick to point out that "the Center of Faith and Justice gives students of all religions a space to interact and participate in programs, clubs, and events." Overall, "everyone is very dedicated to their education, and that motivates all of us together as a family."

Xavier University (OH)

Financial Aid: 513-745-3302 • E-Mail: xuadmit@xavier.edu • Website: www.xavier.edu

THE PRINCETON REVIEW SAYS

Admissions

The school reports that its standardized testing policy for use in admission for Fall 2026 is Test Optional. The Princeton Review suggests that interested applicants consult with the school for the most up-to-date standardized testing policies. *Very important factors considered include:* rigor of secondary school record, academic GPA. *Important factors considered include:* application essay, recommendation(s), extracurricular activities, character/personal qualities. *Other factors considered include:* class rank, standardized test scores, talent/ability, volunteer work, work experience, level of applicant's interest. High school diploma is required and GED is accepted. *Academic units required:* 4 English, 3 math, 3 science, 2 science labs, 2 language (other than English), 3 social studies, 3 history, 5 academic electives, 1 visual/performing arts. *Academic units recommended:* 4 English, 4 math, 4 science, 3 science labs, 3 language (other than English), 4 social studies, 4 history, 5 academic electives, 1 computer science, 2 visual/performing arts.

Financial Aid

Students should submit: FAFSA. Priority filing deadline is 2/15. The Princeton Review suggests that all financial aid forms be submitted as soon as possible. *Need-based scholarships/grants offered:* Federal Pell; Federal SEOG; State scholarships/grants; Private scholarships; United Negro College Fund; College/university scholarship or grant aid from institutional funds. *Loan aid offered:* Federal Direct Subsidized Loans; Federal Direct Unsubsidized Loans; Direct PLUS loans; College/university loans from institutional funds. Admitted students will be notified of awards on a rolling basis. Federal Work-Study Program available. Institutional employment available.

The Inside Word

There should be no major hurdles for above-average students when it comes to gaining admission to Xavier. For select schools within Xavier, it will take a little more legwork; music and theater students must audition, and nursing students must indicate their intent to enroll in the nursing school on the initial application. Look to provide credible demonstrations of commitment to academics and Jesuit ideals of service if you want to win over admissions officers.

THE SCHOOL SAYS

From the Admissions Office

"Founded in 1831, Xavier University is the fourth oldest of the twenty-seven Jesuit colleges and universities in the United States. The Jesuit tradition is evident in the university's core curriculum, degree programs, and involvement opportunities. Xavier is home to approximately 7,000 total students, including 5,200 degree-seeking undergraduates. The student population represents more than forty-five states and thirty foreign countries. Xavier offers more than ninety undergraduate academic majors and more than eighty minors in the College of Arts and Sciences, Williams College of Business, College of Nursing, and the College of Professional Sciences. Most popular majors include business, natural sciences, nursing, liberal arts, education, psychology, biology, and pre-professional study. Other programs of note include University Scholars; Honors AB; Philosophy, Politics, and the Public; Data Science Honors Program; Smith Scholars program; study abroad; service and community-engaged learning. There are more than 100 academic clubs, social and service organizations, and recreational sports activities on campus. Students participate in groups such as student government, campus ministry, performing arts, and intramural sports as well as one of the largest service-oriented Alternative Break clubs in the country. Xavier is a member of the Division I Big East Conference and fields teams in men's and women's basketball, cross-country, track, golf, soccer, swimming, and tennis, as well as men's baseball and women's volleyball. Xavier is situated on more than 180 acres in a residential area of Cincinnati, Ohio. Xavier University offers Test Optional admission."

SELECTIVITY

# of total applicants	11,202
% of total applicants accepted	85
% of total acceptees attending	7
# offered a place on the wait list	768
# admitted from wait list	764

First-Year Profile

Testing policy	Test Optional
Range SAT composite	1130–1300
Range SAT EBRW	560–670
Range SAT math	560–650
Range ACT composite	24–33
% submitting SAT scores	11
% submitting ACT scores	30
Average HS GPA	3.8
% submitting high school GPA	100
% graduated top 10% of class	26
% graduated top 25% of class	56
% graduated top 50% of class	88
% submitting high school rank	27

Important Dates

Early action	
Apply by	11/1
Notified by	Mid December
Regular	
Apply by	2/1
Notified by	Rolling, 10/1
Nonfall registration?	Yes

FINANCIAL FACTS

Annual tuition	$54,530
Food and housing	$11,460
Required fees	$310
Books and supplies	$1,300
Average need-based scholarship (First-year)	$37,257 ($43,615)
% students with need rec. need-based scholarship or grant aid (First-year)	69 (97)
% students with need rec. non-need-based scholarship or grant aid (First-year)	39 (46)
% students with need rec. need-based self-help aid (First-year)	52 (46)
% students rec. any financial aid (First-year)	97 (100)
% UG borrow to pay for school	48
Average cumulative indebtedness	$15,244
% of students with need fully met (First-year)	10 (15)
Average % of student need met (First-year)	78 (83)

Yale University

PO Box 208234, New Haven, CT 06520 • Admissions: 203-432-9316

Survey Snapshot
Great financial aid
Diverse student types interact on campus
Theater is popular

RATINGS

Quality of Life	90
Fire Safety	60*
Green	60*
Academic	91
Profs Interesting	91
Profs Accessible	95
Admissions	99
Financial Aid	99

CAMPUS LIFE

Type of school	Private
Environment	City

Students

Degree-seeking undergrad enrollment	6,636
% male/female/not reported	49/50/1
% from out of state	92
% First-year from public high school	57
% First-year live on campus	100
% Ugrads live on campus	77
# of fraternities (% join)	NR
# of sororities (% join)	NR
% Asian	24
% Black or African American	9
% Hispanic	16
% Native American	1
% Pacific Islander	<1
% Race and/or ethnicity unknown	2
% Two or more races	7
% White	30
% International	11
# of countries represented	118

CAMPUS MENTAL HEALTH SERVICES

Offers mental health/wellness program	Yes
Mental health training available to students	No
Employs Chief Wellness Officer	NR
Peer-to-peer mental health offerings	NR
Counseling center has guidelines or accreditation	No
Mental health/well-being courses	NR

ACADEMICS

% students returning for sophomore year	99
% students graduating within 4 years	53
% students graduating within 6 years	96
Calendar	Semester
Most common class size 10–19.	(45%)

Most Popular Majors

Economics; History; Political Science and Government

STUDENTS SAY "..."

Academics

Listening to Yale students wax rhapsodic about their school, one can be forgiven for wondering whether they aren't actually describing the platonic form of the university. By their own account, students here benefit not only from "amazing academics and extensive resources" that provide "phenomenal in- and out-of-class education," but also from participation in "a student body that is committed to learning and to each other." Unlike some other prestigious, prominent research universities, Yale "places unparalleled focus on undergraduate education," requiring all professors to teach at least one undergraduate course each year. "[You know] the professors actually love teaching, because if they just wanted to do their research, they could have easily gone elsewhere." A residential college system further personalizes the experience. Each residential college "has a Dean and a [Head], each of which is only responsible for 300 to 500 students, so administrative attention is highly specialized and widely available." Students further enjoy access to "a seemingly never-ending supply of resources (they really just love throwing money at us)" that includes "the [13.8] million volumes in our libraries." In short, "the opportunities are truly endless." "The experiences you have here and the people that you meet will change your life and strengthen your dreams," says one student. Looking for the flip side to all this? "If the weather were a bit nicer, that would be excellent," one student offers. Guess that will have to do.

Campus Life

Yale is, of course, extremely challenging academically, but students assure us that "aside from the stress of midterms and finals, life at Yale is relatively carefree." Work doesn't keep undergrads from participating in "a huge variety of activities for fun. There are more than 400 student groups, including singing, dancing, juggling fire, theater...the list goes on. Because of all of these groups, there are shows on-campus all the time, which are a lot of fun and usually free or less than five dollars. On top of that, there are parties and events on campus and off campus, as well as many subsidized trips to New York City and Boston." Many here "are politically active (or at least politically aware)" and "a very large number of students either volunteer or try to get involved in some sort of organization to make a difference in the world." When the weekend comes around, "there are always parties to go to, whether at the frats or in rooms, but there's definitely no pressure to drink if you don't want to. A good friend of mine pledged a frat without drinking and that's definitely not unheard of (but still not common)." The relationship between Yale and the city of New Haven "sometimes leaves a little to be desired, but overall it's a great place to be for four years."

Student Body

A typical Yalie is "tough to define because so much of what makes Yale special is the unique convergence of different students to form one cohesive entity. Nonetheless, the one common characteristic of Yale students is passion—each Yalie is driven and dedicated to what he or she loves most, and it creates a palpable atmosphere of enthusiasm on campus." True enough, the student body represents a wide variety of ethnic, religious, economic, and academic backgrounds, but they all "thrive on learning, whether in a class, from a book, or from a conversation with a new friend." Students here also "tend to do a lot." "Everyone has many activities that they are a part of, which in turn fosters the closely connected feel of the campus." Undergrads tend to lean to the left politically, but for "those whose political views aren't as liberal as the rest of the campus...there are several campus organizations that cater to them."

Yale University

Financial Aid: 203-432-2700 • E-Mail: apply.questions@yale.edu • Website: www.yale.edu

THE PRINCETON REVIEW SAYS

Admissions

The school reports that its standardized testing policy for use in admission for Fall 2026 is Test Flexible. The Princeton Review suggests that interested applicants consult with the school for the most up-to-date standardized testing policies. *Very important factors considered include:* rigor of secondary school record, class rank, academic GPA, application essay, recommendation(s), extracurricular activities, talent/ability, character/personal qualities. *Other factors considered include:* standardized test scores, interview, first generation, alumni/ae relation, geographical residence, state residency, volunteer work, work experience. High school diploma is required and GED is accepted.

Financial Aid

Students should submit: FAFSA; CSS PROFILE. The Princeton Review suggests that all financial aid forms be submitted as soon as possible. *Need-based scholarships/grants offered:* Federal Pell; Federal SEOG; Private scholarships; College/university scholarship or grant aid from institutional funds. *Loan aid offered:* Federal Direct Subsidized Loans; Federal Direct Unsubsidized Loans; Direct PLUS loans; College/university loans from institutional funds. Admitted students will be notified of awards on a rolling basis beginning 12/20. Institutional employment available.

The Inside Word

Yale estimates that over three-quarters of all its applicants are qualified to attend the university, but about five percent get in. That adds up to a lot of broken hearts among kids who, if admitted, could probably handle the academic program. With so many qualified applicants to choose from, Yale can winnow to build an incoming class that is balanced in terms of income level, geographic origin, and academic interest. Legacies (descendants of Yale grads) gain some advantage—although they still need exceptionally strong credentials.

THE SCHOOL SAYS

From the Admissions Office

"The most important questions the admissions committee must resolve are 'Who is likely to make the most of Yale's resources?' and 'Who will contribute significantly to the Yale community?' These questions suggest an approach to evaluating applicants that is more complex than whether Yale would rather admit well-rounded people or those with specialized talents. In selecting a class of 1,650 from roughly 50,000 applicants, the admissions committee looks for academic ability and achievement combined with such personal characteristics as motivation, curiosity, energy, and leadership ability. The nature of these qualities is such that there is no simple profile of grades, scores, interests, and activities that will assure admission. Diversity within the student population is important, and the admissions committee selects a class of able and contributing individuals from a variety of backgrounds and with a broad range of interests and skills."

SELECTIVITY

# of total applicants	50,264
% of total applicants accepted	5
% of total acceptees attending	68
# offered a place on the wait list	944
# admitted from wait list	32

First-Year Profile

Testing policy	Test Flexible
Range SAT composite	1480–1560
Range SAT EBRW	730–780
Range SAT math	740–790
Range ACT composite	33–35
% submitting SAT scores	61
% submitting ACT scores	25
% graduated top 10% of class	96
% graduated top 25% of class	99
% graduated top 50% of class	100
% submitting high school rank	33

Important Dates

Early action	
Apply by	11/1
Notified by	12/15
Regular	
Apply by	1/2
Notified by	4/1
Nonfall registration?	No

FINANCIAL FACTS

Annual tuition	$72,500
Food and housing	$21,600
Books and supplies	$1,000
Average need-based scholarship (First-year)	$72,941 ($74,040)
% students with need rec. need-based scholarship or grant aid (First-year)	100 (100)
% students with need rec. non-need-based scholarship or grant aid (First-year)	1 (1)
% students with need rec. need-based self-help aid (First-year)	80 (69)
% students rec. any financial aid (First-year)	52 (51)
% UG borrow to pay for school	12
Average cumulative indebtedness	$7,265
% of students with need fully met (First-year)	100 (100)
Average % of student need met (First-year)	100 (100)

2027 BEST REGIONAL COLLEGES

In addition to the 392 schools in this book, we salute the following 238 schools that we consider academically outstanding and well worth consideration in your college search. For more information on these schools, visit PrincetonReview.com to find admissions information, costs, and more.

MID-ATLANTIC

Maryland
Hood College
Maryland Institute College of Art
Towson University

Pennsylvania
Albright College
Arcadia University
Chatham University
Chestnut Hill College
Delaware Valley University
Elizabethtown College
King's College
Kutztown University of Pennsylvania
La Roche University
Lebanon Valley College
Messiah University
Misericordia University
Neumann University
PennWest California
Robert Morris University
Seton Hill University
Slippery Rock University of Pennsylvania
University of Pittsburgh at Bradford
Westminster College
Wilkes University
York College of Pennsylvania

Virginia
Averett University
Bridgewater College
Mary Baldwin University
Old Dominion University
Radford University
Sweet Briar College

West Virginia
Concord University
Shepherd University
University of Charleston
West Virginia Wesleyan College

MIDWEST

Illinois
Augustana College
Dominican University
Elmhurst University
Illinois College
Lewis University
Millikin University
Monmouth College
North Central College
Principia College
Rockford University
Southern Illinois University—Carbondale
Western Illinois University

Indiana
Anderson University
Ball State University
Grace College and Seminary
Huntington University
Indiana State University
Manchester University
Saint Mary's College
Trine University
Valparaiso University

Iowa
Briar Cliff University
Drake University
Graceland University
Luther College
Morningside University
Northwestern College
St. Ambrose University
University of Northern Iowa
Wartburg College

Kansas
Baker University
Emporia State University
Pittsburg State University
Sterling College
University of Saint Mary

Michigan
Alma College
Grand Valley State University
Hope College
University of Michigan—Flint
Western Michigan University

Minnesota
Gustavus Adolphus College
Saint Mary's University of Minnesota
St. Catherine University
The College of Saint Scholastica
University of Minnesota, Crookston
University of St. Thomas
Winona State University

Missouri
Columbia College
Southeast Missouri State University
Stephens College
University of Central Missouri
University of Missouri—Kansas City
Westminster College

Nebraska
Doane University
University of Nebraska at Omaha

North Dakota
Mayville State University
University of Jamestown

Ohio
Ashland University
Baldwin Wallace University
Cedarville University
Cleveland Institute of Art
Hiram College
The University of Akron
The University of Findlay
Wright State University

South Dakota
Augustana University

Wisconsin
Carthage College
Edgewood College
Milwaukee School of Engineering
St. Norbert College
University of Wisconsin—Eau Claire
University of Wisconsin—Milwaukee
University of Wisconsin—River Falls

NORTHEAST

Connecticut
Central Connecticut State University
Eastern Connecticut State University

Maine
University of Maine—Fort Kent

Massachusetts
Hult International Business School
Merrimack College
Nichols College
University of Massachusetts—Boston
Wentworth Institute of Technology
Worcester State University

New Hampshire
Keene State College

New Jersey
Ramapo College of New Jersey
Stockton University

New York
Hartwick College
Houghton College
LIM College
Long Island University
Molloy University
Niagara University
Parsons School of Design at The New School
Pratt Institute
Roberts Wesleyan University
Simon's Rock at Bard College
St. John Fisher University
State University of New York—Alfred State College
State University of New York—Brockport
State University of New York—Cortland
State University of New York—Fredonia
State University of New York—Maritime College
State University of New York—New Paltz
State University of New York—Oswego
State University of New York—University at Buffalo
United States Merchant Marine Academy

Rhode Island
Roger Williams University

SOUTH

Alabama
Auburn University at Montgomery
Huntingdon College
Samford University
Talladega College
Troy University—Troy
Tuskegee University

Arkansas
Arkansas State University
Harding University
Hendrix College
Lyon College

Florida
Florida A&M University
Florida Atlantic University
Florida Gulf Coast University
Palm Beach Atlantic University
University of North Florida
University of West Florida

Georgia
Brenau University
Clark Atlanta University
Covenant College
Georgia College & State University
Oglethorpe University
Savannah College of Art and Design
Shorter University
University of West Georgia
Wesleyan College

Kentucky
Kentucky State University
Kentucky Wesleyan College

Louisiana
Centenary College of Louisiana
University of Louisiana at Lafayette
University of New Orleans

Mississippi
Millsaps College

North Carolina
Barton College
Campbell University
Guilford College
Meredith College
University of North Carolina—Wilmington

South Carolina
Anderson University
Coker University
Winthrop University

Tennessee
Belmont University
Carson-Newman University
Christian Brothers University
East Tennessee State University
Fisk University
King University
Lee University
Lipscomb University
Tennessee Technological University
Union University
University of Tennessee at Martin

SOUTHWEST

Arizona
Prescott College

Colorado
Fort Lewis College

New Mexico
New Mexico Institute of Mining and Technology

Oklahoma
Oklahoma Baptist University
Oklahoma City University
Oklahoma State University
Oral Roberts University

Texas
Abilene Christian University
Hardin-Simmons University
Schreiner University
St. Edward's University
Texas Lutheran University
Texas Tech University
The University of Texas at Arlington
University of North Texas

WEST

Alaska
University of Alaska Fairbanks

California
Azusa Pacific University
Biola University
California Institute of the Arts
California State Polytechnic University, Humboldt
California State Polytechnic University, Pomona
California State University, East Bay
California State University, Long Beach
California State University, San Bernardino
Deep Springs College
Menlo College
Otis College of Art and Design
Sonoma State University
University of La Verne
University of the Pacific

Hawaii
Hawai'i Pacific University

Idaho
Northwest Nazarene University
The College of Idaho

Oregon
George Fox University
Linfield University
Willamette University

Utah
Southern Utah University
Utah State University
Weber State University

Washington
The Evergreen State College
Pacific Lutheran University
Seattle Pacific University
University of Washington—Bothell
Whitworth University

INTERNATIONAL

Canada
University of Toronto
McGill University

Ireland
Maynooth University
Trinity College Dublin

PART 4

Indexes

ALPHABETICAL INDEX OF SCHOOLS

INDEX OF SCHOOLS BY LOCATION

INDEX OF SCHOOLS BY TUITION

Price categories are based on figures the schools reported to us in early spring 2026 for tuition and required fees (in-state tuition for public schools) and do not include books, food and housing, transportation, or other expenses.

No Tuition

Less than $9,999

$10,000–$19,999

$60,000–$69,999

OVER $70,000

THE PRINCETON REVIEW NATIONAL COLLEGE COUNSELOR ADVISORY BOARD, 2026–2027

We thank the members of this board for their careful and considered input.

Michael Acquilano, Assistant Head of Upper School and Director of College Guidance, Staten Island Academy, Staten Island, NY

Lee Shulman Bierer, President, Bierer College Consulting, Charlotte, NC

Ellen O'Neill Deitrich, Assistant Head of School for Academics and Dean of College Counseling, St. Mary's Hall, San Antonio, TX

Henry DelAngelo, School Counselor, Joel Barlow High School, Redding, CT

Meghan Garland, College and Career Counselor, Millburn High School, Millburn, NJ

Anne Gregory, School Counselor, Millburn High School, Millburn, NJ

Nancy Griesemer, Independent Educational Consultant and Co-author of *Admission Matters, 5th Edition,* College Explorations LLC, Oakton, VA

Molly Harrington, High School Counselor M–Z, D'Evelyn Junior/Senior High School, Denver, CO

Robert Harry. Associate Director of College Counseling, Kent School, Kent, CT

Jodi Hester, Associate Director of College Counseling, The Westminster School, Atlanta, GA

William Hirt, College Counselor, Professional Children's School, New York, NY

Nikki Lugo Hostnik, Director of College Counseling, Saint Louis Priory School, St. Louis, MO

Marilyn J. Kaufman, M.Ed., Certified College Counselor and Educational Consultant, President, College Admission Consultants, Dallas, TX

Joanne Levy-Prewitt; Independent College Advisor and Co-Founder of Get Going Workshops; Moraga, CA

Dr. Earl R. Macam, College Counselor, Mary Institute and St. Louis Country Day School, St. Louis, MO

Erin McElligott, Director of College & School Counseling, Prospect Hill Academy Charter School, Cambridge, MA

Dr. Niki Mendrinos, Director of School and College Counseling, Bishop Eustace Preparatory School, Pennsauken, NJ

Nancy Ortiz, School Counselor, Innovation High School, Jersey City, NJ

Mary Russell, College and Career Programs Coordinator/Counselor, Corona Del Mar High/Middle School, Newport Beach, CA

Toby Walker, Vice President of BASIS Independent Schools, Redmond, WA

SCHOOL SAYS . . .

In this section you'll find advertisements directly from colleges with information they'd like you to consider about their schools. The editorial in these pages is written by the schools, which pay a fee to offset the cost of printing their advertisements in this section.

The Princeton Review does not charge schools for inclusion in the School Profiles (pp 63–847) section in this book. The company has never required colleges, universities, or any institutions to pay a fee for their profiles or inclusions in our books.

For information about how we selected the 392 outstanding schools in this book, see page 20, "How We Produce This Book."

COMPARISONS FAIL.
THERE'S ONLY ONE BERRY.
STUDENT-FACULTY INTERACTION RANKED IN THE TOP 10% NATIONALLY
National Survey of Student Engagement
REGULARLY RANKED AMONG THE MOST BEAUTIFUL COLLEGES IN AMERICA
1,000+ PROFESSIONAL DEVELOPMENT OPPORTUNITIES THROUGH THE LIFEWORKS PROGRAM
BERRY COLLEGE
berry.edu

FLORIDA SOUTHERN COLLEGE
MOST BEAUTIFUL CAMPUS IN THE NATION
- The Princeton Review
AMONG AMERICA'S TOP COLLEGES
- Forbes
70+ ACADEMIC MAJORS WITH A FOCUS ON ENGAGED LEARNING
THE PRINCETON REVIEW
THE 391 BEST COLLEGES
2026
THE PRINCETON REVIEW
South
BEST REGIONAL COLLEGES
2026
At Florida Southern College, we understand that knowledge is cultivated in the classroom but tested in the real world. Immersive, hands-on experiences, such as internships and research, equip students to lead, succeed, and make an impact in our community and across the globe. All of this is set against the backdrop of our iconic historic campus, where the beauty of Frank Lloyd Wright's architectural masterpiece meets cutting-edge academic and professional development opportunities.
INTERESTED IN FLORIDA SOUTHERN?
Visit our website to learn more about our campus.

FLC
FORT LEWIS COLLEGE®
DURANGO, COLORADO
Look
closer
FULBRIGHT
TOP PRODUCER
U.S. SCHOLAR PROGRAM
2024 • 2025
THE PRINCETON REVIEW
Southwest
2026
BEST REGIONAL COLLEGES
CARNEGIE
Classification
RESEARCH COLLEGES AND UNIVERSITIES
2025
#1
most affordable tuition for Colorado students
Top 10
producer of Ph.D.s in multiple fields
95%
of students participate in undergraduate research
Fort Lewis College sits on a mesa above Durango, Colorado.
Close enough to the city, far enough to think clearly.

Detroit
Chicago

RIT
Rochester Institute of Technology
Built for doers.
An education powered by experience.
At Rochester Institute of Technology, you don't just study your field, you practice it.
With 100+ majors, paid co-ops, internships, research, and accelerated degree options, you'll graduate with real-world experience and a résumé that stands out.
Be on to something amazing.
We invite you to explore RIT.
rit.edu/discover
RIT ESPORTS

SETON HALL UNIVERSITY
1 8 5 6
Ranked a top
11%
for return on investment
#1
national ranking for student support and counseling services
97%
employment rate
98%
students receiving financial aid
TOP 20
Catholic university in America
GREAT MINDS.
Greater purpose.
"Everyone is so supportive and caring. My professors spend lots of extra time with me and really know who I am and care about me. I owe Seton Hall so much because they have made me the person I am today. I have become more confident, open-minded and knowledgeable. I wouldn't be the person I am or have had even half of these experiences if I didn't come to Seton Hall."
KRISTINE MAMANTA
Economics, marketing majors
admissions.shu.edu
thehall@shu.edu
(973) 313-6146

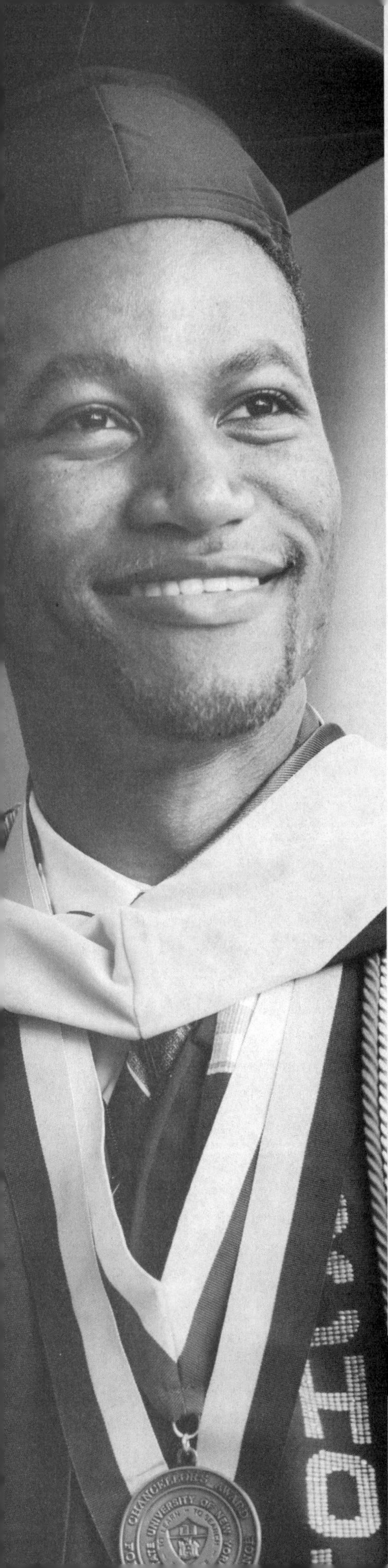

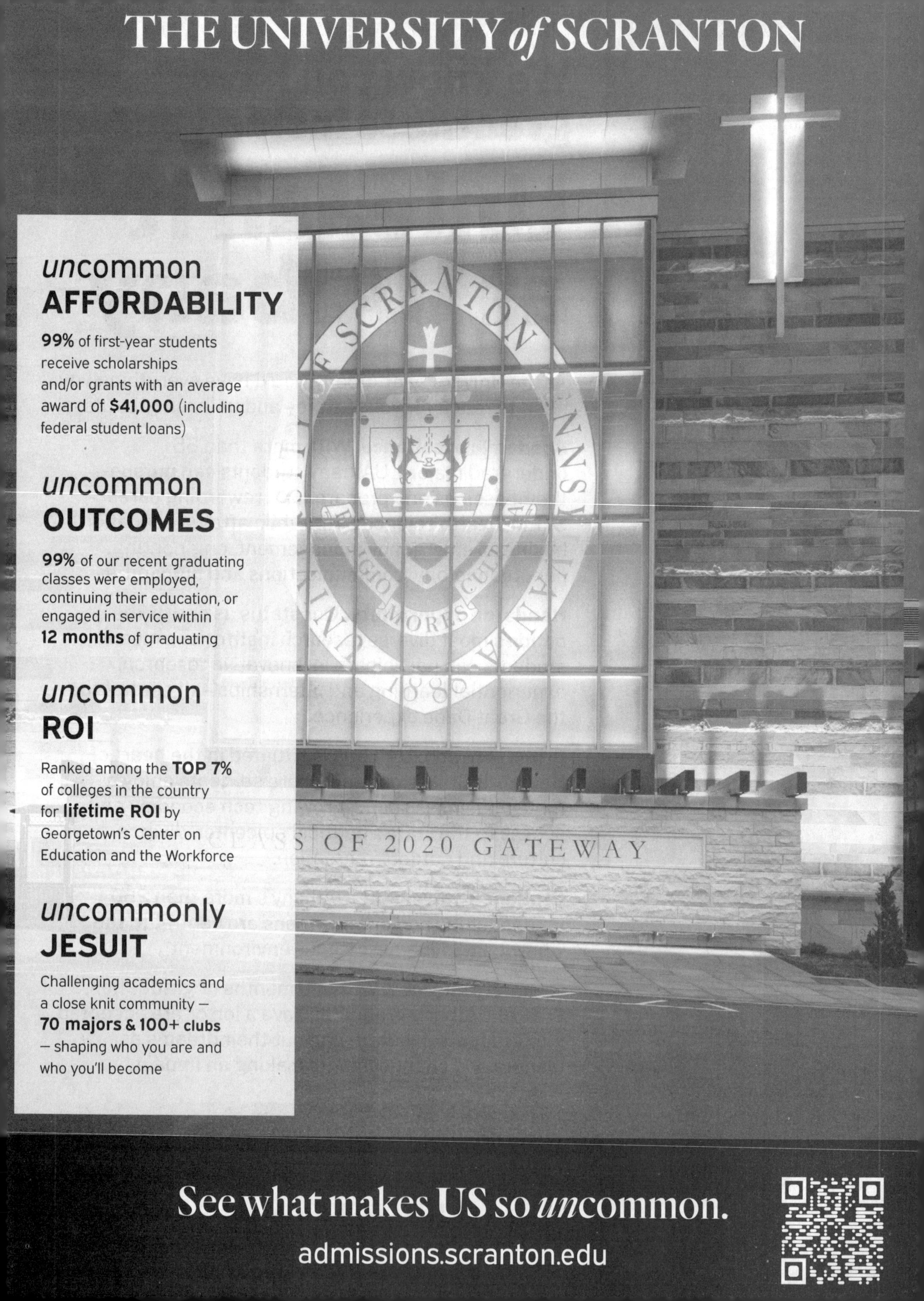
THE UNIVERSITY of SCRANTON
uncommon
AFFORDABILITY
99% of first-year students receive scholarships and/or grants with an average award of $41,000 (including federal student loans)
uncommon
OUTCOMES
99% of our recent graduating classes were employed, continuing their education, or engaged in service within 12 months of graduating
uncommon
ROI
Ranked among the TOP 7% of colleges in the country for lifetime ROI by Georgetown's Center on Education and the Workforce
uncommonly
JESUIT
Challenging academics and a close knit community — 70 majors & 100+ clubs — shaping who you are and who you'll become
UNIVERSITY OF SCRANTON PENNSYLVANIA
RELIGIO MORES CULTURA
1888
OF 2020 GATEWAY
See what makes US so uncommon.
admissions.scranton.edu

Best College Planner

As a bonus for *The Best 392 Colleges*, we've adapted some content from our Complete College Planner book that you can use to help find your best fit school. You can print out additional copies from your free online student tools.

In order to quickly compare schools and narrow down your list, look up the following information for each school. Record your impressions before, during, and after your visit so that you have a clear picture of why your opinion may have changed (so you're not making an in-the-moment decision).

College Name: ____________________

School Stats

Type of school (circle one): Public Private

Environment (circle one): Urban Suburban Rural

Location (City, State): ____________________

Number of students enrolled: ____________________

Percent male/female: ____________________

Student/faculty ratio: ____________________

Average class size: ____________________

Cost per year: ____________________

Academic Stats

Range of SAT scores accepted: ____________________

Range of ACT scores accepted: ____________________

Average GPA of admitted students: ____________________

My ranking (circle one): Reach Good match Safety

Overall Impressions

During my Visit

Answers to my Top 10 Questions:*

1. ______________________________
2. ______________________________
3. ______________________________
4. ______________________________
5. ______________________________
6. ______________________________
7. ______________________________
8. ______________________________
9. ______________________________
10. ______________________________

Campus Visit Notes:

____

____

____

____

____

____

____

____

____

____

____

* To help write your Top 10 Questions, see the following section (on page 884).

Overall Impressions

After my Visit

Academics

1 Not at all impressed — 5 Very impressed

Explanation of ranking: ____________________

____

Programs and Majors of interest: ____________________

____

Student Life

1 Not at all impressed — 5 Very impressed

Explanation of ranking: ____________________

____

Specific student organizations, activities, or opportunities of interest:

____

Campus and Location

1 Not at all impressed — 5 Very impressed

Explanation of ranking: ____________________

____

Ways you could see yourself spending time off campus:

____

____

Do you feel safe on campus and in the surrounding area:

____

Top 10 Questions to Ask on Your College Tour

Touring colleges can be overwhelming; you're seeing and hearing a lot. Use this overall list of big and small questions below to help identify what you most want to know more about. Make sure you ask the same questions at each school, and write them down, so you can most easily compare the results.

1. What are your school's strengths?

- What majors and classes are the most popular?
- What academic support resources are available to students?
- Fill in your own question:
- ____________________
- Fill in your own question:
- ____________________

2. What's your biggest complaint about the school?

- What services could be improved? Are they being improved?
- Is the faculty responsive to student feedback?
- Fill in your own question:
- ____________________
- Fill in your own question:
- ____________________

3. Were you able to get into most of your first-choice classes?

- What is the course selection like?
- Are your professors good teachers?
- Fill in your own question:
- ____________________
- Fill in your own question:
- ____________________

4. Describe your weekly workload.

- Describe the school/social life balance.
- How overwhelmed are students with homework?
- Fill in your own question:
- ____________________
- Fill in your own question:
- ____________________

5. What is the social scene like on campus?

- What is the party culture like on campus?
- What types of activities are popular among students?
- Fill in your own question:
- ____________________
- Fill in your own question:
- ____________________

6. Where are the best places to study?

- Are there places to study at all times of day with available outlets?
- What resources does the library provide to students?
- Fill in your own question:
- ____________________
- Fill in your own question:
- ____________________

7. How would you describe your fellow students?

- How diverse is your campus?
- How involved are students with politics, social justice, and other public issues?
- Fill in your own question:
- ______________________________
- Fill in your own question:
- ______________________________

8. Are there cliques between different groups?

- Describe how the school tries to be inclusive of all types of backgrounds.
- What freshman programs are offered to help new students make friends?
- Fill in your own question:
- ______________________________
- Fill in your own question:
- ______________________________

9. How difficult is it to find internships on campus?

- What types of work experience are available through the college?
- What career counseling services are offered to students?
- Fill in your own question:
- ______________________________
- Fill in your own question:
- ______________________________

10. Do you have a mentor?

- How are students able to form relationships with their professors?
- Describe the relationship between upperclassmen and freshmen.
- Fill in your own question:
- ______________________________
- Fill in your own question:
- ______________________________

Compare Costs

For each school still on your list, fill out the SCHOOL COSTS section to get an overall sense of the sticker price. Then, once you get your financial aid package from the school, add the FINANCIAL AID numbers and calculate the remainder to see how much you have to pay now, and how much debt you'll have. Remember that this is just a calculation for a single year, and college often takes somewhere between 3–6 years. You don't have to choose the school that will cost the least to attend, but you should be sure that it's worth the extra expense for whichever school you do choose.

SCHOOL COSTS

Tuition: $____________

+ Room and Board: $____________

+ Books: $____________

+ Fees: $____________

+ Miscellaneous: $____________

= $____________

FINANCIAL AID

Scholarship: $____________

+ Grant: $____________

+ Federal Loan: $____________

+ Federal Work Study: $____________

= $____________

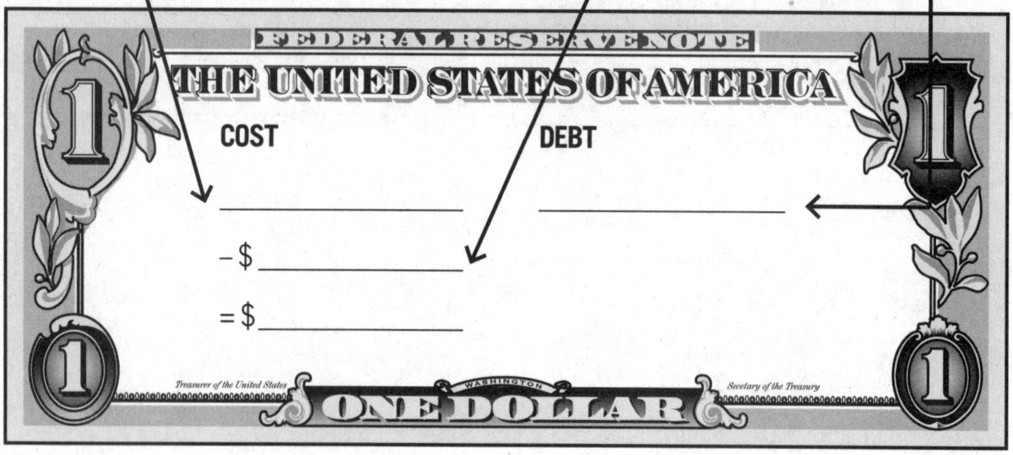

ABOUT THE AUTHORS

Robert Franek, Editor-in-Chief at The Princeton Review, is the company's chief expert on college and higher education issues. Over his 34-year career, he has served as a college admissions administrator, test prep teacher, author, and lecturer. Rob visits more than 50 colleges a year as part of his research for this book. He also oversees the company's line of 150 titles from best-selling college and test-prep guides to study aids books. Rob has also hosted 150+ videos on The Princeton Review's YouTube channel, which has nearly 300K subscribers. Providing timely advice for students and parents on current education topics, the videos have collectively received more than 1,000,000 views. Prior to joining The Princeton Review in 1999, Rob served as a college admissions administrator at Wagner College (New York City) for six years. He earned his BA in Political Science and History at Drew University (Madison, NJ), where he serves as a member of the Board of Trustees. Follow him on X (formerly Twitter) @RobFranek.

David Soto, Senior Director of Data Operations, is a graduate of the Walter Cronkite School of Journalism at Arizona State University. He develops content focused on college admissions, graduate education, and career planning, while also supporting the company website that reaches more than half of all college-bound students. Before joining The Princeton Review in 2001, David worked as a photojournalist for The Arizona Republic in Phoenix. He lives in Brooklyn, NY, with his wife and two sons.

Stephen Koch, Senior Manager of Data Operations, oversees admissions and institutional data workflows that power the company's rankings, guidebooks, APIs, and digital content. Since joining the admissions content team in 2011, he has focused on transforming large-scale survey and institutional data into tools and insights to help students navigate the college search process. He earned a BA in government with a certificate in data science from Wesleyan University. Stephen lives in Brooklyn, NY, with his partner and their dog, Ozzie.

Aaron Riccio, Director of Editorial Admission Content, is a proud graduate of New York's Binghamton University. Since then, he has been working in educational services, and with The Princeton Review as of 2013, where he works to prepare test prep and guidebook content in print and on the web.

Laura Rose, Editor, is a graduate of the School of International Service at American University in Washington, D.C. She has written for numerous magazines and newspapers and has served as marketing director at Eichhorn in San Jose, CA, and editorial director at MetroMedia Inc. before joining The Princeton Review in 2021.